CAME TO US

GREEK

The first translation
from the Hebrew
was the Septuagint

Old

New

LATIN

...Christian
missionaries came to
England bringing the
Bible in Latin.
In the Dark Ages the
monasteries remained
centres of learning

JEROME
*d. 405
revised
Latin Version
using Greek
and
Hebrew texts*

*Codex Sinaiticus
Codex Alexandrinus
Codex Vaticanus*

For the first time
single pages of
papyrus or vellum
were used, and
bound in the form
of a book

**LINDISFARNE
GOSPELS**
698–721

JOHN WYCLIFFE
First English Bible 1384

12th–15th CENTURIES

In the parish churches and
great cathedrals Biblical
truths were conveyed to
an illiterate age in
stained glass,
paintings and sculpture

ERASMUS
*Greek and Latin
New Testament 1516*

15th CENTURY

Scholars fleeing from
Constantinople in 1453
brought the Greek text
of the Bible to the West

WILLIAM TYNDALE
*First printed English
New Testament 1526*

16th CENTURY

From the Elizabethan era
the Bible belonged
to the English home

THE GREAT BIBLE *1539*

17th CENTURY

King James the First
commissioned scholars
to translate the
Authorized Version

THE BISHOPS' BIBLE *1568*

18th & 19th CENTURIES

The influence of the Bible
led to social reform,
by Wilberforce, Fry,
Shaftesbury and others.
Popular education and
the spread of literacy
throughout the world
create a new urgency
for books

THE AUTHORIZED VERSION *1611*

The discovery of hitherto
unknown manuscripts
brought new under-
standing of the
Biblical text and
stimulated many
new translations

20th CENTURY

Modern technology and
science are being
applied to the
new discoveries of
Biblical sources

NEW ENGLISH BIBLE
New Testament 1961

COUNTY COUNCIL OF
THE WEST RIDING OF
YORKSHIRE

THIS BIBLE IS PRESENTED TO

Christopher   Millis

ON ENTERING

Mirfield   Grammar

SCHOOL

EDUCATION DEPARTMENT

THE BIBLE

CONTAINING

THE OLD AND NEW TESTAMENTS

with illustrations by

HORACE KNOWLES

Revised Standard Version

TRANSLATED FROM THE ORIGINAL TONGUES
BEING THE VERSION SET FORTH A.D. 1611
REVISED A.D. 1881–1885 AND A.D. 1901
COMPARED WITH THE MOST ANCIENT AUTHORITIES
AND REVISED A.D. 1952

THE BRITISH & FOREIGN
BIBLE SOCIETY

PUBLISHED IN THE FORMAT OF
THE BIBLE SOCIETY'S
THIRD JUBILEE BIBLE

Edited by

JOHN STIRLING

Specially composed in seven-channel tape at Stephen Austin and Sons, Ltd.,
Hertford, and processed by I.C.T. 1500 computer at Rocappi, Ltd., Sevenoaks.

Printed, bound and published by Collins Clear-type Press.

PRINTED IN GREAT BRITAIN

RS53P-100 M-1967   SBN 564 00101 5

PREFACE

THE Revised Standard Version of the Bible is an authorized revision of the American Standard Version, published in 1901, which was a revision of the King James Version, published in 1611.

The first English version of the Scriptures made by direct translation from the original Hebrew and Greek, and the first to be printed, was the work of William Tyndale. He met bitter opposition. He was accused of wilfully perverting the meaning of the Scriptures, and his New Testaments were ordered to be burned as "untrue translations." He was finally betrayed into the hands of his enemies, and in October 1536, was publicly executed and burned at the stake.

Yet Tyndale's work became the foundation of subsequent English versions, notably those of Coverdale, 1535; Thomas Matthew (probably a pseudonym for John Rogers), 1537; the Great Bible, 1539; the Geneva Bible, 1560; and the Bishops' Bible, 1568. In 1582 a translation of the New Testament, made from the Latin Vulgate by Roman Catholic scholars, was published at Rheims.

The translators who made the King James Version took into account all of these preceding versions; and comparison shows that it owes something to each of them. It kept felicitous phrases and apt expressions, from whatever source, which had stood the test of public usage. It owed most, especially in the New Testament, to Tyndale.

The King James Version had to compete with the Geneva Bible in popular use; but in the end it prevailed, and for more than two and a half centuries no other authorized translation of the Bible into English was made. The King James Version became the "Authorized Version" of the English-speaking peoples.

The King James Version has with good reason been termed "the noblest monument of English prose." Its revisers in 1881 expressed admiration for "its simplicity, its dignity, its power, its happy turns of expression . . . the music of its cadences, and the felicities of its rhythm." It entered, as no other book has, into the making of the personal character and the public institutions of the English-speaking peoples. We owe to it an incalculable debt.

Yet the King James Version has grave defects. By the middle of the nineteenth century, the development of Biblical studies and the discovery of many manuscripts more ancient than those upon which the King James Version was based, made it manifest that these defects are so many and so serious as to call for revision of the English translation. The task was undertaken, by authority of the Church of England, in 1870. The English Revised Version of the Bible was published in 1881–1885; and the American Standard Version, its variant embodying the preferences of the American scholars associated in the work, was published in 1901.

Because of unhappy experience with unauthorized publications in the two decades between 1881 and 1901, which tampered with the text of the English Revised Version in the supposed interest of the American public, the American Standard Version was copyrighted, to protect the text from unauthorized changes. In 1928 this copyright was acquired by the International Council of Religious Education, and thus passed into the ownership of the churches of the United States and Canada which were associated in this Council through their boards of education and publication.

The Council appointed a committee of scholars to have charge of the text of the American Standard Version and to undertake inquiry as to whether further revision was necessary. For more than two years the Committee worked upon the problem of whether or not revision should be undertaken; and if so, what should be its nature and extent. In the end the decision was reached that there is need for a thorough revision of the version of 1901, which will stay as close to the Tyndale-King James tradition as it can in the light of our present knowledge of the Hebrew and Greek texts and their meaning on the one hand, and our present understanding of English on the other.

PREFACE

In 1937 the revision was authorized by vote of the Council, which directed that the resulting version should "embody the best results of modern scholarship as to the meaning of the Scriptures, and express this meaning in English diction which is designed for use in public and private worship and preserve those qualities which have given to the King James Version a supreme place in English literature."

Thirty-two scholars have served as members of the Committee charged with making the revision, and they have secured the review and counsel of an Advisory Board of fifty representatives of the co-operating denominations. The Committee has worked in two sections, one dealing with the Old Testament and one with the New Testament. Each section has submitted its work to the scrutiny of the members of the other section; and the charter of the Committee requires that all changes be agreed upon by a two-thirds vote of the total membership of the Committee. The Revised Standard Version of the New Testament was published in 1946. The publication of the Revised Standard Version of the Bible, containing the Old and New Testaments, was authorized by vote of the National Council of the Churches of Christ in the U.S.A. in 1951.

The problem of establishing the correct Hebrew and Aramaic text of the Old Testament is very different from the corresponding problem in the New Testament. For the New Testament we have a large number of Greek manuscripts, preserving many variant forms of the text. Some of them were made only two or three centuries later than the original composition of the books. For the Old Testament only late manuscripts survive, all (with the exception of the Dead Sea texts of Isaiah and Habakkuk and some fragments of other books) based on a standardized form of the text established many centuries after the books were written.

The present revision is based on the consonantal Hebrew and Aramaic text as fixed early in the Christian era and revised by Jewish scholars (the "Masoretes") of the sixth to ninth centuries. The vowel signs, which were added by the Masoretes, are accepted also in the main, but where a more probable and convincing reading can be obtained by assuming different vowels, this has been done. No notes are given in such cases, because the vowel points are less ancient and reliable than the consonants.

Departures from the consonantal text of the best manuscripts have been made only where it seems clear that errors in copying had been made before the text was standardized. Most of the corrections adopted are based on the ancient versions (translations into Greek, Aramaic, Syriac, and Latin), which were made before the time of the Masoretic revision and therefore reflect earlier forms of the text. In every such instance a footnote specifies the version or versions from which the correction has been derived, and also gives a translation of the Masoretic Text.

Sometimes it is evident that the text has suffered in transmission, but none of the versions provides a satisfactory restoration. Here we can only follow the best judgment of competent scholars as to the most probable reconstruction of the original text. Such corrections are indicated in the footnotes by the abbreviation *Cn*, and a translation of the Masoretic Text is added.

The discovery of the meaning of the text, once the best readings have been established, is aided by many new resources for understanding the original languages. Much progress has been made in the historical and comparative study of these languages. A vast quantity of writings in related Semitic languages, some of them only recently discovered, has greatly enlarged our knowledge of the vocabulary and grammar of Biblical Hebrew and Aramaic. Sometimes the present translation will be found to render a Hebrew word in a sense quite different from that of the traditional interpretation. It has not been felt necessary in such cases to attach a footnote, because no change in the text is involved and it may be assumed that the new rendering was not adopted without convincing evidence. The analysis of religious texts from the ancient Near East has made clearer the significance of ideas and practices recorded in the Old Testament. Many difficulties and obscurities, of course, remain. Where the choice between two meanings is particularly difficult or doubtful, we have given an alternative rendering in a footnote. If in the judgment of the Committee the meaning of a passage is quite uncertain or obscure, either because of corruption in the text or because of the inadequacy of our present knowledge of the language, that fact is indicated by a note. It should not be assumed, however, that the Committee was entirely sure or unanimous concerning every rendering not so indicated. To record all minority views was obviously out of the question.

A major departure from the practice of the American Standard Version is the rendering of the Divine Name, the "Tetragrammaton." The American Standard Version used the term "Jehovah"; the King James Version had employed this in four places, but everywhere else, except in three cases where it was employed as part of a proper name, used the English word LORD (or in certain cases GOD) printed in capitals. The present revision returns to the procedure of the King James Version, which follows the precedent of the ancient Greek and Latin translators and the long established practice in the reading of the Hebrew scriptures in the synagogue. While it is almost if not quite certain that the Name was originally pronounced "Yahweh," this pronunciation was not indicated when the Masoretes added vowel signs to the consonantal Hebrew text. To the four consonants YHWH of the Name, which had come to be regarded as too sacred to be pronounced, they attached vowel signs indicating that in its place should be read the Hebrew word *Adonai* meaning "Lord" (or *Elohim* meaning "God"). The ancient Greek translators substituted the word *Kyrios* (Lord) for the Name. The Vulgate likewise used the Latin word *Dominus*. The form "Jehovah" is of late medieval origin; it is a combination of the consonants of the Divine Name and the vowels attached to it by the Masoretes but belonging to an entirely different word. The sound of Y is represented by J and the sound of W by V, as in Latin. For two reasons the Committee has returned to the more familiar usage of the King James Version: (1) the word "Jehovah" does not accurately represent any form of the Name ever used in Hebrew; and (2) the use of any proper name for the one and only God, as though there were other gods from whom He had to be distinguished, was discontinued in Judaism before the Christian era and is entirely inappropriate for the universal faith of the Christian Church.

The King James Version of the New Testament was based upon a Greek text that was marred by mistakes, containing the accumulated errors of fourteen centuries of manuscript copying. It was essentially the Greek text of the New Testament as edited by Beza, 1589, who closely followed that published by Erasmus, 1516-1535, which was based upon a few medieval manuscripts. The earliest and best of the eight manuscripts which Erasmus consulted was from the tenth century, and he made the least use of it because it differed most from the commonly received text; Beza had access to two manuscripts of great value, dating from the fifth and sixth centuries, but he made very little use of them because they differed from the text published by Erasmus.

We now possess many more ancient manuscripts of the New Testament, and are far better equipped to seek to recover the original wording of the Greek text. The evidence for the text of the books of the New Testament is better than for any other ancient book, both in the number of extant manuscripts and in the nearness of the date of some of these manuscripts to the date when the book was originally written.

The revisers in the 1870's had most of the evidence that we now have for the Greek text, though the most ancient of all extant manuscripts of the Greek New Testament were not discovered until 1931. But they lacked the resources which discoveries within the past eighty years have afforded for understanding the vocabulary, grammar and idioms of the Greek New Testament. An amazing body of Greek papyri has been unearthed in Egypt since the 1870's—private letters, official records, wills, business accounts, petitions, and other such trivial, everyday recordings of the activities of human beings. In 1895 appeared the first of Adolf Deissmann's studies of these ordinary materials. He proved that many words which had hitherto been assumed to belong to what was called "Biblical Greek" were current in the spoken vernacular of the first century A.D. The New Testament was written in the Koine, the common Greek which was spoken and

PREFACE

understood practically everywhere throughout the Roman Empire in the early centuries of the Christian era. This development in the study of New Testament Greek has come since the work on the English Revised Version and the American Standard Version was done, and at many points sheds new light upon the meaning of the Greek text.

A major reason for revision of the King James Version, which is valid for both the Old Testament and the New Testament, is the change since 1611 in English usage. Many forms of expression have become archaic, while still generally intelligible—the use of thou, thee, thy, thine and the verb endings -est and -edst, the verb endings -eth and -th, it came to pass that, whosoever, whatsoever, insomuch that, because that, for that, unto, howbeit, peradventure, holden, aforetime, must needs, would fain, behooved, to you-ward, etc. Other words are obsolete and no longer understood by the common reader. The greatest problem, however, is presented by the English words which are still in constant use but now convey a different meaning from that which they had in 1611 and in the King James Version. These words were once accurate translations of the Hebrew and Greek Scriptures; but now, having changed in meaning, they have become misleading. They no longer say what the King James translators meant them to say.

The King James Version uses the word "let" in the sense of "hinder," "prevent" to mean "precede," "allow" in the sense of "approve," "communicate" for "share," "conversation" for "conduct," "comprehend" for "overcome," "ghost" for "spirit," "wealth" for "well-being," "allege" for "prove," "demand" for "ask," "take no thought" for "be not anxious," "purchase a good degree" for "gain a good standing," etc. The Greek word for "immediately" is translated in the King James Version not only by "immediately" and "straightway" but also by the terms "anon," "by and by," and "presently." There are more than three hundred such English words which are used in the King James Version in a sense substantially different from that which they now convey. It not only does the King James translators no honour, but it is quite unfair to them and to the truth which they understood and expressed, to retain these words which now convey meanings they did not intend.

The Revised Standard Version of the Bible, containing the Old and New Testaments, was published on September 30, 1952, and has met with wide acceptance. This preface does not undertake to set forth in detail the lines along which the revision proceeded. That is done in pamphlets entitled *An Introduction to the Revised Standard Version of the Old Testament* and *An Introduction to the Revised Standard Version of the New Testament*, written by members of the Committee and designed to help the general public to understand the main principles which have guided this comprehensive revision of the King James and American Standard versions.

These principles were reaffirmed by the Committee in 1959, in connection with a study of criticisms and suggestions from various readers. As a result, a few changes have been authorized for the present and subsequent editions. Most of these are corrections of punctuation, capitalization, or footnotes. Some changes of words or phrases are made in the interest of consistency, clarity or accuracy of translation. Examples of such changes are "from," Job 19.26; "bread," Matthew 7.9, 1 Corinthians 10.17; "is he," Matthew 21.9 and parallels; "the Son," Matthew 27.54, Mark 15.39; "ask nothing of me," John 16.23; "for this life only," 1 Corinthians 15.19; "the husband of one wife," 1 Timothy 3.2,12; 5.9; Titus 1.6.

All the reasons which led to the demand for revision of the King James Version in the nineteenth century are still valid, and are even more cogent now than then. We have had a freer charter than our predecessors in the 1870's in that we have not been required, as they were, to limit the language of the English Bible to the vocabulary of the Elizabethan age. But we hope that we have not taken undue advantage of that freedom. The Revised Standard Version is not a new translation in the language of today. It is not a paraphrase which aims at striking idioms. It is a revision which seeks to preserve all that is best in the English

PREFACE

Bible as it has been known and used through the years. It is intended for use in public and private worship, not merely for reading and instruction. We have resisted the temptation to use phrases that are merely current usage, and have sought to put the message of the Bible in simple, enduring words that are worthy to stand in the great Tyndale-King James tradition. We are glad to say, with the King James translators: "Truly (good Christian Reader) we never thought from the beginning, that we should need to make a new Translation, nor yet to make of a bad one a good one . . . but to make a good one better."

The Bible is more than a historical document to be preserved. And it is more than a classic of English literature to be cherished and admired. It is a record of God's dealing with men, of God's revelation of Himself and His will. It records the life and work of Him in whom the Word of God became flesh and dwelt among men. The Bible carries its full message, not to those who regard it simply as a heritage of the past or praise its literary style, but to those who read it that they may discern and understand God's Word to men. That Word must not be disguised in phrases that are no longer clear, or hidden under words that have changed or lost their meaning. It must stand forth in language that is direct and plain and meaningful to people today. It is our hope and our earnest prayer that this Revised Standard Version of the Bible may be used by God to speak to men in these momentous times, and to help them to understand and believe and obey His Word.

ABBREVIATIONS

In the notes to the books of the Old Testament, the following abbreviations are used: Ms for manuscript; Mss for manuscripts. Heb denotes the Hebrew of the consonantal Masoretic Text of the Old Testament; and MT denotes the Hebrew of the pointed Masoretic Text of the Old Testament.

The ancient versions of the Old Testament are indicated by:

Gk   Septuagint, Greek Version of Old Testament
Sam Samaritan Hebrew text of Old Testament
Syr   Syriac Version of Old Testament
Tg   Targum
Vg   Vulgate, Latin Version of Old Testament

Cn indicates a correction made where the text has suffered in transmission and the versions provide no satisfactory restoration but the Committee agrees with the judgment of competent scholars as to the most probable reconstruction of the original text. The reader is referred to the Preface for a statement of policy concerning text and notes.

TO THE READER

You will find a new line of illustration in this Bible. Instead of the usual type of story-picture there are simple little drawings that look more like up-to-date visual aids than illustrations. That is indeed what they are; and they have been fitted into the text just at the place where help is needed.

There are, for example, many little route-maps. The Bible is a great Travel Book, and where so many journeys are made a map is essential. But a general map is often more difficult to read than a page of type. What is wanted for easy reference is a simplified map, or many such maps, each showing only the places mentioned in the text, and if possible also the route taken by the person concerned. To know the distance between the different places would be an advantage. In some cases it adds to the point of the story. So, along with the maps, drawings of milestones have been inserted to give this information.

It is no less important to know when the events about which one is reading took place. A simple artistic design has therefore been devised to show the date. But the use of this Time-signal, as we may call it, has had to be limited to marking the centuries rather than the years. Precise dates could have been given for some of the events, but for many others the specific year has not yet been determined, though scholars have reduced uncertainty to the difference of a few years. There is, however, little doubt about the century to which the great events belong. So we have kept to these broad spans of time. For, although it is often impossible to give the exact date, there is, we feel, some advantage in having at least an indication of the period about which one is reading; and this applies particularly to parts of the Old Testament, where the material does not always run in historical sequence.

When the scene is set in time and place interest is naturally focused on the people who appear in the story. What a strangely mixed company! They crowd in from all sides, people of many nations, who come and go and keep reappearing until the mind is bewildered by their variety and movements. Who are they? How can they be distinguished? By giving each nation an appropriate symbol—a sort of badge or identity flash—so that, when the reader sees it, he knows at once whether it is the Egyptians, the Philistines, the Syrians, or Babylonians who have stepped into the picture.

So much for the foreign nations of the Bible. But what of Israel and Judah, whose complicated fortunes are interlocked in history, and so interwoven in the sacred narrative that it is difficult to separate them. Can anything be done to enable the most casual reader to follow easily the destinies of these two kingdoms? By using a symbol of Jacob's well for Israel, and one of the Gate of Jerusalem for Judah, the separate chapters of their history are plainly displayed.

But more is needed if the history is to become alive. More windows must be put into the pages of letterpress. As one reads, the contour and character of the country must be as clear to the eye as an open landscape. So little sketches have been inserted of the mountains and deserts, valleys and hills that mould the features of the land of this Book. And there are, what might be called, snapshot drawings of the interesting things to be found there, whether by the wayside or in the city streets. It may be a bird or a flower, a beast of burden or a flock of sheep, and perhaps a travelling minstrel or a night watchman.

Here and there are objects of more than passing interest. They have a mission and a message for all mankind, and call for close-up pictures on a larger scale. Such are the early altars of these people of God, the Tabernacle in the wilderness and the Temple on Zion's Hill. Who would not linger at these sacred shrines? Or study in detail these monuments of worship?

In this series of drawings that illustrates the religion of Israel some pictures have been used more than once—a most unusual procedure in modern book production. The repetition is deliberate. It has been done to emphasize the unity and coherence of the sixty-six different books that together make our Bible, and to show the stream of continuity that runs through the Scriptures. By using, for example, one common picture throughout the Bible for the Book of the Law the general reader gathers at once an impression of the place and power of this work in the people's life and history. He realizes that the Book of the Law about which the Psalmist sings, and the Prophets preach, is in effect the Book of the Law that is described in Exodus and discussed by Paul in his Epistles. Later, if the reader wishes, he can with the scholars go more fully into the matter, but for the time being this general idea will serve his purpose. By a similar repetition of pictures the Fall of Jerusalem recorded in the historical books is directly linked with the writings of the Prophets. There are other instances of the same kind.

Many pictures included in this work need no explanation and carry no caption. So close is the connexion between the drawings and the text that the line of letterpress beneath them, or in the adjoining column, will suffice to describe them.

A word about the letterpress and its layout is essential. The text is that of the Revised Standard Version. It is the plain text, without note or comment, and it is complete.

Two changes have been made in the layout of its pages, both with the hope that they will contribute to the easier reading of the Book.

The first is not new. It has often been done, and obviously it meets the needs of modern readers. It is the arrangement of the text in paragraph form instead of the usual division into verses, with headlines to indicate the contents of the main sections, and sub-headings to mark the flow of the story. Great restraint has been exercised to keep the divisions as few as possible, and to use for the headings such words of Scripture as occur in the text.

The second change is a later development in the direction of a simplified page. In order that the reader can more readily distinguish the nature of the material before him two different sizes of type are used, without implying any difference in the value of such material. It is purely a visual aid for the convenience of the reader.

The position becomes clear when we realize how mixed and varied is the material to be found in the Bible. Every kind of literature is there. But whereas in a modern library History is in one section, Law in another, Philosophy in a third, and all the official documents of Church and State are separated from them, in the books of the Bible all these different forms of literature are inextricably woven together. It is this that makes the reading of Scripture so difficult. Surely something can be done, and should be done, to indicate the different types of material without lessening in any way the value of any of them.

Take, for instance, some of the official historic documents preserved in these ancient manuscripts. They may seem strange and obscure to us today. Yet no one would like to lose them. They are an essential part of the Bible's structure. We are drawn to study them as our interest in the volume grows. They are, however, concerned with technical matters that call for specialized critical study. The general reader finds these particular sections dull or puzzling, and could well afford to leave them until he has become acquainted with the main stream of the Book's great story.

When we begin the study of English history we are not, in our first lessons, expected to read through the Domesday Book or Magna Carta. We are, of course, glad to know they are available, and that we could read them if we wished. Under no circumstance would we have them torn from the fabric of British history, for they form a vital part of our inheritance. But they can wait until our interest has matured and our minds have been equipped to deal with them.

So it is with some of the material in the Bible. We cannot part with it without injury to the Divine Revelation. But to meet the needs of the general reader, who may be for the first time taking up the Book, surely we may indicate where these specialized documents are? And this has been done by putting them into smaller type. In the main they cover genealogies, itineraries, building specifications, detailed regulations regarding ancient rites and customs, and a few tribal records of local feuds. But everything essential to the understanding of the message of the Bible has been set in larger type.

LIST OF MAPS AND PLANS

THE OLD TESTAMENT

LIST OF MAPS AND PLANS

THE NEW TESTAMENT

[The illustration on p. 269 is reproduced by permission from the *New Bible Dictionary* (Inter-Varsity Fellowship).]

THE NAMES AND ORDER
OF THE
BOOKS OF THE OLD AND NEW TESTAMENTS

The Books of the Old Testament

The Books of the New Testament

References to quoted and parallel passages are given following the notes on pages where these are relevant The above abbreviations are used for the books of the Bible.

THE NAMES
OF THE
BOOKS OF THE OLD AND NEW TESTAMENTS

ALPHABETICALLY ARRANGED

THE FIRST BOOK OF MOSES
COMMONLY CALLED

GENESIS

IN THE BEGINNING GOD created[a] the heavens and the earth. The earth was without form and void, and darkness was upon the face of the deep; and the Spirit[b] of God was moving over the face of the waters.

3 And God said, "Let there be light"; and 4 there was light. And God saw that the light was good; and God separated the light from 5 the darkness. God called the light Day, and the darkness he called Night. And there was evening and there was morning, one day.

6 And God said, "Let there be a firmament in the midst of the waters, and let it separate the 7 waters from the waters." And God made the firmament and separated the waters which were under the firmament from the waters which were above the firmament. And it was 8 so. And God called the firmament Heaven. And there was evening and there was morning, a second day.

9 And God said, "Let the waters under the heavens be gathered together into one place, and let the dry land appear." And it was so. 10 God called the dry land Earth, and the waters that were gathered together he called 11 Seas. And God saw that it was good. And God said, "Let the earth put forth vegetation, plants yielding seed, and fruit trees bearing fruit in which is their seed, each according to its kind, upon the earth." And it was so. The earth brought forth vege- 12 tation, plants yielding seed according to their own kinds, and trees bearing fruit in which is their seed, each according to its kind. And God saw that it was good. And there was 13 evening and there was morning, a third day.

And God said, "Let there be lights in the 14 firmament of the heavens to separate the day from the night; and let them be for signs and for seasons and for days and years, and let 15 them be lights in the firmament of the heavens to give light upon the earth." And it was so. And God made the two great lights, 16 the greater light to rule the day, and the lesser light to rule the night; he made the stars also. And God set them in the fir- 17 mament of the heavens to give light upon the earth, to rule over the day and over the night, 18 and to separate the light from the darkness. And God saw that it was good. And there 19 was evening and there was morning, a fourth day.

And God said, "Let the waters bring forth 20 swarms of living creatures, and let birds fly above the earth across the firmament of the heavens." So God created the great sea 21 monsters and every living creature that moves, with which the waters swarm, according to their kinds, and every winged bird

[a] Or When God began to create   [b] Or wind
1.1: Jn 1.1.

I

according to its kind. And God saw that it
22 was good. And God blessed them, saying,
"Be fruitful and multiply and fill the waters
in the seas, and let birds multiply on the
23 earth." And there was evening and there was
morning, a fifth day.
24 And God said, "Let the earth bring forth
living creatures according to their kinds:
cattle and creeping things and beasts of the
earth according to their kinds." And it was
25 so. And God made the beasts of the earth
according to their kinds and the cattle according to their kinds, and everything that
creeps upon the ground according to its
kind. And God saw that it was good.
26 Then God said, "Let us make man in our
image, after our likeness; and let them have
dominion over the fish of the sea, and over
the birds of the air, and over the cattle, and
over all the earth, and over every creeping
27 thing that creeps upon the earth." So God
created man in his own image, in the image
of God he created him; male and female he
28 created them. And God blessed them, and
God said to them, "Be fruitful and multiply,
and fill the earth and subdue it; and have
dominion over the fish of the sea and over the
birds of the air and over every living thing
29 that moves upon the earth." And God said,
"Behold, I have given you every plant yielding seed which is upon the face of all the
earth, and every tree with seed in its fruit;
30 you shall have them for food. And to every
beast of the earth, and to every bird of the
air, and to everything that creeps on the
earth, everything that has the breath of life, I
have given every green plant for food." And
31 it was so. And God saw everything that he
had made, and behold, it was very good.
And there was evening and there was morning, a sixth day.

2 Thus the heavens and the earth were
2 finished, and all the host of them. And
on the seventh day God finished his work
which he had done, and he rested on the
seventh day from all his work which he had
3 done. So God blessed the seventh day and
hallowed it, because on it God rested from all
his work which he had done in creation.
4 These are the generations of the heavens
and the earth when they were created.
In the day that the LORD God made the
5 earth and the heavens, when no plant of
the field was yet in the earth and no herb
of the field had yet sprung up—for the LORD
God had not caused it to rain upon the
earth, and there was no man to till the
6 ground; but a mist[c] went up from the earth

and watered the whole face of the ground—
then the LORD God formed man of dust from 7
the ground, and breathed into his nostrils
the breath of life; and man became a living
being. And the LORD God planted a garden 8
in Eden, in the east; and there he put the
man whom he had formed. And out of the 9
ground the LORD God made to grow every
tree that is pleasant to the sight and good for
food, the tree of life also in the midst of the
garden, and the tree of the knowledge of
good and evil.
A river flowed out of Eden to water the 10
garden, and there it divided and became four
rivers. The name of the first is Pishon; it is 11
the one which flows around the whole land of
Hav'ilah, where there is gold; and the gold of 12
that land is good; bdellium and onyx stone
are there. The name of the second river is 13
Gihon; it is the one which flows around the
whole land of Cush. And the name of the 14
third river is Tigris, which flows east
of Assyria. And the fourth river is the
Euphra'tes.
The LORD God took the man and put him 15
in the garden of Eden to till it and keep it.
And the LORD God commanded the man, 16
saying, "You may freely eat of every tree of
the garden; but of the tree of the knowledge 17
of good and evil you shall not eat, for in the
day that you eat of it you shall die."
Then the LORD God said, "It is not good 18
that the man should be alone; I will make
him a helper fit for him." So out of the 19
ground the LORD God formed every beast of
the field and every bird of the air, and
brought them to the man to see what he
would call them; and whatever the man
called every living creature, that was its
name. The man gave names to all cattle, and 20
to the birds of the air, and to every beast of
the field; but for the man there was not
found a helper fit for him. So the LORD God 21
caused a deep sleep to fall upon the man, and
while he slept took one of his ribs and closed
up its place with flesh; and the rib which the 22
LORD God had taken from the man he made
into a woman and brought her to the man.

[c] Or flood
1.26–27: Gen 5.1; Mt 19.4; Mk 10.6; Col 3.10; Jas 3.9.   2.1–3: Ex 20.11.   2.2: Heb 4.4, 10.
2.7: 1 Cor 15.45, 47.   2.9: Rev 2.7; 22.2, 14, 19.

23 Then the man said,

"This at last is bone of my bones
and flesh of my flesh;
she shall be called Woman,[d]
because she was taken out of Man."[e]

24 Therefore a man leaves his father and his mother and cleaves to his wife, and they 25 become one flesh. And the man and his wife were both naked, and were not ashamed.

The fall

3 Now the serpent was more subtle than any other wild creature that the LORD God had made. He said to the woman, "Did God say, 'You shall not eat of any tree of the 2 garden'?" And the woman said to the serpent, "We may eat of the fruit of the trees 3 of the garden; but God said, 'You shall not eat of the fruit of the tree which is in the midst of the garden, neither shall you touch 4 it, lest you die.'" But the serpent said to the 5 woman, "You will not die. For God knows that when you eat of it your eyes will be opened, and you will be like God, knowing 6 good and evil." So when the woman saw that the tree was good for food, and that it was a delight to the eyes, and that the tree was to be desired to make one wise, she took of its fruit and ate; and she also gave some to 7 her husband, and he ate. Then the eyes of both were opened, and they knew that they were naked; and they sewed fig leaves together and made themselves aprons.

8 And they heard the sound of the LORD God walking in the garden in the cool of the day, and the man and his wife hid themselves from the presence of the LORD God among 9 the trees of the garden. But the LORD God called to the man, and said to him, "Where 10 are you?" And he said, "I heard the sound of thee in the garden, and I was afraid, because I was naked; and I hid myself." He 11 said, "Who told you that you were naked? Have you eaten of the tree of which I commanded you not to eat?" The man said, 12 "The woman whom thou gavest to be with me, she gave me fruit of the tree, and I ate." 13 Then the LORD God said to the woman, "What is this that you have done?" The woman said, "The serpent beguiled me, and I ate." The LORD God said to the serpent,

"Because you have done this,
cursed are you above all cattle,
and above all wild animals;
upon your belly you shall go,
and dust you shall eat
all the days of your life.
I will put enmity between you and the 15 woman,
and between your seed and her seed;
he shall bruise your head,
and you shall bruise his heel."

To the woman he said, 16
"I will greatly multiply your pain in childbearing;
in pain you shall bring forth children,
yet your desire shall be for your husband,
and he shall rule over you."

And to Adam he said, 17
"Because you have listened to the voice of your wife,
and have eaten of the tree
of which I commanded you,
'You shall not eat of it,'
cursed is the ground because of you;
in toil you shall eat of it all the days of your life;
thorns and thistles it shall bring forth to 18 you;
and you shall eat the plants of the field.
In the sweat of your face 19
you shall eat bread
till you return to the ground,
for out of it you were taken;
you are dust,
and to dust you shall return."

The man called his wife's name Eve,[f] 20 because she was the mother of all living. And the LORD God made for Adam and for 21 his wife garments of skins, and clothed them.

Then the LORD God said, "Behold, the man 22 has become like one of us, knowing good and evil; and now, lest he put forth his hand and take also of the tree of life, and eat, and live for ever"—therefore the LORD God sent him 23 forth from the garden of Eden, to till the ground from which he was taken. He drove 24 out the man; and at the east of the garden of Eden he placed the cherubim, and a flaming sword which turned every way, to guard the way to the tree of life.

[d] Heb *ishshah*   [e] Heb *ish*   [f] The name in Hebrew resembles the word for *living*
2.24: Mt 19.5; Mk 10.7; 1 Cor 6.16; Eph 5.31.   **3.1:** Rev 12.9; 20.2.   **3.4:** 2 Cor 11.3.   **3.13:** 2 Cor 11.3.
3.14–15: Rev 12.9; 20.2.   **3.17–18:** Heb 6.8.   **3.22, 24:** Rev 2.7; 22.2, 14, 19.

Cain and Abel

4 Now Adam knew Eve his wife, and she conceived and bore Cain, saying, "I have gotten[g] a man with the help of the LORD." 2 And again, she bore his brother Abel. Now Abel was a keeper of sheep, and Cain a 3 tiller of the ground. In the course of time Cain brought to the LORD an offering of the 4 fruit of the ground, and Abel brought of the firstlings of his flock and of their fat portions. And the LORD had regard for Abel 5 and his offering, but for Cain and his offering he had no regard. So Cain was very angry, 6 and his countenance fell. The LORD said to Cain, "Why are you angry, and why has your 7 countenance fallen? If you do well, will you not be accepted? And if you do not do well, sin is couching at the door; its desire is for you, but you must master it." 8 Cain said to Abel his brother, "Let us go out to the field."[h] And when they were in the field, Cain rose up against his brother 9 Abel, and killed him. Then the LORD said to Cain, "Where is Abel your brother?" He said, "I do not know; am I my brother's 10 keeper?" And the LORD said, "What have you done? The voice of your brother's 11 blood is crying to me from the ground. And now you are cursed from the ground, which has opened its mouth to receive your bro- 12 ther's blood from your hand. When you till the ground, it shall no longer yield to you its strength; you shall be a fugitive and a 13 wanderer on the earth." Cain said to the LORD, "My punishment is greater than I can 14 bear. Behold, thou hast driven me this day away from the ground; and from thy face I shall be hidden; and I shall be a fugitive and a wanderer on the earth, and whoever finds me will slay me." Then the LORD said to 15 him, "Not so![i] If any one slays Cain, vengeance shall be taken on him sevenfold." And the LORD put a mark on Cain, lest any who came upon him should kill him. Then 16 Cain went away from the presence of the LORD, and dwelt in the land of Nod,[j] east of Eden.

Cain knew his wife, and she conceived and 17 bore Enoch; and he built a city, and called the name of the city after the name of his son, Enoch. To Enoch was born Irad; and Irad 18 was the father of Me-hu'ja-el, and Me-hu'-ja-el the father of Me-thu'sha-el, and Me-thu'sha-el the father of Lamech. And 19 Lamech took two wives; the name of the one was Adah, and the name of the other Zillah. Adah bore Jabal; he was the father of those 20 who dwell in tents and have cattle. His 21 brother's name was Jubal; he was the father of all those who play the lyre and pipe. Zillah bore Tubal-cain; he was the forger of 22 all instruments of bronze and iron. The sister of Tubal-cain was Na'amah.

Lamech said to his wives: 23
"Adah and Zillah, hear my voice;
    you wives of Lamech, hearken to what I
      say:
I have slain a man for wounding me,
    a young man for striking me.
If Cain is avenged sevenfold, 24
    truly Lamech seventy-sevenfold."
And Adam knew his wife again, and she 25 bore a son and called his name Seth, for she said, "God has appointed for me another child instead of Abel, for Cain slew him." To Seth also a son was born, and he called 26 his name Enosh. At that time men began to call upon the name of the LORD.

Adam's descendants

5 THIS is the book of the genera- tions of Adam. When God created man, he made him in the 2 likeness of God. Male and female he created them, and he blessed them and named them Man when 3 they were created. When Adam had lived a hundred and thirty years, he became the father of a son in his own likeness, after his 4 image, and named him Seth. The days of Adam after he became the father of Seth were eight hundred years; and he had other sons and 5 daughters. Thus all the days that Adam lived were nine hundred and thirty years; and he died.

6 When Seth had lived a hundred and five years, he became the 7 father of Enosh. Seth lived after the birth of Enosh eight hundred and seven years, and had other 8 sons and daughters. Thus all the days of Seth were nine hundred and twelve years; and he died. 9 When Enosh had lived ninety years, he became the father of 10 Kenan. Enosh lived after the birth of Kenan eight hundred and fifteen years, and had other sons 11 and daughters. Thus all the days of Enosh were nine hundred and five years; and he died. 12 When Kenan had lived seventy years, he became the father of 13 Ma-hal'alel. Kenan lived after

the birth of Ma-hal'alel eight hundred and forty years, and had other sons and daughters. Thus 14 all the days of Kenan were nine hundred and ten years; and he died.

When Ma-hal'alel had lived 15 sixty-five years, he became the father of Jared. Ma-hal'alel lived 16 after the birth of Jared eight hundred and thirty years, and had other sons and daughters. Thus 17 all the days of Ma-hal'alel were eight hundred and ninety-five years; and he died.

When Jared had lived a hundred 18 and sixty-two years he became the father of Enoch. Jared lived after 19 the birth of Enoch eight hundred

---

[g] Heb *qanah*, get   [h] Sam Gk Syr Compare Vg: Heb lacks *Let us go out to the field*
[i] Gk Syr Vg: Heb *Therefore*   [j] That is *Wandering*
4.4: Heb 11.4.   **4.8:** 1 Jn 3.12.   **5.1:** Gen 1.27.

years, and had other sons and
20 daughters. Thus all the days of
Jared were nine hundred and
sixty-two years; and he died.
21 When Enoch had lived sixty-five
years, he became the father of
22 Methu'selah. Enoch walked with
God after the birth of Methu'-
selah three hundred years, and
had other sons and daughters.
23 Thus all the days of Enoch were
three hundred and sixty-five
24 years. Enoch walked with God;
and he was not, for God took him.

25 When Methu'selah had lived a
hundred and eighty-seven years,
he became the father of Lamech.
26 Methu'selah lived after the birth
of Lamech seven hundred and
eighty-two years, and had other
27 sons and daughters. Thus all the
days of Methu'selah were nine
hundred and sixty-nine years; and
he died.
28 When Lamech had lived a
hundred and eighty-two years, he
29 became the father of a son, and
called his name Noah, saying,

"Out of the ground which the
LORD has cursed this one shall
bring us relief from our work and
from the toil of our hands."
Lamech lived after the birth of 30
Noah five hundred and ninety-
five years, and had other sons and
daughters. Thus all the days of 31
Lamech were seven hundred and
seventy-seven years; and he died.
After Noah was five hundred 32
years old, Noah became the father
of Shem, Ham, and Japheth.

6 WHEN men began to multiply on the face
of the ground, and daughters were born
2 to them, the sons of God saw that the
daughters of men were fair; and they took to
3 wife such of them as they chose. Then the
LORD said, "My spirit shall not abide in man
for ever, for he is flesh, but his days shall be
4 a hundred and twenty years." The Nephilim
were on the earth in those days, and also
afterward, when the sons of God came in to
the daughters of men, and they bore children
to them. These were the mighty men that
were of old, the men of renown.
5 The LORD saw that the wickedness of man
was great in the earth, and that every imagination of the thoughts of his heart was only
6 evil continually. And the LORD was sorry
that he had made man on the earth, and it
7 grieved him to his heart. So the LORD said,
"I will blot out man whom I have created
from the face of the ground, man and beast
and creeping things and birds of the air, for I
8 am sorry that I have made them." But Noah
found favour in the eyes of the LORD.
9 These are the generations of Noah. Noah
was a righteous man, blameless in his genera-
10 tion; Noah walked with God. And Noah had
three sons, Shem, Ham, and Japheth.

The ark

11 Now the earth was corrupt in God's sight,
12 and the earth was filled with violence. And

God saw the earth, and behold, it was
corrupt; for all flesh had corrupted their way
upon the earth. And God said to Noah, "I 13
have determined to make an end of all flesh;
for the earth is filled with violence through
them; behold, I will destroy them with the
earth. Make yourself an ark of gopher wood; 14
make rooms in the ark, and cover it inside
and out with pitch. This is how you are to 15
make it: the length of the ark three hundred
cubits, its breadth fifty cubits, and its height
thirty cubits. Make a roof[k] for the ark, and 16
finish it to a cubit above; and set the door of
the ark in its side; make it with lower,
second, and third decks. For behold, I will 17
bring a flood of waters upon the earth, to
destroy all flesh in which is the breath of life
from under heaven; everything that is on the
earth shall die. But I will establish my 18
covenant with you; and you shall come into
the ark, you, your sons, your wife, and your
sons' wives with you. And of every living 19
thing of all flesh, you shall bring two of every
sort into the ark, to keep them alive with you;
they shall be male and female. Of the birds 20
according to their kinds, and of the animals
according to their kinds, of every creeping
thing of the ground according to its kind, two
of every sort shall come in to you, to keep
them alive. Also take with you every sort of 21
food that is eaten, and store it up, and it shall
serve as food for you and for them." Noah 22
did this; he did all that God commanded
him.

Then the LORD said to Noah, "Go into the **7**
ark, you and all your household, for I have
seen that you are righteous before me in
this generation. Take with you seven pairs of 2
all clean animals, the male and his mate; and
a pair of the animals that are not clean, the
male and his mate; and seven pairs of the 3
birds of the air also, male and female, to keep

k Or *window*
5.24: Heb 11.5.   6.4: Num 13.33.

their kind alive upon the face of all the earth.
4 For in seven days I will send rain upon the
earth forty days and forty nights; and every
living thing that I have made I will blot out
5 from the face of the ground." And Noah did
all that the LORD had commanded him.
6 Noah was six hundred years old when the
7 flood of waters came upon the earth. And
Noah and his sons and his wife and his sons'
wives with him went into the ark, to escape
8 the waters of the flood. Of clean animals,
and of animals that are not clean, and of
birds, and of everything that creeps on the
9 ground, two and two, male and female, went
into the ark with Noah, as God had com-
10 manded Noah. And after seven days
the waters of the flood came upon the
earth.

The great flood

11 In the six hundredth year of Noah's life, in
the second month, on the seventeenth day
of the month, on that day all the fountains of
the great deep burst forth, and the windows
12 of the heavens were opened. And rain fell
upon the earth forty days and forty nights.
13 On the very same day Noah and his sons,
Shem and Ham and Japheth, and Noah's
wife and the three wives of his sons with
14 them entered the ark, they and every beast
according to its kind, and all the cattle
according to their kinds, and every creeping
thing that creeps on the earth according to its
kind, and every bird according to its kind,
15 every bird of every sort. They went into the
ark with Noah, two and two of all flesh in
16 which there was the breath of life. And they
that entered, male and female of all flesh,
went in as God had commanded him; and
the LORD shut him in.
17 The flood continued forty days upon the
earth; and the waters increased, and bore up
the ark, and it rose high above the earth.
18 The waters prevailed and increased greatly
upon the earth; and the ark floated on the
19 face of the waters. And the waters prevailed
so mightily upon the earth that all the high
mountains under the whole heaven were
20 covered; the waters prevailed above the
mountains, covering them fifteen cubits
21 deep. And all flesh died that moved upon
the earth, birds, cattle, beasts, all swarming
creatures that swarm upon the earth, and
22 every man; everything on the dry land in
23 whose nostrils was the breath of life died. He
blotted out every living thing that was upon
the face of the ground, man and animals and
creeping things and birds of the air; they

were blotted out from the earth. Only Noah
was left, and those that were with him in the
ark. And the waters prevailed upon the earth 24
a hundred and fifty days.

But God remembered Noah and all the 8
beasts and all the cattle that were with him
in the ark. And God made a wind blow over
the earth, and the waters subsided; the foun- 2
tains of the deep and the windows of the
heavens were closed, the rain from the
heavens was restrained, and the waters 3
receded from the earth continually. At the
end of a hundred and fifty days the waters
had abated; and in the seventh month, on 4
the seventeenth day of the month, the ark
came to rest upon the mountains of Ararat.
And the waters continued to abate until the 5
tenth month; in the tenth month, on the first
day of the month, the tops of the mountains
were seen.
At the end of forty days Noah opened the 6
window of the ark which he had made, and 7
sent forth a raven; and it went to and fro
until the waters were dried up from the
earth. Then he sent forth a dove from him, 8
to see if the waters had subsided from the
face of the ground; but the dove found no 9
place to set her foot, and she returned to him
to the ark, for the waters were still on the face
of the whole earth. So he put forth his hand
and took her and brought her into the ark
with him. He waited another seven days, 10
and again he sent forth the dove out of the
ark; and the dove came back to him in the 11
evening, and lo, in her mouth a freshly
plucked olive leaf; so Noah knew that the
waters had subsided from the earth. Then 12
he waited another seven days, and sent forth
the dove; and she did not return to him any
more.
In the six hundred and first year, in the first 13
month, the first day of the month, the waters
were dried from off the earth; and Noah
removed the covering of the ark, and looked,
and behold, the face of the ground was dry.
In the second month, on the twenty-seventh 14
day of the month, the earth was dry. Then 15
God said to Noah, "Go forth from the ark, 16
you and your wife, and your sons and your
sons' wives with you. Bring forth with you 17
every living thing that is with you of all
flesh—birds and animals and every creeping
thing that creeps on the earth—that they may
breed abundantly on the earth, and be
fruitful and multiply upon the earth." So 18
Noah went forth, and his sons and his wife
and his sons' wives with him. And every 19
beast, every creeping thing, and every bird,

7.7: Mt 24.38; Lk 17.27.

everything that moves upon the earth, went forth by families out of the ark.

20 Then Noah built an altar to the LORD, and took of every clean animal and of every clean bird, and offered burnt offerings on the 21 altar. And when the LORD smelled the pleasing odour, the LORD said in his heart, "I will never again curse the ground because of man, for the imagination of man's heart is evil from his youth; neither will I ever again destroy every living creature as I have done. 22 While the earth remains, seedtime and harvest, cold and heat, summer and winter, day and night, shall not cease."

9 And God blessed Noah and his sons, and said to them, "Be fruitful and multiply, 2 and fill the earth. The fear of you and the dread of you shall be upon every beast of the earth, and upon every bird of the air, upon everything that creeps on the ground and all the fish of the sea; into your hand they are 3 delivered. Every moving thing that lives shall be food for you; and as I gave you the 4 green plants, I give you everything. Only you shall not eat flesh with its life, that is, its 5 blood. For your lifeblood I will surely require a reckoning; of every beast I will require it and of man; of every man's brother 6 I will require the life of man. Whoever sheds the blood of man, by man shall his blood be shed; for God made man in his own image. 7 And you, be fruitful and multiply, bring forth abundantly on the earth and multiply in it."

The rainbow

8 Then God said to Noah and to his sons 9 with him, "Behold, I establish my covenant with you and your descendants after you, 10 and with every living creature that is with you, the birds, the cattle, and every beast of the earth with you, as many as came out of 11 the ark.[l] I establish my covenant with you, that never again shall all flesh be cut off by the waters of a flood, and never again shall

there be a flood to destroy the earth." And 12 God said, "This is the sign of the covenant which I make between me and you and every living creature that is with you, for all future generations: I set my bow in the cloud, and it 13 shall be a sign of the covenant between me and the earth. When I bring clouds over the 14 earth and the bow is seen in the clouds, I will 15 remember my covenant which is between me and you and every living creature of all flesh; and the waters shall never again become a flood to destroy all flesh. When the bow is in 16 the clouds, I will look upon it and remember the everlasting covenant between God and every living creature of all flesh that is upon the earth." God said to Noah, "This is the 17 sign of the covenant which I have established between me and all flesh that is upon the earth."

The sons of Noah who went forth from the 18 ark were Shem, Ham, and Japheth. Ham was the father of Canaan. These three were 19 the sons of Noah; and from these the whole earth was peopled.

Noah was the first tiller of the soil. He 20 planted a vineyard; and he drank of the wine, 21 and became drunk, and lay uncovered in his tent. And Ham, the father of Canaan, saw 22 the nakedness of his father, and told his two brothers outside. Then Shem and Japheth 23 took a garment, laid it upon both their shoulders, and walked backward and covered the nakedness of their father; their faces were turned away, and they did not see their father's nakedness. When Noah awoke from 24 his wine and knew what his youngest son had done to him, he said,   25
    "Cursed be Canaan;
        a slave of slaves shall he be to his
            brothers."
He also said,   26
    "Blessed by the LORD my God be Shem;[m]
        and let Canaan be his slave.
    God enlarge Japheth,   27
        and let him dwell in the tents of Shem;
        and let Canaan be his slave."
After the flood Noah lived three hundred 28 and fifty years. All the days of Noah were 29 nine hundred and fifty years; and he died.

---

[l] Gk: Heb repeats *every beast of the earth* [m] Or *Blessed be the* LORD, *the God of Shem*
9.4: Lev 7.26–27; 17.10–14; Deut 12.16, 23.

8   GENESIS 10

Noah's descendants

10 THESE are the generations of the sons of Noah, Shem, Ham, and Japheth; sons were born to them after the flood.

2 The sons of Japheth: Gomer, Magog, Madai, Javan, Tubal, 3 Meshech, and Tiras. The sons of Gomer: Ash'kenaz, Riphath, and 4 Togar'mah. The sons of Javan: Eli'shah, Tarshish, Kittim, and 5 Do'danim. From these the coastland peoples spread. These are the sons of Japheth[n] in their lands, each with his own language, by their families, in their nations.

6 The sons of Ham: Cush, Egypt, 7 Put, and Canaan. The sons of Cush: Seba, Hav'ilah, Sabtah, Ra'amah, and Sab'teca. The sons of Ra'amah: Sheba and Dedan. 8 Cush became the father of Nimrod; he was the first on earth to be 9 a mighty man. He was a mighty hunter before the LORD; therefore it is said, "Like Nimrod a mighty 10 hunter before the LORD." The beginning of his kingdom was

11 Babel, Erech, and Accad, all of them in the land of Shinar. From that land he went to Assyria, and 12 built Nin'eveh, Reho'both-Ir, Calah, and Resen between Nin'eveh and Calah; that is the great 13 city. Egypt became the father of Ludim, An'amim, Leha'bim, 14 Naph-tu'him, Pathru'sim, Caslu'him (whence came the Philistines), and Caph'torim. 15 Canaan became the father of Sidon his first-born, and Heth, 16 and the Jeb'usites, the Amorites, 17 the Gir'gashites, the Hivites, the 18 Arkites, the Sinites, the Ar'vadites, the Zem'arites, and the Ha'mathites. Afterward the families of the Canaanites spread 19 abroad. And the territory of the Canaanites extended from Sidon, in the direction of Gerar, as far as Gaza, and in the direction of Sodom, Gomor'rah, Admah, and 20 Zeboi'im, as far as Lasha. These are the sons of Ham, by their families, their languages, their lands, and their nations. 21 To Shem also, the father of all the children of Eber, the elder

brother of Japheth, children were born. The sons of Shem: Elam, 22 Asshur, Arpach'shad, Lud, and Aram. The sons of Aram: Uz, 23 Hul, Gether, and Mash. Arpach'- 24 shad became the father of Shelah; and Shelah became the father of Eber. To Eber were born two 25 sons: the name of the one was Peleg,[o] for in his days the earth was divided, and his brother's name was Joktan. Joktan became 26 the father of Almo'dad, Sheleph, Hazarma'veth, Jerah, Hador'am, 27 Uzal, Diklah, Obal, Abim'a-el, 28 Sheba, Ophir, Hav'ilah, and 29 Jobab; all these were the sons of Joktan. The territory in which 30 they lived extended from Mesha in the direction of Sephar to the hill country of the east. These are 31 the sons of Shem, by their families, their languages, their lands, and their nations.

These are the families of the sons 32 of Noah, according to their genealogies, in their nations; and from these the nations spread abroad on the earth after the flood.

11 NOW the whole earth had one language 2 and few words. And as men migrated from the east, they found a plain in the land 3 of Shinar and settled there. And they said to one another, "Come, let us make bricks, and burn them thoroughly." And they had brick 4 for stone, and bitumen for mortar. Then they said, "Come, let us build ourselves a city, and a tower with its top in the heavens, and let us make a name for ourselves, lest we be scattered abroad upon the face of the whole earth." And the LORD came down to 5 see the city and the tower, which the sons of men had built. And the LORD said, "Behold, 6 they are one people, and they have all one language; and this is only the beginning of what they will do; and nothing that they propose to do will now be impossible for them. Come, let us go down, and there 7 confuse their language, that they may not understand one another's speech." So the 8 LORD scattered them abroad from there over the face of all the earth, and they left off building the city. Therefore its name was 9 called Babel, because there the LORD confused[p] the language of all the earth; and from there the LORD scattered them abroad over the face of all the earth.

Ancestors of Abraham

10 THESE are the descendants of Shem. When Shem was a hundred years old, he became the father of Arpach'shad two years 11 after the flood; and Shem lived after the birth of Arpach'shad five hundred years, and had other sons and daughters.

12 When Arpach'shad had lived thirty-five years, he became the 13 father of Shelah; and Arpach'shad lived after the birth of Shelah four hundred and three years, and had other sons and daughters.

14 When Shelah had lived thirty 15 years, he became the father of Eber; and Shelah lived after the birth of Eber four hundred and three years, and had other sons and daughters.

16 When Eber had lived thirty-four 17 years, he became the father of Peleg; and Eber lived after the birth of Peleg four hundred and thirty years, and had other sons and daughters.

18 When Peleg had lived thirty 19 years, he became the father of Re'u; and Peleg lived after the birth of Re'u two hundred and

nine years, and had other sons and daughters.

20 When Re'u had lived thirty-two years, he became the father of 21 Serug; and Re'u lived after the birth of Serug two hundred and seven years, and had other sons and daughters.

22 When Serug had lived thirty years, he became the father of 23 Nahor; and Serug lived after the birth of Nahor two hundred years, and had other sons and daughters.

24 When Nahor had lived twenty-nine years, he became the father

---

[n] Compare verses 20, 31. Heb lacks *These are the sons of Japheth*   [o] That is *Division*
[p] Compare Heb *balal*, confuse

25 of Terah; and Nahor lived after the birth of Terah a hundred and nineteen years, and had other sons and daughters.
26 When Terah had lived seventy years, he became the father of Abram, Nahor, and Haran.
27 Now these are the descendants of Terah. Terah was the father of Abram, Nahor, and Haran; and Haran was the father of Lot.
28 Haran died before his father Terah in the land of his birth, in Ur of the Chalde'ans.
29 And Abram and Nahor took wives; the name of Abram's wife was Sar'ai, and the name of Nahor's wife, Milcah, the daughter of Haran the father of Milcah and Iscah.
30 Now Sar'ai was barren; she had no child.
31 Terah took Abram his son and Lot the son of Haran, his grandson, and Sar'ai his daughter-in-law, his son Abram's wife, and they went forth together from Ur of the Chalde'ans to go into the land of Canaan; but when they came to Haran, they settled there.
32 The days of Terah were two hundred and five years; and Terah died in Haran.

GOD CALLS ABRAHAM

12 NOW THE LORD said to Abram, "Go from your country and your kindred and your father's house to the land that I will
2 show you. And I will make of you a great nation, and I will bless you, and make your
3 name great, so that you will be a blessing. I will bless those who bless you, and him who curses you I will curse; and by you all the families of the earth shall bless themselves."[q]
4 So Abram went, as the LORD had told him; and Lot went with him. Abram was seventy-five years old when he departed
5 from Haran. And Abram took Sar'ai his wife, and Lot his brother's son, and all their possessions which they had gathered, and the persons that they had gotten in Haran; and they set forth to go to the land of Canaan. When they had come to the land of Canaan,
6 Abram passed through the land to the place at Shechem, to the oak[r] of Moreh. At that
7 time the Canaanites were in the land. Then the LORD appeared to Abram, and said, "To your descendants I will give this land." So he built there an altar to the LORD, who had
8 appeared to him. Thence he removed to the mountain on the east of Bethel, and pitched his tent, with Bethel on the west and Ai on the east; and there he built an altar to the LORD and called on the name of the LORD. And Abram journeyed on, still going toward 9 the Negeb.

Now there was a famine in the land. So 10 Abram went down to Egypt to sojourn there, for the famine was severe in the land. When 11 he was about to enter Egypt, he said to Sar'ai his wife, "I know that you are a woman beautiful to behold; and when the Egyptians 12 see you, they will say, 'This is his wife'; then they will kill me, but they will let you live. Say you are my sister, that it may go well 13 with me because of you, and that my life may be spared on your account." When Abram 14 entered Egypt the Egyptians saw that the woman was very beautiful. And when the 15 princes of Pharaoh saw her, they praised her to Pharaoh. And the woman was taken into Pharaoh's house. And for her sake he dealt 16 well with Abram; and he had sheep, oxen, he-asses, menservants, maidservants, she-asses, and camels.

But the LORD afflicted Pharaoh and his 17 house with great plagues because of Sar'ai,

q Or *in you all the families of the earth shall be blessed*   *r* Or *terebinth*
12.1: Acts 7.3; Heb 11.8.   12.2: Gen 15.5; 17.4–5; 18.18; 22.17; 28.14; 32.12; 35.11; 46.3.
12.3: Gen 18.18; 22.17–18; 26.4; 28.14; Gal 3.8.
12.7: Gen 13.15; 15.18; 17.8; 24.7; 26.3; 28.4, 13; 35.12; 48.4; Acts 7.5; Gal 3.16.
12.10–20: Gen 20.1–18; 26.7–11.

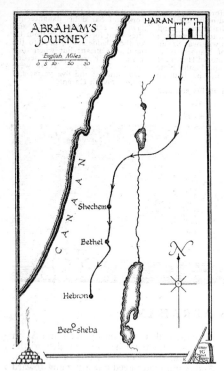

ABRAHAM'S JOURNEY

English Miles
5 5 10   20   30

HARAN

C A N A A N

Shechem

Bethel

Hebron

Beer-sheba

for their possessions were so great that they could not dwell together, and there was strife 7 between the herdsmen of Abram's cattle and the herdsmen of Lot's cattle. At that time the Canaanites and the Per′izzites dwelt in the land.

Then Abram said to Lot, "Let there be no 8 strife between you and me, and between your herdsmen and my herdsmen; for we are kinsmen. Is not the whole land before you? 9 Separate yourself from me. If you take the left hand, then I will go to the right; or if you take the right hand, then I will go to the left." And Lot lifted up his eyes, and saw 10 that the Jordan valley was well watered everywhere like the garden of the LORD, like the land of Egypt, in the direction of Zo′ar; this was before the LORD destroyed Sodom and Gomor′rah. So Lot chose for himself all 11 the Jordan valley, and Lot journeyed east; thus they separated from each other. Abram 12 dwelt in the land of Canaan, while Lot dwelt among the cities of the valley and moved his tent as far as Sodom. Now the men of 13 Sodom were wicked, great sinners against the LORD.

The LORD said to Abram, after Lot had 14 separated from him, "Lift up your eyes, and look from the place where you are, northward and southward and eastward and westward; for all the land which you see I will 15 give to you and to your descendants for ever. I will make your descendants as the dust of 16 the earth; so that if one can count the dust of the earth, your descendants also can be counted. Arise, walk through the length and 17 the breadth of the land, for I will give it to you." So Abram moved his tent, and came 18 and dwelt by the oaks⁸ of Mamre, which are at Hebron; and there he built an altar to the LORD.

18 Abram's wife. So Pharaoh called Abram, and said, "What is this you have done to me? Why did you not tell me that she was 19 your wife? Why did you say, 'She is my sister,' so that I took her for my wife? Now then, here is your wife, take her, and be 20 gone." And Pharaoh gave men orders concerning him; and they set him on the way, with his wife and all that he had.

Abraham and Lot

13 So Abram went up from Egypt, he and his wife, and all that he had, and Lot with him, into the Negeb.
2 Now Abram was very rich in cattle, in
3 silver, and in gold. And he journeyed on from the Negeb as far as Bethel, to the place where his tent had been at the beginning,
4 between Bethel and Ai, to the place where he had made an altar at the first; and there
5 Abram called on the name of the LORD. And Lot, who went with Abram, also had flocks
6 and herds and tents, so that the land could not support both of them dwelling together;

⁸ Or terebinths
13.15: Acts 7.5; Gal 3.16.

In the days of Am′raphel king of Shinar, 14 Ar′i-och king of Ella′sar, Ched-or-lao′mer king of Elam, and Tidal king of Goi′im, these kings made war with Bera king of 2 Sodom, Birsha king of Gomor′rah, Shinab king of Admah, Sheme′ber king of Zeboi′im, and the king of Bela (that is, Zo′ar). And all 3 these joined forces in the Valley of Siddim (that is, the Salt Sea). Twelve years they had 4 served Ched-or-lao′mer, but in the thirteenth year they rebelled. In the fourteenth 5 year Ched-or-lao′mer and the kings who were with him came and subdued the Reph′aim in Ash′teroth-karna′im, the Zuzim in Ham, the Emim in Sha′veh-kiriatha′im, and the Horites in their Mount Se′ir as far as 6 El-paran on the border of the wilderness; then they turned back and came to En-mish′- 7 pat (that is, Kadesh), and subdued all the country of the Amal'ekites, and also the Amorites who dwelt in Haz'azon-ta'mar.

8 Then the king of Sodom, the king of Gomor'rah, the king of Admah, the king of Zeboi'im, and the king of Bela (that is, Zo'ar) went out, and they joined battle in the Valley 9 of Siddim with Ched-or-lao'mer king of Elam, Tidal king of Goi'im, Am'raphel king of Shinar, and Ar'i-och king of Ella'sar, four 10 kings against five. Now the Valley of Siddim was full of bitumen pits; and as the kings of Sodom and Gomor'rah fled, some fell into 11 them, and the rest fled to the mountain. So the enemy took all the goods of Sodom and Gomor'rah, and all their provisions, and 12 went their way; they also took Lot, the son of Abram's brother, who dwelt in Sodom, and his goods, and departed.

13 Then one who had escaped came, and told Abram the Hebrew, who was living by the oaks[8] of Mamre the Amorite, brother of Eshcol and of Aner; these were allies of 14 Abram. When Abram heard that his kinsman had been taken captive, he led forth his trained men, born in his house, three hundred and eighteen of them, and went in 15 pursuit as far as Dan. And he divided his forces against them by night, he and his servants, and routed them and pursued them 16 to Hobah, north of Damascus. Then he brought back all the goods, and also brought back his kinsman Lot with his goods, and the women and the people.

17 After his return from the defeat of Ched-or-lao'mer and the kings who were with him, the king of Sodom went out to meet him at the Valley of Shaveh (that is, the 18 King's Valley). And Melchiz'edek king of Salem brought out bread and wine; he was 19 priest of God Most High. And he blessed him and said,

"Blessed be Abram by God Most High, maker of heaven and earth;
20 and blessed be God Most High, who has delivered your enemies into your hand!"

And Abram gave him a tenth of everything. 21 And the king of Sodom said to Abram, "Give me the persons, but take the goods for 22 yourself." But Abram said to the king of Sodom, "I have sworn to the LORD God 23 Most High, maker of heaven and earth, that I would not take a thread or a sandal-thong or anything that is yours, lest you should say, 'I 24 have made Abram rich.' I will take nothing but what the young men have eaten, and the share of the men who went with me; let Aner, Eshcol, and Mamre take their share."

The covenant

After these things the word of the LORD 15 came to Abram in a vision, "Fear not, Abram, I am your shield; your reward shall be very great." But Abram said, "O Lord 2 GOD, what wilt thou give me, for I continue childless, and the heir of my house is Elie'zer of Damascus?" And Abram said, "Behold, 3 thou hast given me no offspring; and a slave born in my house will be my heir." And 4 behold, the word of the LORD came to him, "This man shall not be your heir; your own son shall be your heir." And he brought him 5 outside and said, "Look toward heaven, and number the stars, if you are able to number them." Then he said to him, "So shall your descendants be." And he believed the LORD; 6 and he reckoned it to him as righteousness.

And he said to him, "I am the LORD who 7 brought you from Ur of the Chalde'ans, to give you this land to possess." But he said, 8 "O Lord GOD, how am I to know that I shall possess it?" He said to him, "Bring me a 9 heifer three years old, a she-goat three years old, a ram three years old, a turtledove, and a young pigeon." And he brought him all 10 these, cut them in two, and laid each half over against the other; but he did not cut the birds in two. And when birds of prey came 11 down upon the carcasses, Abram drove them away.

As the sun was going down, a deep sleep fell 12 on Abram; and lo, a dread and great darkness fell upon him. Then the LORD said 13 to Abram, "Know of a surety that your descendants will be sojourners in a land that is not theirs, and will be slaves there, and they will be oppressed for four hundred years; but I will bring judgment on the 14 nation which they serve, and afterward they shall come out with great possessions. As for 15 yourself, you shall go to your fathers in peace; you shall be buried in a good old age. And they shall come back here in the fourth 16 generation; for the iniquity of the Amorites is not yet complete."

When the sun had gone down and it was 17 dark, behold, a smoking fire pot and a flaming torch passed between these pieces. On that day the LORD made a covenant with 18 Abram, saying, "To your descendants I give this land, from the river of Egypt to the great river, the river Euphra'tes, the land of the 19 Ken'ites, the Ken'izzites, the Kad'monites, the Hittites, the Per'izzites, the Reph'aim, 20 the Amorites, the Canaanites, the Gir'gash- 21 ites and the Jeb'usites."

---

[8] Or terebinths

14.17–20: Heb 7.1–10. 15.4: Gen 17.16, 21; 18.10; 21.2. 15.5: Rom 4.18; Heb 11.12.
15.6: Rom 4.3, 9, 22, 23; Gal 3.6. 15.13–14: Acts 7.6–7. 15.18: Gen 17.2, 7, 9–14, 21.

16 Now Sar'ai, Abram's wife, bore him no children. She had an Egyptian maid 2 whose name was Hagar; and Sar'ai said to Abram, "Behold now, the LORD has prevented me from bearing children; go in to my maid; it may be that I shall obtain children by her." And Abram hearkened to 3 the voice of Sar'ai. So, after Abram had dwelt ten years in the land of Canaan, Sar'ai, Abram's wife, took Hagar the Egyptian, her maid, and gave her to Abram her husband as 4 a wife. And he went in to Hagar, and she conceived; and when she saw that she had conceived, she looked with contempt on her 5 mistress. And Sar'ai said to Abram, "May the wrong done to me be on you! I gave my maid to your embrace, and when she saw that she had conceived, she looked on me with contempt. May the LORD judge between you 6 and me!" But Abram said to Sar'ai, "Behold, your maid is in your power; do to her as you please." Then Sar'ai dealt harshly with her, and she fled from her.

7 The angel of the LORD found her by a spring of water in the wilderness, the spring 8 on the way to Shur. And he said, "Hagar, maid of Sar'ai, where have you come from and where are you going?" She said, "I am 9 fleeing from my mistress Sar'ai." The angel of the LORD said to her, "Return to your 10 mistress, and submit to her." The angel of the LORD also said to her, "I will so greatly multiply your descendants that they cannot 11 be numbered for multitude." And the angel of the LORD said to her, "Behold, you are with child, and shall bear a son; you shall call his name Ish'mael;[t] because the LORD has 12 given heed to your affliction. He shall be a wild ass of a man, his hand against every man and every man's hand against him; and he 13 shall dwell over against all his kinsmen." So she called the name of the LORD who spoke to her, "Thou art a God of seeing"; for she said, "Have I really seen God and remained 14 alive after seeing him?"[u] Therefore the well was called Beer-la'hai-roi;[v] it lies between Kadesh and Bered.

15 And Hagar bore Abram a son; and Abram called the name of his son, whom Hagar 16 bore, Ish'mael. Abram was eighty-six years old when Hagar bore Ish'mael to Abram.

17 When Abram was ninety-nine years old the LORD appeared to Abram, and said to him, "I am God Almighty;[w] walk before 2 me, and be blameless. And I will make my covenant between me and you, and will

multiply you exceedingly." Then Abram fell 3 on his face; and God said to him, "Behold, 4 my covenant is with you, and you shall be the father of a multitude of nations. No longer 5 shall your name be Abram,[x] but your name shall be Abraham;[y] for I have made you the father of a multitude of nations. I will make 6 you exceedingly fruitful; and I will make nations of you, and kings shall come forth from you. And I will establish my covenant 7 between me and you and your descendants after you throughout their generations for an everlasting covenant, to be God to you and to your descendants after you. And I will give 8 to you, and to your descendants after you, the land of your sojournings, all the land of Canaan, for an everlasting possession; and I will be their God."

And God said to Abraham, "As for you, 9 you shall keep my covenant, you and your descendants after you throughout their generations. This is my covenant, which you 10 shall keep, between me and you and your descendants after you: Every male among you shall be circumcised. You shall be 11 circumcised in the flesh of your foreskins, and it shall be a sign of the covenant between me and you. He that is eight days old among 12 you shall be circumcised; every male throughout your generations, whether born in your house, or bought with your money from any foreigner who is not of your offspring, both he that is born in your house 13 and he that is bought with your money, shall be circumcised. So shall my covenant be in your flesh an everlasting covenant. Any 14 uncircumcised male who is not circumcised in the flesh of his foreskin shall be cut off from his people; he has broken my covenant."

And God said to Abraham, "As for Sar'ai 15 your wife, you shall not call her name Sar'ai, but Sarah shall be her name. I will bless her, 16 and moreover I will give you a son by her; I will bless her, and she shall be a mother of nations; kings of peoples shall come from her." Then Abraham fell on his face and 17 laughed, and said to himself, "Shall a child be born to a man who is a hundred years old? Shall Sarah, who is ninety years old, bear a child?" And Abraham said to God, 18 "O that Ish'mael might live in thy sight!" God said, "No, but Sarah your wife shall 19 bear you a son, and you shall call his name Isaac.[z] I will establish my covenant with him as an everlasting covenant for his descendants after him. As for Ish'mael, I 20

---

[t] That is *God hears*   [u] Cn: Heb *have I even here seen after him who sees me?*
[v] That is *the well of one who sees and lives*   [w] Heb *El Shaddai*   [x] That is *exalted father*
[y] Here taken to mean *father of a multitude*   [z] That is *he laughs*
17.5: Rom 4.17.   **17.7:** Lk 1.55; Gal 3.16.   **17.8:** Acts 7.5.   **17.10:** Acts 7.8.   **17.11-14:** Gen 17.24; 21.4.

have heard you; behold, I will bless him and make him fruitful and multiply him exceedingly; he shall be the father of twelve princes, 21 and I will make him a great nation. But I will establish my covenant with Isaac, whom Sarah shall bear to you at this season next year." 22 When he had finished talking with him, 23 God went up from Abraham. Then Abraham took Ish'mael his son and all the slaves born in his house or bought with his money, every male among the men of Abraham's house, and he circumcised the flesh of their foreskins that very day, as God had said to 24 him. Abraham was ninety-nine years old when he was circumcised in the flesh of his 25 foreskin. And Ish'mael his son was thirteen years old when he was circumcised in the 26 flesh of his foreskin. That very day Abraham 27 and his son Ish'mael were circumcised; and all the men of his house, those born in the house and those bought with money from a foreigner, were circumcised with him.

18 And the LORD appeared to him by the oaks[a] of Mamre, as he sat at the door of 2 his tent in the heat of the day. He lifted up his eyes and looked, and behold, three men stood in front of him. When he saw them, he ran from the tent door to meet them, and 3 bowed himself to the earth, and said, "My lord, if I have found favour in your sight, do 4 not pass by your servant. Let a little water be brought, and wash your feet, and rest 5 yourselves under the tree, while I fetch a morsel of bread, that you may refresh yourselves, and after that you may pass on—since you have come to your servant." So they said, 6 "Do as you have said." And Abraham hastened into the tent to Sarah, and said, "Make ready quickly three measures[b] of fine meal, knead it, and make cakes." And 7 Abraham ran to the herd, and took a calf, tender and good, and gave it to the servant, who hastened to prepare it. Then he took 8 curds, and milk, and the calf which he had prepared, and set it before them; and he stood by them under the tree while they ate.

They said to him, "Where is Sarah your 9 wife?" And he said, "She is in the tent." The LORD said, "I will surely return to you 10 in the spring, and Sarah your wife shall have a son." And Sarah was listening at the tent door behind him. Now Abraham and Sarah 11 were old, advanced in age; it had ceased to be with Sarah after the manner of women. So 12 Sarah laughed to herself, saying, "After I have grown old, and my husband is old, shall I have pleasure?" The LORD said to Abra- 13 ham, "Why did Sarah laugh, and say, 'Shall I indeed bear a child, now that I am old?' Is 14 anything too hard[c] for the LORD? At the appointed time I will return to you, in the spring, and Sarah shall have a son." But 15 Sarah denied, saying, "I did not laugh"; for she was afraid. He said, "No, but you did laugh."

The cities of the valley

Then the men set out from there, and they 16 looked toward Sodom; and Abraham went with them to set them on their way. The 17

A family encampment

[a] Or *terebinths*   [b] Heb *seahs*   [c] Or *wonderful*
18.10: Rom 9.9.   **18.12**: 1 Pet 3.6.   **18.14**: Mt 19.26; Mk 10.27; Lk 1.37; Rom 9.9.

LORD said, "Shall I hide from Abraham what
18 I am about to do, seeing that Abraham shall
become a great and mighty nation, and all the
nations of the earth shall bless themselves by
19 him?[d] No, for I have chosen[e] him, that he
may charge his children and his household
after him to keep the way of the LORD by
doing righteousness and justice; so that the
LORD may bring to Abraham what he has
20 promised him." Then the LORD said,
"Because the outcry against Sodom and
Gomor′rah is great and their sin is very
21 grave, I will go down to see whether they
have done altogether according to the outcry
which has come to me; and if not, I will
know."

22 So the men turned from there, and went
toward Sodom; but Abraham still stood
23 before the LORD. Then Abraham drew near,
and said, "Wilt thou indeed destroy the
24 righteous with the wicked? Suppose there
are fifty righteous within the city; wilt thou
then destroy the place and not spare it for the
25 fifty righteous who are in it? Far be it from
thee to do such a thing, to slay the righteous
with the wicked, so that the righteous fare as
the wicked! Far be that from thee! Shall
not the Judge of all the earth do right?"
26 And the LORD said, "If I find at Sodom fifty
righteous in the city, I will spare the whole
27 place for their sake." Abraham answered,
"Behold, I have taken upon myself to speak
to the Lord, I who am but dust and ashes.
28 Suppose five of the fifty righteous are
lacking? Wilt thou destroy the whole city
for lack of five?" And he said, "I will not
29 destroy it if I find forty-five there." Again
he spoke to him, and said, "Suppose forty are
found there." He answered, "For the sake of
30 forty I will not do it." Then he said, "Oh
let not the Lord be angry, and I will
speak. Suppose thirty are found there." He
answered, "I will not do it, if I find thirty
31 there." He said, "Behold, I have taken upon
myself to speak to the Lord. Suppose twenty
are found there." He answered, "For the
32 sake of twenty I will not destroy it." Then
he said, "Oh let not the Lord be angry, and I
will speak again but this once. Suppose ten
are found there." He answered, "For the
33 sake of ten I will not destroy it." And the
LORD went his way, when he had finished
speaking to Abraham; and Abraham returned to his place.

19 The two angels came to Sodom in the
evening; and Lot was sitting in the gate of
Sodom. When Lot saw them, he rose to
meet them, and bowed himself with his face

to the earth, and said, "My lords, turn aside, 2
I pray you, to your servant's house and spend
the night, and wash your feet; then you may
rise up early and go on your way." They
said, "No; we will spend the night in the
street." But he urged them strongly; so they 3
turned aside to him and entered his house;
and he made them a feast, and baked unleavened bread, and they ate. But before 4
they lay down, the men of the city, the men
of Sodom, both young and old, all the people
to the last man, surrounded the house; and 5
they called to Lot, "Where are the men who
came to you tonight? Bring them out to us,
that we may know them." Lot went out of 6
the door to them, shut the door after him,
and said, "I beg you, my brothers, do not act 7
so wickedly. Behold, I have two daughters 8
who have not known man; let me bring them
out to you, and do to them as you please;
only do nothing to these men, for they have
come under the shelter of my roof." But 9
they said, "Stand back!" And they said,
"This fellow came to sojourn, and he would
play the judge! Now we will deal worse with
you than with them." Then they pressed
hard against the man Lot, and drew near to
break the door. But the men put forth their 10
hands and brought Lot into the house to
them, and shut the door. And they struck 11
with blindness the men who were at the door
of the house, both small and great, so that
they wearied themselves groping for the
door.

Then the men said to Lot, "Have you any 12
one else here? Sons-in-law, sons, daughters,
or any one you have in the city, bring them
out of the place; for we are about to destroy 13
this place, because the outcry against its
people has become great before the LORD,
and the LORD has sent us to destroy it." So 14
Lot went out and said to his sons-in-law,
who were to marry his daughters, "Up, get
out of this place; for the LORD is about to
destroy the city." But he seemed to his
sons-in-law to be jesting.

When morning dawned, the angels urged 15
Lot, saying, "Arise, take your wife and your
two daughters who are here, lest you be
consumed in the punishment of the city."
But he lingered; so the men seized him and 16
his wife and his two daughters by the hand,
the LORD being merciful to him, and they
brought him forth and set him outside the
city. And when they had brought them 17
forth, they[f] said, "Flee for your life; do not
look back or stop anywhere in the valley; flee
to the hills, lest you be consumed." And Lot 18
said to them, "Oh, no, my lords; behold, 19
your servant has found favour in your sight,

[d] Or in him all the nations of the earth shall be blessed
18.18: Gen 12.3; Acts 3.25; Gal 3.8.　　[e] Heb known　[f] Gk Syr Vg: Heb he

and you have shown me great kindness in saving my life; but I cannot flee to the hills, lest the disaster overtake me, and I die. Behold, yonder city is near enough to flee to, and it is a little one. Let me escape there—is it not a little one?—and my life will be 1 saved!" He said to him, "Behold, I grant you this favour also, that I will not overthrow 2 the city of which you have spoken. Make haste, escape there; for I can do nothing till you arrive there." Therefore the name of the 3 city was called Zo'ar.⁹ The sun had risen on the earth when Lot came to Zo'ar.

4 Then the LORD rained on Sodom and Gomor'rah brimstone and fire from the 5 LORD out of heaven; and he overthrew those cities, and all the valley, and all the inhabitants of the cities, and what grew on the 6 ground. But Lot's wife behind him looked 7 back, and she became a pillar of salt. And Abraham went early in the morning to the place where he had stood before the LORD; 8 and he looked down toward Sodom and Gomor'rah and toward all the land of the valley, and beheld, and lo, the smoke of the land went up like the smoke of a furnace. 9 So it was that, when God destroyed the cities of the valley, God remembered Abraham, and sent Lot out of the midst of the overthrow, when he overthrew the cities in which Lot dwelt.

10 Now Lot went up out of Zo'ar, and dwelt in the hills with his two daughters, for he was afraid to dwell in Zo'ar; so he dwelt in a cave 11 with his two daughters. And the first-born said to the younger, "Our father is old, and there is not a man on earth to come in to us 12 after the manner of all the earth. Come, let us make our father drink wine, and we will lie with him, that we may preserve offspring 13 through our father." So they made their father drink wine that night; and the first-born went in, and lay with her father; he did not know when she lay down or when she 14 arose. And on the next day, the first-born said to the younger, "Behold, I lay last night with my father; let us make him drink wine tonight also; then you go in and lie with him, that we may preserve offspring through our 15 father." So they made their father drink wine that night also; and the younger arose, and lay with him; and he did not know when 16 she lay down or when she arose. Thus both the daughters of Lot were with child by their 17 father. The first-born bore a son, and called his name Moab; he is the father of the 38 Moabites to this day. The younger also bore a son, and called his name Ben-ammi; he is the father of the Ammonites to this day.

Abraham and Abimelech

From there Abraham journeyed toward 20 the territory of the Negeb, and dwelt between Kadesh and Shur; and he sojourned in Gerar. And Abraham said of Sarah his 2 wife, "She is my sister." And Abim'elech king of Gerar sent and took Sarah. But God 3 came to Abim'elech in a dream by night, and said to him, "Behold, you are a dead man, because of the woman whom you have taken; for she is a man's wife." Now Abim'elech 4 had not approached her; so he said, "Lord, wilt thou slay an innocent people? Did he 5 not himself say to me, 'She is my sister'? And she herself said, 'He is my brother.' In the integrity of my heart and the innocence of my hands I have done this." Then God 6 said to him in the dream, "Yes, I know that you have done this in the integrity of your heart, and it was I who kept you from sinning against me; therefore I did not let you touch her. Now then restore the man's wife; for he 7 is a prophet, and he will pray for you, and you shall live. But if you do not restore her, know that you shall surely die, you, and all that are yours."

So Abim'elech rose early in the morning, 8 and called all his servants, and told them all these things; and the men were very much afraid. Then Abim'elech called Abraham, 9 and said to him, "What have you done to us? And how have I sinned against you, that you have brought on me and my kingdom a great sin? You have done to me things that ought not to be done." And Abim'elech said 10 to Abraham, "What were you thinking of, that you did this thing?" Abraham said, "I 11 did it because I thought, There is no fear of God at all in this place, and they will kill me because of my wife. Besides she is indeed my 12 sister, the daughter of my father but not the daughter of my mother; and she became my wife. And when God caused me to wander 13 from my father's house, I said to her, 'This is the kindness you must do me: at every place to which we come, say of me, He is my brother.'" Then Abim'elech took sheep and 14 oxen, and male and female slaves, and gave them to Abraham, and restored Sarah his wife to him. And Abim'elech said, "Behold, 15 my land is before you; dwell where it pleases you." To Sarah he said, "Behold, I have 16 given your brother a thousand pieces of silver; it is your vindication in the eyes of all who are with you; and before every one you are righted." Then Abraham prayed to 17 God; and God healed Abim'elech, and also healed his wife and female slaves so that they

⁹ That is *Little*
19.24-25: Lk 17.29.   19.26: Lk 17.32.   19.28: Rev 9.2.

18 bore children. For the LORD had closed all the wombs of the house of Abim'elech because of Sarah, Abraham's wife.

ISAAC

21 THE LORD visited Sarah as he had said, and the LORD did to Sarah as he had 2 promised. And Sarah conceived, and bore Abraham a son in his old age at the time of 3 which God had spoken to him. Abraham called the name of his son who was born to 4 him, whom Sarah bore him, Isaac. And Abraham circumcised his son Isaac when he was eight days old, as God had commanded 5 him. Abraham was a hundred years old 6 when his son Isaac was born to him. And Sarah said, "God has made laughter for me; every one who hears will laugh over me." 7 And she said, "Who would have said to Abraham that Sarah would suckle children? Yet I have borne him a son in his old age." 8 And the child grew, and was weaned; and Abraham made a great feast on the day that 9 Isaac was weaned. But Sarah saw the son of Hagar the Egyptian, whom she had borne to 10 Abraham, playing with her son Isaac.[h] So she said to Abraham, "Cast out this slave woman with her son; for the son of this slave woman shall not be heir with my son Isaac." 11 And the thing was very displeasing to 12 Abraham on account of his son. But God said to Abraham, "Be not displeased because of the lad and because of your slave woman; whatever Sarah says to you, do as she tells you, for through Isaac shall your descendants 13 be named. And I will make a nation of the son of the slave woman also, because he is 14 your offspring." So Abraham rose early in the morning, and took bread and a skin of water, and gave it to Hagar, putting it on her shoulder, along with the child, and sent her away. And she departed, and wandered in the wilderness of Beer-sheba. 15 When the water in the skin was gone, she 16 cast the child under one of the bushes. Then she went, and sat down over against him a good way off, about the distance of a bow-shot; for she said, "Let me not look upon the death of the child." And as she sat over against him, the child lifted up his voice[i] and 17 wept. And God heard the voice of the lad; and the angel of God called to Hagar from heaven, and said to her, "What troubles you, Hagar? Fear not; for God has heard the 18 voice of the lad where he is. Arise, lift up the lad, and hold him fast with your hand; for I 19 will make him a great nation." Then God opened her eyes, and she saw a well of water;

and she went, and filled the skin with water, and gave the lad a drink. And God was with 2 the lad, and he grew up; he lived in the wilderness, and became an expert with the bow. He lived in the wilderness of Paran; 2 and his mother took a wife for him from the land of Egypt.

At that time Abim'elech and Phicol the 2 commander of his army said to Abraham, "God is with you in all that you do; now 2 therefore swear to me here by God that you will not deal falsely with me or with my offspring or with my posterity, but as I have dealt loyally with you, you will deal with me and with the land where you have sojourned." And Abraham said, "I will 24 swear."

When Abraham complained to Abim'elech 25 about a well of water which Abim'elech's servants had seized, Abim'elech said, "I do 26 not know who has done this thing; you did not tell me, and I have not heard of it until today." So Abraham took sheep and oxen 27 and gave them to Abim'elech, and the two men made a covenant. Abraham set seven 28 ewe lambs of the flock apart. And Abim'- 29 elech said to Abraham, "What is the meaning of these seven ewe lambs which you have set apart?" He said, "These seven ewe lambs 30 you will take from my hand, that you may be a witness for me that I dug this well." Therefore that place was called Beer-sheba;[j] 31 because there both of them swore an oath. So they made a covenant at Beer-sheba. 32 Then Abim'elech and Phicol the commander of his army rose up and returned to the land of the Philistines. Abraham planted a 33 tamarisk tree in Beer-sheba, and called there on the name of the LORD, the Everlasting God. And Abraham sojourned many days in 34 the land of the Philistines.

Offering of Isaac

After these things God tested Abraham, 22 and said to him, "Abraham!" And he said, "Here am I." He said, "Take your son, 2 your only son Isaac, whom you love, and go to the land of Mori'ah, and offer him there as

[h] Gk Vg: Heb lacks *with her son Isaac*   [i] Gk: Heb *she lifted up her voice*
[j] That is *Well of seven* or *Well of the oath*
21.4: Acts 7.8.   21.10: Gal 4.30.   21.12: Rom 9.7; Heb 11.18.   21.31: Gen 26.33.   22.1–18: Heb 11.17–19.

a burnt offering upon one of the mountains 3 of which I shall tell you." So Abraham rose early in the morning, saddled his ass, and took two of his young men with him, and his son Isaac; and he cut the wood for the burnt offering, and arose and went to the place of 4 which God had told him. On the third day Abraham lifted up his eyes and saw the place 5 afar off. Then Abraham said to his young men, "Stay here with the ass; I and the lad will go yonder and worship, and come again 6 to you." And Abraham took the wood of the burnt offering, and laid it on Isaac his son; and he took in his hand the fire and the knife. 7 So they went both of them together. And Isaac said to his father Abraham, "My father!" And he said, "Here am I, my son." He said, "Behold, the fire and the wood; but where is the lamb for a burnt offering?" 8 Abraham said, "God will provide himself the lamb for a burnt offering, my son." So they went both of them together.

9 When they came to the place of which God had told him, Abraham built an altar there, and laid the wood in order, and bound Isaac his son, and laid him on the altar, upon the 10 wood. Then Abraham put forth his hand, 11 and took the knife to slay his son. But the angel of the LORD called to him from heaven, and said, "Abraham, Abraham!" And he 12 said, "Here am I." He said, "Do not lay your hand on the lad or do anything to him; for now I know that you fear God, seeing you have not withheld your son, your only son, 13 from me." And Abraham lifted up his eyes and looked, and behold, behind him was a ram, caught in a thicket by his horns; and Abraham went and took the ram, and offered it up as a burnt offering instead of his son. 14 So Abraham called the name of that place The LORD will provide;[k] as it is said to this day, "On the mount of the LORD it shall be provided."[l]

15 And the angel of the LORD called to Abra-16 ham a second time from heaven, and said, "By myself I have sworn, says the LORD, because you have done this, and have not 17 withheld your son, your only son, I will indeed bless you, and I will multiply your descendants as the stars of heaven and as the sand which is on the seashore. And your descendants shall possess the gate of their 18 enemies, and by your descendants shall all the nations of the earth bless themselves, 19 because you have obeyed my voice." So Abraham returned to his young men, and they arose and went together to Beer-sheba; and Abraham dwelt at Beer-sheba.

20 Now after these things it was told Abraham,

"Behold, Milcah also has borne children to your brother Nahor: Uz the first-born, Buz 21 his brother, Kemu'el the father of Aram, Chesed, Hazo, Pildash, Jidlaph, and 22 Bethu'el." Bethu'el became the father of 23 Rebekah. These eight Milcah bore to Nahor, Abraham's brother. Moreover, his 24 concubine, whose name was Reumah, bore Tebah, Gaham, Tahash, and Ma'acah.

Sarah lived a hundred and twenty-seven 23 years; these were the years of the life of Sarah. And Sarah died at Kir'iath-ar'ba 2 (that is, Hebron) in the land of Canaan; and Abraham went in to mourn for Sarah and to weep for her. And Abraham rose up from 3 before his dead, and said to the Hittites, "I 4 am a stranger and a sojourner among you; give me property among you for a burying place, that I may bury my dead out of my sight." The Hittites answered Abraham, 5 "Hear us, my lord; you are a mighty prince 6 among us. Bury your dead in the choicest of our sepulchres; none of us will withhold

from you his sepulchre, or hinder you from burying your dead." Abraham rose and 7 bowed to the Hittites, the people of the land. And he said to them, "If you are willing that 8 I should bury my dead out of my sight, hear me, and entreat for me Ephron the son of Zohar, that he may give me the cave of 9 Mach-pe'lah, which he owns; it is at the end of his field. For the full price let him give it to me in your presence as a possession for a burying place." Now Ephron was sitting 10 among the Hittites; and Ephron the Hittite answered Abraham in the hearing of the Hittites, of all who went in at the gate of his city, "No, my lord, hear me; I give you the 11 field, and I give you the cave that is in it; in

k Or see l Or he will be seen
22.9–10, 12: Jas 2.21. 22.16–17: Lk 1.73; Heb 6.13–14; 11.12. 22.18: Acts 3.25; Gal 3.16.
23.4: Heb 11.9, 13.

the presence of the sons of my people I give it
12 to you; bury your dead." Then Abraham
bowed down before the people of the land.
13 And he said to Ephron in the hearing of the
people of the land, "But if you will, hear me;
I will give the price of the field; accept it from
14 me, that I may bury my dead there." Ephron
15 answered Abraham, "My lord, listen to
me; a piece of land worth four hundred
shekels of silver, what is that between you
16 and me? Bury your dead." Abraham agreed
with Ephron; and Abraham weighed out for
Ephron the silver which he had named in the
hearing of the Hittites, four hundred shekels
of silver, according to the weights current
among the merchants.
17 So the field of Ephron in Mach-pe'lah,
which was to the east of Mamre, the field
with the cave which was in it and all the trees
that were in the field, throughout its whole
18 area, was made over to Abraham as a possession in the presence of the Hittites, before all
19 who went in at the gate of his city. After this,
Abraham buried Sarah his wife in the cave of
the field of Mach-pe'lah east of Mamre (that
20 is, Hebron) in the land of Canaan. The field
and the cave that is in it were made over to
Abraham as a possession for a burying place
by the Hittites.

Isaac and Rebekah

24 Now Abraham was old, well advanced in
years; and the LORD had blessed Abra-
2 ham in all things. And Abraham said to his
servant, the oldest of his house, who had
charge of all that he had, "Put your hand
3 under my thigh, and I will make you swear
by the LORD, the God of heaven and of the
earth, that you will not take a wife for my son
from the daughters of the Canaanites, among
4 whom I dwell, but will go to my country and
to my kindred, and take a wife for my son
5 Isaac." The servant said to him, "Perhaps
the woman may not be willing to follow
me to this land; must I then take your son
back to the land from which you came?"
6 Abraham said to him, "See to it that you do
7 not take my son back there. The LORD, the
God of heaven, who took me from my
father's house and from the land of my birth,
and who spoke to me and swore to me, 'To
your descendants I will give this land,' he
will send his angel before you, and you shall
8 take a wife for my son from there. But if the
woman is not willing to follow you, then you
will be free from this oath of mine; only you
9 must not take my son back there." So the
servant put his hand under the thigh of
Abraham his master, and swore to him
concerning this matter.

23.16–17: Acts 7.16.

Then the servant took ten of his master's 10
camels and departed, taking all sorts of
choice gifts from his master; and he arose,
and went to Mesopota'mia, to the city of
Nahor. And he made the camels kneel down 11
outside the city by the well of water at the
time of evening, the time when women go
out to draw water. And he said, "O LORD, 12
God of my master Abraham, grant me success
today, I pray thee, and show steadfast love to
my master Abraham. Behold, I am standing 13
by the spring of water, and the daughters of
the men of the city are coming out to draw
water. Let the maiden to whom I shall say, 14
'Pray let down your jar that I may drink,' and
who shall say, 'Drink, and I will water your
camels'—let her be the one whom thou hast
appointed for thy servant Isaac. By this I
shall know that thou hast shown steadfast
love to my master."
Before he had done speaking, behold, 15
Rebekah, who was born to Bethu'el the son
of Milcah, the wife of Nahor, Abraham's
brother, came out with her water jar upon
her shoulder. The maiden was very fair to 16
look upon, a virgin, whom no man had
known. She went down to the spring, and
filled her jar, and came up. Then the servant 17
ran to meet her, and said, "Pray give me a
little water to drink from your jar." She said, 18
"Drink, my lord"; and she quickly let down
her jar upon her hand, and gave him a drink.
When she had finished giving him a drink, 19
she said, "I will draw for your camels also,
until they have done drinking." So she 20
quickly emptied her jar into the trough and
ran again to the well to draw, and she drew
for all his camels. The man gazed at her in 21
silence to learn whether the LORD had prospered his journey or not.
When the camels had done drinking, the 22
man took a gold ring weighing a half shekel,
and two bracelets for her arms weighing ten
gold shekels, and said, "Tell me whose 23
daughter you are. Is there room in your
father's house for us to lodge in?" She said 24
to him, "I am the daughter of Bethu'el the
son of Milcah, whom she bore to Nahor."
She added, "We have both straw and 25
provender enough, and room to lodge in."
The man bowed his head and worshipped 26
the LORD, and said, "Blessed be the LORD, 27
the God of my master Abraham, who has not
forsaken his steadfast love and his faithfulness toward my master. As for me, the LORD
has led me in the way to the house of my
master's kinsmen."
Then the maiden ran and told her mother's 28
household about these things. Rebekah 29
had a brother whose name was Laban;
and Laban ran out to the man, to the spring.

When he saw the ring, and the bracelets on his sister's arms, and when he heard the words of Rebekah his sister, "Thus the man spoke to me," he went to the man; and behold, he was standing by the camels at the spring. He said, "Come in, O blessed of the LORD; why do you stand outside? For I have prepared the house and a place for the camels." So the man came into the house; and Laban ungirded the camels, and gave him straw and provender for the camels, and water to wash his feet and the feet of the men who were with him. Then food was set before him to eat; but he said, "I will not eat until I have told my errand." He said, "Speak on."

So he said, "I am Abraham's servant. The LORD has greatly blessed my master, and he has become great; he has given him flocks and herds, silver and gold, menservants and maidservants, camels and asses. And Sarah my master's wife bore a son to my master when she was old; and to him he has given all that he has. My master made me swear, saying, 'You shall not take a wife for my son from the daughters of the Canaanites, in whose land I dwell; but you shall go to my father's house and to my kindred, and take a wife for my son.' I said to my master, 'Perhaps the woman will not follow me.' But he said to me, 'The LORD, before whom I walk, will send his angel with you and prosper your way; and you shall take a wife for my son from my kindred and from my father's house; then you will be free from my oath, when you come to my kindred; and if they will not give her to you, you will be free from my oath.'

"I came today to the spring, and said, 'O LORD, the God of my master Abraham, if now thou wilt prosper the way which I go, behold, I am standing by the spring of water; let the young woman who comes out to draw, to whom I shall say, "Pray give me a little water from your jar to drink," and who will say to me, "Drink, and I will draw for your camels also," let her be the woman whom the LORD has appointed for my master's son.'

"Before I had done speaking in my heart, behold, Rebekah came out with her water jar on her shoulder; and she went down to the spring, and drew. I said to her, 'Pray let me drink.' She quickly let down her jar from her shoulder, and said, 'Drink, and I will give your camels drink also.' So I drank, and she gave the camels drink also. Then I asked her, 'Whose daughter are you?' She said, 'The daughter of Bethu'el, Nahor's son, whom Milcah bore to him.' So I put the ring on her nose, and the bracelets on her arms. Then I bowed my head and worshipped the LORD, and blessed the LORD, the God of my master Abraham, who had led me by the right way to take the daughter of my master's kinsman for his son. Now then, if you will deal loyally and truly with my master, tell me; and if not, tell me; that I may turn to the right hand or to the left."

Then Laban and Bethu'el answered, "The thing comes from the LORD; we cannot speak to you bad or good. Behold, Rebekah is before you, take her and go, and let her be the wife of your master's son, as the LORD has spoken."

When Abraham's servant heard their words, he bowed himself to the earth before the LORD. And the servant brought forth jewelry of silver and of gold, and raiment, and gave them to Rebekah; he also gave to her brother and to her mother costly ornaments. And he and the men who were with him ate and drank, and they spent the night there. When they arose in the morning, he said, "Send me back to my master." Her brother and her mother said, "Let the maiden remain with us a while, at least ten days; after that she may go." But he said to them, "Do not delay me, since the LORD has prospered my way; let me go that I may go to my master." They said, "We will call the maiden, and ask her." And they called Rebekah, and said to her, "Will you go with this man?" She said, "I will go." So they sent away Rebekah their sister and her nurse, and Abraham's servant and his men. And they blessed Rebekah, and said to her, "Our sister, be the mother of thousands of ten thousands; and may your descendants possess the gate of those who hate them!" Then Rebekah and her maids arose, and rode upon the camels and followed the man; thus the servant took Rebekah, and went his way.

Now Isaac had come from[n] Beer-la'hai-roi, and was dwelling in the Negeb. And Isaac went out to meditate in the field in the evening; and he lifted up his eyes and looked, and behold there were camels coming. And Rebekah lifted up her eyes, and when she saw Isaac, she alighted from the camel, and said to the servant, "Who is the man yonder, walking in the field to meet us?" The servant said, "It is my master." So she took her veil and covered herself. And the servant told Isaac all the things that he had done. Then Isaac brought her into the tent,[o] and took Rebekah, and she became his wife; and he loved her. So Isaac was comforted after his mother's death.

---

n Syr Tg: Heb *from coming to*　o Heb adds *Sarah his mother*

Death of Abraham

25 Abraham took another wife, whose name
2 was Ketu'rah. She bore him Zimran,
Jokshan, Medan, Mid'ian, Ishbak, and
3 Shu'ah. Jokshan was the father of Sheba and
Dedan. The sons of Dedan were Asshu'rim,
4 Letu'shim, and Le-um'mim. The sons of
Mid'ian were Ephah, Epher, Hanoch,
Abi'da, and Elda'ah. All these were the
5 children of Ketu'rah. Abraham gave all
6 he had to Isaac. But to the sons of his
concubines Abraham gave gifts, and while he
was still living he sent them away from his
son Isaac, eastward to the east country.
7 These are the days of the years of Abraham's life, a hundred and seventy-five years.
8 Abraham breathed his last and died in a good
old age, an old man and full of years, and was
9 gathered to his people. Isaac and Ish'mael
his sons buried him in the cave of Mach-
pe'lah, in the field of Ephron the son of
10 Zohar the Hittite, east of Mamre, the field
which Abraham purchased from the Hittites. There Abraham was buried, with
11 Sarah his wife. After the death of Abraham
God blessed Isaac his son. And Isaac dwelt
at Beer-la'hai-roi.
12 These are the descendants of Ish'mael,
Abraham's son, whom Hagar the Egyptian,
13 Sarah's maid, bore to Abraham. These are
the names of the sons of Ish'mael, named in
the order of their birth: Neba'ioth, the
first-born of Ish'mael, and Kedar, Adbeel,
14, Mibsam, Mishma, Dumah, Massa, Hadad,
15 Tema, Jetur, Naphish, and Ked'emah.
16 These are the sons of Ish'mael and these are
their names, by their villages and by their
encampments, twelve princes according to
17 their tribes. (These are the years of the life
of Ish'mael, a hundred and thirty-seven
years; he breathed his last and died, and was
18 gathered to his kindred.) They dwelt from
Hav'ilah to Shur, which is opposite Egypt
in the direction of Assyria; he settled*p* over
against all his people.

Esau and Jacob

19 These are the descendants of Isaac, Abraham's son: Abraham was the father of Isaac,
20 and Isaac was forty years old when he took to
wife Rebekah, the daughter of Bethu'el the
Aramean of Paddan-aram, the sister of
21 Laban the Aramean. And Isaac prayed to
the LORD for his wife, because she was
barren; and the LORD granted his prayer, and
22 Rebekah his wife conceived. The children
struggled together within her; and she said,

"If it is thus, why do I live?"*q* So she went
to inquire of the LORD. And the LORD said to
her,
"Two nations are in your womb,
   and two peoples, born of you, shall be
     divided;
the one shall be stronger than the other,
   the elder shall serve the younger."
When her days to be delivered were ful- 24
filled, behold, there were twins in her
womb. The first came forth red, all his body 25
like a hairy mantle; so they called his name
Esau. Afterward his brother came forth, and 26
his hand had taken hold of Esau's heel; so his
name was called Jacob.*r* Isaac was sixty
years old when she bore them.
When the boys grew up, Esau was a skilful 27
hunter, a man of the field, while Jacob was a
quiet man, dwelling in tents. Isaac loved 28
Esau, because he ate of his game; but
Rebekah loved Jacob.
Once when Jacob was boiling pottage, Esau 29
came in from the field, and he was famished.
And Esau said to Jacob, "Let me eat some of 30
that red pottage, for I am famished!"
(Therefore his name was called Edom.*s*)
Jacob said, "First sell me your birthright." 31
Esau said, "I am about to die; of what use is a 32
birthright to me?" Jacob said, "Swear to me 33
first."*t* So he swore to him, and sold his
birthright to Jacob. Then Jacob gave Esau 34
bread and pottage of lentils, and he ate and
drank, and rose and went his way. Thus
Esau despised his birthright.

The Philistines

Now there was a famine in the land, besides 26
the former famine that was in the days of
Abraham. And Isaac went to Gerar, to
Abim'elech king of the Philistines. And the 2
LORD appeared to him, and said, "Do not
go down to Egypt; dwell in the land of which
I shall tell you. Sojourn in this land, and I 3
will be with you, and will bless you; for to
you and to your descendants I will give all
these lands, and I will fulfil the oath which
I swore to Abraham your father. I will 4
multiply your descendants as the stars of
heaven, and will give to your descendants all
these lands; and by your descendants all the
nations of the earth shall bless themselves:
because Abraham obeyed my voice and kept 5
my charge, my commandments, my statutes,
and my laws."
So Isaac dwelt in Gerar. When the men of 6
the place asked him about his wife, he said, 7
"She is my sister"; for he feared to say, "My
wife," thinking, "lest the men of the place

---

p Heb *fell*   *q* Syr: Heb obscure   *r* That is *He takes by the heel* or *He supplants*   *s* That is *Red*   *t* Heb *today*
25.13–16: 1 Chron 1.29–31.

should kill me for the sake of Rebekah";
8 because she was fair to look upon. When he had been there a long time, Abim'elech king of the Philistines looked out of a window and
9 saw Isaac fondling Rebekah his wife. So Abim'elech called Isaac, and said, "Behold, she is your wife; how then could you say, 'She is my sister'?" Isaac said to him, "Because I thought, 'Lest I die because of
10 her.'" Abim'elech said, "What is this you have done to us? One of the people might easily have lain with your wife, and you
11 would have brought guilt upon us." So Abim'elech warned all the people, saying, "Whoever touches this man or his wife shall be put to death."

12 And Isaac sowed in that land, and reaped in the same year a hundredfold. The LORD
13 blessed him, and the man became rich, and gained more and more until he became very
14 wealthy. He had possessions of flocks and herds, and a great household, so that the
15 Philistines envied him. (Now the Philistines had stopped and filled with earth all the wells which his father's servants had dug in the
16 days of Abraham his father.) And Abim'-elech said to Isaac, "Go away from us; for you are much mightier than we."
17 So Isaac departed from there, and encamped in the valley of Gerar and dwelt

there. And Isaac dug again the wells of water 18 which had been dug in the days of Abraham his father; for the Philistines had stopped them after the death of Abraham; and he gave them the names which his father had given them. But when Isaac's servants dug 19 in the valley and found there a well of springing water, the herdsmen of Gerar 20 quarrelled with Isaac's herdsmen, saying, "The water is ours." So he called the name of the well Esek,[u] because they contended with him. Then they dug another well, and 21 they quarrelled over that also; so he called its name Sitnah.[v] And he moved from there 22 and dug another well, and over that they did not quarrel; so he called its name Reho'-both,[w] saying, "For now the LORD has made room for us, and we shall be fruitful in the land."

From there he went up to Beer-sheba. 23 And the LORD appeared to him the same night 24 and said, "I am the God of Abraham your father; fear not, for I am with you and will bless you and multiply your descendants for my servant Abraham's sake." So he built an 25 altar there and called upon the name of the LORD, and pitched his tent there. And there Isaac's servants dug a well.

Then Abim'elech went to him from Gerar 26 with Ahuz'zath his adviser and Phicol the commander of his army. Isaac said to them, 27 "Why have you come to me, seeing that you hate me and have sent me away from you?" They said, "We see plainly that the LORD is 28 with you; so we say, let there be an oath between you and us, and let us make a covenant with you, that you will do us no 29

---

u That is *Contention* v That is *Enmity* w That is *Broad places* or *Room* harm, just as we have not touched you and have done to you nothing but good and have sent you away in peace. You are now the 30 blessed of the LORD." So he made them a 31 feast, and they ate and drank. In the morning they rose early and took oath with one another; and Isaac set them on their way, and 32 they departed from him in peace. That same day Isaac's servants came and told him about the well which they had dug, and said to him, 33 "We have found water." He called it Shibah; therefore the name of the city is Beer-sheba to this day.

34 When Esau was forty years old, he took to wife Judith the daughter of Be-e'ri the Hittite, and Bas'emath the daughter of Elon 35 the Hittite; and they made life bitter for Isaac and Rebekah.

JACOB

27 WHEN Isaac was old and his eyes were dim so that he could not see, he called Esau his older son, and said to him, "My son"; 2 and he answered, "Here I am." He said, "Behold, I am old; I do not know the day of 3 my death. Now then, take your weapons, your quiver and your bow, and go out to the 4 field, and hunt game for me, and prepare for me savoury food, such as I love, and bring it to me that I may eat; that I may bless you before I die."

5 Now Rebekah was listening when Isaac spoke to his son Esau. So when Esau went to the field to hunt for game and bring it, 6 Rebekah said to her son Jacob, "I heard your 7 father speak to your brother Esau, 'Bring me game, and prepare for me savoury food, that I may eat it, and bless you before the LORD 8 before I die.' Now therefore, my son, obey 9 my word as I command you. Go to the flock, and fetch me two good kids, that I may

prepare from them savoury food for your father, such as he loves; and you shall bring it 10 to your father to eat, so that he may bless you before he dies." But Jacob said to Rebekah 11 his mother, "Behold, my brother Esau is a hairy man, and I am a smooth man. Perhaps 12 my father will feel me, and I shall seem to be mocking him, and bring a curse upon myself and not a blessing." His mother said to him, 13 "Upon me be your curse, my son; only obey my word, and go, fetch them to me." So he 14 went and took them and brought them to his mother; and his mother prepared savoury food, such as his father loved. Then Re- 15 bekah took the best garments of Esau her older son, which were with her in the house, and put them on Jacob her younger son; and 16 the skins of the kids she put upon his hands and upon the smooth part of his neck; and 17 she gave the savoury food and the bread, which she had prepared, into the hand of her son Jacob.

So he went in to his father, and said, "My 18 father"; and he said, "Here I am; who are you, my son?" Jacob said to his father, "I 19 am Esau your first-born. I have done as you told me; now sit up and eat of my game, that you may bless me." But Isaac said to his son, 20 "How is it that you have found it so quickly, my son?" He answered, "Because the LORD your God granted me success." Then Isaac 21 said to Jacob, "Come near, that I may feel you, my son, to know whether you are really my son Esau or not." So Jacob went near to 22 Isaac his father, who felt him and said, "The voice is Jacob's voice, but the hands are the hands of Esau." And he did not recognise 23 him, because his hands were hairy like his brother Esau's hands; so he blessed him. He 24 said, "Are you really my son Esau?" He answered, "I am." Then he said, "Bring it 25 to me, that I may eat of my son's game and bless you." So he brought it to him, and he ate; and he brought him wine, and he drank. Then his father Isaac said to him, "Come 26 near and kiss me, my son." So he came near 27 and kissed him; and he smelled the smell of his garments, and blessed him, and said,

"See, the smell of my son
    is as the smell of a field which the LORD
      has blessed!
May God give you of the dew of heaven,   28
    and of the fatness of the earth,
    and plenty of grain and wine.
Let peoples serve you,   29
    and nations bow down to you.
Be lord over your brothers,
    and may your mother's sons bow down
      to you.
Cursed be every one who curses you,

and blessed be every one who blesses you!"

10 As soon as Isaac had finished blessing Jacob, when Jacob had scarcely gone out from the presence of Isaac his father, Esau 1 his brother came in from his hunting. He also prepared savoury food, and brought it to his father. And he said to his father, "Let my father arise, and eat of his son's game, 2 that you may bless me." His father Isaac said to him, "Who are you?" He answered, "I am your son, your first-born, Esau." 33 Then Isaac trembled violently, and said, "Who was it then that hunted game and brought it to me, and I ate it all* before you came, and I have blessed him?—yes, and he 34 shall be blessed." When Esau heard the words of his father, he cried out with an exceedingly great and bitter cry, and said to his father, "Bless me, even me also, O my 35 father!" But he said, "Your brother came with guile, and he has taken away your 36 blessing." Esau said, "Is he not rightly named Jacob? For he has supplanted me these two times. He took away my birthright; and behold, now he has taken away my blessing." Then he said, "Have you not 37 reserved a blessing for me?" Isaac answered Esau, "Behold, I have made him your lord, and all his brothers I have given to him for servants, and with grain and wine I have sustained him. What then can I do for you, 38 my son?" Esau said to his father, "Have you but one blessing, my father? Bless me, even me also, O my father." And Esau lifted up his voice and wept.

39 Then Isaac his father answered him:
"Behold, away from* the fatness of the
earth shall your dwelling be,
and away from* the dew of heaven on
high.
40 By your sword you shall live,
and you shall serve your brother;
but when you break loose
you shall break his yoke from your
neck."

41 Now Esau hated Jacob because of the blessing with which his father had blessed him, and Esau said to himself, "The days of mourning for my father are approaching; 42 then I will kill my brother Jacob." But the words of Esau her older son were told to Rebekah; so she sent and called Jacob her younger son, and said to him, "Behold, your brother Esau comforts himself by planning 43 to kill you. Now therefore, my son, obey my voice; arise, flee to Laban my brother in 44 Haran, and stay with him a while, until 45 your brother's fury turns away; until your brother's anger turns away, and he forgets

what you have done to him; then I will send, and fetch you from there. Why should I be bereft of you both in one day?"

Then Rebekah said to Isaac, "I am weary of 46 my life because of the Hittite women. If Jacob marries one of the Hittite women such as these, one of the women of the land, what good will my life be to me?"

Jacob's flight and vision

Then Isaac called Jacob and blessed him, 28 and charged him, "You shall not marry one of the Canaanite women. Arise, go to 2 Paddan-aram to the house of Bethu'el your mother's father; and take as wife from there one of the daughters of Laban your mother's brother. God Almighty* bless you and make 3 you fruitful and multiply you, that you may become a company of peoples. May he give 4 the blessing of Abraham to you and to your descendants with you, that you may take possession of the land of your sojournings which God gave to Abraham!" Thus Isaac 5 sent Jacob away; and he went to Paddan-

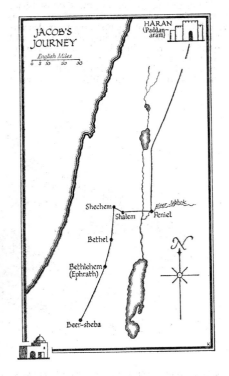

aram to Laban, the son of Bethu'el the Aramean, the brother of Rebekah, Jacob's and Esau's mother.

6 Now Esau saw that Isaac had blessed Jacob and sent him away to Paddan-aram to take a wife from there, and that as he blessed him he charged him, "You shall not marry one of 7 the Canaanite women," and that Jacob had obeyed his father and his mother and gone to 8 Paddan-aram. So when Esau saw that the Canaanite women did not please Isaac his 9 father, Esau went to Ish'mael and took to wife, besides the wives he had, Ma'halath the daughter of Ish'mael Abraham's son, the sister of Neba'ioth.

10 Jacob left Beer-sheba, and went toward 11 Haran. And he came to a certain place, and stayed there that night, because the sun had set. Taking one of the stones of the place, he put it under his head and lay down in that 12 place to sleep. And he dreamed that there was a ladder set up on the earth, and the top of it reached to heaven; and behold, the angels of God were ascending and descend- 13 ing on it! And behold, the Lord stood above it[a] and said, "I am the Lord, the God of Abraham your father and the God of Isaac; the land on which you lie I will give to you 14 and to your descendants; and your descen- dants shall be like the dust of the earth, and you shall spread abroad to the west and to the east and to the north and to the south; and by you and your descendants shall all the families of the earth bless themselves.[b]

Behold, I am with you and will keep you wherever you go, and will bring you back to this land; for I will not leave you until I have done that of which I have spoken to you." Then Jacob awoke from his sleep and said, "Surely the Lord is in this place; and I did not know it." And he was afraid, and said, "How awesome is this place! This is none other than the house of God, and this is the gate of heaven."

Bethel

So Jacob rose early in the morning, and he took the stone which he had put under his head and set it up for a pillar and poured oil on the top of it. He called the name of that place Bethel;[c] but the name of the city was Luz at the first. Then Jacob made a vow, saying, "If God will be with me, and will keep me in this way that I go, and will give me bread to eat and clothing to wear, so that I come again to my father's house in peace, then the Lord shall be my God, and this stone, which I have set up for a pillar, shall be God's house; and of all that thou givest me I will give the tenth to thee."

Laban's daughters

Then Jacob went on his journey, and came to the land of the people of the east. As he looked, he saw a well in the field, and lo, three flocks of sheep lying beside it; for

Bethel

---

[a] Or beside him   [b] Or be blessed   [c] That is The house of God

out of that well the flocks were watered. The
3 stone on the well's mouth was large, and
when all the flocks were gathered there, the
shepherds would roll the stone from the
mouth of the well, and water the sheep, and
put the stone back in its place upon the
mouth of the well.

4 Jacob said to them, "My brothers, where do
you come from?" They said, "We are from
5 Haran." He said to them, "Do you know
Laban the son of Nahor?" They said, "We
6 know him." He said to them, "Is it well with
him?" They said, "It is well; and see,
Rachel his daughter is coming with the
7 sheep!" He said, "Behold, it is still high
day, it is not time for the animals to be
gathered together; water the sheep, and go,
8 pasture them." But they said, "We cannot
until all the flocks are gathered together, and
the stone is rolled from the mouth of the
well; then we water the sheep."

9 While he was still speaking with them,
Rachel came with her father's sheep; for she
10 kept them. Now when Jacob saw Rachel the
daughter of Laban his mother's brother, and
the sheep of Laban his mother's brother,
Jacob went up and rolled the stone from the
well's mouth, and watered the flock of Laban
11 his mother's brother. Then Jacob kissed
12 Rachel, and wept aloud. And Jacob told
Rachel that he was her father's kinsman, and
that he was Rebekah's son; and she ran and
told her father.

13 When Laban heard the tidings of Jacob
his sister's son, he ran to meet him, and
embraced him and kissed him, and brought
him to his house. Jacob told Laban all these
14 things, and Laban said to him, "Surely you
are my bone and my flesh!" And he stayed
with him a month.

15 Then Laban said to Jacob, "Because you
are my kinsman, should you therefore serve
me for nothing? Tell me, what shall your
16 wages be?" Now Laban had two daughters;
the name of the older was Leah, and the
17 name of the younger was Rachel. Leah's
eyes were weak, but Rachel was beautiful and
18 lovely. Jacob loved Rachel; and he said, "I
will serve you seven years for your younger
19 daughter Rachel." Laban said, "It is better
that I give her to you than that I should give
20 her to any other man; stay with me." So
Jacob served seven years for Rachel, and
they seemed to him but a few days because of
the love he had for her.

21 Then Jacob said to Laban, "Give me my
wife that I may go in to her, for my time is
22 completed." So Laban gathered together all
23 the men of the place, and made a feast. But
in the evening he took his daughter Leah and

brought her to Jacob; and he went in to her.
(Laban gave his maid Zilpah to his daughter 24
Leah to be her maid.) And in the morning, 25
behold, it was Leah; and Jacob said to
Laban, "What is this you have done to me?
Did I not serve with you for Rachel? Why
then have you deceived me?" Laban said, 26
"It is not so done in our country, to give the
younger before the first-born. Complete the 27
week of this one, and we will give you the
other also in return for serving me another
seven years." Jacob did so, and completed 28
her week; then Laban gave him his daughter
Rachel to wife. (Laban gave his maid Bilhah 29
to his daughter Rachel to be her maid.) So 30
Jacob went in to Rachel also, and he loved
Rachel more than Leah, and served Laban
for another seven years.

When the LORD saw that Leah was hated, 31
he opened her womb; but Rachel was
barren. And Leah conceived and bore a son, 32
and she called his name Reuben;[d] for she
said, "Because the LORD has looked upon my
affliction; surely now my husband will love
me." She conceived again and bore a son, 33
and said, "Because the LORD has heard[e] that
I am hated, he has given me this son also";
and she called his name Simeon. Again she 34
conceived and bore a son, and said, "Now
this time my husband will be joined[f] to me,
because I have borne him three sons";
therefore his name was called Levi. And she 35
conceived again and bore a son, and said,
"This time I will praise[g] the LORD"; therefore she called his name Judah; then she
ceased bearing.

When Rachel saw that she bore Jacob no **30**
children, she envied her sister; and she said
to Jacob, "Give me children, or I shall
die!" Jacob's anger was kindled against 2
Rachel, and he said, "Am I in the place of
God, who has withheld from you the fruit of
the womb?" Then she said, "Here is my 3
maid Bilhah; go in to her, that she may
bear upon my knees, and even I may have
children through her." So she gave him her 4
maid Bilhah as a wife; and Jacob went in to
her. And Bilhah conceived and bore Jacob a 5
son. Then Rachel said, "God has judged 6
me, and has also heard my voice and given
me a son"; therefore she called his name
Dan.[h] Rachel's maid Bilhah conceived again 7
and bore Jacob a second son. Then Ra- 8
chel said, "With mighty wrestlings I have
wrestled[i] with my sister, and have prevailed"; so she called his name Naph'tali.
When Leah saw that she had ceased bearing 9
children, she took her maid Zilpah and gave
her to Jacob as a wife. Then Leah's maid 10

---

[d] That is *See, a son*   [e] Heb *shama*   [f] Heb *lawah*   [g] Heb *hodah*   [h] That is *He judged*   [i] Heb *niphtal*

11 Zilpah bore Jacob a son. And Leah said,
"Good fortune!" so she called his name
12 Gad.*ʲ* Leah's maid Zilpah bore Jacob a
13 second son. And Leah said, "Happy am I!
For the women will call me happy"; so she
called his name Asher.*ᵏ*
14 In the days of wheat harvest Reuben went
and found mandrakes in the field, and
brought them to his mother Leah. Then
Rachel said to Leah, "Give me, I pray, some
15 of your son's mandrakes." But she said to
her, "Is it a small matter that you have taken
away my husband? Would you take away
my son's mandrakes also?" Rachel said,
"Then he may lie with you tonight for your
16 son's mandrakes." When Jacob came from
the field in the evening, Leah went out to
meet him, and said, "You must come in to
me; for I have hired you with my son's
mandrakes." So he lay with her that night.
17 And God hearkened to Leah, and she con-
18 ceived and bore Jacob a fifth son. Leah said,
"God has given me my hire*ˡ* because I gave
my maid to my husband"; so she called his
19 name Is'sachar. And Leah conceived again,
20 and she bore Jacob a sixth son. Then Leah
said, "God has endowed me with a good
dowry; now my husband will honour*ᵐ* me,
because I have borne him six sons"; so she
21 called his name Zeb'ulun. Afterwards she
bore a daughter, and called her name Dinah.
22 Then God remembered Rachel, and God
23 hearkened to her and opened her womb. She
conceived and bore a son, and said, "God has
24 taken away my reproach"; and she called his
name Joseph,*ⁿ* saying, "May the LORD add
to me another son!"

Jacob and Laban

25 When Rachel had borne Joseph, Jacob said
to Laban, "Send me away, that I may go to
26 my own home and country. Give me my
wives and my children for whom I have
served you, and let me go; for you know the
27 service which I have given you." But Laban
said to him, "If you will allow me to say so, I
have learned by divination that the LORD has
28 blessed me because of you; name your wages,
29 and I will give it." Jacob said to him, "You
yourself know how I have served you, and
30 how your cattle have fared with me. For you
had little before I came, and it has increased
abundantly; and the LORD has blessed you
wherever I turned. But now when shall I
31 provide for my own household also?" He
said, "What shall I give you?" Jacob said,
"You shall not give me anything; if you will
do this for me, I will again feed your flock
32 and keep it: let me pass through all your

flock today, removing from it every speckled
and spotted sheep and every black lamb, and
the spotted and speckled among the goats;
and such shall be my wages. So my honesty 33
will answer for me later, when you come to
look into my wages with you. Every one that
is not speckled and spotted among the goats
and black among the lambs, if found with
me, shall be counted stolen." Laban said, 34
"Good! Let it be as you have said." But 35
that day Laban removed the he-goats that
were striped and spotted, and all the she-goats
that were speckled and spotted, every one
that had white on it, and every lamb that was
black, and put them in charge of his sons;
and he set a distance of three days' journey 36
between himself and Jacob; and Jacob fed
the rest of Laban's flock.
Then Jacob took fresh rods of poplar and 37
almond and plane, and peeled white streaks
in them, exposing the white of the rods. He 38
set the rods which he had peeled in front of
the flocks in the runnels, that is, the watering
troughs, where the flocks came to drink.
And since they bred when they came to
drink, the flocks bred in front of the rods and 39
so the flocks brought forth striped, speckled,
and spotted. And Jacob separated the lambs, 40
and set the faces of the flocks toward the
striped and all the black in the flock of
Laban; and he put his own droves apart, and
did not put them with Laban's flock.
Whenever the stronger of the flock were 41
breeding Jacob laid the rods in the runnels
before the eyes of the flock, that they might
breed among the rods, but for the feebler of 42
the flock he did not lay them there; so the
feebler were Laban's, and the stronger
Jacob's. Thus the man grew exceedingly 43
rich, and had large flocks, maidservants and
menservants, and camels and asses.

Now Jacob heard that the sons of Laban 31
were saying, "Jacob has taken all that was
our father's; and from what was our father's
he has gained all this wealth." And Jacob 2
saw that Laban did not regard him with
favour as before. Then the LORD said to 3
Jacob, "Return to the land of your fathers
and to your kindred, and I will be with
you." So Jacob sent and called Rachel and 4
Leah into the field where his flock was, and 5
said to them, "I see that your father does not
regard me with favour as he did before. But
the God of my father has been with me. You 6
know that I have served your father with all
my strength; yet your father has cheated me 7
and changed my wages ten times, but God
did not permit him to harm me. If he said, 8
'The spotted shall be your wages,' then all

ʲ That is *Fortune*   *ᵏ* That is *Happy*   *ˡ* Heb *sakar*   *ᵐ* Heb *zabal*   *ⁿ* That is *He adds* the flock bore spotted; and if he said, 'The striped shall be your wages,' then all the flock bore striped. Thus God has taken away the cattle of your father, and given them to me. In the mating season of the flock I lifted up my eyes, and saw in a dream that the he-goats which leaped upon the flock were striped, spotted, and mottled. Then the angel of God said to me in the dream, 'Jacob,' and I said, 'Here I am!' And he said, 'Lift up your eyes and see, all the goats that leap upon the flock are striped, spotted, and mottled; for I have seen all that Laban is doing to you. I am the God of Bethel, where you anointed a pillar and made a vow to me. Now arise, go forth from this land, and return to the land of your birth.' " Then Rachel and Leah answered him, "Is there any portion or inheritance left to us in our father's house? Are we not regarded by him as foreigners? For he has sold us, and he has been using up the money given for us. All the property which God has taken away from our father belongs to us and to our children; now then, whatever God has said to you, do."

So Jacob arose, and set his sons and his wives on camels; and he drove away all his cattle, all his livestock which he had gained, the cattle in his possession which he had acquired in Paddan-aram, to go to the land of Canaan to his father Isaac. Laban had gone to shear his sheep, and Rachel stole her father's household gods. And Jacob outwitted Laban the Aramean, in that he did not tell him that he intended to flee. He fled with all that he had, and arose and crossed the Euphra'tes, and set his face toward the hill country of Gilead.

When it was told Laban on the third day that Jacob had fled, he took his kinsmen with him and pursued him for seven days and followed close after him into the hill country of Gilead. But God came to Laban the Aramean in a dream by night, and said to him, "Take heed that you say not a word to Jacob, either good or bad."

And Laban overtook Jacob. Now Jacob had pitched his tent in the hill country, and Laban with his kinsmen encamped in the hill country of Gilead. And Laban said to Jacob, "What have you done, that you have cheated me, and carried away my daughters like captives of the sword? Why did you flee secretly, and cheat me, and did not tell me, so that I might have sent you away with mirth and songs, with tambourine and lyre? And why did you not permit me to kiss my sons and my daughters farewell? Now you have done foolishly. It is in my power to do you harm; but the God of your father spoke to me last night, saying, 'Take heed that you speak to Jacob neither good nor bad.' And now you have gone away because you longed greatly for your father's house, but why did you steal my gods?" Jacob answered Laban, "Because I was afraid, for I thought that you would take your daughters from me by force. Any one with whom you find your gods shall not live. In the presence of our kinsmen point out what I have that is yours, and take it." Now Jacob did not know that Rachel had stolen them.

So Laban went into Jacob's tent, and into Leah's tent, and into the tent of the two maidservants, but he did not find them. And he went out of Leah's tent, and entered Rachel's. Now Rachel had taken the household gods and put them in the camel's saddle, and sat upon them. Laban felt all about the tent, but did not find them. And she said to her father, "Let not my lord be angry that I cannot rise before you, for the way of women is upon me." So he searched, but did not find the household gods.

Then Jacob became angry, and upbraided Laban; Jacob said to Laban, "What is my offence? What is my sin, that you have hotly pursued me? Although you have felt through all my goods, what have you found of all your household goods? Set it here before my kinsmen and your kinsmen, that they may decide between us two. These twenty years I have been with you; your ewes and your she-goats have not miscarried, and I have not eaten the rams of your flocks. That which was torn by wild beasts I did not bring to you; I bore the loss of it myself; of my hand you required it, whether stolen by day or stolen by night. Thus I was; by day the heat consumed me, and the cold by night, and my sleep fled from my eyes. These twenty years I have been in your house; I served you fourteen years for your two daughters, and six years for your flock, and you have changed my wages ten times. If the God of my father, the God of Abraham and the Fear of Isaac, had not been on my side, surely now you would have sent me away empty-handed. God saw my affliction and the labour of my hands, and rebuked you last night."

Then Laban answered and said to Jacob, "The daughters are my daughters, the children are my children, the flocks are my flocks, and all that you see is mine. But what can I do this day to these my daughters, or to their children whom they have borne? Come now, let us make a covenant, you and I; and let it be a witness between you and me." So Jacob took a stone, and set it up as a pillar. And Jacob said to his kinsmen, "Gather stones," and they took stones, and made a heap; and they ate there by the heap.

47 Laban called it Je'gar-sahadu'tha:[o] but
48 Jacob called it Galeed.[p] Laban said, "This
heap is a witness between you and me
49 today." Therefore he named it Galeed, and
the pillar[q] Mizpah,[r] for he said, "The LORD
watch between you and me, when we are
50 absent one from the other. If you ill-treat
my daughters, or if you take wives besides
my daughters, although no man is with us,
remember, God is witness between you and
me."
51 Then Laban said to Jacob, "See this heap
and the pillar, which I have set between you
52 and me. This heap is a witness, and the
pillar is a witness, that I will not pass over
this heap to you, and you will not pass over
this heap and this pillar to me, for harm.
53 The God of Abraham and the God of Nahor,
the God of their father, judge between us."
So Jacob swore by the Fear of his father
54 Isaac, and Jacob offered a sacrifice on the
mountain and called his kinsmen to eat
bread; and they ate bread and tarried all
night on the mountain.
55[s] Early in the morning Laban arose, and
kissed his grandchildren and his daughters
and blessed them; then he departed and
returned home.

Jacob and Esau

32 Jacob went on his way and the angels of
2 God met him; and when Jacob saw them
he said, "This is God's army!" So he called
the name of that place Mahana'im.[t]
3 And Jacob sent messengers before him to
Esau his brother in the land of Se'ir, the
4 country of Edom, instructing them, "Thus
you shall say to my lord Esau: Thus says
your servant Jacob, 'I have sojourned with
5 Laban, and stayed until now; and I have
oxen, asses, flocks, menservants, and maidservants, and I have sent to tell my lord, in
order that I may find favour in your sight.'"
6 And the messengers returned to Jacob,
saying, "We came to your brother Esau, and
he is coming to meet you, and four hundred
7 men with him." Then Jacob was greatly
afraid and distressed; and he divided the
people that were with him, and the flocks and
herds and camels, into two companies,
8 thinking, "If Esau comes to the one company
and destroys it, then the company which is
left will escape."
9 And Jacob said, "O God of my father
Abraham and God of my father Isaac, O
LORD who didst say to me, 'Return to your
country and to your kindred, and I will do
10 you good,' I am not worthy of the least of all
the steadfast love and all the faithfulness
which thou hast shown to thy servant, for

with only my staff I crossed this Jordan; and
now I have become two companies. Deliver
me, I pray thee, from the hand of my
brother, from the hand of Esau, for I fear
him, lest he come and slay us all, the mothers
with the children. But thou didst say, 'I will
do you good, and make your descendants as
the sand of the sea, which cannot be numbered for multitude.'"
So he lodged there that night, and took
from what he had with him a present for his
brother Esau, two hundred she-goats and
twenty he-goats, two hundred ewes and
twenty rams, thirty milch camels and their
colts, forty cows and ten bulls, twenty she-
asses and ten he-asses. These he delivered
into the hand of his servants, every drove by
itself, and said to his servants, "Pass on
before me, and put a space between drove
and drove." He instructed the foremost,
"When Esau my brother meets you, and asks
you, 'To whom do you belong? Where are
you going? And whose are these before
you?' Then you shall say, 'They belong to
your servant Jacob; they are a present sent to
my lord Esau; and moreover he is behind
us.'" He likewise instructed the second and
the third and all who followed the droves,
"You shall say the same thing to Esau when
you meet him, and you shall say, 'Moreover
your servant Jacob is behind us.'" For he
thought, "I may appease him with the
present that goes before me, and afterwards I
shall see his face; perhaps he will accept
me." So the present passed on before him;

and he himself lodged that night in the camp.
2 The same night he arose and took his two
wives, his two maids, and his eleven children,
3 and crossed the ford of the Jabbok. He took
them and sent them across the stream, and
4 likewise everything that he had. And Jacob
was left alone; and a man wrestled with him
5 until the breaking of the day. When the man
saw that he did not prevail against Jacob, he
touched the hollow of his thigh; and Jacob's
thigh was put out of joint as he wrestled with
6 him. Then he said, "Let me go, for the day
is breaking." But Jacob said, "I will not let
7 you go, unless you bless me." And he said to
him, "What is your name?" And he said,
8 "Jacob." Then he said, "Your name shall no
more be called Jacob, but Israel,[u] for you
have striven with God and with men, and
9 have prevailed." Then Jacob said him,
"Tell me, I pray, your name." But he said,
"Why is it that you ask my name?" And
10 there he blessed him. So Jacob called the
name of the place Peni'el,[v] saying, "For I
have seen God face to face, and yet my life is
11 preserved." The sun rose upon him as he
passed Penu'el, limping because of his thigh.
12 Therefore to this day the Israelites do not eat
the sinew of the hip which is upon the hollow
of the thigh, because he touched the hollow
of Jacob's thigh on the sinew of the hip.

33 And Jacob lifted up his eyes and looked,
and behold, Esau was coming, and four
hundred men with him. So he divided the
children among Leah and Rachel and the two
2 maids. And he put the maids with their
children in front, then Leah with her chil-
3 dren, and Rachel and Joseph last of all. He
himself went on before them, bowing himself
to the ground seven times, until he came near
to his brother.
4 But Esau ran to meet him, and embraced
him, and fell on his neck and kissed him, and
5 they wept. And when Esau raised his eyes
and saw the women and children, he said,
"Who are these with you?" Jacob said,
"The children whom God has graciously
6 given your servant." Then the maids drew
near, they and their children, and bowed
7 down; Leah likewise and her children drew
near and bowed down; and last Joseph and
Rachel drew near, and they bowed down.
8 Esau said, "What do you mean by all this
company which I met?" Jacob answered,
"To find favour in the sight of my lord."
9 But Esau said, "I have enough, my brother;
10 keep what you have for yourself." Jacob
said, "No, I pray you, if I have found favour
in your sight, then accept my present from
my hand; for truly to see your face is like

seeing the face of God, with such favour have
you received me. Accept, I pray you, my gift 11
that is brought to you, because God has dealt
graciously with me, and because I have
enough." Thus he urged him, and he took it.
Then Esau said, "Let us journey on our 12
way, and I will go before you." But Jacob 13
said to him, "My lord knows that the
children are frail, and that the flocks and
herds giving suck are a care to me; and if they
are overdriven for one day, all the flocks will
die. Let my lord pass on before his servant, 14
and I will lead on slowly, according to the
pace of the cattle which are before me and
according to the pace of the children, until I
come to my lord in Se'ir."
So Esau said, "Let me leave with you some 15
of the men who are with me." But he said,
"What need is there? Let me find favour in
the sight of my lord." So Esau returned that 16
day on his way to Se'ir. But Jacob journeyed 17
to Succoth,[w] and built himself a house, and
made booths for his cattle; therefore the
name of the place is called Succoth.
And Jacob came safely to the city of 18
Shechem, which is in the land of Canaan, on
his way from Paddan-aram; and he camped
before the city. And from the sons of 19
Hamor, Shechem's father, he bought for a
hundred pieces of money[x] the piece of land
on which he had pitched his tent. There he 20
erected an altar and called it El-Elo'he-
Israel.[y]

Jacob's children

Now Dinah the daughter of Leah, whom 34
she had borne to Jacob, went out to visit
the women of the land; and when Shechem 2
the son of Hamor the Hivite, the prince
of the land, saw her, he seized her and lay
with her and humbled her. And his soul 3
was drawn to Dinah the daughter of Jacob;
he loved the maiden and spoke tenderly to
her. So Shechem spoke to his father Hamor, 4
saying, "Get me this maiden for my wife."
Now Jacob heard that he had defiled his 5
daughter Dinah; but his sons were with his
cattle in the field, so Jacob held his peace
until they came. And Hamor the father of 6
Shechem went out to Jacob to speak with
him. The sons of Jacob came in from the 7
field when they heard of it; and the men were
indignant and very angry, because he had
wrought folly in Israel by lying with Jacob's
daughter, for such a thing ought not to be
done.
But Hamor spoke with them, saying, "The 8
soul of my son Shechem longs for your
daughter; I pray you, give her to him in
marriage. Make marriages with us; give your 9

---

[u] That is *He who strives with God* or *God strives*   [v] That is *The face of God*   [w] That is *Booths*
[x] Heb *a hundred qesitah*   [y] That is *God, the God of Israel*

daughters to us, and take our daughters for
10 yourselves. You shall dwell with us; and the
land shall be open to you; dwell and trade in
11 it, and get property in it." Shechem also said
to her father and to her brothers, "Let me
find favour in your eyes, and whatever you
12 say to me I will give. Ask of me ever so much
as marriage present and gift, and I will give
according as you say to me; only give me the
maiden to be my wife."

13 The sons of Jacob answered Shechem and
his father Hamor deceitfully, because he had
14 defiled their sister Dinah. They said to
them, "We cannot do this thing, to give our
sister to one who is uncircumcised, for that
15 would be a disgrace to us. Only on this
condition will we consent to you: that you
will become as we are and every male of you
16 be circumcised. Then we will give our
daughters to you, and we will take your
daughters to ourselves, and we will dwell
17 with you and become one people. But if you
will not listen to us and be circumcised, then
we will take our daughter, and we will be
gone."

18 Their words pleased Hamor and Hamor's
19 son Shechem. And the young man did not
delay to do the thing, because he had delight
in Jacob's daughter. Now he was the most
20 honoured of all his family. So Hamor and his
son Shechem came to the gate of their city
and spoke to the men of their city, saying,
21 "These men are friendly with us; let them
dwell in the land and trade in it, for behold,
the land is large enough for them; let us take
their daughters in marriage, and let us give
22 them our daughters. Only on this condition
will the men agree to dwell with us, to
become one people: that every male among
us be circumcised as they are circumcised.
23 Will not their cattle, their property and all
their beasts be ours? Only let us agree with
24 them, and they will dwell with us." And all
who went out of the gate of his city hark-
ened to Hamor and his son Shechem; and
every male was circumcised, all who went out
of the gate of his city.
25 On the third day, when they were sore, two
of the sons of Jacob, Simeon and Levi,
Dinah's brothers, took their swords and
came upon the city unawares, and killed all
26 the males. They slew Hamor and his son
Shechem with the sword, and took Dinah out
27 of Shechem's house, and went away. And
the sons of Jacob came upon the slain, and
plundered the city, because their sister had
28 been defiled; they took their flocks and their
herds, their asses, and whatever was in the
29 city and in the field; all their wealth, all their
little ones and their wives, all that was in the

houses, they captured and made their prey.
Then Jacob said to Simeon and Levi, "You 30
have brought trouble on me by making me
odious to the inhabitants of the land, the
Canaanites and the Per'izzites; my numbers
are few, and if they gather themselves against
me and attack me, I shall be destroyed, both
I and my household." But they said, 31
"Should he treat our sister as a harlot?"

An altar to God

God said to Jacob, "Arise, go up to Bethel, 35
and dwell there; and make there an altar
to the God who appeared to you when
you fled from your brother Esau." So Jacob 2
said to his household and to all who were
with him, "Put away the foreign gods that
are among you, and purify yourselves, and
change your garments; then let us arise 3
and go up to Bethel, that I may make there
an altar to the God who answered me in the
day of my distress and has been with me
wherever I have gone." So they gave to 4
Jacob all the foreign gods that they had, and
the rings that were in their ears; and Jacob
hid them under the oak which was near
Shechem.

And as they journeyed, a terror from God 5
fell upon the cities that were round about
them, so that they did not pursue the sons of
Jacob. And Jacob came to Luz (that is, 6
Bethel), which is in the land of Canaan, he
and all the people who were with him, and 7
there he built an altar, and called the place
El-bethel,[a] because there God had revealed
himself to him when he fled from his
brother. And Deb'orah, Rebekah's nurse, 8
died, and she was buried under an oak below
Bethel; so the name of it was called Al'lon-
bacuth.[a]

God appeared to Jacob again, when he 9
came from Paddan-aram, and blessed him.
And God said to him, "Your name is Jacob; 10
no longer shall your name be called Jacob,
but Israel shall be your name." So his name
was called Israel. And God said to him, "I 11
am God Almighty:[b] be fruitful and multiply;
a nation and a company of nations shall come
from you, and kings shall spring from you.
The land which I gave to Abraham and Isaac 12
I will give to you, and I will give the land to
your descendants after you." Then God 13
went up from him in the place where he had
spoken with him. And Jacob set up a pillar 14
in the place where he had spoken with him, a
pillar of stone; and he poured out a drink
offering on it, and poured oil on it. So Jacob 15
called the name of the place where God had
spoken with him, Bethel.
Then they journeyed from Bethel; and 16

---

z That is *God of Bethel*   *a* That is *Oak of weeping*   *b* Heb *El Shaddai* when they were still some distance from Ephrath, Rachel travailed, and she had hard labour. And when she was in her hard labour, the midwife said to her, "Fear not; for now you will have another son." And as her soul was departing (for she died), she called his name Ben-o'ni;° but his father called his name Benjamin.ᵈ So Rachel died, and she was buried on the way to Ephrath (that is, Bethlehem), and Jacob set up a pillar upon her grave; it is the pillar of Rachel's tomb, which is there to this day. Israel journeyed on, and pitched his tent beyond the tower of Eder.

While Israel dwelt in that land Reuben went and lay with Bilhah his father's concubine; and Israel heard of it.

Now the sons of Jacob were twelve. The 23 sons of Leah: Reuben (Jacob's first-born), Simeon, Levi, Judah, Is'sachar, and Zeb'-ulun. The sons of Rachel: Joseph and 24 Benjamin. The sons of Bilhah, Rachel's 25 maid: Dan and Naph'tali. The sons of 26 Zilpah, Leah's maid: Gad and Asher. These were the sons of Jacob who were born to him in Paddan-aram.

And Jacob came to his father Isaac at 27 Mamre, or Kir'iath-ar'ba (that is, Hebron), where Abraham and Isaac had sojourned. Now the days of Isaac were a hundred and 28 eighty years. And Isaac breathed his last; 29 and he died and was gathered to his people, old and full of days; and his sons Esau and Jacob buried him.

Esau's descendants

6 THESE are the descendants of 2 Esau (that is, Edom). Esau took his wives from the Canaanites: Adah the daughter of Elon 15 the Hittite, Oholiba'mah the daughter of Anah the sonᵉ of 3 Zib'eon the Hivite, and Bas'emath, Ish'mael's daughter, the 4 sister of Neba'ioth. And Adah bore to Esau, El'iphaz; Bas'emath 5 bore Reu'el; and Oholiba'mah bore Je'ush, Jalam, and Korah. These are the sons of Esau who were born to him in the land of Canaan.

6 Then Esau took his wives, his sons, his daughters, and all the members of his household, his cattle, all his beasts, and all his property which he had acquired in the land of Canaan; and he went into a land away from his 7 brother Jacob. For their possessions were too great for them to dwell together; the land of their 20 sojournings could not support 8 them because of their cattle. So Esau dwelt in the hill country of 21 Se'ir; Esau is Edom.

9 These are the descendants of Esau the father of the E'domites 22 o in the hill country of Se'ir. These are the names of Esau's sons: 23 El'iphaz the son of Adah the wife of Esau, Reu'el the son of Bas'-1 emath the wife of Esau. The sons 24 of El'iphaz were Teman, Omar, Zepho, Gatam, and Kenaz. 2 (Timna was a concubine of El'iphaz, Esau's son; she bore 25 Am'alek to El'iphaz.) These are the sons of Adah, Esau's wife. 3 These are the sons of Reu'el: 26 Nahath, Zerah, Shammah, and Mizzah. These are the sons of 27 4 Bas'emath, Esau's wife. These

are the sons of Oholiba'mah the daughter of Anah the sonᶠ of Zib'eon, Esau's wife: she bore to Esau Je'ush, Jalam, and Korah.

These are the chiefs of the sons of Esau. The sons of El'iphaz the first-born of Esau: the chiefs 16 Teman, Omar, Zepho, Kenaz, Korah, Gatam, and Am'alek; these are the chiefs of El'iphaz in the land of Edom; they are the 17 sons of Adah. These are the sons of Reu'el, Esau's son: the chiefs Nahath, Zerah, Shammah, and Mizzah; these are the chiefs of Reu'el in the land of Edom; they are the sons of Bas'emath, Esau's 18 wife. These are the sons of Oholiba'mah, Esau's wife: the chiefs Je'ush, Jalam, and Korah; these are the chiefs born of Oholiba'-mah the daughter of Anah, Esau's 19 wife. These are the sons of Esau (that is, Edom), and these are their chiefs.

20 These are the sons of Se'ir the Horite, the inhabitants of the land: Lotan, Shobal, Zib'eon, 21 Anah, Dishon, Ezer, and Dishan; these are the chiefs of the Horites, the sons of Se'ir in the land of 22 Edom. The sons of Lotan were Hori and Heman; and Lotan's 23 sister was Timna. These are the sons of Shobal: Alvan, Man'-ahath, Ebal, Shepho, and Onam. 24 These are the sons of Zib'eon: Ai'ah and Anah; he is the Anah who found the hot springs in the wilderness, as he pastured the 25 asses of Zib'eon his father. These are the children of Anah: Dishon and Oholiba'mah the daughter of Anah. These are the sons 26 of Dishon: Hemdan, Eshban, Ithran, and Cheran. These are 27 the sons of Ezer: Bilhan, Za'avan,

and Akan. These are the sons of 28 Dishan: Uz and Aran. These are 29 the chiefs of the Horites: the chiefs Lotan, Shobal, Zib'eon, Anah, Dishon, Ezer, and Dishan; 30 these are the chiefs of the Horites, according to their clans in the land of Se'ir.

These are the kings who reigned 31 in the land of Edom, before any king reigned over the Israelites. Bela the son of Be'or reigned in 32 Edom, the name of his city being Din'habah. Bela died, and Jo- 33 bab the son of Zerah of Bozrah reigned in his stead. Jobab died, 34 and Husham of the land of the Te'manites reigned in his stead. Husham died, and Hadad the son 35 of Bedad, who defeated Mid'ian in the country of Moab, reigned in his stead, the name of his city being Avith. Hadad died, and 36 Samlah of Masre'kah reigned in his stead. Samlah died, and 37 Sha'ul of Reho'both on the Euphra'tes reigned in his stead. Sha'ul died, and Ba'al-ha'nan 38 the son of Achbor reigned in his stead. Ba'al-ha'nan the 39 son of Achbor died, and Hadar reigned in his stead, the name of his city being Pau; his wife's name was Mehet'abel, the daughter of Matred, daughter of Me'zahab.

These are the names of the chiefs 40 of Esau, according to their fami-lies and their dwelling places, by their names: the chiefs Timna, Alvah, Jetheth, Oholiba'mah, 41 Elah, Pinon, Kenaz, Teman, 42 Mibzar, Mag'diel, and Iram; 43 these are the chiefs of Edom (that is, Esau, the father of Edom), according to their dwelling places in the land of their possession.

c That is Son of my sorrow   d That is Son of the right hand or Son of the South
e Sam Gk Syr: Heb daughter   f Gk Syr: Heb daughter
36.2: Gen 26.34; 28.9.   36.20-28: 1 Chron 1.38-42.   36.31-43: 1 Chron 1.43-53.

Gen **37, 28**

JOSEPH

37 JACOB dwelt in the land of his father's
2 sojournings, in the land of Canaan. This is
the history of the family of Jacob.

Joseph, being seventeen years old, was
shepherding the flock with his brothers; he
was a lad with the sons of Bilhah and Zilpah,
his father's wives; and Joseph brought an ill
3 report of them to their father. Now Israel
loved Joseph more than any other of his
children, because he was the son of his old
age; and he made him a long robe with
4 sleeves. But when his brothers saw that their
father loved him more than all his brothers,
they hated him, and could not speak peaceably to him.
5 Now Joseph had a dream, and when he told
it to his brothers they only hated him the
6 more. He said to them, "Hear this dream
7 which I have dreamed: behold, we were
binding sheaves in the field, and lo, my sheaf
arose and stood upright; and behold, your
sheaves gathered round it, and bowed down
8 to my sheaf." His brothers said to him, "Are
you indeed to reign over us? Or are you
indeed to have dominion over us?" So they
hated him yet more for his dreams and for his
9 words. Then he dreamed another dream,
and told it to his brothers, and said, "Behold,
I have dreamed another dream; and behold,
the sun, the moon, and eleven stars were
10 bowing down to me." But when he told it to
his father and to his brothers, his father
rebuked him, and said to him, "What is this
dream that you have dreamed? Shall I and

your mother and your brothers indeed come
to bow ourselves to the ground before you?"
And his brothers were jealous of him, but his 11
father kept the saying in mind.

Now his brothers went to pasture their 12
father's flock near Shechem. And Israel said 13
to Joseph, "Are not your brothers pasturing
the flock at Shechem? Come, I will send
you to them." And he said to him, "Here I
am." So he said to him, "Go now, see if it is 14
well with your brothers, and with the flock;
and bring me word again." So he sent him
from the valley of Hebron, and he came to
Shechem. And a man found him wandering 15
in the fields; and the man asked him, "What
are you seeking?" "I am seeking my 16
brothers," he said, "tell me, I pray you,
where they are pasturing the flock." And the 17
man said, "They have gone away, for I heard
them say, 'Let us go to Dothan.' " So
Joseph went after his brothers, and found
them at Dothan. They saw him afar off, and 18
before he came near to them they conspired
against him to kill him. They said to one 19
another, "Here comes this dreamer. Come 20
now, let us kill him and throw him into one
of the pits; then we shall say that a wild beast
has devoured him, and we shall see what will
become of his dreams." But when Reuben 21
heard it, he delivered him out of their hands,
saying, "Let us not take his life." And 22
Reuben said to them, "Shed no blood; cast
him into this pit here in the wilderness, but
lay no hand upon him"—that he might
rescue him out of their hand, to restore him
to his father. So when Joseph came to his 23

brothers, they stripped him of his robe, the
24 long robe with sleeves that he wore; and they took him and cast him into a pit. The pit was empty, there was no water in it.

25 Then they sat down to eat; and looking up they saw a caravan of Ish'maelites coming from Gilead, with their camels bearing gum, balm, and myrrh, on their way to carry it 26 down to Egypt. Then Judah said to his brothers, "What profit is it if we slay our 27 brother and conceal his blood? Come, let us sell him to the Ish'maelites, and let not our hand be upon him, for he is our brother, our own flesh." And his brothers heeded him. 28 Then Mid'ianite traders passed by; and they drew Joseph up and lifted him out of the pit, and sold him to the Ish'maelites for twenty shekels of silver; and they took Joseph to Egypt.

29 When Reuben returned to the pit and saw that Joseph was not in the pit, he rent his clothes and returned to his brothers and said, 30 "The lad is gone; and I, where shall I go?" Then they took Joseph's robe, and killed a 31 goat, and dipped the robe in the blood; and 32 they sent the long robe with sleeves and brought it to their father, and said, "This we have found; see now whether it is your son's robe or not." And he recognized it, and said, 33 "It is my son's robe; a wild beast has devoured him; Joseph is without doubt torn to pieces." Then Jacob rent his garments, 34 and put sackcloth upon his loins, and mourned for his son many days. All his sons 35 and all his daughters rose up to comfort him; but he refused to be comforted, and said, "No, I shall go down to Sheol to my son, mourning." Thus his father wept for him. Meanwhile the Mid'ianites had sold him in 36 Egypt to Pot'i-phar, an officer of Pharaoh, the captain of the guard.

Tribal history

38 IT happened at that time that Judah went down from his brothers, and turned in to a certain Adullamite, whose 2 name was Hirah. There Judah saw the daughter of a certain Canaanite whose name was Shu'a; he married her and went in to her, 3 and she conceived and bore a son, 4 and he called his name Er. Again she conceived and bore a son, and 5 she called his name Onan. Yet again she bore a son, and she called his name Shelah. She^g was in Chezib when she bore him. 6 And Judah took a wife for Er his first-born, and her name was 7 Tamar. But Er, Judah's first-born, was wicked in the sight of the LORD; and the LORD slew 8 him. Then Judah said to Onan, "Go in to your brother's wife, and perform the duty of a brother-in-law to her, and raise up off-9 spring for your brother." But Onan knew that the offspring would not be his; so when he went in to his brother's wife he spilled the semen on the ground, lest he should give offspring to his 10 brother. And what he did was displeasing in the sight of the LORD, and he slew him also. 11 Then Judah said to Tamar his daughter-in-law, "Remain a 20 widow in your father's house, till Shelah my son grows up"—for he feared that he would die, like his 21 brothers. So Tamar went and dwelt in her father's house.

12 In course of time the wife of Judah, Shu'a's daughter, died; and when Judah was comforted, he went up to Timnah to his sheepshearers, he and his friend 13 Hirah the Adullamite. And when Tamar was told, "Your father-in-law is going up to Timnah to 14 shear his sheep," she put off her widow's garments, and put on a veil, wrapping herself up, and sat at the entrance to Enaim, which is on the road to Timnah; for she saw that Shelah was grown up, and she had not been given to him 15 in marriage. When Judah saw her, he thought her to be a harlot, 16 for she had covered her face. He went over to her at the road side, and said, "Come, let me come in to you," for he did not know that she was his daughter-in-law. She 17 said, "What will you give me, that you may come in to me?" He answered, "I will send you a kid from the flock." And she said, "Will you give me a pledge, till 18 you send it?" He said, "What pledge shall I give you?" She replied, "Your signet and your cord, and your staff that is in your hand." So he gave them to her, and went in to her, and she con-19 ceived by him. Then she arose and went away, and taking off her veil she put on the garments of her widowhood.

20 When Judah sent the kid by his friend the Adullamite, to receive the pledge from the woman's hand, he could not find her. And 21 he asked the men of the place, "Where is the harlot^h who was at Enaim by the wayside?" And they said, "No harlot^h has been here." So he returned to Judah, 22 and said, "I have not found her; and also the men of the place said, 'No harlot^h has been here.'" And Judah replied, "Let her keep 23 the things as her own, lest we be laughed at; you see, I sent this kid, and you could not find her."

About three months later Judah 24 was told, "Tamar your daughter-in-law has played the harlot; and moreover she is with child by harlotry." And Judah said, "Bring her out, and let her be burned." As she was being 25 brought out, she sent word to her father-in-law, "By the man to whom these belong, I am with child." And she said, "Mark, I pray you, whose these are, the signet and the cord and the staff." Then Judah acknow-26 ledged them and said, "She is more righteous than I, inasmuch as I did not give her to my son Shelah." And he did not lie with her again.

When the time of her delivery 27 came, there were twins in her womb. And when she was in 28 labour, one put out a hand; and the midwife took and bound on his hand a scarlet thread, saying, "This came out first." But as he 29 drew back his hand, behold, his brother came out; and she said, "What a breach you have made for yourself!" Therefore his name was called Perez.^{i} After-30 ward his brother came out with the scarlet thread upon his hand; and his name was called Zerah.

^{g} Gk: Heb *He* ^{h} Or *cult prostitute* ^{i} That is *A breach*

JOSEPH'S
JOURNEY
into
EGYPT

Dothan
Shechem

GOSHEN

EGYPT

N

K

Joseph in Egypt

39 Now Joseph was taken down to Egypt, and Pot′i-phar, an officer of Pharaoh, the captain of the guard, an Egyptian, bought him from the Ish′maelites who had brought 2 him down there. The LORD was with Joseph, and he became a successful man; and he was in the house of his master the 3 Egyptian, and his master saw that the LORD was with him, and that the LORD caused all 4 that he did to prosper in his hands. So Joseph found favour in his sight and attended him, and he made him overseer of his house and put him in charge of all that he 5 had. From the time that he made him overseer in his house and over all that he had the LORD blessed the Egyptian's house for Joseph's sake; the blessing of the LORD was 6 upon all that he had, in house and field. So he left all that he had in Joseph's charge; and having him he had no concern for anything but the food which he ate.

Now Joseph was handsome and good-7 looking. And after a time his master's wife cast her eyes upon Joseph, and said, "Lie 8 with me." But he refused and said to his master's wife, "Lo, having me my master has no concern about anything in the house, and he has put everything that he has in my 9 hand; he is not greater in this house than I am; nor has he kept back anything from me except yourself, because you are his wife; how then can I do this great wickedness, and

39.1-2, 21: Acts 7.9.

sin against God?" And although she spoke 10 to Joseph day after day, he would not listen to her, to lie with her or to be with her. But 11 one day, when he went into the house to do his work and none of the men of the house was there in the house, she caught him by his 12 garment, saying, "Lie with me." But he left his garment in her hand, and fled and got out of the house. And when she saw that he had 13 left his garment in her hand, and had fled out of the house, she called to the men of her 14 household and said to them, "See, he has brought among us a Hebrew to insult us; he came in to me to lie with me, and I cried out 15 with a loud voice; and when he heard that I lifted up my voice and cried, he left his garment with me, and fled and got out of the house." Then she laid up his garment by her 16 until his master came home, and she told him 17 the same story, saying, "The Hebrew servant, whom you have brought among us, came in to me to insult me; but as soon as I 18 lifted up my voice and cried, he left his garment with me, and fled out of the house."

When his master heard the words which his 19 wife spoke to him, "This is the way your servant treated me," his anger was kindled. And Joseph's master took him and put him 20 into the prison, the place where the king's prisoners were confined, and he was there in prison. But the LORD was with Joseph and 21 showed him steadfast love, and gave him favour in the sight of the keeper of the

GENESIS 41

22 prison. And the keeper of the prison committed to Joseph's care all the prisoners who were in the prison; and whatever was done 23 there, he was the doer of it; the keeper of the prison paid no heed to anything that was in Joseph's care, because the LORD was with him; and whatever he did, the LORD made it prosper.

40 Some time after this, the butler of the king of Egypt and his baker offended their 2 lord the king of Egypt. And Pharaoh was angry with his two officers, the chief butler 3 and the chief baker, and he put them in custody in the house of the captain of the guard, in the prison where Joseph was 4 confined. The captain of the guard charged Joseph with them, and he waited on them; and they continued for some time in cus- 5 tody. And one night they both dreamed —the butler and the baker of the king of Egypt, who were confined in the prison —each his own dream, and each dream with 6 its own meaning. When Joseph came to them in the morning and saw them, they 7 were troubled. So he asked Pharaoh's officers who were with him in custody in his master's house, "Why are your faces 8 downcast today?" They said to him, "We have had dreams, and there is no one to interpret them." And Joseph said to them, "Do not interpretations belong to God? Tell them to me, I pray you."

9 So the chief butler told his dream to Joseph, and said to him, "In my dream there was a 10 vine before me, and on the vine there were three branches; as soon as it budded, its blossoms shot forth, and the clusters ripened 11 into grapes. Pharaoh's cup was in my hand; and I took the grapes and pressed them into Pharaoh's cup, and placed the cup in Pha- 12 raoh's hand." Then Joseph said to him, "This is its interpretation: the three 13 branches are three days; within three days Pharaoh will lift up your head and restore you to your office; and you shall place Pharaoh's cup in his hand as formerly, when 14 you were his butler. But remember me, when it is well with you, and do me the kindness, I pray you, to make mention of me to Pharaoh, and so get me out of this house. 15 For I was indeed stolen out of the land of the Hebrews; and here also I have done nothing that they should put me into the dungeon." 16 When the chief baker saw that the interpretation was favourable, he said to Joseph, "I also had a dream: there were three cake 17 baskets on my head, and in the uppermost basket there were all sorts of baked food for Pharaoh, but the birds were eating it out of 18 the basket on my head." And Joseph

answered, "This is its interpretation: the three baskets are three days; within three 19 days Pharaoh will lift up your head—from you!—and hang you on a tree; and the birds will eat the flesh from you."

On the third day, which was Pharaoh's 20 birthday, he made a feast for all his servants, and lifted up the head of the chief butler and the head of the chief baker among his servants. He restored the chief butler to his 21 butlership, and he placed the cup in Pharaoh's hand; but he hanged the chief baker, 22 as Joseph had interpreted to them. Yet the 23 chief butler did not remember Joseph, but forgot him.

After two whole years, Pharaoh dreamed 41 that he was standing by the Nile, and 2 behold, there came up out of the Nile seven cows sleek and fat, and they fed in the reed grass. And behold, seven other cows, 3 gaunt and thin, came up out of the Nile after them, and stood by the other cows on the bank of the Nile. And the gaunt and thin 4 cows ate up the seven sleek and fat cows. And Pharaoh awoke. And he fell asleep and 5 dreamed a second time; and behold, seven ears of grain, plump and good, were growing on one stalk. And behold, after them 6 sprouted seven ears, thin and blighted by the east wind. And the thin ears swallowed up 7 the seven plump and full ears. And Pharaoh awoke, and behold, it was a dream. So in the 8 morning his spirit was troubled; and he sent and called for all the magicians of Egypt and all its wise men; and Pharaoh told them his dream, but there was none who could interpret it[j] to Pharaoh.

Then the chief butler said to Pharaoh, "I 9 remember my faults today. When Pharaoh 10 was angry with his servants, and put me and the chief baker in custody in the house of the captain of the guard, we dreamed on the 11 same night, he and I, each having a dream with its own meaning. A young Hebrew was 12 there with us, a servant of the captain of the guard; and when we told him, he interpreted our dreams to us, giving an interpretation to each man according to his dream. And as he 13 interpreted to us, so it came to pass; I was restored to my office, and the baker was hanged."

Then Pharaoh sent and called Joseph, and 14 they brought him hastily out of the dungeon; and when he had shaved himself and changed his clothes, he came in before Pharaoh. And Pharaoh said to Joseph, "I 15 have had a dream, and there is no one who can interpret it; and I have heard it said of you that when you hear a dream you can interpret it." Joseph answered Pharaoh, "It 16

j Gk: Heb them

is not in me; God will give Pharaoh a
17 favourable answer." Then Pharaoh said
to Joseph, "Behold, in my dream I was
18 standing on the banks of the Nile; and seven
cows, fat and sleek, came up out of the Nile
19 and fed in the reed grass; and seven other
cows came up after them, poor and very
gaunt and thin, such as I had never seen in all
20 the land of Egypt. And the thin and gaunt
21 cows ate up the first seven fat cows, but when
they had eaten them no one would have
known that they had eaten them, for they
were still as gaunt as at the beginning. Then
22 I awoke. I also saw in my dream seven ears
23 growing on one stalk, full and good; and
seven ears, withered, thin, and blighted by
24 the east wind, sprouted after them, and the
thin ears swallowed up the seven good ears.
And I told it to the magicians, but there was
no one who could explain it to me."
25 Then Joseph said to Pharaoh, "The dream
of Pharaoh is one; God has revealed to
26 Pharaoh what he is about to do. The seven
good cows are seven years, and the seven
good ears are seven years; the dream is one.
27 The seven lean and gaunt cows that came up
after them are seven years, and the seven
empty ears blighted by the east wind are also
28 seven years of famine. It is as I told Pharaoh,
God has shown to Pharaoh what he is about
29 to do. There will come seven years of great
30 plenty throughout all the land of Egypt, but
after them there will arise seven years of
famine, and all the plenty will be forgotten
in the land of Egypt; the famine will consume
31 the land, and the plenty will be unknown in
the land by reason of that famine which will
32 follow, for it will be very grievous. And the
doubling of Pharaoh's dream means that the
thing is fixed by God, and God will shortly
33 bring it to pass. Now therefore let Pharaoh
select a man discreet and wise, and set him
34 over the land of Egypt. Let Pharaoh proceed
to appoint overseers over the land, and take
the fifth part of the produce of the land of
Egypt during the seven plenteous years.
35 And let them gather all the food of these
good years that are coming, and lay up grain
under the authority of Pharaoh for food in

the cities, and let them keep it. That food 36
shall be a reserve for the land against the
seven years of famine which are to befall the
land of Egypt, so that the land may not
perish through the famine."

This proposal seemed good to Pharaoh and 37
to all his servants. And Pharaoh said to his 38
servants, "Can we find such a man as this, in
whom is the Spirit of God?" So Pharaoh 39
said to Joseph, "Since God has shown you all
this, there is none so discreet and wise as you
are; you shall be over my house, and all my 40
people shall order themselves as you command; only as regards the throne will I be
greater than you." And Pharaoh said to 41
Joseph, "Behold, I have set you over all the
land of Egypt." Then Pharaoh took his 42
signet ring from his hand and put it on
Joseph's hand, and arrayed him in garments
of fine linen, and put a gold chain about his
neck; and he made him to ride in his second 43
chariot; and they cried before him, "Bow the
knee!"[k] Thus he set him over all the land of
Egypt. Moreover Pharaoh said to Joseph, "I 44
am Pharaoh, and without your consent no
man shall lift up hand or foot in all the land
of Egypt." And Pharaoh called Joseph's 45
name Zaph'enath-pane'ah; and he gave him
in marriage As'enath, the daughter of Poti'-
phera priest of On. So Joseph went out over
the land of Egypt.

Joseph was thirty years old when he entered 46
the service of Pharaoh king of Egypt. And
Joseph went out from the presence of Pharaoh, and went through all the land of
Egypt. During the seven plenteous years the 47
earth brought forth abundantly, and he 48
gathered up all the food of the seven years
when there was plenty[l] in the land of Egypt,
and stored up food in the cities; he stored up
in every city the food from the fields around
it. And Joseph stored up grain in great 49
abundance, like the sand of the sea, until he
ceased to measure it, for it could not be
measured.

Before the year of famine came, Joseph had 50
two sons, whom As'enath, the daughter of
Poti'phera priest of On, bore to him. Joseph 51
called the name of the first-born Manas'-

k *Abrek*, probably an Egyptian word similar in sound to the Hebrew word meaning *to kneel*
l Sam Gk: Heb *which were*
41.38–45: Acts 7.10.

seh,*m* "For," he said, "God has made me
forget all my hardship and all my father's
52 house." The name of the second he called
E'phraim,*n* "For God has made me fruitful
in the land of my affliction."

53 The seven years of plenty that prevailed in
54 the land of Egypt came to an end; and the
seven years of famine began to come, as
Joseph had said. There was famine in all
lands; but in all the land of Egypt there was
55 bread. When all the land of Egypt was
famished, the people cried to Pharaoh for
bread; and Pharaoh said to all the Egyptians,
56 "Go to Joseph; what he says to you, do." So
when the famine had spread over all the land,
Joseph opened all the storehouses,*o* and sold
to the Egyptians, for the famine was severe in
57 the land of Egypt. Moreover, all the earth
came to Egypt to Joseph to buy grain,
because the famine was severe over all the
earth.

Visits of Joseph's brothers

42 When Jacob learned that there was grain
in Egypt, he said to his sons, "Why do
2 you look at one another?" And he said,
"Behold, I have heard that there is grain
in Egypt; go down and buy grain for us
3 there, that we may live, and not die." So ten
of Joseph's brothers went down to buy grain
4 in Egypt. But Jacob did not send Benjamin,
Joseph's brother, with his brothers, for he
5 feared that harm might befall him. Thus the
sons of Israel came to buy among the others
who came, for the famine was in the land of
Canaan.

6 Now Joseph was governor over the land; he
it was who sold to all the people of the land.
And Joseph's brothers came, and bowed
themselves before him with their faces to the
7 ground. Joseph saw his brothers, and knew
them, but he treated them like strangers and
spoke roughly to them. "Where do you
come from?" he said. They said, "From the
8 land of Canaan, to buy food." Thus Joseph
knew his brothers, but they did not know
9 him. And Joseph remembered the dreams
which he had dreamed of them; and he said

to them, "You are spies, you have come to
see the weakness of the land." They said to 10
him, "No, my lord, but to buy food have
your servants come. We are all sons of one 11
man, we are honest men, your servants are
not spies." He said to them, "No, it is the 12
weakness of the land that you have come to
see." And they said, "We, your servants, are 13
twelve brothers, the sons of one man in the
land of Canaan; and behold, the youngest is
this day with our father, and one is no
more." But Joseph said to them, "It is as I 14
said to you, you are spies. By this you shall 15
be tested: by the life of Pharaoh, you shall
not go from this place unless your youngest
brother comes here. Send one of you, and let 16
him bring your brother, while you remain in
prison, that your words may be tested,
whether there is truth in you; or else, by the
life of Pharaoh, surely you are spies." And 17
he put them all together in prison for three
days.

On the third day Joseph said to them, "Do 18
this and you will live, for I fear God: if you 19
are honest men, let one of your brothers
remain confined in your prison, and let the
rest go and carry grain for the famine of your
households, and bring your youngest brother 20
to me; so your words will be verified, and
you shall not die." And they did so. Then 21
they said to one another, "In truth we are
guilty concerning our brother, in that we saw
the distress of his soul, when he besought us
and we would not listen; therefore is this
distress come upon us." And Reuben 22
answered them, "Did I not tell·you not to sin
against the lad? But you would not listen.
So now there comes a reckoning for his
blood." They did not know that Joseph 23
understood them, for there was an inter-
preter between them. Then he turned away 24
from them and wept; and he returned to
them and spoke to them. And he took
Simeon from them and bound him before
their eyes. And Joseph gave orders to fill 25
their bags with grain, and to replace every
man's money in his sack, and to give them
provisions for the journey. This was done
for them.

---

m That is *Making to forget*   *n* From a Hebrew word meaning *to be fruitful*
o Gk Vg Compare Syr: Heb *all that was in them*
41.54: Acts 7.11.   **42.2:** Acts 7.12.   **42.5:** Acts 7.11.

26 Then they loaded their asses with their
27 grain, and departed. And as one of them
opened his sack to give his ass provender at
the lodging place, he saw his money in the
28 mouth of his sack; and he said to his
brothers, "My money has been put back;
here it is in the mouth of my sack!" At this
their hearts failed them, and they turned
trembling to one another, saying, "What is
this that God has done to us?"

29 When they came to Jacob their father in the
land of Canaan, they told him all that had
30 befallen them, saying, "The man, the lord of
the land, spoke roughly to us, and took us to
31 be spies of the land. But we said to him, 'We
32 are honest men, we are not spies; we are
twelve brothers, sons of our father; one is no
more, and the youngest is this day with our
33 father in the land of Canaan.' Then the man,
the lord of the land, said to us, 'By this I shall
know that you are honest men: leave one of
your brothers with me, and take grain for the
famine of your households, and go your way.
34 Bring your youngest brother to me; then I
shall know that you are not spies but honest
men, and I will deliver to you your brother,
and you shall trade in the land.' "

35 As they emptied their sacks, behold, every
man's bundle of money was in his sack; and
when they and their father saw their bundles
36 of money, they were dismayed. And Jacob
their father said to them, "You have bereaved me of my children: Joseph is no
more, and Simeon is no more, and now you
would take Benjamin; all this has come upon
37 me." Then Reuben said to his father, "Slay
my two sons if I do not bring him back to
you; put him in my hands, and I will bring
38 him back to you." But he said, "My son
shall not go down with you, for his brother is
dead, and he only is left. If harm should
befall him on the journey that you are to
make, you would bring down my grey hairs
with sorrow to Sheol."

43 Now the famine was severe in the land.
2 And when they had eaten the grain which
they had brought from Egypt, their father
said to them, "Go again, buy us a little
3 food." But Judah said to him, "The man
solemnly warned us, saying, 'You shall not
see my face, unless your brother is with
4 you.' If you will send our brother with us,
5 we will go down and buy you food; but if you
will not send him, we will not go down, for
the man said to us, 'You shall not see my
face, unless your brother is with you.' "
6 Israel said, "Why did you treat me so ill as to
tell the man that you had another brother?"
7 They replied, "The man questioned us
carefully about ourselves and our kindred,
p Heb *El Shaddai*

saying, 'Is your father still alive? Have you
another brother?' What we told him was in
answer to these questions; could we in any
way know that he would say, 'Bring your
brother down'?" And Judah said to Israel 8
his father, "Send the lad with me, and we
will arise and go, that we may live and not
die, both we and you and also our little ones.
I will be surety for him; of my hand you shall 9
require him. If I do not bring him back to
you and set him before you, then let me bear
the blame for ever; for if we had not delayed, 10
we would now have returned twice."
Then their father Israel said to them, "If it 11
must be so, then do this: take some of the
choice fruits of the land in your bags, and
carry down to the man a present, a little balm
and a little honey, gum, myrrh, pistachio
nuts, and almonds. Take double the money 12
with you; carry back with you the money that
was returned in the mouth of your sacks;
perhaps it was an oversight. Take also your 13
brother, and arise, go again to the man; may 14
God Almighty *p* grant you mercy before the
man, that he may send back your other
brother and Benjamin. If I am bereaved of
my children, I am bereaved." So the men 15
took the present, and they took double the
money with them, and Benjamin; and they
arose and went down to Egypt, and stood
before Joseph.
When Joseph saw Benjamin with them, he 16
said to the steward of his house, "Bring the
men into the house, and slaughter an animal
and make ready, for the men are to dine with
me at noon." The man did as Joseph bade 17
him, and brought the men to Joseph's
house. And the men were afraid because 18
they were brought to Joseph's house, and
they said, "It is because of the money, which
was replaced in our sacks the first time, that
we are brought in, so that he may seek
occasion against us and fall upon us, to make
slaves of us and seize our asses." So they 19
went up to the steward of Joseph's house,
and spoke with him at the door of the house,
and said, "Oh, my lord, we came down the 20
first time to buy food; and when we came to 21
the lodging place we opened our sacks, and
there was every man's money in the mouth of
his sack, our money in full weight; so we
have brought it again with us, and we have 22
brought other money down in our hand to
buy food. We do not know who put our
money in our sacks." He replied, "Rest 23
assured, do not be afraid; your God and the
God of your father must have put treasure in
your sacks for you; I received your money."
Then he brought Simeon out to them. And 24
when the man had brought the men into
Joseph's house, and given them water, and

they had washed their feet, and when he had
25 given their asses provender, they made ready
the present for Joseph's coming at noon, for
they heard that they should eat bread there.
26 When Joseph came home, they brought
into the house to him the present which they
had with them, and bowed down to him to
27 the ground. And he inquired about their
welfare, and said, "Is your father well, the
old man of whom you spoke? Is he still
28 alive?" They said, "Your servant our father
is well, he is still alive." And they bowed
29 their heads and made obeisance. And he
lifted up his eyes, and saw his brother
Benjamin, his mother's son, and said, "Is
this your youngest brother, of whom you
spoke to me? God be gracious to you, my
30 son!" Then Joseph made haste, for his heart
yearned for his brother, and he sought a
place to weep. And he entered his chamber
31 and wept there. Then he washed his face
and came out; and controlling himself he
32 said, "Let food be served." They served him
by himself, and them by themselves, and the
Egyptians who ate with him by themselves,
because the Egyptians might not eat bread
with the Hebrews, for that is an abomination
33 to the Egyptians. And they sat before him,
the first-born according to his birthright and
the youngest according to his youth; and the
men looked at one another in amazement.
34 Portions were taken to them from Joseph's
table, but Benjamin's portion was five times
as much as any of theirs. So they drank and
were merry with him.

44 Then he commanded the steward of his
house, "Fill the men's sacks with food, as
much as they can carry, and put each man's
2 money in the mouth of his sack, and put my
cup, the silver cup, in the mouth of the sack
of the youngest, with his money for the
3 grain." And he did as Joseph told him. As
soon as the morning was light, the men were
4 sent away with their asses. When they had
gone but a short distance from the city,
Joseph said to his steward, "Up, follow after
the men; and when you overtake them, say to
them, 'Why have you returned evil for
good? Why have you stolen my silver cup?*q*
5 Is it not from this that my lord drinks, and by
this that he divines? You have done wrong
in so doing.'"
6 When he overtook them, he spoke to them
7 these words. They said to him, "Why does
my lord speak such words as these? Far be it
from your servants that they should do such
8 a thing! Behold, the money which we found
in the mouth of our sacks, we brought back
to you from the land of Canaan; how then

should we steal silver or gold from your
lord's house? With whomever of your ser- 9
vants it be found, let him die, and we also
will be my lord's slaves." He said, "Let it be 10
as you say: he with whom it is found shall be
my slave, and the rest of you shall
be blameless." Then every man quickly 11
lowered his sack to the ground, and every
man opened his sack. And he searched, 12
beginning with the eldest and ending with
the youngest; and the cup was found in
Benjamin's sack. Then they rent their 13
clothes, and every man loaded his ass, and
they returned to the city.
When Judah and his brothers came to 14
Joseph's house, he was still there; and they
fell before him to the ground. Joseph said to 15
them, "What deed is this that you have
done? Do you not know that such a man as I
can indeed divine?" And Judah said, "What 16
shall we say to my lord? What shall we
speak? Or how can we clear ourselves?
God has found out the guilt of your servants;
behold, we are my lord's slaves, both we and
he also in whose hand the cup has been
found." But he said, "Far be it from me that 17
I should do so! Only the man in whose hand
the cup was found shall be my slave; but as
for you, go up in peace to your father."
Then Judah went up to him and said, "O 18
my lord, let your servant, I pray you, speak a
word in my lord's ears, and let not your anger
burn against your servant; for you are like
Pharaoh himself. My lord asked his ser- 19
vants, saying, 'Have you a father or a
brother?' And we said to my lord, 'We have 20
a father, an old man, and a young brother,
the child of his old age; and his brother is
dead, and he alone is left of his mother's
children; and his father loves him.' Then 21
you said to your servants, 'Bring him down
to me, that I may set my eyes upon him.' We 22
said to my lord, 'The lad cannot leave his
father, for if he should leave his father, his
father would die.' Then you said to your 23
servants, 'Unless your youngest brother
comes down with you, you shall see my face
no more.' When we went back to your 24
servant my father we told him the words of
my lord. And when our father said, 'Go 25
again, buy us a little food,' we said, 'We 26
cannot go down. If our youngest brother
goes with us, then we will go down; for
we cannot see the man's face unless our
youngest brother is with us.' Then your 27
servant my father said to us, 'You know that
my wife bore me two sons; one left me, and I 28
said, Surely he has been torn to pieces; and I
have never seen him since. If you take this 29
one also from me, and harm befalls him, you

---

q Gk Compare Vg: Heb lacks *Why have you stolen my silver cup?*

will bring down my grey hairs in sorrow to
30 Sheol.' Now therefore, when I come to your
servant my father, and the lad is not with us,
then, as his life is bound up in the lad's life,
31 when he sees that the lad is not with us, he
will die; and your servants will bring down
the grey hairs of your servant our father with
32 sorrow to Sheol. For your servant became
surety for the lad to my father, saying, 'If I
do not bring him back to you, then I shall
bear the blame in the sight of my father all
33 my life.' Now therefore, let your servant, I
pray you, remain instead of the lad as a slave
to my lord; and let the lad go back with his
34 brothers. For how can I go back to my father
if the lad is not with me? I fear to see the
evil that would come upon my father."

45 Then Joseph could not control himself
before all those who stood by him; and he
cried, "Make every one go out from me." So
no one stayed with him when Joseph made
2 himself known to his brothers. And he wept
aloud, so that the Egyptians heard it, and the
3 household of Pharaoh heard it. And Joseph
said to his brothers, "I am Joseph; is my
father still alive?" But his brothers could
not answer him, for they were dismayed at
his presence.
4 So Joseph said to his brothers, "Come near
to me, I pray you." And they came near.
And he said, "I am your brother, Joseph,
5 whom you sold into Egypt. And now do not
be distressed, or angry with yourselves,
because you sold me here; for God sent me
6 before you to preserve life. For the famine
has been in the land these two years; and
there are yet five years in which there will be
7 neither ploughing nor harvest. And God
sent me before you to preserve for you a
remnant on earth, and to keep alive for you
8 many survivors. So it was not you who sent
me here, but God; and he has made me a
father to Pharaoh, and lord of all his house
9 and ruler over all the land of Egypt. Make
haste and go up to my father and say to him,
'Thus says your son Joseph, God has made
me lord of all Egypt; come down to me, do
10 not tarry; you shall dwell in the land of
Goshen, and you shall be near me, you and
your children and your children's children,
and your flocks, your herds, and all that you
11 have; and there I will provide for you, for
there are yet five years of famine to come;
lest you and your household, and all that you
12 have, come to poverty.' And now your eyes
see, and the eyes of my brother Benjamin see,
13 that it is my mouth that speaks to you. You
must tell my father of all my splendour in
Egypt, and of all that you have seen. Make

haste and bring my father down here."
Then he fell upon his brother Benjamin's 14
neck and wept; and Benjamin wept upon his
neck. And he kissed all his brothers and 15
wept upon them; and after that his brothers
talked with him.

Pharaoh's invitation

When the report was heard in Pharaoh's 16
house, "Joseph's brothers have come," it
pleased Pharaoh and his servants well. And 17
Pharaoh said to Joseph, "Say to your brothers, 'Do this: load your beasts and go back
to the land of Canaan; and take your father 18
and your households, and come to me, and I
will give you the best of the land of Egypt,
and you shall eat the fat of the land.'
Command them[r] also, 'Do this: take wagons 19
from the land of Egypt for your little ones
and for your wives, and bring your father,
and come. Give no thought to your goods, 20
for the best of all the land of Egypt is
yours.' "
The sons of Israel did so; and Joseph gave 21
them wagons, according to the command of
Pharaoh, and gave them provisions for the
journey. To each and all of them he gave 22
festal garments, but to Benjamin he gave
three hundred shekels of silver and five festal
garments. To his father he sent as follows: 23
ten asses loaded with the good things of
Egypt, and ten she-asses loaded with grain,
bread, and provision for his father on the
journey. Then he sent his brothers away, 24
and as they departed, he said to them, "Do
not quarrel on the way." So they went up 25
out of Egypt, and came to the land of Canaan
to their father Jacob. And they told him, 26
"Joseph is still alive, and he is ruler over all
the land of Egypt." And his heart fainted,
for he did not believe them. But when they 27
told him all the words of Joseph, which he
had said to them, and when he saw the
wagons which Joseph had sent to carry him,
the spirit of their father Jacob revived; and 28
Israel said, "It is enough; Joseph my son is
still alive; I will go and see him before I
die."

God's assurance

So Israel took his journey with all that he **46**
had, and came to Beer-sheba, and offered
sacrifices to the God of his father Isaac. And 2
God spoke to Israel in visions of the night,
and said, "Jacob, Jacob." And he said,
"Here am I." Then he said, "I am God, the 3
God of your father; do not be afraid to go
down to Egypt; for I will there make of you a

---

[r] Compare Gk Vg: Heb *you are commanded*
45.1: Acts 7.13.

great nation. I will go down with you to Egypt, and I will also bring you up again; and Joseph's hand shall close your eyes." 5 Then Jacob set out from Beer-sheba; and the sons of Israel carried Jacob their father, their little ones, and their wives, in the wagons 6 which Pharaoh had sent to carry him. They also took their cattle and their goods, which they had gained in the land of Canaan, and came into Egypt, Jacob and all his offspring with him, his sons, and his sons' sons with 7 him, his daughters, and his sons' daughters; all his offspring he brought with him into Egypt.

Jacob's descendants

8 NOW these are the names of the descendants of Israel, who came into Egypt, Jacob and his sons. Reuben, Jacob's first- 9 born, and the sons of Reuben: Hanoch, Pallu, Hezron, and 10 Carmi. The sons of Simeon: Jemu'el, Jamin, Ohad, Jachin, Zohar, and Sha'ul, the son of a 11 Canaanitish woman. The sons of 12 Levi: Gershon, Kohath, and Merar'i. The sons of Judah: Er, Onan, Shelah, Perez, and Zerah (but Er and Onan died in the land of Canaan); and the sons of Perez 13 were Hezron and Hamul. The sons of Is'sachar: Tola, Puvah, 14 Iob, and Shimron. The sons of Zeb'ulun: Sered, Elon, and Jah'- 15 leel (these are the sons of Leah, whom she bore to Jacob in Pad-dan-aram, together with his daughter Dinah; altogether his sons and his daughters numbered 16 thirty-three). The sons of Gad: Ziph'ion, Haggi, Shuni, Ezbon, 17 Eri, Aro'di, and Are'li. The sons of Asher: Imnah, Ishvah, Ishvi, Beri'ah, with Serah their sister. And the sons of Beri'ah: Heber 18 and Mal'chi-el (these are the sons of Zilpah, whom Laban gave to Leah his daughter; and these she bore to Jacob—sixteen persons). 19 The sons of Rachel, Jacob's wife: 20 Joseph and Benjamin. And to Joseph in the land of Egypt were born Manas'seh and E'phraim, whom As'enath, the daughter of Poti'phera the priest of On, bore 21 to him. And the sons of Benjamin: Bela, Becher, Ashbel, Gera, Na'aman, Ehi, Rosh, Muppim, Huppim, and Ard (these are the sons of Rachel, who 22 were born to Jacob—fourteen persons in all). The sons of Dan: 23 Hushim. The sons of Naph'tali: 24 Jahzeel, Guni, Jezer, and Shillem (these are the sons of Bilhah, 25 whom Laban gave to Rachel his daughter, and these she bore to Jacob—seven persons in all). All 26 the persons belonging to Jacob who came into Egypt, who were his own offspring, not including Jacob's sons' wives, were sixty-six persons in all; and the sons of 27 Joseph, who were born to him in Egypt, were two; all the persons of the house of Jacob, that came into Egypt, were seventy.

Jacob goes to Egypt

28 HE sent Judah before him to Joseph, to appear[s] before him in Goshen; and they 29 came into the land of Goshen. Then Joseph made ready his chariot and went up to meet Israel his father in Goshen; and he presented himself to him, and fell on his neck, and wept 30 on his neck a good while. Israel said to Joseph, "Now let me die, since I have seen your face and know that you are still alive." 31 Joseph said to his brothers and to his father's household, "I will go up and tell Pharaoh, and will say to him, 'My brothers and my father's household, who were in the land of 32 Canaan, have come to me; and the men are shepherds, for they have been keepers of cattle; and they have brought their flocks, and their herds, and all that they have.' 33 When Pharaoh calls you, and says, 'What is 34 your occupation?' you shall say, 'Your servants have been keepers of cattle from our youth even until now, both we and our fathers,' in order that you may dwell in the land of Goshen; for every shepherd is an abomination to the Egyptians."

47 So Joseph went in and told Pharaoh, "My father and my brothers, with their flocks and herds and all that they possess, have come from the land of Canaan; they are now 2 in the land of Goshen." And from among his brothers he took five men and presented them to Pharaoh. Pharaoh said to his 3 brothers, "What is your occupation?" And they said to Pharaoh, "Your servants are shepherds, as our fathers were." They said 4 to Pharaoh, "We have come to sojourn in the land; for there is no pasture for your servants' flocks, for the famine is severe in the land of Canaan; and now, we pray you, let your servants dwell in the land of Goshen." Then Pharaoh said to Joseph, "Your father 5 and your brothers have come to you. The 6 land of Egypt is before you; settle your father and your brothers in the best of the land; let them dwell in the land of Goshen; and if you know any able men among them, put them in charge of my cattle."

Then Joseph brought in Jacob his father, 7 and set him before Pharaoh, and Jacob blessed Pharaoh. And Pharaoh said to Jacob, 8 "How many are the days of the years of your life?" And Jacob said to Pharaoh, "The 9 days of the years of my sojourning are a hundred and thirty years; few and evil have been the days of the years of my life, and they have not attained to the days of the years of the life of my fathers in the days of their sojourning." And Jacob blessed Pharaoh, 10 and went out from the presence of Pharaoh. Then Joseph settled his father and his 11 brothers, and gave them a possession in the land of Egypt, in the best of the land, in the

[s] Sam Syr Compare Gk Vg: Heb *to show the way*
46.6: Acts 7.14–15.　46.8–27: Ex 1.1–4; Num 26.4–50.　46.27: Acts 7.14.

land of Ram′eses, as Pharaoh had com-
12 manded. And Joseph provided his father,
his brothers, and all his father's household
with food, according to the number of their
dependents.

13 Now there was no food in all the land; for
the famine was very severe, so that the land
of Egypt and the land of Canaan languished
14 by reason of the famine. And Joseph
gathered up all the money that was found in
the land of Egypt and in the land of Canaan,
for the grain which they bought; and Joseph
brought the money into Pharaoh's house.
15 And when the money was all spent in the
land of Egypt and in the land of Canaan, all
the Egyptians came to Joseph, and said,
"Give us food; why should we die before
16 your eyes? For our money is gone." And
Joseph answered, "Give your cattle, and I
will give you food in exchange for your cattle,
17 if your money is gone." So they brought
their cattle to Joseph; and Joseph gave them
food in exchange for the horses, the flocks,
the herds, and the asses: and he supplied
them with food in exchange for all their cattle
18 that year. And when that year was ended,
they came to him the following year, and said
to him, "We will not hide from my lord that
our money is all spent; and the herds of cattle
are my lord's; there is nothing left in the
sight of my lord but our bodies and our
19 lands. Why should we die before your eyes,
both we and our land? Buy us and our land
for food, and we with our land will be slaves
to Pharaoh; and give us seed, that we may
live, and not die, and that the land may not
be desolate."
20 So Joseph bought all the land of Egypt for
Pharaoh; for all the Egyptians sold their
fields, because the famine was severe upon
21 them. The land became Pharaoh's; and as
for the people, he made slaves of them[t] from
22 one end of Egypt to the other. Only the land
of the priests he did not buy; for the priests
had a fixed allowance from Pharaoh, and
lived on the allowance which Pharaoh gave
them; therefore they did not sell their land.
23 Then Joseph said to the people, "Behold, I
have this day bought you and your land for
Pharaoh. Now here is seed for you, and you

shall sow the land. And at the harvests you 24
shall give a fifth to Pharaoh, and four
fifths shall be your own, as seed for the field
and as food for yourselves and your households, and as food for your little ones." And 25
they said, "You have saved our lives; may it
please my lord, we will be slaves to Pharaoh."
So Joseph made it a statute concerning the 26
land of Egypt, and it stands to this day, that
Pharaoh should have the fifth; the land of the
priests alone did not become Pharaoh's.
Thus Israel dwelt in the land of Egypt, in 27
the land of Goshen; and they gained possessions in it, and were fruitful and multiplied
exceedingly. And Jacob lived in the land of 28
Egypt seventeen years; so the days of Jacob,
the years of his life, were a hundred and
forty-seven years.
And when the time drew near that Israel 29
must die, he called his son Joseph and said to
him, "If now I have found favour in your
sight, put your hand under my thigh, and
promise to deal loyally and truly with me.
Do not bury me in Egypt, but let me lie with 30
my fathers; carry me out of Egypt and bury
me in their burying place." He answered, "I
will do as you have said." And he said, 31
"Swear to me"; and he swore to him. Then
Israel bowed himself upon the head of his
bed.

After this Joseph was told, "Behold, 48
your father is ill"; so he took with him
his two sons, Manas′seh and E′phraim. And 2
it was told to Jacob, "Your son Joseph has

come to you"; then Israel summoned his strength, and sat up in bed. And Jacob said to Joseph, "God Almighty *u* appeared to me at Luz in the land of Canaan and blessed me, and said to me, 'Behold, I will make you fruitful, and multiply you, and I will make of you a company of peoples, and will give this land to your descendants after you for an 5 everlasting possession.' And now your two sons, who were born to you in the land of Egypt before I came to you in Egypt, are mine; E'phraim and Manas'seh shall be 6 mine, as Reuben and Simeon are. And the offspring born to you after them shall be yours; they shall be called by the name of 7 their brothers in their inheritance. For when I came from Paddan, Rachel to my sorrow died in the land of Canaan on the way, when there was still some distance to go to Ephrath; and I buried her there on the way to Ephrath (that is, Bethlehem)."

8 When Israel saw Joseph's sons, he said, 9 "Who are these?" Joseph said to his father, "They are my sons, whom God has given me here." And he said, "Bring them to me, I 0 pray you, that I may bless them." Now the eyes of Israel were dim with age, so that he could not see. So Joseph brought them near him; and he kissed them and embraced 11 them. And Israel said to Joseph, "I had not thought to see your face; and lo, God has let 12 me see your children also." Then Joseph removed them from his knees, and he bowed 13 himself with his face to the earth. And Joseph took them both, E'phraim in his right hand toward Israel's left hand, and Manas'-seh in his left hand toward Israel's right 14 hand, and brought them near him. And Israel stretched out his right hand and laid it upon the head of E'phraim, who was the younger, and his left hand upon the head of Manas'seh, crossing his hands, for Manas'-15 seh was the first-born. And he blessed Joseph, and said,

"The God before whom my fathers
   Abraham and Isaac walked,
the God who has led me all my life long to
   this day,
16 the angel who has redeemed me from all
   evil, bless the lads;
and in them let my name be perpetuated,
   and the name of my fathers Abraham
   and Isaac;
and let them grow into a multitude in the
   midst of the earth."

17 When Joseph saw that his father laid his right hand upon the head of E'phraim, it displeased him; and he took his father's hand, to remove it from E'phraim's head to 18 Manas'seh's head. And Joseph said to his

father, "Not so, my father; for this one is the first-born; put your right hand upon his head." But his father refused, and said, "I 19 know, my son, I know; he also shall become a people, and he also shall be great; nevertheless his younger brother shall be greater than he, and his descendants shall become a multitude of nations." So he blessed them 20 that day, saying,

"By you Israel will pronounce blessings,
   saying,
'God make you as E'phraim and as
   Manas'seh' ";
and thus he put E'phraim before Manas'seh. Then Israel said to Joseph, "Behold, I am 21 about to die, but God will be with you, and will bring you again to the land of your fathers. Moreover I have given to you rather 22 than to your brothers one mountain slope *v* which I took from the hand of the Amorites with my sword and with my bow."

Jacob's blessing

Then Jacob called his sons, and said, **49** "Gather yourselves together, that I may tell you what shall befall you in days to come.
Assemble and hear, O sons of Jacob,   2
   and hearken to Israel your father.

Reuben, you are my first-born,   3
   my might, and the first fruits of my
      strength,
   pre-eminent in pride and pre-eminent
      in power.
Unstable as water, you shall not have 4
   pre-eminence
   because you went up to your father's
      bed;
   then you defiled it—you *w* went up to my
      couch!

Simeon and Levi are brothers;   5
   weapons of violence are their swords.
O my soul, come not into their council;   6
   O my spirit, *x* be not joined to their
      company;
for in their anger they slay men,
   and in their wantonness they hamstring
      oxen.
Cursed be their anger, for it is fierce;   7
   and their wrath, for it is cruel!
I will divide them in Jacob
   and scatter them in Israel.

Judah, your brothers shall praise you;   8
   your hand shall be on the neck of your
      enemies;
   your father's sons shall bow down be-
      fore you.

u Heb *El Shaddai*   *v* Heb *shekem*, shoulder
w Gk Syr Tg: Heb *he*   *x* Or *glory*

9   Judah is a lion's whelp;
    from the prey, my son, you have gone
    up.
He stooped down, he couched as a lion,
    and as a lioness; who dares rouse him
    up?
10   The sceptre shall not depart from Judah,
    nor the ruler's staff from between his
    feet,
until he comes to whom it belongs;[y]
    and to him shall be the obedience of the
    peoples.
11   Binding his foal to the vine
    and his ass's colt to the choice vine,
he washes his garments in wine
    and his vesture in the blood of grapes;
12   his eyes shall be red with wine,
    and his teeth white with milk.

13   Zeb'ulun shall dwell at the shore of the
    sea;
he shall become a haven for ships,
    and his border shall be at Sidon.

14   Is'sachar is a strong ass,
    crouching between the sheepfolds;
15   he saw that a resting place was good,
    and that the land was pleasant;
so he bowed his shoulder to bear,
    and became a slave at forced labour.

16   Dan shall judge his people
    as one of the tribes of Israel.
17   Dan shall be a serpent in the way,
    a viper by the path,
that bites the horse's heels
    so that his rider falls backward.
18   I wait for thy salvation, O LORD.

19   Raiders[z] shall raid Gad,
    but he shall raid at their heels.

20   Asher's food shall be rich,
    and he shall yield royal dainties.

21   Naph'tali is a hind let loose,
    that bears comely fawns.[a]

22   Joseph is a fruitful bough,
    a fruitful bough by a spring;
his branches run over the wall.
23   The archers fiercely attacked him,
    shot at him, and harassed him sorely;
24   yet his bow remained unmoved,
    his arms[b] were made agile
by the hands of the Mighty One of Jacob
    (by the name of the Shepherd, the Rock
    of Israel),

by the God of your father who will help 25
    you,
by God Almighty[u] who will bless you
    with blessings of heaven above,
blessings of the deep that couches beneath,
    blessings of the breasts and of the
    womb.
The blessings of your father 26
    are mighty beyond the blessings of the
    eternal mountains,[c]
the bounties of the everlasting hills;
may they be on the head of Joseph,
    and on the brow of him who was
    separate from his brothers.

Benjamin is a ravenous wolf, 27
    in the morning devouring the prey,
    and at even dividing the spoil."

Death of Jacob

All these are the twelve tribes of Israel; and 28
this is what their father said to them as he
blessed them, blessing each with the blessing
suitable to him. Then he charged them, and 29
said to them, "I am to be gathered to my
people; bury me with my fathers in the cave
that is in the field of Ephron the Hittite, in 30
the cave that is in the field at Mach-pe'lah, to
the east of Mamre, in the land of Canaan,
which Abraham bought with the field from
Ephron the Hittite to possess as a burying
place. There they buried Abraham and 31
Sarah his wife; there they buried Isaac and
Rebekah his wife; and there I buried
Leah—the field and the cave that is in it were 32
purchased from the Hittites." When Jacob 33
finished charging his sons, he drew up his
feet into the bed, and breathed his last, and
was gathered to his people.

Then Joseph fell on his father's face, and 50
wept over him, and kissed him. And Joseph 2
commanded his servants the physicians to
embalm his father. So the physicians embalmed Israel; forty days were required for 3
it, for so many are required for embalming.
And the Egyptians wept for him seventy
days.

And when the days of weeping for him were 4
past, Joseph spoke to the household of
Pharaoh, saying, "If now I have found favour
in your eyes, speak, I pray you, in the ears of
Pharaoh, saying, My father made me swear, 5
saying, 'I am about to die: in my tomb which
I hewed out for myself in the land of Canaan,
there shall you bury me.' Now therefore let
me go up, I pray you, and bury my father;

---

[y] Syr Compare Tg: Heb *until Shiloh comes* or *until he comes to Shiloh*   [z] Heb *gedud*, a raiding troop
[a] Or *who gives beautiful words*   [b] Heb *the arms of his hands*   [u] Heb *El Shaddai*
[c] Compare Gk: Heb *of my progenitors to*
49.9-10: Num 24.9; Rev 5.5.

6 then I will return." And Pharaoh answered, "Go up, and bury your father, as he made 7 you swear." So Joseph went up to bury his father; and with him went up all the servants of Pharaoh, the elders of his household, and 8 all the elders of the land of Egypt, as well as all the household of Joseph, his brothers, and his father's household; only their children, their flocks, and their herds were left in the 9 land of Goshen. And there went up with him both chariots and horsemen; it was a 10 very great company. When they came to the threshing floor of Atad, which is beyond the Jordan, they lamented there with a very great and sorrowful lamentation; and he made a 11 mourning for his father seven days. When the inhabitants of the land, the Canaanites, saw the mourning on the threshing floor of Atad, they said, "This is a grievous mourning to the Egyptians." Therefore the place was named A'bel-mizraim;[d] it is beyond the 12 Jordan. Thus his sons did for him as he had 13 commanded them; for his sons carried him to the land of Canaan, and buried him in the cave of the field at Mach-pe'lah, to the east of Mamre, which Abraham bought with the field from Ephron the Hittite, to possess as a 14 burying place. After he had buried his father, Joseph returned to Egypt with his brothers and all who had gone up with him to bury his father.

Death of Joseph

15 When Joseph's brothers saw that their father was dead, they said, "It may be that Joseph will hate us and pay us back for all the evil which we did to him." So they sent a 16 message to Joseph, saying, "Your father gave this command before he died, 'Say to Joseph, 17 Forgive, I pray you, the transgression of your brothers and their sin, because they did evil to you.' And now, we pray you, forgive the transgression of the servants of the God of your father." Joseph wept when they spoke to him. His brothers also came and fell down 18 before him, and said, "Behold, we are your servants." But Joseph said to them, "Fear 19 not, for am I in the place of God? As for 20 you, you meant evil against me; but God meant it for good, to bring it about that many people should be kept alive, as they are today. So do not fear; I will provide for you 21 and your little ones." Thus he reassured them and comforted them.

So Joseph dwelt in Egypt, he and his 22 father's house; and Joseph lived a hundred and ten years. And Joseph saw E'phraim's 23 children of the third generation; the children also of Machir the son of Manas'seh were born upon Joseph's knees. And Joseph said 24 to his brothers, "I am about to die; but God will visit you, and bring you up out of this land to the land which he swore to Abraham, to Isaac, and to Jacob." Then Joseph took 25 an oath of the sons of Israel, saying, "God will visit you, and you shall carry up my bones from here." So Joseph died, being 26 a hundred and ten years old; and they embalmed him, and he was put in a coffin in Egypt.

THE SECOND BOOK OF MOSES
COMMONLY CALLED
EXODUS

THESE are the names of the sons of Israel who came to Egypt with Jacob, 2 each with his household: Reuben, 3 Simeon, Levi, and Judah, Is'sachar, 4 Zeb'ulun, and Benjamin, Dan and Naph'- 5 tali, Gad and Asher. All the offspring of Jacob were seventy persons; Joseph was 6 already in Egypt. Then Joseph died, and all 7 his brothers, and all that generation. But the descendants of Israel were fruitful and increased greatly; they multiplied and grew exceedingly strong; so that the land was filled with them.

8 Now there arose a new king over Egypt, 9 who did not know Joseph. And he said to his people, "Behold, the people of Israel are too 10 many and too mighty for us. Come, let us deal shrewdly with them, lest they multiply, and, if war befall us, they join our enemies and fight against us and escape from the 11 land." Therefore they set taskmasters over them to afflict them with heavy burdens; and they built for Pharaoh store-cities, Pithom 12 and Raam'ses. But the more they were oppressed, the more they multiplied and the more they spread abroad. And the Egyptians 13 were in dread of the people of Israel. So they made the people of Israel serve with rigour,

and made their lives bitter with hard service, 14 in mortar and brick, and in all kinds of work in the field; in all their work they made them serve with rigour.

Then the king of Egypt said to the Hebrew 15 midwives, one of whom was named Shiph'- rah and the other Pu'ah, "When you serve as 16 midwife to the Hebrew women, and see them upon the birthstool, if it is a son, you shall kill him; but if it is a daughter, she shall live." But the midwives feared God, and did 17 not do as the king of Egypt commanded them, but let the male children live. So the 18 king of Egypt called the midwives, and said to them, "Why have you done this, and let the male children live?" The midwives said 19 to Pharaoh, "Because the Hebrew women are not like the Egyptian women; for they are vigorous and are delivered before the mid- wife comes to them." So God dealt well with 20 the midwives; and the people multiplied and grew very strong. And because the midwives 21 feared God he gave them families. Then 22 Pharaoh commanded all his people, "Every son that is born to the Hebrews[a] you shall cast into the Nile, but you shall let every daughter live."

a Sam Gk Tg: Heb lacks *to the Hebrews*

1.1–4: Gen 46.8–27; Num 26.4–50.   1.5–8: Acts 7.14–18.   1.10–11, 22: Acts 7.19.

46

MOSES

2 NOW a man from the house of Levi went and took to wife a daughter of Levi. 2 The woman conceived and bore a son; and when she saw that he was a goodly child, she 3 hid him three months. And when she could hide him no longer she took for him a basket made of bulrushes, and daubed it with bitumen and pitch; and she put the child in it and placed it among the reeds at the river's 4 brink. And his sister stood at a distance, to 5 know what would be done to him. Now the daughter of Pharaoh came down to bathe at the river, and her maidens walked beside the river; she saw the basket among the reeds 6 and sent her maid to fetch it. When she opened it she saw the child; and lo, the babe was crying. She took pity on him and said, "This is one of the Hebrews' children." 7 Then his sister said to Pharaoh's daughter, "Shall I go and call you a nurse from the Hebrew women to nurse the child for you?" 8 And Pharaoh's daughter said to her, "Go." So the girl went and called the child's 9 mother. And Pharaoh's daughter said to her, "Take this child away, and nurse him for me, and I will give you your wages." So the 10 woman took the child and nursed him. And the child grew, and she brought him to Pharaoh's daughter, and he became her son; and she named him Moses,[b] for she said, "Because I drew him out[c] of the water."

11 One day, when Moses had grown up, he went out to his people and looked on their burdens; and he saw an Egyptian beating a 12 Hebrew, one of his people. He looked this way and that, and seeing no one he killed the 13 Egyptian and hid him in the sand. When he went out the next day, behold, two Hebrews were struggling together; and he said to the man that did the wrong, "Why do you strike 14 your fellow?" He answered, "Who made you a prince and a judge over us? Do you mean to kill me as you killed the Egyptian?" Then Moses was afraid, and thought, 15 "Surely the thing is known." When Pharaoh heard of it, he sought to kill Moses.

But Moses fled from Pharaoh, and stayed in the land of Mid'ian; and he sat down by a 16 well. Now the priest of Mid'ian had seven daughters; and they came and drew water, and filled the troughs to water their father's 17 flock. The shepherds came and drove them away; but Moses stood up and helped them, 18 and watered their flock. When they came to their father Reu'el, he said, "How is it that 19 you have come so soon today?" They said,

"An Egyptian delivered us out of the hand of the shepherds, and even drew water for us and watered the flock." He said to his 20 daughters, "And where is he? Why have you left the man? Call him, that he may eat bread." And Moses was content to dwell 21 with the man, and he gave Moses his daughter Zippo'rah. She bore a son, and he called 22 his name Gershom; for he said, "I have been a sojourner[d] in a foreign land."

In the course of those many days the king 23 of Egypt died. And the people of Israel groaned under their bondage, and cried out for help, and their cry under bondage came up to God. And God heard their groaning, 24 and God remembered his covenant with Abraham, with Isaac, and with Jacob. And 25 God saw the people of Israel, and God knew their condition.

The angel of the Lord

Now Moses was keeping the flock of his 3 father-in-law, Jethro, the priest of Mid'ian; and he led his flock to the west side of the wilderness, and came to Horeb, the mountain of God. And the angel of the 2 LORD appeared to him in a flame of fire out of the midst of a bush; and he looked, and lo, the bush was burning, yet it was not consumed. And Moses said, "I will turn aside 3 and see this great sight, why the bush is not burnt." When the LORD saw that he turned 4 aside to see, God called to him out of the bush, "Moses, Moses!" And he said, "Here am I." Then he said, "Do not come near; 5 put off your shoes from your feet, for the place on which you are standing is holy ground." And he said, "I am the God of 6 your father, the God of Abraham, the God of Isaac, and the God of Jacob." And Moses hid his face, for he was afraid to look at God.

Then the LORD said, "I have seen the 7 affliction of my people who are in Egypt, and have heard their cry because of their taskmasters; I know their sufferings, and I have 8 come down to deliver them out of the hand of the Egyptians, and to bring them up out of that land to a good and broad land, a land flowing with milk and honey, to the place of the Canaanites, the Hittites, the Amorites, the Per'izzites, the Hivites, and the Jeb'usites. And now, behold, the cry of the 9 people of Israel has come to me, and I have seen the oppression with which the Egyptians oppress them. Come, I will send 10 you to Pharaoh that you may bring forth my people, the sons of Israel, out of Egypt." But 11

b Heb *Mosheh*   c Heb *mashah*   d Heb *ger*
2.2: Acts 7.20; Heb 11.23.   2.5, 10: Acts 7.21.   2.11: Acts 7.23; Heb 11.24.   2.12: Acts 7.24.
2.14: Acts 7.27-28.   2.15, 22: Acts 7.29.   2.24: Acts 7.34.   3.1-4, 17: Ex 6.2-13.   3.2: Acts 7.30.
3.5: Acts 7.33.   3.6: Mt 22.32; Mk 12.26; Lk 20.37; Acts 3.13; 7.32.

Moses said to God, "Who am I that I should go to Pharaoh, and bring the sons of Israel 12 out of Egypt?" He said, "But I will be with you; and this shall be the sign for you, that I have sent you: when you have brought forth the people out of Egypt, you shall serve God upon this mountain."

13 Then Moses said to God, "If I come to the people of Israel and say to them, 'The God of your fathers has sent me to you,' and they ask me, 'What is his name?' what shall I say to 14 them?" God said to Moses, "I AM WHO I AM."[e] And he said, "Say this to the people of 15 Israel, 'I AM has sent me to you.'" God also said to Moses, "Say this to the people of Israel, 'The LORD,[f] the God of your fathers, the God of Abraham, the God of Isaac, and the God of Jacob, has sent me to you': this is my name for ever, and thus I am to be 16 remembered throughout all generations. Go and gather the elders of Israel together, and say to them, 'The LORD, the God of your fathers, the God of Abraham, of Isaac, and of Jacob, has appeared to me, saying, "I have observed you and what has been done to you 17 in Egypt; and I promise that I will bring you up out of the affliction of Egypt, to the land of the Canaanites, the Hittites, the Amorites, the Per'izzites, the Hivites, and the Jeb'usites, a land flowing with milk and 18 honey."' And they will hearken to your voice; and you and the elders of Israel shall go to the king of Egypt and say to him, 'The LORD, the God of the Hebrews, has met with us; and now, we pray you, let us go a three days' journey into the wilderness, that we 19 may sacrifice to the LORD our God.' I know that the king of Egypt will not let you go 20 unless compelled by a mighty hand.[g] So I will stretch out my hand and smite Egypt with all the wonders which I will do in it; 21 after that he will let you go. And I will give this people favour in the sight of the Egyptians; and when you go, you shall not go 22 empty, but each woman shall ask of her neighbour, and of her who sojourns in her house, jewelry of silver and of gold, and clothing, and you shall put them on your sons and on your daughters; thus you shall despoil the Egyptians."

4 Then Moses answered, "But behold, they will not believe me or listen to my voice, for they will say, 'The LORD did not 2 appear to you.'" The LORD said to him, "What is that in your hand?" He said, "A 3 rod." And he said, "Cast it on the ground." So he cast it on the ground, and it became a serpent; and Moses fled from it. But the 4 LORD said to Moses, "Put out your hand, and take it by the tail"—so he put out his hand and caught it, and it became a rod in his hand—"that they may believe that the LORD, 5 the God of their fathers, the God of Abraham, the God of Isaac, and the God of Jacob, has appeared to you." Again, the LORD said 6 to him, "Put your hand into your bosom." And he put his hand into his bosom; and when he took it out, behold, his hand was leprous, as white as snow. Then God said, 7 "Put your hand back into your bosom." So he put his hand back into his bosom; and when he took it out, behold, it was restored like the rest of his flesh. "If they will not 8 believe you," God said, "or heed the first sign, they may believe the latter sign. If they 9 will not believe even these two signs or heed your voice, you shall take some water from the Nile and pour it upon the dry ground; and the water which you shall take from the Nile will become blood upon the dry ground."

But Moses said to the LORD, "Oh, my Lord, 10 I am not eloquent, either heretofore or since thou hast spoken to thy servant; but I am slow of speech and of tongue." Then the 11 LORD said to him, "Who has made man's mouth? Who makes him dumb, or deaf, or seeing, or blind? Is it not I, the LORD? Now therefore go, and I will be with your 12 mouth and teach you what you shall speak." But he said, "Oh, my Lord, send, I pray, 13 some other person." Then the anger of the 14 LORD was kindled against Moses and he said, "Is there not Aaron, your brother, the Levite? I know that he can speak well; and behold, he is coming out to meet you, and when he sees you he will be glad in his heart. And you shall speak to him and put the 15 words in his mouth; and I will be with your mouth and with his mouth, and will teach you what you shall do. He shall speak for 16 you to the people; and he shall be a mouth for you, and you shall be to him as God. And 17 you shall take in your hand this rod, with which you shall do the signs."

Return to Egypt

Moses went back to Jethro his father-in-law 18 and said to him, "Let me go back, I pray, to my kinsmen in Egypt and see whether they are still alive." And Jethro said to Moses, "Go in peace." And the LORD said to Moses 19 in Mid'ian, "Go back to Egypt; for all the men who were seeking your life are dead."

---

[e] Or I AM WHAT I AM or I WILL BE WHAT I WILL BE
[f] The word LORD when spelled with capital letters, stands for the divine name, YHWH, which is here connected with the verb hayah, to be   [g] Gk Vg: Heb no, not by a mighty hand
4.19: Acts 7.34.

0 So Moses took his wife and his sons and set them on an ass, and went back to the land of Egypt; and in his hand Moses took the rod of God.

1 And the LORD said to Moses, "When you go back to Egypt, see that you do before Pharaoh all the miracles which I have put in your power; but I will harden his heart, so that he 2 will not let the people go. And you shall say to Pharaoh, 'Thus says the LORD, Israel is 3 my first-born son, and I say to you, "Let my son go that he may serve me"'; if you refuse to let him go, behold, I will slay your first-born son.'"

4 At a lodging place on the way the LORD met 5 him and sought to kill him. Then Zippo'rah took a flint and cut off her son's foreskin, and touched Moses' feet with it, and said, "Surely you are a bridegroom of blood to 6 me!" So he let him alone. Then it was that she said, "You are a bridegroom of blood," because of the circumcision.

7 The LORD said to Aaron, "Go into the wilderness to meet Moses." So he went, and 8 met him at the mountain of God and kissed him. And Moses told Aaron all the words of the LORD with which he had sent him, and all the signs which he had charged him to do. 9 Then Moses and Aaron went and gathered together all the elders of the people of Israel. 10 And Aaron spoke all the words which the LORD had spoken to Moses, and did the signs 11 in the sight of the people. And the people believed; and when they heard that the LORD had visited the people of Israel and that he had seen their affliction, they bowed their heads and worshipped.

Request to Pharaoh

5 Afterward Moses and Aaron went to Pharaoh and said, "Thus says the LORD, the God of Israel, 'Let my people go, that they may hold a feast to me in the wil- 2 derness.'" But Pharaoh said, "Who is the LORD, that I should heed his voice and let Israel go? I do not know the LORD, and 3 moreover I will not let Israel go." Then they said, "The God of the Hebrews has met with us; let us go, we pray, a three days' journey into the wilderness, and sacrifice to the LORD our God, lest he fall upon us with pestilence 4 or with the sword." But the king of Egypt said to them, "Moses and Aaron, why do you take the people away from their work? Get 5 to your burdens." And Pharaoh said, "Behold, the people of the land are now many and you make them rest from their 6 burdens!" The same day Pharaoh commanded the taskmasters of the people and

their foremen, "You shall no longer give the 7 people straw to make bricks, as heretofore; let them go and gather straw for themselves. But the number of bricks which they made 8 heretofore you shall lay upon them, you shall by no means lessen it; for they are idle; therefore they cry, 'Let us go and offer sacrifice to our God.' Let heavier work be 9 laid upon the men that they may labour at it and pay no regard to lying words."

So the taskmasters and the foremen of the 10 people went out and said to the people, "Thus says Pharaoh, 'I will not give you straw. Go yourselves, get your straw 11 wherever you can find it; but your work will not be lessened in the least.'" So the people 12 were scattered abroad throughout all the land of Egypt, to gather stubble for straw. The 13 taskmasters were urgent, saying, "Complete your work, your daily task, as when there was straw." And the foremen of the people of 14 Israel, whom Pharaoh's taskmasters had set over them, were beaten, and were asked, "Why have you not done all your task of making bricks today, as hitherto?"

Then the foremen of the people of Israel 15 came and cried to Pharaoh, "Why do you deal thus with your servants? No straw is 16 given to your servants, yet they say to us, 'Make bricks!' And behold, your servants are beaten; but the fault is in your own people." But he said, "You are idle, you are 17 idle; therefore you say, 'Let us go and sacrifice to the LORD.' Go now, and work; 18 for no straw shall be given you, yet you shall deliver the same number of bricks." The 19 foremen of the people of Israel saw that they were in evil plight, when they said, "You shall by no means lessen your daily number of bricks." They met Moses and Aaron, who 20 were waiting for them, as they came forth from Pharaoh; and they said to them, "The 21 LORD look upon you and judge, because you have made us offensive in the sight of Pharaoh and his servants, and have put a sword in their hand to kill us."

Then Moses turned again to the LORD and 22 said, "O LORD, why hast thou done evil to this people? Why didst thou ever send me? For since I came to Pharaoh to speak in thy 23 name, he has done evil to this people, and thou hast not delivered thy people at all."

But the LORD said to Moses, "Now you 6 shall see what I will do to Pharaoh; for with a strong hand he will send them out, yea, with a strong hand he will drive them out of his land."

And God said to Moses, "I am the LORD. I 2, appeared to Abraham, to Isaac, and to Jacob, 3

Egyptian gods

have heard the groaning of the people of Israel whom the Egyptians hold in bondage and I have remembered my covenant. Say 6 therefore to the people of Israel, 'I am the LORD, and I will bring you out from under the burdens of the Egyptians, and I will deliver you from their bondage, and I will redeem you with an outstretched arm and with great acts of judgment, and I will take 7 you for my people, and I will be your God; and you shall know that I am the LORD your God, who has brought you out from under the burdens of the Egyptians. And I will 8 bring you into the land which I swore to give to Abraham, to Isaac, and to Jacob; I will give it to you for a possession. I am the LORD.' " Moses spoke thus to the people of 9 Israel; but they did not listen to Moses, because of their broken spirit and their cruel bondage.

And the LORD said to Moses, "Go in, tell 10 Pharaoh king of Egypt to let the people of 11 Israel go out of his land." But Moses said to 12 the LORD, "Behold, the people of Israel have not listened to me; how then shall Pharaoh listen to me, who am a man of uncircumcised lips?" But the LORD spoke to Moses and 13 Aaron, and gave them a charge to the people of Israel and to Pharaoh king of Egypt to bring the people of Israel out of the land of Egypt.

as God Almighty,^h but by my name the LORD I did not make myself known to them. 4 I also established my covenant with them, to give them the land of Canaan, the land in 5 which they dwelt as sojourners. Moreover I

Heads of the families

14 THESE are the heads of their fathers' houses: the sons of Reuben, the first-born of Israel: Hanoch, Pallu, Hezron, and 15 Carmi; these are the families of Reuben. The sons of Simeon: Jemu'el, Jamin, Ohad, Jachin, Zohar, and Sha'ul, the son of a Canaanite woman; these are the 16 families of Simeon. These are the names of the sons of Levi according to their generations: Gershon, Kohath, and Merar'i, the 22 years of the life of Levi being a hundred and thirty-seven years. 17 The sons of Gershon: Libni and 18 Shim'e-i, by their families. The

sons of Kohath; Amram, Izhar, Hebron, and Uz'ziel, the years of 19 the life of Kohath being a hundred and thirty-three years. The sons of Merar'i: Mahli and Mushi. These are the families of 20 the Levites according to their generations. Amram took to wife Joch'ebed his father's sister and she bore him Aaron and Moses, the years of the life of Amram being one hundred and thirty-21 seven years. The sons of Izhar: Korah, Nepheg, and Zichri. And the sons of Uz'ziel: 23 Mi'sha-el, Elza'phan, and Sithri. Aaron took to wife Elish'eba, the daughter of Ammin'adab and the sister of Nahshon; and she bore

him Nadab, Abi'hu, Elea'zar, and Ith'amar. The sons of Korah: 24 Assir, Elka'nah, and Abi'asaph; these are the families of the Ko'rahites. Elea'zar, Aaron's son, 25 took to wife one of the daughters of Pu'ti-el; and she bore him Phin'ehas. These are the heads of the fathers' houses of the Levites by their families.

These are the Aaron and Moses 26 to whom the LORD said: "Bring out the people of Israel from the land of Egypt by their hosts." It 27 was they who spoke to Pharaoh king of Egypt about bringing out the people of Israel from Egypt, this Moses and this Aaron.

Pharaoh's refusal

28 ON the day when the LORD spoke to 29 Moses in the land of Egypt, the LORD said to Moses, "I am the LORD; tell Pharaoh 30 king of Egypt all that I say to you." But Moses said to the LORD, "Behold, I am of

uncircumcised lips; how then shall Pharaoh listen to me?"

And the LORD said to Moses, "See, I 7 make you as God to Pharaoh; and Aaron your brother shall be your prophet. You 2 shall speak all that I command you; and

^h Heb *El Shaddai*
6.14–16: Gen 46.8–11; Num 26.5–14.   6.16–19: Num 3.15–20; 26.57–58; 1 Chron 6.1, 16–19.
6.20–23: Num 26.58–60.

Aaron your brother shall tell Pharaoh to let
3 the people of Israel go out of his land. But I
will harden Pharaoh's heart, and though I
multiply my signs and wonders in the land of
4 Egypt, Pharaoh will not listen to you; then I
will lay my hand upon Egypt and bring forth
my hosts, my people the sons of Israel, out of
the land of Egypt by great acts of judgment.
5 And the Egyptians shall know that I am the
LORD, when I stretch forth my hand upon
Egypt and bring out the people of Israel from
6 among them." And Moses and Aaron did
so; they did as the LORD commanded them.
7 Now Moses was eighty years old, and Aaron
eighty-three years old, when they spoke to
Pharaoh.
8 And the LORD said to Moses and Aaron,
9 "When Pharaoh says to you, 'Prove yourselves by working a miracle,' then you shall
say to Aaron, 'Take your rod and cast it
down before Pharaoh, that it may become a
10 serpent.'" So Moses and Aaron went to
Pharaoh and did as the LORD commanded;
Aaron cast down his rod before Pharaoh and
11 his servants, and it became a serpent. Then
Pharaoh summoned the wise men and the
sorcerers; and they also, the magicians of
12 Egypt, did the same by their secret arts. For
every man cast down his rod, and they
became serpents. But Aaron's rod swallowed
13 up their rods. Still Pharaoh's heart was
hardened, and he would not listen to them;
as the LORD had said.

The plagues

14 Then the LORD said to Moses, "Pharaoh's heart is hardened, he refuses to let the
15 people go. Go to Pharaoh in the morning, as
he is going out to the water; wait for him by
the river's brink, and take in your hand the
16 rod which was turned into a serpent. And
you shall say to him, 'The LORD, the God of
the Hebrews, sent me to you, saying, "Let
my people go, that they may serve me in the
wilderness; and behold, you have not yet
17 obeyed." Thus says the LORD, "By this you
shall know that I am the LORD; behold, I will

strike the water that is in the Nile with the
rod that is in my hand, and it shall be turned
to blood, and the fish in the Nile shall die, 18
and the Nile shall become foul, and the
Egyptians will loathe to drink water from the
Nile."'" And the LORD said to Moses, 19
"Say to Aaron, 'Take your rod and stretch
out your hand over the waters of Egypt, over
their rivers, their canals, and their ponds,
and all their pools of water, that they may
become blood; and there shall be blood
throughout all the land of Egypt, both in
vessels of wood and in vessels of stone.'"
Moses and Aaron did as the LORD com- 20
manded; in the sight of Pharaoh and in the
sight of his servants, he lifted up the rod and
struck the water that was in the Nile, and all
the water that was in the Nile turned to
blood. And the fish in the Nile died; and the 21
Nile became foul, so that the Egyptians could
not drink water from the Nile and there was
blood throughout all the land of Egypt. But 22
the magicians of Egypt did the same by their
secret arts; so Pharaoh's heart remained
hardened, and he would not listen to them;
as the LORD had said. Pharaoh turned and 23
went into his house, and he did not lay even
this to heart. And all the Egyptians dug 24
round about the Nile for water to drink, for
they could not drink the water of the Nile.
Seven days passed after the LORD had 25
struck the Nile.

Then the LORD said to Moses, "Go in to 8[i]
Pharaoh and say to him, 'Thus says the
LORD, "Let my people go, that they may
serve me. But if you refuse to let them go, 2
behold, I will plague all your country with
frogs; the Nile shall swarm with frogs which 3

shall come up into your house, and into your bedchamber and on your bed, and into the houses of your servants and of your people,[j] and into your ovens and your kneading 4 bowls; the frogs shall come up on you and on your people and on all your servants." ' "

5[k] And the LORD said to Moses, "Say to Aaron, 'Stretch out your hand with your rod over the rivers, over the canals, and over the pools, and cause frogs to come upon the land 6 of Egypt!' " So Aaron stretched out his hand over the waters of Egypt; and the frogs 7 came up and covered the land of Egypt. But the magicians did the same by their secret arts, and brought frogs upon the land of Egypt.

8 Then Pharaoh called Moses and Aaron, and said, "Entreat the LORD to take away the frogs from me and from my people; and I will let the people go to sacrifice to the 9 LORD." Moses said to Pharaoh, "Be pleased to command me when I am to entreat, for you and for your servants and for your people, that the frogs be destroyed from you and your houses and be left only in the 10 Nile." And he said, "Tomorrow." Moses said, "Be it as you say, that you may know that there is no one like the LORD our God. 11 The frogs shall depart from you and your houses and your servants and your people; 12 they shall be left only in the Nile." So Moses and Aaron went out from Pharaoh; and Moses cried to the LORD concerning the 13 frogs, as he had agreed with Pharaoh.[l] And the LORD did according to the word of Moses; the frogs died out of the houses and 14 courtyards and out of the fields. And they gathered them together in heaps, and the 15 land stank. But when Pharaoh saw that there was a respite, he hardened his heart, and would not listen to them; as the LORD had said.

16 Then the LORD said to Moses, "Say to Aaron, 'Stretch out your rod and strike the dust of the earth, that it may become gnats 17 throughout all the land of Egypt.' " And they did so; Aaron stretched out his hand with his rod, and struck the dust of the earth, and there came gnats on man and beast; all the dust of the earth became gnats through-18 out all the land of Egypt. The magicians tried by their secret arts to bring forth gnats, but they could not. So there were gnats on 19 man and beast. And the magicians said to Pharaoh, "This is the finger of God." But Pharaoh's heart was hardened, and he would not listen to them; as the LORD had said.

20 Then the LORD said to Moses, "Rise up early in the morning and wait for Pharaoh, as he goes out to the water, and say to him,

'Thus says the LORD, "Let my people go, that they may serve me. Else, if you will not 21 let my people go, behold, I will send swarms of flies on you and your servants and your people, and into your houses; and the houses of the Egyptians shall be filled with swarms of flies, and also the ground on which they stand. But on that day I will set apart the 22 land of Goshen, where my people dwell, so that no swarms of flies shall be there; that you may know that I am the LORD in the midst of the earth. Thus I will put 23 a division[m] between my people and your people. By tomorrow shall this sign be." ' " And the LORD did so; there came great 24 swarms of flies into the house of Pharaoh and into his servants' houses, and in all the land of Egypt the land was ruined by reason of the flies.

Then Pharaoh called Moses and Aaron, and 25 said, "Go, sacrifice to your God within the land." But Moses said, "It would not be 26 right to do so; for we shall sacrifice to the LORD our God offerings abominable to the Egyptians. If we sacrifice offerings abominable to the Egyptians before their eyes, will they not stone us? We must go three days' 27 journey into the wilderness and sacrifice to the LORD our God as he will command us." So Pharaoh said, "I will let you go, to 28 sacrifice to the LORD your God in the wilderness; only you shall not go very far away. Make entreaty for me." Then Moses 29 said, "Behold, I am going out from you and I will pray to the LORD that the swarms of flies may depart from Pharaoh, from his servants, and from his people, tomorrow; only let not Pharaoh deal falsely again by not letting the people go to sacrifice to the LORD." So 30 Moses went out from Pharaoh and prayed to the LORD. And the LORD did as Moses 31 asked, and removed the swarms of flies from Pharaoh, from his servants, and from his people; not one remained. But Pharaoh 32 hardened his heart this time also, and did not let the people go.

Then the LORD said to Moses, "Go in to 9 Pharaoh, and say to him, 'Thus says the LORD, the God of the Hebrews, "Let my people go, that they may serve me. For if 2 you refuse to let them go and still hold them, behold, the hand of the LORD will fall with a 3 very severe plague upon your cattle which are in the field, the horses, the asses, the camels, the herds, and the flocks. But 4 the LORD will make a distinction between the cattle of Israel and the cattle of Egypt, so that nothing shall die of all that belongs to the

---

[j] Gk: Heb *upon your people*   [k] Ch 8.1 in Heb   [l] Or *which he had brought upon Pharaoh*
[m] Gk Vg: Heb *set redemption*

people of Israel." ' " And the LORD set a
time, saying, "Tomorrow the LORD will do
this thing in the land." And on the morrow
the LORD did this thing; all the cattle of the
Egyptians died, but of the cattle of the people
of Israel not one died. And Pharaoh sent,
and behold, not one of the cattle of the
Israelites was dead. But the heart of Pharaoh
was hardened, and he did not let the people
go.

And the LORD said to Moses and Aaron,
"Take handfuls of ashes from the kiln, and
let Moses throw them toward heaven in the
sight of Pharaoh. And it shall become fine
dust over all the land of Egypt, and become
boils breaking out in sores on man and beast
throughout all the land of Egypt." So they
took ashes from the kiln, and stood before
Pharaoh, and Moses threw them toward
heaven, and it became boils breaking out in
sores on man and beast. And the magicians
could not stand before Moses because of the
boils, for the boils were upon the magicians
and upon all the Egyptians. But the LORD
hardened the heart of Pharaoh, and he did
not listen to them; as the LORD had spoken to
Moses.

3 Then the LORD said to Moses, "Rise up
early in the morning and stand before Pharaoh, and say to him, 'Thus says the LORD,
the God of the Hebrews, "Let my people go,
4 that they may serve me. For this time I will
send all my plagues upon your heart, and
upon your servants and your people, that you
may know that there is none like me in all the
5 earth. For by now I could have put forth my
hand and struck you and your people with
pestilence, and you would have been cut off
6 from the earth; but for this purpose have I let
you live, to show you my power, so that my
name may be declared throughout all the
7 earth. You are still exalting yourself against
8 my people, and will not let them go. Behold,
tomorrow about this time I will cause very
heavy hail to fall, such as never has been in
Egypt from the day it was founded until
9 now. Now therefore send, get your cattle
and all that you have in the field into safe
shelter; for the hail shall come down upon
every man and beast that is in the field and is
not brought home, and they shall die." ' "
20 Then he who feared the word of the LORD
among the servants of Pharaoh made his
21 slaves and his cattle flee into the houses; but
he who did not regard the word of the LORD
left his slaves and his cattle in the field.
22 And the LORD said to Moses, "Stretch forth
your hand toward heaven, that there may be
hail in all the land of Egypt, upon man and
beast and every plant of the field, throughout

the land of Egypt." Then Moses stretched 23
forth his rod toward heaven; and the LORD
sent thunder and hail, and fire ran down to
the earth. And the LORD rained hail upon
the land of Egypt; there was hail, and fire 24
flashing continually in the midst of the hail,
very heavy hail, such as had never been in all
the land of Egypt since it became a nation.
The hail struck down everything that was in 25
the field throughout all the land of Egypt,
both man and beast; and the hail struck
down every plant of the field, and shattered
every tree of the field. Only in the land of 26
Goshen, where the people of Israel were,
there was no hail.

Then Pharaoh sent, and called Moses and 27
Aaron, and said to them, "I have sinned this
time; the LORD is in the right, and I and my
people are in the wrong. Entreat the LORD; 28
for there has been enough of this thunder
and hail; I will let you go, and you shall stay
no longer." Moses said to him, "As soon as I 29
have gone out of the city, I will stretch out
my hands to the LORD; the thunder will
cease, and there will be no more hail, that
you may know that the earth is the LORD's.
But as for you and your servants, I know that 30
you do not yet fear the LORD God." (The 31
flax and the barley were ruined, for the
barley was in the ear and the flax was in bud.
But the wheat and the spelt were not ruined, 32
for they are late in coming up.) So Moses 33
went out of the city from Pharaoh, and
stretched out his hands to the LORD; and the
thunder and the hail ceased, and the rain no
longer poured upon the earth. But when 34
Pharaoh saw that the rain and the hail and
the thunder had ceased, he sinned yet again,
and hardened his heart, he and his servants.
So the heart of Pharaoh was hardened, and 35
he did not let the people of Israel go; as the
LORD had spoken through Moses.

Then the LORD said to Moses, "Go 10
in to Pharaoh; for I have hardened
his heart and the heart of his servants, that I
may show these signs of mine among them,
and that you may tell in the hearing of your 2
son and of your son's son how I have made
sport of the Egyptians and what signs I have
done among them; that you may know that I
am the LORD."

So Moses and Aaron went in to Pharaoh, 3
and said to him, "Thus says the LORD, the
God of the Hebrews, 'How long will you
refuse to humble yourself before me? Let
my people go, that they may serve me. For if 4
you refuse to let my people go, behold,
tomorrow I will bring locusts into your

5 country, and they shall cover the face of the land, so that no one can see the land; and they shall eat what is left to you after the hail, and they shall eat every tree of yours which 6 grows in the field, and they shall fill your houses, and the houses of all your servants and of all the Egyptians; as neither your fathers nor your grandfathers have seen, from the day they came on earth to this day.' " Then he turned and went out from Pharaoh.

7 And Pharaoh's servants said to him, "How long shall this man be a snare to us? Let the men go, that they may serve the LORD their God; do you not yet understand that Egypt is 8 ruined?" So Moses and Aaron were brought back to Pharaoh; and he said to them, "Go, serve the LORD your God; but who are to 9 go?" And Moses said, "We will go with our young and our old; we will go with our sons and daughters and with our flocks and herds, 10 for we must hold a feast to the LORD." And he said to them, "The LORD be with you, if ever I let you and your little ones go! Look, 11 you have some evil purpose in mind.ⁿ No! Go, the men among you, and serve the LORD, for that is what you desire." And they were driven out from Pharaoh's presence.

12 Then the LORD said to Moses, "Stretch out your hand over the land of Egypt for the locusts, that they may come upon the land of Egypt, and eat every plant in the land, all 13 that the hail has left." So Moses stretched forth his rod over the land of Egypt, and the LORD brought an east wind upon the land all that day and all that night; and when it was 14 morning the east wind had brought the locusts. And the locusts came up over all the land of Egypt, and settled on the whole country of Egypt, such a dense swarm of locusts as had never been before, nor ever 15 shall be again. For they covered the face of the whole land, so that the land was darkened, and they ate all the plants in the land and all the fruit of the trees which the hail had left; not a green thing remained, neither tree nor plant of the field, through all the 16 land of Egypt. Then Pharaoh called Moses and Aaron in haste, and said, "I have sinned against the LORD your God, and against you. 17 Now therefore, forgive my sin, I pray you, only this once, and entreat the LORD your 18 God only to remove this death from me." So he went out from Pharaoh, and entreated the 19 LORD. And the LORD turned a very strong west wind, which lifted the locusts and drove them into the Red Sea; not a single locust 20 was left in all the country of Egypt. But the LORD hardened Pharaoh's heart, and he did not let the children of Israel go.

Then the LORD said to Moses, "Stretch out 21 your hand toward heaven that there may be darkness over the land of Egypt, a darkness to be felt." So Moses stretched out his hand 22 toward heaven, and there was thick darkness in all the land of Egypt three days; they did 23 not see one another, nor did any rise from his place for three days; but all the people of Israel had light where they dwelt. Then 24 Pharaoh called Moses, and said, "Go, serve the LORD; your children also may go with you; only let your flocks and your herds remain behind." But Moses said, "You 25 must also let us have sacrifices and burnt offerings, that we may sacrifice to the LORD our God. Our cattle also must go with us; 26 not a hoof shall be left behind, for we must take of them to serve the LORD our God, and we do not know with what we must serve the LORD until we arrive there." But the LORD 27 hardened Pharaoh's heart, and he would not let them go. Then Pharaoh said to him, 28 "Get away from me; take heed to yourself; never see my face again; for in the day you see my face you shall die." Moses said, 29 "As you say! I will not see your face again."

The LORD said to Moses, "Yet one plague 1 more I will bring upon Pharaoh and upon Egypt; afterwards he will let you go hence; when he lets you go, he will drive you away completely. Speak now in the hearing of the 2 people, that they ask, every man of his neighbour and every woman of her neighbour, jewelry of silver and of gold." And the LORD 3 gave the people favour in the sight of the Egyptians. Moreover, the man Moses was very great in the land of Egypt, in the sight of Pharaoh's servants and in the sight of the people.

And Moses said, "Thus says the LORD: 4 About midnight I will go forth in the midst of Egypt; and all the first-born in the land of 5 Egypt shall die, from the first-born of Pharaoh who sits upon his throne, even to the first-born of the maidservant who is behind the mill; and all the first-born of the cattle. And there shall be a great cry throughout all 6 the land of Egypt, such as there has never been, nor ever shall be again. But against 7 any of the people of Israel, either man or beast, not a dog shall growl; that you may know that the LORD makes a distinction between the Egyptians and Israel. And all 8 these your servants shall come down to me, and bow down to me, saying, 'Get you out, and all the people who follow you.' And after that I will go out." And he went out

---

ⁿ Heb *before your face*

9 from Pharaoh in hot anger. Then the LORD said to Moses, "Pharaoh will not listen to you; that my wonders may be multiplied in the land of Egypt."
10 Moses and Aaron did all these wonders before Pharaoh; and the LORD hardened Pharaoh's heart, and he did not let the people of Israel go out of his land.

The passover

2 The LORD said to Moses and Aaron in the
2 land of Egypt, "This month shall be for you the beginning of months; it shall be the
3 first month of the year for you. Tell all the congregation of Israel that on the tenth day of this month they shall take every man a lamb according to their fathers' houses, a
4 lamb for a household; and if the household is too small for a lamb, then a man and his neighbour next to his house shall take according to the number of persons; according to what each can eat you shall make your count
5 for the lamb. Your lamb shall be without blemish, a male a year old; you shall take it
6 from the sheep or from the goats; and you shall keep it until the fourteenth day of this month, when the whole assembly of the congregation of Israel shall kill their lambs in
7 the evening.° Then they shall take some of the blood, and put it on the two doorposts and the lintel of the houses in which they eat
8 them. They shall eat the flesh that night, roasted; with unleavened bread and bitter
9 herbs they shall eat it. Do not eat any of it raw or boiled with water, but roasted, its
10 head with its legs and its inner parts. And you shall let none of it remain until the morning, anything that remains until the

Lintel and doorposts

morning you shall burn. In this manner you 11 shall eat it: your loins girded, your sandals on your feet, and your staff in your hand; and you shall eat it in haste. It is the LORD's passover. For I will pass through the land of 12 Egypt that night, and I will smite all the first-born in the land of Egypt, both man and beast; and on all the gods of Egypt I will execute judgments: I am the LORD. The 13 blood shall be a sign for you, upon the houses where you are; and when I see the blood, I will pass over you, and no plague shall fall upon you to destroy you, when I smite the land of Egypt.

"This day shall be for you a memorial day, 14 and you shall keep it as a feast to the LORD; throughout your generations you shall observe it as an ordinance for ever. Seven days 15 you shall eat unleavened bread; on the first day you shall put away leaven out of your houses, for if any one eats what is leavened, from the first day until the seventh day, that person shall be cut off from Israel. On the 16 first day you shall hold a holy assembly, and on the seventh day a holy assembly; no work shall be done on those days; but what every one must eat, that only may be prepared by you. And you shall observe the feast of 17 unleavened bread, for on this very day I brought your hosts out of the land of Egypt: therefore you shall observe this day, throughout your generations, as an ordinance for ever. In the first month, on the 18 fourteenth day of the month at evening, you

Hyssop   Ex 13, 22

° Heb *between the two evenings*
12.13: Heb 11.28.

shall eat unleavened bread, and so until the twenty-first day of the month at evening.

19 For seven days no leaven shall be found in your houses; for if any one eats what is leavened, that person shall be cut off from the congregation of Israel, whether he is a 20 sojourner or a native of the land. You shall eat nothing leavened; in all your dwellings you shall eat unleavened bread."

21 Then Moses called all the elders of Israel, and said to them, "Select lambs for yourselves according to your families, and kill the 22 passover lamb. Take a bunch of hyssop and dip it in the blood which is in the basin, and touch the lintel and the two doorposts with the blood which is in the basin; and none of you shall go out of the door of his house 23 until the morning. For the LORD will pass through to slay the Egyptians; and when he sees the blood on the lintel and on the two doorposts, the LORD will pass over the door, and will not allow the destroyer to enter your 24 houses to slay you. You shall observe this rite as an ordinance for you and for your sons 25 for ever. And when you come to the land which the LORD will give you, as he has 26 promised, you shall keep this service. And when your children say to you, 'What do you 27 mean by this service?' you shall say, 'It is the sacrifice of the LORD's passover, for he passed over the houses of the people of Israel in Egypt, when he slew the Egyptians but spared our houses.'" And the people bowed their heads and worshipped.

28 Then the people of Israel went and did so; as the LORD had commanded Moses and Aaron, so they did.

29 At midnight the LORD smote all the first-born in the land of Egypt, from the first-born of Pharaoh who sat on his throne to the first-born of the captive who was in the dungeon, and all the first-born of the cattle. 30 And Pharaoh rose up in the night, he, and all

his servants, and all the Egyptians; and there was a great cry in Egypt, for there was not a house where one was not dead. And he 31 summoned Moses and Aaron by night, and said, "Rise up, go forth from among my people, both you and the people of Israel; and go, serve the LORD, as you have said. Take your flocks and your herds, as you have 32 said, and be gone; and bless me also!"

And the Egyptians were urgent with the 33 people, to send them out of the land in haste; for they said, "We are all dead men." So 34 the people took their dough before it was leavened, their kneading bowls being bound up in their mantles on their shoulders. The 35 people of Israel had also done as Moses told them, for they had asked of the Egyptians jewelry of silver and of gold, and clothing; and the LORD had given the people favour in 36 the sight of the Egyptians, so that they let them have what they asked. Thus they despoiled the Egyptians.

And the people of Israel journeyed from 37 Ram'eses to Succoth, about six hundred thousand men on foot, besides women and children. A mixed multitude also went up 38 with them, and very many cattle, both flocks and herds. And they baked unleavened cakes 39 of the dough which they had brought out of Egypt, for it was not leavened, because they were thrust out of Egypt and could not tarry, neither had they prepared for themselves any provisions.

The time that the people of Israel dwelt in 40 Egypt was four hundred and thirty years. And at the end of four hundred and thirty 41 years, on that very day, all the hosts of the LORD went out from the land of Egypt. It 42 was a night of watching by the LORD, to bring them out of the land of Egypt; so this same night is a night of watching kept to the LORD by all the people of Israel throughout their generations.

Ordinance of the passover

43 AND the LORD said to Moses and Aaron, "This is the ordinance of the passover: no 44 foreigner shall eat of it; but every slave that is bought for money 45 may eat of it after you have cir-cumcised him. No sojourner or 46 hired servant may eat of it. In one house shall it be eaten; you shall not carry forth any of the flesh outside the house; and you shall 47 not break a bone of it. All the congregation of Israel shall keep 48 it. And when a stranger shall

sojourn with you and would keep the passover to the LORD, let all his males be circumcised, then he may come near and keep it; he shall be as a native of the land. But no uncircumcised person 49 shall eat of it. There shall be one law for the native and for the stranger who sojourns among you."

50 Thus did all the people of Israel; as the LORD commanded Moses 51 and Aaron, so they did. And on that very day the LORD brought the people of Israel out of the land of Egypt by their hosts.

The LORD said to Moses, 13 "Consecrate to me all the first- 2 born; whatever is the first to open the womb among the people of Israel, both of man and of beast, is mine."

And Moses said to the people, 3 "Remember this day, in which you came out from Egypt, out of the house of bondage, for by strength of hand the LORD brought you out from this place; no leavened bread shall be eaten. This day you are to go forth, in 4 the month of Abib. And when 5 the LORD brings you into the land

12.40: Acts 7.6.   12.46: Num 9.12; Jn 19.36.   12.49: Lev 24.22; Num 9.14; 15.15, 16, 29. 13.2, 12, 15: Lk 2.23.

of the Canaanites, the Hittites, the Amorites, the Hivites, and the Jeb'usites, which he swore to your fathers to give you, a land flowing 10 with milk and honey, you shall keep this service in this month. 6 Seven days you shall eat unleavened bread, and on the seventh day there shall be a feast to the 7 LORD. Unleavened bread shall be eaten for seven days; no leavened bread shall be seen with you, and no leaven shall be seen with you in 8 all your territory. And you shall tell your son on that day, 'It is because of what the LORD did for me when I came out of Egypt.' 9 And it shall be to you as a sign on your hand and as a memorial between your eyes, that the law of

the LORD may be in your mouth; for with a strong hand the LORD has brought you out of Egypt. 10 You shall therefore keep this ordinance at its appointed time from year to year. 11 "And when the LORD brings you into the land of the Canaanites, as he swore to you and your fathers, and shall give it to you, you shall 12 set apart to the LORD all that first opens the womb. All the firstlings of your cattle that are males 13 shall be the LORD's. Every firstling of an ass you shall redeem with a lamb, or if you will not redeem it you shall break its neck. Every first-born of man among your sons you shall 14 redeem. And when in time to

come your son asks you, 'What does this mean?' you shall say to him, 'By strength of hand the LORD brought us out of Egypt, from the house of bondage. For 15 when Pharaoh stubbornly refused to let us go, the LORD slew all the first-born in the land of Egypt, both the first-born of man and the first-born of cattle. Therefore I sacrifice to the LORD all the males that first open the womb; but all the first-born of my sons I redeem.' It shall be as a mark on 16 your hand or frontlets between your eyes; for by a strong hand the LORD brought us out of Egypt."

THE EXODUS

17 WHEN Pharaoh let the people go, God did not lead them by way of the land of the Philistines, although that was near; for God said, "Lest the people repent when they 18 see war, and return to Egypt." But God led the people round by the way of the wilderness toward the Red Sea. And the people of Israel went up out of the land of Egypt 19 equipped for battle. And Moses took the bones of Joseph with him; for Joseph had solemnly sworn the people of Israel, saying, "God will visit you; then you must carry my 20 bones with you from here." And they moved on from Succoth, and encamped at Etham, 21 on the edge of the wilderness. And the LORD went before them by day in a pillar of cloud to lead them along the way, and by night in a pillar of fire to give them light, that they 22 might travel by day and by night; the pillar of cloud by day and the pillar of fire by night did not depart from before the people.

14 Then the LORD said to Moses, 'Tell 2 the people of Israel to turn back and encamp in front of Pi-ha-hi'roth, between Migdol and the sea, in front of Ba'al-zephon; you shall encamp over against it, by the sea.

For Pharaoh will say of the people of Israel, 3 'They are entangled in the land; the wilderness has shut them in.' And I will harden 4 Pharaoh's heart, and he will pursue them and I will get glory over Pharaoh and all his host; and the Egyptians shall know that I am the LORD." And they did so.

When the king of Egypt was told that the 5 people had fled, the mind of Pharaoh and his servants was changed toward the people, and they said, "What is this we have done, that we have let Israel go from serving us?" So 6 he made ready his chariot and took his army with him, and took six hundred picked 7 chariots and all the other chariots of Egypt with officers over all of them. And the LORD 8 hardened the heart of Pharaoh king of Egypt and he pursued the people of Israel as they went forth defiantly. The Egyptians pur- 9 sued them, all Pharaoh's horses and chariots and his horsemen and his army, and overtook them encamped at the sea, by Pi-ha-hi'roth, in front of Ba'al-zephon.

When Pharaoh drew near, the people of 10 Israel lifted up their eyes, and behold, the Egyptians were marching after them; and they were in great fear. And the people of

13.19: Gen 50.25.   **14.8:** Acts 13.17.

11 Israel cried out to the LORD; and they said to Moses, "Is it because there are no graves in Egypt that you have taken us away to die in the wilderness? What have you done to us,
12 in bringing us out of Egypt? Is not this what we said to you in Egypt, 'Let us alone and let us serve the Egyptians'? For it would have been better for us to serve the Egyptians than
13 to die in the wilderness." And Moses said to the people, "Fear not, stand firm, and see the salvation of the LORD, which he will work for you today; for the Egyptians whom you see
14 today, you shall never see again. The LORD will fight for you, and you have only to be
15 still." The LORD said to Moses, "Why do you cry to me? Tell the people of Israel to
16 go forward. Lift up your rod, and stretch out your hand over the sea and divide it, that the people of Israel may go on dry ground
17 through the sea. And I will harden the hearts of the Egyptians so that they shall go in after them, and I will get glory over Pharaoh and all his host, his chariots, and his
18 horsemen. And the Egyptians shall know that I am the LORD, when I have gotten glory over Pharaoh, his chariots, and his horsemen."
19 Then the angel of God who went before the host of Israel moved and went behind them; and the pillar of cloud moved from before
20 them and stood behind them, coming between the host of Egypt and the host of Israel. And there was the cloud and the darkness; and the night passed *p* without one coming near the other all night.
21 Then Moses stretched out his hand over the sea; and the LORD drove the sea back by a strong east wind all night, and made the sea
22 dry land, and the waters were divided. And the people of Israel went into the midst of the sea on dry ground, the waters being a wall to them on their right hand and on their left.
23 The Egyptians pursued, and went in after them into the midst of the sea, all Pharaoh's
24 horses, his chariots, and his horsemen. And in the morning watch the LORD in the pillar of fire and of cloud looked down upon the host of the Egyptians, and discomfited the
25 host of the Egyptians, clogging *q* their chariot wheels so that they drove heavily; and the Egyptians said, "Let us flee from before Israel; for the LORD fights for them against the Egyptians."
26 Then the LORD said to Moses, "Stretch out your hand over the sea, that the water may come back upon the Egyptians, upon their
27 chariots, and upon their horsemen." So Moses stretched forth his hand over the sea, and the sea returned to its wonted flow when

the morning appeared; and the Egyptians fled into it, and the LORD routed *r* the Egyptians in the midst of the sea. The waters 28 returned and covered the chariots and the horsemen and all the host *s* of Pharaoh that had followed them into the sea; not so much as one of them remained. But the people of 29 Israel walked on dry ground through the sea, the waters being a wall to them on their right hand and on their left.

Thus the LORD saved Israel that day from 30 the hand of the Egyptians; and Israel saw the Egyptians dead upon the seashore. And 31 Israel saw the great work which the LORD did against the Egyptians, and the people feared the LORD; and they believed in the LORD and in his servant Moses.

Songs of deliverance

Then Moses and the people of Israel sang 15 this song to the LORD, saying,
"I will sing to the LORD, for he has triumphed gloriously;
the horse and his rider *t* he has thrown into the sea.
The LORD is my strength and my song, 2
and he has become my salvation;
this is my God, and I will praise him,
my father's God, and I will exalt him.
The LORD is a man of war; 3
the LORD is his name.

"Pharaoh's chariots and his host he cast 4
into the sea;
and his picked officers are sunk in the Red Sea.
The floods cover them; 5
they went down into the depths like a stone.
Thy right hand, O LORD, glorious in 6 power,
thy right hand, O LORD, shatters the enemy.
In the greatness of thy majesty thou 7 overthrowest thy adversaries;
thou sendest forth thy fury, it consumes them like stubble.
At the blast of thy nostrils the waters piled 8 up,
the floods stood up in a heap;
the deeps congealed in the heart of the sea.
The enemy said, 'I will pursue, I will 9 overtake,
I will divide the spoil, my desire shall have its fill of them.
I will draw my sword, my hand shall destroy them.'

p Gk: Heb *and it lit up the night*   *q* Or *binding*. Sam Gk Syr: Heb *removing*   *r* Heb *shook off*
Gk Syr: Heb *to all the host*   *t* Or *its chariot*
14.12: Ex 16.3; 17.3.

10 Thou didst blow with thy wind, the sea
   covered them;
   they sank as lead in the mighty waters.

11 "Who is like thee, O LORD, among the
      gods?
   Who is like thee, majestic in holiness,
      terrible in glorious deeds, doing won-
      ders?
12 Thou didst stretch out thy right hand,
   the earth swallowed them.

13 "Thou hast led in thy steadfast love the
      people whom thou hast redeemed,
   thou hast guided them by thy strength
      to thy holy abode.
14 The peoples have heard, they tremble;
   pangs have seized on the inhabitants of
      Philistia.
15 Now are the chiefs of Edom dismayed;
      the leaders of Moab, trembling seizes
      them;
   all the inhabitants of Canaan have
      melted away.
16 Terror and dread fall upon them;
   because of the greatness of thy arm, they
      are as still as a stone,
   till thy people, O LORD, pass by,
      till the people pass by whom thou hast
      purchased.
17 Thou wilt bring them in, and plant them
      on thy own mountain,
   the place, O LORD, which thou hast
      made for thy abode,
   the sanctuary, O LORD, which thy hands
      have established.
18 The LORD will reign for ever and ever."

19 For when the horses of Pharaoh with his
   chariots and his horsemen went into the sea,
   the LORD brought back the waters of the sea
   upon them; but the people of Israel walked
20 on dry ground in the midst of the sea. Then
   Miriam, the prophetess, the sister of Aaron,
   took a timbrel in her hand; and all the
   women went out after her with timbrels and
21 dancing. And Miriam sang to them;
   "Sing to the LORD, for he has triumphed
      gloriously;
   the horse and his rider he has thrown into
      the sea."

22 Then Moses led Israel onward from the
   Red Sea, and they went into the wilderness
   of Shur; they went three days in the wil-
23 derness and found no water. When they
   came to Marah, they could not drink the
   water of Marah because it was bitter; there-
24 fore it was named Marah. ᵘ And the people
   murmured against Moses, saying, "What
25 shall we drink?" And he cried to the LORD;
   and the LORD showed him a tree, and he

threw it into the water, and the water became
sweet.
   There the LORD ᵛ made for them a statute
and an ordinance and there he proved them,
saying, "If you will diligently hearken to the 26
voice of the LORD your God, and do that
which is right in his eyes, and give heed to his
commandments and keep all his statutes, I
will put none of the diseases upon you which
I put upon the Egyptians; for I am the LORD,
your healer."
   Then they came to Elim, where there were 27
twelve springs of water and seventy palm
trees; and they encamped there by the water.

Manna

They set out from Elim, and all the 16
congregation of the people of Israel came
to the wilderness of Sin, which is between
Elim and Sinai, on the fifteenth day of the
second month after they had departed from
the land of Egypt. And the whole congrega- 2
tion of the people of Israel murmured against
Moses and Aaron in the wilderness, and said 3
to them, "Would that we had died by the
hand of the LORD in the land of Egypt, when
we sat by the fleshpots and ate bread to the
full; for you have brought us out into this
wilderness to kill this whole assembly with
hunger."
   Then the LORD said to Moses, "Behold, I 4
will rain bread from heaven for you; and the
people shall go out and gather a day's portion
every day, that I may prove them, whether
they will walk in my law or not. On the sixth 5
day, when they prepare what they bring in, it
will be twice as much as they gather daily."
So Moses and Aaron said to all the people of 6
Israel, "At evening you shall know that it was
the LORD who brought you out of the land of
Egypt, and in the morning you shall see the 7
glory of the LORD, because he has heard your
murmurings against the LORD. For what are
we, that you murmur against us?" And 8
Moses said, "When the LORD gives you in
the evening flesh to eat and in the morning
bread to the full, because the LORD has heard
your murmurings which you murmur against
him—what are we? Your murmurings are
not against us but against the LORD."
   And Moses said to Aaron, "Say to the 9
whole congregation of the people of Israel,
'Come near before the LORD, for he has
heard your murmurings.'" And as Aaron 10
spoke to the whole congregation of the
people of Israel, they looked toward
the wilderness, and behold, the glory of the
LORD appeared in the cloud. And the LORD 11
said to Moses, "I have heard the murmur- 12

ᵘ That is *Bitterness*   ᵛ Heb *he*
16.3: Ex 14.12; 17.3.   16.4, 13: Jn 6.31.

Quails

ings of the people of Israel; say to them, 'At twilight you shall eat flesh, and in the morning you shall be filled with bread; then you shall know that I am the LORD your God.' "

13 In the evening quails came up and covered the camp; and in the morning dew lay round 14 about the camp. And when the dew had gone up, there was on the face of the wilderness a fine, flake-like thing, fine as 15 hoarfrost on the ground. When the people of Israel saw it, they said to one another, "What is it?" *w* For they did not know what it was. And Moses said to them, "It is the bread 16 which the LORD has given you to eat. This is what the LORD has commanded: 'Gather of it, every man of you, as much as he can eat; you shall take an omer apiece, according to the number of the persons whom each of you 17 has in his tent.' " And the people of Israel did so; they gathered, some more, some less. 18 But when they measured it with an omer, he that gathered much had nothing over, and he that gathered little had no lack; each gath- 19 ered according to what he could eat. And Moses said to them, "Let no man leave any 20 of it till the morning." But they did not listen to Moses; some left part of it till the morning, and it bred worms and became foul; and Moses was angry with them. 21 Morning by morning they gathered it, each as much as he could eat; but when the sun grew hot, it melted. 22 On the sixth day they gathered twice as much bread, two omers apiece; and when all the leaders of the congregation came and told 23 Moses, he said to them, "This is what the LORD has commanded: 'Tomorrow is a day of solemn rest, a holy sabbath to the LORD; bake what you will bake and boil what you will boil, and all that is left over lay by to be 24 kept till the morning.' " So they laid it by till the morning, as Moses bade them; and it did not become foul, and there were no worms in 25 it. Moses said, "Eat it today, for today is a sabbath to the LORD; today you will not find 26 it in the field. Six days you shall gather it; but on the seventh day, which is a sabbath, 27 there will be none." On the seventh day

some of the people went out to gather, and they found none. And the LORD said to 28 Moses, "How long do you refuse to keep my commandments and my laws? See! The 29 LORD has given you the sabbath, therefore on the sixth day he gives you bread for two days; remain every man of you in his place, let no man go out of his place on the seventh day." So the people rested on the seventh day. 30

Now the house of Israel called its name 31 manna; it was like coriander seed, white, and the taste of it was like wafers, made with honey. And Moses said, "This is what the 32 LORD has commanded: 'Let an omer of it be kept throughout your generations, that they may see the bread with which I fed you in the wilderness, when I brought you out of the land of Egypt.' " And Moses said to Aaron, 33 "Take a jar, and put an omer of manna in it, and place it before the LORD, to be kept throughout your generations." As the LORD 34 commanded Moses, so Aaron placed it be- fore the testimony, to be kept. And the 35 people of Israel ate the manna forty years, till they came to a habitable land; they ate the manna, till they came to the border of the land of Canaan. (An omer is the tenth part of 36 an ephah.)

All the congregation of the people of **17** Israel moved on from the wilderness of Sin by stages, according to the com- mandment of the LORD, and camped at Reph'idim; but there was no water for the people to drink. Therefore the people found 2

Manna, coriander seed (verse 31)

fault with Moses, and said, "Give us water to drink." And Moses said to them, "Why do you find fault with me? Why do you put the 3 LORD to the proof?" But the people thirsted there for water, and the people murmured against Moses, and said, "Why did you bring us up out of Egypt, to kill us and our children 4 and our cattle with thirst?" So Moses cried to the LORD, "What shall I do with this people? They are almost ready to stone 5 me." And the LORD said to Moses, "Pass on before the people, taking with you some of the elders of Israel; and take in your hand the rod with which you struck the Nile, and go. 6 Behold, I will stand before you there on the rock at Horeb; and you shall strike the rock, and water shall come out of it, that the people may drink." And Moses did so, in the sight 7 of the elders of Israel. And he called the name of the place Massah^x and Mer'ibah,^{y} because of the faultfinding of the children of Israel, and because they put the LORD to the proof by saying, "Is the LORD among us or not?"

8 Then came Am'alek and fought with Israel 9 at Reph'idim. And Moses said to Joshua, "Choose for us men, and go out, fight with Am'alek; tomorrow I will stand on the top of 10 the hill with the rod of God in my hand." So Joshua did as Moses told him, and fought with Am'alek; and Moses, Aaron, and Hur 11 went up to the top of the hill. Whenever Moses held up his hand, Israel prevailed; and whenever he lowered his hand, Am'alek 12 prevailed. But Moses' hands grew weary; so they took a stone and put it under him, and he sat upon it, and Aaron and Hur held up his hands, one on one side, and the other on the other side; so his hands were steady until 13 the going down of the sun. And Joshua mowed down Am'alek and his people with the edge of the sword.

14 And the LORD said to Moses, "Write this as a memorial in a book and recite it in the ears of Joshua, that I will utterly blot out the remembrance of Am'alek from under 15 heaven." And Moses built an altar and called the name of it, The LORD is my 16 banner, saying, "A hand upon the banner of the LORD!^{z} The LORD will have war with Am'alek from generation to generation."

Jethro

18 Jethro, the priest of Mid'ian, Moses' father-in-law, heard of all that God had done for Moses and for Israel his people, how the LORD had brought Israel out of 2 Egypt. Now Jethro, Moses' father-in-law,

had taken Zippo'rah, Moses' wife, after he had sent her away, and her two sons, of 3 whom the name of the one was Gershom (for he said, "I have been a sojourner^a in a foreign land"), and the name of the other, 4 Elie'zer^b (for he said, "The God of my father was my help, and delivered me from the sword of Pharaoh"). And Jethro, Moses' 5 father-in-law, came with his sons and his wife to Moses in the wilderness where he was encamped at the mountain of God. And 6 when one told Moses, "Lo,^{c} your father-in-law Jethro is coming to you with your wife and her two sons with her," Moses went out 7 to meet his father-in-law, and did obeisance and kissed him; and they asked each other of their welfare, and went into the tent. Then Moses told his father-in-law all 8 that the LORD had done to Pharaoh and to the Egyptians for Israel's sake, all the hardship that had come upon them in the way, and how the LORD had delivered them. And 9 Jethro rejoiced for all the good which the LORD had done to Israel, in that he had delivered them out of the hand of the Egyptians.

And Jethro said, "Blessed be the LORD,who 10 has delivered you out of the hand of the Egyptians and out of the hand of Pharaoh. Now I know that the LORD is greater than all 11 gods, because he delivered the people from under the hand of the Egyptians,^{d} when they dealt arrogantly with them." And Jethro, 12 Moses' father-in-law, offered^e a burnt offering and sacrifices to God; and Aaron came with all the elders of Israel to eat bread with Moses' father-in-law before God.

On the morrow Moses sat to judge the 13 people, and the people stood about Moses from morning till evening. When Moses' 14 father-in-law saw all that he was doing for the people, he said, "What is this that you are doing for the people? Why do you sit alone, and all the people stand about you from morning till evening?" And Moses said to 15 his father-in-law, "Because the people come to me to inquire of God; when they have a 16 dispute, they come to me and I decide between a man and his neighbour, and I make them know the statutes of God and his decisions." Moses' father-in-law said to 17 him, "What you are doing is not good. You 18 and the people with you will wear yourselves out, for the thing is too heavy for you; you are not able to perform it alone. Listen now 19 to my voice; I will give you counsel, and God be with you! You shall represent the people before God, and bring their cases to God; and you shall teach them the statutes and the 20

---

^{x} That is *Proof* ^{y} That is *Contention* ^{z} Cn: Heb obscure ^{a} Heb *ger* ^{b} Heb *Eli*, my God, *ezer*, help
^{c} Sam Gk Syr: Heb *I* ^{d} Transposing the last clause of v. 10 to v. 11 ^{e} Syr Tg Vg: Heb *took*
17.3: 14.12; 16.3.   17.14: Deut 25.17–19; I Sam 15.2–9.   18.3–4: Acts 7.29.

decisions, and make them know the way in which they must walk and what they must
21 do. Moreover choose able men from all the people, such as fear God, men who are trustworthy and who hate a bribe; and place such men over the people as rulers of thousands, of hundreds, of fifties, and of tens.
22 And let them judge the people at all times; every great matter they shall bring to you, but any small matter they shall decide themselves; so it will be easier for you, and they
23 will bear the burden with you. If you do this, and God so commands you, then you will be able to endure, and all this people also will go to their place in peace."
24 So Moses gave heed to the voice of his father-in-law and did all that he had said.
25 Moses chose able men out of all Israel, and made them heads over the people, rulers of thousands, of hundreds, of fifties, and of tens.
26 And they judged the people at all times; hard cases they brought to Moses, but any small matter they decided themselves.
27 Then Moses let his father-in-law depart, and he went his way to his own country.

AT MOUNT SINAI

19 ON the third new moon after the people of Israel had gone forth out of the land of Egypt, on that day they came into the wilderness of Sinai.
2 And when they set out from Reph'idim and came into the wilderness of Sinai, they encamped in the wilderness; and there Israel encamped before
3 the mountain. And Moses went up to God, and the LORD called to him out of the mountain, saying, "Thus you shall say to the house of Jacob, and tell the people of Israel:
4 You have seen what I did to the Egyptians, and how I bore you on eagles' wings and
5 brought you to myself. Now therefore, if you will obey my voice and keep my covenant, you shall be my own possession among all peoples; for all the earth is mine,
6 and you shall be to me a kingdom of priests and a holy nation. These are the words which you shall speak to the children of Israel."
7 So Moses came and called the elders of the people, and set before them all these words
8 which the LORD had commanded him. And all the people answered together and said, "All that the LORD has spoken we will do." And Moses reported the words of the people
9 to the LORD. And the LORD said to Moses, "Lo, I am coming to you in a thick cloud, that the people may hear when I speak with you, and may also believe you for ever." Then Moses told the words of the people to
10 the LORD. And the LORD said to Moses, "Go to the people and consecrate them today and tomorrow, and let them wash their garments,
11 and be ready by the third day; for on the third day the LORD will come down upon Mount Sinai in the sight of all the people.
12 And you shall set bounds for the people round about, saying, 'Take heed that you do not go up into the mountain or touch the border of it; whoever touches the mountain
13 shall be put to death; no hand shall touch him, but he shall be stoned or shot; whether beast or man, he shall not live.' When the trumpet sounds a long blast, they shall come up to the mountain."
14 So Moses went down from the mountain to the people, and consecrated the people; and they washed their garments.
15 And he said to the people, "Be ready by the third day; do not go near a woman."
16 On the morning of the third day there were thunders and lightnings, and a thick cloud upon the mountain, and a very loud trumpet blast, so that all the people who were in the camp trembled.
17 Then Moses brought the people out of the camp to meet God; and they took their stand at the foot of the mountain.
18 And Mount Sinai was wrapped in smoke, because the LORD descended upon it in fire; and the smoke of it went up like the smoke of a kiln, and the whole mountain quaked greatly.
19 And as the sound of the trumpet grew louder and louder, Moses spoke, and God answered him in thunder.
20 And the LORD came down upon Mount Sinai, to the top of the mountain; and the LORD called Moses to the top of the mountain, and Moses went up.
21 And the LORD said to Moses, "Go down and warn the people, lest they break through to the LORD to gaze and many of them perish.
22 And also let the priests who come near to the LORD consecrate themselves, lest the LORD break out upon them."
23 And Moses said to the LORD, "The people cannot come up to Mount Sinai; for thou thyself didst charge us, saying, 'Set bounds about the mountain, and consecrate it.'"
24 And the LORD said to him, "Go down, and come up bringing Aaron with you; but do not let the priests and the people break through to come up to the LORD, lest he break out against them."
25 So Moses went down to the people and told them.

THE JOURNEY THROUGH
THE WILDERNESS
from
EGYPT TO CANAAN

English Miles

20 And God spoke all these words, saying,
2 "I am the LORD your God, who brought
you out of the land of Egypt, out of the house
of bondage.

"You shall have no other gods before[f] me. 3
"You shall not make for yourself a graven 4
image, or any likeness of anything that is in
heaven above, or that is in the earth beneath

[f] Or besides
20.2–17: Deut 5.6–21.   20.3: Ex 20.23; Deut 5.7.
20.4: Ex 20.23; 34.17; Lev 19.4; 26.1; Deut 4.15–19; 5.8; 27.15.

5 or that is in the water under the earth; you shall not bow down to them or serve them; for I the LORD your God am a jealous God, visiting the iniquity of the fathers upon the children to the third and the fourth genera-
6 tion of those who hate me, but showing steadfast love to thousands of those who love me and keep my commandments.
7 "You shall not take the name of the LORD your God in vain; for the LORD will not hold him guiltless who takes his name in vain.
8 "Remember the sabbath day, to keep it
9 holy. Six days you shall labour, and do all
10 your work; but the seventh day is a sabbath to the LORD your God; in it you shall not do any work, you, or your son, or your daughter, your manservant, or your maidservant, or your cattle, or the sojourner who is within
11 your gates; for in six days the LORD made heaven and earth, the sea, and all that is in them, and rested the seventh day; therefore the LORD blessed the sabbath day and hallowed it.
12 "Honour your father and your mother, that your days may be long in the land which the LORD your God gives you.
"You shall not kill.　　　　　　　　13
"You shall not commit adultery.　　　　14
"You shall not steal.　　　　　　　　15
"You shall not bear false witness against 16 your neighbour.
"You shall not covet your neighbour's 17 house; you shall not covet your neighbour's wife, or his manservant, or his maidservant, or his ox, or his ass, or anything that is your neighbour's."
Now when all the people perceived the 18 thunderings and the lightnings and the sound of the trumpet and the mountain smoking, the people were afraid and trembled; and they stood afar off, and said to 19 Moses, "You speak to us, and we will hear; but let not God speak to us, lest we die." And Moses said to the people, "Do not fear; 20 for God has come to prove you, and that the fear of him may be before your eyes, that you may not sin."

THE BOOK OF THE COVENANT

Worship and justice

21 AND the people stood afar off, while Moses drew near to the thick darkness where God
22 was. And the LORD said to Moses, "Thus you shall say to the people of Israel: 'You have seen for yourselves that I have talked
23 with you from heaven. You shall not make gods of silver to be with me, nor shall you make for your-
24 selves gods of gold. An altar of earth you shall make for me and sacrifice on it your burnt offerings and your peace offerings, your sheep and your oxen; in every place where I cause my name to be remembered I will come to you
25 and bless you. And if you make me an altar of stone, you shall not build it of hewn stones; for if you wield your tool upon it you pro-
26 fane it. And you shall not go up by steps to my altar, that your nakedness be not exposed on it.'

21 "Now these are the ordinances which you shall set before them.
2 When you buy a Hebrew slave, he shall serve six years, and in the seventh he shall go out free, for

3 nothing. If he comes in single he shall go out single; if he comes in married, then his wife shall go out
4 with him. If his master gives him a wife and she bears him sons or daughters, the wife and her children shall be her master's and he
5 shall go out alone. But if the slave plainly says, 'I love my master, my wife, and my children;' I will
6 not go out free,' then his master shall bring him to God, and he shall bring him to the door or the doorpost; and his master shall bore his ear through with an awl; and he shall serve him for life.
7 "When a man sells his daughter as a slave, she shall not go out as
8 the male slaves do. If she does not please her master, who has designated herg for himself, then he shall let her be redeemed; he shall have no right to sell her to a foreign people, since he has dealt
9 faithlessly with her. If he designates her for his son, he shall deal
10 with her as with a daughter. If he takes another wife to himself, he shall not diminish her food, her clothing, or her marital rights.
11 And if he does not do these three things for her, she shall go out for

nothing, without payment of money.
12 "Whoever strikes a man so that he dies shall be put to death. But 13 if he did not lie in wait for him, but God let him fall into his hand, then I will appoint for you a place to which he may flee. But if a man 14 wilfully attacks another to kill him treacherously, you shall take him from my altar, that he may die.
15 "Whoever strikes his father or his mother shall be put to death.
16 "Whoever steals a man, whether he sells him or is found in possession of him, shall be put to death.
17 "Whoever curses his father or his mother shall be put to death.
18 "When men quarrel and one strikes the other with a stone or with his fist and the man does not die but keeps his bed, then if the 19 man rises again and walks abroad with his staff, he that struck him shall be clear; only he shall pay for the loss of his time, and shall have him thoroughly healed.
20 "When a man strikes his slave, male or female, with a rod and the slave dies under his hand, he shall be punished. But if the slave 21 survives a day or two, he is not to

---

g Another reading is *so that he has not designated her*

20.5–6: Ex 23.24; 34.6, 7, 14; Deut 4.24; 5.9–10; 7.9.　20.7: Lev 19.12; Deut 5.11.
20.8: Ex 23.12; 31.12–17; 34.21; 35.2–3; Lev 19.3; Deut 5.12–15.
20.12: Lev 19.3; Deut 5.16; Mt 15.4; Mk 7.10; Eph 6.2.　20.12–16: Mt 19.18–19; Mk 10.19; Lk 18.20.
20.13: Gen 9.6; Ex 21.12; Lev 24.17; Deut 5.17; Mt 5.21; Jas 2.11.　20.13–17: Rom 13.9.
20.14: Lev 20.10; Deut 5.18; Mt 5.27; Rom 7.7.　20.15: Lev 19.11; Deut 5.19.　20.16: Ex 23.1; Deut 5.20.
20.17: Deut 5.21; Rom 7.7.　20.23: Ex 20.3–4; 34.17; Deut 27.15.　20.24: Ex 27.1–8; Deut 12.5; 26.2.
20.25: Deut 27.5–6.　21.2–11: Lev 25.39–46; Deut 15.12–18.
21.12: Ex 20.13; Lev 24.17; Deut 5.17; Mt 5.21.　21.13: Num 35.10–34; Deut 19.1–13; Josh 20.1–9.
21.16: Deut 24.7.　21.17: Lev 20.9; Mt 15.4; Mk 7.10.

be punished; for the slave is his money.

2 "When men strive together, and hurt a woman with child, so that there is a miscarriage, and yet no harm follows, the one who hurt her shall[h] be fined, according as the woman's husband shall lay upon him; and he shall pay as the 3 judges determine. If any harm follows, then you shall give life for 4 life, eye for eye, tooth for tooth, 5 hand for hand, foot for foot, burn for burn, wound for wound, stripe for stripe.

6 "When a man strikes the eye of his slave, male or female, and destroys it, he shall let the slave go 7 free for the eye's sake. If he knocks out the tooth of his slave, male or female, he shall let the slave go free for the tooth's sake.

28 "When an ox gores a man or a woman to death, the ox shall be stoned, and its flesh shall not be eaten; but the owner of the ox 29 shall be clear. But if the ox has been accustomed to gore in the past, and its owner has been warned but has not kept it in, and it kills a man or a woman, the ox shall be stoned, and its owner also 30 shall be put to death. If a ransom is laid on him, then he shall give for the redemption of his life 31 whatever is laid upon him. If it gores a man's son or daughter, he shall be dealt with according to 32 this same rule. If the ox gores a slave, male or female, the owner shall give to their master thirty shekels of silver, and the ox shall be stoned.

33 "When a man leaves a pit open, or when a man digs a pit and does not cover it, and an ox or an ass 34 falls into it, the owner of the pit shall make it good; he shall give money to its owner, and the dead beast shall be his.

35 "When one man's ox hurts another's, so that it dies, then they shall sell the live ox and divide the price of it; and the dead beast 36 also they shall divide. Or if it is known that the ox has been accustomed to gore in the past, and its owner has not kept it in, he shall pay ox for ox, and the dead beast shall be his.

22[i] "If a man steals an ox or a sheep, and kills it or sells it, he shall pay five oxen for an ox, and four sheep for a sheep.[j] He shall make restitution; if he has nothing, then 4 he shall be sold for his theft. If 19 the stolen beast is found alive in his possession, whether it is an ox 20 or an ass or a sheep, he shall pay double.

2[k] "If a thief is found breaking in, and is struck so that he dies, there 3 shall be no bloodguilt for him; but if the sun has risen upon him, there shall be bloodguilt for him.

5 "When a man causes a field or vineyard to be grazed over, or lets his beast loose and it feeds in another man's field, he shall make restitution from the best in his own field and in his own vineyard.

6 "When fire breaks out and catches in thorns so that the stacked grain or the standing grain or the field is consumed, he that kindled the fire shall make full restitution.

7 "If a man delivers to his neighbour money or goods to keep, and it is stolen out of the man's house, then, if the thief is found, he shall 8 pay double. If the thief is not found, the owner of the house shall come near to God, to show whether or not he has put his hand to his neighbour's goods.

9 "For every breach of trust, whether it is for ox, for ass, for sheep, for clothing, or for any kind of lost thing, of which one says, 'This is it,' the case of both parties shall come before God; he whom God shall condemn shall 10 pay double to his neighbour.

"If a man delivers to his neighbour an ass or an ox or a sheep or any beast to keep, and it dies or is 11 hurt or is driven away, without any one seeing it, an oath by the LORD shall be between them both to see whether he has not put his hand to his neighbour's property; and the owner shall accept the oath, and he shall not make res- 12 titution. But if it is stolen from him, he shall make restitution to 13 its owner. If it is torn by beasts, let him bring it as evidence; he shall not make restitution for what has been torn.

14 "If a man borrows anything of his neighbour, and it is hurt or dies, the owner not being with it, 15 he shall make full restitution. If the owner was with it, he shall not make restitution; if it was hired, it came for its hire.[l]

16 "If a man seduces a virgin who is not betrothed, and lies with her, he shall give the marriage present 17 for her, and make her his wife. If her father utterly refuses to give her to him, he shall pay money equivalent to the marriage present for virgins.

18 "You shall not permit a sorceress to live.

19 "Whoever lies with a beast shall be put to death.

20 "Whoever sacrifices to any god, save to the LORD only, shall be utterly destroyed.

"You shall not wrong a stranger 21 or oppress him, for you were strangers in the land of Egypt. You shall not afflict any widow or 22 orphan. If you do afflict them, and they cry out to me, I will 23 surely hear their cry; and my 24 wrath will burn, and I will kill you with the sword, and your wives shall become widows and your children fatherless.

"If you lend money to any of my 25 people with you who is poor, you shall not be to him as a creditor, and you shall not exact interest from him. If ever you take your 26 neighbour's garment in pledge, you shall restore it to him before the sun goes down; for that is his 27 only covering, it is his mantle for his body; in what else shall he sleep? And if he cries to me, I will hear, for I am compassionate.

"You shall not revile God, nor 28 curse a ruler of your people.

"You shall not delay to offer 29 from the fulness of your harvest and from the outflow of your presses.

"The first-born of your sons you 30 shall give to me. You shall do likewise with your oxen and with your sheep: seven days it shall be with its dam; on the eighth day you shall give it to me.

"You shall be men consecrated 31 to me; therefore you shall not eat any flesh that is torn by beasts in the field; you shall cast it to the dogs.

"You shall not utter a false 23 report. You shall not join hands with a wicked man, to be a malicious witness. You shall not fol- 2 low a multitude to do evil; nor shall you bear witness in a suit, turning aside after a multitude, so as to pervert justice; nor shall you 3 be partial to a poor man in his suit.

"If you meet your enemy's ox or 4 his ass going astray, you shall bring it back to him. If you see 5 the ass of one who hates you lying under its burden, you shall refrain from leaving him with it, you shall help him to lift it up.[m]

"You shall not pervert the jus- 6 tice due to your poor in his suit. Keep far from a false charge, and 7 do not slay the innocent and righteous, for I will not acquit the wicked. And you shall take no 8 bribe, for a bribe blinds the officials, and subverts the cause of those who are in the right.

"You shall not oppress a stran- 9 ger; you know the heart of a stranger, for you were strangers in the land of Egypt.

---

h Heb he shall i Ch 21.37 in Heb j Restoring the second half of verse 3 with 4 to their place immediately following verse 1 k Ch 22.1 in Heb l Or it is reckoned in (Heb comes into) its hire m Gk: Heb obscure

21.23-26: Lev 24.19-20; Deut 19.21; Mt 5.38. 22.7-15: Lev 5.14-6.7; Num 5.5-8. 22.16-17: Deut 22.28-29.
22.18: Lev 20.27; Deut 18.10. 22.19: Lev 18.23; 20.15-16; Deut 27.21.
22.21: Ex 23.9; Lev 19.33-34; Deut 27.19.
22.22: Deut 24.17. 22.25-27: Lev 25.36-37; Deut 23.19-20. 22.28: Acts 23.5.
22.29: Ex 13.2, 11-16; 23. 16, 19; Deut 26.2-11. 22.31: Ex 19.6; Lev 7.24; 11.44; 17.15; 19.1.
23.1: Ex 20.16; 23.7; Deut 5.20; 19.15-21. 23.3, 6: Lev 19.15. 23.7: Ex 20.16; 23.1. 23.8: Deut 16.19.
23.9: Ex 22.21; Lev 19.33-34; Deut 27.19.

10 "For six years you shall sow your
11 land and gather in its yield; but
the seventh year you shall let it
rest and lie fallow, that the poor of
your people may eat; and what
they leave the wild beasts may
eat. You shall do likewise with
your vineyard, and with your
olive orchard.
12 "Six days you shall do your
work, but on the seventh day you
shall rest; that your ox and your
ass may have rest, and the son of
your bondmaid, and the alien,
13 may be refreshed. Take heed to
all that I have said to you; and
make no mention of the names of
other gods, nor let such be heard
out of your mouth.
14 "Three times in the year you
15 shall keep a feast to me. You shall
keep the feast of unleavened
bread; as I commanded you, you
shall eat unleavened bread for
seven days at the appointed time
in the month of Abib, for in it you
came out of Egypt. None shall
appear before me empty-handed.
16 You shall keep the feast of harvest, of the first fruits of your
labour, of what you sow in the
field. You shall keep the feast of
ingathering at the end of the year,
when you gather in from the field
17 the fruit of your labour. Three

times in the year shall all your
males appear before the Lord
God.
18 "You shall not offer the blood of
my sacrifice with leavened bread,
or let the fat of my feast remain
until the morning.
19 "The first of the first fruits of
your ground you shall bring into
the house of the Lord your God.
"You shall not boil a kid in its
20 mother's milk.
"Behold, I send an angel before
you, to guard you on the way and
to bring you to the place which I
21 have prepared. Give heed to him
and hearken to his voice, do not
rebel against him, for he will not
pardon your transgression; for my
name is in him.
22 "But if you hearken attentively
to his voice and do all that I say,
then I will be an enemy to your
enemies and an adversary to your
adversaries.
23 "When my angel goes before
you, and brings you to the Amorites, and the Hittites, and the
Per'izzites, and the Canaanites,
the Hivites, and the Jeb'usites,
24 and I blot them out, you shall not
bow down to their gods, nor serve
them, nor do according to their
works, but you shall utterly overthrow them and break their pillars

in pieces. You shall serve the 2
Lord your God, and I[n] will bless
your bread and your water; and I
will take sickness away from the
midst of you. None shall cast her 2
young or be barren in your land; I
will fulfil the number of your
days. I will send my terror before 2
you, and will throw into confusion
all the people against whom you
shall come, and I will make all
your enemies turn their backs to
you. And I will send hornets 2
before you, which shall drive out
Hivite, Canaanite, and Hittite
from before you. I will not drive 2
them out from before you in one
year, lest the land become desolate and the wild beasts multiply
against you. Little by little I will 3
drive them out from before you,
until you are increased and possess the land. And I will set your 3
bounds from the Red Sea to the
sea of the Philistines, and from
the wilderness to the Euphra'tes;
for I will deliver the inhabitants of
the land into your hand, and you
shall drive them out before you.
You shall make no covenant with 3
them or with their gods. They 3
shall not dwell in your land, lest
they make you sin against me; for
if you serve their gods, it will
surely be a snare to you."

The covenant confirmed

24 AND he said to Moses, "Come up to the
Lord, you and Aaron, Nadab, and
Abi'hu, and seventy of the elders of Israel,
2 and worship afar off. Moses alone shall come
near to the Lord; but the others shall not
come near, and the people shall not come up
with him."
3 Moses came and told the people all the
words of the Lord and all the ordinances;
and all the people answered with one voice,
and said, "All the words which the Lord has
4 spoken we will do." And Moses wrote all the
words of the Lord. And he rose early in the
morning, and built an altar at the foot of
the mountain, and twelve pillars, according
5 to the twelve tribes of Israel. And he sent
young men of the people of Israel, who
offered burnt offerings and sacrificed peace
6 offerings of oxen to the Lord. And Moses
took half of the blood and put it in basins,
and half of the blood he threw against the
7 altar. Then he took the book of the covenant, and read it in the hearing of the people;
and they said, "All that the Lord has spoken
8 we will do, and we will be obedient." And

Moses took the blood and threw it upon the
people, and said, "Behold the blood of the
covenant which the Lord has made with you
in accordance with all these words."
Then Moses and Aaron, Nadab, and 9
Abi'hu, and seventy of the elders of Israel
went up, and they saw the God of Israel; and 10
there was under his feet as it were a pavement of sapphire stone, like the very heaven
for clearness. And he did not lay his hand on 11
the chief men of the people of Israel; they
beheld God, and ate and drank.
The Lord said to Moses, "Come up to me 12
on the mountain, and wait there; and I will
give you the tables of stone, with the law and
the commandment, which I have written for
their instruction." So Moses rose with his 13
servant Joshua, and Moses went up into the
mountain of God. And he said to the elders, 14
"Tarry here for us, until we come to you
again; and, behold, Aaron and Hur are with
you; whoever has a cause, let him go to
them."
Then Moses went up on the mountain, and 15
the cloud covered the mountain. The glory 16
of the Lord settled on Mount Sinai, and the
cloud covered it six days; and on the seventh

[n] Gk Vg: Heb he
23.10-11: Lev 25.1-7.   23.12: Ex 20.8-11; 31.15-17; 34.21; 35.2; Deut 5.12-15.
23.14-17: Ex 34.22-24; Lev 23.1-44; Deut 16.1-17.   23.18: Ex 12.10; Ex 34.25; Lev 2.11; Lev 7.15.
23.19: Ex 22.29; 34.26; Deut 14.21; 26.2-11.
24.8: Mt 26.28; Mk 14.24; Lk 22.20; 1 Cor 11.25; Heb 9.20; 10.29.   24.12: 2 Cor 3.3.

day he called to Moses out of the midst of the
17 cloud. Now the appearance of the glory of
the LORD was like a devouring fire on the top
of the mountain in the sight of the people of
18 Israel. And Moses entered the cloud, and
went up on the mountain. And Moses was
on the mountain forty days and forty nights.

25 The LORD said to Moses, "Speak to the
2 people of Israel, that they take for me an
offering; from every man whose heart makes
him willing you shall receive the offering for
3 me. And this is the offering which you shall

receive from them: gold, silver, and bronze,
blue and purple and scarlet stuff and fine 4
twined linen, goats' hair, tanned rams' skins, 5
goatskins, acacia wood, oil for the lamps, 6
spices for the anointing oil and for the
fragrant incense, onyx stones, and stones for 7
setting, for the ephod and for the breastpiece. and let them make me a sanctuary, 8
that I may dwell in their midst. According to 9
all that I show you concerning the pattern of
the tabernacle, and of all its furniture, so you
shall make it.

The pattern of the tabernacle

10 "THEY shall make an ark of
acacia wood; two cubits and a
half shall be its length, a cubit
and a half its breadth, and a
11 cubit and a half its height. And
you shall overlay it with pure
gold, within and without shall you
overlay it, and you shall make
upon it a moulding of gold round
12 about. And you shall cast four
rings of gold for it and put them
on its four feet, two rings on the
one side of it, and two rings on the
13 other side of it. You shall make
14 poles of acacia wood, and overlay
them with gold. And you shall
put the poles into the rings on the
sides of the ark, to carry the ark by
15 them. The poles shall remain in
the rings of the ark; they shall not
16 be taken from it. And you shall
17 put into the ark the testimony
which I shall give you. Then you
shall make a mercy seat° of pure
gold; two cubits and a half shall
be its length, and a cubit and a
18 half its breadth. And you shall
make two cherubim of gold; of
hammered work shall you make
them, on the two ends of the
19 mercy seat. Make one cherub on
the one end, and one cherub
on the other end; of one piece with
the mercy seat shall you make the
20 cherubim on its two ends. The
cherubim shall spread out their
wings above, overshadowing the
mercy seat with their wings, their
faces one to another; toward the
mercy seat shall the faces of the
21 cherubim be. And you shall put
the mercy seat on the top of the
ark; and in the ark you shall put
the testimony that I shall give
22 you. There I will meet with you,
and from above the mercy seat,
from between the two cherubim
that are upon the ark of the
testimony, I will speak with you
of all that I will give you in
commandment for the people of
Israel.
23 "And you shall make a table of
acacia wood; two cubits shall be
its length, a cubit its breadth, and

24 a cubit and a half its height. You
shall overlay it with pure gold,
25 and make a moulding of gold
around it. And you shall make
around it a frame a handbreadth
wide, and a moulding of gold
26 around the frame. And you shall
make for it four rings of gold, and
fasten the rings to the four corners
27 at its four legs. Close to the frame
the rings shall lie, as holders for
28 the poles to carry the table. You
shall make the poles of acacia
wood, and overlay them with
gold, and the table shall be carried
29 with these. And you shall make
its plates and dishes for incense,
and its flagons and bowls with
30 which to pour libations; of pure
gold you shall make them. And
you shall set the bread of the
Presence on the table before me
always.

31 "And you shall make a lampstand of pure gold. The base and
the shaft of the lampstand shall be
made of hammered work; its
cups, its capitals, and its flowers
32 shall be of one piece with it; and
there shall be six branches going
out of its sides, three branches of
the lampstand out of one side of it
and three branches of the lamp-

stand out of the other side of it;
three cups made like almonds, 33
each with capital and flower, on
one branch, and three cups made
like almonds, each with capital
and flower, on the other
branch—so for the six branches
going out of the lampstand; and 34
on the lampstand itself four cups
made like almonds, with their
capitals and flowers, and a capital 35
of one piece with it under each
pair of the six branches going out
from the lampstand. Their capi- 36
tals and their branches shall be of
one piece with it, the whole of it
one piece of hammered work of
pure gold. And you shall make 37
the seven lamps for it; and the
lamps shall be set up so as to give
light upon the space in front of it.
Its snuffers and their trays shall 38
be of pure gold. Of a talent of 39
pure gold shall it be made, with all
these utensils. And see that you 40
make them after the pattern for
them, which is being shown you
on the mountain.

"Moreover you shall make the**26**
tabernacle with ten curtains of
fine twined linen and blue and
purple and scarlet stuff; with
cherubim skilfully worked shall
you make them. The length of 2
each curtain shall be twenty-eight
cubits, and the breadth of each
curtain four cubits; all the curtains shall have one measure.
Five curtains shall be coupled to 3
one another; and the other five
curtains shall be coupled to one
another. And you shall make 4
loops of blue on the edge of the
outmost curtain in the first set;
and likewise you shall make loops
on the edge of the outmost curtain
in the second set. Fifty loops you 5
shall make on the one curtain, and
fifty loops you shall make on the
edge of the curtain that is in the
second set; the loops shall be
opposite one another. And you 6
shall make fifty clasps of gold, and
couple the curtains one to the
other with the clasps, that the
tabernacle may be one whole.

° Or *cover*
25·31: Ex 35·40.   **25.2–8:** Ex 35.4–9.   **25.10–22:** Ex 37.1–9.
25.23–29: Ex 37.10–15.   **25.30:** Ex 39.36; 40.23; Lev 24.5–9.   **25.31–40:** Ex 37.17–24.
25.40: Acts 7.44; Heb 8.5.   **26.1–14:** Ex 36.8–19.

7 "You shall also make curtains of goats' hair for a tent over the tabernacle; eleven curtains shall

8 you make. The length of each curtain shall be thirty cubits, and the breadth of each curtain four cubits; the eleven curtains shall

9 have the same measure. And you shall couple five curtains by themselves, and six curtains by themselves, and the sixth curtain you shall double over at the front

10 of the tent. And you shall make fifty loops on the edge of the curtain that is outmost in one set, and fifty loops on the edge of the curtain which is outmost in the second set.

11 "And you shall make fifty clasps of bronze, and put the clasps into the loops, and couple the tent together that it may be one

12 whole. And the part that remains of the curtains of the tent, the half curtain that remains, shall hang over the back of the tabernacle.

13 And the cubit on the one side, and the cubit on the other side, of what remains in the length of the curtains of the tent shall hang over the sides of the tabernacle, on this side and that side, to cover

14 it. And you shall make for the tent a covering of tanned rams' skins and goatskins.

15 "And you shall make upright frames for the tabernacle of acacia

16 wood. Ten cubits shall be the length of a frame, and a cubit and a half the breadth of each frame.

17 There shall be two tenons in each frame, for fitting together; so shall

18 you do for all the frames of the tabernacle. You shall make the frames for the tabernacle: twenty

19 frames for the south side; and forty bases of silver you shall make under the twenty frames, two bases under one frame for its two tenons, and two bases under another frame for its two tenons;

20 and for the second side of the tabernacle, on the north side

21 twenty frames, and their forty bases of silver, two bases under one frame, and two bases under

22 another frame; and for the rear of the tabernacle westward you shall

23 make six frames. And you shall make two frames for corners of

24 the tabernacle in the rear; they shall be separate beneath, but joined at the top, at the first ring; thus shall it be with both of them; they shall form the two corners.

25 And there shall be eight frames, with their bases of silver, sixteen bases; two bases under one frame, and two bases under another frame.

26 "And you shall make bars of acacia wood, five for the frames of

27 the one side of the tabernacle, and five bars for the frames of the other side of the tabernacle, and five bars for the frames of the side of the tabernacle at the rear

28 westward. The middle bar, halfway up the frames, shall pass

29 through from end to end. You shall overlay the frames with gold, and shall make their rings of gold for holders for the bars; and you shall overlay the bars with gold.

30 And you shall erect the tabernacle according to the plan for it which has been shown you on the mountain.

31 "And you shall make a veil of blue and purple and scarlet stuff and fine twined linen; in skilled work shall it be made, with cheru-

32 bim; and you shall hang it upon four pillars of acacia overlaid with gold, with hooks of gold, upon

33 four bases of silver. And you shall hang the veil from the clasps, and bring the ark of the testimony in thither within the veil; and the veil shall separate for you the holy

34 place from the most holy. You shall put the mercy seat upon the ark of the testimony in the most

35 holy place. And you shall set the table outside the veil, and the lampstand on the south side of the tabernacle opposite the table; and you shall put the table on the north side.

36 "And you shall make a screen for the door of the tent, of blue and purple and scarlet stuff and fine

37 twined linen, embroidered with needlework. And you shall make for the screen five pillars of acacia, and overlay them with gold; their hooks shall be of gold, and you shall cast five bases of bronze for them.

27 "You shall make the altar of acacia wood, five cubits long and five cubits broad; the altar shall be square, and its height shall be

2 three cubits. And you shall make horns for it on its four corners; its horns shall be of one piece with it, and you shall overlay it with

3 bronze. You shall make pots for it to receive its ashes, and shovels and basins and forks and firepans; all its utensils you shall make of

4 bronze. You shall also make for it a grating, a network of bronze; and upon the net you shall make four bronze rings at its four

5 corners. And you shall set it under the ledge of the altar so that the net shall extend halfway down

6 the altar. And you shall make poles for the altar, poles of acacia wood, and overlay them with

7 bronze; and the poles shall be put through the rings, so that the poles shall be upon the two sides of the altar, when it is carried.

8 You shall make it hollow, with boards; as it has been shown you on the mountain, so shall it be made.

9 "You shall make the court of the tabernacle. On the south side the court shall have hangings of fine twined linen a hundred cubits

10 long for one side; their pillars shall be twenty and their bases twenty, of bronze, but the hooks of the pillars and their fillets shall

11 be of silver. And likewise for its length on the north side there shall be hangings a hundred cubits long, their pillars twenty and their bases twenty, of bronze, but the hooks of the pillars and their fillets shall be of silver. And

12 for the breadth of the court on the west side there shall be hangings for fifty cubits, with ten pillars

13 and ten bases. The breadth of the court on the front to the east shall

14 be fifty cubits. The hangings for the one side of the gate shall be fifteen cubits, with three pillars

15 and three bases. On the other side the hangings shall be fifteen cubits, with three pillars and three

16 bases. For the gate of the court there shall be a screen twenty cubits long, of blue and purple and scarlet stuff and fine twined linen, embroidered with needlework; it shall have four pillars and

17 with them four bases. All the pillars around the court shall be filleted with silver; their hooks shall be of silver, and their bases

18 of bronze. The length of the court shall be a hundred cubits, the breadth fifty, and the height five cubits, with hangings of fine twined linen and bases of bronze.

19 All the utensils of the tabernacle for every use, and all its pegs and all the pegs of the court, shall be of bronze.

20 "And you shall command the people of Israel that they bring to you pure beaten olive oil for the light, that a lamp may be set up to

21 burn continually. In the tent of meeting, outside the veil which is before the testimony, Aaron and his sons shall tend it from evening to morning before the LORD. It shall be a statute for ever to be observed throughout their generations by the people of Israel.

Priests

"Then bring near to you Aaron 28 your brother, and his sons with him, from among the people of Israel, to serve me as priests— Aaron and Aaron's sons, Nadab and Abi'hu, Elea'zar and Ith'-

2 amar. And you shall make holy garments for Aaron your brother, for glory and for beauty.

3 And you shall speak to all who have ability, whom I have endowed with an able mind, that they make Aaron's garments to consecrate him for my priest-

4 hood. These are the garments which they shall make: a breastpiece, an ephod, a robe, a coat of chequer work, a turban, and a girdle; they shall make holy garments for Aaron your brother and his sons to serve me as priests.

5 "They shall receive gold, blue and purple and scarlet stuff, and

6 fine twined linen. And they shall make the ephod of gold, of blue and purple and scarlet stuff, and of fine twined linen, skil-

7 fully worked. It shall have two

shoulder-pieces attached to its two edges, that it may be joined 8 together. And the skilfully woven band upon it, to gird it on, shall be of the same workmanship and materials, of gold, blue and purple 9 and scarlet stuff, and fine twined linen. And you shall take two onyx stones, and engrave on them 10 the names of the sons of Israel, six of their names on the one stone, and the names of the remaining six on the other stone, in the order 11 of their birth. As a jeweller engraves signets, so shall you engrave the two stones with the names of the sons of Israel; you 12 shall enclose them in settings of gold filigree. And you shall set the two stones upon the shoulder-pieces of the ephod, as stones of remembrance for the sons of Israel; and Aaron shall bear their names before the LORD upon his two shoulders for 13 remembrance. And you shall 14 make settings of gold filigree, and two chains of pure gold, twisted like cords; and you shall attach the corded chains to the settings.

15 "And you shall make a breastpiece of judgment, in skilled work; like the work of the ephod you shall make it; of gold, blue and purple and scarlet stuff, and 16 fine twined linen shall you make it. It shall be square and double, a span its length and a span its 17 breadth. And you shall set in it four rows of stones. A row of 18 sardius, topaz, and carbuncle shall be the first row; and the second 19 row an emerald, a sapphire, and a diamond; and the third row a 20 jacinth, an agate, and an amethyst; and the fourth row a beryl, an onyx, and a jasper; they 21 shall be set in gold filigree. There shall be twelve stones with their names according to the names of

the sons of Israel; they shall be like signets, each engraved with its name, for the twelve tribes. 22 And you shall make for the breastpiece twisted chains like 23 cords, of pure gold; and you shall make for the breastpiece two rings of gold, and put the two rings on the two edges of the breastpiece. 24 And you shall put the two cords of gold in the two rings at the edges 25 of the breastpiece; the two ends of the two cords you shall attach to the two settings of filigree, and so attach it in front to the 26 shoulder-pieces of the ephod. And you shall make two rings of gold, and put them at the two ends of the breastpiece, on its inside edge next to the ephod. 27 And you shall make two rings of gold, and attach them in front to the lower part of the two shoulder-pieces of the ephod, at its joining above the skilfully 28 woven band of the ephod. And they shall bind the breastpiece by its rings to the rings of the ephod with a lace of blue, that it may lie upon the skilfully woven band of the ephod, and that the breastpiece shall not come loose from 29 the ephod. So Aaron shall bear the names of the sons of Israel in the breastpiece of judgment upon his heart, when he goes into the holy place, to bring them to continual remembrance before the 30 LORD. And in the breastpiece of judgment you shall put the Urim and the Thummim, and they shall be upon Aaron's heart, when he goes in before the LORD; thus Aaron shall bear the judgment of the people of Israel upon his heart before the LORD continually.

31 "And you shall make the robe of 32 the ephod all of blue. It shall have in it an opening for the head, with a woven binding around the opening, like the opening in a garment,[p] that it may not be 33 torn. On its skirts you shall make pomegranates of blue and purple and scarlet stuff, around its skirts, 34 with bells of gold between them, a golden bell and a pomegranate, a golden bell and a pomegranate, 35 round about on the skirts of the robe. And it shall be upon Aaron when he ministers, and its sound shall be heard when he goes into the holy place before the LORD, and when he comes out, lest he die. 36 "And you shall make a plate of pure gold, and engrave on it, like the engraving of a signet, 'Holy to 37 the LORD.' And you shall fasten it on the turban by a lace of blue; it shall be on the front of the 38 turban. It shall be upon Aaron's forehead, and Aaron shall take upon himself any guilt incurred in the holy offering which the people of Israel hallow as their holy gifts; it shall always be upon his forehead, that they may be accepted before the LORD.

"And you shall weave the coat in 39 chequer work of fine linen, and you shall make a turban of fine linen, and you shall make a girdle embroidered with needlework.

"And for Aaron's sons you shall 40 make coats and girdles and caps; you shall make them for glory and beauty. And you shall put them 41 upon Aaron your brother, and upon his sons with him, and shall anoint them and ordain them and consecrate them, that they may serve me as priests. And you shall 42 make for them linen breeches to cover their naked flesh; from the loins to the thighs they shall reach; and they shall be upon 43 Aaron, and upon his sons, when they go into the tent of meeting, or when they come near the altar to minister in the holy place; lest they bring guilt upon themselves and die. This shall be a perpetual statute for him and for his descendants after him.

"Now this is what you shall do 29 to them to consecrate them, that they may serve me as priests. Take one young bull and two 2 rams without blemish, and unleavened bread, unleavened cakes mixed with oil, and unleavened wafers spread with oil. You shall make them of fine wheat flour. And you shall put 3 them in one basket and bring them in the basket, and bring the bull and the two rams. You shall 4 bring Aaron and his sons to the door of the tent of meeting, and wash them with water. And you 5 shall take the garments, and put on Aaron the coat and the robe of the ephod, and the ephod, and the breastpiece, and gird him with the skilfully woven band of the ephod; and you shall set the 6 turban on his head, and put the holy crown upon the turban. And 7 you shall take the anointing oil, and pour it on his head and anoint him. Then you shall bring his 8 sons, and put coats on them, and 9 you shall gird them with girdles[q] and bind caps on them; and the priesthood shall be theirs by a perpetual statute. Thus you shall ordain Aaron and his sons.

Sacrifices

"Then you shall bring the bull 10 before the tent of meeting. Aaron and his sons shall lay their hands upon the head of the bull, and you 11 shall kill the bull before the LORD, at the door of the tent of meeting, and shall take part of the blood of 12 the bull and put it upon the horns of the altar with your finger, and the rest of[r] the blood you shall pour out at the base of the altar. And you shall take all the fat that 13 covers the entrails, and the appendage of the liver, and the two

---

[p] The Hebrew word is of uncertain meaning   [q] Gk: Heb girdles, Aaron and his sons   [r] Heb all
28.15-28: Ex 39.8-21.   28.31-34: Ex 39.22-26.   28.36-37: Ex 39.30-31.   28.39-40, 42: Ex 39.27-29.
29.1-37: Lev 8.1-34.

kidneys with the fat that is on
them, and burn them upon the
14 altar. But the flesh of the bull,
and its skin, and its dung, you
shall burn with fire outside the
camp; it is a sin offering.
15 "Then you shall take one of the
rams, and Aaron and his sons
shall lay their hands upon the
16 head of the ram, and you shall
slaughter the ram, and shall take
its blood and throw it against the
17 altar round about. Then you shall
cut the ram into pieces, and wash
its entrails and its legs, and put
them with its pieces and its head,
18 and burn the whole ram upon the
altar; it is a burnt offering to the
LORD; it is a pleasing odour, an
offering by fire to the LORD.
19 "You shall take the other ram;
and Aaron and his sons shall lay
their hands upon the head of the
20 ram, and you shall kill the ram,
and take part of its blood and put
it upon the tip of the right ear of
Aaron and upon the tips of the
right ears of his sons, and upon
the thumbs of their right hands,
and upon the great toes of their
right feet, and throw the rest of
the blood against the altar round
21 about. Then you shall take part
of the blood that is on the altar,
and of the anointing oil, and
sprinkle it upon Aaron and his
garments, and upon his sons and
his sons' garments with him; and
he and his garments shall be holy,
and his sons and his sons' garments with him.
22 "You shall also take the fat of the
ram, and the fat tail, and the fat
that covers the entrails, and the
appendage of the liver, and the
two kidneys with the fat that is on
them, and the right thigh (for it is
23 a ram of ordination), and one loaf
of bread, and one cake of bread
with oil, and one wafer, out of the
basket of unleavened bread that is
24 before the LORD; and you shall
put all these in the hands of Aaron
and in the hands of his sons, and
wave them for a wave offering
25 before the LORD. Then you shall
take them from their hands, and
burn them on the altar in addition
to the burnt offering, as a pleasing
odour before the LORD; it is an
offering by fire to the LORD.
26 "And you shall take the breast of
the ram of Aaron's ordination and
wave it for a wave offering before
the LORD; and it shall be your
27 portion. And you shall consecrate
the breast of the wave offering,
and the thigh of the priests' portion, which is waved, and which is
offered from the ram of ordination, since it is for Aaron and for
28 his sons. It shall be for Aaron and
his sons as a perpetual due from
the people of Israel, for it is the
priests' portion to be offered by
the people of Israel from their
peace offerings; it is their offering
to the LORD.

29 "The holy garments of Aaron
shall be for his sons after him, to
be anointed in them and ordained
30 in them. The son who is priest in
his place shall wear them seven
days, when he comes into the tent
of meeting to minister in the holy
place.
31 "You shall take the ram of ordination, and boil its flesh in a holy
32 place; and Aaron and his sons
shall eat the flesh of the ram and
the bread that is in the basket, at
the door of the tent of meeting.
33 They shall eat those things with
which atonement was made, to
ordain and consecrate them, but
an outsider shall not eat of them,
34 because they are holy. And if any
of the flesh for the ordination, or
of the bread, remain until the
morning, then you shall burn the
remainder with fire; it shall not be
eaten, because it is holy.
35 "Thus you shall do to Aaron and
to his sons, according to all that I
have commanded you; through
seven days shall you ordain them,
36 and every day you shall offer a
bull as a sin offering for atonement. Also you shall offer a sin
offering for the altar, when you
make atonement for it, and shall
37 anoint it, to consecrate it. Seven
days you shall make atonement
for the altar, and consecrate it,
and the altar shall be most holy;
whatever touches the altar shall
38 become holy.
"Now this is what you shall offer
39 upon the altar: two lambs a year
old day by day continually. One
lamb you shall offer in the morn-
40 ing, and the other lamb you shall
offer in the evening; and with the
first lamb a tenth measure of fine
flour mingled with a fourth of a
hin of beaten oil, and a fourth of a
41 hin of wine for a libation. And
the other lamb you shall offer in
the evening, and shall offer with it
a cereal offering and its libation,
as in the morning, for a pleasing
42 odour, an offering by fire to the
LORD. It shall be a continual
burnt offering throughout your
generations at the door of the tent
of meeting before the LORD,
where I will meet with you, to
43 speak there to you. There I will
meet with the people of Israel,
and it shall be sanctified by my
44 glory; I will consecrate the tent of
meeting and the altar; Aaron also
and his sons I will consecrate, to
45 serve me as priests. And I will
dwell among the people of Israel,
46 and will be their God. And they
shall know that I am the LORD
their God, who brought them
forth out of the land of Egypt that
I might dwell among them; I am
the LORD their God.

30 "You shall make an altar to burn
incense upon; of acacia wood shall
2 you make it. A cubit shall be its
length, and a cubit its breadth; it

shall be square, and two cubits
shall be its height; its horns shall
be of one piece with it. And you
3 shall overlay it with pure gold, its
top and its sides round about and
its horns; and you shall make for
it a moulding of gold round
about. And two golden rings shall
4 you make for it; under its moulding on two opposite sides of it
shall you make them, and they
shall be holders for poles with
which to carry it. You shall make
5 the poles of acacia wood, and
overlay them with gold. And you
6 shall put it before the veil that is
by the ark of the testimony, before
the mercy seat that is over the
testimony, where I will meet with
you. And Aaron shall burn fra-
7 grant incense on it; every
morning when he dresses the
lamps he shall burn it, and when
8 Aaron sets up the lamps in the
evening, he shall burn it, a perpetual incense before the LORD
throughout your generations.
You shall offer no unholy incense
9 thereon, nor burnt offering, nor
cereal offering; and you shall pour
no libation thereon. Aaron shall
10 make atonement upon its horns
once a year; with the blood of the
sin offering of atonement he shall
make atonement for it once in the
year throughout your generations;
it is most holy to the LORD."
The LORD said to Moses, "When
11, you take the census of the people
12 of Israel, then each shall give a
ransom for himself to the LORD
when you number them, that
there be no plague among them
when you number them. Each
13 who is numbered in the census
shall give this: half a shekel according to the shekel of the sanctuary
(the shekel is twenty gerahs), half
a shekel as an offering to the
LORD. Every one who is num-
14 bered in the census, from twenty
years old and upward, shall give
the LORD's offering. The rich
15 shall not give more, and the poor
shall not give less, than the half
shekel, when you give the LORD's
offering to make atonement for
yourselves. And you shall take
16 the atonement money from the
people of Israel, and shall appoint
it for the service of the tent of
meeting; that it may bring the
people of Israel to remembrance
before the LORD, so as to make
atonement for themselves."
The LORD said to Moses, "You
17, shall also make a laver of bronze,
18 with its base of bronze, for washing. And you shall put it between
the tent of meeting and the altar,
and you shall put water in it, with
19 which Aaron and his sons shall
wash their hands and their feet.
When they go into the tent of
20 meeting, or when they come near
the altar to minister, to burn an
offering by fire to the LORD, they
shall wash with water, lest they

29.18: Eph 5.2; Phil 4.18. 29.38-42: Num 28.3-8.
30.1-5: Ex 37.25-28. 30.11-16: Ex 38.25-26.
30.18: Ex 38.8.

21 die. They shall wash their hands and their feet, lest they die: it shall be a statute for ever to them, even to him and his descendants throughout their generations."

22 Moreover, the LORD said to 23 Moses, "Take the finest spices: of liquid myrrh five hundred shekels, and of sweet-smelling cinnamon half as much, that is, two hundred and fifty, and of aromatic cane two hundred and 24 fifty, and of cassia five hundred, according to the shekel of the sanctuary, and of olive oil a hin; 25 and you shall make of these a sacred anointing oil blended as by the perfumer; a holy anointing oil 26 it shall be. And you shall anoint with it the tent of meeting and the 27 ark of the testimony, and the table and all its utensils, and the lampstand and its utensils, and 28 the altar of incense, and the altar of burnt offering with all its uten- 29 sils and the laver and its base; you shall consecrate them, that they may be most holy; whatever touches them will become holy. 30 And you shall anoint Aaron and his sons, and consecrate them, that they may serve me as priests. 31 And you shall say to the people of Israel, 'This shall be my holy anointing oil throughout your 32 generations. It shall not be poured upon the bodies of ordinary men, and you shall make no other like it in composition; it is holy, and it shall be holy to you. 33 Whoever compounds any like it or whoever puts any of it on an outsider shall be cut off from his people.' "

34 And the LORD said to Moses, "Take sweet spices, stacte, and onycha, and galbanum, sweet spices with pure frankincense (of each there shall be an equal part), 35 and make an incense blended as by the perfumer, seasoned with 36 salt, pure and holy; and you shall beat some of it very small, and put part of it before the testimony in the tent of meeting where I shall meet with you; it shall be for you 37 most holy. And the incense which you shall make according to its composition, you shall not make for yourselves; it shall be for 38 you holy to the LORD. Whoever makes any like it to use as perfume shall be cut off from his people."

31 The LORD said to Moses, "See, I 2 have called by name Bez'alel the son of Uri, son of Hur, of the tribe 3 of Judah: and I have filled him with the Spirit of God, with ability and intelligence, with knowledge and all craftsmanship, 4 to devise artistic designs, to work 5 in gold, silver, and bronze, in cutting stones for setting, and in carving wood, for work in every 6 craft. And behold, I have appointed with him Oho'liab, the son of Ahis'amach, of the tribe of Dan; and I have given to all able men ability, that they may make all that I have commanded you: 7 the tent of meeting, and the ark of the testimony, and the mercy seat that is thereon, and all the fur- 8 nishings of the tent, the table and its utensils, and the pure lamp-

stand with all its utensils, and the altar of incense, and the altar of 9 burnt offering with all its utensils, and the laver and its base, and the 10 finely worked garments, the holy garments for Aaron the priest and the garments of his sons, for their service as priests, and the anoint- 11 ing oil and the fragrant incense for the holy place. According to all that I have commanded you they shall do."

And the LORD said to Moses, 12 "Say to the people of Israel, 'You 13 shall keep my sabbaths, for this is a sign between me and you throughout your generations, that you may know that I, the LORD, sanctify you. You shall keep the 14 sabbath, because it is holy for you; every one who profanes it shall be put to death; whoever does any work on it, that soul shall be cut off from among his people. Six days shall work be done, but 15 the seventh day is a sabbath of solemn rest, holy to the LORD; whoever does any work on the sabbath day shall be put to death. Therefore the people of Israel 16 shall keep the sabbath, observing the sabbath throughout their generations, as a perpetual covenant. It is a sign for ever between 17 me and the people of Israel that in six days the LORD made heaven and earth, and on the seventh day he rested, and was refreshed.' "

And he gave to Moses, when he 18 had made an end of speaking with him upon Mount Sinai, the two tables of the testimony, tables of stone, written with the finger of God.

The golden calf

32 WHEN the people saw that Moses delayed to come down from the mountain, the people gathered themselves together to Aaron, and said to him, "Up, make us gods, who shall go before us; as for this Moses, the man who brought us up out of the land of Egypt, we do not know what has become of 2 him." And Aaron said to them, "Take off the rings of gold which are in the ears of your wives, your sons, and your daughters, and 3 bring them to me." So all the people took off the rings of gold which were in their 4 ears, and brought them to Aaron. And he received the gold at their hand, and fashioned it with a graving tool, and made a molten calf; and they said, "These are your gods, O Israel, who brought you up out of 5 the land of Egypt!" When Aaron saw this, he built an altar before it; and Aaron made proclamation and said, "Tomorrow shall be a

feast to the LORD." And they rose up early 6 on the morrow, and offered burnt offerings and brought peace offerings; and the people sat down to eat and drink, and rose up to play.

And the LORD said to Moses, "Go down; 7 for your people, whom you brought up out of the land of Egypt, have corrupted themselves; they have turned aside quickly out of 8 the way which I commanded them; they have made for themselves a molten calf, and have worshipped it and sacrificed to it, and said, 'These are your gods, O Israel, who brought you up out of the land of Egypt!' "

And the LORD said to Moses, "I have seen 9 this people, and behold, it is a stiff-necked people; now therefore let me alone, that my 10 wrath may burn hot against them and I may consume them; but of you I will make a great nation."

But Moses besought the LORD his God, and 11 said, "O LORD, why does thy wrath burn hot

30.22-33: Ex 37.29.　31.1-6: Ex 35.30-36.1.　31.12-17: Ex 20.8; 23.12; 35.2; Deut 5.12-15.
32.1-6: Acts 7.40-41.　32.6: 1 Cor 10.7.　32.9-14: Ex 32.31-35; Num 14.11-25.

against thy people, whom thou hast brought forth out of the land of Egypt with great 12 power and with a mighty hand? Why should the Egyptians say, 'With evil intent did he bring them forth, to slay them in the mountains, and to consume them from the face of the earth'? Turn from thy fierce wrath, and repent of this evil against thy people. 13 Remember Abraham, Isaac, and Israel, thy servants, to whom thou didst swear by thine own self, and didst say to them, 'I will multiply your descendants as the stars of heaven, and all this land that I have promised I will give to your descendants, and they 14 shall inherit it for ever.'" And the LORD repented of the evil which he thought to do to his people.

15 And Moses turned, and went down from the mountain with the two tables of the testimony in his hands, tables that were written on both sides; on the one side and on the 16 other were they written. And the tables were the work of God, and the writing was the writing of God, graven upon the tables. 17 When Joshua heard the noise of the people as they shouted, he said to Moses, "There is a 18 noise of war in the camp." But he said, "It is not the sound of shouting for victory, or the sound of the cry of defeat, but the sound of 19 singing that I hear." And as soon as he came near the camp and saw the calf and the dancing, Moses' anger burned hot, and he threw the tables out of his hands and broke 20 them at the foot of the mountain. And he took the calf which they had made, and burnt it with fire, and ground it to powder, and scattered it upon the water, and made the people of Israel drink it.

21 And Moses said to Aaron, "What did this people do to you that you have brought a 22 great sin upon them?" And Aaron said, "Let not the anger of my lord burn hot; you know the people, that they are set on evil. 23 For they said to me, 'Make us gods, who shall go before us; as for this Moses, the man who brought us up out of the land of Egypt, we do not know what has become of him.' 24 And I said to them, 'Let any who have gold take it off'; so they gave it to me, and I threw it into the fire, and there came out this calf."

25 And when Moses saw that the people had broken loose (for Aaron had let them break loose, to their shame among their enemies), 26 then Moses stood in the gate of the camp, and said, "Who is on the LORD's side? Come to me." And all the sons of Levi 27 gathered themselves together to him. And he said to them, "Thus says the LORD God of Israel, 'Put every man his sword on his side, and go to and fro from gate to gate throughout the camp, and slay every man his brother, and every man his companion, and every man his neighbour.'" And the sons of 28 Levi did according to the word of Moses; and there fell of the people that day about three thousand men. And Moses said, 29 "Today you have ordained yourselves[a] for the service of the LORD, each one at the cost of his son and of his brother, that he may bestow a blessing upon you this day."

Repentance

On the morrow Moses said to the people, 30 "You have sinned a great sin. And now I will go up to the LORD; perhaps I can make atonement for your sin." So Moses returned 31 to the LORD and said, "Alas, this people have sinned a great sin; they have made for themselves gods of gold. But now, if thou 32 wilt forgive their sin—and if not, blot me, I pray thee, out of thy book which thou hast written." But the LORD said to Moses, 33 "Whoever has sinned against me, him will I blot out of my book. But now go, lead the 34 people to the place of which I have spoken to you; behold my angel shall go before you. Nevertheless, in the day when I visit, I will visit their sin upon them."

And the LORD sent a plague upon the 35 people, because they made the calf which Aaron made.

The LORD said to Moses, "Depart, go up 33 hence, you and the people whom you have brought up out of the land of Egypt, to the land of which I swore to Abraham, Isaac, and Jacob, saying, 'To your descendants I will give it.' And I will send an angel before you, 2 and I will drive out the Canaanites, the Amorites, the Hittites, the Per'izzites, the Hivites, and the Jeb'usites. Go up to a land 3 flowing with milk and honey; but I will not go up among you, lest I consume you in the way, for you are a stiff-necked people." When the people heard these evil tidings, 4 they mourned; and no man put on his ornaments. For the LORD had said to Moses, 5 "Say to the people of Israel, 'You are a stiff-necked people; if for a single moment I should go up among you, I would consume you. So now put off your ornaments from you, that I may know what to do with you.'" Therefore the people of Israel 6 stripped themselves of their ornaments, from Mount Horeb onward.

[a] Gk Vg See Tg: Heb *ordain yourselves*

32.23: Acts 7.40. 32.32–33: Rev 3.5. 33.3: Acts 7.51.

7 Now Moses used to take the tent and pitch it outside the camp, far off from the camp; and he called it the tent of meeting. And every one who sought the LORD would go to the tent of meeting, which was outside the 8 camp. Whenever Moses went out to the tent, all the people rose up, and every man stood at his tent door, and looked after Moses, until he had gone into the tent. 9 When Moses entered the tent, the pillar of cloud would descend and stand at the door of the tent, and the LORD would speak with 10 Moses. And when all the people saw the pillar of cloud standing at the door of the tent, all the people would rise up and wor- 11 ship, every man at his tent door. Thus the LORD used to speak to Moses face to face, as a man speaks to his friend. When Moses turned again into the camp, his servant Joshua the son of Nun, a young man, did not depart from the tent.

12 Moses said to the LORD, "See, thou sayest to me, 'Bring up this people'; but thou hast not let me know whom thou wilt send with me. Yet thou hast said, 'I know you by name, and you have also found favour in my 13 sight.' Now therefore, I pray thee, if I have found favour in thy sight, show me now thy ways, that I may know thee and find favour in thy sight. Consider too that this nation is 14 thy people." And he said, "My presence will 15 go with you, and I will give you rest." And he said to him, "If thy presence will not go 16 with me, do not carry us up from here. For how shall it be known that I have found favour in thy sight, I and thy people? Is it not in thy going with us, so that we are distinct, I and thy people, from all other people that are upon the face of the earth?"

17 And the LORD said to Moses, "This very thing that you have spoken I will do; for you have found favour in my sight, and I know 18 you by name." Moses said, "I pray thee, 19 show me thy glory." And he said, "I will make all my goodness pass before you, and will proclaim before you my name 'The LORD'; and I will be gracious to whom I will be gracious, and will show mercy on whom I 20 will show mercy. But," he said, "you cannot see my face; for man shall not see me and 21 live." And the LORD said, "Behold, there is a place by me where you shall stand upon the 22 rock; and while my glory passes by I will put you in a cleft of the rock, and I will cover you with my hand until I have passed by; 23 then I will take away my hand, and you shall see my back; but my face shall not be seen."

The covenant is renewed

The LORD said to Moses, "Cut two tables of **34** stone like the first; and I will write upon the tables the words that were on the first tables, which you broke. Be ready in the morning, 2 and come up in the morning to Mount Sinai, and present yourself there to me on the top of the mountain. No man shall come up with 3 you, and let no man be seen throughout all the mountain; let no flocks or herds feed before that mountain." So Moses cut two 4 tables of stone like the first; and he rose early in the morning and went up on Mount Sinai, as the LORD had commanded him, and took in his hand two tables of stone. And the 5 LORD descended in the cloud and stood with him there, and proclaimed the name of the LORD. The LORD passed before him, and 6 proclaimed, "The LORD, the LORD, a God merciful and gracious, slow to anger, and abounding in steadfast love and faithfulness, keeping steadfast love for thousands, for- 7 giving iniquity and transgression and sin, but who will by no means clear the guilty, visiting the iniquity of the fathers upon the children and the children's children, to the third and the fourth generation." And 8 Moses made haste to bow his head toward the earth, and worshipped. And he said, "If 9 now I have found favour in thy sight, O Lord, let the Lord, I pray thee, go in the midst of us, although it is a stiff-necked people; and pardon our iniquity and our sin, and take us for thy inheritance."

And he said, "Behold, I make a covenant. 10 Before all your people I will do marvels, such as have not been wrought in all the earth or in any nation; and all the people among whom you are shall see the work of the LORD; for it is a terrible thing that I will do with you.

"Observe what I command you this day. 11 Behold, I will drive out before you the Amorites, the Canaanites, the Hittites, the Per'izzites, the Hivites, and the Jeb'usites. Take heed to yourself, lest you make a 12 covenant with the inhabitants of the land whither you go, lest it become a snare in the midst of you. You shall tear down their 13

33.11: Num 12.8; Deut 34.10.   33.19: Rom 9.15.
34.6: Num 14.18; Neh 9.17; Ps 86.15; 103.8; 145.8; Jon 4.2.

altars, and break their pillars, and cut down
14 their Ashe'rim (for you shall worship no
other god, for the LORD, whose name is
15 Jealous, is a jealous God), lest you make a
covenant with the inhabitants of the land,
and when they play the harlot after their gods
and sacrifice to their gods and one invites
16 you, you eat of his sacrifice, and you take of
their daughters for your sons, and their
daughters play the harlot after their gods
and make your sons play the harlot after
their gods.
17 "You shall make for yourself no molten
gods.
18 "The feast of unleavened bread you shall
keep. Seven days you shall eat unleavened
bread, as I commanded you, at the time
appointed in the month Abib; for in the
19 month Abib you came out from Egypt. All
that opens the womb is mine, all your male *t*
20 cattle, the firstlings of cow and sheep. The
firstling of an ass you shall redeem with a
lamb, or if you will not redeem it you shall
break its neck. All the first-born of your sons
you shall redeem. And none shall appear
before me empty.
21 "Six days you shall work, but on the
seventh day you shall rest; in ploughing time
22 and in harvest you shall rest. And you shall
observe the feast of weeks, the first fruits of
wheat harvest, and the feast of ingathering at
23 the year's end. Three times in the year shall
all your males appear before the LORD God,
24 the God of Israel. For I will cast out nations
before you, and enlarge your borders; neither
shall any man desire your land, when you go
up to appear before the LORD your God three
times in the year.
25 "You shall not offer the blood of my

sacrifice with leaven; neither shall the sacrifice
of the feast of the passover be left until the
morning. The first of the first fruits of your 26
ground you shall bring to the house of the
LORD your God. You shall not boil a kid in
its mother's milk."
And the LORD said to Moses, "Write these 27
words; in accordance with these words I have
made a covenant with you and with Israel."
And he was there with the LORD forty days 28
and forty nights; he neither ate bread nor
drank water. And he wrote upon the tables
the words of the covenant, the ten commandments. *u*
When Moses came down from Mount 29
Sinai, with the two tables of the testimony in
his hand as he came down from the mountain, Moses did not know that the skin of his
face shone because he had been talking with
God. And when Aaron and all the people of 30
Israel saw Moses, behold, the skin of his face
shone, and they were afraid to come near
him. But Moses called to them; and Aaron 31
and all the leaders of the congregation
returned to him, and Moses talked with
them. And afterward all the people of Israel 32
came near, and he gave them in commandment all that the LORD had spoken with
him in Mount Sinai. And when Moses had 33
finished speaking with them, he put a veil on
his face; but whenever Moses went in before 34
the LORD to speak with him, he took the veil
off, until he came out; and when he came
out, and told the people of Israel what he was
commanded, the people of Israel saw the face 35
of Moses, that the skin of Moses' face shone;
and Moses would put the veil upon his face
again, until he went in to speak with him.

The building of the tabernacle

35 MOSES assembled all the
congregation of the people
of Israel, and said to them,
"These are the things which the
LORD has commanded you to
2 do. Six days shall work be done,
but on the seventh day you shall
have a holy sabbath of solemn rest
to the LORD; whoever does any
work on it shall be put to death;
3 you shall kindle no fire in all your
habitations on the sabbath day."
4 Moses said to all the congregation of the people of Israel, "This
is the thing which the LORD has
5 commanded. Take from among

you an offering to the LORD;
whoever is of a generous heart, let
6 him bring the LORD's offering:
gold, silver, and bronze; blue and
purple and scarlet stuff and fine
7 twined linen; goats' hair, tanned
rams' skins, and goatskins; acacia
8 wood, oil for the light, spices for
the anointing oil and for the
9 fragrant incense, and onyx stones
and stones for setting, for the
ephod and for the breastpiece.
10 "And let every able man among
you come and make all that the
LORD has commanded: the taber-
11 nacle, its tent and its covering, its
hooks and its frames, its bars, its
12 pillars, and its bases; the ark with

its poles, the mercy seat, and the
veil of the screen; the table with 13
its poles and all its utensils, and
the bread of the Presence; the 14
lampstand also for the light, with
its utensils and its lamps, and the
oil for the light; and the altar of 15
incense, with its poles, and the
anointing oil and the fragrant
incense, and the screen for the
door, at the door of the tabernacle; the altar of burnt offering, 16
with its grating of bronze, its
poles, and all its utensils, the laver
and its base; the hangings of the 17
court, its pillars and its bases, and
the screen for the gate of the
court; the pegs of the tabernacle 18

t Gk Theodotion Vg Tg: Heb uncertain *u* Heb *words*
34.14: Ex 20.5; 34.7; Deut 4.24; 5.9. 34.17: Ex 20.4. 34.18: Ex 12.15-20. 34.19-20: Ex 13.2, 11-16.
34.21: Ex 20.8-10; 23.12; 31.12-17; 35.2; Deut 5.12-15.
34.22-24: Ex 23.14-17; Lev 23.1-44; Deut 16.1-17. 34.25: Ex 12.10; 23.18; Lev 2.11.
34.26: Ex 23.19; Deut 14.21; 26.2-11. 34.29-35: 2 Cor 3.7-16.
35.2-3: Ex 23.12; 31.12-17; 34.21; Deut 5.12-15. 35.4-9: Ex 25.1-9.

and the pegs of the court, and
19 their cords; the finely wrought
garments for ministering in the
holy place, the holy garments for
Aaron the priest, and the garments of his sons, for their service
as priests."
20 Then all the congregation of
the people of Israel departed from
21 the presence of Moses. And
they came, every one whose heart
stirred him, and every one whose
spirit moved him, and brought
the LORD's offering to be used for
the tent of meeting, and for all its
service, and for the holy gar-
22 ments. So they came, both men
and women; all who were of a
willing heart brought brooches
and earrings and signet rings and
armlets, all sorts of gold objects,
every man dedicating an offering
23 of gold to the LORD. And every
man with whom was found blue
or purple or scarlet stuff or fine
linen or goats' hair or tanned
rams' skins or goatskins, brought
24 them. Every one who could make
an offering of silver or bronze
brought it as the LORD's offering;
and every man with whom was
found acacia wood of any use in
25 the work, brought it. And all
women who had ability spun with
their hands, and brought what
they had spun in blue and purple
and scarlet stuff and fine twined
26 linen; all the women whose hearts
were moved with ability spun the
27 goats' hair. And the leaders
brought onyx stones and stones to
be set, for the ephod and for the
28 breastpiece, and spices and oil for
the light, and for the anointing oil,
29 and for the fragrant incense. All
the men and women, the people of
Israel, whose heart moved them
to bring anything for the work
which the LORD had commanded
by Moses to be done, brought it as
their freewill offering to the
LORD.
30 And Moses said to the people of
Israel, "See, the LORD has called
by name Bez'alel the son of Uri,
son of Hur, of the tribe of Judah;
31 and he has filled him with the
Spirit of God, with ability, with
intelligence, with knowledge, and
32 with all craftsmanship, to devise
artistic designs, to work in gold
33 and silver and bronze, in cutting
stones for setting, and in carving
wood, for work in every skilled
34 craft. And he has inspired him to
teach, both him and Oho'liab the
son of Ahis'amach of the tribe of
35 Dan. He has filled them with
ability to do every sort of work
done by a craftsman or by a
designer or by an embroiderer in
blue and purple and scarlet stuff
and fine twined linen, or by a
weaver—by any sort of workman
or skilled designer.

36 "Bez'alel and Oho'liab and every
able man in whom the LORD has
put ability and intelligence to

know how to do any work in the
construction of the sanctuary shall
work in accordance with all that
the LORD has commanded."
2 And Moses called Bez'alel and
Oho'liab and every able man in
whose mind the LORD had put
ability, every one whose heart
stirred him up to come to do the
3 work; and they received from
Moses all the freewill offering
which the people of Israel had
brought for doing the work on the
sanctuary. They still kept bringing him freewill offerings every
4 morning, so that all the able men
who were doing every sort of task
on the sanctuary came, each from
5 the task that he was doing, and
said to Moses, "The people bring
much more than enough for doing
the work which the LORD has
6 commanded us to do." So Moses
gave command, and word was
proclaimed throughout the camp,
"Let neither man nor woman do
anything more for the offering for
the sanctuary." So the people
were restrained from bringing;
7 for the stuff they had was sufficient to do all the work, and more.

The tabernacle

8 And all the able men among the
workmen made the tabernacle
with ten curtains; they were made
of fine twined linen and blue and
purple and scarlet stuff, with
9 cherubim skilfully worked. The
length of each curtain was twenty-eight cubits, and the breadth of
each curtain four cubits; all the
curtains had the same measure.
10 And he coupled five curtains to
one another, and the other five
curtains he coupled to one an-
11 other. And he made loops of blue
on the edge of the outmost curtain
of the first set; likewise he made
them on the edge of the outmost
12 curtain of the second set; he made
fifty loops on the one curtain, and
he made fifty loops on the edge of
the curtain that was in the second
set; the loops were opposite one
13 another. And he made fifty clasps
of gold, and coupled the curtains
one to the other with clasps; so
the tabernacle was one whole.
14 He also made curtains of goats'
hair for a tent over the tabernacle;
15 he made eleven curtains. The
length of each curtain was thirty
cubits, and the breadth of each
curtain four cubits; the eleven
curtains had the same measure.
16 He coupled five curtains by themselves, and six curtains by them-
17 selves. And he made fifty loops
on the edge of the outmost curtain
of the one set, and fifty loops on
the edge of the other connecting
18 curtain. And he made fifty clasps
of bronze to couple the tent
together that it might be one
19 whole. And he made for the tent
a covering of tanned rams' skins
and goatskins.

Then he made the upright 20
frames for the tabernacle of acacia
wood. Ten cubits was the length 21
of a frame, and a cubit and a half
the breadth of each frame. Each 22
frame had two tenons, for fitting
together; he did this for all the
frames of the tabernacle. The 23
frames for the tabernacle he made
thus: twenty frames for the south
side; and he made forty bases of 24
silver under the twenty frames,
two bases under one frame for its
two tenons, and two bases under
another frame for its two tenons.
And for the second side of the 25
tabernacle, on the north side, he
made twenty frames and their 26
forty bases of silver, two bases
under one frame and two bases
under another frame. And for the 27
rear of the tabernacle westward he
made six frames. And he made 28
two frames for corners of the
tabernacle in the rear. And they 29
were separate beneath, but joined
at the top, at the first ring; he
made two of them thus, for the
two corners. There were eight 30
frames with their bases of silver:
sixteen bases, under every frame
two bases.
And he made bars of acacia 31
wood, five for the frames of the
one side of the tabernacle, and 32
five bars for the frames of the
other side of the tabernacle, and
five bars for the frames of the
tabernacle at the rear westward.
And he made the middle bar to 33
pass through from end to end
halfway up the frames. And he 34
overlaid the frames with gold, and
made their rings of gold for
holders for the bars, and overlaid
the bars with gold.
And he made the veil of blue and 35
purple and scarlet stuff and fine
twined linen; with cherubim skilfully worked he made it. And for 36
it he made four pillars of acacia,
and overlaid them with gold; their
hooks were of gold, and he cast for
them four bases of silver. He also 37
made a screen for the door of the
tent, of blue and purple and
scarlet stuff and fine twined linen,
embroidered with needlework;
and its five pillars with their 38
hooks. He overlaid their capitals,
and their fillets were of gold, but
their five bases were of bronze.

The ark

Bez'alel made the ark of acacia **37**
wood; two cubits and a half was

its length, a cubit and a half its breadth, and a cubit and a half its 2 height. And he overlaid it with pure gold within and without, and made a moulding of gold around 3 it. And he cast for it four rings of gold for its four corners, two rings on its one side and two rings on its 4 other side. And he made poles of acacia wood, and overlaid them 5 with gold, and put the poles into the rings on the sides of the ark, to 6 carry the ark. And he made a mercy seat of pure gold; two cubits and a half was its length, and a cubit and a half its breadth. 7 And he made two cherubim of hammered gold; on the two ends 8 of the mercy seat he made them, one cherub on the one end, and one cherub on the other end; of one piece with the mercy seat he made the cherubim on its two 9 ends. The cherubim spread out their wings above, overshadowing the mercy seat with their wings, with their faces one to another; toward the mercy seat were the faces of the cherubim.

10 He also made the table of acacia wood; two cubits was its length, a cubit its breadth, and a cubit and 11 a half its height; and he overlaid it 12 with pure gold, and made a moulding of gold around it. And he made around it a frame a handbreadth wide, and made a moulding of gold around the 13 frame. He cast for it four rings of gold, and fastened the rings to 14 four corners at its four legs. Close to the frame were the rings, as holders for the poles to carry the 15 table. He made the poles of acacia wood to carry the table, and he 16 overlaid them with gold. And he made the vessels of pure gold which were to be upon the table, its plates and dishes for incense, and its bowls and flagons with which to pour libations.

17 He also made the lampstand of pure gold. The base and the shaft of the lampstand were made of hammered work; its cups, its capitals, and its flowers were of 18 one piece with it. And there were six branches going out of its sides, three branches of the lampstand out of one side of it and three 19 branches of the lampstand out of the other side of it; three cups made like almonds, each with capital and flower, on one branch, and three cups made like almonds, each with capital and flower, on the other branch—so for the six branches going out of 20 the lampstand. And on the lampstand itself were four cups made like almonds, with their capitals 21 and flowers, and a capital of one piece with it under each pair of the six branches going out of it. 22 Their capitals and their branches were of one piece with it; the whole of it was one piece of hammered work of pure gold. 23 And he made its seven lamps and

its snuffers and its trays of pure 24 gold. He made it and all its utensils of a talent of pure gold.

The altars

25 He made the altar of incense of acacia wood; its length was a cubit, and its breadth was a cubit; it was square, and two cubits was 26 its height; its horns were of one piece with it. He overlaid it with pure gold, its top, and its sides round about, and its horns; and 27 he made a moulding of gold round about it, and made two rings of gold on it under its moulding, on two opposite sides of it, as holders for the poles with which to carry 28 it. And he made the poles of acacia wood, and overlaid them 29 with gold. He made the holy anointing oil also, and the pure fragrant incense, blended as by the perfumer.

38 He made the altar of burnt offering also of acacia wood; five cubits was its length, and five cubits its breadth; it was square, and three cubits was its height. 2 He made horns for it on its four corners; its horns were of one piece with it, and he overlaid it 3 with bronze. And he made all the utensils of the altar, the pots, the shovels, the basins, the forks, and the firepans: all its utensils he 4 made of bronze. And he made for the altar a grating, a network of bronze, under its ledge, extending 5 halfway down. He cast four rings on the four corners of the bronze 6 grating as holders for the poles; he made the poles of acacia wood, and overlaid them with bronze. 7 And he put the poles through the rings on the sides of the altar, to carry it with them; he made it hollow, with boards.

8 And he made the laver of bronze and its base of bronze, from the mirrors of the ministering women who ministered at the door of the tent of meeting.

9 And he made the court; for the south side the hangings of the court were of fine twined linen, a 10 hundred cubits; their pillars were twenty and their bases twenty, of bronze, but the hooks of the pillars and their fillets were of 11 silver. And for the north side a hundred cubits, their pillars twenty, their bases twenty, of bronze, but the hooks of the pil-

lars and their fillets were of 12 silver. And for the west side were hangings of fifty cubits, their pillars ten, and their sockets ten; the hooks of the pillars and their 13 fillets were of silver. And for the front to the east, fifty cubits. The 14 hangings for one side of the gate were fifteen cubits, with three pillars and three bases. And so 15 for the other side; on this hand and that hand by the gate of the court were hangings of fifteen cubits, with three pillars and three bases. All the hangings round 16 about the court were of fine twined linen. And the bases for 17 the pillars were of bronze, but the hooks of the pillars and their fillets were of silver; the overlaying of their capitals was also of silver, and all the pillars of the court were filleted with silver. And the screen for the gate of 18 the court was embroidered with needlework in blue and purple and scarlet stuff and fine twined linen; it was twenty cubits long and five cubits high in its breadth, corresponding to the hangings of the court. And their pillars were 19 four; their four bases were of bronze, their hooks of silver, and the overlaying of their capitals and their fillets of silver. And all 20 the pegs for the tabernacle and for the court round about were of bronze.

This is the sum of the things for 21 the tabernacle, the tabernacle of the testimony, as they were counted at the commandment of Moses, for the work of the Levites under the direction of Ith′amar the son of Aaron the priest. Bez′alel the son of Uri, son of 22 Hur, of the tribe of Judah, made all that the LORD commanded Moses; and with him was Oho′- 23 liab the son of Ahis′amach, of the tribe of Dan, a craftsman and designer and embroiderer in blue and purple and scarlet stuff and fine twined linen.

All the gold that was used for the 24 work, in all the construction of the sanctuary, the gold from the offering, was twenty-nine talents and seven hundred and thirty shekels, by the shekel of the sanctuary. And the silver from 25 those of the congregation who were numbered was a hundred talents and a thousand seven hundred and seventy-five shekels, by the shekel of the sanctuary: a 26 beka a head (that is, half a shekel, by the shekel of the sanctuary), for every one who was numbered in the census, from twenty years old and upward, for six hundred and three thousand, five hundred and fifty men. The hundred 27 talents of silver were for casting the bases of the sanctuary, and the bases of the veil; a hundred bases for the hundred talents, a talent for a base. And of the thousand 28 seven hundred and seventy-five

37.10–16: Ex 25.23–29.   37.17–24: Ex 25.31–39.   37.25–28: Ex 30.1–5.   38.1–7: Ex 27.1–8.
38.8: Ex 30.18.   38.9–20: Ex 27.9–19.   38.25–26: Ex 30.11–16.

shekels he made hooks for the
pillars, and overlaid their capitals
29 and made fillets for them. And
the bronze that was contributed
was seventy talents, and two
thousand and four hundred shek-
30 els; with it he made the bases for
the door of the tent of meeting,
the bronze altar and the bronze
grating for it and all the utensils of
31 the altar, the bases round about
the court, and the bases of the
gate of the court, all the pegs of
the tabernacle, and all the pegs
round about the court.

*The
table
of
shew-
bread*

39 And of the blue and purple and
scarlet stuff they made finely
wrought garments, for ministering in the holy place; they made
the holy garments for Aaron; as
the LORD had commanded Moses.

The ephod

2 And he made the ephod of gold,
blue and purple and scarlet stuff,
3 and fine twined linen. And gold
leaf was hammered out and cut
into threads to work into the blue
and purple and the scarlet stuff,
and into the fine twined linen, in
4 skilled design. They made for the
ephod shoulder-pieces, joined to
5 it at its two edges. And the
skilfully woven band upon it, to
gird it on, was of the same materials and workmanship; of gold,
blue and purple and scarlet stuff,
and fine twined linen; as the LORD
had commanded Moses.
6 The onyx stones were prepared,
enclosed in settings of gold filigree and engraved like the engrav-
ings of a signet, according to the
7 names of the sons of Israel. And
he set them on the shoulder-
pieces of the ephod, to be stones
of remembrance for the sons of
Israel; as the LORD had commanded Moses.
8 He made the breastpiece, in
skilled work, like the work of the
ephod, of gold, blue and purple
and scarlet stuff, and fine twined
9 linen. It was square; the breastpiece was made double, a span its
length and a span its breadth
10 when doubled. And they set in it
four rows of stones. A row of
sardius, topaz, and carbuncle was
11 the first row; and the second row,
an emerald, a sapphire, and a
12 diamond; and the third row,
a jacinth, an agate, and an
13 amethyst; and the fourth row, a
beryl, an onyx, and a jasper; they
were enclosed in settings of gold
14 filigree. There were twelve stones
with their names according to the
names of the sons of Israel; they
were like signets, each engraved
with its name, for the twelve
15 tribes. And they made on the
breastpiece twisted chains like
16 cords, of pure gold; and they
made two settings of gold filigree
and two gold rings, and put the

two rings on the two edges of the
17 breastpiece; and they put the two
cords of gold in the two rings at
18 the edges of the breastpiece. Two
ends of the two cords they had
attached to the two settings of
filigree; thus they attached it in
front to the shoulder-pieces of the
19 ephod. Then they made two
rings of gold, and put them at the
two ends of the breastpiece, on its
inside edge next to the ephod.
20 And they made two rings of gold,
and attached them in front to the
lower part of the two shoulder-
pieces of the ephod, at its joining
21 above the skilfully woven band of
the ephod. And they bound the
breastpiece by its rings to the
rings of the ephod with a lace of
blue, so that it should lie upon the
skilfully woven band of the
ephod, and that the breastpiece
should not come loose from the
ephod; as the LORD had commanded Moses.
22 He also made the robe of the
23 ephod woven all of blue; and the
opening of the robe in it was like
the opening in a garment, with a
binding around the opening, that
24 it might not be torn. On the skirts

of the robe they made pomegranates of blue and purple and
scarlet stuff and fine twined
linen. They also made bells of 25
pure gold, and put the bells
between the pomegranates upon
the skirts of the robe round about,
between the pomegranates; a bell 26
and a pomegranate, a bell and a
pomegranate round about upon
the skirts of the robe for ministering; as the LORD had commanded
Moses.
They also made the coats, woven 27
of fine linen, for Aaron and his
sons, and the turban of fine linen, 28
and the caps of fine linen, and the
linen breeches of fine twined
linen, and the girdle of fine 29
twined linen and of blue and
purple and scarlet stuff, embroidered with needlework; as the
LORD had commanded Moses.
And they made the plate of the 30
holy crown of pure gold, and
wrote upon it an inscription, like
the engraving of a signet, "Holy
to the LORD." And they tied to it 31
a lace of blue, to fasten it on the
turban above; as the LORD had
commanded Moses.

The altar of incense

39.2-7: Ex 28.6-12. **39.8-21:** Ex 28.15-28. **39.22-26:** Ex 28.31-34. **39.27-29:** Ex 28.39-40, 42.
39.30-31: Ex 28.36-37.

The tabernacle is erected

32 THUS all the work of the tabernacle of the tent of meeting was finished; and the people of Israel had done according to all that the LORD had commanded Moses; so 33 had they done. And they brought the tabernacle to Moses, the tent and all its utensils, its hooks, its frames, its bars, its 34 pillars, and its bases; the covering of tanned rams' skins and goatskins, and the veil of the 35 screen; the ark of the testimony with its poles 36 and the mercy seat; the table with all its 37 utensils, and the bread of the Presence; the lampstand of pure gold and its lamps with the lamps set and all its utensils, and the oil 38 for the light; the golden altar, the anointing oil and the fragrant incense, and the screen 39 for the door of the tent; the bronze altar, and its grating of bronze, its poles, and all its 40 utensils; the laver and its base; the hangings of the court, its pillars, and its bases, and the screen for the gate of the court, its cords, and its pegs; and all the utensils for the service of 41 the tabernacle, for the tent of meeting; the finely worked garments for ministering in the holy place, the holy garments for Aaron the priest, and the garments of his sons to 42 serve as priests. According to all that the LORD had commanded Moses, so the people of 43 Israel had done all the work. And Moses saw all the work, and behold, they had done it; as the LORD had commanded, so had they done it. And Moses blessed them.

40 The LORD said to Moses, "On the first day 2 of the first month you shall erect the taber- 3 nacle of the tent of meeting. And you shall put in it the ark of the testimony, and you 4 shall screen the ark with the veil. And you shall bring in the table, and set its arrange- ments in order; and you shall bring in the 5 lampstand, and set up its lamps. And you shall put the golden altar for incense before the ark of the testimony, and set up the 6 screen for the door of the tabernacle. You shall set the altar of burnt offering before the door of the tabernacle of the tent of meeting, 7 and place the laver between the tent of meeting and the altar, and put water in it. 8 And you shall set up the court round about, and hang up the screen for the gate of the 9 court. Then you shall take the anointing oil, and anoint the tabernacle and all that is in it, and consecrate it and all its furniture; and it 10 shall become holy. You shall also anoint the altar of burnt offering and all its utensils, and consecrate the altar; and the altar shall be 11 most holy. You shall also anoint the laver

and its base, and consecrate it. Then you shall bring Aaron and his sons to the door of the tent of meeting, and shall wash them with water, and put upon Aaron the holy gar- ments, and you shall anoint him and con- secrate him, that he may serve me as priest. You shall bring his sons also and put coats on them, and anoint them, as you anointed their father, that they may serve me as priests: and their anointing shall admit them to a per- petual priesthood throughout their genera- tions."

Thus did Moses; according to all that the LORD commanded him, so he did. And in the first month in the second year, on the first day of the month, the tabernacle was erected. Moses erected the tabernacle; he laid its bases, and set up its frames, and put in its poles, and raised up its pillars; and he spread the tent over the tabernacle, and put the covering of the tent over it, as the LORD had commanded Moses. And he took the testimony and put it into the ark, and put the poles on the ark, and set the mercy seat above on the ark; and he brought the ark into the tabernacle, and set up the veil of the screen, and screened the ark of the testimony; as the LORD had commanded Moses. And he put the table in the tent of meeting, on the north side of the tabernacle, outside the veil, and set the bread in order on it before the LORD; as the LORD had commanded Moses. And he put the lampstand in the tent of meeting, opposite the table on the south side of the tabernacle, and set up the lamps before the LORD; as the LORD had commanded Moses. And he put the golden altar in the tent of meeting before the veil, and burnt fragrant incense upon it; as the LORD had com- manded Moses. And he put in place the screen for the door of the tabernacle. And he set the altar of burnt offering at the door of the tabernacle of the tent of meeting, and offered upon it the burnt offering and the cereal offering; as the LORD had commanded Moses. And he set the laver between the tent of meeting and the altar, and put water in it for washing, with which Moses and Aaron and his sons washed their hands and their feet; when they went into the tent of meeting, and when they approached the altar, they washed; as the LORD commanded Moses. And he erected the court round the tabernacle and the altar, and set up the screen of the gate of the court. So Moses finished the work.

Then the cloud covered the tent of meeting, and the glory of the LORD filled the taber- nacle. And Moses was not able to enter the

39.36: Ex 25.30; 40.23; Lev 24.5–9.   **40.23:** Ex 25.30; 39.36; Lev 24.5–9.   **40.30–32:** Ex 30.18–21.
40.34: Rev 15.8.

tent of meeting, because the cloud abode upon it, and the glory of the LORD filled the
6 tabernacle. Throughout all their journeys, whenever the cloud was taken up from over the tabernacle, the people of Israel would go
7 onward; but if the cloud was not taken up,

then they did not go onward till the day that it was taken up. For throughout all their 38 journeys the cloud of the LORD was upon the tabernacle by day, and fire was in it by night, in the sight of all the house of Israel.

THE THIRD BOOK OF MOSES
COMMONLY CALLED
LEVITICUS

SACRIFICES

THE LORD called Moses, and spoke to him from the 10 tent of meeting, saying,
2 "Speak to the people of Israel, and say to them, When any man of you brings an offering to the LORD, you shall bring your offering of cattle from the herd or from the flock.

The burnt offering

3 "If his offering is a burnt offering from the herd, he shall offer a 13 male without blemish; he shall offer it at the door of the tent of meeting, that he may be accepted
4 before the LORD; he shall lay his hand upon the head of the burnt offering, and it shall be accepted for him to make atonement for 14
5 him. Then he shall kill the bull before the LORD; and Aaron's sons the priests shall present the 15 blood, and throw the blood round about against the altar that is at the door of the tent of meeting.
6 And he shall flay the burnt offer-
7 ing and cut it into pieces; and the 16 sons of Aaron the priest shall put fire on the altar, and lay wood in
8 order upon the fire; and Aaron's 17 sons the priests shall lay the pieces, the head, and the fat, in order upon the wood that is on the
9 fire upon the altar; but its entrails and its legs he shall wash with water. And the priest shall burn

the whole on the altar, as a burnt offering, an offering by fire, a pleasing odour to the LORD.
10 "If his gift for a burnt offering is from the flock, from the sheep or goats, he shall offer a male
11 without blemish; and he shall kill it on the north side of the altar before the LORD, and Aaron's sons the priests shall throw its blood against the altar round
12 about. And he shall cut it into pieces, with its head and its fat, and the priest shall lay them in order upon the wood that is on
13 the fire upon the altar; but the entrails and the legs he shall wash with water. And the priest shall offer the whole, and burn it on the altar; it is a burnt offering, an offering by fire, a pleasing odour to the LORD.
14 "If his offering to the LORD is a burnt offering of birds, then he shall bring his offering of turtle-
15 doves or of young pigeons. And the priest shall bring it to the altar and wring off its head, and burn it on the altar; and its blood shall be drained out on the side of the
16 altar; and he shall take away its crop with the feathers, and cast it beside the altar on the east side, in
17 the place for ashes; he shall tear it by its wings, but shall not divide it asunder. And the priest shall burn it on the altar, upon the wood that is on the fire; it is a burnt offering, an offering by fire, a pleasing odour to the LORD.

The cereal offering

"When any one brings a cereal 2 offering as an offering to the LORD, his offering shall be of fine flour; he shall pour oil upon it, and put frankincense on it, and 2 bring it to Aaron's sons the priests. And he shall take from it a handful of the fine flour and oil, with all of its frankincense; and the priest shall burn this as its memorial portion upon the altar, an offering by fire, a pleasing odour to the LORD. And what is 3 left of the cereal offering shall be for Aaron and his sons; it is a most holy part of the offerings by fire to the LORD.

"When you bring a cereal offer- 4 ing baked in the oven as an offering, it shall be unleavened cakes of fine flour mixed with oil, or unleavened wafers spread with oil. And if your offering is a 5 cereal offering baked on a griddle, it shall be of fine flour unleavened, mixed with oil; you 6 shall break it in pieces, and pour oil on it; it is a cereal offering. And if your offering is a cereal 7 offering cooked in a pan, it shall be made of fine flour with oil. And you shall bring the cereal 8 offering that is made of these things to the LORD; and when it is presented to the priest, he shall bring it to the altar. And the 9 priest shall take from the cereal offering its memorial portion and burn this on the altar, an offering by fire, a pleasing odour to the 10 LORD. And what is left of the cereal offering shall be for Aaron and his sons; it is a most holy part of the offerings by fire to the LORD.

11 "No cereal offering which you bring to the LORD shall be made with leaven; for you shall burn no leaven nor any honey as an offer-

12 ing by fire to the LORD. As an offering of first fruits you may bring them to the LORD, but they shall not be offered on the altar

13 for a pleasing odour. You shall season all your cereal offerings with salt; you shall not let the salt of the covenant with your God be lacking from your cereal offering; with all your offerings you shall offer salt.

14 "If you offer a cereal offering of first fruits to the LORD, you shall offer for the cereal offering of your first fruits crushed new grain from fresh ears, parched with

15 fire. And you shall put oil upon it, and lay frankincense on it; it is

16 a cereal offering. And the priest shall burn as its memorial portion part of the crushed grain and of the oil with all of its frankincense; it is an offering by fire to the LORD.

The peace offering

3 "If a man's offering is a sacrifice of peace offering, if he offers an animal from the herd, male or female, he shall offer it without

2 blemish before the LORD. And he shall lay his hand upon the head of his offering and kill it at the door of the tent of meeting; and Aaron's sons the priests shall throw the blood against the altar

3 round about. And from the sacrifice of the peace offering, as an offering by fire to the LORD, he shall offer the fat covering the entrails and all the fat that is on

4 the entrails, and the two kidneys with the fat that is on them at the loins, and the appendage of the liver which he shall take away

5 with the kidneys. Then Aaron's sons shall burn it on the altar upon the burnt offering, which is upon the wood on the fire; it is an offering by fire, a pleasing odour to the LORD.

6 "If his offering for a sacrifice of peace offering to the LORD is an animal from the flock, male or female, he shall offer it without

7 blemish. If he offers a lamb for his offering, then he shall offer it

8 before the LORD, laying his hand upon the head of his offering and killing it before the tent of meeting; and Aaron's sons shall throw its blood against the altar round

9 about. Then from the sacrifice of the peace offering as an offering by fire to the LORD he shall offer its fat, the fat tail entire, taking it away close by the backbone, and the fat that covers the entrails,

and all the fat that is on the 10 entrails, and the two kidneys with the fat that is on them at the loins, and the appendage of the liver which he shall take away with the 11 kidneys. And the priest shall burn it on the altar as food offered by fire to the LORD.

12 "If his offering is a goat, then he 13 shall offer it before the LORD, and lay his hand upon its head, and kill it before the tent of meeting; and the sons of Aaron shall throw its blood against the altar round 14 about. Then he shall offer from it, as his offering for an offering by fire to the LORD, the fat covering the entrails, and all the fat that 15 is on the entrails, and the two kidneys with the fat that is on them at the loins, and the appendage of the liver which he shall 16 take away with the kidneys. And the priest shall burn them on the altar as food offered by fire for a pleasing odour. All fat is the 17 LORD's. It shall be a perpetual statute throughout your generations, in all your dwelling places, that you eat neither fat nor blood."

The sin offering

4 And the LORD said to Moses, 2 "Say to the people of Israel, If any one sins unwittingly in any of the things which the LORD has commanded not to be done, and 3 does any one of them, if it is the anointed priest who sins, thus bringing guilt on the people, then let him offer for the sin which he has committed a young bull 4 without blemish to the LORD for a sin offering. He shall bring the bull to the door of the tent of meeting before the LORD, and lay his hand on the head of the bull, and kill the bull before the LORD. 5 And the anointed priest shall take some of the blood of the bull and bring it to the tent of meeting; 6 and the priest shall dip his finger in the blood and sprinkle part of the blood seven times before the LORD in front of the veil of the 7 sanctuary. And the priest shall put some of the blood on the horns of the altar of fragrant incense before the LORD which is in the tent of meeting, and the rest of the blood of the bull he shall pour out at the base of the altar of burnt offering which is at the door 8 of the tent of meeting. And all the fat of the bull of the sin offering he shall take from it, the fat that covers the entrails and all the fat 9 that is on the entrails, and the two kidneys with the fat that is on them at the loins, and the appendage of the liver which he shall 10 take away with the kidneys (just as these are taken from the ox of the sacrifice of the peace offerings), and the priest shall burn them upon the altar of burnt offering. 11 But the skin of the bull and all its flesh, with its head, its legs, its

entrails, and its dung, the whole 12 bull he shall carry forth outside the camp to a clean place, where the ashes are poured out, and shall burn it on a fire of wood; where the ashes are poured out it shall be burned.

"If the whole congregation of 13 Israel commits a sin unwittingly and the thing is hidden from the eyes of the assembly, and they do any one of the things which the LORD has commanded not to be done and are guilty; when the sin 14 which they have committed becomes known, the assembly shall offer a young bull for a sin offering and bring it before the tent of meeting; and the elders of 15 the congregation shall lay their hands upon the head of the bull before the LORD, and the bull shall be killed before the LORD. Then the anointed priest shall 16 bring some of the blood of the bull to the tent of meeting, and 17 the priest shall dip his finger in the blood and sprinkle it seven times before the LORD in front of the veil. And he shall put some of 18 the blood on the horns of the altar which is in the tent of meeting before the LORD; and the rest of the blood he shall pour out at the base of the altar of burnt offering which is at the door of the tent of meeting. And all its fat he shall 19 take from it and burn upon the altar. Thus shall he do with the 20 bull; as he did with the bull of the sin offering, so shall he do with this; and the priest shall make atonement for them, and they shall be forgiven. And he shall 21 carry forth the bull outside the camp, and burn it as he burned the first bull; it is the sin offering for the assembly.

"When a ruler sins, doing 22 unwittingly any one of all the things which the LORD his God has commanded not to be done, and is guilty, if the sin which he 23 has committed is made known to him, he shall bring as his offering a goat, a male without blemish, and shall lay his hand upon the 24 head of the goat, and kill it in the place where they kill the burnt offering before the LORD; it is a sin offering. Then the priest shall 25 take some of the blood of the sin offering with his finger and put it on the horns of the altar of burnt offering, and pour out the rest of its blood at the base of the altar of burnt offering. And all its fat he 26 shall burn on the altar, like the fat of the sacrifice of peace offerings; so the priest shall make atonement for him for his sin, and he shall be forgiven.

"If any one of the common 27 people sins unwittingly in doing any one of the things which the LORD has commanded not to be done, and is guilty, when the sin 28 which he has committed is made known to him he shall bring for his offering a goat, a female

without blemish, for his sin which
29 he has committed. And he shall lay his hand on the head of the sin offering, and kill the sin offering in the place of burnt offering.
30 And the priest shall take some of its blood with his finger and put it on the horns of the altar of burnt offering, and pour out the rest of its blood at the base of
31 the altar. And all its fat he shall remove, as the fat is removed from the peace offerings, and the priest shall burn it upon the altar for a pleasing odour to the LORD; and the priest shall make atonement for him, and he shall be forgiven.
32 "If he brings a lamb as his offering for a sin offering, he shall bring a female without blemish,
33 and lay his hand upon the head of the sin offering, and kill it for a sin offering in the place where they
34 kill the burnt offering. Then the priest shall take some of the blood of the sin offering with his finger and put it on the horns of the altar of burnt offering, and pour out the rest of its blood at the base of
35 the altar. And all its fat he shall remove as the fat of the lamb is removed from the sacrifice of peace offerings, and the priest shall burn it on the altar, upon the offerings by fire to the LORD; and the priest shall make atonement for him for the sin which he has committed, and he shall be forgiven.

5 "If any one sins in that he hears a public adjuration to testify and though he is a witness, whether he has seen or come to know the matter, yet does not speak, he
2 shall bear his iniquity. Or if any one touches an unclean thing, whether the carcass of an unclean beast or a carcass of unclean cattle or a carcass of unclean swarming things, and it is hidden from him, and he has become unclean, he
3 shall be guilty. Or if he touches human uncleanness, of whatever sort the uncleanness may be with which one becomes unclean, and it is hidden from him, when he comes to know it he shall be
4 guilty. Or if any one utters with his lips a rash oath to do evil or to do good, any sort of rash oath that men swear, and it is hidden from him, when he comes to know it he shall in any of these be guilty.
5 When a man is guilty in any of these, he shall confess the sin he
6 has committed, and he shall bring his guilt offering to the LORD for the sin which he has committed, a female from the flock, a lamb or a goat, for a sin offering; and the priest shall make atonement for him for his sin.
7 "But if he cannot afford a lamb, then he shall bring, as his guilt offering to the LORD for the sin which he has committed, two

turtledoves or two young pigeons, one for a sin offering and the
8 other for a burnt offering. He shall bring them to the priest, who shall offer first the one for the sin offering; he shall wring its head from its neck, but shall not sever
9 it, and he shall sprinkle some of the blood of the sin offering on the side of the altar, while the rest of the blood shall be drained out at the base of the altar; it is a sin
10 offering. Then he shall offer the second for a burnt offering according to the ordinance; and the priest shall make atonement for him for the sin which he has committed, and he shall be forgiven.
11 "But if he cannot afford two turtledoves or two young pigeons, then he shall bring, as his offering for the sin which he has committed, a tenth of an ephah of fine flour for a sin offering; he shall put no oil upon it, and shall put no frankincense on it, for it is a sin
12 offering. And he shall bring it to the priest, and the priest shall take a handful of it as its memorial portion and burn this on the altar, upon the offerings by fire to the
13 LORD; it is a sin offering. Thus the priest shall make atonement for him for the sin which he has committed in any one of these things, and he shall be forgiven. And the remainder shall be for the priest, as in the cereal offering."

The guilt offering

14, The LORD said to Moses, "If any
15 one commits a breach of faith and sins unwittingly in any of the holy things of the LORD, he shall bring, as his guilt offering to the LORD, a ram without blemish out of the flock, valued by you in shekels of silver, according to the shekel of the sanctuary; it is a guilt offer-
16 ing. He shall also make restitution for what he has done amiss in the holy thing, and shall add a fifth to it and give it to the priest; and the priest shall make atonement for him with the ram of the guilt offering, and he shall be
17 forgiven. "If any one sins, doing any of the things which the Lord has commanded not to be done, though he
18 does not know it, yet he is guilty and shall bear his iniquity. He shall bring to the priest a ram without blemish out of the flock, valued by you at the price for a guilt offering, and the priest shall make atonement for him for the error which he committed unwit-
19 tingly, and he shall be forgiven. It is a guilt offering; he is guilty before the LORD."

6ᵃ The LORD said to Moses, "If any
2 one sins and commits a breach of faith against the LORD by deceiving his neighbour in a matter of

deposit or security, or through robbery, or if he has oppressed his 3 neighbour or has found what was lost and lied about it, swearing falsely—in any of all the things which men do and sin therein, when one has sinned and become 4 guilty, he shall restore what he took by robbery, or what he got by oppression, or the deposit which was committed to him, or the lost thing which he found, or 5 anything about which he has sworn falsely; he shall restore it in full, and shall add a fifth to it, and give it to him to whom it belongs, on the day of his guilt offering. And he shall bring to the priest 6 his guilt offering to the LORD, a ram without blemish out of the flock, valued by you at the price for a guilt offering; and the priest 7 shall make atonement for him before the LORD, and he shall be forgiven for any of the things which one may do and thereby become guilty."

Directions to priests

The LORD said to Moses, 8ᵇ "Command Aaron and his sons, 9 saying, This is the law of the burnt offering. The burnt offering shall be on the hearth upon the altar all night until the morning, and the fire of the altar shall be kept burning on it. And the 10 priest shall put on his linen garment, and put his linen breeches upon his body, and he shall take up the ashes to which the fire has consumed the burnt offering on the altar, and put them beside the altar. Then he shall put off his 11 garments, and put on other garments, and carry forth the ashes outside the camp to a clean place. The fire on the altar shall be kept 12 burning on it, it shall not go out; the priest shall burn wood on it every morning, and he shall lay the burnt offering in order upon it, and shall burn on it the fat of the peace offerings. Fire shall be 13 kept burning upon the altar continually; it shall not go out.
"And this is the law of the cereal 14 offering. The sons of Aaron shall offer it before the LORD, in front of the altar. And one shall take 15 from it a handful of the fine flour of the cereal offering with its oil and all the frankincense which is on the cereal offering, and burn this as its memorial portion on the altar, a pleasing odour to the LORD. And the rest of it Aaron 16 and his sons shall eat; it shall be eaten unleavened in a holy place; in the court of the tent of meeting they shall eat it. It shall not be 17 baked with leaven. I have given it as their portion of my offerings by fire; it is a thing most holy, like the sin offering and the guilt offering. Every male among the 18 children of Aaron may eat of it, as

decreed for ever throughout your generations, from the LORD's offerings by fire; whoever touches them shall become holy."

19, The LORD said to Moses, "This 20 is the offering which Aaron and his sons shall offer to the LORD on the day when he is anointed: a tenth of an ephah of fine flour as a regular cereal offering, half of it in the morning and half in the 21 evening. It shall be made with oil on a griddle; you shall bring it well mixed, in baked[c] pieces like a cereal offering, and offer it for a 22 pleasing odour to the LORD. The priest from among Aaron's sons, who is anointed to succeed him, shall offer it to the LORD as decreed for ever; the whole of it 23 shall be burned. Every cereal offering of a priest shall be wholly burned; it shall not be eaten."

24, The LORD said to Moses, "Say 25 to Aaron and his sons, This is the law of the sin offering. In the place where the burnt offering is killed shall the sin offering be killed before the LORD; it is most 26 holy. The priest who offers it for sin shall eat it; in any holy place it shall be eaten, in the court of 27 the tent of meeting. Whatever[d] touches its flesh shall be holy; and when any of its blood is sprinkled on a garment, you shall wash that on which it was sprinkled in a 28 holy place. And the earthen vessel in which it is boiled shall be broken; but if it is boiled in a bronze vessel, that shall be scoured, and rinsed in water. 29 Every male among the priests may 30 eat of it; it is most holy. But no sin offering shall be eaten from which any blood is brought into the tent of meeting to make atonement in the holy place; it shall be burned with fire.

7 "This is the law of the guilt 2 offering. It is most holy; in the place where they shall kill the burnt offering they shall kill the guilt offering, and its blood shall be thrown on the altar round about. 3 And all its fat shall be offered, the fat tail, the fat that covers the 4 entrails, the two kidneys with the fat that is on them at the loins, and the appendage of the liver which he shall take away with the 5 kidneys; the priest shall burn them on the altar as an offering by fire to the LORD; it is a guilt 6 offering. Every male among the priests may eat of it; it shall be eaten in a holy place; it is most 7 holy. The guilt offering is like the sin offering, there is one law for them; the priest who makes atonement with it shall have it. 8 And the priest who offers any man's burnt offering shall have for himself the skin of the burnt offering which he has offered. 9 And every cereal offering baked in the oven and all that is prepared on a pan or a griddle shall belong 10 to the priest who offers it. And

every cereal offering, mixed with oil or dry, shall be for all the sons of Aaron, one as well as another.

The peace offerings

11 "And this is the law of the sacrifice of peace offerings which 12 one may offer to the LORD. If he offers it for a thanksgiving, then he shall offer with the thank offering unleavened cakes mixed with oil, unleavened wafers spread with oil, and cakes of fine flour 13 well mixed with oil. With the sacrifice of his peace offerings for thanksgiving he shall bring his offering with cakes of leavened 14 bread. And of such he shall offer one cake from each offering, as an offering to the LORD; it shall belong to the priest who throws the blood of the peace offerings. 15 And the flesh of the sacrifice of his peace offerings for thanksgiving shall be eaten on the day of his offering; he shall not leave any 16 of it until the morning. But if the sacrifice of his offering is a votive offering or a freewill offering, it shall be eaten on the day that he offers his sacrifice, and on the morrow what remains of it shall 17 be eaten, but what remains of the flesh of the sacrifice on the third 18 day shall be burned with fire. If any of the flesh of the sacrifice of his peace offering is eaten on the third day, he who offers it shall not be accepted, neither shall it be credited to him; it shall be an abomination, and he who eats of it shall bear his iniquity.

19 "Flesh that touches any unclean thing shall not be eaten; it shall be

burned with fire. All who are clean may eat flesh, but the per- 20 son who eats of the flesh of the sacrifice of the LORD's peace offerings while an uncleanness is on him, that person shall be cut off from his people. And if any 21 one touches an unclean thing, whether the uncleanness of man or an unclean beast or any unclean abomination, and then eats of the flesh of the sacrifice of the LORD's peace offerings, that person shall be cut off from his people."

The LORD said to Moses, "Say 22 to the people of Israel, You shall 23 eat no fat, of ox, or sheep, or goat. The fat of an animal that dies of 24 itself, and the fat of one that is torn by beasts, may be put to any other use, but on no account shall you eat it. For every person who 25 eats of the fat of an animal of which an offering by fire is made to the LORD shall be cut off from his people. Moreover you shall 26 eat no blood whatever, whether of fowl or of animal, in any of your dwellings. Whoever eats any 27 blood, that person shall be cut off from his people."

The LORD said to Moses, "Say to 28 the people of Israel, He that offers 29 the sacrifice of his peace offerings to the LORD shall bring his offering to the LORD; from the sacrifice of his peace offerings he shall 30 bring with his own hands the offerings by fire to the LORD; he shall bring the fat with the breast, that the breast may be waved as a wave offering before the LORD. The priest shall burn the fat on 31 the altar, but the breast shall be for Aaron and his sons. And 32 the right thigh you shall give to the priest as an offering from the sacrifice of your peace offerings; he among the sons of Aaron who 33 offers the blood of the peace offerings and the fat shall have the right thigh for a portion. For the 34 breast that is waved and the thigh that is offered I have taken from the people of Israel, out of the sacrifices of their peace offerings, and have given them to Aaron the priest and to his sons, as a perpetual due from the people of Israel. This is the portion of 35 Aaron and of his sons from the offerings made by fire to the LORD, consecrated to them on the day they were presented to serve as priests of the LORD; the LORD 36 commanded this to be given them by the people of Israel, on the day that they were anointed; it is a perpetual due throughout their generations."

This is the law of the burnt 37 offering, of the cereal offering, of the sin offering, of the guilt offering, of the consecration, and of the peace offerings, which the 38 LORD commanded Moses on Mount Sinai, on the day that he commanded the people of Israel to bring their offerings to the LORD, in the wilderness of Sinai.

---

[c] Meaning of Heb is uncertain   [d] Or *Whoever*

THE PRIESTHOOD

8 THE LORD said to Moses,
2 "Take Aaron and his sons with him, and the garments, and the anointing oil, and the bull of the sin offering, and the two rams, and the basket of unleavened
3 bread; and assemble all the congregation at the door of the tent of
4 meeting." And Moses did as the LORD commanded him; and the congregation was assembled at the door of the tent of meeting.

Consecration

5 And Moses said to the congregation, "This is the thing which the LORD has commanded to be
6 done." And Moses brought Aaron and his sons, and washed
7 them with water. And he put on him the coat, and girded him with the girdle, and clothed him with the robe, and put the ephod upon him, and girded him with the skilfully woven band of the ephod, binding it to him there-
8 with. And he placed the breastpiece on him, and in the breastpiece he put the Urim and the
9 Thummim. And he set the turban upon his head, and on the turban, in front, he set the golden plate, the holy crown, as the LORD commanded Moses.
10 Then Moses took the anointing oil, and anointed the tabernacle and all that was in it, and con-
11 secrated them. And he sprinkled some of it on the altar seven times, and anointed the altar and all its utensils, and the laver and its
12 base, to consecrate them. And he poured some of the anointing oil on Aaron's head, and anointed
13 him, to consecrate him. And Moses brought Aaron's sons, and clothed them with coats, and
14 girded them with girdles, and bound caps on them, as the LORD commanded Moses.
15 Then he brought the bull of the sin offering; and Aaron and his sons laid their hands upon the head of the bull of the sin offer-
16 ing. And Moses killed it, and took the blood, and with his finger put it on the horns of the altar round about, and purified the altar, and poured out the blood at the base of the altar, and con-
17 secrated it, to make atonement for it. And he took all the fat that was on the entrails, and the appendage of the liver, and the two kidneys with their fat, and Moses burned
18 them on the altar. But the bull, and its skin, and its flesh, and its dung, he burned with fire outside the camp, as the LORD commanded Moses.
19 Then he presented the ram of the burnt offering; and Aaron and his sons laid their hands on the
20 head of the ram. And Moses killed it, and threw the blood
21 upon the altar round about. And when the ram was cut into pieces,

Moses burned the head and the
22 pieces and the fat. And when the entrails and the legs were washed with water, Moses burned the whole ram on the altar, as a burnt offering, a pleasing odour, an offering by fire to the LORD, as the LORD commanded Moses.
23 Then he presented the other ram, the ram of ordination; and Aaron and his sons laid their hands on the head of the ram.
24 And Moses killed it, and took some of its blood and put it on the tip of Aaron's right ear and on the thumb of his right hand and on the great toe of his right foot.
25 And Aaron's sons were brought, and Moses put some of the blood on the tips of their right ears and on the thumbs of their right hands and on the great toes of their right feet; and Moses threw the blood
26 upon the altar round about. Then he took the fat, and the fat tail, and all the fat that was on the entrails, and the appendage of the liver, and the two kidneys with
27 their fat, and the right thigh; and out of the basket of unleavened bread which was before the LORD he took one unleavened cake, and one cake of bread with oil, and one wafer, and placed them on the
28 fat and on the right thigh; and he put all these in the hands of Aaron and in the hands of his sons, and waved them as a wave offering
29 before the LORD. Then Moses took them from their hands, and burned them on the altar with the burnt offering, as an ordination offering, a pleasing odour, an offering by fire to the LORD. And
30 Moses took the breast, and waved it for a wave offering before the LORD; it was Moses' portion of the ram of ordination, as the LORD commanded Moses.
31 Then Moses took some of the anointing oil and of the blood which was on the altar, and sprinkled it upon Aaron and his garments, and also upon his sons and his sons' garments; so he consecrated Aaron and his garments, and his sons and his sons' garments with him.
32 And Moses said to Aaron and his sons, "Boil the flesh at the door of the tent of meeting, and there eat it and the bread that is in the basket of ordination offerings, as I commanded, saying, 'Aaron and
33 his sons shall eat it'; and what remains of the flesh and the bread you shall burn with fire. And you
34 shall not go out from the door of the tent of meeting for seven days, until the days of your ordination are completed, for it will take seven days to ordain you. As has been done today, the LORD has commanded to be done to make
35 atonement for you. At the door of the tent of meeting you shall remain day and night for seven days, performing what the LORD
36 has charged, lest you die; for so I am commanded." And Aaron

and his sons did all the things which the LORD commanded by Moses.

Induction

On the eighth day Moses called 9 Aaron and his sons and the elders of Israel; and he said to Aaron, 2 "Take a bull calf for a sin offering, and a ram for a burnt offering, both without blemish, and offer them before the LORD. And say to the people of Israel, 3 'Take a male goat for a sin offering, and a calf and a lamb, both a year old without blemish, for a burnt offering, and an ox and a 4 ram for peace offerings, to sacrifice before the LORD, and a cereal offering mixed with oil; for today the LORD will appear to you.'" And they brought what Moses 5 commanded before the tent of meeting; and all the congregation drew near and stood before the LORD. And Moses said, "This is 6 the thing which the LORD commanded you to do; and the glory of the LORD will appear to you." Then Moses said to Aaron, 7 "Draw near to the altar, and offer your sin offering and your burnt offering, and make atonement for yourself and for the people; and bring the offering of the people, and make atonement for them; as the LORD has commanded."

So Aaron drew near to the altar, 8 and killed the calf of the sin offering, which was for himself. And the sons of Aaron presented 9 the blood to him, and he dipped his finger in the blood and put it on the horns of the altar, and poured out the blood at the base of the altar; but the fat and the 10 kidneys and the appendage of the liver from the sin offering he burned upon the altar, as the LORD commanded Moses. The 11 flesh and the skin he burned with fire outside the camp.

And he killed the burnt offering; 12 and Aaron's sons delivered to him the blood, and he threw it on the altar round about. And they 13 delivered the burnt offering to him, piece by piece, and the head; and he burned them upon the altar. And he washed the entrails 14 and the legs, and burned them with the burnt offering on the altar.

Then he presented the people's 15 offering, and took the goat of the sin offering which was for the people, and killed it, and offered it for sin, like the first sin offering. And he presented the burnt offer- 16 ing, and offered it according to the ordinance. And he presented 17 the cereal offering, and filled his hand from it, and burned it upon the altar, besides the burnt offering of the morning.

He killed the ox also and the 18 ram, the sacrifice of peace offerings for the people; and Aaron's sons delivered to him the blood,

which he threw upon the altar
19 round about, and the fat of the ox
and of the ram, the fat tail, and
that which covers the entrails, and
the kidneys, and the appendage of
20 the liver; and they put the fat
upon the breasts, and he burned
21 the fat upon the altar, but the
breasts and the right thigh Aaron
waved for a wave offering before the LORD; as Moses commanded.
22 Then Aaron lifted up his hands
toward the people and blessed
them; and he came down from
offering the sin offering and the
burnt offering and the peace of-
23 ferings. And Moses and Aaron
went into the tent of meeting; and
when they came out they blessed
the people, and the glory of the
LORD appeared to all the people.
24 And fire came forth from before
the LORD and consumed the burnt
offering and the fat upon the
altar; and when all the people saw
it, they shouted, and fell on their
faces.

Exacting service

10 Now Nadab and Abi'hu, the
sons of Aaron, each took his
censer, and put fire in it, and laid
incense on it, and offered unholy
fire before the LORD, such as he
2 had not commanded them. And
fire came forth from the presence
of the LORD and devoured them,
and they died before the LORD.
3 Then Moses said to Aaron, "This
is what the LORD has said, 'I will
show myself holy among those
who are near me, and before all
the people I will be glori-

fied.'" And Aaron held his
peace.
4 And Moses called Mish'a-el and
Elza'phan, the sons of Uz'ziel the
uncle of Aaron, and said to them,
"Draw near, carry your brethren
from before the sanctuary out of
5 the camp." So they drew near,
and carried them in their coats out
of the camp, as Moses had said.
6 And Moses said to Aaron and to
Elea'zar and Ith'amar, his sons,
"Do not let the hair of your heads
hang loose, and do not rend your
clothes, lest you die, and lest
wrath come upon all the congregation; but your brethren, the
whole house of Israel, may bewail
the burning which the LORD has
7 kindled. And do not go out from
the door of the tent of meeting, lest
you die; for the anointing oil of
the LORD is upon you." And they
did according to the word of
Moses.
8 And the LORD spoke to Aaron,
9 saying, "Drink no wine nor strong
drink, you nor your sons with
you, when you go into the tent of
meeting, lest you die; it shall be a
statute for ever throughout your
10 generations. You are to distinguish between the holy and the
common, and between the un-
11 clean and the clean; and you are to
teach the people of Israel all the
statutes which the LORD has
spoken to them by Moses."
12 And Moses said to Aaron and to
Elea'zar and Ith'amar, his sons
who were left, "Take the cereal
offering that remains of the offerings by fire to the LORD, and eat it
unleavened beside the altar, for it
13 is most holy; you shall eat it in a
holy place, because it is your due

and your sons' due, from the
offerings by fire to the LORD; for
so I am commanded. But the
breast that is waved and the thigh
that is offered you shall eat in any
clean place, you and your sons
and your daughters with you; for
they are given as your due and
your sons' due, from the sacrifices
of the peace offerings of the
people of Israel. The thigh that is
offered and the breast that is
waved they shall bring with the
offerings by fire of the fat, to wave
for a wave offering before the
LORD, and it shall be yours, and
your sons' with you, as a due for
ever; as the LORD has commanded."
15 Now Moses diligently inquired
about the goat of the sin offering,
and behold, it was burned! And
he was angry with Elea'zar and
16 Ith'amar, the sons of Aaron who
were left, saying, "Why have you
not eaten the sin offering in the
place of the sanctuary, since it is a
thing most holy and has been
given to you that you may bear
the iniquity of the congregation,
to make atonement for them
before the LORD? Behold, its
17 blood was not brought into the
inner part of the sanctuary. You
certainly ought to have eaten it in
the sanctuary, as I commanded."
18 And Aaron said to Moses,
"Behold, today they have offered
their sin offering and their burnt
offering before the LORD; and yet
such things as these have befallen
me! If I had eaten the sin offering today, would it have been
acceptable in the sight of the
LORD?" And when Moses heard
20 that, he was content.

Bats and hoopoe   Lev 11, 19

THINGS CLEAN
AND UNCLEAN

11 AND the LORD said to Moses
2   and Aaron, "Say to the
people of Israel, These are the
living things which you may eat
among all the beasts that are on
the earth.

Food

3 "Whatever parts the hoof and is
cloven-footed and chews the cud,
among the animals, you may eat.
4 Nevertheless among those that
chew the cud or part the hoof, you
shall not eat these: The camel,
because it chews the cud but does

not part the hoof, is unclean to
you. And the rock badger, 5
because it chews the cud but does
not part the hoof, is unclean to
you. And the hare, because it 6
chews the cud but does not part
the hoof, is unclean to you. And 7
the swine, because it parts the
hoof and is cloven-footed but does

not chew the cud, is unclean to
8 you. Of their flesh you shall not
eat, and their carcasses you shall
not touch; they are unclean to
you.
9 "These you may eat, of all that
are in the waters. Everything in
the waters that has fins and scales,
whether in the seas or in the
10 rivers, you may eat. But anything
in the seas or the rivers that has
not fins and scales, of the swarming creatures in the waters and of
the living creatures that are in the
waters, is an abomination to you.
11 They shall remain an abomination
to you; of their flesh you shall not
eat, and their carcasses you shall
12 have in abomination. Everything
in the waters that has not fins and
scales is an abomination to you.
13 "And these you shall have in
abomination among the birds,
they shall not be eaten, they are an
14 eagle, the vul-
ture, the osprey, the kite, the
15 falcon according to its kind, every
16 raven according to its kind, the
ostrich, the nighthawk, the sea
gull, the hawk according to its
17 kind, the owl, the cormorant, the
18 ibis, the water hen, the pelican,
19 the carrion vulture, the stork, the
heron according to its kind, the
hoopoe, and the bat.
20 "All winged insects that go upon
all fours are an abomination to
21 you. Yet among the winged
insects that go on all fours you
may eat those which have legs
above their feet, with which to
22 leap on the earth. Of them you
may eat: the locust according to
its kind, the bald locust according
to its kind, the cricket according
to its kind, and the grasshopper
23 according to its kind. But all
other winged insects which have
four feet are an abomination to
24 you. "And by these you shall become
unclean; whoever touches their
carcass shall be unclean until the
25 evening, and whoever carries any
part of their carcass shall wash his
clothes and be unclean until the
26 evening. Every animal which
parts the hoof but is not cloven-
footed or does not chew the cud is
unclean to you; every one who
touches them shall be unclean.
27 And all that go on their paws,
among the animals that go on all
fours, are unclean to you; whoever touches their carcass shall be
28 unclean until the evening, and he
who carries their carcass shall
wash his clothes and be unclean
until the evening; they are unclean to you.
29 "And these are unclean to you
among the swarming things that
swarm upon the earth: the weasel,
the mouse, the great lizard accor-
30 ding to its kind, the gecko, the
land crocodile, the lizard, the sand
31 lizard, and the chameleon. These
are unclean to you among all that
swarm; whoever touches them
when they are dead shall be 46

32 unclean until the evening. And
anything upon which any of them
falls when they are dead shall be
unclean, whether it is an article of
wood or a garment or a skin or a
sack, any vessel that is used for
any purpose; it must be put into
water, and it shall be unclean until
the evening; then it shall be
33 clean. And if any of them falls
into any earthen vessel, all that is
in it shall be unclean, and you
34 shall break it. Any food in it
which may be eaten, upon which
water may come, shall be unclean;
and all drink which may be drunk
from every such vessel shall be
35 unclean. And everything upon
which any part of their carcass
falls shall be unclean; whether
oven or stove, it shall be broken in
pieces; they are unclean, and shall
36 be unclean to you. Nevertheless a
spring or a cistern holding water
shall be clean; but whatever
37 touches their carcass shall be
unclean. And if any part of their
carcass falls upon any seed for
sowing that is to be sown, it is
38 clean; but if water is put on the
seed and any part of their carcass
falls on it, it is unclean to
you.
39 "And if any animal of which you
may eat dies, he who touches its
carcass shall be unclean until the
evening, and he who eats of its
carcass shall wash his clothes and
be unclean until the evening; he
also who carries the carcass shall
wash his clothes and be unclean
41 until the evening. "Every swarming thing that
swarms upon the earth is an
abomination; it shall not be
42 eaten. Whatever goes on its belly,
and whatever goes on all fours, or
whatever has many feet, all the
swarming things that swarm upon
the earth, you shall not eat; for
43 they are an abomination. You
shall not make yourselves abominable with any swarming thing
that swarms; and you shall not
defile yourselves with them, lest
44 you become unclean. For I am
the LORD your God; consecrate
yourselves therefore, and be holy,
for I am holy. You shall not defile
yourselves with any swarming
45 thing that crawls upon the earth.
For I am the LORD who brought
you up out of the land of Egypt, to
be your God; you shall therefore
be holy, for I am holy."
46 This is the law pertaining to

Chameleon and lizard

Lev 11, 30

beast and bird and every living
creature that moves through the
waters and every creature that
47 swarms upon the earth, to make a
distinction between the unclean
and the clean and between the
living creature that may be eaten
and the living creature that may
not be eaten.

Ritual requirements

12 The LORD said to Moses, "Say
to the people of Israel, If a woman
2 conceives, and bears a male child,
then she shall be unclean seven
days; as at the time of her menstruation, she shall be unclean.
3 And on the eighth day the flesh of
his foreskin shall be circumcised.
4 Then she shall continue for
thirty-three days in the blood of
her purifying; she shall not touch
any hallowed thing, nor come into
the sanctuary, until the days of
5 her purifying are completed. But
if she bears a female child, then
she shall be unclean two weeks, as
in her menstruation; and she shall
continue in the blood of her purifying for sixty-six days.
6 "And when the days of her
purifying are completed, whether
for a son or for a daughter, she
shall bring to the priest at the
door of the tent of meeting a lamb
a year old for a burnt offering, and
a young pigeon or a turtledove
7 for a sin offering, and he shall offer
it before the LORD, and make
atonement for her; then she shall
be clean from the flow of her blood.
This is the law for her who bears a
child, either male or female. And
8 if she cannot afford a lamb, then
she shall take two turtledoves or
two young pigeons, one for a
burnt offering and the other for a
sin offering; and the priest shall
make atonement for her, and she
shall be clean."

11.44-45: Lev 19.2; 20.7, 26; 1 Pet 1.16.   12.1-8: Lk 2.22-24.

Leprosy

13 The LORD said to Moses and
2 Aaron, "When a man has on the
skin of his body a swelling or an
eruption or a spot, and it turns
into a leprous disease on the skin
of his body, then he shall be
3 brought to Aaron the priest or to
one of his sons the priests, and
the priest shall examine the diseased spot on the skin of his body;
and if the hair in the diseased spot
has turned white and the disease
appears to be deeper than the skin
of his body, it is a leprous disease;
when the priest has examined him

the skin of his body, and the priest
shall pronounce him unclean; he
12 shall not shut him up, for he is
unclean. And if the leprosy
breaks out in the skin, so that the
leprosy covers all the skin of the
diseased person from head to foot,
13 so far as the priest can see, then
the priest shall make an examination, and if the leprosy has
covered all his body, he shall
pronounce him clean of the dis-
14 ease; it has all turned white, and
he is clean. But when raw flesh
15 appears on him, he shall be
unclean. And the priest shall
examine the raw flesh, and pro-

"Or, when the body has a burn 24
on its skin and the raw flesh of the
burn becomes a spot, reddish-
white or white, the priest shall 25
examine it, and if the hair in the
spot has turned white and it
appears deeper than the skin, then
it is leprosy; it has broken out in
the burn, and the priest shall
pronounce him unclean; it is a
leprous disease. But if the priest 26
examines it, and the hair in the
spot is not white and it is no
deeper than the skin, but is dim,
the priest shall shut him up seven
days, and the priest shall examine 27
him the seventh day; if it is
spreading in the skin, then the
priest shall pronounce him unclean; it is a leprous disease. But 28
if the spot remains in one place
and does not spread in the skin,
but is dim, it is a swelling from
the burn, and the priest shall
pronounce him clean; for it is the
scar of the burn.
"When a man or woman has a 29
disease on the head or the beard,
the priest shall examine the dis- 30
ease; and if it appears deeper than
the skin, and the hair in it is

Lev 11, 9

he shall pronounce him unclean.
4 But if the spot is white in the skin
of his body, and appears no
deeper than the skin, and the hair
in it has not turned white, the
priest shall shut up the diseased
5 person for seven days; and the
priest shall examine him on the
seventh day, and if in his eyes the
disease is checked and the disease
has not spread in the skin, then
the priest shall shut him up seven
6 days more; and the priest shall
examine him again on the seventh
day, and if the diseased spot is
dim and the disease has not
spread in the skin, then the priest
shall pronounce him clean; it is
only an eruption; and he shall
wash his clothes, and be clean.
7 But if the eruption spreads in the
skin, after he has shown himself to
the priest for his cleansing, he
shall appear again before the
8 priest; and the priest shall make
an examination, and if the eruption has spread in the skin, then
the priest shall pronounce him
unclean; it is leprosy.
9 "When a man is afflicted with
leprosy, he shall be brought to the
10 priest; and the priest shall make
an examination, and if there is a
white swelling in the skin, which
has turned the hair white, and
there is quick raw flesh in the
11 swelling, it is a chronic leprosy in

nounce him unclean; raw flesh is
16 unclean, for it is leprosy. But if
the raw flesh turns again and is
changed to white, then he shall
17 come to the priest, and the priest
shall examine him, and if the
disease has turned white, then the
priest shall pronounce the diseased person clean; he is clean.
18 "And when there is in the skin of
one's body a boil that has healed,
19 and in the place of the boil there
comes a white swelling or a reddish-white spot, then it shall be
20 shown to the priest; and the priest
shall make an examination, and if
it appears deeper than the skin
and its hair has turned white, then
the priest shall pronounce him
unclean; it is the disease of leprosy, it has broken out in the boil.
21 But if the priest examines it, and
the hair on it is not white and it is
not deeper than the skin, but is
dim, then the priest shall shut him
22 up seven days; and if it spreads in
the skin, then the priest shall
pronounce him unclean; it is
23 diseased. But if the spot remains
in one place and does not spread,
it is the scar of the boil; and the
priest shall pronounce him clean.

yellow and thin, then the priest
shall pronounce him unclean; it is
an itch, a leprosy of the head or
the beard. And if the priest 31
examines the itching disease, and
it appears no deeper than the skin
and there is no black hair in it,
then the priest shall shut up the
person with the itching disease for
seven days, and on the seventh 32
day the priest shall examine the
disease; and if the itch has not
spread, and there is in it no yellow
hair, and the itch appears to be no
deeper than the skin, then he shall 33
shave himself, but the itch he
shall not shave; and the priest
shall shut up the person with the
itching disease for seven days
more; and on the seventh day the 34
priest shall examine the itch, and
if the itch has not spread in the
skin and it appears to be no
deeper than the skin, then the
priest shall pronounce him clean;
and he shall wash his clothes, and
be clean. But if the itch spreads 35
in the skin after his cleansing,
then the priest shall examine him, 36
and if the itch has spread in the
skin, the priest need not seek for

the yellow hair; he is unclean.
47 But if in his eyes the itch is checked, and black hair has grown in it, the itch is healed, he is clean; and the priest shall pronounce him clean.

48 "When a man or a woman has spots on the skin of the body,
49 white spots, the priest shall make an examination, and if the spots on the skin of the body are of a dull white, it is tetter that has broken out in the skin; he is clean.
40 "If a man's hair has fallen from his head, he is bald but he is clean.
41 And if a man's hair has fallen from his forehead and temples, he has baldness of the forehead but he is clean. But if there is on the bald head or the bald forehead a reddish-white diseased spot, it is leprosy breaking out on his bald head or his
43 bald forehead. Then the priest shall examine him, and if the diseased swelling is reddish-white on his bald head or on his bald forehead, like the appearance of
44 leprosy in the skin of the body, he is a leprous man, he is unclean; the priest must pronounce him unclean; his disease is on his head.
45 "The leper who has the disease shall wear torn clothes and let the hair of his head hang loose, and he shall cover his upper lip and cry,
46 'Unclean, unclean.' He shall remain unclean as long as he has the disease; he is unclean; he shall dwell alone in a habitation outside the camp.

47 "When there is a leprous disease in a garment, whether a woollen
48 or a linen garment, in warp or woof of linen or wool, or in a skin
49 or in anything made of skin, if the disease shows greenish or reddish in the garment, whether in warp or woof or in skin or in anything made of skin, it is a leprous disease and shall be shown to the
50 priest. And the priest shall examine the disease, and shut up that which has the disease for
51 seven days; then he shall examine the disease on the seventh day. If the disease has spread in the garment, in warp or woof, or in the skin, whatever be the use of the skin, the disease is a malignant
52 leprosy; it is unclean. And he shall burn the garment, whether diseased in warp or woof, woollen or linen, or anything of skin, for it is a malignant leprosy; it shall be burned in the fire.
53 "And if the priest examines, and the disease has not spread in the garment in warp or woof or in
54 anything of skin, then the priest shall command that they wash the thing in which is the disease, and he shall shut it up seven
55 days more; and the priest shall examine the diseased thing after it has been washed. And if the diseased spot has not changed its colour, though the disease has not spread, it is unclean; you shall burn it in the fire, whether the

leprous spot is on the back or on the front.
56 "But if the priest examines, and the disease is dim after it is washed, he shall tear the spot out of the garment or the skin or the
57 warp or woof; then if it appears again in the garment, in warp or woof, or in anything of skin, it is spreading; you shall burn with fire that in which is the disease.
58 But the garment, warp or woof, or anything of skin from which the disease departs when you have washed it, shall then be washed a second time, and be clean."
59 This is the law for a leprous disease in a garment of wool or linen, either in warp or woof, or in anything of skin, to decide whether it is clean or unclean.

14 The LORD said to Moses, "This
2 shall be the law of the leper for the day of his cleansing. He shall be
3 brought to the priest; and the priest shall go out of the camp, and the priest shall make an examination. Then, if the leprous
4 disease is healed in the leper, the priest shall command them to take for him who is to be cleansed two
5 living clean birds and cedarwood and scarlet stuff and hyssop; and the priest shall command them to
6 kill one of the birds in an earthen vessel over running water. He shall take the living bird with the cedarwood and the scarlet stuff and the hyssop, and dip them and the living bird in the blood of the
7 bird that was killed over the running water; and he shall sprinkle it seven times upon him who is to be cleansed of leprosy; then he shall pronounce him clean, and
8 shall let the living bird go into the open field. And he who is to be cleansed shall wash his clothes, and shave off all his hair, and bathe himself in water, and he shall be clean; and after that he shall come into the camp, but shall dwell outside his tent seven
9 days. And on the seventh day he shall shave all his hair off his head; he shall shave off his beard and his eyebrows, all his hair. Then he shall wash his clothes, and bathe his body in water, and he shall be clean.
10 "And on the eighth day he shall take two male lambs without blemish, and one ewe lamb a year old without blemish, and a cereal offering of three tenths of an
11 ephah of fine flour mixed with oil, and one log of oil. And the priest who cleanses him shall set the man who is to be cleansed and these things before the LORD, at
12 the door of the tent of meeting. And the priest shall take one of the male lambs, and offer it for a guilt offering, along with the log of oil, and wave them for a wave offering before the LORD; and he
13 shall kill the lamb in the place where they kill the sin offering and the burnt offering, the holy

place; for the guilt offering, like the sin offering, belongs to the priest; it is most holy. The priest
14 shall take some of the blood of the guilt offering, and the priest shall put it on the tip of the right ear of him who is to be cleansed, and on the thumb of his right hand, and on the great toe of his right foot. Then the priest shall take some of
15 the log of oil, and pour it into the palm of his own left hand, and dip
16 his right finger in the oil that is in his left hand, and sprinkle some oil with his finger seven times before the LORD. And some of the
17 oil that remains in his hand the priest shall put on the tip of the right ear of him who is to be cleansed, and on the thumb of his right hand, and on the great toe of his right foot, upon the blood of the guilt offering; and the rest of
18 the oil that is in the priest's hand he shall put on the head of him who is to be cleansed. Then the priest shall make atonement for
19 him before the LORD. The priest shall offer the sin offering, to make atonement for him who is to be cleansed from his uncleanness. And afterward he shall kill the
20 burnt offering; and the priest shall offer the burnt offering and the cereal offering on the altar. Thus the priest shall make atonement for him, and he shall be clean.

"But if he is poor and cannot
21 afford so much, then he shall take one male lamb for a guilt offering to be waved, to make atonement for him, and a tenth of an ephah of fine flour mixed with oil, for a cereal offering, and a log of oil; also two turtledoves or two young
22 pigeons, such as he can afford; the one shall be a sin offering and the other a burnt offering. And on
23 the eighth day he shall bring them for his cleansing to the priest, to the door of the tent of meeting, before the LORD; and the priest
24 shall take the lamb of the guilt offering, and the log of oil, and the priest shall wave them for a wave offering before the LORD. And he shall kill the lamb of the
25 guilt offering; and the priest shall take some of the blood of the guilt offering, and put it on the tip of the right ear of him who is to be cleansed, and on the thumb of his right hand, and on the great toe of his right foot. And the priest
26 shall pour some of the oil into the palm of his own left hand; and
27 shall sprinkle with his right finger some of the oil that is in his left hand seven times before the LORD; and the priest shall put
28 some of the oil that is in his hand on the tip of the right ear of him who is to be cleansed, and on the thumb of his right hand, and the great toe of his right foot, in the place where the blood of the guilt offering was put; and the rest
29 of the oil that is in the priest's hand he shall put on the head of him

who is to be cleansed, to make atonement for him before the 30 LORD. And he shall offer, of the turtledoves or young pigeons such 31 as he can afford, one[x] for a sin offering and the other for a burnt offering, along with a cereal offering; and the priest shall make 32 atonement before the LORD for him who is being cleansed. This is the law for him in whom is a leprous disease, who cannot afford the offerings for his cleansing."

33 The LORD said to Moses and 34 Aaron, "When you come into the land of Canaan, which I give you for a possession, and I put a leprous disease in a house in the 35 land of your possession, then he who owns the house shall come and tell the priest, 'There seems to me to be some sort of disease in 36 my house.' Then the priest shall command that they empty the house before the priest goes to examine the disease, lest all that is in the house be declared unclean; and afterward the priest shall go 37 in to see the house. And he shall examine the disease; and if the disease is in the walls of the house with greenish or reddish spots, and if it appears to be deeper than 38 the surface, then the priest shall go out of the house to the door of the house, and shut up the house 39 seven days. And the priest shall come again on the seventh day, and look; and if the disease has spread in the walls of the house, 40 then the priest shall command that they take out the stones in which is the disease and throw them into an unclean place out-41 side the city; and he shall cause the inside of the house to be scraped round about, and the plaster that they scrape off they shall pour into an unclean place 42 outside the city; then they shall take other stones and put them in the place of those stones, and he shall take other plaster and plaster the house. 43 "If the disease breaks out again in the house, after he has taken out the stones and scraped the 44 house and plastered it, then the priest shall go and look; and if the disease has spread in the house, it is a malignant leprosy in the 45 house; it is unclean. And he shall break down the house, its stones and timber and all the plaster of the house and he shall carry them forth out of the city to an unclean 46 place. Moreover he who enters the house while it is shut up shall 47 be unclean until the evening; and he who lies down in the house shall wash his clothes; and he who eats in the house shall wash his clothes. 48 "But if the priest comes and makes an examination, and the disease has not spread in the house after the house was plastered, then the priest shall pro-

nounce the house clean, for the 49 disease is healed. And for the cleansing of the house he shall take two small birds, with cedarwood and scarlet stuff and hyssop, 50 and shall kill one of the birds in an earthen vessel over running water, 51 and shall take the cedarwood and the hyssop and the scarlet stuff, along with the living bird, and dip them in the blood of the bird that was killed and in the running water, and sprinkle the house 52 seven times. Thus he shall cleanse the house with the blood of the bird, and with the running water, and with the living bird, and with the cedarwood and 53 hyssop and scarlet stuff; and he shall let the living bird go out of the city into the open field; so he shall make atonement for the house, and it shall be clean." 54 This is the law for any leprous 55 disease: for an itch, for leprosy in 56 a garment or in a house, and for a swelling or an eruption or a spot, 57 to show when it is unclean and when it is clean. This is the law for leprosy.

Personal cleanliness

15 The LORD said to Moses and 2 Aaron, "Say to the people of Israel, When any man has a discharge from his body, his 3 discharge is unclean. And this is the law of his uncleanness for a discharge: whether his body runs with his discharge, or his body is stopped from discharge, it is 4 uncleanness in him. Every bed on which he who has the discharge lies shall be unclean; and everything on which he sits shall be 5 unclean. And any one who touches his bed shall wash his clothes, and bathe himself in water, and be unclean until the 6 evening. And whoever sits on anything on which he who has the discharge has sat shall wash his clothes, and bathe himself in water, and be unclean until the 7 evening. And whoever touches the body of him who has the discharge shall wash his clothes, and bathe himself in water, and be 8 unclean until the evening. And if he who has the discharge spits on one who is clean, then he shall wash his clothes, and bathe himself in water, and be unclean until 9 the evening. And any saddle on which he who has the discharge 10 rides shall be unclean. And whoever touches anything that was under him shall be unclean until the evening; and he who carries such a thing shall wash his clothes, and bathe himself in water, and be unclean until the 11 evening. Any one whom he that has the discharge touches without having rinsed his hands in water shall wash his clothes, and bathe himself in water, and be unclean 12 until the evening. And the

earthen vessel which he who has the discharge touches shall be broken; and every vessel of wood shall be rinsed in water. "And when he who has a dis- 13 charge is cleansed of his discharge, then he shall count for himself seven days for his cleansing, and wash his clothes; and he shall bathe his body in running water, and shall be clean. And on 14 the eighth day he shall take two turtledoves or two young pigeons, and come before the LORD to the door of the tent of meeting, and give them to the priest; and the 15 priest shall offer them, one for a sin offering and the other for a burnt offering; and the priest shall make atonement for him before the LORD for his discharge. "And if a man has an emission of 16 semen, he shall bathe his whole body in water, and be unclean until the evening. And every 17 garment and every skin on which the semen comes shall be washed with water, and be unclean until the evening. If a man lies with a 18 woman and has an emission of semen, both of them shall bathe themselves in water, and be unclean until the evening. "When a woman has a discharge 19 of blood which is her regular discharge from her body, she shall be in her impurity for seven days, and whoever touches her shall be unclean until the evening. And 20 everything upon which she lies during her impurity shall be unclean; everything also upon which she sits shall be unclean. And whoever touches her bed 21 shall wash his clothes, and bathe himself in water, and be unclean until the evening. And whoever 22 touches anything upon which she sits shall wash his clothes, and bathe himself in water, and be unclean until the evening; whether it is the bed or anything 23 upon which she sits, when he touches it he shall be unclean until the evening. And if any man 24 lies with her, and her impurity is on him, he shall be unclean seven days; and every bed on which he lies shall be unclean. "If a woman has a discharge of 25 blood for many days, not at the time of her impurity, or if she has a discharge beyond the time of her impurity, all the days of the discharge she shall continue in uncleanness; as in the days of her impurity, she shall be unclean. Every bed on which she lies, all 26 the days of her discharge, shall be to her as the bed of her impurity; and everything on which she sits shall be unclean, as in the uncleanness of her impurity. And 27 whoever touches these things shall be unclean, and shall wash his clothes, and bathe himself in water, and be unclean until the evening. But if she is cleansed of 28 her discharge, she shall count for

---

[x] Gk Syr: Heb afford, [31]such as he can afford, one
15.24: Lev 18.19; 20.18.

herself seven days, and after that she shall be clean. And on the 29 eighth day she shall take two turtledoves or two young pigeons, and bring them to the priest, to the door of the tent of meeting. 30 And the priest shall offer one for a sin offering and the other for a burnt offering; and the priest shall make atonement for her before the LORD for her unclean discharge. 31 "Thus you shall keep the people of Israel separate from their uncleanness, lest they die in their uncleanness by defiling my tabernacle that is in their midst." 32 This is the law for him who has a discharge and for him who has an emission of semen, becoming 33 unclean thereby; also for her who is sick with her impurity; that is, for any one, male or female, who has a discharge, and for the man who lies with a woman who is unclean.

DAY OF ATONEMENT

16 THE LORD spoke to Moses, after the death of the two sons of Aaron, when they drew near 2 before the LORD and died; and the LORD said to Moses, "Tell Aaron your brother not to come at all times into the holy place within the veil, before the mercy seat which is upon the ark, lest he die; for I will appear in the cloud upon 3 the mercy seat. But thus shall Aaron come into the holy place: with a young bull for a sin offering and a ram for a burnt 4 offering. He shall put on the holy linen coat, and shall have the linen breeches on his body, be girded with the linen girdle, and wear the linen turban; these are the holy garments. He shall bathe his

body in water, and then put them 5 on. And he shall take from the congregation of the people of Israel two male goats for a sin offering, and one ram for a burnt offering. 6 "And Aaron shall offer the bull as a sin offering for himself, and shall make atonement for himself 7 and for his house. Then he shall take the two goats, and set them before the LORD at the door of the 8 tent of meeting; and Aaron shall cast lots upon the two goats, one lot for the LORD and the other lot 9 for Aza′zel. And Aaron shall present the goat on which the lot 10 fell for the LORD, and offer it as a sin offering; but the goat on which the lot fell for Aza′zel shall be presented alive before the LORD to make atonement over it, that it may be sent away into the 11 wilderness to Aza′zel. "Aaron shall present the bull as a sin offering for himself, and shall make atonement for himself and for his house; he shall kill the bull 12 as a sin offering for himself. And he shall take a censer full of coals of fire from the altar before the LORD, and two handfuls of sweet incense beaten small; and he shall 13 bring it within the veil and put the incense on the fire before the LORD, that the cloud of the incense may cover the mercy seat which is upon the testimony, lest 14 he die; and he shall take some of the blood of the bull, and sprinkle it with his finger on the front of the mercy seat, and before the mercy seat he shall sprinkle the blood with his finger seven times. 15 "Then he shall kill the goat of the sin offering which is for the people, and bring its blood within the veil, and do with its blood as he did with the blood of the bull,

sprinkling it upon the mercy seat and before the mercy seat; thus he 16 shall make atonement for the holy place, because of the uncleannesses of the people of Israel, and because of their transgressions, all their sins; and so he shall do for the tent of meeting, which abides with them in the midst of their uncleannesses. There shall be no 17 man in the tent of meeting when he enters to make atonement in the holy place until he comes out and has made atonement for himself and for his house and for all the assembly of Israel. Then 18 he shall go out to the altar which is before the LORD and make atonement for it, and shall take some of the blood of the bull and of the blood of the goat, and put it on the horns of the altar round about. And he shall sprinkle 19 some of the blood upon it with his finger seven times, and cleanse it and hallow it from the uncleannesses of the people of Israel. "And when he has made an end 20 of atoning for the holy place and the tent of meeting and the altar, he shall present the live goat; and 21 Aaron shall lay both his hands upon the head of the live goat, and confess over him all the iniquities of the people of Israel, and all their transgressions, all their sins; and he shall put them upon the head of the goat, and send him away into the wilderness by the hand of a man who is in readiness. The goat shall bear all their 22 iniquities upon him to a solitary land; and he shall let the goat go in the wilderness. "Then Aaron shall come into the 23 tent of meeting, and shall put off the linen garments which he put on when he went into the holy place, and shall leave them there;

16.2, 12: Heb 6.19; 9.7, 25.

24 and he shall bathe his body in water in a holy place, and put on his garments, and come forth, and offer his burnt offering and the burnt offering of the people, and make atonement for himself and 25 for the people. And the fat of the sin offering he shall burn upon 26 the altar. And he who lets the goat go to Aza′zel shall wash his clothes and bathe his body in water, and afterward he may come 27 into the camp. And the bull for the sin offering and the goat for the sin offering, whose blood was brought in to make atonement in the holy place, shall be carried forth outside the camp; their skin and their flesh and their dung 28 shall be burned with fire. And he who burns them shall wash his clothes and bathe his body in water, and afterward he may come into the camp.

29 "And it shall be a statute to you for ever that in the seventh month, on the tenth day of the month, you shall afflict yourselves, and shall do no work, either the native or the stranger 30 who sojourns among you; for on this day shall atonement be made for you, to cleanse you; from all your sins you shall be clean before 31 the LORD. It is a sabbath of solemn rest to you, and you shall afflict yourselves; it is a statute for 32 ever. And the priest who is anointed and consecrated as priest in his father's place shall make atonement, wearing the holy linen 33 garments; he shall make atonement for the sanctuary, and he shall make atonement for the tent of meeting and for the altar, and he shall make atonement for the priests and for all the people of 34 the assembly. And this shall be an everlasting statute for you, that atonement may be made for the people of Israel once in the year because of all their sins." And Moses did as the LORD commanded him.

LAW OF HOLINESS

17 AND the LORD said to Moses, 2 "Say to Aaron and his sons, and to all the people of Israel, This is the thing which the LORD has commanded.

Sacrifices

3 "If any man of the house of Israel kills an ox or a lamb or a goat in the camp, or kills it outside 4 the camp, and does not bring it to the door of the tent of meeting, to offer it as a gift to the LORD before the tabernacle of the LORD, bloodguilt shall be imputed to that man; he has shed blood; and that man shall be cut off from among 5 his people. This is to the end that the people of Israel may bring their sacrifices which they slay in the open field, that they may bring them to the LORD, to the priest at the door of the tent of meeting, and slay them as sacri- 6 fices of peace offerings to the LORD; and the priest shall sprinkle the blood on the altar of the LORD at the door of the tent of meeting, and burn the fat for a 7 pleasing odour to the LORD. So they shall no more slay their sacrifices for satyrs, after whom they play the harlot. This shall be a statute for ever to them throughout their generations.

8 "And you shall say to them, Any man of the house of Israel, or of the strangers that sojourn among them, who offers a burnt offering 9 or sacrifice, and does not bring it to the door of the tent of meeting, to sacrifice it to the LORD; that man shall be cut off from his people.

10 "If any man of the house of Israel or of the strangers that sojourn among them eats any blood, I will set my face against that person who eats blood, and will cut him off from among his 11 people. For the life of the flesh is in the blood; and I have given it for you upon the altar to make atonement for your souls; for it is the blood that makes atonement, 12 by reason of the life. Therefore I have said to the people of Israel, No person among you shall eat blood, neither shall any stranger who sojourns among you eat 13 blood. Any man also of the people of Israel, or of the strangers that sojourn among them, who takes in hunting any beast or bird that may be eaten shall pour out its blood and cover it with dust.

14 "For the life of every creature is the blood of it;[e] therefore I have said to the people of Israel, You shall not eat the blood of any creature, for the life of every creature is its blood; whoever eats 15 it shall be cut off. And every person that eats what dies of itself or what is torn by beasts, whether he is a native or a sojourner, shall wash his clothes, and bathe himself in water, and be unclean until the evening; then he shall be 16 clean. But if he does not wash them or bathe his flesh, he shall bear his iniquity."

Marriage

18 And the LORD said to Moses, 2 "Say to the people of Israel, I am 3 the LORD your God. You shall not do as they do in the land of Egypt, where you dwelt, and you shall not do as they do in the land of Canaan, to which I am bringing you. You shall not walk in their statutes. You shall do my ordi- 4 nances and keep my statutes and walk in them. I am the LORD your God. You shall therefore 5 keep my statutes and my ordinances, by doing which a man shall live: I am the LORD.

"None of you shall approach any 6 one near of kin to him to uncover nakedness. I am the LORD. You 7 shall not uncover the nakedness of your father, which is the nakedness of your mother; she is your mother, you shall not uncover her nakedness. You shall not uncover 8 the nakedness of your father's wife; it is your father's nakedness. You shall not uncover 9 the nakedness of your sister, the daughter of your father or the daughter of your mother, whether born at home or born abroad. You shall not uncover the naked- 10 ness of your son's daughter or of your daughter's daughter, for their nakedness is your own nakedness. You shall not uncover 11 the nakedness of your father's wife's daughter, begotten by your father, since she is your sister. You shall not uncover the naked- 12 ness of your father's sister; she is your father's near kinswoman. You shall not uncover the naked- 13 ness of your mother's sister, for she is your mother's near kinswoman. You shall not uncover 14 the nakedness of your father's brother, that is, you shall not approach his wife; she is your aunt. You shall not uncover the 15 nakedness of your daughter-in-law; she is your son's wife, you shall not uncover her nakedness. You shall not uncover the naked- 16 ness of your brother's wife; she is your brother's nakedness. You 17 shall not uncover the nakedness of a woman and of her daughter, and you shall not take her son's daughter or her daughter's daughter to uncover her nakedness; they are your[f] near kinswomen; it is wickedness. And 18 you shall not take a woman as a rival wife to her sister, uncovering her nakedness while her sister is yet alive.

"You shall not approach a 19 woman to uncover her nakedness while she is in her menstrual uncleanness. And you shall not 20 lie carnally with your neighbour's wife, and defile yourself with her. You shall not give any of your 21 children to devote them by fire to Molech, and so profane the name of your God: I am the LORD. You 22 shall not lie with a male as with a woman; it is an abomination.

---

e Gk Syr Compare Vg; Heb for the life of all flesh, its blood is in its life   f Gk: Heb lacks your
16.27: Heb 13.11.   17.10-16: Lev 3.17; 7.26-27; 19.26; Deut 12.16, 23-25.
18.5: Lk 10.28; Rom 10.5; Gal 3.12.   18.7: Lev 20.11.   18.9, 11: Lev 20.17; Deut 27.22.
18.12: Lev 20.19.   18.14: Lev 20.20.   18.15: Lev 20.12.   18.16: Lev 20.21.   18.17: Lev 20.14.
18.19: Lev 15.24; 20.18.   18.21: Lev 20.2-5.   18.22: Lev 20.13; Deut 23.18.

23 And you shall not lie with any beast and defile yourself with it, neither shall any woman give herself to a beast to lie with it: it is perversion.

24 "Do not defile yourselves by any of these things, for by all these the nations I am casting out before

25 you defiled themselves; and the land became defiled, so that I punished its iniquity, and the land

26 vomited out its inhabitants. But you shall keep my statutes and my ordinances and do none of these abominations, either the native or the stranger who sojourns among

27 you (for all of these abominations the men of the land did, who were before you, so that the land

28 became defiled); lest the land vomit you out, when you defile it, as it vomited out the nation that

29 was before you. For whoever shall do any of these abominations, the persons that do them shall be cut off from among their

30 people. So keep my charge never to practise any of these abominable customs which were practised before you, and never to defile yourselves by them: I am the LORD your God."

General statutes

19 And the LORD said to Moses,
2 "Say to all the congregation of the people of Israel, You shall be holy; for I the LORD your God am

3 holy. Every one of you shall revere his mother and his father, and you shall keep my sabbaths: I

4 am the LORD your God. Do not turn to idols or make for yourselves molten gods: I am the LORD your God.

5 "When you offer a sacrifice of peace offerings to the LORD, you

shall offer it so that you may be
6 accepted. It shall be eaten the same day you offer it, or on the morrow; and anything left over until the third day shall be burned
7 with fire. If it is eaten at all on the third day, it is an abomination; it
8 will not be accepted, and every one who eats it shall bear his iniquity, because he has profaned a holy thing of the LORD; and that person shall be cut off from his people.
9 "When you reap the harvest of your land, you shall not reap your field to its very border, neither
10 shall you gather the gleanings after your harvest. And you shall not strip your vineyard bare, neither shall you gather the fallen grapes of your vineyard; you shall leave them for the poor and for the sojourner: I am the LORD your God.
11 "You shall not steal, nor deal falsely, nor lie to one another.
12 And you shall not swear by my name falsely, and so profane the name of your God: I am the LORD.
13 "You shall not oppress your neighbour or rob him. The wages of a hired servant shall not remain with you all night until the morn-
14 ing. You shall not curse the deaf or put a stumbling block before the blind, but you shall fear your God: I am the LORD.
15 "You shall do no injustice in judgment; you shall not be partial to the poor or defer to the great, but in righteousness shall you
16 judge your neighbour. You shall not go up and down as a slanderer among your people, and you shall not stand forth against the life[g] of your neighbour: I am the LORD.
17 "You shall not hate your brother in your heart, but you shall reason with your neighbour, lest you

bear sin because of him. You 18 shall not take vengeance or bear any grudge against the sons of your own people, but you shall love your neighbour as yourself: I am the LORD.

"You shall keep my statutes. 19 You shall not let your cattle breed with a different kind; you shall not sow your field with two kinds of seed; nor shall there come upon you a garment of cloth made of two kinds of stuff.

"If a man lies carnally with a 20 woman who is a slave, betrothed to another man and not yet ransomed or given her freedom, an inquiry shall be held. They shall not be put to death, because she was not free; but he shall 21 bring a guilt offering for himself to the LORD, to the door of the tent of meeting, a ram for a guilt offering. And the priest shall 22 make atonement for him with the ram of the guilt offering before the LORD for his sin which he has committed; and the sin which he has committed shall be forgiven him.

"When you come into the land 23 and plant all kinds of trees for food, then you shall count their fruit as forbidden;[h] three years it shall be forbidden to you, it must not be eaten. And in the fourth 24 year all their fruit shall be holy, an offering of praise to the LORD. But in the fifth year you may eat 25 of their fruit, that they may yield more richly for you: I am the LORD your God.

Lev 11, 18

g Heb *blood*   *h* Heb *their uncircumcision*
18.23: Ex 22.19; Lev 20.15–16; Deut 27.21.
19.2: Lev 11.44–45; 20.7, 26; 1 Pet 1.16.   19.3, 30: Ex 20.8, 12; 23.12; 34.21; Deut 5.12–16.
19.4: Ex 20.4; Lev 26.1; Deut 4.15–19; 27.15.   19.9–10: Lev 23.22; Deut 24.20–21.
19.11: Ex 20.15–16; Deut 5.19.   19.12: Ex 20.7; Deut 5.11; Mt 5.33.
19.13: Deut 24.15; Jas 5.4.   19.14: Deut 27.18.   19.15: Ex 23.6; Deut 1.17.
19.18: Mt 5.43; 19.19; 22.39; Mk 12.31; Lk 10.27; Rom 13.9; Gal 5.14; Jas 2.8.   19.19: Deut 22.9, 11.

26 "You shall not eat any flesh with the blood in it. You shall not practice augury or witchcraft.

27 You shall not round off the hair on your temples or mar the edges

28 of your beard. You shall not make any cuttings in your flesh on account of the dead or tattoo any marks upon you: I am the LORD.

29 "Do not profane your daughter by making her a harlot, lest the land fall into harlotry and the land

30 become full of wickedness. You shall keep my sabbaths and reverence my sanctuary: I am the LORD.

31 "Do not turn to mediums or wizards; do not seek them out, to be defiled by them: I am the LORD your God.

32 "You shall rise up before the hoary head, and honour the face of an old man, and you shall fear your God: I am the LORD.

33 "When a stranger sojourns with you in your land, you shall not do

34 him wrong. The stranger who sojourns with you shall be to you as the native among you, and you shall love him as yourself; for you were strangers in the land of Egypt: I am the LORD your God.

35 "You shall do no wrong in judgment, in measures of length

36 or weight or quantity. You shall have just balances, just weights, a just ephah, and a just hin: I am the LORD your God, who brought

37 you out of the land of Egypt. And you shall observe all my statutes and all my ordinances, and do them: I am the LORD."

20 The LORD said to Moses, "Say

2 to the people of Israel, Any man of the people of Israel, or of the strangers that sojourn in Israel, who gives any of his children to Molech shall be put to death; the people of the land shall stone him

3 with stones. I myself will set my face against that man, and will cut

him off from among his people, because he has given one of his children to Molech, defiling my

4 sanctuary and profaning my holy name. And if the people of the land do at all hide their eyes from that man, when he gives one of his children to Molech, and do not

5 put him to death, then I will set my face against that man and against his family, and will cut them off from among their people, him and all who follow him in playing the harlot after Molech.

6 "If a person turns to mediums and wizards, playing the harlot after them, I will set my face against that person, and will cut him off from among his people.

7 Consecrate yourselves therefore, and be holy; for I am the LORD

8 your God. Keep my statutes, and do them; I am the LORD who

9 sanctify you. For every one who curses his father or his mother shall be put to death; he has cursed his father or his mother, his blood is upon him.

10 "If a man commits adultery with the wife of¹ his neighbour, both the adulterer and the adulteress

11 shall be put to death. The man who lies with his father's wife has uncovered his father's nakedness; both of them shall be put to death,

12 their blood is upon them. If a man lies with his daughter-in-law, both of them shall be put to death; they have committed incest, their blood is upon them.

13 If a man lies with a male as with a woman, both of them have committed an abomination; they shall

14 be put to death, their blood is upon them. If a man takes a wife and her mother also, it is wickedness; they shall be burned with fire, both he and they, that there

15 may be no wickedness among you. If a man lies with a beast, he shall be put to death; and you

shall kill the beast. If a woman 16 approaches any beast and lies with it, you shall kill the woman and the beast; they shall be put to death, their blood is upon them.

"If a man takes his sister, 17 a daughter of his father or a daughter of his mother, and sees her nakedness, and she sees his nakedness, it is a shameful thing, and they shall be cut off in the sight of the children of their people; he has uncovered his sister's nakedness, he shall bear his iniquity. If a man lies with a 18 woman having her sickness, and uncovers her nakedness, he has made naked her fountain, and she has uncovered the fountain of her blood; both of them shall be cut off from among their people. You 19 shall not uncover the nakedness of your mother's sister or of your father's sister, for that is to make naked one's near kin; they shall bear their iniquity. If a man lies 20 with his uncle's wife, he has uncovered his uncle's nakedness; they shall bear their sin, they shall die childless. If a man takes his 21 brother's wife, it is impurity; he has uncovered his brother's nakedness, they shall be childless.

"You shall therefore keep all my 22 statutes and all my ordinances, and do them; that the land where I am bringing you to dwell may not vomit you out. And you shall 23 not walk in the customs of the nation which I am casting out before you; for they did all these things, and therefore I abhorred them. But I have said to you, 24 'You shall inherit their land, and I will give it to you to possess, a land flowing with milk and honey.' I am the LORD your God, who have separated you from the peoples. You shall therefore 25 make a distinction between the clean beast and the unclean, and between the unclean bird and the clean; you shall not make yourselves abominable by beast or by bird or by anything with which the ground teems, which I have set apart for you to hold unclean. You shall be holy to me; for I the 26 LORD am holy, and have separated you from the peoples, that you should be mine.

"A man or a woman who is a 27 medium or a wizard shall be put to death; they shall be stoned with stones, their blood shall be upon them."

Rules for priests

And the LORD said to Moses, 21 "Speak to the priests, the sons of Aaron, and say to them that none

Lev 11, 29, 30

¹ Heb repeats *if a man commits adultery with the wife of*

19.26: Lev 3.17; 7.26–27; 17.10–16; Deut 12.16, 23–25; 18.10.   **19.27–28:** Lev 21.5; Deut 14.1.
19.29: Deut 23.17–18.   **19.30:** Ex 20.8–11; 23.12; 34.21; 35.2–3; Lev 19.3; 26.2; Deut 5.12–15.
19.31: Lev 20.6, 27.   **19.33:** Ex 22.21.   **20.2–5:** Lev 18.21.   **20.6:** Lev 19.31.
20.7: Lev 11.44–45; 19.2; 20.26; I Pet 1.16.   **20.9** Ex 21.17; Deut 27.16.
20.10: Ex 20.14; Lev 18.20; Deut 5.18.   **20.11:** Lev 18.7–8.   **20.12:** Lev 18.15.
20.13: Lev 18.22.   **20.14:** Lev 18.17; Deut 27.23.   **20.15–16:** Lev 18.23.   **20.17:** Lev 18.9.
20.18: Lev 15.24; 18.19.   **20.19:** Lev 18.12–13.   **20.20:** Lev 18.14.   **20.21:** Lev 18.16.
20.26: Lev 20.7.   **20.27:** Lev 19.31; 20.6   **21.1–3:** Ezek 44.25.

of them shall defile himself for the
2 dead among his people, except for
his nearest of kin, his mother, his
father, his son, his daughter, his
3 brother, or his virgin sister (who
is near to him because she has had
no husband; for her he may defile
4 himself). He shall not defile
himself as a husband among his
people and so profane himself.
5 They shall not make tonsures
upon their heads, nor shave off
the edges of their beards, nor
make any cuttings in their flesh.
6 They shall be holy to their God,
and not profane the name of their
God; for they offer the offerings
by fire to the LORD, the bread of
their God; therefore they shall be

blind or lame, or one who has a
mutilated face or a limb too long,
19 or a man who has an injured foot
20 or an injured hand, or a hunch-
back, or a dwarf, or a man with a
defect in his sight or an itching
disease or scabs or crushed tes-

such shall be unclean until the
evening and shall not eat of the
holy things unless he has bathed

Lev 11, 16

7 holy. They shall not marry a 21
harlot or a woman who has been
defiled; neither shall they marry a
woman divorced from her husband; for the priest is holy to his
8 God. You shall consecrate him,
for he offers the bread of your 22
God; he shall be holy to you; for I
the LORD, who sanctify you, am 23
9 holy. And the daughter of any
priest, if she profanes herself by
playing the harlot, profanes her 24
father; she shall be burned with
fire.
10 "The priest who is chief among 22
his brethren, upon whose head 2
the anointing oil is poured, and
who has been consecrated to wear
the garments, shall not let the hair
of his head hang loose, nor rend
11 his clothes; he shall not go in to 3
any dead body, nor defile himself,
even for his father or for his
12 mother; neither shall he go out of
the sanctuary, nor profane the
sanctuary of his God; for the 4
consecration of the anointing oil
of his God is upon him: I am the
13 LORD. And he shall take a wife in
14 her virginity. A widow, or one
divorced, or a woman who has
been defiled, or a harlot, these he 5
shall not marry; but he shall take
to wife a virgin of his own people,
15 that he may not profane his
children among his people; for I 6
am the LORD who sanctify him."
16 And the LORD said to Moses,
17 "Say to Aaron, None of your
descendants throughout their
generations who has a blemish
may approach to offer the bread
18 of his God. For no one who has a
blemish shall draw near, a man

ticles; no man of the descendants
of Aaron the priest who has a
blemish shall come near to offer
the LORD's offerings by fire; since
he has a blemish, he shall not
come near to offer the bread of his
God. He may eat the bread of his
God, both of the most holy and of
the holy things, but he shall not
come near the veil or approach the
altar, because he has a blemish,
that he may not profane my
sanctuaries; for I am the LORD
who sanctify them." So Moses
spoke to Aaron and to his sons
and to all the people of Israel.

And the LORD said to Moses,
"Tell Aaron and his sons to keep
away from the holy things of the
people of Israel, which they
dedicate to me, so that they may
not profane my holy name: I am
the LORD. Say to them, 'If any
one of all your descendants
throughout your generatons approaches the holy things, which
the people of Israel dedicate to the
LORD, while he has an uncleanness, that person shall be cut off
from my presence: I am the
LORD. None of the line of Aaron
who is a leper or suffers a discharge may eat of the holy things
until he is clean. Whoever
touches anything that is unclean
through contact with the dead or a
man who has an emission of
semen, and whoever touches a
creeping thing by which he may
be made unclean or a man from
whom he may take uncleanness,
whatever his uncleanness may
be—the person who touches any

his body in water. When the sun 7
is down he shall be clean; and
afterwards he may eat of the holy
things, because such are his food.
That which dies of itself or is torn 8
by beasts he shall not eat, defiling
himself by it: I am the LORD.'
They shall therefore keep my 9
charge, lest they bear sin for it and
die thereby when they profane it:
I am the LORD who sanctify them.
"An outsider shall not eat of a 10
holy thing. A sojourner of the
priest's or a hired servant shall not
eat of a holy thing; but if a priest 11
buys a slave as his property for
money, the slave may eat of it;
and those that are born in his
house may eat of his food. If a 12
priest's daughter is married to an
outsider she shall not eat of the
offering of the holy things. But if 13
a priest's daughter is a widow or
divorced, and has no child, and
returns to her father's house, as in
her youth, she may eat of her
father's food; yet no outsider shall
eat of it. And if a man eats of a 14
holy thing unwittingly, he shall
add the fifth of its value to it, and
give the holy thing to the priest.
The priests shall not profane the 15
holy things of the people of Israel,
which they offer to the LORD, and 16
so cause them to bear iniquity and
guilt, by eating their holy things:
for I am the LORD who sanctify
them."
And the LORD said to Moses, 17
"Say to Aaron and his sons and all 18
the people of Israel, When any
one of the house of Israel or of the
sojourners in Israel presents his
offering, whether in payment of a
vow or as a freewill offering which
is offered to the LORD as a burnt
offering, to be accepted you shall 19
offer a male without blemish, of
the bulls or the sheep or the
goats. You shall not offer any- 20
thing that has a blemish, for it will
not be acceptable for you. And 21
when any one offers a sacrifice of

21.5: Lev 19.27; Deut 14.1.   **22.12:** Lev 7.31–36.

peace offerings to the LORD, to fulfil a vow or as a freewill offering, from the herd or from the flock, to be accepted it must be perfect; there shall be no
22 blemish in it. Animals blind or disabled or mutilated or having a discharge or an itch or scabs, you shall not offer to the LORD or make of them an offering by fire
23 upon the altar to the LORD. A bull or a lamb which has a part too long or too short you may present for a freewill offering; but for a votive offering it cannot be
24 accepted. Any animal which has its testicles bruised or crushed or torn or cut, you shall not offer to the LORD or sacrifice within your
25 land; neither shall you offer as the bread of your God any such animals gotten from a foreigner. Since there is a blemish in them, because of their mutilation, they will not be accepted for you."
26 And the LORD said to Moses,
27 "When a bull or sheep or goat is born, it shall remain seven days with its mother; and from the eighth day on it shall be acceptable as an offering by fire to the
28 LORD. And whether the mother is a cow or a ewe, you shall not kill both her and her young in one
29 day. And when you sacrifice a sacrifice of thanksgiving to the LORD, you shall sacrifice it so that
30 you may be accepted. It shall be eaten on the same day, you shall leave none of it until morning: I am the LORD.
31 "So you shall keep my commandments and do them: I am
32 the LORD. And you shall not profane my holy name, but I will be hallowed among the people of Israel; I am the LORD who sanc-
33 tify you, who brought you out of the land of Egypt to be your God: I am the LORD."

Sacred calendar

23 The LORD said to Moses, "Say
2 to the people of Israel, The appointed feasts of the LORD

which you shall proclaim as holy convocations, my appointed
3 feasts, are these. Six days shall work be done; but on the seventh day is a sabbath of solemn rest, a holy convocation; you shall do no work; it is a sabbath to the LORD in all your dwellings.
4 "These are the appointed feasts of the LORD, the holy convocations, which you shall proclaim at
5 the time appointed for them. In the first month, on the fourteenth day of the month in the evening,ʲ
6 is the LORD's passover. And on the fifteenth day of the same month is the feast of unleavened bread to the LORD; seven days you
7 shall eat unleavened bread. On the first day you shall have a holy convocation; you shall do no labo-
8 rious work. But you shall present an offering by fire to the LORD seven days; on the seventh day is a holy convocation; you shall do no laborious work."
9 And the LORD said to Moses,
10 "Say to the people of Israel, When you come into the land which I give you and reap its harvest, you shall bring the sheaf of the first fruits of your harvest
11 to the priest; and he shall wave the sheaf before the LORD, that you may find acceptance; on the morrow after the sabbath the
12 priest shall wave it. And on the day when you wave the sheaf, you shall offer a male lamb a year old without blemish as a burnt offer-
13 ing to the LORD. And the cereal offering with it shall be two tenths of an ephah of fine flour mixed with oil, to be offered by fire to the LORD, a pleasing odour; and the drink offering with it shall be
14 of wine, a fourth of a hin. And you shall eat neither bread nor grain parched or fresh until this same day, until you have brought the offering of your God: it is a

statute for ever throughout your generations in all your dwellings.
15 "And you shall count from the morrow after the sabbath, from the day that you brought the sheaf of the wave offering; seven full
16 weeks shall they be, counting fifty days to the morrow after the seventh sabbath; then you shall present a cereal offering of new
17 grain to the LORD. You shall bring from your dwellings two loaves of bread to be waved, made of two tenths of an ephah; they shall be of fine flour, they shall be baked with leaven, as first fruits to
18 the LORD. And you shall present with the bread seven lambs a year old without blemish, and one young bull, and two rams; they shall be a burnt offering to the LORD, with their cereal offering and their drink offerings, an offering by fire, a pleasing odour to the
19 LORD. And you shall offer one male goat for a sin offering, and two male lambs a year old as a
20 sacrifice of peace offerings. And the priest shall wave them with the bread of the first fruits as a wave offering before the LORD, with the two lambs; they shall be holy to the LORD for the priest.
21 And you shall make proclamation on the same day; you shall hold a holy convocation; you shall do no laborious work: it is a statute for ever in all your dwellings throughout your generations.
22 "And when you reap the harvest of your land, you shall not reap your field to its very border, nor shall you gather the gleanings after your harvest; you shall leave them for the poor and for the stranger: I am the LORD your God."
23 And the LORD said to Moses,
24 "Say to the people of Israel, In the seventh month, on the first day of the month, you shall observe a day of solemn rest, a memorial proclaimed with blast of trumpets, a holy convocation.
25 You shall do no laborious work; and you shall present an offering by fire to the LORD."
26 And the LORD said to Moses,
27 "On the tenth day of this seventh month is the day of atonement; it shall be for you a time of holy

Swine, camel, rock badger, and hare   *Lev* 11, 4–7

ʲ Heb *between the two evenings*
23.1–44: Ex 23.14–17; 34.22–24; Deut 16.1–17.   23.22: Lev 19.9–10; Deut 24.20–21.

convocation, and you shall afflict yourselves and present an offering 8 by fire to the LORD. And you shall do no work on this same day; for it is a day of atonement, to make atonement for you before 9 the LORD your God. For whoever is not afflicted on this same day shall be cut off from his people. 0 And whoever does any work on this same day, that person I will destroy from among his people. 1 You shall do no work: it is a statute for ever throughout your generations in all your dwellings. 2 It shall be to you a sabbath of solemn rest, and you shall afflict yourselves; on the ninth day of the month beginning at evening, from evening to evening shall you keep your sabbath."

3 And the LORD said to Moses, 4 "Say to the people of Israel, On the fifteenth day of this seventh month and for seven days is the 5 feast of booths[k] to the LORD. On the first day shall be a holy convocation; you shall do no laborious work. Seven days you shall present offerings by fire to the LORD; on the eighth day you shall hold a holy convocation and present an offering by fire to the LORD; it is a solemn assembly; you shall do no laborious work.

"These are the appointed feasts of the LORD, which you shall proclaim as times of holy convocation, for presenting to the LORD offerings by fire, burnt offerings and cereal offerings, sacrifices and drink offerings, each on its proper day; besides the sabbaths of the LORD, and besides your gifts, and besides all your votive offerings, and besides all your freewill offerings, which you give to the LORD. "On the fifteenth day of the seventh month, when you have gathered in the produce of the land, you shall keep the feast of the LORD seven days; on the first day shall be a sabbath rest, and on the eighth day shall be a solemn rest. And you shall take on the first day the fruit of goodly trees, branches of palm trees, and boughs of leafy trees, and willows of the brook; and you shall rejoice before the LORD your God seven days. You shall keep it as a feast to the LORD seven days in the year; it is a statute for ever throughout your generations; you shall keep it in the seventh month. You shall dwell in booths for seven days; all that are native in Israel shall dwell in booths, that your generations may know that I made the people of Israel dwell in booths when I brought them out of the land of Egypt: I am the LORD your God."

Thus Moses declared to the people of Israel the appointed feasts of the LORD.

Holy things

24 The LORD said to Moses, 2 "Command the people of Israel to bring you pure oil from beaten olives for the lamp, that a light may be kept burning continually. 3 Outside the veil of the testimony, in the tent of meeting, Aaron shall keep it in order from evening to morning before the LORD continually; it shall be a statute for ever throughout your genera-4 tions. He shall keep the lamps in order upon the lampstand of pure gold before the LORD continually. 5 "And you shall take fine flour, and bake twelve cakes of it; two tenths of an ephah shall be in each 6 cake. And you shall set them in two rows, six in a row, upon the 7 table of pure gold. And you shall put pure frankincense with each row, that it may go with the bread as a memorial portion to be offered by fire to the LORD. 8 Every sabbath day Aaron shall set it in order before the LORD continually on behalf of the people of 9 Israel as a covenant for ever. And it shall be for Aaron and his sons, and they shall eat it in a holy place, since it is for him a most holy portion out of the offerings by fire to the LORD, a perpetual due."

10 Now an Israelite woman's son, whose father was an Egyptian, went out among the people of Israel; and the Israelite woman's son and a man of Israel quarrelled 11 in the camp, and the Israelite woman's son blasphemed the Name, and cursed. And they brought him to Moses. His mother's name was Shelo'mith, the daughter of Dibri, of the tribe 12 of Dan. And they put him in custody, till the will of the LORD should be declared to them.

13 And the LORD said to Moses, 14 "Bring out of the camp him who cursed; and let all who heard him lay their hands upon his head, and let all the congregation stone 15 him. And say to the people of Israel, Whoever curses his God 16 shall bear his sin. He who blasphemes the name of the LORD shall be put to death; all the congregation shall stone him; the sojourner as well as the native, when he blasphemes the Name, 17 shall be put to death. He who kills a man shall be put to death. 18 He who kills a beast shall make it 19 good, life for life. When a man causes a disfigurement in his neighbour, as he has done it shall 20 be done to him, fracture for fracture, eye for eye, tooth for tooth; as he has disfigured a man, he 21 shall be disfigured. He who kills a beast shall make it good; and he who kills a man shall be put to 22 death. You shall have one law for

the sojourner and for the native; for I am the LORD your God." So 23 Moses spoke to the people of Israel; and they brought him who had cursed out of the camp, and stoned him with stones. Thus the people of Israel did as the LORD commanded Moses.

Holy times

The LORD said to Moses on 25 Mount Sinai, "Say to the people 2 of Israel, When you come into the land which I give you, the land shall keep a sabbath to the LORD. Six years you shall sow your field, 3 and six years you shall prune your vineyard, and gather in its fruits; but in the seventh year there shall 4 be a sabbath of solemn rest for the land, a sabbath to the LORD; you shall not sow your field or prune your vineyard. What grows of 5 itself in your harvest you shall not reap, and the grapes of your undressed vine you shall not gather; it shall be a year of solemn rest for the land. The sabbath of 6 the land shall provide food for you, for yourself and for your male and female slaves and for your hired servant and the sojourner who lives with you; for your 7 cattle also and for the beasts that are in your land all its yield shall be for food.

"And you shall count seven 8 weeks[l] of years, seven times seven years, so that the time of the seven weeks of years shall be to you forty-nine years. Then you 9 shall send abroad the loud trumpet on the tenth day of the seventh month; on the day of atonement you shall send abroad the trumpet throughout all your land. And 10 you shall hallow the fiftieth year, and proclaim liberty throughout the land to all its inhabitants; it shall be a jubilee for you, when each of you shall return to his property and each of you shall return to his family. A jubilee 11 shall that fiftieth year be to you; in it you shall neither sow, nor reap what grows of itself, nor gather the grapes from the undressed vines. For it is a jubilee; it shall 12 be holy to you; you shall eat what it yields out of the field.

"In this year of jubilee each of 13 you shall return to his property. And if you sell to your neighbour 14 or buy from your neighbour, you shall not wrong one another. According to the number of years 15 after the jubilee, you shall buy from your neighbour, and according to the number of years for crops he shall sell to you. If the 16 years are many you shall increase the price, and if the years are few you shall diminish the price, for it is the number of the crops that he is selling to you. You shall not 17 wrong one another, but you shall

k Or tabernacles   l Or sabbaths
24.1-4: Ex 27.20-21.   24.5-9: Ex 25.30; 39.36; 40.23; Mt 12.4; Mk 2.26; Lk 6.4.
24.19-20: Ex 21.23-25; Deut 19.21; Mt 5.38.   24.22: Ex 12.49; Num 9.14; 15.15-16, 29.
25.2-7: Ex 23.10-11.

fear your God; for I am the LORD your God.

18 "Therefore you shall do my statutes, and keep my ordinances and perform them; so you will 19 dwell in the land securely. The land will yield its fruit, and you 20 will eat your fill, and dwell in it securely. And if you say, 'What shall we eat in the seventh year, if we may not sow or gather in our 21 crop?' I will command my blessing upon you in the sixth year, so 22 that it will bring forth fruit for three years. When you sow in the eighth year, you will be eating old produce; until the ninth year, when its produce comes in, you 23 shall eat the old. The land shall not be sold in perpetuity; for the land is mine; for you are strangers 24 and sojourners with me. And in all the country you possess, you shall grant a redemption of the land.

25 "If your brother becomes poor, and sells part of his property, then his next of kin shall come and 26 redeem what his brother has sold. If a man has no one to redeem it, and then himself becomes prosperous and finds sufficient means 27 to redeem it, let him reckon the years since he sold it and pay back the overpayment to the man to 28 whom he sold it; and he shall return to his property. But if he has not sufficient means to get it back for himself, then what he sold shall remain in the hand of him who bought it until the year of jubilee; in the jubilee it shall be released, and he shall return to his property.

29 "If a man sells a dwelling house in a walled city, he may redeem it within a whole year after its sale; 30 for a full year he shall have the right of redemption. If it is not redeemed within a full year, then the house that is in the walled city shall be made sure in perpetuity to him who bought it, throughout 31 his generations; it shall not be released in the jubilee. But the houses of the villages which have no wall around them shall be reckoned with the fields of the country; they may be redeemed, and they shall be released in the 32 jubilee. Nevertheless the cities of the Levites, the houses in the cities of their possession, the Levites may redeem at any time. 33 And if one of the Levites does not exercise[m] his right of redemption, then the house that was sold in a city of their possession shall be released in the jubilee; for the houses in the cities of the Levites are their possession among the 34 people of Israel. But the fields of common land belonging to their cities may not be sold; for that is their perpetual possession.

35 "And if your brother becomes poor, and cannot maintain himself

with you, you shall maintain him; as a stranger and a sojourner he 36 shall live with you. Take no interest from him or increase, but fear your God; that your brother 37 may live beside you. You shall not lend him your money at interest, nor give him your food for 38 profit. I am the LORD your God, who brought you forth out of the land of Egypt to give you the land of Canaan, and to be your God.

39 "And if your brother becomes poor beside you, and sells himself 40 to you, you shall not make him serve as a slave: he shall be with you as a hired servant and as a sojourner. He shall serve with 41 you until the year of the jubilee; then he shall go out from you, he and his children with him, and go back to his own family, and return to the possession of his fathers. 42 For they are my servants, whom I brought forth out of the land of Egypt; they shall not be sold as 43 slaves. You shall not rule over him with harshness, but shall fear 44 your God. As for your male and female slaves whom you may have: you may buy male and female slaves from among the 45 nations that are round about you. You may also buy from among the strangers who sojourn with you and their families that are with you, who have been born in your land; and they may be your 46 property. You may bequeath them to your sons after you, to inherit as a possession for ever; you may make slaves of them, but over your brethren the people of Israel you shall not rule, one over another, with harshness.

47 "If a stranger or sojourner with you becomes rich, and your brother beside him becomes poor and sells himself to the stranger or sojourner with you, or to a 48 member of the stranger's family, then after he is sold he may be redeemed; one of his brothers 49 may redeem him, or his uncle, or his cousin may redeem him, or a near kinsman belonging to his family may redeem him; or if he grows rich he may redeem him- 50 self. He shall reckon with him who bought him from the year when he sold himself to him until the year of jubilee, and the price of his release shall be according to the number of years; the time he was with his owner shall be rated 51 as the time of a hired servant. If there are still many years, according to them he shall refund out of the price paid for him the price 52 for his redemption. If there remain but a few years until the year of jubilee, he shall make a reckoning with him; according to the years of service due from him 53 he shall refund the money for his redemption. As a servant hired

year by year shall he be with him; he shall not rule with harshness over him in your sight. And if he is not redeemed by these means, then he shall be released in the year of jubilee, he and his children with him. For to me the people of Israel are servants, they are my servants whom I brought forth out of the land of Egypt: I am the LORD your God.

"You shall make for yourselves no idols and erect no graven image or pillar, and you shall not set up a figured stone in your land, to bow down to them; for I am the LORD your God. You shall keep my sabbaths and reverence my sanctuary: I am the LORD.

Promises

"If you walk in my statutes and observe my commandments and do them, then I will give you your rains in their season, and the land shall yield its increase, and the trees of the field shall yield their fruit. And your threshing shall last to the time of vintage, and the vintage shall last to the time for sowing; and you shall eat your bread to the full, and dwell in your land securely. And I will give peace in the land, and you shall lie down, and none shall make you afraid; and I will remove evil beasts from the land, and the sword shall not go through your land. And you shall chase your enemies, and they shall fall before you by the sword. Five of you shall chase a hundred and a hundred of you shall chase ten thousand; and your enemies shall fall before you by the sword. And I will have regard for you and make you fruitful and multiply you, and will confirm my covenant with you. And you shall eat old store long kept, and you shall clear out the old to make way for the new. And I will make my abode among you, and my soul shall not abhor you. And I will walk among you, and will be your God, and you shall be my people. I am the LORD your God, who brought you forth out of the land of Egypt, that you should not be their slaves; and I have broken the bars of your yoke and made you walk erect.

Warnings

"But if you will not hearken to me, and will not do all these commandments, if you spurn my statutes, and if your soul abhors my ordinances, so that you will not do all my commandments, but break my covenant, I will do this to you: I will appoint over you sudden terror, consumption, and

[m] Compare Vg: Heb exercises

25.35: Deut 15.7–11.　25.36: Ex 22.25; Deut 23.19–20.
25.39–43: Ex 21.2–6; Deut 15.12–18.　26.1: Lev 19.4; Ex 20.4, 23; Deut 4.15–18; 27.15.
26.2: Ex 20.8; 23.12; 34.21; 35.2–3; Lev 19.3, 30; Deut 5.12–15.　26.3–13: Deut 7.12–26; 28.1–14.
26.11–12: 2 Cor 6.16.　26.14–45: Deut 28.16–68.

fever that waste the eyes and cause life to pine away. And you shall sow your seed in vain, for your enemies shall eat it; I will set my face against you, and you shall be smitten before your enemies; those who hate you shall rule over 37 you, and you shall flee when none pursues you. And if in spite of this you will not hearken to me, then I will chastise you again sevenfold for your sins, and I will 38 break the pride of your power, and I will make your heavens like iron and your earth like brass; and 39 your strength shall be spent in vain, for your land shall not yield its increase, and the trees of the land shall not yield their fruit.

"Then if you walk contrary to me, and will not hearken to me, I 40 will bring more plagues upon you, sevenfold as many as your sins. And I will let loose the wild beasts among you, which shall rob you of 41 your children, and destroy your cattle, and make you few in number, so that your ways shall become desolate.

"And if by this discipline you are not turned to me, but walk con- 42 trary to me, then I also will walk contrary to you, and I myself will smite you sevenfold for your sins. And I will bring a sword upon 43 you, that shall execute vengeance for the covenant; and if you gather within your cities I will send pestilence among you, and you shall be delivered into the hand of the enemy. When I break your staff of bread, ten women shall bake your bread in one oven, 44 and shall deliver your bread again by weight; and you shall eat, and not be satisfied.

"And if in spite of this you will not hearken to me, but walk con- 45 trary to me, then I will walk contrary to you in fury, and chastise you myself sevenfold for your sins. You shall eat the flesh of your sons, and you shall eat the flesh of your daughters. And I will destroy your high places, and 46 cut down your incense altars, and cast your dead bodies upon the dead bodies of your idols; and my soul shall abhor you. And I will lay your cities waste, and will make your sanctuaries desolate, and I will not smell your pleasing odours. And I will devastate the 27 land, so that your enemies who settle in it shall be astonished at it. And I will scatter you among the nations, and I will unsheathe the sword after you; and your land shall be a desolation, and your cities shall be a waste.

"Then the land shall enjoy[n] its sabbaths as long as it lies desolate, while you are in your enemies' land; then the land shall rest, and enjoy[n] its sabbaths. As long as it lies desolate it shall have rest, the rest which it had not in your sabbaths when you dwelt upon it. And as for those of you that are

left, I will send faintness into their hearts in the lands of their enemies; the sound of a driven leaf shall put them to flight, and they shall flee as one flees from the sword, and they shall fall 37 when none pursues. They shall stumble over one another, as if to escape a sword, though none pursues; and you shall have no power to stand before your enemies. And you shall perish among the nations, and the land 39 of your enemies shall eat you up. And those of you that are left shall pine away in your enemies' lands because of their iniquity; and also because of the iniquities of their fathers they shall pine away like them.

"But if they confess their ini- 40 quity and the iniquity of their fathers in their treachery which they committed against me, and 41 also in walking contrary to me, so that I walked contrary to them and brought them into the land of their enemies; if then their uncircumcised heart is humbled and they make amends for their ini- 42 quity; then I will remember my covenant with Jacob, and I will remember my covenant with Isaac and my covenant with Abraham, and I will remember 43 the land. But the land shall be left by them, and enjoy[n] its sabbaths while it lies desolate without them; and they shall make amends for their iniquity, because they spurned my ordinances, and their soul abhorred my statutes. Yet for all that, when they are in 44 the land of their enemies, I will not spurn them, neither will I abhor them so as to destroy them utterly and break my covenant with them; for I am the LORD 45 their God; but I will for their sake remember the covenant with their forefathers, whom I brought forth out of the land of Egypt in the sight of the nations, that I might be their God: I am the LORD."

These are the statutes and ordi- 46 nances and laws which the LORD made between him and the people of Israel on Mount Sinai by Moses.

Vows and tithes

The LORD said to Moses, "Say 27 to the people of Israel, When a 2 man makes a special vow of persons to the LORD at your valuation, then your valuation of a male 3 from twenty years old up to sixty years old shall be fifty shekels of silver, according to the shekel of the sanctuary. If the person is a 4 female, your valuation shall be thirty shekels. If the person is 5 from five years old up to twenty years old, your valuation shall be for a male twenty shekels, and for a female ten shekels. If the 6 person is from a month old up to five years old, your valuation shall

be for a male five shekels of silver, and for a female your valuation shall be three shekels of silver. And if the person is sixty years old 7 and upward, then your valuation for a male shall be fifteen shekels, and for a female ten shekels. And 8 if a man is too poor to pay your valuation, then he shall bring the person before the priest, and the priest shall value him; according to the ability of him who vowed the priest shall value him.

"If it is an animal such as men 9 offer as an offering to the LORD, all of such that any man gives to the LORD is holy. He shall not 10 substitute anything for it or exchange it, a good for a bad, or a bad for a good; and if he makes any exchange of beast for beast, then both it and that for which it is exchanged shall be holy. And if 11 it is an unclean animal such as is not offered as an offering to the LORD, then the man shall bring the animal before the priest, and 12 the priest shall value it as either good or bad; as you, the priest, value it, so it shall be. But if he 13 wishes to redeem it, he shall add a fifth to the valuation.

"When a man dedicates his 14 house to be holy to the LORD, the priest shall value it as either good or bad; as the priest values it, so it shall stand. And if he who dedi- 15 cates it wishes to redeem his house, he shall add a fifth of the valuation in money to it, and it shall be his.

"If a man dedicates to the LORD 16 part of the land which is his by inheritance, then your valuation shall be according to the seed for it; a sowing of a homer of barley shall be valued at fifty shekels of silver. If he dedicates his field 17 from the year of jubilee, it shall stand at your full valuation; but if 18 he dedicates his field after the jubilee, then the priest shall compute the money-value for it according to the years that remain until the year of jubilee, and a deduction shall be made from your valuation. And if he who 19 dedicates the field wishes to redeem it, then he shall add a fifth of the valuation in money to it, and it shall remain his. But if he 20 does not wish to redeem the field, or if he has sold the field to another man, it shall not be redeemed any more; but the field, 21 when it is released in the jubilee, shall be holy to the LORD, as a field that has been devoted; the priest shall be in possession of it. If he dedicates to the LORD a field 22 which he has bought, which is not a part of his possession by inheritance, then the priest shall com- 23 pute the valuation for it up to the year of jubilee, and the man shall give the amount of the valuation on that day as a holy thing to the LORD. In the year of jubilee the 24 field shall return to him from

whom it was bought, to whom the 28
land belongs as a possession by
25 inheritance. Every valuation shall
be according to the shekel of the
sanctuary: twenty gerahs shall
make a shekel.
26 "But a firstling of animals,
which as a firstling belongs to the
LORD, no man may dedicate;
whether ox or sheep, it is the
27 LORD's. And if it is an unclean 30
animal, then he shall buy it back
at your valuation, and add a fifth
to it; or, if it is not redeemed, 31
it shall be sold at your valuation.

"But no devoted thing that a
man devotes to the LORD, of
anything that he has, whether of
man or beast, or of his inherited
field, shall be sold or redeemed;
every devoted thing is most holy
29 to the LORD. No one devoted,
who is to be utterly destroyed
from among men, shall be ransomed; he shall be put to death.
"All the tithe of the land,
whether of the seed of the land or
of the fruit of the trees, is the
LORD's; it is holy to the LORD. If a
man wishes to redeem any of his

tithe, he shall add a fifth to it.
And all the tithe of herds and 3
flocks, every tenth animal of all
that pass under the herdsman's
staff, shall be holy to the LORD. A
man shall not inquire whether it is
good or bad, neither shall he
exchange it; and if he exchanges
it, then both it and that for which
it is exchanged shall be holy; it
shall not be redeemed."
These are the commandments 3
which the LORD commanded
Moses for the people of Israel on
Mount Sinai.

27.28: Num 18.14.

THE FOURTH BOOK OF MOSES

COMMONLY CALLED

NUMBERS

THE CAMP AT SINAI

THE LORD spoke to Moses in the wilderness of Sinai, in the tent of meeting, on the first day of the second month, in the second year after they had come out of the land of Egypt, 2 saying, "Take a census of all the congregation of the people of Israel, by families, by fathers' houses, according to the number of names, every male, head by 3 head; from twenty years old and upward, all in Israel who are able to go forth to war, you and Aaron shall number them, company by 4 company. And there shall be with you a man from each tribe, each man being the head of the house 5 of his fathers. And these are the names of the men who shall attend you. From Reuben, Eli'zur 6 the son of Shed'eur; from Simeon, Shelu'mi-el the son of 7 Zurishad'dai; from Judah, Nahshon the son of Ammin'adab; 8 from Is'sachar, Nethan'el the son 9 of Zu'ar; from Zeb'ulun, Eli'ab 10 the son of Helon; from the sons of

Joseph, from E'phraim, Elish'ama the son of Ammi'hud, and from Manas'seh, Gama'liel the son of 11 Pedah'zur; from Benjamin, 12 Abi'dan the son of Gideo'ni; from Dan, Ahie'zer the son of Ammi- 13 shad'dai; from Asher, Pa'giel the son of Ochran; from Gad, Eli'- 14 asaph the son of Deu'el; from 15 Naph'tali, Ahi'ra the son of 16 Enan." These were the ones chosen from the congregation, the leaders of their ancestral tribes, the heads of the clans of Israel. 17 Moses and Aaron took these men who have been named, and on the 18 first day of the second month, they assembled the whole congregation together, who registered themselves by families, by fathers' houses, according to the number of names from twenty years old 19 and upward, head by head, as the LORD commanded Moses. So he numbered them in the wilderness of Sinai.
20 The people of Reuben, Israel's first-born, their generations, by their families, by their fathers' houses, according to the number of names, head by head, every

male from twenty years old and upward, all who were able to go forth to war: the number of the 21 tribe of Reuben was forty-six thousand five hundred.
Of the people of Simeon, their 22 generations, by their families, by their fathers' houses, those of them that were numbered, according to the number of names, head by head, every male from twenty years old and upward, all who were able to go forth to war: the number of the tribe of Simeon 23 was fifty-nine thousand three hundred.
Of the people of Gad, their 24 generations, by their families, by their fathers' houses, according to the number of the names, from twenty years old and upward, all who were able to go forth to war: the number of the tribe of Gad 25 was forty-five thousand six hundred and fifty.
Of the people of Judah, their 26 generations, by their families, by their fathers' houses, according to the number of names, from twenty years old and upward, every man able to go forth to war: the 27

1.1-46: Num 26.1-51.

99

number of the tribe of Judah was seventy-four thousand six hundred.

28 Of the people of Is'sachar, their generations, by their families, by their fathers' houses, according to the number of names, from twen- 29 ty years old and upward, every man able to go forth to war: the number of the tribe of Is'sachar was fifty-four thousand four hundred.

30 Of the people of Zeb'ulun, their generations, by their families, by their fathers' houses, according to the number of names, from twen- 31 ty years old and upward, every man able to go forth to war: the number of the tribe of Zeb'ulun was fifty-seven thousand four hundred.

32 Of the people of Joseph, namely, of the people of E'phraim, their generations, by their families, by their fathers' houses, according to the number of names, from twen- 33 ty years old and upward, every man able to go forth to war: the number of the tribe of E'phraim was forty thousand five hundred.

34 Of the people of Manas'seh, their generations, by their fami- lies, by their fathers' houses, according to the number of names, from twenty years old and 35 upward, every man able to go forth to war: the number of the tribe of Manas'seh was thirty-two thousand two hundred.

36 Of the people of Benjamin, their generations, by their families, by their fathers' houses, according to the number of names, from twen- 37 ty years old and upward, every man able to go forth to war: the number of the tribe of Benjamin was thirty-five thousand four hundred.

38 Of the people of Dan, their generations, by their families, by their fathers' houses, according to the number of names, from twen- 39 ty years old and upward, every man able to go forth to war: the number of the tribe of Dan was sixty-two thousand seven hun- dred.

40 Of the people of Asher, their generations, by their families, by their fathers' houses, according to the number of names, from twen- 41 ty years old and upward, every man able to go forth to war: the number of the tribe of Asher was forty-one thousand five hundred.

42 Of the people of Naph'tali, their generations, by their families, by their fathers' houses, according to the number of names, from twen- 43 ty years old and upward, every man able to go forth to war: the number of the tribe of Naph'tali was fifty-three thousand four hundred.

44 These are those who were numbered, whom Moses and Aaron numbered with the help of the leaders of Israel, twelve men, each representing his fathers' 45 house. So the whole number of

the people of Israel, by their fathers' houses, from twenty years old and upward, every man able 46 to go forth to war in Israel— their whole number was six hundred and three thousand five hundred and fifty.

47 But the Levites were not num- bered by their ancestral tribe 48 along with them. For the LORD 49 said to Moses, "Only the tribe of Levi you shall not number, and you shall not take a census of them among the people of Israel; 50 but appoint the Levites over the tabernacle of the testimony, and over all its furnishings, and over all that belongs to it; they are to carry the tabernacle and all its furnishings, and they shall tend it, and shall encamp around the 51 tabernacle. When the tabernacle is to set out, the Levites shall take it down; and when the tabernacle is to be pitched, the Levites shall set it up. And if any one else comes near, he shall be put to 52 death. The people of Israel shall pitch their tents by their com- panies, every man by his own camp and every man by his own 53 standard; but the Levites shall encamp around the tabernacle of the testimony, that there may be no wrath upon the congregation of the people of Israel; and the Levites shall keep charge of the tabernacle of the testimony." 54 Thus did the people of Israel; they did according to all that the LORD commanded Moses.

2 The LORD said to Moses and 2 Aaron, "The people of Israel shall encamp each by his own standard, with the ensigns of their fathers' houses; they shall encamp facing the tent of meeting on every side. 3 Those to encamp on the east side toward the sunrise shall be of the standard of the camp of Judah by their companies, the leader of the people of Judah being Nahshon 4 the son of Ammin'adab, his host as numbered being seventy-four 5 thousand six hundred. Those to encamp next to him shall be the tribe of Is'sachar, the leader of the people of Is'sachar being 6 Nethan'el the son of Zu'ar, his host as numbered being fifty-four 7 thousand four hundred. Then the tribe of Zeb'ulun, the leader of the people of Zeb'ulun being 8 Eli'ab the son of Helon, his host as numbered being fifty-seven 9 thousand four hundred. The whole number of the camp of Judah, by their companies, is a hundred and eighty-six thousand four hundred. They shall set out first on the march.

10 "On the south side shall be the standard of the camp of Reuben by their companies, the leader of the people of Reuben being 11 Eli'zur the son of Shed'eur, his host as numbered being forty-six 12 thousand five hundred. And those to encamp next to him shall

be the tribe of Simeon, the leader of the people of Simeon being Shelu'mi-el the son of Zurishad'- dai, his host as numbered being fifty-nine thousand three hun- dred. Then the tribe of Gad, the leader of the people of Gad being Eli'asaph the son of Reu'el, his host as numbered being forty-five thousand six hundred and fifty. The whole number of the camp of Reuben, by their companies, is a hundred and fifty-one thousand four hundred and fifty. They shall set out second.

"Then the tent of meeting shall set out, with the camp of the Levites in the midst of the camps; as they encamp, so shall they set out, each in position, standard by standard.

"On the west side shall be the standard of the camp of E'phraim by their companies, the leader of the people of E'phraim being Elish'ama the son of Ammi'hud, his host as numbered being forty thousand five hundred. And next to him shall be the tribe of Manas'seh, the leader of the people of Manas'seh being Gama'liel the son of Pedah'zur, his host as numbered being thirty-two thousand two hun- dred. Then the tribe of Ben- jamin, the leader of the people of Benjamin being Abi'dan the son of Gideo'ni, his host as numbered being thirty-five thousand four hundred. The whole number of the camp of E'phraim, by their companies, is a hundred and eight thousand one hundred. They shall set out third on the march.

"On the north side shall be the standard of the camp of Dan by their companies, the leader of the people of Dan being Ahie'zer the son of Ammishad'dai, his host as numbered being sixty-two thousand seven hundred. And those to encamp next to him shall be the tribe of Asher, the leader of the people of Asher being Pa'giel the son of Ochran, his host as numbered being forty-one thousand five hundred. Then the tribe of Naph'tali, the leader of the people of Naph'tali being Ahi'ra the son of Enan, his host as numbered being fifty-three thousand four hundred. The whole number of the camp of Dan is a hundred and fifty-seven thousand six hundred. They shall set out last, standard by standard."

These are the people of Israel as numbered by their fathers' houses; all in the camps who were numbered by their companies were six hundred and three thou- sand five hundred and fifty. But the Levites were not numbered among the people of Israel, as the LORD commanded Moses.

Thus did the people of Israel. According to all that the LORD commanded Moses, so they en- camped by their standards, and so they set out, every one in his family, according to his fathers' house.

Priests and Levites

3 These are the generations of Aaron and Moses at the time when the LORD spoke with Moses 2 on Mount Sinai. These are the names of the sons of Aaron: Nadab the first-born, and Abi'hu, 3 Elea'zar, and Ith'amar; these are the names of the sons of Aaron, the anointed priests, whom he ordained to minister in 4 the priest's office. But Nadab and Abi'hu died before the LORD when they offered unholy fire before the LORD in the wilderness of Sinai; and they had no children. So Elea'zar and Ith'amar served as priests in the lifetime of Aaron their father.

5 And the LORD said to Moses, 6 "Bring the tribe of Levi near, and set them before Aaron the priest, that they may minister to him. 7 They shall perform duties for him and for the whole congregation before the tent of meeting, as they minister at the tabernacle; 8 they shall have charge of all the furnishings of the tent of meeting, and attend to the duties for the people of Israel as they minister at 9 the tabernacle. And you shall give the Levites to Aaron and his sons; they are wholly given to him from among the people of Israel. 10 And you shall appoint Aaron and his sons, and they shall attend to their priesthood; but if any one else comes near, he shall be put to death."

11 And the LORD said to Moses, 12 "Behold, I have taken the Levites from among the people of Israel instead of every first-born that opens the womb among the people of Israel. The Levites 13 shall be mine, for all the first-born are mine; on the day that I slew all the first-born in the land of Egypt, I consecrated for my own all the first-born in Israel, both of man and of beast; they shall be mine: I am the LORD."

14 And the LORD said to Moses in 15 the wilderness of Sinai, "Number

the sons of Levi, by fathers' houses and by families; every male from a month old and 16 upward you shall number." So Moses numbered them according to the word of the LORD, as he was 17 commanded. And these were the sons of Levi by their names: Gershon and Kohath and 18 Merar'i. And these are the names of the sons of Gershon by their families: Libni and Shim'e-i. 19 And the sons of Kohath by their families: Amram, Izhar, Hebron, 20 and Uz'ziel. And the sons of Merar'i by their families: Mahli and Mushi. These are the families of the Levites, by their fathers' houses.

21 Of Gershon were the family of the Libnites and the family of the Shim'e-ites; these were the families of the Gershonites. 22 Their number according to the number of all the males from a month old and upward was[a] seven 23 thousand five hundred. The families of the Gershonites were to encamp behind the tabernacle 24 on the west, with Eli'asaph, son of La'el as head of the fathers' 25 house of the Gershonites. And the charge of the sons of Gershon in the tent of meeting was to be the tabernacle, the tent with its 26 covering, the screen for the door of the tent of meeting, the hangings of the court, the screen for the door of the court which is around the tabernacle and the altar, and its cords; all the service pertaining to these.

27 Of Kohath were the family of the Amramites, and the family of the Iz'harites, and the family of the He'bronites, and the family of the Uzzi'elites; these are the families 28 of the Ko'hathites. According to the number of all the males, from a month old and upward, there were eight thousand six hundred, attending to the duties of the 29 sanctuary. The families of the sons of Kohath were to encamp on the south side of the taber- 30 nacle, with Eliza'phan the son of Uz'ziel as head of the fathers' house of the families of the 31 Ko'hathites. And their charge was to be the ark, the table, the lampstand, the altars, the vessels

of the sanctuary with which the priests minister, and the screen; all the service pertaining to these. And Elea'zar the son of Aaron the 32 priest was to be chief over the leaders of the Levites, and to have oversight of those who had charge of the sanctuary.

Of Merar'i were the family of the 33 Mahlites and the family of the Mushites: these are the families of Merar'i. Their number according 34 to the number of all the males from a month old and upward was six thousand two hundred. And 35 the head of the fathers' house of the families of Merar'i was Zu'riel the son of Ab'ihail; they were to encamp on the north side of the tabernacle. And the appointed 36 charge of the sons of Merar'i was to be the frames of the tabernacle, the bars, the pillars, the bases, and all their accessories; all the service pertaining to these; also the pillars 37 of the court round about, with their bases and pegs and cords.

And those to encamp before the 38 tabernacle on the east, before the tent of meeting toward the sunrise, were Moses and Aaron and his sons, having charge of the rites within the sanctuary, whatever had to be done for the people of Israel; and any one else who came near was to be put to death. All 39 who were numbered of the Levites, whom Moses and Aaron numbered at the commandment of the LORD, by families, all the males from a month old and upward, were twenty-two thousand.

And the LORD said to Moses, 40 "Number all the first-born males of the people of Israel, from a month old and upward, taking their number by names. And you 41 shall take the Levites for me—I am the LORD—instead of all the first-born among the people of Israel, and the cattle of the Levites instead of all the firstlings among the cattle of the people of Israel." So Moses numbered all 42 the first-born among the people of Israel, as the LORD commanded him. And all the first-born males, 43 according to the number of names, from a month old and upward as numbered were twenty-two thousand two hundred and seventy-three.

44 And the LORD said to Moses, 45 "Take the Levites instead of all the first-born among the people of Israel, and the cattle of the Levites instead of their cattle; and 46 the Levites shall be mine: I am the LORD. And for the redemption of the two hundred and seventy-three of the first-born of the people of Israel, over and 47 above the number of the male Levites, you shall take five shekels apiece; reckoning by the shekel of the sanctuary, the shekel of 48 twenty gerahs, you shall take them, and give the money by which the excess number of them 49 is redeemed to Aaron and his sons." So Moses took the redemption money from those 50 who were over and above those redeemed by the Levites; from the first-born of the people of Israel he took the money, one thousand three hundred and sixty-five shekels, reckoned by the 51 shekel of the sanctuary; and Moses gave the redemption money to Aaron and his sons, according to the word of the LORD, as the LORD commanded Moses.

4 The LORD said to Moses and 2 Aaron, "Take a census of the sons of Kohath from among the sons of Levi, by their families and their 3 fathers' houses, from thirty years old up to fifty years old, all who 4 can enter the service, to do the work in the tent of meeting. This is the service of the sons of 5 Kohath in the tent of meeting: the most holy things. When the camp is to set out, Aaron and his sons shall go in and take down the veil 6 of the screen, and cover the ark of the testimony with it; then they shall put on it a covering of goatskin, and spread over that a 7 cloth all of blue, and shall put in its poles. And over the table of the bread of the Presence they shall spread a cloth of blue, and put upon it the plates, the dishes for incense, the bowls, and the flagons for the drink offering; the 8 continual bread also shall be on it; then they shall spread over them a cloth of scarlet, and cover the 9 same with a covering of goatskin, and shall put in its poles. And they shall take a cloth of blue, and cover the lampstand for the light, with its lamps, its snuffers, its trays, and all the vessels for the 10 oil with which it is supplied; and they shall put it with all its uten-

sils in a covering of goatskin and put it upon the carrying frame. 11 And over the golden altar they shall spread a cloth of blue, and cover it with a covering of goat- 12 skin, and shall put in its poles; and they shall take all the vessels of the service which are used in the sanctuary, and put them in a cloth of blue, and cover them with 13 a covering of goatskin, and put them on the carrying frame. And they shall take away the ashes from the altar, and spread a 14 purple cloth over it; and they shall put on it all the utensils of the altar, which are used for the service there, the firepans, the forks, the shovels, and the basins, all the utensils of the altar; and they shall spread upon it a cover- 15 ing of goatskin, and shall put in its poles. And when Aaron and his sons have finished covering the sanctuary and all the furnishings of the sanctuary, as the camp sets out, after that the sons of Kohath shall come to carry these, but they must not touch the holy things, lest they die. These are the things of the tent of meeting which the sons of Kohath are to carry.

16 "And Elea'zar the son of Aaron the priest shall have charge of the oil for the light, the fragrant incense, the continual cereal offering, and the anointing oil, with the oversight of all the tabernacle and all that is in it, of the sanctuary and its vessels."

17 The LORD said to Moses and 18 Aaron, "Let not the tribe of the families of the Ko'hathites be 19 destroyed from among the Levites; but deal thus with them, that they may live and not die when they come near to the most holy things: Aaron and his sons shall go in and appoint them each to his 20 task and to his burden, but they shall not go in to look upon the holy things even for a moment, lest they die."

21 The LORD said to Moses, "Take 22 a census of the sons of Gershon also, by their families and their 23 fathers' houses; from thirty years old up to fifty years old, you shall number them, all who can enter for service, to do the work in the 24 tent of meeting. This is the service of the families of the Gershonites, in serving and bearing 25 burdens: they shall carry the curtains of the tabernacle, and the tent of meeting with its covering, and the covering of goatskin that is on top of it, and the screen for the door of the tent of meeting, 26 and the hangings of the court, and the screen for the entrance of the

gate of the court which is around the tabernacle and the altar, and their cords, and all the equipment for their service; and they shall do all that needs to be done with regard to them. All the service 27 of the sons of the Gershonites shall be at the command of Aaron and his sons, in all that they are to carry, and in all that they have to do; and you shall assign to their charge all that they are to carry. This is the service of the families 28 of the sons of the Gershonites in the tent of meeting, and their work is to be under the oversight of Ith'amar the son of Aaron the priest.

"As for the sons of Merar'i, you 29 shall number them by their families and their fathers' houses; from thirty years old up to fifty 30 years old, you shall number them, every one that can enter the service, to do the work of the tent of meeting. And this is what they 31 are charged to carry, as the whole of their service in the tent of meeting: the frames of the tabernacle, with its bars, pillars, and bases, and the pillars of the 32 court round about with their bases, pegs, and cords, with all their equipment and all their accessories; and you shall assign by name the objects which they are required to carry. This is the 33 service of the families of the sons of Merar'i, the whole of their service in the tent of meeting, under the hand of Ith'amar the son of Aaron the priest."

And Moses and Aaron and the 34 leaders of the congregation numbered the sons of the Ko'hathites, by their families and their fathers' houses, from thirty 35 years old up to fifty years old, every one that could enter the service, for work in the tent of meeting; and their number by 36 families was two thousand seven hundred and fifty. This was 37 the number of the families of the Ko'hathites, all who served in the tent of meeting, whom Moses and Aaron numbered according to the commandment of the LORD by Moses.

The number of the sons of Ger- 38 shon, by their families and their fathers' houses, from thirty years 39 old up to fifty years old, every one that could enter the service for work in the tent of meeting—their 40 number by their families and their fathers' houses was two thousand six hundred and thirty. This was 41 the number of the families of the sons of Gershon, all who served in the tent of meeting, whom Moses and Aaron numbered according to the commandment of the LORD.

The number of the families 42 of the sons of Merar'i, by their families and their fathers' houses, from thirty years old up to fifty 43 years old, every one that could enter the service, for work in the

3.45: Num 3.11–13; 8.18.   4.1–33: Num 1.50–53; 3.5–8, 21–37; 8.19; 18.3–4, 23.
4.34–49: Num 3.15–34.

44 tent of meeting—their number by families was three thousand two 45 hundred. These are those who were numbered of the families of the sons of Merar'i, whom Moses and Aaron numbered according to the commandment of the LORD by Moses.

46 All those who were numbered of the Levites, whom Moses and Aaron and the leaders of Israel numbered, by their families and 47 their fathers' houses, from thirty years old up to fifty years old, every one that could enter to do the work of service and the work 48 of bearing burdens in the tent of meeting, those who were numbered of them were eight thousand five hundred and eighty.

49 According to the commandment of the LORD through Moses they were appointed, each to his task of serving or carrying; thus they were numbered by him, as the LORD commanded Moses.

Various laws

5 The LORD said to Moses, 2 "Command the people of Israel that they put out of the camp every leper, and every one having a discharge, and every one that is unclean through contact with the 3 dead; you shall put out both male and female, putting them outside the camp, that they may not defile their camp, in the midst of which 4 I dwell." And the people of Israel did so, and drove them outside the camp; as the LORD said to Moses, so the people of Israel did.

5 And the LORD said to Moses, 6 "Say to the people of Israel, When a man or woman commits any of the sins that men commit by breaking faith with the LORD, 7 and that person is guilty, he shall confess his sin which he has committed; and he shall make full restitution for his wrong, adding a fifth to it, and giving it to him to 8 whom he did the wrong. But if the man has no kinsman to whom restitution may be made for the wrong, the restitution for wrong shall go to the LORD for the priest, in addition to the ram of atonement with which atonement is 9 made for him. And every offering, all the holy things of the people of Israel, which they bring 10 to the priest, shall be his; and every man's holy things shall be his; whatever any man gives to the priest shall be his."

11 And the LORD said to Moses, 12 "Say to the people of Israel, If any man's wife goes astray and 13 acts unfaithfully against him, if a man lies with her carnally, and it is hidden from the eyes of her husband, and she is undetected though she has defiled herself, and there is no witness against her, since she was not taken in the 14 act; and if the spirit of jealousy comes upon him, and he is jealous of his wife who has defiled herself; or if the spirit of jealousy comes upon him, and he is jealous of his wife, though she has not 15 defiled herself; then the man shall bring his wife to the priest, and bring the offering required of her, a tenth of an ephah of barley meal; he shall pour no oil upon it and put no frankincense on it, for it is a cereal offering of jealousy, a cereal offering of remembrance, bringing iniquity to remembrance.

16 "And the priest shall bring her near, and set her before the LORD; 17 and the priest shall take holy water in an earthen vessel, and take some of the dust that is on the floor of the tabernacle and put 18 it into the water. And the priest shall set the woman before the LORD, and unbind the hair of the woman's head, and place in her hands the cereal offering of remembrance, which is the cereal offering of jealousy. And in his hand the priest shall have the water of bitterness that brings the 19 curse. Then the priest shall make her take an oath, saying, 'If no man has lain with you, and if you have not turned aside to uncleanness, while you were under your husband's authority, be free from this water of bit- 20 terness that brings the curse. But if you have gone astray, though you are under your husband's authority, and if you have defiled yourself, and some man other than your husband has lain with 21 you, then' (let the priest make the woman take the oath of the curse, and say to the woman) 'the LORD make you an execration and an oath among your people, when the LORD makes your thigh fall away 22 and your body swell; may this water that brings the curse pass into your bowels and make your body swell and your thigh fall away.' And the woman shall say, 23 'Amen, Amen.'

"Then the priest shall write these curses in a book, and wash them off into the water of bit- 24 terness; and he shall make the woman drink the water of bitterness that brings the curse, and the water that brings the curse shall enter into her and cause 25 bitter pain. And the priest shall take the cereal offering of jealousy out of the woman's hand, and shall wave the cereal offering before the LORD and bring it to 26 the altar; and the priest shall take a handful of the cereal offering, as its memorial portion, and burn it upon the altar, and afterwards 27 shall make the woman drink the water. And when he has made her drink the water, then, if she has defiled herself and has acted unfaithfully against her husband, the water that brings the curse shall enter into her and cause bitter pain, and her body shall swell, and her thigh shall fall away, and the woman shall become an execration among her 28 people. But if the woman has not defiled herself and is clean, then she shall be free and shall conceive children.

29 "This is the law in cases of jealousy, when a wife, though 30 under her husband's authority, goes astray and defiles herself, or when the spirit of jealousy comes upon a man and he is jealous of his wife; then he shall set the woman before the LORD, and the priest shall execute upon her all 31 this law. The man shall be free from iniquity, but the woman shall bear her iniquity."

Nazirites

And the LORD said to Moses, 6 "Say to the people of Israel, 2 When either a man or a woman makes a special vow, the vow of a Nazirite,[b] to separate himself to the LORD, he shall separate him- 3 self from wine and strong drink; he shall drink no vinegar made from wine or strong drink, and shall not drink any juice of grapes or eat grapes, fresh or dried. All 4 the days of his separation[c] he shall eat nothing that is produced by the grapevine, not even the seeds or the skins.

"All the days of his vow of 5 separation no razor shall come upon his head; until the time is completed for which he separates himself to the LORD, he shall be holy; he shall let the locks of hair of his head grow long.

"All the days that he separates 6 himself to the LORD he shall not go near a dead body. Neither for 7 his father nor for his mother, nor for brother or sister, if they die, shall he make himself unclean; because his separation to God is upon his head. All the days of his 8 separation he is holy to the LORD.

"And if any man dies very sud- 9 denly beside him, and he defiles his consecrated head, then he shall shave his head on the day of his cleansing; on the seventh day he shall shave it. On the eighth 10 day he shall bring two turtledoves or two young pigeons to the priest to the door of the tent of meeting, and the priest shall offer one for a 11 sin offering and the other for a burnt offering, and make atonement for him, because he sinned by reason of the dead body. And he shall consecrate his head that same day, and separate himself to 12 the LORD for the days of his separation, and bring a male lamb a year old for a guilt offering; but the former time shall be void, because his separation was defiled.

"And this is the law for the 13 Nazirite, when the time of his separation has been completed: he shall be brought to the door of

---

b That is *one separated* or *one consecrated*   *c* Or *Naziriteship*
5.2-3: Num 12.14-15.   **5.5-8:** Ex 22.7-15; Lev 6.1-7.   **6.3:** Lk 1.15.   **6.13-21:** Acts 21.24, 26.

14 the tent of meeting, and he shall offer his gift to the LORD, one male lamb a year old without blemish for a burnt offering, and one ewe lamb a year old without blemish as a sin offering, and one ram without blemish as a peace 15 offering, and a basket of unleavened bread, cakes of fine flour mixed with oil, and unleavened wafers spread with oil, and their 16 cereal offering and their drink offerings. And the priest shall present them before the LORD and offer his sin offering and his burnt 17 offering, and he shall offer the ram as a sacrifice of peace offering to the LORD, with the basket of unleavened bread; the priest shall 18 offer also its cereal offering and its drink offering. And the Nazirite shall shave his consecrated head at the door of the tent of meeting, and shall take the hair from his consecrated head and put it on the 19 fire which is under the sacrifice of the peace offering. And the priest shall take the shoulder of the ram, when it is boiled, and one unleavened cake out of the basket, and one unleavened wafer, and shall put them upon the hands of the Nazirite, after he has shaven 20 the hair of his consecration, and the priest shall wave them for a wave offering before the LORD; they are a holy portion for the priest, together with the breast that is waved and the thigh that is offered; and after that the Nazirite may drink wine.
21 "This is the law for the Nazirite who takes a vow. His offering to the LORD shall be according to his vow as a Nazirite, apart from what else he can afford; in accordance with the vow which he takes, so shall he do according to the law for his separation as a Nazirite."
22 The LORD said to Moses, "Say 23 to Aaron and his sons, Thus you shall bless the people of Israel: you shall say to them,

24   The LORD bless you and keep you:
25   The LORD make his face to shine upon you, and be gracious to you:
26   The LORD lift up his countenance upon you, and give you peace.
27 "So shall they put my name upon the people of Israel, and I will bless them."

Transport

7 On the day when Moses had finished setting up the tabernacle, and had anointed and consecrated

it with all its furnishings, and had anointed and consecrated the altar 2 with all its utensils, the leaders of Israel, heads of their fathers' houses, who were over those who were 3 numbered, offered and brought their offerings before the LORD, six covered wagons and twelve oxen, a wagon for every two of the leaders, and for each one an ox; they offered them before the 4 tabernacle. Then the LORD said 5 to Moses, "Accept these from them, that they may be used in doing the service of the tent of meeting, and give them to the Levites, to each man according to 6 his service." So Moses took the wagons and the oxen, and gave 7 them to the Levites. Two wagons and four oxen he gave to the sons of Gershon, according to their 8 service; and four wagons and eight oxen he gave to the sons of Merar'i, according to their service, under the direction of Ith'amar the son of Aaron the 9 priest. But to the sons of Kohath he gave none, because they were charged with the care of the holy things which had to be carried on 10 the shoulder. And the leaders offered offerings for the dedication of the altar on the day it was anointed; and the leaders offered their offering before the altar. 11 And the LORD said to Moses, "They shall offer their offerings, one leader each day, for the dedication of the altar."
12 He who offered his offering the first day was Nahshon the son of Ammin'adab, of the tribe of 13 Judah; and his offering was one silver plate whose weight was a hundred and thirty shekels, one silver basin of seventy shekels, according to the shekel of the sanctuary, both of them full of 14 fine flour mixed with oil for a cereal offering; one golden dish of 15 ten shekels, full of incense; one young bull, one ram, one male lamb a year old, for a burnt 16 offering; one male goat for a sin 17 offering; and for the sacrifice of peace offerings, two oxen, five rams, five male goats, and five male lambs a year old. This was the offering of Nahshon the son of Ammin'adab.
18 On the second day Nethan'el the son of Zu'ar, the leader of Is'- 19 sachar, made an offering; he offered for his offering one silver plate, whose weight was a hundred and thirty shekels, one silver basin of seventy shekels, according to the shekel of the sanc-

tuary, both of them full of fine flour mixed with oil for a cereal offering; one golden dish of ten 20 shekels, full of incense; one young 21 bull, one ram, one male lamb a year old, for a burnt offering; one 22 male goat for a sin offering; and 23 for the sacrifice of peace offerings, two oxen, five rams, five male goats, and five male lambs a year old. This was the offering of Nethan'el the son of Zu'ar.
On the third day Eli'ab the son 24 of Helon, the leader of the men of Zeb'ulun: his offering was one 25 silver plate, whose weight was a hundred and thirty shekels, one silver basin of seventy shekels, according to the shekel of the sanctuary, both of them full of fine flour mixed with oil for a cereal offering; one golden dish of 26 ten shekels, full of incense; one 27 young bull, one ram, one male lamb a year old, for a burnt offering; one male goat for a sin 28 offering; and for the sacrifice of 29 peace offerings, two oxen, five rams, five male goats, and five male lambs a year old. This was the offering of Eli'ab the son of Helon.
On the fourth day Eli'zur the son 30 of Shed'eur, the leader of the men of Reuben: his offering was one 31 silver plate whose weight was a hundred and thirty shekels, one silver basin of seventy shekels, according to the shekel of the sanctuary, both of them full of fine flour mixed with oil for a cereal offering; one golden dish of 32 ten shekels, full of incense; one 33 young bull, one ram, one male lamb a year old, for a burnt offering; one male goat for a sin 34 offering; and for the sacrifice of 35 peace offerings, two oxen, five rams, five male goats, and five male lambs a year old. This was the offering of Eli'zur the son of Shed'eur.
On the fifth day Shelu'mi-el the 39 son of Zurishad'dai, the leader of the men of Simeon: his offering 37 was one silver plate, whose weight was a hundred and thirty shekels, one silver basin of seventy shekels, according to the shekel of the sanctuary, both of them full of fine flour mixed with oil for a cereal offering; one golden dish of 38 ten shekels, full of incense; one 39 young bull, one ram, one male lamb a year old, for a burnt offering; one male goat for a sin 40 offering; and for the sacrifice of 41 peace offerings, two oxen, five rams, five male goats, and five male lambs a year old. This was

the offering of Shelu'mi-el the son of Zurishad'dai.

42 On the sixth day Eli'asaph the son of Deu'el, the leader of the
43 men of Gad: his offering was one silver plate, whose weight was a hundred and thirty shekels, one silver basin of seventy shekels, according to the shekel of the sanctuary, both of them full of
44 fine flour mixed with oil for a cereal offering; one golden dish of
45 ten shekels, full of incense; one young bull, one ram, one male lamb a year old, for a burnt
46 offering; one male goat for a sin
47 offering; and for the sacrifice of peace offerings, two oxen, five rams, five male goats, and five male lambs a year old. This was the offering of Eli'asaph the son of Deu'el.

48 On the seventh day Elish'ama the son of Ammi'hud, the leader
49 of the men of E'phraim: his offering was one silver plate, whose weight was a hundred and thirty shekels, one silver basin of seventy shekels, according to the shekel of the sanctuary, both of
50 them full of fine flour mixed with oil for a cereal offering; one golden dish of ten shekels, full of
51 incense; one young bull, one ram, one male lamb a year old, for a
52 burnt offering; one male goat for a
53 sin offering; and for the sacrifice of peace offerings, two oxen, five rams, five male goats, and five male lambs a year old. This was the offering of Elish'ama the son of Ammi'hud.

54 On the eighth day Gama'liel the son of Pedah'zur, the leader of the
55 men of Manas'seh: his offering was one silver plate, whose weight was a hundred and thirty shekels, one silver basin of seventy shekels, according to the shekel of the sanctuary, both of them full of
56 fine flour mixed with oil for a cereal offering; one golden dish of
57 ten shekels, full of incense; one young bull, one ram, one male lamb a year old, for a burnt
58 offering; one male goat for a sin
59 offering; and for the sacrifice of peace offerings, two oxen, five rams, five male goats, and five male lambs a year old. This was the offering of Gama'liel the son of Pedah'zur.

60 On the ninth day Abi'dan the son of Gideo'ni, the leader of the
61 men of Benjamin: his offering was one silver plate, whose weight was a hundred and thirty shekels, one silver basin of seventy shekels, according to the shekel of the sanctuary, both of them full of
62 fine flour mixed with oil for a cereal offering; one golden dish of

63 ten shekels, full of incense; one young bull, one ram, one male lamb a year old, for a burnt
64 offering; one male goat for a sin
65 offering; and for the sacrifice of peace offerings, two oxen, and five rams, five male goats, and five male lambs a year old. This was the offering of Abi'dan the son of Gideo'ni.

66 On the tenth day Ahie'zer the son of Ammishad'dai, the leader
67 of the men of Dan: his offering was one silver plate, whose weight was a hundred and thirty shekels, one silver basin of seventy shekels, according to the shekel of the sanctuary, both of them full of
68 fine flour mixed with oil for a cereal offering; one golden dish of
69 ten shekels, full of incense; one young bull, one ram, one male lamb a year old, for a burnt
70 offering; one male goat for a sin
71 offering; and for the sacrifice of peace offerings, two oxen, five rams, five male goats, and five male lambs a year old. This was the offering of Ahie'zer the son of Ammishad'dai.

72 On the eleventh day Pa'giel the son of Ochran, the leader of the
73 men of Asher: his offering was one silver plate, whose weight was a hundred and thirty shekels, one silver basin of seventy shekels, according to the shekel of the sanctuary, both of them full of
74 fine flour mixed with oil for a cereal offering; one golden dish of
75 ten shekels, full of incense; one young bull, one ram, one male lamb a year old, for a burnt
76 offering; one male goat for a sin
77 offering; and for the sacrifice of peace offerings, two oxen, five rams, five male goats, and five male lambs a year old. This was the offering of Pa'giel the son of Ochran.

78 On the twelfth day Ahi'ra the son of Enan, the leader of the men
79 of Naph'tali: his offering was one silver plate, whose weight was a

hundred and thirty shekels, one silver basin of seventy shekels, according to the shekel of the sanctuary, both of them full of fine flour mixed with oil for a
80 cereal offering; one golden dish of
81 ten shekels, full of incense; one young bull, one ram, one male lamb a year old, for a burnt
82 offering; one male goat for a sin
83 offering; and for the sacrifice of peace offerings, two oxen, five rams, five male goats, and five male lambs a year old. This was the offering of Ahi'ra the son of Enan.

Dedication

84 This was the dedication offering for the altar, on the day when it was anointed, from the leaders of Israel: twelve silver plates, twelve
85 silver basins, twelve golden dishes, each silver plate weighing a hundred and thirty shekels and each basin seventy, all the silver of the vessels two thousand four hundred shekels according to the
86 shekel of the sanctuary, the twelve golden dishes, full of incense, weighing ten shekels apiece according to the shekel of the sanctuary, all the gold of the dishes being a hundred and twenty
87 shekels; all the cattle for the burnt offering twelve bulls, twelve rams, twelve male lambs a year old, with their cereal offering; and twelve
88 male goats for a sin offering; and all the cattle for the sacrifice of peace offerings twenty-four bulls, the rams sixty, the male goats sixty, the male lambs a year old sixty. This was the dedication offering for the altar, after it was anointed.
89 And when Moses went into the tent of meeting to speak with the LORD, he heard the voice speaking to him from above the mercy seat that was upon the ark of the testimony, from between the two cherubim; and it spoke to him.

Service of priests and Levites

8 Now the LORD said to Moses,
2 "Say to Aaron, When you set up the lamps, the seven lamps shall give light in front of the lamp-stand." And Aaron did so; he set
3 up its lamps to give light in front of the lampstand, as the LORD commanded Moses. And this was
4 the workmanship of the lamp-stand, hammered work of gold; from its base to its flowers, it was hammered work; according to the pattern which the LORD had shown Moses, so he made the lampstand.

Num 8, 2

The Levites

5 And the LORD said to Moses,
6 "Take the Levites from among
the people of Israel, and cleanse
7 them. And thus you shall do to
them, to cleanse them: sprinkle
the water of expiation upon them,
and let them go with a razor over
all their body, and wash their
clothes and cleanse themselves.
8 Then let them take a young bull
and its cereal offering of fine flour
mixed with oil, and you shall take
another young bull for a sin offer-
9 ing. And you shall present the
Levites before the tent of meeting, and assemble the whole congregation of the people of Israel.
10 When you present the Levites
before the LORD, the people of
Israel shall lay their hands upon
11 the Levites, and Aaron shall offer
the Levites before the LORD as a
wave offering from the people of
Israel, that it may be theirs to do
12 the service of the LORD. Then the
Levites shall lay their hands upon
the heads of the bulls; and you
shall offer the one for a sin
offering and the other for a burnt
offering to the LORD, to make
13 atonement for the Levites. And
you shall cause the Levites to
attend Aaron and his sons, and
shall offer them as a wave offering
to the LORD.

Their service

14 "Thus you shall separate the
Levites from among the people of
Israel, and the Levites shall be
15 mine. And after that the Levites
shall go in to do service at the
tent of meeting, when you have
cleansed them and offered them
16 as a wave offering. For they are
wholly given to me from among
the people of Israel; instead of all
that open the womb, the first-
born of all the people of Israel, I
17 have taken them for myself. For
all the first-born among the
people of Israel are mine, both of
man and of beast; on the day that
I slew all the first-born in the land
of Egypt I consecrated them for
18 myself, and I have taken the
Levites instead of all the first-
born among the people of Israel.

19 And I have given the Levites as a
gift to Aaron and his sons from
among the people of Israel, to do
the service for the people of Israel
at the tent of meeting, and to
make atonement for the people of
Israel, that there may be no
plague among the people of Israel
in case the people of Israel should
come near the sanctuary."

Their consecration

20 Thus did Moses and Aaron and
all the congregation of the people
of Israel to the Levites; according
to all that the LORD commanded
Moses concerning the Levites, the
21 people of Israel did to them. And
the Levites purified themselves
from sin, and washed their
clothes; and Aaron offered them
as a wave offering before the
LORD, and Aaron made atonement for them to cleanse them.
22 And after that the Levites went in
to do their service in the tent of
meeting in attendance upon
Aaron and his sons; as the LORD
had commanded Moses concerning the Levites, so they did to
them.

Period of service

23 And the LORD said to Moses,
24 "This is what pertains to the
Levites: from twenty-five years
old and upward they shall go in to
perform the work in the service of
25 the tent of meeting; and from the
age of fifty years they shall
withdraw from the work of the
26 service and serve no more, but
minister to their brethren in the
tent of meeting, to keep the
charge, and they shall do no
service. Thus shall you do to
the Levites in assigning their
duties."

Keeping the passover

9 And the LORD spoke to Moses in
the wilderness of Sinai, in the first
month of the second year after
they had come out of the land of
2 Egypt, saying, "Let the people of
Israel keep the passover at its
3 appointed time. On the fourteenth day of this month, in the

evening, you shall keep it at its
appointed time; according to all
its statutes and all its ordinances
you shall keep it." So Moses told
4 the people of Israel that they
should keep the passover. And
5 they kept the passover in the first
month, on the fourteenth day of
the month, in the evening, in the
wilderness of Sinai; according to
all that the LORD commanded
Moses, so the people of Israel
did. And there were certain men
6 who were unclean through touching the dead body of a man, so
that they could not keep the passover on that day; and they came
before Moses and Aaron on that
day; and those men said to
7 him, "We are unclean through
touching the dead body of a man;
why are we kept from offering the
LORD's offering at its appointed
time among the people of
Israel?" And Moses said to them,
8 "Wait, that I may hear what the
LORD will command concerning
you."

Special cases

The LORD said to Moses, "Say
9 to the people of Israel, If any man
10 of you or of your descendants is
unclean through touching a dead
body, or is afar off on a journey,
he shall still keep the passover to
the LORD. In the second month
11 on the fourteenth day in the
evening they shall keep it; they
shall eat it with unleavened bread
and bitter herbs. They shall leave
12 none of it until the morning, nor
break a bone of it; according to all
the statute for the passover they
shall keep it. But the man who is
13 clean and is not on a journey, yet
refrains from keeping the passover, that person shall be cut off
from his people, because he did
not offer the LORD's offering at its
appointed time; that man shall
bear his sin. And if a stranger
14 sojourns among you, and will
keep the passover to the LORD,
according to the statute of the
passover and according to its ordinance, so shall he do; you shall
have one statute, both for the
sojourner and for the native."

LEAVING SINAI

15 ON the day that the tabernacle was set up,
the cloud covered the tabernacle, the
tent of the testimony; and at evening it was
over the tabernacle like the appearance of fire
16 until morning. So it was continually; the
cloud covered it by day,[d] and the appearance
17 of fire by night. And whenever the cloud
was taken up from over the tent, after that

the people of Israel set out; and in the place
where the cloud settled down, there the
people of Israel encamped. At the command
18 of the LORD the people of Israel set out,
and at the command of the LORD they
encamped; as long as the cloud rested over
the tabernacle, they remained in camp. Even
19 when the cloud continued over the taber-

---

[d] Gk Syr Vg: Heb lacks *by day*
8.6-26: Num 3.5-13.   **8.18**: Num 3.11-13, 45.
9.1-5: Ex 12.1-14, 21-28.   **9.12**: Ex 12.46; Jn 19.36.   **9.15-23**: Ex 40.36-38.

nacle many days, the people of Israel kept the charge of the LORD, and did not set out. 20 Sometimes the cloud was a few days over the tabernacle, and according to the command of the LORD they remained in camp; then according to the command of the LORD they 21 set out. And sometimes the cloud remained from evening until morning; and when the cloud was taken up in the morning, they set out, or if it continued for a day and a night, when the cloud was taken up they set out. 22 Whether it was two days, or a month, or a longer time, that the cloud continued over the tabernacle, abiding there, the people of Israel remained in camp and did not set out; 23 but when it was taken up they set out. At the command of the LORD they encamped, and at the command of the LORD they set out; they kept the charge of the LORD, at the command of the LORD by Moses.

10 The LORD said to Moses, "Make two silver 2 trumpets; of hammered work you shall make them; and you shall use them for summoning the congregation, and for breaking camp. 3 And when both are blown, all the congregation shall gather themselves to you at the 4 entrance of the tent of meeting. But if they blow only one, then the leaders, the heads of the tribes of Israel, shall gather themselves to 5 you. When you blow an alarm, the camps 6 that are on the east side shall set out. And when you blow an alarm the second time, the camps that are on the south side shall set out. An alarm is to be blown whenever they 7 are to set out. But when the assembly is to be gathered together, you shall blow, but you 8 shall not sound an alarm. And the sons of Aaron, the priests, shall blow the trumpets. The trumpets shall be to you for a perpetual 9 statute throughout your generations. And when you go to war in your land against the adversary who oppresses you, then you shall sound an alarm with the trumpets, that you may be remembered before the LORD your God, and you shall be saved from your 10 enemies. On the day of your gladness also, and at your appointed feasts, and at the beginnings of your months, you shall blow the trumpets over your burnt offerings and over the sacrifices of your peace offerings;

they shall serve you for remembrance before your God: I am the LORD your God."

In the second year, in the second month, on 11 the twentieth day of the month, the cloud was taken up from over the tabernacle of the testimony, and the people of Israel set out by 12 stages from the wilderness of Sinai; and the cloud settled down in the wilderness of Paran. They set out for the first time at the 13 command of the LORD by Moses.

Order of the march

The standard of the camp of the men of 14 Judah set out first by their companies; and over their host was Nahshon the son of Ammin'adab. And over the host of the tribe of 15 the men of Is'sachar was Nethan'el the son of Zu'ar. And over the host of the tribe of the 16 men of Zeb'ulun was Eli'ab the son of Helon.

And when the tabernacle was taken down, 17 the sons of Gershon and the sons of Merar'i, who carried the tabernacle, set out. And the 18 standard of the camp of Reuben set out by their companies; and over their host was Eli'zur the son of Shed'eur. And over the 19 host of the tribe of the men of Simeon was Shelu'mi-el the son of Zurishad'dai. And 20 over the host of the tribe of the men of Gad was Eli'asaph the son of Deu'el.

Then the Ko'hathites set out, carrying the 21 holy things, and the tabernacle was set up before their arrival. And the standard of the 22 camp of the men of E'phraim set out by their companies; and over their host was Elish'-ama the son of Ammi'hud. And over the host 23 of the tribe of the men of Manas'seh was Gama'liel the son of Pedah'zur. And over 24 the host of the tribe of the men of Benjamin was Abi'dan the son of Gideo'ni.

Then the standard of the camp of the men 25 of Dan, acting as the rear guard of all the camps, set out by their companies; and over their host was Ahie'zer the son of Ammi-shad'dai. And over the host of the tribe of 26 the men of Asher was Pa'giel the son of Ochran. And over the host of the tribe of the 27 men of Naph'tali was Ahi'ra the son of Enan. This was the order of march of the 28 people of Israel according to their hosts, when they set out.

And Moses said to Hobab the son of Reu'el 29 the Mid'ianite, Moses' father-in-law, "We are setting out for the place of which the LORD said, 'I will give it to you'; come with us, and we will do you good; for the LORD has promised good to Israel." But he said to 30 him, "I will not go; I will depart to my own land and to my kindred." And he said, "Do 31 not leave us, I pray you, for you know how we are to encamp in the wilderness, and you will serve as eyes for us. And if you go with 32 us, whatever good the LORD will do to us, the same will we do to you."

33 So they set out from the mount of the LORD three days' journey; and the ark of the covenant of the LORD went before them three days' journey, to seek out a resting place for 34 them. And the cloud of the LORD was over them by day, whenever they set out from the camp.

35 And whenever the ark set out, Moses said, "Arise, O LORD, and let thy enemies be scattered; and let them that hate thee flee 36 before thee." And when it rested, he said, "Return, O LORD, to the ten thousand thousands of Israel."

Discontent

11 And the people complained in the hearing of the LORD about their misfortunes; and when the LORD heard it, his anger was kindled, and the fire of the LORD burned among them, and consumed some outlying 2 parts of the camp. Then the people cried to Moses; and Moses prayed to the LORD, and 3 the fire abated. So the name of that place was called Tab'erah,[e] because the fire of the LORD burned among them.

4 Now the rabble that was among them had a strong craving; and the people of Israel also wept again, and said, "O that we had meat to 5 eat! We remember the fish we ate in Egypt for nothing, the cucumbers, the melons, the

6 leeks, the onions, and the garlic; but now our strength is dried up, and there is nothing at all but this manna to look at."

7 Now the manna was like coriander seed, 8 and its appearance like that of bdellium. The people went about and gathered it, and ground it in mills or beat it in mortars, and boiled it in pots, and made cakes of it; and the taste of it was like the taste of cakes 9 baked with oil. When the dew fell upon the camp in the night, the manna fell with it.

10 Moses heard the people weeping throughout their families, every man at the door of his tent; and the anger of the LORD blazed 11 hotly, and Moses was displeased. Moses said to the LORD, "Why hast thou dealt ill with

thy servant? And why have I not found favour in thy sight, that thou dost lay the burden of all this people upon me? Did I 12 conceive all this people? Did I bring them forth, that thou shouldst say to me, 'Carry them in your bosom, as a nurse carries the sucking child, to the land which thou didst swear to give their fathers?' Where am I to 13 get meat to give to all this people? For they weep before me and say, 'Give us meat, that we may eat.' I am not able to carry all this 14 people alone, the burden is too heavy for me. If thou wilt deal thus with me, kill me at 15 once, if I find favour in thy sight, that I may not see my wretchedness."

And the LORD said to Moses, "Gather for 16 me seventy men of the elders of Israel, whom you know to be the elders of the people and officers over them; and bring them to the tent of meeting, and let them take their stand there with you. And I will come down and 17 talk with you there; and I will take some of the spirit which is upon you and put it upon them; and they shall bear the burden of the people with you, that you may not bear it yourself alone. And say to the people, 18 'Consecrate yourselves for tomorrow, and you shall eat meat; for you have wept in the hearing of the LORD, saying, "Who will give us meat to eat? For it was well with us in Egypt." Therefore the LORD will give you meat, and you shall eat. You shall not eat 19 one day, or two days, or five days, or ten days, or twenty days, but a whole month, 20 until it comes out at your nostrils and becomes loathsome to you, because you have rejected the LORD who is among you, and have wept before him, saying, "Why did we come forth out of Egypt?"'" But Moses 21 said, "The people among whom I am number six hundred thousand on foot; and thou hast said, 'I will give them meat, that they may eat a whole month!' Shall flocks 22 and herds be slaughtered for them, to suffice them? Or shall all the fish of the sea be gathered together for them, to suffice them?" And the LORD said to Moses, "Is 23 the LORD's hand shortened? Now you shall see whether my word will come true for you or not."

So Moses went out and told the people the 24 words of the LORD; and he gathered seventy men of the elders of the people, and placed them round about the tent. Then the LORD 25 came down in the cloud and spoke to him, and took some of the spirit that was upon him and put it upon the seventy elders; and when the spirit rested upon them, they prophesied. But they did so no more.

e That is Burning
10.35: Ps 68.1–2.   11.4: 1 Cor 10.6.

Now two men remained in the camp, one named Eldad, and the other named Medad, and the spirit rested upon them; they were among those registered, but they had not gone out to the tent, and so they prophesied in the camp. And a young man ran and told Moses, "Eldad and Medad are prophesying in the camp." And Joshua the son of Nun, the minister of Moses, one of his chosen men, said, "My lord Moses, forbid them." But Moses said to him, "Are you jealous for my sake? Would that all the LORD's people were prophets, that the LORD would put his spirit upon them!" And Moses and the elders of Israel returned to the camp.

Quails from the sea

And there went forth a wind from the LORD, and it brought quails from the sea, and let them fall beside the camp, about a day's journey on this side and a day's journey on the other side, round about the camp, and about two cubits above the face of the earth. And the people rose all that day, and all night, and all the next day, and gathered the quails; he who gathered least gathered ten homers; and they spread them out for themselves all around the camp. While the meat was yet between their teeth, before it was consumed, the anger of the LORD was kindled against the people, and the LORD smote the people with a very great plague. Therefore the name of that place was called Kib'roth-hatta'avah,ᶠ because there they buried the people who had the craving. From Kib'roth-hatta'avah the people journeyed to Haze'roth; and they remained at Haze'roth.

Miriam and Aaron

2 Miriam and Aaron spoke against Moses because of the Cushite woman whom he had married, for he had married a Cushite woman; and they said, "Has the LORD indeed spoken only through Moses? Has he not spoken through us also?" And the LORD heard it. Now the man Moses was very meek, more than all men that were on the face of the earth. And suddenly the LORD said to Moses and to Aaron and Miriam, "Come out, you three, to the tent of meeting." And the three of them came out. And the LORD came down in a pillar of cloud, and stood at the door of the tent, and called Aaron and Miriam; and they both came forward. And he said, "Hear my words: If there is a prophet among you, I the

LORD make myself known to him in a vision, I speak with him in a dream. Not so with my 7 servant Moses; he is entrusted with all my house. With him I speak mouth to mouth, 8 clearly, and not in dark speech; and he beholds the form of the LORD. Why then were you not afraid to speak against my servant Moses?"

And the anger of the LORD was kindled 9 against them, and he departed; and when the 10 cloud removed from over the tent, behold, Miriam was leprous, as white as snow. And Aaron turned towards Miriam, and behold, she was leprous. And Aaron said to Moses, 11 "Oh, my lord, do notᵍ punish us because we have done foolishly and have sinned. Let her 12 not be as one dead, of whom the flesh is half consumed when he comes out of his mother's womb." And Moses cried to the LORD, 13 "Heal her, O God, I beseech thee." But the 14 LORD said to Moses, "If her father had but spit in her face, should she not be shamed seven days? Let her be shut up outside the camp seven days, and after that she may be brought in again." So Miriam was shut up 15 outside the camp seven days; and the people did not set out on the march till Miriam was brought in again. After that the people set 16 out from Haze'roth, and encamped in the wilderness of Paran.

Spies sent out

The LORD said to Moses, "Send men to spy 13 out the land of Canaan, which I give to the 2 people of Israel; from each tribe of their fathers shall you send a man, every one a leader among them." So Moses sent them 3 from the wilderness of Paran, according to the command of the LORD, all of them men who were heads of the people of Israel. And 4 these were their names: From the tribe of Reuben, Sham'mu-a the son of Zaccur; from 5 the tribe of Simeon, Shaphat the son of Hori; from the tribe of Judah, Caleb the son of 6 Jephun'neh; from the tribe of Is'sachar, Igal 7 the son of Joseph; from the tribe of 8 E'phraim, Hoshe'a the son of Nun; from the 9 tribe of Benjamin, Palti the son of Raphu; from the tribe of Zeb'ulun, Gad'diel the son 10 of Sodi; from the tribe of Joseph (that is from 11 the tribe of Manas'seh), Gaddi the son of Susi; from the tribe of Dan, Am'miel the son 12 of Gemal'li; from the tribe of Asher, Sethur 13 the son of Michael; from the tribe of 14 Naph'tali, Nahbi the son of Vophsi; from the 15 tribe of Gad, Geu'el the son of Machi. These were the names of the men whom 16

Moses sent to spy out the land. And Moses called Hoshe′a the son of Nun Joshua.

17 Moses sent them to spy out the land of Canaan, and said to them, "Go up into the Negeb yonder, and go up into the hill 18 country, and see what the land is, and whether the people who dwell in it are strong 19 or weak, whether they are few or many, and whether the land that they dwell in is good or bad, and whether the cities that they dwell in 20 are camps or strongholds, and whether the land is rich or poor, and whether there is wood in it or not. Be of good courage, and bring some of the fruit of the land." Now the time was the season of the first ripe grapes. 21 So they went up and spied out the land from the wilderness of Zin to Rehob, near 22 the entrance of Hamath. They went up into the Negeb, and came to Hebron; and Ahi′man, Sheshai, and Talmai, the descendants of Anak, were there. (Hebron was built seven years before Zo′an in Egypt.) 23 And they came to the Valley of Eshcol, and cut down from there a branch with a single cluster of grapes, and they carried it on a pole between two of them; they brought also some 24 pomegranates and figs. That place was called the Valley of Eshcol,[h] because of the cluster which the men of Israel cut down from there.

25 At the end of forty days they returned from 26 spying out the land. And they came to Moses and Aaron and to all the congregation of the people of Israel in the wilderness of Paran, at Kadesh; they brought back word to them and to all the congregation, and showed 27 them the fruit of the land. And they told him, "We came to the land to which you sent us; it flows with milk and honey, and this is 28 its fruit. Yet the people who dwell in the land are strong, and the cities are fortified and very large; and besides, we saw the 29 descendants of Anak there. The Amal′ekites dwell in the land of the Negeb; the Hittites, the Jeb′usites, and the Amorites dwell in the hill country; and the Canaanites dwell by the sea, and along the Jordan."

30 But Caleb quieted the people before Moses, and said, "Let us go up at once, and occupy it; for we are well able to overcome it." 31 Then the men who had gone up with him said, "We are not able to go up against the 32 people; for they are stronger than we." So they brought to the people of Israel an evil report of the land which they had spied out, saying, "The land, through which we have gone, to spy it out, is a land that devours its inhabitants; and all the people that we saw in 33 it are men of great stature. And there we saw

the Nephilim (the sons of Anak, who come from the Nephilim); and we seemed to ourselves like grasshoppers, and so we seemed to them."

Murmurings

Then all the congregation raised a loud cry; 1 and the people wept that night. And all the 2 people of Israel murmured against Moses and Aaron; the whole congregation said to them, "Would that we had died in the land of Egypt! Or would that we had died in this wilderness! Why does the LORD bring us into 3 this land, to fall by the sword? Our wives and our little ones will become a prey; would it not be better for us to go back to Egypt?" And they said to one another, "Let us 4 choose a captain, and go back to Egypt." Then Moses and Aaron fell on their faces 5 before all the assembly of the congregation of the people of Israel. And Joshua the son of 6 Nun and Caleb the son of Jephun′neh, who were among those who had spied out the land, rent their clothes, and said to all the 7 congregation of the people of Israel, "The land, which we passed through to spy it out, is an exceedingly good land. If the LORD 8 delights in us, he will bring us into this land and give it to us, a land which flows with milk and honey. Only, do not rebel against 9 the LORD; and do not fear the people of the land, for they are bread for us; their protection is removed from them, and the LORD is with us; do not fear them." But all the 10 congregation said to stone them with stones. Then the glory of the LORD appeared at the tent of meeting to all the people of Israel. And the LORD said to Moses, "How long will 11 this people despise me? And how long will they not believe in me, in spite of all the signs which I have wrought among them? I will 12 strike them with the pestilence and disinherit them, and I will make of you a nation greater and mightier than they."

Moses' intercession

But Moses said to the LORD, "Then the 13 Egyptians will hear of it, for thou didst bring up this people in thy might from among them, and they will tell the inhabitants of this land. They have heard that thou, O LORD, 14 art in the midst of this people; for thou, O LORD, art seen face to face, and thy cloud stands over them and thou goest before them, in a pillar of cloud by day and in a pillar of fire by night. Now if thou dost kill 15 this people as one man, then the nations who

[h] That is Cluster
13.33: Gen 6.4.   14.3: Acts 7.39.   14.11-25: Ex 32.9-14, 31-35.

6 have heard thy fame will say, 'Because the LORD was not able to bring this people into the land which he swore to give to them, therefore he has slain them in the wil-
7 derness.' And now, I pray thee, let the power of the LORD be great as thou hast
8 promised, saying, 'The LORD is slow to anger, and abounding in steadfast love, forgiving iniquity and transgression, but he will by no means clear the guilty, visiting the iniquity of fathers upon children, upon the third and upon the fourth generation.'
9 Pardon the iniquity of this people, I pray thee, according to the greatness of thy steadfast love, and according as thou hast forgiven this people, from Egypt even until now."

God's judgment

0 Then the LORD said, "I have pardoned,
1 according to your word; but truly, as I live, and as all the earth shall be filled with the
2 glory of the LORD, none of the men who have seen my glory and my signs which I wrought in Egypt and in the wilderness, and yet have put me to the proof these ten times and have
3 not hearkened to my voice, shall see the land which I swore to give to their fathers; and none of those who despised me shall see it.
4 But my servant Caleb, because he has a different spirit and has followed me fully, I will bring into the land into which he went,
5 and his descendants shall possess it. Now, since the Amal′ekites and the Canaanites dwell in the valleys, turn tomorrow and set out for the wilderness by the way to the Red Sea."
6 And the LORD said to Moses and to Aaron,
7 "How long shall this wicked congregation murmur against me? I have heard the murmurings of the people of Israel, which
8 they murmur against me. Say to them, 'As I live', says the LORD, 'What you have said in
9 my hearing I will do to you: your dead bodies shall fall in this wilderness; and of all your number, numbered from twenty years old and upward, who have murmured against
0 me, not one shall come into the land where I swore that I would make you dwell, except Caleb the son of Jephun′neh and Joshua the
1 son of Nun. But your little ones, who you

said would become a prey, I will bring in, and they shall know the land which you have despised. But as for you, your dead bodies 32 shall fall in this wilderness. And your child- 33 ren shall be shepherds in the wilderness forty years, and shall suffer for your faithlessness, until the last of your dead bodies lies in the wilderness. According to the number of the 34 days in which you spied out the land, forty days, for every day a year, you shall bear your iniquity, forty years, and you shall know my displeasure.' I, the LORD, have spoken; 35 surely this will I do to all this wicked congregation that are gathered together against me: in this wilderness they shall come to a full end, and there they shall die."

And the men whom Moses sent to spy out 36 the land, and who returned and made all the congregation to murmur against him by bringing up an evil report against the land, the men who brought up an evil report of the 37 land, died by plague before the LORD. But 38 Joshua the son of Nun and Caleb the son of Jephun′neh remained alive, of those men who went to spy out the land.

Self-willed people

And Moses told these words to all the 39 people of Israel, and the people mourned greatly. And they rose early in the morning, 40 and went up to the heights of the hill country, saying, "See, we are here, we will go up to the place which the LORD has promised; for we have sinned." But Moses 41 said, "Why now are you transgressing the command of the LORD, for that will not succeed? Do not go up lest you be struck 42 down before your enemies, for the LORD is not among you. For there the Amal′ekites 43 and the Canaanites are before you, and you shall fall by the sword; because you have turned back from following the LORD, the LORD will not be with you." But they 44 presumed to go up to the heights of the hill country, although neither the ark of the covenant of the LORD, nor Moses, departed out of the camp. Then the Amal′ekites and 45 the Canaanites who dwelt in that hill country came down, and defeated them and pursued them, even to Hormah.

Supplementary laws

5 THE LORD said to Moses, "Say
2 to the people of Israel, When you come into the land you are to
3 inhabit, which I give you, and you offer to the LORD from the herd or from the flock an offering by fire or a burnt offering, or a sacrifice, to fulfil a vow or as a freewill offering or at your appointed feasts, to make a pleasing odour to
4 the LORD, then he who brings his offering shall offer to the LORD a cereal offering of a tenth of an ephah of fine flour, mixed with a
5 fourth of a hin of oil; and wine for the drink offering, a fourth of a hin, you shall prepare with the burnt offering, or for the sacrifice, for each lamb. Or for a ram, you 6 shall prepare for a cereal offering two tenths of an ephah of fine flour mixed with a third of a hin of oil; and for the drink offering 7 you shall offer a third of a hin of wine, a pleasing odour to the LORD. And when you prepare a 8 bull for a burnt offering, or for a sacrifice, to fulfil a vow, or for

14.22-23: Heb 3.18.   14.29: Heb 3.17.   14.33: Acts 7.36.

9 peace offerings to the LORD, then one shall offer with the bull a cereal offering of three tenths of an ephah of fine flour, mixed with 10 half a hin of oil, and you shall offer for the drink offering half a hin of wine, as an offering by fire, a pleasing odour to the LORD. 11 "Thus it shall be done for each bull or ram, or for each of the 12 male lambs or the kids. According to the number that you prepare, so shall you do with every one according to their 13 number. All who are native shall do these things in this way, in offering an offering by fire, a 14 pleasing odour to the LORD. And if a stranger is sojourning with you, or any one is among you throughout your generations, and he wishes to offer an offering by fire, a pleasing odour to the LORD, 15 he shall do as you do. For the assembly, there shall be one statute for you and for the stranger who sojourns with you, a perpetual statute throughout your generations; as you are, so shall the sojourner be before the LORD. 16 One law and one ordinance shall be for you and for the stranger who sojourns with you."

17, The LORD said to Moses, "Say 18 to the people of Israel, When you come into the land to which I 19 bring you and when you eat of the food of the land, you shall present 20 an offering to the LORD. Of the first of your coarse meal you shall present a cake as an offering; as an offering from the threshing floor, 21 so shall you present it. Of the first of your coarse meal you shall give to the LORD an offering throughout your generations.

22 "But if you err, and do not observe all these commandments which the LORD has spoken to 23 Moses, all that the LORD has commanded you by Moses, from the day that the LORD gave commandment, and onward throughout your generations, 24 then if it was done unwittingly without the knowledge of the congregation, all the congregation shall offer one young bull for a burnt offering, a pleasing odour to the LORD, with its cereal offering and its drink offering, according to the ordinance, and one male 25 goat for a sin offering. And the priest shall make atonement for all the congregation of the people of Israel, and they shall be forgiven; because it was an error, and they have brought their offering, an offering by fire to the LORD, and their sin offering before the LORD, 26 for their error. And all the congregation of the people of Israel shall be forgiven, and the stranger who sojourns among them, because the whole population was involved in the error.

27 "If one person sins unwittingly, he shall offer a female goat a year 28 old for a sin offering. And the priest shall make atonement before the LORD for the person who commits an error, when he sins unwittingly, to make atonement for him; and he shall be 29 forgiven. You shall have one law for him who does anything unwittingly, for him who is native among the people of Israel, and for the stranger who sojourns among them. But the person who 30 does anything with a high hand, whether he is native or a sojour-

ner, reviles the LORD, and that person shall be cut off from among his people. Because he has 31 despised the word of the LORD, and has broken his commandment, that person shall be utterly cut off; his iniquity shall be upon him."

While the people of Israel were 32 in the wilderness, they found a man gathering sticks on the sabbath day. And those who found 33 him gathering sticks brought him to Moses and Aaron, and to all the congregation. They put him in 34 custody, because it had not been made plain what should be done to him. And the LORD said to 35 Moses, "The man shall be put to death; all the congregation shall stone him with stones outside the camp." And all the congregation 36 brought him outside the camp, and stoned him to death with stones, as the LORD commanded Moses.

The LORD said to Moses, "Speak 37 to the people of Israel, and bid 38 them to make tassels on the corners of their garments throughout their generations, and to put upon the tassel of each corner a cord of blue; and it shall be to you a tassel 39 to look upon and remember all the commandments of the LORD, to do them, not to follow after your own heart and your own eyes, which you are inclined to go after wantonly. So you shall remember 40 and do all my commandments, and be holy to your God. I am 41 the LORD your God, who brought you out of the land of Egypt, to be your God: I am the LORD your God."

Moses and Aaron challenged

16 NOW Korah the son of Izhar, son of Kohath, son of Levi, and Dathan and Abi'ram the sons of Eli'ab, and On the son of 2 Peleth, sons of Reuben, took men; and they rose up before Moses, with a number of the people of Israel, two hundred and fifty leaders of the congregation, chosen from 3 the assembly, well-known men; and they assembled themselves together against Moses and against Aaron, and said to them, "You have gone too far! For all the congregation are holy, every one of them, and the LORD is among them; why then do you exalt yourselves above the assembly of the 4 LORD?" When Moses heard it, he fell on his 5 face; and he said to Korah and all his company, "In the morning the LORD will show who is his, and who is holy, and will cause him to come near to him; him whom he will choose he will cause to come near to

him. Do this: take censers, Korah and all his 6 company; put fire in them and put incense 7 upon them before the LORD tomorrow, and the man whom the LORD chooses shall be the holy one. You have gone too far, sons of Levi!" And Moses said to Korah, "Hear 8 now, you sons of Levi: is it too small a thing 9 for you that the God of Israel has separated you from the congregation of Israel, to bring you near to himself, to do service in the tabernacle of the LORD, and to stand before the congregation to minister to them; and 10 that he has brought you near him, and all your brethren the sons of Levi with you? And would you seek the priesthood also? Therefore it is against the LORD that you and 11 all your company have gathered together; what is Aaron that you murmur against him?"

And Moses sent to call Dathan and Abi'ram 12 the sons of Eli'ab; and they said, "We will not come up. Is it a small thing that you 13

15.14: Ex 12.49; Lev 24.22; Num 15.15–16, 29.   15.17–21: Ex 34.26; Lev 23.14.   15.22–26: Lev 4.13–21. 15.27–29: Lev 4.2–12.   15.38–40: Deut 22.12.   16.5: 2 Tim 2.19.

have brought us up out of a land flowing with milk and honey, to kill us in the wilderness, that you must also make yourself a prince 14 over us? Moreover you have not brought us into a land flowing with milk and honey, nor given us inheritance of fields and vineyards. Will you put out the eyes of these men? We will not come up."

15 And Moses was very angry, and said to the LORD, "Do not respect their offering. I have not taken one ass from them, and I have not 16 harmed one of them." And Moses said to Korah, "Be present, you and all your company, before the LORD, you and they, and 17 Aaron, tomorrow; and let every one of you take his censer, and put incense upon it, and

every one of you bring before the LORD his censer, two hundred and fifty censers; you 18 also, and Aaron, each his censer." So every man took his censer, and they put fire in them and laid incense upon them, and they stood at the entrance of the tent of meeting 19 with Moses and Aaron. Then Korah assembled all the congregation against them at the entrance of the tent of meeting. And the glory of the LORD appeared to all the congregation.

20 And the LORD said to Moses and to Aaron, 21 "Separate yourselves from among this congregation, that I may consume them in a 22 moment." And they fell on their faces, and said, "O God, the God of the spirits of all flesh, shall one man sin, and wilt thou be 23 angry with all the congregation?" And the 24 LORD said to Moses, "Say to the congregation, Get away from the dwelling of Korah, Datham, and Abi'ram."

25 Then Moses rose and went to Dathan and Abi'ram; and the elders of Israel followed 26 him. And he said to the congregation, "Depart, I pray you, from the tents of these wicked men, and touch nothing of theirs, lest 27 you be swept away with all their sins." So they got away from about the dwelling of Korah, Dathan, and Abi'ram; and Dathan

and Abi'ram came out and stood at the door of their tents, together with their wives, their sons, and their little ones. And Moses said, 28 "Hereby you shall know that the LORD has sent me to do all these works, and that it has not been of my own accord. If these men die 29 the common death of all men, or if they are visited by the fate of all men, then the LORD has not sent me. But if the LORD creates 30 something new, and the ground opens its mouth, and swallows them up, with all that belongs to them, and they go down alive into Sheol, then you shall know that these men have despised the LORD."

And as he finished speaking all these words, 31 the ground under them split asunder; and 32 the earth opened its mouth and swallowed them up, with their households and all the men that belonged to Korah and all their goods. So they and all that belonged to them 33 went down alive into Sheol; and the earth closed over them, and they perished from the midst of the assembly. And all Israel that 34 were round about them fled at their cry; for they said, "Lest the earth swallow us up!" And fire came forth from the LORD, and 35 consumed the two hundred and fifty men offering the incense.

Then the LORD said to Moses, "Tell Elea'- 36,ⁱ zar the son of Aaron the priest to take up the 37 censers out of the blaze; then scatter the fire far and wide. For they are holy, the censers 38 of these men who have sinned at the cost of their lives; so let them be made into hammered plates as a covering for the altar, for they offered them before the LORD; therefore they are holy. Thus they shall be a sign to the people of Israel." So Elea'zar the priest 39 took the bronze censers, which those who were burned had offered; and they were hammered out as a covering for the altar, to 40 be a reminder to the people of Israel, so that no one who is not a priest, who is not of the descendants of Aaron, should draw near to burn incense before the LORD, lest he become as Korah and as his company—as the LORD said to Elea'zar through Moses.

But on the morrow all the congregation of 41 the people of Israel murmured against Moses and against Aaron, saying, "You have killed the people of the LORD." And when the 42 congregation had assembled against Moses and against Aaron, they turned toward the tent of meeting; and behold, the cloud covered it, and the glory of the LORD appeared. And Moses and Aaron came to 43 the front of the tent of meeting, and the 44 LORD said to Moses, "Get away from the 45 midst of this congregation, that I may consume them in a moment." And they fell on

ⁱ Ch 17.1 in Heb

46 their faces. And Moses said to Aaron, "Take your censer, and put fire therein from off the altar, and lay incense on it, and carry it quickly to the congregation, and make atonement for them; for wrath has gone forth from 47 the LORD, the plague has begun." So Aaron took it as Moses said, and ran into the midst of the assembly; and behold, the plague had already begun among the people; and he put on the incense, and made atonement for the 48 people. And he stood between the dead and 49 the living; and the plague was stopped. Now those who died by the plague were fourteen thousand seven hundred, besides those who 50 died in the affair of Korah. And Aaron returned to Moses at the entrance of the tent of meeting, when the plague was stopped.

Aaron's rod

17 *j* The LORD said to Moses, "Speak to the 2 people of Israel, and get from them rods, one for each fathers' house, from all their leaders according to their fathers' houses, twelve rods. Write each man's name upon his rod, 3 and write Aaron's name upon the rod of Levi. For there shall be one rod for the head 4 of each fathers' house. Then you shall deposit them in the tent of meeting before

the testimony, where I meet with you. And 5 the rod of the man whom I choose shall sprout; thus I will make to cease from me the murmurings of the people of Israel, which they murmur against you." Moses spoke to 6 the people of Israel; and all their leaders gave him rods, one for each leader, according to their fathers' houses, twelve rods; and the rod of Aaron was among their rods. And 7 Moses deposited the rods before the LORD in the tent of the testimony.

And on the morrow Moses went into the 8 tent of the testimony; and behold, the rod of Aaron for the house of Levi had sprouted and put forth buds, and produced blossoms, and it bore ripe almonds. Then Moses 9 brought out all the rods from before the LORD to all the people of Israel; and they looked, and each man took his rod. And the 10 LORD said to Moses, "Put back the rod of Aaron before the testimony, to be kept as a sign for the rebels, that you may make an end of their murmurings against me, lest they die." Thus did Moses; as the LORD com- 11 manded him, so he did.

And the people of Israel said to Moses, 12 "Behold, we perish, we are undone, we are all undone. Every one who comes near, who 13 comes near to the tabernacle of the LORD, shall die. Are we all to perish?"

Law of priests and Levites

18 SO the LORD said to Aaron, "You and your sons and your fathers' house with you shall bear iniquity in connection with the sanctuary; and you and your sons with you shall bear iniquity in connection with your priesthood. 2 And with you bring your brethren also, the tribe of Levi, the tribe of your father, that they may join you, and minister to you while you and your sons with you are before the tent of the testimony. 3 They shall attend you and attend to all duties of the tent; but shall not come near to the vessels of the sanctuary or to the altar, lest they, 4 and you, die. They shall join you, and attend to the tent of meeting, for all the service of the tent; and no one else shall come near you. 5 And you shall attend to the duties of the sanctuary and the duties of the altar, that there be wrath no more upon the people of Israel. 6 And behold, I have taken your brethren the Levites from among the people of Israel; they are a gift to you, given to the LORD, to do the service of the tent of meeting. 7 And you and your sons with you shall attend to your priesthood for all that concerns the altar and that

is within the veil; and you shall serve. I give your priesthood as a gift,*k* and any one else who comes near shall be put to death." 8 Then the LORD said to Aaron, "And behold, I have given you whatever is kept of the offerings made to me, all the consecrated things of the people of Israel; I have given them to you as a portion, and to your sons as a 9 perpetual due. This shall be yours of the most holy things, reserved from the fire; every offering of theirs, every cereal offering of theirs and every sin offering of theirs and every guilt offering of theirs, which they render to me, shall be most 10 holy to you and to your sons. In a most holy place shall you eat of it; every male may eat of it; it is holy 11 to you. This also is yours, the offering of their gift, all the wave offerings of the people of Israel; I have given them to you, and to your sons and daughters with you, as a perpetual due; every one who 12 is clean in your house may eat of it. All the best of the oil, and all the best of the wine and of the grain, the first fruits of what they give to the LORD, I give to you. 13 The first ripe fruits of all that is in their land, which they bring to the

LORD, shall be yours; every one who is clean in your house may eat of it. Every devoted thing in 14 Israel shall be yours. Everything 15 that opens the womb of all flesh, whether man or beast, which they offer to the LORD, shall be yours; nevertheless the first-born of man you shall redeem, and the firstling of unclean beasts you shall redeem. And their redemption 16 price (at a month old you shall redeem them) you shall fix at five shekels in silver, according to the shekel of the sanctuary, which is twenty gerahs. But the firstling of 17 a cow, or the firstling of a sheep, or the firstling of a goat, you shall not redeem; they are holy. You shall sprinkle their blood upon the altar, and shall burn their fat as an offering by fire, a pleasing odour to the LORD; but their flesh shall 18 be yours, as the breast that is waved and as the right thigh are yours. All the holy offerings 19 which the people of Israel present to the LORD I give to you, and to your sons and daughters with you, as a perpetual due; it is a covenant of salt for ever before the LORD for you and for your offspring with you." And the LORD said to 20 Aaron, "You shall have no inheritance in their land, neither shall you have any portion among them; I am your portion and your inheritance among the people of Israel.

21 "To the Levites I have given every tithe in Israel for an inheritance, in return for their service which they serve, their service in 22 the tent of meeting. And henceforth the people of Israel shall not come near the tent of meeting, lest 23 they bear sin and die. But the Levites shall do the service of the tent of meeting, and they shall bear their iniquity; it shall be a perpetual statute throughout your generations; and among the people of Israel they shall have no 24 inheritance. For the tithe of the people of Israel, which they present as an offering to the LORD, I have given to the Levites for an inheritance; therefore I have said of them that they shall have no inheritance among the people of Israel."

25 And the LORD said to Moses, 26 "Moreover you shall say to the Levites, 'When you take from the people of Israel the tithe which I have given you from them for your inheritance, then you shall present an offering from it to the 27 LORD, a tithe of the tithe. And your offering shall be reckoned to you as though it were the grain of the threshing floor, and as the 28 fulness of the wine press. So shall you also present an offering to the LORD from all your tithes, which you receive from the people of Israel; and from it you shall give the LORD's offering to Aaron the 29 priest. Out of all the gifts to you, you shall present every offering due to the LORD, from all the best 30 of them, giving the hallowed part from them.' Therefore you shall say to them, 'When you have offered from it the best of it, then the rest shall be reckoned to the Levites as produce of the threshing floor, and as produce of the 31 wine press; and you may eat it in any place, you and your households; for it is your reward in 32 return for your service in the tent of meeting. And you shall bear no sin by reason of it, when you have offered the best of it. And you

shall not profane the holy things of the people of Israel, lest you die.' "

The red heifer

19 Now the LORD said to Moses 2 and to Aaron, "This is the statute of the law which the LORD has commanded: Tell the people of Israel to bring you a red heifer without defect, in which there is no blemish, and upon which a 3 yoke has never come. And you shall give her to Elea'zar the priest, and she shall be taken outside the camp and slaughtered 4 before him; and Elea'zar the priest shall take some of her blood with his finger, and sprinkle some of her blood toward the front of the tent of meeting seven times. 5 And the heifer shall be burned in his sight; her skin, her flesh, and her blood, with her dung, shall be 6 burned; and the priest shall take cedarwood and hyssop and scarlet stuff, and cast them into the midst of the burning of the heifer. 7 Then the priest shall wash his clothes and bathe his body in water, and afterwards he shall come into the camp; and the priest shall be unclean until eve- 8 ing. He who burns the heifer shall wash his clothes in water and bathe his body in water, and shall 9 be unclean until evening. And a man who is clean shall gather up the ashes of the heifer, and deposit them outside the camp in a clean place; and they shall be kept for the congregation of the people of Israel for the water for impurity, for the removal of sin. 10 And he who gathers the ashes of the heifer shall wash his clothes, and be unclean until evening. And this shall be to the people of Israel, and to the stranger who sojourns among them, a perpetual statute.

Purification

11 "He who touches the dead body of any person shall be unclean 12 seven days; he shall cleanse himself with the water on the third day and on the seventh day, and

so be clean; but if he does not cleanse himself on the third day and on the seventh day, he will not become clean. Whoever 13 touches a dead person, the body of any man who has died, and does not cleanse himself, defiles the tabernacle of the LORD, and that person shall be cut off from Israel; because the water for impurity was not thrown upon him, he shall be unclean; his uncleanness is still on him.

"This is the law when a man dies 14 in a tent: every one who comes into the tent, and every one who is in the tent, shall be unclean seven days. And every open vessel, 15 which has no cover fastened upon it, is unclean. Whoever in the 16 open field touches one who is slain with a sword, or a dead body, or a bone of a man, or a grave, shall be unclean seven days. For the unclean they shall 17 take some ashes of the burnt sin offering, and running water shall be added in a vessel; then a clean 18 person shall take hyssop, and dip it in the water, and sprinkle it upon the tent, and upon all the furnishings, and upon the persons who were there, and upon him who touched the bone, or the slain, or the dead, or the grave; and the clean person shall sprinkle 19 upon the unclean on the third day and on the seventh day; thus on the seventh day he shall cleanse him, and he shall wash his clothes and bathe himself in water, and at evening he shall be clean.

"But the man who is unclean 20 and does not cleanse himself, that person shall be cut off from the midst of the assembly, since he has defiled the sanctuary of the LORD; because the water for impurity has not been thrown upon him, he is unclean. And it 21 shall be a perpetual statute for them. He who sprinkles the water for impurity shall wash his clothes; and he who touches the water for impurity shall be unclean until evening. And what- 22 ever the unclean person touches shall be unclean; and any one who touches it shall be unclean until evening."

WANDERING IN THE WILDERNESS

20 AND the people of Israel, the whole congregation, came into the wilderness of Zin in the first month, and the people stayed in Kadesh; and Miriam died there, and was buried there.

Water from the rock

2 Now there was no water for the congregation; and they assembled themselves together

against Moses and against Aaron. And the 3 people contended with Moses, and said, "Would that we had died when our brethren died before the LORD! Why have you 4 brought the assembly of the LORD into this wilderness, that we should die here, both we and our cattle? And why have you made us 5 come up out of Egypt, to bring us to this evil place? It is no place for grain, or figs, or vines, or pomegranates; and there is no water

6 to drink." Then Moses and Aaron went from the presence of the assembly to the door of the tent of meeting, and fell on their faces. And the glory of the LORD appeared to them,
7, and the LORD said to Moses, "Take the rod,
8 and assemble the congregation, you and Aaron your brother, and tell the rock before their eyes to yield its water; so you shall bring water out of the rock for them; so you shall give drink to the congregation and their
9 cattle." And Moses took the rod from before the LORD, as he commanded him.
10 And Moses and Aaron gathered the assembly together before the rock, and he said to them, "Hear now, you rebels; shall we bring
11 forth water for you out of this rock?" And Moses lifted up his hand and struck the rock with his rod twice; and water came forth abundantly, and the congregation drank, and
12 their cattle. And the LORD said to Moses and Aaron, "Because you did not believe in me, to sanctify me in the eyes of the people of Israel, therefore you shall not bring this assembly into the land which I have given
13 them." These are the waters of Mer'ibah,[l] where the people of Israel contended with the LORD, and he showed himself holy among them.

Israel and Edom

14 Moses sent messengers from Kadesh to the king of Edom, "Thus says your brother Israel: You know all the adversity that has
15 befallen us: how our fathers went down to Egypt, and we dwelt in Egypt a long time; and the Egyptians dealt harshly with us and
16 our fathers; and when we cried to the LORD, he heard our voice, and sent an angel and brought us forth out of Egypt; and here we are in Kadesh, a city on the edge of your
17 territory. Now let us pass through your land. We will not pass through field or vineyard, neither will we drink water from a well; we will go along the King's Highway, we will not turn aside to the right hand or to the left, until we have passed through your terri-
18 tory." But Edom said to him, "You shall not pass through, lest I come out with the
19 sword against you." And the people of Israel said to him, "We will go up by the highway; and if we drink of your water, I and my

cattle, then I will pay for it; let me only pass through on foot, nothing more." But he 20 said, "You shall not pass through." And Edom came out against them with many men, and with a strong force. Thus Edom 21 refused to give Israel passage through his territory; so Israel turned away from him.

Death of Aaron

And they journeyed from Kadesh, and the 22 people of Israel, the whole congregation, came to Mount Hor. And the LORD said to 23 Moses and Aaron at Mount Hor, on the border of the land of Edom, "Aaron shall be 24 gathered to his people; for he shall not enter the land which I have given to the people of Israel, because you rebelled against my command at the waters of Mer'ibah. Take 25 Aaron and Elea'zar his son, and bring them up to Mount Hor; and strip Aaron of his 26 garments, and put them upon Elea'zar his son; and Aaron shall be gathered to his people, and shall die there." Moses did as 27 the LORD commanded; and they went up Mount Hor in the sight of all the congregation. And Moses stripped Aaron of his 28 garments, and put them upon Elea'zar his son; and Aaron died there on the top of the mountain. Then Moses and Elea'zar came down from the mountain. And when all the 29 congregation saw that Aaron was dead, all the house of Israel wept for Aaron thirty days.

When the Canaanite, the king of Arad, who 21 dwelt in the Negeb, heard that Israel was coming by the way of Atharim, he fought against Israel, and took some of them captive. And Israel vowed a vow to the LORD, 2 and said, "If thou wilt indeed give this people into my hand, then I will utterly destroy their cities." And the LORD hear- 3 kened to the voice of Israel, and gave over the Canaanites; and they utterly destroyed them and their cities; so the name of the place was called Hormah.[m]

Bronze serpent

From Mount Hor they set out by the way to 4 the Red Sea, to go around the land of Edom; and the people became impatient on the way. And the people spoke against God and 5 against Moses, "Why have you brought us up out of Egypt to die in the wilderness? For there is no food and no water, and we loathe this worthless food." Then the LORD 6 sent fiery serpents among the people, and they bit the people, so that many people of

---

7 Israel died. And the people came to Moses, and said, "We have sinned, for we have spoken against the LORD and against you; pray to the LORD, that he take away the serpents from us." So Moses prayed for the 8 people. And the LORD said to Moses, "Make a fiery serpent, and set it on a pole; and every one who is bitten, when he sees it, shall 9 live." So Moses made a bronze serpent, and set it on a pole; and if a serpent bit any man, he would look at the bronze serpent and live.

To the plains of Moab

10 And the people of Israel set out, and 11 encamped in Oboth. And they set out from Oboth, and encamped at I'ye-ab'arim, in the wilderness which is opposite Moab, toward 12 the sunrise. From there they set out, and 13 encamped in the Valley of Zered. From there they set out, and encamped on the other side of the Arnon, which is in the wilderness, that extends from the boundary of the Amorites; for the Arnon is the boundary of Moab, between Moab and the Amo- 14 rites. Wherefore it is said in the Book of the Wars of the LORD,

"Waheb in Suphah,
    and the valleys of the Arnon,
15   and the slope of the valleys
    that extends to the seat of Ar,
    and leans to the border of Moab."

16 And from there they continued to Beer;[n] that is the well of which the LORD said to Moses, "Gather the people together, and I 17 will give them water." Then Israel sang this song:

"Spring up, O well!—Sing to it!—
18   the well which the princes dug,
    which the nobles of the people delved,
    with the sceptre and with their staves."

And from the wilderness they went on to 19 Mat'tanah, and from Mat'tanah to Nahal'iel, 20 and from Nahal'iel to Bamoth, and from Bamoth to the valley lying in the region of Moab by the top of Pisgah which looks down upon the desert.[o]

21 Then Israel sent messengers to Sihon king 22 of the Amorites, saying, "Let me pass through your land; we will not turn aside into field or vineyard; we will not drink the water of a well; we will go by the King's Highway, until we have passed through your 23 territory." But Sihon would not allow Israel to pass through his territory. He gathered all his men together, and went out against Israel to the wilderness, and came to Jahaz, and 24 fought against Israel. And Israel slew him

with the edge of the sword, and took possession of his land from the Arnon to the Jabbok, as far as to the Ammonites; for Jazer was the boundary of the Ammonites.[p] And 25 Israel took all these cities, and Israel settled in all the cities of the Amorites, in Heshbon, and in all its villages. For Heshbon was the 26 city of Sihon the king of the Amorites, who had fought against the former king of Moab and taken all his land out of his hand, as far as the Arnon. Therefore the ballad singers 27 say,

"Come to Heshbon, let it be built, let the city of Sihon be established.
For fire went forth from Heshbon, flame 28 from the city of Sihon.
It devoured Ar of Moab,
    the lords of the heights of the Arnon.
Woe to you, O Moab!   29
    You are undone, O people of Chemosh!
He has made his sons fugitives,
    and his daughters captives,
    to an Amorite king, Sihon.
So their posterity perished from Hesh- 30 bon,[q] as far as Dibon,
    and we laid waste until fire spread to Med'eba."[r]

Thus Israel dwelt in the land of the Amor- 31 ites. And Moses sent to spy out Jazer; and 32 they took its villages, and dispossessed the Amorites that were there. Then they turned 33 and went up by the way to Bashan; and Og the king of Bashan came out against them, he and all his people, to battle at Ed're-i. But 34 the LORD said to Moses, "Do not fear him; for I have given him into your hand, and all his people, and his land; and you shall do to him as you did to Sihon king of the Amorites, who dwelt at Heshbon." So they slew him, 35 and his sons, and all his people, until there was not one survivor left to him; and they possessed his land.

Balak and Balaam

Then the people of Israel set out, and 22 encamped in the plains of Moab beyond the Jordan at Jericho. And Balak the son of 2 Zippor saw all that Israel had done to the Amorites. And Moab was in great dread of 3 the people, because they were many; Moab was overcome with fear of the people of Israel. And Moab said to the elders of 4 Mid'ian, "This horde will now lick up all that is round about us, as the ox licks up the grass of the field." So Balak the son of Zippor, who was king of Moab at that time, sent messengers to Balaam the son of Be'or at 5

---

n That is Well   o Or Jeshimon   p Gk: Heb the boundary of the Ammonites was strong
q Gk: Heb we have shot at them. Heshbon has perished
r Compare Sam and Gk: Heb we have laid waste to Nophah which to Medeba
21.21-30: Deut 2.26-37.   21.33-35: Deut 3.1-7.   22.1: Num 33.48.

Pethor, which is near the River, in the land of
Amaw to call him, saying, "Behold, a people
has come out of Egypt; they cover the face of
the earth, and they are dwelling opposite
6 me. Come now, curse this people for me,
since they are too mighty for me; perhaps I
shall be able to defeat them and drive them
from the land; for I know that he whom you
bless is blessed, and he whom you curse is
cursed."
7 So the elders of Moab and the elders of
Mid′ian departed with the fees for divination
in their hand; and they came to Balaam, and
8 gave him Balak's message. And he said to
them, "Lodge here this night, and I will
bring back word to you, as the LORD speaks
to me"; so the princes of Moab stayed with
9 Balaam. And God came to Balaam and said,
10 "Who are these men with you?" And
Balaam said to God, "Balak the son of
Zippor, king of Moab, has sent to me, saying,
11 'Behold, a people has come out of Egypt, and
it covers the face of the earth; now come,
curse them for me; perhaps I shall be able to
fight against them and drive them out.'"
12 God said to Balaam, "You shall not go with
them; you shall not curse the people, for they
13 are blessed." So Balaam rose in the morning, and said to the princes of Balak, "Go to
your own land; for the LORD has refused to
14 let me go with you." So the princes of Moab
rose and went to Balak, and said, "Balaam
refuses to come with us."
15 Once again Balak sent princes, more in
number and more honourable than they.
16 And they came to Balaam and said to him,
"Thus says Balak the son of Zippor: 'Let
17 nothing hinder you from coming to me; for I
will surely do you great honour, and whatever you say to me I will do; come, curse this
18 people for me.'" But Balaam answered and
said to the servants of Balak, "Though Balak
were to give me his house full of silver and
gold, I could not go beyond the command of
19 the LORD my God, to do less or more. Pray
now, tarry here this night also, that I may
know what more the LORD will say to me."
20 And God came to Balaam at night and said to
him, "If the men have come to call you, rise,
go with them; but only what I bid you, that
shall you do."
21 So Balaam rose in the morning, and saddled
his ass, and went with the princes of Moab.
22 But God's anger was kindled because he
went; and the angel of the LORD took his
stand in the way as his adversary. Now he
was riding on the ass, and his two servants
23 were with him. And the ass saw the angel of
the LORD standing in the road, with a drawn
sword in his hand; and the ass turned aside
out of the road, and went into the field; and
Balaam struck the ass, to turn her into the

road. Then the angel of the LORD stood in a 24
narrow path between the vineyards, with a
wall on either side. And when the ass saw 25
the angel of the LORD, she pushed against the
wall, and pressed Balaam's foot against the
wall; so he struck her again. Then the angel 26
of the LORD went ahead, and stood in a
narrow place, where there was no way to turn
either to the right or to the left. When the 27
ass saw the angel of the LORD, she lay down
under Balaam; and Balaam's anger was
kindled, and he struck the ass with his staff.
Then the LORD opened the mouth of the ass, 28
and she said to Balaam, "What have I done
to you, that you have struck me these three
times?" And Balaam said to the ass, 29
"Because you have made sport of me. I wish
I had a sword in my hand, for then I would
kill you." And the ass said to Balaam, "Am I 30
not your ass, upon which you have ridden all
your life long to this day? Was I ever
accustomed to do so to you?" And he said,
"No."
Then the LORD opened the eyes of Balaam, 31
and he saw the angel of the LORD standing in
the way, with his drawn sword in his hand;
and he bowed his head, and fell on his face.
And the angel of the LORD said to him, "Why 32
have you struck your ass these three times?
Behold, I have come forth to withstand you,
because your way is perverse before me; and 33
the ass saw me, and turned aside before me
these three times. If she had not turned
aside from me, surely just now I would have
slain you and let her live." Then Balaam 34
said to the angel of the LORD, "I have sinned,
for I did not know that thou didst stand in
the road against me. Now therefore, if it is
evil in thy sight, I will go back again." And 35
the angel of the LORD said to Balaam, "Go
with the men; but only the word which I bid
you, that shall you speak." So Balaam went
on with the princes of Balak.
When Balak heard that Balaam had come, 36
he went out to meet him at the city of Moab,
on the boundary formed by the Arnon, at the

37 extremity of the boundary. And Balak said to Balaam, "Did I not send to you to call you? Why did you not come to me? Am I 38 not able to honour you?" Balaam said to Balak, "Lo, I have come to you! Have I now any power at all to speak anything? The word that God puts in my mouth, that must 39 I speak." Then Balaam went with Balak, 40 and they came to Kir′iath-hu′zoth. And Balak sacrificed oxen and sheep, and sent to Balaam and to the princes who were with him. 41 And on the morrow Balak took Balaam and brought him up to Bamoth-ba′al; and from there he saw the nearest of the people.

23 And Balaam said to Balak, "Build for me here seven altars, and provide for me here 2 seven bulls and seven rams." Balak did as Balaam had said; and Balak and Balaam 3 offered on each altar a bull and a ram. And Balaam said to Balak, "Stand beside your burnt offering, and I will go; perhaps the LORD will come to meet me; and whatever he shows me I will tell you." And he went to a 4 bare height. And God met Balaam; and Balaam said to him, "I have prepared the seven altars, and I have offered upon each 5 altar a bull and a ram." And the LORD put a word in Balaam's mouth, and said, "Return 6 to Balak, and thus you shall speak." And he returned to him, and lo, he and all the princes of Moab were standing beside his 7 burnt offering. And Balaam took up his discourse, and said,

"From Aram Balak has brought me,
the king of Moab from the eastern mountains:
'Come, curse Jacob for me,
and come, denounce Israel!'
8 How can I curse whom God has not cursed?
How can I denounce whom the LORD has not denounced?
9 For from the top of the mountains I see him,
from the hills I behold him;
lo, a people dwelling alone,
and not reckoning itself among the nations!
10 Who can count the dust of Jacob,
or number the fourth part[s] of Israel?
Let me die the death of the righteous,
and let my end be like his!"

11 And Balak said to Balaam, "What have you done to me? I took you to curse my enemies, and behold, you have done nothing but bless 12 them." And he answered, "Must I not take heed to speak what the LORD puts in my mouth?"

And Balak said to him, "Come with me to 13 another place, from which you may see them; you shall see only the nearest of them, and shall not see them all; then curse them for me from there." And he took him to the field of 14 Zophim, to the top of Pisgah, and built seven altars, and offered a bull and a ram on each altar. Balaam said to Balak, "Stand here 15 beside your burnt offering, while I meet the LORD yonder." And the LORD met Balaam, 16 and put a word in his mouth, and said, "Return to Balak, and thus shall you speak." And he came to him, and, lo, he was standing 17 beside his burnt offering, and the princes of Moab with him. And Balak said to him, "What has the LORD spoken?" And Balaam 18 took up his discourse, and said,

"Rise, Balak, and hear;
hearken to me, O son of Zippor:
God is not man, that he should lie, 19
or a son of man, that he should repent.
Has he said, and will he not do it?
Or has he spoken, and will he not fulfil it?
Behold, I received a command to bless: 20
he has blessed, and I cannot revoke it.
He has not beheld misfortune in Jacob; 21
nor has he seen trouble in Israel.
The LORD their God is with them,
and the shout of a king is among them.
God brings them out of Egypt; 22
they have as it were the horns of the wild ox.
For there is no enchantment against Jacob, 23
no divination against Israel;
now it shall be said of Jacob and Israel,
'What has God wrought!'
Behold, a people! As a lioness it rises up 24
and as a lion it lifts itself;
it does not lie down till it devours the prey,
and drinks the blood of the slain."

And Balak said to Balaam, "Neither curse 25 them at all, nor bless them at all." But 26 Balaam answered Balak, "Did I not tell you, 'All that the LORD says, that I must do'?" And Balak said to Balaam, "Come now, I will 27 take you to another place; perhaps it will please God that you may curse them for me from there." So Balak took Balaam to the 28 top of Pe′or, that overlooks the desert.[t] And 29 Balaam said to Balak, "Build for me here seven altars, and provide for me here seven bulls and seven rams." And Balak did as 30 Balaam had said, and offered a bull and a ram on each altar.

When Balaam saw that it pleased the LORD 24 to bless Israel, he did not go, as at other times, to look for omens, but set his face toward the wilderness. And Balaam lifted up 2

s Or *dust clouds*   t Or *Jeshimon*

his eyes, and saw Israel encamping tribe by
tribe. And the Spirit of God came upon
3 him, and he took up his discourse, and
said,
"The oracle of Balaam the son of Be'or,
the oracle of the man whose eye is
opened, "
4   the oracle of him who hears the words of
God,
who sees the vision of the Almighty,
falling down, but having his eyes uncovered:
5   how fair are your tents, O Jacob,
your encampments, O Israel!
6   Like valleys that stretch afar,
like gardens beside a river,
like aloes that the LORD has planted,
like cedar trees beside the waters.
7   Water shall flow from his buckets,
and his seed shall be in many waters,
his king shall be higher than Agag,
and his kingdom shall be exalted.
8   God brings him out of Egypt,
he has as it were the horns of the wild ox,
he shall eat up the nations his adversaries,
and shall break their bones in pieces,
and pierce them through with his arrows.
9   He couched, he lay down like a lion,
and like a lioness; who will rouse him up?
Blessed be every one who blesses you,
and cursed be every one who curses you."
10 And Balak's anger was kindled against
Balaam, and he struck his hands together;
and Balak said to Balaam, "I called you to
curse my enemies, and behold, you have
11 blessed them these three times. Therefore
now flee to your place; I said, 'I will certainly
honour you,' but the LORD has held you back
12 from honour." And Balaam said to Balak,
"Did I not tell your messengers whom you
13 sent to me, 'If Balak should give me his
house full of silver and gold, I would not be
able to go beyond the word of the LORD, to
do either good or bad of my own will; what
14 the LORD speaks, that will I speak'? And
now, behold, I am going to my people; come,
I will let you know what this people will do to
15 your people in the latter days." And he took
up his discourse, and said,
"The oracle of Balaam the son of Be'or,
the oracle of the man whose eye is
opened, "
16   the oracle of him who hears the words of
God,
and knows the knowledge of the Most
High,
who sees the vision of the Almighty,
falling down, but having his eyes uncovered:

I see him, but not now;   17
I behold him, but not nigh:
a star shall come forth out of Jacob,
and a sceptre shall rise out of Israel;
it shall crush the forehead *v* of Moab,
and break down all the sons of Sheth.
Edom shall be dispossessed,   18
Se'ir also, his enemies, shall be dispossessed,
while Israel does valiantly.
By Jacob shall dominion be exercised,   19
and the survivors of cities be destroyed!"
Then he looked on Am'alek, and took up his   20
discourse, and said,
"Am'alek was the first of the nations,
but in the end he shall come to destruction."
And he looked on the Ken'ite, and took up   21
his discourse, and said,
"Enduring is your dwelling place,
and your nest is set in the rock;
nevertheless Kain shall be wasted.   22
How long shall Asshur take you away
captive?"
And he took up his discourse, and said,   23
"Alas, who shall live when God does this?
But ships shall come from Kittim   24
and shall afflict Asshur and Eber;
and he also shall come to destruction."
Then Balaam rose, and went back to his   25
place; and Balak also went his way.

Israel and Moab

While Israel dwelt in Shittim the people 25
began to play the harlot with the daughters of
Moab. These invited the people to the 2
sacrifices of their gods, and the people ate,
and bowed down to their gods. So Israel 3
yoked himself to Ba'al of Pe'or. And the
anger of the LORD was kindled against Israel;
and the LORD said to Moses, "Take all the 4
chiefs of the people, and hang them in the
sun before the LORD, that the fierce anger of
the LORD may turn away from Israel." And 5
Moses said to the judges of Israel, "Every
one of you slay his men who have yoked
themselves to Ba'al of Pe'or."

The Midianites

And behold, one of the people of Israel 6
came and brought a Mid'ianite woman to his
family, in the sight of Moses and in the sight
of the whole congregation of the people of
Israel, while they were weeping at the door of
the tent of meeting. When Phin'ehas the son 7
of Elea'zar, son of Aaron the priest, saw it, he

u Or *closed* or *perfect*   *v* Heb *corners* (of the head)
24.9: Gen 49.9.

rose and left the congregation, and took a spear in his hand and went after the man of Israel into the inner room, and pierced both of them, the man of Israel and the woman, through her body. Thus the plague was stayed from the people of Israel. Nevertheless those that died by the plague were twenty-four thousand.

, And the LORD said to Moses, "Phin'ehas the son of Elea'zar, son of Aaron the priest, has turned back my wrath from the people of Israel, in that he was jealous with my jealousy among them, so that I did not consume the people of Israel in my jealousy. Therefore say, 'Behold, I give to him my covenant of peace; and it shall be to him, and to his descendants after him, the covenant of a perpetual priesthood, because he was jealous for his God, and made atonement for the people of Israel.'"

The name of the slain man of Israel, who 14 was slain with the Mid'ianite woman, was Zimri the son of Salu, head of a fathers' house belonging to the Simeonites. And the 15 name of the Mid'ianite woman who was slain was Cozbi the daughter of Zur, who was the head of the people of a fathers' house in Mid'ian.

And the LORD said to Moses, "Harass the 16, Mid'ianites, and smite them; for they have 17, harassed you with their wiles, with which 18 they beguiled you in the matter of Pe'or, and in the matter of Cozbi, the daughter of the prince of Mid'ian, their sister, who was slain on the day of the plague on account of Pe'or."

Census of the people

3 AFTER the plague the LORD said to Moses and to Elea'zar the son of Aaron, the priest, "Take a census of all the congregation of the people of Israel, 10 from twenty years old and upward, by their fathers' houses, all in Israel who are able to go forth to war." And Moses and Elea'zar the priest spoke with them in the plains of Moab by the Jordan at Jericho, saying, "Take a census of the people,[w] from 12 twenty years old and upward," as the LORD commanded Moses. The people of Israel, who came forth out of the land of Egypt, were:

5 Reuben, the first-born of Israel; the sons of Reuben: of Hanoch, the family of the Ha'nochites; of Pallu, the family of the Pal'luites; of Hezron, the family of the Hez'ronites; of Carmi, the family of the Carmites. These are the families of the Reubenites; and their number was forty-three thousand seven hundred and thirty. And the sons of Pallu: Eli'ab. The sons of Eli'ab: Nem'u-el,

Dathan, and Abi'ram. These are the Dathan and Abi'ram, chosen from the congregation, who contended against Moses and Aaron in the company of Korah, when they contended against the LORD, and the earth opened its mouth and swallowed them up together with Korah, when that company died, when the fire devoured two hundred and fifty men; and they 11 became a warning. Notwithstanding, the sons of Korah did not die.

The sons of Simeon according to 12 their families: of Nem'u-el, the family of the Nem'uelites; of Jamin, the family of the Ja'minites; of Jachin, the family of the 13 Ja'chinites; of Zerah, the family of the Zer'ahites; of Sha'ul, the family of the Sha'ulites. These 14 are the families of the Simeonites, twenty-two thousand two hundred.

The sons of Gad according to 15 their families: of Zephon, the family of the Ze'phonites; of Haggi, the family of the Haggites; of Shuni, the family of the Shunites; of Ozni, the family of the 16 Oznites; of Eri, the family of the

Erites; of Ar'od, the family of the 17 Ar'odites; of Are'li, the family of the Are'lites. These are the fami-18 lies of the sons of Gad according to their number, forty thousand five hundred.

The sons of Judah were Er and 19 Onan; and Er and Onan died in the land of Canaan. And the sons 20 of Judah according to their families were: of Shelah, the family of the Shela'nites; of Perez, the family of the Per'ezites; of Zerah, the family of the Zer'ahites. And 21 the sons of Perez were: of Hezron, the family of the Hez'ronites; of Hamul, the family of the Ha-mu'lites. These are the families of 22 Judah according to their number, seventy-six thousand five hundred.

The sons of Is'sachar according 23 to their families: of Tola, the family of the To'laites; of Puvah, 24 the family of the Punites; of Jashub, the family of the Jash'-ubites; of Shimron, the family of the Shim'ronites. These are the 25 families of Is'sachar according to their number, sixty-four thousand three hundred.

The sons of Zeb'ulun, according 26

The wilderness

[w] Supplying *take a census of the people* Compare verse 2
26.5–51: Num 1.20–46.

to their families: of Sered, the
family of the Ser'edites; of Elon,
the family of the E'lonites; of
Jahleel, the family of the Jah'leel-
27 ites. These are the families of the
Zebu'lunites according to their
number, sixty thousand five
hundred.

28 The sons of Joseph according to
their families: Manas'seh and
29 E'phraim. The sons of Manas'-
seh: of Machir, the family of the
Machirites; and Machir was the
father of Gilead; of Gilead,
30 the family of the Gileadites. These
are the sons of Gilead: of Ie'zer,
the family of the Ie'zerites; of
Helek, the family of the He'lek-
31 ites; and of As'ri-el, the family of
the As'rielites; and of Shechem,
the family of the She'chemites;
32 and of Shemi'da, the family of the
Shemi'daites; and of Hepher, the
33 family of the He'pherites. Now
Zelo'phehad the son of Hepher
had no sons, but daughters: and
the names of the daughters of
Zelo'phehad were Mahlah, Noah,
Hoglah, Milcah, and Tirzah.
34 These are the families of Manas'-
seh; and their number was fifty-
two thousand seven hundred.

35 These are the sons of E'phraim
according to their families: of
Shuthe'lah, the family of the
Shuthe'lahites; of Becher, the
family of the Be'cherites; of
Tahan, the family of the Ta'han-
36 ites. And these are the sons of
Shuthe'lah: of Eran, the family of
37 the E'ranites. These are the
families of the sons of E'phraim
according to their number,
thirty-two thousand five hundred. These are the sons of
Joseph according to their families.

38 The sons of Benjamin according
to their families: of Bela, the
family of the Be'la-ites; of Ashbel,
the family of the Ash'belites; of
Ahi'ram, the family of the Ahi'-
39 ramites; of Shephu'pham, the
family of the Shu'phamites; of
Hupham, the family of the
40 Hu'phamites. And the sons of
Bela were Ard and Na'aman: of
Ard, the family of the Ard'ites;
of Na'aman, the family of the
41 Na'amites. These are the sons of
Benjamin according to their families; and their number was forty-
five thousand six hundred.

42 These are the sons of Dan according to their families: of Shuham,
the family of the Shu'hamites.
These are the families of Dan
43 according to their families. All
the families of the Shu'hamites,
according to their number, were
sixty-four thousand four hundred.

44 The sons of Asher according to
their families: of Imnah, the
family of the Imnites; of Ishvi,
the family of the Ishvites; of
Beri'ah, the family of the Beri'-
45 ites. Of the sons of Beri'ah: of
Heber, the family of the He'ber-
ites; of Mal'chi-el, the family of
46 the Mal'chi-elites. And the name
of the daughter of Asher was
47 Serah. These are the families of
the sons of Asher according to
their number, fifty-three thousand four hundred.

48 The sons of Naph'tali according
to their families: of Jahzeel, the
family of the Jah'zeelites; of
Guni, the family of the Gunites;
49 of Jezer, the family of the Je'zerites; of Shillem, the family of the
50 Shil'lemites. These are the families of Naph'tali according to their
families; and their number was
forty-five thousand four hundred.

51 This was the number of the
people of Israel, six hundred and
one thousand seven hundred and
thirty.

52 The LORD said to Moses: "To
53 these the land shall be divided for
inheritance according to the
54 number of names. To a large
tribe you shall give a large inheritance, and to a small tribe you
shall give a small inheritance;
every tribe shall be given its
inheritance according to its
55 numbers. But the land shall be
divided by lot; according to the
names of the tribes of their fathers
56 they shall inherit. Their inheritance shall be divided according
to lot between the larger and the
smaller."

57 These are the Levites as numbered according to their families:
of Gershon, the family of the
Gershonites; of Kohath, the family of the Ko'hathites; of Merar'i,
the family of the Merar'ites.
58 These are the families of Levi: the
family of the Libnites, the family
of the He'bronites, the family of
the Mahlites, the family of
the Mushites, the family of the
Ko'rahites. And Kohath was the
59 father of Amram. The name of
Amram's wife was Joch'ebed the
daughter of Levi, who was born to
Levi in Egypt; and she bore to
Amram Aaron and Moses and
60 Miriam their sister. And to
Aaron were born Nadab, Abi'hu,
61 Elea'zar and Ith'amar. But
Nadab and Abi'hu died when
they offered unholy fire before the
62 LORD. And those numbered of
them were twenty-three thousand, every male from a month
old and upward; for they were not
numbered among the people of

Israel, because there was no inheritance given to them among
the people of Israel.

63 These were those numbered by
Moses and Elea'zar the priest,
who numbered the people of
Israel in the plains of Moab by the
Jordan at Jericho. But among
64 these there was not a man of those
numbered by Moses and Aaron
the priest, who had numbered the
people of Israel in the wilderness
of Sinai. For the LORD had said
65 of them, "They shall die in the
wilderness." There was not left a
man of them, except Caleb the
son of Jephun'neh and Joshua the
son of Nun.

Inheritance of daughters

27 Then drew near the daughters
of Zelo'phehad the son of
Hepher, son of Gilead, son of
Machir, son of Manas'seh, from
the families of Manas'seh the son
of Joseph. The names of his
daughters were: Mahlah, Noah,
Hoglah, Milcah, and Tirzah.
2 And they stood before Moses, and
before Elea'zar the priest, and
before the leaders and all the
congregation, at the door of the
tent of meeting, saying, "Our
3 father died in the wilderness; he
was not among the company of
those who gathered themselves
together against the LORD in the
company of Korah, but died for
his own sin; and he had no sons.
4 Why should the name of our
father be taken away from his
family, because he had no son?
Give to us a possession among our
father's brethren."
5 Moses brought their case before
the LORD. And the LORD said
6 to Moses, "The daughters of
7 Zelo'phehad are right; you shall
give them possession of an inheritance among their father's brethren and cause the inheritance of
their father to pass to them. And
8 you shall say to the people of
Israel, 'If a man dies, and has
no son, then you shall cause
his inheritance to pass to his
9 daughter. And if he has no
daughter, then you shall give his
10 inheritance to his brothers. And
if he has no brothers, then you
shall give his inheritance to his
11 father's brothers. And if his
father has no brothers, then you
shall give his inheritance to his
kinsman that is next to him of his
family, and he shall possess it.
And it shall be to the people of
Israel a statute and ordinance, as
the LORD commanded Moses.'"

Moses and Joshua

12 THE LORD said to Moses, "Go up into this
mountain of Ab'arim, and see the land
which I have given to the people of Israel.
13 And when you have seen it, you also shall be
gathered to your people, as your brother
14 Aaron was gathered, because you rebelled

26.57-62: Num 1.47-49.   26.64-65: Num 14.26-35.   27.1-11: Num 36.1-12.
27.12-14: Deut 3.23-27; 32.48-52.

against my word in the wilderness of Zin during the strife of the congregation, to sanctify me at the waters before their eyes." (These are the waters of Mer'ibah of Kadesh 15 in the wilderness of Zin.) Moses said to the 16 LORD, "Let the LORD, the God of the spirits of all flesh, appoint a man over the congrega- 17 tion, who shall go out before them and come in before them, who shall lead them out and bring them in; that the congregation of the LORD may not be as sheep which have no 18 shepherd." And the LORD said to Moses, "Take Joshua the son of Nun, a man in whom is the spirit, and lay your hand upon 19 him; cause him to stand before Elea'zar the priest and all the congregation, and you shall commission him in their sight. You shall 20 invest him with some of your authority, that all the congregation of the people of Israel may obey. And he shall stand before Elea'- 21 zar the priest, who shall inquire for him by the judgment of the Urim before the LORD; at his word they shall go out, and at his word they shall come in, both he and all the people of Israel with him, the whole congregation." And Moses did as the LORD commanded 22 him; he took Joshua and caused him to stand before Elea'zar the priest and the whole congregation, and he laid his hands upon 23 him, and commissioned him as the LORD directed through Moses.

A calendar of offerings

28 THE LORD said to Moses, 2 "Command the people of Israel, and say to them, 'My offering, my food for my offerings by fire, my pleasing odour, you shall take heed to offer to me in its 3 due season.' And you shall say to them, This is the offering by fire which you shall offer to the LORD: two male lambs a year old without blemish, day by day, as a con- 4 tinual offering. The one lamb you shall offer in the morning, and the other lamb you shall offer 5 in the evening; also a tenth of an ephah of fine flour for a cereal offering, mixed with a fourth of a 6 hin of beaten oil. It is a continual burnt offering, which was or- dained at Mount Sinai for a pleasing odour, an offering by fire 7 to the LORD. Its drink offering shall be a fourth of a hin for each lamb; in the holy place you shall pour out a drink offering of strong 8 drink to the LORD. The other lamb you shall offer in the even- ing; like the cereal offering of the morning, and like its drink offering, you shall offer it as an offering by fire, a pleasing odour to the LORD.

9 "On the sabbath day two male lambs a year old without blemish, and two tenths of an ephah of fine flour for a cereal offering, mixed 10 with oil, and its drink offering: this is the burnt offering of every sabbath, besides the continual burnt offering and its drink offering.

11 "At the beginnings of your months you shall offer a burnt offering to the LORD: two young bulls, one ram, seven male lambs 12 a year old without blemish; also three tenths of an ephah of fine flour for a cereal offering, mixed with oil, for each bull; and two tenths of fine flour for a cereal offering, mixed with oil, for the

13 one ram; and a tenth of fine flour mixed with oil as a cereal offering for every lamb; for a burnt offer- ing of pleasing odour, an offering 14 by fire to the LORD. Their drink offerings shall be half a hin of wine for a bull, a third of a hin for a ram, and a fourth of a hin for a lamb; this is the burnt offering of each month throughout the 15 months of the year. Also one male goat for a sin offering to the LORD; it shall be offered besides the continual burnt offering and its drink offering.

16 "On the fourteenth day of the first month is the LORD's pass- 17 over. And on the fifteenth day of this month is a feast; seven days shall unleavened bread be eaten. 18 On the first day there shall be a holy convocation: you shall do no 19 laborious work, but offer an offer- ing by fire, a burnt offering to the LORD: two young bulls, one ram, and seven male lambs a year old; see that they are without blemish; 20 also their cereal offering of fine flour mixed with oil; three tenths of an ephah shall you offer for a 21 bull, and two tenths for a ram; a tenth shall you offer for each of 22 the seven lambs; also one male goat for a sin offering, to make 23 atonement for you. You shall offer these besides the burnt offering of the morning, which is 24 for a continual burnt offering. In the same way you shall offer daily, for seven days, the food of an offering by fire, a pleasing odour to the LORD; it shall be offered besides the continual burnt offer- 25 ing and its drink offering. And on the seventh day you shall have a holy convocation; you shall do no laborious work.

26 "On the day of the first fruits, when you offer a cereal offering of new grain to the LORD at your feast of weeks, you shall have a holy convocation; you shall do no 27 laborious work, but offer a burnt

offering, a pleasing odour to the LORD: two young bulls, one ram, seven male lambs a year old; also 28 their cereal offering of fine flour mixed with oil, three tenths of an ephah for each bull, two tenths for 29 one ram, a tenth for each of the seven lambs; with one male 30 goat, to make atonement for you. Besides the continual burnt offer- 31 ing and its cereal offering, you shall offer them and their drink offering. See that they are with- out blemish.

29 "On the first day of the seventh month you shall have a holy con- vocation; you shall do no labori- ous work. It is a day for you to blow the trumpets, and you shall 2 offer a burnt offering, a pleasing odour to the LORD: one young bull, one ram, seven male lambs a year old without blemish; also 3 their cereal offering of fine flour mixed with oil, three tenths of an ephah for the bull, two tenths for the ram, and one tenth for each of 4 the seven lambs; with one male 5 goat for a sin offering, to make atonement for you; besides the 6 burnt offering of the new moon, and its cereal offering, and the continual burnt offering and its cereal offering, and their drink offering, according to the ordi- nance for them, a pleasing odour, an offering by fire to the LORD.

"On the tenth day of this sev- 7 enth month you shall have a holy convocation, and afflict your- selves; you shall do no work, but 8 you shall offer a burnt offering to the LORD, a pleasing odour: one young bull, one ram, seven male lambs a year old; they shall be to you without blemish; and their 9 cereal offering of fine flour mixed with oil, three tenths of an ephah for the bull, two tenths for the one ram, a tenth for each of the seven 10 lambs: also one male goat for a sin 11 offering, besides the sin offering

27.18-23: Deut 3.28. 28.3-8: Ex 29.38-42. 28.16: Ex 12.1-14, 21-27; Lev 23.5; Deut 16.1-2, 5-7.
28.17-25: Ex 12.15-20; Lev 23.6-8; Deut 16.3-4, 8. 28.26-31: Ex 23.16; 34.22; Lev 23.15-21; Deut 16.9-12.
29.1-6: Ex 23.16; 34.22; Lev 23.23-25. 29.7-11: Lev 16.29-34; 23.26-32.

of atonement, and the continual 32
burnt offering and its cereal
offering, and their drink offerings. 33

12 "On the fifteenth day of the
seventh month you shall have a
holy convocation; you shall do no
laborious work, and you shall
keep a feast to the LORD seven 34
13 days; and you shall offer a burnt
offering, an offering by fire, a
pleasing odour to the LORD, thirteen young bulls, two rams,
fourteen male lambs a year old;
they shall be without blemish; 35
14 and their cereal offering of fine
flour mixed with oil, three tenths
of an ephah for each of the thirteen bulls, two tenths for each of 36
15 the two rams, and a tenth for each
16 of the fourteen lambs; also one
male goat for a sin offering, 37
besides the continual burnt offering, its cereal offering and its
drink offering.
17 "On the second day twelve 38
young bulls, two rams, fourteen
male lambs a year old without
18 blemish, with the cereal offering
and the drink offerings for the 39
bulls, for the rams, and for the
lambs, by number, according to
19 the ordinance; also one male goat
for a sin offering, besides the continual burnt offering and its cereal
offering, and their drink offerings. 40
20 "On the third day eleven bulls,
two rams, fourteen male lambs a
21 year old without blemish, with the
cereal offering and the drink
offerings for the bulls, for the
rams, and for the lambs, by
number, according to the ordi- 30
22 nance; also one male goat for a sin
offering, besides the continual
burnt offering and its cereal
offering and its drink offering. 2
23 "On the fourth day ten bulls,
two rams, fourteen male lambs a
24 year old without blemish, with the 3
cereal offering and the drink
offerings for the bulls, for the
rams, and for the lambs, by
number, according to the ordi-
25 nance; also one male goat for a sin 4
offering, besides the continual
burnt offering, its cereal offering
and its drink offering.
26 "On the fifth day nine bulls, two
rams, fourteen male lambs a year
27 old without blemish, with the 5
cereal offering and the drink
offerings for the bulls, for the
rams, and for the lambs, by
number, according to the ordi-
28 nance; also one male goat for a sin
offering; besides the continual
burnt offerings and its cereal 6
offering and its drink offering.
29 "On the sixth day eight bulls,
two rams, fourteen male lambs a
30 year old without blemish, with the 7
cereal offering and the drink
offerings for the bulls, for the
rams, and for the lambs, by
number, according to the ordi-
31 nance; also one male goat for a sin 8
offering; besides the continual
burnt offering, its cereal offering,
and its drink offerings.

"On the seventh day seven bulls,
two rams, fourteen male lambs a
year old without blemish, with the
cereal offering and the drink
offerings for the bulls, for the
rams, and for the lambs, by
number, according to the ordinance; also one male goat for a sin
offering; besides the continual
burnt offering, its cereal offering,
and its drink offering.
"On the eighth day you shall
have a solemn assembly: you shall
do no laborious work, but you
shall offer a burnt offering, an
offering by fire, a pleasing odour
to the LORD: one bull, one ram,
seven male lambs a year old
without blemish, and the cereal
offering and the drink offerings
for the bull, for the ram, and for
the lambs, by number, according
to the ordinance; also one male
goat for a sin offering; besides
the continual burnt offering and
its cereal offering and its drink
offering.
"These you shall offer to the
LORD at your appointed feasts, in
addition to your votive offerings
and your freewill offerings, for
your burnt offerings, and for
your cereal offerings, and for your
drink offerings, and for your
peace offerings."
And Moses told the people of
Israel everything just as the LORD
had commanded Moses.

Vows

Moses said to the heads of the
tribes of the people of Israel,
"This is what the LORD has
commanded. When a man vows a
vow to the LORD, or swears an
oath to bind himself by a pledge,
he shall not break his word; he
shall do according to all that
proceeds out of his mouth. Or
when a woman vows a vow to the
LORD, and binds herself by a
pledge, while within her father's
house, in her youth, and her
father hears of her vow and of her
pledge by which she has bound
herself, and says nothing to her;
then all her vows shall stand, and
every pledge by which she has
bound herself shall stand. But
if her father expresses disapproval
to her on the day that he hears of
it, no vow of hers, no pledge by
which she has bound herself, shall
stand; and the LORD will forgive
her, because her father opposed
her. And if she is married to a
husband, while under her vows or
any thoughtless utterance of her
lips by which she has bound
herself, and her husband hears of
it, and says nothing to her on the
day that he hears; then her vows
shall stand, and her pledges by
which she has bound herself shall
stand. But if, on the day that her
husband comes to hear of it, he
expresses disapproval, then he
shall make void her vow which

was on her, and the thoughtless
utterance of her lips, by which she
bound herself; and the LORD will
forgive her. But any vow of a 9
widow or of a divorced woman,
anything by which she has bound
herself shall stand against her.
And if she vowed in her hus- 10
band's house, or bound herself by
a pledge with an oath, and her 11
husband heard of it, and said
nothing to her, and did not
oppose her; then all her vows shall
stand, and every pledge by which
she bound herself shall stand.
But if her husband makes them 12
null and void on the day that
he hears them, then whatever
proceeds out of her lips concerning her vows, or concerning her
pledge of herself, shall not stand:
her husband has made them void,
and the LORD will forgive her.
Any vow and any binding oath to 13
afflict herself, her husband may
establish, or her husband may
make void. But if her husband 14
says nothing to her from day to
day, then he establishes all her
vows, or all her pledges that are
upon her; he has established
them, because he said nothing to
her on the day that he heard of
them. But if he makes them null 15
and void after he has heard of
them, then he shall bear her iniquity."
These are the statutes which the 16
LORD commanded Moses, as
between a man and his wife,
and between a father and his
daughter, while in her youth,
within her father's house.

Spoils of war

The LORD said to Moses, 31
"Avenge the people of Israel on 2
the Mid'ianites; afterward you
shall be gathered to your people."
And Moses said to the people, 3
"Arm men from among you for the
war, that they may go against
Mid'ian, to execute the LORD's
vengeance on Mid'ian. You shall 4
send a thousand from each of the
tribes of Israel to the war." So 5
there were provided, out of the
thousands of Israel, a thousand
from each tribe, twelve thousand
armed for war. And Moses sent 6
them to the war, a thousand from
each tribe, together with Phin'ehas
the son of Elea'zar the priest, with
the vessels of the sanctuary and the
trumpets for the alarm in his
hand.   They warred against 7
Mid'ian, as the LORD commanded
Moses, and slew every male.
They slew the kings of Mid'ian 8
with the rest of their slain, Evi,
Rekem, Zur, Hur, and Reba, the
five kings of Mid'ian; and they
also slew Balaam the son of Be'or
with the sword. And the people 9
of Israel took captive the women
of Mid'ian and their little ones;
and they took as booty all their
cattle, their flocks, and all their

10 goods. All their cities in the places where they dwelt, and all their encampments, they burned 11 with fire, and took all the spoil and all the booty, both of man and 12 of beast. Then they brought the captives and the booty and the spoil to Moses, and to Elea′zar the priest, and to the congregation of the people of Israel, at the camp on the plains of Moab by the Jordan at Jericho.

13 Moses, and Elea′zar the priest, and all the leaders of the congregation, went forth to meet 14 them outside the camp. And Moses was angry with the officers of the army, the commanders of thousands and the commanders of 15 hundreds, who had come from service in the war. Moses said to 16 them, "Have you let all the women live? Behold, these caused the people of Israel, by the counsel of Balaam, to act treacherously against the LORD in the matter of Pe′or, and so the plague 17 came among the congregation of the LORD. Now therefore, kill every male among the little ones, and kill every woman who has 18 known man by lying with him. But all the young girls who have not known man by lying with 19 him, keep alive for yourselves. Encamp outside the camp seven days; whoever of you has killed any person, and whoever has touched any slain, purify yourselves and your captives on the 20 third day and on the seventh day. You shall purify every garment, every article of skin, all work of goats' hair, and every article of 21 wood." And Elea′zar the priest said to the men of war who had gone to battle: "This is the statute of the 22 law which the LORD has commanded Moses: only the gold, the silver, the bronze, the iron, the 23 tin, and the lead, everything that can stand the fire, you shall pass through the fire, and it shall be clean. Nevertheless it shall also be purified with the water of impurity; and whatever cannot 24 stand the fire, you shall pass through the water. You must wash your clothes on the seventh day, and you shall be clean; and afterward you shall come into the camp."

25 The LORD said to Moses, "Take 26 the count of the booty that was taken, both of man and of beast, you and Elea′zar the priest and the heads of the fathers' houses of 27 the congregation; and divide the booty into two parts, between the 28 warriors who went out to battle and all the congregation. And levy for the LORD a tribute from the men of war who went out to battle, one out of five hundred, of the persons and of the oxen and of 29 the asses and of the flocks; take it from their half, and give it to Elea′zar the priest as an offering 30 to the LORD. And from the

people of Israel's half you shall take one drawn out of every fifty, of the persons, of the oxen, of the asses, and of the flocks, of all the cattle, and give them to the Le-31 vites who have charge of the tabernacle of the LORD." And Moses and Elea′zar the priest did 32 as the LORD commanded Moses. Now the booty remaining of the spoil that the men of war took 33 was: six hundred and seventy-five thousand sheep, seventy-two 34 thousand cattle, sixty-one thou-35 sand asses, and thirty-two thousand persons in all, women who 36 had not known man by lying with him. And the half, the portion of those who had gone out to war, was in number three hundred and 37 thirty-seven thousand five hundred sheep, and the LORD's tri-38 bute of sheep was six hundred and seventy-five. The cattle were thirty-six thousand, of which the LORD's tribute was seventy-two. 39 The asses were thirty thousand five hundred, of which the LORD's 40 tribute was sixty-one. The persons were sixteen thousand, of which the LORD's tribute was 41 thirty-two persons. And Moses gave the tribute, which was the offering for the LORD, to Elea′zar the priest, as the LORD commanded Moses.

42 From the people of Israel's half, which Moses separated from that of the men who had gone to 43 war—now the congregation's half was three hundred and thirty-seven thousand five hundred 44 sheep, thirty-six thousand cattle, 45 and thirty thousand five hundred 46 asses, and sixteen thousand per-47 sons—from the people of Israel's half Moses took one of every fifty, both of persons and of beasts, and gave them to the Levites who had charge of the tabernacle of the LORD; as the LORD commanded Moses.

48 Then the officers who were over the thousands of the army, the captains of thousands and the captains of hundreds, came near 49 to Moses, and said to Moses, "Your servants have counted the men of war who are under our command, and there is not a man 50 missing from us. And we have brought the LORD's offering, what each man found, articles of gold, armlets and bracelets, signet rings, earrings, and beads, to make atonement for ourselves 51 before the LORD." And Moses and Elea′zar the priest received from them the gold, all wrought 52 articles. And all the gold of the offering that they offered to the LORD, from the commanders of thousands and the commanders of hundreds, was sixteen thousand seven hundred and fifty shekels. 53 (The men of war had taken booty, 54 every man for himself.) And Moses and Elea′zar the priest received the gold from the commanders of thousands and of

hundreds, and brought it into the tent of meeting, as a memorial for the people of Israel before the LORD.

Settlements of tribes

32 Now the sons of Reuben and the sons of Gad had a very great multitude of cattle; and they saw the land of Jazer and the land of Gilead, and behold, the place was 2 a place for cattle. So the sons of Gad and the sons of Reuben came and said to Moses and to Elea′zar the priest and to the leaders of the congregation, "At′aroth, Dibon, 3 Jazer, Nimrah, Heshbon, Elea′-4 leh, Sebam, Nebo, and Be′on, the land which the LORD smote before the congregation of Israel, is a land for cattle; and your servants 5 have cattle." And they said, "If we have found favour in your sight, let this land be given to your servants for a possession; do not take us across the Jordan." 6 But Moses said to the sons of Gad and to the sons of Reuben, "Shall your brethren go to the 7 war while you sit here? Why will you discourage the heart of the people of Israel from going over into the land which the LORD has given them? Thus did your 8 fathers, when I sent them from Ka′desh-bar′nea to see the land. For when they went up to the 9 Valley of Eshcol, and saw the land, they discouraged the heart of the people of Israel from going into the land which the LORD had given them. And the LORD's 10 anger was kindled on that day, and he swore, saying, 'Surely 11 none of the men who came up out of Egypt, from twenty years old and upward, shall see the land which I swore to give to Abraham, to Isaac, and to Jacob, because they have not wholly followed me; none except Caleb 12 the son of Jephun′neh the Ken′-izzite and Joshua the son of Nun, for they have wholly followed the LORD.' And the LORD's anger was 13 kindled against Israel, and he made them wander in the wilderness forty years, until all the generation that had done evil in the sight of the LORD was consumed. And behold, you have 14 risen in your fathers' stead, a brood of sinful men, to increase still more the fierce anger of the LORD against Israel! For if you 15 turn away from following him, he will again abandon them in the wilderness; and you will destroy all this people."

16 Then they came near to him, and said, "We will build sheepfolds here for our flocks, and cities for 17 our little ones, but we will take up arms, ready to go before the people of Israel, until we have brought them to their place; and our little ones shall live in the fortified cities because of the inhabitants of the land. We will 18

31.16: Rev 2.14.

Num 32, 6

not return to our homes until the people of Israel have inherited 19 each his inheritance. For we will not inherit with them on the other side of the Jordan and beyond; because our inheritance has come to us on this side of the Jordan to 20 the east." So Moses said to them, "If you will do this, if you will take up arms to go before the 21 LORD for the war, and every armed man of you will pass over the Jordan before the LORD, until he has driven out his enemies 22 from before him and the land is subdued before the LORD; then after that you shall return and be free of obligation to the LORD and to Israel; and this land shall be 23 your possession before the LORD. But if you will not do so, behold, you have sinned against the LORD; and be sure your sin will find you 24 out. Build cities for your little ones, and folds for your sheep; and do what you have promised." 25 And the sons of Gad and the sons of Reuben said to Moses, "Your servants will do as my lord com- 26 mands. Our little ones, our wives, our flocks, and all our cattle, shall remain there in the cities of 27 Gilead; but your servants will pass over, every man who is armed for war, before the LORD to battle, as my lord orders." 28 So Moses gave command concerning them to Elea'zar the priest, and to Joshua the son of Nun, and to the heads of the fathers' houses of the tribes of 29 people of Israel. And Moses said to them, "If the sons of Gad and the sons of Reuben, every man who is armed to battle before the LORD, will pass with you over the Jordan and the land shall be subdued before you, then you shall 30 give them the land of Gilead for a possession; but if they will not pass over with you armed, they shall have possessions among you 31 in the land of Canaan." And the sons of Gad and the sons of Reuben answered, "As the LORD has said to your servants, so we 32 will do. We will pass over armed before the LORD into the land of Canaan, and the possession of our

inheritance shall remain with us beyond the Jordan."

33 And Moses gave to them, to the sons of Gad and to the sons of Reuben and to the half-tribe of Manas'seh the son of Joseph, the kingdom of Sihon king of the Amorites and the kingdom of Og king of Bashan, the land and its cities with their territories, the cities of the land throughout the 34 country. And the sons of Gad built Dibon, At'aroth, Aro'er, 35 At'roth-sho'phan, Jazer, Jog'- 36 behah, Beth-nim'rah and Beth-ha'ran, fortified cities, and 37 folds for sheep. And the sons of Reuben built Heshbon, Elea'leh, 38 Kiriatha'im, Nebo, and Ba'al-me'on (their names to be changed), and Sibmah; and they gave other names to the cities 39 which they built. And the sons of Machir the son of Manas'seh went to Gilead and took it, and dispossessed the Amorites who 40 were in it. And Moses gave Gilead to Machir the son of Manas'seh, and he settled in it. 41 And Ja'ir the son of Manas'seh went and took their villages, and 42 called them Hav'voth-ja'ir.*ⱽ* And Nobah went and took Kenath and its villages, and called it Nobah, after his own name.

Itinerary of the journey

33 These are the stages of the people of Israel, when they went forth out of the land of Egypt by 2 their hosts under the leadership of Moses and Aaron. Moses wrote down their starting places, stage by stage, by command of the LORD; and these are their stages 3 according to their starting places. They set out from Ram'eses in the first month, on the fifteenth day of the first month; on the day after the passover the people of Israel went out triumphantly in the sight of all the Egyptians, 4 while the Egyptians were burying all their first-born, whom the LORD had struck down among them; upon their gods also the LORD executed judgments. 5 So the people of Israel set out

from Ram'eses, and encamped at 6 Succoth. And they set out from Succoth, and encamped at Etham, which is on the edge of the wil- 7 derness. And they set out from Etham, and turned back to Pi-ha-hi'roth, which is east of Ba'al-ze'phon; and they en- 8 camped before Migdol. And they set out from before Hahi'-roth, and passed through the midst of the sea into the wilderness, and they went a three days' journey in the wilderness of 9 Etham, and encamped at Marah. And they set out from Marah, and came to Elim; at Elim there were twelve springs of water and seventy palm trees, and they 10 encamped there. And they set out from Elim, and encamped by the 11 Red Sea. And they set out from the Red Sea, and encamped in the 12 wilderness of Sin. And they set out from the wilderness of Sin, 13 and encamped at Dophkah. And they set out from Dophkah, and 14 encamped at Alush. And they set out from Alush, and encamped at Reph'idim, where there was no water for the people to drink. 15 And they set out from Reph'-idim, and encamped in the wil- 16 derness of Sinai. And they set out from the wilderness of Sinai, 17 and encamped at Kib'roth-hatta'avah. And they set out from Kib'roth-hatta'avah, and en- 18 camped at Haze'roth. And they set out from Haze'roth, and 19 encamped at Rithmah. And they set out from Rithmah, and 20 encamped at Rim'mon-per'ez. And they set out from Rim'mon-per'ez, and encamped at Libnah. 21 And they set out from Libnah, 22 and encamped at Rissah. And they set out from Rissah, and 23 encamped at Kehela'thah. And they set out from Kehela'thah, and encamped at Mount She- 24 pher. And they set out from Mount Shepher, and encamped at 25 Hara'dah. And they set out from Hara'dah, and encamped at 26 Makhe'loth. And they set out from Makhe'loth, and encamped 27 at Tahath. And they set out from Tahath, and encamped at Terah.

ⱽ That is the villages of Jair

28 And they set out from Terah, and 29 encamped at Mithkah. And they set out from Mithkah, and 30 encamped at Hashmo′nah. And they set out from Hashmo′nah, 31 and encamped at Mose′roth. And they set out from Mose′roth, 32 and encamped at Bene-ja′akan. And they set out from Bene-ja′akan, and encamped at Hor-haggid′gad. 33 And they set out from Hor-haggid′gad, and encamped at Jot′ba- 34 thah. And they set out from 35 Jot′bathah, and encamped at Abro′nah. And they set out from 36 Abro′nah, and encamped at E′zion-ge′ber. And they set out from E′zion-ge′ber, and encamped in the 37 wilderness of Zin (that is, Kadesh). And they set out from Kadesh, and encamped at Mount Hor, on the edge of the land of Edom.

38 And Aaron the priest went up Mount Hor at the command of the LORD, and died there, in the fortieth year after the people of Israel had come out of the land of Egypt, on the first day of the fifth 39 month. And Aaron was a hundred and twenty-three years old when he died on Mount Hor.

40 And the Canaanite, the king of Arad, who dwelt in the Negeb in the land of Canaan, heard of the coming of the people of Israel.

41 And they set out from Mount Hor, and encamped at Zal- 42 mo′nah. And they set out from Zalmo′nah, and encamped at 43 Punon. And they set out from Punon, and encamped at Oboth. 44 And they set out from Oboth, and encamped at I′ye-ab′arim, in the 45 territory of Moab. And they set out from I′yim, and encamped at 46 Dibon-gad. And they set out from Dibon-gad, and encamped 47 at Al′mon-diblatha′im. And they set out from Al′mon-diblatha′im, and encamped in the mountains 48 of Ab′arim, before Nebo. And they set out from the mountains of Ab′arim, and encamped in the plains of Moab by the Jordan at 49 Jericho; they encamped by the Jordan from Beth-jesh′amoth as far as Abel-shittim in the plains of Moab.

Division of Canaan

50 And the LORD said to Moses in the plains of Moab by the Jordan 51 at Jericho, "Say to the people of Israel, When you pass over the Jordan into the land of Canaan, 52 then you shall drive out all the inhabitants of the land from before you, and destroy all their figured stones, and destroy all their molten images, and demo- 53 lish all their high places; and you shall take possession of the land and settle in it, for I have given the land to you to possess it. 54 You shall inherit the land by lot according to your families; to a large tribe you shall give a large in-heritance, and to a small tribe you shall give a small inheritance; wherever the lot falls to any man, that shall be his; according to the tribes of your fathers you shall 55 inherit. But if you do not drive out the inhabitants of the land from before you, then those of them whom you let remain shall be as pricks in your eyes and thorns in your sides, and they 56 shall trouble you in the land where you dwell. And I will do to you as I thought to do to them."

34 The LORD said to Moses, 2 "Command the people of Israel, and say to them, When you enter the land of Canaan (this is the land that shall fall to you for an inheritance, the land of Canaan in 3 its full extent), your south side shall be from the wilderness of Zin along the side of Edom, and your southern boundary shall be from the end of the Salt Sea on 4 the east; and your boundary shall turn south of the ascent of Akrab′bim, and cross to Zin, and its end shall be south of Ka′-desh-bar′nea; then it shall go on to Ha′zar-ad′dar, and pass along to 5 Azmon; and the boundary shall turn from Azmon to the Brook of Egypt, and its termination shall be at the sea.

6 "For the western boundary, you shall have the Great Sea and its[z] coast; this shall be your western boundary.

7 "This shall be your northern boundary: from the Great Sea you shall mark out your line to 8 Mount Hor; from Mount Hor you shall mark it out to the entrance of Hamath, and the end of the boundary shall be at Zedad; 9 then the boundary shall extend to Ziphron, and its end shall be at Hazar-enan; this shall be your northern boundary.

10 "You shall mark out your eastern boundary from Hazar-enan to 11 Shepham; and the boundary shall go down from Shepham to Riblah on the east side of A′in; and the boundary shall go down, and reach to the shoulder of the sea of 12 Chin′nereth on the east; and the boundary shall go down to the Jordan, and its end shall be at the Salt Sea. This shall be your land with its boundaries all round."

13 Moses commanded the people of Israel, saying, "This is the land which you shall inherit by lot, which the LORD has commanded to give to the nine tribes and to 14 the half-tribe; for the tribe of the sons of Reuben by fathers' houses and the tribe of the sons of Gad by their fathers' houses have received their inheritance, and also the half-tribe of Manas′seh; 15 the two tribes and the half-tribe have received their inheritance beyond the Jordan at Jericho eastward, toward the sunrise."

The LORD said to Moses, 16 "These are the names of the men 17 who shall divide the land to you for inheritance: Elea′zar the priest and Joshua the son of Nun. You 18 shall take one leader of every tribe, to divide the land for inheritance. These are the names of the 19 men: Of the tribe of Judah, Caleb the son of Jephun′neh. Of the 20 tribe of the sons of Simeon, Shemu′el the son of Ammi′hud. Of the tribe of Benjamin, Eli′dad 21 the son of Chislon. Of the tribe 22 of the sons of Dan a leader, Bukki the son of Jogli. Of the sons of 23 Joseph: of the tribe of the sons of Manas′seh a leader, Han′niel the son of Ephod. And of the tribe of 24 the sons of E′phraim a leader, Kemu′el the son of Shiphtan. Of 25 the tribe of the sons of Zeb′ulun a leader, Eliza′phan the son of Parnach. Of the tribe of the sons 26 of Is′sachar a leader, Pal′tiel the son of Azzan. And of the tribe of 27 the sons of Asher a leader, Ahi′hud the son of Shelo′mi. Of 28 the tribe of the sons of Naph′tali a leader, Pedah′el the son of Ammi′hud. These are the men 29 whom the LORD commanded to divide the inheritance for the people of Israel in the land of Canaan."

Cities for Levites

The LORD said to Moses in the **35** plains of Moab by the Jordan at Jericho, "Command the people of 2 Israel, that they give to the Levites, from the inheritance of their possession, cities to dwell in; and you shall give to the Levites pasture lands round about the cities. The cities shall be theirs to 3 dwell in, and their pasture lands shall be for their cattle and for their livestock and for all their beasts. The pasture lands of the 4 cities, which you shall give to the Levites, shall reach from the wall of the city outward a thousand cubits all round. And you shall 5 measure, outside the city, for the east side two thousand cubits, and for the south side two thousand cubits, and for the west side two thousand cubits, and for the north side two thousand cubits, the city being in the middle; this shall belong to them as pasture land for their cities. The cities which you 6 give to the Levites shall be the six cities of refuge, where you shall permit the manslayer to flee, and in addition to them you shall give forty-two cities. All the cities 7 which you give to the Levites shall be forty-eight, with their pasture lands. And as for the 8 cities which you shall give from the possession of the people of Israel, from the larger tribes you shall take many, and from the smaller tribes you shall take few; each, in proportion to the

z Syr: Heb lacks *its*
33.38–39: Num 20.23–29; Deut 10.6.   33.52: Ex 23.24; Deut 7.5; 12.3.   34.3–5: Josh 15.1–4.
34.13–15: Josh 14.1–5.   35.1–8: Lev 25.32–34; Josh 21.1–42.   35.6, 9–34: Deut 19.1–13.

inheritance which it inherits, shall give of its cities to the Levites."

Cities of refuge

9 And the LORD said to Moses, 10 "Say to the people of Israel, When you cross the Jordan into 11 the land of Canaan, then you shall select cities to be cities of refuge for you, that the manslayer who 12 kills any person without intent may flee there. The cities shall be for you a refuge from the avenger, that the manslayer may not die 13 until he stands before the congregation for judgment. And the cities which you give shall be your 14 six cities of refuge. You shall give three cities beyond the Jordan, and three cities in the land of Canaan, to be cities of refuge. 15 These six cities shall be for refuge for the people of Israel, and for the stranger and for the sojourner among them, that any one who kills any person without intent may flee there.

16 "But if he struck him down with an instrument of iron, so that he died, he is a murderer; the mur-17 derer shall be put to death. And if he struck him down with a stone in the hand, by which a man may die, and he died, he is a murderer; the murderer shall be put to 18 death. Or if he struck him down with a weapon of wood in the hand, by which a man may die, and he died, he is a murderer; the murderer shall be put to death. 19 The avenger of blood shall himself put the murderer to death; when he meets him, he shall put 20 him to death. And if he stabbed him from hatred, or hurled at him, lying in wait, so that he died, 21 or in enmity struck him down with his hand, so that he died, then he who struck the blow shall be put to death; he is a murderer; the avenger of blood shall put the murderer to death, when he meets him.

22 "But if he stabbed him suddenly without enmity, or hurled any-thing on him without lying in 23 wait, or used a stone, by which a man may die, and without seeing him cast it upon him, so that he died, though he was not his enemy, and did not seek his harm; 24 then the congregation shall judge between the manslayer and the

25 avenger of blood, in accordance with these ordinances; and the congregation shall rescue the manslayer from the hand of the avenger of blood, and the con-gregation shall restore him to his city of refuge, to which he had fled, and he shall live in it until 26 the death of the high priest who was anointed with the holy oil. 26 But if the manslayer shall at any time go beyond the bounds of his city of refuge to which he fled, 27 and the avenger of blood finds him outside the bounds of his city of refuge, and the avenger of blood slays the manslayer, he shall 28 not be guilty of blood. For the man must remain in his city of refuge until the death of the high priest; but after the death of the high priest the manslayer may return to the land of his posses-sion.

29 "And these things shall be for a statute and ordinance to you throughout your generations in all 30 your dwellings. If any one kills a person, the murderer shall be put to death on the evidence of wit-nesses; but no person shall be put to death on the testimony of one 31 witness. Moreover you shall accept no ransom for the life of a murderer, who is guilty of death; 32 but he shall be put to death. And you shall accept no ransom for him who has fled to his city of refuge, that he may return to dwell in the land before the death 33 of the high priest. You shall not thus pollute the land in which you live; for blood pollutes the land, and no expiation can be made for the land, for the blood that is shed in it, except by the blood of him 34 who shed it. You shall not defile the land in which you live, in the midst of which I dwell; for I the LORD dwell in the midst of the people of Israel."

Inheritance of daughters

36 The heads of the fathers' houses of the families of the sons of Gilead the son of Machir, son of Manas'seh, of the fathers' houses of the sons of Joseph, came near and spoke before Moses and before the leaders, the heads of 2 the fathers' houses of the people of Israel; they said, "The LORD commanded my lord to give the

land for inheritance by lot to the people of Israel; and my lord was commanded by the LORD to give the inheritance of Zelo'phehad 3 our brother to his daughters. But if they are married to any of the sons of the other tribes of the people of Israel then their inheri-tance will be taken from the inheritance of our fathers, and added to the inheritance of the tribe to which they belong; so it will be taken away from the lot of our inheritance. And when the 4 jubilee of the people of Israel comes, then their inheritance will be added to the inheritance of the tribe to which they belong; and their inheritance will be taken from the inheritance of the tribe of our fathers."

5 And Moses commanded the people of Israel according to the word of the LORD, saying, "The tribe of the sons of Joseph is right. This is what the LORD commands 6 concerning the daughters of Zelo'phehad, 'Let them marry whom they think best; only, they shall marry within the family of the tribe of their father. The 7 inheritance of the people of Israel shall not be transferred from one tribe to another; for every one of the people of Israel shall cleave to the inheritance of the tribe of his fathers. And every daughter who 8 possesses an inheritance in any tribe of the people of Israel shall be wife to one of the family of the tribe of her father, so that every one of the people of Israel may possess the inheritance of his fathers. So no inheritance shall 9 be transferred from one tribe to another; for each of the tribes of the people of Israel shall cleave to its own inheritance.' "

10 The daughters of Zelo'phehad did as the LORD commanded Moses; for Mahlah, Tirzah, Hog-11 lah, Milcah, and Noah, the daughters of Zelo'phehad, were married to sons of their father's 12 brothers. They were married into the families of the sons of Manas'seh the son of Joseph, and their inheritance remained in the tribe of the family of their father.

13 These are the commandments and the ordinances which the LORD commanded by Moses to the people of Israel in the plains of Moab by the Jordan at Jericho.

THE FIFTH BOOK OF MOSES

COMMONLY CALLED

DEUTERONOMY

THESE are the words that Moses spoke to all Israel beyond the Jordan in the wilderness, in the Arabah over against Suph, between Paran and Tophel, Laban, 2 Haze′roth, and Di′-zahab. It is eleven days' journey from Horeb by the way of Mount 3 Se′ir to Ka′desh-bar′nea. And in the fortieth year, on the first day of the eleventh month, Moses spoke to the people of Israel according to all that the LORD had given him in 4 commandment to them, after he had defeated Sihon the king of the Amorites, who lived in Heshbon, and Og the king of Bashan, who lived in Ash′taroth and in Ed′re-i. 5 Beyond the Jordan, in the land of Moab, Moses undertook to explain this law, saying, 6 "The LORD our God said to us in Horeb, 'You have stayed long enough at this moun- 7 tain; turn and take your journey, and go to the hill country of the Amorites, and to all their neighbours in the Arabah, in the hill country and in the lowland, and in the Negeb, and by the seacoast, the land of the Canaanites, and Lebanon, as far as the great 8 river, the river Euphra′tes. Behold, I have set the land before you; go in and take possession of the land which the LORD swore to your fathers, to Abraham, to Isaac, and to Jacob, to give to them and to their descendants after them.' 9 "At that time I said to you, 'I am not able 10 alone to bear you; the LORD your God has multiplied you, and behold, you are this day as the stars of heaven for multitude. May the 11 LORD, the God of your fathers, make you a thousand times as many as you are, and bless you, as he has promised you! How can I 12 bear alone the weight and burden of you and your strife? Choose wise, understanding, 13 and experienced men, according to your tribes, and I will appoint them as your heads.' And you answered me, 'The thing 14 that you have spoken is good for us to do.' So I took the heads of your tribes, wise and 15 experienced men, and set them as heads over you, commanders of thousands, commanders of hundreds, commanders of fifties, commanders of tens, and officers, throughout your tribes. And I charged your judges at 16 that time, 'Hear the cases between your brethren, and judge righteously between a man and his brother or the alien that is with him. You shall not be partial in judgment; 17 you shall hear the small and the great alike; you shall not be afraid of the face of man, for the judgment is God's; and the case that is too hard for you, you shall bring to me, and I will hear it.' And I commanded you at that 18 time all the things that you should do.

"And we set out from Horeb, and went 19 through all that great and terrible wilderness which you saw, on the way to the hill country of the Amorites, as the LORD our God commanded us; and we came to Ka′desh-bar′nea. And I said to you, 'You have come 20 to the hill country of the Amorites, which the

1.9-15: Num 11.10-25. 1.16-18: Ex 18.25-26

129

21 LORD our God gives us. Behold, the LORD your God has set the land before you; go up, take possession, as the LORD, the God of your fathers, has told you; do not fear or be 22 dismayed.' Then all of you came near me, and said, 'Let us send men before us, that they may explore the land for us, and bring us word again of the way by which we must go up and 23 the cities into which we shall come.' The thing seemed good to me, and I took twelve 24 men of you, one man for each tribe; and they turned and went up into the hill country, and came to the Valley of Eshcol and spied it out. 25 And they took in their hands some of the fruit of the land and brought it down to us, and brought us word again, and said, 'It is a good land which the LORD our God gives us.' 26 "Yet you would not go up, but rebelled against the command of the LORD your God; 27 and you murmured in your tents, and said, 'Because the LORD hated us he has brought us forth out of the land of Egypt, to give us into the hand of the Amorites, to destroy us. 28 Whither are we going up? Our brethren have made our hearts melt, saying, "The people are greater and taller than we; the cities are great and fortified up to heaven; , and moreover we have seen the sons of the 29 Anakim there."' Then I said to you, 'Do 30 not be in dread or afraid of them. The LORD your God who goes before you will himself fight for you, just as he did for you in Egypt 31 before your eyes, and in the wilderness, where you have seen how the LORD your God bore you, as a man bears his son, in all the way that you went until you came to this 32 place.' Yet in spite of this word you did not 33 believe the LORD your God, who went before you in the way to seek you out a place to pitch your tents, in fire by night, to show you by what way you should go, and in the cloud by day.
34 "And the LORD heard your words, and was 35 angered, and he swore, 'Not one of these men of this evil generation shall see the good land 36 which I swore to give to your fathers, except Caleb the son of Jephun'neh; he shall see it, and to him and to his children I will give the land upon which he has trodden, because he 37 has wholly followed the LORD!' The LORD was angry with me also on your account, and 38 said, 'You also shall not go in there; Joshua the son of Nun, who stands before you, he shall enter; encourage him, for he shall cause 39 Israel to inherit it. Moreover your little ones, who you said would become a prey, and your children, who this day have no knowledge of good or evil, shall go in there, and to them I will give it, and they shall 40 possess it. But as for you, turn, and

journey into the wilderness in the direction of the Red Sea.'
41 "Then you answered me, 'We have sinned against the LORD; we will go up and fight, just as the LORD our God commanded us.' And every man of you girded on his weapons of war, and thought it easy to go up into the hill country. And the LORD said to me, 'Say 42 to them, Do not go up or fight, for I am not in the midst of you; lest you be defeated before your enemies.' So I spoke to you, and 43 you would not hearken; but you rebelled against the command of the LORD, and were presumptuous and went up into the hill country. Then the Amorites who lived in that 44 hill country came out against you and chased you as bees do and beat you down in Se'ir as far as Hormah. And you returned 45 and wept before the LORD; but the LORD did not hearken to your voice or give ear to you. So you remained at Kadesh many days, the 46 days that you remained there.

"Then we turned, and journeyed into the 2 wilderness in the direction of the Red Sea, as the LORD told me; and for many days we went about Mount Se'ir. Then the LORD 2 said to me, 'You have been going about this 3 mountain country long enough; turn northward. And command the people, You are 4 about to pass through the territory of your brethren the sons of Esau, who live in Se'ir; and they will be afraid of you. So take good heed; do not contend with them; for I will 5 not give you any of their land, no, not so much as for the sole of the foot to tread on, because I have given Mount Se'ir to Esau as a possession. You shall purchase food from 6 them for money, that you may eat; and you shall also buy water of them for money, that you may drink. For the LORD your God has 7 blessed you in all the work of your hands; he knows your going through this great wilderness; these forty years the LORD your God has been with you; you have lacked nothing.' So we went on, away from our brethren the 8 sons of Esau who live in Se'ir, away from the Arabah road from Elath and E'zion-ge'ber.
"And we turned and went in the direction of the wilderness of Moab. And the LORD 9 said to me, 'Do not harass Moab or contend with them in battle, for I will not give you any of their land for a possession, because I have given Ar to the sons of Lot for a possession.' (The Emim formerly lived 10 there, a people great and many, and tall as the Anakim; like the Anakim they are also known 11 as Reph'aim, but the Moabites call them Emim. The Horites also lived in Se'ir 12

formerly, but the sons of Esau dispossessed them, and destroyed them from before them, and settled in their stead; as Israel did to the land of their possession, which the LORD 3 gave to them.) 'Now rise up, and go over the brook Zered.' So we went over the brook 4 Zered. And the time from our leaving Ka′desh-bar′nea until we crossed the brook Zered was thirty-eight years, until the entire generation, that is, the men of war, had perished from the camp, as the LORD had 5 sworn to them. For indeed the hand of the LORD was against them, to destroy them from the camp, until they had perished.

6 "So when all the men of war had perished 7 and were dead from among the people, the 8 LORD said to me, 'This day you are to pass 9 over the boundary of Moab at Ar; and when you approach the frontier of the sons of Ammon, do not harass them or contend with them, for I will not give you any of the land of the sons of Ammon as a possession, because I have given it to the sons of Lot for 20 a possession.' (That also is known as a land of Reph′aim; Reph′aim formerly lived there, but the Ammonites called them Zamzum′- 21 mim, a people great and many, and tall as the Anakim; but the LORD destroyed them before them; and they dispossessed them, 22 and settled in their stead; as he did for the sons of Esau, who live in Se′ir, when he destroyed the Horites before them, and they dispossessed them, and settled in their stead 23 even to this day. As for the Avvim, who lived in villages as far as Gaza, the Caph′- torim, who came from Caphtor, destroyed 24 them and settled in their stead.) 'Rise up, take your journey, and go over the valley of the Arnon; behold, I have given into your hand Sihon the Amorite, king of Heshbon, and his land; begin to take possession, and 25 contend with him in battle. This day I will begin to put the dread and fear of you upon the peoples that are under the whole heaven, who shall hear the report of you and shall tremble and be in anguish because of you.'

26 "So I sent messengers from the wilderness of Ked′emoth to Sihon the king of Heshbon, 27 with words of peace, saying, 'Let me pass through your land; I will go only by the road, I will turn aside neither to the right nor to 28 the left. You shall sell me food for money, that I may eat, and give me water for money, that I may drink; only let me pass through on 29 foot, as the sons of Esau who live in Se′ir and the Moabites who live in Ar did for me, until I go over the Jordan into the land which the 30 LORD our God gives to us.' But Sihon the king of Heshbon would not let us pass by him; for the LORD your God hardened his

spirit and made his heart obstinate, that he might give him into your hand, as at this day. And the LORD said to me, 31 'Behold, I have begun to give Sihon and his land over to you; begin to take possession, that you may occupy his land.' Then Sihon 32 came out against us, he and all his people, to battle at Jahaz. And the LORD our God gave 33 him over to us; and we defeated him and his sons and all his people. And we captured all 34 his cities at that time and utterly destroyed every city, men, women, and children; we left none remaining; only the cattle we took 35 as spoil for ourselves, with the booty of the cities which we captured. From Aro′er, 36 which is on the edge of the valley of the Arnon, and from the city that is in the valley, as far as Gilead, there was not a city too high for us; the LORD our God gave all into our hands. Only to the land of the sons of 37 Ammon you did not draw near, that is, to all the banks of the river Jabbok and the cities of the hill country, and wherever the LORD our God forbade us.

"Then we turned and went up the way to 3 Bashan; and Og the king of Bashan came out against us, he and all his people, to battle at Ed′re-i. But the LORD said to me, 'Do not 2 fear him; for I have given him and all his people and his land into your hand; and you shall do to him as you did to Sihon the king of the Amorites, who dwelt at Heshbon.' So the LORD our God gave into our hand 3 Og also, the king of Bashan, and all his people; and we smote him until no survivor was left to him. And we took all his cities at 4 that time—there was not a city which we did not take from them—sixty cities, the whole region of Argob, the kingdom of Og in Bashan. All these were cities fortified with 5 high walls, gates, and bars, besides very many unwalled villages. And we utterly 6 destroyed them, as we did to Sihon the king of Heshbon, destroying every city, men, women, and children. But all the cattle and 7 the spoil of the cities we took as our booty. So we took the land at that time out of the 8 hand of the two kings of the Amorites who were beyond the Jordan, from the valley of the Arnon to Mount Hermon (the Sido′nians 9 call Hermon Sirion, while the Amorites call it Senir), all the cities of the tableland and all 10 Gilead and all Bashan, as far as Sal′ecah and Ed′re-i, cities of the kingdom of Og in Bashan. (For only Og the king of Bashan 11 was left of the remnant of the Reph′aim; behold, his bedstead was a bedstead of iron; is it not in Rabbah of the Ammonites? Nine

2.26–37: Num 21.21–32.   3.1–11: Num 21.33–35.

cubits was its length, and four cubits its breadth, according to the common cubit.*)

12 "When we took possession of this land at that time, I gave to the Reubenites and the Gadites the territory beginning at Aro'er, which is on the edge of the valley of the Arnon, and half the hill country of Gilead
13 with its cities; the rest of Gilead, and all Bashan, the kingdom of Og, that is, all the region of Argob, I gave to the half-tribe of Manas'seh. (The whole of that Bashan is
14 called the land of Reph'aim. Ja'ir the Manas'site took all the region of Argob, that is, Bashan, as far as the border of the Gesh'urites and the Maac'athites, and called the villages after his own name, Hav'voth-
15 ja'ir, as it is to this day.) To Machir I gave
16 Gilead, and to the Reubenites and the Gadites I gave the territory from Gilead as far as the valley of the Arnon, with the middle of the valley as a boundary, as far over as the river Jabbok, the boundary of
17 Ammonites; the Arabah also, with the Jordan as the boundary, from Chin'nereth as far as the sea of the Arabah, the Salt Sea, under the slopes of Pisgah on the east.
18 "And I commanded you at that time, saying, 'The LORD your God has given you this land to possess; all your men of valour shall pass over armed before your brethren
19 the people of Israel. But your wives, your little ones, and your cattle (I know that you have many cattle) shall remain in the cities
20 which I have given you, until the LORD gives

rest to your brethren, as to you, and they also occupy the land which the LORD your God gives them beyond the Jordan; then you shall return every man to his possession which I have given you.' And I commanded Joshua at that time, 'Your eyes have seen all that the LORD your God has done to these two kings; so will the LORD do to all the kingdoms into which you are going over. You shall not fear them; for it is the LORD your God who fights for you.'

"And I besought the LORD at that time, saying, 'O Lord GOD, thou hast only begun to show thy servant thy greatness and thy mighty hand; for what god is there in heaven or on earth who can do such works and mighty acts as thine? Let me go over, I pray, and see the good land beyond the Jordan, that goodly hill country, and Lebanon.' But the LORD was angry with me on your account, and would not hearken to me; and the LORD said to me, 'Let it suffice you; speak no more to me of this matter. Go up to the top of Pisgah, and lift up your eyes westward and northward and southward and eastward, and behold it with your eyes; for you shall not go over this Jordan. But charge Joshua, and encourage and strengthen him; for he shall go over at the head of this people, and he shall put them in possession of the land which you shall see.' So we remained in the valley opposite Beth-pe'or.

"And now, O Israel, give heed to the statutes and the ordinances which I teach

The Sea of the Arabah, the Salt Sea   *Deut 3, 17*

you, and do them; that you may live, and go in and take possession of the land which the LORD, the God of your fathers, gives you.
2 You shall not add to the word which I command you, nor take from it; that you may keep the commandments of the LORD your
3 God which I command you. Your eyes have seen what the LORD did at Ba'al-pe'or; for the LORD your God destroyed from among you all the men who followed the Ba'al of
4 Pe'or; but you who held fast to the LORD
5 your God are all alive this day. Behold, I have taught you statutes and ordinances, as the LORD my God commanded me, that you should do them in the land which you are
6 entering to take possession of it. Keep them and do them; for that will be your wisdom and your understanding in the sight of the peoples, who, when they hear all these statutes, will say, 'Surely this great nation is a
7 wise and understanding people.' For what great nation is there that has a god so near to it as the LORD our God is to us, whenever we
8 call upon him? And what great nation is there, that has statutes and ordinances so righteous as all this law which I set before you this day?
9 "Only take heed, and keep your soul diligently, lest you forget the things which your eyes have seen, and lest they depart from your heart all the days of your life; make them known to your children and your
10 children's children—how on the day that you stood before the LORD your God at Horeb, the LORD said to me, 'Gather the people to me, that I may let them hear my words, so that they may learn to fear me all the days that they live upon the earth, and that they
11 may teach their children so.' And you came near and stood at the foot of the mountain, while the mountain burned with fire to the heart of heaven, wrapped in darkness, cloud,
12 and gloom. Then the LORD spoke to you out of the midst of the fire; you heard the sound of words, but saw no form; there was only a
13 voice. And he declared to you his covenant, which he commanded you to perform, that is, the ten commandments;[b] and he wrote
14 them upon two tables of stone. And the LORD commanded me at that time to teach you statutes and ordinances, that you might do them in the land which you are going over to possess.
15 "Therefore take good heed to yourselves. Since you saw no form on the day that the LORD spoke to you at Horeb out of the midst
16 of the fire, beware lest you act corruptly by making a graven image for yourselves, in the form of any figure, the likeness of male or

female, the likeness of any beast that is on the 17 earth, the likeness of any winged bird that flies in the air, the likeness of anything that 18 creeps on the ground, the likeness of any fish that is in the water under the earth. And 19 beware lest you lift up your eyes to heaven, and when you see the sun and the moon and the stars, all the host of heaven, you be drawn away and worship them and serve them, things which the LORD your God has allotted to all the peoples under the whole heaven. But the LORD has taken you, and brought 20 you forth out of the iron furnace, out of Egypt, to be a people of his own possession, as at this day. Furthermore the LORD was 21 angry with me on your account, and he swore that I should not cross the Jordan, and that I should not enter the good land which the LORD your God gives you for an inheritance. For I must die in this land, I must not go 22 over the Jordan; but you shall go over and take possession of that good land. Take heed 23 to yourselves, lest you forget the covenant of the LORD your God, which he made with you, and make a graven image in the form of anything which the LORD your God has forbidden you. For the LORD your God is a 24 devouring fire, a jealous God.
"When you beget children and children's 25 children, and have grown old in the land, if you act corruptly by making a graven image in the form of anything, and by doing what is evil in the sight of the LORD your God, so as to provoke him to anger, I call heaven and 26 earth to witness against you this day, that you will soon utterly perish from the land which you are going over the Jordan to possess; you will not live long upon it, but will be utterly destroyed. And the LORD will scatter you 27 among the peoples, and you will be left few in number among the nations where the LORD will drive you. And there you will 28 serve gods of wood and stone, the work of men's hands, that neither see, nor hear, nor eat, nor smell. But from there you will seek 29 the LORD your God, and you will find him, if you search after him with all your heart and with all your soul. When you are in tribu- 30 lation, and all these things come upon you in the latter days, you will return to the LORD your God and obey his voice, for the LORD 31 your God is a merciful God; he will not fail you or destroy you or forget the covenant with your fathers which he swore to them.
"For ask now of the days that are past, 32 which were before you, since the day that God created man upon the earth, and ask from one end of heaven to the other, whether such a great thing as this has ever happened

b Heb words
4.2: Rev 22.18–19.   4.9–14: Ex 19.1–21.   4.24: Heb 12.29.

33 or was ever heard of. Did any people ever hear the voice of a god speaking out of the midst of the fire, as you have heard, and still
34 live? Or has any god ever attempted to go and take a nation for himself from the midst of another nation, by trials, by signs, by wonders, and by war, by a mighty hand and an outstretched arm, and by great terrors, according to all that the LORD your God did
35 for you in Egypt before your eyes? To you it was shown, that you might know that the LORD is God; there is no other besides him.
36 Out of heaven he let you hear his voice, that he might discipline you; and on earth he let you see his great fire, and you heard his
37 words out of the midst of the fire. And because he loved your fathers and chose their descendants after them, and brought you out of Egypt with his own presence, by his great
38 power, driving out before you nations greater and mightier than yourselves, to bring you in, to give you their land for an inheritance,
39 as at this day; know therefore this day, and lay it to your heart, that the LORD is God in heaven above and on the earth beneath; there
40 is no other. Therefore you shall keep his statutes and his commandments, which I command you this day, that it may go well with you, and with your children after you, and that you may prolong your days in the land which the LORD your God gives you for ever."
41 Then Moses set apart three cities in the east
42 beyond the Jordan, that the manslayer might flee there, who kills his neighbour unintentionally, without being at enmity with him in time past, and that by fleeing to one of these
43 cities he might save his life: Bezer in the wilderness on the tableland for the Reubenites, and Ramoth in Gilead for the Gadites, and Golan in Bashan for the Manas'sites.

THIS IS THE LAW

44 THIS is the law which Moses set before
45 the children of Israel; these are the testimonies, the statutes, and the ordinances, which Moses spoke to the children of Israel
46 when they came out of Egypt, beyond the Jordan in the valley opposite Beth-pe'or, in the land of Sihon the king of the Amorites, who lived at Heshbon, whom Moses and the children of Israel defeated when they came
47 out of Egypt. And they took possession of his land and the land of Og the king of Bashan, the two kings of the Amorites, who
48 lived to the east beyond the Jordan; from Aro'er, which is on the edge of the valley of the Arnon, as far as Mount Sirion⁰ (that is,

Hermon), together with all the Arabah on the east side of the Jordan as far as the Sea of the Arabah, under the slopes of Pisgah.

And Moses summoned all Israel, and said to them, "Hear, O Israel, the statutes and the ordinances which I speak in your hearing this day, and you shall learn them and be careful to do them. The LORD our God made a covenant with us in Horeb. Not with our fathers did the LORD make this covenant, but with us, who are all of us here alive this day. The LORD spoke with you face to face at the mountain, out of the midst of the fire, while I stood between the LORD and you at that time, to declare to you the word of the LORD; for you were afraid because of the fire, and you did not go up into the mountain. He said:

"'I am the LORD your God, who brought you out of the land of Egypt, out of the house of bondage.

"'You shall have no other gods before[d] me.

"'You shall not make for yourself a graven image, or any likeness of anything that is in heaven above, or that is on the earth beneath, or that is in the water under the earth; you shall not bow down to them or serve them; for I the LORD your God am a jealous God, visiting the iniquity of the fathers upon the children to the third and fourth generation of those who hate me, but showing steadfast love to thousands of those who love me and keep my commandments.

"'You shall not take the name of the LORD your God in vain: for the LORD will not hold him guiltless who takes his name in vain.

"'Observe the sabbath day, to keep it holy, as the LORD your God commanded you. Six days you shall labour, and do all your work; but the seventh day is a sabbath to the LORD your God; in it you shall not do any work, you, or your son, or your daughter, or your manservant, or your maidservant, or your ox, or your ass, or any of your cattle, or the sojourner who is within your gates, that your manservant and your maidservant may rest as well as you. You shall remember that you were a servant in the land of Egypt, and the LORD your God brought you out thence with a mighty hand and an outstretched arm; therefore the LORD your God commanded you to keep the sabbath day.

"'Honour your father and your mother, as the LORD your God commanded you; that your days may be prolonged, and that it may go well with you, in the land which the LORD your God gives you.

⁰ Syr: Heb *Sion*   d Or *besides*
4.35: Mk 12.32.   4.41–43: Num 35.6, 9–34; Deut 19.2–13; Josh 20.7–9.   5.6–21: Ex 20.2–17.
5.14: Ex 20.8–11; 23.12.   5.16: Mt 15.4; Mk 7.10; Eph 6.2–3.   5.16–20: Mt 19.18–19; Mk 10.19; Lk 18.20.

" 'You shall not kill.

" 'Neither shall you commit adultery.

" 'Neither shall you steal.

" 'Neither shall you bear false witness against your neighbour.

" 'Neither shall you covet your neighbour's wife; and you shall not desire your neighbour's house, his field, or his manservant, or his maidservant, his ox, or his ass, or anything that is your neighbour's.'

"These words the LORD spoke to all your assembly at the mountain out of the midst of the fire, the cloud, and the thick darkness, with a loud voice; and he added no more. And he wrote them upon two tables of stone, and gave them to me. And when you heard the voice out of the midst of the darkness, while the mountain was burning with fire, you came near to me, all the heads of your tribes, and your elders; and you said, 'Behold, the LORD our God has shown us his glory and greatness, and we have heard his voice out of the midst of the fire; we have this day seen God speak with man and man still live. Now therefore why should we die? For this great fire will consume us; if we hear the voice of the LORD our God any more, we shall die. For who is there of all flesh, that has heard the voice of the living God speaking out of the midst of fire, as we have, and has still lived? Go near, and hear all that the LORD our God will say; and speak to us all that the LORD our God will speak to you; and we will hear and do it.'

"And the LORD heard your words, when you spoke to me; and the LORD said to me, 'I have heard the words of this people, which they have spoken to you; they have rightly said all that they have spoken. Oh that they had such a mind as this always, to fear me and to keep all my commandments, that it might go well with them and with their children for ever! Go and say to them, "Return to your tents." But you, stand here by me, and I will tell you all the commandment and the statutes and the ordinances which you shall teach them, that they may do them in the land which I give them to possess.' You shall be careful to do therefore as the LORD your God has commanded you; you shall not turn aside to the right hand or to the left. You shall walk in all the way which the LORD your God has commanded you, that you may live, and that it may go well with you, and that you may live long in the land which you shall possess.

"Now this is the commandment, the sta- 6 tutes and the ordinances which the LORD your God commanded me to teach you, that you may do them in the land to which you are going over, to possess it; that you may 2 fear the LORD your God, you and your son and your son's son, by keeping all his statutes and his commandments, which I command you, all the days of your life; and that your days may be prolonged. Hear therefore, O 3 Israel, and be careful to do them; that it may go well with you, and that you may multiply greatly, as the LORD, the God of your fathers, has promised you, in a land flowing with milk and honey.

"Hear, O Israel: The LORD our God is one 4 LORD;[e] and you shall love the LORD your 5 God with all your heart, and with all your soul, and with all your might. And these 6 words which I command you this day shall be upon your heart; and you shall teach them 7 diligently to your children, and shall talk of them when you sit in your house, and when you walk by the way, and when you lie down, and when you rise. And you shall bind them 8 as a sign upon your hand, and they shall be as frontlets between your eyes. And you shall 9 write them on the doorposts of your house and on your gates.

"And when the LORD your God brings you 10 into the land which he swore to your fathers, to Abraham, to Isaac, and to Jacob, to give you, with great and goodly cities, which you did not build, and houses full of all good 11 things, which you did not fill, and cisterns hewn out, which you did not hew, and vineyards and olive trees, which you did not plant, and when you eat and are full, then 12 take heed lest you forget the LORD, who brought you out of the land of Egypt, out of the house of bondage. You shall fear the 13 LORD your God; you shall serve him, and swear by his name. You shall not go after 14 other gods, of the gods of the peoples who are round about you; for the LORD your God in 15 the midst of you is a jealous God; lest the anger of the LORD your God be kindled against you, and he destroy you from off the face of the earth.

"You shall not put the LORD your God to 16 the test, as you tested him at Massah. You 17 shall diligently keep the commandments of the LORD your God, and his testimonies, and his statutes, which he has commanded you. And you shall do what is right and good in 18 the sight of the LORD, that it may go well with you, and that you may go in and take

---

[e] Or the LORD our God, the LORD is one   Or the LORD is our God, the LORD is one   Or the LORD is our God, the LORD alone

5.17-18: Jas 2.11.   5.17-21: Rom 13.9.   5.18: Mt 5.27; Rom 7.2.   5.21: Rom 7.7.   5.22-27: Ex 20.18-21.   6.4-5: Mt 22.37; Mk 12.29-30; Lk 10.27.   6.6-9: Deut 6.20-25; 11.18-20.   6.8: Ex 13.9, 16; Deut 11.18.   6.13: Mt 4.10; Lk 4.8.   6.16: Mt 4.7; Lk 4.12.

gives them over to you, and you defeat them; then you must utterly destroy them; you shall make no covenant with them, and show no mercy to them. You shall not make 3 marriages with them, giving your daughters to their sons or taking their daughters for your sons. For they would turn away your 4 sons from following me, to serve other gods; then the anger of the LORD would be kindled against you, and he would destroy you quickly. But thus shall you deal with them: 5 you shall break down their altars, and dash in pieces their pillars, and hew down their Ashe′rim, and burn their graven images with fire.

"For you are a people holy to the LORD your 6 God; the LORD your God has chosen you to be a people for his own possession, out of all the peoples that are on the face of the earth. It was not because you were more in number 7 than any other people that the LORD set his love upon you and chose you, for you were the fewest of all peoples; but it is because the 8 LORD loves you, and is keeping the oath which he swore to your fathers, that the LORD has brought you out with a mighty hand, and redeemed you from the house of bondage, from the hand of Pharaoh king of Egypt. Know therefore that the LORD your 9 God is God, the faithful God who keeps covenant and steadfast love with those who love him and keep his commandments, to a thousand generations, and requites to their 10 face those who hate him, by destroying them; he will not be slack with him who hates him, he will requite him to his face. You shall 11 therefore be careful to do the commandment, and the statutes, and the ordinances, which I command you this day.

"And because you hearken to these ordi- 12 nances, and keep and do them, the LORD your God will keep with you the covenant and the steadfast love which he swore to your fathers to keep; he will love you, bless you, 13 and multiply you; he will also bless the fruit of your body and the fruit of your ground, your grain and your wine and your oil, the increase of your cattle and the young of your flock, in the land which he swore to your fathers to give you. You shall be blessed 14 above all peoples; there shall not be male or female barren among you, or among your cattle. And the LORD will take away from 15 you all sickness; and none of the evil diseases of Egypt, which you knew, will he inflict upon you, but he will lay them upon all who hate you. And you shall destroy all the 16 peoples that the LORD your God will give over to you, your eye shall not pity them;

possession of the good land which the LORD
19 swore to give to your fathers by thrusting out all your enemies from before you, as the LORD has promised.
20 "When your son asks you in time to come, 'What is the meaning of the testimonies and the statutes and the ordinances which the
21 LORD our God has commanded you?' then you shall say to your son, 'We were Pharaoh's slaves in Egypt; and the LORD brought
22 us out of Egypt with a mighty hand; and the LORD showed signs and wonders, great and grievous, against Egypt and against Pharaoh
23 and all his household, before our eyes; and he brought us out from there, that he might bring us in and give us the land which he
24 swore to give to our fathers. And the LORD commanded us to do all these statutes, to fear the LORD our God, for our good always, that he might preserve us alive, as at this day.
25 And it will be righteousness for us, if we are careful to do all this commandment before the LORD our God, as he has commanded us.'

7 "When the LORD your God brings you into the land which you are entering to take possession of it, and clears away many nations before you, the Hittites, the Gir′gashites, the Amorites, the Canaanites, the Per′izzites, the Hivites, and the Jeb′usites, seven nations greater and mightier than
2 yourselves, and when the LORD your God

neither shall you serve their gods, for that would be a snare to you.

"If you say in your heart, 'These nations are greater than I; how can I dispossess them?' you shall not be afraid of them, but you shall remember what the LORD your God did to Pharaoh and to all Egypt, the great trials which your eyes saw, the signs, the wonders, the mighty hand, and the outstretched arm, by which the LORD your God brought you out; so will the LORD your God do to all the peoples of whom you are afraid. Moreover the LORD your God will send hornets among them, until those who are left and hide themselves from you are destroyed. You shall not be in dread of them; for the LORD your God is in the midst of you, a great and terrible God. The LORD your God will clear away these nations before you little by little; you may not make an end of them at once,[j] lest the wild beasts grow too numerous for you. But the LORD your God will give them over to you, and throw them into great confusion, until they are destroyed. And he will give their kings into your hand, and you shall make their names perish from under heaven; not a man shall be able to stand against you, until you have destroyed them. The graven images of their gods you shall burn with fire; you shall not covet the silver or the gold that is on them, or take it for yourselves, lest you be ensnared by it; for it is an abomination to the LORD your God. And you shall not bring an abominable thing into your house, and become accursed like it; you shall utterly detest and abhor it; for it is an accursed thing.

"All the commandment which I command you this day you shall be careful to do, that you may live and multiply, and go in and possess the land which the LORD swore to give to your fathers. And you shall remember all the way which the LORD your God has led you these forty years in the wilderness, that he might humble you, testing you to know what was in your heart, whether you would keep his commandments, or not. And he humbled you and let you hunger and fed you with manna, which you did not know, nor did your fathers know; that he might make you know that man does not live by bread alone, but that man lives by everything that proceeds out of the mouth of the LORD. Your clothing did not wear out upon you, and your foot did not swell, these forty years. Know then in your heart that, as a man disciplines his son, the LORD your God disciplines you. So you shall keep the

commandments of the LORD your God, by walking in his ways and by fearing him. For the LORD your God is bringing you into a good land, a land of brooks of water, of fountains and springs, flowing forth in valleys and hills, a land of wheat and barley, of vines and fig trees and pomegranates, a land of olive trees and honey, a land in which you will eat bread without scarcity, in which you will lack nothing, a land whose stones are iron, and out of whose hills you can dig copper. And you shall eat and be full, and you shall bless the LORD your God for the good land he has given you.

"Take heed lest you forget the LORD your God, by not keeping his commandments and his ordinances and his statutes, which I command you this day: lest, when you have eaten and are full, and have built goodly houses and live in them, and when your herds and flocks multiply, and your silver and gold is multiplied, and all that you have is multiplied, then your heart be lifted up, and you forget the LORD your God, who brought you out of the land of Egypt, out of the house of bondage, who led you through the great and terrible wilderness, with its fiery serpents and scorpions and thirsty ground where there was no water, who brought you water out of the flinty rock, who fed you in the wilderness with manna which your fathers did not know, that he might humble you and test you, to do you good in the end. Beware lest you say in your heart, 'My power and the might of my hand have gotten me this wealth.' You shall remember the LORD your God, for it is he who gives you power to get wealth; that he may confirm his covenant which he swore to your fathers, as at this day. And if you forget the LORD your God and go after other gods and serve them and worship them, I solemnly warn you this day that you shall surely perish. Like the nations that the LORD makes to perish before you, so shall you perish, because you would not obey the voice of the LORD your God.

"Hear, O Israel; you are to pass over the Jordan this day, to go in to dispossess nations greater and mightier than yourselves, cities great and fortified up to heaven, a people great and tall, the sons of the Anakim, whom you know, and of whom you have heard it said, 'Who can stand before the sons of Anak?' Know therefore this day that he who goes over before you as a devouring fire is the LORD your God; he will destroy them and subdue them before you; so you shall drive them out, and make them perish quickly, as the LORD has promised you.

4 "Do not say in your heart, after the LORD your God has thrust them out before you, 'It is because of my righteousness that the LORD has brought me in to possess this land'; whereas it is because of the wickedness of these nations that the LORD is driving them 5 out before you. Not because of your righteousness or the uprightness of your heart are you going in to possess their land; but because of the wickedness of these nations the LORD your God is driving them out from before you, and that he may confirm the word which the LORD swore to your fathers, to Abraham, to Isaac, and to Jacob.

6 "Know therefore, that the LORD your God is not giving you this good land to possess because of your righteousness; for you are a 7 stubborn people. Remember and do not forget how you provoked the LORD your God to wrath in the wilderness; from the day you came out of the land of Egypt, until you came to this place, you have been rebellious against 8 the LORD. Even at Horeb you provoked the LORD to wrath, and the LORD was so angry with you that he was ready to destroy you. 9 When I went up the mountain to receive the tables of stone, the tables of the covenant which the LORD made with you, I remained on the mountain forty days and forty nights; 10 I neither ate bread nor drank water. And the LORD gave me the two tables of stone written with the finger of God; and on them were all the words which the LORD had spoken with you on the mountain out of the midst of the 11 fire on the day of the assembly. And at the end of forty days and forty nights the LORD gave me the two tables of stone, the tables of 12 the covenant. Then the LORD said to me, 'Arise, go down quickly from here; for your people whom you have brought from Egypt have acted corruptly; they have turned aside quickly out of the way which I commanded them; they have made themselves a molten image.'

13 "Furthermore the LORD said to me, 'I have seen this people, and behold, it is a stubborn 14 people; let me alone, that I may destroy them and blot out their name from under heaven; and I will make of you a nation mightier and 15 greater than they.' So I turned and came down from the mountain, and the mountain was burning with fire; and the two tables of 16 the covenant were in my two hands. And I looked, and behold, you had sinned against the LORD your God; you had made yourselves a molten calf; you had turned aside quickly from the way which the LORD had 17 commanded you. So I took hold of the two

tables, and cast them out of my two hands, and broke them before your eyes. Then I lay prostrate before the LORD as before, forty days and forty nights; I neither ate bread nor drank water, because of all the sin which you had committed, in doing what was evil in the sight of the LORD, to provoke him to anger. For I was afraid of the anger and hot 19 displeasure which the LORD bore against you, so that he was ready to destroy you. But the LORD hearkened to me that time also. And 20 the LORD was so angry with Aaron that he was ready to destroy him; and I prayed for Aaron also at the same time. Then I took the 21 sinful thing, the calf which you had made, and burned it with fire and crushed it, grinding it very small, until it was as fine as dust; and I threw the dust of it into the brook that descended out of the mountain.

"At Tab'erah also, and at Massah, and at 22 Kib'roth-hatta'avah, you provoked the LORD to wrath. And when the LORD sent you from 23 Ka'desh-bar'nea, saying, 'Go up and take possession of the land which I have given you,' then you rebelled against the commandment of the LORD your God, and did not believe him or obey his voice. You have 24 been rebellious against the LORD from the day that I knew you.

"So I lay prostrate before the LORD for 25 these forty days and forty nights, because the LORD had said he would destroy you. And I 26 prayed to the LORD, 'O Lord GOD, destroy not thy people and thy heritage, whom thou hast redeemed through thy greatness, whom thou hast brought out of Egypt with a mighty hand. Remember thy servants, Abraham, 27 Isaac, and Jacob; do not regard the stubbornness of this people, or their wickedness, or their sin, lest the land from which thou 28 didst bring us say, "Because the LORD was not able to bring them into the land which he promised them, and because he hated them, he has brought them out to slay them in the wilderness." For they are thy people and thy 29 heritage, whom thou didst bring out by thy great power and by thy outstretched arm.'

"At that time the LORD said to me, 'Hew 10 two tables of stone like the first, and come up to me on the mountain, and make an ark of wood. And I will write on the tables the 2 words that were on the first tables which you broke, and you shall put them in the ark.' So 3 I made an ark of acacia wood, and hewed two tables of stone like the first, and went up the mountain with the two tables in my hand. And he wrote on the tables, as at the first 4 writing, the ten commandments[g] which the LORD had spoken to you on the mountain out of the midst of the fire on the day of the assembly; and the LORD gave them to me. Then I turned and came down from the mountain, and put the tables in the ark which I had made; and there they are, as the LORD commanded me.

(The people of Israel journeyed from Be-er′oth Bene-ja′akan[h] to Mose′rah. There Aaron died, and there he was buried; and his son Elea′zar ministered as priest in his stead. From there they journeyed to Gud′godah, and from Gud′godah to Jot′bathah, a land with brooks of water. At that time the LORD set apart the tribe of Levi to carry the ark of the covenant of the LORD, to stand before the LORD to minister to him and to bless in his name, to this day. Therefore Levi has no portion or inheritance with his brothers; the LORD is his inheritance, as the LORD your God said to him.)

"I stayed on the mountain, as at the first time, forty days and forty nights, and the LORD hearkened to me that time also; the LORD was unwilling to destroy you. And the LORD said to me, 'Arise, go on your journey at the head of the people, that they may go in and possess the land, which I swore to their fathers to give them.'

2 "And now, Israel, what does the LORD your God require of you, but to fear the LORD your God, to walk in all his ways, to love 3 him, to serve the LORD your God with all your heart and with all your soul, and to keep the commandments and statutes of the LORD, 4 which I command you this day for your good? Behold, to the LORD your God belong heaven and the heaven of heavens, the earth 5 with all that is in it; yet the LORD set his heart in love upon your fathers and chose their descendants after them, you above all 6 peoples, as at this day. Circumcise therefore the foreskin of your heart, and be no longer 7 stubborn. For the LORD your God is God of gods and LORD of lords, the great, the mighty, and the terrible God, who is not 8 partial and takes no bribe. He executes justice for the fatherless and the widow, and loves the sojourner, giving him food and 9 clothing. Love the sojourner therefore; for you were sojourners in the land of Egypt. 20 You shall fear the LORD your God; you shall serve him and cleave to him, and by his name 21 you shall swear. He is your praise; he is your God, who has done for you these great and 22 terrible things which your eyes have seen. Your fathers went down to Egypt seventy persons; and now the LORD your God has

made you as the stars of heaven for multitude.

11 "You shall therefore love the LORD your God, and keep his charge, his statutes, his ordinances, and his commandments always. 2 And consider this day (since I am not speaking to your children who have not known or seen it), consider the discipline[i] of 3 the LORD your God, his greatness, his mighty hand and his outstretched arm, his signs and his deeds which he did in Egypt to Pharaoh the king of Egypt and to all his land; and 4 what he did to the army of Egypt, to their horses and to their chariots; how he made the water of the Red Sea overflow them as they pursued after you, and how the LORD has 5 destroyed them to this day; and what he did to you in the wilderness, until you came to 6 this place; and what he did to Dathan and Abi′ram the sons of Eli′ab, son of Reuben; how the earth opened its mouth and swallowed them up, with their households, their tents, and every living thing that followed 7 them, in the midst of all Israel; for your eyes have seen all the great work of the LORD which he did.

8 "You shall therefore keep all the commandment which I command you this day, that you may be strong, and go in and take possession of the land which you are going 9 over to possess, and that you may live long in the land which the LORD swore to your fathers to give to them and to their descendants, a land flowing with milk and honey. 10 For the land which you are entering to take possession of it is not like the land of Egypt, from which you have come, where you sowed your seed and watered it with your feet, like a 11 garden of vegetables; but the land which you are going over to possess is a land of hills and valleys, which drinks water by the rain from 12 heaven, a land which the LORD your God cares for; the eyes of the LORD your God are always upon it, from the beginning of the year to the end of the year.

13 "And if you will obey my commandments which I command you this day, to love the LORD your God, and to serve him with all 14 your heart and with all your soul, he[i] will give the rain for your land in its season, the early rain and the later rain, that you may gather in your grain and your wine and your 15 oil. And he[j] will give grass in your fields for your cattle, and you shall eat and be full. 16 Take heed lest your heart be deceived, and you turn aside and serve other gods and 17 worship them, and the anger of the LORD be kindled against you, and he shut up the

Mount Ebal and Mount Gerizim   *Deut 11, 29*

heavens, so that there be no rain, and the land yield no fruit, and you perish quickly off the good land which the LORD gives you.

18 "You shall therefore lay up these words of mine in your heart and in your soul; and you shall bind them as a sign upon your hand, and they shall be as frontlets between your 19 eyes. And you shall teach them to your children, talking of them when you are sitting in your house, and when you are walking by the way, and when you lie down, 20 and when you rise. And you shall write them upon the doorposts of your house and upon 21 your gates, that your days and the days of your children may be multiplied in the land which the LORD swore to your fathers to give them, as long as the heavens are above the 22 earth. For if you will be careful to do all this commandment which I command you to do, loving the LORD your God, walking in all his 23 ways, and cleaving to him, then the LORD will drive out all these nations before you, and you will dispossess nations greater and 24 mightier than yourselves. Every place on which the sole of your foot treads shall be yours; your territory shall be from the wilderness and Lebanon and from the River, the

river Euphra′tes, to the western sea. No man shall be able to stand against you; the LORD your God will lay the fear of you and the dread of you upon all the land that you shall tread, as he promised you.

"Behold, I set before you this day a blessing and a curse: the blessing, if you obey the commandments of the LORD your God, which I command you this day, and the curse, if you do not obey the commandments of the LORD your God, but turn aside from the way which I command you this day, to go after other gods which you have not known. And when the LORD your God brings you into the land which you are entering to take possession of it, you shall set the blessing on Mount Ger′izim and the curse on Mount Ebal. Are they not beyond the Jordan, west of the road, toward the going down of the sun, in the land of the Canaanites who live in the Arabah, over against Gilgal, beside the oak[k] of Moreh ? For you are to pass over the Jordan to go in to take possession of the land which the LORD your God gives you; and when you possess it and live in it, you shall be careful to do all the statutes and the ordinances which I set before you this day.

[k] Gk Syr: See Gen 12.6. Heb *oaks* or *terebinths*

THE BOOK
OF THE
COVENANT

Statutes and ordinances

12 "THESE are the statutes and
ordinances which you shall
be careful to do in the land which
the LORD, the God of your
fathers, has given you to possess,
all the days that you live upon the
earth.

Religious statutes

2 "You shall surely destroy all the
places where the nations whom
you shall dispossess served their
gods, upon the high mountains
and upon the hills and under
3 every green tree; you shall tear
down their altars, and dash in
pieces their pillars, and burn their
Ashe′rim with fire; you shall hew
down the graven images of their
gods, and destroy their name out
4 of that place. You shall not do so
5 to the LORD your God. But you
shall seek the place which the
LORD your God will choose out of
all your tribes to put his name and
make his habitation there; thither
6 you shall go, and thither you shall
bring your burnt offerings and
your sacrifices, your tithes and the
offering that you present, your
votive offerings, your freewill
offerings, and the firstlings of
7 your herd and of your flock; and
there you shall eat before the
LORD your God, and you shall
rejoice, you and your households,
in all that you undertake, in which
the LORD your God has blessed
8 you. You shall not do according
to all that we are doing here this
day, every man doing whatever is
9 right in his own eyes; for you have
not as yet come to the rest and to
the inheritance which the LORD
10 your God gives you. But when
you go over the Jordan, and live in
the land which the LORD your
God gives you to inherit, and so
that you live in safety, then to the
11 place which the LORD your God
will choose, to make his name
dwell there, thither you shall
bring all that I command you:
your burnt offerings and your

sacrifices, your tithes and the
offering that you present, and all
your votive offerings which you
12 vow to the LORD. And you shall
rejoice before the LORD your God,
you and your sons and your
daughters, your menservants and
your maidservants, and the Levite
that is within your towns, since he
has no portion or inheritance with
13 you. Take heed that you do not
offer your burnt offerings at every
14 place that you see; but at the place
which the LORD will choose in one
of your tribes, there you shall
offer your burnt offerings, and
there you shall do all that I am
commanding you.
15 "However, you may slaughter
and eat flesh within any of your
towns, as much as you desire,
according to the blessing of the
LORD your God which he has
given you; the unclean and the
16 clean may eat of it, as of the
gazelle and as of the hart. Only
you shall not eat the blood; you
17 shall pour it out upon the earth
like water. You may not eat
within your towns the tithe of
your grain or of your wine or of
your oil, or the firstlings of your
herd or of your flock, or any of
your votive offerings which you
vow, or your freewill offerings, or
18 the offering that you present; but
you shall eat them before the
LORD your God in the place
which the LORD your God will
choose, you and your son and
your daughter, your manservant
and your maidservant, and the
Levite who is within your towns;
and you shall rejoice before the
LORD your God in all that you
19 undertake. Take heed that you
do not forsake the Levite as long
as you live in your land.
20 "When the LORD your God
enlarges your territory, as he has
promised you, and you say, 'I will
eat flesh,' because you crave flesh,
you may eat as much flesh as you
21 desire. If the place which the
LORD your God will choose to put
his name there is too far from you,
then you may kill any of your herd

or your flock, which the LORD has
given you, as I have commanded
you; and you may eat within your
towns as much as you desire. Just 22
as the gazelle or the hart is eaten,
so you may eat of it; the unclean
and the clean alike may eat of it.
Only be sure that you do not eat 23
the blood; for the blood is the life,
and you shall not eat the life with
the flesh. You shall not eat it; you 24
shall pour it out upon the earth
like water. You shall not eat it; 25
that all may go well with you and
with your children after you,
when you do what is right in the
sight of the LORD. But the holy 26
things which are due from you,
and your votive offerings, you
shall take, and you shall go to the
place which the LORD will choose,
and offer your burnt offerings, the 27
flesh and the blood, on the altar of
the LORD your God; the blood of
your sacrifices shall be poured out
on the altar of the LORD your
God, but the flesh you may eat.
Be careful to heed all these words 28
which I command you, that it
may go well with you and with
your children after you for ever,
when you do what is good and
right in the sight of the LORD your
God.
"When the LORD your God cuts 29
off before you the nations whom
you go in to dispossess, and you
dispossess them and dwell in their
land, take heed that you be not 30
ensnared to follow them, after
they have been destroyed before
you, and that you do not inquire
about their gods, saying, 'How
did these nations serve their
gods?'—that I also may do likewise.' You shall not do so to 31
the LORD your God; for every
abominable thing which the LORD
hates they have done for their
gods; for they even burn their
sons and their daughters in the
fire to their gods.
"Everything that I command 32[1]
you you shall be careful to do; you
shall not add to it or take from it.

"If a prophet arises among you, 13
or a dreamer of dreams, and gives
you a sign or a wonder, and the 2
sign or wonder which he tells you
comes to pass, and if he says, 'Let
us go after other gods,' which you
have not known, 'and let us serve
them,' you shall not listen to the 3
words of that prophet or to that
dreamer of dreams; for the LORD
your God is testing you, to know
whether you love the LORD your
God with all your heart and with
all your soul. You shall walk after 4
the LORD your God and fear him,
and keep his commandments and
obey his voice, and you shall serve
him and cleave to him. But that 5
prophet or that dreamer of
dreams shall be put to death,
because he has taught rebellion
against the LORD your God, who
brought you out of the land of

[1] Ch 13.1 in Heb
12.1–28: Ex 20.24.   12.16, 23: Lev 17.10–14; 19.26.   12.29–32: Ex 23.24; 34.12–14; Num 33.52.

Egypt and redeemed you out of the house of bondage, to make you leave the way in which the LORD your God commanded you to walk. So you shall purge the evil from the midst of you.

6 "If your brother, the son of your mother, or your son, or your daughter, or the wife of your bosom, or your friend who is as your own soul, entices you secretly, saying, 'Let us go and serve other gods,' which neither you nor your fathers have known,

7 some of the gods of the peoples that are round about you, whether near you or far off from you, from the one end of the earth to the

8 other, you shall not yield to him or listen to him, nor shall your eye pity him, nor shall you spare him,

9 nor shall you conceal him; but you shall kill him; your hand shall be first against him to put him to death, and afterwards the hand of

10 all the people. You shall stone him to death with stones, because he sought to draw you away from the LORD your God, who brought you out of the land of Egypt, out

11 of the house of bondage. And all Israel shall hear, and fear, and never again do any such wickedness as this among you.

12 "If you hear in one of your cities, which the LORD your God gives

13 you to dwell there, that certain base fellows have gone out among you and have drawn away the inhabitants of the city, saying, 'Let us go and serve other gods,'

14 which you have not known, then you shall inquire and make search and ask diligently; and behold, if it be true and certain that such an abominable thing has been done

15 among you, you shall surely put the inhabitants of that city to the sword, destroying it utterly, all who are in it and its cattle, with

16 the edge of the sword. You shall gather all its spoil into the midst of its open square, and burn the city and all its spoil with fire, as a whole burnt offering to the LORD your God; it shall be a heap for ever, it shall not be built again.

17 None of the devoted things shall cleave to your hand; that the LORD may turn from the fierceness of his anger, and show you mercy, and have compassion on you, and multiply you, as he

18 swore to your fathers, if you obey the voice of the LORD your God, keeping all his commandments which I command you this day, and doing what is right in the sight of the LORD your God.

14 "You are the sons of the LORD your God; you shall not cut yourselves or make any baldness on

2 your foreheads for the dead. For you are a people holy to the LORD your God, and the LORD has chosen you to be a people for his own possession, out of all the peoples that are on the face of the earth.

3 "You shall not eat any abomi-

4 nable thing. These are the animals you may eat: the ox, the

5 sheep, the goat, the hart, the gazelle, the roebuck, the wild goat, the ibex, the antelope, and

6 the mountain-sheep. Every animal that parts the hoof and has the hoof cloven in two, and chews the cud, among the animals, you

7 may eat. Yet of those that chew the cud or have the hoof cloven you shall not eat these: the camel, the hare, and the rock badger, because they chew the cud but do not part the hoof, are unclean for

8 you. And the swine, because it parts the hoof but does not chew the cud, is unclean for you. Their flesh you shall not eat, and their carcasses you shall not touch.

Rock badgers   *Deut* **14, 7**

9 "Of all that are in the waters you may eat these: whatever has fins

10 and scales you may eat. And whatever does not have fins and scales you shall not eat; it is unclean for you.

11 "You may eat all clean birds.

12 But these are the ones which you shall not eat: the eagle, the vul-

13 ture, the osprey, the buzzard, the

14 kite, after their kinds; every raven

15 after its kind; the ostrich, the nighthawk, the sea gull, the hawk,

16 after their kinds; the little owl and the great owl, the water hen

17 and the pelican, the carrion vul-

18 ture and the cormorant, the stork, the heron, after their kinds; the

19 hoopoe and the bat. And all winged insects are unclean for

20 you; they shall not be eaten. All clean winged things you may eat.

21 "You shall not eat anything that dies of itself; you may give it to the alien who is within your towns, that he may eat it, or you may sell it to a foreigner; for you are a people holy to the LORD your God.

"You shall not boil a kid in its mother's milk.

22 "You shall tithe all the yield of your seed, which comes forth

from the field year by year. And before the LORD your God, in the place which he will choose, to make his name dwell there, you shall eat the tithe of your grain, of your wine, and of your oil, and the firstlings of your herd and flock; that you may learn to fear the LORD your God always. And if the way is too long for you, so that you are not able to bring the tithe, when the LORD your God blesses you, because the place is too far from you, which the LORD your God chooses, to set his name there, then you shall turn it into money, and bind up the money in your hand, and go to the place which the LORD your God chooses, and spend the money for whatever you desire, oxen, or sheep, or wine or strong drink, whatever your appetite craves; and you shall eat there before the LORD your God and rejoice, you and your household. And you shall not forsake the Levite who is within your towns, for he has no portion or inheritance with you.

"At the end of every three years you shall bring forth all the tithe of your produce in the same year, and lay it up within your towns; and the Levite, because he has no portion or inheritance with you, and the sojourner, the fatherless, and the widow, who are within your towns, shall come and eat and be filled; that the LORD your God may bless you in all the work of your hands that you do.

15 "At the end of every seven years you shall grant a release. And this

2 is the manner of the release: every creditor shall release what he has lent to his neighbour; he shall not exact it of his neighbour, his brother, because the LORD's re-

3 lease has been proclaimed. Of a foreigner you may exact it; but whatever of yours is with your

4 brother your hand shall release. But there will be no poor among you (for the LORD will bless you in the land which the LORD your God gives you for an inheritance

5 to possess), if only you will obey the voice of the LORD your God, being careful to do all this commandment which I command you

6 this day. For the LORD your God will bless you, as he promised you, and you shall lend to many nations, but you shall not borrow; and you shall rule over many nations, but they shall not rule over you.

7 "If there is among you a poor man, one of your brethren, in any of your towns within your land which the LORD your God gives you, you shall not harden your heart or shut your hand against

8 your poor brother, but you shall open your hand to him, and lend him sufficient for his need, what-

14.1: Lev 19.28.   **14.2:** Ex 19.5–6; Deut 26.19; Tit 2.14; 1 Pet 2.9; Rev 1.6; 5.10.   **14.3–20:** Lev 11.2–23.
14.21: Ex 23.19; 34.26; Lev 11.39–40; 17.15.   **14.22–29:** Lev 27.30–33; Num 18.21–32.

9 ever it may be. Take heed lest there be a base thought in your heart, and you say, 'The seventh year, the year of release is near,' and your eye be hostile to your poor brother, and you give him nothing, and he cry to the LORD against you, and it be sin in you. 10 You shall give to him freely, and your heart shall not be grudging when you give to him; because for this the LORD your God will bless

The owl and hawk   *Deut* 14, 15–16

you in all your work and in all that 19 you undertake. For the poor will never cease out of the land; therefore I command you, You shall open wide your hand to your brother, to the needy and to the poor, in the land.

12 "If your brother, a Hebrew man, or a Hebrew woman, is sold to you, he shall serve you six years, and in the seventh year you shall 13 let him go free from you. And when you let him go free from you, you shall not let him go 14 empty-handed; you shall furnish him liberally out of your flock, out of your threshing floor, and out of your wine press; as the LORD your 15 God has blessed you, you shall give to him. You shall remember that you were a slave in the land of Egypt, and the LORD your God 16 redeemed you; therefore I command you this today. But if he says to you, 'I will not go out from you,' because he loves you and your household, since he fares 17 well with you, then you shall take an awl, and thrust it through his ear into the door, and he shall be your bondman for ever. And to your bondwoman you shall do 18 likewise. It shall not seem hard to you, when you let him go free from you; for at half the cost of a hired servant he has served you six years. So the LORD your God will bless you in all that you do.

19 "All the firstling males that are born of your herd and flock you shall consecrate to the LORD your God; you shall do no work with the firstling of your herd, nor shear the firstling of your flock. 20 You shall eat it, you and your household, before the LORD your God year by year at the place 21 which the LORD will choose. But if it has any blemish, if it is lame or blind, or has any serious blemish whatever, you shall not sacrifice it to the LORD your God. 22 You shall eat it within your towns; the unclean and the clean alike may eat it, as though it were 23 a gazelle or a hart. Only you shall not eat its blood; you shall pour it out on the ground like water.

16 "Observe the month of Abib, and keep the passover to the LORD your God; for in the month of Abib the LORD your God brought 2 you out of Egypt by night. And you shall offer the passover sacrifice to the LORD your God, from the flock or the herd, at the place which the LORD will choose, to 3 make his name dwell there. You shall eat no leavened bread with it; seven days you shall eat it with unleavened bread, the bread of affliction—for you came out of the land of Egypt in hurried flight—that all the days of your life you may remember the day

when you came out of the land of Egypt. No leaven shall be seen 4 with you in all your territory for seven days; nor shall any of the flesh which you sacrifice on the evening of the first day remain all night until morning. You may 5 not offer the passover sacrifice within any of your towns which the LORD your God gives you; but 6 at the place which the LORD your God will choose, to make his name dwell in it, there you shall offer the passover sacrifice, in the evening at the going down of the sun, at the time you came out of Egypt. And you shall boil it and 7 eat it at the place which the LORD your God will choose; and in the morning you shall turn and go to your tents. For six days you shall 8 eat unleavened bread; and on the seventh day there shall be a solemn assembly to the LORD your God; you shall do no work on it.

"You shall count seven weeks; 9 begin to count the seven weeks from the time you first put the sickle to the standing grain. Then 10 you shall keep the feast of weeks to the LORD your God with the tribute of a freewill offering from your hand, which you shall give as the LORD your God blesses you; and you shall rejoice before the 11 LORD your God, you and your son and your daughter, your manservant and your maidservant, the Levite who is within your towns, the sojourner, the fatherless, and the widow who are among you, at the place which the LORD your God will choose, to make his name dwell there. You shall 12 remember that you were a slave in Egypt; and you shall be careful to observe these statutes.

"You shall keep the feast of 13 booths seven days, when you make your ingathering from your threshing floor and your wine press; you shall rejoice in your 14 feast, you and your son and your daughter, your manservant and your maidservant, the Levite, the

sojourner, the fatherless, and the widow who are within your
15 towns. For seven days you shall keep the feast to the LORD your God at the place which the LORD will choose; because the LORD your God will bless you in all your produce and in all the work of your hands, so that you will be altogether joyful.

16 "Three times a year all your males shall appear before the LORD your God at the place which he will choose: at the feast of unleavened bread, at the feast of weeks, and at the feast of booths. They shall not appear before the
17 LORD empty-handed; every man shall give as he is able, according to the blessing of the LORD your God which he has given you.

Civil statutes

18 "You shall appoint judges and officers in all your towns which the LORD your God gives you, according to your tribes; and they shall judge the people with right-
19 eous judgment. You shall not pervert justice; you shall not show partiality; and you shall not take a bribe, for a bribe blinds the eyes of the righteous and subverts the cause
20 of the righteous. Justice, and only justice, you shall follow, that you may live and inherit the land which the LORD your God gives you.
21 "You shall not plant any tree as an Ashe'rah beside the altar of the LORD your God which you shall
22 make. And you shall not set up a pillar, which the LORD your God hates.

17 "You shall not sacrifice to the LORD your God an ox or a sheep in which is a blemish, any defect whatever; for that is an abomination to the LORD your God.
2 "If there is found among you, within any of your towns which the LORD your God gives you, a man or woman who does what is evil in the sight of the LORD your God, in transgressing his coven-
3 ant, and has gone and served other gods and worshipped them, or the sun or the moon or any of the host of heaven, which I have
4 forbidden, and it is told you and you hear of it; then you shall inquire diligently, and if it is true and certain that such an abominable thing has been done in Israel,
5 then you shall bring forth to your gates that man or woman who has done this evil thing, and you shall stone that man or woman to death
6 with stones. On the evidence of two witnesses or of three witnesses he that is to die shall be put to death; a person shall not be put to death on the evidence of one
7 witness. The hand of the witnesses shall be first against him to put him to death, and afterward

Osprey   *Deut* 14, 12

the hand of all the people. So you shall purge the evil from the midst of you.
8 "If any case arises requiring decision between one kind of homicide and another, one kind of legal right and another, or one kind of assault and another, any case within your towns which is too difficult for you, then you shall arise and go up to the place which the LORD your God will
9 choose, and coming to the Levitical priests, and to the judge who is in office in those days, you shall consult them, and they shall de-
10 clare to you the decision. Then you shall do according to what they declare to you from that place which the LORD will choose; and you shall be careful to do according to all that they direct
11 you; according to the instructions which they give you, and according to the decision which they pronounce to you, you shall do; you shall not turn aside from the verdict which they declare to you, either to the right hand or to the
12 left. The man who acts presumptuously, by not obeying the priest who stands to minister there before the LORD your God, or the judge, that man shall die; so you shall purge the evil from Israel.
13 And all the people shall hear, and fear, and not act presumptuously again.
14 "When you come to the land which the LORD your God gives you, and you possess it and dwell in it, and then say, 'I will set a king over me, like all the nations
15 that are round about me'; you may indeed set as king over you him whom the LORD your God will choose. One from among your brethren you shall set as king over you; you may not put a foreigner over you, who is not
16 your brother. Only he must not multiply horses for himself, or cause the people to return to Egypt in order to multiply horses, since the LORD has said to you, 'You shall never return that way

again.' And he shall not multiply wives for himself, lest his heart turn away; nor shall he greatly multiply for himself silver and gold.
"And when he sits on the throne of his kingdom, he shall write for himself in a book a copy of this law, from that which is in charge of the Levitical priests; and it shall be with him, and he shall read in it all the days of his life, that he may learn to fear the LORD his God, by keeping all the words of this law and these statutes, and doing them; that his heart may not be lifted up above his brethren, and that he may not turn aside from the commandment, either to the right hand or to the left; so that he may continue long in his kingdom, he and his children, in Israel.

"The Levitical priests, that is, all the tribe of Levi, shall have no portion or inheritance with Israel; they shall eat the offerings by fire to the LORD, and his rightful dues. They shall have no inheritance among their brethren; the LORD is their inheritance, as he promised them. And this shall be the priests' due from the people, from those offering a sacrifice, whether it be ox or sheep; they shall give to the priest the shoulder and the two cheeks and the stomach. The first fruits of your grain, of your wine and of your oil, and the first of the fleece of your sheep, you shall give him. For the LORD your God has chosen him out of all your tribes, to stand and minister in the name of the LORD, him and his sons for ever.
"And if a Levite comes from any of your towns out of all Israel, where he lives—and he may come when he desires—to the place which the LORD will choose, then he may minister in the name of the LORD his God, like all his fellow-Levites who stand to minister there before the LORD. They shall have equal portions to eat, besides what he receives from the sale of his patrimony.[m]
"When you come into the land which the LORD your God gives you, you shall not learn to follow the abominable practices of those nations. There shall not be found among you any one who burns his son or his daughter as an offering,[n] any one who practises divination, a soothsayer, or an augur, or a sorcerer, or a charmer, or a medium, or a wizard, or a necromancer. For whoever does these things is an abomination to the LORD; and because of these abominable practices the LORD your God is driving them out before you. You shall be blameless before the LORD your God.

---

[m] Heb obscure   [n] Heb *makes his son or his daughter pass through the fire*
16.19: Ex 23.6–9; Lev 19.15.   **16.21–22:** Lev 26.1.   **17.1:** Lev 22.17–24.   **17.2–7:** Ex 22.20.
17.6: Num 35.30; Deut 19.15; Mt 18.16; 2 Cor 13.1; 1 Tim 5.19; Heb 10.28.   **17.7:** Deut 19.19; 1 Cor 5.13.
18.1–8: Num 18.20–24.   **18.10–11:** Ex 22.18; Lev 19.26, 31; 20.6, 27.   **18.13:** Mt 5.48.

4 For these nations, which you are about to dispossess, give heed to soothsayers and to diviners; but as for you, the LORD your God has not allowed you so to do.

5 "The LORD your God will raise up for you a prophet like me from among you, from your breth-
6 ren—him you shall heed—just as you desired of the LORD your God at Horeb on the day of the assembly, when you said, 'Let me not hear again the voice of the LORD my God, or see this great
7 fire any more, lest I die.' And the LORD said to me, 'They have rightly said all that they have
8 spoken. I will raise up for them a prophet like you from among their brethren; and I will put my words in his mouth, and he shall speak to them all that I command
9 him. And whoever will not give heed to my words which he shall speak in my name, I myself will
10 require it of him. But the prophet who presumes to speak a word in my name which I have not com-manded him to speak, or who speaks in the name of other gods,
11 that same prophet shall die.' And if you say in your heart, 'How may we know the word which the
12 LORD has not spoken?'—when a prophet speaks in the name of the LORD, if the word does not come to pass or come true, that is a word which the LORD has not spoken; the prophet has spoken it presumptuously, you need not be afraid of him.

Criminal law

19 "When the LORD your God cuts off the nations whose land the LORD your God gives you, and you dispossess them and dwell in their cities and in their houses,
2 you shall set apart three cities for you in the land which the LORD your God gives you to possess.
3 You shall prepare the roads, and divide into three parts the area of the land which the LORD your God gives you as a possession, so that any manslayer can flee to them.
4 "This is the provision for the manslayer, who by fleeing there may save his life. If any one kills his neighbour unintentionally without having been at enmity
5 with him in time past—as when a man goes into the forest with his neighbour to cut wood, and his hand swings the axe to cut down a tree, and the head slips from the handle and strikes his neighbour so that he dies—he may flee to one of these cities and save his
6 life; lest the avenger of blood in hot anger pursue the manslayer and overtake him, because the way is long, and wound him mortally, though the man did not

Eagle   *Deut* **14**, 12

enmity with his neighbour in time
7 past. Therefore I command you, You shall set apart three cities.
8 And if the LORD your God en-larges your border, as he has sworn to your fathers, and gives you all the land which he pro-mised to give to your fathers—
9 provided you are careful to keep all this commandment, which I command you this day, by loving the Lord your God and by walking ever in his ways—then
10 you shall add three other cities to these three, lest innocent blood be shed in your land which the LORD your God gives you for an inheri-tance, and so the guilt of blood-shed be upon you.
11 "But if any man hates his neigh-bour, and lies in wait for him, and attacks him, and wounds him mortally so that he dies, and the man flees into one of these cities,
12 then the elders of his city shall send and fetch him from there, and hand him over to the avenger of blood, so that he may die.
13 Your eye shall not pity him, but you shall purge the guilt of innocent blood° from Israel, so that it may be well with you.
14 "In the inheritance which you will hold in the land that the LORD your God gives you to possess, you shall not remove your neigh-bour's landmark, which the men of old have set.
15 "A single witness shall not pre-vail against a man for any crime or for any wrong in connection with any offence that he has com-mitted; only on the evidence of two witnesses, or of three wit-nesses, shall a charge be sus-
16 tained. If a malicious witness rises against any man to accuse

him of wrongdoing, then both
17 parties to the dispute shall appear before the LORD, before the priests and the judges who are in office in those days; the judges
18 shall inquire diligently; and if the witness is a false witness and has accused his brother falsely, then
19 you shall do to him as he had meant to do to his brother; so you shall purge the evil from the midst of you. And the rest shall hear,
20 and fear, and shall never again commit any such evil among you. Your eye shall not pity; it shall be
21 life for life, eye for eye, tooth for tooth, hand for hand, foot for foot.

"When you go forth to war **20** against your enemies, and see horses and chariots and an army larger than your own, you shall not be afraid of them; for the LORD your God is with you, who brought you up out of the land of Egypt. And when you draw near
2 to the battle, the priest shall come forward and speak to the people, and shall say to them, 'Hear, O
3 Israel, you draw near this day to battle against your enemies: let not your heart faint; do not fear, or tremble, or be in dread of them; for the LORD your God is
4 he that goes with you, to fight for you against your enemies, to give you the victory.' Then the offi-
5 cers shall speak to the people, saying, 'What man is there that has built a new house and has not dedicated it? Let him go back to his house, lest he die in the battle and another man dedicate it. And
6 what man is there that has planted a vineyard and has not enjoyed its fruit? Let him go back to his house, lest he die in the battle and another man enjoy its fruit. And
7 what man is there that has be-trothed a wife and has not taken her? Let him go back to his house, lest he die in the battle and another man take her.' And the
8 officers shall speak further to the people, and say, 'What man is there that is fearful and faint-hearted? Let him go back to his house, lest the heart of his fellows melt as his heart.' And when the
9 officers have made an end of speaking to the people, then commanders shall be appointed at the head of the people.
10 "When you draw near to a city to fight against it, offer terms of
11 peace to it. And if its answer to you is peace and it opens to you, then all the people who are found in it shall do forced labour for you
12 and shall serve you. But if it makes no peace with you, but makes war against you, then you
13 shall besiege it; and when the LORD your God gives it into your hand you shall put all its males to the sword, but the women and the
14

° Or *the blood of the innocent*

18.15-19: Acts 3.22-23; 7.37. **19.1-13:** Ex 21.12-14; Num 35.
19.15: Num 35.30; Deut 17.6; Mt 18.16; 2 Cor 13.1; 1 Tim 5.19; Heb 10.28.
19.16-20: Ex 20.16; 23.1; Lev 19.16; Deut 5.20. **19.19:** 1 Cor 5.13.
19.21: Ex 21.23-25; Lev 24.20; Mt 5.38.

little ones, the cattle, and everything else in the city, all its spoil, you shall take as booty for yourselves; and you shall enjoy the spoil of your enemies, which the LORD your God has given you. 15 Thus you shall do to all the cities which are very far from you, which are not cities of the nations 16 here. But in the cities of these peoples that the LORD your God gives you for an inheritance, you shall save alive nothing that 17 breathes, but you shall utterly destroy them, the Hittites and the Amorites, the Canaanites and the Per'izzites, the Hivites and the Jeb'usites, as the LORD your God 18 has commanded; that they may not teach you to do according to all their abominable practices which they have done in the service of their gods, and so to sin against the LORD your God.

19 "When you besiege a city for a long time, making war against it in order to take it, you shall not destroy its trees by wielding an axe against them; for you may eat of them, but you shall not cut them down. Are the trees in the field men that they should be 20 besieged by you? Only the trees which you know are not trees for food you may destroy and cut down that you may build siegeworks against the city that makes war with you, until it falls.

21 "If in the land which the LORD your God gives you to possess, any one is found slain, lying in the open country, and it is not known 2 who killed him, then your elders and your judges shall come forth, and they shall measure the distance to the cities which are 3 around him that is slain; and the elders of the city which is nearest to the slain man shall take a heifer which has never been worked and which has not been pulled in the yoke. 4 And the elders of that city shall bring the heifer down to a valley with running water, which is neither ploughed nor sown, and shall break the heifer's neck there 5 in the valley. And the priests the sons of Levi shall come forward, for the LORD your God has chosen them to minister to him and to bless in the name of the LORD, and by their word every dispute 22 and every assault shall be settled. 6 And all the elders of that city nearest to the slain man shall wash 23 their hands over the heifer whose 7 neck was broken in the valley; and they shall testify, 'Our hands did not shed this blood, neither did 8 our eyes see it shed. Forgive, O LORD, thy people Israel, whom thou hast redeemed, and set not the guilt of innocent blood in the 22 midst of thy people Israel; but let the guilt of blood be forgiven 9 them.' So you shall purge the guilt of innocent blood from your midst, when you do what is right

in the sight of the LORD.

10 "When you go forth to war against your enemies, and the LORD your God gives them into your hands, and you take them 11 captive, and see among the captives a beautiful woman, and you have desire for her and would take 12 her for yourself as wife, then you shall bring her home to your house, and she shall shave her 13 head and pare her nails. And she shall put off her captive's garb, and shall remain in your house and bewail her father and her mother a full month; after that you may go in to her, and be her husband, and she shall be your 14 wife. Then, if you have no delight in her, you shall let her go where she will; but you shall not sell her for money, you shall not treat her as a slave, since you have humiliated her.

Other statutes

15 "If a man has two wives, the one loved and the other disliked, and they have borne him children, both the loved and the disliked, and if the first-born son is hers 16 that is disliked, then on the day when he assigns his possessions as an inheritance to his sons, he may not treat the son of the loved as the first-born in preference to the 17 first-born, who is the son of the disliked, who is the son of the disliked, who is the son of the disliked, by giving him a double portion of all that he has, for he is the first issue of his strength; the right of the first-born is his. 18 "If a man has a stubborn and rebellious son, who will not obey the voice of his father or the voice of his mother, and, though they chastise him, will not give heed to 19 them, then his father and his mother shall take hold of him and bring him out to the elders of his city at the gate of the place where 20 he lives, and they shall say to the elders of his city, 'This our son is stubborn and rebellious, he will not obey our voice; he is a glutton 21 and a drunkard.' Then all the men of the city shall stone him to death with stones; so you shall purge the evil from your midst; and all Israel shall hear, and fear.

22 "And if a man has committed a crime punishable by death and he is put to death, and you hang him 23 on a tree, his body shall not remain all night upon the tree, but you shall bury him the same day, for a hanged man is accursed by God; you shall not defile your land which the LORD your God gives you for an inheritance.

22 "You shall not see your brother's ox or his sheep go astray, and withhold your help *p* from them; you shall take them back to 2 your brother. And if he is not near you, or if you do not know

him, you shall bring it home to your house, and it shall be with you until your brother seeks it; then you shall restore it to him. And so you shall do with his ass; so you shall do with his garment; so you shall do with any lost thing of your brother's, which he loses and you find; you may not withhold your help. You shall not see your brother's ass or his ox fallen down by the way, and withhold your help *p* from them; you shall help him to lift them up again.

"A woman shall not wear anything that pertains to a man, nor shall a man put on a woman's garment; for whoever does these things is an abomination to the LORD your God.

"If you chance to come upon a bird's nest, in any tree or on the ground, with young ones or eggs and the mother sitting upon the young or upon the eggs, you shall not take the mother with the young; you shall let the mother go, but the young you may take to yourself; that it may go well with you, and that you may live long.

"When you build a new house, you shall make a parapet for your roof, that you may not bring the guilt of blood upon your house, if any one fall from it.

"You shall not sow your vineyard with two kinds of seed, lest the whole yield be forfeited to the sanctuary,*q* the crop which you have sown and the yield of the vineyard. You shall not plough with an ox and an ass together. You shall not wear a mingled stuff, wool and linen together.

"You shall make yourself tassels on the four corners of your cloak with which you cover yourself.

"If any man takes a wife, and goes in to her, and then spurns her, and charges her with shameful conduct, and brings an evil name upon her, saying, 'I took this woman, and when I came near her, I did not find in her the tokens of virginity,' then the father of the young woman and her mother shall take and bring out the tokens of her virginity to the elders of the city in the gate; and the father of the young woman shall say to the elders, 'I gave my daughter to this man to wife, and he spurns her; and lo, he has made shameful charges against her, saying, "I did not find in your daughter the tokens of virginity." And yet these are the tokens of my daughter's virginity.' And they shall spread the garment before the elders of the city. Then the elders of that city shall take the man and whip him; and they shall fine him a hundred shekels of silver, and give them to the father of the young woman, because he has brought an evil name upon a virgin of Israel; and she shall be

---

p Heb *hide yourself*   *q* Heb *become holy*

21.18–21: Ex 20.12; 21.15, 17; Lev 20.9; Deut 5.16; 27.16.   21.22: Acts 5.30; 10.39.   21.23: Gal 3.13.
22.1–4: Ex 23.4–5.   22.9–11: Lev 19.19.   22.12: Num 15.37–41.

'You shall not plough with an ox and an ass together'   Deut **22**, 10

his wife; he may not put her away all his days. But if the thing is true, that the tokens of virginity were not found in the young woman, then they shall bring out the young woman to the door of her father's house, and the men of her city shall stone her to death with stones, because she has wrought folly in Israel by playing the harlot in her father's house; so you shall purge the evil from the midst of you.

2 "If a man is found lying with the wife of another man, both of them shall die, the man who lay with the woman, and the woman; so you shall purge the evil from Israel.

3 "If there is a betrothed virgin, and a man meets her in the city 4 and lies with her, then you shall bring them both out to the gate of that city, and you shall stone them to death with stones, the young woman because she did not cry for help though she was in the city, and the man because he violated his neighbour's wife; so you shall purge the evil from the midst of you.

5 "But if in the open country a man meets a young woman who is betrothed, and the man seizes her and lies with her, then only the man who lay with her shall die. 6 But to the young woman you shall do nothing; in the young woman there is no offence punishable by death, for this case is like that of a man attacking and murdering his 7 neighbour; because he came upon her in the open country, and though the betrothed young woman cried for help there was no one to rescue her.

8 "If a man meets a virgin who is not betrothed, and seizes her and 9 lies with her, and they are found, then the man who lay with her

shall give to the father of the young woman fifty shekels of silver, and she shall be his wife, because he has violated her; he may not put her away all his days. 30 "A man shall not take his father's wife, nor shall he uncover her who is his father's.[s]

23 "He whose testicles are crushed or whose male member is cut off shall not enter the assembly of the LORD.

2 "No bastard shall enter the assembly of the LORD; even to the tenth generation none of his descendants shall enter the assembly of the LORD.

3 "No Ammonite or Moabite shall enter the assembly of the LORD; even to the tenth generation none belonging to them shall enter the assembly of the LORD for ever; 4 because they did not meet you with bread and with water on the way, when you came forth out of Egypt, and because they hired against you Balaam the son of Be'or from Pethor of Mesopo-ta'mia, to curse you. Neverthe-5 less the LORD your God would not hearken to Balaam; but the LORD your God turned the curse into a blessing for you, because the 6 LORD your God loved you. You shall not seek their peace or their prosperity all your days for ever.

7 "You shall not abhor an E'dom-ite, for he is your brother; you shall not abhor an Egyptian, because you were a sojourner in 8 his land. The children of the third generation that are born to them may enter the assembly of the LORD.

9 "When you go forth against your enemies and are in camp, then you shall keep yourself from every evil thing.

"If there is among you any man 10 who is not clean by reason of what chances to him by night, then he shall go outside the camp, he shall not come within the camp; but 11 when evening comes on, he shall bathe himself in water, and when the sun is down, he may come within the camp.

"You shall have a place outside 12 the camp and you shall go out to it; and you shall have a stick with 13 your weapons; and when you sit down outside, you shall dig a hole with it, and turn back and cover up your excrement. Because the 14 LORD your God walks in the midst of your camp, to save you and to give up your enemies before you, therefore your camp must be holy, that he may not see anything indecent among you, and turn away from you.

"You shall not give up to his 15 master a slave who has escaped from his master to you; he shall 16 dwell with you, in your midst, in the place which he shall choose within one of your towns, where it pleases him best; you shall not oppress him.

"There shall be no cult prosti-17 tute of the daughters of Israel, neither shall there be a cult prosti-tute of the sons of Israel. You 18 shall not bring the hire of a harlot, or the wages of a dog,[t] into the house of the LORD your God in payment for any vow; for both of these are an abomination to the LORD your God.

"You shall not lend upon inter-19 est to your brother, interest on money, interest on victuals, interest on anything that is lent for interest. To a foreigner you 20 may lend upon interest, but to your brother you shall not lend upon interest; that the LORD your God may bless you in all that you

---

[r] Ch 23.1 in Heb   [s] Heb *uncover his father's skirt*   [t] Or *sodomite*
22.21: 1 Cor 5.13.   **22.22–27:** Ex 20.14; Lev 18.20; 20.10; Deut 5.18.   **22.24:** 1 Cor 5.13.
22.28–29: Ex 22.16–17.   **23.19:** Ex 22.26; Lev 25.35–37.

undertake in the land which you are entering to take possession of it.

21 "When you make a vow to the LORD your God, you shall not be slack to pay it; for the LORD your God will surely require it of you, 22 and it would be sin in you. But if you refrain from vowing, it shall 23 be no sin in you. You shall be careful to perform what has passed your lips, for you have voluntarily vowed to the LORD your God what you have promised with your mouth.

24 "When you go into your neighbour's vineyard, you may eat your fill of grapes, as many as you wish, but you shall not put any in your 25 vessel. When you go into your neighbour's standing grain, you may pluck the ears with your hand, but you shall not put a sickle to your neighbour's standing grain.

24 "When a man takes a wife and marries her, if then she finds no favour in his eyes because he has found some indecency in her, and he writes her a bill of divorce and puts it in her hand and sends her out of his house, and she departs 2 out of his house, and if she goes and becomes another man's 3 wife, and the latter husband dislikes her and writes her a bill of divorce and puts it in her hand and sends her out of his house, or if the latter husband dies, who 4 took her to be his wife, then her former husband, who sent her away, may not take her again to be his wife, after she has been 20 defiled; for that is an abomination before the LORD, and you shall not bring guilt upon the land which the LORD your God gives you for 21 an inheritance.

5 "When a man is newly married, he shall not go out with the army or be charged with any business; he shall be free at home one year, to be happy with his wife whom he has taken.

6 "No man shall take a mill or an upper millstone in pledge; for he would be taking a life in pledge.

7 "If a man is found stealing one of his brethren, the people of Israel, and if he treats him as a slave or sells him, then that thief shall die; so you shall purge the evil from the midst of you.

8 "Take heed, in an attack of leprosy, to be very careful to do according to all that the Levitical priests shall direct you; as I commanded them, so you shall be 9 careful to do. Remember what the LORD your God did to Miriam on the way as you came forth out of Egypt.

10 "When you make your neighbour a loan of any sort, you shall

not go into his house to fetch his 11 pledge. You shall stand outside, and the man to whom you make 12 the loan shall bring the pledge out to you. And if he is a poor man, you shall not sleep in his pledge; 13 when the sun goes down, you shall restore to him the pledge that he may sleep in his cloak and bless you; and it shall be right-14 eousness to you before the LORD your God.

"You shall not oppress a hired servant who is poor and needy, whether he is one of your brethren or one of the sojourners who are in your land within your 15 towns; you shall give him his hire on the day he earns it, before the sun goes down (for he is poor, and sets his heart upon it); lest he cry against you to the LORD, and it be 16 sin in you.

"The fathers shall not be put to death for the children, nor shall the children be put to death for the fathers; every man shall be put to death for his own sin.

17 "You shall not pervert the justice due to the sojourner or to the fatherless, or take a widow's 18 garment in pledge; but you shall remember that you were a slave in Egypt and the LORD your God redeemed you from there; there-19 fore I command you to do this.

"When you reap your harvest in your field, and have forgotten a sheaf in the field, you shall not go back to get it; it shall be for the sojourner, the fatherless, and the widow; that the LORD your God may bless you in all the work of 20 your hands. When you beat your olive trees, you shall not go over the boughs again; it shall be for the sojourner, the fatherless, 21 and the widow. When you gather the grapes of your vineyard, you shall not glean it afterward; it shall be for the sojourner, the fatherless, 22 and the widow. You shall remember that you were a slave in the land of Egypt; therefore I command you to do this.

25 "If there is a dispute between men, and they come into court, and the judges decide between them, acquitting the innocent and 2 condemning the guilty, then if the guilty man deserves to be beaten, the judge shall cause him to lie down and be beaten in his presence with a number of stripes in 3 proportion to his offence. Forty stripes may be given him, but not more; lest, if one should go on to beat him with more stripes than these, your brother be degraded in your sight.

4 "You shall not muzzle an ox when it treads out the grain.

5 "If brothers dwell together, and one of them dies and has no son,

the wife of the dead shall not be married outside the family to a stranger; her husband's brother shall go in to her, and take her as his wife, and perform the duty of a husband's brother to her. And the first son whom she bears shall succeed to the name of his brother who is dead, that his name may not be blotted out of Israel. And if the man does not wish to take his brother's wife, then his brother's wife shall go up to the gate to the elders, and say, 'My husband's brother refuses to perpetuate his brother's name in Israel; he will not perform the duty of a husband's brother to me.' Then the elders of his city shall call him, and speak to him: and if he persists, saying, 'I do not wish to take her,' then his brother's wife shall go up to him in the presence of the elders, and pull his sandal off his foot, and spit in his face; and she shall answer and say, 'So shall it be done to the man who does not build up his brother's house.' And the name of his house[u] shall be called in Israel, The house of him that had his sandal pulled off.

"When men fight with one another, and the wife of the one draws near to rescue her husband from the hand of him who is beating him, and puts out her hand and seizes him by the private parts, then you shall cut off her hand; your eye shall have no pity.

"You shall not have in your bag two kinds of weights, a large and a small. You shall not have in your house two kinds of measures, a large and a small. A full and just weight you shall have, a full and just measure you shall have; that your days may be prolonged in the land which the LORD your God gives you. For all who do such things, all who act dishonestly, are an abomination to the LORD your God.

"Remember how Am'alek did to you on the way as you came out of Egypt, how he attacked you on the way, when you were faint and weary, and cut off at your rear all who lagged behind you; and he did not fear God. Therefore when the LORD your God has given you rest from all your enemies round about, in the land which the LORD your God gives you for an inheritance to possess, you shall blot out the remembrance of Am'alek from under heaven; you shall not forget.

The promised land

"When you come into the land **2** which the LORD your God gives you for an inheritance, and have

u Heb its name
23.21-23: Num 30.2-16. 24.1: Mt 5.31; 19.7; Mk 10.4. 24.6, 10-13: Ex 22.26-27.
24.7: Ex 21.16; 1 Cor 5.13. 24.8-9: Lev 13-14. 24.14-15: Lev 19.13; Jas 5.4.
24.17-18: Ex 22.21-24; 23.9; Lev 19.33-34. 24.19-22: Lev 19.9-10; 23.22. 25.4: 1 Cor 9.9; 1 Tim 5.18.
25.5-6: Mt 22.24; Mk 12.19; Lk 20.28. 25.13-16: Lev 19.35-36. 25.17-19: Ex 17.14; 1 Sam 15.
26.1-11: Ex 22.29; 23.19; 34.26; Num 18.12-13.

taken possession of it, and live in it, you shall take some of the first of all the fruit of the ground, which you harvest from your land that the LORD your God gives you, and you shall put it in a basket, and you shall go to the place which the LORD your God will choose, to make his name to dwell there. And you shall go to the priest who is in office at that time, and say to him, 'I declare this day to the LORD your God that I have come into the land which the LORD swore to our fathers to give to us.' Then the priest shall take the basket from your hand, and set it down before the altar of the LORD your God.

"And you shall make response before the LORD your God, 'A wandering Aramean was my father; and he went down into Egypt and sojourned there, few in number; and there he became a nation, great, mighty, and populous. And the Egyptians treated us harshly, and afflicted us, and laid upon us hard bondage. Then we cried to the LORD the God of our fathers, and the LORD heard our voice, and saw our affliction, our toil, and our oppression; and the LORD brought us out of Egypt with a mighty hand and an

9 outstretched arm, with great terror, with signs and wonders; and he brought us into this place and 10 gave us this land, a land flowing with milk and honey. And behold, now I bring the first of the fruit of the ground, which thou, O LORD, hast given me.' And you shall set it down before 11 the LORD your God, and worship before the LORD your God; and you shall rejoice in all the good which the LORD your God has given to you and to your house, you, and the Levite, and the sojourner who is among you.

12 "When you have finished paying all the tithe of your produce in the third year, which is the year of tithing, giving it to the Levite, the sojourner, the fatherless, and the 13 widow, that they may eat within your towns and be filled, then you shall say before the LORD your God, 'I have removed the sacred portion out of my house, and moreover I have given it to the Levite, the sojourner, the fatherless, and the widow, according to all thy commandment which thou hast commanded me; I have not 14 gotten them; I have not eaten of the tithe while I was mourning, or

removed any of it while I was unclean, or offered any of it to the dead; I have obeyed the voice of the LORD my God, I have done according to all that thou hast commanded me. Look down 15 from thy holy habitation, from heaven, and bless thy people Israel and the ground which thou hast given us, as thou didst swear to our fathers, a land flowing with milk and honey.'

"This day the LORD your God 16 commands you to do these statutes and ordinances; you shall therefore be careful to do them with all your heart and with all your soul. You have declared this 17 day concerning the LORD that he is your God, and that you will walk in his ways, and keep his statutes and his commandments and his ordinances, and will obey his voice; and the LORD has de- 18 clared this day concerning you that you are a people for his own possession, as he has promised you, and that you are to keep all his commandments, that he will 19 set you high above all nations that he has made, in praise and in fame and in honour, and that you shall be a people holy to the LORD your God, as he has spoken."

THE PEOPLE OF GOD

NOW Moses and the elders of Israel commanded the people, saying, "Keep all the commandment which I command you this day. And on the day you pass over the Jordan to the land which the LORD your God gives you, you shall set up large stones, and plaster them with plaster; and you shall write upon them all the words of this law, when you pass over to enter the land which the LORD your God gives you, a land flowing with milk and honey, as the LORD, the God of your fathers, has promised you. And when you have passed over the Jordan, you shall set up these stones, concerning which I command you this day, on Mount Ebal, and you shall plaster them with plaster. And there you shall build an altar to the LORD your God, an altar of stones; you shall lift up no iron tool upon them. You shall build an altar to the LORD your God of unhewn v stones; and you shall offer burnt offerings on it to the LORD your God; and you shall sacrifice peace offerings, and shall eat there; and you shall rejoice before the LORD your God. And you shall write upon the stones all the words of this law very plainly."

And Moses and the Levitical priests said to 9 all Israel, "Keep silence and hear, O Israel: this day you have become the people of the LORD your God. You shall therefore obey 10 the voice of the LORD your God, keeping his commandments and his statutes, which I command you this day."

"And Moses charged the people the same 11 day, saying, "When you have passed over the 12 Jordan, these shall stand upon Mount Ger'izim to bless the people: Simeon, Levi, Judah, Is'sachar, Joseph, and Benjamin. And these shall stand upon Mount Ebal for 13 the curse: Reuben, Gad, Asher, Zeb'ulun, Dan, and Naph'tali. And the Levites shall 14 declare to all the men of Israel with a loud voice:

" 'Cursed be the man who makes a graven 15 or molten image, an abomination to the LORD, a thing made by the hands of a craftsman, and sets it up in secret.' And all the people shall answer and say, 'Amen.'

" 'Cursed be he who dishonours his father 16 or his mother.' And all the people shall say, 'Amen.'

" 'Cursed be he who removes his neigh- 17 bour's landmark.' And all the people shall say, 'Amen.'

v Heb whole
27.15: Ex 20.4, 23; 34.17; Lev 19.4; 26.1; Deut 4.16, 23, 25; 5.8; 7.25.
27.16: Ex 20.12; 21.15, 17; Lev 20.9; Deut 5.16; 21.18–21.

150 DEUTERONOMY 28

18 " 'Cursed be he who misleads a blind man on the road.' And all the people shall say, 'Amen.'
19 " 'Cursed be he who perverts the justice due to the sojourner, the fatherless, and the widow.' And all the people shall say, 'Amen.'
20 " 'Cursed be he who lies with his father's wife, because he has uncovered her who is his father's.'*w* And all the people shall say, 'Amen.'
21 " 'Cursed be he who lies with any kind of beast.' And all the people shall say, 'Amen.'
22 " 'Cursed be he who lies with his sister, whether the daughter of his father or the daughter of his mother.' And all the people shall say, 'Amen.'
23 " 'Cursed be he who lies with his mother-in-law.' And all the people shall say, 'Amen.'
24 " 'Cursed be he who slays his neighbour in secret.' And all the people shall say, 'Amen.'
25 " 'Cursed be he who takes a bribe to slay an innocent person.' And all the people shall say, 'Amen.'
26 " 'Cursed be he who does not confirm the words of this law by doing them.' And all the people shall say, 'Amen.'

28 "And if you obey the voice of the LORD your God, being careful to do all his commandments which I command you this day, the LORD your God will set you high above 2 all the nations of the earth. And all these blessings shall come upon you and overtake you, if you obey the voice of the LORD your 3 God. Blessed shall you be in the city, and 4 blessed shall you be in the field. Blessed shall be the fruit of your body, and the fruit of your ground, and the fruit of your beasts, the increase of your cattle, and the young of 5 your flock. Blessed shall be your basket and 6 your kneading-trough. Blessed shall you be when you come in, and blessed shall you be when you go out.
7 "The LORD will cause your enemies who rise against you to be defeated before you; they shall come out against you one way, and 8 flee before you seven ways. The LORD will command the blessing upon you in your barns, and in all that you undertake; and he will bless you in the land which the LORD 9 your God gives you. The LORD will establish you as a people holy to himself, as he has sworn to you, if you keep the commandments of the LORD your God, and walk in his ways. 10 And all the peoples of the earth shall see that you are called by the name of the LORD; and

they shall be afraid of you. And the LORD will make you abound in prosperity, in the fruit of your body, and in the fruit of your cattle, and in the fruit of your ground, within the land which the LORD swore to your fathers to give you. The LORD will open to you his good treasury the heavens, to give the rain of your land in its season and to bless all the work of your hands; and you shall lend to many nations, but you shall not borrow. And the LORD will make you the head, and not the tail; and you shall tend upward only, and not downward; if you obey the commandments of the LORD your God, which I command you this day, being careful to do them, and if you do not turn aside from any of the words which I command you this day, to the right hand or to the left, to go after other gods to serve them.
"But if you will not obey the voice of the LORD your God or be careful to do all his commandments and his statutes which I command you this day, then all these curses shall come upon you and overtake you. Cursed shall you be in the city, and cursed shall you be in the field. Cursed shall be your basket and your kneading-trough. Cursed shall be the fruit of your body, and the fruit of your ground, the increase of your cattle, and the young of your flock. Cursed shall you be when you come in, and cursed shall you be when you go out.
"The LORD will send upon you curses, confusion, and frustration, in all that you undertake to do, until you are destroyed and perish quickly, on account of the evil of your doings, because you have forsaken me. The LORD will make the pestilence cleave to you until he has consumed you off the land which you are entering to take possession of it. The LORD will smite you with consumption, and with fever, inflammation, and fiery heat, and with drought,*x* and with blasting, and with mildew; they shall pursue you until you perish. And the heavens over your head shall be brass, and the earth under you shall be iron. The LORD will make the rain of your land powder and dust; from heaven it shall come down upon you until you are destroyed.
"The LORD will cause you to be defeated before your enemies; you shall go out one way against them, and flee seven ways before them; and you shall be a horror to all the kingdoms of the earth. And your dead body shall be food for all birds of the air, and for the beasts of the earth; and there shall be no one to frighten them away. The LORD will

w Heb *uncovered his father's skirt*   *x* Another reading is *sword*
27.18: Lev 19.14.   27.19: Ex 22.21–24; 23.9; Lev 19.33–34; Deut 24.17–18.
27.20: Lev 18.8; 20.11; Deut 22.30.   27.21: Ex 22.19; Lev 18.23; 20.15.   27.22: Lev 18.9; 20.17.
27.23: Lev 18.17; 20.14.   27.26: Gal 3.10.   28: Lev 26.3–45.

smite you with the boils of Egypt, and with the ulcers and the scurvy and the itch, of which you cannot be healed. The LORD will smite you with madness and blindness and confusion of mind; and you shall grope at noonday, as the blind grope in darkness, and you shall not prosper in your ways; and you shall be only oppressed and robbed continually, and there shall be no one to help you. You shall betroth a wife, and another man shall lie with her; you shall build a house, and you shall not dwell in it; you shall plant a vineyard, and you shall not use the fruit of it. Your ox shall be slain before your eyes, and you shall not eat of it; your ass shall be violently taken away before your face, and shall not be restored to you; your sheep shall be given to your enemies, and there shall be no one to help you. Your sons and your daughters shall be given to another people, while your eyes look on and fail with longing for them all the day; and it shall not be in the power of your hand to prevent it. A nation which you have not known shall eat up the fruit of your ground and of all your labours; and you shall be only oppressed and crushed continually; so that you shall be driven mad by the sight which your eyes shall see. The LORD will smite you on the knees and on the legs with grievous boils of which you cannot be healed, from the sole of your foot to the crown of your head.

"The LORD will bring you, and your king whom you set over you, to a nation that neither you nor your fathers have known; and there you shall serve other gods, of wood and stone. And you shall become a horror, a proverb, and a byword, among all the peoples where the LORD will lead you away. You shall carry much seed into the field, and shall gather little in; for the locust shall consume it. You shall plant vineyards and dress them, but you shall neither drink of the wine nor gather the grapes; for the worm shall eat them. You shall have olive trees throughout all your territory, but you shall not anoint yourself with the oil; for your olives shall drop off. You shall beget sons and daughters, but they shall not be yours; for they shall go into captivity. All your trees and the fruit of your ground the locust shall possess. The sojourner who is among you shall mount above you higher and higher;

and you shall come down lower and lower. He shall lend to you, and you shall not lend 44 to him; he shall be the head, and you shall be the tail. All these curses shall come upon you 45 and pursue you and overtake you, till you are destroyed, because you did not obey the voice of the LORD your God, to keep his commandments and his statutes which he commanded you. They shall be upon you as 46 a sign and a wonder, and upon your descendants for ever.

"Because you did not serve the LORD your 47 God with joyfulness and gladness of heart, by reason of the abundance of all things, therefore you shall serve your enemies whom 48 the LORD will send against you, in hunger and thirst, in nakedness, and in want of all things; and he will put a yoke of iron upon your neck, until he has destroyed you. The 49 LORD will bring a nation against you from afar, from the end of the earth, as swift as the eagle flies, a nation whose language you do not understand, a nation of stern coun- 50 tenance, who shall not regard the person of the old or show favour to the young, and 51 shall eat the offspring of your cattle and the fruit of your ground, until you are destroyed; who also shall not leave you grain, wine, or oil, the increase of your cattle or the young of your flock, until they have caused you to perish. They shall besiege you in all your 52 towns, until your high and fortified walls, in which you trusted, come down throughout all your land; and they shall besiege you in all your towns throughout all your land, which the LORD your God has given you. And you 53 shall eat the offspring of your own body, the flesh of your sons and daughters, whom the LORD your God has given you, in the siege and in the distress with which your enemies shall distress you. The man who is the most 54 tender and delicately bred among you will grudge food to his brother, to the wife of his bosom, and to the last of the children who remain to him; so that he will not give to any 55 of them any of the flesh of his children whom he is eating, because he has nothing left him, in the siege and in the distress with which your enemy shall distress you in all your towns. The most tender and delicately bred 56 woman among you, who would not venture to set the sole of her foot upon the ground because she is so delicate and tender, will

grudge to the husband of her bosom, to her
57 son and to her daughter, her afterbirth that
comes out from between her feet and her
children whom she bears, because she will
eat them secretly, for want of all things, in
the siege and in the distress with which your
enemy shall distress you in your towns.

Words of warning

58 "If you are not careful to do all the words of
this law which are written in this book, that
you may fear this glorious and awful name,
59 the LORD your God, then the LORD will bring
on you and your offspring extraordinary
afflictions, afflictions severe and lasting, and
60 sicknesses grievous and lasting. And he will
bring upon you again all the diseases of
Egypt, which you were afraid of; and they
61 shall cleave to you. Every sickness also, and
every affliction which is not recorded in the
book of this law, the LORD will bring upon
62 you, until you are destroyed. Whereas you
were as the stars of heaven for multitude, you
shall be left few in number; because you did
not obey the voice of the LORD your God.
63 And as the LORD took delight in doing you
good and multiplying you, so the LORD will
take delight in bringing ruin upon you and
destroying you; and you shall be plucked off
the land which you are entering to take
64 possession of it. And the LORD will scatter
you among all peoples, from one end of the
earth to the other; and there you shall serve
other gods, of wood and stone, which neither
65 you nor your fathers have known. And
among these nations you shall find no ease,
and there shall be no rest for the sole of your
foot; but the LORD will give you there a
trembling heart, and failing eyes, and a
66 languishing soul; your life shall hang in
doubt before you; night and day you shall be
in dread, and have no assurance of your life.
67 In the morning, you shall say, 'Would it were
evening!' and at evening you shall say,
'Would it were morning!' because of the
dread which your heart shall fear, and the
68 sights which your eyes shall see. And
the LORD will bring you back in ships to Egypt,
a journey which I promised that you should
never make again; and there you shall offer
yourselves for sale to your enemies as male
and female slaves, but no man will buy you."

A last appeal

29[y] These are the words of the covenant which
the LORD commanded Moses to make with
the people of Israel in the land of Moab,

besides the covenant which he had made
with them at Horeb.

And Moses summoned all Israel and said to
them: "You have seen all that the LORD did
before your eyes in the land of Egypt, to
Pharaoh and to all his servants and to all his
land, the great trials which your eyes saw,
the signs, and those great wonders; but to
this day the LORD has not given you a mind
to understand, or eyes to see, or ears to hear.
I have led you forty years in the wilderness;
your clothes have not worn out upon you,
and your sandals have not worn off your feet;
you have not eaten bread, and you have not
drunk wine or strong drink; that you may
know that I am the LORD your God. And
when you came to this place, Sihon the king
of Heshbon and Og the king of Bashan came
out against us to battle, but we defeated
them; we took their land, and gave it for an
inheritance to the Reubenites, the Gadites,
and the half-tribe of the Manas'sites. Therefore be careful to do the words of this
covenant, that you may prosper[a] in all that
you do.

"You stand this day all of you before the
LORD your God; the heads of your tribes,[b]
your elders, and your officers, all the men of
Israel, your little ones, your wives, and the
sojourner who is in your camp, both he who
hews your wood and he who draws your
water, that you may enter into the sworn
covenant of the LORD your God, which the
LORD your God makes with you this day;
that he may establish you this day as his
people, and that he may be your God, as he
promised you, and as he swore to your
fathers, to Abraham, to Isaac, and to Jacob.
Nor is it with you only that I make this sworn
covenant, but with him who is not here with
us this day as well as with him who stands
here with us this day before the LORD our
God.

"You know how we dwelt in the land of
Egypt, and how we came through the midst
of the nations through which you passed; and
you have seen their detestable things, their
idols of wood and stone, of silver and gold,
which were among them. Beware lest there
be among you a man or woman or family or
tribe, whose heart turns away this day from
the LORD our God to go and serve the gods of
those nations; lest there be among you a root
bearing poisonous and bitter fruit, one who,
when he hears the words of this sworn
covenant, blesses himself in his heart, saying,
'I shall be safe, though I walk in the stubbornness of my heart.' This would lead to
the sweeping away of moist and dry alike.

y Ch 28.69 in Heb   z Ch 29.1 in Heb   a Or deal wisely   b Gk Syr: Heb your heads, your tribes
29.4: Rom 11.8.   29.18: Acts 8.23; Heb 12.15.

The LORD would not pardon him, but rather the anger of the LORD and his jealousy would smoke against that man, and the curses written in this book would settle upon him, and the LORD would blot out his name from under heaven. And the LORD would single him out from all the tribes of Israel for calamity, in accordance with all the curses of the covenant written in this book of the law. And the generation to come, your children who rise up after you, and the foreigner who comes from a far land, would say, when they see the afflictions of that land and the sicknesses with which the LORD has made it sick—the whole land brimstone and salt, and a burnt-out waste, unsown, and growing nothing, where no grass can sprout, an overthrow like that of Sodom and Gomor′-rah, Admah and Zeboi′im, which the LORD overthrew in his anger and wrath—yea, all the nations would say, 'Why has the LORD done thus to this land? What means the heat of this great anger?' Then men would say, 'It is because they forsook the covenant of the LORD, the God of their fathers, which he made with them when he brought them out of the land of Egypt, and went and served other gods and worshipped them, gods whom they had not known and whom he had not allotted to them; therefore the anger of the LORD was kindled against this land, bringing upon it all the curses written in this book; and the LORD uprooted them from their land in anger and fury and great wrath, and cast them into another land, as at this day.'

"The secret things belong to the LORD our God; but the things that are revealed belong to us and to our children for ever, that we may do all the words of this law.

) "And when all these things come upon you, the blessing and the curse, which I have set before you, and you call them to mind among all the nations where the LORD your God has driven you, and return to the LORD your God, you and your children, and obey his voice in all that I command you this day, with all your heart and with all your soul; then the LORD your God will restore your fortunes, and have compassion upon you, and he will gather you again from all the peoples where the LORD your God has scattered you. If your outcasts are in the uttermost parts of heaven, from there the LORD your God will gather you, and from there he will fetch you; and the LORD your God will bring you into the land which your fathers possessed, that you may possess it; and he will make you more prosperous and numerous than your fathers. And the LORD 6 your God will circumcise your heart and the heart of your offspring, so that you will love the LORD your God with all your heart and with all your soul, that you may live. And 7 the LORD your God will put all these curses upon your foes and enemies who persecuted you. And you shall again obey the voice of 8 the LORD, and keep all his commandments which I command you this day. The LORD 9 your God will make you abundantly prosperous in all the work of your hand, in the fruit of your body, and in the fruit of your cattle, and in the fruit of your ground; for the LORD will again take delight in prospering you, as he took delight in your fathers, if you 10 obey the voice of the LORD your God, to keep his commandments and his statutes which are written in this book of the law, if you turn to the LORD your God with all your heart and with all your soul.

"For this commandment which I command 11 you this day is not too hard for you, neither is it far off. It is not in heaven, that you should 12 say, 'Who will go up for us to heaven, and bring it to us, that we may hear it and do it?' Neither is it beyond the sea, that you should 13 say, 'Who will go over the sea for us, and bring it to us, that we may hear it and do it?' But the word is very near you; it is in your 14 mouth and in your heart, so that you can do it.

"See, I have set before you this day life and 15 good, death and evil. If you obey the 16 commandments of the LORD your God⁰ which I command you this day, by loving the LORD your God, by walking in his ways, and by keeping his commandments and his statutes and his ordinances, then you shall live and multiply, and the LORD your God will bless you in the land which you are entering to take possession of it. But if your heart 17 turns away, and you will not hear, but are drawn away to worship other gods and serve them, I declare to you this day, that you shall 18 perish; you shall not live long in the land which you are going over the Jordan to enter and possess. I call heaven and earth to 19 witness against you this day, that I have set before you life and death, blessing and curse; therefore choose life, that you and your descendants may live, loving the LORD your 20 God, obeying his voice, and cleaving to him; for that means life to you and length of days, that you may dwell in the land which the LORD swore to your fathers, to Abraham, to Isaac, and to Jacob, to give them."

⁰ Gk: Heb lacks *If you obey the commandments of the* LORD *your God*
30.4: Mt 24.31; Mk 13.27.   30.12-13: Rom 10.6-7.   30.14: Rom 10.8.

31 So Moses continued to speak these words to ² all Israel. And he said to them, "I am a hundred and twenty years old this day; I am no longer able to go out and come in. The LORD has said to me, 'You shall not go over ³ this Jordan.' The LORD your God himself will go over before you; he will destroy these nations before you, so that you shall dispossess them; and Joshua will go over at your ⁴ head, as the LORD has spoken. And the LORD will do to them as he did to Sihon and Og, the kings of the Amorites, and to their land, ⁵ when he destroyed them. And the LORD will give them over to you, and you shall do to them according to all the commandment ⁶ which I have commanded you. Be strong and of good courage, do not fear or be in dread of them: for it is the LORD your God who goes with you; he will not fail you or forsake you."

⁷ Then Moses summoned Joshua, and said to him in the sight of all Israel, "Be strong and of good courage; for you shall go with this people into the land which the LORD has sworn to their fathers to give them; and you ⁸ shall put them in possession of it. It is the LORD who goes before you; he will be with you, he will not fail you or forsake you; do not fear or be dismayed."

⁹ And Moses wrote this law, and gave it to the priests the sons of Levi, who carried the ark of the covenant of the LORD, and to all the ¹⁰ elders of Israel. And Moses commanded them, "At the end of every seven years, at the set time of the year of release, at the feast of ¹¹ booths, when all Israel comes to appear before the LORD your God at the place which he will choose, you shall read this law before ¹² all Israel in their hearing. Assemble the people, men, women, and little ones, and the sojourner within your towns, that they may hear and learn to fear the LORD your God, and be careful to do all the words of this law, ¹³ and that their children, who have not known it, may hear and learn to fear the LORD your God, as long as you live in the land which you are going over the Jordan to possess."

¹⁴ And the LORD said to Moses, "Behold, the days approach when you must die; call Joshua, and present yourselves in the tent of meeting, that I may commission him." And Moses and Joshua went and presented them- ¹⁵ selves in the tent of meeting. And the LORD appeared in the tent in a pillar of cloud; and the pillar of cloud stood by the door of the tent.

¹⁶ And the LORD said to Moses, "Behold, you are about to sleep with your fathers; then this people will rise and play the harlot after the strange gods of the land, where they go to be among them, and they will forsake me and break my covenant which I have made with them. Then my anger will be kindled against them in that day, and I will forsake them and hide my face from them, and they will be devoured; and many evils and troubles will come upon them, so that they will say in that day, 'Have not these evils come upon us because our God is not among us?' And I will surely hide my face in that day on account of all the evil which they have done, because they have turned to other gods. Now therefore write this song, and teach it to the people of Israel; put it in their mouths, that this song may be a witness for me against the people of Israel. For when I have brought them into the land flowing with milk and honey, which I swore to give to their fathers, and they have eaten and are full and grown fat, they will turn to other gods and serve them, and despise me and break my covenant. And when many evils and troubles have come upon them, this song shall confront them as a witness (for it will live unforgotten in the mouths of their descendants); for I know the purposes which they are already forming, before I have brought them into the land that I swore to give." So Moses wrote this song the same day, and taught it to the people of Israel.

And the LORD commissioned Joshua the son of Nun and said, "Be strong and of good courage; for you shall bring the children of Israel into the land which I swore to give them: I will be with you."

The written word

When Moses had finished writing the words of this law in a book, to the very end, Moses commanded the Levites who carried the ark of the covenant of the LORD, "Take this book of the law, and put it by the side of the ark of the covenant of the LORD your God, that it may be there for a witness against you. For I know how rebellious and stubborn you are; behold, while I am yet alive with you, today you have been rebellious against the LORD; how much more after my death! Assemble to me all the elders of your tribes, and your officers, that I may speak these words in their ears and call heaven and earth to witness against them. For I know that after my death you will surely act corruptly, and turn aside from the way which I have commanded you; and in the days to come evil will befall you, because you will do what is evil in the sight of the

Lord, provoking him to anger through the work of your hands."

30 Then Moses spoke the words of this song until they were finished, in the ears of all the assembly of Israel:

THE SONG OF MOSES

32 "GIVE ear, O heavens, and I will speak;
    and let the earth hear the words of
    my mouth.

2 May my teaching drop as the rain,
    my speech distil as the dew,
    as the gentle rain upon the tender grass,
    and as the showers upon the herb.

3 For I will proclaim the name of the Lord.
    Ascribe greatness to our God!

4 "The Rock, his work is perfect;
    for all his ways are justice.
    A God of faithfulness and without iniquity,
    just and right is he.

5 They have dealt corruptly with him,
    they are no longer his children because of
    their blemish;
    they are a perverse and crooked genera-
    tion.

6 Do you thus requite the Lord,
    you foolish and senseless people?
    Is not he your father, who created you,
    who made you and established you?

7 Remember the days of old,
    consider the years of many generations;
    ask your father, and he will show you;
    your elders, and they will tell you.

8 When the Most High gave to the nations
    their inheritance,
    when he separated the sons of men,
    he fixed the bounds of the peoples
    according to the number of the sons of
    God.[d]

9 For the Lord's portion is his people,
    Jacob his allotted heritage.

10 "He found him in a desert land,
    and in the howling waste of the wil-
    derness;
    he encircled him, he cared for him,
    he kept him as the apple of his eye.

11 Like an eagle that stirs up its nest,
    that flutters over its young,
    spreading out its wings, catching them,
    bearing them on its pinions,

12 the Lord alone did lead him,
    and there was no foreign god with him.

13 He made him ride on the high places of the
    earth,
    and he ate the produce of the field;

and he made him suck honey out of the
    rock,
    and oil out of the flinty rock.

14 Curds from the herd, and milk from the
    flock,
    with fat of lambs and rams,
    herds of Bashan and goats,
    with the finest of the wheat—
    and of the blood of the grape you drank
    wine.

15 "But Jesh'urun waxed fat, and kicked;
    you waxed fat, you grew thick, you
    became sleek;
    then he forsook God who made him,
    and scoffed at the Rock of his salvation.

16 They stirred him to jealousy with strange
    gods;
    with abominable practices they provoked
    him to anger.

17 They sacrificed to demons which were no
    gods,
    to gods they had never known,
    to new gods that had come in of late,
    whom your fathers had never dreaded.

18 You were unmindful of the Rock that
    begot[e] you,
    and you forgot the God who gave you
    birth.

19 "The Lord saw it, and spurned them,
    because of the provocation of his sons
    and his daughters.

20 And he said, 'I will hide my face from
    them,
    I will see what their end will be,
    for they are a perverse generation,
    children in whom is no faithfulness.

21 They have stirred me to jealousy with
    what is no god;
    they have provoked me with their idols.
    So I will stir them to jealousy with those
    who are no people;
    I will provoke them with a foolish nation.

22 For a fire is kindled by my anger,
    and it burns to the depths of Sheol,
    devours the earth and its increase,
    and sets on fire the foundations of the
    mountains.

23 "'And I will heap evils upon them;
    I will spend my arrows upon them;

24 they shall be wasted with hunger,
    and devoured with burning heat
    and poisonous pestilence;
    and I will send the teeth of beasts against
    them,
    with venom of crawling things of the dust.

25 In the open the sword shall bereave,

[d] Compare Gk: Heb *Israel*   [e] Or *bore*
32.5: Phil 2.15.   32.17: 1 Cor 10.20.   32.21: Rom 10.19; 11.11; 1 Cor 10.22.

and in the chambers shall be terror,
destroying both young man and virgin,
the sucking child with the man of grey
hairs.

26 I would have said, "I will scatter them
afar,
I will make the remembrance of them
cease from among men",

27 had I not feared provocation by the
enemy,
lest their adversaries should judge amiss,
lest they should say, "Our hand is
triumphant,
the LORD has not wrought all this." '

28 "For they are a nation void of counsel,
and there is no understanding in them.

29 If they were wise, they would understand
this,
they would discern their latter end!

30 How should one chase a thousand,
and two put ten thousand to flight,
unless their Rock had sold them,
and the LORD had given them up?

31 For their rock is not as our Rock,
even our enemies themselves being
judges.

32 For their vine comes from the vine of
Sodom,
and from the fields of Gomor'rah;
their grapes are grapes of poison,
their clusters are bitter;

33 their wine is the poison of serpents,
and the cruel venom of asps.

34 "Is not this laid up in store with me,
sealed up in my treasuries?

35 Vengeance is mine, and recompense,
for the time when their foot shall slip;
for the day of their calamity is at hand,
and their doom comes swiftly.

36 For the LORD will vindicate his people
and have compassion on his servants,
when he sees that their power is gone,
and there is none remaining, bond or free.

37 Then he will say, 'Where are their gods,
the rock in which they took refuge,

38 who ate the fat of their sacrifices,
and drank the wine of their drink
offering?
Let them rise up and help you,
let them be your protection!

39 " 'See now that I, even I, am he,
and there is no god beside me;
I kill and I make alive;
I wound and I heal;
and there is none that can deliver out of
my hand.

For I lift up my hand to heaven,   40
and swear, As I live for ever,
if I whet my glittering sword,[f]   41
and my hand takes hold on judgment,
I will take vengeance on my adversaries,
and will requite those who hate me.
I will make my arrows drunk with blood,   42
and my sword shall devour flesh—
with the blood of the slain and the
captives,
from the long-haired heads of the enemy.'

"Praise his people, O you nations;   43
for he avenges the blood of his servants,
and takes vengeance on his adversaries,
and makes expiation for the land of his
people."[g]

Moses came and recited all the words of this   44
song in the hearing of the people, he and
Joshua[h] the son of Nun. And when Moses   45
had finished speaking all these words to all
Israel, he said to them, "Lay to heart all the   46
words which I enjoin upon you this day, that
you may command them to your children,
that they may be careful to do all the words
of this law. For it is no trifle for you, but it is   47
your life, and thereby you shall live long in
the land which you are going over the Jordan
to possess."

And the LORD said to Moses that very day,   48
"Ascend this mountain of the Ab'arim,   49
Mount Nebo, which is in the land of Moab,
opposite Jericho; and view the land of
Canaan, which I give to the people of Israel
for a possession; and die on the mountain   50
which you ascend, and be gathered to your
people, as Aaron your brother died in Mount
Hor and was gathered to his people; because   51
you broke faith with me in the midst of the
people of Israel at the waters of Meribath-
ka'desh, in the wilderness of Zin; because
you did not revere me as holy in the midst of
the people of Israel. For you shall see the   52
land before you; but you shall not go there,
into the land which I give to the people of
Israel."

THE BLESSING OF MOSES

THIS is the blessing with which Moses   33
the man of God blessed the children of
Israel before his death. He said,   2
"The LORD came from Sinai,
and dawned from Se'ir upon us;[i]
he shone forth from Mount Paran,
he came from the ten thousands of holy
ones,
with flaming fire[j] at his right hand.
Yea, he loved his people;[k]   3

f Heb the lightning of my sword   g Gk Vg: Heb his land his people   h Gk Syr Vg: Heb Hoshea
i Gk Syr Vg: Heb them   j The meaning of the Hebrew word is uncertain   k Gk: Heb peoples
32.35: Rom 12.19; Heb 10.30.   32.43: Rom 15.10; Heb 1.6 (Septuagint); Rev 6.10; 19.2

all those consecrated to him were in his[l]
    hand;
so they followed[m] in thy steps,
    receiving direction from thee,
4 when Moses commanded us a law,
    as a possession for the assembly of Jacob.
5 Thus the LORD became king in Jesh'urun,
    when the heads of the people were
       gathered,
    all the tribes of Israel together.

6 "Let Reuben live, and not die,
    nor let his men be few."

7 And this he said of Judah:
    "Hear, O LORD, the voice of Judah,
    and bring him in to his people.
    With thy hands contend[n] for him,
    and be a help against his adversaries."

8 And of Levi he said,
    "Give to Levi[o] thy Thummim,
    and thy Urim to thy godly one,
    whom thou didst test at Massah,
    with whom thou didst strive at the waters
      of Mer'ibah;
9 who said of his father and mother,
    'I regard them not';
    he disowned his brothers,
    and ignored his children.
    For they observed thy word,
    and kept thy covenant.
10 They shall teach Jacob thy ordinances,
    and Israel thy law;
    they shall put incense before thee,
    and whole burnt offering upon thy altar.
11 Bless, O LORD, his substance,
    and accept the work of his hands;
    crush the loins of his adversaries,
    of those that hate him, that they rise not
      again."

12 Of Benjamin he said,
    "The beloved of the LORD,
    he dwells in safety by him;
    he encompasses him all the day long,
    and makes his dwelling between his
      shoulders."

13 And of Joseph he said,
    "Blessed by the LORD be his land,
    with the choicest gifts of heaven above,[p]
    and of the deep that couches beneath,
14 with the choicest fruits of the sun,
    and the rich yield of the months,
15 with the finest produce of the ancient
      mountains,
    and the abundance of the everlasting
      hills,

with the best gifts of the earth and its 16
    fulness,
    and the favour of him that dwelt in the
      bush.
Let these come upon the head of Joseph,
    and upon the crown of the head of him
      that is prince among his brothers.
His firstling bull has majesty,   17
    and his horns are the horns of a wild ox;
    with them he shall push the peoples,
    all of them, to the ends of the earth;
    such are the ten thousands of E'phraim,
    and such are the thousands of Manas'-
      seh."

And of Zeb'ulun he said,   18
    "Rejoice, Zeb'ulun, in your going out;
    and Is'sachar, in your tents.
They shall call peoples to their mountain; 19
    there they offer right sacrifices;
    for they suck the affluence of the seas
    and the hidden treasures of the sand."

And of Gad he said,   20
    "Blessed be he who enlarges Gad!
    Gad couches like a lion,
    he tears the arm, and the crown of the
      head.
He chose the best of the land for himself, 21
    for there a commander's portion was
      reserved;
    and he came to the heads of the people,
    with Israel he executed the commands
    and just decrees of the LORD."

And of Dan he said,   22
    "Dan is a lion's whelp,
    that leaps forth from Bashan."

And of Naph'tali he said,   23
    "O Naph'tali, satisfied with favour,
    and full of the blessing of the LORD,
    possess the lake and the south."

And of Asher he said,   24

---

[l] Heb thy [m] The meaning of the Hebrew word is uncertain [n] Cn: Heb *with his hands he contended*
[o] Gk: Heb lacks *Give to Levi* [p] Two Heb Mss and Tg: Heb *with the dew*

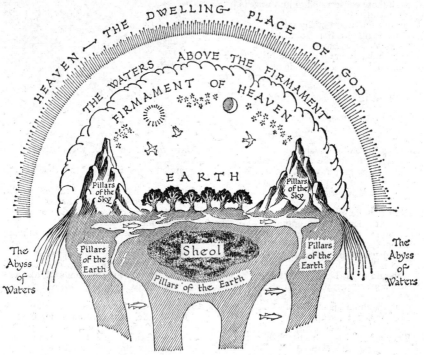

Early conception of the universe

"Blessed above sons be Asher;
  let him be the favourite of his brothers,
  and let him dip his foot in oil.
25 Your bars shall be iron and bronze;
  and as your days, so shall your strength be.

26 "There is none like God, O Jesh'urun,
  who rides through the heavens to your
    help,
  and in his majesty through the skies.
27 The eternal God is your dwelling place,
  and underneath are the everlasting arms.
  And he thrust out the enemy before you,
  and said, Destroy.
28 So Israel dwelt in safety,
  the fountain of Jacob alone,
  in a land of grain and wine;
  yea, his heavens drop down dew.
29 Happy are you, O Israel! Who is like you,
  a people saved by the LORD,
  the shield of your help,
  and the sword of your triumph!
  Your enemies shall come fawning to you;
  and you shall tread upon their high
    places."

The death of Moses

And Moses went up from the plains of 34
Moab to Mount Nebo, to the top of Pisgah,
which is opposite Jericho. And the LORD
showed him all the land, Gilead as far as Dan,
all Naph'tali, the land of E'phraim and 2
Manas'seh, all the land of Judah as far as the
Western Sea, the Negeb, and the Plain, that 3
is, the valley of Jericho the city of palm trees,
as far as Zo'ar. And the LORD said to him, 4
"This is the land of which I swore to
Abraham, to Isaac, and to Jacob, 'I will give
it to your descendants.' I have let you see it
with your eyes, but you shall not go over
there." So Moses the servant of the LORD 5
died there in the land of Moab, according to
the word of the LORD, and he buried him in 6
the valley in the land of Moab opposite
Beth-pe'or; but no man knows the place of
his burial to this day. Moses was a hundred 7
and twenty years old when he died; his eye
was not dim, nor his natural force abated.
And the people of Israel wept for Moses in 8
the plains of Moab thirty days; then the days

of weeping and mourning for Moses were ended.

9 And Joshua the son of Nun was full of the spirit of wisdom, for Moses had laid his hands upon him; so the people of Israel obeyed him, and did as the LORD had 10 commanded Moses. And there has not arisen a prophet since in Israel like Moses, whom the LORD knew face to face, none like 11 him for all the signs and the wonders which the LORD sent him to do in the land of Egypt, to Pharaoh and to all his servants and to all his land, and for all the mighty power and all 12 the great and terrible deeds which Moses wrought in the sight of all Israel.

THE BOOK OF

JOSHUA

THE PROMISED LAND

AFTER the death of Moses the servant of the LORD, the LORD said to Joshua the son of Nun, Moses' mini-
2 ster, "Moses my servant is dead; now therefore arise, go over this Jordan, you and all this people, into the land which I am
3 giving to them, to the people of Israel. Every place that the sole of your foot will tread upon I have given to you, as I promised to
4 Moses. From the wilderness and this Lebanon as far as the great river, the river Euphra'tes, all the land of the Hittites to the Great Sea toward the going down of the sun
5 shall be your territory. No man shall be able to stand before you all the days of your life; as I was with Moses, so I will be with you; I
6 will not fail you or forsake you. Be strong and of good courage; for you shall cause this people to inherit the land which I swore to

their fathers to give them. Only be strong 7 and very courageous, being careful to do according to all the law which Moses my servant commanded you; turn not from it to the right hand or to the left, that you may have good success wherever you go. This 8 book of the law shall not depart out of your mouth, but you shall meditate on it day and night, that you may be careful to do according to all that is written in it; for then you shall make your way prosperous, and then you shall have good success. Have I not 9 commanded you? Be strong and of good courage; be not frightened, neither be dismayed; for the LORD your God is with you wherever you go."

Then Joshua commanded the officers of the 10 people, "Pass through the camp, and command the people, 'Prepare your provisions; 11 for within three days you are to pass over this Jordan, to go in to take possession of the land

34.10: Num 12.6–8. 1.5: Heb 13.5.

which the LORD your God gives you to possess.' "

12 And to the Reubenites, the Gadites, and the half-tribe of Manas′seh Joshua said,
13 "Remember the word which Moses the servant of the LORD commanded you, saying, 'The LORD your God is providing you a place
14 of rest, and will give you this land.' Your wives, your little ones, and your cattle shall remain in the land which Moses gave you beyond the Jordan; but all the men of valour among you shall pass over armed before your
15 brethren and shall help them, until the LORD gives rest to your brethren as well as to you, and they also take possession of the land which the LORD your God is giving them; then you shall return to the land of your possession, and shall possess it, the land which Moses the servant of the LORD gave you beyond the Jordan toward the sunrise."
16 And they answered Joshua, "All that you have commanded us we will do, and
17 wherever you send us we will go. Just as we obeyed Moses in all things, so we will obey you; only may the LORD your God be with
18 you, as he was with Moses! Whoever rebels against your commandment and disobeys your words, whatever you command him, shall be put to death. Only be strong and of good courage."

Spies sent out

2 And Joshua the son of Nun sent two men secretly from Shittim as spies, saying, "Go, view the land, especially Jericho." And they went, and came into the house of a harlot whose name was Rahab, and lodged there.
2 And it was told the king of Jericho, "Behold, certain men of Israel have come here tonight
3 to search out the land." Then the king of Jericho sent to Rahab, saying, "Bring forth the men that have come to you, who entered your house; for they have come to search out
4 all the land." But the woman had taken the two men and hidden them; and she said, "True, men came to me, but I did not know
5 where they came from; and when the gate was to be closed, at dark, the men went out; where the men went I do not know; pursue them
6 quickly, for you will overtake them." But she had brought them up to the roof, and hid them with the stalks of flax which she had laid
7 in order on the roof. So the men pursued after them on the way to the Jordan as far as the fords; and as soon as the pursuers had gone out, the gate was shut.
8 Before they lay down, she came up to them
9 on the roof, and said to the men, "I know that the LORD has given you the land, and

that the fear of you has fallen upon us, and that all the inhabitants of the land melt away before you. For we have heard how the 10 LORD dried up the water of the Red Sea before you when you came out of Egypt, and what you did to the two kings of the Amorites that were beyond the Jordan, to Sihon and Og, whom you utterly destroyed. And 11 as soon as we heard it, our hearts melted, and there was no courage left in any man, because of you; for the LORD your God is he who is God in heaven above and on earth beneath. Now then, swear to me by the LORD that as I 12 have dealt kindly with you, you also will deal kindly with my father's house, and give me a sure sign, and save alive my father and 13 mother, my brothers and sisters, and all who belong to them, and deliver our lives from death." And the men said to her, "Our life 14 for yours! If you do not tell this business of ours, then we will deal kindly and faithfully with you when the LORD gives us the land."

Then she let them down by a rope through 15 the window, for her house was built into the city wall, so that she dwelt in the wall. And 16 she said to them, "Go into the hills, lest the pursuers meet you; and hide yourselves there three days, until the pursuers have returned; then afterward you may go your way." The 17 men said to her, "We will be guiltless with respect to this oath of yours which you have made us swear. Behold, when we come into 18 the land, you shall bind this scarlet cord in the window through which you let us down; and you shall gather into your house your father and mother, your brothers, and all your father's household. If any one goes out 19 of the doors of your house into the street, his blood shall be upon his head, and we shall be guiltless; but if a hand is laid upon any one who is with you in the house, his blood shall be on our head. But if you tell this business 20 of ours, then we shall be guiltless with respect to your oath which you have made us swear." And she said, "According to your 21 words, so be it." Then she sent them away, and they departed; and she bound the scarlet cord in the window.

They departed, and went into the hills, and 22 remained there three days, until the pursuers returned; for the pursuers had made search all along the way and found nothing. Then 23 the two men came down again from the hills, and passed over and came to Joshua the son of Nun; and they told him all that had befallen them. And they said to Joshua, 24 "Truly the LORD has given all the land into our hands; and moreover all the inhabitants of the land are fainthearted because of us."

Crossing the Jordan

3 Early in the morning Joshua rose and set out from Shittim, with all the people of Israel; and they came to the Jordan, and **2** lodged there before they passed over. At the end of three days the officers went through **3** the camp and commanded the people, "When you see the ark of the covenant of the LORD your God being carried by the Levitical priests, then you shall set out from your **4** place and follow it, that you may know the way you shall go, for you have not passed this way before. Yet there shall be a space between you and it, a distance of about two **5** thousand cubits; do not come near it." And Joshua said to the people, "Sanctify yourselves; for tomorrow the LORD will do won-**6** ders among you." And Joshua said to the priests, "Take up the ark of the covenant, and pass on before the people." And they took up the ark of the covenant, and went before the people.

7 And the LORD said to Joshua, "This day I will begin to exalt you in the sight of all Israel, that they may know that, as I was with **8** Moses, so I will be with you. And you shall command the priests who bear the ark of the covenant, 'When you come to the brink of the waters of the Jordan, you shall stand still **9** in the Jordan.'" And Joshua said to the people of Israel, "Come hither, and hear the **10** words of the LORD your God." And Joshua said, "Hereby you shall know that the living God is among you, and that he will without fail drive out from before you the Canaanites, the Hittites, the Hivites, the Per'izzites, the Gir'gashites, the Amorites, and the Jeb'us-**11** ites. Behold, the ark of the covenant of the Lord of all the earth is to pass over before **12** you into the Jordan. Now therefore take twelve men from the tribes of Israel, from **13** each tribe a man. And when the soles of the feet of the priests who bear the ark of the Lord, the Lord of all the earth, shall rest in the waters of the Jordan, the waters of the Jordan shall be stopped from flowing, and the waters coming down from above shall stand in one heap."

14 So, when the people set out from their tents, to pass over the Jordan with the priests bearing the ark of the covenant before the **15** people, and when those who bore the ark had come to the Jordan, and the feet of the priests bearing the ark were dipped in the brink of the water (the Jordan overflows all its banks **16** throughout the time of harvest), the waters coming down from above stood and rose up in a heap far off, at Adam, the city that is beside Zarethan, and those flowing down toward the sea of the Arabah, the Salt Sea, were wholly cut off; and the people passed over opposite Jericho. And while all Israel **17** were passing over on dry ground, the priests who bore the ark of the covenant of the LORD stood on dry ground in the midst of the Jordan, until all the nation finished passing over the Jordan.

When all the nation had finished passing **4** over the Jordan, the LORD said to Joshua, "Take twelve men from the people, from **2** each tribe a man, and command them, 'Take **3** twelve stones from here out of the midst of the Jordan, from the very place where the priests' feet stood, and carry them over with you, and lay them down in the place where you lodge tonight.'" Then Joshua called the **4** twelve men from the people of Israel, whom he had appointed, a man from each tribe; and **5** Joshua said to them, "Pass on before the ark of the LORD your God into the midst of the Jordan, and take up each of you a stone upon his shoulder, according to the number of the tribes of the people of Israel, that this **6** may be a sign among you, when your children ask in time to come, 'What do those stones mean to you?' Then you shall tell **7** them that the waters of the Jordan were cut off before the ark of the covenant of the LORD; when it passed over the Jordan, the waters of the Jordan were cut off. So these stones shall be to the people of Israel a memorial for ever."

And the men of Israel did as Joshua com-**8** manded, and took up twelve stones out of the midst of the Jordan, according to the number of the tribes of the people of Israel, as the LORD told Joshua; and they carried them over with them to the place where they lodged, and laid them down there. And **9** Joshua set up twelve stones in the midst of the Jordan, in the place where the feet of the priests bearing the ark of the covenant had stood; and they are there to this day. For the **10** priests who bore the ark stood in the midst of the Jordan, until everything was finished that the LORD commanded Joshua to tell the people, according to all that Moses had commanded Joshua.

The people passed over in haste; and when **11** all the people had finished passing over, the ark of the LORD and the priests passed over before the people. The sons of Reuben and **12** the sons of Gad and the half-tribe of Manas'seh passed over armed before the people of Israel, as Moses had bidden them; about forty thousand ready armed for war **13** passed over before the LORD for battle, to the plains of Jericho. On that day the LORD **14** exalted Joshua in the sight of all Israel; and they stood in awe of him, as they had stood in awe of Moses, all the days of his life.

And the LORD said to Joshua, "Command **15,**

16 the priests who bear the ark of the testimony
17 to come up out of the Jordan." Joshua
therefore commanded the priests, "Come up
18 out of the Jordan." And when the priests
bearing the ark of the covenant of the LORD
came up from the midst of the Jordan, and
the soles of the priests' feet were lifted up
on dry ground, the waters of the Jordan
returned to their place and overflowed all its
banks, as before.

19 The people came up out of the Jordan on
the tenth day of the first month, and they
encamped in Gilgal on the east border of
20 Jericho. And those twelve stones, which
they took out of the Jordan, Joshua set up in
21 Gilgal. And he said to the people of Israel,
"When your children ask their fathers in
time to come, 'What do these stones mean?'
22 then you shall let your children know, 'Israel
23 passed over this Jordan on dry ground.' For
the LORD your God dried up the waters of
the Jordan for you until you passed over,
as the LORD your God did to the Red Sea,
which he dried up for us until we passed
24 over, so that all the peoples of the earth may
know that the hand of the LORD is mighty;
that you may fear the LORD your God for
ever."

5 When all the kings of the Amorites that
were beyond the Jordan to the west, and all
the kings of the Canaanites that were by the
sea, heard that the LORD had dried up the
waters of the Jordan for the people of Israel
until they had crossed over, their heart
melted, and there was no longer any spirit in
them, because of the people of Israel.

2 At that time the LORD said to Joshua,
"Make flint knives and circumcise the people

of Israel again the second time." So Joshua 3
made flint knives, and circumcised the
people of Israel at Gibeath-haaraloth.[a] And 4
this is the reason why Joshua circumcised
them: all the males of the people who came
out of Egypt, all the men of war, had died on
the way in the wilderness after they had come
out of Egypt. Though all the people who 5
came out had been circumcised, yet all the
people that were born on the way in the
wilderness after they had come out of Egypt
had not been circumcised. For the people of 6
Israel walked forty years in the wilderness,
till all the nation, the men of war that came
forth out of Egypt, perished, because they
did not hearken to the voice of the LORD; to
them the LORD swore that he would not let
them see the land which the LORD had sworn
to their fathers to give us, a land flowing with
milk and honey. So it was their children, 7
whom he raised up in their stead, that Joshua
circumcised; for they were uncircumcised,
because they had not been circumcised on
the way.

When the circumcising of all the nation was 8
done, they remained in their places in the
camp till they were healed. And the LORD 9
said to Joshua, "This day I have rolled away
the reproach of Egypt from you." And so
the name of that place is called Gilgal[b] to this
day.

While the people of Israel were encamped 10
in Gilgal they kept the passover on the
fourteenth day of the month at evening in the
plains of Jericho. And on the morrow after 11
the passover, on that very day, they ate of the
produce of the land, unleavened cakes and
parched grain. And the manna ceased on the 12
morrow, when they ate of the produce of the

a That is *the hill of the foreskins*   b From Heb *galal*, to roll land; and the people of Israel had manna no more, but ate of the fruit of the land of Canaan that year.

Fall of Jericho

13 When Joshua was by Jericho, he lifted up his eyes and looked, and behold, a man stood before him with his drawn sword in his hand; and Joshua went to him and said to him, "Are you for us, or for our adversaries?" 14 And he said, "No; but as commander of the army of the LORD I have now come." And Joshua fell on his face to the earth, and worshipped, and said to him, "What does my 15 lord bid his servant?" And the commander of the LORD's army said to Joshua, "Put off your shoes from your feet; for the place where you stand is holy." And Joshua did so.

the covenant of the LORD following them. And the armed men went before the priests 9 who blew the trumpets, and the rear guard came after the ark, while the trumpets blew continually. But Joshua commanded the 10 people, "You shall not shout or let your voice be heard, neither shall any word go out of your mouth, until the day I bid you shout; then you shall shout." So he caused the ark 11 of the LORD to compass the city, going about it once; and they came into the camp, and spent the night in the camp.

Then Joshua rose early in the morning, and 12 the priests took up the ark of the LORD. And 13 the seven priests bearing the seven trumpets of rams' horns before the ark of the LORD passed on, blowing the trumpets continually; and the armed men went before them, and the rear guard came after the ark of the LORD, while the trumpets blew continually.

6 Now Jericho was shut up from within and from without because of the people of Israel; 2 none went out, and none came in. And the LORD said to Joshua, "See, I have given into your hand Jericho, with its king and mighty 3 men of valour. You shall march around the city, all the men of war going around the city 4 once. Thus shall you do for six days. And seven priests shall bear seven trumpets of rams' horns before the ark; and on the seventh day you shall march around the city seven times, the priests blowing the trum-5 pets. And when they make a long blast with the ram's horn, as soon as you hear the sound of the trumpet, then all the people shall shout with a great shout; and the wall of the city will fall down flat, and the people shall go up 6 every man straight before him." So Joshua the son of Nun called the priests and said to them, "Take up the ark of the covenant, and let seven priests bear seven trumpets of rams' 7 horns before the ark of the LORD." And he said to the people, "Go forward; march around the city, and let the armed men pass on before the ark of the LORD."

8 And as Joshua had commanded the people, the seven priests bearing the seven trumpets of rams' horns before the LORD went forward, blowing the trumpets, with the ark of

And the second day they marched around the 14 city once, and returned into the camp. So they did for six days.

On the seventh day they rose early at the 15 dawn of day, and marched around the city in the same manner seven times: it was only on that day that they marched around the city seven times. And at the seventh time, when 16 the priests had blown the trumpets, Joshua said to the people, "Shout; for the LORD has given you the city. And the city and all that 17 is within it shall be devoted to the LORD for destruction; only Rahab the harlot and all who are with her in her house shall live, because she hid the messengers that we sent. But you, keep yourselves from the things 18 devoted to destruction, lest when you have devoted them you take any of the devoted things and make the camp of Israel a thing for destruction, and bring trouble upon it. But all silver and gold, and vessels of bronze 19 and iron, are sacred to the LORD; they shall go into the treasury of the LORD." So the 20 people shouted, and the trumpets were blown. As soon as the people heard the sound of the trumpet, the people raised a great shout, and the wall fell down flat, so that the people went up into the city, every man straight before him, and they took the

21 city. Then they utterly destroyed all in the city, both men and women, young and old, oxen, sheep, and asses, with the edge of the sword.

22 And Joshua said to the two men who had spied out the land, "Go into the harlot's house, and bring out from it the woman, and all who belong to her, as you swore to her."

23 So the young men who had been spies went in, and brought out Rahab, and her father and mother and brothers and all who belonged to her; and they brought all her kindred, and set them outside the camp of

24 Israel. And they burned the city with fire, and all within it; only the silver and gold, and the vessels of bronze and of iron, they put into the treasury of the house of the LORD.

25 But Rahab the harlot, and her father's household, and all who belonged to her, Joshua saved alive; and she dwelt in Israel to this day, because she hid the messengers whom Joshua sent to spy out Jericho.

26 Joshua laid an oath upon them at that time, saying, "Cursed before the LORD be the man that rises up and rebuilds this city, Jericho.

At the cost of his first-born shall he lay its foundation,

And at the cost of his youngest son shall he set up its gates."

27 So the LORD was with Joshua; and his fame was in all the land.

Ai is destroyed

7 But the people of Israel broke faith in regard to the devoted things; for Achan the son of Carmi, son of Zabdi, son of Zerah, of the tribe of Judah, took some of the devoted things; and the anger of the LORD burned against the people of Israel.

2 Joshua sent men from Jericho to Ai, which is near Beth-a'ven, east of Bethel, and said to them, "Go up and spy out the land." And

3 the men went up and spied out Ai. And they returned to Joshua, and said to him, "Let not all the people go up, but let about two or three thousand men go up and attack Ai; do

not make the whole people toil up there, for they are but few." So about three thousand 4 went up there from the people; and they fled before the men of Ai, and the men of Ai 5 killed about thirty-six men of them, and chased them before the gate as far as Sheb'arim, and slew them at the descent. And the hearts of the people melted, and became as water.

Then Joshua rent his clothes, and fell to the 6 earth upon his face before the ark of the LORD until the evening, he and the elders of Israel; and they put dust upon their heads. And Joshua said, "Alas, O Lord GOD, why 7 hast thou brought this people over the Jordan at all, to give us into the hands of the Amorites, to destroy us? Would that we had been content to dwell beyond the Jordan! O 8 Lord, what can I say, when Israel has turned their backs before their enemies! For the 9 Canaanites and all the inhabitants of the land will hear of it, and will surround us, and cut off our name from the earth; and what wilt thou do for thy great name?"

The LORD said to Joshua, "Arise, why have 10 you thus fallen upon your face? Israel has 11 sinned; they have transgressed my covenant which I commanded them; they have taken some of the devoted things; they have stolen, and lied, and put them among their own stuff. Therefore the people of Israel cannot 12 stand before their enemies; they turn their backs before their enemies, because they have become a thing for destruction. I will be with you no more, unless you destroy the devoted things from among you. Up, 13 sanctify the people, and say, 'Sanctify yourselves for tomorrow; for thus says the LORD, God of Israel, "There are devoted things in the midst of you, O Israel; you cannot stand before your enemies, until you take away the devoted things from among you." In the 14 morning therefore you shall be brought near by your tribes; and the tribe which the LORD takes shall come near by families; and the family which the LORD takes shall come near by households; and the household which the LORD takes shall come near man by man. And he who is taken with the devoted things 15 shall be burned with fire, he and all that he has, because he has transgressed the covenant of the LORD, and because he has done a shameful thing in Israel.' "

So Joshua rose early in the morning, and 16 brought Israel near tribe by tribe, and the tribe of Judah was taken; and he brought 17 near the families of Judah, and the family of the Zer'ahites was taken; and he brought near the family of the Zer'ahites man by man, and Zabdi was taken; and he brought 18

near his household man by man, and Achan the son of Carmi, son of Zabdi, son of Zerah,
19 of the tribe of Judah, was taken. Then Joshua said to Achan, "My son, give glory to the LORD God of Israel, and render praise to him; and tell me now what you have done; do
20 not hide it from me." And Achan answered Joshua, "Of a truth I have sinned against the LORD God of Israel, and this is what I did:
21 when I saw among the spoil a beautiful mantle from Shinar, and two hundred shekels of silver, and a bar of gold weighing fifty shekels, then I coveted them, and took them; and behold, they are hidden in the earth inside my tent, with the silver underneath."
22 So Joshua sent messengers, and they ran to the tent; and behold, it was hidden in his tent
23 with the silver underneath. And they took them out of the tent and brought them to Joshua and all the people of Israel; and they
24 laid them down before the LORD. And Joshua and all Israel with him took Achan the son of Zerah, and the silver and the mantle and the bar of gold, and his sons and daughters, and his oxen and asses and sheep, and his tent, and all that he had; and they brought them up to the Valley of Achor.
25 And Joshua said, "Why did you bring trouble on us? The LORD brings trouble on you today." And all Israel stoned him with stones; they burned them with fire, and
26 stoned them with stones. And they raised over him a great heap of stones that remains to this day; then the LORD turned from his burning anger. Therefore to this day the name of that place is called the Valley of Achor.*c*

8 And the LORD said to Joshua, "Do not fear or be dismayed; take all the fighting men with you, and arise, go up to Ai; see, I have given into your hand the king of Ai, and his
2 people, his city, and his land; and you shall do to Ai and its king as you did to Jericho and its king; only its spoil and its cattle you shall take as booty for yourselves; lay an ambush against the city, behind it."
3 So Joshua arose, and all the fighting men, to go up to Ai; and Joshua chose thirty thousand mighty men of valour, and sent
4 them forth by night. And he commanded them, "Behold, you shall lie in ambush against the city, behind it; do not go very far from the city, but hold yourselves all in
5 readiness; and I, and all the people who are with me, will approach the city. And when they come out against us, as before, we shall
6 flee before them; and they will come out after us, till we have drawn them away from the

city; for they will say, 'They are fleeing from us, as before.' So we will flee from them;
7 then you shall rise up from the ambush, and seize the city; for the LORD your God will
8 give it into your hand. And when you have taken the city, you shall set the city on fire, doing as the LORD has bidden; see, I have
9 commanded you." So Joshua sent them forth; and they went to the place of ambush, and lay between Bethel and Ai, to the west of Ai; but Joshua spent that night among the people.
10 And Joshua arose early in the morning and mustered the people, and went up, with the elders of Israel, before the people to Ai. And
11 all the fighting men who were with him went up, and drew near before the city, and encamped on the north side of Ai, with a ravine between them and Ai. And he took
12 about five thousand men, and set them in ambush between Bethel and Ai, to the west

of the city. So they stationed the forces, the
13 main encampment which was north of the city and its rear guard west of the city. But Joshua spent that night in the valley. And
14 when the king of Ai saw this he and all his people, the men of the city, made haste and went out early to the descent*d* toward the Arabah to meet Israel in battle; but he did not know that there was an ambush against
15 him behind the city. And Joshua and all Israel made a pretence of being beaten before them, and fled in the direction of the wil-
16 derness. So all the people who were in the city were called together to pursue them, and as they pursued Joshua they were drawn
17 away from the city. There was not a man left in Ai or Bethel, who did not go out after Israel; they left the city open, and pursued Israel.
18 Then the LORD said to Joshua, "Stretch out the javelin that is in your hand toward Ai; for I will give it into your hand." And Joshua stretched out the javelin that was in his hand
19 toward the city. And the ambush rose quickly out of their place, and as soon as he had stretched out his hand, they ran and entered the city and took it; and they made

c That is *Trouble*   *d* Cn: Heb *appointed time*

20 haste to set the city on fire. So when the men of Ai looked back, behold, the smoke of the city went up to heaven; and they had no power to flee this way or that, for the people that fled to the wilderness turned back upon
21 the pursuers. And when Joshua and all Israel saw that the ambush had taken the city, and that the smoke of the city went up, then they turned back and smote the men of
22 Ai. And the others came forth from the city against them; so they were in the midst of Israel, some on this side, and some on that side; and Israel smote them, until there was
23 left none that survived or escaped. But the king of Ai they took alive, and brought him to Joshua.
24 When Israel had finished slaughtering all the inhabitants of Ai in the open wilderness where they pursued them and all of them to the very last had fallen by the edge of the sword, all Israel returned to Ai, and smote it
25 with the edge of the sword. And all who fell that day, both men and women, were twelve
26 thousand, all the people of Ai. For Joshua did not draw back his hand, with which he stretched out the javelin, until he had utterly
27 destroyed all the inhabitants of Ai. Only the cattle and the spoil of that city Israel took as their booty, according to the word of the
28 LORD which he commanded Joshua. So Joshua burned Ai, and made it for ever a
29 heap of ruins, as it is to this day. And he hanged the king of Ai on a tree until evening; and at the going down of the sun Joshua commanded, and they took his body down from the tree, and cast it at the entrance of the gate of the city, and raised over it a great heap of stones, which stands there to this day.
30 Then Joshua built an altar in Mount Ebal to
31 the LORD, the God of Israel, as Moses the servant of the LORD had commanded the people of Israel, as it is written in the book of the law of Moses, "an altar of unhewn stones, upon which no man has lifted an iron tool"; and they offered on it burnt offerings to the
32 LORD, and sacrificed peace offerings. And there, in the presence of the people of Israel, he wrote upon the stones a copy of the law of
33 Moses, which he had written. And all Israel, sojourner as well as home-born, with their elders and officers and their judges, stood on opposite sides of the ark before the Levitical priests who carried the ark of the covenant of the LORD, half of them in front of Mount Ger'izim and half of them in front of Mount Ebal, as Moses the servant of the LORD had commanded at the first, that they should
34 bless the people of Israel. And afterward he read all the words of the law, the blessing and

the curse, according to all that is written in the book of the law. There was not a word of 35 all that Moses commanded which Joshua did not read before all the assembly of Israel, and the women, and the little ones, and the sojourners who lived among them.

When all the kings who were beyond the 9 Jordan in the hill country and in the lowland all along the coast of the Great Sea toward Lebanon, the Hittites, the Amorites, the Canaanites, the Per'izzites, the Hivites, and the Jeb'usites, heard of this, they gathered 2 together with one accord to fight Joshua and Israel.

The Gibeonites

But when the inhabitants of Gibeon heard 3 what Joshua had done to Jericho and to Ai, they on their part acted with cunning, and 4 went and made ready provisions, and took worn-out sacks upon their asses, and wine-skins, worn-out and torn and mended, with 5 worn-out, patched sandals on their feet, and worn-out clothes; and all their provisions were dry and mouldy. And they went to 6 Joshua in the camp at Gilgal, and said to him and to the men of Israel, "We have come from a far country; so now make a covenant with us." But the men of Israel said to the 7 Hivites, "Perhaps you live among us; then how can we make a covenant with you?" They said to Joshua, "We are your ser- 8 vants." And Joshua said to them, "Who are you? And where do you come from?" They said to him, "From a very far country 9 your servants have come, because of the name of the LORD your God; for we have heard a report of him, and all that he did in Egypt, and all that he did to the two kings of 10 the Amorites who were beyond the Jordan, Sihon the king of Heshbon, and Og king of Bashan, who dwelt in Ash'taroth. And our 11 elders and all the inhabitants of our country said to us, 'Take provisions in your hand for the journey, and go to meet them, and say to them, "We are your servants; come now, make a covenant with us." ' Here is our 12 bread; it was still warm when we took it from our houses as our food for the journey, on the day we set forth to come to you, but now, behold, it is dry and mouldy; these wineskins 13 were new when we filled them, and behold, they are burst; and these garments and shoes of ours are worn out from the very long journey." So the men partook of their 14 provisions, and did not ask direction from the LORD. And Joshua made peace with 15 them, and made a covenant with them, to let

JOSHUA'S
CAMPAIGNS
1
In the South
Scale of Miles
0   5   10   15   20

The
Great
Sea

Mt Ebal

●Adam

Bethel
●Ai
Jericho●
Valley of Ajalon
Gibeon
Valley of Achor
Gilgal
●Shittim

Beth-horon●

●Azekah
Mt Pisgah

●Eglon
●Lachish
●Hebron

Salt Sea

them live; and the leaders of the congregation swore to them.

16 At the end of three days after they had made a covenant with them, they heard that they were their neighbours, and that they dwelt 17 among them. And the people of Israel set out and reached their cities on the third day. Now their cities were Gibeon, Chephi'rah, 18 Be-er'oth, and Kir'iath-je'arim. But the people of Israel did not kill them, because the leaders of the congregation had sworn to them by the LORD, the God of Israel. Then all the congregation murmured against the 19 leaders. But all the leaders said to all the congregation, "We have sworn to them by the LORD, the God of Israel, and now we may 20 not touch them. This we will do to them, and let them live, lest wrath be upon us, because of the oath which we swore to 21 them." And the leaders said to them, "Let them live." So they became hewers of wood and drawers of water for all the congregation, as the leaders had said of them.

22 Joshua summoned them, and he said to them, "Why did you deceive us, saying, 'We are very far from you,' when you dwell 23 among us? Now therefore you are cursed, and some of you shall always be slaves, hewers of wood and drawers of water for the 24 house of my God." They answered Joshua, "Because it was told to your servants for a certainty that the LORD your God had

commanded his servant Moses to give you all the land, and to destroy all the inhabitants of the land from before you; so we feared greatly for our lives because of you, and did this thing. And now, behold, we are in your 25 hand: do as it seems good and right in your sight to do to us." So he did to them, and 26 delivered them out of the hand of the people of Israel; and they did not kill them. But 27 Joshua made them that day hewers of wood and drawers of water for the congregation and for the altar of the LORD, to continue to this day, in the place which he should choose.

A memorable day

When Ado'ni-ze'dek king of Jerusalem 10 heard how Joshua had taken Ai, and had utterly destroyed it, doing to Ai and its king as he had done to Jericho and its king, and how the inhabitants of Gibeon had made peace with Israel and were among them, he *x* 2 feared greatly, because Gibeon was a great city, like one of the royal cities, and because it was greater than Ai, and all its men were mighty. So Ado'ni-ze'dek king of Jerusalem 3 sent to Hoham king of Hebron, to Piram king of Jarmuth, to Japhi'a king of Lachish, and to Debir king of Eglon, saying, "Come up to 4 me, and help me, and let us smite Gibeon; for it has made peace with Joshua and with the people of Israel." Then the five kings of 5

x Heb *they*

the Amorites, the king of Jerusalem, the king of Hebron, the king of Jarmuth, the king of Lachish, and the king of Eglon, gathered their forces, and went up with all their armies and encamped against Gibeon, and made war against it.

6 And the men of Gibeon sent to Joshua at the camp in Gilgal, saying, "Do not relax your hand from your servants; come up to us quickly, and save us, and help us; for all the kings of the Amorites that dwell in the hill 7 country are gathered against us." So Joshua went up from Gilgal, he and all the people of war with him, and all the mighty men of 8 valour. And the LORD said to Joshua, "Do not fear them, for I have given them into your hands; there shall not a man of them 9 stand before you." So Joshua came upon them suddenly, having marched up all night 10 from Gilgal. And the LORD threw them into a panic before Israel, who slew them with a great slaughter at Gibeon, and chased them

by the way of the ascent of Beth-horon, and smote them as far as Aze′kah and Makke′- 11 dah. And as they fled before Israel, while they were going down the ascent of Beth-horon, the LORD threw down great stones from heaven upon them as far as Aze′kah, and they died; there were more who died because of the hailstones than the men of Israel killed with the sword.

12 Then spoke Joshua to the LORD in the day when the LORD gave the Amorites over to the men of Israel; and he said in the sight of Israel,

"Sun, stand thou still at Gibeon,
and thou Moon in the valley of Ai′jalon."

13 And the sun stood still, and the moon stayed,
until the nation took vengeance on their enemies.

Is this not written in the Book of Jashar? The sun stayed in the midst of heaven, and did not hasten to go down for about a whole 14 day. There has been no day like it before or since, when the LORD hearkened to the voice of a man; for the LORD fought for Israel. 15 Then Joshua returned, and all Israel with him, to the camp at Gilgal.

16 These five kings fled, and hid themselves in the cave at Makke′dah. And it was told 17 Joshua, "The five kings have been found, hidden in the cave at Makke′dah." And 18 Joshua said, "Roll great stones against the mouth of the cave, and set men by it to guard them; but do not stay there yourselves, 19 pursue your enemies, fall upon their rear, do not let them enter their cities; for the LORD your God has given them into your hand." When Joshua and the men of Israel had 20 finished slaying them with a very great slaughter, until they were wiped out, and when the remnant which remained of them had entered into the fortified cities, all the 21 people returned safe to Joshua in the camp at Makke′dah; not a man moved his tongue against any of the people of Israel.

Then Joshua said, "Open the mouth of the 22 cave, and bring those five kings out to me from the cave." And they did so, and 23 brought those five kings out to him from the cave, the king of Jerusalem, the king of Hebron, the king of Jarmuth, the king of Lachish, and the king of Eglon. And when 24 they brought those kings out to Joshua, Joshua summoned all the men of Israel, and said to the chiefs of the men of war who had gone with him, "Come near, put your feet upon the necks of these kings." Then they came near, and put their feet on their necks. And Joshua said to them, "Do not be afraid 25 or dismayed; be strong and of good courage; for thus the LORD will do to all your enemies against whom you fight." And afterward 26 Joshua smote them and put them to death, and he hung them on five trees. And they hung upon the trees until evening; but at the 27 time of the going down of the sun, Joshua commanded, and they took them down from the trees, and threw them into the cave where they had hidden themselves, and they set great stones against the mouth of the cave, which remain to this very day.

Completing the conquest

And Joshua took Makke′dah on that day, 28 and smote it and its king with the edge of the sword; he utterly destroyed every person in it, he left none remaining; and he did to the king of Makke′dah as he had done to the king of Jericho.

Then Joshua passed on from Makke′dah, 29 and all Israel with him, to Libnah, and fought against Libnah; and the LORD gave it 30 also and its king into the hand of Israel; and he smote it with the edge of the sword, and every person in it; he left none remaining in it; and he did to its king as he had done to the king of Jericho.

And Joshua passed on from Libnah, and all 31 Israel with him, to Lachish, and laid siege to

32 it, and assaulted it: and the LORD gave Lachish into the hand of Israel, and he took it on the second day, and smote it with the edge of the sword, and every person in it, as he had done to Libnah.

33 Then Horam king of Gezer came up to help Lachish; and Joshua smote him and his people, until he left none remaining.

34 And Joshua passed on with all Israel from Lachish to Eglon; and they laid siege to it,

35 and assaulted it; and they took it on that day, and smote it with the edge of the sword; and every person in it he utterly destroyed that day, as he had done to Lachish.

36 Then Joshua went up with all Israel from

37 Eglon to Hebron; and they assaulted it, and took it, and smote it with the edge of the sword, and its king and its towns, and every person in it; he left none remaining, as he had done to Eglon, and utterly destroyed it with every person in it.

38 Then Joshua, with all Israel, turned back to

39 Debir and assaulted it, and he took it with its king and all its towns; and they smote them with the edge of the sword, and utterly destroyed every person in it; he left none remaining; as he had done to Hebron and to Libnah and its king, so he did to Debir and to its king.

40 So Joshua defeated the whole land, the hill country and the Negeb and the lowland and the slopes, and all their kings; he left none remaining, but utterly destroyed all that breathed, as the LORD God of Israel com-

41 manded. And Joshua defeated them from Ka'desh-bar'nea to Gaza, and all the country

42 of Goshen, as far as Gibeon. And Joshua took all these kings and their land at one time, because the LORD God of Israel fought

43 for Israel. Then Joshua returned, and all Israel with him, to the camp at Gilgal.

11 When Jabin king of Hazor heard of this, he sent to Jobab king of Madon, and to the king of Shimron, and to the king of Ach'shaph,

2 and to the kings who were in the northern hill country, and in the Arabah south of Chin'neroth, and in the lowland, and in

3 Naphoth-dor on the west, to the Canaanites in the east and the west, the Amorites, the Hittites, the Per'izzites, and the Jeb'usites in the hill country, and the Hivites under

4 Hermon in the land of Mizpah. And they came out, with all their troops, a great host, in number like the sand that is upon the seashore, with very many horses and char-

5 iots. And all these kings joined their forces, and came and encamped together at the waters of Merom, to fight with Israel.

6 And the LORD said to Joshua, "Do not be afraid of them, for tomorrow at this time I will give over all of them, slain, to Israel; you

JOSHUA'S CAMPAIGNS 2 In the North

The Great Sea

Misrephoth-maim

Hazor

Waters of Merom

Achshaph

Madon

Sea of Chinnereth

Mt Carmel

Lasharon

Dor

Megiddo

Taanach

Scale of Miles
0 5 10 15

Shechem

shall hamstring their horses, and burn their chariots with fire." So Joshua came sud- 7 denly upon them with all his people of war, by the waters of Merom, and fell upon them. And the LORD gave them into the hand of 8 Israel, who smote them and chased them as far as Great Sidon and Mis'rephoth-ma'im, and eastward as far as the valley of Mizpeh; and they smote them, until they left none remaining. And Joshua did to them as the 9 LORD bade him; he hamstrung their horses, and burned their chariots with fire.

And Joshua turned back at that time, and 10 took Hazor, and smote its king with the sword; for Hazor formerly was the head of all those kingdoms. And they put to the sword 11 all who were in it, utterly destroying them; there was none left that breathed, and he burned Hazor with fire. And all the cities of 12 those kings, and all their kings, Joshua took, and smote them with the edge of the sword, utterly destroying them, as Moses the servant of the LORD had commanded. But none 13 of the cities that stood on mounds did Israel burn, except Hazor only; that Joshua burned. And all the spoil of these cities and 14 the cattle, the people of Israel took for their booty; but every man they smote with the edge of the sword, until they had destroyed them, and they did not leave any that breathed. As the LORD had commanded 15

Moses his servant, so Moses commanded Joshua, and so Joshua did; he left nothing undone of all that the LORD had commanded Moses.

16 So Joshua took all that land, the hill country and all the Negeb and all the land of Goshen and the lowland and the Arabah and the hill 17 country of Israel and its lowland from Mount Halak, that rises toward Se'ir, as far as Ba'al-gad in the valley of Lebanon below Mount Hermon. And he took all their kings, and smote them, and put them to death. 18 Joshua made war a long time with all those 19 kings. There was not a city that made peace with the people of Israel, except the Hivites, the inhabitants of Gibeon; they took all in 20 battle. For it was the LORD's doing to harden their hearts that they should come against

Israel in battle, in order that they should be utterly destroyed, and should receive no mercy but be exterminated, as the LORD commanded Moses.

And Joshua came at that time, and wiped out the Anakim from the hill country, from Hebron, from Debir, from Anab, and from all the hill country of Judah, and from all the hill country of Israel; Joshua utterly destroyed them with their cities. There was none of the Anakim left in the land of the people of Israel; only in Gaza, in Gath, and in Ashdod, did some remain. So Joshua took the whole land, according to all that the LORD had spoken to Moses; and Joshua gave it for an inheritance to Israel according to their tribal allotments. And the land had rest from war.

CONQUERED KINGS

12 NOW these are the kings of the land, whom the people of Israel defeated, and took possession of their land beyond the Jordan toward the sunrising, from the valley of the Arnon to Mount Hermon, with all the Arabah 2 eastward: Sihon king of the Amorites who dwelt at Heshbon, and ruled from Aro'er, which is on the edge of the valley of the Arnon, and from the middle of the valley as far as the river Jabbok, the boundary of the Ammonites, that is, half of 3 Gilead, and the Arabah to the Sea of Chin'neroth eastward, and in the direction of Beth-jesh'-imoth, to the sea of the Arabah, the Salt Sea, southward to the 4 foot of the slopes of Pisgah; and the Og[e] king of Bashan, one of the remnant of the Reph'aim, who dwelt at Ash'taroth and at Ed're-i 5 and ruled over Mount Hermon and Sal'ecah and all Bashan to the boundary of the Gesh'urites and the Ma-ac'athites, and over half of Gilead to the boundary of Sihon 6 king of Heshbon. Moses, the servant of the LORD, and the people of Israel defeated them;

and Moses the servant of the LORD gave their land for a possession to the Reubenites and the Gadites and the half-tribe of Manas'seh.

7 And these are the kings of the land whom Joshua and the people of Israel defeated on the west side of the Jordan, from Ba'al-gad in the valley of Lebanon to Mount Halak, that rises toward Se'ir (and Joshua gave their land to the tribes of Israel as a possession 8 according to their allotments, in the hill country, in the lowland, in the Arabah, in the slopes, in the wilderness, and in the Negeb, the land of the Hittites, the Amorites, the Canaanites, the Per'izzites, the Hivites, and the Jeb'usites): the 9 king of Jericho, one; the king of Ai, which is beside Bethel, one; 10 the king of Jerusalem, one; the 11 king of Hebron, one; the king of Jarmuth, one; the king of 12 Lachish, one; the king of Eglon, 13 one; the king of Gezer, one; the king of Debir, one; the king of 14 Geder, one; the king of Hormah, 15 one; the king of Arad, one; the king of Libnah, one; the king of 16 Adullam, one; the king of Mak-ke'dah, one; the king of Bethel, 17 one; the king of Tap'pu-ah, one;

the king of Hepher, one; the 1 king of Aphek, one; the king of Lashar'on, one; the king of 1 Madon, one; the king of Hazor, one; the king of Shim'ron-2 me'ron, one; the king of Ach'-shaph, one; the king of Ta'anach, 2 one; the king of Megid'do, one; the king of Kedesh, one; the king 2 of Jok'ne-am in Carmel, one; the 2 king of Dor in Naphath-dor, one; the king of Goi'im in Galilee,[f] one; the king of Tirzah, one: in 2 all, thirty-one kings.

DIVISION OF THE LAND

NOW Joshua was old and 13 advanced in years; and the LORD said to him, "You are old and advanced in years, and there remains yet very much land to be possessed. This is the land that 2 yet remains: all the regions of the Philistines, and all those of the Gesh'urites (from the Shihor, 3 which is east of Egypt, northward to the boundary of Ekron, it is reckoned as Canaanite; there are

---

[e] Gk: Heb the boundary of Og   [f] Gk: Heb Gilgal

five rulers of the Philistines, those of Gaza, Ashdod, Ash'kelon, Gath, and Ekron), and those of 4 the Avvim, in the south, all the land of the Canaanites, and Me-ar'ah which belongs to the Sido'nians, to Aphek, to the 5 boundary of the Amorites, and the land of the Geb'alites, and all Lebanon, toward the sunrising, from Ba'al-gad below Mount Hermon to the entrance of 6 Hamath, all the inhabitants of the hill country from Lebanon to Mis'rephoth-ma'im, even all the Sido'nians. I will myself drive them out from before the people of Israel; only allot the land to Israel for an inheritance, as I have 7 commanded you. Now therefore divide this land for an inheritance to the nine tribes and half the tribe of Manas'seh.'

8 With the other half of the tribe of Manas'seh[g] the Reubenites and the Gadites received their inheritance, which Moses gave them, beyond the Jordan eastward, as Moses the servant of the LORD 9 gave them: from Aro'er, which is on the edge of the valley of the Arnon, and the city that is in the middle of the valley, and all the tableland of Med'eba as far as 10 Dibon; and all the cities of Sihon king of the Amorites, who reigned in Heshbon, as far as the boun-
11 dary of the Ammonites; and Gilead, and the region of the Gesh'urites and Ma-ac'athites, and all Mount Hermon, and all 12 Bashan to Sal'ecah; all the kingdom of Og in Bashan, who reigned in Ash'taroth and in Ed're-i (he alone was left of the remnant of the Reph'aim); these 13 Moses had defeated and driven out. Yet the people of Israel did not drive out the Gesh'urites or the Ma-ac'athites; but Geshur and Ma'acath dwell in the midst of Israel to this day.
14 To the tribe of Levi alone Moses gave no inheritance; the offerings by fire to the LORD God of Israel are their inheritance, as he said to him.

In the East

15 And Moses gave an inheritance to the tribe of the Reubenites 16 according to their families. So their territory was from Aro'er, which is on the edge of the valley of the Arnon, and the city that is in the middle of the valley, and all 17 the tableland by Med'eba; with Heshbon, and all its cities that are in the tableland; Dibon, and Ba'moth-ba'al, and Beth-ba'al-
18 me'on, and Jahaz, and Ked'-
19 emoth, and Meph'a-ath, and Kiriatha'im, and Sibmah, and Zer'eth-sha'har on the hill of the 20 valley, and Beth-pe'or, and the slopes of Pisgah, and Beth-jesh'-
21 imoth, that is, all the cities of the tableland, and all the kingdom of

Sihon king of the Amorites, who reigned in Heshbon, whom Moses defeated with the leaders of Mid'ian, Evi and Rekem and Zur and Hur and Reba, the princes of Sihon, who dwelt in the land. 22 Balaam also, the son of Be'or, the soothsayer, the people of Israel killed with the sword among the 23 rest of their slain. And the border of the people of Reuben was the Jordan as a boundary. This was the inheritance of the Reubenites, according to their families with their cities and villages.
24 And Moses gave an inheritance also to the tribe of the Gadites, 25 according to their families. Their territory was Jazer, and all the cities of Gilead, and half the land of the Ammonites, to Aro'er, 26 which is east of Rabbah, and from Heshbon to Ra'math-miz'peh and Bet'onim, and from Mahana'im to 27 the territory of Debir,[h] and in the valley Beth-ha'ram, Beth-nim'rah, Succoth, and Zaphon, the rest of the kingdom of Sihon king of Heshbon, having the Jordan as a boundary, to the lower end of the Sea of Chin'nereth, eastward beyond the Jordan. 28 This is the inheritance of the Gadites according to their families, with their cities and villages.
29 And Moses gave an inheritance to the half-tribe of Manas'seh; it was allotted to the half-tribe of the Manas'sites according to their 30 families. Their region extended from Mahana'im, through all Bashan, the whole kingdom of Og king of Bashan, and all the towns of Ja'ir, which are in Bashan, sixty 31 cities, and half Gilead, and Ash'taroth, and Ed're-i, the cities of the kingdom of Og in Bashan; these were allotted to the people of Machir the son of Manas'seh for the half of the Machirites according to their families.
32 These are the inheritances which Moses distributed in the plains of Moab, beyond the Jordan east of 33 Jericho. But to the tribe of Levi Moses gave no inheritance; the LORD God of Israel is their inheritance, as he said to them.

In the West

14 And these are the inheritances which the people of Israel received in the land of Canaan, which Elea'zar the priest, and Joshua the son of Nun, and the heads of the fathers' houses of the 2 tribes of the people of Israel distributed to them. Their inheritance was by lot, as the LORD had commanded Moses for 3 the nine and one half tribes. For Moses had given an inheritance to the two and one half tribes beyond the Jordan; but to the Levites he gave no inheritance 4 among them. For the people of Joseph were two tribes,

Manas'seh and E'phraim; and no portion was given to the Levites in the land, but only cities to dwell in, with their pasture lands for their cattle and their sub-5 stance. The people of Israel did as the LORD commanded Moses; they allotted the land.

6 Then the people of Judah came to Joshua at Gilgal; and Caleb the son of Jephun'neh the Ken'izzite said to him, "You know what the LORD said to Moses the man of God in Ka'desh-bar'nea concern-7 ing you and me. I was forty years old when Moses the servant of the LORD sent me from Ka'desh-bar'nea to spy out the land; and I brought him word 8 again as it was in my heart. But my brethren who went up with me made the heart of the people melt; yet I wholly followed the 9 LORD my God. And Moses swore on that day, saying, 'Surely the land on which your foot has trodden shall be an inheritance for you and your children for ever, because you have wholly followed 10 the LORD my God.' And now, behold, the LORD has kept me alive, as he said, these forty-five years since the time that the LORD spoke this word to Moses, while Israel walked in the wilder-11 ness; and now, lo, I am this day eighty-five years old. I am still as strong to this day as I was in the day that Moses sent me; my strength now is as my strength was then, for war, and for going 12 and coming. So now give me this hill country of which the LORD spoke on that day; for you heard on that day how the Anakim were there, with great fortified cities: it may be that the LORD will be with me, and I shall drive them out as the LORD said."
13 Then Joshua blessed him; and he gave Hebron to Caleb the son of Jephun'neh for an inheritance. 14 So Hebron became the inheritance of Caleb the son of Jephun'neh the Ken'izzite to this day, because he wholly followed the LORD, the God of Israel. Now the 15 name of Hebron formerly was Kir'iath-ar'ba;[i] this Arba was the greatest man among the Anakim. And the land had rest from war.

15 The lot for the tribe of the people of Judah according to their families reached southward to the boundary of Edom, to the wilderness of Zin at the farthest 2 south. And their south boundary ran from the end of the Salt Sea, from the bay that faces south-3 ward; it goes out southward of the ascent of Akrab'bim, passes along to Zin, and goes up south of Ka'desh-bar'nea, along by Hezron, up to Addar, turns about 4 to Karka, passes along to Azmon, goes out by the Brook of Egypt, and comes to its end at the

---

g Cn: Heb *With it*   h Gk Syr Vg: Heb *Lidebir*   i That is *The city of Arba*
14.6-15: Num 13.6, 30; 14.6, 24, 30.

sea. This shall be your south 5 boundary. And the east boundary is the Salt Sea, to the mouth of the Jordan. And the boundary on the north side runs from the bay of the sea at the mouth of 6 Jordan; and the boundary goes up to Beth-hoglah, and passes along north of Beth-arabah; and the boundary goes up to the stone of 7 Bohan the son of Reuben; and the boundary goes up to Debir from the Valley of Achor, and so northward, turning toward Gilgal, which is opposite the ascent of Adum'mim, which is on the south side of the valley; and the boundary passes along to the waters of En-she'mesh, and ends 8 at En-ro'gel; then the boundary goes up by the valley of the son of Hinnom at the southern shoulder of the Jeb'usite (that is, Jerusalem); and the boundary goes up to the top of the mountain that lies over against the valley of Hinnom, on the west, at the northern end of the valley of 9 Reph'aim; then the boundary extends from the top of the mountain to the spring of the Waters of Nephto'ah, and from there to the cities of Mount Ephron; then the boundary bends round to Ba'alah (that is, Kir'- 10 iath-je'arim); and the boundary circles west of Ba'alah to Mount Se'ir, passes along to the northern shoulder of Mount Je'arim (that is, Ches'alon), and goes down to Beth-she'mesh, and passes along 11 by Timnah; the boundary goes out to the shoulder of the hill north of Ekron, then the boundary bends round to Shik'- keron, and passes along to Mount Ba'alah, and goes out to Jabneel; then the boundary comes to an 12 end at the sea. And the west boundary was the Great Sea with its coast-line. This is the boundary round about the people of Judah according to their families 13 According to the commandment of the LORD to Joshua, he gave to Caleb the son of Jephun'neh a portion among the people of Judah, Kir'iath-ar'ba, that is, Hebron (Arba was the father of 14 Anak). And Caleb drove out from there the three sons of Anak, Sheshai and Ahi'man and Talmai, 15 the descendants of Anak. And he went up from there against the inhabitants of Debir; now the name of Debir formerly was 16 Kir'iath-se'pher. And Caleb said, "Whoever smites Kir'iath- se'pher and takes it, to him will I give Achsah my daughter as 17 wife." And Oth'ni-el the son of Kenaz, the brother of Caleb, took it; and he gave him Achsah his 18 daughter as wife. When she came to him, she urged him to ask her father for a field; and she alighted 19 from her ass, and Caleb said to her, "What do you wish?" She said to him, "Give me a present; since you have set me in the land

of the Negeb, give me also springs of water." And Caleb gave her the upper springs and the lower springs.

20 This is the inheritance of the tribe of the people of Judah according to their families.

21 The cities belonging to the tribe of the people of Judah in the extreme South, toward the boundary of Edom, were Kabzeel, Eder, 22 Jagur, Kinah, Dimo'nah, Ada'- 23 dah, Kedesh, Hazor, Ithnan, 24 Ziph, Telem, Bealoth, Ha'zor- 25 hadat'tah, Ker'ioth-hezron (that 26 is, Hazor), Amam, Shema, Mola'- 27 dah, Ha'zar-gad'dah, Heshmon, 28 Beth-pelet, Hazar-shu'al, Beer- 29 sheba. Biziothi'ah, Ba'alah, I'im, 30 Ezem, Elto'lad, Chesil, Hormah, 31 Ziklag, Madman'nah, Sansan'- 32 nah, Leba'oth, Shilhim, A'in, and

Rimmon: in all, twenty-nine cities, with their villages.

And in the lowland, Esh'ta-ol, 33 Zorah, Ashnah, Zano'ah, En- 34 gan'nim, Tap'pu-ah, Enam, Jar- 35 muth, Adullam, Socoh, Aze'kah, 36 Sha-ara'im, Aditha'im, Gede'rah, Gederotha'im: fourteen cities with their villages.

Zenan, Hadash'ah, Mig'dal-gad, 37 Di'lean, Mizpeh, Jok'theel, La- 38 chish, Bozkath, Eglon, Cabbon, 39 Lahmam, Chitlish, Gede'roth, 40 Beth-da'gon, Na'-amah, and 41 Makke'dah: sixteen cities with their villages.

Libnah, Ether, Ashan, Iphtah, 42 Ashnah, Nezib, Kei'lah, Achzib, 43 and Mare'shah: nine cities with 44 their villages.

Ekron, with its towns and its 45 villages; from Ekron to the sea, all 46

15.14–19: Judg 1.10–15, 20.

that were by the side of Ashdod, with their villages.

Ashdod, its towns and its villages; Gaza, its towns and its villages; to the Brook of Egypt, and the Great Sea with its coast-line.

And in the hill country, Shamir, Jattir, Socoh, Dannah, Kir'iath-san'nah (that is, Debir), Anab, Esh'temoh, Anim, Goshen, Holon, and Giloh: eleven cities with their villages.

Arab, Dumah, Eshan, Janim, Beth-tap'pu-ah, Aphe'kah, Hum-tah, Kir'iath-ar'ba (that is, Hebron), and Zi'or: nine cities with their villages.

Ma'on, Carmel, Ziph, Juttah, Jezreel, Jok'de-am, Zano'ah, Kain, Gib'e-ah, and Timnah: ten cities with their villages.

Halhul, Beth-zur, Gedor, Ma'arath, Beth-anoth, and El'tekon: six cities with their villages.

Kir'iath-ba'al (that is, Kir'iath-je'arim), and Rabbah: two cities with their villages.

In the wilderness, Beth-arabah, Middin, Seca'cah, Nibshan, the City of Salt, and En-ge'di: six cities with their villages.

But the Jeb'usites, the inhabitants of Jerusalem, the people of Judah could not drive out; so the Jeb'usites dwell with the people of Judah at Jerusalem to this day.

16 The allotment of the descendants of Joseph went from the Jordan by Jericho, east of the waters of Jericho, into the wilderness, going up from Jericho into the hill country to Bethel; 2 then going from Bethel to Luz, it passes along to At'aroth, the territory of the Archites; then it goes 3 down westward to the territory of the Japh'letites, as far as the territory of Lower Beth-horon, then to Gezer, and it ends at the sea. 4 The people of Joseph, Manas'seh and E'phraim, received their inheritance.

5 The territory of the E'phraimites by their families was as follows: the boundary of their inheritance on the east was At'aroth-ad'dar as 6 far as Upper Beth-horon, and the boundary goes thence to the sea; on the north is Michme'thath; then on the east the boundary turns round toward Ta'anath-shi'loh, and passes along beyond 7 it on the east to Jano'ah, then it goes down from Jano'ah to At'aroth and to Na'arah, and touches Jericho, ending at the 8 Jordan. From Tap'pu-ah the boundary goes westward to the brook Kanah, and ends at the sea. Such is the inheritance of the tribe of the E'phraimites by their 9 families, together with the towns which were set apart for the E'phraimites within the inheritance of the Manas'sites, all those towns with their villages. How-

ever they did not drive out the Canaanites that dwelt in Gezer: so the Canaanites have dwelt in the midst of E'phraim to this day but have become slaves to do forced labour.

17 Then allotment was made to the tribe of Manas'seh, for he was the first-born of Joseph. To Machir the first-born of Manas'seh, the father of Gilead, were allotted Gilead and Bashan, because he 2 was a man of war. And allotments were made to the rest of the tribe of Manas'seh, by their families, Abi-e'zer, Helek, As'ri-el, Shechem, Hepher, and Shemi'da; these were the male descendants of Manas'seh the son of Joseph, by their families. 3 Now Zelo'phe-had the son of Hepher, son of Gilead, son of Machir, son of Manas'seh, had no sons, but only daughters; and these are the names of his daughters: Mahlah, Noah, Hoglah, Milcah, and Tirzah. 4 They came before Elea'zar the priest and Joshua the son of Nun and the leaders, and said, "The LORD commanded Moses to give us an inheritance along with our brethren." So according to the commandment of the LORD he gave them an inheritance among 5 the brethren of their father. Thus there fell to Manas'seh ten portions, besides the land of Gilead and Bashan, which is on the other 6 side of the Jordan; because the daughters of Manas'seh received an inheritance along with his sons. The land of Gilead was allotted to the rest of the Manas'-sites.

7 The territory of Manas'seh reached from Asher to Michme'-thath, which is east of Shechem; then the boundary goes along southward to the inhabitants of 8 En-tap'pu-ah. The land of Tap'-pu-ah belonged to Manas'seh, but the town of Tap'pu-ah on the boundary of Manas'seh belonged 9 to the sons of E'phraim. Then the boundary went down to the brook Kanah. The cities here, to the south of the brook, among the cities of Manas'seh, belong to E'phraim. Then the boundary of Manas'seh goes on the north side 10 of the brook and ends at the sea; the land to the south being E'phraim's, and that to the north being Manas'seh's, with the sea forming its boundary; on the north Asher is reached, and on the 11 east Is'sachar. Also in Is'sachar and in Asher Manas'seh had Beth-she'an and its villages, and Ib'le-am and its villages, and the inhabitants of Dor and its villages, and the inhabitants of En-dor and its villages, and the inhabitants of Ta'anach and its villages, and the inhabitants of Megid'do and its villages; the third is Naphath.[j] 12 Yet the sons of Manas'seh could

not take possession of those cities; but the Canaanites persisted in dwelling in that land. But when 13 the people of Israel grew strong, they put the Canaanites to forced labour, and did not utterly drive them out.

And the tribe of Joseph spoke to 14 Joshua, saying, "Why have you given me but one lot and one portion as an inheritance, although I am a numerous people, since hitherto the LORD has blessed me?" And Joshua said to 15 them, "If you are a numerous people, go up to the forest, and there clear ground for yourselves in the land of the Per'izzites and the Reph'aim, since the hill country of E'phraim is too narrow for you." The tribe of Joseph 16 said, "The hill country is not enough for us; yet all the Canaanites who dwell in the plain have chariots of iron, both those in Beth-she'an and its villages and those in the Valley of Jezreel." Then Joshua said to the house 17 of Joseph, to E'phraim and Manas'seh, "You are a numerous people, and have great power; you shall not have one lot only, but the 18 hill country shall be yours, for though it is a forest, you shall clear it and possess it to its farthest borders; for you shall drive out the Canaanites, though they have chariots of iron, and though they are strong."

The tent of meeting

Then the whole congregation of **18** the people of Israel assembled at Shiloh, and set up the tent of meeting there; the land lay subdued before them.

There remained among the 2 people of Israel seven tribes whose inheritance had not yet been apportioned. So Joshua said 3 to the people of Israel, "How long will you be slack to go in and take possession of the land, which the LORD, the God of your fathers, has given you? Provide three 4 men from each tribe, and I will send them out that they may set out and go up and down the land, writing a description of it with a view to their inheritances, and then come to me. They shall 5 divide it into seven portions, Judah continuing in his territory on the south, and the house of Joseph in their territory on the north. And you shall describe the 6 land in seven divisions and bring the description here to me; and I will cast lots for you here before the LORD our God. The Levites 7 have no portion among you, for the priesthood of the LORD is their heritage; and Gad and Reuben and half the tribe of Manas'seh have received their inheritance beyond the Jordan eastward, which Moses the servant of the LORD gave them."

j Heb obscure
15.63: Judg 1.21; 2 Sam 5.6.   **16.10:** Judg 1.29.   **17.3-4:** Num 26.33; 27.1-7.   **17.11-13:** Judg 1.27-28.

8 So the men started on their way; and Joshua charged those who went to write the description of the land, saying, "Go up and down and write a description of the land, and come again to me; and I will cast lots for you here 9 before the LORD in Shiloh." So the men went and passed up and down in the land and set down in a book a description of it by towns in seven divisions; then they came to Joshua in the camp at Shiloh, 10 and Joshua cast lots for them in Shiloh before the LORD; and there Joshua apportioned the land to the people of Israel, to each his portion.

11 The lot of the tribe of Benjamin according to its families came up, and the territory allotted to it fell between the tribe of Judah and 12 the tribe of Joseph. On the north side their boundary began at the Jordan; then the boundary goes up to the shoulder north of Jericho, then up through the hill country westward; and it ends at 13 the wilderness of Beth-a'ven. From there the boundary passes along southward in the direction of Luz, to the shoulder of Luz (the same is Bethel), then the boundary goes down to At'aroth-ad'dar, upon the mountain that lies south of Lower Beth-horon. 14 Then the boundary goes in another direction, turning on the western side southward from the mountain that lies to the south, opposite Beth-horon, and it ends at Kir'iath-ba'al (that is, Kir'iath-je'arim), a city belonging to the tribe of Judah. This forms 15 the western side. And the southern side begins at the outskirts of Kir'iath-je'arim; and the boundary goes from there to Ephron,[k] to the spring of the 16 Waters of Nephto'ah; then the boundary goes down to the border of the mountain that overlooks the valley of the son of Hinnom, which is at the north end of the valley of Reph'aim; and it then goes down the valley of Hinnom, south of the shoulder of the Jeb'usites, and downward to 17 En-ro'gel; then it bends in a northerly direction going on to En-she'mesh, and thence goes to Geli'loth, which is opposite the ascent of Adum'mim; then it goes down to the Stone of Bohan the 18 son of Reuben; and passing on to the north of the shoulder of Beth-arabah[l] it goes down to 19 Arabah; then the boundary passes on to the north of the shoulder of Beth-hoglah; and the boundary ends at the northern bay of the Salt Sea, at the south end of the Jordan: this is the southern 20 border. The Jordan forms its boundary on the eastern side. This is the inheritance of the tribe of Benjamin, according to its families, boundary by boundary round about.

21 Now the cities of the tribe of Benjamin according to their families were Jericho, Beth-ho-glah, Emek-ke'ziz, Beth-arabah, 22 Zemara'im, Bethel, Avvim, 23 Parah, Ophrah, Che'phar-am'moni, Ophni, Geba—twelve 24 cities with their villages: Gibeon, 25 Ramah, Be-er'oth, Mizpeh, 26 Chephi'rah, Mozah, Rekem, 27 Irpeel, Tar'alah, Zela, Ha-eleph, Jebus[m] (that is, Jerusalem), Gib'e-ah[n] and Kir'iath-je'-arim[o]—fourteen cities with their villages. This is the inheritance of the tribe of Benjamin according to its families.

19 The second lot came out for Simeon, for the tribe of Simeon, according to its families; and its inheritance was in the midst of the inheritance of the tribe of Judah. 2 And it had for its inheritance Beer-sheba, Sheba, Mola'dah, 3 Hazar-shu'al, Balah, Ezem, 4 Elto'lad, Bethul, Hormah, Ziklag, 5 Beth-mar'caboth, Ha'zar-su'sah, 6 Beth-leba'oth, and Sharu'hen —thirteen cities with their vil-7 lages; En-rim'mon, Ether, and Ashan—four cities with their vil-8 lages; together with all the villages round about these cities as far as Ba'alath-beer, Ramah of the Negeb. This was the inheritance of the tribe of Simeon according 9 to its families. The inheritance of the tribe of Simeon formed part of the territory of Judah; because the portion of the tribe of Judah was too large for them, the tribe of Simeon obtained an inheritance in the midst of their inheritance.

10 The third lot came up for the tribe of Zeb'ulun, according to its families. And the territory of its inheritance reached as far as 11 Sarid; then its boundary goes up westward, and on to Mar'eal, and touches Dab'besheth, then the brook which is east of Jok'ne-am; 12 from Sarid it goes in the other direction eastward toward the sunrise to the boundary of Chis'-loth-ta'bor; thence it goes to Dab'erath, then up to Japhi'a; 13 from there it passes along on the east toward the sunrise to Gath-hepher, to Eth-kazin, and going on to Rimmon it bends toward 14 Ne'ah; then on the north the boundary turns about to Han'-nathon, and it ends at the valley of 15 Iph'tahel; and Kattath, Na'halal, Shimron, I'dalah, and Beth-lehem—twelve cities with their 16 villages. This is the inheritance of the tribe of Zeb'ulun, according to its families—these cities with their villages.

17 The fourth lot came out for Is'sachar, for the tribe of Is'-sachar, according to its families. 18 Its territory included Jezreel, Chesul'loth, Shunem, Haph'-19 ara-im, Shion, Ana'harath, Rab-20 bith, Kish'ion, Ebez, Remeth, 21 En-gan'nim, En-had'dah, Beth-

paz'zez; the boundary also 22 touches Tabor, Shahazu'mah, and Beth-she'mesh, and its boundary ends at the Jordan —sixteen cities with their vil-23 lages. This is the inheritance of the tribe of Is'sachar, according to its families—the cities with their villages.

The fifth lot came out for the 24 tribe of Asher according to its families. Its territory included 25 Helkath, Hali, Beten, Ach'shaph, 26 Allam'melech, Amad, and Mish-al; on the west it touches Carmel and Shihor-lib'nath, then it turns 27 eastward, it goes to Beth-da'gon, and touches Zeb'ulun and the valley of Iph'tah-el northward to Beth-emek and Nei'el; then it 28 continues in the north to Cabul, Ebron, Rehob, Ham'mon, Kanah, as far as Sidon the Great; then 29 the boundary turns to Ramah, reaching to the fortified city of Tyre; then the boundary turns to Hosah, and it ends at the sea; Mahalab,[p] Achzib, Ummah, 30 Aphek and Rehob—twenty-two cities with their villages. This is 31 the inheritance of the tribe of Asher according to its families —these cities with their villages.

The sixth lot came out for the 32 tribe of Naph'tali, for the tribe of Naph'tali, according to its families. And its boundary ran 33 from Heleph, from the oak in Za-anan'nim, and Ad'ami-nekeb, and Jabneel, as far as Lakkum; and it ended at the Jordan; then 34 the boundary turns westward to Az'noth-tabor, and goes from there to Hukkok, touching Zeb'-ulun at the south, and Asher on the west, and Judah on the east at the Jordan. The fortified cities 35 are Ziddim, Zer, Hammath, Rakkath, Chin'nereth, Ad'amah, 36 Ramah, Hazor, Kedesh, Ed're-i, 37 En-ha'zor, Yiron, Mig'dal-el, 38 Horem, Beth-anath, and Beth-she'mesh—nineteen cities with 39 their villages. This is the inheritance of the tribe of Naph'tali according to its families—the cities with their villages.

The seventh lot came out for the 40 tribe of Dan, according to its families. And the territory of its 41 inheritance included Zorah, Esh'-ta-ol, Ir-she'mesh, Sha-alab'bin, 42 Ai'jalon, Ithlah, Elon, Timnah, 43 Ekron, El'tekeh, Gib'bethon, 44 Ba'alath, Jehud, Bene-be'rak, 45 Gath-rim'mon, and Me-jar'kon 46 and Rakkon with the territory over against Joppa. When the 47 territory of the Danites was lost to them, the Danites went up and fought against Leshem, and after capturing it and putting it to the sword they took possession of it and settled in it, calling Leshem, Dan, after the name of Dan their ancestor. This is the inheritance 48 of the tribe of Dan, according to their families—these cities with their villages.

k Cn See 15.9. Heb westward   l Gk: Heb to the shoulder over against the Arabah
m Gk Syr Vg: Heb the Jebusite   n Heb Gibeath   o Gk: Heb Kiriath   p Cn Compare Gk: Heb Mehebel
19.47: Judg 18.27–31.

49 When they had finished distributing the several territories of the land as inheritances, the people of Israel gave an inheritance among them to Joshua the 50 son of Nun. By command of the LORD they gave him the city which he asked, Tim′nath-se′rah in the hill country of E′phraim; and he rebuilt the city, and settled in it.

51 These are the inheritances which Elea′zar the priest and Joshua the son of Nun and the heads of the fathers' houses of the tribes of the people of Israel distributed by lot at Shiloh before the LORD, at the door of the tent of meeting. So they finished dividing the land.

Cities of refuge

20 Then the LORD said to Joshua, 2 "Say to the people of Israel, 'Appoint the cities of refuge, of which I spoke to you through 3 Moses, that the manslayer who kills any person without intent or unwittingly may flee there; they shall be for you a refuge from the 4 avenger of blood. He shall flee to one of these cities and shall stand at the entrance of the gate of the city, and explain his case to the elders of that city; then they shall take him into the city, and give him a place, and he shall remain 5 with them. And if the avenger of blood pursues him, they shall not give up the slayer into his hand; because he killed his neighbour unwittingly, having had no enmity against him in times past. 6 And he shall remain in that city until he has stood before the congregation for judgment, until the death of him who is high priest at the time: then the slayer may go again to his own town and his own home, to the town from which he fled.' "

7 So they set apart Kedesh in Galilee in the hill country of Naph′tali, and Shechem in the hill country of E′phraim, and Kir′iath-ar′ba (that is, Hebron) in 8 the hill country of Judah. And beyond the Jordan east of Jericho, they appointed Bezer in the wilderness on the tableland, from the tribe of Reuben, and Ramoth in Gilead, from the tribe of Gad, and Golan in Bashan, from the tribe of 9 Manas′seh. These were the cities designated for all the people of Israel, and for the stranger sojourning among them, that any one who killed a person without intent could flee there, so that he might not die by the hand of the avenger of blood, till he stood before the congregation.

Cities for Levites

21 Then the heads of the fathers' houses of the Levites came to Elea′zar the priest and to Joshua the son of Nun and to the heads of the fathers' houses of the tribes 2 of the people of Israel; and they said to them at Shiloh in the land of Canaan, "The LORD commanded through Moses that we be given cities to dwell in, along with their pasture lands for our 3 cattle." So by command of the LORD the people of Israel gave to the Levites the following cities and pasture lands out of their inheritance.

4 The lot came out for the families of the Ko′hathites. So those Levites who were descendants of Aaron the priest received by lot from the tribes of Judah, Simeon, and Benjamin, thirteen cities.

5 And the rest of the Ko′hathites received by lot from the families of the tribes of E′phraim, from the tribe of Dan and the half-tribe of Manas′seh, ten cities.

6 The Gershonites received by lot from the families of the tribe of Is′sachar, from the tribe of Asher, from the tribe of Naph′tali, and from the half-tribe of Manas′seh in Bashan, thirteen cities.

7 The Merar′ites according to their families received from the tribe of Reuben, the tribe of Gad, and the tribe of Zeb′ulun, twelve cities.

8 These cities and their pasture lands the people of Israel gave by lot to the Levites, as the LORD had commanded through Moses.

9 Out of the tribe of Judah and the tribe of Simeon they gave the following cities mentioned by 10 name, which went to the descendants of Aaron, one of the families of the Ko′hathites who belonged to the Levites; since the 11 lot fell to them first. They gave them Kir′iath-ar′ba (Arba being the father of Anak), that is Hebron, in the hill country of Judah, along with the pasture 12 lands round about it. But the fields of the city and its villages had been given to Caleb the son of Jephun′neh as his possession. 13 And to the descendants of Aaron the priest gave Hebron, the city of refuge for the slayer, with its pasture lands, Libnah with its 14 pasture lands, Jattir with its pasture lands, Eshtemo′a with 15 its pasture lands, Holon with its pasture lands, Debir with its 16 pasture lands, A′in with its pasture lands, Juttah with its pasture lands, Beth-she′mesh with its pasture lands—nine cities out of 17 these two tribes; then out of the tribe of Benjamin, Gibeon with its pasture lands, Geba with its pas- 18 ture lands, An′athoth with its pasture lands, and Almon with its 19 pasture lands—four cities. The cities of the descendants of Aaron, the priests, were in all thirteen cities with their pasture lands.

20 As to the rest of the Ko′hathites belonging to the Ko′hathite families of the Levites, the cities allotted to them were out of the tribe of E′phraim. To them were 21 given Shechem, the city of refuge for the slayer, with its pasture lands in the hill country of E′phraim, Gezer with its pasture lands, Kib′zaim with its pas- 22 ture lands, Beth-horon with its 23 pasture lands—four cities; and out of the tribe of Dan, El′teke with its pasture lands, Gib′bethon with its pasture lands Ai′jalon with its pasture lands, 24 Gath-rim′mon with its pasture lands—four cities; and out of 25 half-tribe of Manas′seh, Ta′anach with its pasture lands, and Gath-rim′mon with its pasture lands—two cities. The cities of 26 the families of the rest of the Ko′hathites were ten in all with their pasture lands.

And to the Gershonites, one of 27 the families of the Levites, were given out of the half-tribe of Manas′seh, Golan in Bashan with its pasture lands, the city of refuge for the slayer, and Be-esh′terah with its pasture lands—two cities; and out of the tribe of Is′sachar, 28 Kish′ion with its pasture lands, Dab′erath with its pasture lands, Jarmuth with its pasture 29 lands, En-gan′nim with its pasture lands—four cities; and out of 30 the tribe of Asher, Mishal with its pasture lands, Abdon with its pasture lands, Helkath with 31 its pasture lands, and Rehob with its pasture lands—four cities; and 32 out of the tribe of Naph′tali, Kedesh in Galilee with its pasture lands, the city of refuge for the slayer, Ham′moth-dor with its pasture lands, and Kartan with its pasture lands—three cities. The 33 cities of the several families of the Gershonites were in all thirteen cities with their pasture lands.

And to the rest of the Levites, 34 the Merar′ite families, were given out of the tribe of Zeb′ulun, Jok′ne-am with its pasture lands, Kartah with its pasture lands, Dimnah with its pasture 35 lands, Na′halal with its pasture lands—four cities; and out of the 36 tribe of Reuben, Bezer with its pasture lands, Jahaz with its pasture lands, Ked′emoth with its pas- 37 ture lands, and Meph′a-ath with its pasture lands—four cities; and out of the tribe of Gad, 38 Ramoth in Gilead with its pasture lands, the city of refuge for the slayer, Mahana′im with its pasture lands, Heshbon with its pas- 39 ture lands, Jazer with its pasture lands—four cities in all. As for 40 the cities of the several Merar′ite families, that is, the remainder of the families of the Levites, those allotted to them were in all twelve cities.

The cities of the Levites in the 41 midst of the possession of the people of Israel were in all forty-eight cities with their pasture lands. These cities had each its 42 pasture lands round about it; so it was with all these cities.

20.2–9: Num 35.6–34; Deut 4.41–43; 19.1–13.   21.1–42: Num 35.1–8; 1 Chron 6.54–81.

REST AND PEACE

43 THUS the LORD gave to Israel all the land
which he swore to give to their fathers;
and having taken possession of it, they settled
44 there. And the LORD gave them rest on every
side just as he had sworn to their fathers; not
one of all their enemies had withstood them,
for the LORD had given all their enemies
45 into their hands. Not one of all the good
promises which the LORD had made to the
house of Israel had failed; all came to pass.

22 Then Joshua summoned the Reubenites,
and the Gadites, and the half-tribe of
2 Manas′seh, and said to them, "You have kept
all that Moses the servant of the LORD
commanded you, and have obeyed my voice
3 in all that I have commanded you; you have
not forsaken your brethren these many days,
down to this day, but have been careful to
4 keep the charge of the LORD your God. And
now the LORD your God has given rest
to your brethren, as he promised them;
therefore turn and go to your home in the
land where your possession lies, which
Moses the servant of the LORD gave you on
5 the other side of the Jordan. Take good care
to observe the commandment and the law
which Moses the servant of the LORD commanded you, to love the LORD your God, and
to walk in all his ways, and to keep his
commandments, and to cleave to him, and to
serve him with all your heart and with all
6 your soul." So Joshua blessed them, and
sent them away; and they went to their
homes.
7 Now to the one half of the tribe of
Manas′seh Moses had given a possession in
Bashan; but to the other half Joshua had
given a possession beside their brethren in
the land west of the Jordan. And when
Joshua sent them away to their homes and
8 blessed them, he said to them, "Go back to
your homes with much wealth, and with very
many cattle, with silver, gold, bronze, and
iron, and with much clothing; divide the
spoil of your enemies with your brethren."
9 So the Reubenites and the Gadites and the
half-tribe of Manas′seh returned home, parting from the people of Israel at Shiloh, which
is in the land of Canaan, to go to the land of
Gilead, their own land of which they had
possessed themselves by command of the
LORD through Moses.

Altar of witness

10 And when they came to the region about the
Jordan, that lies in the land of Canaan, the

Reubenites and the Gadites and the half-
tribe of Manas′seh built there an altar by the
Jordan, an altar of great size. And the people 11
of Israel heard say, "Behold, the Reubenites and the Gadites and the half-tribe of
Manas′seh have built an altar at the frontier
of the land of Canaan, in the region about the
Jordan, on the side that belongs to the people
of Israel." And when the people of Israel 12
heard of it, the whole assembly of the people
of Israel gathered at Shiloh, to make war
against them.
Then the people of Israel sent to the 13
Reubenites and the Gadites and the half-
tribe of Manas′seh, in the land of Gilead,
Phin′ehas the son of Elea′zar the priest, and 14
with him ten chiefs, one from each of the
tribal families of Israel, every one of them the
head of a family among the clans of Israel.
And they came to the Reubenites, the 15
Gadites, and the half-tribe of Manas′seh, in
the land of Gilead, and they said to them,
"Thus says the whole congregation of the 16
LORD, 'What is this treachery which you
have committed against the God of Israel in
turning away this day from following the
LORD, by building yourselves an altar this
day in rebellion against the LORD? Have we 17
not had enough of the sin at Pe′or from
which even yet we have not cleansed ourselves, and for which there came a plague
upon the congregation of the LORD, that you 18
must turn away this day from following the
LORD? And if you rebel against the LORD
today he will be angry with the whole
congregation of Israel tomorrow. But now, if 19
your land is unclean, pass over into the
LORD's land where the LORD's tabernacle
stands, and take for yourselves a possession

22.1–34: Num 32.20–22; Josh 1.12–18.

among us; only do not rebel against the LORD, or make us as rebels by building yourselves an altar other than the altar of the LORD our God. Did not Achan the son of Zerah break faith in the matter of the devoted things, and wrath fell upon all the congregation of Israel? And he did not perish alone for his iniquity.'"

Then the Reubenites, the Gadites, and the half-tribe of Manas′seh said in answer to the heads of the families of Israel, "The Mighty One, God, the LORD! The Mighty One, God, the LORD! He knows; and let Israel itself know! If it was in rebellion or in breach of faith toward the LORD, spare us not today for building an altar to turn away from following the LORD; or if we did so to offer burnt offerings or cereal offerings or peace offerings on it, may the LORD himself take vengeance. Nay, but we did it from fear that in time to come your children might say to our children, 'What have you to do with the LORD, the God of Israel? For the LORD has made the Jordan a boundary between us and you, you Reubenites and Gadites; you have no portion in the LORD.' So your children might make our children cease to worship the LORD. Therefore we said, 'Let us now build an altar, not for burnt offering, nor for sacrifice, but to be a witness between us and you, and between the generations after us, that we do perform the service of the LORD in his presence with our burnt offerings and sacrifices and peace offerings; lest your children say to our children in time to come, "You have no portion in the LORD."' And we thought, If this should be said to us or to our descendants in time to come, we should say, 'Behold the copy of the altar of the LORD, which our fathers made, not for burnt offerings, nor for sacrifice, but to be a witness between us and you.' Far be it from us that we should rebel against the LORD, and turn away this day from following the LORD by building an altar for burnt offering, cereal offering, or sacrifice, other than the altar of the LORD our God that stands before his tabernacle!"

When Phin′ehas the priest and the chiefs of the congregation, the heads of the families of Israel who were with him, heard the words that the Reubenites and the Gadites and the Manas′sites spoke, it pleased them well. And Phin′ehas the son of Elea′zar the priest said to the Reubenites and the Gadites and the Manas′sites, "Today we know that the LORD is in the midst of us, because you have not committed this treachery against the LORD; now you have saved the people of Israel from the hand of the LORD."

Then Phin′ehas the son of Elea′zar the priest, and the chiefs, returned from the Reubenites and the Gadites in the land of Gilead to the land of Canaan, to the people of Israel, and brought back word to them. And the report pleased the people of Israel; and the people of Israel blessed God and spoke no more of making war against them, to destroy the land where the Reubenites and the Gadites were settled. The Reubenites and the Gadites called the altar Witness; "For," said they, "it is a witness between us that the LORD is God."

Joshua's farewell

A long time afterward, when the LORD had given rest to Israel from all their enemies round about, and Joshua was old and well advanced in years, Joshua summoned all Israel, their elders and heads, their judges and officers, and said to them, "I am now old and well advanced in years; and you have seen all that the LORD your God has done to all these nations for your sake, for it is the LORD your God who has fought for you. Behold, I have allotted to you as an inheritance for your tribes those nations that remain, along with all the nations that I have already cut off, from the Jordan to the Great Sea in the west. The LORD your God will push them back before you, and drive them out of your sight; and you shall possess their land, as the LORD your God promised you. Therefore be very steadfast to keep and do all that is written in the book of the law of Moses, turning aside from it neither to the right hand nor to the left, that you may not be mixed with these nations left here among you, or make mention of the names of their gods, or swear by them, or serve them, or bow down yourselves to them, but cleave to the LORD your God as you have done to this day. For the LORD has driven out before you great and strong nations; and as for you, no man has been able to withstand you to this day. One man of you puts to flight a thousand, since it is the LORD your God who fights for you, as he promised you. Take good heed to yourselves, therefore, to love the LORD your God. For if you turn back, and join the remnant of these nations left here among you, and make marriages with them, so that you marry their women and they yours, know assuredly that the LORD your God will not continue to drive out these nations before you; but they shall be a snare and a trap for you, a scourge on your sides, and thorns in your eyes, till you perish from off this good land which the LORD your God has given you.

"And now I am about to go the way of all the earth, and you know in your hearts and souls, all of you, that not one thing has failed

of all the good things which the LORD your God promised concerning you; all have come to pass for you, not one of them has failed.
15 But just as all the good things which the LORD your God promised concerning you have been fulfilled for you, so the LORD will bring upon you all the evil things, until he have destroyed you from off this good land
16 which the LORD your God has given you, if you transgress the covenant of the LORD your God, which he commanded you, and go and serve other gods and bow down to them. Then the anger of the LORD will be kindled against you, and you shall perish quickly from off the good land which he has given to you."

24 Then Joshua gathered all the tribes of Israel to Shechem, and summoned the elders, the heads, the judges, and the officers of Israel; and they presented themselves before God.
2 And Joshua said to all the people, "Thus says the LORD, the God of Israel, 'Your fathers lived of old beyond the Euphra'tes, Terah, the father of Abraham and of Nahor; and
3 they served other gods. Then I took your father Abraham from beyond the River and led him through all the land of Canaan, and made his offspring many. I gave him Isaac;
4 and to Isaac I gave Jacob and Esau. And I gave Esau the hill country of Se'ir to possess, but Jacob and his children went down to
5 Egypt. And I sent Moses and Aaron, and I plagued Egypt with what I did in the midst of it; and afterwards I brought you out.
6 Then I brought your fathers out of Egypt, and you came to the sea; and the Egyptians pursued your fathers with chariots and
7 horsemen to the Red Sea. And when they cried to the LORD, he put darkness between you and the Egyptians, and made the sea come upon them and cover them; and your eyes saw what I did to Egypt; and you lived
8 in the wilderness a long time. Then I brought you to the land of the Amorites, who lived on the other side of the Jordan; they fought with you, and I gave them into your hand, and you took possession of their land,
9 and I destroyed them before you. Then Balak the son of Zippor, king of Moab, arose and fought against Israel; and he sent and invited Balaam the son of Be'or to curse you,
10 but I would not listen to Balaam; therefore he blessed you; so I delivered you out of his
11 hand. And you went over the Jordan and came to Jericho, and the men of Jericho fought against you, and also the Amorites, the Per'izzites, the Canaanites, the Hittites, the Gir'gashites, the Hivites, and the Jeb'usites; and I gave them into your hand.
12 And I sent the hornet before you, which drove them out before you, the two kings of

the Amorites; it was not by your sword or by your bow. I gave you a land on which you 13 had not laboured, and cities which you had not built, and you dwell therein; you eat the fruit of vineyards and oliveyards which you did not plant.'

"Now therefore fear the LORD, and serve 14 him in sincerity and in faithfulness; put away the gods which your fathers served beyond the River, and in Egypt, and serve the LORD. And if you be unwilling to serve the LORD, 15 choose this day whom you will serve, whether the gods your fathers served in the region beyond the River, or the gods of the Amorites in whose land you dwell; but as for me and my house, we will serve the LORD."

Then the people answered, "Far be it from 16 us that we should forsake the LORD, to serve other gods; for it is the LORD our God who 17 brought us and our fathers up from the land of Egypt, out of the house of bondage, and who did those great signs in our sight, and preserved us in all the way that we went, and among all the peoples through whom we passed; and the LORD drove out before us all 18 the peoples, the Amorites who lived in the land; therefore we also will serve the LORD, for he is our God."

But Joshua said to the people, "You cannot 19 serve the LORD; for he is a holy God; he is a jealous God; he will not forgive your transgressions or your sins. If you forsake the 20 LORD and serve foreign gods, then he will turn and do you harm, and consume you, after having done you good." And the 21 people said to Joshua, "Nay; but we will serve the LORD." Then Joshua said to the 22 people, "You are witnesses against yourselves that you have chosen the LORD, to serve him." And they said, "We are witnesses." He said, "Then put away the 23 foreign gods which are among you, and incline your heart to the LORD, the God of Israel." And the people said to Joshua, 24 "The LORD our God we will serve, and his voice we will obey." So Joshua made a 25 covenant with the people that day, and made statutes and ordinances for them at Shechem. And Joshua wrote these words in 26 the book of the law of God; and he took a great stone, and set it up there under the oak in the sanctuary of the LORD. And Joshua 27 said to all the people, "Behold, this stone shall be a witness against us; for it has heard all the words of the LORD which he spoke to us; therefore it shall be a witness against you, lest you deal falsely with your God." So 28 Joshua sent the people away, every man to his inheritance.

After these things Joshua the son of Nun, 29 the servant of the LORD, died, being a hundred and ten years old. And they buried 30 him in his own inheritance at Tim'nath-se'rah, which is in the hill country of E'phraim, north of the mountain of Ga'ash.

And Israel served the LORD all the days of Joshua, and all the days of the elders who outlived Joshua and had known all the work which the LORD did for Israel.

The bones of Joseph which the people of Israel brought up from Egypt were buried at Shechem, in the portion of ground which Jacob bought from the sons of Hamor the father of Shechem for a hundred pieces of money;[q] it became an inheritance of the descendants of Joseph.

And Elea'zar the son of Aaron died; and 33 they buried him at Gib'e-ah, the town of Phin'ehas his son, which had been given him in the hill country of E'phraim.

THE BOOK OF

JUDGES

TRIBAL CONQUESTS

AFTER the death of Joshua the people of Israel inquired of the LORD, "Who shall go up first for us against the Canaanites, to fight against them?" The LORD said, "Judah shall go up; behold, I have given the land into his hand." And Judah said to Simeon his brother, "Come up with me into the territory allotted to me, that we may fight against the Canaanites; and I likewise will go with you into the territory allotted to you." So Simeon went with him. Then Judah went up and the LORD gave the Canaanites and the Per'izzites into their hand; and they defeated ten thousand of them at Bezek. They came upon 5 Ado'ni-be'zek at Bezek, and fought against him, and defeated the Canaanites and the Per'izzites. Ado'ni-be'zek fled; but they 6 pursued him, and caught him, and cut off his thumbs and his great toes. And 7 Ado'ni-be'zek said, "Seventy kings with their thumbs and their great toes cut off used to pick up scraps under my table; as I have done, so God has requited me." And they brought him to Jerusalem, and he died there.

And the men of Judah fought against 8 Jerusalem, and took it, and smote it with the edge of the sword, and set the city on fire.

---

[q] Heb qesitah
24.32: Gen 50.24–25; Ex 13.19; Acts 7.16.

9 And afterward the men of Judah went down to fight against the Canaanites who dwelt in the hill country, in the Negeb, and in
10 the lowland. And Judah went against the Canaanites who dwelt in Hebron (now the name of Hebron was formerly Kir′iath-ar′ba); and they defeated Sheshai and Ahi′man and Talmai.
11 From there they went against the inhabitants of Debir. The name of Debir was
12 formerly Kir′iath-se′pher. And Caleb said, "He who attacks Kir′iath-se′pher and takes it, I will give him Achsah my daughter as
13 wife." And Oth′ni-el the son of Kenaz, Caleb's younger brother, took it; and he gave
14 him Achsah his daughter as wife. When she came to him, she urged him to ask her father for a field; and she alighted from her ass, and
15 Caleb said to her, "What do you wish?" She said to him, "Give me a present; since you have set me in the land of the Negeb, give me also springs of water." And Caleb gave her the upper springs and the lower springs.
16 And the descendants of the Ken′ite, Moses' father-in-law, went up with the people of Judah from the city of palms into the wilderness of Judah, which lies in the Negeb near Arad; and they went and settled with
17 the people. And Judah went with Simeon his brother, and they defeated the Canaanites who inhabited Zephath, and utterly destroyed it. So the name of the city was
18 called Hormah. Judah also took Gaza with its territory, and Ash′kelon with its territory,
19 and Ekron with its territory. And the LORD was with Judah, and he took possession of the hill country, but he could not drive out the inhabitants of the plain, because they had
20 chariots of iron. And Hebron was given to Caleb, as Moses had said; and he drove out
21 from it the three sons of Anak. But the people of Benjamin did not drive out the Jeb′usites who dwelt in Jerusalem; so the Jeb′usites have dwelt with the people of Benjamin in Jerusalem to this day.
22 The house of Joseph also went up against
23 Bethel; and the LORD was with them. And the house of Joseph sent to spy out Bethel. (Now the name of the city was formerly
24 Luz.) And the spies saw a man coming out of the city, and they said to him, "Pray, show us the way into the city, and we will deal
25 kindly with you." And he showed them the way into the city; and they smote the city with the edge of the sword, but they let the
26 man and all his family go. And the man went to the land of the Hittites and built a city, and called its name Luz; that is its name to this day.

Manas′seh did not drive out the inhabitants of Beth-she′an and its villages, or Ta′anach and its villages, or the inhabitants of Dor and its villages, or the inhabitants of Ib′le-am and its villages, or the inhabitants of Megid′do and its villages; but the Canaanites persisted in dwelling in that land. When Israel grew strong, they put the Canaanites to forced labour, but did not utterly drive them out.

And E′phraim did not drive out the Canaanites who dwelt in Gezer; but the Canaanites dwelt in Gezer among them.

Zeb′ulun did not drive out the inhabitants of Kitron, or the inhabitants of Na′halol; but the Canaanites dwelt among them, and became subject to forced labour.

Asher did not drive out the inhabitants of Acco, or the inhabitants of Sidon, or of Ahlab, or of Achzib, or of Helbah, or of Aphik, or of Rehob; but the Asherites dwelt among the Canaanites, the inhabitants of the land; for they did not drive them out.

Naph′tali did not drive out the inhabitants of Beth-she′mesh, or the inhabitants of Beth-anath, but dwelt among the Canaanites, the inhabitants of the land; nevertheless the inhabitants of Beth-she′mesh and of Beth-anath became subject to forced labour for them.

The Amorites pressed the Danites back into the hill country, for they did not allow them to come down to the plain; the Amorites persisted in dwelling in Har-heres, in Ai′jalon, and in Sha-al′bim, but the hand of the house of Joseph rested heavily upon them, and they became subject to forced labour. And the border of the Amorites ran from the ascent of Akrab′bim, from Sela and upward.

The angel of the Lord

Now the angel of the LORD went up from Gilgal to Bochim. And he said, "I brought you up from Egypt, and brought you into the land which I swore to give to your fathers. I said, 'I will never break my covenant with you, and you shall make no covenant with the inhabitants of this land; you shall break down their altars.' But you have not obeyed my command. What is this you have done? So now I say, I will not drive them out before you; but they shall become adversaries[a] to you, and their gods shall be a snare to you." When the angel of the LORD spoke these words to all the people of Israel, the people lifted up their voices and wept. And they called the name of that place Bochim;[b] and they sacrificed there to the LORD.

[a] Vg Old Latin Compare Gk: Heb *sides*   [b] That is *Weepers*
1.10: Josh 15.13–19.   1.10–15: Josh 15.14–19.   1.20: Josh 15.14.   1.21: Josh 15.63.
1.27–28: Josh 17.11–13.   1.29: Josh 16.10.

When Joshua dismissed the people, the people of Israel went each to his inheritance to take possession of the land. And the people served the LORD all the days of Joshua, and all the days of the elders who outlived Joshua, who had seen all the great work which the LORD had done for Israel. And Joshua the son of Nun, the servant of the LORD, died at the age of one hundred and ten years. And they buried him within the bounds of his inheritance in Tim'nath-he'res, in the hill country of E'phraim, north of the mountain of Ga'ash. And all that generation also were gathered to their fathers; and there arose another generation after them, who did not know the LORD or the work which he had done for Israel. And the people of Israel did what was evil in the sight of the LORD and served the Ba'als; and they forsook the LORD, the God of their fathers, who had brought them out of the land of Egypt; they went after other gods, from among the gods of the peoples who were round about them, and bowed down to them; and they provoked the LORD to anger. They forsook the LORD, and served the Ba'als and the Ash'taroth. So the anger of the LORD was kindled against Israel, and he gave them over to plunderers, who plundered them; and he sold them into the power of their enemies round about, so that they could no longer withstand their enemies. Whenever they marched out, the hand of the LORD was against them for evil, as the LORD had warned, and as the LORD had sworn to them; and they were in sore straits.

6 Then the LORD raised up judges, who saved them out of the power of those who plundered them. And yet they did not listen to their judges; for they played the harlot after other gods and bowed down to them; they soon turned aside from the way in which their fathers had walked, who had obeyed the commandments of the LORD, and they did not do so. Whenever the LORD raised up judges for them, the LORD was with the judge, and he saved them from the hand of their enemies all the days of the judge; for the LORD was moved to pity by their groaning because of those who afflicted and oppressed them. But whenever the judge died, they turned back and behaved worse than their fathers, going after other gods, serving them and bowing down to them; they did not drop any of their practices or their stubborn ways. So the anger of the LORD was kindled against Israel; and he said, "Because this people have transgressed my covenant which I commanded their fathers, and have not obeyed my voice, I will not henceforth

drive out before them any of the nations that Joshua left when he died, that by them I may test Israel, whether they will take care to walk in the way of the LORD as their fathers did, or not." So the LORD left those nations, not driving them out at once, and he did not give them into the power of Joshua.

Now these are the nations which the LORD 3 left, to test Israel by them, that is, all in Israel who had no experience of any war in Canaan; it was only that the generations of the people 2 of Israel might know war, that he might teach war to such at least as had not known it before. These are the nations: the five lords 3 of the Philistines, and all the Canaanites, and the Sido'nians, and the Hivites who dwelt on Mount Lebanon, from Mount Ba'al-her'mon as far as the entrance of Hamath. They were 4 for the testing of Israel, to know whether Israel would obey the commandments of the LORD, which he commanded their fathers by Moses. So the people of Israel dwelt among 5 the Canaanites, the Hittites, the Amorites, the Per'izzites, the Hivites, and the Jeb'usites; and they took their daughters to them- 6 selves for wives, and their own daughters they gave to their sons; and they served their gods.

OTHNIEL

AND the people of Israel did what was evil 7 in the sight of the LORD, forgetting the LORD their God, and serving the Ba'als and the Ashe'roth. Therefore the anger of the 8 LORD was kindled against Israel, and he sold them into the hand of Cu'shan-rishatha'im king of Mesopota'mia; and the people of Israel served Cu'shan-rishatha'im eight years. But when the people of Israel cried to 9 the LORD, the LORD raised up a deliverer for the people of Israel, who delivered them, Oth'ni-el the son of Kenaz, Caleb's younger brother. The Spirit of the LORD came upon 10 him, and he judged Israel; he went out to war, and the LORD gave Cu'shan-rishatha'im king of Mesopota'mia into his hand; and his hand prevailed over Cu'shan-rishatha'im. So the land had rest forty years. Then 11 Oth'ni-el the son of Kenaz died.

EHUD

AND the people of Israel again did what 12 was evil in the sight of the LORD; and the LORD strengthened Eglon the king of Moab against Israel, because they had done what was evil in the sight of the LORD. He 13 gathered to himself the Ammonites and the

Amal'ekites, and went and defeated Israel; and they took possession of the city of
14 palms. And the people of Israel served Eglon the king of Moab eighteen years.
15 But when the people of Israel cried to the LORD, the LORD raised up for them a deliverer, Ehud, the son of Gera, the Benjaminite, a left-handed man. The people of Israel sent tribute by him to Eglon the king
16 of Moab. And Ehud made for himself a sword with two edges, a cubit in length; and he girded it on his right thigh under his
17 clothes. And he presented the tribute to Eglon king of Moab. Now Eglon was a very
18 fat man. And when Ehud had finished presenting the tribute, he sent away the
19 people that carried the tribute. But he himself turned back at the sculptured stones near Gilgal, and said, "I have a secret message for you, O king." And he commanded, "Silence." And all his attendants
20 went out from his presence. And Ehud came to him, as he was sitting alone in his cool roof chamber. And Ehud said, "I have a message from God for you." And he arose from his
21 seat. And Ehud reached with his left hand, took the sword from his right thigh, and
22 thrust it into his belly; and the hilt also went in after the blade, and the fat closed over the blade, for he did not draw the sword out of
23 his belly; and the dirt came out. Then Ehud went out into the vestibule,ᶜ and closed the doors of the roof chamber upon him, and locked them.
24 When he had gone, the servants came; and when they saw that the doors of the roof chamber were locked, they thought, "He is only relieving himself in the closet of the cool
25 chamber." And they waited till they were utterly at a loss; but when he still did not open the doors of the roof chamber, they took the key and opened them; and there lay their lord dead on the floor.
26 Ehud escaped while they delayed, and passed beyond the sculptured stones, and
27 escaped to Se-i'rah. When he arrived, he sounded the trumpet in the hill country of E'phraim; and the people of Israel went down with him from the hill country, having
28 him at their head. And he said to them, "Follow after me; for the LORD has given your enemies the Moabites into your hand." So they went down after him, and seized the fords of the Jordan against the Moabites, and
29 allowed not a man to pass over. And they killed at that time about ten thousand of the Moabites, all strong, able-bodied men; not a
30 man escaped. So Moab was subdued that day under the hand of Israel. And the land had rest for eighty years.

ᶜ The meaning of the Hebrew word is unknown

After him was Shamgar the son of Anath, 31 who killed six hundred of the Philistines with an oxgoad; and he too delivered Israel.

DEBORAH

AND the people of Israel again did what 4 was evil in the sight of the LORD, after Ehud died. And the LORD sold them into the 2 hand of Jabin king of Canaan, who reigned in Hazor; the commander of his army was Sis'era, who dwelt in Haro'sheth-ha-goi'im. Then the people of Israel cried to the LORD 3 for help; for he had nine hundred chariots of iron, and oppressed the people of Israel cruelly for twenty years.

Now Deb'orah, a prophetess, the wife of 4 Lap'pidoth, was judging Israel at that time. She used to sit under the palm of Deb'- 5 orah between Ramah and Bethel in the hill country of E'phraim; and the people of Israel came up to her for judgment. She sent and 6 summoned Barak the son of Abin'o-am from Kedesh in Naph'tali, and said to him, "The LORD, the God of Israel, commands you, 'Go, gather your men at Mount Tabor, taking ten thousand from the tribe of Naph'tali and the tribe of Zeb'ulun. And I 7 will draw out Sis'era, the general of Jabin's army, to meet you by the river Kishon with his chariots and his troops; and I will give him into your hand.'" Barak said to her, "If 8 you will go with me, I will go; but if you will not go with me, I will not go." And she said, 9

"I will surely go with you; nevertheless, the road on which you are going will not lead to your glory, for the LORD will sell Sis′era into the hand of a woman." Then Deb′orah arose, and went with Barak to Kedesh. And Barak summoned Zeb′ulun and Naph′tali to Kedesh; and ten thousand men went up at his heels; and Deb′orah went up with him.

Now Heber the Ken′ite had separated from the Ken′ites, the descendants of Hobab the father-in-law of Moses, and had pitched his tent as far away as the oak in Za-anan′nim, which is near Kedesh.

When Sis′era was told that Barak the son of Abin′o-am had gone up to Mount Tabor, Sis′era called out all his chariots, nine hundred chariots of iron, and all the men who were with him, from Haro′sheth-ha-goi′im to the river Kishon. And Deb′orah said to Barak, "Up! For this is the day in which the LORD has given Sis′era into your hand. Does not the LORD go out before you?" So Barak went down from Mount Tabor with ten thousand men following him. And the LORD routed Sis′era and all his chariots and all his army before Barak at the edge of the sword; and Sis′era alighted from his chariot and fled away on foot. And Barak pursued the chariots and the army to Haro′sheth-ha-goi′im, and all the army of Sis′era fell by the edge of the sword; not a man was left.

But Sis′era fled away on foot to the tent of Ja′el, the wife of Heber the Ken′ite; for there was peace between Jabin the king of Hazor and the house of Heber the Ken′ite. And Ja′el came out to meet Sis′era, and said to him, "Turn aside, my lord, turn aside to me; have no fear." So he turned aside to her into the tent, and she covered him with a rug. And he said to her, "Pray, give me a little water to drink; for I am thirsty." So she opened a skin of milk and gave him a drink and covered him. And he said to her, "Stand at the door of the tent, and if any man comes and asks you, 'Is any one here?' say, No." But Ja′el the wife of Heber took a tent peg, and took a hammer in her hand, and went softly to him and drove the peg into his temple, till it went down into the ground, as he was lying fast asleep from weariness. So he died. And behold, as Barak pursued Sis′era, Ja′el went out to meet him, and said to him, "Come, and I will show you the man whom you are seeking." So he went in to her tent; and there lay Sis′era dead, with the tent peg in his temple.

So on that day God subdued Jabin the king of Canaan before the people of Israel. And the hand of the people of Israel bore harder and harder on Jabin the king of Canaan, until they destroyed Jabin king of Canaan.

Song of Deborah

Then sang Deb′orah and Barak the son of 5 Abin′o-am on that day:
"That the leaders took the lead in Israel, 2
   that the people offered themselves willingly,
   bless[d] the LORD!

"Hear, O kings; give ear, O princes; 3
   to the LORD I will sing,
   I will make melody to the LORD, the God of Israel.

"LORD, when thou didst go forth from 4
   Se′ir,
   when thou didst march from the region of Edom,
the earth trembled,
   and the heavens dropped,
   yea, the clouds dropped water.
The mountains quaked before the LORD, 5
   yon Sinai before the LORD, the God of Israel.

"In the days of Shamgar, son of Anath, 6
   in the days of Ja′el, caravans ceased
   and travellers kept to the byways.
The peasantry ceased in Israel, they ceased 7
   until you arose, Deb′orah,
   arose as a mother in Israel.
When new gods were chosen, 8
   then war was in the gates.
Was shield or spear to be seen
   among forty thousand in Israel?
My heart goes out to the commanders of 9
   Israel
   who offered themselves willingly among the people.
   Bless the LORD.

"Tell of it, you who ride on tawny asses, 10
   you who sit on rich carpets[e]
   and you who walk by the way.
To the sound of musicians[e] at the watering 11
   places,
   there they repeat the triumphs of the LORD,
   the triumphs of his peasantry in Israel.

"Then down to the gates marched the people of the LORD.

"Awake, awake, Deb′orah! 12
   Awake, awake, utter a song!
Arise, Barak, lead away your captives,

---

[d] Or You who offered yourselves willingly among the people, bless
[e] The meaning of the Hebrew word is uncertain

O son of Abin'o-am.

13 Then down marched the remnant of the
    noble;
    the people of the LORD marched down for
        him*f* against the mighty.
14 From E'phraim they set out thither*x* into
    the valley,*g*
    following you, Benjamin, with your
        kinsmen;
    from Machir marched down the com-
        manders,
    and from Zeb'ulun those who bear the
        marshal's staff;
15 the princes of Is'sachar came with
    Deb'orah,
    and Is'sachar faithful to Barak;
    into the valley they rushed forth at his
        heels.
    Among the clans of Reuben
        there were great searchings of heart.
16 Why did you tarry among the sheepfolds,
    to hear the piping for the flocks?
    Among the clans of Reuben
        there were great searchings of heart.
17 Gilead stayed beyond the Jordan;
    and Dan, why did he abide with the
        ships?
    Asher sat still at the coast of the sea,
        settling down by his landings.
18 Zeb'ulun is a people that jeoparded their
    lives to the death;
    Naph'tali too, on the heights of the field.

19 "The kings came, they fought;
    then fought the kings of Canaan,
    at Ta'anach, by the waters of Megid'do;
    they got no spoils of silver.
20 From heaven fought the stars,
    from their courses they fought against
        Sis'era.
21 The torrent Kishon swept them away,
    the onrushing torrent, the torrent
        Kishon.
    March on, my soul, with might!

22 "Then loud beat the horses' hoofs
    with the galloping, galloping of his steeds.

23 "Curse Meroz, says the angel of the LORD,
    curse bitterly its inhabitants,
    because they came not to the help of the
        LORD,
    to the help of the LORD against the
        mighty.

24 "Most blessed of women be Ja'el,
    the wife of Heber the Ken'ite,
    of tent-dwelling women most blessed.
25 He asked water and she gave him milk,

she brought him curds in a lordly bowl.
20 She put her hand to the tent peg
    and her right hand to the workmen's
        mallet;
    she struck Sis'era a blow,
    she crushed his head,
    she shattered and pierced his temple.
27 He sank, he fell,
    he lay still at her feet;
    at her feet he sank, he fell;
    where he sank, there he fell dead.

28 "Out of the window she peered,
    the mother of Sis'era gazed*h* through the
        lattice;
    'Why is his chariot so long in coming?
    Why tarry the hoofbeats of his chariots?'
29 Her wisest ladies make answer,
    nay, she gives answer to herself,
    'Are they not finding and dividing the
30   spoil?—
    A maiden or two for every man;
    spoil of dyed stuffs for Sis'era,
    spoil of dyed stuffs embroidered,
    two pieces of dyed work embroidered for
        my neck as spoil?'

31 "So perish all thine enemies, O LORD!
    But thy friends be like the sun as he rises
        in his might."

And the land had rest for forty years.

GIDEON

THE people of Israel did what was evil in 6
the sight of the LORD; and the LORD gave
them into the hand of Mid'ian seven years.
And the hand of Mid'ian prevailed over 2
Israel; and because of Mid'ian the people of
Israel made for themselves the dens which
are in the mountains, and the caves and the
strongholds. For whenever the Israelites put 3
in seed the Mid'ianites and the Amal'ekites
and the people of the East would come up
and attack them; they would encamp against 4
them and destroy the produce of the land, as
far as the neighbourhood of Gaza, and leave
no sustenance in Israel, and no sheep or ox or
ass. For they would come up with their 5
cattle and their tents, coming like locusts for
number; both they and their camels could
not be counted; so that they wasted the land
as they came in. And Israel was brought 6
very low because of Mid'ian; and the people
of Israel cried for help to the LORD.

When the people of Israel cried to the LORD 7
on account of the Mid'ianites, the LORD sent 8
a prophet to the people of Israel; and he said

f Gk: Heb *me*   *x* Cn: Heb *From Ephraim their root*   *g* Gk: Heb *in Amalek*
h Gk Compare Tg: Heb *exclaimed*
5.31: Rev 1.16.

to them, "Thus says the LORD, the God of Israel: I led you up from Egypt, and brought you out of the house of bondage; and I delivered you from the hand of the Egyptians, and from the hand of all who oppressed you, and drove them out before you, and gave you their land; and I said to you, 'I am the LORD your God; you shall not pay reverence to the gods of the Amorites, in whose land you dwell.' But you have not given heed to my voice."

Gideon's call

Now the angel of the LORD came and sat under the oak at Ophrah, which belonged to Jo′ash the Abiez′rite, as his son Gideon was beating out wheat in the wine press, to hide it from the Mid′ianites. And the angel of the LORD appeared to him and said to him, "The LORD is with you, you mighty man of valour." And Gideon said to him, "Pray, sir, if the LORD is with us, why then has all this befallen us? And where are all his wonderful deeds which our fathers recounted to us, saying, 'Did not the LORD bring us up from Egypt?' But now the LORD has cast us off, and given us into the hand of Mid′ian." And the LORD turned to him and said, "Go in this might of yours and deliver Israel from the hand of Mid′ian; do not I send you?" And he said to him, "Pray, Lord, how can I deliver Israel? Behold, my clan is the weakest in Manas′seh, and I am the least in my family." And the LORD said to him, "But I will be with you, and you shall smite the Mid′ianites as one man." And he said to him, "If now I have found favour with thee, then show me a sign that it is thou who speakest with me. Do not depart from here, I pray thee, until I come to thee, and bring out my present, and set it before thee." And he said, "I will stay till you return."

So Gideon went into his house and prepared a kid, and unleavened cakes from an ephah of flour; the meat he put in a basket, and the broth he put in a pot, and brought them to him under the oak and presented them. And the angel of God said to him, "Take the meat and the unleavened cakes, and put them on this rock, and pour the broth over them." And he did so. Then the angel of the LORD reached out the tip of the staff that was in his hand, and touched the meat and the unleavened cakes; and there sprang up fire from the rock and consumed the flesh and the unleavened cakes; and the angel of the LORD vanished from his sight. Then Gideon perceived that he was the angel of the LORD; and Gideon said, "Alas, O Lord GOD! For now I have seen the angel of the LORD face to face." But the LORD said to him, "Peace be to you; do not fear, you shall not die." Then Gideon built an altar there to the LORD, and called it, The LORD is peace. To this day it still stands at Ophrah, which belongs to the Abiez′rites.

That night the LORD said to him, "Take your father's bull, the second bull seven years old, and pull down the altar of Ba′al which your father has, and cut down the Ashe′rah that is beside it; and build an altar to the LORD your God on the top of the stronghold here, with stones laid in due order; then take the second bull, and offer it as a burnt offering with the wood of the Ashe′rah which you shall cut down." So Gideon took ten men of his servants, and did as the LORD had told him; but because he was too afraid of his family and the men of the town to do it by day, he did it by night.

When the men of the town rose early in the morning, behold, the altar of Ba′al was broken down, and the Ashe′rah beside it was cut down, and the second bull was offered upon the altar which had been built. And they said to one another, "Who has done this thing?" And after they had made search and inquired, they said, "Gideon the son of Jo′ash has done this thing." Then the men of the town said to Jo′ash, "Bring out your son, that he may die, for he has pulled down the altar of Ba′al and cut down the Ashe′rah beside it." But Jo′ash said to all who were arrayed against him, "Will you contend for Ba′al? Or will you defend his cause? Whoever contends for him shall be put to death by morning. If he is a god, let him contend for himself, because his altar has been pulled down." Therefore on that day he was called Jerubba′al, that is to say, "Let Ba′al contend against him," because he pulled down his altar.

Then all the Mid′ianites and the Amal′ekites and the people of the East came together, and crossing the Jordan they encamped in the Valley of Jezreel. But the Spirit of the LORD took possession of Gideon; and he sounded the trumpet, and the Abiez′rites were called out to follow him. And he sent messengers throughout all Manas′seh; and they too were called out to follow him. And he sent messengers to Asher, Zeb′ulun, and

OPHRAH
13
MILES
JERUSALEM

Naph'tali; and they went up to meet them.

36 Then Gideon said to God, "If thou wilt deliver Israel by my hand, as thou hast said,
37 behold, I am laying a fleece of wool on the threshing floor; if there is dew on the fleece alone, and it is dry on all the ground, then I shall know that thou wilt deliver Israel by my
38 hand, as thou hast said." And it was so. When he rose early next morning and squeezed the fleece, he wrung enough dew from the fleece to fill a bowl with water.
39 Then Gideon said to God, "Let not thy anger burn against me, let me speak but this once; pray, let me make trial only this once with the fleece; pray, let it be dry only on the fleece, and on all the ground let there be
40 dew." And God did so that night; for it was dry on the fleece only, and on all the ground there was dew.

Gideon's victories

7 Then Jerubba'al (that is, Gideon) and all the people who were with him rose early and encamped beside the spring of Harod; and the camp of Mid'ian was north of them, by the hill of Moreh, in the valley.
2 The LORD said to Gideon, "The people with you are too many for me to give the Mid'ianites into their hand, lest Israel vaunt themselves against me, saying, 'My own
3 hand has delivered me.' Now therefore proclaim in the ears of the people, saying, 'Whoever is fearful and trembling, let him return home.'" And Gideon tested them;[i] twenty-two thousand returned, and ten thousand remained.
4 And the LORD said to Gideon, "The people are still too many; take them down to the water and I will test them for you there; and he of whom I say to you, 'This man shall go with you,' shall go with you; and any of whom I say to you, 'This man shall not go
5 with you,' shall not go." So he brought the people down to the water; and the LORD said to Gideon, "Every one that laps the water with his tongue, as a dog laps, you shall set by himself; likewise every one that kneels
6 down to drink." And the number of those that lapped, putting their hands to their mouths, was three hundred men; but all the rest of the people knelt down to drink water.
7 And the LORD said to Gideon, "With the three hundred men that lapped I will deliver you, and give the Mid'ianites into your hand; and let all the others go every man to his
8 home." So he took the jars of the people from their hands,[j] and their trumpets; and he sent all the rest of Israel every man to his tent, but retained the three hundred men;

and the camp of Mid'ian was below him in the valley.

That same night the LORD said to him, 9 "Arise, go down against the camp; for I have given it into your hand. But if you fear to go down, go down to the camp with Purah your servant; and you shall hear what they say, and afterward your hands shall be strengthened to go down against the camp." Then he went down with Purah his servant to the outposts of the armed men that were in the camp. And the Mid'ianites and the Amal'ekites and all the people of the East lay along the valley like locusts for multitude; and their camels were without number, as the sand which is upon the seashore for multitude. When Gideon came, behold, a man was telling a dream to his comrade; and he said, "Behold, I dreamed a dream; and lo, a cake of barley bread tumbled into the camp of Mid'ian, and came to the tent, and struck it so that it fell, and turned it upside down, so that the tent lay flat." And his comrade answered, "This is no other than the sword of Gideon the son of Jo'ash, a man of Israel; into his hand God has given Mid'ian and all the host."

When Gideon heard the telling of the dream and its interpretation, he worshipped; and he returned to the camp of Israel, and said, "Arise; for the LORD has given the host of Mid'ian into your hand." And he divided the three hundred men into three companies, and put trumpets into the hands of all of

---

[i] Cn: Heb *and depart from Mount Gilead*   [j] Cn: Heb *the people took provisions in their hands*

them and empty jars, with torches inside the
7 jars. And he said to them, "Look at me, and
do likewise; when I come to the outskirts of
8 the camp, do as I do. When I blow the
trumpet, I and all who are with me, then
blow the trumpets also on every side of all
the camp, and shout, 'For the LORD and for
Gideon.'"

9 So Gideon and the hundred men who were
with him came to the outskirts of the camp at
the beginning of the middle watch, when
they had just set the watch; and they blew
the trumpets and smashed the jars that were
10 in their hands. And the three companies
blew the trumpets and broke the jars, holding in their left hands the torches, and in
their right hands the trumpets to blow; and
they cried, "A sword for the LORD and for
11 Gideon!" They stood every man in his place
round about the camp, and all the army ran;
12 they cried out and fled. When they blew the
three hundred trumpets, the LORD set every
man's sword against his fellow and against all
the army; and the army fled as far as
Beth-shit'tah toward Zer'erah,[k] as far as the
13 border of A'bel-meho'lah, by Tabbath. And
the men of Israel were called out from
Naph'tali and from Asher and from all
Manas'seh, and they pursued after Mid'ian.

14 And Gideon sent messengers throughout all
the hill country of E'phraim, saying, "Come
down against the Mid'ianites and seize the
waters against them, as far as Beth-bar'ah,
and also the Jordan." So all the men of
E'phraim were called out, and they seized the
waters as far as Beth-bar'ah, and also the
15 Jordan. And they took the two princes of
Mid'ian, Oreb and Zeeb; they killed Oreb at
the rock of Oreb, and Zeeb they killed at the
wine press of Zeeb, as they pursued Mid'ian;
and they brought the heads of Oreb and Zeeb
to Gideon beyond the Jordan.

8 And the men of E'phraim said to him,
"What is this that you have done to us, not
to call us when you went to fight with
Mid'ian?" And they upbraided him vio-
2 lently. And he said to them, "What have I
done now in comparison with you? Is not
the gleaning of the grapes of E'phraim better
3 than the vintage of Abi-e'zer? God has
given into your hands the princes of Mid'ian,
Oreb and Zeeb; what have I been able to do
in comparison with you?" Then their anger
against him was abated, when he had said
this.

4 And Gideon came to the Jordan and passed
over, he and the three hundred men who
5 were with him, faint yet pursuing. So he said
to the men of Succoth, "Pray, give loaves of
bread to the people who follow me; for they
are faint, and I am pursuing after Zebah and
Zalmun'na, the kings of Mid'ian." And the 6
officials of Succoth said, "Are Zebah and
Zalmun'na already in your hand, that we
should give bread to your army?" And 7
Gideon said, "Well then, when the LORD has
given Zebah and Zalmun'na into my hand, I
will flail your flesh with the thorns of the
wilderness and with briers." And from there 8
he went up to Penu'el, and spoke to them in
the same way; and the men of Penu'el
answered him as the men of Succoth had
answered. And he said to the men of 9
Penu'el, "When I come again in peace, I will
break down this tower."

Now Zebah and Zalmun'na were in Karkor 10
with their army, about fifteen thousand men,
all who were left of all the army of the people
of the East; for there had fallen a hundred
and twenty thousand men who drew the
sword. And Gideon went up by the caravan 11
route east of Nobah and Jog'behah, and
attacked the army; for the army was off its
guard. And Zebah and Zalmun'na fled; and 12
he pursued them and took the two kings of
Mid'ian, Zebah and Zalmun'na, and he
threw all the army into a panic.

Then Gideon the son of Jo'ash returned 13
from the battle by the ascent of Heres. And 14
he caught a young man of Succoth, and
questioned him; and he wrote down for him
the officials and elders of Succoth, seventy-
seven men. And he came to the men of 15
Succoth, and said, "Behold Zebah and
Zalmun'na, about whom you taunted me,
saying, 'Are Zebah and Zalmun'na already in
your hand, that we should give bread to your
men who are faint?'" And he took the 16
elders of the city and he took thorns of the
wilderness and briers and with them taught
the men of Succoth. And he broke down the 17
tower of Penu'el, and slew the men of the
city.

Then he said to Zebah and Zalmun'na, 18
"Where are the men whom you slew at
Tabor?" They answered, "As you are, so
were they, every one of them; they resembled
the sons of a king." And he said, "They 19
were my brothers, the sons of my mother; as
the LORD lives, if you had saved them alive, I
would not slay you." And he said to Jether 20
his first-born, "Rise, and slay them." But
the youth did not draw his sword; for he was
afraid, because he was still a youth. Then 21
Zebah and Zalmun'na said, "Rise yourself,
and fall upon us; for as the man is, so is his
strength." And Gideon arose and slew
Zebah and Zalmun'na; and he took the

[k] Another reading is Zeredah

crescents that were on the necks of their camels.

22 Then the men of Israel said to Gideon, "Rule over us, you and your son and your grandson also; for you have delivered us out 23 of the hand of Mid'ian." Gideon said to them, "I will not rule over you, and my son will not rule over you; the LORD will rule 24 over you." And Gideon said to them, "Let me make a request of you; give me every man of you the earrings of his spoil." (For they had golden earrings, because they were

buried in the tomb of Jo'ash his father, at Ophrah of the Abiez'rites.

As soon as Gideon died, the people of Israel turned again and played the harlot after the Ba'als, and made Ba'al-be'rith their god. And the people of Israel did not remember the LORD their God, who had rescued them from the hand of all their enemies on every

Judges 9, 10

side; and they did not show kindness to the family of Jerubba'al (that is, Gideon) in return for all the good that he had done to Israel.

Gideon's son

Now Abim'elech the son of Jerubba'al went to Shechem to his mother's kinsmen and said to them and to the whole clan of his mother's family, "Say in the ears of all the citizens of 2 Shechem, 'Which is better for you, that all seventy of the sons of Jerubba'al rule over you, or that one rule over you?' Remember also that I am your bone and your flesh." And his mother's kinsmen spoke all these 3 words on his behalf in the ears of all the men of Shechem; and their hearts inclined to follow Abim'elech, for they said, "He is our brother." And they gave him seventy pieces 4 of silver out of the house of Ba'al-be'rith with which Abim'elech hired worthless and reckless fellows, who followed him. And he went 5 to his father's house at Ophrah, and slew his brothers the sons of Jerubba'al, seventy men, upon one stone; but Jotham the youngest son of Jerubba'al was left, for he hid himself. And all the citizens of Shechem came to- 6 gether, and all Beth-millo, and they went and made Abim'elech king, by the oak of the pillar at Shechem.

25 Ish'maelites.) And they answered, "We will willingly give them." And they spread a garment, and every man cast in it the ear- 26 rings of his spoil. And the weight of the golden earrings that he requested was one thousand seven hundred shekels of gold; besides the crescents and the pendants and the purple garments worn by the kings of Mid'ian, and besides the collars that were 27 about the necks of their camels. And Gideon made an ephod of it and put it in his city, in Ophrah; and all Israel played the harlot after it there, and it became a snare to Gideon and 28 to his family. So Mid'ian was subdued before the people of Israel, and they lifted up their heads no more. And the land had rest forty years in the days of Gideon.

29 Jerubba'al the son of Jo'ash went and dwelt 30 in his own house. Now Gideon had seventy sons, his own offspring, for he had many 31 wives. And his concubine who was in Shechem also bore him a son, and he called 32 his name Abim'elech. And Gideon the son of Jo'ash died in a good old age, and was

When it was told to Jotham, he went and 7 stood on the top of Mount Ger'izim, and cried aloud and said to them, "Listen to me, you men of Shechem, that God may listen to

8 you. The trees once went forth to anoint a
king over them; and they said to the olive
9 tree, 'Reign over us.' But the olive tree said
to them, 'Shall I leave my fatness, by which
gods and men are honoured, and go to sway
10 over the trees?' And the trees said to the fig
11 tree, 'Come you, and reign over us.' But the
fig tree said to them, 'Shall I leave my
sweetness and my good fruit, and go to sway
12 over the trees?' And the trees said to the
13 vine, 'Come you, and reign over us.' But the
vine said to them, 'Shall I leave my wine
which cheers gods and men, and go to sway
14 over the trees?' Then all the trees said to the
bramble, 'Come you, and reign over us.'

15 And the bramble said to the trees, 'If in good
faith you are anointing me king over you,
then come and take refuge in my shade; but
if not, let fire come out of the bramble and
devour the cedars of Lebanon.'
16 "Now therefore, if you acted in good faith
and honour when you made Abim′elech
king, and if you have dealt well with Jerub-
ba′al and his house, and have done to him as
17 his deeds deserved— for my father fought for
you, and risked his life, and rescued you from
18 the hand of Mid′ian; and you have risen up
against my father's house this day, and have
slain his sons, seventy men on one stone, and
have made Abim′elech, the son of his maidservant, king over the citizens of Shechem,
19 because he is your kinsman— if you then
have acted in good faith and honour with
Jerubba′al and with his house this day, then
rejoice in Abim′elech, and let him also rejoice
20 in you; but if not, let fire come out from
Abim′elech, and devour the citizens of
Shechem, and Beth-millo; and let fire come
out from the citizens of Shechem, and from
21 Beth-millo, and devour Abim′elech." And
Jotham ran away and fled, and went to Beer
and· dwelt there, for fear of Abim′elech his
brother.

The men of Shechem

22 Abim′elech ruled over Israel three years.
23 And God sent an evil spirit between Abim′-
elech and the men of Shechem; and the
men of Shechem dealt treacherously with
Abim′elech; that the violence done to the 24
seventy sons of Jerubba′al might come and
their blood be laid upon Abim′elech their
brother, who slew them, and upon the men
of Shechem, who strengthened his hands to
slay his brothers. And the men of Shechem 25
put men in ambush against him on the
mountain tops, and they robbed all who
passed by them along that way; and it was
told Abim′elech.
And Ga′al the son of Ebed moved into 26
Shechem with his kinsmen; and the men of
Shechem put confidence in him. And they 27
went out into the field, and gathered the
grapes from their vineyards and trod them,
and held festival, and went into the house of
their god, and ate and drank and reviled
Abim′elech. And Ga′al the son of Ebed said, 28
"Who is Abim′elech, and who are we of
Shechem, that we should serve him? Did
not the son of Jerubba′al and Zebul his
officer serve the men of Hamor the father of
Shechem? Why then should we serve him?
Would that this people were under my hand! 29
then I would remove Abim′elech. I would
say[l] to Abim′elech, 'Increase your army, and
come out.' "
When Zebul the ruler of the city heard the 30
words of Ga′al the son of Ebed, his anger
was kindled. And he sent messengers to 31
Abim′elech at Aru′mah,[m] saying, "Behold,
Ga′al the son of Ebed and his kinsmen have
come to Shechem, and they are stirring up[n]
the city against you. Now therefore, go by 32
night, you and the men that are with you,
and lie in wait in the fields. Then in the 33
morning, as soon as the sun is up, rise early
and rush upon the city; and when he and the
men that are with him come out against you,
you may do to them as occasion offers."
And Abim′elech and all the men that were 34
with him rose up by night, and laid wait
against Shechem in four companies. And 35
Ga′al the son of Ebed went out and stood in
the entrance of the gate of the city; and
Abim′elech and the men that were with him
rose from the ambush. And when Ga′al saw 36
the men, he said to Zebul, "Look, men are
coming down from the mountain tops!"
And Zebul said to him, "You see the shadow
of the mountains as if they were men." Ga′al 37
spoke again and said, "Look, men are coming
down from the centre of the land, and one
company is coming from the direction of the
Diviners' Oak." Then Zebul said to him, 38
"Where is your mouth now, you who said,
'Who is Abim′elech, that we should serve
him?' Are not these the men whom you

despised? Go out now and fight with
39 them." And Ga'al went out at the head of
the men of Shechem, and fought with
40 Abim'elech. And Abim'elech chased him,
and he fled before him; and many fell
wounded, up to the entrance of the gate.
41 And Abim'elech dwelt at Aru'mah; and
Zebul drove out Ga'al and his kinsmen, so
that they could not live on at Shechem.
42 On the following day the men went out into
43 the fields. And Abim'elech was told. He
took his men and divided them into three
companies, and laid wait in the fields; and he
looked and saw the men coming out of the
city, and he rose against them and slew
44 them. Abim'elech and the company[o] that
was with him rushed forward and stood at
the entrance of the gate of the city, while the
two companies rushed upon all who were in
45 the fields and slew them. And Abim'elech
fought against the city all that day; he took
the city, and killed the people that were in it;
and he razed the city and sowed it with salt.
46 When all the people of the Tower of
Shechem heard of it, they entered the strong-
47 hold of the house of El-be'rith. Abim'elech
was told that all the people of the Tower of
48 Shechem were gathered together. And
Abim'elech went up to Mount Zalmon, he
and all the men that were with him; and
Abim'elech took an axe in his hand, and cut
down a bundle of brushwood, and took it up
and laid it on his shoulder. And he said to
the men that were with him, "What you have
seen me do, make haste to do, as I have
49 done." So every one of the people cut down
his bundle and following Abim'elech put it
against the stronghold, and they set the
stronghold on fire over them, so that all the
people of the Tower of Shechem also died,
about a thousand men and women.
50 Then Abim'elech went to Thebez, and
51 encamped against Thebez, and took it. But
there was a strong tower within the city, and
all the people of the city fled to it, all the men
and women, and shut themselves in; and
52 they went to the roof of the tower. And
Abim'elech came to the tower, and fought
against it, and drew near to the door of the
53 tower to burn it with fire. And a certain
woman threw an upper millstone upon
Abim'elech's head, and crushed his skull.
54 Then he called hastily to the young man his
armour-bearer, and said to him, "Draw your
sword and kill me, lest men say of me, 'A
woman killed him.' " And his young man
55 thrust him through, and he died. And when
the men of Israel saw that Abim'elech was
dead, they departed every man to his home.
56 Thus God requited the crime of Abim'elech,

which he committed against his father in
killing his seventy brothers; and God also 5
made all the wickedness of the men of
Shechem fall back upon their heads, and
upon them came the curse of Jotham the son
of Jerubba'al.

Minor judges

After Abim'elech there arose to deliver 1
Israel Tola the son of Pu'ah, son of Dodo, a
man of Is'sachar; and he lived at Shamir in
the hill country of E'phraim. And he judged 2
Israel twenty-three years. Then he died, and
was buried at Shamir.

After him arose Ja'ir the Gileadite, who 3
judged Israel twenty-two years. And he had 4
thirty sons who rode on thirty asses; and they
had thirty cities, called Hav'voth-ja'ir to this
day, which are in the land of Gilead. And 5
Ja'ir died, and was buried in Kamon.

Serving other gods

And the people of Israel again did what was 6
evil in the sight of the LORD, and served the
Ba'als and the Ash'taroth, the gods of Syria,
the gods of Sidon, the gods of Moab, the
gods of the Ammonites, and the gods of the
Philistines; and they forsook the LORD, and
did not serve him. And the anger of the 7

LORD was kindled against Israel, and he sold
them into the hand of the Philistines and
into the hand of the Ammonites, and they 8
crushed and oppressed the children of Israel
that year. For eighteen years they oppressed
all the people of Israel that were beyond the
Jordan in the land of the Amorites, which is
in Gilead. And the Ammonites crossed the 9
Jordan to fight also against Judah and against
Benjamin and against the house of E'phraim;
so that Israel was sorely distressed.

And the people of Israel cried to the LORD, 10
saying, "We have sinned against thee, because we have forsaken our God and have
served the Ba'als." And the LORD said to the 11
people of Israel, "Did I not deliver you from
the Egyptians and from the Amorites, from
the Ammonites and from the Philistines?

[o] Vg and some Mss of Gk: Heb *companies*

The Sido'nians also, and the Amal'ekites, and the Ma'onites, oppressed you; and you cried to me, and I delivered you out of their hand. Yet you have forsaken me and served other gods; therefore I will deliver you no more. Go and cry to the gods whom you have chosen; let them deliver you in the time of your distress." And the people of Israel said to the LORD, "We have sinned; do to us whatever seems good to thee; only deliver us, we pray thee, this day." So they put away the foreign gods from among them and served the LORD; and he became indignant over the misery of Israel.

The Ammonites

Then the Ammonites were called to arms, and they encamped in Gilead; and the people of Israel came together, and they encamped at Mizpah. And the people, the leaders of Gilead, said one to another, "Who is the man that will begin to fight against the Ammonites? He shall be head over all the inhabitants of Gilead."

JEPHTHAH

1 NOW Jephthah the Gileadite was a mighty warrior, but he was the son of a harlot. Gilead was the father of Jephthah. And Gilead's wife also bore him sons; and when his wife's sons grew up, they thrust Jephthah out, and said to him, "You shall not inherit in our father's house; for you are the son of another woman." Then Jephthah fled from his brothers, and dwelt in the land of Tob; and worthless fellows collected round Jephthah, and went raiding with him.

4 After a time the Ammonites made war 5 against Israel. And when the Ammonites made war against Israel, the elders of Gilead went to bring Jephthah from the land of 6 Tob; and they said to Jephthah, "Come and be our leader, that we may fight with the 7 Ammonites." But Jephthah said to the elders of Gilead, "Did you not hate me, and drive me out of my father's house? Why have you come to me now when you are in 8 trouble?" And the elders of Gilead said to Jephthah, "That is why we have turned to you now, that you may go with us and fight with the Ammonites, and be our head over 9 all the inhabitants of Gilead." Jephthah said to the elders of Gilead, "If you bring me home again to fight with the Ammonites, and the LORD gives them over to me, I will be 10 your head." And the elders of Gilead said to Jephthah, "The LORD will be witness between us; we will surely do as you say." 11 So Jephthah went with the elders of Gilead, and the people made him head and leader

over them; and Jephthah spoke all his words before the LORD at Mizpah.

Then Jephthah sent messengers to the king 12 of the Ammonites and said, "What have you against me, that you have come to me to fight against my land?" And the king of the 13 Ammonites answered the messengers of Jephthah, "Because Israel on coming from Egypt took away my land, from the Arnon to the Jabbok and to the Jordan; now therefore restore it peaceably." And Jephthah 14 sent messengers again to the king of the Ammonites and said to him, "Thus says 15 Jephthah: Israel did not take away the land of Moab or the land of the Ammonites, but 16 when they came up from Egypt, Israel went through the wilderness to the Red Sea and came to Kadesh. Israel then sent messengers 17 to the king of Edom, saying, 'Let us pass, we pray, through your land'; but the king of Edom would not listen. And they sent also to the king of Moab, but he would not consent. So Israel remained at Kadesh. Then they journeyed through the wilderness, 18 and went around the land of Edom and the land of Moab, and arrived on the east side of the land of Moab, and camped on the other side of the Arnon; but they did not enter the territory of Moab, for the Arnon was the boundary of Moab. Israel then sent messen- 19 gers to Sihon king of the Amorites, king of Heshbon; and Israel said to him, 'Let us pass, we pray, through your land to our country.' But Sihon did not trust Israel to 20 pass through his territory; so Sihon gathered all his people together, and encamped at Jahaz, and fought with Israel. And the 21 LORD, the God of Israel, gave Sihon and all his people into the hand of Israel, and they defeated them; so Israel took possession of all the land of the Amorites, who inhabited that country. And they took possession of all the 22 territory of the Amorites from the Arnon to the Jabbok and from the wilderness to the Jordan. So then the LORD, the God of Israel, 23 dispossessed the Amorites from before his people Israel; and are you to take possession of them? Will you not possess what 24 Chemosh your god gives you to possess? And all that the LORD our God has dispossessed before us, we will possess. Now 25 are you any better than Balak the son of Zippor, king of Moab? Did he ever strive against Israel, or did he ever go to war with them? While Israel dwelt in Heshbon and 26 its villages, and in Aro'er and its villages, and in all the cities that are on the banks of the Arnon, three hundred years, why did you not recover them within that time? I therefore 27 have not sinned against you, and you do me wrong by making war on me; the LORD, the Judge, decide this day between the people of

28 Israel and the people of Ammon." But the king of the Ammonites did not heed the message of Jephthah which he sent to him.

Jephthah's vow and victory

29 Then the Spirit of the LORD came upon Jephthah, and he passed through Gilead and Manas'seh, and passed on to Mizpah of Gilead, and from Mizpah of Gilead he 30 passed on to the Ammonites. And Jephthah made a vow to the LORD, and said, "If thou 31 wilt give the Ammonites into my hand, then whoever comes forth from the doors of my house to meet me, when I return victorious from the Ammonites, shall be the LORD's, and I will offer him up for a burnt offering." 32 So Jephthah crossed over to the Ammonites to fight against them; and the LORD gave 33 them into his hand. And he smote them from Aro'er to the neighbourhood of Minnith, twenty cities, and as far as Abel-keramim, with a very great slaughter. So the Ammonites were subdued before the people of Israel.

34 Then Jephthah came to his home at Mizpah; and behold, his daughter came out to meet him with timbrels and with dances; she was his only child; beside her he had 35 neither son nor daughter. And when he saw her, he rent his clothes, and said, "Alas, my daughter! you have brought me very low, and you have become the cause of great trouble to me; for I have opened my mouth to the LORD, and I cannot take back my 36 vow." And she said to him, "My father, if you have opened your mouth to the LORD, do to me according to what has gone forth from your mouth, now that the LORD has avenged you on your enemies, on the Ammonites." 37 And she said to her father, "Let this thing be done for me; let me alone two months, that I may go and wander *p* on the mountains, and bewail my virginity, I and my companions." 38 And he said, "Go." And he sent her away for two months; and she departed, she and her companions, and bewailed her virginity 39 upon the mountains. And at the end of two months, she returned to her father, who did with her according to his vow which he had made. She had never known a man. And it 40 became a custom in Israel that the daughters of Israel went year by year to lament the daughter of Jephthah the Gileadite four days in the year.

Shibboleth

12 The men of E'phraim were called to arms, and they crossed to Zaphon and said to

Jephthah, "Why did you cross over to fight against the Ammonites, and did not call us to go with you? We will burn your house over you with fire." And Jephthah said to them, "I and my people had a great feud with the Ammonites; and when I called you, you did not deliver me from their hand. And when I saw that you would not deliver me, I took my life in my hand, and crossed over against the Ammonites, and the LORD gave them into my hand; why then have you come up to me this day, to fight against me?" Then Jephthah gathered all the men of Gilead and fought with E'phraim; and the men of Gilead smote E'phraim, because they said, "You are fugitives of E'phraim, you Gileadites, in the midst of E'phraim and Manas'seh." And the Gileadites took the fords of the Jordan against the E'phraimites. And when any of the fugitives of E'phraim said, "Let me go over," the men of Gilead said to him, "Are you an E'phraimite?" When he said, "No," they said to him, "Then say Shibboleth," and he said, "Sibboleth," for he could not pronounce it right; then they seized him and slew him at the fords of the Jordan. And there fell at that time forty-two thousand of the E'phraimites

Jephthah judged Israel six years. Then Jephthah the Gileadite died, and was buried in his city in Gilead.*q*

Minor judges

After him Ibzan of Bethlehem judged Israel. He had thirty sons; and thirty daughters he gave in marriage outside his clan, and thirty daughters he brought in from outside for his sons. And he judged Israel seven years. Then Ibzan died, and was buried at Bethlehem.

After him Elon the Zeb'ulunite judged Israel; and he judged Israel ten years. Then Elon the Zeb'ulunite died, and was buried at Ai'jalon in the land of Zeb'ulun.

After him Abdon the son of Hillel the Pir'athonite judged Israel. He had forty sons and thirty grandsons, who rode on seventy asses; and he judged Israel eight years. Then Abdon the son of Hillel the Pir'athonite died, and was buried at Pir'athon in the land of E'phraim, in the hill country of the Amal'ekites.

SAMSON

AND the people of Israel again did what) was evil in the sight of the LORD; and the LORD gave them into the hand of the Philistines for forty years.

---

p Cn: Heb *go down*   *q* Gk: Heb *in the cities of Gilead*

2 And there was a certain man of Zorah, of the tribe of the Danites, whose name was Mano'ah; and his wife was barren and had 3 no children. And the angel of the LORD appeared to the woman and said to her, "Behold, you are barren and have no children; but you shall conceive and bear a son. 4 Therefore beware, and drink no wine or 5 strong drink, and eat nothing unclean, for lo, you shall conceive and bear a son. No razor shall come upon his head, for the boy shall be a Nazirite to God from birth; and he shall begin to deliver Israel from the hand of the 6 Philistines." Then the woman came and told her husband, "A man of God came to me, and his countenance was like the countenance of the angel of God, very terrible; I did not ask him whence he was, and he did 7 not tell me his name; but he said to me, 'Behold, you shall conceive and bear a son; so then drink no wine or strong drink, and eat nothing unclean, for the boy shall be a Nazirite to God from birth to the day of his death.' "

8 Then Mano'ah entreated the LORD, and said, "O, LORD, I pray thee, let the man of God whom thou didst send come again to us, and teach us what we are to do with the boy 9 that will be born." And God listened to the voice of Mano'ah, and the angel of God came again to the woman as she sat in the field; but 10 Mano'ah her husband was not with her. And the woman ran in haste and told her husband, "Behold, the man who came to me the 11 other day has appeared to me." And Mano'ah arose and went after his wife, and came to the man and said to him, "Are you the man who spoke to this woman?" And he 12 said, "I am." And Mano'ah said, "Now when your words come true, what is to be the boy's manner of life, and what is he to do?" 13 And the angel of the LORD said to Mano'ah, "Of all that I said to the woman let her 14 beware. She may not eat of anything that comes from the vine, neither let her drink wine or strong drink, or eat any unclean thing; all that I commanded her let her observe."

15 Mano'ah said to the angel of the LORD, "Pray, let us detain you, and prepare a kid 16 for you." And the angel of the LORD said to Mano'ah, "If you detain me, I will not eat of your food; but if you make ready a burnt offering, then offer it to the LORD." (For Mano'ah did not know that he was the angel 17 of the LORD.) And Mano'ah said to the angel of the LORD, "What is your name, so that, when your words come true, we may honour 18 you?" And the angel of the LORD said to

him, "Why do you ask my name, seeing it is wonderful?" So Mano'ah took the kid with 19 the cereal offering, and offered it upon the rock to the LORD, to him who works[r] wonders.[s] And when the flame went up toward 20 heaven from the altar, the angel of the LORD ascended in the flame of the altar while Mano'ah and his wife looked on; and they fell on their faces to the ground.

The angel of the LORD appeared no more to 21 Mano'ah and to his wife. Then Mano'ah knew that he was the angel of the LORD. And 22 Mano'ah said to his wife, "We shall surely die, for we have seen God." But his wife said 23 to him, "If the LORD had meant to kill us, he would not have accepted a burnt offering and a cereal offering at our hands, or shown us all these things, or now announced to us such things as these." And the woman bore a son, 24 and called his name Samson; and the boy grew, and the LORD blessed him. And the 25 Spirit of the LORD began to stir him in Ma'haneh-dan, between Zorah and Esh'ta-ol.

Among the Philistines

Samson went down to Timnah, and at 14 Timnah he saw one of the daughters of the Philistines. Then he came up, and told 2 his father and mother, "I saw one of the daughters of the Philistines at Timnah; now get her for me as my wife." But his father 3 and mother said to him, "Is there not a woman among the daughters of your kinsmen, or among all our people, that you must go to take a wife from the uncircumcised Philistines?" But Samson said to his father, "Get her for me; for she pleases me well." His father and mother did not know that it 4 was from the LORD; for he was seeking an occasion against the Philistines. At that time the Philistines had dominion over Israel.

Then Samson went down with his father 5 and mother to Timnah, and he came to the vineyards of Timnah. And behold, a young lion roared against him; and the Spirit of the 6 LORD came mightily upon him, and he tore the lion asunder as one tears a kid; and he had nothing in his hand. But he did not tell his father or his mother what he had done. Then he went down and talked with the 7 woman; and she pleased Samson well. And 8 after a while he returned to take her; and he turned aside to see the carcass of the lion, and behold, there was a swarm of bees in the body of the lion, and honey. He scraped it 9 out into his hands, and went on, eating as he went; and he came to his father and mother,

SAMSON'S
EXPLOITS   DAN
Valley of
Sorel Eshtaol
Zorah Lehi
Timnah
The
Great Ashkelon
Sea Gaza
PHILISTINES
The Great Sea

and gave some to them, and they ate. But he did not tell them that he had taken the honey from the carcass of the lion.

10 And his father went down to the woman, and Samson made a feast there; for so the 11 young men used to do. And when the people saw him, they brought thirty companions to 12 be with him. And Samson said to them, "Let me now put a riddle to you; if you can tell me what it is, within the seven days of the feast, and find it out, then I will give you thirty linen garments and thirty festal gar- 13 ments; but if you cannot tell me what it is, then you shall give me thirty linen garments and thirty festal garments." And they said to him, "Put your riddle, that we may hear it." 14 And he said to them,

"Out of the eater came something to eat.
Out of the strong came something sweet."

And they could not in three days tell what the riddle was.

15 On the fourth[t] day they said to Samson's wife, "Entice your husband to tell us what the riddle is, lest we burn you and your father's house with fire. Have you invited us 16 here to impoverish us?" And Samson's wife wept before him, and said, "You only hate me, you do not love me; you have put a riddle to my countrymen, and you have not told me what it is." And he said to her, "Behold, I have not told my father nor my 17 mother, and shall I tell you?" She wept before him the seven days that their feast lasted; and on the seventh day he told her, because she pressed him hard. Then she told 18 the riddle to her countrymen. And the men of the city said to him on the seventh day before the sun went down,

"What is sweeter than honey?
What is stronger than a lion?"

And he said to them,

"If you had not ploughed with my heifer, you would not have found out my riddle."

And the Spirit of the LORD came mightily upon him, and he went down to Ashʹkelon and killed thirty men of the town, and took their spoil and gave the festal garments to those who had told the riddle. In hot anger he went back to his father's house. And Samson's wife was given to his companion, who had been his best man.

After a while, at the time of wheat harvest, 1 Samson went to visit his wife with a kid; and he said, "I will go in to my wife in the chamber." But her father would not allow him to go in. And her father said, "I really 2 thought that you utterly hated her; so I gave her to your companion. Is not her younger sister fairer than she? Pray take her instead." And Samson said to them, "This 3 time I shall be blameless in regard to the Philistines, when I do them mischief." So 4 Samson went and caught three hundred foxes, and took torches; and he turned them tail to tail, and put a torch between each pair of tails. And when he had set fire to the 5 torches, he let the foxes go into the standing grain of the Philistines, and burned up the shocks and the standing grain, as well as the olive orchards. Then the Philistines said, 6 "Who has done this?" And they said, "Samson, the son-in-law of the Timnite, because he has taken his wife and given her to his companion." And the Philistines came up, and burned her and her father with fire. And Samson said to them, "If this is what 7 you do, I swear I will be avenged upon you, and after that I will quit." And he smote 8 them hip and thigh with great slaughter; and he went down and stayed in the cleft of the rock of Etam.

Then the Philistines came up and en- 9 camped in Judah, and made a raid on Lehi. And the men of Judah said, "Why have you 1 come up against us?" They said, "We have come up to bind Samson, to do to him as he did to us." Then three thousand men of 1 Judah went down to the cleft of the rock of Etam, and said to Samson, "Do you not know that the Philistines are rulers over us? What then is this that you have done to us?" And he said to them, "As they did to me, so have I done to them." And they said to him, 1 "We have come down to bind you, that we may give you into the hands of the Philistines." And Samson said to them, "Swear to me that you will not fall upon me yourselves." They said to him, "No; we will only 1 bind you and give you into their hands; we will not kill you." So they bound him with

[t] Gk Syr: Heb seventh

PHILISTINES

two new ropes, and brought him up from the rock.

4 When he came to Lehi, the Philistines came shouting to meet him; and the Spirit of the LORD came mightily upon him, and the ropes which were on his arms became as flax that has caught fire, and his bonds melted off his 5 hands. And he found a fresh jawbone of an ass, and put out his hand and seized it, and 5 with it he slew a thousand men. And Samson said,

"With the jawbone of an ass,
heaps upon heaps,
with the jawbone of an ass
have I slain a thousand men."

7 When he had finished speaking, he threw away the jawbone out of his hand; and that place was called Ra′math-le′hi. *u*
8 And he was very thirsty, and he called on the LORD and said, "Thou hast granted this great deliverance by the hand of thy servant; and shall I now die of thirst, and fall into the 9 hands of the uncircumcised?" And God split open the hollow place that is at Lehi, and there came water from it; and when he drank, his spirit returned, and he revived. Therefore the name of it was called En-hak′- 0 kore; *v* it is at Lehi to this day. And he judged Israel in the days of the Philistines twenty years.

16 Samson went to Gaza, and there he saw a 2 harlot, and he went in to her. The Gazites were told, "Samson has come here," and they surrounded the place and lay in wait for him all night at the gate of the city. They kept quiet all night, saying, "Let us wait till the light of the morning; then we will kill 3 him." But Samson lay till midnight, and at midnight he arose and took hold of the doors of the gate of the city and the two posts, and pulled them up, bar and all, and put them on his shoulders and carried them to the top of the hill that is before Hebron.

Delilah

4 After this he loved a woman in the valley of 5 Sorek, whose name was Deli′lah. And the lords of the Philistines came to her and said to her, "Entice him, and see wherein his

great strength lies, and by what means we may overpower him, that we may bind him to subdue him; and we will each give you eleven hundred pieces of silver." And 6 Deli′lah said to Samson, "Please tell me wherein your great strength lies, and how you might be bound, that one could subdue you." And Samson said to her, "If they bind 7 me with seven fresh bowstrings which have not been dried, then I shall become weak, and be like any other man." Then the lords 8 of the Philistines brought her seven fresh bowstrings which had not been dried, and she bound him with them. Now she had 9 men lying in wait in an inner chamber. And she said to him, "The Philistines are upon you, Samson!" But he snapped the bow-strings, as a string of tow snaps when it touches the fire. So the secret of his strength was not known.

And Deli′lah said to Samson, "Behold, you 10 have mocked me, and told me lies; please tell me how you might be bound." And he said 11 to her, "If they bind me with new ropes that have not been used, then I shall become weak, and be like any other man." So 12 Deli′lah took new ropes and bound him with them, and said to him, "The Philistines are upon you, Samson!" And the men lying in wait were in an inner chamber. But he snapped the ropes off his arms like a thread.

And Deli′lah said to Samson, "Until now 13 you have mocked me, and told me lies; tell me how you might be bound." And he said to her, "If you weave the seven locks of my head with the web and make it tight with the pin, then I shall become weak, and be like any other man." So while he slept, Deli′lah 14 took the seven locks of his head and wove them into the web. *w* And she made them tight with the pin, and said to him, "The Philistines are upon you, Samson!" But he awoke from his sleep, and pulled away the pin, the loom, and the web.

And she said to him, "How can you say, 'I 15 love you,' when your heart is not with me ? You have mocked me these three times, and you have not told me wherein your great strength lies." And when she pressed him 16 hard with her words day after day, and urged him, his soul was vexed to death. And he 17 told her all his mind, and said to her, "A razor has never come upon my head; for I have been a Nazirite to God from my mother's womb. If I be shaved, then my strength will leave me, and I shall become weak, and be like any other man."

When Deli′lah saw that he had told her all 18 his mind, she sent and called the lords of the

---

u That is *The hill of the jawbone*   *v* That is *The spring of him who called*
w Compare Gk: Heb lacks *and make it tight . . . into the web*

Philistines, saying, "Come up this once, for he has told me all his mind." Then the lords of the Philistines came up to her, and
19 brought the money in their hands. She made him sleep upon her knees; and she called a man, and had him shave off the seven locks of his head. Then she began to torment him,
20 and his strength left him. And she said, "The Philistines are upon you, Samson!" And he awoke from his sleep, and said, "I will go out as at other times, and shake myself free." And he did not know that the
21 LORD had left him. And the Philistines seized him and gouged out his eyes, and brought him down to Gaza, and bound him with bronze fetters; and he ground at the mill
22 in the prison. But the hair of his head began to grow again after it had been shaved.

23 Now the lords of the Philistines gathered to offer a great sacrifice to Dagon their god, and to rejoice; for they said, "Our god has given
24 Samson our enemy into our hand." And when the people saw him, they praised their god; for they said, "Our god has given our enemy into our hand, the ravager of our country, who has slain many of us." And
25 when their hearts were merry, they said, "Call Samson, that he may make sport for us." So they called Samson out of the prison, and he made sport before them. They made him stand between the pillars; and Samson said
26 to the lad who held him by the hand, "Let me feel the pillars on which the house rests, that I may lean against them." Now the
27 house was full of men and women; all the lords of the Philistines were there, and on the roof there were about three thousand men and women, who looked on while Samson made sport.

Then Samson called to the LORD and said,
28 "O Lord GOD, remember me, I pray thee, and strengthen me, I pray thee, only this once, O God, that I may be avenged upon the Philistines for one of my two eyes." And
29 Samson grasped the two middle pillars upon which the house rested, and he leaned his weight upon them, his right hand on the one and his left hand on the other. And Samson
30 said, "Let me die with the Philistines." Then he bowed with all his might; and the house fell upon the lords and upon all the people that were in it. So the dead whom he slew at his death were more than those whom he had slain during his life. Then his
31 brothers and all his family came down and took him and brought him up and buried him between Zorah and Esh'ta-ol in the tomb of Mano'ah his father. He had judged Israel twenty years.

THE DANITES

17 THERE was a man of the hill country of E'phraim, whose
2 name was Micah. And he said to his mother, "The eleven hundred pieces of silver which were taken from you, about which you uttered a curse, and also spoke it in my ears, behold, the silver is with me; I took it." And his mother said, "Blessed be my son
3 by the LORD." And he restored the eleven hundred pieces of silver to his mother; and his mother said, "I consecrate the silver to the LORD from my hand for my son, to make a graven image and a molten image; now therefore I will restore it to you."
4 So when he restored the money to his mother, his mother took two hundred pieces of silver, and gave it to the silversmith, who made it into a graven image and a molten image; and it was in the house of
5 Micah. And the man Micah had a shrine, and he made an ephod and teraphim, and installed one of his
6 sons, who became his priest. In those days there was no king in Israel; every man did what was right in his own eyes.
7 Now there was a young man of Bethlehem in Judah, of the family of Judah, who was a Levite; and
8 he sojourned there. And the man departed from the town of Bethlehem in Judah, to live where he could find a place; and as he journeyed, he came to the hill country of E'phraim to the house
9 of Micah. And Micah said to him, "From where do you come?" And he said to him, "I am a Levite of Bethlehem in Judah, and I am going to sojourn
10 where I may find a place." And Micah said to him, "Stay with me, and be to me a father and a priest, and I will give you ten pieces of silver a year, and a suit of
11 apparel, and your living." x And the Levite was content to dwell with the man; and the young man became to him like one of his
12 sons. And Micah installed the Levite, and the young man became his priest, and was in the
13 house of Micah. Then Micah said, "Now I know that the LORD will prosper me, because I have a Levite as priest."

In those days there was no king
18 in Israel. And in those days the tribe of the Danites was seeking for itself an inheritance to dwell in; for until then no inheritance among the tribes of Israel had fallen to them. So the Danites
2 sent five able men from the whole number of their tribe, from Zorah and from Esh'ta-ol, to spy out the land and to explore it; and they said to them, "Go and explore the land." And they came to the hill country of E'phraim, to the house of Micah, and lodged there. When they were by the house of
3 Micah, they recognized the voice of the young Levite; and they turned aside and said to him, "Who brought you here? What are you doing in this place? What is your business here?" And he
4 said to them, "Thus and thus has Micah dealt with me: he has hired me, and I have become his priest." And they said to him,
5

x Heb living, and the Levite went

"Inquire of God, we pray thee, that we may know whether the journey on which we are setting out will succeed." And the priest said to them, "Go in peace. The journey on which you go is under the eye of the LORD."

7 Then the five men departed, and came to La'ish, and saw the people who were there, how they dwelt in security, after the manner of the Sido'nians, quiet and unsuspecting, lacking[v] nothing that is in the earth, and possessing wealth, and how they were far from the Sido'nians and had no 8 dealings with any one. And when they came to their brethren at Zorah and Esh'ta-ol, their brethren said to them, "What do you 9 report?" They said, "Arise, and let us go up against them; for we have seen the land, and behold, it is very fertile. And will you do nothing? Do not be slow to go, and enter in and possess the land. 10 When you go, you will come to an unsuspecting people. The land is broad; yea, God has given it into your hands, a place where there is no lack of anything that is in the earth."

11 And six hundred men of the tribe of Dan, armed with weapons of war, set forth from Zorah and 12 Esh'ta-ol, and went up and encamped at Kir'iath-je'arim in Judah. On this account that place is called Ma'haneh-dan[z] to this 13 day; behold, it is west of Kir'iath-je'arim. And they passed on from there to the hill country of E'phraim, and came to the house of Micah.

14 Then the five men who had gone to spy out the country of La'ish said to their brethren, "Do you know that in these houses there are an ephod, teraphim, a graven 15 image, and a molten image? Now therefore consider what you will do." And they turned aside thither, and came to the house of the young Levite, at the home of Micah, and asked him of his 16 welfare. Now the six hundred men of the Danites, armed with their weapons of war, stood by the 17 entrance of the gate; and the five men who had gone to spy out the land went up, and entered and took the graven image, the ephod, the teraphim, and the molten image, while the priest stood by the entrance of the gate with the six hundred men armed with 18 weapons of war. And when these went into Micah's house and took the graven image, the ephod, the teraphim, and the molten image, the priest said to them, "What are 19 you doing?" And they said to him, "Keep quiet, put your hand upon your mouth, and come with us, and be to us a father and a priest. Is it better for you to be priest to the house of one man, or to be priest to a tribe and family in

20 Israel?" And the priest's heart was glad; he took the ephod, and the teraphim, and the graven image, and went in the midst of the people.
21 So they turned and departed, putting the little ones and the cattle and the goods in front of 22 them. When they were a good way from the home of Micah, the men who were in the houses near Micah's house were called out, and they overtook the Danites. 23 And they shouted to the Danites, who turned round and said to Micah, "What ails you that you come with such a company?" 24 And he said, "You take my gods which I made, and the priest, and go away, and what have I left?" How then do you ask me, 'What 25 ails you?'" And the Danites said to him, "Do not let your voice be heard among us, lest angry fellows fall upon you, and you lose your life with the lives of your house- 26 hold." Then the Danites went their way; and when Micah saw that they were too strong for him, he turned and went back to his home.
27 And taking what Micah had made, and the priest who belonged to him, the Danites came to La'ish, to a people quiet and unsuspecting, and smote them with the edge of the sword, and burned the city with fire. 28 And there was no deliverer because it was far from Sidon, and they had no dealings with any one. It was in the valley which belongs to Beth-re'hob. And they rebuilt the city, and dwelt in it. 29 And they named the city Dan, after the name of Dan their ancestor, who was born to Israel; but the name of the city was 30 La'ish at the first. And the Danites set up the graven image for themselves; and Jonathan the son of Gershom, son of Moses,[a] and his sons were priests to the 31 tribe of the Danites until the day of the captivity of the land. So they set up Micah's graven image which he made, as long as the house of God was at Shiloh.

THE BENJAMINITES

19 IN those days, when there was no king in Israel, a certain Levite was sojourning in the remote parts of the hill country of E'phraim, who took to himself a concubine from Bethlehem in 2 Judah. And his concubine became angry with[b] him, and she went away from him to her father's house at Bethlehem in Judah, and was there some four 3 months. Then her husband arose and went after her, to speak kindly to her and bring her back. He had with him his servant and a couple of asses. And he came[c] to

her father's house; and when the girl's father saw him, he came with joy to meet him. And his 4 father-in-law, the girl's father, made him stay, and he remained with him three days; so they ate and drank, and lodged there. And 5 on the fourth day they arose early in the morning, and he prepared to go; but the girl's father said to his son-in-law, "Strengthen your heart with a morsel of bread, and after that you may go." So the 6 two men sat and ate and drank together; and the girl's father said to the man, "Be pleased to spend the night, and let your heart be merry." And when the man rose 7 up to go, his father-in-law urged him, till he lodged there again. And on the fifth day he arose early 8 in the morning to depart; and the girl's father said, "Strengthen your heart, and tarry until the day declines." So they ate, both of them. And when the man and his 9 concubine and his servant rose up to depart, his father-in-law, the girl's father, said to him, "Behold, now the day has waned toward evening; pray tarry all night. Behold, the day draws to its close; lodge here and let your heart be merry; and tomorrow you shall arise early in the morning for your journey, and go home."
But the man would not spend 10 the night; he rose up and departed, and arrived opposite Jebus (that is, Jerusalem). He had with him a couple of saddled asses, and his concubine was with him. When they were near Jebus, 11 the day was far spent, and the servant said to his master, "Come now, let us turn aside to this city of the Jeb'usites, and spend the night in it." And his master said 12 to him, "We will not turn aside into the city of foreigners, who do not belong to the people of Israel; but we will pass on to Gib'e-ah." And he said to his servant, "Come 13 and let us draw near to one of these places, and spend the night at Gib'e-ah or at Ramah." So 14 they passed on and went their way; and the sun went down on them near Gib'e-ah, which belongs to Benjamin, and they 15 turned aside there, to go in and spend the night at Gib'e-ah. And he went in and sat down in the open square of the city; for no man took them into his house to spend the night.
And behold, an old man was 16 coming from his work in the field at evening; the man was from the hill country of E'phraim, and he was sojourning in Gib'e-ah; the men of the place were Benjaminites. And he lifted up his eyes, 17 and saw the wayfarer in the open square of the city; and the old man said, "Where are you going? and whence do you come?" And 18 he said to him, "We are passing

v Cn Compare 18.10. The Hebrew text is uncertain   z That is Camp of Dan
a Another reading is Manasseh   b Gk Old Latin: Heb played the harlot against   c Gk: Heb she brought him
18.7: Judg 18.27-28.

from Bethlehem in Judah to the remote parts of the hill country of E'phraim, from which I come. I went to Bethlehem in Judah; and I am going to my home;[d] and nobody takes me into his house."

19 We have straw and provender for our asses, with bread and wine for me and your maidservant and the young man with your servants; there is no lack of anything."

20 And the old man said, "Peace be to you; I will care for all your wants; only, do not spend the

21 night in the square." So he brought him into his house, and gave the asses provender; and they washed their feet, and ate and drank.

22 As they were making their hearts merry, behold, the men of the city, base fellows, beset the house round about, beating on the door; and they said to the old man, the master of the house, "Bring out the man who came into your house, that we may know him."

23 And the man, the master of the house, went out to them and said to them, "No, my brethren, do not act so wickedly; seeing that this man has come into my house,

24 do not do this vile thing. Behold, here are my virgin daughter and his concubine; let me bring them out now. Ravish them and do with them what seems good to you; but against this man do not

25 do so vile a thing." But the men would not listen to him. So the man seized his concubine, and put her out to them; and they knew her, and abused her all night until the morning. And as the dawn began to break, they let her go.

26 And as morning appeared, the woman came and fell down at the door of the man's house where her master was, till it was light.

27 And her master rose up in the morning, and when he opened the doors of the house and went out to go on his way, behold, there was his concubine lying at the door of the house, with her hands on the

28 threshold. He said to her, "Get up, let us be going." But there was no answer. Then he put her upon the ass; and the man rose up

29 and went away to his home. And when he entered his house, he took a knife, and laying hold of his concubine he divided her, limb by limb, into twelve pieces, and sent her throughout all the territory of

30 Israel. And all who saw it said, "Such a thing has never happened or been seen from the day that the people of Israel came up out of the land of Egypt until this day; consider it, take counsel, and speak."

20 Then all the people of Israel came out, from Dan to Beer-sheba, including the land of Gilead, and the congregation assembled as one

2 man to the LORD at Mizpah. And the chiefs of all the people, of all the tribes of Israel, presented

themselves in the assembly of the people of God, four hundred thousand men on foot that drew

3 the sword. (Now the Benjamin-ites heard that the people of Israel had gone up to Mizpah.) And the people of Israel said, "Tell us, how was this wickedness brought

4 to pass?" And the Levite, the husband of the woman who was murdered, answered and said "I came to Gib'e-ah that belongs to Benjamin, I and my concubine, to

5 spend the night. And the men of Gib'e-ah rose against me, and beset the house round about me by night; they meant to kill me, and they ravished my con-

6 cubine, and she is dead. And I took my concubine and cut her in pieces, and sent her throughout all the country of the inheritance of Israel; for they have committed abomination and wantonness in

7 Israel. Behold, you people of Israel, all of you, give your advice and counsel here."

8 And all the people arose as one man, saying, "We will not any of us go to his tent, and none of us

9 will return to his house. But now this is what we will do to Gib'e-ah: we will go up against it

10 by lot, and we will take ten men of a hundred throughout all the tribes of Israel, and a hundred of a thousand, and a thousand of ten thousand, to bring provisions for the people, that when they come they may requite Gib'e-ah of Ben-jamin, for all the wanton crime which they have committed in

11 Israel." So all the men of Israel gathered against the city, united as one man.

12 And the tribes of Israel sent men through all the tribe of Benjamin, saying, "What wickedness is this that has taken place among you?

13 Now therefore give up the men, the base fellows in Gib'e-ah, that we may put them to death, and put away evil from Israel." But the Benjaminites would not listen to the voice of their brethren, the

14 people of Israel. And the Benjam-inites came together out of the cities to Gib'e-ah, to go out to battle against the people of Israel.

15 And the Benjaminites mustered out of their cities on that day twenty-six thousand men that drew the sword, besides the inhabitants of Gib'e-ah, who mustered seven hundred picked

16 men. Among all these were seven hundred picked men who were left-handed; every one could sling a stone at a hair, and not miss.

17 And the men of Israel, apart from Benjamin, mustered four hundred thousand men that drew sword; all these were men of war.

18 The people of Israel arose and went up to Bethel, and inquired of God, "Which of us shall go up first to battle against the Benjam-inites?" And the LORD said, "Judah shall go up first."

19 Then the people of Israel rose

in the morning, and encamped against Gib'e-ah. And the men of

20 Israel went out to battle against Benjamin; and the men of Israel drew up the battle line against them at Gib'e-ah. The Benjamin-

21 ites came out of Gib'e-ah, and felled to the ground on that day twenty-two thousand men of the Israelites. But the people, the

22 men of Israel, took courage, and again formed the battle line in the same place where they had formed it on the first day. And

23 the people of Israel went up and wept before the LORD until the evening; and they inquired of the LORD, "Shall we again draw near to battle against our brethren the Benjaminites?" And the LORD said, "Go up against them."

24 So the people of Israel came near against the Benjaminites the

25 second day. And Benjamin went out against them out of Gib'e-ah the second day, and felled to the ground eighteen thousand men of the people of Israel; all these were men who drew the sword. Then

26 all the people of Israel, the whole army, went up and came to Bethel and wept; they sat there before the LORD, and fasted that day until evening, and offered burnt offerings and peace offerings before the LORD. And the people

27 of Israel inquired of the LORD (for the ark of the covenant of God was there in those days, and

28 Phin'ehas the son of Elea'zar, son of Aaron, ministered before it in those days), saying, "Shall we yet again go out to battle against our brethren the Benjaminites, or shall we cease?" And the LORD said, "Go up; for tomorrow I will give them into your hand."

29 So Israel set men in ambush

30 round about Gib'e-ah. And the people of Israel went up against the Benjaminites on the third day, and set themselves in array against Gib'e-ah, as at other

31 times. And the Benjaminites went out against the people, and were drawn away from the city; and as at other times they began to smite and kill some of the people, in the highways, one of which goes up to Bethel and the other to Gib'e-ah, and in the open country, about thirty men of

32 Israel. And the Benjaminites said, "They are routed before us, as at the first." But the men of Israel said, "Let us flee, and draw them away from the city to the

33 highways." And all the men of Israel rose up out of their place, and set themselves in array at Ba'al-ta'mar; and the men of Israel who were in ambush rushed out of their place west[e] of Geba.

34 And there came against Gib'e-ah ten thousand picked men out of all Israel, and the battle was hard; but the Benjaminites did not know that disaster was close upon them. And the LORD defeated

35 Benjamin before Israel; and the

---

d Gk Compare 19.29. Heb *to the house of the* LORD   *e* Gk Vg: Heb *in the plain* men of Israel destroyed twenty-five thousand one hundred men of Benjamin that day; all these were 6 men who drew the sword. So the Benjaminites saw that they were defeated.

7 The men of Israel gave ground to Benjamin, because they trusted to the men in ambush whom they had set against Gib′e-ah. And the men in ambush made haste and rushed upon Gib′e-ah; the men in ambush moved out and smote all 8 the city with the edge of the sword. Now the appointed signal between the men of Israel and the men in ambush was that when they made a great cloud of smoke 9 rise up out of the city the men of Israel should turn in battle. Now Benjamin had begun to smite and kill about thirty men of Israel; they said, "Surely they are smitten down before us, as in the 10 first battle." But when the signal began to rise out of the city in a column of smoke, the Benjamin-

ites looked behind them; and behold, the whole of the city went 41 up in smoke to heaven. Then the men of Israel turned, and the men of Benjamin were dismayed, for they saw that disaster was close 42 upon them. Therefore they turned their backs before the men of Israel in the direction of the wilderness; but the battle overtook them, and those who came out of the cities destroyed them in 43 the midst of them. Cutting down[f] the Benjaminites, they pursued them and trod them down from Nohah[g] as far as opposite 44 Gib′e-ah on the east. Eighteen thousand men of Benjamin fell, all 45 of them men of valour. And they turned and fled toward the wilderness to the rock of Rimmon; five thousand men of them were cut down in the highways, and they were pursued hard to Gidom, and two thousand men of 46 them were slain. So all who fell that day of Benjamin were

twenty-five thousand men that drew the sword, all of them men of valour. But six hundred men 47 turned and fled toward the wilderness to the rock of Rimmon, and abode at the rock of Rimmon four months. And the men of 48 Israel turned back against the Benjaminites, and smote them with the edge of the sword, men and beasts and all that they found. And all the towns which they found they set on fire.

Now the men of Israel had **21** sworn at Mizpah, "No one of us shall give his daughter in marriage to Benjamin." And the people 2 came to Bethel, and sat there till evening before God, and they lifted up their voices and wept bitterly. And they said, "O LORD, 3 the God of Israel, why has this come to pass in Israel, that there should be today one tribe lacking in Israel?" And on the morrow 4 the people rose early, and built

Bethlehem

there an altar, and offered burnt 12 offerings and peace offerings.

5 And the people of Israel said, "Which of all the tribes of Israel did not come up in the assembly to the LORD?" For they had taken a great oath concerning him who did not come up to the LORD to Mizpah, saying, "He shall be 6 put to death." And the people of Israel had compassion for Benjamin their brother, and said, "One tribe is cut off from Israel 7 this day. What shall we do for wives for those who are left, since we have sworn by the LORD that we will not give them any of our daughters for wives?"

8 And they said, "What one is there of the tribes of Israel that did not come up to the LORD to Mizpah?" And behold, no one had come to the camp from Ja'besh-gil'ead, to the assembly. 9 For when the people were mustered, behold, not one of the inhabitants of Ja'besh-gil'ead was 10 there. So the congregation sent thither twelve thousand of their bravest men, and commanded them, "Go and smite the inhabitants of Ja'besh-gil'ead with the edge of the sword; also the women 11 and the little ones. This is what you shall do; every male and every woman that has lain with a male

you shall utterly destroy." And they found among the inhabitants of Ja'besh-gil'ead four hundred young virgins who had not known man by lying with him; and they brought them to the camp at 13 Shiloh, which is in the land of Canaan.

Then the whole congregation sent word to the Benjaminites who were at the rock of Rimmon, and proclaimed peace to them. 14 And Benjamin returned at that time; and they gave them the women whom they had saved alive of the women of Ja'besh-gil'ead; but they did not suffice 15 for them. And the people had compassion on Benjamin because the LORD had made a breach in the tribes of Israel.

16 Then the elders of the congregation said, "What shall we do for wives for those who are left, since the women are destroyed out of 17 Benjamin?" And they said, "There must be an inheritance for the survivors of Benjamin, that a tribe be not blotted out from 18 Israel. Yet we cannot give them wives of our daughters." For the people of Israel had sworn, "Cursed be he who gives a wife 19 to Benjamin." So they said, "Behold, there is the yearly feast of the LORD at Shiloh, which is

north of Bethel, on the east of the highway that goes up from Bethel to Shechem, and south of Lebo'nah." And they com- 2 manded the Benjaminites, saying, "Go and lie in wait in the vineyards, and watch; if the daughters 2 of Shiloh come out to dance in the dances, then come out of the vineyards and seize each man his wife from the daughters of Shiloh, and go to the land of Benjamin. And when their fathers or their 2 brothers come to complain to us, we will say to them, 'Grant them graciously to us; because we did not take for each man of them his wife in battle, neither did you give them to them, else you would now be guilty.'" And the Benjamin- 2 ites did so, and took their wives, according to their number, from the dancers whom they carried off; then they went and returned to their inheritance, and rebuilt the towns, and dwelt in them. And the people of Israel departed 2 from there at that time, every man to his tribe and family, and they went out from there every man to his inheritance.

In those days there was no king 2 in Israel; every man did what was right in his own eyes.

THE BOOK OF
RUTH

IN the days when the judges ruled there was a famine in the land, and a certain man of Bethlehem in Judah went to sojourn in the country of Moab, he and his 2 wife and his two sons. The name of the man was Elim'elech and the name of his wife Na'omi, and the names of his two sons were Mahlon and Chil'ion; they were Eph'rathites from Bethlehem in Judah. They went into the country of Moab and remained there. 3 But Elim'elech, the husband of Na'omi, died, and she was left with her two sons. 4 These took Moabite wives; the name of one was Orpah and the name of the other Ruth. 5 They lived there about ten years; and both

Mahlon and Chil'ion died, so that the woman was bereft of her two sons and her husband.

Then she started with her daughters-in-law 6 to return from the country of Moab, for she had heard in the country of Moab that the LORD had visited his people and given them food. So she set out from the place where 7 she was, with her two daughters-in-law, and they went on the way to return to the land of Judah. But Na'omi said to her two daugh- 8 ters-in-law, "Go, return each of you to her mother's house. May the LORD deal kindly with you, as you have dealt with the dead and with me. The LORD grant that you may find 9 a home, each of you in the house of her husband!" Then she kissed them, and they lifted up their voices and wept. And they 10 said to her, "No, we will return with you to your people." But Na'omi said, "Turn back, 11 my daughters, why will you go with me? Have I yet sons in my womb that they may become your husbands? Turn back, my 12 daughters, go your way, for I am too old to have a husband. If I should say I have hope, even if I should have a husband this night and should bear sons, would you therefore 13

wait till they were grown? Would you therefore refrain from marrying? No, my daughters, for it is exceedingly bitter to me for your sake that the hand of the LORD has 4 gone forth against me." Then they lifted up their voices and wept again; and Orpah kissed her mother-in-law, but Ruth clung to her.
5 And she said, "See, your sister-in-law has gone back to her people and to her gods; 6 return after your sister-in-law." But Ruth said, "Entreat me not to leave you or to return from following you; for where you go I will go, and where you lodge I will lodge; your people shall be my people, and your 7 God my God; where you die I will die, and there will I be buried. May the LORD do so to me and more also if even death parts me 8 from you." And when Na′omi saw that she was determined to go with her, she said no more.
9 So the two of them went on until they came to Bethlehem. And when they came to Bethlehem, the whole town was stirred because of them; and the women said, "Is 10 this Na′omi?" She said to them, "Do not call me Na′omi,[a] call me Mara,[b] for the 11 Almighty has dealt very bitterly with me. I went away full, and the LORD has brought me back empty. Why call me Na′omi, when the LORD has afflicted[c] me and the Almighty has brought calamity upon me?"
12 So Na′omi returned, and Ruth the Moabitess her daughter-in-law with her, who returned from the country of Moab. And they came to Bethlehem at the beginning of barley harvest.

Ruth and Boaz

2 Now Na′omi had a kinsman of her husband's, a man of wealth, of the family of 2 Elim′elech, whose name was Bo′az. And Ruth the Moabitess said to Na′omi, "Let me go to the field, and glean among the ears of grain after him in whose sight I shall find favour." And she said to her, "Go, my 3 daughter." So she set forth and went and gleaned in the field after the reapers; and she happened to come to the part of the field belonging to Bo′az, who was of the family of 4 Elim′elech. And behold, Bo′az came from Bethlehem; and he said to the reapers, "The LORD be with you!" And they answered, 5 "The LORD bless you." Then Bo′az said to his servant who was in charge of the reapers, 6 "Whose maiden is this?" And the servant who was in charge of the reapers answered, "It is the Moabite maiden, who came back

with Na′omi from the country of Moab. She 7 said, 'Pray, let me glean and gather among the sheaves after the reapers.' So she came, and she has continued from early morning until now, without resting even for a moment."[d]
Then Bo′az said to Ruth, "Now, listen, my 8 daughter, do not go to glean in another field or leave this one, but keep close to my maidens. Let your eyes be upon the field 9 which they are reaping, and go after them. Have I not charged the young men not to molest you? And when you are thirsty, go to the vessels and drink what the young men have drawn." Then she fell on her face, 10 bowing to the ground, and said to him, "Why have I found favour in your eyes, that you should take notice of me, when I am a foreigner?" But Bo′az answered her, "All 11 that you have done for your mother-in-law since the death of your husband has been fully told me, and how you left your father and mother and your native land and came to a people that you did not know before. The 12 LORD recompense you for what you have done, and a full reward be given you by the LORD, the God of Israel, under whose wings you have come to take refuge!" Then she 13 said, "You are most gracious to me, my lord, for you have comforted me and spoken kindly to your maidservant, though I am not one of your maidservants."
And at mealtime Bo′az said to her, "Come 14 here, and eat some bread, and dip your morsel in the wine." So she sat beside the reapers, and he passed to her her parched grain; and she ate until she was satisfied, and she had some left over. When she rose to glean, 15 Bo′az instructed his young men, saying, "Let her glean even among the sheaves, and do not reproach her. And also pull out some from 16 the bundles for her, and leave it for her to glean, and do not rebuke her."
So she gleaned in the field until evening; 17 then she beat out what she had gleaned, and it was about an ephah of barley. And she 18 took it up and went into the city; she showed her mother-in-law what she had gleaned, and she also brought out and gave her what food she had left over after being satisfied. And 19 her mother-in-law said to her, "Where did you glean today? And where have you worked? Blessed be the man who took notice of you." So she told her mother-in-law with whom she had worked, and said, "The man's name with whom I worked today is Bo′az." And Na′omi said to her 20 daughter-in-law, "Blessed be he by the LORD, whose kindness has not forsaken the

---

[a] That is *Pleasant*   [b] That is *Bitter*   [c] Gk Syr Vg: Heb *testified against*
[d] Compare Gk Vg: the meaning of the Hebrew text is uncertain

living or the dead!" Na'omi also said to her, "The man is a relative of ours, one of our 21 nearest kin." And Ruth the Moabitess said, "Besides, he said to me, 'You shall keep close by my servants, till they have finished all my 22 harvest.'" And Na'omi said to Ruth, her daughter-in-law, "It is well, my daughter, that you go out with his maidens, lest in 23 another field you be molested." So she kept close to the maidens of Bo'az, gleaning until the end of the barley and wheat harvests; and she lived with her mother-in-law.

Naomi's advice

3 Then Na'omi her mother-in-law said to her, "My daughter, should I not seek a home 2 for you, that it may be well with you? Now is not Bo'az our kinsman, with whose maidens you were? See, he is winnowing 3 barley tonight at the threshing floor. Wash therefore and anoint yourself, and put on your best clothes and go down to the threshing floor; but do not make yourself known to the man until he has finished eating 4 and drinking. But when he lies down, observe the place where he lies; then, go and uncover his feet and lie down; and he will tell 5 you what to do." And she replied, "All that you say I will do."
6 So she went down to the threshing floor and did just as her mother-in-law had told her. 7 And when Bo'az had eaten and drunk, and his heart was merry, he went to lie down at the end of the heap of grain. Then she came softly, and uncovered his feet, and lay down. 8 At midnight the man was startled, and turned over, and behold, a woman lay at his 9 feet! He said, "Who are you?" And she answered, "I am Ruth, your maidservant; spread your skirt over your maidservant, for 10 you are next of kin." And he said, "May you be blessed by the LORD, my daughter; you have made this last kindness greater than the first, in that you have not gone after young 11 men, whether poor or rich. And now, my daughter, do not fear, I will do for you all that you ask, for all my fellow townsmen 12 know that you are a woman of worth. And now it is true that I am a near kinsman, yet 13 there is a kinsman nearer than I. Remain this night, and in the morning, if he will do the part of the next of kin for you, well; let him do it; but if he is not willing to do the part of the next of kin for you, then, as the LORD lives, I will do the part of the next of kin for you. Lie down until the morning." 14 So she lay at his feet until the morning, but arose before one could recognize another;

and he said, "Let it not be known that the woman came to the threshing floor." And he 15 said, "Bring the mantle you are wearing and hold it out." So she held it, and he measured out six measures of barley, and laid it upon her; then she went into the city. And when 16 she came to her mother-in-law, she said, "How did you fare, my daughter?" Then she told her all that the man had done for her, saying, "These six measures of barley he 17 gave to me, for he said, 'You must not go back empty-handed to your mother-in-law.'" She replied, "Wait, my daughter, 18 until you learn how the matter turns out, for the man will not rest, but will settle the matter today."

Ruth's marriage

And Bo'az went up to the gate and sat down 4 there; and behold, the next of kin, of whom Bo'az had spoken, came by. So Bo'az said, "Turn aside, friend; sit down here"; and he turned aside and sat down. And he took ten 2 men of the elders of the city, and said, "Sit down here"; so they sat down. Then he said 3 to the next of kin, "Na'omi, who has come back from the country of Moab, is selling the parcel of land which belonged to our kinsman Elim'elech. So I thought I would tell 4 you of it, and say, Buy it in the presence of those sitting here, and in the presence of the elders of my people. If you will redeem it, redeem it; but if you will not, tell me, that I may know, for there is no one besides you to redeem it, and I come after you." And he said, "I will redeem it." Then Bo'az said, 5 "The day you buy the field from the hand of Na'omi, you are also buying Ruth[e] the Moabitess, the widow of the dead, in order to restore the name of the dead to his inheritance." Then the next of kin said, "I cannot 6 redeem it for myself, lest I impair my own inheritance. Take my right of redemption yourself, for I cannot redeem it."
Now this was the custom in former times in 7 Israel concerning redeeming and exchanging: to confirm a transaction, the one drew off his sandal and gave it to the other, and this was the manner of attesting in Israel. So 8 when the next of kin said to Bo'az, "Buy it for yourself," he drew off his sandal. Then 9 Bo'az said to the elders and all the people, "You are witnesses this day that I have bought from the hand of Na'omi all that belonged to Elim'elech and all that belonged to Chil'ion and to Mahlon. Also Ruth the 10 Moabitess, the widow of Mahlon, I have bought to be my wife, to perpetuate the name

[e] Old Latin Vg: Heb of Naomi and from Ruth 4.7: Deut 25.8-10.

of the dead in his inheritance, that the name of the dead may not be cut off from among his brethren and from the gate of his native 1 place; you are witnesses this day." Then all the people who were at the gate, and the elders, said, "We are witnesses. May the LORD make the woman, who is coming into your house, like Rachel and Leah, who together built up the house of Israel. May you prosper in Eph'rathah and be renowned 2 in Bethlehem; and may your house be like the house of Perez, whom Tamar bore to Judah, because of the children that the LORD will give you by this young woman."

3 So Bo'az took Ruth and she became his wife; and he went in to her, and the LORD gave her conception, and she bore a son. 4 Then the women said to Na'omi, "Blessed be the LORD, who has not left you this day without next of kin; and may his name be renowned in Israel! He shall be to you a 15 restorer of life and a nourisher of your old age; for your daughter-in-law who loves you, who is more to you than seven sons, has borne him." Then Na'omi took the child 16 and laid him in her bosom, and became his nurse. And the women of the neighbour- 17 hood gave him a name, saying, "A son has been born to Na'omi." They named him Obed; he was the father of Jesse, the father of David.

Now these are the descendants of Perez: 18 Perez was the father of Hezron, Hezron of 19 Ram, Ram of Ammin'adab, Ammin'adab 20 of Nahshon, Nahshon of Salmon, Salmon of 21 Bo'az, Bo'az of Obed, Obed of Jesse, and 22 Jesse of David.

THE FIRST BOOK OF

SAMUEL

THERE was a certain man of Rama-
tha'im-zo'phim of the hill country
of E'phraim, whose name was Elka'-
nah the son of Jero'ham, son of Eli'hu,
son of Tohu, son of Zuph, an E'phraimite.
2 He had two wives; the name of the one
was Hannah, and the name of the other
Penin'nah. And Penin'nah had children, but
Hannah had no children.
3 Now this man used to go up year by year

from his city to worship and to sacrifice to
the LORD of hosts at Shiloh, where the two
sons of Eli, Hophni and Phin'ehas, were
priests of the LORD. On the day when 4
Elka'nah sacrificed, he would give portions
to Penin'nah his wife and to all her sons and
daughters; and, although[a] he loved Hannah, 5
he would give Hannah only one portion,
because the LORD had closed her womb.
And her rival used to provoke her sorely, to 6

[a] Gk: Heb obscure

irritate her, because the LORD had closed her
7 womb. So it went on year by year; as often
as she went up to the house of the LORD, she
used to provoke her. Therefore Hannah
8 wept and would not eat. And Elka′nah, her
husband, said to her, "Hannah, why do you
weep? And why do you not eat? And why
is your heart sad? Am I not more to you
than ten sons?"

Hannah's prayer

9 After they had eaten and drunk in Shiloh,
Hannah rose. Now Eli the priest was sitting
on the seat beside the doorpost of the temple
10 of the LORD. She was deeply distressed and
11 prayed to the LORD, and wept bitterly. And
she vowed a vow and said, "O LORD of hosts,
if thou wilt indeed look on the affliction of
thy maidservant, and remember me, and not
forget thy maidservant, but wilt give to thy
maidservant a son, then I will give him to the
LORD all the days of his life, and no razor
shall touch his head."
12 As she continued praying before the LORD,
13 Eli observed her mouth. Hannah was speaking in her heart; only her lips moved, and her
voice was not heard; therefore Eli took her to
14 be a drunken woman. And Eli said to her,
"How long will you be drunken? Put away
15 your wine from you." But Hannah
answered, "No, my lord, I am a woman
sorely troubled; I have drunk neither wine
nor strong drink, but I have been pouring
16 out my soul before the LORD. Do not regard
your maidservant as a base woman, for all
along I have been speaking out of my great
17 anxiety and vexation." Then Eli answered,
"Go in peace, and the God of Israel grant
your petition which you have made to him."
18 And she said, "Let your maidservant find
favour in your eyes." Then the woman went
her way and ate, and her countenance was no
longer sad.
19 They rose early in the morning and worshipped before the LORD; then they went
back to their house at Ramah. And Elka′nah
knew Hannah his wife, and the LORD re-
20 membered her; and in due time Hannah
conceived and bore a son, and she called his
name Samuel, for she said, "I have asked
him of the LORD."
21 And the man Elka′nah and all his house
went up to offer to the LORD the yearly
22 sacrifice, and to pay his vow. But Hannah
did not go up, for she said to her husband,
"As soon as the child is weaned, I will bring
him, that he may appear in the presence of
the LORD, and abide there for ever."

Elka′nah her husband said to her, "Do what 23
seems best to you, wait until you have
weaned him; only, may the LORD establish
his word." So the woman remained and
nursed her son, until she weaned him. And 24
when she had weaned him, she took him up
with her, along with a three-year-old bull,[b]
an ephah of flour, and a skin of wine; and she
brought him to the house of the LORD at
Shiloh; and the child was young. Then they 25
slew the bull, and they brought the child to
Eli. And she said, "Oh, my lord! As you 26
live, my lord, I am the woman who was
standing here in your presence, praying to
the LORD. For this child I prayed; and the 27
LORD has granted me my petition which I
made to him. Therefore I have lent him to 28
the LORD; as long as he lives, he is lent to the
LORD."
And they[c] worshipped the LORD there.

Hannah also prayed and said,   2
  "My heart exults in the LORD;
    my strength is exalted in the LORD.
My mouth derides my enemies,
  because I rejoice in thy salvation.

"There is none holy like the LORD,   2
  there is none besides thee;
  there is no rock like our God.
Talk no more so very proudly,   3
  let not arrogance come from your mouth;
for the LORD is a God of knowledge,
  and by him actions are weighed.
The bows of the mighty are broken,   4
  but the feeble gird on strength.
Those who were full have hired them-   5
    selves out for bread,
  but those who were hungry have ceased
    to hunger.
The barren has borne seven,
  but she who has many children is forlorn.
The LORD kills and brings to life;   6
  he brings down to Sheol and raises up.
The LORD makes poor and makes rich;   7
  he brings low, he also exalts.
He raises up the poor from the dust;   8
  he lifts the needy from the ash heap,

b Gk Syr: Heb three bulls   c Heb he
2.1–10: Lk 1.46–55.

to make them sit with princes and inherit
a seat of honour.
For the pillars of the earth are the LORD's,
and on them he has set the world.

9   "He will guard the feet of his faithful ones;
but the wicked shall be cut off in darkness;
for not by might shall a man prevail.
10   The adversaries of the LORD shall be
broken to pieces;
against them he will thunder in heaven.
The LORD will judge the ends of the earth;
he will give strength to his king,
and exalt the power of his anointed."
11   Then Elka′nah went home to Ramah. And
the boy ministered to the LORD, in the
presence of Eli the priest.

The sons of Eli

12   Now the sons of Eli were worthless men;
13   they had no regard for the LORD. The
custom of the priests with the people was
that when any man offered sacrifice, the
priest's servant would come, while the meat
was boiling, with a three-pronged fork in his
14   hand, and he would thrust it into the pan, or
kettle, or cauldron, or pot; all that the fork
brought up the priest would take for himself.[d] So they did at Shiloh to all the
15   Israelites who came there. Moreover, before
the fat was burned, the priest's servant would
come and say to the man who was sacrificing,
"Give meat for the priest to roast; for he will
not accept boiled meat from you, but raw."
16   And if the man said to him, "Let them burn
the fat first, and then take as much as you
wish," he would say, "No, you must give it
now; and if not, I will take it by force."
17   Thus the sin of the young men was very great
in the sight of the LORD; for the men treated
the offering of the LORD with contempt.

Samuel and Eli

18   Samuel was ministering before the LORD, a
19   boy girded with a linen ephod. And his
mother used to make for him a little robe and
take it to him each year, when she went up
with her husband to offer the yearly sacrifice.
20   Then Eli would bless Elka′nah and his wife,
and say, "The LORD give you children by
this woman for the loan which she lent to[e]
the LORD"; so then they would return to
their home.
21   And the LORD visited Hannah, and she
conceived and bore three sons and two
daughters. And the boy Samuel grew in the
presence of the LORD.

Now Eli was very old, and he heard all that
his sons were doing to all Israel, and how
they lay with the women who served at the
entrance to the tent of meeting. And he said
to them, "Why do you do such things? For
I hear of your evil dealings from all the
people. No, my sons; it is no good report
that I hear the people of the LORD spreading
abroad. If a man sins against a man, God
will mediate for him; but if a man sins
against the LORD, who can intercede for
him?" But they would not listen to the voice
of their father; for it was the will of the LORD
to slay them.

Now the boy Samuel continued to grow
both in stature and in favour with the LORD
and with men.

And there came a man of God to Eli, and
said to him, "Thus the LORD has said, 'I
revealed[f] myself to the house of your father
when they were in Egypt subject to the house
of Pharaoh. And I chose him out of all the
tribes of Israel to be my priest, to go up to
my altar, to burn incense, to wear an ephod
before me; and I gave to the house of your
father all my offerings by fire from the
people of Israel. Why then look with greedy
eye at[g] my sacrifices and my offerings which
I commanded, and honour your sons above
me by fattening yourselves upon the choicest
parts of every offering of my people Israel?'
Therefore the LORD the God of Israel declares: 'I promised that your house and the
house of your father should go in and out
before me for ever'; but now the LORD
declares: 'Far be it from me; for those who
honour me I will honour, and those who
despise me shall be lightly esteemed.
Behold, the days are coming, when I will cut
off your strength and the strength of your
father's house, so that there will not be an old
man in your house. Then in distress you will
look with envious eye on all the prosperity
which shall be bestowed upon Israel; and
there shall not be an old man in your house
for ever. The man of you whom I shall not
cut off from my altar shall be spared to weep
out his[h] eyes and grieve his[h] heart; and all
the increase of your house shall die by the
sword of men.[i] And this which shall befall
your two sons, Hophni and Phin′ehas, shall
be the sign to you: both of them shall die on
the same day. And I will raise up for myself
a faithful priest, who shall do according to
what is in my heart and in my mind; and I
will build him a sure house, and he shall go in
and out before my anointed for ever. And
every one who is left in your house shall
come to implore him for a piece of silver or a

---

[d] Gk Syr Vg: Heb *with it*   [e] Or *for the petition which she asked of*   [f] Gk Tg: Heb *Did I reveal*
[g] Or *treat with scorn* Gk: Heb *kick at*   [h] Gk: Heb *your*   [i] Gk: Heb *die as men*
2.26: Lk 2.52.

loaf of bread, and shall say, "Put me, I pray you, in one of the priest's places, that I may eat a morsel of bread." ' "

The call of Samuel

3 Now the boy Samuel was ministering to the LORD under Eli. And the word of the LORD was rare in those days; there was no frequent vision.

2 At that time Eli, whose eyesight had begun to grow dim, so that he could not see, was

3 lying down in his own place; the lamp of God had not yet gone out, and Samuel was lying down within the temple of the LORD, where

4 the ark of God was. Then the LORD called, "Samuel! Samuel!"[j] and he said, "Here I

5 am!" and ran to Eli, and said, "Here I am, for you called me." But he said, "I did not call; lie down again." So he went and lay

6 down. And the LORD called again, "Samuel!" And Samuel arose and went to Eli, and said, "Here I am, for you called me." But he said, "I did not call, my son; lie

7 down again." Now Samuel did not yet know the LORD, and the word of the LORD had not

8 yet been revealed to him. And the LORD called Samuel again the third time. And he arose and went to Eli, and said, "Here I am, for you called me." Then Eli perceived that

9 the LORD was calling the boy. Therefore Eli said to Samuel, "Go, lie down; and if he calls you, you shall say, 'Speak, LORD, for thy servant hears.'" So Samuel went and lay down in his place.

10 And the LORD came and stood forth, calling as at other times, "Samuel! Samuel!" And Samuel said, "Speak, for thy servant hears."

11 Then the LORD said to Samuel, "Behold, I am about to do a thing in Israel, at which the two ears of every one that hears it will tingle.

12 On that day I will fulfil against Eli all that I have spoken concerning his house, from

13 beginning to end. And I tell him that I am about to punish his house for ever, for the iniquity which he knew, because his sons were blaspheming God,[k] and he did not

14 restrain them. Therefore I swear to the house of Eli that the iniquity of Eli's house shall not be expiated by sacrifice or offering for ever."

15 Samuel lay until morning; then he opened the doors of the house of the LORD. And Samuel was afraid to tell the vision to Eli.

16 But Eli called Samuel and said, "Samuel, my

17 son." And he said, "Here I am." And Eli said, "What was it that he told you? Do not hide it from me. May God do so to you and more also, if you hide anything from me of all

18 that he told you." So Samuel told him

everything and hid nothing from him. And he said, "It is the LORD; let him do what seems good to him."

19 And Samuel grew, and the LORD was with him and let none of his words fall to the

20 ground. And all Israel from Dan to Beersheba knew that Samuel was established as

21 a prophet of the LORD. And the LORD appeared again at Shiloh, for the LORD revealed himself to Samuel at Shiloh by the word of the LORD.

SAMUEL and the ARK OF THE LORD

The Great Sea

Aphek
Eben-ezer •Shiloh
Ramathaim-zophim
•Ekron •Mizpah
•Ashdod Kiriath-jearim
Beth-shemesh
Gath
•Gaza
Salt Sea

4 And the word of Samuel came to all Israel. Now Israel went out to battle against the Philistines; they encamped at Ebene'zer, and

2 the Philistines encamped at Aphek. The Philistines drew up in line against Israel, and when the battle spread, Israel was defeated by the Philistines, who slew about four thousand men on the field of battle. And

3 when the troops came to the camp, the elders of Israel said, "Why has the LORD put us to rout today before the Philistines? Let us bring the ark of the covenant of the LORD here from Shiloh, that he may come among us and save us from the power of our

4 enemies." So the people sent to Shiloh, and brought from there the ark of the covenant of the LORD of hosts, who is enthroned on the cherubim; and the two sons of Eli, Hophni and Phin'ehas, were there with the ark of the covenant of God.

5 When the ark of the covenant of the LORD came into the camp, all Israel gave a mighty

6 shout, so that the earth resounded. And when the Philistines heard the noise of the shouting, they said, "What does this great shouting in the camp of the Hebrews mean?" And when they learned that the ark

7 of the LORD had come to the camp, the Philistines were afraid; for they said, "A god

---

j Gk See 3.10: Heb *the LORD called Samuel*   k Another reading is *for themselves*

PHILISTINES

has come into the camp." And they said, "Woe to us! For nothing like this has 8 happened before. Woe to us! Who can deliver us from the power of these mighty gods? These are the gods who smote the Egyptians with every sort of plague in the 9 wilderness. Take courage, and acquit yourselves like men, O Philistines, lest you become slaves to the Hebrews as they have been to you; acquit yourselves like men and fight."

10 So the Philistines fought, and Israel was defeated, and they fled, every man to his home; and there was a very great slaughter, for there fell of Israel thirty thousand foot 11 soldiers. And the ark of God was captured; and the two sons of Eli, Hophni and Phin'-ehas, were slain.

12 A man of Benjamin ran from the battle line, and came to Shiloh the same day, with his clothes rent and with earth upon his head. 13 When he arrived, Eli was sitting upon his seat by the road watching, for his heart trembled for the ark of God. And when the man came into the city and told the news, all 14 the city cried out. When Eli heard the sound of the outcry, he said, "What is this uproar?" Then the man hastened and came 15 and told Eli. Now Eli was ninety-eight years old and his eyes were set, so that he could not 16 see. And the man said to Eli, "I am he who has come from the battle; I fled from the battle today." And he said, "How did it go, 17 my son?" He who brought the tidings answered and said, "Israel has fled before the Philistines, and there has also been a great slaughter among the people; your two sons also, Hophni and Phin'ehas, are dead, and 18 the ark of God has been captured." When he mentioned the ark of God, Eli fell over backward from his seat by the side of the gate; and his neck was broken and he died, for he was an old man, and heavy. He had judged Israel forty years.

19 Now his daughter-in-law, the wife of Phin'ehas, was with child, about to give birth. And when she heard the tidings that the ark of God was captured, and that her father-in-law and her husband were dead, she bowed and gave birth; for her pains came 20 upon her. And about the time of her death the women attending her said to her, "Fear not, for you have borne a son." But she did 21 not answer or give heed. And she named the

child Ich'abod, saying, "The glory has departed from Israel!" because the ark of God had been captured and because of her father-in-law and her husband. And she 2 said, "The glory has departed from Israel, for the ark of God has been captured."

When the Philistines captured the ark of 5 God, they carried it from Ebene'zer to 2 Ashdod; then the Philistines took the ark of God and brought it into the house of Dagon and set it up beside Dagon. And when the 3 people of Ashdod rose early the next day, behold, Dagon had fallen face downward on the ground before the ark of the LORD. So they took Dagon and put him back in his place. But when they rose early on the next 4 morning, behold, Dagon had fallen face downward on the ground before the ark of the LORD, and the head of Dagon and both his hands were lying cut off upon the threshold; only the trunk of Dagon was left to him. This is why the priests of Dagon and 5 all who enter the house of Dagon do not tread on the threshold of Dagon in Ashdod to this day.

The hand of the LORD was heavy upon the 6 people of Ashdod, and he terrified and afflicted them with tumours, both Ashdod and its territory. And when the men of 7 Ashdod saw how things were, they said, "The ark of the God of Israel must not remain with us; for his hand is heavy upon us and upon Dagon our god." So they sent and 8 gathered together all the lords of the Philistines, and said, "What shall we do with the ark of the God of Israel?" They answered, "Let the ark of the God of Israel be brought around to Gath." So they brought the ark of the God of Israel there. But after they had 9 brought it around, the hand of the LORD was against the city, causing a very great panic, and he afflicted the men of the city, both young and old, so that tumours broke out upon them. So they sent the ark of God to 1 Ekron. But when the ark of God came to Ekron, the people of Ekron cried out, "They have brought around to us the ark of the God of Israel to slay us and our people." They 1 sent therefore and gathered together all the lords of the Philistines, and said, "Send away the ark of the God of Israel, and let it return to its own place, that it may not slay us and our people." For there was a deathly panic throughout the whole city. The hand of God 2 was very heavy there; the men who did not die were stricken with tumours, and the cry of the city went up to heaven.

6 The ark of the LORD was in the country of 2 the Philistines seven months. And the Philistines called for the priests and the diviners and said, "What shall we do with the ark of the LORD? Tell us with what we shall send it 3 to its place." They said, "If you send away the ark of the God of Israel, do not send it empty, but by all means return him a guilt offering. Then you will be healed, and it will be known to you why his hand does not turn 4 away from you." And they said, "What is the guilt offering that we shall return to him?" They answered, "Five golden tumours and five golden mice, according to the number of the lords of the Philistines; for the same plague was upon all of you and 5 upon your lords. So you must make images of your tumours and images of your mice that ravage the land, and give glory to the God of Israel; perhaps he will lighten his hand from off you and your gods and your 6 land. Why should you harden your hearts as the Egyptians and Pharaoh hardened their hearts? After he had made sport of them, did not they let the people go, and they 7 departed? Now then, take and prepare a new cart and two milch cows upon which there has never come a yoke, and yoke the cows to the cart, but take their calves home, 8 away from them. And take the ark of the LORD and place it on the cart, and put in a box at its side the figures of gold, which you are returning to him as a guilt offering. 9 Then send it off, and let it go its way. And watch; if it goes up on the way to its own land, to Beth-she′mesh, then it is he who has done us this great harm; but if not, then we shall know that it is not his hand that struck us, it happened to us by chance." 10 The men did so, and took two milch cows and yoked them to the cart, and shut up their 11 calves at home. And they put the ark of the LORD on the cart, and the box with the golden mice and the images of their 12 tumours. And the cows went straight in the direction of Beth-she′mesh along one

highway, lowing as they went; they turned neither to the right nor to the left, and the lords of the Philistines went after them as far as the border of Beth-she′mesh. Now the 13 people of Beth-she′mesh were reaping their wheat harvest in the valley; and when they lifted up their eyes and saw the ark, they rejoiced to see it. The cart came into the 14 field of Joshua of Beth-she′mesh, and stopped there. A great stone was there; and they split up the wood of the cart and offered the cows as a burnt offering to the LORD. And the Levites took down the ark of the 15 LORD and the box that was beside it, in which were the golden figures, and set them upon the great stone; and the men of Beth-she′mesh offered burnt offerings and sacrificed sacrifices on that day to the LORD. And 16 when the five lords of the Philistines saw it, they returned that day to Ekron.

These are the golden tumours, which the 17 Philistines returned as a guilt offering to the LORD: one for Ashdod, one for Gaza, one for Ash′kelon, one for Gath, one for Ekron; also 18 the golden mice, according to the number of all the cities of the Philistines belonging to the five lords, both fortified cities and unwalled villages. The great stone, beside which they set down the ark of the LORD, is a witness to this day in the field of Joshua of Beth-she′mesh.

And he slew some of the men of Beth- 19 she′mesh, because they looked into the ark of the LORD; he slew seventy men of them,ˣ and the people mourned because the LORD had made a great slaughter among the people. Then the men of Beth-she′mesh said, "Who 20 is able to stand before the LORD, this holy God? And to whom shall he go up away from us?" So they sent messengers to the 21 inhabitants of Kir′iath-je′arim, saying, "The Philistines have returned the ark of the LORD. Come down and take it up to you."

And the men of Kir′iath-je′arim came and **7** took up the ark of the LORD, and brought it to the house of Abin′adab on the hill; and

ˣ Cn: Heb *of the people seventy men, fifty thousand men*

they consecrated his son, Elea′zar, to have
2 charge of the ark of the LORD. From the day
that the ark was lodged at Kir′iath-je′arim, a
long time passed, some twenty years, and all
the house of Israel lamented after the
LORD.

Samuel rules Israel

3 Then Samuel said to all the house of Israel,
"If you are returning to the LORD with all
your heart, then put away the foreign gods
and the Ash′taroth from among you, and
direct your heart to the LORD, and serve him
only, and he will deliver you out of the hand
4 of the Philistines." So Israel put away the
Ba′als and the Ash′taroth, and they served
the LORD only.
5 Then Samuel said, "Gather all Israel at
Mizpah, and I will pray to the LORD for
6 you." So they gathered at Mizpah, and drew
water and poured it out before the LORD, and
fasted on that day, and said there, "We have
sinned against the LORD." And Samuel
7 judged the people of Israel at Mizpah. Now
when the Philistines heard that the people of
Israel had gathered at Mizpah, the lords of
the Philistines went up against Israel. And
when the people of Israel heard of it they
8 were afraid of the Philistines. And the
people of Israel said to Samuel, "Do not
cease to cry to the LORD our God for us, that
he may save us from the hand of the Philis-
9 tines." So Samuel took a sucking lamb and
offered it as a whole burnt offering to the
LORD; and Samuel cried to the LORD for
10 Israel, and the LORD answered him. As
Samuel was offering up the burnt offering,
the Philistines drew near to attack Israel; but
the LORD thundered with a mighty voice that
day against the Philistines and threw them
into confusion; and they were routed before
11 Israel. And the men of Israel went out of

Kiriath-jearim

Mizpah and pursued the Philistines, and
smote them, as far as below Beth-car.
Then Samuel took a stone and set it up 12
between Mizpah and Jesh′anah,[l] and called
its name Ebene′zer;[m] for he said, "Hitherto
the LORD has helped us." So the Philistines 1
were subdued and did not again enter the
territory of Israel. And the hand of the LORD
was against the Philistines all the days of
Samuel. The cities which the Philistines had 1
taken from Israel were restored to Israel,
from Ekron to Gath; and Israel rescued their
territory from the hand of the Philistines.
There was peace also between Israel and the
Amorites.
Samuel judged Israel all the days of his life. 1
And he went on a circuit year by year to 1
Bethel, Gilgal, and Mizpah; and he judged
Israel in all these places. Then he would 1
come back to Ramah, for his home was there,
and there also he administered justice to
Israel. And he built there an altar to the
LORD.

Demand for a king

When Samuel became old, he made his sons 8
judges over Israel. The name of his first- 2
born son was Jo′el, and the name of
his second, Abi′jah; they were judges in

---

[l] Gk Syr: Heb *Shen*   [m] That is *Stone of help*

3 Beer-sheba. Yet his sons did not walk in his ways, but turned aside after gain; they took bribes and perverted justice.

4 Then all the elders of Israel gathered 5 together and came to Samuel at Ramah, and said to him, "Behold, you are old and your sons do not walk in your ways; now appoint for us a king to govern us like all the 6 nations." But the thing displeased Samuel when they said, "Give us a king to govern 7 us." And Samuel prayed to the LORD. And the LORD said to Samuel, "Hearken to the voice of the people in all that they say to you; for they have not rejected you, but they have rejected me from being king over them. 8 According to all the deeds which they have done to me,^{n} from the day I brought them up out of Egypt even to this day, forsaking me and serving other gods, so they are also doing 9 to you. Now then, hearken to their voice; only, you shall solemnly warn them, and show them the ways of the king who shall reign over them."

10 So Samuel told all the words of the LORD to the people who were asking a king from him. 11 He said, "These will be the ways of the king who will reign over you: he will take your sons and appoint them to his chariots and to be his horsemen, and to run before his 12 chariots; and he will appoint for himself commanders of thousands and commanders of fifties, and some to plough his ground and to reap his harvest, and to make his implements of war and the equipment of his 13 chariots. He will take your daughters to be 14 perfumers and cooks and bakers. He will take the best of your fields and vineyards and olive orchards and give them to his servants. 15 He will take the tenth of your grain and of your vineyards and give it to his officers and 16 to his servants. He will take your menservants and maidservants, and the best of your cattle^o and your asses, and put them to 17 his work. He will take the tenth of your 18 flocks, and you shall be his slaves. And in that day you will cry out because of your king, whom you have chosen for yourselves; but the LORD will not answer you in that day."

19 But the people refused to listen to the voice of Samuel; and they said, "No! but we will 20 have a king over us, that we also may be like all the nations, and that our king may govern us and go out before us and fight our 21 battles." And when Samuel had heard all the words of the people, he repeated them in 22 the ears of the LORD. And the LORD said to Samuel, "Hearken to their voice, and make them a king." Samuel then said to the men of Israel, "Go every man to his city."

SAUL

THERE was a man of Benjamin whose 9 name was Kish, the son of Abi'el, son of Zeror, son of Beco'rath, son of Aphi'ah, a Benjaminite, a man of wealth; and he had a 2 son whose name was Saul, a handsome young man. There was not a man among the people of Israel more handsome than he; from his shoulders upward he was taller than any of the people.

Now the asses of Kish, Saul's father, were 3 lost. So Kish said to Saul his son, "Take one of the servants with you, and arise, go and look for the asses." And they^p passed 4 through the hill country of E'phraim and passed through the land of Shal'ishah, but they did not find them. And they passed through the land of Sha'alim, but they were not there. Then they passed through the land of Benjamin, but did not find them.

When they came to the land of Zuph, Saul 5 said to his servant who was with him, "Come, let us go back, lest my father cease to care about the asses and become anxious about us." But he said to him, "Behold, 6 there is a man of God in this city, and he is a man that is held in honour; all that he says comes true. Let us go there; perhaps he can tell us about the journey on which we have set out." Then Saul said to his servant, "But 7 if we go, what can we bring the man? For the bread in our sacks is gone, and there is no present to bring to the man of God. What have we?" The servant answered Saul 8 again, "Here, I have with me the fourth part of a shekel of silver, and I will give it to the man of God, to tell us our way." (Formerly 9 in Israel, when a man went to inquire of God, he said, "Come, let us go to the seer"; for he who is now called a prophet was formerly called a seer.) And Saul said to his 10 servant, "Well said; come, let us go." So they went to the city where the man of God was. As they went up the hill to the city, they 11 met young maidens coming out to draw water, and said to them, "Is the seer here?" They answered, "He is; behold, he is just 12 ahead of you. Make haste; he has come just now to the city, because the people have a sacrifice today on the high place. As soon as 13 you enter the city, you will find him, before he goes up to the high place to eat; for the people will not eat till he comes, since he must bless the sacrifice; afterward those eat who are invited. Now go up, for you will meet him immediately." So they went up to 14 the city. As they were entering the city, they saw Samuel coming out toward them on his way up to the high place.

^{n} Gk: Heb lacks *to me* ^{o} Gk: Heb *young men* ^{p} Gk Vg: Heb *he*

15 Now the day before Saul came, the LORD
16 had revealed to Samuel: "Tomorrow about
this time I will send to you a man from the
land of Benjamin, and you shall anoint him
to be prince over my people Israel. He shall
save my people from the hand of the Philistines; for I have seen the affliction of^q my
people, because their cry has come to me."
17 When Samuel saw Saul, the LORD told him,
"Here is the man of whom I spoke to you!
He it is who shall rule over my people."
18 Then Saul approached Samuel in the gate,
and said, "Tell me where is the house of the
19 seer?" Samuel answered Saul, "I am the
seer; go up before me to the high place, for
today you shall eat with me, and in the
morning I will let you go and will tell you all
20 that is on your mind. As for your asses that
were lost three days ago, do not set your
mind on them, for they have been found.
And for whom is all that is desirable in
Israel? Is it not for you and for all your
21 father's house?" Saul answered, "Am I not
a Benjaminite, from the least of the tribes of
Israel? And is not my family the humblest
of all the families of the tribe of Benjamin?
Why then have you spoken to me in this
way?"
22 Then Samuel took Saul and his servant and
brought them into the hall and gave them a
place at the head of those who had been
23 invited, who were about thirty persons. And
Samuel said to the cook, "Bring the portion I
gave you, of which I said to you, 'Put it
24 aside.'" So the cook took up the leg and the
upper portion^r and set them before Saul; and
Samuel said, "See, what was kept is set
before you. Eat; because it was kept for you
until the hour appointed, that you might eat
with the guests."^{s}
25 So Saul ate with Samuel that day. And
when they came down from the high place
into the city, a bed was spread for Saul^t upon
26 the roof, and he lay down to sleep. Then at
the break of dawn^u Samuel called to Saul
upon the roof, "Up, that I may send you on
your way." So Saul arose, and both he and
Samuel went out into the street.
27 As they were going down to the outskirts of
the city, Samuel said to Saul, "Tell the
servant to pass on before us, and when he has
passed on stop here yourself for a while, that
I may make known to you the word of God."

The anointed king

10 Then Samuel took a vial of oil and poured it
on his head, and kissed him and said, "Has

not the LORD anointed you to be prince over
his people Israel? And you shall reign over
the people of the LORD and you will save
them from the hand of their enemies round
about. And this shall be the sign to you that
the LORD has anointed you to be prince^w over
his heritage. When you depart from me 2
today you will meet two men by Rachel's
tomb in the territory of Benjamin at Zelzah,
and they will say to you, 'The asses which
you went to seek are found, and now your
father has ceased to care about the asses and
is anxious about you, saying, "What shall I
do about my son?"' Then you shall go on 3
from there further and come to the oak of
Tabor; three men going up to God at Bethel
will meet you there, one carrying three kids,
another carrying three loaves of bread, and
another carrying a skin of wine. And they 4
will greet you and give you two loaves of
bread, which you shall accept from their
hand. After that you shall come to Gib'- 5
eath-elohim,^{x} where there is a garrison of the
Philistines; and there, as you come to the
city, you will meet a band of prophets
coming down from the high place with harp,
tambourine, flute, and lyre before them,
prophesying. Then the spirit of the LORD 6
will come mightily upon you, and you shall
prophesy with them and be turned into
another man. Now when these signs meet 7
you, do whatever your hand finds to do, for
God is with you. And you shall go down 8
before me to Gilgal; and behold, I am
coming to you to offer burnt offerings and to
sacrifice peace offerings. Seven days you
shall wait, until I come to you and show you
what you shall do."
When he turned his back to leave Samuel, 9
God gave him another heart; and all these
signs came to pass that day. When they came 10
to Gib'e-ah,^{z} behold, a band of prophets met
him; and the spirit of God came mightily
upon him, and he prophesied among them.
And when all who knew him before saw how 11
he prophesied with the prophets, the people
said to one another, "What has come over the
son of Kish? Is Saul also among the prophets?" And a man of the place answered, 12
"And who is their father?" Therefore it
became a proverb, "Is Saul also among the
prophets?" When he had finished prophe- 13
sying, he came to the high place.
Saul's uncle said to him and to his servant, 14
"Where did you go?" And he said, "To seek
the asses; and when we saw they were not to
be found, we went to Samuel." And Saul's 15
uncle said, "Pray, tell me what Samuel said

16 to you." And Saul said to his uncle, "He told us plainly that the asses had been found." But about the matter of the kingdom, of which Samuel had spoken, he did not tell him anything.

17 Now Samuel called the people together to
18 the LORD at Mizpah; and he said to the people of Israel, "Thus says the LORD, the God of Israel, 'I brought up Israel out of Egypt, and I delivered you from the hand of the Egyptians and from the hand of all the
19 kingdoms that were oppressing you.' But you have this day rejected your God, who saves you from all your calamities and your distresses; and you have said, 'No! but set a king over us.' Now therefore present yourselves before the LORD by your tribes and by your thousands."
20 Then Samuel brought all the tribes of Israel

I Sam 10, 25

near, and the tribe of Benjamin was taken by
21 lot. He brought the tribe of Benjamin near by its families, and the family of the Matrites was taken by lot; finally he brought the family of the Matrites near man by man,[a] and Saul the son of Kish was taken by lot. But when they sought him, he could not be
22 found. So they inquired again of the LORD, "Did the man come hither?"[b] and the LORD said, "Behold, he has hidden himself among
23 the baggage." Then they ran and fetched him from there; and when he stood among the people, he was taller than any of the
24 people from his shoulders upward. And Samuel said to all the people, "Do you see him whom the LORD has chosen? There is none like him among all the people." And all the people shouted, "Long live the king!"
25 Then Samuel told the people the rights and duties of the kingship; and he wrote them in a book and laid it up before the LORD. Then Samuel sent all the people away, each one to

his home. Saul also went to his home at
26 Gib'e-ah, and with him went men of valour whose hearts God had touched. But some
27 worthless fellows said, "How can this man save us?" And they despised him, and brought him no present. But he held his peace.

Then Nahash the Ammonite went up and
11 besieged Ja'besh-gil'ead; and all the men of Jabesh said to Nahash, "Make a treaty with us, and we will serve you." But Nahash the
2 Ammonite said to them, "On this condition I will make a treaty with you, that I gouge out all your right eyes, and thus put disgrace upon all Israel." The elders of Jabesh said to
3 him, "Give us seven days respite that we may send messengers through all the territory of Israel. Then, if there is no one to save us, we will give ourselves up to you." When the
4 messengers came to Gib'e-ah of Saul, they reported the matter in the ears of the people; and all the people wept aloud.

Now Saul was coming from the field behind
5 the oxen; and Saul said, "What ails the people, that they are weeping?" So they told him the tidings of the men of Jabesh. And
6 the spirit of God came mightily upon Saul when he heard these words, and his anger was greatly kindled. He took a yoke of oxen,
7 and cut them in pieces and sent them throughout all the territory of Israel by the hand of messengers, saying, "Whoever does not come out after Saul and Samuel, so shall it be done to his oxen!" Then the dread of the LORD fell upon the people, and they came out as one man. When he mustered them at
8 Bezek, the men of Israel were three hundred thousand, and the men of Judah thirty thousand. And they said to the messengers
9 who had come, "Thus shall you say to the men of Ja'besh-gil'ead: 'Tomorrow, by the time the sun is hot, you shall have deliverance.'" When the messengers came and told the men of Jabesh, they were glad. There-
10 fore the men of Jabesh said, "Tomorrow we will give ourselves up to you, and you may do to us whatever seems good to you." And on
11 the morrow Saul put the people in three companies; and they came into the midst of the camp in the morning watch, and cut down the Ammonites until the heat of the day; and those who survived were scattered, so that no two of them were left together.

Then the people said to Samuel, "Who is it
12 that said, 'Shall Saul reign over us?' Bring the men, that we may put them to death."
13 But Saul said, "Not a man shall be put to death this day, for today the LORD has wrought deliverance in Israel." Then
14

---

[a] Gk: Heb lacks *finally . . . man by man* [b] Gk: Heb *Is there yet a man to come hither?*

Samuel said to the people, "Come, let us go
15 to Gilgal and there renew the kingdom." So
all the people went to Gilgal, and there they
made Saul king before the LORD in Gilgal.
There they sacrificed peace offerings before
the LORD, and there Saul and all the men of
Israel rejoiced greatly.

Samuel's farewell

12 And Samuel said to all Israel, "Behold, I
have hearkened to your voice in all that you
have said to me, and have made a king over
2 you. And now, behold, the king walks before
you; and I am old and grey, and behold, my
sons are with you; and I have walked before
3 you from my youth until this day. Here I
am; testify against me before the LORD and
before his anointed. Whose ox have I
taken? Or whose ass have I taken? Or
whom have I defrauded? Whom have I
oppressed? Or from whose hand have I
taken a bribe to blind my eyes with it?
Testify against me[c] and I will restore it to
4 you." They said, "You have not defrauded
us or oppressed us or taken anything from
5 any man's hand." And he said to them,
"The LORD is witness against you, and his
anointed is witness this day, that you have
not found anything in my hand." And they
said, "He is witness."
6 And Samuel said to the people, "The LORD
is witness,[d] who appointed Moses and Aaron
and brought your fathers up out of the land
7 of Egypt. Now therefore stand still, that I
may plead with you before the LORD concerning all the saving deeds of the LORD
which he performed for you and for your
8 fathers. When Jacob went into Egypt and
the Egyptians oppressed them,[e] then your
fathers cried to the LORD and the LORD sent
Moses and Aaron, who brought forth your
fathers out of Egypt, and made them dwell in
9 this place. But they forgot the LORD their
God; and he sold them into the hand of
Sis′era, commander of the army of Jabin king
of[f] Hazor, and into the hand of the Philistines, and into the hand of the king of Moab,
10 and they fought against them. And they
cried to the LORD, and said, 'We have sinned,
because we have forsaken the LORD, and have
served the Ba′als and the Ash′taroth; but
now deliver us out of the hand of our
11 enemies, and we will serve thee.' And the
LORD sent Jerubba′al and Barak,[g] and
Jephthah, and Samuel, and delivered you out
of the hand of your enemies on every side;
12 and you dwelt in safety. And when you saw
that Nahash the king of the Ammonites came

SAMUEL and SAUL

The Great Sea

Bezek• •Jabesh-gilead

•Ophrah
Bethel• •Beth-aven
Aijalon• •Mich-•Gilgal
Mizpah• mash•Ramah
Gibeah•

against you, you said to me, 'No, but a king
shall reign over us,' when the LORD your
God was your king. And now behold the 13
king whom you have chosen, for whom you
have asked; behold, the LORD has set a king
over you. If you will fear the LORD and serve 14
him and hearken to his voice and not rebel
against the commandment of the LORD, and
if both you and the king who reigns over you
will follow the LORD your God, it will be
well; but if you will not hearken to the voice 15
of the LORD, but rebel against the commandment of the LORD, then the hand of the
LORD will be against you and your king.[h]
Now therefore stand still and see this great 16
thing, which the LORD will do before your
eyes. Is it not wheat harvest today? I will 17
call upon the LORD, that he may send
thunder and rain; and you shall know and see
that your wickedness is great, which you
have done in the sight of the LORD, in asking
for yourselves a king." So Samuel called 18
upon the LORD, and the LORD sent thunder
and rain that day; and all the people greatly
feared the LORD and Samuel.
And all the people said to Samuel, "Pray for 19
your servants to the LORD your God, that we
may not die; for we have added to all our sins
this evil, to ask for ourselves a king." And 20
Samuel said to the people, "Fear not; you
have done all this evil, yet do not turn aside
from following the LORD, but serve the LORD
with all your heart; and do not turn aside 21
after[i] vain things which cannot profit or save,
for they are vain. For the LORD will not cast 22
away his people, for his great name's sake,
because it has pleased the LORD to make you
a people for himself. Moreover as for me, far 23
be it from me that I should sin against the
LORD by ceasing to pray for you; and I will

[c] Gk: Heb lacks *Testify against me*   [d] Gk: Heb lacks *is witness*
[e] Gk: Heb lacks *and the Egyptians oppressed them*   [f] Gk: Heb lacks *Jabin king of*   [g] Gk Syr: Heb *Bedan*
[h] Gk: Heb *fathers*   [i] Gk Syr Tg Vg: Heb *because after*

instruct you in the good and the right way.
4 Only fear the LORD, and serve him faithfully
with all your heart; for consider what great
5 things he has done for you. But if you still do
wickedly, you shall be swept away, both you
and your king."

Saul's disobedience

3 Saul was . . .ʲ years old when he began to
reign; and he reigned . . . and twoᵏ years over
Israel.
2 Saul chose three thousand men of Israel;
two thousand were with Saul in Michmash
and the hill country of Bethel, and a thous-
and were with Jonathan in Gib'e-ah of
Benjamin; the rest of the people he sent
3 home, every man to his tent. Jonathan
defeated the garrison of the Philistines which
was at Geba; and the Philistines heard of it.
And Saul blew the trumpet throughout all
the land, saying, "Let the Hebrews hear."
4 And all Israel heard it said that Saul had
defeated the garrison of the Philistines, and
also that Israel had become odious to the
Philistines. And the people were called out
to join Saul at Gilgal.
5 And the Philistines mustered to fight with
Israel, thirty thousand chariots, and six
thousand horsemen, and troops like the sand
on the seashore in multitude; they came up
and encamped in Michmash, to the east of
6 Beth-a'ven. When the men of Israel saw that
they were in straits (for the people were hard
pressed), the people hid themselves in caves
and in holes and in rocks and in tombs and in
7 cisterns, or crossed the fords of the Jordanˡ to
the land of Gad and Gilead. Saul was still at
Gilgal, and all the people followed him
trembling.
8 He waited seven days, the time appointed
by Samuel; but Samuel did not come to
Gilgal, and the people were scattering from
9 him. So Saul said, "Bring the burnt offering
here to me, and the peace offerings." And he
10 offered the burnt offering. As soon as he had
finished offering the burnt offering, behold,
Samuel came; and Saul went out to meet him
11 and salute him. Samuel said, "What have
you done?" And Saul said, "When I saw
that the people were scattering from me, and
that you did not come within the days
appointed, and that the Philistines had
12 mustered at Michmash, I said, 'Now the
Philistines will come down upon me at
Gilgal, and I have not entreated the favour of
the LORD'; so I forced myself, and offered
13 the burnt offering." And Samuel said to
Saul, "You have done foolishly; you have not

kept the commandment of the LORD your
God, which he commanded you; for now the
LORD would have established your kingdom
over Israel for ever. But now your kingdom 14
shall not continue; the LORD has sought out a
man after his own heart; and the LORD has
appointed him to be prince over his people,
because you have not kept what the LORD
commanded you." And Samuel arose, and 15
went up from Gilgal to Gib'e-ah of Benjamin.

And Saul numbered the people who were
present with him, about six hundred men.
And Saul, and Jonathan his son, and the 16
people who were present with them, stayed
in Geba of Benjamin; but the Philistines
encamped in Michmash. And raiders came 17
out of the camp of the Philistines in three
companies; one company turned toward
Ophrah, to the land of Shu'al, another 18
company turned toward Beth-horon, and
another company turned toward the border
that looks down upon the valley of Zebo'im
toward the wilderness.
Now there was no smith to be found 19
throughout all the land of Israel; for the
Philistines said, "Lest the Hebrews make
themselves swords or spears"; but every one 20
of the Israelites went down to the Philistines
to sharpen his ploughshare, his mattock, his
axe, or his sickle;ᵐ and the charge was a pim 21
for the ploughshares and for the mattocks,
and a third of a shekel for sharpening the
axes and for setting the goads.ⁿ So on the 22
day of the battle there was neither sword nor
spear found in the hand of any of the people
with Saul and Jonathan; but Saul and
Jonathan his son had them. And the garrison 23
of the Philistines went out to the pass of
Michmash.

Jonathan's exploit

One day Jonathan the son of Saul said to the 14
young man who bore his armour, "Come, let
us go over to the Philistine garrison on
yonder side." But he did not tell his father.
Saul was staying in the outskirts of Gib'e-ah 2

ʲ The number is lacking in Heb   ᵏ Two is not the entire number. Something has dropped out.
ˡ Cn: Heb Hebrews crossed the Jordan   ᵐ Gk: Heb ploughshare   ⁿ The Heb of this verse is obscure
13.14: Acts 13.22.

Mattock   *I Sam* 13, 20

under the pomegranate tree which is at Migron; the people who were with him were

3 about six hundred men, and Ahi′jah the son of Ahi′tub, Ich′abod's brother, son of Phin′ehas, son of Eli, the priest of the LORD in Shiloh, wearing an ephod. And the people

4 did not know that Jonathan had gone. In the pass,° by which Jonathan sought to go over to the Philistine garrison, there was a rocky crag on the one side and a rocky crag on the other side; the name of the one was Bozez, and the

5 name of the other Seneh. The one crag rose on the north in front of Michmash, and the other on the south in front of Geba.

6 And Jonathan said to the young man who bore his armour, "Come, let us go over to the garrison of these uncircumcised; it may be that the LORD will work for us; for nothing can hinder the LORD from saving by many or

7 by few." And his armour-bearer said to him, "Do all that your mind inclines to;ᵖ behold, I am with you, as is your mind so is mine."�q

8 Then said Jonathan, "Behold, we will cross over to the men, and we will show ourselves

9 to them. If they say to us, 'Wait until we come to you,' then we will stand still in our

10 place, and we will not go up to them. But if they say, 'Come up to us,' then we will go up; for the LORD has given them into our hand.

11 And this shall be the sign to us." So both of them showed themselves to the garrison of the Philistines; and the Philistines said, "Look, Hebrews are coming out of the holes

12 where they have hid themselves." And the men of the garrison hailed Jonathan and his armour-bearer, and said, "Come up to us, and we will show you a thing." And Jonathan said to his armour-bearer, "Come up after me; for the LORD has given them into

13 the hand of Israel." Then Jonathan climbed up on his hands and feet, and his armour-bearer after him. And they fell before Jonathan, and his armour-bearer killed them

14 after him; and that first slaughter, which Jonathan and his armour-bearer made, was of about twenty men within as it were half a

15 furrow's length in an acreʳ of land. And there was a panic in the camp, in the field, and among all the people; the garrison and

even the raiders trembled; the earth quaked; and it became a very great panic.

And the watchmen of Saul in Gib′e-ah of Benjamin looked; and behold, the multitude was surging hither and thither.ˢ Then Saul said to the people who were with him, "Number and see who has gone from us." And when they had numbered, behold, Jonathan and his armour-bearer were not there. And Saul said to Ahi′jah, "Bring hither the ark of God." For the ark of God went at that time with the people of Israel. And while Saul was talking to the priest, the tumult in the camp of the Philistines increased more and more; and Saul said to the priest, "Withdraw your hand." Then Saul and all the people who were with him rallied and went into the battle; and behold, every man's sword was against his fellow, and there was very great confusion. Now the Hebrews who had been with the Philistines before that time and who had gone up with them into the camp, even they also turned to be withᵗ the Israelites who were with Saul and Jonathan. Likewise, when all the men of Israel who had hid themselves in the hill country of E′phraim heard that the Philistines were fleeing, they too followed hard after them in the battle. So the LORD delivered Israel that day; and the battle passed beyond Beth-a′ven.

And the men of Israel were distressed that day; for Saul laid an oath on the people, saying, "Cursed be the man who eats food until it is evening and I am avenged on my enemies." So none of the people tasted food. And all the peopleᵘ came into the forest; and there was honey on the ground. And when the people entered the forest, behold, the honey was dropping, but no man put his hand to his mouth; for the people feared the oath. But Jonathan had not heard his father charge the people with the oath; so he put forth the tip of the staff that was in his hand, and dipped it in the honeycomb, and put his hand to his mouth; and his eyes became bright. Then one of the people said, "Your father strictly charged the people with an oath, saying, 'Cursed be the man who eats food this day.'" And the people were faint. Then Jonathan said, "My father has troubled the land; see how my eyes have become bright, because I tasted a little of this honey. How much better if the people had eaten freely today of the spoil of their enemies which they found; for now the slaughter among the Philistines has not been great."

They struck down the Philistines that day

° Heb *between the passes* ᵖ Gk: Heb *Do all that is in your mind. Turn* q Gk: Heb lacks *so is mine*
ʳ Heb *yoke* ˢ Gk: Heb *they went and thither* ᵗ Gk Syr Vg Tg: Heb *round about, they also, to be with*
ᵘ Heb *land*

from Michmash to Ai'jalon. And the people
2 were very faint; the people flew upon the
spoil, and took sheep and oxen and calves,
and slew them on the ground; and the people
3 ate them with the blood. Then they told
Saul, "Behold, the people are sinning against
the LORD, by eating with the blood." And he
said, "You have dealt treacherously; roll a
4 great stone to me here."ᵛ And Saul said,
"Disperse yourselves among the people, and
say to them, 'Let every man bring his ox or
his sheep, and slay them here, and eat; and
do not sin against the LORD by eating with
the blood.'" So every one of the people
5 brought his ox with him that night, and slew
them there. And Saul built an altar to the
LORD; it was the first altar that he built to the
LORD.
6 Then Saul said, "Let us go down after the
Philistines by night and despoil them until
the morning light; let us not leave a man of
them." And they said, "Do whatever seems
good to you." But the priest said, "Let
7 us draw near hither to God." And Saul
inquired of God, "Shall I go down after the
Philistines? Wilt thou give them into the
hand of Israel?" But he did not answer him
8 that day. And Saul said, "Come hither, all
you leaders of the people; and know and see
9 how this sin has arisen today. For as the
LORD lives who saves Israel, though it be in
Jonathan my son, he shall surely die." But
there was not a man among all the people
10 that answered him. Then he said to all
Israel, "You shall be on one side, and I and
Jonathan my son will be on the other side."
And the people said to Saul, "Do what seems
11 good to you." Therefore Saul said, "O LORD
God of Israel, why hast thou not answered
thy servant this day? If this guilt is in me or
in Jonathan my son, O LORD, God of Israel,
give Urim; but if this guilt is in thy people
Israel,ʷ give Thummim." And Jonathan
and Saul were taken, but the people escaped.
12 Then Saul said, "Cast the lot between me
and my son Jonathan." And Jonathan was
taken.
13 Then Saul said to Jonathan, "Tell me what
you have done." And Jonathan told him, "I
tasted a little honey with the tip of the staff
that was in my hand; here I am, I will die."
44 And Saul said, "God do so to me and more
45 also; you shall surely die, Jonathan." Then
the people said to Saul, "Shall Jonathan die,

who has wrought this great victory in
Israel? Far from it! As the LORD lives,
there shall not one hair of his head fall to the
ground; for he has wrought with God this
day." So the people ransomed Jonathan,
that he did not die. Then Saul went up from 46
pursuing the Philistines; and the Philistines
went to their own place.
When Saul had taken the kingship over 47
Israel, he fought against all his enemies on
every side, against Moab, against the
Ammonites, against Edom, against the kings
of Zobah, and against the Philistines;
wherever he turned he put them to the
worse. And he did valiantly, and smote the 48
Amal'ekites, and delivered Israel out of
the hands of those who plundered them.
Now the sons of Saul were Jonathan, Ishvi, 49
and Mal'chishu'a; and the names of his two
daughters were these: the name of the
first-born was Merab, and the name of the
younger Michal; and the name of Saul's wife 50
was Ahin'o-am the daughter of Ahim'a-az.
And the name of the commander of his army
was Abner the son of Ner, Saul's uncle; Kish 51
was the father of Saul, and Ner the father of
Abner was the son of Abi'el.
There was hard fighting against the Philis- 52
tines all the days of Saul; and when Saul saw
any strong man, or any valiant man, he
attached him to himself.

The Amalekites

And Samuel said to Saul, "The LORD sent 15
me to anoint you king over his people Israel;
now therefore hearken to the words of the
LORD. Thus says the LORD of hosts, 'I 2
will punish what Am'alek did to Israel in
opposing them on the way, when they came
up out of Egypt. Now go and smite Am'alek, 3
and utterly destroy all that they have; do not
spare them, but kill both man and woman,
infant and suckling, ox and sheep, camel and
ass.'"
So Saul summoned the people, and 4
numbered them in Tela'im, two hundred
thousand men on foot, and ten thousand men
of Judah. And Saul came to the city of 5
Am'alek, and lay in wait in the valley. And 6
Saul said to the Ken'ites, "Go, depart, go
down from among the Amal'ekites, lest I
destroy you with them; for you showed
kindness to all the people of Israel when they
came up out of Egypt." So the Ken'ites
departed from among the Amal'ekites. And 7
Saul defeated the Amal'ekites, from Hav'ilah
as far as Shur, which is east of Egypt. And 8
he took Agag the king of the Amal'ekites

ᵛ Gk: Heb *this day*   ʷ Vg Compare Gk: Heb *Saul said to the* LORD, *the God of Israel*
14.49: 1 Sam 31.2; 1 Chron 10.2.

alive, and utterly destroyed all the people 9 with the edge of the sword. But Saul and the people spared Agag, and the best of the sheep and of the oxen and of the fatlings, and the lambs, and all that was good, and would not utterly destroy them; all that was despised and worthless they utterly destroyed.

10, The word of the LORD came to Samuel: "I 11 repent that I have made Saul king; for he has turned back from following me, and has not performed my commandments." And Samuel was angry; and he cried to the LORD 12 all night. And Samuel rose early to meet Saul in the morning; and it was told Samuel, "Saul came to Carmel, and behold, he set up a monument for himself and turned, and 13 passed on, and went down to Gilgal." And Samuel came to Saul, and Saul said to him, "Blessed be you to the LORD; I have performed the commandment of the LORD."

14 And Samuel said, "What then is this bleating of the sheep in my ears, and the lowing of the 15 oxen which I hear?" Saul said, "They have brought them from the Amal′ekites; for the people spared the best of the sheep and of the oxen, to sacrifice to the LORD your God; and 16 the rest we have utterly destroyed." Then Samuel said to Saul, "Stop! I will tell you what the LORD said to me this night." And he said to him, "Say on."

17 And Samuel said, "Though you are little in your own eyes, are you not the head of the tribes of Israel? The LORD anointed you 18 king over Israel. And the LORD sent you on a mission, and said, 'Go, utterly destroy the sinners, the Amal′ekites, and fight against 19 them until they are consumed.' Why then did you not obey the voice of the LORD? Why did you swoop on the spoil, and do what was evil in the sight of the LORD?" 20 And Saul said to Samuel, "I have obeyed the voice of the LORD, I have gone on the mission on which the LORD sent me, I have brought Agag the king of Am′alek, and I have utterly 21 destroyed the Amal′ekites. But the people took of the spoil, sheep and oxen, the best of the things devoted to destruction, to sacrifice 22 to the LORD your God in Gilgal." And Samuel said,

"Has the LORD as great delight in burnt
    offerings and sacrifices,
as in obeying the voice of the LORD?
Behold, to obey is better than sacrifice,
    and to hearken than the fat of rams.
23 For rebellion is as the sin of divination,
    and stubbornness is as iniquity and
       idolatry.
Because you have rejected the word of the
    LORD,
he has also rejected you from being king."

And Saul said to Samuel, "I have sinned; 24 for I have transgressed the commandment of the LORD and your words, because I feared the people and obeyed their voice. Now 25 therefore, I pray, pardon my sin, and return with me, that I may worship the LORD." And Samuel said to Saul, "I will not return 26 with you; for you have rejected the word of the LORD, and the LORD has rejected you from being king over Israel." As Samuel 27 turned to go away, Saul laid hold upon the skirt of his robe, and it tore. And Samuel 28 said to him, "The LORD has torn the kingdom of Israel from you this day, and has given it to a neighbour of yours, who is better than you. And also the Glory of Israel will 29 not lie or repent; for he is not a man, that he should repent." Then he said, "I have 30 sinned; yet honour me now before the elders of my people and before Israel, and return with me, that I may worship the LORD your God." So Samuel turned back after Saul; 31 and Saul worshipped the LORD.

Then Samuel said, "Bring here to me Agag 32 the king of the Amal′ekites." And Agag came to him cheerfully. Agag said, "Surely the bitterness of death is past." And Samuel 33 said, "As your sword has made women childless, so shall your mother be childless among women." And Samuel hewed Agag in pieces before the LORD in Gilgal.

Then Samuel went to Ramah; and Saul 34 went up to his house in Gib′e-ah of Saul. And Samuel did not see Saul again until the 35 day of his death, but Samuel grieved over Saul. And the LORD repented that he had made Saul king over Israel.

DAVID

THE LORD said to Samuel, "How long will 1 you grieve over Saul, seeing I have rejected him from being king over Israel? Fill your horn with oil, and go; I will send you to Jesse the Bethlehemite, for I have provided for myself a king among his sons." And Samuel said, "How can I go? If Saul 2 hears it, he will kill me." And the LORD said, "Take a heifer with you, and say, 'I have come to sacrifice to the LORD.' And invite 3 Jesse to the sacrifice, and I will show you what you shall do; and you shall anoint for me him whom I name to you." Samuel did 4 what the LORD commanded, and came to Bethlehem. The elders of the city came to meet him trembling, and said, "Do you come peaceably?" And he said, "Peaceably; I 5 have come to sacrifice to the LORD; consecrate yourselves, and come with me to the sacrifice." And he consecrated Jesse and his sons, and invited them to the sacrifice.

When they came, he looked on Eli'ab and thought, "Surely the LORD'S anointed is before him." But the LORD said to Samuel, "Do not look on his appearance or on the height of his stature, because I have rejected him; for the LORD sees not as man sees; man looks on the outward appearance, but the LORD looks on the heart." Then Jesse called Abin'adab, and made him pass before

DAVID'S
EARLY
DAYS

The
Great
Sea

●Ekron   Ramah
          ●Naioth
Azekah Bethlehem
  Valley of Elah ●Socoh
Gath●

N

Samuel. And he said, "Neither has the LORD chosen this one." Then Jesse made Shammah pass by. And he said, "Neither has the LORD chosen this one." And Jesse made seven of his sons pass before Samuel. And Samuel said to Jesse, "The LORD has not chosen these." And Samuel said to Jesse, "Are all your sons here?" And he said, "There remains yet the youngest, but behold, he is keeping the sheep." And Samuel said to Jesse, "Send and fetch him; for we will not sit down till he comes here." 2 And he sent, and brought him in. Now he was ruddy, and had beautiful eyes, and was handsome. And the LORD said, "Arise, 3 anoint him; for this is he." Then Samuel took the horn of oil, and anointed him in the midst of his brothers; and the Spirit of the LORD came mightily upon David from that day forward. And Samuel rose up, and went to Ramah.

4 Now the Spirit of the LORD departed from Saul, and an evil spirit from the LORD 5 tormented him. And Saul's servants said to him, "Behold now, an evil spirit from God is 6 tormenting you. Let our lord now command your servants, who are before you, to seek out a man who is skilful in playing the lyre; and when the evil spirit from God is upon 17 you, he will play it, and you will be well." So Saul said to his servants, "Provide for me a

man who can play well, and bring him to me." One of the young men answered, 18 "Behold, I have seen a son of Jesse the Bethlehemite, who is skilful in playing, a man of valour, a man of war, prudent in speech, and a man of good presence; and the LORD is with him." Therefore Saul sent 19 messengers to Jesse, and said, "Send me David your son, who is with the sheep." And Jesse took an ass laden with bread, and a 20 skin of wine and a kid, and sent them by David his son to Saul. And David came to 21 Saul, and entered his service. And Saul loved him greatly, and he became his armour-bearer. And Saul sent to Jesse, 22 saying, "Let David remain in my service, for he has found favour in my sight." And 23 whenever the evil spirit from God was upon Saul, David took the lyre and played it with his hand; so Saul was refreshed, and was well, and the evil spirit departed from him.

David slays Goliath

Now the Philistines gathered their armies 17 for battle; and they were gathered at Socoh, which belongs to Judah, and encamped between Socoh and Aze'kah, in E'phes-dam'mim. And Saul and the men of Israel 2 were gathered, and encamped in the valley of Elah, and drew up in line of battle against the Philistines. And the Philistines stood on the 3 mountain on the one side, and Israel stood on the mountain on the other side, with a valley between them. And there came out from the 4 camp of the Philistines a champion named Goliath, of Gath, whose height was six cubits and a span. He had a helmet of bronze on his 5 head, and he was armed with a coat of mail, and the weight of the coat was five thousand shekels of bronze. And he had greaves of 6 bronze upon his legs, and a javelin of bronze slung between his shoulders. And the shaft 7 of his spear was like a weaver's beam, and his spear's head weighed six hundred shekels of iron; and his shield-bearer went before him. He stood and shouted to the ranks of Israel, 8 "Why have you come out to draw up for battle? Am I not a Philistine, and are you not servants of Saul? Choose a man for yourselves, and let him come down to me. If 9 he is able to fight with me and kill me, then we will be your servants; but if I prevail against him and kill him, then you shall be our servants and serve us." And the Philis- 10 tine said, "I defy the ranks of Israel this day; give me a man, that we may fight together." When Saul and all Israel heard these words 11 of the Philistine, they were dismayed and greatly afraid.

Now David was the son of an Eph'rathite of 12 Bethlehem in Judah, named Jesse, who had

eight sons. In the days of Saul the man was
13 already old and advanced in years.ᵃ The
three eldest sons of Jesse had followed Saul
to the battle; and the names of his three sons
who went to the battle were Eli′ab the
first-born, and next to him Abin′adab,
14 and the third Shammah. David was the
15 youngest; the three eldest followed Saul, but
David went back and forth from Saul to feed
16 his father's sheep at Bethlehem. For forty
days the Philistine came forward and took his
stand, morning and evening.
17 And Jesse said to David his son, "Take for
your brothers an ephah of this parched grain,
and these ten loaves, and carry them quickly
18 to the camp to your brothers; also take these
ten cheeses to the commander of their
thousand. See how your brothers fare, and
bring some token from them."
19 Now Saul, and they, and all the men of
Israel, were in the valley of Elah, fighting
20 with the Philistines. And David rose early in
the morning, and left the sheep with a
keeper, and took the provisions, and went, as
Jesse had commanded him; and he came to
the encampment as the host was going forth
21 to the battle line, shouting the war cry. And
Israel and the Philistines drew up for battle,
22 army against army. And David left the
things in charge of the keeper of the baggage,
and ran to the ranks, and went and greeted
23 his brothers. As he talked with them,
behold, the champion, the Philistine of Gath,
Goliath by name, came up out of the ranks of
the Philistines, and spoke the same words as
before. And David heard him.
24 All the men of Israel, when they saw the
man, fled from him, and were much afraid.
25 And the men of Israel said, "Have you seen
this man who has come up? Surely he has
come up to defy Israel; and the man who kills
him, the king will enrich with great riches,
and will give him his daughter, and make his
26 father's house free in Israel." And David
said to the men who stood by him, "What
shall be done for the man who kills this
Philistine, and takes away the reproach from
Israel? For who is this uncircumcised Philistine, that he should defy the armies of the
27 living God?" And the people answered him
in the same way, "So shall it be done to the
man who kills him."
28 Now Eli′ab his eldest brother heard when
he spoke to the men; and Eli′ab's anger was
kindled against David, and he said, "Why
have you come down? And with whom have
you left those few sheep in the wilderness? I
know your presumption, and the evil of your
heart; for you have come down to see the
29 battle." And David said, "What have I done

I Sam 17, 34

now? Was it not but a word?" And he 30
turned away from him toward another, and
spoke in the same way; and the people
answered him again as before.
When the words which David spoke were 31
heard, they repeated them before Saul; and
he sent for him. And David said to Saul, 32
"Let no man's heart fail because of him; your
servant will go and fight with this Philistine." And Saul said to David, "You are not 33
able to go against this Philistine to fight with
him; for you are but a youth, and he has been
a man of war from his youth." But David 34
said to Saul, "Your servant used to keep
sheep for his father; and when there came a
lion, or a bear, and took a lamb from the
flock, I went after him and smote him and 35
delivered it out of his mouth; and if he arose
against me, I caught him by his beard, and
smote him and killed him. Your servant has 36
killed both lions and bears; and this uncircumcised Philistine shall be like one of them,
seeing he has defied the armies of the living
God." And David said, "The LORD who 37
delivered me from the paw of the lion and
from the paw of the bear, will deliver me
from the hand of this Philistine." And Saul
said to David, "Go, and the LORD be with
you!" Then Saul clothed David with his 38
armour; he put a helmet of bronze on his
head, and clothed him with a coat of mail.
And David girded his sword over his armour, 39
and he tried in vain to go, for he was not used
to them. Then David said to Saul, "I cannot
go with these; for I am not used to them."
And David put them off. Then he took his 40
staff in his hand, and chose five smooth
stones from the brook, and put them in his
shepherd's bag or wallet; his sling was in his
hand, and he drew near to the Philistine.
And the Philistine came on and drew near 41
to David, with his shield-bearer in front of
him. And when the Philistine looked, and 42
saw David, he disdained him; for he was but
a youth, ruddy and comely in appearance.
And the Philistine said to David, "Am I a 43
dog, that you come to me with sticks?" And
the Philistine cursed David by his gods. The 44
Philistine said to David, "Come to me, and I
will give your flesh to the birds of the air and
to the beasts of the field." Then David said 45

ᵃ Gk Syr: Heb *among men*

to the Philistine, "You come to me with a sword and with a spear and with a javelin; but I come to you in the name of the LORD of hosts, the God of the armies of Israel, whom
5 you have defied. This day the LORD will deliver you into my hand, and I will strike you down, and cut off your head; and I will give the dead bodies of the host of the Philistines this day to the birds of the air and to the wild beasts of the earth; that all the earth may know that there is a God in Israel,
7 and that all this assembly may know that the LORD saves not with sword and spear; for the battle is the LORD's and he will give you into our hand."
8 When the Philistine arose and came and drew near to meet David, David ran quickly toward the battle line to meet the Philistine.
9 And David put his hand in his bag and took out a stone, and slung it, and struck the Philistine on his forehead; the stone sank into his forehead, and he fell on his face to the ground.
10 So David prevailed over the Philistine with a sling and with a stone, and struck the Philistine, and killed him; there was no
11 sword in the hand of David. Then David ran and stood over the Philistine, and took his sword and drew it out of its sheath, and killed him, and cut off his head with it. When the Philistines saw that their champion was dead,
12 they fled. And the men of Israel and Judah rose with a shout and pursued the Philistines as far as Gath[v] and the gates of Ekron, so that the wounded Philistines fell on the way from
13 Sha-ara′im as far as Gath and Ekron. And the Israelites came back from chasing the Philistines, and they plundered their camp.
14 And David took the head of the Philistine and brought it to Jerusalem; but he put his armour in his tent.
15 When Saul saw David go forth against the Philistine, he said to Abner, the commander of the army, "Abner, whose son is this youth?" And Abner said, "As your soul
16 lives, O king, I cannot tell." And the king said, "Inquire whose son the stripling is."
17 And as David returned from the slaughter of the Philistine, Abner took him, and brought him before Saul with the head of the Philistine in his hand. And Saul said to him, 58 "Whose son are you, young man?" And David answered, "I am the son of your servant Jesse the Bethlehemite."

David and Jonathan

When he had finished speaking to Saul, the 18 soul of Jonathan was knit to the soul of David, and Jonathan loved him as his own soul. And Saul took him that day, and would 2 not let him return to his father's house. Then Jonathan made a covenant with David, 3 because he loved him as his own soul. And 4 Jonathan stripped himself of the robe that was upon him, and gave it to David, and his armour, and even his sword and his bow and his girdle. And David went out and was 5 successful wherever Saul sent him; so that Saul set him over the men of war. And this was good in the sight of all the people and also in the sight of Saul's servants.

As they were coming home, when David 6 returned from slaying the Philistine, the women came out of all the cities of Israel, singing and dancing, to meet King Saul, with timbrels, with songs of joy, and with instruments[z] of music. And the women sang 7 to one another as they made merry,

"Saul has slain his thousands,
and David his ten thousands."

And Saul was very angry, and this saying 8 displeased him; he said, "They have ascribed to David ten thousands, and to me they have ascribed thousands; and what more can he have but the kingdom?" And Saul eyed 9 David from that day on.

And on the morrow an evil spirit from God 10 rushed upon Saul, and he raved within his house, while David was playing the lyre, as he did day by day. Saul had his spear in his hand; and Saul cast the spear, for he thought, 11 "I will pin David to the wall." But David evaded him twice.

Saul was afraid of David, because the LORD 12 was with him but had departed from Saul. So Saul removed him from his presence, and 13 made him a commander of a thousand; and he went out and came in before the people. And David had success in all his under- 14 takings; for the LORD was with him. And 15 when Saul saw that he had great success, he stood in awe of him. But all Israel and Judah 16 loved David; for he went out and came in before them.

Then Saul said to David, "Here is my elder 17 daughter Merab; I will give her to you for a wife; only be valiant for me and fight the

LORD's battles." For Saul thought, "Let not
my hand be upon him, but let the hand of the
18 Philistines be upon him." And David said to
Saul, "Who am I, and who are my kinsfolk,
my father's family in Israel, that I should be
19 son-in-law to the king?" But at the time
when Merab, Saul's daughter, should have
been given to David, she was given to
A′dri-el the Meho′lathite for a wife.
20 Now Saul's daughter Michal loved David;
and they told Saul, and the thing pleased
21 him. Saul thought, "Let me give her to him,
that she may be a snare for him, and that the
hand of the Philistines may be against him."
Therefore Saul said to David a second time,[a]
22 "You shall now be my son-in-law." And
Saul commanded his servants, "Speak to
David in private and say, 'Behold, the king
has delight in you, and all his servants love
you; now then become the king's son-
23 in-law.'" And Saul's servants spoke
those words in the ears of David. And David
said, "Does it seem to you a little thing to
become the king's son-in-law, seeing that I
24 am a poor man and of no repute?" And the
servants of Saul told him, "Thus and so did
25 David speak." Then Saul said, "Thus shall
you say to David, 'The king desires no
marriage present except a hundred foreskins
of the Philistines, that he may be avenged of
the king's enemies.'" Now Saul thought to
make David fall by the hand of the Philis-
26 tines. And when his servants told David
these words, it pleased David well to be the
king's son-in-law. Before the time had
27 expired, David arose and went, along with
his men, and killed two hundred of the
Philistines; and David brought their foreskins, which were given in full number to the
king, that he might become the king's son-
in-law. And Saul gave him his daughter
28 Michal for a wife. But when Saul saw and
knew that the LORD was with David, and that
29 all Israel[b] loved him, Saul was still more
afraid of David. So Saul was David's enemy
continually.
30 Then the princes of the Philistines came out
to battle, and as often as they came out David
had more success than all the servants of
Saul; so that his name was highly esteemed.

19 And Saul spoke to Jonathan his son and to
all his servants, that they should kill David.

But Jonathan, Saul's son, delighted much in
David. And Jonathan told David, "Saul my 2
father seeks to kill you; therefore take heed to
yourself in the morning, stay in a secret place
and hide yourself; and I will go out and stand 3
beside my father in the field where you are,
and I will speak to my father about you; and
if I learn anything I will tell you." And 4
Jonathan spoke well of David to Saul his
father, and said to him, "Let not the king sin
against his servant David; because he has not
sinned against you, and because his deeds
have been of good service to you; for he took 5
his life in his hand and he slew the Philistine,
and the LORD wrought a great victory for all
Israel. You saw it, and rejoiced; why then
will you sin against innocent blood by killing
David without cause?" And Saul hearkened 6
to the voice of Jonathan; Saul swore, "As the
LORD lives, he shall not be put to death."
And Jonathan called David, and Jonathan 7
showed him all these things. And Jonathan
brought David to Saul, and he was in his
presence as before.

And there was war again; and David went 8
out and fought with the Philistines, and
made a great slaughter among them, so that
they fled before him. Then an evil spirit 9
from the LORD came upon Saul, as he sat in
his house with his spear in his hand; and
David was playing the lyre. And Saul sought 10
to pin David to the wall with the spear; but
he eluded Saul, so that he struck the spear
into the wall. And David fled, and escaped.

That night Saul[z] sent messengers to 11
David's house to watch him, that he might
kill him in the morning. But Michal,
David's wife, told him, "If you do not save
your life tonight, tomorrow you will be
killed." So Michal let David down through 12
the window; and he fled away and escaped.
Michal took an image[c] and laid it on the bed 13
and put a pillow[d] of goats' hair at its head,
and covered it with the clothes. And when 14
Saul sent messengers to take David, she said,
"He is sick." Then Saul sent the messengers 15
to see David, saying, "Bring him up to me in
the bed, that I may kill him." And when the 16
messengers came in, behold, the image[c] was
in the bed, with the pillow[d] of goats' hair at
its head. Saul said to Michal, "Why have 17
you deceived me thus, and let my enemy go,
so that he has escaped?" And Michal

---

[a] Heb *by two*   [b] Gk: Heb *Michal, Saul's daughter*   [z] Gk Old Latin: Heb *escaped that night.* 11 *And Saul*
[c] Heb *teraphim*   [d] The meaning of the Hebrew word is uncertain

answered Saul, "He said to me, 'Let me go; why should I kill you?'"

8 Now David fled and escaped, and he came to Samuel at Ramah, and told him all that Saul had done to him. And he and Samuel 9 went and dwelt at Nai′oth. And it was told Saul, "Behold, David is at Nai′oth in 10 Ramah." Then Saul sent messengers to take David; and when they saw the company of the prophets prophesying, and Samuel standing as head over them, the Spirit of God came upon the messengers of Saul, and 11 they also prophesied. When it was told Saul, he sent other messengers, and they also prophesied. And Saul sent messengers again the third time, and they also prophesied. 12 Then he himself went to Ramah, and came to the great well that is in Secu; and he asked, "Where are Samuel and David?" And one said, "Behold, they are at Nai′oth in 13 Ramah." And he went from′ there to Nai′oth in Ramah; and the Spirit of God came upon him also, and as he went he prophesied, until he came to Nai′oth in 14 Ramah. And he too stripped off his clothes, and he too prophesied before Samuel, and lay naked all that day and all that night. Hence it is said, "Is Saul also among the prophets?"

20 Then David fled from Nai′oth in Ramah, and came and said before Jonathan, "What have I done? What is my guilt? And what is my sin before your father, that he seeks my 2 life?" And he said to him, "Far from it! You shall not die. Behold, my father does nothing either great or small without disclosing it to me; and why should my father 3 hide this from me? It is not so." But David replied,ᵍ "Your father knows well that I have found favour in your eyes; and he thinks, 'Let not Jonathan know this, lest he be grieved.' But truly, as the LORD lives and as your soul lives, there is but a step between 4 me and death." Then said Jonathan to David, "Whatever you say, I will do for 5 you." David said to Jonathan, "Behold, tomorrow is the new moon, and I should not fail to sit at table with the king; but let me go, that I may hide myself in the field till the 6 third day at evening. If your father misses me at all, then say, 'David earnestly asked leave of me to run to Bethlehem his city; for there is a yearly sacrifice there for all the 7 family.' If he says, 'Good!' it will be well with your servant; but if he is angry, then know that evil is determined by him. 8 Therefore deal kindly with your servant, for

you have brought your servant into a sacred covenantʰ with you. But if there is guilt in me, slay me yourself; for why should you bring me to your father?" And Jonathan 9 said, "Far be it from you! If I knew that it was determined by my father that evil should come upon you, would I not tell you?" 10 Then said David to Jonathan, "Who will tell me if your father answers you roughly?" And Jonathan said to David, "Come, let us 11 go out into the field." So they both went out into the field.

And Jonathan said to David, "The LORD, 12 the God of Israel, be witness!ⁱ When I have sounded my father, about this time tomorrow, or the third day, behold, if he is well disposed toward David, shall I not then send and disclose it to you? But should it 13 please my father to do you harm, the LORD do so to Jonathan, and more also, if I do not disclose it to you, and send you away, that you may go in safety. May the LORD be with you, as he has been with my father. If I am 14 still alive, show me the loyal love of the LORD, that I may not die;ʲ and do not cut off 15 your loyalty from my house for ever. When the LORD cuts off every one of the enemies of David from the face of the earth, let not the 16 name of Jonathan be cut off from the house of David.ᵏ And may the LORD take vengeance on David's enemies." And Jonathan 17 made David swear again by his love for him; for he loved him as he loved his own soul.

Then Jonathan said to him, "Tomorrow is 18 the new moon; and you will be missed, because your seat will be empty. And on the 19 third day you will be greatly missed;ˡ then go to the place where you hid yourself when the matter was in hand, and remain beside yonder stone heap.ᵐ And I will shoot three 20 arrows to the side of it, as though I shot at a mark. And behold, I will send the lad, 21 saying, 'Go, find the arrows.' If I say to the lad, 'Look, the arrows are on this side of you, take them,' then you are to come, for, as the LORD lives, it is safe for you and there is no danger. But if I say to the youth, 'Look, 22 the arrows are beyond you,' then go; for the LORD has sent you away. And as for the 23 matter of which you and I have spoken, behold, the LORD is between you and me for ever."

So David hid himself in the field; and when 24 the new moon came, the king sat down to eat food. The king sat upon his seat, as at other 25 times, upon the seat by the wall; Jonathan sat opposite,ⁿ and Abner sat by Saul's side, but David's place was empty.

ʲ Gk: Heb lacks *from*   ᵍ Gk: Heb *swore again*   ʰ Heb *a covenant of the* LORD   ⁱ Heb lacks *be witness*
ʲ Heb uncertain   ᵏ Gk: Heb *earth, and Jonathan made a covenant with the house of David*
ˡ Gk: Heb *go down quickly*   ᵐ Gk: Heb *the stone Ezel*   ⁿ Cn See Gk: Heb *stood up*
19.23–24: 1 Sam 10.10–12.

26 Yet Saul did not say anything that day; for he thought, "Something has befallen him; he is
27 not clean, surely he is not clean." But on the second day, the morrow after the new moon, David's place was empty. And Saul said to Jonathan his son, "Why has not the son of Jesse come to the meal, either yesterday or
28 today?" Jonathan answered Saul, "David earnestly asked leave of me to go to Beth-
29 lehem; he said, 'Let me go; for our family holds a sacrifice in the city, and my brother has commanded me to be there. So now, if I have found favour in your eyes, let me get away, and see my brothers.' For this reason he has not come to the king's table."
30 Then Saul's anger was kindled against Jonathan, and he said to him, "You son of a perverse, rebellious woman, do I not know that you have chosen the son of Jesse to your own shame, and to the shame of your
31 mother's nakedness? For as long as the son of Jesse lives upon the earth, neither you nor your kingdom shall be established. Therefore send and fetch him to me, for he
32 shall surely die." Then Jonathan answered Saul his father, "Why should he be put to
33 death? What has he done?" But Saul cast his spear at him to smite him; so Jonathan knew that his father was determined to put
34 David to death. And Jonathan rose from the table in fierce anger and ate no food the second day of the month, for he was grieved for David, because his father had disgraced him.
35 In the morning Jonathan went out into the field to the appointment with David, and
36 with him a little lad. And he said to his lad, "Run and find the arrows which I shoot." As the lad ran, he shot an arrow beyond him.

37 And when the lad came to the place of the arrow which Jonathan had shot, Jonathan called after the lad and said, "Is not the
38 arrow beyond you?" And Jonathan called after the lad, "Hurry, make haste, stay not." So Jonathan's lad gathered up the arrows,
39 and came to his master. But the lad knew nothing; only Jonathan and David knew the
40 matter. And Jonathan gave his weapons to his lad, and said to him, "Go and carry them
41 to the city." And as soon as the lad had gone, David rose from beside the stone heap⁰ and fell on his face to the ground, and bowed three times; and they kissed one another,

and wept with one another, until David recovered himself.ᵖ Then Jonathan said to 42 David, "Go in peace, forasmuch as we have sworn both of us in the name of the LORD, saying, 'The LORD shall be between me and you, and between my descendants and your descendants, for ever.'" And he rose and departed; and Jonathan went into the city.�q

David and Saul

Then came David to Nob to Ahim′elech2 the priest; and Ahim′elech came to meet David trembling, and said to him, "Why are you alone, and no one with you?" And 2 David said to Ahim′elech the priest, "The king has charged me with a matter, and said to me, 'Let no one know anything of the matter about which I send you, and with which I have charged you.' I have made an appointment with the young men for such and such a place. Now then, what have you 3 at hand? Give me five loaves of bread, or whatever is here." And the priest answered 4 David, "I have no common bread at hand, but there is holy bread; if only the young men have kept themselves from women." And David answered the priest, "Of a truth 5 women have been kept from us as always when I go on an expedition; the vessels of the young men are holy, even when it is a common journey; how much more today will their vessels be holy?" So the priest gave 6 him the holy bread; for there was no bread there but the bread of the Presence, which is removed from before the LORD, to be replaced by hot bread on the day it is taken away.

Now a certain man of the servants of Saul 7 was there that day, detained before the LORD; his name was Do′eg the E′domite, the chief of Saul's herdsmen.

And David said to Ahim′elech, "And have 8 you not here a spear or a sword at hand? For I have brought neither my sword nor my weapons with me, because the king's business required haste." And the priest said, 9 "The sword of Goliath the Philistine, whom you killed in the valley of Elah, behold, it is here wrapped in a cloth behind the ephod; if you will take that, take it, for there is none but that here." And David said, "There is none like that; give it to me."

And David rose and fled that day from 10 Saul, and went to A′chish the king of Gath. And the servants of A′chish said to him, "Is 11 not this David the king of the land? Did they not sing to one another of him in dances,

---

⁰ Gk: Heb *from beside the south*   ᵖ Or *exceeded*   q This sentence is Ch 21.1 in Heb   ʳ Ch 21.2 in Heb
21.11: I Sam 18.7; 29.5.

'Saul has slain his thousands,
and David his ten thousands'?"

2 And David took these words to heart, and
was much afraid of A'chish the king of Gath.
3 So he changed his behaviour before them,
and feigned himself mad in their hands, and
made marks on the doors of the gate, and let
4 his spittle run down his beard. Then said
A'chish to his servants, "Lo, you see the man
is mad; why then have you brought him to
5 me? Do I lack madmen, that you have
brought this fellow to play the madman in
my presence? Shall this fellow come into my
house?"

:2 David departed from there and escaped to
the cave of Adullam; and when his brothers
and all his father's house heard it, they went
2 down there to him. And every one who was
in distress, and every one who was in debt,
and every one who was discontented, gathered to him; and he became captain over
them. And there were with him about four
hundred men.
3 And David went from there to Mizpeh of
Moab; and he said to the king of Moab,
"Pray let my father and my mother stay⁸ with
you, till I know what God will do for me."
4 And he left them with the king of Moab, and
they stayed with him all the time that David
5 was in the stronghold. Then the prophet
Gad said to David, "Do not remain in the
stronghold; depart, and go into the land of
Judah." So David departed, and went into
the forest of Hereth.
6 Now Saul heard that David was discovered,
and the men who were with him. Saul was
sitting at Gib'e-ah, under the tamarisk tree
on the height, with his spear in his hand, and
all his servants were standing about him.
7 And Saul said to his servants who stood
about him, "Hear now, you Benjaminites;
will the son of Jesse give every one of you
fields and vineyards, will he make you all
commanders of thousands and commanders
8 of hundreds, that all of you have conspired
against me? No one discloses to me when
my son makes a league with the son of Jesse,
none of you is sorry for me or discloses to me
that my son has stirred up my servant against
9 me, to lie in wait, as at this day." Then
answered Do'eg the E'domite, who stood by
the servants of Saul, "I saw the son of Jesse
coming to Nob, to Ahim'elech the son of
10 Ahi'tub, and he inquired of the LORD for
him, and gave him provisions, and gave him
the sword of Goliath the Philistine."
11 Then the king sent to summon Ahim'elech
the priest, the son of Ahi'tub, and all his
father's house, the priests who were at Nob;

and all of them came to the king. And Saul 12
said, "Hear now, son of Ahi'tub." And he
answered, "Here I am, my lord." And Saul 13
said to him, "Why have you conspired
against me, you and the son of Jesse, in that
you have given him bread and a sword, and
have inquired of God for him, so that he has
risen against me, to lie in wait, as at this
day?" Then Ahim'elech answered the king, 14
"And who among all your servants is so
faithful as David, who is the king's son-in-
law, and captain over⁴ your bodyguard, and
honoured in your house? Is today the first 15
time that I have inquired of God for him?
No! Let not the king impute anything to his
servant or to all the house of my father; for
your servant has known nothing of all this,
much or little." And the king said, "You 16
shall surely die, Ahim'elech, you and all your
father's house." And the king said to the 17
guard who stood about him, "Turn and kill
the priests of the LORD; because their hand
also is with David, and they knew that he
fled, and did not disclose it to me." But the
servants of the king would not put forth their
hand to fall upon the priests of the LORD.
Then the king said to Do'eg, "You turn and 18
fall upon the priests." And Do'eg the
E'domite turned and fell upon the priests,
and he killed on that day eighty-five persons
who wore the linen ephod. And Nob, the city 19
of the priests, he put to the sword; both men
and women, children and sucklings, oxen,
asses and sheep, he put to the sword.
But one of the sons of Ahim'elech the son of 20
Ahi'tub, named Abi'athar, escaped and fled
after David. And Abi'athar told David that 21
Saul had killed the priests of the LORD. And 22
David said to Abi'athar, "I knew on that day,
when Do'eg the E'domite was there, that he
would surely tell Saul. I have occasioned the
death of all the persons of your father's
house. Stay with me, fear not; for he that 23
seeks my life seeks your life; with me you
shall be in safekeeping."

Now they told David, "Behold, the Philis-23
tines are fighting against Kei'lah, and are
robbing the threshing floors." Therefore 2
David inquired of the LORD, "Shall I go and
attack these Philistines?" And the LORD
said to David, "Go and attack the Philistines
and save Kei'lah." But David's men said to 3
him, "Behold, we are afraid here in Judah;
how much more then if we go to Kei'lah
against the armies of the Philistines?" Then 4
David inquired of the LORD again. And the
LORD answered him, "Arise, go down to
Kei'lah; for I will give the Philistines into
your hand." And David and his men went to 5

⁸ Syr Vg: Heb *come out*   ⁴ Gk Tg: Heb *and has turned aside to*

Kei′lah, and fought with the Philistines, and brought away their cattle, and made a great slaughter among them. So David delivered the inhabitants of Kei′lah.

6 When Abi′athar the son of Ahim′elech fled to David to Kei′lah, he came down with an 7 ephod in his hand. Now it was told Saul that David had come to Kei′lah. And Saul said, "God has given him into my hand; for he has shut himself in by entering a town that has 8 gates and bars." And Saul summoned all the people to war, to go down to Kei′lah, to 9 besiege David and his men. David knew that Saul was plotting evil against him; and he said to Abi′athar the priest, "Bring the ephod 10 here." Then said David, "O LORD, the God of Israel, thy servant has surely heard that Saul seeks to come to Kei′lah, to destroy the 11 city on my account. Will the men of Kei′lah surrender me into his hand? Will Saul come down, as thy servant has heard? O LORD, the God of Israel, I beseech thee, tell thy servant." And the LORD said, "He will come 12 down." Then said David, "Will the men of Kei′lah surrender me and my men into the hand of Saul?" And the LORD said, "They 13 will surrender you." Then David and his men, who were about six hundred, arose and departed from Kei′lah, and they went wherever they could go. When Saul was told that David had escaped from Kei′lah, he gave up 14 the expedition. And David remained in the strongholds in the wilderness, in the hill country of the Wilderness of Ziph. And Saul sought him every day, but God did not give him into his hand.

15 And David was afraid because[u] Saul had come out to seek his life. David was in 16 the Wildnerness of Ziph at Horesh. And Jonathan, Saul's son, rose, and went to David at Horesh, and strengthened his hand 17 in God. And he said to him, "Fear not; for the hand of Saul my father shall not find you; you shall be king over Israel, and I shall be next to you; Saul my father also knows 18 this." And the two of them made a covenant before the LORD; David remained at Horesh, and Jonathan went home.

19 Then the Ziphites went up to Saul at Gib′e-ah, saying, "Does not David hide among us in the strongholds at Horesh, on the hill of Hachi′lah, which is south of 20 Jeshi′mon? Now come down, O king, according to all your heart's desire to come down; and our part shall be to surrender him 21 into the king's hand." And Saul said, "May you be blessed by the LORD; for you have had 22 compassion on me. Go, make yet more sure; know and see the place where his haunt is,

and who has seen him there; for it is told me that he is very cunning. See therefore, and take note of all the lurking places where he hides, and come back to me with sure information. Then I will go with you; and if he is in the land, I will search him out among all the thousands of Judah." And they arose, and went to Ziph ahead of Saul.

Now David and his men were in the wilderness of Ma′on, in the Arabah to the south of Jeshi′mon. And Saul and his men 2 went to seek him. And David was told; therefore he went down to the rock which is[v] in the wilderness of Ma′on. And when Saul heard that, he pursued after David in the wilderness of Ma′on. Saul went on one side of the mountain, and David and his men on the other side of the mountain; and David was making haste to get away from Saul, as Saul and his men were closing in upon David and his men to capture them, when a mes- 2 senger came to Saul, saying, "Make haste and come; for the Philistines have made a raid upon the land." So Saul returned from pursuing after David, and went against the Philistines; therefore that place was called the Rock of Escape. And David went up 2 from there, and dwelt in the strongholds of En-ge′di.

When Saul returned from following the 24 Philistines, he was told, "Behold, David is in the wilderness of En-ge′di." Then Saul took 2 three thousand chosen men out of all Israel, and went to seek David and his men in front of the Wildgoats' Rocks. And he came to the 3 sheepfolds by the way, where there was a cave; and Saul went in to relieve himself. Now David and his men were sitting in the innermost parts of the cave. And the men of 4 David said to him, "Here is the day of which the LORD said to you, 'Behold, I will give your enemy into your hand, and you shall do to him as it shall seem good to you.' " Then David arose and stealthily cut off the skirt of Saul's robe. And afterward David's heart 5 smote him, because he had cut off Saul's skirt. He said to his men, "The LORD forbid 6

u Or saw that   v Gk: Heb and dwelt   w Ch 24.1 in Heb
24.1–22: 1 Sam 26.1–25.

A town that has gates   I Sam **23, 7**

that I should do this thing to my lord, the
LORD's anointed, to put forth my hand
against him, seeing he is the LORD's
7 anointed." So David persuaded his men
with these words, and did not permit them to
attack Saul. And Saul rose up and left the
cave, and went upon his way.
8 Afterward David also arose, and went out
of the cave, and called after Saul, "My lord
the king!" And when Saul looked behind
him, David bowed with his face to the earth,
9 and did obeisance. And David said to Saul,
"Why do you listen to the words of men who
10 say, 'Behold, David seeks your hurt'? Lo,
this day your eyes have seen how the LORD
gave you today into my hand in the cave; and
some bade me kill you, but I *x* spared you. I
said, 'I will not put forth my hand against my
11 lord; for he is the LORD's anointed.' See, my
father, see the skirt of your robe in my hand;
for by the fact that I cut off the skirt of your
robe, and did not kill you, you may know and
see that there is no wrong or treason in my
hands. I have not sinned against you, though
12 you hunt my life to take it. May the LORD
judge between me and you, and may the LORD
avenge me upon you; but my hand shall not
13 be against you. As the proverb of the
ancients says, 'Out of the wicked comes forth
wickedness'; but my hand shall not be
14 against you. After whom has the king of
Israel come out? After whom do you
pursue? After a dead dog! After a flea!
15 May the LORD therefore be judge, and give
sentence between me and you, and see to it,

and plead my cause, and deliver me from
your hand."
    When David had finished speaking these 16
words to Saul, Said said, "Is this your voice,
my son David?" And Saul lifted up his
voice and wept. He said to David, "You are 17
more righteous than I; for you have repaid
me good, whereas I have repaid you evil.
And you have declared this day how you 18
have dealt well with me, in that you did not
kill me when the LORD put me into your
hands. For if a man finds his enemy, will he 19
let him go away safe? So may the LORD
reward you with good for what you have
done to me this day. And now, behold, I 20
know that you shall surely be king, and that
the kingdom of Israel shall be established in
your hand. Swear to me therefore by the 21
LORD that you will not cut off my descendants after me, and that you will not destroy
my name out of my father's house." And 22
David swore this to Saul. Then Saul went
home; but David and his men went up to the
stronghold.

David and Abigail

    Now Samuel died; and all Israel assembled 25
and mourned for him, and they buried him
in his house at Ramah.
    Then David rose and went down to the
wilderness of Paran. And there was a man in 2
Ma'on, whose business was in Carmel. The
man was very rich; he had three thousand
sheep and a thousand goats. He was shearing his sheep in Carmel. Now the name of 3
the man was Nabal, and the name of his wife
Ab'igail. The woman was of good understanding and beautiful, but the man was
churlish and ill-behaved; he was a Calebite.

x Gk Syr Tg: Heb *you*

4 David heard in the wilderness that Nabal was
5 shearing his sheep. So David sent ten young
men; and David said to the young men, "Go
up to Carmel, and go to Nabal, and greet him
6 in my name. And thus you shall salute him:
'Peace be to you, and peace be to your house,
7 and peace be to all that you have. I hear that
you have shearers; now your shepherds have
been with us, and we did them no harm, and
they missed nothing, all the time they were in
8 Carmel. Ask your young men, and they will
tell you. Therefore let my young men find
favour in your eyes; for we come on a feast
day. Pray, give whatever you have at hand to
your servants and to your son David.' "
9 When David's young men came, they said
all this to Nabal in the name of David; and
10 then they waited. And Nabal answered
David's servants, "Who is David? Who is
the son of Jesse? There are many servants
nowadays who are breaking away from their
11 masters. Shall I take my bread and my water
and my meat that I have killed for my
shearers, and give it to men who come from I
12 do not know where?" So David's young
men turned away, and came back and told
13 him all this. And David said to his men,
"Every man gird on his sword!" And every
man of them girded on his sword; David also
girded on his sword; and about four hundred
men went up after David, while two hundred
remained with the baggage.
14 But one of the young men told Ab'igail,
Nabal's wife, "Behold, David sent messengers out of the wilderness to salute our
15 master; and he railed at them. Yet the men
were very good to us, and we suffered no
harm, and we did not miss anything when we
were in the fields, as long as we went with
16 them; they were a wall to us both by night
and by day, all the while we were with them
17 keeping the sheep. Now therefore know this
and consider what you should do; for evil is
determined against our master and against all
his house, and he is so ill-natured that one
cannot speak to him."
18 Then Ab'igail made haste, and took two
hundred loaves, and two skins of wine, and
five sheep ready dressed, and five measures
of parched grain, and a hundred clusters of
raisins, and two hundred cakes of figs, and
19 laid them on asses. And she said to her
young men, "Go on before me; behold, I
come after you." But she did not tell her
20 husband Nabal. And as she rode on the ass,
and came down under cover of the mountain,
behold, David and his men came down
21 toward her; and she met them. Now David
had said, "Surely in vain have I guarded all
that this fellow has in the wilderness, so that

nothing was missed of all that belonged to
him; and he has returned me evil for good.
God do so to David[v] and more also, if by
morning I leave so much as one male of all
who belong to him."
When Ab'igail saw David, she made haste,
and alighted from the ass, and fell before
David on her face, and bowed to the ground.
She fell at his feet and said, "Upon me alone,
my lord, be the guilt; pray let your handmaid
speak in your ears, and hear the words of
your handmaid. Let not my lord regard this
ill-natured fellow, Nabal; for as his name is,
so is he; Nabal[z] is his name, and folly is with
him; but I your handmaid did not see the
young men of my lord, whom you sent.
Now then, my lord, as the LORD lives, and
as your soul lives, seeing the LORD has
restrained you from bloodguilt, and from
taking vengeance with your own hand, now
then let your enemies and those who seek to
do evil to my lord be as Nabal. And now let
this present which your servant has brought
to my lord be given to the young men who
follow my lord. Pray forgive the trespass of
your handmaid; for the LORD will certainly
make my lord a sure house, because my lord
is fighting the battles of the LORD; and evil
shall not be found in you so long as you live.
If men rise up to pursue you and to seek your
life, the life of my lord shall be bound in the
bundle of the living in the care of the LORD
your God; and the lives of your enemies he
shall sling out as from the hollow of a sling.
And when the LORD has done to my lord
according to all the good that he has spoken
concerning you, and has appointed you
prince over Israel, my lord shall have no
cause of grief, or pangs of conscience, for
having shed blood without cause or for my
lord taking vengeance himself. And when
the LORD has dealt well with my lord, then
remember your handmaid."
And David said to Ab'igail, "Blessed be the
LORD, the God of Israel, who sent you this
day to meet me! Blessed be your discretion,
and blessed be you, who have kept me this
day from bloodguilt and from avenging
myself with my own hand! For as surely as
the LORD the God of Israel lives, who has
restrained me from hurting you, unless you
had made haste and come to meet me, truly
by morning there had not been left to Nabal
so much as one male." Then David received
from her hand what she had brought him;
and he said to her, "Go up in peace to your
house; see, I have hearkened to your voice,
and I have granted your petition."
And Ab'igail came to Nabal; and, lo, he was
holding a feast in his house, like the feast of a

---

king. And Nabal's heart was merry within him, for he was very drunk; so she told him 7 nothing at all until the morning light. And in the morning, when the wine had gone out of Nabal, his wife told him these things, and his heart died within him, and he became as a 8 stone. And about ten days later the LORD smote Nabal; and he died.

9 When David heard that Nabal was dead, he said, "Blessed be the LORD who has avenged the insult I received at the hand of Nabal, and has kept back his servant from evil; the LORD has returned the evil-doing of Nabal upon his own head." Then David sent and 10 wooed Ab'igail, to make her his wife. And when the servants of David came to Ab'igail at Carmel, they said to her, "David has sent us to you to take you to him as his wife." 11 And she rose and bowed with her face to the ground, and said, "Behold, your handmaid is a servant to wash the feet of the servants of 12 my lord." And Ab'igail made haste and rose and mounted on an ass, and her five maidens attended her; she went after the messengers of David, and became his wife.

13 David also took Ahin'o-am of Jezreel; and 14 both of them became his wives. Saul had given Michal his daughter, David's wife, to Palti the son of La'ish, who was of Gallim.

David spares Saul

26 Then the Ziphites came to Saul at Gib'e-ah, saying, "Is not David hiding himself on the hill of Hachi'lah, which is on the east of 2 Jeshi'mon?" So Saul arose and went down to the wilderness of Ziph, with three thousand chosen men of Israel, to seek David in 3 the wilderness of Ziph. And Saul encamped on the hill of Hachi'lah, which is beside the road on the east of Jeshi'mon. But David remained in the wilderness; and when he saw that Saul came after him into the wilderness, 4 David sent out spies, and learned of a 5 certainty that Saul had come. Then David rose and came to the place where Saul had encamped; and David saw the place where Saul lay, with Abner the son of Ner, the commander of his army; Saul was lying within the encampment, while the army was encamped around him.

6 Then David said to Ahim'elech the Hittite, and to Jo'ab's brother Abi'shai the son of Zeru'iah, "Who will go down with me into the camp to Saul?" And Abi'shai said, "I 7 will go down with you." So David and Abi'shai went to the army by night; and there lay Saul sleeping within the encampment, with his spear stuck in the ground at

his head; and Abner and the army lay around him. Then said Abi'shai to David, "God has 8 given your enemy into your hand this day; now therefore let me pin him to the earth with one stroke of the spear, and I will not strike him twice." But David said to 9 Abi'shai, "Do not destroy him; for who can put forth his hand against the LORD's anointed, and be guiltless?" And David 10 said, "As the LORD lives, the LORD will smite him; or his day shall come to die; or he shall go down into battle and perish. The LORD 11 forbid that I should put forth my hand against the LORD's anointed; but take now the spear that is at his head, and the jar of water, and let us go." So David took the 12 spear and the jar of water from Saul's head; and they went away. No man saw it, or knew it, nor did any awake; for they were all asleep, because a deep sleep from the LORD had fallen upon them.

Then David went over to the other side, 13 and stood afar off on the top of the mountain, with a great space between them; and David 14 called to the army, and to Abner the son of Ner, saying, "Will you not answer, Abner?" Then Abner answered, "Who are you that calls to the king?" And David said to Abner, 15 "Are you not a man? Who is like you in Israel? Why then have you not kept watch over your lord the king? For one of the people came in to destroy the king your lord. This thing that you have done is not good. 16 As the LORD lives, you deserve to die, because you have not kept watch over your lord, the LORD's anointed. And now see where the king's spear is, and the jar of water that was at his head."

Saul recognised David's voice, and said, "Is 17 this your voice, my son David?" And David said, "It is my voice, my lord, O king." And 18 he said, "Why does my lord pursue after his servant? For what have I done? What guilt is on my hands? Now therefore let my lord 19 the king hear the words of his servant. If it is the LORD who has stirred you up against me, may he accept an offering; but if it is men, may they be cursed before the LORD, for they have driven me out this day that I should have no share in the heritage of the LORD, saying, 'Go, serve other gods.' Now there- 20 fore, let not my blood fall to the earth away from the presence of the LORD; for the king of Israel has come out to seek my life,ᵃ like one who hunts a partridge in the mountains."

Then Saul said, "I have done wrong; 21 return, my son David, for I will no more do you harm, because my life was precious in

F your eyes this day; behold, I have played the
22 fool, and have erred exceedingly." And
David made answer, "Here is the spear, O
king! Let one of the young men come over
23 and fetch it. The LORD rewards every man
for his righteousness and his faithfulness; for
the LORD gave you into my hand today, and I
would not put forth my hand against the
24 LORD's anointed. Behold, as your life was
precious this day in my sight, so may my life
be precious in the sight of the LORD, and may
25 he deliver me out of all tribulation." Then
Saul said to David, "Blessed be you, my son
David! You will do many things and will
succeed in them." So David went his way,
and Saul returned to his place.

27 And David said in his heart, "I shall now
perish one day by the hand of Saul; there is
nothing better for me than that I should
escape to the land of the Philistines; then
Saul will despair of seeking me any longer
within the borders of Israel, and I shall
2 escape out of his hand." So David arose and
went over, he and the six hundred men who
were with him, to A'chish the son of Ma'och,
3 king of Gath. And David dwelt with A'chish
at Gath, he and his men, every man with his
household, and David with his two wives,
Ahin'o-am of Jezreel, and Ab'igail of
4 Carmel, Nabal's widow. And when it was
told Saul that David had fled to Gath, he
sought for him no more.
5 Then David said to A'chish, "If I have
found favour in your eyes, let a place be
given me in one of the country towns, that I
may dwell there; for why should your servant
6 dwell in the royal city with you?" So
that day A'chish gave him Ziklag; therefore
Ziklag has belonged to the kings of Judah to
7 this day. And the number of the days that
David dwelt in the country of the Philistines
was a year and four months.
8 Now David and his men went up, and made
raids upon the Gesh'urites, the Gir'zites, and
the Amal'ekites; for these were the inhabitants of the land from of old, as far as Shur,
9 to the land of Egypt. And David smote the
land, and left neither man nor woman alive,
but took away the sheep, the oxen, the asses,
the camels, and the garments, and came back
10 to A'chish. When A'chish asked, "Against
whom[b] have you made a raid today?" David
would say, "Against the Negeb of Judah," or
"Against the Negeb of the Jerah'meelites,"
or, "Against the Negeb of the Ken'ites."
11 And David saved neither man nor woman
alive, to bring tidings to Gath, thinking,
"Lest they should tell about us, and say, 'So
David has done.'" Such was his custom all

the while he dwelt in the country of the
Philistines. And A'chish trusted David,
thinking, "He has made himself utterly
abhorred by his people Israel; therefore he
shall be my servant always."

In those days the Philistines gathered their
forces for war, to fight against Israel. And
A'chish said to David, "Understand that you
and your men are to go out with me in the
army." David said to A'chish, "Very well,
you shall know what your servant can do."
And A'chish said to David, "Very well, I will
make you my bodyguard for life."

Now Samuel had died, and all Israel had
mourned for him and buried him in Ramah,
his own city. And Saul had put the mediums
and the wizards out of the land. The Philistines assembled, and came and encamped at
Shunem; and Saul gathered all Israel, and
they encamped at Gilbo'a. When Saul saw
the army of the Philistines, he was afraid, and
his heart trembled greatly. And when Saul
inquired of the LORD, the LORD did not
answer him, either by dreams, or by Urim, or
by prophets. Then Saul said to his servants,
"Seek out for me a woman who is a medium
that I may go to her and inquire of her."
And his servants said to him, "Behold, there
is a medium at Endor."

The witch of Endor

So Saul disguised himself and put on other 8
garments, and went, he and two men with
him; and they came to the woman by night.
And he said, "Divine for me by a spirit, and

---

b Gk Vg: Heb lacks whom

bring up for me whomever I shall name to
9 you." The woman said to him, "Surely you
know what Saul has done, how he has cut off
the mediums and the wizards from the land.
Why then are you laying a snare for my life to
10 bring about my death?" But Saul swore to
her by the LORD, "As the LORD lives, no
punishment shall come upon you for this
11 thing." Then the woman said, "Whom shall
I bring up for you?" He said, "Bring up
12 Samuel for me." When the woman saw
Samuel, she cried out with a loud voice; and
the woman said to Saul, "Why have you
13 deceived me? You are Saul." The king said
to her, "Have no fear; what do you see?"
And the woman said to Saul, "I see a god
14 coming up out of the earth." He said to her,
"What is his appearance?" And she said,
"An old man is coming up; and he is
wrapped in a robe." And Saul knew that it
was Samuel, and he bowed with his face to
the ground, and did obeisance.
15 Then Samuel said to Saul, "Why have you
disturbed me by bringing me up?" Saul
answered, "I am in great distress; for the
Philistines are warring against me, and God
has turned away from me and answers me no
more, either by prophets or by dreams;
therefore I have summoned you to tell me
16 what I shall do." And Samuel said, "Why
then do you ask me, since the LORD has
turned from you and become your enemy?
17 The LORD has done to you as he spoke by
me; for the LORD has torn the kingdom out of
your hand, and given it to your neighbour,
18 David. Because you did not obey the voice
of the LORD, and did not carry out his fierce
wrath against Am'alek, therefore the LORD
19 has done this thing to you this day. Moreover the LORD will give Israel also with
you into the hand of the Philistines; and
tomorrow you and your sons shall be with
me; the LORD will give the army of Israel also
into the hand of the Philistines."
20 Then Saul fell at once full length upon the
ground, filled with fear because of the words
of Samuel; and there was no strength in him,
for he had eaten nothing all day and all
21 night. And the woman came to Saul, and
when she saw that he was terrified, she
said to him, "Behold, your handmaid has
hearkened to you; I have taken my life in my
hand, and have hearkened to what you have
22 said to me. Now therefore, you also hearken
to your handmaid; let me set a morsel of
bread before you; and eat, that you may have
23 strength when you go on your way." He
refused, and said, "I will not eat." But his
servants, together with the woman, urged
him; and he hearkened to their words. So he

arose from the earth, and sat upon the bed.
Now the woman had a fatted calf in the 24
house, and she quickly killed it, and she took
flour, and kneaded it and baked unleavened
bread of it, and she put it before Saul and his 25
servants; and they ate. Then they rose and
went away that night.

David and his men

Now the Philistines gathered all their forces 29
at Aphek; and the Israelites were encamped
by the fountain which is in Jezreel. As the 2
lords of the Philistines were passing on by
hundreds and by thousands, and David and
his men were passing on in the rear with
A'chish, the commanders of the Philistines 3
said, "What are these Hebrews doing
here?" And A'chish said to the commanders
of the Philistines, "Is not this David, the
servant of Saul, king of Israel, who has been
with me now for days and years, and since he
deserted to me I have found no fault in him
to this day." But the commanders of the 4
Philistines were angry with him; and the
commanders of the Philistines said to him,
"Send the man back, that he may return to
the place to which you have assigned him; he
shall not go down with us to battle, lest in the
battle he become an adversary to us. For
how could this fellow reconcile himself to his
lord? Would it not be with the heads of the
men here? Is not this David, of whom they 5
sing to one another in dances,
'Saul has slain his thousands,
and David his ten thousands'?"
Then A'chish called David and said to him, 6
"As the LORD lives, you have been honest,
and to me it seems right that you should
march out and in with me in the campaign;
for I have found nothing wrong in you from
the day of your coming to me to this day.
Nevertheless the lords do not approve of
you. So go back now; and go peaceably, that 7
you may not displease the lords of the
Philistines." And David said to A'chish, 8
"But what have I done? What have you
found in your servant from the day I entered
your service until now, that I may not go and
fight against the enemies of my lord the
king?" And A'chish made answer to David, 9
"I know that you are as blameless in my sight
as an angel of God; nevertheless the commanders of the Philistines have said, 'He
shall not go up with us to the battle.' Now 10
then rise early in the morning with the
servants of your lord who came with you;
and start early in the morning, and depart as
soon as you have light." So David set out 11
with his men early in the morning, to return

to the land of the Philistines. But the Philistines went up to Jezreel.

30 Now when David and his men came to Ziklag on the third day, the Amal'ekites had made a raid upon the Negeb and upon Ziklag. They had overcome Ziklag, and 2 burned it with fire, and taken captive the women and all[c] who were in it, both small and great; they killed no one, but carried

strengthened himself in the LORD his God. And David said to Abi'athar the priest, the son of Ahim'elech, "Bring me the ephod." So Abi'athar brought the ephod to David. And David inquired of the LORD, "Shall I pursue after this band? Shall I overtake them?" He answered him, "Pursue; for you shall surely overtake and shall surely rescue." So David set out, and the six hundred men who were with him, and they came to the brook Besor, where those stayed who were left behind. But David went on with the pursuit, he and four hundred men; two hundred stayed behind, who were too exhausted to cross the brook Besor.

They found an Egyptian in the open country, and brought him to David; and they gave him bread and he ate, they gave him water to drink, and they gave him a piece of a cake of figs and two clusters of raisins. And when he had eaten, his spirit revived; for he had not eaten bread or drunk water for three days and three nights. And David said to him, "To whom do you belong? And where are you from?" He said, "I am a young man of Egypt, servant to an Amal'ekite; and my master left me behind because I fell sick three days ago. We had made a raid upon the Negeb of the Cher'ethites and upon that which belongs to Judah and upon the Negeb of Caleb; and we burned Ziklag with fire." And David said to him, "Will you take me

3 them off, and went their way. And when David and his men came to the city, they found it burned with fire, and their wives 4 and sons and daughters taken captive. Then David and the people who were with him raised their voices and wept, until they had 5 no more strength to weep. David's two wives also had been taken captive, Ahin'o-am of Jezreel, and Ab'igail the widow of Nabal 6 of Carmel. And David was greatly distressed; for the people spoke of stoning him, because all the people were bitter in soul, each for his sons and daughters. But David

down to this band?" And he said, "Swear to me by God, that you will not kill me, or deliver me into the hands of my master, and I will take you down to this band."

And when he had taken him down, behold, 16 they were spread abroad over all the land, eating and drinking and dancing, because of all the great spoil they had taken from the land of the Philistines and from the land of Judah. And David smote them from twilight 17 until the evening of the next day; and not a man of them escaped, except four hundred young men, who mounted camels and fled.

[c] Gk: Heb lacks *and all*

8 David recovered all that the Amal′ekites had
taken; and David rescued his two wives.
9 Nothing was missing, whether small or great,
sons or daughters, spoil or anything that had
0 been taken; David brought back all. David
also captured all the flocks and herds; and
the people drove those cattle before him,[a]
and said, "This is David's spoil."

Dividing the spoil

1 Then David came to the two hundred men,
who had been too exhausted to follow David,
and who had been left at the brook Besor;
and they went out to meet David and to meet
the people who were with him; and when
David drew near to the people he saluted
2 them. Then all the wicked and base fellows
among the men who had gone with David
said, "Because they did not go with us, we
will not give them any of the spoil which we
have recovered, except that each man may
lead away his wife and children, and
3 depart." But David said, "You shall not do
so, my brothers, with what the LORD has
given us; he has preserved us and given into
our hand the band that came against us.
4 Who would listen to you in this matter? For
as his share is who goes down into the battle,
so shall his share be who stays by the
5 baggage; they shall share alike." And from
that day forward he made it a statute and an
ordinance for Israel to this day.
6 When David came to Ziklag, he sent part of
the spoil to his friends, the elders of Judah,
saying, "Here is a present for you from the
7 spoil of the enemies of the LORD"; it was for
those in Bethel, in Ramoth of the Negeb, in
8 Jattir, in Aro′er, in Siphmoth, in Eshtemo′a,
9 in Racal, in the cities of the Jerah′meelites, in
0 the cities of the Ken′ites, in Hormah, in
1 Borash′an, in A′thach, in Hebron, for all the
places where David and his men had roamed.

The death of Saul

Now the Philistines fought against Israel;**31**
and the men of Israel fled before the Philistines, and fell slain on Mount Gilbo′a. And 2
the Philistines overtook Saul and his sons;
and the Philistines slew Jonathan and
Abin′adab and Mal′chishu′a, the sons of
Saul. The battle pressed hard upon Saul, 3
and the archers found him; and he was badly
wounded by the archers. Then Saul said to 4
his armour-bearer, "Draw your sword, and
thrust me through with it, lest these uncircumcised come and thrust me through, and
make sport of me." But his armour-bearer
would not; for he feared greatly. Therefore
Saul took his own sword, and fell upon it.
And when his armour-bearer saw that Saul 5
was dead, he also fell upon his sword, and
died with him. Thus Saul died, and his three 6
sons, and his armour-bearer, and all his men,
on the same day together. And when the 7
men of Israel who were on the other side of
the valley and those beyond the Jordan saw
that the men of Israel had fled and that Saul
and his sons were dead, they forsook their

---

[a] Cn: Heb *they drove before those cattle*
31.1–13: 2 Sam 1.6–10; 1 Chron 10.1–12.

cities and fled; and the Philistines came and dwelt in them.

8 On the morrow, when the Philistines came to strip the slain, they found Saul and his 9 three sons fallen on Mount Gilbo′a. And they cut off his head, and stripped off his armour, and sent messengers throughout the land of the Philistines, to carry the good news 10 to their idols[e] and to the people. They put his armour in the temple of Ash′taroth;

and they fastened his body to the wall of Beth-shan. But when the inhabitants of 11 Ja′besh-gil′ead heard what the Philistines had done to Saul, all the valiant men arose, 12 and went all night, and took the body of Saul and the bodies of his sons from the wall of Beth-shan; and they came to Jabesh and burnt them there. And they took their bones 13 and buried them under the tamarisk tree in Jabesh, and fasted seven days.

THE SECOND BOOK OF

SAMUEL

AFTER the death of Saul, when David had returned from the slaughter of the Amal′ekites, David remained two 2 days in Ziklag; and on the third day, behold, a man came from Saul's camp, with his clothes rent and earth upon his head. And when he came to David, he fell to the ground 3 and did obeisance. David said to him, "Where do you come from?" And he said to him, "I have escaped from the camp of 4 Israel." And David said to him, "How did it go? Tell me." And he answered, "The people have fled from the battle, and many of the people also have fallen and are dead; and Saul and his son Jonathan are also dead." 5 Then David said to the young man who told him, "How do you know that Saul and his 6 son Jonathan are dead?" And the young man who told him said, "By chance I happened to be on Mount Gilbo′a; and there was Saul leaning upon his spear; and lo, the chariots and the horsemen were close upon 7 him. And when he looked behind him, he

saw me, and called to me. And I answered, 'Here I am.' And he said to me, 'Who are 8 you?' I answered him, 'I am an Amal′- ekite.' And he said to me, 'Stand beside me 9 and slay me; for anguish has seized me, and yet my life still lingers.' So I stood beside 10 him, and slew him, because I was sure that he could not live after he had fallen; and I took the crown which was on his head and the armlet which was on his arm, and I have brought them here to my lord."

Then David took hold of his clothes, and 11 rent them; and so did all the men who were with him; and they mourned and wept and 12 fasted until evening for Saul and for Jona- than his son and for the people of the LORD and for the house of Israel, because they had fallen by the sword. And David said to the 13 young man who told him, "Where do you come from?" And he answered, "I am the son of a sojourner, an Amal′ekite." David 14 said to him, "How is it you were not afraid to put forth your hand to destroy the LORD's

---

[e] Gk Compare 1 Chron 10.9: Heb *to the house of their idols*
1.6–10: 1 Sam 31.1–13; 1 Chron 10.1–12.

15 anointed?" Then David called one of the young men and said, "Go, fall upon him."
16 And he smote him so that he died. And David said to him, "Your blood be upon your head; for your own mouth has testified against you, saying, 'I have slain the LORD's anointed.'"

David's lament

17 And David lamented with this lamentation
18 over Saul and Jonathan his son, and he said it*a* should be taught to the people of Judah; behold, it is written in the Book of Jashar.*b* He said:

19 "Thy glory, O Israel, is slain upon thy high places!
How are the mighty fallen!

20 Tell it not in Gath,
publish it not in the streets of Ash′kelon;
lest the daughters of the Philistines rejoice,
lest the daughters of the uncircumcised exult.

21 "Ye mountains of Gilbo′a,
let there be no dew or rain upon you,
nor upsurging of the deep!*c*
For there the shield of the mighty was defiled,
the shield of Saul, not anointed with oil.

22 "From the blood of the slain,
from the fat of the mighty,
the bow of Jonathan turned not back,
and the sword of Saul returned not empty.

23 "Saul and Jonathan, beloved and lovely!
In life and in death they were not divided;
they were swifter than eagles,
they were stronger than lions.

24 "Ye daughters of Israel, weep over Saul,
who clothed you daintily in scarlet,
who put ornaments of gold upon your apparel.

25 "How are the mighty fallen
in the midst of the battle!

"Jonathan lies slain upon thy high places.
26 I am distressed for you, my brother Jonathan;
very pleasant have you been to me;
your love to me was wonderful,
passing the love of women.

27 "How are the mighty fallen,
and the weapons of war perished!"

King of Judah

After this David inquired of the LORD, 2 "Shall I go up into any of the cities of Judah?" And the LORD said to him, "Go up." David said, "To which shall I go up?" And he said, "To Hebron." So David went 2 up there, and his two wives also, Ahin′o-am of Jezreel, and Ab′igail the widow of Nabal of Carmel. And David brought up his men 3 who were with him, every one with his household; and they dwelt in the towns of Hebron. And the men of Judah came, and 4 there they anointed David king over the house of Judah.

When they told David, "It was the men of Ja′besh-gil′ead who buried Saul," David 5 sent messengers to the men of Ja′besh-gil′ead, and said to them, "May you be blessed by the LORD, because you showed this loyalty to Saul your lord, and buried him! Now may the LORD show steadfast 6 love and faithfulness to you! And I will do good to you because you have done this thing. Now therefore let your hands be 7 strong, and be valiant; for Saul your lord is dead, and the house of Judah has anointed me king over them."

The end of Saul's house

Now Abner the son of Ner, commander of 8 Saul's army, had taken Ish-bo′sheth the son of Saul, and brought him over to Mahana′im; and he made him king over Gilead 9 and the Ash′urites and Jezreel and E′phraim and Benjamin and all Israel. Ish-bo′sheth, 10 Saul's son, was forty years old when he began to reign over Israel, and he reigned two years. But the house of Judah followed David. And the time that David was king in 11 Hebron over the house of Judah was seven years and six months.

Abner the son of Ner, and the servants of 12 Ish-bo′sheth the son of Saul, went out from Mahana′im to Gibeon. And Jo′ab the son of 13 Zeru′iah, and the servants of David, went out and met them at the pool of Gibeon; and they sat down, the one on the one side of the pool, and the other on the other side of the pool. And Abner said to Jo′ab, "Let the 14 young men arise and play before us." And Jo′ab said, "Let them arise." Then they 15 arose and passed over by number, twelve for Benjamin and Ish-bo′sheth the son of Saul, and twelve of the servants of David. And 16 each caught his opponent by the head, and thrust his sword in his opponent's side; so they fell down together. Therefore that place was called Hel′kath-hazzu′rim,*d* which

---

a Gk: Heb *the Bow*   *b* Or *The upright*   *c* Cn: Heb *fields of offerings*   *d* That is *the field of sword-edges*

17 is at Gibeon. And the battle was very fierce that day; and Abner and the men of Israel were beaten before the servants of David.
18 And the three sons of Zeru'iah were there, Jo'ab, Abi'shai, and As'ahel. Now As'ahel
19 was as swift of foot as a wild gazelle; and

As'ahel pursued Abner, and as he went he turned neither to the right hand nor to the
20 left from following Abner. Then Abner looked behind him and said, "Is it you, As'ahel?" And he answered, "It is I."
21 Abner said to him, "Turn aside to your right hand or to your left, and seize one of the young men, and take his spoil." But As'ahel would not turn aside from following him.
22 And Abner said again to As'ahel, "Turn aside from following me; why should I smite you to the ground? How then could I lift up
23 my face to your brother Jo'ab?" But he refused to turn aside; therefore Abner smote him in the belly with the butt of his spear, so that the spear came out at his back; and he fell there, and died where he was. And all who came to the place where As'ahel had fallen and died, stood still.
24 But Jo'ab and Abi'shai pursued Abner; and as the sun was going down they came to the hill of Ammah, which lies before Gi'ah on
25 the way to the wilderness of Gibeon. And the Benjaminites gathered themselves together behind Abner, and became one band, and took their stand on the top of a hill.
26 Then Abner called to Jo'ab, "Shall the sword devour for ever? Do you not know that the end will be bitter? How long will it be before you bid your people turn from the
27 pursuit of their brethren?" And Jo'ab said, "As God lives, if you had not spoken, surely the men would have given up the pursuit of
28 their brethren in the morning." So Jo'ab

blew the trumpet; and all the men stopped, and pursued Israel no more, nor did they fight any more.
29 And Abner and his men went all that night through the Arabah; they crossed the Jordan, and marching the whole forenoon they came to Mahana'im. 30 Jo'ab returned from the pursuit of Abner; and when he had gathered all the people together, there were missing of David's servants nineteen men besides As'ahel. 31 But the servants of David had slain of Benjamin three hundred and sixty of Abner's men. 32 And they took up As'ahel, and buried him in the tomb of his father, which was at Bethlehem. And Jo'ab and his men marched all night, and the day broke upon them at Hebron.

There was a long war between the house of 3 Saul and the house of David; and David grew stronger and stronger, while the house of Saul became weaker and weaker.
2 And sons were born to David at Hebron: his first-born was Amnon, of Ahin'o-am of Jezreel; and his second, Chil'e-ab, of Ab'igail 3 the widow of Nabal of Carmel; and the third, Ab'salom the son of Ma'acah the daughter of Talmai king of Geshur; and the fourth, 4 Adoni'jah the son of Haggith; and the fifth, Shephati'ah the son of Abi'tal; and the sixth, 5 Ith're-am, of Eglah, David's wife. These were born to David in Hebron.
6 While there was war between the house of Saul and the house of David, Abner was making himself strong in the house of Saul. 7 Now Saul had a concubine, whose name was Rizpah, the daughter of Ai'ah; and Ishbo'sheth said to Abner, "Why have you gone in to my father's concubine?" 8 Then Abner was very angry over the words of Ish-bo'sheth, and said, "Am I a dog's head of Judah? This day I keep showing loyalty to the house of Saul your father, to his brothers, and to his friends, and have not given you into the hand of David; and yet you charge me today with a fault concerning a woman. 9 God do so to Abner, and more also, if I do not accomplish for David what the LORD has 10 sworn to him, to transfer the kingdom from the house of Saul, and set up the throne of David over Israel and over Judah, from Dan to Beer-sheba." 11 And Ish-bo'sheth could not answer Abner another word, because he feared him.

David, Abner, and Joab

12 And Abner sent messengers to David at Hebron,[e] saying, "To whom does the land

---

[e] Gk: Heb *where he was*
3.2–5: 1 Chron 3.1–4.

Hebron

belong? Make your covenant with me, and behold, my hand shall be with you to bring
13 over all Israel to you." And he said, "Good; I will make a covenant with you; but one thing I require of you; that is, you shall not see my face, unless you first bring Michal, Saul's daughter, when you come to see my
14 face." Then David sent messengers to Ish-bo′sheth Saul's son, saying, "Give me my wife Michal, whom I betrothed at the price of a hundred foreskins of the Philis-
15 tines." And Ish-bo′sheth sent, and took her from her husband Pal′tiel the son of La′ish.
16 But her husband went with her, weeping after her all the way to Bahu′rim. Then Abner said to him, "Go, return"; and he returned.

17 And Abner conferred with the elders of Israel, saying, "For some time past you have
18 been seeking David as king over you. Now then bring it about; for the Lord has promised David, saying, 'By the hand of my servant David I will save my people Israel from the hand of the Philistines, and from
19 the hand of all their enemies.'" Abner also spoke to Benjamin; and then Abner went to tell David at Hebron all that Israel and the whole house of Benjamin thought good to do.
20 When Abner came with twenty men to David at Hebron, David made a feast for
21 Abner and the men who were with him. And Abner said to David, "I will arise and go, and will gather all Israel to my lord the king, that they may make a covenant with you, and that you may reign over all that your heart

desires." So David sent Abner away; and he went in peace.

Just then the servants of David arrived with 22 Jo′ab from a raid, bringing much spoil with them. But Abner was not with David at Hebron, for he had sent him away, and he had gone in peace. When Jo′ab and all the 23 army that was with him came, it was told Jo′ab, "Abner the son of Ner came to the king, and he has let him go, and he has gone in peace." Then Jo′ab went to the king and 24 said, "What have you done? Behold, Abner came to you; why is it that you have sent him away, so that he is gone? You know that 25 Abner the son of Ner came to deceive you, and to know your going out and your coming in, and to know all that you are doing."

When Jo′ab came out from David's pre- 26 sence, he sent messengers after Abner, and they brought him back from the cistern of Sirah; but David did not know about it. And 27 when Abner returned to Hebron, Jo′ab took him aside into the midst of the gate to speak with him privately, and there he smote him in the belly, so that he died, for the blood of As′ahel his brother. Afterward, when David 28 heard of it, he said, "I and my kingdom are for ever guiltless before the Lord for the blood of Abner the son of Ner. May it fall 29 upon the head of Jo′ab, and upon all his father's house; and may the house of Jo′ab never be without one who has a discharge, or who is leprous, or who holds a spindle, or who is slain by the sword, or who lacks bread!" So Jo′ab and Abi′shai his brother 30 slew Abner, because he had killed their brother As'ahel in the battle at Gibeon.

31 Then David said to Jo'ab and to all the people who were with him, "Rend your clothes, and gird on sackcloth, and mourn before Abner." And King David followed 32 the bier. They buried Abner at Hebron; and the king lifted up his voice and wept at the grave of Abner; and all the people wept.

33 And the king lamented for Abner, saying, "Should Abner die as a fool dies?

34 Your hands were not bound,
    your feet were not fettered;
    as one falls before the wicked
    you have fallen."

And all the people wept again over him. 35 Then all the people came to persuade David to eat bread while it was yet day; but David swore, saying, "God do so to me and more also, if I taste bread or anything else till the 36 sun goes down!" And all the people took notice of it, and it pleased them; as everything that the king did pleased all the 37 people. So all the people and all Israel understood that day that it had not been the 38 king's will to slay Abner the son of Ner. And the king said to his servants, "Do you not know that a prince and a great man has fallen 39 this day in Israel? And I am this day weak, though anointed king; these men the sons of Zeru'iah are too hard for me. The LORD requite the evildoer according to his wickedness!"

4 When Ish-bo'sheth, Saul's son, heard that Abner had died at Hebron, his courage 2 failed, and all Israel was dismayed. Now Saul's son had two men who were captains of raiding bands; the name of the one was Ba'anah, and the name of the other Rechab, sons of Rimmon a man of Benjamin from Be-er'oth (for the Be-er'oth also is reckoned to 3 Benjamin; the Be-er'othites fled to Gitta'im, and have been sojourners there to this day).

4 Jonathan, the son of Saul, had a son who was crippled in his feet. He was five years old when the news about Saul and Jonathan came from Jezreel; and his nurse took him up, and fled; and, as she fled in her haste, he fell, and became lame. And his name was Mephib'osheth.

5 Now the sons of Rimmon the Be-er'othite, Rechab and Ba'anah, set out, and about the heat of the day they came to the house of Ish-bo'sheth, as he was taking his noonday 6 rest. And behold, the doorkeeper of the house had been cleaning wheat, but she grew drowsy and slept; so Rechab and Ba'anah his 7 brother slipped in.ᶠ When they came into the house, as he lay on his bed in his bedchamber, they smote him, and slew him, and beheaded him. They took his head, and went by the way of the Arabah all night, and 8 brought the head of Ish-bo'sheth to David at Hebron. And they said to the king, "Here is the head of Ish-bo'sheth, the son of Saul, your enemy, who sought your life; the LORD has avenged my lord the king this day on Saul and on his offspring." But David 9 answered Rechab and Ba'anah his brother, the sons of Rimmon the Be-er'othite, "As the LORD lives, who has redeemed my life out of every adversity, when one told me, 'Behold, 10 Saul is dead,' and thought he was bringing good news, I seized him and slew him at Ziklag, which was the reward I gave him for his news. How much more, when wicked 11 men have slain a righteous man in his own house upon his bed, shall I not now require his blood at your hand, and destroy you from the earth?" And David commanded his 12 young men, and they killed them, and cut off their hands and feet, and hanged them beside the pool at Hebron. But they took the head of Ish-bo'sheth, and buried it in the tomb of Abner at Hebron.

King over all Israel

Then all the tribes of Israel came to David 5 at Hebron, and said, "Behold, we are your bone and flesh. In times past, when Saul was 2 king over us, it was you that led out and brought in Israel; and the LORD said to you, 'You shall be shepherd of my people Israel, and you shall be prince over Israel.'" So all 3 the elders of Israel came to the king at Hebron, and King David made a covenant with them at Hebron before the LORD, and they anointed David king over Israel. David 4 was thirty years old when he began to reign, and he reigned forty years. At Hebron he 5 reigned over Judah seven years and six months; and at Jerusalem he reigned over all Israel and Judah thirty-three years.

Capture of Jerusalem

And the king and his men went to Jeru- 6 salem against the Jeb'usites, the inhabitants of the land, who said to David, "You will not come in here, but the blind and the lame will ward you off"—thinking, "David cannot come in here." Nevertheless David took the 7 stronghold of Zion, that is, the city of David. And David said on that day, "Whoever 8 would smite the Jeb'usites, let him get up the water shaft to attack the lame and the blind,

ᶠ Gk: Heb 6 And hither they came into the midst of the house fetching wheat; and they smote him in the belly; and Rechab and Baanah his brother escaped

5.1–3: 1 Chron 11.1–3.   5.4–5: 1 Chron 3.4.   5.6–10: 1 Chron 11.4–9.

who are hated by David's soul." Therefore it is said, "The blind and the lame shall not come into the house." And David dwelt in the stronghold, and called it the city of David. And David built the city round about from the Millo inward. And David became greater and greater, for the LORD, the God of hosts, was with him.

And Hiram king of Tyre sent messengers to David, and cedar trees, also carpenters and masons who built David a house. And David perceived that the LORD had established him king over Israel, and that he had exalted his kingdom for the sake of his people Israel.

And David took more concubines and wives from Jerusalem, after he came from Hebron; and more sons and daughters were born to David. And these are the names of those who were born to him in Jerusalem: Sham′mu-a, Shobab, Nathan, Solomon, Ibhar, Eli′shu-a, Nepheg, Japhi′a, Elish′ama, Eli′ada, and Eliph′elet.

When the Philistines heard that David had been anointed king over Israel, all the Philistines went up in search of David; but David heard of it and went down to the stronghold. Now the Philistines had come and spread out in the valley of Reph′aim. And David inquired of the LORD, "Shall I go up against the Philistines? Wilt thou give them into my hand?" And the LORD said to David, "Go up; for I will certainly give the Philistines

into your hand." And David came to Ba′-20 al-pera′zim, and David defeated them there; and he said, "The LORD has broken through[g] my enemies before me, like a bursting flood." Therefore the name of that place is called Ba′al-pera′zim.[h] And the Philistines 21 left their idols there, and David and his men carried them away.

And the Philistines came up yet again, and 22 spread out in the valley of Reph′aim. And 23 when David inquired of the LORD, he said, "You shall not go up; go around to their rear, and come upon them opposite the balsam trees. And when you hear the sound of 24 marching in the tops of the balsam trees, then bestir yourself; for then the LORD has gone out before you to smite the army of the Philistines." And David did as the LORD 25 commanded him, and smote the Philistines from Geba to Gezer.

The ark of the Lord

David again gathered all the chosen men of 6 Israel, thirty thousand. And David arose 2 and went with all the people who were with him from Ba′ale-judah, to bring up from there the ark of God, which is called by the name of the LORD of hosts who sits enthroned on the cherubim. And they car- 3 ried the ark of God upon a new cart, and brought it out of the house of Abin′adab

which was on the hill; and Uzzah and Ahi'o,[t]
the sons of Abin'adab, were driving the new
4 cart[j] with the ark of God; and Ahi'o[t] went
5 before the ark. And David and all the house
of Israel were making merry before the LORD
with all their might, with songs[k] and lyres
and harps and tambourines and castanets and
cymbals.
6 And when they came to the threshing floor
of Nacon, Uzzah put out his hand to the ark
of God and took hold of it, for the oxen
7 stumbled. And the anger of the LORD was
kindled against Uzzah; and God smote him
there because he put forth his hand to the
ark;[l] and he died there beside the ark of
8 God. And David was angry because the
LORD had broken forth upon Uzzah; and that
place is called Pe'rez-uz'zah,[m] to this day.
9 And David was afraid of the LORD that day;
and he said, "How can the ark of the LORD
10 come to me?" So David was not willing to
take the ark of the LORD into the city of
David; but David took it aside to the house
11 of O'bed-e'dom the Gittite. And the ark
of the LORD remained in the house of
O'bed-e'dom the Gittite three months; and
the LORD blessed O'bed-e'dom and all his
household.
12 And it was told King David, "The LORD
has blessed the household of O'bed-e'dom
and all that belongs to him, because of the
ark of God." So David went and brought up
the ark of God from the house of O'bed-
e'dom to the city of David with rejoicing;
13 and when those who bore the ark of the LORD
had gone six paces, he sacrificed an ox and a
14 fatling. And David danced before the LORD
with all his might; and David was girded
15 with a linen ephod. So David and all the
house of Israel brought up the ark of the
LORD with shouting, and with the sound of
the horn.
16 As the ark of the LORD came into the city of
David, Michal the daughter of Saul looked
out of the window, and saw King David
leaping and dancing before the LORD; and
17 she despised him in her heart. And they
brought in the ark of the LORD, and set it in
its place, inside the tent which David had
pitched for it; and David offered burnt
offerings and peace offerings before the
18 LORD. And when David had finished offering the burnt offerings and the peace offerings, he blessed the people in the name of
19 the LORD of hosts, and distributed among
all the people, the whole multitude of Israel,
both men and women, to each a cake of

bread, a portion of meat,[n] and a cake of
raisins. Then all the people departed, each
to his house.
And David returned to bless his household.
But Michal the daughter of Saul came out to
meet David, and said, "How the king of
Israel honoured himself today, uncovering
himself today before the eyes of his servants'
maids, as one of the vulgar fellows shame-
lessly uncovers himself!" And David said to
Michal, "It was before the LORD, who chose
me above your father, and above all his
house, to appoint me as prince over Israel,
the people of the LORD—and I will make
merry before the LORD. I will make myself
yet more contemptible than this, and I will
be abased in your[o] eyes; but by the maids of
whom you have spoken, by them I shall be
held in honour." And Michal the daughter
of Saul had no child to the day of her death.

The house of the Lord

Now when the king dwelt in his house, and
the LORD had given him rest from all his
enemies round about, the king said to
Nathan the prophet, "See now, I dwell in a
house of cedar, but the ark of God dwells in a
tent." And Nathan said to the king, "Go, do
all that is in your heart; for the LORD is with
you."
But that same night the word of the LORD
came to Nathan, "Go and tell my servant
David, 'Thus says the LORD: Would you
build me a house to dwell in? I have not
dwelt in a house since the day I brought up
the people of Israel from Egypt to this day,
but I have been moving about in a tent for
my dwelling. In all places where I have
moved with all the people of Israel, did I
speak a word with any of the judges[p] of
Israel, whom I commanded to shepherd my
people Israel, saying, "Why have you not
built me a house of cedar?" ' Now therefore
thus you shall say to my servant David,
'Thus says the LORD of hosts, I took you
from the pasture, from following the sheep,
that you should be prince over my people
Israel; and I have been with you wherever
you went, and have cut off all your enemies
from before you; and I will make for you a
great name, like the name of the great ones of
the earth. And I will appoint a place for my
people Israel, and will plant them, that they
may dwell in their own place, and be disturbed no more; and violent men shall afflict
them no more, as formerly, from the time

[t] Or and his brother
[j] Compare Gk: Heb the new cart, and brought it out of the house of Abinadab which was on the hill
[k] Gk 1 Chron 13.8: Heb fir trees   [l] 1 Chron 13.10: Heb uncertain
[m] That is The breaking forth upon Uzzah   [n] Vg: Heb uncertain   [o] Gk: Heb my   [p] 1 Chron 17.6: Heb tribes
6.12–19: 1 Chron 15.1–16.3.   7.1–29: 1 Chron 17.1–27.

B. C.

1,000~900

that I appointed judges over my people Israel; and I will give you rest from all your enemies. Moreover the LORD declares to you that the LORD will make you a house. When your days are fulfilled and you lie down with your fathers, I will raise up your offspring after you, who shall come forth from your body, and I will establish his kingdom. He shall build a house for my name, and I will establish the throne of his kingdom for ever. I will be his father, and he shall be my son. When he commits iniquity, I will chasten him with the rod of men, with the stripes of the sons of men; but I will not take[q] my steadfast love from him, as I took it from Saul, whom I put away from before you. And your house and your kingdom shall be made sure for ever before me; your throne shall be established for ever.' " In accordance with all these words, and in accordance with all this vision, Nathan spoke to David.

Then King David went in and sat before the LORD, and said, "Who am I, O Lord GOD, and what is my house, that thou hast brought me thus far? And yet this was a small thing in thy eyes, O Lord GOD; thou hast spoken also of thy servant's house for a great while to come, and hast shown me future generations,[r] O Lord GOD! And what more can David say to thee? For thou knowest thy servant, O Lord GOD! Because of thy promise, and according to thy own heart, thou hast wrought all this greatness, to make thy servant know it. Therefore thou art great, O LORD God; for there is none like thee, and there is no God besides thee, according to all that we have heard with our ears. What other[s] nation on earth is like thy people Israel, whom God went to redeem to be his people, making himself a name, and doing for them[t] great and terrible things, by driving out[u] before his people a nation and its gods?[v] And thou didst establish for thyself thy people Israel to be thy people for ever; and thou, O LORD, didst become their God. And now, O LORD God, confirm for

ever the word which thou hast spoken concerning thy servant and concerning his house, and do as thou hast spoken; and thy 26 name be magnified for ever, saying, 'The LORD of hosts is God over Israel,' and the house of thy servant David will be established before thee. For thou, O LORD of 27 hosts, the God of Israel, hast made this revelation to thy servant, saying, 'I will build you a house'; therefore thy servant has found courage to pray this prayer to thee. And 28 now, O Lord GOD, thou art God, and thy words are true, and thou hast promised this good thing to thy servant; now therefore may 29 it please thee to bless the house of thy servant, that it may continue for ever before thee; for thou, O Lord GOD, hast spoken, and with thy blessing shall the house of thy servant be blessed for ever."

Enemies and friends

After this David defeated the Philis- 8 tines and subdued them, and David took Meth′eg-am′mah out of the hand of the Philistines.

And he defeated Moab, and measured them 2 with a line, making them lie down on the ground; two lines he measured to be put to death, and one full line to be spared. And the Moabites became servants to David and brought tribute.

David also defeated Hadade′zer the son of 3 Rehob, king of Zobah, as he went to restore his power at the river Euphra′tes. And 4 David took from him a thousand and seven hundred horsemen, and twenty thousand foot soldiers; and David hamstrung all the chariot horses, but left enough for a hundred chariots. And when the Syrians of 5 Damascus came to help Hadade′zer king of Zobah, David slew twenty-two thousand men of the Syrians. Then David put garri- 6 sons in Aram of Damascus; and the Syrians became servants to David and brought tribute. And the LORD gave victory to David

---

[q] Gk Syr Vg 1 Chron 17.13: Heb *shall not depart*   [r] Cn: Heb *this is the law for man*
[s] Gk: Heb *one*   [t] Heb *you*   [u] Gk 1 Chron 17.21: Heb *for your land*
[v] Heb *before thy people, whom thou didst redeem for thyself from Egypt, nations and its gods*
7.14: Heb 1.5.   8.1-14: 1 Chron 18.1-13.

7 wherever he went. And David took the shields of gold which were carried by the servants of Hadade′zer, and brought them to 8 Jerusalem. And from Betah and from Bero′thai, cities of Hadade′zer, King David took very much bronze.

9 When To′i king of Hamath heard that David had defeated the whole army of 10 Hadade′zer, To′i sent his son Joram to King David, to greet him, and to congratulate him because he had fought against Hadade′zer and defeated him; for Hadade′zer had often been at war with To′i. And Joram brought with him articles of silver, of gold, and of 11 bronze; these also King David dedicated to the LORD, together with the silver and gold which he dedicated from all the nations 12 he subdued, from Edom, Moab, the Ammonites, the Philistines, Am′alek, and from the spoil of Hadade′zer the son of Rehob, king of Zobah.

13 And David won a name for himself. When he returned, he slew eighteen thousand 14 Edomites ^{w} in the Valley of Salt. And he put garrisons in Edom; throughout all Edom he put garrisons, and all the Edomites became David's servants. And the LORD gave victory to David wherever he went.

15 So David reigned over all Israel; and David administered justice and equity to all his 16 people. And Jo′ab the son of Zeru′iah was over the army; and Jehosh′aphat the son of 17 Ahi′lud was recorder; and Zadok the son of Ahi′tub and Ahim′elech the son of Abi′athar 18 were priests; and Serai′ah was secretary; and Benai′ah the son of Jehoi′ada was over ^{x} the Cher′ethites and the Pel′ethites; and David's sons were priests.

9 And David said, "Is there still any one left of the house of Saul, that I may show him 2 kindness for Jonathan's sake?" Now there was a servant of the house of Saul whose name was Ziba, and they called him to David; and the king said to him, "Are you Ziba?" And he said, "Your servant is he." 3 And the king said, "Is there not still some one of the house of Saul, that I may show the kindness of God to him?" Ziba said to the king, "There is still a son of Jonathan; he is 4 crippled in his feet." The king said to him, "Where is he?" And Ziba said to the king, "He is in the house of Machir the son of 5 Am′miel, at Lo-debar." Then King David sent and brought him from the house of Machir the son of Am′miel, at Lo-debar. 6 And Mephib′osheth the son of Jonathan, son of Saul, came to David, and fell on his face and did obeisance. And David said,

"Mephib′osheth!" And he answered, "Behold, your servant." And David said to him, "Do not fear; for I will show you kindness for the sake of your father Jonathan, and I will restore to you all the land of Saul your father; and you shall eat at my table always." And he did obeisance, and said, "What is your servant, that you should look upon a dead dog such as I?"

Then the king called Ziba, Saul's servant, and said to him, "All that belonged to Saul and to all his house I have given to your master's son. And you and your sons and your servants shall till the land for him, and shall bring in the produce, that your master's son may have bread to eat; but Mephib′osheth your master's son shall always eat at my table." Now Ziba had fifteen sons and twenty servants. Then Ziba said to the king, "According to all that my lord the king commands his servant, so will your servant do." So Mephib′osheth ate at David's ^{y} table, like one of the king's sons. And Mephib′osheth had a young son, whose name was Mica. And all who dwelt in Ziba's house became Mephib′osheth's servants. So Mephib′osheth dwelt in Jerusalem; for he ate always at the king's table. Now he was lame in both his feet.

After this the king of the Ammonites died, 1 and Hanun his son reigned in his stead. And 2 David said, "I will deal loyally with Hanun the son of Nahash, as his father dealt loyally with me." So David sent by his servants to console him concerning his father. And David's servants came into the land of the Ammonites. But the princes of the 3 Ammonites said to Hanun their lord, "Do you think because David has sent comforters to you, that he is honouring your father? Has not David sent his servants to you to search the city, and to spy it out, and to overthrow it?" So Hanun took David's 4 servants, and shaved off half the beard of each, and cut off their garments in the middle, at their hips, and sent them away. When it was told David, he sent to meet 5 them, for the men were greatly ashamed. And the king said, "Remain at Jericho until your beards have grown, and then return."

When the Ammonites saw that they had 6 become odious to David, the Ammonites sent and hired the Syrians of Beth-re′hob, and the Syrians of Zobah, twenty thousand foot soldiers, and the king of Ma′acah with a thousand men, and the men of Tob, twelve thousand men. And when David heard of it, 7 he sent Jo′ab and all the host of the mighty

---

^{w} Gk: Heb *returned from smiting eighteen thousand Syrians*
^{x} Syr Tg Vg 20.23; 1 Chron 18.17: Heb lacks *was over* ^{y} Gk: Heb *my*
8.15–18: 2 Sam 20.23–26; 1 Chron 18.14–17.   **10.1–19:** 1 Chron 19.1–19.

men. And the Ammonites came out and drew up in battle array at the entrance of the gate; and the Syrians of Zobah and of Rehob, and the men of Tob and Ma′acah, were by themselves in the open country.

When Jo′ab saw that the battle was set against him both in front and in the rear, he chose some of the picked men of Israel, and arrayed them against the Syrians; the rest of his men he put in the charge of Abi′shai his brother, and he arrayed them against the Ammonites. And he said, "If the Syrians are too strong for me, then you shall help me; but if the Ammonites are too strong for you, then I will come and help you. Be of good courage, and let us play the man for our people, and for the cities of our God; and may the LORD do what seems good to him." So Jo′ab and the people who were with him drew near to battle against the Syrians; and they fled before him. And when the Ammonites saw that the Syrians fled, they likewise fled before Abi′shai, and entered the city. Then Jo′ab returned from fighting against the Ammonites, and came to Jerusalem.

But when the Syrians saw that they had been defeated by Israel, they gathered themselves together. And Hadade′zer sent, and brought out the Syrians who were beyond the Euphra′tes;[z] and they came to Helam, with Shobach the commander of the army of Hadade′zer at their head. And when it was told David, he gathered all Israel together, and crossed the Jordan, and came to Helam. And the Syrians arrayed themselves against David, and fought with him. And the Syrians fled before Israel; and David slew of the Syrians the men of seven hundred chariots, and forty thousand horsemen, and wounded Shobach the commander of their army, so that he died there. And when all the kings who were servants of Hadade′zer saw that they had been defeated by Israel, they made peace with Israel, and became subject to them. So the Syrians feared to help the Ammonites any more.

David and Bathsheba

1 In the spring of the year, the time when kings go forth to battle, David sent Jo′ab, and his servants with him, and all Israel; and they ravaged the Ammonites, and besieged Rabbah. But David remained at Jerusalem.

It happened, late one afternoon, when David arose from his couch and was walking upon the roof of the king's house, that he saw from the roof a woman bathing; and the woman was very beautiful. And David sent 3 and inquired about the woman. And one said, "Is not this Bathshe′ba, the daughter of Eli′am, the wife of Uri′ah the Hittite?" So 4 David sent messengers, and took her; and she came to him, and he lay with her. (Now she was purifying herself from her uncleanness.) Then she returned to her house. And 5 the woman conceived; and she sent and told David, "I am with child."

So David sent word to Jo′ab, "Send me 6 Uri′ah the Hittite." And Jo′ab sent Uri′ah to David. When Uri′ah came to him, David 7 asked how Jo′ab was doing, and how the people fared, and how the war prospered. Then David said to Uri′ah, "Go down to 8 your house, and wash your feet." And Uri′ah went out of the king's house, and there followed him a present from the king. But Uri′ah slept at the door of the king's 9 house with all the servants of his lord, and did not go down to his house. When they 10 told David, "Uri′ah did not go down to his house," David said to Uri′ah, "Have you not come from a journey? Why did you not go down to your house?" Uri′ah said to David, 11 "The ark and Israel and Judah dwell in booths; and my lord Jo′ab and the servants of my lord are camping in the open field; shall I then go to my house, to eat and to drink, and to lie with my wife? As you live, and as your soul lives, I will not do this thing." Then 12 David said to Uri′ah, "Remain here today also, and tomorrow I will let you depart." So Uri′ah remained in Jerusalem that day, and the next. And David invited him, and he ate 13 in his presence and drank, so that he made him drunk; and in the evening he went out to lie on his couch with the servants of his lord, but he did not go down to his house.

In the morning David wrote a letter to 14 Jo′ab, and sent it by the hand of Uri′ah. In 15 the letter he wrote, "Set Uri′ah in the forefront of the hardest fighting, and then draw back from him, that he may be struck down, and die." And as Jo′ab was besieging 16 the city, he assigned Uri′ah to the place where he knew there were valiant men. And 17 the men of the city came out and fought with Jo′ab; and some of the servants of David

among the people fell. Uri'ah the Hittite was
18 slain also. Then Jo'ab sent and told David
19 all the news about the fighting; and he
instructed the messenger, "When you have
finished telling all the news about the fight-
20 ing to the king, then, if the king's anger rises,
and if he says to you, 'Why did you go so
near the city to fight? Did you not know
21 that they would shoot from the wall? Who
killed Abim'elech the son of Jerub'besheth?
Did not a woman cast an upper millstone
upon him from the wall, so that he died at
Thebez? Why did you go so near the wall?'
then you shall say, 'Your servant Uri'ah the
Hittite is dead also.' "
22 So the messenger went, and came and told
23 David all that Jo'ab had sent him to tell. The
messenger said to David, "The men gained
an advantage over us, and came out against
us in the field; but we drove them back to the
24 entrance of the gate. Then the archers shot
at your servants from the wall; some of the
king's servants are dead; and your servant
25 Uri'ah the Hittite is dead also." David said
to the messenger, "Thus shall you say to
Jo'ab, 'Do not let this matter trouble you, for
the sword devours now one and now another;
strengthen your attack upon the city, and
overthrow it.' And encourage him."
26 When the wife of Uri'ah heard that Uri'ah
her husband was dead, she made lamentation
27 for her husband. And when the mourning
was over, David sent and brought her to his
house, and she became his wife, and bore
him a son. But the thing that David had
done displeased the LORD.

12 And the LORD sent Nathan to David. He
came to him, and said to him, "There were
two men in a certain city, the one rich and
2 the other poor. The rich man had very many
3 flocks and herds; but the poor man had
nothing but one little ewe lamb, which he
had bought. And he brought it up, and it
grew up with him and with his children; it
used to eat of his morsel, and drink from his
cup, and lie in his bosom, and it was like a
4 daughter to him. Now there came a traveller
to the rich man, and he was unwilling to take
one of his own flock or herd to prepare for
the wayfarer who had come to him, but he
took the poor man's lamb, and prepared it for
5 the man who had come to him." Then
David's anger was greatly kindled against the
man; and he said to Nathan, "As the LORD
lives, the man who has done this deserves to
6 die; and he shall restore the lamb fourfold,
because he did this thing, and because he had
no pity."

Nathan said to David, "You are the man.
Thus says the LORD, the God of Israel, 'I
anointed you king over Israel, and I delivered you out of the hand of Saul; and I gave
you your master's house, and your master's
wives into your bosom, and gave you the
house of Israel and of Judah; and if this were
too little, I would add to you as much more.
Why have you despised the word of the
LORD, to do what is evil in his sight? You
have smitten Uri'ah the Hittite with the
sword, and have taken his wife to be your
wife, and have slain him with the sword of
the Ammonites. Now therefore the sword
shall never depart from your house, because
you have despised me, and have taken the
wife of Uri'ah the Hittite to be your wife.'
Thus says the LORD, 'Behold, I will raise up
evil against you out of your own house; and I
will take your wives before your eyes, and
give them to your neighbour, and he shall lie
with your wives in the sight of this sun. For
you did it secretly; but I will do this thing
before all Israel, and before the sun.' "
David said to Nathan, "I have sinned against
the LORD." And Nathan said to David,
"The LORD also has put away your sin; you
shall not die. Nevertheless, because by this
deed you have utterly scorned the LORD,*a* the
child that is born to you shall die." Then
Nathan went to his house.

And the LORD struck the child that Uri'ah's
wife bore to David, and it became sick.
David therefore besought God for the child;
and David fasted, and went in and lay all
night upon the ground. And the elders of his
house stood beside him, to raise him from the
ground; but he would not, nor did he eat
food with them. On the seventh day the
child died. And the servants of David feared
to tell him that the child was dead; for they
said, "Behold, while the child was yet alive,
we spoke to him, and he did not listen to us;
how then can we say to him the child is
dead? He may do himself some harm." But
when David saw that his servants were
whispering together, David perceived that
the child was dead; and David said to his
servants, "Is the child dead?" They said,
"He is dead." Then David arose from the
earth, and washed, and anointed himself, and
changed his clothes; and he went into the
house of the LORD, and worshipped; he then
went to his own house; and when he asked,
they set food before him, and he ate. Then
his servants said to him, "What is this thing
that you have done? You fasted and wept
for the child while it was alive; but when the
child died, you arose and ate food." He said,
"While the child was still alive, I fasted and

House-tops of an Eastern city

Family problems

wept; for I said, 'Who knows whether the LORD will be gracious to me, that the
23 child may live?' But now he is dead; why should I fast? Can I bring him back again? I shall go to him, but he will not return to me."

24 Then David comforted his wife, Bathshe′ba, and went in to her, and lay with her; and she bore a son, and he called his name
25 Solomon. And the LORD loved him, and sent a message by Nathan the prophet; so he called his name Jedidi′ah,[b] because of the LORD.

26 Now Jo′ab fought against Rabbah of the
27 Ammonites, and took the royal city. And Jo′ab sent messengers to David, and said, "I have fought against Rabbah; moreover, I
28 have taken the city of waters. Now, then, gather the rest of the people together, and encamp against the city, and take it; lest I take the city, and it be called by my name."
29 So David gathered all the people together and went to Rabbah, and fought against it
30 and took it. And he took the crown of their king[c] from his head; the weight of it was a talent of gold, and in it was a precious stone; and it was placed on David's head. And he brought forth the spoil of the city, a very
31 great amount. And he brought forth the people who were in it, and set them to labour with saws and iron picks and iron axes, and made them toil at[d] the brick-kilns; and thus he did to all the cities of the Ammonites. Then David and all the people returned to Jerusalem.

Now Ab′salom, David's son, had a beautiful 13 sister, whose name was Tamar; and after a time Amnon, David's son, loved her. And 2 Amnon was so tormented that he made himself ill because of his sister Tamar; for she was a virgin, and it seemed impossible to Amnon to do anything to her. But Amnon 3 had a friend, whose name was Jon′adab, the son of Shim′e-ah, David's brother; and Jon′adab was a very crafty man. And he said 4 to him, "O son of the king, why are you so haggard morning after morning? Will you not tell me?" Amnon said to him, "I love Tamar, my brother Ab′salom's sister." Jon′adab said to him, "Lie down on your 5 bed, and pretend to be ill; and when your father comes to see you, say to him, 'Let my sister Tamar come and give me bread to eat, and prepare the food in my sight, that I may see it, and eat it from her hand.' " So 6 Amnon lay down, and pretended to be ill; and when the king came to see him, Amnon said to the king, "Pray let my sister Tamar come and make a couple of cakes in my sight, that I may eat from her hand."

Then David sent home to Tamar, saying, 7 "Go to your brother Amnon's house, and prepare food for him." So Tamar went to 8 her brother Amnon's house, where he was lying down. And she took dough, and kneaded it, and made cakes in his sight, and baked the cakes. And she took the pan 9 and emptied it out before him, but he refused to eat. And Amnon said, "Send out every one from me." So every one went out from him. Then Amnon said to Tamar, "Bring 10 the food into the chamber, that I may eat from your hand." And Tamar took the cakes she had made, and brought them into the

---

[b] That is *beloved of the* LORD   [c] Or *Milcom* See Zeph 1.5.   [d] Cn: Heb *pass through*
12.26–31: 1 Chron 20.1–3.

11 chamber to Amnon her brother. But when she brought them near him to eat, he took hold of her, and said to her, "Come, lie with 12 me, my sister." She answered him, "No, my brother, do not force me; for such a thing is not done in Israel; do not do this wanton 13 folly. As for me, where could I carry my shame? And as for you, you would be as one of the wanton fools in Israel. Now therefore, I pray you, speak to the king; for he will not 14 withhold me from you." But he would not listen to her; and being stronger than she, he forced her, and lay with her.

15 Then Amnon hated her with very great hatred; so that the hatred with which he hated her was greater than the love with which he had loved her. And Amnon said to 16 her, "Arise, be gone." But she said to him, "No, my brother; for this wrong in sending me away is greater than the other which you did to me."[e] But he would not listen to her. 17 He called the young man who served him and said, "Put this woman out of my pre- 18 sence, and bolt the door after her." Now she was wearing a long robe with sleeves; for thus were the virgin daughters of the king clad of old.[f] So his servant put her out, and 19 bolted the door after her. And Tamar put ashes on her head, and rent the long robe which she wore; and she laid her hand on her head, and went away, crying aloud as she went.

20 And her brother Ab'salom said to her, "Has Amnon your brother been with you? Now hold your peace, my sister; he is your brother; do not take this to heart." So Tamar dwelt, a desolate woman, in her 21 brother Ab'salom's house. When King David heard of all these things, he was very 22 angry. But Ab'salom spoke to Amnon neither good nor bad; for Ab'salom hated Amnon, because he had forced his sister Tamar.

23 After two full years Ab'salom had sheep-shearers at Ba'al-ha'zor, which is near E'phraim, and Ab'salom invited all the king's 24 sons. And Ab'salom came to the king, and said, "Behold, your servant has sheep-shearers; pray let the king and his servants go 25 with your servant." But the king said to Ab'salom, "No, my son, let us not all go, lest we be burdensome to you." He pressed him, but he would not go but gave him his 26 blessing. Then Ab'salom said, "If not, pray let my brother Amnon go with us." And the king said to him, "Why should he go with 27 you?" But Ab'salom pressed him until he let Amnon and all the king's sons go with 28 him. Then Ab'salom commanded his ser-

vants, "Mark when Amnon's heart is merry with wine, and when I say to you, 'Strike Amnon,' then kill him. Fear not; have I not commanded you? Be courageous and be valiant." So the servants of Ab'salom did to 29 Amnon as Ab'salom had commanded. Then all the king's sons arose, and each mounted his mule and fled.

While they were on the way, tidings came to 30 David, "Ab'salom has slain all the king's sons, and not one of them is left." Then the 31 king arose, and rent his garments, and lay on the earth; and all his servants who were standing by rent their garments. But 32 Jon'adab the son of Shim'e-ah, David's brother, said, "Let not my lord suppose that they have killed all the young men the king's sons, for Amnon alone is dead, for by the command of Ab'salom this has been determined from the day he forced his sister Tamar. Now therefore let not my lord the 33 king so take it to heart as to suppose that all the king's sons are dead; for Amnon alone is dead."

But Ab'salom fled. And the young man 34 who kept the watch lifted up his eyes, and looked, and behold, many people were coming from the Horona'im road[g] by the side of the mountain. And Jon'adab said to 35 the king, "Behold, the king's sons have come; as your servant said, so it has come about." And as soon as he had finished 36 speaking, behold, the king's sons came, and lifted up their voice and wept; and the king also and all his servants wept very bitterly.

But Ab'salom fled, and went to Talmai the 37 son of Ammi'hud, king of Geshur. And David mourned for his son day after day. So 38 Ab'salom fled, and went to Geshur, and was there three years. And the spirit[h] of the king 39 longed to go forth to Ab'salom; for he was comforted about Amnon, seeing he was dead.

Now Jo'ab the son of Zeru'iah perceived 14 that the king's heart went out to Ab'salom. And Jo'ab sent to Teko'a, and fetched from 2 there a wise woman, and said to her, "Pretend to be a mourner, and put on mourning garments; do not anoint yourself with oil, but behave like a woman who has been mourning many days for the dead; and go to the king, 3 and speak thus to him." So Jo'ab put the words in her mouth.

When the woman of Teko'a came to the 4 king, she fell on her face to the ground, and did obeisance, and said, "Help, O king." And the king said to her, "What is your 5 trouble?" She answered, "Alas, I am a widow; my husband is dead. And your 6

[e] Cn Compare Gk Vg: Heb *No, for this great wrong in sending me away is (worse) than the other which you did to me*   [f] Cn: Heb *clad in robes*   [g] Cn Compare Gk: Heb *the road behind him*   [h] Gk: Heb *David*

handmaid had two sons, and they quarrelled with one another in the field; there was no one to part them, and one struck the other 7 and killed him. And now the whole family has risen against your handmaid, and they say, 'Give up the man who struck his brother, that we may kill him for the life of his brother whom he slew'; and so they would destroy the heir also. Thus they would quench my coal which is left, and leave to my husband neither name nor remnant upon the face of the earth."

8 Then the king said to the woman, "Go to your house, and I will give orders concerning 9 you." And the woman of Teko′a said to the king, "On me be the guilt, my lord the king, and on my father's house; let the king and his 10 throne be guiltless." The king said, "If any one says anything to you, bring him to me, 11 and he shall never touch you again." Then she said, "Pray let the king invoke the LORD your God, that the avenger of blood slay no more, and my son be not destroyed." He said, "As the LORD lives, not one hair of your son shall fall to the ground."

2 Then the woman said, "Pray let your handmaid speak a word to my lord the 3 king." He said, "Speak." And the woman said, "Why then have you planned such a thing against the people of God? For in giving this decision the king convicts himself, inasmuch as the king does not bring his 4 banished one home again. We must all die, we are like water spilt on the ground, which cannot be gathered up again; but God will not take away the life of him who devises[f] means not to keep his banished one an 5 outcast. Now I have come to say this to my lord the king because the people have made me afraid; and your handmaid thought, 'I will speak to the king; it may be that the king 6 will perform the request of his servant. For the king will hear, and deliver his servant from the hand of the man who would destroy me and my son together from the heritage of 7 God.' And your handmaid thought, 'The word of my lord the king will set me at rest'; for my lord the king is like the angel of God to discern good and evil. The LORD your God be with you!"

8 Then the king answered the woman, "Do not hide from me anything I ask you." And the woman said, "Let my lord the king 9 speak." The king said, "Is the hand of Jo′ab with you in all this?" The woman answered and said, "As surely as you live, my lord the king, one cannot turn to the right hand or to the left from anything that my lord the king has said. It was your servant Jo′ab who bade me; it was he who put all these words in the

mouth of your handmaid. In order to change 20 the course of affairs your servant Jo′ab did this. But my lord has wisdom like the wisdom of the angel of God to know all things that are on the earth."

Then the king said to Jo′ab, "Behold now, I 21 grant this; go, bring back the young man Ab′salom." And Jo′ab fell on his face to the 22 ground, and did obeisance, and blessed the king; and Jo′ab said, "Today your servant knows that I have found favour in your sight, my lord the king, in that the king has granted the request of his servant." So Jo′ab arose 23 and went to Geshur, and brought Ab′salom to Jerusalem. And the king said, "Let him 24 dwell apart in his own house; he is not to come into my presence." So Ab′salom dwelt apart in his own house, and did not come into the king's presence.

Now in all Israel there was no one so much 25 to be praised for his beauty as Ab′salom; from the sole of his foot to the crown of his head there was no blemish in him. And 26 when he cut the hair of his head (for at the end of every year he used to cut it; when it was heavy on him, he cut it), he weighed the hair of his head, two hundred shekels by the king's weight. There were born to Ab′salom 27 three sons, and one daughter whose name was Tamar; she was a beautiful woman.

So Ab′salom dwelt two full years in Jeru- 28 salem, without coming into the king's presence. Then Ab′salom sent for Jo′ab, to send 29 him to the king; but Jo′ab would not come to him. And he sent a second time, but Jo′ab would not come. Then he said to his ser- 30 vants, "See, Jo′ab's field is next to mine, and he has barley there; go and set it on fire." So Ab′salom's servants set the field on fire. Then Jo′ab arose and went to Ab′salom at his 31 house, and said to him, "Why have your servants set my field on fire?" Ab′salom 32 answered Jo′ab, "Behold, I sent word to you, 'Come here, that I may send you to the king, to ask, "Why have I come from Geshur? It would be better for me to be there still." Now therefore let me go into the presence of the king; and if there is guilt in me, let him kill me.' " Then Jo′ab went to the king, and 33 told him; and he summoned Ab′salom. So he came to the king, and bowed himself on

[f] Cn: Heb *and he devises*

DAVID'S KINGDOM

The Great Sea

Abel-beth-maachah
•Dan

BASHAN

GESHUR

GILEAD

River Jordan

Mahanaim

AMMON

Baal-hazor
Gibeon
Gibeah
Gilgal
Rabbah
Jerusalem □ Bahurim
Valley of Rephaim
Adullam
•Bethlehem
Gath
Tekoa'
Hebron

PHILISTINES

MOAB

•Beer-sheba

E D O M

N

would give him justice." And whenever a man came near to do obeisance to him, he would put out his hand, and take hold of him, and kiss him. Thus Ab′salom did to all of Israel who came to the king for judgment; so Ab′salom stole the hearts of the men of Israel.

And at the end of four[j] years Ab′salom said to the king, "Pray let me go and pay my vow, which I have vowed to the LORD, in Hebron. For your servant vowed a vow while I dwelt at Geshur in Aram, saying, 'If the LORD will indeed bring me back to Jerusalem, then I will offer worship to the LORD.'" The king said to him, "Go in peace." So he arose, and went to Hebron. But Ab′salom sent secret messengers throughout all the tribes of Israel, saying, "As soon as you hear the sound of the trumpet, then say, 'Ab′salom is king at Hebron!'" With Ab′salom went two hundred men from Jerusalem who were invited guests, and they went in their simplicity, and knew nothing. And while Ab′salom was offering the sacrifices, he sent for[k] Ahith′ophel the Gi′lonite, David's counsellor, from his city Giloh. And the conspiracy grew strong, and the people with Ab′salom kept increasing.

And a messenger came to David, saying, "The hearts of the men of Israel have gone after Ab′salom." Then David said to all his servants who were with him at Jerusalem, "Arise, and let us flee; or else there will be no escape for us from Ab′salom; go in haste, lest he overtake us quickly, and bring down evil upon us, and smite the city with the edge of the sword." And the king's servants said to the king, "Behold, your servants are ready to do whatever my lord the king decides." So the king went forth, and all his household after him. And the king left ten concubines to keep the house. And the king went forth, and all the people after him; and they halted at the last house. And all his servants passed by him; and all the Cher′ethites, and all the Pel′ethites, and all the six hundred Gittites who had followed him from Gath, passed on before the king.

Then the king said to It′tai the Gittite, "Why do you also go with us? Go back, and stay with the king; for you are a foreigner, and also an exile from[l] your home. You came only yesterday, and shall I today make you wander about with us, seeing I go I know not where? Go back, and take your brethren with you; and may the LORD show[m] steadfast love and faithfulness to you." But It′tai answered the king, "As the LORD lives, and as my lord the king lives, wherever my lord the king shall be, whether for death or for

his face to the ground before the king; and the king kissed Ab′salom.

Absalom's revolt

15 After this Ab′salom got himself a chariot and horses, and fifty men to run before him. 2 And Ab′salom used to rise early and stand beside the way of the gate; and when any man had a suit to come before the king for judgment, Ab′salom would call to him, and say, "From what city are you?" And when he said, "Your servant is of such and such a 3 tribe in Israel," Ab′salom would say to him, "See, your claims are good and right; but there is no man deputed by the king to hear 4 you." Ab′salom said moreover, "Oh that I were judge in the land! Then every man with a suit or cause might come to me, and I

ʲ Gk Syr: Heb forty   ᵏ Or sent   ˡ Gk Syr Vg: Heb to   ᵐ Gk: Heb lacks may the LORD show

2 life, there also will your servant be." And David said to It′tai, "Go then, pass on." So It′tai the Gittite passed on, with all his men and all the little ones who were with him.

3 And all the country wept aloud as all the people passed by, and the king crossed the brook Kidron, and all the people passed on toward the wilderness.

4 And Abi′athar came up, and lo, Zadok came also, with all the Levites, bearing the ark of the covenant of God; and they set down the ark of God, until the people had all passed

5 out of the city. Then the king said to Zadok, "Carry the ark of God back into the city. If I find favour in the eyes of the LORD, he will bring me back and let me see both it and his

6 habitation; but if he says, 'I have no pleasure in you,' behold, here I am, let him do to me

7 what seems good to him." The king also said to Zadok the priest, "Look,ⁿ go back to the city in peace, you and Abi′athar,ᵒ with your two sons, Ahim′a-az your son, and Jonathan

8 the son of Abi′athar. See, I will wait at the fords of the wilderness, until word comes

9 from you to inform me." So Zadok and Abi′athar carried the ark of God back to Jerusalem; and they remained there.

David's flight

30 But David went up the ascent of the Mount of Olives, weeping as he went, barefoot and with his head covered; and all the people who were with him covered their heads, and they

31 went up, weeping as they went. And it was told David, "Ahith′ophel is among the conspirators with Ab′salom." And David said, "O LORD, I pray thee, turn the counsel of Ahith′ophel into foolishness."

32 When David came to the summit, where God was worshipped, behold, Hushai the Archite came to meet him with his coat rent

33 and earth upon his head. David said to him, "If you go on with me, you will be a burden

34 to me. But if you return to the city, and say to Ab′salom, 'I will be your servant, O king; as I have been your father's servant in time past, so now I will be your servant,' then you will defeat for me the counsel of Ahith′-

35 ophel. Are not Zadok and Abi′athar the priests with you there? So whatever you hear from the king's house, tell it to Zadok

36 and Abi′athar the priests. Behold, their two sons are with them there, Ahim′a-az, Zadok's son, and Jonathan, Abi′athar's son; and by them you shall send to me everything you

37 hear." So Hushai, David's friend, came into the city, just as Ab′salom was entering Jerusalem.

When David had passed a little beyond the 16 summit, Ziba the servant of Mephib′osheth met him, with a couple of asses saddled, bearing two hundred loaves of bread, a hundred bunches of raisins, a hundred of summer fruits, and a skin of wine. And the 2 king said to Ziba, "Why have you brought these?" Ziba answered, "The asses are for the king's household to ride on, the bread and summer fruit for the young men to eat, and the wine for those who faint in the wilderness to drink." And the king said, 3 "And where is your master's son?" Ziba said to the king, "Behold, he remains in Jerusalem; for he said, 'Today the house of Israel will give me back the kingdom of my father.'" Then the king said to Ziba, 4 "Behold, all that belonged to Mephib′osheth is now yours." And Ziba said, "I do obeisance; let me ever find favour in your sight, my lord the king."

When King David came to Bahu′rim, there 5 came out a man of the family of the house of Saul, whose name was Shim′e-i, the son of Gera; and as he came he cursed continually. And he threw stones at David, and at all the 6 servants of King David; and all the people and all the mighty men were on his right hand and on his left. And Shim′e-i said as he 7 cursed, "Begone, begone, you man of blood, you worthless fellow! The LORD has 8 avenged upon you all the blood of the house of Saul, in whose place you have reigned; and the LORD has given the kingdom into the hand of your son Ab′salom. See, your ruin is on you; for you are a man of blood."

Then Abi′shai the son of Zeru′iah said to 9 the king, "Why should this dead dog curse my lord the king? Let me go over and take off his head." But the king said, "What have 10 I to do with you, you sons of Zeru′iah? If he is cursing because the LORD has said to him, 'Curse David,' who then shall say, 'Why have you done so?'" And David said to 11 Abi′shai and to all his servants, "Behold, my own son seeks my life; how much more now may this Benjaminite! Let him alone, and let him curse; for the LORD has bidden him. It may be that the LORD will look upon my 12 affliction,ᵖ and that the LORD will repay me with good for this cursing of me today." So 13 David and his men went on the road, while Shim′e-i went along on the hillside opposite him and cursed as he went, and threw stones at him and flung dust. And the king, and all 14 the people who were with him, arrived weary at the Jordan;�q and there he refreshed himself.

ⁿ Gk: Heb *Are you a seer* or *Do you see?*   ᵒ Cn: Heb lacks *and Abiathar*
ᵖ Gk Vg: Heb *iniquity*   �q Gk: Heb lacks *at the Jordan*

15 Now Ab′salom and all the people, the men of Israel, came to Jerusalem, and Ahith′ophel
16 with him. And when Hushai the Archite, David's friend, came to Ab′salom, Hushai said to Ab′salom, "Long live the king! Long
17 live the king!" And Ab′salom said to Hushai, "Is this your loyalty to your friend? Why
18 did you not go with your friend?" And Hushai said to Ab′salom, "No; for whom the LORD and this people and all the men of Israel have chosen, his I will be, and with
19 him I will remain. And again, whom should I serve? Should it not be his son? As I have served your father, so I will serve you."
20 Then Ab′salom said to Ahith′ophel, "Give
21 your counsel; what shall we do?" Ahith′ophel said to Ab′salom, "Go in to your father's concubines, whom he has left to keep the house; and all Israel will hear that you have made yourself odious to your father, and the hands of all who are with you will be
22 strengthened." So they pitched a tent for Ab′salom upon the roof; and Ab′salom went in to his father's concubines in the sight of all
23 Israel. Now in those days the counsel which Ahith′ophel gave was as if one consulted the oracle[r] of God; so was all the counsel of Ahith′ophel esteemed, both by David and by Ab′salom.

17 Moreover Ahith′ophel said to Ab′salom, "Let me choose twelve thousand men, and I
2 will set out and pursue David tonight. I will come upon him while he is weary and discouraged, and throw him into a panic; and all the people who are with him will flee.
3 I will strike down the king only, and I will bring all the people back to you as a bride comes home to her husband. You seek the life of only one man,[s] and all the people will
4 be at peace." And the advice pleased Ab′salom and all the elders of Israel.
5 Then Ab′salom said, "Call Hushai the Archite also, and let us hear what he has to
6 say." And when Hushai came to Ab′salom, Ab′salom said to him, "Thus has Ahith′ophel spoken; shall we do as he advises? If
7 not, you speak." Then Hushai said to Ab′salom, "This time the counsel which
8 Ahith′ophel has given is not good." Hushai said moreover, "You know that your father and his men are mighty men, and that they are enraged, like a bear robbed of her cubs in the field. Besides, your father is expert in war; he will not spend the night with the
9 people. Behold, even now he has hidden himself in one of the pits, or in some other place. And when some of the people fall[t] at the first attack, whoever hears it will say,

'There has been a slaughter among the people who follow Ab′salom.' Then even the
10 valiant man, whose heart is like the heart of a lion, will utterly melt with fear; for all Israel knows that your father is a mighty man, and that those who are with him are valiant men.
11 But my counsel is that all Israel be gathered to you, from Dan to Beer-sheba, as the sand by the sea for multitude, and that you go to battle in person. So we shall come upon him
12 in some place where he is to be found, and we shall light upon him as the dew falls on the ground; and of him and all the men with him not one will be left. If he withdraws into a
13 city, then all Israel will bring ropes to that city, and we shall drag it into the valley, until not even a pebble is to be found there." And
14 Ab′salom and all the men of Israel said, "The counsel of Hushai the Archite is better than the counsel of Ahith′ophel." For the LORD had ordained to defeat the good counsel of Ahith′ophel, so that the LORD might bring evil upon Ab′salom.
15 Then Hushai said to Zadok and Abi′athar the priests, "Thus and so did Ahith′ophel counsel Ab′salom and the elders of Israel; and thus and so have I counselled. Now
16 therefore send quickly and tell David, 'Do not lodge tonight at the fords of the wilderness, but by all means pass over; lest the king and all the people who are with him be swallowed up.'" Now Jonathan and
17 Ahim′a-az were waiting at En-ro′gel; a maidservant used to go and tell them, and they would go and tell King David; for they must not be seen entering the city. But a lad saw
18 them, and told Ab′salom; so both of them went away quickly, and came to the house of a man at Bahu′rim, who had a well in his courtyard; and they went down into it. And
19 the woman took and spread a covering over the well's mouth, and scattered grain upon it; and nothing was known of it. When Ab′-
20 salom's servants came to the woman at the house, they said, "Where are Ahim′a-az and Jonathan?" And the woman said to them, "They have gone over the brook[u] of water." And when they had sought and could not find them, they returned to Jerusalem.
21 After they had gone, the men came up out of the well, and went and told King David. They said to David, "Arise, and go quickly over the water; for thus and so has Ahith′ophel counselled against you." Then David
22 arose, and all the people who were with him, and they crossed the Jordan; by daybreak not one was left who had not crossed the Jordan.
23 When Ahith′ophel saw that his counsel was not followed, he saddled his ass, and went off

[r] Heb word   [s] Gk: Heb like the return of the whole (is) the man whom you seek
[t] Or when he falls upon them   [u] The meaning of the Hebrew word is uncertain

home to his own city. And he set his house in order, and hanged himself; and he died, and was buried in the tomb of his father.

4 Then David came to Mahana'im. And Ab'salom crossed the Jordan with all the men 5 of Israel. Now Ab'salom had set Ama'sa over the army instead of Jo'ab. Ama'sa was the son of a man named Ithra the Ish'maelite,*v* who had married Ab'igal the daughter of Nahash, sister of Zeru'iah, Jo'ab's 6 mother. And Israel and Ab'salom encamped in the land of Gilead.

7 When David came to Mahana'im, Shobi the son of Nahash from Rabbah of the Ammonites, and Machir the son of Am'miel from Lo-debar, and Barzil'lai the Gileadite 8 from Ro'gelim, brought beds, basins, and earthen vessels, wheat, barley, meal, parched 9 grain, beans and lentils,*w* honey and curds and sheep and cheese from the herd, for David and the people with him to eat; for they said, "The people are hungry and weary and thirsty in the wilderness."

8 Then David mustered the men who were with him, and set over them commanders of thousands and commanders of hundreds. 2 And David sent forth the army, one third under the command of Jo'ab, one third under the command of Abi'shai the son of Zeru'iah, Jo'ab's brother, and one third under the command of It'tai the Gittite. And the king said to the men, "I myself will 3 also go out with you." But the men said, "You shall not go out. For if we flee, they will not care about us. If half of us die, they will not care about us. But you are worth ten thousand of us;*x* therefore it is better that 4 you send us help from the city." The king said to them, "Whatever seems best to you I will do." So the king stood at the side of the gate, while all the army marched out by 5 hundreds and by thousands. And the king ordered Jo'ab and Abi'shai and It'tai, "Deal gently for my sake with the young man Ab'salom." And all the people heard when the king gave orders to all the commanders about Ab'salom.

6 So the army went out into the field against Israel; and the battle was fought in the forest 7 of E'phraim. And the men of Israel were defeated there by the servants of David, and the slaughter there was great on that day, 8 twenty thousand men. The battle spread over the face of all the country; and the forest devoured more people that day than the sword.

Death of Absalom

And Ab'salom chanced to meet the servants 9 of David. Ab'salom was riding upon his mule, and the mule went under the thick branches of a great oak, and his head caught fast in the oak, and he was left hanging*v* between heaven and earth, while the mule that was under him went on. And a certain 10 man saw it, and told Jo'ab, "Behold, I saw Ab'salom hanging in an oak." Jo'ab said to 11 the man who told him, "What, you saw him! Why then did you not strike him there to the ground? I would have been glad to give you ten pieces of silver and a girdle." But the man said to Jo'ab, "Even if I felt in 12 my hand the weight of a thousand pieces of silver, I would not put forth my hand against the king's son; for in our hearing the king commanded you and Abi'shai and It'tai, 'For my sake protect the young man Ab'salom.' On the other hand, if I had dealt treacher- 13 ously against his life*z* (and there is nothing hidden from the king), then you yourself would have stood aloof." Jo'ab said, "I will 14 not waste time like this with you." And he took three darts in his hand, and thrust them into the heart of Ab'salom, while he was still alive in the oak. And ten young men, Jo'ab's 15 armour-bearers, surrounded Ab'salom and struck him, and killed him.

Then Jo'ab blew the trumpet, and the 16 troops came back from pursuing Israel; for Jo'ab restrained them. And they took 17 Ab'salom, and threw him into a great pit in

---

v 1 Chron 2.17: Heb *Israelite*   *w* Heb *lentils and parched grain*
x Gk Vg Symmachus: Heb *for now there are ten thousand such as we*   *y* Gk Syr Tg: Heb *was put*
z Another reading is *at the risk of my life*

the forest, and raised over him a very great heap of stones; and all Israel fled every one to 18 his own home. Now Ab′salom in his lifetime had taken and set up for himself the pillar which is in the King's Valley, for he said, "I have no son to keep my name in remembrance"; he called the pillar after his own name, and it is called Ab′salom's monument to this day.

19 Then said Ahim′a-az the son of Zadok, "Let me run, and carry tidings to the king that the LORD has delivered him from the 20 power of his enemies." And Jo′ab said to him, "You are not to carry tidings today; you may carry tidings another day, but today you shall carry no tidings, because the king's son 21 is dead." Then Jo′ab said to the Cushite, "Go, tell the king what you have seen." The 22 Cushite bowed before Jo′ab, and ran. Then Ahim′a-az the son of Zadok said again to Jo′ab, "Come what may, let me also run after the Cushite." And Jo′ab said, "Why will you run, my son, seeing that you will have no 23 reward for the tidings?" "Come what may," he said, "I will run." So he said to him, "Run." Then Ahim′a-az ran by the way of the plain, and outran the Cushite.

24 Now David was sitting between the two gates; and the watchman went up to the roof of the gate by the wall, and when he lifted up his eyes and looked, he saw a man running 25 alone. And the watchman called out and told the king. And the king said, "If he is alone, there are tidings in his mouth." And he 26 came apace, and drew near. And the watchman saw another man running; and the watchman called to the gate and said, "See, another man running alone!" The king said, 27 "He also brings tidings." And the watchman said, "I think the running of the foremost is like the running of Ahim′a-az the son of Zadok." And the king said, "He is a good man, and comes with good tidings." 28 Then Ahim′a-az cried out to the king, "All is well." And he bowed before the king with his face to the earth, and said, "Blessed be the LORD your God, who has delivered up the men who raised their hand against my

lord the king." And the king said, "Is it well 2 with the young man Ab′salom?" Ahim′a-az answered, "When Jo′ab sent your servant,[a] I saw a great tumult, but I do not know what it was." And the king said, "Turn aside, and 3 stand here." So he turned aside, and stood still.

And behold, the Cushite came; and the 3 Cushite said, "Good tidings for my lord the king! For the LORD has delivered you this day from the power of all who rose up against you." The king said to the Cushite, "Is it 3 well with the young man Ab′salom?" And the Cushite answered, "May the enemies of my lord the king, and all who rise up against you for evil, be like that young man." And 3 the king was deeply moved, and went up to the chamber over the gate, and wept; and as he went, he said, "O my son Ab′salom, my son, my son Ab′salom! Would I had died instead of you, O Ab′salom, my son, my son!"[b]

It was told Jo′ab, "Behold, the king 19 is weeping and mourning for Ab′salom." So the victory that day was turned into 2 mourning for all the people; for the people heard that day, "The king is grieving for his son." And the people stole into the city that 3 day as people steal in who are ashamed when they flee in battle. The king covered his face, 4 and the king cried with a loud voice, "O my son Ab′salom, O Ab′salom, my son, my son!" Then Jo′ab came into the house to the 5 king, and said, "You have today covered with shame the faces of all your servants, who have this day saved your life, and the lives of your sons and your daughters, and the lives of your wives and your concubines, because 6 you love those who hate you and hate those who love you. For you have made it clear today that commanders and servants are nothing to you; for today I perceive that if Ab′salom were alive and all of us were dead today, then you would be pleased. Now 7 therefore arise, go out and speak kindly to your servants; for I swear by the LORD, if you do not go, not a man will stay with you this night; and this will be worse for you than all the evil that has come upon you from your youth until now." Then the king arose, and 8 took his seat in the gate. And the people were all told, "Behold, the king is sitting in the gate"; and all the people came before the king.

Now Israel had fled every man to his own home. And all the people were at strife 9 throughout all the tribes of Israel, saying, "The king delivered us from the hand of our enemies, and saved us from the hand of the

Philistines; and now he has fled out of the land from Ab'salom. But Ab'salom, whom we anointed over us, is dead in battle. Now therefore why do you say nothing about bringing the king back?"

11 And King David sent this message to Zadok and Abi'athar the priests, "Say to the elders of Judah, 'Why should you be the last to bring the king back to his house, when the word of all Israel has come to the king?[c] 12 You are my kinsmen, you are my bone and my flesh; why then should you be the last to 13 bring back the king?' And say to Ama'sa, 'Are you not my bone and my flesh? God do so to me, and more also, if you are not commander of my army henceforth in place 14 of Jo'ab.'" And he swayed the heart of all the men of Judah as one man; so that they sent word to the king, "Return, both you and 15 all your servants." So the king came back to the Jordan; and Judah came to Gilgal to meet the king and to bring the king over the Jordan.

David's return

16 And Shim'e-i the son of Gera, the Benjaminite, from Bahu'rim, made haste to come down with the men of Judah to meet King 17 David; and with him were a thousand men from Benjamin. And Ziba the servant of the house of Saul, with his fifteen sons and his twenty servants, rushed down to the Jordan 18 before the king, and they crossed the ford[d] to bring over the king's household, and to do his pleasure. And Shim'e-i the son of Gera fell down before the king, as he was about to 19 cross the Jordan, and said to the king, "Let not my lord hold me guilty or remember how your servant did wrong on the day my lord the king left Jerusalem; let not the king bear 20 it in mind. For your servant knows that I have sinned; therefore, behold, I have come this day, the first of all the house of Joseph to come down to meet my lord the king."

Abi'shai the son of Zeru'iah answered, 21 "Shall not Shim'e-i be put to death for this, because he cursed the LORD's anointed?" But David said, "What have I to do with 22 you, you sons of Zeru'iah, that you should this day be as an adversary to me? Shall any one be put to death in Israel this day? For do I not know that I am this day king over Israel?" And the king said to Shim'e-i, 23 "You shall not die." And the king gave him his oath.

And Mephib'osheth the son of Saul came 24 down to meet the king; he had neither dressed his feet, nor trimmed his beard, nor washed his clothes, from the day the king departed until the day he came back in safety. And when he came from[e] Jerusalem 25 to meet the king, the king said to him, "Why did you not go with me, Mephib'osheth?" He answered, "My lord, O king, my servant 26 deceived me; for your servant said to him, 'Saddle an ass for me,[f] that I may ride upon it and go with the king.' For your servant is lame. He has slandered your servant to my 27 lord the king. But my lord the king is like the angel of God; do therefore what seems good to you. For all my father's house were but 28 men doomed to death before my lord the king; but you set your servant among those who eat at your table. What further right have I, then, to cry to the king?" And the 29 king said to him, "Why speak any more of your affairs? I have decided: you and Ziba shall divide the land." And Mephib'osheth 30 said to the king, "Oh, let him take it all, since my lord the king has come safely home."

Now Barzil'lai the Gileadite had come 31 down from Ro'gelim; and he went on with the king to the Jordan, to escort him over the Jordan. Barzil'lai was a very aged man, 32 eighty years old; and he had provided the king with food while he stayed at Maha-na'im; for he was a very wealthy man. And 33 the king said to Barzil'lai, "Come over with me, and I will provide for you with me in

c Gk: Heb to the king, to his house   d Cn: Heb the ford crossed   e Heb to
f Gk Syr Vg: Heb said, I will saddle an ass for myself

34 Jerusalem." But Barzil'lai said to the king, "How many years have I still to live, that I
35 should go up with the king to Jerusalem? I am this day eighty years old; can I discern what is pleasant and what is not? Can your servant taste what he eats or what he drinks? Can I still listen to the voice of singing men and singing women? Why then should your servant be an added burden to my lord the
36 king? Your servant will go a little way over the Jordan with the king. Why should the king recompense me with such a reward?
37 Pray let your servant return, that I may die in my own city, near the grave of my father and my mother. But here is your servant Chimham; let him go over with my lord the king; and do for him whatever seems good to
38 you." And the king answered, "Chimham shall go over with me, and I will do for him whatever seems good to you; and all that you
39 desire of me I will do for you." Then all the people went over the Jordan, and the king went over; and the king kissed Barzil'lai and blessed him, and he returned to his own
40 home. The king went on to Gilgal, and Chimham went on with him; all the people of Judah, and also half the people of Israel, brought the king on his way.
41 Then all the men of Israel came to the king, and said to the king, "Why have our brethren the men of Judah stolen you away, and brought the king and his household over the
42 Jordan, and all David's men with him?" All the men of Judah answered the men of Israel, "Because the king is near of kin to us. Why then are you angry over this matter? Have we eaten at all at the king's expense? Or has
43 he given us any gift?" And the men of Israel answered the men of Judah, "We have ten shares in the king, and in David also we have more than you. Why then did you despise us? Were we not the first to speak of bringing back our king?" But the words of the men of Judah were fiercer than the words of the men of Israel.

20 Now there happened to be there a worthless fellow, whose name was Sheba, the son of Bichri, a Benjaminite; and he blew the trumpet, and said,

"We have no portion in David,
    and we have no inheritance in the son of Jesse;
every man to his tents, O Israel!"

2 So all the men of Israel withdrew from David, and followed Sheba the son of Bichri; but the men of Judah followed their king steadfastly from the Jordan to Jerusalem.
3 And David came to his house at Jerusalem;

and the king took the ten concubines whom he had left to care for the house, and put them in a house under guard, and provided for them, but did not go in to them. So they were shut up until the day of their death, living as if in widowhood.

Then the king said to Ama'sa, "Call the 4 men of Judah together to me within three days, and be here yourself." So Ama'sa went 5 to summon Judah; but he delayed beyond the set time which had been appointed him. And David said to Abi'shai, "Now Sheba the 6 son of Bichri will do us more harm than Ab'salom; take your lord's servants and pursue him, lest he get himself fortified cities, and cause us trouble."[g] And there 7 went out after Abi'shai, Jo'ab[h] and the Cher'ethites and the Pel'ethites, and all the mighty men; they went out from Jerusalem to pursue Sheba the son of Bichri. When 8 they were at the great stone which is in Gibeon, Ama'sa came to meet them. Now Jo'ab was wearing a soldier's garment, and over it was a girdle with a sword in its sheath fastened upon his loins, and as he went forward it fell out. And Jo'ab said to Ama'sa, 9 "Is it well with you, my brother?" And Jo'ab took Ama'sa by the beard with his right hand to kiss him. But Ama'sa did not 10 observe the sword which was in Jo'ab's hand; so Jo'ab struck him with it in the body, and shed his bowels to the ground, without striking a second blow; and he died.

Then Jo'ab and Abi'shai his brother pursued Sheba the son of Bichri. And one of 11 Jo'ab's men took his stand by Ama'sa, and said, "Whoever favours Jo'ab, and whoever is for David, let him follow Jo'ab." And 12 Ama'sa lay wallowing in his blood in the highway. And any one who came by, seeing him, stopped;[i] and when the man saw that all the people stopped, he carried Ama'sa out of the highway into the field, and threw a garment over him. When he was taken out of 13 the highway, all the people went on after Jo'ab to pursue Sheba the son of Bichri.

And Sheba passed through all the tribes of 14 Israel to Abel of Beth-ma'acah;[j] and all the Bichrites[k] assembled, and followed him in. And all the men who were with Jo'ab came 15 and besieged him in Abel of Beth-ma'acah; they cast up a mound against the city, and it stood against the rampart; and they were battering the wall, to throw it down. Then a 16 wise woman called from the city, "Hear! Hear! Tell Jo'ab, 'Come here, that I may speak to you.'" And he came near her; and 17 the woman said, "Are you Jo'ab?" He answered, "I am." Then she said to him,

"Listen to the words of your maidservant." And he answered, "I am listening." Then she said, "They were wont to say in old time, 'Let them but ask counsel at Abel'; and so they settled a matter. I am one of those who are peaceable and faithful in Israel; you seek to destroy a city which is a mother in Israel; why will you swallow up the heritage of the LORD?" Jo'ab answered, "Far be it from me, far be it, that I should swallow up or destroy! That is not true. But a man of the hill country of E'phraim, called Sheba the son of Bichri, has lifted up his hand against King David; give up him alone, and I will withdraw from the city." And the woman said to Jo'ab, "Behold, his head shall be thrown to you over the wall." Then the woman went to all the people in her wisdom. And they cut off the head of Sheba the son of Bichri, and threw it out to Jo'ab. So he blew the trumpet, and they dispersed from the city, every man to his home. And Jo'ab returned to Jerusalem to the king.

Now Jo'ab was in command of all the army of Israel; and Benai'ah the son of Jehoi'ada was in command of the Cher'ethites and the Pel'ethites; and Ado'ram was in charge of the forced labour; and Jehosh'aphat the son of Ahi'lud was the recorder; and Sheva was secretary; and Zadok and Abi'athar were priests; and Ira the Ja'irite was also David's priest.

A famine

Now there was a famine in the days of David for three years, year after year; and David sought the face of the LORD. And the LORD said, "There is blood guilt on Saul and on his house, because he put the Gib'eonites to death." So the king called the Gib'eonites.[i] Now the Gib'eonites were not of the people of Israel, but of the remnant of the Amorites; although the people of Israel had sworn to spare them, Saul had sought to slay them in his zeal for the people of Israel and Judah. And David said to the Gib'eonites, "What shall I do for you? And how shall I make expiation, that you may bless the heritage of the LORD?" The Gib'eonites said to him, "It is not a matter of silver or gold between us and Saul or his house; neither is it for us to put any man to death in Israel." And he said, "What do you say that I shall do for you?" They said to the king, "The man who consumed us and planned to destroy us, so that we should have no place in all the territory of Israel, let seven of his sons

be given to us, so that we may hang them up before the LORD at Gibeon on the mountain of the LORD."[m] And the king said, "I will give them."

But the king spared Mephib'osheth, the son 7 of Saul's son Jonathan, because of the oath of the LORD which was between them, between David and Jonathan the son of Saul. The 8 king took the two sons of Rizpah the daughter of Ai'ah, whom she bore to Saul, Armo'ni and Mephib'osheth; and the five sons of Merab[n] the daughter of Saul, whom she bore to A'dri-el the son of Barzil'lai the Meho'lathite; and he gave them into the 9 hands of the Gib'eonites, and they hanged them on the mountain before the LORD, and the seven of them perished together. They were put to death in the first days of harvest, at the beginning of barley harvest.

Then Rizpah the daughter of Ai'ah took 10 sackcloth, and spread it for herself on the rock, from the beginning of harvest until rain fell upon them from the heavens; and she did not allow the birds of the air to come upon them by day, or the beasts of the field by night. When David was told what Rizpah 11 the daughter of Ai'ah, the concubine of Saul, had done, David went and took the bones of 12 Saul and the bones of his son Jonathan from the men of Ja'besh-gil'ead, who had stolen them from the public square of Beth-shan, where the Philistines had hanged them, on the day the Philistines killed Saul on Gilbo'a; and he brought up from there the bones of 13 Saul and the bones of his son Jonathan; and they gathered the bones of those who were hanged. And they buried the bones of Saul 14 and his son Jonathan in the land of Benjamin in Zela, in the tomb of Kish his father; and they did all that the king commanded. And after that God heeded supplications for the land.

The Philistines had war again with Israel, 15 and David went down together with his servants, and they fought against the Philistines; and David grew weary. And Ish'- 16 bi-be'nob, one of the descendants of the giants, whose spear weighed three hundred shekels of bronze, and who was girded with a new sword, thought to kill David. But 17 Abi'shai the son of Zeru'iah came to his aid, and attacked the Philistine and killed him. Then David's men adjured him, "You shall no more go out with us to battle, lest you quench the lamp of Israel."

After this there was again war with the 18 Philistines at Gob; then Sib'becai the Hu'- shathite slew Saph, who was one of the

i Heb *the Gibeonites and said to them*
m Cn Compare Gk and 21.9: Heb *at Gibeah of Saul, the chosen of the* LORD
n Two Hebrew Mss Gk: Heb *Michal*
20.23–26: 2 Sam 8.15–18; 1 Chron 18.14–17. 21.18–22: 1 Chron 20.4–8.

19 descendants of the giants. And there was again war with the Philistines at Gob; and Elha′nan the son of Ja′are-or′egim, the Bethlehemite, slew Goliath the Gittite, the shaft of whose spear was like a weaver's
20 beam. And there was again war at Gath, where there was a man of great stature, who had six fingers on each hand, and six toes on each foot, twenty-four in number; and he
21 also was descended from the giants. And when he taunted Israel, Jonathan the son of
22 Shim′e-i, David's brother, slew him. These four were descended from the giants in Gath; and they fell by the hand of David and by the hand of his servants.

Hymn of praise

22 And David spoke to the LORD the words of this song on the day when the LORD delivered him from the hand of all his enemies, and from the hand of Saul. He said,
2   "The LORD is my rock, and my fortress, and my deliverer,
3   my° God, my rock, in whom I take refuge, my shield and the horn of my salvation, my stronghold and my refuge, my saviour; thou savest me from violence.
4   I call upon the LORD, who is worthy to be praised, and I am saved from my enemies.

5   "For the waves of death encompassed me, the torrents of perdition assailed me;
6   the cords of Sheol entangled me, the snares of death confronted me.

7   "In my distress I called upon the LORD; to my God I called. From his temple he heard my voice, and my cry came to his ears.

8   "Then the earth reeled and rocked; the foundations of the heavens trembled

and quaked, because he was angry.
9 Smoke went up from his nostrils, and devouring fire from his mouth; glowing coals flamed forth from him.
10 He bowed the heavens, and came down; thick darkness was under his feet.
11 He rode on a cherub, and flew; he was seen upon the wings of the wind.
12 He made darkness around him his canopy, thick clouds, a gathering of water.
13 Out of the brightness before him coals of fire flamed forth.
14 The LORD thundered from heaven, and the Most High uttered his voice.
15 And he sent out arrows, and scattered them; lightning, and routed them.
16 Then the channels of the sea were seen, the foundations of the world were laid bare, at the rebuke of the LORD, at the blast of the breath of his nostrils.

17 "He reached from on high, he took me, he drew me out of many waters.
18 He delivered me from my strong enemy, from those who hated me; for they were too mighty for me.
19 They came upon me in the day of my calamity; but the LORD was my stay.
20 He brought me forth into a broad place; he delivered me, because he delighted in me.

21 "The LORD rewarded me according to my righteousness; according to the cleanness of my hands he recompensed me.
22 For I have kept the ways of the LORD, and have not wickedly departed from my God.
23 For all his ordinances were before me, and from his statutes I did not turn aside.
24 I was blameless before him, and I kept myself from guilt.
25 Therefore the LORD has recompensed me according to my righteousness, according to my cleanness in his sight.

26 "With the loyal thou dost show thyself loyal; with the blameless man thou dost show thyself blameless;
27 with the pure thou dost show thyself pure, and with the crooked thou dost show thyself perverse.

° Gk Ps 18.2: Heb lacks my
22.2–51: Ps 18.2–50.

28 Thou dost deliver a humble people,
but thy eyes are upon the haughty to
bring them down.
29 Yea, thou art my lamp, O LORD,
and my God lightens my darkness.
30 Yea, by thee I can crush a troop,
and by my God I can leap over a wall.
31 This God—his way is perfect;
the promise of the LORD proves true;
he is a shield for all those who take
refuge in him.

32 "For who is God, but the LORD?
And who is a rock, except our God?
33 This God is my strong refuge,
and has made*p* my*q* way safe.
34 He made my*q* feet like hinds' feet,
and set me secure on the heights.
35 He trains my hands for war,
so that my arms can bend a bow of
bronze.
36 Thou hast given me the shield of thy
salvation,
and thy help*r* made me great.
37 Thou didst give a wide place for my steps
under me,
and my feet*s* did not slip;
38 I pursued my enemies and destroyed
them,
and did not turn back until they were
consumed.
39 I consumed them; I thrust them through,
so that they did not rise;
they fell under my feet.
40 For thou didst gird me with strength for
the battle;
thou didst make my assailants sink
under me.
41 Thou didst make my enemies turn their
backs to me,
those who hated me, and I destroyed
them.
42 They looked, but there was none to save;
they cried to the LORD, but he did not
answer them.
43 I beat them fine as the dust of the earth,
I crushed them and stamped them down
like the mire of the streets.

44 "Thou didst deliver me from strife with
the peoples;*t*
thou didst keep me as the head of the
nations;
people whom I had not known served me.
45 Foreigners came cringing to me;
as soon as they heard of me, they obeyed
me.
46 Foreigners lost heart,
and came trembling*u* out of their fastnesses.

47 "The LORD lives; and blessed be my rock,
and exalted be my God, the rock of my
salvation,
48 the God who gave me vengeance
and brought down peoples under me,
49 who brought me out from my enemies;
thou didst exalt me above my adversaries,
thou didst deliver me from men of
violence.

50 "For this I will extol thee, O LORD, among
the nations,
and sing praises to thy name.
51 Great triumphs he gives*v* to his king,
and shows steadfast love to his anointed,
to David, and his descendants for ever."

David's last words

23 Now these are the last words of David:
The oracle of David, the son of Jesse,
the oracle of the man who was raised on
high,
the anointed of the God of Jacob,
the sweet psalmist of Israel:*w*

2 "The Spirit of the LORD speaks by me,
his word is upon my tongue.
3 The God of Israel has spoken,
the Rock of Israel has said to me:
When one rules justly over men,
ruling in the fear of God,
4 he dawns on them like the morning light,
like the sun shining forth upon a cloud-
less morning,
like rain*x* that makes grass to sprout
from the earth.
5 Yea, does not my house stand so with
God?
For he has made with me an everlasting
covenant,
ordered in all things and secure.
For will he not cause to prosper
all my help and my desire?
6 But godless men*y* are all like thorns that
are thrown away;
for they cannot be taken with the hand;
7 but the man who touches them
arms himself with iron and the shaft of a
spear,
and they are utterly consumed with
fire."*z*

p Ps 18.32: Heb *set free*   *q* Another reading is *his*   *r* Or *gentleness*   *s* Heb *ankles*
t Gk: Heb *from strife with my people*   *u* Ps 18.45: Heb *girded themselves*
v Another reading is *He is a tower of salvation*   *w* Or *the favourite of the songs of Israel*   *x* Heb *from rain*
y Heb *worthlessness*   *z* Heb *fire in the sitting*
22.50: Rom 15.9.

David's mighty men

8 These are the names of the mighty men whom David had: Josheb-basshe'beth a Tah-che'monite; he was chief of the three;[a] he wielded his spear[b] against eight hundred whom he slew at one time.

9 And next to him among the three mighty men was Elea'zar the son of Dodo, son of Aho'hi. He was with David when they defied the Philistines who were gathered there for battle, and the men of Israel 10 withdrew. He rose and struck down the Philistines until his hand was weary, and his hand cleaved to the sword; and the LORD wrought a great victory that day; and the men returned after him only to strip the slain.

11 And next to him was Shammah, the son of Agee the Har'arite. The Philistines gathered together at Lehi, where there was a plot of ground full of lentils; and the men fled from 12 the Philistines. But he took his stand in the midst of the plot, and defended it, and slew the Philistines; and the LORD wrought a great victory.

13 And three of the thirty chief men went down, and came about harvest time to David at the cave of Adullam, when a band of Philistines was encamped in the valley of 14 Reph'aim. David was then in the stronghold; and the garrison of the Philistines 15 was then at Bethlehem. And David said longingly, "O that some one would give me water to drink from the well of Bethlehem 16 which is by the gate!" Then the three mighty men broke through the camp of the Philistines, and drew water out of the well of Bethlehem which was by the gate, and took and brought it to David. But he would not 17 drink of it; he poured it out to the LORD, and said, "Far be it from me, O LORD, that I should do this. Shall I drink the blood of the men who went at the risk of their lives?" Therefore he would not drink it. These things did the three mighty men.

18 Now Abi'shai, the brother of Jo'ab, the son of Zeru'iah, was chief of the thirty.[c] And he wielded his spear against three hundred men and slew them, and won a name beside the 19 three. He was the most renowned of the thirty,[d] and became their commander; but he did not attain to the three.

20 And Benai'ah the son of Jehoi'ada was a valiant man[e] of Kabzeel, a doer of great deeds; he smote two ariels[f] of Moab. He also went down and slew a lion in a pit on a 21 day when snow had fallen. And he slew an

Egyptian, a handsome man. The Egyptian had a spear in his hand; but Benai'ah went down to him with a staff, and snatched the spear out of the Egyptian's hand, and slew him with his own spear. These things did 22 Benai'ah the son of Jehoi'ada, and won a name beside the three mighty men. He was 23 renowned among the thirty, but he did not attain to the three. And David set him over his bodyguard.

As'ahel the brother of Jo'ab was one of 24 the thirty; Elha'nan the son of Dodo of Bethlehem, Shammah of Harod, Eli'ka 25 of Harod, Helez the Paltite, Ira the son 26 of Ikkesh of Teko'a, Abi-e'zer, of An'- 27 athoth, Mebun'nai the Hu'shathite, Zalmon 28 the Aho'hite, Ma'harai of Netoph'ah, Heleb 29 the son of Ba'anah of Netoph'ah, It'tai the son of Ri'bai of Gib'e-ah of the Benjaminites, Benai'ah of Pir'athon, Hid'dai of the brooks 30 of Ga'ash, Abial'bon the Ar'bathite, 31 Az'maveth of Bahu'rim, Eli'ahba of 32 Sha-al'bon, the sons of Jashen, Jonathan, Shammah the Har'arite, Ahi'am the son of 33 Sharar the Har'arite, Eliph'elet the son of 34 Ahas'bai of Ma'acah, Eli'am the son of Ahith'ophel of Gilo, Hezro[g] of Carmel, 35 Pa'arai the Arbite, Igal the son of Nathan 36 of Zobah, Bani the Gadite, Zelek the 37

---

a Or *captains*   *b* 1 Chron 11.11: Heb obscure   *c* Two Hebrew Mss Syr: MT *three*
d 1 Chron 11.25: Heb *Was he the most renowned of the three?*   *e* Another reading is *the son of Ish-hai*
f The meaning of the word *ariel* is unknown   *g* Another reading is *Hezrai*
23.8–39: 1 Chron 11.10–41.

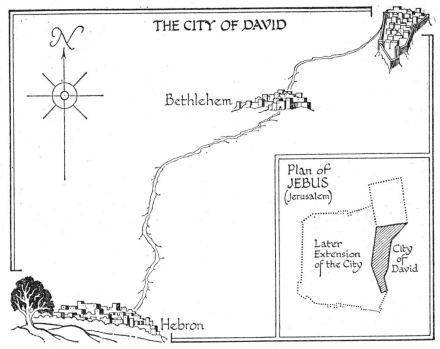

The city David captured and made the capital of his Kingdom

Ammonite, Na′harai of Be-er′oth, the armour-bearer of Jo′ab the son of Zeru′iah, 38,Ira the Ithrite, Gareb the Ithrite, Uri′ah the 39 Hittite: thirty-seven in all.

Numbering the people

24 Again the anger of the LORD was kindled against Israel, and he incited David against them, saying, "Go, number Israel and 2 Judah." So the king said to Jo′ab and the commanders of the army,ʰ who were with him, "Go through all the tribes of Israel, from Dan to Beer-sheba, and number the people, that I may know the number of the 3 people." But Jo′ab said to the king, "May the LORD your God add to the people a hundred times as many as they are, while the eyes of my lord the king still see it; but why does my lord the king delight in this thing?" 4 But the king's word prevailed against Jo′ab and the commanders of the army. So Jo′ab and the commanders of the army went out from the presence of the king to number the people of Israel. They crossed the Jordan, 5 and began from Aro′er,ⁱ and from the city that is in the middle of the valley, toward Gad and on to Jazer. Then they came to 6 Gilead, and to Kadesh in the land of the Hittites;ʲ and they came to Dan, and from Danᵏ they went around to Sidon, and came 7 to the fortress of Tyre and to all the cities of the Hivites and Canaanites; and they went out to the Negeb of Judah at Beer-sheba. So 8 when they had gone through all the land, they came to Jerusalem at the end of nine months and twenty days. And Jo′ab gave the 9 sum of the numbering of the people to the king: in Israel there were eight hundred thousand valiant men who drew the sword, and the men of Judah were five hundred thousand.

But David's heart smote him after he had 10 numbered the people. And David said to the LORD, "I have sinned greatly in what I have done. But now, O LORD, I pray thee, take away the iniquity of thy servant; for I have done very foolishly." And when David arose 11

ʰ 1 Chron 21.2. Gk: Heb *to Joab the commander of the army*   ⁱ Gk: Heb *encamped in Aroer*
ʲ Gk: Heb *to the land of Tahtim-hodshi*   ᵏ Cn Compare Gk: Heb *they came to Dan-jaan and*
24.1-25: 1 Chron 21.1-27.

in the morning, the word of the LORD came to the prophet Gad, David's seer, saying, 12 "Go and say to David, 'Thus says the LORD, Three things I offer[i] you; choose one of 13 them, that I may do it to you.'" So Gad came to David and told him, and said to him, "Shall three[m] years of famine come to you in your land? Or will you flee three months before your foes while they pursue you? Or shall there be three days' pestilence in your land? Now consider, and decide what answer I shall return to him who sent me." 14 Then David said to Gad, "I am in great distress; let us fall into the hand of the LORD, for his mercy is great; but let me not fall into the hand of man."

15 So the LORD sent a pestilence upon Israel from the morning until the appointed time; and there died of the people from Dan to 16 Beer-sheba seventy thousand men. And when the angel stretched forth his hand toward Jerusalem to destroy it, the LORD repented of the evil, and said to the angel who was working destruction among the people, "It is enough; now stay your hand." And the angel of the LORD was by the threshing floor of Arau'nah the Jeb'usite. 17 Then David spoke to the LORD when he saw the angel who was smiting the people, and said, "Lo, I have sinned, and I have done wickedly; but these sheep, what have they done? Let thy hand, I pray thee, be against me and against my father's house."

An altar to the Lord

And Gad came that day to David, and said 18 to him, "Go up, rear an altar to the LORD on the threshing floor of Arau'nah the Jeb'usite." So David went up at Gad's 19 word, as the LORD commanded. And when 20 Arau'nah looked down, he saw the king and his servants coming on toward him; and Arau'nah went forth, and did obeisance to the king with his face to the ground. And 21 Arau'nah said, "Why has my lord the king come to his servant?" David said, "To buy the threshing floor of you, in order to build an altar to the LORD, that the plague may be averted from the people." Then Arau'nah 22 said to David, "Let my lord the king take and offer up what seems good to him; here are the oxen for the burnt offering, and the threshing sledges and the yokes of the oxen for the wood. All this, O king, Arau'nah 23 gives to the king." And Arau'nah said to the king, "The LORD your God accept you." But the king said to Arau'nah, "No, but I 24 will buy it of you for a price; I will not offer burnt offerings to the LORD my God which cost me nothing." So David bought the threshing floor and the oxen for fifty shekels of silver. And David built there an altar to 25 the LORD, and offered burnt offerings and peace offerings. So the LORD heeded supplications for the land, and the plague was averted from Israel.

THE FIRST BOOK OF THE

KINGS

NOW King David was old and advanced in years; and although they covered him with clothes, he could not get warm. Therefore his servants said to him, "Let a young maiden be sought for my lord the king, and let her wait upon the king, and be his nurse; let her lie in your bosom, that my lord the king may be warm." So they sought for a beautiful maiden throughout all the territory of Israel, and found Ab'ishag the Shu'nammite, and brought her to the king. The maiden was very beautiful; and she became the king's nurse and ministered to him; but the king knew her not.

David's successor

5 Now Adoni'jah the son of Haggith exalted himself, saying, "I will be king"; and he prepared for himself chariots and horsemen, and fifty men to run before him. His father had never at any time displeased him by asking, "Why have you done thus and so?" He was also a very handsome man; and he was born next after Ab'salom. He conferred with Jo'ab the son of Zeru'iah and with Abi'athar the priest; and they followed Adoni'jah and helped him. But Zadok the priest, and Benai'ah the son of Jehoi'ada, and Nathan the prophet, and Shim'e-i, and Re'i, and David's mighty men were not with Adoni'jah. Adoni'jah sacrificed sheep, oxen, and fatlings by the Serpent's Stone, which is beside En-ro'gel, and he invited all his brothers, the king's sons, and all the royal officials of Judah, but he did not invite Nathan the 10 prophet or Benai'ah or the mighty men or Solomon his brother.

Then Nathan said to Bathshe'ba the mother 11 of Solomon, "Have you not heard that Adoni'jah the son of Haggith has become king and David our lord does not know it? Now therefore come, let me give you 12 counsel, that you may save your own life and the life of your son Solomon. Go in at once 13 to King David, and say to him, 'Did you not, my lord the king, swear to your maidservant, saying, "Solomon your son shall reign after me, and he shall sit upon my throne"? Why then is Adoni'jah king?' Then while you are 14 still speaking with the king, I also will come in after you and confirm your words."

So Bathshe'ba went to the king into his 15 chamber (now the king was very old, and Ab'ishag the Shu'nammite was ministering to the king). Bathshe'ba bowed and did 16 obeisance to the king, and the king said, "What do you desire?" She said to him, 17 "My lord, you swore to your maidservant by the LORD your God, saying, 'Solomon your son shall reign after me, and he shall sit upon my throne.' And now, behold, Adoni'jah is 18 king, although you, my lord the king, do not know it. He has sacrificed oxen, fatlings, and 19 sheep in abundance, and has invited all the sons of the king, Abi'athar the priest, and Jo'ab the commander of the army; but Solomon your servant he has not invited. And now, my lord the king, the eyes of all 20

261

Israel are upon you, to tell them who shall sit on the throne of my lord the king after him.
21 Otherwise it will come to pass, when my lord the king sleeps with his fathers, that I and my son Solomon will be counted offenders."
22 While she was still speaking with the king,
23 Nathan the prophet came in. And they told the king, "Here is Nathan the prophet." And when he came in before the king, he bowed before the king, with his face to the
24 ground. And Nathan said, "My lord the king, have you said, 'Adoni'jah shall reign after me, and he shall sit upon my throne'?
25 For he has gone down this day, and has sacrificed oxen, fatlings, and sheep in abundance, and has invited all the king's sons, Jo'ab the commander*a* of the army, and Abi'athar the priest; and behold, they are eating and drinking before him, and saying,
26 'Long live King Adoni'jah!' But me, your servant, and Zadok the priest, and Benai'ah the son of Jehoi'ada, and your servant
27 Solomon, he has not invited. Has this thing been brought about by my lord the king and you have not told your servants who should sit on the throne of my lord the king after him?"
28 Then King David answered, "Call Bath-she'ba to me." So she came into the king's
29 presence, and stood before the king. And the king swore, saying, "As the LORD lives, who has redeemed my soul out of every adversity,
30 as I swore to you by the LORD, the God of Israel, saying, 'Solomon your son shall reign after me, and he shall sit upon my throne in
31 my stead'; even so will I do this day." Then Bathshe'ba bowed with her face to the ground, and did obeisance to the king, and said, "May my lord King David live for ever!"
32 King David said, "Call to me Zadok the priest, Nathan the prophet, and Benai'ah the son of Jehoi'ada." So they came before
33 the king. And the king said to them, "Take with you the servants of your lord, and cause Solomon my son to ride on my own mule,
34 and bring him down to Gihon; and let Zadok the priest and Nathan the prophet there anoint him king over Israel; then blow the trumpet, and say, 'Long live King
35 Solomon!' You shall then come up after him, and he shall come and sit upon my throne; for he shall be king in my stead; and I have appointed him to be ruler over Israel
36 and over Judah." And Benai'ah the son of Jehoi'ada answered the king, "Amen! May the LORD, the God of my lord the king, say
37 so. As the LORD has been with my lord the king, even so may he be with Solomon, and

make his throne greater than the throne of my lord King David."
38 So Zadok the priest, Nathan the prophet, and Benai'ah the son of Jehoi'ada, and the Cher'ethites and the Pel'ethites, went down and caused Solomon to ride on King David's mule, and brought him to Gihon. There
39 Zadok the priest took the horn of oil from the tent, and anointed Solomon. Then they blew the trumpet; and all the people said, "Long live King Solomon!" And all the
40 people went up after him, playing on pipes, and rejoicing with great joy, so that the earth was split by their noise.
41 Adoni'jah and all the guests who were with him heard it as they finished feasting. And when Jo'ab heard the sound of the trumpet, he said, "What does this uproar in the city
42 mean?" While he was still speaking, behold, Jonathan the son of Abi'athar the priest came; and Adoni'jah said, "Come in, for you are a worthy man and bring good news."
43 Jonathan answered Adoni'jah, "No, for our lord King David has made Solomon king;
44 and the king has sent with him Zadok the priest, Nathan the prophet, and Benai'ah the son of Jehoi'ada, and the Cher'ethites and the Pel'ethites; and they have caused him to ride on the king's mule; and Zadok the priest
45 and Nathan the prophet have anointed him king at Gihon; and they have gone up from there rejoicing, so that the city is in an uproar. This is the noise that you have
46 heard. Solomon sits upon the royal throne.
47 Moreover the king's servants came to congratulate our lord King David, saying, 'Your God make the name of Solomon more famous than yours, and make his throne greater than your throne.' And the king
48 bowed himself upon the bed. And the king also said, 'Blessed be the LORD, the God of Israel, who has granted one of my offspring*b* to sit on my throne this day, my own eyes seeing it.' "
49 Then all the guests of Adoni'jah trembled, and rose, and each went his own way. And
50 Adoni'jah feared Solomon; and he arose, and went, and caught hold of the horns of the
51 altar. And it was told Solomon, "Behold, Adoni'jah fears King Solomon; for, lo, he has laid hold of the horns of the altar, saying, 'Let King Solomon swear to me first that he will not slay his servant with the sword.' "
52 And Solomon said, "If he prove to be a worthy man, not one of his hairs shall fall to the earth; but if wickedness is found in him, he shall die." So King Solomon sent, and they
53 brought him down from the altar. And he came and did obeisance to King Solomon; and Solomon said to him, "Go to your house."

a Gk: Heb *commanders* *b* Gk: Heb *one*

David's charge to Solomon

When David's time to die drew near, he charged Solomon his son, saying, "I am about to go the way of all the earth. Be strong, and show yourself a man, and keep the charge of the LORD your God, walking in his ways and keeping his statutes, his commandments, his ordinances, and his testimonies, as it is written in the law of Moses, that you may prosper in all that you do and wherever you turn; that the LORD may establish his word which he spoke concerning me, saying, 'If your sons take heed to their way, to walk before me in faithfulness with all their heart and with all their soul, there shall not fail you a man on the throne of Israel.'

"Moreover you know also what Jo'ab the son of Zeru'iah did to me, how he dealt with the two commanders of the armies of Israel, Abner the son of Ner, and Ama'sa the son of Jether, whom he murdered, avenging[c] in time of peace blood which had been shed in war, and putting innocent blood[d] upon the girdle about my[e] loins, and upon the sandals on my[e] feet. Act therefore according to your wisdom, but do not let his grey head go down to Sheol in peace. But deal loyally with the sons of Barzil'lai the Gileadite, and let them be among those who eat at your table; for with such loyalty they met me when I fled from Ab'salom your brother. And there is also with you Shim'e-i the son of Gera, the Benjaminite from Bahu'rim, who cursed me with a grievous curse on the day when I went to Mahana'im; but when he came down to meet me at the Jordan, I swore to him by the LORD, saying, 'I will not put you to death with the sword.' Now therefore hold him not guiltless, for you are a wise man; you will know what you ought to do to him, and you shall bring his grey head down with blood to Sheol."

Then David slept with his fathers, and was buried in the city of David. And the time that David reigned over Israel was forty years; he reigned seven years in Hebron, and thirty-three years in Jerusalem. So Solomon sat upon the throne of David his father; and his kingdom was firmly established.

Then Adoni'jah the son of Haggith came to Bathshe'ba the mother of Solomon. And she said, "Do you come peaceably?" He said, "Peaceably." Then he said, "I have something to say to you." She said, "Say on." He said, "You know that the kingdom was mine, and that all Israel fully expected me to reign; however the kingdom has turned about and become my brother's, for it was his from the LORD. And now I have one 16 request to make of you; do not refuse me." She said to him, "Say on." And he said, 17 "Pray ask King Solomon—he will not refuse you—to give me Ab'ishag the Shu'nammite as my wife." Bathshe'ba said, "Very well; I 18 will speak for you to the king."

So Bathshe'ba went to King Solomon, to 19 speak to him on behalf of Adoni'jah. And the king rose to meet her, and bowed down to her; then he sat on his throne, and had a seat brought for the king's mother; and she sat on his right. Then she said, "I have one small 20 request to make of you; do not refuse me." And the king said to her, "Make your request, my mother; for I will not refuse you." She said, "Let Ab'ishag the Shu'- 21 nammite be given to Adoni'jah your brother as his wife." King Solomon answered his 22 mother, "And why do you ask Ab'ishag the Shu'nammite for Adoni'jah? Ask for him the kingdom also; for he is my elder brother, and on his side are Abi'athar[f] the priest and Jo'ab the son of Zeru'iah." Then King 23 Solomon swore by the LORD, saying, "God do so to me and more also if this word does not cost Adoni'jah his life! Now therefore as 24 the LORD lives, who has established me, and placed me on the throne of David my father, and who has made me a house, as he promised, Adoni'jah shall be put to death this day." So King Solomon sent Benai'ah 25 the son of Jehoi'ada; and he struck him down, and he died.

And to Abi'athar the priest the king said, 26 "Go to An'athoth, to your estate; for you deserve death. But I will not at this time put you to death, because you bore the ark of the Lord GOD before David my father, and because you shared in all the affliction of my father." So Solomon expelled Abi'athar 27 from being priest to the LORD, thus fulfilling the word of the LORD which he had spoken concerning the house of Eli in Shiloh.

When the news came to Jo'ab—for Jo'ab 28 had supported Adoni'jah although he had not supported Ab'salom—Jo'ab fled to the tent of the LORD and caught hold of the horns of the altar. And when it was told 29 King Solomon, "Jo'ab has fled to the tent of the LORD, and behold, he is beside the altar," Solomon sent Benai'ah the son of Jehoi'ada, saying, "Go, strike him down." So Benai'ah 30 came to the tent of the LORD, and said to him, "The king commands, 'Come forth.'" But he said, "No, I will die here." Then Benai'ah brought the king word again, saying, "Thus said Jo'ab, and thus he

---

[c] Gk: Heb *placing*   [d] Gk: Heb *blood of war*   [e] Gk: Heb *his*
[f] Gk Syr Vg: Heb *and for him and for Abiathar*
2.12: 1 Chron 29.23.

31 answered me." The king replied to him, "Do as he has said, strike him down and bury him; and thus take away from me and from my father's house the guilt for the blood
32 which Jo'ab shed without cause. The LORD will bring back his bloody deeds upon his own head, because, without the knowledge of my father David, he attacked and slew with the sword two men more righteous and better than himself, Abner the son of Ner, commander of the army of Israel, and Ama'sa the son of Jether, commander of the
33 army of Judah. So shall their blood come back upon the head of Jo'ab and upon the head of his descendants for ever; but to David, and to his descendants, and to his house, and to his throne, there shall be peace
34 from the LORD for evermore." Then Benai'ah the son of Jehoi'ada went up, and struck him down and killed him; and he was buried in his own house in the wilderness.
35 The king put Benai'ah the son of Jehoi'ada over the army in place of Jo'ab, and the king put Zadok the priest in the place of Abi'-athar.
36 Then the king sent and summoned Shim'e-i, and said to him, "Build yourself a house in Jerusalem, and dwell there, and do not go forth from there to any place
37 whatever. For on the day you go forth, and cross the brook Kidron, know for certain that you shall die; your blood shall be upon your
38 own head." And Shim'e-i said to the king, "What you say is good; as my lord the king has said, so will your servant do." So Shim'e-i dwelt in Jerusalem many days.
39 But it happened at the end of three years that two of Shim'e-i's slaves ran away to A'chish, son of Ma'acah, king of Gath. And when it was told Shim'e-i, "Behold, your
40 slaves are in Gath," Shim'e-i arose and saddled an ass, and went to Gath to A'chish,

to seek his slaves; Shim'e-i went and brought his slaves from Gath. And when Solomon was told that Shim'e-i had gone from Jerusalem to Gath and returned, the king sent and summoned Shim'e-i, and said to him, "Did I not make you swear by the LORD, and solemnly admonish you, saying, 'Know for certain that on the day you go forth and go to any place whatever, you shall die'? And you said to me, 'What you say is good; I obey.' Why then have you not kept your oath to the LORD and the commandment with which I charged you?" The king also said to Shim'e-i, "You know in your own heart all the evil that you did to David my father; so the LORD will bring back your evil upon your own head. But King Solomon shall be blessed, and the throne of David shall be established before the LORD for ever." Then the king commanded Benai'ah the son of Jehoi'ada; and he went out and struck him down, and he died.

So the kingdom was established in the hand of Solomon.

Marriage to Pharaoh's daughter

Solomon made a marriage alliance with Pharaoh king of Egypt; he took Pharaoh's daughter, and brought her into the city of David, until he had finished building his own house and the house of the LORD and the wall around Jerusalem. The people were sacrificing at the high places, however, because no house had yet been built for the name of the LORD.

Solomon loved the LORD, walking in the statutes of David his father; only, he sacrificed and burnt incense at the high places. And the king went to Gibeon to sacrifice there, for that was the great high place;

3.4–15: 2 Chron 1.3–13.

Solomon used to offer a thousand burnt offerings upon that altar.

Solomon's choice of wisdom

5 At Gibeon the LORD appeared to Solomon in a dream by night; and God said, "Ask 5 what I shall give you." And Solomon said, "Thou hast shown great and steadfast love to thy servant David my father, because he walked before thee in faithfulness, and in righteousness, and in uprightness of heart toward thee; and thou hast kept for him this great and steadfast love, and hast given him a 7 son to sit on his throne this day. And now, O LORD my God, thou hast made thy servant king in place of David my father, although I am but a little child; I do not know how to go 8 out or come in. And thy servant is in the midst of thy people whom thou hast chosen, a great people, that cannot be numbered or 9 counted for multitude. Give thy servant therefore an understanding mind to govern thy people, that I may discern between good and evil; for who is able to govern this thy great people?"

10 It pleased the LORD that Solomon had asked 11 this. And God said to him, "Because you have asked this, and have not asked for yourself long life or riches or the life of your enemies, but have asked for yourself under-12 standing to discern what is right, behold, I now do according to your word. Behold, I give you a wise and discerning mind, so that none like you has been before you and none 13 like you shall arise after you. I give you also what you have not asked, both riches and honour, so that no other king shall compare 14 with you, all your days. And if you will walk in my ways, keeping my statutes and my commandments, as your father David walked, then I will lengthen your days."

15 And Solomon awoke, and behold, it was a dream. Then he came to Jerusalem, and stood before the ark of the covenant of the LORD, and offered up burnt offerings and peace offerings, and made a feast for all his servants.

16 Then two harlots came to the king, and 17 stood before him. The one woman said, "Oh, my lord, this woman and I dwell in the same house; and I gave birth to a child while 18 she was in the house. Then on the third day after I was delivered, this woman also gave birth; and we were alone; there was no one else with us in the house, only we two were in 19 the house. And this woman's son died in the 20 night, because she lay on it. And she arose at midnight, and took my son from beside me, while your maidservant slept, and laid it in her bosom, and laid her dead son in my 21 bosom. When I rose in the morning to nurse

my child, behold, it was dead; but when I looked at it closely in the morning, behold, it was not the child that I had borne." But the 22 other woman said, "No, the living child is mine, and the dead child is yours." The first said, "No, the dead child is yours, and the living child is mine." Thus they spoke before the king.

Then the king said, "The one says, 'This is 23 my son that is alive, and your son is dead'; and the other says, 'No; but your son is dead, and my son is the living one.'" And the king 24 said, "Bring me a sword." So a sword was brought before the king. And the king said, 25 "Divide the living child in two, and give half to the one, and half to the other." Then the 26 woman whose son was alive said to the king, because her heart yearned for her son, "Oh, my lord, give her the living child, and by no means slay it." But the other said, "It shall be neither mine nor yours; divide it." Then 27 the king answered and said, "Give the living child to the first woman, and by no means slay it; she is its mother." And all Israel 28 heard of the judgment which the king had rendered; and they stood in awe of the king, because they perceived that the wisdom of God was in him, to render justice.

Solomon's princes

King Solomon was king over all Israel, and 4 these were his high officials: Azari′ah the son 2 of Zadok was the priest; Eliho′reph and 3 Ahi′jah the sons of Shisha were secretaries; Jehosh′aphat the son of Ahi′lud was recorder; Benai′ah the son of Jehoi′ada was in 4 command of the army; Zadok and Abi′athar were priests; Azari′ah the son of Nathan was 5 over the officers; Zabud the son of Nathan was priest and king's friend; Ahi′shar was in 6 charge of the palace; and Adoni′ram the son of Abda was in charge of the forced labour.

Solomon had twelve officers over all Israel, 7 who provided food for the king and his household; each man had to make provision for one month in the year. These were their 8 names: Ben-hur, in the hill country of E′phraim; Ben-deker, in Makaz, Sha-al′bim, 9 Beth-she′mesh, and E′lon-beth-ha′nan; Ben-hesed, in Arub′both (to him belonged 10 Socoh and all the land of Hepher); Ben- 11 abin′adab, in all Naphath-dor (he had Taphath the daughter of Solomon as his wife); Ba′ana the son of Ahi′lud, in Ta′anach, 12 Megid′do, and all Beth-she′an which is beside Zarethan below Jezreel, and from Beth-she′an to A′bel-meho′lah, as far as the other side of Jok′meam; Ben-geber, in 13 Ramoth-gilead (he had the villages of Ja′ir the son of Manas′seh, which are in Gilead, and he had the region of Argob, which is in

Bashan, sixty great cities with walls and
14 bronze bars); Ahin′adab the son of Iddo, in
15 Mahana′im; Ahim′a-az, in Naph′tali (he had
taken Bas′emath the daughter of Solomon as
16 his wife); Ba′ana the son of Hushai, in Asher
17 and Bealoth; Jehosh′aphat the son of
18 Paru′ah, in Is′sachar; Shim′e-i the son of
19 Ela, in Benjamin; Geber the son of Uri, in
the land of Gilead, the country of Sihon king
of the Amorites and of Og king of Bashan.
And there was one officer in the land of
Judah.
20 Judah and Israel were as many as the sand
by the sea; they ate and drank and were
21 *g* happy. Solomon ruled over all the kingdoms from the Euphra′tes to the land of the
Philistines and to the border of Egypt; they
brought tribute and served Solomon all the
days of his life.
22 Solomon's provision for one day was thirty
23 cors of fine flour, and sixty cors of meal, ten
fat oxen, and twenty pasture-fed cattle, a
hundred sheep, besides harts, gazelles,
24 roebucks, and fatted fowl. For he had
dominion over all the region west of the
Euphra′tes from Tiphsah to Gaza, over all
the kings west of the Euphra′tes; and he had
25 peace on all sides round about him. And
Judah and Israel dwelt in safety, from Dan
even to Beer-sheba, every man under his vine
and under his fig tree, all the days of
26 Solomon. Solomon also had forty thousand
stalls of horses for his chariots, and twelve
27 thousand horsemen. And those officers
supplied provisions for King Solomon, and
for all who came to King Solomon's table,
each one in his month; they let nothing be
28 lacking. Barley also and straw for the horses
and swift steeds they brought to the place
where it was required, each according to his
charge.
29 And God gave Solomon wisdom and understanding beyond measure, and largeness of
30 mind like the sand on the seashore, so that
Solomon's wisdom surpassed the wisdom of
all the people of the east, and all the wisdom
31 of Egypt. For he was wiser than all other
men, wiser than Ethan the Ez′rahite, and
Heman, Calcol, and Darda, the sons of
Mahol; and his fame was in all the nations
32 round about. He also uttered three thousand
proverbs; and his songs were a thousand and
33 five. He spoke of trees, from the cedar that is
in Lebanon to the hyssop that grows out of
the wall; he spoke also of beasts, and of birds,
34 and of reptiles, and of fish. And men came
from all peoples to hear the wisdom of
Solomon, and from all the kings of the earth,
who had heard of his wisdom.

Building the temple

Now Hiram king of Tyre sent his servants
to Solomon, when he heard that they had
anointed him king in place of his father; for
Hiram always loved David. And Solomon
sent word to Hiram, "You know that David
my father could not build a house for the
name of the LORD his God because of the
warfare with which his enemies surrounded
him, until the LORD put them under the soles
of his feet. But now the LORD my God has
given me rest on every side; there is neither
adversary nor misfortune. And so I purpose
to build a house for the name of the LORD my
God, as the LORD said to David my father,
'Your son, whom I will set upon your throne
in your place, shall build the house for my
name.' Now therefore command that cedars
of Lebanon be cut for me; and my servants
will join your servants, and I will pay you for
your servants such wages as you set; for
you know that there is no one among us
who knows how to cut timber like the
Sido′nians."

When Hiram heard the words of Solomon,
he rejoiced greatly, and said, "Blessed be the
LORD this day, who has given to David a wise
son to be over this great people." And
Hiram sent to Solomon, saying, "I have
heard the message which you have sent to
me; I am ready to do all you desire in the
matter of cedar and cypress timber. My
servants shall bring it down to the sea from
Lebanon; and I will make it into rafts to go
by sea to the place you direct, and I will have
them broken up there, and you shall receive
it; and you shall meet my wishes by providing food for my household." So Hiram
supplied Solomon with all the timber of
cedar and cypress that he desired, while
Solomon gave Hiram twenty thousand cors
of wheat as food for his household,
and twenty thousand*i* cors of beaten oil.
Solomon gave this to Hiram year by year.
And the LORD gave Solomon wisdom, as he
promised him; and there was peace between
Hiram and Solomon; and the two of them
made a treaty.

King Solomon raised a levy of forced labour
out of all Israel; and the levy numbered
thirty thousand men. And he sent them to
Lebanon, ten thousand a month in relays;
they would be a month in Lebanon and two
months at home; Adoni′ram was in charge of
the levy. Solomon also had seventy thousand
burden-bearers and eighty thousand hewers
of stone in the hill country, besides
Solomon's three thousand three hundred

g Ch 5.1 in Heb   *h* Ch 5.15 in Heb   *i* Gk: Heb *twenty*
5.2–11: 2 Chron 2.3–16.   5.5: 2 Chron 2.1.   5.15–16: 2 Chron 2.2, 18.

and the men of Gebal did the hewing and prepared the timber and the stone to build the house.

chief officers who were over the work, who had charge of the people who carried on the work. At the king's command, they quarried out great, costly stones in order to lay the foundation of the house with dressed stones. So Solomon's builders and Hiram's builders

In the four hundred and eightieth year after **6** the people of Israel came out of the land of Egypt, in the fourth year of Solomon's reign over Israel, in the month of Ziv, which is the second month, he began to build the house of the LORD.

THE HOUSE OF THE LORD

THE house which ᵇKing Solomon built for the LORD was sixty cubits long, twenty cubits wide, and thirty cubits high. The vestibule in front of 11 the nave of the house was twenty cubits long, equal to the width of the house, and ten cubits deep in front of the house. And he made for the house windows with recessed frames. He also built a structure against the wall of the house, running round the walls of 13 the house, both the nave and the inner sanctuary; and he made side chambers all around. The lowest storyʲ was five cubits broad, the 14 middle one was six cubits broad, 15 and the third was seven cubits broad; for around the outside of the house he made offsets on the wall in order that the supporting beams should not be inserted into the walls of the house.

When the house was built, it was 16 with stone prepared at the quarry; so that neither hammer nor axe nor any tool of iron was heard in the temple, while it was being built.

The entrance for the lowestᵏ story was on the south side of the house; and one went up by stairs 18 to the middle story, and from the middle story to the third. So he built the house, and finished it; 19 and he made the ceiling of the house of beams and planks of cedar. He built the structure

against the whole house, each storyˡ five cubits high, and it was joined to the house with timbers of cedar.

Now the word of the LORD came 11 to Solomon, "Concerning this house which you are building, if you will walk in my statutes and obey my ordinances and keep all my commandments and walk in them, then I will establish my word with you, which I spoke to 13 David your father. And I will dwell among the children of Israel, and will not forsake my people Israel."

So Solomon built the house, and 14 finished it. He lined the walls of 15 the house on the inside with boards of cedar; from the floor of the house to the raftersᵐ of the ceiling, he covered them on the inside with wood; and he covered the floor of the house with boards 16 of cypress. He built twenty cubits of the rear of the house with boards of cedar from the floor to the rafters,ᵐ and he built this within as an inner sanctuary, as 17 the most holy place. The house, that is, the nave in front of the inner sanctuary, was forty cubits long. The cedar within the house 19 was carved in the form of gourds and open flowers; all was cedar, no stone was seen. The inner sanctuary he prepared in the innermost part of the house, to set there the ark of the covenant of

the LORD. The inner sanctuaryⁿ 20 was twenty cubits long, twenty cubits wide, and twenty cubits high; and he overlaid it with pure gold. He also madeᵒ an altar of cedar. And Solomon overlaid the 21 inside of the house with pure gold, and he drew chains of gold across, in front of the inner sanctuary, and overlaid it with gold. And he overlaid the whole house 22 with gold, until all the house was finished. Also the whole altar that belonged to the inner sanctuary he overlaid with gold.

In the inner sanctuary he made 23 two cherubim of olivewood, each ten cubits high. Five cubits was 24 the length of one wing of the cherub, and five cubits the length of the other wing of the cherub; it was ten cubits from the tip of one wing to the tip of the other. The 25 other cherub also measured ten cubits; both cherubim had the same measure and the same form. The height of one cherub was ten 26 cubits, and so was that of the other cherub. He put the cheru- 27 bim in the innermost part of the house; and the wings of the cherubim were spread out so that a wing of one touched the one wall, and a wing of the other cherub touched the other wall; their other wings touched each other in the middle of the house. And he overlaid the cherubim 28 with gold.

ʲ Gk: Heb *structure*   ᵏ Gk Tg: Heb *middle*   ˡ Heb lacks *each story*   ᵐ Gk: Heb *walls*
ⁿ Vg: Heb *and before the inner sanctuary*   ᵒ Gk: Heb *covered*
6.1-28: 2 Chron 3.1-13; Acts 7.47.

29 He carved all the walls of the house round about with carved figures of cherubim and palm trees and open flowers, in the 30 inner and outer rooms. The floor of the house he overlaid with gold in the inner and outer rooms.

31 For the entrance to the inner sanctuary he made doors of olive-wood; the lintel and the doorposts 32 formed a pentagon.[p] He covered the two doors of olivewood with carvings of cherubim, palm trees, and open flowers; he overlaid them with gold, and spread gold upon the cherubim and upon the palm trees.

33 So also he made for the entrance to the nave doorposts of olive- 34 wood, in the form of a square, and two doors of cypress wood; the two leaves of the one door were folding, and the two leaves of 35 other door were folding. On them he carved cherubim and palm trees and open flowers; and he overlaid them with gold evenly applied upon the carved work. 36 He built the inner court with three courses of hewn stone and one course of cedar beams.

37 In the fourth year the foundation of the house of the LORD was laid, 38 in the month of Ziv. And in the eleventh year, in the month of Bul, which is the eighth month, the house was finished in all its parts, and according to all its specifications. He was seven years in building it.

Solomon's house

7 Solomon was building his own house thirteen years, and he finished his entire house.

2 He built the House of the Forest of Lebanon; its length was a hundred cubits, and its breadth fifty cubits, and its height thirty cubits, and it was built upon three[q] rows of cedar pillars, with cedar beams upon the pillars. 3 And it was covered with cedar above the chambers that were upon the forty-five pillars, fifteen 4 in each row. There were window frames in three rows, and window opposite window in three tiers. 5 All the doorways and windows[r] had square frames, and window was opposite window in three tiers.

6 And he made the Hall of Pillars; its length was fifty cubits, and its breadth thirty cubits; there was a porch in front with pillars, and a canopy before them.

7 And he made the Hall of the Throne where he was to pronounce judgment, even the Hall of Judgment; it was finished with cedar from floor to rafters.[s] 8 His own house where he was to dwell, in the other court back of the hall, was of like workmanship. Solomon also made a house like this hall for Pharaoh's daughter whom he had taken in marriage.

9 All these were made of costly stones, hewn according to measure, sawed with saws, back and front, even from the foundation to the coping, and from the court of the house of the LORD[t] to 10 the great court. The foundation was of costly stones, huge stones, stones of eight and ten cubits. 11 And above were costly stones, hewn according to measurement, 12 and cedar. The great court had three courses of hewn stone round about, and a course of cedar beams; so had the inner court of the house of the LORD, and the vestibule of the house.

Temple furniture

13 And King Solomon sent and 14 brought Hiram from Tyre. He was the son of a widow of the tribe of Naph'tali, and his father was a man of Tyre, a worker in bronze; and he was full of wisdom, understanding, and skill, for making any work in bronze. He came to King Solomon, and did all his work.

15 He cast two pillars of bronze. Eighteen cubits was the height of one pillar, and a line of twelve cubits measured its circumference; it was hollow, and its 16 thickness was four fingers; the second pillar was the same.[u] He also made two capitals of molten bronze, to set upon the tops of the pillars; the height of the one capital was five cubits, and the height of the other capital was five 17 cubits. Then he made two[v] nets of chequer work with wreaths of chain work for the capitals upon the tops of the pillars; a net[w] for the one capital, and a net[w] for the 18 other capital. Likewise he made pomegranates;[x] in two rows round about upon the one network, to cover the capital that was upon the top of the pillar; and he did the same with the other 19 capital. Now the capitals that were upon the tops of the pillars in the vestibule were of lily-work, 20 four cubits. The capitals were upon the two pillars and also above the rounded projection which was beside the network; there were two hundred pomegranates, in two rows round about; and so with the other 21 capital. He set up the pillars at the vestibule of the temple; he set up the pillar on the south and called its name Jachin; and he set up the pillar on the north and 22 called its name Bo'az. And upon the tops of the pillars was lily-

work. Thus the work of the pillars was finished.

Then he made the molten sea; it was round, ten cubits from brim to brim, and five cubits high, and a line of thirty cubits measured its circumference. Under its brim were gourds, for thirty[y] cubits, compassing the sea round about; the gourds were in two rows, cast with it when it was cast. It stood upon twelve oxen, three facing north, three facing west, three facing south, and three facing east; the sea was set upon them, and all their hinder parts were inward. Its thickness was a handbreadth; and its brim was made like the brim of a cup, like the flower of a lily; it held two thousand baths.

He also made the ten stands of bronze; each stand was four cubits long, four cubits wide, and three cubits high. This was the construction of the stands: they had panels, and the panels were set in the frames and on the panels that were set in the frames were lions, oxen, and cherubim. Upon the frames, both above and below the lions and oxen, there were wreaths of bevelled work. Moreover each stand had four bronze wheels and axles of bronze; and at the four corners were supports for a laver. The supports were cast, with wreaths at the side of each. Its opening was within a crown which projected upward one cubit; its opening was round, as a pedestal is made, a cubit and a half deep. At its opening there were carvings; and its panels were square, not round. And the four wheels were underneath the panels; the axles of the wheels were of one piece with the stands; and the height of a wheel was a cubit and a half. The wheels were made like a chariot wheel; their axles, their rims, their spokes, and their hubs, were all cast. There were four supports at the four corners of each stand; the supports were of one piece with the stands. And on the top of the stand there was a round band half a cubit high; and on the top of the stand its stays and its panels were of one piece with it. And on the surfaces of its stays and on its panels, he carved cherubim, lions, and palm trees, according to the space of each, with wreaths round about. After this manner he made the ten stands; all of them were cast alike, of the same measure and the same form.

And he made ten lavers of bronze; each laver held forty baths, each laver measured four cubits, and there was a laver for each of the ten stands. And he set the stands, five on the south side of the house, and five on the north

[p] Heb obscure   [q] Gk: Heb four   [r] Gk: Heb posts   [s] Syr Vg: Heb floor   [t] With 7.12: Heb from the outside
[u] Tg Syr Compare Gk and Jer 52.21: Heb and a line of twelve cubits measured the circumference of the second pillar
[v] Gk: Heb lacks he made two   [w] Gk: Heb seven   [x] With two Mss Compare Gk: Heb pillars   [y] Heb ten
7.15-21: 2 Chron 3.15-17.   7.23-26: 2 Chron 4.2-5.   7.38-51: 2 Chron 4.6-5.1.

SOLOMON'S
TEMPLE

side of the house; and he set the sea on the south-east corner of the house.

40 Hiram also made the pots, the shovels, and the basins. So Hiram finished all the work that he did for King Solomon on the 41 house of the LORD: the two pillars, the two bowls of the bowls that were on the tops of the pillars, and the two networks to cover the two bowls of the capitals that were on the tops of the 42 pillars; and the four hundred pomegranates for the two networks, two rows of pomegranates for each network, to cover the two

bowls of the capitals that were 43 upon the pillars; the ten stands, and the ten lavers upon the 44 stands; and the one sea, and the twelve oxen underneath the sea.
45 Now the pots, the shovels, and the basins, all these vessels in the house of the LORD, which Hiram made for King Solomon, were of 46 burnished bronze. In the plain of the Jordan the king cast them, in the clay ground between Succoth 47 and Zarethan. And Solomon left all the vessels unweighed, because there were so many of them; the weight of the bronze was not found out.

So Solomon made all the vessels 48 that were in the house of the LORD: the golden altar, the golden table for the bread of the Presence, the lamp-stands of pure 49 gold, five on the south side and five on the north, before the inner sanctuary; the flowers, the lamps, and the tongs, of gold; the cups, 50 snuffers, basins, dishes for incense, and firepans, of pure gold; and the sockets of gold, for the doors of the innermost part of the house, the most holy place, and for the doors of the nave of the temple.

The dedication

51 THUS all the work that King Solomon did on the house of the LORD was finished. And Solomon brought in the things which David his father had dedicated, the silver, the gold, and the vessels, and stored them in the treasuries of the house of the LORD.

Then Solomon assembled the elders of 8 Israel and all the heads of the tribes, the leaders of the fathers' houses of the people of Israel, before King Solomon in Jerusalem, to bring up the ark of the covenant of the LORD out of the city of David, which is Zion. And 2 all the men of Israel assembled to King Solomon at the feast in the month Eth'anim, 3 which is the seventh month. And all the elders of Israel came, and the priests took up 4 the ark. And they brought up the ark of the LORD, the tent of meeting, and all the holy vessels that were in the tent; the priests and 5 the Levites brought them up. And King Solomon and all the congregation of Israel, who had assembled before him, were with him before the ark, sacrificing so many sheep and oxen that they could not be counted or 6 numbered. Then the priests brought the ark of the covenant of the LORD to its place, in the inner sanctuary of the house, in the most holy place, underneath the wings of the 7 cherubim. For the cherubim spread out their wings over the place of the ark, so that the cherubim made a covering above the ark 8 and its poles. And the poles were so long that the ends of the poles were seen from the holy place before the inner sanctuary; but they could not be seen from outside; and 9 they are there to this day. There was nothing in the ark except the two tables of stone which Moses put there at Horeb, where the LORD made a covenant with the people of Israel, when they came out of the land of 10 Egypt. And when the priests came out of the holy place, a cloud filled the house of the 11 LORD, so that the priests could not stand to minister because of the cloud; for the glory of the LORD filled the house of the LORD.

12 Then Solomon said,
"The LORD has set the sun in the heavens,
but* has said that he would dwell in thick darkness.
13 I have built thee an exalted house,
a place for thee to dwell in for ever."
14 Then the king faced about, and blessed all the assembly of Israel, while all the assembly 15 of Israel stood. And he said, "Blessed be the LORD, the God of Israel, who with his hand has fulfilled what he promised with his 16 mouth to David my father, saying, 'Since the day that I brought my people Israel out of Egypt, I chose no city in all the tribes of Israel in which to build a house, that my name might be there; but I chose David to be 17 over my people Israel.' Now it was in the heart of David my father to build a house for 18 the name of the LORD, the God of Israel. But the LORD said to David my father, 'Whereas it was in your heart to build a house for my name, you did well that it was in your heart, 19 nevertheless you shall not build the house, but your son who shall be born to you shall 20 build the house for my name.' Now the LORD has fulfilled his promise which he made; for I have risen in the place of David my father, and sit on the throne of Israel, as the LORD promised, and I have built the house for the name of the LORD, the God of Israel. And there I have provided a place for 21 the ark, in which is the covenant of the LORD which he made with our fathers, when he brought them out of the land of Egypt."

Solomon's prayer

Then Solomon stood before the altar of the 22 LORD in the presence of all the assembly of Israel, and spread forth his hands toward heaven; and said, "O LORD, God of Israel, 23 there is no God like thee, in heaven above or on earth beneath, keeping covenant and showing steadfast love to thy servants who walk before thee with all their heart; who 24 hast kept with thy servant David my father what thou didst declare to him; yea, thou didst speak with thy mouth, and with thy hand hast fulfilled it this day. Now 25 therefore, O LORD, God of Israel, keep with thy servant David my father what thou hast promised him, saying, 'There shall never fail you a man before me to sit upon the throne of Israel, if only your sons take heed to their way, to walk before me as you have walked before me.' Now therefore, O God of 26 Israel, let thy word be confirmed, which thou hast spoken to thy servant David my father.

"But will God indeed dwell on the earth? 27 Behold, heaven and the highest heaven cannot contain thee; how much less this house which I have built! Yet have regard to 28 the prayer of thy servant and to his supplication, O LORD my God, hearkening to the cry and to the prayer which thy servant prays before thee this day; that thy eyes may be 29 open night and day toward this house, the place of which thou hast said, 'My name shall be there,' that thou mayest hearken to the prayer which thy servant offers toward this place. And hearken thou to the supplication 30 of thy servant and of thy people Israel, when they pray toward this place; yea, hear thou in heaven thy dwelling place; and when thou hearest, forgive.

"If a man sins against his neighbour and is 31 made to take an oath, and comes and swears his oath before thine altar in this house, then 32 hear thou in heaven, and act, and judge thy servants, condemning the guilty by bringing his conduct upon his own head, and vindicating the righteous by rewarding him according to his righteousness.

"When thy people Israel are defeated 33

---

* Gk: Heb lacks *has set the sun in the heavens, but*
8.10-11: 2 Chron 5.13-14; Rev 15.8.   8.12-50: 2 Chron 6.1-39.

before the enemy because they have sinned against thee, if they turn again to thee, and acknowledge thy name, and pray and make supplication to thee in this house; then hear thou in heaven, and forgive the sin of thy people Israel, and bring them again to the land which thou gavest to their fathers.

⁵ "When heaven is shut up and there is no rain because they have sinned against thee, if they pray toward this place, and acknowledge thy name, and turn from their sin, when thou dost afflict them, then hear thou in heaven, and forgive the sin of thy servants, thy people Israel, when thou dost teach them the good way in which they should walk; and grant rain upon thy land, which thou hast given to thy people as an inheritance.

⁷ "If there is famine in the land, if there is pestilence or blight or mildew or locust or caterpillar; if their enemy besieges them in any[a] of their cities; whatever plague, whatever sickness there is; whatever prayer, whatever supplication is made by any man or by all thy people Israel, each knowing the affliction of his own heart and stretching out his hands toward this house; then hear thou in heaven thy dwelling place, and forgive, and act, and render to each whose heart thou knowest, according to all his ways (for thou, thou only, knowest the hearts of all the children of men); that they may fear thee all the days that they live in the land which thou gavest to our fathers.

¹ "Likewise when a foreigner, who is not of thy people Israel, comes from a far country for thy name's sake (for they shall hear of thy great name, and thy mighty hand, and of thy outstretched arm), when he comes and prays toward this house, hear thou in heaven thy dwelling place, and do according to all for which the foreigner calls to thee; in order that all the peoples of the earth may know thy name and fear thee, as do thy people Israel, and that they may know that this house which I have built is called by thy name.

⁴ "If thy people go out to battle against their enemy, by whatever way thou shalt send them, and they pray to the LORD toward the city which thou hast chosen and the house which I have built for thy name, then hear thou in heaven their prayer and their supplication, and maintain their cause.

⁶ "If they sin against thee—for there is no man who does not sin—and thou art angry with them, and dost give them to an enemy, so that they are carried away captive to the land of the enemy, far off or near; yet if they lay it to heart in the land to which they have been carried captive, and repent, and make supplication to thee in the land of their captors, saying, 'We have sinned, and have acted perversely and wickedly'; if they repent 48 with all their mind and with all their heart in the land of their enemies, who carried them captive, and pray to thee toward their land, which thou gavest to their fathers, the city which thou hast chosen, and the house which I have built for thy name; then hear thou in 49 heaven thy dwelling place their prayer and their supplication, and maintain their cause and forgive thy people who have sinned 50 against thee, and all their transgressions which they have committed against thee; and grant them compassion in the sight of those who carried them captive, that they may have compassion on them (for they are thy people, 51 and thy heritage, which thou didst bring out of Egypt, from the midst of the iron furnace). Let thy eyes be open to the supplica- 52 tion of thy servant, and to the supplication of thy people Israel, giving ear to them whenever they call to thee. For thou didst 53 separate them from among all the peoples of the earth, to be thy heritage, as thou didst declare through Moses, thy servant, when thou didst bring our fathers out of Egypt, O Lord GOD."

Solomon's blessing

Now as Solomon finished offering all this 54 prayer and supplication to the LORD, he arose from before the altar of the LORD, where he had knelt with hands outstretched toward heaven; and he stood, and blessed all the 55 assembly of Israel with a loud voice, saying, "Blessed be the LORD who has given rest to 56 his people Israel, according to all that he promised; not one word has failed of all his good promise, which he uttered by Moses his servant. The LORD our God be with us, as 57 he was with our fathers; may he not leave us or forsake us; that he may incline our hearts 58 to him, to walk in all his ways, and to keep his commandments, his statutes, and his ordinances, which he commanded our fathers. Let these words of mine, wherewith I have 59 made supplication before the LORD, be near to the LORD our God day and night, and may he maintain the cause of his servant, and the cause of his people Israel, as each day requires; that all the peoples of the earth may 60 know that the LORD is God; there is no other. Let your heart therefore be wholly 61 true to the LORD our God, walking in his statutes and keeping his commandments, as at this day."

Then the king, and all Israel with him, 62

63 offered sacrifice before the LORD. Solomon offered as peace offerings to the LORD twenty-two thousand oxen and a hundred and twenty thousand sheep. So the king and all the people of Israel dedicated the house of 64 the LORD. The same day the king consecrated the middle of the court that was before the house of the LORD; for there he offered the burnt offering and the cereal offering and the fat pieces of the peace offerings, because the bronze altar that was before the LORD was too small to receive the burnt offering and the cereal offering and the fat pieces of the peace offerings. 65 So Solomon held the feast at that time, and all Israel with him, a great assembly, from the entrance of Hamath to the Brook of Egypt, before the LORD our God, seven 66 days.[b] On the eighth day he sent the people away; and they blessed the king, and went to their homes joyful and glad of heart for all the goodness that the LORD had shown to David his servant and to Israel his people.

God's covenant

9 When Solomon had finished building the house of the LORD and the king's house and 2 all that Solomon desired to build, the LORD appeared to Solomon a second time, as he 3 had appeared to him at Gibeon. And the LORD said to him, "I have heard your prayer and your supplication, which you have made before me; I have consecrated this house which you have built, and put my name there for ever; my eyes and my heart will be there 4 for all time. And as for you, if you will walk before me, as David your father walked, with integrity of heart and uprightness, doing according to all that I have commanded you, and keeping my statutes and my ordinances, 5 then I will establish your royal throne over Israel for ever, as I promised David your father, saying, 'There shall not fail you a man 6 upon the throne of Israel.' But if you turn aside from following me, you or your children, and do not keep my commandments and my statutes which I have set before you, but go and serve other gods and 7 worship them, then I will cut off Israel from the land which I have given them; and the house which I have consecrated for my name I will cast out of my sight; and Israel will become a proverb and a byword among all 8 peoples. And this house will become a heap of ruins;[c] everyone passing by it will be astonished, and will hiss; and they will say, 'Why has the LORD done thus to this land 9 and to this house?' Then they will say,

'Because they forsook the LORD their God who brought their fathers out of the land of Egypt, and laid hold on other gods, and worshipped them and served them; therefore the LORD has brought all this evil upon them.'"

Cities and ships

At the end of twenty years, in which Solomon had built the two houses, the house of the LORD and the king's house, and Hiram king of Tyre had supplied Solomon with cedar and cypress timber and gold, as much as he desired, King Solomon gave to Hiram twenty cities in the land of Galilee. But when Hiram came from Tyre to see the cities which Solomon had given him, they did not please him. Therefore he said, "What kind of cities are these which you have given me, my brother?" So they are called the land of Cabul to this day. Hiram had sent to the king one hundred and twenty talents of gold.

And this is the account of the forced labour which King Solomon levied to build the house of the LORD and his own house and the Millo and the wall of Jerusalem and Hazor and Megiddo and Gezer (Pharaoh king of Egypt had gone up and captured Gezer and burnt it with fire, and had slain the Canaanites who dwelt in the city, and had given it as dowry to his daughter, Solomon's wife; so Solomon rebuilt Gezer) and Lower Bethhoron and Ba'alath and Tamar in the wilderness, in the land of Judah,[d] and all the store-cities that Solomon had, and the cities for his chariots, and the cities for his horsemen, and whatever Solomon desired to build in Jerusalem, in Lebanon, and in all the land of his dominion. All the people who were left of the Amorites, the Hittites, the Per'izzites, the Hivites, and the Jeb'usites, who were not of the people of Israel—their descendants who were left after them in the land, whom the people of Israel were unable to destroy utterly—these Solomon made a forced levy of slaves, and so they are to this day. But of the people of Israel Solomon made no slaves; they were the soldiers, they were his officials, his commanders, his captains, his chariot commanders and his horsemen.

These were the chief officers who were over Solomon's work: five hundred and fifty, who had charge of the people who carried on the work.

But Pharaoh's daughter went up from the city of David to her own house which

[b] Gk: Heb seven days and seven days, fourteen days [c] Syr Old Latin: Heb high [d] Heb lacks of Judah
9.1–9: 2 Chron 7.11–22. 9.10–28: 2 Chron 8.1–18.

Solomon had built for her; then he built the Millo.

25 Three times a year Solomon used to offer up burnt offerings and peace offerings upon the altar which he built to the LORD, burning incense*e* before the LORD. So he finished the house.

26 King Solomon built a fleet of ships at E'zion-ge'ber, which is near Eloth on the shore of the Red Sea, in the land of Edom.

27 And Hiram sent with the fleet his servants, seamen who were familiar with the sea,

28 together with the servants of Solomon; and they went to Ophir, and brought from there gold, to the amount of four hundred and twenty talents; and they brought it to King Solomon.

The queen of Sheba

10 Now when the queen of Sheba heard of the fame of Solomon concerning the name of the LORD, she came to test him with hard

2 questions. She came to Jerusalem with a very great retinue, with camels bearing spices, and very much gold, and precious stones; and when she came to Solomon, she

3 told him all that was on her mind. And Solomon answered all her questions; there was nothing hidden from the king which he

could not explain to her. And when the 4 queen of Sheba had seen all the wisdom of Solomon, the house that he had built, the 5 food of his table, the seating of his officials, and the attendance of his servants, their clothing, his cupbearers, and his burnt offerings which he offered at the house of the LORD, there was no more spirit in her.

And she said to the king, "The report was 6 true which I heard in my own land of your affairs and of your wisdom, but I did not 7 believe the reports until I came and my own eyes had seen it; and, behold, the half was not told me; your wisdom and prosperity surpass the report which I heard. Happy are 8 your wives!*f* Happy are these your servants, who continually stand before you and hear your wisdom! Blessed be the LORD your 9 God, who has delighted in you and set you on the throne of Israel! Because the LORD loved Israel for ever, he has made you king, that you may execute justice and righteousness." Then she gave the king a hundred 10 and twenty talents of gold, and a very great quantity of spices, and precious stones; never again came such an abundance of spices as these which the queen of Sheba gave to King Solomon.

Moreover the fleet of Hiram, which 11 brought gold from Ophir, brought from

e Gk: Heb *burning incense with it which*   *f* Gk Syr: Heb *men*
10.1-29: 2 Chron 9.1-28.

Ophir a very great amount of almug wood
12 and precious stones. And the king made of
the almug wood supports for the house of the
LORD, and for the king's house, lyres also and
harps for the singers; no such almug wood
has come or been seen, to this day.

13 And King Solomon gave to the queen of
Sheba all that she desired, whatever she
asked besides what was given her by the
bounty of King Solomon. So she turned and
went back to her own land, with her servants.

Wealth and splendour

14 Now the weight of gold that came to
Solomon in one year was six hundred and
15 sixty-six talents of gold, besides that which
came from the traders and from the traffic of
the merchants, and from all the kings of
Arabia and from the governors of the land.
16 King Solomon made two hundred large
shields of beaten gold; six hundred shekels of
17 gold went into each shield. And he made
three hundred shields of beaten gold; three
minas of gold went into each shield; and the
king put them in the House of the Forest of
18 Lebanon. The king also made a great ivory
throne, and overlaid it with the finest gold.
19 The throne had six steps, and at the back of
the throne was a calf's head, and on each side
of the seat were arm rests and two lions
20 standing beside the arm rests, while twelve
lions stood there, one on each end of a step
on the six steps. The like of it was never
21 made in any kingdom. All King Solomon's
drinking vessels were of gold, and all the
vessels of the House of the Forest of
Lebanon were of pure gold; none were of
silver, it was not considered as anything in
22 the days of Solomon. For the king had a fleet
of ships of Tarshish at sea with the fleet of
Hiram. Once every three years the fleet of
ships of Tarshish used to come bringing
gold, silver, ivory, apes, and peacocks. [g]
23 Thus King Solomon excelled all the kings
24 of the earth in riches and in wisdom. And
the whole earth sought the presence of
Solomon to hear his wisdom, which God had
25 put into his mind. Every one of them
brought his present, articles of silver and
gold, garments, myrrh, spices, horses, and
mules, so much year by year.
26 And Solomon gathered together chariots
and horsemen; he had fourteen hundred
chariots and twelve thousand horsemen,
whom he stationed in the chariot cities and
27 with the king in Jerusalem. And the king
made silver as common in Jerusalem as
stone, and he made cedar as plentiful as the
28 sycamore of the Shephe'lah. And Solomon's

import of horses was from Egypt and Ku'e,
and the king's traders received them from
Ku'e at a price. A chariot could be imported [29]
from Egypt for six hundred shekels of silver,
and a horse for a hundred and fifty; and so
through the king's traders they were exported to all the kings of the Hittites and the
kings of Syria.

Solomon's fall

Now King Solomon loved many foreign [1]
women: the daughter of Pharaoh, and
Moabite, Ammonite, E'domite, Sido'nian,
and Hittite women, from the nations con- [2]
cerning which the LORD had said to the
people of Israel, "You shall not enter into
marriage with them, neither shall they with
you, for surely they will turn away your heart
after their gods"; Solomon clung to these in
love. He had seven hundred wives, prin- [3]
cesses, and three hundred concubines; and
his wives turned away his heart. For when [4]
Solomon was old his wives turned away his
heart after other gods; and his heart was not
wholly true to the LORD his God, as was the
heart of David his father. For Solomon went [5]
after Ash'toreth the goddess of the Sido'-
nians, and after Milcom the abomination of
the Ammonites. So Solomon did what was [6]
evil in the sight of the LORD, and did not
wholly follow the LORD, as David his father
had done. Then Solomon built a high place [7]
for Chemosh the abomination of Moab, and
for Molech the abomination of the Ammonites, on the mountain east of Jerusalem.
And so he did for all his foreign wives, [8]
who burned incense and sacrificed to their
gods.
And the LORD was angry with Solomon, [9]
because his heart had turned away from the
LORD, the God of Israel, who had appeared
to him twice, and had commanded him [10]
concerning this thing, that he should not go
after other gods; but he did not keep what
the LORD commanded. Therefore the LORD [11]
said to Solomon, "Since this has been your
mind and you have not kept my covenant and
my statutes which I have commanded you, I
will surely tear the kingdom from you and
will give it to your servant. Yet for the sake [12]
of David your father I will not do it in your
days, but I will tear it out of the hand of your
son. However I will not tear away all the [13]
kingdom; but I will give one tribe to your
son, for the sake of David my servant and for
the sake of Jerusalem which I have chosen."
And the LORD raised up an adversary [14]
against Solomon, Hadad the E'domite; he
was of the royal house in Edom. For when [15]

[g] Or baboons

David was in Edom, and Jo'ab the commander of the army went up to bury the slain, he slew every male in Edom (for Jo'ab and all Israel remained there six months, until he had cut off every male in Edom); but Hadad fled to Egypt, together with certain Edomites of his father's servants, Hadad being yet a little child. They set out from Mid'ian and came to Paran, and took men with them from Paran and came to Egypt, to Pharaoh king of Egypt, who gave him a house, and assigned him an allowance of food, and gave him land. And Hadad found great favour in the sight of Pharaoh, so that he gave him in marriage the sister of his own wife, the sister of Tah'penes the queen. And the sister of Tah'penes bore him Genu'-bath his son, whom Tah'penes weaned in Pharaoh's house; and Genu'bath was in Pharaoh's house among the sons of Pharaoh. But when Hadad heard in Egypt that David slept with his fathers and that Jo'ab the commander of the army was dead, Hadad said to Pharaoh, "Let me depart, that I may go to my own country." But Pharaoh said to him, "What have you lacked with me that you are now seeking to go to your own country?" And he said to him, "Only let me go."

God also raised up as an adversary to him, Rezon the son of Eli'ada, who had fled from his master Hadade'zer king of Zobah. And he gathered men about him and became leader of a marauding band, after the slaughter by David; and they went to Damascus, and dwelt there, and made him king in Damascus. He was an adversary of Israel all the days of Solomon, doing mischief as Hadad did; and he abhorred Israel, and reigned over Syria.

Jeroboam's revolt

Jerobo'am the son of Nebat, an E'phraimite of Zer'edah, a servant of Solomon, whose mother's name was Zeru'ah, a widow, also lifted up his hand against the king. And this was the reason why he lifted up his hand against the king. Solomon built the Millo, and closed up the breach of the city of David his father. The man Jerobo'am was very able, and when Solomon saw that the young man was industrious he gave him charge over all the forced labour of the house of Joseph. And at that time, when Jerobo'am went out of Jerusalem, the prophet Ahi'jah the Shi'lonite found him on the road. Now Ahi'jah had clad himself with a new garment; and the two of them were alone in the open country. Then Ahi'jah laid hold of the new garment that was on him, and tore it into twelve pieces. And he said to Jerobo'am, "Take for yourself ten pieces; for thus says the LORD, the God of Israel, 'Behold, I am about to tear the kingdom from the hand of Solomon, and will give you ten tribes (but he shall have one tribe, for the sake of my servant David and for the sake of Jerusalem, the city which I have chosen out of all the tribes of Israel), because he has[h] forsaken me, and worshipped Ash'toreth the goddess of the Sido'nians, Chemosh the god of Moab, and Milcom the god of the Ammonites, and has[h] not walked in my ways, doing what is right in my sight and keeping my statutes and my ordinances, as David his father did. Nevertheless I will not take the whole kingdom out of his hand; but I will make him ruler all the days of his life, for the sake of David my servant whom I chose, who kept my commandments and my statutes; but I will take the kingdom out of his son's hand, and will give it to you, ten tribes. Yet to his son I will give one tribe, that David my servant may always have a lamp before me in Jerusalem, the city where I have chosen to put my name. And I will take you, and you shall reign over all that your soul desires, and you shall be king over Israel. And if you will hearken to all that I command you, and will walk in my ways, and do what is right in my eyes by keeping my statutes and my commandments, as David my servant did, I will be with you, and will build you a sure house, as I built for David, and I will give Israel to you. And I will for this afflict the descendants of David, but not for ever.' " Solomon sought therefore to kill Jerobo'am; but Jerobo'am arose, and fled into Egypt, to Shishak king of Egypt, and was in Egypt until the death of Solomon.

Now the rest of the acts of Solomon, and all that he did, and his wisdom, are they not written in the book of the acts of Solomon? And the time that Solomon reigned in Jerusalem over all Israel was forty years. And Solomon slept with his fathers, and was buried in the city of David his father; and Rehobo'am his son reigned in his stead.

THE KINGDOM DIVIDED

REHOBO'AM went to Shechem, for all Israel had come to Shechem to make him king. And when Jerobo'am the son of Nebat heard of it (for he was still in Egypt, whither he had fled from King Solomon),

[h] Gk Syr Vg: Heb *they have*
11.42-43: 2 Chron 9.30-31. 12.1-19: 2 Chron 10.1-19.

S.B.—G

3 then Jerobo'am returned from¹ Egypt. And they sent and called him; and Jerobo'am and all the assembly of Israel came and said to
4 Rehobo'am, "Your father made our yoke heavy. Now therefore lighten the hard service of your father and his heavy yoke
5 upon us, and we will serve you." He said to them, "Depart for three days, then come again to me." So the people went away.
6 Then King Rehobo'am took counsel with the old men, who had stood before Solomon his father while he was yet alive, saying, "How do you advise me to answer this
7 people?" And they said to him, "If you will be a servant to this people today and serve them, and speak good words to them when you answer them, then they will be your
8 servants for ever." But he forsook the counsel which the old men gave him, and took counsel with the young men who had grown up with him and stood before him.
9 And he said to them, "What do you advise that we answer this people who have said to me, 'Lighten the yoke that your father put
10 upon us'?" And the young men who had grown up with him said to him, "Thus shall you speak to this people who said to you, 'Your father made our yoke heavy, but do you lighten it for us'; thus shall you say to them, 'My little finger is thicker than my
11 father's loins. And now, whereas my father laid upon you a heavy yoke, I will add to your yoke. My father chastised you with whips, but I will chastise you with scorpions.'"
12 So Jerobo'am and all the people came to Rehobo'am the third day, as the king said,
13 "Come to me again the third day." And the king answered the people harshly, and forsaking the counsel which the old men had
14 given him, he spoke to them according to the counsel of the young men, saying, "My father made your yoke heavy, but I will add to your yoke; my father chastised you with whips, but I will chastise you with scor-
15 pions." So the king did not hearken to the people; for it was a turn of affairs brought about by the LORD that he might fulfil his word, which the LORD spoke by Ahi'jah the Shi'lonite to Jerobo'am the son of Nebat.
16 And when all Israel saw that the king did not hearken to them, the people answered the king,

"What portion have we in David?
We have no inheritance in the son of Jesse.
To your tents, O Israel!
Look now to your own house, David."

17 So Israel departed to their tents. But Reho-

bo'am reigned over the people of Israel who dwelt in the cities of Judah. Then King Rehobo'am sent Ado'ram, who was taskmaster over the forced labour, and all Israel stoned him to death with stones. And King Rehobo'am made haste to mount his chariot, to flee to Jerusalem. So Israel has been in rebellion against the house of David to this day. And when all Israel heard that Jerobo'am had returned, they sent and called him to the assembly and made him king over all Israel. There was none that followed the house of David, but the tribe of Judah only.

When Rehobo'am came to Jerusalem, he assembled all the house of Judah, and the tribe of Benjamin, a hundred and eighty thousand chosen warriors, to fight against the house of Israel, to restore the kingdom to Rehobo'am the son of Solomon. But the word of God came to Shemai'ah the man of God: "Say to Rehobo'am the son of Solomon, king of Judah, and to all the house of Judah and Benjamin, and to the rest of the people, 'Thus says the LORD, You shall not go up or fight against your kinsmen the people of Israel. Return every man to his home, for this thing is from me.' " So they hearkened to the word of the LORD, and went home again, according to the word of the LORD.

Then Jerobo'am built Shechem in the hill country of E'phraim, and dwelt there; and he went out from there and built Penu'el.

Golden calves

And Jerobo'am said in his heart, "Now the kingdom will turn back to the house of David; if this people go up to offer sacrifices in the house of the LORD at Jerusalem, then the heart of this people will turn again to their lord, to Rehobo'am king of Judah, and they will kill me and return to Rehobo'am king of Judah." So the king took counsel, and made two calves of gold. And he said to the people, "You have gone up to Jerusalem long enough. Behold your gods, O Israel, who brought you up out of the land of Egypt." And he set one in Bethel, and the other he put in Dan. And this thing became a sin, for the people went to the one at Bethel and to the other as far as Dan.ʲ He also made houses on high places, and appointed priests from among all the people, who were not of the Levites. And Jerobo'am appointed a feast on the fifteenth day of the eighth month like the feast that was in Judah, and he offered sacrifices upon the altar; so he did in Bethel, sacrificing to the calves that he had

¹ Gk Vg Compare 2 Chron 10.2: Heb *dwelt in*   ʲ Gk: Heb *went to the one as far as Dan*
12.22–24: 2 Chron 11.1–4.

made. And he placed in Bethel the priests of the high places that he had made. He went up to the altar which he had made in Bethel on the fifteenth day in the eighth month, in the month which he had devised of his own heart; and he ordained a feast for the people of Israel, and went up to the altar to burn incense.

At Bethel's altar

And behold, a man of God came out of Judah by the word of the LORD to Bethel. Jerobo′am was standing by the altar to burn incense. And the man cried against the altar by the word of the LORD, and said, "O altar, altar, thus says the LORD: 'Behold, a son shall be born to the house of David, Josi′ah by name; and he shall sacrifice upon you the priests of the high places who burn incense upon you, and men's bones shall be burned upon you.' " And he gave a sign the same day, saying, "This is the sign that the LORD has spoken: 'Behold, the altar shall be torn down, and the ashes that are upon it shall be poured out.' " And when the king heard the saying of the man of God, which he cried against the altar at Bethel, Jerobo′am stretched out his hand from the altar, saying, "Lay hold of him." And his hand, which he stretched out against him, dried up, so that he could not draw it back to himself. The altar also was torn down, and the ashes poured out from the altar, according to the sign which the man of God had given by the word of the LORD. And the king said to the man of God, "Entreat now the favour of the LORD your God, and pray for me, that my hand may be restored to me." And the man of God entreated the LORD; and the king's hand was restored to him, and became as it was before. And the king said to the man of God, "Come home with me, and refresh yourself, and I will give you a reward." And the man of God said to the king, "If you give me half your house, I will not go in with you. And I will not eat bread or drink water in this place; for so was it commanded me by the word of the LORD, saying, 'You shall neither eat bread, nor drink water, nor return by the way that you came.' " So he went another way, and did not return by the way that he came to Bethel.

Now there dwelt an old prophet in Bethel. And his sons[k] came and told him all that the man of God had done that day in Bethel; the words also which he had spoken to the king, they told to their father. And their father said to them, "Which way did he go?" And his sons showed him the way which the man

THE TWO KINGDOMS

The Great Sea

ISRAEL
Samaria
Shechem
Bethel
JERUSALEM
JUDAH

of God who came from Judah had gone. And he said to his sons, "Saddle the ass for 13 me." So they saddled the ass for him and he mounted it. And he went after the man of 14 God, and found him sitting under an oak; and he said to him, "Are you the man of God who came from Judah?" And he said, "I am." Then he said to him, "Come home 15 with me and eat bread." And he said, "I 16 may not return with you, or go in with you; neither will I eat bread nor drink water with you in this place; for it was said to me by the 17 word of the LORD, 'You shall neither eat bread nor drink water there, nor return by the way that you came.' " And he said to 18 him, "I also am a prophet as you are, and an angel spoke to me by the word of the LORD, saying, 'Bring him back with you into your house that he may eat bread and drink water.' " But he lied to him. So he went 19 back with him, and ate bread in his house, and drank water.

And as they sat at the table, the word of the 20 LORD came to the prophet who had brought him back; and he cried to the man of God 21 who came from Judah, "Thus says the LORD, 'Because you have disobeyed the word of the LORD, and have not kept the commandment

---

[k] Gk Syr Vg: Heb son

which the LORD your God commanded you,
22 but have come back, and have eaten bread
and drunk water in the place of which he said
to you, "Eat no bread, and drink no water";
your body shall not come to the tomb of your
23 fathers.' " And after he had eaten bread and
drunk, he saddled the ass for the prophet
24 whom he had brought back. And as he went
away a lion met him on the road and killed
him. And his body was thrown in the road,
and the ass stood beside it; the lion also stood
25 beside the body. And behold, men passed
by, and saw the body thrown in the road, and
the lion standing by the body. And they
came and told it in the city where the old
prophet dwelt.
26 And when the prophet who had brought
him back from the way heard of it, he said,
"It is the man of God, who disobeyed the
word of the LORD; therefore the LORD has
given him to the lion, which has torn him and
slain him, according to the word which the
27 LORD spoke to him." And he said to his
sons, "Saddle the ass for me." And they
28 saddled it. And he went and found his body
thrown in the road, and the ass and the lion
standing beside the body. The lion had not
29 eaten the body or torn the ass. And the
prophet took up the body of the man of God
and laid it upon the ass, and brought it back
30 to the city,[1] to mourn and to bury him. And
he laid the body in his own grave; and they
mourned over him, saying, "Alas, my
31 brother!" And after he had buried him, he
said to his sons, "When I die, bury me in the
grave in which the man of God is buried; lay
32 my bones beside his bones. For the saying
which he cried by the word of the LORD
against the altar in Bethel, and against all the
houses of the high places which are in the
cities of Samar'ia, shall surely come to pass."

After this thing Jerobo'am did not turn
from his evil way, but made priests for the
high places again from among all the people;
any who would, he consecrated to be priests
of the high places. And this thing became sin
to the house of Jerobo'am, so as to cut it
off and to destroy it from the face of the
earth.

Jeroboam's son

At that time Abi'jah the son of Jerobo'am
fell sick. And Jerobo'am said to his wife,
"Arise, and disguise yourself, that it be not
known that you are the wife of Jerobo'am,
and go to Shiloh; behold, Ahi'jah the
prophet is there, who said of me that I should
be king over this people. Take with you ten
loaves, some cakes, and a jar of honey, and go
to him; he will tell you what shall happen to
the child."
Jerobo'am's wife did so; she arose, and went
to Shiloh, and came to the house of Ahi'jah.
Now Ahi'jah could not see, for his eyes were
dim because of his age. And the LORD said to
Ahi'jah, "Behold, the wife of Jerobo'am is
coming to inquire of you concerning her son;
for he is sick. Thus and thus shall you say to
her."
When she came, she pretended to be
another woman. But when Ahi'jah heard the
sound of her feet, as she came in at the door,
he said, "Come in, wife of Jerobo'am; why
do you pretend to be another? For I am
charged with heavy tidings for you. Go, tell
Jerobo'am, 'Thus says the LORD, the God of
Israel: "Because I exalted you from among
the people, and made you leader over my
people Israel, and tore the kingdom away
from the house of David and gave it to you;
and yet you have not been like my servant
David, who kept my commandments, and
followed me with all his heart, doing only
that which was right in my eyes, but you
have done evil above all that were before you
and have gone and made for yourself other
gods, and molten images, provoking me to
anger, and have cast me behind your back;
therefore behold, I will bring evil upon the
house of Jerobo'am, and will cut off from
Jerobo'am every male, both bond and free in
Israel, and will utterly consume the house of
Jerobo'am, as a man burns up dung until it is
all gone. Any one belonging to Jerobo'am
who dies in the city the dogs shall eat; and
any one who dies in the open country the
birds of the air shall eat; for the LORD has
spoken it." ' Arise therefore, go to your
house. When your feet enter the city, the

---

[1] Gk: Heb *he came to the city of the old prophet*

3 child shall die. And all Israel shall mourn for him, and bury him; for he only of Jerobo'am shall come to the grave, because in him there is found something pleasing to the LORD, the God of Israel, in the house of Jerobo'am.
4 Moreover the LORD will raise up for himself a king over Israel, who shall cut off the house
5 of Jerobo'am today. And henceforth[m] the LORD will smite Israel, as a reed is shaken in the water, and root up Israel out of this good land which he gave to their fathers, and scatter them beyond the Euphra'tes, because they have made their Ashe'rim,
6 provoking the LORD to anger. And he will give Israel up because of the sins of Jero-

bo'am, which he sinned and which he made Israel to sin."

17 Then Jerobo'am's wife arose, and departed, and came to Tirzah. And as she came to the
18 threshold of the house, the child died. And all Israel buried him and mourned for him, according to the word of the LORD, which he spoke by his servant Ahi'jah the prophet.
19 Now the rest of the acts of Jerobo'am, how he warred and how he reigned, behold, they are written in the Book of the Chronicles of
20 the Kings of Israel. And the time that Jerobo'am reigned was twenty-two years; and he slept with his fathers, and Nadab his son reigned in his stead.

JUDAH—Rehoboam

1 Now Rehobo'am the son of Solomon reigned in Judah. Rehobo'am was forty-one years old when he began to reign, and he reigned seventeen years in Jerusalem, the city which the LORD had chosen out of all the tribes of Israel, to put his name there. His
2 mother's name was Na'amah the Ammonitess. And Judah did what was evil in the sight of the LORD, and they provoked him to jealousy with their sins which they committed, more than all that their fathers had
3 done. For they also built for themselves high places, and pillars, and Ashe'rim on every
4 high hill and under every green tree; and there were also male cult prostitutes in the land. They did according to all the abominations of the nations which the LORD drove out before the people of Israel.
5 In the fifth year of King Rehobo'am, Shishak king of Egypt came up against
6 Jerusalem; he took away the treasures of the house of the LORD and the treasures of the king's house; he took away everything. He also took away all the shields of gold which
7 Solomon had made; and King Rehobo'am made in their stead shields of bronze, and committed them to the hands of the officers

of the guard, who kept the door of the king's house. And as often as the king went into the
28 house of the LORD, the guard bore them and brought them back to the guardroom.
29 Now the rest of the acts of Rehobo'am, and all that he did, are they not written in the Book of the Chronicles of the Kings of
30 Judah? And there was war between Rehobo'am and Jerobo'am continually. And
31 Rehobo'am slept with his fathers and was buried with his fathers in the city of David. His mother's name was Na'amah the Ammonitess. And Abi'jam his son reigned in his stead.

Abijam

15 Now in the eighteenth year of King Jerobo'am the son of Nebat, Abi'jam began to
2 reign over Judah. He reigned for three years in Jerusalem. His mother's name was Ma'acah the daughter of Abish'alom. And
3 he walked in all the sins which his father did before him; and his heart was not wholly true to the LORD his God, as the heart of David
4 his father. Nevertheless for David's sake the LORD his God gave him a lamp in Jerusalem, setting up his son after him, and establishing
5 Jerusalem; because David did what was right

in the eyes of the LORD, and did not turn aside from anything that he commanded him all the days of his life, except in the matter of 6 Uri'ah the Hittite. Now there was war between Rehobo'am and Jerobo'am all the 7 days of his life. The rest of the acts of Abi'jam, and all that he did, are they not written in the Book of the Chronicles of the Kings of Judah? And there was war 8 between Abi'jam and Jerobo'am. And Abi'jam slept with his fathers; and they buried him in the city of David. And Asa his son reigned in his stead.

Asa

9 In the twentieth year of Jerobo'am king of 10 Israel Asa began to reign over Judah, and he reigned forty-one years in Jerusalem. His mother's name was Ma'acah the daughter of

An eastern street

11 Abish'alom. And Asa did what was right in the eyes of the LORD, as David his father had 12 done. He put away the male cult prostitutes out of the land, and removed all the idols that

his fathers had made. He also removed 1 Ma'acah his mother from being queen mother because she had an abominable image made for Ashe'rah; and Asa cut down her image and burned it at the brook Kidron. But the high places were not taken 1 away. Nevertheless the heart of Asa was wholly true to the LORD all his days. And he 1 brought into the house of the LORD the votive gifts of his father and his own votive gifts, silver, and gold, and vessels.

And there was war between Asa and 1 Ba'asha king of Israel all their days. Ba'asha 1 king of Israel went up against Judah, and built Ramah, that he might permit no one to go out or come in to Asa king of Judah. Then Asa took all the silver and the gold that 1 were left in the treasures of the house of the LORD and the treasures of the king's house, and gave them into the hands of his servants; and King Asa sent them to Ben-ha'dad the son of Tabrim'mon, the son of He'zi-on, king of Syria, who dwelt in Damascus, saying, "Let there be a league between me 1 and you, as between my father and your father: behold, I am sending to you a present of silver and gold; go, break your league with Ba'asha king of Israel, that he may withdraw from me." And Ben-ha'dad hearkened to 20 King Asa, and sent the commanders of his armies against the cities of Israel, and conquered I'jon, Dan, A'bel-beth-ma'acah, and all Chin'neroth, with all the land of Naph'tali. And when Ba'asha heard of it, he 21 stopped building Ramah, and he dwelt in Tirzah. Then King Asa made a proclama- 22 tion to all Judah, none was exempt, and they carried away the stones of Ramah and its timber, with which Ba'asha had been building; and with them King Asa built Geba of Benjamin and Mizpah. Now the 23 rest of all the acts of Asa, all his might, and all that he did, and the cities which he built, are they not written in the Book of the Chronicles of the Kings of Judah? But in his old age he was diseased in his feet. And Asa 24 slept with his fathers, and was buried with his fathers in the city of David his father; and Jehosh'aphat his son reigned in his stead.

ISRAEL—Nadab

Nadab the son of Jerobo'am began to reign 25 over Israel in the second year of Asa king of Judah; and he reigned over Israel two years. He did what was evil in the sight of 26 the LORD, and walked in the way of his father, and in his sin which he made Israel to sin.

Baasha

7 Ba'asha the son of Ahi'jah, of the house of Is'sachar, conspired against him; and Ba'asha struck him down at Gib'bethon, which belonged to the Philistines; for Nadab and all Israel were laying siege to Gib'-
8 bethon. So Ba'asha killed him in the third year of Asa king of Judah, and reigned in his
9 stead. And as soon as he was king, he killed all the house of Jerobo'am; he left to the house of Jerobo'am not one that breathed, until he had destroyed it, according to the word of the LORD which he spoke by his
10 servant Ahi'jah the Shi'lonite; it was for the sins of Jerobo'am which he sinned and which he made Israel to sin, and because of the anger to which he provoked the LORD, the God of Israel.
11 Now the rest of the acts of Nadab, and all that he did, are they not written in the Book of the Chronicles of the Kings of Israel?
12 And there was war between Asa and Ba'asha king of Israel all their days.
13 In the third year of Asa king of Judah, Ba'asha the son of Ahi'jah began to reign over all Israel at Tirzah, and reigned
14 twenty-four years. He did what was evil in the sight of the LORD, and walked in the way of Jerobo'am and in his sin which he made Israel to sin.

Jehu

16 And the word of the LORD came to Jehu the son of Hana'ni against Ba'asha, saying,
2 "Since I exalted you out of the dust and made you leader over my people Israel, and you have walked in the way of Jerobo'am, and have made my people Israel to sin, provoking me to anger with their sins,
3 behold, I will utterly sweep away Ba'asha and his house, and I will make your house like the house of Jerobo'am the son of
4 Nebat. Any one belonging to Ba'asha who

dies in the city the dogs shall eat; and any one of his who dies in the field the birds of the air shall eat."
5 Now the rest of the acts of Ba'asha, and what he did, and his might, are they not written in the Book of the Chronicles of the Kings of Israel? And Ba'asha slept with his 6 fathers, and was buried at Tirzah; and Elah his son reigned in his stead. Moreover the 7 word of the LORD came by the prophet Jehu the son of Hana'ni against Ba'asha and his house, both because of all the evil that he did in the sight of the LORD, provoking him to anger with the work of his hands, in being like the house of Jerobo'am, and also because he destroyed it.

Civil war in Israel

In the twenty-sixth year of Asa king of 8 Judah, Elah the son of Ba'asha began to reign over Israel in Tirzah, and reigned two years. But his servant Zimri, commander of half his 9 chariots, conspired against him. When he was at Tirzah, drinking himself drunk in the house of Arza, who was over the household in Tirzah, Zimri came in and struck him 10 down and killed him, in the twenty-seventh year of Asa king of Judah, and reigned in his stead.
When he began to reign, as soon as he had 11 seated himself on his throne, he killed all the house of Ba'asha; he did not leave him a single male of his kinsmen or his friends. Thus Zimri destroyed all the house of 12 Ba'asha, according to the word of the LORD, which he spoke against Ba'asha by Jehu the prophet, for all the sins of Ba'asha and the 13 sins of Elah his son which they sinned, and which they made Israel to sin, provoking the LORD God of Israel to anger with their idols. Now the rest of the acts of Elah, and all that 14 he did, are they not written in the Book of the Chronicles of the Kings of Israel?
In the twenty-seventh year of Asa king of 15

B. C.
900~800

Judah, Zimri reigned seven days in Tirzah.
Now the troops were encamped against
Gib'bethon, which belonged to the Philis-
16 tines, and the troops who were encamped
heard it said, "Zimri has conspired, and he
has killed the king"; therefore all Israel made
Omri, the commander of the army, king over
17 Israel that day in the camp. So Omri went
up from Gib'bethon, and all Israel with him,
18 and they besieged Tirzah. And when Zimri
saw that the city was taken, he went into the
citadel of the king's house, and burned the
king's house over him with fire, and died,
19 because of his sins which he committed,
doing evil in the sight of the LORD, walking
in the way of Jerobo'am, and for his sin
which he committed, making Israel to sin.
20 Now the rest of the acts of Zimri, and the
conspiracy which he made, are they not
written in the Book of the Chronicles of the
Kings of Israel?

Omri

21 Then the people of Israel were divided into
two parts; half of the people followed Tibni
the son of Ginath, to make him king, and half
22 followed Omri. But the people who followed
Omri overcame the people who followed
Tibni the son of Ginath; so Tibni died, and
23 Omri became king. In the thirty-first year of
Asa king of Judah, Omri began to reign over
Israel, and reigned for twelve years; six years
24 he reigned in Tirzah. He bought the hill of
Samar'ia from Shemer for two talents of
silver; and he fortified the hill, and called the
name of the city which he built, Samar'ia,
after the name of Shemer, the owner of the
hill.
25 Omri did what was evil in the sight of the
LORD, and did more evil than all who were
26 before him. For he walked in all the way of
Jerobo'am the son of Nebat, and in the sins
which he made Israel to sin, provoking the
LORD, the God of Israel, to anger by their
27 idols. Now the rest of the acts of Omri which
he did, and the might that he showed, are

they not written in the Book of the Chronicles of the Kings of Israel? And Omri slept 28
with his fathers, and was buried in Samar'ia;
and Ahab his son reigned in his stead.

Ahab

In the thirty-eighth year of Asa king of 29
Judah, Ahab the son of Omri began to reign
over Israel, and Ahab the son of Omri
reigned over Israel in Samar'ia twenty-two
years. And Ahab the son of Omri did evil in 30
the sight of the LORD more than all that were
before him. And as if it had been a light 31
thing for him to walk in the sins of Jerobo'am
the son of Nebat, he took for wife Jez'ebel
the daughter of Ethba'al king of the Sido'-
nians, and went and served Ba'al, and worshipped him. He erected an altar for Ba'al in 32
the house of Ba'al, which he built in
Samar'ia. And Ahab made an Ashe'rah. 33
Ahab did more to provoke the LORD, the
God of Israel, to anger than all the kings of
Israel who were before him. In his days 34
Hi'el of Bethel built Jericho; he laid its
foundation at the cost of Abi'ram his first-
born, and set up its gates at the cost of his
youngest son Segub, according to the word
of the LORD, which he spoke by Joshua the
son of Nun.

ELIJAH

NOW Eli'jah the Tishbite, of Tishbe[n] in 17
Gilead, said to Ahab, "As the LORD the
God of Israel lives, before whom I stand,
there shall be neither dew nor rain these
years, except by my word." And the word of 2
the LORD came to him, "Depart from here 3
and turn eastward, and hide yourself by the
brook Cherith, that is east of the Jordan.
You shall drink from the brook, and I have 4
commanded the ravens to feed you there."
So he went and did according to the word of 5
the LORD; he went and dwelt by the brook
Cherith that is east of the Jordan. And the 6

Samaria was a fortified city built on a hill

ravens brought him bread and meat in the morning, and bread and meat in the evening; 7 and he drank from the brook. And after a while the brook dried up, because there was no rain in the land.

At Zarephath

8 Then the word of the LORD came to him, 9 "Arise, go to Zar′ephath, which belongs to Sidon, and dwell there. Behold, I have 10 commanded a widow there to feed you." So he arose and went to Zar′ephath; and when he came to the gate of the city, behold, a widow was there gathering sticks; and he called to her and said, "Bring me a little 11 water in a vessel, that I may drink." And as she was going to bring it, he called to her and said, "Bring me a morsel of bread in your 12 hand." And she said, "As the LORD your God lives, I have nothing baked, only a handful of meal in a jar, and a little oil in a cruse; and now, I am gathering a couple of sticks, that I may go in and prepare it for myself and my son, that we may eat it, and 13 die." And Eli′jah said to her, "Fear not; go and do as you have said; but first make me a little cake of it and bring it to me, and afterward make for yourself and your son. 14 For thus says the LORD the God of Israel, 'The jar of meal shall not be spent, and the cruse of oil shall not fail, until the day that 15 the LORD sends rain upon the earth.'" And she went and did as Eli′jah said; and she, and he, and her household ate for many days. 16 The jar of meal was not spent, neither did the cruse of oil fail, according to the word of the LORD which he spoke by Eli′jah.

After this the son of the woman, the 17 mistress of the house, became ill; and his illness was so severe that there was no breath left in him. And she said to Eli′jah, "What 18 have you against me, O man of God? You have come to me to bring my sin to remembrance, and to cause the death of my son!" And he said to her, "Give me your son." 19 And he took him from her bosom, and carried him up into the upper chamber, where he lodged, and laid him upon his own bed. And he cried to the LORD, "O LORD my 20 God, hast thou brought calamity even upon the widow with whom I sojourn, by slaying her son?" Then he stretched himself upon 21 the child three times, and cried to the LORD, "O LORD my God, let this child's soul come into him again." And the LORD hearkened to 22 the voice of Eli′jah; and the soul of the child came into him again, and he revived. And 23 Eli′jah took the child, and brought him down from the upper chamber into the house, and delivered him to his mother; and Eli′jah said, "See, your son lives." And the woman said 24 to Eli′jah, "Now I know that you are a man of God, and that the word of the LORD in your mouth is truth."

In Samaria

After many days the word of the LORD came 18 to Eli′jah, in the third year, saying, "Go, show yourself to Ahab; and I will send rain upon the earth." So Eli′jah went to show 2 himself to Ahab. Now the famine was severe in Samar′ia. And Ahab called Obadi′ah, who 3 was over the household. (Now Obadi′ah revered the LORD greatly; and when Jez′ebel 4

17.8–16: Lk 4.25–26.   **17.18:** Mt 8.29; Mk 1.24; Jn 2.4.

cut off the prophets of the LORD, Obadi'ah took a hundred prophets and hid them by fifties in a cave, and fed them with bread and 5 water.) And Ahab said to Obadi'ah, "Go through the land to all the springs of water and to all the valleys; perhaps we may find grass and save the horses and mules alive, 6 and not lose some of the animals." So they divided the land between them to pass through it; Ahab went in one direction by himself, and Obadi'ah went in another direction by himself.

7 And as Obadi'ah was on the way, behold, Eli'jah met him; and Obadi'ah recognized him, and fell on his face, and said, "Is it you, 8 my lord Eli'jah?" And he answered, "It is I. Go, tell your lord, 'Behold, Eli'jah is 9 here.'" And he said, "Wherein have I sinned, that you would give your servant into 10 the hand of Ahab, to kill me? As the LORD

answered, "I have not troubled Israel; but you have, and your father's house, because you have forsaken the commandments of the LORD and followed the Ba'als. Now therefore send and gather all Israel to me at Mount Carmel, and the four hundred and fifty prophets of Ba'al and the four hundred prophets of Ashe'rah, who eat at Jez'ebel's table."

Mount Carmel

So Ahab sent to all the people of Israel, and 2 gathered the prophets together at Mount Carmel. And Eli'jah came near to all the 2 people, and said, "How long will you go limping with two different opinions? If the LORD is God, follow him; but if Ba'al, then follow him." And the people did not answer

your God lives, there is no nation or kingdom whither my lord has not sent to seek you; and when they would say, 'He is not here,' he would take an oath of the kingdom or nation, 11 that they had not found you. And now you say, 'Go, tell your lord, "Behold, Eli'jah is 12 here."' And as soon as I have gone from you, the Spirit of the LORD will carry you whither I know not; and so, when I come and tell Ahab and he cannot find you, he will kill me, although I your servant have revered the 13 LORD from my youth. Has it not been told my lord what I did when Jez'ebel killed the prophets of the LORD, how I hid a hundred men of the LORD's prophets by fifties in a cave, and fed them with bread and water? 14 And now you say, 'Go, tell your lord, "Behold, Eli'jah is here"'; and he will kill 15 me." And Eli'jah said, "As the LORD of hosts lives, before whom I stand, I will surely 16 show myself to him today." So Obadi'ah went to meet Ahab, and told him; and Ahab went to meet Eli'jah.

17 When Ahab saw Eli'jah, Ahab said to him, 18 "Is it you, you troubler of Israel?" And he

him a word. Then Eli'jah said to the people, 22 "I, even I only, am left a prophet of the LORD; but Ba'al's prophets are four hundred and fifty men. Let two bulls be given to 23 us; and let them choose one bull for themselves, and cut it in pieces and lay it on the wood, but put no fire to it; and I will prepare the other bull and lay it on the wood, and put no fire to it. And you call on the 24 name of your god and I will call on the name of the LORD; and the God who answers by fire, he is God." And all the people answered, "It is well spoken." Then Eli'jah 25 said to the prophets of Ba'al, "Choose for yourselves one bull and prepare it first, for you are many; and call on the name of your god, but put no fire to it." And they took the 26 bull which was given them, and they prepared it, and called on the name of Ba'al from morning until noon, saying, "O Ba'al, answer us!" But there was no voice, and no one answered. And they limped about the altar which they had made. And at noon 27 Eli'jah mocked them, saying, "Cry aloud, for he is a god; either he is musing, or he has

gone aside, or he is on a journey, or perhaps
28 he is asleep and must be awakened." And
they cried aloud, and cut themselves after
their custom with swords and lances, until
29 the blood gushed out upon them. And as
midday passed, they raved on until the time
of the offering of the oblation, but there was
no voice; no one answered, no one heeded.
30 Then Eli′jah said to all the people, "Come
near to me"; and all the people came near to
him. And he repaired the altar of the LORD
31 that had been thrown down; Eli′jah took
twelve stones, according to the number of the
tribes of the sons of Jacob, to whom the word
of the LORD came, saying, "Israel shall be
32 your name"; and with the stones he built an
altar in the name of the LORD. And he made
a trench about the altar, as great as would
33 contain two measures of seed. And he put
the wood in order, and cut the bull in pieces
and laid it on the wood. And he said, "Fill
four jars with water, and pour it on the burnt
34 offering, and on the wood." And he said,
"Do it a second time"; and they did it a
second time. And he said, "Do it a third
35 time"; and they did it a third time. And the
water ran round about the altar, and filled
the trench also with water.
36 And at the time of the offering of the
oblation, Eli′jah the prophet came near and
said, "O LORD, God of Abraham, Isaac, and
Israel, let it be known this day that thou art
God in Israel, and that I am thy servant, and
that I have done all these things at thy word.
37 Answer me, O LORD, answer me, that this
people may know that thou, O LORD, art
God, and that thou hast turned their hearts
38 back." Then the fire of the LORD fell, and
consumed the burnt offering, and the wood,
and the stones, and the dust, and licked up
39 the water that was in the trench. And when
all the people saw it, they fell on their faces;
and they said, "The LORD, he is God; the
40 LORD, he is God." And Eli′jah said to them,
"Seize the prophets of Ba′al; let not one of
them escape." And they seized them; and
Eli′jah brought them down to the brook
Kishon, and killed them there.
41 And Eli′jah said to Ahab, "Go up, eat and
drink; for there is a sound of the rushing
42 of rain." So Ahab went up to eat and to
drink. And Eli′jah went up to the top of
Carmel; and he bowed himself down upon
the earth, and put his face between his
43 knees. And he said to his servant, "Go up
now, look toward the sea." And he went up
and looked, and said, "There is nothing."
44 And he said, "Go again seven times." And
at the seventh time he said, "Behold, a little
cloud like a man's hand is rising out of the

sea." And he said, "Go up, say to Ahab,
'Prepare your chariot and go down, lest the
rain stop you.'" And in a little while the 45
heavens grew black with clouds and wind,
and there was a great rain. And Ahab rode
and went to Jezreel. And the hand of the 46
LORD was on Eli′jah; and he girded up his
loins and ran before Ahab to the entrance of
Jezreel.

On Mount Horeb

Ahab told Jez′ebel all that Eli′jah had done,19
and how he had slain all the prophets with
the sword. Then Jez′ebel sent a messenger 2
to Eli′jah, saying, "So may the gods do to
me, and more also, if I do not make your life
as the life of one of them by this time
tomorrow." Then he was afraid, and he 3
arose and went for his life, and came to
Beer-sheba, which belongs to Judah, and left
his servant there.
But he himself went a day's journey into the 4
wilderness, and came and sat down under a
broom tree; and he asked that he might die,
saying, "It is enough; now, O LORD, take
away my life; for I am no better than my
fathers." And he lay down and slept under a 5
broom tree; and behold, an angel touched
him, and said to him, "Arise and eat." And 6
he looked, and behold, there was at his head a
cake baked on hot stones and a jar of water.
And he ate and drank, and lay down again.
And the angel of the LORD came again a 7
second time, and touched him, and said,
"Arise and eat, else the journey will be too
great for you." And he arose, and ate and 8
drank, and went in the strength of that food
forty days and forty nights to Horeb the
mount of God.
And there he came to a cave, and lodged 9
there; and behold, the word of the LORD
came to him, and he said to him, "What are
you doing here, Eli′jah?" He said, "I have 10
been very jealous for the LORD, the God of
hosts; for the people of Israel have forsaken
thy covenant, thrown down thy altars, and
slain thy prophets with the sword; and I,
even I only, am left; and they seek my life, to
take it away." And he said, "Go forth, and 11
stand upon the mount before the LORD."
And behold, the LORD passed by, and a great
and strong wind rent the mountains, and
broke in pieces the rocks before the LORD,
but the LORD was not in the wind; and after
the wind an earthquake, but the LORD was
not in the earthquake; and after the earth- 12
quake a fire, but the LORD was not in the fire;
and after the fire a still small voice. And 13
when Eli′jah heard it, he wrapped his face in

19.10: Rom 11.2–3.

his mantle and went out and stood at the entrance of the cave. And behold, there came a voice to him, and said, "What are you 14 doing here, Eli'jah?" He said, "I have been very jealous for the LORD, the God of hosts; for the people of Israel have forsaken thy covenant, thrown down thy altars, and slain thy prophets with the sword; and I, even I only, am left; and they seek my life, to take it

SYRIA

15 away." And the LORD said to him, "Go, return on your way to the wilderness of Damascus; and when you arrive, you shall 16 anoint Haz'ael to be king over Syria; and Jehu the son of Nimshi you shall anoint to be king over Israel; and Eli'sha the son of Shaphat of A'bel-meho'lah you shall anoint 17 to be prophet in your place. And him who escapes from the sword of Haza'el shall Jehu slay; and him who escapes from the sword of 18 Jehu shall Eli'sha slay. Yet I will leave seven thousand in Israel, all the knees that have not bowed to Ba'al, and every mouth that has not kissed him."

Call of Elisha

19 So he departed from there, and found Eli'sha the son of Shaphat, who was ploughing, with twelve yoke of oxen before him, and he was with the twelfth. Eli'jah passed by 20 him and cast his mantle upon him. And he left the oxen, and ran after Eli'jah, and said, "Let me kiss my father and my mother, and then I will follow you." And he said to him, "Go back again; for what have I done to 21 you?" And he returned from following him, and took the yoke of oxen, and slew them, and boiled their flesh with the yokes of the oxen, and gave it to the people, and they ate. Then he arose and went after Eli'jah, and ministered to him.

Syria attacks Israel

20 Ben-ha'dad the king of Syria gathered all his army together; thirty-two kings were with him, and horses and chariots; and he went up and besieged Samar'ia, and fought 2 against it. And he sent messengers into the

city to Ahab king of Israel, and said to him, "Thus says Ben-ha'dad: 'Your silver and 3 your gold are mine; your fairest wives and children also are mine.'" And the king of 4 Israel answered, "As you say, my lord, O king, I am yours, and all that I have." The 5 messengers came again, and said, "Thus says Ben-ha'dad: 'I sent to you, saying, "Deliver to me your silver and your gold, your wives and your children"; nevertheless I will send 6 my servants to you tomorrow about this time, and they shall search your house and the houses of your servants, and lay hands on whatever pleases them,º and take it away.'"

Then the king of Israel called all the elders 7 of the land, and said, "Mark, now, and see how this man is seeking trouble; for he sent to me for my wives and my children, and for my silver and my gold, and I did not refuse him." And all the elders and all the people 8 said to him, "Do not heed or consent." So 9 he said to the messengers of Ben-ha'dad, "Tell my lord the king, 'All that you first demanded of your servant I will do; but this thing I cannot do.'" And the messengers departed and brought him word again. Ben-ha'dad sent to him and said, "The gods 10 do so to me, and more also, if the dust of Samar'ia shall suffice for handfuls for all the people who follow me." And the king of 11 Israel answered, "Tell him, 'Let not him that girds on his armour boast himself as he that puts it off.'" When Ben-ha'dad heard this 12 message as he was drinking with the kings in the booths, he said to his men, "Take your positions." And they took their positions against the city.

And behold, a prophet came near to Ahab 13 king of Israel and said, "Thus says the LORD, Have you seen all this great multitude? Behold, I will give it into your hand this day; and you shall know that I am the LORD." And Ahab said, "By whom?" He said, 14 "Thus says the LORD, By the servants of the governors of the districts." Then he said, "Who shall begin the battle?" He answered, "You." Then he mustered the servants of 15 the governors of the districts, and they were two hundred and thirty-two; and after them he mustered all the people of Israel, seven thousand.

And they went out at noon, while Ben-ha'- 16 dad was drinking himself drunk in the booths, he and the thirty-two kings who helped him. The servants of the governors 17 of the districts went out first. And Ben-ha'dad sent out scouts, and they reported to him, "Men are coming out from Samar'ia." He said, "If they have come out for peace, 18

take them alive; or if they have come out for
war, take them alive."

So these went out of the city, the servants of
the governors of the districts, and the army
which followed them. And each killed his
man; the Syrians fled and Israel pursued
them, but Ben-ha′dad king of Syria escaped
on a horse with horsemen. And the king of
Israel went out, and captured *p* the horses
and chariots, and killed the Syrians with a
great slaughter.

Then the prophet came near to the king of
Israel, and said to him, "Come, strengthen
yourself, and consider well what you have to
do; for in the spring the king of Syria will
come up against you."

And the servants of the king of Syria said to
him, "Their gods are gods of the hills, and so
they were stronger than we; but let us fight
against them in the plain, and surely we shall
be stronger than they. And do this: remove
the kings, each from his post, and put
commanders in their places; and muster an
army like the army that you have lost, horse
for horse, and chariot for chariot; then we
will fight against them in the plain, and
surely we shall be stronger than they." And
he hearkened to their voice, and did so.

In the spring Ben-ha′dad mustered the
Syrians, and went up to Aphek, to fight
against Israel. And the people of Israel were
mustered, and were provisioned, and went
against them; the people of Israel encamped
before them like two little flocks of goats, but
the Syrians filled the country. And a man of
God came near and said to the king of Israel,
"Thus says the LORD, 'Because the Syrians
have said, "The LORD is a god of the hills but
he is not a god of the valleys," therefore I will
give all this great multitude into your hand,
and you shall know that I am the LORD.' "

And they encamped opposite one another
seven days. Then on the seventh day the
battle was joined; and the people of Israel
smote of the Syrians a hundred thousand
foot soldiers in one day. And the rest fled
into the city of Aphek; and the wall fell upon
twenty-seven thousand men that were left.

Ben-ha′dad also fled, and entered an inner
chamber in the city. And his servants said to
him, "Behold now, we have heard that the
kings of the house of Israel are merciful
kings; let us put sackcloth on our loins and
ropes upon our heads, and go out to the king
of Israel; perhaps he will spare your life." So
they girded sackcloth on their loins, and put
ropes on their heads, and went to the king of
Israel and said, "Your servant Ben-ha′dad
says, 'Pray, let me live.' " And he said,
"Does he still live? He is my brother."

Now the men were watching for an omen,
and they quickly took it up from him and
said, "Yes, your brother Ben-ha′dad." Then
he said, "Go and bring him." Then Ben-
ha′dad came forth to him; and he caused him
to come up into the chariot. And Ben-ha′dad
said to him, "The cities which my father took
from your father I will restore; and you may
establish bazaars for yourself in Damascus,
as my father did in Samar′ia." And Ahab
said, "I will let you go on these terms." So
he made a covenant with him and let him go.

And a certain man of the sons of the
prophets said to his fellow at the command of
the LORD, "Strike me, I pray." But the man
refused to strike him. Then he said to him,
"Because you have not obeyed the voice of
the LORD, behold, as soon as you have gone
from me, a lion shall kill you." And as soon
as he had departed from him, a lion met him
and killed him. Then he found another man,
and said, "Strike me, I pray." And the man
struck him, smiting and wounding him. So
the prophet departed, and waited for the king
by the way, disguising himself with a
bandage over his eyes. And as the king
passed, he cried to the king and said, "Your
servant went out into the midst of the battle;
and behold, a soldier turned and brought a
man to me, and said, 'Keep this man; if by
any means he be missing, your life shall be
for his life, or else you shall pay a talent of

p Gk: Heb *smote*

40 silver.' And as your servant was busy here and there, he was gone." The king of Israel said to him, "So shall your judgment be; you
41 yourself have decided it." Then he made haste to take the bandage away from his eyes; and the king of Israel recognised him as one
42 of the prophets. And he said to him, "Thus says the LORD, 'Because you have let go out of your hand the man whom I had devoted to destruction, therefore your life shall go for his life, and your people for his people.'"
43 And the king of Israel went to his house resentful and sullen, and came to Samar'ia.

Naboth's vineyard

21 Now Naboth the Jez'reelite had a vineyard in Jezreel, beside the palace of Ahab king of
2 Samar'ia. And after this Ahab said to Naboth, "Give me your vineyard, that I may have it for a vegetable garden, because it is near my house; and I will give you a better vineyard for it; or, if it seems good to you, I
3 will give you its value in money." But Naboth said to Ahab, "The LORD forbid that I should give you the inheritance of my
4 fathers." And Ahab went into his house vexed and sullen because of what Naboth the Jez'reelite had said to him; for he had said, "I will not give you the inheritance of my fathers." And he lay down on his bed, and turned away his face, and would eat no food.
5 But Jez'ebel his wife came to him, and said to him, "Why is your spirit so vexed that you
6 eat no food?" And he said to her, "Because I spoke to Naboth the Jez'reelite, and said to him, 'Give me your vineyard for money; or else, if it please you, I will give you another vineyard for it'; and he answered, 'I will not
7 give you my vineyard.'" And Jez'ebel his wife said to him, "Do you now govern Israel? Arise, and eat bread, and let your heart be cheerful; I will give you the vineyard of Naboth the Jez'reelite."
8 So she wrote letters in Ahab's name and sealed them with his seal, and she sent the letters to the elders and the nobles who dwelt
9 with Naboth in his city. And she wrote in the letters, "Proclaim a fast, and set Naboth
10 on high among the people; and set two base fellows opposite him, and let them bring a charge against him, saying, 'You have cursed God and the king.' Then take him out, and
11 stone him to death." And the men of his city, the elders and the nobles who dwelt in his city, did as Jez'ebel had sent word to them. As it was written in the letters which
12 she had sent to them, they proclaimed a fast, and set Naboth on high among the people.
13 And the two base fellows came in and sat

opposite him; and the base fellows brought a charge against Naboth, in the presence of the people, saying, "Naboth cursed God and the king." So they took him outside the city, and stoned him to death with stones. Then they sent to Jez'ebel, saying, "Naboth has been stoned; he is dead."

As soon as Jez'ebel heard that Naboth had been stoned and was dead, Jez'ebel said to Ahab, "Arise, take possession of the vineyard of Naboth the Jez'reelite, which he refused to give you for money; for Naboth is not alive, but dead." And as soon as Ahab heard that Naboth was dead, Ahab arose to go down to the vineyard of Naboth the Jez'reelite, to take possession of it.

Elijah denounces Ahab

Then the word of the LORD came to Eli'jah the Tishbite, saying, "Arise, go down to meet Ahab king of Israel, who is in Samar'ia; behold, he is in the vineyard of Naboth, where he has gone to take possession. And you shall say to him, 'Thus says the LORD, "Have you killed, and also take possession?"'" And you shall say to him, 'Thus says the LORD: "In the place where dogs licked up the blood of Naboth shall dogs lick your own blood."'"

Ahab said to Eli'jah, "Have you found me, O my enemy?" He answered, "I have found you, because you have sold yourself to do what is evil in the sight of the LORD. Behold, I will bring evil upon you; I will utterly sweep you away, and will cut off from Ahab every male, bond or free, in Israel; and I will make your house like the house of Jerobo'am the son of Nebat, and like the house of Ba'asha the son of Ahi'jah, for the anger to which you have provoked me, and because you have made Israel to sin. And of Jez'ebel the LORD also said, 'The dogs shall eat Jez'ebel within the bounds of Jezreel.' Any one belonging to Ahab who dies in the city the dogs shall eat; and any one of his who dies in the open country the birds of the air shall eat."

(There was none who sold himself to do what was evil in the sight of the LORD like Ahab, whom Jez'ebel his wife incited. He did very abominably in going after idols, as the Amorites had done, whom the LORD cast out before the people of Israel.)

And when Ahab heard those words, he rent 27 his clothes, and put sackcloth upon his flesh, and fasted and lay in sackcloth, and went about dejectedly. And the word of the LORD 28 came to Eli'jah the Tishbite, saying, "Have 29 you seen how Ahab has humbled himself

Entrance to a vineyard

before me? Because he has humbled himself before me, I will not bring the evil in his days; but in his son's days I will bring the evil upon his house."

The death of Ahab

22 For three years Syria and Israel continued 2 without war. But in the third year Jehosh'-aphat the king of Judah came down to the 3 king of Israel. And the king of Israel said to his servants, "Do you know that Ramoth-gilead belongs to us, and we keep quiet and do not take it out of the hand of the king of 4 Syria?" And he said to Jehosh'aphat, "Will you go with me to battle at Ramoth-gilead?" And Jehosh'aphat said to the king of Israel, "I am as you are, my people as your people, my horses as your horses." 5 And Jehosh'aphat said to the king of Israel, "Inquire first for the word of the LORD."

Then the king of Israel gathered the pro- 6 phets together, about four hundred men, and said to them, "Shall I go to battle against Ramoth-gilead, or shall I forbear?" And they said, "Go up; for the Lord will give it into the hand of the king." But Jehosh'aphat 7 said, "Is there not here another prophet of the LORD of whom we may inquire?" And 8 the king of Israel said to Jehosh'aphat, "There is yet one man by whom we may inquire of the LORD, Micai'ah the son of Imlah; but I hate him, for he never prophesies good concerning me, but evil." And Jehosh'aphat said, "Let not the king say so." Then the king of Israel summoned an officer 9 and said, "Bring quickly Micai'ah the son of Imlah." Now the king of Israel and 10 Jehosh'aphat the king of Judah were sitting on their thrones, arrayed in their robes, at the threshing floor at the entrance of the gate of Samar'ia; and all the prophets were prophesying before them. And Zedeki'ah the son of 11 Chena'anah made for himself horns of iron, and said, "Thus says the LORD, 'With these you shall push the Syrians until they are destroyed.'" And all the prophets prophe- 12 sied so, and said, "Go up to Ramoth-gilead and triumph; the LORD will give it into the hand of the king."

And the messenger who went to summon 13 Micai'ah said to him, "Behold, the words of the prophets with one accord are favourable to the king; let your word be like the word of one of them, and speak favourably." But 14 Micai'ah said, "As the LORD lives, what the LORD says to me, that I will speak." And 15 when he had come to the king, the king said to him, "Micai'ah, shall we go to Ramoth-gilead to battle, or shall we forbear?" And he answered him, "Go up and triumph; the LORD will give it into the hand of the king." But the king said to him, "How many times 16 shall I adjure you that you speak to me nothing but the truth in the name of the LORD?" And he said, "I saw all Israel 17 scattered upon the mountains, as sheep that have no shepherd; and the LORD said, 'These have no master; let each return to his home in peace.'" And the king of Israel said to 18 Jehosh'aphat, "Did I not tell you that he would not prophesy good concerning me, but evil?" And Micai'ah said, "Therefore hear 19 the word of the LORD: I saw the LORD sitting on his throne, and all the host of heaven standing beside him on his right hand and on his left; and the LORD said, 'Who will entice 20 Ahab, that he may go up and fall at Ramoth-gilead?' And one said one thing, and another said another. Then a spirit came 21 forward and stood before the LORD, saying,

22 'I will entice him.' And the LORD said to
him, 'By what means?' And he said, 'I will
go forth, and will be a lying spirit in the
mouth of all his prophets.' And he said,
'You are to entice him, and you shall suc-
23 ceed; go forth and do so.' Now therefore
behold, the LORD has put a lying spirit in the
mouth of all these your prophets; the LORD
has spoken evil concerning you."
24 Then Zedeki′ah the son of Chena′anah
came near and struck Micai′ah on the cheek,
and said, "How did the Spirit of the LORD go
25 from me to speak to you?" And Micai′ah
said, "Behold, you shall see on that day when
you go into an inner chamber to hide
26 yourself." And the king of Israel said,
"Seize Micai′ah, and take him back to Amon
the governor of the city and to Jo′ash the
27 king's son; and say, 'Thus says the king,
"Put this fellow in prison, and feed him with
scant fare of bread and water, until I come in
28 peace."'" And Micai′ah said, "If you
return in peace, the LORD has not spoken by
me." And he said, "Hear, all you peoples!"
29 So the king of Israel and Jehosh′aphat the
king of Judah went up to Ramoth-gilead.
30 And the king of Israel said to Jehosh′aphat,
"I will disguise myself and go into battle, but
you wear your robes." And the king of Israel
31 disguised himself and went into battle. Now
the king of Syria had commanded the
thirty-two captains of his chariots, "Fight
with neither small nor great, but only with
32 the king of Israel." And when the captains
of the chariots saw Jehosh′aphat, they said,
"It is surely the king of Israel." So they
turned to fight against him; and Jehosh′-
33 aphat cried out. And when the captains of
the chariots saw that it was not the king of

Israel, they turned back from pursuing him.
But a certain man drew his bow at a venture,
and struck the king of Israel between the
scale armour and the breastplate; therefore
he said to the driver of his chariot, "Turn
about, and carry me out of the battle, for I
am wounded." And the battle grew hot that
day, and the king was propped up in his
chariot facing the Syrians, until at evening he
died; and the blood of the wound flowed into
the bottom of the chariot. And about sunset
a cry went through the army, "Every man to
his city, and every man to his country!"
So the king died, and was brought to
Samar′ia; and they buried the king in
Samar′ia. And they washed the chariot by
the pool of Samar′ia, and the dogs licked up
his blood, and the harlots washed themselves
in it, according to the word of the LORD
which he had spoken. Now the rest of the
acts of Ahab, and all that he did, and the
ivory house which he built, and all the cities
that he built, are they not written in the Book
of the Chronicles of the Kings of Israel? So
Ahab slept with his fathers; and Ahazi′ah his
son reigned in his stead.

The two kingdoms

Jehosh′aphat the son of Asa began to reign
over Judah in the fourth year of Ahab king of
Israel. Jehosh′aphat was thirty-five years old
when he began to reign, and he reigned
twenty-five years in Jerusalem. His mother's
name was Azu′bah the daughter of Shilhi.
He walked in all the way of Asa his father;
he did not turn aside from it, doing what was
right in the sight of the LORD; yet the high
places were not taken away, and the people
still sacrificed and burned incense on the
high places. Jehosh′aphat also made peace
with the king of Israel.
Now the rest of the acts of Jehosh′aphat,
and his might that he showed, and how he
warred, are they not written in the Book of
the Chronicles of the Kings of Judah? And
the remnant of the male cult prostitutes who
remained in the days of his father Asa, he
exterminated from the land.
There was no king in Edom; a deputy was
king. Jehosh′aphat made ships of Tarshish
to go to Ophir for gold; but they did not go,
for the ships were wrecked at E′zion-ge′ber.
Then Ahazi′ah the son of Ahab said to
Jehosh′aphat, "Let my servants go with your
servants in the ships," but Jehosh′aphat was
not willing. And Jehosh′aphat slept with his
fathers, and was buried with his fathers in
the city of David his father; and Jeho′ram his
son reigned in his stead.

Ahazi′ah the son of Ahab began to reign over Israel in Samar′ia in the seventeenth year of Jehosh′aphat king of Judah, and he reigned two years over Israel. He did what was evil in the sight of the LORD, and walked in the way of his father, and in the way of his mother, and in the way of Jerobo′am the son of Nebat, who made Israel to sin. He served 53 Ba′al and worshipped him, and provoked the LORD, the God of Israel, to anger in every way that his father had done.

Damascus, the capital of Syria

THE SECOND BOOK OF THE

KINGS

FTER the death of Ahab, Moab
rebelled against Israel.
2 Now Ahazi′ah fell through the lattice
in his upper chamber in Samar′ia, and lay sick;
so he sent messengers, telling them, "Go,
inquire of Ba′al-ze′bub, the god of Ekron,
whether I shall recover from this sickness."

Elijah and the messengers

3 But the angel of the LORD said to Eli′jah the
Tishbite, "Arise, go up to meet the messengers of the king of Samar′ia, and say to them,
'Is it because there is no God in Israel that
you are going to inquire of Ba′al-ze′bub, the
4 god of Ekron?' Now therefore thus says
the LORD, 'You shall not come down from
the bed to which you have gone, but you
shall surely die.'" So Eli′jah went.
5 The messengers returned to the king, and
he said to them, "Why have you returned?"
6 And they said to him, "There came a man to
meet us, and said to us, 'Go back to the king

who sent you, and say to him, Thus says the
LORD, Is it because there is no God in Israel
that you are sending to inquire of Ba′al-
ze′bub, the god of Ekron? Therefore you
shall not come down from the bed to which
you have gone, but shall surely die.'" He 7
said to them, "What kind of man was he who
came to meet you and told you these
things?" They answered him, "He wore a 8
garment of haircloth, with a girdle of leather
about his loins." And he said, "It is Eli′jah
the Tishbite."
Then the king sent to him a captain of fifty 9
men with his fifty. He went up to Eli′jah,
who was sitting on the top of a hill, and said
to him, "O man of God, the king says, 'Come
down.'" But Eli′jah answered the captain of 10
fifty, "If I am a man of God, let fire come
down from heaven and consume you and
your fifty." Then fire came down from
heaven, and consumed him and his fifty.
Again the king sent to him another captain 11
of fifty men with his fifty. And he went up[a]

---

[a] Gk Compare verses 9, 13: Heb *answered*
1.10–12: Lk 9.54; Rev 11.5; 20.9.

nd said to him, "O man of God, this is the
ing's order, 'Come down quickly!'" But
li'jah answered them, "If I am a man of
God, let fire come down from heaven and
onsume you and your fifty." Then the fire
f God came down from heaven and con-
umed him and his fifty.

Again the king sent the captain of a third
ifty with his fifty. And the third captain of
ifty went up, and came and fell on his knees
before Eli'jah, and entreated him, "O man of
God, I pray you, let my life, and the life of
hese fifty servants of yours, be precious in
your sight. Lo, fire came down from heaven,
nd consumed the two former captains of
ifty men with their fifties; but now let my
ife be precious in your sight." Then the
ngel of the LORD said to Eli'jah, "Go down
with him; do not be afraid of him." So he
arose and went down with him to the king,
and said to him, "Thus says the LORD,
'Because you have sent messengers to inquire
of Ba'al-ze'bub, the god of Ekron,—is it
because there is no God in Israel to inquire
of his word?—therefore you shall not come
down from the bed to which you have gone,
but you shall surely die.'"

So he died according to the word of the
LORD which Eli'jah had spoken. Jeho'ram,
his brother,[b] became king in his stead in the
second year of Jeho'ram the son of Jehosh'-
aphat, king of Judah, because Ahazi'ah had
no son. Now the rest of the acts of Ahazi'ah
which he did, are they not written in the
Book of the Chronicles of the Kings of
Israel?

Elijah taken up to heaven

Now when the LORD was about to take
Eli'jah up to heaven by a whirlwind, Eli'jah
and Eli'sha were on their way from Gilgal.
And Eli'jah said to Eli'sha, "Tarry here, I
pray you; for the LORD has sent me as far as
Bethel." But Eli'sha said, "As the LORD
lives, and as you yourself live, I will not leave
you." So they went down to Bethel. And
the sons of the prophets who were in Bethel
came out to Eli'sha, and said to him, "Do
you know that today the LORD will take away
your master from over you?" And he said,
"Yes, I know it; hold your peace."

Eli'jah said to him, "Eli'sha, tarry here, I
pray you; for the LORD has sent me to
Jericho." But he said, "As the LORD lives,
and as you yourself live, I will not leave
you." So they came to Jericho. The sons of
the prophets who were at Jericho drew near
to Eli'sha, and said to him, "Do you know

that today the LORD will take away your
master from over you?" And he answered,
"Yes, I know it; hold your peace."

Then Eli'jah said to him, "Tarry here, I 6
pray you; for the LORD has sent me to the
Jordan." But he said, "As the LORD lives,
and as you yourself live, I will not leave
you." So the two of them went on. Fifty 7
men of the sons of the prophets also went,
and stood at some distance from them, as
they both were standing by the Jordan.
Then Eli'jah took his mantle, and rolled it 8
up, and struck the water, and the water was
parted to the one side and to the other, till
the two of them could go over on dry ground.

When they had crossed, Eli'jah said to 9
Eli'sha, "Ask what I shall do for you, before
I am taken from you." And Eli'sha said, "I
pray you, let me inherit a double share of
your spirit." And he said, "You have asked a 10
hard thing; yet, if you see me as I am being
taken from you, it shall be so for you; but if
you do not see me, it shall not be so." And as 11
they still went on and talked, behold, a
chariot of fire and horses of fire separated the
two of them. And Eli'jah went up by a
whirlwind into heaven. And Eli'sha saw it 12
and he cried, "My father, my father! the
chariots of Israel and its horsemen!" And he
saw him no more.

Then he took hold of his own clothes and
rent them in two pieces. And he took up the 13
mantle of Eli'jah that had fallen from him,
and went back and stood on the bank of the
Jordan. Then he took the mantle of Eli'jah 14
that had fallen from him, and struck the
water, saying, "Where is the LORD, the God
of Eli'jah?" And when he had struck the
water, the water was parted to the one side
and to the other; and Eli'sha went over.

ELISHA

NOW when the sons of the prophets who 15
were at Jericho saw him over against
them, they said, "The spirit of Eli'jah rests
on Eli'sha." And they came to meet him,
and bowed to the ground before him. And 16
they said to him, "Behold now, there are
with your servants fifty strong men; pray, let
them go, and seek your master; it may be that
the Spirit of the LORD has caught him up and
cast him upon some mountain or into some
valley." And he said, "You shall not send."
But when they urged him till he was 17
ashamed, he said, "Send." They sent therefore fifty men; and for three days they sought
him but did not find him. And they came 18
back to him, while he tarried at Jericho, and

b Gk Syr: Heb lacks *his brother*
2.11: Rev 11.12.

he said to them, "Did I not say to you, Do not go?"

Elisha purifies water

19 Now the men of the city said to Eli′sha, "Behold, the situation of this city is pleasant, as my lord sees; but the water is bad, and the
20 land is unfruitful." He said, "Bring me a new bowl, and put salt in it." So they
21 brought it to him. Then he went to the spring of water and threw salt in it, and said, "Thus says the LORD, I have made this water wholesome; henceforth neither death nor
22 miscarriage shall come from it." So the water has been wholesome to this day, according to the word which Eli′sha spoke.
23 He went up from there to Bethel; and while he was going up on the way, some small boys came out of the city and jeered at him, saying, "Go up, you baldhead! Go up, you
24 baldhead!" And he turned around, and when he saw them, he cursed them in the name of the LORD. And two she-bears came out of the woods and tore forty-two of the
25 boys. From there he went on to Mount Carmel, and thence he returned to Samar′ia.

3 In the eighteenth year of Jehosh′aphat king of Judah, Jeho′ram the son of Ahab became king over Israel in Samar′ia, and he reigned
2 twelve years. He did what was evil in the sight of the LORD, though not like his father and mother, for he put away the pillar of
3 Ba′al which his father had made. Nevertheless he clung to the sin of Jerobo′am the son of Nebat, which he made Israel to sin; he did not depart from it.

Elisha fills the water trenches

4 Now Mesha king of Moab was a sheep breeder; and he had to deliver annually[c] to the king of Israel a hundred thousand lambs, and the wool of a hundred thousand rams.
5 But when Ahab died, the king of Moab
6 rebelled against the king of Israel. So King Jeho′ram marched out of Samar′ia at that
7 time and mustered all Israel. And he went and sent word to Jehosh′aphat king of Judah, "The king of Moab has rebelled against me; will you go with me to battle against Moab?" And he said, "I will go; I am as you are, my people as your people, my horses as
8 your horses." Then he said, "By which way shall we march?" Jeho′ram answered, "By the way of the wilderness of Edom."
9 So the king of Israel went with the king of Judah and the king of Edom. And when they had made a circuitous march of seven days,

[c] Tg: **Heb** lacks *annually*

there was no water for the army or for the beasts which followed them. Then the king of Israel said, "Alas! The LORD has called these three kings to give them into the hand of Moab." And Jehosh′aphat said, "Is there no prophet of the LORD here, through whom we may inquire of the LORD?" Then one of the king of Israel's servants answered, "Eli′sha the son of Shaphat is here, who poured water on the hands of Eli′jah." And Jehosh′aphat said, "The word of the LORD is with him." So the king of Israel and Jehosh′aphat and the king of Edom went down to him.

MOAB

And Eli′sha said to the king of Israel, "What have I to do with you? Go to the prophets of your father and the prophets of your mother." But the king of Israel said to him, "No; it is the LORD who has called these three kings to give them into the hand of Moab." And Eli′sha said, "As the LORD of hosts lives, whom I serve, were it not that I have regard for Jehosh′aphat the king of Judah, I would neither look at you, nor see you. But now bring me a minstrel." And when the minstrel played, the power of the LORD came upon him. And he said, "Thus says the LORD, 'I will make this dry stream-bed full of pools.' For thus says the LORD, 'You shall not see wind or rain, but that stream-bed shall be filled with water, so that you shall drink, you, your cattle, and your beasts.' This is a light thing in the sight of the LORD; he will also give the Moabites into your hand, and you shall conquer every fortified city, and every choice city, and shall fell every good tree, and stop up all springs of water, and ruin every good piece of land with stones." The next morning, about the time of offering the sacrifice, behold, water came from the direction of Edom, till the country was filled with water.

When all the Moabites heard that the kings had come up to fight against them, all who were able to put on armour, from the youngest to the oldest, were called out, and were drawn up at the frontier. And when they rose early in the morning, and the sun shone upon the water, the Moabites saw the water opposite them as red as blood. And they said, "This is blood; the kings have surely fought together, and slain one another. Now then, Moab, to the spoil!" 4 But when they came to the camp of Israel, the Israelites rose and attacked the Moabites, till they fled before them; and they went forward, slaughtering the Moabites as they 5 went.*d* And they overthrew the cities, and on every good piece of land every man threw a stone, until it was covered; they stopped every spring of water, and felled all the good trees; till only its stones were left in Kirhar'eseth, and the slingers surrounded and 6 conquered it. When the king of Moab saw that the battle was going against him, he took with him seven hundred swordsmen to break through, opposite the king of Edom; but they 7 could not. Then he took his eldest son who was to reign in his stead, and offered him for a burnt offering upon the wall. And there came great wrath upon Israel; and they withdrew from him and returned to their own land.

Vessels of oil

4 Now the wife of one of the sons of the prophets cried to Eli'sha, "Your servant my husband is dead; and you know that your servant feared the LORD, but the creditor has come to take my two children to be his 2 slaves." And Eli'sha said to her, "What shall I do for you? Tell me; what have you in the house?" And she said, "Your maidservant has nothing in the house, except a jar of oil." 3 Then he said, "Go outside, borrow vessels of all your neighbours, empty vessels and not 4 too few. Then go in, and shut the door upon yourself and your sons, and pour into all these vessels; and when one is full, set it 5 aside." So she went from him and shut the door upon herself and her sons; and as she poured they brought the vessels to her. 6 When the vessels were full, she said to her son, "Bring me another vessel." And he said to her, "There is not another." Then the oil 7 stopped flowing. She came and told the man of God, and he said, "Go, sell the oil and pay

your debts, and you and your sons can live on the rest."

The Shunammite's son

One day Eli'sha went on to Shunem, where 8 a wealthy woman lived, who urged him to eat some food. So whenever he passed that way, he would turn in there to eat food. And she 9 said to her husband, "Behold now, I perceive that this is a holy man of God, who is continually passing our way. Let us make a small 10 roof chamber with walls, and put there for him a bed, a table, a chair, and a lamp, so that whenever he comes to us, he can go in there."

One day he came there, and he turned into 11 the chamber and rested there. And he said to 12 Geha'zi his servant, "Call this Shu'nammite." When he had called her, she stood before him. And he said to him, "Say now to 13 her, See, you have taken all this trouble for us; what is to be done for you? Would you have a word spoken on your behalf to the king or to the commander of the army?" She answered, "I dwell among my own people." And he said, "What then is to be 14 done for her?" Geha'zi answered, "Well, she has no son, and her husband is old." He 15 said, "Call her." And when he had called her, she stood in the doorway. And he said, 16 "At this season, when the time comes round, you shall embrace a son." And she said, "No, my lord, O man of God; do not lie to your maidservant." But the woman con- 17 ceived, and she bore a son about that time the following spring, as Eli'sha had said to her.

When the child had grown, he went out one 18 day to his father among the reapers. And he 19 said to his father, "Oh, my head, my head!" The father said to his servant, "Carry him to his mother." And when he had lifted him, 20 and brought him to his mother, the child sat on her lap till noon, and then he died. And 21 she went up and laid him on the bed of the man of God, and shut the door upon him, and went out. Then she called to her 22 husband, and said, "Send me one of the servants and one of the asses, that I may quickly go to the man of God, and come back again." And he said, "Why will you go to 23 him today? It is neither new moon nor sabbath." She said, "It will be well." Then 24 she saddled the ass, and she said to her servant, "Urge the beast on; do not slacken the pace for me unless I tell you." So she set 25 out, and came to the man of God at Mount Carmel.

When the man of God saw her coming, he said to Geha'zi his servant, "Look, yonder is

d Gk: Heb uncertain

26 the Shu′nammite; run at once to meet her, and say to her, Is it well with you? Is it well with your husband? Is it well with the child?" And she answered, "It is well."
27 And when she came to the mountain to the man of God, she caught hold of his feet. And Geha′zi came to thrust her away. But the man of God said, "Let her alone, for she is in bitter distress; and the LORD has hidden it
28 from me, and has not told me." Then she said, "Did I ask my lord for a son? Did I not
29 say, Do not deceive me?" He said to Geha′zi, "Gird up your loins, and take my staff in your hand, and go. If you meet any one, do not salute him; and if any one salutes you, do not reply; and lay my staff upon the
30 face of the child." Then the mother of the child said, "As the LORD lives, and as you yourself live, I will not leave you." So he
31 arose and followed her. Geha′zi went on ahead and laid the staff upon the face of the child, but there was no sound or sign of life. Therefore he returned to meet him, and told him, "The child has not awaked."
32 When Eli′sha came into the house, he saw
33 the child lying dead on his bed. So he went in and shut the door upon the two of them,
34 and prayed to the LORD. Then he went up and lay upon the child, putting his mouth upon his mouth, his eyes upon his eyes, and his hands upon his hands; and as he stretched himself upon him, the flesh of the
35 child became warm. Then he got up again, and walked once to and fro in the house, and went up, and stretched himself upon him; the child sneezed seven times, and the child
36 opened his eyes. Then he summoned Geha′zi and said, "Call this Shu′nammite." So he called her. And when she came to him,
37 he said, "Take up your son." She came and fell at his feet, bowing to the ground; then she took up her son and went out.

38 And Eli′sha came again to Gilgal when there was a famine in the land. And as the sons of the prophets were sitting before him, he said to his servant, "Set on the great pot, and boil pottage for the sons of the
39 prophets." One of them went out into the field to gather herbs, and found a wild vine and gathered from it his lap full of wild gourds, and came and cut them up into the pot of pottage, not knowing what they were.
40 And they poured out for the men to eat. But while they were eating of the pottage, they cried out, "O man of God, there is death in
41 the pot!" And they could not eat it. He said, "Then bring meal." And he threw it into the pot, and said, "Pour out for the men, that they may eat." And there was no harm in the pot.

A man came from Ba′al-shal′ishah, bringing the man of God bread of the first fruits, twenty loaves of barley, and fresh ears of grain in his sack. And Eli′sha said, "Give to the men, that they may eat." But his servant said, "How am I to set this before a hundred men?" So he repeated, "Give them to the men, that they may eat, for thus says the LORD, 'They shall eat and have some left.'" So he set it before them. And they ate, and had some left, according to the word of the LORD.

Naaman the leper healed

Na′aman, commander of the army of the 5 king of Syria, was a great man with his master and in high favour, because by him the LORD had given victory to Syria. He was a mighty man of valour, but he was a leper. Now the Syrians on one of their raids had 2 carried off a little maid from the land of Israel, and she waited on Na′aman's wife. She said to her mistress, "Would that my 3 lord were with the prophet who is in Samar′ia! He would cure him of his leprosy." So Na′aman went in and told his 4 lord, "Thus and so spoke the maiden from the land of Israel." And the king of Syria 5 said, "Go now, and I will send a letter to the king of Israel."
So he went, taking with him ten talents of silver, six thousand shekels of gold, and ten festal garments. And he brought the letter to 6 the king of Israel, which read, "When this letter reaches you, know that I have sent to you Na′aman my servant, that you may cure him of his leprosy." And when the king of 7 Israel read the letter, he rent his clothes and said, "Am I God, to kill and to make alive, that this man sends word to me to cure a man of his leprosy? Only consider, and see how he is seeking a quarrel with me."
But when Eli′sha the man of God heard that 8 the king of Israel had rent his clothes, he sent to the king, saying, "Why have you rent your clothes? Let him come now to me, that he may know that there is a prophet in Israel." So Na′aman came with his horses and chari- 9 ots, and halted at the door of Eli′sha's house. And Eli′sha sent a messenger to him, 10 saying, "Go and wash in the Jordan seven times, and your flesh shall be restored, and you shall be clean." But Na′aman was angry, 11 and went away, saying, "Behold, I thought that he would surely come out to me, and stand, and call on the name of the LORD his God, and wave his hand over the place, and cure the leper. Are not Aba′na[e] and Pharpar, 12 the rivers of Damascus, better than all the

waters of Israel? Could I not wash in them, and be clean?" So he turned and went away
3 in a rage. But his servants came near and said to him, "My father, if the prophet had commanded you to do some great thing, would you not have done it? How much rather, then, when he says to you, 'Wash, and
4 be clean'?" So he went down and dipped himself seven times in the Jordan, according to the word of the man of God; and his flesh was restored like the flesh of a little child, and he was clean.
5 Then he returned to the man of God, he and all his company, and he came and stood before him; and he said, "Behold, I know that there is no God in all the earth but in Israel; so accept now a present from your
6 servant." But he said, "As the LORD lives, whom I serve, I will receive none." And he
7 urged him to take it, but he refused. Then Na′aman said, "If not, I pray you, let there be given to your servant two mules' burden of earth; for henceforth your servant will not offer burnt offering or sacrifice to any god
8 but the LORD. In this matter may the LORD pardon your servant: when my master goes into the house of Rimmon to worship there, leaning on my arm, and I bow myself in the house of Rimmon, when I bow myself in the house of Rimmon, the LORD pardon your
9 servant in this matter." He said to him, "Go in peace."

Elisha's servant

But when Na′aman had gone from him a
10 short distance, Geha′zi, the servant of Eli′sha the man of God, said, "See, my master has spared this Na′aman the Syrian, in not accepting from his hand what he brought. As the LORD lives, I will run after him, and
11 get something from him." So Geha′zi followed Na′aman. And when Na′aman saw some one running after him, he alighted from the chariot to meet him, and said, "Is all
12 well?" And he said, "All is well. My master has sent me to say, 'There have just now come to me from the hill country of E′phraim two young men of the sons of the prophets; pray, give them a talent of silver
23 and two festal garments.'" And Na′aman said, "Be pleased to accept two talents." And he urged him, and tied up two talents of silver in two bags, with two festal garments, and laid them upon two of his servants; and
24 they carried them before Geha′zi. And when he came to the hill, he took them from their hand, and put them in the house; and he sent the men away, and they departed. He went
25 in, and stood before his master, and Eli′sha said to him, "Where have you been, Geha′zi?" And he said, "Your servant went

nowhere." But he said to him, "Did I not go 26 with you in spirit when the man turned from his chariot to meet you? Was it a time to accept money and garments, olive orchards and vineyards, sheep and oxen, menservants and maidservants? Therefore the leprosy of 27 Na′aman shall cleave to you, and to your descendants for ever." So he went out from his presence a leper, as white as snow.

The borrowed axe

Now the sons of the prophets said to 6 Eli′sha, "See, the place where we dwell under your charge is too small for us. Let us 2 go to the Jordan, and each of us get there a log, and let us make a place for us to dwell there." And he answered, "Go." Then one 3 of them said, "Be pleased to go with your servants." And he answered, "I will go." So 4 he went with them. And when they came to the Jordan, they cut down trees. But as one 5 was felling a log, his axe head fell into the water; and he cried out, "Alas, my master! It was borrowed." Then the man of God 6 said, "Where did it fall?" When he showed him the place, he cut off a stick, and threw it in there, and made the iron float. And he 7 said, "Take it up." So he reached out his hand and took it.

Elisha and the Syrians

Once when the king of Syria was warring 8 against Israel, he took counsel with his servants, saying, "At such and such a place shall be my camp." But the man of God sent 9 word to the king of Israel, "Beware that you do not pass this place, for the Syrians are

SYRIA

10 going down there." And the king of Israel sent to the place of which the man of God told him. Thus he used to warn him, so that he saved himself there more than once or twice.

11 And the mind of the king of Syria was greatly troubled because of this thing; and he called his servants and said to them, "Will you not show me who of us is for the king of
12 Israel?" And one of his servants said, "None, my lord, O king; but Eli'sha, the prophet who is in Israel, tells the king of Israel the words that you speak in your
13 bedchamber." And he said, "Go and see where he is, that I may send and seize him." It was told him, "Behold, he is in Dothan."
14 So he sent there horses and chariots and a great army; and they came by night, and surrounded the city.

15 When the servant of the man of God rose early in the morning and went out, behold, an army with horses and chariots was round about the city. And the servant said, "Alas,
16 my master! What shall we do?" He said, "Fear not, for those who are with us are more
17 than those who are with them." Then Eli'sha prayed, and said, "O LORD, I pray thee, open his eyes that he may see." So the LORD opened the eyes of the young man, and he saw; and behold, the mountain was full of horses and chariots of fire round about
18 Eli'sha. And when the Syrians came down against him, Eli'sha prayed to the LORD, and said, "Strike this people, I pray thee, with blindness." So he struck them with blindness in accordance with the prayer of
19 Eli'sha. And Eli'sha said to them, "This is not the way, and this is not the city; follow me, and I will bring you to the man whom you seek." And he led them to Samar'ia.
20 As soon as they entered Samar'ia, Eli'sha said, "O LORD, open the eyes of these men, that they may see." So the LORD opened their eyes, and they saw; and lo, they were in
21 the midst of Samar'ia. When the king of Israel saw them he said to Eli'sha, "My father, shall I slay them? Shall I slay
22 them?" He answered, "You shall not slay them. Would you slay those whom you have taken captive with your sword and with your bow? Set bread and water before them, that they may eat and drink and go to their

master." So he prepared for them a great 2 feast; and when they had eaten and drunk, he sent them away, and they went to their master. And the Syrians came no more on raids into the land of Israel.

The siege of Samaria

Afterward Ben-ha'dad king of Syria mus- 2 tered his entire army, and went up, and besieged Samar'ia. And there was a great 2 famine in Samar'ia, as they besieged it, until an ass's head was sold for eighty shekels of silver, and the fourth part of a kab of dove's dung for five shekels of silver. Now as the 2 king of Israel was passing by upon the wall, a woman cried out to him, saying, "Help, my lord, O king!" And he said, "If the LORD 2 will not help you, whence shall I help you? From the threshing floor, or from the wine press?" And the king asked her, "What is 2 your trouble?" She answered, "This woman said to me, 'Give your son, that we may eat him today, and we will eat my son tomorrow.' So we boiled my son, and ate 2 him. And on the next day I said to her, 'Give your son, that we may eat him'; but she has hidden her son." When the king heard the 3 words of the woman he rent his clothes —now he was passing by upon the wall—and the people looked, and behold, he had sackcloth beneath upon his body—and he 3 said, "May God do so to me, and more also, if the head of Eli'sha the son of Shaphat remains on his shoulders today." Eli'sha was sitting in his house, and the 3 elders were sitting with him. Now the king had despatched a man from his presence; but before the messenger arrived Eli'sha said to the elders, "Do you see how this murderer has sent to take off my head? Look, when the messenger comes, shut the door, and hold the door fast against him. Is not the sound of his master's feet behind him?" And while he was still speaking with them, 3 the king[f] came down to him and said, "This trouble is from the LORD! Why should I wait for the LORD any longer?"

But Eli'sha said, "Hear the word of the 7 LORD: thus says the LORD, Tomorrow about this time a measure of fine meal shall be sold for a shekel, and two measures of barley for a shekel, at the gate of Samar'ia." Then the 2 captain on whose hand the king leaned said to the man of God, "If the LORD himself should make windows in heaven, could this thing be?" But he said, "You shall see it with your own eyes, but you shall not eat of it."

f See 7.2: Heb messenger

Flight of the Syrians

Now there were four men who were lepers at the entrance to the gate; and they said to one another, "Why do we sit here till we die? If we say, 'Let us enter the city,' the famine is in the city, and we shall die there; and if we sit here, we die also. So now come, let us go over to the camp of the Syrians; if they spare our lives we shall live, and if they kill us we shall but die." So they arose at twilight to go to the camp of the Syrians; but when they came to the edge of the camp of the Syrians, behold, there was no one there. For the Lord had made the army of the Syrians hear the sound of chariots, and of horses, the sound of a great army, so that they said to one another, "Behold, the king of Israel has hired against us the kings of the Hittites and the kings of Egypt to come upon us." So they fled away in the twilight and forsook their tents, their horses, and their asses, leaving the camp as it was, and fled for their lives. And when these lepers came to the edge of the camp, they went into a tent, and ate and drank, and they carried off silver and gold and clothing, and went and hid them; then they came back, and entered another tent, and carried off things from it, and went and hid them.

Then they said to one another, "We are not doing right. This day is a day of good news; if we are silent and wait until the morning light, punishment will overtake us; now therefore come, let us go and tell the king's household." So they came and called to the gatekeepers of the city, and told them, "We came to the camp of the Syrians, and behold, there was no one to be seen or heard there, nothing but the horses tied, and the asses tied, and the tents as they were." Then the gatekeepers called out, and it was told within the king's household. And the king rose in the night, and said to his servants, "I will tell you what the Syrians have prepared against us. They know that we are hungry; therefore they have gone out of the camp to hide themselves in the open country, thinking, 'When they come out of the city, we shall take them alive and get into the city.'" And one of his servants said, "Let some men take five of the remaining horses, seeing that those who are left here will fare like the whole multitude of Israel that have already perished; let us send and see." So they took two mounted men, and the king sent them after the army of the Syrians, saying, "Go and see." So they went after them as far as the Jordan; and, lo, all the way was littered with garments and equipment which the Syrians had thrown away in their haste. And the messengers returned, and told the king.

Then the people went out, and plundered the camp of the Syrians. So a measure of fine meal was sold for a shekel, and two measures of barley for a shekel, according to the word of the Lord. Now the king had appointed the captain on whose hand he leaned to have charge of the gate; and the people trod upon him in the gate, so that he died, as the man of God had said when the king came down to him. For when the man of God had said to the king, "Two measures of barley shall be sold for a shekel, and a measure of fine meal for a shekel, about this time tomorrow in the gate of Samar′ia," the captain had answered the man of God, "If the Lord himself should make windows in heaven, could such a thing be?" And he had said, "You shall see it with your own eyes, but you shall not eat of it." And so it happened to him, for the people trod upon him in the gate and he died.

The Shunammite woman's estate

Now Eli′sha had said to the woman whose son he had restored to life, "Arise, and depart with your household, and sojourn wherever you can; for the Lord has called for a famine, and it will come upon the land for seven years." So the woman arose, and did according to the word of the man of God; she went with her household and sojourned in the land of the Philistines seven years. And at the end of the seven years, when the woman returned from the land of the Philistines, she went forth to appeal to the king for her house and her land. Now the king was talking with Geha′zi the servant of the man of God, saying, "Tell me all the great things that Eli′sha has done." And while he was telling the king how Eli′sha had restored the dead to life, behold, the woman whose son he had restored to life appealed to the king for her house and her land. And Geha′zi said, "My lord, O king, here is the woman, and here is her son whom Eli′sha restored to life." And when the king asked the woman, she told him. So the king appointed an official for her, saying, "Restore all that was hers, together with all the produce of the fields from the day that she left the land until now."

Elisha and Hazael

7 Now Eli'sha came to Damascus. Ben-ha'dad the king of Syria was sick; and when it was told him, "The man of God has come
8 here," the king said to Haz'ael, "Take a present with you and go to meet the man of God, and inquire of the LORD through him, saying, 'Shall I recover from this sick-
9 ness?'" So Haz'ael went to meet him, and took a present with him, all kinds of goods of Damascus, forty camel loads. When he came and stood before him, he said, "Your son Ben-ha'dad king of Syria has sent me to you, saying, 'Shall I recover from this sick-
10 ness?'" And Eli'sha said to him, "Go, say to him, 'You shall certainly recover'; but the LORD has shown me that he shall certainly
11 die." And he fixed his gaze and stared at him, until he was ashamed. And the man of
12 God wept. And Haz'ael said, "Why does my lord weep?" He answered, "Because I know the evil that you will do to the people of Israel; you will set on fire their fortresses, and you will slay their young men with the sword, and dash in pieces their little ones,
13 and rip up their women with child." And Haz'ael said, "What is your servant, who is but a dog, that he should do this great thing?" Eli'sha answered, "The LORD has shown me that you are to be king over
14 Syria." Then he departed from Eli'sha, and came to his master, who said to him, "What did Eli'sha say to you?" And he answered, "He told me that you would certainly
15 recover." But on the morrow he took the coverlet and dipped it in water and spread it over his face, till he died. And Haz'ael became king in his stead.

16 In the fifth year of Joram the son of Ahab, king of Israel,[g] Jeho'ram the son of Jehosh'-
17 aphat, king of Judah, began to reign. He was thirty-two years old when he became king, and he reigned eight years in Jerusalem.
18 And he walked in the way of the kings of Israel, as the house of Ahab had done, for the daughter of Ahab was his wife. And he did

what was evil in the sight of the LORD. Yet the LORD would not destroy Judah, for the sake of David his servant, since he promised to give a lamp to him and to his sons for ever.
20 In his days Edom revolted from the rule of Judah, and set up a king of their own. Then
21 Joram passed over to Za'ir with all his chariots, and rose by night, and he and his chariot commanders smote the Edomites who had surrounded him; but his army fled home. So Edom revolted from the rule of
22 Judah to this day. Then Libnah revolted at the same time. Now the rest of the acts of
23 Joram, and all that he did, are they not written in the Book of the Chronicles of the Kings of Judah? So Joram slept with his
24 fathers, and was buried with his fathers in the city of David; and Ahazi'ah his son reigned in his stead.
25 In the twelfth year of Joram the son of Ahab, king of Israel, Ahazi'ah the son of Jeho'ram, king of Judah, began to reign.
26 Ahazi'ah was twenty-two years old when he began to reign, and he reigned one year in Jerusalem. His mother's name was Athali'ah; she was a grand-daughter of Omri king of Israel. He also walked in the way of
27 the house of Ahab, and did what was evil in the sight of the LORD, as the house of Ahab had done, for he was son-in-law to the house of Ahab.
28 He went with Joram the son of Ahab to make war against Haz'ael king of Syria at Ramoth-gilead, where the Syrians wounded Joram. And King Joram returned to be
29 healed in Jezreel of the wounds which the Syrians had given him at Ramah, when he fought against Haz'ael king of Syria. And Ahazi'ah the son of Jeho'ram king of Judah went down to see Joram the son of Ahab in Jezreel, because he was sick.

Then Eli'sha the prophet called one of the sons of the prophets and said to him, "Gird up your loins, and take this flask of oil in your hand, and go to Ramoth-gilead. And when you arrive, look there for Jehu the son of Jehosh'aphat, son of Nimshi; and go in and bid him rise from among his fellows, and lead him to an inner chamber. Then take the flask of oil, and pour it on his head, and say, 'Thus says the LORD, I anoint you king over Israel.' Then open the door and flee; do not tarry."

So the young man, the prophet,[h] went to Ramoth-gilead. And when he came, behold, the commanders of the army were in council; and he said, "I have an errand to you, O commander." And Jehu said, "To which of

---

[g] Gk Syr: Heb *Israel, Jehoshaphat being king of Judah*
[h] Gk Syr: Heb *the young man, the young man, the prophet*
8.17–23: 2 Chron 21.5–10, 20.   8.24–29: 2 Chron 22.1–6.   9.1–10.36: 2 Chron 22.7–9.

flask of oil, and pour it on his head, and say, 'Thus says the LORD, I anoint you king over Israel.' Then open the door and flee; do not tarry."

So the young man, the prophet,[h] went to Ramoth-gilead. And when he came, behold, the commanders of the army were in council; and he said, "I have an errand to you, O commander." And Jehu said, "To which of us all?" And he said, "To you, O commander." So he arose, and went into the house; and the young man poured the oil on his head, saying to him, "Thus says the LORD the God of Israel, I anoint you king over the people of the LORD, over Israel. And you shall strike down the house of Ahab your master, that I may avenge on Jez'ebel the blood of my servants the prophets, and the blood of all the servants of the LORD. For the whole house of Ahab shall perish; and I will cut off from Ahab every male, bond or free, in Israel. And I will make the house of Ahab like the house of Jerobo'am the son of Nebat, and like the house of Ba'asha the son of Ahi'jah. And the dogs shall eat Jez'ebel in the territory of Jezreel, and none shall bury her." Then he opened the door, and fled.

When Jehu came out to the servants of his master, they said to him, "Is all well? Why did this mad fellow come to you?" And he said to them, "You know the fellow and his talk." And they said, "That is not true; tell us now." And he said, "Thus and so he spoke to me, saying, 'Thus says the LORD, I anoint you king over Israel.'" Then in haste every man of them took his garment, and put it under him on the bare[i] steps, and they blew the trumpet, and proclaimed, "Jehu is king."

Thus Jehu the son of Jehosh'aphat the son of Nimshi conspired against Joram. (Now Joram with all Israel had been on guard at Ramoth-gilead against Haz'ael king of Syria; but King Joram had returned to be healed in Jezreel of the wounds which the Syrians had given him, when he fought with Haz'ael king of Syria.) So Jehu said, "If this is your mind, then let no one slip out of the city to go and tell the news in Jezreel." Then Jehu mounted his chariot, and went to Jezreel, for Joram lay there. And Ahazi'ah king of Judah had come down to visit Joram.

Now the watchman was standing on the tower in Jezreel, and he spied the company of Jehu as he came, and said, "I see a company." And Joram said, "Take a horseman, and send to meet them, and let him say, 'Is it peace?'" So a man on horseback went to meet him, and said, "Thus says the king, 'Is it peace?'" And Jehu said, "What have you to do with peace? Turn round and ride behind me." And the watchman reported, saying, "The messenger reached them, but he is not coming back." Then he sent out a second horseman, who came to them, and said, "Thus the king has said, 'Is it peace?'" And Jehu answered, "What have you to do with peace? Turn round and ride behind me." Again the watchman reported, "He reached them, but he is not coming back. And the driving is like the driving of Jehu the son of Nimshi; for he drives furiously."

Joram said, "Make ready." And they made ready his chariot. Then Joram king of Israel and Ahazi'ah king of Judah set out, each in his chariot, and went to meet Jehu, and met him at the property of Naboth the Jez'reelite. And when Joram saw Jehu, he said, "Is it peace, Jehu?" He answered, "What peace can there be, so long as the harlotries and the sorceries of your mother Jez'ebel are so many?" Then Joram reined about and fled, saying to Ahazi'ah, "Treachery, O Ahazi'ah!" And Jehu drew his bow with his full strength, and shot Joram between the shoulders, so that the arrow pierced his heart, and he sank in his chariot. Jehu said to Bidkar his aide, "Take him up, and cast him on the plot of ground belonging to Naboth the Jez'reelite; for remember, when you and I rode side by side behind Ahab his father, how the LORD uttered this oracle against him: 'As surely as I saw yesterday the blood of Naboth and the blood of his sons—says the LORD—I will requite you on this plot of ground.' Now therefore take him up and cast him on the plot of ground, in accordance with the word of the LORD."

When Ahazi'ah the king of Judah saw this, he fled in the direction of Beth-haggan. And Jehu pursued him, and said, "Shoot him also"; and they shot him[j] in the chariot at the ascent of Gur, which is by Ib'le-am. And he fled to Megid'do, and died there. His servants carried him in a chariot to Jerusalem, and buried him in his tomb with his fathers in the city of David.

In the eleventh year of Joram the son of Ahab, Ahazi'ah began to reign over Judah.

When Jehu came to Jezreel, Jez'ebel heard of it; and she painted her eyes, and adorned her head, and looked out of the window. And as Jehu entered the gate, she said, "Is it peace, you Zimri, murderer of your master?" And he lifted up his face to the window, and said, "Who is on my side? Who?" Two or three eunuchs looked out at

---

h Gk Syr: Heb the young man, the young man, the prophet   i The meaning of the Hebrew word is uncertain
j Syr Vg Compare Gk: Heb lacks and they shot him
9.26: 1 Kings 21.19.

33 him. He said, "Throw her down." So they threw her down; and some of her blood spattered on the wall and on the horses, and 34 they trampled on her. Then he went in and ate and drank; and he said, "See now to this cursed woman, and bury her; for she is a 35 king's daughter." But when they went to bury her, they found no more of her than the skull and the feet and the palms of her 36 hands. When they came back and told him, he said, "This is the word of the LORD, which he spoke by his servant Eli′jah the Tishbite, 'In the territory of Jezreel the dogs 37 shall eat the flesh of Jez′ebel; and the corpse of Jez′ebel shall be as dung upon the face of the field in the territory of Jezreel, so that no one can say, This is Jez′ebel.' "

10 Now Ahab had seventy sons in Samar′ia. So Jehu wrote letters, and sent them to Samar′ia, to the rulers of the city,*k* and to the elders, and to the guardians of the sons of 2 Ahab, saying, "Now then, as soon as this letter comes to you, seeing your master's sons are with you, and there are with you chariots and horses, fortified cities also, and weapons, 3 select the best and fittest of your master's sons and set him on his father's throne, and 4 fight for your master's house." But they were exceedingly afraid, and said, "Behold, the two kings could not stand before him; 5 how then can we stand?" So he who was over the palace, and he who was over the city, together with the elders and the guardians, sent to Jehu, saying, "We are your servants, and we will do all that you bid us. We will not make any one king; do whatever is good 6 in your eyes." Then he wrote to them a second letter, saying, "If you are on my side, and if you are ready to obey me, take the heads of your master's sons, and come to me at Jezreel tomorrow at this time." Now the king's sons, seventy persons, were with the great men of the city, who were bringing 7 them up. And when the letter came to them, they took the king's sons, and slew them, seventy persons, and put their heads in baskets, and sent them to him at Jezreel. 8 When the messenger came and told him, "They have brought the heads of the king's sons," he said, "Lay them in two heaps at the entrance of the gate until the morning." 9 Then in the morning, when he went out, he stood, and said to all the people, "You are innocent. It was I who conspired against my master, and slew him; but who struck down 10 all these? Know then that there shall fall to the earth nothing of the word of the LORD, which the LORD spoke concerning the house

of Ahab; for the LORD has done what he said by his servant Eli′jah." So Jehu slew all that remained of the house of Ahab in Jezreel, all his great men, and his familiar friends, and his priests, until he left him none remaining.

Then he set out and went to Samar′ia. On the way, when he was at Beth-eked of the Shepherds, Jehu met the kinsmen of Ahazi′ah king of Judah, and he said, "Who are you?" And they answered, "We are the kinsmen of Ahazi′ah, and we came down to visit the royal princes and the sons of the queen mother." He said, "Take them alive." And they took them alive, and slew them at the pit of Beth-eked, forty-two persons, and he spared none of them.

And when he departed from there, he met Jehon′adab the son of Rechab coming to meet him; and he greeted him, and said to him, "Is your heart true to my heart as mine is to yours?"*l* And Jehon′adab answered, "It is." Jehu said,*m* "If it is, give me your hand." So he gave him his hand. And Jehu took him up with him into the chariot. And he said, "Come with me, and see my zeal for the LORD." So he*n* had him ride in his chariot. And when he came to Samar′ia, he slew all that remained to Ahab in Samar′ia, till he had wiped them out, according to the word of the LORD which he spoke to Eli′jah.

Then Jehu assembled all the people, and said to them, "Ahab served Ba′al a little; but Jehu will serve him much. Now therefore

call to me all the prophets of Ba′al, all his worshippers and all his priests; let none be missing, for I have a great sacrifice to offer to Ba′al; whoever is missing shall not live." But Jehu did it with cunning in order to destroy the worshippers of Ba′al. And Jehu ordered, "Sanctify a solemn assembly for Ba′al." So they proclaimed it. And Jehu sent throughout all Israel; and all the worshippers of Ba′al came, so that there was not a man left who did not come. And they entered the house of Ba′al, and the house of Ba′al was filled from one end to the other. He said to him who was in charge of the wardrobe, "Bring out the vestments for all the worshippers of

k Gk Vg: Heb *Jezreel*   *l* Gk: Heb *Is it right with your heart, as my heart is with your heart?*   *m* Gk: Heb lacks *Jehu said*   *n* Gk Syr Tg: Heb *they*
9.36: 1 Kings 21.23.

Ba′al." So he brought out the vestments for
3 them. Then Jehu went into the house of
Ba′al with Jehon′adab the son of Rechab;
and he said to the worshippers of Ba′al,
"Search, and see that there is no servant of
the LORD here among you, but only the
24 worshippers of Ba′al." Then he° went in to
offer sacrifices and burnt offerings.

Now Jehu had stationed eighty men outside, and said, "The man who allows any of
those whom I give into your hands to escape
25 shall forfeit his life." So as soon as he had
made an end of offering the burnt offering,
Jehu said to the guard and to the officers,
"Go in and slay them; let not a man escape."
So when they put them to the sword, the
guard and the officers cast them out and
went into the inner room ᵖ of the house of
26 Ba′al and they brought out the pillar that was
27 in the house of Ba′al, and burned it. And
they demolished the pillar of Ba′al, and
demolished the house of Ba′al, and made it a
latrine to this day.
28, Thus Jehu wiped out Ba′al from Israel. But
29 Jehu did not turn aside from the sins of
Jerobo′am the son of Nebat, which he made
Israel to sin, the golden calves that were in
30 Bethel, and in Dan. And the LORD said to
Jehu, "Because you have done well in carrying out what is right in my eyes, and have
done to the house of Ahab according to all
that was in my heart, your sons of the fourth
generation shall sit on the throne of Israel."
31 But Jehu was not careful to walk in the law of
the LORD the God of Israel with all his heart;
he did not turn from the sins of Jerobo′am,
which he made Israel to sin.
32 In those days the LORD began to cut off
parts of Israel. Haz′ael defeated them
33 throughout the territory of Israel: from the
Jordan eastward, all the land of Gilead,
the Gadites, and the Reubenites, and the
Manas′sites, from Aro′er, which is by the
valley of the Arnon, that is, Gilead and
34 Bashan. Now the rest of the acts of Jehu,
and all that he did, and all his might, are they
not written in the Book of the Chronicles of
35 the Kings of Israel? So Jehu slept with his
fathers, and they buried him in Samar′ia. And
36 Jeho′ahaz his son reigned in his stead. The
time that Jehu reigned over Israel in
Samar′ia was twenty-eight years.

Athaliah

11 Now when Athali′ah the mother of Ahazi′-
ah saw that her son was dead, she arose and
2 destroyed all the royal family. But Jehosh′-
eba, the daughter of King Joram, sister of

Ahazi′ah, took Jo′ash the son of Ahazi′ah,
and stole him away from among the king's
sons who were about to be slain, and she putᑫ
him and his nurse in a bedchamber. Thus
sheʳ hid him from Athali′ah, so that he was
not slain; and he remained with her six years, 3
hid in the house of the LORD, while Athali′ah
reigned over the land.

But in the seventh year Jehoi′ada sent and 4
brought the captains of the Carites and of the
guards, and had them come to him in the
house of the LORD; and he made a covenant
with them and put them under oath in the
house of the LORD, and he showed them the
king's son. And he commanded them, "This 5
is the thing that you shall do: one third of
you, those who come off duty on the sabbath
and guard the king's house (another third 6
being at the gate Sur and a third at the gate
behind the guards), shall guard the palace;
and the two divisions of you, which come on 7
duty in force on the sabbath and guard the
house of the LORD,ˢ shall surround the king, 8
each with his weapons in his hand; and
whoever approaches the ranks is to be slain.
Be with the king when he goes out and when
he comes in."

The captains did according to all that 9
Jehoi′ada the priest commanded, and each
brought his men who were to go off duty on
the sabbath, with those who were to come on
duty on the sabbath, and came to Jehoi′ada
the priest. And the priest delivered to the 10
captains the spears and shields that had been
King David's, which were in the house of the
LORD; and the guards stood, every man with 11
his weapons in his hand, from the south side
of the house to the north side of the house,
around the altar and the house.ᵗ Then he 12
brought out the king's son, and put the
crown upon him, and gave him the testimony; and they proclaimed him king, and
anointed him; and they clapped their hands,
and said, "Long live the king!"

When Athali′ah heard the noise of the 13
guard and of the people, she went into the
house of the LORD to the people; and when 14
she looked, there was the king standing by
the pillar, according to the custom, and the
captains and the trumpeters beside the king,
and all the people of the land rejoicing and

° Gk Compare verse 25: Heb *they*   ᵖ Cn: Heb *city*   ᑫ With 2 Chron 22.11: Heb lacks *and she put*
ʳ Gk Syr Vg Compare 2 Chron 22.11: Heb *they*   ˢ Heb *the LORD to the king*   ᵗ Heb *the house to the king*
11.1-20: 2 Chron 22.10-23.21.

blowing trumpets. And Athali′ah rent her
clothes, and cried, "Treason! Treason!"
15 Then Jehoi′ada the priest commanded the
captains who were set over the army, "Bring
her out between the ranks; and slay with the
sword any one who follows her." For the
priest said, "Let her not be slain in the house
16 of the LORD." So they laid hands on her; and
she went through the horses' entrance to the
king's house, and there she was slain.
17   And Jehoi′ada made a covenant between the
LORD and the king and people, that they
should be the LORD's people; and also
18 between the king and the people. Then all
the people of the land went to the house of
Ba′al, and tore it down; his altars and his
images they broke in pieces, and they slew
Mattan the priest of Ba′al before the altars.
And the priest posted watchmen over the
19 house of the LORD. And he took the captains, the Carites, the guards, and all the
people of the land; and they brought the king
down from the house of the LORD, marching
through the gate of the guards to the king's
house. And he took his seat on the throne of
20 the kings. So all the people of the land
rejoiced; and the city was quiet after
Athali′ah had been slain with the sword at
the king's house.
21 [u] Jeho′ash was seven years old when he
began to reign.

Jehoash

12 In the seventh year of Jehu Jeho′ash began
to reign, and he reigned forty years in
Jerusalem. His mother's name was Zib′iah
2 of Beer-sheba. And Jeho′ash did what was
right in the eyes of the LORD all his days,
because Jehoi′ada the priest instructed him.

Nevertheless the high places were not taken 3
away; the people continued to sacrifice and
burn incense on the high places.
Jeho′ash said to the priests, "All the money 4
of the holy things which is brought into
the house of the LORD, the money for which
each man is assessed—the money from the
assessment of persons—and the money
which a man's heart prompts him to bring
into the house of the LORD, let the priests 5
take, each from his acquaintance; and let
them repair the house wherever any need of
repairs is discovered." But by the twenty- 6
third year of King Jeho′ash the priests had
made no repairs on the house. Therefore 7
King Jeho′ash summoned Jehoi′ada the
priest and the other priests and said to them,
"Why are you not repairing the house? Now
therefore take no more money from your
acquaintances, but hand it over for the repair
of the house." So the priests agreed that 8
they should take no more money from the
people, and that they should not repair the
house.
Then Jehoi′ada the priest took a chest, and 9
bored a hole in the lid of it, and set it beside
the altar on the right side as one entered the
house of the LORD; and the priests who
guarded the threshold put in it all the money
that was brought into the house of the LORD.
And whenever they saw that there was much 10
money in the chest, the king's secretary and
the high priest came up and they counted
and tied up in bags the money that was found
in the house of the LORD. Then they would 11
give the money that was weighed out into the
hands of the workmen who had the oversight
of the house of the LORD; and they paid it out
to the carpenters and the builders who
worked upon the house of the LORD, and to 12
the masons and the stonecutters, as well as to
buy timber and quarried stone for making
repairs on the house of the LORD, and for any
outlay upon the repairs of the house. But 13
there were not made for the house of the
LORD basins of silver, snuffers, bowls,
trumpets, or any vessels of gold, or of silver,
from the money that was brought into the
house of the LORD, for that was given to the 14
workmen who were repairing the house of
the LORD with it. And they did not ask an 15
accounting from the men into whose hand
they delivered the money to pay out to the
workmen, for they dealt honestly. The 16
money from the guilt offerings and
the money from the sin offerings was not
brought into the house of the LORD; it
belonged to the priests.
At that time Haz′ael king of Syria went up 17

and fought against Gath, and took it. But when Haz'ael set his face to go up against 8 Jerusalem, Jeho'ash king of Judah took all the votive gifts that Jehosh'aphat and Jeho'ram and Ahazi'ah, his fathers, the kings of Judah, had dedicated, and his own votive gifts, and all the gold that was found in the treasuries of the house of the LORD and of the king's house, and sent these to Haz'ael king of Syria. Then Haz'ael went away from Jerusalem.

9 Now the rest of the acts of Jo'ash, and all that he did, are they not written in the Book of the Chronicles of the Kings of Judah? 10 His servants arose and made a conspiracy, and slew Jo'ash in the house of Millo, on 11 way that goes down to Silla. It was Jo'zacar the son of Shim'eath and Jeho'zabad the son of Shomer, his servants, who struck him down, so that he died. And they buried him with his fathers in the city of David, and Amazi'ah his son reigned in his stead.

ISRAEL

Jehoahaz, son of Jehu

13 In the twenty-third year of Jo'ash the son of Ahazi'ah, king of Judah, Jeho'ahaz the son of Jehu began to reign over Israel in Samar'ia, 2 and he reigned seventeen years. He did what was evil in the sight of the LORD, and followed the sins of Jerobo'am the son of Nebat, which he made Israel to sin; he did 3 not depart from them. And the anger of the LORD was kindled against Israel, and he gave them continually into the hand of Haz'ael king of Syria and into the hand of Ben-ha'-4 dad the son of Haz'ael. Then Jeho'ahaz besought the LORD, and the LORD hearkened to him; for he saw the oppression of Israel, how the king of Syria oppressed them. 5 (Therefore the LORD gave Israel a saviour, so that they escaped from the hand of the Syrians; and the people of Israel dwelt in 6 their homes as formerly. Nevertheless they did not depart from the sins of the house of Jerobo'am, which he made Israel to sin, but walked[v] in them; and the Ashe'rah also 7 remained in Samar'ia.) For there was not left to Jeho'ahaz an army of more than fifty horsemen and ten chariots and ten thousand footmen; for the king of Syria had destroyed

them and made them like the dust at threshing. Now the rest of the acts of Jeho'ahaz 8 and all that he did, and his might, are they not written in the Book of the Chronicles of the Kings of Israel? So Jeho'ahaz slept 9 with his fathers, and they buried him in Samar'ia; and Jo'ash his son reigned in his stead.

Jehoash

In the thirty-seventh year of Jo'ash king of 10 Judah Jeho'ash the son of Jeho'ahaz began to reign over Israel in Samar'ia, and he reigned sixteen years. He also did what was evil in 11 the sight of the LORD; he did not depart from all the sins of Jerobo'am the son of Nebat, which he made Israel to sin, but he walked in them. Now the rest of the acts of Jo'ash, and 12 all that he did, and the might with which he fought against Amazi'ah king of Judah, are they not written in the Book of the Chronicles of the Kings of Israel? So Jo'ash slept 13 with his fathers, and Jerobo'am sat upon his throne; and Jo'ash was buried in Samar'ia with the kings of Israel.

Death of Elisha

Now when Eli'sha had fallen sick with the 14 illness of which he was to die, Jo'ash king of Israel went down to him, and wept before him, crying, "My father, my father! The chariots of Israel and its horsemen!" And 15 Eli'sha said to him, "Take a bow and arrows"; so he took a bow and arrows. Then 16 he said to the king of Israel, "Draw the bow"; and he drew it. And Eli'sha laid his hands upon the king's hands. And he said, 17 "Open the window eastward"; and he opened it. Then Eli'sha said, "Shoot"; and he shot. And he said, "The LORD's arrow of victory, the arrow of victory over Syria! For you shall fight the Syrians in Aphek until you have made an end of them." And he said, 18 "Take the arrows"; and he took them. And he said to the king of Israel, "Strike the ground with them"; and he struck three times, and stopped. Then the man of God 19 was angry with him, and said, "You should have struck five or six times; then you would have struck down Syria until you had made an end of it, but now you will strike down Syria only three times."

So Eli'sha died, and they buried him. Now 20 bands of Moabites used to invade the land in the spring of the year. And as a man was 21 being buried, lo, a marauding band was seen and the man was cast into the grave of Eli'sha; and as soon as the man touched the

v Gk Syr Tg Vg: Heb *he walked*

B. C.
800~700

bones of Eli'sha, he revived, and stood on his feet.

22 Now Haz'ael king of Syria oppressed Israel 23 all the days of Jeho'ahaz. But the LORD was gracious to them and had compassion on them, and he turned toward them, because of his covenant with Abraham, Isaac, and Jacob, and would not destroy them; nor has he cast them from his presence until now. 24 When Haz'ael king of Syria died, Ben-ha'dad his son became king in his stead. 25 Then Jeho'ash the son of Jeho'ahaz took again from Ben-ha'dad the son of Haz'ael the cities which he had taken from Jeho'ahaz his father in war. Three times Jo'ash defeated him and recovered the cities of Israel.

JUDAH

Amaziah

14 In the second year of Jo'ash the son of Jo'ahaz, king of Israel, Amazi'ah the son of 2 Jo'ash, king of Judah, began to reign. He was twenty-five years old when he began to reign, and he reigned twenty-nine years in Jerusalem. His mother's name was Jeho-3 ad'din of Jerusalem. And he did what was right in the eyes of the LORD, yet not like David his father; he did in all things as Jo'ash 4 his father had done. But the high places were not removed; the people still sacrificed 5 and burned incense on the high places. And as soon as the royal power was firmly in his hand he killed his servants who had slain the 6 king his father. But he did not put to death the children of the murderers; according to what is written in the book of the law of Moses, where the LORD commanded, "The fathers shall not be put to death for the children, or the children be put to death for the fathers; but every man shall die for his own sin."

He killed ten thousand Edomites in the 7 Valley of Salt and took Sela by storm, and called it Jok'theel, which is its name to this day.

Then Amazi'ah sent messengers to Jeho'ash 8 the son of Jeho'ahaz, son of Jehu, king of Israel, saying, "Come, let us look one another in the face." And Jeho'ash king of 9 Israel sent word to Amazi'ah king of Judah, "A thistle on Lebanon sent to a cedar on Lebanon, saying, 'Give your daughter to my son for a wife'; and a wild beast of Lebanon passed by and trampled down the thistle. You have indeed smitten Edom, and your 10 heart has lifted you up. Be content with your glory, and stay at home; for why should you provoke trouble so that you fall, you and Judah with you?"

But Amazi'ah would not listen. So Jeho'ash 11 king of Israel went up, and he and Amazi'ah king of Judah faced one another in battle at Beth-she'mesh, which belongs to Judah. And Judah was defeated by Israel, and every 12 man fled to his home. And Jeho'ash king of 13 Israel captured Amazi'ah king of Judah, the son of Jeho'ash, son of Ahazi'ah, at Beth-she'mesh, and came to Jerusalem, and broke down the wall of Jerusalem for four hundred cubits, from the E'phraim Gate to the Corner Gate. And he seized all the gold 14 and silver, and all the vessels that were found in the house of the LORD and in the treasuries of the king's house, also hostages, and he returned to Samar'ia.

Now the rest of the acts of Jeho'ash which 15 he did, and his might, and how he fought with Amazi'ah king of Judah, are they not written in the Book of the Chronicles of the Kings of Israel? And Jeho'ash slept with his 16 fathers, and was buried in Samar'ia with the kings of Israel; and Jerobo'am his son reigned in his stead.

Azariah (Uzziah: II Chron. 26, 1)

Amazi'ah the son of Jo'ash, king of Judah, 17 lived fifteen years after the death of Jeho'ash son of Jeho'ahaz, king of Israel. Now the 18 rest of the deeds of Amazi'ah, are they not

14.2–6: 2 Chron 25.1–4.   14.7: 2 Chron 25.11.   14.8–14: 2 Chron 25.17–24.   14.17–20: 2 Chron 25.25–28.

written in the Book of the Chronicles of the
9 Kings of Judah? And they made a conspiracy against him in Jerusalem, and he fled
to Lachish. But they sent after him to
10 Lachish, and slew him there. And they
brought him upon horses; and he was buried
in Jerusalem with his fathers in the city of
11 David. And all the people of Judah took
Azari'ah, who was sixteen years old, and
made him king instead of his father
12 Amazi'ah. He built Elath and restored it to
Judah, after the king slept with his fathers.

ISRAEL

Jeroboam II

23 In the fifteenth year of Amazi'ah the son of
Jo'ash, king of Judah, Jerobo'am the son of
Jo'ash, king of Israel, began to reign in
Samar'ia, and he reigned forty-one years.
24 And he did what was evil in the sight of the
LORD; he did not depart from all the sins of
Jerobo'am the son of Nebat, which he made
25 Israel to sin. He restored the border of Israel
from the entrance of Hamath as far as the Sea
of the Arabah, according to the word of the
LORD, the God of Israel, which he spoke by
his servant Jonah the son of Amit'tai, the
26 prophet, who was from Gath-hepher. For
the LORD saw that the affliction of Israel was
very bitter, for there was none left, bond or
27 free, and there was none to help Israel. But
the LORD had not said that he would blot out
the name of Israel from under heaven, so he
saved them by the hand of Jerobo'am the son
of Jo'ash.

Zechariah

28 Now the rest of the acts of Jerobo'am, and
all that he did, and his might, how he fought,
and how he recovered for Israel Damascus
and Hamath, which had belonged to Judah,
are they not written in the Book of the
29 Chronicles of the Kings of Israel? And
Jerobo'am slept with his fathers, the kings of
Israel, and Zechari'ah his son reigned in his
stead.

Judah's kings

15 In the twenty-seventh year of Jerobo'am

JUDAH

king of Israel Azari'ah the son of Amazi'ah,
king of Judah, began to reign. He was 2
sixteen years old when he began to reign, and
he reigned fifty-two years in Jerusalem. His
mother's name was Jecoli'ah of Jerusalem.
And he did what was right in the eyes of the 3
LORD, according to all that his father
Amazi'ah had done. Nevertheless the high 4
places were not taken away; the people still
sacrificed and burned incense on the high
places. And the LORD smote the king, so that 5
he was a leper to the day of his death, and he
dwelt in a separate house. And Jotham the
king's son was over the household, governing
the people of the land. Now the rest of the 6
acts of Azari'ah, and all that he did, are they
not written in the Book of the Chronicles of
the Kings of Judah? And Azari'ah slept 7
with his fathers, and they buried him with
his fathers in the city of David, and Jotham
his son reigned in his stead.

Israel's last kings

In the thirty-eighth year of Azari'ah king of 8
Judah Zechari'ah the son of Jerobo'am
reigned over Israel in Samar'ia six months.
And he did what was evil in the sight of the 9
LORD, as his fathers had done. He did not
depart from the sins of Jerobo'am the son of
Nebat, which he made Israel to sin. Shallum 10
the son of Jabesh conspired against him, and
struck him down at Ib'le-am,ʷ and killed
him, and reigned in his stead. Now the rest 11
of the deeds of Zechari'ah, behold, they are
written in the Book of the Chronicles of the
Kings of Israel. (This was the promise of the 12
LORD which he gave to Jehu, "Your sons
shall sit upon the throne of Israel to the
fourth generation." And so it came to pass.)
Shallum the son of Jabesh began to reign in 13
the thirty-ninth year of Uzzi'ah king of
Judah, and he reigned one month in
Samar'ia. Then Men'ahem the son of Gadi 14
came up from Tirzah and came to Samar'ia,
and he struck down Shallum the son of
Jabesh in Samar'ia and slew him, and
reigned in his stead. Now the rest of the 15
deeds of Shallum, and the conspiracy which
he made, behold, they are written in the

ʷ Gk Compare 9.27: Heb *before the people*
14.21–22: 2 Chron 26.1–2.   **15.2–3:** 2 Chron 26.3–4.   **15.5–7:** 2 Chron 26.20–23.

ISRAEL

Book of the Chronicles of the Kings of
16 Israel. At that time Men'ahem sacked
Tap'pu-ah[x] and all who were in it and its
territory from Tirzah on; because they did
not open it to him, therefore he sacked it, and
he ripped up all the women in it who were
with child.
17 In the thirty-ninth year of Azari'ah king of
Judah Men'ahem the son of Gadi began to
reign over Israel, and he reigned ten years in
18 Samar'ia. And he did what was evil in the
sight of the LORD; he did not depart all his
days from all the sins of Jerobo'am the son of
19 Nebat, which he made Israel to sin. Pul the
king of Assyria came against the land; and
Men'ahem gave Pul a thousand talents of
silver, that he might help him to confirm his
20 hold of the royal power. Men'ahem exacted
the money from Israel, that is, from all the
wealthy men, fifty shekels of silver from
every man, to give to the king of Assyria. So
the king of Assyria turned back, and did not
21 stay there in the land. Now the rest of the
deeds of Men'ahem, and all that he did, are
they not written in the Book of the Chroni-
22 cles of the Kings of Israel? And Men'ahem
slept with his fathers, and Pekahi'ah his son
reigned in his stead.
23 In the fiftieth year of Azari'ah king of Judah
Pekahi'ah the son of Men'ahem began to
reign over Israel in Samar'ia, and he reigned
24 two years. And he did what was evil in the
sight of the LORD; he did not turn away from
the sins of Jerobo'am the son of Nebat,
25 which he made Israel to sin. And Pekah the
son of Remali'ah, his captain, conspired
against him with fifty men of the Gileadites,
and slew him in Samar'ia, in the citadel of
the king's house;[y] he slew him, and reigned
26 in his stead. Now the rest of the deeds of
Pekahi'ah, and all that he did, behold, they
are written in the Book of the Chronicles of
the Kings of Israel.
27 In the fifty-second year of Azari'ah king of
Judah Pekah the son of Remali'ah began to
reign over Israel in Samar'ia, and reigned
28 twenty years. And he did what was evil in
the sight of the LORD; he did not depart from
the sins of Jerobo'am the son of Nebat,
which he made Israel to sin.

In the days of Pekah king of Israel 29
Tig'lath-pile'ser king of Assyria came and
captured I'jon, A'bel-beth-ma'acah, Jano'ah,
Kedesh, Hazor, Gilead, and Galilee, all the
land of Naph'tali; and he carried the people
captive to Assyria. Then Hoshe'a the son of 30
Elah made a conspiracy against Pekah the
son of Remali'ah, and struck him down, and
slew him, and reigned in his stead, in the
twentieth year of Jotham the son of Uzzi'ah.
Now the rest of the acts of Pekah, and all that 31
he did, behold, they are written in the Book
of the Chronicles of the Kings of Israel.

JUDAH

Jotham

In the second year of Pekah the son of 32
Remali'ah, king of Israel, Jotham the son of
Uzzi'ah, king of Judah, began to reign. He 33
was twenty-five years old when he began to
reign, and he reigned sixteen years in Jerusalem. His mother's name was Jeru'sha the
daughter of Zadok. And he did what was 34
right in the eyes of the LORD, according to all
that his father Uzzi'ah had done. Neverthe- 35
less the high places were not removed; the
people still sacrificed and burned incense on
the high places. He built the upper gate of
the house of the LORD. Now the rest of the 36
acts of Jotham, and all that he did, are they
not written in the Book of the Chronicles of
the Kings of Judah? In those days the LORD 37
began to send Rezin the king of Syria and
Pekah the son of Remali'ah against Judah.
Jotham slept with his fathers, and was buried 38
with his fathers in the city of David his
father; and Ahaz his son reigned in his stead.

Ahaz

In the seventeenth year of Pekah the son of 16
Remali'ah, Ahaz the son of Jotham, king of
Judah, began to reign. Ahaz was twenty 2
years old when he began to reign, and he
reigned sixteen years in Jerusalem. And he
did not do what was right in the eyes of the
LORD his God, as his father David had done,
but he walked in the way of the kings of 3
Israel. He even burned his son as an

---

[x] Compare Gk: Heb *Tiphsah*　[y] Heb adds *Argob and Arieh*, which probably belong to the list of places in verse 29
15.33–35: 2 Chron 27.1–3.　15.38: 2 Chron 27.9.　16.2–4: 2 Chron 28.1–4.

offering,[z] according to the abominable practices of the nations whom the LORD drove out
4 before the people of Israel. And he sacrificed and burned incense on the high places, and on the hills, and under every green tree.
5 Then Rezin king of Syria and Pekah the son of Remali′ah, king of Israel, came up to wage war on Jerusalem, and they besieged Ahaz
6 but could not conquer him. At that time[a] the king of Edom[b] recovered Elath for Edom,[b] and drove the men of Judah from Elath; and the Edomites came to Elath,
7 where they dwell to this day. So Ahaz sent messengers to Tig′lath-pile′ser king of Assyria, saying, "I am your servant and your son. Come up, and rescue me from the hand of the king of Syria and from the hand of
8 king of Israel, who are attacking me." Ahaz also took the silver and gold that was found in the house of the LORD and in the treasures of the king's house, and sent a present to the
9 king of Assyria. And the king of Assyria hearkened to him; the king of Assyria marched up against Damascus, and took it, carrying its people captive to Kir, and he killed Rezin.
10 When King Ahaz went to Damascus to meet Tig′lath-pile′ser king of Assyria, he saw the altar that was at Damascus. And King Ahaz sent to Uri′ah the priest a model of the altar, and its pattern, exact in all its details.
11 And Uri′ah the priest built the altar; in accordance with all that King Ahaz had sent from Damascus, so Uri′ah the priest made it, before King Ahaz arrived from Damascus.
12 And when the king came from Damascus, the king viewed the altar. Then the king
13 drew near to the altar, and went up on it, and burned his burnt offering and his cereal offering, and poured his drink offering, and threw the blood of his peace offerings upon
14 the altar. And the bronze altar which was before the LORD he removed from the front of the house, from the place between his altar and the house of the LORD, and put it on the
15 north side of his altar. And King Ahaz commanded Uri′ah the priest, saying, "Upon the great altar burn the morning burnt offering, and the evening cereal offering, and the king's burnt offering, and his cereal offering, with the burnt offering of all the people of the land, and their cereal offering, and their drink offering; and throw upon it all the blood of the burnt offering, and all the blood of the sacrifice; but the bronze altar shall be for me to inquire by."
16 Uri′ah the priest did all this, as King Ahaz commanded.
17 And King Ahaz cut off the frames of the stands, and removed the laver from them, and he took down the sea from off the bronze oxen that were under it, and put it upon a pediment of stone. And the covered way for 18 the sabbath which had been built inside the palace, and the outer entrance for the king he removed from[c] the house of the LORD, because of the king of Assyria. Now the rest 19 of the acts of Ahaz which he did, are they not written in the Book of the Chronicles of the Kings of Judah? And Ahaz slept with his 20 fathers, and was buried with his fathers in the city of David; and Hezeki′ah his son reigned in his stead.

FALL OF SAMARIA

In the twelfth year of Ahaz king of Judah 17 Hoshe′a the son of Elah began to reign in Samar′ia over Israel, and he reigned nine years. And he did what was evil in the sight 2 of the LORD, yet not as the kings of Israel who were before him. Against him came up 3 Shalmane′ser king of Assyria; and Hoshe′a became his vassal, and paid him tribute. But 4 the king of Assyria found treachery in Hoshe′a; for he had sent messengers to So, king of Egypt, and offered no tribute to the king of Assyria, as he had done year by year; therefore the king of Assyria shut him up, and bound him in prison. Then the king of 5 Assyria invaded all the land and came to Samar′ia, and for three years he besieged it. In the ninth year of Hoshe′a the king of 6 Assyria captured Samar′ia, and he carried the Israelites away to Assyria, and placed them in Halah, and on the Habor, the river of Gozan, and in the cities of the Medes. And this was so, because the people of 7 Israel had sinned against the LORD their God, who had brought them up out of the land of Egypt from under the hand of Pharaoh king of Egypt, and had feared other gods and walked in the customs of the 8 nations whom the LORD drove out before the people of Israel, and in the customs which the kings of Israel had introduced.[d] And the 9 people of Israel did secretly against the LORD their God things that were not right. They built for themselves high places at all their

[z] Or *made his son to pass through the fire* [a] Heb *At that time Rezin* [b] Heb *Aram* (Syria)
[c] Cn: Heb *turned to* [d] Heb obscure
16.20: 2 Chron 28.27.

towns, from watchtower to fortified city;
10 they set up for themselves pillars and
Ashe'rim on every high hill and under every
11 green tree; and there they burned incense on
all the high places, as the nations did whom
the LORD carried away before them. And
they did wicked things, provoking the LORD
12 to anger, and they served idols, of which the
LORD had said to them, "You shall not do
13 this." Yet the LORD warned Israel and
Judah by every prophet and every seer,
saying, "Turn from your evil ways and keep
my commandments and my statutes, in
accordance with all the law which I commanded your fathers, and which I sent to you
14 by my servants the prophets." But they
would not listen, but were stubborn, as their
fathers had been, who did not believe in the
15 LORD their God. They despised his statutes,
and his covenant that he made with their
fathers, and the warnings which he gave
them. They went after false idols, and
became false, and they followed the nations
that were round about them, concerning
whom the LORD had commanded them that
16 they should not do like them. And they
forsook all the commandments of the LORD
their God, and made for themselves molten
images of two calves; and they made an
Ashe'rah, and worshipped all the host of
17 heaven, and served Ba'al. And they burned
their sons and their daughters as offerings,[e]
and used divination and sorcery, and sold
themselves to do evil in the sight of the
18 LORD, provoking him to anger. Therefore
the LORD was very angry with Israel, and
removed them out of his sight; none was left
but the tribe of Judah only.
19 Judah also did not keep the commandments of the LORD their God, but walked in
the customs which Israel had introduced.
20 And the LORD rejected all the descendants of
Israel, and afflicted them, and gave them into
the hand of spoilers, until he had cast them
out of his sight.
21 When he had torn Israel from the house of
David they made Jerobo'am the son of Nebat

king. And Jerobo'am drove Israel from
following the LORD and made them commit
great sin. The people of Israel walked in all 22
the sins which Jerobo'am did; they did not
depart from them, until the LORD removed 23
Israel out of his sight, as he had spoken by all
his servants the prophets. So Israel was
exiled from their own land to Assyria until
this day.
And the king of Assyria brought people 24
from Babylon, Cuthah, Avva, Hamath, and
Sepharva'im, and placed them in the cities of
Samar'ia instead of the people of Israel; and
they took possession of Samar'ia, and dwelt
in its cities. And at the beginning of their 25
dwelling there, they did not fear the LORD;
therefore the LORD sent lions among them,
which killed some of them. So the king of 26
Assyria was told, "The nations which you
have carried away and placed in the cities of
Samar'ia do not know the law of the god of
the land; therefore he has sent lions among
them, and behold, they are killing them,
because they do not know the law of the god
of the land." Then the king of Assyria 27
commanded, "Send there one of the priests
whom you carried away thence; and let him[f]
go and dwell there, and teach them the law of
the god of the land." So one of the priests 28
whom they had carried away from Samar'ia
came and dwelt in Bethel, and taught them
how they should fear the LORD.
But every nation still made gods of its own, 29
and put them in the shrines of the high places
which the Samaritans had made, every
nation in the cities in which they dwelt; the 30
men of Babylon made Suc'coth-be'noth, the
men of Cuth made Nergal, the men of
Hamath made Ashi'ma, and the Av'vites 31
made Nibhaz and Tartak; and the Sephar'-
vites burned their children in the fire to
Adram'melech and Anam'melech, the gods
of Sepharva'im. They also feared the LORD, 32
and appointed from among themselves all
sorts of people as priests of the high places,
who sacrificed for them in the shrines of the
high places. So they feared the LORD but 33

---

[e] Or *made their sons and their daughters pass through the fire*   [f] Syr Vg: Heb *them*

also served their own gods, after the manner of the nations from among whom they had been carried away. To this day they do according to the former manner.

They do not fear the LORD, and they do not follow the statutes or the ordinances or the law or the commandment which the LORD commanded the children of Jacob, whom he named Israel. The LORD made a covenant with them, and commanded them, "You shall not fear other gods or bow yourselves to them or serve them or sacrifice to them; but you shall fear the LORD, who brought you out of the land of Egypt with great power and with an outstretched arm; you shall bow yourselves to him, and to him you shall sacrifice. And the statutes and the ordinances and the law and the commandment which he wrote for you, you shall always be careful to do. You shall not fear other gods, and you shall not forget the covenant that I have made with you. You shall not fear other gods, but you shall fear the LORD your God, and he will deliver you out of the hand of all your enemies." However they would not listen, but they did according to their former manner.

So these nations feared the LORD, and also served their graven images; their children likewise, and their children's children—as their fathers did, so they do to this day.

JUDAH—Hezekiah

8 IN the third year of Hoshe'a son of Elah, king of Israel, Hezeki'ah the son of Ahaz, king of Judah, began to reign. He was twenty-five years old when he began to reign, and he reigned twenty-nine years in Jerusalem. His mother's name was Abi the daughter of Zechari'ah. And he did what was right in the eyes of the LORD, according to all that David his father had done. He removed the high places, and broke the pillars, and cut down the Ashe'rah. And he broke in pieces the bronze serpent that Moses had made, for until those days the people of Israel had burned incense to it; it was called Nehush'tan. He trusted in the LORD the God of Israel; so that there was none like him among all the kings of Judah after him, nor among those who were before him. For he held fast to the LORD; he did not depart from following him, but kept the commandments which the LORD commanded Moses. And the LORD was with him; wherever he went forth, he prospered. He rebelled against the king of Assyria, and would not serve him. He smote the Philistines as far as Gaza and its territory, from watchtower to fortified city.

9 In the fourth year of King Hezeki'ah, which was the seventh year of Hoshe'a son of Elah, king of Israel, Shalmane'ser king of Assyria came up against Samar'ia and besieged it and at the end of three years he took it. In the sixth year of Hezeki'ah, which was the ninth year of Hoshe'a king of Israel, Samar'ia was taken. The king of Assyria carried the Israelites away to Assyria, and put them in Halah, and on the Habor, the river of Gozan, and in the cities of the Medes, because they did not obey the voice of the LORD their God but transgressed his covenant, even all that Moses the servant of the LORD commanded; they neither listened nor obeyed.

Assyria's threat

In the fourteenth year of King Hezeki'ah Sennach'erib king of Assyria came up against all the fortified cities of Judah and took them. And Hezeki'ah king of Judah sent to the king of Assyria at Lachish, saying, "I have done wrong; withdraw from me; whatever you impose on me I will bear." And the king of Assyria required of Hezeki'ah king of Judah three hundred talents of silver and thirty talents of gold. And Hezeki'ah gave him all the silver that was found in the house of the LORD, and in the treasuries of the king's house. At that time

18.1–3: 2 Chron 29.1–2. 18.13–19.37: 2 Chron 32.1–21; Is 36.1–37.38.

Hezeki′ah stripped the gold from the doors
of the temple of the LORD, and from the
doorposts which Hezeki′ah king of Judah
had overlaid and gave it to the king of
17 Assyria. And the king of Assyria sent the
Tartan, the Rab′saris, and the Rab′-
shakeh with a great army from Lachish to
King Hezeki′ah at Jerusalem. And they
went up and came to Jerusalem. When they
arrived, they came and stood by the conduit
of the upper pool, which is on the highway to
18 the Fuller's Field. And when they called for
the king, there came out to them Eli′akim the
son of Hilki′ah, who was over the household,
and Shebnah the secretary, and Jo′ah the son
of Asaph, the recorder.

19 And the Rab′shakeh said to them, "Say to
Hezeki′ah, 'Thus says the great king, the
king of Assyria: On what do you rest this
20 confidence of yours? Do you think that
mere words are strategy and power for war?
On whom do you now rely, that you have
21 rebelled against me? Behold, you are relying
now on Egypt, that broken reed of a staff,
which will pierce the hand of any man who
leans on it. Such is Pharaoh king of Egypt to
22 all who rely on him. But if you say to me,
"We rely on the LORD our God," is it not he
whose high places and altars Hezeki′ah has
removed, saying to Judah and to Jerusalem,
"You shall worship before this altar in
23 Jerusalem"? Come now, make a wager with
my master the king of Assyria: I will give you
two thousand horses, if you are able on your
24 part to set riders upon them. How then can
you repulse a single captain among the least
of my master's servants, when you rely on
Egypt for chariots and for horsemen?
25 Moreover, is it without the LORD that I have
come up against this place to destroy it?
The LORD said to me, Go up against this
land, and destroy it.' "
26 Then Eli′akim the son of Hilki′ah, and
Shebnah, and Jo′ah, said to the Rab′shakeh,
"Pray, speak to your servants in the Aramaic
language, for we understand it; do not speak
to us in the language of Judah within the
hearing of the people who are on the wall."
27 But the Rab′shakeh said to them, "Has my

master sent me to speak these words to your
master and to you, and not to the men sitting
on the wall, who are doomed with you to eat
their own dung and to drink their own
urine?"

Then the Rab′shakeh stood and called out
in a loud voice in the language of Judah:
"Hear the word of the great king, the king of
Assyria! Thus says the king: 'Do not let
Hezeki′ah deceive you, for he will not be able
to deliver you out of my hand. Do not let
Hezeki′ah make you to rely on the LORD by
saying, The LORD will surely deliver us, and
this city will not be given into the hand of the
king of Assyria.' Do not listen to Hezeki′ah;
for thus says the king of Assyria: 'Make your
peace with me and come out to me; then
every one of you will eat of his own vine, and
every one of his own fig tree, and every one
of you will drink the water of his own cistern;
until I come and take you away to a land like
your own land, a land of grain and wine, a
land of bread and vineyards, a land of olive
trees and honey, that you may live, and not
die. And do not listen to Hezeki′ah when he
misleads you by saying, The LORD will
deliver us. Has any of the gods of the nations
ever delivered his land out of the hand of the
king of Assyria? Where are the gods of
Hamath and Arpad? Where are the gods of
Sepharva′im, Hena, and Ivvah? Have they
delivered Samar′ia out of my hand? Who
among all the gods of the countries have
delivered their countries out of my hand, that
the LORD should deliver Jerusalem out of my
hand?' "

But the people were silent and answered
him not a word, for the king's command was,
"Do not answer him." Then Eli′akim the
son of Hilki′ah, who was over the household,
and Shebna the secretary, and Jo′ah the son
of Asaph, the recorder, came to Hezeki′ah
with their clothes rent, and told him the
words of the Rab′shakeh.

When King Hezeki′ah heard it, he rent his
clothes, and covered himself with sackcloth,
and went into the house of the LORD. And he

sent Eli′akim, who was over the household, and Shebna the secretary, and the senior priests, covered with sackcloth, to the
3 prophet Isaiah the son of Amoz. They said to him, "Thus says Hezeki′ah, This day is a day of distress, of rebuke, and of disgrace; children have come to the birth, and there is
4 no strength to bring them forth. It may be that the LORD your God heard all the words of the Rab′shakeh, whom his master the king of Assyria has sent to mock the living God, and will rebuke the words which the LORD your God has heard; therefore lift up your prayer for the remnant that is left."

Isaiah's counsel

5 When the servants of King Hezeki′ah came
6 to Isaiah, Isaiah said to them, "Say to your master, 'Thus says the LORD: Do not be afraid because of the words that you have heard, with which the servants of the king of
7 Assyria have reviled me. Behold, I will put a spirit in him, so that he shall hear a rumour and return to his own land; and I will cause him to fall by the sword in his own land.' "
8 The Rab′shakeh returned, and found the king of Assyria fighting against Libnah; for
9 he heard that the king had left Lachish. And when the king heard concerning Tirha′kah king of Ethiopia, "Behold, he has set out to fight against you," he sent messengers again
10 to Hezeki′ah, saying, "Thus shall you speak to Hezeki′ah king of Judah: 'Do not let your God on whom you rely deceive you by promising that Jerusalem will not be given
11 into the hand of the king of Assyria. Behold, you have heard what the kings of Assyria have done to all lands, destroying them
12 utterly. And shall you be delivered? Have the gods of the nations delivered them, the nations which my fathers destroyed, Gozan, Haran, Rezeph, and the people of Eden who
13 were in Telas′sar? Where is the king of Hamath, the king of Arpad, the king of the city of Sepharva′im, the king of Hena, or the king of Ivvah?' "
14 Hezeki′ah received the letter from the hand of the messengers, and read it; and Hezeki′ah went up to the house of the LORD, and spread it before the LORD. And Hezeki′ah prayed 15 before the LORD, and said: "O LORD the God of Israel, who art enthroned above the cherubim, thou art the God, thou alone, of all the kingdoms of the earth; thou hast made heaven and earth. Incline thy ear, O LORD, 16 and hear; open thy eyes, O LORD, and see; and hear the words of Sennach′erib, which he has sent to mock the living God. Of a 17 truth, O LORD, the kings of Assyria have laid waste the nations and their lands, and 18 have cast their gods into the fire; for they were no gods, but the work of men's hands, wood and stone; therefore they were destroyed. So now, O LORD our God, save us, I 19 beseech thee, from his hand, that all the kingdoms of the earth may know that thou, O LORD, art God alone."

Then Isaiah the son of Amoz sent to 20 Hezeki′ah, saying, "Thus says the LORD, the God of Israel: Your prayer to me about Sennach′erib king of Assyria I have heard. This is the word that the LORD has spoken 21 concerning him:

"She despises you, she scorns you—
   the virgin daughter of Zion;
she wags her head behind you—
   the daughter of Jerusalem.

"Whom have you mocked and reviled? 22
   Against whom have you raised your
      voice
and haughtily lifted your eyes?
   Against the Holy One of Israel!
By your messengers you have mocked the 23
   Lord,
   and you have said, 'With my many
      chariots
I have gone up the heights of the
   mountains,
   to the far recesses of Lebanon;
I felled its tallest cedars,
   its choicest cypresses;
I entered its farthest retreat,
   its densest forest.
I dug wells   24
   and drank foreign waters,

and I dried up with the sole of my
   foot
all the streams of Egypt.'

25 "Have you not heard
       that I determined it long ago?
    I planned from days of old
       what now I bring to pass,
    that you should turn fortified cities
       into heaps of ruins,
26 while their inhabitants, shorn of strength,
       are dismayed and confounded,
    and have become like plants of the field,
       and like tender grass,
    like grass on the housetops;
       blighted before it is grown?

27 "But I know your sitting down
       and your going out and coming in,
       and your raging against me.
28 Because you have raged against me
       and your arrogance has come into my
          ears,
    I will put my hook in your nose
       and my bit in your mouth,
    and I will turn you back on the way
       by which you came.

29 "And this shall be the sign for you: this year
    you shall eat what grows of itself, and in the
    second year what springs of the same; then in
    the third year sow, and reap, and plant
30 vineyards, and eat their fruit. And the
    surviving remnant of the house of Judah
    shall again take root downward, and bear
31 fruit upward; for out of Jerusalem shall go
    forth a remnant, and out of Mount Zion a
    band of survivors. The zeal of the LORD will
    do this.
32 "Therefore thus says the LORD concerning
    the king of Assyria, He shall not come into
    this city or shoot an arrow there, or come
    before it with a shield or cast up a siege
33 mound against it. By the way that he came,
    by the same he shall return, and he shall not
34 come into this city, says the LORD. For I will
    defend this city to save it, for my own sake
    and for the sake of my servant David."

Jerusalem delivered

35 And that night the angel of the LORD went
    forth, and slew a hundred and eighty-five
    thousand in the camp of the Assyrians; and
    when men arose early in the morning,
36 behold, these were all dead bodies. Then
    Sennach'erib king of Assyria departed, and
37 went home, and dwelt at Nin'eveh. And as
    he was worshipping in the house of Nisroch

his god, Adram'melech and Share'zer, his
sons, slew him with the sword, and escaped
into the land of Ararat. And E'sar-had'don
his son reigned in his stead.

Hezekiah's sickness

In those days Hezeki'ah became sick and
was at the point of death. And Isaiah the
prophet the son of Amoz came to him, and
said to him, "Thus says the LORD, 'Set your
house in order; for you shall die, you shall
not recover.'" Then Hezeki'ah turned his
face to the wall, and prayed to the LORD,
saying, "Remember now, O LORD, I beseech
thee, how I have walked before thee in
faithfulness and with a whole heart, and have
done what is good in thy sight." And
Hezeki'ah wept bitterly. And before Isaiah
had gone out of the middle court, the word of
the LORD came to him: "Turn back, and say
to Hezeki'ah the prince of my people, Thus
says the LORD, the God of David your father:
I have heard your prayer, I have seen your
tears; behold, I will heal you; on the third
day you shall go up to the house of the
LORD. And I will add fifteen years to your
life. I will deliver you and this city out of the
hand of the king of Assyria, and I will defend
this city for my own sake and for my servant
David's sake." And Isaiah said, "Bring a
cake of figs. And let them take and lay it on
the boil, that he may recover."
And Hezeki'ah said to Isaiah, "What shall
be the sign that the LORD will heal me, and
that I shall go up to the house of the LORD on
the third day?" And Isaiah said, "This is
the sign to you from the LORD, that the LORD
will do the thing that he has promised: shall
the shadow go forward ten steps, or go back
ten steps?" And Hezeki'ah answered, "It is
an easy thing for the shadow to lengthen ten
steps; rather let the shadow go back ten
steps." And Isaiah the prophet cried to the
LORD; and he brought the shadow back ten
steps, by which the sun[g] had declined on
the dial of Ahaz.

Letters from Babylon

At that time Mero'dach-bal'adan the son of
Bal'adan, king of Babylon, sent envoys with
letters and a present to Hezeki'ah; for he
heard that Hezeki'ah had been sick. And
Hezeki'ah welcomed them, and he showed
them all his treasure house, the silver, the
gold, the spices, the precious oil, his
armoury, all that was found in his storehouses; there was nothing in his house or in

[g] Syr See Is 38.8 and Tg: Heb lacks *the sun*
20.1–21: 2 Chron 32.24–33; Is 38. 1–39.8.

B. C.
700~600

all his realm that Hezeki'ah did not show them.

Isaiah's prophecy

Then Isaiah the prophet came to King Hezeki'ah, and said to him, "What did these men say? And whence did they come to you?" And Hezeki'ah said, "They have come from a far country, from Babylon." He said, "What have they seen in your house?" And Hezeki'ah answered, "They have seen all that is in my house; there is nothing in my storehouses that I did not show them."

Then Isaiah said to Hezeki'ah, "Hear the word of the LORD: Behold, the days are coming, when all that is in your house, and that which your fathers have stored up till this day, shall be carried to Babylon; nothing shall be left, says the LORD. And some of your own sons, who are born to you, shall be taken away; and they shall be eunuchs in the palace of the king of Babylon." Then said Hezeki'ah to Isaiah, "The word of the LORD which you have spoken is good." For he thought, "Why not, if there will be peace and security in my days?"

The rest of the deeds of Hezeki'ah, and all his might, and how he made the pool and the conduit and brought water into the city, are they not written in the Book of the Chronicles of the Kings of Judah? And Hezeki'ah slept with his fathers; and Manas'seh his son reigned in his stead.

Manasseh

1 Manas'seh was twelve years old when he began to reign, and he reigned fifty-five years in Jerusalem. His mother's name was
2 Heph'zibah. And he did what was evil in the sight of the LORD, according to the abominable practices of the nations whom the LORD drove out before the people of
3 Israel. For he rebuilt the high places which Hezeki'ah his father had destroyed; and he erected altars for Ba'al, and made an Ashe'rah, as Ahab king of Israel had done, and worshipped all the host of heaven, and

served them. And he built altars in the house 4 of the LORD, of which the LORD had said, "In Jerusalem will I put my name." And he 5 built altars for all the host of heaven in the two courts of the house of the LORD. And he 6 burned his son as an offering, and practised soothsaying and augury, and dealt with mediums and with wizards. He did much evil in the sight of the LORD, provoking him to anger. And the graven image of Ashe'rah 7 that he had made he set in the house of which the LORD said to David and to Solomon his son, "In this house, and in Jerusalem, which I have chosen out of all the tribes of Israel, I will put my name for ever; and I will not 8 cause the feet of Israel to wander any more out of the land which I gave to their fathers, if only they will be careful to do according to all that I have commanded them, and according to all the law that my servant Moses commanded them." But they did not listen, 9 and Manas'seh seduced them to do more evil than the nations had done whom the LORD destroyed before the people of Israel.

And the LORD said by his servants the 10 prophets, "Because Manas'seh king of Judah 11 has committed these abominations, and has done things more wicked than all that the Amorites did, who were before him, and has made Judah also to sin with his idols; therefore thus says the LORD, the God of 12 Israel, Behold, I am bringing upon Jerusalem and Judah such evil that the ears of every one who hears of it will tingle. And I 13 will stretch over Jerusalem the measuring line of Samar'ia, and the plummet of the house of Ahab; and I will wipe Jerusalem as one wipes a dish, wiping it and turning it upside down. And I will cast off the remnant 14 of my heritage, and give them into the hand of their enemies, and they shall become a prey and a spoil to all their enemies, because 15 they have done what is evil in my sight and have provoked me to anger, since the day their fathers came out of Egypt, even to this day."

Moreover Manas'seh shed very much 16 innocent blood, till he had filled Jerusalem from one end to another, besides the sin

21.1–9: 2 Chron 33.1–9.

which he made Judah to sin so that they did what was evil in the sight of the LORD.

17 Now the rest of the acts of Manas'seh, and all that he did, and the sin that he committed, are they not written in the Book of the 18 Chronicles of the Kings of Judah? And Manas'seh slept with his fathers, and was buried in the garden of his house, in the garden of Uzza; and Amon his son reigned in his stead.

Amon

19 Amon was twenty-two years old when he began to reign, and he reigned two years in Jerusalem. His mother's name was Meshul'lemeth the daughter of Haruz of 20 Jotbah. And he did what was evil in the sight of the LORD, as Manas'seh his father had 21 done. He walked in all the way in which his father walked, and served the idols that his 22 father served, and worshipped them; he forsook the LORD, the God of his fathers, and 23 did not walk in the way of the LORD. And the servants of Amon conspired against him, 24 and killed the king in his house. But the people of the land slew all those who had conspired against King Amon, and the people of the land made Josi'ah his son king 25 in his stead. Now the rest of the acts of Amon which he did, are they not written in the Book of the Chronicles of the Kings of 26 Judah? And he was buried in his tomb in the garden of Uzza; and Josi'ah his son reigned in his stead.

Josiah

22 Josi'ah was eight years old when he began to reign, and he reigned thirty-one years in Jerusalem. His mother's name was Jedi'dah 2 the daughter of Adai'ah of Bozkath. And he did what was right in the eyes of the LORD, and walked in all the way of David his father, and he did not turn aside to the right hand or to the left.

The repair of the temple

3 In the eighteenth year of King Josi'ah, the king sent Shaphan the son of Azali'ah, son of Meshul'lam, the secretary, to the house of 4 the LORD, saying, "Go up to Hilki'ah the high priest, that he may reckon the amount of the money which has been brought into the house of the LORD, which the keepers of the threshold have collected from the people; 5 and let it be given into the hand of the workmen who have the oversight of the house of the LORD; and let them give it to

the workmen who are at the house of the LORD, repairing the house, that is, to the carpenters, and to the builders, and to the masons, as well as for buying timber and quarried stone to repair the house. But no accounting shall be asked from them for the money which is delivered into their hand, for they deal honestly."

The book of the law

8 And Hilki'ah the high priest said to Shaphan the secretary, "I have found the book of the law in the house of the LORD." And Hilki'ah gave the book to Shaphan, and 9 he read it. And Shaphan the secretary came to the king, and reported to the king, "Your servants have emptied out the money that was found in the house, and have delivered it into the hand of the workmen who have the oversight of the house of the LORD." Then 10 Shaphan the secretary told the king, "Hilki'ah the priest has given me a book." And Shaphan read it before the king.

11 And when the king heard the words of the book of the law, he rent his clothes. And the 12 king commanded Hilki'ah the priest, and Ahi'kam the son of Shaphan, and Achbor the son of Micai'ah, and Shaphan the secretary, and Asa'iah the king's servant, saying, "Go, 13 inquire of the LORD for me, and for the people, and for all Judah, concerning the words of this book that has been found; for great is the wrath of the LORD that is kindled against us, because our fathers have not obeyed the words of this book, to do according to all that is written concerning us."

14 So Hilki'ah the priest, and Ahi'kam, and Achbor, and Shaphan, and Asa'iah went to Huldah the prophetess, the wife of Shallum the son of Tikvah, son of Harhas, keeper of the wardrobe (now she dwelt in Jerusalem in the Second Quarter); and they talked with her. And she said to them, "Thus says the 15 LORD, the God of Israel: 'Tell the man who sent you to me, Thus says the LORD, Behold, 16 I will bring evil upon this place and upon its

inhabitants, all the words of the book which the king of Judah has read. Because they have forsaken me and have burned incense to other gods, that they might provoke me to anger with all the work of their hands, therefore my wrath will be kindled against this place, and it will not be quenched. But as to the king of Judah, who sent you to inquire of the LORD, thus shall you say to him, Thus says the LORD, the God of Israel: Regarding the words which you have heard, because your heart was penitent, and you humbled yourself before the LORD, when you heard how I spoke against this place, and against its inhabitants, that they should become a desolation and a curse, and you have rent your clothes and wept before me, I also have heard you, says the LORD. Therefore, behold, I will gather you to your fathers, and you shall be gathered to your grave in peace, and your eyes shall not see all the evil which I will bring upon this place.' " And they brought back word to the king.

23 Then the king sent, and all the elders of Judah and Jerusalem were gathered to him. And the king went up to the house of the LORD, and with him all the men of Judah and all the inhabitants of Jerusalem, and the priests and the prophets, all the people, both small and great; and he read in their hearing all the words of the book of the covenant which had been found in the house of the LORD. And the king stood by the pillar and made a covenant before the LORD, to walk after the LORD and to keep his commandments and his testimonies and his statutes, with all his heart and all his soul, to perform the words of this covenant that were written in this book; and all the people joined in the covenant.

Josiah's reforms

4 And the king commanded Hilki′ah, the high priest, and the priests of the second order, and the keepers of the threshold, to bring out of the temple of the LORD all the vessels made for Ba′al, for Ashe′rah, and for all the host of heaven; he burned them outside Jerusalem in the fields of the Kidron, and carried their ashes to Bethel. And he deposed the idolatrous priests whom the kings of Judah had ordained to burn incense in the high places at the cities of Judah and round about Jerusalem; those also who burned incense to Ba′al, to the sun, and the moon, and the constellations, and all the host of the heavens. And he brought out the Ashe′rah from the house of the LORD, outside Jerusalem, to the brook Kidron, and burned it at the brook Kidron, and beat it to dust and cast the dust of it upon the graves of the common people. And he broke down the houses of the male cult prostitutes which were in the house of the LORD, where the women wove hangings for the Ashe′rah. And he brought all the priests out of the cities of Judah, and defiled the high places where the priests had burned incense, from Geba to Beer-sheba; and he broke down the high places of the gates that were at the entrance of the gate of Joshua the governor of the city, which were on one's left at the gate of the city. However, the priests of the high places did not come up to the altar of the LORD in Jerusalem, but they ate unleavened bread among their brethren. And he defiled Topheth, which is in the valley of the sons of Hinnom, that no one might burn his son or his daughter as an offering to Molech. And he removed the horses that the kings of Judah had dedicated to the sun, at the entrance to the house of the LORD, by the chamber of Nathan-melech the chamberlain, which was in the precincts;[h] and he burned the chariots of the sun with fire. And the altars on the roof of the upper chamber of Ahaz, which the kings of Judah had made, and the altars which Manas′seh had made in the two courts of the house of the LORD, he pulled down and broke in pieces,[i] and cast the dust of them into the brook Kidron. And the king defiled the high places that were east of Jerusalem, to the south of the mount of corruption, which Solomon the king of Israel had built for Ash′toreth the abomination of the Sido′nians, and for Chemosh the abomination of Moab, and for Milcom the abomination of the Ammonites. And he broke in pieces the pillars, and cut down the Ashe′rim, and filled their places with the bones of men.

Moreover the altar at Bethel, the high place erected by Jerobo′am the son of Nebat, who made Israel to sin, that altar with the high place he pulled down and he broke in pieces its stones,[j] crushing them to dust; also he burned the Ashe′rah. And as Josi′ah turned, he saw the tombs there on the mount; and he sent and took the bones out of the tombs, and burned them upon the altar, and defiled it, according to the word of the LORD which the man of God proclaimed, who had predicted these things. Then he said, "What is yonder monument that I see?" And the men of the city told him, "It is the tomb of the man of God who came from Judah and predicted

---

[h] The meaning of the Hebrew word is uncertain   [i] Heb *pieces from there*
[j] Gk: Heb *he burned the high place*
23.4–20: 2 Chron 34.3–7.

these things which you have done against the
18 altar at Bethel." And he said, "Let him be;
let no man move his bones." So they let his
bones alone, with the bones of the prophet
19 who came out of Samar′ia. And all the
shrines also of the high places that were in
the cities of Samar′ia, which kings of Israel
had made, provoking the LORD to anger,
Josi′ah removed; he did to them according to
20 all that he had done at Bethel. And he slew
all the priests of the high places who were
there, upon the altars, and burned the bones
of men upon them. Then he returned to
Jerusalem.
21 And the king commanded all the people,
"Keep the passover to the LORD your God,
as it is written in this book of the covenant."
22 For no such passover had been kept since the
days of the judges who judged Israel, or
during all the days of the kings of Israel or of
23 the kings of Judah; but in the eighteenth year
of King Josi′ah this passover was kept to the
LORD in Jerusalem.
24 Moreover Josi′ah put away the mediums
and the wizards and the teraphim and the
idols and all the abominations that were seen
in the land of Judah and in Jerusalem, that he
might establish the words of the law which
were written in the book that Hilki′ah the
priest found in the house of the LORD.
25 Before him there was no king like him, who
turned to the LORD with all his heart and
with all his soul and with all his might,
according to all the law of Moses; nor did any
like him arise after him.
26 Still the LORD did not turn from the
fierceness of his great wrath, by which his
anger was kindled against Judah, because of
all the provocations with which Manas′seh
27 had provoked him. And the LORD said, "I
will remove Judah also out of my sight, as I
have removed Israel, and I will cast off this
city which I have chosen, Jerusalem, and the
house of which I said, My name shall be
there."
28 Now the rest of the acts of Josi′ah, and all
that he did, are they not written in the Book
29 of the Chronicles of the Kings of Judah? In
his days Pharaoh Neco king of Egypt went
up to the king of Assyria to the river
Euphra′tes. King Josi′ah went to meet him;
and Pharaoh Neco slew him at Megid′do,
30 when he saw him. And his servants carried
him dead in a chariot from Megid′do, and
brought him to Jerusalem, and buried him in
his own tomb. And the people of the land
took Jeho′ahaz the son of Josi′ah, and
anointed him, and made him king in his
father's stead.

Jehoahaz

31 Jeho′ahaz was twenty-three years old when
he began to reign, and he reigned three
months in Jerusalem. His mother's name
was Hamu′tal the daughter of Jeremiah of
32 Libnah. And he did what was evil in the
sight of the LORD, according to all that his
33 fathers had done. And Pharaoh Neco put
him in bonds at Riblah in the land of
Hamath, that he might not reign in Jerusalem, and laid upon the land a tribute of a
hundred talents of silver and a talent of gold.
34 And Pharaoh Neco made Eli′akim the son of
Josi′ah king in the place of Josi′ah his father,
and changed his name to Jehoi′akim. But he
took Jeho′ahaz away; and he came to Egypt,
35 and died there. And Jehoi′akim gave the
silver and the gold to Pharaoh, but he taxed
the land to give the money according to the
command of Pharaoh. He exacted the silver
and the gold of the people of the land, from
every one according to his assessment, to give
it to Pharaoh Neco.
36 Jehoi′akim was twenty-five years old when
he began to reign, and he reigned eleven
years in Jerusalem. His mother's name was
Zebi′dah the daughter of Peda′iah of
37 Rumah. And he did what was evil in the
sight of the LORD, according to all that his
fathers had done.

Jehoiakim

24 In his days Nebuchadnez′zar king of
Babylon came up, and Jehoi′akim became his
servant three years; then he turned and
2 rebelled against him. And the LORD sent
against him bands of the Chalde′ans, and
bands of the Syrians, and bands of the
Moabites, and bands of the Ammonites, and
sent them against Judah to destroy it, according to the word of the LORD which he spoke
3 by his servants the prophets. Surely this
came upon Judah at the command of the
LORD, to remove them out of his sight, for
4 the sins of Manas′seh, according to all that he
had done, and also for the innocent blood
that he had shed; for he filled Jerusalem with
innocent blood, and the LORD would not
5 pardon. Now the rest of the deeds of
Jehoi′akim, and all that he did, are they not
written in the Book of the Chronicles of the
6 Kings of Judah? So Jehoi′akim slept with
his fathers, and Jehoi′achin his son reigned in
7 his stead. And the king of Egypt did not
come again out of his land, for the king of
Babylon had taken all that belonged to the

B. C. 600~500

king of Egypt from the Brook of Egypt to the river Euphra′tes.

Jehoiachin

8 Jehoi′achin was eighteen years old when he became king, and he reigned three months in Jerusalem. His mother's name was Nehush′ta the daughter of Elna′than of
9 Jerusalem. And he did what was evil in the sight of the LORD, according to all that his father had done.

FALL OF JERUSALEM

10 At that time the servants of Nebuchadnez′zar king of Babylon came up to
11 Jerusalem, and the city was besieged. And Nebuchadnez′zar king of Babylon came to the city, while his servants were besieging it;
12 and Jehoi′achin the king of Judah gave himself up to the king of Babylon, himself, and his mother, and his servants, and his princes, and his palace officials. The king of Babylon took him prisoner in the eighth year
13 of his reign, and carried off all the treasures of the house of the LORD, and the treasures of the king's house, and cut in pieces all the vessels of gold in the temple of the LORD, which Solomon king of Israel had made, as
14 the LORD had foretold. He carried away all

Jerusalem, and all the princes, and all the mighty men of valour, ten thousand captives, and all the craftsmen and the smiths; none remained, except the poorest people of the land. And he carried away Jehoi′achin to 15 Babylon; the king's mother, the king's wives, his officials, and the chief men of the land, he took into captivity from Jerusalem to Babylon. And the king of Babylon brought 16 captive to Babylon all the men of valour, seven thousand, and the craftsmen and the smiths, one thousand, all of them strong and fit for war. And the king of Babylon made 17 Mattani′ah, Jehoi′achin's uncle, king in his stead, and changed his name to Zedeki′ah.

Zedeki′ah was twenty-one years old when 18 he became king, and he reigned eleven years in Jerusalem. His mother's name was Hamu′tal the daughter of Jeremiah of Libnah. And he did what was evil in the 19 sight of the LORD, according to all that Jehoi′akim had done. For because of the 20 anger of the LORD it came to the point in Jerusalem and Judah that he cast them out from his presence.

And Zedeki′ah rebelled against the king of Babylon.

And in the ninth year of his reign, in the 25 tenth month, on the tenth day of the month, Nebuchadnez′zar king of Babylon came with all his army against Jerusalem, and laid siege

to it; and they built siegeworks against it
2 round about. So the city was besieged till the
3 eleventh year of King Zedeki′ah. On the
ninth day of the fourth month the famine was
so severe in the city that there was no food
4 for the people of the land. Then a breach
was made in the city; the king with all the
men of war fled[k] by night by the way of the
gate between the two walls, by the king's
garden, though the Chalde′ans were around
the city. And they went in the direction of
5 the Arabah. But the army of the Chalde′ans
pursued the king, and overtook him in the
plains of Jericho; and all his army was
6 scattered from him. Then they captured the
king, and brought him up to the king of
Babylon at Riblah, who passed sentence
7 upon him. They slew the sons of Zedeki′ah
before his eyes, and put out the eyes of
Zedeki′ah, and bound him in fetters, and
took him to Babylon.
8 In the fifth month, on the seventh day of
the month—which was the nineteenth year
of King Nebuchadnez′zar, king of Babylon—Nebu′zarad′an, the captain of the bodyguard, a servant of the king of Babylon, came
9 to Jerusalem. And he burned the house of
the LORD, and the king's house and all the
houses of Jerusalem; every great house he
10 burned down. And all the army of the
Chalde′ans, who were with the captain of the
guard, broke down the walls around Jeru-
11 salem. And the rest of the people who were
left in the city and the deserters who had
deserted to the king of Babylon, together
with the rest of the multitude, Nebu′zarad′an
the captain of the guard carried into exile.
12 But the captain of the guard left some of the
poorest of the land to be vinedressers and
ploughmen.
13 And the pillars of bronze that were in the
house of the LORD, and the stands and
the bronze sea that were in the house of the
LORD, the Chalde′ans broke in pieces, and
14 carried the bronze to Babylon. And they
took away the pots, and the shovels, and the
snuffers, and the dishes for incense and all
the vessels of bronze used in the temple
15 service, the firepans also, and the bowls.
What was of gold the captain of the guard
took away as gold, and what was of silver, as
16 silver. As for the two pillars, the one sea, and
the stands, which Solomon had made for the
house of the LORD, the bronze of all these
17 vessels was beyond weight. The height of
the one pillar was eighteen cubits, and upon
it was a capital of bronze; the height of the
capital was three cubits; a network and
pomegranates, all of bronze, were upon the
capital round about. And the second pillar
had the like, with the network.

18 And the captain of the guard took Serai′ah
the chief priest, and Zephani′ah the second
priest, and the three keepers of the threshold;
19 and from the city he took an officer who had
been in command of the men of war, and five
men of the king's council who were found in
the city; and the secretary of the commander
of the army who mustered the people of the
land; and sixty men of the people of the land
who were found in the city. And Nebu-
20 zarad′an the captain of the guard took them,
and brought them to the king of Babylon at
Riblah. And the king of Babylon smote
21 them, and put them to death at Riblah in the
land of Hamath. So Judah was taken into
exile out of its land.

22 And over the people who remained in the
land of Judah, whom Nebuchadnez′zar king
of Babylon had left, he appointed Gedali′ah
the son of Ahi′kam, son of Shaphan, gover-
23 nor. Now when all the captains of the forces
in the open country[l] and their men heard
that the king of Babylon had appointed
Gedali′ah governor, they came with their
men to Gedali′ah at Mizpah, namely,
Ish′mael the son of Nethani′ah, and Joha′nan
the son of Kare′ah, and Serai′ah the son of
Tanhu′meth the Netoph′athite, and Ja-
azani′ah the son of the Ma-ac′athite. And
24 Gedali′ah swore to them and their men,
saying, "Do not be afraid because of the
Chalde′an officials; dwell in the land, and
serve the king of Babylon, and it shall be well
25 with you." But in the seventh month, Ish′mael the son of Nethani′ah, son of
Elish′ama, of the royal family, came with ten
men, and attacked and killed Gedali′ah and
the Jews and the Chalde′ans who were with
26 him at Mizpah. Then all the people, both
small and great, and the captains of the forces
arose, and went to Egypt; for they were
afraid of the Chalde′ans.

27 And in the thirty-seventh year of the exile
of Jehoi′achin king of Judah, in the twelfth
month, on the twenty-seventh day of the
month, Evil-mero′dach king of Babylon, in
the year that he began to reign, graciously
freed Jehoi′achin king of Judah from prison;
28 and he spoke kindly to him, and gave him a
seat above the seats of the kings who were
29 with him in Babylon. So Jehoi′achin put off
his prison garments. And every day of his
30 life he dined regularly at the king's table; and
for his allowance, a regular allowance was
given him by the king, every day a portion, as
long as he lived.

---

[k] Gk Compare Jer 39.4; 52.7: Heb lacks *the king* and *fled*   [l] With Jer 40.7: Heb lacks *in the open country*
25.22–26: Jer 40.7–43.7.   **25.27–30:** Jer 52.31–34.

Babylon

THE FIRST BOOK OF THE
CHRONICLES

OFFICIAL LISTS

Adam's descendants

2 ADAM, Seth, Enosh; Kenan,
3 Mahal'alel, Jared; Enoch,
Methu'selah, Lamech;
4 Noah, Shem, Ham, and Japheth.
5 The sons of Japheth: Gomer,
Magog, Madai, Javan, Tubal,
6 Meshech, and Tiras. The sons of
Gomer: Ash'kenaz, Diphath, and
7 Togar'mah. The sons of Javan:
Eli'shah, Tarshish, Kittim, and
Ro'danim.
8 The sons of Ham: Cush, Egypt,
9 Put, and Canaan. The sons of
Cush: Seba, Hav'i-lah, Sabta,
Ra'ama, and Sab'teca. The sons
of Ra'amah: Sheba and Dedan.
10 Cush was the father of Nimrod;
he began to be a mighty one in the
earth.
11 Egypt was the father of Ludim,
An'amim, Leha'bim, Naph-tu'-
12 him, Pathru'sim, Caslu'him
(whence came the Philistines), and
Caph'torim.
13 Canaan was the father of Sidon
14 his first-born, and Heth, and
the Jeb'usites, the Amorites, the
15 Gir'gashites, the Hivites, the
16 Arkites, the Sinites, the Ar'vadites, the Zem'arites, and the
Ha'mathites.
17 The sons of Shem: Elam, Asshur, Arpach'shad, Lud, Aram,
Uz, Hul, Gether, and Meshech.
18 Arpach'shad was the father of
Shelah; and Shelah was the father
19 of Eber. To Eber were born two
sons: the name of the one was
Peleg (for in his days the earth
was divided), and the name of his
20 brother Joktan. Joktan was the
father of Almo'dad, Sheleph,
21 Hazarma'veth, Jerah, Hador'am,
22 Uzal, Diklah, Ebal, Abim'a-el,
23 Sheba, Ophir, Hav'i-lah, and
Jobab; all these were the sons of
Joktan.
24 Shem, Arpach'shad, Shelah;

25 Eber, Peleg, Re'u; Serug,
26 Nahor, Terah; Abram, that is,
27 Abraham.
28 The sons of Abraham: Isaac and
29 Ish'mael. These are their genealogies: the first-born of Ish'mael,
Neba'ioth; and Kedar, Adbeel,
30 Mibsam, Mishma, Dumah,
31 Massa, Hadad, Tema, Jetur,
Naphish, and Ked'emah. These
32 are the sons of Ish'mael. The
sons of Ketu'rah, Abraham's
concubine: she bore Zimran, Jokshan, Medan, Mid'ian, Ishbak,
and Shuah. The sons of Jokshan:
33 Sheba and Dedan. The sons of
Mid'ian: Ephah, Epher, Hanoch,
Abi'da, and Elda'ah. All these
were the descendants of Ketu'rah.
34 Abraham was the father of
Isaac. The sons of Isaac: Esau
35 and Israel. The sons of Esau:
El'iphaz, Reu'el, Je'ush, Jalam,
36 and Korah. The sons of El'iphaz:
Teman, Omar, Zephi, Gatam,
Kenaz, Timna, and Am'alek.
37 The sons of Reu'el: Nahath,
Zerah, Shammah, and Mizzah.
38 The sons of Se'ir: Lotan,
Shobal, Zib'eon, Anah, Dishon,
39 Ezer, and Dishan. The sons of
Lotan: Hori and Homam; and
40 Lotan's sister was Timna. The
sons of Shobal: Al'ian, Man'-
ahath, Ebal, Shephi, and Onam.
41 The sons of Zib'eon: Ai'ah and
Anah. The sons of Anah:
Dishon. The sons of Dishon:
42 Hamran, Eshban, Ithran, and
Cheran. The sons of Ezer:
Bilhan, Za'avan, and Ja'akan. The
sons of Dishan: Uz and Aran.

Kings of Edom

43 These are the kings who reigned
in the land of Edom before any
king reigned over the Israelites:
Bela the son of Be'or, the name of
44 whose city was Din'habah. When
Bela died, Jobab the son of Zerah
of Bozrah reigned in his stead.

When Jobab died, Husham of the 4
land of the Te'manites reigned in
his stead. When Husham died, 46
defeated Mid'ian in the country of
Moab, reigned in his stead; and
the name of his city was Avith.
When Hadad died, Samlah of 47
Masre'kah reigned in his stead.
When Samlah died, Sha'ul of 48
Reho'both on the Euphra'tes
reigned in his stead. When Sha'ul 49
died, Ba'al-ha'nan, the son of
Achbor, reigned in his stead.
When Ba'al-ha'nan died, Hadad 50
reigned in his stead; and the name
of his city was Pa'i, and his wife's
name Mehet'abel the daughter of
Matred, the daughter of Me'-
zahab. And Hadad died.   51
The chiefs of Edom were: chiefs
Timna, Al'iah, Jetheth, Oholi- 52
ba'mah, Elah, Pinon, Kenaz, 53
Teman, Mibzar, Mag'diel, and 54
Iram; these are the chiefs of
Edom.

Sons of Israel

These are the sons of Israel: 2
Reuben, Simeon, Levi, Judah,
Is'sachar, Zeb'ulun, Dan, Joseph, 2
Benjamin, Naph'tali, Gad, and
Asher. The sons of Judah: Er, 3
Onan, and Shelah; these three
Bath-shu'a the Canaanitess bore
to him. Now Er, Judah's first-
born, was wicked in the sight of
the LORD, and he slew him. His 4
daughter-in-law Tamar also bore
him Perez and Zerah. Judah had
five sons in all.
The sons of Perez: Hezron and 5
Hamul. The sons of Zerah: 6
Zimri, Ethan, Heman, Calcol, and
Dara, five in all. The sons of 7
Carmi: Achar, the troubler of
Israel, who transgressed in the
matter of the devoted thing; and 8
Ethan's son was Azari'ah.
The sons of Hezron, that were 9
born to him: Jerah'meel, Ram,

1.1-54: Gen 5; 10; 11; 25; 36.   2.1-2: Gen 35.23-26.   2.3-4: Gen 38.3-7, 29-30; Num 26.19-20.
2.5: Gen 46.12; Num 26.21.   2.6-8: Josh 7.1; 1 Kings 4.31.

and Chelu'bai. Ram was the father of Ammin'adab, and Ammin'adab was the father of Nahshon, prince of the sons of Judah. Nahshon was the father of Salma, Salma of Bo'az, Bo'az of Obed, Obed of Jesse. Jesse the father of Eli'ab his first-born, Abin'adab the second, Shim'e-a the third, Nethan'el the fourth, Raddai the fifth, Ozem the sixth, David the seventh; and their sisters were Zeru'iah and Ab'igail. The sons of Zeru'iah: Abi'shai, Jo'ab, and As'ahel, three. Ab'igail bore Ama'sa, and the father of Ama'sa was Jether the Ish'maelite.

Caleb the son of Hezron had children by his wife Azu'bah, and by Jer'ioth; and these were her sons: Jesher, Shobab, and Ardon. When Azu'bah died, Caleb married Ephrath, who bore him Hur. Hur was the father of Uri, and Uri was the father of Bez'alel.

Afterward Hezron went in to the daughter of Machir the father of Gilead, whom he married when he was sixty years old; and she bore him Segub; and Segub was the father of Ja'ir, who had twenty-three cities in the land of Gilead. But Geshur and Aram took from them Havvothja'ir, Kenath and its villages, sixty towns. All these were descendants of Machir, the father of Gilead. After the death of Hezron, Caleb went in to Eph'rathah,ᵃ the wife of Hezron his father, and she bore him Ashhur, the father of Teko'a.

The sons of Jerah'meel, the first-born of Hezron: Ram, his first-born, Bunah, Oren, Ozem, and Ahi'jah. Jerah'meel also had another wife, whose name was At'arah; she was the mother of Onam. The sons of Ram, the first-born of Jerah'meel: Ma'az, Jamin, and Eker. The sons of Onam: Sham'mai and Jada. The sons of Sham'mai: Nadab and Abi'shur. The name of Abi'shur's wife was Ab'ihail, and she bore him Ahban and Molid. The sons of Nadab: Seled and Ap'pa-im; and Seled died childless. The sons of Ap'pa-im: Ishi. The sons of Ishi: Sheshan. The sons of Sheshan: Ahlai. The sons of Jada, Sham'mai's brother: Jether and Jonathan; and Jether died childless. The sons of Jonathan: Peleth and Zaza. These were the descendants of Jerah'meel. Now Sheshan had no sons, only daughters; but Sheshan had an Egyptian slave, whose name was Jarha. So Sheshan gave his daughter in marriage to Jarha his slave; and she bore him Attai. Attai was the father of Nathan and Nathan of Zabad, and the father of Ephlal, and Ephlal of Obed. Obed was the father of Jehu, and Jehu of Azari'ah. Azari'ah was the father of Helez, and Helez of Ele-a'sah. Ele-a'sah was the father of Sismai, and Sismai of Shallum. Shallum was the father of Jekami'ah, and Jekami'ah of Elish'ama.

The sons of Caleb the brother of Jerah'meel: Mare'shahᵇ his first-born, who was the father of Ziph. The sons of Mare'shah: Hebron.ᶜ The sons of Hebron: Korah, Tap'pu-ah, Rekem, and Shema. Shema was the father of Raham, the father of Jor'ke-am; and Rekem was the father of Sham'mai. The son of Sham'mai: Ma'on; and Ma'on was the father of Beth-zur. Ephah also, Caleb's concubine, bore Haran, Moza, and Gazez; and Haran was the father of Gazez. The sons of Jah'dai: Regem, Jotham, Geshan, Pelet, Ephah, and Sha'aph. Ma'acah, Caleb's concubine, bore Sheber and Tir'hanah. She also bore Sha'aph the father of Madman'nah, Sheva the father of Machbe'nah and the father of Gib'e-a; and the daughter of Caleb was Achsah. These were the descendants of Caleb.

The sonsᵈ of Hur the first-born of Eph'rathah: Shobal the father of Kir'iath-je'arim, Salma, father of Bethlehem, and Hareph the father of Beth-gader. Shobal the father of Kir'iath-je'arim had other sons: Haro'eh, half of the Menu'hoth. And the families of Kir'iath-je'arim: the Ithrites, the Puthites, the Shu'ma-thites, and the Mish'ra-ites; from these came the Zo'rathites and the Esh'taol-ites. The sons of Salma: Bethlehem, the Netoph'athites, At'roth-beth-jo'ab, and half of the Man'aha'thites, the Zorites. The families also of the scribes that dwelt at Jabez: the Ti'rathites, the Shim'eathites, and the Su'cath-ites. These are the Ken'ites who came from Hammath, the father of the house of Rechab.

House of David

3 These are the sons of David that were born to him in Hebron: the first-born Amnon, by Ahin'o-am the Jez'reelitess; the second Daniel, by Ab'igail the Car'mel-itess; the third Ab'salom, whose mother was Ma'acah, the daughter of Talmai, king of Geshur; the fourth Adoni'jah, whose mother was Haggith; the fifth Shepha-ti'ah, by Abi'tal; the sixth Ith'ream, by his wife Eglah; six were born to him in Hebron, where he reigned for seven years and six months. And he reigned thirty-three years in Jerusalem. These were born to him in Jeru-salem: Shim'e-a, Shobab, Nathan, and Solomon, four by Bath-shu'a, the daughter of Am'miel; then Ibhar, Elish'ama, Eliph'elet, Nogah, Nepheg, Japhi'a, Elish'ama, Eli'ada, and Eliph'elet, nine. All these were David's sons, besides the sons of the concubines; and Tamar was their sister.

The descendants of Solomon: Rehobo'am, Abi'jah his son, Asa his son, Jehosh'aphat his son, Joram his son, Ahazi'ah his son, Jo'ash his son, Amazi'ah his son, Azari'ah his son, Jotham his son, Ahaz his son, Hezeki'ah his son, Manas'seh his son, Amon his son, Josi'ah his son. The sons of Josi'ah: Joha'nan the first-born, the second Jehoi'akim, the third Zedeki'ah, the fourth Shal-lum. The descendants of Jehoi'-akim: Jeconi'ah his son, Zedeki'ah his son; and the sons of Je-coni'ah, the captive: She-al'ti-el his son, Malchi'ram, Peda'iah, She-naz'zar, Jekami'ah, Hosh'ama, and Nedabi'ah; and the sons of Peda'-iah: Zerub'babel and Shim'e-i; and the sons of Zerub'babel: Meshul'lam and Hanani'ah, and Shelo'mith was their sister; and Hashu'bah, Ohel, Berechi'ah, Hasadi'ah, and Ju'shab-he'sed, five. The sons of Hanani'ah: Pelati'ah and Jeshai'ah, his sonᵉ Repha'iah, his sonᵉ Arnan, his sonᵉ Obadi'ah, his sonᵉ Shecani'-ah. The sons of Shecani'ah: Shemai'ah. And the sons of Shemai'ah: Hattush, Igal, Bari'-ah, Neari'ah, and Shaphat, six. The sons of Neari'ah: Eli-o-e'nai, Hizki'ah, and Azri'kam, three. The sons of Eli-o-e'nai: Hodavi'ah, Eli'ashib, Pelai'ah, Akkub, Joha'nan, Dela'iah, and Ana'ni, seven.

Sons of Judah

The sons of Judah: Perez, Hezron, Carmi, Hur, and Shobal. Re-a'iah the son of Shobal was the father of Jahath, and Jahath was the father of Ahu'mai and Lahad. These were the families of the Zo'rathites. These were the sonsᶠ of Etam: Jezreel, Ishma, and Idbash; and the name of their sister was Haz-zelelpo'ni, and Penu'el was the father of Gedor, and Ezer the father of Hushah. These were the sons of Hur, the first-born of Eph'rathah, the father of Bethlehem. Ashhur, the father of Teko'a, had two wives, Helah and Na'arah; Na'arah bore him Ahuz'zam, Hepher, Te'meni, and Haahash'tari. These were the sons of Na'arah. The sons of Helah: Zereth, Izhar, and Eth-nan. Koz was the father of Anub, Zobe'bah, and the families of Ahar'hel the son of Harum. Jabez was more honourable than his brothers; and his mother called his name Jabez, saying, "Because I bore him in pain." Jabez called on the God of Israel, saying, "Oh

---

ᵃ Gk Vg: Heb *in Caleb Ephrathah*   ᵇ Gk: Heb *Mesha*   ᶜ Heb *the father of Hebron*   ᵈ Gk Vg: Heb *son*
ᵉ Gk Compare Syr Vg: Heb *sons of*   ᶠ Gk Compare Vg: Heb *father*
3.1–9: 2 Sam 3.2–5; 5.14–16; 1 Chron 14.3–7.   3.4: 2 Sam 5.4–5.

that thou wouldst bless me and enlarge my border, and that thy hand might be with me, and that thou wouldst keep me from harm so that it might not hurt me!" And God granted what he asked. 11 Chelub, the brother of Shuhah, was the father of Mehir, who was 12 the father of Beth-ra'pha, Pase'ah, and Tehin'nah the father of Irna'hash. These are the men of 13 Recah. The sons of Kenaz: Oth'ni-el and Serai'ah; and the sons of Oth'ni-el: Hathath and 14 Meo'nothai.g Meo'nothai was the father of Ophrah; and Serai'ah was the father of Jo'ab the father of Ge-har'ashim,h so-called be- 15 cause they were craftsmen. The sons of Caleb the son of Jephun'neh: Iru, Elah, and Na'am; and 16 the sons of Elah: Kenaz. The sons of Jehal'lelel: Ziph, Ziphah, 17 Tir'i-a, and As'arel. The sons of Ezrah: Jether, Mered, Epher, and Jalon. These are the sons of Bith'i-ah, the daughter of Pharaoh, whom Mered married;i and she conceived and borej Miriam, Sham'mai, and Ishbah, the father 18 of Eshtemo'a. And his Jewish wife bore Jered the father of Gedor, Heber the father of Soco, and Jeku'thiel the father of 19 Zano'ah. The sons of the wife of Hodi'ah, the sister of Naham, were the fathers of Kei'lah the Garmite and Eshtemo'a the 20 Ma-ac'athite. The sons of Shimon: Amnon, Rinnah, Benha'nan, and Tilon. The sons of Ishi: Zoheth and Ben-zo'heth. 21 The sons of Shelah the son of Judah: Er the father of Lecah, La'adah the father of Mare'shah, and the families of the house of linen workers at Beth-ashbe'a; 22 and Jokim, and the men of Coze'ba, and Jo'ash, and Saraph, who ruled in Moab and returned to Lehemk (now the records are 23 ancient). These were the potters and inhabitants of Neta'im and Gede'rah; they dwelt there with the king for his work.

Sons of Simeon

24 The sons of Simeon: Nem'u-el, Jamin, Jarib, Zerah, Sha'ul; 25 Shallum was his son, Mibsam his 26 son, Mishma his son. The sons of Mishma: Ham'mu-el his son, Zaccur his son, Shim'e-i his son. 27 Shim'e-i had sixteen sons and six daughters; but his brothers had not many children, nor did all their family multiply like the men 28 of Judah. They dwelt in Beersheba, Mola'dah, Ha'zar-shu'al, 29 Bilhah, Ezem, Tolad, Bethu'el, 30 Hormah, Ziklag, Beth-mar'ca- 31 both, Ha'zar-su'sim, Beth-biri, and Sha-ara'im. These were their 32 cities until David reigned. And their villages were Etam, A'in, Rimmon, Tochen, and Ashan, 33 five cities, along with all their villages which were round about these cities as far as Ba'al. These were their settlements, and they kept a genealogical record. 34 Mesho'bab, Jamlech, Joshah the 35 son of Amazi'ah, Jo'el, Jehu the son of Joshibi'ah, son of Serai'- 36 ah, son of As'i-el, Eli-o-e'nai, Ja-ako'bah, Jeshohai'ah, Asa'iah, 37 Ad'i-el, Jesim'i-el, Benai'ah, Ziza the son of Shiphi, son of Allon, son of Jedai'ah, son of Shimri, son 38 of Shemai'ah—these mentioned by name were princes in their families, and their fathers' houses 39 increased greatly. They journeyed to the entrance of Gedor, to 40 the east side of the valley, to seek pasture for their flocks, where they found rich, good pasture, and the land was very broad, quiet, and peaceful; for the former inhabitants there belonged to 41 Ham. These, registered by name, came in the days of Hezeki'ah, king of Judah, and destroyed their tents and the Me-u'nim who were found there, and exterminated them to this day, and settled in their place, because there was pasture there for their flocks. 42 And some of them, five hundred men of the Simeonites, went to Mount Se'ir, having as their leaders Pelati'ah, Neari'ah, Repha'iah, and Uz'ziel, the sons 43 of Ishi; and they destroyed the remnant of the Amal'ekites that had escaped, and they have dwelt there to this day.

Sons of Reuben

5 The sons of Reuben the firstborn of Israel (for he was the first-born; but because he polluted his father's couch, his birthright was given to the sons of Joseph the son of Israel, so that he is not enrolled in the genealogy according to the birthright; 2 though Judah became strong among his brothers and a prince was from him, yet the birthright 3 belonged to Joseph), the sons of Reuben, the first-born of Israel: Hanoch, Pallu, Hezron, and 4 Carmi. The sons of Jo'el: Shemai'ah his son, Gog his son, 5 Shim'e-i his son, Micah his son, Re-a'iah his son, Ba'al his 6 son, Be-e'rah his son, whom Til'gath-pilne'ser king of Assyria carried away into exile; he was a 7 chieftain of the Reubenites. And his kinsmen by their families, when the genealogy of their generations was reckoned: the chief, Je-i'el, 8 and Zechari'ah, and Bela the son of Azaz, son of Shema, son of Jo'el, who dwelt in Aro'er, as far 9 as Nebo and Ba'al-me'on. He also dwelt to the east as far as the entrance of the desert this side of the Euphra'tes, because their cattle had multiplied in the land of Gilead. And in the days of Saul they made war on the Hagrites, who fell by their hand; and they dwelt in their tents throughout all the region east of Gilead.

The sons of Gad dwelt over against them in the land of Bashan as far as Sal'ecah: Jo'el the chief, Shapham the second, Ja'nai, and Shaphat in Bashan. And their kinsmen according to their fathers' houses: Michael, Meshul'lam, Sheba, Jo'rai, Jacan, Zi'a, and Eber, seven. These were the sons of Ab'ihail the son of Huri, son of Jaro'ah, son of Gilead, son of Michael, son of Jeshish'ai, son of Jahdo, son of Buz; Ahi the son of Ab'di-el, son of Guni, was chief in their fathers' houses; and they dwelt in Gilead, in Bashan and in its towns, and in all the pasture lands of Sharon to their limits. All of these were enrolled by genealogies in the days of Jotham king of Judah, and in the days of Jerobo'am king of Israel.

The Reubenites, the Gadites, and the half-tribe of Manas'seh had valiant men, who carried shield and sword, and drew the bow, expert in war, forty-four thousand seven hundred and sixty, ready for service. They made war upon the Hagrites, Jetur, Naphish, and Nodab; and when they received help against them, the Hagrites and all who were with them were given into their hands, for they cried to God in the battle, and he granted their entreaty because they trusted in him. They carried off their livestock: fifty thousand of their camels, two hundred and fifty thousand sheep, two thousand asses, and a hundred thousand men alive. For many fell slain, because the war was of God. And they dwelt in their place until the exile.

The members of the half-tribe of Manas'seh dwelt in the land; they were very numerous from Bashan to Ba'al-her'mon, Senir, and Mount Hermon. These were the heads of their fathers' houses: Epher,m Ishi, Eli'el, Az'ri-el, Jeremiah, Hodavi'ah, and Jah'di-el, mighty warriors, famous men, heads of their fathers' houses. But they transgressed against the God of their fathers, and played the harlot after the gods of the peoples of the land, whom God had destroyed before them. So the God of Israel stirred up the spirit of Pul king of Assyria, the spirit of Til'gath-pilneser king of Assyria, and he carried them away, namely, the Reubenites, the Gadites, and the half-tribe of Manas'seh, and

---

g Gk Vg: Heb lacks Meonothai   h That is Valley of craftsmen
i The clause: These are . . . married is transposed from verse 18   j Heb lacks and bore
k Vg Compare Gk: Heb and Jashubi-lahem   l Or matters   m Gk Vg: Heb and Epher
4.24: Gen 46.10; Ex 6.15; Num 26.12–13.   4.28–33: Josh 19.2–8.   5.1–26: Gen 46.9; Num 26.5–6.

brought them to Halah, Habor,
Hara, and the river Gozan, to this
day.

Sons of Levi

[n] The sons of Levi: Gershom,
Kohath, and Merar'i. The sons
of Kohath: Amram, Izhar, He-
bron, and Uz'ziel. The children
of Amram: Aaron, Moses, and
Miriam. The sons of Aaron:
Nadab, Abi'hu, Elea'zar, and
Ith'amar. Elea'zar was the father
of Phin'ehas, Phin'ehas of
Abishu'a, Abishu'a of Bukki,
Bukki of Uzzi, Uzzi of Zerahi'ah,
Zerahi'ah of Mera'ioth, Mera'ioth
of Amari'ah, Amari'ah of Ahi'tub,
Ahi'tub of Zadok, Zadok of
Ahim'a-az, Ahim'a-az of Aza-
ri'ah, Azari'ah of Joha'nan, and
Joha'nan of Azari'ah (it was he
who served as priest in the house
that Solomon built in Jerusalem).
Azari'ah was the father of Ama-
ri'ah, Amari'ah of Ahi'tub,
Ahi'tub of Zadok, Zadok of
Shallum, Shallum of Hilki'ah,
Hilki'ah of Azari'ah, Azari'ah of
Sera'iah, Sera'iah of Jehoz'adak;
and Jehoz'adak went into exile
when the LORD sent Judah and
Jerusalem into exile by the hand
of Nebuchadnez'zar.

50 The sons of Levi: Gershom,
Kohath, and Merar'i. And these
are the names of the sons of
Gershom: Libni and Shim'e-i.
The sons of Kohath: Amram,
Izhar, Hebron, and Uz'ziel. The
sons of Merar'i: Mahli and
Mushi. These are the families of
the Levites according to their
fathers. Of Gershom: Libni his
son, Jahath his son, Zimmah his
son, Jo'ah his son, Iddo his son,
Zerah his son, Je-ath'erai his son.
The sons of Kohath: Ammin'-
adab his son, Korah his son, Assir
his son, Elka'nah his son, Ebi'-
asaph his son, Assir his son,
Tahath his son, Uri'el his son,
Uzzi'ah his son, and Sha'ul his
son. The sons of Elka'nah:
Ama'sai and Ahi'moth, Elka'nah
his son, Zophai his son, Nahath
his son, Eli'ab his son, Jero'-
ham his son, Elka'nah his son.
The sons of Samuel: Jo'el[p] his
first-born, the second Abi'jah.[q]
The sons of Merar'i: Mahli,
Libni his son, Shim'e-i his son,
Uzzah his son, Shim'e-a his son,
Haggi'ah his son, and Asa'iah his
son.

These are the men whom David
put in charge of the service of
song in the house of the LORD,
after the ark rested there. They
ministered with song before the
tabernacle of the tent of meeting,
until Solomon had built the house
of the LORD in Jerusalem; and
they performed their service in
due order. These are the men
who served and their sons. Of the
sons of the Ko'hathites: Heman

the singer the son of Jo'el, son of
34 Samuel, son of Elka'nah, son of
35 Jero'ham, son of Eli'el, son
of To'ah, son of Zuph, son of
36 Elka'nah, son of Mahath, son of
Ama'sai, son of Elka'nah, son
37 of Jo'el, son of Azari'ah, son of
Zephani'ah, son of Tahath, son of
38 Assir, son of Ebi'asaph, son
of Korah, son of Izhar, son of
39 Kohath, son of Levi, son of Israel;
and his brother Asaph, who stood
on his right hand, namely, Asaph
40 the son of Berechi'ah, son of
Shim'e-a, son of Michael, son of
41 Ba-ase'iah, son of Malchi'jah, son
of Ethni, son of Zerah, son of
42 Adai'ah, son of Ethan, son of
Zimmah, son of Shim'e-i, son
43 of Jahath, son of Gershom, son of
44 Levi. On the left hand were their
brethren the sons of Merar'i:
Ethan the son of Kishi, son of
45 Abdi; son of Malluch, son of
Hashabi'ah, son of Amazi'ah, son
46 of Hilki'ah, son of Amzi, son of
47 Bani, son of Shemer, son
of Mahli, son of Mushi, son of
48 Merar'i, son of Levi; and their
brethren the Levites were appointed for all the service of the
tabernacle of the house of God.

Sons of Aaron

49 But Aaron and his sons made
offerings upon the altar of burnt
offering and upon the altar of
incense for all the work of the
most holy place, and to make
50 atonement for Israel, according to
all that Moses the servant of God
had commanded. These are the
sons of Aaron: Elea'zar his son,
Phin'ehas his son, Abishu'a his
51 son, Bukki his son, Uzzi his son,
52 Zerahi'ah his son, Mera'ioth his
53 son, Amari'ah his son, Ahi'tub his
son, Zadok his son, Ahim'a-az
his son.

54 These are their dwelling places
according to their settlements
within their borders: to the
sons of Aaron of the families
of Ko'hathites, for theirs was the
55 lot, to them they gave Hebron in
the land of Judah and its sur-
56 rounding pasture lands, but the
fields of the city and its villages
57 they gave to Caleb the son of
Jephun'neh. To the sons of
Aaron they gave the cities
of refuge: Hebron, Libnah with
its pasture lands, Jattir, Eshtemo'a with its pasture lands,
58 Hilen with its pasture lands,
59 Debir with its pasture lands, Ashan with its pasture lands, and
Beth-she'mesh with its pasture
60 lands; and from the tribe of Benjamin, Geba with its pasture
lands, Al'emeth with its pasture
lands, and An'athoth with its
pasture lands. All their cities
throughout their families were
61 thirteen.

To the rest of the Ko'hathites
were given by lot out of the family

of the tribe, out of the half-tribe,
the half of Manas'seh, ten cities.
62 To the Gershomites according to
their families were allotted thirteen cities out of the tribes of
Is'sachar, Asher, Naph'tali, and
63 Manas'seh in Bashan. To the
Merar'ites according to their
families were allotted twelve cities
out of the tribes of Reuben, Gad,
64 and Zeb'ulun. So the people of
Israel gave the Levites the cities
65 with their pasture lands. They
also gave them by lot out of the
tribes of Judah, Simeon, and Benjamin these cities which are men-
66 tioned by name.
And some of the families of the
sons of Kohath had cities of their
67 territory out of the tribe of
E'phraim. They were given the
cities of refuge: Shechem with its
pasture lands in the hill country of
68 E'phraim, Gezer with its pasture
lands, Jok'meam with its pas-
69 ture lands, Ai'jalon with its pasture lands, Gath-rim'mon with its
70 pasture lands, and out of the
half-tribe of Manas'seh, Aner
with its pasture lands, and Bil'e-
am with its pasture lands, for the
rest of the families of the Ko'-
hathites.
71 To the Gershomites were given
out of the half-tribe of Manas'-
seh: Golan in Bashan with its
pasture lands and Ash'taroth with
72 its pasture lands; and out of the
tribe of Is'sachar: Kedesh with its
pasture lands, Dab'erath with its
73 pasture lands, Ramoth with
its pasture lands, and Anem with
74 its pasture lands; out of the tribe
of Asher: Mashal with its pasture
lands, Abdon with its pasture
75 lands, Hukok with its pasture lands, and Rehob with its
76 pasture lands; and out of the tribe
of Naph'tali: Kedesh in Galilee
with its pasture lands, Ham'mon
with its pasture lands, and Kiri-
77 atha'im with its pasture lands. To
the rest of the Merar'ites were
allotted out of the tribe of
Zeb'ulun: Rim'mono with its
pasture lands, Tabor with its
78 pasture lands, and beyond the
Jordan at Jericho, on the east side
of the Jordan, out of the tribe of
Reuben: Bezer in the steppe with
its pasture lands, Jahzah with its
79 pasture lands, Ked'emoth with its
pasture lands, and Meph'a-ath
80 with its pasture lands; and out of
the tribe of Gad: Ramoth in
Gilead with its pasture lands,
Mahana'im with its pasture lands,
81 Heshbon with its pasture
lands, and Jazer with its pasture
lands.

Sons of Issachar

7 The sons[r] of Is'sachar: Tola,
Pu'ah, Jashub, and Shimron,
2 four. The sons of Tola: Uzzi,
Repha'iah, Je'ri-el, Jah'mai,

---

[n] Ch 5.27 in Heb   [o] Ch 6.1 in Heb   [p] Gk Syr Compare verse 33 and 1 Sam 8.2: Heb lacks *Joel*
[q] Heb *and Abijah*   [r] Syr Compare Vg: Heb *and to the sons*
6.1–15: Gen 46.11; Ex 6.16–20; Num 3.2.   6.16–53: Ex 6.16–24.   6.54–81: Josh 21.1–42.

Ibsam, and Shemu′el, heads of their fathers′ houses, namely of Tola, mighty warriors of their generations, their number in the days of David being twenty-two 3 thousand six hundred. The sons of Uzzi: Izrahi′ah. And the sons of Izrahi′ah: Michael, Obadi′ah, Jo′el, and Isshi′ah, five, all of 4 them chief men; and along with them, by their generations, according to their fathers′ houses, were units of the army for war, thirty-six thousand, for they had 5 many wives and sons. Their kinsmen belonging to all the families of Is′sachar were in all eighty-seven thousand mighty warriors, enrolled by genealogy.

Benjamin and Naphtali

6 The sons of Benjamin: Bela, 7 Becher, and Jedi′a-el, three. The sons of Bela: Ezbon, Uzzi, Uz′ziel, Jer′imoth, and Iri, five, heads of fathers′ houses, mighty warriors; and their enrolment by genealogies was twenty-two 8 thousand and thirty-four. The sons of Becher: Zemi′rah, Jo′ash, Elie′zer, Eli-o-e′nai, Omri, Jer′-emoth, Abi′jah, An′athoth, and Al′emeth. All these were the sons 9 of Becher; and their enrolment by genealogies, according to their generations, as heads of their fathers′ houses, mighty warriors, was twenty thousand two hun-10 dred. The sons of Jedi′a-el: Bilhan. And the sons of Bilhan: Je′ush, Benjamin, Ehud, Chena′-anah, Zethan, Tarshish, and 11 Ahish′ahar. All these were the sons of Jedi′a-el according to the heads of their fathers′ houses, mighty warriors, seventeen thousand and two hundred, ready for 12 service in war. And Shuppim and Huppim were the sons of Ir, Hushim the sons of Aher. 13 The sons of Naph′tali: Jah′zi-el, Guni, Jezer, and Shallum, the offspring of Bilhah.

Joseph′s family

14 The sons of Manas′seh: As′ri-el, whom his Aramean concubine bore; she bore Machir the father 15 of Gilead. And Machir took a wife for Huppim and for Shuppim. The name of his sister was Ma′acah. And the name of the second was Zelo′phehad; and 16 Zelo′phehad had daughters. And Ma′acah the wife of Machir bore a son, and she called his name Peresh; and the name of his brother was Sheresh; and his sons 17 were Ulam and Rakem. The sons of Ulam: Bedan. These were the sons of Gilead the son of Machir, 18 son of Manas′seh. And his sister Hammo′lecheth bore Ishhod, 19 Abie′zer, and Mahlah. The sons of Shemi′da were Ahi′an, Shechem, Likhi, and Ani′am.

20 The sons of E′phraim: Shuthe′-lah, and Bered his son, Tahath his 21 son, Ele-a′dah his son, Tahath his son, Zabad his son, Shuthe′lah his son, and Ezer and E′le-ad, whom the men of Gath who were born in the land slew, because 22 they came down to raid their cattle. And E′phraim their father mourned many days, and his 23 brothers came to comfort him. And E′phraim went in to his wife, and she conceived and bore a son; and he called his name Beri′ah, because evil had befallen his 24 house. His daughter was She′-erah, who built both Lower and Upper Beth-horon, and Uz′zen-25 she′erah. Rephah was his son, 26 Resheph his son, Telah his son, Tahan his son, Ladan his son, Ammi′hud his son, Elish′ama his 27 son, Nun his son, Joshua his son. 28 Their possessions and settlements were Bethel and its towns, and eastward Na′aran, and westward Gezer and its towns, Shechem and its towns, and Ayyah and its 29 towns; also along the borders of the Manas′sites, Beth-she′an and its towns, Ta′anach and its towns, Megid′do and its towns, Dor and its towns. In these dwelt the sons of Joseph the son of Israel.

Sons of Asher

30 The sons of Asher: Imnah, Ishvah, Ishvi, Beri′ah, and their 31 sister Serah. The sons of Beri′ah: Heber and Mal′chi-el, who was 32 the father of Bir′zaith. Heber was the father of Japhlet, Shomer, Hotham, and their sister Shu′a. 33 The sons of Japhlet: Pasach, Bimhal, and Ashvath. These are 34 the sons of Japhlet. The sons of Shemer his brother: Rohgah, 35 Jehub′bah, and Aram. The sons of Helem his brother: Zophah, 36 Imna, Shelesh, and Amal. The sons of Zophah: Su′ah, Har′-37 nepher, Shu′al, Beri, Imrah, 38 Bezer, Hod, Shamma, Shilshah, Ithran, and Be-e′ra. The sons of 39 Jether: Jephun′neh, Pispa, and 40 Ara. The sons of Ulla: Arah, Han′niel, and Rizi′a. All of these were men of Asher, heads of fathers′ houses, approved, mighty warriors, chief of the princes. Their number enrolled by genealogies, for service in war, was twenty-six thousand men.

Tribe of Benjamin

8 Benjamin was the father of Bela his first-born, Ashbel the second, 2 Ahar′ah the third, Nohah the 3 fourth and Rapha the fifth. And 4 Bela had sons: Addar, Gera, 5 Abi′hud, Abishu′a, Na′aman, 6 Aho′ah, Gera, Shephu′phan, and Huram. These are the sons of Ehud (they were heads of fathers′ houses of the inhabitants of Geba, and they were carried into exile to

Man′ahath): Na′aman,ᵍ Ahi′jah and Gera, that is, Heglam,ᵗ who was the father of Uzza and Ahi′hud. And Shahara′im had sons in the country of Moab after he had sent away Hushim and Ba′ara his wives. He had sons by Hodesh his wife: Jobab, Zib′i-a, Mesha, Malcam, Je′uz, Sachi′a, and Mirmah. These were his sons, heads of fathers′ houses. He also had sons by Hushim: Abi′tub and Elpa′al. The sons of Elpa′al: Eber, Misham, and Shemed, who built Ono and Lod with its towns, and Beri′ah and Shema (they were heads of fathers′ houses of the inhabitants of Ai′jalon, who put to flight the inhabitants of Gath); and Ahi′o, Shashak, and Jer′-emoth. Zebadi′ah, Arad, Eder, Michael, Ishpah, and Joha were sons of Beri′ah. Zebadi′ah, Meshul′lam, Hizki, Heber, Ish′-merai, Izli′ah, and Jobab were the sons of Elpa′al. Jakim, Zichri, Zabdi, Elie′nai, Zil′le-thai, Eli′el, Adai′ah, Bera′iah, and Shimrath were the sons of Shim′e-i. Ishpan, Eber, Eli′el, Abdon, Zichri, Hanan, Hanani′ah, Elam, Anthothi′jah, Iphde′iah, and Penu′el were the sons of Shashak. Sham′sherai, Shehari′ah, Athali′ah, Ja-areshi′ah, Eli′jah, and Zichri were the sons of Jero′ham. These were the heads of fathers′ houses, according to their generations, chief men. These dwelt in Jerusalem.

Je-i′elᵘ the father of Gibeon dwelt in Gibeon, and the name of his wife was Ma′acah. His first-born son: Abdon, then Zur, Kish, Ba′al, Nadab, Gedor, Ahi′o, Zecher, and Mikloth (he was the father of Shim′e-ah). Now these also dwelt opposite their kinsmen in Jerusalem, with their kinsmen.

House of Saul

Ner was the father of Kish, Kish of Saul, Saul of Jonathan, Mal′-chishu′a, Abin′adab, and Esh-ba′al; and the son of Jonathan was Mer′ib-ba′al; and Mer′ib-ba′al was the father of Micah. The sons of Micah: Pithon, Melech, Tare′a, and Ahaz. Ahaz was the father of Jeho′addah; and Jeho′-addah was the father of Al′emeth, Az′maveth, and Zimri; Zimri was the father of Moza. Moza was the father of Bin′e-a; Raphah was his son, Ele-a′sah his son, Azel his son. Azel had six sons, and these are their names: Azri′kam, Bo′cheru, Ish′mael, She-ari′ah, Obadi′ah, and Hanan. All these were the sons of Azel. The sons of Eshek his brother: Ulam his first-born, Je′ush the second, and Eliph′elet the third. The sons of Ulam were men who were mighty warriors, bowmen, having many sons and grandsons, one hundred and fifty. All these were Benjaminites.

ᵍ Heb and Naaman   ᵗ Or he carried them into exile
ᵘ Compare 9.35: Heb lacks Jeiel

Inhabitants of Jerusalem

So all Israel was enrolled by genealogies; and these are written in the Book of the Kings of Israel. And Judah was taken into exile in Babylon because of their unfaithfulness. Now the first to dwell again in their possessions in their cities were Israel, the priests, the Levites, and the temple servants. And some of the people of Judah, Benjamin, E'phraim, and Manas'seh dwelt in Jerusalem: Uthai the son of Ammi'hud, son of Omri, son of Imri, son of Bani, from the sons of Perez the son of Judah. And of the Shi'lonites: Asa'iah the first-born, and his sons. Of the sons of Zerah: Jeu'el and their kinsmen, six hundred and ninety. Of the Benjaminites: Sallu the son of Meshul'lam, son of Hodavi'ah, son of Hassenu'ah, Ibne'iah the son of Jero'ham, Elah the son of Uzzi, son of Michri, and Meshul'lam, the son of Shephati'ah, son of Reu'el, son of Ibni'jah; and their kinsmen according to their generations, nine hundred and fifty-six. All these were heads of fathers' houses according to their fathers' houses.

Of the priests: Jedai'ah, Jehoi'-arib, Jachin, and Azari'ah the son of Hilki'ah, son of Meshul'lam, son of Zadok, son of Mera'ioth, son of Ahi'tub, the chief officer of the house of God; and Adai'ah the son of Jero'ham, son of Pashhur, son of Malchi'jah, and Ma'asai the son of Ad'i-el, son of Jah'-zerah, son of Meshul'lam, son of Meshil'lemith, son of Immer; besides their kinsmen, heads of their fathers' houses, one thousand seven hundred and sixty, very able men for the work of the service of the house of God.

Of the Levites: Shemai'ah the son of Hasshub, son of Azri'kam, son of Hashabi'ah, of the sons of Merar'i; and Bakbak'kar, Heresh, Galal, and Mattani'ah the son of Mica, son of Zichri, son of Asaph; and Obadi'ah the son of She-mai'ah, son of Galal, son of Jedu'thun, and Berechi'ah the son of Asa, son of Elka'nah, who dwelt in the villages of the Netoph'athites.

The gatekeepers were: Shallum, Akkub, Talmon, Ahi'man, and their kinsmen (Shallum being the chief), stationed hitherto in the king's gate on the east side. These were the gatekeepers of the

19 camp of the Levites. Shallum the son of Ko're, son of Ebi'asaph, son of Korah, and his kinsmen of his fathers' house, the Ko'rahites, were in charge of the work of the service, keepers of the thresholds of the tent, as their fathers had been in charge of the camp of the LORD, keepers of the entrance. 20 And Phin'ehas the son of Elea'zar was the ruler over them in time past; the LORD was with him. 21 Zechari'ah the son of Meshele-mi'ah was gatekeeper at the entrance of the tent of meeting. 22 All these, who were chosen as gatekeepers at the thresholds, were two hundred and twelve. They were enrolled by genealogies in their villages. David and Samuel the seer established them 23 in their office of trust. So they and their sons were in charge of the gates of the house of the LORD, that is, the house of the 24 tent, as guards. The gatekeepers were on the four sides, east, west, 25 north, and south; and their kinsmen who were in their villages were obliged to come in every seven days, from time to 26 time, to be with these; for the four chief gatekeepers, who were Levites, were in charge of the chambers and the treasures of the 27 house of God. And they lodged round about the house of God; for upon them lay the duty of watching, and they had charge of opening it every morning. 28 Some of them had charge of the utensils of service, for they were required to count them when they were brought in and taken out. 29 Others of them were appointed over the furniture, and over all the holy utensils, also over the fine flour, the wine, the oil, the in-30 cense, and the spices. Others, of the sons of the priests, prepared 31 the mixing of the spices, and Mattithi'ah, one of the Levites, the first-born of Shallum the Ko'rahite, was in charge of 32 making the flat cakes. Also some of their kinsmen of the Ko'hath-ites had charge of the showbread, to prepare it every sabbath. 33 Now these are the singers, the heads of fathers' houses of the Levites, dwelling in the chambers of the temple free from other service, for they were on duty day 34 and night. These were heads of fathers' houses of the Levites, according to their generations, leaders, who lived in Jerusalem.

In Gibeon

In Gibeon dwelt the father of 35 Gibeon, Je-i'el, and the name of his wife was Ma'acah, and his 36 first-born son Abdon, then Zur, Kish, Ba'al, Ner, Nadab, Gedor, 37 Ahi'o, Zechari'ah, and Mikloth; and Mikloth was the father of 38 Shim'e-am; and these also dwelt opposite their kinsmen in Jerusalem, with their kinsmen. Ner 39 was the father of Kish, Kish of Saul, Saul of Jonathan, Mal'chi-shu'a, Abin'adab, and Esh-ba'al; and the son of Jonathan was 40 Mer'ib-ba'al; and Mer'ib-ba'al was the father of Micah. The 41 sons of Micah: Pithon, Melech, Tah're-a, and Ahaz;[v] and Ahaz 42 was the father of Jarah, and Jarah of Al'emeth, Az'maveth, and Zimri; and Zimri was the father of Moza. Moza was the father of 43 Bin'e-a; and Repha'iah was his son, Ele-a'sah his son, Azel his son. Azel had six sons and these 44 are their names: Azri'kam, Bo'-cheru, Ish'mael, Sheari'ah, Obadi'ah, and Hanan; these were the sons of Azel.

THE CITY
OF
DAVID

B.C.
1000–
900

From Saul to David

10 NOW the Philistines fought against Israel; and the men of Israel fled before the Philistines, and fell slain on Mount Gilbo′a. 2 And the Philistines overtook Saul and his sons; and the Philistines slew Jonathan and Abin′adab and Mal′chishu′a, the sons of 3 Saul. The battle pressed hard upon Saul, and the archers found him; and he was 4 wounded by the archers. Then Saul said to his armour-bearer, "Draw your sword, and thrust me through with it, lest these uncircumcised come and make sport of me." But his armour-bearer would not; for he feared greatly. Therefore Saul took his own sword, 5 and fell upon it. And when his armour-bearer saw that Saul was dead, he also fell 6 upon his sword, and died. Thus Saul died; he and his three sons and all his house died 7 together. And when all the men of Israel who were in the valley saw that the army[w] had fled and that Saul and his sons were dead, they forsook their cities and fled; and the Philistines came and dwelt in them.

8 On the morrow, when the Philistines came to strip the slain, they found Saul and his 9 sons fallen on Mount Gilbo′a. And they stripped him and took his head and his armour, and sent messengers throughout the land of the Philistines, to carry the good news 10 to their idols and to the people. And they put his armour in the temple of their gods, and fastened his head in the temple of 11 Dagon. But when all Ja′besh-gil′ead heard all 12 that the Philistines had done to Saul, all the valiant men arose, and took away the body of Saul and the bodies of his sons, and brought them to Jabesh. And they buried their bones under the oak in Jabesh, and fasted seven days.

So Saul died for his unfaithfulness; he was unfaithful to the LORD in that he did not keep the command of the LORD, and also consulted a medium, seeking guidance, and did not seek guidance from the LORD. Therefore the LORD slew him, and turned the kingdom over to David the son of Jesse.

From Hebron to Jerusalem

Then all Israel gathered together to David 1 at Hebron, and said, "Behold, we are your bone and flesh. In times past, even when 2 Saul was king, it was you that led out and brought in Israel; and the LORD your God said to you, 'You shall be shepherd of my people Israel, and you shall be prince over my people Israel.'" So all the elders of 3 Israel came to the king at Hebron; and David made a covenant with them at Hebron before the LORD, and they anointed David king over Israel, according to the word of the LORD by Samuel.

And David and all Israel went to Jerusalem, 4 that is Jebus, where the Jeb′usites were, the inhabitants of the land. The inhabitants of 5 Jebus said to David, "You will not come in here." Nevertheless David took the stronghold of Zion, that is, the city of David. David said, "Whoever shall smite the 6 Jeb′usites first shall be chief and commander." And Jo′ab the son of Zeru′iah went up first, so he became chief. And 7 David dwelt in the stronghold; therefore it was called the city of David. And he built 8 the city round about from the Millo in complete circuit; and Jo′ab repaired the rest of the city. And David became greater 9 and greater, for the LORD of hosts was with him.

[w] Heb *they*   10.1–12: 1 Sam 31.1–13.   11.1–3: 2 Sam 5.1–3.   11.4–9: 2 Sam 5.6–10.

David's mighty men

NOW these are the chiefs of David's mighty men, who gave him strong support in his kingdom, together with all Israel, to make him king, according to the word of the LORD concerning Israel. 1 This is an account of David's mighty men: Jasho'be-am, a Hach'monite, was chief of the three;[x] he wielded his spear against three hundred whom he slew at one time. 2 And next to him among the three mighty men was Elea'zar the son 3 of Dodo, the Aho'hite. He was with David at Pas-dam'mim when the Philistines were gathered there for battle. There was a plot of ground full of barley, and the men fled from the Philistines; 4 but he[y] took his[y] stand in the midst of the plot, and defended it, and slew the Philistines; and the LORD saved them by a great victory. 5 Three of the thirty chief men went down to the rock to David at the cave of Adullam, when the army of Philistines was encamped 6 in the valley of Reph'aim. David was then in the stronghold; and the garrison of the Philistines was 7 then at Bethlehem. And David said longingly, "O that some one would give me water to drink from the well of Bethlehem which 8 is by the gate!" Then the three mighty men broke through the camp of the Philistines, and drew water out of the well of Bethlehem which was by the gate, and took and brought it to David. But David would not drink of it; he 9 poured it out to the LORD, and said, "Far be it from me before my God that I should do this. Shall I drink the life-blood of these men? For at the risk of their lives they brought it." Therefore he would not drink it. These things did the three mighty men.

20 Now Abi'shai, the brother of Jo'ab, was chief of the thirty.[z] And he wielded his spear against three hundred men and slew them, and won a name beside the 21 three. He was the most renowned[a] of the thirty,[z] and became their commander; but he did not attain to the three. 22 And Benai'ah the son of Jehoi'ada was a valiant man[b] of Kabzeel, a doer of great deeds; he smote two ariels[c] of Moab. He also went down and slew a lion in a pit on a 23 day when snow had fallen. And he slew an Egyptian, a man of great stature, five cubits tall. The Egyptian had in his hand a spear like a weaver's beam; but Benai'-ah went down to him with a staff, and snatched the spear out of the

Egyptian's hand, and slew him 24 with his own spear. These things did Benai'ah the son of Jehoi'ada, and won a name beside the three 25 mighty men. He was renowned among the thirty, but he did not attain to the three. And David set him over his bodyguard. 26 The mighty men of the armies were As'ahel the brother of Jo'-ab, Elha'nan the son of Dodo of Bethlehem, Shammoth of 28 Harod,[d] Helez the Pel'onite, Ira the son of Ikkesh of Teko'a, 29 Abi-e'zer of An'athoth, Sib'becai the Hu'shathite, I'lai the Aho'- 30 hite, Ma'harai of Netoph'ah, Heled the son of Ba'anah of 31 Netoph'ah, Ithai the son of Ri'bai of Gib'eah of the Benjaminites, 32 Benai'ah of Pir'athon, Hurai of the brooks of Ga'ash, Abi'el the 33 Ar'bathite, Az'maveth of Baha'-rum, Eli'ahba of Sha-al'bon, 34 Hashem[e] the Gi'zonite, Jonathan the son of Shagee the Har'arite, 35 Ahi'am the son of Sachar the Har'arite, Eli'phal the son of Ur, 36 Hepher the Meche'rathite, Ahi'- 37 jah the Pel'onite, Hezro of Carmel, Na'arai the son of Ezbai, 38 Jo'el the brother of Nathan, 39 Mibhar the son of Hagri, Zelek the Ammonite, Na'harai of Be-er'oth, the armour-bearer of 40 Jo'ab the son of Zeru'iah, Ira the 41 Ithrite, Gareb the Ithrite, Uri'ah the Hittite, Zabad the son of 42 Ahlai, Ad'ina the son of Shiza the Reubenite, a leader of the Reu-benites, and thirty with him, 43 Hanan the son of Ma'acah, and 44 Josh'aphat the Mithnite, Uzzi'a the Ash'terathite, Shama and Je-i'el the sons of Hotham 45 Aro'erite, Jedi'a-el the son of Shimri, and Joha his brother, the 46 Tizite, Eli'el the Ma'havite, and Jer'ibai, and Joshavi'ah, the sons of El-na'am, and Ithmah the 47 Moabite, Eli'el, and Obed, and Ja-a'si-el the Mezo'ba-ite.

12 Now these are the men who came to David at Ziklag, while he could not move about freely because of Saul the son of Kish; and they were among the mighty men who helped him in war. 2 They were bowmen, and could shoot arrows and sling stones with either the right or the left hand; they were Benjaminites, Saul's 3 kinsmen. The chief was Ahie'-zer, then Jo'ash, both sons of Shema'ah of Gib'e-ah; also Je'zi-el and Pelet the sons of Az'maveth; Bera'cah, Jehu of 4 An'athoth, Ishma'iah of Gibeon, a mighty man among the thirty and a leader over the thirty; Jeremiah,[f] Jahazi'el, Joha'nan, 5 Jo'zabad of Gede'rah, Elu'zai,[g] Jer'imoth, Beali'ah, Shemari'ah, Shephati'ah the Har'uphite;

Elka'nah, Isshi'ah, Az'arel, 6 Jo-e'zer, and Jasho'be-am, the Ko'rahites; and Jo-e'lah and 7 Zebadi'ah, the sons of Jero'ham of Gedor.

From the Gadites there went 8 over to David at the stronghold in the wilderness mighty and experienced warriors, expert with shield and spear, whose faces were like the faces of lions, and who were swift as gazelles upon the mountains: Ezer the chief, Oba- 9 di'ah second, Eli'ab third, Mishman'nah fourth, Jeremiah 10 fifth, Attai sixth, Eli'el seventh, 11 Joha'nan eighth, Elza'bad ninth, 12 Jeremiah tenth, Mach'bannai 13 eleventh. These Gadites were 14 officers of the army, the lesser over a hundred and the greater over a thousand. These are the 15 men who crossed the Jordan in the first month, when it was over-flowing all its banks, and put to flight all those in the valleys, to the east and to the west.

And some of the men of Ben- 16 jamin and Judah came to the stronghold to David. David went 17 out to meet them and said to them, "If you have come to me in friendship to help me, my heart will be knit to you; but if to betray me to my adversaries, although there is no wrong in my hands, then may the God of our fathers see and rebuke you." Then the 18 Spirit came upon Ama'sai, chief of the thirty, and he said

"We are yours, O David;
    and with you, O son of Jesse!
Peace, peace to you,
    and peace to your helpers!
For your God helps you."

Then David received them, and made them officers of his troops. Some of the men of Manas'seh 19 deserted to David when he came with the Philistines for the battle against Saul. (Yet he did not help them, for the rulers of the Philis-tines took counsel and sent him away, saying, "At peril to our heads he will desert to his master Saul.") As he went to Ziklag 20 these men of Manas'seh deserted to him: Adnah, Jo'zabad, Jedi'-a-el, Michael, Jo'zabad, Eli'hu, and Zil'le-thai, chiefs of thou-sands in Manas'seh. They helped 21 David against the band of raid-ers;[h] for they were all mighty men of valour, and were commanders in the army. For from day to day 22 men kept coming to David to help him, until there was a great army, like an army of God.

These are the numbers of the 23 divisions of the armed troops, who came to David in Hebron, to turn the kingdom of Saul over to him, according to the word of the

---

[x] Compare 2 Sam 23.8: Heb *thirty* or *captains*   [y] Compare 2 Sam 23.12: Heb *they . . . their*
[z] Syr: Heb *three*   [a] Compare 2 Sam 23.19: Heb *more renowned among the two*
[b] Syr: Heb *the son of a valiant man*   [c] The meaning of the word *ariel* is unknown
[d] Compare 2 Sam 23.25: Heb *the Harorite*   [e] Compare Gk and 2 Sam 23.32: Heb *the sons of Hashem*
[f] Heb verse 5   [g] Heb verse 6   [h] Or *as officers of his troops*
11.10–47: 2 Sam 23.8–39.

LORD. The men of Judah bearing shield and spear were six thousand eight hundred armed troops. Of the Simeonites, mighty men of valour for war, seven thousand one hundred. Of the Levites four thousand six hundred. The prince Jehoi'ada, of the house of Aaron, and with him three thousand seven hundred. Zadok, a young man mighty in valour, and twenty-two commanders from his own father's house. Of the Benjaminites, the kinsmen of Saul, three thousand, of whom the majority had hitherto kept their allegiance to the house of Saul. Of the E'phraimites twenty thousand eight hundred, mighty men of valour, famous men in their fathers' houses. Of the half-tribe of Manas'seh eighteen thousand, who were expressly named to come and make David king. Of Is'sachar men who had understanding of the times, to know what Israel ought to do, two hundred chiefs, and all their kinsmen under their command. Of Zeb'ulun fifty thousand seasoned troops, equipped for battle with all the weapons of war, to help David[i] with singleness of purpose. Of Naph'tali a thousand commanders with whom were thirty-seven thousand men armed with shield and spear. Of the Danites twenty-eight thousand six hundred men equipped for battle. Of Asher forty thousand seasoned troops ready for battle. Of the Reubenites and Gadites and the half-tribe of Manas'seh from beyond the Jordan, one hundred and twenty thousand men armed with all the weapons of war.

All these, men of war, arrayed in battle order, came to Hebron with full intent to make David king over all Israel; likewise all the rest of Israel were of a single mind to make David king. And they were there with David for three days, eating and drinking, for their brethren had made preparation for them. And also their neighbours, from as far as Is'sachar and Zeb'ulun and Naph'tali, came bringing food on asses and on camels and on mules and on oxen, abundant provisions of meal, cakes of figs, clusters of raisins, and wine and oil, oxen and sheep, for there was joy in Israel.

THE ARK OF THE LORD IS BROUGHT TO JERUSALEM

A solemn journey

13 DAVID consulted with the commanders of thousands and of hundreds, with every leader. And David said to all the assembly of Israel, "If it seems good to you, and if it is the will of the LORD our God, let us send abroad to our brethren who remain in all the land of Israel, and with them to the priests and Levites in the cities that have pasture lands, that they may come together to us. Then let us bring again the ark of our God to us; for we neglected it in the days of Saul." All the assembly agreed to do so, for the thing was right in the eyes of all the people. So David assembled all Israel from the Shihor of Egypt to the entrance of Hamath, to bring the ark of God from Kir'iath-je'arim. And David and all Israel went up to Ba'alah, that is, to Kir'iath-je'arim which belongs to Judah, to bring up from there the ark of God, which is called by the name of the LORD who sits enthroned above the cherubim. And they carried the ark of God upon a new cart, from the house of Abin'adab, and Uzzah and Ahi'o[j] were driving the cart. And David and all Israel were making merry before God with all their might, with song and lyres and harps and tambourines and cymbals and trumpets.

And when they came to the threshing floor of Chidon, Uzzah put out his hand to hold the ark, for the oxen stumbled. And the anger of the LORD was kindled against Uzzah; and he smote him because he put forth his hand to the ark; and he died there before God. And David was angry because the LORD had broken forth upon Uzzah; and that place is called Pe'rez-uz'za[k] to this day. And David was afraid of God that day; and he said, "How can I bring the ark of God home to me?" So David did not take the ark home into the city of David, but took it aside to the house of O'bed-e'dom the Gittite. And the ark of God remained with the household of O'bed-e'dom in his house three months; and the LORD blessed the household of O'bed-e'dom and all that he had.

Gifts from Tyre

And Hiram king of Tyre sent messengers to David, and cedar trees, also masons and carpenters to build a house for him. And David perceived that the LORD had established him king over Israel, and that his kingdom was highly exalted for the sake of his people Israel.

[i] Gk: Heb lacks David   [j] Or and his brother   [k] That is The breaking forth upon Uzzah
13.1–14: 2 Sam 6.1–11.   14.1–2: 2 Sam 5.11–12.

David's family

3 And David took more wives in Jerusalem, and David begot more sons and daughters.
4 These are the names of the children whom he had in Jerusalem: Sham'mu-a, Shobab,
5 Nathan, Solomon, Ibhar, Eli'shu-a, El'pelet,
6 Nogah, Nepheg, Japhi'a, Elish'ama, Beeli'-
7 ada, and Eliph'elet.

David's victories

8 When the Philistines heard that David had been anointed king over all Israel, all the Philistines went up in search of David; and David heard of it and went out against them.
9 Now the Philistines had come and made a
10 raid in the valley of Reph'aim. And David inquired of God, "Shall I go up against the Philistines? Wilt thou give them into my hand?" And the LORD said to him, "Go up,
11 and I will give them into your hand." And he went up to Ba'al-pera'zim, and David defeated them there; and David said, "God has broken through[l] my enemies by my hand, like a bursting flood." Therefore the name of that place is called Ba'al-pera'zim.[m]
12 And they left their gods there, and David gave command, and they were burned.
13 And the Philistines yet again made a raid in
14 the valley. And when David again inquired of God, God said to him, "You shall not go up after them; go around and come upon
15 them opposite the balsam trees. And when you hear the sound of marching in the tops of the balsam trees, then go out to battle; for God has gone out before you to smite the
16 army of the Philistines." And David did as God commanded him, and they smote the
17 Philistine army from Gibeon to Gezer. And the fame of David went out into all lands, and the LORD brought the fear of him upon all nations.

The ark of the Lord

15 David built houses for himself in the city of David; and he prepared a place for the ark of
2 God, and pitched a tent for it. Then David said, "No one but the Levites may carry the ark of God, for the LORD chose them to carry the ark of the LORD and to minister to him
3 for ever." And David assembled all Israel at Jerusalem, to bring up the ark of the LORD to
4 its place, which he had prepared for it. And David gathered together the sons of Aaron
5 and the Levites: of the sons of Kohath, Uri'el the chief, with a hundred and twenty
6 of his brethren; of the sons of Merar'i,

Asa'iah the chief, with two hundred and twenty of his brethren; of the sons of 7 Gershom, Jo'el the chief, with a hundred and thirty of his brethren; of the sons of 8 Eliza'phan, Shemai'ah the chief, with two hundred of his brethren; of the sons of 9 Hebron, Eli'el the chief, with eighty of his brethren; of the sons of Uz'ziel, Ammin'adab 10 the chief, with a hundred and twelve of his brethren. Then David summoned the 11 priests Zadok and Abi'athar, and the Levites Uri'el, Asa'iah, Jo'el, Shemai'ah, Eli'el, and Ammin'adab, and said to them, "You are the 12 heads of the fathers' houses of the Levites; sanctify yourselves, you and your brethren, so that you may bring up the ark of the LORD, the God of Israel, to the place that I have prepared for it. Because you did not carry it 13 the first time,[n] the LORD our God broke forth upon us, because we did not care for it in the way that is ordained." So the priests 14 and the Levites sanctified themselves to bring up the ark of the LORD, the God of Israel. And the Levites carried the ark of 15 God upon their shoulders with the poles, as Moses had commanded according to the word of the LORD.

David also commanded the chiefs of the 16 Levites to appoint their brethren as the singers who should play loudly on musical instruments, on harps and lyres and cymbals, to raise sounds of joy. So the Levites 17 appointed Heman the son of Jo'el; and of his brethren Asaph the son of Berechi'ah; and of the sons of Merar'i, their brethren, Ethan the son of Kusha'iah; and with them their 18 brethren of the second order, Zechari'ah, Ja-a'ziel, Shemir'amoth, Jehi'el, Unni, Eli'ab, Benai'ah, Ma-asei'ah, Mattithi'ah, Eliph'elehu, and Mikne'iah, and the gatekeepers O'bed-e'dom and Je-i'el. The 19 singers, Heman, Asaph, and Ethan, were to sound bronze cymbals; Zechari'ah, A'zi-el, 20 Shemir'amoth, Jehi'el, Unni, Eli'ab, Ma-asei'ah, and Benai'ah were to play harps according to Al'amoth; but Mattithi'ah, 21 Eliph'elehu, Mikne'iah, O'bed-e'dom,

[l] Heb *paraz*   [m] That is *Lord of breaking through*   [n] The meaning of the Hebrew word is uncertain
14.3–7: 1 Chron 3.5–8; 2 Sam 5.14–16.   14.8–12: 2 Sam 5.17–21.   14.13–16: 2 Sam 5.22–25.
15.1–16.3: 2 Sam 6.12–19.

Je-i'el, and Azazi'ah were to lead with lyres
22 according to the Shem'inith. Chenani'ah,
leader of the Levites in music, should direct
23 the music, for he understood it. Berechi'ah
and Elka'nah were to be gatekeepers for the
24 ark. Shebani'ah, Josh'aphat, Nethan'el,
Ama'sai, Zechari'ah, Benai'ah, and Elie'zer,
the priests, should blow the trumpets before
the ark of God. O'bed-e'dom and Jehi'ah
also were to be gatekeepers for the ark.
25 So David and the elders of Israel, and the
commanders of thousands, went to bring up
the ark of the covenant of the LORD from the
26 house of O'bed-e'dom with rejoicing. And
because God helped the Levites who were
carrying the ark of the covenant of the LORD,
they sacrificed seven bulls and seven rams.
27 David was clothed with a robe of fine linen,
as also were all the Levites who were carrying
the ark, and the singers, and Chenani'ah the
leader of the music of the singers; and David
28 wore a linen ephod. So all Israel brought up
the ark of the covenant of the LORD with
shouting, to the sound of the horn, trumpets,
and cymbals, and made loud music on harps
and lyres.
29 And as the ark of the covenant of the LORD
came to the city of David, Michal came to the
daughter of Saul looked out of the window,
and saw King David dancing and making
merry; and she despised him in her heart.

16 And they brought in the ark of God, and set
it inside the tent which David had pitched
for it; and they offered burnt offerings and
2 peace offerings before God. And when
David had finished offering the burnt offerings and the peace offerings, he blessed the
3 people in the name of the LORD, and
distributed to all Israel, both men and
women, to each a loaf of bread, a portion of
meat,[o] and a cake of raisins.
4 Moreover he appointed certain of the Levites as ministers before the ark of the LORD,
to invoke, to thank, and to praise the LORD,
5 the God of Israel. Asaph was the chief, and
second to him were Zechari'ah, Je-i'el,
Shemir'amoth, Jehi'el, Mattithi'ah, Eli'ab,
Benai'ah, O'bed-e'dom, and Je-i'el, who

were to play harps and lyres; Asaph was to
sound the cymbals, and Benai'ah and Jaha- 6
zi'el the priests were to blow trumpets
continually, before the ark of the covenant of
God.

Psalm of praise

Then on that day David first appointed that 7
thanksgiving be sung to the LORD by Asaph
and his brethren.

O give thanks to the LORD, call on his 8
    name,
    make known his deeds among the
    peoples!
Sing to him, sing praises to him,   9
    tell of all his wonderful works!
Glory in his holy name;   1
    let the hearts of those who seek the
    LORD rejoice!
Seek the LORD and his strength,   1
    seek his presence continually!
Remember the wonderful works that he 1
    has done,
    the wonders he wrought, the judgments
    he uttered,
O offspring of Abraham his servant,   1
    sons of Jacob, his chosen ones!

He is the LORD our God;   1
    his judgments are in all the earth.
He is mindful of his covenant for ever,   1
    of the word that he commanded, for a
    thousand generations,
the covenant which he made with 16
    Abraham,
    his sworn promise to Isaac,
which he confirmed as a statute to Jacob, 17
    as an everlasting covenant to Israel,
saying, "To you I will give the land of 18
    Canaan,
    as your portion for an inheritance."

When they were few in number,   19
    and of little account, and sojourners in
    it,
wandering from nation to nation,   20
    from one kingdom to another people,

---

[o] Compare Gk Syr Vg: Heb uncertain
16.8–22: Ps 105.1–15.

he allowed no one to oppress them;
  he rebuked kings on their account,
saying, "Touch not my anointed ones,
  do my prophets no harm!"

Sing to the LORD, all the earth!
  Tell of his salvation from day to day.
Declare his glory among the nations,
  his marvellous works among all the
    peoples!
For great is the LORD, and greatly to be
    praised,
  and he is to be held in awe above all
    gods.
For all the gods of the peoples are idols;
  but the LORD made the heavens.
Honour and majesty are before him;
  strength and joy are in his place.

Ascribe to the LORD, O families of the
    peoples,
  ascribe to the LORD glory and strength!
Ascribe to the LORD the glory due his name;
  bring an offering, and come before him!
Worship the LORD in holy array;
  tremble before him, all the earth;
  yea, the world stands firm, never to be
    moved.
Let the heavens be glad, and let the earth
    rejoice,
  and let them say among the nations,
    "The LORD reigns!"
Let the sea roar, and all that fills it,
  let the field exult, and everything in it!
Then shall the trees of the wood sing for
    joy
  before the LORD, for he comes to judge
    the earth.
O give thanks to the LORD, for he is good;
  for his steadfast love endures for ever!

Say also:

"Deliver us, O God of our salvation,
  and gather and save us from among the
    nations,
that we may give thanks to thy holy name,
  and glory in thy praise.
Blessed be the LORD, the God of Israel,   36
  from everlasting to everlasting!"
Then all the people said "Amen!" and
praised the LORD.

So David left Asaph and his brethren there 37
before the ark of the covenant of the LORD to
minister continually before the ark as each
day required, and also O'bed-e'dom and his *p* 38
sixty-eight brethren; while O'bed-e'dom, the
son of Jedu'thun, and Hosah were to be
gatekeepers. And he left Zadok the priest 39
and his brethren the priests before the
tabernacle of the LORD in the high place that
was at Gibeon, to offer burnt offerings to the 40
LORD upon the altar of burnt offering continually morning and evening, according to
all that is written in the law of the LORD
which he commanded Israel. With them 41
were Heman and Jedu'thun, and the rest of
those chosen and expressly named to give
thanks to the LORD, for his steadfast love
endures for ever. Heman and Jedu'thun had 42
trumpets and cymbals for the music and
instruments for sacred song. The sons of
Jedu'thun were appointed to the gate.

Then all the people departed each to his 43
house, and David went home to bless his
household.

The house of the Lord

Now when David dwelt in his house, David 17
said to Nathan the prophet, "Behold, I dwell
in a house of cedar, but the ark of the
covenant of the LORD is under a tent." And 2
Nathan said to David, "Do all that is in your
heart, for God is with you."

3 But that same night the word of the LORD
4 came to Nathan, "Go and tell my servant
David, 'Thus says the LORD: You shall not
5 build me a house to dwell in. For I have not
dwelt in a house since the day I led up Israel
to this day, but I have gone from tent to tent
6 and from dwelling to dwelling. In all places
where I have moved with all Israel, did I
speak a word with any of the judges of Israel,
whom I commanded to shepherd my people,
saying, "Why have you not built me a house
7 of cedar?"' Now therefore thus shall you
say to my servant David, 'Thus says the
LORD of hosts, I took you from the pasture,
from following the sheep, that you should be
8 prince over my people Israel; and I have
been with you wherever you went, and have
cut off all your enemies from before you; and
I will make for you a name, like the name of
9 the great ones of the earth. And I will
appoint a place for my people Israel, and will
plant them, that they may dwell in their own
place, and be disturbed no more; and violent
men shall waste them no more, as formerly,
10 from the time that I appointed judges over
my people Israel; and I will subdue all your
enemies. Moreover I declare to you that the
11 LORD will build you a house. When your
days are fulfilled to go to be with your
fathers, I will raise up your offspring after
you, one of your own sons, and I will
12 establish his kingdom. He shall build a
house for me, and I will establish his throne
13 for ever. I will be his father, and he shall be
my son; I will not take my steadfast love
from him, as I took it from him who was
14 before you, but I will confirm him in my
house and in my kingdom for ever and his
15 throne shall be established for ever.'" In
accordance with all these words, and in
accordance with all this vision, Nathan spoke
to David.
16 Then King David went in and sat before
the LORD, and said, "Who am I, O LORD
God, and what is my house, that thou hast
17 brought me thus far? And this was a small
thing in thy eyes, O God; thou hast also
spoken of thy servant's house for a great
while to come, and hast shown me future
18 generations,*q* O LORD God! And what more
can David say to thee for honouring thy
19 servant? For thou knowest thy servant. For
thy servant's sake, O LORD, and according to
thy own heart, thou hast wrought all this
greatness, in making known all these great
20 things. There is none like thee, O LORD, and
there is no God besides thee, according to all
21 that we have heard with our ears. What
other*r* nation on earth is like thy people

Israel, whom God went to redeem to be his
people, making for thyself a name for great
and terrible things, in driving out nations
before thy people whom thou didst redeem
from Egypt? And thou didst make thy*s*
people Israel to be thy people for ever; and
thou, O LORD, didst become their God. And*s*
now, O LORD, let the word which thou hast
spoken concerning thy servant and concerning his house be established for ever, and do
as thou hast spoken; and thy name will be
established and magnified for ever, saying,
'The LORD of hosts, the God of Israel, is
Israel's God,' and the house of thy servant
David will be established before thee. For*s*
thou, my God, hast revealed to thy servant
that thou wilt build a house for him; therefore thy servant has found courage to pray
before thee. And now, O LORD, thou art*s*
God, and thou hast promised this good thing
to thy servant; now therefore may it please*s*
thee to bless the house of thy servant, that it
may continue for ever before thee; for what
thou, O LORD, hast blessed is blessed for
ever."

David's conquests

After this David defeated the Philistines 1
and subdued them, and he took Gath and its
villages out of the hand of the Philistines.
And he defeated Moab, and the Moabites 2
became servants to David and brought
tribute.
David also defeated Hadade′zer king of 3
Zobah, toward Hamath, as he went to set up
his monument*s* at the river Eu-phra′tes. And 4
David took from him a thousand chariots,
seven thousand horsemen, and twenty thousand foot soldiers; and David hamstrung all
the chariot horses, but left enough for a
hundred chariots. And when the Syrians of 5
Damascus came to help Hadade′zer king of
Zobah, David slew twenty-two thousand
men of the Syrians. Then David put gar- 6
risons*t* in Syria of Damascus; and the Syrians
became servants to David, and brought
tribute. And the LORD gave victory to David
wherever he went. And David took the 7
shields of gold which were carried by the
servants of Hadade′zer, and brought them to
Jerusalem. And from Tibhath and from 8
Cun, cities of Hadade′zer, David took very
much bronze; with it Solomon made the
bronze sea and the pillars and the vessels of
bronze.
When To′u king of Hamath heard that 9
David had defeated the whole army of
Hadade′zer, king of Zobah, he sent his son 10

---

q Cn: Heb uncertain   *r* Gk Vg: Heb *one*   *s* Heb *hand*   *t* Gk Vg 2 Sam 8.6 Compare Syr: Heb lacks *garrisons*
18.1–13: 2 Sam 8.1–14.

Hador'am to King David, to greet him, and to congratulate him because he had fought against Hadade'zer and defeated him; for Hadade'zer had often been at war with To'u. And he sent all sorts of articles of gold, of silver, and of bronze; these also King David dedicated to the Lord, together with the silver and gold which he had carried off from all the nations, from Edom, Moab, the Ammonites, the Philistines, and Am'alek.

And Abi'shai, the son of Zeru'iah, slew eighteen thousand E'domites in the Valley of Salt. And he put garrisons in Edom; and all the E'domites became David's servants. And the Lord gave victory to David wherever he went.

So David reigned over all Israel; and he administered justice and equity to all his people. And Jo'ab the son of Zeru'iah was over the army; and Jehosh'aphat the son of Ahi'lud was recorder; and Zadok the son of Ahi'tub and Ahim'elech the son of Abi'athar were priests; and Shavsha was secretary; and Benai'ah the son of Jehoi'ada was over the Cher'ethites and the Pel'ethites; and David's sons were the chief officials in the service of the king.

9 Now after this Nahash the king of the Ammonites died, and his son reigned in his stead. And David said, "I will deal loyally with Hanun the son of Nahash, for his father dealt loyally with me." So David sent messengers to console him concerning his father. And David's servants came to Hanun in the land of the Ammonites, to console him. But the princes of the Ammonites said to Hanun, "Do you think, because David has sent comforters to you, that he is honouring your father? Have not his servants come to you to search and to overthrow and to spy out the land?" So Hanun took David's servants, and shaved them, and cut off their garments in the middle, at their hips, and sent them away; and they departed. When David was told concerning the men, he sent to meet them, for the men were greatly ashamed. And the king said, "Remain at Jericho until your beards have grown, and then return."

When the Ammonites saw that they had made themselves odious to David, Hanun and the Ammonites sent a thousand talents of silver to hire chariots and horsemen from Mesopota'mia, from Aram-ma'acah, and from Zobah. They hired thirty-two thousand chariots and the king of Ma'acah with his army, who came and encamped before Med'eba. And the Ammonites were mus-

tered from their cities and came to battle. When David heard of it, he sent Jo'ab and all 8 the army of the mighty men. And the 9 Ammonites came out and drew up in battle array at the entrance of the city, and the kings who had come were by themselves in the open country.

When Jo'ab saw that the battle was set 10 against him both in front and in the rear, he chose some of the picked men of Israel, and arrayed them against the Syrians; the rest of 11 his men he put in the charge of Abi'shai his brother, and they were arrayed against the Ammonites. And he said, "If the Syrians are 12 too strong for me, then you shall help me; but if the Ammonites are too strong for you, then I will help you. Be of good courage, and 13 let us play the man for our people, and for the cities of our God; and may the Lord do what seems good to him." So Jo'ab and the 14 people who were with him drew near before the Syrians for battle; and they fled before him. And when the Ammonites saw that the 15 Syrians fled, they likewise fled before Abi'shai, Jo'ab's brother, and entered the city. Then Jo'ab came to Jerusalem.

But when the Syrians saw that they had 16 been defeated by Israel, they sent messengers and brought out the Syrians who were beyond the Euphra'tes, with Shophach the commander of the army of Hadade'zer at their head. And when it was told David, he 17 gathered all Israel together, and crossed the Jordan, and came to them, and drew up his forces against them. And when David set the battle in array against the Syrians, they fought with him. And the Syrians fled 18 before Israel; and David slew of the Syrians the men of seven thousand chariots, and forty thousand foot soldiers, and killed also Shophach the commander of their army. And when the servants of Hadade'zer saw 19 that they had been defeated by Israel, they made peace with David, and became subject to him. So the Syrians were not willing to help the Ammonites any more.

In the spring of the year, the time when 20 kings go forth to battle, Jo'ab led out the army, and ravaged the country of the Ammonites, and came and besieged Rabbah. But David remained at Jerusalem. And Jo'ab smote Rabbah, and overthrew it. And David took the crown of their king" 2 from his head; he found that it weighed a talent of gold, and in it was a precious stone; and it was placed on David's head. And he brought forth the spoil of the city, a very great amount. And he brought forth the 3

---

people who were in it, and set them to labour ^{v} with saws and iron picks and axes; ^{w} and thus David did to all the cities of the Ammonites. Then David and all the people returned to Jerusalem.

4 And after this there arose war with the Philistines at Gezer; then Sib′becai the Hu′shathite slew Sip′pai, who was one of the descendants of the giants; and the Philistines 5 were subdued. And there was again war with the Philistines; and Elha′nan the son of Ja′ir slew Lahmi the brother of Goliath the Gittite, the shaft of whose spear was like a 6 weaver's beam. And there was again war at Gath, where there was a man of great stature, who had six fingers on each hand, and six toes on each foot, twenty-four in number; and he also was descended from the giants. 7 And when he taunted Israel, Jonathan the son of Shim′e-a, David's brother, slew him. 8 These were descended from the giants in Gath; and they fell by the hand of David and by the hand of his servants.

A cause of trespass

21 Satan stood up against Israel, and incited 2 David to number Israel. So David said to Jo′ab and the commanders of the army, "Go, number Israel, from Beer-sheba to Dan, and bring me a report, that I may know their 3 number." But Jo′ab said, "May the LORD add to his people a hundred times as many as they are! Are they not, my lord the king, all of them my lord's servants? Why then should my lord require this? Why should he 4 bring guilt upon Israel?" But the king's word prevailed against Jo′ab. So Jo′ab departed and went throughout all Israel, and 5 came back to Jerusalem. And Jo′ab gave the sum of the numbering of the people to David. In all Israel there were one million one hundred thousand men who drew the sword, and in Judah four hundred and 6 seventy thousand who drew the sword. But he did not include Levi and Benjamin in the numbering, for the king's command was abhorrent to Jo′ab.

7 But God was displeased with this thing, and 8 he smote Israel. And David said to God, "I have sinned greatly in that I have done this thing. But now, I pray thee, take away the iniquity of thy servant; for I have done very 9 foolishly." And the LORD spoke to Gad, 10 David's seer, saying, "Go and say to David, 'Thus says the LORD, Three things I offer you; choose one of them, that I may do it to 11 you.'" So Gad came to David and said to him, "Thus says the LORD, 'Take which you

will: either three years of famine; or three months of devastation by your foes, while the sword of your enemies overtakes you; or else three days of the sword of the LORD, pestilence upon the land, and the angel of the LORD destroying throughout all the territory of Israel.' Now decide what answer I shall return to him who sent me." Then David said to Gad, "I am in great distress; let me fall into the hand of the LORD, for his mercy is very great; but let me not fall into the hand of man."

So the LORD sent a pestilence upon Israel; and there fell seventy thousand men of Israel. And God sent the angel to Jerusalem to destroy it; but when he was about to destroy it, the LORD saw, and he repented of the evil; and he said to the destroying angel, "It is enough; now stay your hand." And the angel of the LORD was standing by the threshing floor of Ornan the Jeb′usite. And David lifted his eyes and saw the angel of the LORD standing between earth and heaven, and in his hand a drawn sword stretched out over Jerusalem. Then David and the elders, clothed in sackcloth, fell upon their faces. And David said to God, "Was it not I who gave command to number the people? It is I who have sinned and done very wickedly. But these sheep, what have they done? Let thy hand, I pray thee, O LORD my God, be against me and against my father's house; but let not the plague be upon thy people."

An altar to the Lord

Then the angel of the LORD commanded Gad to say to David that David should go up and rear an altar to the LORD on the threshing floor of Ornan the Jeb′usite. So David went up at Gad's word, which he had spoken in the name of the LORD. Now Ornan was threshing wheat; he turned and saw the angel, and his four sons who were with him hid themselves. As David came to Ornan, Ornan looked and saw David and went forth from the threshing floor, and did obeisance to David with his face to the ground. And David said to Ornan, "Give me the site of the threshing floor that I may build on it an altar to the LORD—give it to me at its full price—that the plague may be averted from the people." Then Ornan said to David, "Take it; and let my lord the king do what seems good to him; see, I give the oxen for burnt offerings, and the threshing sledges for the wood, and the wheat for a cereal offering. I give it all." But King David said to Ornan, "No, but I will buy it

^{v} Compare 2 Sam 12.31: Heb *he sawed* ^{w} Compare 2 Sam 12.31: Heb *saws*   20.4–8: 2 Sam 21.18–22.   **21.1–27: 2 Sam 24.1–25.**

for the full price; I will not take for the LORD what is yours, nor offer burnt offerings which cost me nothing." So David paid Ornan six hundred shekels of gold by weight for the site. And David built there an altar to the LORD and presented burnt offerings and peace offerings, and called upon the LORD, and he answered him with fire from heaven upon the altar of burnt offering. Then the LORD commanded the angel; and he put his sword back into its sheath.

At that time, when David saw that the LORD had answered him at the threshing floor of Ornan the Jeb′usite, he made his sacrifices there. For the tabernacle of the LORD, which Moses had made in the wilderness, and the altar of burnt offering were at that time in the high place at Gibeon; but David could not go before it to inquire of God, for he was afraid of the sword of the angel of the LORD.

2 Then David said, "Here shall be the house of the LORD God and here the altar of burnt offering for Israel."

Plans for the temple

David commanded to gather together the aliens who were in the land of Israel, and he set stonecutters to prepare dressed stones for building the house of God. David also provided great stores of iron for nails for the doors of the gates and for clamps, as well as bronze in quantities beyond weighing, and cedar timbers without number; for the Sido′-nians and Tyrians brought great quantities of cedar to David. For David said, "Solomon my son is young and inexperienced, and the house that is to be built for the LORD must be exceedingly magnificent, of fame and glory throughout all lands; I will therefore make preparation for it." So David provided materials in great quantity before his death.

Then he called for Solomon his son, and charged him to build a house for the LORD, the God of Israel. David said to Solomon, "My son, I had it in my heart to build a house to the name of the LORD my God. But the word of the LORD came to me, saying, 'You have shed much blood and have waged great wars; you shall not build a house to my name, because you have shed so much blood before me upon the earth. Behold, a son shall be born to you; he shall be a man of peace. I will give him peace from all his enemies round about; for his name shall be Solomon, and I will give peace and quiet to Israel in his days. He shall build a house for my name. He shall be my son, and I will be his father, and I will establish his royal throne in Israel for ever.' Now, my son, the

LORD be with you, so that you may succeed in building the house of the LORD your God, as he has spoken concerning you. Only, may the LORD grant you discretion and under-standing, that when he gives you charge over Israel you may keep the law of the LORD your God. Then you will prosper if you are careful to observe the statutes and the ordi-nances which the LORD commanded Moses for Israel. Be strong, and of good courage. Fear not; be not dismayed. With great pains I have provided for the house of the LORD a hundred thousand talents of gold, a million talents of silver, and bronze and iron beyond weighing, for there is so much of it; timber and stone too I have provided. To these you must add. You have an abundance of workmen: stonecutters, masons, carpenters, and all kinds of craftsmen without number, skilled in working gold, silver, bronze, and iron. Arise and be doing! The LORD be with you!"

David also commanded all the leaders of Israel to help Solomon his son, saying, "Is

Towards the temple

not the LORD your God with you? And has he not given you peace on every side? For he has delivered the inhabitants of the land into my hand; and the land is subdued before 19 the LORD and his people. Now set your mind and heart to seek the LORD your God. Arise and build the sanctuary of the LORD God, so that the ark of the covenant of the LORD and the holy vessels of God may be brought into a house built for the name of the LORD."

TEMPLE AREA

TEMPLE APPOINTMENTS

23 WHEN David was old and full of days, he made Solomon his son king over Israel.

Priests and Levites

2 David assembled all the leaders of Israel and the priests and the 3 Levites. The Levites, thirty years old and upward, were numbered, 4 and the total was thirty-eight thousand men. "Twenty-four thousand of these," David said, "shall have charge of the work in the house of the LORD, six thou- 5 sand shall be officers and judges, four thousand gatekeepers, and four thousand shall offer praises to the LORD with the instruments which I have made for praise." 6 And David organized them in divisions corresponding to the sons of Levi: Gershom, Kohath, and Merar′i.

7 The sons of Gershom[x] were 8 Ladan and Shim′e-i. The sons of Ladan: Jehi′el the chief, and 9 Zetham, and Jo′el, three. The sons of Shim′e-i: Shelo′moth, Ha′zi-el, and Haran, three. These were the heads of the 10 fathers' houses of Ladan. And the sons of Shim′e-i: Jahath, Zina, and Je′ush, and Beri′ah. 11 These four were the sons of Shim′e-i. Jahath was the chief, and Zizah the second; but Je′ush and Beri′ah had not many sons, therefore they became a father's house in one reckoning. 12 The sons of Kohath: Amram, Izhar, Hebron, and Uz′ziel, four. 13 The sons of Amram: Aaron and Moses. Aaron was set apart to consecrate the most holy things, that he and his sons for ever should burn incense before the LORD, and minister to him and pronounce blessings in his name 14 for ever. But the sons of Moses the man of God were named 15 among the tribe of Levi. The

sons of Moses: Gershom and Elie′zer. The sons of Gershom: Sheb′uel the chief. The sons of Elie′zer: Rehabi′ah the chief; Elie′zer had no other sons, but the sons of Rehabi′ah were very many. The sons of Izhar: Shelo′mith the chief. The sons of Hebron: Jeri′ah the chief, Amari′ah the second, Jahazi′el the third, and Jekame′am the fourth. The sons of Uz′ziel: Micah the chief and Isshi′ah the second.

The sons of Merar′i: Mahli and Mushi. The sons of Mahli: Elea′zar and Kish. Elea′zar died having no sons, but only daughters; their kinsmen, the sons of Kish, married them. The sons of Mushi: Mahli, Eder, and Jer′emoth, three.

These were the sons of Levi by their fathers' houses, the heads of fathers' houses as they were registered according to the number of the names of the individuals from twenty years old and upward who were to do the work for the service

of the house of the LORD. For 13
David said, "The LORD, the God
of Israel, has given peace to his
people; and he dwells in Jerusalem for ever. And so the 15
Levites no longer need to carry
the tabernacle or any of the things 16
for its service"—for by the last 17
words of David these were the
number of the Levites from 18
twenty years old and up-
ward—"but their duty shall be to 19
assist the sons of Aaron for the
service of the house of the LORD,
having the care of the courts and
the chambers, the cleansing of all
that is holy, and any work for the
service of the house of God; to
assist also with the showbread, the
flour for the cereal offering, the 20
wafers of unleavened bread, the
baked offering, the offering mixed
with oil, and all measures of
quantity or size. And they shall
stand every morning, thanking 22
and praising the LORD, and likewise at evening, and whenever 23
burnt offerings are offered to the
LORD on sabbaths, new moons,
and feast days, according to the 24
number required of them, continually before the LORD. Thus 25
they shall keep charge of the tent
of meeting and the sanctuary, and 26
shall attend the sons of Aaron,
their brethren, for the service of 27
the house of the LORD."

28
4 The divisions of the sons of
Aaron were these. The sons of
Aaron: Nadab, Abi′hu, Elea′zar, 30
and Ith′amar. But Nadab and
Abi′hu died before their father,
and had no children, so Elea′zar
and Ith′amar became the priests. 31
3 With the help of Zadok of the
sons of Elea′zar, and Ahim′elech
of the sons of Ith′amar, David
organized them according to the
appointed duties in their service.
4 Since more chief men were found
among the sons of Elea′zar than
among the sons of Ith′amar, they
organized them under sixteen
heads of fathers' houses of the
sons of Elea′zar, and eight of the 25
5 sons of Ith′amar. They organized
them by lot, all alike, for there
were officers of the sanctuary and
officers of God among both the
sons of Elea′zar and the sons of
6 Ith′amar. And the scribe She-
mai′ah the son of Nethan′el, a
Levite, recorded them in the 2
presence of the king, and the
princes, and Zadok the priest, and
Ahim′elech the son of Abi′athar,
and the heads of the fathers'
houses of the priests and of the 3
Levites; one father's house being
chosen for Elea′zar and one chosen for Ith′amar.
7 The first lot fell to Jehoi′arib, 4
8 the second to Jedai′ah, the third
to Harim, the fourth to Se-o′rim,
9 the fifth to Malchi′jah, the sixth
2 to Mi′jamin, the seventh to
1 Hakkoz, the eighth to Abi′jah, the
ninth to Jeshua, the tenth to
2 Shecani′ah, the eleventh to Eli′-

ashib, the twelfth to Jakim, the
thirteenth to Huppah, the fourteenth to Jesheb′e-ab, the fifteenth to Bilgah, the sixteenth
to Immer, the seventeenth to
Hezir, the eighteenth to Hap′piz-
zez, the nineteenth to Pethahi′ah,
the twentieth to Jehez′kel, the
twenty-first to Jachin, the twenty-second to Gamul, the twenty-
third to Dela′iah, the twenty-
fourth to Maazi′ah. These had as
their appointed duty in their
service to come into the house of
the LORD according to the procedure established for them by
Aaron their father, as the LORD
God of Israel had commanded
him.
And of the rest of the sons of
Levi: of the sons of Amram,
Shu′ba-el; of the sons of Shu′-
ba-el, Jehde′iah. Of Rehabi′ah:
of the sons of Rehabi′ah, Isshi′ah
the chief. Of the Iz′harites,
Shelo′moth; of the sons of
Shelo′moth, Jahath. The sons of
Hebron:ʸ Jeri′ah the chief,ᶻ
Amari′ah the second, Jahazi′el the
third, Jekame′am the fourth. The
sons of Uz′ziel, Micah; of the sons
of Micah, Shamir. The brother
of Micah, Isshi′ah; of the sons of
Isshi′ah, Zechari′ah. The sons of
Merar′i: Mahli and Mushi. The
sons of Ja-azi′ah: Beno. The sons
of Merar′i: of Ja-azi′ah, Beno,
Shoham, Zaccur, and Ibri. Of
Mahli: Elea′zar, who had no
sons. Of Kish, the sons of Kish:
Jerah′meel. The sons of Mushi:
Mahli, Eder, and Jer′imoth.
These were the sons of the Levites according to their fathers'
houses. These also, the head
of each father's house and his
younger brother alike, cast lots,
just as their brethren in the
presence of King
David, Zadok, Ahim′elech, and
the heads of fathers' houses of the
priests and of the Levites.

Musicians and singers

25 David and the chiefs of the
service also set apart for the
service certain of the sons of
Asaph, and of Heman, and of
Jedu′thun, who should prophesy
with lyres, with harps, and with
cymbals. The list of those who
did the work and of their duties
was: Of the sons of Asaph:
Zaccur, Joseph, Nethani′ah, and
Ashare′lah, sons of Asaph, under
the direction of Asaph, who
prophesied under the direction of
the king. Of Jedu′thun, the sons
of Jedu′thun: Gedali′ah, Zeri,
Jeshai′ah, Shim′e-i,ᵃ Hashabi′ah,
and Mattithi′ah, six, under the
direction of their father Jedu′-
thun, who prophesied with the
lyre in thanksgiving and praise to
the LORD. Of Heman, the sons of
Heman: Bukki′ah, Mattani′ah,
Uz′ziel, Sheb′uel, and Jer′imoth,
Hanani′ah, Hana′ni, Eli′athah,
Giddal′ti, and Romam′ti-e′zer,

Joshbekash′ah, Mallo′thi, Hothir,
Maha′zi-oth. All these were the 5
sons of Heman, the king's seer,
according to the promise of God
to exalt him; for God had given
Heman fourteen sons and three
daughters. They were all under 6
the direction of their father in the
music in the house of the LORD
with cymbals, harps, and lyres for
the service of the house of God.
Asaph, Jedu′thun, and Heman
were under the order of the king.
The number of them along with 7
their brethren, who were trained
in singing to the LORD, all who
were skilful, was two hundred and
eighty-eight. And they cast lots 8
for their duties, small and great,
teacher and pupil alike.
The first lot fell for Asaph to 9
Joseph; the second to Gedali′ah,
to him and his brethren and his
sons, twelve; the third to Zaccur, 10
his sons and his brethren, twelve;
the fourth to Izri, his sons and his 11
brethren, twelve; the fifth to 12
Nethani′ah, his sons and his
brethren, twelve; the sixth to 13
Bukki′ah, his ʹsons and his brethren, twelve; the seventh to Jesh- 14
are′lah, his sons and his brethren, twelve; the eighth to Jesh- 15
ai′ah, his sons and his brethren,
twelve; the ninth to Mattani′ah, 16
his sons and his brethren, twelve;
the tenth to Shim′e-i, his sons and 17
his brethren, twelve; the elev- 18
enth to Az′arel, his sons and his
brethren, twelve; the twelfth to 19
Hashabi′ah, his sons and his
brethren, twelve; to the thir- 20
teenth, Shu′ba-el, his sons and
his brethren, twelve; to the 21
fourteenth, Mattithi′ah, his sons
and his brethren, twelve; to the 22
fifteenth, to Jer′emoth, his sons
and his brethren, twelve; to the 23
sixteenth, to Hanani′ah, his sons
and his brethren, twelve; to the 24
seventeenth, to Joshbekash′ah, his
sons and his brethren, twelve; to 25
the eighteenth, to Hana′ni, his
sons and his brethren, twelve; to 26
the nineteenth, to Mallo′thi, his
sons and his brethren, twelve; to 27
the twentieth, to Eli′athah, his
sons and his brethren, twelve; to 28
the twenty-first, to Hothir, his
sons and his brethren, twelve; to 29
the twenty-second, to Giddal′ti,
his sons and his brethren, twelve;
to the twenty-third, to Maha′zi- 30
oth, his sons and his brethren,
twelve; to the twenty-fourth, to 31
Romam′ti-e′zer, his sons and his
brethren, twelve.

Officers and judges

As for the divisions of the gate- 26
keepers: of the Ko′rahites,
Meshelemi′ah the son of Ko′re, of
the sons of Asaph. And Meshel- 2
emi′ah had sons: Zechari′ah the
first-born, Jedi′a-el the second,
Zebadi′ah the third, Jath′ni-el the
fourth, Elam the fifth, Jehoha′- 3
nan the sixth, El′ieho-e′nai the
seventh. And O′bed-e′dom had 4

ʸ See 23.19: Heb lacks *Hebron*   ᶻ See 23.19: Heb lacks *the chief*   ᵃ One Ms: Gk: Heb lacks *Shimei*

sons: Shemai'ah the first-born, Jeho'zabad the second, Jo'ah the third, Sachar the fourth, Neth-
5 an'el the fifth, Am'miel the sixth, Is'sachar the seventh, Pe-ul'lethai the eighth; for God blessed him.
6 Also to his son Shemai'ah were sons born who were rulers in their fathers' houses, for they were men
7 of great ability. The sons of Shemai'ah: Othni, Reph'a-el, Obed, and Elza'bad, whose brethren were able men, Eli'hu and
8 Semachi'ah. All these were of the sons of O'bed-e'dom with their sons and brethren, able men qualified for the service; sixty-
9 two of O'bed-e'dom. And Meshelemi'ah had sons and brethren, able men, eighteen.
10 And Hosah, of the sons of Merar'i, had sons: Shimri the chief (for though he was not the first-born, his father made him
11 chief), Hilki'ah the second, Tebali'ah the third, Zechari'ah the fourth: all the sons and brethren of Hosah were thirteen.
12 These divisions of the gatekeepers, corresponding to their chief men, had duties, just as their brethren did, ministering in the
13 house of the LORD; and they cast lots by fathers' houses, small and
14 great alike, for their gates. The lot for the east fell to Shelemi'ah. They cast lots also for his son Zechari'ah, a shrewd counsellor, and his lot came out for the
15 north. O'bed-e'dom's came out for the south, and to his sons was
16 allotted the storehouse. For Shuppim and Hosah it came out for the west, at the gate of Shal'lecheth on the road that goes up. Watch corresponded to watch.
17 On the east there were six each day,[b] on the north four each day, on the south four each day, as well as two and two at the storehouse;
18 and for the parbar[c] on the west there were four at the road and
19 two at the parbar. These were the divisions of the gatekeepers among the Ko'rahites and the sons of Merar'i.
20 And of the Levites, Ahi'jah had charge of the treasuries of the house of God and the treasuries of
21 the dedicated gifts. The sons of Ladan, the sons of the Gershonites belonging to Ladan, the heads of the fathers' houses belonging to Ladan the Gershonite: Jehi'eli.[d]
22 The sons of Jehi'eli, Zetham and Jo'el his brother, were in charge of the treasuries of the house of
23 the LORD. Of the Amramites, the Iz'harites, the He'bronites, and
24 the Uz'zielites—and Sheb'uel the son of Gershom, son of Moses, was chief officer in charge of the
25 treasuries. His brethren: from Elie'zer were his son Rehabi'ah, and his son Jeshai'ah, and his son Joram, and his son Zichri, and his
26 son Shelo'moth. This Shelo'-

moth and his brethren were in charge of all the treasuries of the dedicated gifts which David the king, and the heads of the fathers' houses, and the officers of the thousands and the hundreds, and the commanders of the army, had
27 dedicated. From spoil won in battles they dedicated gifts for the maintenance of the house of
28 the LORD. Also all that Samuel the seer, and Saul the son of Kish, and Abner the son of Ner, and Jo'ab the son of Zeru'iah had dedicated—all dedicated gifts were in the care of Shelo'moth[e] and his brethren.
29 Of the Iz'harites, Chenani'ah and his sons were appointed to outside duties for Israel, as offi-
30 cers and judges. Of the He'bronites, Hashabi'ah and his brethren, one thousand seven hundred men of ability, had the oversight of Israel westward of the Jordan for all the work of the LORD and for
31 the service of the king. Of the He'bronites, Jeri'jah was chief of the He'bronites of whatever genealogy or fathers' houses. (In the fortieth year of David's reign search was made and men of great ability among them were found at
32 Jazer in Gilead.) King David appointed him and his brethren, two thousand seven hundred men of ability, heads of fathers' houses, to have the oversight of the Reubenites, the Gadites, and the half-tribe of the Manas'sites for everything pertaining to God and for the affairs of the king.

Overseers

27 This is the list of the people of Israel, the heads of fathers' houses, the commanders of thousands and hundreds, and their officers who served the king in all matters concerning the divisions that came and went, month after month throughout the year, each division numbering twenty-four
2 thousand: Jasho'be-am the son of Zab'di-el was in charge of the first division in the first month; in his division
3 were twenty-four thousand. He was a descendant of Perez, and was chief of all the commanders of the army for the first month.
4 Dodai the Aho'hite[f] was in charge of the division of the second month; in his division were twen-
5 ty-four thousand. The third commander, for the third month, was Benai'ah, the son of Jehoi'ada the priest, as chief; in his division
6 were twenty-four thousand. This is the Benai'ah who was a mighty man of the thirty and in command of the thirty; Ammiz'abad his son was in charge of his division.[g]
7 As'ahel the brother of Jo'ab was fourth, for the fourth month, and his son Zebadi'ah after him; in his division were twenty-four

thousand. The fifth commander, for the fifth month, was Shamhuth, the Iz'rahite; in his division were twenty-four thousand. Sixth, for the sixth month, was Ira, the son of Ikkesh the Teko'ite; in his division were twenty-four thousand. Seventh, for the seventh month, was Helez the Pel'onite, of the sons of E'phraim; in his division were twenty-four thousand. Eighth, for the eighth month, was Sib'becai the Hu'shathite, of the Zer'ahites; in his division were twenty-four thousand. Ninth, for the ninth month, was Abi-e'zer of An'athoth, a Benjaminite; in his division were twenty-four thousand. Tenth, for the tenth month, was Ma'harai of Netoph'ah, of the Zer'ahites; in his division were twenty-four thousand. Eleventh, for the eleventh month, was Benai'ah of Pir'athon, of the sons of E'phraim; in his division were twenty-four thousand. Twelfth, for the twelfth month, was Heldai the Netoph'athite, of Oth'ni-el; in his division were twenty-four thousand.

Over the tribes of Israel, for the Reubenites Elie'zer the son of Zichri was chief officer; for the Simeonites, Shephati'ah the son of Ma'acah; for Levi, Hashabi'ah the son of Kemu'el; for Aaron, Zadok; for Judah, Eli'hu, one of David's brothers; for Is'sachar, Omri the son of Michael; for Zeb'ulun, Ishma'iah the son of Obadi'ah; for Naph'tali, Jer'emoth the son of Az'ri-el; for the E'phraimites, Hoshe'a the son of Azazi'ah; for the half-tribe of Manas'seh, Jo'el the son of Peda'iah; for the half-tribe of Manas'seh in Gilead, Iddo the son of Zechari'ah; for Benjamin, Ja-a'si-el the son of Abner; for Dan, Az'arel the son of Jero'ham. These were the leaders of the tribes of Israel. David did not number those below twenty years of age, for the LORD had promised to make Israel as many as the stars of heaven. Jo'ab the son of Zeru'iah began to number, but did not finish; yet wrath came upon Israel for this, and the number was not entered in the chronicles of King David.

Over the king's treasuries was Az'maveth the son of Ad'i-el; and over the treasuries in the country, in the cities, in the villages and in the towers, was Jonathan the son of Uzzi'ah; and over those who did the work of the field for tilling the soil was Ezri the son of Chelub; and over the vineyards was Shim'e-i the Ra'mathite; and over the produce of the vineyards for the wine cellars was Zabdi the Shiphmite. Over the olive and sycamore trees in the Sheph'elah was Ba'al-ha'nan the Gede'rite; and over the stores of oil was

---

[b] Gk: Heb Levites   [c] The meaning of the word parbar is unknown
[d] The Hebrew text of verse 21 is confused   [e] Heb Shelomith
[f] Gk: Heb Ahohite and his division and Mikloth the chief officer   [g] Gk Vg: Heb was his division

9 Jo'ash. Over the herds that
pastured in Sharon was Shitrai
the Sharonite; over the herds in
the valleys was Shaphat the son of
0 Adlai. Over the camels was Obil
the Ish'maelite; and over the
she-asses was Jehde'iah the
Meron'othite. Over the flocks 33

31 was Jaziz the Hagrite. All these
were stewards of King David's
property. 32 Jonathan, David's uncle, was a
counsellor, being a man of understanding and a scribe; he and
Jehi'el the son of Hach'moni
attended the king's sons. Ahith'-

ophel was the king's counsellor,
and Hushai the Archite was the
king's friend. Ahith'ophel was 34
succeeded by Jehoi'ada the son of
Benai'ah, and Abi'athar. Jo'ab
was commander of the king's
army.

David's last words

28 DAVID assembled at Jerusalem all the
officials of Israel, the officials of the
tribes, the officers of the divisions that served
the king, the commanders of thousands, the
commanders of hundreds, the stewards of all
the property and cattle of the king and his
sons, together with the palace officials, the
mighty men, and all the seasoned warriors.
2 Then King David rose to his feet and said:
"Hear me, my brethren and my people. I
had it in my heart to build a house of rest for
the ark of the covenant of the LORD, and for
the footstool of our God; and I made prepa-
3 rations for building. But God said to me,
'You may not build a house for my name, for
4 you are a warrior and have shed blood.' Yet
the LORD God of Israel chose me from all my
father's house to be king over Israel for ever;
for he chose Judah as leader, and in the house
of Judah my father's house, and among my
father's sons he took pleasure in me to make
5 me king over all Israel. And of all my sons
(for the LORD has given me many sons) he
has chosen Solomon my son to sit upon the
throne of the kingdom of the LORD over
6 Israel. He said to me, 'It is Solomon your
son who shall build my house and my courts,
for I have chosen him to be my son, and I
7 will be his father. I will establish his
kingdom for ever if he continues resolute in
keeping my commandments and my ordi-
8 nances, as he is today.' Now therefore in the
sight of all Israel, the assembly of the LORD,
and in the hearing of our God, observe and
seek out all the commandments of the LORD
your God; that you may possess this good
land, and leave it for an inheritance to your
children after you for ever.
9 "And you, Solomon my son, know the God
of your father, and serve him with a whole
heart and with a willing mind; for the LORD
searches all hearts, and understands every
plan and thought. If you seek him, he will be
found by you; but if you forsake him, he will
10 cast you off for ever. Take heed now, for the
LORD has chosen you to build a house for the
sanctuary; be strong, and do it."
11 Then David gave Solomon his son the plan
of the vestibule of the temple, and of its

houses, its treasuries, its upper rooms, and its
inner chambers, and of the room for the
mercy seat; and the plan of all that he had in 12
mind for the courts of the house of the LORD,
all the surrounding chambers, the treasuries
of the house of God, and the treasuries for
dedicated gifts; for the divisions of the 13
priests and of the Levites, and all the work of
the service in the house of the LORD; for all
the vessels for the service in the house of the
LORD, the weight of gold for all golden 14
vessels for each service, the weight of silver
vessels for each service, the weight of the 15
golden lampstands and their lamps, the
weight of gold for each lampstand and its
lamps, the weight of silver for a lampstand
and its lamps, according to the use of each
lampstand in the service, the weight of gold 16
for each table for the showbread, the silver
for the silver tables, and pure gold for the 17
forks, the basins, and the cups; for the golden
bowls and the weight of each; for the silver
bowls and the weight of each; for the altar of 18
incense made of refined gold, and its weight;
also his plan for the golden chariot of
the cherubim that spread their wings and
covered the ark of the covenant of the LORD.
All this he made clear by the writing from the 19
hand of the LORD concerning it,[h] all the work
to be done according to the plan.
Then David said to Solomon his son, "Be 20
strong and of good courage, and do it. Fear
not, be not dismayed; for the LORD God,
even my God, is with you. He will not fail
you or forsake you, until all the work for the
service of the house of the LORD is finished.
And behold the divisions of the priests and 21
the Levites for all the service of the house of
God; and with you in all the work will be
every willing man who has skill for any kind
of service; also the officers and all the people
will be wholly at your command."

And David the king said to all the assembly, 29
"Solomon my son, whom alone God has
chosen, is young and inexperienced, and the
work is great; for the palace will not be for
man but for the LORD God. So I have 2
provided for the house of my God, so far as I
was able, the gold for the things of gold, the
silver for the things of silver, and the bronze

[h] Cn: Heb *upon me*

for the things of bronze, the iron for the things of iron, and wood for the things of wood, besides great quantities of onyx and stones for setting, antimony, coloured stones, all sorts of precious stones, and marble. 3 Moreover, in addition to all that I have provided for the holy house, I have a treasure of my own of gold and silver, and because of my devotion to the house of my God I give it 4 to the house of my God: three thousand talents of gold, of the gold of Ophir, and seven thousand talents of refined silver, for 5 overlaying the walls of the house, and for all the work to be done by craftsmen, gold for the things of gold and silver for the things of silver. Who then will offer willingly, consecrating himself today to the Lord?"

6 Then the heads of fathers' houses made their freewill offerings, as did also the leaders of the tribes, the commanders of thousands and of hundreds, and the officers over the 7 king's work. They gave for the service of the house of God five thousand talents and ten thousand darics of gold, ten thousand talents of silver, eighteen thousand talents of bronze, 8 and a hundred thousand talents of iron. And whoever had precious stones gave them to the treasury of the house of the Lord, in the 9 care of Jehi'el the Gershonite. Then the people rejoiced because these had given willingly, for with a whole heart they had offered freely to the Lord; David the king also rejoiced greatly.

David gives thanks to God

10 Therefore David blessed the Lord in the presence of all the assembly; and David said: "Blessed art thou, O Lord, the God of Israel 11 our father, for ever and ever. Thine, O Lord, is the greatness, and the power, and the glory, and the victory, and the majesty; for all that is in the heavens and in the earth is thine; thine is the kingdom, O Lord, and 12 thou art exalted as head above all. Both riches and honour come from thee, and thou rulest over all. In thy hand are power and might; and in thy hand it is to make great and 13 to give strength to all. And now we thank thee, our God, and praise thy glorious name. 14 "But who am I, and what is my people, that we should be able thus to offer willingly? For all things come from thee, and of 15 thy own have we given thee. For we are strangers before thee, and sojourners, as all our fathers were; our days on the earth are 16 like a shadow, and there is no abiding.ⁱ O Lord our God, all this abundance that we

have provided for building thee a house for thy holy name comes from thy hand and is all thy own. I know, my God, that thou triest the heart, and hast pleasure in uprightness; in the uprightness of my heart I have freely offered all these things, and now I have seen thy people, who are present here, offering freely and joyously to thee. O Lord, the God of Abraham, Isaac, and Israel, our fathers, keep for ever such purposes and thoughts in the hearts of thy people, and direct their hearts toward thee. Grant to Solomon my son that with a whole heart he may keep thy commandments, thy testimonies, and thy statutes, performing all, and that he may build the palace for which I have made provision."

Then David said to all the assembly, "Bless the Lord your God." And all the assembly blessed the Lord, the God of their fathers, and bowed their heads, and worshipped the Lord, and did obeisance to the king. And they performed sacrifices to the Lord, and on the next day offered burnt offerings to the Lord, a thousand bulls, a thousand rams, and a thousand lambs, with their drink offerings, and sacrifices in abundance for all Israel; and they ate and drank before the Lord on that day with great gladness.

And they made Solomon the son of David king the second time, and they anointed him as prince for the Lord, and Zadok as priest. Then Solomon sat on the throne of the Lord as king instead of David his father; and he prospered, and all Israel obeyed him. All the leaders and the mighty men, and also all the sons of King David, pledged their allegiance to King Solomon. And the Lord gave Solomon great repute in the sight of all Israel, and bestowed upon him such royal majesty as had not been on any king before him in Israel.

Thus David the son of Jesse reigned over all Israel. The time that he reigned over Israel was forty years; he reigned seven years in Hebron, and thirty-three years in Jerusalem. Then he died in a good old age, full of days, riches, and honour; and Solomon his son reigned in his stead. Now the acts of King David, from first to last, are written in the Chronicles of Samuel the seer, and in the Chronicles of Nathan the prophet, and in the Chronicles of Gad the seer, with accounts of all his rule and his might and of the circumstances that came upon him and upon Israel, and upon all the kingdoms of the countries.

ⁱ Gk Vg: Heb *hope*
29.23: 1 Kings 2.12.

THE SECOND BOOK OF THE

CHRONICLES

SOLOMON the son of David established himself in his kingdom, and the LORD his God was with him and made him exceedingly great.

2 Solomon spoke to all Israel, to the commanders of thousands and of hundreds, to the judges, and to all the leaders in all Israel,
3 the heads of fathers' houses. And Solomon, and all the assembly with him, went to the high place that was at Gibeon; for the tent of meeting of God, which Moses the servant of the LORD had made in the wilderness, was
4 there. (But David had brought up the ark of God from Kir′iath-je′arim to the place that David had prepared for it, for he had pitched
5 a tent for it in Jerusalem.) Moreover the bronze altar that Bez′alel the son of Uri, son of Hur, had made, was there before the tabernacle of the LORD. And Solomon and
6 the assembly sought the LORD. And Solomon went up there to the bronze altar before the LORD, which was at the tent of meeting, and offered a thousand burnt offerings upon it.

7 In that night God appeared to Solomon, and said to him, "Ask what I shall give
8 you." And Solomon said to God, "Thou hast shown great and steadfast love to David my father, and hast made me king in his
9 stead. O LORD God, let thy promise to David my father be now fulfilled, for thou hast made me king over a people as many as
10 the dust of the earth. Give me now wisdom and knowledge to go out and come in before this people, for who can rule this thy people,
11 that is so great?" God answered Solomon, "Because this was in your heart, and you

have not asked possessions, wealth, honour, or the life of those who hate you, and have not even asked long life, but have asked wisdom and knowledge for yourself that you may rule my people over whom I have made you king, wisdom and knowledge are granted 12 to you. I will also give you riches, possessions, and honour, such as none of the kings had who were before you, and none after you shall have the like." So Solomon came from*a* 13 the high place at Gibeon, from before the tent of meeting, to Jerusalem. And he reigned over Israel.

Solomon gathered together chariots and 14 horsemen; he had fourteen hundred chariots and twelve thousand horsemen, whom he stationed in the chariot cities and with the king in Jerusalem. And the king made silver 15 and gold as common in Jerusalem as stone, and he made cedar as plentiful as the sycamore of the Shephe′lah. And Solomon's 16 import of horses was from Egypt and Ku′e, and the king's traders received them from Ku′e for a price. They imported a chariot 17 from Egypt for six hundred shekels of silver, and a horse for a hundred and fifty; likewise through them these were exported to all the kings of the Hittites and the kings of Syria.

BUILDING THE TEMPLE

NOW Solomon purposed to build a 2*b* temple for the name of the LORD, and a royal palace for himself. And Solomon 2*c* assigned seventy thousand men to bear burdens and eighty thousand to quarry in the

a Gk Vg: Heb *to*   *b* Ch 1.18 in Heb   *c* Ch 2.1 in Heb
1.3-13: 1 Kings 3.4-15.   **1.14-17:** 1 Kings 10.26-29.   **2.1:** 1 Kings 5.5.
2.2: 1 Kings 5.15-16; 1 Chron 2.18.

343

hill country, and three thousand six hundred
3 to oversee them. And Solomon sent word to Huram the king of Tyre: "As you dealt with David my father and sent him cedar to build himself a house to dwell in, so deal with me.
4 Behold, I am about to build a house for the name of the LORD my God and dedicate it to him for the burning of incense of sweet spices before him, and for the continual offering of the showbread, and for burnt offerings morning and evening, on the sabbaths and the new moons and the appointed feasts of the LORD our God, as ordained for
5 ever for Israel. The house which I am to build will be great, for our God is greater
6 than all gods. But who is able to build him a house, since heaven, even highest heaven, cannot contain him? Who am I to build a house for him, except as a place to burn
7 incense before him? So now send me a man skilled to work in gold, silver, bronze, and iron, and in purple, crimson, and blue fabrics, trained also in engraving, to be with the skilled workers who are with me in Judah and Jerusalem, whom David my father
8 provided. Send me also cedar, cypress, and algum timber from Lebanon, for I know that your servants know how to cut timber in Lebanon. And my servants will be with your
9 servants, to prepare timber for me in abundance, for the house I am to build will
10 be great and wonderful. I will give for your servants, the hewers who cut timber, twenty thousand cors of crushed wheat, twenty thousand cors of barley, twenty thousand baths of wine, and twenty thousand baths of oil."

Then Huram the king of Tyre answered in a letter which he sent to Solomon, "Because the LORD loves his people he has made you king over them." Huram also said, "Blessed be the LORD God of Israel, who made heaven and earth, who has given King David a wise son, endued with discretion and understanding, who will build a temple for the LORD, and a royal palace for himself.

"Now I have sent a skilled man, endued with understanding, Huram-abi, the son of a woman of the daughters of Dan, and his father was a man of Tyre. He is trained to work in gold, silver, bronze, iron, stone, and wood, and in purple, blue, and crimson fabrics and fine linen, and to do all sorts of engraving and execute any design that may be assigned him, with your craftsmen, the craftsmen of my lord, David your father. Now therefore the wheat and barley, oil and wine, of which my lord has spoken, let him send to his servants; and we will cut whatever timber you need from Lebanon, and bring it to you in rafts by sea to Joppa, so that you may take it up to Jerusalem."

Foreign labour

Then Solomon took a census of all the aliens who were in the land of Israel, after the census of them which David his father had taken; and there were found a hundred and fifty-three thousand six hundred. Seventy thousand of them he assigned to bear burdens, eighty thousand to quarry in the hill country, and three thousand six hundred as overseers to make the people work.

THE TEMPLE BUILDING

3 THEN Solomon began to build the house of the LORD in Jerusalem on Mount Mori'ah, where the LORD had appeared to David his father, at the place that David had appointed, on the
2 threshing floor of Ornan the Jeb'usite. He began to build in the second month of the fourth
3 year of his reign. These are Solomon's measurements[d] for building the house of God: the length, in cubits of the old standard, was sixty cubits, and the
4 breadth twenty cubits. The vestibule in front of the nave of the house was twenty cubits long, equal to the width of the house;[e] and its height was a hundred and twenty cubits. He overlaid it on
5 the inside with pure gold. The nave he lined with cypress, and

covered it with fine gold, and
6 made palms and chains on it. He adorned the house with settings of precious stones. The gold was
7 gold of Parva'im. So he lined the house with gold—its beams, its thresholds, its walls, and its doors; and he carved cherubim on the walls.
8 And he made the most holy place; its length, corresponding to the breadth of the house, was twenty cubits, and its breadth was twenty cubits; he overlaid it with six hundred talents of fine gold.
9 The weight of the nails was one shekel[f] to fifty shekels of gold. And he overlaid the upper chambers with gold.
10 In the most holy place he made two cherubim of wood[g] and over-
11 laid[h] them with gold. The wings of the cherubim together extended twenty cubits: one wing of the one, of five cubits, touched

the wall of the house, and its other wing, of five cubits, touched the wing of the other cherub; and of this cherub, one wing, of five cubits, touched the wall of the house, and the other wing, also of five cubits, was joined to the wing of the first cherub. The wings of these cherubim extended twenty cubits; the cherubim[i] stood on their feet, facing the nave. And he made the veil of blue and purple and crimson fabrics and fine linen, and worked cherubim on it.

In front of the house he made two pillars thirty-five cubits high, with a capital of five cubits on the top of each. He made chains like a necklace[j] and put them on the tops of the pillars; and he made a hundred pomegranates, and put them on the chains. He set up the pillars in front of the temple, one on the south, the other on the

---

[d] Syr: Heb foundations   [e] 1 Kings 6.3: Heb uncertain   [f] Compare Gk: Heb lacks one shekel
[g] Gk: Heb uncertain   [h] Heb they overlaid   [i] Heb they   [j] Cn: Heb in the inner sanctuary
2.3–16: 1 Kings 5.2–11.   3.1–13: 1 Kings 6.1–28.   3.15–17: 1 Kings 7.15–21.

north; that on the south he called
Jachin, and that on the north
Bo′az.

Temple furniture

He made an altar of bronze,
twenty cubits long, and twenty
cubits wide, and ten cubits high.
2 Then he made the molten sea; it
was round, ten cubits from brim
to brim, and five cubits high, and
a line of thirty cubits measured its
3 circumference. Under it were
figures of gourds,[k] for thirty[l]
cubits, compassing the sea round
about; the gourds[k] were in two
rows, cast with it when it was
4 cast. It stood upon twelve oxen,
three facing north, three facing
west, three facing south, and three
facing east; the sea was set upon
them, and all their hinder parts
5 were inward. Its thickness was a
handbreadth; and its brim was
made like the brim of a cup, like
the flower of a lily; it held over
6 three thousand baths. He also
made ten lavers in which to wash,
and set five on the south side, and
five on the north side. In these
they were to rinse off what was
used for the burnt offering, and
the sea was for the priests to wash
in.
7 And he made ten golden lampstands as prescribed, and set them
in the temple, five on the south
8 side and five on the north. He
also made ten tables, and placed
them in the temple, five on the
south side and five on the north.
And he made a hundred basins of
9 gold. He made the court of the
priests, and the great court, and
doors for the court, and overlaid

High priest

10 their doors with bronze; and he
set the sea at the southeast corner
of the house.
11 Huram also made the pots, the
shovels, and the basins. So
Huram finished the work that he
did for King Solomon on the
12 house of God: the two pillars, the
bowls, and the two capitals on
the top of the pillars; and the two
networks to cover the two bowls
of the capitals that were on the top

of the pillars; and the four hun- 13
dred pomegranates for the two
networks, two rows of pomegranates for each network, to
cover the two bowls of the capitals
that were upon the pillars. He 14
made the stands also, and the
lavers upon the stands, and the 15
one sea, and the twelve oxen
underneath it. The pots, the 16
shovels, the forks, and all the
equipment for these Huram-abi
made of burnished bronze for
King Solomon for the house of
the LORD. In the plain of the 17
Jordan the king cast them, in the
clay ground between Succoth and
Zer′edah. Solomon made all 18
these things in great quantities, so
that the weight of the bronze was
not ascertained.
So Solomon made all the things 19
that were in the house of God: the
golden altar, the tables for the
bread of the Presence, the lamp- 20
stands and their lamps of pure
gold to burn before the inner
sanctuary, as prescribed; the 21
flowers, the lamps, and the tongs,
of purest gold; the snuffers, 22
basins, dishes for incense, and
firepans, of pure gold; and the
sockets[m] of the temple, for the
inner doors to the most holy place
and for the doors of the nave of
the temple were of gold.

Thus all the work that Solomon **5**
did for the house of the LORD was
finished. And Solomon brought
in the things which David his
father had dedicated, and stored
the silver, the gold, and all the
vessels in the treasuries of the
house of God.

The dedication

2 THEN Solomon assembled the elders of
Israel and all the heads of the tribes, the
leaders of the fathers' houses of the people of
Israel, in Jerusalem, to bring up the ark of
the covenant of the LORD out of the city
3 of David, which is Zion. And all the men of
Israel assembled before the king at the feast
4 which is in the seventh month. And all the

elders of Israel came, and the Levites took up
the ark. And they brought up the ark, the 5
tent of meeting, and all the holy vessels that
were in the tent; the priests and the Levites
brought them up. And King Solomon and 6
all the congregation of Israel, who had
assembled before him, were before the ark,
sacrificing so many sheep and oxen that they
could not be counted or numbered. So the 7
priests brought the ark of the covenant of the
LORD to its place, in the inner sanctuary
of the house, in the most holy place, underneath the wings of the cherubim. For the 8
cherubim spread out their wings over the
place of the ark, so that the cherubim made a
covering above the ark and its poles. And the 9
poles were so long that the ends of the poles
were seen from the holy place before the
inner sanctuary; but they could not be seen
from outside; and they are there to this day.
There was nothing in the ark except the two 10

[k] 1 Kings 7.24: Heb *oxen* [l] Compare verse 2: Heb *ten* [m] 1 Kings 7.50: Heb *the door of the house*
4.2–5: 1 Kings 7.23–26. 4.6–5.1: 1 Kings 7.38–51.

tables which Moses put there at Horeb, where the LORD made a covenant with the people of Israel, when they came out of
11 Egypt. Now when the priests came out of the holy place (for all the priests who were present had sanctified themselves, without
12 regard to their divisions; and all the Levitical singers, Asaph, Heman, and Jedu'thun, their sons and kinsmen, arrayed in fine linen with cymbals, harps, and lyres, stood east of the altar with a hundred and twenty priests who
13 were trumpeters; and it was the duty of the trumpeters and singers to make themselves heard in unison in praise and thanksgiving to the LORD), and when the song was raised, with trumpets and cymbals and other musical instruments, in praise to the LORD,
"For he is good,
     for his steadfast love endures for ever,"
the house, the house of the LORD, was filled
14 with a cloud, so that the priests could not stand to minister because of the cloud; for the glory of the LORD filled the house of God.

6 Then Solomon said,
"The LORD has said that he would dwell in thick darkness.
2   I have built thee an exalted house,
      a place for thee to dwell in for ever."
3 Then the king faced about, and blessed all the assembly of Israel, while all the assembly
4 of Israel stood. And he said, "Blessed be the LORD, the God of Israel, who with his hand
5 has fulfilled what he promised with his mouth to David my father, saying, 'Since the day that I brought my people out of the land of Egypt, I chose no city in all the tribes of Israel in which to build a house, that my name might be there, and I chose no man as
6 prince over my people Israel; but I have chosen Jerusalem that my name may be there and I have chosen David to be over my
7 people Israel.' Now it was in the heart of David my father to build a house for the
8 name of the LORD, the God of Israel. But the LORD said to David my father, 'Whereas it was in your heart to build a house for my name, you did well that it was in your heart;
9 nevertheless you shall not build the house, but your son who shall be born to you shall
10 build the house for my name.' Now the LORD has fulfilled his promise which he made; for I have risen in the place of David my father, and sit on the throne of Israel, as the LORD promised, and I have built the house for the name of the LORD, the God of
11 Israel. And there I have set the ark, in which is the covenant of the LORD which he made with the people of Israel."

Solomon's prayer

Then Solomon stood before the altar of the LORD in the presence of all the assembly of Israel, and spread forth his hands. Solomon had made a bronze platform five cubits long, five cubits wide, and three cubits high, and had set it in the court; and he stood upon it. Then he knelt upon his knees in the presence of all the assembly of Israel, and spread forth his hands toward heaven; and said, "O LORD, God of Israel, there is no God like thee, in heaven or on earth, keeping covenant and showing steadfast love to thy servants who walk before thee with all their heart; who hast kept with thy servant David my father what thou didst declare to him; yea, thou didst speak with thy mouth, and with thy hand hast fulfilled it this day. Now therefore, O LORD, God of Israel, keep with thy servant David my father what thou hast promised him, saying, 'There shall never fail you a man before me to sit upon the throne of Israel, if only your sons take heed to their way, to walk in my law as you have walked before me.' Now therefore, O LORD, God of Israel, let thy word be confirmed, which thou hast spoken to thy servant David.

"But will God dwell indeed with man on the earth? Behold, heaven and the highest heaven cannot contain thee; how much less this house which I have built! Yet have I regard to the prayer of thy servant and to his supplication, O LORD my God, hearkening to the cry and to the prayer which thy servant prays before thee; that thy eyes may be open day and night toward this house, the place where thou hast promised to set thy name, that thou mayest hearken to the prayer which thy servant offers toward this place. And hearken thou to the supplications of thy servant and of thy people Israel, when they pray toward this place; yea, hear thou from heaven thy dwelling place; and when thou hearest, forgive.

"If a man sins against his neighbour and is made to take an oath, and comes and swears his oath before thy altar in this house, then hear thou from heaven, and act, and judge thy servants, requiting the guilty by bringing his conduct upon his own head, and vindicating the righteous by rewarding him according to his righteousness.

"If thy people Israel are defeated before the enemy because they have sinned against thee, when they turn again and acknowledge thy name, and pray and make supplication to thee in this house, then hear thou from heaven, and forgive the sin of thy people Israel, and bring them again to the land which thou gavest to them and to their fathers.

26 "When heaven is shut up and there is no rain because they have sinned against thee, if they pray toward this place, and acknowledge thy name, and turn from their sin, when thou 27 dost afflict them, then hear thou in heaven, and forgive the sin of thy servants, thy people Israel, when thou dost teach them the good way[n] in which they should walk; and grant rain upon thy land, which thou hast given to thy people as an inheritance.

28 "If there is famine in the land, if there is pestilence or blight or mildew or locust or caterpillar; if their enemies besiege them in any of their cities; whatever plague, whatever 29 sickness there is; whatever prayer, whatever supplication is made by any man or by all thy people Israel, each knowing his own affliction, and his own sorrow and stretching out 30 his hands toward this house; then hear thou from heaven thy dwelling place, and forgive, and render to each whose heart thou knowest, according to all his ways (for thou, thou only, knowest the hearts of the children 31 of men); that they may fear thee and walk in thy ways all the days that they live in the land which thou gavest to our fathers.

32 "Likewise when a foreigner, who is not of thy people Israel, comes from a far country for the sake of thy great name, and thy mighty hand, and thy outstretched arm, when he comes and prays toward this house, 33 hear thou from heaven thy dwelling place, and do according to all for which the foreigner calls to thee; in order that all the peoples of the earth may know thy name and fear thee, as do thy people Israel, and that they may know that this house which I have built is called by thy name.

34 "If thy people go out to battle against their enemies, by whatever way thou shalt send them, and they pray to thee toward this city which thou hast chosen and the house which 35 I have built for thy name, then hear thou from heaven their prayer and their supplication, and maintain their cause.

36 "If they sin against thee—for there is no man who does not sin—and thou art angry with them, and dost give them to an enemy, so that they are carried away captive to a land 37 far or near; yet if they lay it to heart in the land to which they have been carried captive, and repent, and make supplication to thee in the land of their captivity, saying, 'We have sinned, and have acted perversely and 38 wickedly'; if they repent with all their mind and with all their heart in the land of their captivity, to which they were carried captive,

and pray toward their land, which thou gavest to their fathers, the city which thou hast chosen, and the house which I have built for thy name, then hear thou from heaven 39 thy dwelling place their prayer and their supplications, and maintain their cause and forgive thy people who have sinned against thee. Now, O my God, let thy eyes be open 40 and thy ears attentive to a prayer of this place.

"And now arise, O LORD God, and go to 41
   thy resting place,
   thou and the ark of thy might.
Let thy priests, O LORD God, be clothed
   with salvation,
   and let thy saints rejoice in thy goodness.
O LORD God, do not turn away the face of 42
   thy anointed one!
Remember thy steadfast love for David
   thy servant."

The glory of the Lord

When Solomon had ended his prayer, fire 7 came down from heaven and consumed the burnt offering and the sacrifices, and the glory of the LORD filled the temple. And 2 the priests could not enter the house of the LORD, because the glory of the LORD filled the LORD's house. When all the children of 3 Israel saw the fire come down and the glory of the LORD upon the temple, they bowed down with their faces to the earth on the pavement, and worshipped and gave thanks to the LORD, saying,
   "For he is good,
   for his steadfast love endures for ever."
Then the king and all the people offered 4 sacrifice before the LORD. King Solomon 5 offered as a sacrifice twenty-two thousand oxen and a hundred and twenty thousand sheep. So the king and all the people dedicated the house of God. The priests 6 stood at their posts; the Levites also, with the instruments for music to the LORD which King David had made for giving thanks to the LORD—for his steadfast love endures for ever—whenever David offered praises by their ministry; opposite them the priests sounded trumpets; and all Israel stood.

And Solomon consecrated the middle of 7 the court that was before the house of the LORD; for there he offered the burnt offering and the fat of the peace offerings, because the bronze altar Solomon had made could not hold the burnt offering and the cereal offering and the fat.

At that time Solomon held the feast for 8

[n] Gk Syr Vg: Heb *toward the good way*
6.41-42: Ps 132.8-10.   7.4-10: 1 Kings 8.62-66.

seven days, and all Israel with him, a very great congregation, from the entrance of 9 Hamath to the Brook of Egypt. And on the eighth day they held a solemn assembly; for they had kept the dedication of the altar 10 seven days and the feast seven days. On the twenty-third day of the seventh month he sent the people away to their homes, joyful and glad of heart for the goodness that the LORD had shown to David and to Solomon and to Israel his people.

The divine covenant

11 Thus Solomon finished the house of the LORD and the king's house; all that Solomon had planned to do in the house of the LORD and in his own house he successfully 12 accomplished. Then the LORD appeared to Solomon in the night and said to him: "I have heard your prayer, and have chosen this place for myself as a house of sacrifice. 13 When I shut up the heavens so that there is no rain, or command the locust to devour the 14 land, or send pestilence among my people, if my people who are called by my name humble themselves, and pray and seek my face, and turn from their wicked ways, then I will hear from heaven, and will forgive their 15 sin and heal their land. Now my eyes will be open and my ears attentive to the prayer that 16 is made in this place. For now I have chosen and consecrated this house that my name may be there for ever; my eyes and my heart 17 will be there for all time. And as for you, if you walk before me, as David your father walked, doing according to all that I have commanded you and keeping my statutes 18 and my ordinances, then I will establish your royal throne, as I covenanted with David your father, saying, 'There shall not fail you a man to rule Israel.'

19 "But if you° turn aside and forsake my statutes and my commandments which I have set before you, and go and serve other 20 gods and worship them, then I will pluck you ᵖ up from the land which I have given you; ᵖ and this house, which I have consecrated for my name, I will cast out of my sight, and will make it a proverb and a byword among all peoples. And at this 21 house, which is exalted, every one passing by will be astonished, and say, 'Why has the LORD done thus to this land and to this house?' Then they will say, 'Because they forsook the 22 LORD the God of their fathers who brought them out of the land of Egypt, and laid hold on other gods, and worshipped them and served them; therefore he has brought all this evil upon them.' "

SOLOMON'S REIGN

AT the end of twenty years, in which 8 Solomon had built the house of the LORD and his own house, Solomon rebuilt 2 the cities which Huram had given to him, and settled the people of Israel in them. And Solomon went to Ha′math-zo′bah, and 3 took it. He built Tadmor in the wilderness 4 and all the store-cities which he built in Hamath. He also built Upper Beth-horon 5 and Lower Beth-horon, fortified cities with walls, gates, and bars, and Ba′alath, and all 6 the store-cities that Solomon had, and all the cities for his chariots, and the cities for his horsemen, and whatever Solomon desired to build in Jerusalem, in Lebanon, and in all the land of his dominion. All the people who 7 were left of the Hittites, the Amorites, the Per′izzites, the Hivites, and the Jeb′usites, who were not of Israel, from their descen- 8 dants who were left after them in the land, whom the people of Israel had not destroyed—these Solomon made a forced levy and so they are to this day. But of the people 9 of Israel Solomon made no slaves for his work; they were soldiers, and his officers, the commanders of his chariots, and his horsemen. And these were the chief officers of 10 King Solomon, two hundred and fifty, who exercised authority over the people. Solomon brought Pharaoh's daughter up 11 from the city of David to the house which he had built for her, for he said, "My wife shall not live in the house of David king of Israel, for the places to which the ark of the LORD has come are holy." Then Solomon offered up burnt offerings 12 to the LORD upon the altar of the LORD which he had built before the vestibule, as the duty 13 of each day required, offering according to the commandment of Moses for the sabbaths, the new moons, and the three annual feasts—the feast of unleavened bread, the feast of weeks, and the feast of tabernacles. According to the ordinance of David his 14 father, he appointed the divisions of the priests for their service, and the Levites for

---

° The word *you* is plural here   ᵖ Heb *them*
7.11–22: 1 Kings 9.1–9.   8.1–18: 1 Kings 9.10–28.

their offices of praise and ministry before the priests as the duty of each day required, and the gatekeepers in their divisions for the several gates; for so David the man of God 5 had commanded. And they did not turn aside from what the king had commanded the priests and Levites concerning any matter and concerning the treasuries.

6 Thus was accomplished all the work of Solomon from*q* the day the foundation of the house of the LORD was laid until it was finished. So the house of the LORD was completed.

7 Then Solomon went to E'zion-ge'ber and Eloth on the shore of the sea, in the land of 8 Edom. And Huram sent him by his servants ships and servants familiar with the sea, and they went to Ophir together with the servants of Solomon, and fetched from there four hundred and fifty talents of gold and brought it to King Solomon.

The queen of Sheba

9 Now when the queen of Sheba heard of the fame of Solomon she came to Jerusalem to test him with hard questions, having a very great retinue and camels bearing spices and very much gold and precious stones. When 2 she came to Solomon, she told him all that was on her mind. And Solomon answered all her questions; there was nothing hidden from Solomon which he could not explain to 3 her. And when the queen of Sheba had seen the wisdom of Solomon, the house that he had built, the food of his table, the seating of 4 his officials, and the attendance of his servants, and their clothing, his cupbearers, and their clothing, and his burnt offerings which he offered at the house of the LORD, there was no more spirit in her.

And she said to the king, "The report was 5 true which I heard in my own land of your affairs and of your wisdom, but I did not 6 believe the*r* reports until I came and my own eyes had seen it; and behold, half the greatness of your wisdom was not told me; you surpass the report which I heard. Happy are your wives!*s* Happy are these 7 your servants, who continually stand before you and hear your wisdom! Blessed be the 8 LORD your God, who has delighted in you and set you on his throne as king for the LORD your God! Because your God loved Israel and would establish them for ever, he has made you king over them, that you may execute justice and righteousness." Then 9 she gave the king a hundred and twenty talents of gold, and a very great quantity of spices, and precious stones: there were no spices such as those which the queen of Sheba gave to King Solomon.

Moreover the servants of Huram and the 10 servants of Solomon, who brought gold from Ophir, brought algum wood and precious stones. And the king made of the algum 11 wood steps*t* for the house of the LORD and for the king's house, lyres also and harps for the singers; there never was seen the like of them before in the land of Judah.

q Gk Syr Vg: Heb *to* *r* Heb *their* *s* Gk Compare 1 Kings 10.8: Heb *men*
t Gk Vg: The meaning of the Hebrew word is uncertain
9.1–28: 1 Kings 10.1–29.

Solomon's wisdom

Thus King Solomon excelled all the kings 22
of the earth in riches and in wisdom. And all 23
the kings of the earth sought the presence of
Solomon to hear his wisdom, which God had
put into his mind. Every one of them 24
brought his present, articles of silver and of
gold, garments, myrrh, spices, horses, and
mules, so much year by year. And Solomon 25
had four thousand stalls for horses and
chariots, and twelve thousand horsemen,
whom he stationed in the chariot cities and
with the king in Jerusalem. And he ruled 26
over all the kings from the Euphra'tes to the
land of the Philistines, and to the border of
Egypt. And the king made silver as common 27
in Jerusalem as stone, and cedar as plentiful
as the sycamore of the Shephe'lah. And 28
horses were imported for Solomon from
Egypt and from all lands.

12 And King Solomon gave to the queen of
Sheba all that she desired, whatever she
asked besides what she had brought to the
king. So she turned and went back to her
own land, with her servants.

Solomon's wealth

13 Now the weight of gold that came to
Solomon in one year was six hundred and
14 sixty-six talents of gold, besides that which
the traders and merchants brought; and all
the kings of Arabia and the governors of the
land brought gold and silver to Solomon.
15 King Solomon made two hundred large
shields of beaten gold; six hundred shekels of
16 beaten gold went into each shield. And he
made three hundred shields of beaten gold;
three hundred shekels of gold went into each
shield; and the king put them in the House of
17 the Forest of Lebanon. The king also made a
great ivory throne, and overlaid it with pure
18 gold. The throne had six steps and a footstool of gold, which were attached to the
throne, and on each side of the seat were arm
rests and two lions standing beside the arm
19 rests, while twelve lions stood there, one on
each end of a step on the six steps. The like
20 of it was never made in any kingdom. All
King Solomon's drinking vessels were of
gold, and all the vessels of the House of the
Forest of Lebanon were of pure gold; silver
was not considered as anything in the days of
21 Solomon. For the king's ships went to
Tarshish with the servants of Huram; once
every three years the ships of Tarshish used
to come bringing gold, silver, ivory, apes,
and peacocks. [u]

The Extent of
SOLOMON'S
EMPIRE

PHOENICIA

Tyre • Dan

The
Great
Sea

EGYPTIAN

Gibeon
• Anathoth
Jerusalem
• Gath

Beer-sheba

EGYPT

Ezion-geber • Elath

N

[u] Or baboons

Now the rest of the acts of Solomon, from first to last, are they not written in the history of Nathan the prophet, and in the prophecy of Ahi'jah the Shi'lonite, and in the visions of Iddo the seer concerning Jerobo'am the son of Nebat? Solomon reigned in Jerusalem over all Israel forty years. And Solomon slept with his fathers, and was buried in the city of David his father; and Rehobo'am his son reigned in his stead.

THE KINGDOM OF JUDAH

REHOBO'AM went to Shechem, for all Israel had come to Shechem to make him king. And when Jerobo'am the son of Nebat heard of it (for he was in Egypt, whither he had fled from King Solomon), then Jerobo'am returned from Egypt. And they sent and called him; and Jerobo'am and all Israel came and said to Rehobo'am, "Your father made our yoke heavy. Now therefore lighten the hard service of your father and his heavy yoke upon us, and we will serve you." He said to them, "Come to me again in three days." So the people went away.

King Rehoboam

Then King Rehobo'am took counsel with the old men, who had stood before Solomon his father while he was yet alive, saying, "How do you advise me to answer this people?" And they said to him, "If you will be kind to this people and please them, and speak good words to them, then they will be your servants for ever." But he forsook the counsel which the old men gave him, and took counsel with the young men who had grown up with him and stood before him. And he said to them, "What do you advise that we answer this people who have said to me, 'Lighten the yoke that your father put upon us'?" And the young men who had grown 10 up with him said to him, "Thus shall you speak to the people who said to you, 'Your father made our yoke heavy, but do you lighten it for us'; thus shall you say to them, 'My little finger is thicker than my father's loins. And now, whereas my father laid upon 11 you a heavy yoke, I will add to your yoke. My father chastised you with whips, but I will chastise you with scorpions.' "

So Jerobo'am and all the people came to 12 Rehobo'am the third day, as the king said, "Come to me again the third day." And the 13 king answered them harshly, and forsaking the counsel of the old men, King Rehobo'am 14 spoke to them according to the counsel of the young men, saying, "My father made your yoke heavy, but I will add to it; my father chastised you with whips, but I will chastise you with scorpions." So the king did not 15 hearken to the people; for it was a turn of affairs brought about by God that the LORD might fulfil his word, which he spoke by Ahi'jah the Shi'lonite to Jerobo'am the son of Nebat.

Revolt of ten tribes

And when all Israel saw that the king did 16 not hearken to them, the people answered the king,

"What portion have we in David?
     We have no inheritance in the son of Jesse.
Each of you to your tents, O Israel!
     Look now to your own house, David."

So all Israel departed to their tents. But 17 Rehobo'am reigned over the people of Israel who dwelt in the cities of Judah. Then King 18 Rehobo'am sent Hador'am, who was taskmaster over the forced labour, and the people of Israel stoned him to death with stones. And King Rehobo'am made haste to mount his chariot, to flee to Jerusalem. So Israel 19 has been in rebellion against the house of David to this day.

9.30–31: 1 Kings 11.42–48.   10.1–19: 1 Kings 12.1–19.

JERUSALEM THE CAPITAL OF JUDAH

Fortified cities

11 WHEN Rehobo'am came to Jerusalem, he assembled the house of Judah, and Benjamin, a hundred and eighty thousand chosen warriors, to fight against Israel, to 2 restore the kingdom to Rehobo'am. But the word of the LORD came to Shemai'ah the 3 man of God: "Say to Rehobo'am the son of Solomon king of Judah, and to all Israel in 4 Judah and Benjamin, 'Thus says the LORD, You shall not go up or fight against your brethren. Return every man to his home, for this thing is from me.'" So they hearkened to the word of the LORD, and returned and did not go against Jerobo'am.

5 Rehobo'am dwelt in Jerusalem, and he 6 built cities for defence in Judah. He built 7 Bethlehem, Etam, Teko'a, Beth-zur, Soco, 8 Adullam, Gath, Mare'shah, Ziph, 9,Adora'im, Lachish, Aze'kah, Zorah, Ai'- 10 jalon, and Hebron, fortified cities which are 11 in Judah and in Benjamin. He made the fortresses strong, and put commanders in 12 them, and stores of food, oil, and wine. And he put shields and spears in all the cities, and made them very strong. So he held Judah and Benjamin.

13 And the priests and the Levites that were in all Israel resorted to him from all places 14 where they lived. For the Levites left their common lands and their holdings and came to Judah and Jerusalem, because Jerobo'am and his sons cast them out from serving as 15 priests of the LORD, and he appointed his own priests for the high places, and for the satyrs, and for the calves which he had 16 made. And those who had set their hearts to seek the LORD God of Israel came after them from all the tribes of Israel to Jerusalem to sacrifice to the LORD, the God of their 17 fathers. They strengthened the kingdom of Judah, and for three years they made Rehobo'am the son of Solomon secure, for they walked for three years in the way of David and Solomon.

18 Rehobo'am took as wife Ma'halath the daughter of Jer'imoth the son of David, and of Ab'ihail the daughter of Eli'ab the son of 19 Jesse; and she bore him sons, Je'ush, 20 Shemari'ah, and Zaham. After her he took Ma'acah the daughter of Ab'salom, who bore him Abi'jah, Attai, Ziza, and Shelo'mith. 21 Rehobo'am loved Ma'acah the daughter of Ab'salom above all his wives and concubines (he took eighteen wives and sixty concubines, and had twenty-eight sons and sixty daugh-

ters); and Rehobo'am appointed Abi'jah the son of Ma'acah as chief prince among his brothers, for he intended to make him king. And he dealt wisely, and distributed some of his sons through all the districts of Judah and Benjamin, in all the fortified cities; and he gave them abundant provisions, and procured wives for them. [v]

Attacked by Egypt

When the rule of Rehobo'am was estab- 1 lished and was strong, he forsook the law of the LORD, and all Israel with him. In the fifth year of King Rehobo'am, because they had been unfaithful to the LORD, Shishak king of Egypt came up against Jerusalem with twelve hundred chariots and sixty thousand horsemen. And the people were without number who came with him from Egypt—Libyans, Suk'ki-im, and Ethiopians. And he took the fortified cities of Judah and came as far as Jerusalem. Then Shemai'ah the prophet came to Rehobo'am and to the princes of Judah, who had gathered at Jerusalem because of Shishak, and said to them, "Thus says the LORD, 'You abandoned me, so I have abandoned you to the hand of Shishak.'" Then the princes of Israel and the king humbled themselves and said, "The LORD is righteous." When the LORD saw that they humbled themselves, the word of the LORD came to Shemai'ah: "They have humbled themselves; I will not destroy them, but I will grant them some deliverance, and my wrath shall not be poured out upon Jerusalem by the hand of Shishak. Nevertheless they shall be servants to him, 8 that they may know my service and the service of the kingdoms of the countries."

So Shishak king of Egypt came up against 9 Jerusalem; he took away the treasures of the house of the LORD and the treasures of the king's house; he took away everything. He also took away the shields of gold which Solomon had made; and King Rehobo'am made in their stead shields of bronze, and committed them to the hands of the officers of the guard, who kept the door of the king's house. And as often as the king went into the house of the LORD, the guard came and bore them, and brought them back to the guardroom. And when he humbled himself the wrath of the LORD turned from him, so as not to make a complete destruction; moreover, conditions were good in Judah.

So King Rehobo'am established himself in 1

Jerusalem and reigned. Rehobo'am was forty-one years old when he began to reign, and he reigned seventeen years in Jerusalem, the city which the LORD had chosen out of all the tribes of Israel to put his name there. His mother's name was Na'amah the Ammonit-
14 ess. And he did evil, for he did not set his heart to seek the LORD.

15 Now the acts of Rehobo'am, from first to last, are they not written in the chronicles of Shemai'ah the prophet and of Iddo the seer?[w] There were continual wars between
16 Rehobo'am and Jerobo'am. And Rehobo'am slept with his fathers, and was buried in the city of David; and Abi'jah his son reigned in his stead.

Abijah's reign

13 In the eighteenth year of King Jerobo'am
2 Abi'jah began to reign over Judah. He reigned for three years in Jerusalem. His mother's name was Micai'ah the daughter of Uri'el of Gib'e-ah.

Now there was war between Abi'jah and
3 Jerobo'am. Abi'jah went out to battle having an army of valiant men of war, four hundred thousand picked men; and Jerobo'am drew up his line of battle against him with eight hundred thousand picked mighty warriors.
4 Then Abi'jah stood up on Mount Zemara'im which is in the hill country of E'phraim, and said, "Hear me, O Jerobo'am and all Israel!
5 Ought you not to know that the LORD God of Israel gave the kingship over Israel for ever to David and his sons by a covenant of salt?
6 Yet Jerobo'am the son of Nebat, a servant of Solomon the son of David, rose up and
7 rebelled against his lord; and certain worthless scoundrels gathered about him and defied Rehobo'am the son of Solomon, when Rehobo'am was young and irresolute and could not withstand them.
8 "And now you think to withstand the kingdom of the LORD in the hand of the sons of David, because you are a great multitude and have with you the golden calves which Jerobo'am made you for gods. Have you not 9 driven out the priests of the LORD, the sons of Aaron, and the Levites, and made priests for yourselves like the peoples of other lands? Whoever comes to consecrate himself with a young bull or seven rams becomes a priest of what are no gods. But as for us, 10 the LORD is our God, and we have not forsaken him. We have priests ministering to the LORD who are sons of Aaron, and Levites for their service. They offer to the LORD 11 every morning and every evening burnt offerings and incense of sweet spices, set out the showbread on the table of pure gold, and care for the golden lampstand that its lamps may burn every evening; for we keep the charge of the LORD our God, but you have forsaken him. Behold, God is with us at our 12 head, and his priests with their battle trumpets to sound the call to battle against you. O sons of Israel, do not fight against the LORD, the God of your fathers; for you cannot succeed."

Jerobo'am had sent an ambush around to 13 come on them from behind; thus his troops[x] were in front of Judah, and the ambush was behind them. And when Judah looked, 14 behold, the battle was before and behind them; and they cried to the LORD, and the priests blew the trumpets. Then the men of 15 Judah raised the battle shout. And when the men of Judah shouted, God defeated Jerobo'am and all Israel before Abi'jah and Judah. The men of Israel fled before 16 Judah, and God gave them into their hand. Abi'jah and his people slew them with a great 17 slaughter; so there fell slain of Israel five hundred thousand picked men. Thus the 18 men of Israel were subdued at that time, and the men of Judah prevailed, because they relied upon the LORD, the God of their fathers. And Abi'jah pursued Jerobo'am, 19 and took cities from him, Bethel with its villages and Jesh'anah with its villages and Ephron[y] with its villages. Jerobo'am did not 20

---

[w] Heb *seer, to enrol oneself*   [x] Heb *they*   [y] Another reading is *Ephrain*
13.1–2: 1 Kings 15.1–2, 7.

recover his power in the days of Abi'jah; and 21 the LORD smote him, and he died. But Abi'jah grew mighty. And he took fourteen wives, and had twenty-two sons and sixteen 22 daughters. The rest of the acts of Abi'jah, his ways and his sayings, are written in the story of the prophet Iddo.

Asa

14ᶻ So Abi'jah slept with his fathers, and they buried him in the city of David; and Asa his son reigned in his stead. In his days the land 2ᵃhad rest for ten years. And Asa did what was good and right in the eyes of the LORD 3 his God. He took away the foreign altars and the high places, and broke down the pillars 4 and hewed down the Ashe'rim, and commanded Judah to seek the LORD, the God of their fathers, and to keep the law and the 5 commandment. He also took out of all the cities of Judah the high places and the incense altars. And the kingdom had rest 6 under him. He built fortified cities in Judah, for the land had rest. He had no war in those 7 years, for the LORD gave him peace. And he said to Judah, "Let us build these cities, and surround them with walls and towers, gates and bars; the land is still ours, because we have sought the LORD our God; we have sought him, and he has given us peace on every side." So they built and prospered. 8 And Asa had an army of three hundred thousand from Judah, armed with bucklers and spears, and two hundred and eighty thousand men from Benjamin, that carried shields and drew bows; all these were mighty men of valour. 9   Zerah the Ethiopian came out against them with an army of a million men and three hundred chariots, and came as far as 10 Mare'shah. And Asa went out to meet him, and they drew up their lines of battle in the 11 valley of Zeph'athah at Mare'shah. And Asa cried to the LORD his God, "O LORD, there is none like thee to help, between the mighty and the weak. Help us, O LORD our God, for we rely on thee, and in thy name we have come against this multitude. O LORD, thou art our God; let not man prevail against 12 thee." So the LORD defeated the Ethiopians before Asa and before Judah, and the Ethio- 13 pians fled. Asa and the people that were with him pursued them as far as Gerar, and the Ethiopians fell until none remained alive; for they were broken before the LORD and his army. The men of Judahᵇ carried away very 14 much booty. And they smote all the cities round about Gerar, for the fear of the LORD

was upon them. They plundered all the cities, for there was much plunder in them. And they smote the tents of those who had 15 cattle,ᶜ and carried away sheep in abundance and camels. Then they returned to Jerusalem.

The prophecy of Azariah

The Spirit of God came upon Azari'ah the **15** son of Oded, and he went out to meet Asa, 2 and said to him, "Hear me, Asa, and all Judah and Benjamin: The LORD is with you, while you are with him. If you seek him, he will be found by you, but if you forsake him, he will forsake you. For a long time Israel 3 was without the true God, and without a teaching priest, and without law; but when in 4 their distress they turned to the LORD, the God of Israel, and sought him, he was found by them. In those times there was no peace 5 to him who went out or to him who came in, for great disturbances afflicted all the inhabitants of the lands. They were broken in 6 pieces, nation against nation and city against city, for God troubled them with every sort of distress. But you, take courage! Do not 7 let your hands be weak, for your work shall be rewarded."

When Asa heard these words, the prophecy 8 of Azari'ah the son of Oded,ᵈ he took courage, and put away the abominable idols from all the land of Judah and Benjamin and from the cities which he had taken in the hill country of E'phraim, and he repaired the altar of the LORD that was in front of the vestibule of the house of the LORD.ᵉ And he gathered 9 all Judah and Benjamin, and those from E'phraim, Manas'seh, and Simeon who were sojourning with them, for great numbers had deserted to him from Israel when they saw that the LORD his God was with him. They 10 were gathered at Jerusalem in the third month of the fifteenth year of the reign of Asa. They sacrificed to the LORD on that 11 day, from the spoil which they had brought, seven hundred oxen and seven thousand sheep. And they entered into a covenant to 12 seek the LORD, the God of their fathers, with all their heart and with all their soul; and that 13 whoever would not seek the LORD, the God of Israel, should be put to death, whether young or old, man or woman. They took 14 oath to the LORD with a loud voice, and with shouting, and with trumpets, and with horns. And all Judah rejoiced over the oath; 15 for they had sworn with all their heart, and had sought him with their whole desire, and

---

ᶻ Ch 13.23 in Heb   ᵃ Ch 14.1 in Heb   ᵇ Heb *they*   ᶜ Heb obscure
ᵈ Compare Syr Vg: Heb *the prophecy, Oded the prophet*   ᵉ Heb *the vestibule of the* LORD
14.1–5: 1 Kings 15.8–12.

B. C.
900~800

he was found by them, and the LORD gave them rest round about.

16 Even Ma′acah, his mother, King Asa removed from being queen mother because she had made an abominable image for Ashe′rah. Asa cut down her image, crushed 17 it, and burned it at the brook Kidron. But the high places were not taken out of Israel. Nevertheless the heart of Asa was blameless 18 all his days. And he brought into the house of God the votive gifts of his father and his own votive gifts, silver, and gold, and 19 vessels. And there was no more war until the thirty-fifth year of the reign of Asa.

16 In the thirty-sixth year of the reign of Asa, Ba′asha king of Israel went up against Judah, and built Ramah, that he might permit no one to go out or come in to Asa king of 2 Judah. Then Asa took silver and gold from the treasures of the house of the LORD and the king's house, and sent them to Ben-ha′dad king of Syria, who dwelt in Damas-3 cus, saying, "Let there be a league between me and you, as between my father and your father; behold, I am sending to you silver and gold; go, break your league with Ba′asha king of Israel, that he may withdraw from 4 me." And Ben-ha′dad hearkened to King Asa, and sent the commanders of his armies against the cities of Israel, and they conquered I′jon, Dan, A′bel-ma′im, and all the 5 store-cities of Naph′tali. And when Ba′asha heard of it, he stopped building Ramah, and 6 let his work cease. Then King Asa took all Judah, and they carried away the stones of Ramah and its timber, with which Ba′asha had been building, and with them he built Geba and Mizpah.

7 At that time Hana′ni the seer came to Asa king of Judah, and said to him, "Because you relied on the king of Syria, and did not rely on the LORD your God, the army of the king 8 of Syria has escaped you. Were not the Ethiopians and the Libyans a huge army with exceedingly many chariots and horsemen? Yet because you relied on the LORD, 9 he gave them into your hand. For the eyes of the LORD run to and fro throughout the whole earth, to show his might in behalf of those whose heart is blameless toward him. You have done foolishly in this; for from now on you will have wars." Then Asa 10 was angry with the seer, and put him in the stocks, in prison, for he was in a rage with him because of this. And Asa inflicted cruelties upon some of the people at the same time.

The acts of Asa, from first to last, are 11 written in the Book of the Kings of Judah and Israel. In the thirty-ninth year of his 12 reign Asa was diseased in his feet, and his disease became severe; yet even in his disease he did not seek the LORD, but sought help from physicians. And Asa slept with his 13 fathers, dying in the forty-first year of his reign. They buried him in the tomb which 14 he had hewn out for himself in the city of David. They laid him on a bier which had been filled with various kinds of spices prepared by the perfumer's art; and they made a very great fire in his honour.

Jehoshaphat

Jehosh′aphat his son reigned in his stead, **17** and strengthened himself against Israel. He 2 placed forces in all the fortified cities of Judah, and set garrisons in the land of Judah, and in the cities of E′phraim which Asa his father had taken. The LORD was with Je- 3 hosh′aphat, because he walked in the earlier ways of his father;*f* he did not seek the Ba′als, but sought the God of his father 4 and walked in his commandments, and not according to the ways of Israel. Therefore 5 the LORD established the kingdom in his hand; and all Judah brought tribute to Jehosh′aphat; and he had great riches and honour. His heart was courageous in the 6 ways of the LORD; and furthermore he took the high places and the Ashe′rim out of Judah.

In the third year of his reign he sent his 7 princes, Ben-hail, Obadi′ah, Zechari′ah, Nethan′el, and Micai′ah, to teach in the cities

---

f Another reading is *his father David*

8 of Judah; and with them the Levites, Shemai′ah, Nethani′ah, Zebadi′ah, As′ahel, Shemir′amoth, Jehon′athan, Adoni′jah, Tobi′jah, and Tobadoni′jah; and with these Levites, the priests Elish′ama and Jeho′ram.
9 And they taught in Judah, having the book of

the law of the LORD with them; they went about through all the cities of Judah and taught among the people.
10 And the fear of the LORD fell upon all the kingdoms of the lands that were round about Judah, and they made no war against
11 Jehosh′aphat. Some of the Philistines brought Jehosh′aphat presents, and silver for tribute; and the Arabs also brought him seven thousand seven hundred rams and seven thousand seven hundred he-goats.
12 And Jehosh′aphat grew steadily greater. He
13 built in Judah fortresses and store-cities, and he had great stores in the cities of Judah. He had soldiers, mighty men of valour, in Jeru-
14 salem. This was the muster of them by fathers′ houses: Of Judah, the commanders of thousands: Adnah the commander, with three hundred thousand mighty men of
15 valour, and next to him Jehoha′nan the commander, with two hundred and eighty
16 thousand, and next to him Amasi′ah the son of Zichri, a volunteer for the service of the LORD, with two hundred thousand mighty
17 men of valour. Of Benjamin: Eli′ada, a mighty man of valour, with two hundred thousand men armed with bow and shield,
18 and next to him Jeho′zabad with a hundred
19 and eighty thousand armed for war. These were in the service of the king, besides those whom the king had placed in the fortified cities throughout all Judah.

Now Jehosh′aphat had great riches and 1 honour; and he made a marriage alliance with Ahab. After some years he went down 2 to Ahab in Samar′ia. And Ahab killed an abundance of sheep and oxen for him and for the people who were with him, and induced him to go up against Ramoth-gilead. Ahab 3 king of Israel said to Jehosh′aphat king of Judah, "Will you go with me to Ramoth-gilead?" He answered him, "I am as you are, my people as your people. We will be with you in the war."

The prophecy of Micaiah

And Jehosh′aphat said to the king of Israel, 4 "Inquire first for the word of the LORD." Then the king of Israel gathered the 5 prophets together, four hundred men, and said to them, "Shall we go to battle against Ramoth-gilead, or shall I forbear?" And they said, "Go up; for God will give it into the hand of the king." But Jehosh′aphat 6 said, "Is there not here another prophet of the LORD of whom we may inquire?" And 7 the king of Israel said to Jehosh′aphat, "There is yet one man by whom we may inquire of the LORD, Micai′ah the son of Imlah; but I hate him, for he never prophesies good concerning me, but always evil." And Jehosh′aphat said, "Let not the king say so." Then the king of Israel summoned an 8 officer and said, "Bring quickly Micai′ah the son of Imlah." Now the king of Israel and 9 Jehosh′aphat the king of Judah were sitting on their thrones, arrayed in their robes; and they were sitting at the threshing floor at the entrance of the gate of Samar′ia; and all the prophets were prophesying before them. And Zedeki′ah the son of Chena′anah made 10 for himself horns of iron, and said, "Thus says the LORD, 'With these you shall push the Syrians until they are destroyed.' " And all 11 the prophets prophesied so, and said, "Go up to Ramoth-gilead and triumph; the LORD will give it into the hand of the king."
And the messenger who went to summon 12 Micai′ah said to him, "Behold, the words of the prophets with one accord are favourable to the king; let your word be like the word of one of them, and speak favourably." But 13 Micai′ah said, "As the LORD lives, what my God says, that I will speak." And when he 14 had come to the king, the king said to him, "Micai′ah, shall we go to Ramoth-gilead to battle, or shall I forbear?" And he answered, "Go up and triumph; they will be given into your hand." But the king said to 15 him, "How many times shall I adjure you that you speak to me nothing but the truth in

5 the name of the LORD?" And he said, "I saw all Israel scattered upon the mountains, as sheep that have no shepherd; and the LORD said, 'These have no master; let each return 7 to his home in peace.'" And the king of Israel said to Jehosh′aphat, "Did I not tell you that he would not prophesy good concer- 8 ning me, but evil?" And Micai′ah said, "Therefore hear the word of the LORD: I saw the LORD sitting on his throne, and all the host of heaven standing on his right hand and 9 on his left; and the LORD said, 'Who will entice Ahab the king of Israel, that he may go up and fall at Ramoth-gilead?' And one said 0 one thing, and another said another. Then a spirit came forward and stood before the LORD, saying, 'I will entice him.' And the 1 LORD said to him, 'By what means?' And he said, 'I will go forth, and will be a lying spirit in the mouth of all his prophets.' And he said, 'You are to entice him, and you shall 2 succeed; go forth and do so.' Now therefore behold, the LORD has put a lying spirit in the mouth of these your prophets; the LORD has spoken evil concerning you."

3 Then Zedeki′ah the son of Chena′anah came near and struck Micai′ah on the cheek, and said, "Which way did the Spirit of the 4 LORD go from me to speak to you?" And Micai′ah said, "Behold, you shall see on that day when you go into an inner chamber to 5 hide yourself." And the king of Israel said, "Seize Micai′ah, and take him back to Amon the governor of the city and to Jo′ash the 6 king's son; and say, 'Thus says the king, Put this fellow in prison, and feed him with scant fare of bread and water, until I return in 7 peace.'" And Micai′ah said, "If you return in peace, the LORD has not spoken by me." And he said, "Hear, all you peoples!"

8 So the king of Israel and Jehosh′aphat the king of Judah went up to Ramoth-gilead. 9 And the king of Israel said to Jehosh′aphat, "I will disguise myself and go into battle, but you wear your robes." And the king of Israel disguised himself; and they went into battle. 0 Now the king of Syria had commanded the captains of his chariots, "Fight with neither small nor great, but only with the king of 1 Israel." And when the captains of the chariots saw Jehosh′aphat, they said, "It is the king of Israel." So they turned to fight against him; and Jehosh′aphat cried out, and the LORD helped him. God drew them away 2 from him, for when the captains of the chariots saw that it was not the king of Israel, 3 they turned back from pursuing him. But a certain man drew his bow at a venture, and struck the king of Israel between the scale armour and the breastplate; therefore he said to the driver of his chariot, "Turn about, and carry me out of the battle, for I am

wounded." And the battle grew hot that 34 day, and the king of Israel propped himself up in his chariot facing the Syrians until evening; then at sunset he died.

Jehosh′aphat the king of Judah returned in 19 safety to his house in Jerusalem. But Jehu 2 the son of Hana′ni the seer went out to meet him, and said to King Jehosh′aphat, "Should you help the wicked and love those who hate the LORD? Because of this, wrath has gone out against you from the LORD. Nevertheless 3 some good is found in you, for you destroyed the Ashe′rahs out of the land, and have set your heart to seek God."

Jehosh′aphat dwelt at Jerusalem; and he 4 went out again among the people, from Beer-sheba to the hill country of E′phraim, and brought them back to the LORD, the God of their fathers. He appointed judges in the 5 land in all the fortified cities of Judah, city by city, and said to the judges, "Consider what 6 you do, for you judge not for man but for the LORD; he is with you in giving judgment. Now then, let the fear of the LORD be upon 7 you; take heed what you do, for there is no perversion of justice with the LORD our God, or partiality, or taking bribes."

Moreover in Jerusalem Jehosh′aphat ap- 8 pointed certain Levites and priests and heads of families of Israel, to give judgment for the LORD and to decide disputed cases. They had their seat at Jerusalem. And he 9 charged them: "Thus you shall do in the fear of the LORD, in faithfulness, and with your whole heart: whenever a case comes to you 10 from your brethren who live in their cities,

Levite and priest

concerning bloodshed, law or commandment, statutes or ordinances, then you shall
instruct them, that they may not incur guilt
before the LORD and wrath may not come
upon you and your brethren. Thus you shall
11 do, and you will not incur guilt. And behold,
Amari′ah the chief priest is over you in all
matters of the LORD; and Zebadi′ah the son
of Ish′mael, the governor of the house of
Judah, in all the king's matters; and the
Levites will serve you as officers. Deal
courageously, and may the LORD be with the
upright!"

20 After this the Moabites and Ammonites,
and with them some of the Me-u′nites,^g came
2 against Jehosh′aphat for battle. Some men
came and told Jehosh′aphat, "A great multitude is coming against you from Edom,^h
from beyond the sea; and, behold, they are in
3 Haz′azon-ta′mar" (that is, En-ge′di). Then
Jehosh′aphat feared, and set himself to seek
the LORD, and proclaimed a fast throughout
4 all Judah. And Judah assembled to seek help
from the LORD; from all the cities of Judah
they came to seek the LORD.

Jehoshaphat's prayer

5 And Jehosh′aphat stood in the assembly of
Judah and Jerusalem, in the house of the
6 LORD, before the new court, and said, "O
LORD, God of our fathers, art thou not God
in heaven? Dost thou not rule over all the
kingdoms of the nations? In thy hand are
power and might, so that none is able to
7 withstand thee. Didst thou not, O our God,
drive out the inhabitants of this land before
thy people Israel, and give it for ever to the
8 descendants of Abraham thy friend? And
they have dwelt in it, and have built thee in it
9 a sanctuary for thy name, saying, 'If evil
comes upon us, the sword, judgment,ⁱ or
pestilence, or famine, we will stand before
this house, and before thee, for thy name is in
this house, and cry to thee in our affliction,
10 and thou wilt hear and save.' And now
behold, the men of Ammon and Moab and
Mount Se′ir, whom thou wouldest not let
Israel invade when they came from the land
of Egypt, and whom they avoided and did
11 not destroy—behold, they reward us by
coming to drive us out of thy possession,
12 which thou hast given us to inherit. O our
God, wilt thou not execute judgment upon
them? For we are powerless against this
great multitude that is coming against us.
We do not know what to do, but our eyes are
upon thee."

Meanwhile all the men of Judah stood 1
before the LORD, with their little ones, their
wives, and their children. And the Spirit of 1
the LORD came upon Jahazi′el the son of
Zechari′ah, son of Benai′ah, son of Je-i′el,
son of Mattani′ah, a Levite of the sons of
Asaph, in the midst of the assembly. And he 1
said, "Hearken, all Judah and inhabitants of
Jerusalem, and King Jehosh′aphat: Thus
says the LORD to you, 'Fear not, and be not
dismayed at this great multitude; for the
battle is not yours but God's. Tomorrow 1
go down against them; behold, they will
come up by the ascent of Ziz; you will find
them at the end of the valley, east of the
wilderness of Jeru′el. You will not need to 1
fight in this battle; take your position, stand
still, and see the victory of the LORD on your
behalf, O Judah and Jerusalem.' Fear not,
and be not dismayed; tomorrow go out
against them, and the LORD will be with you."
Then Jehosh′aphat bowed his head with his 1
face to the ground, and all Judah and the
inhabitants of Jerusalem fell down before
the LORD, worshipping the LORD. And 1
the Levites, of the Ko′hathites and the
Ko′rahites, stood up to praise the LORD, the
God of Israel, with a very loud voice.

And they rose early in the morning and 2
went out into the wilderness of Teko′a;
and as they went out, Jehosh′aphat stood and
said, "Hear me, Judah and inhabitants of
Jerusalem! Believe in the LORD your God,
and you will be established; believe his
prophets, and you will succeed." And when 2
he had taken counsel with the people, he
appointed those who were to sing to the
LORD and praise him in holy array, as they
went before the army, and say,
"Give thanks to the LORD,
for his steadfast love endures for ever."
And when they began to sing and praise, the 2
LORD set an ambush against the men of
Ammon, Moab, and Mount Se′ir, who had
come against Judah, so that they were
routed. For the men of Ammon and Moab 2
rose against the inhabitants of Mount Se′ir,
destroying them utterly, and when they had
made an end of the inhabitants of Se′ir, they
all helped to destroy one another.

When Judah came to the watchtower of the 2
wilderness, they looked toward the multitude; and behold, they were dead bodies
lying on the ground; none had escaped.
When Jehosh′aphat and his people came to 2
take the spoil from them, they found cattle^j
in great numbers, goods, clothing, and precious things, which they took for themselves
until they could carry no more. They were

^g Compare 26.7: Heb *Ammonites*   ^h One Ms: Heb *Aram* (Syria)   ⁱ Or *the sword of judgment*
^j Gk: Heb *among them*
20.7: Jas 2.23.

three days in taking the spoil, it was so much. On the fourth day they assembled in the Valley of Bera'cah,[k] for there they blessed the LORD; therefore the name of that place has been called the Valley of Bera'cah to this day. Then they returned, every man of Judah and Jerusalem, and Jehosh'aphat at their head, returning to Jerusalem with joy, for the LORD had made them rejoice over their enemies. They came to Jerusalem, with harps and lyres and trumpets, to the house of the LORD. And the fear of God came on all the kingdoms of the countries when they heard that the LORD had fought against the enemies of Israel. So the realm of Jehosh'-aphat was quiet, for his God gave him rest round about.

Thus Jehosh'aphat reigned over Judah. He was thirty-five years old when he began to reign, and he reigned twenty-five years in Jerusalem. His mother's name was Azu'bah the daughter of Shilhi. He walked in the way of Asa his father and did not turn aside from it; he did what was right in the sight of the LORD. The high places, however, were not taken away; the people had not yet set their hearts upon the God of their fathers. Now the rest of the acts of Jehosh'aphat, from first to last, are written in the chronicles of Jehu the son of Hana'ni, which are recorded in the Book of the Kings of Israel. After this Jehosh'aphat king of Judah joined with Ahazi'ah king of Israel, who did wickedly. He joined him in building ships to go to Tarshish, and they built the ships in E'zion-ge'ber. Then Elie'zer the son of Dodav'ahu of Mare'shah prophesied against Jehosh'aphat, saying, "Because you have joined with Ahazi'ah, the LORD will destroy what you have made." And the ships were wrecked and were not able to go to Tarshish.

Jehoram

Jehosh'aphat slept with his fathers, and was buried with his fathers in the city of David; and Jeho'ram his son reigned in his stead. He had brothers, the sons of Jehosh'aphat: Azari'ah, Jehi'el, Zechari'ah, Azari'ah, Michael, and Shephati'ah; all these were the sons of Jehosh'aphat king of Judah. Their father gave them great gifts, of silver, gold, and valuable possessions, together with fortified cities in Judah; but he gave the kingdom to Jeho'ram, because he was the first-born. When Jeho'ram had ascended the throne of his father and was established, he slew all his brothers with the sword, and also some of the princes of Israel. Jeho'ram

was thirty-two years old when he became king, and he reigned eight years in Jerusalem. And he walked in the way of the kings of Israel, as the house of Ahab had done; for the daughter of Ahab was his wife. And he did what was evil in the sight of the LORD. Yet the LORD would not destroy the house of David, because of the covenant which he had made with David, and since he had promised to give a lamp to him and to his sons for ever.

In his days Edom revolted from the rule of Judah, and set up a king of their own. Then Jeho'ram passed over with his commanders and all his chariots, and he rose by night and smote the E'domites who had surrounded him and his chariot commanders. So Edom revolted from the rule of Judah to this day. At that time Libnah also revolted from his rule, because he had forsaken the LORD, the God of his fathers.

Moreover he made high places in the hill country of Judah, and led the inhabitants of Jerusalem into unfaithfulness, and made Judah go astray. And a letter came to him from Eli'jah the prophet, saying, "Thus says the LORD, the God of David your father, 'Because you have not walked in the ways of Jehosh'aphat your father, or in the ways of Asa king of Judah, but have walked in the way of the kings of Israel, and have led Judah and the inhabitants of Jerusalem into unfaithfulness, as the house of Ahab led Israel into unfaithfulness, and also you have killed your brothers, of your father's house, who were better than yourself; behold, the LORD will bring a great plague on your people, your children, your wives, and all your possessions, and you yourself will have a severe sickness with a disease of your bowels, until your bowels come out because of the disease, day by day.'"

And the LORD stirred up against Jeho'ram the anger of the Philistines and of the Arabs who are near the Ethiopians; and they came up against Judah, and invaded it, and carried away all the possessions they found that belonged to the king's house, and also his sons and his wives, so that no son was left to him except Jeho'ahaz, his youngest son.

And after all this the LORD smote him in his bowels with an incurable disease. In course of time, at the end of two years, his bowels came out because of the disease, and he died in great agony. His people made no fire in his honour, like the fires made for his fathers. He was thirty-two years old when he began to reign, and he reigned eight years in Jerusalem; and he departed with no one's regret. They buried him in the city

A city gate of Jerusalem

of David, but not in the tombs of the kings.

Ahaziah

22 And the inhabitants of Jerusalem made Ahazi′ah his youngest son king in his stead; for the band of men that came with the Arabs to the camp had slain all the older sons. So Ahazi′ah the son of Jeho′ram king of Judah 2 reigned. Ahazi′ah was forty-two years old when he began to reign, and he reigned one year in Jerusalem. His mother's name was 3 Athali′ah, the granddaughter of Omri. He also walked in the ways of the house of Ahab, for his mother was his counsellor in doing 4 wickedly. He did what was evil in the sight of the LORD, as the house of Ahab had done; for after the death of his father they were his 5 counsellors, to his undoing. He even followed their counsel, and went with Jeho′ram the son of Ahab king of Israel to make war against Haz′ael king of Syria at Ramoth-gilead. And the Syrians wounded Joram, 6 and he returned to be healed in Jezreel of the wounds which he had received at Ramah, when he fought against Haz′ael king of Syria. And Ahazi′ah the son of Jeho′ram king of Judah went down to see Joram the son of Ahab in Jezreel, because he was sick. 7 But it was ordained by God that the downfall of Ahazi′ah should come about through his going to visit Joram. For when he came there he went out with Jeho′ram to meet Jehu the son of Nimshi, whom the LORD had anointed to destroy the house of 8 Ahab. And when Jehu was executing judgment upon the house of Ahab, he met

the princes of Judah and the sons of Ahazi′ah's brothers, who attended Ahazi′ah, and he killed them. He searched for 9 Ahazi′ah, and he was captured while hiding in Samar′ia, and he was brought to Jehu and put to death. They buried him, for they said, "He is the grandson of Jehosh′aphat, who sought the LORD with all his heart." And the house of Ahazi′ah had no one able to rule the kingdom.

Athaliah

Now when Athali′ah the mother of Aha- 10 zi′ah saw that her son was dead, she arose and destroyed all the royal family of the house of Judah. But Jeho-shab′e-ath, the 11 daughter of the king, took Jo′ash the son of Ahazi′ah, and stole him away from among the king's sons who were about to be slain, and she put him and his nurse in a bed-chamber. Thus Jeho-shab′e-ath, the daughter of King Jeho′ram and wife of Jehoi′ada the priest, because she was a sister of Ahazi′ah, hid him from Athali′ah, so that she did not slay him; and he remained with them 12 six years, hid in the house of God, while Athali′ah reigned over the land.

But in the seventh year Jehoi′ada took **23** courage, and entered into a compact with the commanders of hundreds, Azari′ah the son of Jero′ham, Ish′mael the son of Jehoha′nan, Azari′ah the son of Obed, Ma-asei′ah the son of Adai′ah, and Elisha′phat the son of Zichri. And they went about through Judah 2 and gathered the Levites from all the cities of Judah, and the heads of fathers' houses of

Israel, and they came to Jerusalem. And all the assembly made a covenant with the king in the house of God. And Jehoi′ada[l] said to them, "Behold, the king's son! Let him reign, as the LORD spoke concerning the sons of David. This is the thing that you shall do: of you priests and Levites who come off duty on the sabbath, one third shall be gatekeepers, and one third shall be at the king's house and one third at the Gate of the Foundation; and all the people shall be in the courts of the house of the LORD. Let no one enter the house of the LORD except the priests and ministering Levites; they may enter, for they are holy, but all the people shall keep the charge of the LORD. The Levites shall surround the king, each with his weapons in his hand; and whoever enters the house shall be slain. Be with the king when he comes in, and when he goes out."

The Levites and all Judah did according to all that Jehoi′ada the priest commanded. They each brought his men, who were to go off duty on the sabbath, with those who were to come on duty on the sabbath; for Jehoi′ada the priest did not dismiss the divisions. And Jehoi′ada the priest delivered to the captains the spears and the large and small shields that had been King David's, which were in the house of God; and he set all the people as a guard for the king, every man with his weapon in his hand, from the south side of the house to the north side of the house, around the altar and the house. Then he brought out the king's son, and put the crown upon him, and gave him the testimony; and they proclaimed him king, and Jehoi′ada and his sons anointed him, and they said, "Long live the king."

When Athali′ah heard the noise of the people running and praising the king, she went into the house of the LORD to the people; and when she looked, there was the king standing by his pillar at the entrance, and the captains and the trumpeters beside the king, and all the people of the land rejoicing and blowing trumpets, and the singers with their musical instruments leading in the celebration. And Athali′ah rent her clothes, and cried, "Treason! Treason!" Then Jehoi′ada the priest brought out the captains who were set over the army, saying to them, "Bring her out between the ranks; any one who follows her is to be slain with the sword." For the priest said, "Do not slay her in the house of the LORD." So they laid hands on her; and she went into the entrance of the horse gate of the king's house, and they slew her there.

And Jehoi′ada made a covenant between 16 himself and all the people and the king that they should be the LORD's people. Then all 17 the people went to the house of Ba′al, and tore it down; his altars and his images they broke in pieces, and they slew Mattan the priest of Ba′al before the altars. And 18 Jehoi′ada posted watchmen for the house of the LORD under the direction of the Levitical priests and the Levites whom David had organized to be in charge of the house of the LORD, to offer burnt offerings to the LORD, as it is written in the law of Moses, with rejoicing and with singing, according to the order of David. He stationed the gatekeepers 19 at the gates of the house of the LORD so that no one should enter who was in any way unclean. And he took the captains, the 20 nobles, the governors of the people, and all the people of the land; and they brought the king down from the house of the LORD, marching through the upper gate to the king's house. And they set the king upon the royal throne. So all the people of the land 21 rejoiced; and the city was quiet, after Athali′ah had been slain with the sword.

Joash

Jo′ash was seven years old when he began to 24 reign, and he reigned forty years in Jerusalem; his mother's name was Zib′iah of Beer-sheba. And Jo′ash did what was right 2 in the eyes of the LORD all the days of Jehoi′ada the priest. Jehoi′ada got for him 3 two wives, and he had sons and daughters.

After this Jo′ash decided to restore the 4 house of the LORD. And he gathered the 5 priests and the Levites, and said to them, "Go out to the cities of Judah, and gather from all Israel money to repair the house of your God from year to year; and see that you hasten the matter." But the Levites did not hasten it. So the king summoned Jehoi′ada 6 the chief, and said to him, "Why have you not required the Levites to bring in from Judah and Jerusalem the tax levied by Moses, the servant of the LORD, on[m] the congregation of Israel for the tent of testimony?" For the sons of Athali′ah, that 7 wicked woman, had broken into the house of God; and had also used all the dedicated things of the house of the LORD for the Ba′als.

So the king commanded, and they made a 8 chest, and set it outside the gate of the house of the LORD. And proclamation was made 9 throughout Judah and Jerusalem, to bring in for the LORD the tax that Moses the servant

---

l Heb *he*   m Compare Vg: Heb *and*
24.1–14: 2 Kings 11.21–12.14.

of God laid upon Israel in the wilderness.
10 And all the princes and all the people rejoiced and brought their tax and dropped it
11 into the chest until they had finished. And whenever the chest was brought to the king's officers by the Levites, when they saw that there was much money in it, the king's secretary and the officer of the chief priest would come and empty the chest and take it and return it to its place. Thus they did day after day, and collected money in
12 abundance. And the king and Jehoi′ada gave it to those who had charge of the work of the house of the LORD, and they hired masons and carpenters to restore the house of the LORD, and also workers in iron and bronze to
13 repair the house of the LORD. So those who were engaged in the work laboured, and the repairing went forward in their hands, and they restored the house of God to its proper
14 condition and strengthened it. And when they had finished, they brought the rest of the money before the king and Jehoi′ada, and with it were made utensils for the house of the LORD, both for the service and for the burnt offerings, and dishes for incense, and vessels of gold and silver. And they offered burnt offerings in the house of the LORD continually all the days of Jehoi′ada.
15 But Jehoi′ada grew old and full of days, and died; he was a hundred and thirty years old
16 at his death. And they buried him in the city of David among the kings, because he had done good in Israel, and toward God and his house.
17 Now after the death of Jehoi′ada the princes of Judah came and did obeisance to the king;
18 then the king hearkened to them. And they forsook the house of the LORD, the God of their fathers, and served the Ashe′rim and the idols. And wrath came upon Judah and
19 Jerusalem for this their guilt. Yet he sent prophets among them to bring them back to the LORD; these testified against them, but they would not give heed.
20 Then the Spirit of God took possession of[n] Zechari′ah the son of Jehoi′ada the priest; and he stood above the people, and said

to them, "Thus says God, 'Why do you transgress the commandments of the LORD, so that you cannot prosper? Because you have forsaken the LORD, he has forsaken you.'" But they conspired against him, and by command of the king they stoned him with stones in the court of the house of the LORD. Thus Jo′ash the king did not remember the kindness which Jehoi′ada, Zechari′ah's father, had shown him, but killed his son. And when he was dying, he said, "May the LORD see and avenge!"

At the end of the year the army of the Syrians came up against Jo′ash. They came to Judah and Jerusalem, and destroyed all the princes of the people from among the people, and sent all their spoil to the king of Damascus. Though the army of the Syrians had come with few men, the LORD delivered into their hand a very great army, because they had forsaken the LORD, the God of their fathers. Thus they executed judgment on Jo′ash.

When they had departed from him, leaving him severely wounded, his servants conspired against him because of the blood of the son[o] of Jehoi′ada the priest, and slew him on his bed. So he died; and they buried him in the city of David, but they did not bury him in the tombs of the kings. Those who conspired against him were Zabad the son of Shim′e-ath the Ammonitess, and Jeho′zabad the son of Shimrith the Moabitess. Accounts of his sons, and of the many oracles against him, and of the rebuilding[p] of the house of God are written in the Commentary on the Book of the Kings. And Amazi′ah his son reigned in his stead.

Amaziah

Amazi′ah was twenty-five years old when he began to reign, and he reigned twenty-nine years in Jerusalem. His mother's name was Jeho-ad′dan of Jerusalem. And he did what was right in the eyes of the LORD, yet not with a blameless heart. And as soon as the royal power was firmly in his hand he

---

[n] Heb *clothed itself with*   [o] Gk Vg: Heb *sons*   [p] Heb *founding*
24.23–26: 2 Kings 12.17–18, 20–21.   25.1–4: 2 Kings 14.2–6.

killed his servants who had slain the king his
father. But he did not put their children to
death, according to what is written in the
law, in the book of Moses, where the LORD
commanded, "The fathers shall not be put to
death for the children, or the children be put
to death for the fathers; but every man shall
die for his own sin."

Then Amazi'ah assembled the men of
Judah, and set them by fathers' houses under
commanders of thousands and of hundreds
for all Judah and Benjamin. He mustered
those twenty years old and upward, and
found that they were three hundred thousand picked men, fit for war, able to handle
spear and shield. He hired also a hundred
thousand mighty men of valour from Israel
for a hundred talents of silver. But a man of
God came to him and said, "O king, do not
let the army of Israel go with you, for the
LORD is not with Israel, with all these
E'phraimites. But if you suppose that in this
way you will be strong for war,^{q} God will cast
you down before the enemy; for God has
power to help or to cast down." And
Amazi'ah said to the man of God, "But what
shall we do about the hundred talents which
I have given to the army of Israel?" The
man of God answered, "The LORD is able to
give you much more than this." Then
Amazi'ah discharged the army that had come
to him from E'phraim, to go home again.
And they became very angry with Judah, and
returned home in fierce anger. But Amazi'ah
took courage, and led out his people, and
went to the Valley of Salt and smote ten
thousand men of Se'ir. The men of Judah
captured another ten thousand alive, and
took them to the top of a rock and threw
them down from the top of the rock; and
they were all dashed to pieces. But the men
of the army whom Amazi'ah sent back, not
letting them go with him to battle, fell upon
the cities of Judah, from Samar'ia to Beth-
horon, and killed three thousand people in
them, and took much spoil.

After Amazi'ah came from the slaughter of
the E'domites, he brought the gods of the
men of Se'ir, and set them up as his gods,
and worshipped them, making offerings to
them. Therefore the LORD was angry with
Amazi'ah and sent to him a prophet, who
said to him, "Why have you resorted to the
gods of a people, which did not deliver their
own people from your hand?" But as he was
speaking the king said to him, "Have we
made you a royal counsellor? Stop! Why
should you be put to death?" So the
prophet stopped, but said, "I know that God

has determined to destroy you, because you
have done this and have not listened to my
counsel."

Then Amazi'ah king of Judah took counsel 17
and sent to Jo'ash the son of Jeho'ahaz, son
of Jehu, king of Israel, saying, "Come, let us
look one another in the face." And Jo'ash 18
the king of Israel sent word to Amazi'ah king
of Judah, "A thistle on Lebanon sent to
a cedar on Lebanon, saying, 'Give your
daughter to my son for a wife'; and a wild
beast of Lebanon passed by and trampled
down the thistle. You say, 'See, I have 19
smitten Edom,' and your heart has lifted you
up in boastfulness. But now stay at home;
why should you provoke trouble so that you
fall, you and Judah with you?"

But Amazi'ah would not listen; for it was of 20
God, in order that he might give them into
the hand of their enemies, because they had
sought the gods of Edom. So Jo'ash king of 21
Israel went up; and he and Amazi'ah king of
Judah faced one another in battle at
Beth-she'mesh, which belongs to Judah.
And Judah was defeated by Israel, and every 22
man fled to his home. And Jo'ash king of 23
Israel captured Amazi'ah king of Judah, the
son of Jo'ash, son of Ahazi'ah, at Beth-
she'mesh, and brought him to Jerusalem,
and broke down the wall of Jerusalem for
four hundred cubits, from the E'phraim
Gate to the Corner Gate. And he seized all 24
the gold and silver, and all the vessels that
were found in the house of God, and
O'bed-e'dom with them; he seized also the
treasuries of the king's house, and hostages,
and he returned to Samar'ia.

Amazi'ah the son of Jo'ash king of Judah 25
lived fifteen years after the death of Jo'ash
the son of Jeho'ahaz, king of Israel. Now the 26
rest of the deeds of Amazi'ah, from first to
last, are they not written in the Book of the
Kings of Judah and Israel? From the time 27
when he turned away from the LORD they
made a conspiracy against him in Jerusalem,
and he fled to Lachish. But they sent after
him to Lachish, and slew him there. And 28
they brought him upon horses; and he was
buried with his fathers in the city of David.

Uzziah

And all the people of Judah took Uzzi'ah, **26**
who was sixteen years old, and made him
king instead of his father Amazi'ah. He built 2
Eloth and restored it to Judah, after the king
slept with his fathers. Uzzi'ah was sixteen 3
years old when he began to reign, and he
reigned fifty-two years in Jerusalem. His

---

^{q} Gk: Heb *But if you go, act, be strong for the battle*
25.11: 2 Kings 14.7.   25.17-20, 21-24: 2 Kings 14.8-14.   25.25-28: 2 Kings 14.17-20.
26.1-4: 2 Kings 14.21-22; 15.2-3.

mother's name was Jecoli′ah of Jerusalem.
4 And he did what was right in the eyes of the
LORD, according to all that his father
5 Amazi′ah had done. He set himself to
seek God in the days of Zechari′ah, who
instructed him in the fear of God; and as
long as he sought the LORD, God made him
prosper.
6 He went out and made war against the
Philistines, and broke down the wall of Gath
and the wall of Jabneh and the wall of
Ashdod; and he built cities in the territory of
Ashdod and elsewhere among the Philis-
7 tines. God helped him against the Philistines, and against the Arabs that dwelt in
8 Gurba′al, and against the Me-u′nites. The
Ammonites paid tribute to Uzzi′ah, and his
fame spread even to the border of Egypt, for
9 he became very strong. Moreover Uzzi′ah
built towers in Jerusalem at the Corner Gate
and at the Valley Gate and at the Angle, and
10 fortified them. And he built towers in the
wilderness, and hewed out many cisterns, for
he had large herds, both in the Shephe′lah
and in the plain, and he had farmers and
vinedressers in the hills and in the fertile
11 lands, for he loved the soil. Moreover
Uzzi′ah had an army of soldiers, fit for war,
in divisions according to the numbers in the
muster made by Je-i′el the secretary and
Ma-asei′ah the officer, under the direction of
Hanani′ah, one of the king's commanders.
12 The whole number of the heads of fathers'
houses of mighty men of valour was two
13 thousand six hundred. Under their command was an army of three hundred and
seven thousand five hundred, who could
make war with mighty power, to help the
14 king against the enemy. And Uzzi′ah
prepared for all the army shields, spears,
helmets, coats of mail, bows, and stones for
15 slinging. In Jerusalem he made engines,
invented by skilful men, to be on the towers
and the corners, to shoot arrows and great
stones. And his fame spread far, for he was
marvellously helped, till he was strong.
16 But when he was strong he grew proud, to
his destruction. For he was false to the LORD
his God, and entered the temple of the LORD
17 to burn incense on the altar of incense. But
Azari′ah the priest went in after him, with
eighty priests of the LORD who were men of
18 valour; and they withstood King Uzzi′ah,
and said to him, "It is not for you, Uzzi′ah,
to burn incense to the LORD, but for the
priests the sons of Aaron, who are consecrated to burn incense. Go out of the
sanctuary; for you have done wrong, and it
will bring you no honour from the LORD
19 God." Then Uzzi′ah was angry. Now he

had a censer in his hand to burn incense, and
when he became angry with the priests
leprosy broke out on his forehead, in the
presence of the priests in the house of the
LORD, by the altar of incense. And Azari′ah
the chief priest, and all the priests, looked at
him, and behold, he was leprous in his
forehead! And they thrust him out quickly,
and he himself hastened to go out, because
the LORD had smitten him. And King
Uzzi′ah was a leper to the day of his death,
and being a leper dwelt in a separate house,
for he was excluded from the house of the
LORD. And Jotham his son was over the
king's household, governing the people of
the land.
    Now the rest of the acts of Uzzi′ah, from
first to last, Isaiah the prophet the son of
Amoz wrote. And Uzzi′ah slept with his
fathers, and they buried him with his fathers
in the burial field which belonged to the
kings, for they said, "He is a leper." And
Jotham his son reigned in his stead.

Jotham

Jotham was twenty-five years old when he 2
began to reign, and he reigned sixteen years
in Jerusalem. His mother's name was Jeru′-
shah the daughter of Zadok. And he did
what was right in the eyes of the LORD
according to all that his father Uzzi′ah had
done—only he did not invade the temple of
the LORD. But the people still followed
corrupt practices. He built the upper gate of 3
the house of the LORD, and did much
building on the wall of Ophel. Moreover he 4
built cities in the hill country of Judah, and
forts and towers on the wooded hills. He 5
fought with the king of the Ammonites and
prevailed against them. And the Ammonites
gave him that year a hundred talents of
silver, and ten thousand cors of wheat and
ten thousand of barley. The Ammonites
paid him the same amount in the second and
the third years. So Jotham became mighty, 6

because he ordered his ways before the LORD his God. Now the rest of the acts of Jotham, and all his wars, and his ways, behold, they are written in the Book of the Kings of Israel and Judah. He was twenty-five years old when he began to reign, and he reigned sixteen years in Jerusalem. And Jotham slept with his fathers, and they buried him in the city of David; and Ahaz his son reigned in his stead.

Ahaz

3 Ahaz was twenty years old when he began to reign, and he reigned sixteen years in Jerusalem. And he did not do what was right in the eyes of the LORD, like his father David, but walked in the ways of the kings of Israel. He even made molten images for the Ba′als; and he burned incense in the valley of the son of Hinnom, and burned his sons as an offering, according to the abominable practices of the nations whom the LORD drove out before the people of Israel. And he sacrificed and burned incense on the high places, and on the hills, and under every green tree.

Therefore the LORD his God gave him into the hand of the king of Syria, who defeated him and took captive a great number of his people and brought them to Damascus. He was also given into the hand of the king of Israel, who defeated him with great slaughter. For Pekah the son of Remali′ah slew a hundred and twenty thousand in Judah in one day, all of them men of valour, because they had forsaken the LORD, the God of their fathers. And Zichri, a mighty man of E′phraim, slew Ma-asei′ah the king's son and Azri′kam the commander of the palace and Elka′nah the next in authority to the king. The men of Israel took captive two hundred thousand of their kinsfolk, women, sons, and daughters; they also took much spoil from them and brought the spoil to Samar′ia. But a prophet of the LORD was there, whose name was Oded; and he went out to meet the army that came to Samar′ia, and said to them, "Behold, because the LORD, the God of your fathers, was angry with Judah, he gave them into your hand, but you have slain them in a rage which has reached up to heaven. And now you intend to subjugate the people of Judah and Jerusalem, male and female, as your slaves. Have you not sins of your own against the LORD your God? Now hear me, and send back the captives from your kinsfolk whom you have taken, for the fierce wrath of the LORD is upon you." Certain chiefs also of the men of E′phraim, Azari′ah

the son of Joha′nan, Berechi′ah the son of Meshil′lemoth, Jehizki′ah the son of Shallum, and Ama′sa the son of Hadlai, stood up against those who were coming from the war, and said to them, "You shall 13 not bring the captives in here, for you propose to bring upon us guilt against the LORD in addition to our present sins and guilt. For our guilt is already great, and there is fierce wrath against Israel." So the 14 armed men left the captives and the spoil before the princes and all the assembly. And 15 the men who have been mentioned by name rose and took the captives, and with the spoil they clothed all that were naked among them; they clothed them, gave them sandals, provided them with food and drink, and anointed them; and carrying all the feeble among them on asses, they brought them to their kinsfolk at Jericho, the city of palm trees. Then they returned to Samar′ia.

At that time King Ahaz sent to the king^r of 16 Assyria for help. For the E′domites had 17 again invaded and defeated Judah, and carried away captives. And the Philistines had 18 made raids on the cities in the Shephe′lah and the Negeb of Judah, and had taken Beth-she′mesh, Ai′jalon, Gede′roth, Soco with its villages, Timnah with its villages, and Gimzo with its villages; and they settled there. For the LORD brought Judah low 19 because of Ahaz king of Israel, for he had dealt wantonly in Judah and had been faithless to the LORD. So Til′gath-pilne′ser king 20 of Assyria came against him, and afflicted him instead of strengthening him. For Ahaz 21 took from the house of the LORD and the house of the king and of the princes, and gave tribute to the king of Assyria; but it did not help him.

In the time of his distress he became yet 22 more faithless to the LORD—this same King Ahaz. For he sacrificed to the gods of 23 Damascus which had defeated him, and said, "Because the gods of the kings of Syria helped them, I will sacrifice to them that they may help me." But they were the ruin of him, and of all Israel. And Ahaz gathered 24 together the vessels of the house of God and cut in pieces the vessels of the house of God, and he shut up the doors of the house of the LORD; and he made himself altars in every corner of Jerusalem. In every city of Judah 25 he made high places to burn incense to other gods, provoking to anger the LORD, the God of his fathers. Now the rest of his acts and all 26 his ways, from first to last, behold, they are written in the Book of the Kings of Judah and Israel. And Ahaz slept with his fathers, 27 and they buried him in the city, in Jerusalem, for they did not bring him into the tombs of the kings of Israel. And Hezeki′ah his son reigned in his stead.

Hezekiah

29 Hezeki′ah began to reign when he was twenty-five years old, and he reigned twenty-nine years in Jerusalem. His mother's name was Abi′jah the daughter of
2 Zechari′ah. And he did what was right in the eyes of the LORD, according to all that David his father had done.

3 In the first year of his reign, in the first month, he opened the doors of the house of
4 the LORD, and repaired them. He brought in the priests and the Levites, and assembled
5 them in the square on the east, and said to them, "Hear me, Levites! Now sanctify yourselves, and sanctify the house of the LORD, the God of your fathers, and carry out
6 the filth from the holy place. For our fathers have been unfaithful and have done what was evil in the sight of the LORD our God; they have forsaken him, and have turned away their faces from the habitation of the LORD,
7 and turned their backs. They also shut the doors of the vestibule and put out the lamps, and have not burned incense or offered burnt offerings in the holy place to the God of
8 Israel. Therefore the wrath of the LORD came on Judah and Jerusalem, and he has made them an object of horror, of astonishment, and of hissing, as you see with your
9 own eyes. For lo, our fathers have fallen by the sword and our sons and our daughters
10 and our wives are in captivity for this. Now it is in my heart to make a covenant with the LORD, the God of Israel, that his fierce anger
11 may turn away from us. My sons, do not now be negligent, for the LORD has chosen you to stand in his presence, to minister to him, and to be his ministers and burn incense to him."

The temple cleansed

12 Then the Levites arose, Mahath the son of Ama′sai, and Jo′el the son of Azari′ah, of the sons of the Ko′hathites; and of the sons of Merar′i, Kish the son of Abdi, and Azari′ah the son of Jehal′lelel; and of the Gershonites, Jo′ah the son of Zimmah, and Eden the son
13 of Jo′ah; and of the sons of Eliza′phan, Shimri and Jeu′el; and of the sons of Asaph,
14 Zechari′ah and Mattani′ah; and of the sons of Heman, Jehu′el and Shim′e-i; and of the sons of Jedu′thun, Shemai′ah and Uz′ziel.
15 They gathered their brethren, and sanctified

themselves, and went in as the king had commanded, by the words of the LORD, to cleanse the house of the LORD. The priests went into the inner part of the house of the LORD to cleanse it, and they brought out all the uncleanness that they found in the temple of the LORD into the court of the house of the LORD; and the Levites took it and carried it out to the brook Kidron. They 17 began to sanctify on the first day of the first month, and on the eighth day of the month they came to the vestibule of the LORD; then for eight days they sanctified the house of the LORD, and on the sixteenth day of the first month they finished. Then they went in to 18 Hezeki′ah the king and said, "We have cleansed all the house of the LORD, the altar of burnt offering and all its utensils, and the table for the showbread and all its utensils. All the utensils which King Ahaz discarded 19 in his reign when he was faithless, we have made ready and sanctified; and behold, they are before the altar of the LORD."

Then Hezeki′ah the king rose early and 20 gathered the officials of the city, and went up to the house of the LORD. And they brought 21 seven bulls, seven rams, seven lambs, and seven he-goats for a sin offering for the kingdom and for the sanctuary and for Judah. And he commanded the priests the sons of Aaron to offer them on the altar of the LORD. So they killed the bulls, and 22 the priests received the blood and threw it against the altar; and they killed the rams and their blood was thrown against the altar; and they killed the lambs and their blood was thrown against the altar. Then the he-goats 23 for the sin offering were brought to the king and the assembly, and they laid their hands upon them, and the priests killed them and 24 made a sin offering with their blood on the altar, to make atonement for all Israel. For the king commanded that the burnt offering and the sin offering should be made for all Israel.

And he stationed the Levites in the house of 25

the LORD with cymbals, harps, and lyres, according to the commandment of David and of Gad the king's seer and of Nathan the prophet; for the commandment was from the LORD through his prophets. The Levites stood with the instruments of David, and the priests with the trumpets. Then Hezeki′ah commanded that the burnt offering be offered on the altar. And when the burnt offering began, the song to the LORD began also, and the trumpets, accompanied by the instruments of David king of Israel. The whole assembly worshipped, and the singers sang, and the trumpeters sounded; all this continued until the burnt offering was finished. When the offering was finished, the king and all who were present with him bowed themselves and worshipped. And Hezeki′ah the king and the princes commanded the Levites to sing praises to the LORD with the words of David and of Asaph the seer. And they sang praises with gladness, and they bowed down and worshipped. Then Hezeki′ah said, "You have now consecrated yourselves to the LORD; come near, bring sacrifices and thank offerings to the house of the LORD." And the assembly brought sacrifices and thank offerings; and all who were of a willing heart brought burnt offerings. The number of the burnt offerings which the assembly brought was seventy bulls, a hundred rams, and two hundred lambs; all these were for a burnt offering to the LORD. And the consecrated offerings were six hundred bulls and three thousand sheep. But the priests were too few and could not flay all the burnt offerings, so until other priests had sanctified themselves their brethren the Levites helped them, until the work was finished—for the Levites were more upright in heart than the priests in sanctifying themselves. Besides the great number of burnt offerings there was the fat of the peace offerings, and there were the libations for the burnt offerings. Thus the service of the house of the LORD was restored. And Hezeki′ah and all the people rejoiced because of what God had done for the people; for the thing came about suddenly.

The passover renewed

30 Hezeki′ah sent to all Israel and Judah, and wrote letters also to E′phraim and Manas′seh, that they should come to the house of the LORD at Jerusalem, to keep the passover to the LORD the God of Israel. For the king and his princes and all the assembly in Jerusalem had taken counsel to keep the passover in the second month—for they could not keep it in its time because the priests had not sanctified themselves in sufficient number, nor had the people assembled in Jerusalem—and the plan seemed right to the king and all the assembly. So they decreed to make a proclamation throughout all Israel, from Beer-sheba to Dan, that the people should come and keep the passover to the LORD the God of Israel, at Jerusalem; for they had not kept it in great numbers as prescribed. So couriers went throughout all Israel and Judah with letters from the king and his princes, as the king had commanded, saying, "O people of Israel, return to the LORD, the God of Abraham, Isaac, and Israel, that he may turn again to the remnant of you who have escaped from the hand of the kings of Assyria. Do not be like your fathers and your brethren, who were faithless to the LORD God of their fathers, so that he made them a desolation, as you see. Do not now be stiff-necked as your fathers were, but yield yourselves to the LORD, and come to his sanctuary, which he has sanctified for ever, and serve the LORD your God, that his fierce anger may turn away from you. For if you return to the LORD, your brethren and your children will find compassion with their captors, and return to this land. For the LORD your God is gracious and merciful, and will not turn away his face from you, if you return to him."

So the couriers went from city to city through the country of E′phraim and Manas′seh, and as far as Zeb′ulun; but they laughed them to scorn, and mocked them. Only a few men of Asher, of Manas′seh, and of Zeb′ulun humbled themselves and came to Jerusalem. The hand of God was also upon Judah to give them one heart to do what the king and the princes commanded by the word of the LORD. And many people came together in Jerusalem to keep the feast of unleavened bread in the second month, a very great assembly. They set to work and removed the altars that were in Jerusalem, and all the altars for burning incense they took away and threw into the Kidron valley. And they killed the passover lamb on the fourteenth day of the second month. And the priests and the Levites were put to shame, so that they sanctified themselves, and brought burnt

16 offerings into the house of the LORD. They took their accustomed posts according to the law of Moses the man of God; the priests sprinkled the blood which they received from 17 the hand of the Levites. For there were many in the assembly who had not sanctified themselves; therefore the Levites had to kill the passover lamb for every one who was not 18 clean, to make it holy to the LORD. For a multitude of the people, many of them from E'phraim, Manas'seh, Is'sachar, and Zeb'-ulun, had not cleansed themselves, yet they ate the passover otherwise than as prescribed. For Hezeki'ah had prayed for them, saying, "The good LORD pardon every 19 one who sets his heart to seek God, the LORD the God of his fathers, even though not according to the sanctuary's rules of clean-20 ness." And the LORD heard Hezeki'ah, and 21 healed the people. And the people of Israel that were present at Jerusalem kept the feast of unleavened bread seven days with great gladness; and the Levites and the priests praised the LORD day by day, singing with all 22 their might[s] to the LORD. And Hezeki'ah spoke encouragingly to all the Levites who showed good skill in the service of the LORD. So the people ate the food of the festival for seven days, sacrificing peace offerings and giving thanks to the LORD the God of their fathers.

23 Then the whole assembly agreed together to keep the feast for another seven days; so they kept it for another seven days with glad-24 ness. For Hezeki'ah king of Judah gave the assembly a thousand bulls and seven thousand sheep for offerings, and the princes gave the assembly a thousand bulls and ten thousand sheep. And the priests sanctified 25 themselves in great numbers. The whole assembly of Judah, and the priests and the Levites, and the whole assembly that came out of Israel, and the sojourners who came out of the land of Israel, and the sojourners 26 who dwelt in Judah, rejoiced. So there was great joy in Jerusalem, for since the time of Solomon the son of David king of Israel there had been nothing like this in Jeru-27 salem. Then the priests and the Levites arose and blessed the people, and their voice was heard, and their prayer came to his holy habitation in heaven.

31 Now when all this was finished, all Israel who were present went out to the cities of Judah and broke in pieces the pillars and hewed down the Ashe'rim and broke down the high places and the altars throughout all Judah and Benjamin, and in E'phraim and Manas'seh, until they had destroyed them all. Then all the people of Israel returned to their cities, every man to his possession.

Tithes and offerings

And Hezeki'ah appointed the divisions of 2 the priests and of the Levites, division by division, each according to his service, the priests and the Levites, for burnt offerings and peace offerings, to minister in the gates of the camp of the LORD and to give thanks and praise. The contribution of the king 3 from his own possessions was for the burnt offerings: the burnt offerings of morning and evening, and the burnt offerings for the sabbaths, the new moons, and the appointed feasts, as it is written in the law of the LORD. And he commanded the people who lived in 4 Jerusalem to give the portion due to the priests and the Levites, that they might give themselves to the law of the LORD. As soon 5 as the command was spread abroad, the people of Israel gave in abundance the first fruits of grain, wine, oil, honey, and of all the produce of the field; and they brought in abundantly the tithe of everything. And the 6 people of Israel and Judah who lived in the cities of Judah also brought in the tithe of cattle and sheep, and the dedicated things[t] which had been consecrated to the LORD their God, and laid them in heaps. In the 7 third month they began to pile up the heaps, and finished them in the seventh month. When Hezeki'ah and the princes came and 8 saw the heaps, they blessed the LORD and his people Israel. And Hezeki'ah questioned the 9 priests and the Levites about the heaps. Azari'ah the chief priest, who was of the 1 house of Zadok, answered him, "Since they began to bring the contributions into the house of the LORD we have eaten and had enough and have plenty left; for the LORD has blessed his people, so that we have this great store left."

Then Hezeki'ah commanded them to 1 prepare chambers in the house of the LORD; and they prepared them. And they faithfully 1 brought in the contributions, the tithes and the dedicated things. The chief officer in charge of them was Conani'ah the Levite, with Shim'e-i his brother as second; while 1 Jehi'el, Azazi'ah, Nahath, As'ahel, Jer'imoth, Jo'zabad, Eli'el, Ismachi'ah, Mahath, and Benai'ah were overseers assisting Conani'ah and Shim'e-i his brother, by the appoint-ment of Hezeki'ah the king and Azari'ah the chief officer of the house of God. And Ko're 1 the son of Imnah the Levite, keeper of the east gate, was over the freewill offerings to God, to apportion the contribution reserved

---

[s] Compare 1 Chron 13.8: Heb *with instruments of might*   [t] Heb *the tithe of the dedicated things*

for the LORD and the most holy offerings. Eden, Mini'amin, Jeshua, Shemai'ah, Amari'ah, and Shecani'ah were faithfully assisting him in the cities of the priests, to distribute the portions to their brethren, old and young alike, by divisions, except those enrolled by genealogy, males from three years old and upwards, all who entered the house of the LORD as the duty of each day required, for their service according to their offices, by their divisions. The enrolment of the priests was according to their fathers' houses; that of the Levites from twenty years old and upwards was according to their offices, by their divisions. The priests were enrolled with all their little children, their wives, their sons, and their daughters, the whole multitude; for they were faithful in keeping themselves holy. And for the sons of Aaron, the priests, who were in the fields of common land belonging to their cities, there were men in the several cities who were designated by name to distribute portions to every male among the priests and to every one among the Levites who was enrolled. Thus Hezeki'ah did throughout all Judah; and he did what was good and right and faithful before the LORD his God. And every work that he undertook in the service of the house of God and in accordance with the law and the commandments, seeking his God, he did with all his heart, and prospered.

Jerusalem threatened

32 After these things and these acts of faithfulness Sennach'erib king of Assyria came and invaded Judah and encamped against the fortified cities, thinking to win them for himself. And when Hezeki'ah saw that Sennach'erib had come and intended to fight against Jerusalem, he planned with his officers and his mighty men to stop the water of the springs that were outside the city; and they helped him. A great many people were gathered, and they stopped all the springs and the brook that flowed through the land, saying, "Why should the kings of Assyria come and find much water?" He set to work resolutely and built up all the wall that was broken down, and raised towers upon it,ᵘ and outside it he built another wall; and he strengthened the Millo in the city of David. He also made weapons and shields in abundance. And he set combat commanders over the people, and gathered them together to him in the square at the gate of the city and spoke encouragingly to them, saying, "Be strong and of good courage. Do not be afraid or dismayed before the king of Assyria and all the horde that is with him; for there is one greater with us than with him. With him is an arm of flesh; but with us is the LORD our God, to help us and to fight our battles." And the people took confidence from the words of Hezeki'ah king of Judah.

After this Sennach'erib king of Assyria, who was besieging Lachish with all his forces, sent his servants to Jerusalem to Hezeki'ah king of Judah and to all the people of Judah that were in Jerusalem, saying, "Thus says Sennach'erib king of Assyria, 'On what are you relying, that you stand siege in Jerusalem? Is not Hezeki'ah misleading you, that he may give you over to die by famine and by thirst, when he tells you, "The LORD our God will deliver us from the hand of the king of Assyria"? Has not this same Hezeki'ah taken away his high places and his altars and commanded Judah and Jerusalem, "Before one altar you shall worship, and upon it you shall burn your sacrifices"? Do you not know what I and my fathers have done to all the peoples of other lands? Were the gods of the nations of those lands at all able to deliver their lands out of my hand? Who among all the gods of those nations which my fathers utterly destroyed was able to deliver his people from my hand, that your God should be able to

ᵘ Vg: Heb *and raised upon the towers*
32.1: 2 Kings 18.13.   **32.9–21:** 2 Kings 18.17–19.37.

15 deliver you from my hand? Now therefore do not let Hezeki'ah deceive you or mislead you in this fashion, and do not believe him, for no god of any nation or kingdom has been able to deliver his people from my hand or from the hand of my fathers. How much less will your God deliver you out of my hand!'"

16 And his servants said still more against the Lord GOD and against his servant Heze-

17 ki'ah. And he wrote letters to cast contempt on the LORD the God of Israel and to speak against him, saying, "Like the gods of the nations of the lands who have not delivered their people from my hands, so the God of Hezeki'ah will not deliver his people from

18 my hand." And they shouted it with a loud voice in the language of Judah to the people of Jerusalem who were upon the wall, to frighten and terrify them, in order that they

19 might take the city. And they spoke of the God of Jerusalem as they spoke of the gods of the peoples of the earth, which are the work of men's hands.

Jerusalem delivered

20 Then Hezeki'ah the king and Isaiah the prophet, the son of Amoz, prayed because of

21 this and cried to heaven. And the LORD sent an angel, who cut off all the mighty warriors and commanders and officers in the camp of the king of Assyria. So he returned with shame of face to his own land. And when he came into the house of his god, some of his own sons struck him down there with the

22 sword. So the LORD saved Hezeki'ah and the inhabitants of Jerusalem from the hand of Sennach'erib king of Assyria and from the hand of all his enemies; and he gave them

23 rest on every side. And many brought gifts to the LORD to Jerusalem and precious things to Hezeki'ah king of Judah, so that he was exalted in the sight of all nations from that time onward.

24 In those days Hezeki'ah became sick and was at the point of death, and he prayed to the LORD; and he answered him and gave

25 him a sign. But Hezeki'ah did not make return according to the benefit done to him, for his heart was proud. Therefore wrath came upon him and Judah and Jerusalem.

26 But Hezeki'ah humbled himself for the pride of his heart, both he and the inhabitants of Jerusalem, so that the wrath of the LORD did not come upon them in the days of Hezeki'ah.

27 And Hezeki'ah had very great riches and honour; and he made for himself treasuries for silver, for gold, for precious stones, for spices, for shields, and for all kinds of costly vessels; storehouses also for the yield of 2 grain, wine, and oil; and stalls for all kinds of cattle, and sheepfolds. He likewise provided 2 cities for himself, and flocks and herds in abundance; for God had given him very great possessions. This same Hezeki'ah 3 closed the upper outlet of the waters of Gihon and directed them down to the west side of the city of David. And Hezeki'ah prospered in all his works. And so in the 3 matter of the envoys of the princes of Babylon, who had been sent to him to inquire about the sign that had been done in the land, God left him to himself, in order to try him and to know all that was in his heart.

Now the rest of the acts of Hezeki'ah, and 3 his good deeds, behold, they are written in the vision of Isaiah the prophet the son of Amoz, in the Book of the Kings of Judah and Israel. And Hezeki'ah slept with his fathers, 3 and they buried him in the ascent of the tombs of the sons of David; and all Judah and the inhabitants of Jerusalem did him honour at his death. And Manas'seh his son reigned in his stead.

Manasseh

Manas'seh was twelve years old when he 3: began to reign, and he reigned fifty-five years in Jerusalem. He did what was evil in 2 the sight of the LORD, according to the abominable practices of the nations whom the LORD drove out before the people of Israel. For he rebuilt the high places which 3 his father Hezeki'ah had broken down, and erected altars to the Ba'als, and made Ashe'rahs, and worshipped all the host of heaven, and served them. And he built altars 4 in the house of the LORD, of which the LORD had said, "In Jerusalem shall my name be for

B. C.
700~600

ever." And he built altars for all the host of heaven in the two courts of the house of the LORD. And he burned his sons as an offering in the valley of the son of Hinnom, and practised soothsaying and augury and sorcery, and dealt with mediums and with wizards. He did much evil in the sight of the LORD, provoking him to anger. And the image of the idol which he had made he set in the house of God, of which God said to David and to Solomon his son, "In this house, and in Jerusalem, which I have chosen out of all the tribes of Israel, I will put my name for ever; and I will no more remove the foot of Israel from the land which I appointed for your fathers, if only they will be careful to do all that I have commanded them, all the law, the statutes, and the ordinances given through Moses." Manas′seh seduced Judah and the inhabitants of Jerusalem, so that they did more evil than the nations whom the LORD destroyed before the people of Israel. The LORD spoke to Manas′seh and to his people, but they gave no heed. Therefore the LORD brought upon them the commanders of the army of the king of Assyria, who took Manas′seh with hooks and bound him with fetters of bronze and brought him to Babylon. And when he was in distress he entreated the favour of the LORD his God and humbled himself greatly before the God of his fathers. He prayed to him, and God received his entreaty and heard his supplication and brought him again to Jerusalem into his kingdom. Then Manas′seh knew that the LORD was God.

Afterwards he built an outer wall for the city of David west of Gihon, in the valley, and for the entrance into the Fish Gate, and carried it round Ophel, and raised it to a very great height; he also put commanders of the army in all the fortified cities in Judah. And he took away the foreign gods and the idol from the house of the LORD, and all the altars that he had built on the mountain of the house of the LORD and in Jerusalem, and he threw them outside of the city. He also

restored the altar of the LORD and offered upon it sacrifices of peace offerings and of thanksgiving; and he commanded Judah to serve the LORD the God of Israel. Nevertheless the people still sacrificed at the high places, but only to the LORD their God.

Now the rest of the acts of Manas′seh, and his prayer to his God, and the words of the seers who spoke to him in the name of the LORD the God of Israel, behold, they are in the Chronicles of the Kings of Israel. And his prayer, and how God received his entreaty, and all his sin and his faithlessness, and the sites on which he built high places and set up the Ashe′rim and the images, before he humbled himself, behold, they are written in the Chronicles of the Seers.[v] So Manas′seh slept with his fathers, and they buried him in his house; and Amon his son reigned in his stead.

Amon

Amon was twenty-two years old when he began to reign, and he reigned two years in Jerusalem. He did what was evil in the sight of the LORD, as Manas′seh his father had done. Amon sacrificed to all the images that Manas′seh his father had made, and served them. And he did not humble himself before the LORD, as Manas′seh his father had humbled himself, but this Amon incurred guilt more and more. And his servants conspired against him and killed him in his house. But the people of the land slew all those who had conspired against King Amon; and the people of the land made Josi′ah his son king in his stead.

Josiah

Josi′ah was eight years old when he began to reign, and he reigned thirty-one years in Jerusalem. He did what was right in the eyes of the LORD, and walked in the ways of David his father; and he did not turn aside to the right or to the left. For in the eighth year of his reign, while he was yet a boy, he began to

v One Ms: Gk: Heb of Hozai
33.20: 2 Kings 21.18.   33.21-25: 2 Kings 21.19-24.   34.1-2: 2 Kings 22.1-2.   34.3-7: 2 Kings 23.4-20.

seek the God of David his father; and in the twelfth year he began to purge Judah and Jerusalem of the high places, the Ashe′rim, 4 and the graven and the molten images. And they broke down the altars of the Ba′als in his presence; and he hewed down the incense altars which stood above them; and he broke in pieces the Ashe′rim and the graven and the molten images, and he made dust of them and strewed it over the graves of those who 5 had sacrificed to them. He also burned the bones of the priests on their altars, and 6 purged Judah and Jerusalem. And in the cities of Manas′seh, E′phraim, and Simeon, and as far as Naph′tali, in their ruins ^{w} round 7 about, he broke down the altars, and beat the Ashe′rim and the images into powder, and hewed down all the incense altars throughout all the land of Israel. Then he returned to Jerusalem.

8 Now in the eighteenth year of his reign, when he had purged the land and the house, he sent Shaphan the son of Azali′ah, and Ma-asei′ah the governor of the city, and Jo′ah the son of Jo′ahaz, the recorder, to repair the house of the LORD his God. 9 They came to Hilki′ah the high priest and delivered the money that had been brought into the house of God, which the Levites, the keepers of the threshold, had collected from Manas′seh and E′phraim and from all the remnant of Israel and from all Judah and Benjamin and from the inhabitants of Jeru- 10 salem. They delivered it to the workmen who had the oversight of the house of the LORD; and the workmen who were working in the house of the LORD gave it for repairing 11 and restoring the house. They gave it to the carpenters and the builders to buy quarried stone, and timber for binders and beams for the buildings which the kings of Judah had 12 let go to ruin. And the men did the work faithfully. Over them were set Jahath and Obadi′ah the Levites, of the sons of Merar′i, and Zechari′ah and Meshul′lam, of the sons of the Ko′hathites, to have oversight. The Levites, all who were skilful with instru- 13 ments of music, were over the burden bearers and directed all who did work in every kind of service; and some of the Levites were scribes, and officials, and gatekeepers.

The book of the law found

14 While they were bringing out the money that had been brought into the house of the LORD, Hilki′ah the priest found the book of the law of the LORD given through Moses.

Then Hilki′ah said to Shaphan the secretary, » "I have found the book of the law in the house of the LORD"; and Hilki′ah gave the book to Shaphan. Shaphan brought the » book to the king, and further reported to the king, "All that was committed to your servants they are doing. They have emptied » out the money that was found in the house of the LORD and have delivered it into the hand of the overseers and the workmen." Then » Shaphan the secretary told the king, "Hilki′ah the priest has given me a book." And Shaphan read it before the king.

When the king heard the words of the law » he rent his clothes. And the king com- 2 manded Hilki′ah, Ahi′kam the son of Shaphan, Abdon the son of Micah, Shaphan the secretary, and Asa′iah, the king's servant, saying, "Go, inquire of the LORD for me and 2 for those who are left in Israel and in Judah, concerning the words of the book that has been found; for great is the wrath of the LORD that is poured out on us, because our fathers have not kept the word of the LORD, to do according to all that is written in this book."

So Hilki′ah and those whom the king had 2 sent ^{x} went to Huldah the prophetess, the wife of Shallum the son of Tokhath, son of Hasrah, keeper of the wardrobe (now she dwelt in Jerusalem in the Second Quarter) and spoke to her to that effect. And she said 2 to them, "Thus says the LORD, the God of Israel: 'Tell the man who sent you to me, Thus says the LORD, Behold, I will bring evil 2 upon this place and upon its inhabitants, all the curses that are written in the book which was read before the king of Judah. Because 2 they have forsaken me and have burned incense to other gods, that they might pro- voke me to anger with all the works of their hands, therefore my wrath will be poured out upon this place and will not be quenched. But to the king of Judah, who sent you to 2 inquire of the LORD, thus shall you say to him, Thus says the LORD, the God of Israel: Regarding the words which you have heard, 2 because your heart was penitent and you humbled yourself before God when you heard his words against this place and its inhabitants, and you have humbled yourself before me, and have rent your clothes and wept before me, I also have heard you, says the LORD. Behold, I will gather you to your 2 fathers, and you shall be gathered to your grave in peace, and your eyes shall not see all the evil which I will bring upon this place and its inhabitants.'" And they brought back word to the king.

---

^{w} Heb uncertain ^{x} Syr Vg: Heb lacks *had sent*
34.8–12: 2 Kings 22.3–7.

The covenant renewed

Then the king sent and gathered together all the elders of Judah and Jerusalem. And the king went up to the house of the LORD, with all the men of Judah and the inhabitants of Jerusalem and the priests and the Levites, all the people both great and small; and he read in their hearing all the words of the book of the covenant which had been found in the house of the LORD. And the king stood in his place and made a covenant before the LORD, to walk after the LORD and to keep his commandments and his testimonies and his statutes, with all his heart and all his soul, to perform the words of the covenant that were written in this book. Then he made all who were present in Jerusalem and in Benjamin stand to it. And the inhabitants of Jerusalem did according to the covenant of God, the God of their fathers. And Josi′ah took away all the abominations from all the territory that belonged to the people of Israel, and made all who were in Israel serve the LORD their God. All his days they did not turn away from following the LORD the God of their fathers.

5 Josi′ah kept a passover to the LORD in Jerusalem; and they killed the passover lamb on the fourteenth day of the first month. He appointed the priests to their offices and encouraged them in the service of the house of the LORD. And he said to the Levites who taught all Israel and who were holy to the LORD, "Put the holy ark in the house which Solomon the son of David, king of Israel, built; you need no longer carry it upon your shoulders. Now serve the LORD your God and his people Israel. Prepare yourselves according to your fathers' houses by your divisions, following the directions of David king of Israel and the directions of Solomon his son. And stand in the holy place according to the groupings of the fathers' houses of your brethren the lay people, and let there be for each a part of a father's house of the Levites.*y* And kill the passover lamb, and sanctify yourselves, and prepare for your brethren, to do according to the word of the LORD by Moses."

Then Josi′ah contributed to the lay people, as passover offerings for all that were present, lambs and kids from the flock to the number of thirty thousand, and three thousand bulls; these were from the king's possessions. And his princes contributed willingly to the people, to the priests, and to the Levites. Hilki′ah, Zechari′ah, and

Jehi′el, the chief officers of the house of God, gave to the priests for the passover offerings two thousand six hundred lambs and kids and three hundred bulls. Conani′ah 9 also, and Shemai′ah and Nethan′el his brothers, and Hashabi′ah and Je-i′el and Jo′zabad, the chiefs of the Levites, gave to the Levites for the passover offerings five thousand lambs and kids and five hundred bulls.

When the service had been prepared for, 10 the priests stood in their place, and the Levites in their divisions according to the king's command. And they killed the pass- 11 over lamb, and the priests sprinkled the blood which they received from them while the Levites flayed the victims. And they set 12 aside the burnt offerings that they might distribute them according to the groupings of the fathers' houses of the lay people, to offer to the LORD, as it is written in the book of Moses. And so they did with the bulls. And 13 they roasted the passover lamb with fire according to the ordinance; and they boiled the holy offerings in pots, in cauldrons, and in pans, and carried them quickly to all the lay people. And afterward they prepared for 14 themselves and for the priests, because the priests the sons of Aaron were busied in offering the burnt offerings and the fat parts until night; so the Levites prepared for themselves and for the priests the sons of Aaron. The singers, the sons of Asaph, were 15 in their place according to the command of David, and Asaph, and Heman, and Jedu′-thun the king's seer; and the gatekeepers were at each gate; they did not need to depart from their service, for their brethren the Levites prepared for them.

So all the service of the LORD was prepared 16 that day, to keep the passover and to offer burnt offerings on the altar of the LORD, according to the command of King Josi′ah. And the people of Israel who were present 17 kept the passover at that time, and the feast of unleavened bread seven days. No pass- 18 over like it had been kept in Israel since the days of Samuel the prophet; none of the kings of Israel had kept such a passover as was kept by Josi′ah, and the priests and the Levites, and all Judah and Israel who were present, and the inhabitants of Jerusalem. In 19 the eighteenth year of the reign of Josi′ah this passover was kept.

Death of Josiah

After all this, when Josi′ah had prepared the 20 temple, Neco king of Egypt went up to fight

y Heb obscure
35.1-19: 2 Kings 23.21-23.

at Car'chemish on the Euphra'tes and
21 Josi'ah went out against him. But he sent
envoys to him, saying, "What have we to do
with each other, king of Judah? I am not
coming against you this day, but against the
house with which I am at war; and God has
commanded me to make haste. Cease
opposing God, who is with me, lest he
22 destroy you." Nevertheless Josi'ah would
not turn away from him, but disguised
himself in order to fight with him. He did
not listen to the words of Neco from the
mouth of God, but joined battle in the plain
23 of Megid'do. And the archers shot King
Josi'ah; and the king said to his servants,
"Take me away, for I am badly wounded."
24 So his servants took him out of the chariot
and carried him in his second chariot and
brought him to Jerusalem. And he died, and
was buried in the tombs of his fathers. All
Judah and Jerusalem mourned for Josi'ah.
25 Jeremiah also uttered a lament for Josi'ah;
and all the singing men and singing women
have spoken of Josi'ah in their laments to this
day. They made these an ordinance in
Israel; behold, they are written in the
26 Laments. Now the rest of the acts of Josi'ah,
and his good deeds according to what is
27 written in the law of the LORD, and his acts,
first and last, behold, they are written in the
Book of the Kings of Israel and Judah.

Under Egypt

36 The people of the land took Jeho'ahaz the
son of Josi'ah and made him king in his
2 father's stead in Jerusalem. Jeho'ahaz was

twenty-three years old when he began to
reign; and he reigned three months in Jerusalem. Then the king of Egypt deposed him
in Jerusalem and laid upon the land a tribute
of a hundred talents of silver and a talent of
gold. And the king of Egypt made Eli'akim
his brother king over Judah and Jerusalem,

THE DEATH
of
JOSIAH

Carchemish

River Euphrates

*The
Great
Sea*

o Damascus

o Megiddo

◎ Jerusalem

Scale of Miles

0 25 50 100 200

EGYPT

B. C.
600~500

and changed his name to Jehoi'akim; but Neco took Jeho'ahaz his brother and carried him to Egypt.

Attacked by Babylon

Jehoi'akim was twenty-five years old when he began to reign, and he reigned eleven years in Jerusalem. He did what was evil in the sight of the LORD his God. Against him came up Nebuchadnez'zar king of Babylon, and bound him in fetters to take him to Babylon. Nebuchadnez'zar also carried part of the vessels of the house of the LORD to Babylon and put them in his palace in Babylon. Now the rest of the acts of Jehoi'-akim, and the abominations which he did, and what was found against him, behold, they are written in the Book of the Kings of Israel and Judah; and Jehoi'achin his son reigned in his stead.

Jehoi'achin was eight years old when he began to reign, and he reigned three months and ten days in Jerusalem. He did what was evil in the sight of the LORD. In the spring of the year King Nebuchadnez'zar sent and brought him to Babylon, with the precious vessels of the house of the LORD, and made his brother Zedeki'ah king over Judah and Jerusalem.

Zedeki'ah was twenty-one years old when he began to reign, and he reigned eleven years in Jerusalem. He did what was evil in the sight of the LORD his God. He did not humble himself before Jeremiah the prophet,

who spoke from the mouth of the LORD. He 13 also rebelled against King Nebuchadnez'zar, who had made him swear by God; he stiffened his neck and hardened his heart against turning to the LORD, the God of Israel. All the leading priests and the people 14 likewise were exceedingly unfaithful, following all the abominations of the nations; and they polluted the house of the LORD which he had hallowed in Jerusalem.

The LORD, the God of their fathers, sent 15 persistently to them by his messengers, because he had compassion on his people and on his dwelling place; but they kept mocking 16 the messengers of God, despising his words, and scoffing at his prophets, till the wrath of the LORD rose against his people, till there was no remedy.

The captivity

Therefore he brought up against them the 17 king of the Chalde'ans, who slew their young men with the sword in the house of their sanctuary, and had no compassion on young man or virgin, old man or aged; he gave them all into his hand. And all the vessels of 18 the house of God, great and small, and the treasures of the house of the LORD, and the treasures of the king and of his princes, all these he brought to Babylon. And they 19 burned the house of God, and broke down the wall of Jerusalem, and burned all its palaces with fire, and destroyed all its precious vessels. He took into exile in Babylon 20

36.5–8: 2 Kings 23.36–24.6.   36.9–10: 2 Kings 24.8–17.
36.11–21: 2 Kings 24.18–25.21.

Babylon—The city of the captivity

those who had escaped from the sword, and they became servants to him and to his sons until the establishment of the kingdom of 21 Persia, to fulfil the word of the LORD by the mouth of Jeremiah, until the land had enjoyed its sabbaths. All the days that it lay desolate it kept sabbath, to fulfil seventy years.

The return

22 Now in the first year of Cyrus king of Persia, that the word of the LORD by the mouth of Jeremiah might be accomplished, the LORD stirred up the spirit of Cyrus king of Persia so that he made a proclamation throughout all his kingdom and also put it in writing: "Thus says Cyrus king of Persia, 'The LORD, the God of heaven, has given me all the kingdoms of the earth, and he has charged me to build him a house at Jerusalem, which is in Judah. Whoever is among you of all his people, may the LORD his God be with him. Let him go up.' "

36.22–23: Ezra 1.1–3.

THE BOOK OF

EZRA

IN the first year of Cyrus king of Persia, that the word of the LORD by the mouth of Jeremiah might be accomplished, the LORD stirred up the spirit of Cyrus king of Persia so that he made a proclamation throughout all his kingdom and also put it in writing:

2 "Thus says Cyrus king of Persia: The LORD, the God of heaven, has given me all the kingdoms of the earth, and he has charged me to build him a house at Jerusalem, which 3 is in Judah. Whoever is among you of all his people, may his God be with him, and let him go up to Jerusalem, which is in Judah, and rebuild the house of the LORD, the God of Israel—he is the God who is in Jerusalem; 4 and let each survivor, in whatever place he sojourns, be assisted by the men of his place with silver and gold, with goods and with beasts, besides freewill offerings for the house of God which is in Jerusalem."

5 Then rose up the heads of the fathers' houses of Judah and Benjamin, and the priests and the Levites, every one whose spirit God had stirred to go up to rebuild the house of the LORD which is in Jerusalem; and 6 all who were about them aided them with vessels of silver, with gold, with goods, with beasts, and with costly wares, besides all that was freely offered. Cyrus the king also 7 brought out the vessels of the house of the LORD which Nebuchadnez'zar had carried away from Jerusalem and placed in the house of his gods. Cyrus king of Persia brought 8 these out in charge of Mith'redath the treasurer, who counted them out to Shesh-baz'zar the prince of Judah. And this was 9 the number of them: a thousand[a] basins of gold, a thousand basins of silver, twenty-nine censers, thirty bowls of gold, two thousand[b] 10 four hundred and ten bowls of silver, and a thousand other vessels; all the vessels of gold 11 and of silver were five thousand four hundred and sixty-nine.[c] All these did Shesh-baz'zar bring up, when the exiles were brought up from Babylonia to Jerusalem.

ZERUBBABEL'S COMPANY

2 NOW these were the people of the province who came up out of the captivity of those exiles whom Nebuchadnez'zar the king of Babylonia had carried captive to Babylonia; they returned to Jeru-salem and Judah, each to his own 2 town. They came with Zerub'-babel, Jeshua, Nehemi'ah, Serai'-ah, Re-el-ai'ah, Mor'decai, Bil-shan, Mispar, Big'vai, Rehum, and Ba'anah.

The number of the men of the 3 people of Israel: the sons of Parosh, two thousand one hun-dred and seventy-two. The sons 4 of Shephati'ah, three hundred and seventy-two. The sons of 5 Arah, seven hundred and seventy-five. The sons of Pa'hath-mo'ab, 6 namely the sons of Jeshua and Jo'ab, two thousand eight hun-dred and twelve. The sons of 7 Elam, one thousand two hundred

[a] 1 Esdras 2.13: Heb thirty   [b] 1 Esdras 2.13: Heb of a second sort
[c] 1 Esdras 2.14: Heb five thousand four hundred
1.1–3: 2 Chron 36.22–23; Ezra 5.13; 6.3. 2.1–70: Neh 7.6–73.

8 and fifty-four. The sons of Zattu, 9 nine hundred and forty-five. The sons of Zac'cai, seven hundred 10 and sixty. The sons of Bani, six 11 hundred and forty-two. The sons of Be'bai, six hundred and 12 twenty-three. The sons of Azgad, one thousand two hundred and 13 twenty-two. The sons of Adoni'-kam, six hundred and sixty-six. 14 The sons of Big'vai, two thousand 15 and fifty-six. The sons of Adin, 16 four hundred and fifty-four. The sons of Ater, namely of Hezeki'ah, 17 ninety-eight. The sons of Be'zai, three hundred and twenty-three. 18 The sons of Jorah, one hundred 19 and twelve. The sons of Hashum, two hundred and twenty-three. 20 The sons of Gibbar, ninety-five. 21 The sons of Bethlehem, one 22 hundred and twenty-three. The 23 men of Netoph'ah, fifty-six. The men of An'athoth, one hundred 24 and twenty-eight. The sons of 25 Az'maveth, forty-two. The sons of Kir'iath-ar'im, Chephi'rah, and Be-er'oth, seven hundred and 26 forty-three. The sons of Ramah and Geba, six hundred and twen-27 ty-one. The men of Michmas, one hundred and twenty-two. 28 The men of Bethel and Ai, two 29 hundred and twenty-three. The 30 sons of Nebo, fifty-two. The sons of Magbish, one hundred and 31 fifty-six. The sons of the other Elam, one thousand two hun-32 dred and fifty-four. The sons of Harim, three hundred and 33 twenty. The sons of Lod, Hadid, and Ono, seven hundred and 34 twenty-five. The sons of Jericho, three hundred and forty-five. 35 The sons of Sena'ah, three thousand six hundred and thirty. 36 The priests: the sons of Jedai'ah, of the house of Jeshua, nine 37 hundred and seventy-three. The sons of Immer, one thousand and 38 fifty-two. The sons of Pashhur, one thousand two hundred and

39 forty-seven. The sons of Harim, one thousand and seventeen. 40 The Levites: the sons of Jeshua and Kad'mi-el, of the sons of 41 Hodavi'ah, seventy-four. The singers: the sons of Asaph, one 42 hundred and twenty-eight. The sons of the gatekeepers: the sons of Shallum, the sons of Ater, the sons of Talmon, the sons of Akkub, the sons of Hati'ta, and the sons of Sho'bai, in all one hundred and thirty-nine. 43 The temple servants:[d] the sons of Ziha, the sons of Hasu'pha, the 44 sons of Tabba'oth, the sons of Keros, the sons of Si'aha, the sons 45 of Padon, the sons of Leba'nah, the sons of Hag'abah, the sons of 46 Akkub, the sons of Hagab, the sons of Shamlai, the sons of 47 Hanan, the sons of Giddel, the sons of Gahar, the sons of 48 Re-ai'ah, the sons of Rezin, the sons of Neko'da, the sons of 49 Gazzam, the sons of Uzza, the sons of Pase'ah, the sons of Besai, 50 the sons of Asnah, the sons of Me-u'nim, the sons of Nephi'sim, 51 the sons of Bakbuk, the sons of Haku'pha, the sons of Harhur, the 52 sons of Bazluth, the sons of Mehi'da, the sons of Harsha, the 53 sons of Barkos, the sons of Sis'era, 54 the sons of Temah, the sons of Nezi'ah, and the sons of Hati'pha. 55 The sons of Solomon's servants: the sons of So'tai, the sons of Hasso'phereth, the sons of 56 Peru'da, the sons of Ja'alah, the sons of Darkon, the sons of 57 Giddel, the sons of Shephati'ah, the sons of Hattil, the sons of Po'chereth-hazzeba'im, and the sons of Ami. 58 All the temple servants[d] and the sons of Solomon's servants were three hundred and ninety-two. 59 The following were those who came up from Tel-me'lah, Tel-har'sha, Cherub, Addan, and Immer, though they could not

prove their fathers' houses or their descent, whether they belonged to Israel: the sons of 60 Dela'iah, the sons of Tobi'ah, and the sons of Neko'da, six hundred and fifty-two. Also, of the sons of 61 the priests: the sons of Habai'ah, the sons of Hakkoz, and the sons of Barzil'lai (who had taken a wife from the daughters of Barzil'lai the Gileadite, and was called by their name). These sought their 62 registration among those enrolled in the genealogies, but they were not found there, and so they were excluded from the priesthood as unclean; the governor told them 63 that they were not to partake of the most holy food, until there should be a priest to consult Urim and Thummim.

The whole assembly together 64 was forty-two thousand three hundred and sixty, besides their 65 menservants and maidservants, of whom there were seven thousand three hundred and thirty-seven; and they had two hundred male and female singers. Their horses 66 were seven hundred and thirty-six, their mules were two hundred and forty-five, their camels were 67 four hundred and thirty-five, and their asses were six thousand seven hundred and twenty.

Some of the heads of families, 68 when they came to the house of the LORD which is in Jerusalem, made freewill offerings for the house of God, to erect it on its 69 site; according to their ability they gave to the treasury of the work sixty-one thousand darics of gold, five thousand minas of silver, and one hundred priests' garments.

The priests, the Levites, and 70 some of the people lived in Jerusalem and its vicinity;[e] and the singers, the gatekeepers, and the temple servants lived in their towns, and all Israel in their towns.

The return to Jerusalem

3 WHEN the seventh month came, and the sons of Israel were in the towns, the people gathered as one man to Jerusalem. 2 Then arose Jeshua the son of Jo'zadak, with his fellow priests, and Zerub'babel the son of She-al'ti-el with his kinsmen, and they built the altar of the God of Israel, to offer burnt offerings upon it, as it is written in the law of 3 Moses the man of God. They set the altar in its place, for fear was upon them because of the peoples of the lands, and they offered burnt offerings upon it to the LORD, burnt 4 offerings morning and evening. And they kept the feast of booths, as it is written, and

offered the daily burnt offerings by number according to the ordinance, as each day required, and after that the continual burnt 5 offerings, the offerings at the new moon and at all the appointed feasts of the LORD, and the offerings of every one who made a freewill offering to the LORD. From the first 6 day of the seventh month they began to offer burnt offerings to the LORD. But the foundation of the temple of the LORD was not yet laid. So they gave money to the masons and 7 the carpenters, and food, drink, and oil to the Sido'nians and the Tyrians to bring cedar trees from Lebanon to the sea, to Joppa, according to the grant which they had from Cyrus king of Persia.

---

d Heb *nethinim*   *e* 1 Esdras 5.46: Heb lacks *lived in Jerusalem and its vicinity*

Rebuilding the temple

Now in the second year of their coming to the house of God at Jerusalem, in the second month, Zerub′babel the son of She-al′ti-el and Jeshua the son of Jo′zadak made a beginning, together with the rest of their brethren, the priests and the Levites and all who had come to Jerusalem from the captivity. They appointed the Levites, from twenty years old and upward, to have the oversight of the work of the house of the LORD. And Jeshua with his sons and his kinsmen, and Kad′mi-el and his sons, the sons of Judah, together took the oversight of the workmen in the house of God, along with the sons of Hen′adad and the Levites, their sons and kinsmen.

And when the builders laid the foundation of the temple of the LORD, the priests in their vestments came forward with trumpets, and the Levites, the sons of Asaph, with cymbals, to praise the LORD, according to the directions of David king of Israel; and they sang responsively, praising and giving thanks to the LORD,

"For he is good,
    for his steadfast love endures for ever
        toward Israel."

And all the people shouted with a great shout, when they praised the LORD, because the foundation of the house of the LORD was laid. But many of the priests and Levites and heads of fathers' houses, old men who had seen the first house, wept with a loud voice when they saw the foundation of this house being laid, though many shouted aloud for joy; so that the people could not distinguish the sound of the joyful shout from the sound of the people's weeping, for the people shouted with a great shout, and the sound was heard afar.

The work hindered

Now when the adversaries of Judah and Benjamin heard that the returned exiles were building a temple to the LORD, the God of Israel, they approached Zerub′babel and the heads of fathers' houses and said to them, "Let us build with you; for we worship your God as you do, and we have been sacrificing to him ever since the days of E′sar-had′don king of Assyria who brought us here." But Zerub′babel, Jeshua, and the rest of the heads of fathers' houses in Israel said to them, "You have nothing to do with us in building a house to our God; but we alone will build to the LORD, the God of Israel, as King Cyrus the king of Persia has commanded us."

Then the people of the land discouraged the 4 people of Judah, and made them afraid to build, and hired counsellors against them to 5 frustrate their purpose, all the days of Cyrus king of Persia, even until the reign of Darius king of Persia.

And in the reign of Ahasu-e′rus, in the 6 beginning of his reign, they wrote an accusation against the inhabitants of Judah and Jerusalem.

And in the days of Ar-ta-xerx′es, Bishlam 7 and Mith′redath and Ta′be-el and the rest of their associates wrote to Ar-ta-xerx′es king of Persia; the letter was written in Aramaic and translated.[f] Rehum the commander and 8 Shim′shai the scribe wrote a letter against Jerusalem to Ar-ta-xerx′es the king as follows—then wrote Rehum the commander, and 9 Shim′shai the scribe, and the rest of their associates, the judges, the governors, the officials, the Persians, the men of Erech, the Babylonians, the men of Susa, that is, the Elamites, and the rest of the nations whom 10 the great and noble Osnap′par deported and settled in the cities of Samar′ia and in the rest of the province Beyond the River, and now this is a copy of the letter that they 11 sent—"To Ar-ta-xerx′es the king: Your servants, the men of the province Beyond the River, send greeting. And now be it known 12 to the king that the Jews who came up from you to us have gone to Jerusalem. They are rebuilding that rebellious and wicked city; they are finishing the walls and repairing the foundations. Now be it known to the king 13 that, if this city is rebuilt and the walls finished, they will not pay tribute, custom, or toll, and the royal revenue will be impaired. Now because we eat the salt of the palace and 14 it is not fitting for us to witness the king's dishonour, therefore we send and inform the king, in order that search may be made in the 15 book of the records of your fathers. You will find in the book of the records and learn that this city is a rebellious city, hurtful to kings and provinces, and that sedition was stirred up in it from of old. That was why this city was laid waste. We make known to the king 16 that, if this city is rebuilt and its walls finished, you will then have no possession in the province Beyond the River."

The king sent an answer: "To Rehum the 17 commander and Shim′shai the scribe and the rest of their associates who live in Samar′ia and in the rest of the province Beyond the River, greeting. And now the letter which 18

---

[f] Heb adds *in Aramaic*, indicating that 4.8–6.18 is in Aramaic. Another interpretation is *The letter was written in the Aramaic script and set forth in the Aramaic language.*

you sent to us has been plainly read before
19 me. And I made a decree, and search has
been made, and it has been found that this
city from of old has risen against kings, and
that rebellion and sedition have been made in
20 it. And mighty kings have been over Jerusalem, who ruled over the whole province
Beyond the River, to whom tribute, custom,
21 and toll were paid. Therefore make a decree
that these men be made to cease, and that
this city be not rebuilt, until a decree is made
22 by me. And take care not to be slack in this
matter; why should damage grow to the hurt
of the king?"
23 Then, when the copy of King Ar-ta-xerx'es'
letter was read before Rehum and Shim'shai
the scribe and their associates, they went in
haste to the Jews at Jerusalem and by force
24 and power made them cease. Then the work
on the house of God which is in Jerusalem
stopped; and it ceased until the second year
of the reign of Darius king of Persia.

The work resumed

5 Now the prophets, Haggai and Zechari'ah
the son of Iddo, prophesied to the Jews who
were in Judah and Jerusalem, in the name of
2 the God of Israel who was over them. Then
Zerub'babel the son of She-al'ti-el and
Jeshua the son of Jo'zadak arose and began to
rebuild the house of God which is in Jerusalem; and with them were the prophets of
God, helping them.
3 At the same time Tat'tenai the governor of
the province Beyond the River and She'-
thar-boz'enai and their associates came to
them and spoke to them thus, "Who gave
you a decree to build this house and to finish
4 this structure?" They[g] also asked them this,
"What are the names of the men who are
5 building this building?" But the eye of their
God was upon the elders of the Jews, and
they did not stop them till a report should
reach Darius and then answer be returned by
letter concerning it.
6 The copy of the letter which Tat'tenai the
governor of the province Beyond the River

and She'thar-boz'enai and his associates the
governors who were in the province Beyond
the River sent to Darius the king; they sent 7
him a report, in which was written as follows: "To Darius the king, all peace. Be it 8
known to the king that we went to the
province of Judah, to the house of the great
God. It is being built with huge stones, and
timber is laid in the walls; this work goes on
diligently and prospers in their hands. Then 9
we asked those elders and spoke to them
thus, 'Who gave you a decree to build this
house and to finish this structure?' We also 10
asked them their names, for your information, that we might write down the names
of the men at their head. And this was their 11
reply to us: 'We are the servants of the God
of heaven and earth, and we are rebuilding
the house that was built many years ago,
which a great king of Israel built and finished. But because our fathers had angered 12
the God of heaven, he gave them into the
hand of Nebuchadnez'zar king of Babylon,
the Chalde'an, who destroyed this house and
carried away the people to Babylonia.
However in the first year of Cyrus king of 13
Babylon, Cyrus the king made a decree that
this house of God should be rebuilt. And the 14
gold and silver vessels of the house of God,
which Nebuchadnez'zar had taken out of the
temple that was in Jerusalem and brought
into the temple of Babylon, these Cyrus the
king took out of the temple of Babylon, and
they were delivered to one whose name was
Shesh-baz'zar, whom he had made governor;
and he said to him, "Take these vessels, go 15
and put them in the temple which is in
Jerusalem, and let the house of God be
rebuilt on its site.' Then this Shesh-baz'zar 16
came and laid the foundations of the house of
God which is in Jerusalem; and from that
time until now it has been in building, and it
is not yet finished.' Therefore, if it seem 17
good to the king, let search be made in the
royal archives there in Babylon, to see
whether a decree was issued by Cyrus the
king for the rebuilding of this house of God
in Jerusalem. And let the king send us his
pleasure in this matter."

g Gk Syr: Aramaic *We*
5.1: Hag 1.1; Zech 1.1.   **5.13:** Ezra 1.1; 6.3.

The king's decree

Then Darius the king made a decree, and search was made in Babylonia, in the house of the archives where the documents were stored. And in Ecbat'ana, the capital which is in the province of Media, a scroll was found on which this was written: "A record. In the first year of Cyrus the king, Cyrus the king issued a decree: Concerning the house of God at Jerusalem, let the house be rebuilt, the place where sacrifices are offered and burnt offerings are brought; its height shall be sixty cubits and its breadth sixty cubits, with three courses of great stones and one course of timber; let the cost be paid from the royal treasury. And also let the gold and silver vessels of the house of God, which Nebuchadnez'zar took out of the temple that is in Jerusalem and brought to Babylon, be restored and brought back to the temple which is in Jerusalem, each to its place; you shall put them in the house of God."

"Now therefore, Tat'tenai, governor of the province Beyond the River, She'thar-boz'enai, and your associates the governors who are in the province Beyond the River, keep away; let the work on this house of God alone; let the governor of the Jews and the elders of the Jews rebuild this house of God on its site. Moreover I make a decree regarding what you shall do for these elders of the Jews for the rebuilding of this house of God; the cost is to be paid to these men in full and without delay from the royal revenue, the tribute of the province from Beyond the River. And whatever is needed—young bulls, rams, or sheep for burnt offerings to the God of heaven, wheat, salt, wine, or oil, as the priests at Jerusalem require—let that be given to them day by day without fail, that they may offer pleasing sacrifices to the God of heaven, and pray for the life of the king and his sons. Also I make a decree that if any one alters this edict, a beam shall be pulled out of his house, and he shall be impaled upon it, and his house shall be made a dunghill. May the God who has caused his name to dwell there overthrow any king or people that shall put forth a hand to alter this, or to destroy this house of God which is in Jerusalem. I Darius make a decree; let it be done with all diligence."

Then, according to the word sent by Darius 13 the king, Tat'tenai, the governor of the province Beyond the River, She'thar-boz'enai, and their associates did with all diligence what Darius the king had ordered. And the elders of the Jews built and pros- 14 pered, through the prophesying of Haggai the prophet and Zechari'ah the son of Iddo. They finished their building by command of the God of Israel and by decree of Cyrus and Darius and Ar-ta-xerx'es king of Persia; and 15 this house was finished on the third day of the month of Adar, in the sixth year of the reign of Darius the king.

The feast of dedication

And the people of Israel, the priests and the 16 Levites, and the rest of the returned exiles, celebrated the dedication of this house of God with joy. They offered at the dedication 17 of this house of God one hundred bulls, two hundred rams, four hundred lambs, and as a sin offering for all Israel twelve he-goats, according to the number of the tribes of Israel. And they set the priests in their 18 divisions and the Levites in their courses, for the service of God at Jerusalem, as it is written in the book of Moses.

On the fourteenth day of the first month 19 the returned exiles kept the passover. For 20 the priests and the Levites had purified themselves together; all of them were clean. So they killed the passover lamb for all the returned exiles, for their fellow priests, and for themselves; it was eaten by the people of 21 Israel who had returned from exile, and also by every one who had joined them and separated himself from the pollutions of the peoples of the land to worship the LORD, the God of Israel. And they kept the feast of 22 unleavened bread seven days with joy; for the LORD had made them joyful, and had turned the heart of the king of Assyria to them, so that he aided them in the work of the house of God, the God of Israel.

EZRA

NOW after this, in the reign of Ar- 7 ta-xerx'es king of Persia, Ezra the son of Serai'ah, son of Azari'ah, son of Hilki'ah, son 2 of Shallum, son of Zadok, son of Ahi'tub, son 3 of Amari'ah, son of Azari'ah, son of Mera'ioth, son of Zerahi'ah, son of Uzzi, son 4

5 of Bukki, son of Abishu'a, son of Phin'ehas, son of Elea'zar, son of Aaron the chief
6 priest—this Ezra went up from Babylonia. He was a scribe skilled in the law of Moses which the LORD the God of Israel had given; and the king granted him all that he asked, for the hand of the LORD his God was upon him.
7 And there went up also to Jerusalem, in the seventh year of Ar-ta-xerx'es the king, some of the people of Israel, and some of the priests and Levites, the singers and gate-
8 keepers, and the temple servants. And he came to Jerusalem in the fifth month, which
9 was in the seventh year of the king; for on the first day of the first month he began[h] to go up from Babylonia, and on the first day of the fifth month he came to Jerusalem, for the
10 good hand of his God was upon him. For Ezra had set his heart to study the law of the LORD, and to do it, and to teach his statutes and ordinances in Israel.

Letter of authority

11 This is a copy of the letter which King Ar-ta-xerx'es gave to Ezra the priest, the scribe, learned in matters of the commandments of the LORD and his statutes for
12 Israel: "Ar-ta-xerx'es, king of kings, to Ezra the priest, the scribe of the law of the God of
13 heaven.[i] And now I make a decree that any one of the people of Israel or their priests or Levites in my kingdom, who freely offers to
14 go to Jerusalem, may go with you. For you are sent by the king and his seven counsellors to make inquiries about Judah and Jerusalem according to the law of your God, which is in
15 your hand, and also to convey the silver and gold which the king and his counsellors have freely offered to the God of Israel, whose
16 dwelling is in Jerusalem, with all the silver and gold which you shall find in the whole province of Babylonia, and with the freewill offerings of the people and the priests, vowed willingly for the house of their God which is
17 in Jerusalem. With this money, then, you shall with all diligence buy bulls, rams, and lambs, with their cereal offerings and their drink offerings, and you shall offer them upon the altar of the house of your God
18 which is in Jerusalem. Whatever seems good

to you and your brethren to do with the rest of the silver and gold, you may do, according to the will of your God. The vessels that have been given you for the service of the house of your God, you shall deliver before the God of Jerusalem. And whatever else is required for the house of your God, which you have occasion to provide, you may provide it out of the king's treasury.

"And I, Ar-ta-xerx'es the king, make a decree to all the treasurers in the province Beyond the River: Whatever Ezra the priest, the scribe of the law of the God of heaven, requires of you, be it done with all diligence, up to a hundred talents of silver, a hundred cors of wheat, a hundred baths of wine, a hundred baths of oil, and salt without prescribing how much. Whatever is commanded by the God of heaven, let it be done in full for the house of the God of heaven, lest his wrath be against the realm of the king and his sons. We also notify you that it shall not be lawful to impose tribute, custom, or toll upon any one of the priests, the Levites, the singers, the doorkeepers, the temple servants, or other servants of this house of God.

"And you, Ezra, according to the wisdom of your God which is in your hand, appoint magistrates and judges who may judge all the people in the province Beyond the River, all such as know the laws of your God; and those who do not know them, you shall teach. Whoever will not obey the law of your God and the law of the king, let judgment be strictly executed upon him, whether for death or for banishment or for confiscation of his goods or for imprisonment."

Blessed be the LORD, the God of our fathers, who put such a thing as this into the heart of the king, to beautify the house of the LORD which is in Jerusalem, and who extended to me his steadfast love before the king and his counsellors, and before all the king's mighty officers. I took courage, for the hand of the LORD my God was upon me, and I gathered leading men from Israel to go up with me.

Ancient seals

[h] Vg See Syr: Heb *that was the foundation of the going up*   [i] Aram adds a word of uncertain meaning

EZRA'S COMPANY

THESE are the heads of their fathers' houses, and this is the genealogy of those who went up with me from Babylonia, in the reign of Ar-ta-xerx'es the king: Of the sons of Phin'ehas, Gershom. Of the sons of Ith'amar, Daniel. Of the sons of David, Hattush, of the sons of Shecani'ah. Of the sons of Parosh, Zechari'ah, with whom were registered one hundred and fifty men. Of the sons of Pa'hath-mo'ab, El'ieho-e'nai the son of Zerahi'ah, and with him two 5 hundred men. Of the sons of Zattu,[j] Shecani'ah the son of Jahazi'el, and with him three 6 hundred men. Of the sons of Adin, Ebed the son of Jonathan, 7 and with him fifty men. Of the sons of Elam, Jeshai'ah the son of Athali'ah, and with him seventy 8 men. Of the sons of Shephati'ah, Zebadi'ah the son of Michael, and 9 with him eighty men. Of the sons of Jo'ab, Obadi'ah the son of Jehi'el, and with him two hun- 10 dred and eighteen men. Of the sons of Bani,[k] Shelo'mith the son of Josiphi'ah, and with him a hundred and sixty men. Of the 11 sons of Be'bai, Zechari'ah, the son of Be'bai, and with him twenty-eight men. Of the sons of 12 Azgad, Joha'nan the son of Hak'katan, and with him a hundred and ten men. Of the sons of 13 Adoni'kam, those who came later, their names being Eliph'elet, Jeu'el, and Shemai'ah, and with them sixty men. Of the sons of 14 Big'vai, Uthai and Zaccur, and with them seventy men.

The journey

I GATHERED them to the river that runs to Aha'va, and there we encamped three days. As I reviewed the people and the priests, I found there none of the sons of Levi. Then I sent for Elie'zer, Ar'i-el, Shemai'ah, Elna'than, Jarib, Elna'than, Nathan, Zechari'ah, and Meshul'lam, leading men, and for Joi'arib and Elna'than, who were men of insight, and sent them to Iddo, the leading man at the place Casiph'ia, telling them what to say to Iddo and his brethren the temple servants[i] at the place Casiph'ia, namely, to send us ministers for the house of our God. And by the good hand of our God upon us, they brought us a man of discretion, of the sons of Mahli the son of Levi, son of Israel, namely Sherebi'ah with his sons and kinsmen, eighteen; also Hashabi'ah and with him Jeshai'ah of the sons of Merar'i, with his kinsmen and their sons, twenty; besides two hundred and twenty of the temple servants, whom David and his officials had set apart to attend the Levites. These were all mentioned by name.

Prayer on the way

Then I proclaimed a fast there, at the river Aha'va, that we might humble ourselves before our God, to seek from him a straight way for ourselves, our children, and all our goods. For I was ashamed to ask the king for a band of soldiers and horsemen to protect us against the enemy on our way; since we had told the king, "The hand of our God is for good upon all that seek him, and the power of his wrath is against all that forsake him." So we fasted and besought our God for this, and he listened to our entreaty.

Then I set apart twelve of the leading priests: Sherebi'ah, Hashabi'ah, and ten of their kinsmen with them. And I weighed out to them the silver and the gold and the vessels, the offering for the house of our God which the king and his counsellors and his lords and all Israel there present had offered; I weighed out into their hand six hundred 26 and fifty talents of silver, and silver vessels worth a hundred talents, and a hundred talents of gold, twenty bowls of gold worth a 27 thousand darics, and two vessels of fine bright bronze as precious as gold. And I said 28 to them, "You are holy to the LORD, and the vessels are holy; and the silver and the gold are a freewill offering to the LORD, the God of your fathers. Guard them and keep them 29 until you weigh them before the chief priests and the Levites and the heads of fathers' houses in Israel at Jerusalem, within the chambers of the house of the LORD." So the 30 priests and the Levites took over the weight of the silver and the gold and the vessels, to bring them to Jerusalem, to the house of our God.

In Jerusalem

Then we departed from the river Aha'va on 31 the twelfth day of the first month, to go to Jerusalem; the hand of our God was upon us, and he delivered us from the hand of the enemy and from ambushes by the way. We 32 came to Jerusalem, and there we remained three days. On the fourth day, within the 33 house of our God, the silver and the gold and the vessels were weighed into the hands of Mer'emoth the priest, son of Uri'ah, and with him was Elea'zar the son of Phin'ehas, and with them were the Levites, Jo'zabad the son of Jeshua and No-adi'ah the son of Bin'nui. The whole was counted and 34 weighed, and the weight of everything was recorded.

An offering to God

At that time those who had come from 35 captivity, the returned exiles, offered burnt

---

[j] Gk 1 Esdras 8.32: Heb lacks *of Zattu*   [k] Gk 1 Esdras 8.36: Heb lacks *Bani*   Heb *nethinim*

Probable route of Ezra's company

offerings to the God of Israel, twelve bulls
for all Israel, ninety-six rams, seventy-seven
lambs, and as a sin offering twelve he-goats;
all this was a burnt offering to the LORD.
36 They also delivered the king's commissions
to the king's satraps and to the governors of
the province Beyond the River; and they
aided the people and the house of God.

Mixed marriages

9 After these things had been done, the
officials approached me and said, "The
people of Israel and the priests and the
Levites have not separated themselves from
the peoples of the lands with their abominations, from the Canaanites, the Hittites, the
Per'izzites, the Jeb'usites, the Ammonites,
the Moabites, the Egyptians, and the Amor-
2 ites. For they have taken some of their
daughters to be wives for themselves and for
their sons; so that the holy race has mixed
itself with the peoples of the lands. And in
this faithlessness the hand of the officials and
chief men has been foremost." When I
heard this, I rent my garments and my
mantle, and pulled hair from my head and
beard, and sat appalled. Then all who
trembled at the words of the God of Israel,
because of the faithlessness of the returned
exiles, gathered round me while I sat
appalled until the evening sacrifice. And at
the evening sacrifice I rose from my fasting,
with my garments and my mantle rent, and
fell upon my knees and spread out my hands
to the LORD my God, saying:

"O my God, I am ashamed and blush to lift
my face to thee, my God, for our iniquities
have risen higher than our heads, and our
guilt has mounted up to the heavens. From
the days of our fathers to this day we have
been in great guilt; and for our iniquities we,
our kings, and our priests have been given
into the hand of the kings of the lands, to the
sword, to captivity, to plundering, and to
utter shame, as at this day. But now for a
brief moment favour has been shown by the

LORD our God, to leave us a remnant, and to give us a secure hold*m* within his holy place, that our God may brighten our eyes and grant us a little reviving in our bondage. For we are bondmen; yet our God has not forsaken us in our bondage, but has extended to us his steadfast love before the kings of Persia, to grant us some reviving to set up the house of our God, to repair its ruins, and to give us protection*n* in Judea and Jerusalem.

"And now, O our God, what shall we say after this? For we have forsaken thy commandments, which thou didst command by thy servants the prophets, saying, 'The land which you are entering, to take possession of it, is a land unclean with the pollutions of the peoples of the lands, with their abominations which have filled it from end to end with their uncleanness. Therefore give not your daughters to their sons, neither take their daughters for your sons, and never seek their peace or prosperity, that you may be strong, and eat the good of the land, and leave it for an inheritance to your children for ever.' And after all that has come upon us for our evil deeds and for our great guilt, seeing that thou, our God, hast punished us less than our iniquities deserved and hast given us such a remnant as this, shall we break thy commandments again and intermarry with the peoples who practise these abominations? Wouldst thou not be angry with us till thou wouldst consume us, so that there should be no remnant, nor any to escape? O LORD the God of Israel, thou art just, for we are left a remnant that has escaped, as at this day. Behold, we are before thee in our guilt, for none can stand before thee because of this."

10 While Ezra prayed and made confession, weeping and casting himself down before the house of God, a very great assembly of men, women, and children, gathered to him out of Israel; for the people wept bitterly. And Shecani'ah the son of Jehi'el, of the sons of Elam, addressed Ezra: "We have broken faith with our God and have married foreign women from the peoples of the land, but even now there is hope for Israel in spite of this. Therefore let us make a covenant with our God to put away all these wives and their children, according to the counsel of my lord and of those who tremble at the commandment of our God; and let it be done according to the law. Arise, for it is your task, and we are with you; be strong and do

it." Then Ezra arose and made the leading 5 priests and Levites and all Israel take oath that they would do as had been said. So they took the oath.

A great assembly

Then Ezra withdrew from before the house 6 of God, and went to the chamber of Jehoha'nan the son of Eli'ashib, where he spent the night,*o* neither eating bread nor drinking water; for he was mourning over the faithlessness of the exiles. And a proclamation 7 was made throughout Judah and Jerusalem to all the returned exiles that they should assemble at Jerusalem, and that if any one 8 did not come within three days, by order of the officials and the elders all his property should be forfeited, and he himself banned from the congregation of the exiles.

Then all the men of Judah and Benjamin 9 assembled at Jerusalem within the three days; it was the ninth month, on the twentieth day of the month. And all the people sat in the open square before the house of God, trembling because of this matter and because of the heavy rain. And Ezra the 10 priest stood up and said to them, "You have trespassed and married foreign women, and so increased the guilt of Israel. Now then 11 make confession to the LORD the God of your fathers, and do his will; separate yourselves from the peoples of the land and from the foreign wives." Then all the assembly 12 answered with a loud voice, "It is so; we must do as you have said. But the people are 13 many, and it is a time of heavy rain; we cannot stand in the open. Nor is this a work for one day or for two; for we have greatly transgressed in this matter. Let our officials 14 stand for the whole assembly; let all in our cities who have taken foreign wives come at appointed times, and with them the elders and judges of every city, till the fierce wrath of our God over this matter be averted from us." Only Jonathan the son of As'ahel and 15 Jahzei'ah the son of Tikvah opposed this, and Meshul'lam and Shab'bethai the Levite supported them.

Then the returned exiles did so. Ezra the 16 priest selected men,*p* heads of fathers' houses, according to their fathers' houses, each of them designated by name. On the first day of the tenth month they sat down to examine the matter; and by the first day 17 of the first month they had come to the end of all the men who had married foreign women.

---

m Heb *nail* or *tent-pin*   *n* Heb *a wall*   *o* 1 Esdras 9.2: Heb *where he went*
p 1 Esdras 9.16 Syr: Heb *and there were selected Ezra*, etc.

18 OF the sons of the priests who had married foreign women were found Ma-asei′ah, Elie′zer, Jarib, and Gedali′ah, of the sons of Jeshua the son of Jo′zadak and 19 his brethren. They pledged themselves to put away their wives, and their guilt offering was a ram of the flock for their guilt. 20 Of the sons of Immer: Hana′ni 21 and Zebadi′ah. Of the sons of Harim: Ma-asei′ah, Eli′jah, Shemai′ah, Jehi′el, and Uzzi′ah. 22 Of the sons of Pashhur: Eli-o-e′nai, Ma-asei′ah, Ish′mael, Nethan′el, Jo′zabad, and Ela′sah. 23 Of the Levites: Jo′zabad, Shim′e-i, Kelai′ah (that is, Keli′ta), Pethahi′ah, Judah, and 24 Elie′zer. Of the singers: Eli′-

ashib. Of the gatekeepers: Shallum, Telem, and Uri. 25 And of Israel: of the sons of Parosh: Rami′ah, Izzi′ah, Malchi′jah, Mi′jamin, Elea′zar, 26 Hashabi′ah,�q and Benai′ah. Of the sons of Elam: Mattani′ah, Zechari′ah, Jehi′el, Abdi, Jer′-27 emoth, and Eli′jah. Of the sons of Zattu: Eli-o-e′nai, Eli′ashib, Mattani′ah, Jer′emoth, Zabad, 28 and Azi′za. Of the sons of Be′bai were Jehoha′nan, Hanani′ah, 29 Zab′bai, and Ath′lai. Of the sons of Bani were Meshul′lam, Malluch, Adai′ah, Jashub, She′al, and 30 Jer′emoth. Of the sons of Pa′hath-mo′ab: Adna, Chelal, Benai′ah, Ma-asei′ah, Mattani′ah, Bez′alel, Bin′nui, and Manas′seh. 31 Of the sons of Harim: Elie′zer,

Isshi′jah, Malchi′jah, Shemai′ah, Shim′e-on, Benjamin, Malluch, 32 and Shemari′ah. Of the sons of 33 Hashum: Matte′nai, Mat′tattah, Zabad, Eliph′elet, Jer′emai, Manas′seh, and Shim′e-i. Of the 34 sons of Bani: Ma-ada′i, Amram, Uel, Benai′ah, Bedei′ah, Chel′uhi, 35 Vani′ah, Mer′emoth, Eli′ashib, 36 Mattani′ah, Matte′nai, Ja′asu. Of 37 the sons of Bin′nuiʳ: Shim′e-i, 38 Shelemi′ah, Nathan, Adai′ah, 39 Machnad′ebai, Shashai, Sha′rai, 40 Az′arel, Shelemi′ah, Shemari′ah, 41 Shallum, Amari′ah, and Joseph. 42 Of the sons of Nebo: Je-i′el, 43 Mattithi′ah, Zabad, Zebi′na, Jaddai, Jo′el, and Benai′ah. All 44 these had married foreign women, and they put them away with their children.ˢ

THE BOOK OF

NEHEMIAH

THE words of Nehemi′ah the son of Hacali′ah.

Now it happened in the month of Chislev, in the twentieth year, as I was in Susa 2 the capital, that Hana′ni, one of my brethren, came with certain men out of Judah; and I asked them concerning the Jews that survived, who had escaped exile, and concerning 3 Jerusalem. And they said to me, "The

survivors there in the province who escaped exile are in great trouble and shame; the wall of Jerusalem is broken down, and its gates are destroyed by fire."

When I heard these words I sat down and 4 wept, and mourned for days; and I continued fasting and praying before the God of heaven. And I said, "O LORD God of 5 heaven, the great and terrible God who keeps

�q 1 Esdras 9.26 Gk: Heb Malchijah   ʳ Gk: Heb Bani, Binnui   ˢ 1 Esdras 9.36: Heb obscure covenant and steadfast love with those who love him and keep his commandments; let thy ear be attentive, and thy eyes open, to hear the prayer of thy servant which I now pray before thee day and night for the people of Israel thy servants, confessing the sins of the people of Israel, which we have sinned against thee. Yea, I and my father's house have sinned. We have acted very corruptly against thee, and have not kept the commandments, the statutes, and the ordinances which thou didst command thy servant Moses. Remember the word which thou didst command thy servant Moses, saying, 'If you are unfaithful, I will scatter you among the peoples; but if you return to me and keep my commandments and do them, though your dispersed be under the farthest skies, I will gather them thence and bring them to the place which I have chosen, to make my name dwell there.' They are thy servants and thy people, whom thou hast redeemed by thy great power and by thy strong hand. O Lord, let thy ear be attentive to the prayer of thy servant, and to the prayer of thy servants who delight to fear thy name; and give success to thy servant today, and grant him mercy in the sight of this man."

Now I was cupbearer to the king.

The king's commission

2 In the month of Nisan, in the twentieth year of King Ar-ta-xerx´es, when wine was before him, I took up the wine and gave it to the king. Now I had not been sad in his presence. And the king said to me, "Why is your face sad, seeing you are not sick? This is nothing else but sadness of the heart." Then I was very much afraid. I said to the king, "Let the king live for ever! Why should not my face be sad, when the city, the place of my fathers' sepulchres, lies waste, and its gates have been destroyed by fire?" Then the king said to me, "For what do you make request?" So I prayed to the God of heaven. And I said to the king, "If it pleases the king, and if your servant has found favour in your sight, that you send me to Judah, to the city of my fathers' sepulchres, that I may rebuild it." And the king said to me (the queen sitting beside him), "How long will you be gone, and when will you return?" So it pleased the king to send me; and I set him a time. And I said to the king, "If it pleases the king, let letters be given me to the governors of the province Beyond the River, that they may let me pass through until I come to Judah; and a letter to Asaph, the keeper of the king's forest, that he may give me timber to make beams for the gates

of the fortress of the temple, and for the wall of the city, and for the house which I shall occupy." And the king granted me what I asked, for the good hand of my God was upon me.

Then I came to the governors of the province Beyond the River, and gave them the king's letters. Now the king had sent with me officers of the army and horsemen. But when Sanbal´lat the Hor´onite and Tobi´ah the servant, the Ammonite, heard this, it displeased them greatly that some one had come to seek the welfare of the children of Israel.

Nehemiah surveys Jerusalem

So I came to Jerusalem and was there three days. Then I arose in the night, I and a few men with me; and I told no one what my God had put into my heart to do for Jerusalem. There was no beast with me but the beast on which I rode. I went out by night by the Valley Gate to the Jackal's Well and to the Dung Gate, and I inspected the walls of Jerusalem which were broken down and its gates which had been destroyed by fire. Then I went on to the Fountain Gate and to the King's Pool; but there was no place for the beast that was under me to pass. Then I went up in the night by the valley and inspected the wall; and I turned back and entered by the Valley Gate, and so returned. And the officials did not know where I had gone or what I was doing; and I had not yet told the Jews, the priests, the nobles, the officials, and the rest that were to do the work. Then I said to them, "You see the trouble we are in, how Jerusalem lies in ruins with its gates burned. Come, let us build the wall of Jerusalem, that we may no longer suffer disgrace." And I told them of the hand of my God which had been upon me for good, and also of the words which the king had spoken to me. And they said, "Let us rise up and build." So they strengthened their hands for the good work.

Opposition

But when Sanbal´lat the Hor´onite and Tobi´ah the servant, the Ammonite, and Geshem the Arab heard of it, they derided us and despised us and said, "What is this thing that you are doing? Are you rebelling against the king?" Then I replied to them, "The God of heaven will make us prosper, and we his servants will arise and build; but you have no portion or right or memorial in Jerusalem."

JERUSALEM
Its Ancient Walls
and Gates

thousand cubits of the wall, as far as the Dung Gate.

Malchi′jah the son of Rechab, ruler of the district of[d] Beth-hac-che′rem, repaired the Dung Gate; he rebuilt it and set its doors, its bolts, and its bars.

And Shallum the son of Col-ho′zeh, ruler of the district of[d] Mizpah, repaired the Fountain Gate; he rebuilt it and covered it and set its doors, its bolts, and its bars; and he built the wall of the Pool of Shelah of the king's garden, as far as the stairs that go down from the City of David. After him Nehemi′ah the son of Azbuk, ruler of half the district of[d] Beth-zur, repaired to a point opposite the sepulchres of David, to the artificial pool, and to the house of the mighty men. After him the Levites repaired: Rehum the son of Bani; next to him Hashabi′ah, ruler of half the district of[d] Kei′lah, repaired for his district. After him their brethren repaired: Bav′vai the son of Hen′adad, ruler of half the district of[d] Kei′lah; next to him Ezer the son of Jeshua, ruler of Mizpah, repaired another section opposite the ascent to the armoury at the Angle. After him Baruch the son of Zab′bai repaired another section from the Angle to the door of the house of Eli′ashib the high priest. After him Mer′emoth the son of Uri′ah, son of Hakkoz repaired another section from the door of the house of Eli′ashib to the end of the house of Eli′ashib. After him the priests, the men of the Plain, repaired. After them Benjamin and Hasshub repaired opposite their house. After them Azari′ah the son of Ma-asei′ah, son of Anani′ah repaired beside his own house. After him Bin′nui the son of Hen′adad repaired another section, from the house of Azari′ah to the Angle and to the corner. Palal the son of Uzai repaired opposite the Angle and the tower projecting from the upper house of the king at the court of the guard. After him Peda′iah the son of Parosh and the temple servants living[e] on Ophel repaired to a point opposite the Water Gate on the east and the projecting tower. After him the Teko′-ites repaired another section opposite the great projecting tower as far as the wall of Ophel.

Above the Horse Gate the priests repaired, each one opposite his own house. After them Zadok the son of Immer repaired opposite his own house. After him Shemai′ah the son of Sheca-ni′ah, the keeper of the East Gate, repaired. After him Hanani′ah the son of Shelemi′ah and Hanun the sixth son of Zalaph repaired another section. After him Meshul′lam the son of Berechi′ah repaired opposite his chamber.

SPECIFICATION OF WORK

3 THEN Eli′ashib the high priest rose up with his brethren the priests and they built the Sheep Gate. They consecrated it and set its doors; they consecrated it as far as the Tower of the Hundred, as far as the Tower of Han′anel. 2 And next to him the men of Jericho built. And next to them[a] Zaccur the son of Imri built.

3 And the sons of Hassena′ah built the Fish Gate; they laid its beams and set its doors, its bolts, and its 4 bars. And next to them Mer′emoth the son of Uri′ah, son of Hakkoz repaired. And next to them Meshul′lam the son of Bere-chi′ah, son of Meshez′abel repaired. And next to them Zadok 5 the son of Ba′ana repaired. And next to them the Teko′ites repaired; but their nobles did not put their necks to the work of their Lord.[b]

6 And Joi′ada the son of Pase′-ah and Meshul′lam the son of Besodei′ah repaired the Old Gate; they laid its beams and set its

7 doors, its bolts, and its bars. And next to them repaired Melati′ah the Gib′eonite and Jadon the Meron′othite, the men of Gibeon and of Mizpah, who were under the jurisdiction of the governor of the province Beyond the River. 8 Next to them Uz′ziel the son of Harhai′ah, goldsmiths, repaired. Next to him Hanani′ah, one of the perfumers, repaired; and they restored[c] Jerusalem as far as the 9 Broad Wall. Next to them Repha′iah the son of Hur, ruler of half the district of[d] Jerusalem, 10 repaired. Next to them Jedai′ah the son of Haru′maph repaired opposite his house; and next to him Hattush the son of Hashab-11 nei′ah repaired. Malchi′jah the son of Harim and Hasshub the son of Pa′hath-mo′ab repaired another section and the Tower of 12 the Ovens. Next to him Shallum the son of Hallo′hesh, ruler of half the district of[d] Jerusalem, repaired, he and his daughters.

13 Hanun and the inhabitants of Zano′ah repaired the Valley Gate; they rebuilt it and set its doors, its bolts, and its bars, and repaired a

1 After him Malchi'jah, one of the goldsmiths, repaired as far as the house of the temple servants and of the merchants, opposite the Muster Gate,^f and to the upper 32 chamber of the corner. And between the upper chamber of the corner and the Sheep Gate the goldsmiths and the merchants repaired.

Hostility to the work

1^g NOW when Sanbal'lat heard that we were building the wall, he was angry and greatly enraged, and he ridiculed the 2 Jews. And he said in the presence of his brethren and of the army of Samar'ia, "What are these feeble Jews doing? Will they restore things? Will they sacrifice? Will they finish up in a day? Will they revive the heaps of rubbish, and 3 burned ones at that?" Tobi'ah the Ammonite was by him, and he said, "Yes, what they are building—if a fox goes up on it he will 4 break down their stone wall!" Hear, O our God, for we are despised; turn back their taunt upon their own heads, and give them up to be plundered in a land where they are 5 captives. Do not cover their guilt, and let not their sin be blotted out from thy sight; for they have provoked thee to anger before the builders. 6 So we built the wall; and all the wall was joined together to half its height. For the people had a mind to work.

7^h But when Sanbal'lat and Tobi'ah and the Arabs and the Ammonites and the Ash'-dodites heard that the repairing of the walls of Jerusalem was going forward and that the breaches were beginning to be closed, they 8 were very angry; and they all plotted together to come and fight against Jerusalem 9 and to cause confusion in it. And we prayed to our God, and set a guard as a protection against them day and night.

Nehemiah's response

10 But Judah said, "The strength of the burden-bearers is failing, and there is much rubbish; we are not able to work on the 11 wall." And our enemies said, "They will not know or see till we come into the midst of them and kill them and stop the work." 12 When the Jews who lived by them came they said to us ten times, "From all the places where they liveⁱ they will come up against us."^j So in the lowest parts of the space 13 behind the wall, in open places, I stationed the people according to their families, with their swords, their spears, and their bows. And I looked, and arose, and said to the 14 nobles and to the officials and to the rest of the people, "Do not be afraid of them. Remember the Lord, who is great and terrible, and fight for your brethren, your sons, your daughters, your wives, and your homes."

When our enemies heard that it was known 15 to us and that God had frustrated their plan, we all returned to the wall, each to his work. From that day on, half of my servants 16 worked on construction, and half held the spears, shields, bows, and coats of mail; and the leaders stood behind all the house of Judah, who were building on the wall. 17 Those who carried burdens were laden in such a way that each with one hand laboured on the work and with the other held his weapon. And each of the builders had his 18 sword girded at his side while he built. The man who sounded the trumpet was beside me. And I said to the nobles and to the 19 officials and to the rest of the people, "The work is great and widely spread, and we are separated on the wall, far from one another. In the place where you hear the sound of the 20 trumpet, rally to us there. Our God will fight for us."

So we laboured at the work, and half of 21 them held the spears from the break of dawn till the stars came out. I also said to the 22 people at that time, "Let every man and his servant pass the night within Jerusalem, that they may be a guard for us by night and may labour by day." So neither I nor my 23 brethren nor my servants nor the men of the guard who followed me, none of us took off our clothes; each kept his weapon in his hand.^k

A cry of the people

Now there arose a great outcry of the people 5 and of their wives against their Jewish brethren. For there were those who said, 2 "With our sons and our daughters, we are many; let us get grain, that we may eat and

---

^f Or Hammiphkad Gate   ^g Ch 3.33 in Heb   ^h Ch 4.1 in Heb   ⁱ Cn: Heb *you return*
^j Compare Gk Syr: Heb uncertain   ^k Cn: Heb *each his weapon the water*

3 keep alive." There were also those who said, "We are mortgaging our fields, our vine-
4 yards, and our houses to get grain because of the famine." And there were those who said, "We have borrowed money for the king's tax
5 upon our fields and our vineyards. Now our flesh is as the flesh of our brethren, our children are as their children; yet we are forcing our sons and our daughters to be slaves, and some of our daughters have already been enslaved; but it is not in our power to help it, for other men have our fields and our vineyards."
6 I was very angry when I heard their outcry
7 and these words. I took counsel with myself, and I brought charges against the nobles and the officials. I said to them, "You are exacting interest, each from his brother." And I held a great assembly against them,
8 and said to them, "We, as far as we are able, have bought back our Jewish brethren who have been sold to the nations; but you even sell your brethren that they may be sold to us!" They were silent, and could not find a
9 word to say. So I said, "The thing that you are doing is not good. Ought you not to walk in the fear of our God to prevent the taunts
10 of the nations our enemies? Moreover I and my brethren and my servants are lending them money and grain. Let us leave off this
11 interest. Return to them this very day their fields, their vineyards, their olive orchards, and their houses, and the hundredth of money, grain, wine, and oil which you have
12 been exacting of them." Then they said, "We will restore these and require nothing from them. We will do as you say." And I called the priests, and took an oath of them to
13 do as they had promised. I also shook out my lap and said, "So may God shake out every man from his house and from his labour who does not perform this promise. So may he be shaken out and emptied." And all the assembly said "Amen" and praised the LORD. And the people did as they had promised.
14 Moreover from the time that I was appointed to be their governor in the land of Judah, from the twentieth year to the thirty-second year of Ar-ta-xerx'es the king, twelve years, neither I nor my brethren ate
15 the food allowance of the governor. The former governors who were before me laid heavy burdens upon the people, and took from them food and wine, besides forty shekels of silver. Even their servants lorded it over the people. But I did not do so,
16 because of the fear of God. I also held to the work on this wall, and acquired no land; and all my servants were gathered there for the

work. Moreover there were at my table a 17 hundred and fifty men, Jews and officials, besides those who came to us from the nations which were about us. Now that 18 which was prepared for one day was one ox and six choice sheep; fowls likewise were prepared for me, and every ten days skins of wine in abundance; yet with all this I did not demand the food allowance of the governor, because the servitude was heavy upon this people. Remember for my good, O my God, 19 all that I have done for this people.

More opposition

Now when it was reported to Sanbal'lat and 6 Tobi'ah and to Geshem the Arab and to the rest of our enemies that I had built the wall and that there was no breach left in it (although up to that time I had not set up the doors in the gates), Sanbal'lat and Geshem 2 sent to me, saying, "Come and let us meet together in one of the villages in the plain of Ono." But they intended to do me harm. And I sent messengers to them, saying, "I 3 am doing a great work and I cannot come down. Why should the work stop while I leave it and come down to you?" And they 4 sent to me four times in this way and I answered them in the same manner. In the 5 same way Sanbal'lat for the fifth time sent his servant to me with an open letter in his hand. In it was written, "It is reported 6 among the nations, and Geshem[1] also says it, that you and the Jews intend to rebel; that is why you are building the wall; and you wish to become their king, according to this report. And you have also set up prophets to 7 proclaim concerning you in Jerusalem, 'There is a king in Judah.' And now it will be reported to the king according to these words. So now come, and let us take counsel together." Then I sent to him, saying, "No 8 such things as you say have been done, for you are inventing them out of your own mind." For they all wanted to frighten us, 9 thinking, "Their hands will drop from the work, and it will not be done." But now, O God, strengthen thou my hands.

Now when I went into the house of 10 Shemai'ah the son of Dela'iah, son of Mehet'abel, who was shut up, he said, "Let us meet together in the house of God, within the temple, and let us close the doors of the temple; for they are coming to kill you, at night they are coming to kill you." But I 11 said, "Should such a man as I flee? And what man such as I could go into the temple and live?[m] I will not go in." And I under- 12 stood, and saw that God had not sent him, but he had pronounced the prophecy against me because Tobi′ah and Sanbal′lat had hired him. For this purpose he was hired, that I should be afraid and act in this way and sin, and so they could give me an evil name, in order to taunt me. Remember Tobi′ah and Sanbal′lat, O my God, according to these things that they did, and also the prophetess No-adi′ah and the rest of the prophets who wanted to make me afraid.

The wall finished

So the wall was finished on the twenty-fifth day of the month Elul, in fifty-two days. And when all our enemies heard of it, all the nations round about us were afraid[n] and fell greatly in their own esteem; for they perceived that this work had been accomplished with the help of our God. Moreover in those days the nobles of Judah sent many letters to Tobi′ah, and Tobi′ah's letters came to them. For many in Judah were bound by oath to him, because he was the son-in-law of Shecani′ah the son of Arah: and his son Jehoha′nan had taken the daughter of Meshul′lam the son of Berechi′ah as his wife. Also they spoke of his good deeds in 19 my presence, and reported my words to him. And Tobi′ah sent letters to make me afraid.

Now when the wall had been built and I had 7 set up the doors, and the gatekeepers, and the singers, and the Levites had been appointed, I gave my brother Hana′ni and Hanani′ah 2 the governor of the castle charge over Jerusalem, for he was a more faithful and God-fearing man than many. And I said to 3 them, "Let not the gates of Jerusalem be opened until the sun is hot; and while they are still standing guard[o] let them shut and bar the doors. Appoint guards from among the inhabitants of Jerusalem, each to his station and each opposite his own house." The city was wide and large, but the people 4 within it were few and no houses had been built.

REGISTER OF THE EXILES

THEN God put it into my mind 20 to assemble the nobles and the 21 officials and the people to be enrolled by genealogy. And I 22 found the book of the genealogy 23 of those who came up at the first, and I found written in it: 24 These were the people of the 25 province who came up out of the 26 captivity of those exiles whom Nebuchadnez′zar the king of 27 Babylon had carried into exile; they returned to Jerusalem and 28 Judah, each to his town. They 29 came with Zerub′babel, Jeshua, Nehemi′ah, Azari′ah, Ra-ami′ah, Naham′ani, Mor′decai, Bilshan, 30 Mis′pereth, Big′vai, Nehum, Ba′anah. 31 The number of the men of the people of Israel: the sons of 32 Parosh, two thousand a hundred and seventy-two. The sons of 33 Shephati′ah, three hundred and 34 seventy-two. The sons of Arah, six hundred and fifty-two. The 35 sons of Pa′hath-mo′ab, namely the sons of Jeshua and Jo′ab, two 36 thousand eight hundred and eighteen. The sons of Elam, a 37 thousand two hundred and fifty-four. The sons of Zattu, eight 38 hundred and forty-five. The sons of Zac′cai, seven hundred and sixty. The sons of Bin′nui, six 39 hundred and forty-eight. The sons of Be′bai, six hundred and 40 twenty-eight. The sons of Azgad, two thousand three hundred and 41 twenty-two. The sons of

Adoni′kam, six hundred and 19 sixty-seven. The sons of Big′vai, two thousand and sixty-seven. The sons of Adin, six hundred 20 and fifty-five. The sons of Ater, 21 namely of Hezeki′ah, ninety-eight. The sons of Hashum, three 22 hundred and twenty-eight. The sons of Be′zai, three hundred and 23 twenty-four. The sons of Hariph, 24 a hundred and twelve. The sons 25 of Gibeon, ninety-five. The men 26 of Bethlehem and Netoph′ah, a hundred and eighty-eight. The 27 men of An′athoth, a hundred and 28 twenty-eight. The men of 29 Beth-az′maveth, forty-two. The men of Kir′iath-je′arim, Cheph-i′rah, and Be-er′oth, seven hun- 30 dred and forty-three. The men of Ramah and Geba, six hundred 31 and twenty-one. The men of Michmas, a hundred and twen- 32 ty-two. The men of Bethel and Ai, a hundred and twenty-three. The men of the other Nebo, 33 fifty-two. The sons of the other 34 Elam, a thousand two hun- dred and fifty-four. The sons 35 of Harim, three hundred and 36 twenty. The sons of Jericho, three hundred and forty-five. The sons of Lod, Hadid, and 37 Ono, seven hundred and twen- ty-one. The sons of Sena′ah, 38 three thousand nine hundred and thirty. The priests: the sons of Jedai′ah, 39 namely the house of Jeshua, nine hundred and seventy-three. The 40 sons of Immer, a thousand and fifty-two. The sons of Pashhur, a 41 thousand two hundred and forty-

seven. The sons of Harim, a 42 thousand and seventeen. The Levites: the sons of Jeshua, 43 namely of Kad′mi-el of the sons of Ho′devah, seventy-four. The 44 singers: the sons of Asaph, a hundred and forty-eight. The 45 gatekeepers: the sons of Shallum, the sons of Ater, the sons of Talmon, the sons of Akkub, the sons of Hati′ta, the sons of Sho′bai, a hundred and thirty-eight. The temple servants:[p] the sons 46 of Ziha, the sons of Hasu′pha, the sons of Tabba′oth, the sons of 47 Keros, the sons of Si′a, the sons of Padon, the sons of Leba′na, the 48 sons of Hag′aba, the sons of Shal- mai, the sons of Hanan, the sons 49 of Giddel, the sons of Gahar, the 50 sons of Re-ai′ah, the sons of Rezin, the sons of Neko′da, the 51 sons of Gazzam, the sons of Uzza, the sons of Pase′ah, the sons of 52 Besai, the sons of Me-u′nim, the sons of Nephush′esim, the sons of 53 Bakbuk, the sons of Haku′pha, the sons of Harhur, the sons of 54 Bazlith, the sons of Mehi′da, the sons of Harsha, the sons of 55 Barkos, the sons of Sis′era, the sons of Temah, the sons of 56 Nezi′ah, the sons of Hati′pha. The sons of Solomon's servants: 57 the sons of So′tai, the sons of So′phereth, the sons of Peri′da, the sons of Ja′ala, the sons of 58 Darkon, the sons of Giddel, the 59 sons of Shephati′ah, the sons of Hattil, the sons of Po′chereth- hazzeba′im, the sons of Amon. All the temple servants and the 60

[n] Another reading is *saw*   [o] Heb obscure   [p] Heb *nethinim*
7.6–73: Ezra 2.1–70.

sons of Solomon's servants were
three hundred and ninety-two.
61 The following were those who
came up from Tel-me'lah, Tel-
har'sha, Cherub, Addon, and
Immer, but they could not prove
their fathers' houses nor their
descent, whether they belonged to
62 Israel: the sons of Dela'iah, the
sons of Tobi'ah, the sons of
Neko'da, six hundred and forty-
63 two. Also, of the priests: the sons
of Hobai'ah, the sons of Hakkoz,
the sons of Barzil'lai (who had
taken a wife of the daughters of
Barzil'lai the Gileadite and was
64 called by their name). These
sought their registration among
those enrolled in the genealogies,
but it was not found there, so they
were excluded from the priest-

65 hood as unclean; the governor
told them that they were not to
partake of the most holy food,
until a priest with Urim and
Thummim should arise.
66 The whole assembly together
was forty-two thousand three
67 hundred and sixty, besides their
menservants and maidservants, of
whom there were seven thousand
three hundred and thirty-seven;
and they had two hundred and
forty-five singers, male and female.
68 Their horses were seven hundred
and thirty-six, their mules two
69 hundred and forty-five,^{q} their
camels four hundred and thirty-
five, and their asses six thousand
seven hundred and twenty.
70 Now some of the heads of
fathers' houses gave to the work.

The governor gave to the treasury
a thousand darics of gold, fifty
basins, five hundred and thirty
priests' garments. And some of 7
the heads of fathers' houses gave
into the treasury of the work
twenty thousand darics of gold
and two thousand two hundred
minas of silver. And what the rest 7
of the people gave was twenty
thousand darics of gold, two
thousand minas of silver, and
sixty-seven priests' garments.
So the priests, the Levites, the 7
gatekeepers, the singers, some of
the people, the temple servants,
and all Israel, lived in their towns.
And when the seventh month
had come, the children of Israel
were in their towns.

A GREAT ASSEMBLY

8 AND all the people gathered as one man
into the square before the Water Gate; and
they told Ezra the scribe to bring the book of
the law of Moses which the LORD had given
2 to Israel. And Ezra the priest brought the
law before the assembly, both men and
women and all who could hear with understanding, on the first day of the seventh
3 month. And he read from it facing the
square before the Water Gate from early
morning until midday, in the presence of the
men and the women and those who could
understand; and the ears of all the people
4 were attentive to the book of the law. And
Ezra the scribe stood on a wooden pulpit
which they had made for the purpose; and
beside him stood Mattithi'ah, Shema,
Anai'ah, Uri'ah, Hilki'ah, and Ma-asei'ah on
his right hand; and beside him stood Peda'iah, Mish'a-el,
Malchi'jah, Hashum, Hash-bad'danah,
Zechari'ah, and Meshul'lam on his left
5 hand. And Ezra opened the book in the sight
of all the people, for he was above all the
people; and when he opened it all the people
6 stood. And Ezra blessed the LORD, the great
God; and all the people answered, "Amen,
Amen," lifting up their hands; and they
bowed their heads and worshipped the LORD
7 with their faces to the ground. Also Jeshua,
Bani, Sherebi'ah, Jamin, Akkub, Shab'-
bethai, Hodi'ah, Ma-asei'ah, Keli'ta, Azari'-
ah, Jo'zabad, Hanan, Pelai'ah, the Levites,^{r}
helped the people to understand the law,
while the people remained in their places.
8 And they read from the book, from the law of
God, clearly;^{s} and they gave the sense, so
that the people understood the reading.
9 And Nehemi'ah, who was the governor, and

Ezra the priest and scribe, and the Levites
who taught the people said to all the people,
"This day is holy to the LORD your God; do
not mourn or weep." For all the people wept
when they heard the words of the law. Then ︎
he said to them, "Go your way, eat the fat
and drink sweet wine and send portions to
him for whom nothing is prepared; for this
day is holy to our Lord; and do not be
grieved, for the joy of the LORD is your
strength." So the Levites stilled all the ︎
people, saying, "Be quiet, for this day is
holy; do not be grieved." And all the people ︎
went their way to eat and drink and to send
portions and to make great rejoicing, because
they had understood the words that were
declared to them.
On the second day the heads of fathers' ︎
houses of all the people, with the priests and

^{q} Ezra 2.66 and the margins of some Hebrew Mss: Heb lacks *their horses . . . forty-five*
^{r} 1 Esdras 9.48 Vg: Heb *and the Levites* ^{s} Or *with interpretation*

the Levites, came together to Ezra the scribe in order to study the words of the law. And they found it written in the law that the LORD had commanded by Moses that the people of Israel should dwell in booths during the feast of the seventh month, and that they should publish and proclaim in all their towns and in Jerusalem, "Go out to the hills and bring branches of olive, wild olive, myrtle, palm, and other leafy trees to make booths, as it is written." So the people went out and brought them and made booths for themselves, each on his roof, and in their courts and in the courts of the house of God, and in the square at the Water Gate and in the square at the Gate of E'phraim. And all the assembly of those who had returned from the captivity made booths and dwelt in the booths; for from the days of Jeshua the son of Nun to that day the people of Israel had not done so. And there was very great rejoicing. And day by day, from the first day to the last day, he read from the book of the law of God. They kept the feast seven days; and on the eighth day there was a solemn assembly, according to the ordinance.

Now on the twenty-fourth day of this month the people of Israel were assembled with fasting and in sackcloth, and with earth upon their heads. And the Israelites separated themselves from all foreigners, and stood and confessed their sins and the iniquities of their fathers. And they stood up in their place and read from the book of the law of the LORD their God for a fourth of the day; for another fourth of it they made confession and worshipped the LORD their God. Upon the stairs of the Levites stood Jeshua, Bani, Kad'mi-el, Shebani'ah, Bunni, Sherebi'ah, Bani, and Chena'ni; and they cried with a loud voice to the LORD their God. Then the Levites, Jeshua, Kad'mi-el, Bani, Hashabnei'ah, Sherebi'ah, Hodi'ah, Shebani'ah, and Pethahi'ah, said, "Stand up and bless the LORD your God from everlasting to everlasting. Blessed be thy glorious name which is exalted above all blessing and praise."

The confession

And Ezra said:[t] "Thou art the LORD, thou alone; thou hast made heaven, the heaven of heavens, with all their host, the earth and all that is on it, the seas and all that is in them; and thou preservest all of them; and the host of heaven worships thee. Thou art the LORD, the God who didst choose Abram and bring him forth out of Ur of the Chalde'ans and give him the name Abraham; and thou didst

find his heart faithful before thee, and didst make with him the covenant to give to his descendants the land of the Canaanite, the Hittite, the Amorite, the Per'izzite, the Jeb'usite, and the Gir'gashite; and thou hast fulfilled thy promise, for thou art righteous.

"And thou didst see the affliction of our 9 fathers in Egypt and hear their cry at the Red Sea, and didst perform signs and wonders 10 against Pharaoh and all his servants and all the people of his land, for thou knewest that they acted insolently against our fathers; and thou didst get thee a name, as it is to this day. And thou didst divide the sea before 11 them, so that they went through the midst of the sea on dry land; and thou didst cast their pursuers into the depths, as a stone into mighty waters. By a pillar of cloud thou 12 didst lead them in the day, and by a pillar of fire in the night to light for them the way in which they should go. Thou didst come 13 down upon Mount Sinai, and speak with them from heaven and give them right ordinances and true laws, good statutes and commandments, and thou didst make known 14 to them thy holy sabbath and command them commandments and statutes and a law by Moses thy servant. Thou didst give them 15 bread from heaven for their hunger and bring forth water for them from the rock for their thirst, and thou didst tell them to go in to possess the land which thou hadst sworn to give them.

"But they and our fathers acted presump- 16 tuously and stiffened their neck and did not obey thy commandments; they refused to 17 obey, and were not mindful of the wonders which thou didst perform among them; but they stiffened their neck and appointed a leader to return to their bondage in Egypt. But thou art a God ready to forgive, gracious and merciful, slow to anger and abounding in steadfast love, and didst not forsake them. Even when they had made for themselves a 18 molten calf and said, 'This is your God who brought you up out of Egypt,' and had committed great blasphemies, thou in thy 19 great mercies didst not forsake them in the wilderness; the pillar of cloud which led them in the way did not depart from them by day, nor the pillar of fire by night which lighted for them the way by which they should go. Thou gavest thy good Spirit to 20 instruct them, and didst not withhold thy manna from their mouth, and gavest them water for their thirst. Forty years didst thou 21 sustain them in the wilderness, and they lacked nothing; their clothes did not wear out and their feet did not swell. And thou didst 22 give them kingdoms and peoples, and didst

Jerusalem

allot to them every corner; so they took possession of the land of Sihon king of Heshbon and the land of Og king of Bashan. 23 Thou didst multiply their descendants as the stars of heaven, and thou didst bring them into the land which thou hadst told their 24 fathers to enter and possess. So the descendants went in and possessed the land, and thou didst subdue before them the inhabitants of the land, the Canaanites, and didst give them into their hands, with their kings and the peoples of the land, that they might 25 do with them as they would. And they captured fortified cities and a rich land, and took possession of houses full of all good things, cisterns hewn out, vineyards, olive orchards and fruit trees in abundance; so they ate, and were filled and became fat, and delighted themselves in thy great goodness. 26 "Nevertheless they were disobedient and rebelled against thee and cast thy law behind their back and killed thy prophets, who had warned them in order to turn them back to thee, and they committed great blasphemies. 27 Therefore thou didst give them into the hand of their enemies, who made them suffer; and in the time of their suffering they cried to thee and thou didst hear them from heaven; and according to thy great mercies thou didst give them saviours who saved them from the 28 hand of their enemies. But after they had rest they did evil again before thee, and thou didst abandon them to the hand of their enemies, so that they had dominion over them; yet when they turned and cried to thee thou didst hear from heaven, and many times thou didst deliver them according to thy 29 mercies. And thou didst warn them in order to turn them back to thy law. Yet they acted presumptuously and did not obey thy commandments, but sinned against thy ordinances, by the observance of which a man

shall live, and turned a stubborn shoulder and stiffened their neck and would not obey. Many years thou didst bear with them, and 30 didst warn them by thy Spirit through thy prophets; yet they would not give ear. Therefore thou didst give them into the hand of the peoples of the lands. Nevertheless in 31 thy great mercies thou didst not make an end of them or forsake them; for thou art a gracious and merciful God.

Sealing the covenant

"Now therefore, our God, the great and 32 mighty and terrible God, who keepest covenant and steadfast love, let not all the hardship seem little to thee that has come upon us, upon our kings, our princes, our priests, our prophets, our fathers, and all thy people, since the time of the kings of Assyria until this day. Yet thou hast been just in all 33 that has come upon us, for thou hast dealt faithfully and we have acted wickedly; our 34 kings, our princes, our priests, and our fathers have not kept thy law or heeded thy commandments and thy warnings which thou didst give them. They did not serve 35 thee in their kingdom, and in thy great goodness which thou gavest them, and in the large and rich land which thou didst set before them; and they did not turn from their wicked works. Behold, we are slaves 36 this day; in the land that thou gavest to our fathers to enjoy its fruit and its good gifts, behold, we are slaves. And its rich yield goes 37 to the kings whom thou hast set over us because of our sins; they have power also over our bodies and over our cattle at their pleasure, and we are in great distress." Because of all this we make a firm 38 covenant and write it, and our princes, our Levites, and our priests set their seal to it.

u Ch 10.1 in Heb

Those who sealed the covenant

THOSE who set their seal are Nehemi'ah the governor, the son of Hacali'ah, Zedeki'ah, Serai'ah, Azari'ah, Jeremiah, Pashhur, Amari'ah, Malchi'jah, 35 Hattush, Shebani'ah, Malluch, Harim, Mer'emoth, Obadi'ah, Daniel, Gin'nethon, Baruch, Meshul'lam, Abi'jah, Mi'jamin, 36 Ma-azi'ah, Bil'gai, Shemai'ah; these are the priests. And the Levites: Jeshua the son of Azani'ah, Bin'nui of the sons of Hen'adad, Kad'mi-el; and their brethren, Shebani'ah, Hodi'ah, Keli'ta, Pelai'ah, Hanan, Mica, 37 Rehob, Hashabi'ah, Zaccur, Sherebi'ah, Shebani'ah, Hodi'ah, Bani, Beni'nu. The chiefs of the people: Parosh, Pa'hath-mo'ab, Elam, Zattu, Bani, Bunni, Azgad, Be'bai, Adoni'jah, Big'vai, Adin, Ater, Hezeki'ah, Azzur, Hodi'ah, Hashum, Be'zai, 38 Hariph, An'athoth, Ne'bai, Mag'piash, Meshul'lam, Hezir, Meshez'abel, Zadok, Jad'du-a, Pelati'ah, Hanan, Anai'ah, Hoshe'a, Hanani'ah, Hasshub, Hallo'hesh, Pi'lha, Shobek, Rehum, Hashab'nah, Ma-asei'ah, 39 Ahi'ah, Hanan, Anan, Malluch, Harim, Ba'anah.

Special obligations

The rest of the people, the priests, the Levites, the gatekeepers, the singers, the temple servants, and all who have separated themselves from the peoples of the lands to the law of God, their wives, their sons, their daughters, all who have knowledge and understanding, join with their brethren, their nobles, and enter into a curse and an oath to walk in God's law which was given by Moses the servant of God, and to observe and do all the commandments of the LORD our Lord and his ordinances and his statutes. We will not give our daughters to the peoples of the land or take their daughters for our sons; and if the peoples of the land bring in wares or any grain on the sabbath day to sell, we will not buy from them on the sabbath or on a holy day; and we will forego the crops of the seventh year and the exaction of every debt.

We also lay upon ourselves the obligation to charge ourselves yearly with the third part of a shekel for the service of the house of our God: for the showbread, the continual cereal offering, the continual burnt offering, the sabbaths, the new moons, the appointed feasts, the holy things, and the sin offerings to make atonement for Israel, and for all the work of the house of our God. We have likewise cast lots, the priests, the Levites, and the people, for the wood offering, to bring it into the house of our God, according to our fathers' houses, at times appointed, year by year, to burn upon the altar of the LORD our God, as it is written in the law. We obligate ourselves to bring the first fruits of our ground and the first fruits of all fruit of every tree, year by year, to the house of the LORD; also to bring to the house of our God, to the priests who minister in the house of our God, the first-born of our sons and of our cattle, as it is written in the law, and the firstlings of our herds and of our flocks; and to bring the first of our coarse meal, and our contributions, the fruit of every tree, the wine and the oil, to the priests, to the chambers of the house of our God; and to bring to the Levites the tithes from our ground, for it is the Levites who collect the tithes in all our rural towns. And the priest, the son of Aaron, shall be with the Levites when the Levites receive the tithes; and the Levites shall bring up the tithe of the tithes to the house of our God, to the chambers, to the storehouse. For the people of Israel and the sons of Levi shall bring the contribution of grain, wine, and oil to the chambers, where are the vessels of the sanctuary, and the priests that minister, and the gatekeepers and the singers. We will not neglect the house of our God.

INHABITANTS OF JERUSALEM

11 NOW the leaders of the people lived in Jerusalem; and the rest of the people cast lots to bring one out of ten to live in Jerusalem the holy city, while nine tenths remained in the other towns. And 2 the people blessed all the men who willingly offered to live in Jerusalem.

3 These are the chiefs of the province who lived in Jerusalem; but in the towns of Judah every one lived on his property in their towns: Israel, the priests, the Levites, the temple servants, and the descendants of Solomon's servants. And in Jerusalem lived 4 certain of the sons of Judah and of the sons of Benjamin. Of the sons of Judah: Athai'ah the son of Uzzi'ah, son of Zechari'ah, son of Amari'ah, son of Shephati'ah, son of Ma-hal'alel, of the sons of Perez; and Ma-asei'ah son of 5 Baruch, son of Col-ho'zeh, son of Hazai'ah, son of Adai'ah, son of Joi'arib, son of Zechari'ah, son of the Shi'lonite. All the sons 6 of Perez who lived in Jerusalem were four hundred and sixty-eight valiant men.

7 And these are the sons of Benjamin: Sallu the son of Meshul'lam, son of Jo'ed, son of Peda'iah, son of Kola'iah, son of Ma-asei'ah, son of Ith'i-el, son of Jeshai'ah. And after him Gabba'i, 8 Sal'lai, nine hundred and twenty-eight. Jo'el the son of Zichri 9 was their overseer; and Judah the son of Hassenu'ah was second over the city.

Of the priests: Jedai'ah the son 10 of Joi'arib, Jachin, Serai'ah the 11 son of Hilki'ah, son of Meshul'lam, son of Zadok, son of Mera'ioth, son of Ahi'tub, ruler of the house of God, and their brethren 12 who did the work of the house, eight hundred and twenty-two; and Adai'ah the son of Jero'ham, son of Pelali'ah, son of Amzi, son of Zechari'ah, son of Pashhur, son of Malchi'jah, and his brethren, 13 heads of fathers' houses, two hundred and forty-two; and Amash'sai, the son of Az'arel, son of Ah'zai, son of Meshil'lemoth, son of Immer, and their brethren, 14 mighty men of valour, a hundred and twenty-eight; their overseer was Zab'di-el the son of Haggedo'lim.

And of the Levites: Shemai'ah 15 the son of Hasshub, son of Azri'kam, son of Hashabi'ah, son of Bunni; and Shab'bethai and 16 Jo'zabad, of the chiefs of the Levites, who were over the outside work of the house of God; and Mattani'ah the son of Mica, 17 son of Zabdi, son of Asaph, who was the leader to begin the thanksgiving in prayer, and Bakbuki'ah, the second among his brethren; and Abda the son of Sham'mu-a, son of Galal, son of Jedu'thun. All the Levites in the 18 holy city were two hundred and eighty-four.

The gatekeepers, Akkub, Talmon and their brethren, who kept 19 watch at the gates, were a hundred and seventy-two.

In other towns

And the rest of Israel, and of the 20 priests and the Levites, were in all the towns of Judah, every one in his inheritance. But the temple 21 servants lived on Ophel; and Ziha and Gishpa were over the temple servants.

The overseer of the Levites in 22 Jerusalem was Uzzi the son of Bani, son of Hashabi'ah, son of Mattani'ah, son of Mica, of the sons of Asaph, the singers, over the work of the house of God. For there was a command from 23 the king concerning them, and a settled provision for the singers, as every day required. And 24 Pethahi'ah the son of Meshez'-abel, of the sons of Zerah the son of Judah, was at the king's hand in all matters concerning the people.

And as for the villages, with their 25 fields, some of the people of Judah lived in Kir'iath-ar'ba and its villages, and in Dibon and its

villages, and in Jekab'zeel and its
26 villages, and in Jeshua and in
27 Mola'dah and Beth-pelet, in
Ha'zar-shu'al, in Beer-sheba and
28 its villages, in Ziklag, in Meco'-
29 nah and its villages, in En-
rim'mon, in Zorah, in Jarmuth,
30 Zano'ah, Adullam, and their villages, Lachish and its fields, and
Aze'kah and its villages. So they
encamped from Beer-sheba to the
31 valley of Hinnom. The people of
Benjamin also lived from Geba
onward, at Michmash, Ai'ja,
32 Bethel and its villages, An'athoth,
33 Nob, Anani'ah, Hazor, Ramah,
34 Gitta'im, Hadid, Zebo'im, Neb-
35 al'lat, Lod, and Ono, the valley of
36 craftsmen. And certain divisions
of the Levites in Judah were
joined to Benjamin.

Zerubbabel's company

12 These are the priests and the
Levites who came up with Zerub'babel the son of She-al'ti-el,
and Jeshua: Serai'ah, Jeremiah,
2 Ezra, Amari'ah, Malluch, Hat-
3 tush, Shecani'ah, Rehum, Mer'-
4 emoth, Iddo, Gin'nethoi, Abi'jah,

5 Mi'jamin, Ma-adi'ah, Bilgah,
6 Shemai'ah, Joi'arib, Jedai'ah,
7 Sallu, Amok, Hilki'ah, Jedai'ah.
These were the chiefs of the
priests and of their brethren in the
days of Jeshua.
8 And the Levites: Jeshua, Bin'-
nui, Kad'mi-el, Sherebi'ah,
Judah, and Mattani'ah, who with
his brethren was in charge of the
9 songs of thanksgiving. And Bakbuki'ah and Unno their brethren
stood opposite them in the ser-
10 vice. And Jeshua was the father
of Joi'akim, Joi'akim the father of
Eli'ashib, Eli'ashib the father
11 of Joi'ada, Joi'ada the father of
Jonathan, and Jonathan the father
of Jad'du-a.
12 And in the days of Joi'akim were
priests, heads of fathers' houses:
of Serai'ah, Merai'ah; of Jere-
13 miah, Hanani'ah; of Ezra, Meshul'lam; of Amari'ah, Jeho-
14 ha'nan; of Mal'luchi, Jonathan; of
15 Shebani'ah, Joseph; of Harim,
16 Adna; of Mera'ioth, Hel'kai; of
Iddo, Zechari'ah; of Gin'nethon,
17 Meshul'lam; of Abi'jah, Zichri; of
Mini'amin, of Moadi'ah, Pil'tai;
18 of Bilgah, Sham'mu-a; of Shem-

ai'ah, Jehon'athan; of Joi'arib,
Matte'nai; of Jedai'ah, Uzzi; of
Sal'lai, Kal'lai; of Amok, Eber; of
Hilki'ah, Hashabi'ah; of Jedai'ah,
Nethan'el.
As for the Levites, in the days of
Eli'ashib, Joi'ada, Joha'nan, and
Jad'du-a, there were recorded the
heads of fathers' houses; also the
priests until the reign of Darius
the Persian. The sons of Levi,
heads of fathers' houses, were
written in the Book of the Chronicles until the days of Joha'nan the
son of Eli'ashib. And the chiefs of
the Levites: Hashabi'ah, Sherebi'ah, and Jeshua the son of
Kad'mi-el, with their brethren
over against them, to praise and to
give thanks, according to the
commandment of David the man
of God, watch corresponding to
watch. Mattani'ah, Bakbuki'ah,
Obadi'ah, Meshul'lam, Talmon,
and Akkub were gatekeepers
standing guard at the storehouses
of the gates. These were in the
days of Joi'akim the son of Jeshua
son of Jo'zadak, and in the days of
Nehemi'ah the governor and of
Ezra the priest the scribe.

AT THE DEDICATION

27 AND at the dedication of the wall of
Jerusalem they sought the Levites in all
their places, to bring them to Jerusalem to
celebrate the dedication with gladness, with
thanksgivings and with singing, with cym-
28 bals, harps, and lyres. And the sons of the
singers gathered together from the circuit
29 round Jerusalem and from the villages of the
Netoph'athites; also from Beth-gilgal and
from the region of Geba and Az'maveth; for
the singers had built for themselves villages
30 around Jerusalem. And the priests and the
Levites purified themselves; and they purified the people and the gates and the wall.
31 Then I brought up the princes of Judah
upon the wall, and appointed two great
companies which gave thanks and went
in procession. One went to the right upon
32 the wall to the Dung Gate; and after them
went Hoshai'ah and half of the princes of
33 Judah, and Azari'ah, Ezra, Meshul'lam,
34 Judah, Benjamin, Shemai'ah, and Jeremiah,
35 and certain of the priests' sons with trumpets:
Zechari'ah the son of Jonathan, son of
Shemai'ah, son of Mattani'ah, son of
36 Micai'ah, son of Zaccur, son of Asaph; and
his kinsmen, Shemai'ah, Az'arel, Mil'alai,

Gil'alai, Ma'ai, Nethan'el, Judah, and
Hana'ni, with the musical instruments of
David the man of God; and Ezra the scribe
went before them. At the Fountain Gate
they went up straight before them by the
stairs of the city of David, at the ascent of the
wall, above the house of David, to the Water
Gate on the east.
The other company of those who gave
thanks went to the left, and I followed them
with half of the people, upon the wall, above
the Tower of the Ovens, to the Broad Wall,
and above the Gate of E'phraim, and by the
Old Gate, and by the Fish Gate and
the Tower of Han'anel and the Tower of the
Hundred, to the Sheep Gate; and they came
to a halt at the Gate of the Guard. So both
companies of those who gave thanks stood in
the house of God, and I and half of the
officials with me; and the priests Eli'akim,
Ma-asei'ah, Mini'amin, Micai'ah, Eli-o-e'nai,
Zechari'ah, and Hanani'ah, with trumpets;
and Ma-asei'ah, Shemai'ah, Elea'zar, Uzzi,
Jehoha'nan, Malchi'jah, Elam, and Ezer.
And the singers sang with Jezrahi'ah as their
leader. And they offered great sacrifices that
day and rejoiced, for God had made them
rejoice with great joy; the women and
children also rejoiced. And the joy of Jerusalem was heard afar off.
On that day men were appointed over the
chambers for the stores, the contributions,
the first fruits, and the tithes, to gather into
them the portions required by the law for the
priests and for the Levites according to the
fields of the towns; for Judah rejoiced over

the priests and the Levites who ministered. And they performed the service of their God and the service of purification, as did the singers and the gatekeepers, according to the command of David and his son Solomon. For in the days of David and Asaph of old there was a chief of the singers, and there were songs of praise and thanksgiving to God. And all Israel in the days of Zerub'-babel and in the days of Nehemi'ah gave the daily portions for the singers and the gate-keepers; and they set apart that which was for the Levites; and the Levites set apart that which was for the sons of Aaron.

Nehemiah's reforms

3 On that day they read from the book of Moses in the hearing of the people; and in it was found written that no Ammonite or Moabite should ever enter the assembly of God; for they did not meet the children of Israel with bread and water, but hired Balaam against them to curse them—yet our God turned the curse into a blessing. When the people heard the law, they separated from Israel all those of foreign descent.

Now before this, Eli'ashib the priest, who was appointed over the chambers of the house of our God, and who was connected with Tobi'ah, prepared for Tobi'ah a large chamber where they had previously put the cereal offering, the frankincense, the vessels, and the tithes of grain, wine, and oil, which were given by commandment to the Levites, singers, and gatekeepers, and the contribu-tions for the priests. While this was taking place I was not in Jerusalem, for in the thirty-second year of Ar-ta-xerx'es king of Babylon I went to the king. And after some time I asked leave of the king and came to Jerusalem, and I then discovered the evil that Eli'ashib had done for Tobi'ah, preparing for him a chamber in the courts of the house of God. And I was very angry, and I threw all the household furniture of Tobi'ah out of the chamber. Then I gave orders and they cleansed the chambers; and I brought back thither the vessels of the house of God, with the cereal offering and the frankincense.

I also found out that the portions of the Levites had not been given to them; so that the Levites and the singers, who did the work, had fled each to his field. So I remonstrated with the officials and said, "Why is the house of God forsaken?" And I gathered them together and set them in their stations. Then all Judah brought the tithe of the grain, wine, and oil into the storehouses. And I appointed as treasurers over the storehouses Shelemi'ah the priest, Zadok the scribe, and Peda'iah of the Levites, and as their assistant Hanan the son of Zaccur, son of Mattani'ah, for they were counted faith-ful; and their duty was to distribute to their brethren. Remember me, O my God, con- 14 cerning this, and wipe not out my good deeds that I have done for the house of my God and for his service.

Keeping the sabbath

In those days I saw in Judah men treading 15 wine presses on the sabbath, and bringing in heaps of grain and loading them on asses; and also wine, grapes, figs, and all kinds of burdens, which they brought into Jerusalem on the sabbath day; and I warned them on the day when they sold food. Men of Tyre 16 also, who lived in the city, brought in fish and all kinds of wares and sold them on the sabbath to the people of Judah, and in Jerusalem. Then I remonstrated with the 17 nobles of Judah and said to them, "What is this evil thing which you are doing, pro-faning the sabbath day? Did not your 18 fathers act in this way, and did not our God bring all this evil on us and on this city? Yet you bring more wrath upon Israel by pro-faning the sabbath."

When it began to be dark at the gates of 19 Jerusalem before the sabbath, I commanded that the doors should be shut and gave orders that they should not be opened until after the sabbath. And I set some of my servants over the gates, that no burden might be brought in on the sabbath day. Then the merchants 20 and sellers of all kinds of wares lodged outside Jerusalem once or twice. But I 21 warned them and said to them, "Why do you lodge before the wall? If you do so again I will lay hands on you." From that time on they did not come on the sabbath. And I 22 commanded the Levites that they should purify themselves and come and guard the gates, to keep the sabbath day holy. Remember this also in my favour, O my God, and spare me according to the greatness of thy steadfast love.

In those days also I saw the Jews who had 23 married women of Ashdod, Ammon, and Moab; and half of their children spoke the 24 language of Ashdod, and they could not speak the language of Judah, but the language of each people. And I contended 25 with them and cursed them and beat some of them and pulled out their hair; and I made them take oath in the name of God, saying, "You shall not give your daughters to their sons, or take their daughters for your sons or

13.1: Deut 23.3-5.

26 for yourselves. Did not Solomon king of Israel sin on account of such women? Among the many nations there was no king like him, and he was beloved by his God, and God made him king over all Israel; nevertheless foreign women made even him to sin. 27 Shall we then listen to you and do all this great evil and act treacherously against our God by marrying foreign women?" 28 And one of the sons of Jehoi′ada, the son of Eli′ashib the high priest, was the son-in-law of Sanbal′lat the Hor′onite; therefore I chased him from me. Remember them, O my God, because they have defiled the priesthood and the covenant of the priesthood and the Levites.

29 Thus I cleansed them from everything foreign, and I established the duties of the priests and Levites, each in his work; and I 31 provided for the wood offering, at appointed times, and for the first fruits. Remember me, O my God, for good.

THE BOOK OF

ESTHER

IN the days of Ahasu-e′rus, the Ahasu-e′rus who reigned from India to Ethiopia over one hundred and twenty-seven provinces, in those days when King Ahasu-e′rus sat on his royal throne in Susa the capital, in the third year of his reign he gave a banquet for all his princes and servants, the army chiefs[a] of Persia and Media and the nobles and governors of the provinces being before him, while he showed the riches of his royal glory and the splendour and pomp of his majesty for many days, a hundred and eighty days. And when these days were completed, the king gave for all the people present in Susa the capital, both great and small, a banquet lasting for seven days, in the court of the garden of the king's palace. There were white cotton curtains and blue hangings caught up with cords of fine linen and purple to silver rings[b] and marble pillars, and also couches of gold and silver on a mosaic pavement of porphyry, marble, mother-of-pearl and precious stones. Drinks were served in golden goblets, goblets of different kinds, and the royal wine was lavished according to the bounty of the king. And drinking was according to the law, no one was compelled; for the king had given orders to all the officials of his palace to do as every man desired. Queen Vashti also gave a banquet for the women in the palace which belonged to King Ahasu-e′rus.

On the seventh day, when the heart of the king was merry with wine, he commanded Mehu′man, Biztha, Harbo′na, Bigtha and Abag′tha, Zethar and Carkas, the seven eunuchs who served King Ahasu-e′rus as chamberlains, to bring Queen Vashti before 11 the king with her royal crown, in order to show the peoples and the princes her beauty; for she was fair to behold. But Queen Vashti 12 refused to come at the king's command conveyed by the eunuchs. At this the king was enraged, and his anger burned within him.

Then the king said to the wise men who 13 knew the times—for this was the king's procedure toward all who were versed in law and judgment, the men next to him being 14 Carshe′na, Shethar, Adma′tha, Tarshish, Meres, Marse′na, and Memu′can, the seven princes of Persia and Media, who saw the king's face, and sat first in the kingdom—: "According to the law, what is to be done to 15 Queen Vashti, because she has not performed the command of King Ahasu-e′rus conveyed by the eunuchs?" Then Memu′- 16 can said in presence of the king and the princes, "Not only to the king has Queen Vashti done wrong, but also to all the princes and all the peoples who are in all the provinces of King Ahasu-e′rus. For this 17 deed of the queen will be made known to all women, causing them to look with contempt upon their husbands, since they will say, 'King Ahasu-e′rus commanded Queen Vashti to be brought before him, and she did not come.' This very day the ladies of Persia 18 and Media who have heard of the queen's

[a] Heb the army   [b] Or rods

behaviour will be telling it to all the king's princes, and there will be contempt and
19 wrath in plenty. If it please the king, let a royal order go forth from him, and let it be written among the laws of the Persians and the Medes so that it may not be altered, that Vashti is to come no more before King Ahasu-e′rus; and let the king give her royal position to another who is better than she.
20 So when the decree made by the king is proclaimed throughout all his kingdom, vast as it is, all women will give honour to their
21 husbands, high and low." This advice pleased the king and the princes, and the
22 king did as Memu′can proposed; he sent letters to all the royal provinces, to every province in its own script and to every people in its own language, that every man be lord in his own house and speak according to the language of his people.

Esther crowned

2 After these things, when the anger of King Ahasu-e′rus had abated, he remembered Vashti and what she had done and what had
2 been decreed against her. Then the king's servants who attended him said, "Let beautiful young virgins be sought out for the
3 king. And let the king appoint officers in all the provinces of his kingdom to gather all the beautiful young virgins to the harem in Susa the capital, under custody of Hegai the king's eunuch who is in charge of the women; let
4 their ointments be given them. And let the maiden who pleases the king be queen instead of Vashti." This pleased the king, and he did so.
5 Now there was a Jew in Susa the capital whose name was Mor′decai, the son of Ja′ir, son of Shim′e-i, son of Kish, a Benjaminite,
6 who had been carried away from Jerusalem among the captives carried away with Jeconi′ah king of Judah, whom Nebuchad-nez′zar king of Babylon had carried away.
7 He had brought up Hadas′sah, that is Esther, the daughter of his uncle, for she had neither father nor mother; the maiden was beautiful and lovely, and when her father and her mother died, Mor′decai adopted her as his
8 own daughter. So when the king's order and his edict were proclaimed, and when many maidens were gathered in Susa the capital in custody of Hegai, Esther also was taken into the king's palace and put in custody of Hegai
9 who had charge of the women. And the maiden pleased him and won his favour; and he quickly provided her with her ointments and her portion of food, and with seven chosen maids from the king's palace, and

advanced her and her maids to the best place in the harem. Esther had not made known her people or kindred, for Mor′decai had charged her not to make it known. And every day Mor′decai walked in front of the court of the harem, to learn how Esther was and how she fared.

Now when the turn came for each maiden to go in to King Ahasu-e′rus, after being twelve months under the regulations for the women, since this was the regular period of their beautifying, six months with oil of myrrh and six months with spices and ointments for women—when the maiden went in to the king in this way she was given whatever she desired to take with her from the harem to the king's palace. In the evening she went, and in the morning she came back to the second harem in custody of Sha-ash′gaz the king's eunuch who was in charge of the concubines; she did not go in to the king again, unless the king delighted in her and she was summoned by name.

When the turn came for Esther the daughter of Ab′ihail the uncle of Mor′decai, who had adopted her as his own daughter, to go in to the king, she asked for nothing except what Hegai the king's eunuch, who had charge of the women, advised. Now Esther found favour in the eyes of all who saw her. And when Esther was taken to King Ahasu-e′rus into his royal palace in the tenth month, which is the month of Tebeth, in the seventh year of his reign, the king loved Esther more than all the women, and she found grace and favour in his sight more than all the virgins, so that he set the royal crown on her head and made her queen instead of Vashti. Then the king gave a great banquet to all his princes and servants; it was Esther's banquet. He also granted a remission of taxes[c] to the provinces, and gave gifts with royal liberality.

When the virgins were gathered together the second time, Mor′decai was sitting at the king's gate. Now Esther had not made known her kindred or her people, as Mor′decai had charged her; for Esther obeyed Mor′decai just as when she was brought up by him. And in those days, as Mor′decai was sitting at the king's gate, Bigthan and Teresh, two of the king's eunuchs, who guarded the threshold, became angry and sought to lay hands on King Ahasu-e′rus. And this came to the knowledge of Mor′-decai, and he told it to Queen Esther, and Esther told the king in the name of Mor′-decai. When the affair was investigated and found to be so, the men were both hanged on the gallows. And it was recorded in the Book

c Or a holiday

of the Chronicles in the presence of the king.

Haman's plot

3 After these things King Ahasu-e'rus promoted Haman the Ag'agite, the son of Hammeda'tha, and advanced him and set his seat above all the princes who were with 2 him. And all the king's servants who were at the king's gate bowed down and did obeisance to Haman; for the king had so commanded concerning him. But Mor'decai 3 did not bow down or do obeisance. Then the king's servants who were at the king's gate said to Mor'decai, "Why do you transgress 4 the king's command?" And when they spoke to him day after day and he would not listen to them, they told Haman, in order to see whether Mor'decai's words would avail; 5 for he had told them that he was a Jew. And when Haman saw that Mor'decai did not bow down or do obeisance to him, Haman 6 was filled with fury. But he disdained to lay hands on Mor'decai alone. So, as they had made known to him the people of Mor'decai, Haman sought to destroy all the Jews, the people of Mor'decai, throughout the whole kingdom of Ahasu-e'rus.

7 In the first month, which is the month of Nisan, in the twelfth year of King Ahasu-e'rus, they cast Pur, that is the lot, before Haman day after day; and they cast it month after month till the twelfth month, which is 8 the month of Adar. Then Haman said to King Ahasu-e'rus, "There is a certain people scattered abroad and dispersed among the peoples in all the provinces of your kingdom; their laws are different from those of every other people, and they do not keep the king's laws, so that it is not for the king's profit to 9 tolerate them. If it please the king, let it be decreed that they be destroyed, and I will pay ten thousand talents of silver into the hands of those who have charge of the king's business, that they may put it into the king's 10 treasuries." So the king took his signet ring from his hand and gave it to Haman the Ag'agite, the son of Hammeda'tha, the 11 enemy of the Jews. And the king said to Haman, "The money is given to you, the people also, to do with them as it seems good to you."

12 Then the king's secretaries were summoned on the thirteenth day of the first month, and an edict, according to all that Haman commanded, was written to the king's satraps and to the governors over all the provinces and to the princes of all the peoples, to every province in its own script and every people in its own language; it was written in the name of King Ahasu-e'rus and sealed with the king's ring. Letters were sent by couriers to 13 all the king's provinces, to destroy, to slay, and to annihilate all Jews, young and old, women and children, in one day, the thirteenth day of the twelfth month, which is the month of Adar, and to plunder their goods. A copy of the document was to be 14 issued as a decree in every province by proclamation to all the peoples to be ready for that day. The couriers went in haste by 15 order of the king, and the decree was issued in Susa the capital. And the king and Haman sat down to drink; but the city of Susa was perplexed.

When Mor'decai learned all that had been 4 done, Mor'decai rent his clothes and put on sackcloth and ashes, and went out into the midst of the city, wailing with a loud and bitter cry; he went up to the entrance of the 2 king's gate, for no one might enter the king's gate clothed with sackcloth. And in every 3 province, wherever the king's command and his decree came, there was great mourning among the Jews, with fasting and weeping and lamenting, and most of them lay in sackcloth and ashes.

When Esther's maids and her eunuchs came 4 and told her, the queen was deeply distressed; she sent garments to clothe Mor'decai, so that he might take off his sackcloth, but he would not accept them. Then Esther 5 called for Hathach, one of the king's eunuchs, who had been appointed to attend her, and ordered him to go to Mor'decai to learn what this was and why it was. Hathach 6 went out to Mor'decai in the open square of the city in front of the king's gate, and 7 Mor'decai told him all that had happened to him, and the exact sum of money that Haman had promised to pay into the king's treasuries for the destruction of the Jews. Mor'decai also gave him a copy of 8 the written decree issued in Susa for their destruction, that he might show it to Esther and explain it to her and charge her to go to the king to make supplication to him and entreat him for her people. And Hathach 9 went and told Esther what Mor'decai had said. Then Esther spoke to Hathach and 10 gave him a message for Mor'decai, saying, "All the king's servants and the people of the 11 king's provinces know that if any man or woman goes to the king inside the inner court without being called, there is but one law; all alike are to be put to death, except the one to whom the king holds out the golden sceptre that he may live. And I have not been called to come in to the king these thirty days." And they told Mor'decai what Esther had 12 said. Then Mor'decai told them to return 13 answer to Esther, "Think not that in the

king's palace you will escape any more than
14 all the other Jews. For if you keep silence at
such a time as this, relief and deliverance will
rise for the Jews from another quarter, but
you and your father's house will perish. And
who knows whether you have not come to the
15 kingdom for such a time as this?" Then
16 Esther told them to reply to Mor'decai, "Go,
gather all the Jews to be found in Susa, and
hold a fast on my behalf, and neither eat nor
drink for three days, night or day. I and my
maids will also fast as you do. Then I will go
to the king, though it is against the law; and
17 if I perish, I perish." Mor'decai then went
away and did everything as Esther had
ordered him.

Esther's request

5 On the third day Esther put on her royal
robes and stood in the inner court of the
king's palace, opposite the king's hall. The
king was sitting on his royal throne inside
the palace opposite the entrance to the
2 palace; and when the king saw Queen Esther
standing in the court, she found favour in his
sight and he held out to Esther the golden
sceptre that was in his hand. Then Esther
approached and touched the top of the
3 sceptre. And the king said to her, "What is
it, Queen Esther? What is your request? It
shall be given you, even to the half of my
4 kingdom." And Esther said, "If it please the
king, let the king and Haman come this day
to a dinner that I have prepared for the
5 king." Then said the king, "Bring Haman
quickly, that we may do as Esther desires."
So the king and Haman came to the dinner
6 that Esther had prepared. And as they were
drinking wine, the king said to Esther,
"What is your petition? It shall be granted
you. And what is your request? Even to the
half of my kingdom, it shall be fulfilled."
7 But Esther said, "My petition and my
8 request is: If I have found favour in the sight
of the king, and if it please the king to grant
my petition and fulfil my request, let the king
and Haman come tomorrow*d* to the dinner
which I will prepare for them, and tomorrow
I will do as the king has said."

9 And Haman went out that day joyful and
glad of heart. But when Haman saw Mor'-
decai in the king's gate, that he neither rose
nor trembled before him, he was filled with
10 wrath against Mor'decai. Nevertheless
Haman restrained himself, and went home;
and he sent and fetched his friends and his
11 wife Zeresh. And Haman recounted to them
the splendour of his riches, the number of his

sons, all the promotions with which the king
had honoured him, and how he had advanced
him above the princes and the servants of the
king. And Haman added, "Even Queen ▶
Esther let no one come with the king to the
banquet she prepared but myself. And
tomorrow also I am invited by her together
with the king. Yet all this does me no good, ▶
so long as I see Mor'decai the Jew sitting at
the king's gate." Then his wife Zeresh and 1
all his friends said to him, "Let a gallows
fifty cubits high be made, and in the morning
tell the king to have Mor'decai hanged upon
it; then go merrily with the king to the
dinner." This counsel pleased Haman, and
he had the gallows made.

On that night the king could not sleep; 6
and he gave orders to bring the book of
memorable deeds, the chronicles, and they
were read before the king. And it was found 2
written how Mor'decai had told about
Bigthana and Teresh, two of the king's
eunuchs, who guarded the threshold, and
who had sought to lay hands upon King
Ahasu-e'rus. And the king said, "What 3
honour or dignity has been bestowed on
Mor'decai for this?" The king's servants
who attended him said, "Nothing has been
done for him." And the king said, "Who is 4
in the court?" Now Haman had just entered
the outer court of the king's palace to speak
to the king about having Mor'decai hanged
on the gallows that he had prepared for him.
So the king's servants told him, "Haman is 5
there, standing in the court." And the king
said, "Let him come in." So Haman came 6
in, and the king said to him, "What shall be
done to the man whom the king delights to
honour?" And Haman said to himself,
"Whom would the king delight to honour
more than me?" And Haman said to the 7
king, "For the man whom the king delights
to honour, let royal robes be brought, which 8
the king has worn, and the horse which the
king has ridden, and on whose head a royal
crown is set; and let the robes and the horse 9
be handed over to one of the king's most
noble princes; let him*e* array the man whom
the king delights to honour, and let him*e*
conduct the man on horseback through the
open square of the city, proclaiming before
him: 'Thus shall it be done to the man whom
the king delights to honour.'" Then the 10
king said to Haman, "Make haste, take the
robes and the horse, as you have said, and do
so to Mor'decai the Jew who sits at the king's
gate. Leave out nothing that you have
mentioned." So Haman took the robes and 11

---

d Gk: Heb lacks *tomorrow*   *e* Heb *them*
5.3, 6: Mk 6.23.

the horse, and he arrayed Mor'decai and made him ride through the open square of the city, proclaiming, "Thus shall it be done to the man whom the king delights to honour."
Then Mor'decai returned to the king's gate. But Haman hurried to his house, mourning and with his head covered. And Haman told his wife Zeresh and all his friends everything that had befallen him. Then his wise men and his wife Zeresh said to him, "If Mor'decai, before whom you have begun to fall, is of the Jewish people, you will not prevail against him but will surely fall before him."

4 While they were yet talking with him, the king's eunuchs arrived and brought Haman in haste to the banquet that Esther had prepared.

7 So the king and Haman went in to feast **2** with Queen Esther. And on the second day, as they were drinking wine, the king again said to Esther, "What is your petition, Queen Esther? It shall be granted you. And what is your request? Even to the half of my **3** kingdom, it shall be fulfilled." Then Queen Esther answered, "If I have found favour in your sight, O king, and if it please the king, let my life be given me at my petition, and **4** my people at my request. For we are sold, I and my people, to be destroyed, to be slain, and to be annihilated. If we had been sold merely as slaves, men and women, I would have held my peace; for our affliction is not to be compared with the loss to the king." **5** Then King Ahasu-e'rus said to Queen Esther, "Who is he, and where is he, that **6** would presume to do this?" And Esther said, "A foe and enemy! This wicked Haman!" Then Haman was in terror before **7** the king and the queen. And the king rose from the feast in wrath and went into the palace garden; but Haman stayed to beg his life from Queen Esther, for he saw that evil was determined against him by the king. **8** And the king returned from the palace garden to the place where they were drinking wine, as Haman was falling on the couch where Esther was; and the king said, "Will he even assault the queen in my presence, in my own house?" As the words left the mouth of the king, they covered Haman's **9** face. Then said Harbo'na, one of the eunuchs in attendance on the king, "Moreover, the gallows which Haman has prepared for Mor'decai, whose word saved the king, is standing in Haman's house, fifty cubits **10** high." And the king said, "Hang him on that." So they hanged Haman on the gallows which he had prepared for Mor'decai. Then the anger of the king abated.

Mordecai honoured

On that day King Ahasu-e'rus gave to **8** Queen Esther the house of Haman, the enemy of the Jews. And Mor'decai came before the king, for Esther had told what he was to her; and the king took off his signet **2** ring, which he had taken from Haman, and gave it to Mor'decai. And Esther set Mor'decai over the house of Haman.
Then Esther spoke again to the king; she **3** fell at his feet and besought him with tears to avert the evil design of Haman the Ag'agite and the plot which he had devised against the Jews. And the king held out the golden **4** sceptre to Esther, and Esther rose and stood **5** before the king. And she said, "If it please the king, and if I have found favour in his sight, and if the thing seem right before the king, and I be pleasing in his eyes, let an order be written to revoke the letters devised by Haman the Ag'agite, the son of Hammeda'tha, which he wrote to destroy the Jews who are in all the provinces of the king. For **6** how can I endure to see the calamity that is coming to my people? Or how can I endure to see the destruction of my kindred?" Then King Ahasu-e'rus said to Queen **7** Esther and to Mor'decai the Jew, "Behold, I have given Esther the house of Haman, and they have hanged him on the gallows, because he would lay hands on the Jews. And you may write as you please with regard **8** to the Jews, in the name of the king, and seal it with the king's ring; for an edict written in the name of the king and sealed with the king's ring cannot be revoked."
The king's secretaries were summoned at **9** that time, in the third month, which is the month of Sivan, on the twenty-third day; and an edict was written according to all that Mor'decai commanded concerning the Jews to the satraps and the governors and the princes of the provinces from India to Ethiopia, a hundred and twenty-seven provinces, to every province in its own script and to every people in its own language, and also to the Jews in their script and their language. The writing was in the name of King Ahasu- **10** e'rus and sealed with the king's ring, and letters were sent by mounted couriers riding on swift horses that were used in the king's service, bred from the royal stud. By these **11** the king allowed the Jews who were in every city to gather and defend their lives, to destroy, to slay, and to annihilate any armed force of any people or province that might

7.2: Mk 6.23.

attack them, with their children and women,
12 and to plunder their goods, upon one day
throughout all the provinces of King Ahasu-
e'rus, on the thirteenth day of the twelfth
13 month, which is the month of Adar. A copy
of what was written was to be issued as a
decree in every province, and by proclamation to all peoples, and the Jews were to be
ready on that day to avenge themselves upon
14 their enemies. So the couriers, mounted on
their swift horses that were used in the king's
service, rode out in haste, urged by the king's
command; and the decree was issued in Susa
the capital.
15 Then Mor'decai went out from the presence of the king in royal robes of blue and
white, with a great golden crown and a
mantle of fine linen and purple, while the
16 city of Susa shouted and rejoiced. The Jews
had light and gladness and joy and honour.
17 And in every province and in every city,
wherever the king's command and his edict
came, there was gladness and joy among the
Jews, a feast and a holiday. And many from
the peoples of the country declared themselves Jews, for the fear of the Jews had fallen
upon them.

9 Now in the twelfth month, which is the
month of Adar, on the thirteenth day of the
same, when the king's command and edict
were about to be executed, on the very day
when the enemies of the Jews hoped to get
the mastery over them, but which had been
changed to a day when the Jews should get
2 the mastery over their foes, the Jews
gathered in their cities throughout all the
provinces of King Ahasu-e'rus to lay hands
on such as sought their hurt. And no one
could make a stand against them, for the fear
3 of them had fallen upon all peoples. All the
princes of the provinces and the satraps and
the governors and the royal officials also
helped the Jews, for the fear of Mor'decai
4 had fallen upon them. For Mor'decai was
great in the king's house, and his fame spread
throughout all the provinces; for the man
Mor'decai grew more and more powerful.
5 So the Jews smote all their enemies with the
sword, slaughtering, and destroying them,
and did as they pleased to those who hated
6 them. In Susa the capital itself the Jews slew
7 and destroyed five hundred men, and also
slew Par-shan-da'tha and Dalphon and
8 Aspa'tha and Pora'tha and Ada'lia and
9 Arida'tha and Parmash'ta and Ar'isai
10 and Ar'idai and Vaiza'tha, the ten sons of
Haman the son of Hammeda'tha, the enemy
of the Jews; but they laid no hand on the
plunder.
11 That very day the number of those slain in
Susa the capital was reported to the king.

And the king said to Queen Esther, "In Susa 1
the capital the Jews have slain five hundred
men and also the ten sons of Haman. What
then have they done in the rest of the king's
provinces! Now what is your petition? It
shall be granted you. And what further is
your request? It shall be fulfilled." And 1
Esther said, "If it please the king, let the
Jews who are in Susa be allowed tomorrow
also to do according to this day's edict. And
let the ten sons of Haman be hanged on the
gallows." So the king commanded this to be 1
done; a decree was issued in Susa, and the
ten sons of Haman were hanged. The Jews 1
who were in Susa gathered also on the
fourteenth day of the month of Adar and
they slew three hundred men in Susa; but
they laid no hands on the plunder.
Now the other Jews who were in the king's 1
provinces also gathered to defend their lives,
and got relief from their enemies, and slew
seventy-five thousand of those who hated
them; but they laid no hands on the plunder.
This was on the thirteenth day of the month 1
of Adar, and on the fourteenth day they
rested and made that a day of feasting and
gladness. But the Jews who were in Susa 1
gathered on the thirteenth day and on the
fourteenth, and rested on the fifteenth day,
making that a day of feasting and gladness.
Therefore the Jews of the villages, who live 1
in the open towns, hold the fourteenth day of
the month of Adar as a day for gladness and
feasting and holiday-making, and a day on
which they send choice portions to one
another.

The feast of Purim

And Mor'decai recorded these things, and 20
sent letters to all the Jews who were in all the
provinces of King Ahasu-e'rus, both near
and far, enjoining them that they should keep 21
the fourteenth day of the month Adar and
also the fifteenth day of the same, year by
year, as the days on which the Jews got relief 22
from their enemies, and as the month that
had been turned for them from sorrow into
gladness and from mourning into a holiday;
that they should make them days of feasting
and gladness, days for sending choice portions to one another and gifts to the poor.
So the Jews undertook to do as they had 23
begun, and as Mor'decai had written to
them. For Haman the Ag'agite, the son of 24
Hammeda'tha, the enemy of all the Jews, had
plotted against the Jews to destroy them, and
had cast Pur, that is the lot, to crush and
destroy them; but when Esther came before 25
the king, he gave orders in writing that his
wicked plot which he had devised against the
Jews should come upon his own head, and

that he and his sons should be hanged on the gallows. Therefore they called these days Purim, after the term Pur. And therefore, because of all that was written in this letter, and of what they had faced in this matter, and of what had befallen them, the Jews ordained and took it upon themselves and their descendants and all who joined them, that without fail they would keep these two days according to what was written and at the time appointed every year, that these days should be remembered and kept throughout every generation, in every family, province, and city, and that these days of Purim should never fall into disuse among the Jews, nor should the commemoration of these days cease among their descendants. Then Queen Esther, the daughter of Ab'ihail, and Mor'decai the Jew gave full written authority, confirming this second letter about Purim. Letters were sent to all the Jews, to the hundred and twenty-seven provinces of the kingdom of Ahasu-e'rus, in words of peace and truth, that these days of 31 Purim should be observed at their appointed seasons, as Mor'decai the Jew and Queen Esther enjoined upon the Jews, and as they had laid down for themselves and for their descendants, with regard to their fasts and their lamenting. The command of Queen 32 Esther fixed these practices of Purim, and it was recorded in writing.

King Ahasu-e'rus laid tribute on the land **10** and on the coastlands of the sea. And all the 2 acts of his power and might, and the full account of the high honour of Mor'decai, to which the king advanced him, are they not written in the Book of the Chronicles of the kings of Media and Persia? For Mor'decai 3 the Jew was next in rank to King Ahasu-e'rus, and he was great among the Jews and popular with the multitude of his brethren, for he sought the welfare of his people and spoke peace to all his people.

THE BOOK OF

JOB

THERE was a man in the land of Uz, whose name was Job; and that man was blameless and upright, one who feared 2 God, and turned away from evil. There were born to him seven sons and three daughters. 3 He had seven thousand sheep, three thousand camels, five hundred yoke of oxen, and five hundred she-asses, and very many servants; so that this man was the greatest of 4 all the people of the east. His sons used to go and hold a feast in the house of each on his day; and they would send and invite their 5 three sisters to eat and drink with them. And when the days of the feast had run their course, Job would send and sanctify them, and he would rise early in the morning and offer burnt offerings according to the number of them all; for Job said, "It may be that my sons have sinned, and cursed God in their hearts." Thus Job did continually.

Job's character

6 Now there was a day when the sons of God came to present themselves before the LORD, 7 and Satan*a* also came among them. The LORD said to Satan, "Whence have you come?" Satan answered the LORD, "From going to and fro on the earth, and from 8 walking up and down on it." And the LORD said to Satan, "Have you considered my servant Job, that there is none like him on the earth, a blameless and upright man, who 9 fears God and turns away from evil?" Then Satan answered the LORD, "Does Job fear 10 God for naught? Hast thou not put a hedge about him and his house and all that he has, on every side? Thou hast blessed the work

of his hands, and his possessions have increased in the land. But put forth thy hand 11 now, and touch all that he has, and he will curse thee to thy face." And the LORD said 12 to Satan, "Behold, all that he has is in your power; only upon himself do not put forth your hand." So Satan went forth from the presence of the LORD.

Job's afflictions

Now there was a day when his sons and 13 daughters were eating and drinking wine in their eldest brother's house; and there came a 14 messenger to Job, and said, "The oxen were ploughing and the asses feeding beside them; and the Sabe'ans fell upon them and took 15 them, and slew the servants with the edge of the sword; and I alone have escaped to tell you." While he was yet speaking, there came 16 another, and said, "The fire of God fell from heaven and burned up the sheep and the servants, and consumed them; and I alone have escaped to tell you." While he was yet 17 speaking, there came another, and said, "The Chalde'ans formed three companies, and made a raid upon the camels and took them, and slew the servants with the edge of the sword; and I alone have escaped to tell you." While he was yet speaking, there came 18 another, and said, "Your sons and daughters were eating and drinking wine in their eldest brother's house; and behold, a great wind 19 came across the wilderness, and struck the four corners of the house, and it fell upon the young people, and they are dead; and I alone have escaped to tell you."

Then Job arose, and rent his robe, and 20

a Heb *the adversary*

406

shaved his head, and fell upon the ground, and worshipped. And he said, "Naked I came from my mother's womb, and naked shall I return; the LORD gave, and the LORD has taken away; blessed be the name of the LORD."

In all this Job did not sin or charge God with wrong.

Again there was a day when the sons of God came to present themselves before the LORD, and Satan also came among them to present himself before the LORD. And the LORD said to Satan, "Whence have you come?" Satan answered the LORD, "From going to and fro on the earth, and from walking up and down on it." And the LORD said to Satan, "Have you considered my servant Job, that there is none like him on the earth, a blameless and upright man, who fears God and turns away from evil? He still holds fast his integrity, although you moved me against him, to destroy him without cause." Then Satan answered the LORD, "Skin for skin! All that a man has he will give for his life. But put forth thy hand now, and touch his bone and his flesh, and he will curse thee to thy face." And the LORD said to Satan, "Behold, he is in your power; only spare his life."

So Satan went forth from the presence of 7 the LORD, and afflicted Job with loathsome sores from the sole of his foot to the crown of his head. And he took a potsherd with which 8 to scrape himself, and sat among the ashes.

Then his wife said to him, "Do you still 9 hold fast your integrity? Curse God, and die." But he said to her, "You speak as one 10 of the foolish women would speak. Shall we receive good at the hand of God, and shall we not receive evil?" In all this Job did not sin with his lips.

Job's friends

Now when Job's three friends heard of all 11 this evil that had come upon him, they came each from his own place, El'iphaz the Te'manite, Bildad the Shuhite, and Zophar the Na'amathite. They made an appointment together to come to condole with him and comfort him. And when they saw him 12 from afar, they did not recognise him; and they raised their voices and wept; and they rent their robes and sprinkled dust upon their heads toward heaven. And they sat 13 with him on the ground seven days and seven nights, and no one spoke a word to him, for they saw that his suffering was very great.

THE DEBATE

JOB'S OUTBURST

3 After this Job opened his mouth and cursed
2 the day of his birth. And Job said:
3   "LET the day perish wherein I was
          born,
       and the night which said,
        'A man-child is conceived.'
4   Let that day be darkness!
       May God above not seek it,
         nor light shine upon it.
5   Let gloom and deep darkness claim it.
       Let clouds dwell upon it;
         let the blackness of the day terrify it.
6   That night—let thick darkness seize it!
       let it not rejoice among the days of the
          year,
       let it not come into the number of the
          months.
7   Yea, let that night be barren;
       let no joyful cry be heard[b] in it.
8   Let those curse it who curse the day,
       who are skilled to rouse up Leviathan.
9   Let the stars of its dawn be dark;
       let it hope for light, but have none,
         nor see the eyelids of the morning;

       because it did not shut the doors of my 10
          mother's womb,
       nor hide trouble from my eyes.

       "Why did I not die at birth,   11
       come forth from the womb and expire?
       Why did the knees receive me?   12
       Or why the breasts, that I should suck?
       For then I should have lain down and been 13
          quiet;
       I should have slept; then I should have
          been at rest,
       with kings and counsellors of the earth   14
       who rebuilt ruins for themselves,
       or with princes who had gold,   15
       who filled their houses with silver.
       Or why was I not as a hidden untimely 16
          birth,
       as infants that never see the light?
       There the wicked cease from troubling,   17
       and there the weary are at rest.
       There the prisoners are at ease together; 18
       they hear not the voice of the task-
          master.
       The small and the great are there,   19
       and the slave is free from his master.

[b] Heb come
3.3–19: Jer 20.14–18.

20 "Why is light given to him that is in
       misery,
       and life to the bitter in soul,
21 who long for death, but it comes not,
       and dig for it more than for hid
       treasures;
22 who rejoice exceedingly,
       and are glad, when they find the grave?
23 Why is light given to a man whose way is
       hid,
       whom God has hedged in?
24 For my sighing comes as^c my bread,
       and my groanings are poured out like
       water.
25 For the thing that I fear comes upon me,
       and what I dread befalls me.
26 I am not at ease, nor am I quiet;
       I have no rest; but trouble comes."

ELIPHAZ SPEAKS

4 Then El'iphaz the Te'manite answered:
2 "IF one ventures a word with you, will
       you be offended?
       Yet who can keep from speaking?
3 Behold, you have instructed many,
       and you have strengthened the weak
       hands.
4 Your words have upheld him who was
       stumbling,
       and you have made firm the feeble
       knees.
5 But now it has come to you, and you are
       impatient;
       it touches you, and you are dismayed.
6 Is not your fear of God your confidence,
       and the integrity of your ways your
       hope?

7 "Think now, who that was innocent ever
       perished?
       Or where were the upright cut off?
8 As I have seen, those who plough iniquity
       and sow trouble reap the same.
9 By the breath of God they perish,
       and by the blast of his anger they are
       consumed.
10 The roar of the lion, the voice of the fierce
       lion,
       the teeth of the young lions, are broken.
11 The strong lion perishes for lack of prey,
       and the whelps of the lioness are
       scattered.

12 "Now a word was brought to me stealthily,
       my ear received the whisper of it.
13 Amid thoughts from visions of the night,
       when deep sleep falls on men,
14 dread came upon me, and trembling,

which made all my bones shake.
A spirit glided past my face;
       the hair of my flesh stood up.
It stood still,
       but I could not discern its appearance.
A form was before my eyes;
       there was silence, then I heard a voice:
'Can mortal man be righteous before^d
       God?
Can a man be pure before^d his Maker?
Even in his servants he puts no trust,   1
       and his angels he charges with error;
how much more those who dwell in houses 1
       of clay,
       whose foundation is in the dust,
       who are crushed before the moth.
Between morning and evening they are 2
       destroyed;
       they perish for ever without any regard-
       ing it.
If their tent-cord is plucked up within 2
       them,
       do they not die, and that without
       wisdom?'

"Call now; is there any one who will 5
       answer you?
       To which of the holy ones will you
       turn?
Surely vexation kills the fool,   2
       and jealousy slays the simple.
I have seen the fool taking root,   3
       but suddenly I cursed his dwelling.
His sons are far from safety,   4
       they are crushed in the gate,
       and there is no one to deliver them.
His harvest the hungry eat,   5
       and he takes it even out of thorns;^{e}
       and the thirsty^f pant after his^g wealth.
For affliction does not come from the dust, 6
       nor does trouble sprout from the
       ground;
but man is born to trouble   7
       as the sparks fly upward.

"As for me, I would seek God,   8
       and to God would I commit my cause;
who does great things and unsearchable,   9
       marvellous things without number:
he gives rain upon the earth   10
       and sends waters upon the fields;
he sets on high those who are lowly,   11
       and those who mourn are lifted to
       safety.
He frustrates the devices of the crafty,   12
       so that their hands achieve no success.
He takes the wise in their own craftiness;   13
       and the schemes of the wily are brought
       to a quick end.

^{c} Heb before ^{d} Or more than ^{e} Heb obscure ^{f} Aquila Symmachus Syr Vg: Heb snare ^{g} Heb their
5.12–13: 1 Cor 3.19.

They meet with darkness in the daytime,
and grope at noonday as in the night.
But he saves the fatherless from their
mouth,[h]
the needy from the hand of the mighty.
So the poor have hope,
and injustice shuts her mouth.

"Behold, happy is the man whom God
reproves;
therefore despise not the chastening of
the Almighty.
For he wounds, but he binds up;
he smites, but his hands heal.
He will deliver you from six troubles;
in seven there shall no evil touch you.
In famine he will redeem you from death,
and in war from the power of the sword.
You shall be hid from the scourge of the
tongue,
and shall not fear destruction when it
comes.
At destruction and famine you shall laugh,
and shall not fear the beasts of the earth.
For you shall be in league with the stones
of the field,
and the beasts of the field shall be at
peace with you.
You shall know that your tent is safe,
and you shall inspect your fold and miss
nothing.
You shall know also that your descendants
shall be many,
and your offspring as the grass of the
earth.
You shall come to your grave in ripe old
age,
as a shock of grain comes up to the
threshing floor in its season.
Lo, this we have searched out; it is true.
Hear, and know it for your good."[i]

JOB'S REPLY

Then Job answered:
"O THAT my vexation were weighed,
and all my calamity laid in the
balances!
For then it would be heavier than the sand
of the sea;
therefore my words have been rash.
For the arrows of the Almighty are in me;
my spirit drinks their poison;
the terrors of God are arrayed against
me.
Does the wild ass bray when he has grass,
or the ox low over his fodder?
Can that which is tasteless be eaten without salt,

or is there any taste in the slime of the
purslane?[j]
My appetite refuses to touch them;   7
they are as food that is loathsome to
me.[k]

"O that I might have my request,   8
and that God would grant my desire;
that it would please God to crush me,   9
that he would let loose his hand and cut
me off!
This would be my consolation;   10
I would even exult[l] in pain unsparing;
for I have not denied the words of the
Holy One.
What is my strength, that I should wait?   11
And what is my end, that I should be
patient?
Is my strength the strength of stones,   12
or is my flesh bronze?
In truth I have no help in me,   13
and any resource is driven from me.

"He who withholds[m] kindness from a   14
friend
forsakes the fear of the Almighty.
My brethren are treacherous as a torrent-   15
bed,
as freshets that pass away,

which are dark with ice,   16
and where the snow hides itself.
In time of heat they disappear;   17
when it is hot, they vanish from their
place.
The caravans turn aside from their course;   18
they go up into the waste, and perish.
The caravans of Tema look,   19
the travellers of Sheba hope.
They are disappointed because they were   20
confident;
they come thither and are confounded.
Such you have now become to me;[n]   21
you see my calamity, and are afraid.
Have I said, 'Make me a gift'?   22
Or, 'From your wealth offer a bribe for
me'?
Or, 'Deliver me from the adversary's   23
hand'?
Or, 'Ransom me from the hand of
oppressors'?

"Teach me, and I will be silent;   24
make me understand how I have erred.

[h] Cn: Heb uncertain   [i] Heb *for yourself*   [j] The meaning of the Hebrew word is uncertain
[k] Heb obscure   [l] The meaning of the Hebrew word is uncertain   [m] Syr Vg Compare Tg: Heb obscure
[n] Cn Compare Gk Syr: Heb obscure

25 How forceful are honest words!
   But what does reproof from you
   reprove?

26 Do you think that you can reprove words,
   when the speech of a despairing man is
   wind?

27 You would even cast lots over the fatherless,

   and bargain over your friend.

28 "But now, be pleased to look at me;
   for I will not lie to your face.

29 Turn, I pray, let no wrong be done.
   Turn now, my vindication is at stake.

30 Is there any wrong on my tongue?
   Cannot my taste discern calamity?

7 "Has not man a hard service upon earth,
   and are not his days like the days of a
   hireling?

2 Like a slave who longs for the shadow,
   and like a hireling who looks for his
   wages,

3 so I am allotted months of emptiness,
   and nights of misery are apportioned to
   me.

4 When I lie down I say, 'When shall I
   arise?'
   But the night is long,
   and I am full of tossing till the dawn.

5 My flesh is clothed with worms and dirt;
   my skin hardens, then breaks out afresh.

6 My days are swifter than a weaver's
   shuttle,
   and come to their end without hope.

7 "Remember that my life is a breath;
   my eye will never again see good.

8 The eye of him who sees me will behold
   me no more;
   while thy eyes are upon me, I shall be
   gone.

9 As the cloud fades and vanishes,
   so he who goes down to Sheol does not
   come up;

10 he returns no more to his house,
   nor does his place know him any more.

11 "Therefore I will not restrain my mouth;
   I will speak in the anguish of my spirit;
   I will complain in the bitterness of my
   soul.

12 Am I the sea, or a sea monster,
   that thou settest a guard over me?

13 When I say, 'My bed will comfort me,
   my couch will ease my complaint,'

14 then thou dost scare me with dreams
   and terrify me with visions,

15 so that I would choose strangling
   and death rather than my bones.

I loathe my life; I would not live for ever. 16
Let me alone, for my days are a breath.

What is man, that thou dost make so much 17
of him,
and that thou dost set thy mind upon
him,

dost visit him every morning,   18
and test him every moment?

How long wilt thou not look away from me, 19
nor let me alone till I swallow my
spittle?

If I sin, what do I do to thee, thou watcher 20
of men?
Why hast thou made me thy mark?
Why have I become a burden to thee?

Why dost thou not pardon my trans-   21
gression
and take away my iniquity?

For now I shall lie in the earth;
thou wilt seek me, but I shall not be."

BILDAD'S SPEECH

Then Bildad the Shuhite answered: 8
"HOW long will you say these things, 2
and the words of your mouth be a
great wind?

Does God pervert justice?   3
Or does the Almighty pervert the right?

If your children have sinned against him, 4
he has delivered them into the power of
their transgression.

If you will seek God   5
and make supplication to the Almighty,

if you are pure and upright,   6
surely then he will rouse himself for you
and reward you with a rightful habitation.

And though your beginning was small,   7
your latter days will be very great.

"For inquire, I pray you, of bygone ages, 8
and consider what the fathers have
found;

for we are but of yesterday, and know 9
nothing,
for our days on earth are a shadow.

Will they not teach you, and tell you,   10
and utter words out of their understanding?

"Can papyrus grow where there is no 11
marsh?
Can reeds flourish where there is no
water?

While yet in flower and not cut down,   12
they wither before any other plant.

Such are the paths of all who forget God; 13
the hope of the godless man shall perish.

His confidence breaks in sunder,   14

and his trust is a spider's web.*o*

He leans against his house, but it does not stand;
he lays hold of it, but it does not endure.
He thrives before the sun,
and his shoots spread over his garden.
His roots twine about the stoneheap;
he lives among the rocks.*p*
If he is destroyed from his place,
then it will deny him, saying,
'I have never seen you.'
Behold, this is the joy of his way;
and out of the earth others will spring.

"Behold, God will not reject a blameless man,
nor take the hand of evildoers.
He will yet fill your mouth with laughter,
and your lips with shouting.
Those who hate you will be clothed with shame,
and the tent of the wicked will be no more."

JOB'S REPLY

Then Job answered:
"TRULY I know that it is so:
But how can a man be just before God?
If one wished to contend with him,
one could not answer him once in a thousand times.
He is wise in heart, and mighty in strength
—who has hardened himself against him, and succeeded?—
he who removes mountains, and they know it not,
when he overturns them in his anger;
who shakes the earth out of its place,
and its pillars tremble;
who commands the sun, and it does not rise;
who seals up the stars;

8 who alone stretched out the heavens,
and trampled the waves of the sea;*q*
9 who made the Bear and Orion,

the Plei'ades and the chambers of the south;
who does great things beyond under- 10
standing,
and marvellous things without number.
Lo, he passes by me, and I see him not; 11
he moves on, but I do not perceive him.
Behold, he snatches away; who can hinder 12
him?
Who will say to him, 'What doest thou'?

"God will not turn back his anger; 13
beneath him bowed the helpers of Rahab.
How then can I answer him, 14
choosing my words with him?
Though I am innocent, I cannot answer 15
him;
I must appeal for mercy to my accuser.*r*
If I summoned him and he answered me, 16
I would not believe that he was listening to my voice.
For he crushes me with a tempest, 17
and multiplies my wounds without cause;
he will not let me get my breath, 18
but fills me with bitterness.
If it is a contest of strength, behold him! 19
If it is a matter of justice, who can summon him?*s*
Though I am innocent, my own mouth 20
would condemn me;
though I am blameless, he would prove me perverse.
I am blameless; I regard not myself; 21
I loathe my life.
It is all one; therefore I say, 22
he destroys both the blameless and the wicked.
When disaster brings sudden death, 23
he mocks at the calamity*t* of the innocent.
The earth is given into the hand of the 24
wicked;
he covers the faces of its judges—
if it is not he, who then is it?

"My days are swifter than a runner; 25
they flee away, they see no good.
They go by like skiffs of reed, 26
like an eagle swooping on the prey.
If I say, 'I will forget my complaint, 27
I will put off my sad countenance, and be of good cheer,'
I become afraid of all my suffering, 28
for I know thou wilt not hold me innocent.
I shall be condemned; 29
why then do I labour in vain?

---

o Heb *house* *p* Gk Vg: Heb uncertain *q* Or *trampled the back of the sea dragon* *r* Or *for my right*
s Compare Gk: Heb *me*. The text of the verse is uncertain
t The meaning of the Hebrew word is uncertain

30   If I wash myself with snow,
     and cleanse my hands with lye,
31   yet thou wilt plunge me into a pit,
     and my own clothes will abhor me.
32   For he is not a man, as I am, that I might answer him,
     that we should come to trial together.
33   There is no[u] umpire between us,
     who might lay his hand upon us both.
34   Let him take his rod away from me,
     and let not dread of him terrify me.
35   Then I would speak without fear of him,
     for I am not so in myself.

10   "I loathe my life;
     I will give free utterance to my complaint;
     I will speak in the bitterness of my soul.
2   I will say to God, Do not condemn me;
     let me know why thou dost contend against me.
3   Does it seem good to thee to oppress,
     to despise the work of thy hands
     and favour the designs of the wicked?
4   Hast thou eyes of flesh?
     Dost thou see as man sees?
5   Are thy days as the days of man,
     or thy years as man's years,
6   that thou dost seek out my iniquity
     and search for my sin,
7   although thou knowest that I am not guilty,
     and there is none to deliver out of thy hand?
8   Thy hands fashioned and made me;
     and now thou dost turn about and destroy me.[v]
9   Remember that thou hast made me of clay;[w]
     and wilt thou turn me to dust again?
10   Didst thou not pour me out like milk
     and curdle me like cheese?
11   Thou didst clothe me with skin and flesh,
     and knit me together with bones and sinews.
12   Thou hast granted me life and steadfast love;
     and thy care has preserved my spirit.
13   Yet these things thou didst hide in thy heart;
     I know that this was thy purpose.
14   If I sin, thou dost mark me,
     and dost not acquit me of my iniquity.
15   If I am wicked, woe to me!
     If I am righteous, I cannot lift up my head,

for I am filled with disgrace
     and look upon my affliction.
And if I lift myself up,[x] thou dost hunt me like a lion,
     and again work wonders against me;
thou dost renew thy witnesses against me,
     and increase thy vexation toward me;
     thou dost bring fresh hosts against me.[y]

"Why didst thou bring me forth from the womb?
     Would that I had died before any eye had seen me,
and were as though I had not been,
     carried from the womb to the grave.
Are not the days of my life few?[z]
     Let me alone, that I may find a little comfort[a]
before I go whence I shall not return,
     to the land of gloom and deep darkness,
the land of gloom[b] and chaos,
     where light is as darkness."

ZOPHAR'S SPEECH

Then Zophar the Na'amathite answered:
"SHOULD a multitude of words go unanswered,
     and a man full of talk be vindicated?
Should your babble silence men,
     and when you mock, shall no one shame you?
For you say, 'My doctrine is pure,
     and I am clean in God's eyes.'
But oh, that God would speak,
     and open his lips to you,
and that he would tell you the secrets of wisdom!
     For he is manifold in understanding.[c]
Know then that God exacts of you less than your guilt deserves.

"Can you find out the deep things of God?
     Can you find out the limit of the Almighty?
It is higher than heaven[d]—what can you do?
     Deeper than Sheol—what can you know?
Its measure is longer than the earth,
     and broader than the sea.
If he passes through, and imprisons,
     and calls to judgment, who can hinder him?
For he knows worthless men;

[u] Another reading is *Would that there were*
[v] Cn Compare Gk Syr: Heb *made me together round about and thou dost destroy me*
[w] Gk: Heb *like clay*   [x] Syr: Heb *he lifts himself up*
[y] Cn Compare Gk: Heb *changes and a host are with me*
[z] Cn Compare Gk Syr: Heb *Are not my days few? Let him cease*
[a] Heb *brighten up*   [b] Heb *gloom as darkness, deep darkness*   [c] Heb obscure   [d] Heb *The heights of heaven*

when he sees iniquity, will he not consider it?

2 But a stupid man will get understanding,
when a wild ass's colt is born a man.

3 "If you set your heart aright,
you will stretch out your hands toward
him.

4 If iniquity is in your hand, put it far away,
and let not wickedness dwell in your
tents.

5 Surely then you will lift up your face
without blemish;
you will be secure, and will not fear.

6 You will forget your misery;
you will remember it as waters that have
passed away.

7 And your life will be brighter than the
noonday;
its darkness will be like the morning.

8 And you will have confidence, because
there is hope;
you will be protected[e] and take your rest
in safety.

9 You will lie down, and none will make you
afraid;
many will entreat your favour.

20 But the eyes of the wicked will fail;
all way of escape will be lost to them,
and their hope is to breathe their last."

JOB'S REPLY

12 Then Job answered:

2 "NO doubt you are the people,
and wisdom will die with you.

3 But I have understanding as well as you;
I am not inferior to you.
Who does not know such things as
these?

4 I am a laughingstock to my friends;
I, who called upon God and he
answered me,
a just and blameless man, am a
laughingstock.

5 In the thought of one who is at ease
there is contempt for misfortune;
it is ready for those whose feet slip.

6 The tents of robbers are at peace,
and those who provoke God are secure,
who bring their god in their hand.[f]

7 "But ask the beasts, and they will teach
you;
the birds of the air, and they will tell
you;

8 or the plants of the earth,[g] and they will
teach you;
and the fish of the sea will declare to you.

9 Who among all these does not know

that the hand of the LORD has done
this?

10 In his hand is the life of every living thing
and the breath of all mankind.

11 Does not the ear try words
as the palate tastes food?

12 Wisdom is with the aged,
and understanding in length of days.

13 "With God[h] are wisdom and might;
he has counsel and understanding.

14 If he tears down, none can rebuild;
if he shuts a man in, none can open.

15 If he withholds the waters, they dry up;
if he sends them out, they overwhelm
the land.

16 With him are strength and wisdom;
the deceived and the deceiver are his.

17 He leads counsellors away stripped,
and judges he makes fools.

18 He looses the bonds of kings,
and binds a waistcloth on their loins.

19 He leads priests away stripped,
and overthrows the mighty.

20 He deprives of speech those who are
trusted,
and takes away the discernment of the
elders.

21 He pours contempt on princes,
and looses the belt of the strong.

22 He uncovers the deeps out of darkness,
and brings deep darkness to light.

23 He makes nations great, and he destroys
them:
he enlarges nations, and leads them
away.

24 He takes away understanding from the
chiefs of the people of the earth,
and makes them wander in a pathless
waste.

25 They grope in the dark without light;
and he makes them stagger like a
drunken man.

13 "Lo, my eye has seen all this,
my ear has heard and understood it.

2 What you know, I also know;
I am not inferior to you.

3 But I would speak to the Almighty,
and I desire to argue my case with God.

4 As for you, you whitewash with lies;
worthless physicians are you all.

5 Oh that you would keep silent,
and it would be your wisdom!

6 Hear now my reasoning,
and listen to the pleadings of my lips.

7 Will you speak falsely for God,
and speak deceitfully for him?

8 Will you show partiality toward him,
will you plead the case for God?

---

e Or *you will look around*   f Hebrew uncertain   g Or *speak to the earth*   h Heb *him*

9   Will it be well with you when he searches
     you out?
     Or can you deceive him, as one deceives
     a man?

10   He will surely rebuke you
     if in secret you show partiality.

11   Will not his majesty terrify you,
     and the dread of him fall upon you?

12   Your maxims are proverbs of ashes,
     your defences are defences of clay.

13   "Let me have silence, and I will speak,
     and let come on me what may.

14   I will take^i my flesh in my teeth,
     and put my life in my hand.

15   Behold, he will slay me; I have no hope;
     yet I will defend my ways to his face.

16   This will be my salvation,
     that a godless man shall not come before
     him.

17   Listen carefully to my words,
     and let my declaration be in your ears.

18   Behold, I have prepared my case;
     I know that I shall be vindicated.

19   Who is there that will contend with me?
     For then I would be silent and die.

20   Only grant two things to me,
     then I will not hide myself from thy face:

21   withdraw thy hand far from me,
     and let not dread of thee terrify me.

22   Then call, and I will answer;
     or let me speak, and do thou reply to me.

23   How many are my iniquities and my sins?
     Make me know my transgression and
     my sin.

24   Why dost thou hide thy face,
     and count me as thy enemy?

25   Wilt thou frighten a driven leaf
     and pursue dry chaff?

26   For thou writest bitter things against me,
     and makest me inherit the iniquities of
     my youth.

27   Thou puttest my feet in the stocks,
     and watchest all my paths;
     thou settest a bound to the soles of my
     feet.

28   Man^j wastes away like a rotten thing,
     like a garment that is moth-eaten.

14   "Man that is born of a woman is of few
     days, and full of trouble.

2   He comes forth like a flower, and withers;
he flees like a shadow, and continues
not.

3   And dost thou open thy eyes upon such a
one
     and bring him^k into judgment with
     thee?

4   Who can bring a clean thing out of an
unclean?
     There is not one.

5   Since his days are determined,
     and the number of his months is with
     thee,
     and thou hast appointed his bounds
     that he cannot pass,

6   look away from him, and desist,^{l}
     that he may enjoy, like a hireling, his
     day.

7   "For there is hope for a tree,
     if it be cut down, that it will sprout
     again,
     and that its shoots will not cease.

8   Though its root grow old in the earth,
     and its stump die in the ground,

9   yet at the scent of water it will bud
     and put forth branches like a young
     plant.

10   But man dies, and is laid low;
     man breathes his last, and where is he?

11   As waters fail from a lake,
     and a river wastes away and dries up,

12   so man lies down and rises not again;
     till the heavens are no more he will not
     awake,
     or be roused out of his sleep.

13   Oh that thou wouldest hide me in Sheol,
     that thou wouldest conceal me until thy
     wrath be past,
     that thou wouldest appoint me a set
     time, and remember me!

14   If a man die, shall he live again?
     All the days of my service I would wait,
     till my release should come.

15   Thou wouldest call, and I would answer
     thee;
     thou wouldest long for the work of thy
     hands.

16   For then thou wouldest number my steps,
     thou wouldest not keep watch over my
     sin;

^{i} Gk: Heb *Why should I take?* ^{j} Heb *He* ^{k} Gk Syr Vg: Heb *me* ^{l} Cn: Heb *that he may desist*

my transgression would be sealed up in a
bag,
and thou wouldest cover over my iniquity.

"But the mountain falls and crumbles
away,
and the rock is removed from its place;
the waters wear away the stones;
the torrents wash away the soil of the
earth;
so thou destroyest the hope of man.
Thou prevailest for ever against him, and
he passes;
thou changest his countenance, and
sendest him away.
His sons come to honour, and he does not
know it;
they are brought low, and he perceives it
not.
He feels only the pain of his own body,
and he mourns only for himself."

ELIPHAZ SPEAKS

5 Then Eli'phaz the Te'manite answered:
"SHOULD a wise man answer with
windy knowledge,
and fill himself with the east wind?
Should he argue in unprofitable talk,
or in words with which he can do no
good?
But you are doing away with the fear of
God,
and hindering meditation before God.
For your iniquity teaches your mouth,
and you choose the tongue of the crafty.
Your own mouth condemns you, and not I;
your own lips testify against you.

"Are you the first man that was born?
Or were you brought forth before the
hills?
Have you listened in the council of God?
And do you limit wisdom to yourself?
What do you know that we do not know?
What do you understand that is not
clear to us?
Both the grey-haired and the aged are
among us,
older than your father.
Are the consolations of God too small for
you,
or the word that deals gently with you?
Why does your heart carry you away,
and why do your eyes flash,
that you turn your spirit against God,
and let such words go out of your
mouth?

What is man, that he can be clean?   14
Or he that is born of a woman, that he
can be righteous?
Behold, God puts no trust in his holy ones, 15
and the heavens are not clean in his
sight;
how much less one who is abominable and 16
corrupt,
a man who drinks iniquity like water!

"I will show you, hear me;   17
and what I have seen I will declare
(what wise men have told,   18
and their fathers have not hidden,
to whom alone the land was given,   19
and no stranger passed among them).
The wicked man writhes in pain all his 20
days,
through all the years that are laid up for
the ruthless.
Terrifying sounds are in his ears;   21
in prosperity the destroyer will come
upon him.
He does not believe that he will return out 22
of darkness,
and he is destined for the sword.
He wanders abroad for bread, saying, 23
'Where is it?'
He knows that a day of darkness is ready
at his hand;
distress and anguish terrify him;   24
they prevail against him, like a king
prepared for battle.
Because he has stretched forth his hand 25
against God,
and bids defiance to the Almighty,
running stubbornly against him   26
with a thick-bossed shield;
because he has covered his face with his fat, 27
and gathered fat upon his loins,
and has lived in desolate cities,   28
in houses which no man should inhabit,
which were destined to become heaps of
ruins;
he will not be rich, and his wealth will not 29
endure,
nor will he strike root in the earth;[m]
he will not escape from darkness;   30
the flame will dry up his shoots,
and his blossom[n] will be swept away[o] by
the wind.
Let him not trust in emptiness, deceiving 31
himself;
for emptiness will be his recompense.
It will be paid in full before his time,   32
and his branch will not be green.
He will shake off his unripe grape, like the 33
vine,
and cast off his blossom, like the olive
tree.

[m] Vg: Heb obscure   [n] Gk: Heb *mouth*   [o] Cn: Heb *will depart*

34 For the company of the godless is barren,
    and fire consumes the tents of bribery.
35 They conceive mischief and bring forth evil
    and their heart prepares deceit."

JOB'S REPLY

16 Then Job answered:
2   "I HAVE heard many such things;
    miserable comforters are you all.
3 Shall windy words have an end?
    Or what provokes you that you answer?
4 I also could speak as you do,
    if you were in my place;
    I could join words together against you,
    and shake my head at you.
5 I could strengthen you with my mouth,
    and the solace of my lips would assuage your pain.

6 "If I speak, my pain is not assuaged,
    and if I forbear, how much of it leaves me?
7 Surely now God has worn me out;
    he has ^{p} made desolate all my company.
8 And the has ^{p} shrivelled me up,
    which is a witness against me;
    and my leanness has risen up against me,
    it testifies to my face.
9 He has torn me in his wrath, and hated me;
    he has gnashed his teeth at me;
    my adversary sharpens his eyes against me.
10 Men have gaped at me with their mouth,
    they have struck me insolently upon the cheek,
    they mass themselves together against me.
11 God gives me up to the ungodly,
    and casts me into the hands of the wicked.
12 I was at ease, and he broke me asunder;
    he seized me by the neck and dashed me to pieces;
    he set me up as his target,
13 his archers surround me.
    He slashes open my kidneys, and does not spare;
    he pours out my gall on the ground.
14 He breaks me with breach upon breach;
    he runs upon me like a warrior.
15 I have sewed sackcloth upon my skin,
    and have laid my strength in the dust.
16 My face is red with weeping,
    and on my eyelids is deep darkness;
17 although there is no violence in my hands,
    and my prayer is pure.

"O earth, cover not my blood,
    and let my cry find no resting place.
Even now, behold, my witness is in heaven,
    and he that vouches for me is on high.
My friends scorn me;
    my eye pours out tears to God,
that he would maintain the right of a man with God,
    like ^{q} that of a man with his neighbour.
For when a few years have come
    I shall go the way whence I shall not return.

"My spirit is broken, my days are extinct,
    the grave is ready for me.
Surely there are mockers about me,
    and my eye dwells on their provocation.

"Lay down a pledge for me with thyself;
    who is there that will give surety for me?
Since thou hast closed their minds to understanding,
    therefore thou wilt not let them triumph.
He who informs against his friends to get a share of their property,
    the eyes of his children will fail.

"He has made me a byword of the peoples,
    and I am one before whom men spit.
My eye has grown dim from grief,
    and all my members are like a shadow.
Upright men are appalled at this,
    and the innocent stirs himself up against the godless.
Yet the righteous holds to his way,
    and he that has clean hands grows stronger and stronger.
But you, come on again, all of you,
    and I shall not find a wise man among you.
My days are past, my plans are broken off,
    the desires of my heart.
They make night into day;
    'The light,' they say, 'is near to the darkness.' ^{r}
If I look for Sheol as my house,
    if I spread my couch in darkness,
if I say to the pit, 'You are my father,'
    and to the worm, 'My mother,' or 'My sister,'
where then is my hope?
    Who will see my hope?
Will it go down to the bars of Sheol?
    Shall we descend together into the dust?"

^{p} Heb *thou hast* ^{q} Syr Vg Tg: Heb *and* ^{r} Heb obscure

BILDAD'S SPEECH

Then Bildad the Shuhite answered:

"HOW long will you hunt for words?
Consider, and then we will speak.
Why are we counted as cattle?
Why are we stupid in your sight?
You who tear yourself in your anger,
shall the earth be forsaken for you,
or the rock be removed out of its place?

"Yea, the light of the wicked is put out,
and the flame of his fire does not shine.
The light is dark in his tent,
and his lamp above him is put out.
His strong steps are shortened
and his own schemes throw him down.
For he is cast into a net by his own feet,
and he walks on a pitfall.
A trap seizes him by the heel,
a snare lays hold of him.
A rope is hid for him in the ground,
a trap for him in the path.
Terrors frighten him on every side,
and chase him at his heels.
His strength is hunger-bitten,
and calamity is ready for his stumbling.
By disease his skin is consumed,[s]
the first-born of death consumes his
limbs.
He is torn from the tent in which he
trusted,
and is brought to the king of terrors.
In his tent dwells that which is none of his;
brimstone is scattered upon his habitation.
His roots dry up beneath,
and his branches wither above.
His memory perishes from the earth,
and he has no name in the street.
He is thrust from light into darkness,
and driven out of the world.
He has no offspring or descendant among
his people,
and no survivor where he used to live.
They of the west are appalled at his day,
and horror seizes them of the east.
Surely such are the dwellings of the
ungodly,
such is the place of him who knows not
God."

JOB'S REPLY

Then Job answered:

"HOW long will you torment me,
and break me in pieces with
words?
These ten times you have cast reproach
upon me;

are you not ashamed to wrong me?
And even if it be true that I have erred, 4
my error remains with myself.
If indeed you magnify yourselves against 5
me,
and make my humiliation an argument
against me,
know then that God has put me in the 6
wrong,
and closed his net about me.
Behold, I cry out, 'Violence!' but I am not 7
answered;
I call aloud, but there is no justice.
He has walled up my way, so that I cannot 8
pass,
and he has set darkness upon my paths.
He has stripped from me my glory, 9
and taken the crown from my head.
He breaks me down on every side, and I 10
am gone,
and my hope has he pulled up like a tree.
He has kindled his wrath against me, 11
and counts me as his adversary.
His troops come on together; 12
they have cast up siegeworks[t] against
me,
and encamp round about my tent.

"He has put my brethren far from me, 13
and my acquaintances are wholly
estranged from me.
My kinsfolk and my close friends have 14
failed me;
the guests in my house have forgotten 15
me;
my maidservants count me as a stranger;
I have become an alien in their eyes.
I call to my servant, but he gives me no 16
answer;
I must beseech him with my mouth.
I am repulsive to my wife, 17
loathsome to the sons of my own
mother.
Even young children despise me; 18
when I rise they talk against me.
All my intimate friends abhor me, 19
and those whom I loved have turned
against me.
My bones cleave to my skin and to my 20
flesh,
and I have escaped by the skin of my
teeth.
Have pity on me, have pity on me, 21
O you my friends,
for the hand of God has touched me!
Why do you, like God, pursue me? 22
Why are you not satisfied with my
flesh?

"Oh that my words were written! 23

---

[s] Cn: Heb *it consumes the limbs of his skin*   [t] Heb *their way*

²⁴ Oh that they were inscribed in a book!
Oh that with an iron pen and lead
they were graven in the rock for ever!
²⁵ For I know that my Redeemer^u lives,
and at last he will stand upon the earth;^v
²⁶ and after my skin has been thus destroyed,
then from^w my flesh I shall see God,^x
²⁷ whom I shall see on my side,^y
and my eyes shall behold, and not
another.
My heart faints within me!
²⁸ If you say, 'How we will pursue him!'
and, 'The root of the matter is found in
him';
²⁹ be afraid of the sword,
for wrath brings the punishment of the
sword,
that you may know there is a judgment."

ZOPHAR'S SPEECH

²⁰ Then Zophar the Na'amathite answered:
² "THEREFORE my thoughts answer
me,
because of my haste within me.
³ I hear censure which insults me,
and out of my understanding a spirit
answers me.
⁴ Do you not know this from of old,
since man was placed upon earth,
⁵ that the exulting of the wicked is short,
and the joy of the godless but for a
moment?
⁶ Though his height mount up to the
heavens,
and his head reach to the clouds,
⁷ he will perish for ever like his own dung;
those who have seen him will say,
'Where is he?'
⁸ He will fly away like a dream, and not be
found;
he will be chased away like a vision of
the night.
⁹ The eye which saw him will see him no
more,
nor will his place any more behold him.
¹⁰ His children will seek the favour of the
poor,

and his hands will give back his
wealth.
His bones are full of youthful vigour,
but it will lie down with him in the dust.

"Though wickedness is sweet in his
mouth,
though he hides it under his tongue,
though he is loath to let it go,
and holds it in his mouth,
yet his food is turned in his stomach;
it is the gall of asps within him.
He swallows down riches and vomits them
up again;
God casts them out of his belly.
He will suck the poison of asps;
the tongue of a viper will kill him.
He will not look upon the rivers,
the streams flowing with honey and
curds.
He will give back the fruit of his toil,
and will not swallow it down;
from the profit of his trading
he will get no enjoyment.
For he has crushed and abandoned the
poor,
he has seized a house which he did not
build.

"Because his greed knew no rest,
he will not save anything in which he
delights.
There was nothing left after he had eaten;
therefore his prosperity will not endure.
In the fullness of his sufficiency he will be
in straits;
all the force of misery will come upon
him.
To fill his belly to the full
God^z will send his fierce anger into
him,
and rain it upon him as his food.^a
He will flee from an iron weapon;
a bronze arrow will strike him through.
It is drawn forth and comes out of his
body,
the glittering point comes out of his gall;
terrors come upon him.
Utter darkness is laid up for his treasures;
a fire not blown upon will devour him;
what is left in his tent will be consumed.
The heavens will reveal his iniquity,
and the earth will rise up against him.
The possessions of his house will be
carried away,
dragged off in the day of God's^b wrath.
This is the wicked man's portion from
God,
the heritage decreed for him by God."

^u Or *Vindicator*   ^v Or *dust*   ^w Or *without*   ^x The meaning of this verse is uncertain   ^y Or *for myself*
^z Heb *he*   ^a Cn: Heb *in his flesh*   ^b Heb *his*

JOB 22

JOB'S REPLY

Then Job answered:
"LISTEN carefully to my words,
   and let this be your consolation.
Bear with me, and I will speak,
   and after I have spoken, mock on.
As for me, is my complaint against man?
   Why should I not be impatient?
Look at me, and be appalled,
   and lay your hand upon your mouth.
When I think of it I am dismayed,
   and shuddering seizes my flesh.
Why do the wicked live,
   reach old age, and grow mighty in power?
Their children are established in their presence,
   and their offspring before their eyes.
Their houses are safe from fear,
   and no rod of God is upon them.
Their bull breeds without fail;
   their cow calves, and does not cast her calf.
They send forth their little ones like a flock,
   and their children dance.
They sing to the tambourine and the lyre,
   and rejoice to the sound of the pipe.
They spend their days in prosperity,
   and in peace they go down to Sheol.
They say to God, 'Depart from us!
   We do not desire the knowledge of thy ways.
What is the Almighty, that we should serve him?
   And what profit do we get if we pray to him?'
Behold, is not their prosperity in their hand?
   The counsel of the wicked is far from me.

"How often is it that the lamp of the wicked is put out?
   That their calamity comes upon them?
   That God[c] distributes pains in his anger?

You say, 'God stores up their iniquity for 19 their sons.'
Let him recompense it to themselves,
   that they may know it.
Let their own eyes see their destruction, 20
   and let them drink of the wrath of the Almighty.
For what do they care for their houses 21 after them,
   when the number of their months is cut off?
Will any teach God knowledge, 22
   seeing that he judges those that are on high?
One dies in full prosperity, 23
   being wholly at ease and secure,
his body[d] full of fat 24
   and the marrow of his bones moist.
Another dies in bitterness of soul, 25
   never having tasted of good.
They lie down alike in the dust, 26
   and the worms cover them.

"Behold, I know your thoughts, 27
   and your schemes to wrong me.
For you say, 'Where is the house of the 28 prince?
   Where is the tent in which the wicked dwelt?'
Have you not asked those who travel the 29 roads,
   and do you not accept their testimony
that the wicked man is spared in the day of 30 calamity,
   that he is rescued in the day of wrath?
Who declares his way to his face, 31
   and who requites him for what he has done?
When he is borne to the grave, 32
   watch is kept over his tomb.
The clods of the valley are sweet to him; 33
   all men follow after him,
   and those who go before him are innumerable.
How then will you comfort me with empty 34 nothings?
   There is nothing left of your answers but falsehood."

ELIPHAZ SPEAKS

Then Eliphaz the Temanite answered: 22
"CAN a man be profitable to God? 2
   Surely he who is wise is profitable to himself.
Is it any pleasure to the Almighty if you 3 are righteous,
   or is it gain to him if you make your ways blameless?

8   That they are like straw before the wind,
   and like chaff that the storm carries away?

c Heb he   d The meaning of the Hebrew word is uncertain
22.2-3: Job 35.6-8.

4 Is it for your fear of him that he reproves
     you,
       and enters into judgment with you?
5 Is not your wickedness great?
       There is no end to your iniquities.
6 For you have exacted pledges of your
     brothers for nothing,
       and stripped the naked of their clothing.
7 You have given no water to the weary to
     drink,
       and you have withheld bread from the
       hungry.
8 The man with power possessed the land,
       and the favoured man dwelt in it.
9 You have sent widows away empty,
       and the arms of the fatherless were
       crushed.
10 Therefore snares are round about you,
       and sudden terror overwhelms you;
11 your light is darkened, so that^e you cannot
     see,
       and a flood of water covers you.

12 "Is not God high in the heavens?
       See the highest stars, how lofty they are!
13 Therefore you say, 'What does God
     know?
       Can he judge through the deep dark-
       ness?
14 Thick clouds enwrap him, so that he does
     not see,
       and he walks on the vault of heaven.'
15 Will you keep to the old way
       which wicked men have trod?
16 They were snatched away before their
     time;
       their foundation was washed away.
17 They said to God, 'Depart from us,'
       and 'What can the Almighty do to us?'^{f}
18 Yet he filled their houses with good
     things—
       but the counsel of the wicked is far from
       me.
19 The righteous see it and are glad;
       the innocent laugh them to scorn,
20 saying, 'Surely our adversaries are cut off,
       and what they left the fire has con-
       sumed.'

21 "Agree with God, and be at peace;
       thereby good will come to you.
22 Receive instruction from his mouth,
       and lay up his words in your heart.
23 If you return to the Almighty and humble
     yourself,^{g}
       if you remove unrighteousness far from
       your tents,
24 if you lay gold in the dust,

and gold of Ophir among the stones of
       the torrent bed,
     and if the Almighty is your gold,
       and your precious silver;
     then you will delight yourself in the
       Almighty,
       and lift up your face to God.
   You will make your prayer to him, and he
       will hear you;
       and you will pay your vows.
   You will decide on a matter, and it will be
       established for you,
       and light will shine on your ways.
   For God abases the proud,^{h}
       but he saves the lowly.
   He delivers the innocent man;^{i}
       you will be delivered through the
       cleanness of your hands."

JOB'S REPLY

Then Job answered:

  "TODAY also my complaint is bitter,^{j}
       his^k hand is heavy in spite of my
       groaning.
   Oh, that I knew where I might find him,
       that I might come even to his seat!
   I would lay my case before him
       and fill my mouth with arguments.
   I would learn what he would answer me,
       and understand what he would say to
       me.
   Would he contend with me in the great-
       ness of his power?
       No; he would give heed to me.
   There an upright man could reason with
       him,
       and I should be acquitted for ever by my
       judge.

   "Behold, I go forward, but he is not there;
       and backward, but I cannot perceive
       him;
   on the left hand I seek him,^{l} but I cannot
       behold him;
       I^m turn to the right hand, but I cannot
       see him.
   But he knows the way that I take;
       when he has tried me, I shall come forth
       as gold.
   My foot has held fast to his steps;
       I have kept his way and have not turned
       aside.
   I have not departed from the command-
       ment of his lips;
       I have treasured in^n my bosom the
       words of his mouth.

^{e} Cn Compare Gk: Heb *or darkness* ^{f} Gk Syr: Heb *them* ^{g} Gk: Heb *you will be built up*
^{h} Cn: Heb *when they abased you said, Proud* ^{i} Gk Syr Vg: Heb *him that is not innocent*
^{j} Syr Vg Tg: Heb *rebellious* ^{k} Gk Syr: Heb *my* ^{l} Compare Syr: Heb *on the left hand when he works*
^{m} Syr Vg: Heb *he* ^{n} Gk Vg: Heb *from*

But he is unchangeable and who can turn
  him?
What he desires, that he does.
For he will complete what he appoints for
  me;
  and many such things are in his mind.
Therefore I am terrified at his presence;
  when I consider, I am in dread of him.
God has made my heart faint;
  the Almighty has terrified me;
for I am[o] hemmed in by darkness,
  and thick darkness covers my face.[p]

"Why are not times of judgment kept by
  the Almighty,
  and why do those who know him never
    see his days?
Men remove landmarks;
  they seize flocks and pasture them.
They drive away the ass of the fatherless;
  they take the widow's ox for a pledge.
They thrust the poor off the road;
  the poor of the earth all hide them-
    selves.
Behold, like wild asses in the desert
  they go forth to their toil,
seeking prey in the wilderness
  as food[q] for their children.
They gather their[r] fodder in the field
  and they glean the vineyard of the
    wicked man.
They lie all night naked, without clothing,
  and have no covering in the cold.
They are wet with the rain of the mountains,
  and cling to the rock for want of shelter.
(There are those who snatch the fatherless
  child from the breast,
  and take in pledge the infant of the
    poor.)
They go about naked, without clothing;
  hungry, they carry the sheaves;
among the olive rows of the wicked[s] they
  make oil;
  they tread the wine presses, but suffer
    thirst.
From out of the city the dying groan,
  and the soul of the wounded cries for
    help;
  yet God pays no attention to their
    prayer.

"There are those who rebel against the
  light,
  who are not acquainted with its ways,
  and do not stay in its paths.
The murderer rises in the dark,[t]
  that he may kill the poor and needy;

  and in the night he is as a thief.
The eye of the adulterer also waits for the 15
  twilight,
  saying, 'No eye will see me';
  and he disguises his face.
In the dark they dig through houses;   16
  by day they shut themselves up;
  they do not know the light.
For deep darkness is morning to all of 17
  them;
  for they are friends with the terrors of
    deep darkness.

"You say, 'They are swiftly carried away 18
  upon the face of the waters;
  their portion is cursed in the land;
  no treader turns toward their vine-
    yards.
Drought and heat snatch away the snow 19
  waters;
  so does Sheol those who have sinned.
The squares of the town[u] forget them;   20
  their name[v] is no longer remembered;
  so wickedness is broken like a tree.'

"They feed on the barren childless 21
  woman,
  and do no good to the widow.
Yet God[w] prolongs the life of the mighty 22
  by his power;
  they rise up when they despair of life.
He gives them security, and they are 23
  supported;
  and his eyes are upon their ways.
They are exalted a little while, and then 24
  are gone;
  they wither and fade like the mallow;[x]
  they are cut off like the heads of grain.
If it is not so, who will prove me a liar, 25
  and show that there is nothing in what I
    say?"

BILDAD'S SPEECH

Then Bildad the Shuhite answered: 25
"DOMINION and fear are with 2
  God;[y]
  he makes peace in his high heaven.
Is there any number to his armies?   3
  Upon whom does his light not arise?
How then can man be righteous before 4
  God?
  How can he who is born of woman be
    clean?
Behold, even the moon is not bright   5
  and the stars are not clean in his sight;
  how much less man, who is a maggot,   6
  and the son of man, who is a worm!"

---

[o] With one Ms: Heb *am not*   [p] Vg: Heb *from my face*   [q] Heb *food to him*   [r] Heb *his*   [s] Heb *their olive rows*
[t] Cn: Heb *at the light*   [u] Cn: Heb obscure   [v] Cn: Heb *a worm*   [w] Heb *he*   [x] Gk: Heb *all*   [y] Heb *him*

JOB'S REPLY

26 Then Job answered:

2 "How you have helped him who has
no power!
How you have saved the arm that has no
strength!

3 How you have counselled him who has no
wisdom,
and plentifully declared sound knowledge!

4 With whose help have you uttered words,
and whose spirit has come forth from
you?

5 The shades below tremble,
the waters and their inhabitants.

6 Sheol is naked before God,
and Abaddon has no covering.

7 He stretches out the north over the void,
and hangs the earth upon nothing.

8 He binds up the waters in his thick clouds,
and the cloud is not rent under them.

9 He covers the face of the moon,^{g}
and spreads over it his cloud.

10 He has described a circle upon the face of
the waters
at the boundary between light and darkness.

11 The pillars of heaven tremble,
and are astounded at his rebuke.

12 By his power he stilled the sea;
by his understanding he smote Rahab.

13 By his wind the heavens were made fair;
his hand pierced the fleeing serpent.

14 Lo, these are but the outskirts of his ways;
and how small a whisper do we hear of
him!
But the thunder of his power who can
understand?"

27 And Job again took up his discourse, and
said:

2 "As God lives, who has taken away my
right,
and the Almighty, who has made my
soul bitter;

3 as long as my breath is in me,

and the spirit of God is in my nostrils;
my lips will not speak falsehood,
and my tongue will not utter deceit.

Far be it from me to say that you are right;
till I die I will not put away my integrity
from me.

I hold fast my righteousness, and will not
let it go;
my heart does not reproach me for any
of my days.

"Let my enemy be as the wicked,
and let him that rises up against me be
as the unrighteous.

For what is the hope of the godless when
God cuts him off,
when God takes away his life?

Will God hear his cry,
when trouble comes upon him?

Will he take delight in the Almighty?
Will he call upon God at all times?

I will teach you concerning the hand of
God;
what is with the Almighty I will not
conceal.

Behold, all of you have seen it yourselves;
why then have you become altogether
vain?

"This is the portion of a wicked man with
God,
and the heritage which oppressors receive
from the Almighty:

If his children are multiplied, it is for the
sword;
and his offspring have not enough to eat.

Those who survive him the pestilence
buries,
and their widows make no lamentation.

Though he heap up silver like dust,
and pile up clothing like clay;

he may pile it up, but the just will wear it,
and the innocent will divide the silver.

The house which he builds is like a
spider's web,^{a}
like a booth which a watchman makes.

He goes to bed rich, but will do so no
more;^{b}
he opens his eyes, and his wealth is
gone.

Terrors overtake him like a flood;
in the night a whirlwind carries him off.

The east wind lifts him up and he is gone;
it sweeps him out of his place.

It^c hurls at him without pity;
he flees from its^d power in headlong
flight.

It^c claps its^d hands at him,
and hisses at him from its^d place.

---

^{g} Or *his throne*　^{a} Cn Compare Gk Syr: Heb *He builds his house like the moth*
^{b} Gk Compare Syr: Heb *shall not be gathered*　^{c} Or *He* (that is, God)　^{d} Or *his*

8 "Surely there is a mine for silver,
and a place for gold which they refine.
9 Iron is taken out of the earth,
and copper is smelted from the ore.
3 Men put an end to darkness,
and search out to the farthest bound
the ore in gloom and deep darkness.
4 They open shafts in a valley away from
where men live;
they are forgotten by travellers,
they hang afar from men, they swing to
and fro.
5 As for the earth, out of it comes bread;
but underneath it is turned up as by fire.
6 Its stones are the place of sapphires,[e]
and it has dust of gold.

7 "That path no bird of prey knows,
and the falcon's eye has not seen it.
8 The proud beasts have not trodden it;
the lion has not passed over it.

9 "Man puts his hand to the flinty rock,
and overturns mountains by the roots.
10 He cuts out channels in the rocks,
and his eye sees every precious thing.
11 He binds up the streams so that they do
not trickle,
and the thing that is hid he brings forth
to light.

12 "But where shall wisdom be found?
And where is the place of understanding?
13 Man does not know the way to it,[f]
and it is not found in the land of the
living.
14 The deep says, 'It is not in me,'
and the sea says, 'It is not with me.'
15 It cannot be gotten for gold,
and silver cannot be weighed as its
price.
16 It cannot be valued in the gold of Ophir,
in precious onyx or sapphire.[g]
17 Gold and glass cannot equal it,
nor can it be exchanged for jewels of fine
gold.
18 No mention shall be made of coral or of
crystal;
the price of wisdom is above pearls.
19 The topaz of Ethiopia cannot compare
with it,
nor can it be valued in pure gold.

20 "Whence then comes wisdom?
And where is the place of understanding?
21 It is hid from the eyes of all living,
and concealed from the birds of the air.
22 Abaddon and Death say,

'We have heard a rumour of it with our
ears.'

23 "God understands the way to it,
and he knows its place.
24 For he looks to the ends of the earth,
and sees everything under the heavens.
25 When he gave to the wind its weight,
and meted out the waters by measure;
26 when he made a decree for the rain,
and a way for the lightning of the
thunder;
27 then he saw it and declared it;
he established it, and searched it out.
28 And he said to man,
'Behold, the fear of the Lord, that is
wisdom;
and to depart from evil is understanding.'"

29 And Job again took up his discourse, and
said:
2 "Oh, that I were as in the months of old,
as in the days when God watched over
me;
3 when his lamp shone upon my head,
and by his light I walked through
darkness;
4 as I was in my autumn days,
when the friendship of God was upon
my tent;
5 when the Almighty was yet with me,
when my children were about me;
6 when my steps were washed with milk,
and the rock poured out for me streams
of oil!
7 When I went out to the gate of the city,
when I prepared my seat in the square,
8 the young men saw me and withdrew,
and the aged rose and stood;
9 the princes refrained from talking,
and laid their hand on their mouth;
10 the voice of the nobles was hushed,
and their tongue cleaved to the roof of
their mouth.
11 When the ear heard, it called me blessed,
and when the eye saw, it approved;
12 because I delivered the poor who cried,
and the fatherless who had none to help
him.
13 The blessing of him who was about to
perish came upon me,
and I caused the widow's heart to sing
for joy.
14 I put on righteousness, and it clothed
me;
my justice was like a robe and a turban.
15 I was eyes to the blind,
and feet to the lame.
16 I was a father to the poor,

[e] Or lapis lazuli   [f] Gk: Heb its price   [g] Or lapis lazuli

and I searched out the cause of him
whom I did not know.

17 I broke the fangs of the unrighteous,
and made him drop his prey from his
teeth.

18 Then I thought, 'I shall die in my nest,
and I shall multiply my days as the sand,

19 my roots spread out to the waters,
with the dew all night on my branches,

20 my glory fresh with me,
and my bow ever new in my hand.'

21 "Men listened to me, and waited,
and kept silence for my counsel.

22 After I spoke they did not speak again,
and my word dropped upon them.

23 They waited for me as for the rain;
and they opened their mouths as for the
spring rain.

24 I smiled on them when they had no
confidence;
and the light of my countenance they
did not cast down.

25 I chose their way, and sat as chief,
and I dwelt like a king among his troops,
like one who comforts mourners.

30 "But now they make sport of me,
men who are younger than I,
whose fathers I would have disdained
to set with the dogs of my flock.

2 What could I gain from the strength of
their hands,
men whose vigour is gone?

3 Through want and hard hunger
they gnaw the dry and desolate ground;[h]

4 they pick mallow and the leaves of bushes,
and to warm themselves the roots of the
broom.

5 They are driven out from among men;
they shout after them as after a thief.

6 In the gullies of the torrents they must
dwell,
in holes of the earth and of the rocks.

7 Among the bushes they bray;
under the nettles they huddle together.

8 A senseless, a disreputable brood,
they have been whipped out of the land.

9 "And now I have become their song,
I am a byword to them.

They abhor me, they keep aloof from me;
they do not hesitate to spit at the sight of
me.

Because God has loosed my cord and
humbled me,
they have cast off restraint in my
presence.

On my right hand the rabble rise,
they drive me[i] forth,
they cast up against me their ways of
destruction.

They break up my path,
they promote my calamity;
no one restrains[j] them.

As through[k] a wide breach they come;
amid the crash they roll on.

Terrors are turned upon me;
my honour is pursued as by the wind,
and my prosperity has passed away like
a cloud.

"And now my soul is poured out within 16
me;
days of affliction have taken hold of me.

The night racks my bones, 17
and the pain that gnaws me takes no
rest.

With violence it seizes my garment;[l] 18
it binds me about like the collar of my
tunic.

God has cast me into the mire, 19
and I have become like dust and ashes.

I cry to thee and thou dost not answer me; 20
I stand, and thou dost not[m] heed me.

Thou hast turned cruel to me; 21
with the might of thy hand thou dost
persecute me.

Thou liftest me up on the wind, 22
thou makest me ride on it,
and thou tossest me about in the roar of
the storm.

Yea, I know that thou wilt bring me to 23
death,
and to the house appointed for all living.

"Yet does not one in a heap of ruins 24
stretch out his hand,
and in his disaster cry for help?[n]

Did not I weep for him whose day was 25
hard?
Was not my soul grieved for the poor?

But when I looked for good, evil came; 26
and when I waited for light, darkness
came.

My heart is in turmoil, and is never still; 27
days of affliction come to meet me.

I go about blackened, but not by the sun; 28
I stand up in the assembly, and cry for
help.

---

[h] Heb *ground yesterday waste*   [i] Heb *my feet*   [j] Cn: Heb *helps*   [k] Cn: Heb *like*
[l] Gk: Heb *my garment is disfigured*   [m] One Heb Ms and Vg: Heb lacks *not*   [n] Cn: Heb obscure

I am a brother of jackals,
and a companion of ostriches.
My skin turns black and falls from me,
and my bones burn with heat.
My lyre is turned to mourning,
and my pipe to the voice of those who
weep.

1 "I have made a covenant with my eyes;
how then could I look upon a virgin?
2 What would be my portion from God
above,
and my heritage from the Almighty on
high?
3 Does not calamity befall the unrighteous,
and disaster the workers of iniquity?
4 Does not he see my ways,
and number all my steps?

5 "If I have walked with falsehood,
and my foot has hastened to deceit;
6 (Let me be weighed in a just balance,
and let God know my integrity!)
7 if my step has turned aside from the way,
and my heart has gone after my eyes,
and if any spot has cleaved to my hands;
8 then let me sow, and another eat;
and let what grows for me be rooted out.

9 "If my heart has been enticed to a woman,
and I have lain in wait at my neighbour's door;
10 then let my wife grind for another,
and let others bow down upon her.
11 For that would be a heinous crime;
that would be an iniquity to be punished
by the judges;
12 for that would be a fire which consumes
unto Abaddon,
and it would burn to the root all my
increase.

13 "If I have rejected the cause of my manservant or my maidservant,
when they brought a complaint against
me;
14 what then shall I do when God rises up?
When he makes inquiry, what shall I
answer him?
15 Did not he who made me in the womb
make him?
And did not one fashion us in the
womb?

16 "If I have withheld anything that the poor
desired,
or have caused the eyes of the widow to
fail,
17 or have eaten my morsel alone,

and the fatherless has not eaten of it
18 (for from his youth I reared him as a
father,
and from his mother's womb I guided
him*);
19 if I have seen any one perish for lack of
clothing,
or a poor man without covering;
20 if his loins have not blessed me,
and if he was not warmed with the fleece
of my sheep;
21 if I have raised my hand against the
fatherless,
because I saw help in the gate;
22 then let my shoulder blade fall from my
shoulder,
and let my arm be broken from its
socket.
23 For I was in terror of calamity from God,
and I could not have faced his majesty.

24 "If I have made gold my trust,
or called fine gold my confidence;
25 if I have rejoiced because my wealth was
great,
or because my hand had gotten much;
26 if I have looked at the sun* when it shone,
or the moon moving in splendour,
27 and my heart has been secretly enticed,
and my mouth has kissed my hand;
28 this also would be an iniquity to be
punished by the judges,
for I should have been false to God
above.

29 "If I have rejoiced at the ruin of him that
hated me,
or exulted when evil overtook him
30 (I have not let my mouth sin
by asking for his life with a curse);
31 if the men of my tent have not said,
'Who is there that has not been filled
with his meat?'
32 (the sojourner has not lodged in the
street;
I have opened my doors to the wayfarer);
33 if I have concealed my transgressions from
men,*
by hiding my iniquity in my bosom,
34 because I stood in great fear of the multitude,
and the contempt of families terrified
me,
so that I kept silence, and did not go out
of doors—
35 Oh, that I had one to hear me!
(Here is my signature! let the Almighty
answer me!)

---

* Cn: Heb *for from my youth he grew up to me as a father, and from my mother's womb I guided her*
* Heb *the light*   * Cn: Heb *like men* or *like Adam*

Oh, that I had the indictment written by
  my adversary!
36 Surely I would carry it on my shoulder;
    I would bind it on me as a crown;
37 I would give him an account of all my
    steps;
    like a prince I would approach him.

38 "If my land has cried out against me,
    and its furrows have wept together;
39 if I have eaten its yield without payment,
    and caused the death of its owners;
40 let thorns grow instead of wheat,
    and foul weeds instead of barley."

The words of Job are ended.

ELIHU'S INTRUSION

32 So these three men ceased to answer Job,
  because he was righteous in his own eyes.
2 Then Eli′hu the son of Bar′achel the Buzite,
  of the family of Ram, became angry. He was
  angry at Job because he justified himself
3 rather than God; he was angry also at Job's
  three friends because they had found no
  answer, although they had declared Job to be
4 in the wrong. Now Eli′hu had waited to
  speak to Job because they were older than
5 he. And when Eli′hu saw that there was no
  answer in the mouth of these three men, he
  became angry.
6 And Eli′hu the son of Bar′achel the Buzite
  answered:
  "I AM young in years,
    and you are aged;
  therefore I was timid and afraid
    to declare my opinion to you.
7 I said, 'Let days speak,
    and many years teach wisdom.'
8 But it is the spirit in a man,
    the breath of the Almighty,
    that makes him understand.
9 It is not the old[r] that are wise,
    nor the aged that understand what is
    right.
10 Therefore I say, 'Listen to me;
    let me also declare my opinion.'

11 "Behold, I waited for your words,
    I listened for your wise sayings,
    while you searched out what to say.
12 I gave you my attention,
    and, behold, there was none that con-
    futed Job,
    or that answered his words, among you.
13 Beware lest you say, 'We have found
    wisdom;
    God may vanquish him, not man.'
14 He has not directed his words against me,

and I will not answer him with your
  speeches.

"They are discomfited, they answer no 15
  more;
  they have not a word to say.
And shall I wait, because they do not 16
  speak,
  because they stand there, and answer no
  more?
I also will give my answer; 17
  I also will declare my opinion.
For I am full of words, 18
  the spirit within me constrains me.
Behold, my heart is like wine that has no 19
  vent;
  like new wineskins, it is ready to burst.
I must speak, that I may find relief; 20
  I must open my lips and answer.
I will not show partiality to any person 21
  or use flattery toward any man.
For I do not know how to flatter, 22
  else would my Maker soon put an end to
  me.

"But now, hear my speech, O Job, 33
  and listen to all my words.
Behold, I open my mouth; 2
  the tongue in my mouth speaks.
My words declare the uprightness of my 3
  heart,
  and what my lips know they speak
  sincerely.
The spirit of God has made me, 4
  and the breath of the Almighty gives me
  life.
Answer me, if you can; 5
  set your words in order before me; take
  your stand.
Behold, I am toward God as you are; 6
  I too was formed from a piece of clay.
Behold, no fear of me need terrify you; 7
  my pressure will not be heavy upon
  you.

"Surely, you have spoken in my hearing, 8
  and I have heard the sound of your
  words.
You say, 'I am clean, without trans- 9
  gression;
  I am pure, and there is no inquity in me.
Behold, he finds occasions against me, 10
  he counts me as his enemy;
he puts my feet in the stocks, 11
  and watches all my paths.'

"Behold, in this you are not right. I will 12
  answer you.
  God is greater than man.
Why do you contend against him, 13

r Gk Syr Vg: Heb many

saying, 'He will answer none of my[s]
words'?

4 For God speaks in one way,
and in two, though man does not perceive it.

5 In a dream, in a vision of the night,
when deep sleep falls upon men,
while they slumber on their beds,

6 then he opens the ears of men,
and terrifies them with warnings,

7 that he may turn man aside from his
deed,
and cut off[t] pride from man;

18 he keeps back his soul from the Pit,
his life from perishing by the sword.

19 "Man is also chastened with pain upon his
bed,
and with continual strife in his bones;

20 so that his life loathes bread,
and his appetite dainty food.

21 His flesh is so wasted away that it cannot
be seen;
and his bones which were not seen stick
out.

22 His soul draws near the Pit,
and his life to those who bring death.

23 If there be for him an angel,
a mediator, one of the thousand,
to declare to man what is right for him;

24 and he is gracious to him, and says,
'Deliver him from going down into the
Pit,
I have found a ransom;

25 let his flesh become fresh with youth;
let him return to the days of his youthful
vigour';

26 then man prays to God, and he accepts
him,
he comes into his presence with joy.
He recounts[u] to men his salvation,

27 and he sings before men, and says:
'I sinned, and perverted what was right,
and it was not requited to me.

28 He has redeemed my soul from going
down into the Pit,
and my life shall see the light.'

29 "Behold, God does all these things,
twice, three times, with a man,

30 to bring back his soul from the Pit,
that he may see the light of life.[v]

31 Give heed, O Job, listen to me;
be silent, and I will speak.

32 If you have anything to say, answer
me;
speak, for I desire to justify you.

33 If not, listen to me;
be silent, and I will teach you wisdom."

Then Eli′hu said:

34

2 "Hear my words, you wise men,
and give ear to me, you who know;

3 for the ear tests words
as the palate tastes food.

4 Let us choose what is right;
let us determine among ourselves what
is good.

5 For Job has said, 'I am innocent,
and God has taken away my right;

6 in spite of my right I am counted a liar;
my wound is incurable, though I am
without transgression.'

7 What man is like Job,
who drinks up scoffing like water,

8 who goes in company with evildoers
and walks with wicked men?

9 For he has said, 'It profits a man nothing
that he should take delight in God.'

10 "Therefore, hear me, you men of understanding,
far be it from God that he should do
wickedness,
and from the Almighty that he should
do wrong.

11 For according to the work of a man he will
requite him,
and according to his ways he will make it
befall him.

12 Of a truth, God will not do wickedly,
and the Almighty will not pervert justice.

13 Who gave him charge over the earth
and who laid on him[w] the whole world?

14 If he should take back his spirit[x] to
himself,
and gather to himself his breath,

15 all flesh would perish together,
and man would return to dust.

16 "If you have understanding, hear this;
listen to what I say.

17 Shall one who hates justice govern?
Will you condemn him who is righteous
and mighty,

18 who says to a king, 'Worthless one,'
and to nobles, 'Wicked man';

19 who shows no partiality to princes,
nor regards the rich more than the poor,
for they are all the work of his hands?

20 In a moment they die;
at midnight the people are shaken and
pass away,
and the mighty are taken away by no
human hand.

21 "For his eyes are upon the ways of a man,
and he sees all his steps.

---

[s] Compare Gk: Heb *his*   [t] Cn: Heb *hide*   [u] Cn: Heb *returns*
[v] Syr: Heb *to be lighted with the light of life*   [w] Heb lacks *on him*   [x] Heb *his heart his spirit*

22 There is no gloom or deep darkness
where evildoers may hide themselves.
23 For he has not appointed a time[y] for any
man
to go before God in judgment.
24 He shatters the mighty without investigation,
and sets others in their place.
25 Thus, knowing their works,
he overturns them in the night,
and they are crushed.
26 He strikes them for their wickedness
in the sight of men,
27 because they turned aside from following
him,
and had no regard for any of his ways,
28 so that they caused the cry of the poor to
come to him,
and he heard the cry of the afflicted—
29 When he is quiet, who can condemn?
When he hides his face, who can behold
him,
whether it be a nation or a man?—
30 that a godless man should not reign,
that he should not ensnare the people.

31 "For has any one said to God,
'I have borne chastisement; I will not
offend any more;
32 teach me what I do not see;
if I have done iniquity, I will do it no
more'?
33 Will he then make requital to suit you,
because you reject it?
For you must choose, and not I;
therefore declare what you know.
34 Men of understanding will say to me,
and the wise man who hears me will say:
35 'Job speaks without knowledge,
his words are without insight.'
36 Would that Job were tried to the end,
because he answers like wicked men.
37 For he adds rebellion to his sin;
he claps his hands among us,
and multiplies his words against God."

35 And Eli′hu said:
2 "Do you think this to be just?
Do you say, 'It is my right before God,'
3 that you ask, 'What advantage have I?
How am I better off than if I had
sinned?'
4 I will answer you
and your friends with you.
5 Look at the heavens, and see;
and behold the clouds, which are higher
than you.
6 If you have sinned, what do you accomplish against him?

And if your transgressions are multiplied, what do you do to him?
7 If you are righteous, what do you give to
him;
or what does he receive from your
hand?
8 Your wickedness concerns a man like
yourself,
and your righteousness a son of man.

9 "Because of the multitude of oppressions
people cry out;
they call for help because of the arm of
the mighty.
10 But none says, 'Where is God my Maker,
who gives songs in the night,

11 who teaches us more than the beasts of the
earth,
and makes us wiser than the birds of the
air?'
12 There they cry out, but he does not
answer,
because of the pride of evil men.
13 Surely God does not hear an empty cry,
nor does the Almighty regard it.
14 How much less when you say that you do
not see him,
that the case is before him, and you are
waiting for him!
15 And now, because his anger does not
punish,
and he does not greatly heed transgression,[a]
16 Job opens his mouth in empty talk,
he multiplies words without knowledge."

And Eli′hu continued, and said: **36**
2 "Bear with me a little, and I will show you,
for I have yet something to say on God's
behalf.
3 I will fetch my knowledge from afar,
and ascribe righteousness to my Maker.
4 For truly my words are not false;
one who is perfect in knowledge is with
you.

5 "Behold, God is mighty, and does not
despise any;

---

[y] Cn: Heb *yet*   [z] The Hebrew of verses 29–33 is obscure
[a] Theodotion Symmachus Compare Vg: The meaning of the Hebrew word is uncertain
35.6–8: Job 22.2–3.

he is mighty in strength of understanding.

6 He does not keep the wicked alive,
but gives the afflicted their right.

7 He does not withdraw his eyes from the righteous,
but with kings upon the throne
he sets them for ever, and they are exalted.

8 And if they are bound in fetters
and caught in the cords of affliction,

9 then he declares to them their work
and their transgressions, that they are behaving arrogantly.

10 He opens their ears to instruction,
and commands that they return from iniquity.

11 If they hearken and serve him,
they complete their days in prosperity,
and their years in pleasantness.

12 But if they do not hearken, they perish by the sword,
and die without knowledge.

13 "The godless in heart cherish anger;
they do not cry for help when he binds them.

14 They die in youth,
and their life ends in shame.[b]

15 He delivers the afflicted by their affliction,
and opens their ear by adversity.

16 He also allured you out of distress
into a broad place where there was no cramping,
and what was set on your table was full of fatness.

17 "But you are full of the judgment on the wicked;
judgment and justice seize you.

18 Beware lest wrath entice you into scoffing;
and let not the greatness of the ransom turn you aside.

19 Will your cry avail to keep you from distress,
or all the force of your strength?

20 Do not long for the night,
when peoples are cut off in their place.

21 Take heed, do not turn to iniquity,
for this you have chosen rather than affliction.

22 Behold, God is exalted in his power;
who is a teacher like him?

23 Who has prescribed for him his way,
or who can say, 'Thou hast done wrong'?

24 "Remember to extol his work,
of which men have sung.

25 All men have looked on it;
man beholds it from afar.

26 Behold, God is great, and we know him not;
the number of his years is unsearchable.

27 For he draws up the drops of water,
he[c] distils his mist in rain

28 which the skies pour down,
and drop upon man abundantly.

29 Can any one understand the spreading of the clouds,
the thunderings of his pavilion?

30 Behold, he scatters his lightning about him,
and covers the roots of the sea.

31 For by these he judges peoples;
he gives food in abundance.

32 He covers his hands with the lightning,
and commands it to strike the mark.

33 Its crashing declares concerning him,
who is jealous with anger against iniquity.

37 "At this also my heart trembles,
and leaps out of its place.

2 Hearken to the thunder of his voice
and the rumbling that comes from his mouth.

3 Under the whole heaven he lets it go,
and his lightning to the corners of the earth.

4 After it his voice roars;
he thunders with his majestic voice
and he does not restrain the lightnings[d]
when his voice is heard.

5 God thunders wondrously with his voice;
he does great things which we cannot comprehend.

6 For to the snow he says, 'Fall on the earth';
and to the shower and the rain,[e]
'Be strong.'

7 He seals up the hand of every man,
that all men may know his work.[f]

8 Then the beasts go into their lairs,
and remain in their dens.

9 From its chamber comes the whirlwind,
and cold from the scattering winds.

10 By the breath of God ice is given,
and the broad waters are frozen fast.

11 He loads the thick cloud with moisture;
the clouds scatter his lightning.

12 They turn round and round by his guidance,
to accomplish all that he commands them
on the face of the habitable world.

13 Whether for correction, or for his land,
or for love, he causes it to happen.

b Heb *among the cult prostitutes*   c Cn: Heb *they distil*   d Heb *them*
e Cn Compare Syr: Heb *shower of rain and shower of rains*
f Vg Compare Syr Tg: Heb *that all men whom he has made may know it*

14 "Hear this, O Job;
    stop and consider the wondrous works
    of God.
15 Do you know how God lays his command
    upon them,
    and causes the lightning of his cloud to
    shine ?
16 Do you know the balancings of the clouds,
    the wondrous works of him who is
    perfect in knowledge,
17 you whose garments are hot
    when the earth is still because of the
    south wind ?
18 Can you, like him, spread out the skies,
    hard as a molten mirror ?
19 Teach us what we shall say to him;
    we cannot draw up our case because of
    darkness.
20 Shall it be told him that I would speak ?
    Did a man ever wish that he would be
    swallowed up ?

21 "And now men cannot look on the light
    when it is bright in the skies,
    when the wind has passed and cleared
    them.
22 Out of the north comes golden splendour;
    God is clothed with terrible majesty.
23 The Almighty—we cannot find him;
    he is great in power and justice,
    and abundant righteousness he will not
    violate.
24 Therefore men fear him;
    he does not regard any who are wise in
    their own conceit."

THE LORD ANSWERS JOB

38 Then the LORD answered Job out of the
whirlwind:
2 "WHO is this that darkens counsel by
    words without knowledge ?
3 Gird up your loins like a man,
    I will question you, and you shall
    declare to me.

4 "Where were you when I laid the founda-
    tion of the earth ?
    Tell me, if you have understanding.
5 Who determined its measurements—surely
    you know!
    Or who stretched the line upon it ?
6 On what were its bases sunk,
    or who laid its cornerstone,
7 when the morning stars sang together,
    and all the sons of God shouted for joy ?

8 "Or who shut in the sea with doors,
    when it burst forth from the womb;

9 when I made clouds its garment,
    and thick darkness its swaddling band,
10 and prescribed bounds for it,
    and set bars and doors,
11 and said, 'Thus far shall you come, and no
    farther,
    and here shall your proud waves be
    stayed' ?

12 "Have you commanded the morning since
    your days began,
    and caused the dawn to know its place,
13 that it might take hold of the skirts of the
    earth,
    and the wicked be shaken out of it ?
14 It is changed like clay under the seal,
    and it is dyed⁹ like a garment.
15 From the wicked their light is withheld,
    and their uplifted arm is broken.

16 "Have you entered into the springs of the
    sea,
    or walked in the recesses of the deep ?
17 Have the gates of death been revealed to
    you,
    or have you seen the gates of deep
    darkness ?
18 Have you comprehended the expanse of
    the earth ?
    Declare, if you know all this.

19 "Where is the way to the dwelling of
    light,
    and where is the place of darkness,
20 that you may take it to its territory
    and that you may discern the paths to its
    home ?
21 You know, for you were born then,
    and the number of your days is great!

22 "Have you entered the storehouses of the
    snow,
    or have you seen the storehouses of the
    hail,
23 which I have reserved for the time of
    trouble,
    for the day of battle and war ?
24 What is the way to the place where the
    light is distributed,
    or where the east wind is scattered upon
    the earth ?

25 "Who has cleft a channel for the torrents
    of rain,
    and a way for the thunderbolt,
26 to bring rain on a land where no man is,
    on the desert in which there is no man;
27 to satisfy the waste and desolate land,
    and to make the ground put forth grass ?

⁹ Cn: Heb *they stand forth*
38.10: Jer 5.22.

"Has the rain a father,
    or who has begotten the drops of dew?
From whose womb did the ice come forth,
    and who has given birth to the hoarfrost
        of heaven?
The waters become hard like stone,
    and the face of the deep is frozen.

"Can you bind the chains of the Plei′ades,
    or loose the cords of Orion?
Can you lead forth the Maz′zaroth in their
        season,
    or can you guide the Bear with its
        children?
Do you know the ordinances of the
        heavens?
    Can you establish their rule on the
        earth?

"Can you lift up your voice to the clouds,
    that a flood of waters may cover you?
Can you send forth lightnings, that they
        may go
    and say to you, 'Here we are'?
Who has put wisdom in the clouds,[h]
    or given understanding to the mists?[h]
Who can number the clouds by wisdom?
    Or who can tilt the waterskins of the
        heavens,
when the dust runs into a mass
    and the clods cleave fast together?

"Can you hunt the prey for the lion,
    or satisfy the appetite of the young
        lions,
when they crouch in their dens,
    or lie in wait in their covert?
Who provides for the raven its prey,
    when its young ones cry to God,
    and wander about for lack of food?

"Do you know when the mountain goats
        bring forth?
    Do you observe the calving of the
        hinds?
Can you number the months that they
        fulfil,
    and do you know the time when they
        bring forth,
when they crouch, bring forth their
        offspring,
    and are delivered of their young?
Their young ones become strong, they
        grow up in the open;
    they go forth, and do not return to them.

"Who has let the wild ass go free?
    Who has loosed the bonds of the swift
        ass,

Goat and kids   Job 39, 1

to whom I have given the steppe for his 6
        home,
    and the salt land for his dwelling place?
He scorns the tumult of the city;   7
    he hears not the shouts of the driver.
He ranges the mountains as his pasture,   8
    and he searches after every green thing.

"Is the wild ox willing to serve you?   9
    Will he spend the night at your crib?
Can you bind him in the furrow with   10
        ropes,
    or will he harrow the valleys after you?
Will you depend on him because his   11
        strength is great,
    and will you leave to him your labour?
Do you have faith in him that he will   12
        return,
    and bring your grain to your threshing
        floor?[i]

"The wings of the ostrich wave proudly;   13
    but are they the pinions and plumage of
        love?[j]
For she leaves her eggs to the earth,   14
    and lets them be warmed on the ground,
forgetting that a foot may crush them,   15
    and that the wild beast may trample
        them.
She deals cruelly with her young,   16
    as if they were not hers;
    though her labour be in vain, yet she has
        no fear;
because God has made her forget wisdom,   17
    and given her no share in under-
        standing.
When she rouses herself to flee,[k]   18
    she laughs at the horse and his rider.

"Do you give the horse his might?   19

[h] The meaning of the Hebrew word is uncertain   [i] Heb *your grain and your threshing floor*
[j] Heb obscure   [k] Heb obscure

Do you clothe his neck with strength?[1]

20 Do you make him leap like the locust?
His majestic snorting is terrible.

21 He paws[m] in the valley, and exults in his strength;
he goes out to meet the weapons.

22 He laughs at fear, and is not dismayed;
he does not turn back from the sword.

23 Upon him rattle the quiver,
the flashing spear and the javelin.

24 With fierceness and rage he swallows the ground;
he cannot stand still at the sound of the trumpet.

25 When the trumpet sounds, he says 'Aha!'
He smells the battle from afar,
the thunder of the captains, and the shouting.

26 "Is it by your wisdom that the hawk soars,
and spreads his wings toward the south?

27 Is it at your command that the eagle mounts up
and makes his nest on high?

28 On the rock he dwells and makes his home
in the fastness of the rocky crag.

29 Thence he spies out the prey;
his eyes behold it afar off.

30 His young ones suck up blood;
and where the slain are, there is he."

40 And the LORD said to Job:

2 "Shall a faultfinder contend with the Almighty?
He who argues with God, let him answer it."

JOB'S REPLY

3 Then Job answered the LORD:

4 "BEHOLD, I am of small account;
what shall I answer thee?
I lay my hand on my mouth.

5 I have spoken once, and I will not answer;
twice, but I will proceed no further."

THE LORD'S ANSWER

6 Then the LORD answered Job out of the whirlwind:

7 "GIRD up your loins like a man;
I will question you, and you declare to me.

8 Will you even put me in the wrong?
Will you condemn me that you may be justified?

9 Have you an arm like God,
and can you thunder with a voice like his?

"Deck yourself with majesty and dignity;
clothe yourself with glory and splendour.

Pour forth the overflowings of your anger,
and look on every one that is proud, and abase him.

Look on every one that is proud, and bring him low;
and tread down the wicked where they stand.

Hide them all in the dust together;
bind their faces in the world below.[n]

Then will I also acknowledge to you,
that your own right hand can give you victory.

"Behold, Be′hemoth,[o]
which I made as I made you;
he eats grass like an ox.

Behold, his strength in his loins,
and his power in the muscles of his belly.

He makes his tail stiff like a cedar;
the sinews of his thighs are knit together.

His bones are tubes of bronze,
his limbs like bars of iron.

"He is the first of the works[p] of God;
let him who made him bring near his sword!

For the mountains yield food for him
where all the wild beasts play.

Under the lotus plants he lies,
in the covert of the reeds and in the marsh.

For his shade the lotus trees cover him;
the willows of the brook surround him.

Behold, if the river is turbulent he is not frightened;
he is confident though Jordan rushes against his mouth.

Can one take him with hooks,[q]
or pierce his nose with a snare?

"Can you draw out Leviathan[s] with a fishhook,
or press down his tongue with a cord?

Can you put a rope in his nose,
or pierce his jaw with a hook?

Will he make many supplications to you?

---

[l] Tg: The meaning of the Hebrew word is obscure   [m] Gk Syr Vg: Heb *they dig*   [n] Heb *hidden place*
[o] Or *the hippopotamus*   [p] Heb *ways*   [q] Cn: Heb *in his eyes*   [r] Ch 40.25 in Heb   [s] Or *the crocodile*

Will he speak to you soft words?
Will he make a covenant with you
    to take him for your servant for ever?
Will you play with him as with a bird,
    or will you put him on leash for your
    maidens?
Will traders bargain over him?
    Will they divide him up among the
    merchants?
Can you fill his skin with harpoons,
    or his head with fishing spears?
Lay hands on him;
    think of the battle; you will not do it
    again!
Behold, the hope of a man is dis-
    appointed;
    he is laid low even at the sight of him.
No one is so fierce that he dares to stir him
    up.
    Who then is he that can stand before
    me?
Who has given to me,[u] that I should repay
    him?
    Whatever is under the whole heaven is
    mine.

"I will not keep silence concerning his
    limbs,
    or his mighty strength, or his goodly
    frame.
Who can strip off his outer garment?
    Who can penetrate his double coat of
    mail?[v]
Who can open the doors of his face?
    Round about his teeth is terror.
His back[w] is made of rows of shields,
    shut up closely as with a seal.
One is so near to another
    that no air can come between them.
They are joined one to another;
    they clasp each other and cannot be
    separated.
His sneezings flash forth light,
    and his eyes are like the eyelids of the
    dawn.
Out of his mouth go flaming torches;
    sparks of fire leap forth.

Out of his nostrils comes forth smoke,   20
    as from a boiling pot and burning
    rushes.
His breath kindles coals,   21
    and a flame comes forth from his
    mouth.
In his neck abides strength,   22
    and terror dances before him.
The folds of his flesh cleave together,   23
    firmly cast upon him and immovable.
His heart is hard as a stone,   24
    hard as the nether millstone.
When he raises himself up the mighty[x] are 25
    afraid;
    at the crashing they are beside them-
    selves.
Though the sword reaches him, it does not   26
    avail;
    nor the spear, the dart, or the javelin.
He counts iron as straw,   27
    and bronze as rotten wood.
The arrow cannot make him flee;   28
    for him slingstones are turned to
    stubble.
Clubs are counted as stubble;   29
    he laughs at the rattle of javelins.
His underparts are like sharp potsherds;   30
    he spreads himself like a threshing
    sledge on the mire.
He makes the deep boil like a pot;   31
    he makes the sea like a pot of ointment.
Behind him he leaves a shining wake;   32
    one would think the deep to be hoary.
Upon earth there is not his like,   33
    a creature without fear.
He beholds everything that is high;   34
    he is king over all the sons of pride."

JOB'S REPLY

Then Job answered the LORD: 42
    "I KNOW that thou canst do all things,   2
        and that no purpose of thine can be
        thwarted.
'Who is this that hides counsel without   3
    knowledge?'
Therefore I have uttered what I did not
    understand,
    things too wonderful for me,
    which I did not know.
'Hear, and I will speak;   4
    I will question you, and you declare to
    me.'
I had heard of thee by the hearing of the   5
    ear,
    but now my eye sees thee;
therefore I despise myself,   6
    and repent in dust and ashes."

---

[t] Ch 41.1 in Heb   [u] The meaning of the Hebrew is uncertain
[v] Gk: Heb bridle   [w] Cn Compare Gk Vg: Heb pride   [x] Or gods
41.11: Rom 11.35.

THE EPILOGUE

7 AFTER the Lord had spoken these words to Job, the Lord said to El'iphaz the Te'manite: "My wrath is kindled against you and against your two friends; for you have not spoken of me what is right, as my servant
8 Job has. Now therefore take seven bulls and seven rams, and go to my servant Job, and offer up for yourselves a burnt offering; and my servant Job shall pray for you, for I will accept his prayer not to deal with you according to your folly; for you have not spoken of me what is right, as my servant Job
9 has." So El'iphaz the Te'manite and Bildad the Shuhite and Zophar the Na'amathite went and did what the Lord had told them; and the Lord accepted Job's prayer.
10 And the Lord restored the fortunes of Job, when he had prayed for his friends; and the Lord gave Job twice as much as he had
11 before. Then came to him all his brothers and sisters and all who had known him before, and ate bread with him in his house; and they showed him sympathy and comforted him for all the evil that the Lord had brought upon him; and each of them gave him a piece of money *y* and a ring of gold. And the Lord blessed the latter days of Job more than his beginning; and he had fourteen thousand sheep, six thousand camels, a thousand yoke of oxen, and a thousand she-asses. He had also seven sons and three daughters. And he called the name of the first Jemi'mah; and the name of the second Kezi'ah; and the name of the third Ker'en-hap'puch. And in all the land there were no women so fair as Job's daughters; and their father gave them inheritance among their brothers. And after this Job lived a hundred and forty years, and saw his sons, and his sons' sons, four generations. And Job died, an old man, and full of days.

y Heb *qesitah*

THE PSALMS

BOOK I

1 BLESSED is the man
who walks not in the counsel of the
wicked,
nor stands in the way of sinners,
nor sits in the seat of scoffers;
2 but his delight is in the law of the LORD,
and on his law he meditates day and night.
3 He is like a tree
planted by streams of water,
that yields its fruit in its season,
and its leaf does not wither.
In all that he does, he prospers.

4 The wicked are not so,
but are like chaff which the wind drives
away.
5 Therefore the wicked will not stand in the
judgment,
nor sinners in the congregation of the
righteous;
6 for the LORD knows the way of the righteous,
but the way of the wicked will perish.

2 WHY do the nations conspire,
and the peoples plot in vain?
2 The kings of the earth set themselves,
and the rulers take counsel together,
against the LORD and his anointed, saying,
3 "Let us burst their bonds asunder,
and cast their cords from us."

4 He who sits in the heavens laughs;
the LORD has them in derision.
5 Then he will speak to them in his wrath,
and terrify them in his fury, saying,
6 "I have set my king
on Zion, my holy hill."

7 I will tell of the decree of the LORD:
He said to me, "You are my son,
today I have begotten you.
8 Ask of me, and I will make the nations your
heritage,
and the ends of the earth your possession.
9 You shall break them with a rod of iron,
and dash them in pieces like a potter's
vessel."

10 Now therefore, O kings, be wise;
be warned, O rulers of the earth.
11 Serve the LORD with fear,
with trembling kiss his feet,[a]

lest he be angry, and you perish in the way; 12
for his wrath is quickly kindled.

Blessed are all who take refuge in him.

A Psalm of David, when he fled from Absalom his son.
3 O LORD, how many are my foes!
Many are rising against me;
many are saying of me, 2
there is no help for him in God. *Selah*

But thou, O LORD, art a shield about me, 3
my glory, and the lifter of my head.
I cry aloud to the LORD, 4
and he answers me from his holy hill.
Selah

I lie down and sleep; 5
I wake again, for the LORD sustains me.
I am not afraid of ten thousands of people 6
who have set themselves against me round
about.

Arise, O LORD! 7
Deliver me, O my God!
For thou dost smite all my enemies on the
cheek,
thou dost break the teeth of the wicked.
Deliverance belongs to the LORD; 8
thy blessing be upon thy people! *Selah*

a Cn: The Hebrew of this line is uncertain
1.1–3: Jer 17.7–8.   2.1–2: Acts 4.25–26.   2.7: Mt 3.17; Acts 13.33; Heb 1.5; 5.5; 2 Pet 1.17.
2.8–9: Rev 2.26; 12.5; 19.15.

To the choirmaster: with stringed instruments.
A Psalm of David.

4 ANSWER me when I call, O God of my
right!
Thou hast given me room when I was in
distress.
Be gracious to me, and hear my prayer.

2 O men, how long shall my honour suffer
shame?
How long will you love vain words, and
seek after lies?   *Selah*
3 But know that the LORD has set apart the
godly for himself;
the LORD hears when I call to him.

4 Be angry, but sin not;
commune with your own hearts on your
beds, and be silent.   *Selah*
5 Offer right sacrifices,
and put your trust in the LORD.

6 There are many who say, "O that we might
see some good!
Lift up the light of thy countenance upon
us, O LORD!"
7 Thou hast put more joy in my heart
than they have when their grain and wine
abound.

8 In peace I will both lie down and sleep;
for thou alone, O LORD, makest me dwell
in safety.

To the choirmaster: for the flutes.
A Psalm of David.

5 GIVE ear to my words, O LORD;
give heed to my groaning.
2 Hearken to the sound of my cry,
my King and my God,
for to thee do I pray.
3 O LORD, in the morning thou dost hear my
voice;
in the morning I prepare a sacrifice for
thee, and watch.

4 For thou art not a God who delights in
wickedness;
evil may not sojourn with thee.
5 The boastful may not stand before thy eyes;
thou hatest all evildoers.
6 Thou destroyest those who speak lies;
the LORD abhors bloodthirsty and deceitful men.

7 But I through the abundance of thy steadfast
love
will enter thy house,

I will worship toward thy holy temple in the
fear of thee.
Lead me, O LORD, in thy righteousness
because of my enemies;
make thy way straight before me.

For there is no truth in their mouth;
their heart is destruction,
their throat is an open sepulchre,
they flatter with their tongue.
Make them bear their guilt, O God;
let them fall by their own counsels;
because of their many transgressions cast
them out,
for they have rebelled against thee.

But let all who take refuge in thee rejoice,
let them ever sing for joy;
and do thou defend them,
that those who love thy name may exult in
thee.
For thou dost bless the righteous, O LORD;
thou dost cover him with favour as with a
shield.

To the choirmaster: with stringed instruments;
according to the Sheminith. A Psalm of David.

6 O LORD, rebuke me not in thy anger,
nor chasten me in thy wrath.
Be gracious to me, O LORD, for I am 2
languishing;
O LORD, heal me, for my bones are
troubled.
My soul also is sorely troubled.   3
But thou, O LORD—how long?

Turn, O LORD, save my life;   4
deliver me for the sake of thy steadfast
love.
For in death there is no remembrance of 5
thee;
in Sheol who can give thee praise?

I am weary with my moaning;   6
every night I flood my bed with tears;
I drench my couch with my weeping.
My eye wastes away because of grief,   7
it grows weak because of all my foes.

Depart from me, all you workers of evil; 8
for the LORD has heard the sound of my
weeping.
The LORD has heard my supplication;   9
the LORD accepts my prayer.
All my enemies shall be ashamed and sorely 10
troubled;
they shall turn back, and be put to shame
in a moment.

4.4: Eph 4.26.   5.9: Rom 3.13.   6.8: Mt 7.23; Lk 13.27.

A Shiggaion of David, which he sang to the LORD
concerning Cush a Benjaminite.

7 O LORD my God, in thee do I take
refuge;
save me from all my pursuers, and
deliver me,
lest like a lion they rend me,
dragging me away, with none to rescue.

O LORD my God, if I have done this,
if there is wrong in my hands,
if I have requited my friend with evil
or plundered my enemy without cause,
let the enemy pursue me and overtake me,
and let him trample my life to the
ground,
and lay my soul in the dust.   *Selah*

6 Arise, O LORD, in thy anger,
lift thyself up against the fury of my
enemies;
awake, O my God;[b] thou hast appointed a
judgment.
7 Let the assembly of the peoples be gathered
about thee;
and over it take thy seat[c] on high.
8 The LORD judges the peoples;
judge me, O LORD, according to my
righteousness
and according to the integrity that is in
me.

9 O let the evil of the wicked come to an
end,
but establish thou the righteous,
thou who triest the minds and hearts,
thou righteous God.
10 My shield is with God,
who saves the upright in heart.
11 God is a righteous judge,
and a God who has indignation every day.

12 If a man[d] does not repent, God[d] will whet his
sword;
he has bent and strung his bow;
13 he has prepared his deadly weapons,
making his arrows fiery shafts.
14 Behold, the wicked man conceives evil,
and is pregnant with mischief,
and brings forth lies.
15 He makes a pit, digging it out,
and falls into the hole which he has made.
16 His mischief returns upon his own head,
and on his own pate his violence descends.

17 I will give to the LORD the thanks due to his
righteousness,
and I will sing praise to the name of the
LORD, the Most High.

To the choirmaster: according to the Gittith.
A Psalm of David.

8 O LORD, our Lord,
how majestic is thy name in all the
earth!

Thou whose glory above the heavens is
chanted
by the mouth of babes and infants, 2
thou hast founded a bulwark because of thy
foes,
to still the enemy and the avenger.

When I look at thy heavens, the work of thy 3
fingers,

the moon and the stars which thou hast
established;
what is man that thou art mindful of him, 4
and the son of man that thou dost care for
him?

Yet thou hast made him little less than God, 5
and dost crown him with glory and
honour.
Thou hast given him dominion over the 6
works of thy hands;
thou hast put all things under his feet,
all sheep and oxen, 7
and also the beasts of the field,
the birds of the air, and the fish of the sea, 8
whatever passes along the paths of the sea.

O LORD, our Lord, 9
how majestic is thy name in all the earth!

b Or for me   c Cn: Heb return   d Heb he
7.9: Rev 2.23.   8.2: Mt 21.16.   8.4-6: Job 7.17-18; Ps 144.3; Heb 2.6-8.   8.6: 1 Cor 15.27; Eph 1.22.

To the choirmaster: according to Muth-labben.
A Psalm of David.

9 I WILL give thanks to the LORD with my
whole heart;
I will tell of all thy wonderful deeds.
2 I will be glad and exult in thee,
I will sing praise to thy name, O Most
High.

3 When my enemies turned back,
they stumbled and perished before thee.
4 For thou hast maintained my just cause;
thou hast sat on the throne giving
righteous judgment.
5 Thou hast rebuked the nations, thou hast
destroyed the wicked;
thou hast blotted out their name for ever
and ever.
6 The enemy have vanished in everlasting
ruins;
their cities thou hast rooted out;
the very memory of them has perished.

7 But the LORD sits enthroned for ever,
he has established his throne for judgment;
8 and he judges the world with righteousness,
he judges the peoples with equity.

9 The LORD is a stronghold for the oppressed,
a stronghold in times of trouble.
10 And those who know thy name put their
trust in thee,
for thou, O LORD, hast not forsaken those
who seek thee.

11 Sing praises to the LORD, who dwells in
Zion!
Tell among the peoples his deeds!
12 For he who avenges blood is mindful of
them;
he does not forget the cry of the afflicted.

13 Be gracious to me, O LORD!
Behold what I suffer from those who hate
me,
O thou who liftest me up from the gates of
death,
14 that I may recount all thy praises,
that in the gates of the daughter of Zion
I may rejoice in thy deliverance.

15 The nations have sunk in the pit which they
made;
in the net which they hid has their own
foot been caught.
16 The LORD has made himself known, he has
executed judgment;

the wicked are snared in the work of their
own hands.   *Higgaion. Selah*

The wicked shall depart to Sheol,
all the nations that forget God.

For the needy shall not always be forgotten,
and the hope of the poor shall not perish
for ever.

Arise, O LORD! Let not man prevail;
let the nations be judged before thee!
Put them in fear, O LORD!
Let the nations know that they are but
men!   *Selah*

10 WHY dost thou stand afar off, O
LORD?
Why dost thou hide thyself in times of
trouble?
In arrogance the wicked hotly pursue the
poor;
let them be caught in the schemes which
they have devised.

For the wicked boasts of the desires of his
heart,
and the man greedy for gain curses and
renounces the LORD.
In the pride of his countenance the wicked
does not seek him;
all his thoughts are, "There is no God."

His ways prosper at all times;
thy judgments are on high, out of his sight;
as for all his foes, he puffs at them.
He thinks in his heart, "I shall not be moved;
throughout all generations I shall not meet
adversity."

His mouth is filled with cursing and deceit
and oppression;
under his tongue are mischief and iniquity.
He sits in ambush in the villages;
in hiding places he murders the innocent.

His eyes stealthily watch for the hapless,
he lurks in secret like a lion in his covert;
he lurks that he may seize the poor,
he seizes the poor when he draws him into
his net.

The hapless is crushed, sinks down,
and falls by his might.
He thinks in his heart, "God has forgotten,
he has hidden his face, he will never see
it."

Arise, O LORD; O God, lift up thy hand;
forget not the afflicted.

9.8: Acts 17.31. 10.7: Rom 3.14.

Why does the wicked renounce God,
and say in his heart, "Thou wilt not call to
account"?

Thou dost see; yea, thou dost note trouble
and vexation,
that thou mayest take it into thy hands;
the hapless commits himself to thee;
thou hast been the helper of the fatherless.

Break thou the arm of the wicked and
evildoer;
seek out his wickedness till thou find none.
, The Lord is king for ever and ever;
the nations shall perish from his land.

, O Lord, thou wilt hear the desire of the
meek;
thou wilt strengthen their heart,
thou wilt incline thy ear
8 to do justice to the fatherless and the
oppressed,
so that man who is of the earth may strike
terror no more.

To the choirmaster. Of David.

11 IN the Lord I take refuge;
how can you say to me,
"Flee like a bird to the mountains;*
2 for lo, the wicked bend the bow,
they have fitted their arrow to the string,
to shoot in the dark at the upright in
heart;
3 if the foundations are destroyed,
what can the righteous do"?

4 The Lord is in his holy temple,
the Lord's throne is in heaven;
his eyes behold, his eyelids test, the
children of men.
5 The Lord tests the righteous and the wicked,
and his soul hates him that loves violence.
6 On the wicked he will rain coals of fire and
brimstone;
a scorching wind shall be the portion of
their cup.
7 For the Lord is righteous, he loves righteous
deeds;
the upright shall behold his face.

*To the choirmaster: according to the Sheminith.
A Psalm of David.*

12 HELP, Lord; for there is no longer
any that is godly;
for the faithful have vanished from among
the sons of men.
2 Every one utters lies to his neighbour;
with flattering lips and a double heart they
speak.

May the Lord cut off all flattering lips,   3
the tongue that makes great boasts,
those who say, "With our tongue we will 4
prevail,
our lips are with us; who is our master?"

"Because the poor are despoiled, because the 5
needy groan,
I will now arise," says the Lord;
"I will place him in the safety for which he
longs."
The promises of the Lord are promises that 6
are pure,
silver refined in a furnace on the ground,
purified seven times.

Do thou, O Lord, protect us,   7
guard us ever from this generation.
On every side the wicked prowl,   8
as vileness is exalted among the sons of
men.

To the choirmaster. A Psalm of David.

13 HOW long, O Lord? Wilt thou forget
me for ever?
How long wilt thou hide thy face from
me?
How long must I bear pain* in my soul,   2
and have sorrow in my heart all the day?
How long shall my enemy be exalted over
me?

Consider and answer me, O Lord my God; 3
lighten my eyes, lest I sleep the sleep of
death;
lest my enemy say, "I have prevailed over 4
him";
lest my foes rejoice because I am shaken.

But I have trusted in thy steadfast love;   5
my heart shall rejoice in thy salvation.
I will sing to the Lord,   6
because he has dealt bountifully with
me.

To the choirmaster. Of David.

14 THE fool says in his heart,
"There is no God."
They are corrupt, they do abominable
deeds,
there is none that does good.

The Lord looks down from heaven upon the 2
children of men,
to see if there are any that act wisely,
that seek after God.

They have all gone astray, they are all alike 3
corrupt;

---

* Gk Syr Jerome Tg: Heb *flee to your mountain, O bird*   † Syr: Heb *hold counsels*
14.1–3: Rom 3.10–12.   14.1–7: Ps 53.1–6.

there is none that does good,
no, not one.

4 Have they no knowledge, all the evildoers
who eat up my people as they eat bread,
and do not call upon the LORD?

5 There they shall be in great terror,
for God is with the generation of the
righteous.
6 You would confound the plans of the poor,
but the LORD is his refuge.

7 O that deliverance for Israel would come out
of Zion!
When the LORD restores the fortunes of his
people,
Jacob shall rejoice, Israel shall be glad.

A Psalm of David.

15 O LORD, who shall sojourn in thy
tent?
Who shall dwell on thy holy hill?

2 He who walks blamelessly, and does what is
right,
and speaks truth from his heart;
3 who does not slander with his tongue,
and does no evil to his friend,
nor takes up a reproach against his neighbour;
4 in whose eyes a reprobate is despised,
but who honours those who fear the LORD;
who swears to his own hurt and does not
change;
5 who does not put out his money at interest,
and does not take a bribe against the
innocent.

He who does these things shall never be
moved.

A Miktam of David.

16 PRESERVE me, O God, for in thee I
take refuge.
2 I say to the LORD, "Thou art my Lord;
I have no good apart from thee."[g]

3 As for the saints in the land, they are the
noble,
in whom is all my delight.

4 Those who choose another god multiply
their sorrows;[h]
their libations of blood I will not pour out
or take their names upon my lips.

5 The LORD is my chosen portion and my cup;
thou holdest my lot.

The lines have fallen for me in pleasant 6
places;
yea, I have a goodly heritage.

I bless the LORD who gives me counsel; 7
in the night also my heart instructs me.
I keep the LORD always before me; 8
because he is at my right hand, I shall not
be moved.

Therefore my heart is glad, and my soul 9
rejoices;
my body also dwells secure.
For thou dost not give me up to Sheol, 10
or let thy godly one see the Pit.

Thou dost show me the path of life; 11
in thy presence there is fullness of joy,
in thy right hand are pleasures for evermore.

A Prayer of David.

17 HEAR a just cause, O LORD;
attend to my cry!
Give ear to my prayer from lips free of
deceit!
From thee let my vindication come! 2
Let thy eyes see the right!

If thou triest my heart, if thou visitest me by 3
night,
if thou testest me, thou wilt find no
wickedness in me;
my mouth does not transgress.
With regard to the works of men, 4
by the word of thy lips
I have avoided the ways of the violent.
My steps have held fast to thy paths, 5
my feet have not slipped.

I call upon thee, for thou wilt answer me, 6
O God;
incline thy ear to me, hear my words.
Wondrously show thy steadfast love, 7
O saviour of those who seek refuge
from their adversaries at thy right hand.

Keep me as the apple of the eye; 8
hide me in the shadow of thy wings,
from the wicked who despoil me, 9
my deadly enemies who surround me.

They close their hearts to pity; 10
with their mouths they speak arrogantly.
They track me down; now they surround 11
me;
they set their eyes to cast me to the
ground.

---

[g] Jerome Tg: The meaning of the Hebrew is uncertain
16.8-11: Acts 2.25-28, 31. **16.10:** Acts 13.35.

[h] Cn: The meaning of the Hebrew is uncertain

They are like a lion eager to tear,
as a young lion lurking in ambush.

Arise, O LORD! confront them, overthrow them!
Deliver my life from the wicked by thy sword,
from men by thy hand, O LORD,
from men whose portion in life is of the world.
May their belly be filled with what thou hast stored up for them;
may their children have more than enough;
may they leave something over to their babes.

As for me, I shall behold thy face in righteousness;
when I awake, I shall be satisfied with beholding thy form.

To the choirmaster. A Psalm of David the servant of the LORD, who addressed the words of this song to the LORD on the day when the LORD delivered him from the hand of all his enemies, and from the hand of Saul. He said:

18 I LOVE thee, O LORD, my strength.
The LORD is my rock, and my fortress, and my deliverer,
my God, my rock, in whom I take refuge,
my shield, and the horn of my salvation, my stronghold.
3 I call upon the LORD, who is worthy to be praised,
and I am saved from my enemies.

4 The cords of death encompassed me,
the torrents of perdition assailed me;
5 the cords of Sheol entangled me,
the snares of death confronted me.

6 In my distress I called upon the LORD;
to my God I cried for help.
From his temple he heard my voice,
and my cry to him reached his ears.

7 Then the earth reeled and rocked;
the foundations also of the mountains trembled
and quaked, because he was angry.
8 Smoke went up from his nostrils,
and devouring fire from his mouth;
glowing coals flamed forth from him.
9 He bowed the heavens, and came down;
thick darkness was under his feet.
10 He rode on a cherub, and flew;
he came swiftly upon the wings of the wind.

He made darkness his covering around 11 him,
his canopy thick clouds dark with water.
Out of the brightness before him   12
there broke through his clouds
hailstones and coals of fire.
The LORD also thundered in the heavens, 13
and the Most High uttered his voice,
hailstones and coals of fire.
And he sent out his arrows, and scattered 14 them;
he flashed forth lightnings, and routed them.
Then the channels of the sea were seen,   15
and the foundations of the world were laid bare,
at thy rebuke, O LORD,
at the blast of the breath of thy nostrils.

He reached from on high, he took me,   16
he drew me out of many waters.
He delivered me from my strong enemy,   17
and from those who hated me;
for they were too mighty for me.
They came upon me in the day of my 18 calamity;
but the LORD was my stay.
He brought me forth into a broad 19 place;
he delivered me, because he delighted in me.

The LORD rewarded me according to my 20 righteousness;
according to the cleanness of my hands he recompensed me.
For I have kept the ways of the LORD,   21
and have not wickedly departed from my God.
For all his ordinances were before me,   22
and his statutes I did not put away from me.
I was blameless before him,   23
and I kept myself from guilt.
Therefore the LORD has recompensed me 24
according to my righteousness,
according to the cleanness of my hands in his sight.
With the loyal thou dost show thyself 25 loyal;
with the blameless man thou dost show thyself blameless;
with the pure thou dost show thyself 26 pure;
and with the crooked thou dost show thyself perverse.
For thou dost deliver a humble people;   27
but the haughty eyes thou dost bring down.
Yea, thou dost light my lamp;   28

18.1–50: 2 Sam 22.2–51.

the LORD my God
lightens my dark-
ness.

29 Yea, by thee I can
crush a troop;
and by my God
I can leap over a
wall.

30 This God—his way is perfect;
the promise of the LORD proves true;
he is a shield for all those who take refuge
in him.

31 For who is God, but the LORD?
And who is a rock, except our God?—

32 the God who girded me with strength,
and made my way safe.

33 He made my feet like hinds' feet,
and set me secure on the heights.

34 He trains my hands for war,
so that my arms can bend a bow of bronze.

35 Thou hast given me the shield of thy
salvation,
and thy right hand supported me,
and thy help*i* made me great.

36 Thou didst give a wide place for my steps
under me,
and my feet did not slip.

37 I pursued my enemies and overtook them;
and did not turn back till they were
consumed.

38 I thrust them through, so that they were not
able to rise;
they fell under my feet.

39 For thou didst gird me with strength for the
battle;
thou didst make my assailants sink under
me.

40 Thou didst make my enemies turn their
backs to me,
and those who hated me I destroyed.

41 They cried for help, but there was none to
save,
they cried to the LORD, but he did not
answer them.

42 I beat them fine as dust before the wind;
I cast them out like the mire of the
streets.

43 Thou didst deliver me from strife with the
peoples;*j*
thou didst make me the head of the
nations;
people whom I had not known served me.

44 As soon as they heard of me they obeyed
me;
foreigners came cringing to me.

45 Foreigners lost heart,
and came trembling out of their fastnesses.

The LORD lives; and blessed be my rock,
and exalted be the God of my salvation,
the God who gave me vengeance
and subdued peoples under me;
who delivered me from my enemies;
yea, thou didst exalt me above my adversaries;
thou didst deliver me from men of violence.

For this I will extol thee, O LORD, among the
nations,
and sing praises to thy name.
Great triumphs he gives to his king,   5
and shows steadfast love to his anointed,
to David and his descendants for ever.

To the choirmaster. A Psalm of David.

19 THE heavens are telling the glory of
God;
and the firmament proclaims his handi-
work.
Day to day pours forth speech,   2
and night to night declares knowledge.
There is no speech, nor are there words;   3
their voice is not heard;
yet their voice*k* goes out through all the 4
earth,
and their words to the end of the world.

In them he has set a tent for the sun,
which comes forth like a bridegroom leaving 5
his chamber,
and like a strong man runs its course with
joy.
Its rising is from the end of the heavens,   6
and its circuit to the end of them;
and there is nothing hid from its heat.

The law of the LORD is perfect,   7
reviving the soul;
the testimony of the LORD is sure,
making wise the simple;
the precepts of the LORD are right,   8
rejoicing the heart;
the commandment of the LORD is pure,
enlightening the eyes;
the fear of the LORD is clean,   9
enduring for ever;
the ordinances of the LORD are true,
and righteous altogether.
More to be desired are they than gold,   10
even much fine gold;
sweeter also than honey
and drippings of the honeycomb.

Moreover by them is thy servant warned;   11
in keeping them there is great reward.
But who can discern his errors?   12

i Or *gentleness*   *j* Gk Tg‡ Heb *people*   *k* Gk Jerome Compare Syr: Heb *line*
18.49: Rom 15.9.   **19.4:** Rom 10.18.

Clear thou me from hidden faults.

3 Keep back thy servant also from presumptuous sins;
let them not have dominion over me!
Then I shall be blameless,
and innocent of great transgression.

4 Let the words of my mouth and the meditation of my heart
be acceptable in thy sight,
O Lord, my rock and my redeemer.

To the choirmaster. A Psalm of David.

20 THE Lord answer you in the day of trouble!
The name of the God of Jacob protect you!

2 May he send you help from the sanctuary,
and give you support from Zion!

3 May he remember all your offerings,
and regard with favour your burnt sacrifices! *Selah*

4 May he grant you your heart's desire,
and fulfil all your plans!

5 May we shout for joy over your victory,

and in the name of our God set up our banners!
May the Lord fulfil all your petitions!

6 Now I know that the Lord will help his anointed;
he will answer him from his holy heaven
with mighty victories by his right hand.

7 Some boast of chariots, and some of horses;
but we boast of the name of the Lord our God.

8 They will collapse and fall;
but we shall rise and stand upright.

9 Give victory to the king, O Lord;
answer us when we call.[l]

To the choirmaster. A Psalm of David.

21 IN thy strength the king rejoices, O Lord;
and in thy help how greatly he exults!

2 Thou hast given him his heart's desire,

and hast not withheld the request of his lips. *Selah*

3 For thou dost meet him with goodly blessings;
thou dost set a crown of fine gold upon his head.

4 He asked life of thee; thou gavest it to him,
length of days for ever and ever.

5 His glory is great through thy help;
splendour and majesty thou dost bestow upon him.

6 Yea, thou dost make him most blessed for ever;
thou dost make him glad with the joy of thy presence.

7 For the king trusts in the Lord;
and through the steadfast love of the Most High he shall not be moved.

8 Your hand will find out all your enemies;
your right hand will find out those who hate you.

9 You will make them as a blazing oven when you appear.
The Lord will swallow them up in his wrath;
and fire will consume them.

10 You will destroy their offspring from the earth,
and their children from among the sons of men.

11 If they plan evil against you,
if they devise mischief, they will not succeed.

12 For you will put them to flight;
you will aim at their faces with your bows.

13 Be exalted, O Lord, in thy strength!
We will sing and praise thy power.

To the choirmaster: according to the Hind of the Dawn.
A Psalm of David.

22 MY God, my God, why hast thou forsaken me?
Why art thou so far from helping me, from the words of my groaning?

2 O my God, I cry by day, but thou dost not answer;
and by night, but find no rest.

3 Yet thou art holy,
enthroned on the praises of Israel.

4 In thee our fathers trusted;
they trusted, and thou didst deliver them.

5 To thee they cried, and were saved;
in thee they trusted, and were not disappointed.

---

l Gk: Heb *give victory, O* Lord, *let the King answer us when we call*
22.1: Mt 27.46; Mk 15.34.

6 But I am a worm, and no man;
     scorned by men, and despised by the
     people.
7 All who see me mock at me,
     they make mouths at me, they wag their
     heads;
8 "He committed his cause to the LORD; let
     him deliver him,
     let him rescue him, for he delights in
     him!"

9 Yet thou art he who took me from the womb;
     thou didst keep me safe upon my mother's
     breasts.
10 Upon thee was I cast from my birth,
     and since my mother bore me thou hast
     been my God.
11 Be not far from me,
     for trouble is near
     and there is none to help.

12 Many bulls encompass me,
     strong bulls of Bashan surround me;
13 they open wide their mouths at me,
     like a ravening and roaring lion.

14 I am poured out like water,
     and all my bones are out of joint;
     my heart is like wax,
     it is melted within my breast;
15 my strength is dried up like a potsherd,
     and my tongue cleaves to my jaws;
     thou dost lay me in the dust of death.

16 Yea, dogs are round about me;
     a company of evildoers encircle me;
     they have pierced[m] my hands and feet—
17 I can count all my bones—
     they stare and gloat over me;
18 they divide my garments among them,
     and for my raiment they cast lots.

19 But thou, O LORD, be not far off!
     O thou my help, hasten to my aid!
20 Deliver my soul from the sword,
     my life[n] from the power of the dog!
21 Save me from the mouth of the lion,
     my afflicted soul[o] from the horns of the
     wild oxen!

22 I will tell of thy name to my brethren;
     in the midst of the congregation I will
     praise thee:
23 You who fear the LORD, praise him!
     all you sons of Jacob, glorify him,
     and stand in awe of him, all you sons of
     Israel!

For he has not despised or abhorred 2
     the affliction of the afflicted;
and he has not hid his face from him,
     but has heard, when he cried to him.

From thee comes my praise in the great 2
     congregation;
my vows I will pay before those who fear
     him.
The afflicted[p] shall eat and be satisfied; 2
     those who seek him shall praise the LORD!
May your hearts live for ever!

All the ends of the earth shall remember 2
     and turn to the LORD;
and all the families of the nations
     shall worship before him.[q]
For dominion belongs to the LORD, 2
     and he rules over the nations.

Yea, to him[r] shall all the proud of the earth 2
     bow down;
     before him shall bow all who go down to
     the dust,
     and he who cannot keep himself alive.
Posterity shall serve him; 3
     men shall tell of the Lord to the coming
     generation,
and proclaim his deliverance to a people yet 3
     unborn,
     that he has wrought it.

A Psalm of David.

23 THE LORD is my shepherd, I shall not
     want;
he makes me lie down in green pastures. 2
He leads me beside still waters;[s]
     he restores my soul.[t] 3
He leads me in paths of righteousness[u]
     for his name's sake.

---

m Gk Syr Jerome: Heb *like a lion*   n Heb *my only one*   o Gk Syr: Heb *thou hast answered me*
p Or *poor*   q Gk Syr Jerome: Heb *thee*   r Cn: Heb *they have eaten and*   s Heb *the waters of rest*
t Or *life*   u Or *right paths*
22.7–8: Mt 27.39, 43; Mk 15.29; Lk 23.35.   22.18: Mt 27.35; Mk 15.24; Lk 23.34; Jn 19.24.
22.22: Heb 2.12.   23.2: Rev 7.17.

Even though I walk through the valley of the
    shadow of death,[v]
I fear no evil;
for thou art with me;
    thy rod and thy staff,
    they comfort me.

Thou preparest a table before me
    in the presence of my enemies;
thou anointest my head with oil,
    my cup overflows.
Surely[w] goodness and mercy[x] shall follow
    me
all the days of my life;
and I shall dwell in the house of the LORD
    for ever.[y]

A Psalm of David.

24 THE earth is the LORD's and the
    fullness thereof,
    the world and those who dwell therein;
for he has founded it upon the seas,
    and established it upon the rivers.

Who shall ascend the hill of the LORD?
    And who shall stand in his holy place?
He who has clean hands and a pure heart,
    who does not lift up his soul to what is
    false,
    and does not swear deceitfully.
He will receive blessing from the LORD,
    and vindication from the God of his
    salvation.
Such is the generation of those who seek
    him,
    who seek the face of the God of Jacob.[z]
                                    Selah

Lift up your heads, O gates!
    and be lifted up, O ancient doors!
    that the King of glory may come in.
Who is the King of glory?
    The LORD, strong and mighty,
    the LORD, mighty in battle!
Lift up your heads, O gates!
    and be lifted up,[a] O ancient doors!
    that the King of glory may come in.
Who is this King of glory?
    The LORD of hosts,
    he is the King of glory!   *Selah*

A Psalm of David.

25 TO thee, O LORD, I lift up my soul.
    O my God, in thee I trust,
let me not be put to shame;
let not my enemies exult over me.

Yea, let none that wait for thee be put to 3
    shame;
    let them be ashamed who are wantonly
    treacherous.

Make me to know thy ways, O LORD;   4
    teach me thy paths.
Lead me in thy truth, and teach me,   5
    for thou art the God of my salvation;
    for thee I wait all the day long.

Be mindful of thy mercy, O LORD,   6
    and of thy steadfast love,
    for they have been from of old.
Remember not the sins of my youth, or 7
    my transgressions;
    according to thy steadfast love remember
    me,
    for thy goodness' sake, O LORD!

Good and upright is the LORD;   8
    therefore he instructs sinners in the way.
He leads the humble in what is right,   9
    and teaches the humble his way.
All the paths of the LORD are steadfast love 10
    and faithfulness,
    for those who keep his covenant and his
    testimonies.

For thy name's sake, O LORD,   11
    pardon my guilt, for it is great.
Who is the man that fears the LORD?   12
    Him will he instruct in the way that he
    should choose.
He himself shall abide in prosperity,   13
    and his children shall possess the land.
The friendship of the LORD is for those who 14
    fear him,
    and he makes known to them his covenant.
My eyes are ever toward the LORD,   15
    for he will pluck my feet out of the net.
Turn thou to me, and be gracious to me; 16
    for I am lonely and afflicted.
Relieve the troubles of my heart,   17
    and bring me[b] out of my distresses.
Consider my affliction and my trouble,   18
    and forgive all my sins.

Consider how many are my foes,   19
    and with what violent hatred they hate me.
Oh guard my life, and deliver me;   20
    let me not be put to shame, for I take
    refuge in thee.
May integrity and uprightness preserve me, 21
    for I wait for thee.

Redeem Israel, O God,   22
    out of all his troubles.

v Or *the valley of deep darkness*   w Or *Only*   x Or *kindness*   y Or *as long as I live*
z Gk Syr: Heb *thy face, O Jacob*   a Gk Syr Jerome Tg Compare verse 7: Heb *lift up*
b Or *The troubles of my heart are enlarged; bring me*
24.1: 1 Cor 10.26.   24.4: Mt 5.8.

A Psalm of David.

26 VINDICATE me, O LORD,
for I have walked in my integrity,
and I have trusted in the LORD without
wavering.

2 Prove me, O LORD, and try me;
test my heart and my mind.

3 For thy steadfast love is before my eyes,
and I walk in faithfulness to thee.[c]

4 I do not sit with false men,
nor do I consort with dissemblers;

5 I hate the company of evildoers,
and I will not sit with the wicked.

6 I wash my hands in innocence,
and go about thy altar, O LORD,

7 singing aloud a song of thanksgiving,
and telling all thy wondrous deeds.

8 O LORD, I love the habitation of thy house,
and the place where thy glory dwells.

9 Sweep me not away with sinners,
nor my life with bloodthirsty men,

10 men in whose hands are evil devices,
and whose right hands are full of bribes.

11 But as for me, I walk in my integrity;
redeem me, and be gracious to me.

12 My foot stands on level ground;
in the great congregation I will bless the
LORD.

A Psalm of David.

27 THE LORD is my light and my salvation;
whom shall I fear?
The LORD is the stronghold[d] of my life;
of whom shall I be afraid?

2 When evildoers assail me,
uttering slanders against me,[e]
my adversaries and foes,
they shall stumble and fall.

3 Though a host encamp against me,
my heart shall not fear;
though war arise against me,
yet I will be confident.

4 One thing have I asked of the LORD,
that will I seek after;
that I may dwell in the house of the LORD
all the days of my life,
to behold the beauty of the LORD,
and to inquire in his temple.

5 For he will hide me in his shelter
in the day of trouble;

he will conceal me under the cover of his
tent,
he will set me high upon a rock.

And now my head shall be lifted up   6
above my enemies round about me;
and I will offer in his tent
sacrifices with shouts of joy;
I will sing and make melody to the LORD.

Hear, O LORD, when I cry aloud,   7
be gracious to me and answer me!
Thou hast said, "Seek ye my face."   8
My heart says to thee,
"Thy face, LORD, do I seek."
Hide not thy face from me.   9

Turn not thy servant away in anger,
thou who hast been my help.
Cast me not off, forsake me not,
O God of my salvation!
For my father and my mother have forsaken 10
me,
but the LORD will take me up.

Teach me thy way, O LORD;   1
and lead me on a level path
because of my enemies.
Give me not up to the will of my adversaries; 1
for false witnesses have risen against me,
and they breathe out violence.

I believe that I shall see the goodness of the 1
LORD
in the land of the living!
Wait for the LORD;   1
be strong, and let your heart take courage;
yea, wait for the LORD!

A Psalm of David.

28 TO thee, O LORD, I call;
my rock, be not deaf to me,
lest, if thou be silent to me,
I become like those who go down to the
Pit.
Hear the voice of my supplication,   2
as I cry to thee for help,
as I lift up my hands
toward thy most holy sanctuary.[f]

Take me not off with the wicked,   3
with those who are workers of evil,
who speak peace with their neighbours,
while mischief is in their hearts.
Requite them according to their work,   4
and according to the evil of their deeds;
requite them according to the work of their
hands;
render them their due reward.

---

[c] Or *in thy faithfulness*   [d] Or *refuge*   [e] Heb *to eat up my flesh*   [f] Heb *thy innermost sanctuary*

5 Because they do not regard the works of the
  LORD,
    or the work of his hands,
  he will break them down and build them up
    no more.

6 Blessed be the LORD!
    for he has heard the voice of my suppli-
    cations.
7 The LORD is my strength and my shield;
    in him my heart trusts;
  so I am helped, and my heart exults,
    and with my song I give thanks to him.
8 The LORD is the strength of his people,
    he is the saving refuge of his anointed.
9 O save thy people, and bless thy heritage;
    be thou their shepherd, and carry them for
    ever.

A Psalm of David.

29 ASCRIBE to the LORD, O heavenly
    beings,*ᵍ*
  ascribe to the LORD glory and strength.
2 Ascribe to the LORD the glory of his name;
    worship the LORD in holy array.

3 The voice of the LORD is upon the waters;
    the God of glory thunders,
    the LORD, upon many waters.
4 The voice of the LORD is powerful,
    the voice of the LORD is full of majesty.

5 The voice of the LORD breaks the cedars,
    the LORD breaks the cedars of Lebanon.
6 He makes Lebanon to skip like a calf,
    and Sirion like a young wild ox.

7 The voice of the LORD flashes forth flames of
    fire.
8 The voice of the LORD shakes the wilderness,
    the LORD shakes the wilderness of Kadesh.

9 The voice of the LORD makes the oaks to
    whirl,*ʰ*
    and strips the forest bare;
    and in his temple all cry, "Glory!"

10 The LORD sits enthroned over the flood;
    the LORD sits enthroned as king for ever.
11 May the LORD give strength to his people!
    May the LORD bless his people with peace!

A Psalm of David.
A song at the dedication of the temple.

30 I WILL extol thee, O LORD, for thou
    hast drawn me up,
  and hast not let my foes rejoice over me.
2 O LORD my God, I cried to thee for help,
    and thou hast healed me.

O LORD, thou hast brought up my soul from 3
  Sheol,
    restored me to life from among those gone
    down to the Pit.*ⁱ*

Sing praises to the LORD, O you his saints, 4
    and give thanks to his holy name.
For his anger is but for a moment, 5
    and his favour is for a lifetime.
Weeping may tarry for the night,
    but joy comes with the morning.

As for me, I said in my prosperity, 6
    "I shall never be moved."
By thy favour, O LORD, 7
    thou hadst established me as a strong
    mountain;
  thou didst hide thy face,
    I was dismayed.

To thee, O LORD, I cried; 8
    and to the LORD I made supplication:
"What profit is there in my death, 9
    if I go down to the Pit?
Will the dust praise thee?
    Will it tell of thy faithfulness?
Hear, O LORD, and be gracious to me! 10
    O LORD, be thou my helper!"

Thou hast turned for me my mourning into 11
    dancing;
    thou hast loosed my sackcloth
    and girded me with gladness,
that my soul*ʲ* may praise thee and not be 12
    silent.
    O LORD my God, I will give thanks to thee
    for ever.

To the choirmaster. A Psalm of David.

31 IN thee, O LORD, do I seek refuge;
    let me never be put to shame;
  in thy righteousness deliver me!
Incline thy ear to me, 2
    rescue me speedily!
Be thou a rock of refuge for me,
    a strong fortress to save me!

Yea, thou art my rock and my fortress; 3
    for thy name's sake lead me and guide me,
take me out of the net which is hidden for 4
    me,
    for thou art my refuge.
Into thy hand I commit my spirit; 5
    thou hast redeemed me, O LORD, faithful
    God.

Thou hatest*ᵏ* those who pay regard to vain 6
    idols;
    but I trust in the LORD.

ᵍ Heb *sons of gods*   *ʰ* Or *makes the hinds to calve*   *ⁱ* Or *that I should not go down to the Pit*
ʲ Heb *that glory*   *ᵏ* With one Heb Ms Gk Syr Jerome: Heb *I hate*
31.5: Lk 23.46.

7 I will rejoice and be glad for thy steadfast
love,
   because thou hast seen my affliction,
   thou hast taken heed of my adversities,
8 and hast not delivered me into the hand of
the enemy;
   thou hast set my feet in a broad place.

9 Be gracious to me, O Lord, for I am in
distress;
   my eye is wasted from grief,
   my soul and my body also.
10 For my life is spent with sorrow,
   and my years with sighing;
   my strength fails because of my misery,[l]
   and my bones waste away.

11 I am the scorn of all my adversaries,
   a horror[m] to my neighbours,
   an object of dread to my acquaintances;
   those who see me in the street flee from
me.
12 I have passed out of mind like one who is
dead;
   I have become like a broken vessel.
13 Yea, I hear the whispering of many—
   terror on every side!—
   as they scheme together against me,
   as they plot to take my life.

14 But I trust in thee, O Lord,
   I say, "Thou art my God."

15 My times are in thy hand;
   deliver me from the hand of my enemies
and persecutors!
16 Let thy face shine on thy servant;
   save me in thy steadfast love!
17 Let me not be put to shame, O Lord,
   for I call on thee;
   let the wicked be put to shame,
   let them go dumbfounded to Sheol.
18 Let the lying lips be dumb,
   which speak insolently against the righteous
in pride and contempt.

19 O how abundant is thy goodness,
   which thou hast laid up for those who fear
thee,
   and wrought for those who take refuge in
thee,

in the sight of the sons of men!
In the covert of thy presence thou hidest 2
them
   from the plots of men;
   thou holdest them safe under thy shelter
   from the strife of tongues.

Blessed be the Lord,   2
   for he has wondrously shown his steadfast
love to me
   when I was beset as in a besieged city.
I had said in my alarm,   2
   "I am driven far[n] from thy sight."
But thou didst hear my supplications,
   when I cried to thee for help.

Love the Lord, all you his saints!
   The Lord preserves the faithful,
   but abundantly requites him who acts
haughtily.
Be strong, and let your heart take courage, 2
   all you who wait for the Lord!

A Psalm of David. A Maskil.

32 BLESSED is he whose transgression
   is forgiven,
   whose sin is covered.
Blessed is the man to whom the Lord 2
   imputes no iniquity,
   and in whose spirit there is no deceit.

When I declared not my sin, my body wasted 3
away
   through my groaning all day long.
For day and night thy hand was heavy upon 4
me;
   my strength was dried up[o] as by the heat of
summer.   *Selah*

I acknowledged my sin to thee,   5
   and I did not hide my iniquity;
I said, "I will confess my transgressions to
the Lord";
   then thou didst forgive the guilt of my
sin.   *Selah*

Therefore let every one who is godly   6
   offer prayer to thee;
at a time of distress,[p] in the rush of great
waters,
   they shall not reach him.
Thou art a hiding place for me,   7
   thou preservest me from trouble;
   thou dost encompass me with deliverance.[q]
                      Selah

I will instruct you and teach you   8
   the way you should go;

---

[l] Gk Syr: Heb *iniquity*   [m] Cn: Heb *exceedingly*   [n] Another reading is *cut off*
[o] Heb obscure   [p] Cn: Heb *at a time of finding only*   [q] Cn: Heb *shouts of deliverance*
31.13: Jer 6.25; 20.3, 10; 46.5; 49.29.   **32.1-2:** Rom 4.7-8.

I will counsel you with my eye upon you.
9 Be not like a horse or a mule, without
    understanding,
    which must be curbed with bit and bridle,
    else it will not keep with you.

10 Many are the pangs of the wicked;
    but steadfast love surrounds him who
        trusts in the LORD.
11 Be glad in the LORD, and rejoice, O
        righteous,
    and shout for joy, all you upright in heart!

33 REJOICE in the LORD, O you righteous!
Praise befits the upright.
2 Praise the LORD with the lyre,
    make melody to him with the harp of ten
        strings!
3 Sing to him a new song,
    play skilfully on the strings, with loud
        shouts.

4 For the word of the LORD is upright;
    and all his work is done in faithfulness.
5 He loves righteousness and justice;
    the earth is full of the steadfast love of the
        LORD.

6 By the word of the LORD the heavens were
        made,
    and all their host by the breath of his
        mouth.
7 He gathered the waters of the sea as in a
        bottle;
    he put the deeps in storehouses.

8 Let all the earth fear the LORD,
    let all the inhabitants of the world stand in
        awe of him!
9 For he spoke, and it came to be;
    he commanded, and it stood forth.

10 The LORD brings the counsel of the nations
        to naught;
    he frustrates the plans of the peoples.
11 The counsel of the LORD stands for ever,
    the thoughts of his heart to all generations.
12 Blessed is the nation whose God is the LORD,
    the people whom he has chosen as his
        heritage!

13 The LORD looks down from heaven,
    he sees all the sons of men;
14 from where he sits enthroned he looks forth
    on all the inhabitants of the earth,
15 he who fashions the hearts of them all,
    and observes all their deeds.

A king is not saved by his great army;   16
    a warrior is not delivered by his great
        strength.
The war horse is a vain hope for victory,   17

and by its great might it cannot save.

Behold, the eye of the LORD is on those who   18
    fear him,
    on those who hope in his steadfast love,
that he may deliver their soul from death,   19
    and keep them alive in famine.

Our soul waits for the LORD;   20
    he is our help and shield.
Yea, our heart is glad in him,   21
    because we trust in his holy name.
Let thy steadfast love, O LORD, be upon us,   22
    even as we hope in thee.

*A Psalm of David, when he feigned madness before
Abimelech, so that he drove him out, and he went away.*

34 I WILL bless the LORD at all times;
    his praise shall continually be in my
        mouth.
My soul makes its boast in the LORD;   2
    let the afflicted hear and be glad.
O magnify the LORD with me,   3
    and let us exalt his name together!

I sought the LORD, and he answered me,   4
    and delivered me from all my fears.
Look to him, and be radiant;   5
    so your[r] faces shall never be ashamed.
This poor man cried, and the LORD heard   6
    him,
    and saved him out of all his troubles.
The angel of the LORD encamps   7
    around those who fear him, and delivers
        them.
O taste and see that the LORD is good!   8

[r] Gk Syr Jerome: Heb *their*
34.8: 1 Pet 2.3.

Happy is the man who takes refuge in
  him!

9 O fear the LORD, you his saints,
  for those who fear him have no want!
10 The young lions suffer want and hunger;
  but those who seek the LORD lack no good
  thing.

11 Come, O sons, listen to me,
  I will teach you the fear of the LORD.
12 What man is there who desires life,
  and covets many days, that he may enjoy
  good?
13 Keep your tongue from evil,
  and your lips from speaking deceit.
14 Depart from evil, and do good;
  seek peace, and pursue it.

15 The eyes of the LORD are toward the
  righteous,
  and his ears toward their cry.
16 The face of the LORD is against evildoers,
  to cut off the remembrance of them from
  the earth.
17 When the righteous cry for help,
  the LORD hears,
  and delivers them out of all their troubles.
18 The LORD is near to the brokenhearted,
  and saves the crushed in spirit.

19 Many are the afflictions of the righteous;
  but the LORD delivers him out of them all.
20 He keeps all his bones;
  not one of them is broken.
21 Evil shall slay the wicked;
  and those who hate the righteous will be
  condemned.
22 The LORD redeems the life of his servants;
  none of those who take refuge in him will
  be condemned.

A Psalm of David.

35 CONTEND, O LORD, with those who
  contend with me;
  fight against those who fight against me!
2 Take hold of shield and buckler,
  and rise for my help!
3 Draw the spear and javelin
  against my pursuers!
  Say to my soul,
  "I am your deliverance!"

4 Let them be put to shame and dishonour
  who seek after my life!
  Let them be turned back and confounded
  who devise evil against me!
5 Let them be like chaff before the wind,
  with the angel of the LORD driving them on!

Let their way be dark and slippery,   6
  with the angel of the LORD pursuing them!

For without cause they hid their net for me;   7
  without cause they dug a pit[s] for my life.
Let ruin come upon them unawares!   8
And let the net which they hid ensnare them;
  let them fall therein to ruin!

Then my soul shall rejoice in the LORD,   9
  exulting in his deliverance.
All my bones shall say,   10
  "O LORD, who is like thee,
  thou who deliverest the weak
  from him who is too strong for him,
  the weak and needy from him who despoils
  him?"

Malicious witnesses rise up;   11
  they ask me of things that I know not.
They requite me evil for good;   12
  my soul is forlorn.
But I, when they were sick—   13
  I wore sackcloth,
  I afflicted myself with fasting.
I prayed with head bowed[t] on my bosom,
  as though I grieved for my friend or my 14
  brother;
I went about as one who laments his mother,
  bowed down and in mourning.

But at my stumbling they gathered in glee,   15
  they gathered together against me;
cripples whom I knew not
  slandered me without ceasing;
they impiously mocked more and more,[u]   16
  gnashing at me with their teeth.

How long, O LORD, wilt thou look on?   17
  Rescue me from their ravages,
  my life from the lions!
Then I will thank thee in the great congrega-   18
  tion;
  in the mighty throng I will praise thee.

Let not those rejoice over me   19
  who are wrongfully my foes,
and let not those wink the eye
  who hate me without cause.

---

[s] The word *pit* is transposed from the preceding line   [t] Or *My prayer turned back*
[u] Cn Compare Gk: Heb *like the profanest of mockers of a cake*
34.12-16: 1 Pet 3.10-12. 35.19: Ps 69.4; Jn 15.25.

20 For they do not speak peace,
    but against those who are quiet in the land
    they conceive words of deceit.
21 They open wide their mouths against me;
    they say, "Aha, Aha!
    our eyes have seen it!"

22 Thou hast seen, O LORD; be not silent!
    O Lord, be not far from me!
23 Bestir thyself, and awake for my right,
    for my cause, my God and my Lord!
24 Vindicate me, O LORD, my God, according
    to thy righteousness;
    and let them not rejoice over me!
25 Let them not say to themselves,
    "Aha, we have our heart's desire!"
    Let them not say, "We have swallowed him
    up."

26 Let them be put to shame and confusion
    altogether
    who rejoice at my calamity!
    Let them be clothed with shame and dis-
    honour
    who magnify themselves against me!

27 Let those who desire my vindication
    shout for joy and be glad,
    and say evermore,
    "Great is the LORD,
    who delights in the welfare of his servant!"
28 Then my tongue shall tell of thy righteousness
    and of thy praise all the day long.

How precious is thy steadfast love, O God! 7
    The children of men take refuge in the
    shadow of thy wings.
They feast on the abundance of thy house, 8
    and thou givest them drink from the river
    of thy delights.
For with thee is the fountain of life; 9
    in thy light do we see light.

O continue thy steadfast love to those who 10
    know thee,
    and thy salvation to the upright of heart!
Let not the foot of arrogance come upon 11
    me,
    nor the hand of the wicked drive me away.
There the evildoers lie prostrate, 12
    they are thrust down, unable to rise.

*To the choirmaster. A Psalm of David, the servant of
the LORD.*

36

TRANSGRESSION speaks to the
    wicked
deep in his heart;
there is no fear of God
    before his eyes.
2 For he flatters himself in his own eyes
    that his iniquity cannot be found out and
    hated.
3 The words of his mouth are mischief and
    deceit;
    he has ceased to act wisely and do good.
4 He plots mischief while on his bed;
    he sets himself in a way that is not good;
    he spurns not evil.

5 Thy steadfast love, O LORD, extends to the
    heavens,
    thy faithfulness to the clouds.
6 Thy righteousness is like the mountains of
    God,
    thy judgments are like the great deep;
    man and beast thou savest, O LORD.

A Psalm of David.

37

FRET not yourself because of the
    wicked,
    be not envious of wrongdoers!
For they will soon fade like the grass, 2
    and wither like the green herb.

Trust in the LORD, and do good; 3
    so you will dwell in the land, and enjoy
    security.
Take delight in the LORD, 4
    and he will give you the desires of your
    heart.

Commit your way to the LORD; 5
    trust in him, and he will act.
He will bring forth your vindication as the 6
    light,
    and your right as the noonday.

Be still before the LORD, and wait patiently 7
    for him;
    fret not yourself over him who prospers in
    his way,
    over the man who carries out evil devices!

36.1: Rom 3.18.

8 Refrain from anger, and forsake wrath!
  Fret not yourself; it tends only to evil.
9 For the wicked shall be cut off;
  but those who wait for the LORD shall
    possess the land.

10 Yet a little while, and the wicked will be no
    more;
    though you look well at his place, he will
      not be there.
11 But the meek shall possess the land,
    and delight themselves in abundant pros-
      perity.

12 The wicked plots against the righteous,
    and gnashes his teeth at him;
13 but the LORD laughs at the wicked,
    for he sees that his day is coming.

14 The wicked draw the sword and bend their
      bows,
    to bring down the poor and needy,
    to slay those who walk uprightly;
15 their sword shall enter their own heart,
    and their bows shall be broken.

16 Better is a little that the righteous has
    than the abundance of many wicked.
17 For the arms of the wicked shall be broken;
    but the LORD upholds the righteous.

18 The LORD knows the days of the blameless,
    and their heritage will abide for ever;
19 they are not put to shame in evil times,
    in the days of famine they have abundance.
20 But the wicked perish;
    the enemies of the LORD are like the glory
      of the pastures,
    they vanish—like smoke they vanish away.

21 The wicked borrows, and cannot pay back,
    but the righteous is generous and gives;
22 for those blessed by the LORD shall possess
      the land,
    but those cursed by him shall be cut off.

23 The steps of a man are from the LORD,
    and he establishes him in whose way he
      delights;
24 though he fall, he shall not be cast headlong,
    for the LORD is the stay of his hand.

25 I have been young, and now am old;
    yet I have not seen the righteous forsaken
      or his children begging bread.
26 He is ever giving liberally and lending,
    and his children become a blessing.

27 Depart from evil, and do good;

so shall you abide for ever.
For the LORD loves justice;   28
  he will not forsake his saints.

The righteous shall be preserved for ever,
  but the children of the wicked shall be cut
    off.
The righteous shall possess the land,   29
  and dwell upon it for ever.

The mouth of the righteous utters wisdom,   30
  and his tongue speaks justice.
The law of his God is in his heart;   31
  his steps do not slip.

The wicked watches the righteous,   32
  and seeks to slay him.
The LORD will not abandon him to his   33
    power,
  or let him be condemned when he is
    brought to trial.

Wait for the LORD, and keep to his way,   34
  and he will exalt you to possess the land;
  you will look on the destruction of the
    wicked.

I have seen a wicked man overbearing,   35
  and towering like a cedar of Lebanon.*
Again I* passed by, and, lo, he was no more;   36
  though I sought him, he could not be
    found.

Mark the blameless man, and behold the   37
    upright,
  for there is posterity for the man of peace.
But transgressors shall be altogether des-   38
    troyed;
  the posterity of the wicked shall be cut off.

The salvation of the righteous is from the   39
    LORD;
  he is their refuge in the time of trouble.
The LORD helps them and delivers them;   40
  he delivers them from the wicked, and
    saves them,
  because they take refuge in him.

A Psalm of David, for the memorial offering.

38 O LORD, rebuke me not in thy anger,
     nor chasten me in thy wrath!
For thy arrows have sunk into me,   2
  and thy hand has come down on me.

There is no soundness in my flesh   3
  because of thy indignation;
there is no health in my bones
  because of my sin.

*ᵛ Gk: Heb obscure   ʷ Gk Syr Jerome: Heb *he*
37.11: Mt 5.5.

For my iniquities have gone over my head;
 they weigh like a burden too heavy for me.

My wounds grow foul and fester
 because of my foolishness,
I am utterly bowed down and prostrate;
 all the day I go about mourning.
For my loins are filled with burning,
 and there is no soundness in my flesh.
I am utterly spent and crushed;
 I groan because of the tumult of my heart.

Lord, all my longing is known to thee,
 my sighing is not hidden from thee.
My heart throbs, my strength fails me;
 and the light of my eyes—it also has gone
 from me.
My friends and companions stand aloof from
 my plague,
 and my kinsmen stand afar off.

12 Those who seek my life lay their snares,
 those who seek my hurt speak of ruin,
 and meditate treachery all the day long.

13 But I am like a deaf man, I do not hear,
 like a dumb man who does not open his
 mouth.
14 Yea, I am like a man who does not hear,
 and in whose mouth are no rebukes.

15 But for thee, O LORD, do I wait;
 it is thou, O LORD my God, who wilt
 answer.
16 For I pray, "Only let them not rejoice over
 me,
 who boast against me when my foot slips!"

17 For I am ready to fall,
 and my pain is ever with me.
18 I confess my iniquity,
 I am sorry for my sin.
19 Those who are my foes without cause[x] are
 mighty,
 and many are those who hate me wrongfully.
20 Those who render me evil for good
 are my adversaries because I follow after
 good.

21 Do not forsake me, O LORD!
 O my God, be not far from me!
22 Make haste to help me,
 O Lord, my salvation!

To the choirmaster: to Jeduthun. A Psalm of David.

39 I SAID, "I will guard my ways,
 that I may not sin with my tongue;
I will bridle[y] my mouth,
 so long as the wicked are in my presence."

I was dumb and silent,   2
 I held my peace to no avail;
my distress grew worse,
 my heart became hot within me.   3
As I mused, the fire burned;
 then I spoke with my tongue:

"LORD, let me know my end,   4
 and what is the measure of my days;
 let me know how fleeting my life is!
Behold, thou hast made my days a few 5
 handbreadths,
 and my lifetime is as nothing in thy sight.
Surely every man stands as a mere breath!
                                          Selah
Surely man goes about as a shadow!   6
Surely for naught are they in turmoil;
 man heaps up, and knows not who will
 gather!

"And now, Lord, for what do I wait?   7
 My hope is in thee.
Deliver me from all my transgressions.   8
 Make me not the scorn of the fool!
I am dumb, I do not open my mouth;   9
 for it is thou who hast done it.
Remove thy stroke from me;   10
 I am spent by the blows[z] of thy hand.
When thou dost chasten man   11
 with rebukes for sin,
thou dost consume like a moth what is dear
 to him;
 surely every man is a mere breath!   *Selah*

"Hear my prayer, O LORD,   12
 and give ear to my cry;
 hold not thy peace at my tears!
For I am thy passing guest,
 a sojourner, like all my fathers.
Look away from me, that I may know 13
 gladness,
 before I depart and be no more!"

To the choirmaster. A Psalm of David.

40 I WAITED patiently for the LORD;
 he inclined to me and heard my cry.
He drew me up from the desolate pit,[a]   2
 out of the miry bog,
and set my feet upon a rock,
 making my steps secure.
He put a new song in my mouth,   3
 a song of praise to our God.
Many will see and fear,
 and put their trust in the LORD.

Blessed is the man who makes   4
 the LORD his trust,
who does not turn to the proud,
 to those who go astray after false gods!
Thou hast multiplied, O LORD my God,   5

x Cn: Heb living   y Heb muzzle   z Heb hostility   a Cn: Heb pit of tumult

thy wondrous deeds and thy thoughts
toward us;
none can compare with thee!
Were I to proclaim and tell of them,
they would be more than can be numbered.

6 Sacrifice and offering thou dost not desire;
but thou hast given me an open ear.[b]
Burnt offering and sin offering
thou hast not required.
7 Then I said, "Lo, I come;
in the roll of the book it is written of me;
8 I delight to do thy will, O my God;
thy law is within my heart."

9 I have told the glad news of deliverance
in the great congregation;
lo, I have not restrained my lips,
as thou knowest, O LORD.
10 I have not hid thy saving help within my
heart,
I have spoken of thy faithfulness and thy
salvation;
I have not concealed thy steadfast love and
thy faithfulness
from the great congregation.

11 Do not thou, O LORD, withhold
thy mercy from me,
let thy steadfast love and thy faithfulness
ever preserve me!
12 For evils have encompassed me
without number;
my iniquities have overtaken me,
till I cannot see;
they are more than the hairs of my head;
my heart fails me.

13 Be pleased, O LORD, to deliver me!
O LORD, make haste to help me!
14 Let them be put to shame and confusion
altogether
who seek to snatch away my life;
let them be turned back and brought to
dishonour
who desire my hurt!
15 Let them be appalled because of their
shame
who say to me, "Aha, Aha!"

16 But may all who seek thee
rejoice and be glad in thee;
may those who love thy salvation
say continually, "Great is the LORD!"
17 As for me, I am poor and needy;
but the Lord takes thought for me.
Thou art my help and my deliverer;
do not tarry, O my God!

To the choirmaster. A Psalm of David.

41 BLESSED is he who considers the
poor![c]
The LORD delivers him in the day of
trouble;
the LORD protects him and keeps him alive;
he is called blessed in the land;
thou dost not give him up to the will of his
enemies.
The LORD sustains him on his sickbed;
in his illness thou healest all his infirmities.[d]

As for me, I said, "O LORD, be gracious to
me;
heal me, for I have sinned against thee!"
My enemies say of me in malice:
"When will he die, and his name perish?"
And when one comes to see me, he utters
empty words,
while his heart gathers mischief;
when he goes out, he tells it abroad.
All who hate me whisper together about me;
they imagine the worst for me.

They say, "A deadly thing has fastened upon
him;
he will not rise again from where he lies."
Even my bosom friend in whom I trusted,
who ate of my bread, has lifted his heel
against me.
But do thou, O LORD, be gracious to me,
and raise me up, that I may requite them!

By this I know that thou art pleased with
me,
in that my enemy has not triumphed over
me.
But thou hast upheld me because of my
integrity,
and set me in thy presence for ever.

Blessed be the LORD, the God of Israel,
from everlasting to everlasting!
Amen and Amen.

BOOK II

To the choirmaster. A Maskil of the sons of Korah.

42 AS a hart longs
for flowing streams,
so longs my soul
for thee, O God.
My soul thirsts for God,
for the living God.
When shall I come and behold
the face of God?

[b] Heb *ears thou hast dug for me*   [c] Or *weak*   [d] Heb *thou changest all his bed*
40.6–8: Heb 10.5–9.   **40.13–17:** Ps 70.1–5.   **41.9:** Jn 13.18.

My tears have been my food
    day and night,
while men say to me continually,
    "Where is your God?"

These things I remember,
    as I pour out my soul:
how I went with the throng,
    and led them in procession to the house of
        God,
with glad shouts and songs of thanksgiving,
    a multitude keeping festival.
Why are you cast down, O my soul,
    and why are you disquieted within me?
Hope in God; for I shall again praise him,
    my help and my God.

My soul is cast down within me,
    therefore I remember thee
from the land of Jordan and of Hermon,
    from Mount Mizar.
Deep calls to deep
    at the thunder of thy cataracts;
all thy waves and thy billows
    have gone over me.
By day the LORD commands his steadfast
    love;
    and at night his song is with me,
    a prayer to the God of my life.

I say to God, my rock:
    "Why hast thou forgotten me?
Why go I mourning
    because of the oppression of the enemy?"
As with a deadly wound in my body,
    my adversaries taunt me,
while they say to me continually,
    "Where is your God?"

Why are you cast down, O my soul,

and why are you disquieted within me?
Hope in God; for I shall again praise him,
    my help and my God.

43 VINDICATE me, O God, and defend
    my cause
against an ungodly people;
from deceitful and unjust men
    deliver me!
For thou art the God in whom I take refuge; 2
    why hast thou cast me off?
Why go I mourning
    because of the oppression of the enemy?

Oh send out thy light and thy truth;   3
    let them lead me,
let them bring me to thy holy hill
    and to thy dwelling!
Then I will go to the altar of God,   4
    to God my exceeding joy;
and I will praise thee with the lyre,
    O God, my God.

Why are you cast down, O my soul,   5
    and why are you disquieted within me?
Hope in God; for I shall again praise him,
    my help and my God.

To the choirmaster. A Maskil of the sons of Korah.
44 WE have heard with our ears, O God,
    our fathers have told us,
what deeds thou didst perform in their days,
    in the days of old:
thou with thy own hand didst drive out the 2
    nations,
    but them thou didst plant;
thou didst afflict the peoples,
    but them thou didst set free;
for not by their own sword did they win the 3
    land,
    nor did their own arm give them victory;
but thy right hand, and thy arm,
    and the light of thy countenance;
    for thou didst delight in them.

Thou art my King and my God,   4
    who ordainest[e] victories for Jacob.
Through thee we push down our foes;   5
    through thy name we tread down our
        assailants.
For not in my bow do I trust,   6
    nor can my sword save me.
But thou hast saved us from our foes,   7
    and hast put to confusion those who hate
        us.
In God we have boasted continually,   8
    and we will give thanks to thy name for
        ever.   *Selah*

Yet thou hast cast us off and abased us,   9

e Gk Syr: Heb *Thou art my King, O God; ordain*

and hast not gone out with our armies.
10 Thou hast made us turn back from the foe;
    and our enemies have gotten spoil.
11 Thou hast made us like sheep for slaughter,
    and hast scattered us among the nations.
12 Thou hast sold thy people for a trifle,
    demanding no high price for them.

13 Thou hast made us the taunt of our neigh-
    bours,
    the derision and scorn of those about us.
14 Thou hast made us a byword among the
    nations,
    a laughingstock[f] among the peoples.
15 All day long my disgrace is before me,
    and shame has covered my face,
16 at the words of the taunters and revilers,
    at the sight of the enemy and the avenger.

17 All this has come upon us,
    though we have not forgotten thee,
    or been false to thy covenant.
18 Our heart has not turned back,
    nor have our steps departed from thy way,
19 that thou shouldst have broken us in the
    place of jackals,
    and covered us with deep darkness.

20 If we had forgotten the name of our God,
    or spread forth our hands to a strange god,
21 would not God discover this?
    For he knows the secrets of the heart.
22 Nay, for thy sake we are slain all the day
    long,
    and accounted as sheep for the slaughter.

23 Rouse thyself! Why sleepest thou, O Lord?
    Awake! Do not cast us off for ever!
24 Why dost thou hide thy face?
    Why dost thou forget our affliction and
    oppression?
25 For our soul is bowed down to the dust;
    our body cleaves to the ground.
26 Rise up, come to our help!
    Deliver us for the sake of thy steadfast
    love!

*To the choirmaster: according to Lilies. A Maskil of
the sons of Korah; a love song.*

45 MY heart overflows with a goodly
    theme;
    I address my verses to the king;
    my tongue is like the pen of a ready
    scribe.

2 You are the fairest of the sons of men;
    grace is poured upon your lips;
    therefore God has blessed you for ever.
3 Gird your sword upon your thigh,

O mighty one,
    in your glory and majesty!

In your majesty ride forth victoriously
    for the cause of truth and to defend[g] the
    right;
    let your right hand teach you dread deeds!
Your arrows are sharp
    in the heart of the king's enemies;
    the peoples fall under you.

Your divine throne[h] endures for ever and
    ever.
    Your royal sceptre is a sceptre of equity;
    you love righteousness and hate wicked-
    ness.
Therefore God, your God, has anointed you
    with the oil of gladness above your fellows;

Myrrh

your robes are all fragrant with myrrh and
    aloes and cassia.
From ivory palaces stringed instruments
    make you glad;
    daughters of kings are among your ladies
    of honour;
    at your right hand stands the queen in gold
    of Ophir.

Hear, O daughter, consider, and incline your
    ear;
    forget your people and your father's
    house;

---

[f] Heb *a shaking of the head*   [g] Cn: Heb *and the meekness of*
[h] Or *Your throne is a throne of God*, or *Thy throne, O God*
44.22: Rom 8.36.   45.6-7: Heb 1.8-9.

and the king will desire your beauty.
Since he is your lord, bow to him;
the people[i] of Tyre will sue your favour
with gifts,
the richest of the people with all kinds of
wealth.

The princess is decked in her chamber with
gold-woven robes;[j]
in many-coloured robes she is led to the
king,
with her virgin companions, her escort,[k] in
her train.
With joy and gladness they are led along
as they enter the palace of the king.

Instead of your fathers shall be your sons;
you will make them princes in all the earth.
I will cause your name to be celebrated in all
generations;
therefore the peoples will praise you for
ever and ever.

*To the choirmaster. A Psalm of the sons of Korah.
According to Alamoth. A song.*

46 GOD is our refuge and strength,
a very present[l] help in trouble.
Therefore we will not fear though the earth
should change,
though the mountains shake in the heart of
the sea;
though its waters roar and foam,
though the mountains tremble with its
tumult.   *Selah*

There is a river whose streams make glad the
city of God,
the holy habitation of the Most High.
God is in the midst of her, she shall not be
moved;
God will help her right early.
The nations rage, the kingdoms totter;
he utters his voice, the earth melts.
The LORD of hosts is with us;
the God of Jacob is our refuge.[m]   *Selah*

Come, behold the works of the LORD,
how he has wrought desolations in the
earth.
He makes wars cease to the end of the
earth;
he breaks the bow, and shatters the spear,
he burns the chariots with fire!
"Be still, and know that I am God.
I am exalted among the nations,
I am exalted in the earth!"
The LORD of hosts is with us;
the God of Jacob is our refuge.[m]   *Selah*

To the choirmaster. A Psalm of the sons of Korah.

47 CLAP your hands, all peoples!
Shout to God with loud songs of joy!
For the LORD, the Most High, is terrible,   2
a great king over all the earth.
He subdued peoples under us,   3
and nations under our feet.
He chose our heritage for us,   4
the pride of Jacob whom he loves.   *Selah*

God has gone up with a shout,   5
the LORD with the sound of a trumpet.
Sing praises to God, sing praises!   6
Sing praises to our King, sing praises!
For God is the king of all the earth;   7
sing praises with a psalm![n]

God reigns over the nations;   8
God sits on his holy throne.
The princes of the peoples gather   9
as the people of the God of Abraham.
For the shields of the earth belong to God;
he is highly exalted!

A song. A Psalm of the sons of Korah.

48 GREAT is the LORD and greatly to be
praised
in the city of our God!
His holy mountain, beautiful in elevation,   2
is the joy of all the earth,
Mount Zion, in the far north,
the city of the great King.
Within her citadels God   3
has shown himself a sure defence.

For lo, the kings assembled,   4
they came on together.
As soon as they saw it, they were astounded, 5
they were in panic, they took to flight;
trembling took hold of them there,   6
anguish as of a woman in travail.
By the east wind thou didst shatter   7
the ships of Tarshish.
As we have heard, so have we seen   8
in the city of the LORD of hosts,
in the city of our God,
which God establishes for ever.   *Selah*

We have thought on thy steadfast love, 9
O God,
in the midst of thy temple.
As thy name, O God,   10
so thy praise reaches to the ends of the
earth.
Thy right hand is filled with victory;
let Mount Zion be glad!   11
Let the daughters of Judah rejoice
because of thy judgments!

---

[i] Heb *daughter*   [j] Or *people. All glorious is the princess within, gold embroidery is her clothing*
[k] Heb *those brought to you*   [l] Or *well proved*   [m] Or *fortress*   [n] Heb *Maskil*
48.2: Mt 5.35.

12 Walk about Zion, go round about her,
   number her towers,
13 consider well her ramparts,
   go through her citadels;
   that you may tell the next generation
14   that this is God,
   our God for ever and ever.
   He will be our guide for ever.

To the choirmaster. A Psalm of the sons of Korah.

49 HEAR this, all peoples!
   Give ear, all inhabitants of the
   world,
2 both low and high,
   rich and poor together!
3 My mouth shall speak wisdom;
   the meditation of my heart shall be understanding.
4 I will incline my ear to a proverb;
   I will solve my riddle to the music of the
   lyre.

5 Why should I fear in times of trouble,
   when the iniquity of my persecutors
   surrounds me,
6 men who trust in their wealth
   and boast of the abundance of their
   riches?
7 Truly no man can ransom himself,*o*
   or give to God the price of his life,
8 for the ransom of his*p* life is costly,
   and can never suffice,
9 that he should continue to live on for ever,
   and never see the Pit.

10 Yea, he shall see that even the wise die,
   the fool and the stupid alike must perish
   and leave their wealth to others.
11 Their graves*q* are their homes for ever,
   their dwelling places to all generations,
   though they named lands their own.
12 Man cannot abide in his pomp,
   he is like the beasts that perish.

13 This is the fate of those who have foolish
   confidence,
   the end of those*r* who are pleased with
   their portion.   *Selah*
14 Like sheep they are appointed for Sheol;
   Death shall be their shepherd;
   straight to the grave they descend,*s*
   and their form shall waste away;
   Sheol shall be their home.*t*
15 But God will ransom my soul from the power
   of Sheol,
   for he will receive me.   *Selah*

16 Be not afraid when one becomes rich,

when the glory*u* of his house increases.
For when he dies he will carry nothing away;
   his glory*u* will not go down after him.
Though, while he lives, he counts himself
   happy,
and though a man gets praise when he does
   well for himself,
he will go to the generation of his fathers,
   who will never more see the light.
Man cannot abide in his pomp,
   he is like the beasts that perish.

A Psalm of Asaph.

50 THE Mighty One, God the LORD,
   speaks and summons the earth
from the rising of the sun to its setting.
Out of Zion, the perfection of beauty,
   God shines forth.

Our God comes, he does not keep silence,
   before him is a devouring fire,
   round about him a mighty tempest.
He calls to the heavens above
   and to the earth, that he may judge his
   people:
"Gather to me my faithful ones,
   who made a covenant with me by sacrifice!"
The heavens declare his righteousness,
   for God himself is judge!   *Selah*

"Hear, O my people, and I will speak,
   O Israel, I will testify against you.
   I am God, your God.
I do not reprove you for your sacrifices;
   your burnt offerings are continually before
   me.
I will accept no bull from your house,
   nor he-goat from your folds.
For every beast of the forest is mine,
   the cattle on a thousand hills.
I know all the birds of the air,*v*
   and all that moves in the field is mine.

"If I were hungry, I would not tell you;
   for the world and all that is in it is mine.
Do I eat the flesh of bulls,
   or drink the blood of goats?
Offer to God a sacrifice of thanksgiving,*w*
   and pay your vows to the Most High;
and call upon me in the day of trouble;
   I will deliver you, and you shall glorify
   me."

But to the wicked God says:
   "What right have you to recite my
   statutes,
   or take my covenant on your lips?

---

o Another reading is *no man can ransom his brother*   *p* Gk: Heb *their*
q Gk Syr Compare Tg: Heb *their inward* (thought)   *r* Tg: Heb *after them*
s Cn: Heb *the upright shall have dominion over them in the morning*   *t* Heb uncertain   *u* Or *wealth*
v Gk Syr Tg: Heb *mountains*   *w* Or *make thanksgiving your sacrifice to God*

For you hate discipline,
  and you cast my words behind you.
If you see a thief, you are a friend of his;
  and you keep company with adulterers.

"You give your mouth free rein for evil,
  and your tongue frames deceit.
You sit and speak against your brother;
  you slander your own mother's son.
These things you have done and I have been
    silent;
  you thought that I was one like yourself.
But now I rebuke you, and lay the charge
  before you.

"Mark this, then, you who forget God,
  lest I rend, and there be none to deliver!
He who brings thanksgiving as his sacrifice
    honours me;
  to him who orders his way aright
    I will show the salvation of God!"

Hyssop   Ps 51, 7

*To the choirmaster. A Psalm of David, when Nathan
the prophet came to him, after he had gone in to
Bathsheba.*

51 HAVE mercy on me, O God,
      according to thy steadfast love;
  according to thy abundant mercy
    blot out my transgressions.
Wash me thoroughly from my iniquity,
  and cleanse me from my sin!

For I know my transgressions,
  and my sin is ever before me.
Against thee, thee only, have I sinned,
  and done that which is evil in thy sight,
so that thou art justified in thy sentence
  and blameless in thy judgment.
Behold, I was brought forth in iniquity,
  and in sin did my mother conceive me.

Behold, thou desirest truth in the inward
    being;
  therefore teach me wisdom in my secret
    heart.
Purge me with hyssop, and I shall be clean;
  wash me, and I shall be whiter than snow.
Fill ^{x} me with joy and gladness;
  let the bones which thou hast broken
    rejoice.
Hide thy face from my sins,
  and blot out all my iniquities.

Create in me a clean heart, O God,
  and put a new and right ^{y} spirit within me.
Cast me not away from thy presence,
  and take not thy holy Spirit from me.
Restore to me the joy of thy salvation,
  and uphold me with a willing spirit.

Then I will teach transgressors thy ways,   13
  and sinners will return to thee.
Deliver me from bloodguiltiness, ^{z} O God, 14
  thou God of my salvation,
  and my tongue will sing aloud of thy
    deliverance.

O Lord, open thou my lips,   15
  and my mouth shall show forth thy praise.
For thou hast no delight in sacrifice;   16
  were I to give a burnt offering,
    thou wouldst not be pleased.
The sacrifice acceptable to God ^{a} is a broken 17
    spirit;
  a broken and contrite heart, O God, thou
    wilt not despise.

Do good to Zion in thy good pleasure;   18
  rebuild the walls of Jerusalem,
then wilt thou delight in right sacrifices, 19
  in burnt offerings and whole burnt offer-
    ings;
  then bulls will be offered on thy altar.

*To the choirmaster. A Maskil of David, when Doeg,
the Edomite, came and told Saul, "David has come
to the house of Ahimelech."*

52 WHY do you boast, O mighty man,
      of mischief done against the godly? ^{b}
  All the day you are plotting destruction.   2
Your tongue is like a sharp razor,
  you worker of treachery.
You love evil more than good,   3
  and lying more than speaking the truth.
                                    Selah

You love all words that devour,   4
  O deceitful tongue.

^{x} Syr: Heb *Make to hear* ^{y} Or *steadfast* ^{z} Or *death* ^{a} Or *My sacrifice, O God*
^{b} Cn Compare Syr: Heb *the kindness of God*
51.4: Rom 3.4.

5 But God will break you down for ever;
  he will snatch and tear you from your
    tent;
  he will uproot you from the land of the
    living.   *Selah*
6 The righteous shall see, and fear,
  and shall laugh at him, saying,
7 "See the man who would not make God his
    refuge,
  but trusted in the abundance of his
    riches,
  and sought refuge in his wealth!"*c*

8 But I am like a green olive tree
    in the house of God.
  I trust in the steadfast love of God
    for ever and ever.
9 I will thank thee for ever,
    because thou hast done it.
  I will proclaim*d* thy name, for it is good,
    in the presence of the godly.

To the choirmaster: according to Mahalath. A Maskil
of David.

53   THE fool says in his heart,
       "There is no God."
  They are corrupt, doing abominable ini-
    quity;
  there is none that does good.

2 God looks down from heaven
    upon the sons of men
  to see if there are any that are wise,
    that seek after God.

3 They have all fallen away;
    they are all alike depraved;
  there is none that does good,
    no, not one.

4 Have those who work evil no understanding,
  who eat up my people as they eat bread,
  and do not call upon God?

5 There they are, in great terror,
    in terror such as has not been!
  For God will scatter the bones of the
    ungodly;*e*
  they will be put to shame,*f* for God has
    rejected them.

6 O that deliverance for Israel would come
    from Zion!
  When God restores the fortunes of his
    people,
  Jacob will rejoice and Israel be glad.

To the choirmaster: with stringed instruments. A
Maskil of David, when the Ziphites went and told
Saul, "David is in hiding among us."

54   SAVE me, O God, by thy name,
       and vindicate me by thy might.
  Hear my prayer, O God;
    give ear to the words of my mouth.

For insolent*g* men have risen against me,
    ruthless men seek my life;
  they do not set God before them.   *Selah*

Behold, God is my helper;
    the LORD is the upholder*h* of my life.
  He will requite my enemies with evil;
    in thy faithfulness put an end to them.

With a freewill offering I will sacrifice to
    thee;
  I will give thanks to thy name, O LORD, for
    it is good.
For thou hast delivered me from every
    trouble,
  and my eye has looked in triumph on my
    enemies.

To the choirmaster: with stringed instruments.
A Maskil of David.

55   GIVE ear to my prayer, O God;
       and hide not thyself from my
    supplication!
  Attend to me, and answer me;
    I am overcome by my trouble.
  I am distraught by the noise of the enemy,
    because of the oppression of the wicked.
  For they bring*i* trouble upon me,
    and in anger they cherish enmity against
    me.

My heart is in anguish within me,
    the terrors of death have fallen upon me.
  Fear and trembling come upon me,
    and horror overwhelms me.
  And I say, "O that I had wings like a dove!
    I would fly away and be at rest;
  yea, I would wander afar,
    I would lodge in the wilderness,   *Selah*
  I would haste to find me a shelter
    from the raging wind and tempest."

Destroy their plans,*j* O Lord, confuse their
    tongues;
  for I see violence and strife in the city.
  Day and night they go around it on its
    walls;
  and mischief and trouble are within it,
    ruin is in its midst;

c Syr Tg: Heb *his destruction*   *d* Cn: Heb *wait for*
e Cn Compare Gk Syr: Heb *him who encamps against you*   *f* Gk: Heb *you will put to shame*
g Another reading is *strangers*   *h* Gk Syr Jerome: Heb *of* or *with those who uphold*
i Cn Compare Gk: Heb *they cause to totter*   *j* Tg: Heb lacks *their plans*
53.1-3: Rom 3.10-12.   **53.1-6:** Ps 14.1-7.

oppression and fraud
   do not depart from its market place.

It is not an enemy who taunts me—
   then I could bear it;
it is not an adversary who deals insolently
    with me—
   then I could hide from him.
But it is you, my equal,
   my companion, my familiar friend.
We used to hold sweet converse together;
   within God's house we walked in fellow-
    ship.
Let death[k] come upon them;
   let them go down to Sheol alive;
   let them go away in terror into their
    graves.[l]

But I call upon God;
   and the LORD will save me.
Evening and morning and at noon
   I utter my complaint and moan,
   and he will hear my voice.
He will deliver my soul in safety
   from the battle that I wage,
   for many are arrayed against me.
God will give ear, and humble them,
   he who is enthroned from of old;
because they keep no law,[m]
   and do not fear God.   *Selah*

My companion stretched out his hand
   against his friends,
   he violated his covenant.
His speech was smoother than butter,
   yet war was in his heart;
his words were softer than oil,
   yet they were drawn swords.

Cast your burden[n] on the LORD,
   and he will sustain you;
he will never permit
   the righteous to be moved.

But thou, O God, wilt cast them down
   into the lowest pit;
men of blood and treachery
   shall not live out half their days.
But I will trust in thee.

*To the choirmaster: according to the Dove on Far-
off Terebinths. A Miktam of David, when the
Philistines seized him in Gath.*

56 BE gracious to me, O God,
     for men trample upon me;
   all day long foemen oppress me;
my enemies trample upon me all day long,
   for many fight against me proudly.
When I am afraid,

I put my trust in thee.
In God, whose word I praise,   4
   in God I trust without a fear.
What can flesh do to me?

All day long they seek to injure my cause; 5
   all their thoughts are against me for evil.
They band themselves together, they 6
    lurk,
   they watch my steps.
As they have waited for my life,
   so recompense[o] them for their crime;   7
   in wrath cast down the peoples, O God!

Thou hast kept count of my tossings;   8
   put thou my tears in thy bottle!
   Are they not in thy book?
Then my enemies will be turned back 9
   in the day when I call.
   This I know, that[p] God is for me.
In God, whose word I praise,   10
   in the LORD, whose word I praise,
in God I trust without a fear.   11
   What can man do to me?

My vows to thee I must perform, O God; 12
   I will render thank offerings to thee.
For thou hast delivered my soul from 13
    death,
   yea, my feet from falling,
that I may walk before God
   in the light of life.

*To the choirmaster: according to Do Not Destroy.
A Miktam of David, when he fled from Saul, in the
cave.*

57 BE merciful to me, O God,
     be merciful to me,
   for in thee my soul takes refuge;
in the shadow of thy wings I will take refuge,
   till the storms of destruction pass by.
I cry to God Most High,   2
   to God who fulfils his purpose for me.
He will send from heaven and save me, 3
   he will put to shame those who trample
    upon me.   *Selah*
God will send forth his steadfast love and his
   faithfulness!

I lie in the midst of lions   4
   that greedily devour[q] the sons of men;
their teeth are spears and arrows,
   their tongues sharp swords.

Be exalted, O God, above the heavens! 5
   Let thy glory be over all the earth!

They set a net for my steps;   6
   my soul was bowed down.

---

[k] Or *desolations*   [l] Cn: Heb *evils are in their habitation, in their midst*   [m] Or *do not change*
[n] Or *what he has given you*   [o] Cn: Heb *deliver*   [p] Or *because*   [q] Cn: Heb *are aflame*
55.22: 1 Pet 5.7.

They dug a pit in my way,
but they have fallen into it themselves.
Selah

7 My heart is steadfast, O God,
my heart is steadfast!
I will sing and make melody!
8   Awake, my soul!
Awake, O harp and lyre!
I will awake the dawn!
9 I will give thanks to thee, O Lord, among the
peoples;
I will sing praises to thee among the
nations.
10 For thy steadfast love is great to the heavens,
thy faithfulness to the clouds.

11 Be exalted, O God, above the heavens!
Let thy glory be over all the earth!

*To the choirmaster: according to Do Not Destroy.
A Miktam of David.*

58 DO you indeed decree what is right,
you gods?[r]
Do you judge the sons of men uprightly?
2 Nay, in your hearts you devise wrongs;
your hands deal out violence on earth.

3 The wicked go astray from the womb,
they err from their birth, speaking lies.
4 They have venom like the venom of a
serpent,
like the deaf adder that stops its ear,
5 so that it does not hear the voice of charmers
or of the cunning enchanter.

6 O God, break the teeth in their mouths;
tear out the fangs of the young lions, O
LORD!
7 Let them vanish like water that runs away;
like grass let them be trodden down and
wither.[s]
8 Let them be like the snail which dissolves
into slime,
like the untimely birth that never sees the
sun.
9 Sooner than your pots can feel the heat of
thorns,
whether green or ablaze, may he sweep
them away!

10 The righteous will rejoice when he sees the
vengeance;
he will bathe his feet in the blood of the
wicked.
11 Men will say, "Surely there is a reward for
the righteous;
surely there is a God who judges on
earth."

*To the choirmaster: according to Do Not Destroy.
A Miktam of David, when Saul sent men to watch
his house in order to kill him.*

59 DELIVER me from my enemies, O
my God,
protect me from those who rise up against
me,
deliver me from those who work evil,
and save me from bloodthirsty men.

For, lo, they lie in wait for my life;
fierce men band themselves against me.
For no transgression or sin of mine, O LORD,
for no fault of mine, they run and make
ready.

Rouse thyself, come to my help, and see!
Thou, LORD God of hosts, art God of
Israel.
Awake to punish all the nations;
spare none of those who treacherously plot
evil.   *Selah*

Each evening they come back,
howling like dogs
and prowling about the city.
There they are, bellowing with their
mouths,
and snarling with[t] their lips—
for "Who," they think, "will hear us?"

But thou, O LORD, dost laugh at them;
thou dost hold all the nations in derision.
O my Strength, I will sing praises to thee;[u]
for thou, O God, art my fortress.
My God in his steadfast love will meet
me;
my God will let me look in triumph on my
enemies.

Slay them not, lest my people forget;
make them totter by thy power,
and bring them down,
O Lord, our shield!
For the sin of their mouths, the words of
their lips,
let them be trapped in their pride.
For the cursing and lies which they utter,
consume them in wrath,
consume them till they are no more,
that men may know that God rules over
Jacob
to the ends of the earth.   *Selah*

Each evening they come back,
howling like dogs
and prowling about the city.
They roam about for food,
and growl if they do not get their fill.

r Or *mighty lords*   s Cn: Heb uncertain   t Cn: Heb *swords in*   u Syr: Heb *I will watch for thee*
57.7-11: Ps 108.1-5.

6 But I will sing of thy might;
  I will sing aloud of thy steadfast love in the
    morning.
For thou hast been to me a fortress
  and a refuge in the day of my distress.
7 O my Strength, I will sing praises to thee,
  for thou, O God, art my fortress,
  the God who shows me steadfast love.

*To the choirmaster: according to Shushan Eduth.
A Miktam of David; for instruction; when he strove
with Aram-naharaim and with Aram-zobah, and
when Joab on his return killed twelve thousand of
Edom in the Valley of Salt.*

60 O GOD, thou hast rejected us,
      broken our defences;
  thou hast been angry; oh, restore us.
2 Thou hast made the land to quake, thou hast
    rent it open;
  repair its breaches, for it totters.
3 Thou hast made thy people suffer hard
    things;
  thou hast given us wine to drink that made
    us reel.

4 Thou hast set up a banner for those who fear
    thee,
  to rally to it from the bow.*v*   *Selah*
5 That thy beloved may be delivered,
  give victory by thy right hand and answer
    us!

6 God has spoken in his sanctuary:*w*
  "With exultation I will divide up Shechem
  and portion out the Vale of Succoth.
7 Gilead is mine; Manas′seh is mine;
  E′phraim is my helmet;
  Judah is my sceptre.
8 Moab is my washbasin;
  upon Edom I cast my shoe;
  over Philistia I shout in triumph."

9 Who will bring me to the fortified city?
  Who will lead me to Edom?
10 Hast thou not rejected us, O God?
  Thou dost not go forth, O God, with our
    armies.
11 O grant us help against the foe,
  for vain is the help of man!
12 With God we shall do valiantly;
  it is he who will tread down our foes.

*To the choirmaster: with stringed instruments. A Psalm
of David.*

61 HEAR my cry, O God,
      listen to my prayer;
2 from the end of the earth I call to thee,
  when my heart is faint.

Lead thou me
  to the rock that is higher than I;
for thou art my refuge,   3
  a strong tower against the enemy.

Let me dwell in thy tent for ever!   4
  Oh to be safe under the shelter of thy
    wings!   *Selah*
For thou, O God, hast heard my vows,   5
  thou hast given me the heritage of those
    who fear thy name.

Prolong the life of the king;   6
  may his years endure to all generations!
May he be enthroned for ever before God;   7
  bid steadfast love and faithfulness watch
    over him!

So will I ever sing praises to thy name,   8
  as I pay my vows day after day.

*To the choirmaster: according to Jeduthun. A Psalm of
David.*

62 FOR God alone my soul waits in
      silence;
  from him comes my salvation.
He only is my rock and my salvation,   2
  my fortress; I shall not be greatly moved.

How long will you set upon a man   3
  to shatter him, all of you,
  like a leaning wall, a tottering fence?
They only plan to thrust him down from his 4
    eminence.
  They take pleasure in falsehood.
They bless with their mouths,
  but inwardly they curse.   *Selah*

For God alone my soul waits in silence,   5
  for my hope is from him.
He only is my rock and my salvation,   6
  my fortress; I shall not be shaken.
On God rests my deliverance and my 7
    honour;
  my mighty rock, my refuge is God.

Trust in him at all times, O people;   8
  pour out your heart before him;
  God is a refuge for us.   *Selah*

v Gk Syr Jerome: Heb *truth*   *w* Or *by his holiness*
60.5–12: Ps 108.6–13.

9 Men of low estate are but a breath,
  men of high estate are a delusion;
in the balances they go up;
  they are together lighter than a breath.
10 Put no confidence in extortion,
  set no vain hopes on robbery;
  if riches increase, set not your heart on
    them.

11 Once God has spoken;
  twice have I heard this;
that power belongs to God;
12 and that to thee, O Lord, belongs steadfast
    love.
  For thou dost requite a man
    according to his work.

*A Psalm of David, when he was in the Wilderness of
Judah.*

63 O GOD, thou art my God, I seek thee,
     my soul thirsts for thee;
my flesh faints for thee,
  as in a dry and weary land where no water
    is.
2 So I have looked upon thee in the sanctuary,
  beholding thy power and glory.
3 Because thy steadfast love is better than life,
  my lips will praise thee.
4 So I will bless thee as long as I live;
  I will lift up my hands and call on thy
    name.

5 My soul is feasted as with marrow and fat,
  and my mouth praises thee with joyful
    lips,
6 when I think of thee upon my bed,
  and meditate on thee in the watches of the
    night;
7 for thou hast been my help,
  and in the shadow of thy wings I sing for
    joy.
8 My soul clings to thee;
  thy right hand upholds me.

9 But those who seek to destroy my life
  shall go down into the depths of the earth;
10 they shall be given over to the power of the
    sword,
  they shall be prey for jackals.
11 But the king shall rejoice in God;
  all who swear by him shall glory;
  for the mouths of liars will be stopped.

To the choirmaster. A Psalm of David.

64 HEAR my voice, O God, in my
     complaint;
  preserve my life from dread of the enemy,
2 hide me from the secret plots of the wicked,
  from the scheming of evildoers,

who whet their tongues like swords,   3
  who aim bitter words like arrows,
shooting from ambush at the blameless, 4
  shooting at him suddenly and without
    fear.
They hold fast to their evil purpose;   5
  they talk of laying snares secretly,
thinking, "Who can see us?ˣ
  Who can search out our crimes?ʸ   6
We have thought out a cunningly conceived
    plot."
  For the inward mind and heart of a man
    are deep!

But God will shoot his arrow at them;   7
  they will be wounded suddenly.
Because of their tongue he will bring them to 8
    ruin;ᶻ
  all who see them will wag their heads.
Then all men will fear;   9
  they will tell what God has wrought,
  and ponder what he has done.

Let the righteous rejoice in the LORD, 10
  and take refuge in him!
Let all the upright in heart glory!

To the choirmaster. A Psalm of David. A song.

65 PRAISE is due to thee,
     O God, in Zion;
and to thee shall vows be performed,
  O thou who hearest prayer!   2
To thee shall all flesh come
  on account of sins.   3
When our transgressions prevail over us,ᵃ
  thou dost forgive them.
Blessed is he whom thou dost choose and 4
    bring near,
  to dwell in thy courts!
We shall be satisfied with the goodness of thy
    house,
  thy holy temple!

By dread deeds thou dost answer us with 5
    deliverance,
  O God of our salvation,
who art the hope of all the ends of the
    earth,
  and of the farthest seas;
who by thy strength hast established the 6
    mountains,
  being girded with might;
who dost still the roaring of the seas, 7
  the roaring of their waves,
  the tumult of the peoples;
so that those who dwell at earth's farthest 8
    bounds
  are afraid at thy signs;

ˣ Syr: Heb *them*   ʸ Cn: Heb *they search out crimes*
ᶻ Cn: Heb *They will bring him to ruin, their tongue being against them*   ᵃ Gk: Heb *me*
62.12: Jer 17.10; Rev 2.23; 22.12.

thou makest the outgoings of the morning
and the evening
to shout for joy.

Thou visitest the earth and waterest it,
thou greatly enrichest it;
the river of God is full of water;
thou providest their grain,
for so thou hast prepared it.
Thou waterest its furrows abundantly,
settling its ridges,
softening it with showers,
and blessing its growth.
Thou crownest the year with thy bounty;
the tracks of thy chariot drip with fatness.
The pastures of the wilderness drip,
the hills gird themselves with joy,
the meadows clothe themselves with flocks,
the valleys deck themselves with grain,
they shout and sing together for joy.

To the choirmaster. A song. A Psalm.

66 MAKE a joyful noise to God,
all the earth;
sing the glory of his name;
give to him glorious praise!
Say to God, "How terrible are thy deeds!
So great is thy power that thy enemies
cringe before thee.
All the earth worships thee;
they sing praises to thee,
sing praises to thy name." *Selah*

5 Come and see what God has done:
he is terrible in his deeds among men.
6 He turned the sea into dry land;
men passed through the river on foot.
There did we rejoice in him,
7 who rules by his might for ever,

whose eyes keep watch on the nations—
let not the rebellious exalt themselves.
Selah

Bless our God, O peoples,   8
let the sound of his praise be heard,
who has kept us among the living,   9
and has not let our feet slip.
For thou, O God, hast tested us;   10
thou hast tried us as silver is tried.
Thou didst bring us into the net;   11
thou didst lay affliction on our loins;
thou didst let men ride over our heads;   12
we went through fire and through water;
yet thou hast brought us forth to a spacious
place.[b]

I will come into thy house with burnt 13
offerings;
I will pay thee my vows,
that which my lips uttered   14
and my mouth promised when I was in
trouble.
I will offer to thee burnt offerings of fatlings, 15
with the smoke of the sacrifice of rams;
I will make an offering of bulls and
goats.   *Selah*

Come and hear, all you who fear God,   16
and I will tell what he has done for me.
I cried aloud to him,   17
and he was extolled with my tongue.
If I had cherished iniquity in my heart,   18
the LORD would not have listened.
But truly God has listened;   19
he has given heed to the voice of my
prayer.

Blessed be God,   20
because he has not rejected my prayer
or removed his steadfast love from me!

b Cn Compare Gk Syr Jerome Tg: Heb *saturation*

To the choirmaster: with stringed instruments.
A Psalm. A song.

67 MAY God be gracious to us and bless
us
and make his face to shine upon us,
                                                Selah
2 that thy way may be known upon earth,
thy saving power among all nations.
3 Let the peoples praise thee, O God;
let all the peoples praise thee!

4 Let the nations be glad and sing for joy,
for thou dost judge the peoples with equity
and guide the nations upon earth.   *Selah*
5 Let the peoples praise thee, O God;
let all the peoples praise thee!

6 The earth has yielded its increase;
God, our God, has blessed us.
7 God has blessed us;
let all the ends of the earth fear him!

To the choirmaster. A Psalm of David. A song.

68 LET God arise, let his enemies be
scattered;
let those who hate him flee before him!
2 As smoke is driven away, so drive them
away;
as wax melts before fire,
let the wicked perish before God!
3 But let the righteous be joyful;
let them exult before God;
let them be jubilant with joy!

4 Sing to God, sing praises to his name;
lift up a song to him who rides upon the
clouds;[c]
his name is the LORD, exult before him!

5 Father of the fatherless and protector of
widows
is God in his holy habitation.
6 God gives the desolate a home to dwell in;
he leads out the prisoners to prosperity;
but the rebellious dwell in a parched land.

7 O God, when thou didst go forth before thy
people,
when thou didst march through the
wilderness,   *Selah*
8 the earth quaked, the heavens poured down
rain,
at the presence of God;
yon Sinai quaked at the presence of God,
the God of Israel.
9 Rain in abundance, O God, thou didst shed
abroad;
thou didst restore thy heritage as it
languished;

thy flock found a dwelling in it;   10
in thy goodness, O God, thou didst
provide for the needy.

The Lord gives the command;   11
great is the host of those who bore the
tidings:
"The kings of the armies, they flee, they   12
flee!"
The women at home divide the spoil,
though they stay among the sheepfolds—   13
the wings of a dove covered with silver,
its pinions with green gold.
When the Almighty scattered kings there,   14
snow fell on Zalmon.

O mighty mountain, mountain of Bashan;   15
O many-peaked mountain, mountain of
Bashan!
Why look you with envy, O many-peaked   16
mountain,
at the mount which God desired for his
abode,
yea, where the LORD will dwell for ever?

With mighty chariotry, twice ten thousand,   17
thousands upon thousands,
the Lord came from Sinai into the holy
place.[d]
Thou didst ascend the high mount,   18
leading captives in thy train,
and receiving gifts among men,
even among the rebellious, that the LORD
God may dwell there.

Blessed be the Lord,   19
who daily bears us up;
God is our salvation.   *Selah*
Our God is a God of salvation;   20
and to GOD, the Lord, belongs escape from
death.

But God will shatter the heads of his   21
enemies,
the hairy crown of him who walks in his
guilty ways.
The Lord said,   22
"I will bring them back from Bashan,
I will bring them back from the depths of
the sea,
that you may bathe[e] your feet in blood,   23
that the tongues of your dogs may have
their portion from the foe."

Thy solemn processions are seen,[f] O God,   24
the processions of my God, my King, into
the sanctuary—
the singers in front, the minstrels last,   25
between them maidens playing timbrels:

[c] Or *cast up a highway for him who rides through the deserts*
[d] Cn: Heb *The Lord among them Sinai in the holy place*   [e] Gk Syr Tg: Heb *shatter*   [f] Or *have been seen*
68.18: Eph 4.8.

"Bless God in the great congregation,
   the LORD, O you who are of Israel's
   fountain!"
There is Benjamin, the least of them, in the
   lead,
   the princes of Judah in their throng,
   the princes of Zeb′ulun, the princes of
   Naph′tali.

Summon thy might, O God;
   show thy strength, O God, thou who hast
   wrought for us.
Because of thy temple at Jerusalem
   kings bear gifts to thee.
Rebuke the beasts that dwell among the
   reeds,
   the herd of bulls with the calves of the
   peoples.
Trample[g] under foot those who lust after
   tribute;
   scatter the peoples who delight in war.[h]
Let bronze be brought from Egypt;
   let Ethiopia hasten to stretch out her hands
   to God.

Sing to God, O kingdoms of the earth;
   sing praises to the Lord,   *Selah*
to him who rides in the heavens, the ancient
   heavens;
   lo, he sends forth his voice, his mighty
   voice.
Ascribe power to God,
   whose majesty is over Israel,
   and his power is in the skies.
Terrible is God in his[i] sanctuary,
   the God of Israel,
   he gives power and strength to his people.

Blessed be God!

*To the choirmaster: according to Lilies. A Psalm of
   David.*

69 SAVE me, O God!
       For the waters have come up to my
   neck.
I sink in deep mire,
   where there is no foothold;
I have come into deep waters,
   and the flood sweeps over me.
I am weary with my crying;
   my throat is parched.
My eyes grow dim
   with waiting for my God.

More in number than the hairs of my head
   are those who hate me without cause;
mighty are those who would destroy me,
   those who attack me with lies.
What I did not steal

must I now restore?
O God, thou knowest my folly;   5
   the wrongs I have done are not hidden
   from thee.

Let not those who hope in thee be put to   6
   shame through me,
   O Lord GOD of hosts;
let not those who seek thee be brought to
   dishonour through me,
   O God of Israel.
For it is for thy sake that I have borne   7
   reproach,
   that shame has covered my face.
I have become a stranger to my brethren,   8
   an alien to my mother's sons.

For zeal for thy house has consumed me,   9
   and the insults of those who insult thee
   have fallen on me.
When I humbled[j] my soul with fasting,   10
   it became my reproach.
When I made sackcloth my clothing,   11
   I became a byword to them.
I am the talk of those who sit in the gate,   12
   and the drunkards make songs about me.

But as for me, my prayer is to thee, O LORD. 13
   At an acceptable time, O God,
   in the abundance of thy steadfast love
   answer me.
With thy faithful help rescue me   14
   from sinking in the mire;
let me be delivered from my enemies
   and from the deep waters.
Let not the flood sweep over me,   15
   or the deep swallow me up,
   or the pit close its mouth over me.

Answer me, O LORD, for thy steadfast love is 16
   good;
   according to thy abundant mercy, turn to
   me.
Hide not thy face from thy servant;   17
   for I am in distress, make haste to answer
   me.
Draw near to me, redeem me,   18
   set me free because of my enemies!

Thou knowest my reproach,   19
   and my shame and my dishonour;
   my foes are all known to thee.
Insults have broken my heart,   20
   so that I am in despair.
I looked for pity, but there was none;
   and for comforters, but I found none.
They gave me poison for food,   21
   and for my thirst they gave me vinegar to
   drink.

[g] Cn: Heb *trampling*   [h] The Hebrew of verse 30 is obscure   [i] Gk: Heb *from thy*
[j] Gk Syr: Heb *I wept with fasting my soul* or *I made my soul mourn with fasting*
69.4: Ps 35.19; Jn 15.25.   69.9: Jn 2.17; Rom 15.3.   69.21: Mt 27.34, 48; Mk 15.36; Lk 23.36; Jn 19.29.

22 Let their own table before them become a
       snare;
    let their sacrificial feasts[k] be a trap.
23 Let their eyes be darkened, so that they
       cannot see;
    and make their loins tremble continually.
24 Pour out thy indignation upon them,
    and let thy burning anger overtake them.
25 May their camp be a desolation,
    let no one dwell in their tents.
26 For they persecute him whom thou hast
       smitten,
    and him[l] whom thou hast wounded, they
       afflict still more.[m]
27 Add to them punishment upon punishment;
    may they have no acquittal from thee.
28 Let them be blotted out of the book of the
       living;
    let them not be enrolled among the
       righteous.

29 But I am afflicted and in pain;
    let thy salvation, O God, set me on high!

30 I will praise the name of God with a
       song;
    I will magnify him with thanksgiving.
31 This will please the LORD more than an ox
    or a bull with horns and hoofs.
32 Let the oppressed see it and be glad;
    you who seek God, let your hearts revive.
33 For the LORD hears the needy,
    and does not despise his own that are in
       bonds.

34 Let heaven and earth praise him,
    the seas and everything that moves
       therein.
35 For God will save Zion
    and rebuild the cities of Judah;
    and his servants shall dwell[n] there and
       possess it;
36   the children of his servants shall inherit it,
    and those who love his name shall dwell in
       it.

To the choirmaster. A Psalm of David, for the
memorial offering.

70 BE pleased, O God, to deliver me!
       O LORD, make haste to help me!
2 Let them be put to shame and confusion
    who seek my life!
Let them be turned back and brought to
    dishonour
    who desire my hurt!
3 Let them be appalled because of their
    shame
    who say, "Aha, Aha!"

May all who seek thee
    rejoice and be glad in thee!
May those who love thy salvation
    say evermore, "God is great!"
But I am poor and needy;
    hasten to me, O God!
Thou art my help and my deliverer;
    O LORD, do not tarry!

71 IN thee, O LORD, do I take refuge;
       let me never be put to shame!
In thy righteousness deliver me and rescue
       me;
    incline thy ear to me, and save me!
Be thou to me a rock of refuge,
    a strong fortress,[o] to save me,
    for thou art my rock and my fortress.
Rescue me, O my God, from the hand of the
       wicked,
    from the grasp of the unjust and cruel
       man.
For thou, O Lord, art my hope,
    my trust, O LORD, from my youth.
Upon thee I have leaned from my birth;
    thou art he who took me from my mother's
       womb.
My praise is continually of thee.

I have been as a portent to many;
    but thou art my strong refuge.
My mouth is filled with thy praise,
    and with thy glory all the day.
Do not cast me off in the time of old age;
    forsake me not when my strength is spent.
For my enemies speak concerning me,
    those who watch for my life consult
       together,
and say, "God has forsaken him;
    pursue and seize him,
    for there is none to deliver him."

O God, be not far from me;
    O my God, make haste to help me!
May my accusers be put to shame and
       consumed;
    with scorn and disgrace may they be
       covered
    who seek my hurt.
But I will hope continually,
    and will praise thee yet more and more.
My mouth will tell of thy righteous acts,
    of thy deeds of salvation all the day,
    for their number is past my knowledge.
With the mighty deeds of the Lord GOD I
       will come,
    I will praise thy righteousness, thine
       alone.

[k] Tg: Heb *for security* [l] One Ms Tg Compare Syr: Heb *those* [m] Gk Syr: Heb *recount the pain of*
[n] Syr: Heb *and they shall dwell* [o] Gk Compare 31.3: Heb *to come continually thou hast commanded*
69.22–23: Rom 11.9–10. **69.24:** Rev 16.1. **69.25:** Acts 1.20.
69.28: Rev 3.5; 13.8; 17.8; 20.12, 15; 21.27. **70.1–5:** Ps 40.13–17.

O God, from my youth thou hast taught me,
and I still proclaim thy wondrous deeds.
So even to old age and grey hairs,
O God, do not forsake me,
till I proclaim thy might
to all the generations to come. [p]
Thy power and thy righteousness, O God,
reach the high heavens.

Thou who hast done great things,
O God, who is like thee?
Thou who hast made me see many sore
troubles
wilt revive me again;
from the depths of the earth
thou wilt bring me up again.
Thou wilt increase my honour,
and comfort me again.

I will also praise thee with the harp
for thy faithfulness, O my God;
I will sing praises to thee with the lyre,
O Holy One of Israel.
My lips will shout for joy,
when I sing praises to thee;
my soul also, which thou hast rescued.
And my tongue will talk of thy righteous help
all the day long,
for they have been put to shame and
disgraced
who sought to do me hurt.

A Psalm of Solomon.

72 GIVE the king thy justice, O God,
and thy righteousness to the royal
son!
2 May he judge thy people with righteousness,
and thy poor with justice!
3 Let the mountains bear prosperity for the
people,
and the hills, in righteousness!
4 May he defend the cause of the poor of the
people,
give deliverance to the needy,
and crush the oppressor!

5 May he live[q] while the sun endures,
and as long as the moon, throughout all
generations!
6 May he be like rain that falls on the mown
grass,
like showers that water the earth!
7 In his days may righteousness flourish,
and peace abound, till the moon be no
more!

8 May he have dominion from sea to sea,
and from the River to the ends of the
earth!

May his foes[r] bow down before him,   9
and his enemies lick the dust!
May the kings of Tarshish and of the isles   10
render him tribute,
may the kings of Sheba and Seba bring gifts!
May all kings fall down before him,   11
all nations serve him!

For he delivers the needy when he calls,   12
the poor and him who has no helper.
He has pity on the weak and the needy,   13
and saves the lives of the needy.
From oppression and violence he redeems   14
their life;
and precious is their blood in his sight.

Long may he live,   15
may gold of Sheba be given to him!
May prayer be made for him continually,
and blessings invoked for him all the day!
May there be abundance of grain in the land; 16
on the tops of the mountains may it wave;
may its fruit be like Lebanon;
and may men blossom forth from the cities
like the grass of the field!
May his name endure for ever,   17
his fame continue as long as the sun!
May men bless themselves by him,
all nations call him blessed!

Blessed be the LORD, the God of Israel,   18
who alone does wondrous things.
Blessed be his glorious name for ever;   19
may his glory fill the whole earth!
Amen and Amen!

The prayers of David, the son of Jesse, are 20
ended.

BOOK III

A Psalm of Asaph.

73 TRULY God is good to the upright,
to those who are pure in heart.[s]
But as for me, my feet had almost stumbled, 2
my steps had well nigh slipped.
For I was envious of the arrogant,   3
when I saw the prosperity of the wicked.

For they have no pangs;   4
their bodies are sound and sleek.
They are not in trouble as other men are;   5
they are not stricken like other men.
Therefore pride is their necklace;   6
violence covers them as a garment.
Their eyes swell out with fatness,   7
their hearts overflow with follies.

---

[p] Gk Compare Syr: Heb *to a generation, to all that come*   [q] Gk: Heb *may they fear thee*
[r] Cn: Heb *those who dwell in the wilderness*
[s] Or *Truly God is good to Israel, to those who are pure in heart*

8 They scoff and speak with malice;
   loftily they threaten oppression.
9 They set their mouths against the heavens,
   and their tongue struts through the earth.
10 Therefore the people turn and praise them;[t]
   and find no fault in them.[u]
11 And they say, "How can God know?
   Is there knowledge in the Most High?"
12 Behold, these are the wicked;
   always at ease, they increase in riches.
13 All in vain have I kept my heart clean
   and washed my hands in innocence.
14 For all the day long I have been stricken,
   and chastened every morning.

15 If I had said, "I will speak thus,"
   I would have been untrue to the generation
   of thy children.
16 But when I thought how to understand this,
   it seemed to me a wearisome task,

17 until I went into the sanctuary of God;
   then I perceived their end.
18 Truly thou dost set them in slippery
   places;
   thou dost make them fall to ruin.
19 How they are destroyed in a moment,
   swept away utterly by terrors!
20 They are[v] like a dream when one awakes,
   on awaking you despise their phantoms.

21 When my soul was embittered,
   when I was pricked in heart,
22 I was stupid and ignorant,
   I was a beast toward thee.
23 Nevertheless I am continually with thee;
   thou dost hold my right hand.
24 Thou dost guide me with thy counsel,
   and afterward thou wilt receive me to
   glory.[w]
25 Whom have I in heaven but thee?
   And there is nothing upon earth that I
   desire besides thee.
26 My flesh and my heart fail,
   but God is the strength[x] of my heart and
   my portion for ever.

For lo, those who are far from thee shall 27
   perish;
   thou dost put an end to those who are false
   to thee.
But for me it is good to be near God;   28
   I have made the Lord GOD my refuge,
   that I may tell of all thy works.

A Maskil of Asaph.

74 O GOD, why dost thou cast us off for
   ever?
Why does thy anger smoke against the
   sheep of thy pasture?
Remember thy congregation, which thou 2
   hast gotten of old,
   which thou hast redeemed to be the tribe
   of thy heritage!
Remember Mount Zion, where thou hast
   dwelt.
Direct thy steps to the perpetual ruins;   3
   the enemy has destroyed everything in the
   sanctuary!

Thy foes have roared in the midst of thy holy 4
   place;
   they set up their own signs for signs.
At the upper entrance they hacked the 5
   wooden trellis with axes.[y]
And then all its carved wood   6
   they broke down with hatchets and
   hammers.
They set thy sanctuary on fire;   7
   to the ground they desecrated the dwelling
   place of thy name.
They said to themselves, "We will utterly 8
   subdue them";
   they burned all the meeting places of God
   in the land.

We do not see our signs;   9
   there is no longer any prophet,
   and there is none among us who knows
   how long.
How long, O God, is the foe to scoff?   10
   Is the enemy to revile thy name for ever?
Why dost thou hold back thy hand,   11
   why dost thou keep thy right hand in[z] thy
   bosom?

Yet God my King is from of old,   12
   working salvation in the midst of the earth.
Thou didst divide the sea by thy might;   13
   thou didst break the heads of the dragons
   on the waters.
Thou didst crush the heads of Leviathan,   14
   thou didst give him as food[a] for the
   creatures of the wilderness.
Thou didst cleave open springs and brooks;   15
   thou didst dry up ever-flowing streams.

t Cn: Heb *his people return hither*   *u* Cn: Heb *abundant waters are drained by them*   *v* Cn: Heb *Lord*
w Or *honour*   *x* Heb *rock*   *y* Cn Compare Gk Syr: Heb uncertain
z Cn: Heb *consume thy right hand from*   *a* Heb *food for the people*

6 Thine is the day, thine also the night;
    thou hast established the luminaries and
    the sun.
7 Thou hast fixed all the bounds of the earth;
    thou hast made summer and winter.

8 Remember this, O LORD, how the enemy
    scoffs,
    and an impious people reviles thy name.
9 Do not deliver the soul of thy dove to the
    wild beasts;
    do not forget the life of thy poor for ever.
20 Have regard for thy[b] covenant;
    for the dark places of the land are full of
    the habitations of violence.
21 Let not the downtrodden be put to shame;
    let the poor and needy praise thy name.

22 Arise, O God, plead thy cause;
    remember how the impious scoff at thee all
    the day!
23 Do not forget the clamour of thy foes,
    the uproar of thy adversaries which goes
    up continually!

*To the choirmaster: according to Do Not Destroy.
A Psalm of Asaph. A song.*

75 WE give thanks to thee, O God; we
    give thanks;
    we call on thy name and recount[c] thy
    wondrous deeds.

2 At the set time which I appoint
    I will judge with equity.
3 When the earth totters, and all its inhabi-
    tants,
    it is I who keep steady its pillars.   *Selah*
4 I say to the boastful, "Do not boast,"
    and to the wicked, "Do not lift up your
    horn;
5 do not lift up your horn on high,
    or speak with insolent neck."

6 For not from the east or from the west
    and not from the wilderness comes lifting
    up;
7 but it is God who executes judgment,
    putting down one and lifting up another.
8 For in the hand of the LORD there is a cup,
    with foaming wine, well mixed;
    and he will pour a draught from it,

and all the wicked of the earth
    shall drain it down to the dregs.

But I will rejoice[d] for ever,   9
    I will sing praises to the God of Jacob.
All the horns of the wicked he[e] will cut off, 10
    but the horns of the righteous shall be
    exalted.

*To the choirmaster: with stringed instruments. A Psalm
of Asaph. A song.*

76 IN Judah God is known,
    his name is great in Israel.
His abode has been established in Salem,   2
    his dwelling place in Zion.
There he broke the flashing arrows,   3
    the shield, the sword, and the weapons of
    war.   *Selah*

Glorious art thou, more majestic   4
    than the everlasting mountains.[f]
The stouthearted were stripped of their   5
    spoil;
    they sank into sleep;
all the men of war
    were unable to use their hands.
At thy rebuke, O God of Jacob,   6
    both rider and horse lay stunned.

But thou, terrible art thou!   7
    Who can stand before thee
    when once thy anger is roused?
From the heavens thou didst utter judgment; 8
    the earth feared and was still,
when God arose to establish judgment   9
    to save all the oppressed of the earth.
                                  Selah

Surely the wrath of men shall praise thee; 10
    the residue of wrath thou wilt gird upon
    thee.
Make your vows to the LORD your God, and 11
    perform them;
    let all around him bring gifts
    to him who is to be feared,
who cuts off the spirit of princes,   12
    who is terrible to the kings of the earth.

*To the choirmaster: according to Jeduthun. A Psalm of
Asaph.*

77 I CRY aloud to God,
    aloud to God, that he may hear me.
In the day of my trouble I seek the Lord; 2
    in the night my hand is stretched out
    without wearying;
    my soul refuses to be comforted.

I think of God, and I moan;   3
    I meditate, and my spirit faints. *Selah*

---

[b] Gk Syr: Heb *the*   [c] Syr Compare Gk: Heb *and near is thy name. They recount*   [d] Gk: Heb *declare*
[e] Heb *I*   [f] Gk: Heb *the mountains of prey*

4 Thou dost hold my eyelids from closing;
   I am so troubled that I cannot speak.
5 I consider the days of old,
   I remember the years long ago.
6 I commune*g* with my heart in the night;
   I meditate and search my spirit:*h*
7 "Will the Lord spurn for ever,
   and never again be favourable?
8 Has his steadfast love for ever ceased?
   Are his promises at an end for all time?
9 Has God forgotten to be gracious?
   Has he in anger shut up his com-
     passion?"   *Selah*
10 And I say, "It is my grief
   that the right hand of the Most High has
    changed."

11 I will call to mind the deeds of the LORD;
   yea, I will remember thy wonders of old.
12 I will meditate on all thy work,
   and muse on thy mighty deeds.
13 Thy way, O God, is holy.
   What god is great like our God?
14 Thou art the God who workest wonders,
   who hast manifested thy might among the
    peoples.
15 Thou didst with thy arm redeem thy
    people,
   the sons of Jacob and Joseph.   *Selah*

16 When the waters saw thee, O God,
   when the waters saw thee, they were
    afraid,
   yea, the deep trembled.
17 The clouds poured out water;
   the skies gave forth thunder;
   thy arrows flashed on every side.
18 The crash of thy thunder was in the
    whirlwind;
   thy lightnings lighted up the world;
   the earth trembled and shook.
19 Thy way was through the sea,
   thy path through the great waters;
   yet thy footprints were unseen.
20 Thou didst lead thy people like a flock
   by the hand of Moses and Aaron.

A Maskil of Asaph.

78 GIVE ear, O my people, to my
    teaching;
incline your ears to the words of my
  mouth!
2 I will open my mouth in a parable;
   I will utter dark sayings from of old,
3 things that we have heard and known,
   that our fathers have told us.
4 We will not hide them from their children,
   but tell to the coming generation

the glorious deeds of the LORD, and his
   might,
   and the wonders which he has wrought.

He established a testimony in Jacob,   5
   and appointed a law in Israel,
which he commanded our fathers
   to teach to their children;
that the next generation might know them, 6
   the children yet unborn,
and arise and tell them to their children,
   so that they should set their hope in God, 7
and not forget the works of God,
   but keep his commandments;
and that they should not be like their fathers, 8
   a stubborn and rebellious generation,
a generation whose heart was not steadfast,
   whose spirit was not faithful to God.

The E′phraimites, armed with*i* the bow,   9
   turned back on the day of battle.
They did not keep God's covenant,   10
   but refused to walk according to his law.
They forgot what he had done,   11
   and the miracles that he had shown them.
In the sight of their fathers he wrought 12
   marvels
   in the land of Egypt, in the fields of Zo′an.
He divided the sea and let them pass through 13
   it,
   and made the waters stand like a heap.
In the daytime he led them with a cloud,   14
   and all the night with a fiery light.
He cleft rocks in the wilderness,   15
   and gave them drink abundantly as from
    the deep.
He made streams come out of the rock,   16
   and caused waters to flow down like rivers.

Yet they sinned still more against him,   17
   rebelling against the Most High in the
    desert.
They tested God in their heart   18
   by demanding the food they craved.
They spoke against God, saying,   19
   "Can God spread a table in the wilder-
    ness?
He smote the rock so that water gushed out 20
   and streams overflowed.
Can he also give bread,
   or provide meat for his people?"

Therefore, when the LORD heard, he was 21
   full of wrath;
   a fire was kindled against Jacob,
   his anger mounted against Israel;
because they had no faith in God,   22
   and did not trust his saving power.
Yet he commanded the skies above,   23

g Gk Syr: Heb *my music*   *h* Syr Jerome: Heb *my spirit searches*   *i* Heb *armed with shooting*
78.2: Mt 13.35.

and opened the doors of heaven;
and he rained down upon them manna to eat,
and gave them the grain of heaven.
Man ate of the bread of the angels;
he sent them food in abundance.
He caused the east wind to blow in the heavens,
and by his power he led out the south wind;
he rained flesh upon them like dust,
winged birds like the sand of the seas;
he let them fall in the midst of their camp,
all around their habitations.
And they ate and were well filled,
for he gave them what they craved.
But before they had sated their craving,
while the food was still in their mouths,
the anger of God rose against them
and he slew the strongest of them,
and laid low the picked men of Israel.

In spite of all this they still sinned;
despite his wonders they did not believe.
So he made their days vanish like a breath,
and their years in terror.
When he slew them, they sought for him;
they repented and sought God earnestly.
They remembered that God was their rock,
the Most High God their redeemer.
But they flattered him with their mouths;
they lied to him with their tongues.
Their heart was not steadfast toward him;
they were not true to his covenant.
Yet he, being compassionate,
forgave their iniquity,
and did not destroy them;
he restrained his anger often,
and did not stir up all his wrath.
He remembered that they were but flesh,
a wind that passes and comes not again.
How often they rebelled against him in the wilderness
and grieved him in the desert!
They tested him again and again,
and provoked the Holy One of Israel.
They did not keep in mind his power,
or the day when he redeemed them from the foe;
when he wrought his signs in Egypt,
and his miracles in the fields of Zo'an.
He turned their rivers to blood,
so that they could not drink of their streams.
He sent among them swarms of flies, which devoured them,
and frogs, which destroyed them.
He gave their crops to the caterpillar,
and the fruit of their labour to the locust.
He destroyed their vines with hail,
and their sycamores with frost.

He gave over their cattle to the hail, 48
and their flocks to thunderbolts.
He let loose on them his fierce anger, 49
wrath, indignation, and distress,
a company of destroying angels.
He made a path for his anger; 50
he did not spare them from death,
but gave their lives over to the plague.
He smote all the first-born in Egypt, 51
the first issue of their strength in the tents of Ham.
Then he led forth his people like sheep, 52
and guided them in the wilderness like a flock.
He led them in safety, so that they were not 53
afraid;
but the sea overwhelmed their enemies.
And he brought them to his holy land, 54
to the mountain which his right hand had won.
He drove out nations before them; 55
he apportioned them for a possession
and settled the tribes of Israel in their tents.

Yet they tested and rebelled against the Most 56
High God,
and did not observe his testimonies,
but turned away and acted treacherously like 57
their fathers;
they twisted like a deceitful bow.
For they provoked him to anger with their 58
high places;
they moved him to jealousy with their graven images.
When God heard, he was full of wrath, 59
and he utterly rejected Israel.
He forsook his dwelling at Shiloh, 60
the tent where he dwelt among men,
and delivered his power to captivity, 61
his glory to the hand of the foe.
He gave his people over to the sword, 62
and vented his wrath on his heritage.
Fire devoured their young men, 63
and their maidens had no marriage song.
Their priests fell by the sword, 64
and their widows made no lamentation.
Then the Lord awoke as from sleep, 65
like a strong man shouting because of wine.
And he put his adversaries to rout; 66
he put them to everlasting shame.

He rejected the tent of Joseph, 67
he did not choose the tribe of E'phraim;
but he chose the tribe of Judah, 68
Mount Zion, which he loves.
He built his sanctuary like the high heavens, 69
like the earth, which he has founded for ever.

8.24: Jn 6.31. 78.37: Acts 8.21.

70 He chose David his servant,
    and took him from the sheepfolds;
71 from tending the ewes that had young he
    brought him
    to be the shepherd of Jacob his people,
    of Israel his inheritance.
72 With upright heart he tended them,
    and guided them with skilful hand.

A Psalm of Asaph.

79 O GOD, the heathen have come into
    thy inheritance;
    they have defiled thy holy temple;
    they have laid Jerusalem in ruins.
2 They have given the bodies of thy servants
    to the birds of the air for food,
    the flesh of thy saints to the beasts of the
    earth.
3 They have poured out their blood like water
    round about Jerusalem,
    and there was none to bury them.
4 We have become a taunt to our neighbours,
    mocked and derided by those round about
    us.

5 How long, O LORD? Wilt thou be angry for
    ever?

Will thy jealous wrath burn like fire?
Pour out thy anger on the nations
    that do not know thee,
and on the kingdoms
    that do not call on thy name!
For they have devoured Jacob,
    and laid waste his habitation.

Do not remember against us the iniquities o
    our forefathers;
    let thy compassion come speedily to mee
    us,
    for we are brought very low.
Help us, O God of our salvation,
    for the glory of thy name;
deliver us, and forgive our sins,
    for thy name's sake!
Why should the nations say,
    "Where is their God?"
Let the avenging of the outpoured blood o
    thy servants
    be known among the nations before ou
    eyes!

Let the groans of the prisoners come befor
    thee;
    according to thy great power preserve
    those doomed to die!

Return sevenfold into the bosom of our
neighbours
the taunts with which they have taunted
thee, O Lord!
Then we thy people, the flock of thy pasture,
will give thanks to thee for ever;
from generation to generation we will
recount thy praise.

*To the choirmaster: according to Lilies. A testimony of
Asaph. A Psalm.*

80 GIVE ear, O Shepherd of Israel,
thou who leadest Joseph like a flock!
Thou who art enthroned upon the cherubim,
shine forth
before E'phraim and Benjamin and
Manas'seh!
Stir up thy might,
and come to save us!

Restore us, O God;
let thy face shine, that we may be saved!

O LORD God of hosts,
how long wilt thou be angry with thy
people's prayers?
Thou hast fed them with the bread of tears,
and given them tears to drink in full
measure.
Thou dost make us the scorn[j] of our neighbours;
and our enemies laugh among themselves.

Restore us, O God of hosts;
let thy face shine, that we may be saved!

Thou didst bring a vine out of Egypt;
thou didst drive out the nations and plant it.
Thou didst clear the ground for it;
it took deep root and filled the land.
The mountains were covered with its shade,
the mighty cedars with its branches;
it sent out its branches to the sea,
and its shoots to the River.
Why then hast thou broken down its walls,
so that all who pass along the way pluck its
fruit?
The boar from the forest ravages it,
and all that move in the field feed on it.

Turn again, O God of hosts!
Look down from heaven, and see;
have regard for this vine,
the stock which thy right hand planted.[k]
They have burned it with fire, they have cut
it down;
may they perish at the rebuke of thy
countenance!

But let thy hand be upon the man of thy right 17
hand,
the son of man whom thou hast made
strong for thyself!
Then we will never turn back from thee;   18
give us life, and we will call on thy name!

Restore us, O LORD God of hosts!   19
let thy face shine, that we may be saved!

*To the choirmaster: according to the Gittith. A Psalm
of Asaph.*

81 SING aloud to God our strength;
shout for joy to the God of Jacob!
Raise a song, sound the timbrel,   2
the sweet lyre with the harp.
Blow the trumpet at the new moon,   3
at the full moon, on our feast day.
For it is a statute for Israel,   4
an ordinance of the God of Jacob.
He made it a decree in Joseph,   5
when he went out over[l] the land of Egypt.

I hear a voice I had not known:
"I relieved your[m] shoulder of the burden; 6
your[m] hands were freed from the basket.
In distress you called, and I delivered 7
you;
I answered you in the secret place of
thunder;
I tested you at the waters of Mer'ibah.
                                    Selah
Hear, O my people, while I admonish you! 8
O Israel, if you would but listen to me!
There shall be no strange god among you;   9
you shall not bow down to a foreign god.
I am the LORD your God,   10
who brought you up out of the land of
Egypt.
Open your mouth wide, and I will fill it.

"But my people did not listen to my 11
voice;
Israel would have none of me.
So I gave them over to their stubborn 12
hearts,
to follow their own counsels.
O that my people would listen to me,   13
that Israel would walk in my ways!
I would soon subdue their enemies,   14
and turn my hand against their foes.
Those who hate the LORD would cringe 15
toward him,
and their fate would last for ever.
I would feed you[n] with the finest of the 16
wheat,
and with honey from the rock I would
satisfy you."

j Syr: Heb *strife*   *k* Heb *planted and upon the son whom thou hast reared for thyself*
l Or *against*   *m* Heb *his*   *n* Cn Compare verse 16b: Heb *he would feed him*

A Psalm of Asaph.

82 GOD has taken his place in the divine council;
in the midst of the gods he holds judgment:

2 "How long will you judge unjustly
and show partiality to the wicked?   *Selah*

3 Give justice to the weak and the fatherless;
maintain the right of the afflicted and the destitute.

4 Rescue the weak and the needy;
deliver them from the hand of the wicked."

5 They have neither knowledge nor understanding,
they walk about in darkness;
all the foundations of the earth are shaken.

6 I say, "You are gods,
sons of the Most High, all of you;

7 nevertheless, you shall die like men,
and fall like any prince."[o]

8 Arise, O God, judge the earth;
for to thee belong all the nations!

A song. A Psalm of Asaph.

83 O GOD, do not keep silence;
do not hold thy peace or be still, O God!

2 For lo, thy enemies are in tumult;
those who hate thee have raised their heads.

3 They lay crafty plans against thy people;
they consult together against thy protected ones.

4 They say, "Come, let us wipe them out as a nation;
let the name of Israel be remembered no more!"

5 Yea, they conspire with one accord;
against thee they make a covenant—

6 the tents of Edom and the Ish'maelites,
Moab and the Hagrites,

7 Gebal and Ammon and Am'alek,
Philistia with the inhabitants of Tyre;

8 Assyria also has joined them;
they are the strong arm of the children of Lot.   *Selah*

9 Do to them as thou didst to Mid'ian,
as to Sis'era and Jabin at the river Kishon,

10 who were destroyed at En-dor,
who became dung for the ground.

11 Make their nobles like Oreb and Zeeb,
all their princes like Zebah and Zalmun'na;

who said, "Let us take possession for ourselves
of the pastures of God."

O my God, make them like whirling dust,[p]
like chaff before the wind.
As fire consumes the forest,
as the flame sets the mountains ablaze,
so do thou pursue them with thy tempest
and terrify them with thy hurricane!
Fill their faces with shame,
that they may seek thy name, O LORD.
Let them be put to shame and dismayed for ever;
let them perish in disgrace.
Let them know that thou alone,
whose name is the LORD,
art the Most High over all the earth.

To the choirmaster: according to the Gittith. A Psalm of the sons of Korah.

84 HOW lovely is thy dwelling place,
O LORD of hosts!
My soul longs, yea, faints
for the courts of the LORD;
my heart and flesh sing for joy to the living God.

Even the sparrow finds a home,
and the swallow a nest for herself,
where she may lay her young,
at thy altars, O LORD of hosts,
my King and my God.
Blessed are those who dwell in thy house,
ever singing thy praise!   *Selah*

Blessed are the men whose strength is in thee,
in whose heart are the highways to Zion.[q]

---

o Or fall as one man, O princes   *p Or a tumbleweed*   *q* Heb lacks *to Zion*
82.6: Jn 10.34.

As they go through the valley of Baca
  they make it a place of springs;
  the early rain also covers it with pools.
They go from strength to strength;
  the God of gods will be seen in Zion.

O Lord God of hosts, hear my prayer;
  give ear, O God of Jacob!   *Selah*
Behold our shield, O God;
  look upon the face of thine anointed!

For a day in thy courts is better
  than a thousand elsewhere.
I would rather be a doorkeeper in the house
    of my God
  than dwell in the tents of wickedness.
For the Lord God is a sun and shield;
  he bestows favour and honour.
No good thing does the Lord withhold
  from those who walk uprightly.
O Lord of hosts,
  blessed is the man who trusts in thee!

To the choirmaster. A Psalm of the sons of Korah.

85 LORD, thou wast favourable to thy
        land;
  'thou didst restore the fortunes of Jacob.
Thou didst forgive the iniquity of thy
    people;
  thou didst pardon all their sin.   *Selah*
Thou didst withdraw all thy wrath;
  thou didst turn from thy hot anger.

Restore us again, O God of our salvation,
  and put away thy indignation toward us!
Wilt thou be angry with us for ever?
  Wilt thou prolong thy anger to all genera-
    tions?
Wilt thou not revive us again,
  that thy people may rejoice in thee?
Show us thy steadfast love, O Lord,
  and grant us thy salvation.

Let me hear what God the Lord will speak,
  for he will speak peace to his people,
  to his saints, to those who turn to him in
    their hearts.[r]
Surely his salvation is at hand for those who
    fear him,
  that glory may dwell in our land.

Steadfast love and faithfulness will meet;
  righteousness and peace will kiss each
    other.
Faithfulness will spring up from the ground,
  and righteousness will look down from the
    sky.
Yea, the Lord will give what is good,

[r] Gk: Heb *but let them not turn back to folly*

and our land will yield its increase.
Righteousness will go before him,   13
  and make his footsteps a way.

A Prayer of David.

86 INCLINE thy ear, O Lord, and
        answer me,
  for I am poor and needy.
Preserve my life, for I am godly;   2
  save thy servant who trusts in thee.
Thou art my God; be gracious to me, O   3
    Lord,
  for to thee do I cry all the day.
Gladden the soul of thy servant,   4
  for to thee, O Lord, do I lift up my soul.
For thou, O Lord, art good and forgiving,   5
  abounding in steadfast love to all who call
    on thee.
Give ear, O Lord, to my prayer;   6
  hearken to my cry of supplication.
In the day of my trouble I call on thee,   7
  for thou dost answer me.

There is none like thee among the gods, O   8
    Lord,
  nor are there any works like thine.
All the nations thou hast made shall come   9
  and bow down before thee, O Lord,
  and shall glorify thy name.
For thou art great and doest wondrous   10
    things,
  thou alone art God.
Teach me thy way, O Lord,   11
  that I may walk in thy truth;
  unite my heart to fear thy name.
I give thanks to thee, O Lord my God, with 12
  my whole heart,
  and I will glorify thy name for ever.
For great is thy steadfast love toward me; 13
  thou hast delivered my soul from the
    depths of Sheol.

O God, insolent men have risen up against 14
    me;
  a band of ruthless men seek my life,
  and they do not set thee before them.
But thou, O Lord, art a God merciful and   15
    gracious,
  slow to anger and abounding in steadfast
    love and faithfulness.
Turn to me and take pity on me;   16
  give thy strength to thy servant,
  and save the son of thy handmaid.
Show me a sign of thy favour,   17
  that those who hate me may see and be put
    to shame
  because thou, Lord, hast helped me and
    comforted me.

A Psalm of the sons of Korah. A song.

87 ON the holy mount stands the city he
founded;
2   the Lord loves the gates of Zion
more than all the dwelling places of Jacob.
3 Glorious things are spoken of you,
O city of God.   *Selah*

4 Among those who know me I mention Rahab
and Babylon;
behold, Philistia and Tyre, with Ethiopia—
"This one was born there," they say.
5 And of Zion it shall be said,
"This one and that one were born in her";
for the Most High himself will establish
her.
6 The Lord records as he registers the peoples,
"This one was born there."   *Selah*

7 Singers and dancers alike say,
"All my springs are in you."

*A song. A Psalm of the sons of Korah. To the choir-
master: according to Mahalath Leannoth. A Maskil
of Heman the Ezrahite.*

88 O LORD, my God, I call for help[s] by
day;
I cry out in the night before thee.
2 Let my prayer come before thee,
incline thy ear to my cry!

3 For my soul is full of troubles,
and my life draws near to Sheol.
4 I am reckoned among those who go down to
the Pit;
I am a man who has no strength,
5 like one forsaken among the dead,
like the slain that lie in the grave,
like those whom thou dost remember no
more,
for they are cut off from thy hand.
6 Thou hast put me in the depths of the Pit,
in the regions dark and deep.
7 Thy wrath lies heavy upon me,
and thou dost overwhelm me with all thy
waves.   *Selah*
8 Thou hast caused my companions to shun
me;
thou hast made me a thing of horror to
them.
I am shut in so that I cannot escape;
9   my eye grows dim through sorrow.
Every day I call upon thee, O LORD;
I spread out my hands to thee.
10 Dost thou work wonders for the dead?
Do the shades rise up to praise thee?
Selah

Is thy steadfast love declared in the grave,
or thy faithfulness in Abaddon?
Are thy wonders known in the darkness,
or thy saving help in the land of forget-
fulness?

But I, O LORD, cry to thee;
in the morning my prayer comes before
thee.
O LORD, why dost thou cast me off?
Why dost thou hide thy face from me?
Afflicted and close to death from my youth
up,
I suffer thy terrors; I am helpless.[t]
Thy wrath has swept over me;
thy dread assaults destroy me.
They surround me like a flood all day long;
they close in upon me together.
Thou hast caused lover and friend to shun
me;
my companions are in darkness.

A Maskil of Ethan the Ezrahite.

89 I WILL sing of thy steadfast love,
O LORD,[u] for ever;
with my mouth I will proclaim thy faithfulness to all generations.
For thy steadfast love was established for 2
ever,
thy faithfulness is firm as the heavens.
Thou hast said, "I have made a covenant 3
with my chosen one,
I have sworn to David my servant:
'I will establish your descendants for ever, 4
and build your throne for all generations.'"   *Selah*

Let the heavens praise thy wonders, O LORD, 5
thy faithfulness in the assembly of the holy
ones!
For who in the skies can be compared to the 6
LORD?
Who among the heavenly beings[v] is like
the LORD,
a God feared in the council of the holy ones, 7
great and terrible[w] above all that are round
about him?
O LORD God of hosts,   8
who is mighty as thou art, O LORD,
with thy faithfulness round about thee?
Thou dost rule the raging of the sea;   9
when its waves rise, thou stillest them.
Thou didst crush Rahab like a carcass,   10
thou didst scatter thy enemies with thy
mighty arm.
The heavens are thine, the earth also is thine; 11
the world and all that is in it, thou hast
founded them.

s Cn: Heb O LORD, *God of my salvation*   *t* The meaning of the Hebrew word is uncertain
u Gk: Heb *the steadfast love of the LORD*   *v* Or *sons of gods*   *w* Gk Syr: Heb *greatly terrible*
89.3–4: Ps 132.11; Acts 2.30.

The north and the south, thou hast created
  them;
  Tabor and Hermon joyously praise thy
  name.
Thou hast a mighty arm;
  strong is thy hand, high thy right hand.
Righteousness and justice are the foundation
  of thy throne;
  steadfast love and faithfulness go before
  thee.
Blessed are the people who know the festal
  shout,
  who walk, O LORD, in the light of thy
  countenance,
who exult in thy name all the day,
  and extol* thy righteousness.
For thou art the glory of their strength;
  by thy favour our horn is exalted.
For our shield belongs to the LORD,
  our king to the Holy One of Israel.

Of old thou didst speak in a vision
  to thy faithful one, and say:
"I have set the crown* upon one who is
  mighty,
  I have exalted one chosen from the people.
I have found David, my servant;
  with my holy oil I have anointed him;
so that my hand shall ever abide with
  him,
  my arm also shall strengthen him.
The enemy shall not outwit him,
  the wicked shall not humble him.
I will crush his foes before him
  and strike down those who hate him.
My faithfulness and my steadfast love shall
  be with him,
  and in my name shall his horn be exalted.
I will set his hand on the sea
  and his right hand on the rivers.
He shall cry to me, 'Thou art my Father,
  my God, and the Rock of my salvation.'
And I will make him the first-born,
  the highest of the kings of the earth.
My steadfast love I will keep for him for
  ever,
  and my covenant will stand firm for him.
I will establish his line for ever
  and his throne as the days of the heavens.
If his children forsake my law
  and do not walk according to my ordinances,
if they violate my statutes
  and do not keep my commandments,
then I will punish their transgression with
  the rod
  and their iniquity with scourges;
but I will not remove from him my steadfast
  love,
  or be false to my faithfulness.

I will not violate my covenant,   34
  or alter the word that went forth from my
  lips.
Once for all I have sworn by my holiness; 35
  I will not lie to David.
His line shall endure for ever,   36
  his throne as long as the sun before me.
Like the moon it shall be established for 37
  ever;
  it shall stand firm while the skies
  endure."*   Selah

But now thou hast cast off and rejected,   38
  thou art full of wrath against thy
  anointed.
Thou hast renounced the covenant with thy 39
  servant;
  thou hast defiled his crown in the dust.
Thou hast breached all his walls;   40
  thou hast laid his strongholds in ruins.
All that pass by despoil him;   41
  he has become the scorn of his neighbours.
Thou hast exalted the right hand of his 42
  foes;
  thou hast made all his enemies rejoice.
Yea, thou hast turned back the edge of his 43
  sword,
  and thou hast not made him stand in
  battle.
Thou hast removed the sceptre from his 44
  hand,*
  and cast his throne to the ground.
Thou hast cut short the days of his youth; 45
  thou hast covered him with shame. Selah

How long, O LORD? Wilt thou hide thyself 46
  for ever?
  How long will thy wrath burn like fire?
Remember, O Lord,* what the measure of 47
  life is,
  for what vanity thou hast created all the
  sons of men!
What man can live and never see death?   48
  Who can deliver his soul from the power of
  Sheol?   Selah

Lord, where is thy steadfast love of old,   49
  which by thy faithfulness thou didst swear
  to David?
Remember, O Lord, how thy servant is 50
  scorned;
  how I bear in my bosom the insults* of the
  peoples,
with which thy enemies taunt, O LORD,   51
  with which they mock the footsteps of thy
  anointed.

Blessed be the LORD for ever!   52
  Amen and Amen.

x Cn: Heb *are exalted in*   *y* Cn: Heb *help*   *z* Cn: Heb *the witness in the skies is sure*
a Cn: Heb *removed his cleanness*   *b* Cn: Heb *I*   *c* Cn: Heb *all of many*
89.20: Acts 13.22.   89.27: Rev 1.5.

BOOK IV

A prayer of Moses, the man of God.

90 LORD, thou hast been our dwelling place[d]
in all generations.
2 Before the mountains were brought forth,
    or ever thou hadst formed the earth and
    the world,
    from everlasting to everlasting thou art
    God.

3 Thou turnest man back to the dust,
    and sayest, "Turn back, O children of
    men!"
4 For a thousand years in thy sight
    are but as yesterday when it is past,
    or as a watch in the night.

5 Thou dost sweep men away; they are like a
    dream,
    like grass which is renewed in the
    morning:
6 in the morning it flourishes and is renewed;
    in the evening it fades and withers.

7 For we are consumed by thy anger;
    by thy wrath we are overwhelmed.
8 Thou hast set our iniquities before thee,
    our secret sins in the light of thy coun-
    tenance.

9 For all our days pass away under thy wrath,
    our years come to an end[e] like a sigh.
10 The years of our life are threescore and ten,
    or even by reason of strength fourscore;
    yet their span[f] is but toil and trouble;
    they are soon gone, and we fly away.
11 Who considers the power of thy anger,
    and thy wrath according to the fear of
    thee?

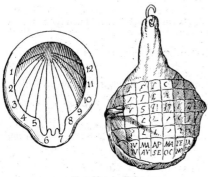

Portable sun-dials

So teach us to number our days   1
    that we may get a heart of wisdom.

Return, O LORD! How long?   1;
    Have pity on thy servants!
Satisfy us in the morning with thy steadfast 1
    love,
    that we may rejoice and be glad all our
    days.
Make us glad as many days as thou hast 1;
    afflicted us,
    and as many years as we have seen evil.
Let thy work be manifest to thy servants,   1
    and thy glorious power to their children.
Let the favour of the Lord our God be upon 1;
    us,
    and establish thou the work of our hands
    upon us,
    yea, the work of our hands establish thou
    it.

91 HE who dwells in the shelter of the
    Most High,
    who abides in the shadow of the Almighty,
will say to the LORD, "My refuge and my 2
    fortress;
    my God, in whom I trust."
For he will deliver you from the snare of the 3
    fowler
    and from the deadly pestilence;
he will cover you with his pinions,   4
    and under his wings you will find refuge;
    his faithfulness is a shield and buckler.
You will not fear the terror of the night,   5
    nor the arrow that flies by day,
nor the pestilence that stalks in darkness,   6
    nor the destruction that wastes at noonday.

A thousand may fall at your side,   7
    ten thousand at your right hand;
    but it will not come near you.
You will only look with your eyes   8
    and see the recompense of the wicked.

Because you have made the LORD your 9
    refuge,[g]
    the Most High your habitation,
no evil shall befall you,   10
    no scourge come near your tent.

For he will give his angels charge of 11
    you
    to guard you in all your ways.
On their hands they will bear you up,   12
    lest you dash your foot against a stone.
You will tread on the lion and the adder,   13
    the young lion and the serpent you will
    trample under foot.

[d] Another reading is *refuge*   [e] Syr: Heb *we bring our years to an end*
[f] Cn Compare Gk Syr Jerome Tg: Heb *pride*   [g] Cn: Heb *Because thou,* LORD, *art my refuge; you have made*
90.4: 2 Pet 3.8.   **91.11–12:** Mt 4.6; Lk 4.10–11.   **91.13:** Lk 10.19.

14 Because he cleaves to me in love, I will
    deliver him;
    I will protect him, because he knows my
    name.
15 When he calls to me, I will answer him;
    I will be with him in trouble,
    I will rescue him and honour him.
16 With long life I will satisfy him,
    and show him my salvation.

A Psalm. A song for the Sabbath.

92 IT is good to give thanks to the LORD,
    to sing praises to thy name, O Most
    High;
2 to declare thy steadfast love in the morning,
    and thy faithfulness by night,
3 to the music of the lute and the harp,
    to the melody of the lyre.
4 For thou, O LORD, hast made me glad by thy
    work;
    at the works of thy hands I sing for joy.

5 How great are thy works, O LORD!
    Thy thoughts are very deep!
6 The dull man cannot know,
    the stupid cannot understand this:
7 that, though the wicked sprout like grass
    and all evildoers flourish,
    they are doomed to destruction for ever,
8   but thou, O LORD, art on high for ever.
9 For, lo, thy enemies, O LORD,
    for, lo, thy enemies shall perish;
    all evildoers shall be scattered.

10 But thou hast exalted my horn like that of the
    wild ox;
    thou hast poured over me[h] fresh oil.
11 My eyes have seen the downfall of my
    enemies,
    my ears have heard the doom of my evil
    assailants.
12 The righteous flourish like the palm tree,
    and grow like a cedar in Lebanon.
13 They are planted in the house of the LORD,
    they flourish in the courts of our God.
14 They still bring forth fruit in old age,
    they are ever full of sap and green,
15 to show that the LORD is upright;
    he is my rock, and there is no unrighteous-
    ness in him.

93 THE LORD reigns; he is robed in
    majesty;
    the LORD is robed, he is girded with
    strength.
Yea, the world is established; it shall never
    be moved;

thy throne is established from of old;   2
thou art from everlasting.

The floods have lifted up, O LORD,   3
    the floods have lifted up their voice,
    the floods lift up their roaring.
Mightier than the thunders of many waters,   4
    mightier than the waves[i] of the sea,
    the LORD on high is mighty!

Thy decrees are very sure;   5
    holiness befits thy house,
    O LORD, for evermore.

94 O LORD, thou God of vengeance,
    thou God of vengeance, shine forth!
Rise up, O judge of the earth;   2
    render to the proud their deserts!
O LORD, how long shall the wicked,   3
    how long shall the wicked exult?

They pour out their arrogant words,   4
    they boast, all the evildoers.
They crush thy people, O LORD,   5
    and afflict thy heritage.
They slay the widow and the sojourner,   6
    and murder the fatherless;
and they say, "The LORD does not see;   7
    the God of Jacob does not perceive."

Understand, O dullest of the people!   8
    Fools, when will you be wise?
He who planted the ear, does he not hear?   9
He who formed the eye, does he not see?
He who chastens the nations, does he not   10
    chastise?
He who teaches men knowledge,
    the LORD, knows the thoughts of man,   11
    that they are but a breath.

Blessed is the man whom thou dost chasten,   12
    O LORD,
    and whom thou dost teach out of thy law
to give him respite from days of trouble,   13
    until a pit is dug for the wicked.
For the LORD will not forsake his people;   14
    he will not abandon his heritage;
for justice will return to the righteous,   15
    and all the upright in heart will follow it.

Who rises up for me against the wicked?   16
    Who stands up for me against evildoers?
If the LORD had not been my help,   17
    my soul would soon have dwelt in the land
    of silence.
When I thought, "My foot slips,"   18
    thy steadfast love, O LORD, held me up.
When the cares of my heart are many,   19

[h] Syr: Heb uncertain   [i] Cn: Heb *mighty the waves*
94.11: 1 Cor 3.20.

thy consolations cheer my soul.
20 Can wicked rulers be allied with thee,
   who frame mischief by statute?
21 They band together against the life of the
      righteous,
   and condemn the innocent to death.
22 But the LORD has become my stronghold,
   and my God the rock of my refuge.
23 He will bring back on them their iniquity
   and wipe them out for their wickedness;
   the LORD our God will wipe them out.

95 O COME, let us sing to the LORD;
   let us make a joyful noise to the rock
   of our salvation!
2 Let us come into his presence with thanks-
     giving;
   let us make a joyful noise to him with
     songs of praise!
3 For the LORD is a great God,
   and a great King above all gods.
4 In his hand are the depths of the earth;
   the heights of the mountains are his also.
5 The sea is his, for he made it;
   for his hands formed the dry land.

6 O come, let us worship and bow down,
   let us kneel before the LORD, our Maker!
7 For he is our God,
   and we are the people of his pasture,
   and the sheep of his hand.

O that today you would hearken to his voice!
8   Harden not your hearts, as at Mer'ibah,
     as on the day at Massah in the wilderness,
9 when your fathers tested me,
     and put me to the proof, though they had
       seen my work.
10 For forty years I loathed that generation
     and said, "They are a people who err in
       heart,
     and they do not regard my ways."
11 Therefore I swore in my anger
     that they should not enter my rest.

96 O SING to the LORD a new song;
   sing to the LORD, all the earth!
2 Sing to the LORD, bless his name;
   tell of his salvation from day to day.
3 Declare his glory among the nations,
   his marvellous works among all the
     peoples!
4 For great is the LORD, and greatly to be
     praised;
   he is to be feared above all gods.
5 For all the gods of the peoples are idols;
   but the LORD made the heavens.

Honour and majesty are before him;   6
   strength and beauty are in his sanctuary.

Ascribe to the LORD, O families of the   7
     peoples,
   ascribe to the LORD glory and strength!
Ascribe to the LORD the glory due his name; 8
   bring an offering, and come into his
     courts!
Worship the LORD in holy array;   9
   tremble before him, all the earth!

Say among the nations, "The LORD reigns!   10
   Yea, the world is established, it shall never
     be moved;
   he will judge the peoples with equity."
Let the heavens be glad, and let the earth 11
     rejoice;
   let the sea roar, and all that fills it;
   let the field exult, and everything in it!   12
Then shall all the trees of the wood sing for
     joy
   before the LORD, for he comes,   13
   for he comes to judge the earth.
He will judge the world with righteousness,
   and the peoples with his truth.

97 THE LORD reigns; let the earth rejoice;
   let the many coastlands be glad!
Clouds and thick darkness are round about   2
     him;
   righteousness and justice are the founda-
     tion of his throne.
Fire goes before him,   3
   and burns up his adversaries round about.
His lightnings lighten the world;   4
   the earth sees and trembles.
The mountains melt like wax before the   5
     LORD,
   before the Lord of all the earth.

The heavens proclaim his righteousness;   6
   and all the peoples behold his glory.
All worshippers of images are put to shame, 7
   who make their boast in worthless idols;
   all gods bow down before him.
Zion hears and is glad,   8
   and the daughters of Judah rejoice,
   because of thy judgments, O God.
For thou, O LORD, art most high over all the 9
     earth;
   thou art exalted far above all gods.

The LORD loves those who hate evil;[j]   10
   he preserves the lives of his saints;
   he delivers them from the hand of the
     wicked.
Light dawns[k] for the righteous,   11

j Cn: Heb *You who love the LORD hate evil*   k Gk Syr Jerome: Heb *is sown*
95.7-11: Heb 3.7-11; 4.3-11.   **96.1-13**: 1 Chron 16.23-33.   **97.7**: Heb 1.6.

and joy for the upright in heart.
2 Rejoice in the LORD, O you righteous,
and give thanks to his holy name!

A Psalm.

98 O SING to the LORD a new song,
for he has done marvellous things!
His right hand and his holy arm
have gotten him victory.
2 The LORD has made known his victory,
he has revealed his vindication in the sight
of the nations.
3 He has remembered his steadfast love and
faithfulness
to the house of Israel.
All the ends of the earth have seen
the victory of our God.

4 Make a joyful noise to the LORD, all the
earth;
break forth into joyous song and sing
praises!
5 Sing praises to the LORD with the lyre,
with the lyre and the sound of melody!
6 With trumpets and the sound of the horn
make a joyful noise before the King, the
LORD!

7 Let the sea roar, and all that fills it;
the world and those who dwell in it!
8 Let the floods clap their hands;
let the hills sing for joy together
9 before the LORD, for he comes to judge the
earth.
He will judge the world with righteousness,
and the peoples with equity.

99 THE LORD reigns; let the peoples
tremble!
He sits enthroned upon the cherubim; let
the earth quake!
2 The LORD is great in Zion;
he is exalted over all the peoples.
3 Let them praise thy great and terrible name!
Holy is he!
4 Mighty King,[l] lover of justice,
thou hast established equity;
thou hast executed justice
and righteousness in Jacob.
5 Extol the LORD our God;
worship at his footstool!
Holy is he!

6 Moses and Aaron were among his priests,
Samuel also was among those who called
on his name.
They cried to the LORD, and he answered
them.
7 He spoke to them in the pillar of cloud;

they kept his testimonies,
and the statutes that he gave them.

O LORD our God, thou didst answer them; 8
thou wast a forgiving God to them,
but an avenger of their wrongdoings.
Extol the LORD our God, 9
and worship at his holy mountain;
for the LORD our God is holy!

A Psalm for the thank offering.

100 MAKE a joyful noise to the LORD,
all the lands![m]
Serve the LORD with gladness! 2
Come into his presence with singing!

Know that the LORD is God! 3
It is he that made us, and we are his;[n]
we are his people, and the sheep of his
pasture.

Enter his gates with thanksgiving, 4
and his courts with praise!
Give thanks to him, bless his name!

For the LORD is good; 5
his steadfast love endures for ever,
and his faithfulness to all generations.

A Psalm of David.

101 I WILL sing of loyalty and of
justice;
to thee, O LORD, I will sing.
I will give heed to the way that is blameless. 2
Oh when wilt thou come to me?

I will walk with integrity of heart
within my house;
I will not set before my eyes 3
anything that is base.

I hate the work of those who fall away;
it shall not cleave to me.
Perverseness of heart shall be far from me; 4
I will know nothing of evil.

Him who slanders his neighbour secretly 5
I will destroy.
The man of haughty looks and arrogant heart
I will not endure.

I will look with favour on the faithful in the 6
land,
that they may dwell with me;
he who walks in the way that is blameless
shall minister to me.

No man who practises deceit 7
shall dwell in my house;

---

[l] Cn: Heb *and the king's strength*   [m] Heb *land* or *earth*   [n] Another reading is *and not we ourselves*

no man who utters lies
  shall continue in my presence.

8 Morning by morning I will destroy
    all the wicked in the land,
  cutting off all the evildoers
    from the city of the LORD.

---

*A prayer of one afflicted, when he is faint and pours out
his complaint before the LORD.*

102 HEAR my prayer, O LORD;
      let my cry come to thee!
2 Do not hide thy face from me
    in the day of my distress!
  Incline thy ear to me;
    answer me speedily in the day when I call!
3 For my days pass away like smoke,
    and my bones burn like a furnace.
4 My heart is smitten like grass, and withered;
    I forget to eat my bread.
5 Because of my loud groaning
    my bones cleave to my flesh.
6 I am like a vulture[o] of the wilderness,

      like an owl of the waste places;
7 I lie awake,
    I am like a lonely bird on the housetop.
8 All the day my enemies taunt me,
    those who deride me use my name for a
    curse.
9 For I eat ashes like bread,
    and mingle tears with my drink,
10 because of thy indignation and anger;
    for thou hast taken me up and thrown me
    away.
11 My days are like an evening shadow;
    I wither away like grass.

12 But thou, O LORD, art enthroned for ever;
    thy name endures to all generations.
13 Thou wilt arise and have pity on Zion;
    it is the time to favour her;
    the appointed time has come.
14 For thy servants hold her stones dear,
    and have pity on her dust.

The nations will fear the name of the LORD, 15
    and all the kings of the earth thy glory.
For the LORD will build up Zion, 16
    he will appear in his glory;
he will regard the prayer of the destitute, 17
    and will not despise their supplication.

Let this be recorded for a generation to 18
    come,
  so that a people yet unborn may praise the
    LORD:
that he looked down from his holy height, 19
    from heaven the LORD looked at the
    earth,
to hear the groans of the prisoners, 20
    to set free those who were doomed to die;
that men may declare in Zion the name of the 21
    LORD,
    and in Jerusalem his praise,
when peoples gather together, 22
    and kingdoms, to worship the LORD.

He has broken my strength in mid-course; 23
    he has shortened my days.
"O my God," I say, "take me not hence 24
    in the midst of my days,
thou whose years endure
    throughout all generations!"

Of old thou didst lay the foundation of the 25
    earth,
    and the heavens are the work of thy hands.
They will perish, but thou dost endure; 26
    they will all wear out like a garment.
Thou changest them like raiment,
    and they pass away;
  but thou art the same, and thy years have 27
    no end.
The children of thy servants shall dwell 28
    secure;
    their posterity shall be established before
    thee.

A Psalm of David.

103 BLESS the LORD, O my soul;
      and all that is within me,
      bless his holy name!
Bless the LORD, O my soul, 2
    and forget not all his benefits,
who forgives all your iniquity, 3
    who heals all your diseases,
who redeems your life from the Pit, 4
    who crowns you with steadfast love and
    mercy,
who satisfies you with good as long as you 5
    live[p]
  so that your youth is renewed like the
    eagle's.

---

[o] The meaning of the Hebrew word is uncertain   [p] Heb uncertain
102.25-27: Heb 1.10-12.

The LORD works vindication
and justice for all who are oppressed.
He made known his ways to Moses,
his acts to the people of Israel.
The LORD is merciful and gracious,
slow to anger and abounding in steadfast
love.
He will not always chide,
nor will he keep his anger for ever.
He does not deal with us according to our
sins,
nor requite us according to our iniquities.
For as the heavens are high above the earth,
so great is his steadfast love toward those
who fear him;
as far as the east is from the west,
so far does he remove our transgressions
from us.
As a father pities his children,
so the LORD pities those who fear him.
For he knows our frame;
he remembers that we are dust.

As for man, his days are like grass;
he flourishes like a flower of the field;
for the wind passes over it, and it is gone,
and its place knows it no more.
But the steadfast love of the LORD is from
everlasting to everlasting
upon those who fear him,
and his righteousness to children's children,
to those who keep his covenant
and remember to do his commandments.
The LORD has established his throne in the
heavens,
and his kingdom rules over all.
Bless the LORD, O you his angels,
you mighty ones who do his word,
hearkening to the voice of his word!
Bless the LORD, all his hosts,
his ministers that do his will!
Bless the LORD, all his works,
in all places of his dominion.
Bless the LORD, O my soul!

104 BLESS the LORD, O my soul!
O LORD my God, thou art very
great!
Thou art clothed with honour and majesty,
2   who coverest thyself with light as with a
garment,
who hast stretched out the heavens like a
tent,
3   who hast laid the beams of thy chambers
on the waters,
who makest the clouds thy chariot,

who ridest on the wings of the wind,
who makest the winds thy messengers,   4
fire and flame thy ministers.

Thou didst set the earth on its foundations,   5
so that it should never be shaken.
Thou didst cover it with the deep as with a   6
garment;
the waters stood above the mountains.
At thy rebuke they fled;   7
at the sound of thy thunder they took to
flight.
The mountains rose, the valleys sank down   8
to the place which thou didst appoint for
them.
Thou didst set a bound which they should   9
not pass,
so that they might not again cover the
earth.

Thou makest springs gush forth in the   10
valleys;
they flow between the hills,
they give drink to every beast of the field;   11
the wild asses quench their thirst.
By them the birds of the air have their   12
habitation;
they sing among the branches.
From thy lofty abode thou waterest the   13
mountains;
the earth is satisfied with the fruit of thy
work.

Thou dost cause the grass to grow for the   14
cattle,
and plants for man to cultivate,[q]
that he may bring forth food from the earth,
and wine to gladden the heart of man,   15
oil to make his face shine,
and bread to strengthen man's heart.
The trees of the LORD are watered abun-   16
dantly,
the cedars of Lebanon which he planted.
In them the birds build their nests;   17
the stork has her home in the fir trees.
The high mountains are for the wild goats;   18
the rocks are a refuge for the badgers.
Thou hast made the moon to mark the   19
seasons;
the sun knows its time for setting.
Thou makest darkness, and it is night,   20
when all the beasts of the forest creep
forth.
The young lions roar for their prey,   21
seeking their food from God.
When the sun rises, they get them away   22
and lie down in their dens.
Man goes forth to his work   23
and to his labour until the evening.

---

[q] Or fodder for the animals that serve man
103.8: Jas 5.11.   **103.17:** Lk 1.50.   **104.4:** Heb 1.7.   **104.12:** Mt 13.32; Mk 4.32; Lk 13.19.

Ps **104**, 23

24 O Lord, how manifold are thy works!
    In wisdom hast thou made them all;
    the earth is full of thy creatures.
25 Yonder is the sea, great and wide,
    which teems with things innumerable,
    living things both small and great.
26 There go the ships,
    and Leviathan which thou didst form to
    sport in it.

27 These all look to thee,
    to give them their food in due season.
28 When thou givest to them, they gather it
    up;
    when thou openest thy hand, they are filled
    with good things.
29 When thou hidest thy face, they are dis-
    mayed;
    when thou takest away their breath, they
    die
    and return to their dust.
30 When thou sendest forth thy Spirit,ʳ they are
    created;
    and thou renewest the face of the ground.

31 May the glory of the Lord endure for ever,
    may the Lord rejoice in his works,
32 who looks on the earth and it trembles,

who touches the mountains and they
    smoke!
I will sing to the Lord as long as I live;
    I will sing praise to my God while I have
    being.
May my meditation be pleasing to him,
    for I rejoice in the Lord.
Let sinners be consumed from the earth,
    and let the wicked be no more!
Bless the Lord, O my soul!
Praise the Lord!

105 O GIVE thanks to the Lord,
        call on his name,
    make known his deeds among the peoples!
Sing to him, sing praises to him,
    tell of all his wonderful works!
Glory in his holy name;
    let the hearts of those who seek the Lord
    rejoice!
Seek the Lord and his strength,
    seek his presence continually!
Remember the wonderful works that he has
    done,
    his miracles, and the judgments he uttered,
O offspring of Abraham his servant,
    sons of Jacob, his chosen ones!

ʳ Or *breath*
105.1–15: 1 Chron 16.8–22.

He is the LORD our God;
   his judgments are in all the earth.
He is mindful of his covenant for ever,
   of the word that he commanded, for a
    thousand generations,
the covenant which he made with Abraham,
   his sworn promise to Isaac,
which he confirmed to Jacob as a statute,
   to Israel as an everlasting covenant,
saying, "To you I will give the land of
   Canaan
as your portion for an inheritance."

When they were few in number,
   of little account, and sojourners in it,
wandering from nation to nation,
   from one kingdom to another people,
he allowed no one to oppress them;
   he rebuked kings on their account,
saying, "Touch not my anointed ones,
   do my prophets no harm!"

When he summoned a famine on the land,
   and broke every staff of bread,
he had sent a man ahead of them,
   Joseph, who was sold as a slave.
His feet were hurt with fetters,
   his neck was put in a collar of iron;
until what he had said came to pass
   the word of the LORD tested him.
The king sent and released him,
   the ruler of the peoples set him free;
he made him lord of his house,
   and ruler of all his possessions,
to instruct[s] his princes at his pleasure,
   and to teach his elders wisdom.

Then Israel came to Egypt;
   Jacob sojourned in the land of Ham.
And the LORD made his people very fruitful,
   and made them stronger than their foes.
He turned their hearts to hate his people,
   to deal craftily with his servants.

He sent Moses his servant,
   and Aaron whom he had chosen.
They wrought his signs among them,
   and miracles in the land of Ham.
He sent darkness, and made the land dark;
   they rebelled[t] against his words.
He turned their waters into blood,
   and caused their fish to die.
Their land swarmed with frogs,
   even in the chambers of their kings.
He spoke, and there came swarms of flies,
   and gnats throughout their country.
He gave them hail for rain,
   and lightning that flashed through their
    land.

He smote their vines and fig trees,   33
   and shattered the trees of their country.
He spoke, and the locusts came,   34
   and young locusts without number;
which devoured all the vegetation in their 35
   land,
   and ate up the fruit of their ground.
He smote all the first-born in their land,   36
   the first issue of all their strength.

Then he led forth Israel with silver and gold, 37
   and there was none among his tribes who
    stumbled.
Egypt was glad when they departed,   38
   for dread of them had fallen upon it.
He spread a cloud for a covering,   39
   and fire to give light by night.
They asked, and he brought quails,   40
   and gave them bread from heaven in
    abundance.
He opened the rock, and water gushed forth; 41
   it flowed through the desert like a river.
For he remembered his holy promise,   42
   and Abraham his servant.

So he led forth his people with joy,   43
   his chosen ones with singing.
And he gave them the lands of the nations; 44
   and they took possession of the fruit of the
    peoples' toil,
to the end that they should keep his statutes, 45
   and observe his laws.
Praise the LORD!

106 PRAISE the LORD!
    O give thanks to the LORD,
   for he is good;
   for his steadfast love endures for ever!
Who can utter the mighty doings of the 2
   LORD,
   or show forth all his praise?
Blessed are they who observe justice,   3
   who do righteousness at all times!

Remember me, O LORD, when thou showest 4
   favour to thy people;
   help me when thou deliverest them;
that I may see the prosperity of thy chosen 5
   ones,
   that I may rejoice in the gladness of thy
    nation,
   that I may glory with thy heritage.
Both we and our fathers have sinned;   6
   we have committed iniquity, we have done
    wickedly.
Our fathers, when they were in Egypt,   7
   did not consider thy wonderful works;
they did not remember the abundance of thy
   steadfast love,

---

[s] Gk Syr Jerome: Heb *to bind*   [t] Cn Compare Gk Syr: Heb *they did not rebel*
105.8–9: Lk 1.72–73.   **106.1:** 1 Chron 16.34.

but rebelled against the Most High[u] at the Red Sea.

8 Yet he saved them for his name's sake,
    that he might make known his mighty power.

9 He rebuked the Red Sea, and it became dry;
    and he led them through the deep as through a desert.

10 So he saved them from the hand of the foe,
    and delivered them from the power of the enemy.

11 And the waters covered their adversaries;
    not one of them was left.

12 Then they believed his words;
    they sang his praise.

13 But they soon forgot his works;
    they did not wait for his counsel.

14 But they had a wanton craving in the wilderness,
    and put God to the test in the desert;

15 he gave them what they asked,
    but sent a wasting disease among them.

16 When men in the camp were jealous of Moses
    and Aaron, the holy one of the LORD,

17 the earth opened and swallowed up Dathan,
    and covered the company of Abi'ram.

18 Fire also broke out in their company;
    the flame burned up the wicked.

19 They made a calf in Horeb
    and worshipped a molten image.

20 They exchanged the glory of God
    for the image of an ox that eats grass.

21 They forgot God, their Saviour,
    who had done great things in Egypt,

22 wondrous works in the land of Ham,
    and terrible things by the Red Sea.

23 Therefore he said he would destroy them—
    had not Moses, his chosen one,
    stood in the breach before him,
    to turn away his wrath from destroying them.

24 Then they despised the pleasant land,
    having no faith in his promise.

25 They murmured in their tents,
    and did not obey the voice of the LORD.

26 Therefore he raised his hand and swore to them
    that he would make them fall in the wilderness,

27 and would disperse[v] their descendants among the nations,
    scattering them over the lands.

28 Then they attached themselves to the Ba'al of Pe'or,
    and ate sacrifices offered to the dead;

29 they provoked the LORD to anger with their doings,
    and a plague broke out among them.

30 Then Phin'ehas stood up and interposed,
    and the plague was stayed.

31 And that has been reckoned to him as righteousness
    from generation to generation for ever.

32 They angered him at the waters of Mer'ibah,
    and it went ill with Moses on their account;

33 for they made his spirit bitter,
    and he spoke words that were rash.

34 They did not destroy the peoples,
    as the LORD commanded them,

35 but they mingled with the nations
    and learned to do as they did.

36 They served their idols,
    which became a snare to them.

37 They sacrificed their sons
    and their daughters to the demons;

38 they poured out innocent blood,
    the blood of their sons and daughters,
    whom they sacrificed to the idols of Canaan;
    and the land was polluted with blood.

39 Thus they became unclean by their acts,
    and played the harlot in their doings.

40 Then the anger of the LORD was kindled against his people,
    and he abhorred his heritage;

41 he gave them into the hand of the nations,
    so that those who hated them ruled over them.

42 Their enemies oppressed them,
    and they were brought into subjection under their power.

43 Many times he delivered them,
    but they were rebellious in their purposes,
    and were brought low through their iniquity.

44 Nevertheless he regarded their distress,
    when he heard their cry.

45 He remembered for their sake his covenant,
    and relented according to the abundance of his steadfast love.

46 He caused them to be pitied
    by all those who held them captive.

47 Save us, O LORD our God,
    and gather us from among the nations,
    that we may give thanks to thy holy name
    and glory in thy praise.

---

[u] Cn Compare 78.17, 56: Heb *at the sea*   [v] Syr Compare Ezek 20.23: Heb *cause to fall*
106.47-48: 1 Chron 16.35-36.

Blessed be the LORD, the God of Israel,
   from everlasting to everlasting!
And let all the people say, "Amen!"
   Praise the LORD!

BOOK V

107 O GIVE thanks to the LORD,
         for he is good;
   for his steadfast love endures for ever!
Let the redeemed of the LORD say so,
   whom he has redeemed from trouble
and gathered in from the lands,
   from the east and from the west,
   from the north and from the south.

Some wandered in desert wastes,
   finding no way to a city to dwell in;
hungry and thirsty,
   their soul fainted within them.
Then they cried to the LORD in their trouble,
   and he delivered them from their distress;
   he led them by a straight way,
   till they reached a city to dwell in.
Let them thank the LORD for his steadfast
      love,
   for his wonderful works to the sons of
      men!
For he satisfies him who is thirsty,
   and the hungry he fills with good things.

Some sat in darkness and in gloom,
   prisoners in affliction and in irons,
for they had rebelled against the words of
      God,
   and spurned the counsel of the Most High.
Their hearts were bowed down with hard
      labour;
   they fell down, with none to help.
Then they cried to the LORD in their trouble,
   and he delivered them from their distress;

he brought them out of darkness and gloom, 14
   and broke their bonds asunder.
Let them thank the LORD for his steadfast 15
      love,
   for his wonderful works to the sons of
      men!
For he shatters the doors of bronze,   16
   and cuts in two the bars of iron.

Some were sick *w* through their sinful ways, 17
   and because of their iniquities suffered
      affliction;
they loathed any kind of food,   18
   and they drew near to the gates of death.
Then they cried to the LORD in their trouble, 19
   and he delivered them from their distress;
he sent forth his word, and healed them,   20
   and delivered them from destruction.
Let them thank the LORD for his steadfast 21
      love,
   for his wonderful works to the sons of
      men!
And let them offer sacrifices of thanksgiving, 22
   and tell of his deeds in songs of joy!

Some went down to the sea in ships,   23
   doing business on the great waters;
they saw the deeds of the LORD,   24
   his wondrous works in the deep.
For he commanded, and raised the stormy 25
      wind,
   which lifted up the waves of the sea.

w Cn: Heb *fools*

26 They mounted up to heaven, they went
    down to the depths;
  their courage melted away in their evil
    plight;
27 they reeled and staggered like drunken men,
    and were at their wits' end.
28 Then they cried to the LORD in their trouble,
    and he delivered them from their distress;
29 he made the storm be still,
    and the waves of the sea were hushed.
30 Then they were glad because they had quiet,
    and he brought them to their desired
    haven.
31 Let them thank the LORD for his steadfast
    love,
  for his wonderful works to the sons of
    men!
32 Let them extol him in the congregation of the
    people,
  and praise him in the assembly of the
    elders.

33 He turns rivers into a desert,
    springs of water into thirsty ground,
34 a fruitful land into a salty waste,
    because of the wickedness of its inhabi-
    tants.
35 He turns a desert into pools of water,
    a parched land into springs of water.
36 And there he lets the hungry dwell,
    and they establish a city to live in;
37 they sow fields, and plant vineyards,
    and get a fruitful yield.
38 By his blessing they multiply greatly;
    and he does not let their cattle decrease.

39 When they are diminished and brought low
    through oppression, trouble, and sorrow,
40 he pours contempt upon princes
    and makes them wander in trackless
    wastes;
41 but he raises up the needy out of affliction,
    and makes their families like flocks.
42 The upright see it and are glad;
    and all wickedness stops its mouth.
43 Whoever is wise, let him give heed to these
    things;
  let men consider the steadfast love of the
    LORD.

A song. A Psalm of David.

108 MY heart is steadfast, O God,
    my heart is steadfast!
I will sing and make melody!
  Awake, my soul!
2 Awake, O harp and lyre!
  I will awake the dawn!
3 I will give thanks to thee, O LORD, among the
    peoples,

I will sing praises to thee among the
    nations.
For thy steadfast love is great above the
    heavens,
  thy faithfulness reaches to the clouds.

Be exalted, O God, above the heavens!
  Let thy glory be over all the earth!
That thy beloved may be delivered,
  give help by thy right hand, and answer
    me!

God has promised in his sanctuary:*
  "With exultation I will divide up Shechem,
    and portion out the Vale of Succoth.
Gilead is mine; Manas′seh is mine;
  E′phraim is my helmet;
  Judah my sceptre.
Moab is my washbasin;
  upon Edom I cast my shoe;
  over Philistia I shout in triumph."

Who will bring me to the fortified city?
  Who will lead me to Edom?
Hast thou not rejected us, O God?
  Thou dost not go forth, O God, with our
    armies.
O grant us help against the foe,
  for vain is the help of man!
With God we shall do valiantly;
  it is he who will tread down our foes.

To the choirmaster. A Psalm of David.

109 BE not silent, O God of my praise!
    For wicked and deceitful mouths are 2
    opened against me,
  speaking against me with lying tongues.
They beset me with words of hate,   3
  and attack me without cause.
In return for my love they accuse me,   4
  even as I make prayer for them.*
So they reward me evil for good,   5
  and hatred for my love.

Appoint a wicked man against him;   6
  let an accuser bring him to trial.*
When he is tried, let him come forth guilty; 7
  let his prayer be counted as sin!
May his days be few;   8
  may another seize his goods!
May his children be fatherless,   9
  and his wife a widow!
May his children wander about and beg;   10
  may they be driven out of* the ruins they
    inhabit!
May the creditor seize all that he has; 11
  may strangers plunder the fruits of his
    toil!

2 Let there be none to extend kindness to him,
   nor any to pity his fatherless children!
3 May his posterity be cut off;
   may his name be blotted out in the second
      generation!
4 May the iniquity of his fathers be remem-
      bered before the LORD,
   and let not the sin of his mother be blotted
      out!
5 Let them be before the LORD continually;
   and may his[b] memory be cut off from the
      earth!
6 For he did not remember to show kindness,
   but pursued the poor and needy
   and the brokenhearted to their death.
7 He loved to curse; let curses come on him!
   He did not like blessing; may it be far from
      him!
8 He clothed himself with cursing as his coat,
   may it soak into his body like water,
   like oil into his bones!
9 May it be like a garment which he wraps
      round him,
   like a belt with which he daily girds
      himself!

10 May this be the reward of my accusers from
      the LORD,
   of those who speak evil against my life!
11 But thou, O GOD my Lord,
   deal on my behalf for thy name's sake;
   because thy steadfast love is good, deliver
      me!
12 For I am poor and needy,
   and my heart is stricken within me.
13 I am gone, like a shadow at evening;
   I am shaken off like a locust.
14 My knees are weak through fasting;
   my body has become gaunt.
15 I am an object of scorn to my accusers;
   when they see me, they wag their heads.

16 Help me, O LORD my God!
   Save me according to thy steadfast love!
17 Let them know that this is thy hand;
   thou, O LORD, hast done it!
18 Let them curse, but do thou bless!
   Let my assailants be put to shame;[c] may
      thy servant be glad!
19 May my accusers be clothed with dishonour!
   may they be wrapped in their own shame
      as in a mantle!

30 With my mouth I will give great thanks to
      the LORD;
   I will praise him in the midst of the
      throng.
31 For he stands at the right hand of the needy,

to save him from those who condemn him
   to death.

A Psalm of David.

110 THE LORD says to my lord:
   "Sit at my right hand,
till I make your enemies your footstool."

The LORD sends forth from Zion   2
   your mighty sceptre.
   Rule in the midst of your foes!
Your people will offer themselves freely 3
   on the day you lead your host
   upon the holy mountains.[d]
From the womb of the morning
   like dew your youth[e] will come to you.
The LORD has sworn   4
   and will not change his mind,
"You are a priest for ever
   after the order of Melchiz'edek."

The Lord is at your right hand;   5
   he will shatter kings on the day of his
      wrath.
He will execute judgment among the nations, 6
   filling them with corpses;
he will shatter chiefs[f]
   over the wide earth.
He will drink from the brook by the way; 7
   therefore he will lift up his head.

111 PRAISE the LORD.
   I will give thanks to the LORD
   with my whole heart,
   in the company of the upright,
   in the congregation.
Great are the works of the LORD,   2
   studied by all who have pleasure in them.
Full of honour and majesty is his work, 3
   and his righteousness endures for ever.
He has caused his wonderful works to be 4
      remembered;
   the LORD is gracious and merciful.
He provides food for those who fear him; 5
   he is ever mindful of his covenant.
He has shown his people the power of his 6
      works,
   in giving them the heritage of the nations.
The works of his hands are faithful and just; 7
   all his precepts are trustworthy,
they are established for ever and ever, 8
   to be performed with faithfulness and
      uprightness.
He sent redemption to his people;   9
   he has commanded his covenant for ever.
   Holy and terrible is his name!

---

[b] Gk: Heb *their*   [c] Gk: Heb *they have arisen and have been put to shame*
[d] Another reading is *in holy array*   [e] Cn: Heb *the dew of your youth*   [f] Or *the head*
109.25: Mt 27.39; Mk 15.29.   110.1: Mt 22.44; 26.64; Mk 12.36; 14.62; 16.19; Lk 20.42-43; 22.69; Acts
2.34; 1 Cor 15.25; Eph 1.20; Col 3.1; Heb 1.3, 13; 10.12-13; 12.2.   110.4: Heb 5.6, 10; 6.20; 7.11, 15, 21.

10 The fear of the LORD is the beginning of
    wisdom;
        a good understanding have all those who
        practise it.
        His praise endures for ever!

112 PRAISE the LORD.
        Blessed is the man who fears the
    LORD,
        who greatly delights in his command-
        ments!
2 His descendants will be mighty in the land;
        the generation of the upright will be
        blessed.
3 Wealth and riches are in his house;
        and his righteousness endures for ever.
4 Light rises in the darkness for the upright;
        the LORD[g] is gracious, merciful, and
        righteous.
5 It is well with the man who deals generously
        and lends,
        who conducts his affairs with justice.
6 For the righteous will never be moved;
        he will be remembered for ever.
7 He is not afraid of evil tidings;
        his heart is firm, trusting in the LORD.
8 His heart is steady, he will not be afraid,
        until he sees his desire on his adversaries.
9 He has distributed freely, he has given to the
        poor;
        his righteousness endures for ever;
        his horn is exalted in honour.
10 The wicked man sees it and is angry;
        he gnashes his teeth and melts away;
        the desire of the wicked man comes to
        naught.

113 PRAISE the LORD!
        Praise, O servants of the LORD,
    praise the name of the LORD!

2 Blessed be the name of the LORD
        from this time forth and for evermore!
3 From the rising of the sun to its setting
        the name of the LORD is to be praised!
4 The LORD is high above all nations,
        and his glory above the heavens!

5 Who is like the LORD our God,
        who is seated on high,
6 who looks far down
        upon the heavens and the earth?
7 He raises the poor from the dust,
        and lifts the needy from the ash heap,
8 to make them sit with princes,
        with the princes of his people.
9 He gives the barren woman a home,
        making her the joyous mother of children.
        Praise the LORD!

114 WHEN Israel went forth from
        Egypt,
        the house of Jacob from a people of strange
        language,
Judah became his sanctuary,   2
        Israel his dominion.

The sea looked and fled,   3
        Jordan turned back.
The mountains skipped like rams,   4
        the hills like lambs.

What ails you, O sea, that you flee?   5
        O Jordan, that you turn back?
O mountains, that you skip like rams?   6
        O hills, like lambs?

Tremble, O earth, at the presence of the 7
    LORD,
        at the presence of the God of Jacob,
who turns the rock into a pool of water,   8
        the flint into a spring of water.

115 NOT to us, O LORD, not to us,
        but to thy name give glory,
for the sake of thy steadfast love
        and thy faithfulness!
Why should the nations say,   2
        "Where is their God?"

Our God is in the heavens;   3
        he does whatever he pleases.
Their idols are silver and gold,   4
        the work of men's hands.
They have mouths, but do not speak;   5
        eyes, but do not see.
They have ears, but do not hear;   6
        noses, but do not smell.
They have hands, but do not feel;   7
        feet, but do not walk;
        and they do not make a sound in their
        throat.
Those who make them are like them;   8
        so are all who trust in them.

O Israel, trust in the LORD!   9
        He is their help and their shield.
O house of Aaron, put your trust in the 10
    LORD!
        He is their help and their shield.
You who fear the LORD, trust in the LORD! 11
        He is their help and their shield.

The LORD has been mindful of us; he will 12
        bless us;
        he will bless the house of Israel;
        he will bless the house of Aaron;
he will bless those who fear the LORD,   13
        both small and great.

g Gk: Heb lacks the LORD
112.9: 2 Cor 9.9.   115.4–8: Ps 135.15–18.   115.13: Rev 11.18; 19.5.

4 May the LORD give you increase,
   you and your children!
5 May you be blessed by the LORD,
   who made heaven and earth!

6 The heavens are the LORD's heavens,
   but the earth he has given to the sons of
      men.
7 The dead do not praise the LORD,
   nor do any that go down into silence.
8 But we will bless the LORD
   from this time forth and for evermore.
   Praise the LORD!

116

I LOVE the LORD, because he has
   heard
   my voice and my supplications.
2 Because he inclined his ear to me,
   therefore I will call on him as long as I live.
3 The snares of death encompassed me;
   the pangs of Sheol laid hold on me;
   I suffered distress and anguish.
4 Then I called on the name of the LORD:
   "O LORD, I beseech thee, save my life!"

5 Gracious is the LORD, and righteous;
   our God is merciful.
6 The LORD preserves the simple;
   when I was brought low, he saved me.
7 Return, O my soul, to your rest;
   for the LORD has dealt bountifully with you.

8 For thou hast delivered my soul from death,
   my eyes from tears,
   my feet from stumbling;
9 I walk before the LORD
   in the land of the living.
10 I kept my faith, even when I said,
   "I am greatly afflicted";
11 I said in my consternation,
   "Men are all a vain hope."

12 What shall I render to the LORD
   for all his bounty to me?
13 I will lift up the cup of salvation
   and call on the name of the LORD,
14 I will pay my vows to the LORD
   in the presence of all his people.
15 Precious in the sight of the LORD
   is the death of his saints.
16 O LORD, I am thy servant;
   I am thy servant, the son of thy handmaid.
   Thou hast loosed my bonds.
17 I will offer to thee the sacrifice of thanks-
      giving
   and call on the name of the LORD.
18 I will pay my vows to the LORD
   in the presence of all his people,

in the courts of the house of the LORD,   19
   in your midst, O Jerusalem.
Praise the LORD!

117

PRAISE the LORD, all nations!
   Extol him, all peoples!
For great is his steadfast love toward us;   2
   and the faithfulness of the LORD endures
      for ever.
Praise the LORD!

118

O GIVE thanks to the LORD, for he
   is good;
   his steadfast love endures for ever!

Let Israel say,   2
   "His steadfast love endures for ever."
Let the house of Aaron say,   3
   "His steadfast love endures for ever."
Let those who fear the LORD say,   4
   "His steadfast love endures for ever."

Out of my distress I called on the LORD;   5
   the LORD answered me and set me free.
With the LORD on my side I do not fear.   6
   What can man do to me?
The LORD is on my side to help me;   7
   I shall look in triumph on those who hate
      me.
It is better to take refuge in the LORD   8
   than to put confidence in man.
It is better to take refuge in the LORD   9
   than to put confidence in princes.

All nations surrounded me;   10
   in the name of the LORD I cut them off!
They surrounded me, surrounded me on   11
      every side;
   in the name of the LORD I cut them off!
They surrounded me like bees,   12
   they blazed[h] like a fire of thorns;
   in the name of the LORD I cut them off!
I was pushed hard,[i] so that I was falling,   13
   but the LORD helped me.
The LORD is my strength and my song;   14
   he has become my salvation.

Hark, glad songs of victory   15
   in the tents of the righteous:
"The right hand of the LORD does valiantly,
   the right hand of the LORD is exalted,   16
   the right hand of the LORD does vali-
      antly!"
I shall not die, but I shall live,   17
   and recount the deeds of the LORD.
The LORD has chastened me sorely,   18
   but he has not given me over to death.

---

h Gk: Heb *were extinguished*   i Gk Syr Jerome: Heb *thou didst push me hard*
116.10: 2 Cor 4.13.   117.1: Rom 15.11.   118.6: Heb 13.6.

19 Open to me the gates of righteousness,
   that I may enter through them
   and give thanks to the LORD.

20 This is the gate of the LORD;
   the righteous shall enter through it.

21 I thank thee that thou hast answered me
   and hast become my salvation.
22 The stone which the builders rejected
   has become the head of the corner.
23 This is the LORD's doing;
   it is marvellous in our eyes.
24 This is the day which the LORD has made;
   let us rejoice and be glad in it.
25 Save us, we beseech thee, O LORD!
   O LORD, we beseech thee, give us success!

26 Blessed be he who enters in the name of the
   LORD!
   We bless you from the house of the LORD.
27 The LORD is God,
   and he has given us light.
   Bind the festal procession with branches,
   up to the horns of the altar!

28 Thou art my God, and I will give thanks to
   thee;
   thou art my God, I will extol thee.

29 O give thanks to the LORD, for he is good;
   for his steadfast love endures for ever!

119 BLESSED are those whose way is
   blameless,
   who walk in the law of the LORD!
2 Blessed are those who keep his testimonies,
   who seek him with their whole heart,

who also do no wrong,   3
   but walk in his ways!
Thou hast commanded thy precepts   4
   to be kept diligently.
O that my ways may be steadfast   5
   in keeping thy statutes!
Then I shall not be put to shame,   6
   having my eyes fixed on all thy commandments.
I will praise thee with an upright heart,   7
   when I learn thy righteous ordinances.
I will observe thy statutes;   8
   O forsake me not utterly!

How can a young man keep his way pure? 9
   By guarding it according to thy word.
With my whole heart I seek thee;   10
   let me not wander from thy command-
   ments!
I have laid up thy word in my heart,   11
   that I might not sin against thee.
Blessed be thou, O LORD;   12
   teach me thy statutes!
With my lips I declare   13
   all the ordinances of thy mouth.
In the way of thy testimonies I delight   14
   as much as in all riches.
I will meditate on thy precepts,   15
   and fix my eyes on thy ways.
I will delight in thy statutes;   16
   I will not forget thy word.

Deal bountifully with thy servant,   17
   that I may live and observe thy word.
Open my eyes, that I may behold   18
   wondrous things out of thy law.
I am a sojourner on earth;   19
   hide not thy commandments from me!
My soul is consumed with longing   20
   for thy ordinances at all times.
Thou dost rebuke the insolent, accursed 21
   ones,
   who wander from thy commandments;
take away from me their scorn and contempt, 22
   for I have kept thy testimonies.
Even though princes sit plotting against me, 23
   thy servant will meditate on thy statutes.
Thy testimonies are my delight,   24
   they are my counsellors.

My soul cleaves to the dust;   25
   revive me according to thy word!
When I told of my ways, thou didst answer 26
   me;
   teach me thy statutes!
Make me understand the way of thy pre- 27
   cepts,
   and I will meditate on thy wondrous
   works.

28 My soul melts away for sorrow;
    strengthen me according to thy word!
29 Put false ways far from me;
    and graciously teach me thy law!
30 I have chosen the way of faithfulness,
    I set thy ordinances before me.
31 I cleave to thy testimonies, O LORD;
    let me not be put to shame!
32 I will run in the way of thy commandments
    when thou enlargest my understanding!

33 Teach me, O LORD, the way of thy statutes;
    and I will keep it to the end.
34 Give me understanding, that I may keep thy
    law
    and observe it with my whole heart.
35 Lead me in the path of thy commandments,
    for I delight in it.
36 Incline my heart to thy testimonies,
    and not to gain!
37 Turn my eyes from looking at vanities;
    and give me life in thy ways.
38 Confirm to thy servant thy promise,
    which is for those who fear thee.
39 Turn away the reproach which I dread;
    for thy ordinances are good.
40 Behold, I long for thy precepts;
    in thy righteousness give me life!

41 Let thy steadfast love come to me, O LORD,
    thy salvation according to thy promise;
42 then shall I have an answer for those who
    taunt me,
    for I trust in thy word.
43 And take not the word of truth utterly out of
    my mouth,
    for my hope is in thy ordinances.
44 I will keep thy law continually,
    for ever and ever;
45 and I shall walk at liberty,
    for I have sought thy precepts.
46 I will also speak of thy testimonies before
    kings,
    and shall not be put to shame;
47 for I find my delight in thy commandments,
    which I love.
48 I revere thy commandments, which I love,
    and I will meditate on thy statutes.

49 Remember thy word to thy servant,
    in which thou hast made me hope.
50 This is my comfort in my affliction
    that thy promise gives me life.
51 Godless men utterly deride me,
    but I do not turn away from thy law.
52 When I think of thy ordinances from of old,
    I take comfort, O LORD.
53 Hot indignation seizes me because of the
    wicked,
    who forsake thy law.
54 Thy statutes have been my songs
    in the house of my pilgrimage.

I remember thy name in the night, O LORD, 55
    and keep thy law.
This blessing has fallen to me, 56
    that I have kept thy precepts.

The LORD is my portion; 57
    I promise to keep thy words.
I entreat thy favour with all my heart; 58
    be gracious to me according to thy
    promise.
When I think of thy ways, 59
    I turn my feet to thy testimonies;
I hasten and do not delay 60
    to keep thy commandments.
Though the cords of the wicked ensnare me, 61
    I do not forget thy law.
At midnight I rise to praise thee, 62
    because of thy righteous ordinances.
I am a companion of all who fear thee, 63
    of those who keep thy precepts.
The earth, O LORD, is full of thy steadfast 64
    love;
    teach me thy statutes!

Thou hast dealt well with thy servant, 65
    O LORD, according to thy word.
Teach me good judgment and knowledge, 66
    for I believe in thy commandments.
Before I was afflicted I went astray; 67
    but now I keep thy word.
Thou art good and doest good; 68
    teach me thy statutes.
The godless besmear me with lies, 69
    but with my whole heart I keep thy
    precepts;
their heart is gross like fat, 70
    but I delight in thy law.
It is good for me that I was afflicted, 71
    that I might learn thy statutes.
The law of thy mouth is better to me 72
    than thousands of gold and silver pieces.

Thy hands have made and fashioned me; 73
    give me understanding that I may learn
    thy commandments.
Those who fear thee shall see me and rejoice, 74
    because I have hoped in thy word.
I know, O LORD, that thy judgments are 75
    right,
    and that in faithfulness thou hast afflicted
    me.
Let thy steadfast love be ready to comfort 76
    me
    according to thy promise to thy servant.
Let thy mercy come to me, that I may live; 77
    for thy law is my delight.
Let the godless be put to shame, 78
    because they have subverted me with
    guile;
    as for me, I will meditate on thy precepts.
Let those who fear thee turn to me, 79
    that they may know thy testimonies.

80 May my heart be blameless in thy
      statutes,
   that I may not be put to shame!

81 My soul languishes for thy salvation;
   I hope in thy word.
82 My eyes fail with watching for thy
      promise;
   I ask, "When wilt thou comfort me?"
83 For I have become like a wineskin in the
      smoke,
   yet I have not forgotten thy statutes.
84 How long must thy servant endure?
   When wilt thou judge those who persecute
      me?
85 Godless men have dug pitfalls for me,
   men who do not conform to thy law.
86 All thy commandments are sure;
   they persecute me with falsehood; help
      me!
87 They have almost made an end of me on
      earth;
   but I have not forsaken thy precepts.
88 In thy steadfast love spare my life,
   that I may keep the testimonies of thy
      mouth.

89 For ever, O LORD, thy word
   is firmly fixed in the heavens.
90 Thy faithfulness endures to all generations;
   thou hast established the earth, and it
      stands fast.
91 By thy appointment they stand this day;
   for all things are thy servants.
92 If thy law had not been my delight,
   I should have perished in my affliction.
93 I will never forget thy precepts;
   for by them thou hast given me life.
94 I am thine, save me;
   for I have sought thy precepts.
95 The wicked lie in wait to destroy me;
   but I consider thy testimonies.
96 I have seen a limit to all perfection,
   but thy commandment is exceedingly
      broad.

97 Oh, how I love thy law!
   It is my meditation all the day.
98 Thy commandment makes me wiser than
      my enemies,
   for it is ever with me.
99 I have more understanding than all my
      teachers,
   for thy testimonies are my meditation.
100 I understand more than the aged,
   for I keep thy precepts.
101 I hold back my feet from every evil way,
   in order to keep thy word.
102 I do not turn aside from thy ordinances,
   for thou hast taught me.
103 How sweet are thy words to my taste,
   sweeter than honey to my mouth!

104 Through thy precepts I get understanding;
   therefore I hate every false way.

105 Thy word is a lamp to my feet
   and a light to my path.
106 I have sworn an oath and confirmed it,
   to observe thy righteous ordinances.
107 I am sorely afflicted;
   give me life, O LORD, according to thy
      word!
108 Accept my offerings of praise, O LORD,
   and teach me thy ordinances.
109 I hold my life in my hand continually,
   but I do not forget thy law.
110 The wicked have laid a snare for me,
   but I do not stray from thy precepts.
111 Thy testimonies are my heritage for
      ever;
   yea, they are the joy of my heart.
112 I incline my heart to perform thy statutes
   for ever, to the end.

113 I hate double-minded men,
   but I love thy law.
114 Thou art my hiding place and my shield;
   I hope in thy word.
115 Depart from me, you evildoers,
   that I may keep the commandments of my
      God.
116 Uphold me according to thy promise, that I
      may live,
   and let me not be put to shame in my
      hope!
117 Hold me up, that I may be safe
   and have regard for thy statutes con-
      tinually!
118 Thou dost spurn all who go astray from thy
      statutes;
   yea, their cunning is in vain.
119 All the wicked of the earth thou dost count
      as dross;
   therefore I love thy testimonies.
120 My flesh trembles for fear of thee,
   and I am afraid of thy judgments.

121 I have done what is just and right;
   do not leave me to my oppressors.
122 Be surety for thy servant for good;
   let not the godless oppress me.
123 My eyes fail with watching for thy
      salvation,
   and for the fulfilment of thy righteous
      promise.
124 Deal with thy servant according to thy
      steadfast love,
   and teach me thy statutes.
125 I am thy servant; give me understanding,
   that I may know thy testimonies!
126 It is time for the LORD to act,
   for thy law has been broken.
127 Therefore I love thy commandments
   above gold, above fine gold.

Therefore I direct my steps by all thy
    precepts;[j]
I hate every false way.

Thy testimonies are wonderful;
    therefore my soul keeps them.
The unfolding of thy words gives light;
    it imparts understanding to the simple.
With open mouth I pant,
    because I long for thy commandments.
Turn to me and be gracious to me,
    as is thy wont toward those who love thy
    name.
Keep steady my steps according to thy
    promise,
    and let no iniquity get dominion over me.
Redeem me from man's oppression,
    that I may keep thy precepts.
Make thy face shine upon thy servant,
    and teach me thy statutes.
My eyes shed streams of tears,
    because men do not keep thy law.

Righteous art thou, O LORD,
    and right are thy judgments.
Thou hast appointed thy testimonies in
    righteousness
    and in all faithfulness.
My zeal consumes me,
    because my foes forget thy words.
Thy promise is well tried,
    and thy servant loves it.
I am small and despised,
    yet I do not forget thy precepts.
Thy righteousness is righteous for
    ever,
    and thy law is true.
Trouble and anguish have come upon me,
    but thy commandments are my delight.
Thy testimonies are righteous for
    ever;
    give me understanding that I may live.

With my whole heart I cry; answer me, O
    LORD!
    I will keep thy statutes.
I cry to thee; save me,
    that I may observe thy testimonies.
I rise before dawn and cry for help;
    I hope in thy words.
My eyes are awake before the watches of
    the night,
    that I may meditate upon thy promise.
Hear my voice in thy steadfast love;
    O LORD, in thy justice preserve my life.
They draw near who persecute me with evil
    purpose;
    they are far from thy law.
But thou art near, O LORD,
    and all thy commandments are true.

Long have I known from thy testimonies   152
    that thou hast founded them for ever.

Look on my affliction and deliver me,   153
    for I do not forget thy law.
Plead my cause and redeem me;   154
    give me life according to thy promise!
Salvation is far from the wicked,   155
    for they do not seek thy statutes.
Great is thy mercy, O LORD;   156
    give me life according to thy justice.
Many are my persecutors and my   157
    adversaries,
    but I do not swerve from thy testimonies.
I look at the faithless with disgust,   158
    because they do not keep thy commands.
Consider how I love thy precepts!   159
    Preserve my life according to thy steadfast
    love.
The sum of thy word is truth;   160
    and every one of thy righteous ordinances
    endures for ever.

Princes persecute me without cause,   161
    but my heart stands in awe of thy words.
I rejoice at thy word   162
    like one who finds great spoil.
I hate and abhor falsehood,   163
    but I love thy law.
Seven times a day I praise thee   164
    for thy righteous ordinances.
Great peace have those who love thy   165
    law;
    nothing can make them stumble.
I hope for thy salvation, O LORD,   166
    and I do thy commandments.
My soul keeps thy testimonies;   167

Ps 119, 176

I love them exceedingly.
168 I keep thy precepts and testimonies,
for all my ways are before thee.

169 Let my cry come before thee, O LORD;
give me understanding according to thy
word!
170 Let my supplication come before thee;
deliver me according to thy word.
171 My lips will pour forth praise
that thou dost teach me thy statutes.
172 My tongue will sing of thy word,
for all thy commandments are right.
173 Let thy hand be ready to help me,
for I have chosen thy precepts.
174 I long for thy salvation, O LORD,
and thy law is my delight.
175 Let me live, that I may praise thee,
and let thy ordinances help me.
176 I have gone astray like a lost sheep; seek thy
servant,
for I do not forget thy commandments.

A Song of ascents.

120 IN my distress I cry to the LORD,
that he may answer me:
2 "Deliver me, O LORD,
from lying lips,
from a deceitful tongue."

3 What shall be given to you?
And what more shall be done to you,
you deceitful tongue?
4 A warrior's sharp arrows,
with glowing coals of the broom tree!

5 Woe is me, that I sojourn in Meshech,
that I dwell among the tents of Kedar!
6 Too long have I had my dwelling
among those who hate peace.
7 I am for peace;
but when I speak,
they are for war!

A Song of ascents.

121 I LIFT up my eyes to the hills.
From whence does my help
come?
2 My help comes from the LORD,
who made heaven and earth.

3 He will not let your foot be moved,
he who keeps you will not slumber.
4 Behold, he who keeps Israel
will neither slumber nor sleep.

5 The LORD is your keeper;
the LORD is your shade
on your right hand.
6 The sun shall not smite you by day,
nor the moon by night.

The LORD will keep you from all evil;
he will keep your life.
The LORD will keep
your going out and your coming in
from this time forth and for evermore.

A Song of ascents. Of David.

122 I WAS glad when they said to me,
"Let us go to the house of the
LORD!"
Our feet have been standing
within your gates, O Jerusalem!

Jerusalem, built as a city
which is bound firmly together,
to which the tribes go up,
the tribes of the LORD,
as was decreed for Israel,
to give thanks to the name of the LORD.
There thrones for judgment were set,
the thrones of the house of David.

Pray for the peace of Jerusalem!
"May they prosper who love you!
Peace be within your walls,
and security within your towers!"
For my brethren and companions' sake
I will say, "Peace be within you!"
For the sake of the house of the LORD our
God,
I will seek your good.

A Song of ascents.

123 TO thee I lift up my eyes,
O thou who art enthroned in the
heavens!
Behold, as the eyes of servants
look to the hand of their master,
as the eyes of a maid
to the hand of her mistress,
so our eyes look to the LORD our God,
till he have mercy upon us.

Have mercy upon us, O LORD, have mercy 3
upon us,
for we have had more than enough of
contempt.
Too long our soul has been sated 4
with the scorn of those who are at ease,
the contempt of the proud.

A Song of ascents. Of David.

124 IF it had not been the LORD who
was on our side,
let Israel now say—
if it had not been the LORD who was on our 2
side,
when men rose up against us,
then they would have swallowed us up alive, 3
when their anger was kindled against us;
then the flood would have swept us away, 4
the torrent would have gone over us;

hen over us would have gone
  the raging waters.

Blessed be the Lord,
  who has not given us
  as prey to their teeth!
We have escaped as a bird
  from the snare of the fowlers;
the snare is broken,
  and we have escaped!

Our help is in the name of the Lord,
  who made heaven and earth.

A Song of ascents.

125 THOSE who trust in the Lord are
        like Mount Zion,
  which cannot be moved, but abides for
    ever.
As the mountains are round about Jeru-
    salem,
  so the Lord is round about his people,
  from this time forth and for evermore.
For the sceptre of wickedness shall not rest
  upon the land allotted to the righteous,
lest the righteous put forth
  their hands to do wrong.
Do good, O Lord, to those who are good,
  and to those who are upright in their
    hearts!
But those who turn aside upon their crooked
    ways
  the Lord will lead away with evildoers!
Peace be in Israel!

A Song of ascents.

126 WHEN the Lord restored the
        fortunes of Zion,[k]
  we were like those who dream.
2 Then our mouth was filled with laughter,
  and our tongue with shouts of joy;
then they said among the nations,
  "The Lord has done great things for
    them."
3 The Lord has done great things for us;
  we are glad.

4 Restore our fortunes, O Lord,
  like the watercourses in the Negeb!
5 May those who sow in tears
  reap with shouts of joy!
6 He that goes forth weeping,
  bearing the seed for sowing,
shall come home with shouts of joy,
  bringing his sheaves with him.

A Song of ascents. Of Solomon.

127 UNLESS the Lord builds the
        house,
  those who build it labour in vain.

Unless the Lord watches over the city,
  the watchman stays awake in vain.
It is in vain that you rise up early and go late 2
    to rest,
eating the bread of anxious toil;
  for[l] he gives to his beloved sleep.

Lo, sons are a heritage from the Lord,   3
  the fruit of the womb a reward.
Like arrows in the hand of a warrior   4
  are the sons of one's youth.
Happy is the man who has   5
  his quiver full of them!
He shall not be put to shame
  when he speaks with his enemies in the
    gate.

A Song of ascents.

128 BLESSED is every one who fears
        the Lord,
  who walks in his ways!
You shall eat the fruit of the labour of your 2
    hands;
  you shall be happy, and it shall be well
    with you.

Your wife will be like a fruitful vine   3
    within your house;
your children will be like olive shoots
    around your table.
Lo, thus shall the man be blessed   4
  who fears the Lord.

The Lord bless you from Zion!   5
  May you see the prosperity of Jerusalem
    all the days of your life!
May you see your children's children!   6
  Peace be upon Israel!

A Song of ascents.

129 "SORELY have they afflicted me
        from my youth,"
  let Israel now say—
"Sorely have they afflicted me from my 2
    youth,
  yet they have not prevailed against me.
The ploughers ploughed upon my back;   3
  they made long their furrows."
The Lord is righteous;   4
  he has cut the cords of the wicked.
May all who hate Zion   5
  be put to shame and turned backward!
Let them be like the grass on the housetops, 6
  which withers before it grows up,
with which the reaper does not fill his 7
    hand
  or the binder of sheaves his bosom,
while those who pass by do not say,   8
  "The blessing of the Lord be upon you!
  We bless you in the name of the Lord!"

---

k Or *brought back those who returned to Zion*   l Another reading is *so*

A Song of ascents.

130 OUT of the depths I cry to thee, O
LORD!
2 Lord, hear my voice!
Let thy ears be attentive
to the voice of my supplications!

3 If thou, O LORD, shouldst mark iniquities,
Lord, who could stand?
4 But there is forgiveness with thee,
that thou mayest be feared.

5 I wait for the LORD, my soul waits,
and in his word I hope;
6 my soul waits for the LORD
more than watchmen for the morning,
more than watchmen for the morning.

7 O Israel, hope in the LORD!
For with the LORD there is steadfast love,
and with him is plenteous redemption.
8 And he will redeem Israel
from all his iniquities.

A Song of ascents. Of David.

131 O LORD, my heart is not lifted up,
my eyes are not raised too high;
I do not occupy myself with things
too great and too marvellous for me.
2 But I have calmed and quieted my soul,
like a child quieted at its mother's breast;
like a child that is quieted is my soul.

3 O Israel, hope in the LORD
from this time forth and for evermore.

A Song of ascents.

132 REMEMBER, O LORD, in David's
favour,
all the hardships he endured;
2 how he swore to the LORD
and vowed to the Mighty One of Jacob,
3 "I will not enter my house
or get into my bed;
4 I will not give sleep to my eyes
or slumber to my eyelids,
5 until I find a place for the LORD,
a dwelling place for the Mighty One of
Jacob."

6 Lo, we heard of it in Eph'rathah,
we found it in the fields of Ja'ar.
7 "Let us go to his dwelling place;
let us worship at his footstool!"

8 Arise, O LORD, and go to thy resting place,
thou and the ark of thy might.
9 Let thy priests be clothed with righteousness,

and let thy saints shout for joy.
For thy servant David's sake
do not turn away the face of thy anointed
one.

The LORD swore to David a sure oath
from which he will not turn back:
"One of the sons of your body
I will set on your throne.
If your sons keep my covenant
and my testimonies which I shall teach
them,
their sons also for ever
shall sit upon your throne."

For the LORD has chosen Zion;
he has desired it for his habitation:
"This is my resting place for ever;
here I will dwell, for I have desired it.
I will abundantly bless her provisions;
I will satisfy her poor with bread.
Her priests I will clothe with salvation,
and her saints will shout for joy.
There I will make a horn to sprout for
David;
I have prepared a lamp for my anointed.
His enemies I will clothe with shame,
but upon himself his crown will shed its
lustre."

A Song of ascents. Of David.

133 BEHOLD, how good and pleasant
it is
when brothers dwell in unity!
It is like the precious oil upon the head,
running down upon the beard,
upon the beard of Aaron,
running down on the collar of his robes!
It is like the dew of Hermon,
which falls on the mountains of Zion!
For there the LORD has commanded the
blessing,
life for evermore.

A Song of ascents.

134 COME, bless the LORD,
all you servants of the LORD,
who stand by night in the house of the
LORD!
Lift up your hands to the holy place,
and bless the LORD!

May the LORD bless you from Zion,
he who made heaven and earth!

135 PRAISE the LORD.
Praise the name of the LORD,
give praise, O servants of the LORD,

130.3: Ps 143.2; Rom 3.20; Gal 2.16.   132.11: Ps 89.3-4; Acts 2.30.

you that stand in the house of the LORD,
  in the courts of the house of our God!
Praise the LORD, for the LORD is good;
  sing to his name, for he is gracious!
For the LORD has chosen Jacob for himself,
  Israel as his own possession.

For I know that the LORD is great,
  and that our Lord is above all gods.
Whatever the LORD pleases he does,
  in heaven and on earth,
  in the seas and all deeps.
He it is who makes the clouds rise at the end
  of the earth,
  who makes lightnings for the rain
  and brings forth the wind from his
  storehouses.

He it was who smote the first-born of Egypt,
  both of man and of beast;
who in thy midst, O Egypt,
  sent signs and wonders
  against Pharaoh and all his servants;
who smote many nations
  and slew mighty kings,
Sihon, king of the Amorites,
  and Og, king of Bashan,
  and all the kingdoms of Canaan,
and gave their land as a heritage,
  a heritage to his people Israel.

Thy name, O LORD, endures for ever,
  thy renown, O LORD, throughout all ages.
For the LORD will vindicate his people,
  and have compassion on his servants.

The idols of the nations are silver and gold,
  the work of men's hands.
They have mouths, but they speak not,
  they have eyes, but they see not,
they have ears, but they hear not,
  nor is there any breath in their mouths.
Like them be those who make them!—
  yea, every one who trusts in them!

O house of Israel, bless the LORD!
  O house of Aaron, bless the LORD!
O house of Levi, bless the LORD!
  You that fear the LORD, bless the LORD!
Blessed be the LORD from Zion,
  he who dwells in Jerusalem!
Praise the LORD!

136 O GIVE thanks to the LORD, for he
     is good,
  for his steadfast love endures for ever.
O give thanks to the God of gods,
  for his steadfast love endures for ever.
O give thanks to the Lord of lords,

for his steadfast love endures for ever;

to him who alone does great wonders,   4
  for his steadfast love endures for ever;
to him who by understanding made the 5
  heavens,
  for his steadfast love endures for ever;
to him who spread out the earth upon the 6
  waters,
  for his steadfast love endures for ever;
to him who made the great lights,   7
  for his steadfast love endures for ever;
the sun to rule over the day,   8
  for his steadfast love endures for ever;
the moon and stars to rule over the night, 9
  for his steadfast love endures for ever;

to him who smote the first-born of Egypt, 10
  for his steadfast love endures for ever;
and brought Israel out from among them, 11
  for his steadfast love endures for ever;
with a strong hand and an outstretched arm, 12
  for his steadfast love endures for ever;
to him who divided the Red Sea in sunder, 13
  for his steadfast love endures for ever;
and made Israel pass through the midst of it, 14
  for his steadfast love endures for ever;
but overthrew Pharaoh and his host in the 15
  Red Sea,
  for his steadfast love endures for ever;
to him who led his people through the 16
  wilderness,
  for his steadfast love endures for ever;
to him who smote great kings,   17
  for his steadfast love endures for ever;
and slew famous kings,   18
  for his steadfast love endures for ever;
Sihon, king of the Amorites,   19
  for his steadfast love endures for ever;
and Og, king of Bashan,   20
  for his steadfast love endures for ever;
and gave their land as a heritage,   21
  for his steadfast love endures for ever;
a heritage to Israel his servant,   22
  for his steadfast love endures for ever.

It is he who remembered us in our low estate, 23
  for his steadfast love endures for ever;
and rescued us from our foes,   24
  for his steadfast love endures for ever;
he who gives food to all flesh,   25
  for his steadfast love endures for ever.

O give thanks to the God of heaven,   26
  for his steadfast love endures for ever.

137 BY the waters[m] of Babylon,
     there we sat down and wept,
  when we remembered Zion.

[m] Heb streams
135.14: Heb 10.30. 135.15–18: Ps 115.4–8.

and they shall sing of the ways of the LORD,
   for great is the glory of the LORD.
For though the LORD is high, he regards the lowly;
   but the haughty he knows from afar.

Though I walk in the midst of trouble,
   thou dost preserve my life;
thou dost stretch out thy hand against the wrath of my enemies,
   and thy right hand delivers me.
The LORD will fulfil his purpose for me;
   thy steadfast love, O LORD, endures for ever.
   Do not forsake the work of thy hands.

2 On the willows[n] there
   we hung up our lyres.
3 For there our captors
   required of us songs,
and our tormentors, mirth, saying,
   "Sing us one of the songs of Zion!"

4 How shall we sing the LORD's song
   in a foreign land?
5 If I forget you, O Jerusalem,
   let my right hand wither!
6 Let my tongue cleave to the roof of my mouth,
   if I do not remember you,
if I do not set Jerusalem
   above my highest joy!

7 Remember, O LORD, against the E′domites
   the day of Jerusalem,
how they said, "Rase it, rase it!
   Down to its foundations!"
8 O daughter of Babylon, you devastator![o]
   Happy shall he be who requites you
   with what you have done to us!
9 Happy shall he be who takes your little ones
   and dashes them against the rock!

A Psalm of David.

138 I GIVE thee thanks, O LORD, with my whole heart;
   before the gods I sing thy praise;
2 I bow down toward thy holy temple
   and give thanks to thy name for thy steadfast love and thy faithfulness;
for thou hast exalted above everything
   thy name and thy word.[p]
3 On the day I called, thou didst answer me,
   my strength of soul thou didst increase.[q]

4 All the kings of the earth shall praise thee, O LORD,
   for they have heard the words of thy mouth;

To the choirmaster. A Psalm of David.

139 O LORD, thou hast searched me and known me!
Thou knowest when I sit down and when I rise up;
   thou discernest my thoughts from afar.
Thou searchest out my path and my lying down,
   and art acquainted with all my ways.
Even before a word is on my tongue,
   lo, O LORD, thou knowest it altogether.
Thou dost beset me behind and before,
   and layest thy hand upon me.
Such knowledge is too wonderful for me;
   it is high, I cannot attain it.

Whither shall I go from thy Spirit?
   Or whither shall I flee from thy presence?
If I ascend to heaven, thou art there!
   If I make my bed in Sheol, thou art there!
If I take the wings of the morning
   and dwell in the uttermost parts of the sea,
even there thy hand shall lead me,
   and thy right hand shall hold me.
If I say, "Let only darkness cover me,
   and the light about me be night,"
even the darkness is not dark to thee,
   the night is bright as the day;
   for darkness is as light with thee.

For thou didst form my inward parts,
   thou didst knit me together in my mother's womb.
I praise thee, for thou art fearful and wonderful.[r]
   Wonderful are thy works!
Thou knowest me right well;
   my frame was not hidden from thee,
when I was being made in secret,
   intricately wrought in the depths of the earth.
Thy eyes beheld my unformed substance;

[n] Or *poplars*   [o] Or *you who are devastated*   [p] Cn: Heb *thou hast exalted thy word above all thy name*
[q] Syr Compare Gk Tg: Heb *thou didst make me arrogant in my soul with strength*
[r] Cn Compare Gk Syr Jerome: Heb *fearful things I am wonderful*

They make their tongue sharp as a serpent's, 3
and under their lips is the poison of
vipers.   *Selah*

Guard me, O LORD, from the hands of the 4
wicked;
preserve me from violent men,
who have planned to trip up my feet.
Arrogant men have hidden a trap for me, 5
and with cords they have spread a net, *w*
by the wayside they have set snares for
me.   *Selah*

I say to the LORD, Thou art my God;   6
give ear to the voice of my supplications, O
LORD!
O LORD, my Lord, my strong deliverer, 7
thou hast covered my head in the day of
battle.
Grant not, O LORD, the desires of the 8
wicked;
do not further his evil plot!   *Selah*

Those who surround me lift up their head, *x* 9
let the mischief of their lips overwhelm
them!
Let burning coals fall upon them!   10
Let them be cast into pits, no more to
rise!
Let not the slanderer be established in the 11
land;
let evil hunt down the violent man
speedily!

I know that the LORD maintains the cause of 12
the afflicted,
and executes justice for the needy.
Surely the righteous shall give thanks to thy 13
name;
the upright shall dwell in thy presence.

in thy book were written, every one of
them,
the days that were formed for me,
when as yet there was none of them.
7 How precious to me are thy thoughts, O
God!
How vast is the sum of them!
8 If I would count them, they are more than
the sand.
When I awake, I am still with thee. *s*

9 O that thou wouldst slay the wicked, O God,
and that men of blood would depart from
me,
10 men who maliciously defy thee,
who lift themselves up against thee for
evil! *t*
11 Do I not hate them that hate thee, O LORD?
And do I not loathe them that rise up
against thee?
12 I hate them with perfect hatred;
I count them my enemies.
13 Search me, O God, and know my heart!
Try me and know my thoughts!
14 And see if there be any wicked *u* way in me,
and lead me in the way everlasting! *v*

To the choirmaster. A Psalm of David.

140 DELIVER me, O LORD, from evil
men;
preserve me from violent men,
2 who plan evil things in their heart,
and stir up wars continually.

A Psalm of David.

141 I CALL upon thee, O LORD; make
haste to me!
Give ear to my voice, when I call to thee!
Let my prayer be counted as incense before 2
thee,
and the lifting up of my hands as an
evening sacrifice!
Set a guard over my mouth, O LORD,   3
keep watch over the door of my lips!
Incline not my heart to any evil,   4
to busy myself with wicked deeds
in company with men who work iniquity;
and let me not eat of their dainties!

Let a good man strike or rebuke me in 5
kindness,

s Or were I to come to the end I would still be with thee   t Cn: Heb uncertain   u Heb hurtful
v Or the ancient way. Compare Jer 6.16.   w Or they have spread cords as a net
x Cn Compare Gk: Heb those who surround me are uplifted in head
140.3: Rom 3.13.   **141.2:** Rev 5.8; 8.3-4.

but let the oil of the wicked never anoint
my head;ʸ
for my prayer is continuallyᶻ
against their wicked deeds.

6 When they are given over to those who shall
condemn them,
then they shall learn that the word of the
LORD is true.

7 As a rock which one cleaves and shatters on
the land,
so shall their bones be strewn at the mouth
of Sheol.ᵃ

8 But my eyes are toward thee, O LORD God;
in thee I seek refuge; leave me not
defenceless!

9 Keep me from the trap which they have laid
for me,
and from the snares of evildoers!

10 Let the wicked together fall into their own
nets,
while I escape.

A Maskil of David, when he was in the cave. A Prayer.

142 I CRY with my voice to the LORD,
with my voice I make supplication to the LORD,

2 I pour out my complaint before him,
I tell my trouble before him.

3 When my spirit is faint,
thou knowest my way!

In the path where I walk
they have hidden a trap for me.

4 I look to the right and watch,ᵇ
but there is none who takes notice of me;
no refuge remains to me,
no man cares for me.

5 I cry to thee, O LORD;
I say, Thou art my refuge,
my portion in the land of the living.

6 Give heed to my cry;
for I am brought very low!

Deliver me from my persecutors;
for they are too strong for me!

7 Bring me out of prison,
that I may give thanks to thy name!
The righteous will surround me;
for thou wilt deal bountifully with me.

A Psalm of David.

143 HEAR my prayer, O LORD;
give ear to my supplications!
In thy faithfulness answer me,
in thy righteousness!

2 Enter not into judgment with thy servant;

for no man living is righteous before thee.

3 For the enemy has pursued me;
he has crushed my life to the ground;
he has made me sit in darkness like those
long dead.

4 Therefore my spirit faints within me;
my heart within me is appalled.

5 I remember the days of old,
I meditate on all that thou hast done;
I muse on what thy hands have wrought.

6 I stretch out my hands to thee;
my soul thirsts for thee like a parched
land.   *Selah*

7 Make haste to answer me, O LORD!
My spirit fails!
Hide not thy face from me,
lest I be like those who go down to the Pit.

8 Let me hear in the morning of thy steadfast
love,
for in thee I put my trust.
Teach me the way I should go,
for to thee I lift up my soul.

9 Deliver me, O LORD, from my enemies!
I have fled to thee for refuge!ᶜ

10 Teach me to do thy will,
for thou art my God!
Let thy good spirit lead me
on a level path!

11 For thy name's sake, O LORD, preserve my
life!
In thy righteousness bring me out of
trouble!

12 And in thy steadfast love cut off my enemies,
and destroy all my adversaries,
for I am thy servant.

A Psalm of David.

144 BLESSED be the LORD, my rock,
who trains my hands for war,
and my fingers for battle;

2 my rockᵈ and my fortress,
my stronghold and my deliverer,
my shield and he in whom I take refuge,
who subdues the peoples under him.ᵉ

3 O LORD, what is man that thou dost regard
him,
or the son of man that thou dost think of
him?

4 Man is like a breath,
his days are like a passing shadow.

5 Bow thy heavens, O LORD, and come down!
Touch the mountains that they smoke!

ʸ Gk: Heb obscure   ᶻ Cn: Heb *for continually and my prayer*   ᵃ The Hebrew of verses 5-7 is obscure
ᵇ Or *Look to the right and watch*   ᶜ One Heb Ms Gk: Heb *to thee I have hidden*
ᵈ With Ps 18.2, 2 Sam 22.2: Heb *my steadfast love*   ᵉ Another reading is *my people under me*
143.2: Ps 130.3; Rom 3.20; Gal 2.16.

5 Flash forth the lightning and scatter them,
    send out thy arrows and rout them!
7 Stretch forth thy hand from on high,
    rescue me and deliver me from the many
        waters,
    from the hand of aliens,
8 whose mouths speak lies,
    and whose right hand is a right hand of
        falsehood.

9 I will sing a new song to thee, O God;
    upon a ten-stringed harp I will play to
        thee,
10 who givest victory to kings,
    who rescuest David thy[f] servant.
11 Rescue me from the cruel sword,
    and deliver me from the hand of aliens,
    whose mouths speak lies,
    and whose right hand is a right hand of
        falsehood.

12 May our sons in their youth
    be like plants full grown,
    our daughters like corner pillars
        cut for the structure of a palace;
13 may our garners be full,
    providing all manner of store;
    may our sheep bring forth thousands
        and ten thousands in our fields;
14 may our cattle be heavy with young,
    suffering no mischance or failure in
        bearing;
    may there be no cry of distress in our
        streets!
15 Happy the people to whom such blessings fall!
    Happy the people whose God is the LORD!

A Song of praise. Of David.

145 I WILL extol thee, my God and
        King,
    and bless thy name for ever and ever.
2 Every day I will bless thee,
    and praise thy name for ever and ever.
3 Great is the LORD, and greatly to be praised,
    and his greatness is unsearchable.

4 One generation shall laud thy works to
        another,
    and shall declare thy mighty acts.
5 On the glorious splendour of thy majesty,
    and on thy wondrous works, I will
        meditate.
6 Men shall proclaim the might of thy terrible
        acts,
    and I will declare thy greatness.
7 They shall pour forth the fame of thy
        abundant goodness,
    and shall sing aloud of thy righteousness.

8 The LORD is gracious and merciful,

slow to anger and abounding in steadfast
    love.
The LORD is good to all,   9
    and his compassion is over all that he has
        made.

All thy works shall give thanks to thee, O 10
    LORD,
    and all thy saints shall bless thee!
They shall speak of the glory of thy kingdom, 11
    and tell of thy power,
to make known to the sons of men thy[f] 12
    mighty deeds,
    and the glorious splendour of thy[f]
        kingdom.
Thy kingdom is an everlasting kingdom,   13
    and thy dominion endures
        throughout all generations.

The LORD is faithful in all his words,
    and gracious in all his deeds.[g]
The LORD upholds all who are falling,   14
    and raises up all who are bowed down.
The eyes of all look to thee,   15
    and thou givest them their food in due
        season.
Thou openest thy hand,   16
    thou satisfiest the desire of every living
        thing.
The LORD is just in all his ways,   17
    and kind in all his doings.
The LORD is near to all who call upon him,   18
    to all who call upon him in truth.
He fulfils the desire of all who fear him,   19
    he also hears their cry, and saves them.
The LORD preserves all who love him;   20
    but all the wicked he will destroy.

My mouth will speak the praise of the LORD, 21
    and let all flesh bless his holy name for
        ever and ever.

146 PRAISE the LORD!
        Praise the LORD, O my soul!
I will praise the LORD as long as I live;   2
    I will sing praises to my God while I have
        being.

Put not your trust in princes,   3
    in a son of man, in whom there is no help.
When his breath departs he returns to his 4
    earth;
    on that very day his plans perish.

Happy is he whose help is the God of 5
    Jacob,
    whose hope is in the LORD his God,
who made heaven and earth,   6
    the sea, and all that is in them;
who keeps faith for ever;

---

f Heb *his*   *g* These two lines are supplied by one Hebrew Ms, Gk and Syr

7 who executes justice for the oppressed;
who gives food to the hungry.

The LORD sets the prisoners free;
8   the LORD opens the eyes of the blind.
The LORD lifts up those who are bowed
down;
the LORD loves the righteous.
9 The LORD watches over the sojourners,
he upholds the widow and the fatherless;
but the way of the wicked he brings to
ruin.

10 The LORD will reign for ever,
thy God, O Zion, to all generations.
Praise the LORD!

147   PRAISE the LORD!
For it is good to sing praises to
our God;
for he is gracious, and a song of praise is
seemly.
2 The LORD builds up Jerusalem;
he gathers the outcasts of Israel.
3 He heals the brokenhearted,
and binds up their wounds.
4 He determines the number of the stars,
he gives to all of them their names.
5 Great is our LORD, and abundant in power;
his understanding is beyond measure.
6 The LORD lifts up the downtrodden,
he casts the wicked to the ground.

7 Sing to the LORD with thanksgiving;
make melody to our God upon the lyre!
8 He covers the heavens with clouds,
he prepares rain for the earth,
he makes grass grow upon the hills.
9 He gives to the beasts their food,
and to the young ravens which cry.
10 His delight is not in the strength of the
horse,
nor his pleasure in the legs of a man;
11 but the LORD takes pleasure in those who fear
him,
in those who hope in his steadfast love.

12 Praise the LORD, O Jerusalem!
Praise your God, O Zion!
13 For he strengthens the bars of your gates;
he blesses your sons within you.
14 He makes peace in your borders;
he fills you with the finest of the wheat.
15 He sends forth his command to the earth;
his word runs swiftly.
16 He gives snow like wool;
he scatters hoarfrost like ashes.
17 He casts forth his ice like morsels;
who can stand before his cold?
18 He sends forth his word, and melts them;

ʰ Or he set a law which cannot pass away

he makes his wind blow, and the waters
flow.
He declares his word to Jacob,   19
his statutes and ordinances to Israel.
He has not dealt thus with any other 20
nation;
they do not know his ordinances.
Praise the LORD!

148   PRAISE the LORD!
Praise the LORD from the heavens,
praise him in the heights!
Praise him, all his angels,   2
praise him, all his host!

Praise him, sun and moon,   3
praise him, all you shining stars!
Praise him, you highest heavens,   4
and you waters above the heavens!

Let them praise the name of the LORD!   5
For he commanded and they were created.
And he established them for ever and ever; 6
he fixed their bounds which cannot be
passed.ʰ

Praise the LORD from the earth,   7
you sea monsters and all deeps,
fire and hail, snow and frost,   8
stormy wind fulfilling his command!

Mountains and all hills,   9
fruit trees and all cedars!
Beasts and all cattle,   10
creeping things and flying birds!

Kings of the earth and all peoples,   11
princes and all rulers of the earth!
Young men and maidens together,   12
old men and children!

Let them praise the name of the LORD,   13
for his name alone is exalted;
his glory is above earth and heaven.
He has raised up a horn for his people,   14
praise for all his saints,
for the people of Israel who are near to
him.
Praise the LORD!

149   PRAISE the LORD!
Sing to the LORD a new song,
his praise in the assembly of the faithful!
Let Israel be glad in his Maker,   2
let the sons of Zion rejoice in their King!
Let them praise his name with dancing,   3
making melody to him with timbrel and
lyre!
For the LORD takes pleasure in his people; 4
he adorns the humble with victory.

5 Let the faithful exult in glory;
  let them sing for joy on their couches.
6 Let the high praises of God be in their
  throats
  and two-edged swords in their hands,
7 to wreak vengeance on the nations
  and chastisement on the peoples,
8 to bind their kings with chains
  and their nobles with fetters of iron,
9 to execute on them the judgment written!
  This is glory for all his faithful ones.
  Praise the LORD!

150 PRAISE the LORD!
    Praise God in his sanctuary;

praise him in his mighty firmament!
Praise him for his mighty deeds;   2
  praise him according to his exceeding
  greatness!

Praise him with trumpet sound;   3
  praise him with lute and harp!
Praise him with timbrel and dance;   4
  praise him with strings and pipe!
Praise him with sounding cymbals;   5
  praise him with loud clashing cymbals!
Let everything that breathes praise the 6
  LORD!
Praise the LORD!

Trumpets   *Cornets*   *Drums*   *Cymbals and bells*

THE
PROVERBS

THE proverbs of Solomon, son of
  David, king of Israel:

2 That men may know wisdom and instruction,
  understand words of insight,
3 receive instruction in wise dealing,
  righteousness, justice, and equity;
4 that prudence may be given to the simple,
  knowledge and discretion to the youth—
5 the wise man also may hear and increase in
  learning,
  and the man of understanding acquire skill,
6 to understand a proverb and a figure,
  the words of the wise and their riddles.

7 The fear of the LORD is the beginning of
  knowledge;
  fools despise wisdom and instruction.

8 Hear, my son, your father's instruction,

and reject not your mother's teaching;
for they are a fair garland for your head,   9
  and pendants for your neck.
My son, if sinners entice you,   10
  do not consent.
If they say, "Come with us, let us lie in wait 11
  for blood,
  let us wantonly ambush the innocent;
like Sheol let us swallow them alive   12
  and whole, like those who go down to the
    Pit;
we shall find all precious goods,   13
  we shall fill our houses with spoil;
throw in your lot among us,   14
  we will all have one purse"—
my son, do not walk in the way with them,   15
  hold back your foot from their paths;
for their feet run to evil,   16
  and they make haste to shed blood.
For in vain is a net spread   17,

in the sight of any bird;
18 but these men lie in wait for their own blood,
they set an ambush for their own lives.
19 Such are the ways of all who get gain by violence;
it takes away the life of its possessors.

The cry of wisdom

20 Wisdom cries aloud in the street;
in the markets she raises her voice;
21 on the top of the walls[a] she cries out;
at the entrance of the city gates she speaks:
22 "How long, O simple ones, will you love being simple?
How long will scoffers delight in their scoffing
and fools hate knowledge?
23 Give heed[b] to my reproof;
behold, I will pour out my thoughts[c] to you;
I will make my words known to you.
24 Because I have called and you refused to listen,
have stretched out my hand and no one has heeded,
25 and you have ignored all my counsel
and would have none of my reproof,
26 I also will laugh at your calamity;
I will mock when panic strikes you,
27 when panic strikes you like a storm,
and your calamity comes like a whirlwind,
when distress and anguish come upon you.
28 Then they will call upon me, but I will not answer;
they will seek me diligently but will not find me.
29 Because they hated knowledge
and did not choose the fear of the LORD,
30 would have none of my counsel,
and despised all my reproof,
31 therefore they shall eat the fruit of their way
and be sated with their own devices.
32 For the simple are killed by their turning away,
and the complacence of fools destroys them;
33 but he who listens to me will dwell secure
and will be at ease, without dread of evil."

2 My son, if you receive my words
and treasure up my commandments with you,
2 making your ear attentive to wisdom
and inclining your heart to understanding;
3 yes, if you cry out for insight
and raise your voice for understanding,
4 if you seek it like silver
and search for it as for hidden treasures;

then you will understand the fear of the 5 LORD
and find the knowledge of God.
For the LORD gives wisdom; 6
from his mouth come knowledge and understanding;
he stores up sound wisdom for the upright; 7
he is a shield to those who walk in integrity,
guarding the paths of justice 8
and preserving the way of his saints.
Then you will understand righteousness and 9 justice
and equity, every good path;
for wisdom will come into your heart, 10
and knowledge will be pleasant to your soul;
discretion will watch over you; 11
understanding will guard you;
delivering you from the way of evil, 12
from men of perverted speech,
who forsake the paths of uprightness 13
to walk in the ways of darkness,
who rejoice in doing evil 14
and delight in the perverseness of evil;
men whose paths are crooked, 15
and who are devious in their ways.

You will be saved from the loose[d] woman, 16
from the adventuress[e] with her smooth words,
who forsakes the companion of her youth 17
and forgets the covenant of her God;
for her house sinks down to death, 18
and her paths to the shades;
none who go to her come back 19
nor do they regain the paths of life.

So you will walk in the way of good men 20
and keep to the paths of the righteous.
For the upright will inhabit the land, 21
and men of integrity will remain in it;
but the wicked will be cut off from the land, 22
and the treacherous will be rooted out of it.

My son, do not forget my teaching, 3
but let your heart keep my commandments;
for length of days and years of life 2
and abundant welfare will they give you.

Let not loyalty and faithfulness forsake you; 3
bind them about your neck,
write them on the tablet of your heart.
So you will find favour and good repute[f] 4
in the sight of God and man.

Trust in the LORD with all your heart, 5
and do not rely on your own insight.

In all your ways acknowledge him,
  and he will make straight your paths.
Be not wise in your own eyes;
  fear the LORD, and turn away from evil.
It will be healing to your flesh*g*
  and refreshment*h* to your bones.

Honour the LORD with your substance

  and with the first fruits of all your
    produce;
then your barns will be filled with plenty,
  and your vats will be bursting with wine.

My son, do not despise the LORD's discipline
  or be weary of his reproof,
for the LORD reproves him whom he loves,
  as a father the son in whom he delights.

Happy is the man who finds wisdom,
  and the man who gets understanding,
for the gain from it is better than gain from
    silver
  and its profit better than gold.
She is more precious than jewels,
  and nothing you desire can compare with
    her.
Long life is in her right hand;
  in her left hand are riches and honour.
Her ways are ways of pleasantness,
  and all her paths are peace.
She is a tree of life to those who lay hold of
    her;
  those who hold her fast are called happy.

The LORD by wisdom founded the earth;
  by understanding he established the
    heavens;
by his knowledge the deeps broke forth,
  and the clouds drop down the dew.

My son, keep sound wisdom and discretion;
  let them not escape from your sight,*i*
and they will be life for your soul
  and adornment for your neck.
Then you will walk on your way securely
  and your foot will not stumble.
If you sit down,*j* you will not be afraid;
  when you lie down, your sleep will be
    sweet.
Do not be afraid of sudden panic,

or of the ruin*k* of the wicked, when it
    comes;
for the LORD will be your confidence   26
  and will keep your foot from being caught.
Do not withhold good from those to whom it*l* 27
    is due,
  when it is in your power to do it.

Do not say to your neighbour, "Go, and 28
    come again,
  tomorrow I will give it"—when you have
    it with you.
Do not plan evil against your neighbour   29
  who dwells trustingly beside you.
Do not contend with a man for no reason,   30
  when he has done you no harm.
Do not envy a man of violence   31
  and do not choose any of his ways;
for the perverse man is an abomination to the 32
    LORD,
  but the upright are in his confidence.
The LORD's curse is on the house of the 33
    wicked,
  but he blesses the abode of the righteous.
Toward the scorners he is scornful,   34
  but to the humble he shows favour.
The wise will inherit honour,   35
  but fools get*m* disgrace.

A father's instruction

Hear, O sons, a father's instruction,   **4**
  and be attentive, that you may gain*n*
    insight;
for I give you good precepts: 2
  do not forsake my teaching.
When I was a son with my father,   3
  tender, the only one in the sight of my
    mother,
he taught me, and said to me,   4
  "Let your heart hold fast my words;
  keep my commandments, and live;
do not forget, and do not turn away from the 5
    words of my mouth.
  Get wisdom; get insight.*o*
Do not forsake her, and she will keep you; 6
  love her, and she will guard you.
The beginning of wisdom is this: 7
  Get wisdom,
  and whatever you get, get insight.
Prize her highly,*p* and she will exalt you; 8
  she will honour you if you embrace her.
She will place on your head a fair garland; 9
  she will bestow on you a beautiful crown."

Hear, my son, and accept my words,   10
  that the years of your life may be many.
I have taught you the ways of wisdom;   11

---

g Heb *navel*   *h* Or *medicine*   *i* Reversing the order of the clauses   *j* Gk: Heb *lie down*   *k* Heb *storm*
l Heb *Do not withhold good from its owners*   *m* Cn: Heb *exalt*   *n* Heb *know*
o Reversing the order of the lines   *p* The meaning of the Hebrew is uncertain
3.7: Rom 12.16.   **3.11-12**: Heb 12.5-6.   **3.34** (Gk): Jas 4.6; 1 Pet 5.5.

Prov 4, 9

I have led you in the paths of uprightness.
12 When you walk, your step will not be hampered;
and if you run, you will not stumble.
13 Keep hold of instruction, do not let go;
guard her, for she is your life.
14 Do not enter the path of the wicked,
and do not walk in the way of evil men.
15 Avoid it; do not go on it;
turn away from it and pass on.
16 For they cannot sleep unless they have done wrong;
they are robbed of sleep unless they have made some one stumble.
17 For they eat the bread of wickedness
and drink the wine of violence.
18 But the path of the righteous is like the light of dawn,
which shines brighter and brighter until full day.
19 The way of the wicked is like deep darkness;
they do not know over what they stumble.

20 My son, be attentive to my words;
incline your ear to my sayings.
21 Let them not escape from your sight;
keep them within your heart.
22 For they are life to him who finds them,
and healing to all his flesh.
23 Keep your heart with all vigilance;
for from it flow the springs of life.
24 Put away from you crooked speech,
and put devious talk far from you.
25 Let your eyes look directly forward,
and your gaze be straight before you.
26 Take heed to*q* the path of your feet,
then all your ways will be sure.
27 Do not swerve to the right or to the left;
turn your foot away from evil.

5 My son, be attentive to my wisdom,
incline your ear to my understanding;
2 that you may keep discretion,
and your lips may guard knowledge.
3 For the lips of a loose woman drip honey,
and her speech*r* is smoother than oil;
4 but in the end she is bitter as wormwood,

sharp as a two-edged sword.
Her feet go down to death;
her steps follow the path to*s* Sheol;
she does not take heed to*t* the path of life;
her ways wander, and she does not know it.

And now, O sons, listen to me,
and do not depart from the words of my mouth.
Keep your way far from her,
and do not go near the door of her house;
lest you give your honour to others
and your years to the merciless;
lest strangers take their fill of your strength,*u*
and your labours go to the house of an alien;
and at the end of your life you groan,
when your flesh and body are consumed;
and you say, "How I hated discipline,
and my heart despised reproof!
I did not listen to the voice of my teachers
or incline my ear to my instructors.
I was at the point of utter ruin
in the assembled congregation."

Drink water from your own cistern,
flowing water from your own well.
Should your springs be scattered abroad,
streams of water in the streets?
Let them be for yourself alone,
and not for strangers with you.
Let your fountain be blessed,
and rejoice in the wife of your youth,
a lovely hind, a graceful doe.
Let her affection fill you at all times with delight,
be infatuated always with her love.
Why should you be infatuated, my son, with a loose woman
and embrace the bosom of an adventuress?
For a man's ways are before the eyes of the LORD,
and he watches*v* all his paths.
The iniquities of the wicked ensnare him,
and he is caught in the toils of his sin.
He dies for lack of discipline,
and because of his great folly he is lost.

My son, if you have become surety for your 6 neighbour,
have given your pledge for a stranger;
if you are snared in the utterance of your lips,*w*
caught in the words of your mouth;
then do this, my son, and save yourself,
for you have come into your neighbour's power:

q The meaning of the Hebrew word is uncertain
t The meaning of the Hebrew word is uncertain
v The meaning of the Hebrew word is uncertain
4.26 (Gk): Heb 12.13.
r Heb *palate*   *s* Heb *lay hold of*
u Or *wealth*
w Cn Compare Gk Syr: Heb *the words of your mouth*

go, hasten,[x] and importune your neighbour.
Give your eyes no sleep
    and your eyelids no slumber;
save yourself like a gazelle from the hunter,[y]
    like a bird from the hand of the fowler.

Go to the ant, O sluggard;
    consider her ways, and be wise.
Without having any chief,
    officer or ruler,
she prepares her food in summer,
    and gathers her sustenance in harvest.
How long will you lie there, O sluggard?
    When will you arise from your sleep?
A little sleep, a little slumber,
    a little folding of the hands to rest,
and poverty will come upon you like a
        vagabond,
    and want like an armed man.

A worthless person, a wicked man,
    goes about with crooked speech,
winks with his eyes, scrapes[z] with his feet,
    points with his finger,
with perverted heart devises evil,
    continually sowing discord;
therefore calamity will come upon him
        suddenly;
    in a moment he will be broken beyond
        healing.

There are six things which the LORD hates,
    seven which are an abomination to him:
haughty eyes, a lying tongue,
    and hands that shed innocent blood,
a heart that devises wicked plans,
    feet that make haste to run to evil,
a false witness who breathes out lies,
    and a man who sows discord among
        brothers.

My son, keep your father's commandment,
    and forsake not your mother's teaching.
Bind them upon your heart always;
    tie them about your neck.
When you walk, they[a] will lead you;
    when you lie down, they[a] will watch over
        you;
    and when you awake, they[a] will talk with
        you.
For the commandment is a lamp and the
        teaching a light,
    and the reproofs of discipline are the way
        of life,
to preserve you from the evil woman,
    from the smooth tongue of the adven-
        turess.
Do not desire her beauty in your heart,

and do not let her capture you with her
        eyelashes;
for a harlot may be hired for a loaf of bread,[b] 26
    but an adulteress[c] stalks a man's very life.
Can a man carry fire in his bosom   27
    and his clothes not be burned?
Or can one walk upon hot coals   28
    and his feet not be scorched?
So is he who goes in to his neighbour's wife; 29
    none who touches her will go unpunished.
Do not men despise[d] a thief if he steals   30
    to satisfy his appetite when he is hungry?
And if he is caught, he will pay sevenfold;   31
    he will give all the goods of his house.
He who commits adultery has no sense;   32
    he who does it destroys himself.
Wounds and dishonour will he get,   33
    and his disgrace will not be wiped away.
For jealousy makes a man furious,   34
    and he will not spare when he takes
        revenge.
He will accept no compensation,   35
    nor be appeased though you multiply gifts.

My son, keep my words   **7**
    and treasure up my commandments with
        you;
keep my commandments and live,   2
    keep my teachings as the apple of your eye;
bind them on your fingers,   3
    write them on the tablet of your heart.
Say to wisdom, "You are my sister,"   4
    and call insight your intimate friend;
to preserve you from the loose woman,   5
    from the adventuress with her smooth
        words.

For at the window of my house   6
    I have looked out through my lattice,
and I have seen among the simple,   7
    I have perceived among the youths,
    a young man without sense,
passing along the street near her corner,   8
    taking the road to her house
in the twilight, in the evening,   9
    at the time of night and darkness.

And lo, a woman meets him,   10
    dressed as a harlot, wily of heart.[e]
She is loud and wayward,   11
    her feet do not stay at home;
now in the street, now in the market,   12
    and at every corner she lies in wait.
She seizes him and kisses him,   13
    and with impudent face she says to him:
"I had to offer sacrifices,   14
    and today I have paid my vows;
so now I have come out to meet you,   15
    to seek you eagerly, and I have found you.

---

[x] Or *humble yourself*   [y] Cn: Heb *hand*   [z] Or *taps*   [a] Heb *it*
[b] Cn Compare Gk Syr Vg Tg: Heb *for because of a harlot to a piece of bread*   [c] Heb *a man's wife*
[d] Or *Men do not despise*   [e] The meaning of the Hebrew is uncertain

16 I have decked my couch with coverings,
    coloured spreads of Egyptian linen;
17 I have perfumed my bed with myrrh,
    aloes, and cinnamon.
18 Come, let us take our fill of love till morning;
    let us delight ourselves with love.
19 For my husband is not at home;
    he has gone on a long journey;
20 he took a bag of money with him;
    at full moon he will come home."

21 With much seductive speech she persuades
    him;
    with her smooth talk she compels him.
22 All at once he follows her,
    as an ox goes to the slaughter,
    or as a stag is caught fast[f]
23   till an arrow pierces its entrails;
    as a bird rushes into a snare;
    he does not know that it will cost him his
    life.

24 And now, O sons, listen to me,
    and be attentive to the words of my mouth.
25 Let not your heart turn aside to her ways,
    do not stray into her paths;
26 for many a victim has she laid low;
    yea, all her slain are a mighty host.
27 Her house is the way to Sheol,
    going down to the chambers of death.

Wisdom and folly

8 Does not wisdom call,
    does not understanding raise her voice?
2 On the heights beside the way,
    in the paths she takes her stand;
3 beside the gates in front of the town,
    at the entrance of the portals she cries
    aloud:
4 "To you, O men, I call,
    and my cry is to the sons of men.
5 O simple ones, learn prudence;
    O foolish men, pay attention.
6 Hear, for I will speak noble things,
    and from my lips will come what is right;
7 for my mouth will utter truth;
    wickedness is an abomination to my lips.
8 All the words of my mouth are righteous;
    there is nothing twisted or crooked in
    them.
9 They are all straight to him who understands
    and right to those who find knowledge.
10 Take my instruction instead of silver,
    and knowledge rather than choice gold;
11 for wisdom is better than jewels,
    and all that you may desire cannot com-
    pare with her.
12 I, wisdom, dwell in prudence,[g]

and I find knowledge and discretion.
The fear of the LORD is hatred of evil.
Pride and arrogance and the way of evil
    and perverted speech I hate.
I have counsel and sound wisdom,
    I have insight, I have strength.
By me kings reign,
    and rulers decree what is just;
by me princes rule,
    and nobles govern[h] the earth.
I love those who love me,
    and those who seek me diligently find me.
Riches and honour are with me,
    enduring wealth and prosperity.
My fruit is better than gold, even fine gold,
    and my yield than choice silver.
I walk in the way of righteousness,
    in the paths of justice,
endowing with wealth those who love me,
    and filling their treasuries.

"The LORD created me at the beginning of
    his work,[i]
    the first of his acts of old.
Ages ago I was set up,
    at the first, before the beginning of the
    earth.
When there were no depths I was brought 2
    forth,
    when there were no springs abounding
    with water.
Before the mountains had been shaped,
    before the hills, I was brought forth; 2
before he had made the earth with its fields,[j]
    or the first of the dust[j] of the world.
When he established the heavens, I was 2
    there,
    when he drew a circle on the face of the
    deep,
when he made firm the skies above, 2
    when he established[j] the fountains of the
    deep,
when he assigned to the sea its limit, 2
    so that the waters might not transgress his
    command,
when he marked out the foundations of the
    earth,
    then I was beside him, like a master 3
    workman;[k]
and I was daily his[l] delight,
    rejoicing before him always,
rejoicing in his inhabited world 3
    and delighting in the sons of men.

"And now, my sons, listen to me: 3
    happy are those who keep my ways.
Hear instruction and be wise, 3
    and do not neglect it.
Happy is the man who listens to me, 34

---

[f] Cn Compare Gk: Heb uncertain   [g] Heb obscure   [h] Gk: Heb *all the governors of*   [i] Heb *way*
[j] The meaning of the Hebrew is uncertain   [k] Another reading is *little child*   [l] Gk: Heb lacks *his*
8.1–3: Prov 1.20–21.

watching daily at my gates,
  waiting beside my doors.
For he who finds me finds life
  and obtains favour from the LORD;
but he who misses me injures himself;
  all who hate me love death."

Wisdom has built her house,
  she has set up*m* her seven pillars.
She has slaughtered her beasts,
  she has mixed her wine,
  she has also set her table.
She has sent out her maids to call
  from the highest places in the town,
"Whoever is simple, let him turn in here!"
To him who is without sense she says,

"Come, eat of my bread
  and drink of the wine I have mixed.
Leave simpleness,*n* and live,
  and walk in the way of insight."

He who corrects a scoffer gets himself abuse,
  and he who reproves a wicked man incurs
    injury.
Do not reprove a scoffer, or he will hate you;
  reprove a wise man, and he will love you.
Give instruction*o* to a wise man, and he will
    be still wiser;
  teach a righteous man and he will increase
    in learning.
The fear of the LORD is the beginning of
    wisdom,
  and the knowledge of the Holy One is
    insight.
For by me your days will be multiplied,
  and years will be added to your life.
If you are wise, you are wise for yourself;
  if you scoff, you alone will bear it.

A foolish woman is noisy;
  she is wanton*p* and knows no shame.*q*
She sits at the door of her house,
  she takes a seat on the high places of the
    town,
calling to those who pass by,
  who are going straight on their way,
"Whoever is simple, let him turn in here!"

And to him who is without sense she says,
"Stolen water is sweet,   17
  and bread eaten in secret is pleasant."
But he does not know that the dead*r* are 18
    there,
  that her guests are in the depths of Sheol.

PROVERBS OF SOLOMON

THE proverbs of Solomon.   **10**
  A wise son makes a glad father,
  but a foolish son is a sorrow to his mother.
Treasures gained by wickedness do not 2
    profit,
  but righteousness delivers from death.
The LORD does not let the righteous go 3
    hungry,
  but he thwarts the craving of the wicked.
A slack hand causes poverty,   4
  but the hand of the diligent makes rich.
A son who gathers in summer is prudent,   5
  but a son who sleeps in harvest brings
    shame.
Blessings are on the head of the righteous, 6
  but the mouth of the wicked conceals
    violence.
The memory of the righteous is a blessing,   7
  but the name of the wicked will rot.
The wise of heart will heed commandments,   8
  but a prating fool will come to ruin.
He who walks in integrity walks securely,   9
  but he who perverts his ways will be found
    out.
He who winks the eye causes trouble,   10
  but he who boldly reproves makes peace.*s*
The mouth of the righteous is a fountain of 11
    life,
  but the mouth of the wicked conceals
    violence.
Hatred stirs up strife,   12
  but love covers all offences.
On the lips of him who has understanding 13
    wisdom is found,
  but a rod is for the back of him who lacks
    sense.
Wise men lay up knowledge,   14
  but the babbling of a fool brings ruin near.
A rich man's wealth is his strong city;   15
  the poverty of the poor is their ruin.
The wage of the righteous leads to life,   16
  the gain of the wicked to sin.
He who heeds instruction is on the path to 17
    life,
  but he who rejects reproof goes astray.
He who conceals hatred has lying lips,   18
  and he who utters slander is a fool.

m Gk Syr Tg: Heb *hewn*   *n* Gk Syr Vg Tg: Heb *simple ones*   *o* Heb lacks *instruction*
p Cn Compare Syr Vg: The meaning of the Hebrew is uncertain
q Gk Syr: The meaning of the Hebrew is uncertain   *r* Heb *shades*
s Gk: Heb *but a prating fool will come to ruin*
10.12: Jas 5.20; 1 Pet 4.8.

19 When words are many, transgression is not
      lacking,
      but he who restrains his lips is prudent.
20 The tongue of the righteous is choice silver;
      the mind of the wicked is of little worth.
21 The lips of the righteous feed many,
      but fools die for lack of sense.
22 The blessing of the LORD makes rich,
      and he adds no sorrow with it.[t]
23 It is like sport to a fool to do wrong,
      but wise conduct is pleasure to a man of
      understanding.
24 What the wicked dreads will come upon him,
      but the desire of the righteous will be
      granted.
25 When the tempest passes, the wicked is no
      more,
      but the righteous is established for ever.
26 Like vinegar to the teeth, and smoke to the
      eyes,
      so is the sluggard to those who send him.
27 The fear of the LORD prolongs life,
      but the years of the wicked will be short.
28 The hope of the righteous ends in gladness,
      but the expectation of the wicked comes to
      naught.
29 The LORD is a stronghold to him whose way
      is upright,
      but destruction to evildoers.
30 The righteous will never be removed,
      but the wicked will not dwell in the land.
31 The mouth of the righteous brings forth
      wisdom,
      but the perverse tongue will be cut off.
32 The lips of the righteous know what is
      acceptable,
      but the mouth of the wicked, what is
      perverse.

11 A false balance is an abomination to the
      LORD,
      but a just weight is his delight.
2 When pride comes, then comes disgrace;
      but with the humble is wisdom.
3 The integrity of the upright guides them,
      but the crookedness of the treacherous
      destroys them.
4 Riches do not profit in the day of wrath,
      but righteousness delivers from death.
5 The righteousness of the blameless keeps his
      way straight,
      but the wicked falls by his own wicked-
      ness.
6 The righteousness of the upright delivers
      them,
      but the treacherous are taken captive by
      their lust.
7 When the wicked dies, his hope perishes,
      and the expectation of the godless comes to
      naught.

The righteous is delivered from trouble,
      and the wicked gets into it instead.
With his mouth the godless man would
      destroy his neighbour,
      but by knowledge the righteous are
      delivered.
When it goes well with the righteous, the city
      rejoices;
      and when the wicked perish there are
      shouts of gladness.
By the blessing of the upright a city is
      exalted,
      but it is overthrown by the mouth of the
      wicked.
He who belittles his neighbour lacks sense,
      but a man of understanding remains silent.
He who goes about as a talebearer reveals
      secrets,
      but he who is trustworthy in spirit keeps a
      thing hidden.
Where there is no guidance, a people falls;
      but in an abundance of counsellors there is
      safety.
He who gives surety for a stranger will smart
      for it,
      but he who hates suretyship is secure.
A gracious woman gets honour,
      and violent men get riches.
A man who is kind benefits himself,
      but a cruel man hurts himself.
A wicked man earns deceptive wages,
      but one who sows righteousness gets a sure
      reward.
He who is steadfast in righteousness will live,
      but he who pursues evil will die.
Men of perverse mind are an abomination to
      the LORD,
      but those of blameless ways are his delight.
Be assured, an evil man will not go un-
      punished,
      but those who are righteous will be
      delivered.
Like a gold ring in a swine's snout
      is a beautiful woman without discretion.
The desire of the righteous ends only in
      good;
      the expectation of the wicked in wrath.
One man gives freely, yet grows all the
      richer;
      another withholds what he should give,
      and only suffers want.
A liberal man will be enriched,
      and one who waters will himself be
      watered.
The people curse him who holds back grain,
      but a blessing is on the head of him who
      sells it.
He who diligently seeks good seeks favour,
      but evil comes to him who searches for it.
He who trusts in his riches will wither,[u]

but the righteous will flourish like a green
  leaf.
He who troubles his household will inherit
  wind,
  and the fool will be servant to the wise.
The fruit of the righteous is a tree of life,
  but lawlessness *v* takes away lives.
If the righteous is requited on earth,
  how much more the wicked and the
  sinner!

2 Whoever loves discipline loves knowledge,
  but he who hates reproof is stupid.
2 A good man obtains favour from the LORD,
  but a man of evil devices he condemns.
3 A man is not established by wickedness,
  but the root of the righteous will never be
  moved.
4 A good wife is the crown of her husband,
  but she who brings shame is like rottenness in his bones.
5 The thoughts of the righteous are just;
  the counsels of the wicked are treacherous.
6 The words of the wicked lie in wait for blood,
  but the mouth of the upright delivers men.
7 The wicked are overthrown and are no more,
  but the house of the righteous will stand.
8 A man is commended according to his good
  sense,
  but one of perverse mind is despised.
9 Better is a man of humble standing who
  works for himself
  than one who plays the great man but lacks
  bread.
10 A righteous man has regard for the life of his
  beast,
  but the mercy of the wicked is cruel.

1 He who tills his land will have plenty of
  bread,
  but he who follows worthless pursuits has
  no sense.
2 The strong tower of the wicked comes to
  ruin,
  but the root of the righteous stands firm. *w*
3 An evil man is ensnared by the transgression
  of his lips,
  but the righteous escapes from trouble.
4 From the fruit of his words a man is satisfied
  with good,

and the work of a man's hand comes back
  to him.
The way of a fool is right in his own eyes, 15
  but a wise man listens to advice.
The vexation of a fool is known at once, 16
  but the prudent man ignores an insult.
He who speaks the truth gives honest 17
  evidence,
  but a false witness utters deceit.
There is one whose rash words are like sword 18
  thrusts,
  but the tongue of the wise brings healing.
Truthful lips endure for ever, 19
  but a lying tongue is but for a moment.
Deceit is in the heart of those who devise 20
  evil,
  but those who plan good have joy.
No ill befalls the righteous, 21
  but the wicked are filled with trouble.
Lying lips are an abomination to the LORD, 22
  but those who act faithfully are his delight.
A prudent man conceals his knowledge, 23
  but fools *x* proclaim their folly.
The hand of the diligent will rule, 24
  while the slothful will be put to forced
  labour.
Anxiety in a man's heart weighs him down, 25
  but a good word makes him glad.
A righteous man turns away from evil, *y* 26
  but the way of the wicked leads them
  astray.
A slothful man will not catch his prey, *z* 27
  but the diligent man will get precious
  wealth. *a*
In the path of righteousness is life, 28
  but the way of error leads to death. *b*

A wise son hears his father's instruction, **13**
  but a scoffer does not listen to rebuke.
From the fruit of his mouth a good man eats 2
  good,
  but the desire of the treacherous is for
  violence.
He who guards his mouth preserves his life; 3
  he who opens wide his lips comes to ruin.
The soul of the sluggard craves, and gets 4
  nothing,
  while the soul of the diligent is richly
  supplied.
A righteous man hates falsehood, 5
  but a wicked man acts shamefully and
  disgracefully.
Righteousness guards him whose way is 6
  upright,
  but sin overthrows the wicked.
One man pretends to be rich, yet has 7
  nothing;

v Cn Compare Gk Syr: Heb *a wise man*   *w* Cn: The Hebrew of verse 12 is obscure
x Heb *the heart of fools*   *y* Cn: The meaning of the Hebrew is uncertain
z Cn Compare Gk Syr: The meaning of the Hebrew is uncertain
a Cn: The meaning of the Hebrew is uncertain   *b* Cn: The meaning of the Hebrew is uncertain
11.31 (Gk): 1 Pet 4.18.

another pretends to be poor, yet has great
wealth.

8 The ransom of a man's life is his wealth,
but a poor man has no means of redemption.*c*

9 The light of the righteous rejoices,
but the lamp of the wicked will be put out.

10 By insolence the heedless make strife,
but with those who take advice is wisdom.

11 Wealth hastily gotten*d* will dwindle,
but he who gathers little by little will
increase it.

12 Hope deferred makes the heart sick,
but a desire fulfilled is a tree of life.

13 He who despises the word brings destruction
on himself,
but he who respects the commandment
will be rewarded.

14 The teaching of the wise is a fountain of life,
that one may avoid the snares of death.

15 Good sense wins favour,
but the way of the faithless is their ruin.*e*

16 In everything a prudent man acts with
knowledge,
but a fool flaunts his folly.

17 A bad messenger plunges men into trouble,
but a faithful envoy brings healing.

18 Poverty and disgrace come to him who
ignores instruction,
but he who heeds reproof is honoured.

19 A desire fulfilled is sweet to the soul;
but to turn away from evil is an abomination to fools.

20 He who walks with wise men becomes wise,
but the companion of fools will suffer
harm.

21 Misfortune pursues sinners,
but prosperity rewards the righteous.

22 A good man leaves an inheritance to his
children's children,
but the sinner's wealth is laid up for the
righteous.

23 The fallow ground of the poor yields much
food,
but it is swept away through injustice.

24 He who spares the rod hates his son,
but he who loves him is diligent to discipline him.

25 The righteous has enough to satisfy his
appetite,
but the belly of the wicked suffers want.

14 Wisdom*f* builds her house,
but folly with her own hands tears it down.

2 He who walks in uprightness fears the LORD,
but he who is devious in his ways despises
him.

3 The talk of a fool is a rod for his back,*g*

but the lips of the wise will preserve them.

4 Where there are no oxen, there is no*h* grain;
but abundant crops come by the strength
of the ox.

5 A faithful witness does not lie,
but a false witness breathes out lies.

6 A scoffer seeks wisdom in vain,
but knowledge is easy for a man of
understanding.

7 Leave the presence of a fool,
for there you do not meet words of
knowledge.

8 The wisdom of a prudent man is to discern
his way,
but the folly of fools is deceiving.

9 God scorns the wicked,*i*
but the upright enjoy his favour.

10 The heart knows its own bitterness,
and no stranger shares its joy.

11 The house of the wicked will be destroyed,
but the tent of the upright will flourish.

12 There is a way which seems right to a man,
but its end is the way to death.*j*

13 Even in laughter the heart is sad,
and the end of joy is grief.

14 A perverse man will be filled with the fruit of
his ways,
and a good man with the fruit of his
deeds.*k*

15 The simple believes everything,
but the prudent looks where he is going.

16 A wise man is cautious and turns away from
evil,
but a fool throws off restraint and is
careless.

17 A man of quick temper acts foolishly,
but a man of discretion is patient.*l*

18 The simple acquire folly,
but the prudent are crowned with
knowledge.

19 The evil bow down before the good,
the wicked at the gates of the righteous.

20 The poor is disliked even by his neighbour,
but the rich has many friends.

21 He who despises his neighbour is a sinner,
but happy is he who is kind to the poor.

22 Do they not err that devise evil?
Those who devise good meet loyalty and
faithfulness.

23 In all toil there is profit,
but mere talk tends only to want.

24 The crown of the wise is their wisdom,*m*
but folly is the garland*n* of fools.

25 A truthful witness saves lives,
but one who utters lies is a betrayer.

26 In the fear of the LORD one has strong
confidence,
and his children will have a refuge.

c Cn: Heb *does not hear rebuke*   *d* Gk Vg: Heb *from vanity*   *e* Cn Compare Gk Syr Vg Tg: Heb *is enduring*
f Heb *Wisdom of women*   *g* Cn: Heb *a rod of pride*   *h* Cn: Heb *a manger of*   *i* Cn: Heb obscure
j Heb *ways of death*   *k* Cn: Heb *from upon him*   *l* Gk: Heb *is hated*   *m* Cn Compare Gk: Heb *riches*
n Cn: Heb *folly*

The fear of the LORD is a fountain of life,
   that one may avoid the snares of death.
In a multitude of people is the glory of a
   king,
   but without people a prince is ruined.
He who is slow to anger has great understanding,
   but he who has a hasty temper exalts folly.
A tranquil mind gives life to the flesh,
   but passion makes the bones rot.
He who oppresses a poor man insults his
   Maker,
   but he who is kind to the needy honours
   him.
The wicked is overthrown through his
   evil-doing,
   but the righteous finds refuge through his
   integrity.[o]
Wisdom abides in the mind of a man of
   understanding,
   but it is not [p] known in the heart of fools.
Righteousness exalts a nation,
   but sin is a reproach to any people.
A servant who deals wisely has the king's
   favour,
   but his wrath falls on one who acts
   shamefully.

A soft answer turns away wrath,
   but a harsh word stirs up anger.
The tongue of the wise dispenses knowledge,[q]
   but the mouths of fools pour out folly.
The eyes of the LORD are in every place,
   keeping watch on the evil and the good.
A gentle tongue is a tree of life,
   but perverseness in it breaks the spirit.
A fool despises his father's instruction,
   but he who heeds admonition is prudent.
In the house of the righteous there is much
   treasure,
   but trouble befalls the income of the
   wicked.
The lips of the wise spread knowledge;
   not so the minds of fools.
The sacrifice of the wicked is an abomination
   to the LORD,
   but the prayer of the upright is his delight.
The way of the wicked is an abomination to
   the LORD,
   but he loves him who pursues righteousness.
There is severe discipline for him who
   forsakes the way;
   he who hates reproof will die.
Sheol and Abaddon lie open before the
   LORD,
   how much more the hearts of men!
A scoffer does not like to be reproved;

he will not go to the wise.
A glad heart makes a cheerful countenance, 13
   but by sorrow of heart the spirit is
   broken.
The mind of him who has understanding 14
   seeks knowledge,
   but the mouths of fools feed on folly.
All the days of the afflicted are evil,   15
   but a cheerful heart has a continual feast.
Better is a little with the fear of the LORD 16
   than great treasure and trouble with it.
Better is a dinner of herbs where love is 17
   than a fatted ox and hatred with it.
A hot-tempered man stirs up strife,   18
   but he who is slow to anger quiets contention.
The way of a sluggard is overgrown with 19
   thorns,
   but the path of the upright is a level
   highway.
A wise son makes a glad father,   20
   but a foolish man despises his mother.
Folly is a joy to him who has no sense,   21
   but a man of understanding walks aright.
Without counsel plans go wrong,   22
   but with many advisers they succeed.
To make an apt answer is a joy to a man,   23
   and a word in season, how good it is!
The wise man's path leads upward to life,   24
   that he may avoid Sheol beneath.
The LORD tears down the house of the 25
   proud,
   but maintains the widow's boundaries.
The thoughts of the wicked are an abomina- 26
   tion to the LORD,
   the words of the pure are pleasing to him.[r]
He who is greedy for unjust gain makes 27
   trouble for his household,
   but he who hates bribes will live.
The mind of the righteous ponders how to 28
   answer,
   but the mouth of the wicked pours out evil
   things.
The LORD is far from the wicked,   29
   but he hears the prayer of the righteous.
The light of the eyes rejoices the heart,   30
   and good news refreshes[s] the bones.
He whose ear heeds wholesome admonition 31
   will abide among the wise.
He who ignores instruction despises himself, 32
   but he who heeds admonition gains understanding.
The fear of the LORD is instruction in 33
   wisdom,
   and humility goes before honour.

The plans of the mind belong to man,   **16**
   but the answer of the tongue is from the
   LORD.

---

[o] Gk Syr: Heb *in his death*   [p] Gk Syr: Heb lacks *not*   [q] Cn: Heb *makes knowledge good*
[r] Cn Compare Gk: Heb *pleasant words are pure*   [s] Heb *makes fat*

2 All the ways of a man are pure in his own
  eyes,
    but the LORD weighs the spirit.
3 Commit your work to the LORD,
    and your plans will be established.
4 The LORD has made everything for its
  purpose,
    even the wicked for the day of trouble.
5 Every one who is arrogant is an abomination
  to the LORD;
    be assured, he will not go unpunished.
6 By loyalty and faithfulness iniquity is atoned
  for,
    and by the fear of the LORD a man avoids
    evil.
7 When a man's ways please the LORD,
    he makes even his enemies to be at peace
    with him.
8 Better is a little with righteousness
    than great revenues with injustice.
9 A man's mind plans his way,
    but the LORD directs his steps.
10 Inspired decisions are on the lips of a king;
    his mouth does not sin in judgment.
11 A just balance and scales are the LORD's;
    all the weights in the bag are his work.
12 It is an abomination to kings to do evil,
    for the throne is established by righteous-
    ness.
13 Righteous lips are the delight of a king,
    and he loves him who speaks what is right.
14 A king's wrath is a messenger of death,
    and a wise man will appease it.
15 In the light of a king's face there is life,
    and his favour is like the clouds that bring
    the spring rain.
16 To get wisdom is better^t than gold;
    to get understanding is to be chosen rather
    than silver.
17 The highway of the upright turns aside from
  evil;
    he who guards his way preserves his life.
18 Pride goes before destruction,
    and a haughty spirit before a fall.
19 It is better to be of a lowly spirit with the
  poor
    than to divide the spoil with the proud.
20 He who gives heed to the word will prosper,
    and happy is he who trusts in the LORD.
21 The wise of heart is called a man of discernment,
    and pleasant speech increases persuasive-
    ness.
22 Wisdom is a fountain of life to him who has
  it,
    but folly is the chastisement of fools.
23 The mind of the wise makes his speech
  judicious,
    and adds persuasiveness to his lips.
24 Pleasant words are like a honeycomb,

sweetness to the soul and health to the
  body.
There is a way which seems right to a man, 2
  but its end is the way to death.^{u}
A worker's appetite works for him; 2
  his mouth urges him on.
A worthless man plots evil, 2
  and his speech is like a scorching fire.
A perverse man spreads strife, 2
  and a whisperer separates close friends.
A man of violence entices his neighbour 2
  and leads him in a way that is not good.
He who winks his eyes plans^v perverse 3
  things,
  he who compresses his lips brings evil to
  pass.
A hoary head is a crown of glory; 3
  it is gained in a righteous life.
He who is slow to anger is better than the 3
  mighty,
  and he who rules his spirit than he who
  takes a city.
The lot is cast into the lap, 33
  but the decision is wholly from the LORD.

Better is a dry morsel with quiet 17
  than a house full of feasting with strife.
A slave who deals wisely will rule over a son 2
  who acts shamefully,
  and will share the inheritance as one of the
  brothers.
The crucible is for silver, and the furnace is 3
  for gold,
  and the LORD tries hearts.
An evildoer listens to wicked lips; 4
  and a liar gives heed to a mischievous
  tongue.
He who mocks the poor insults his Maker; 5
  he who is glad at calamity will not go
  unpunished.
Grandchildren are the crown of the aged, 6
  and the glory of sons is their fathers.
Fine speech is not becoming to a fool; 7
  still less is false speech to a prince.
A bribe is like a magic stone in the eyes of 8
  him who gives it;
  wherever he turns he prospers.
He who forgives an offence seeks love, 9
  but he who repeats a matter alienates a
  friend.
A rebuke goes deeper into a man of under- 10
  standing
  than a hundred blows into a fool.
An evil man seeks only rebellion, 11
  and a cruel messenger will be sent against
  him.
Let a man meet a she-bear robbed of her 12
  cubs,
  rather than a fool in his folly.
If a man returns evil for good, 13

^{t} Gk Syr Vg Tg: Heb *how much better* ^{u} Heb *ways of death* ^{v} Gk Syr Vg Tg: Heb *to plan*

evil will not depart from his house.
4 The beginning of strife is like letting out
water;
so quit before the quarrel breaks out.
5 He who justifies the wicked and he who
condemns the righteous
are both alike an abomination to the Lord.
16 Why should a fool have a price in his hand to
buy wisdom,
when he has no mind?
17 A friend loves at all times,
and a brother is born for adversity.
18 A man without sense gives a pledge,
and becomes surety in the presence of his
neighbour.
19 He who loves transgression loves strife;
he who makes his door high seeks
destruction.
20 A man of crooked mind does not prosper,
and one with a perverse tongue falls into
calamity.
21 A stupid son is a grief to a father;
and the father of a fool has no joy.
22 A cheerful heart is a good medicine,
but a downcast spirit dries up the bones.
23 A wicked man accepts a bribe from the
bosom
to pervert the ways of justice.
24 A man of understanding sets his face toward
wisdom,
but the eyes of a fool are on the ends of the
earth.
25 A foolish son is a grief to his father
and bitterness to her who bore him.
26 To impose a fine on a righteous man is not
good;
to flog noble men is wrong.
27 He who restrains his words has knowledge,
and he who has a cool spirit is a man of
understanding.
28 Even a fool who keeps silent is considered
wise;
when he closes his lips, he is deemed
intelligent.

18 He who is estranged [w] seeks pretexts [x]
to break out against all sound judgment.
2 A fool takes no pleasure in understanding,
but only in expressing his opinion.
3 When wickedness comes, contempt comes
also;
and with dishonour comes disgrace.
4 The words of a man's mouth are deep
waters;
the fountain of wisdom is a gushing
stream.
5 It is not good to be partial to a wicked man,
or to deprive a righteous man of justice.
6 A fool's lips bring strife,

and his mouth invites a flogging.
A fool's mouth is his ruin, 7
and his lips are a snare to himself.
The words of a whisperer are like delicious 8
morsels;
they go down into the inner parts of the
body.
He who is slack in his work 9
is a brother to him who destroys.
The name of the Lord is a strong tower; 10
the righteous man runs into it and is safe.
A rich man's wealth is his strong city, 11
and like a high wall protecting him. [y]
Before destruction a man's heart is haughty, 12
but humility goes before honour.
If one gives answer before he hears, 13
it is his folly and shame.
A man's spirit will endure sickness; 14
but a broken spirit who can bear?
An intelligent mind acquires knowledge, 15
and the ear of the wise seeks knowledge.
A man's gift makes room for him 16
and brings him before great men.
He who states his case first seems right, 17
until the other comes and examines him.
The lot puts an end to disputes 18
and decides between powerful contenders.
A brother helped is like a strong city, [z] 19
but quarrelling is like the bars of a castle.
From the fruit of his mouth a man is 20
satisfied;
he is satisfied by the yield of his lips.
Death and life are in the power of the tongue, 21
and those who love it will eat its fruits.
He who finds a wife finds a good thing, 22
and obtains favour from the Lord.
The poor use entreaties, 23
but the rich answer roughly.
There are [a] friends who pretend to be 24
friends, [b]
but there is a friend who sticks closer than
a brother.

Better is a poor man who walks in his 19
integrity
than a man who is perverse in speech, and
is a fool.
It is not good for a man to be without 2
knowledge,

[w] Heb separated   [x] Gk Vg: Heb desire   [y] Or in his imagination
[z] Gk Syr Vg Tg: The meaning of the Hebrew is uncertain   [a] Syr Tg: Heb A man of
[b] Cn Compare Syr Vg Tg: Heb to be broken

and he who makes haste with his feet
misses his way.

3 When a man's folly brings his way to ruin,
his heart rages against the LORD.

4 Wealth brings many new friends,
but a poor man is deserted by his friend.

5 A false witness will not go unpunished,
and he who utters lies will not escape.

6 Many seek the favour of a generous man,
and every one is a friend to a man who
gives gifts.

7 All a poor man's brothers hate him;
how much more do his friends go far from
him!
He pursues them with words, but does not
have them.[c]

8 He who gets wisdom loves himself;
he who keeps understanding will prosper.

9 A false witness will not go unpunished,
and he who utters lies will perish.

10 It is not fitting for a fool to live in luxury,
much less for a slave to rule over princes.

11 Good sense makes a man slow to anger,
and it is his glory to overlook an offence.

12 A king's wrath is like the growling of a lion,
but his favour is like dew upon the grass.

13 A foolish son is ruin to his father,
and a wife's quarrelling is a continual
dripping of rain.

14 House and wealth are inherited from fathers,
but a prudent wife is from the LORD.

15 Slothfulness casts into a deep sleep,
and an idle person will suffer hunger.

16 He who keeps the commandment keeps his
life;
he who despises the word[d] will die.

17 He who is kind to the poor lends to the LORD,
and he will repay him for his deed.

18 Discipline your son while there is hope;
do not set your heart on his destruction.

19 A man of great wrath will pay the penalty;
for if you deliver him, you will only have to
do it again.[e]

20 Listen to advice and accept instruction,
that you may gain wisdom for the future.

21 Many are the plans in the mind of a man,
but it is the purpose of the LORD that will
be established.

22 What is desired in a man is loyalty,
and a poor man is better than a liar.

23 The fear of the LORD leads to life;
and he who has it rests satisfied;
he will not be visited by harm.

24 The sluggard buries his hand in the dish,
and will not even bring it back to his
mouth.

25 Strike a scoffer, and the simple will learn
prudence;
reprove a man of understanding,
and he will gain knowledge.

He who does violence to his father and chases 2
away his mother
is a son who causes shame and brings
reproach.

Cease, my son, to hear instruction 2
only to stray from the words of knowledge.

A worthless witness mocks at justice, 2
and the mouth of the wicked devours
iniquity.

Condemnation is ready for scoffers, 2
and flogging for the backs of fools.

Wine is a mocker, strong drink a brawler; 2
and whoever is led astray by it is not wise.

The dread wrath of a king is like the growling 2
of a lion;
he who provokes him to anger forfeits his
life.

It is an honour for a man to keep aloof from 3
strife;
but every fool will be quarrelling.

The sluggard does not plough in the autumn; 4
he will seek at harvest and have nothing.

The purpose in a man's mind is like deep 5
water,
but a man of understanding will draw it
out.

Many a man proclaims his own loyalty, 6
but a faithful man who can find?

A righteous man who walks in his integrity— 7
blessed are his sons after him!

A king who sits on the throne of judgment 8
winnows all evil with his eyes.

Who can say, "I have made my heart clean; 9
I am pure from my sin"?

Diverse weights and diverse measures 10
are both alike an abomination to the LORD.

Even a child makes himself known by his 11
acts,
whether what he does is pure and right.

The hearing ear and the seeing eye, 12
the LORD has made them both.

Love not sleep, lest you come to poverty; 13
open your eyes, and you will have plenty of
bread.

"It is bad, it is bad," says the buyer; 14
but when he goes away, then he boasts.

There is gold, and abundance of costly 15
stones;
but the lips of knowledge are a precious
jewel.

Take a man's garment when he has given 16
surety for a stranger,
and hold him in pledge when he gives
surety for foreigners.

Bread gained by deceit is sweet to a man, 17
but afterward his mouth will be full of
gravel.

Plans are established by counsel; 18
by wise guidance wage war.

---

[c] Heb uncertain   [d] Cn Compare 13.13: Heb *his ways*   [e] Heb obscure

He who goes about gossiping reveals secrets;
therefore do not associate with one who
speaks foolishly.
If one curses his father or his mother,
his lamp will be put out in utter darkness.
An inheritance gotten hastily in the
beginning
will in the end not be blessed.
Do not say, "I will repay evil";
wait for the LORD, and he will help you.
Diverse weights are an abomination to the
LORD,
and false scales are not good.
A man's steps are ordered by the LORD;
how then can man understand his way?
It is a snare for a man to say rashly, "It is
holy,"
and to reflect only after making his vows.
A wise king winnows the wicked,
and drives the wheel over them.
The spirit of man is the lamp of the LORD,
searching all his innermost parts.
Loyalty and faithfulness preserve the king,
and his throne is upheld by righteousness.[f]
The glory of young men is their strength,
but the beauty of old men is their grey
hair.
Blows that wound cleanse away evil;
strokes make clean the innermost parts.

The king's heart is a stream of water in the
hand of the LORD;
he turns it wherever he will.
Every way of a man is right in his own
eyes,
but the LORD weighs the heart.
To do righteousness and justice
is more acceptable to the LORD than
sacrifice.
Haughty eyes and a proud heart,
the lamp of the wicked, are sin.
The plans of the diligent lead surely to
abundance,
but every one who is hasty comes only to
want.
The getting of treasures by a lying tongue
is a fleeting vapour and a snare of death.
The violence of the wicked will sweep them
away,
because they refuse to do what is just.
The way of the guilty is crooked,
but the conduct of the pure is right.
It is better to live in a corner of the housetop
than in a house shared with a contentious
woman.
The soul of the wicked desires evil;
his neighbour finds no mercy in his eyes.
When a scoffer is punished, the simple
becomes wise;

when a wise man is instructed, he gains
knowledge.
The righteous observes the house of the 12
wicked;
the wicked are cast down to ruin.
He who closes his ear to the cry of the poor 13
will himself cry out and not be heard.
A gift in secret averts anger;   14
and a bribe in the bosom, strong wrath.
When justice is done, it is a joy to the 15
righteous,
but dismay to evildoers.
A man who wanders from the way of 16
understanding
will rest in the assembly of the dead.
He who loves pleasure will be a poor man; 17
he who loves wine and oil will not be rich.
The wicked is a ransom for the righteous, 18
and the faithless for the upright.
It is better to live in a desert land   19
than with a contentious and fretful
woman.
Precious treasure remains[g] in a wise man's 20
dwelling,
but a foolish man devours it.
He who pursues righteousness and kindness 21
will find life[h] and honour.
A wise man scales the city of the mighty 22
and brings down the stronghold in which
they trust.
He who keeps his mouth and his tongue   23
keeps himself out of trouble.
"Scoffer" is the name of the proud, haughty 24
man
who acts with arrogant pride.
The desire of the sluggard kills him   25
for his hands refuse to labour.
All day long the wicked covets,[i]   26
but the righteous gives and does not hold
back.
The sacrifice of the wicked is an abomina- 27
tion;
how much more when he brings it with
evil intent.
A false witness will perish,   28
but the word of a man who hears will
endure.
A wicked man puts on a bold face,   29
but an upright man considers[j] his ways.
No wisdom, no understanding, no counsel, 30
can avail against the LORD.
The horse is made ready for the day of battle, 31
but the victory belongs to the LORD.

A good name is to be chosen rather than 22
great riches,
and favour is better than silver or gold.
The rich and the poor meet together;   2
the LORD is the maker of them all.

---

[f] Gk: Heb loyalty   [g] Gk: Heb and oil   [h] Gk: Heb life and righteousness
[i] Gk: Heb all day long he covets covetously   [j] Another reading is establishes

3 A prudent man sees danger and hides
    himself;
    but the simple go on, and suffer for it.
4 The reward for humility and fear of the
    LORD
    is riches and honour and life.
5 Thorns and snares are in the way of the
    perverse;
    he who guards himself will keep far from
    them.
6 Train up a child in the way he should go,
    and when he is old he will not depart from
    it.
7 The rich rules over the poor,
    and the borrower is the slave of the lender.
8 He who sows injustice will reap calamity,
    and the rod of his fury will fail.
9 He who has a bountiful eye will be blessed,
    for he shares his bread with the poor.
10 Drive out a scoffer, and strife will go out,
    and quarrelling and abuse will cease.
11 He who loves purity of heart,
    and whose speech is gracious, will have the
    king as his friend.
12 The eyes of the LORD keep watch over
    knowledge,
    but he overthrows the words of the
    faithless.
13 The sluggard says, "There is a lion outside!
    I shall be slain in the streets!"
14 The mouth of a loose woman is a deep pit;
    he with whom the LORD is angry will fall
    into it.
15 Folly is bound up in the heart of a child,
    but the rod of discipline drives it far from
    him.
16 He who oppresses the poor to increase his
    own wealth,
    or gives to the rich, will only come to want.

WORDS OF THE WISE

17 INCLINE your ear, and hear the words of
    the wise,
    and apply your mind to my knowledge;
18 for it will be pleasant if you keep them within
    you,
    if all of them are ready on your lips.
19 That your trust may be in the LORD,
    I have made them known to you today,
    even to you.

20 Have I not written for you thirty sayings
    of admonition and knowledge,
21 to show you what is right and true,
    that you may give a true answer to those
    who sent you?

22 Do not rob the poor, because he is poor,

or crush the afflicted at the gate;
for the LORD will plead their cause
    and despoil of life those who despoil them.
Make no friendship with a man given to
    anger,
    nor go with a wrathful man,
lest you learn his ways
    and entangle yourself in a snare.
Be not one of those who give pledges,
    who become surety for debts.
If you have nothing with which to pay,
    why should your bed be taken from under
    you?

Remove not the ancient landmark
    which your fathers have set.
Do you see a man skilful in his work?
    he will stand before kings;
    he will not stand before obscure men.

When you sit down to eat with a ruler,
    observe carefully what[k] is before you;
and put a knife to your throat
    if you are a man given to appetite.
Do not desire his delicacies,
    for they are deceptive food.
Do not toil to acquire wealth;
    be wise enough to desist.
When your eyes light upon it, it is gone;
    for suddenly it takes to itself wings,
    flying like an eagle toward heaven.
Do not eat the bread of a man who is stingy,
    do not desire his delicacies;
for he is like one who is inwardly reckoning.[l]
    "Eat and drink!" he says to you;
    but his heart is not with you.
You will vomit up the morsels which you
    have eaten,
    and waste your pleasant words.
Do not speak in the hearing of a fool,
    for he will despise the wisdom of your
    words.
Do not remove an ancient landmark
    or enter the fields of the fatherless;
for their Redeemer is strong;
    he will plead their cause against you.
Apply your mind to instruction
    and your ear to words of knowledge.
Do not withhold discipline from a child;
    if you beat him with a rod, he will not
    die.
If you beat him with the rod
    you will save his life from Sheol.
My son, if your heart is wise,

---

[k] Or who   [l] Heb obscure
22.8 (Gk): 1 Cor 9.7.

my heart too will be glad.
My soul will rejoice
    when your lips speak what is right.
Let not your heart envy sinners,
    but continue in the fear of the LORD all the
        day.
Surely there is a future,
    and your hope will not be cut off.

Hear, my son, and be wise,
    and direct your mind in the way.
Be not among winebibbers,
    or among gluttonous eaters of meat;
for the drunkard and the glutton will come
        to poverty,
    and drowsiness will clothe a man with
        rags.

Hearken to your father who begot you,
    and do not despise your mother when she
        is old.
Buy truth, and do not sell it;
    buy wisdom, instruction, and under-
        standing.
The father of the righteous will greatly
        rejoice;
    he who begets a wise son will be glad in
        him.
Let your father and mother be glad,
    let her who bore you rejoice.

My son, give me your heart,
    and let your eyes observe[m] my ways.
For a harlot is a deep pit;
    an adventuress is a narrow well.
She lies in wait like a robber
    and increases the faithless among men.

Who has woe? Who has sorrow?
    Who has strife? Who has complaining?
Who has wounds without cause?
    Who has redness of eyes?
Those who tarry long over wine,
    those who go to try mixed wine.
Do not look at wine when it is red,
    when it sparkles in the cup
    and goes down smoothly.
At the last it bites like a serpent,
    and stings like an adder.
Your eyes will see strange things,
    and your mind utter perverse things.
You will be like one who lies down in the
        midst of the sea,
    like one who lies on the top of a mast.[n]
"They struck me," you will say,[o]
    "but I was not hurt;
    they beat me, but I did not feel it.
When shall I awake?
    I will seek another drink."

Be not envious of evil men,   24
    nor desire to be with them;
for their minds devise violence,   2
    and their lips talk of mischief.

By wisdom a house is built,   3
    and by understanding it is established;
by knowledge the rooms are filled   4
    with all precious and pleasant riches.
A wise man is mightier than a strong man,[p] 5
    and a man of knowledge than he who has
        strength;
for by wise guidance you can wage your war, 6
    and in abundance of counsellors there is
        victory.
Wisdom is too high for a fool;   7
    in the gate he does not open his mouth.

He who plans to do evil   8
    will be called a mischief-maker.
The devising of folly is sin,   9
    and the scoffer is an abomination to men.

If you faint in the day of adversity,   10
    your strength is small.
Rescue those who are being taken away to 11
        death;
    hold back those who are stumbling to the
        slaughter.
If you say, "Behold, we did not know this," 12
    does not he who weighs the heart perceive
        it?
Does not he who keeps watch over your soul
        know it,
    and will he not requite man according to
        his work?

My son, eat honey, for it is good,   13
    and the drippings of the honeycomb are
        sweet to your taste.
Know that wisdom is such to your soul;   14
    if you find it, there will be a future,
    and your hope will not be cut off.

Lie not in wait as a wicked man against the 15
        dwelling of the righteous;
    do not violence to his home;
for a righteous man falls seven times, and 16
        rises again;
    but the wicked are overthrown by
        calamity.

Do not rejoice when your enemy falls,   17
    and let not your heart be glad when he
        stumbles;
lest the LORD see it, and be displeased,   18
    and turn away his anger from him.

Fret not yourself because of evildoers,   19

[m] Another reading is *delight in*   [n] Heb obscure   [o] Gk Syr Vg Tg: Heb lacks *you will say*
[p] Gk Compare Syr Tg: Heb *is in strength*

and be not envious of the wicked;
20 for the evil man has no future;
     the lamp of the wicked will be put out.

21 My son, fear the LORD and the king,
     and do not disobey either of them;[q]
22 for disaster from them will rise suddenly,
     and who knows the ruin that will come
     from them both?

23   These also are sayings of the wise.

     Partiality in judging is not good.
24 He who says to the wicked, "You are
     innocent,"
     will be cursed by peoples, abhorred by
     nations;
25 but those who rebuke the wicked will have
     delight,
     and a good blessing will be upon them.
26 He who gives a right answer
     kisses the lips.

27 Prepare your work outside,
     get everything ready for you in the field;
     and after that build your house.

28 Be not a witness against your neighbour
     without cause,
     and do not deceive with your lips.
29 Do not say, "I will do to him as he has done
     to me;
     I will pay the man back for what he has
     done."

30 I passed by the field of a sluggard,
     by the vineyard of a man without sense;

31 and lo, it was all overgrown with thorns;
     the ground was covered with nettles,
     and its stone wall was broken down.
32 Then I saw and considered it;
     I looked and received instruction.
33 A little sleep, a little slumber,
     a little folding of the hands to rest,
34 and poverty will come upon you like a
     robber,
     and want like an armed man.

PROVERBS OF SOLOMON

25 THESE also are proverbs of Solomon
which the men of Hezeki′ah king of
Judah copied.

It is the glory of God to conceal things,
     but the glory of kings is to search things
     out.
As the heavens for height, and the earth for
     depth,
     so the mind of kings is unsearchable.
Take away the dross from the silver,
     and the smith has material for a vessel;
take away the wicked from the presence of
     the king,
     and his throne will be established in
     righteousness.
Do not put yourself forward in the king's
     presence
     or stand in the place of the great;
for it is better to be told, "Come up
     here,"
     than to be put lower in the presence of the
     prince.

What your eyes have seen
     do not hastily bring into court;   8
for[r] what will you do in the end,
     when your neighbour puts you to shame?
Argue your case with your neighbour 9
     himself,
     and do not disclose another's secret;
lest he who hears you bring shame upon you, 10
     and your ill repute have no end.
A word fitly spoken 11
     is like apples of gold in a setting of
     silver.
Like a gold ring or an ornament of gold 12
     is a wise reprover to a listening ear.
Like the cold of snow in the time of harvest 13
     is a faithful messenger to those who send
     him,
     he refreshes the spirit of his masters.
Like clouds and wind without rain 14
     is a man who boasts of a gift he does not
     give.

With patience a ruler may be persuaded, 15
     and a soft tongue will break a bone.
If you have found honey, eat only enough for 16
     you,
     lest you be sated with it and vomit it.
Let your foot be seldom in your neighbour's 17
     house,
     lest he become weary of you and hate you.
A man who bears false witness against his 18
     neighbour
     is like a war club, or a sword, or a sharp
     arrow.
Trust in a faithless man in time of trouble 19
     is like a bad tooth or a foot that slips.
He who sings songs to a heavy heart 20
     is like one who takes off a garment on a
     cold day,
     and like vinegar on a wound.[s]

q Gk: Heb *do not associate with those who change*   r Cn: Heb *lest*   s Gk: Heb *lye*

If your enemy is hungry, give him bread to
eat;
and if he is thirsty, give him water to
drink;
for you will heap coals of fire on his head,
and the LORD will reward you.
The north wind brings forth rain;
and a backbiting tongue, angry looks.
It is better to live in a corner of the housetop
than in a house shared with a contentious
woman.
Like cold water to a thirsty soul,
so is good news from a far country.
Like a muddied spring or a polluted fountain
is a righteous man who gives way before
the wicked.
It is not good to eat much honey,
so be sparing of complimentary words.[t]
A man without self-control
is like a city broken into and left without
walls.

Like snow in summer or rain in harvest,
so honour is not fitting for a fool.
Like a sparrow in its flitting, like a swallow in
its flying,
a curse that is causeless does not alight.
A whip for the horse, a bridle for the ass,
and a rod for the back of fools.
Answer not a fool according to his folly,
lest you be like him yourself.
Answer a fool according to his folly,
lest he be wise in his own eyes.
He who sends a message by the hand of a fool
cuts off his own feet and drinks violence.
Like a lame man's legs, which hang useless,
is a proverb in the mouth of fools.
Like one who binds the stone in the sling
is he who gives honour to a fool.
Like a thorn that goes up into the hand of a
drunkard
is a proverb in the mouth of fools.
Like an archer who wounds everybody
is he who hires a passing fool or
drunkard.[u]
Like a dog that returns to his vomit
is a fool that repeats his folly.
Do you see a man who is wise in his own
eyes?
There is more hope for a fool than for him.
The sluggard says, "There is a lion in the
road!
There is a lion in the streets!"
As a door turns on its hinges,
so does a sluggard on his bed.
The sluggard buries his hand in the dish;
it wears him out to bring it back to his
mouth.
The sluggard is wiser in his own eyes

than seven men who can answer discreetly.
He who meddles in a quarrel not his own   17
is like one who takes a passing dog by the
ears.
Like a madman who throws firebrands,   18
arrows, and death,
is the man who deceives his neighbour   19
and says, "I am only joking!"
For lack of wood the fire goes out;   20
and where there is no whisperer, quarrelling
ceases.
As charcoal to hot embers and wood to fire,   21
so is a quarrelsome man for kindling strife.
The words of a whisperer are like delicious   22
morsels;
they go down into the inner parts of the
body.
Like the glaze[v] covering an earthen vessel   23
are smooth[w] lips with an evil heart.
He who hates, dissembles with his lips   24
and harbours deceit in his heart;
when he speaks graciously, believe him not,   25
for there are seven abominations in his
heart;
though his hatred be covered with guile,   26
his wickedness will be exposed in the
assembly.
He who digs a pit will fall into it,   27
and a stone will come back upon him who
starts it rolling.
A lying tongue hates its victims,   28
and a flattering mouth works ruin.

Do not boast about tomorrow,   **27**
for you do not know what a day may bring
forth.
Let another praise you, and not your own   2
mouth;
a stranger, and not your own lips.
A stone is heavy, and sand is weighty,   3
but a fool's provocation is heavier than
both.
Wrath is cruel, anger is overwhelming;   4
but who can stand before jealousy?
Better is open rebuke   5
than hidden love.
Faithful are the wounds of a friend;   6
profuse are the kisses of an enemy.
He who is sated loathes honey,   7
but to one who is hungry everything bitter
is sweet.
Like a bird that strays from its nest,   8
is a man who strays from his home.
Oil and perfume make the heart glad,   9
but the soul is torn by trouble.[x]
Your friend, and your father's friend, do not   10
forsake;
and do not go to your brother's house in
the day of your calamity.

---

[t] Cn Compare Gk Syr Tg: Heb *searching out their glory is glory*   [u] The Hebrew text of this verse is uncertain
[v] Cn: Heb *silver of dross*   [w] Gk: Heb *burning*   [x] Gk: Heb *the sweetness of his friend from hearty counsel*
25.21–22: Rom 12.20.   26.11: 2 Pet 2.22.

Better is a neighbour who is near
than a brother who is far away.
11 Be wise, my son, and make my heart glad,
that I may answer him who reproaches me.
12 A prudent man sees danger and hides
himself;
but the simple go on, and suffer for it.
13 Take a man's garment when he has given
surety for a stranger,
and hold him in pledge when he gives
surety for foreigners.[y]
14 He who blesses his neighbour with a loud
voice,
rising early in the morning,
will be counted as cursing.
15 A continual dripping on a rainy day
and a contentious woman are alike;
16 to restrain her is to restrain the wind[z]
or to grasp oil in his right hand.
17 Iron sharpens iron,
and one man sharpens another.
18 He who tends a fig tree will eat its fruit,
and he who guards his master will be
honoured.
19 As in water face answers to face,
so the mind of man reflects the man.
20 Sheol and Abaddon are never satisfied,
and never satisfied are the eyes of man.
21 The crucible is for silver, and the furnace is
for gold,
and a man is judged by his praise.
22 Crush a fool in a mortar with a pestle
along with crushed grain,
yet his folly will not depart from him.

23 Know well the condition of your flocks,
and give attention to your herds;
24 for riches do not last for ever;
and does a crown endure to all generations?
25 When the grass is gone, and the new growth
appears,
and the herbage of the mountains is
gathered,
26 the lambs will provide your clothing,
and the goats the price of a field;
27 there will be enough goats' milk for your
food,
for the food of your household
and maintenance for your maidens.

28 The wicked flee when no one pursues,
but the righteous are bold as a lion.
2 When a land transgresses
it has many rulers;
but with men of understanding and knowledge
its stability will long continue.
3 A poor man who oppresses the poor
is a beating rain that leaves no food.

Those who forsake the law praise the wicked,
but those who keep the law strive against
them.
Evil men do not understand justice,
but those who seek the LORD understand it
completely.
Better is a poor man who walks in his
integrity
than a rich man who is perverse in his
ways.
He who keeps the law is a wise son,
but a companion of gluttons shames his
father.
He who augments his wealth by interest and
increase
gathers it for him who is kind to the poor.
If one turns away his ear from hearing the
law,
even his prayer is an abomination.
He who misleads the upright into an evil
way
will fall into his own pit;
but the blameless will have a goodly
inheritance.
A rich man is wise in his own eyes,
but a poor man who has understanding
will find him out.
When the righteous triumph, there is great
glory;
but when the wicked rise, men hide
themselves.
He who conceals his transgressions will not
prosper,
but he who confesses and forsakes them
will obtain mercy.
Blessed is the man who fears the LORD
always;
but he who hardens his heart will fall into
calamity.
Like a roaring lion or a charging bear
is a wicked ruler over a poor people.
A ruler who lacks understanding is a cruel
oppressor;
but he who hates unjust gain will prolong
his days.
If a man is burdened with the blood of
another,
let him be a fugitive until death;
let no one help him.
He who walks in integrity will be delivered,
but he who is perverse in his ways will fall
into a pit.[a]
He who tills his land will have plenty of
bread,
but he who follows worthless pursuits will
have plenty of poverty.
A faithful man will abound with blessings,
but he who hastens to be rich will not go
unpunished.
To show partiality is not good;

[y] Vg and 20.16: Heb *a foreign woman*   [z] Heb obscure   [a] Syr: Heb *in one*

but for a piece of bread a man will do wrong.

2 A miserly man hastens after wealth, and does not know that want will come upon him.

3 He who rebukes a man will afterward find more favour than he who flatters with his tongue.

4 He who robs his father or his mother and says, "That is no transgression," is the companion of a man who destroys.

5 A greedy man stirs up strife, but he who trusts in the LORD will be enriched.

6 He who trusts in his own mind is a fool; but he who walks in wisdom will be delivered.

7 He who gives to the poor will not want, but he who hides his eyes will get many a curse.

8 When the wicked rise, men hide themselves, but when they perish, the righteous increase.

29 He who is often reproved, yet stiffens his neck will suddenly be broken beyond healing.

2 When the righteous are in authority, the people rejoice; but when the wicked rule, the people groan.

3 He who loves wisdom makes his father glad, but one who keeps company with harlots squanders his substance.

4 By justice a king gives stability to the land, but one who exacts gifts ruins it.

5 A man who flatters his neighbour spreads a net for his feet.

6 An evil man is ensnared in his transgression, but a righteous man sings and rejoices.

7 A righteous man knows the rights of the poor; a wicked man does not understand such knowledge.

8 Scoffers set a city aflame, but wise men turn away wrath.

9 If a wise man has an argument with a fool, the fool only rages and laughs, and there is no quiet.

10 Bloodthirsty men hate one who is blameless, and the wicked[b] seek his life.

11 A fool gives full vent to his anger, but a wise man quietly holds it back.

12 If a ruler listens to falsehood, all his officials will be wicked.

13 The poor man and the oppressor meet together; the LORD gives light to the eyes of both.

14 If a king judges the poor with equity

his throne will be established for ever.

15 The rod and reproof give wisdom, but a child left to himself brings shame to his mother.

16 When the wicked are in authority, transgression increases; but the righteous will look upon their downfall.

17 Discipline your son, and he will give you rest; he will give delight to your heart.

18 Where there is no prophecy the people cast off restraint, but blessed is he who keeps the law.

19 By mere words a servant is not disciplined, for though he understands, he will not give heed.

20 Do you see a man who is hasty in his words? There is more hope for a fool than for him.

21 He who pampers his servant from childhood, will in the end find him his heir.[c]

22 A man of wrath stirs up strife, and a man given to anger causes much transgression.

23 A man's pride will bring him low, but he who is lowly in spirit will obtain honour.

24 The partner of a thief hates his own life; he hears the curse, but discloses nothing.

25 The fear of man lays a snare, but he who trusts in the LORD is safe.

26 Many seek the favour of a ruler, but from the LORD a man gets justice.

27 An unjust man is an abomination to the righteous, but he whose way is straight is an abomination to the wicked.

WORDS OF AGUR

30 THE words of Agur son of Jakeh of Massa.[d]

The man says to Ith'i-el, to Ith'i-el and Ucal:[e]

2 Surely I am too stupid to be a man. I have not the understanding of a man.

3 I have not learned wisdom, nor have I knowledge of the Holy One.

4 Who has ascended to heaven and come down? Who has gathered the wind in his fists? Who has wrapped up the waters in a garment? Who has established all the ends of the earth? What is his name, and what is his son's name? Surely you know!

b Cn: Heb *upright*   c The meaning of the Hebrew word is uncertain   d Or *the oracle*
e The Hebrew of this verse is obscure

5 Every word of God proves true;
  he is a shield to those who take refuge in
    him.
6 Do not add to his words,
  lest he rebuke you, and you be found a liar.

7 Two things I ask of thee;
  deny them not to me before I die:
8 Remove far from me falsehood and lying;
  give me neither poverty nor riches;
  feed me with the food that is needful for
    me,
9 lest I be full, and deny thee,
  and say, "Who is the Lord?"
  or lest I be poor, and steal,
  and profane the name of my God.

10 Do not slander a servant to his master,
  lest he curse you, and you be held guilty.

11 There are those who curse their fathers
  and do not bless their mothers.
12 There are those who are pure in their own
    eyes
  but are not cleansed of their filth.
13 There are those—how lofty are their eyes,
  how high their eyelids lift!
14 There are those whose teeth are swords,
  whose teeth are knives,
  to devour the poor from off the earth,
  the needy from among men.

15 The leech[f] has two daughters;
  "Give, give," they cry.
  Three things are never satisfied;
  four never say, "Enough":
16 Sheol, the barren womb,
  the earth ever thirsty for water,
  and the fire which never says, "Enough."[g]

17 The eye that mocks a father
  and scorns to obey a mother
  will be picked out by the ravens of the valley
  and eaten by the vultures.

18 Three things are too wonderful for me;
  four I do not understand:
19 the way of an eagle in the sky,
  the way of a serpent on a rock,
  the way of a ship on the high seas,
  and the way of a man with a maiden.

20 This is the way of an adulteress:
  she eats, and wipes her mouth,
  and says, "I have done no wrong."

21 Under three things the earth trembles;
  under four it cannot bear up:
22 a slave when he becomes king,

and a fool when he is filled with food;
an unloved woman when she gets a husband, 2
  and a maid when she succeeds her
    mistress.

Four things on earth are small, 2
  but they are exceedingly wise:
the ants are a people not strong, 2
  yet they provide their food in the summer;
the badgers are a people not mighty, 2
  yet they make their homes in the rocks;
the locusts have no king, 2
  yet all of them march in rank;
the lizard you can take in your hands, 2
  yet it is in kings' palaces.

Three things are stately in their tread; 2
  four are stately in their stride:
the lion, which is mightiest among beasts 3
  and does not turn back before any;
the strutting cock,[h] the he-goat, 3
  and a king striding before[i] his people.

If you have been foolish, exalting yourself, 32
  or if you have been devising evil,
  put your hand on your mouth.
For pressing milk produces curds, 33
  pressing the nose produces blood,
  and pressing anger produces strife.

WORDS OF LEMUEL

THE words of Lemuel, king of Massa,[j] 31
which his mother taught him:

What, my son? What, son of my womb? 2
  What, son of my vows?
Give not your strength to women, 3
  your ways to those who destroy kings.
It is not for kings, O Lemuel, 4
  it is not for kings to drink wine,
  or for rulers to desire[k] strong drink;
lest they drink and forget what has been 5
    decreed,
  and pervert the rights of all the afflicted.
Give strong drink to him who is perishing, 6
  and wine to those in bitter distress;
let them drink and forget their poverty, 7
  and remember their misery no more.
Open your mouth for the dumb, 8
  for the rights of all who are left desolate.[l]
Open your mouth, judge righteously, 9
  maintain the rights of the poor and needy.

The good wife

A good wife who can find? 10
  She is far more precious than jewels.

f The meaning of the Hebrew word is uncertain g Heb obscure h Gk Syr Tg Compare Vg: Heb obscure
i The meaning of the Hebrew is uncertain j Or King Lemuel, the oracle k Cn: Heb where
l Heb are sons of passing away

The heart of her husband trusts in her,
and he will have no lack of gain.
She does him good, and not harm,
all the days of her life.
She seeks wool and flax,
and works with willing hands.
She is like the ships of the merchant,
she brings her food from afar.
She rises while it is yet night
and provides food for her household
and tasks for her maidens.
She considers a field and buys it;
with the fruit of her hands she plants a
vineyard.
She girds her loins with strength and makes
her arms strong.
She perceives that her merchandise is profitable.
Her lamp does not go out at night.
She puts her hands to the distaff,
and her hands hold the spindle.
She opens her hand to the poor,
and reaches out her hands to the needy.
She is not afraid of snow for her household,

for all her household are clothed in scarlet.
She makes herself coverings; 22
her clothing is fine linen and purple.
Her husband is known in the gates, 23
when he sits among the elders of the land.
She makes linen garments and sells them; 24
she delivers girdles to the merchant.
Strength and dignity are her clothing, 25
and she laughs at the time to come.
She opens her mouth with wisdom, 26
and the teaching of kindness is on her
tongue.
She looks well to the ways of her household, 27
and does not eat the bread of idleness.
Her children rise up and call her blessed; 28
her husband also, and he praises her:
"Many women have done excellently, 29
but you surpass them all."
Charm is deceitful, and beauty is vain, 30
but a woman who fears the LORD is to be
praised.
Give her of the fruit of her hands, 31
and let her works praise her in the gates.

ECCLESIASTES

OR,

THE PREACHER

THE words of the Preacher,[a] the son of
David, king in Jerusalem.
2 Vanity of vanities, says the Preacher,
vanity of vanities! All is vanity.
3 What does man gain by all the toil
at which he toils under the sun?
4 A generation goes, and a generation comes,
but the earth remains for ever.
5 The sun rises and the sun goes down,
and hastens to the place where it rises.
6 The wind blows to the south,
and goes round to the north;
round and round goes the wind,
and on its circuits the wind returns.
7 All streams run to the sea,
but the sea is not full;
to the place where the streams flow,
there they flow again.
8 All things are full of weariness;
a man cannot utter it;
the eye is not satisfied with seeing,

Eccl **12,** 6

nor the ear filled with hearing.
What has been is what will be, 9
and what has been done is what will be done;
and there is nothing new under the sun.
Is there a thing of which it is said, 10
"See, this is new"?

[a] Heb *Koheleth*

It has been already,
in the ages before us.

11 There is no remembrance of former
things,
nor will there be any remembrance
of later things yet to happen
among those who come after.

The vanity of knowledge

12 I the Preacher have been king over Israel in
13 Jerusalem. And I applied my mind to seek
and to search out by wisdom all that is done
under heaven; it is an unhappy business that
God has given to the sons of men to be busy
14 with. I have seen everything that is done
under the sun; and behold, all is vanity and a
striving after wind.[b]

15 What is crooked cannot be made straight,
and what is lacking cannot be numbered.

16 I said to myself, "I have acquired great
wisdom, surpassing all who were over Jerusalem before me; and my mind has had great
17 experience of wisdom and knowledge." And
I applied my mind to know madness and to
know madness and folly. I perceived that
this also is but a striving after wind.

18 For in much wisdom is much vexation,
and he who increases knowledge increases
sorrow.

The vanity of pleasure

2 I said to myself, "Come now, I will make a
test of pleasure; enjoy yourself." But
2 behold, this also was vanity. I said of
laughter, "It is mad," and of pleasure,
3 "What use is it?" I searched with my mind
how to cheer my body with wine—my mind
still guiding me with wisdom—and how to
lay hold on folly, till I might see what was
good for the sons of men to do under heaven
4 during the few days of their life. I made
great works; I built houses and planted
5 vineyards for myself; I made myself gardens
and parks, and planted in them all kinds of
6 fruit trees. I made myself pools from which
7 to water the forest of growing trees. I bought
male and female slaves, and had slaves who
were born in my house; I had also great
possessions of herds and flocks, more than
8 any who had been before me in Jerusalem. I
also gathered for myself silver and gold and
the treasure of kings and provinces; I got
singers, both men and women, and many
concubines,[c] man's delight.
9 So I became great and surpassed all who

were before me in Jerusalem; also my
wisdom remained with me. And whatever
my eyes desired I did not keep from them; I
kept my heart from no pleasure, for my heart
found pleasure in all my toil, and this was my
reward for all my toil. Then I considered all
that my hands had done and the toil I had
spent in doing it, and behold, all was vanity
and a striving after wind, and there was
nothing to be gained under the sun.

So I turned to consider wisdom and madness and folly; for what can the man do who
comes after the king? Only what he has
already done. Then I saw that wisdom
excels folly as light excels darkness. The
wise man has his eyes in his head, but the
fool walks in darkness; and yet I perceived
that one fate comes to all of them. Then I
said to myself, "What befalls the fool will
befall me also; why then have I been so very
wise?" And I said to myself that this also is
vanity. For of the wise man as of the fool
there is no enduring remembrance, seeing
that in the days to come all will have been
long forgotten. How the wise man dies just
like the fool! So I hated life, because what is
done under the sun was grievous to me; for
all is vanity and a striving after wind.

The vanity of work and riches

I hated all my toil in which I had toiled
under the sun, seeing that I must leave it to
the man who will come after me; and who
knows whether he will be a wise man or a
fool? Yet he will be master of all for which I
toiled and used my wisdom under the sun.
This also is vanity. So I turned about and
gave my heart up to despair over all the toil
of my labours under the sun, because
sometimes a man who has toiled with
wisdom and knowledge and skill must leave
all to be enjoyed by a man who did not toil
for it. This also is vanity and a great evil.
What has a man from all the toil and strain
with which he toils beneath the sun? For all
his days are full of pain, and his work is a
vexation; even in the night his mind does not
rest. This also is vanity.

There is nothing better for a man than that
he should eat and drink, and find enjoyment
in his toil. This also, I saw, is from the hand
of God; for apart from him[d] who can eat or
who can have enjoyment? For to the man
who pleases him God gives wisdom and
knowledge and joy; but to the sinner he gives
the work of gathering and heaping, only to
give to one who pleases God. This also is
vanity and a striving after wind.

For everything there is a season, and a time for every matter under heaven:

 a time to be born, and a time to die;
 a time to plant, and a time to pluck up what is planted;
 a time to kill, and a time to heal;
 a time to break down, and a time to build up;
 a time to weep, and a time to laugh;
 a time to mourn, and a time to dance;
 a time to cast away stones, and a time to gather stones together;
 a time to embrace, and a time to refrain from embracing;
 a time to seek, and a time to lose;
 a time to keep, and a time to cast away;
 a time to rend, and a time to sew;
 a time to keep silence, and a time to speak;
 a time to love, and a time to hate;
 a time for war, and a time for peace.

9 What gain has the worker from his toil? 10 I have seen the business that God has given 11 to the sons of men to be busy with. He has made everything beautiful in its time; also he has put eternity into man's mind, yet so that he cannot find out what God has done from 12 the beginning to the end. I know that there is nothing better for them than to be happy and enjoy themselves as long as they live; 13 also that it is God's gift to man that every one should eat and drink and take pleasure in all 14 his toil. I know that whatever God does endures for ever; nothing can be added to it, nor anything taken from it; God has made it so, in order that men should fear before him. 15 That which is, already has been; that which is to be, already has been; and God seeks what has been driven away.

16 Moreover I saw under the sun that in the place of justice, even there was wickedness, and in the place of righteousness, even there 17 was wickedness. I said in my heart, God will judge the righteous and the wicked, for he has appointed a time for every matter, and 18 for every work. I said in my heart with regard to the sons of men that God is testing them to show them that they are but beasts. 19 For the fate of the sons of men and the fate of beasts is the same; as one dies, so dies the other. They all have the same breath, and man has no advantage over the beasts; for all 20 is vanity. All go to one place; all are from the 21 dust, and all turn to dust again. Who knows whether the spirit of man goes upward and the spirit of the beast goes down to the 22 earth? So I saw that there is nothing better than that a man should enjoy his work, for that is his lot; who can bring him to see what will be after him?

Again I saw all the oppressions that are 4 practised under the sun. And behold, the tears of the oppressed, and they had no one to comfort them! On the side of their oppressors there was power, and there was no one to comfort them. And I thought the 2 dead who are already dead more fortunate than the living who are still alive; but better 3 than both is he who has not yet been, and has not seen the evil deeds that are done under the sun.

Then I saw that all toil and all skill in work 4 come from a man's envy of his neighbour. This also is vanity and a striving after wind.

The fool folds his hands, and eats his own 5 flesh.

Better is a handful of quietness than two 6 hands full of toil and a striving after wind.

Again, I saw vanity under the sun: a person 7, who has no one, either son or brother, yet 8 there is no end to all his toil, and his eyes are never satisfied with riches, so that he never asks, "For whom am I toiling and depriving myself of pleasure?" This also is vanity and an unhappy business.

Two are better than one, because they have 9 a good reward for their toil. For if they fall, 10 one will lift up his fellow; but woe to him who is alone when he falls and has not another to lift him up. Again, if two lie 11 together, they are warm; but how can one be warm alone? And though a man might 12 prevail against one who is alone, two will withstand him. A threefold cord is not quickly broken.

Better is a poor and wise youth than an old 13 and foolish king, who will no longer take advice, even though he had gone from prison 14 to the throne or in his own kingdom had been born poor. I saw all the living who move 15 about under the sun, as well as that[e] youth, who was to stand in his place; there was no 16 end of all the people; he was over all of them. Yet those who come later will not rejoice in him. Surely this also is vanity and a striving after wind.

Guard your steps when you go to the house 5[f] of God; to draw near to listen is better than to offer the sacrifice of fools; for they do not know that they are doing evil. Be not rash 2[g] with your mouth, nor let your heart be hasty to utter a word before God, for God is in heaven, and you upon earth; therefore let your words be few.

For a dream comes with much business, 3 and a fool's voice with many words.

When you vow a vow to God, do not delay 4 paying it; for he has no pleasure in fools. Pay what you vow. It is better that you should 5

---

not vow than that you should vow and not
6 pay. Let not your mouth lead you into sin,
and do not say before the messenger[h] that it
was a mistake; why should God be angry at
your voice, and destroy the work of your
hands ?

7 For when dreams increase, empty words
grow many:[i] but do you fear God.

8 If you see in a province the poor oppressed
and justice and right violently taken away, do
not be amazed at the matter; for the high
official is watched by a higher, and there are
9 yet higher ones over them. But in all, a king
is an advantage to a land with cultivated
fields.[j]

10 He who loves money will not be satisfied
with money; nor he who loves wealth, with
gain: this also is vanity.

11 When goods increase, they increase who eat
them; and what gain has their owner but to
see them with his eyes ?

12 Sweet is the sleep of a labourer, whether he
eats little or much; but the surfeit of the rich
will not let him sleep.

13 There is a grievous evil which I have seen
under the sun: riches were kept by their
14 owner to his hurt, and those riches were lost
in a bad venture; and he is father of a son,
15 but he has nothing in his hand. As he came
from his mother's womb he shall go again,
naked as he came, and shall take nothing for
his toil, which he may carry away in his
16 hand. This also is a grievous evil: just as he
came, so shall he go; and what gain has he
17 that he toiled for the wind, and spent all his
days in darkness and grief,[k] in much vexation
and sickness and resentment ?

18 Behold, what I have seen to be good and to
be fitting is to eat and drink and find
enjoyment in all the toil with which one toils
under the sun the few days of his life which
19 God has given him, for this is his lot. Every
man also to whom God has given wealth and
possessions and power to enjoy them, and to
accept his lot and find enjoyment in his
20 toil—this is the gift of God. For he will not
much remember the days of his life because
God keeps him occupied with joy in his
heart.

6 There is an evil which I have seen under the
2 sun, and it lies heavy upon men: a man to
whom God gives wealth, possessions, and
honour, so that he lacks nothing of all that he
desires, yet God does not give him power to
enjoy them, but a stranger enjoys them; this
3 is vanity; it is a sore affliction. If a man
begets a hundred children, and lives many
years, so that the days of his years are many,

but he does not enjoy life's good things, and
also has no burial, I say that an untimely
birth is better off than he. For it comes into 4
vanity and goes into darkness, and in darkness its name is covered; moreover it has not 5
seen the sun or known anything; yet it finds
rest rather than he. Even though he should 6
live a thousand years twice told, yet enjoy no
good—do not all go to the one place ?

All the toil of man is for his mouth, yet his 7
appetite is not satisfied. For what advantage 8
has the wise man over the fool? And what
does the poor man have who knows how to
conduct himself before the living? Better is 9
the sight of the eyes than the wandering of
desire; this also is vanity and a striving after
wind.

Whatever has come to be has already been 1
named, and it is known what man is, and that
he is not able to dispute with one stronger
than he. The more words, the more vanity, 1
and what is man the better? For who knows 1
what is good for man while he lives the few
days of his vain life, which he passes like a
shadow? For who can tell man what will be
after him under the sun ?

The vanity of fame

A good name is better than precious **7**
   ointment;
   and the day of death, than the day of
     birth.
It is better to go to the house of 2
   mourning
than to go to the house of feasting;
for this is the end of all men,
   and the living will lay it to heart.
Sorrow is better than laughter,   3
   for by sadness of countenance the heart
     is made glad.
The heart of the wise is in the house of 4
   mourning;
   but the heart of fools is in the house of
     mirth.
It is better for a man to hear the rebuke of 5
   the wise
than to hear the song of fools.
For as the crackling of thorns under a 6
   pot,
   so is the laughter of the fools;
   this also is vanity.
Surely oppression makes the wise man 7
   foolish,
   and a bribe corrupts the mind.
Better is the end of a thing than its 8
   beginning;
   and the patient in spirit is better than
     the proud in spirit.

---

[h] Or *angel*   [i] Or *For in a multitude of dreams there is futility, and ruin in a flood of words*
[j] Or *The profit of the land is among all of them; a cultivated field has a king*
[k] Gk: Heb *all his days also he eats in darkness*

Be not quick to anger,
for anger lodges in the bosom of fools.
Say not, "Why were the former days
better than these?"
For it is not from wisdom that you ask
this.
Wisdom is good with an inheritance,
an advantage to those who see the sun.
For the protection of wisdom is like the
protection of money;
and the advantage of knowledge is that
wisdom preserves the life of him who
has it.
Consider the work of God;
who can make straight what he has made
crooked?
In the day of prosperity be joyful, and in the
day of adversity consider; God has made the
one as well as the other, so that man may not
find out anything that will be after him.

In my vain life I have seen everything; there
is a righteous man who perishes in his
righteousness, and there is a wicked man who
prolongs his life in his evil-doing. Be not
righteous overmuch, and do not make
yourself overwise; why should you destroy
yourself? Be not wicked overmuch, neither
be a fool; why should you die before your
time? It is good that you should take hold of
this, and from that withhold not your hand;
for he who fears God shall come forth from
them all.
Wisdom gives strength to the wise man
more than ten rulers that are in a city.
Surely there is not a righteous man on earth
who does good and never sins.
Do not give heed to all the things that men
say, lest you hear your servant cursing you;
your heart knows that many times you have
yourself cursed others.

The quest for wisdom

All this I have tested by wisdom; I said, "I
will be wise"; but it was far from me. That
which is, is far off, and deep, very deep; who
can find it out? I turned my mind to know
and to search out and to seek wisdom and the
sum of things, and to know the wickedness of
folly and the foolishness which is madness.
And I found more bitter than death the
woman whose heart is snares and nets, and
whose hands are fetters; he who pleases God
escapes her, but the sinner is taken by her.
Behold, this is what I found, says the
Preacher, adding one thing to another to find
the sum, which my mind has sought repeatedly, but I have not found. One man among
a thousand I found, but a woman among all
these I have not found. Behold, this alone I

found, that God made man upright, but they
have sought out many devices.

Who is like the wise man?   8
And who knows the interpretation of a
thing?
A man's wisdom makes his face shine,
and the hardness of his countenance is
changed.
Keep[1] the king's command, and because of 2
your sacred oath be not dismayed; go from 3
his presence, do not delay when the matter is
unpleasant, for he does whatever he pleases.
For the word of the king is supreme, and who 4
may say to him, "What are you doing?" He 5
who obeys a command will meet no harm,
and the mind of a wise man will know the
time and way. For every matter has its time 6
and way, although man's trouble lies heavy
upon him. For he does not know what is to 7
be, for who can tell him how it will be? No 8
man has power to retain the spirit, or
authority over the day of death; there is no
discharge from war, nor will wickedness
deliver those who are given to it. All this I 9
observed while applying my mind to all that
is done under the sun, while man lords it
over man to his hurt.
Then I saw the wicked buried; they used to 10
go in and out of the holy place, and were
praised in the city where they had done such
things. This also is vanity. Because sentence 11
against an evil deed is not executed speedily,
the heart of the sons of men is fully set to do
evil. Though a sinner does evil a hundred 12
times and prolongs his life, yet I know that it
will be well with those who fear God,
because they fear before him; but it will not 13
be well with the wicked, neither will he
prolong his days like a shadow, because he
does not fear before God.
There is a vanity which takes place on earth, 14
that there are righteous men to whom it
happens according to the deeds of the
wicked, and there are wicked men to whom it
happens according to the deeds of the
righteous. I said that this also is vanity. And 15
I commend enjoyment, for man has no good
thing under the sun but to eat, and drink,
and enjoy himself, for this will go with him in
his toil through the days of life which God
gives him under the sun.
When I applied my mind to know wisdom, 16
and to see the business that is done on earth,
how neither day nor night one's eyes see
sleep; then I saw all the work of God, that man 17
cannot find out the work that is done under
the sun. However much man may toil in seeking, he will not find it out; even though a wise
man claims to know, he cannot find it out.

[1] Heb inserts an *I*

9 But all this I laid to heart, examining it all, how the righteous and the wise and their deeds are in the hand of God; whether it is love or hate man does not know. Everything

2 before them is vanity,[m] since one fate comes to all, to the righteous and the wicked, to the good and the evil,[n] to the clean and the unclean, to him who sacrifices and him who does not sacrifice. As is the good man, so is the sinner; and he who swears is as he who

3 shuns an oath. This is an evil in all that is done under the sun, that one fate comes to all; also the hearts of men are full of evil, and madness is in their hearts while they live, and

4 after that they go to the dead. But he who is joined with all the living has hope, for a

5 living dog is better than a dead lion. For the living know that they will die, but the dead know nothing, and they have no more reward; but the memory of them is lost.

6 Their love and their hate and their envy have already perished, and they have no more for ever any share in all that is done under the sun.

7 Go, eat your bread with enjoyment, and drink your wine with a merry heart; for God has already approved what you do.

8 Let your garments be always white; let not oil be lacking on your head.

9 Enjoy life with the wife whom you love, all the days of your vain life which he has given you under the sun, because that is your portion in life and in your toil at which

10 you toil under the sun. Whatever your hand finds to do, do it with your might; for there is no work or thought or knowledge or wisdom in Sheol, to which you are going.

11 Again I saw that under the sun the race is not to the swift, nor the battle to the strong, nor bread to the wise, nor riches to the intelligent, nor favour to the men of skill; but

12 time and chance happen to them all. For man does not know his time. Like fish which are taken in an evil net, and like birds which are caught in a snare, so the sons of men are snared at an evil time, when it suddenly falls upon them.

13 I have also seen this example of wisdom under the sun, and it seemed great to me.

There was a little city with few men in it; and a great king came against it and besieged it, building great siegeworks against it. But there was found in it a poor wise man, and he by his wisdom delivered the city. Yet no one remembered that poor man. But I say that wisdom is better than might, though the poor man's wisdom is despised, and his words are not heeded.

The words of the wise heard in quiet are better than the shouting of a ruler among fools. Wisdom is better than weapons of war, but one sinner destroys much good.

Dead flies make the perfumer's ointment
   give off an evil odour;
  so a little folly outweighs wisdom and
   honour.
A wise man's heart inclines him toward the
   right,
  but a fool's heart toward the left.
Even when the fool walks on the road, he
   lacks sense,
  and he says to every one that he is a fool.
If the anger of the ruler rises against you,
   do not leave your place,
  for deference will make amends for great
   offences.
There is an evil which I have seen under the sun, as it were an error proceeding from the ruler: folly is set in many high places, and the rich sit in a low place. I have seen slaves on horses, and princes walking on foot like slaves.
He who digs a pit will fall into it;
  and a serpent will bite him who breaks
   through a wall.
He who quarries stones is hurt by them;
  and he who splits logs is endangered by
   them.
If the iron is blunt, and one does not whet
   the edge,
  he must put forth more strength;
  but wisdom helps one to succeed.
If the serpent bites before it is charmed,
  there is no advantage in a charmer.

The words of a wise man's mouth win him
   favour,
  but the lips of a fool consume him.
The beginning of the words of his mouth
   is foolishness,
  and the end of his talk is wicked
   madness.
A fool multiplies words,
  though no man knows what is to be,
  and who can tell him what will be after
   him?
The toil of a fool wearies him,

---

[m] Syr Compare Gk: Heb *Everything before them is everything*   [n] Gk Syr Vg: Heb *lacks and the evil*

so that he does not know the way to the city.

Woe to you, O land, when your king is a child,
and your princes feast in the morning!
Happy are you, O land, when your king is the son of free men,
and your princes feast at the proper time,
for strength, and not for drunkenness!
Through sloth the roof sinks in,
and through indolence the house leaks.
Bread is made for laughter,
and wine gladdens life,
and money answers everything.
Even in your thought, do not curse the king,
nor in your bedchamber curse the rich;
for a bird of the air will carry your voice,
or some winged creature tell the matter.

1 Cast your bread upon the waters,
for you will find it after many days.
2 Give a portion to seven, or even to eight,
for you know not what evil may happen on earth.
3 If the clouds are full of rain,
they empty themselves on the earth;
and if a tree falls to the south or to the north,
in the place where the tree falls, there it will lie.
4 He who observes the wind will not sow;
and he who regards the clouds will not reap.
5 As you do not know how the spirit comes to the bones in the womb⁰ of a woman with child, so you do not know the work of God who makes everything.
6 In the morning sow your seed, and at evening withhold not your hand; for you do not know which will prosper, this or that, or whether both alike will be good.
7 Light is sweet, and it is pleasant for the eyes to behold the sun.
8 For if a man lives many years, let him rejoice in them all; but let him remember that the days of darkness will be many. All that comes is vanity.
9 Rejoice, O young man, in your youth, and

let your heart cheer you in the days of your youth; walk in the ways of your heart and the sight of your eyes. But know that for all these things God will bring you into judgment.
10 Remove vexation from your mind, and put away pain from your body; for youth and the dawn of life are vanity.

12 Remember also your Creator in the days of your youth, before the evil days come, and the years draw nigh, when you will say, "I have no pleasure in them"; 2 before the sun and the light and the moon and the stars are darkened and the clouds return after the rain; 3 in the day when the keepers of the house tremble, and the strong men are bent, and the grinders cease because they are few, and those that look through the windows are dimmed, and the doors on the street are shut; 4 when the sound of the grinding is low, and one rises up at the voice of a bird, and all the daughters of song are brought low; 5 they are afraid also of what is high, and terrors are in the way; the almond tree blossoms, the grasshopper drags itself along ᵖ and desire fails; because man goes to his eternal home, and the mourners go about the streets; 6 before the silver cord is snapped,�q or the golden bowl is broken, or the pitcher is broken at the fountain, or the wheel broken at the cistern, 7 and the dust returns to the earth as it was, and the spirit returns to God who gave it. 8 Vanity of vanities, says the Preacher; all is vanity.
9 Besides being wise, the Preacher also taught the people knowledge, weighing and studying and arranging proverbs with great care. 10 The Preacher sought to find pleasing words, and uprightly he wrote words of truth. 11 The sayings of the wise are like goads, and like nails firmly fixed are the collected sayings which are given by one Shepherd. 12 My son, beware of anything beyond these. Of making many books there is no end, and much study is a weariness of the flesh.
13 The end of the matter; all has been heard. Fear God, and keep his commandments; for this is the whole duty of man.ʳ 14 For God will bring every deed into judgment, withˢ every secret thing, whether good or evil.

⁰ Or *As you do not know the way of the wind, or how the bones grow in the womb*   ᵖ Or *is a burden*
q Syr Vg Compare Gk: Heb *is removed*   ʳ Or *the duty of all men*   ˢ Or *into the judgment on*

THE SONG OF SOLOMON

THE Song of Songs, which is Solomon's.

2 O that you*a* would kiss me with the kisses of
　your*b* mouth!
For your love is better than wine,
3 　your anointing oils are fragrant,
　your name is oil poured out;
　　therefore the maidens love you.
4 Draw me after you, let us make haste.
　　The king has brought me into his chambers.
　We will exult and rejoice in you;
　　we will extol your love more than wine;
　　rightly do they love you.

5 I am very dark, but comely,
　　O daughters of Jerusalem,
　like the tents of Kedar,
　　like the curtains of Solomon.
6 Do not gaze at me because I am swarthy,
　　because the sun has scorched me.
　My mother's sons were angry with me,
　　they made me keeper of the vineyards;
　　but, my own vineyard I have not kept!
7 Tell me, you whom my soul loves,
　　where you pasture your flock,
　　where you make it lie down at noon;
　for why should I be like one who wanders*c*
　　beside the flocks of your companions?

8 If you do not know,
　　O fairest among women,
　follow in the tracks of the flock,
　　and pasture your kids
　　beside the shepherds' tents.

9 I compare you, my love,
　　to a mare of Pharaoh's chariots.
10 Your cheeks are comely with ornaments,
　　your neck with strings of jewels.
11 We will make you ornaments of gold,
　　studded with silver.

12 While the king was on his couch,
　　my nard gave forth its fragrance.
13 My beloved is to me a bag of myrrh,
　　that lies between my breasts.
14 My beloved is to me a cluster of henna
　　blossoms
　　in the vineyards of En-ge'di.

15 Behold, you are beautiful, my love;
　　behold, you are beautiful;
　　your eyes are doves.
16 Behold, you are beautiful, my beloved,
　　truly lovely.
Our couch is green;
17 　the beams of our house are cedar,
　　our rafters*d* are pine.

2 I am a rose*e* of Sharon,
　　a lily of the valleys.

2 As a lily among brambles,
　　so is my love among maidens.

3 As an apple tree among the trees of the wood,
　　so is my beloved among young men.
With great delight I sat in his shadow,
　　and his fruit was sweet to my taste.
4 He brought me to the banqueting house,
　　and his banner over me was love.
5 Sustain me with raisins,
　　refresh me with apples;
　　for I am sick with love.
6 O that his left hand were under my head,
　　and that his right hand embraced me!
7 I adjure you, O daughters of Jerusalem,
　　by the gazelles or the hinds of the field,
　that you stir not up nor awaken love
　　until it please.

8 The voice of my beloved!
　　Behold, he comes,
　leaping upon the mountains,
　　bounding over the hills.
9 My beloved is like a gazelle,
　　or a young stag.
Behold, there he stands
　　behind our wall,
　gazing in at the windows,
　　looking through the lattice.
10 My beloved speaks and says to me:
"Arise, my love, my fair one,
　　and come away;
11 for lo, the winter is past,
　　the rain is over and gone.
12 The flowers appear on the earth,
　　the time of singing has come,
and the voice of the turtledove
　　is heard in our land.
13 The fig tree puts forth its figs,

---

a Heb *he*　*b* Heb *his*　*c* Gk Syr Vg: Heb *is veiled*　*d* The meaning of the Hebrew word is uncertain
e Heb *crocus*

and the vines are in blossom;
  they give forth fragrance.
Arise, my love, my fair one,
  and come away.
O my dove, in the clefts of the rock,
  in the covert of the cliff,
let me see your face,
  let me hear your voice,
for your voice is sweet,
  and your face is comely.
5 Catch us the foxes,
  the little foxes,
that spoil the vineyards,
  for our vineyards are in blossom."

16 My beloved is mine and I am his,
  he pastures his flock among the lilies.
17 Until the day breathes
  and the shadows flee,
turn, my beloved, be like a gazelle,
  or a young stag upon rugged[f] mountains.

3 Upon my bed by night
  I sought him whom my soul loves;
I sought him, but found him not;
  I called him, but he gave no answer.[g]
2 "I will rise now and go about the city,
  in the streets and in the squares;
I will seek him whom my soul loves."
  I sought him, but found him not.
3 The watchmen found me,
  as they went about in the city.
"Have you seen him whom my soul loves?"
4 Scarcely had I passed them,
  when I found him whom my soul loves.
I held him, and would not let him go
  until I had brought him into my mother's
    house,
  and into the chamber of her that conceived
    me.
5 I adjure you, O daughters of Jerusalem,
  by the gazelles or the hinds of the field,
that you stir not up nor awaken love until it
    please.

6 What is that coming up from the wilderness,
  like a column of smoke,
perfumed with myrrh and frankincense,
  with all the fragrant powders of the
    merchant?
7 Behold, it is the litter of Solomon!
  About it are sixty mighty men
of the mighty men of Israel,
8 all girt with swords
  and expert in war,
each with his sword at his thigh,
  against alarms by night.
9 King Solomon made himself a palanquin
  from the wood of Lebanon.

10 He made its posts of silver,
  its back of gold, its seat of purple;
it was lovingly wrought within[h]
  by the daughters of Jerusalem.
11 Go forth, O daughters of Zion,
  and behold King Solomon,
with the crown with which his mother
    crowned him
on the day of his wedding,
  on the day of the gladness of his heart.

4 Behold, you are beautiful, my love,
  behold, you are beautiful!
Your eyes are doves
  behind your veil.
Your hair is like a flock of goats,
  moving down the slopes of Gilead.
2 Your teeth are like a flock of shorn ewes
  that have come up from the washing,
all of which bear twins,
  and not one among them is bereaved.
3 Your lips are like a scarlet thread,
  and your mouth is lovely.
Your cheeks are like halves of a pomegranate
  behind your veil.
4 Your neck is like the tower of David,
  built for an arsenal,[i]
whereon hang a thousand bucklers,
  all of them shields of warriors.
5 Your two breasts are like two fawns,
  twins of a gazelle,
  that feed among the lilies.
6 Until the day breathes
  and the shadows flee,
I will hie me to the mountain of myrrh
  and the hill of frankincense.
7 You are all fair, my love;
  there is no flaw in you.
8 Come with me from Lebanon, my bride;
  come with me from Lebanon.
Depart[j] from the peak of Ama'na,
  from the peak of Senir and Hermon,
from the dens of lions,
  from the mountains of leopards.

9 You have ravished my heart, my sister, my
    bride,
  you have ravished my heart with a glance
    of your eyes,
  with one jewel of your necklace.
10 How sweet is your love, my sister, my bride!
  how much better is your love than wine,
  and the fragrance of your oils than any
    spice!
11 Your lips distil nectar, my bride;
  honey and milk are under your tongue;
  the scent of your garments is like the scent
    of Lebanon.
12 A garden locked is my sister, my bride,

---

f The meaning of the Hebrew word is unknown   g Gk: Heb lacks this line
h The meaning of the Hebrew is uncertain   i The meaning of the Hebrew word is uncertain   j Or Look

a garden locked, a fountain sealed.

13 Your shoots are an orchard of pomegranates
  with all choicest fruits,
  henna with nard,

14 nard and saffron, calamus and cinnamon,
  with all trees of frankincense,
  myrrh and aloes,
  with all chief spices—

15 a garden fountain, a well of living water,
  and flowing streams from Lebanon.

16 Awake, O north wind,
  and come, O south wind!
Blow upon my garden,
  let its fragrance be wafted abroad.
Let my beloved come to his garden,
  and eat its choicest fruits.

5 I come to my garden, my sister, my bride,
  I gather my myrrh with my spice,
  I eat my honeycomb with my honey,
  I drink my wine with my milk.

Eat, O friends, and drink:
  drink deeply, O lovers!

2 I slept, but my heart was awake.
Hark! my beloved is knocking.
"Open to me, my sister, my love,
  my dove, my perfect one;
for my head is wet with dew,
  my locks with the drops of the night."

3 I had put off my garment,
  how could I put it on?
I had bathed my feet,
  how could I soil them?

4 My beloved put his hand to the latch,
  and my heart was thrilled within me.

5 I arose to open to my beloved,
  and my hands dripped with myrrh,
my fingers with liquid myrrh,
  upon the handles of the bolt.

6 I opened to my beloved,
  but my beloved had turned and gone.
My soul failed me when he spoke.
I sought him, but found him not;
  I called him, but he gave no answer.

7 The watchmen found me,
  as they went about in the city;
they beat me, they wounded me,
  they took away my mantle,
  those watchmen of the walls.

8 I adjure you, O daughters of Jerusalem,
  if you find my beloved,
that you tell him
  I am sick with love.

9 What is your beloved more than another
  beloved,

O fairest among women?
What is your beloved more than another
  beloved,
  that you thus adjure us?

My beloved is all radiant and ruddy,   10
  distinguished among ten thousand.

His head is the finest gold;   11
  his locks are wavy,
  black as a raven.

His eyes are like doves   12
  beside springs of water,
bathed in milk,
  fitly set. *k*

His cheeks are like beds of spices,   13
  yielding fragrance.
His lips are lilies,
  distilling liquid myrrh.

His arms are rounded gold,   14
  set with jewels.
His body is ivory work, *l*
  encrusted with sapphires. *m*

His legs are alabaster columns,   15
  set upon bases of gold.
His appearance is like Lebanon,
  choice as the cedars.

His speech is most sweet,   16
  and he is altogether desirable.
This is my beloved and this is my friend,
  O daughters of Jerusalem.

Whither has your beloved gone,   **6**
  O fairest among women?
Whither has your beloved turned,
  that we may seek him with you?

My beloved has gone down to his garden,   2
  to the beds of spices,
to pasture his flock in the gardens,
  and to gather lilies.

I am my beloved's and my beloved is mine; 3
  he pastures his flock among the lilies.

You are beautiful as Tirzah, my love,   4
  comely as Jerusalem,
  terrible as an army with banners.

Turn away your eyes from me,   5
  for they disturb me—
Your hair is like a flock of goats,
  moving down the slopes of Gilead.
Your teeth are like a flock of ewes,   6
  that have come up from the washing,
all of them bear twins,
  not one among them is bereaved.
Your cheeks are like halves of a pomegranate 7
  behind your veil.
There are sixty queens and eighty con-   8
  cubines,
  and maidens without number.

k The meaning of the Hebrew is uncertain   *l* The meaning of the Hebrew word is uncertain
m Heb *lapis lazuli*

9 My dove, my perfect one, is only one,
   the darling of her mother,
   flawless to her that bore her.
The maidens saw her and called her happy;
   the queens and concubines also, and they
     praised her.
10 "Who is this that looks forth like the dawn,
   fair as the moon, bright as the sun,
   terrible as an army with banners?"

11 I went down to the nut orchard,
   to look at the blossoms of the valley,
to see whether the vines had budded,
   whether the pomegranates were in bloom.
12 Before I was aware, my fancy set me
   in a chariot beside my prince. [n]

13 Return, return, O Shu'lammite,
   return, return, that we may look upon you.

Why should you look upon the Shu'lammite,
   as upon a dance before two armies? [p]

7 How graceful are your feet in sandals,
   O queenly maiden!
Your rounded thighs are like jewels,
   the work of a master hand.
2 Your navel is a rounded bowl
   that never lacks mixed wine.
Your belly is a heap of wheat,
   encircled with lilies.
3 Your two breasts are like two fawns,
   twins of a gazelle.
4 Your neck is like an ivory tower.
Your eyes are pools in Heshbon,
   by the gate of Bath-rab'bim.
Your nose is like a tower of Lebanon,
   overlooking Damascus.
5 Your head crowns you like Carmel,
   and your flowing locks are like purple;
   a king is held captive in the tresses. [q]

6 How fair and pleasant you are,
   O loved one, delectable maiden! [r]
7 You are stately [s] as a palm tree,
   and your breasts are like its clusters.
8 I say I will climb the palm tree
   and lay hold of its branches.
Oh, may your breasts be like clusters of the
     vine,
   and the scent of your breath like apples,
9 and your kisses [t] like the best wine
   that goes down [u] smoothly,
   gliding over lips and teeth. [v]

10 I am my beloved's,
   and his desire is for me.
11 Come, my beloved,

let us go forth into the fields,
   and lodge in the villages;
let us go out early to the vineyards,   12
   and see whether the vines have budded,
whether the grape blossoms have opened
   and the pomegranates are in bloom.
There I will give you my love.
The mandrakes give forth fragrance,   13
   and over our doors are all choice fruits,
new as well as old,
   which I have laid up for you, O my beloved.

O that you were like a brother to me,   8
   that nursed at my mother's breast!
If I met you outside, I would kiss you,
   and none would despise me.
I would lead you and bring you   2
   into the house of my mother,
   and into the chamber of her that conceived
     me. [w]
I would give you spiced wine to drink,
   the juice of my pomegranates.
O that his left hand were under my head,   3
   and that his right hand embraced me!
I adjure you, O daughters of Jerusalem,   4
   that you stir not up nor awaken love
   until it please.

Who is that coming up from the wilderness,   5
   leaning upon her beloved?

Under the apple tree I awakened you.
There your mother was in travail with you,
   there she who bore you was in travail.

Set me as a seal upon your heart,   6
   as a seal upon your arm;
for love is strong as death,
   jealousy is cruel as the grave.
Its flashes are flashes of fire,
   a most vehement flame.
Many waters cannot quench love,   7
   neither can floods drown it.
If a man offered for love
   all the wealth of his house,

---

n Cn: The meaning of the Hebrew is uncertain   *o* Ch 7.1 in Heb   *p* Or *dance of Mahanaim*
q The meaning of the Hebrew word is uncertain   *r* Syr: Heb *in delights*   *s* Heb *This your stature is*
t Heb *palate*   *u* Heb *down for my lover*   *v* Gk Syr Vg: Heb *lips of sleepers*
w Gk Syr: Heb *mother; she* (or *you*) *will teach me*

it would be utterly scorned.

8 We have a little sister,
    and she has no breasts.
What shall we do for our sister,
    on the day when she is spoken for?
9 If she is a wall,
    we will build upon her a battlement of
        silver;
but if she is a door,
    we will enclose her with boards of cedar.
10 I was a wall,
    and my breasts were like towers;
then I was in his eyes
    as one who brings *x* peace.

11 Solomon had a vineyard at Ba'al-ha'mon;

he let out the vineyard to keepers;
    each one was to bring for its fruit a
        thousand pieces of silver.
My vineyard, my very own, is for myself;   12
    you, O Solomon, may have the thousand,
    and the keepers of the fruit two hun-
        dred.

O you who dwell in the gardens,   13
    my companions are listening for your
        voice;
    let me hear it.

Make haste, my beloved,   14
    and be like a gazelle
or a young stag
    upon the mountains of spices.

THE BOOK OF

ISAIAH

CONCERNING THE FALL OF JUDAH

THE vision of Isaiah the son of Amoz,
which he saw concerning Judah and
Jerusalem in the days of Uzzi'ah,
Jotham, Ahaz, and Hezeki'ah, kings of Judah.
2   Hear, O heavens, and give ear, O earth;
    for the LORD has spoken:
"Sons have I reared and brought up,
    but they have rebelled against me.
3   The ox knows its owner,
    and the ass its master's crib;
but Israel does not know,
    my people does not understand."

4   Ah, sinful nation,
    a people laden with iniquity,
offspring of evildoers,

sons who deal corruptly!
They have forsaken the LORD,
    they have despised the Holy One of
        Israel,
they are utterly estranged.

Why will you still be smitten,   5
    that you continue to rebel?
The whole head is sick,
    and the whole heart faint.
From the sole of the foot even to the 6
        head,
    there is no soundness in it,
but bruises and sores
    and bleeding wounds;
they are not pressed out, or bound up,

x Or *finds*

or softened with oil.

7 Your country lies desolate,
    your cities are burned with fire;
in your very presence
    aliens devour your land;
    it is desolate, as overthrown by aliens.
8 And the daughter of Zion is left
    like a booth in a vineyard,
like a lodge in a cucumber field,
    like a besieged city.

9 If the LORD of hosts
    had not left us a few survivors,
we should have been like Sodom,
    and become like Gomor'rah.

10 Hear the word of the LORD,
    you rulers of Sodom!
Give ear to the teaching of our God,
    you people of Gomor'rah!
11 "What to me is the multitude of your
    sacrifices?
says the LORD;
I have had enough of burnt offerings of
    rams
and the fat of fed beasts;
I do not delight in the blood of bulls,
    or of lambs, or of he-goats.

12 "When you come to appear before me,
    who requires of you
    this trampling of my courts?
13 Bring no more vain offerings;
    incense is an abomination to me.
New moon and sabbath and the calling of
    assemblies—
    I cannot endure iniquity and solemn
    assembly.
14 Your new moons and your appointed feasts
    my soul hates;
they have become a burden to me,
    I am weary of bearing them.
15 When you spread forth your hands,
    I will hide my eyes from you;
even though you make many prayers,
    I will not listen;
    your hands are full of blood.
16 Wash yourselves; make yourselves clean;
    remove the evil of your doings
    from before my eyes;
cease to do evil,
17   learn to do good;
seek justice,
    correct oppression;
defend the fatherless,
    plead for the widow.

18 "Come now, let us reason together,
    says the LORD:

though your sins are like scarlet,
    they shall be as white as snow;
though they are red like crimson,
    they shall become like wool.
19 If you are willing and obedient,
    you shall eat the good of the land;
20 but if you refuse and rebel,
    you shall be devoured by the sword;
    for the mouth of the LORD has spoken."

21 How the faithful city
    has become a harlot,
    she that was full of justice!
Righteousness lodged in her,
    but now murderers.
22 Your silver has become dross,
    your wine mixed with water.
23 Your princes are rebels
    and companions of thieves.
Every one loves a bribe
    and runs after gifts.
They do not defend the fatherless,
    and the widow's cause does not come to
    them.

24 Therefore the Lord says,
    the LORD of hosts,
    the Mighty One of Israel:
"Ah, I will vent my wrath on my enemies,
    and avenge myself on my foes.
25 I will turn my hand against you
    and will smelt away your dross as with
    lye
    and remove all your alloy.
26 And I will restore your judges as at the
    first,
    and your counsellors as at the begin-
    ning.
Afterward you shall be called the city of
    righteousness,
    the faithful city."

27 Zion shall be redeemed by justice,
    and those in her who repent, by
    righteousness.
28 But rebels and sinners shall be destroyed
    together,
    and those who forsake the LORD shall be
    consumed.
29 For you shall be ashamed of the oaks
    in which you delighted;
and you shall blush for the gardens
    which you have chosen.
30 For you shall be like an oak
    whose leaf withers,
    and like a garden without water.
31 And the strong shall become tow,
    and his work a spark,
and both of them shall burn together,
    with none to quench them.

1.9: Rom 9.29.

Jerusalem

2 The word which Isaiah the son of Amoz
saw concerning Judah and Jerusalem.

2   It shall come to pass in the latter days
     that the mountain of the house of the
     Lord
   shall be established as the highest of the
     mountains,
     and shall be raised above the hills;
   and all the nations shall flow to it,

3   and many peoples shall come, and say:
   "Come, let us go up to the mountain of the
     Lord,
     to the house of the God of Jacob;
   that he may teach us his ways
     and that we may walk in his paths."
   For out of Zion shall go forth the law,
     and the word of the Lord from Jeru-
     salem.

4   He shall judge between the nations,
     and shall decide for many peoples;
   and they shall beat their swords into
     ploughshares,
     and their spears into pruning hooks;
   nation shall not lift up sword against
     nation,
     neither shall they learn war any more.

5   O house of Jacob,
     come, let us walk
     in the light of the Lord.

6   For thou hast rejected thy people,
     the house of Jacob,
   because they are full of diviners[a] from the
     east
     and of soothsayers like the Philistines,
     and they strike hands with foreigners.

7   Their land is filled with silver and gold,
     and there is no end to their treasures;
   their land is filled with horses,
     and there is no end to their chariots.

8   Their land is filled with idols;
     they bow down to the work of their
     hands,
     to what their own fingers have made.

9   So man is humbled,
     and men are brought low—
     forgive them not!

10   Enter into the rock,
     and hide in the dust
   from before the terror of the Lord,
     and from the glory of his majesty.

11   The haughty looks of man shall be brought
     low,
     and the pride of men shall be humbled;
   and the Lord alone will be exalted in that
     day.

   For the Lord of hosts has a day   1
     against all that is proud and lofty,
     against all that is lifted up and high;[b]
  against all the cedars of Lebanon,   1
     lofty and lifted up;
     and against all the oaks of Bashan;
  against all the high mountains,   1
     and against all the lofty hills;
  against every high tower,   1
     and against every fortified wall;
  against all the ships of Tarshish,   16
     and against all the beautiful craft.
  And the haughtiness of man shall be   1
     humbled,
     and the pride of men shall be brought
     low;
     and the Lord alone will be exalted in
     that day.
  And the idols shall utterly pass away.   1
  And men shall enter the caves of the   1
     rocks
     and the holes of the ground,
  from before the terror of the Lord,
     and from the glory of his majesty,
     when he rises to terrify the earth.

  In that day men will cast forth   20
     their idols of silver and their idols of
     gold,
     which they made for themselves to wor-
     ship,
     to the moles and to the bats,
  to enter the caverns of the rocks   21
     and the clefts of the cliffs,
  from before the terror of the Lord,
     and from the glory of his majesty,
     when he rises to terrify the earth.
  Turn away from man   22
     in whose nostrils is breath,
     for of what account is he?

  For, behold, the Lord, the Lord of hosts, 3
     is taking away from Jerusalem and from
     Judah
  stay and staff,
     the whole stay of bread,
     and the whole stay of water;
  the mighty man and the soldier,   2
     the judge and the prophet,
     the diviner and the elder,
  the captain of fifty   3
     and the man of rank,
     the counsellor and the skilful magician
     and the expert in charms.
  And I will make boys their princes,   4
     and babes shall rule over them.
  And the people will oppress one another,   5
     every man his fellow
     and every man his neighbour;

---

[a] Cn: Heb lacks *of diviners*   [b] Cn Compare Gk: Heb *low*
2.2–4: Mic 4.1–3.

the youth will be insolent to the elder,
    and the base fellow to the honourable.

6 When a man takes hold of his brother
        in the house of his father, saying:
    "You have a mantle;
        you shall be our leader,
    and this heap of ruins
        shall be under your rule";
7 in that day he will speak out, saying:
    "I will not be a healer;
        in my house there is neither bread nor
            mantle;
    you shall not make me
        leader of the people."
8 For Jerusalem has stumbled,
        and Judah has fallen;
    because their speech and their deeds are
            against the LORD,
        defying his glorious presence.

9 Their partiality witnesses against them;
        they proclaim their sin like Sodom,
        they do not hide it.
    Woe to them!
        For they have brought evil upon
            themselves.
10 Tell the righteous that it shall be well with
        them,
        for they shall eat the fruit of their
            deeds.
11 Woe to the wicked! It shall be ill with
        him,
        for what his hands have done shall be
            done to him.
12 My people—children are their oppressors,
        and women rule over them.
    O my people, your leaders mislead you,
        and confuse the course of your paths.

13 The LORD has taken his place to contend,
        he stands to judge his people.[c]
14 The LORD enters into judgment
        with the elders and princes of his
            people:
    "It is you who have devoured the
        vineyard,
        the spoil of the poor is in your
            houses.
15 What do you mean by crushing my
        people,
    by grinding the face of the poor?"
        says the Lord GOD of hosts.

The daughters of Zion

The LORD said: 16
    Because the daughters of Zion are haughty
        and walk with outstretched necks,
        glancing wantonly with their eyes,
    mincing along as they go,
        tinkling with their feet;
    the Lord will smite with a scab   17
        the heads of the daughters of Zion,
        and the LORD will lay bare their secret
            parts.

In that day the Lord will take away the 18
finery of the anklets, the headbands, and the
crescents; the pendants, the bracelets, and 19
the scarfs; the headdresses, the armlets, the 20
sashes, the perfume boxes, and the amulets;
the signet rings and nose rings; the festal 21
robes, the mantles, the cloaks, and the 22
handbags; the garments of gauze, the linen 23
garments, the turbans, and the veils.
    Instead of perfume there will be rotten- 24
        ness;
        and instead of a girdle, a rope;
    and instead of well-set hair, baldness;
        and instead of a rich robe, a girding of
            sackcloth;
    instead of beauty, shame.[d]
    Your men shall fall by the sword   25
        and your mighty men in battle.
    And her gates shall lament and mourn;   26
        ravaged, she shall sit upon the ground.

And seven women shall take hold of one 4
man in that day, saying, "We will eat our
own bread and wear our own clothes, only let
us be called by your name; take away our
reproach."

In that day the branch of the LORD shall be 2
beautiful and glorious, and the fruit of the
land shall be the pride and glory of the
survivors of Israel. And he who is left in 3
Zion and remains in Jerusalem will be called
holy, every one who has been recorded for
life in Jerusalem, when the Lord shall have 4
washed away the filth of the daughters of
Zion and cleansed the bloodstains of Jerusalem from its midst by a spirit of judgment
and by a spirit of burning. Then the LORD 5
will create over the whole site of Mount Zion
and over her assemblies a cloud by day, and
smoke and the shining of a flaming fire by
night; for over all the glory there will be a
canopy and a pavilion. It will be for a shade 6
by day from the heat, and for a refuge and a
shelter from the storm and rain.

_____
_c_ Gk Syr: Heb _judge peoples_   _d_ One ancient Ms: Heb lacks _shame_
4.2: Jer 23.5; 33.15; Zech 3.8; 6.12.

A parable

5 Let me sing for my beloved
    a love song concerning his vineyard:
My beloved had a vineyard
    on a very fertile hill.
2 He digged it and cleared it of stones,
    and planted it with choice vines;
he built a watchtower in the midst of it,
    and hewed out a wine vat in it;
and he looked for it to yield grapes,
    but it yielded wild grapes.

3 And now, O inhabitants of Jerusalem
    and men of Judah,
judge, I pray you, between me
    and my vineyard.
4 What more was there to do for my
    vineyard,
    that I have not done in it?
When I looked for it to yield grapes,
    why did it yield wild grapes?

5 And now I will tell you
    what I will do to my vineyard.
I will remove its hedge,
    and it shall be devoured;
I will break down its wall,
    and it shall be trampled down.
6 I will make it a waste;
    it shall not be pruned or hoed,
    and briers and thorns shall grow up;
I will also command the clouds
    that they rain no rain upon it.

7 For the vineyard of the LORD of hosts
    is the house of Israel,
and the men of Judah
    are his pleasant planting;
and he looked for justice,
    but behold, bloodshed;
for righteousness,
    but behold, a cry!

8 Woe to those who join house to house,
    who add field to field,
until there is no more room,
    and you are made to dwell alone
in the midst of the land.
The LORD of hosts has sworn in my 9
    hearing:
"Surely many houses shall be desolate,
    large and beautiful houses, without
    inhabitant.
For ten acres of vineyard shall yield but 10
    one bath,
    and a homer of seed shall yield but an
    ephah."

Woe to those who rise early in the 11
    morning,
    that they may run after strong drink,
who tarry late into the evening
    till wine inflames them!
They have lyre and harp, 12
    timbrel and flute and wine at their
    feasts;
but they do not regard the deeds of the
    LORD,
    or see the work of his hands.

Therefore my people go into exile for want 13
    of knowledge;
their honoured men are dying of hunger,
    and their multitude is parched with
    thirst.
Therefore Sheol has enlarged its appetite 14
    and opened its mouth beyond measure,
and the nobility of Jerusalem[e] and her
    multitude go down,
    her throng and he who exults in her.
Man is bowed down, and men are brought 15
    low,
    and the eyes of the haughty are
    humbled.
But the LORD of hosts is exalted in justice, 16
    and the Holy God shows himself holy in
    righteousness.
Then shall the lambs graze as in their 17
    pasture,
fatlings and kids[f] shall feed among the
    ruins.

Woe to those who draw iniquity with cords 18
    of falsehood,
    who draw sin as with cart ropes,
who say: "Let him make haste, 19
    let him speed his work
    that we may see it;
let the purpose of the Holy One of Israel
    draw near,
    and let it come, that we may know it!"
Woe to those who call evil good 20
    and good evil,
who put darkness for light
    and light for darkness,
who put bitter for sweet

---

[e] Heb *her nobility* [f] Cn Compare Gk: Heb *aliens*
5.1–7: Mt 21.33–46; Mk 12.1–12; Lk 20.9–19.

and sweet for bitter!
Woe to those who are wise in their own
    eyes,
    and shrewd in their own sight!
Woe to those who are heroes at drinking
    wine,
    and valiant men in mixing strong drink,
who acquit the guilty for a bribe,
    and deprive the innocent of his right!

Therefore, as the tongue of fire devours
    the stubble,
    and as dry grass sinks down in the flame,
so their root will be as rottenness,
    and their blossom go up like dust;
for they have rejected the law of the LORD
    of hosts,
    and have despised the word of the Holy
    One of Israel.
Therefore the anger of the LORD was
    kindled against his people,
    and he stretched out his hand against
    them and smote them,
    and the mountains quaked;
and their corpses were as refuse
    in the midst of the streets.
For all this his anger is not turned away
    and his hand is stretched out still.

He will raise a signal for a nation afar off,
    and whistle for it from the ends of the
    earth;
and lo, swiftly, speedily it comes!
None is weary, none stumbles,
    none slumbers or sleeps,
not a waistcloth is loose,
    not a sandal-thong broken;
their arrows are sharp,
    all their bows bent,
their horses' hoofs seem like flint,
    and their wheels like the whirlwind.
Their roaring is like a lion,
    like young lions they roar;
they growl and seize their prey,
    they carry it off, and none can rescue.
They will growl over it on that day,
    like the roaring of the sea.
And if one look to the land,
    behold, darkness and distress;
    and the light is darkened by its clouds.

Isaiah's vision and call

6 In the year that King Uzzi'ah died I saw the
  Lord sitting upon a throne, high and lifted
2 up; and his train filled the temple. Above
him stood the seraphim; each had six wings:
with two he covered his face, and with two he

covered his feet, and with two he flew. And 3
one called to another and said:
    "Holy, holy, holy is the LORD of hosts;
    the whole earth is full of his glory."
And the foundations of the thresholds shook 4
at the voice of him who called, and the house
was filled with smoke. And I said: "Woe is 5
me! For I am lost; for I am a man of unclean
lips, and I dwell in the midst of a people of
unclean lips; for my eyes have seen the King,
the LORD of hosts!"
    Then flew one of the seraphim to me, 6
having in his hand a burning coal which he
had taken with tongs from the altar. And he 7
touched my mouth, and said: "Behold, this
has touched your lips; your guilt is taken
away, and your sin forgiven." And I heard 8
the voice of the Lord saying, "Whom shall I
send, and who will go for us?" Then I said,
"Here am I! Send me." And he said, "Go, 9
and say to this people:
    'Hear and hear, but do not understand;
    see and see, but do not perceive.'
Make the heart of this people fat,   10
    and their ears heavy,
    and shut their eyes;
lest they see with their eyes,
    and hear with their ears,
and understand with their hearts,
    and turn and be healed."
Then I said, "How long, O Lord?" 11
And he said:
    "Until cities lie waste
    without inhabitant,
and houses without men,
    and the land is utterly desolate,
and the LORD removes men far away,   12
    and the forsaken places are many in the
    midst of the land.
And though a tenth remain in it,   13
    it will be burned again,
like a terebinth or an oak,
    whose stump remains standing
    when it is felled."
The holy seed is its stump.

ISAIAH AND AHAZ

IN the days of Ahaz the son of Jotham, son 7
of Uzzi'ah, king of Judah, Rezin the king
of Syria and Pekah the son of Remali'ah the
king of Israel came up to Jerusalem to wage
war against it, but they could not conquer it.
When the house of David was told, "Syria is 2
in league with E'phraim," his heart and the
heart of his people shook as the trees of the
forest shake before the wind.
    And the LORD said to Isaiah, "Go forth to 3
meet Ahaz, you and She'ar-jash'ub [g] your son,

---

g That is *A remnant shall return*
6.3: Rev 4.8.   **6.4:** Rev 15.8.   **6.9-10:** Mt 13.14-15; Mk 4.12; Lk 8.10; Jn 12.39-41; Acts 28.26-27.

at the end of the conduit of the upper pool on
4 the highway to the Fuller's Field, and say to
him, 'Take heed, be quiet, do not fear, and
do not let your heart be faint because of these
two smouldering stumps of firebrands, at the
fierce anger of Rezin and Syria and the son of
5 Remali′ah. Because Syria, with E′phraim
and the son of Remali′ah, has devised evil
6 against you, saying, "Let us go up against
Judah and terrify it, and let us conquer it for
ourselves, and set up the son of Ta′be-el as
7 king in the midst of it," thus says the Lord
God:

  It shall not stand,
    and it shall not come to pass.
8 For the head of Syria is Damascus,
    and the head of Damascus is Rezin.
(Within sixty-five years E′phraim will be
broken to pieces so that it will no longer be a
people.)
9 And the head of E′phraim is Samar′ia,
    and the head of Samar′ia is the son of
    Remali′ah.
  If you will not believe,
    surely you shall not be established.' "

The sign Immanuel

10, Again the Lord spoke to Ahaz, "Ask a sign
11 of the Lord your God; let it be deep as Sheol
12 or high as heaven." But Ahaz said, "I will
not ask, and I will not put the Lord to the
13 test." And he said, "Hear then, O house of
David! Is it too little for you to weary men,
14 that you weary my God also? Therefore the
Lord himself will give you a sign. Behold, a
young woman[h] shall conceive and bear[i] a
15 son, and shall call his name Imman′u-el.[j] He
shall eat curds and honey when he knows
how to refuse the evil and choose the good.
16 For before the child knows how to refuse the
evil and choose the good, the land before
whose two kings you are in dread will be
17 deserted. The Lord will bring upon you and
upon your people and upon your father's
house such days as have not come since the
day that E′phraim departed from Judah—the
king of Assyria."
18 In that day the Lord will whistle for the fly
which is at the sources of the streams of
Egypt, and for the bee which is in the land of
19 Assyria. And they will all come and settle in
the steep ravines, and in the clefts of the
rocks, and on all the thornbushes, and on all
the pastures.
20 In that day the Lord will shave with a razor
which is hired beyond the River—with the
king of Assyria—the head and the hair of the
feet, and it will sweep away the beard also.

In that day a man will keep alive a young
cow and two sheep; and because of the
abundance of milk which they give, he will
eat curds; for every one that is left in the land
will eat curds and honey.

In that day every place where there used to
be a thousand vines, worth a thousand
shekels of silver, will become briers and
thorns. With bow and arrows men will come
there, for all the land will be briers and
thorns; and as for all the hills which used to
be hoed with a hoe, you will not come there
for fear of briers and thorns; but they will
become a place where cattle are let loose and
where sheep tread.

Then the Lord said to me, "Take a large
tablet and write upon it in common charac-
ters, 'Belonging to Ma′her-shal′al-hash′-
baz.' "[k] And I got reliable witnesses, Uri′ah
the priest and Zechari′ah the son of Jeberechi′-
ah, to attest for me. And I went to the
prophetess, and she conceived and bore a
son. Then the Lord said to me, "Call his
name Ma′her-shal′al-hash′-baz; for before
the child knows how to cry 'My father' or
'My mother,' the wealth of Damascus and
the spoil of Samar′ia will be carried away
before the king of Assyria."

The Lord spoke to me again: "Because this
people have refused the waters of Shilo′ah
that flow gently, and melt in fear before[l]
Rezin and the son of Remali′ah; therefore,
behold, the Lord is bringing up against them
the waters of the River, mighty and many,
the king of Assyria and all his glory; and it
will rise over all its channels and go over all
its banks; and it will sweep on into Judah, it
will overflow and pass on, reaching even to
the neck; and its outspread wings will fill the
breadth of your land, O Imman′u-el."

  Be broken, you peoples, and be dismayed;
    give ear, all you far countries;
  gird yourselves and be dismayed;
  gird yourselves and be dismayed.
  Take counsel together, but it will come to
    naught;
  speak a word, but it will not stand,
    for God is with us.[m]
For the Lord spoke thus to me with his
strong hand upon me, and warned me not to
walk in the way of this people, saying: "Do
not call conspiracy all that this people call
conspiracy, and do not fear what they fear,
nor be in dread. But the Lord of hosts, him
you shall regard as holy; let him be your fear,
and let him be your dread. And he will
become a sanctuary, and a stone of offence,

[h] Or virgin   [i] Or is with child and shall bear   [j] That is God is with us
[k] That is The spoil speeds, the prey hastes   [l] Cn: Heb rejoices in   [m] Heb immanu el
7.14: Mt 1.23.   8.12–13: 1 Pet 3.14–15.   8.14: Rom 9.32–33; 1 Pet 2.8.

and a rock of stumbling to both houses of Israel, a trap and a snare to the inhabitants of 5 Jerusalem. And many shall stumble thereon; they shall fall and be broken; they shall be snared and taken."

6 Bind up the testimony, seal the teaching 7 among my disciples. I will wait for the LORD, who is hiding his face from the house 8 of Jacob, and I will hope in him. Behold, I and the children whom the LORD has given me are signs and portents in Israel from the LORD of hosts, who dwells on Mount Zion. 9 And when they say to you, "Consult the mediums and the wizards who chirp and mutter," should not a people consult their God? Should they consult the dead on 10 behalf of the living? To the teaching and to the testimony! Surely for this word which 11 they speak there is no dawn. They will pass through the land, *n* greatly distressed and hungry; and when they are hungry, they will be enraged and will curse *o* their king and 12 their God, and turn their faces upward; and they will look to the earth, but behold, distress and darkness, the gloom of anguish; and they will be thrust into thick darkness.

The Prince of Peace

9 *p* But there will be no gloom for her that was in anguish. In the former time he brought into contempt the land of Zeb'ulun and the land of Naph'tali, but in the latter time he will make glorious the way of the sea, the land beyond the Jordan, Galilee of the nations.
2 *q* The people who walked in darkness
    have seen a great light;
those who dwelt in a land of deep darkness,
    on them has light shined.
3 Thou hast multiplied the nation,
    thou hast increased its joy;
they rejoice before thee
    as with joy at the harvest,
    as men rejoice when they divide the spoil.
4 For the yoke of his burden,
    and the staff for his shoulder,
    the rod of his oppressor,
thou hast broken as on the day of Mid'ian.
5 For every boot of the tramping warrior in battle tumult
    and every garment rolled in blood
    will be burned as fuel for the fire.
6 For to us a child is born,
    to us a son is given;

and the government will be upon his shoulder,
    and his name will be called
"Wonderful Counsellor, Mighty God,
    Everlasting Father, Prince of Peace."
7 Of the increase of his government and of peace
    there will be no end,
upon the throne of David, and over his kingdom,
    to establish it, and to uphold it
with justice and with righteousness
    from this time forth and for evermore.
The zeal of the LORD of hosts will do this.

ISRAEL

8 THE Lord has sent a word against Jacob,
    and it will light upon Israel;
9 and all the people will know,
    E'phraim and the inhabitants of Samar'ia,
who say in pride and in arrogance of heart:
10 "The bricks have fallen,
    but we will build with dressed stones;
the sycamores have been cut down,
    but we will put cedars in their place."
11 So the LORD raises adversaries *r* against them,
    and stirs up their enemies.
12 The Syrians on the east and the Philistines on the west
    devour Israel with open mouth.
For all this his anger is not turned away
    and his hand is stretched out still.

13 The people did not turn to him who smote them,
    nor seek the LORD of hosts.
14 So the LORD cut off from Israel head and tail,
    palm branch and reed in one day—
15 the elder and honoured man is the head,
    and the prophet who teaches lies is the tail;
16 for those who lead this people lead them astray,
    and those who are led by them are swallowed up.
17 Therefore the Lord does not rejoice over their young men,

---

n Heb *it* *o* Or *curse by* *p* Ch 8.23 in Heb *q* Ch 9.1 in Heb *r* Cn: Heb *the adversaries of Rezin*
8.17–18: Heb 2.13. 9.1–2: Mt 4.15–16; Lk 1.79.

and has no compassion on their fatherless and widows;
for every one is godless and an evildoer,
and every mouth speaks folly.
For all this his anger is not turned away
and his hand is stretched out still.

18 For wickedness burns like a fire,
it consumes briers and thorns;
it kindles the thickets of the forest,
and they roll upward in a column of
smoke.
19 Through the wrath of the LORD of hosts
the land is burned,
and the people are like fuel for the fire;
no man spares his brother.
20 They snatch on the right, but are still
hungry,
and they devour on the left, but are not
satisfied;
each devours his neighbour's[s] flesh,
21 Manas'seh E'phraim, and E'phraim
Manas'seh,
and together they are against Judah.
For all this his anger is not turned away
and his hand is stretched out still.

10 Woe to those who decree iniquitous
decrees,
and the writers who keep writing oppression,
2 to turn aside the needy from justice
and to rob the poor of my people of their
right,
that widows may be their spoil,
and that they may make the fatherless
their prey!
3 What will you do on the day of punishment,
in the storm which will come from afar?
To whom will you flee for help,
and where will you leave your wealth?
4 Nothing remains but to crouch among the
prisoners
or fall among the slain.
For all this his anger is not turned away
and his hand is stretched out still.

Assyria

5 AH, Assyria, the rod of my anger,
the staff of my fury![t]
6 Against a godless nation I send him,
and against the people of my wrath I
command him,
to take spoil and seize plunder,
and to tread them down like the mire of
the streets.
7 But he does not so intend,

ASSYRIA

and his mind does not so think;
but it is in his mind to destroy,
and to cut off nations not a few;
for he says:
"Are not my commanders all kings?
Is not Calno like Car'chemish?
Is not Hamath like Arpad?
Is not Samar'ia like Damascus?
As my hand has reached to the kingdoms
of the idols
whose graven images were greater than
those of Jerusalem and Samar'ia,
shall I not do to Jerusalem and her idols
as I have done to Samar'ia and her
images?"

When the Lord has finished all his work on
Mount Zion and on Jerusalem he[u] will
punish the arrogant boasting of the king of
Assyria and his haughty pride. For he says:
"By the strength of my hand I have done it,
and by my wisdom, for I have understanding;
I have removed the boundaries of peoples,
and have plundered their treasures;
like a bull I have brought down those
who sat on thrones.
My hand has found like a nest
the wealth of the peoples;
and as men gather eggs that have been
forsaken
so I have gathered all the earth;
and there was none that moved a wing,
or opened the mouth, or chirped."

Shall the axe vaunt itself over him who
hews with it,
or the saw magnify itself against him
who wields it?
As if a rod should wield him who lifts it,
or as if a staff should lift him who is not
wood!
Therefore the Lord, the LORD of hosts,
will send wasting sickness among his
stout warriors,
and under his glory a burning will be
kindled,
like the burning of fire.
The light of Israel will become a fire,
and his Holy One a flame;

---

[s] Tg Compare Gk: Heb *the flesh of his arm*   [t] Heb *a staff it is in their hand my fury*   [u] Heb *I*
10.5-34: Nahum; Zeph 2.13-15.

and it will burn and devour
  his thorns and briers in one day.
The glory of his forest and of his fruitful
    land
  the LORD will destroy, both soul and
    body,
  and it will be as when a sick man wastes
    away.
The remnant of the trees of his forest will
    be so few
  that a child can write them down.

In that day the remnant of Israel and the
survivors of the house of Jacob will no more
lean upon him that smote them, but will lean
upon the LORD, the Holy One of Israel, in
truth. A remnant will return, the remnant of
Jacob, to the mighty God. For though your
people Israel be as the sand of the sea, only a
remnant of them will return. Destruction is
decreed, overflowing with righteousness.
For the Lord, the LORD of hosts, will make a
full end, as decreed, in the midst of all the
earth.
  Therefore thus says the Lord, the LORD of
hosts: "O my people, who dwell in Zion, be
not afraid of the Assyrians when they smite
with the rod and lift up their staff against you
as the Egyptians did. For in a very little
while my indignation will come to an end,
and my anger will be directed to their
destruction. And the LORD of hosts will
wield against them a scourge, as when he
smote Mid'ian at the rock of Oreb; and his
rod will be over the sea, and he will lift it as
he did in Egypt. And in that day his burden
will depart from your shoulder, and his yoke
will be destroyed from your neck."

  He has gone up from Rimmon,ᵛ
    he has come to Ai'ath;
  he has passed through Migron,
    at Michmash he stores his baggage;
  they have crossed over the pass,
    at Geba they lodge for the night;
  Ramah trembles,
    Gib'e-ah of Saul has fled.
  Cry aloud, O daughter of Gallim!
    Hearken, O La'ishah!
    Answer her, O An'athoth!
  Madme'nah is in flight,
    the inhabitants of Gebim flee for safety.
  This very day he will halt at Nob,
    he will shake his fist
    at the mount of the daughter of Zion,
    the hill of Jerusalem.

  Behold, the Lord, the LORD of hosts

will lop the boughs with terrifying
    power;
the great in height will be hewn down,
  and the lofty will be brought low.
He will cut down the thickets of the forest 34
  with an axe,
  and Lebanon with its majestic trees ʷ
    will fall.

JUDAH

The root and branch

THERE shall come forth a shoot from the 11
    stump of Jesse,
  and a branch shall grow out of his roots.
And the Spirit of the LORD shall rest upon 2
    him,
  the spirit of wisdom and understanding,
  the spirit of counsel and might,
  the spirit of knowledge and the fear of
    the LORD.
And his delight shall be in the fear of the 3
  LORD.

He shall not judge by what his eyes see,
  or decide by what his ears hear;
but with righteousness he shall judge the 4
    poor,
  and decide with equity for the meek of
    the earth;
and he shall smite the earth with the rod of
    his mouth,
  and with the breath of his lips he shall
    slay the wicked.
Righteousness shall be the girdle of his 5
    waist,
  and faithfulness the girdle of his loins.

The wolf shall dwell with the lamb,   6
  and the leopard shall lie down with the
    kid,
and the calf and the lion and the fatling
    together,
  and a little child shall lead them.
The cow and the bear shall feed;   7
  their young shall lie down together;
  and the lion shall eat straw like the ox.
The sucking child shall play over the hole 8
    of the asp,
  and the weaned child shall put his hand
    on the adder's den.

ᵛ Cn: Heb *and his yoke from your neck, and a yoke will be destroyed because of fatness*
ʷ Cn Compare Gk Vg: Heb *with a majestic one*
10.22–23: Rom 9.27–28. **11.1**: Is 11.10; Rom 15.12. **11.2**: 1 Pet 4.14. **11.5**: Eph 6.14.
11.6–9: Is 65.25; Hab 2.14.

9 They shall not hurt or destroy
   in all my holy mountain;
for the earth shall be full of the knowledge
   of the LORD
   as the waters cover the sea.

10 In that day the root of Jesse shall stand as an
   ensign to the peoples; him shall the nations
   seek, and his dwellings shall be glorious.

11 In that day the Lord will extend his hand
   yet a second time to recover the remnant
   which is left of his people, from Assyria,
   from Egypt, from Pathros, from Ethiopia,
   from Elam, from Shinar, from Hamath,
   and from the coastlands of the sea.

12 He will raise an ensign for the nations,
   and will assemble the outcasts of Israel,
   and gather the dispersed of Judah
      from the four corners of the earth.

13 The jealousy of E′phraim shall depart,
   and those who harass Judah shall be cut
      off;
E′phraim shall not be jealous of Judah,
   and Judah shall not harass E′phraim.

14 But they shall swoop down upon the
      shoulder of the Philistines in the west,
   and together they shall plunder the
      people of the east.
They shall put forth their hand against
      Edom and Moab,
   and the Ammonites shall obey them.

15 And the LORD will utterly destroy
   the tongue of the sea of Egypt;
and will wave his hand over the River
   with his scorching wind,

and smite it into seven channels
   that men may cross dryshod.
And there will be a highway from Assyria
   for the remnant which is left of his
      people,
as there was for Israel
   when they came up from the land of
      Egypt.

You will say in that day:
"I will give thanks to thee, O LORD,
   for though thou wast angry with me,
thy anger turned away,
   and thou didst comfort me.

"Behold, God is my salvation;
   I will trust, and will not be afraid;
for the LORD GOD is my strength and my
      song,
   and he has become my salvation."

With joy you will draw water from the wells 3
of salvation. And you will say in that day: 4
"Give thanks to the LORD,
   call upon his name;
make known his deeds among the nations,
   proclaim that his name is exalted.

"Sing praises to the LORD, for he has done 5
      gloriously;
   let this be known[x] in all the earth.
Shout, and sing for joy, O inhabitant of 6
      Zion,
   for great in your midst is the Holy One
      of Israel."

CONCERNING THE NATIONS

BABYLON

13 THE oracle concerning Babylon which
   Isaiah the son of Amoz saw.
2 On a bare hill raise a signal,
   cry aloud to them;
wave the hand for them to enter
   the gates of the nobles.
3 I myself have commanded my consecrated
      ones,
   have summoned my mighty men to
      execute my anger,
   my proudly exulting ones.

Hark, a tumult on the mountains 4
   as of a great multitude!
Hark, an uproar of kingdoms,
   of nations gathering together!
The LORD of hosts is mustering
   a host for battle.
They come from a distant land, 5
   from the end of the heavens,
the LORD and the weapons of his
      indignation,
   to destroy the whole earth.

Wail, for the day of the LORD is near; 6
   as destruction from the Almighty it will
      come!
Therefore all hands will be feeble, 7
   and every man's heart will melt,
   and they will be dismayed. 8
Pangs and agony will seize them;

---

[x] Or *this is made known*
11.10: Is 11.1; Rom 15.12.   13.1–14.23: Is 47; Jer 50–51; Hab 1–2.

they will be in anguish like a woman in travail.
They will look aghast at one another; their faces will be aflame.

9 Behold, the day of the LORD comes, cruel, with wrath and fierce anger, to make the earth a desolation and to destroy its sinners from it.

10 For the stars of the heavens and their constellations will not give their light; the sun will be dark at its rising and the moon will not shed its light.

11 I will punish the world for its evil, and the wicked for their iniquity; I will put an end to the pride of the arrogant, and lay low the haughtiness of the ruthless.

12 I will make men more rare than fine gold, and mankind than the gold of Ophir.

13 Therefore I will make the heavens tremble, and the earth will be shaken out of its place, at the wrath of the LORD of hosts in the day of his fierce anger.

14 And like a hunted gazelle, or like sheep with none to gather them, every man will turn to his own people, and every man will flee to his own land.

15 Whoever is found will be thrust through, and whoever is caught will fall by the sword.

16 Their infants will be dashed in pieces before their eyes; their houses will be plundered and their wives ravished.

17 Behold, I am stirring up the Medes against them, who have no regard for silver and do not delight in gold.

18 Their bows will slaughter the young men; they will have no mercy on the fruit of the womb; their eyes will not pity children.

19 And Babylon, the glory of kingdoms, the splendour and pride of the Chaldeʹans, will be like Sodom and Gomorʹrah when God overthrew them.

20 It will never be inhabited or dwelt in for all generations; no Arab will pitch his tent there, no shepherds will make their flocks lie down there.

21 But wild beasts will lie down there,

and its houses will be full of howling creatures;
there ostriches will dwell, and there satyrs will dance.
22 Hyenas will cry in its towers, and jackals in the pleasant palaces; its time is close at hand and its days will not be prolonged.

14 The LORD will have compassion on Jacob and will again choose Israel, and will set them in their own land, and aliens will join them and will cleave to the house of Jacob. 2 And the peoples will take them and bring them to their place, and the house of Israel will possess them in the LORD's land as male and female slaves; they will take captive those who were their captors, and rule over those who oppressed them.

3 When the LORD has given you rest from your pain and turmoil and the hard service with which you were made to serve, 4 you will take up this taunt against the king of Babylon:
"How the oppressor has ceased, the insolent fury[v] ceased!
5 The LORD has broken the staff of the wicked, the sceptre of rulers,
6 that smote the peoples in wrath with unceasing blows, that ruled the nations in anger with unrelenting persecution.
7 The whole earth is at rest and quiet; they break forth into singing.
8 The cypresses rejoice at you, the cedars of Lebanon, saying, 'Since you were laid low, no hewer comes up against us.'
9 Sheol beneath is stirred up to meet you when you come, it rouses the shades to greet you, all who were leaders of the earth; it raises from their thrones all who were kings of the nations.
10 All of them will speak and say to you:
'You too have become as weak as we! You have become like us!'
11 Your pomp is brought down to Sheol, the sound of your harps; maggots are the bed beneath you, and worms are your covering.

12 "How you are fallen from heaven, O Day Star, son of Dawn! How you are cut down to the ground, you who laid the nations low!
13 You said in your heart,

v One ancient Ms Compare Gk Syr Vg: The meaning of the Hebrew word is uncertain
13.10: Mt 24.29; Mk 13.24; Rev 6.12; 8.12.   13.21: Rev 18.2.

'I will ascend to heaven;
above the stars of God
I will set my throne on high;
I will sit on the mount of assembly
in the far north;

14 I will ascend above the heights of the clouds,
I will make myself like the Most High.'

15 But you are brought down to Sheol,
to the depths of the Pit.

16 Those who see you will stare at you,
and ponder over you:
'Is this the man who made the earth tremble,
who shook kingdoms,

17 who made the world like a desert
and overthrew its cities,
who did not let his prisoners go home?'

18 All the kings of the nations lie in glory,
each in his own tomb;

19 but you are cast out, away from your sepulchre,
like a loathed untimely birth,[z]
clothed with the slain, those pierced by the sword,
who go down to the stones of the Pit,
like a dead body trodden under foot.

20 You will not be joined with them in burial,
because you have destroyed your land,
you have slain your people.

"May the descendants of evildoers
nevermore be named!

21 Prepare slaughter for his sons
because of the guilt of their fathers,
lest they rise and possess the earth,
and fill the face of the world with cities."

22 "I will rise up against them," says the LORD of hosts, "and will cut off from Babylon name and remnant, offspring and posterity,

23 says the LORD. And I will make it a possession of the hedgehog, and pools of water, and I will sweep it with the broom of destruction, says the LORD of hosts."

ASSYRIA

24 THE LORD of hosts has sworn:
"As I have planned,
so shall it be,
and as I have purposed,
so shall it stand,

25 that I will break the Assyrian in my land,
and upon my mountains trample him under foot;
and his yoke shall depart from them,

and his burden from their shoulder."

26 This is the purpose that is purposed
concerning the whole earth;
and this is the hand that is stretched out
over all the nations.

27 For the LORD of hosts has purposed,
and who will annul it?
His hand is stretched out,
and who will turn it back?

PHILISTIA

28 IN the year that King Ahaz died came this oracle:

29 "Rejoice not, O Philistia, all of you,
that the rod which smote you is broken,
for from the serpent's root will come forth an adder,
and its fruit will be a flying serpent.

30 And the first-born of the poor will feed,
and the needy lie down in safety;
but I will kill your root with famine,
and your remnant I[a] will slay.

31 Wail, O gate; cry, O city;
melt in fear, O Philistia, all of you!
For smoke comes out of the north,
and there is no straggler in his ranks."

32 What will one answer the messengers of the nation?
"The LORD has founded Zion,
and in her the afflicted of his people find refuge."

MOAB

15 AN oracle concerning Moab.
Because Ar is laid waste in a night
Moab is undone;
because Kir is laid waste in a night
Moab is undone.

2 The daughter of Dibon[b] has gone up
to the high places to weep;
over Nebo and over Med'eba
Moab wails.
On every head is baldness,
every beard is shorn;

3 in the streets they gird on sackcloth;
on the housetops and in the squares
every one wails and melts in tears.

4 Heshbon and Elea'leh cry out,
their voice is heard as far as Jahaz;

[z] Cn Compare Tg Symmachus: Heb a loathed branch   [a] One ancient Ms Vg: Heb he
[b] Cn: Heb the house and Dibon
14.29–31: Jer 47; Ezek 25.15–17; Joel 3.4–8; Amos 1.6–8; Zeph 2.4–7; Zech 9.5–7.
15–16: Is 25.10–12; Jer 48; Ezek 25.8–11; Amos 2.1–3; Zeph 2.8–11.

therefore the armed men of Moab cry
aloud;
his soul trembles.
5 My heart cries out for Moab;
his fugitives flee to Zo'ar,
to Eg'lath-shelish'iyah.
For at the ascent of Luhith
they go up weeping;
on the road to Horona'im
they raise a cry of destruction;
6 the waters of Nimrim
are a desolation;
the grass is withered, the new growth fails,
the verdure is no more.
7 Therefore the abundance they have gained
and what they have laid up
they carry away
over the Brook of the Willows.
8 For a cry has gone
round the land of Moab;
the wailing reaches to Egla'im,
the wailing reaches to Beer-e'lim.
9 For the waters of Dibon^c are full of blood;
yet I will bring upon Dibon^c even more,
a lion for those of Moab who escape,
for the remnant of the land.

16 They have sent lambs
to the ruler of the land,
from Sela, by way of the desert,
to the mount of the daughter of Zion.
2 Like fluttering birds,
like scattered nestlings,
so are the daughters of Moab
at the fords of the Arnon.
3 "Give counsel,
grant justice;
make your shade like night
at the height of noon;
hide the outcasts,
betray not the fugitive;
4 let the outcasts of Moab
sojourn among you;
be a refuge to them
from the destroyer.
When the oppressor is no more,
and destruction has ceased,
and he who tramples under foot
has vanished from the land,
5 then a throne will be established in
steadfast love
and on it will sit in faithfulness
in the tent of David
one who judges and seeks justice
and is swift to do righteousness."

6 We have heard of the pride of Moab,
how proud he was;
of his arrogance, his pride, and his
insolence—
his boasts are false.
Therefore let Moab wail,   7
let every one wail for Moab.
Mourn, utterly stricken,
for the raisin-cakes of Kir-har'eseth.

For the fields of Heshbon languish,   8
and the vine of Sibmah;
the lords of the nations
have struck down its branches,
which reached to Jazer
and strayed to the desert;
its shoots spread abroad
and passed over the sea.
Therefore I weep with the weeping of 9
Jazer
for the vine of Sibmah;
I drench you with my tears,
O Heshbon and Elea'leh;
for upon your fruit and your harvest
the battle shout has fallen.
And joy and gladness are taken away   10
from the fruitful field;
and in the vineyards no songs are sung,
no shouts are raised;
no treader treads out wine in the presses;
the vintage shout is hushed.^{d}
Therefore my soul moans like a lyre for 11
Moab,
and my heart for Kir-he'res.
And when Moab presents himself, when he 12
wearies himself upon the high place, when he
comes to his sanctuary to pray, he will not
prevail.
This is the word which the LORD spoke 13
concerning Moab in the past. But now the 14
LORD says, "In three years, like the years of a
hireling, the glory of Moab will be brought
into contempt, in spite of all his great
multitude, and those who survive will be
very few and feeble."

DAMASCUS

AN oracle concerning Damascus.   17
Behold, Damascus will cease to be a city,
and will become a heap of ruins.
Her cities will be deserted for ever;^{e} 2
they will be for flocks,
which will lie down, and none will make
them afraid.
The fortress will disappear from E'ph- 3
raim,
and the kingdom from Damascus;
and the remnant of Syria will be

^{c} One ancient Ms Vg Compare Syr: Heb *Dimon* ^{d} Gk: Heb *I have hushed*
^{e} Cn Compare Gk: Heb *the cities of Aroer are deserted*
17.1–3: Jer 49.23–27; Amos 1.3–5; Zech 9.1.

like the glory of the children of Israel,
    says the LORD of hosts.

4 And in that day
    the glory of Jacob will be brought low,
    and the fat of his flesh will grow lean.
5 And it shall be as when the reaper gathers
      standing grain
    and his arm harvests the ears,
    and as when one gleans the ears of grain
    in the Valley of Reph'aim.
6 Gleanings will be left in it,
    as when an olive tree is beaten—
    two or three berries
    in the top of the highest bough,
    four or five
      on the branches of a fruit tree,
      says the LORD God of Israel.

7 In that day men will regard their Maker,
and their eyes will look to the Holy One of
8 Israel; they will not have regard for the
altars, the work of their hands, and they will
not look to what their own fingers have
made, either the Ashe'rim or the altars of
incense.
9 In that day their strong cities will be like the
deserted places of the Hivites and the Amorites,*f* which they deserted because of the
children of Israel, and there will be desolation.

10 For you have forgotten the God of your
      salvation,
    and have not remembered the Rock of
      your refuge;
    therefore, though you plant pleasant plants
    and set out slips of an alien god,
11 though you make them grow on the day
      that you plant them,
    and make them blossom in the morning
      that you sow;
    yet the harvest will flee away
    in a day of grief and incurable pain.

12 Ah, the thunder of many peoples,
    they thunder like the thundering of the
      sea!
    Ah, the roar of nations,
    they roar like the roaring of mighty
      waters!
13 The nations roar like the roaring of many
      waters,
    but he will rebuke them, and they will
      flee far away,
    chased like chaff on the mountains before
      the wind
    and whirling dust before the storm.
14 At evening time, behold, terror!

Before morning, they are no more!
This is the portion of those who despoil us,
    and the lot of those who plunder us.

ETHIOPIA

AH, land of whirring wings   18
    which is beyond the rivers of Ethiopia;
which sends ambassadors by the Nile,   2
    in vessels of papyrus upon the waters!
Go, you swift messengers,
    to a nation, tall and smooth,
    to a people feared near and far,
    a nation mighty and conquering,
    whose land the rivers divide.

All you inhabitants of the world,   3
    you who dwell on the earth,
    when a signal is raised on the mountains,
      look!
    When a trumpet is blown, hear!
For thus the LORD said to me: 4
"I will quietly look from my dwelling
    like clear heat in sunshine,
    like a cloud of dew in the heat of
      harvest."
For before the harvest, when the blossom 5
    is over,
    and the flower becomes a ripening
      grape,
    he will cut off the shoots with pruning
      hooks,
    and the spreading branches he will hew
      away.
They shall all of them be left   6
    to the birds of prey of the mountains
    and to the beasts of the earth.
And the birds of prey will summer upon
      them,
    and all the beasts of the earth will winter
      upon them.

At that time gifts will be brought to the 7
LORD of hosts
    from a people tall and smooth,
    from a people feared near and far,
    a nation mighty and conquering,
    whose land the rivers divide,
to Mount Zion, the place of the name of the
LORD of hosts.

EGYPT

AN oracle concerning Egypt.   19
    Behold, the LORD is riding on a swift
      cloud
    and comes to Egypt;
    and the idols of Egypt will tremble at his
      presence,

f Cn Compare Gk: Heb *the wood and the highest bough*
18: Zeph 2.12.   **19:** Jer 46; Ezek 29–32; Zech 14.18–19.

and the heart of the Egyptians will melt
within them.
2 And I will stir up Egyptians against
Egyptians,
and they will fight, every man against
his brother
and every man against his neighbour,
city against city, kingdom against
kingdom;
3 and the spirit of the Egyptians within them
will be emptied out,
and I will confound their plans;
and they will consult the idols and the
sorcerers,
and the mediums and the wizards;
4 and I will give over the Egyptians
into the hand of a hard master;
and a fierce king will rule over them,
says the Lord, the LORD of hosts.

5 And the waters of the Nile will be dried
up,
and the river will be parched and dry;
6 and its canals will become foul,
and the branches of Egypt's Nile will
diminish and dry up,
reeds and rushes will rot away.
7 There will be bare places by the Nile,
on the brink of the Nile,
and all that is sown by the Nile will dry up,
be driven away, and be no more.
8 The fishermen will mourn and lament,
all who cast hook in the Nile;
and they will languish
who spread nets upon the water.
9 The workers in combed flax will be in
despair,
and the weavers of white cotton.
10 Those who are the pillars of the land will
be crushed,
and all who work for hire will be
grieved.

11 The princes of Zo'an are utterly foolish;
the wise counsellors of Pharaoh give
stupid counsel.
How can you say to Pharaoh,
"I am a son of the wise,
a son of ancient kings"?
12 Where then are your wise men?
Let them tell you and make known
what the LORD of hosts has purposed
against Egypt.

The princes of Zo'an have become fools, 13
and the princes of Memphis are
deluded;
those who are the cornerstones of her
tribes
have led Egypt astray.
The LORD has mingled within her   14
a spirit of confusion;
and they have made Egypt stagger in all
her doings
as a drunken man staggers in his vomit.
And there will be nothing for Egypt   15
which head or tail, palm branch or reed,
may do.

In that day the Egyptians will be like 16
women, and tremble with fear before the
hand which the LORD of hosts shakes over
them. And the land of Judah will become a 17
terror to the Egyptians; every one to whom it
is mentioned will fear because of the purpose
which the LORD of hosts has purposed
against them.
In that day there will be five cities in the 18
land of Egypt which speak the language of
Canaan and swear allegiance to the LORD of
hosts. One of these will be called the City
of the Sun.
In that day there will be an altar to the 19
LORD in the midst of the land of Egypt, and a
pillar to the LORD at its border. It will be a 20
sign and a witness to the LORD of hosts in the
land of Egypt; when they cry to the LORD
because of oppressors he will send them a
saviour, and will defend and deliver them.
And the LORD will make himself known to 21
the Egyptians; and the Egyptians will know
the LORD in that day and worship with
sacrifice and burnt offering, and they will
make vows to the LORD and perform them.
And the LORD will smite Egypt, smiting and 22
healing, and they will return to the LORD,
and he will heed their supplications and heal
them.
In that day there will be a highway from 23
Egypt to Assyria, and the Assyrian will come
into Egypt, and the Egyptian into Assyria,
and the Egyptians will worship with the
Assyrians.
In that day Israel will be the third with 24
Egypt and Assyria, a blessing in the midst of
the earth, whom the LORD of hosts has 25
blessed, saying, "Blessed be Egypt my
people, and Assyria the work of my hands,
and Israel my heritage."

In the year that the commander in chief, 20
who was sent by Sargon the king of Assyria,
came to Ashdod and fought against it and
took it,—at that time the LORD had spoken 2
by Isaiah the son of Amoz, saying, "Go, and
loose the sackcloth from your loins and take

off your shoes from your feet," and he had
3 done so, walking naked and barefoot—the
Lord said, "As my servant Isaiah has walked
naked and barefoot for three years as a sign
4 and a portent against Egypt and Ethiopia, so
shall the king of Assyria lead away the
Egyptians captives and the Ethiopians exiles,
both the young and the old, naked and
barefoot, with buttocks uncovered, to the
5 shame of Egypt. Then they shall be dismayed and confounded because of Ethiopia
6 their hope and of Egypt their boast. And the
inhabitants of this coastland will say in that
day, 'Behold, this is what has happened to
those in whom we hoped and to whom we
fled for help to be delivered from the king of
Assyria! And we, how shall we escape?'"

BABYLON

21 THE oracle concerning the wilderness of
the sea.
> As whirlwinds in the Negeb sweep on,
>   it comes from the desert,
>   from a terrible land.
2 A stern vision is told to me;
>   the plunderer plunders,
>   and the destroyer destroys.
> Go up, O Elam,
>   lay siege, O Media;
> all the sighing she has caused
>   I bring to an end.
3 Therefore my loins are filled with anguish;
>   pangs have seized me,
> like the pangs of a woman in travail;
> I am bowed down so that I cannot hear,
>   I am dismayed so that I cannot see.
4 My mind reels, horror has appalled me;
>   the twilight I longed for
> has been turned for me into trembling.
5 They prepare the table,
>   they spread the rugs,
>   they eat, they drink.
> Arise, O princes,
>   oil the shield!
6 For thus the Lord said to me:
> "Go, set a watchman,
>   let him announce what he sees.
7 When he sees riders, horsemen in pairs,
>   riders on asses, riders on camels,
> let him listen diligently,
>   very diligently."

ᵍ One ancient Ms: Heb *a lion*

Then he who saw ᵍ cried: 8
> "Upon a watchtower I stand, O Lord,
>   continually by day,
> and at my post I am stationed
>   whole nights.
> And, behold, here come riders,   9
>   horsemen in pairs!"
> And he answered,
>   "Fallen, fallen is Babylon;
> and all the images of her gods
>   he has shattered to the ground."
> O my threshed and winnowed one,   10
>   what I have heard from the Lord of
> hosts,
> the God of Israel, I announce to you.

DUMAH

> THE oracle concerning Dumah.   11
> One is calling to me from Se'ir,
>   "Watchman, what of the night?
>   Watchman, what of the night?"
> The watchman says: 12
> "Morning comes, and also the night.
>   If you will inquire, inquire;
>   come back again."

ARABIA

> THE oracle concerning Arabia.   13
> In the thickets in Arabia you will lodge,
>   O caravans of De'danites.
> To the thirsty bring water,   14
>   meet the fugitive with bread,
>   O inhabitants of the land of Tema.
> For they have fled from the swords,   15
>   from the drawn sword,

Watchman, what of the night?   v. 11

from the bent bow,
and from the press of battle.
For thus the Lord said to me, "Within a year, according to the years of a hireling, all the glory of Kedar will come to an end; and the remainder of the archers of the mighty men of the sons of Kedar will be few; for the LORD, the God of Israel, has spoken."

JUDAH

JERUSALEM

2 THE oracle concerning the valley of vision.
What do you mean that you have gone up,
all of you, to the housetops,
you who are full of shoutings,
tumultuous city, exultant town?
Your slain are not slain with the sword
or dead in battle.
All your rulers have fled together,
without the bow they were captured.
All of you who were found were captured,
though they had fled far away.[h]
Therefore I said:
"Look away from me,
let me weep bitter tears;
do not labour to comfort me
for the destruction of the daughter of
my people."

5 For the Lord GOD of hosts has a day
of tumult and trampling and confusion
in the valley of vision,
a battering down of walls
and a shouting to the mountains.
6 And Elam bore the quiver
with chariots and horsemen,[i]
and Kir uncovered the shield.
7 Your choicest valleys were full of chariots,
and the horsemen took their stand at the
gates.
8 He has taken away the covering of
Judah.

In that day you looked to the weapons of the
9 House of the Forest, and you saw that the
breaches of the city of David were many, and
you collected the waters of the lower pool,
10 and you counted the houses of Jerusalem,
and you broke down the houses to fortify the
11 wall. You made a reservoir between the two
walls for the water of the old pool. But you did not look to him who did it, or have regard for him who planned it long ago.

In that day the Lord GOD of hosts 12
called to weeping and mourning,
to baldness and girding with sackcloth;
and behold, joy and gladness, 13
slaying oxen and killing sheep,
eating flesh and drinking wine.
"Let us eat and drink,
for tomorrow we die."
The LORD of hosts has revealed himself in 14
my ears:
"Surely this iniquity will not be forgiven
you
till you die,"
says the Lord GOD of hosts.

Thus says the Lord GOD of hosts, "Come, 15
go to this steward, to Shebna, who is over the
household, and say to him: What have you to 16
do here and whom have you here, that you
have hewn here a tomb for yourself, you who
hew a tomb on the height, and carve a
habitation for yourself in the rock? Behold, 17
the LORD will hurl you away violently, O you
strong man. He will seize firm hold on you,
and whirl you round and round, and throw 18
you like a ball into a wide land; there you
shall die, and there shall be your splendid
chariots, you shame of your master's house.
I will thrust you from your office, and you 19
will be cast down from your station. In that 20
day I will call my servant Eli′akim the son of
Hilki′ah, and I will clothe him with your 21
robe, and will bind your girdle on him, and
will commit your authority to his hand; and
he shall be a father to the inhabitants of
Jerusalem and to the house of Judah. And I 22
will place on his shoulder the key of the
house of David; he shall open, and none shall
shut; and he shall shut, and none shall open.
And I will fasten him like a peg in a sure 23
place, and he will become a throne of honour
to his father's house. And they will hang on 24
him the whole weight of his father's house,
the offspring and issue, every small vessel,
from the cups to all the flagons. In that day, 25
says the LORD of hosts, the peg that was
fastened in a sure place will give way; and it
will be cut down and fall, and the burden
that was upon it will be cut off, for the LORD
has spoken."

TYRE

THE oracle concerning Tyre.   **23**
Wail, O ships of Tarshish,

h Gk Syr Vg: Heb *from far away*   i The Hebrew of this line is obscure
22.22: Rev 3.7.   **23:** Ezek 26.1–28.19; Joel 3.4–8; Amos 1.9–10; Zech 9.3–4.

TYRE

for Tyre is laid waste, without house or
    haven!
From the land of Cyprus
    it is revealed to them.

2 Be still, O inhabitants of the coast,
        O merchants of Sidon;
    your messengers passed over the sea[j]

3 and were on many waters;
    your revenue was the grain of Shihor,
        the harvest of the Nile;
    you were the merchant of the nations.

4 Be ashamed, O Sidon, for the sea has
        spoken,
    the stronghold of the sea, saying:
    "I have neither travailed nor given birth,
    I have neither reared young men
        nor brought up virgins."

5 When the report comes to Egypt,
    they will be in anguish over the report
        about Tyre.

6 Pass over to Tarshish,
    wail, O inhabitants of the coast!

7 Is this your exultant city
    whose origin is from days of old,
    whose feet carried her
        to settle afar?

8 Who has purposed this
    against Tyre, the bestower of crowns,
    whose merchants were princes,
        whose traders were the honoured of the
            earth?

9 The LORD of hosts has purposed it,
        to defile the pride of all glory,
        to dishonour all the honoured of the
            earth.

10 Overflow your land like the Nile,
        O daughter of Tarshish;
    there is no restraint any more.

11 He has stretched out his hand over the sea,
    he has shaken the kingdoms;
    the LORD has given command concerning
        Canaan
    to destroy its strongholds.

12 And he said:
    "You will no more exult,
        O oppressed virgin daughter of Sidon;
    arise, pass over to Cyprus,
        even there you will have no rest."

13 Behold the land of the Chalde'ans! This is
    the people; it was not Assyria. They des-

tined Tyre for wild beasts. They erected
their siege towers, they razed her palaces,
they made her a ruin.[k]

Wail, O ships of Tarshish,   1
    for your stronghold is laid waste.
In that day Tyre will be forgotten for seventy 1
years, like the days of one king. At the end of
seventy years, it will happen to Tyre as in the
song of the harlot:
    "Take a harp,   1
        go about the city,
        O forgotten harlot!
    Make sweet melody,
        sing many songs,
        that you may be remembered."

At the end of seventy years, the LORD will 1
visit Tyre, and she will return to her hire, and
will play the harlot with all the kingdoms
of the world upon the face of the earth. Her 1
merchandise and her hire will be dedicated to
the LORD; it will not be stored or hoarded,
but her merchandise will supply abundant
food and fine clothing for those who dwell
before the LORD.

THE WHOLE WORLD

BEHOLD, the LORD will lay waste the 2
        earth and make it desolate,
    and he will twist its surface and scatter
        its inhabitants.
And it shall be, as with the people, so with 2
        the priest;
    as with the slave, so with his master;
    as with the maid, so with her mistress;
as with the buyer, so with the seller;
    as with the lender, so with the borrower;
    as with the creditor, so with the debtor.
The earth shall be utterly laid waste and 3
        utterly despoiled;
    for the LORD has spoken this word.

The earth mourns and withers,   4
    the world languishes and withers;
    the heavens languish together with the
        earth.
The earth lies polluted   5
    under its inhabitants;
for they have transgressed the laws,
    violated the statutes,
    broken the everlasting covenant.
Therefore a curse devours the earth,   6
    and its inhabitants suffer for their guilt;
therefore the inhabitants of the earth are
        scorched,
    and few men are left.
The wine mourns,   7
    the vine languishes,
    all the merry-hearted sigh.

[j] One ancient Ms: Heb *who passed over the sea, they replenished you*
[k] The Hebrew of this verse is obscure
23.17: Rev 17.2.

The mirth of the timbrels is stilled,
  the noise of the jubilant has ceased,
  the mirth of the lyre is stilled.
No more do they drink wine with singing;
  strong drink is bitter to those who drink
    it.
The city of chaos is broken down,
  every house is shut up so that none can
    enter.
There is an outcry in the streets for lack of
    wine;
  all joy has reached its eventide;
  the gladness of the earth is banished.
Desolation is left in the city,
  the gates are battered into ruins.
For thus it shall be in the midst of the
    earth
    among the nations,
  as when an olive tree is beaten,
    as at the gleaning when the vintage is
      done.

They lift up their voices, they sing for joy;
  over the majesty of the LORD they shout
    from the west.
Therefore in the east give glory to the
    LORD;
  in the coastlands of the sea, to the name
    of the LORD, the God of Israel.
From the ends of the earth we hear songs
    of praise,
  of glory to the Righteous One.
But I say, "I pine away,
  I pine away. Woe is me!
For the treacherous deal treacherously,
  the treacherous deal very treacher-
    ously."

Terror, and the pit, and the snare
  are upon you, O inhabitant of the earth!
He who flees at the sound of the terror
  shall fall into the pit;
and he who climbs out of the pit
  shall be caught in the snare.
For the windows of heaven are opened,
  and the foundations of the earth
    tremble.
The earth is utterly broken,
  the earth is rent asunder,
  the earth is violently shaken.

The earth staggers like a drunken man, 20
  it sways like a hut;
its transgression lies heavy upon it,
  and it falls, and will not rise again.

On that day the LORD will punish   21
  the host of heaven, in heaven,
  and the kings of the earth, on the earth.
They will be gathered together   22
  as prisoners in a pit;
they will be shut up in a prison,
  and after many days they will be
    punished.
Then the moon will be confounded,   23
  and the sun ashamed;
for the LORD of hosts will reign
  on Mount Zion and in Jerusalem
and before his elders he will manifest his
  glory.

Songs of deliverance

O LORD, thou art my God;   **25**
  I will exalt thee, I will praise thy name;
for thou hast done wonderful things,
  plans formed of old, faithful and sure.
For thou hast made the city a heap,   2
  the fortified city a ruin;
the palace of aliens is a city no more,
  it will never be rebuilt.
Therefore strong peoples will glorify thee; 3
  cities of ruthless nations will fear thee.
For thou hast been a stronghold to the 4
    poor,
  a stronghold to the needy in his distress,
  a shelter from the storm and a shade
    from the heat;
for the blast of the ruthless is like a storm
    against a wall,
  like heat in a dry place.   5
Thou dost subdue the noise of the aliens;
  as heat by the shade of a cloud,
  so the song of the ruthless is stilled.

On this mountain the LORD of hosts will 6
make for all peoples a feast of fat things, a
feast of wine on the lees, of fat things full of
marrow, of wine on the lees well refined.
And he will destroy on this mountain the 7
covering that is cast over all peoples, the veil

8 that is spread over all nations. He will swallow up death for ever, and the Lord GOD will wipe away tears from all faces, and the reproach of his people he will take away from all the earth; for the LORD has spoken.
9 It will be said on that day, "Lo, this is our God; we have waited for him, that he might save us. This is the LORD; we have waited for him; let us be glad and rejoice in his salvation."
10 For the hand of the LORD will rest on this mountain, and Moab shall be trodden down in his place, as straw is trodden down in a
11 dung-pit. And he will spread out his hands in the midst of it as a swimmer spreads his hands out to swim; but the LORD will lay low his pride together with the skill[l] of his
12 hands. And the high fortifications of his walls he will bring down, lay low, and cast to the ground, even to the dust.

National hopes

26 In that day this song will be sung in the land of Judah:
"We have a strong city;
he sets up salvation
as walls and bulwarks.
2 Open the gates,
that the righteous nation which keeps faith
may enter in.
3 Thou dost keep him in perfect peace,
whose mind is stayed on thee,
because he trusts in thee.
4 Trust in the LORD for ever,
for the LORD GOD
is an everlasting rock.
5 For he has brought low
the inhabitants of the height,
the lofty city.
He lays it low, lays it low to the ground,
casts it to the dust.
6 The foot tramples it,
the feet of the poor,
the steps of the needy."

7 The way of the righteous is level;
thou[m] dost make smooth the path of the righteous.
8 In the path of thy judgments,
O LORD, we wait for thee;
thy memorial name
is the desire of our soul.
9 My soul yearns for thee in the night,
my spirit within me earnestly seeks thee.
For when thy judgments are in the earth,
the inhabitants of the world learn righteousness.

If favour is shown to the wicked,
he does not learn righteousness;
in the land of uprightness he deals perversely
and does not see the majesty of the LORD.
O LORD, thy hand is lifted up,
but they see it not.
Let them see thy zeal for thy people, and be ashamed.
Let the fire for thy adversaries consume them.
O LORD, thou wilt ordain peace for us,
thou hast wrought for us all our works.
O LORD our God,
other lords besides thee have ruled over us,
but thy name alone we acknowledge.
They are dead, they will not live;
they are shades, they will not arise;
to that end thou hast visited them with destruction
and wiped out all remembrance of them.
But thou hast increased the nation, O LORD,
thou hast increased the nation; thou art glorified;
thou hast enlarged all the borders of the land.

O LORD, in distress they sought thee,
they poured out a prayer[n]
when thy chastening was upon them.
Like a woman with child,
who writhes and cries out in her pangs,
when she is near her time,
so were we because of thee, O LORD;
we were with child, we writhed,
we have as it were brought forth wind.
We have wrought no deliverance in the earth,
and the inhabitants of the world have not fallen.
Thy dead shall live, their bodies[o] shall rise.
O dwellers in the dust, awake and sing for joy!
For thy dew is a dew of light,
and on the land of the shades thou wilt let it fall.

Come, my people, enter your chambers,
and shut your doors behind you;
hide yourselves for a little while
until the wrath is past.
For behold, the LORD is coming forth out of his place
to punish the inhabitants of the earth for their iniquity,

---

[l] The meaning of the Hebrew word is uncertain   [m] Cn Compare Gk: Heb *thou (that art) upright*
[n] Heb uncertain   [o] Cn Compare Syr Tg: Heb *my body*
25.8: I Cor 15.54; Rev 7.17; 21.4.   **25.10–12:** Is 15–16; Jer 48; Ezek 25.8–11; Amos 2.1–3; Zeph 2.8–11.

and the earth will disclose the blood shed
  upon her,
and will no more cover her slain.

In that day the LORD with his hard and
great and strong sword will punish Leviathan
the fleeing serpent, Leviathan the twisting
serpent, and he will slay the dragon that is in
the sea.

In that day:
"A pleasant vineyard, sing of it!
 I, the LORD, am its keeper;
 every moment I water it.
Lest any one harm it,
 I guard it night and day;
 I have no wrath.
Would that I had thorns and briers to
  battle!
 I would set out against them,
 I would burn them up together.
Or let them lay hold of my protection,
 let them make peace with me,
 let them make peace with me."

In days to come *p* Jacob shall take root,
 Israel shall blossom and put forth
  shoots,
 and fill the whole world with fruit.

Has he smitten them as he smote those
 who smote them?
 Or have they been slain as their slayers
  were slain?
Measure by measure,*q* by exile thou didst
 contend with them;
 he removed them with his fierce blast in
  the day of the east wind.
Therefore by this the guilt of Jacob will be
 expiated,
 and this will be the full fruit of the
  removal of his sin:
when he makes all the stones of the altars
 like chalkstones crushed to pieces,
 no Ashe'rim or incense altars will
  remain standing.
For the fortified city is solitary,
 a habitation deserted and forsaken, like
  the wilderness;
there the calf grazes,
 there he lies down, and strips its
  branches.
When its boughs are dry, they are broken;
 women come and make a fire of them.
For this is a people without discernment;
 therefore he who made them will not
  have compassion on them,
 he that formed them will show them no
  favour.

In that day from the river Euphra'tes to the 12
Brook of Egypt the LORD will thresh out the
grain, and you will be gathered one by one, O
people of Israel. And in that day a great 13
trumpet will be blown, and those who were
lost in the land of Assyria and those who
were driven out to the land of Egypt will
come and worship the LORD on the holy
mountain at Jerusalem.

WOE to the proud crown of the drunkards 28
 of E'phraim,
 and to the fading flower of its glorious
  beauty,
 which is on the head of the rich valley of
  those overcome with wine!
Behold, the Lord has one who is mighty 2
 and strong;
 like a storm of hail, a destroying
  tempest,
like a storm of mighty, overflowing
  waters,
 he will cast down to the earth with
  violence.
The proud crown of the drunkards of 3
 E'phraim
 will be trodden under foot;
and the fading flower of its glorious 4
 beauty,
 which is on the head of the rich valley,
will be like a first-ripe fig before the
  summer:
 when a man sees it, he eats it up
 as soon as it is in his hand.

In that day the LORD of hosts will be a 5
 crown of glory,
 and a diadem of beauty, to the remnant
  of his people;
and a spirit of justice to him who sits in 6
 judgment,
 and strength to those who turn back the
  battle at the gate.

These also reel with wine   7
 and stagger with strong drink;
the priest and the prophet reel with strong
  drink,
 they are confused with wine,
 they stagger with strong drink;
they err in vision,

they stumble in giving judgment.

8 For all tables are full of vomit,
no place is without filthiness.

9 "Whom will he teach knowledge,
and to whom will he explain the message?
Those who are weaned from the milk,
those taken from the breast?

10 For it is precept upon precept, precept
upon precept,
line upon line, line upon line,
here a little, there a little."

11 Nay, but by men of strange lips
and with an alien tongue
the LORD will speak to this people,

12 to whom he has said,
"This is rest;
give rest to the weary;
and this is repose";
yet they would not hear.

13 Therefore the word of the LORD will be to
them
precept upon precept, precept upon
precept,
line upon line, line upon line,
here a little, there a little;
that they may go, and fall backward,
and be broken, and snared, and taken.

14 Therefore hear the word of the LORD, you
scoffers,
who rule this people in Jerusalem!

15 Because you have said, "We have made a
covenant with death,
and with Sheol we have an agreement;

when the overwhelming scourge passes
through
it will not come to us;
for we have made lies our refuge,
and in falsehood we have taken shelter";

16 therefore thus says the Lord GOD,
"Behold, I am laying in Zion for a
foundation
a stone, a tested stone,
a precious cornerstone, of a sure foundation:
'He who believes will not be in haste.'

17 And I will make justice the line,
and righteousness the plummet;
and hail will sweep away the refuge of
lies,
and waters will overwhelm the shelter."

18 Then your covenant with death will be
annulled,
and your agreement with Sheol will not
stand;
when the overwhelming scourge passes
through
you will be beaten down by it.

19 As often as it passes through it will take
you;
for morning by morning it will pass
through,
by day and by night;
and it will be sheer terror to understand
the message.

20 For the bed is too short to stretch oneself
on it,
and the covering too narrow to wrap
oneself in it.

21 For the LORD will rise up as on Mount
Pera'zim,

An eastern threshing-floor

Isa **28,** 27–28

28.11–12: 1 Cor 14.21.   28.12: Mt 11.29.   28.16: Rom 9.33; 10.11; 1 Pet 2.4–6.

he will be wroth as in the valley of
Gibeon;
to do his deed—strange is his deed!
and to work his work—alien is his work!
Now therefore do not scoff,
lest your bonds be made strong;
for I have heard a decree of destruction
from the Lord GOD of hosts upon the
whole land.

Give ear, and hear my voice;
hearken, and hear my speech.
Does he who ploughs for sowing plough
continually?
does he continually open and harrow his
ground?
When he has levelled its surface,
does he not scatter dill, sow cummin,
and put in wheat in rows
and barley in its proper place,
and spelt as the border?
For he is instructed aright;
his God teaches him.

Dill is not threshed with a threshing
sledge,
nor is a cart wheel rolled over cummin;
but dill is beaten out with a stick,
and cummin with a rod.
Does one crush bread grain?
No, he does not thresh it for ever;
when he drives his cart wheel over it
with his horses, he does not crush it.
This also comes from the LORD of hosts;
he is wonderful in counsel,
and excellent in wisdom.

JERUSALEM

29 HO Ariel, Ariel,
the city where David encamped!
Add year to year;
let the feasts run their round.
2   Yet I will distress Ariel,
and there shall be moaning and lamentation,
and she shall be to me like an Ariel.
3   And I will encamp against you round
about,
and will besiege you with towers
and I will raise siegeworks against you.
4   Then deep from the earth you shall
speak,
from low in the dust your words shall
come;
your voice shall come from the ground like
the voice of a ghost,
and your speech shall whisper out of the
dust.

But the multitude of your foes[r] shall be 5
like small dust,
and the multitude of the ruthless like
passing chaff.
And in an instant, suddenly,
you will be visited by the LORD of hosts 6
with thunder and with earthquake and
great noise,
with whirlwind and tempest, and the
flame of a devouring fire.
And the multitude of all the nations that 7
fight against Ariel,
all that fight against her and her
stronghold and distress her,
shall be like a dream, a vision of the
night.
As when a hungry man dreams he is eating 8
and awakes with his hunger not
satisfied,
or as when a thirsty man dreams he is
drinking
and awakes faint, with his thirst not
quenched,
so shall the multitude of all the nations be
that fight against Mount Zion.

Stupefy yourselves and be in a stupor,   9
blind yourselves and be blind!
Be drunk, but not with wine;
stagger, but not with strong drink!
For the LORD has poured out upon you   10
a spirit of deep sleep,
and has closed your eyes, the prophets,
and covered your heads, the seers.
And the vision of all this has become to you 11
like the words of a book that is sealed. When
men give it to one who can read, saying,
"Read this," he says, "I cannot, for it is
sealed." And when they give the book to one 12
who cannot read, saying, "Read this," he
says, "I cannot read."

And the Lord said: 13
"Because this people draw near with their
mouth
and honour me with their lips,
while their hearts are far from me,
and their fear of me is a commandment of
men learned by rote;
therefore, behold, I will again   14
do marvellous things with this people,
wonderful and marvellous;
and the wisdom of their wise men shall
perish,
and the discernment of their discerning
men shall be hid."

Woe to those who hide deep from the 15
LORD their counsel,

---

[r] Cn: Heb *strangers*
29.13: Mt 15.8–9; Mk 7.6–7.   **29.14:** 1 Cor 1.19.

whose deeds are in the dark,
and who say, "Who sees us?
Who knows us?"

16 You turn things upside down!
Shall the potter be regarded as the clay;
that the thing made should say of its
maker,
"He did not make me";
or the thing formed say of him who formed
it,
"He has no understanding"?

17 Is it not yet a very little while
until Lebanon shall be turned into a
fruitful field,
and the fruitful field shall be regarded as
a forest?

18 In that day the deaf shall hear
the words of a book,
and out of their gloom and darkness
the eyes of the blind shall see.

19 The meek shall obtain fresh joy in the
LORD,
and the poor among men shall exult in
the Holy One of Israel.

20 For the ruthless shall come to naught and
the scoffer cease,
and all who watch to do evil shall be cut
off,

21 who by a word make a man out to be an
offender,
and lay a snare for him who reproves in
the gate,
and with an empty plea turn aside him
who is in the right.

22 Therefore thus says the LORD, who
redeemed Abraham, concerning the house of
Jacob:
"Jacob shall no more be ashamed,
no more shall his face grow pale.

23 For when he sees his children,
the work of my hands, in his midst,
they will sanctify my name;
they will sanctify the Holy One of Jacob,
and will stand in awe of the God of
Israel.

24 And those who err in spirit will come to
understanding,
and those who murmur will accept
instruction."

Relations with Egypt

30 "Woe to the rebellious children," says the
LORD,
"who carry out a plan, but not mine;
and who make a league, but not of my
spirit,

that they may add sin to sin;
who set out to go down to Egypt,
without asking for my counsel,
to take refuge in the protection of Pharaoh,
and to seek shelter in the shadow of
Egypt!
Therefore shall the protection of Pharaoh
turn to your shame,
and the shelter in the shadow of Egypt
to your humiliation.
For though his officials are at Zo'an
and his envoys reach Ha'nes,
every one comes to shame
through a people that cannot profit
them,
that brings neither help nor profit,
but shame and disgrace."

An oracle on the beasts of the Negeb.
Through a land of trouble and anguish,
from where come the lioness and the
lion,
the viper and the flying serpent,
they carry their riches on the backs of
asses,
and their treasures on the humps of
camels,
to a people that cannot profit them.
For Egypt's help is worthless and empty, 7
therefore I have called her
"Rahab who sits still."

And now, go, write it before them on a 8
tablet,
and inscribe it in a book,
that it may be for the time to come
as a witness for ever.
For they are a rebellious people, 9
lying sons,
sons who will not hear
the instruction of the LORD;
who say to the seers, "See not"; 1
and to the prophets, "Prophesy not to us
what is right;
speak to us smooth things,
prophesy illusions,
leave the way, turn aside from the path, 1
let us hear no more of the Holy One of
Israel."
Therefore thus says the Holy One of 1
Israel,
"Because you despise this word,
and trust in oppression and perverseness,
and rely on them;
therefore this iniquity shall be to you 1
like a break in a high wall, bulging out,
and about to collapse,
whose crash comes suddenly, in an
instant;

and its breaking is like that of a potter's
vessel
which is smashed so ruthlessly
that among its fragments not a sherd is
found
with which to take fire from the hearth,
or to dip up water out of the cistern."

For thus said the Lord GOD, the Holy One
of Israel,
"In returning and rest you shall be
saved;
in quietness and in trust shall be your
strength."
And you would not, but you said,
"No! We will speed upon horses,"
therefore you shall speed away;
and, "We will ride upon swift steeds,"
therefore your pursuers shall be swift.
A thousand shall flee at the threat of one,
at the threat of five you shall flee,
till you are left
like a flagstaff on the top of a mountain,
like a signal on a hill.

Therefore the LORD waits to be gracious to
you;
therefore he exalts himself to show
mercy to you.
For the LORD is a God of justice;
blessed are all those who wait for him.
Yea, O people in Zion who dwell at Jerusalem; you shall weep no more. He will
surely be gracious to you at the sound of your
cry; when he hears it, he will answer you.
And though the Lord give you the bread of
adversity and the water of affliction, yet your
Teacher will not hide himself any more, but
your eyes shall see your Teacher. And your
ears shall hear a word behind you, saying,
"This is the way, walk in it," when you turn
to the right or when you turn to the left.
Then you will defile your silver-covered
graven images and your gold-plated molten
images. You will scatter them as unclean
things; you will say to them, "Begone!"
And he will give rain for the seed with
which you sow the ground, and grain, the
produce of the ground, which will be rich
and plenteous. In that day your cattle will
graze in large pastures; and the oxen and the
asses that till the ground will eat salted
provender, which has been winnowed with
shovel and fork. And upon every lofty
mountain and every high hill there will be
brooks running with water, in the day of the
great slaughter, when the towers fall.
Moreover the light of the moon will be as the
light of the sun, and the light of the sun will
be sevenfold, as the light of seven days, in the
day when the LORD binds up the hurt of his
people, and heals the wounds inflicted by his
blow.

Behold, the name of the LORD comes from 27
far,
burning with his anger, and in thick
rising smoke;
his lips are full of indignation,
and his tongue is like a devouring fire;
his breath is like an overflowing stream 28
that reaches up to the neck;
to sift the nations with the sieve of destruction,
and to place on the jaws of the peoples a
bridle that leads astray.

You shall have a song as in the night when a 29
holy feast is kept; and gladness of heart, as
when one sets out to the sound of the flute to
go to the mountain of the LORD, to the Rock
of Israel. And the LORD will cause his 30
majestic voice to be heard and the
descending blow of his arm to be seen, in
furious anger and a flame of devouring fire,
with a cloudburst and tempest and hailstones. The Assyrians will be terror-stricken 31
at the voice of the LORD, when he smites with
his rod. And every stroke of the staff of 32
punishment which the LORD lays upon them
will be to the sound of timbrels and lyres;
battling with brandished arm he will fight
with them. For a burning place* has long 33
been prepared; yea, for the king† it is made
ready, its pyre made deep and wide, with fire
and wood in abundance; the breath of the
LORD, like a stream of brimstone, kindles it.

Woe to those who go down to Egypt for 31
help
and rely on horses,
who trust in chariots because they are
many
and in horsemen because they are very
strong,
but do not look to the Holy One of Israel
or consult the LORD!
And yet he is wise and brings disaster, 2
he does not call back his words,
but will arise against the house of the
evildoers,
and against the helpers of those who
work iniquity.
The Egyptians are men, and not God; 3
and their horses are flesh, and not
spirit.
When the LORD stretches out his hand,
the helper will stumble, and he who is
helped will fall,
and they will all perish together.

* Or *Topheth* † Or *Molech*

4 For thus the LORD said to me,
As a lion or a young lion growls over his
prey,
and when a band of shepherds is called
forth against him
is not terrified by their shouting
or daunted at their noise,
so the LORD of hosts will come down
to fight upon Mount Zion and upon its
hill.
5 Like birds hovering, so the LORD of hosts
will protect Jerusalem;
he will protect and deliver it,
he will spare and rescue it.

6 Turn to him from whom you [u] have deeply
7 revolted, O people of Israel. For in that day
every one shall cast away his idols of silver
and his idols of gold, which your hands have
sinfully made for you.
8 "And the Assyrian shall fall by a sword,
not of man;
and a sword, not of man, shall devour
him;
and he shall flee from the sword,
and his young men shall be put to forced
labour.
9 His rock shall pass away in terror,
and his officers desert the standard in
panic,"
says the LORD, whose fire is in Zion,
and whose furnace is in Jerusalem.

32 Behold, a king will reign in righteousness,
and princes will rule in justice.
2 Each will be like a hiding place from the
wind,
a covert from the tempest,
like streams of water in a dry place,
like the shade of a great rock in a weary
land.
3 Then the eyes of those who see will not be
closed,
and the ears of those who hear will
hearken.
4 The mind of the rash will have good
judgment,
and the tongue of the stammerers will
speak readily and distinctly.
5 The fool will no more be called noble,
nor the knave said to be honourable.
6 For the fool speaks folly,
and his mind plots iniquity:
to practise ungodliness,
to utter error concerning the LORD,
to leave the craving of the hungry
unsatisfied,
and to deprive the thirsty of drink.
7 The knaveries of the knave are evil;
he devises wicked devices

to ruin the poor with lying words,
even when the plea of the needy is right.
But he who is noble devises noble things,
and by noble things he stands.

Women of Jerusalem

Rise up, you women who are at ease, hear
my voice;
you complacent daughters, give ear to
my speech.
In little more than a year
you will shudder, you complacent
women;
for the vintage will fail,
the fruit harvest will not come.
Tremble, you women who are at ease,
shudder, you complacent ones;
strip, and make yourselves bare,
and gird sackcloth upon your loins.
Beat upon your breasts for the pleasant
fields,
for the fruitful vine,
for the soil of my people
growing up in thorns and briers;
yea, for all the joyous houses
in the joyful city.
For the palace will be forsaken,
the populous city deserted;
the hill and the watchtower
will become dens for ever,
a joy of wild asses,
a pasture of flocks;
until the Spirit is poured upon us from on
high,
and the wilderness becomes a fruitful
field,
and the fruitful field is deemed a forest.
Then justice will dwell in the wilderness,
and righteousness abide in the fruitful
field.
And the effect of righteousness will be
peace,
and the result of righteousness, quietness and trust for ever.
My people will abide in a peaceful
habitation,
in secure dwellings, and in quiet resting
places.
And the forest will utterly go down, [v]
and the city will be utterly laid low.
Happy are you who sow beside all waters,
who let the feet of the ox and the ass
range free.

Woe to you, destroyer,
who yourself have not been destroyed;
you treacherous one,
with whom none has dealt treacherously!

---

[u] Heb *they*   [v] Cn: Heb *And it will hail when the forest comes down*

When you have ceased to destroy,
  you will be destroyed;
and when you have made an end of dealing
    treacherously,
  you will be dealt with treacherously.

O LORD, be gracious to us; we wait for
    thee.
  Be our arm every morning,
  our salvation in the time of trouble.
At the thunderous noise peoples flee,
  at the lifting up of thyself nations are
    scattered;
and spoil is gathered as the caterpillar
    gathers;
  as locusts leap, men leap upon it.

The LORD is exalted, for he dwells on
    high;
  he will fill Zion with justice and
    righteousness;
and he will be the stability of your
    times,
  abundance of salvation, wisdom, and
    knowledge;
  the fear of the LORD is his treasure.

Behold, the valiant ones _w_ cry without;
  the envoys of peace weep bitterly.
The highways lie waste,
  the wayfaring man ceases.
Covenants are broken,
  witnesses _x_ are despised,
  there is no regard for man.

The land mourns and languishes;   9
  Lebanon is confounded and withers
    away;
Sharon is like a desert;
  and Bashan and Carmel shake off their
    leaves.

"Now I will arise," says the LORD,   10
  "now I will lift myself up;
  now I will be exalted.
You conceive chaff, you bring forth 11
    stubble;
  your breath is a fire that will consume
    you.
And the peoples will be as if burned to 12
    lime,
  like thorns cut down, that are burned in
    the fire."

Hear, you who are far off, what I have 13
    done;
  and you who are near, acknowledge my
    might.
The sinners in Zion are afraid;   14
  trembling has seized the godless:
"Who among us can dwell with the
    devouring fire?
  Who among us can dwell with everlast-
    ing burnings?"
He who walks righteously and speaks 15
    uprightly,
  who despises the gain of oppressions,
  who shakes his hands, lest they hold a
    bribe,

Isa 30, 6

_w_ The meaning of the Hebrew word is uncertain   _x_ One ancient Ms: Heb _cities_

who stops his ears from hearing of
   bloodshed
and shuts his eyes from looking upon
   evil,

16 he will dwell on the heights;
    his place of defence will be the fortresses
     of rocks;
    his bread will be given him, his water
     will be sure.

17 Your eyes will see the king in his beauty;
    they will behold a land that stretches
     afar.

18 Your mind will muse on the terror:
    "Where is he who counted, where is he
     who weighed the tribute?
    Where is he who counted the towers?"

19 You will see no more the insolent people,
    the people of an obscure speech which
     you cannot comprehend,
    stammering in a tongue which you
     cannot understand.

20 Look upon Zion, the city of our appointed
    feasts!
    Your eyes will see Jerusalem,
    a quiet habitation, an immovable tent,
    whose stakes will never be plucked up,
    nor will any of its cords be broken.

21 But there the LORD in majesty will be for
    us
    a place of broad rivers and streams,
    where no galley with oars can go,
    nor stately ship can pass.

22 For the LORD is our judge, the LORD is our
    ruler,
    the LORD is our king; he will save us.

23 Your tackle hangs loose;
    it cannot hold the mast firm in its place,
    or keep the sail spread out.

    Then prey and spoil in abundance will be
     divided;
    even the lame will take the prey.

24 And no inhabitant will say, "I am sick";
    the people who dwell there will be
     forgiven their iniquity.

The day of the Lord

34 Draw near, O nations, to hear,
    and hearken, O peoples!
    Let the earth listen, and all that fills it;
    the world, and all that comes from it.

2 For the LORD is enraged against all the
    nations,
    and furious against all their host,
    he has doomed them, has given them
     over for slaughter.

Their slain shall be cast out,
   and the stench of their corpses shall
    rise;
   the mountains shall flow with their
    blood.
All the host of heaven shall rot away,
   and the skies roll up like a scroll.
All their host shall fall,
   as leaves fall from the vine,
   like leaves falling from the fig tree.

For my sword has drunk its fill in the
   heavens;
   behold, it descends for judgment upon
    Edom,
   upon the people I have doomed.
The LORD has a sword; it is sated with
   blood,
   it is gorged with fat,
   with the blood of lambs and goats,
   with the fat of the kidneys of rams.
For the LORD has a sacrifice in Bozrah,
   a great slaughter in the land of Edom.
Wild oxen shall fall with them,
   and young steers with the mighty bulls.
Their land shall be soaked with blood,
   and their soil made rich with fat.

For the LORD has a day of vengeance,
   a year of recompense for the cause of
    Zion.
And the streams of Edom[y] shall be turned
   into pitch,
   and her soil into brimstone;
   her land shall become burning pitch.
Night and day it shall not be quenched;
   its smoke shall go up for ever.
From generation to generation it shall lie
   waste;
   none shall pass through it for ever and
    ever.
But the hawk and the porcupine shall
   possess it,
   the owl and the raven shall dwell in it.
He shall stretch the line of confusion over
   it,
   and the plummet of chaos over[z] its
    nobles.
They shall name it No Kingdom There,
   and all its princes shall be nothing.

Thorns shall grow over its strongholds,
   nettles and thistles in its fortresses.
It shall be the haunt of jackals,
   an abode for ostriches.
And wild beasts shall meet with hyenas,
   the satyr shall cry to his fellow;
yea, there shall the night hag alight,
   and find for herself a resting place.

y Heb her streams   z Heb lacks over
34: Is 63.1–6; Jer 49.7–22; Ezek 25.12–14; 35; Amos 1.11–12; Obad; Mal 1.2–5.   34.4: Rev 6.13–14.
34.9–10: Rev 19.3.

15 There shall the owl nest and lay
    and hatch and gather her young in her
       shadow;
    yea, there shall the kites be gathered,
       each one with her mate.

16 Seek and read from the book of the LORD:
    Not one of these shall be missing;
    none shall be without her mate.
    For the mouth of the LORD has com-
       manded,
    and his Spirit has gathered them.

17 He has cast the lot for them,
    his hand has portioned it out to them
       with the line;
    they shall possess it for ever,
    from generation to generation they shall
       dwell in it.

The glory of the Lord

35 The wilderness and the dry land shall be
    glad,
    the desert shall rejoice and blossom;

like the crocus it shall blossom abundantly, 2
    and rejoice with joy and singing.
The glory of Lebanon shall be given to it,
    the majesty of Carmel and Sharon.
They shall see the glory of the LORD,
    the majesty of our God.

Strengthen the weak hands,   3
    and make firm the feeble knees.
Say to those who are of a fearful heart,   4
    "Be strong, fear not!
Behold, your God
    will come with vengeance,
    with the recompense of God.
    He will come and save you."

Then the eyes of the blind shall be opened, 5
    and the ears of the deaf unstopped;
then shall the lame man leap like a hart,   6
    and the tongue of the dumb sing for joy.
For waters shall break forth in the
       wilderness,
    and streams in the desert;
the burning sand shall become a pool,   7
    and the thirsty ground springs of water;
the haunt of jackals shall become a
       swamp,*a*
    the grass shall become reeds and rushes.

And a highway shall be there,   8
    and it shall be called the Holy Way;
the unclean shall not pass over it,*b*
    and fools shall not err therein.
No lion shall be there,   9
    nor shall any ravenous beast come up on
       it;
they shall not be found there,
    but the redeemed shall walk there.
And the ransomed of the LORD shall 10
       return,
    and come to Zion with singing;
everlasting joy shall be upon their heads;
    they shall obtain joy and gladness,
    and sorrow and sighing shall flee away.

ISAIAH AND HEZEKIAH

36 IN the fourteenth year of King Hezeki'-
    ah, Sennach'erib king of Assyria came up
against all the fortified cities of Judah and
2 took them. And the king of Assyria sent the
Rab'shakeh from Lachish to King Hezeki'ah
at Jerusalem, with a great army. And he
stood by the conduit of the upper pool on the
3 highway to the Fuller's Field. And there
came out to him Eli'akim the son of Hilki'ah,
who was over the household, and Shebna the

secretary, and Jo'ah the son of Asaph, the
recorder.

The Assyrian threat

And the Rab'shakeh said to them, "Say to 4
Hezeki'ah, 'Thus says the great king, the
king of Assyria: On what do you rest this
confidence of yours? Do you think that 5
mere words are strategy and power for war?

---

a Cn: Heb *in the haunt of jackals is her resting place*   *b* Heb *it and he is for them a wayfarer*
35.3: Heb 12.12.   35.5-6: Mt 11.5; Lk 7.22.   36.1-38.8, 21-22: 2 Kings 18.13-20.11; 2 Chron 32.1-24.

On whom do you now rely, that you have
6 rebelled against me? Behold, you are relying
on Egypt, that broken reed of a staff, which
will pierce the hand of any man who leans on
it. Such is Pharaoh king of Egypt to all who
7 rely on him. But if you say to me, "We rely
on the LORD our God," is it not he whose
high places and altars Hezeki′ah has
removed, saying to Judah and to Jerusalem,
"You shall worship before this altar"?
8 Come now, make a wager with my master the
king of Assyria: I will give you two thousand
horses, if you are able on your part to set
9 riders upon them. How then can you repulse
a single captain among the least of my
master's servants, when you rely on Egypt
10 for chariots and for horsemen? Moreover, is
it without the LORD that I have come up
against this land to destroy it? The LORD
said to me, Go up against this land, and
destroy it.'"
11 Then Eli′akim, Shebna, and Jo′ah said to
the Rab′shakeh, "Pray, speak to your servants in Aramaic, for we understand it; do
not speak to us in the language of Judah
within the hearing of the people who are on
12 the wall." But the Rab′shakeh said, "Has
my master sent me to speak these words to
your master and to you, and not to the men
sitting on the wall, who are doomed with you
to eat their own dung and drink their own
urine?"
13 Then the Rab′shakeh stood and called out
in a loud voice in the language of Judah:
"Hear the words of the great king, the king of
14 Assyria! Thus says the king: 'Do not let
Hezeki′ah deceive you, for he will not be able
15 to deliver you. Do not let Hezeki′ah make
you rely on the LORD by saying, "The LORD
will surely deliver us; this city will not be
given into the hand of the king of Assyria."
16 Do not listen to Hezeki′ah; for thus says the
king of Assyria: Make your peace with me
and come out to me; then every one of you
will eat of his own vine, and every one of his
own fig tree, and every one of you will drink
17 the water of his own cistern; until I come and
take you away to a land like your own land, a

land of grain and wine, a land of bread and
vineyards. Beware lest Hezeki′ah mislead
you by saying, "The LORD will deliver us."
18 Has any of the gods of the nations delivered
his land out of the hand of the king of
19 Assyria? Where are the gods of Hamath and
Arpad? Where are the gods of Sepharva′-
im? Have they delivered Samar′ia out of my
20 hand? Who among all the gods of these
countries have delivered their countries out
of my hand, that the LORD should deliver
Jerusalem out of my hand?'"
21 But they were silent and answered him not a
word, for the king's command was, "Do not
22 answer him." Then Eli′akim the son of
Hilki′ah, who was over the household, and
Shebna the secretary, and Jo′ah the son of
Asaph, the recorder, came to Hezeki′ah with
their clothes rent, and told him the words of
the Rab′shakeh.

When King Hezeki′ah heard it, he rent his **3**
clothes, and covered himself with sackcloth,
and went into the house of the LORD. And he **2**
sent Eli′akim, who was over the household,
and Shebna the secretary, and the senior
priests, clothed with sackcloth, to the
prophet Isaiah the son of Amoz. They said **3**
to him, "Thus says Hezeki′ah, 'This day is a
day of distress, of rebuke, and of disgrace;
children have come to the birth, and there is
no strength to bring them forth. It may be **4**
that the LORD your God heard the words of
the Rab′shakeh, whom his master the king of
Assyria has sent to mock the living God, and
will rebuke the words which the LORD your
God has heard; therefore lift up your prayer
for the remnant that is left.'"
When the servants of King Hezeki′ah came **5**
to Isaiah, Isaiah said to them, "Say to your **6**
master, 'Thus says the LORD: Do not be
afraid because of the words that you have
heard, with which the servants of the king of
Assyria have reviled me. Behold, I will put a **7**
spirit in him, so that he shall hear a rumour,
and return to his own land; and I will make
him fall by the sword in his own land.'"

The Rab'shakeh returned, and found the king of Assyria fighting against Libnah; for he had heard that the king had left Lachish. Now the king heard concerning Tirha'kah king of Ethiopia, "He has set out to fight against you." And when he heard it, he sent messengers to Hezeki'ah, saying, "Thus shall you speak to Hezeki'ah king of Judah: 'Do not let your God on whom you rely deceive you by promising that Jerusalem will not be given into the hand of the king of Assyria. Behold, you have heard what the kings of Assyria have done to all lands, destroying them utterly. And shall you be delivered? Have the gods of the nations delivered them, the nations which my fathers destroyed, Gozan, Haran, Rezeph, and the people of Eden who were in Telas'sar? Where is the king of Hamath, the king of Arpad, the king of the city of Sepharva'im, the king of Hena, or the king of Ivvah?'"

Hezekiah's prayer

Hezeki'ah received the letter from the hand of the messengers, and read it; and Hezeki'ah went up to the house of the LORD, and spread it before the LORD. And Hezeki'ah prayed to the LORD: "O LORD of hosts, God of Israel, who art enthroned above the cherubim, thou art the God, thou alone, of all the kingdoms of the earth; thou hast made heaven and earth. Incline thy ear, O LORD, and hear; open thy eyes, O LORD, and see; and hear all the words of Sennach'erib, which he has sent to mock the living God. Of a truth, O LORD, the kings of Assyria have laid waste all the nations and their lands, and have cast their gods into the fire; for they were no gods, but the work of men's hands, wood and stone; therefore they were destroyed. So now, O LORD our God, save us from his hand, that all the kingdoms of the earth may know that thou alone art the LORD."

Then Isaiah the son of Amoz sent to Hezeki'ah, saying, "Thus says the LORD, the God of Israel: Because you have prayed to me concerning Sennach'erib king of Assyria, this is the word that the LORD has spoken concerning him:

'She despises you, she scorns you—
the virgin daughter of Zion;
she wags her head behind you—
the daughter of Jerusalem.

'Whom have you mocked and reviled?
Against whom have you raised your voice
and haughtily lifted your eyes?
Against the Holy One of Israel!

By your servants you have mocked the 24
Lord,
and you have said, With my many chariots
I have gone up the heights of the mountains,
to the far recesses of Lebanon;
I felled its tallest cedars,
its choicest cypresses;
I came to its remotest height,
its densest forest.
I dug wells 25
and drank waters,
and I dried up with the sole of my foot
all the streams of Egypt.

'Have you not heard 26
that I determined it long ago?
I planned from days of old
what now I bring to pass,
that you should make fortified cities
crash into heaps of ruins,
while their inhabitants, shorn of strength, 27
are dismayed and confounded,
and have become like plants of the field
and like tender grass,
like grass on the housetops,
blighted[c] before it is grown.

'I know your sitting down 28
and your going out and coming in,
and your raging against me.
Because you have raged against me 29
and your arrogance has come to my ears,
I will put my hook in your nose
and my bit in your mouth,
and I will turn you back on the way
by which you came.'

"And this shall be the sign for you: this year 30 eat what grows of itself, and in the second year what springs of the same; then in the third year sow and reap, and plant vineyards, and eat their fruit. And the surviving rem- 31 nant of the house of Judah shall again take root downward, and bear fruit upward; for 32 out of Jerusalem shall go forth a remnant, and out of Mount Zion a band of survivors. The zeal of the LORD of hosts will accomplish this.

"Therefore thus says the LORD concerning 33 the king of Assyria: He shall not come into this city, or shoot an arrow there, or come before it with a shield, or cast up a siege mound against it. By the way that he came, 34 by the same he shall return, and he shall not come into this city, says the LORD. For I will 35 defend this city to save it, for my own sake and for the sake of my servant David."

c With 2 Kings 19.26: Heb *field*

36 And the angel of the LORD went forth, and slew a hundred and eighty-five thousand in the camp of the Assyrians; and when men arose early in the morning, behold, these 37 were all dead bodies. Then Sennach′erib king of Assyria departed, and went home and 38 dwelt at Nin′eveh. And as he was worshipping in the house of Nisroch his god, Adram′melech and Share′zer, his sons, slew him with the sword, and escaped into the land of Ararat. And E′sar-had′don his son reigned in his stead.

Hezekiah's sickness

38 In those days Hezeki′ah became sick and was at the point of death. And Isaiah the prophet the son of Amoz came to him, and said to him, "Thus says the LORD: Set your house in order; for you shall die, you shall 2 not recover." Then Hezeki′ah turned his 3 face to the wall, and prayed to the LORD, and said, "Remember now, O LORD, I beseech thee, how I have walked before thee in faithfulness and with a whole heart, and have done what is good in thy sight." And 4 Hezeki′ah wept bitterly. Then the word of 5 the LORD came to Isaiah: "Go and say to Hezeki′ah, Thus says the LORD, the God of David your father: I have heard your prayer, I have seen your tears; behold, I will add

fifteen years to your life. I will deliver you and this city out of the hand of the king of Assyria, and defend this city.

"This is the sign to you from the LORD, that the LORD will do this thing that he has promised: Behold, I will make the shadow cast by the declining sun on the dial of Ahaz turn back ten steps." So the sun turned back on the dial the ten steps by which it had declined. [d]

Hymn of thanksgiving

A writing of Hezeki′ah king of Judah, after he had been sick and had recovered from his sickness:
    I said, In the noontide of my days
        I must depart;
    I am consigned to the gates of Sheol
        for the rest of my years.
    I said, I shall not see the LORD
        in the land of the living;
    I shall look upon man no more
        among the inhabitants of the world.
    My dwelling is plucked up and removed
        from me
        like a shepherd's tent;
    like a weaver I have rolled up my life;
        he cuts me off from the loom;
    from day to night thou dost bring me to an
        end; [e]

[d] The Hebrew of this verse is obscure   [e] Heb uncertain

I cry for help[f] until morning;
  like a lion he breaks all my bones;
    from day to night thou dost bring me to
      an end.[g]

4 Like a swallow or a crane[g] I clamour,
    I moan like a dove.
  My eyes are weary with looking upward.
    O Lord, I am oppressed; be thou my
      security!
5 But what can I say? For he has spoken to
    me,
    and he himself has done it.
  All my sleep has fled[h]
    because of the bitterness of my soul.

6 O Lord, by these things men live,
    and in all these is the life of my spirit.[i]
  Oh, restore me to health and make me
    live!
7 Lo, it was for my welfare
    that I had great bitterness;
  but thou hast held back[j] my life
    from the pit of destruction,
  for thou hast cast all my sins
    behind thy back.
8 For Sheol cannot thank thee,
    death cannot praise thee;
  those who go down to the pit cannot hope
    for thy faithfulness.
9 The living, the living, he thanks thee,
    as I do this day;
  the father makes known to the children
    thy faithfulness.

20 The Lord will save me,
    and we will sing to stringed instru-
      ments[k]
  all the days of our life,
    at the house of the Lord.

21 Now Isaiah had said, "Let them take a cake
of figs, and apply it to the boil, that he may
22 recover." Hezeki′ah also had said, "What is
the sign that I shall go up to the house of the
Lord?"

Towards the captivity

39 At that time Mero′dach-bal′adan the son of
Bal′adan, king of Babylon, sent envoys with
letters and a present to Hezeki′ah, for he
heard that he had been sick and had
2 recovered. And Hezeki′ah welcomed them;
and he showed them his treasure house, the
silver, the gold, the spices, the precious oil,
his whole armoury, all that was found in his
storehouses. There was nothing in his house
or in all his realm that Hezeki′ah did not

show them. Then Isaiah the prophet came 3
to King Hezeki′ah, and said to him, "What
did these men say? And whence did they
come to you?" Hezeki′ah said, "They have
come to me from a far country, from
Babylon." He said, "What have they seen in 4
your house?" Hezeki′ah answered, "They
have seen all that is in my house; there is
nothing in my storehouses that I did not
show them."

Then Isaiah said to Hezeki′ah, "Hear the 5
word of the Lord of hosts: Behold, the days 6
are coming, when all that is in your house,
and that which your fathers have stored up
till this day, shall be carried to Babylon;
nothing shall be left, says the Lord. And 7
some of your own sons, who are born to you,
shall be taken away; and they shall be
eunuchs in the palace of the king of
Babylon." Then said Hezeki′ah to Isaiah, 8
"The word of the Lord which you have
spoken is good." For he thought, "There
will be peace and security in my days."

f Cn: Heb obscure g Heb uncertain h Cn Compare Syr: Heb I will walk slowly all my years
i Heb uncertain j Cn Compare Gk Vg: Heb loved k Heb my stringed instruments
39.1–8: 2 Kings 20.12–19; 2 Chron 32.31.

CONCERNING THE RETURN
TO JERUSALEM

B. C.
600–500

40   COMFORT, comfort my people,
     says your God.
2   Speak tenderly to Jerusalem,
     and cry to her
   that her warfare[1] is ended,
     that her iniquity is pardoned,
   that she has received from the LORD's
     hand
     double for all her sins.

3   A voice cries:
   "In the wilderness prepare the way of the
     LORD,
     make straight in the desert a highway for
     our God.
4   Every valley shall be lifted up,
     and every mountain and hill be made
     low;
   the uneven ground shall become level,
     and the rough places a plain.
5   And the glory of the LORD shall be
     revealed,
     and all flesh shall see it together,
     for the mouth of the LORD has spoken."

6   A voice says, "Cry!"
   And I said, "What shall I cry?"
   All flesh is grass,
     and all its beauty is like the flower of the
     field.
7   The grass withers, the flower fades,
     when the breath of the LORD blows
     upon it;
     surely the people is grass.
8   The grass withers, the flower fades;
     but the word of our God will stand for
     ever.

Behold your God

9   Get you up to a high mountain,
     O Zion, herald of good tidings;[m]
   lift up your voice with strength,
     O Jerusalem, herald of good tidings,[n]
   lift it up, fear not;
   say to the cities of Judah,
     "Behold your God!"
10   Behold, the Lord GOD comes with might,
     and his arm rules for him;
   behold, his reward is with him,
     and his recompense before him.
11   He will feed his flock like a shepherd,

he will gather the lambs in his arms,
he will carry them in his bosom,
   and gently lead those that are with
   young.

Who has measured the waters in the
   hollow of his hand   12
   and marked off the heavens with a span,
enclosed the dust of the earth in a measure
   and weighed the mountains in scales
   and the hills in a balance?
Who has directed the Spirit of the LORD,   13
   or as his counsellor has instructed him?
Whom did he consult for his enlighten-   14
   ment,
   and who taught him the path of justice,
and taught him knowledge,
   and showed him the way of understanding?
Behold, the nations are like a drop from a   15
   bucket,
   and are accounted as the dust on the
   scales;
   behold, he takes up the isles like fine
   dust.
Lebanon would not suffice for fuel,   16
   nor are its beasts enough for a burnt
   offering.
All the nations are as nothing before   17
   him,
   they are accounted by him as less than
   nothing and emptiness.

To whom then will you liken God,   18
   or what likeness compare with him?
The idol! a workman casts it,   19
   and a goldsmith overlays it with gold,
   and casts for it silver chains.
He who is impoverished[o] chooses for an   20
   offering
   wood that will not rot;
he seeks out a skilful craftsman
   to set up an image that will not move.

Have you not known? Have you not   21
   heard?
   Has it not been told you from the
   beginning?
   Have you not understood from the
   foundations of the earth?
It is he who sits above the circle of the   22
   earth,

[1] Or *time of service*   [m] Or *O herald of good tidings to Zion*   [n] Or *O herald of good tidings to Jerusalem*
[o] Heb uncertain
40.3: Mt 3.3; Mk 1.3; Lk 3.4; Jn 1.23.   **40.4–5:** Lk 3.5–6.   **40.6–8:** 1 Pet 1.24–25.
40.9: Is 52.7; Nah 1.15; Acts 10.36; Rom 10.15.   **40.10:** Rev 22.7, 12.   **40.13:** Rom 11.34; 1 Cor 2.16.

and its inhabitants are like grasshoppers;
who stretches out the heavens like a
curtain,
and spreads them like a tent to dwell in;
who brings princes to naught,
and makes the rulers of the earth as
nothing.

Scarcely are they planted, scarcely sown,
scarcely has their stem taken root in the
earth,
when he blows upon them, and they
wither,
and the tempest carries them off like
stubble.

To whom then will you compare me,
that I should be like him? says the
Holy One.
Lift up your eyes on high and see:
who created these?
He who brings out their host by number,
calling them all by name;
by the greatness of his might,
and because he is strong in power
not one is missing.

Why do you say, O Jacob,
and speak, O Israel,
"My way is hid from the LORD,
and my right is disregarded by my
God"?
Have you not known? Have you not
heard?
The LORD is the everlasting God,
the Creator of the ends of the earth.
He does not faint or grow weary,
his understanding is unsearchable.
He gives power to the faint,
and to him who has no might he
increases strength.
Even youths shall faint and be weary,
and young men shall fall exhausted;
but they who wait for the LORD shall
renew their strength,
they shall mount up with wings like
eagles,
they shall run and not be weary,
they shall walk and not faint.

41 Listen to me in silence, O coastlands;
let the peoples renew their strength;
let them approach, then let them speak;
let us together draw near for judgment.

2 Who stirred up one from the east
whom victory meets at every step?
He gives up nations before him,
so that he tramples kings under foot;

he makes them like dust with his sword,
like driven stubble with his bow.
He pursues them and passes on safely,   3
by paths his feet have not trod.
Who has performed and done this,   4
calling the generations from the beginning?
I, the LORD, the first,
and with the last; I am He.

The coastlands have seen and are afraid,   5
the ends of the earth tremble;
they have drawn near and come.
Every one helps his neighbour,   6
and says to his brother, "Take
courage!"
The craftsman encourages the goldsmith,   7
and he who smooths with the hammer
him who strikes the anvil,
saying of the soldering, "It is good";
and they fasten it with nails so that it
cannot be moved.

Appeal to exiles

But you, Israel, my servant,   8
Jacob, whom I have chosen,
the offspring of Abraham, my friend;
you whom I took from the ends of the   9
earth,
and called from its farthest corners,
saying to you, "You are my servant,
I have chosen you and not cast you off";
fear not, for I am with you,   10
be not dismayed, for I am your God;
I will strengthen you, I will help you,
I will uphold you with my victorious
right hand.

Behold, all who are incensed against you   11
shall be put to shame and confounded;
those who strive against you
shall be as nothing and shall perish.
You shall seek those who contend with   12
you,
but you shall not find them;
those who war against you
shall be as nothing at all.
For I, the LORD your God,   13
hold your right hand;
it is I who say to you, "Fear not,
I will help you."

Fear not, you worm Jacob,   14
you men of Israel!
I will help you, says the LORD;
your Redeemer is the Holy One of
Israel.
Behold, I will make of you a threshing   15
sledge,

41.8: Jas 2.23.   41.8–9: Lk 1.54; Heb 2.16.   41.10: Acts 18.10.

Isa **40**, 11

new, sharp, and having teeth;
you shall thresh the mountains and crush
   them,
and you shall make the hills like chaff;
16   you shall winnow them and the wind shall
   carry them away,
   and the tempest shall scatter them.
And you shall rejoice in the LORD;
   in the Holy One of Israel you shall
   glory.

17   When the poor and needy seek water,
   and there is none,
   and their tongue is parched with thirst,
   I the LORD will answer them,
   I the God of Israel will not forsake
   them.
18   I will open rivers on the bare heights,
   and fountains in the midst of the valleys;
   I will make the wilderness a pool of water,
   and the dry land springs of water.
19   I will put in the wilderness the cedar,
   the acacia, the myrtle, and the olive;
   I will set in the desert the cypress,
   the plane and the pine together;
20   that men may see and know,
   may consider and understand together,
   that the hand of the LORD has done this,
   the Holy One of Israel has created it.

Challenge to nations

21   Set forth your case, says the LORD;
   bring your proofs, says the King of
   Jacob.
22   Let them bring them, and tell us
   what is to happen.
   Tell us the former things, what they are,
   that we may consider them,

that we may know their outcome;
   or declare to us the things to come.
Tell us what is to come hereafter,
   that we may know that you are gods;
do good, or do harm,
   that we may be dismayed and terrified.
Behold, you are nothing,
   and your work is naught;
   an abomination is he who chooses you.

I stirred up one from the north, and he has
   come,
   from the rising of the sun, and he shall
   call on my name;
he shall trample *p* on rulers as on mortar,
   as the potter treads clay.
Who declared it from the beginning, that
   we might know,
   and beforetime, that we might say, "He
   is right"?
There was none who declared it, none who
   proclaimed,
   none who heard your words.
I first have declared it to Zion, *q*
   and I give to Jerusalem a herald of good
   tidings.
But when I look there is no one;
   among these there is no counsellor
   who, when I ask, gives an answer.
Behold, they are all a delusion;
   their works are nothing;
   their molten images are empty wind.

Behold my servant

Behold my servant, whom I uphold,   42
   my chosen, in whom my soul delights;
I have put my Spirit upon him,
   he will bring forth justice to the nations.

p Cn: Heb *come*   *q* Cn: Heb *first to Zion, Behold, behold them*
42.1–4: Mt 12.18–21.

He will not cry or lift up his voice,
  or make it heard in the street;
a bruised reed he will not break,
  and a dimly burning wick he will not
    quench;
  he will faithfully bring forth justice.
He will not fail[r] or be discouraged[s]
  till he has established justice in the
    earth;
  and the coastlands wait for his law.

Thus says God, the LORD,
  who created the heavens and stretched
    them out,
  who spread forth the earth and what
    comes from it,
who gives breath to the people upon it
  and spirit to those who walk in it:
"I am the LORD, I have called you in
    righteousness,
  I have taken you by the hand and kept
    you;
I have given you as a covenant to the
    people,
  a light to the nations,
  to open the eyes that are blind,
to bring out the prisoners from the dun-
    geon,
  from the prison those who sit in dark-
    ness.
I am the LORD, that is my name;
  my glory I give to no other,
  nor my praise to graven images.
Behold, the former things have come to
    pass,
  and new things I now declare;
before they spring forth
  I tell you of them."

Sing to the LORD a new song,
  his praise from the end of the earth!
Let the sea roar[t] and all that fills it,
  the coastlands and their inhabitants.
Let the desert and its cities lift up their
    voice,
  the villages that Kedar inhabits;
let the inhabitants of Sela sing for
    joy,
  let them shout from the top of the
    mountains.
Let them give glory to the LORD,
  and declare his praise in the coast-
    lands.
The LORD goes forth like a mighty man,
  like a man of war he stirs up his fury;
he cries out, he shouts aloud,
  he shows himself mighty against his
    foes.

For a long time I have held my peace,   14
  I have kept still and restrained myself;
now I will cry out like a woman in
    travail,
  I will gasp and pant.
I will lay waste mountains and hills,   15
  and dry up all their herbage;
I will turn the rivers into islands,
  and dry up the pools.
And I will lead the blind   16
  in a way that they know not,
in paths that they have not known
  I will guide them.
I will turn the darkness before them into
    light,
  the rough places into level ground.
These are the things I will do,
  and I will not forsake them.
They shall be turned back and utterly put   17
    to shame,
  who trust in graven images,
who say to molten images,
  "You are our gods."

Hear, you deaf;   18
  and look, you blind, that you may see!
Who is blind but my servant,   19
  or deaf as my messenger whom I send?
Who is blind as my dedicated one,
  or blind as the servant of the LORD?
He sees[u] many things, but does not   20
    observe them;
  his ears are open, but he does not hear.
The LORD was pleased, for his righteous-   21
    ness' sake,
  to magnify his law and make it glorious.
But this is a people robbed and plundered,   22
  they are all of them trapped in holes
  and hidden in prisons;
they have become a prey with none to
    rescue,
  a spoil with none to say, "Restore!"
Who among you will give ear to this,   23
  will attend and listen for the time to
    come?
Who gave up Jacob to the spoiler,   24
  and Israel to the robbers?
Was it not the LORD, against whom we
    have sinned,
  in whose ways they would not walk,
  and whose law they would not obey?
So he poured upon him the heat of his   25
    anger
  and the might of battle;
it set him on fire round about, but he did
    not understand;
  it burned him, but he did not take it to
    heart.

---

[r] Or *burn dimly*   [s] Or *bruised*   [t] Cn Compare Ps 96.11; 98.7: Heb *Those who go down to the sea*
[u] Heb *you see*
42.5: Acts 17.24-25.   **42.6:** Is 49.6; Lk 2.32; Acts 13.47; 26.23.   **42.7:** Acts 26.18.
42.16: Acts 26.18.

43 But now thus says the LORD,
    he who created you, O Jacob,
    he who formed you, O Israel:
"Fear not, for I have redeemed you;
    I have called you by name, you are
    mine.
2 When you pass through the waters I will
    be with you;
    and through the rivers, they shall not
    overwhelm you;
when you walk through fire you shall not
    be burned,
    and the flame shall not consume you.
3 For I am the LORD your God,
    the Holy One of Israel, your Saviour.
I give Egypt as your ransom,
    Ethiopia and Seba in exchange for you.
4 Because you are precious in my eyes,
    and honoured, and I love you,
I give men in return for you,
    peoples in exchange for your life.
5 Fear not, for I am with you;
    I will bring your offspring from the
    east,
    and from the west I will gather you;
6 I will say to the north, Give up,
    and to the south, Do not withhold;
bring my sons from afar
    and my daughters from the end of the
    earth,
7 every one who is called by my name,
    whom I created for my glory,
    whom I formed and made."

8 Bring forth the people who are blind, yet
    have eyes,
    who are deaf, yet have ears!
9 Let all the nations gather together,
    and let the peoples assemble.
Who among them can declare this,
    and show us the former things?
Let them bring their witnesses to justify
    them,
    and let them hear and say, It is true.
10 "You are my witnesses," says the LORD,
    "and my servant whom I have chosen,
that you may know and believe me
    and understand that I am He.
Before me no god was formed,
    nor shall there be any after me.
11 I, I am the LORD,
    and besides me there is no saviour.
12 I declared and saved and proclaimed,
    when there was no strange god among
    you;
    and you are my witnesses," says the
    LORD.
13 "I am God, and also henceforth I am
    He;

there is none who can deliver from my
    hand;
I work and who can hinder it?"

Fall of Babylon

Thus says the LORD,
    your Redeemer, the Holy One of Israel:
"For your sake I will send to Babylon
    and break down all the bars,
    and the shouting of the Chalde'ans will
    be turned to lamentations. *v*
I am the LORD, your Holy One,
    the Creator of Israel, your King."
Thus says the LORD,
    who makes a way in the sea,
    a path in the mighty waters,
who brings forth chariot and horse,
    army and warrior;
they lie down, they cannot rise,
    they are extinguished, quenched like a
    wick:
"Remember not the former things,
    nor consider the things of old.
Behold, I am doing a new thing;
    now it springs forth, do you not perceive
    it?
I will make a way in the wilderness
    and rivers in the desert.
The wild beasts will honour me,
    the jackals and the ostriches;
for I give water in the wilderness,
    rivers in the desert,
to give drink to my chosen people,
    the people whom I formed for myself
that they might declare my praise.

"Yet you did not call upon me, O Jacob;
    but you have been weary of me, O
    Israel!
You have not brought me your sheep for
    burnt offerings,
    or honoured me with your sacrifices.
I have not burdened you with offerings,
    or wearied you with frankincense.
You have not bought me sweet cane with
    money,
    or satisfied me with the fat of your
    sacrifices.
But you have burdened me with your sins,
    you have wearied me with your ini-
    quities.

"I, I am He
    who blots out your transgressions for
    my own sake,
    and I will not remember your sins.
Put me in remembrance, let us argue
    together;

v Heb obscure
43.5: Acts 18.10.

set forth your case, that you may be
proved right.
Your first father sinned,
and your mediators transgressed against
me.
Therefore I profaned the princes of the
sanctuary,
I delivered Jacob to utter destruction
and Israel to reviling.

"But now hear, O Jacob my servant,
Israel whom I have chosen!
Thus says the LORD who made you,
who formed you from the womb and
will help you:
Fear not, O Jacob my servant,
Jesh´urun whom I have chosen.
For I will pour water on the thirsty land,
and streams on the dry ground;
I will pour my Spirit upon your descen-
dants,
and my blessing on your offspring.
They shall spring up like grass amid
waters,^{w}
like willows by flowing streams.
This one will say, 'I am the LORD's,'
another will call himself by the name of
Jacob,
and another will write on his hand, 'The
LORD's,'
and surname himself by the name of
Israel."

Thus says the LORD, the King of Israel
and his Redeemer, the LORD of hosts:
"I am the first and I am the last;
besides me there is no god.
Who is like me? Let him proclaim it,
let him declare and set it forth before
me.
Who has announced from of old the things
to come?^{x}
Let them tell us^y what is yet to be.
Fear not, nor be afraid;
have I not told you from of old and
declared it?
And you are my witnesses!
Is there a God besides me?
There is no Rock; I know not any."

Folly of idolatry

All who make idols are nothing, and the
things they delight in do not profit; their
witnesses neither see nor know, that they
may be put to shame. Who fashions a god or
casts an image, that is profitable for
nothing? Behold, all his fellows shall be put
to shame, and the craftsmen are but men; let

them all assemble, let them stand forth, they
shall be terrified, they shall be put to shame
together.
The ironsmith fashions it^z and works it over 12
the coals; he shapes it with hammers, and
forges it with his strong arm; he becomes
hungry and his strength fails, he drinks no
water and is faint. The carpenter stretches a 13
line, he marks it out with a pencil; he
fashions it with planes, and marks it with a
compass; he shapes it into the figure of a
man, with the beauty of a man, to dwell in
a house. He cuts down cedars; or he chooses a 14
holm tree or an oak and lets it grow strong
among the trees of the forest; he plants a
cedar and the rain nourishes it. Then it 15
becomes fuel for a man; he takes a part of it
and warms himself, he kindles a fire and
bakes bread; also he makes a god and worships it, he makes it a graven image and falls
down before it. Half of it he burns in the 16
fire; over the half he eats flesh, he roasts meat
and is satisfied; also he warms himself and
says, "Aha, I am warm, I have seen the
fire!" And the rest of it he makes into a god, 17
his idol; and falls down to it and worships it;
he prays to it and says, "Deliver me, for thou
art my god!"
They know not, nor do they discern; for he 18
has shut their eyes, so that they cannot see,
and their minds, so that they cannot understand. No one considers, nor is there 19
knowledge or discernment to say, "Half of it
I burned in the fire, I also baked bread on its
coals, I roasted flesh and have eaten; and
shall I make the residue of it an abomination? Shall I fall down before a block of
wood?" He feeds on ashes; a deluded mind 20
has led him astray, and he cannot deliver
himself or say, "Is there not a lie in my right
hand?"

Let the universe rejoice

Remember these things, O Jacob,   21
and Israel, for you are my servant;
I formed you, you are my servant;
O Israel, you will not be forgotten by
me.
I have swept away your transgressions like 22
a cloud,
and your sins like mist;
return to me, for I have redeemed you.

Sing, O heavens, for the LORD has done 23
it;
shout, O depths of the earth;
break forth into singing, O mountains,
O forest, and every tree in it!

---

^{w} Gk Compare Tg: Heb *They shall spring up in among grass*
^{x} Cn: Heb *from my placing an eternal people and things to come* ^{y} Tg: Heb *them* ^{z} Cn: Heb *an axe*
44.6: Is 48.12; Rev 1.17; 2.8; 22.13.   **44.23:** Jer 51.48; Rev 12.12; 18.20.

For the LORD has redeemed Jacob,
and will be glorified in Israel.

The choice of Cyrus

24 Thus says the LORD, your Redeemer,
who formed you from the womb:
"I am the LORD, who made all things,
who stretched out the heavens alone,
who spread out the earth—Who was
with me?[a]—
25 who frustrates the omens of liars,
and makes fools of diviners;
who turns wise men back,
and makes their knowledge foolish;
26 who confirms the word of his servant,
and performs the counsel of his messengers;
who says of Jerusalem, 'She shall be
inhabited,'
and of the cities of Judah, 'They shall be
built,
and I will raise up their ruins';
27 who says to the deep, 'Be dry,
I will dry up your rivers';
28 who says of Cyrus, 'He is my shepherd,
and he shall fulfil all my purpose';
saying of Jerusalem, 'She shall be built,'
and of the temple, 'Your foundation
shall be laid.' "

The call of Cyrus

45 Thus says the LORD to his anointed, to
Cyrus,
whose right hand I have grasped,
to subdue nations before him
and ungird the loins of kings,
to open doors before him
that gates may not be closed:
2 "I will go before you
and level the mountains,[b]
I will break in pieces the doors of bronze
and cut asunder the bars of iron,
3 I will give you the treasures of darkness
and the hoards in secret places,
that you may know that it is I, the LORD,

the God of Israel, who call you by your
name.
For the sake of my servant Jacob,
and Israel my chosen,
I call you by your name,
I surname you, though you do not know
me.
I am the LORD, and there is no other,
besides me there is no God;
I gird you, though you do not know me,
that men may know, from the rising of the
sun
and from the west, that there is none
besides me;
I am the LORD, and there is no other.
I form light and create darkness,
I make weal and create woe,
I am the LORD, who do all these things.

"Shower, O heavens, from above,
and let the skies rain down righteousness;
let the earth open, that salvation may
sprout forth,[c]
and let it cause righteousness to spring
up also;
I the LORD have created it.

"Woe to him who strives with his Maker,
an earthern vessel with the potter![d]
Does the clay say to him who fashions it,
'What are you making'?
or 'Your work has no handles'?
Woe to him who says to a father, 'What
are you begetting?'
or to a woman, 'With what are you in
travail?' "
Thus says the LORD,
the Holy One of Israel, and his Maker:
"Will you question me[e] about my
children,
or command me concerning the work of
my hands?
I made the earth,
and created man upon it;
it was my hands that stretched out the
heavens,
and I commanded all their host.
I have aroused him in righteousness,
and I will make straight all his ways;
he shall build my city
and set my exiles free,
not for price or reward,"
says the LORD of hosts.

Thus says the LORD:
"The wealth of Egypt and the merchandise of Ethiopia,

---

[a] Another reading is *who spread out the earth by myself*   [b] One ancient Ms Gk: Heb *the swellings*
[c] One ancient Ms: Heb *that they may bring forth salvation*   [d] Cn: Heb *potsherds* or *potters*
[e] Cn: Heb *Ask me of things to come*
44.25: 1 Cor 1.20.   45.9: Is 29.16; Rom 9.20.   45.14: 1 Cor 14.25.

and the Sabe'ans, men of stature,
shall come over to you and be yours,
   they shall follow you;
   they shall come over in chains and bow
      down to you.
They will make supplication to you,
      saying:
   'God is with you only, and there is no
      other,
      no god besides him.' "
5 Truly, thou art a God who hidest thyself,
   O God of Israel, the Saviour.
6 All of them are put to shame and con-
      founded,
   the makers of idols go in confusion
      together.
7 But Israel is saved by the LORD
   with everlasting salvation;
   you shall not be put to shame or con-
      founded
   to all eternity.

8 For thus says the LORD,
   who created the heavens
      (he is God!),
   who formed the earth and made it
      (he established it;
   he did not create it a chaos,
      he formed it to be inhabited!):
   "I am the LORD, and there is no other.
19 I did not speak in secret,
      in a land of darkness;
   I did not say to the offspring of Jacob,
      'Seek me in chaos.'
   I the LORD speak the truth,
      I declare what is right.

20 "Assemble yourselves and come,
      draw near together,
   you survivors of the nations!
   They have no knowledge
   who carry about their wooden idols,
   and keep on praying to a god
      that cannot save.
21 Declare and present your case;
   let them take counsel together!
   Who told this long ago?
      Who declared it of old?
   Was it not I, the LORD?
   And there is no other god besides me,
   a righteous God and a Saviour;
      there is none besides me.

22 "Turn to me and be saved,
      all the ends of the earth!
   For I am God, and there is no other.
23 By myself I have sworn,
   from my mouth has gone forth in
      righteousness
   a word that shall not return:

'To me every knee shall bow,
   every tongue shall swear.'

"Only in the LORD, it shall be said of me, 24
   are righteousness and strength;
to him shall come and be ashamed,
   all who were incensed against him.
In the LORD all the offspring of Israel   25
   shall triumph and glory."

Gods of Babylon

Bel bows down, Nebo stoops,   **46**
   their idols are on beasts and cattle;
these things you carry are loaded as
   burdens on weary beasts.
They stoop, they bow down together,   2
   they cannot save the burden,
   but themselves go into captivity.

"Hearken to me, O house of Jacob,   3
   all the remnant of the house of Israel,
who have been borne by me from your
      birth,
   carried from the womb;
even to your old age I am He,   4
   and to grey hairs I will carry you.
I have made, and I will bear;
   I will carry and will save.

"To whom will you liken me and make me 5
      equal,
   and compare me, that we may be alike?
Those who lavish gold from the purse,   6
   and weigh out silver in the scales,
hire a goldsmith, and he makes it into a
      god;
   then they fall down and worship!
They lift it upon their shoulders, they 7
      carry it,
   they set it in its place, and it stands
      there;
   it cannot move from its place.
If one cries to it, it does not answer
   or save him from his trouble.

"Remember this and consider,   8
   recall it to mind, you transgressors,
   remember the former things of old;   9
for I am God, and there is no other;
   I am God, and there is none like me,
declaring the end from the beginning   10
   and from ancient times things not yet
      done,
saying, 'My counsel shall stand,
   and I will accomplish all my purpose,'
calling a bird of prey from the east,   11
   the man of my counsel from a far
      country.

45.17: Heb 5.9.   45.21: Acts 15.18.   45.23: Rom 14.11; Phil 2.10–11.

I have spoken, and I will bring it to pass;
I have purposed, and I will do it.

12 "Hearken to me, you stubborn of heart,
    you who are far from deliverance:
13 I bring near my deliverance, it is not far
    off,
    and my salvation will not tarry;
    I will put salvation in Zion,
    for Israel my glory."

Doom of Babylon

47 Come down and sit in the dust,
    O virgin daughter of Babylon;
    sit on the ground without a throne,
    O daughter of the Chalde´ans!
    For you shall no more be called
    tender and delicate.
2   Take the millstones and grind meal,
    put off your veil,
    strip off your robe, uncover your legs,
    pass through the rivers.
3   Your nakedness shall be uncovered,
    and your shame shall be seen.
    I will take vengeance,
    and I will spare no man.
4   Our Redeemer—the LORD of hosts is his
    name—
    is the Holy One of Israel.

5   Sit in silence, and go into darkness,
    O daughter of the Chalde´ans;
    for you shall no more be called
    the mistress of kingdoms.
6   I was angry with my people,
    I profaned my heritage;
    I gave them into your hand,
    you showed them no mercy;
    on the aged you made your yoke

exceedingly heavy.
You said, "I shall be mistress for ever,"   7
so that you did not lay these things to
heart
or remember their end.

Now therefore hear this, you lover of 8
pleasures,
who sit securely,
who say in your heart,
"I am, and there is no one besides me;
I shall not sit as a widow
or know the loss of children":
These two things shall come to you   9
in a moment, in one day;
the loss of children and widowhood
shall come upon you in full measure,
in spite of your many sorceries
and the great power of your enchantments.

You felt secure in your wickedness,   10
you said, "No one sees me";
your wisdom and your knowledge
led you astray,
and you said in your heart,
"I am, and there is no one besides me."
But evil shall come upon you,   11
for which you cannot atone;
disaster shall fall upon you,
which you will not be able to expiate;
and ruin shall come on you suddenly,
of which you know nothing.

Stand fast in your enchantments   12
and your many sorceries,
with which you have laboured from
your youth;
perhaps you may be able to succeed,
perhaps you may inspire terror.

47: Is 13.1–14.23; Jer 50–51; Hab 1–2.   47.8: Rev 18.7.   47.9: Rev 18.8.

You are wearied with your many counsels;
  let them stand forth and save you,
those who divide the heavens,
  who gaze at the stars,
who at the new moons predict
  what*f* shall befall you.

Behold, they are like stubble,
  the fire consumes them;
they cannot deliver themselves
  from the power of the flame.
No coal for warming oneself is this,
  no fire to sit before!
Such to you are those with whom you have
    laboured,
  who have trafficked with you from your
    youth;
they wander about each in his own
    direction;
  there is no one to save you.

Israel's obstinacy

8 Hear this, O house of Jacob,
    who are called by the name of Israel,
    and who came forth from the loins*g* of
      Judah;
  who swear by the name of the LORD,
    and confess the God of Israel,
    but not in truth or right.
2 For they call themselves after the holy city,
    and stay themselves on the God of
      Israel;
  the LORD of hosts is his name.

3 "The former things I declared of old,
    they went forth from my mouth and I
      made them known;
  then suddenly I did them and they came
    to pass.
4 Because I know that you are obstinate,
    and your neck is an iron sinew
    and your forehead brass,
5 I declared them to you from of old,
    before they came to pass I announced
      them to you,
  lest you should say, 'My idol did them,
    my graven image and my molten image
    commanded them.'

6 "You have heard; now see all this;
    and will you not declare it?
  From this time forth I make you hear new
    things,
    hidden things which you have not
      known.
7 They are created now, not long ago;
    before today you have never heard of
      them,

  lest you should say, 'Behold, I knew
    them.'
You have never heard, you have never 8
    known,
  from of old your ear has not been
    opened.
For I knew that you would deal very
    treacherously,
  and that from birth you were called a
    rebel.

"For my name's sake I defer my anger, 9
  for the sake of my praise I restrain it for
    you,
  that I may not cut you off.
Behold, I have refined you, but not like*h* 10
    silver;
  I have tried you in the furnace of
    affliction.
For my own sake, for my own sake, I do it, 11
  for how should my name*i* be profaned?
  My glory I will not give to another.

"Hearken to me, O Jacob,   12
  and Israel, whom I called!
I am He, I am the first,
  and I am the last.
My hand laid the foundation of the earth, 13
  and my right hand spread out the
    heavens;
when I call to them,
  they stand forth together.

"Assemble, all of you, and hear!   14
  Who among them has declared these
    things?
The LORD loves him;
  he shall perform his purpose on
    Babylon,
  and his arm shall be against the Chal-
    de'ans.
I, even I, have spoken and called him, 15
  I have brought him, and he will prosper
    in his way.
Draw near to me, hear this: 16
  from the beginning I have not spoken in
    secret,
  from the time it came to be I have been
    there."
And now the Lord GOD has sent me and
  his Spirit.

Thus says the LORD,   17
  your Redeemer, the Holy One of Israel:
"I am the LORD your God,
  who teaches you to profit,
  who leads you in the way you should go.
O that you had hearkened to my 18
  commandments!

---

f Gk Syr Compare Vg: Heb *from what*   *g* Cn: Heb *waters*   *h* Cn: Heb *with*
i Gk Old Latin: Heb lacks *my name*
48.12: Is 44.6; Rev 1.17; 2.8; 22.13.

Then your peace would have been like a river,
and your righteousness like the waves of the sea;

19 your offspring would have been like the sand,
and your descendants like its grains;
their name would never be cut off
or destroyed from before me."

20 Go forth from Babylon, flee from Chaldeʹa,
declare this with a shout of joy, proclaim it,
send it forth to the end of the earth;
say, "The LORD has redeemed his servant Jacob!"

21 They thirsted not when he led them through the deserts;
he made water flow for them from the rock;
he cleft the rock and the water gushed out.

22 "There is no peace," says the LORD, "for the wicked."

The servant's commission

49 Listen to me, O coastlands,
and hearken, you peoples from afar.
The LORD called me from the womb,
from the body of my mother he named my name.

2 He made my mouth like a sharp sword,
in the shadow of his hand he hid me;
he made me a polished arrow,
in his quiver he hid me away.

3 And he said to me, "You are my servant,
Israel, in whom I will be glorified."

4 But I said, "I have laboured in vain,
I have spent my strength for nothing and vanity;
yet surely my right is with the LORD,
and my recompense with my God."

5 And now the LORD says,
who formed me from the womb to be his servant,
to bring Jacob back to him,
and that Israel might be gathered to him,
for I am honoured in the eyes of the LORD,
and my God has become my strength—

6 he says:
"It is too light a thing that you should be my servant
to raise up the tribes of Jacob
and to restore the preserved of Israel;
I will give you as a light to the nations,

that my salvation may reach to the end of the earth."

7 Thus says the LORD,
the Redeemer of Israel and his Holy One,
to one deeply despised, abhorred by the nations,
the servant of rulers:
"Kings shall see and arise;
princes, and they shall prostrate themselves;
because of the LORD, who is faithful,
the Holy One of Israel, who has chosen you."

8 Thus says the LORD:
"In a time of favour I have answered you,
in a day of salvation I have helped you;
I have kept you and given you
as a covenant to the people,
to establish the land,
to apportion the desolate heritages;

9 saying to the prisoners, 'Come forth,'
to those who are in darkness, 'Appear.'
They shall feed along the ways,
on all bare heights shall be their pasture;

10 they shall not hunger or thirst,
neither scorching wind nor sun shall smite them,
for he who has pity on them will lead them,
and by springs of water will guide them.

11 And I will make all my mountains a way,
and my highways shall be raised up.

12 Lo, these shall come from afar,
and lo, these from the north and from the west,
and these from the land of Syene."ʲ

13 Sing for joy, O heavens, and exult, O earth;
break forth, O mountains, into singing!
For the LORD has comforted his people,
and will have compassion on his afflicted.

14 But Zion said, "The LORD has forsaken me,
my Lord has forgotten me."

15 "Can a woman forget her sucking child,
that she should have no compassion on the son of her womb?
Even these may forget,
yet I will not forget you.

16 Behold, I have graven you on the palms of my hands;
your walls are continually before me.

17 Your builders outstrip your destroyers,

ʲ Cn: Heb Sinim
49.1: Jer 1.5; Gal 1.15.   49.4: Phil 2.16.   49.6: Is 42.6; Lk 2.32; Acts 13.47; 26.23.   49.8: 2 Cor 6.2.
49.10: Rev 7.16.   49.13: Is 44.23; Jer 51.48; Rev 12.12; 18.20.

and those who laid you waste go forth
from you.
8 Lift up your eyes round about and see;
they all gather, they come to you.
As I live, says the LORD,
you shall put them all on as an
ornament,
you shall bind them on as a bride does.

9 "Surely your waste and your desolate
places
and your devastated land—
surely now you will be too narrow for your
inhabitants,
and those who swallowed you up will be
far away.
10 The children born in the time of your
bereavement
will yet say in your ears:
'The place is too narrow for me;
make room for me to dwell in.'
11 Then you will say in your heart:
'Who has borne me these?
I was bereaved and barren,
exiled and put away,
but who has brought up these?
Behold, I was left alone;
whence then have these come?' "

22 Thus says the Lord GOD:
"Behold, I will lift up my hand to the
nations,
and raise my signal to the peoples;
and they shall bring your sons in their
bosom,
and your daughters shall be carried on
their shoulders.
23 Kings shall be your foster fathers,
and their queens your nursing mothers.
With their faces to the ground they shall
bow down to you,
and lick the dust of your feet.
Then you will know that I am the LORD;
those who wait for me shall not be put to
shame."

24 Can the prey be taken from the mighty,
or the captives of a tyrant[k] be rescued?
25 Surely, thus says the LORD:
"Even the captives of the mighty shall be
taken,
and the prey of the tyrant be rescued,
for I will contend with those who contend
with you,
and I will save your children.
26 I will make your oppressors eat their own
flesh,
and they shall be drunk with their own
blood as with wine.

Then all flesh shall know
that I am the LORD your Saviour,
and your Redeemer, the Mighty One of
Jacob."

Thus says the LORD: 50
"Where is your mother's bill of divorce,
with which I put her away?
Or which of my creditors is it
to whom I have sold you?
Behold, for your iniquities you were sold,
and for your transgressions your mother
was put away.
Why, when I came, was there no man?   2
When I called, was there no one to
answer?
Is my hand shortened, that it cannot
redeem?
Or have I no power to deliver?
Behold, by my rebuke I dry up the sea,
I make the rivers a desert;
their fish stink for lack of water,
and die of thirst.
I clothe the heavens with blackness,   3
and make sackcloth their covering."

The servant's endowment

The Lord GOD has given me   4
the tongue of those who are taught,
that I may know how to sustain with a
word
him that is weary.
Morning by morning he wakens,
he wakens my ear
to hear as those who are taught.
The Lord GOD has opened my ear,   5
and I was not rebellious,
I turned not backward.
I gave my back to the smiters,   6
and my cheeks to those who pulled out
the beard;
I hid not my face
from shame and spitting.

For the Lord GOD helps me;   7
therefore I have not been confounded;
therefore I have set my face like a flint,
and I know that I shall not be put to
shame;
he who vindicates me is near.   8
Who will contend with me?
Let us stand up together.
Who is my adversary?
Let him come near to me.
Behold, the Lord GOD helps me;   9
who will declare me guilty?

---

[k] One ancient Ms Syr Vg: Heb *righteous man*
50.8–9: Rom 8.33; Heb 1.11.

Behold, all of them will wear out like a garment;
the moth will eat them up.

10 Who among you fears the LORD
and obeys the voice of his servant,
who walks in darkness
and has no light,
yet trusts in the name of the LORD
and relies upon his God?

11 Behold, all you who kindle a fire,
who set brands alight![l]
Walk by the light of your fire,
and by the brands which you have kindled!
This shall you have from my hand:
you shall lie down in torment.

51 "Hearken to me, you who pursue deliverance,
you who seek the LORD;
look to the rock from which you were hewn,
and to the quarry from which you were digged.

2 Look to Abraham your father
and to Sarah who bore you;
for when he was but one I called him,
and I blessed him and made him many.

3 For the LORD will comfort Zion;
he will comfort all her waste places,
and will make her wilderness like Eden,
her desert like the garden of the LORD;
joy and gladness will be found in her,
thanksgiving and the voice of song.

4 "Listen to me, my people,
and give ear to me, my nation;
for a law will go forth from me,
and my justice for a light to the peoples.

5 My deliverance draws near speedily,
my salvation has gone forth,
and my arms will rule the peoples;
the coastlands wait for me,
and for my arm they hope.

6 Lift up your eyes to the heavens,
and look at the earth beneath;
for the heavens will vanish like smoke,
the earth will wear out like a garment,
and they who dwell in it will die like gnats;[m]
but my salvation will be for ever,
and my deliverance will never be ended.

7 "Hearken to me, you who know righteousness,
the people in whose heart is my law;
fear not the reproach of men,
and be not dismayed at their revilings.

For the moth will eat them up like a 8 garment,
and the worm will eat them like wool;
but my deliverance will be for ever,
and my salvation to all generations."

The arm of the Lord

Awake, awake, put on strength, 9
O arm of the LORD;
awake, as in days of old,
the generations of long ago.
Was it not thou that didst cut Rahab in pieces,
that didst pierce the dragon?
Was it not thou that didst dry up the sea, 10
the waters of the great deep;
that didst make the depths of the sea a way
for the redeemed to pass over?
And the ransomed of the LORD shall 11 return,
and come to Zion with singing;
everlasting joy shall be upon their heads;
they shall obtain joy and gladness,
and sorrow and sighing shall flee away.

"I, I am he that comforts you; 12
who are you that you are afraid of man who dies,
of the son of man who is made like grass,
and have forgotten the LORD, your Maker, 13
who stretched out the heavens
and laid the foundations of the earth,
and fear continually all the day
because of the fury of the oppressor,
when he sets himself to destroy?
And where is the fury of the oppressor?
He who is bowed down shall speedily be 14 released;
he shall not die and go down to the Pit,
neither shall his bread fail.
For I am the LORD your God, 15
who stirs up the sea so that its waves roar—
the LORD of hosts is his name.
And I have put my words in your mouth, 16
and hid you in the shadow of my hand,
stretching out[n] the heavens
and laying the foundations of the earth,
and saying to Zion, 'You are my people.'"

Rouse yourself, rouse yourself, 17
stand up, O Jerusalem,
you who have drunk at the hand of the LORD
the cup of his wrath,
who have drunk to the dregs
the bowl of staggering.

---

[l] Syr: Heb *gird yourselves with brands*   [m] Or *in like manner*   [n] Syr: Heb *plant*
51.6: Heb 1.11.

There is none to guide her
   among all the sons she has borne;
there is none to take her by the hand
   among all the sons she has brought up.
These two things have befallen you—
   who will condole with you?—
devastation and destruction, famine and
   sword;
who will comfort you?[o]
Your sons have fainted,
   they lie at the head of every street
   like an antelope in a net;
they are full of the wrath of the LORD,
   the rebuke of your God.

Therefore hear this, you who are afflicted,
   who are drunk, but not with wine:
Thus says your Lord, the LORD,
   your God who pleads the cause of his
     people:
"Behold, I have taken from your hand
   the cup of staggering;
the bowl of my wrath
   you shall drink no more;
and I will put it into the hand of your
   tormentors,
   who have said to you,
   'Bow down, that we may pass over';
and you have made your back like the
   ground
   and like the street for them to pass
   over."

2 Awake, awake,
   put on your strength, O Zion;
put on your beautiful garments,
   O Jerusalem, the holy city;
for there shall no more come into you
   the uncircumcised and the unclean.
Shake yourself from the dust, arise,
   O captive[p] Jerusalem;
loose the bonds from your neck,
   O captive daughter of Zion.

3 For thus says the LORD: "You were sold for
nothing, and you shall be redeemed without
4 money. For thus says the Lord GOD: My
people went down at the first into Egypt to
sojourn there, and the Assyrian oppressed
5 them for nothing. Now therefore what have
I here, says the LORD, seeing that my people
are taken away for nothing? Their rulers
wail, says the LORD, and continually all the
6 day my name is despised. Therefore my
people shall know my name; therefore in that
day they shall know that it is I who speak;
here am I."

How beautiful upon the mountains   7
   are the feet of him who brings good
     tidings,
who publishes peace, who brings good
   tidings of good,
who publishes salvation,
   who says to Zion, "Your God reigns."
Hark, your watchmen lift up their voice,   8
   together they sing for joy;
for eye to eye they see
   the return of the LORD to Zion.
Break forth together into singing,   9
   you waste places of Jerusalem;
for the LORD has comforted his people,
   he has redeemed Jerusalem.
The LORD has bared his holy arm   10
   before the eyes of all the nations;
and all the ends of the earth shall see
   the salvation of our God.

Depart, depart, go out thence,   11
   touch no unclean thing;
go out from the midst of her, purify
   yourselves,
you who bear the vessels of the LORD.
For you shall not go out in haste,   12
   and you shall not go in flight,
for the LORD will go before you,
   and the God of Israel will be your rear
   guard.

The suffering servant

Behold, my servant shall prosper,   13
   he shall be exalted and lifted up,
   and shall be very high.
As many were astonished at him[q]—   14
   his appearance was so marred,
     beyond human semblance,
   and his form beyond that of the sons of
     men—
so shall he startle[r] many nations;   15
   kings shall shut their mouths because of
     him;
for that which has not been told them they
   shall see,
   and that which they have not heard they
   shall understand.

Who has believed what we have heard?   53
   And to whom has the arm of the LORD
   been revealed?
For he grew up before him like a young   2
   plant,
   and like a root out of dry ground;
he had no form or comeliness that we
   should look at him,

o One ancient Ms Gk Syr Vg: Heb *how may I comfort you*   p Cn: Heb *sit*   q Syr Tg: Heb *you*
r The meaning of the Hebrew word is uncertain
52.1: Rev 21.27.   52.5: Rom 2.24.   52.7: Acts 10.36; Rom 10.15; Eph 6.15.   52.10: Lk 2.30; 3.6.
52.11: 2 Cor 6.17.   52.15: Rom 15.21.   53.1: Jn 12.38; Rom 10.16.

and no beauty that we should desire
him.

3 He was despised and rejected[s] by men;
a man of sorrows,[t] and acquainted with
grief;[u]
and as one from whom men hide their
faces
he was despised, and we esteemed him
not.

4 Surely he has borne our griefs[v]
and carried our sorrows;[w]
yet we esteemed him stricken,
smitten by God, and afflicted.

5 But he was wounded for our transgressions,
he was bruised for our iniquities;
upon him was the chastisement that made
us whole,
and with his stripes we are healed.

6 All we like sheep have gone astray;
we have turned every one to his own
way;
and the LORD has laid on him
the iniquity of us all.

7 He was oppressed, and he was afflicted,
yet he opened not his mouth;
like a lamb that is led to the slaughter,
and like a sheep that before its shearers
is dumb,
so he opened not his mouth.

8 By oppression and judgment he was taken
away;
and as for his generation, who considered

that he was cut off out of the land of the
living,
stricken for the transgression of my
people?
And they made his grave with the wicked 9
and with a rich man in his death,
although he had done no violence,
and there was no deceit in his mouth.

Yet it was the will of the LORD to bruise 10
him;
he has put him to grief;[x]
when he makes himself[y] an offering for
sin,
he shall see his offspring, he shall
prolong his days;
the will of the LORD shall prosper in his
hand;
he shall see the fruit of the travail of his 11
soul and be satisfied;
by his knowledge shall the righteous one,
my servant,
make many to be accounted righteous;
and he shall bear their iniquities.
Therefore I will divide him a portion with 12
the great,
and he shall divide the spoil with the
strong;
because he poured out his soul to death,
and was numbered with the transgressors;
yet he bore the sin of many,
and made intercession for the transgressors.

Jerusalem's future

"Sing, O barren one, who did not bear; 54
break forth into singing and cry aloud,
you who have not been in travail!
For the children of the desolate one will be
more
than the children of her that is married,
says the LORD.
Enlarge the place of your tent, 2
and let the curtains of your habitations
be stretched out;
hold not back, lengthen your cords
and strengthen your stakes.
For you will spread abroad to the right and 3
to the left,
and your descendants will possess the
nations
and will people the desolate cities.

"Fear not, for you will not be ashamed; 4
be not confounded, for you will not be
put to shame;

[s] Or forsaken   [t] Or pains   [u] Or sickness   [v] Or sicknesses   [w] Or pains   [x] Heb made him sick
[y] Vg: Heb thou makest his soul
53.4: Mt 8.17.   53.5–6: I Pet 2.24–25.   53.7–8: Acts 8.32–33.   53.9: I Pet 2.22.
53.12: Lk 22.37.   54.1: Gal 4.27.

for you will forget the shame of your
youth,
and the reproach of your widowhood
you will remember no more.

5 For your Maker is your husband,
the LORD of hosts is his name;
and the Holy One of Israel is your
Redeemer,
the God of the whole earth he is called.

6 For the LORD has called you
like a wife forsaken and grieved in spirit,
like a wife of youth when she is cast
off,
says your God.

7 For a brief moment I forsook you,
but with great compassion I will gather
you.

8 In overflowing wrath for a moment
I hid my face from you,
but with everlasting love I will have
compassion on you,
says the LORD, your Redeemer.

9 "For this is like the days of Noah to me:
as I swore that the waters of Noah
should no more go over the earth,
so I have sworn that I will not be angry
with you
and will not rebuke you.

0 For the mountains may depart
and the hills be removed,
but my steadfast love shall not depart from
you,
and my covenant of peace shall not be
removed,
says the LORD, who has compassion on
you.

11 "O afflicted one, storm-tossed, and not
comforted,
behold, I will set your stones in
antimony,
and lay your foundations with
sapphires.ᶻ

12 I will make your pinnacles of agate,
your gates of carbuncles,
and all your wall of precious stones.

13 All your sons shall be taught by the LORD,
and great shall be the prosperity of your
sons.

14 In righteousness you shall be established;
you shall be far from oppression, for you
shall not fear;
and from terror, for it shall not come
near you.

15 If any one stirs up strife,
it is not from me;
whoever stirs up strife with you
shall fall because of you.

Behold, I have created the smith   16
who blows the fire of coals,
and produces a weapon for its purpose.
I have also created the ravager to destroy;
no weapon that is fashioned against you 17
shall prosper,
and you shall confute every tongue that
rises against you in judgment.
This is the heritage of the servants of the
LORD
and their vindication from me, says the
LORD."

Divine invitation to return

"Ho, every one who thirsts,   **55**
come to the waters;
and he who has no money,
come, buy and eat!
Come, buy wine and milk
without money and without price.
Why do you spend your money for that 2
which is not bread,
and your labour for that which does not
satisfy?
Hearken diligently to me, and eat what is
good,
and delight yourselves in fatness.
Incline your ear, and come to me;   3
hear, that your soul may live;
and I will make with you an everlasting
covenant,
my steadfast, sure love for David.
Behold, I made him a witness to the 4
peoples,
a leader and commander for the peoples.
Behold, you shall call nations that you 5
know not,
and nations that knew you not shall run
to you,
because of the LORD your God, and of the
Holy One of Israel,
for he has glorified you.

"Seek the LORD while he may be found,   6
call upon him while he is near;
let the wicked forsake his way,   7
and the unrighteous man his thoughts;
let him return to the LORD, that he may
have mercy on him,
and to our God, for he will abundantly
pardon.
For my thoughts are not your thoughts,   8
neither are your ways my ways, says the
LORD.
For as the heavens are higher than the 9
earth,
so are my ways higher than your ways
and my thoughts than your thoughts.

10 "For as the rain and the snow come down
        from the heaven,
      and return not thither but water the
        earth,
    making it bring forth and sprout,
      giving seed to the sower and bread to the
        eater,
11 so shall my word be that goes forth from
      my mouth;
    it shall not return to me empty,
    but it shall accomplish that which I
      purpose,
      and prosper in the thing for which I sent
        it.

12 "For you shall go out in joy,
      and be led forth in peace;
    the mountains and the hills before you
      shall break forth into singing,
      and all the trees of the field shall clap
        their hands.
13 Instead of the thorn shall come up the
      cypress;
      instead of the brier shall come up the
        myrtle;
    and it shall be to the LORD for a memorial,
      for an everlasting sign which shall not be
        cut off."

56 Thus says the LORD:
      "Keep justice, and do righteousness,
      for soon my salvation will come,
      and my deliverance be revealed.
2 Blessed is the man who does this,

and the son of man who holds it fast,
who keeps the sabbath, not profaning it,
    and keeps his hand from doing any
      evil."

Let not the foreigner who has joined 3
    himself to the LORD say,
  "The LORD will surely separate me from
    his people";
and let not the eunuch say,
  "Behold, I am a dry tree."
For thus says the LORD: 4
"To the eunuchs who keep my sabbaths,
    who choose the things that please me
      and hold fast my covenant,
I will give in my house and within my walls 5
    a monument and a name
    better than sons and daughters;
I will give them an everlasting name
    which shall not be cut off.

"And the foreigners who join themselves 6
    to the LORD,
    to minister to him, to love the name of
      the LORD,
    and to be his servants,
every one who keeps the sabbath, and does
      not profane it,
    and holds fast my covenant—
these I will bring to my holy mountain,   7
    and make them joyful in my house of
      prayer;
their burnt offerings and their sacrifices
    will be accepted on my altar;
for my house shall be called a house of
      prayer
    for all peoples.
Thus says the Lord GOD,   8
    who gathers the outcasts of Israel,
I will gather yet others to him
    besides those already gathered." a

All you beasts of the field, come to 9
      devour—
    all you beasts in the forest.
His watchmen are blind,   10
    they are all without knowledge;
they are all dumb dogs,
    they cannot bark;
dreaming, lying down,
    loving to slumber.
The dogs have a mighty appetite;   11
    they never have enough.
The shepherds also have no under-
      standing;
    they have all turned to their own way,
    each to his own gain, one and all.
"Come," they say, "let us b get wine,   12
    let us fill ourselves with strong drink;

a Heb his gathered ones   b One ancient Ms Syr Vg Tg: Heb me
55.10: 2 Cor 9.10.   56.7: Mt 21.13; Mk 11.17; Lk 19.46.

and tomorrow will be like this day,
    great beyond measure."

The righteous man perishes,
    and no one lays it to heart;
devout men are taken away,
    while no one understands.
For the righteous man is taken away from
    calamity,
    he enters into peace;
they rest in their beds
    who walk in their uprightness.
But you, draw near hither,
    sons of the sorceress,
offspring of the adulterer and the harlot.
Of whom are you making sport?
    Against whom do you open your mouth
      wide
    and put out your tongue?
Are you not children of transgression,
    the offspring of deceit,
you who burn with lust among the oaks,
    under every green tree;
who slay your children in the valleys,
    under the clefts of the rocks?
Among the smooth stones of the valley is
    your portion;
    they, they, are your lot;
to them you have poured out a drink
    offering,
    you have brought a cereal offering.
    Shall I be appeased for these things?
Upon a high and lofty mountain
    you have set your bed,
    and thither you went up to offer
      sacrifice.
Behind the door and the doorpost
    you have set up your symbol;
for, deserting me, you have uncovered
    your bed,
    you have gone up to it,
    you have made it wide;
and you have made a bargain for yourself
    with them,
    you have loved their bed,
    you have looked on nakedness.^{c}
You journeyed to Molech^d with oil
    and multiplied your perfumes;
you sent your envoys far off,
    and sent down even to Sheol.
You were wearied with the length of your
    way,
    but you did not say, "It is hopeless";
you found new life for your strength,
    and so you were not faint.

Whom did you dread and fear,
    so that you lied,
    and did not remember me,

did not give me a thought?
Have I not held my peace, even for a long
    time,
    and so you do not fear me?
I will tell of your righteousness and your 12
    doings,
    but they will not help you.
When you cry out, let your collection of 13
    idols deliver you!
The wind will carry them off,
    a breath will take them away.
But he who takes refuge in me shall
    possess the land,
    and shall inherit my holy mountain.

And it shall be said,   14
"Build up, build up, prepare the way,
    remove every obstruction from my
    people's way."
For thus says the high and lofty One   15
    who inhabits eternity, whose name is
    Holy:
"I dwell in the high and holy place,
    and also with him who is of a contrite
    and humble spirit,
to revive the spirit of the humble,
    and to revive the heart of the contrite.
For I will not contend for ever,   16
    nor will I always be angry;
for from me proceeds the spirit,
    and I have made the breath of life.
Because of the iniquity of his covetousness 17
    I was angry,
    I smote him, I hid my face and was
    angry;
    but he went on backsliding in the way of
    his own heart.
I have seen his ways, but I will heal him; 18
    I will lead him and requite him with
    comfort,
    creating for his mourners the fruit of the
    lips.
Peace, peace, to the far and to the near, 19
    says the LORD;
    and I will heal him.
But the wicked are like the tossing sea;   20
    for it cannot rest,
    and its waters toss up mire and dirt.
There is no peace, says my God, for the 21
    wicked."

"Cry aloud, spare not,   **58**
    lift up your voice like a trumpet;
declare to my people their transgression,
    to the house of Jacob their sins.
Yet they seek me daily,   2
    and delight to know my ways,
as if they were a nation that did righteous-
    ness

---

^{c} The meaning of the Hebrew is uncertain ^{d} Or *the king*
57.15: Mt 5.3. **57.19**: Acts 2.39; Eph 2.13, 17.

and did not forsake the ordinance of
   their God;
they ask of me righteous judgments,
   they delight to draw near to God.

3 'Why have we fasted, and thou seest it
   not?
   Why have we humbled ourselves, and
     thou takest no knowledge of it?'
Behold, in the day of your fast you seek
   your own pleasure,[e]
   and oppress all your workers.
4 Behold, you fast only to quarrel and to
   fight
   and to hit with wicked fist.
Fasting like yours this day
   will not make your voice to be heard on
   high.
5 Is such the fast that I choose,
   a day for a man to humble himself?
Is it to bow down his head like a rush,
   and to spread sackcloth and ashes under
   him?
Will you call this a fast,
   and a day acceptable to the LORD?

6 "Is not this the fast that I choose:
   to loose the bonds of wickedness,
   to undo the thongs of the yoke,
to let the oppressed go free,
   and to break every yoke?
7 Is it not to share your bread with the
   hungry,
   and bring the homeless poor into your
   house;
when you see the naked, to cover him,
   and not to hide yourself from your own
   flesh?
8 Then shall your light break forth like the
   dawn,
   and your healing shall spring up
   speedily;
your righteousness shall go before you,
   the glory of the LORD shall be your rear
   guard.
9 Then you shall call, and the LORD will
   answer;
   you shall cry, and he will say, Here I am.

"If you take away from the midst of you
   the yoke,
   the pointing of the finger, and speaking
   wickedness,
10 if you pour yourself out for the hungry
   and satisfy the desire of the afflicted,
then shall your light rise in the darkness
   and your gloom be as the noonday.
11 And the LORD will guide you continually,
   and satisfy your desire with good
   things,[f]

and make your bones strong;
and you shall be like a watered garden,
   like a spring of water,
   whose waters fail not.
And your ancient ruins shall be rebuilt;
   you shall raise up the foundations of
   many generations;
you shall be called the repairer of the
   breach,
   the restorer of streets to dwell in.

"If you turn back your foot from the
   sabbath,
   from doing your pleasure[g] on my holy
   day,
and call the sabbath a delight
   and the holy day of the LORD honourable;
if you honour it, not going your own ways,
   or seeking your own pleasure,[h] or
   talking idly;
then you shall take delight in the LORD,
   and I will make you ride upon the
   heights of the earth;
I will feed you with the heritage of Jacob
   your father,
   for the mouth of the LORD has spoken."

Behold, the LORD's hand is not shortened,
   that it cannot save,
   or his ear dull, that it cannot hear;
but your iniquities have made a separation
   between you and your God,
and your sins have hid his face from you
   so that he does not hear.
For your hands are defiled with blood
   and your fingers with iniquity;
your lips have spoken lies,
   your tongue mutters wickedness.
No one enters suit justly,
   no one goes to law honestly;
they rely on empty pleas, they speak
   lies,
   they conceive mischief and bring forth
   iniquity.
They hatch adders' eggs,
   they weave the spider's web;
he who eats their eggs dies,
   and from one which is crushed a viper is
   hatched.
Their webs will not serve as clothing;
   men will not cover themselves with what
   they make.
Their works are works of iniquity,
   and deeds of violence are in their hands.
Their feet run to evil,
   and they make haste to shed innocent
   blood;
their thoughts are thoughts of iniquity,

---

[e] Or pursue your own business   [f] The meaning of the Hebrew word is uncertain
[g] Or business   [h] Or pursuing your own business
58.6: Acts 8.23.   **59.7–8:** Rom 3.15–17.

desolation and destruction are in their
highways.

8 The way of peace they know not,
and there is no justice in their paths;
they have made their roads crooked,
no one who goes in them knows peace.

9 Therefore justice is far from us,
and righteousness does not overtake us;
we look for light, and behold, darkness,
and for brightness, but we walk in
gloom.

10 We grope for the wall like the blind,
we grope like those who have no eyes;
we stumble at noon as in the twilight,
among those in full vigour we are like
dead men.

11 We all growl like bears,
we moan and moan like doves;
we look for justice, but there is none;
for salvation, but it is far from us.

12 For our transgressions are multiplied
before thee,
and our sins testify against us;
for our transgressions are with us,
and we know our iniquities:

13 transgressing, and denying the LORD,
and turning away from following our
God,
speaking oppression and revolt,
conceiving and uttering from the heart
lying words.

14 Justice is turned back,
and righteousness stands afar off;
for truth has fallen in the public squares,
and uprightness cannot enter.

15 Truth is lacking,
and he who departs from evil makes
himself a prey.

The LORD saw it, and it displeased him
that there was no justice.

16 He saw that there was no man,
and wondered that there was no one to
intervene;
then his own arm brought him victory,
and his righteousness upheld him.

17 He put on righteousness as a breastplate,
and a helmet of salvation upon his head;
he put on garments of vengeance for
clothing,
and wrapped himself in fury as a mantle.

18 According to their deeds, so will he repay,
wrath to his adversaries, requital to his
enemies;
to the coastlands he will render requital.

19 So they shall fear the name of the LORD
from the west,
and his glory from the rising of the sun;

for he will come like a rushing stream,
which the wind of the LORD drives.

"And he will come to Zion as Redeemer, 20
to those in Jacob who turn from transgression, says the LORD.
"And as for me, this is my covenant with 21
them, says the LORD: my spirit which is upon
you, and my words which I have put in your
mouth, shall not depart out of your mouth,
or out of the mouth of your children, or out
of the mouth of your children's children, says
the LORD, from this time forth and for
evermore."

The new Jerusalem

Arise, shine; for your light has come,   **60**
and the glory of the LORD has risen upon
you.
For behold, darkness shall cover the earth, 2
and thick darkness the peoples;
but the LORD will arise upon you,
and his glory will be seen upon you.
And nations shall come to your light,   3
and kings to the brightness of your
rising.

Lift up your eyes round about, and see;   4
they all gather together, they come to
you;
your sons shall come from far,
and your daughters shall be carried in
the arms.
Then you shall see and be radiant,   5
your heart shall thrill and rejoice;[i]
because the abundance of the sea shall be
turned to you,
the wealth of the nations shall come to
you.
A multitude of camels shall cover you,   6
the young camels of Mid'ian and
Ephah;
all those from Sheba shall come.
They shall bring gold and frankincense,
and shall proclaim the praise of the
LORD.
All the flocks of Kedar shall be gathered to 7
you,
the rams of Nebai'oth shall minister to
you;
they shall come up with acceptance on my
altar,
and I will glorify my glorious house.

Who are these that fly like a cloud,   8
and like doves to their windows?
For the coastlands shall wait for me,   9
the ships of Tarshish first,

[i] Heb be enlarged
59.17: Eph 6.14, 17; 1 Thess 5.8.   59.19: Mt 8.11; Lk 13.29.   59.20–21: Rom 11.26–27.   60.6: Mt 2.11.

and your Redeemer, the Mighty One of
Jacob.

Instead of bronze I will bring gold,   17
   and instead of iron I will bring silver;
instead of wood, bronze,
   instead of stones, iron.
I will make your overseers peace
   and your taskmasters righteousness.
Violence shall no more be heard in your 18
   land,
   devastation or destruction within your
   borders;
you shall call your walls Salvation,
   and your gates Praise.

The sun shall be no more   19
   your light by day,
nor for brightness shall the moon
   give light to you by night;[j]
but the LORD will be your everlasting light,
   and your God will be your glory.
Your sun shall no more go down,   20
   nor your moon withdraw itself;
for the LORD will be your everlasting light,
   and your days of mourning shall be
   ended.
Your people shall all be righteous;   21
   they shall possess the land for ever,
the shoot of my planting, the work of my
   hands,
   that I might be glorified.
The least one shall become a clan,   22
   and the smallest one a mighty nation;
I am the LORD;
   in its time I will hasten it.

The Lord's anointed

The Spirit of the Lord GOD is upon me, **61**
   because the LORD has anointed me
to bring good tidings to the afflicted;[k]
   he has sent me to bind up the brokenhearted,
to proclaim liberty to the captives,
   and the opening of the prison[l] to those
   who are bound;
to proclaim the year of the LORD's favour, 2
   and the day of vengeance of our God;
   to comfort all who mourn;
to grant to those who mourn in Zion— 3
   to give them a garland instead of ashes,
the oil of gladness instead of mourning,
   the mantle of praise instead of a faint
   spirit;
that they may be called oaks of righteousness,
   the planting of the LORD, that he may be
   glorified.

to bring your sons from far,
   their silver and gold with them,
for the name of the LORD your God,
   and for the Holy One of Israel,
   because he has glorified you.

10 Foreigners shall build up your walls,
   and their kings shall minister to you;
for in my wrath I smote you,
   but in my favour I have had mercy on
   you.

11 Your gates shall be open continually;
   day and night they shall not be shut;
that men may bring to you the wealth of
   the nations,
   with their kings led in procession.

12 For the nation and kingdom
   that will not serve you shall perish;
   those nations shall be utterly laid waste.

13 The glory of Lebanon shall come to you,
   the cypress, the plane, and the pine,
to beautify the place of my sanctuary;
   and I will make the place of my feet
   glorious.

14 The sons of those who oppressed you
   shall come bending low to you;
and all who despised you
   shall bow down at your feet;
they shall call you the City of the LORD,
   the Zion of the Holy One of Israel.

15 Whereas you have been forsaken and
   hated,
   with no one passing through,
I will make you majestic for ever,
   a joy from age to age.

16 You shall suck the milk of nations,
   you shall suck the breast of kings;
and you shall know that I, the LORD, am
   your Saviour

---

[j] One ancient Ms Gk Old Latin Tg: Heb lacks *by night*   [k] Or *poor*
[l] Or *the opening of the eyes:* Heb *the opening*
60.11: Rev 21.25-26. 60.14: Rev 3.9. 60.19: Rev 21.23; 22.5. 61.1-2: Mt 11.5; Lk 4.18-19; 7.22.

4 They shall build up the ancient ruins,
   they shall raise up the former devastations;
they shall repair the ruined cities,
   the devastations of many generations.

5 Aliens shall stand and feed your flocks,
   foreigners shall be your ploughmen and vinedressers;
6 but you shall be called the priests of the LORD,
   men shall speak of you as the ministers of our God;
you shall eat the wealth of the nations,
   and in their riches you shall glory.
7 Instead of your shame you shall have a double portion,
   instead of dishonour you[m] shall rejoice in your[n] lot;
therefore in your[n] land you[m] shall possess a double portion;
   yours[o] shall be everlasting joy.

8 For I the LORD love justice,
   I hate robbery and wrong;[p]
I will faithfully give them their recompense,
   and I will make an everlasting covenant with them.
9 Their descendants shall be known among the nations,
   and their offspring in the midst of the peoples;
all who see them shall acknowledge them,
   that they are a people whom the LORD has blessed.

10 I will greatly rejoice in the LORD,
   my soul shall exult in my God;
for he has clothed me with the garments of salvation,
   he has covered me with the robe of righteousness,
as a bridegroom decks himself with a garland,
   and as a bride adorns herself with her jewels.
11 For as the earth brings forth its shoots,
   and as a garden causes what is sown in it to spring up,
so the Lord GOD will cause righteousness and praise
   to spring forth before all the nations.

62 For Zion's sake I will not keep silent,
   and for Jerusalem's sake I will not rest,
until her vindication goes forth as brightness,

and her salvation as a burning torch.
The nations shall see your vindication, 2
   and all the kings your glory;
and you shall be called by a new name
   which the mouth of the LORD will give.
You shall be a crown of beauty in the hand 3
   of the LORD,
   and a royal diadem in the hand of your God.
You shall no more be termed Forsaken,[q] 4
   and your land shall no more be termed Desolate;[r]
but you shall be called My delight is in her,[s]
   and your land Married;[t]
for the LORD delights in you,
   and your land shall be married.
For as a young man marries a virgin, 5
   so shall your sons marry you,
and as the bridegroom rejoices over the bride,
   so shall your God rejoice over you.

Upon your walls, O Jerusalem, 6
   I have set watchmen;
all the day and all the night
   they shall never be silent.
You who put the LORD in remembrance,
   take no rest,
and give him no rest 7
   until he establishes Jerusalem
   and makes it a praise in the earth.
The LORD has sworn by his right hand 8
   and by his mighty arm:
"I will not again give your grain
   to be food for your enemies,
and foreigners shall not drink your wine
   for which you have laboured;
but those who garner it shall eat it and 9
   praise the LORD,
and those who gather it shall drink it
   in the courts of my sanctuary."

Go through, go through the gates, 10
   prepare the way for the people;
build up, build up the highway,
   clear it of stones,
lift up an ensign over the peoples.
Behold, the LORD has proclaimed 11
   to the end of the earth:
Say to the daughter of Zion,
   "Behold, your salvation comes;
behold, his reward is with him,
   and his recompense before him."
And they shall be called The holy 12
   people,
   The redeemed of the LORD;
and you shall be called Sought out,
   a city not forsaken.

[m] Heb *they*   [n] Heb *their*   [o] Heb *theirs*   [p] Or *robbery with a burnt offering*   [q] Heb *Azubah*
[r] Heb *Shemamah*   [s] Heb *Hephzibah*   [t] Heb *Beulah*
61.6: Ex 19.6; 1 Pet 2.5; Rev 1.6; 5.10; 20.6.   62.2: Rev 2.17.

A day of judgment

63 Who is this that comes from Edom,
   in crimsoned garments from Bozrah,
he that is glorious in his apparel,
   marching in the greatness of his
     strength?

"It is I, announcing vindication,
   mighty to save."

2   Why is thy apparel red,
   and thy garments like his that treads in
     the wine press?

3   "I have trodden the wine press alone,
   and from the peoples no one was with
     me;
I trod them in my anger
   and trampled them in my wrath;
their lifeblood is sprinkled upon my
     garments,
   and I have stained all my raiment.
4   For the day of vengeance was in my heart,
   and my year of redemption[u] has come.
5   I looked, but there was no one to help;
   I was appalled, but there was no one to
     uphold;
so my own arm brought me victory,
   and my wrath upheld me.
6   I trod down the peoples in my anger,
   I made them drunk in my wrath,
   and I poured out their lifeblood on the
     earth."

7   I will recount the steadfast love of the
     LORD,
   the praises of the LORD,
according to all that the LORD has granted
     us,
   and the great goodness to the house of
     Israel
which he has granted them according to
     his mercy,
   according to the abundance of his
     steadfast love.
8   For he said, Surely they are my people,
   sons who will not deal falsely;
   and he became their Saviour.
9   In all their affliction he was afflicted,[v]
   and the angel of his presence saved
     them;
in his love and in his pity he redeemed
     them;
   he lifted them up and carried them all
     the days of old.

10   But they rebelled
   and grieved his holy Spirit;

therefore he turned to be their enemy,
   and himself fought against them.
Then he remembered the days of old,   11
   of Moses his servant.
Where is he who brought up out of the sea
   the shepherds of his flock?
Where is he who put in the midst of them
   his holy Spirit,
who caused his glorious arm   12
   to go at the right hand of Moses,
who divided the waters before them
   to make for himself an everlasting name,
   who led them through the depths?   13
Like a horse in the desert,
   they did not stumble.
Like cattle that go down into the valley,   14
   the Spirit of the LORD gave them rest.
So thou didst lead thy people,
   to make for thyself a glorious name.

Look down from heaven and see,   15
   from thy holy and glorious habitation.
Where are thy zeal and thy might?
   The yearning of thy heart and thy
     compassion
   are withheld from me.
For thou art our Father,   16
   though Abraham does not know us
   and Israel does not acknowledge us;
thou, O LORD, art our Father,
   our Redeemer from of old is thy name.
O LORD, why dost thou make us err from   17
   thy ways
   and harden our heart, so that we fear
     thee not?
Return for the sake of thy servants,
   the tribes of thy heritage.
Thy holy people possessed thy sanctuary a 18
   little while;
   our adversaries have trodden it down.
We have become like those over whom   19
   thou hast never ruled,
   like those who are not called by thy
     name.

O that thou wouldst rend the heavens and **64**
   come down,
   that the mountains might quake at thy
     presence—
as when fire kindles brushwood   2[w]
   and the fire causes water to boil—
to make thy name known to thy adver-
     saries,
   and that the nations might tremble at
     thy presence!
When thou didst terrible things which we 3
   looked not for,
   thou camest down, the mountains
     quaked at thy presence.

[u] Or *the year of my redeemed*   [v] Another reading is *he did not afflict*   [w] Ch 64.1 in Heb
63.1–6: Is 34; Jer 49.7–22; Ezek 25.12–14; 35; Amos 1.11–12; Obad; Mal 1.2–5.   **63.3:** Rev 19.15.
63.11: Heb 13.20.   **64.4:** 1 Cor 2.9.

4 From of old no one has heard
  or perceived by the ear,
no eye has seen a God besides thee,
  who works for those who wait for him.
5 Thou meetest him that joyfully works
    righteousness,
  those that remember thee in thy ways.
Behold, thou wast angry, and we sinned;
  in our sins we have been a long time,
  and shall we be saved? *z*
6 We have all become like one who is
    unclean,
  and all our righteous deeds are like a
    polluted garment.
We all fade like a leaf,
  and our iniquities, like the wind, take us
    away.
7 There is no one that calls upon thy name,
  that bestirs himself to take hold of thee;
for thou hast hid thy face from us,
  and hast delivered*v* us into the hand of
    our iniquities.

8 Yet, O LORD, thou art our Father;
  we are the clay, and thou art our potter;
  we are all the work of thy hand.
9 Be not exceedingly angry, O LORD,
  and remember not iniquity for ever.
  Behold, consider, we are all thy people.
10 Thy holy cities have become a wilderness,
  Zion has become a wilderness,
  Jerusalem a desolation.
11 Our holy and beautiful house,
  where our fathers praised thee,
has been burned by fire,
  and all our pleasant places have become
    ruins.
12 Wilt thou restrain thyself at these things,
    O LORD?
  Wilt thou keep silent, and afflict us
    sorely?

65 I was ready to be sought by those who did
    not ask for me;
  I was ready to be found by those who
    did not seek me.
I said, "Here am I, here am I,"
  to a nation that did not call on my name.
2 I spread out my hands all the day
  to a rebellious people,
who walk in a way that is not good,
  following their own devices;
3 a people who provoke me
  to my face continually,
sacrificing in gardens
  and burning incense upon bricks;
4 who sit in tombs,
  and spend the night in secret places;
who eat swine's flesh,

and broth of abominable things is in
    their vessels;
who say, "Keep to yourself,   5
  do not come near me, for I am set apart
    from you."
These are a smoke in my nostrils,
  a fire that burns all the day.
Behold, it is written before me: 6
  "I will not keep silent, but I will
    repay,
yea, I will repay into their bosom
  their*z* iniquities and their*z* fathers' 7
    iniquities together,
                              says the LORD;
because they burned incense upon the
    mountains
  and reviled me upon the hills,
I will measure into their bosom
  payment for their former doings."

Thus says the LORD: 8
"As the wine is found in the cluster,
  and they say, 'Do not destroy it,
    for there is a blessing in it,'
so I will do for my servants' sake,
  and not destroy them all.
I will bring forth descendants from Jacob, 9
  and from Judah inheritors of my
    mountains;
my chosen shall inherit it,
  and my servants shall dwell there.
Sharon shall become a pasture for flocks, 10
  and the Valley of Achor a place for herds
    to lie down,
  for my people who have sought me.
But you who forsake the LORD,   11
  who forget my holy mountain,
who set a table for Fortune
  and fill cups of mixed wine for Destiny;
I will destine you to the sword,   12
  and all of you shall bow down to the
    slaughter;
because, when I called, you did not
    answer,
  when I spoke, you did not listen,
but you did what was evil in my eyes,
  and chose what I did not delight in."

Therefore thus says the Lord GOD: 13
"Behold, my servants shall eat,
  but you shall be hungry;
behold, my servants shall drink,
  but you shall be thirsty;
behold, my servants shall rejoice,
  but you shall be put to shame;
behold, my servants shall sing for gladness 14
    of heart,
  but you shall cry out for pain of heart,
  and shall wail for anguish of spirit.

---

z Hebrew obscure   *v* Gk Syr Old Latin Tg: Heb *melted*   *z* Gk Syr: Heb *your*
65.1-2: Rom 10.20-21.

15 You shall leave your name to my chosen
      for a curse,
    and the Lord GOD will slay you;
    but his servants he will call by a
      different name.
16 So that he who blesses himself in the land
      shall bless himself by the God of truth,
    and he who takes an oath in the land
      shall swear by the God of truth;
    because the former troubles are forgotten
      and are hid from my eyes.

17 "For behold, I create new heavens and a new
      earth;
    and the former things shall not be
      remembered
      or come into mind.
18 But be glad and rejoice for ever
      in that which I create;
    for behold, I create Jerusalem a rejoicing,
      and her people a joy.
19 I will rejoice in Jerusalem,
      and be glad in my people;
    no more shall be heard in it the sound of
      weeping
    and the cry of distress.
20 No more shall there be in it
      an infant that lives but a few days,
    or an old man who does not fill out his
      days,
    for the child shall die a hundred years old,
      and the sinner a hundred years old shall
      be accursed.
21 They shall build houses and inhabit them;
      they shall plant vineyards and eat their
      fruit.
22 They shall not build and another inhabit;
      they shall not plant and another eat;
    for like the days of a tree shall the days of
      my people be,
    and my chosen shall long enjoy the work
      of their hands.
23 They shall not labour in vain,
      or bear children for calamity;[a]
    for they shall be the offspring of the
      blessed of the LORD,
    and their children with them.
24 Before they call I will answer,
      while they are yet speaking I will hear.
25 The wolf and the lamb shall feed together,
      the lion shall eat straw like the ox;
    and dust shall be the serpent's food.
    They shall not hurt or destroy
      in all my holy mountain,
                        says the LORD."

66 Thus says the LORD:
      "Heaven is my throne
        and the earth is my footstool;

what is the house which you would build
  for me,
and what is the place of my rest?
All these things my hand has made,   2
  and so all these things are mine,[b]
                            says the LORD.
But this is the man to whom I will look,
  he that is humble and contrite in
    spirit,
  and trembles at my word.

"He who slaughters an ox is like him who 3
    kills a man;
  he who sacrifices a lamb, like him who
    breaks a dog's neck;
he who presents a cereal offering, like him
    who offers swine's blood;
  he who makes a memorial offering of
    frankincense, like him who blesses an
    idol.
These have chosen their own ways,
  and their soul delights in their abomin-
    ations;
I also will choose affliction for them,   4
  and bring their fears upon them;
because, when I called, no one answered,
  when I spoke they did not listen;
but they did what was evil in my eyes,
  and chose that in which I did not
    delight."

Hear the word of the LORD,   5
  you who tremble at his word:
"Your brethren who hate you
  and cast you out for my name's sake
have said, 'Let the LORD be glorified,
  that we may see your joy';
but it is they who shall be put to
    shame.

"Hark, an uproar from the city!   6
  A voice from the temple!
The voice of the LORD,
  rendering recompense to his enemies!

"Before she was in labour   7
  she gave birth;
before her pain came upon her
  she was delivered of a son.
Who has heard such a thing?   8
  Who has seen such things?
Shall a land be born in one day?
  Shall a nation be brought forth in one
    moment?
For as soon as Zion was in labour
  she brought forth her sons.
Shall I bring to the birth and not cause to 9
    bring forth?
                        says the LORD;

---

a Or *sudden terror*   b Gk Syr: Heb *came to be*
65.17: Is 66.22; 2 Pet 3.13; Rev 21.1.   65.25: Is 11.6–9.   66.1–2: Mt 5.34; Acts 7.49–50.
66.6: Rev 16.1, 17.   66.7: Rev 12.5.

shall I, who cause to bring forth, shut the
    womb?
    says your God.

"Rejoice with Jerusalem, and be glad for
        her,
    all you who love her;
rejoice with her in joy,
    all you who mourn over her;
that you may suck and be satisfied
    with her consoling breasts;
that you may drink deeply with delight
    from the abundance of her glory."

For thus says the LORD:
"Behold, I will extend prosperity to her
        like a river,
    and the wealth of the nations like an
        overflowing stream;
and you shall suck, you shall be carried
    upon her hip,
    and dandled upon her knees.
As one whom his mother comforts,
    so I will comfort you;
    you shall be comforted in Jerusalem.
You shall see, and your heart shall
        rejoice;
    your bones shall flourish like the grass;
and it shall be known that the hand of the
    LORD is with his servants,
    and his indignation is against his
        enemies.

"For behold, the LORD will come in fire,
    and his chariots like the stormwind,
to render his anger in fury,
    and his rebuke with flames of fire.
For by fire will the LORD execute
        judgment,
    and by his sword, upon all flesh;
    and those slain by the LORD shall be
        many.

"Those who sanctify and purify themselves 17
to go into the gardens, following one in the
midst, eating swine's flesh and the abomination and mice, shall come to an end together, says the LORD.

"For I know^c their works and their 18
thoughts, and I am^d coming to gather all
nations and tongues; and they shall come and
shall see my glory, and I will set a sign among 19
them. And from them I will send survivors
to the nations, to Tarshish, Put,^{e} and Lud,
who draw the bow, to Tubal and Javan, to
the coastlands afar off, that have not heard
my fame or seen my glory; and they shall
declare my glory among the nations. And 20
they shall bring all your brethren from all the
nations as an offering to the LORD, upon
horses, and in chariots, and in litters, and
upon mules, and upon dromedaries, to my
holy mountain Jerusalem, says the LORD, just
as the Israelites bring their cereal offering in
a clean vessel to the house of the LORD. And 21
some of them also I will take for priests and
for Levites, says the LORD.

"For as the new heavens and the new earth 22
    which I will make
shall remain before me, says the LORD;
    so shall your descendants and your
        name remain.
From new moon to new moon,   23
    and from sabbath to sabbath,
all flesh shall come to worship before me,
    says the LORD.

"And they shall go forth and look on the 24
dead bodies of the men that have rebelled
against me; for their worm shall not die, their
fire shall not be quenched, and they shall be
an abhorrence to all flesh."

Jerusalem

THE BOOK OF

JEREMIAH

THE words of Jeremiah, the son of Hilki′ah, of the priests who were in An′athoth in the land of Benjamin, to 2 whom the word of the LORD came in the days of Josi′ah the son of Amon, king of Judah, in 3 the thirteenth year of his reign. It came also in the days of Jehoi′akim the son of Josi′ah, king of Judah, and until the end of the eleventh year of Zedeki′ah, the son of Josi′ah, king of Judah, until the captivity of Jerusalem in the fifth month.

The prophet's call

4 Now the word of the LORD came to me saying,
5 "Before I formed you in the womb I knew you,
and before you were born I consecrated you;
I appointed you a prophet to the nations."
6 Then I said, "Ah, Lord GOD! Behold, I do not know how to speak, for I am only a 7 youth." But the LORD said to me,
"Do not say, 'I am only a youth';
for to all to whom I send you you shall go,
and whatever I command you you shall speak.
8 Be not afraid of them,
for I am with you to deliver you,
says the LORD."

Then the LORD put forth his hand and 9 touched my mouth; and the LORD said to me,
"Behold, I have put my words in your mouth.
See, I have set you this day over nations 10 and over kingdoms,
to pluck up and to break down,
to destroy and to overthrow,
to build and to plant."
And the word of the LORD came to me, 11 saying, "Jeremiah, what do you see?" And I said, "I see a rod of almond."ᵃ Then the 12 LORD said to me, "You have seen well, for I am watchingᵇ over my word to perform it."
The word of the LORD came to me a second 13 time, saying, "What do you see?" And I said, "I see a boiling pot, facing away from the north." Then the LORD said to me, "Out 14 of the north evil shall break forth upon all the inhabitants of the land. For, lo, I am calling 15 all the tribes of the kingdoms of the north, says the LORD; and they shall come and every one shall set his throne at the entrance of the gates of Jerusalem, against all its walls round about, and against all the cities of Judah. And I will utter my judgments against them, 16 for all their wickedness in forsaking me; they have burned incense to other gods, and worshipped the works of their own hands. But you, gird up your loins; arise, and say to 17 them everything that I command you. Do not be dismayed by them, lest I dismay you

ᵃ Heb shaqed ᵇ Heb shoqed
1.5: Is 49.1; Gal 1.15. 1.8: Is 43.5; Acts 18.9-10. 1.10: Rev 10.11.

before them. And I, behold, I make you this day a fortified city, an iron pillar, and bronze walls, against the whole land, against the kings of Judah, its princes, its priests, and the people of the land. They will fight against you; but they shall not prevail against you, for I am with you, says the LORD, to deliver you."

THE WORD OF THE LORD TO JUDAH

THE word of the LORD came to me, saying, "Go and proclaim in the hearing of Jerusalem, Thus says the LORD,

I remember the devotion of your youth,
    your love as a bride,
how you followed me in the wilderness,
    in a land not sown.
Israel was holy to the LORD,
    the first fruits of his harvest.
All who ate of it became guilty;
    evil came upon them,"
                    says the LORD.

Hear the word of the LORD, O house of Jacob, and all the families of the house of Israel. Thus says the LORD:
"What wrong did your fathers find in me
    that they went far from me,
and went after worthlessness, and became worthless?
They did not say, 'Where is the LORD
    who brought us up from the land of Egypt,
who led us in the wilderness,
    in a land of deserts and pits,
in a land of drought and deep darkness,
    in a land that none passes through,
    where no man dwells?'
And I brought you into a plentiful land
    to enjoy its fruits and its good things.
But when you came in you defiled my land,
    and made my heritage an abomination.
The priests did not say, 'Where is the LORD?'
Those who handle the law did not know me;
    the rulers[c] transgressed against me;
the prophets prophesied by Ba'al,
    and went after things that do not profit.

The divine appeal

"Therefore I still contend with you,
                    says the LORD,
    and with your children's children I will contend.
For cross to the coasts of Cyprus and see,

B. C.
700–600

or send to Kedar and examine with care;
    see if there has been such a thing.
Has a nation changed its gods,   11
    even though they are no gods?
But my people have changed their glory
    for that which does not profit.
Be appalled, O heavens, at this,   12
    be shocked, be utterly desolate,
                    says the LORD,
for my people have committed two evils: 13
    they have forsaken me,
the fountain of living waters,
    and hewed out cisterns for themselves,
broken cisterns,
    that can hold no water.

"Is Israel a slave? Is he a homeborn   14
    servant?
Why then has he become a prey?
The lions have roared against him,   15
    they have roared loudly.
They have made his land a waste;
    his cities are in ruins, without inhabitant.
Moreover, the men of Memphis and   16
    Tah'panhes
have broken the crown of your head.
Have you not brought this upon yourself   17
    by forsaking the LORD your God,
    when he led you in the way?
And now what do you gain by going to   18
    Egypt,
    to drink the waters of the Nile?
Or what do you gain by going to Assyria,
    to drink the waters of the Euphra'tes?
Your wickedness will chasten you,   19
    and your apostasy will reprove you.
Know and see that it is evil and bitter
    for you to forsake the LORD your God;
    the fear of me is not in you,
                    says the Lord GOD of hosts.

"For long ago you broke your yoke   20
    and burst your bonds;
    and you said, 'I will not serve.'
Yea, upon every high hill
    and under every green tree
    you bowed down as a harlot.
Yet I planted you a choice vine,   21
    wholly of pure seed.
How then have you turned degenerate
    and become a wild vine?
Though you wash yourself with lye   22
    and use much soap,

---

c Heb *shepherds*

the stain of your guilt is still before me,
　　says the Lord GOD.

23 How can you say, 'I am not defiled,
　　I have not gone after the Ba′als'?
　Look at your way in the valley;
　　know what you have done—
　a restive young camel interlacing her
　　tracks,
24 a wild ass used to the wilderness,
　　in her heat sniffing the wind!
　Who can restrain her lust?
　None who seek her need weary them-
　　selves;
　　in her month they will find her.
25 Keep your feet from going unshod
　　and your throat from thirst.
　But you said, 'It is hopeless,
　　for I have loved strangers,
　　and after them I will go.'

26 "As a thief is shamed when caught,
　　so the house of Israel shall be shamed:
　they, their kings, their princes,
　　their priests, and their prophets,
27 who say to a tree, 'You are my father,'
　　and to a stone, 'You gave me birth.'
　For they have turned their back to me,
　　and not their face.
　But in the time of their trouble they say,
　　'Arise and save us!'
28 But where are your gods
　　that you made for yourself?
　Let them arise, if they can save you,
　　in your time of trouble;
　for as many as your cities
　　are your gods, O Judah.

29 "Why do you complain against me?
　　You have all rebelled against me,
　　　says the LORD.
30 In vain have I smitten your children,
　　they took no correction;
　your own sword devoured your prophets
　　like a ravening lion.
31 And you, O generation, heed the word of
　　the LORD.
　Have I been a wilderness to Israel,
　　or a land of thick darkness?
　Why then do my people say, 'We are free,
　　we will come no more to thee'?
32 Can a maiden forget her ornaments,
　　or a bride her attire?
　Yet my people have forgotten me
　　days without number.

33 "How well you direct your course
　　to seek lovers!
　So that even to wicked women
　　you have taught your ways.
34 Also on your skirts is found

the lifeblood of guiltless poor;
you did not find them breaking in.
　Yet in spite of all these things
you say, 'I am innocent;
　surely his anger has turned from me.'
Behold, I will bring you to judgment
　for saying, 'I have not sinned.'
How lightly you gad about,
　changing your way!
You shall be put to shame by Egypt
　as you were put to shame by Assyria.
From it too you will come away
　with your hands upon your head,
for the LORD has rejected those in whom
　you trust,
　and you will not prosper by them.

"If[d] a man divorces his wife
　and she goes from him
and becomes another man's wife,
　will he return to her?
Would not that land be greatly polluted?
You have played the harlot with many
　lovers;
　and would you return to me?
　　　　　　　　　　says the LORD.
Lift up your eyes to the bare heights, and
　see!
Where have you not been lain with?
By the waysides you have sat awaiting
　lovers
　like an Arab in the wilderness.
You have polluted the land
　with your vile harlotry.
Therefore the showers have been with-
　held,
　and the spring rain has not come;
yet you have a harlot's brow,
　you refuse to be ashamed.
Have you not just now called to me,
　'My father, thou art the friend of my
　　youth—
will he be angry for ever,
　will he be indignant to the end?'
Behold, you have spoken,
　but you have done all the evil that you
　　could."

Israel and Judah

　The LORD said to me in the days of King
Josi′ah: "Have you seen what she did, that
faithless one, Israel, how she went up on
every high hill and under every green tree,
and there played the harlot? And I thought,
'After she has done all this she will return to
me'; but she did not return, and her false
sister Judah saw it. She saw that for all the
adulteries of that faithless one, Israel, I had

---

[d] Gk Syr: Heb *Saying, If*

sent her away with a decree of divorce; yet her false sister Judah did not fear, but she too went and played the harlot. Because harlotry was so light to her, she polluted the land, committing adultery with stone and tree.

Jer I, II

Yet for all this her false sister Judah did not return to me with her whole heart, but in pretence, says the LORD."

And the LORD said to me, "Faithless Israel has shown herself less guilty than false Judah. Go, and proclaim these words toward the north, and say,

'Return, faithless Israel,
                  says the LORD.
I will not look on you in anger,
  for I am merciful,
                  says the LORD;
I will not be angry for ever.
Only acknowledge your guilt,
  that you rebelled against the LORD your God
and scattered your favours among
  strangers under every green tree,
  and that you have not obeyed my voice,
                  says the LORD.
Return, O faithless children,
                  says the LORD;
  for I am your master;
I will take you, one from a city and two
  from a family,
  and I will bring you to Zion.

" 'And I will give you shepherds after my own heart, who will feed you with knowledge and understanding. And when you have multiplied and increased in the land, in those days, says the LORD, they shall no more say, "The ark of the covenant of the LORD." It shall not come to mind, or be remembered, or missed; it shall not be made again. At that time Jerusalem shall be called the throne of the LORD, and all nations shall gather to it, to the presence of the LORD in Jerusalem, and they shall no more stubbornly follow their own evil heart. In those days the house of Judah shall join the house of Israel, and together they shall come from the land of the

north to the land that I gave your fathers for a heritage.

" 'I thought   19
  how I would set you among my sons,
and give you a pleasant land,
  a heritage most beauteous of all nations.
And I thought you would call me, My Father,
  and would not turn from following me.
Surely, as a faithless wife leaves her   20
  husband,
so have you been faithless to me, O house
  of Israel,
              says the LORD.' "

A voice on the bare heights is heard,   21
  the weeping and pleading of Israel's sons,
because they have perverted their way,
  they have forgotten the LORD their God.
"Return, O faithless sons,   22
  I will heal your faithlessness."
"Behold, we come to thee;
  for thou art the LORD our God.
Truly the hills are a delusion,   23
  the orgies on the mountains.
Truly in the LORD our God
  is the salvation of Israel.
"But from our youth the shameful thing has 24 devoured all for which our fathers laboured, their flocks and their herds, their sons and their daughters. Let us lie down in our 25 shame, and let our dishonour cover us; for we have sinned against the LORD our God, we and our fathers, from our youth even to this day; and we have not obeyed the voice of the LORD our God."

"If you return, O Israel,   **4**
              says the LORD,
  to me you should return.
If you remove your abominations from my
  presence,
  and do not waver,
and if you swear, 'As the LORD lives,'   2
  in truth, in justice, and in uprightness,
then nations shall bless themselves in him,
  and in him shall they glory."
For thus says the LORD to the men of Judah 3 and to the inhabitants of Jerusalem:

"Break up your fallow ground,
and sow not among thorns.
4 Circumcise yourselves to the LORD,
remove the foreskin of your hearts,
O men of Judah and inhabitants of
Jerusalem;
lest my wrath go forth like fire,
and burn with none to quench it,
because of the evil of your doings."

The coming judgment

5 Declare in Judah, and proclaim in Jerusalem, and say,
"Blow the trumpet through the land;
cry aloud and say,
'Assemble, and let us go
into the fortified cities!'
6 Raise a standard toward Zion,
flee for safety, stay not,
for I bring evil from the north,
and great destruction.
7 A lion has gone up from his thicket,
a destroyer of nations has set out;
he has gone forth from his place
to make your land a waste;
your cities will be ruins
without inhabitant.
8 For this gird you with sackcloth,
lament and wail;
for the fierce anger of the LORD
has not turned back from us."

9 "In that day, says the LORD, courage shall
fail both king and princes; the priests shall be
appalled and the prophets astounded."
10 Then I said, "Ah, Lord GOD, surely thou
hast utterly deceived this people and Jerusalem, saying, 'It shall be well with you';
whereas the sword has reached their very
life."

11 At that time it will be said to this people and
to Jerusalem, "A hot wind from the bare
heights in the desert toward the daughter of
12 my people, not to winnow or cleanse, a wind
too full for this comes for me. Now it is I
who speak in judgment upon them."
13 Behold, he comes up like clouds,
his chariots like the whirlwind;
his horses are swifter than eagles—
woe to us, for we are ruined!
14 O Jerusalem, wash your heart from
wickedness,
that you may be saved.
How long shall your evil thoughts
lodge within you?
15 For a voice declares from Dan
and proclaims evil from Mount E'phraim.
16 Warn the nations that he is coming;
announce to Jerusalem,

"Besiegers come from a distant land;
they shout against the cities of Judah.
Like keepers of a field are they against her
round about,
because she has rebelled against me,
             says the LORD.
Your ways and your doings
have brought this upon you.
This is your doom, and it is bitter;
it has reached your very heart."

The prophet's grief

My anguish, my anguish! I writhe in
pain!
Oh, the walls of my heart!
My heart is beating wildly;
I cannot keep silent;
for I hear the sound of the trumpet,
the alarm of war.
Disaster follows hard on disaster,
the whole land is laid waste.
Suddenly my tents are destroyed,
my curtains in a moment.
How long must I see the standard,
and hear the sound of the trumpet?
"For my people are foolish,
they know me not;
they are stupid children,
they have no understanding.
They are skilled in doing evil,
but how to do good they know not."

I looked on the earth, and lo, it was waste
and void;
and to the heavens, and they had no
light.
I looked on the mountains, and lo, they
were quaking,
and all the hills moved to and fro.
I looked, and lo, there was no man,
and all the birds of the air had fled.
I looked, and lo, the fruitful land was a
desert,
and all its cities were laid in ruins
before the LORD, before his fierce anger.
For thus says the LORD, "The whole land
shall be a desolation; yet I will not make a
full end.
For this the earth shall mourn,
and the heavens above be black;
for I have spoken, I have purposed;
I have not relented nor will I turn
back."

At the noise of horseman and archer
every city takes to flight;
they enter thickets; they climb among
rocks;
all the cities are forsaken,
and no man dwells in them.
And you, O desolate one,

what do you mean that you dress in scarlet,
that you deck yourself with ornaments
of gold,
that you enlarge your eyes with paint?
In vain you beautify yourself.
Your lovers despise you;
they seek your life.
31 For I heard a cry as of a woman in travail,
anguish as of one bringing forth her
first child,
the cry of the daughter of Zion gasping for
breath,
stretching out her hands,
"Woe is me! I am fainting before murderers."

A hopeless outlook

5 Run to and fro through the streets of
Jerusalem,
look and take note!
Search her squares to see
if you can find a man,
one who does justice
and seeks truth;
that I may pardon her.
2 Though they say, "As the LORD lives,"
yet they swear falsely.
3 O LORD, do not thy eyes look for truth?
Thou hast smitten them,
but they felt no anguish;
thou hast consumed them,
but they refused to take correction.
They have made their faces harder than
rock;
they have refused to repent.
4 Then I said, "These are only the poor,
they have no sense;
for they do not know the way of the LORD,
the law of their God.
5 I will go to the great,
and will speak to them;
for they know the way of the LORD,
the law of their God."
But they all alike had broken the yoke,
they had burst the bonds.
6 Therefore a lion from the forest shall slay
them,
a wolf from the desert shall destroy
them.
A leopard is watching against their cities,
every one who goes out of them shall be
torn in pieces;
because their transgressions are many,
their apostasies are great.
7 "How can I pardon you?
Your children have forsaken me,

and have sworn by those who are no
gods.
When I fed them to the full,
they committed adultery
and trooped to the houses of harlots.
They were well-fed lusty stallions,   8
each neighing for his neighbour's wife.
Shall I not punish them for these things? 9
says the LORD;
and shall I not avenge myself
on a nation such as this?

"Go up through her vine-rows and 10
destroy,
but make not a full end;
strip away her branches,
for they are not the LORD's.
For the house of Israel and the house of 11
Judah
have been utterly faithless to me,
says the LORD.
They have spoken falsely of the LORD,   12
and have said, 'He will do nothing;
no evil will come upon us,
nor shall we see sword or famine.
The prophets will become wind;   13
the word is not in them.
Thus shall it be done to them!' "

The Lord's agents

Therefore thus says the LORD, the God of 14
hosts:
"Because they[e] have spoken this word,
behold, I am making my words in your
mouth a fire,
and this people wood, and the fire shall
devour them.
Behold, I am bringing upon you   15
a nation from afar, O house of Israel,
says the LORD.
It is an enduring nation,
it is an ancient nation,
a nation whose language you do not know,
nor can you understand what they say.
Their quiver is like an open tomb,   16
they are all mighty men.
They shall eat up your harvest and your 17
food;
they shall eat up your sons and your
daughters;
they shall eat up your flocks and your
herds;
they shall eat up your vines and your fig
trees;
your fortified cities in which you trust
they shall destroy with the sword."

"But even in those days, says the LORD, I 18
will not make a full end of you. And when 19

e Heb you

your people say, 'Why has the LORD our God done all these things to us?' you shall say to them, 'As you have forsaken me and served foreign gods in your land, so you shall serve strangers in a land that is not yours.' "

20 Declare this in the house of Jacob,
   proclaim it in Judah:
21 "Hear this, O foolish and senseless people,
   who have eyes, but see not,
   who have ears, but hear not.
22 Do you not fear me? says the LORD;
   Do you not tremble before me?
   I placed the sand as the bound for the sea,
   a perpetual barrier which it cannot pass;
   though the waves toss, they cannot prevail,
   though they roar, they cannot pass over it.
23 But this people has a stubborn and rebellious heart;
   they have turned aside and gone away.
24 They do not say in their hearts,
   'Let us fear the LORD our God,
   who gives the rain in its season,
   the autumn rain and the spring rain,
   and keeps for us
   the weeks appointed for the harvest.'
25 Your iniquities have turned these away,
   and your sins have kept good from you.
26 For wicked men are found among my people;
   they lurk like fowlers lying in wait.[f]
   They set a trap;
   they catch men.
27 Like a basket full of birds,
   their houses are full of treachery;
   therefore they have become great and rich,
28 they have grown fat and sleek.
   They know no bounds in deeds of wickedness;
   they judge not with justice
   the cause of the fatherless, to make it prosper,
   and they do not defend the rights of the needy.
29 Shall I not punish them for these things?
                                    says the LORD,
   and shall I not avenge myself
   on a nation such as this?"

30 An appalling and horrible thing
   has happened in the land:
31 the prophets prophesy falsely,
   and the priests rule at their direction;
   my people love to have it so,
   but what will you do when the end comes?

The city is besieged

Flee for safety, O people of Benjamin,   6
   from the midst of Jerusalem!
Blow the trumpet in Teko'a,
   and raise a signal on Beth-hac-che'rem;
for evil looms out of the north,
   and great destruction.
The comely and delicately bred I will   2
   destroy,
   the daughter of Zion.
Shepherds with their flocks shall come   3
   against her;
   they shall pitch their tents around her,
   they shall pasture, each in his place.
"Prepare war against her;   4
   up, and let us attack at noon!"
"Woe to us, for the day declines,
   for the shadows of evening lengthen!"
"Up, and let us attack by night,   5
   and destroy her palaces!"

For thus says the LORD of hosts: 6
   "Hew down her trees;
   cast up a siege mound against Jerusalem.
This is the city which must be punished;
   there is nothing but oppression within her.
As a well keeps its water fresh,   7
   so she keeps fresh her wickedness;
violence and destruction are heard within her;
   sickness and wounds are ever before me.
Be warned, O Jerusalem,   8
   lest I be alienated from you;
   lest I make you a desolation,
   an uninhabited land."

Thus says the LORD of hosts: 9
   "Glean[g] thoroughly as a vine
   the remnant of Israel;
like a grape-gatherer pass your hand again
   over its branches."
To whom shall I speak and give warning, 10
   that they may hear?
Behold, their ears are closed,[h]
   they cannot listen;
behold, the word of the LORD is to them an
   object of scorn,
   they take no pleasure in it.
Therefore I am full of the wrath of the 11
   LORD;
   I am weary of holding it in.
"Pour it out upon the children in the street,
   and upon the gatherings of young men, also;
both husband and wife shall be taken,

[f] Heb uncertain   [g] Cn: Heb they shall glean   [h] Heb uncircumcised
5.21: Is 6.9–10; Mt 13.10–15; Mk 8.17–18.

the old folk and the very aged.
Their houses shall be turned over to others,
    their fields and wives together;
for I will stretch out my hand
    against the inhabitants of the land,"
                                    says the LORD.
"For from the least to the greatest of them,
    every one is greedy for unjust gain;
and from prophet to priest,
    every one deals falsely.
They have healed the wound of my people lightly,
    saying, 'Peace, peace,'
    when there is no peace.
Were they ashamed when they committed abomination?
    No, they were not at all ashamed;
    they did not know how to blush.
Therefore they shall fall among those who fall;
    at the time that I punish them,
    they shall be overthrown,"
                                    says the LORD.

Thus says the LORD:
"Stand by the roads, and look,
    and ask for the ancient paths,
where the good way is; and walk in it,
    and find rest for your souls.
But they said, 'We will not walk in it.'
I set watchmen over you, saying,
    'Give heed to the sound of the trumpet!'
But they said, 'We will not give heed.'
Therefore hear, O nations,
    and know, O congregation, what will happen to them.
Hear, O earth; behold, I am bringing evil upon this people,
    the fruit of their devices,
because they have not given heed to my words;
    and as for my law, they have rejected it.
To what purpose does frankincense come to me from Sheba,
    or sweet cane from a distant land?
Your burnt offerings are not acceptable,
    nor your sacrifices pleasing to me.
Therefore thus says the LORD:
'Behold, I will lay before this people
    stumbling blocks against which they shall stumble;
fathers and sons together,
    neighbour and friend shall perish.' "

Thus says the LORD:
"Behold, a people is coming from the north country,
    a great nation is stirring from the farthest parts of the earth.

They lay hold on bow and spear, 23
    they are cruel and have no mercy,
    the sound of them is like the roaring sea;
they ride upon horses,
    set in array as a man for battle,
    against you, O daughter of Zion!"
We have heard the report of it, 24
    our hands fall helpless;
anguish has taken hold of us,
    pain as of a woman in travail.
Go not forth into the field, 25
    nor walk on the road;
for the enemy has a sword,
    terror is on every side.
O daughter of my people, gird on sack- 26
    cloth,
    and roll in ashes;
make mourning as for an only son,
    most bitter lamentation;
for suddenly the destroyer
    will come upon us.

"I have made you an assayer and tester 27
    among my people,
    that you may know and assay their ways.
They are all stubbornly rebellious, 28
    going about with slanders;
they are bronze and iron,
    all of them act corruptly.
The bellows blow fiercely, 29
    the lead is consumed by the fire;
in vain the refining goes on,
    for the wicked are not removed.
Refuse silver they are called, 30
    for the LORD has rejected them."

The temple proclamation

The word that came to Jeremiah from the 7
LORD: "Stand in the gate of the LORD's 2
house, and proclaim there this word, and say,
Hear the word of the LORD, all you men of
Judah who enter these gates to worship the
LORD. Thus says the LORD of hosts, the God 3
of Israel, Amend your ways and your doings,
and I will let you dwell in this place. Do not 4
trust in these deceptive words: 'This is the
temple of the LORD, the temple of the LORD,
the temple of the LORD.'
"For if you truly amend your ways and your 5
doings, if you truly execute justice one with
another, if you do not oppress the alien, the 6
fatherless or the widow, or shed innocent
blood in this place, and if you do not go after
other gods to your own hurt, then I will let 7
you dwell in this place, in the land that I gave
of old to your fathers for ever.
"Behold, you trust in deceptive words to no 8
avail. Will you steal, murder, commit 9

adultery, swear falsely, burn incense to Ba′al, and go after other gods that you have not 10 known, and then come and stand before me in this house, which is called by my name, and say, 'We are delivered!'—only to go on 11 doing all these abominations? Has this house, which is called by my name, become a den of robbers in your eyes? Behold, I 12 myself have seen it, says the LORD. Go now to my place that was in Shiloh, where I made my name dwell at first, and see what I did to it for the wickedness of my people Israel. 13 And now, because you have done all these things, says the LORD, and when I spoke to you persistently you did not listen, and when 14 I called you, you did not answer, therefore I will do to the house which is called by my name, and in which you trust, and to the place which I gave to you and to your fathers, 15 as I did to Shiloh. And I will cast you out of my sight, as I cast out all your kinsmen, all the offspring of E′phraim.

16 "As for you, do not pray for this people, or lift up cry or prayer for them, and do not 17 intercede with me, for I do not hear you. Do you not see what they are doing in the cities of Judah and in the streets of Jerusalem? 18 The children gather wood, the fathers kindle fire, and the women knead dough, to make cakes for the queen of heaven; and they pour out drink offerings to other gods, to provoke 19 me to anger. Is it I whom they provoke? says the LORD. Is it not themselves, to their 20 own confusion? Therefore thus says the Lord GOD: Behold, my anger and my wrath will be poured out on this place, upon man and beast, upon the trees of the field and the fruit of the ground; it will burn and not be quenched."

21 Thus says the LORD of hosts, the God of Israel: "Add your burnt offerings to your 22 sacrifices, and eat the flesh. For in the day that I brought them out of the land of Egypt, I did not speak to your fathers or command them concerning burnt offerings and sacri- 23 fices. But this command I gave them, 'Obey my voice, and I will be your God, and you shall be my people; and walk in all the way that I command you, that it may be well with 24 you.' But they did not obey or incline their ear, but walked in their own counsels and the stubbornness of their evil hearts, and went 25 backward and not forward. From the day that your fathers came out of the land of Egypt to this day, I have persistently sent all my servants the prophets to them, day after 26 day; yet they did not listen to me, or incline their ear, but stiffened their neck. They did worse than their fathers.

Let Jerusalem mourn

"So you shall speak all these words to them, but they will not listen to you. You shall call to them, but they will not answer you. And you shall say to them, 'This is the nation that did not obey the voice of the LORD their God, and did not accept discipline; truth has perished; it is cut off from their lips.

Cut off your hair and cast it away;
    raise a lamentation on the bare heights,
for the LORD has rejected and forsaken
    the generation of his wrath.'

"For the sons of Judah have done evil in my sight, says the LORD; they have set their abominations in the house which is called by my name, to defile it. And they have built the high place[i] of Topheth, which is in the valley of the son of Hinnom, to burn their sons and their daughters in the fire; which I did not command, nor did it come into my mind. Therefore, behold, the days are coming, says the LORD, when it will no more be called Topheth, or the valley of the son of Hinnom, but the valley of Slaughter: for they will bury in Topheth, because there is no room elsewhere. And the dead bodies of this people will be food for the birds of the air, and for the beasts of the earth; and none will frighten them away. And I will make to cease from the cities of Judah and from the streets of Jerusalem the voice of mirth and the voice of gladness, the voice of the bridegroom and the voice of the bride; for the land shall become a waste.

"At that time, says the LORD, the bones of the kings of Judah, the bones of its princes, the bones of the priests, the bones of the prophets, and the bones of the inhabitants of Jerusalem shall be brought out of their tombs; and they shall be spread before the sun and the moon and all the host of heaven, which they have loved and served, which they have gone after, and which they have sought and worshipped; and they shall not be gathered or buried; they shall be as dung on the surface of the ground. Death shall be preferred to life by all the remnant that remains of this evil family in all the places where I have driven them, says the LORD of hosts.

No man repented

"You shall say to them, Thus says the
    LORD:
When men fall, do they not rise again?
If one turns away, does he not return?

Why then has this people turned away
   in perpetual backsliding?
They hold fast to deceit,
   they refuse to return.
I have given heed and listened,
   but they have not spoken aright;
no man repents of his wickedness,
   saying, 'What have I done?'
Every one turns to his own course,
   like a horse plunging headlong into
     battle.
Even the stork in the heavens
   knows her times;
and the turtledove, swallow, and crane[j]
   keep the time of their coming;
but my people know not
   the ordinance of the Lord.

"How can you say, 'We are wise,
   and the law of the Lord is with us'?
But, behold, the false pen of the scribes
   has made it into a lie.
The wise men shall be put to shame,
   they shall be dismayed and taken;
lo, they have rejected the word of the
    Lord,
   and what wisdom is in them?
Therefore I will give their wives to others
   and their fields to conquerors,
because from the least to the greatest
   every one is greedy for unjust gain;
from prophet to priest
   every one deals falsely.
They have healed the wound of my people
    lightly,
   saying, 'Peace, peace,'
   when there is no peace.
Were they ashamed when they committed
    abomination?
   No, they were not at all ashamed;
   they did not know how to blush.
Therefore they shall fall among the fallen;
   when I punish them, they shall be
    overthrown,
                 says the Lord.
When I would gather them, says the Lord,
   there are no grapes on the vine,

nor figs on the fig tree;
even the leaves are withered,
   and what I gave them has passed away
    from them."[k]

Why do we sit still?
Gather together, let us go into the fortified
    cities
   and perish there;
for the Lord our God has doomed us to
    perish,
   and has given us poisoned water to
    drink,
   because we have sinned against the
    Lord.
We looked for peace, but no good came,
   for a time of healing, but behold, terror.

"The snorting of their horses is heard
    from Dan;
at the sound of the neighing of their
    stallions
   the whole land quakes.
They come and devour the land and all
    that fills it,
   the city and those who dwell in it.
For behold, I am sending among you
    serpents,
adders which cannot be charmed,
   and they shall bite you,"
                 says the Lord.

The prophet's sorrow

My grief is beyond healing,[l]
   my heart is sick within me.

---

[j] The meaning of the Hebrew word is uncertain   [k] Heb uncertain   [l] Cn Compare Gk: Heb uncertain

19 Hark, the cry of the daughter of my people
 from the length and breadth of the land:
"Is the LORD not in Zion?
 Is her King not in her?"
"Why have they provoked me to anger
 with their graven images,
 and with their foreign idols?"
20 "The harvest is past, the summer is ended,
 and we are not saved."
21 For the wound of the daughter of my
 people is my heart wounded,
 I mourn, and dismay has taken hold on
 me.

22 Is there no balm in Gilead?
 Is there no physician there?
Why then has the health of the daughter of
 my people
 not been restored?
9[m] O that my head were waters,
 and my eyes a fountain of tears,
that I might weep day and night
 for the slain of the daughter of my
 people!

2[n] O that I had in the desert
 a wayfarers' lodging place,
that I might leave my people
 and go away from them!
For they are all adulterers,
 a company of treacherous men.
3 They bend their tongue like a bow;
 falsehood and not truth has grown
 strong[o] in the land;
for they proceed from evil to evil,
 and they do not know me, says the
 LORD.

4 Let every one beware of his neighbour,
 and put no trust in any brother;
for every brother is a supplanter,
 and every neighbour goes about as a
 slanderer.
5 Every one deceives his neighbour,
 and no one speaks the truth;
they have taught their tongue to speak
 lies;
 they commit iniquity and are too weary
 to repent.[p]
6 Heaping oppression upon oppression, and
 deceit upon deceit,
 they refuse to know me, says the LORD.

7 Therefore thus says the LORD of hosts:
"Behold, I will refine them and test them,
 for what else can I do, because of my
 people?
8 Their tongue is a deadly arrow;
 it speaks deceitfully;

with his mouth each speaks peaceably to
 his neighbour,
 but in his heart he plans an ambush for
 him.
Shall I not punish them for these things? 9
 says the LORD;
 and shall I not avenge myself
 on a nation such as this?

"Take up[q] weeping and wailing for the 10
 mountains,
 and a lamentation for the pastures of the
 wilderness,
because they are laid waste so that no one
 passes through,
 and the lowing of cattle is not heard;
both the birds of the air and the beasts
 have fled and are gone.
I will make Jerusalem a heap of ruins, 11
 a lair of jackals;
and I will make the cities of Judah a
 desolation,
 without inhabitant."

Who is the man so wise that he can 12
understand this? To whom has the mouth
of the LORD spoken, that he may declare it?
Why is the land ruined and laid waste like a
wilderness, so that no one passes through?
And the LORD says: "Because they have 13
forsaken my law which I set before them, and
have not obeyed my voice, or walked in
accord with it, but have stubbornly followed 14
their own hearts and have gone after
the Ba'als, as their fathers taught them.
Therefore thus says the LORD of hosts, the 15
God of Israel: Behold, I will feed this people
with wormwood, and give them poisonous
water to drink. I will scatter them among the 16
nations whom neither they nor their fathers
have known; and I will send the sword after
them, until I have consumed them."

Thus says the LORD of hosts: 17
"Consider, and call for the mourning
 women to come;
 send for the skilful women to come;
let them make haste and raise a wailing 18
 over us,
 that our eyes may run down with tears,
 and our eyelids gush with water.
For a sound of wailing is heard from 19
 Zion:
'How we are ruined!
We are utterly shamed,
because we have left the land,
 because they have cast down our
 dwellings.'"

[m] Ch 8.23 in Heb [n] Ch 9.1 in Heb [o] Gk: Heb *and not for truth they have grown strong*
[p] Cn Compare Gk: Heb *your dwelling* [q] Gk Syr: Heb *I will take up*

Hear, O women, the word of the LORD,
   and let your ear receive the word of his
      mouth;
teach to your daughters a lament,
   and each to her neighbour a dirge.
For death has come up into our windows,
   it has entered our palaces,
cutting off the children from the streets
   and the young men from the squares.
Speak, "Thus says the LORD:
'The dead bodies of men shall fall
   like dung upon the open field,
like sheaves after the reaper,
   and none shall gather them.' "

Thus says the LORD: "Let not the wise man
glory in his wisdom, let not the mighty man
glory in his might, let not the rich man glory
in his riches; but let him who glories glory in
this, that he understands and knows me, that
I am the LORD who practise steadfast love,
justice, and righteousness in the earth; for in
these things I delight, says the LORD."
"Behold, the days are coming, says the
LORD, when I will punish all those who are
circumcised but yet uncircumcised—Egypt,
Judah, Edom, the sons of Ammon, Moab,
and all who dwell in the desert that cut the
corners of their hair; for all these nations are
uncircumcised, and all the house of Israel is
uncircumcised in heart."

The only true God

) Hear the word which the LORD speaks to
you, O house of Israel.
   Thus says the LORD:
   "Learn not the way of the nations,
      nor be dismayed at the signs of the
         heavens
      because the nations are dismayed at
         them,
   for the customs of the peoples are false.
A tree from the forest is cut down,
   and worked with an axe by the hands of
      a craftsman.
Men deck it with silver and gold;
   they fasten it with hammer and nails
      so that it cannot move.
Their idols[r] are like scarecrows in a
      cucumber field,
   and they cannot speak;
they have to be carried,
   for they cannot walk.
Be not afraid of them,
   for they cannot do evil,
   neither is it in them to do good."

There is none like thee, O LORD;   6
   thou art great, and thy name is great in
      might.
Who would not fear thee, O King of the 7
   nations?
   For this is thy due;
for among all the wise ones of the nations
   and in all their kingdoms
   there is none like thee.
They are both stupid and foolish;   8
   the instruction of idols is but wood!
Beaten silver is brought from Tarshish,   9
   and gold from Uphaz.
They are the work of the craftsman and of
   the hands of the goldsmith;
   their clothing is violet and purple;
   they are all the work of skilled men.
But the LORD is the true God;   10
   he is the living God and the everlasting
      King.
At his wrath the earth quakes,
   and the nations cannot endure his
      indignation.

Thus shall you say to them: "The gods who 11
did not make the heavens and the earth shall
perish from the earth and from under the
heavens."[s]

It is he who made the earth by his power, 12
   who established the world by his
      wisdom,
   and by his understanding stretched out
      the heavens.
When he utters his voice there is a tumult 13
   of waters in the heavens,
   and he makes the mist rise from the ends
      of the earth.
He makes lightnings for the rain,
   and he brings forth the wind from his
      storehouses.
Every man is stupid and without know- 14
   ledge;
   every goldsmith is put to shame by his
      idols;
for his images are false,
   and there is no breath in them.
They are worthless, a work of delusion; 15
   at the time of their punishment they
      shall perish.
Not like these is he who is the portion of 16
   Jacob,
for he is the one who formed all things,
   and Israel is the tribe of his inheritance;
   the LORD of hosts is his name.

Gather up your bundle from the ground, 17
   O you who dwell under siege!

---

[r] Heb *They*   [s] This verse is in Aramaic
9.24: 1 Cor 1.31; 2 Cor 10.17.   **9.26:** Acts 7.51.

18 For thus says the LORD:
   "Behold, I am slinging out the inhabitants
       of the land
       at this time,
   and I will bring distress on them,
       that they may feel it."

19 Woe is me because of my hurt!
       My wound is grievous.
   But I said, "Truly this is an affliction,
       and I must bear it."

20 My tent is destroyed,
       and all my cords are broken;
   my children have gone from me,
       and they are not;
   there is no one to spread my tent again,
       and to set up my curtains.

21 For the shepherds are stupid,
       and do not inquire of the LORD;
   therefore they have not prospered,
       and all their flock is scattered.

22 Hark, a rumour! Behold, it comes!—
       a great commotion out of the north
       country
   to make the cities of Judah a desolation,
       a lair of jackals.

23 I know, O LORD, that the way of man is
       not in himself,
       that it is not in man who walks to direct
       his steps.

24 Correct me, O LORD, but in just measure;
       not in thy anger, lest thou bring me to
       nothing.

25 Pour out thy wrath upon the nations that
       know thee not,
       and upon the peoples that call not on thy
       name;
   for they have devoured Jacob;
       they have devoured him and consumed
       him,
       and have laid waste his habitation.

The covenant recalled

11 The word that came to Jeremiah from the
2 LORD: "Hear the words of this covenant, and
   speak to the men of Judah and the inhabi-
3 tants of Jerusalem. You shall say to them,
   Thus says the LORD, the God of Israel:
   Cursed be the man who does not heed the
4 words of this covenant which I commanded
   your fathers when I brought them out of the
   land of Egypt, from the iron furnace, saying,
   Listen to my voice, and do all that I command you. So shall you be my people, and I

will be your God, that I may perform the
oath which I swore to your fathers, to give
them a land flowing with milk and honey, as
at this day." Then I answered, "So be it,
LORD."

   And the LORD said to me, "Proclaim all
these words in the cities of Judah, and in the
streets of Jerusalem: Hear the words of this
covenant and do them. For I solemnly
warned your fathers when I brought them up
out of the land of Egypt, warning them
persistently, even to this day, saying, Obey
my voice. Yet they did not obey or incline
their ear, but every one walked in the
stubbornness of his evil heart. Therefore I
brought upon them all the words of this
covenant, which I commanded them to do,
but they did not."

   Again the LORD said to me, "There is revolt
among the men of Judah and the inhabitants
of Jerusalem. They have turned back to the
iniquities of their forefathers, who refused to
hear my words; they have gone after other
gods to serve them; the house of Israel and
the house of Judah have broken my covenant
which I made with their fathers. Therefore,
thus says the LORD, Behold, I am bringing
evil upon them which they cannot escape;
though they cry to me, I will not listen to
them. Then the cities of Judah and the
inhabitants of Jerusalem will go and cry to
the gods to whom they burn incense, but
they cannot save them in the time of their
trouble. For your gods have become as many
as your cities, O Judah; and as many as the
streets of Jerusalem are the altars you have
set up to shame, altars to burn incense to
Ba'al.

   "Therefore do not pray for this people, or
lift up a cry or prayer on their behalf, for I
will not listen when they call to me in the
time of their trouble. What right has my
beloved in my house, when she has done vile
deeds? Can vows[f] and sacrificial flesh avert
your doom? Can you then exult? The
LORD once called you, 'A green olive tree,
fair with goodly fruit'; but with the roar of a
great tempest he will set fire to it, and its
branches will be consumed. The LORD of
hosts, who planted you, has pronounced evil
against you, because of the evil which the
house of Israel and the house of Judah have
done, provoking me to anger by burning
incense to Ba'al."

A plot against the prophet

   The LORD made it known to me and I
   knew;

---

f Gk: Heb *many*
10.25: 1 Thess 4.5; Rev 16.1.

then thou didst show me their evil
deeds.
But I was like a gentle lamb
led to the slaughter.
I did not know it was against me
they devised schemes, saying,
"Let us destroy the tree with its fruit,
let us cut him off from the land of the
living,
that his name be remembered no more."
But, O LORD of hosts, who judgest
righteously,
who triest the heart and the mind,
let me see thy vengeance upon them,
for to thee have I committed my cause.
Therefore thus says the LORD concerning
the men of An'athoth, who seek your life,
and say, "Do not prophesy in the name of the
LORD, or you will die by our hand"—therefore thus says the LORD of hosts: "Behold, I
will punish them; the young men shall die by
the sword; their sons and their daughters
shall die by famine; and none of them shall
be left. For I will bring evil upon the men of
An'athoth, the year of their punishment."

The prophet's problem

2 Righteous art thou, O LORD,
when I complain to thee;
yet I would plead my case before thee.
Why does the way of the wicked prosper?
Why do all who are treacherous thrive?
Thou plantest them, and they take root;
they grow and bring forth fruit;
thou art near in their mouth
and far from their heart.
But thou, O LORD, knowest me;
thou seest me, and triest my mind
toward thee.
Pull them out like sheep for the slaughter,
and set them apart for the day of
slaughter.
How long will the land mourn,
and the grass of every field wither?
For the wickedness of those who dwell in
it
the beasts and the birds are swept away,
because men said, "He will not see our
latter end."

"If you have raced with men on foot, and
they have wearied you,
how will you compete with horses?
And if in a safe land you fall down,
how will you do in the jungle of the
Jordan?
For even your brothers and the house of
your father,

even they have dealt treacherously with
you;
they are in full cry after you;
believe them not,
though they speak fair words to you."

"I have forsaken my house,   7
I have abandoned my heritage;
I have given the beloved of my soul
into the hands of her enemies.
My heritage has become to me   8
like a lion in the forest,
she has lifted up her voice against me;
therefore I hate her.
Is my heritage to me like a speckled bird of 9
prey?
Are the birds of prey against her round
about?
Go, assemble all the wild beasts;
bring them to devour.
Many shepherds have destroyed my 10
vineyard,
they have trampled down my portion,
they have made my pleasant portion
a desolate wilderness.
They have made it a desolation;   11
desolate, it mourns to me.
The whole land is made desolate,
but no man lays it to heart.
Upon all the bare heights in the desert   12
destroyers have come;
for the sword of the LORD devours
from one end of the land to the other;
no flesh has peace.
They have sown wheat and have reaped 13
thorns,
they have tired themselves out but profit
nothing.
They shall be ashamed of their [u]
harvests
because of the fierce anger of the
LORD."

Thus says the LORD concerning all my evil 14
neighbours who touch the heritage which I
have given my people Israel to inherit:
"Behold, I will pluck them up from their
land, and I will pluck up the house of Judah
from among them. And after I have plucked 15
them up, I will again have compassion on
them, and I will bring them again each to his
heritage and each to his land. And it shall 16
come to pass, if they will diligently learn the
ways of my people, to swear by my name, 'As
the LORD lives,' even as they taught my
people to swear by Ba'al, then they shall be
built up in the midst of my people. But 17
if any nation will not listen, then I will
utterly pluck it up and destroy it, says the
LORD."

[u] Heb *your*

Parable of the waistcloth

13 Thus said the Lord to me, "Go and buy a linen waistcloth, and put it on your loins, and 2 do not dip it in water." So I bought a waistcloth according to the word of the 3 Lord, and put it on my loins. And the word of the Lord came to me a second time, 4 "Take the waistcloth which you have bought, which is upon your loins, and arise, go to the Euphra'tes, and hide it there in a 5 cleft of the rock." So I went, and hid it by the Euphra'tes, as the Lord commanded 6 me. And after many days the Lord said to me, "Arise, go to the Euphra'tes, and take from there the waistcloth which I com-7 manded you to hide there." Then I went to the Euphra'tes, and dug, and I took the waistcloth from the place where I had hidden it. And behold, the waistcloth was spoiled; it was good for nothing. 8 Then the word of the Lord came to me: 9 "Thus says the Lord: Even so will I spoil the pride of Judah and the great pride of 10 Jerusalem. This evil people, who refuse to hear my words, who stubbornly follow their own heart and have gone after other gods to serve them and worship them, shall be like this waistcloth, which is good for nothing. 11 For as the waistcloth clings to the loins of a man, so I made the whole house of Israel and the whole house of Judah cling to me, says the Lord, that they might be for me a people, a name, a praise, and a glory, but they would not listen.

Coming disaster

12 "You shall speak to them this word: 'Thus says the Lord, the God of Israel, "Every jar

shall be filled with wine." ' And they will say to you, 'Do we not indeed know that every jar will be filled with wine?' Then you shall say to them, 'Thus says the Lord: Behold, I will fill with drunkenness all the inhabitants of this land: the kings who sit on David's throne, the priests, the prophets, and all the inhabitants of Jerusalem. And I will dash them one against another, fathers and sons together, says the Lord. I will not pity or spare or have compassion, that I should not destroy them.' "

Hear and give ear; be not proud,
    for the Lord has spoken.
Give glory to the Lord your God
    before he brings darkness,
before your feet stumble
    on the twilight mountains,
and while you look for light
    he turns it into gloom
    and makes it deep darkness.
But if you will not listen,
    my soul will weep in secret for your
      pride;
my eyes will weep bitterly and run down
    with tears,
    because the Lord's flock has been taken
      captive.

Say to the king and the queen mother:
    "Take a lowly seat,
for your beautiful crown
    has come down from your head." *v*
The cities of the Negeb are shut up,
    with none to open them;
all Judah is taken into exile,
    wholly taken into exile.

The leopard's spots

"Lift up your eyes and see
    those who come from the north.
Where is the flock that was given you,
    your beautiful flock?
What will you say when they set as head
    over you
    those whom you yourself have taught
    to be friends to you?
Will not pangs take hold of you,
    like those of a woman in travail?
And if you say in your heart,
    'Why have these things come upon me?'
it is for the greatness of your iniquity
    that your skirts are lifted up,
    and you suffer violence.
Can the Ethiopian change his skin
    or the leopard his spots?
Then also you can do good
    who are accustomed to do evil.

v Gk Syr Vg: Heb obscure

I will scatter you[w] like chaff
    driven by the wind from the desert.
This is your lot,
    the portion I have measured out to you,
      says the LORD,
because you have forgotten me
    and trusted in lies.
I myself will lift up your skirts over your
      face,
    and your shame will be seen.
I have seen your abominations,
    your adulteries and neighings,
      your lewd harlotries,
    on the hills in the field.
Woe to you, O Jerusalem!
    How long will it be
    before you are made clean?"

A great drought

4 The word of the LORD which came to
Jeremiah concerning the drought:
  "Judah mourns
    and her gates languish;
  her people lament on the ground,
    and the cry of Jerusalem goes up.
  Her nobles send their servants for water;
    they come to the cisterns,
  they find no water,
    they return with their vessels empty;
  they are ashamed and confounded
    and cover their heads.
  Because of the ground which is dismayed,
    since there is no rain on the land,
  the farmers are ashamed,
    they cover their heads.
  Even the hind in the field forsakes her
      newborn calf
    because there is no grass.
  The wild asses stand on the bare heights,
    they pant for air like jackals;
  their eyes fail
    because there is no herbage."

  "Though our iniquities testify against us,
    act, O LORD, for thy name's sake;
  for our backslidings are many,
    we have sinned against thee.

O thou hope of Israel,   8
    its saviour in time of trouble,
why shouldst thou be like a stranger in the
      land,
    like a wayfarer who turns aside to tarry
      for a night?
Why shouldst thou be like a man confused, 9
    like a mighty man who cannot save?
Yet thou, O LORD, art in the midst of us,
    and we are called by thy name;
    leave us not."

Thus says the LORD concerning this 10
    people:
  "They have loved to wander thus,
    they have not restrained their feet;
  therefore the LORD does not accept them,
    now he will remember their iniquity
    and punish their sins."

The LORD said to me: "Do not pray for the 11
welfare of this people. Though they fast, I 12
will not hear their cry, and though they offer
burnt offering and cereal offering, I will not
accept them; but I will consume them by the
sword, by famine, and by pestilence."
Then I said: "Ah, Lord GOD, behold, the 13
prophets say to them, 'You shall not see the
sword, nor shall you have famine, but I will
give you assured peace in this place.'" And 14
the LORD said to me: "The prophets are
prophesying lies in my name; I did not send
them, nor did I command them or speak to
them. They are prophesying to you a lying
vision, worthless divination, and the deceit of
their own minds. Therefore thus says the 15
LORD concerning the prophets who prophesy
in my name although I did not send them,
and who say, 'Sword and famine shall not
come on this land': By sword and famine
those prophets shall be consumed. And the 16
people to whom they prophesy shall be cast
out in the streets of Jerusalem, victims of
famine and sword, with none to bury
them—them, their wives, their sons, and
their daughters. For I will pour out their
wickedness upon them.

"You shall say to them this word: 17
  'Let my eyes run down with tears night
      and day,
    and let them not cease,
  for the virgin daughter of my people is
      smitten with a great wound,
    with a very grievous blow.
  If I go out into the field,   18
    behold, those slain by the sword!
  And if I enter the city,
    behold, the diseases of famine!

[w] Heb *them*
14.12: Rev 6.8.

For both prophet and priest ply their trade
    through the land,
    and have no knowledge.' "

19 Hast thou utterly rejected Judah?
    Does thy soul loathe Zion?
    Why hast thou smitten us
      so that there is no healing for us?
    We looked for peace, but no good came;
      for a time of healing, but behold, terror.
20 We acknowledge our wickedness, O LORD,
    and the iniquity of our fathers,
      for we have sinned against thee.
21 Do not spurn us, for thy name's sake;
    do not dishonour thy glorious throne;
    remember and do not break thy
      covenant with us.
22 Are there any among the false gods of the
      nations that can bring rain?
    Or can the heavens give showers?
    Art thou not he, O LORD our God?
    We set our hope on thee,
      for thou doest all these things.

15 Then the LORD said to me, "Though
Moses and Samuel stood before me, yet
my heart would not turn toward this people.
Send them out of my sight, and let them
2 go! And when they ask you, 'Where shall
we go?' you shall say to them, 'Thus says
the LORD:

    "Those who are for pestilence, to pesti-
      lence,
    and those who are for the sword, to the
      sword;
    those who are for famine, to famine,
    and those who are for captivity, to
      captivity." '
3 "I will appoint over them four kinds of
destroyers, says the LORD: the sword to slay,
the dogs to tear, and the birds of the air
and the beasts of the earth to devour and
4 destroy. And I will make them a horror to all
the kingdoms of the earth because of what
Manas'seh the son of Hezeki'ah, king of
Judah, did in Jerusalem.

5 "Who will have pity on you, O Jerusalem,
    or who will bemoan you?
    Who will turn aside
      to ask about your welfare?
6 You have rejected me, says the LORD,
    you keep going backward;
    so I have stretched out my hand against
      you and destroyed you;—
    I am weary of relenting.
7 I have winnowed them with a winnowing
      fork
    in the gates of the land;

I have bereaved them, I have destroyed
    my people;
    they did not turn from their ways.
I have made their widows more in number
    than the sand of the seas;
I have brought against the mothers of
    young men
    a destroyer at noonday;
I have made anguish and terror
    fall upon them suddenly.
She who bore seven has languished;
    she has swooned away;
    her sun went down while it was yet day;
    she has been shamed and disgraced.
And the rest of them I will give to the
    sword
    before their enemies,"
                      says the LORD.

The prophet's lament

    Woe is me, my mother, that you bore me, a
man of strife and contention to the whole
land! I have not lent, nor have I borrowed,
yet all of them curse me. So let it be, O
LORD,ˣ if I have not entreatedʸ thee for their
good, if I have not pleaded with thee on
behalf of the enemy in the time of trouble
and in the time of distress! Can one break
iron, iron from the north, and bronze?
    "Your wealth and your treasures I will give
as spoil, without price, for all your sins,
throughout all your territory. I will make
you serve your enemies in a land which you
do not know, for in my anger a fire is kindled
which shall burn for ever."

O LORD, thou knowest;
    remember me and visit me,
      and take vengeance for me on my
      persecutors.
In thy forbearance take me not away;
    know that for thy sake I bear reproach.
Thy words were found, and I ate them,
    and thy words became to me a joy
    and the delight of my heart;
for I am called by thy name,
    O LORD, God of hosts.
I did not sit in the company of merry-
      makers,
    nor did I rejoice;
I sat alone, because thy hand was upon me,
    for thou hadst filled me with indig-
      nation.
Why is my pain unceasing,
    my wound incurable,
    refusing to be healed?
Wilt thou be to me like a deceitful brook,
    like waters that fail?

ˣ Gk Old Latin: Heb *the* LORD *said*   ʸ Cn: Heb obscure
15.2: Rev 13.10.

Therefore thus says the LORD:
"If you return, I will restore you,
and you shall stand before me.
If you utter what is precious, and not what
is worthless,
you shall be as my mouth.
They shall turn to you,
but you shall not turn to them.
And I will make you to this people
a fortified wall of bronze;
they will fight against you,
but they shall not prevail over you,
for I am with you
to save you and deliver you,
says the LORD.
I will deliver you out of the hand of the
wicked,
and redeem you from the grasp of the
ruthless."

6 The word of the LORD came to me: "You shall not take a wife, nor shall you have sons or daughters in this place. For thus says the LORD concerning the sons and daughters who are born in this place, and concerning the mothers who bore them and the fathers who begot them in this land: They shall die of deadly diseases. They shall not be lamented, nor shall they be buried; they shall be as dung on the surface of the ground. They shall perish by the sword and by famine, and their dead bodies shall be food for the birds of the air and for the beasts of the earth.

5 "For thus says the LORD: Do not enter the house of mourning, or go to lament, or bemoan them; for I have taken away my peace from this people, says the LORD, my steadfast love and mercy. Both great and small shall die in this land; they shall not be buried, and no one shall lament for them or cut himself or make himself bald for them. No one shall break bread for the mourner, to comfort him for the dead; nor shall any one give him the cup of consolation to drink for his father or his mother. You shall not go into the house of feasting to sit with them, to eat and drink. For thus says the LORD of hosts, the God of Israel: Behold, I will make to cease from this place, before your eyes and in your days, the voice of mirth and the voice of gladness, the voice of the bridegroom and the voice of the bride.

10 "And when you tell this people all these words, and they say to you, 'Why has the LORD pronounced all this great evil against us? What is our iniquity? What is the sin that we have committed against the LORD our God?' then you shall say to them: 'Because

your fathers have forsaken me, says the LORD, and have gone after other gods and have served and worshipped them, and have forsaken me and have not kept my law, and **12** because you have done worse than your fathers, for behold, every one of you follows his stubborn evil will, refusing to listen to me; therefore I will hurl you out of this land **13** into a land which neither you nor your fathers have known, and there you shall serve other gods day and night, for I will show you no favour.'

"Therefore, behold, the days are coming, **14** says the LORD, when it shall no longer be said, 'As the LORD lives who brought up the people of Israel out of the land of Egypt,' but **15** 'As the LORD lives who brought up the people of Israel out of the north country and out of all the countries where he had driven them.' For I will bring them back to their own land which I gave to their fathers.

"Behold, I am sending for many fishers, **16** says the LORD, and they shall catch them; and afterwards I will send for many hunters, and they shall hunt them from every mountain and every hill, and out of the clefts of the rocks. For my eyes are upon all their ways; **17** they are not hid from me, nor is their iniquity concealed from my eyes. And[z] I will doubly **18** recompense their iniquity and their sin, because they have polluted my land with the carcasses of their detestable idols, and have filled my inheritance with their abominations."

O LORD, my strength and my stronghold, **19**
my refuge in the day of trouble,
to thee shall the nations come
from the ends of the earth and say:
"Our fathers have inherited naught but
lies,
worthless things in which there is no
profit.
Can man make for himself gods?   **20**
Such are no gods!"

"Therefore, behold, I will make them **21** know, this once I will make them know my power and my might, and they shall know that my name is the LORD."

A pen of iron

"The sin of Judah is written with a pen of **17** iron; with a point of diamond it is engraved on the tablet of their heart, and on the horns of their altars, while their children remember **2** their altars and their Ashe'rim, beside every green tree, and on the high hills, on the **3**

Jer 17, 1

mountains in the open country. Your wealth and all your treasures I will give for spoil as the price of your sin[a] throughout all your
4 territory. You shall loosen your hand[b] from your heritage which I gave to you, and I will make you serve your enemies in a land which you do not know, for in my anger a fire is kindled which shall burn for ever."

Trust in the Lord

5 Thus says the LORD:
   "Cursed is the man who trusts in man
     and makes flesh his arm,
     whose heart turns away from the LORD.
6 He is like a shrub in the desert,
     and shall not see any good come.
   He shall dwell in the parched places of the
     wilderness,
     in an uninhabited salt land.

7 "Blessed is the man who trusts in the
     LORD,
     whose trust is the LORD.
8 He is like a tree planted by water,
     that sends out its roots by the stream,
   and does not fear when heat comes,
     for its leaves remain green,
   and is not anxious in the year of drought,
     for it does not cease to bear fruit."

9 The heart is deceitful above all things,
     and desperately corrupt;
     who can understand it?
10 "I the LORD search the mind
     and try the heart,
   to give to every man according to his
     ways,
     according to the fruit of his doings."

Like the partridge that gathers a brood
     which she did not hatch,
   so is he who gets riches but not by right;
   in the midst of his days they will leave him,
     and at his end he will be a fool.

A glorious throne set on high from the
     beginning
   is the place of our sanctuary.
O LORD, the hope of Israel,
     all who forsake thee shall be put to
     shame;
those who turn away from thee[c] shall be
     written in the earth,
     for they have forsaken the LORD, the
     fountain of living water.

Heal me, O LORD, and I shall be healed;
     save me, and I shall saved;
     for thou art my praise.
Behold, they say to me,
     "Where is the word of the LORD?
     Let it come!"
I have not pressed thee to send evil,
     nor have I desired the day of disaster,
     thou knowest;
that which came out of my lips
     was before thy face.
Be not a terror to me;
     thou art my refuge in the day of evil.
Let those be put to shame who persecute
     me,
   but let me not be put to shame;
let them be dismayed,
     but let me not be dismayed;
bring upon them the day of evil;
     destroy them with double destruction!

Keep the sabbath

Thus said the LORD to me: "Go and stand in the Benjamin[d] Gate, by which the kings of Judah enter and by which they go out, and in all the gates of Jerusalem, and say: 'Hear the word of the LORD, you kings of Judah, and all Judah, and all the inhabitants of Jerusalem, who enter by these gates. Thus says the LORD: Take heed for the sake of your lives, and do not bear a burden on the sabbath day or bring it in by the gates of Jerusalem. And do not carry a burden out of your houses on the sabbath or do any work, but keep the sabbath day holy, as I commanded your fathers. Yet they did not listen or incline their ear, but stiffened their neck, that they might not hear and receive instruction.
" 'But if you listen to me, says the LORD, and bring in no burden by the gates of this city on the sabbath day, but keep the sabbath

---

[a] Cn: Heb *your high places for sin*   [b] Cn: Heb *and in you*   [c] Heb *me*   [d] Cn: Heb *sons of people*
17.7–8: Ps 1.1–3.   17.10: Ps 62.12; Rev 2.23; 22.12.

day holy and do no work on it, then there shall enter by the gates of this city kings*e* who sit on the throne of David, riding in chariots and on horses, they and their princes, the men of Judah and the inhabitants of Jerusalem; and this city shall be inhabited for ever. And people shall come from the cities of Judah and the places round about Jerusalem, from the land of Benjamin, from the Shephe'lah, from the hill country, and from the Negeb, bringing burnt offerings and sacrifices, cereal offerings and frankincense, and bringing thank offerings to the house of the LORD. But if you do not listen to me, to keep the sabbath day holy, and not to bear a burden and enter by the gates of Jerusalem on the sabbath day, then I will kindle a fire in its gates, and it shall devour the palaces of Jerusalem and shall not be quenched.' "

Parable of the potter

8 The word that came to Jeremiah from the 2 LORD: "Arise, and go down to the potter's house, and there I will let you hear my 3 words." So I went down to the potter's house, and there he was working at his 4 wheel. And the vessel he was making of clay was spoiled in the potter's hand, and he reworked it into another vessel, as it seemed good to the potter to do.

5, Then the word of the LORD came to me: "O 6 house of Israel, can I not do with you as this potter has done? says the LORD. Behold, like the clay in the potter's hand, so are you in my hand, O house of Israel. If at any time I 7 declare concerning a nation or a kingdom, that I will pluck up and break down and destroy it, and if that nation, concerning 8 which I have spoken, turns from its evil, I will repent of the evil that I intended to do to it. And if at any time I declare concerning a 9 nation or a kingdom that I will build and plant it, and if it does evil in my sight, not 10 listening to my voice, then I will repent of the good which I had intended to do to it. Now, therefore, say to the men of Judah and 11 the inhabitants of Jerusalem: 'Thus says the LORD, Behold, I am shaping evil aganst you and devising a plan against you. Return, every one from his evil way, and amend your ways and your doings.'

"But they say, 'That is in vain! We will 12 follow our own plans, and will every one act according to the stubbornness of his evil heart.'

"Therefore thus says the LORD: 13
   Ask among the nations,
      who has heard the like of this?
The virgin Israel
      has done a very horrible thing.
Does the snow of Lebanon leave   14
      the crags of Sirion?*f*
Do the mountain*g* waters run dry,*h*
      the cold flowing streams?
But my people have forgotten me,   15
      they burn incense to false gods;
they have stumbled*i* in their ways,
      in the ancient roads,
and have gone into bypaths,
      not the highway,
making their land a horror,   16
      a thing to be hissed at for ever.
Every one who passes by it is horrified
      and shakes his head.
Like the east wind I will scatter them 17
      before the enemy.
I will show them my back, not my face,
      in the day of their calamity."

Enemies of the prophet

Then they said, "Come, let us make plots 18 against Jeremiah, for the law shall not perish from the priest, nor counsel from the wise, nor the word from the prophet. Come, let us smite him with the tongue, and let us not heed any of his words."

Give heed to me, O LORD,   19
      and hearken to my plea.*j*
Is evil a recompense for good?   20
      Yet they have dug a pit for my life.

---

e Cn: Heb *kings and princes*   *f* Cn: Heb *the field*   *g* Cn: Heb *foreign*   *h* Cn: Heb *Are . . . plucked up?*
i Gk Syr Vg: Heb *they made them stumble*   *j* Gk Compare Syr Tg: Heb *my adversaries*
18.6: Rom 9.21.

Remember how I stood before thee
  to speak good for them,
  to turn away thy wrath from them.
21 Therefore deliver up their children to
    famine;
  give them over to the power of the
    sword,
  let their wives become childless and
    widowed.
  May their men meet death by pesti-
    lence,
  their youths be slain by the sword in
    battle.
22 May a cry be heard from their houses,
  when thou bringest the marauder sud-
    denly upon them!
  For they have dug a pit to take me,
  and laid snares for my feet.
23 Yet, thou, O LORD, knowest
  all their plotting to slay me.
  Forgive not their iniquity,
  nor blot out their sin from thy sight.
  Let them be overthrown before thee;
  deal with them in the time of thine
    anger.

Broken pottery

19 Thus said the LORD, "Go, buy a potter's
earthen flask, and take some of the elders of
2 the people and some of the senior priests, and
go out to the valley of the son of Hinnom, at
the entry of the Potsherd Gate, and proclaim
3 there the words that I tell you. You shall say,
'Hear the word of the LORD, O kings of
Judah and inhabitants of Jerusalem. Thus
says the LORD of hosts, the God of Israel,
Behold, I am bringing such evil upon this
place that the ears of every one who hears of
4 it will tingle. Because the people have
forsaken me, and have profaned this place by
burning incense in it to other gods whom
neither they nor their fathers nor the kings
of Judah have known; and because they have
filled this place with the blood of innocents,
5 and have built the high places of Ba'al to
burn their sons in the fire as burnt offerings
to Ba'al, which I did not command or decree,
6 nor did it come into my mind; therefore,
behold, days are coming, says the LORD,
when this place shall no more be called
Topheth, or the valley of the son of Hinnom,
7 but the valley of Slaughter. And in this place
I will make void the plans of Judah and
Jerusalem, and will cause their people to fall
by the sword before their enemies, and by
the hand of those who seek their life. I will
give their dead bodies for food to the birds of
8 the air and to the beasts of the earth. And I
will make this city a horror, a thing to be

hissed at; every one who passes by it will be
horrified and will hiss because of all its
disasters. And I will make them eat the flesh
of their sons and their daughters, and every
one shall eat the flesh of his neighbour in the
siege and in the distress, with which their
enemies and those who seek their life afflict
them.'
  "Then you shall break the flask in the sight
of the men who go with you, and shall say to
them, 'Thus says the LORD of hosts: So will I
break this people and this city, as one breaks
a potter's vessel, so that it can never
be mended. Men shall bury in Topheth
because there will be no place else to bury.
Thus will I do to this place, says the LORD,
and to its inhabitants, making this city like
Topheth. The houses of Jerusalem and the
houses of the kings of Judah—all the houses
upon whose roofs incense has been burned to
all the host of heaven, and drink offerings
have been poured out to other gods—shall be
defiled like the place of Topheth.' "
  Then Jeremiah came from Topheth, where
the LORD had sent him to prophesy, and he
stood in the court of the LORD's house, and
said to all the people: "Thus says the LORD
of hosts, the God of Israel, Behold, I am
bringing upon this city and upon all its towns
all the evil that I have pronounced against it,
because they have stiffened their neck,
refusing to hear my words."

Jeremiah in the stocks

Now Pashhur the priest, the son of Immer, 2
who was chief officer in the house of the
LORD, heard Jeremiah prophesying these
things. Then Pashhur beat Jeremiah the 2
prophet, and put him in the stocks that were
in the upper Benjamin Gate of the house of
the LORD. On the morrow, when Pashhur 3
released Jeremiah from the stocks, Jeremiah
said to him, "The LORD does not call your
name Pashhur, but Terror on every side.
For thus says the LORD: Behold, I will make 4
you a terror to yourself and to all your
friends. They shall fall by the sword of their
enemies while you look on. And I will give
all Judah into the hand of the king of
Babylon; he shall carry them captive to
Babylon, and shall slay them with the sword.
Moreover, I will give all the wealth of the 5
city, all its gains, all its prized belongings,
and all the treasures of the kings of Judah
into the hand of their enemies, who shall
plunder them, and seize them, and carry
them to Babylon. And you, Pashhur, and all 6
who dwell in your house, shall go into
captivity; to Babylon you shall go; and there

you shall die, and there you shall be buried, you and all your friends, to whom you have prophesied falsely."

O LORD, thou hast deceived me,
  and I was deceived;
thou art stronger than I,
  and thou hast prevailed.
I have become a laughingstock all the day;
  every one mocks me.
For whenever I speak, I cry out,
  I shout, "Violence and destruction!"
For the word of the LORD has become for me
  a reproach and derision all day long.
If I say, "I will not mention him,
  or speak any more in his name,"
there is in my heart as it were a burning fire
  shut up in my bones,
and I am weary with holding it in,
  and I cannot.
For I hear many whispering.
  Terror is on every side!
"Denounce him! Let us denounce him!"
  say all my familiar friends,
  watching for my fall.
"Perhaps he will be deceived,
  then we can overcome him,
  and take our revenge on him."
But the LORD is with me as a dread warrior;
  therefore my persecutors will stumble,
  they will not overcome me.
They will be greatly shamed,
  for they will not succeed.
Their eternal dishonour
  will never be forgotten.
O LORD of hosts, who triest the righteous,
  who seest the heart and the mind,
let me see thy vengeance upon them,
  for to thee have I committed my cause.

Sing to the LORD;
  praise the LORD!
For he has delivered the life of the needy
  from the hand of evildoers.

Cursed be the day
  on which I was born!
The day when my mother bore me,
  let it not be blessed!
Cursed be the man
  who brought the news to my father,
"A son is born to you,"
  making him very glad.
Let that man be like the cities
  which the LORD overthrew without pity;
let him hear a cry in the morning
  and an alarm at noon,

because he did not kill me in the womb; 17
  so my mother would have been my grave,
  and her womb for ever great.
Why did I come forth from the womb 18
  to see toil and sorrow,
  and spend my days in shame?

Jerusalem besieged

This is the word which came to Jeremiah 21 from the LORD, when King Zedeki′ah sent to him Pashhur the son of Malchi′ah and Zephani′ah the priest, the son of Ma-asei′ah, saying, "Inquire of the LORD for us, for 2 Nebuchadrez′zar king of Babylon is making war against us; perhaps the LORD will deal with us according to all his wonderful deeds, and will make him withdraw from us."

Then Jeremiah said to them: "Thus you 3 shall say to Zedeki′ah, 'Thus says the LORD, 4 the God of Israel: Behold, I will turn back the weapons of war which are in your hands and with which you are fighting against the king of Babylon and against the Chalde′ans who are besieging you outside the walls; and I will bring them together into the midst of this city. I myself will fight against you with 5 outstretched hand and strong arm, in anger, and in fury, and in great wrath. And I will 6 smite the inhabitants of this city, both man and beast; they shall die of a great pestilence. Afterward, says the LORD, I will give 7 Zedeki′ah king of Judah, and his servants, and the people in this city who survive the pestilence, sword, and famine, into the hand of Nebuchadrez′zar king of Babylon and into the hand of their enemies, into the hand of those who seek their lives. He shall smite them with the edge of the sword; he shall not pity them, or spare them, or have compassion.'

"And to this people you shall say: 'Thus 8 says the LORD: Behold, I set before you the way of life and the way of death. He who 9 stays in this city shall die by the sword, by famine, and by pestilence; but he who goes out and surrenders to the Chalde′ans who are besieging you shall live and shall have his life as a prize of war. For I have set my face 10 against this city for evil and not for good, says the LORD: it shall be given into the hand of the king of Babylon, and he shall burn it with fire.'

"And to the house of the king of Judah say, 11 'Hear the word of the LORD, O house of 12 David! Thus says the LORD:
  "'Execute justice in the morning,
    and deliver from the hand of the oppressor

20.14–18: Job 3.3–19.

him who has been robbed,
lest my wrath go forth like fire,
and burn with none to quench it,
because of your evil doings.' "

13   "Behold, I am against you, O inhabitant of
the valley,
O rock of the plain,
says the LORD;
you who say, 'Who shall come down
against us,
or who shall enter our habitations ?'
14   I will punish you according to the fruit of
your doings,
says the LORD;
I will kindle a fire in her forest,
and it shall devour all that is round
about her."

Unworthy rulers

22 Thus says the LORD: "Go down to the
house of the king of Judah, and speak there
2 this word, and say, 'Hear the word of the
LORD, O King of Judah, who sit on the
throne of David, you, and your servants, and
3 your people who enter these gates. Thus
says the LORD: Do justice and righteousness,
and deliver from the hand of the oppressor
him who has been robbed. And do no wrong
or violence to the alien, the fatherless, and
the widow, nor shed innocent blood in this
4 place. For if you will indeed obey this word,
then there shall enter the gates of this house
kings who sit on the throne of David, riding
in chariots and on horses, they, and their
5 servants, and their people. But if you will
not heed these words, I swear by myself, says
the LORD, that this house shall become a
6 desolation. For thus says the LORD concerning the house of the king of Judah:
" 'You are as Gilead to me,
as the summit of Lebanon,
yet surely I will make you a desert,
an uninhabited city.[k]
7   I will prepare destroyers against you,
each with his weapons;
and they shall cut down your choicest
cedars,
and cast them into the fire.
8   " 'And many nations will pass by this city,
and every man will say to his neighbour,
"Why has the LORD dealt thus with this great
9 city ?" And they will answer, "Because they
forsook the covenant of the LORD their God,
and worshipped other gods and served
them." ' "

10   Weep not for him who is dead,

nor bemoan him;
but weep bitterly for him who goes away,
for he shall return no more
to see his native land.
For thus says the LORD concerning Shallum
the son of Josi'ah, king of Judah, who
reigned instead of Josi'ah his father, and who
went away from this place: "He shall return
here no more, but in the place where they
have carried him captive, there shall he die,
and he shall never see this land again."

"Woe to him who builds his house by
unrighteousness,
and his upper rooms by injustice;
who makes his neighbour serve him for
nothing,
and does not give him his wages;
who says, 'I will build myself a great
house
with spacious upper rooms,'
and cuts out windows for it,
panelling it with cedar,
and painting it with vermilion.
Do you think you are a king
because you compete in cedar ?
Did not your father eat and drink
and do justice and righteousness ?
Then it was well with him.
He judged the cause of the poor and
needy;
then it was well.
Is not this to know me ?
says the LORD.
But you have eyes and heart
only for your dishonest gain,
for shedding innocent blood,
and for practising oppression and
violence."
Therefore thus says the LORD concerning
Jehoi'akim the son of Josi'ah, king of
Judah:
"They shall not lament for him, saying,
'Ah my brother!' or 'Ah sister!'
They shall not lament for him, saying,
'Ah lord!' or 'Ah his majesty!'
With the burial of an ass he shall be
buried,
dragged and cast forth beyond the gates
of Jerusalem."

"Go up to Lebanon, and cry out,
and lift up your voice in Bashan;
cry from Ab'arim,
for all your lovers are destroyed.
I spoke to you in your prosperity,
but you said, 'I will not listen.'
This has been your way from your youth,
that you have not obeyed my voice.

[k] Cn: Heb cities
22.5: Mt 23.38; Lk 13.35.

2 The wind shall shepherd all your
shepherds,
and your lovers shall go into captivity;
then you will be ashamed and confounded
because of all your wickedness.

3 O inhabitant of Lebanon,
nested among the cedars,
how you will groan[l] when pangs come
upon you,
pain as of a woman in travail!"

4 "As I live, says the LORD, though Coni′ah
the son of Jehoi′akim, king of Judah, were

the signet ring on my right hand, yet I would
5 tear you off and give you into the hand of
those who seek your life, into the hand of
those of whom you are afraid, even into the
hand of Nebuchadrez′zar king of Babylon
6 and into the hand of the Chalde′ans. I will
hurl you and the mother who bore you into
another country, where you were not born,
7 and there you shall die. But to the land to
which they will long to return, there they
shall not return."

8 Is this man Coni′ah a despised, broken
pot,
a vessel no one cares for?
Why are he and his children hurled and cast
into a land which they do not know?

9 O land, land, land,
hear the word of the LORD!

30 Thus says the LORD:
"Write this man down as childless,
a man who shall not succeed in his days;
for none of his offspring shall succeed
in sitting on the throne of David,
and ruling again in Judah."

23 "Woe to the shepherds who destroy and
scatter the sheep of my pasture!" says the
2 LORD. Therefore thus says the LORD, the
God of Israel, concerning the shepherds who

care for my people: "You have scattered my
flock, and have driven them away, and you
have not attended to them. Behold, I will
attend to you for your evil doings, says the
LORD. Then I will gather the remnant of my 3
flock out of all the countries where I have
driven them, and I will bring them back to
their fold, and they shall be fruitful and
multiply. I will set shepherds over them who 4
will care for them, and they shall fear no
more, nor be dismayed, neither shall any be
missing, says the LORD.

"Behold, the days are coming, says the 5
LORD, when I will raise up for David a
righteous Branch, and he shall reign as king
and deal wisely, and shall execute justice and
righteousness in the land. In his days Judah 6
will be saved, and Israel will dwell securely.
And this is the name by which he will be
called: 'The LORD is our righteousness.'

"Therefore, behold, the days are coming, 7
says the LORD, when men shall no longer say,
'As the LORD lives who brought up the
people of Israel out of the land of Egypt,' but 8
'As the LORD lives who brought up and led
the descendants of the house of Israel out of
the north country and out of all the countries
where he[m] had driven them.' Then they
shall dwell in their own land."

Unworthy prophets and priests

Concerning the prophets: 9
My heart is broken within me,
all my bones shake;
I am like a drunken man,
like a man overcome by wine,
because of the LORD
and because of his holy words.
For the land is full of adulterers; 10
because of the curse the land mourns,
and the pastures of the wilderness are
dried up.
Their course is evil,
and their might is not right.
"Both prophet and priest are ungodly; 11
even in my house I have found their
wickedness,
says the LORD.
Therefore their way shall be to them 12
like slippery paths in the darkness,
into which they shall be driven and fall;
for I will bring evil upon them
in the year of their punishment,
says the LORD.
In the prophets of Samar′ia 13
I saw an unsavoury thing:
they prophesied by Ba′al
and led my people Israel astray.

14 But in the prophets of Jerusalem
  I have seen a horrible thing:
  they commit adultery and walk in lies;
  they strengthen the hands of evildoers,
  so that no one turns from his
    wickedness;
  all of them have become like Sodom to me,
  and its inhabitants like Gomor'rah."

15 Therefore thus says the LORD of hosts
  concerning the prophets:
  "Behold, I will feed them with worm-
    wood,
  and give them poisoned water to drink;
  for from the prophets of Jerusalem
  ungodliness has gone forth into all the
    land."

16 Thus says the LORD of hosts: "Do not listen
  to the words of the prophets who prophesy to
  you, filling you with vain hopes; they speak
  visions of their own minds, not from the
17 mouth of the LORD. They say continually to
  those who despise the word of the LORD, 'It
  shall be well with you'; and to every one who
  stubbornly follows his own heart, they say,
  'No evil shall come upon you.' "

18 For who among them has stood in the
  council of the LORD
  to perceive and to hear his word,
  or who has given heed to his word and
    listened ?

19 Behold, the storm of the LORD !
  Wrath has gone forth,
  a whirling tempest;
  it will burst upon the head of the
    wicked.

20 The anger of the LORD will not turn back
  until he has executed and accomplished
  the intents of his mind.
  In the latter days you will understand it
    clearly.

21 "I did not send the prophets,
  yet they ran;
  I did not speak to them,
  yet they prophesied.

22 But if they had stood in my council,
  then they would have proclaimed my
    words to my people,
  and they would have turned them from
    their evil way,
  and from the evil of their doings.

23 "Am I a God at hand, says the LORD, and
24 not a God afar off ? Can a man hide himself
  in secret places so that I cannot see him ? says
  the LORD. Do I not fill heaven and earth ?
25 says the LORD. I have heard what the
  prophets have said who prophesy lies in my

name, saying, 'I have dreamed, I have
dreamed!' How long shall there be lies[n] in 26
the heart of the prophets who prophesy lies,
and who prophesy the deceit of their own
heart, who think to make my people forget 27
my name by their dreams which they tell one
another, even as their fathers forgot my name
for Ba'al ? Let the prophet who has a dream 28
tell the dream, but let him who has my word
speak my word faithfully. What has straw in
common with wheat ? says the LORD. Is not 29
my word like fire, says the LORD, and like a
hammer which breaks the rock in pieces ?
Therefore, behold, I am against the pro- 30
phets, says the LORD, who steal my words
from one another. Behold, I am against the 31
prophets, says the LORD, who use their
tongues and say, 'Says the LORD.' Behold, I 32
am against those who prophesy lying dreams,
says the LORD, and who tell them and lead
my people astray by their lies and their
recklessness, when I did not send them or
charge them; so they do not profit this people
at all, says the LORD.

"When one of this people, or a prophet, or a 33
priest asks you, 'What is the burden of the
LORD ?' you shall say to them, 'You are the
burden,[o] and I will cast you off, says
the LORD.' And as for the prophet, priest, or 34
one of the people who says, 'The burden of
the LORD,' I will punish that man and his
household. Thus shall you say, every one to 35
his neighbour and every one to his brother,
'What has the LORD answered ?' or 'What has
the LORD spoken ?' But 'the burden of the 36
LORD' you shall mention no more, for the
burden is every man's own word, and you
pervert the words of the living God, the
LORD of hosts, our God. Thus you shall say 37
to the prophet, 'What has the LORD answered
you ?' or 'What has the LORD spoken ?' But 38
if you say, 'The burden of the LORD,' thus
says the LORD, 'Because you have said these
words, "The burden of the LORD," when I
sent to you, saying, "You shall not say, 'The
burden of the LORD,' " therefore, behold, I 39
will surely lift you up and cast you away from
my presence, you and the city which I gave
to you and your fathers. And I will bring 40
upon you everlasting reproach and perpetual
shame, which shall not be forgotten.' "

Parable of the figs

After Nebuchadrez'zar king of Babylon had 24
taken into exile from Jerusalem Jeconi'ah
the son of Jehoi'akim, king of Judah,
together with the princes of Judah, the
craftsmen, and the smiths, and had brought
them to Babylon, the LORD showed me this

---

[n] Cn Compare Syr: Heb obscure   [o] Gk Vg: Heb *What burden*

upon them, until they shall be utterly destroyed from the land which I gave to them and their fathers."

The fall of Judah

The word that came to Jeremiah concerning **25** all the people of Judah, in the fourth year of Jehoi′akim the son of Josi′ah, king of Judah (that was the first year of Nebuchadrez′zar king of Babylon), which Jeremiah the 2 prophet spoke to all the people of Judah and all the inhabitants of Jerusalem: "For 3 twenty-three years, from the thirteenth year of Josi′ah the son of Amon, king of Judah, to this day, the word of the LORD has come to me, and I have spoken persistently to you, but you have not listened. You have neither 4 listened nor inclined your ears to hear, although the LORD persistently sent to you all his servants the prophets, saying, 'Turn now, 5 every one of you, from his evil way and wrong doings, and dwell upon the land which the LORD has given to you and your fathers from of old and for ever; do not go 6 after other gods to serve and worship them, or provoke me to anger with the work of your hands. Then I will do you no harm.' Yet 7 you have not listened to me, says the LORD, that you might provoke me to anger with the work of your hands to your own harm.

"Therefore thus says the LORD of hosts: 8 Because you have not obeyed my words, behold, I will send for all the tribes of the 9 north, says the LORD, and for Nebuchadrez′zar the king of Babylon, my servant, and I will bring them against this land and its inhabitants, and against all these nations round about; I will utterly destroy them, and make them a horror, a hissing, and an everlasting reproach.*q* Moreover, I will 10 banish from them the voice of mirth and the voice of gladness, the voice of the bridegroom and the voice of the bride, the grinding of the millstones and the light of the lamp. This whole land shall become a ruin 11 and a waste, and these nations shall serve the king of Babylon seventy years. Then after 12 seventy years are completed, I will punish the king of Babylon and that nation, the land of the Chalde′ans, for their iniquity, says the LORD, making the land an everlasting waste. I will bring upon that land all the words 13 which I have uttered against it, everything written in this book, which Jeremiah prophesied against all the nations. For many 14 nations and great kings shall make slaves even of them; and I will recompense them

vision: Behold, two baskets of figs placed before the temple of the LORD. One basket had very good figs, like first-ripe figs, but the other basket had very bad figs, so bad that they could not be eaten. And the LORD said to me, "What do you see, Jeremiah?" I said, "Figs, the good figs very good, and the bad figs very bad, so bad that they cannot be eaten."

Then the word of the LORD came to me: "Thus says the LORD, the God of Israel: Like these good figs, so I will regard as good the exiles from Judah, whom I have sent away from this place to the land of the Chalde′ans. I will set my eyes upon them for good, and I will bring them back to this land. I will build them up, and not tear them down; I will plant them, and not uproot them. I will give them a heart to know that I am the LORD; and they shall be my people and I will be their God, for they shall return to me with their whole heart.

"But thus says the LORD: Like the bad figs which are so bad they cannot be eaten, so will I treat Zedeki′ah the king of Judah, his princes, the remnant of Jerusalem who remain in this land, and those who dwell in the land of Egypt. I will make them a horror *p* to all the kingdoms of the earth, to be a reproach, a byword, a taunt, and a curse in all the places where I shall drive them. And I will send sword, famine, and pestilence

p Compare Gk: Heb *horror for evil*   *q* Gk Compare Syr: Heb *desolations*
25.10: Jer 7.34; 16.9; Rev 18.23.

according to their deeds and the work of their hands.''

The doom of the nations

15 Thus the LORD, the God of Israel, said to me: "Take from my hand this cup of the wine of wrath, and make all the nations to 16 whom I send you drink it. They shall drink and stagger and be crazed because of the sword which I am sending among them."

17 So I took the cup from the LORD's hand, and made all the nations to whom the LORD 18 sent me drink it: Jerusalem and the cities of Judah, its kings and princes, to make them a desolation and a waste, a hissing and a curse, 19 as at this day; Pharaoh king of Egypt, his 20 servants, his princes, all his people, and all the foreign folk among them; all the kings of the land of Uz and all the kings of the land of the Philistines (Ash′kelon, Gaza, Ekron, 21 and the remnant of Ashdod); Edom, Moab, 22 and the sons of Ammon; all the kings of Tyre, all the kings of Sidon, and the kings of the 23 coastland across the sea; Dedan, Tema, Buz, 24 and all who cut the corners of their hair; all the kings of Arabia and all the kings of the 25 mixed tribes that dwell in the desert; all the kings of Zimri, all the kings of Elam, and all 26 the kings of Media; all the kings of the north, far and near, one after another, and all the kingdoms of the world which are on the face of the earth. And after them the king of Babylon[r] shall drink.

27 "Then you shall say to them, 'Thus says the LORD of hosts, the God of Israel: Drink, be drunk and vomit, fall and rise no more, because of the sword which I am sending among you.' 28 "And if they refuse to accept the cup from your hand to drink, then you shall say to them, 'Thus says the LORD of hosts: You 29 must drink! For behold, I begin to work evil at the city which is called by my name, and shall you go unpunished? You shall not go unpunished, for I am summoning a sword against all the inhabitants of the earth, says the LORD of hosts.'

"You, therefore, shall prophesy against them all these words, and say to them:
'The LORD will roar from on high,
    and from his holy habitation utter his voice;
he will roar mightily against his fold,
    and shout, like those who tread grapes,
    against all the inhabitants of the earth.
The clamour will resound to the ends of the earth,
    for the LORD has an indictment against the nations;
he is entering into judgment with all flesh,
    and the wicked he will put to the sword,
                    says the LORD.'

"Thus says the LORD of hosts:
Behold, evil is going forth
    from nation to nation,
and a great tempest is stirring
    from the farthest parts of the earth!
"And those slain by the LORD on that day shall extend from one end of the earth to the other. They shall not be lamented, or gathered, or buried; they shall be dung on the surface of the ground.
"Wail, you shepherds, and cry,
    and roll in ashes, you lords of the flock,
for the days of your slaughter and dispersion have come,
    and you shall fall like choice rams.[s]
No refuge will remain for the shepherds,
    nor escape for the lords of the flock.
Hark, the cry of the shepherds,
    and the wail of the lords of the flock!
For the LORD is despoiling their pasture,
    and the peaceful folds are devastated,
    because of the fierce anger of the LORD.
Like a lion he has left his covert,
    for their land has become a waste
because of the sword of the oppressor,
    and because of his fierce anger."

EVENTS IN THE LIFE OF THE PROPHET (Chaps. 26–45)

Attacked in the temple

26 IN the beginning of the reign of Jehoi′- akim the son of Josi′ah, king of Judah, this 2 word came from the LORD, "Thus says the LORD: Stand in the court of the LORD's house, and speak to all the cities of Judah which come to worship in the house of the LORD all the words that I command you to 3 speak to them; do not hold back a word. It may be they will listen, and every one turn from his evil way, that I may repent of the evil which I intend to do to them because of their evil doings. You shall say to them, 'Thus says the LORD: If you will not listen to me, to walk in my law which I have set before you, and to heed the words of my servants the prophets whom I send to you urgently, though you have not heeded, then I will make this house like Shiloh, and I will make

---

r Heb *Sheshach*, a cipher for Babylon   s Gk: Heb *a choice vessel*
25.15: Jer 51.7; Rev 14.8, 10; 16.19; 17.4; 18.3.

this city a curse for all the nations of the earth.' "

The priests and the prophets and all the people heard Jeremiah speaking these words in the house of the LORD. And when Jeremiah had finished speaking all that the LORD had commanded him to speak to all the people, then the priests and the prophets and all the people laid hold of him, saying, "You shall die! Why have you prophesied in the name of the LORD, saying, 'This house shall be like Shiloh, and this city shall be desolate, without inhabitant'?" And all the people gathered about Jeremiah in the house of the LORD.

When the princes of Judah heard these things, they came up from the king's house to the house of the LORD and took their seat in the entry of the New Gate of the house of the LORD. Then the priests and the prophets said to the princes and to all the people, "This man deserves the sentence of death, because he has prophesied against this city, as you have heard with your own ears."

Then Jeremiah spoke to all the princes and all the people, saying, "The LORD sent me to prophesy against this house and this city all the words you have heard. Now therefore amend your ways and your doings, and obey the voice of the LORD your God, and the LORD will repent of the evil which he has pronounced against you. But as for me, behold, I am in your hands. Do with me as seems good and right to you. Only know for certain that if you put me to death, you will bring innocent blood upon yourselves and upon this city and its inhabitants, for in truth the LORD sent me to you to speak all these words in your ears."

Then the princes and all the people said to the priests and the prophets, "This man does not deserve the sentence of death, for he has spoken to us in the name of the LORD our God." And certain of the elders of the land arose and spoke to all the assembled people, saying, "Micah of Mo′resheth prophesied in the days of Hezeki′ah king of Judah, and said to all the people of Judah: 'Thus says the LORD of hosts,

Zion shall be ploughed as a field;
Jerusalem shall become a heap of ruins,
and the mountain of the house a wooded height.'

Did Hezeki′ah king of Judah and all Judah put him to death? Did he not fear the LORD and entreat the favour of the LORD, and did not the LORD repent of the evil which he had pronounced against them? But we are about to bring great evil upon ourselves."

There was another man who prophesied in 20 the name of the LORD, Uri′ah the son of Shemai′ah from Kir′iath-je′arim. He prophesied against this city and against this land in words like those of Jeremiah. And 21 when King Jehoi′akim, with all his warriors and all the princes, heard his words, the king sought to put him to death; but when Uri′ah heard of it, he was afraid and fled and escaped to Egypt. Then King Jehoi′akim 22 sent to Egypt certain men, Elna′than the son of Achbor and others with him, and they 23 fetched Uri′ah from Egypt and brought him to King Jehoi′akim, who slew him with the sword and cast his dead body into the burial place of the common people.

But the hand of Ahi′kam the son of 24 Shaphan was with Jeremiah so that he was not given over to the people to be put to death.

A yoke on the prophet's neck

In the beginning of the reign of Zedeki′ah[t] **27** the son of Josi′ah, king of Judah, this word came to Jeremiah from the LORD. Thus the 2 LORD said to me: "Make yourself thongs and yoke-bars, and put them on your neck. Send 3 word[u] to the king of Edom, the king of Moab, the king of the sons of Ammon, the king of Tyre, and the king of Sidon by the hand of the envoys who have come to Jerusalem to Zedeki′ah king of Judah. Give 4 them this charge for their masters: 'Thus says the LORD of hosts, the God of Israel: This is what you shall say to your masters: "It 5 is I who by my great power and my out-stretched arm have made the earth, with the men and animals that are on the earth, and I give it to whomever it seems right to me. Now 6 I have given all these lands into the hand of Nebuchadnez′zar, the king of Babylon, my servant, and I have given him also the beasts of the field to serve him. All the nations shall 7 serve him and his son and his grandson, until the time of his own land comes; then many nations and great kings shall make him their slave.

" ' "But if any nation or kingdom will not 8 serve this Nebuchadnez′zar king of Babylon, and put its neck under the yoke of the king of Babylon, I will punish that nation with the sword, with famine, and with pestilence, says the LORD, until I have consumed it by his hand. So do not listen to your prophets, 9 your diviners, your dreamers,[v] your sooth-sayers, or your sorcerers, who are saying to you, 'You shall not serve the king of Babylon.' For it is a lie which they are 10 prophesying to you, with the result that you

t Another reading is *Jehoiakim*   u Cn: Heb *send them*   v Gk Syr Vg: Heb *dreams*

---

will be removed far from your land, and I
11 will drive you out, and you will perish. But
any nation which will bring its neck under
the yoke of the king of Babylon and serve
him, I will leave on its own land, to till it and
dwell there, says the LORD." ' "
12 To Zedeki′ah king of Judah I spoke in like
manner: "Bring your necks under the yoke
of the king of Babylon, and serve him and his
13 people, and live. Why will you and your
people die by the sword, by famine, and by
pestilence, as the LORD has spoken concerning any nation which will not serve the king
14 of Babylon? Do not listen to the words of
the prophets who are saying to you, 'You
shall not serve the king of Babylon,' for it is a
15 lie which they are prophesying to you. I
have not sent them, says the LORD, but they
are prophesying falsely in my name, with the
result that I will drive you out and you will
perish, you and the prophets who are
prophesying to you."
16 Then I spoke to the priests and to all this
people, saying, "Thus says the LORD: Do not
listen to the words of your prophets who are
prophesying to you, saying, 'Behold, the

vessels of the LORD's house will now shortly
be brought back from Babylon,' for it is a lie
17 which they are prophesying to you. Do not
listen to them; serve the king of Babylon and
live. Why should this city become a desola-
18 tion? If they are prophets, and if the word of
the LORD is with them, then let them intercede with the LORD of hosts, that the vessels
which are left in the house of the LORD, in
the house of the king of Judah, and in
19 Jerusalem may not go to Babylon. For thus
says the LORD of hosts concerning the pillars,
the sea, the stands, and the rest of the vessels
20 which are left in this city, which Nebuchad-
nez′zar king of Babylon did not take away,
when he took into exile from Jerusalem to
Babylon Jeconi′ah the son of Jehoi′akim,
king of Judah, and all the nobles of Judah
21 and Jerusalem—thus says the LORD of hosts,
the God of Israel, concerning the vessels
which are left in the house of the LORD, in
the house of the king of Judah, and in
22 Jerusalem: They shall be carried to Babylon
and remain there until the day when I give
attention to them, says the LORD. Then I
will bring them back and restore them to this
place."

In that same year, at the beginning of the
reign of Zedeki′ah king of Judah, in the fifth
month of the fourth year, Hanani′ah the son
of Azzur, the prophet from Gibeon, spoke to
me in the house of the LORD, in the presence
of the priests and all the people, saying,
"Thus says the LORD of hosts, the God of
Israel: I have broken the yoke of the king of
Babylon. Within two years I will bring back
to this place all the vessels of the LORD's
house, which Nebuchadnez′zar king of
Babylon took away from this place and
carried to Babylon. I will also bring back to
this place Jeconi′ah the son of Jehoi′akim,
king of Judah, and all the exiles from Judah
who went to Babylon, says the LORD, for I
will break the yoke of the king of Babylon."

Then the prophet Jeremiah spoke to Ha-
nani′ah the prophet in the presence of the
priests and all the people who were standing
in the house of the LORD; and the prophet
Jeremiah said, "Amen! May the LORD do
so; may the LORD make the words which you
have prophesied come true, and bring back
to this place from Babylon the vessels of the
house of the LORD, and all the exiles. Yet
hear now this word which I speak in your
hearing and in the hearing of all the people.
The prophets who preceded you and me
from ancient times prophesied war, famine,
and pestilence against many countries and
great kingdoms. As for the prophet who
prophesies peace, when the word of that
prophet comes to pass, then it will be known
that the LORD has truly sent the prophet."

Then the prophet Hanani′ah took the
yoke-bars from the neck of Jeremiah the
prophet, and broke them. And Hanani′ah
spoke in the presence of all the people,
saying, "Thus says the LORD: Even so will I
break the yoke of Nebuchadnez′zar king of
Babylon from the neck of all the nations
within two years." But Jeremiah the prophet
went his way.

Sometime after the prophet Hanani′ah had
broken the yoke-bars from off the neck of
Jeremiah the prophet, the word of the LORD
came to Jeremiah: "Go, tell Hanani′ah,
'Thus says the LORD: You have broken
wooden bars, but I *w* will make in their place
bars of iron. For thus says the LORD of hosts,
the God of Israel: I have put upon the neck
of all these nations an iron yoke of servitude
to Nebuchadnez′zar king of Babylon, and
they shall serve him, for I have given to him
even the beasts of the field.' " And Jeremiah
the prophet said to the prophet Hanani′ah,
"Listen, Hanani′ah, the LORD has not sent
you, and you have made this people trust in a
lie. Therefore thus says the LORD: 'Behold,

---

w Gk: Heb *you*

I will remove you from the face of the earth. This very year you shall die, because you have uttered rebellion against the LORD.' "

In that same year, in the seventh month, the prophet Hanani'ah died.

Letter to the exiles

9 These are the words of the letter which Jeremiah the prophet sent from Jerusalem to the elders[x] of the exiles, and to the priests, the prophets, and all the people, whom Nebuchadnez'zar had taken into exile from Jerusalem to Babylon. This was after King Jeconi'ah, and the queen mother, the eunuchs, the princes of Judah and Jerusalem, the craftsmen, and the smiths had departed from Jerusalem. The letter was sent by the hand of Ela'sah the son of Shaphan and Gemari'ah the son of Hilki'ah, whom Zedeki'ah king of Judah sent to Babylon to Nebuchadnez'zar king of Babylon. It said: 4 "Thus says the LORD of hosts, the God of Israel, to all the exiles whom I have sent into 5 exile from Jerusalem to Babylon: Build houses and live in them; plant gardens and 6 eat their produce. Take wives and have sons and daughters; take wives for your sons, and give your daughters in marriage, that they may bear sons and daughters; multiply there, 7 and do not decrease. But seek the welfare of the city where I have sent you into exile, and pray to the LORD on its behalf, for in its 8 welfare you will find your welfare. For thus says the LORD of hosts, the God of Israel: Do not let your prophets and your diviners who are among you deceive you, and do not listen 9 to the dreams which they dream,[y] for it is a lie which they are prophesying to you in my name; I did not send them, says the LORD. 10 "For thus says the LORD: When seventy years are completed for Babylon, I will visit you, and I will fulfil to you my promise and 11 bring you back to this place. For I know the plans I have for you, says the LORD, plans for welfare and not for evil, to give you a future 12 and a hope. Then you will call upon me and come and pray to me, and I will hear you. 13 You will seek me and find me; when you seek 14 me with all your heart, I will be found by you, says the LORD, and I will restore your fortunes and gather you from all the nations and all the places where I have driven you, says the LORD, and I will bring you back to the place from which I sent you into exile. 15 "Because you have said, 'The LORD has raised up prophets for us in Babylon,' 16 —Thus says the LORD concerning the king who sits on the throne of David, and concerning all the people who dwell in this city, your kinsmen who did not go out with you into exile: 'Thus says the LORD of hosts, 17 Behold, I am sending on them sword, famine, and pestilence, and I will make them like vile figs which are so bad they cannot be eaten. I will pursue them with sword, 18 famine, and pestilence, and will make them a horror to all the kingdoms of the earth, to be a curse, a terror, a hissing, and a reproach among all the nations where I have driven them, because they did not heed my words, 19 says the LORD, which I persistently sent to you by my servants the prophets, but you would not listen, says the LORD.'—Hear the 20 word of the LORD, all you exiles whom I sent away from Jerusalem to Babylon: 'Thus says 21 the LORD of hosts, the God of Israel, concerning Ahab the son of Kola'iah and Zedeki'ah the son of Ma-asei'ah, who are prophesying a lie to you in my name: Behold, I will deliver them into the hand of Nebuchadrez'zar king of Babylon, and he shall slay them before your eyes. Because of 22 them this curse shall be used by all the exiles from Judah in Babylon: "The LORD make you like Zedeki'ah and Ahab, whom the king of Babylon roasted in the fire," because they 23 have committed folly in Israel, they have committed adultery with their neighbours' wives, and they have spoken in my name lying words which I did not command them. I am the one who knows, and I am witness, says the LORD.' "

Concerning Shemaiah

To Shemai'ah of Nehel'am you shall say: 24 "Thus says the LORD of hosts, the God of 25 Israel: You have sent letters in your name to all the people who are in Jerusalem, and to Zephani'ah the son of Ma-asei'ah the priest, and to all the priests, saying, 'The LORD has 26 made you priest instead of Jehoi'ada the priest, to have charge in the house of the LORD over every madman who prophesies, to put him in the stocks and collar. Now why 27

have you not rebuked Jeremiah of An'athoth who is prophesying to you? For he has sent 28 to us in Babylon, saying, "Your exile will be long; build houses and live in them, and plant gardens and eat their produce." ' "

Zephani'ah the priest read this letter in the 29 hearing of Jeremiah the prophet. Then the 30

x Gk: Heb the rest of the elders   y Cn: Heb your dreams which you cause to dream

31 word of the LORD came to Jeremiah: "Send
to all the exiles, saying, 'Thus says the LORD
concerning Shemai′ah of Nehel′am: Because
Shemai′ah has prophesied to you when I did
not send him, and has made you trust in a lie,
32 therefore thus says the LORD: Behold, I will
punish Shemai′ah of Nehel′am and his
descendants; he shall not have any one living
among this people to see² the good that I will
do to my people, says the LORD, for he has
talked rebellion against the LORD.' "

Return from exile promised

30 The word that came to Jeremiah from the
2 LORD: "Thus says the LORD, the God of
Israel: Write in a book all the words that I
3 have spoken to you. For behold, days are
coming, says the LORD, when I will restore
the fortunes of my people, Israel and Judah,
says the LORD, and I will bring them back to
the land which I gave to their fathers, and
they shall take possession of it."
4 These are the words which the LORD spoke
concerning Israel and Judah:
5 "Thus says the LORD:
　We have heard a cry of panic,
　　of terror, and no peace.
6 Ask now, and see,
　　can a man bear a child?
　Why then do I see every man
　　with his hands on his loins like a woman
　　　in labour?
　Why has every face turned pale?
7 Alas! that day is so great
　　there is none like it;
　it is a time of distress for Jacob;
　　yet he shall be saved out of it.
8 "And it shall come to pass in that day, says
the LORD of hosts, that I will break the yoke
from off their* neck, and I will burst their*
bonds, and strangers shall no more make
9 servants of them.ᵇ But they shall serve the
LORD their God and David their king, whom
I will raise up for them.

10 "Then fear not, O Jacob my servant, says
　　the LORD,

　nor be dismayed, O Israel;
for lo, I will save you from afar,
　and your offspring from the land of their
　　captivity.
Jacob shall return and have quiet and ease,
　and none shall make him afraid.
For I am with you to save you,
　　　　　　　　　　　says the LORD;
I will make a full end of all the nations
　among whom I scattered you,
　but of you I will not make a full end.
I will chasten you in just measure,
　and I will by no means leave you
　　unpunished.

"For thus says the LORD:
Your hurt is incurable,
　and your wound is grievous.
There is none to uphold your cause,
　no medicine for your wound,
　no healing for you.
All your lovers have forgotten you;
　they care nothing for you;
for I have dealt you the blow of an enemy,
　the punishment of a merciless foe,
because your guilt is great,
　because your sins are flagrant.
Why do you cry out over your hurt?
　Your pain is incurable.
Because your guilt is great,
　because your sins are flagrant,
　I have done these things to you.
Therefore all who devour you shall be
　　devoured,
　and all your foes, every one of them,
　　shall go into captivity;
those who despoil you shall become a
　　spoil,
　and all who prey on you I will make a
　　prey.
For I will restore health to you,
　and your wounds I will heal,
　　　　　　　　　　　says the LORD,
because they have called you an outcast:
　'It is Zion, for whom no one cares!'

"Thus says the LORD:
Behold, I will restore the fortunes of the
　　tents of Jacob,
　and have compassion on his dwellings;
the city shall be rebuilt upon its mound,
　and the palace shall stand where it used
　　to be.
Out of them shall come songs of thanks-
　　giving,
　and the voices of those who make merry.
I will multiply them, and they shall not be
　　few;
　I will make them honoured, and they
　　shall not be small.

---

² Gk: Heb *and he shall not see*　　* Gk Old Latin: Heb *your*　　ᵇ Heb *make a servant of him*

Their children shall be as they were of old,
    and their congregation shall be estab-
      lished before me;
and I will punish all who oppress them.
Their prince shall be one of themselves,
    their ruler shall come forth from their
      midst;
I will make him draw near, and he shall
    approach me,
    for who would dare of himself to
      approach me ?
                    says the LORD.
And you shall be my people,
    and I will be your God."

Behold the storm of the LORD!
    Wrath has gone forth,
a whirling tempest;
    it will burst upon the head of the
      wicked.
The fierce anger of the LORD will not turn
    back
    until he has executed and accomplished
    the intents of his mind.
In the latter days you will understand this.

1 "At that time, says the LORD, I will be the
God of all the families of Israel, and they
shall be my people."
    Thus says the LORD:
"The people who survived the sword
    found grace in the wilderness;
when Israel sought for rest,
    the LORD appeared to him[c] from afar.
I have loved you with an everlasting love;
    therefore I have continued my faith-
      fulness to you.
Again I will build you, and you shall be
    built,
    O virgin Israel!
Again you shall adorn yourself with
    timbrels,
    and shall go forth in the dance of the
      merrymakers.
Again you shall plant vineyards
    upon the mountains of Samar′ia;
the planters shall plant,
    and shall enjoy the fruit.
For there shall be a day when watchmen
    will call
    in the hill country of E′phraim:
'Arise, and let us go up to Zion,
    to the LORD our God.' "

For thus says the LORD:
"Sing aloud with gladness for Jacob,
    and raise shouts for the chief of the
      nations;
proclaim, give praise, and say,

'The LORD has saved his people,
    the remnant of Israel.'
Behold, I will bring them from the north 8
    country,
    and gather them from the farthest parts
      of the earth,
among them the blind and the lame,
    the woman with child and her who is in
      travail, together;
    a great company, they shall return
      here.
With weeping they shall come, 9
    and with consolations[d] I will lead them
      back,
I will make them walk by brooks of water,
    in a straight path in which they shall not
      stumble;
for I am a father to Israel,
    and E′phraim is my first-born.

"Hear the word of the LORD, O nations, 10
    and declare it in the coastlands afar
      off;
say, 'He who scattered Israel will gather
    him,
    and will keep him as a shepherd keeps
      his flock.'
For the LORD has ransomed Jacob, 11
    and has redeemed him from hands too
      strong for him.
They shall come and sing aloud on the 12
    height of Zion,
    and they shall be radiant over the
      goodness of the LORD,
over the grain, the wine, and the oil,
    and over the young of the flock and the
      herd;
their life shall be like a watered garden,
    and they shall languish no more.
Then shall the maidens rejoice in the 13
    dance,
    and the young men and the old shall be
      merry.
I will turn their mourning into joy,
    I will comfort them, and give them
      gladness for sorrow.
I will feast the soul of the priests with 14
    abundance,
    and my people shall be satisfied with my
      goodness,"
                    says the LORD.

Thus says the LORD: 15
"A voice is heard in Ramah,
    lamentation and bitter weeping.
Rachel is weeping for her children;
    she refuses to be comforted for her
      children,
    because they are not."

[c] Gk: Heb *me*   [d] Gk Compare Vg Tg: Heb *supplications*
31.15: Mt 2.18.

16 Thus says the LORD:
  "Keep your voice from weeping,
    and your eyes from tears;
  for your work shall be rewarded,
                says the LORD,
    and they shall come back from the land
      of the enemy.
17 There is hope for your future,
                says the LORD,
    and your children shall come back to
      their own country.
18 I have heard E′phraim bemoaning,
  'Thou hast chastened me, and I was
      chastened,
    like an untrained calf;
  bring me back that I may be restored,
    for thou art the LORD my God.
19 For after I had turned away I repented;
    and after I was instructed, I smote upon
      my thigh;
  I was ashamed, and I was confounded,
    because I bore the disgrace of my
      youth.'
20 Is E′phraim my dear son?
    Is he my darling child?
  For as often as I speak against him,
    I do remember him still.
  Therefore my heart yearns for him;
    I will surely have mercy on him,
                says the LORD.

21 "Set up waymarks for yourself,
    make yourself guideposts;
  consider well the highway,
    the road by which you went.
  Return, O virgin Israel,
    return to these your cities.
22 How long will you waver,
    O faithless daughter?
  For the LORD has created a new thing on
      the earth:
    a woman protects a man."

23 Thus says the LORD of hosts, the God of
  Israel: "Once more they shall use these
  words in the land of Judah and in its cities,
  when I restore their fortunes:
  'The LORD bless you, O habitation of
      righteousness,
    O holy hill!'
24 And Judah and all its cities shall dwell there
  together, and the farmers and those who
25 wander[e] with their flocks. For I will satisfy
  the weary soul, and every languishing soul I
  will replenish."
26 Thereupon I awoke and looked, and my
  sleep was pleasant to me.
27 "Behold, the days are coming, says the
  LORD, when I will sow the house of Israel

and the house of Judah with the seed of man
and the seed of beast. And it shall come to
pass that as I have watched over them to
pluck up and break down, to overthrow,
destroy, and bring evil, so I will watch over
them to build and to plant, says the LORD.
In those days they shall no longer say:
  'The fathers have eaten sour grapes,
    and the children's teeth are set on edge.'
But every one shall die for his own sin; each
man who eats sour grapes, his teeth shall be
set on edge.

The new covenant

"Behold, the days are coming, says the
LORD, when I will make a new covenant with
the house of Israel and the house of Judah,
not like the covenant which I made with their
fathers when I took them by the hand to
bring them out of the land of Egypt, my
covenant which they broke, though I was
their husband, says the LORD. But this is the
covenant which I will make with the house of
Israel after those days, says the LORD: I will
put my law within them, and I will write it
upon their hearts; and I will be their God,
and they shall be my people. And no longer
shall each man teach his neighbour and each
his brother, saying, 'Know the LORD,' for
they shall all know me, from the least of them
to the greatest, says the LORD; for I will
forgive their iniquity, and I will remember
their sin no more."

Thus says the LORD,
  who gives the sun for light by day
    and the fixed order of the moon
    and the stars for light by night,
  who stirs up the sea so that its waves
      roar—
    the LORD of hosts is his name:
  "If this fixed order departs
    from before me, says the LORD,
  then shall the descendants of Israel cease
    from being a nation before me for ever."

Thus says the LORD:
  "If the heavens above can be measured,
    and the foundations of the earth below
      can be explored,
  then I will cast off all the descendants of
      Israel
    for all that they have done,
                says the LORD."

"Behold, the days are coming, says the
LORD, when the city shall be rebuilt for
the LORD from the tower of Hanan′el to the

---

e Cn Compare Syr Vg Tg: Heb *and they shall wander*
31.31: Lk 22.20; 1 Cor 11.25.   **31.31-34:** Jer 32.38-40; Heb 8.8-12; 10.16-17.

Corner Gate. And the measuring line shall go out farther, straight to the hill Gareb, and shall then turn to Go'ah. The whole valley of the dead bodies and the ashes, and all the fields as far as the brook Kidron, to the corner of the Horse Gate toward the east, shall be sacred to the LORD. It shall not be uprooted or overthrown any more for ever."

Jeremiah buys a field

2 The word that came to Jeremiah from the LORD in the tenth year of Zedeki'ah king of Judah, which was the eighteenth year of Nebuchadrez'zar. At that time the army of the king of Babylon was besieging Jerusalem, and Jeremiah the prophet was shut up in the court of the guard which was in the palace of the king of Judah. For Zedeki'ah king of Judah had imprisoned him, saying, "Why do you prophesy and say, 'Thus says the LORD: Behold, I am giving this city into the hand of the king of Babylon, and he shall take it; Zedeki'ah king of Judah shall not escape out of the hand of the Chalde'ans, but shall surely be given into the hand of the king of Babylon, and shall speak with him face to face and see him eye to eye; and he shall take Zedeki'ah to Babylon, and there he shall remain until I visit him, says the LORD; though you fight against the Chalde'ans, you shall not succeed'?"

Jeremiah said, "The word of the LORD came to me: Behold, Han'amel the son of Shallum your uncle will come to you and say, 'Buy my field which is at An'athoth, for the right of redemption by purchase is yours.' Then Han'amel my cousin came to me in the court of the guard, in accordance with the word of the LORD, and said to me, 'Buy my field which is at An'athoth in the land of Benjamin, for the right of possession and redemption is yours; buy it for yourself.' Then I knew that this was the word of the LORD.

"And I bought the field at An'athoth from Han'amel my cousin, and weighed out the money to him, seventeen shekels of silver. I signed the deed, sealed it, got witnesses, and weighed the money on scales. Then I took the sealed deed of purchase, containing the terms and conditions, and the open copy; and I gave the deed of purchase to Baruch the son of Neri'ah son of Mahsei'ah, in the presence of Han'amel my cousin, in the presence of the witnesses who signed the deed of purchase, and in the presence of all the Jews who were sitting in the court of the guard. I charged Baruch in their presence, saying, 'Thus says the LORD of hosts, the God of Israel: Take these deeds, both this sealed deed of purchase and this open deed, and put them in an earthenware vessel, that they may last for a long time. For thus says 15 the LORD of hosts, the God of Israel: Houses and fields and vineyards shall again be bought in this land.'

"After I had given the deed of purchase to 16 Baruch the son of Neri'ah, I prayed to the LORD, saying: 'Ah Lord GOD! It is thou 17 who hast made the heavens and the earth by thy great power and by thy outstretched arm! Nothing is too hard for thee, who 18 showest steadfast love to thousands, but dost requite the guilt of fathers to their children after them, O great and mighty God whose name is the LORD of hosts, great in counsel 19 and mighty in deed; whose eyes are open to all the ways of men, rewarding every man according to his ways and according to the fruit of his doings; who hast shown signs and 20 wonders in the land of Egypt, and to this day in Israel and among all mankind, and hast made thee a name, as at this day. Thou didst 21 bring thy people Israel out of the land of Egypt with signs and wonders, with a strong hand and outstretched arm, and with great terror; and thou gavest them this land, which 22 thou didst swear to their fathers to give them, a land flowing with milk and honey; and they 23 entered and took possession of it. But they did not obey thy voice or walk in thy law; they did nothing of all thou didst command them to do. Therefore thou hast made all this evil come upon them. Behold, the siege 24 mounds have come up to the city to take it, and because of sword and famine and pestilence the city is given into the hands of the Chalde'ans who are fighting against it. What thou didst speak has come to pass, and behold, thou seest it. Yet thou, O Lord GOD, 25 hast said to me, "Buy the field for money and get witnesses"—though the city is given into the hands of the Chalde'ans.' "

The word of the LORD came to Jeremiah: 26 "Behold, I am the LORD, the God of all flesh; 27 is anything too hard for me? Therefore, 28 thus says the LORD: Behold, I am giving this city into the hands of the Chalde'ans and into the hand of Nebuchadrez'zar king of Babylon, and he shall take it. The Chal- 29 de'ans who are fighting against this city shall come and set this city on fire, and burn it, with the houses on whose roofs incense has been offered to Ba'al and drink offerings have been poured out to other gods, to provoke me to anger. For the sons of Israel 30 and the sons of Judah have done nothing but evil in my sight from their youth; the sons of Israel have done nothing but provoke me to anger by the work of their hands, says the LORD. This city has aroused my anger and 31 wrath, from the day it was built to this day, so that I will remove it from my sight

32 because of all the evil of the sons of Israel and the sons of Judah which they did to provoke me to anger—their kings and their princes, their priests and their prophets, the men of Judah and the inhabitants of Jerusalem.
33 They have turned to me their back and not their face; and though I have taught them persistently they have not listened to receive
34 instruction. They set up their abominations in the house which is called by my name, to
35 defile it. They built the high places of Ba'al in the valley of the son of Hinnom, to offer up their sons and daughters to Molech, though I did not command them, nor did it enter into my mind, that they should do this abomination, to cause Judah to sin.
36 "Now therefore thus says the LORD, the God of Israel, concerning this city of which you say, 'It is given into the hand of the king of Babylon by sword, by famine, and by
37 pestilence': Behold, I will gather them from all the countries to which I drove them in my anger and my wrath and in great indignation; I will bring them back to this place, and I
38 will make them dwell in safety. And they shall be my people, and I will be their God.
39 I will give them one heart and one way, that they may fear me for ever, for their own good
40 and the good of their children after them. I will make with them an everlasting covenant, that I will not turn away from doing good to them; and I will put the fear of me in their
41 hearts, that they may not turn from me. I will rejoice in doing them good, and I will plant them in this land in faithfulness, with all my heart and all my soul.
42 "For thus says the LORD: Just as I have brought all this great evil upon this people, so I will bring upon them all the good that I
43 promise them. Fields shall be bought in this land of which you are saying, It is a desolation, without man or beast; it is given into
44 the hands of the Chalde'ans. Fields shall be bought for money, and deeds shall be signed and sealed and witnessed, in the land of Benjamin, in the places about Jerusalem, and in the cities of Judah, in the cities of the hill country, in the cities of the Shephe'lah, and in the cities of the Negeb; for I will restore their fortunes, says the LORD."

Shut up in prison

33 The word of the LORD came to Jeremiah a second time, while he was still shut up in the
2 court of the guard: "Thus says the LORD who made the earth,[f] the LORD who formed
3 it to establish it—the LORD is his name: Call to me and I will answer you, and will tell you

great and hidden things which you have not known. For thus says the LORD, the God of 4 Israel, concerning the houses of this city and the houses of the kings of Judah which were torn down to make a defence against the siege mounds and before the sword:[g] The 5 Chalde'ans are coming in to fight[h] and to fill them with the dead bodies of men whom I shall smite in my anger and my wrath, for I have hidden my face from this city because of all their wickedness. Behold, I will bring to 6 it health and healing, and I will heal them and reveal to them abundance[i] of prosperity and security. I will restore the fortunes of 7 Judah and the fortunes of Israel, and rebuild them as they were at first. I will cleanse 8 them from all the guilt of their sin against me, and I will forgive all the guilt of their sin and rebellion against me. And this city[j] shall 9 be to me a name of joy, a praise and a glory before all the nations of the earth who shall hear of all the good that I do for them; they shall fear and tremble because of all the good and all the prosperity I provide for it.

"Thus says the LORD: In this place of 10 which you say, 'It is a waste without man or beast,' in the cities of Judah and the streets of Jerusalem that are desolate, without man or inhabitant or beast, there shall be heard again the voice of mirth and the voice of gladness, 11 the voice of the bridegroom and the voice of the bride, the voices of those who sing, as they bring thank offerings to the house of the LORD:

'Give thanks to the LORD of hosts,
  for the LORD is good,
    for his steadfast love endures for
      ever!'

For I will restore the fortunes of the land as at first, says the LORD.

"Thus says the LORD of hosts: In this place 12 which is waste, without man or beast, and in all of its cities, there shall again be habitations of shepherds resting their flocks. In the 13 cities of the hill country, in the cities of the Shephe'lah, and in the cities of the Negeb, in the land of Benjamin, the places about Jerusalem, and in the cities of Judah, flocks shall again pass under the hands of the one who counts them, says the LORD.

"Behold, the days are coming, says the 14 LORD, when I will fulfil the promise I made to the house of Israel and the house of Judah. In those days and at that time I will 15 cause a righteous Branch to spring forth for David; and he shall execute justice and righteousness in the land. In those days 16 Judah will be saved and Jerusalem will dwell securely. And this is the name by which it

---

f Gk: Heb it   g Heb obscure   h Cn: Heb They are coming in to fight against the Chaldeans   i Heb uncertain
j Heb and it
32.38–40: Jer 31.31–34.   33.15: Is 4.2; Jer 23.5; Zech 3.8; 6.12.

will be called: 'The LORD is our righteousness.'

"For thus says the LORD: David shall never lack a man to sit on the throne of the house of Israel, and the Levitical priests shall never lack a man in my presence to offer burnt offerings, to burn cereal offerings, and to make sacrifices for ever."

The word of the LORD came to Jeremiah: "Thus says the LORD: If you can break my covenant with the day and my covenant with the night, so that day and night will not come at their appointed time, then also my covenant with David my servant may be broken, so that he shall not have a son to reign on his throne, and my covenant with the Levitical priests my ministers. As the host of heaven cannot be numbered and the sands of the sea cannot be measured, so I will multiply the descendants of David my servant, and the Levitical priests who minister to me."

The word of the LORD came to Jeremiah: "Have you not observed what these people are saying, 'The LORD has rejected the two families which he chose'? Thus they have despised my people so that they are no longer a nation in their sight. Thus says the LORD: If I have not established my covenant with day and night and the ordinances of heaven and earth, then I will reject the descendants of Jacob and David my servant and will not choose one of his descendants to rule over the seed of Abraham, Isaac, and Jacob. For I will restore their fortunes, and will have mercy upon them."

The king rebuked

34 The word which came to Jeremiah from the LORD, when Nebuchadrez'zar king of Babylon and all his army and all the kingdoms of the earth under his dominion and the peoples were fighting against Jerusalem and all of its cities: "Thus says the LORD, the God of Israel: Go and speak to Zedeki'ah king of Judah and say to him, 'Thus says the LORD: Behold, I am giving this city into the hand of the king of Babylon, and he shall burn it with fire. You shall not escape from his hand, but shall surely be captured and delivered into his hand; you shall see the king of Babylon eye to eye and speak with him face to face; and you shall go to Babylon.' Yet hear the word of the LORD, O Zedeki'ah king of Judah! Thus says the LORD concerning you: 'You shall not die by the sword. You shall die in peace. And as spices were burned for your fathers, the former kings who were before you, so men shall burn spices for you and lament for you, saying, "Alas, lord!"' For I have spoken the word, says the LORD."

Then Jeremiah the prophet spoke all these 6 words to Zedeki'ah king of Judah, in Jerusalem, when the army of the king of Babylon 7 was fighting against Jerusalem and against all the cities of Judah that were left, Lachish and Aze'kah; for these were the only fortified cities of Judah that remained.

The word which came to Jeremiah from the 8 LORD, after King Zedeki'ah had made a covenant with all the people in Jerusalem to make a proclamation of liberty to them, that 9 every one should set free his Hebrew slaves, male and female, so that no one should enslave a Jew, his brother. And they obeyed, 10 all the princes and all the people who had entered into the covenant that every one would set free his slave, male or female, so that they would not be enslaved again; they obeyed and set them free. But afterward 11 they turned around and took back the male and female slaves they had set free, and brought them into subjection as slaves. The 12 word of the LORD came to Jeremiah from the LORD: "Thus says the LORD, the God of 13 Israel: I made a covenant with your fathers when I brought them out of the land of Egypt, out of the house of bondage, saying, 'At the end of six*k* years each of you must set 14 free the fellow Hebrew who has been sold to you and has served you six years; you must set him free from your service.' But your fathers did not listen to me or incline their ears to me. You recently repented and did 15 what was right in my eyes by proclaiming liberty, each to his neighbour, and you made a covenant before me in the house which is called by my name; but then you turned 16 around and profaned my name when each of you took back his male and female slaves, whom you had set free according to their desire, and you brought them into subjection to be your slaves. Therefore, thus says the 17 LORD: You have not obeyed me by proclaiming liberty, every one to his brother and to his neighbour; behold, I proclaim to you liberty to the sword, to pestilence, and to famine, says the LORD. I will make you a horror to all the kingdoms of the earth. And 18 the men who transgressed my covenant and did not keep the terms of the covenant which they made before me, I will make like*l* the calf which they cut in two and passed between its parts—the princes of Judah, the 19 princes of Jerusalem, the eunuchs, the priests, and all the people of the land who passed between the parts of the calf; and I 20 will give them into the hand of their enemies

---

k Gk: Heb *seven*   *l* Cn: Heb lacks *like*

and into the hand of those who seek their lives. Their dead bodies shall be food for the birds of the air and the beasts of the earth.

21 And Zedeki′ah king of Judah, and his princes I will give into the hand of their enemies and into the hand of those who seek their lives, into the hand of the army of the king of Babylon which has withdrawn from you.

22 Behold, I will command, says the LORD, and will bring them back to this city; and they will fight against it, and take it, and burn it

with fire. I will make the cities of Judah a desolation without inhabitant.''

The Rechabites commended

35 The word which came to Jeremiah from the LORD in the days of Jehoi′akim the son of

2 Josi′ah, king of Judah: ''Go to the house of the Re′chabites, and speak with them, and bring them to the house of the LORD, into one of the chambers; then offer them wine to

3 drink.'' So I took Ja-azani′ah the son of Jeremiah, son of Habazzini′ah, and his brothers, and all his sons, and the whole

4 house of the Re′chabites. I brought them to the house of the LORD into the chamber of the sons of Hanan the son of Igdali′ah, the man of God, which was near the chamber of the princes, above the chamber of Ma-asei′ah the son of Shallum, keeper of the threshold.

5 Then I set before the Re′chabites pitchers full of wine, and cups; and I said to them,

6 ''Drink wine.'' But they answered, ''We will drink no wine, for Jon′adab the son of Rechab, our father, commanded us, 'You shall not drink wine, neither you nor your

7 sons for ever; you shall not build a house; you shall not sow seed; you shall not plant or have a vineyard; but you shall live in tents all

your days, that you may live many days in the land where you sojourn.' We have 8 obeyed the voice of Jon′adab the son of Rechab, our father, in all that he commanded us, to drink no wine all our days, ourselves, our wives, our sons, or our daughters, and 9 not to build houses to dwell in. We have no vineyard or field or seed; but we have lived in 10 tents, and have obeyed and done all that Jon′adab our father commanded us. But 11 when Nebuchadrez′zar king of Babylon came up against the land, we said, 'Come, and let us go to Jerusalem for fear of the army of the Chalde′ans and the army of the Syrians.' So we are living in Jerusalem.''

Then the word of the LORD came to 12 Jeremiah: ''Thus says the LORD of hosts, the 13 God of Israel: Go and say to the men of Judah and the inhabitants of Jerusalem, Will you not receive instruction and listen to my words? says the LORD. The command which 14 Jon′adab the son of Rechab gave to his sons, to drink no wine, has been kept; and they drink none to this day, for they have obeyed their father's command. I have spoken to you persistently, but you have not listened to me. I have sent to you all my servants the 15 prophets, sending them persistently, saying, 'Turn now every one of you from his evil way, and amend your doings, and do not go after other gods to serve them, and then you shall dwell in the land which I gave to you and your fathers.' But you did not incline your ear or listen to me. The sons of 16 Jon′adab the son of Rechab have kept the command which their father gave them, but this people has not obeyed me. Therefore, 17 thus says the LORD, the God of hosts, the God of Israel: Behold, I am bringing on Judah and all the inhabitants of Jerusalem all the evil that I have pronounced against them; because I have spoken to them and they have not listened, I have called to them and they have not answered.''

But to the house of the Re′chabites Jere- 18 miah said, ''Thus says the LORD of hosts, the God of Israel: Because you have obeyed the command of Jon′adab your father, and kept all his precepts, and done all that he commanded you, therefore thus says the 19 LORD of hosts, the God of Israel: Jon′adab the son of Rechab shall never lack a man to stand before me.''

The burning of the scroll

In the fourth year of Jehoi′akim the son of 36 Josi′ah, king of Judah, this word came to Jeremiah from the LORD: ''Take a scroll and 2 write on it all the words that I have spoken to you against Israel and Judah and all the nations, from the day I spoke to you, from

3 the days of Josi'ah until today. It may be that the house of Judah will hear all the evil which I intend to do to them, so that every one may turn from his evil way, and that I may forgive their iniquity and their sin."

4 Then Jeremiah called Baruch the son of Neri'ah, and Baruch wrote upon a scroll at the dictation of Jeremiah all the words of the

5 LORD which he had spoken to him. And Jeremiah ordered Baruch, saying, "I am debarred from going to the house of the

6 LORD; so you are to go, and on a fast day in the hearing of all the people in the LORD's house you shall read the words of the LORD from the scroll which you have written at my dictation. You shall read them also in the hearing of all the men of Judah who come out

7 of their cities. It may be that their supplication will come before the LORD, and that every one will turn from his evil way, for great is the anger and wrath that the LORD

8 has pronounced against this people." And Baruch the son of Neri'ah did all that Jeremiah the prophet ordered him about reading from the scroll the words of the LORD in the LORD's house.

9 In the fifth year of Jehoi'akim the son of Josi'ah, king of Judah, in the ninth month, all the people in Jerusalem and all the people who came from the cities of Judah to Jerusalem proclaimed a fast before the LORD.

10 Then, in the hearing of all the people, Baruch read the words of Jeremiah from the scroll, in the house of the LORD, in the chamber of Gemari'ah the son of Shaphan the secretary, which was in the upper court, at the entry of the New Gate of the LORD's house.

11 When Micai'ah the son of Gemari'ah, son of Shaphan, heard all the words of the LORD

12 from the scroll, he went down to the king's house, into the secretary's chamber; and all the princes were sitting there: Elish'ama the secretary, Delai'ah the son of Shemai'ah, Elna'than the son of Achbor, Gemari'ah the son of Shaphan, Zedeki'ah the son

13 of Hanani'ah, and all the princes. And Micai'ah told them all the words that he had heard, when Baruch read the scroll in the

14 hearing of the people. Then all the princes sent Jehu'di the son of Nethani'ah, son of Shelemi'ah, son of Cushi, to say to Baruch, "Take in your hand the scroll that you read in the hearing of the people, and come." So Baruch the son of Neri'ah took the scroll in

15 his hand and came to them. And they said to him, "Sit down and read it." So Baruch read

16 it to them. When they heard all the words, they turned one to another in fear; and they said to Baruch, "We must report all these

17 words to the king." Then they asked Baruch, "Tell us, how did you write all these

words? Was it at his dictation?" Baruch 18 answered them, "He dictated all these words to me, while I wrote them with ink on the scroll." Then the princes said to Baruch, 19 "Go and hide, you and Jeremiah, and let no one know where you are."

So they went into the court to the king, 20 having put the scroll in the chamber of Elish'ama the secretary; and they reported all the words to the king. Then the king sent 21 Jehu'di to get the scroll, and he took it from the chamber of Elish'ama the secretary; and Jehu'di read it to the king and all the princes who stood beside the king. It was the ninth 22 month, and the king was sitting in the winter house and there was a fire burning in the brazier before him. As Jehu'di read three or 23 four columns, the king would cut them off

with a penknife and throw them into the fire in the brazier, until the entire scroll was consumed in the fire that was in the brazier. Yet neither the king, nor any of his servants 24 who heard all these words, was afraid, nor did they rend their garments. Even when 25 Elna'than and Delai'ah and Gemari'ah urged the king not to burn the scroll, he would not listen to them. And the king commanded 26 Jerah'meel the king's son and Serai'ah the son of Az'ri-el and Shelemi'ah the son of Abdeel to seize Baruch the secretary and Jeremiah the prophet, but the LORD hid them.

Now, after the king had burned the scroll 27 with the words which Baruch wrote at Jeremiah's dictation, the word of the LORD came to Jeremiah: "Take another scroll and 28 write on it all the former words that were in the first scroll, which Jehoi'akim the king of

29 Judah has burned. And concerning Jehoi'-akim king of Judah you shall say, 'Thus says the LORD, You have burned this scroll, saying, "Why have you written in it that the king of Babylon will certainly come and destroy this land, and will cut off from it man 30 and beast?" Therefore thus says the LORD concerning Jehoi'akim king of Judah, He shall have none to sit upon the throne of David, and his dead body shall be cast out to 31 the heat by day and the frost by night. And I will punish him and his offspring and his servants for their iniquity; I will bring upon them, and upon the inhabitants of Jerusalem, and upon the men of Judah, all the evil that I have pronounced against them, but they would not hear.' "

32 Then Jeremiah took another scroll and gave it to Baruch the scribe, the son of Neri'ah, who wrote on it at the dictation of Jeremiah all the words of the scroll which Jehoi'akim king of Judah had burned in the fire; and many similar words were added to them.

The king's appeal

37 Zedeki'ah the son of Josi'ah, whom Nebuchadrez'zar king of Babylon made king in the land of Judah, reigned instead of 2 Coni'ah the son of Jehoi'akim. But neither he nor his servants nor the people of the land listened to the words of the LORD which he spoke through Jeremiah the prophet.

3 King Zedeki'ah sent Jehu'cal the son of Shelemi'ah, and Zephani'ah the priest, the son of Ma-asei'ah, to Jeremiah the prophet, saying, "Pray for us to the LORD our God." 4 Now Jeremiah was still going in and out among the people, for he had not yet been 5 put in prison. The army of Pharaoh had come out of Egypt; and when the Chalde'ans who were besieging Jerusalem heard news of them, they withdrew from Jerusalem.

6 Then the word of the LORD came to 7 Jeremiah the prophet: "Thus says the LORD, God of Israel: Thus shall you say to the king of Judah who sent you to me to inquire of me, 'Behold, Pharaoh's army which came to help you is about to return to Egypt, to its 8 own land. And the Chalde'ans shall come back and fight against this city; they shall 9 take it and burn it with fire. Thus says the LORD, Do not deceive yourselves, saying, "The Chalde'ans will surely stay away from 10 us," for they will not stay away. For even if you should defeat the whole army of Chalde'ans who are fighting against you, and there remained of them only wounded men, every man in his tent, they would rise up and burn this city with fire.' "

Jeremiah imprisoned

Now when the Chalde'an army had with- 11 drawn from Jerusalem at the approach of Pharaoh's army, Jeremiah set out from Jeru- 12 salem to go to the land of Benjamin to receive his portion[m] there among the people. When 13 he was at the Benjamin Gate, a sentry there named Iri'jah the son of Shelemi'ah, son of Hanani'ah, seized Jeremiah the prophet, saying, "You are deserting to the Chal- de'ans." And Jeremiah said, "It is false; 14 I am not deserting to the Chalde'ans." But Iri'jah would not listen to him, and seized Jeremiah and brought him to the princes. And the princes were enraged at Jeremiah, 15 and they beat him and imprisoned him in the house of Jonathan the secretary, for it had been made a prison.

When Jeremiah had come to the dungeon 16 cells, and remained there many days, King 17 Zedeki'ah sent for him, and received him. The king questioned him secretly in his house, and said, "Is there any word from the LORD?" Jeremiah said, "There is." Then he said, "You shall be delivered into the hand of the king of Babylon." Jeremiah also said to 18 King Zedeki'ah, "What wrong have I done to you or your servants or this people, that you have put me in prison? Where are your 19 prophets who prophesied to you, saying, 'The king of Babylon will not come against you and against this land'? Now hear, I pray 20 you, O my lord the king: let my humble plea come before you, and do not send me back to the house of Jonathan the secretary, lest I die there." So King Zedeki'ah gave orders, and 21 they committed Jeremiah to the court of the guard; and a loaf of bread was given him daily from the bakers' street, until all the bread of the city was gone. So Jeremiah remained in the court of the guard.

Condemned to death

Now Shephati'ah the son of Mattan, Geda- 38 li'ah the son of Pashhur, Jucal the son of Shelemi'ah, and Pashhur the son of Malchi'ah heard the words that Jeremiah was saying to all the people, "Thus says the 2 LORD, He who stays in this city shall die by the sword, by famine, and by pestilence; but he who goes out to the Chalde'ans shall live; he shall have his life as a prize of war, and live. Thus says the LORD, This city shall 3 surely be given into the hand of the army of the king of Babylon and be taken." Then the 4 princes said to the king, "Let this man be put to death, for he is weakening the hands of the soldiers who are left in this city, and the

---

[m] Heb obscure

hands of all the people, by speaking such words to them. For this man is not seeking the welfare of this people, but their harm." 5 King Zedeki'ah said, "Behold, he is in your hands; for the king can do nothing against 6 you." So they took Jeremiah and cast him into the cistern of Malchi'ah, the king's son, which was in the court of the guard, letting Jeremiah down by ropes. And there was no water in the cistern, but only mire, and Jeremiah sank in the mire.

Rescued by an Ethiopian

7 When E'bed-mel'ech the Ethiopian, a eunuch, who was in the king's house, heard that they had put Jeremiah into the cistern—the king was sitting in the Benjamin 8 Gate—E'bed-mel'ech went from the king's 9 house and said to the king, "My lord the king, these men have done evil in all that they did to Jeremiah the prophet by casting him into the cistern; and he will die there of hunger, for there is no bread left in the 10 city." Then the king commanded E'bed-mel'ech, the Ethiopian, "Take three men with you from here, and lift Jeremiah the prophet out of the cistern before he dies." 11 So E'bed-mel'ech took the men with him and went to the house of the king, to a wardrobe of[n] the storehouse, and took from there old rags and worn-out clothes, which he let down 12 to Jeremiah in the cistern by ropes. Then E'bed-mel'ech the Ethiopian said to Jeremiah, "Put the rags and clothes between your armpits and the ropes." Jeremiah did 13 so. Then they drew Jeremiah up with ropes and lifted him out of the cistern. And Jeremiah remained in the court of the guard.

A secret interview

14 King Zedeki'ah sent for Jeremiah the prophet and received him at the third entrance of the temple of the LORD. The king said to Jeremiah, "I will ask you a 15 question; hide nothing from me." Jeremiah said to Zedeki'ah, "If I tell you, will you not be sure to put me to death? And if I give you 16 counsel, you will not listen to me." Then King Zedeki'ah swore secretly to Jeremiah, "As the LORD lives, who made our souls, I will not put you to death or deliver you into the hand of these men who seek your life." 17 Then Jeremiah said to Zedeki'ah, "Thus says the LORD, the God of hosts, the God of Israel, If you will surrender to the princes of the king of Babylon, then your life shall be spared, and this city shall not be burned with 18 fire, and you and your house shall live. But if

you do not surrender to the princes of the king of Babylon, then this city shall be given into the hand of the Chalde'ans, and they shall burn it with fire, and you shall not escape from their hand." King Zedeki'ah 19 said to Jeremiah, "I am afraid of the Jews who have deserted to the Chalde'ans, lest I be handed over to them and they abuse me." Jeremiah said, "You shall not be given to 20 them. Obey now the voice of the LORD in what I say to you, and it shall be well with you, and your life shall be spared. But if you 21 refuse to surrender, this is the vision which the LORD has shown to me: Behold, all the 22 women left in the house of the king of Judah were being led out to the princes of the king of Babylon and were saying,

'Your trusted friends have deceived you
    and prevailed against you;
now that your feet are sunk in the mire,
    they turn away from you.'

All your wives and your sons shall be led out 23 to the Chalde'ans, and you yourself shall not escape from their hand, but shall be seized by the king of Babylon; and this city shall be burned with fire."

Then Zedeki'ah said to Jeremiah, "Let no 24 one know of these words and you shall not die. If the princes hear that I have spoken 25 with you and come to you and say to you, 'Tell us what you said to the king and what the king said to you; hide nothing from us and we will not put you to death,' then you 26 shall say to them, 'I made a humble plea to the king that he would not send me back to the house of Jonathan to die there.'" Then 27 all the princes came to Jeremiah and asked him, and he answered them as the king had instructed him. So they left off speaking with him, for the conversation had not been overheard. And Jeremiah remained in the 28 court of the guard until the day that Jerusalem was taken.

Jerusalem destroyed

In the ninth year of Zedeki'ah king of 39 Judah, in the tenth month, Nebuchadrez'zar king of Babylon and all his army came against Jerusalem and besieged it; in the 2 eleventh year of Zedeki'ah, in the fourth month, on the ninth day of the month, a breach was made in the city. When Jeru- 3 salem was taken,[o] all the princes of the king of Babylon came and sat in the middle gate: Ner'gal-share'zer, Sam'gar-ne'bo, Sar'se-chim the Rab'saris, Ner'gal-share'zer the Rabmag, with all the rest of the officers of the king of Babylon. When Zedeki'ah king 4 of Judah and all the soldiers saw them, they

---

_n_ Cn: Heb _to under_   _o_ This clause has been transposed from the end of Chapter 38 fled, going out of the city at night by way of the king's garden through the gate between the two walls; and they went toward the 5 Arabah. But the army of the Chalde'ans pursued them, and overtook Zedeki'ah in the plains of Jericho; and when they had taken him, they brought him up to Nebuchadrez'zar king of Babylon, at Riblah, in the land of Hamath; and he passed sentence upon 6 him. The king of Babylon slew the sons of Zedeki'ah at Riblah before his eyes; and the king of Babylon slew all the nobles of Judah. 7 He put out the eyes of Zedeki'ah, and bound 8 him in fetters to take him to Babylon. The Chalde'ans burned the king's house and the house of the people, and broke down the 9 walls of Jerusalem. Then Nebu'zarad'an, the captain of the guard, carried into exile to Babylon the rest of the people who were left in the city, those who had deserted to him, 10 and the people who remained. Nebu'zarad'an, the captain of the guard, left in the land of Judah some of the poor people who owned nothing, and gave them vineyards and fields at the same time.

Jeremiah spared

11 Nebuchadrez'zar king of Babylon gave command concerning Jeremiah through Nebu'zarad'an, the captain of the guard, 12 saying, "Take him, look after him well and do him no harm, but deal with him as he tells 13 you." So Nebu'zarad'an the captain of the guard, Nebushaz'ban the Rab'saris, Ner'-gal-share'zer the Rabmag, and all the chief 14 officers of the king of Babylon sent and took Jeremiah from the court of the guard. They entrusted him to Gedali'ah the son of Ahi'kam, son of Shaphan, that he should take him home. So he dwelt among the people. 15 The word of the LORD came to Jeremiah while he was shut up in the court of the 16 guard: "Go, and say to E'bed-mel'ech the Ethiopian, 'Thus says the LORD of hosts, the God of Israel: Behold, I will fulfil my words against this city for evil and not for good, and they shall be accomplished before 17 you on that day. But I will deliver you on that day, says the LORD, and you shall not be given into the hand of the men of whom you are 18 afraid. For I will surely save you, and you shall not fall by the sword; but you shall have your life as a prize of war, because you have put your trust in me, says the LORD.' "

Jeremiah stays with the remnant

40 The word that came to Jeremiah from the LORD after Nebu'zarad'an the captain of the guard had let him go from Ramah, when he took him bound in chains along with all the captives of Jerusalem and Judah who were being exiled to Babylon. The captain of the 2 guard took Jeremiah and said to him, "The LORD your God pronounced this evil against this place; the LORD has brought it about, 3 and has done as he said. Because you sinned against the LORD, and did not obey his voice, this thing has come upon you. Now, behold, 4 I release you today from the chains on your hands. If it seems good to you to come with me to Babylon, come, and I will look after you well; but if it seems wrong to you to come with me to Babylon, do not come. See, the whole land is before you; go wherever you think it good and right to go. If you 5 remain, *p* then return to Gedali'ah the son of Ahi'kam, son of Shaphan, whom the king of Babylon appointed governor of the cities of Judah, and dwell with him among the people; or go wherever you think it right to go." So the captain of the guard gave him an allowance of food and a present, and let him go. Then Jeremiah went to Gedali'ah the son 6 of Ahi'kam, at Mizpah, and dwelt with him among the people who were left in the land. When all the captains of the forces in the open 7 country and their men heard that the king of Babylon had appointed Gedali'ah the son of Ahi'kam governor in the land, and had committed to him men, women, and children, those of the poorest of the land who had not been taken into exile to Babylon, they 8 went to Gedali'ah at Mizpah—Ish'mael the son of Nethani'ah, Joha'nan the son of Kare'ah, Serai'ah the son of Tanhu'meth, the sons of Ephai the Netoph'athite, Jezani'ah the son of the Ma-ac'athite, they and their men. Gedali'ah the son of 9 Ahi'kam, son of Shaphan, swore to them and their men, saying, "Do not be afraid to serve the Chalde'ans. Dwell in the land, and serve the king of Babylon, and it shall be well with you. As for me, I will dwell at Mizpah, to 10 stand for you before the Chalde'ans who will come to us; but as for you, gather wine and summer fruits and oil, and store them in your vessels, and dwell in your cities that you have taken." Likewise, when all the Jews who 11 were in Moab and among the Ammonites and in Edom and in other lands heard that the king of Babylon had left a remnant in Judah and had appointed Gedali'ah the son of Ahi'kam, son of Shaphan, as governor over them, then all the Jews returned from 12 all the places to which they had been driven and came to the land of Judah, to Gedali'ah at Mizpah; and they gathered wine and summer fruits in great abundance.

p Syr: Heb obscure

Murder of the governor

13 Now Joha'nan the son of Kare'ah and all the leaders of the forces in the open country
14 came to Gedali'ah at Mizpah and said to him, "Do you know that Ba'alis the king of the Ammonites has sent Ish'mael the son of Nethani'ah to take your life?" But Geda-li'ah the son of Ahi'kam would not be-
15 lieve them. Then Joha'nan the son of Kare'ah spoke secretly to Gedali'ah at Mizpah, "Let me go and slay Ish'mael the son of Nethani'ah, and no one will know it. Why should he take your life, so that all the Jews who are gathered about you would be scattered, and the remnant of Judah would
16 perish?" But Gedali'ah the son of Ahi'kam said to Joha'nan the son of Kare'ah, "You shall not do this thing, for you are speaking falsely of Ish'mael."

41 In the seventh month, Ish'mael the son of Nethani'ah, son of Elish'ama, of the royal family, one of the chief officers of the king, came with ten men to Gedali'ah the son of Ahi'kam, at Mizpah. As they ate bread
2 together there at Mizpah, Ish'mael the son of Nethani'ah and the ten men with him rose up and struck down Gedali'ah the son of Ahi'kam, son of Shaphan, with the sword, and killed him, whom the king of Babylon
3 had appointed governor in the land. Ish'-mael also slew all the Jews who were with Gedali'ah at Mizpah, and the Chalde'an soldiers who happened to be there.
4 On the day after the murder of Gedali'ah,
5 before any one knew of it, eighty men arrived from Shechem and Shiloh and Samar'ia, with their beards shaved and their clothes torn, and their bodies gashed, bringing cereal offerings and incense to present at the temple
6 of the LORD. And Ish'mael the son of Nethani'ah came out from Mizpah to meet them, weeping as he came. As he met them, he said to them, "Come in to Gedali'ah the son
7 of Ahi'kam." When they came into the city, Ish'mael the son of Nethani'ah and the men with him slew them, and cast them into
8 a cistern. But there were ten men among them who said to Ish'mael, "Do not kill us, for we have stores of wheat, barley, oil, and honey hidden in the fields." So he refrained and did not kill them with their companions.
9 Now the cistern into which Ish'mael cast all the bodies of the men whom he had slain was the large cistern*q* which King Asa had made for defence against Ba'asha king of Israel; Ish'mael the son of Nethani'ah filled it with
10 the slain. Then Ish'mael took captive all the rest of the people who were in Mizpah, the king's daughters and all the people who were left at Mizpah, whom Nebu'zarad'an, the captain of the guard, had committed to Gedali'ah the son of Ahi'kam. Ish'mael the son of Nethani'ah took them captive and set out to cross over to the Ammonites.

11 But when Joha'nan the son of Kare'ah and all the leaders of the forces with him heard of all the evil which Ish'mael the son of Netha-
12 ni'ah had done, they took all their men and went to fight against Ish'mael the son of Nethani'ah. They came upon him at the
13 great pool which is in Gibeon. And when all the people who were with Ish'mael saw Joha'nan the son of Kare'ah and all the leaders of the forces with him, they rejoiced.
14 So all the people whom Ish'mael had carried away captive from Mizpah turned about and came back, and went to Joha'nan the son of
15 Kare'ah. But Ish'mael the son of Nethani'ah escaped from Joha'nan with eight men, and
16 went to the Ammonites. Then Joha'nan the son of Kare'ah and all the leaders of the forces with him took all the rest of the people whom Ish'mael the son of Nethani'ah had carried away captive*r* from Mizpah after he had slain Gedali'ah the son of Ahi'kam —soldiers, women, children, and eunuchs,

q Gk: Heb *he had slain by the hand of Gedaliah*   *r* Cn: Heb *whom he recovered from Ishmael*

whom Joha'nan brought back from Gibeon.
17 And they went and stayed at Geruth Chimham near Bethlehem, intending to go to
18 Egypt because of the Chalde'ans; for they were afraid of them, because Ish'mael the son of Nethani'ah had slain Gedali'ah the son of Ahi'kam, whom the king of Babylon had made governor over the land.

Jeremiah's counsel

42 Then all the commanders of the forces, and Joha'nan the son of Kare'ah and Azari'ah[s] the son of Hoshai'ah, and all the people from
2 the least to the greatest, came near and said to Jeremiah the prophet, "Let our supplication come before you, and pray to the LORD your God for us, for all this remnant (for we are left but a few of many, as your eyes see
3 us), that the LORD your God may show us the way we should go, and the thing that we
4 should do." Jeremiah the prophet said to them, "I have heard you; behold, I will pray to the LORD your God according to your request, and whatever the LORD answers you I will tell you; I will keep nothing back from
5 you." Then they said to Jeremiah, "May the LORD be a true and faithful witness against us if we do not act according to all the word with which the LORD your God sends you to
6 us. Whether it is good or evil, we will obey the voice of the LORD our God to whom we are sending you, that it may be well with us when we obey the voice of the LORD our God."

7 At the end of ten days the word of the LORD
8 came to Jeremiah. Then he summoned Joha'nan the son of Kare'ah and all the commanders of the forces who were with him, and all the people from the least to the
9 greatest, and said to them, "Thus says the LORD, the God of Israel, to whom you sent me to present your supplication before him:
10 If you will remain in this land, then I will build you up and not pull you down; I will plant you, and not pluck you up; for I repent
11 of the evil which I did to you. Do not fear the king of Babylon, of whom you are afraid; do not fear him, says the LORD, for I am with you, to save you and to deliver you from his
12 hand. I will grant you mercy, that he may have mercy on you and let you remain in
13 your own land. But if you say, 'We will not remain in this land,' disobeying the voice of
14 the LORD your God and saying, 'No, we will go to the land of Egypt, where we shall not see war, or hear the sound of the trumpet, or be hungry for bread, and we will dwell
15 there,' then hear the word of the LORD, O remnant of Judah. Thus says the LORD of

hosts, the God of Israel: If you set your faces to enter Egypt and go to live there, then the 16 sword which you fear shall overtake you there in the land of Egypt; and the famine of which you are afraid shall follow hard after you to Egypt; and there you shall die. All the 17 men who set their faces to go to Egypt to live there shall die by the sword, by famine, and by pestilence; they shall have no remnant or survivor from the evil which I will bring upon them.

"For thus says the LORD of hosts, the God 18 of Israel: As my anger and my wrath were poured out on the inhabitants of Jerusalem, so my wrath will be poured out on you when you go to Egypt. You shall become an execration, a horror, a curse, and a taunt. You shall see this place no more. The LORD 19 has said to you, O remnant of Judah, 'Do not go to Egypt.' Know for a certainty that I have warned you this day that you have gone 20 astray at the cost of your lives. For you sent me to the LORD your God, saying, 'Pray for us to the LORD our God, and whatever the LORD our God says declare to us and we will do it.' And I have this day declared it to you, 21 but you have not obeyed the voice of the LORD your God in anything that he sent me to tell you. Now therefore know for a 22 certainty that you shall die by the sword, by famine, and by pestilence in the place where you desire to go to live."

Jeremiah taken to Egypt

When Jeremiah finished speaking to all the 43 people all these words of the LORD their God, with which the LORD their God had sent him to them, Azari'ah the son of Hoshai'ah and 2 Joha'nan the son of Kare'ah and all the insolent men said to Jeremiah, "You are telling a lie. The LORD our God did not send you to say, 'Do not go to Egypt to live there'; but Baruch the son of Neri'ah has set you 3 against us, to deliver us into the hand of the Chalde'ans, that they may kill us or take us into exile in Babylon." So Joha'nan the son 4 of Kare'ah and all the commanders of the forces and all the people did not obey the voice of the LORD, to remain in the land of Judah. But Joha'nan the son of Kare'ah and 5 all the commanders of the forces took all the remnant of Judah who had returned to live in the land of Judah from all the nations to which they had been driven—the men, the 6 women, the children, the princesses, and every person whom Nebu'zarad'an the captain of the guard had left with Gedali'ah the son of Ahi'kam, son of Shaphan; also Jeremiah the prophet and Baruch the son of

7 Neri'ah. And they came into the land of Egypt, for they did not obey the voice of the Lord. And they arrived at Tah'panhes.

8 Then the word of the Lord came to 9 Jeremiah in Tah'panhes: "Take in your hands large stones, and hide them in the mortar in the pavement which is at the entrance to Pharaoh's palace in Tah'panhes, 10 in the sight of the men of Judah, and say to them, 'Thus says the Lord of hosts, the God of Israel: Behold, I will send and take Nebuchadrez'zar the king of Babylon, my servant, and he*t* will set his throne above these stones which I have hid, and he will 11 spread his royal canopy over them. He shall come and smite the land of Egypt, giving to the pestilence those who are doomed to the pestilence, to captivity those who are doomed to captivity, and to the sword those who are 12 doomed to the sword. He*u* shall kindle a fire in the temples of the gods of Egypt; and he shall burn them and carry them away captive; and he shall clean the land of Egypt, as a shepherd cleans his cloak of vermin; and he 13 shall go away from there in peace. He shall break the obelisks of Heliop'olis which is in the land of Egypt; and the temples of the gods of Egypt he shall burn with fire.'"

The prophet in Egypt

44 The word that came to Jeremiah concerning all the Jews that dwelt in the land of Egypt, at Migdol, at Tah'panhes, at Memphis, and 2 in the land of Pathros, "Thus says the Lord of hosts, the God of Israel: You have seen all the evil that I brought upon Jerusalem and upon all the cities of Judah. Behold, this day they are a desolation, and no one dwells in 3 them, because of the wickedness which they committed, provoking me to anger, in that they went to burn incense and serve other gods that they knew not, neither they, nor 4 you, nor your fathers. Yet I persistently sent to you all my servants the prophets, saying, 'Oh, do not do this abominable thing that I 5 hate!' But they did not listen or incline their ear, to turn from their wickedness and burn 6 no incense to other gods. Therefore my wrath and my anger were poured forth and kindled in the cities of Judah and in the streets of Jerusalem; and they became a 7 waste and a desolation, as at this day. And now thus says the Lord God of hosts, the God of Israel: Why do you commit this great evil against yourselves, to cut off from you man and woman, infant and child, from the midst of Judah, leaving you no remnant? 8 Why do you provoke me to anger with the works of your hands, burning incense to

other gods in the land of Egypt where you have come to live, that you may be cut off and become a curse and a taunt among all the nations of the earth? Have you forgotten the 9 wickedness of your fathers, the wickedness of the kings of Judah, the wickedness of their*v* wives, your own wickedness, and the wickedness of your wives, which they committed in the land of Judah and in the streets of Jerusalem? They have not humbled themselves even to this day, nor have they 10 feared, nor walked in my law and my statutes which I set before you and before your fathers.

"Therefore thus says the Lord of hosts, the 11 God of Israel: Behold, I will set my face against you for evil, to cut off all Judah. I 12 will take the remnant of Judah who have set their faces to come to the land of Egypt to live, and they shall all be consumed; in the land of Egypt they shall fall; by the sword and by famine they shall be consumed; from the least to the greatest, they shall die by the sword and by famine; and they shall become an execration, a horror, a curse, and a taunt. I will punish those who dwell in the land of 13 Egypt, as I have punished Jerusalem, with the sword, with famine, and with pestilence, so that none of the remnant of Judah who 14 have come to live in the land of Egypt shall escape or survive or return to the land of Judah, to which they desire to return to dwell

---

t Gk Syr: Heb *I*   *u* Gk Syr Vg: Heb *I*   *v* Heb *his* there; for they shall not return, except some fugitives."

A protest

15 Then all the men who knew that their wives had offered incense to other gods, and all the women who stood by, a great assembly, all the people who dwelt in Pathros in the land 16 of Egypt, answered Jeremiah: "As for the word which you have spoken to us in the name of the LORD, we will not listen to you. 17 But we will do everything that we have vowed, burn incense to the queen of heaven and pour out libations to her, as we did, both we and our fathers, our kings and our princes, in the cities of Judah and in the streets of Jerusalem; for then we had plenty 18 of food, and prospered, and saw no evil. But since we left off burning incense to the queen of heaven and pouring out libations to her, we have lacked everything and have been consumed by the sword and by famine." 19 And the women said,[w] "When we burned incense to the queen of heaven and poured out libations to her, was it without our husbands' approval that we made cakes for her bearing her image and poured out libations to her?"

The prophet's answer

20 Then Jeremiah said to all the people, men and women, all the people who had given 21 him this answer: "As for the incense that you burned in the cities of Judah and in the streets of Jerusalem, you and your fathers, your kings and your princes, and the people of the land, did not the LORD remember it?[x] 22 Did it not come into his mind? The LORD could no longer bear your evil doings and the abominations which you committed; therefore your land has become a desolation and a waste and a curse, without inhabitant, 23 as it is this day. It is because you burned incense, and because you sinned against the LORD and did not obey the voice of the LORD or walk in his law and in his statutes and in his testimonies, that this evil has befallen you, as at this day." 24 Jeremiah said to all the people and all the women, "Hear the word of the LORD, all you 25 of Judah who are in the land of Egypt, Thus says the LORD of hosts, the God of Israel:

You and your wives have declared with your mouths, and have fulfilled it with your hands, saying, 'We will surely perform our vows that we have made, to burn incense to the queen of heaven and to pour out libations to her.' Then confirm your vows and perform your vows! Therefore hear the word of 26 the LORD, all you of Judah who dwell in the land of Egypt: Behold, I have sworn by my great name, says the LORD, that my name shall no more be invoked by the mouth of any man of Judah in all the land of Egypt, saying, 'As the Lord GOD lives.' Behold, I 27 am watching over them for evil and not for good; all the men of Judah who are in the land of Egypt shall be consumed by the sword and by famine, until there is an end of them. And those who escape the sword shall 28 return from the land of Egypt to the land of Judah, few in number; and all the remnant of Judah, who came to the land of Egypt to live, shall know whose word will stand, mine or theirs. This shall be the sign to you, says the 29 LORD, that I will punish you in this place, in order that you may know that my words will surely stand against you for evil: Thus says 30 the LORD, Behold, I will give Pharaoh Hophra king of Egypt into the hand of his enemies and into the hand of those who seek his life, as I gave Zedeki'ah king of Judah into the hand of Nebuchadrez'zar king of Babylon, who was his enemy and sought his life."

A word for Baruch

The word that Jeremiah the prophet spoke 45 to Baruch the son of Neri'ah, when he wrote these words in a book at the dictation of Jeremiah, in the fourth year of Jehoi'akim the son of Josi'ah, king of Judah: "Thus says 2 the LORD, the God of Israel, to you, O Baruch: You said, 'Woe is me! for the LORD 3 has added sorrow to my pain; I am weary with my groaning, and I find no rest.' Thus 4 shall you say to him, Thus says the LORD: Behold, what I have built I am breaking down, and what I have planted I am plucking up—that is, the whole land. And do you seek 5 great things for yourself? Seek them not; for, behold, I am bringing evil upon all flesh, says the LORD; but I will give you your life as a prize of war in all places to which you may go."

---

[w] Compare Syr: Heb lacks *And the women said* [x] Syr: Heb *them*

CONCERNING THE NATIONS

46 THE word of the LORD which came to Jeremiah the prophet concerning the nations.

EGYPT

2 About Egypt. Concerning the army of Pharaoh Neco, king of Egypt, which was by the river Euphra'tes at Car'chemish and which Nebuchadrez'zar king of Babylon defeated in the fourth year of Jehoi'akim the son of Josi'ah, king of Judah:

3 "Prepare buckler and shield,
    and advance for battle!
4 Harness the horses;
    mount, O horsemen!
Take your stations with your helmets,
    polish your spears,
    put on your coats of mail!
5 Why have I seen it?
They are dismayed
    and have turned backward.
Their warriors are beaten down,
    and have fled in haste;
they look not back—
    terror on every side!
                says the LORD.
6 The swift cannot flee away,
    nor the warrior escape;
in the north by the river Euphra'tes
    they have stumbled and fallen.

7 "Who is this, rising like the Nile,
    like rivers whose waters surge?
8 Egypt rises like the Nile,
    like rivers whose waters surge.
He said, I will rise, I will cover the earth,
    I will destroy cities and their inhabitants.
9 Advance, O horses,
    and rage, O chariots!
Let the warriors go forth:
    men of Ethiopia and Put who handle the shield,
    men of Lud, skilled in handling the bow.
10 That day is the day of the Lord GOD of hosts,
    a day of vengeance,
    to avenge himself on his foes.

The sword shall devour and be sated,
    and drink its fill of their blood.
For the Lord GOD of hosts holds a sacrifice
    in the north country by the river Euphra'tes.
Go up to Gilead, and take balm,   11
    O virgin daughter of Egypt!
In vain you have used many medicines;
    there is no healing for you.
The nations have heard of your shame,   12
    and the earth is full of your cry;
for warrior has stumbled against warrior;
    they have both fallen together."

The word which the LORD spoke to 13 Jeremiah the prophet about the coming of Nebuchadrez'zar king of Babylon to smite the land of Egypt:

"Declare in Egypt, and proclaim in 14 Migdol;
proclaim in Memphis and Tah'panhes;
Say, 'Stand ready and be prepared,
    for the sword shall devour round about you.'
Why has Apis fled?[y]   15
    Why did not your bull stand?
    Because the LORD thrust him down.
Your multitude stumbled[z] and fell,   16
    and they said one to another,
'Arise, and let us go back to our own people
    and to the land of our birth,
because of the sword of the oppressor.'
Call the name of Pharaoh, king of Egypt, 17
    'Noisy one who lets the hour go by.'

"As I live, says the King,   18
    whose name is the LORD of hosts,
like Tabor among the mountains,
    and like Carmel by the sea, shall one come.
Prepare yourselves baggage for exile,   19
    O inhabitants of Egypt!
For Memphis shall become a waste,
    a ruin, without inhabitant.

"A beautiful heifer is Egypt,   20
    but a gadfly from the north has come upon her.
Even her hired soldiers in her midst   21
    are like fatted calves;
yea, they have turned and fled together,
    they did not stand;
for the day of their calamity has come upon them,
    the time of their punishment.

---

y Gk: Heb *Why was it swept away*   *z* Gk: Heb *He made many stumble*
46: Is 19; Ezek 29–32; Zech 14.18–19.   **46.5**: Ps 31.13; Jer 6.25; 20.3, 10; 49.29.

22 "She makes a sound like a serpent gliding
          away;
      for her enemies march in force,
   and come against her with axes,
      like those who fell trees.
23 They shall cut down her forest,
                          says the LORD,
      though it is impenetrable,
   because they are more numerous than
          locusts;
      they are without number.
24 The daughter of Egypt shall be put to
          shame,
      she shall be delivered into the hand of a
          people from the north."

25 The LORD of hosts, the God of Israel, said:
"Behold, I am bringing punishment upon
Amon of Thebes, and Pharaoh, and Egypt
and her gods and her kings, upon Pharaoh
26 and those who trust in him. I will deliver
them into the hand of those who seek their
life, into the hand of Nebuchadrez′zar king
of Babylon and his officers. Afterward
Egypt shall be inhabited as in the days of old,
says the LORD.

27 "But fear not, O Jacob my servant,
      nor be dismayed, O Israel;
   for lo, I will save you from afar,
      and your offspring from the land of their
          captivity.
   Jacob shall return and have quiet and
          ease,
      and none shall make him afraid.
28 Fear not, O Jacob my servant,
                          says the LORD,
      for I am with you.
   I will make a full end of all the nations
      to which I have driven you,
      but of you I will not make a full end.
   I will chasten you in just measure,
      and I will by no means leave you
          unpunished."

PHILISTIA

47 The word of the LORD that came to Jeremiah the prophet concerning the Philistines,
before Pharaoh smote Gaza.
2 "Thus says the LORD:
   Behold, waters are rising out of the
          north,
      and shall become an overflowing
          torrent;
   they shall overflow the land and all that
          fills it,
      the city and those who dwell in it.
   Men shall cry out,

and every inhabitant of the land shall
      wail.
   At the noise of the stamping of the hoofs of 3
          his stallions,
      at the rushing of his chariots, at the
          rumbling of their wheels,
   the fathers look not back to their children,
      so feeble are their hands,
   because of the day that is coming to 4
          destroy
      all the Philistines,
   to cut off from Tyre and Sidon
      every helper that remains.
   For the LORD is destroying the Philistines,
      the remnant of the coastland of Caphtor.
   Baldness has come upon Gaza,   5
      Ash′kelon has perished.
   O remnant of the Anakim,[a]
      how long will you gash yourselves?
   Ah, sword of the LORD!   6
      How long till you are quiet?
   Put yourself into your scabbard,
      rest and be still!
   How can it[b] be quiet,   7
      when the LORD has given it a charge?
   Against Ash′kelon and against the seashore
      he has appointed it."

MOAB

Concerning Moab.   48
Thus says the LORD of hosts, the God of
Israel:
   "Woe to Nebo, for it is laid waste!
      Kiriatha′im is put to shame, it is taken;
   the fortress is put to shame and broken
          down;
      the renown of Moab is no more.   2
   In Heshbon they planned evil against her:
      'Come, let us cut her off from being a
          nation!'
   You also, O Madmen, shall be brought to
          silence;
      the sword shall pursue you.

   "Hark! a cry from Horona′im,   3
      'Desolation and great destruction!'
   Moab is destroyed;   4
      a cry is heard as far as Zo′ar.[c]
   For at the ascent of Luhith   5
      they go up weeping;[d]
   for at the descent of Horona′im

a Gk: Heb their valley b Gk Vg: Heb you c Gk: Heb her little ones d Cn: Heb weeping goes up with weeping
47: Is 14.29–31; Ezek 25.15–17; Amos 1.6–8; Zeph 2.4–7; Zech 9.5–7.
48: Is 15–16; 25.10–12; Ezek 25.8–11; Amos 2.1–3; Zeph 2.8–11.

JEREMIAH 48

they have heard the cry[e] of destruction.

6 Flee! Save yourselves!
Be like a wild ass[f] in the desert!

7 For, because you trusted in your strongholds[g] and your treasures,
you also shall be taken;
and Chemosh shall go forth into exile,
with his priests and his princes.

8 The destroyer shall come upon every city,
and no city shall escape;
the valley shall perish,
and the plain shall be destroyed,
as the LORD has spoken.

9 "Give wings to Moab,
for she would fly away;
her cities shall become a desolation,
with no inhabitant in them.

10 "Cursed is he who does the work of the
LORD with slackness; and cursed is he who
keeps back his sword from bloodshed.

11 "Moab has been at ease from his youth
and has settled on his lees;
he has not been emptied from vessel to
vessel,
nor has he gone into exile;
so his taste remains in him,
and his scent is not changed.

12 "Therefore, behold, the days are coming,
says the LORD, when I shall send to him
tilters who will tilt him, and empty his
13 vessels, and break his[h] jars in pieces. Then
Moab shall be ashamed of Chemosh, as the
house of Israel was ashamed of Bethel, their
confidence.

14 "How do you say, 'We are heroes
and mighty men of war'?

15 The destroyer of Moab and his cities has
come up,
and the choicest of his young men have
gone down to slaughter,
says the King, whose name is the LORD
of hosts.

16 The calamity of Moab is near at hand
and his affliction hastens apace.

17 Bemoan him, all you who are round about
him,
and all who know his name;
say, 'How the mighty sceptre is broken,
the glorious staff!'

18 "Come down from your glory,
and sit on the parched ground,
O inhabitant of Dibon!
For the destroyer of Moab has come up
against you;

he has destroyed your strongholds.

19 Stand by the way and watch,
O inhabitant of Aro'er!
Ask him who flees and her who escapes;
say, 'What has happened?'

20 Moab is put to shame, for it is broken;
wail and cry!
Tell it by the Arnon,
that Moab is laid waste.

21 "Judgment has come upon the tableland,
upon Holon, and Jahzah, and Meph'a-ath,
22 and Dibon, and Nebo, and Beth-diblatha'im,
23 and Kiriatha'im, and Beth-ga'mul, and
24 Beth-me'on, and Ker'ioth, and Bozrah, and
all the cities of the land of Moab, far
25 and near. The horn of Moab is cut off, and
his arm is broken, says the LORD.

26 "Make him drunk, because he magnified
himself against the LORD; so that Moab shall
wallow in his vomit, and he too shall be held
27 in derision. Was not Israel a derision to
you? Was he found among thieves, that
whenever you spoke of him you wagged your
head?

28 "Leave the cities, and dwell in the rock,
O inhabitants of Moab!
Be like the dove that nests
in the sides of the mouth of a gorge.
29 We have heard of the pride of Moab—
he is very proud—
of his loftiness, his pride, and his
arrogance,
and the haughtiness of his heart.
30 I know his insolence, says the LORD;
his boasts are false,
his deeds are false.
31 Therefore I wail for Moab;
I cry out for all Moab;
for the men of Kir-he'res I mourn.
32 More than for Jazer I weep for you,
O vine of Sibmah!
Your branches passed over the sea,
reached as far as Jazer;[i]
upon your summer fruits and your vintage
the destroyer has fallen.
33 Gladness and joy have been taken away
from the fruitful land of Moab;
I have made the wine cease from the wine
presses;
no one treads them with shouts of joy;
the shouting is not the shout of joy.

34 "Heshbon and Elea'leh cry out;[j] as far as
Jahaz they utter their voice, from Zo'ar to
Horona'im and Eg'lath-shelish'iyah. For the
waters of Nimrim also have become deso-
35 late. And I will bring to an end in Moab,

---

[e] Gk Compare Is 15.5: Heb *the distress of the cry* [f] Gk Aquila: Heb *like Aroer* [g] Gk: Heb *works*
[h] Gk Aquila: Heb *their* [i] Cn: Heb *the sea of Jazer* [j] Cn: Heb *From the cry of Heshbon to Elealeh*

says the LORD, him who offers sacrifice in the high place and burns incense to his god.

36 Therefore my heart moans for Moab like a flute, and my heart moans like a flute for the men of Kir-he´res; therefore the riches they gained have perished.

37 "For every head is shaved and every beard cut off; upon all the hands are gashes, and on
38 the loins is sackcloth. On all the housetops of Moab and in the squares there is nothing but lamentation; for I have broken Moab like a vessel for which no one cares, says the LORD.

39 How it is broken! How they wail! How Moab has turned his back in shame! So Moab has become a derision and a horror to all that are round about him."

40 For thus says the LORD:
"Behold, one shall fly swiftly like an eagle,
and spread his wings against Moab;
41 the cities shall be taken
and the strongholds seized.
The heart of the warriors of Moab shall be in that day
like the heart of a woman in her pangs;
42 Moab shall be destroyed and be no longer a people,
because he magnified himself against the LORD.
43 Terror, pit, and snare
are before you, O inhabitant of Moab!
says the LORD.
44 He who flees from the terror
shall fall into the pit,
and he who climbs out of the pit
shall be caught in the snare.
For I will bring these things[k] upon Moab
in the year of their punishment,
says the LORD.

45 "In the shadow of Heshbon
fugitives stop without strength;
for a fire has gone forth from Heshbon,
a flame from the house of Sihon;
it has destroyed the forehead of Moab,
the crown of the sons of tumult.
46 Woe to you, O Moab!
The people of Chemosh is undone;
for your sons have been taken captive,
and your daughters into captivity.
47 Yet I will restore the fortunes of Moab
in the latter days, says the LORD."
Thus far is the judgment on Moab.

AMMON

49 Concerning the Ammonites.
Thus says the LORD:
"Has Israel no sons?
Has he no heir?

Why then has Milcom dispossessed Gad,
and his people settled in its cities?
2 Therefore, behold, the days are coming,
says the LORD,
when I will cause the battle cry to be heard
against Rabbah of the Ammonites;
it shall become a desolate mound,
and its villages shall be burned with fire;
then Israel shall dispossess those who dispossessed him,
says the LORD.

3 "Wail, O Heshbon, for Ai is laid waste!
Cry, O daughters of Rabbah!
Gird yourselves with sackcloth,
lament, and run to and fro among the hedges!
For Milcom shall go into exile,
with his priests and his princes.
4 Why do you boast of your valleys,[l]
O faithless daughter,
who trusted in her treasures, saying,
'Who will come against me?'
5 Behold, I will bring terror upon you,
says the Lord GOD of hosts,
from all who are round about you,
and you shall be driven out, every man straight before him,
with none to gather the fugitives.
6 But afterward I will restore the fortunes of the Ammonites, says the LORD."

EDOM

7 Concerning Edom.
Thus says the LORD of hosts:
"Is wisdom no more in Teman?
Has counsel perished from the prudent?
Has their wisdom vanished?
8 Flee, turn back, dwell in the depths,
O inhabitants of Dedan!
For I will bring the calamity of Esau upon him,
the time when I punish him.
9 If grape-gatherers came to you,
would they not leave gleanings?
If thieves came by night,
would they not destroy only enough for themselves?
10 But I have stripped Esau bare,
I have uncovered his hiding places,
and he is not able to conceal himself.
His children are destroyed, and his brothers,
and his neighbours; and he is no more.
11 Leave your fatherless children, I will keep them alive;
and let your widows trust in me."

[k] Gk Syr: Heb *to her*   [l] Heb *valleys, your valley flows*
49.1-6: Ezek 21.28-32; 25.1-7; Amos 1.13-15; Zeph 2.8-11.
49.7-22: Is 34; 63.1-6; Ezek 25.12-14; 35; Amos 1.11-12; Obad; Mal 1.2-5.

2 For thus says the LORD: "If those who did not deserve to drink the cup must drink it, will you go unpunished? You shall not go 3 unpunished, but you must drink. For I have sworn by myself, says the LORD, that Bozrah shall become a horror, a taunt, a waste, and a curse; and all her cities shall be perpetual wastes."

4 I have heard tidings from the LORD,
   and a messenger has been sent among
      the nations:
   "Gather yourselves together and come
      against her,
   and rise up for battle!"
5 For behold, I will make you small among
      the nations,
   despised among men.
6 The horror you inspire has deceived you,
   and the pride of your heart,
   you who live in the clefts of the rock,[m]
      who hold the height of the hill.
   Though you make your nest as high as the
      eagle's,
   I will bring you down from there,
                     says the LORD.
17 "Edom shall become a horror; every one
   who passes by it will be horrified and will
18 hiss because of all its disasters. As when
   Sodom and Gomor'rah and their neighbour
   cities were overthrown, says the LORD, no
   man shall dwell there, no man shall sojourn
19 in her. Behold, like a lion coming up from
   the jungle of the Jordan against a strong
   sheepfold, I will suddenly make them[n] run
   away from her; and I will appoint over her
   whomever I choose. For who is like me?
   Who will summon me? What shepherd can
20 stand before me? Therefore hear the plan
   which the LORD has made against Edom and
   the purposes which he has formed against the
   inhabitants of Teman: Even the little ones of
   the flock shall be dragged away; surely their
21 fold shall be appalled at their fate. At the
   sound of their fall the earth shall tremble; the
   sound of their cry shall be heard at the Red
22 Sea. Behold, one shall mount up and fly
   swiftly like an eagle, and spread his wings
   against Bozrah, and the heart of the warriors
   of Edom shall be in that day like the heart of
   a woman in her pangs."

DAMASCUS

23 Concerning Damascus.
   "Hamath and Arpad are confounded,
      for they have heard evil tidings;
   they melt in fear, they are troubled like the
      sea[o]
         which cannot be quiet.

DAMASCUS

Damascus has become feeble, she turned 24
      to flee,
   and panic seized her;
anguish and sorrows have taken hold of
      her,
   as of a woman in travail.
How the famous city is forsaken,[p]   25
   the joyful city![q]
Therefore her young men shall fall in her 26
      squares,
   and all her soldiers shall be destroyed in
      that day,
                     says the LORD of hosts.
And I will kindle a fire in the wall of 27
      Damascus,
   and it shall devour the strongholds of
      Ben-ha'dad."

KEDAR

Concerning Kedar and the kingdoms 28
of Hazor which Nebuchadrez'zar king of
Babylon smote.
Thus says the LORD:
   "Rise up, advance against Kedar!
      Destroy the people of the east!
   Their tents and their flocks shall be taken, 29
      their curtains and all their goods;
   their camels shall be borne away from
      them,
   and men shall cry to them: 'Terror on
      every side!'
Flee, wander far away, dwell in the depths, 30
   O inhabitants of Hazor!
                     says the LORD.
For Nebuchadrez'zar king of Babylon
   has made a plan against you,
   and formed a purpose against you.

"Rise up, advance against a nation at ease, 31
   that dwells securely,
                     says the LORD,
that has no gates or bars,
   that dwells alone.
Their camels shall become booty,   32
   their herds of cattle a spoil.
I will scatter to every wind
   those who cut the corners of their hair,
and I will bring their calamity
   from every side of them,
                     says the LORD.
Hazor shall become a haunt of jackals, 33
   an everlasting waste;

---

m Or Sela   n Gk Syr: Heb him   o Cn: Heb there is trouble in the sea   p Vg: Heb not forsaken
q Syr Vg Tg: Heb city of my joy
49.23-27: Is 17.1-3; Amos 1.3-5; Zech 9.1.   49.29: Ps 31.13; Jer 6.25; 20.3, 10; 46.5.

no man shall dwell there,
no man shall sojourn in her."

ELAM

34 The word of the LORD that came to Jeremiah the prophet concerning Elam, in the beginning of the reign of Zedeki′ah king of Judah.
35 Thus says the LORD of hosts: "Behold, I will break the bow of Elam, the mainstay of
36 their might; and I will bring upon Elam the four winds from the four quarters of heaven; and I will scatter them to all those winds, and there shall be no nation to which those driven
37 out of Elam shall not come. I will terrify Elam before their enemies, and before those who seek their life; I will bring evil upon them, my fierce anger, says the LORD. I will send the sword after them, until I have
38 consumed them; and I will set my throne in Elam, and destroy their king and princes, says the LORD.
39 "But in the latter days I will restore the fortunes of Elam, says the LORD."

BABYLON

50 The word which the LORD spoke concerning Babylon, concerning the land of the Chalde′ans, by Jeremiah the prophet:
2   "Declare among the nations and proclaim,
    set up a banner and proclaim,
    conceal it not, and say:
'Babylon is taken,
    Bel is put to shame,
    Mer′odach is dismayed.
Her images are put to shame,
    her idols are dismayed.'
3 "For out of the north a nation has come up against her, which shall make her land a desolation, and none shall dwell in it; both man and beast shall flee away.

4 "In those days and in that time, says the LORD, the people of Israel and the people of Judah shall come together, weeping as they come; and they shall seek the LORD their
5 God. They shall ask the way to Zion, with faces turned toward it, saying, 'Come, let us join ourselves to the LORD in an everlasting covenant which will never be forgotten.'

"My people have been lost sheep; their 6 shepherds have led them astray, turning them away on the mountains; from mountain to hill they have gone, they have forgotten their fold. All who found them have 7 devoured them, and their enemies have said, 'We are not guilty, for they have sinned against the LORD, their true habitation, the LORD, the hope of their fathers.'

"Flee from the midst of Babylon, and go 8 out of the land of the Chalde′ans, and be as he-goats before the flock. For behold, I am 9 stirring up and bringing against Babylon a company of great nations, from the north country; and they shall array themselves against her; from there she shall be taken. Their arrows are like a skilled warrior who does not return empty-handed. Chalde′a 10 shall be plundered; all who plunder her shall be sated, says the LORD.

"Though you rejoice, though you exult, 11
    O plunderers of my heritage,
though you are wanton as a heifer at grass,
    and neigh like stallions,
your mother shall be utterly shamed, 12
    and she who bore you shall be disgraced.
Lo, she shall be the last of the nations,
    a wilderness dry and desert.
Because of the wrath of the LORD she shall 13
    not be inhabited,
    but shall be an utter desolation;
every one who passes by Babylon shall be
    appalled,
    and hiss because of all her wounds.
Set yourselves in array against Babylon 14
    round about,
    all you that bend the bow;
shoot at her, spare no arrows,
    for she has sinned against the LORD.
Raise a shout against her round about, 15
    she has surrendered;
    her bulwarks have fallen,
    her walls are thrown down.
For this is the vengeance of the LORD:
    take vengeance on her,
    do to her as she has done.
Cut off from Babylon the sower, 16
    and the one who handles the sickle in
    time of harvest;
because of the sword of the oppressor,
    every one shall turn to his own people,
    and every one shall flee to his own land.

"Israel is a hunted sheep driven away by 17 lions. First the king of Assyria devoured him, and now at last Nebuchadrez′zar king of Babylon has gnawed his bones. Therefore, 18 thus says the LORD of hosts, the God of

50–51: Is 13.1–14.23; 47; Hab 1–2.   50.8: Jer 51.6, 9, 45; 2 Cor 6.17; Rev 18.4.

Israel: Behold, I am bringing punishment on the king of Babylon and his land, as I punished the king of Assyria. I will restore Israel to his pasture, and he shall feed on Carmel and in Bashan, and his desire shall be satisfied on the hills of E'phraim and in Gilead. In those days and in that time, says the LORD, iniquity shall be sought in Israel, and there shall be none; and sin in Judah, and none shall be found; for I will pardon those whom I leave as a remnant.

"Go up against the land of Meratha'im,[r] and against the inhabitants of Pekod.[s] Slay, and utterly destroy after them,
                    says the LORD,
and do all that I have commanded you.
The noise of battle is in the land,
    and great destruction!
How the hammer of the whole earth
    is cut down and broken!
How Babylon has become
    a horror among the nations!
I set a snare for you and you were taken, O Babylon,
    and you did not know it;
you were found and caught,
    because you strove against the LORD.
The LORD has opened his armoury,
    and brought out the weapons of his wrath,
for the Lord GOD of hosts has a work to do
    in the land of the Chalde'ans.
Come against her from every quarter;
    open her granaries;
pile her up like heaps of grain, and destroy her utterly;
    let nothing be left of her.
Slay all her bulls,
    let them go down to the slaughter.
Woe to them, for their day has come,
    the time of their punishment.

"Hark! they flee and escape from the land of Babylon, to declare in Zion the vengeance of the LORD our God, vengeance for his temple.

"Summon archers against Babylon, all those who bend the bow. Encamp round about her; let no one escape. Requite her according to her deeds, do to her according to all that she has done; for she has proudly defied the LORD, the Holy One of Israel. Therefore her young men shall fall in her squares, and all her soldiers shall be destroyed on that day, says the LORD.

"Behold, I am against you, O proud one, says the Lord GOD of hosts;

for your day has come,
    the time when I will punish you.
The proud one shall stumble and fall,   32
    with none to raise him up,
and I will kindle a fire in his cities,
    and it will devour all that is round about him.

"Thus says the LORD of hosts: The people 33 of Israel are oppressed, and the people of Judah with them; all who took them captive have held them fast, they refuse to let them go. Their Redeemer is strong; the LORD of 34 hosts is his name. He will surely plead their cause, that he may give rest to the earth, but unrest to the inhabitants of Babylon.

"A sword upon the Chalde'ans, says the 35 LORD,
    and upon the inhabitants of Babylon,
    and upon her princes and her wise men!
A sword upon the diviners,   36
    that they may become fools!
A sword upon her warriors,
    that they may be destroyed!
A sword upon her horses and upon her 37 chariots,
    and upon all the foreign troops in her midst,
    that they may become women!
A sword upon all her treasures,
    that they may be plundered!
A drought upon her waters,   38
    that they may be dried up!
For it is a land of images,
    and they are mad over idols.

"Therefore wild beasts shall dwell with 39 hyenas in Babylon, and ostriches shall dwell in her; she shall be peopled no more for ever, nor inhabited for all generations. As when 40 God overthrew Sodom and Gomor'rah and their neighbour cities, says the LORD, so no man shall dwell there, and no son of man shall sojourn in her.

"Behold, a people comes from the north; 41
    a mighty nation and many kings
    are stirring from the farthest parts of the earth.
They lay hold of bow and spear;   42
    they are cruel, and have no mercy.
The sound of them is like the roaring of the sea;
    they ride upon horses,
arrayed as a man for battle
    against you, O daughter of Babylon!

"The king of Babylon heard the report of 43 them,

---

[r] Or Double Rebellion   [s] Or Punishment

and his hands fell helpless;
  anguish seized him,
    pain as of a woman in travail.

44 "Behold, like a lion coming up from the
jungle of the Jordan against a strong sheepfold, I will suddenly make them run away
from her; and I will appoint over her
whomever I choose. For who is like me?
Who will summon me? What shepherd can
45 stand before me? Therefore hear the plan
which the LORD has made against Babylon,
and the purposes which he has formed
against the land of the Chalde'ans: Surely
the little ones of their flock shall be dragged
away; surely their fold shall be appalled at
46 their fate. At the sound of the capture of
Babylon the earth shall tremble, and her cry
shall be heard among the nations."

51 Thus says the LORD:
  "Behold, I will stir up the spirit of a
    destroyer
    against Babylon,
    against the inhabitants of Chalde'a;[t]
2 and I will send to Babylon winnowers,
    and they shall winnow her,
    and they shall empty her land,
  when they come against her from every
    side
    on the day of trouble.
3 Let not the archer bend his bow,
    and let him not stand up in his coat of
    mail.
  Spare not her young men;
    utterly destroy all her host.
4 They shall fall down slain in the land of
    the Chalde'ans,
    and wounded in her streets.
5 For Israel and Judah have not been
    forsaken
    by their God, the LORD of hosts;
  but the land of the Chalde'ans[u] is full of
    guilt
    against the Holy One of Israel.

6 "Flee from the midst of Babylon,
    let every man save his life!
  Be not cut off in her punishment,
  for this is the time of the LORD's
    vengeance,
    the requital he is rendering her.
7 Babylon was a golden cup in the LORD's
    hand,
    making all the earth drunken;
  the nations drank of her wine,
    therefore the nations went mad.
8 Suddenly Babylon has fallen and been
    broken;

    wail for her!
  Take balm for her pain;
    perhaps she may be healed.
9 We would have healed Babylon,
    but she was not healed.
  Forsake her, and let us go
    each to his own country;
  for her judgment has reached up to heaven
    and has been lifted up even to the
    skies.
10 The LORD has brought forth our vindi-
    cation;
  come, let us declare in Zion
    the work of the LORD our God.

11 "Sharpen the arrows!
    Take up the shields!
The LORD has stirred up the spirit of the
kings of the Medes, because his purpose
concerning Babylon is to destroy it, for that
is the vengeance of the LORD, the vengeance
for his temple.
12 Set up a standard against the walls of
    Babylon;
  make the watch strong;
  set up watchmen;
    prepare the ambushes;
  for the LORD has both planned and done
    what he spoke concerning the inhabi-
    tants of Babylon.
13 O you who dwell by many waters,
    rich in treasures,
  your end has come,
    the thread of your life is cut.
14 The LORD of hosts has sworn by himself:
Surely I will fill you with men, as many as
    locusts,
  and they shall raise the shout of victory
    over you.

15 "It is he who made the earth by his power,
  who established the world by his wis-
    dom,
  and by his understanding stretched out the
    heavens.
16 When he utters his voice there is a tumult
    of waters in the heavens,
  and he makes the mist rise from the ends
    of the earth.
  He makes lightnings for the rain,
    and he brings forth the wind from his
    storehouses.
17 Every man is stupid and without know-
    ledge;
  every goldsmith is put to shame by his
    idols;
  for his images are false,
    and there is no breath in them.
18 They are worthless, a work of delusion;

[t] Heb Leb-qamai, a cipher for Chaldea   [u] Heb their land
51.6, 9, 45: Jer 50.8; 2 Cor 6.17; Rev 18.4.   51.7–8: Jer 25.15; Rev 14.8, 10; 16.19; 17.4; 18.3.
51.13: Rev 17.1.

at the time of their punishment they
shall perish.

9 Not like these is he who is the portion of
Jacob,
  for he is the one who formed all things,
and Israel is the tribe of his inheritance;
  the LORD of hosts is his name.

0 "You are my hammer and weapon of war:
  with you I break nations in pieces;
    with you I destroy kingdoms;
1 with you I break in pieces the horse and
    his rider;
    with you I break in pieces the chariot
      and the charioteer;
2 with you I break in pieces man and woman;
    with you I break in pieces the old man
      and the youth;
    with you I break in pieces the young man
      and the maiden;
3 with you I break in pieces the shepherd
      and his flock;
    with you I break in pieces the farmer and
      his team;
    with you I break in pieces governors and
      commanders.

24 "I will requite Babylon and all the inhabitants of Chalde′a before your very eyes for all
the evil that they have done in Zion, says the
LORD.

25 "Behold, I am against you, O destroying
    mountain,
                    says the LORD,
  which destroys the whole earth;
I will stretch out my hand against you,
  and roll you down from the crags,
  and make you a burnt mountain.
26 No stone shall be taken from you for a
    corner
  and no stone for a foundation,
but you shall be a perpetual waste,
                    says the LORD.

27 "Set up a standard on the earth,
  blow the trumpet among the nations;
prepare the nations for war against her,
  summon against her the kingdoms,
  Ararat, Minni, and Ash′kenaz;
appoint a marshal against her,
  bring up horses like bristling locusts.
28 Prepare the nations for war against her,
  the kings of the Medes, with their
    governors and deputies,
  and every land under their dominion.
29 The land trembles and writhes in pain,
  for the LORD's purposes against Babylon
    stand,
  to make the land of Babylon a desolation,

without inhabitant.
The warriors of Babylon have ceased 30
  fighting,
  they remain in their strongholds;
their strength has failed,
  they have become women;
her dwellings are on fire,
  her bars are broken.
One runner runs to meet another,   31
  and one messenger to meet another,
to tell the king of Babylon
  that his city is taken on every side;
the fords have been seized,   32
  the bulwarks are burned with fire,
  and the soldiers are in panic.
For thus says the LORD of hosts, the God 33
    of Israel:
The daughter of Babylon is like a thresh-
    ing floor
  at the time when it is trodden;
yet a little while
  and the time of her harvest will come."

"Nebuchadrez′zar the king of Babylon has 34
    devoured me,
  he has crushed me;
he has made me an empty vessel,
  he has swallowed me like a monster;
he has filled his belly with my delicacies,
  he has rinsed me out.
The violence done to me and to my 35
    kinsmen be upon Babylon,"
  let the inhabitant of Zion say.
"My blood be upon the inhabitants of
    Chalde′a,"
  let Jerusalem say.
Therefore thus says the LORD: 36
"Behold, I will plead your cause
  and take vengeance for you.
I will dry up her sea
  and make her fountain dry;
and Babylon shall become a heap of ruins, 37
  the haunt of jackals,
a horror and a hissing,
  without inhabitant.

"They shall roar together like lions; 38
  they shall growl like lions' whelps.
While they are inflamed I will prepare 39
    them a feast
  and make them drunk, till they swoon
    away ᵛ
and sleep a perpetual sleep
  and not wake, says the LORD.
I will bring them down like lambs to the 40
    slaughter,
  like rams and he-goats.

"How Babylon ʷ is taken,   41
  the praise of the whole earth seized!

ᵛ Gk Vg: Heb *rejoice*   ʷ Heb *Sheshach*, a cipher for Babylon

How Babylon has become
a horror among the nations!

42 The sea has come up on Babylon;
she is covered with its tumultuous
waves.

43 Her cities have become a horror,
a land of drought and a desert,
a land in which no one dwells,
and through which no son of man
passes.

44 And I will punish Bel in Babylon,
and take out of his mouth what he has
swallowed.
The nations shall no longer flow to him;
the wall of Babylon has fallen.

45 "Go out of the midst of her, my people!
Let every man save his life
from the fierce anger of the LORD!

46 Let not your heart faint, and be not fearful
at the report heard in the land,
when a report comes in one year
and afterward a report in another year,
and violence is in the land,
and ruler is against ruler.

47 "Therefore, behold, the days are coming
when I will punish the images of
Babylon;
her whole land shall be put to shame,
and all her slain shall fall in the midst of
her.

48 Then the heavens and the earth,
and all that is in them,
shall sing for joy over Babylon;
for the destroyers shall come against
them out of the north,
says the LORD.

49 Babylon must fall for the slain of Israel,
as for Babylon have fallen the slain of all
the earth.

50 "You that have escaped from the sword,
go, stand not still!
Remember the LORD from afar,
and let Jerusalem come into your mind:

51 'We are put to shame, for we have heard
reproach;
dishonour has covered our face,
for aliens have come
into the holy places of the LORD's
house.'

52 "Therefore, behold, the days are coming,
says the LORD,
when I will execute judgment upon her
images,
and through all her land
the wounded shall groan.

Though Babylon should mount up to 53
heaven,
and though she should fortify her strong
height,
yet destroyers would come from me upon
her,
says the LORD.

"Hark! a cry from Babylon! 54
The noise of great destruction from the
land of the Chalde'ans!
For the LORD is laying Babylon waste, 55
and stilling her mighty voice.
Their waves roar like many waters,
the noise of their voice is raised;
for a destroyer has come upon her, 56
upon Babylon;
her warriors are taken,
their bows are broken in pieces;
for the LORD is a God of recompense,
he will surely requite.
I will make drunk her princes and her wise 57
men,
her governors, her commanders, and
her warriors;
they shall sleep a perpetual sleep and not
wake,
says the King, whose name is the LORD
of hosts.

"Thus says the LORD of hosts: 58
The broad wall of Babylon
shall be levelled to the ground
and her high gates
shall be burned with fire.
The peoples labour for naught,
and the nations weary themselves only
for fire."

The word which Jeremiah the prophet 59
commanded Serai'ah the son of Neri'ah, son
of Mahsei'ah, when he went with Zedeki'ah
king of Judah to Babylon, in the fourth year
of his reign. Serai'ah was the quartermaster.
Jeremiah wrote in a book all the evil that 60
should come upon Babylon, all these words
that are written concerning Babylon. And 61
Jeremiah said to Serai'ah: "When you come
to Babylon, see that you read all these words,
and say, 'O LORD, thou hast said concerning 62
this place that thou wilt cut it off, so that
nothing shall dwell in it, neither man nor
beast, and it shall be desolate for ever.'
When you finish reading this book, bind a 63
stone to it, and cast it into the midst of the
Euphra'tes, and say, 'Thus shall Babylon 64
sink, to rise no more, because of the evil that
I am bringing upon her.' " *z*
Thus far are the words of Jeremiah.

---

z Gk: Heb *upon her. And they shall weary themselves*
51.48: Is 44.23; Rev 12.12; 18.20.   **51.63–64**: Rev 18.21.

JUDAH

Judah made captive

2 Zedeki′ah was twenty-one years old when he became king; and he reigned eleven years in Jerusalem. His mother's name was Hamu′tal the daughter of Jeremiah of 2 Libnah. And he did what was evil in the sight of the LORD, according to all that 3 Jehoi′akim had done. Surely because of the anger of the LORD things came to such a pass in Jerusalem and Judah that he cast them out from his presence.

And Zedeki′ah rebelled against the king of 4 Babylon. And in the ninth year of his reign, in the tenth month, on the tenth day of the month, Nebuchadrez′zar king of Babylon came with all his army against Jerusalem, and they laid siege to it and built siegeworks 5 against it round about. So the city was besieged till the eleventh year of King 6 Zedeki′ah. On the ninth day of the fourth month the famine was so severe in the city, that there was no food for the people of the 7 land. Then a breach was made in the city; and all the men of war fled and went out from the city by night by the way of a gate between the two walls, by the king's garden, while the Chalde′ans were round about the city. And they went in the direction of 8 Arabah. But the army of the Chalde′ans pursued the king, and overtook Zedeki′ah in the plains of Jericho; and all his army was 9 scattered from him. Then they captured the king, and brought him up to the king of Babylon at Riblah in the land of Hamath, 10 and he passed sentence upon him. The king of Babylon slew the sons of Zedeki′ah before his eyes, and also slew all the princes of 11 Judah at Riblah. He put out the eyes of Zedeki′ah, and bound him in fetters, and the king of Babylon took him to Babylon, and put him in prison till the day of his death.

12 In the fifth month, on the tenth day of the month—which was the nineteenth year of King Nebu′zarad′zar, king of Babylon— Nebu′zarad′an the captain of the bodyguard who served the king of Babylon, entered 13 Jerusalem. And he burned the house of the LORD, and the king's house and all the houses of Jerusalem; every great house he burned 14 down. And all the army of the Chalde′ans, who were with the captain of the guard, broke down all the walls round about Jerusalem. And Nebu′zarad′an the captain of the 15 guard carried away captive some of the poorest of the people and the rest of the people who were left in the city and the deserters who had deserted to the king of Babylon, together with the rest of the artisans. But Nebu′zarad′an the captain of the 16 guard left some of the poorest of the land to be vinedressers and ploughmen.

And the pillars of bronze that were in the 17 house of the LORD, and the stands and the bronze sea that were in the house of the LORD, the Chalde′ans broke in pieces, and carried all the bronze to Babylon. And they 18 took away the pots, and the shovels, and the snuffers, and the basins, and the dishes for incense, and all the vessels of bronze used in the temple service; also the small bowls, and 19 the firepans, and the basins, and the pots, and the lampstands, and the dishes for incense, and the bowls for libation. What was of gold the captain of the guard took away as gold, and what was of silver, as silver. As for the two pillars, the one sea, the 20 twelve bronze bulls which were under the sea,[v] and the stands, which Solomon the king had made for the house of the LORD, the bronze of all these things was beyond weight. As for the pillars, the height of 21 the one pillar was eighteen cubits, its circumference was twelve cubits, and its thickness was four fingers, and it was hollow. Upon it was a capital of bronze; the height of 22 the one capital was five cubits; a network and pomegranates, all of bronze, were upon the capital round about. And the second pillar had the like, with pomegranates. There were 23 ninety-six pomegranates on the sides; all the pomegranates were a hundred upon the network round about.

And the captain of the guard took Serai′ah 24 the chief priest, and Zephani′ah the second priest, and the three keepers of the threshold; and from the city he took an officer who had 25 been in command of the men of war, and seven men of the king's council, who were found in the city; and the secretary of the commander of the army who mustered the people of the land; and sixty men of the people of the land, who were found in the midst of the city. And Nebu′zarad′an the 26 captain of the guard took them, and brought them to the king of Babylon at Riblah. And 27 the king of Babylon smote them, and put them to death at Riblah in the land of Hamath. So Judah was carried captive out of its land.

This is the number of the people whom 28

v Heb lacks the sea
52: 2 Kings 24.18–25. 30; 2 Chron 36.11–13.

Nebuchadrez′zar carried away captive: in the seventh year, three thousand and twenty-
29 three Jews; in the eighteenth year of Nebuchadrez′zar he carried away captive from Jerusalem eight hundred and thirty-
30 two persons; in the twenty-third year of Nebuchadrez′zar, Nebu′zarad′an the captain of the guard carried away captive of the Jews seven hundred and forty-five persons; all the persons were four thousand and six hundred.
31 And in the thirty-seventh year of the captivity of Jehoi′achin king of Judah, in the twelfth month, on the twenty-fifth day of the month, E′vil-mero′dach king of Babylon, in the year that he became king, lifted up the head of Jehoi′achin king of Judah and
32 brought him out of prison; and he spoke kindly to him, and gave him a seat above the seats of the kings who were with him in

Babylon. So Jehoi′achin put off his prison 3 garments. And every day of his life he dined regularly at the king's table; as for his 3 allowance, a regular allowance was given him by the king according to his daily need, until the day of his death as long as he lived.

THE LAMENTATIONS

OF JEREMIAH

HOW lonely sits the city
    that was full of people!
  How like a widow has she become,
she that was great among the nations!
She that was a princess among the cities
  has become a vassal.

2 She weeps bitterly in the night,
    tears on her cheeks;
among all her lovers
  she has none to comfort her;
all her friends have dealt treacherously with her,
  they have become her enemies.

3 Judah has gone into exile because of affliction
  and hard servitude;
she dwells now among the nations,
  but finds no resting place;
her pursuers have all overtaken her
  in the midst of her distress.

4 The roads to Zion mourn,
    for none come to the appointed feasts;

all her gates are desolate,
  her priests groan;
her maidens have been dragged away,[a]
  and she herself suffers bitterly.

Her foes have become the head,   5
  her enemies prosper,
because the LORD has made her suffer
  for the multitude of her transgressions;
her children have gone away,
  captives before the foe.

From the daughter of Zion has departed   6
  all her majesty.
Her princes have become like harts
  that find no pasture;
they fled without strength
  before the pursuer.

Jerusalem remembers   7
  in the days of her affliction and bitterness[b]
all the precious things
  that were hers from days of old.
When her people fell into the hand of the foe,
  and there was none to help her,

[a] Gk Old Latin: Heb *afflicted*   [b] Cn: Heb *wandering*

the foe gloated over her,
   mocking at her downfall.

8 Jerusalem sinned grievously,
   therefore she became filthy;
all who honoured her despise her,
   for they have seen her nakedness;
yea, she herself groans,
   and turns her face away.

9 Her uncleanness was in her skirts;
   she took no thought of her doom;
therefore her fall is terrible,
   she has no comforter.
"O LORD, behold my affliction,
   for the enemy has triumphed!"

10 The enemy has stretched out his hands
   over all her precious things;
yea, she has seen the nations
   invade her sanctuary,
those whom thou didst forbid
   to enter thy congregation.

11 All her people groan
   as they search for bread;
they trade their treasures for food
   to revive their strength.
"Look, O LORD, and behold,
   for I am despised."

12 "Is it nothing to you,*c* all you who pass by?
   Look and see
if there is any sorrow like my sorrow
   which was brought upon me,
which the LORD inflicted
   on the day of his fierce anger.

13 "From on high he sent fire;
   into my bones*d* he made it descend;
he spread a net for my feet;
   he turned me back;
he has left me stunned,
   faint all the day long.

14 "My transgressions were bound*e* into a
   yoke;
   by his hand they were fastened together;
they were set upon my neck;
   he caused my strength to fail;
the Lord gave me into the hands
   of those whom I cannot withstand.

15 "The Lord flouted all my mighty men
   in the midst of me;
he summoned an assembly against me
   to crush my young men;
the Lord has trodden as in a wine press
   the virgin daughter of Judah.

"For these things I weep;   16
   my eyes flow with tears;
for a comforter is far from me,
   one to revive my courage;
my children are desolate,
   for the enemy has prevailed."

Zion stretches out her hands,   17
   but there is none to comfort her;
the LORD has commanded against Jacob
   that his neighbours should be his foes;
Jerusalem has become
   a filthy thing among them.

"The LORD is in the right,   18
   for I have rebelled against his word;
but hear, all you peoples,
   and behold my suffering;
my maidens and my young men
   have gone into captivity.

"I called to my lovers   19
   but they deceived me;
my priests and elders
   perished in the city,
while they sought food
   to revive their strength.

"Behold, O LORD, for I am in distress,   20
   my soul is in tumult,
my heart is wrung within me,
   because I have been very rebellious.
In the street the sword bereaves;
   in the house it is like death.

"Hear*f* how I groan;   21
   there is none to comfort me.
All my enemies have heard of my trouble;
   they are glad that thou hast done it.
Bring thou*g* the day thou hast announced,
   and let them be as I am.

"Let all their evil doing come before thee;   22
   and deal with them
as thou hast dealt with me
   because of all my transgressions;
for my groans are many
   and my heart is faint."

H OW the Lord in his anger   2
   has set the daughter of Zion under a
   cloud!
He has cast down from heaven to earth
   the splendour of Israel;
he has not remembered his footstool
   in the day of his anger.

The Lord has destroyed without mercy   2
   all the habitations of Jacob;

c Heb uncertain   *d* Gk: Heb *bones and*   *e* Cn: Heb uncertain
f Gk Syr: Heb *they heard*   *g* Syr: Heb *thou hast brought*

in his wrath he has broken down
  the strongholds of the daughter of Judah;
he has brought down to the ground in
    dishonour
  the kingdom and its rulers.

3 He has cut down in fierce anger
    all the might of Israel;
he has withdrawn from them his right hand
    in the face of the enemy;
he has burned like a flaming fire in Jacob,
    consuming all around.

4 He has bent his bow like an enemy,
    with his right hand set like a foe;
and he has slain all the pride of our
    eyes
  in the tent of the daughter of Zion;
he has poured out his fury like fire.

5 The Lord has become like an enemy,
    he has destroyed Israel;
he has destroyed all its palaces,
    laid in ruins its strongholds;
and he has multiplied in the daughter of
    Judah
  mourning and lamentation.

6 He has broken down his booth like that of a
    garden,
  laid in ruins the place of his appointed
    feasts;
the Lord has brought to an end in Zion
    appointed feast and sabbath,
and in his fierce indignation has spurned
    king and priest.

7 The Lord has scorned his altar,
    disowned his sanctuary;
he has delivered into the hand of the enemy
    the walls of her palaces;
a clamour was raised in the house of the
    Lord
  as on the day of an appointed feast.

8 The Lord determined to lay in ruins
    the wall of the daughter of Zion;
he marked it off by the line;
    he restrained not his hand from destroy-
      ing;
he caused rampart and wall to lament,
    they languish together.

9 Her gates have sunk into the ground;
    he has ruined and broken her bars;
her king and princes are among the
    nations;
  the law is no more,
and her prophets obtain
  no vision from the Lord.

The elders of the daughter of Zion   1
  sit on the ground in silence;
they have cast dust on their heads
  and put on sackcloth;
the maidens of Jerusalem
  have bowed their heads to the ground.

My eyes are spent with weeping;   1
  my soul is in tumult;
my heart is poured out in grief[h]
  because of the destruction of the daughter
    of my people,
because infants and babes faint
  in the streets of the city.

They cry to their mothers,   1.
  "Where is bread and wine?"
as they faint like wounded men
  in the streets of the city,
as their life is poured out
  on their mothers' bosom.

What can I say for you, to what compare 1
    you,
  O daughter of Jerusalem?
What can I liken to you, that I may comfort
    you,
  O virgin daughter of Zion?
For vast as the sea is your ruin;
  who can restore you?

Your prophets have seen for you   1₄
  false and deceptive visions;
they have not exposed your iniquity
  to restore your fortunes,
but have seen for you oracles
  false and misleading.

All who pass along the way   15
  clap their hands at you;
they hiss and wag their heads
  at the daughter of Jerusalem;
"Is this the city which was called
  the perfection of beauty,
  the joy of all the earth?"

All your enemies   16
  rail against you;
they hiss, they gnash their teeth,
  they cry: "We have destroyed her!
Ah, this is the day we longed for;
  now we have it; we see it!"

The Lord has done what he purposed,   17
  has carried out his threat;
as he ordained long ago,
  he has demolished without pity;
he has made the enemy rejoice over
    you,
  and exalted the might of your foes.

Cry aloud[i] to the Lord!
    O[j] daughter of Zion!
Let tears stream down like a torrent
    day and night!
Give yourself no rest,
    your eyes no respite!

Arise, cry out in the night,
    at the beginning of the watches!
Pour out your heart like water
    before the presence of the Lord!
Lift your hands to him
    for the lives of your children,
who faint for hunger
    at the head of every street.

Look, O LORD, and see!
    With whom hast thou dealt thus?
Should women eat their offspring,
    the children of their tender care?
Should priest and prophet be slain
    in the sanctuary of the Lord?

In the dust of the streets
    lie the young and the old;
my maidens and my young men
    have fallen by the sword;
in the day of thy anger thou hast slain them,
    slaughtering without mercy.

Thou didst invite as to the day of an
        appointed feast
    my terrors on every side;
and on the day of the anger of the LORD
    none escaped or survived;
those whom I dandled and reared
    my enemy destroyed.

3 I AM the man who has seen affliction
        under the rod of his wrath;
2 he has driven and brought me
    into darkness without any light;
3 surely against me he turns his hand
    again and again the whole day long.

4 He has made my flesh and my skin waste
        away,
    and broken my bones;
5 he has besieged and enveloped me
    with bitterness and tribulation;
6 he has made me dwell in darkness
    like the dead of long ago.

7 He has walled me about so that I cannot
        escape;
    he has put heavy chains on me;
8 though I call and cry for help,
    he shuts out my prayer;
9 he has blocked my ways with hewn stones,
    he has made my paths crooked.

He is to me like a bear lying in wait,   10
    like a lion in hiding;
he led me off my way and tore me to pieces; 11
    he has made me desolate;
he bent his bow and set me   12
    as a mark for his arrow.

He drove into my heart   13
    the arrows of his quiver;
I have become the laughingstock of all   14
        peoples,
    the burden of their songs all day long.
He has filled me with bitterness,   15
    he has sated me with wormwood.

He has made my teeth grind on gravel,   16
    and made me cower in ashes;
my soul is bereft of peace,   17
    I have forgotten what happiness is;
so I say, "Gone is my glory,   18
    and my expectation from the LORD."

Remember my affliction and my bitterness,[k] 19
    the wormwood and the gall!
My soul continually thinks of it   20
    and is bowed down within me.
But this I call to mind,   21
    and therefore I have hope:

The steadfast love of the LORD never   22
    ceases,[l]
    his mercies never come to an end;
they are new every morning;   23
    great is thy faithfulness.
"The LORD is my portion," says my soul,   24
    "therefore I will hope in him."

The LORD is good to those who wait for   25
        him,
    to the soul that seeks him.
It is good that one should wait quietly   26
    for the salvation of the LORD.
It is good for a man that he bear   27
    the yoke in his youth.

Let him sit alone in silence   28
    when he has laid it on him;
let him put his mouth in the dust—   29
    there may yet be hope;
let him give his cheek to the smiter,   30
    and be filled with insults.

For the Lord will not   31
    cast off for ever,
but, though he cause grief, he will have 32
        compassion
    according to the abundance of his steadfast
        love;
for he does not willingly afflict   33
    or grieve the sons of men.

---

[i] Cn: Heb *Their heart cried*   [j] Cn: Heb *O wall of*   [k] Cn: Heb *wandering*   [l] Syr Tg: Heb *we are not cut off*

34 To crush under foot
    all the prisoners of the earth,
35 to turn aside the right of a man
    in the presence of the Most High,
36 to subvert a man in his cause,
    the Lord does not approve.

37 Who has commanded and it came to pass,
    unless the Lord has ordained it?
38 Is it not from the mouth of the Most High
    that good and evil come?
39 Why should a living man complain,
    a man, about the punishment of his sins?

40 Let us test and examine our ways,
    and return to the LORD!
41 Let us lift up our hearts and hands
    to God in heaven:
42 "We have transgressed and rebelled,
    and thou hast not forgiven.

43 "Thou hast wrapped thyself with anger and
        pursued us,
    slaying without pity;
44 thou hast wrapped thyself with a cloud
    so that no prayer can pass through.
45 Thou hast made us offscouring and refuse
    among the peoples.

46 "All our enemies
    rail against us;
47 panic and pitfall have come upon us,
    devastation and destruction;
48 my eyes flow with rivers of tears
    because of the destruction of the daughter
        of my people.

49 "My eyes will flow without ceasing,
    without respite,
50 until the LORD from heaven
    looks down and sees;
51 my eyes cause me grief
    at the fate of all the maidens of my city.

52 "I have been hunted like a bird
    by those who were my enemies without
        cause;
53 they flung me alive into the pit
    and cast stones on me;
54 water closed over my head;
    I said, 'I am lost.'

55 "I called on thy name, O LORD,
    from the depths of the pit;
56 thou didst hear my plea, 'Do not close
    thine ear to my cry for help!'ᵐ
57 Thou didst come near when I called on
        thee;
    thou didst say, 'Do not fear!'

"Thou hast taken up my cause, O Lord,
    thou hast redeemed my life.
Thou hast seen the wrong done to me, O
    LORD;
    judge thou my cause.
Thou hast seen all their vengeance,
    all their devices against me.

"Thou hast heard their taunts, O LORD,
    all their devices against me.
The lips and thoughts of my assailants
    are against me all the day long.
Behold their sitting and their rising;
    I am the burden of their songs.

"Thou wilt requite them, O LORD,
    according to the work of their hands.
Thou wilt give them dullness of heart;
    thy curse will be on them.
Thou wilt pursue them in anger and destroy
        them
    from under thy heavens, O LORD."ⁿ

HOW the gold has grown dim,   4
    how the pure gold is changed!
The holy stones lie scattered
    at the head of every street.

The precious sons of Zion,   2
    worth their weight in fine gold,
how they are reckoned as earthen pots,
    the work of a potter's hands!

Even the jackals give the breast   3
    and suckle their young,
but the daughter of my people has become
        cruel,
    like the ostriches in the wilderness.

The tongue of the nursling cleaves   4
    to the roof of its mouth for thirst;
the children beg for food,
    but no one gives to them.

Those who feasted on dainties   5
    perish in the streets;
those who were brought up in purple
    lie on ash heaps.

For the chastisementᵒ of the daughter of my 6
        people has been greater
    than the punishmentᵖ of Sodom,
which was overthrown in a moment,
    no hand being laid on it.ᑫ

Her princes were purer than snow,   7
    whiter than milk;
their bodies were more ruddy than coral,

ᵐ Heb uncertain   ⁿ Syr Compare Gk Vg: Heb *the heavens of the* LORD   ᵒ Or *iniquity*   ᵖ Or *sin*
ᑫ Heb uncertain

the beauty of their form[r] was like sapphire.[s]

8 Now their visage is blacker than soot,
   they are not recognised in the streets;
 their skin has shrivelled upon their bones,
   it has become as dry as wood.

9 Happier were the victims of the sword
   than the victims of hunger,
 who pined away, stricken
   by want of the fruits of the field.

10 The hands of compassionate women
   have boiled their own children;
 they became their food
   in the destruction of the daughter of my people.

11 The LORD gave full vent to his wrath,
   he poured out his hot anger;
 and he kindled a fire in Zion,
   which consumed its foundations.

12 The kings of the earth did not believe,
   or any of the inhabitants of the world,
 that foe or enemy could enter
   the gates of Jerusalem.

13 This was for the sins of her prophets
   and the iniquities of her priests,
 who shed in the midst of her
   the blood of the righteous.

14 They wandered, blind, through the streets,
   so defiled with blood
 that none could touch
   their garments.

15 "Away! Unclean!" men cried at them;
   "Away! Away! Touch not!"
 So they became fugitives and wanderers;
   men said among the nations,
   "They shall stay with us no longer."

16 The LORD himself has scattered them,
   he will regard them no more;
 no honour was shown to the priests,
   no favour to the elders.

17 Our eyes failed, ever watching
   vainly for help;
 in our watching[t] we watched
   for a nation which could not save.

18 Men dogged our steps
   so that we could not walk in our streets;
 our end drew near; our days were numbered;
   for our end had come.

Our pursuers were swifter   19
   than the vultures in the heavens;
 they chased us on the mountains,
   they lay in wait for us in the wilderness.

The breath of our nostrils, the LORD's 20
   anointed,
   was taken in their pits,
 he of whom we said, "Under his shadow
   we shall live among the nations."

Rejoice and be glad, O daughter of Edom,   21
   dweller in the land of Uz;
 but to you also the cup shall pass;
   you shall become drunk and strip yourself
   bare.

The punishment of your iniquity, O daughter 22
   of Zion, is accomplished,
   he will keep you in exile no longer;
 but your iniquity, O daughter of Edom, he
   will punish,
   he will uncover your sins.

R EMEMBER, O LORD, what has befallen **5**
   us;
   behold, and see our disgrace!
Our inheritance has been turned over to 2
   strangers,
   our homes to aliens.
We have become orphans, fatherless;   3
   our mothers are like widows.
We must pay for the water we drink,   4
   the wood we get must be bought.
With a yoke[u] on our necks we are hard 5
   driven;
   we are weary, we are given no rest.
We have given the hand to Egypt,   6
   and to Assyria, to get bread enough.
Our fathers sinned, and are no more;   7
   and we bear their iniquities.
Slaves rule over us;   8
   there is none to deliver us from their hand.
We get our bread at the peril of our lives, 9
   because of the sword in the wilderness.
Our skin is hot as an oven   10
   with the burning heat of famine.
Women are ravished in Zion,   11
   virgins in the towns of Judah.
Princes are hung up by their hands;   12
   no respect is shown to the elders.
Young men are compelled to grind at the 13
   mill;
   and boys stagger under loads of wood.
The old men have quit the city gate,   14
   the young men their music.
The joy of our hearts has ceased;   15
   our dancing has been turned to mourning.
The crown has fallen from our head;   16
   woe to us, for we have sinned!

---

[r] Heb uncertain   [s] Heb *lapis lazuli*   [t] Heb uncertain   [u] Symmachus: Heb lacks *with a yoke*

17 For this our heart has become sick,
   for these things our eyes have grown dim,
18 for Mount Zion which lies desolate;
   jackals prowl over it.

19 But thou, O LORD, dost reign for ever;
   thy throne endures to all generations.

Why dost thou forget us for ever,   20
   why dost thou so long forsake us?
Restore us to thyself, O LORD, that we may 21
   be restored!
Renew our days as of old!
Or hast thou utterly rejected us?   22
   Art thou exceedingly angry with us?

THE BOOK OF

EZEKIEL

IN the thirtieth year, in the fourth month, on the fifth day of the month, as I was among the exiles by the river Chebar, the heavens were opened, and I saw visions 2 of God. On the fifth day of the month (it was the fifth year of the exile of King Jehoi'- 3 achin), the word of the LORD came to Ezekiel the priest, the son of Buzi, in the land of the Chalde'ans by the river Chebar; and the hand of the LORD was upon him there.

Ezekiel's vision

4 As I looked, behold, a stormy wind came out of the north, and a great cloud, with brightness round about it, and fire flashing forth continually, and in the midst of the fire, 5 as it were gleaming bronze. And from the midst of it came the likeness of four living creatures. And this was their appearance: 6 they had the form of men, but each had four faces, and each of them had four wings.

Their legs were straight, and the soles of 7 their feet were like the sole of a calf's foot; and they sparkled like burnished bronze. Under their wings on their four sides they 8 had human hands. And the four had their faces and their wings thus: their wings 9 touched one another; they went every one straight forward, without turning as they went. As for the likeness of their faces, each 10 had the face of a man in front;[a] the four had the face of a lion on the right side, the four had the face of an ox on the left side, and the four had the face of an eagle at the back.[b] Such were their faces. And their wings were 11 spread out above; each creature had two wings, each of which touched the wing of another, while two covered their bodies. And each went straight forward; wherever 12 the spirit would go, they went, without turning as they went. In the midst of[c] the 13 living creatures there was something that looked like burning coals of fire, like torches

---

[a] Cn: Heb lacks *in front*   [b] Cn: Heb lacks *at the back*   [c] Gk Old Latin: Heb *And the likeness of*
1.1: Rev 19.11.   1.5, 18: Rev 4.6.   1.10: Rev 4.7.   1.13: Rev 4.5.

moving to and fro among the living creatures; and the fire was bright, and out of the
4 fire went forth lightning. And the living creatures darted to and fro, like a flash of lightning.

5 Now as I looked at the living creatures, I saw a wheel upon the earth beside the living creatures, one for each of the four of them. [d]
6 As for the appearance of the wheels and their construction: their appearance was like the gleaming of a chrysolite; and the four had the same likeness, their construction being as it
7 were a wheel within a wheel. When they went, they went in any of their four direc-
8 tions[e] without turning as they went. The four wheels had rims and they had spokes;[f] and their rims were full of eyes round about.
9 And when the living creatures went, the wheels went beside them; and when the living creatures rose from the earth, the
10 wheels rose. Wherever the spirit would go, they went, and the wheels rose along with them; for the spirit of the living creatures
11 was in the wheels. When those went, these went; and when those stood, these stood; and when those rose from the earth, the wheels rose along with them; for the spirit of the living creatures was in the wheels.
22 Over the heads of the living creatures there was the likeness of a firmament, shining like crystal,[g] spread out above their heads.
23 And under the firmament their wings were stretched out straight, one toward another; and each creature had two wings covering its
24 body. And when they went, I heard the sound of their wings like the sound of many waters, like the thunder of the Almighty, a sound of tumult like the sound of a host; when they stood still, they let down their
25 wings. And there came a voice from above the firmament over their heads; when they stood still, they let down their wings.
26 And above the firmament over their heads there was the likeness of a throne, in appearance like sapphire;[h] and seated above the likeness of a throne was a likeness as it were
27 of a human form. And upward from what had the appearance of his loins I saw as it were gleaming bronze, like the appearance of fire enclosed round about; and downward from what had the appearance of his loins I saw as it were the appearance of fire, and
28 there was brightness round about him.[i] Like the appearance of the bow that is in the cloud on the day of rain, so was the appearance of the brightness round about.

Such was the appearance of the likeness of the glory of the LORD. And when I saw it, I fell upon my face, and I heard the voice of one speaking.

Ezekiel's call

2 And he said to me, "Son of man, stand
2 upon your feet, and I will speak with you." And when he spoke to me, the Spirit entered into me and set me upon my feet; and I heard
3 him speaking to me. And he said to me, "Son of man, I send you to the people of Israel, to a nation[j] of rebels, who have rebelled against me; they and their fathers have transgressed against me to this very
4 day. The people also are impudent and stubborn: I send you to them; and you shall
5 say to them, 'Thus says the Lord GOD.' And whether they hear or refuse to hear (for they are a rebellious house) they will know that
6 there has been a prophet among them. And you, son of man, be not afraid of them, nor be afraid of their words, though briers and thorns are with you and you sit upon scorpions; be not afraid of their words, nor be dismayed at their looks, for they are a
7 rebellious house. And you shall speak my words to them, whether they hear or refuse to hear; for they are a rebellious house.
8 "But you, son of man, hear what I say to you; be not rebellious like that rebellious house; open your mouth, and eat what I give
9 you." And when I looked, behold, a hand was stretched out to me, and, lo, a written scroll was in it; and he spread it before me;
10 and it had writing on the front and on the back, and there were written on it words of lamentation and mourning and woe.

3 And he said to me, "Son of man, eat what is offered to you; eat this scroll, and go, speak
2 to the house of Israel." So I opened my mouth, and he gave me the scroll to eat. And
3 he said to me, "Son of man, eat this scroll that I give you and fill your stomach with it." Then I ate it; and it was in my mouth as sweet as honey.
4 And he said to me, "Son of man, go, get you to the house of Israel, and speak with my
5 words to them. For you are not sent to a people of foreign speech and a hard language,
6 but to the house of Israel—not to many peoples of foreign speech and a hard language, whose words you cannot understand. Surely, if I sent you to such, they would
7 listen to you. But the house of Israel will not listen to you; for they are not willing to listen to me; because all the house of Israel are of a

[d] Heb of their faces [e] Heb on their four sides [f] Cn: Heb uncertain [g] Gk: Heb awesome crystal
[h] Heb lapis lazuli [i] Or it [j] Syr: Heb nations
1.18: Ezek 10.12; Rev 4.8. 1.24: Ezek 43.2; Rev 1.15; 14.2; 19.6. 1.26: Rev 1.13; 4.2.
2.8–3.3: Rev 5.1; 10.8–10.

hard forehead and of a stubborn heart.
8 Behold, I have made your face hard against
their faces, and your forehead hard against
9 their foreheads. Like adamant harder than
flint have I made your forehead; fear them
not, nor be dismayed at their looks, for they
10 are a rebellious house." Moreover he said to
me, "Son of man, all my words that I shall
speak to you receive in your heart, and hear
11 with your ears. And go, get you to the exiles,
to your people, and say to them, 'Thus says
the Lord GOD'; whether they hear or refuse
to hear."
12 Then the Spirit lifted me up, and as the
glory of the LORD arose[k] from its place, I
heard behind me the sound of a great
13 earthquake; it was the sound of the wings of
the living creatures as they touched one
another, and the sound of the wheels beside
them, that sounded like a great earthquake.
14 The Spirit lifted me up and took me away,
and I went in bitterness in the heat of my
spirit, the hand of the LORD being strong
15 upon me; and I came to the exiles at
Tela'bib, who dwelt by the river Chebar.[l]
And I sat there overwhelmed among them
seven days.

Ezekiel's mission

16 And at the end of seven days, the word of
17 the LORD came to me: "Son of man, I have
made you a watchman for the house of Israel;
whenever you hear a word from my mouth,
18 you shall give them warning from me. If I
say to the wicked, 'You shall surely die,' and
you give him no warning, nor speak to warn
the wicked from his wicked way, in order to
save his life, that wicked man shall die in his
iniquity; but his blood I will require at your
19 hand. But if you warn the wicked, and he

B. C.
600–500

does not turn from his wickedness, or from
his wicked way, he shall die in his iniquity;
but you will have saved your life. Again, if a 2
righteous man turns from his righteousness
and commits iniquity, and I lay a stumbling
block before him, he shall die; because you
have not warned him, he shall die for his sin,
and his righteous deeds which he has done
shall not be remembered; but his blood I will
require at your hand. Nevertheless if you 2
warn the righteous man not to sin, and he does
not sin, he shall surely live, because he took
warning; and you will have saved your life."
And the hand of the LORD was there upon 22
me; and he said to me, "Arise, go forth into
the plain,[m] and there I will speak with you."
So I arose and went forth into the plain;[m] 23
and, lo, the glory of the LORD stood there,
like the glory which I had seen by the river
Chebar; and I fell on my face. But the Spirit 24
entered into me, and set me upon my feet;
and he spoke with me and said to me, "Go,
shut yourself within your house. And you, O 25
son of man, behold, cords will be placed
upon you, and you shall be bound with them,
so that you cannot go out among the people;
and I will make your tongue cleave to the 26
roof of your mouth, so that you shall be
dumb and unable to reprove them; for they
are a rebellious house. But when I speak 27
with you, I will open your mouth, and you
shall say to them, 'Thus says the Lord GOD';
he that will hear, let him hear; and he that
will refuse to hear, let him refuse; for they
are a rebellious house.

BEFORE THE FALL OF JERUSALEM

Symbols of its fall

4 "AND you, O son of man, take a brick and
lay it before you, and portray upon it a
2 city, even Jerusalem; and put siegeworks
against it, and build a siege wall against it, and
cast up a mound against it; set camps also
against it, and plant battering rams against it
3 round about. And take an iron plate, and place
it as an iron wall between you and the city; and
set your face toward it, and let it be in a state
of siege, and press the siege against it. This
is a sign for the house of Israel.

"Then lie upon your left side, and I will lay 4
the punishment of the house of Israel upon
you;[n] for the number of the days that you lie
upon it, you shall bear their punishment.
For I assign to you a number of days, three 5
hundred and ninety days, equal to the
number of the years of their punishment; so
long shall you bear the punishment of the
house of Israel. And when you have com- 6
pleted these, you shall lie down a second
time, but on your right side, and bear the
punishment of the house of Judah; forty days
I assign you, a day for each year. And you 7

[k] Cn: Heb *blessed be the glory of the* LORD
[l] Heb *Chebar, and to where they dwelt.* Another reading is *Chebar, and I sat where they sat*   [m] Or *valley*
[n] Cn: Heb *you shall lay . . . upon it*
3.16–21: Ezek 33.1–9.

all set your face toward the siege of
Jerusalem, with your arm bared; and you
shall prophesy against the city. And, behold,
I will put cords upon you, so that you cannot
turn from one side to the other, till you have
completed the days of your siege.
"And you, take wheat and barley, beans and
lentils, millet and spelt, and put them into a
single vessel, and make bread of them.
During the number of days that you lie upon
your side, three hundred and ninety days,
you shall eat it. And the food which you eat

Ancient weights

shall be by weight, twenty shekels a day;
once a day you shall eat it. And water you
shall drink by measure, the sixth part of a
hin; once a day you shall drink. And you
shall eat it as a barley cake, baking it in their
sight on human dung." And the LORD said,
"Thus shall the people of Israel eat their
bread unclean, among the nations whither I
will drive them." Then I said, "Ah Lord
GOD! behold, I have never defiled myself;
from my youth up till now I have never eaten
what died of itself or was torn by beasts, nor
has foul flesh come into my mouth." Then
he said to me, "See, I will let you have cow's
dung instead of human dung, on which you
may prepare your bread." Moreover he said
to me, "Son of man, behold, I will break the
staff of bread in Jerusalem; they shall eat
bread by weight and with fearfulness; and
they shall drink water by measure and in
dismay. I will do this that they may lack
bread and water, and look at one another in
dismay, and waste away under their punishment.

"And you, O son of man, take a sharp
sword; use it as a barber's razor and pass it
over your head and your beard; then take
balances for weighing, and divide the hair. A
third part you shall burn in the fire in the
midst of the city, when the days of the siege
are completed; and a third part you shall take
and strike with the sword round about the
city; and a third part you shall scatter to the
wind, and I will unsheathe the sword after
them. And you shall take from these a small
number, and bind them in the skirts of your

robe. And of these again you shall take some, 4
and cast them into the fire, and burn them in
the fire; from there a fire will come forth into
all the house of Israel.

The city's destruction

"Thus says the Lord GOD: This is Jeru- 5
salem; I have set her in the centre of the
nations, with countries round about her.
And she has wickedly rebelled against my 6
ordinances[o] more than the nations, and
against my statutes more than the countries
round about her, by rejecting my ordinances
and not walking in my statutes. Therefore 7
thus says the Lord GOD: Because you are
more turbulent than the nations that are
round about you, and have not walked in my
statutes or kept my ordinances, but have
acted[p] according to the ordinances of the
nations that are round about you; therefore 8
thus says the Lord GOD: Behold, I, even I,
am against you; and I will execute judgments
in the midst of you in the sight of the
nations. And because of all your abomina- 9
tions I will do with you what I have never yet
done, and the like of which I will never do

again. Therefore fathers shall eat their sons 10
in the midst of you, and sons shall eat their
fathers; and I will execute judgments on you,
and any of you who survive I will scatter to
all the winds. Wherefore, as I live, says the 11
Lord GOD, surely, because you have defiled
my sanctuary with all your detestable things

Or *changed my ordinances into wickedness*   p Another reading is *and have not acted* and with all your abominations, therefore I will cut you down;[q] my eye will not spare, 12 and I will have no pity. A third part of you shall die of pestilence and be consumed with famine in the midst of you; a third part shall fall by the sword round about you; and a third part I will scatter to all the winds and will unsheathe the sword after them. 13 "Thus shall my anger spend itself, and I will vent my fury upon them and satisfy myself; and they shall know that I, the LORD, have spoken in my jealousy, when I spend 14 my fury upon them. Moreover I will make you a desolation and an object of reproach among the nations round about you and in 15 the sight of all that pass by. You shall be[r] a reproach and a taunt, a warning and a horror, to the nations round about you, when I execute judgments on you in anger and fury, and with furious chastisements—I, the 16 LORD, have spoken—when I loose against you[s] my deadly arrows of famine, arrows for destruction, which I will loose to destroy you, and when I bring more and more famine 17 upon you, and break your staff of bread. I will send famine and wild beasts against you, and they will rob you of your children; pestilence and blood shall pass through you; and I will bring the sword upon you. I, the LORD, have spoken."

The desolation of the land

6 The word of the LORD came to me: "Son of 2 man, set your face toward the mountains of 3 Israel, and prophesy against them, and say, You mountains of Israel, hear the word of

the Lord GOD! Thus says the Lord GOD to the mountains and the hills, to the ravines and the valleys: Behold, I, even I, will bring a sword upon you, and I will destroy your high places. Your altars shall become desolate, and your incense altars shall be broken; and I will cast down your slain before your idols. And I will lay the dead bodies of the people of Israel before their idols; and I will scatter your bones round about your altars. Wherever you dwell your cities shall be waste and your high places ruined, so that your altars will be waste and ruined,[t] your idols broken and destroyed, your incense altars cut down, and your works wiped out. And the slain shall fall in the midst of you, and you shall know that I am the LORD.

"Yet I will leave some of you alive. When you have among the nations some who escape the sword, and when you are scattered through the countries, then those of you who escape will remember me among the nations where they are carried captive, when I have broken[u] their wanton heart which has departed from me, and blinded their eyes which turn wantonly after their idols; and they will be loathsome in their own sight for the evils which they have committed, for all their abominations. And they shall know that I am the LORD; I have not said in vain

that I would do this evil to them."

Thus says the Lord GOD: "Clap your hands, and stamp your foot, and say, Alas because of all the evil abominations of the house of Israel; for they shall fall by the sword, by famine, and by pestilence. He that is far off shall die of pestilence; and he that is near shall fall by the sword; and he that is left and is preserved shall die of famine. Thus I will spend my fury upon them. And you shall know that I am the LORD, when their

[q] Another reading is *I will withdraw*   [r] Gk Syr Vg Tg: Heb *And it shall be*   [s] Heb *them*
[t] Syr Vg Tg: Heb *and be made guilty*   [u] Syr Vg Tg: Heb *I have been broken*
6.9: Ezek 20.43; 36.31.

ain lie among their idols round about their
tars, upon every high hill, on all the
ountain tops, under every green tree, and
ader every leafy oak, wherever they offered
easing odour to all their idols. And I will
retch out my hand against them, and make
e land desolate and waste, throughout all
eir habitations, from the wilderness to
iblah.[v] Then they will know that I am the
ORD."

day of doom

The word of the LORD came to me: "And
ou, O son of man, thus says the Lord GOD
 the land of Israel: An end! The end has
me upon the four corners of the land.
Now the end is upon you, and I will let loose
y anger upon you, and will judge you
cording to your ways; and I will punish
ou for all[ʸ] your abominations. And my eye
ill not spare you, nor will I have pity; but I
ill punish you for your ways, while your
bominations are in your midst. Then you
ill know that I am the LORD.

"Thus says the Lord GOD: Disaster after
isaster! Behold, it comes. An end has
ome, the end has come; it has awakened
gainst you. Behold, it comes. Your doom[w]
as come to you, O inhabitant of the land;
he time has come, the day is near, a day of
umult, and not of joyful shouting upon the
ountains. · Now I will soon pour out my
rath upon you, and spend my anger against
ou, and judge you according to your ways;
nd I will punish you for all your abomina-
ons. And my eye will not spare, nor will I
ave pity; I will punish you according to
our ways, while your abominations are in
our midst. Then you will know that I am
he LORD, who smite.

"Behold, the day! Behold, it comes! Your
oom[w] has come, injustice[x] has blossomed,
ride has budded. Violence has grown up
nto a rod of wickedness; none of them shall
emain, nor their abundance, nor their
vealth; neither shall there be pre-eminence
mong them.[ʸ] The time has come, the day
raws near. Let not the buyer rejoice, nor the
eller mourn, for wrath is upon all their
nultitude. For the seller shall not return to
vhat he has sold, while they live. For wrath[z]
s upon all their multitude; it shall not turn
ack; and because of his iniquity, none can
naintain his life.[a]

"They have blown the trumpet and made
ll ready; but none goes to battle, for my
vrath is upon all their multitude. The sword

is without, pestilence and famine are within;
he that is in the field dies by the sword; and
him that is in the city famine and pestilence
devour. And if any survivors escape, they 16
will be on the mountains, like doves of the
valleys, all of them moaning, every one over
his iniquity. All hands are feeble, and all 17
knees weak as water. They gird themselves 18
with sackcloth, and horror covers them;
shame is upon all faces, and baldness on all
their heads. They cast their silver into the 19
streets, and their gold is like an unclean
thing; their silver and gold are not able to
deliver them in the day of the wrath of the
LORD; they cannot satisfy their hunger or fill
their stomachs with it. For it was the
stumbling block of their iniquity. Their[b] 20
beautiful ornament they used for vainglory,
and they made their abominable images and
their detestable things of it; therefore I will
make it an unclean thing to them. And I will 21
give it into the hands of foreigners for a prey,
and to the wicked of the earth for a spoil; and
they shall profane it. I will turn my face 22
from them, that they may profane my precious[c] place; robbers shall enter and profane
it, and make a desolation.[d] 23

"Because the land is full of bloody crimes
and the city is full of violence, I will bring the 24
worst of the nations to take possession of
their houses; I will put an end to their proud
might, and their holy places shall be profaned. When anguish comes, they will seek 25
peace, but there shall be none. . Disaster 26
comes upon disaster, rumour follows
rumour; they seek a vision from the prophet,
but the law perishes from the priest, and

Buyer and seller   v. 12

Another reading is *Diblah*   [w] The meaning of the Hebrew word is uncertain   [x] Or *the rod*
The Hebrew of verse 11 is uncertain   [z] Cn: Heb *vision*   [a] Heb obscure   [b] Syr Symmachus: Heb *Its*
Or *secret*   [d] Cn: Heb *make the chain*
.2: Rev 7.1; 20.8.

27 counsel from the elders. The king mourns, the prince is wrapped in despair, and the hands of the people of the land are palsied by terror. According to their way I will do to them, and according to their own judgments I will judge them; and they shall know that I am the LORD."

Abominations in the temple

8 In the sixth year, in the sixth month, on the fifth day of the month, as I sat in my house, with the elders of Judah sitting before me, the hand of the Lord GOD fell there upon 2 me. Then I beheld, and, lo, a form that had the appearance of a man;*e* below what appeared to be his loins it was fire, and above his loins it was like the appearance of 3 brightness, like gleaming bronze. He put forth the form of a hand, and took me by a lock of my head; and the Spirit lifted me up between earth and heaven, and brought me in visions of God to Jerusalem, to the entrance of the gateway of the inner court that faces north, where was the seat of the image of jealousy, which provokes to 4 jealousy. And behold, the glory of the God of Israel was there, like the vision that I saw in the plain.

5 Then he said to me, "Son of man, lift up your eyes now in the direction of the north." So I lifted up my eyes toward the north, and behold, north of the altar gate, in the 6 entrance, was this image of jealousy. And he said to me, "Son of man, do you see what they are doing, the great abominations that the house of Israel are committing here, to drive me far from my sanctuary? But you will see still greater abominations."

7 And he brought me to the door of the court; and when I looked, behold, there was a hole 8 in the wall. Then said he to me, "Son of man, dig in the wall"; and when I dug in the 9 wall, lo, there was a door. And he said to me, "Go in, and see the vile abominations which 10 they are committing here." So I went in and saw; and there, portrayed upon the wall round about, were all kinds of creeping things, and loathsome beasts, and all the 11 idols of the house of Israel. And before them stood seventy men of the elders of the house of Israel, with Ja-azani′ah the son of Shaphan standing among them. Each had his censer in his hand, and the smoke of the 12 cloud of incense went up. Then he said to me, "Son of man, have you seen what the elders of the house of Israel are doing in the dark, every man in his room*f* of pictures? For they say, 'The LORD does not see us, the

LORD has forsaken the land.'" He said also to me, "You will see still greater abominations which they commit."

Then he brought me to the entrance of the north gate of the house of the LORD; and behold, there sat women weeping for Tammuz. Then he said to me, "Have you seen this, O son of man? You will see still greater abominations than these."

And he brought me into the inner court of the house of the LORD; and behold, at the door of the temple of the LORD, between the porch and the altar, were about twenty-five men, with their backs to the temple of the LORD, and their faces toward the east, worshipping the sun toward the east. Then he said to me,"Have you seen this, O son of man? Is it too slight a thing for the house of Judah to commit the abominations which they commit here, that they should fill the land with violence, and provoke me further to anger? Lo, they put the branch to their nose. Therefore I will deal in wrath; my eye will not spare, nor will I have pity; and though they cry in my ears with a loud voice I will not hear them."

Slaughter of the people

Then he cried in my ears with a loud voice saying, "Draw near, you executioners of the city, each with his destroying weapon in his hand." And lo, six men came from the direction of the upper gate, which faces north, every man with his weapon for slaughter in his hand, and with them was a man clothed in linen, with a writing case at his side. And they went in and stood beside the bronze altar.

Now the glory of the God of Israel had gone up from the cherubim on which it rested to the threshold of the house; and he called to the man clothed in linen, who had the writing case at his side. And the LORD said to him, "Go through the city, through Jerusalem, and put a mark upon the foreheads of the men who sigh and groan over all the abominations that are committed in it." And to the others he said in my hearing, "Pass through the city after him, and smite; your eye shall not spare, and you shall show no pity; slay old men outright, young men and maidens, little children and women, but touch no one upon whom is the mark. And begin at my sanctuary." So they began with the elders who were before the house. Then he said to them, "Defile the house, and fill the courts with the slain. Go forth." So they went forth, and smote in the city. And while

---

e Gk: Heb *fire*   *f* Gk Syr Vg Tg: Heb *rooms*
9.4, 6: 1 Pet 4.17; Rev 7.3; 9.4; 14.1.

ey were smiting, and I was left alone, I fell on my face, and cried, "Ah Lord God! It thou destroy all that remains of Israel in e outpouring of thy wrath upon Jeru- lem?"

Then he said to me, "The guilt of the house Israel and Judah is exceedingly great; the nd is full of blood, and the city full of justice; for they say, 'The Lord has for- ken the land, and the Lord does not see.' s for me, my eye will not spare, nor will I ive pity, but I will requite their deeds upon eir heads."

And lo, the man clothed in linen, with the riting case at his side, brought back word, ying, "I have done as thou didst command e."

urning of the city

Then I looked, and behold, on the fir- nament that was over the heads of the herubim there appeared above them some- hing like a sapphire, in form resembling a hrone. And he said to the man clothed in inen, "Go in among the whirling wheels inderneath the cherubim; fill your hands vith burning coals from between the cheru- im, and scatter them over the city." And he went in before my eyes. Now the herubim were standing on the south side of he house, when the man went in; and a loud filled the inner court. And the glory of he Lord went up from the cherubim to the hreshold of the house; and the house was illed with the cloud, and the court was full of he brightness of the glory of the Lord. And he sound of the wings of the cherubim was heard as far as the outer court, like the voice of God Almighty when he speaks.

And when he commanded the man clothed in linen, "Take fire from between the whirl- ing wheels, from between the cherubim," he went in and stood beside a wheel. And a cherub stretched forth his hand from between the cherubim to the fire that was between the cherubim, and took some of it, and put it into the hands of the man clothed in linen, who took it and went out. The cherubim appeared to have the form of a human hand under their wings.

And I looked, and behold, there were four wheels beside the cherubim, one beside each cherub; and the appearance of the wheels was like sparkling chrysolite. And as for their appearance, the four had the same likeness, as if a wheel were within a wheel. When they went, they went in any of their four directions[g] without turning as they

went, but in whatever direction the front wheel faced the others followed without turning as they went. And[h] their rims, and 12 their spokes,[i] and the wheels were full of eyes round about—the wheels that the four of them had. As for the wheels, they were 13 called in my hearing the whirling wheels. And every one had four faces: the first face 14 was the face of the cherub, and the second face was the face of a man, and the third the face of a lion, and the fourth the face of an eagle.

And the cherubim mounted up. These 15 were the living creatures that I saw by the river Chebar. And when the cherubim went, 16 the wheels went beside them; and when the cherubim lifted up their wings to mount up from the earth, the wheels did not turn from beside them. When they stood still, these 17 stood still, and when they mounted up, these mounted up with them; for the spirit of the living creatures[j] was in them.

Then the glory of the Lord went forth from 18 the threshold of the house, and stood over the cherubim. And the cherubim lifted up their 19 wings and mounted up from the earth in my sight as they went forth, with the wheels beside them; and they stood at the door of the east gate of the house of the Lord; and the glory of the God of Israel was over them.

These were the living creatures that I saw 20 underneath the God of Israel by the river Chebar; and I knew that they were cherubim. Each had four faces, and each 21 four wings, and underneath their wings the semblance of human hands. And as for the 22 likeness of their faces, they were the very faces whose appearance I had seen by the river Chebar. They went every one straight forward.

Abandoned by God

The Spirit lifted me up, and brought me to **11** the east gate of the house of the Lord, which faces east. And behold, at the door of the gateway there were twenty-five men; and I saw among them Ja-azani′ah the son of Azzur, and Pelati′ah the son of Benai′ah, princes of the people. And he said to me, 2 "Son of man, these are the men who devise iniquity and who give wicked counsel in this city; who say, 'The time is not near[k] to build 3 houses; this city is the cauldron, and we are the flesh.' Therefore prophesy against them, 4 prophesy, O son of man."

And the Spirit of the Lord fell upon me, 5 and he said to me, "Say, Thus says the Lord: So you think, O house of Israel; for I

g Heb on their four sides   h Gk: Heb And their whole body and   i Heb spokes and their wings   j Or of life
k Or Is not the time near . . . ?
10.1: Rev 4.2.   10.2: Rev 8.5.   10.12: Ezek 1.18; Rev 4.8.   10.14: Ezek 1.10; Rev 4.7.

know the things that come into your mind.

6 You have multiplied your slain in this city, and have filled its streets with the slain.

7 Therefore thus says the Lord God: Your slain whom you have laid in the midst of it, they are the flesh, and this city is the cauldron; but you shall be brought forth out

8 of the midst of it. You have feared the sword; and I will bring the sword upon you,

9 says the Lord God. And I will bring you forth out of the midst of it, and give you into the hands of foreigners, and execute judg-

10 ments upon you. You shall fall by the sword; I will judge you at the border of Israel; and

11 you shall know that I am the LORD. This city shall not be your cauldron, nor shall you be the flesh in the midst of it; I will judge you at

12 the border of Israel; and you shall know that I am the LORD; for you have not walked in my statutes, nor executed my ordinances, but have acted according to the ordinances of the nations that are round about you."

13 And it came to pass, while I was prophesying, that Pelati′ah the son of Benai′ah died. Then I fell down upon my face, and cried with a loud voice, and said, "Ah Lord God! wilt thou make a full end of the remnant of Israel?"

14 And the word of the LORD came to me:

15 "Son of man, your brethren, even your brethren, your fellow exiles,[l] the whole house of Israel, all of them, are those of whom the inhabitants of Jerusalem have said, 'They have gone far from the LORD; to us this land

16 is given for a possession.' Therefore say, 'Thus says the Lord God: Though I removed them far off among the nations, and though I scattered them among the countries, yet I have been a sanctuary to them for a while[m] in the countries where they

17 have gone.' Therefore say, 'Thus says the Lord God: I will gather you from the peoples, and assemble you out of the countries where you have been scattered, and I

18 will give you the land of Israel.' And when they come there, they will remove from it all its detestable things and all its abominations.

19 And I will give them one[n] heart, and put a new spirit within them; I will take the stony heart out of their flesh and give them a heart

20 of flesh, that they may walk in my statutes and keep my ordinances and obey them; and they shall be my people, and I will be their

21 God. But as for those[o] whose heart goes after their detestable things and their abominations, I will requite their deeds upon their own heads, says the Lord God."

22 Then the cherubim lifted up their wings, with the wheels beside them; and the glory of

the God of Israel was over them. And the glory of the LORD went up from the midst of the city, and stood upon the mountain which is on the east side of the city. And the Spirit lifted me up and brought me in the vision by the Spirit of God into Chalde′a, to the exiles. Then the vision that I had seen went up from me. And I told the exiles all the things that the LORD had showed me.

The march of exiles

The word of the LORD came to me: "Son of man, you dwell in the midst of a rebellious house, who have eyes to see, but see not, who have ears to hear, but hear not; for they are a rebellious house. Therefore, son of man, prepare for yourself an exile's baggage, and go into exile by day in their sight; you shall go like an exile from your place to another place in their sight. Perhaps they will understand, though[p] they are a rebellious house. You shall bring out your baggage by day in their sight, as baggage for exile; and you shall

Babylon

[l] Gk Syr: Heb *men of your kindred*   [m] Or *in small measure*   [n] Another reading is *a new*
[o] Cn: Heb *To the heart of their detestable things and their abominations their heart goes*   [p] Or *will see that*
11.19: Ezek 18.31; 36.26; 2 Cor 3.3.   12.2: Mk 8.18.

go forth yourself at evening in their sight, as men do who must go into exile. Dig through the wall in their sight, and go*q* out through it. In their sight you shall lift the baggage upon your shoulder, and carry it out in the dark; you shall cover your face, that you may not see the land; for I have made you a sign for the house of Israel."

And I did as I was commanded. I brought out my baggage by day, as baggage for exile, and in the evening I dug through the wall with my own hands; I went forth in the dark, carrying my outfit upon my shoulder in their sight.

In the morning the word of the LORD came to me: "Son of man, has not the house of Israel, the rebellious house, said to you, 'What are you doing?' Say to them, 'Thus says the Lord GOD: This oracle concerns the prince in Jerusalem and all the house of Israel who are in it.'*r* Say, 'I am a sign for you: as I have done, so shall it be done to them; they shall go into exile, into captivity.' And the prince who is among them shall lift his baggage upon his shoulder in the dark, and shall go forth; he*s* shall dig through the wall and go*t* out through it; he shall cover his face, that he may not see the land with his eyes. And I will spread my net over him, and he shall be taken in my snare; and I will bring him to Babylon in the land of the Chalde´ans, yet he shall not see it; and he shall die there. And I will scatter toward every wind all who are round about him, his helpers*u* and all his troops; and I will unsheathe the sword after them. And they shall know that I am the LORD, when I disperse them among the nations and scatter them through the countries. But I will let a few of them escape from the sword, from famine and pestilence, that they may confess all their abominations among the nations where they go, and may know that I am the LORD."

Moreover the word of the LORD came to me: "Son of man, eat your bread with quaking, and drink water with trembling and with fearfulness; and say of the people of the land, Thus says the Lord GOD concerning the inhabitants of Jerusalem in the land of Israel: They shall eat their bread with fearfulness, and drink water in dismay, because their land will be stripped of all it contains, on account of the violence of all those who dwell in it. And the inhabited cities shall be laid waste, and the land shall become a desolation; and you shall know that I am the LORD."

And the word of the LORD came to me:

"Son of man, what is this proverb that you have about the land of Israel, saying, 'The days grow long, and every vision comes to naught'? Tell them therefore, 'Thus says the Lord GOD: I will put an end to this proverb, and they shall no more use it as a proverb in Israel.' But say to them, The days are at hand, and the fulfilment*v* of every vision. For there shall be no more any false vision or flattering divination within the house of Israel. But I the LORD will speak the word which I will speak, and it will be performed. It will no longer be delayed, but in your days, O rebellious house, I will speak the word and perform it, says the Lord GOD."

Again the word of the LORD came to me: "Son of man, behold, they of the house of Israel say, 'The vision that he sees is for many days hence, and he prophesies of times far off.' Therefore say to them, Thus says the Lord GOD: None of my words will be delayed any longer, but the word which I speak will be performed, says the Lord GOD."

Woe to the false prophets

The word of the LORD came to me: "Son of man, prophesy against the prophets of Israel, prophesy*w* and say to those who prophesy out of their own minds: 'Hear the word of the LORD!' Thus says the Lord GOD, Woe to the foolish prophets who follow their own spirit, and have seen nothing! Your prophets have been like foxes among ruins, O Israel. You have not gone up into the breaches, or built up a wall for the house of Israel, that it might stand in battle in the day of the LORD. They have spoken falsehood and divined a lie; they say, 'Says the LORD,' when the LORD has not sent them, and yet they expect him to fulfil their word. Have you not seen a delusive vision, and uttered a lying divination, whenever you have said, 'Says the LORD,' although I have not spoken?"

Therefore thus says the Lord GOD: "Because you have uttered delusions and seen lies, therefore behold, I am against you, says the Lord GOD. My hand will be against the prophets who see delusive visions and who give lying divinations; they shall not be in the council of my people, nor be enrolled in the register of the house of Israel, nor shall they enter the land of Israel; and you shall know that I am the Lord GOD. Because, yea, because they have misled my people, saying, 'Peace,' when there is no peace; and because,

when the people build a wall, these prophets
11 daub it with whitewash; say to those who
daub it with whitewash that it shall fall!
There will be a deluge of rain,* great hailstones will fall, and a stormy wind break out;
12 and when the wall falls, will it not be said to
you, 'Where is the daubing with which you
13 daubed it?' Therefore thus says the Lord
God: I will make a stormy wind break out in
my wrath; and there shall be a deluge of rain
in my anger, and great hailstones in wrath to
14 destroy it. And I will break down the wall
that you have daubed with whitewash, and
bring it down to the ground, so that its
foundation will be laid bare; when it falls,
you shall perish in the midst of it; and you
15 shall know that I am the Lord. Thus will I
spend my wrath upon the wall, and upon
those who have daubed it with whitewash;
and I will say to you, The wall is no more,
16 nor those who daubed it, the prophets of
Israel who prophesied concerning Jerusalem
and saw visions of peace for her, when there
was no peace, says the Lord God.
17 "And you, son of man, set your face against
the daughters of your people, who prophesy
out of their own minds; prophesy against
18 them and say, Thus says the Lord God: Woe
to the women who sew magic bands upon all
wrists, and make veils for the heads of
persons of every stature, in the hunt for
souls! Will you hunt down souls belonging
to my people, and keep other souls alive for
19 your profit? You have profaned me among
my people for handfuls of barley and for
pieces of bread, putting to death persons who
should not die and keeping alive persons who
should not live, by your lies to my people,
who listen to lies.
20 "Wherefore thus says the Lord God:
Behold, I am against your magic bands with
which you hunt the souls,y and I will tear
them from your arms; and I will let the souls
21 that you hunt go freez like birds. Your veils
also I will tear off, and deliver my people out
of your hand, and they shall be no more in
your hand as prey; and you shall know that
22 I am the Lord. Because you have disheartened the righteous falsely, although I
have not disheartened him, and you have
encouraged the wicked, that he should not
turn from his wicked way to save his life;
23 therefore you shall no more see delusive
visions nor practise divination; I will deliver
my people out of your hand. Then you will
know that I am the Lord."

The certainty of judgment
14 Then came certain of the elders of Israel to

me, and sat before me. And the word of the 2
Lord came to me: "Son of man, these men 3
have taken their idols into their hearts, and
set the stumbling block of their iniquity
before their faces; should I let myself be
inquired of at all by them? Therefore speak 4
to them, and say to them, Thus says the Lord
God: Any man of the house of Israel who
takes his idols into his heart and sets the
stumbling block of his iniquity before his
face, and yet comes to the prophet, I the
Lord will answer him myselfa because of the
multitude of his idols, that I may lay hold of 5
the hearts of the house of Israel, who are all
estranged from me through their idols.
"Therefore say to the house of Israel, Thus 6
says the Lord God: Repent and turn away
from your idols; and turn away your faces
from all your abominations. For any one of 7
the house of Israel, or of the strangers that
sojourn in Israel, who separates himself from
me, taking his idols into his heart and putting
the stumbling block of his iniquity before his
face, and yet comes to a prophet to inquire
for himself of me, I the Lord will answer
him myself; and I will set my face against 8
that man, I will make him a sign and a
byword and cut him off from the midst of my
people; and you shall know that I am the
Lord. And if the prophet be deceived and 9
speak a word, I, the Lord, have deceived that
prophet, and I will stretch out my hand
against him, and will destroy him from the
midst of my people Israel. And they shall 10
bear their punishment—the punishment of
the prophet and the punishment of the
inquirer shall be alike—that the house of 11
Israel may go no more astray from me, nor
defile themselves any more with all their
transgressions, but that they may be my
people and I may be their God, says the Lord
God."
And the word of the Lord came to me: 12
"Son of man, when a land sins against me by 13
acting faithlessly, and I stretch out my hand
against it, and break its staff of bread and
send famine upon it, and cut off from it man
and beast, even if these three men, Noah, 14
Daniel, and Job, were in it, they would
deliver but their own lives by their righteousness, says the Lord God. If I cause wild 15
beasts to pass through the land, and they
ravage it, and it be made desolate, so that no
man may pass through because of the beasts;
even if these three men were in it, as I live, 16
says the Lord God, they would deliver
neither sons nor daughters; they alone would
be delivered, but the land would be desolate.
Or if I bring a sword upon that land, and say, 17
Let a sword go through the land; and I cut

18 off from it man and beast; though these three men were in it, as I live, says the Lord GOD, they would deliver neither sons nor daugh-
19 ters, but they alone would be delivered. Or if I send a pestilence into that land, and pour out my wrath upon it with blood, to cut off
20 from it man and beast; even if Noah, Daniel, and Job were in it, as I live, says the Lord GOD, they would deliver neither son nor daughter; they would deliver but their own lives by their righteousness.
21 "For thus says the Lord GOD: How much more when I send upon Jerusalem my four sore acts of judgment, sword, famine, evil beasts, and pestilence, to cut off from it man
22 and beast! Yet, if there should be left in it any survivors to lead out sons and daughters, when they come forth to you, and you see their ways and their doings, you will be consoled for the evil that I have brought upon Jerusalem, for all that I have brought
23 upon it. They will console you, when you see their ways and their doings; and you shall know that I have not done without cause all that I have done in it, says the Lord GOD."

Jerusalem a fruitless vine

15 And the word of the LORD came to me:
2 "Son of man, how does the wood of the vine surpass any wood, the vine branch which is among the trees of the forest? Is wood taken 3 from it to make anything? Do men take a peg from it to hang any vessel on? Lo, it is 4 given to the fire for fuel; when the fire has consumed both ends of it, and the middle of it is charred, is it useful for anything? Behold, when it was whole, it was used for 5 nothing; how much less, when the fire has consumed it and it is charred, can it ever be used for anything! Therefore thus says the 6 Lord GOD: Like the wood of the vine among the trees of the forest, which I have given to the fire for fuel, so will I give up the inhabitants of Jerusalem. And I will set my 7 face against them; though they escape from the fire, the fire shall yet consume them; and you will know that I am the LORD, when I set my face against them. And I will make the 8 land desolate, because they have acted faithlessly, says the Lord GOD."

A foundling

Again the word of the LORD came to me: 16 "Son of man, make known to Jerusalem her 2 abominations, and say, Thus says the Lord 3 GOD to Jerusalem: Your origin and your birth are of the land of the Canaanites; your father was an Amorite, and your mother a Hittite. And as for your birth, on the day 4 you were born your navel string was not cut, nor were you washed with water to cleanse you, nor rubbed with salt, nor swathed with bands. No eye pitied you, to do any of these 5 things to you out of compassion for you; but you were cast out on the open field, for you were abhorred, on the day that you were born.
"And when I passed by you, and saw you 6 weltering in your blood, I said to you in your blood, 'Live, and grow up'ᵇ like a plant of the 7 field.' And you grew up and became tall and arrived at full maidenhood;ᶜ your breasts were formed, and your hair had grown; yet you were naked and bare.
"When I passed by you again and looked 8 upon you, behold, you were at the age for love; and I spread my skirt over you, and covered your nakedness: yea, I plighted my troth to you and entered into a covenant with you, says the Lord GOD, and you became mine. Then I bathed you with water 9 and washed off your blood from you, and anointed you with oil. I clothed you also 10 with embroidered cloth and shod you with leather, I swathed you in fine linen and covered you with silk. And I decked you 11 with ornaments, and put bracelets on your arms, and a chain on your neck. And I put a 12 ring on your nose, and earrings in your ears,

---

ᵇ Gk Syr: Heb *I made you a myriad*   ᶜ Cn: Heb *ornament of ornaments*
14.21: Rev 6.8.   **16.3**: Ezek 16.45.

13 and a beautiful crown upon your head. Thus
you were decked with gold and silver; and
your raiment was of fine linen, and silk,
and embroidered cloth; you ate fine flour and
honey and oil. You grew exceedingly beauti-
14 ful, and came to regal estate. And your
renown went forth among the nations because of your beauty, for it was perfect
through the splendour which I had bestowed
upon you, says the Lord God.

Shameful ingratitude

15 "But you trusted in your beauty, and played
the harlot because of your renown, and
lavished your harlotries on any passer-by.
16 You took some of your garments, and made
for yourself gaily decked shrines, and on
them played the harlot; the like has never
17 been, nor ever shall be. You also took your
fair jewels of my gold and of my silver, which
I had given you, and made for yourself
images of men, and with them played the
18 harlot; and you took your embroidered
garments to cover them, and set my oil and
19 my incense before them. Also my bread
which I gave you—I fed you with fine flour
and oil and honey—you set before them for a
20 pleasing odour, says the Lord God.[d] And
you took your sons and your daughters,
whom you had borne to me, and these you
sacrificed to them to be devoured. Were
21 your harlotries so small a matter that you
slaughtered my children and delivered them
22 up as an offering by fire to them? And in all
your abominations and your harlotries you
did not remember the days of your youth,
when you were naked and bare, weltering in
your blood.
23 "And after all your wickedness (woe, woe to
24 you! says the Lord God), you built yourself a
vaulted chamber, and made yourself a lofty
25 place in every square; at the head of every
street you built your lofty place and prosti-
tuted your beauty, offering yourself to any
passer-by, and multiplying your harlotry.
26 You also played the harlot with the Egyptians, your lustful neighbours, multiplying
your harlotry, to provoke me to anger.
27 Behold, therefore, I stretched out my hand
against you, and diminished your allotted
portion, and delivered you to the greed of
your enemies, the daughters of the Philistines, who were ashamed of your lewd
28 behaviour. You played the harlot also with
the Assyrians, because you were insatiable;
yea, you played the harlot with them, and
29 still you were not satisfied. You multiplied
your harlotry also with the trading land of

Chalde'a; and even with this you were not
satisfied.
"How lovesick is your heart, says the Lord 30
God, seeing you did all these things, the
deeds of a brazen harlot; building your 31
vaulted chamber at the head of every street,
and making your lofty place in every square.
Yet you were not like a harlot, because you
scorned hire. Adulterous wife, who receives 32
strangers instead of her husband! Men give 33
gifts to all harlots; but you gave your gifts to
all your lovers, bribing them to come to you
from every side for your harlotries. So you 34
were different from other women in your
harlotries: none solicited you to play the
harlot; and you gave hire, while no hire was
given to you; therefore you were different.
"Wherefore, O harlot, hear the word of the 35
Lord: Thus says the Lord God, Because 36
your shame was laid bare and your nakedness
uncovered in your harlotries with your
lovers, and because of all your idols, and
because of the blood of your children that
you gave to them, therefore, behold, I will 37
gather all your lovers, with whom you took
pleasure, all those you loved and all those you
loathed; I will gather them against you from
every side, and will uncover your nakedness
to them, that they may see all your
nakedness. And I will judge you as women 38
who break wedlock and shed blood are
judged, and bring upon you the blood of
wrath and jealousy. And I will give you into 39
the hand of your lovers, and they shall throw
down your vaulted chamber and break down
your lofty places; they shall strip you of your
clothes and take your fair jewels, and leave
you naked and bare. They shall bring up a 40
host against you, and they shall stone you
and cut you to pieces with their swords. And 41
they shall burn your houses and execute
judgments upon you in the sight of many
women; I will make you stop playing the
harlot, and you shall also give hire no more.
So will I satisfy my fury on you, and my 42
jealousy shall depart from you; I will be
calm, and will no more be angry. Because 43
you have not remembered the days of your
youth, but have enraged me with all these
things; therefore, behold, I will requite your
deeds upon your head, says the Lord God.
"Have you not committed lewdness in
addition to all your abominations? Behold, 44
every one who uses proverbs will use this
proverb about you, 'Like mother, like
daughter.' You are the daughter of your 45
mother, who loathed her husband and her
children; and you are the sister of your
sisters, who loathed their husbands and their

[d] Syr: Heb and it was, says the Lord God
16.45: Ezek 16.3.

children. Your mother was a Hittite and
46 your father an Amorite. And your elder
sister is Samar′ia, who lived with her
daughters to the north of you; and her
younger sister, who lived to the south of you,
47 is Sodom with her daughters. Yet you were
not content to walk in their ways, or do
according to their abominations; within a
very little time you were more corrupt than
48 they in all your ways. As I live, says the
Lord God, your sister Sodom and her
daughters have not done as you and your
49 daughters have done. Behold, this was the
guilt of your sister Sodom: she and her
daughters had pride, surfeit of food, and
prosperous ease, but did not aid the poor
50 and needy. They were haughty, and did
abominable things before me; therefore I
51 removed them, when I saw it. Samar′ia has
not committed half your sins; you have
committed more abominations than they,
and have made your sisters appear righteous
by all the abominations which you have
52 committed. Bear your disgrace, you also, for
you have made judgment favourable to your
sisters; because of your sins in which you
acted more abominably than they, they are
more in the right than you. So be ashamed,
you also, and bear your disgrace, for you
have made your sisters appear righteous.
53 "I will restore their fortunes, both the
fortunes of Sodom and her daughters, and
the fortunes of Samar′ia and her daughters,
and I will restore your own fortunes in the
54 midst of them, that you may bear your
disgrace and be ashamed of all that you have
55 done, becoming a consolation to them. As
for your sisters, Sodom and her daughters
shall return to their former estate, and
Samar′ia and her daughters shall return to
their former estate; and you and your
daughters shall return to your former estate.
56 Was not your sister Sodom a byword in your
57 mouth in the day of your pride, before your
wickedness was uncovered? Now you have
become like her[e] an object of reproach for the
daughters of Edom[f] and all her neighbours,
and for the daughters of the Philistines, those
58 round about who despise you. You bear the
penalty of your lewdness and your abominations, says the Lord.
59 "Yea, thus says the Lord God: I will deal
with you as you have done, who have des-
60 pised the oath in breaking the covenant, yet
I will remember my covenant with you in the
days of your youth, and I will establish with
61 you an everlasting covenant. Then you will
remember your ways, and be ashamed when
I[g] take your sisters, both your elder and your

younger, and give them to you as daughters,
but not on account of the covenant with you.
I will establish my covenant with you, and 62
you shall know that I am the Lord, that you 63
may remember and be confounded, and
never open your mouth again because of your
shame, when I forgive you all that you have
done, says the Lord God."

The eagle and the cedar

The word of the Lord came to me: "Son of **17**
man, propound a riddle, and speak an alle- 2
gory to the house of Israel; say, Thus says 3
the Lord God: A great eagle with great
wings and long pinions, rich in plumage of
many colours, came to Lebanon and took the
top of the cedar; he broke off the topmost of 4
its young twigs and carried it to a land of
trade, and set it in a city of merchants. Then 5
he took of the seed of the land and planted it
in fertile soil; he placed it beside abundant
waters. He set it like a willow twig, and it 6
sprouted and became a low spreading vine,
and its branches turned toward him, and its
roots remained where it stood. So it became
a vine, and brought forth branches and put
forth foliage.
"But there was another great eagle with 7
great wings and much plumage; and behold,
this vine bent its roots toward him, and shot
forth its branches toward him that he might
water it. From the bed where it was planted
he transplanted it[h] to good soil by abundant 8
waters, that it might bring forth branches,
and bear fruit, and become a noble vine.
Say, Thus says the Lord God: Will it 9
thrive? Will he not pull up its roots and cut
off its branches,[i] so that all its fresh sprout-
ing leaves wither? It will not take a strong
arm or many people to pull it from its roots.
Behold, when it is transplanted, will it 10
thrive? Will it not utterly wither when the
east wind strikes it—wither away on the bed
where it grew?"
Then the word of the Lord came to me: 11
"Say now to the rebellious house, Do you not 12
know what these things mean? Tell them,
Behold, the king of Babylon came to Jerusalem, and took her king and her princes and
brought them to him to Babylon. And he 13
took one of the seed royal and made a
covenant with him, putting him under oath.
(The chief men of the land he had taken
away, that the kingdom might be humble and 14
not lift itself up, and that by keeping his
covenant it might stand.) But he rebelled 15
against him by sending ambassadors to
Egypt, that they might give him horses and a

---

[e] Cn: Heb uncertain   [f] Another reading is *Aram*   [g] Syr: Heb *you*   [h] Cn: Heb *it was transplanted*
[i] Cn: Heb *fruit*

large army. Will he succeed? Can a man escape who does such things? Can he break 16 the covenant and yet escape? As I live, says the Lord GOD, surely in the place where the king dwells who made him king, whose oath he despised, and whose covenant with him he 17 broke, in Babylon he shall die. Pharaoh with his mighty army and great company will not

help him in war, when mounds are cast up and siege walls built to cut off many lives. 18 Because he despised the oath and broke the covenant, because he gave his hand and yet did all these things, he shall not escape. 19 Therefore thus says the Lord GOD: As I live, surely my oath which he despised, and my covenant which he broke, I will requite upon 20 his head. I will spread my net over him, and he shall be taken in my snare, and I will bring him to Babylon and enter into judgment with him there for the treason he has committed 21 against me. And all the pick^j of his troops shall fall by the sword, and the survivors shall be scattered to every wind; and you shall know that I, the LORD, have spoken."

22 Thus says the Lord GOD: "I myself will take a sprig from the lofty top of the cedar, and will set it out; I will break off from the topmost of its young twigs a tender one, and I myself will plant it upon a high and lofty 23 mountain; on the mountain height of Israel will I plant it, that it may bring forth boughs and bear fruit, and become a noble cedar; and under it will dwell all kinds of beasts;^{k} in the shade of its branches birds of every sort 24 will nest. And all the trees of the field shall know that I the LORD bring low the high tree, and make high the low tree, dry up the green tree, and make the dry tree flourish. I the LORD have spoken, and I will do it."

Personal responsibility

18 The word of the LORD came to me again: 2 "What do you mean by repeating this proverb concerning the land of Israel, 'The fathers have eaten sour grapes, and the 3 children's teeth are set on edge'? As I live, says the Lord GOD, this proverb shall no 4 more be used by you in Israel. Behold, all souls are mine; the soul of the father as well

as the soul of the son is mine: the soul that sins shall die.

"If a man is righteous and does what is 5 lawful and right—if he does not eat upon the 6 mountains or lift up his eyes to the idols of the house of Israel, does not defile his neighbour's wife or approach a woman in her time of impurity, does not oppress any one, 7 but restores to the debtor his pledge, commits no robbery, gives his bread to the hungry and covers the naked with a garment, does not lend at interest or take any increase, 8 withholds his hand from iniquity, executes true justice between man and man, walks in 9 my statutes, and is careful to observe my ordinances^l—he is righteous, he shall surely live, says the Lord GOD.

"If he begets a son who is a robber, a 10 shedder of blood,^{m} who does none of these 11 duties, but eats upon the mountains, defiles his neighbour's wife, oppresses the poor and 12 needy, commits robbery, does not restore the pledge, lifts up his eyes to the idols, commits abomination, lends at interest, and takes 13 increase; shall he then live? He shall not live. He has done all these abominable

---

^{j} Another reading is *fugitives* ^{k} Gk: Heb lacks *all kinds of beasts* ^{l} Gk: Heb *has kept my ordinances, to deal truly* ^{m} Heb *blood, and he does any of these things*
17.23: Ezek 31.6; Mt 13.32; Mk 4.32; Lk 13.19.   **18.2**: Jer 31.29.   **18.4**: Ezek 18.20.

things; he shall surely die; his blood shall be upon himself.

"But if this man begets a son who sees all the sins which his father has done, and fears, and does not do likewise, who does not eat upon the mountains or lift up his eyes to the idols of the house of Israel, does not defile his neighbour's wife, does not wrong any one, exacts no pledge, commits no robbery, but gives his bread to the hungry and covers the naked with a garment, withholds his hand from iniquity,[n] takes no interest or increase, observes my ordinances, and walks in my statutes; he shall not die for his father's iniquity; he shall surely live. As for his father, because he practised extortion, robbed his brother, and did what is not good among his people, behold, he shall die for his iniquity.

"Yet you say, 'Why should not the son suffer for the iniquity of the father?' When the son has done what is lawful and right, and has been careful to observe all my statutes, he shall surely live. The soul that sins shall die. The son shall not suffer for the iniquity of the father, nor the father suffer for the iniquity of the son; the righteousness of the righteous shall be upon himself, and the wickedness of the wicked shall be upon himself.

"But if a wicked man turns away from all his sins which he has committed and keeps all my statutes and does what is lawful and right, he shall surely live; he shall not die. None of the transgressions which he has committed shall be remembered against him; for the righteousness which he has done he shall live. Have I any pleasure in the death of the wicked, says the Lord GOD, and not rather that he should turn from his way and live? But when a righteous man turns away from his righteousness and commits iniquity and does the same abominable things that the wicked man does, shall he live? None of the righteous deeds which he has done shall be remembered; for the treachery of which he is guilty and the sin he has committed, he shall die.

"Yet you say, 'The way of the Lord is not just.' Hear now, O house of Israel: Is my way not just? Is it not your ways that are not just? When a righteous man turns away from his righteousness and commits iniquity, he shall die for it; for the iniquity which he has committed he shall die. Again, when a wicked man turns away from the wickedness he has committed and does what is lawful and right, he shall save his life. Because he considered and turned away from all the transgressions which he had committed, he shall surely live, he shall not die. Yet the house of Israel says, 'The way of the Lord is not just.' O house of Israel, are my ways not just? Is it not your ways that are not just?

"Therefore I will judge you, O house of Israel, every one according to his ways, says the Lord GOD. Repent and turn from all your transgressions, lest iniquity be your ruin.[o] Cast away from you all the transgressions which you have committed against me, and get yourselves a new heart and a new spirit! Why will you die, O house of Israel? For I have no pleasure in the death of any one, says the Lord GOD; so turn, and live."

A lamentation

And you, take up a lamentation for the princes of Israel, and say:

> What a lioness was your mother
>   among lions!
> She couched in the midst of young lions,
>   rearing her whelps.
> And she brought up one of her whelps;
>   he became a young lion,
> and he learned to catch prey;
>   he devoured men.
> The nations sounded an alarm against him;
>   he was taken in their pit;
> and they brought him with hooks
>   to the land of Egypt.
> When she saw that she was baffled,[p]
>   that her hope was lost,
> she took another of her whelps
>   and made him a young lion.
> He prowled among the lions;
>   he became a young lion,
> and he learned to catch prey;
>   he devoured men.
> And he ravaged their strongholds,[q]
>   and laid waste their cities;
> and the land was appalled and all who were in it
>   at the sound of his roaring.
> Then the nations set against him
>   snares[r] on every side;
> they spread their net over him;
>   he was taken in their pit.
> With hooks they put him in a cage,
>   and brought him to the king of Babylon;
> they brought him into custody,
>   that his voice should no more be heard
>   upon the mountains of Israel.
>
> Your mother was like a vine in a vineyard[s]
>   transplanted by the water,
> fruitful and full of branches

---

[n] Gk: Heb *the poor* [o] Or *so that they shall not be a stumbling block of iniquity to you* [p] Heb *had waited*
[q] Tg Compare Theodotion: Heb *knew his widows* [r] Cn: Heb *from the provinces* [s] Cn: Heb *in your blood*
18.20: Ezek 18.4. **18.23:** Ezek 18.32; 33.11. **18.31:** Ezek 11.19; 36.26. **18.32:** Ezek 18.23; 33.11.

by reason of abundant water.

11 Its strongest stem became
a ruler's sceptre;
it towered aloft
among the thick boughs;
it was seen in its height
with the mass of its branches.

12 But the vine was plucked up in fury,
cast down to the ground;
the east wind dried it up;
its fruit was stripped off,
its strong stem was withered;
the fire consumed it.

13 Now it is transplanted in the wilderness,
in a dry and thirsty land.

14 And fire has gone out from its stem,
has consumed its branches and fruit,
so that there remains in it no strong stem,
no sceptre for a ruler.

This is a lamentation, and has become a lamentation.

A long record of sin

20 In the seventh year, in the fifth month, on the tenth day of the month, certain of the elders of Israel came to inquire of the LORD,
2 and sat before me. And the word of the
3 LORD came to me: "Son of man, speak to the elders of Israel, and say to them, Thus says the Lord GOD, Is it to inquire of me that you come? As I live, says the Lord GOD, I will
4 not be inquired of by you. Will you judge them, son of man, will you judge them? Then let them know the abominations of
5 their fathers, and say to them, Thus says the Lord GOD: On the day when I chose Israel, I swore to the seed of the house of Jacob, making myself known to them in the land of Egypt, I swore to them, saying, I am the
6 LORD your God. On that day I swore to them that I would bring them out of the land of Egypt into a land that I had searched out for them, a land flowing with milk and
7 honey, the most glorious of all lands. And I said to them, Cast away the detestable things your eyes feast on, every one of you, and do not defile yourselves with the idols of Egypt;
8 I am the LORD your God. But they rebelled against me and would not listen to me; they did not every man cast away the detestable things their eyes feasted on, nor did they forsake the idols of Egypt. "Then I thought I would pour out my wrath upon them and spend my anger against them in the midst of the land of
9 Egypt. But I acted for the sake of my name, that it should not be profaned in the sight of the nations among whom they dwelt, in whose sight I made myself known to them in
10 bringing them out of the land of Egypt. So I

led them out of the land of Egypt and brought them into the wilderness. I gave them my statutes and showed them my ordinances, by whose observance man shall live. Moreover I gave them my sabbaths, as a sign between me and them, that they might know that I the LORD sanctify them. But the house of Israel rebelled against me in the wilderness; they did not walk in my statutes but rejected my ordinances, by whose observance man shall live; and my sabbaths they greatly profaned.

"Then I thought I would pour out my wrath upon them in the wilderness, to make a full end of them. But I acted for the sake of my name, that it should not be profaned in the sight of the nations, in whose sight I had brought them out. Moreover I swore to them in the wilderness that I would not bring them into the land which I had given them, a land flowing with milk and honey, the most glorious of all lands, because they rejected my ordinances and did not walk in my statutes, and profaned my sabbaths; for their heart went after their idols. Nevertheless my eye spared them, and I did not destroy them or make a full end of them in the wilderness.

"And I said to their children in the wilderness, Do not walk in the statutes of your fathers, nor observe their ordinances, nor defile yourselves with their idols. I the LORD am your God; walk in my statutes, and be careful to observe my ordinances, and hallow my sabbaths that they may be a sign between me and you, that you may know that I the LORD am your God. But the children rebelled against me; they did not walk in my statutes, and were not careful to observe my ordinances, by whose observance man shall live; they profaned my sabbaths.

"Then I thought I would pour out my wrath upon them and spend my anger against them in the wilderness. But I withheld my hand, and acted for the sake of my name, that it should not be profaned in the sight of the nations, in whose sight I had brought them out. Moreover I swore to them in the wilderness that I would scatter them among the nations and disperse them through the countries, because they had not executed my ordinances, but had rejected my statutes and profaned my sabbaths, and their eyes were set on their fathers' idols. Moreover I gave them statutes that were not good and ordinances by which they could not have life; and I defiled them through their very gifts in making them offer by fire all their first-born, that I might horrify them; I did it that they might know that I am the LORD.

"Therefore, son of man, speak to the house of Israel and say to them, Thus says the Lord

GOD: In this again your fathers blasphemed me, by dealing treacherously with me. For when I had brought them into the land which I swore to give them, then wherever they saw any high hill or any leafy tree, there they offered their sacrifices and presented the provocation of their offering; there they sent up their soothing odours, and there they poured out their drink offerings. (I said to them, What is the high place to which you go? So its name is called Bamah*t* to this day.) Wherefore say to the house of Israel, Thus says the Lord GOD: Will you defile yourselves after the manner of your fathers and go astray after their detestable things? When you offer your gifts and sacrifice your sons by fire, you defile yourselves with all your idols to this day. And shall I be inquired of by you, O house of Israel? As I live, says the Lord GOD, I will not be inquired of by you.

"What is in your mind shall never happen—the thought, 'Let us be like the nations, like the tribes of the countries, and worship wood and stone.'

"As I live, says the Lord GOD, surely with a mighty hand and an outstretched arm, and with wrath poured out, I will be king over you. I will bring you out from the peoples and gather you out of the countries where you are scattered, with a mighty hand and an outstretched arm, and with wrath poured out; and I will bring you into the wilderness of the peoples, and there I will enter into judgment with you face to face. As I entered into judgment with your fathers in the wilderness of the land of Egypt, so I will enter into judgment with you, says the Lord GOD. I will make you pass under the rod, and I will let you go in by number.*u* I will purge out the rebels from among you, and those who transgress against me; I will bring them out of the land where they sojourn, but they shall not enter the land of Israel. Then you will know that I am the LORD.

"As for you, O house of Israel, thus says the Lord GOD: Go serve every one of you his idols, now and hereafter, if you will not listen to me; but my holy name you shall no more profane with your gifts and your idols.

"For on my holy mountain, the mountain height of Israel, says the Lord GOD, there all the house of Israel, all of them, shall serve me in the land; there I will accept them, and there I will require your contributions and the choicest of your gifts, with all your sacred offerings. As a pleasing odour I will accept you, when I bring you out from the peoples, and gather you out of the countries where

you have been scattered; and I will manifest my holiness among you in the sight of the nations. And you shall know that I am the 42 LORD, when I bring you into the land of Israel, the country which I swore to give to your fathers. And there you shall remember 43 your ways and all the doings with which you have polluted yourselves; and you shall loathe yourselves for all the evils that you have committed. And you shall know that I 44 am the LORD, when I deal with you for my name's sake, not according to your evil ways, nor according to your corrupt doings, O house of Israel, says the Lord GOD."

And the word of the LORD came to me: 45 *v* "Son of man, set your face toward the south, 46 preach against the south, and prophesy against the forest land in the Negeb; say to 47 the forest of the Negeb, Hear the word of the LORD: Thus says the Lord GOD, Behold, I will kindle a fire in you, and it shall devour every green tree in you and every dry tree; the blazing flame shall not be quenched, and all faces from south to north shall be scorched by it. All flesh shall see that I 48 the LORD have kindled it; it shall not be quenched." Then I said, "Ah Lord GOD! 49 they are saying of me, 'Is he not a maker of allegories?'"

The sword of justice

The word of the LORD came to me: "Son 21 *w* of man, set your face toward Jerusalem and 2 preach against the sanctuaries; prophesy against the land of Israel and say to the land 3 of Israel, Thus says the LORD: Behold, I am against you, and will draw forth my sword out of its sheath, and will cut off from you both righteous and wicked. Because I will 4 cut off from you both righteous and wicked, therefore my sword shall go out of its sheath against all flesh from south to north; and all 5 flesh shall know that I the LORD have drawn my sword out of its sheath; it shall not be sheathed again. Sigh therefore, son of man; 6 sigh with breaking heart and bitter grief before their eyes. And when they say to you, 7 'Why do you sigh?' you shall say, 'Because of the tidings. When it comes, every heart will melt and all hands will be feeble, every spirit will faint and all knees will be weak as water. Behold, it comes and it will be fulfilled,'" says the Lord GOD.

And the word of the LORD came to me: 8 "Son of man, prophesy and say, Thus says 9 the Lord, Say:
A sword, a sword is sharpened
    and also polished,

---

t That is *High Place*   *u* Gk: Heb *bring you into the bond of the covenant*   *v* Ch 21.1 in Heb
w Ch 21.6 in Heb
20.41: Eph 5.2; Phil 4.18.   **20.43:** Ezek 6.9; 36.31.

10 sharpened for slaughter,
     polished to flash like lightning!
Or do we make mirth? You have despised
the rod, my son, with everything of wood.
11 So the sword is given to be polished, that it
may be handled; it is sharpened and polished
12 to be given into the hand of the slayer. Cry
and wail, son of man, for it is against my
people; it is against all the princes of Israel;
they are delivered over to the sword with my
people. Smite therefore upon your thigh.
13 For it will not be a testing—what could it
do if you despise the rod?" says the Lord
God.
14 "Prophesy therefore, son of man; clap your
hands and let the sword come down twice,
yea thrice, the sword for those to be slain; it
is the sword for the great slaughter, which
15 encompasses them, that their hearts may
melt, and many fall at all their gates. I have
given the glittering sword; ah! it is made like
16 lightning, it is polished *x* for slaughter. Cut
sharply to right *y* and left where your edge is
17 directed. I also will clap my hands, and I

will satisfy my fury; I the Lord have
spoken."
The word of the Lord came to me again:
"Son of man, mark two ways for the sword of
the king of Babylon to come; both of them
shall come forth from the same land. And
make a signpost, make it at the head of the
way to a city; mark a way for the sword to
come to Rabbah of the Ammonites and to
Judah and to *z* Jerusalem the fortified. For
the king of Babylon stands at the parting of
the way, at the head of the two ways, to use
divination; he shakes the arrows, he consults
the teraphim, he looks at the liver. Into his
right hand comes the lot for Jerusalem, *a* to
open the mouth with a cry, *b* to lift up the
voice with shouting, to set battering rams
against the gates, to cast up mounds, to build
siege towers. But to them it will seem like a
false divination; they have sworn solemn
oaths; but he brings their guilt to remembrance, that they may be captured.
"Therefore thus says the Lord God:
Because you have made your guilt to be

The green trees   Ezek 20, 47

remembered, in that your transgressions are
uncovered, so that in all your doings your
sins appear—because you have come to
remembrance, you shall be taken in them. *c*
And you, O unhallowed wicked one, prince
of Israel, whose day has come, the time of
your final punishment, thus says the Lord
God: Remove the turban, and take off the
crown; things shall not remain as they are;
exalt that which is low, and abase that which
is high. A ruin, ruin, ruin I will make it;
there shall not be even a trace *d* of it until he
comes whose right it is; and to him I will give
it.
"And you, son of man, prophesy, and say,
Thus says the Lord God concerning the
Ammonites, and concerning their reproach;
say, A sword, a sword is drawn for the
slaughter, it is polished to glitter *e* and to flash
like lightning—while they see for you false
visions, while they divine lies for you—to be

x Tg: Heb *wrapped up*   *y* Gk Syr Vg: Heb *right, set*   *z* Gk Syr: Heb *in*
a Heb *Jerusalem, to set battering rams*   *b* Gk: Heb *with slaughter*   *c* Gk: Heb *with the hand*
d Cn: Heb *not even this*   *e* Cn: Heb *to contain*
21.28-32: Jer 49.1-6; Ezek 25.1-7; Amos 1.13-15; Zeph 2.8-11.

laid on the necks of the unhallowed wicked, whose day has come, the time of their final punishment. Return it to its sheath. In the place where you were created, in the land of your origin, I will judge you. And I will pour out my indignation upon you; I will blow upon you with the fire of my wrath; and I will deliver you into the hands of brutal men, skilful to destroy. You shall be fuel for the fire; your blood shall be in the midst of the land; you shall be no more remembered; for I the LORD have spoken."

The city of blood

22 Moreover the word of the LORD came to me, saying, "And you, son of man, will you judge, will you judge the bloody city? Then declare to her all her abominable deeds. You shall say, Thus says the Lord GOD: A city that sheds blood in the midst of her, that her time may come, and that makes idols to defile herself! You have become guilty by the blood which you have shed, and defiled by the idols which you have made; and you have brought your day near, the appointed time^f of your years has come. Therefore I have made you a reproach to the nations, and a mocking to all the countries. Those who are near and those who are far from you will mock you, you infamous one, full of tumult. "Behold, the princes of Israel in you, every one according to his power, have been bent on shedding blood. Father and mother are treated with contempt in you; the sojourner suffers extortion in your midst; the fatherless and the widow are wronged in you. You have despised my holy things, and profaned my sabbaths. There are men in you who slander to shed blood, and men in you who eat upon the mountains; men commit lewdness in your midst. In you men uncover their fathers' nakedness; in you they humble women who are unclean in their impurity. One commits abomination with his neighbour's wife; another lewdly defiles his daughter-in-law; another in you defiles his sister, his father's daughter. In you men take bribes to shed blood; you take interest and increase and make gain of your neighbours by extortion; and you have forgotten me, says the Lord GOD. "Behold, therefore, I strike my hands together at the dishonest gain which you have made, and at the blood which has been in the midst of you. Can your courage endure, or can your hands be strong, in the days that I shall deal with you? I the LORD have spoken, and I will do it. I will scatter you among the nations and disperse you through the countries, and I will consume your filthiness out of you. And I^g shall be profaned through you in the sight of the nations; and you shall know that I am the LORD."

And the word of the LORD came to me: "Son of man, the house of Israel has become dross to me; all of them, silver^h and bronze and tin and iron and lead in the furnace, have become dross. Therefore thus says the Lord GOD: Because you have all become dross, therefore, behold, I will gather you into the midst of Jerusalem. As men gather silver and bronze and iron and lead and tin into a furnace, to blow the fire upon it in order to melt it; so I will gather you in my anger and in my wrath, and I will put you in and, melt you. I will gather you and blow upon you with the fire of my wrath, and you shall be melted in the midst of it. As silver is melted in a furnace, so you shall be melted in the midst of it; and you shall know that I the LORD have poured out my wrath upon you."

And the word of the LORD came to me: "Son of man, say to her, You are a land that is not cleansed, or rained upon in the day of indignation. Her princes^i in the midst of her are like a roaring lion tearing the prey; they have devoured human lives; they have taken treasure and precious things; they have made many widows in the midst of her. Her priests have done violence to my law and have profaned my holy things; they have made no distinction between the holy and the common, neither have they taught the difference between the unclean and the clean, and they have disregarded my sabbaths, so that I am profaned among them. Her princes in the midst of her are like wolves tearing the prey, shedding blood, destroying lives to get dishonest gain. And her prophets have daubed for them with whitewash, seeing false visions and divining lies for them, saying, 'Thus says the Lord GOD,' when the LORD has not spoken. The people of the land have practised extortion and committed robbery; they have oppressed the poor and needy, and have extorted from the sojourner without redress. And I sought for a man among them who should build up the wall and stand in the breach before me for the land, that I should not destroy it; but I found none. Therefore I have poured out my indignation upon them; I have consumed them with the fire of my wrath; their way have I requited upon their heads, says the Lord GOD."

---

^{f} Two Mss Gk Syr Vg Tg: Heb *until* ^{g} Gk Syr Vg: Heb *you*
^{h} Transposed from the end of the verse. Compare verse 20 ^{i} Gk: Heb *a conspiracy of her prophets*

The two sisters

23 The word of the LORD came to me: "Son of
2 man, there were two women, the daughters
3 of one mother; they played the harlot in
Egypt; they played the harlot in their youth;
there their breasts were pressed and their
4 virgin bosoms handled. Oho'lah was the
name of the elder and Ohol'ibah the name of
her sister. They became mine, and they bore
sons and daughters. As for their names,
Oho'lah is Samar'ia, and Ohol'ibah is Jerusalem.
5 "Oho'lah played the harlot while she was
mine; and she doted on her lovers the
6 Assyrians, warriors clothed in purple,
governors and commanders, all of them
desirable young men, horsemen riding on
7 horses. She bestowed her harlotries upon
them, the choicest men of Assyria all of
them; and she defiled herself with all the
8 idols of every one on whom she doted. She
did not give up her harlotry which she had
practised since her days in Egypt; for in her
youth men had lain with her and handled her
virgin bosom and poured out their lust upon
9 her. Therefore I delivered her into the
hands of her lovers, into the hands of the
10 Assyrians, upon whom she doted. These
uncovered her nakedness; they seized her
sons and her daughters; and her they slew
with the sword; and she became a byword
among women, when judgment had been
executed upon her.
11 "Her sister Ohol'ibah saw this, yet she was
more corrupt than she in her doting and in
her harlotry, which was worse than that of
12 her sister. She doted upon the Assyrians,
governors and commanders, warriors clothed
in full armour, horsemen riding on horses, all
13 of them desirable young men. And I saw
that she was defiled; they both took the same
14 way. But she carried her harlotry further;
she saw men portrayed upon the wall, the
images of the Chalde'ans portrayed in ver-
15 milion, girded with belts on their loins, with
flowing turbans on their heads, all of them
looking like officers, a picture of Babylonians
16 whose native land was Chalde'a. When she
saw them she doted upon them, and sent
17 messengers to them in Chalde'a. And the
Babylonians came to her into the bed of love,
and they defiled her with their lust; and after
she was polluted by them, she turned from
18 them in disgust. When she carried on her
harlotry so openly and flaunted her nakedness, I turned in disgust from her, as I had
19 turned from her sister. Yet she increased her
harlotry, remembering the days of her youth,

when she played the harlot in the land of
Egypt and doted upon her paramours there, 20
whose members were like those of asses, and
whose issue was like that of horses. Thus 21
you longed for the lewdness of your youth,
when the Egyptians[j] handled your bosom
and pressed[k] your young breasts."
Therefore, O Ohol'ibah, thus says the Lord 22
GOD: "Behold, I will rouse against you your
lovers from whom you turned in disgust, and
I will bring them against you from every
side: the Babylonians and all the Chalde'ans, 23
Pekod and Sho'a and Ko'a, and all the
Assyrians with them, desirable young men,
governors and commanders all of them,
officers and warriors,[l] all of them riding on
horses. And they shall come against you 24
from the north[m] with chariots and wagons
and a host of peoples; they shall set themselves against you on every side with buckler,
shield, and helmet, and I will commit the
judgment to them, and they shall judge you
according to their judgments. And I will 25
direct my indignation against you, that they
may deal with you in fury. They shall cut off
your nose and your ears, and your survivors
shall fall by the sword. They shall seize your
sons and your daughters, and your survivors
shall be devoured by fire. They shall also 26
strip you of your clothes and take away your
fine jewels. Thus I will put an end to your 27
lewdness and your harlotry brought from the
land of Egypt; so that you shall not lift up
your eyes to the Egyptians or remember
them any more. For thus says the Lord 28
GOD: Behold, I will deliver you into the
hands of those whom you hate, into the
hands of those from whom you turned in
disgust; and they shall deal with you in 29

---

[j] Two Mss: Heb *from Egypt*   [k] Cn: Heb *for the sake of*   [l] Compare verses 6 and 12: Heb *called*
[m] Gk: The meaning of the Hebrew word is unknown

hatred, and take away all the fruit of your labour, and leave you naked and bare, and the nakedness of your harlotry shall be uncovered. Your lewdness and your harlotry have brought this upon you, because you played the harlot with the nations, and polluted yourself with their idols. You have gone the way of your sister; therefore I will give her cup into your hand. Thus says the Lord GOD:

"You shall drink your sister's cup
  which is deep and large;
you shall be laughed at and held in
    derision,
  for it contains much;
you will be filled with drunkenness and
    sorrow.
A cup of horror and desolation,
  is the cup of your sister Samar′ia;
you shall drink it and drain it out,
  and pluck out your hair,ⁿ
  and tear your breasts;
for I have spoken, says the Lord GOD.

5 Therefore thus says the Lord GOD: Because you have forgotten me and cast me behind your back, therefore bear the consequences of your lewdness and harlotry."

6 The LORD said to me: "Son of man, will you judge Oho′lah and Ohol′ibah? 7 declare to them their abominable deeds. For they have committed adultery, and blood is upon their hands; with their idols they have committed adultery; and they have even offered up to them for food the sons whom 8 they had borne to me. Moreover this they have done to me: they have defiled my sanctuary on the same day and profaned my 9 sabbaths. For when they had slaughtered their children in sacrifice to their idols, on the same day they came into my sanctuary to profane it. And lo, this is what they did in 10 my house. They even sent for men to come from far, to whom a messenger was sent, and lo, they came. For them you bathed yourself, painted your eyes, and decked 11 yourself with ornaments; you sat upon a stately couch, with a table spread before it on which you had placed my incense and my 12 oil. The sound of a carefree multitude was with her; and with men of the common sort drunkardsᵒ were brought from the wilderness; and they put bracelets upon the hands of the women, and beautiful crowns upon their heads.

43 "Then I said, Do not men now commit adulteryᵖ when they practise harlotry with 44 her? For they have gone in to her, as men go in to a harlot. Thus they went into Oho′lah

and to Ohol′ibah to commit lewdness.�q But 45 righteous men shall pass judgment on them with the sentence of adulteresses, and with the sentence of women that shed blood; because they are adulteresses, and blood is upon their hands."

For thus says the Lord GOD: "Bring up a 46 host against them, and make them an object of terror and a spoil. And the host shall stone 47 them and despatch them with their swords; they shall slay their sons and their daughters, and burn up their houses. Thus will I put an 48 end to lewdness in the land, that all women may take warning and not commit lewdness as you have done. And your lewdness shall 49 be requited upon you, and you shall bear the penalty for your sinful idolatry; and you shall know that I am the Lord GOD."

The end of the siege

In the ninth year, in the tenth month, on 24 the tenth day of the month, the word of the LORD came to me: "Son of man, write down 2 the name of this day, this very day. The king of Babylon has laid siege to Jerusalem this very day. And utter an allegory to the 3 rebellious house and say to them, Thus says the Lord GOD:

Set on the pot, set it on,
  pour in water also;
put in it the pieces of flesh,   4
  all the good pieces, the thigh and the
    shoulder;
  fill it with choice bones.
Take the choicest one of the flock,   5
  pile the logsʳ under it;
boil its pieces,ˢ
  seetheᵗ also its bones in it.

"Therefore thus says the Lord GOD: Woe 6 to the bloody city, to the pot whose rust is in it, and whose rust has not gone out of it! Take out of it piece after piece, without making any choice.ᵘ For the blood she has 7 shed is still in the midst of her; she put it on the bare rock, she did not pour it upon the ground to cover it with dust. To rouse my 8 wrath, to take vengeance, I have set on the bare rock the blood she has shed, that it may not be covered. Therefore thus says the 9 Lord GOD: Woe to the bloody city! I also will make the pile great. Heap on the logs, 10 kindle the fire, boil well the flesh, and empty out the broth,ᵛ and let the bones be burned up. Then set it empty upon the coals, that it 11 may become hot, and its copper may burn, that its filthiness may be melted in it, its rust consumed. In vain I have wearied myself;ʷ 12

ⁿ Compare Syr: Heb *gnaw its sherds*   ᵒ Heb uncertain   ᵖ Compare Gk: Heb obscure
q Gk: Heb *a woman of lewdness*   ʳ Compare verse 10: Heb *the bones*   ˢ Two Mss: Heb *its boilings*
ᵗ Cn: Heb *its bones seethe*   ᵘ Heb *no lot has fallen upon it*   ᵛ Compare Gk: Heb *mix the spices*
ʷ Cn: Heb uncertain

13 its thick rust does not go out of it by fire. Its rust is your filthy lewdness. Because I would have cleansed you and you were not cleansed from your filthiness, you shall not be cleansed any more till I have satisfied my 14 fury upon you. I the LORD have spoken; it shall come to pass, I will do it; I will not go back, I will not spare, I will not repent; according to your ways and your doings I will judge you, says the Lord GOD."

15 Also the word of the LORD came to me: 16 "Son of man, behold, I am about to take the delight of your eyes away from you at a stroke; yet you shall not mourn or weep nor 17 shall your tears run down. Sigh, but not aloud; make no mourning for the dead. Bind on your turban, and put your shoes on your feet; do not cover your lips, nor eat the bread 18 of mourners." *ˣ* So I spoke to the people in the morning, and at evening my wife died. And on the next morning I did as I was commanded.

19 And the people said to me, "Will you not tell us what these things mean for us, that 20 you are acting thus?" Then I said to them, 21 "The word of the LORD came to me: 'Say to the house of Israel, Thus says the Lord GOD: Behold, I will profane my sanctuary, the pride of your power, the delight of your eyes, and the desire of your soul; and your sons and your daughters whom you left behind shall fall by the sword. And you shall do as I 22 have done; you shall not cover your lips, nor eat the bread of mourners. *ˣ* Your turbans 23 shall be on your heads and your shoes on your feet; you shall not mourn or weep, but you shall pine away in your iniquities and groan to one another. Thus shall Ezekiel be 24 to you a sign; according to all that he has done you shall do. When this comes, then you will know that I am the Lord GOD.'

"And you, son of man, on the day when I 25 take from them their stronghold, their joy and glory, the delight of their eyes and their heart's desire, and also their sons and daughters, on that day a fugitive will come to 26 you to report to you the news. On that day 27 your mouth will be opened to the fugitive, and you shall speak and be no longer dumb. So you will be a sign to them; and they will know that I am the LORD."

JUDGMENT ON THE NATIONS

AMMON

25 THE word of the LORD came to me: "Son 2 of man, set your face toward the Ammo-3 nites, and prophesy against them. Say to the Ammonites, Hear the word of the Lord GOD: Thus says the Lord GOD, Because you said, 'Aha!' over my sanctuary when it was profaned, and over the land of Israel when it was made desolate, and over the house of 4 Judah when it went into exile; therefore I am handing you over to the people of the East for a possession, and they shall set their encampments among you and make their dwellings in your midst; they shall eat your fruit, and they shall drink your milk. I will 5 make Rabbah a pasture for camels and the cities of the Ammonites *ʸ* a fold for flocks. Then you will know that I am the LORD. For 6 thus says the Lord GOD: Because you have clapped your hands and stamped your feet and rejoiced with all the malice within you against the land of Israel, therefore, behold, I 7 have stretched out my hand against you, and will hand you over as spoil to the nations; and I will cut you off from the peoples and will make you perish out of the countries; I will destroy you. Then you will know that I am the LORD.

MOAB

8 "Thus says the Lord God: Because Moab[z] said, Behold, the house of Judah is like all the 9 other nations, therefore I will lay open the flank of Moab from the cities[a] on its frontier, the glory of the country, Beth-jesh′imoth, 10 Ba′al-me′on, and Kiriatha′im. I will give it along with the Ammonites to the people of the East as a possession, that it[b] may be 11 remembered no more among the nations, and I will execute judgments upon Moab. Then they will know that I am the Lord.

EDOM

12 "Thus says the Lord God: Because Edom acted revengefully against the house of Judah and has grievously offended in taking 13 vengeance upon them, therefore thus says the Lord God, I will stretch out my hand against Edom, and cut off from it man and beast; and I will make it desolate; from Teman even to Dedan they shall fall by the 14 sword. And I will lay my vengeance upon Edom by the hand of my people Israel; and they shall do in Edom according to my anger and according to my wrath; and they shall know my vengeance, says the Lord God.

PHILISTIA

15 "Thus says the Lord God: Because the Philistines acted revengefully and took vengeance with malice of heart to destroy in 16 never-ending enmity; therefore thus says the Lord God, Behold, I will stretch out my hand against the Philistines, and I will cut off the Cher′ethites, and destroy the rest of the 17 sea coast. I will execute great vengeance upon them with wrathful chastisements. Then they will know that I am the Lord, when I lay my vengeance upon them."

TYRE

26 In the eleventh year, on the first day of the month, the word of the Lord came to me: 2 "Son of man, because Tyre said concerning Jerusalem, 'Aha, the gate of the peoples is

broken, it has swung open to me; I shall be replenished, now that she is laid waste,' therefore thus says the Lord God: Behold, I 3 am against you, O Tyre, and will bring up many nations against you, as the sea brings up its waves. They shall destroy the walls of 4 Tyre, and break down her towers; and I will scrape her soil from her, and make her a bare rock. She shall be in the midst of the sea a 5 place for the spreading of nets; for I have spoken, says the Lord God; and she shall become a spoil to the nations; and her 6 daughters on the mainland shall be slain by the sword. Then they will know that I am the Lord.

"For thus says the Lord God: Behold, I 7 will bring upon Tyre from the north Nebuchadrez′zar king of Babylon, king of kings, with horses and chariots, and with horsemen and a host of many soldiers. He 8 will slay with the sword your daughters on the mainland; he will set up a siege wall against you, and throw up a mound against you, and raise a roof of shields against you. He will direct the shock of his battering rams 9 against your walls, and with his axes he will break down your towers. His horses will be 10 so many that their dust will cover you; your walls will shake at the noise of the horsemen and wagons and chariots, when he enters your gates as one enters a city which has been breached. With the hoofs of his horses he 11 will trample all your streets; he will slay your people with the sword; and your mighty pillars will fall to the ground. They will 12 make a spoil of your riches and a prey of your merchandise; they will break down your walls and destroy your pleasant houses; your stones and timber and soil they will cast into the midst of the waters. And I will stop the 13 music of your songs, and the sound of your lyres shall be heard no more. I will make you 14 a bare rock; you shall be a place for the spreading of nets; you shall never be rebuilt; for I the Lord have spoken, says the Lord God.

"Thus says the Lord God to Tyre: Will not 15 the coastlands shake at the sound of your fall, when the wounded groan, when slaughter is made in the midst of you? Then all the 16 princes of the sea will step down from their thrones, and remove their robes, and strip off their embroidered garments; they will clothe themselves with trembling; they will sit upon the ground and tremble every moment, and be appalled at you. And they will raise a 17 lamentation over you, and say to you,

z Gk Old Latin: Heb *Moab and Seir*   a Heb *cities from its cities*   b Cn: Heb *the Ammonites*
25.8–11: Is 15–16; 25.10–12; Jer 48; Amos 2.1–3; Zeph 2.8–11.
25.12–14: Is 34; 63.1–6; Jer 49.7–22; Ezek 35; Amos 1.11–12; Obad; Mal 1.2–5.
25.15–17: Is 14.29–31; Jer 47; Amos 1.6–8; Zeph 2.4–7; Zech 9.5–7.
26.1–28.19: Is 23; Joel 3.4–8; Amos 1.9–10; Zech 9.3–4.   26.13: Rev 18.22.   26.16–17: Rev 18.9–10.

'How you have vanished[c] from the seas,
  O city renowned,
that was mighty on the sea,
  you and your inhabitants,
who imposed your terror
  on all the mainland![d]
18 Now the isles tremble
  on the day of your fall;
yea, the isles that are in the sea
  are dismayed at your passing.'

19 "For thus says the Lord GOD: When I make you a city laid waste, like the cities that are not inhabited, when I bring up the deep over you, and the great waters cover you, 20 then I will thrust you down with those who descend into the Pit, to the people of old, and I will make you to dwell in the nether world, among primeval ruins, with those who go down to the Pit, so that you will not be inhabited or have a place[e] in the land of 21 living. I will bring you to a dreadful end, and you shall be no more; though you be sought for, you will never be found again, says the Lord GOD."

27 The word of the LORD came to me: "Now 2 you, son of man, raise a lamentation over 3 Tyre, and say to Tyre, who dwells at the entrance to the sea, merchant of the peoples on many coastlands, thus says the Lord GOD:
"O Tyre, you have said,
  'I am perfect in beauty.'
4 Your borders are in the heart of the seas;
  your builders made perfect your beauty.
5 They made all your planks
  of fir trees from Senir;
they took a cedar from Lebanon
  to make a mast for you.
6 Of oaks of Bashan
  they made your oars;
they made your deck of pines
  from the coasts of Cyprus,
  inlaid with ivory.
7 Of fine embroidered linen from Egypt
  was your sail,
  serving as your ensign;
blue and purple from the coasts of Eli'shah
  was your awning.
8 The inhabitants of Sidon and Arvad
  were your rowers;
skilled men of Zemer[f] were in you,
  they were your pilots.
9 The elders of Gebal and her skilled men
  were in you,
    caulking your seams;
all the ships of the sea with their mariners
  were in you,

to barter for your wares.
10 "Persia and Lud and Put were in your army as your men of war; they hung the shield and helmet in you; they gave you splendour. 11 The men of Arvad and Helech[g] were upon your walls round about, and men of Gamad were in your towers; they hung their shields upon your walls round about; they made perfect your beauty. 12 "Tarshish trafficked with you because of your great wealth of every kind; silver, iron, tin, and lead they exchanged for your wares. 13 Javan, Tubal, and Meshech traded with you; they exchanged the persons of men and vessels of bronze for your merchandise. 14 Beth-togar'mah exchanged for your wares horses, war horses, and mules. 15 The men of Rhodes[h] traded with you; many coastlands were your own special markets, they brought you in payment ivory tusks and ebony. 16 Edom[i] trafficked with you because of your abundant goods; they exchanged for your wares emeralds, purple, embroidered work, fine linen, coral, and agate. 17 Judah and the land of Israel traded with you; they exchanged for your merchandise wheat, olives and early figs,[j] honey, oil, and balm. 18 Damascus trafficked with you for your abundant goods, because of your great wealth of every kind; wine of Helbon, and white wool, and 19 wine[k] from Uzal they exchanged for your wares; wrought iron, cassia, and calamus were bartered for your merchandise. 20 Dedan traded with you in saddlecloths for riding. 21 Arabia and all the princes of Kedar were your favoured dealers in lambs, rams, and goats; in these they trafficked with you. 22 The traders of Sheba and Ra'amah traded with you; they exchanged for your wares the best of all kinds of spices, and all precious stones, and gold. 23 Haran, Canneh, Eden,[l] Asshur, and Chilmad traded with you. 24 These traded with you in choice garments, in clothes of blue and embroidered work, and in carpets of coloured stuff, bound with cords and made secure; in these they traded with you.[m] 25 The ships of Tarshish travelled for you with your merchandise.[n]

"So you were filled and heavily laden
  in the heart of the seas.
Your rowers have brought you out 26
  into the high seas.
The east wind has wrecked you
  in the heart of the seas.
Your riches, your wares, your merchan- 27
  dise,

---

[e] Gk Old Latin Aquila: Heb *vanished, O inhabited one*,   [d] Cn: Heb *her inhabitants*   [e] Gk: Heb *I will give beauty*
[f] Compare Gen 10.18: Heb *your skilled men, O Tyre*   [g] Or *and your army*   [h] Gk: Heb *Dedan*
[i] Another reading is *Ara* [n]   [j] Cn: Heb *wheat of minnith and pannag*   [k] Gk: Heb *Vedan and Javan*
[l] Cn: Heb *Eden the traders of Sheba*   [m] Cn: Heb *in your market*   [n] Cn: Heb *your travellers your merchandise*
27.13: Rev 18.13.   27.27–36: Rev 18.9–19.

your mariners and your pilots,
your caulkers, your dealers in merchandise,
  and all your men of war who are in
    you,
with all your company
  that is in your midst,
sink into the heart of the seas
  on the day of your ruin.
28 At the sound of the cry of your pilots
  the countryside shakes,
29 and down from their ships
  come all that handle the oar.
The mariners and all the pilots of the
    sea
  stand on the shore
30 and wail aloud over you,
  and cry bitterly.
They cast dust on their heads
  and wallow in ashes;
31 they make themselves bald for you,
  and gird themselves with sackcloth,
  and they weep over you in bitterness of
    soul,
  with bitter mourning.
32 In their wailing they raise a lamentation
    for you,
  and lament over you:
  'Who was ever destroyed⁰ like Tyre
  in the midst of the sea?
33 When your wares came from the seas,
  you satisfied many peoples;
  with your abundant wealth and mer-
    chandise
  you enriched the kings of the earth.
34 Now you are wrecked by the seas,
  in the depths of the waters;
  your merchandise and all your crew
  have sunk with you.
35 All the inhabitants of the coastlands
  are appalled at you;
  and their kings are horribly afraid,
  their faces are convulsed.
36 The merchants among the peoples hiss at
    you;
  you have come to a dreadful end
  and shall be no more for ever.' "

The king of Tyre

The word of the LORD came to me: "Son of 28
man, say to the prince of Tyre, Thus says the 2
Lord GOD:
"Because your heart is proud,
  and you have said, 'I am a god,
I sit in the seat of the gods,
  in the heart of the seas,'
yet you are but a man, and no god,
  though you consider yourself as wise as
    a god—
you are indeed wiser than Daniel;   3
  no secret is hidden from you;
by your wisdom and your understanding 4
  you have gotten wealth for yourself,
and have gathered gold and silver
  into your treasuries;
by your great wisdom in trade   5
  you have increased your wealth,
  and your heart has become proud in
    your wealth—
therefore thus says the Lord GOD: 6
"Because you consider yourself
  as wise as a god,
therefore, behold, I will bring strangers 7
  upon you,
  the most terrible of the nations;
and they shall draw their swords against
  the beauty of your wisdom
  and defile your splendour.
They shall thrust you down into the Pit, 8
  and you shall die the death of the slain
  in the heart of the seas.
Will you still say, 'I am a god,'   9
  in the presence of those who slay you,
though you are but a man, and no god,
  in the hands of those who wound you?
You shall die the death of the uncircum- 10
  cised
  by the hand of foreigners;
  for I have spoken, says the Lord GOD."
Moreover the word of the LORD came to 11
me: "Son of man, raise a lamentation over 12
the king of Tyre, and say to him, Thus says
the Lord GOD:
"You were the signet of perfection,ᵖ
  full of wisdom
  and perfect in beauty.
You were in Eden, the garden of God;   13
  every precious stone was your covering,
carnelian, topaz, and jasper,
  chrysolite, beryl, and onyx,
sapphire,�q carbuncle, and emerald;
  and wrought in gold were your settings
  and your engravings.ʳ
On the day that you were created
  they were prepared.
With an anointed guardian cherub I 14

⁰ Tg Vg: Heb *like silence*   ᵖ Heb obscure   q Or *lapis lazuli*   ʳ Heb uncertain
28.2: Dan 11.36; 2 Thess 2.4; Rev 13.5.

placed you;[8]
you were on the holy mountain of God;
in the midst of the stones of fire you
walked.

15 You were blameless in your ways
from the day you were created,
till iniquity was found in you.

16 In the abundance of your trade
you were filled with violence, and you
sinned;
so I cast you as a profane thing from the
mountain of God,
and the guardian cherub drove you out
from the midst of the stones of fire.

17 Your heart was proud because of your
beauty;
you corrupted your wisdom for the sake
of your splendour.
I cast you to the ground;
I exposed you before kings,
to feast their eyes on you.

18 By the multitude of your iniquities,
in the unrighteousness of your trade
you profaned your sanctuaries;
so I brought forth fire from the midst of
you;
it consumed you,
and I turned you to ashes upon the earth
in the sight of all who saw you.

19 All who know you among the peoples
are appalled at you;
you have come to a dreadful end
and shall be no more for ever."

20, The word of the LORD came to me: "Son
21 of man, set your face toward Sidon, and
22 prophesy against her and say, Thus says the
Lord GOD:
"Behold, I am against you, O Sidon,
and I will manifest my glory in the
midst of you.
And they shall know that I am the LORD
when I execute judgments in her,
and manifest my holiness in her;

23 for I will send pestilence into her,
and blood into her streets;
and the slain shall fall in the midst of her,
by the sword that is against her on every
side.
Then they will know that I am the LORD.

24 "And for the house of Israel there shall be
no more a brier to prick or a thorn to hurt
them among all their neighbours who have
treated them with contempt. Then they will
know that I am the Lord GOD.

25 "Thus says the Lord GOD: When I gather
the house of Israel from the peoples among
whom they are scattered, and manifest my
holiness in them in the sight of the nations,
then they shall dwell in their own land which

I gave to my servant Jacob. And they shall 26
dwell securely in it, and they shall build
houses and plant vineyards. They shall
dwell securely, when I execute judgments
upon all their neighbours who have treated
them with contempt. Then they will know
that I am the LORD their God."

EGYPT

In the tenth year, in the tenth month, on the 29
twelfth day of the month, the word of the
LORD came to me: "Son of man, set your 2
face against Pharaoh king of Egypt, and
prophesy against him and against all Egypt;
speak, and say, Thus says the Lord GOD: 3
"Behold, I am against you,
Pharaoh king of Egypt,
the great dragon that lies
in the midst of his streams,
that says, 'My Nile is my own;
I made it.'[t]
I will put hooks in your jaws, 4
and make the fish of your streams stick
to your scales;
and I will draw you up out of the midst of
your streams,
with all the fish of your streams
which stick to your scales.
And I will cast you forth into the 5
wilderness,
you and all the fish of your streams;
you shall fall upon the open field,
and not be gathered and buried.
To the beasts of the earth and to the birds
of the air
I have given you as food.
"Then all the inhabitants of Egypt shall 6
know that I am the LORD. Because you[u]
have been a staff of reed to the house of
Israel; when they grasped you with the hand, 7
you broke, and tore all their shoulders; and
when they leaned upon you, you broke, and
made all their loins to shake;[v] therefore thus 8
says the Lord GOD: Behold, I will bring a
sword upon you, and will cut off from you
man and beast; and the land of Egypt shall be 9
a desolation and a waste. Then they will
know that I am the LORD.
"Because you[w] said, 'The Nile is mine, and
I made it,' therefore, behold, I am against 10
you, and against your streams, and I will

[8] Heb uncertain   [t] Syr Compare Gk: Heb *I have made myself*   [u] Gk Syr Vg: Heb *they*   [v] Syr: Heb *stand*
[w] Gk Syr Vg: Heb *he*
28.20–26: Joel 3.4–8; Zech 9.2.   29–32: Is 19; Jer 46; Zech 14.18–19.

make the land of Egypt an utter waste and desolation, from Migdol to Syene, as far as the border of Ethiopia. No foot of man shall pass through it, and no foot of beast shall pass through it; it shall be uninhabited forty years. And I will make the land of Egypt a desolation in the midst of desolated countries; and her cities shall be a desolation forty years among cities that are laid waste. I will scatter the Egyptians among the nations, and disperse them among the countries.

"For thus says the Lord GOD: At the end of forty years I will gather the Egyptians from the peoples among whom they were scattered; and I will restore the fortunes of Egypt, and bring them back to the land of Pathros, the land of their origin; and there they shall be a lowly kingdom. It shall be the most lowly of the kingdoms, and never again exalt itself above the nations; and I will make them so small that they will never again rule over the nations. And it shall never again be the reliance of the house of Israel, recalling their iniquity, when they turn to them for aid. Then they will know that I am the Lord GOD."

In the twenty-seventh year, in the first month, on the first day of the month, the word of the LORD came to me: "Son of man, Nebuchadrez'zar king of Babylon made his army labour hard against Tyre; every head was made bald and every shoulder was rubbed bare; yet neither he nor his army got anything from Tyre to pay for the labour that he had performed against it. Therefore thus says the Lord GOD: Behold, I will give the land of Egypt to Nebuchadrez'zar king of Babylon; and he shall carry off its wealth[x] and despoil it and plunder it; and it shall be the wages for his army. I have given him the land of Egypt as his recompense for which he laboured, because they worked for me, says the Lord GOD.

"On that day I will cause a horn to spring forth to the house of Israel, and I will open your lips among them. Then they will know that I am the LORD."

Desolation of Egypt

The word of the LORD came to me: "Son of 30 man, prophesy, and say, Thus says the Lord 2 GOD:

"Wail, 'Alas for the day!'
For the day is near, 3
the day of the LORD is near;
it will be a day of clouds,
a time of doom for the nations.
A sword shall come upon Egypt, 4
and anguish shall be in Ethiopia,
when the slain fall in Egypt,
and her wealth is carried away,
and her foundations are torn down.
Ethiopia, and Put, and Lud, and all Arabia, 5
and Libya,[y] and the people of the land that is
in league, shall fall with them by the sword.

"Thus says the LORD: 6
Those who support Egypt shall fall,
and her proud might shall come down;
from Migdol to Syene
they shall fall within her by the sword,
says the Lord GOD.
And she[z] shall be desolated in the midst of 7
desolated countries
and her cities shall be in the midst of
cities that are laid waste.
Then they will know that I am the LORD, 8
when I have set fire to Egypt,
and all her helpers are broken.
"On that day swift[a] messengers shall go 9
forth from me to terrify the unsuspecting
Ethiopians; and anguish shall come upon
them on the day of Egypt's doom; for, lo, it
comes!

"Thus says the Lord GOD: 10
I will put an end to the wealth[b] of Egypt,
by the hand of Nebuchadrez'zar king of
Babylon.
He and his people with him, the most 11
terrible of the nations,
shall be brought in to destroy the land;
and they shall draw their swords against
Egypt,

---

[x] Or multitude [y] Gk Compare Syr Vg: Heb Cub [z] Gk: Heb they [a] Gk Syr: Heb in ships [b] Or multitude

and fill the land with the slain.

12 And I will dry up the Nile,
and will sell the land into the hand of
evil men;
I will bring desolation upon the land and
everything in it,
by the hand of foreigners;
I, the LORD, have spoken.

13 "Thus says the Lord GOD:
I will destroy the idols,
and put an end to the images, in
Memphis;
there shall no longer be a prince in the land
of Egypt;
so I will put fear in the land of Egypt.

14 I will make Pathros a desolation,
and will set fire to Zo'an,
and will execute acts of judgment upon
Thebes.

15 And I will pour my wrath upon Pelusium,
the stronghold of Egypt,
and cut off the multitude of Thebes.

16 And I will set fire to Egypt;
Pelusium shall be in great agony;
Thebes shall be breached,
and its walls broken down.[c]

17 The young men of On and of Pibe'seth
shall fall by the sword;
and the women shall go into captivity.

18 At Tehaph'nehes the day shall be dark,
when I break there the dominion of
Egypt,
and her proud might shall come to an end;
she shall be covered by a cloud,
and her daughters shall go into captivity.

19 Thus I will execute acts of judgment upon
Egypt.
Then they will know that I am the
LORD."

20 In the eleventh year, in the first month, on
the seventh day of the month, the word of the
21 LORD came to me: "Son of man, I have
broken the arm of Pharaoh king of Egypt;
and lo, it has not been bound up, to heal it by

binding it with a bandage, so that it may
become strong to wield the sword. Therefore thus says the Lord GOD: Behold, I am
against Pharaoh king of Egypt, and will break
his arms, both the strong arm and the one
that was broken; and I will make the sword
fall from his hand. I will scatter the
Egyptians among the nations, and disperse
them throughout the lands. And I will
strengthen the arms of the king of Babylon,
and put my sword in his hand; but I will
break the arms of Pharaoh, and he will groan
before him like a man mortally wounded. I
will strengthen the arms of the king of
Babylon, but the arms of Pharaoh shall fall;
and they shall know that I am the LORD.
When I put my sword into the hand of the
king of Babylon, he shall stretch it out
against the land of Egypt; and I will scatter the Egyptians among the nations and
disperse them throughout the countries.
Then they will know that I am the LORD."

Pharaoh's greatness

In the eleventh year, in the third month, on
the first day of the month, the word of the
LORD came to me: "Son of man, say to
Pharaoh king of Egypt and to his multitude:
"Whom are you like in your greatness?
Behold, I will liken you to[d] a cedar in
Lebanon,
with fair branches and forest shade,
and of great height,
its top among the clouds.[e]
The waters nourished it,
the deep made it grow tall,
making its rivers flow[f]
round the place of its planting,
sending forth its streams
to all the trees of the forest.
So it towered high
above all the trees of the forest;
its boughs grew large
and its branches long,
from abundant water in its shoots.

---

[c] Cn: Heb *and Memphis, distresses by day*   [d] Cn: Heb *Behold, Assyria*   [e] Gk: Heb *thick boughs*
[f] Gk: Heb *going*

All the birds of the air
    made their nests in its boughs;
under its branches all the beasts of the
    field
    brought forth their young;
and under its shadow
    dwelt all great nations.
It was beautiful in its greatness,
    in the length of its branches;
for its roots went down
    to abundant waters.
The cedars in the garden of God could not
    rival it,
    nor the fir trees equal its boughs;
the plane trees were as nothing
    compared with its branches;
no tree in the garden of God
    was like it in beauty.
I made it beautiful
    in the mass of its branches,
and all the trees of Eden envied it,
    that were in the garden of God.
"Therefore thus says the Lord GOD:
Because it^g towered high and set its top
among the clouds,^{h} and its heart was proud
of its height, I will give it into the hand of a
mighty one of the nations; he shall surely
deal with it as its wickedness deserves. I
have cast it out. Foreigners, the most ter-
ible of the nations, will cut it down and leave
t. On the mountains and in all the valleys its
branches will fall, and its boughs will lie
broken in all the watercourses of the land;
and all the peoples of the earth will go from
its shadow and leave it. Upon its ruin will
dwell all the birds of the air, and upon its
branches will be all the beasts of the field.
All this is in order that no trees by the waters
may grow to lofty height or set their tops
among the clouds,^{h} and that no trees that
drink water may reach up to them in height;
for they are all given over to death, to the
nether world among mortal men, with those
who go down to the Pit.
"Thus says the Lord GOD: When it goes
down to Sheol I will make the deep mourn
for^i it, and restrain its rivers, and many
waters shall be stopped; I will clothe
Lebanon in gloom for it, and all the trees of
the field shall faint because of it. I will make
the nations quake at the sound of its fall,
when I cast it down to Sheol with those who
go down to the Pit; and all the trees of Eden,
the choice and best of Lebanon, all that drink
water, will be comforted in the nether world.
They also shall go down to Sheol with it, to
those who are slain by the sword; yea, those
who dwelt under its shadow among the
nations shall perish.^{j} Whom are you thus

like in glory and in greatness among the trees
of Eden? You shall be brought down with
the trees of Eden to the nether world; you
shall lie among the uncircumcised, with
those who are slain by the sword.
"This is Pharaoh and all his multitude, says
the Lord GOD."

Pharaoh's doom

In the twelfth year, in the twelfth month, on 32
the first day of the month, the word of the
LORD came to me: "Son of man, raise a 2
lamentation over Pharaoh king of Egypt, and
say to him:
"You consider yourself a lion among the
    nations,
    but you are like a dragon in the seas;
you burst forth in your rivers,
    trouble the waters with your feet,
    and foul their rivers.
Thus says the Lord GOD: 3
    I will throw my net over you
    with a host of many peoples;
    and I^k will haul you up in my dragnet.
And I will cast you on the ground,   4
    on the open field I will fling you,
and will cause all the birds of the air to
    settle on you,
    and I will gorge the beasts of the whole
    earth with you.
I will strew your flesh upon the moun- 5
    tains,
    and fill the valleys with your carcass.^{l}
I will drench the land even to the moun- 6
    tains
    with your flowing blood;
    and the watercourses will be full of
    you.
When I blot you out, I will cover the 7
    heavens,
    and make their stars dark;
I will cover the sun with a cloud,
    and the moon shall not give its light.
All the bright lights of heaven   8
    will I make dark over you,
    and put darkness upon your land,
                            says the Lord GOD.
"I will trouble the hearts of many peoples, 9
when I carry you captive^m among the
nations, into the countries which you have
not known. I will make many peoples 10
appalled at you, and their kings shall shudder
because of you, when I brandish my sword
before them; they shall tremble every
moment, every one for his own life, on the
day of your downfall. For thus says the Lord 11
GOD: The sword of the king of Babylon shall
come upon you. I will cause your multitude 12

---

^{g} Syr Vg: Heb *you* ^{h} Gk: Heb *thick boughs* ^{i} Gk: Heb *mourn for, I have covered* ^{j} Compare Gk: Heb obscure
^{k} Gk Vg: Heb *they* ^{l} Symmachus Syr Vg: Heb *your height* ^{m} Gk: Heb *bring your destruction*
31.6: Ezek 17.23; Dan 4.12–21; Mt 13.32; Mk 4.32; Lk 13.19.   31.8: (Gk): Rev 2.7.

to fall by the swords of mighty ones, all of them most terrible among the nations.

"They shall bring to naught the pride of Egypt,
and all its multitude shall perish.

13 I will destroy all its beasts
from beside many waters;
and no foot of man shall trouble them any more,
nor shall the hoofs of beasts trouble them.

14 Then I will make their waters clear,
and cause their rivers to run like oil,
says the Lord GOD.

15 When I make the land of Egypt desolate
and when the land is stripped of all that fills it,
when I smite all who dwell in it,
then they will know that I am the LORD.

16 This is a lamentation which shall be chanted; the daughters of the nations shall chant it; over Egypt, and over all her multitude, shall they chant it, says the Lord GOD."

17 In the twelfth year, in the first month,[n] on the fifteenth day of the month, the word of 18 the LORD came to me: "Son of man, wail over the multitude of Egypt, and send them down, her and the daughters of majestic nations, to the nether world, to those who have gone down to the Pit:

19 'Whom do you surpass in beauty?
Go down, and be laid with the uncircumcised.'

20 They shall fall amid those who are slain by the sword,[o] and with her shall lie all her 21 multitudes.[p] The mighty chiefs shall speak of them, with their helpers, out of the midst of Sheol: 'They have come down, they lie still, the uncircumcised, slain by the sword.'

22 "Assyria is there, and all her company, their graves round about her, all of them slain, 23 fallen by the sword; whose graves are set in the uttermost parts of the Pit, and her company is round about her grave; all of them slain, fallen by the sword, who spread terror in the land of the living.

"Elam is there, and all her multitude about her grave; all of them slain, fallen by the sword, who went down uncircumcised into the nether world, who spread terror in the land of the living, and they bear their shame with those who go down to the Pit. They have made her a bed among the slain with all her multitude, their graves round about her, all of them uncircumcised, slain by the sword; for terror of them was spread in the land of the living, and they bear their shame with those who go down to the Pit; they are placed among the slain.

"Meshech and Tubal are there, and all their multitude, their graves round about them, all of them uncircumcised, slain by the sword, for they spread terror in the land of the living. And they do not lie with the fallen mighty men of old[q] who went down to Sheol with their weapons of war, whose swords were laid under their heads, and whose shields[r] are upon their bones; for the terror of the mighty men was in the land of the living. So you shall be broken and lie among the uncircumcised, with those who are slain by the sword.

"Edom is there, her kings and all her princes, who for all their might are laid with those who are slain by the sword; they lie with the uncircumcised, with those who go down to the Pit.

"The princes of the north are there, all of them, and all the Sido'nians, who have gone down in shame with the slain, for all the terror which they caused by their might; they lie uncircumcised with those who are slain by the sword, and bear their shame with those who go down to the Pit.

"When Pharaoh sees them, he will comfort himself for all his multitude, Pharaoh and all his army, slain by the sword, says the Lord GOD. For he[s] spread terror in the land of the living; therefore he shall be laid among the uncircumcised, with those who are slain by the sword, Pharaoh and all his multitude, says the Lord GOD."

AFTER THE FALL OF JERUSALEM

33 THE word of the LORD came to me: "Son 2 of man, speak to your people and say to them, If I bring the sword upon a land, and the people of the land take a man from among them, and make him their watchman; 3 and if he sees the sword coming upon the land and blows the trumpet and warns the 4 people; then if any one who hears the sound

of the trumpet does not take warning, and the sword comes and takes him away, his blood shall be upon his own head. He heard the sound of the trumpet, and did not take warning; his blood shall be upon himself. But if he had taken warning, he would have saved his life. But if the watchman sees the sword coming and does not blow the

---

[n] Gk: Heb lacks *in the first month*   [o] Gk Syr: Heb *sword, the sword is delivered*
[p] Gk: Heb *they have drawn her away and all her multitudes*   [q] Gk Old Latin: Heb *of the uncircumcised*
[r] Cn: Heb *iniquities*   [s] Cn: Heb *I*
33.1–9: Ezek 3.16–21.

umpet, so that the people are not warned,
nd the sword comes, and takes any one of
hem; that man is taken away in his iniquity,
ut his blood I will require at the watch-
an's hand.

'So you, son of man, I have made a
atchman for the house of Israel; whenever
ou hear a word from my mouth, you shall
ive them warning from me. If I say to the
icked, O wicked man, you shall surely die,
nd you do not speak to warn the wicked to
urn from his way, that wicked man shall die
n his iniquity, but his blood I will require at
our hand. But if you warn the wicked to
urn from his way, and he does not turn from
is way; he shall die in his iniquity, but you
ill have saved your life.

"And you, son of man, say to the house of
srael, Thus have you said: 'Our transgres-
ions and our sins are upon us, and we waste
way because of them; how then can we
ve?' Say to them, As I live, says the Lord
GOD, I have no pleasure in the death of the
icked, but that the wicked turn from his
ay and live; turn back, turn back from your
vil ways; for why will you die, O house of
srael? And you, son of man, say to your
eople, The righteousness of the righteous
hall not deliver him when he transgresses;
nd as for the wickedness of the wicked, he
hall not fall by it when he turns from his
ickedness; and the righteous shall not be
ble to live by his righteousness^t when he
ins. Though I say to the righteous that
e shall surely live, yet if he trusts in his
ighteousness and commits iniquity, none of
is righteous deeds shall be remembered; but
n the iniquity that he has committed he shall
lie. Again, though I say to the wicked, 'You
shall surely die,' yet if he turns from his sin
nd does what is lawful and right, if the
wicked restores the pledge, gives back what
he has taken by robbery, and walks in the
statutes of life, committing no iniquity; he
shall surely live, he shall not die. None of
the sins that he has committed shall be
remembered against him; he has done what
is lawful and right, he shall surely
live.

"Yet your people say, 'The way of the Lord
is not just'; when it is their own way that is
not just. When the righteous turns from his
righteousness, and commits iniquity, he shall
die for it. And when the wicked turns from
his wickedness, and does what is lawful and
right, he shall live by it. Yet you say, 'The
way of the Lord is not just.' O house of
Israel, I will judge each of you according to
his ways."

News of Jerusalem

In the twelfth year of our exile, in the tenth 21 month, on the fifth day of the month, a man who had escaped from Jerusalem came to me and said, "The city has fallen." Now the 22 hand of the LORD had been upon me the evening before the fugitive came; and he had opened my mouth by the time the man came to me in the morning; so my mouth was opened, and I was no longer dumb.

The word of the LORD came to me: "Son of 23, man, the inhabitants of these waste places in 24 the land of Israel keep saying, 'Abraham was only one man, yet he got possession of the land; but we are many; the land is surely given us to possess.' Therefore say to them, 25 Thus says the Lord GOD: You eat flesh with the blood, and lift up your eyes to your idols, and shed blood; shall you then possess the land? You resort to the sword, you commit 26 abominations and each of you defiles his neighbour's wife; shall you then possess the land? Say this to them, Thus says the Lord 27 GOD: As I live, surely those who are in the waste places shall fall by the sword; and him that is in the open field I will give to the beasts to be devoured; and those who are in strongholds and in caves shall die by pestilence. And I will make the land a desolation 28 and a waste; and her proud might shall come to an end; and the mountains of Israel shall be so desolate that none will pass through. Then they will know that I am the LORD, 29 when I have made the land a desolation and a waste because of all their abominations which they have committed.

"As for you, son of man, your people who 30 talk together about you by the walls and at the doors of the houses, say to one another, each to his brother, 'Come, and hear what the word is that comes forth from the LORD.' And they come to you as people come, and 31 they sit before you as my people, and they hear what you say but they will not do it; for with their lips they show much love, but their heart is set on their gain. And, lo, you 32 are to them like one who sings love songs^u with a beautiful voice and plays well on an instrument, for they hear what you say, but they will not do it. When this comes—and 33 come it will!—then they will know that a prophet has been among them."

Government to be replaced

The word of the LORD came to me: "Son of 34 man, prophesy against the shepherds of 2 Israel, prophesy, and say to them, even to the shepherds, Thus says the Lord GOD: Ho, shepherds of Israel who have been feeding yourselves! Should not shepherds feed the 3 sheep? You eat the fat, you clothe yourselves with the wool, you slaughter the fat- 4 lings; but you do not feed the sheep. The weak you have not strengthened, the sick you have not healed, the crippled you have not bound up, the strayed you have not brought back, the lost you have not sought, and with 5 force and harshness you have ruled them. So they were scattered, because there was no shepherd; and they became food for all the 6 wild beasts. My sheep were scattered, they wandered over all the mountains and on every high hill; my sheep were scattered over all the face of the earth, with none to search or seek for them.

7 "Therefore, you shepherds, hear the word 8 of the LORD: As I live, says the Lord GOD, because my sheep have become a prey, and my sheep have become food for all the wild beasts, since there was no shepherd; and because my shepherds have not searched for my sheep, but the shepherds have fed themselves, and have not fed my sheep; 9 therefore, you shepherds, hear the word of 10 the LORD: Thus says the Lord GOD, Behold, I am against the shepherds; and I will require my sheep at their hand, and put a stop to their feeding the sheep; no longer shall the shepherds feed themselves. I will rescue my sheep from their mouths, that they may not be food for them.

11 "For thus says the Lord GOD: Behold, I, I myself will search for my sheep, and will seek them out. As a shepherd seeks out his flock when some of his sheep *v* have been scattered abroad, so will I seek out my sheep; and I will rescue them from all places where they have been scattered on a day of clouds and thick darkness. And I will bring them out from the peoples, and gather them from the countries, and will bring them into their own land; and I will feed them on the mountains of Israel, by the fountains, and in all the inhabited places of the country. I will feed them with good pasture, and upon the mountain heights of Israel shall be their pasture; there they shall lie down in good grazing land, and on fat pasture they shall feed on the mountains of Israel. I myself will be the shepherd of my sheep, and I will make them lie down, says the Lord GOD. I will seek the lost, and I will bring back the strayed, and I will bind up the crippled, and I will strengthen the weak, and the fat and the strong I will watch over; *w* I will feed them in justice.

"As for you, my flock, thus says the Lord GOD: Behold, I judge between sheep and sheep, rams and he-goats. Is it not enough for you to feed on the good pasture, that you must tread down with your feet the rest of your pasture; and to drink of clear water, that you must foul the rest with your feet? And must my sheep eat what you have trodden with your feet, and drink what you have fouled with your feet?

"Therefore, thus says the Lord GOD to

Ezek 33, 30

them: Behold, I, I myself will judge between
21 the fat sheep and the lean sheep. Because
you push with side and shoulder, and thrust
at all the weak with your horns, till you have
22 scattered them abroad, I will save my flock,
they shall no longer be a prey; and I will
23 judge between sheep and sheep. And I will
set up over them one shepherd, my servant
David, and he shall feed them: he shall feed
24 them and be their shepherd. And I, the
LORD, will be their God, and my servant
David shall be prince among them; I, the
LORD, have spoken.

25 "I will make with them a covenant of peace
and banish wild beasts from the land, so that
they may dwell securely in the wilderness
26 and sleep in the woods. And I will make
them and the places round about my hill a
blessing; and I will send down the showers in
their season; they shall be showers of bless-
27 ing. And the trees of the field shall yield
their fruit, and the earth shall yield its
increase, and they shall be secure in their
land; and they shall know that I am the
LORD, when I break the bars of their yoke,
and deliver them from the hand of those who
28 enslaved them. They shall no more be a prey
to the nations, nor shall the beasts of the land
devour them; they shall dwell securely, and
29 none shall make them afraid. And I will
provide for them prosperous *ˣ* plantations so
that they shall no more be consumed with
hunger in the land, and no longer suffer the
30 reproach of the nations. And they shall know
that I, the LORD their God, am with them,
and that they, the house of Israel, are my
31 people, says the Lord GOD. And you are my
sheep, the sheep of my pasture, *ʸ* and I am
your God, says the Lord GOD."

Land to be restored

35 The word of the LORD came to me: "Son of
2 man, set your face against Mount Se'ir, and
3 prophesy against it, and say to it, Thus says
the Lord GOD: Behold, I am against you,
Mount Se'ir, and I will stretch out my hand
against you, and I will make you a desolation
4 and a waste. I will lay your cities waste, and
you shall become a desolation; and you shall
5 know that I am the LORD. Because you
cherished perpetual enmity, and gave over
the people of Israel to the power of the sword
at the time of their calamity, at the time of
6 their final punishment; therefore, as I live,
says the Lord GOD, I will prepare you for
blood, and blood shall pursue you; because
you are guilty of blood, *ᶻ* therefore blood shall
7 pursue you. I will make Mount Se'ir a waste

and a desolation; and I will cut off from it all
who come and go. And I will fill your 8
mountains with the slain; on your hills and in
your valleys and in all your ravines those
slain with the sword shall fall. I will make 9
you a perpetual desolation, and your cities
shall not be inhabited. Then you will know
that I am the LORD.

"Because you said, 'These two nations and 10
these two countries shall be mine, and we
will take possession of them,'—although the
LORD was there—therefore, as I live, says the 11
Lord GOD, I will deal with you according to
the anger and envy which you showed
because of your hatred against them; and I
will make myself known among you, *ᵃ* when I
judge you. And you shall know that I, the 12
LORD, have heard all the revilings which you
uttered against the mountains of Israel,
saying, 'They are laid desolate, they are given
us to devour.' And you magnified yourselves 13
against me with your mouth, and multiplied
your words against me; I heard it. Thus says 14
the Lord GOD: For the rejoicing of the whole
earth I will make you desolate. As you 15
rejoiced over the inheritance of the house of
Israel, because it was desolate, so I will deal
with you; you shall be desolate, Mount Se'ir,
and all Edom, all of it. Then they will know
that I am the LORD.

"And you, son of man, prophesy to the 36
mountains of Israel, and say, O mountains of
Israel, hear the word of the LORD. Thus says 2
the Lord GOD: Because the enemy said of
you, 'Aha!' and, 'The ancient heights have
become our possession,' therefore prophesy, 3
and say, Thus says the Lord GOD: Because,
yea, because they made you desolate, and
crushed you from all sides, so that you
became the possession of the rest of the
nations, and you became the talk and evil
gossip of the people; therefore, O mountains 4
of Israel, hear the word of the Lord GOD:
Thus says the Lord GOD to the mountains
and the hills, the ravines and the valleys, the
desolate wastes and the deserted cities, which
have become a prey and derision to the rest
of the nations round about; therefore thus 5
says the Lord GOD: I speak in my hot
jealousy against the rest of the nations, and
against all Edom, who gave my land to
themselves as a possession with wholehearted
joy and utter contempt, that they might
possess *ᵇ* it and plunder it. Therefore 6
prophesy concerning the land of Israel, and
say to the mountains and hills, to the ravines
and valleys, Thus says the Lord GOD:

ˣ Gk Syr Old Latin: Heb *for renown*   *ʸ* Gk Old Latin: Heb *pasture you are men*
ᶻ Gk: Heb *you have hated blood*   *ᵃ* Gk: Heb *them*   *ᵇ* One Ms: Heb *drive out*
34.23: Ezek 37.24.

Behold, I speak in my jealous wrath, because you have suffered the reproach of the 7 nations; therefore thus says the Lord GOD: I swear that the nations that are round about you shall themselves suffer reproach.

8   "But you, O mountains of Israel, shall shoot forth your branches, and yield your fruit to my people Israel; for they will soon come 9 home. For, behold, I am for you, and I will turn to you, and you shall be tilled and sown; 10 and I will multiply men upon you, the whole house of Israel, all of it; the cities shall be 11 inhabited and the waste places rebuilt; and I will multiply upon you man and beast; and they shall increase and be fruitful; and I will cause you to be inhabited as in your former times, and will do more good to you than ever before. Then you will know that I am 12 the LORD. Yea, I will let men walk upon you, even my people Israel; and they shall possess you, and you shall be their inheritance, and you shall no longer bereave them of 13 children. Thus says the Lord GOD: Because men say to you, 'You devour men, and you 14 bereave your nation of children,' therefore you shall no longer devour men and no longer bereave your nation of children, says 15 the Lord GOD; and I will not let you hear any more the reproach of the nations, and you shall no longer bear the disgrace of the peoples and no longer cause your nation to stumble, says the Lord GOD."

People to be renewed

16, The word of the LORD came to me: "Son of 17 man, when the house of Israel dwelt in their own land, they defiled it by their ways and their doings; their conduct before me was like the uncleanness of a woman in her 18 impurity. So I poured out my wrath upon them for the blood which they had shed in the land, for the idols with which they had 19 defiled it. I scattered them among the nations, and they were dispersed through the countries; in accordance with their conduct 20 and their deeds I judged them. But when they came to the nations, wherever they came, they profaned my holy name, in that men said of them, 'These are the people of the LORD, and yet they had to go out of his 21 land.' But I had concern for my holy name, which the house of Israel caused to be profaned among the nations to which they came.

22   "Therefore say to the house of Israel, Thus says the Lord GOD: It is not for your sake, O house of Israel, that I am about to act, but for the sake of my holy name, which you have profaned among the nations to which you came. And I will vindicate the holiness of 2 my great name, which has been profaned among the nations, and which you have profaned among them; and the nations will know that I am the LORD, says the Lord GOD, when through you I vindicate my holiness before their eyes. For I will take 24 you from the nations, and gather you from all the countries, and bring you into your own land. I will sprinkle clean water upon 25 you, and you shall be clean from all your uncleannesses, and from all your idols I will cleanse you. A new heart I will give you, and 26 a new spirit I will put within you; and I will take out of your flesh the heart of stone and give you a heart of flesh. And I will put my 27 spirit within you, and cause you to walk in my statutes and be careful to observe my ordinances. You shall dwell in the land 28 which I gave to your fathers; and you shall be my people, and I will be your God. And I 29 will deliver you from all your uncleannesses; and I will summon the grain and make it abundant and lay no famine upon you. I will 30 make the fruit of the tree and the increase of the field abundant, that you may never again suffer the disgrace of famine among the nations. Then you will remember your evil 31 ways, and your deeds that were not good; and you will loathe yourselves for your iniquities and your abominable deeds. It is 32 not for your sake that I will act, says the Lord GOD; let that be known to you. Be ashamed and confounded for your ways, O house of Israel.

"Thus says the Lord GOD: On the day that 33 I cleanse you from all your iniquities, I will cause the cities to be inhabited, and the waste places shall be rebuilt. And the land that was 34 desolate shall be tilled, instead of being the desolation that it was in the sight of all who passed by. And they will say, 'This land that 35 was desolate has become like the garden of Eden; and the waste and desolate and ruined cities are now inhabited and fortified.' Then 36 the nations that are left round about you shall know that I, the LORD, have rebuilt the ruined places, and replanted that which was desolate; I, the LORD, have spoken, and I will do it.

"Thus says the Lord GOD: This also I will 37 let the house of Israel ask me to do for them: to increase their men like a flock. Like the 38 flock for sacrifices,[c] like the flock at Jerusalem during her appointed feasts, so shall the waste cities be filled with flocks of men. Then they will know that I am the LORD."

c Heb flock of holy things
36.26: Ezek 11.19; 18.31; 2 Cor 3.3.   36.27: Ezek 37.14; 1 Thess 4.8.   36.31: Ezek 6.9; 20.43.

The breath of the Lord

37 The hand of the Lord was upon me, and he brought me out by the Spirit of the Lord, and set me down in the midst of the valley;[d] 2 it was full of bones. And he led me round among them; and behold, there were very many upon the valley;[d] and lo, they were 3 very dry. And he said to me, "Son of man, can these bones live?" And I answered, "O 4 Lord God, thou knowest." Again he said to me, "Prophesy to these bones, and say to them, O dry bones, hear the word of the 5 Lord. Thus says the Lord God to these bones: Behold, I will cause breath[e] to enter 6 you, and you shall live. And I will lay sinews upon you, and will cause flesh to come upon you, and cover you with skin, and put breath[e] in you, and you shall live; and you shall know that I am the Lord."

7 So I prophesied as I was commanded; and as I prophesied, there was a noise, and behold, a rattling; and the bones came 8 together, bone to its bone. And as I looked, there were sinews on them, and flesh had come upon them, and skin had covered them; but there was no breath in them. 9 Then he said to me, "Prophesy to the breath, prophesy, son of man, and say to the breath,[f] Thus says the Lord God: Come from the four winds, O breath,[f] and breathe upon 10 these slain, that they may live." So I prophesied as he commanded me, and the breath came into them, and they lived, and stood upon their feet, an exceedingly great host.

11 Then he said to me, "Son of man, these bones are the whole house of Israel. Behold, they say, 'Our bones are dried up, and our 12 hope is lost; we are clean cut off.' Therefore prophesy, and say to them, Thus says the Lord God: Behold, I will open your graves, and raise you from your graves, O my people; and I will bring you home into the 13 land of Israel. And you shall know that I am the Lord, when I open your graves, and raise 14 you from your graves, O my people. And I will put my Spirit within you, and you shall live, and I will place you in your own land; then you shall know that I, the Lord, have spoken, and I have done it, says the Lord."

15, The word of the Lord came to me: "Son of 16 man, take a stick and write on it, 'For Judah, and the children of Israel associated with him'; then take another stick and write upon it, 'For Joseph (the stick of E'phraim) and all 17 the house of Israel associated with him'; and join them together into one stick, that they 18 may become one in your hand. And when your people say to you, 'Will you not show us what you mean by these?' say to them, Thus 19 says the Lord God: Behold, I am about to take the stick of Joseph (which is in the hand of E'phraim) and the tribes of Israel associated with him; and I will join[g] with it the stick of Judah, and make them one stick, that they may be one in my hand. When the 20 sticks on which you write are in your hand before their eyes, then say to them, Thus 21 says the Lord God: Behold, I will take the people of Israel from the nations among which they have gone, and will gather them from all sides, and bring them to their own land; and I will make them one nation in the 22 land, upon the mountains of Israel; and one king shall be king over them all; and they shall be no longer two nations, and no longer divided into two kingdoms. They shall not 23 defile themselves any more with their idols and their detestable things, or with any of their transgressions; but I will save them from all the backslidings in which they have sinned, and will cleanse them; and they shall be my people, and I will be their God.

"My servant David shall be king over them; 24 and they shall all have one shepherd. They shall follow my ordinances and be careful to observe my statutes. They shall dwell in the 25 land where your fathers dwelt that I gave to my servant Jacob; they and their children and their children's children shall dwell there for ever; and David my servant shall be their prince for ever. I will make a covenant of 26 peace with them; it shall be an everlasting covenant with them; and I will bless[h] them and multiply them, and will set my sanctuary in the midst of them for evermore. My 27 dwelling place shall be with them; and I will be their God, and they shall be my people. Then the nations will know that I the Lord 28 sanctify Israel, when my sanctuary is in the midst of them for evermore."

Final triumph

The word of the Lord came to me: "Son of **38** man, set your face toward Gog, of the land of 2 Magog, the chief prince of Meshech and Tubal, and prophesy against him and say, 3 Thus says the Lord God: Behold, I am against you, O Gog, chief prince of Meshech and Tubal; and I will turn you about, and 4 put hooks into your jaws, and I will bring you forth, and all your army, horses and horsemen, all of them clothed in full armour, a great company, all of them with buckler and shield, wielding swords; Persia, Cush, 5 and Put are with them, all of them with

---

[d] Or plain   [e] Or spirit   [f] Or wind or spirit   [g] Heb join them   [h] Tg: Heb give
37.5, 10: Rev 11.11.   **37.14:** Ezek 36.27; 1 Thess 4.8.   **37.26:** Heb 13.20.
37.27: Ex 25.8; 29.45; Lev 26.12; Jer 31.1; 2 Cor 6.16; Rev 21.3.   **38.2, 9, 15:** Rev 20.8.

6 shield and helmet; Gomer and all his hordes; Beth-togar′mah from the uttermost parts of the north with all his hordes—many peoples are with you.

7 "Be ready and keep ready, you and all the hosts that are assembled about you, and be a
8 guard for them. After many days you will be mustered; in the latter years you will go against the land that is restored from war, the land where people were gathered from many nations upon the mountains of Israel, which had been a continual waste; its people were brought out from the nations and now dwell
9 securely, all of them. You will advance, coming on like a storm, you will be like a cloud covering the land, you and all your hordes, and many peoples with you.

Gog's evil scheme

10 "Thus says the Lord GOD: On that day thoughts will come into your mind, and you
11 will devise an evil scheme and say, 'I will go up against the land of unwalled villages; I will fall upon the quiet people who dwell securely, all of them dwelling without walls,
12 and having no bars or gates'; to seize spoil and carry off plunder; to assail the waste places which are now inhabited, and the people who were gathered from the nations, who have gotten cattle and goods, who dwell
13 at the centre of the earth. Sheba and Dedan and the merchants of Tarshish and all its villages will say to you, 'Have you come to seize spoil? Have you assembled your hosts to carry off plunder, to carry away silver and gold, to take away cattle and goods, to seize great spoil?'

14 "Therefore, son of man, prophesy, and say to Gog, Thus says the Lord GOD: On that day when my people Israel are dwelling
15 securely, you will bestir yourself[i] and come from your place out of the uttermost parts of the north, you and many peoples with you, all of them riding on horses, a great host, a
16 mighty army; you will come up against my people Israel, like a cloud covering the land. In the latter days I will bring you against my land, that the nations may know me, when through you, O Gog, I vindicate my holiness before their eyes.

17 "Thus says the Lord GOD: Are you he of whom I spoke in former days by my servants the prophets of Israel, who in those days prophesied for years that I would bring you
18 against them? But on that day, when Gog shall come against the land of Israel, says the
19 Lord GOD, my wrath will be roused. For in my jealousy and in my blazing wrath I

declare, On that day there shall be a great
20 shaking in the land of Israel; the fish of the sea, and the birds of the air, and the beasts of the field, and all creeping things that creep on the ground, and all the men that are upon the face of the earth, shall quake at my presence, and the mountains shall be thrown down, and the cliffs shall fall, and every wall shall tumble to the ground. I will summon
21 every kind of terror[j] against Gog,[k] says the Lord GOD; every man's sword will be against his brother. With pestilence and bloodshed I
22 will enter into judgment with him; and I will rain upon him and his hordes and the many peoples that are with him, torrential rains and hailstones, fire and brimstone. So I will
23 show my greatness and my holiness and make myself known in the eyes of many nations. Then they will know that I am the LORD.

39 "And you, son of man, prophesy against Gog, and say, Thus says the Lord GOD: Behold, I am against you, O Gog, chief prince of Meshech and Tubal; and I will
2 turn you about and drive you forward, and bring you up from the uttermost parts of the north, and lead you against the mountains of Israel; then I will strike your bow from your
3 left hand, and will make your arrows drop out of your right hand. You shall fall upon
4 the mountains of Israel, you and all your hordes and the peoples that are with you; I will give you to birds of prey of every sort and to the wild beasts to be devoured. You
5 shall fall in the open field; for I have spoken, says the Lord GOD. I will send fire on
6 Magog and on those who dwell securely in the coastlands; and they shall know that I am the LORD.

7 "And my holy name I will make known in the midst of my people Israel; and I will not let my holy name be profaned any more; and the nations shall know that I am the LORD, the Holy One in Israel. Behold, it is coming
8 and it will be brought about, says the Lord GOD. That is the day of which I have spoken.

9 "Then those who dwell in the cities of Israel will go forth and make fires of the weapons and burn them, shields and bucklers, bows and arrows, handpikes and spears, and they will make fires of them for seven
10 years; so that they will not need to take wood out of the field or cut down any out of the forests, for they will make their fires of the weapons; they will despoil those who despoiled them, and plunder those who plundered them, says the Lord GOD.

i Gk: Heb *will you not know?*   *j* Gk: Heb *a sword to all my mountains*   *k* Heb *him*
38.22: Rev 8.7; 14.10.   39.4, 17–20: Rev 19.17, 18, 21.

11 "On that day I will give to Gog a place for burial in Israel, the Valley of the Travellers[1] east of the sea; it will block the travellers, for there Gog and all his multitude will be buried; it will be called the Valley of 12 Hamon-gog.[m] For seven months the house of Israel will be burying them, in order to 13 cleanse the land. All the people of the land will bury them; and it will redound to their honour on the day that I show my glory, says

and all the nations shall see my judgment which I have executed, and my hand which I have laid on them. The house of Israel shall 22 know that I am the LORD their God, from that day forward. And the nations shall 23 know that the house of Israel went into captivity for their iniquity, because they dealt so treacherously with me that I hid my face from them and gave them into the hand of their adversaries, and they all fell by the

The land of Israel

14 the Lord GOD. They will set apart men to pass through the land continually and bury[n] those remaining upon the face of the land, so as to cleanse it; at the end of seven months 15 they will make their search. And when these pass through the land and any one sees a man's bone, he shall set up a sign by it, till the buriers have buried it in the Valley of 16 Hamon-gog. (A city Hamo'nah[o] is there also.) Thus shall they cleanse the land.

17 "As for you, son of man, thus says the Lord GOD: Speak to the birds of every sort and to all beasts of the field, 'Assemble and come, gather from all sides to the sacrificial feast which I am preparing for you, a great sacrificial feast upon the mountains of Israel, 18 and you shall eat flesh and drink blood. You shall eat the flesh of the mighty, and drink the blood of the princes of the earth—of rams, of lambs, and of goats, of bulls, all of 19 them fatlings of Bashan. And you shall eat fat till you are filled, and drink blood till you 20 are drunk, at the sacrificial feast which I am preparing for you. And you shall be filled at my table with horses and riders, with mighty men and all kinds of warriors,' says the Lord GOD.

21 "And I will set my glory among the nations;

sword. I dealt with them according to their 24 uncleanness and their transgressions, and hid my face from them.

"Therefore thus says the Lord GOD: Now I 25 will restore the fortunes of Jacob, and have mercy upon the whole house of Israel; and I will be jealous for my holy name. They shall 26 forget their shame, and all the treachery they have practised against me, when they dwell securely in their land with none to make them afraid, when I have brought them back 27 from the peoples and gathered them from their enemies' lands, and through them have vindicated my holiness in the sight of many nations. Then they shall know that I am the 28 LORD their God because I sent them into exile among the nations, and then gathered them into their own land. I will leave none of them remaining among the nations any more; and I will not hide my face any more 29 from them, when I pour out my Spirit upon the house of Israel, says the Lord GOD."

[1] Or Abarim   [m] That is the multitude of Gog   [n] Gk Syr: Heb bury the travellers
[o] That is Multitude

THE TEMPLE OF THE HOLY CITY

40 IN the twenty-fifth year of our exile, at the beginning of the year, on the tenth day of the month, in the fourteenth year after the city was conquered, on that very day, the 2 hand of the LORD was upon me, and brought me in the visions of God into the land of Israel, and set me down upon a very high mountain, on which was a structure like a 3 city opposite me.*ᵖ* When he brought me there, behold, there was a man, whose appearance was like bronze, with a line of flax and a measuring reed in his hand; and he 4 was standing in the gateway. And the man said to me, "Son of man, look with your eyes, and hear with your ears, and set your mind upon all that I shall show you, for you were brought here in order that I might show it to you; declare all that you see to the house of Israel."

The temple buildings

5 And behold, there was a wall all around the outside of the temple area, and the length of the measuring reed in the man's hand was six long cubits, each being a cubit and a handbreadth in length; so he measured the thickness of the wall, one reed; and the height, one reed. Then he went into the 6 gateway facing east, going up its steps, and measured the threshold of the gate, one reed deep;*�q* and the side rooms, one reed long, and 7 one reed broad; and the space between the side rooms, five cubits; and the threshold of the gate by the vestibule of the gate at the inner end, one reed. Then he measured the 8 vestibule of the gateway, eight cubits; and its 9 jambs, two cubits; and the vestibule of the gate was at the inner end. And there were 10 three side rooms on either side of the east gate; the three were of the same size; and the jambs on either side were of the same size. Then he measured the breadth of the 11 opening of the gateway, ten cubits; and the breadth of the gateway, thirteen cubits. There was a barrier before the side rooms, 12 one cubit on either side; and the side rooms were six cubits on either side. Then he 13 measured the gate from the back*ʳ* of the one side room to the back*ʳ* of the other, a breadth of five and twenty cubits, from door to door. He measured also the vestibule, twenty 14 cubits; and round about the vestibule of the gateway was the court.*ˢ* From the front of 15 the gate at the entrance to the end of the inner vestibule of the gate was fifty cubits. And the gateway had windows round about, 16 narrowing inwards into their jambs in the side rooms, and likewise the vestibule had windows round about inside, and on the jambs were palm trees.

Then he brought me into the outer court; 17 and behold, there were chambers and a pavement, round about the court; thirty chambers fronted on the pavement. And the 18 pavement ran along the side of the gates, corresponding to the length of the gates; this was the lower pavement. Then he measured 19

ᵖ Gk: Heb *on the south*   �q Heb *deep, and one threshold, one reed deep*   ʳ Compare Gk: Heb *roof*
ˢ Compare Gk: Heb *and he made the jambs sixty cubits, and to the jamb of the court was the gateway round about*
40.1–43.17: 1 Kings 6–7; 2 Chron 3–4.   40.2: Rev 21.10.   40.3, 5: Rev 21.15.

the distance from the inner front of[t] the lower gate to the outer front of the inner court, a hundred cubits.

Then he went before me to the north, and behold, there was a gate[u] which faced toward the north, belonging to the outer court. He measured its length and its breadth. Its side rooms, three on either side, and its jambs and its vestibule were of the same size as those of the first gate; its length was fifty cubits, and its breadth twenty-five cubits. And its windows, its vestibule, and its palm trees were of the same size as those of the gate which faced toward the east; and seven steps led up to it; and its vestibule was on the inside. And opposite the gate on the north, as on the east, was a gate to the inner court; and he measured from gate to gate, a hundred cubits.

And he led me toward the south, and behold, there was a gate on the south; and he measured its jambs and its vestibule; they had the same size as the others. And there were windows round about in it and in its vestibule, like the windows of the others; its length was fifty cubits, and its breadth twenty-five cubits. And there were seven steps leading up to it, and its vestibule was on the inside; and it had palm trees on its jambs, one on either side. And there was a gate on the south of the inner court; and he measured from gate to gate toward the south, a hundred cubits.

Then he brought me to the inner court by the south gate, and he measured the south gate; it was of the same size as the others. Its side rooms, its jambs, and its vestibule were of the same size as the others; and there were windows round about in it and in its vestibule; its length was fifty cubits, and its breadth twenty-five cubits. And there were vestibules round about, twenty-five cubits long and five cubits broad. Its vestibule faced the outer court, and palm trees were on its jambs, and its stairway had eight steps.

Then he brought me to the inner court on the east side, and he measured the gate; it was of the same size as the others. Its side rooms, its jambs, and its vestibule were of the same size as the others; and there were windows round about in it and in its vestibule; its length was fifty cubits, and its breadth twenty-five cubits. Its vestibule faced the outer court, and it had palm trees on its jambs, one on either side; and its stairway had eight steps.

Then he brought me to the north gate, and

he measured it; it had the same size as the others. Its side rooms, its jambs, and its vestibule were of the same size as the others;[v] and it had windows round about; its length was fifty cubits, and its breadth twenty-five cubits. Its vestibule[w] faced the outer court, and it had palm trees on its jambs, one on either side; and its stairway had eight steps.

The tables

There was a chamber with its door in the vestibule of the gate,[x] where the burnt offering was to be washed. And in the vestibule of the gate were two tables on either side, on which the burnt offering and the sin offering and the guilt offering were to be slaughtered. And on the outside of the vestibule[y] at the entrance of the north gate were two tables; and on the other side of the vestibule of the gate were two tables. Four tables were on the inside, and four tables on the outside of the side of the gate, eight tables, on which the sacrifices were to be slaughtered. And there were also four tables of hewn stone for the burnt offering, a cubit and a half long, and a cubit and a half broad, and one cubit high, on which the instruments were to be laid with which the burnt offerings and the sacrifices were slaughtered. And hooks, a hand-breadth long, were fastened round about within. And on the tables the flesh of the offering was to be laid.

Then he brought me from without into the inner court, and behold, there were two chambers[z] in the inner court, one[a] at the side of the north gate facing south, the other at the side of the south[b] gate facing north. And he said to me, This chamber which faces south is for the priests who have charge of the temple, and the chamber which faces north is for the priests who have charge of the altar; these are the sons of Zadok, who alone among the sons of Levi may come near to the LORD to minister to him. And he measured the court, a hundred cubits long, and a hundred cubits broad, foursquare; and the altar was in front of the temple.

Then he brought me to the vestibule of the temple and measured the jambs of the vestibule, five cubits on either side; and the breadth of the gate was fourteen cubits; and the sidewalls of the gate were three cubits[c] on either side. The length of the vestibule was twenty cubits, and the breadth twelve[d]

[t] Compare Gk: Heb *from before* [u] Gk: Heb *a hundred cubits on the east and on the north.* [20] *And the gate*
[v] One Ms Compare verses 29 and 33: Heb lacks *were of the same size as the others*
[w] Gk Vg Compare verses 26, 31, 34: Heb *jambs* [x] Cn: Heb *at the jambs of the gates*
[y] Cn: Heb *to him who goes up* [z] Gk: Heb *and from without to the inner gate were chambers for singers*
[a] Gk: Heb *which* [b] Gk: Heb *east* [c] Gk: Heb *and the breadth of the gates was three cubits* [d] Gk: Heb *eleven*

cubits; and ten steps led up[e] to it; and there were pillars beside the jambs on either side.

The holy of holies

41 Then he brought me to the nave, and measured the jambs; on each side six cubits 2 was the breadth of the jambs.[f] And the breadth of the entrance was ten cubits; and the sidewalls of the entrance were five cubits on either side; and he measured the length of the nave, forty cubits, and its breadth, twenty 3 cubits. Then he went into the inner room and measured the jambs of the entrance, two cubits; and the breadth of the entrance, six cubits; and the sidewalls[g] of the entrance, 4 seven cubits. And he measured the length of the room, twenty cubits, and its breadth, twenty cubits, beyond the nave. And he said to me, This is the most holy place.

5 Then he measured the wall of the temple, six cubits thick; and the breadth of the side chambers, four cubits, round about the 6 temple. And the side chambers were in three stories, one over another, thirty in each story. There were offsets[h] all around the wall of the temple to serve as supports for the side chambers, so that they should not be 7 supported by the wall of the temple. And the side chambers became broader as they rose[i] from story to story, corresponding to the enlargement of the offset[j] from story to story round about the temple; on the side of the temple a stairway led upward, and thus one went up from the lowest story to the top 8 story through the middle story. I saw also that the temple had a raised platform round about; the foundations of the side chambers 9 measured a full reed of six long cubits. The thickness of the outer wall of the side chambers was five cubits; and the part of the platform which was left free was five cubits.[k] Between the platform[l] of the temple 10 and the chambers of the court was a breadth of twenty cubits round about the temple on 11 every side. And the doors of the side chambers opened on the part of the platform that was left free, one door toward the north, and another door toward the south; and the breadth of the part that was left free was five cubits round about.

12 The building that was facing the temple yard on the west side was seventy cubits broad; and the wall of the building was five cubits thick round about, and its length ninety cubits.

Then he measured the temple, a hundred cubits long; and the yard and the building with its walls, a hundred cubits long; also the breadth of the east front of the temple and the yard, a hundred cubits.

Interior of the temple

Then he measured the length of the building facing the yard which was at the west and its walls[m] on either side, a hundred cubits.

The nave of the temple and the inner room and the outer[n] vestibule were panelled[o] round about all three had windows with recessed[p] frames. Over against the threshold the temple was panelled with wood round about, from the floor up to the windows (now the windows were covered), to the space above the door, even to the inner room, and on the outside. And on all the walls round about in the inner room and the nave were carved likenesses[q] of cherubim and palm trees, a palm tree between cherub and cherub. Every cherub had two faces: the face of a man toward the palm tree on the one side, and the face of a young lion toward the palm tree on the other side. They were carved on the whole temple round about; from the floor to above the door cherubim and palm trees were carved on the wall.[r]

The doorposts of the nave were squared; and in front of the holy place was something resembling an altar of wood, three cubits high, two cubits long, and two cubits broad; its corners, its base,[t] and its walls were of wood. He said to me, "This is the table which is before the LORD." The nave and the holy place had each a double door. The doors had two leaves apiece, two swinging leaves for each door. And on the doors of the nave were carved cherubim and palm trees, such as were carved on the walls; and there was a canopy of wood in front of the vestibule outside. And there were recessed windows and palm trees on either side, on the sidewalls of the vestibule.[u]

Then he led me out into the inner[v] court, 42 toward the north, and he brought me to the chambers which were opposite the temple yard and opposite the building on the north. The length of the building which was on the

---

[e] Gk: Heb *and by steps which went up*　[f] Compare Gk: Heb *tent*　[g] Gk: Heb *breadth*
[h] Gk Compare 1 Kings 6.6: Heb *they entered*　[i] Cn: Heb *it was surrounded*
[j] Gk: Heb *for the encompassing of the temple*　[k] Syr: Heb lacks *five cubits*
[l] Cn: Heb *house of the side chambers*　[m] Cn: The meaning of the Hebrew term is unknown
[n] Gk: Heb *of the court*　[o] Gk: Heb *the thresholds*
[p] Cn Compare Gk 1 Kings 6.4: The meaning of the Hebrew term is unknown
[q] Cn: Heb *measures and carved*　[r] Cn Compare verse 25: Heb *and the wall*　[s] Gk: Heb lacks *two cubits broad*
[t] Gk: Heb *length*　[u] Cn: Heb *vestibule. And the side chambers of the temple and the canopies*　[v] Gk: Heb *outer*

orth side[w] was[x] a hundred cubits, and the breadth fifty cubits. Adjoining the twenty cubits which belonged to the inner court, and facing the pavement which belonged to the outer court, was gallery[y] against gallery[y] in three stories. And before the chambers was a passage inward, ten cubits wide and a hundred cubits long,[z] and their doors were on the north. Now the upper chambers were narrower, for the galleries[y] took more away from them than from the lower and middle chambers in the building. For they were in three stories, and they had no pillars like the pillars of the outer[a] court; hence the upper chambers were set back from the ground more than the lower and the middle ones. And there was a wall outside parallel to the chambers, toward the outer court, opposite the chambers, fifty cubits long. For the chambers on the outer court were fifty cubits long, while those opposite the temple were a hundred cubits long. Below these chambers was an entrance on the east side, as one enters them from the outer court, where the outside wall begins.[b]

On the south[c] also, opposite the yard and opposite the building, there were chambers with a passage in front of them; they were similar to the chambers on the north, of the same length and breadth, with the same exits[d] and arrangements and doors. And below the south chambers was an entrance on the east side, where one enters the passage, and opposite them was a dividing wall.[e]

Then he said to me, "The north chambers and the south chambers opposite the yard are the holy chambers, where the priests who approach the LORD shall eat the most holy offerings; there they shall put the most holy offerings—the cereal offering, the sin offering, and the guilt offering, for the place is holy. When the priests enter the holy place, they shall not go out of it into the outer court without laying there the garments in which they minister, for these are holy; they shall put on other garments before they go near to that which is for the people."

The whole enclosure

Now when he had finished measuring the interior of the temple area, he led me out by the gate which faced east, and measured the

temple area round about. He measured the 16 east side with the measuring reed, five hundred cubits by the measuring reed. Then he turned and measured[f] the north 17 side, five hundred cubits by the measuring reed. Then he turned and measured[f] the 18 south side, five hundred cubits by the measuring reed. Then he turned to the west 19 side and measured, five hundred cubits by the measuring reed. He measured it on the 20 four sides. It had a wall around it, five hundred cubits long and five hundred cubits broad, to make a separation between the holy and the common.

The return of the Lord

Afterward he brought me to the gate, the **43** gate facing east. And behold, the glory of the 2 God of Israel came from the east; and the sound of his coming was like the sound of many waters; and the earth shone with his glory. And[g] the vision I saw was like the 3 vision which I had seen when he came to destroy the city, and[h] like the vision which I had seen by the river Chebar; and I fell upon my face. As the glory of the LORD entered 4 the temple by the gate facing east, the Spirit 5 lifted me up, and brought me into the inner court; and behold, the glory of the LORD filled the temple.

While the man was standing beside me, I 6 heard one speaking to me out of the temple; and he said to me, "Son of man, this is the 7 place of my throne and the place of the soles of my feet, where I will dwell in the midst of the people of Israel for ever. And the house of Israel shall no more defile my holy name, neither they, nor their kings, by their harlotry, and by the dead bodies[i] of their kings, by setting their threshold by my threshold 8 and their doorposts beside my doorposts, with only a wall between me and them. They have defiled my holy name by their abominations which they have committed, so I have consumed them in my anger. Now let 9 them put away their idolatry and the dead bodies[i] of their kings far from me, and I will dwell in their midst for ever.

"And you, son of man, describe to the 10 house of Israel the temple and its appearance and plan,[j] that they may be ashamed of their iniquities. And if they are ashamed of all 11 that they have done, portray[k] the temple, its

---

[w] Gk: Heb *door*   [x] Gk: Heb *before the length*   [y] The meaning of the Hebrew word is unknown
[z] Gk Syr: Heb *a way of one cubit*   [a] Gk: Heb lacks *outer*
[b] Cn Compare Gk: Heb *in the breadth of the wall of the court*   [c] Gk: Heb *east*   [d] Heb *and all their exits*
[e] Cn: Heb *And according to the entrances of the chambers that were toward the south was an entrance at the head of the way, the way before the dividing wall toward the east as one enters them*
[f] Gk: Heb *measuring reed round about. He measured*   [g] Gk: Heb *And like the vision*
[h] Syr: Heb *and the visions*   [i] Or *the monuments*   [j] Gk: Heb *the temple that they may measure the pattern*
[k] Gk: Heb *the form of*
43.2: Ezek 1.24; Rev 1.15; 14.2; 19.6.

arrangement, its exits and its entrances, and its whole form; and make known to them all its ordinances and all its laws; and write it down in their sight, so that they may observe and perform all its laws[l] and all its ordi-
12 nances. This is the law of the temple: the whole territory round about upon the top of the mountain shall be most holy. Behold, this is the law of the temple.

The altar

13 "These are the dimensions of the altar by cubits (the cubit being a cubit and a handbreadth): its base shall be one cubit high,[m] and one cubit broad, with a rim of one span around its edge. And this shall be the
14 height[n] of the altar: from the base on the ground to the lower ledge, two cubits, with a breadth of one cubit; and from the smaller ledge to the larger ledge, four cubits, with a
15 breadth of one cubit; and the altar hearth, four cubits; and from the altar hearth projecting upward, four horns, one cubit
16 high.[o] The altar hearth shall be square,
17 twelve cubits long by twelve broad. The ledge also shall be square, fourteen cubits long by fourteen broad, with a rim around it half a cubit broad, and its base one cubit round about. The steps of the altar shall face east."
18 And he said to me, "Son of man, thus says the Lord GOD: These are the ordinances for the altar: On the day when it is erected for offering burnt offerings upon it and for
19 throwing blood against it, you shall give to the Levitical priests of the family of Zadok, who draw near to me to minister to me, says
20 the Lord GOD, a bull for a sin offering. And you shall take some of its blood, and put it on the four horns of the altar, and on the four corners of the ledge, and upon the rim round about; thus you shall cleanse the altar and
21 make atonement for it. You shall also take the bull of the sin offering, and it shall be burnt in the appointed place belonging to the
22 temple, outside the sacred area. And on the second day you shall offer a he-goat without blemish for a sin offering; and the altar shall be cleansed, as it was cleansed with the bull.
23 When you have finished cleansing it, you shall offer a bull without blemish and a ram
24 from the flock without blemish. You shall present them before the LORD, and the priests shall sprinkle salt upon them and offer them up as a burnt offering to the
25 LORD. For seven days you shall provide daily a goat for a sin offering; also a bull and

a ram from the flock, without blemish, shall be provided. Seven days shall they make atonement for the altar and purify it, and so consecrate it. And when they have completed these days, then from the eighth day onward the priests shall offer upon the altar your burnt offerings and your peace offerings; and I will accept you, says the Lord GOD."

Temple officers

Then he brought me back to the outer gate of the sanctuary, which faces east; and it was shut. And he[p] said to me, "This gate shall remain shut; it shall not be opened, and no one shall enter by it; for the LORD, the God of Israel, has entered by it; therefore it shall remain shut. Only the prince may sit in it to eat bread before the LORD; he shall enter by way of the vestibule of the gate, and shall go out by the same way."

Then he brought me by way of the north gate to the front of the temple; and I looked, and behold, the glory of the LORD filled the temple of the LORD; and I fell upon my face. And the LORD said to me, "Son of man, mark well, see with your eyes, and hear with your ears all that I shall tell you concerning all the ordinances of the temple of the LORD and all its laws; and mark well those who may be admitted to[q] the temple and all those who are to be excluded from the sanctuary. And say to the rebellious house,[r] to the house of Israel, Thus says the Lord GOD: O house of Israel, let there be an end to all your abominations, in admitting foreigners, uncircumcised in heart and flesh, to be in my sanctuary, profaning it,[s] when you offer to me my food, the fat and the blood. You[t] have broken my covenant, in addition to all your abominations. And you have not kept charge of my holy things; but you have set foreigners to keep my charge in my sanctuary.

The Levites

"Therefore[u] thus says the Lord GOD: No foreigner, uncircumcised in heart and flesh, of all the foreigners who are among the people of Israel, shall enter my sanctuary. But the Levites who went far from me, going astray from me after their idols when Israel went astray, shall bear their punishment. They shall be ministers in my sanctuary, having oversight at the gates of the temple, and serving in the temple; they shall slay the

---

[l] Compare Gk: Heb *its whole form*   [m] Gk: Heb lacks *high*   [n] Gk: Heb *back*   [o] Gk: Heb lacks *one cubit high*
[p] Cn: Heb *the LORD*   [q] Cn: Heb *the entrance of*   [r] Gk: Heb lacks *house*   [s] Gk: Heb *it my temple*
[t] Gk Syr Vg: Heb *they*   [u] Gk: Heb *for you*
44.4: Rev 15.8.

burnt offering and the sacrifice for the people, and they shall attend on the people, to serve them. Because they ministered to them before their idols and became a stumbling block of iniquity to the house of Israel, therefore I have sworn concerning them, says the Lord GOD, that they shall bear their punishment. They shall not come near to me, to serve me as priest, nor come near any of my sacred things and the things that are most sacred; but they shall bear their shame, because of the abominations which they have committed. Yet I will appoint them to keep charge of the temple, to do all its service and all that is to be done in it.

Priest and Levite

The priests

5 "But the Levitical priests, the sons of Zadok, who kept the charge of my sanctuary when the people of Israel went astray from me, shall come near to me to minister to me; and they shall attend on me to offer me the fat and the blood, says the Lord GOD; they shall enter my sanctuary, and they shall approach my table, to minister to me, and they shall keep my charge. When they enter the gates of the inner court, they shall wear linen garments; they shall have nothing of wool on them, while they minister at the gates of the inner court, and within. They shall have linen turbans upon their heads, and linen breeches upon their loins; they shall not gird themselves with anything that causes sweat. And when they go out into the outer court to the people, they shall put off the garments in which they have been ministering, and lay them in the holy chambers; and they shall put on other garments, lest they communicate holiness to the people with their garments. They shall not shave 20 their heads or let their locks grow long; they shall only trim the hair of their heads. No 21 priest shall drink wine, when he enters the inner court. They shall not marry a widow, 22 or a divorced woman, but only a virgin of the stock of the house of Israel, or a widow who is the widow of a priest. They shall teach my 23 people the difference between the holy and the common, and show them how to distinguish between the unclean and the clean. In 24 a controversy they shall act as judges, and they shall judge it according to my judgments. They shall keep my laws and my statutes in all my appointed feasts, and they shall keep my sabbaths holy. They shall not 25 defile themselves by going near to a dead person; however, for father or mother, for son or daughter, for brother or unmarried sister they may defile themselves. After he is 26 defiled,^{v} he shall count for himself seven days, and then he shall be clean.^{w} And on 27 the day that he goes into the holy place, into the inner court, to minister in the holy place, he shall offer his sin offering, says the Lord GOD.

"They shall have no^x inheritance; I am 28 their inheritance: and you shall give them no possession in Israel; I am their possession. They shall eat the cereal offering, the sin 29 offering, and the guilt offering; and every devoted thing in Israel shall be theirs. And 30 the first of all the first fruits of all kinds, and every offering of all kinds from all your offerings, shall belong to the priests; you shall also give to the priests the first of your coarse meal, that a blessing may rest on your house. The priests shall not eat of anything, 31 whether bird or beast, that has died of itself or is torn.

"When you allot the land as a possession, **45** you shall set apart for the LORD a portion of the land as a holy district, twenty-five thousand cubits long and twenty^y thousand cubits broad; it shall be holy throughout its whole extent. Of this a square plot of five 2 hundred by five hundred cubits shall be for the sanctuary, with fifty cubits for an open space around it. And in the holy district you 3 shall measure off a section twenty-five thousand cubits long and ten thousand broad, in which shall be the sanctuary, the most holy place. It shall be the holy portion 4 of the land; it shall be for the priests, who

---

^{v} Syr: Heb *cleansed* ^{w} Syr: Heb lacks *and then he shall be clean* ^{x} Vg: Heb *as an* ^{y} Gk: Heb *ten* minister in the sanctuary and approach the LORD to minister to him; and it shall be a place for their houses and a holy place for the sanctuary. Another section, twenty-five thousand cubits long and ten thousand cubits broad, shall be for the Levites who minister at the temple, as their possession for cities to live in.[z]

6 "Alongside the portion set apart as the holy district you shall assign for the possession of the city an area five thousand cubits broad, and twenty-five thousand cubits long; it shall belong to the whole house of Israel.

The prince's portion

7 "And to the prince shall belong the land on both sides of the holy district and the property of the city, alongside the holy district and the property of the city, on the west and on the east, corresponding in length to one of the tribal portions, and extending from the western to the eastern boundary of 8 the land. It is to be his property in Israel. And my princes shall no more oppress my people; but they shall let the house of Israel have the land according to their tribes.

9 "Thus says the Lord GOD: Enough, O princes of Israel! Put away violence and oppression, and execute justice and righteousness; cease your evictions of my people, says the Lord GOD.

10 "You shall have just balances, a just ephah, 11 and a just bath. The ephah and the bath shall be of the same measure, the bath containing one tenth of a homer, and the ephah one tenth of a homer; the homer shall 12 be the standard measure. The shekel shall be twenty gerahs; five shekels shall be five shekels, and ten shekels shall be ten shekels, and your mina shall be fifty shekels.[a]

13 "This is the offering which you shall make: one sixth of an ephah from each homer of wheat, and one sixth of an ephah from each 14 homer of barley, and as the fixed portion of oil,[b] one tenth of a bath from each cor (the 15 cor,[c] like the homer, contains ten baths); and one sheep from every flock of two hundred, from the families[d] of Israel. This is the offering for cereal offerings, burnt offerings, and peace offerings, to make atonement for 16 them, says the Lord GOD. All the people of the land shall give[e] this offering to the prince 17 in Israel. It shall be the prince's duty to furnish the burnt offerings, cereal offerings, and drink offerings, at the feasts, the new moons, and the sabbaths, all the appointed feasts of the house of Israel: he shall provide

the sin offerings, cereal offerings, burnt offerings, and peace offerings, to make atonement for the house of Israel.

The festivals

"Thus says the Lord GOD: In the first month, on the first day of the month, you shall take a young bull without blemish, and cleanse the sanctuary. The priest shall take some of the blood of the sin offering and put it on the doorposts of the temple, the four corners of the ledge of the altar, and the posts of the gate of the inner court. You shall do the same on the seventh day of the month for any one who has sinned through error or ignorance; so you shall make atonement for the temple.

"In the first month, on the fourteenth day of the month, you shall celebrate the feast of the passover, and for seven days unleavened bread shall be eaten. On that day the prince shall provide for himself and all the people of the land a young bull for a sin offering. And on the seven days of the festival he shall provide as a burnt offering to the LORD seven young bulls and seven rams without blemish, on each of the seven days; and a he-goat daily for a sin offering. And he shall provide as a cereal offering an ephah for each bull, an ephah for each ram, and a hin of oil to each ephah. In the seventh month, on the fifteenth day of the month and for the seven days of the feast, he shall make the same provision for sin offerings, burnt offerings, and cereal offerings, and for the oil.

The sabbath

"Thus says the Lord GOD: The gate of the 4 inner court that faces east shall be shut on the six working days; but on the sabbath day it shall be opened and on the day of the new moon it shall be opened. The prince shall 2 enter by the vestibule of the gate from without, and shall take his stand by the post of the gate. The priests shall offer his burnt offering and his peace offerings, and he shall worship at the threshold of the gate. Then he shall go out, but the gate shall not be shut until evening. The people of the land shall 3 worship at the entrance of that gate before the LORD on the sabbaths and on the new moons. The burnt offering that the prince 4 offers to the LORD on the sabbath day shall be six lambs without blemish and a ram without blemish; and the cereal offering with 5 the ram shall be an ephah, and the cereal offering with the lambs shall be as much as

[z] Gk: Heb twenty chambers   [a] Gk: Heb twenty shekels, twenty-five shekels, fifteen shekels shall be your mina
[b] Cn: Heb oil, the bath the oil   [c] Vg: Heb homer   [d] Gk: Heb watering places
[e] Gk Compare Syr: Heb shall be to

he is able, together with a hin of oil to each ephah.

The new moon

5 "On the day of the new moon he shall offer a young bull without blemish, and six lambs and a ram, which shall be without blemish;
7 as a cereal offering he shall provide an ephah with the bull and an ephah with the ram, and with the lambs as much as he is able, to-
8 gether with a hin of oil to each ephah. When the prince enters, he shall go in by the vestibule of the gate, and he shall go out by the same way.

9 "When the people of the land come before the LORD at the appointed feasts, he who enters by the north gate to worship shall go out by the south gate; and he who enters by the south gate shall go out by the north gate: no one shall return by way of the gate by which he entered, but each shall go out
10 straight ahead. When they go in, the prince shall go in with them; and when they go out, he shall go out.

11 "At the feasts and the appointed seasons the cereal offering with a young bull shall be an ephah, and with a ram an ephah, and with the lambs as much as one is able to give,
12 together with a hin of oil to an ephah. When the prince provides a freewill offering, either a burnt offering or peace offerings as a freewill offering to the LORD, the gate facing east shall be opened for him; and he shall offer his burnt offering or his peace offerings as he does on the sabbath day. Then he shall go out, and after he has gone out the gate shall be shut.

The daily offering

13 "He shall provide a lamb a year old without blemish for a burnt offering to the LORD daily; morning by morning he shall provide
14 it. And he shall provide a cereal offering with it morning by morning, one sixth of an ephah, and one third of a hin of oil to moisten the flour, as a cereal offering to the LORD; this is the ordinance for the continual burnt
15 offering.[f] Thus the lamb and the meal offering and the oil shall be provided, morning by morning, for a continual burnt offering.

16 "Thus says the Lord GOD: If the prince makes a gift to any of his sons out of[g] his inheritance, it shall belong to his sons, it is
17 their property by inheritance. But if he makes a gift out of his inheritance to one of his servants, it shall be his to the year of

liberty; then it shall revert to the prince; only his sons may keep a gift from his inheritance. The prince shall not take any of 18 the inheritance of the people, thrusting them out of their property; he shall give his sons their inheritance out of his own property, so that none of my people shall be dispossessed of his property."

The temple kitchens

Then he brought me through the entrance, 19 which was at the side of the gate, to the north row of the holy chambers for the priests; and there I saw a place at the extreme western end of them. And he said to me, "This is the 20 place where the priests shall boil the guilt offering and the sin offering, and where they shall bake the cereal offering, in order not to bring them out into the outer court and so communicate holiness to the people."

Then he brought me forth to the outer 21 court, and led me to the four corners of the court; and in each corner of the court there was a court—in the four corners of the court 22 were small[h] courts, forty cubits long and thirty broad; the four were of the same size. On the inside, around each of the four courts 23 was a row of masonry, with hearths made at the bottom of the rows round about. Then 24 he said to me, "These are the kitchens where those who minister at the temple shall boil the sacrifices of the people."

The river of life

Then he brought me back to the door of the **47** temple; and behold, water was issuing from below the threshold of the temple toward the east (for the temple faced east); and the water was flowing down from below the south end of the threshold of the temple, south of the altar. Then he brought me out by way of the 2 north gate, and led me round on the outside to the outer gate, that faces toward the east;[i] and the water was coming out on the south side.

Going on eastward with a line in his hand, 3 the man measured a thousand cubits, and then led me through the water; and it was ankle-deep. Again he measured a thousand, 4 and led me through the water; and it was knee-deep. Again he measured a thousand, and led me through the water; and it was up to the loins. Again he measured a thousand, 5 and it was a river that I could not pass through, for the water had risen; it was deep enough to swim in, a river that could not be

f Cn: Heb *perpetual ordinances continually*   g Gk: Heb *it is his inheritance*
h Gk Syr Vg: The meaning of the Hebrew word is uncertain   i Heb obscure
47.1–2: Zech 14.8; Rev 22.1–2.   S.B.–Q

6 passed through. And he said to me, "Son of
man, have you seen this?"

Then he led me back along the bank of the
7 river. As I went back, I saw upon the bank
of the river very many trees on the one side
8 and on the other. And he said to me, "This
water flows toward the eastern region and
goes down into the Arabah; and when it
enters the stagnant waters of the sea,^{j} the
9 water will become fresh. And wherever the
river^k goes every living creature which
swarms will live, and there will be very many
fish; for this water goes there, that the waters
of the sea^l may become fresh; so everything
10 will live where the river goes. Fishermen
will stand beside the sea; from En-ge′di to
En-eg′laim it will be a place for the spreading
of nets; its fish will be of very many kinds,
11 like the fish of the Great Sea. But its swamps
and marshes will not become fresh; they are
12 to be left for salt. And on the banks, on both
sides of the river, there will grow all kinds of
trees for food. Their leaves will not wither
nor their fruit fail, but they will bear fresh
fruit every month, because the water for
them flows from the sanctuary. Their fruit
will be for food, and their leaves for healing."

Boundaries of the land

Thus says the Lord God: "These are the
boundaries by which you shall divide the
land for inheritance among the twelve tribes
of Israel. Joseph shall have two portions.
And you shall divide it equally; I swore to
give it to your fathers, and this land shall fall
to you as your inheritance.

"This shall be the boundary of the land: On
the north side, from the Great Sea by way of
Hethlon to the entrance of Hamath, and on
to Zedad,^{m} Bero′thah, Sib′raim (which lies
on the border between Damascus and
Hamath), as far as Hazer-hatticon, which is
on the border of Hauran. So the boundary
shall run from the sea to Hazar-e′non, which
is on the northern border of Damascus, with
the border of Hamath to the north.^{n} This
shall be the north side.

"On the east side, the boundary shall run
from Hazar-e′non^o between Hauran and
Damascus;^{n} along the Jordan between Gilead and the land of Israel; to the eastern sea
and as far as Tamar.^{p} This shall be the east
side.

"On the south side, it shall run from Tamar

Ezek 47, 10

^{j} Compare Syr: Heb *into the sea to the sea those that were made to issue forth* ^{k} Gk Syr Vg Tg: Heb *two rivers*
^{l} Compare Syr: Heb lacks *the waters of the sea* ^{m} Gk: Heb *the entrance of Zedad, Hamath* ^{n} Heb obscure
^{o} Cn: Heb lacks *Hazar-enon* ^{p} Compare Syr: Heb *you shall measure*

as far as the waters of Meribath-ka'desh, thence along the Brook of Egypt to the Great Sea. This shall be the south side.

"On the west side, the Great Sea shall be the boundary to a point opposite the entrance of Hamath. This shall be the west side.

"So you shall divide this land among you according to the tribes of Israel. You shall allot it as an inheritance for yourselves and for the aliens who reside among you and have begotten children among you. They shall be to you as native-born sons of Israel; with you they shall be allotted an inheritance among the tribes of Israel. In whatever tribe the alien resides, there you shall assign him his inheritance, says the Lord GOD.

Tribal allotments

8 "These are the names of the tribes: Beginning at the northern border, from the sea by way^q of Hethlon to the entrance of Hamath, as far as Hazar-e'non (which is on the northern border of Damascus over against Hamath), and^r extending from the east side to the west,^{s} Dan, one portion. Adjoining the territory of Dan, from the east side to the west, Asher, one portion. Adjoining the territory of Asher, from the east side to the west, Naph'tali, one portion. Adjoining the territory of Naph'tali, from the east side to the west, Manas'seh, one portion. Adjoining the territory of Manas'seh, from the east side to the west, E'phraim, one portion. Adjoining the territory of E'phraim, from the east side to the west, Reuben, one portion. Adjoining the territory of Reuben, from the east side to the west, Judah, one portion.

"Adjoining the territory of Judah, from the east side to the west, shall be the portion which you shall set apart, twenty-five thousand cubits in breadth, and in length equal to one of the tribal portions, from the east side to the west, with the sanctuary in the midst of it. The portion which you shall set apart for the LORD shall be twenty-five thousand cubits in length, and twenty^t thousand in breadth. These shall be the allotments of the holy portion: the priests shall have an allotment measuring twenty-five thousand cubits on the northern side, ten thousand cubits in breadth on the western side, ten thousand in breadth on the eastern side, and twenty-five thousand in length on the southern side, with the sanctuary of the LORD in the midst of it. This shall be for the consecrated priests, the sons^u of Zadok, who kept my charge, who did not go astray when

the people of Israel went astray, as the Levites did. And it shall belong to them as a 12 special portion from the holy portion of the land, a most holy place, adjoining the territory of the Levites. And alongside the 13 territory of the priests, the Levites shall have an allotment twenty-five thousand cubits in length and ten thousand in breadth. The whole length shall be twenty-five thousand cubits and the breadth twenty^v thousand. They shall not sell or exchange any of it; they 14 shall not alienate this choice portion of the land, for it is holy to the LORD.

"The remainder, five thousand cubits in 15 breadth and twenty-five thousand in length, shall be for ordinary use for the city, for dwellings and for open country. In the midst of it shall be the city; and these shall be its 16 dimensions: the north side four thousand five hundred cubits, the south side four thousand five hundred, the east side four thousand five hundred, and the west side four thousand and five hundred. And the 17 city shall have open land: on the north two hundred and fifty cubits, on the south two hundred and fifty, on the east two hundred and fifty, and on the west two hundred and fifty. The remainder of the length alongside 18 the holy portion shall be ten thousand cubits to the east, and ten thousand to the west, and it shall be alongside the holy portion. Its produce shall be food for the workers of the city. And the workers of the city, from all 19 the tribes of Israel, shall till it. The whole 20 portion which you shall set apart shall be twenty-five thousand cubits square, that is, the holy portion together with the property of the city.

"What remains on both sides of the holy 21 portion and of the property of the city shall belong to the prince. Extending from the twenty-five thousand cubits of the holy portion to the east border, and westward from the twenty-five thousand cubits to the west border, parallel to the tribal portions, it shall belong to the prince. The holy portion with the sanctuary of the temple in its midst, and the property of the Levites and the 22 property of the city,^{w} shall be in the midst of that which belongs to the prince. The portion of the prince shall lie between the territory of Judah and the territory of Benjamin.

"As for the rest of the tribes: from the east 23 side to the west, Benjamin, one portion. Adjoining the territory of Benjamin, from 24 the east side to the west, Simeon, one portion. Adjoining the territory of Simeon, 25

---

^{q} Compare 47.15: Heb *by the side of the way* ^{r} Cn: Heb *and they shall be his*
^{s} Gk Compare verses 2–8: Heb *the east side the west* ^{t} Compare 45.1: Heb *ten* ^{u} One Ms Gk: Heb *of the sons*
^{v} Gk: Heb *ten* ^{w} Cn: Heb *and from the property of the Levites and from the property of the city*
48.16: Rev 21.16.

from the east side to the west, Is'sachar,
26 one portion. Adjoining the territory of
Is'sachar, from the east side to the west,
27 Zeb'ulun, one portion. Adjoining the territory of Zeb'ulun, from the east side to the
28 west, Gad, one portion. And adjoining the
territory of Gad to the south, the boundary
shall run from Tamar to the waters of
Meribath-ka'desh, thence along the Brook of
29 Egypt to the Great Sea. This is the land
which you shall allot as an inheritance among
the tribes of Israel, and these are their several
portions, says the Lord GOD.

The gates of the city

30 "These shall be the exits of the city: On the
north side, which is to be four thousand five
hundred cubits by measure, three gates, the
gate of Reuben, the gate of Judah, and the
gate of Levi, the gates of the city being
named after the tribes of Israel. On the east
side, which is to be four thousand five
hundred cubits, three gates, the gate of
Joseph, the gate of Benjamin, and the gate of
Dan. On the south side, which is to be four
thousand five hundred cubits by measure,
three gates, the gate of Simeon, the gate of
Is'sachar, and the gate of Zeb'ulun. On the
west side, which is to be four thousand five
hundred cubits, three gates,^{x} the gate of
Gad, the gate of Asher, and the gate of
Naph'tali. The circumference of the city
shall be eighteen thousand cubits. And the
name of the city henceforth shall be, The
LORD is there."

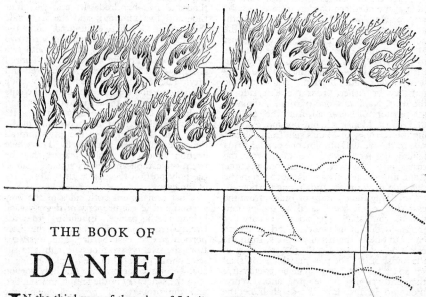

THE BOOK OF

DANIEL

IN the third year of the reign of Jehoi'-
akim king of Judah, Nebuchadnez'zar
king of Babylon came to Jerusalem and
2 besieged it. And the Lord gave Jehoi'akim
king of Judah into his hand, with some of the
vessels of the house of God; and he brought
them to the land of Shinar, to the house of
his god, and placed the vessels in the treasury
3 of his god. Then the king commanded
Ash'penaz, his chief eunuch, to bring some
of the people of Israel, both of the royal
family and of the nobility, youths without
blemish, handsome and skilful in all wisdom,
endowed with knowledge, understanding
learning, and competent to serve in the king's
palace, and to teach them the letters and
language of the Chalde'ans. The king
assigned them a daily portion of the rich food
which the king ate, and of the wine which he
drank. They were to be educated for three
years, and at the end of that time they were to
stand before the king. Among these were

Daniel, Hanani′ah, Mish′a-el, and Azari′ah of the tribe of Judah. And the chief of the eunuchs gave them names: Daniel he called Belteshaz′zar, Hanani′ah he called Shadrach, Mish′a-el he called Meshach, and Azari′ah he called Abed′nego.

But Daniel resolved that he would not defile himself with the king's rich food, or with the wine which he drank; therefore he asked the chief of the eunuchs to allow him not to defile himself. And God gave Daniel favour and compassion in the sight of the chief of the eunuchs; and the chief of the eunuchs said to Daniel, "I fear lest my lord the king, who appointed your food and your drink, should see that you were in poorer condition than the youths who are of your own age. So you would endanger my head with the king." Then Daniel said to the steward whom the chief of the eunuchs had appointed over Daniel, Hanani′ah, Mish′a-el, and Azari′ah, "Test your servants for ten days; let us be given vegetables to eat and water to drink. Then let our appearance and the appearance of the youths who eat the king's rich food be observed by you, and according to what you see deal with your servants." So he hearkened to them in this matter, and tested them for ten days. At the end of ten days it was seen that they were better in appearance and fatter in flesh than all the youths who ate the king's rich food. So the steward took away their rich food and the wine they were to drink, and gave them vegetables.

As for these four youths, God gave them learning and skill in all letters and wisdom; and Daniel had understanding in all visions and dreams. At the end of the time, when the king had commanded that they should be brought in, the chief of the eunuchs brought them in before Nebuchadnez′zar. And the king spoke with them, and among them all none was found like Daniel, Hanani′ah, Mish′a-el, and Azari′ah; therefore they stood before the king. And in every matter of wisdom and understanding concerning which the king inquired of them, he found them ten times better than all the magicians and enchanters that were in all his kingdom. And Daniel continued until the first year of King Cyrus.

NEBUCHADNEZZAR'S DREAM

2 IN the second year of the reign of Nebuchadnez′zar, Nebuchadnez′zar had dreams; and his spirit was troubled, and his sleep left him. Then the king commanded

Cameo Portrait of Nebuchadnezzar

that the magicians, the enchanters, the sorcerers, and the Chalde′ans be summoned, to tell the king his dreams. So they came in and stood before the king. And the king said 3 to them, "I had a dream, and my spirit is troubled to know the dream." Then the 4 Chalde′ans said to the king,[a] "O king, live for ever! Tell your servants the dream, and we will show the interpretation." The king 5 answered the Chalde′ans, "The word from me is sure: if you do not make known to me the dream and its interpretation, you shall be torn limb from limb, and your houses shall be laid in ruins. But if you show the dream 6 and its interpretation, you shall receive from me gifts and rewards and great honour. Therefore show me the dream and its interpretation." They answered a second 7 time, "Let the king tell his servants the dream, and we will show its interpretation." The king answered, "I know with certainty 8 that you are trying to gain time, because you see that the word from me is sure that if you 9 do not make the dream known to me, there is but one sentence for you. You have agreed to speak lying and corrupt words before me till the times change. Therefore tell me the dream, and I shall know that you can show me its interpretation." The Chalde′ans 10 answered the king, "There is not a man on earth who can meet the king's demand; for no great and powerful king has asked such a thing of any magician or enchanter or Chalde′an. The thing that the king asks is 11 difficult, and none can show it to the king except the gods, whose dwelling is not with flesh."

Because of this the king was angry and very 12 furious, and commanded that all the wise men of Babylon be destroyed. So the decree 13 went forth that the wise men were to be slain, and they sought Daniel and his companions, to slay them. Then Daniel replied with 14 prudence and discretion to Ar′i-och, the captain of the king's guard, who had gone out to slay the wise men of Babylon; he said to 15 Ar′i-och, the king's captain, "Why is the decree of the king so severe?" Then Ar′i-och made the matter known to Daniel. And Daniel went in and besought the king to 16 appoint him a time, that he might show to the king the interpretation.

a Heb adds *in Aramaic*, indicating that the text from this point to the end of chapter 7 is in Aramaic

17 Then Daniel went to his house and made the matter known to Hanani'ah, Mish'a-el,
18 and Azari'ah, his companions, and told them to seek mercy of the God of heaven concerning this mystery, so that Daniel and his companions might not perish with the rest of
19 the wise men of Babylon. Then the mystery was revealed to Daniel in a vision of the night. Then Daniel blessed the God of heaven.
20 Daniel said:

"Blessed be the name of God for ever and ever,
    to whom belong wisdom and might.
21 He changes times and seasons;
    he removes kings and sets up kings;
    he gives wisdom to the wise
    and knowledge to those who have understanding;
22 he reveals deep and mysterious things;
    he knows what is in the darkness,
    and the light dwells with him.
23 To thee, O God of my fathers,
    I give thanks and praise,
    for thou hast given me wisdom and strength,
    and hast now made known to me what we asked of thee,
    for thou hast made known to us the king's matter."

24 Therefore Daniel went in to Ar'i-och, whom the king had appointed to destroy the wise men of Babylon; he went and said thus to him, "Do not destroy the wise men of Babylon; bring me in before the king, and I will show him the interpretation."
25 Then Ar'i-och brought in Daniel before the king in haste, and said thus to him: "I have found among the exiles from Judah a man who can make known to the king the inter-
26 pretation." The king said to Daniel, whose name was Belteshaz'zar, "Are you able to make known to me the dream that I have
27 seen and its interpretation?" Daniel answered the king, "No wise men, enchanters, magicians, or astrologers can show to the king the mystery which the king
28 has asked, but there is a God in heaven who reveals mysteries, and he has made known to King Nebuchadnez'zar what will be in the latter days. Your dream and the visions of
29 your head as you lay in bed are these: To you, O king, as you lay in bed came thoughts of what would be hereafter, and he who reveals mysteries made known to you what is
30 to be. But as for me, not because of any wisdom that I have more than all the living has this mystery been revealed to me, but in order that the interpretation may be made

known to the king, and that you may know the thoughts of your mind.

31 "You saw, O king, and behold, a great image. This image, mighty and of exceeding brightness, stood before you, and its appearance was frightening.
32 The head of this image was of fine gold, its breast and arms of silver, its belly and thighs of bronze,
33 its legs of iron, its feet partly of iron and partly of clay.
34 As you looked, a stone was cut out by no human hand, and it smote the image on its feet of iron and clay, and broke them in pieces;
35 then the iron, the clay, the bronze, the silver, and the gold, all together were broken in pieces, and became like the chaff of the summer threshing floors; and the wind carried them away, so that not a trace of them could be found. But the stone that struck the image became a great mountain and filled the whole earth.

36 "This was the dream; now we will tell the king its interpretation.
37 You, O king, the king of kings, to whom the God of heaven has given the kingdom, the power, and the might, and the glory,
38 and into whose hand he has given, wherever they dwell, the sons of men, the beasts of the field, and the birds of the air, making you rule over them all—you are the head of gold.
39 After you shall arise another kingdom inferior to you, and yet a third kingdom of bronze, which shall rule over all the earth.
40 And there shall be a fourth kingdom, strong as iron, because iron breaks to pieces and shatters all things; and like iron which crushes, it shall break and crush all these.
41 And as you saw the feet and toes partly of potter's clay and partly of iron, it shall be a divided kingdom; but some of the firmness of iron shall be in it, just as you saw iron mixed with the miry clay.
42 And as the toes of the feet were partly iron and partly clay, so the kingdom shall be partly strong and partly brittle.
43 As you saw the iron mixed with miry clay, so they will mix with one another in marriage,[b] but they will not hold together, just as iron does not mix with clay.
44 And in the days of those kings the God of heaven will set up a kingdom which shall never be destroyed, nor shall its sovereignty be left to another people. It shall break in pieces all these kingdoms and bring them to an end, and it shall stand for ever;
45 just as you saw that a stone was cut from a mountain by no human hand, and that it broke in pieces the iron, the bronze, the clay, the silver, and the gold. A great God has made known to the king what shall be hereafter. The dream is certain, and its interpretation sure."

46 Then King Nebuchadnez'zar fell upon his

b Aram by the seed of men
2.44: Rev 11.15.

face, and did homage to Daniel, and commanded that an offering and incense be offered up to him. The king said to Daniel, "Truly, your God is God of gods and Lord of kings, and a revealer of mysteries, for you have been able to reveal this mystery." Then the king gave Daniel high honours and many great gifts, and made him ruler over the whole province of Babylon, and chief prefect over all the wise men of Babylon. Daniel made request of the king, and he appointed Shadrach, Meshach, and Abed'nego over the affairs of the province of Babylon; but Daniel remained at the king's court.

THE GOLDEN IMAGE

KING Nebuchadnez'zar made an image of gold, whose height was sixty cubits and its breadth six cubits. He set it up on the plain of Dura, in the province of Babylon. Then King Nebuchadnez'zar sent to assemble the satraps, the prefects, and the governors, the counsellors, the treasurers, the justices, the magistrates, and all the officials of the provinces to come to the dedication of the image which King Nebuchadnez'zar had set up. Then the satraps, the prefects, and the governors, the counsellors, the treasurers, the justices, the magistrates, and all the officials of the provinces, were assembled for the dedication of the image that King Nebuchadnez'zar had set up; and they stood before the image that Nebuchadnez'zar had set up. And the herald proclaimed aloud, "You are commanded, O peoples, nations, and languages, that when you hear the sound of the horn, pipe, lyre, trigon, harp, bagpipe, and every kind of music, you are to fall down and worship the golden image that King Nebuchadnez'zar has set up; and whoever does not fall down and worship shall immediately be cast into a burning fiery furnace." Therefore, as soon as all the peoples heard the sound of the horn, pipe, lyre, trigon, harp, bagpipe, and every kind of music, all the peoples, nations, and languages fell down and worshipped the golden image which King Nebuchadnez'zar had set up.

God's heroes

Therefore at that time certain Chalde'ans came forward and maliciously accused the Jews. They said to King Nebuchadnez'zar, "O king, live for ever! You, O king, have made a decree, that every man who hears the sound of the horn, pipe, lyre, trigon, harp, bagpipe, and every kind of music, shall fall down and worship the golden image; and whoever does not fall down and worship shall be cast into a burning fiery furnace. There are certain Jews whom you have appointed over the affairs of the province of Babylon: Shadrach, Meshach, and Abed'nego. These men, O king, pay no heed to you; they do not serve your gods or worship the golden image which you have set up."

Then Nebuchadnez'zar in furious rage commanded that Shadrach, Meshach, and Abed'nego be brought. Then they brought these men before the king. Nebuchadnez'zar said to them, "Is it true, O Shadrach, Meshach, and Abed'nego, that you do not serve my gods or worship the golden image which I have set up? Now if you are ready when you hear the sound of the horn, pipe, lyre, trigon, harp, bagpipe, and every kind of music, to fall down and worship the image which I have made, well and good; but if you do not worship, you shall immediately be cast into a burning fiery furnace; and who is the god that will deliver you out of my hands?"

Shadrach, Meshach, and Abed'nego answered the king, "O Nebuchadnez'zar, we have no need to answer you in this matter. If it be so, our God whom we serve is able to deliver us from the burning fiery furnace; and he will deliver us out of your hand, O king.[c] But if not, be it known to you, O king, that we will not serve your gods or worship the golden image which you have set up."

The fiery furnace

Then Nebuchadnez'zar was full of fury, and the expression of his face was changed against Shadrach, Meshach, and Abed'nego. He ordered the furnace heated seven times more than it was wont to be heated. And he ordered certain mighty men of his army to bind Shadrach, Meshach, and Abed'nego, and to cast them into the burning fiery furnace. Then these men were bound in their mantles,[d] their tunics,[d] their hats, and their other garments, and they were cast into the burning fiery furnace. Because the king's order was strict and the furnace very hot, the flame of the fire slew those men who took up Shadrach, Meshach, and Abed'nego. And these three men, Shadrach, Meshach, and Abed'nego, fell bound into the burning fiery furnace.

---

[c] Or *Behold, our God . . . king.* Or *If our God is able to deliver us, he will deliver us from the burning fiery furnace and out of your hand, O king.*   [d] The meaning of the Aramaic word is uncertain
3.5–6: Rev 13.15.

24 Then King Nebuchadnez'zar was astonished and rose up in haste. He said to his
counsellors, "Did we not cast three men
bound into the fire?" They answered the
25 king, "True, O king." He answered, "But I
see four men loose, walking in the midst of
the fire, and they are not hurt; and the
appearance of the fourth is like a son of the
gods."
26 Then Nebuchadnez'zar came near to the
door of the burning fiery furnace and said,
"Shadrach, Meshach, and Abed'nego, servants of the Most High God, come forth, and
come here!" Then Shadrach, Meshach, and
27 Abed'nego came out from the fire. And the
satraps, the prefects, the governors, and the
king's counsellors gathered together and saw
that the fire had not had any power over the
bodies of those men; the hair of their heads
was not singed, their mantles^d were not
harmed, and no smell of fire had come upon
28 them. Nebuchadnez'zar said, "Blessed be
the God of Shadrach, Meshach, and Abed'-
nego, who has sent his angel and delivered
his servants, who trusted in him, and set at
naught the king's command, and yielded up
their bodies rather than serve and worship
29 any god except their own God. Therefore I
make a decree: Any people, nation, or
language that speaks anything against the
God of Shadrach, Meshach, and Abed'nego
shall be torn limb from limb, and their
houses laid in ruins; for there is no other god
30 who is able to deliver in this way." Then the
king promoted Shadrach, Meshach, and
Abed'nego in the province of Babylon.

SIGNS AND WONDERS

4^e KING Nebuchadnez'zar to all peoples,
nations, and languages, that dwell in all
2 the earth: Peace be multiplied to you! It has
seemed good to me to show the signs and
wonders that the Most High God has
wrought toward me.
3   How great are his signs,
        how mighty his wonders!
    His kingdom is an everlasting kingdom,
        and his dominion is from generation to
            generation.
4^f I, Nebuchadnez'zar, was at ease in my
5 house and prospering in my palace. I had a
dream which made me afraid; as I lay in bed
the fancies and the visions of my head
6 alarmed me. Therefore I made a decree that
all the wise men of Babylon should be
brought before me, that they might make
known to me the interpretation of the
7 dream. Then the magicians, the enchanters,

the Chalde'ans, and the astrologers came in;
and I told them the dream, but they could
not make known to me its interpretation. At 8
last Daniel came in before me—he who was
named Belteshaz'zar after the name of my
god, and in whom is the spirit of the holy
gods^g—and I told him the dream, saying, "O 9
Belteshaz'zar, chief of the magicians, because
I know that the spirit of the holy gods^g is in
you and that no mystery is difficult for you,
here is^h the dream which I saw; tell me its
interpretation. The visions of my head as I 10
lay in bed were these: I saw, and behold, a
tree in the midst of the earth; and its height
was great. The tree grew and became strong, 11
and its top reached to heaven, and it was
visible to the end of the whole earth. Its 12
leaves were fair and its fruit abundant, and in
it was food for all. The beasts of the field
found shade under it, and the birds of the air
dwelt in its branches, and all flesh was fed
from it.
"I saw in the visions of my head as I lay in 13
bed, and behold, a watcher, a holy one, came
down from heaven. He cried aloud and said 14
thus, 'Hew down the tree and cut off its
branches, strip off its leaves and scatter its
fruit; let the beasts flee from under it and the
birds from its branches. But leave the stump 15
of its roots in the earth, bound with a band of
iron and bronze, amid the tender grass of the
field. Let him be wet with the dew of
heaven; let his lot be with the beasts in the
grass of the earth; let his mind be changed 16
from a man's, and let a beast's mind be given
to him; and let seven times pass over him.
The sentence is by the decree of the 17
watchers, the decision by the word of the
holy ones, to the end that the living may
know that the Most High rules the kingdom
of men, and gives it to whom he will, and sets
over it the lowliest of men.' This dream I, 18
King Nebuchadnez'zar, saw. And you, O
Belteshaz'zar, declare the interpretation,
because all the wise men of my kingdom are
not able to make known to me the interpretation, but you are able, for the spirit of the
holy gods^i is in you."
Then Daniel, whose name was Belte- 19
shaz'zar, was dismayed for a moment, and his
thoughts alarmed him. The king said,
"Belteshaz'zar, let not the dream or the
interpretation alarm you." Belteshaz'zar
answered, "My lord, may the dream be for
those who hate you and its interpretation for
your enemies! The tree you saw, which 20
grew and became strong, so that its top
reached to heaven, and it was visible to the
end of the whole earth; whose leaves were 21

---

^{d} The meaning of the Aramaic word is uncertain ^{e} Ch 3.31 in Aram ^{f} Ch 4.1 in Aram
^{g} Or *Spirit of the holy God* ^{h} Cn: Aram *visions of* ^{i} Or *Spirit of the holy God*
4.12, 21: Ezek 17.23; 31.6; Mt 13.32; Mk 4.32; Lk 13.19.

fair and its fruit abundant, and in which was food for all; under which beasts of the field found shade, and in whose branches the 22 birds of the air dwelt—it is you, O king, who have grown and become strong. Your greatness has grown and reaches to heaven, and your dominion to the ends of the earth. 23 And whereas the king saw a watcher, a holy one, coming down from heaven and saying, 'Hew down the tree and destroy it, but leave the stump of its roots in the earth, bound with a band of iron and bronze, in the tender grass of the field; and let him be wet with the dew of heaven; and let his lot be with the beasts of the field, till seven times pass over 24 him'; this is the interpretation, O king: It is a decree of the Most High, which has come 25 upon my lord the king, that you shall be driven from among men, and your dwelling shall be with the beasts of the field; you shall be made to eat grass like an ox, and you shall be wet with the dew of heaven, and seven times shall pass over you, till you know that the Most High rules the kingdom of men, 26 and gives it to whom he will. And as it was commanded to leave the stump of the roots of the tree, your kingdom shall be sure for you from the time that you know that 27 Heaven rules. Therefore, O king, let my counsel be acceptable to you; break off your sins by practising righteousness, and your iniquities by showing mercy to the oppressed, that there may perhaps be a lengthening of your tranquillity."

28 All this came upon King Nebuchadnez'zar. 29 At the end of twelve months he was walking on the roof of the royal palace of Babylon, 30 and the king said, "Is not this great Babylon, which I have built by my mighty power as a royal residence and for the glory of my 31 majesty?" While the words were still in the king's mouth, there fell a voice from heaven, "O King Nebuchadnez'zar, to you it is spoken: The kingdom has departed from 32 you, and you shall be driven from among men, and your dwelling shall be with the beasts of the field; and you shall be made to eat grass like an ox; and seven times shall

pass over you, until you have learned that the Most High rules the kingdom of men and gives it to whom he will." Immediately the 33 word was fulfilled upon Nebuchadnez'zar. He was driven from among men, and ate grass like an ox, and his body was wet with the dew of heaven till his hair grew as long as eagles' feathers, and his nails were like birds' claws.

At the end of the days I, Nebuchadnez'zar, 34 lifted my eyes to heaven, and my reason returned to me, and I blessed the Most High, and praised and honoured him who lives for ever;

for his dominion is an everlasting dominion,
    and his kingdom endures from genera-tion to generation;
all the inhabitants of the earth are 35 accounted as nothing;
    and he does according to his will in the host of heaven
    and among the inhabitants of the earth;
and none can stay his hand
    or say to him, "What doest thou?"

At the same time my reason returned to me; 36 and for the glory of my kingdom, my majesty and splendour returned to me. My counsellors and my lords sought me, and I was established in my kingdom, and still more greatness was added to me. Now I, 37 Nebuchadnez'zar, praise and extol and honour the King of heaven; for all his works are right and his ways are just; and those who walk in pride he is able to abase.

BELSHAZZAR'S FEAST

KING Belshaz'zar made a great feast for a 5 thousand of his lords, and drank wine in front of the thousand.

Belshaz'zar, when he tasted the wine, 2 commanded that the vessels of gold and of silver which Nebuchadnez'zar his father had taken out of the temple in Jerusalem be brought, that the king and his lords, his wives, and his concubines might drink from

3 them. Then they brought in the golden and silver vessels[j] which had been taken out of the temple, the house of God in Jerusalem; and the king and his lords, his wives, and his 4 concubines drank from them. They drank wine, and praised the gods of gold and silver, bronze, iron, wood, and stone.

5 Immediately the fingers of a man's hand appeared and wrote on the plaster of the wall of the king's palace, opposite the lampstand; 6 and the king saw the hand as it wrote. Then the king's colour changed, and his thoughts alarmed him; his limbs gave way, and his 7 knees knocked together. The king cried aloud to bring in the enchanters, the Chalde'ans, and the astrologers. The king said to the wise men of Babylon, "Whoever reads this writing, and shows me its interpretation, shall be clothed with purple, and have a chain of gold about his neck, and shall be the third ruler in the kingdom." 8 Then all the king's wise men came in, but they could not read the writing or make 9 known to the king the interpretation. Then King Belshaz'zar was greatly alarmed, and his colour changed; and his lords were perplexed.

10 The queen, because of the words of the king and his lords, came into the banqueting hall; and the queen said, "O king, live for ever! Let not your thoughts alarm you or your 11 colour change. There is in your kingdom a man in whom is the spirit of the holy gods.[k] In the days of your father light and understanding and wisdom, like the wisdom of the gods, were found in him, and King Nebuchadnez'zar, your father, made him chief of the magicians, enchanters, Chalde'ans, and 12 astrologers,[l] because an excellent spirit, knowledge, and understanding to interpret dreams, explain riddles, and solve problems were found in this Daniel, whom the king named Belteshaz'zar. Now let Daniel be called, and he will show the interpretation."

13 Then Daniel was brought in before the king. The king said to Daniel, "You are that Daniel, one of the exiles of Judah, whom the 14 king my father brought from Judah. I have heard of you that the spirit of the holy gods[k] is in you, and that light and understanding 15 and excellent wisdom are found in you. Now the wise men, the enchanters, have been brought in before me to read this writing and make known to me its interpretation; but they could not show the interpretation of the 16 matter. But I have heard that you can give interpretations and solve problems. Now if you can read the writing and make known to me its interpretation, you shall be clothed with purple, and have a chain of gold about

your neck, and shall be the third ruler in the kingdom."

Then Daniel answered before the king, 17 "Let your gifts be for yourself, and give your rewards to another; nevertheless I will read the writing to the king and make known to him the interpretation. O king, the Most 18 High God gave Nebuchadnez'zar your father kingship and greatness and glory and majesty; and because of the greatness that he 19 gave him, all peoples, nations, and languages trembled and feared before him; whom he would he slew, and whom he would he kept alive; whom he would he raised up, and whom he would he put down. But when his 20 heart was lifted up and his spirit was hardened so that he dealt proudly, he was deposed from his kingly throne, and his glory was taken from him; he was driven from 21 among men, and his mind was made like that of a beast, and his dwelling was with the wild asses; he was fed grass like an ox, and his body was wet with the dew of heaven, until he knew that the Most High God rules the kingdom of men, and sets over it whom he will. And you his son, Belshaz'zar, have not 22 humbled your heart, though you knew all this, but you have lifted up yourself against 23 the Lord of heaven; and the vessels of his house have been brought in before you, and you and your lords, your wives, and your concubines have drunk wine from them; and you have praised the gods of silver and gold, of bronze, iron, wood, and stone, which do not see or hear or know, but the God in whose hand is your breath, and whose are all your ways, you have not honoured.

The writing on the wall

"Then from his presence the hand was sent, 24 and this writing was inscribed. And this is 25 the writing that was inscribed: MENE, MENE, TEKEL, and PARSIN. This is the interpretation 26 of the matter: MENE, God has numbered the days of your kingdom and brought it to an end; TEKEL, you have been weighed in the 27 balances and found wanting; PERES, your 28 kingdom is divided and given to the Medes and Persians."

Then Belshaz'zar commanded, and Daniel 29 was clothed with purple, a chain of gold was put about his neck, and proclamation was made concerning him, that he should be the third ruler in the kingdom.

That very night Belshaz'zar the Chalde'an 30 king was slain. And Darius the Mede 31 received the kingdom, being about sixty-two years old.

---

[j] Theodotion Vg: Aram golden vessels   [k] Or Spirit of the holy God   [l] Aram repeats the king your father

THE DEN OF LIONS

6 IT pleased Darius to set over the kingdom a hundred and twenty satraps, to be 2 throughout the whole kingdom; and over them three presidents, of whom Daniel was one, to whom these satraps should give account, so that the king might suffer no 3 loss. Then this Daniel became distinguished above all the other presidents and satraps, because an excellent spirit was in him; and the king planned to set him over the whole 4 kingdom. Then the presidents and the satraps sought to find a ground for complaint against Daniel with regard to the kingdom; but they could find no ground for complaint or any fault, because he was faithful, and no 5 error or fault was found in him. Then these men said, "We shall not find any ground for complaint against this Daniel unless we find it in connection with the law of his God." 6 Then these presidents and satraps came by agreement[m] to the king and said to him, "O 7 King Darius, live for ever! All the presidents of the kingdom, the prefects and the satraps, the counsellors and the governors are agreed that the king should establish an ordinance and enforce an interdict, that whoever makes petition to any god or man for thirty days, except to you, O king, shall 8 be cast into the den of lions. Now, O king, establish the interdict and sign the document, so that it cannot be changed, according to the law of the Medes and the Persians, which cannot be revoked." 9 Therefore King Darius signed the document and interdict. 10 When Daniel knew that the document had been signed, he went to his house where he had windows in his upper chamber open toward Jerusalem; and he got down upon his knees three times a day and prayed and gave thanks before his God, as he had done 11 previously. Then these men came by agreement[m] and found Daniel making petition and supplication before his God. 12 Then they came near and said before the king, concerning the interdict, "O king! Did you not sign an interdict, that any man who makes petition to any god or man within thirty days except to you, O king, shall be cast into the den of lions?" The king answered, "The thing stands fast, according to the law of the Medes and Persians, which 13 cannot be revoked." Then they answered before the king, "That Daniel, who is one of the exiles from Judah, pays no heed to you, O king, or the interdict you have signed, but makes his petition three times a day."

Then the king, when he heard these words, 14 was much distressed, and set his mind to deliver Daniel; and he laboured till the sun went down to rescue him. Then these men 15 came by agreement[m] to the king, and said to the king, "Know, O king, that it is a law of the Medes and Persians that no interdict or ordinance which the king establishes can be changed."

Then the king commanded, and Daniel was 16 brought and cast into the den of lions. The king said to Daniel, "May your God, whom you serve continually, deliver you!" And a 17 stone was brought and laid upon the mouth of the den, and the king sealed it with his own signet and with the signet of his lords, that nothing might be changed concerning Daniel. Then the king went to his palace, 18 and spent the night fasting; no diversions were brought to him, and sleep fled from him.

Then, at break of day, the king arose and 19 went in haste to the den of lions. When he 20 came near to the den where Daniel was, he cried out in a tone of anguish and said to Daniel, "O Daniel, servant of the living God, has your God, whom you serve continually, been able to deliver you from the lions?" Then Daniel said to the king, "O king, live 21 for ever! My God sent his angel and shut 22 the lions' mouths, and they have not hurt me, because I was found blameless before him; and also before you, O king, I have done no wrong." Then the king was exceedingly 23 glad, and commanded that Daniel be taken up out of the den. So Daniel was taken up out of the den, and no kind of hurt was found upon him, because he had trusted in his God. And the king commanded, and those 24 men who had accused Daniel were brought and cast into the den of lions—they, their children, and their wives; and before they reached the bottom of the den the lions overpowered them and broke all their bones in pieces.

Then King Darius wrote to all the peoples, 25 nations, and languages that dwell in all the earth: "Peace be multiplied to you. I make a 26 decree, that in all my royal dominion men tremble and fear before the God of Daniel,

for he is the living God,
   enduring for ever;
his kingdom shall never be destroyed,
   and his dominion shall be to the end.
He delivers and rescues,   27
   he works signs and wonders
     in heaven and on earth,
he who has saved Daniel
   from the power of the lions."

[m] Or *thronging*
6.22: 2 Tim 4.17.

28 So this Daniel prospered during the reign of Darius and the reign of Cyrus the Persian.

DANIEL'S VISIONS

Four great beasts

7 IN the first year of Belshaz´zar king of Babylon, Daniel had a dream and visions of his head as he lay in his bed. Then he wrote down the dream, and told the sum of 2 the matter. Daniel said, "I saw in my vision by night, and behold, the four winds of 3 heaven were stirring up the great sea. And four great beasts came up out of the sea, 4 different from one another. The first was like a lion and had eagles' wings. Then as I looked its wings were plucked off, and it was lifted up from the ground and made to stand upon two feet like a man; and the mind of a 5 man was given to it. And behold, another beast, a second one, like a bear. It was raised up on one side; it had three ribs in its mouth between its teeth; and it was told, 'Arise, 6 devour much flesh.' After this I looked, and lo, another, like a leopard, with four wings of a bird on its back; and the beast had four 7 heads; and dominion was given to it. After this I saw in the night visions, and behold, a fourth beast, terrible and dreadful and ex-

ceedingly strong; and it had great iron teeth; it devoured and broke in pieces, and stamped the residue with its feet. It was different from all the beasts that were before it; and it had ten horns. I considered the horns, and 8 behold, there came up among them another horn, a little one, before which three of the first horns were plucked up by the roots; and behold, in this horn were eyes like the eyes of a man, and a mouth speaking great things. As I looked,   9

thrones were placed
     and one that was ancient of days took his
        seat;
   his raiment was white as snow,
     and the hair of his head like pure wool;
   his throne was fiery flames,
     its wheels were burning fire.
   A stream of fire issued   10
     and came forth from before him;
   a thousand thousands served him,
     and ten thousand times ten thousand
        stood before him;
   the court sat in judgment,
     and the books were opened.
I looked then because of the sound of the 11 great words which the horn was speaking. And as I looked, the beast was slain, and its body destroyed and given over to be burned

The windswept sea   *Dan 7, 2*

7.3: Rev 13.1.   7.3, 7, 21: Rev 11.7.   7.4-6: Rev 13.2.   7.7: Rev 12.3; 13.1; 17.3.   7.8, 11: Rev 13.5.
7.9: Rev 1.14; 20.4, 11.   7.10: Rev 5.11; 20.12.

with fire. As for the rest of the beasts, their dominion was taken away, but their lives were prolonged for a season and a time. I saw in the night visions,

and behold, with the clouds of heaven
there came one like a son of man,
and he came to the Ancient of Days
and was presented before him.
And to him was given dominion
and glory and kingdom,
that all peoples, nations, and languages
should serve him;
his dominion is an everlasting dominion,
which shall not pass away,
and his kingdom one
that shall not be destroyed.

"As for me, Daniel, my spirit within me was anxious and the visions of my head alarmed me. I approached one of those who stood there and asked him the truth concerning all this. So he told me, and made known to me the interpretation of the things. 'These four great beasts are four kings who shall arise out of the earth. But the saints of the Most High shall receive the kingdom, and possess the kingdom for ever, for ever and ever.'

"Then I desired to know the truth concerning the fourth beast, which was different from all the rest, exceedingly terrible, with its teeth of iron and claws of bronze; and which devoured and broke in pieces, and stamped the residue with its feet; and concerning the ten horns that were on its head, and the other horn which came up and before which three of them fell, the horn which had eyes and a mouth that spoke great things, and which seemed greater than its fellows. As I looked, this horn made war with the saints, and prevailed over them, until the Ancient of Days came, and judgment was given for the saints of the Most High, and the time came when the saints received the kingdom.

"Thus he said: 'As for the fourth beast,
there shall be a fourth kingdom on earth,
which shall be different from all the
kingdoms,
and it shall devour the whole earth,
and trample it down, and break it to
pieces.
As for the ten horns,
out of this kingdom
ten kings shall arise,
and another shall arise after them;
he shall be different from the former ones,
and shall put down three kings.
He shall speak words against the Most
High,
and shall wear out the saints of the Most
High,

and shall think to change the times and
the law;
and they shall be given into his hand
for a time, two times, and half a time.
But the court shall sit in judgment,   26
and his dominion shall be taken away,
to be consumed and destroyed to the
end.
And the kingdom and the dominion   27
and the greatness of the kingdoms under
the whole heaven
shall be given to the people of the saints
of the Most High;
their kingdom shall be an everlasting
kingdom,
and all dominions shall serve and obey
them.'

"Here is the end of the matter. As for me, 28 Daniel, my thoughts greatly alarmed me, and my colour changed; but I kept the matter in my mind."

A ram and a goat

In the third year of the reign of King 8 Belshaz'zar a vision appeared to me, Daniel, after that which appeared to me at the first. And I saw in the vision; and when I saw, I 2 was in Susa the capital, which is in the province of Elam; and I saw in the vision, and I was at the river U'lai. I raised my eyes 3 and saw, and behold, a ram standing on the bank of the river. It had two horns; and both horns were high, but one was higher than the other, and the higher one came up last. I saw 4 the ram charging westward and northward and southward; no beast could stand before him, and there was no one who could rescue from his power; he did as he pleased and magnified himself.

As I was considering, behold, a he-goat 5 came from the west across the face of the whole earth, without touching the ground; and the goat had a conspicuous horn between his eyes. He came to the ram with the two 6 horns, which I had seen standing on the bank of the river, and he ran at him in his mighty wrath. I saw him come close to the ram, and 7 he was enraged against him and struck the ram and broke his two horns; and the ram had no power to stand before him, but he cast him down to the ground and trampled upon him; and there was no one who could rescue the ram from his power. Then the 8 he-goat magnified himself exceedingly; but when he was strong, the great horn was broken, and instead of it there came up four conspicuous horns toward the four winds of heaven.

9 Out of one of them came forth a little horn, which grew exceedingly great toward the south, toward the east, and toward the
10 glorious land. It grew great, even to the host of heaven; and some of the host of the stars it cast down to the ground, and trampled upon
11 them. It magnified itself, even up to the Prince of the host; and the continual burnt offering was taken away from him, and the
12 place of his sanctuary was overthrown. And the host was given over to it together with the continual burnt offering through transgression;[n] and truth was cast down to the ground, and the horn acted and prospered.
13 Then I heard a holy one speaking; and another holy one said to the one that spoke, "For how long is the vision concerning the continual burnt offering, the transgression that makes desolate, and the giving over of the sanctuary and host to be trampled under
14 foot?"[o] And he said to him,[p] "For two thousand and three hundred evenings and mornings; then the sanctuary shall be restored to its rightful state."
15 When I, Daniel, had seen the vision, I sought to understand it; and behold, there stood before me one having the appearance
16 of a man. And I heard a man's voice between the banks of the U'lai, and it called, "Gabriel, make this man understand the vision."
17 So he came near where I stood; and when he came, I was frightened and fell upon my face. But he said to me, "Understand, O son of man, that the vision is for the time of the end."
18 As he was speaking to me, I fell into a deep sleep with my face to the ground; but he
19 touched me and set me on my feet. He said, "Behold, I will make known to you what shall be at the latter end of the indignation; for it pertains to the appointed time of the
20 end. As for the ram which you saw with the two horns, these are the kings of Media and
21 Persia. And the he-goat[q] is the king of Greece; and the great horn between his eyes
22 is the first king. As for the horn that was broken, in place of which four others arose, four kingdoms shall arise from his[r] nation,
23 but not with his power. And at the latter end of their rule, when the transgressors have reached their full measure, a king of bold countenance, one who understands riddles,
24 shall arise. His power shall be great,[s] and he shall cause fearful destruction, and shall succeed in what he does, and destroy mighty
25 men and the people of the saints. By his cunning he shall make deceit prosper under his hand, and in his own mind he shall

magnify himself. Without warning he shall destroy many; and he shall even rise up against the Prince of princes; but, by no human hand, he shall be broken. The vision of the evenings and the mornings which has been told is true; but seal up the vision, for it pertains to many days hence."

And I, Daniel, was overcome and lay sick for some days; then I rose and went about the king's business; but I was appalled by the vision and did not understand it.

The time of restoration

In the first year of Darius the son of Ahasu-e'rus, by birth a Mede, who became king over the realm of the Chalde'ans—in the first year of his reign, I, Daniel, perceived in the books the number of years which, according to the word of the LORD to Jeremiah the prophet, must pass before the end of the desolations of Jerusalem, namely, seventy years.

Then I turned my face to the Lord God, seeking him by prayer and supplications with fasting and sackcloth and ashes. I prayed to the LORD my God, and made confession, saying, "O Lord, the great and terrible God, who keepest covenant and steadfast love with those who love him and keep his commandments, we have sinned and done wrong and acted wickedly and rebelled, turning aside from thy commandments and ordinances; we have not listened to thy servants the prophets, who spoke in thy name to our kings, our princes, and our fathers, and to all the people of the land. To thee, O Lord, belongs righteousness, but to us confusion of face, as at this day, to the men of Judah, to the inhabitants of Jerusalem, and to all Israel, those that are near and those that are far away, in all the lands to which thou hast driven them, because of the treachery which they have committed against thee. To us, O Lord, belongs confusion of face, to our kings, to our princes, and to our fathers, because we have sinned against thee. To the Lord our God belong mercy and forgiveness; because we have rebelled against him, and have not obeyed the voice of the LORD our God by following his laws, which he set before us by his servants the prophets. All Israel has transgressed thy law and turned aside, refusing to obey thy voice. And the curse and oath which are written in the law of Moses the servant of God have been poured out upon us, because we have sinned against him. He has confirmed his words, which he

---

[n] Heb obscure   [o] Heb obscure   [p] Theodotion Gk Syr Vg: Heb *me*
[q] Or *shaggy he-goat*   [r] Theodotion Gk Vg: Heb *the*
[s] Theodotion and Beatty papyrus of Gk: Heb repeats *but not with his power* from verse 22
8.10: Rev 12.4.   **8.13:** Lk 21.24.

spoke against us and against our rulers who ruled us, by bringing upon us a great calamity; for under the whole heaven there has not been done the like of what has been done against Jerusalem. As it is written in the law of Moses, all this calamity has come upon us, yet we have not entreated the favour of the LORD our God, turning from our iniquities and giving heed to thy truth. Therefore the LORD has kept ready the calamity and has brought it upon us; for the LORD our God is righteous in all the works which he has done, and we have not obeyed his voice. And now, O LORD our God, who didst bring thy people out of the land of Egypt with a mighty hand, and hast made thee a name, as at this day, we have sinned, we have done wickedly. O Lord, according to all thy righteous acts, let thy anger and thy wrath turn away from thy city Jerusalem, thy holy hill; because for our sins, and for the iniquities of our fathers, Jerusalem and thy people have become a byword among all who are round about us. Now therefore, O our God, hearken to the prayer of thy servant and to his supplications, and for thy own sake, O Lord,[t] cause thy face to shine upon thy sanctuary, which is desolate. O my God, incline thy ear and hear; open thy eyes and behold our desolations, and the city which is called by thy name; for we do not present our supplications before thee on the ground of our righteousness, but on the ground of thy great mercy. O LORD, hear; O LORD, forgive; O LORD, give heed and act; delay not, for thy own sake, O my God, because thy city and thy people are called by thy name."

While I was speaking and praying, confessing my sin and the sin of my people Israel, and presenting my supplication before the LORD my God for the holy hill of my God; while I was speaking in prayer, the man Gabriel, whom I had seen in the vision at the first, came to me in swift flight at the time of the evening sacrifice. He came[u] and he said to me, "O Daniel, I have now come out to give you wisdom and understanding. At the beginning of your supplications a word went forth, and I have come to tell it to you, for you are greatly beloved; therefore consider the word and understand the vision.

"Seventy weeks of years are decreed concerning your people and your holy city, to finish the transgression, to put an end to sin, and to atone for iniquity, to bring in everlasting righteousness, to seal both vision and prophet, and to anoint a most holy place.[v] Know therefore and understand that from

the going forth of the word to restore and build Jerusalem to the coming of an anointed one, a prince, there shall be seven weeks. Then for sixty-two weeks it shall be built again with squares and moat, but in a troubled time. And after the sixty-two 26 weeks, an anointed one shall be cut off, and shall have nothing; and the people of the prince who is to come shall destroy the city and the sanctuary. Its[w] end shall come with a flood, and to the end there shall be war; desolations are decreed. And he shall make a 27 strong covenant with many for one week; and for half of the week he shall cause sacrifice and offering to cease; and upon the wing of abominations shall come one who makes desolate, until the decreed end is poured out on the desolator."

The end of the age

In the third year of Cyrus king of Persia a **10** word was revealed to Daniel, who was named Belteshaz'zar. And the word was true, and it was a great conflict. And he understood the word and had understanding of the vision.

In those days I, Daniel, was mourning for 2 three weeks. I ate no delicacies, no meat or 3 wine entered my mouth, nor did I anoint myself at all, for the full three weeks. On the 4 twenty-fourth day of the first month, as I was standing on the bank of the great river, that is, the Tigris, I lifted up my eyes and 5 looked, and behold, a man clothed in linen, whose loins were girded with gold of Uphaz. His body was like beryl, his face like the 6 appearance of lightning, his eyes like flaming torches, his arms and legs like the gleam of burnished bronze, and the sound of his words like the noise of a multitude. And I, 7 Daniel, alone saw the vision, for the men who were with me did not see the vision, but a great trembling fell upon them, and they fled to hide themselves. So I was left alone and 8 saw this great vision, and no strength was left in me; my radiant appearance was fearfully changed, and I retained no strength. Then I 9 heard the sound of his words; and when I heard the sound of his words, I fell on my face in a deep sleep with my face to the ground.

And behold, a hand touched me and set me 10 trembling on my hands and knees. And he 11 said to me, "O Daniel, man greatly beloved, give heed to the words that I speak to you, and stand upright, for now I have been sent to you." While he was speaking this word to me, I stood up trembling. Then he said to 12 me, "Fear not, Daniel, for from the first day

---

t Theodotion Vg Compare Syr: Heb *for the Lord's sake*   u Gk Syr: Heb *made to understand*
v Or *thing* or *one*   w Or *his*
9.27: Dan 11.31; 12.11; Mt 24.15; Mk 13.14.   **10.5-6:** Rev 1.13–14; 2.18.

that you set your mind to understand and humbled yourself before your God, your words have been heard, and I have come
13 because of your words. The prince of the kingdom of Persia withstood me twenty-one days; but Michael, one of the chief princes, came to help me, so I left him there with the
14 prince of the kingdom of Persia *x* and came to make you understand what is to befall your people in the latter days. For the vision is for days yet to come."
15 When he had spoken to me according to these words, I turned my face toward the
16 ground and was dumb. And behold, one in the likeness of the sons of men touched my lips; then I opened my mouth and spoke. I said to him who stood before me, "O my
17 lord, by reason of the vision pains have come upon me, and I retain no strength. How can my lord's servant talk with my lord? For now no strength remains in me, and no breath is left in me."
18 Again one having the appearance of a man
19 touched me and strengthened me. And he said, "O man greatly beloved, fear not, peace be with you; be strong and of good courage." And when he spoke to me, I was strengthened and said, "Let my lord speak,
20 for you have strengthened me." Then he said, "Do you know why I have come to you? But now I will return to fight against the prince of Persia; and when I am through with him, lo, the prince of Greece will come.
21 But I will tell you what is inscribed in the book of truth: there is none who contends by my side against these except Michael, your prince.

11 "And as for me, in the first year of Darius the Mede, I stood up to confirm and strengthen him.
2 "And now I will show you the truth. Behold, three more kings shall arise in Persia; and a fourth shall be far richer than all of them; and when he has become strong through his riches, he shall stir up all against
3 the kingdom of Greece. Then a mighty king shall arise, who shall rule with great domin-
4 ion and do according to his will. And when he has arisen, his kingdom shall be broken and divided toward the four winds of heaven, but not to his posterity, nor according to the dominion with which he ruled; for his kingdom shall be plucked up and go to others besides these.
5 "Then the king of the south shall be strong, but one of his princes shall be stronger than he and his dominion shall be a great

dominion. After some years they shall make an alliance, and the daughter of the king of the south shall come to the king of the north to make peace; but she shall not retain the strength of her arm, and he and his offspring shall not endure; but she shall be given up, and her attendants, her child, and he who got possession of *y* her.

"In those times a branch *z* from her roots shall arise in his place; he shall come against the army and enter the fortress of the king of the north, and he shall deal with them and shall prevail. He shall also carry off to Egypt their gods with their molten images and with their precious vessels of silver and of gold; and for some years he shall refrain from attacking the king of the north. Then the latter shall come into the realm of the king of the south but shall return into his own land.

"His sons shall wage war and assemble a multitude of great forces, which shall come on and overflow and pass through, and again shall carry the war as far as his fortress. Then the king of the south, moved with anger, shall come out and fight with the king of the north; and he shall raise a great multitude, but it shall be given into his hand. And when the multitude is taken, his heart shall be exalted, and he shall cast down tens of thousands, but he shall not prevail. For the king of the north shall again raise a multitude, greater than the former; and after some years *a* he shall come on with a great army and abundant supplies.

"In those times many shall rise against the king of the south; and the men of violence among your own people shall lift themselves up in order to fulfil the vision; but they shall fail. Then the king of the north shall come and throw up siegeworks, and take a well-fortified city. And the forces of the south shall not stand, or even his picked troops, for there shall be no strength to stand. But he who comes against him shall do according to his own will, and none shall stand before him; and he shall stand in the glorious land, and all of it shall be in his power. He shall set his face to come with the strength of his whole kingdom, and he shall bring terms of peace *b* and perform them. He shall give him the daughter of women to destroy the kingdom; *c* but it shall not stand or be to his advantage. Afterward he shall turn his face to the coastlands, and shall take many of them; but a commander shall put an end to his insolence; indeed *d* he shall turn his insolence back upon him. Then he shall turn *x* his face back toward the fortresses of his own

---

x Theodotion Compare Gk: Heb *I was left there with the kings of Persia*   *y* Or *supported*
z Gk: Heb *from a branch*   *a* Heb *at the end of the times years*   *b* Gk: Heb *upright ones*
c Heb *her* or *it*   *d* Heb obscure
10.13, 21: Rev 12.7.

land; but he shall stumble and fall, and shall not be found.

o "Then shall arise in his place one who shall send an exactor of tribute through the glory of the kingdom; but within a few days he shall be broken, neither in anger nor in battle. In his place shall arise a contemptible person to whom royal majesty has not been given; he shall come in without warning and obtain the kingdom by flatteries. Armies shall be utterly swept away before him and broken, and the prince of the covenant also. And from the time that an alliance is made with him he shall act deceitfully; and he shall become strong with a small people. Without warning he shall come into the richest parts[e] of the province; and he shall do what neither his fathers nor his fathers' fathers have done, scattering among them plunder, spoil, and goods. He shall devise plans against strongholds, but only for a time. And he shall stir up his power and his courage against the king of the south with a great army; and the king of the south shall wage war with an exceedingly great and mighty army; but he shall not stand, for plots shall be devised against him. Even those who eat his rich food shall be his undoing; his army shall be swept away, and many shall fall down slain. And as for the two kings, their minds shall be bent on mischief; they shall speak lies at the same table, but to no avail; for the end is yet to be at the time appointed. And he shall return to his land with great substance, but his heart shall be set against the holy covenant. And he shall work his will, and return to his own land.

9 "At the time appointed he shall return and come into the south; but it shall not be this time as it was before. For ships of Kittim shall come against him, and he shall be afraid and withdraw, and shall turn back and be enraged and take action against the holy covenant. He shall turn back and give heed to those who forsake the holy covenant. Forces from him shall appear and profane the temple and fortress, and shall take away the continual burnt offering. And they shall set up the abomination that makes desolate. He shall seduce with flattery those who violate the covenant; but the people who know their God stand firm and take action. And those among the people who are wise shall make many understand, though they shall fall by sword and flame, by captivity and plunder, for some days. When they fall, they shall receive a little help. And many shall join themselves to them with flattery; and some of those who are wise shall

fall, to refine and to cleanse them[f] and to make them white, until the time of the end, for it is yet for the time appointed.

"And the king shall do according to his will; 36 he shall exalt himself and magnify himself above every god, and shall speak astonishing things against the God of gods. He shall prosper till the indignation is accomplished; for what is determined shall be done. He 37 shall give no heed to the gods of his fathers, or to the one beloved by women; he shall not give heed to any other god, for he shall magnify himself above all. He shall honour 38 the god of fortresses instead of these; a god whom his fathers did not know he shall honour with gold and silver, with precious stones and costly gifts. He shall deal with the 39 strongest fortresses by the help of a foreign god; those who acknowledge him he shall magnify with honour. He shall make them rulers over many and shall divide the land for a price.

"At the time of the end the king of the south 40 shall attack[g] him; but the king of the north shall rush upon him like a whirlwind, with chariots and horsemen, and with many ships; and he shall come into countries and shall overflow and pass through. He shall come 41 into the glorious land. And tens of thousands shall fall, but these shall be delivered out of his hand: Edom and Moab and the main part of the Ammonites. He shall 42 stretch out his hand against the countries, and the land of Egypt shall not escape. He 43 shall become ruler of the treasures of gold and of silver, and all the precious things of Egypt; and the Libyans and the Ethiopians shall follow in his train. But tidings from the 44 east and the north shall alarm him, and he shall go forth with great fury to exterminate and utterly destroy many. And he shall pitch 45 his palatial tents between the sea and the glorious holy mountain; yet he shall come to his end, with none to help him.

"At that time shall arise Michael, the great 12 prince who has charge of your people. And there shall be a time of trouble, such as never has been since there was a nation till that time; but at that time your people shall be delivered, every one whose name shall be found written in the book. And many of 2 those who sleep in the dust of the earth shall awake, some to everlasting life, and some to shame and everlasting contempt. And those 3 who are wise shall shine like the brightness of the firmament; and those who turn many to righteousness, like the stars for ever and ever. But you, Daniel, shut up the words, 4 and seal the book, until the time of the end.

e Or among the richest men f Gk: Heb among them g Heb thrust at
11.31: Dan 9.27; 12.11; Mt 24.15; Mk 13.14. 11.36: Ezek 28.2; 2 Thess 2.4; Rev 13.5.
12.1: Mt 24.21; Mk 13.19; Rev 12.7; 16.18. 12.2: Mt 25.46. 12.3: Mt 13.43. 12.4: Rev 22.10.

Many shall run to and fro, and knowledge shall increase."

5 Then I Daniel looked, and behold, two others stood, one on this bank of the stream
6 and one on that bank of the stream. And I[h] said to the man clothed in linen, who was above the waters of the stream, "How long shall it be till the end of these wonders?"
7 The man clothed in linen, who was above the waters of the stream, raised his right hand and his left hand toward heaven; and I heard him swear by him who lives for ever that it would be for a time, two times, and half a time; and that when the shattering of the power of the holy people comes to an end all these
8 things would be accomplished. I heard, but I did not understand. Then I said, "O my

lord, what shall be the issue of these things?" He said, "Go your way, Daniel, 9 for the words are shut up and sealed until the time of the end. Many shall purify 10 themselves, and make themselves white, and be refined; but the wicked shall do wickedly; and none of the wicked shall understand; but those who are wise shall understand. And 11 from the time that the continual burnt offering is taken away, and the abomination that makes desolate is set up, there shall be a thousand two hundred and ninety days. Blessed is he who waits and comes to the 12 thousand three hundred and thirty-five days. But go your way till the end; and you 13 shall rest, and shall stand in your allotted place at the end of the days."

THE BOOK OF
HOSEA

Hos 3, 2

THE word of the LORD that came to Hose′a the son of Be-e′ri, in the days of Uzzi′ah, Jotham, Ahaz, and Hezeki′ah, kings of Judah, and in the days of Jerobo′am the son of Jo′ash, king of Israel.
2 When the LORD first spoke through Hose′a, the LORD said to Hose′a, "Go, take to yourself a wife of harlotry and have children of harlotry, for the land commits great
3 harlotry by forsaking the LORD." So he went and took Gomer the daughter of Dibla′im, and she conceived and bore him a son.
4 And the LORD said to him, "Call his name Jezreel; for yet a little while, and I will

punish the house of Jehu for the blood of Jezreel, and I will put an end to the kingdom of the house of Israel. And on that day, I will 5 break the bow of Israel in the valley of Jezreel."

She conceived again and bore a daughter. 6 And the LORD said to him, "Call her name Not pitied, for I will no more have pity on the house of Israel, to forgive them at all. But I will have pity on the house of Judah, 7 and I will deliver them by the LORD their God; I will not deliver them by bow, nor by sword, nor by war, nor by horses, nor by horsemen."

[h] Gk Vg: Heb *he*
12.7: Rev 4.9; 10.5; 12.14. 12.11: Dan 9.27; 11.31; Mt 24.15; Mk 13.14. 1.6, 9: Hos 2.23; 1 Pet 2.10.

When she had weaned Not pitied, she conceived and bore a son. And the LORD said, "Call his name Not my people, for you are not my people and I am not your God."[a]

[b] Yet the number of the people of Israel shall be like the sand of the sea, which can be neither measured nor numbered; and in the place where it was said to them, "You are not my people," it shall be said to them, "Sons of the living God." And the people of Judah and the people of Israel shall be gathered together, and they shall appoint for themselves one head; and they shall go up from the land, for great shall be the day of Jezreel.

[c] Say to your brother,[d] "My people," and to your sister,[e] "She has obtained pity."

Israel, a faithless wife

[2] "Plead with your mother, plead—
for she is not my wife,
and I am not her husband—
that she put away her harlotry from her face,
and her adultery from between her breasts;

[3] lest I strip her naked
and make her as in the day she was born,
and make her like a wilderness,
and set her like a parched land,
and slay her with thirst.

[4] Upon her children also I will have no pity,
because they are children of harlotry.

[5] For their mother has played the harlot;
she that conceived them has acted shamefully.
For she said, 'I will go after my lovers,
who give me my bread and my water,
my wool and my flax, my oil and my drink.'

[6] Therefore I will hedge up her[f] way with thorns;
and I will build a wall against her,
so that she cannot find her paths.

[7] She shall pursue her lovers,
but not overtake them;
and she shall seek them,
but shall not find them.
Then she shall say, 'I will go
and return to my first husband,
for it was better with me then than now.'

[8] And she did not know
that it was I who gave her
the grain, the wine, and the oil,
and who lavished upon her silver
and gold which they used for Ba'al.

[9] Therefore I will take back
my grain in its time,
and my wine in its season;
and I will take away my wool and my flax,
which were to cover her nakedness.

[10] Now I will uncover her lewdness
in the sight of her lovers,
and no one shall rescue her out of my hand.

[11] And I will put an end to all her mirth,
her feasts, her new moons, her sabbaths,
and all her appointed feasts.

[12] And I will lay waste her vines and her fig trees,
of which she said,
'These are my hire,
which my lovers have given me.'
I will make them a forest,
and the beasts of the field shall devour them.

[13] And I will punish her for the feast days of the Ba'als
when she burned incense to them
and decked herself with her ring and jewelry,
and went after her lovers,
and forgot me, says the LORD.

[14] "Therefore, behold, I will allure her,
and bring her into the wilderness,
and speak tenderly to her.

[15] And there I will give her her vineyards,
and make the Valley of Achor a door of hope.
And there she shall answer as in the days of her youth,
as at the time when she came out of the land of Egypt.

[16] "And in that day, says the LORD, you will call me, 'My husband,' and no longer will you call me, 'My Ba'al.' [17] For I will remove the names of the Ba'als from her mouth, and they shall be mentioned by name no more. [18] And I will make for you[g] a covenant on that day with the beasts of the field, the birds of the air, and the creeping things of the ground; and I will abolish[h] the bow, the sword, and war from the land; and I will make you lie down in safety. [19] And I will betroth you to me for ever; I will betroth you to me in righteousness and in justice, in steadfast love, and in mercy. [20] I will betroth you to me in faithfulness; and you shall know the LORD.

[21] "And in that day, says the LORD,
I will answer the heavens
and they shall answer the earth;

[22] and the earth shall answer the grain, the wine, and the oil,
and they shall answer Jezreel;[i]

---

[a] Gk: Heb *I am not yours*   [b] Ch 2.1 in Heb   [c] Ch 2.3 in Heb   [d] Gk: Heb *brothers*   [e] Gk Vg: Heb *sisters*
[f] Gk Syr: Heb *your*   [g] Heb *them*   [h] Heb *break*   [i] That is *God sows*
1.10: Rom 9.26.   **2.1, 23**: Rom 9.25; 1 Pet 2.10.

23 and I will sow him[j] for myself in the
land.
And I will have pity on Not pitied,
    and I will say to Not my people, 'You
    are my people';
and he shall say, 'Thou art my God.' "

Her purchase price

3 And the LORD said to me, "Go again, love a
woman who is beloved of a paramour and is
an adulteress; even as the LORD loves the
people of Israel, though they turn to other
2 gods and love cakes of raisins." So I bought
her for fifteen shekels of silver and a homer
3 and a lethech of barley. And I said to her,
"You must dwell as mine for many days; you
shall not play the harlot, or belong to another
man; so will I also be to you."

Israel's return

4 For the children of Israel shall dwell many
days without king or prince, without sacrifice
5 or pillar, without ephod or teraphim. Afterward the children of Israel shall return and
seek the LORD their God, and David their
king; and they shall come in fear to the LORD
and to his goodness in the latter days.

The Lord's controversy

4 Hear the word of the LORD, O people of
    Israel;
        for the LORD has a controversy with the
        inhabitants of the land.
    There is no faithfulness or kindness,
        and no knowledge of God in the land;
2 there is swearing, lying, killing, stealing,
        and committing adultery;
    they break all bounds and murder
        follows murder.
3 Therefore the land mourns,
    and all who dwell in it languish,
and also the beasts of the field,
    and the birds of the air;
    and even the fish of the sea are taken
    away.

4 Yet let no one contend,
    and let none accuse,
    for with you is my contention, O priest.[k]
5 You shall stumble by day,
    the prophet also shall stumble with you
        by night;
    and I will destroy your mother.
6 My people are destroyed for lack of know-
        ledge;
    because you have rejected knowledge,

I reject you from being a priest to me.
And since you have forgotten the law of
    your God,
I also will forget your children.

The more they increased, 7
    the more they sinned against me;
    I will change their glory into shame.
They feed on the sin of my people; 8
    they are greedy for their iniquity.
And it shall be like people, like priest; 9
    I will punish them for their ways,
    and requite them for their deeds.
They shall eat, but not be satisfied; 10
    they shall play the harlot, but not
    multiply;
because they have forsaken the LORD
    to cherish harlotry.

Wine and new wine 11
    take away the understanding.
My people inquire of a thing of wood, 12
    and their staff gives them oracles.
For a spirit of harlotry has led them astray,
    and they have left their God to play the
    harlot.
They sacrifice on the tops of the moun- 13
    tains,
    and make offerings upon the hills,
under oak, poplar, and terebinth,
    because their shade is good.

Therefore your daughters play the harlot,
    and your brides commit adultery.
I will not punish your daughters when 14
    they play the harlot,
    nor your brides when they commit
    adultery;
for the men themselves go aside with
    harlots,
    and sacrifice with cult prostitutes,
and a people without understanding shall
    come to ruin.

Though you play the harlot, O Israel, 15
    let not Judah become guilty.
Enter not into Gilgal,
    nor go up to Beth-a'ven,
    and swear not, "As the LORD lives."
Like a stubborn heifer, 16
    Israel is stubborn;
can the LORD now feed them
    like a lamb in a broad pasture?

E'phraim is joined to idols, 17
    let him alone.
A band[l] of drunkards, they give them- 18
    selves to harlotry;
    they love shame more than their glory.[m]

---

[j] Cn: Heb *her* [k] Cn: Heb uncertain [l] Cn: Heb uncertain
[m] Cn Compare Gk: Heb of this line uncertain

19   A wind has wrapped them[n] in its wings,
     and they shall be ashamed because of
     their altars.[o]

Against priests and kings

5   Hear this, O priests!
     Give heed, O house of Israel!
     Hearken, O house of the king!
     For the judgment pertains to you;
     for you have been a snare at Mizpah,
     and a net spread upon Tabor.
2   And they have made deep the pit of
     Shittim;[p]
     but I will chastise all of them.
3   I know E'phraim,
     and Israel is not hid from me;
     for now, O E'phraim, you have played the
     harlot,
     Israel is defiled.
4   Their deeds do not permit them
     to return to their God.
     For the spirit of harlotry is within them,
     and they know not the LORD.
5   The pride of Israel testifies to his face;
     E'phraim[q] shall stumble in his guilt;
     Judah also shall stumble with them.
6   With their flocks and herds they shall go
     to seek the LORD,
     but they will not find him;
     he has withdrawn from them.
7   They have dealt faithlessly with the LORD;
     for they have borne alien children.
     Now the new moon shall devour them
     with their fields.

8   Blow the horn in Gib'e-ah,
     the trumpet in Ramah.
     Sound the alarm at Beth-a'ven;
     tremble,[r] O Benjamin!
9   E'phraim shall become a desolation
     in the day of punishment;
     among the tribes of Israel
     I declare what is sure.
10   The princes of Judah have become
     like those who remove the landmark;
     upon them I will pour out
     my wrath like water.
11   E'phraim is oppressed, crushed in judg-
     ment,
     because he was determined to go after
     vanity.[s]
12   Therefore I am like a moth to E'phraim,
     and like dry rot to the house of Judah.

13   When E'phraim saw his sickness,
     and Judah his wound,
     then E'phraim went to Assyria,
     and sent to the great king.[t]
     But he is not able to cure you
     or heal your wound.
14   For I will be like a lion to E'phraim,
     and like a young lion to the house of
     Judah.
     I, even I, will rend and go away,
     I will carry off, and none shall rescue.

A brief repentance

15   I will return again to my place,
     until they acknowledge their guilt and
     seek my face,
     and in their distress they seek me,
     saying,
6   "Come, let us return to the LORD;
     for he has torn, that he may heal us;
     he has stricken, and he will bind us up.
2   After two days he will revive us;
     on the third day he will raise us up,
     that we may live before him.
3   Let us know, let us press on to know the
     LORD;
     his going forth is sure as the dawn;
     he will come to us as the showers,
     as the spring rains that water the earth."

4   What shall I do with you, O E'phraim?
     What shall I do with you, O Judah?
     Your love is like a morning cloud,
     like the dew that goes early away.
5   Therefore I have hewn them by the
     prophets,
     I have slain them by the words of my
     mouth,
     and my judgment goes forth as the
     light.[u]
6   For I desire steadfast love and not
     sacrifice,
     the knowledge of God, rather than
     burnt offerings.

7   But at[v] Adam they transgressed the
     covenant;
     there they dealt faithlessly with me.
8   Gilead is a city of evildoers,
     tracked with blood.
9   As robbers lie in wait[w] for a man,
     so the priests are banded together;[x]
     they murder on the way to Shechem,
     yea, they commit villainy.
10   In the house of Israel I have seen a
     horrible thing;
     E'phraim's harlotry is there, Israel is
     defiled.

---

[n] Heb *her*   [o] Gk Syr: Heb *sacrifices*   [p] Cn: Heb uncertain   [q] Heb *Israel and Ephraim*
[r] Cn Compare Gk: Heb *after you*   [s] Gk: Heb *a command*   [t] Cn: Heb *a king that will contend*
[u] Gk Syr: Heb *thy judgment goes forth*   [v] Cn: Heb *like*   [w] Cn: Heb uncertain   [x] Syr: Heb *a company*
6.6: Mt 9.13; 12.7.

11 For you also, O Judah, a harvest is
       appointed.

Ephraim a half-baked cake

   When I would restore the fortunes of my
         people,
7   when I would heal Israel,
    the corruption of E'phraim is revealed,
       and the wicked deeds of Samar'ia;
    for they deal falsely,
       the thief breaks in,
       and the bandits raid without.
2 But they do not consider
       that I remember all their evil works.
    Now their deeds encompass them,
       they are before my face.
3 By their wickedness they make the king
         glad,
       and the princes by their treachery.
4 They are all adulterers;
       they are like a heated oven,
    whose baker ceases to stir the fire,
       from the kneading of the dough until it
         is leavened.
5 On the day of our king the princes
         became sick with the heat of wine;
       he stretched out his hand with mockers.
6 For like an oven their hearts burn^y with
         intrigue;
       all night their anger smoulders;
       in the morning it blazes like a flaming
         fire.
7 All of them are hot as an oven,
       and they devour their rulers.
    All their kings have fallen;
       and none of them calls upon me.

8 E'phraim mixes himself with the peoples;
       E'phraim is a cake not turned.
9 Aliens devour his strength,
       and he knows it not;
    grey hairs are sprinkled upon him,
       and he knows it not.
10 The pride of Israel witnesses against
         him;
       yet they do not return to the LORD their
         God,
       nor seek him, for all this.

11 E'phraim is like a dove,
       silly and without sense,
       calling to Egypt, going to Assyria.
12 As they go, I will spread over them my
         net;
    I will bring them down like birds of the
       air;
    I will chastise them for their wicked
       deeds.^{z}

Woe to them, for they have strayed from 1
       me!
    Destruction to them, for they have
       rebelled against me!
    I would redeem them,
       but they speak lies against me.

    They do not cry to me from the heart,   1
       but they wail upon their beds;
    for grain and wine they gash themselves,
       they rebel against me.
    Although I trained and strengthened their 1
       arms,
       yet they devise evil against me.
    They turn to Ba'al;^{a} 1
       they are like a treacherous bow,
    their princes shall fall by the sword
       because of the insolence of their tongue.
    This shall be their derision in the land of
       Egypt.

Reaping the whirlwind

    Set the trumpet to your lips,   8
       for^b a vulture is over the house of the
         LORD,
    because they have broken my covenant,
       and transgressed my law.
    To me they cry,   2
       My God, we Israel know thee.
    Israel has spurned the good;   3
       the enemy shall pursue him.

    They made kings, but not through me.   4
       They set up princes, but without my
         knowledge.
    With their silver and gold they made idols
       for their own destruction.
    I have^c spurned your calf, O Samar'ia. 5
       My anger burns against them.
    How long will it be
       till they are pure in Israel?^{d} 6

    A workman made it;
       it is not God.
    The calf of Samar'ia
       shall be broken to pieces.^{e}

    For they sow the wind,   7
       and they shall reap the whirlwind.
    The standing grain has no heads,
       it shall yield no meal;
    if it were to yield,
       aliens would devour it.
    Israel is swallowed up;   8
       already they are among the nations
         as a useless vessel.
    For they have gone up to Assyria,   9
       a wild ass wandering alone;

---

^{y} Gk Syr: Heb *brought near* ^{z} Cn: Heb *according to the report to their congregation* ^{a} Cn: Heb uncertain
^{b} Cn: Heb *as* ^{c} Heb *He has* ^{d} Gk: Heb *for from Israel* ^{e} Or *shall go up in flames*

E'phraim has hired lovers.
Though they hire allies among the nations,
  I will soon gather them up.
And they shall cease[f] for a little while
  from anointing[g] king and princes.

Because E'phraim has multiplied altars for
    sinning,
  they have become to him altars for
    sinning.
Were I to write for him my laws by ten
    thousands,
  they would be regarded as a strange
    thing.
They love sacrifice;[h]
  they sacrifice flesh and eat it;
  but the LORD has no delight in them.
Now he will remember their iniquity,
  and punish their sins;
  they shall return to Egypt.
For Israel has forgotten his Maker,
  and built palaces;
and Judah has multiplied fortified cities;
  but I will send a fire upon his cities,
  and it shall devour his strongholds.

Days of recompense

9 Rejoice not, O Israel!
  Exult not[i] like the peoples;
for you have played the harlot, forsaking
    your God.
You have loved a harlot's hire
  upon all threshing floors.
2 Threshing floor and winevat shall not feed
    them,
  and the new wine shall fail them.
3 They shall not remain in the land of the
    LORD;
  but E'phraim shall return to Egypt,
  and they shall eat unclean food in
    Assyria.

4 They shall not pour libations of wine to
    the LORD;
  and they shall not please him with their
    sacrifices.
Their bread[j] shall be like mourners' bread;
  all who eat of it shall be defiled;
for their bread shall be for their hunger
    only;
  it shall not come to the house of the
    LORD.

5 What will you do on the day of appointed
    festival,
  and on the day of the feast of the LORD?
6 For behold, they are going to Assyria;[k]
  Egypt shall gather them,

Memphis shall bury them.
Nettles shall possess their precious things
    of silver;
  thorns shall be in their tents.

7 The days of punishment have come,
  the days of recompense have come;
  Israel shall know it.
The prophet is a fool,
  the man of the spirit is mad,
because of your great iniquity
  and great hatred.
8 The prophet is the watchman of E'phraim,
  the people of my God,
yet a fowler's snare is on all his ways,
  and hatred in the house of his God.
9 They have deeply corrupted themselves
  as in the days of Gib'e-ah:
he will remember their iniquity,
  he will punish their sins.

10 Like grapes in the wilderness,
  I found Israel.
Like the first fruit on the fig tree,
  in its first season,
  I saw your fathers.
But they came to Ba'al-pe'or,
  and consecrated themselves to Ba'al,[l]
  and became detestable like the thing
    they loved.
11 E'phraim's glory shall fly away like a
  bird—

no birth, no pregnancy, no conception!
12 Even if they bring up children,
  I will bereave them till none is left.
Woe to them
  when I depart from them!
13 E'phraim's sons, as I have seen, are
  destined for a prey;[m]
  E'phraim must lead forth his sons to
    slaughter.
14 Give them, O LORD—

[f] Gk: Heb begin   [g] Gk: Heb burden   [h] Cn: Heb uncertain   [i] Gk: Heb to exultation   [j] Cn: Heb to them
[k] Cn: Heb from destruction   [l] Heb shame   [m] Cn Compare Gk: Heb uncertain
8.14: Amos 1.4, 7, 10, 12, 14; 2.2, 5.   9.7: Lk 21.22.

what wilt thou give?
Give them a miscarrying womb
　　and dry breasts.

15 Every evil of theirs is in Gilgal;
　　there I began to hate them.
　　Because of the wickedness of their deeds
　　　I will drive them out of my house.
　　I will love them no more;
　　　all their princes are rebels.

16 E'phraim is stricken,
　　　their root is dried up,
　　　they shall bear no fruit.
　　Even though they bring forth,
　　　I will slay their beloved children.

17 My God will cast them off,
　　　because they have not hearkened to him;
　　　they shall be wanderers among the
　　　nations.

A false heart

10 Israel is a luxuriant vine
　　that yields its fruit.
　　The more his fruit increased
　　　the more altars he built;
　　as his country improved
　　　he improved his pillars.

2 Their heart is false;
　　　now they must bear their guilt.
　　The LORD[n] will break down their altars,
　　　and destroy their pillars.

3 For now they will say:
　　　"We have no king,
　　for we fear not the LORD,
　　　and a king, what could he do for us?"

4 They utter mere words;
　　　with empty oaths they make covenants;
　　so judgment springs up like poisonous
　　　weeds
　　　in the furrows of the field.

5 The inhabitants of Samar'ia tremble
　　　for the calf[o] of Beth-a'ven.
　　Its people shall mourn for it,
　　　and its idolatrous priests shall wail[p] over
　　　it,
　　over its glory which has departed from
　　　it.

6 Yea, the thing itself shall be carried to
　　　Assyria,
　　　as tribute to the great king.[q]
　　E'phraim shall be put to shame,
　　　and Israel shall be ashamed of his idol.[r]

7 Samar'ia's king shall perish,
　　　like a chip on the face of the waters.

The high places of Aven, the sin of Israel, 8
　　shall be destroyed.
Thorn and thistle shall grow up
　　on their altars;
and they shall say to the mountains, Cover
　　us,
and to the hills, Fall upon us.

From the days of Gib'e-ah, you have 9
　　sinned, O Israel;
　　there they have continued.
　　Shall not war overtake them in Gib'e-
　　ah?
I will come[s] against the wayward people to 10
　　chastise them;
　　and nations shall be gathered against
　　them
　　when they are chastised[t] for their double
　　iniquity.

E'phraim was a trained heifer 11
　　that loved to thresh,
　　and I spared her fair neck;
but I will put E'phraim to the yoke,
　Judah must plough,
　Jacob must harrow for himself.
Sow for yourselves righteousness, 12
　reap the fruit[u] of steadfast love;
　break up your fallow ground,
for it is the time to seek the LORD,
　that he may come and rain salvation
　upon you.

You have ploughed iniquity, 13
　you have reaped injustice,
　you have eaten the fruit of lies.
Because you have trusted in your chariots[v]
　and in the multitude of your warriors,
therefore the tumult of war shall arise 14
　among your people,
　and all your fortresses shall be des-
　troyed,
as Shalman destroyed Beth-ar'bel on the
　day of battle;
　mothers were dashed in pieces with
　their children.
Thus it shall be done to you, O house of 15
　Israel,[w]
　because of your great wickedness.
In the storm[x] the king of Israel
　shall be utterly cut off.

The Father's love

When Israel was a child, I loved him, 11
　and out of Egypt I called my son.
The more I[y] called them, 2
　the more they went from me;[z]

---

[n] Heb he　[o] Gk Syr: Heb calves　[p] Cn: Heb exult　[q] Cn: Heb a king that will contend　[r] Cn: Heb counsel
[s] Cn Compare Gk: Heb in my desire　[t] Gk: Heb bound　[u] Gk: Heb according to　[v] Gk: Heb way
[w] Gk: Heb O Bethel　[x] Cn: Heb dawn　[y] Gk: Heb they　[z] Gk: Heb them
10.8: Lk 23.30; Rev 6.16.　10.12: 2 Cor 9.10.　11.1: Mt 2.15.

they kept sacrificing to the Ba'als,
and burning incense to idols.

3 Yet it was I who taught E'phraim to walk,
I took them up in my[a] arms;
but they did not know that I healed
them.

4 I led them with cords of compassion,[b]
with the bands of love,
and I became to them as one
who eases the yoke on their jaws,
and I bent down to them and fed them.

5 They shall return to the land of Egypt,
and Assyria shall be their king,
because they have refused to return to
me.

6 The sword shall rage against their cities,
consume the bars of their gates,
and devour them in their fortresses.[c]

7 My people are bent on turning away from
me;[d]
so they are appointed to the yoke,
and none shall remove it.

8 How can I give you up, O E'phraim!
How can I hand you over, O Israel!
How can I make you like Admah!
How can I treat you like Zeboi'im!
My heart recoils within me,
my compassion grows warm and tender.

9 I will not execute my fierce anger,
I will not again destroy E'phraim;
for I am God and not man,
the Holy One in your midst,
and I will not come to destroy.[e]

10 They shall go after the LORD,
he will roar like a lion;
yea, he will roar,
and his sons shall come trembling from
the west;

11 they shall come trembling like birds from
Egypt,
and like doves from the land of Assyria;
and I will return them to their homes,
says the LORD.

12[f] E'phraim has encompassed me with lies,
and the house of Israel with deceit;
but Judah is still known by[g] God,
and is faithful to the Holy One.

Israel's past experiences

12 E'phraim herds the wind,
and pursues the east wind all day long;
they multiply falsehood and violence;
they make a bargain with Assyria,

and oil is carried to Egypt.

2 The LORD has an indictment against
Judah,
and will punish Jacob according to his
ways,
and requite him according to his deeds.

3 In the womb he took his brother by the
heel,
and in his manhood he strove with God.

4 He strove with the angel and prevailed,
he wept and sought his favour.
He met God at Bethel,
and there God spoke with him[h]—

5 the LORD the God of hosts,
the LORD is his name:

6 "So you, by the help of your God, return,
hold fast to love and justice,
and wait continually for your God."

7 A trader, in whose hands are false
balances,
he loves to oppress.

8 E'phraim has said, "Ah, but I am rich,
I have gained wealth for myself";
but all his riches can never offset[i]
the guilt he has incurred.

9 I am the LORD your God
from the land of Egypt;
I will again make you dwell in tents,
as in the days of the appointed feast.

10 I spoke to the prophets;
it was I who multiplied visions,
and through the prophets gave parables.

11 If there is iniquity in Gilead
they shall surely come to naught;
if in Gilgal they sacrifice bulls,
their altars also shall be like stone heaps
on the furrows of the field.

12 (Jacob fled to the land of Aram,
there Israel did service for a wife,
and for a wife he herded sheep.)

13 By a prophet the LORD brought Israel up
from Egypt,
and by a prophet he was preserved.

14 E'phraim has given bitter provocation;
so his LORD will leave his bloodguilt
upon him,
and will turn back upon him his reproaches.

The only Saviour

13 When E'phraim spoke, men trembled;
he was exalted in Israel;
but he incurred guilt through Ba'al and
died.

2 And now they sin more and more,
   and make for themselves molten images,
idols skilfully made of their silver,
   all of them the work of craftsmen.
Sacrifice to these, they say.[j]
Men kiss calves!
3 Therefore they shall be like the morning mist
   or like the dew that goes early away,
like the chaff that swirls from the
   threshing floor
or like smoke from a window.

4 I am the LORD your God
   from the land of Egypt;
you know no God but me,
   and besides me there is no saviour.
5 It was I who knew you in the wilderness,
   in the land of drought;
6 but when they had fed[k] to the full,
   they were filled, and their heart was
      lifted up;
   therefore they forgot me.
7 So I will be to them like a lion,
   like a leopard I will lurk beside the way.
8 I will fall upon them like a bear robbed of
      her cubs,
   I will tear open their breast,
and there I will devour them like a lion,
   as a wild beast would rend them.

9 I will destroy you, O Israel;
   who[l] can help you?
10 Where[m] now is your king, to save you;
   where are all[n] your princes,[o] to defend
      you[p]—
   those of whom you said,
   "Give me a king and princes"?
11 I have given you kings in my anger,
   and I have taken them away in my wrath.

12 The iniquity of E'phraim is bound up,
   his sin is kept in store.
13 The pangs of childbirth come for him,
   but he is an unwise son;
for now he does not present himself
   at the mouth of the womb.

14 Shall I ransom them from the power of
      Sheol?
   Shall I redeem them from Death?
O Death, where[q] are your plagues?
O Sheol, where[q] is your destruction?
   Compassion is hid from my eyes.

15 Though he may flourish as the reed plant,[r]
   the east wind, the wind of the LORD,
      shall come,

rising from the wilderness;
and his fountain shall dry up,
   his spring shall be parched;
it shall strip his treasury
   of every precious thing.
Samar'ia shall bear her guilt, 16
   because she has rebelled against her God;
they shall fall by the sword,
   their little ones shall be dashed in pieces,
   and their pregnant women ripped open.

Return, O Israel

Return, O Israel, to the LORD your God, 1
   for you have stumbled because of your
      iniquity.
Take with you words 2
   and return to the LORD;
say to him,
   "Take away all iniquity;
accept that which is good
   and we will render
   the fruit[t] of our lips.
Assyria shall not save us, 3
   we will not ride upon horses;
and we will say no more, 'Our God,'
   to the work of our hands.
In thee the orphan finds mercy."

I will heal their faithlessness; 4
   I will love them freely,
   for my anger has turned from them.
I will be as the dew to Israel; 5
   he shall blossom as the lily,
   he shall strike root as the poplar;[u]
his shoots shall spread out; 6
   his beauty shall be like the olive,
   and his fragrance like Lebanon.
They shall return and dwell beneath my[v] 7
      shadow,
   they shall flourish as a garden;[w]
they shall blossom as the vine,
   their fragrance shall be like the wine of
      Lebanon.

O E'phraim, what have I to do with idols? 8
   It is I who answer and look after you.[x]
I am like an evergreen cypress,
   from me comes your fruit.

Whoever is wise, let him understand these 9
      things;
   whoever is discerning, let him know
      them;
for the ways of the LORD are right,
   and the upright walk in them,
   but transgressors stumble in them.

---

[j] Gk: Heb *to these they say sacrifices of*　[k] Cn: Heb *according to their pasture*　[l] Gk Syr: Heb *for in me*
[m] Gk Syr Vg: Heb *I will be*　[n] Cn: Heb *in all*　[o] Cn: Heb *cities*　[p] Cn Compare Gk: Heb *and your judges*
[q] Gk Syr: Heb *I will be*　[r] Cn: Heb *among brothers*　[s] Ch 14.1 in Heb　[t] Gk Syr: Heb *bulls*
[u] Cn: Heb *Lebanon*　[v] Heb *his*　[w] Cn: Heb *they shall grow grain*　[x] Heb *him*
13.14: 1 Cor 15.55.　**14.2:** Heb 13.15.　**14.9:** Acts 13.10.

THE BOOK OF

JOEL

THE word of the LORD that came to
Jo′el, the son of Pethu′el:

2 Hear this, you aged men,
　give ear, all inhabitants of the land!
Has such a thing happened in your days,
　or in the days of your fathers?
3 Tell your children of it,
　and let your children tell their children,
　and their children another generation.

4 What the cutting locust left,
　the swarming locust has eaten.
What the swarming locust left,
　the hopping locust has eaten,
and what the hopping locust left,
　the destroying locust has eaten.

5 Awake, you drunkards, and weep;
　and wail, all you drinkers of wine,
because of the sweet wine,
　for it is cut off from your mouth.
6 For a nation has come up against my land,
　powerful and without number;
its teeth are lions' teeth,
　and it has the fangs of a lioness.
7 It has laid waste my vines,
　and splintered my fig trees;
it has stripped off their bark and thrown it
　down;
　their branches are made white.

Lament like a virgin girded with sackcloth 8
　for the bridegroom of her youth.
The cereal offering and the drink offering 9
　are cut off
　from the house of the LORD.
The priests mourn,
　the ministers of the LORD.
The fields are laid waste, 10
　the ground mourns;
because the grain is destroyed,
　the wine fails,
　the oil languishes.

Be confounded, O tillers of the soil, 11
　wail, O vinedressers,
for the wheat and the barley;
　because the harvest of the field has
　perished.
The vine withers, 12
　the fig tree languishes.
Pomegranate, palm, and apple,
　all the trees of the field are withered;
and gladness fails
　from the sons of men.

The day of the Lord

Gird on sackcloth and lament, O priests, 13
　wail, O ministers of the altar.
Go in, pass the night in sackcloth,
　O ministers of my God!

1.6: Rev 9.8.

Because cereal offering and drink offering
    are withheld from the house of your
    God.

14   Sanctify a fast,
    call a solemn assembly.
   Gather the elders
    and all the inhabitants of the land
   to the house of the LORD your God;
    and cry to the LORD.

15   Alas for the day!
   For the day of the LORD is near,
    and as destruction from the Almighty it
     comes.

16   Is not the food cut off
    before our eyes,
   joy and gladness
    from the house of our God?

17   The seed shrivels under the clods,^{a}
    the storehouses are desolate;
   the granaries are ruined
    because the grain has failed.

18   How the beasts groan!
    The herds of cattle are perplexed
   because there is no pasture for them;
    even the flocks of sheep are dismayed.

19   Unto thee, O LORD, I cry.
   For fire has devoured
    the pastures of the wilderness,
   and flame has burned
    all the trees of the field.

20   Even the wild beasts cry to thee
    because the water brooks are dried up,
   and fire has devoured
    the pastures of the wilderness.

2   Blow the trumpet in Zion;
    sound the alarm on my holy mountain!
   Let all the inhabitants of the land tremble,
    for the day of the LORD is coming, it is
     near,

2   a day of darkness and gloom,
    a day of clouds and thick darkness!
   Like blackness there is spread upon the
    mountains
   a great and powerful people;
    their like has never been from of old,
    nor will be again after them
    through the years of all generations.

3   Fire devours before them,
    and behind them a flame burns.
   The land is like the garden of Eden before
    them,
    but after them a desolate wilderness,
    and nothing escapes them.

Joel 2, 1

Their appearance is like the appearance of
   horses,
   and like war horses they run.
As with the rumbling of chariots,
   they leap on the tops of the mountains,
like the crackling of a flame of fire
   devouring the stubble,
like a powerful army
   drawn up for battle.

Before them peoples are in anguish,
   all faces grow pale.
Like warriors they charge,
   like soldiers they scale the wall.
They march each on his way,
   they do not swerve^b from their paths.
They do not jostle one another,
   each marches in his path;
they burst through the weapons
   and are not halted.
They leap upon the city,
   they run upon the walls;
they climb up into the houses,
   they enter through the windows like a
    thief.

The earth quakes before them,
   the heavens tremble.

^{a} Heb uncertain ^{b} Gk Syr Vg: Heb *take a pledge*
2.4–5: Rev 9.7, 9. **2.10**: Rev 9.2.

The sun and the moon are darkened,
  and the stars withdraw their shining.
The LORD utters his voice
  before his army,
for his host is exceedingly great;
  he that executes his word is powerful.
For the day of the LORD is great and very
    terrible;
  who can endure it?

2 "Yet even now," says the LORD,
  "return to me with all your heart,
with fasting, with weeping, and with
    mourning;
3 and rend your hearts and not your
    garments."
Return to the LORD, your God,
  for he is gracious and merciful,
slow to anger, and abounding in steadfast
    love,
  and repents of evil.
4 Who knows whether he will not turn and
    repent,
  and leave a blessing behind him,
a cereal offering and a drink offering
  for the LORD, your God?

5 Blow the trumpet in Zion;
  sanctify a fast;
call a solemn assembly;
6   gather the people.
Sanctify the congregation;
  assemble the elders;
gather the children,
  even nursing infants.
Let the bridegroom leave his room,
  and the bride her chamber.

17 Between the vestibule and the altar
  let the priests, the ministers of the
    LORD, weep
and say, "Spare thy people, O LORD,
  and make not thy heritage a reproach,
  a byword among the nations.
Why should they say among the peoples,
  'Where is their God?'"

18 Then the LORD became jealous for his
    land,
  and had pity on his people.
19 The LORD answered and said to his people,
  "Behold, I am sending to you
    grain, wine, and oil,
    and you will be satisfied;
and I will no more make you
  a reproach among the nations.

20 "I will remove the northerner far from
    you,

and drive him into a parched and
    desolate land,
his front into the eastern sea,
  and his rear into the western sea;
the stench and foul smell of him will rise,
  for he has done great things.

21 "Fear not, O land;
  be glad and rejoice,
  for the LORD has done great things!
22 Fear not, you beasts of the field,
  for the pastures of the wilderness are
    green;
the tree bears its fruit,
  the fig tree and vine give their full yield.

23 "Be glad, O sons of Zion,
  and rejoice in the LORD, your God;
for he has given the early rain for your
    vindication,
he has poured down for you abundant
    rain,
  the early and the latter rain, as before.

24 "The threshing floors shall be full of grain,
  the vats shall overflow with wine and oil.
25 I will restore to you the years
  which the swarming locust has eaten,
the hopper, the destroyer, and the cutter,
  my great army, which I sent among you.

26 "You shall eat in plenty and be satisfied,
  and praise the name of the LORD your
    God,
  who has dealt wondrously with you.
And my people shall never again be put to
    shame.
27 You shall know that I am in the midst of
    Israel,
  and that I, the LORD, am your God and
    there is none else.
And my people shall never again be put to
    shame.

28 "And it shall come to pass afterward,
  that I will pour out my spirit on all
    flesh;
your sons and your daughters shall
    prophesy,
  your old men shall dream dreams,
  and your young men shall see visions.
29 Even upon the menservants and maid-
    servants
  in those days, I will pour out my
    spirit.

30 "And I will give portents in the heavens and
on the earth, blood and fire and columns of
smoke. 31 The sun shall be turned to darkness,

c Ch 3.1 in Heb
2.11: Rev 6.17.   2.28-32: Acts 2.17-21.   2.31: Rev 6.12.

and the moon to blood, before the great and
32 terrible day of the LORD comes. And it shall
come to pass that all who call upon the name
of the LORD shall be delivered; for in Mount
Zion and in Jerusalem there shall be those
who escape, as the LORD has said, and among
the survivors shall be those whom the LORD
calls.

The valley of decision

3 *d* "For behold, in those days and at that
time, when I restore the fortunes of Judah
2 and Jerusalem, I will gather all the nations
and bring them down to the valley of
Jehosh'aphat, and I will enter into judgment
with them there, on account of my people
and my heritage Israel, because they have
scattered them among the nations, and have
3 divided up my land, and have cast lots for my
people, and have given a boy for a harlot, and
have sold a girl for wine, and have drunk it.
4 "What are you to me, O Tyre and Sidon,
and all the regions of Philistia? Are you
paying me back for something? If you are
paying me back, I will requite your deed
upon your own head swiftly and speedily.
5 For you have taken my silver and my gold,
and have carried my rich treasures into your
6 temples.*e* You have sold the people of Judah
and Jerusalem to the Greeks, removing them
7 far from their own border. But now I will
stir them up from the place to which you
have sold them, and I will requite your deed
8 upon your own head. I will sell your sons
and your daughters into the hand of the sons
of Judah, and they will sell them to the
Sabe'ans, to a nation far off; for the LORD has
spoken."

9 Proclaim this among the nations:
   Prepare war,
      stir up the mighty men
   Let all the men of war draw near,
      let them come up.
10 Beat your ploughshares into swords,
      and your pruning hooks into spears;
   let the weak say, "I am a warrior."

11 Hasten and come,
      all you nations round about,
      gather yourselves there.
   Bring down thy warriors, O LORD.

Let the nations bestir themselves,   12
   and come up to the valley of Jehosh'-
      aphat;
for there I will sit to judge
   all the nations round about.

Put in the sickle,   13
   for the harvest is ripe.
Go in, tread,
   for the wine press is full.
The vats overflow,
   for their wickedness is great.

Multitudes, multitudes,   14
   in the valley of decision!
For the day of the LORD is near
   in the valley of decision.
The sun and the moon are darkened,   15
   and the stars withdraw their shining.

And the LORD roars from Zion,   16
   and utters his voice from Jerusalem,
   and the heavens and the earth shake.
But the LORD is a refuge to his people,
   a stronghold to the people of Israel.

"So you shall know that I am the LORD 17
      your God,
   who dwell in Zion, my holy mountain.
And Jerusalem shall be holy
   and strangers shall never again pass
      through it.

"And in that day   18
the mountains shall drip sweet wine,
   and the hills shall flow with milk,
and all the stream beds of Judah shall flow
      with water;
and a fountain shall come forth from the
      house of the LORD
   and water the valley of Shittim.

"Egypt shall become a desolation   19
   and Edom a desolate wilderness,
for the violence done to the people of
      Judah,
   because they have shed innocent blood
      in their land.
But Judah shall be inhabited for ever,   20
   and Jerusalem to all generations.
I will avenge their blood, and I will not 21
      clear the guilty,*f*
   for the LORD dwells in Zion."

d Ch 4.1 in Heb   *e* Or *palaces*   *f* Gk Syr: Heb *I will hold innocent their blood which I have not held innocent*
2.32: Rom 10.13.   3.4–8: Is 23; Ezek 26.1–28.19; Amos 1.9–10; Zech 9.3–4; Ezek 28.20–26; Zech 9.2;
Is 14.29–31; Jer 47; Ezek 25.15–17; Amos 1.6–8; Zeph 2.4–7; Zech 9.5–7.   3.10: Is 2.4; Mic 4.3.
3.13: Mk 4.29; Rev 14.15, 18–19.   3.16: Amos 1.2.   3.18: Ezek 47.1–12; Amos 9.13; Zech 14.8; Rev 22.1.

THE BOOK OF
AMOS

GOD AND THE NATIONS

THE words of Amos, who was
among the shepherds of Teko′a,
which he saw concerning Israel in
the days of Uzzi′ah king of Judah and in
the days of Jerobo′am the son of Jo′ash,
king of Israel, two years*a* before the
2 earthquake. And he said:
"The LORD roars from Zion,
    and utters his voice from Jeru-
    salem;
the pastures of the shepherds mourn,
    and the top of Carmel withers."

Damascus

3   Thus says the LORD:
"For three transgressions of
    Damascus,
    and for four, I will not revoke the
    punishment;*b*
because they have threshed Gilead
    with threshing sledges of iron.
4   So I will send a fire upon the house of
    Haz′ael,
    and it shall devour the strongholds of
    Ben-ha′dad.
5   I will break the bar of Damascus,
    and cut off the inhabitants from the
    Valley of Aven,*c*

and him that holds the sceptre
    from Beth-eden;
and the people of Syria shall go
    into exile to Kir,"
            says the LORD.

Gaza

Thus says the LORD: 6
"For three transgressions of Gaza,
    and for four, I will not revoke the
    punishment;*b*
because they carried into exile a whole
    people
    to deliver them up to Edom.
So I will send a fire upon the wall of 7
    Gaza,
    and it shall devour her strongholds.
I will cut off the inhabitants from Ashdod, 8
    and him that holds the sceptre from
    Ash′kelon;
I will turn my hand against Ekron;
    and the remnant of the Philistines shall
    perish,"
            says the Lord GOD.

Tyre

Thus says the LORD: 9
"For three transgressions of Tyre,
    and for four, I will not revoke the
    punishment;*b*
because they delivered up a whole people
    to Edom,
    and did not remember the covenant of
    brotherhood.
So I will send a fire upon the wall of 10
    Tyre,
    and it shall devour her strongholds."

Edom

Thus says the LORD: 11
"For three transgressions of Edom,
    and for four, I will not revoke the
    punishment;*b*
because he pursued his brother with the
    sword,
    and cast off all pity,
and his anger tore perpetually,
    and he kept his wrath*d* for ever.
So I will send a fire upon Teman,   12
    and it shall devour the strongholds of
    Bozrah."

---

a Or *during two years* *b* Heb *cause it to return* *c* Or *On* *d* Gk Syr Vg: Heb *his wrath kept*
1.2: Joel 3.16.   1.3–5: Is 17.1–3; Jer 49.23–27; Zech 9.1.
1.6–8: Is 14.29–31; Jer 47; Ezek 25.15–17; Joel 3.4–8; Zeph 2.4–7; Zech 9.5–7.
1.9–10: Is 23; Ezek 26.1–28.19; Joel 3.4–8; Zech 9.3–4.
1.11–12: Is 34; 63.1–6; Jer 49.7–22; Ezek 25.12–14; 35; Obad; Mal 1.2–5.

Ammon

13 Thus says the LORD:
"For three transgressions of the Ammonites,
and for four, I will not revoke the
punishment;*
because they have ripped up women with
child in Gilead,
that they might enlarge their border.
14 So I will kindle a fire in the wall of
Rabbah,
and it shall devour her strongholds,
with shouting in the day of battle,
with a tempest in the day of the whirlwind;
15 and their king shall go into exile,
he and his princes together,"
says the LORD.

Moab

2 Thus says the LORD:
"For three transgressions of Moab,
and for four, I will not revoke the
punishment;*
because he burned to lime
the bones of the king of Edom.
2 So I will send a fire upon Moab,
and it shall devour the strongholds of
Ker′ioth,
and Moab shall die amid uproar,
amid shouting and the sound of the
trumpet;
3 I will cut off the ruler from its midst,
and will slay all its princes with him,"
says the LORD.

Judah

4 Thus says the LORD:
"For three transgressions of Judah,
and for four, I will not revoke the
punishment;*
because they have rejected the law of the
LORD,
and have not kept his statutes,
but their lies have led them astray,
after which their fathers walked.
5 So I will send a fire upon Judah,
and it shall devour the strongholds of
Jerusalem."

Israel

6 Thus says the LORD:
"For three transgressions of Israel,
and for four, I will not revoke the
punishment;*

because they sell the righteous for silver,
and the needy for a pair of shoes—
they that trample the head of the poor into 7
the dust of the earth,
and turn aside the way of the afflicted;
a man and his father go in to the same
maiden,
so that my holy name is profaned;
they lay themselves down beside every altar 8
upon garments taken in pledge;
and in the house of their God they drink
the wine of those who have been fined.

"Yet I destroyed the Amorite before them, 9
whose height was like the height of the
cedars,
and who was as strong as the oaks;
I destroyed his fruit above,
and his roots beneath.
Also I brought you up out of the land of 10
Egypt,
and led you forty years in the
wilderness,
to possess the land of the Amorite.
And I raised up some of your sons for 11
prophets,
and some of your young men for
Nazirites.
Is it not indeed so, O people of Israel?"
says the LORD.

"But you made the Nazirites drink wine, 12
and commanded the prophets,
saying, 'You shall not prophesy.'

"Behold, I will press you down in your 13
place,
as a cart full of sheaves presses down.
Flight shall perish from the swift,   14
and the strong shall not retain his
strength,
nor shall the mighty save his life;
he who handles the bow shall not stand, 15
and he who is swift of foot shall not save
himself,
nor shall he who rides the horse save his
life;
and he who is stout of heart among the 16
mighty
shall flee away naked in that day,"
says the LORD.

GOD AND ISRAEL

HEAR this word that the LORD has spoken 3
against you, O people of Israel, against
the whole family which I brought up out of
the land of Egypt:

---

e Heb *cause it to return*
1.13–15: Jer 49.1–6; Ezek 21.28–32; 25.1–7; Zeph 2.8–11.
2.1–3: Is 15–16; 25.10–12; Jer 48; Ezek 25.8–11; Zeph 2.8–11.

2 "You only have I known
    of all the families of the earth;
  therefore I will punish you
    for all your iniquities.

3 "Do two walk together,
    unless they have made an appointment?
4 Does a lion roar in the forest,
    when he has no prey?
  Does a young lion cry out from his den,
    if he has taken nothing?
5 Does a bird fall in a snare on the earth,
    when there is no trap for it?
  Does a snare spring up from the ground,
    when it has taken nothing?
6 Is a trumpet blown in a city,
    and the people are not afraid?
  Does evil befall a city,
    unless the LORD has done it?
7 Surely the Lord GOD does nothing,
    without revealing his secret
    to his servants the prophets.
8 The lion has roared;
    who will not fear?
  The Lord GOD has spoken;
    who can but prophesy?"

9 Proclaim to the strongholds in Assyria,[f]
    and to the strongholds in the land of
    Egypt,
  and say, "Assemble yourselves upon the
    mountains of Samar'ia,
  and see the great tumults within her,
    and the oppressions in her midst."
10 "They do not know how to do right," says
    the LORD,
    "those who store up violence and rob-
    bery in their strongholds."
11 Therefore thus says the Lord GOD:
  "An adversary shall surround the
    land,
  and bring down your defences from you,
    and your strongholds shall be plun-
    dered."

12 Thus says the LORD: "As the shepherd
  rescues from the mouth of the lion two legs,
  or a piece of an ear, so shall the people of
  Israel who dwell in Samar'ia be rescued, with
  the corner of a couch and part[g] of a bed."

13 "Hear, and testify against the house of
    Jacob,"
    says the Lord GOD, the God of hosts,
14 "that on the day I punish Israel for his
    transgressions,
  I will punish the altars of Bethel,
    and the horns of the altar shall be cut off
    and fall to the ground.

I will smite the winter house with the 15
    summer house;
  and the houses of ivory shall perish,
  and the great houses[h] shall come to an
    end,"
                          says the LORD.

The women of Samaria

"Hear this word, you cows of Bashan,   4
    who are in the mountain of Samar'ia,
  who oppress the poor, who crush the
    needy,
  who say to their husbands,
    'Bring, that we may drink!'
The Lord GOD has sworn by his holiness 2
  that, behold, the days are coming upon
    you,
  when they shall take you away with hooks,
    even the last of you with fishhooks.
And you shall go out through the 3
    breaches,
    every one straight before her;
  and you shall be cast forth into
    Harmon,"
                          says the LORD.

"Come to Bethel, and transgress;   4
    to Gilgal, and multiply transgression;
  bring your sacrifices every morning,
    your tithes every three days;
  offer a sacrifice of thanksgiving of that 5
    which is leavened,
  and proclaim freewill offerings, publish
    them;
  for so you love to do, O people of
    Israel!"
                          says the Lord GOD.

"I gave you cleanness of teeth in all your 6
    cities,
  and lack of bread in all your places,
    yet you did not return to me,"
                          says the LORD.

"And I also withheld the rain from you   7
    when there were yet three months to the
      harvest;
  I would send rain upon one city,
    and send no rain upon another city;
  one field would be rained upon,
    and the field on which it did not rain
      withered;
  so two or three cities wandered to one city 8
    to drink water, and were not satisfied;
  yet you did not return to me,"
                          says the LORD.

"I smote you with blight and mildew;   9

<hr>

f Gk: Heb Ashdod   g The meaning of the Hebrew word is uncertain   h Or many houses
3.7: Rev 10.7.

I laid waste[i] your gardens and your
vineyards;
your fig trees and your olive trees the
locust devoured;
yet you did not return to me,"
says the LORD.

10 "I sent among you a pestilence after the
manner of Egypt;
I slew your young men with the sword;
I carried away your horses;[j]
and I made the stench of your camp go
up into your nostrils;
yet you did not return to me,"
says the LORD.

11 "I overthrew some of you,
as when God overthrew Sodom and
Gomor'rah,
and you were as a brand plucked out of
the burning;
yet you did not return to me,"
says the LORD.

12 "Therefore thus I will do to you, O
Israel;
because I will do this to you,
prepare to meet your God, O Israel!"

13 For lo, he who forms the mountains, and
creates the wind,
and declares to man what is his thought;
who makes the morning darkness,
and treads on the heights of the earth—
the LORD, the God of hosts, is his name!

The worshippers of Bethel

5 Hear this word which I take up over you in
lamentation, O house of Israel:
2 "Fallen, no more to rise,
is the virgin Israel;
forsaken on her land,
with none to raise her up."

3 For thus says the Lord GOD:
"The city that went forth a thousand
shall have a hundred left,
and that which went forth a hundred
shall have ten left
to the house of Israel."

4 For thus says the LORD to the house of
Israel:
"Seek me and live;
5 but do not seek Bethel,
and do not enter into Gilgal
or cross over to Beer-sheba;
for Gilgal shall surely go into exile,
and Bethel shall come to naught."

Seek the LORD and live,   6
lest he break out like fire in the house of
Joseph,
and it devour, with none to quench it for
Bethel,
O you who turn justice to wormwood,   7
and cast down righteousness to the
earth!

He who made the Plei'ades and Orion,   8
and turns deep darkness into the morning,
and darkens the day into night,
who calls for the waters of the sea,
and pours them out upon the surface of
the earth,
the LORD is his name,
who makes destruction flash forth against 9
the strong,
so that destruction comes upon the
fortress.

They hate him who reproves in the gate,   10
and they abhor him who speaks the
truth.
Therefore because you trample upon the 11
poor
and take from him exactions of wheat,
you have built houses of hewn stone,
but you shall not dwell in them;
you have planted pleasant vineyards,
but you shall not drink their wine.
For I know how many are your trans-   12
gressions,
and how great are your sins—
you who afflict the righteous, who take a
bribe,
and turn aside the needy in the gate.
Therefore he who is prudent will keep   13
silent in such a time;
for it is an evil time.

Seek good, and not evil,   14
that you may live;
and so the LORD, the God of hosts, will be
with you,
as you have said.
Hate evil, and love good,   15
and establish justice in the gate;
it may be that the LORD, the God of hosts,
will be gracious to the remnant of
Joseph.

Therefore thus says the LORD, the God of 16
hosts, the Lord:
"In all the squares there shall be
wailing;
and in all the streets they shall say,
'Alas! alas!'"
They shall call the farmers to mourning

[i] Cn: Heb the multitude of   [j] Heb with the captivity of your horses

and to wailing those who are skilled in
lamentation,

17 and in all vineyards there shall be wailing,
for I will pass through the midst of
you,"

says the LORD.

18 Woe to you who desire the day of the
LORD!
Why would you have the day of the
LORD?
It is darkness, and not light;

19 as if a man fled from a lion,
and a bear met him;
or went into the house and leaned with his
hand against the wall,
and a serpent bit him.

20 Is not the day of the LORD darkness, and
not light,
and gloom with no brightness in it?

21 "I hate, I despise your feasts,
and I take no delight in your solemn
assemblies.

22 Even though you offer me your burnt
offerings and cereal offerings,
I will not accept them,
and the peace offerings of your fatted
beasts
I will not look upon.

23 Take away from me the noise of your
songs;
to the melody of your harps I will not
listen.

24 But let justice roll down like waters,
and righteousness like an everflowing
stream.

25 "Did you bring to me sacrifices and offerings the forty years in the wilderness, O
26 house of Israel? You shall take up Sakkuth
your king, and Kaiwan your star-god, your
images,^{k} which you made for yourselves;
27 therefore I will take you into exile beyond
Damascus," says the LORD, whose name is
the God of hosts.

The rulers at ease

6 "Woe to those who are at ease in Zion,
and to those who feel secure on the
mountain of Samar'ia,
the notable men of the first of the
nations,
to whom the house of Israel come!

2 Pass over to Calneh, and see;
and thence go to Hamath the great;
then go down to Gath of the Philistines.
Are they better than these kingdoms?

Or is their territory greater than your
territory,

3 O you who put far away the evil day,
and bring near the seat of violence?

4 "Woe to those who lie upon beds of
ivory,
and stretch themselves upon their
couches,
and eat lambs from the flock,
and calves from the midst of the stall;

5 who sing idle songs to the sound of the
harp,
and like David invent for themselves
instruments of music;

6 who drink wine in bowls,
and anoint themselves with the finest
oils,
but are not grieved over the ruin of
Joseph!

7 Therefore they shall now be the first of
those to go into exile,
and the revelry of those who stretch
themselves shall pass away."

8 The Lord GOD has sworn by himself
(says the LORD, the God of hosts):
"I abhor the pride of Jacob,
and hate his strongholds;
and I will deliver up the city and all that
is in it."

9 And if ten men remain in one house, they
10 shall die. And when a man's kinsman, he
who burns him,^{l} shall take him up to bring
the bones out of the house, and shall say to
him who is in the innermost parts of the
house, "Is there still any one with you?" he
shall say, "No"; and he shall say, "Hush!
We must not mention the name of the
LORD."

11 For behold, the LORD commands,
and the great house shall be smitten into
fragments,
and the little house into bits.

12 Do horses run upon rocks?
Does one plough the sea with oxen?
But you have turned justice into poison
and the fruit of righteousness into
wormwood—

13 you who rejoice in Lo-debar,^{m}
who say, "Have we not by our own
strength
taken Karnaim^n for ourselves?"

14 "For behold, I will raise up against you a
nation,
O house of Israel," says the LORD, the
God of hosts;

---

^{k} Heb *your images, your star-god* ^{l} Or *who makes a burning for him* ^{m} Or *a thing of naught* ^{n} Or *horns*
5.25–27: Acts 7.42–43.

"and they shall oppress you from the
entrance of Hamath
to the Brook of the Arabah."

VISIONS OF JUDGMENT

Locusts

7 THUS the Lord GOD showed me: behold,
he was forming locusts in the beginning
of the shooting up of the latter growth; and
lo, it was the latter growth after the king's
2 mowings. When they had finished eating the
grass of the land, I said,
"O Lord GOD, forgive, I beseech thee!
How can Jacob stand?
He is so small!"
3 The LORD repented concerning this;
"It shall not be," said the LORD.

Fire

4 Thus the Lord GOD showed me: behold,
the Lord GOD was calling for a judgment by
fire, and it devoured the great deep and was
5 eating up the land. Then I said,
"O Lord GOD, cease, I beseech thee!
How can Jacob stand?
He is so small!"
6 The LORD repented concerning this;
"This also shall not be," said the Lord
GOD.

The plumb line

7 He showed me: behold, the Lord was
standing beside a wall built with a plumb
8 line, with a plumb line in his hand. And the
LORD said to me, "Amos, what do you see?"
And I said, "A plumb line." Then the Lord
said,
"Behold, I am setting a plumb line
in the midst of my people Israel;
I will never again pass by them;
9 the high places of Isaac shall be made
desolate,
and the sanctuaries of Israel shall be laid
waste,
and I will rise against the house of
Jerobo'am with the sword."

AMOS AT BETHEL

10 Then Amazi'ah the priest of Bethel sent to
Jerobo'am king of Israel, saying, "Amos has
conspired against you in the midst of the
house of Israel; the land is not able to bear all
11 his words. For thus Amos has said,

'Jerobo'am shall die by the sword,
and Israel must go into exile
away from his land.'"
And Amazi'ah said to Amos, "O seer, go, flee 12
away to the land of Judah, and eat bread
there, and prophesy there; but never again 13
prophesy at Bethel, for it is the king's
sanctuary, and it is a temple of the
kingdom."
Then Amos answered Amazi'ah, "I am no 14
prophet, nor a prophet's son;[o] but I am a
herdsman, and a dresser of sycamore trees,
and the LORD took me from following the 15
flock, and the LORD said to me, 'Go,
prophesy to my people Israel.'
"Now therefore hear the word of the 16
LORD.
You say, 'Do not prophesy against Israel,
and do not preach against the house of
Isaac.'
Therefore thus says the LORD: 17
'Your wife shall be a harlot in the city,
and your sons and your daughters shall
fall by the sword,
and your land shall be parcelled out by
line;
you yourself shall die in an unclean land,
and Israel shall surely go into exile away
from its land.'"

A basket of fruit

Thus the Lord GOD showed me: behold, a 8
basket of summer fruit.[p] And he said, 2
"Amos, what do you see?" And I said, "A
basket of summer fruit."[p] Then the LORD
said to me,
"The end[q] has come upon my people
Israel;
I will never again pass by them.
The songs of the temple[r] shall become 3
wailings in that day,"
says the Lord GOD;
"the dead bodies shall be many;
in every place they shall be cast out in
silence."[s]

Hear this, you who trample upon the 4
needy,
and bring the poor of the land to an end,
saying, "When will the new moon be over, 5
that we may sell grain?
And the sabbath,
that we may offer wheat for sale,
that we may make the ephah small and the
shekel great,
and deal deceitfully with false balances,
that we may buy the poor for silver 6
and the needy for a pair of sandals,
and sell the refuse of the wheat?"

---

[o] Or one of the sons of the prophets　[p] Heb qayits　[q] Heb qets　[r] Or palace　[s] Or be silent!

7 The LORD has sworn by the pride of
    Jacob:
  "Surely I will never forget any of their
    deeds.
8 Shall not the land tremble on this account,
  and every one mourn who dwells in it,
and all of it rise like the Nile,
    and be tossed about and sink again, like
    the Nile of Egypt?"

9 "And on that day," says the Lord GOD,
  "I will make the sun go down at noon,
    and darken the earth in broad daylight.
10 I will turn your feasts into mourning,
  and all your songs into lamentation;
I will bring sackcloth upon all loins,
  and baldness on every head;
I will make it like the mourning for an only
    son,
  and the end of it like a bitter day.

11 "Behold, the days are coming," says the
    Lord GOD,
  "when I will send a famine on the land;
not a famine of bread, nor a thirst for
    water,
but of hearing the words of the LORD.
12 They shall wander from sea to sea,
  and from north to east;
they shall run to and fro, to seek the word
    of the LORD,
  but they shall not find it.

13 "In that day the fair virgins and the young
    men
  shall faint for thirst.
14 Those who swear by Ash′imah of
    Samar′ia,
and say, 'As thy god lives, O Dan,'
and, 'As the way of Beer-sheba lives,'
  they shall fall, and never rise again."

The Lord at the altar

9 I saw the LORD standing beside[t] the altar,
and he said:
  "Smite the capitals until the thresholds
    shake,
    and shatter them on the heads of all the
    people;[u]
and what are left of them I will slay with
    the sword;
    not one of them shall flee away,
    not one of them shall escape.

2 "Though they dig into Sheol,
  from there shall my hand take them;
though they climb up to heaven,
  from there I will bring them down.

Though they hide themselves on the top of 3
    Carmel,
  from there I will search out and take
    them;
and though they hide from my sight at the
    bottom of the sea,
  there I will command the serpent, and it
    shall bite them.
And though they go into captivity before 4
    their enemies,
  there I will command the sword, and it
    shall slay them;
and I will set my eyes upon them
  for evil and not for good."

The Lord, GOD of hosts,   5
he who touches the earth and it melts,
  and all who dwell in it mourn,
and all of it rises like the Nile,
  and sinks again, like the Nile of Egypt;
who builds his upper chambers in the 6
    heavens,
  and founds his vault upon the earth;
who calls for the waters of the sea,
  and pours them out upon the surface of
    the earth—
the LORD is his name.

"Are you not like the Ethiopians to me, 7
  O people of Israel?" says the LORD.
"Did I not bring up Israel from the land of
    Egypt,
  and the Philistines from Caphtor and
    the Syrians from Kir?
Behold, the eyes of the Lord GOD are upon 8
    the sinful kingdom,
  and I will destroy it from the surface of
    the ground;
except that I will not utterly destroy the
    house of Jacob,"
               says the LORD.

"For lo, I will command,   9
  and shake the house of Israel among all
    the nations
as one shakes with a sieve,
  but no pebble shall fall upon the earth.
All the sinners of my people shall die by 10
    the sword,
  who say, 'Evil shall not overtake or meet
    us.'

"In that day I will raise up   11
  the booth of David that is fallen
and repair its breaches,
  and raise up its ruins,
  and rebuild it as in the days of old;
that they may possess the remnant of 12
    Edom

---

t Or *upon* u Heb *all of them*
9.11–12: Acts 15.16–17.

and all the nations who are called by my
name,"
says the LORD who does this.

13   "Behold, the days are coming," says the
LORD,
"when the ploughman shall overtake the
reaper
and the treader of grapes him who sows
the seed;
the mountains shall drip sweet wine,
and all the hills shall flow with it.
14   I will restore the fortunes of my people
Israel,

and they shall rebuild the ruined cities
and inhabit them;
they shall plant vineyards and drink their
wine,
and they shall make gardens and eat
their fruit.
I will plant them upon their land,   1
and they shall never again be plucked
up
out of the land which I have given
them,"
says the LORD your God.

THE BOOK OF
OBADIAH

T HE vision of Obadi′ah.

Edom

Thus says the Lord GOD concerning
Edom:
We have heard tidings from the LORD,
and a messenger has been sent among
the nations:
"Rise up! let us rise against her for
battle!"
2   Behold, I will make you small among the
nations,
you shall be utterly despised.
3   The pride of your heart has deceived you,
you who live in the clefts of the rock, *a*
whose dwelling is high,
who say in your heart,
"Who will bring me down to the
ground?"
4   Though you soar aloft like the eagle,
though your nest is set among the
stars,
thence I will bring you down,
says the LORD.

5   If thieves came to you,
if plunderers by night—
how you have been destroyed!—
would they not steal only enough for
themselves?
If grape gatherers came to you,
would they not leave gleanings?
6   How Esau has been pillaged,

his treasures sought out!
All your allies have deceived you,   7
they have driven you to the border;
your confederates have prevailed against
you;

a Or Sela
9.13: Joel 3.18.   **1–21:** Is 34; 63.1–6; Jer 49.7–22; Ezek 25.12–14; 35; Amos 1.11–12; Mal 1.2–5.

your trusted friends have set a trap
    under you—
there is no understanding of it.
Will I not on that day, says the LORD,
    destroy the wise men out of Edom,
    and understanding out of Mount Esau?
And your mighty men shall be dismayed,
    O Teman,
    so that every man from Mount Esau will
        be cut off by slaughter.
For the violence done to your brother
    Jacob,
    shame shall cover you,
    and you shall be cut off for ever.
On the day that you stood aloof,
    on the day that strangers carried off his
        wealth,
and foreigners entered his gates
    and cast lots for Jerusalem,
    you were like one of them.
But you should not have gloated over the
    day of your brother
    in the day of his misfortune;
you should not have rejoiced over the
    people of Judah
    in the day of their ruin;
you should not have boasted
    in the day of distress.
You should not have entered the gate of
    my people
    in the day of his calamity;
you should not have gloated over his
    disaster
    in the day of his calamity;
you should not have looted his goods
    in the day of his calamity.
You should not have stood at the parting
    of the ways
    to cut off his fugitives;
you should not have delivered up his
    survivors
    in the day of distress.

The day of the Lord

For the day of the LORD is near upon all 15
    the nations.
As you have done, it shall be done to you,
    your deeds shall return on your own
        head.
For as you have drunk upon my holy 16
    mountain,
all the nations round about shall drink;
they shall drink, and stagger,[b]
    and shall be as though they had not
        been.
But in Mount Zion there shall be those 17
    that escape,
    and it shall be holy;
and the house of Jacob shall possess their
    own possessions.
The house of Jacob shall be a fire,   18
    and the house of Joseph a flame,
    and the house of Esau stubble;
they shall burn them and consume them,
    and there shall be no survivor to the
        house of Esau;
        for the LORD has spoken.
Those of the Negeb shall possess Mount 19
    Esau,
    and those of the Shephe'lah the land of
        the Philistines;
they shall possess the land of E'phraim and
    the land of Samar'ia
    and Benjamin shall possess Gilead.
The exiles in Halah[c] who are of the people 20
    of Israel
    shall possess[d] Phoeni'cia as far as
        Zar'ephath;
and the exiles of Jerusalem who are in
    Sephar'ad
    shall possess the cities of the Negeb.
Saviours shall go up to Mount Zion   21
    to rule Mount Esau;
    and the kingdom shall be the LORD's.

b Cn: Heb swallow   c Cn: Heb this army   d Cn: Heb which

Joppa

THE BOOK OF
JONAH

NOW the word of the LORD came to Jonah the son of Amit'tai, saying,
2 "Arise, go to Nin'eveh, that great city, and cry against it; for their wickedness
3 has come up before me." But Jonah rose to flee to Tarshish from the presence of the LORD. He went down to Joppa and found a ship going to Tarshish; so he paid the fare, and went on board, to go with them to Tarshish, away from the presence of the LORD.

4 But the LORD hurled a great wind upon the sea, and there was a mighty tempest on the sea, so that the ship threatened to break up.
5 Then the mariners were afraid, and each cried to his god; and they threw the wares that were in the ship into the sea, to lighten it for them. But Jonah had gone down into the inner part of the ship and had lain down, and
6 was fast asleep. So the captain came and said to him, "What do you mean, you sleeper? Arise, call upon your god! Perhaps the god will give a thought to us, that we do not perish."

7 And they said to one another, "Come, let us cast lots, that we may know on whose account this evil has come upon us." So they
8 cast lots, and the lot fell upon Jonah. Then they said to him, "Tell us on whose account this evil has come upon us. What is your occupation? And whence do you come? What is your country? And of what people
9 are you?" And he said to them, "I am a Hebrew; and I fear the LORD, the God of heaven, who made the sea and the dry land."
10 Then the men were exceedingly afraid, and said to him, "What is this that you have

done!" For the men knew that he was fleeing from the presence of the LORD, because he had told them.

Then they said to him, "What shall we do to you, that the sea may quiet down for us?" For the sea grew more and more tempestuous. He said to them, "Take me up and throw me into the sea; then the sea will quiet down for you; for I know it is because of me that this great tempest has come upon you." Nevertheless the men rowed hard to bring the ship back to land, but they could not, for the sea grew more and more tempestuous against them. Therefore they cried to the LORD, "We beseech thee, O LORD, let us not perish for this man's life, and lay not on us innocent blood; for thou, O LORD, hast done as it pleased thee." So they took up Jonah and threw him into the sea; and the sea ceased from its raging. Then the men feared the LORD exceedingly, and they offered a sacrifice to the LORD and made vows.

The prophet's prayer

And the LORD appointed a great fish to swallow up Jonah; and Jonah was in the belly of the fish three days and three nights.

Then Jonah prayed to the LORD his God from the belly of the fish, saying,

"I called to the LORD, out of my distress,
    and he answered me;
out of the belly of Sheol I cried,
    and thou didst hear my voice.
For thou didst cast me into the deep,
    into the heart of the seas,

---

a Ch 2.1 in Heb
1.17: Mt 12.40.

and the flood was round about me;
all thy waves and thy billows
    passed over me.
Then I said, 'I am cast out
    from thy presence;
how shall I again look
    upon thy holy temple?'
The waters closed in over me,
    the deep was round about me;
weeds were wrapped about my head
    at the roots of the mountains.
I went down to the land
    whose bars closed upon me for ever;
yet thou didst bring up my life from the
    Pit,
    O Lord my God.

When my soul fainted within me,   7
    I remembered the Lord;
and my prayer came to thee,
    into thy holy temple.
Those who pay regard to vain idols   8
    forsake their true loyalty.
But I with the voice of thanksgiving   9
    will sacrifice to thee;
    what I have vowed I will pay.
    Deliverance belongs to the Lord!"
And the Lord spoke to the fish, and it 10
vomited out Jonah upon the dry land.

The prophet's obedience

Then the word of the Lord came to Jonah **3**
the second time, saying, "Arise, go to Nin'- 2
eveh, that great city, and proclaim to it the
message that I tell you." So Jonah arose and 3
went to Nin'eveh, according to the word of
the Lord. Now Nin'eveh was an exceedingly great city, three days' journey in
breadth. Jonah began to go into the city, 4
going a day's journey. And he cried, "Yet
forty days, and Nin'eveh shall be over-

Nineveh, the capital of Assyria

5 thrown!" And the people of Nin'eveh believed God; they proclaimed a fast, and put on sackcloth, from the greatest of them to the least of them.

6 Then tidings reached the king of Nin'eveh, and he arose from his throne, removed his robe, and covered himself with sackcloth, 7 and sat in ashes. And he made proclamation and published through Nin'eveh, "By the decree of the king and his nobles: Let neither man nor beast, herd nor flock, taste any- 8 thing; let them not feed, or drink water, but let man and beast be covered with sackcloth, and let them cry mightily to God; yea, let every one turn from his evil way and from 9 the violence which is in his hands. Who knows, God may yet repent and turn from his fierce anger, so that we perish not?"

10 When God saw what they did, how they turned from their evil way, God repented of the evil which he had said he would do to them; and he did not do it.

The prophet's education

4 But it displeased Jonah exceedingly, and he 2 was angry. And he prayed to the LORD and said, "I pray thee, LORD, is not this what I said when I was yet in my country? That is why I made haste to flee to Tarshish; for I knew that thou art a gracious God and merciful, slow to anger, and abounding in steadfast love, and repentest of evil. There- 3 fore now, O LORD, take my life from me, I beseech thee, for it is better for me to die than to live." And the LORD said, "Do you 4 do well to be angry?" Then Jonah went out 5 of the city and sat to the east of the city, and made a booth for himself there. He sat under it in the shade, till he should see what would become of the city.

And the LORD God appointed a plant,[b] and 6 made it come up over Jonah, that it might be a shade over his head, to save him from his discomfort. So Jonah was exceedingly glad because of the plant.[b] But when dawn came 7 up the next day, God appointed a worm which attacked the plant,[b] so that it with- ered. When the sun rose, God appointed a 8 sultry east wind, and the sun beat upon the head of Jonah so that he was faint; and he asked that he might die, and said, "It is better for me to die than to live." But God 9 said to Jonah, "Do you do well to be angry for the plant?"[b] And he said, "I do well to be angry, angry enough to die." And the 10 LORD said, "You pity the plant,[b] for which you did not labour, nor did you make it grow, which came into being in a night, and perished in a night. And should not I pity 11 Nin'eveh, that great city, in which there are more than a hundred and twenty thousand persons who do not know their right hand from their left, and also much cattle?"

THE BOOK OF
MICAH

THE word of the LORD that came to Micah of Mo'resheth in the days of Jotham, Ahaz, and Hezeki'ah, kings of Judah, which he saw concerning Samar'ia and Jerusalem.

The house of Israel

2 Hear, you peoples, all of you;
hearken, O earth, and all that is in it;
and let the Lord GOD be a witness against you,
the Lord from his holy temple.
3 For behold, the LORD is coming forth out of his place,
and will come down and tread upon the high places of the earth.
4 And the mountains will melt under him

and the valleys will be cleft,
like wax before the fire,
like waters poured down a steep place.
All this is for the transgression of Jacob 5
and for the sins of the house of Israel.
What is the transgression of Jacob?
Is it not Samar'ia?
And what is the sin of the house[a] of Judah?
Is it not Jerusalem?
Therefore I will make Samar'ia a heap in 6
the open country,
a place for planting vineyards;
and I will pour down her stones into the valley,
and uncover her foundations.
All her images shall be beaten to pieces, 7
all her hires shall be burned with fire,

---

[b] Heb qiqayon, probably *the castor oil plant*   [a] Gk Tg Compare Syr: Heb *what are the high places*
3.9: Joel 2.14.   **4.2:** Ex 34.6.   **1.2:** 1 Kings 22.28.

do not come forth;
the wailing of Beth-e′zel
shall take away from you its standing
place.
For the inhabitants of Maroth   12
wait anxiously for good,
because evil has come down from the
LORD
to the gate of Jerusalem.
Harness the steeds to the chariots,   13
inhabitants of Lachish;
you were[c] the beginning of sin
to the daughter of Zion,
for in you were found
the transgressions of Israel.
Therefore you shall give parting gifts 14
to Mo′resheth-gath;
the houses of Achzib shall be a deceitful
thing
to the kings of Israel.
I will again bring a conqueror upon you, 15
inhabitants of Mare′shah;
the glory of Israel
shall come to Adullam.
Make yourselves bald and cut off your 16
hair,
for the children of your delight;
make yourselves as bald as the eagle,
for they shall go from you into exile.

To men in power

Woe to those who devise wickedness   **2**
and work evil upon their beds!
When the morning dawns, they perform it,
because it is in the power of their hand.
They covet fields, and seize them;   2
and houses, and take them away;
they oppress a man and his house,
a man and his inheritance.
Therefore thus says the LORD: 3
Behold, against this family I am devising
evil,
from which you cannot remove your
necks;
and you shall not walk haughtily,
for it will be an evil time.
In that day they shall take up a taunt song 4
against you,
and wail with bitter lamentation,
and say, "We are utterly ruined;
he changes the portion of my people;
how he removes it from me!
Among our captors[d] he divides our
fields."
Therefore you will have none to cast the 5
line by lot
in the assembly of the LORD.

"Do not preach"—thus they preach—   6

and all her idols I will lay waste;
for from the hire of a harlot she gathered
them,
and to the hire of a harlot they shall
return.

8   For this I will lament and wail;
I will go stripped and naked;
I will make lamentation like the jackals,
and mourning like the ostriches.
9   For her wound[b] is incurable;
and it has come to Judah,
it has reached to the gate of my people,
to Jerusalem.

The house of Judah

10   Tell it not in Gath,
weep not at all;
in Beth-le-aph′rah
roll yourselves in the dust.
11   Pass on your way,
inhabitants of Shaphir,
in nakedness and shame;
the inhabitants of Za′anan

---

[b] Gk Syr Vg: Heb *wounds*   [c] Cn: Heb *it was*   [d] Cn: Heb *the rebellious*

"one should not preach of such things;
   disgrace will not overtake us."
7 Should this be said, O house of Jacob?
   Is the Spirit of the LORD impatient?
   Are these his doings?
Do not my words do good
   to him who walks uprightly?
8 But you rise against my people[e] as an
   enemy;
   you strip the robe from the peaceful,[f]
from those who pass by trustingly
   with no thought of war.
9 The women of my people you drive out
   from their pleasant houses;
from their young children you take away
   my glory for ever.
10 Arise and go,
   for this is no place to rest;
because of uncleanness that destroys
   with a grievous destruction.
11 If a man should go about and utter wind
   and lies,
   saying, "I will preach to you of wine and
   strong drink,"
   he would be the preacher for this
   people!

12 I will surely gather all of you, O Jacob,
   I will gather the remnant of Israel;
I will set them together
   like sheep in a fold,
like a flock in its pasture,
   a noisy multitude of men.
13 He who opens the breach will go up before
   them;
   they will break through and pass the
   gate,
   going out by it.
Their king will pass on before them,
   the LORD at their head.

Jerusalem, city of blood

3 And I said:
   Hear, you heads of Jacob
   and rulers of the house of Israel!
Is it not for you to know justice?—
2   you who hate the good and love the
   evil,
who tear the skin from off my people,
   and their flesh from off their bones;
3 who eat the flesh of my people,
   and flay their skin from off them,
and break their bones in pieces,
   and chop them up like meat[g] in a kettle,
   like flesh in a cauldron.

4 Then they will cry to the LORD,
   but he will not answer them;

he will hide his face from them at that
   time,
because they have made their deeds evil.

Thus says the LORD concerning the 5
   prophets
   who lead my people astray,
who cry "Peace"
   when they have something to eat,
but declare war against him
   who puts nothing into their mouths.
Therefore it shall be night to you, without 6
   vision,
   and darkness to you, without divination.
The sun shall go down upon the prophets,
   and the day shall be black over them;
the seers shall be disgraced,   7
   and the diviners put to shame;
they shall all cover their lips,
   for there is no answer from God.
But as for me, I am filled with power, 8
   with the Spirit of the LORD,
   and with justice and might,
to declare to Jacob his transgression
   and to Israel his sin.

Hear this, you heads of the house of Jacob 9
   and rulers of the house of Israel,
who abhor justice
   and pervert all equity,
who build Zion with blood   10
   and Jerusalem with wrong.
Its heads give judgment for a bribe, 11
   its priests teach for hire,
   its prophets divine for money;
yet they lean upon the LORD and say,
   "Is not the LORD in the midst of us?
   No evil shall come upon us."
Therefore because of you   12
   Zion shall be ploughed as a field;
Jerusalem shall become a heap of ruins,
   and the mountain of the house a wooded
   height.

Jerusalem, city of God

It shall come to pass in the latter days 4
   that the mountain of the house of the
   LORD
shall be established as the highest of the
   mountains,
   and shall be raised up above the hills;
and peoples shall flow to it,
   and many nations shall come, and say: 2
"Come, let us go up to the mountain of the
   LORD,
   to the house of the God of Jacob;
that he may teach us his ways
   and we may walk in his paths."

[e] Cn: Heb *yesterday my people rose*   [f] Cn: Heb *from before a garment*   [g] Gk: Heb *as*
4.1–3: Is 2.2–4.

For out of Zion shall go forth the law,
  and the word of the LORD from
    Jerusalem.
3 He shall judge between many peoples,
  and shall decide for strong nations afar
    off;
  and they shall beat their swords into
    ploughshares,
  and their spears into pruning hooks;
nation shall not lift up sword against
  nation,
  neither shall they learn war any more;
4 but they shall sit every man under his vine
  and under his fig tree,
  and none shall make them afraid;
for the mouth of the LORD of hosts has
  spoken.

5 For all the peoples walk
  each in the name of its god,
but we will walk in the name of the LORD
  our God
    for ever and ever.

6 In that day, says the LORD,
  I will assemble the lame
and gather those who have been driven
  away,
  and those whom I have afflicted;
7 and the lame I will make the remnant;
  and those who were cast off, a strong
    nation;
and the LORD will reign over them in
  Mount Zion
    from this time forth and for evermore.

8 And you, O tower of the flock,
  hill of the daughter of Zion,
to you shall it come,
  the former dominion shall come,
  the kingdom of the daughter of
    Jerusalem.

9 Now why do you cry aloud?
  Is there no king in you?
Has your counsellor perished,
  that pangs have seized you like a woman
    in travail?
10 Writhe and groan,[h] O daughter of Zion,
  like a woman in travail;
for now you shall go forth from the city
  and dwell in the open country;
  you shall go to Babylon.
There you shall be rescued,
  there the LORD will redeem you
    from the hand of your enemies.

11 Now many nations
  are assembled against you,

saying, "Let her be profaned,
  and let our eyes gaze upon Zion."
But they do not know   12
  the thoughts of the LORD,
they do not understand his plan,
  that he has gathered them as sheaves to
    the threshing floor.
Arise and thresh,   13
  O daughter of Zion,
for I will make your horn iron
  and your hoofs bronze;
you shall beat in pieces many peoples,
  and shall[i] devote their gain to the
    LORD,
  their wealth to the Lord of the whole
    earth.

Now you are walled about with a wall;[k] 5[j]
  siege is laid against us;
with a rod they strike upon the cheek
  the ruler of Israel.

Little town of Bethlehem

But you, O Bethlehem Eph'rathah,   2[l]
  who are little to be among the clans of
    Judah,
from you shall come forth for me
  one who is to be ruler in Israel,
whose origin is from of old,
  from ancient days.
Therefore he shall give them up until the 3
  time
  when she who is in travail has brought
    forth;
then the rest of his brethren shall return
  to the people of Israel.
And he shall stand and feed his flock in the 4
  strength of the LORD,
  in the majesty of the name of the LORD
    his God.
And they shall dwell secure, for now
  he shall be great
    to the ends of the earth.

And this shall be peace,   5
  when the Assyrian comes into our land
  and treads upon our soil,[m]
that we will raise against him seven
  shepherds
  and eight princes of men;
they shall rule the land of Assyria with the 6
  sword,
  and the land of Nimrod with the drawn
    sword;[n]
and they[o] shall deliver us from the
  Assyrian
when he comes into our land
  and treads within our border.

[h] Heb uncertain   [i] Gk Syr Tg: Heb *I will*   [j] Ch 4.14 in Heb   [k] Cn Compare Gk: Heb obscure
[l] Ch 5.1 in Heb   [m] Gk: Heb *in our palaces*   [n] Cn: Heb *in its entrances*   [o] Heb *he*
4.4: Zech 3.10.   5.2: Mt 2.6; Jn 7.42.

7 Then the remnant of Jacob shall be
   in the midst of many peoples
like dew from the LORD,
   like showers upon the grass,
which tarry not for men
   nor wait for the sons of men.
8 And the remnant of Jacob shall be among
   the nations,
   in the midst of many peoples,
like a lion among the beasts of the
   forest,
   like a young lion among the flocks of
   sheep,
which, when it goes through, treads down
   and tears in pieces, and there is none to
   deliver.
9 Your hand shall be lifted up over your
   adversaries,
   and all your enemies shall be cut off.

10 And in that day, says the LORD,
   I will cut off your horses from among
   you
   and will destroy your chariots;
11 and I will cut off the cities of your land
   and throw down all your strongholds;
12 and I will cut off sorceries from your hand,
   and you shall have no more soothsayers;
13 and I will cut off your images
   and your pillars from among you,
and you shall bow down no more
   to the work of your hands;
14 and I will root out your Ashe′rim from
   among you
   and destroy your cities.

And in anger and wrath I will execute 15
   vengeance
upon the nations that did not obey.

Hear what the LORD says: **6**
Arise, plead your case before the mountains,
   and let the hills hear your voice.
Hear, you mountains, the controversy of 2
   the LORD,
   and you enduring foundations of the
   earth;
for the LORD has a controversy with his
   people,
   and he will contend with Israel.

"O my people, what have I done to you? 3
   In what have I wearied you? Answer
   me!
For I brought you up from the land of 4
   Egypt,
   and redeemed you from the house of
   bondage;
and I sent before you Moses,
   Aaron, and Miriam.
O my people, remember what Balak king 5
   of Moab devised,
   and what Balaam the son of Be′or
   answered him,
and what happened from Shittim to
   Gilgal,
   that you may know the saving acts of the
   LORD."

"With what shall I come before the LORD, 6
   and bow myself before God on high?
Shall I come before him with burnt
   offerings,
   with calves a year old?
Will the LORD be pleased with thousands 7
   of rams,
   with ten thousands of rivers of oil?
Shall I give my first-born for my transgression,
   the fruit of my body for the sin of my
   soul?"
He has showed you, O man, what is good; 8
   and what does the LORD require of you
but to do justice, and to love kindness,[p]
   and to walk humbly with your God?

The Lord's call to the city

The voice of the LORD cries to the city— 9
   and it is sound wisdom to fear thy name:
"Hear, O tribe and assembly of the city![q]
Can I forget[r] the treasures of wicked- 10
   ness in the house of the wicked,
   and the scant measure that is accursed?

---

[p] Or *steadfast love*   [q] Cn Compare Gk: Heb *and who has appointed it yet*   [r] Cn: Heb uncertain

11 Shall I acquit the man with wicked scales
and with a bag of deceitful weights?

12 Your[s] rich men are full of violence;
your[s] inhabitants speak lies,
and their tongue is deceitful in their
mouth.

13 Therefore I have begun[t] to smite you,
making you desolate because of your
sins.

14 You shall eat, but not be satisfied,
and there shall be hunger in your inward
parts;
you shall put away, but not save,
and what you save I will give to the
sword.

15 You shall sow, but not reap;
you shall tread olives, but not anoint
yourselves with oil;
you shall tread grapes, but not drink
wine.

16 For you have kept the statutes of Omri,[u]
and all the works of the house of Ahab;
and you have walked in their counsels;
that I may make you a desolation, and
your[v] inhabitants a hissing;
so you shall bear the scorn of the
peoples."[w]

7 Woe is me! For I have become
as when the summer fruit has been
gathered,
as when the vintage has been gleaned:
there is no cluster to eat,
no first-ripe fig which my soul desires.

2 The godly man has perished from the
earth,
and there is none upright among men;
they all lie in wait for blood,
and each hunts his brother with a net.

3 Their hands are upon what is evil, to do it
diligently;
the prince and the judge ask for a bribe,
and the great man utters the evil desire of
his soul;
thus they weave it together.

4 The best of them is like a brier,
the most upright of them a thorn hedge.
The day of their[x] watchmen, of their[x]
punishment, has come;
now their confusion is at hand.

5 Put no trust in a neighbour,
have no confidence in a friend;
guard the doors of your mouth
from her who lies in your bosom;

6 for the son treats the father with contempt,
the daughter rises up against her
mother,
the daughter-in-law against her mother-
in-law;

a man's enemies are the men of his own
house.

7 But as for me, I will look to the LORD,
I will wait for the God of my salvation;
my God will hear me.

Trust in God

8 Rejoice not over me, O my enemy;
when I fall, I shall rise;
when I sit in darkness,
the LORD will be a light to me.

9 I will bear the indignation of the LORD
because I have sinned against him,
until he pleads my cause
and executes judgment for me.
He will bring me forth to the light;
I shall behold his deliverance.

10 Then my enemy will see,
and shame will cover her who said to
me,
"Where is the LORD your God?"
My eyes will gloat over her;
now she will be trodden down
like the mire of the streets.

11 A day for the building of your walls!
In that day the boundary shall be far
extended.

12 In that day they will come to you,
from Assyria to[y] Egypt,
and from Egypt to the River,
from sea to sea and from mountain to
mountain.

13 But the earth will be desolate
because of its inhabitants,
for the fruit of their doings.

14 Shepherd thy people with thy staff,
the flock of thy inheritance,
who dwell alone in a forest
in the midst of a garden land;
let them feed in Bashan and Gilead
as in the days of old.

15 As in the days when you came out of the
land of Egypt
I will show them[z] marvellous things.

16 The nations shall see and be ashamed
of all their might;
they shall lay their hands on their
mouths;
their ears shall be deaf;

17 they shall lick the dust like a serpent,
like the crawling things of the earth;
they shall come trembling out of their
strongholds,

[s] Heb *whose*   [t] Gk Syr Vg: Heb *have made sick*   [u] Gk Syr Vg Tg: Heb *the statutes of Omri are kept*
[v] Heb *its*   [w] Gk: Heb *my people*   [x] Heb *your*   [y] Cn: Heb *and cities of*   [z] Heb *him*
7.6: Mt 10.21, 35–36; Mk 13.12; Lk 12.53.

they shall turn in dread to the LORD our God,
and they shall fear because of thee.

18 Who is a God like thee, pardoning iniquity
and passing over transgression
for the remnant of his inheritance?
He does not retain his anger for ever
because he delights in steadfast love.

He will again have compassion upon us, 19
he will tread our iniquities under foot.
Thou wilt cast all our[a] sins
into the depths of the sea.
Thou wilt show faithfulness to Jacob 20
and steadfast love to Abraham,
as thou hast sworn to our fathers
from the days of old.

THE BOOK OF

NAHUM

AN oracle concerning Nin′eveh. The
book of the vision of Nahum of
Elkosh.

The wrath of God

2 The LORD is a jealous God and avenging,
the LORD is avenging and wrathful;
the LORD takes vengeance on his
adversaries
and keeps wrath for his enemies.
3 The LORD is slow to anger and of great
might,
and the LORD will by no means clear the
guilty.

His way is in whirlwind and storm,

and the clouds are the dust of his
feet.
He rebukes the sea and makes it dry, 4
he dries up all the rivers;
Bashan and Carmel wither,
the bloom of Lebanon fades.
The mountains quake before him, 5
the hills melt;
the earth is laid waste before him,
the world and all that dwell therein.

Who can stand before his indignation? 6
Who can endure the heat of his
anger?
His wrath is poured out like fire,
and the rocks are broken asunder by
him.
The LORD is good, 7
a stronghold in the day of trouble;
he knows those who take refuge in
him.
But with an overflowing flood 8

---

he will make a full end of his adversaries,[a]
and will pursue his enemies into
darkness.

9 What do you plot against the LORD?
He will make a full end;
he will not take vengeance[b] twice on his
foes.[c]

o Like entangled thorns they are consumed,[d]
like dry stubble.

11 Did one not[e] come out from you,
who plotted evil against the LORD,
and counselled villainy?

12 Thus says the LORD,
"Though they be strong and many,[f]
they will be cut off and pass away.
Though I have afflicted you,
I will afflict you no more.

13 And now I will break his yoke from off you
and will burst your bonds asunder."

14 The LORD has given commandment about
you:
"No more shall your name be perpetuated;
from the house of your gods I will cut off
the graven image and the molten image.
I will make your grave, for you are vile."

15[g] Behold, on the mountains the feet of him
who brings good tidings,
who proclaims peace!
Keep your feasts, O Judah,
fulfil your vows,
for never again shall the wicked come
against you,
he is utterly cut off.

2 The shatterer has come up against you.
Man the ramparts;
watch the road;
gird your loins;
collect all your strength.

2 (For the LORD is restoring the majesty of
Jacob
as the majesty of Israel,
for plunderers have stripped them
and ruined their branches.)

Attack on Nineveh

3 The shield of his mighty men is red,
his soldiers are clothed in scarlet.

The chariots flash like flame[h]
when mustered in array;
the chargers[i] prance.

The chariots rage in the streets,   4
they rush to and fro through the
squares;
they gleam like torches,
they dart like lightning.

The officers are summoned,   5
they stumble as they go,
they hasten to the wall,
the mantelet is set up.

The river gates are opened,   6
the palace is in dismay;
its mistress[j] is stripped, she is carried off, 7
her maidens lamenting,
moaning like doves,
and beating their breasts.

Nin'eveh is like a pool   8
whose waters[k] run away.
"Halt! Halt!" they cry;
but none turns back.

Plunder the silver,   9
plunder the gold!
There is no end of treasure,
or wealth of every precious thing.

Desolate! Desolation and ruin!   10
Hearts faint and knees tremble,
anguish is on all loins,
all faces grow pale!

Where is the lions' den,   11
the cave[i] of the young lions,
where the lion brought his prey,
where his cubs were, with none to
disturb?

The lion tore enough for his whelps   12
and strangled prey for his lionesses;
he filled his caves with prey
and his dens with torn flesh.

Behold, I am against you, says the LORD of 13
hosts, and I will burn your[m] chariots in
smoke, and the sword shall devour your
young lions; I will cut off your prey from the
earth, and the voice of your messengers shall
no more be heard.

The end of Nineveh

Woe to the bloody city,   3
all full of lies and booty—
no end to the plunder!
The crack of whip, and rumble of wheel, 2
galloping horse and bounding chariot!
Horsemen charging,   3

---

[a] Gk: Heb *her place*   [b] Gk: Heb *rise up*   [c] Cn: Heb *distress*
[d] Heb *are consumed, drunken as with their drink*   [e] Cn: Heb *fully*   [f] Heb uncertain   [g] Ch 2.1 in Heb
[h] Cn: The meaning of the Hebrew word is uncertain   [i] Cn Compare Gk Syr: Heb *cypresses*
[j] The meaning of the Hebrew is uncertain
[k] Cn Compare Gk: Heb *from the days that she has become, and they*   [l] Cn: Heb *pasture*   [m] Heb *her*
1.15: Is 40.9; 52.7; Acts 10.36; Rom 10.15.

flashing sword and glittering spear,
  hosts of slain,
    heaps of corpses,
  dead bodies without end—
    they stumble over the bodies!
4 And all for the countless harlotries of the
    harlot,
  graceful and of deadly charms,
who betrays nations with her harlotries,
  and peoples with her charms.

5 Behold, I am against you,
  says the LORD of hosts,
    and will lift up your skirts over your
      face;
  and I will let nations look on your
    nakedness
  and kingdoms on your shame.
6 I will throw filth at you
  and treat you with contempt,
  and make you a gazingstock.
7 And all who look on you will shrink from
    you and say,
  Wasted is Nin'eveh; who will bemoan
    her?
  whence shall I seek comforters for her? [n]

8 Are you better than Thebes [o]
  that sat by the Nile,
with water around her,
  her rampart a sea,
  and water her wall?
9 Ethiopia was her strength,
  Egypt too, and that without limit;
  Put and the Libyans were her [p] helpers.

10 Yet she was carried away,
  she went into captivity;
her little ones were dashed in pieces
  at the head of every street;
for her honoured men lots were cast,
  and all her great men were bound in
    chains.
11 You also will be drunken,
  you will be dazed;
  you will seek

a refuge from the enemy.
All your fortresses are like fig trees   12
  with first-ripe figs—
if shaken they fall
  into the mouth of the eater.
Behold, your troops   13
  are women in your midst.
The gates of your land
  are wide open to your foes;
  fire has devoured your bars.

Draw water for the siege,   14
  strengthen your forts;
go into the clay,
  tread the mortar,
  take hold of the brick mould!
There will the fire devour you,   15
  the sword will cut you off.
It will devour you like the locust.

Multiply yourselves like the locust,
  multiply like the grasshopper!
You increased your merchants   16
  more than the stars of the heavens.
  The locust spreads its wings and flies
    away.
Your princes are like grasshoppers,   17
  your scribes [q] like clouds of locusts
settling on the fences
  in a day of cold—
when the sun rises, they fly away;
  no one knows where they are.

Your shepherds are asleep,
  O king of Assyria;   18
  your nobles slumber.
Your people are scattered on the
    mountains
  with none to gather them.
There is no assuaging your hurt,   19
  your wound is grievous.
All who hear the news of you
  clap their hands over you.
For upon whom has not come
  your unceasing evil?

[n] Gk: Heb *you*   [o] Heb *No-amon*   [p] Gk: Heb *your*   [q] Or *marshals*

THE BOOK OF
HABAKKUK

T HE oracle of God which Habak′kuk
the prophet saw.

2 O LORD, how long shall I cry for help,
and thou wilt not hear?
Or cry to thee "Violence!"
and thou wilt not save?
3 Why dost thou make me see wrongs
and look upon trouble?
Destruction and violence are before me;
strife and contention arise.
4 So the law is slacked
and justice never goes forth.
For the wicked surround the righteous,
so justice goes forth perverted.

5 Look among the nations, and see;
wonder and be astounded.
For I am doing a work in your days
that you would not believe if told.
6 For lo, I am rousing the Chalde′ans,
that bitter and hasty nation,
who march through the breadth of the
earth,
to seize habitations not their own.
7 Dread and terrible are they;
their justice and dignity proceed from
themselves.
8 Their horses are swifter than leopards,
more fierce than the evening wolves;
their horsemen press proudly on.
Yea, their horsemen come from afar;
they fly like an eagle swift to
devour.
9 They all come for violence;
terror[a] of them goes before them.
They gather captives like sand.
10 At kings they scoff,
and of rulers they make sport.
They laugh at every fortress,
for they heap up earth and take it.
11 Then they sweep by like the wind and go
on,
guilty men, whose own might is their
god!

12 Art thou not from everlasting,
O LORD my God, my Holy One?
We shall not die.
O LORD, thou hast ordained them as a
judgment;
and thou, O Rock, hast established them
for chastisement.

Thou who art of purer eyes than to behold 13
evil
and canst not look on wrong,
why dost thou look on faithless men,
and art silent when the wicked swallows
up
the man more righteous than he?
For thou makest men like the fish of the 14
sea,
like crawling things that have no ruler.
He brings all of them up with a hook, 15
he drags them out with his net,
he gathers them in his seine;
so he rejoices and exults.
Therefore he sacrifices to his net 16
and burns incense to his seine;
for by them he lives in luxury,[b]
and his food is rich.
Is he then to keep on emptying his net, 17
and mercilessly slaying nations for ever?

The prophet's watchtower

I will take my stand to watch, 2
and station myself on the tower,
and look forth to see what he will say to
me,
and what I will answer concerning my
complaint.
And the LORD answered me: 2
"Write the vision;

---

a Cn: Heb uncertain   b Heb his portion is fat
1-2: Is 13.1–14.23; 47; Jer 50–51.   1.5: Acts 13.41.   1.6: Rev 20.9.   2.1: Is 21.8.

make it plain upon tablets,
so he may run who reads it.

3 For still the vision awaits its time;
it hastens to the end—it will not lie.
If it seem slow, wait for it;
it will surely come, it will not delay.

4 Behold, he whose soul is not upright in
him shall fail,[c]
but the righteous shall live by his faith.[d]

5 Moreover, wine is treacherous;
the arrogant man shall not abide.[e]
His greed is as wide as Sheol;
like death he has never enough.
He gathers for himself all nations,
and collects as his own all peoples."

6 Shall not all these take up their taunt
against him, in scoffing derision of him, and
say,
"Woe to him who heaps up what is not his
own—
for how long?—
and loads himself with pledges!"

7 Will not your debtors suddenly arise,
and those awake who will make you
tremble?
Then you will be booty for them.

8 Because you have plundered many
nations,
all the remnant of the peoples shall
plunder you,
for the blood of men and violence to the
earth,
to cities and all who dwell therein.

9 Woe to him who gets evil gain for his
house,
to set his nest on high,
to be safe from the reach of harm!

10 You have devised shame to your house
by cutting off many peoples;
you have forfeited your life.

11 For the stone will cry out from the wall,
and the beam from the woodwork
respond.

12 Woe to him who builds a town with blood,
and founds a city on iniquity!

13 Behold, is it not from the LORD of hosts
that peoples labour only for fire,
and nations weary themselves for
naught?

14 For the earth will be filled
with the knowledge of the glory of the
LORD,
as the waters cover the sea.

15 Woe to him who makes his neighbours
drink

of the cup of his wrath,[f] and makes them
drunk,
to gaze on their shame!
You will be sated with contempt instead of 16
glory.
Drink, yourself, and stagger![g]
The cup in the LORD's right hand
will come around to you,
and shame will come upon your glory!
The violence done to Lebanon will 17
overwhelm you;
the destruction of the beasts will terrify
you,[h]
for the blood of men and violence to the
earth,
to cities and all who dwell therein.

What profit is an idol   18
when its maker has shaped it,
a metal image, a teacher of lies?
For the workman trusts in his own
creation
when he makes dumb idols!
Woe to him who says to a wooden thing, 19
Awake;
to a dumb stone, Arise!
Can this give revelation?
Behold, it is overlaid with gold and silver,
and there is no breath at all in it.

But the LORD is in his holy temple;   20
let all the earth keep silence before
him.

The prophet's prayer

A prayer of Habak'kuk the prophet, accor- 3
ding to Shigion'oth.
O LORD, I have heard the report of thee, 2
and thy work, O LORD, do I fear.
In the midst of the years renew it;
in the midst of the years make it known;
in wrath remember mercy.
God came from Teman, 3
and the Holy One from Mount Paran.
His glory covered the heavens,
and the earth was full of his praise.
Selah
His brightness was like the light, 4
rays flashed from his hand;
and there he veiled his power.
Before him went pestilence, 5
and plague followed close behind.
He stood and measured the earth; 6
he looked and shook the nations;
then the eternal mountains were scattered,
the everlasting hills sank low.
His ways were as of old.
I saw the tents of Cushan in affliction; 7

<hr>

[c] Cn: Heb *is puffed up*   [d] Or *faithfulness*   [e] The Hebrew of these two lines is obscure
[f] Cn: Heb *joining to your wrath*   [g] Cn Compare Gk Syr: Heb *be uncircumcised*   [h] Gk Syr: Heb *them*
2.3: Heb 10.37.   2.4: Rom 1.17; Gal 3.11; Heb 10.38–39.   2.14: Is 11.9.   2.20: Zeph 1.7; Zech 2.13.

the curtains of the land of Mid'ian did
tremble.
Was thy wrath against the rivers, O LORD?
Was thy anger against the rivers,
or thy indignation against the sea,
when thou didst ride upon thy horses,
upon thy chariot of victory?
Thou didst strip the sheath from thy bow,
and put the arrows to the string.[i]
Selah
Thou didst cleave the earth with rivers.
The mountains saw thee, and writhed;
the raging waters swept on;
the deep gave forth its voice,
it lifted its hands on high.
The sun and moon stood still in their
habitation[j]
at the light of thine arrows as they sped,
at the flash of thy glittering spear.
Thou didst bestride the earth in fury,
thou didst trample the nations in anger.
Thou wentest forth for the salvation of thy
people,
for the salvation of thy anointed.
Thou didst crush the head of the wicked,[k]
laying him bare from thigh to neck.[l]
Selah
Thou didst pierce with thy[m] shafts the
head of his warriors,[n]

who came like a whirlwind to scatter me,
rejoicing as if to devour the poor in
secret.
Thou didst trample the sea with thy 15
horses,
the surging of mighty waters.

I hear, and my body trembles,   16
my lips quiver at the sound;
rottenness enters into my bones,
my steps totter[o] beneath me.
I will quietly wait for the day of trouble
to come upon people who invade us.

Though the fig tree do not blossom,   17
nor fruit be on the vines,
the produce of the olive fail
and the fields yield no food,
the flock be cut off from the fold
and there be no herd in the stalls,
yet I will rejoice in the LORD,   18
I will joy in the God of my salvation.
GOD, the Lord, is my strength;   19
he makes my feet like hinds' feet,
he makes me tread upon my high places.

To the choirmaster: with stringed[p] instruments.

THE BOOK OF
ZEPHANIAH

THE word of the LORD which came to
Zephani'ah the son of Cushi, son of
Gedali'ah, son of Amari'ah, son of
Hezeki'ah, in the days of Josi'ah the son
of Amon, king of Judah.

The day of the Lord

2 "I will utterly sweep away everything
from the face of the earth," says the
LORD.
3 "I will sweep away man and beast;
I will sweep away the birds of the air
and the fish of the sea.
I will overthrow[a] the wicked;
I will cut off mankind
from the face of the earth," says the
LORD.
4 "I will stretch out my hand against Judah,
and against all the inhabitants of
Jerusalem;

and I will cut off from this place the
remnant of Ba'al
and the name of the idolatrous priests;[b]
those who bow down on the roofs   5
to the host of the heavens;
those who bow down and swear to the
LORD

---

[i] Cn: Heb obscure   [j] Heb uncertain   [k] Cn: Heb *head from the house of the wicked*   [l] Heb obscure   [m] Heb *his*
[n] Vg Compare Gk Syr: Heb uncertain   [o] Cn Compare Gk: Heb *I tremble because*   [p] Heb *my stringed*
[a] Cn: Heb *the stumbling blocks*   [b] Compare Gk: Heb *idolatrous priests with the priests*

and yet swear by Milcom;
6 those who have turned back from following the LORD,
who do not seek the LORD or inquire of
him."

7 Be silent before the Lord GOD!
For the day of the LORD is at hand;
the LORD has prepared a sacrifice
and consecrated his guests.
8 And on the day of the LORD's sacrifice—
"I will punish the officials and the king's
sons
and all who array themselves in foreign
attire.
9 On that day I will punish
every one who leaps over the threshold,
and those who fill their master's house
with violence and fraud."

10 "On that day," says the LORD,
"a cry will be heard from the Fish Gate,
a wail from the Second Quarter,
a loud crash from the hills.
11 Wail, O inhabitants of the Mortar!
For all the traders are no more;
all who weigh out silver are cut off.
12 At that time I will search Jerusalem with
lamps,
and I will punish the men
who are thickening upon their lees,
those who say in their hearts,
'The LORD will not do good,
nor will he do ill.'
13 Their goods shall be plundered,
and their houses laid waste.
Though they build houses,
they shall not inhabit them;
though they plant vineyards,
they shall not drink wine from them."

14 The great day of the LORD is near,
near and hastening fast;
the sound of the day of the LORD is bitter,
the mighty man cries aloud there.
15 A day of wrath is that day,
a day of distress and anguish,
a day of ruin and devastation,
a day of darkness and gloom,
a day of clouds and thick darkness,
16 a day of trumpet blast and battle cry
against the fortified cities
and against the lofty battlements.

17 I will bring distress on men,
so that they shall walk like the blind,
because they have sinned against the
LORD;
their blood shall be poured out like dust,

and their flesh like dung.
Neither their silver nor their gold
shall be able to deliver them
on the day of the wrath of the LORD.
In the fire of his jealous wrath,
all the earth shall be consumed;
for a full, yea, sudden end
he will make of all the inhabitants of the
earth.

Come together and hold assembly, 2
O shameless nation,
before you are driven away 2
like the drifting chaff,ᶜ
before there comes upon you
the fierce anger of the LORD,
before there comes upon you
the day of the wrath of the LORD.
Seek the LORD, all you humble of the land, 3
who do his commands;
seek righteousness, seek humility;
perhaps you may be hidden
on the day of the wrath of the LORD.
For Gaza shall be deserted, 4
and Ash'kelon shall become a desolation;
Ashdod's people shall be driven out at
noon,
and Ekron shall be uprooted.

Philistia

Woe to you inhabitants of the sea coast, 5
you nation of the Cher'ethites!
The word of the LORD is against you,
O Canaan, land of the Philistines;
and I will destroy you till no inhabitant
is left.
And you, O sea coast, shall be pastures, 6
meadows for shepherds
and folds for flocks.
The sea coast shall become the possession 7
of the remnant of the house of Judah,
on which they shall pasture,
and in the houses of Ash'kelon
they shall lie down at evening.
For the LORD their God will be mindful of
them
and restore their fortunes.

Moab and Ammon

"I have heard the taunts of Moab 8
and the revilings of the Ammonites,
how they have taunted my people
and made boasts against their territory.
Therefore, as I live," says the LORD of 9
hosts,
the God of Israel,

ᶜ Cn Compare Gk Syr: Heb *before a decree is born; like chaff a day has passed away*
1.7: Hab 2.20; Zech 2.13. 2.4-7: Is 14.29-31; Jer 47; Ezek 25.15-17; Joel 3.4-8; Amos 1.6-8; Zech 9.5-7.
2.8-11: Is 15-16; 25.10-12; Jer 48; Ezek 25.8-11; Amos 2.1-3.

"Moab shall become like Sodom,
and the Ammonites like Gomor'rah,
a land possessed by nettles and salt pits,
and a waste for ever.
The remnant of my people shall plunder
them,
and the survivors of my nation shall
possess them."
This shall be their lot in return for their
pride,
because they scoffed and boasted
against the people of the LORD of hosts.
The LORD will be terrible against them;
yea, he will famish all the gods of the
earth,
and to him shall bow down,
each in its place,
all the lands of the nations.

Ethiopia and Assyria

You also, O Ethiopians,
shall be slain by my sword.

And he will stretch out his hand against
the north,
and destroy Assyria;
and he will make Nin'eveh a desolation,
a dry waste like the desert.
Herds shall lie down in the midst of her,
all the beasts of the field; *d*
the vulture *e* and the hedgehog
shall lodge in her capitals;
the owl *f* shall hoot in the window,
the raven *g* croak on the threshold;
for her cedar work will be laid bare.
This is the exultant city
that dwelt secure,
that said to herself,
"I am and there is none else."
What a desolation she has become,
a lair for wild beasts!
Every one who passes by her
hisses and shakes his fist.

Jerusalem's danger

Woe to her that is rebellious and defiled,
the oppressing city!
She listens to no voice,
she accepts no correction.
She does not trust in the LORD,
she does not draw near to her God.

Her officials within her
are roaring lions;
her judges are evening wolves
that leave nothing till the morning.
Her prophets are wanton,

faithless men;
her priests profane what is sacred,
they do violence to the law.
The LORD within her is righteous,   5
he does no wrong;
every morning he shows forth his justice,
each dawn he does not fail;
but the unjust knows no shame.

"I have cut off nations;   6
their battlements are in ruins;
I have laid waste their streets
so that none walks in them;
their cities have been made desolate,
without a man, without an inhabitant.
I said, 'Surely she will fear me,   7
she will accept correction;
she will not lose sight *h*
of all that I have enjoined upon her.'
But all the more they were eager
to make all their deeds corrupt."

Jerusalem's deliverance

"Therefore wait for me," says the LORD,   8
"for the day when I arise as a witness.
For my decision is to gather nations,
to assemble kingdoms,
to pour out upon them my indignation,
all the heat of my anger;
for in the fire of my jealous wrath
all the earth shall be consumed.

"Yea, at that time I will change the speech 9
of the peoples
to a pure speech,
that all of them may call on the name of the
LORD
and serve him with one accord.
From beyond the rivers of Ethiopia   10
my suppliants, the daughter of my
dispersed ones,
shall bring my offering.

"On that day you shall not be put to shame 11
because of the deeds by which you have
rebelled against me;
for then I will remove from your midst
your proudly exultant ones,
and you shall no longer be haughty
in my holy mountain.
For I will leave in the midst of you   12
a people humble and lowly.
They shall seek refuge in the name of the
LORD,
those who are left in Israel;   13
they shall do no wrong
and utter no lies,
nor shall there be found in their mouth

---

d Tg Compare Gk: Heb *nation*   *e* The meaning of the Hebrew word is uncertain   *f* Cn: Heb *a voice*
g Gk Vg: Heb *desolation*   *h* Gk Syr: Heb *and her dwelling will not be cut off*
2.12: Is 18.   2.13–15: Is 10.5–34; Nahum.   3.13: Rev 14.5.

a deceitful tongue.
For they shall pasture and lie down,
    and none shall make them afraid."

14 Sing aloud, O daughter of Zion;
        shout, O Israel!
    Rejoice and exult with all your heart,
        O daughter of Jerusalem!
15 The LORD has taken away the judgments
        against you,
    he has cast out your enemies.
    The King of Israel, the LORD, is in your
        midst;
    you shall fear evil no more.
16 On that day it shall be said to Jerusalem:
    "Do not fear, O Zion;
    let not your hands grow weak.
7 The LORD, your God, is in your midst,
    a warrior who gives victory;

he will rejoice over you with gladness,
    he will renew you[i] in his love;
he will exult over you with loud singing
    as on a day of festival.[j]
"I will remove disaster[k] from you,
    so that you will not bear reproach for it.
Behold, at that time I will deal
    with all your oppressors.
And I will save the lame
    and gather the outcast,
and I will change their shame into praise
    and renown in all the earth.
At that time I will bring you home,
    at the time when I gather you together;
yea, I will make you renowned and praised
    among all the peoples of the earth,
when I restore your fortunes
    before your eyes," says the LORD.

THE BOOK OF
HAGGAI

This house in ruins

IN the second year of Darius the king, in
the sixth month, on the first day of
the month, the word of the LORD came
by Haggai the prophet to Zerub'babel the
son of She-al'ti-el, governor of Judah, and
to Joshua the son of Jehoz'adak, the high
2 priest, "Thus says the LORD of hosts: This
people say the time has not yet come to
3 rebuild the house of the LORD." Then the
word of the LORD came by Haggai the
4 prophet, "Is it a time for you yourselves to
dwell in your panelled houses, while this
5 house lies in ruins? Now therefore

thus says the LORD of hosts: Consider
how you have fared. You have sown much, 6
and harvested little; you eat, but you never
have enough; you drink, but you never have
your fill; you clothe yourselves, but no one is
warm; and he who earns wages earns wages
to put them into a bag with holes.
"Thus says the LORD of hosts: Consider 7
how you have fared. Go up to the hills and 8
bring wood and build the house, that I may
take pleasure in it and that I may appear in
my glory, says the LORD. You have looked 9
for much, and, lo, it came to little; and when
you brought it home, I blew it away. Why?
says the LORD of hosts. Because of my house

that lies in ruins, while you busy yourselves each with his own house. Therefore the heavens above you have withheld the dew, and the earth has withheld its produce. And I have called for a drought upon the land and the hills, upon the grain, the new wine, the oil, upon what the ground brings forth, upon men and cattle, and upon all their labours." Then Zerub'babel the son of She-al'ti-el, and Joshua the son of Jehoz'adak, the high priest, with all the remnant of the people, obeyed the voice of the LORD their God, and the words of Haggai the prophet, as the LORD their God had sent him; and the people feared before the LORD. Then Haggai, the messenger of the LORD, spoke to the people with the LORD's message, "I am with you, says the LORD." And the LORD stirred up the spirit of Zerub'babel the son of She-al'ti-el, governor of Judah, and the spirit of Joshua the son of Jehoz'adak, the high priest, and the spirit of all the remnant of the people; and they came and worked on the house of the LORD of hosts, their God, on the twenty-fourth day of the month, in the sixth month.

Recall its former glory

2 In the second year of Darius the king, in the seventh month, on the twenty-first day of the month, the word of the LORD came by Haggai the prophet, "Speak now to Zerub'babel the son of She-al'ti-el, governor of Judah, and to Joshua the son of Jehoz'adak, the high priest, and to all the remnant of the people, and say, 'Who is left among you that saw this house in its former glory? How do you see it now? Is it not in your sight as nothing? Yet now take courage, O Zerub'babel, says the LORD; take courage, O Joshua, son of Jehoz'adak, the high priest; take courage, all you people of the land, says the LORD; work, for I am with you, says the LORD of hosts, according to the promise that I made you when you came out of Egypt. My Spirit abides among you; fear not. For thus says the LORD of hosts: Once again, in a little while, I will shake the heavens and the earth and the sea and the dry land; and I will shake all nations, so that the treasures of all nations shall come in, and I will fill this house with splendour, says the LORD of hosts. The silver is mine, and the gold is mine, says the LORD of hosts. The latter splendour of this house shall be greater than the former, says the LORD of hosts; and in this place I will give prosperity, says the LORD of hosts.'"

On the twenty-fourth day of the ninth month, in the second year of Darius, the word of the LORD came by Haggai the prophet, "Thus says the LORD of hosts: Ask the priests to decide this question, 'If one carries holy flesh in the skirt of his garment, and touches with his skirt bread, or pottage, or wine, or oil, or any kind of food, does it become holy?'" The priests answered, "No." Then said Haggai, "If one who is unclean by contact with a dead body touches any of these, does it become unclean?" The priests answered, "It does become unclean."

Then Haggai said, "So is it with this people, and with this nation before me, says the LORD; and so with every work of their hands; and what they offer there is unclean. Pray now, consider what will come to pass from this day onward. Before a stone was placed upon a stone in the temple of the LORD, how did you fare?ª When one came to a heap of twenty measures, there were but ten; when one came to the winevat to draw fifty measures, there were but twenty. I smote you and all the products of your toil with blight and mildew and hail; yet you did not return to me, says the LORD.

Build for a great future

"Consider from this day onward, from the

ª Gk: Heb *since they were*
2.6: Heb 12.26.

twenty-fourth day of the ninth month. Since the day that the foundation of the LORD's 19 temple was laid, consider: Is the seed yet in the barn? Do the vine, the fig tree, the pomegranate, and the olive tree still yield nothing? From this day on I will bless you."
20 The word of the LORD came a second time to Haggai on the twenty-fourth day of the 21 month, "Speak to Zerub'babel, governor of Judah, saying, I am about to shake the 22 heavens and the earth, and to overthrow the throne of kingdoms; I am about to destroy the strength of the kingdoms of the nations, and overthrow the chariots and their riders; and the horses and their riders shall go down, every one by the sword of his fellow. On that day, says the LORD of hosts, I will take you, O Zerub'babel my servant, the son of She-al'ti-el, says the LORD, and make you like a signet ring; for I have chosen you, says the LORD of hosts."

ZECHARIAH

Call to repentance

IN the eighth month, in the second year of Darius, the word of the LORD came to Zechari'ah the son of Berechi'ah, son of 2 Iddo, the prophet, saying, "The LORD was 3 very angry with your fathers. Therefore say to them, Thus says the LORD of hosts: Return to me, says the LORD of hosts, and I 4 will return to you, says the LORD of hosts. Be not like your fathers, to whom the former prophets cried out, 'Thus says the LORD of hosts, Return from your evil ways and from your evil deeds.' But they did not hear or 5 heed me, says the LORD. Your fathers, where are they? And the prophets, do they live for 6 ever? But my words and my statutes, which I commanded my servants the prophets, did they not overtake your fathers? So they repented and said, As the LORD of hosts purposed to deal with us for our ways and deeds, so has he dealt with us."

Among the myrtle trees

ON the twenty-fourth day of the eleventh 7 month which is the month of Shebat, in the second year of Darius, the word of the LORD came to Zechari'ah the son of Berechi'ah, son of Iddo, the prophet; and 8 Zechari'ah said, "I saw in the night, and behold, a man riding upon a red horse! He was standing among the myrtle trees in the glen; and behind him were red, sorrel, and white horses. Then I said, 'What are these, 9 my lord?' The angel who talked with me said to me, 'I will show you what they are.' So the man who was standing among the 10 myrtle trees answered, 'These are they whom the LORD has sent to patrol the earth.' And 11 they answered the angel of the LORD who was standing among the myrtle trees, 'We have patrolled the earth, and behold, all the earth remains at rest.' Then the angel of the LORD 12 said, 'O LORD of hosts, how long wilt thou have no mercy on Jerusalem and the cities of Judah, against which thou hast had indignation these seventy years?' And the LORD answered gracious and comforting words to the angel who talked with me. So the angel who talked with me said to me, 'Cry out, Thus says the LORD of hosts: I am exceedingly jealous for Jerusalem and for Zion. And I am very angry with the nations that are at ease; for while I was angry but a little they furthered the disaster. Therefore, thus says the LORD, I have returned to Jerusalem with compassion; my house shall be built in it, says the LORD of hosts, and the measuring line shall be stretched out over Jerusalem. Cry again, Thus says the LORD of hosts: My cities shall again overflow with prosperity, and the LORD will again comfort Zion and again choose Jerusalem.' "

Four horns

8ª And I lifted my eyes and saw, and behold, four horns! And I said to the angel who talked with me, "What are these?" And he answered me, "These are the horns which have scattered Judah, Israel, and Jerusalem." Then the LORD showed me four smiths. And I said, "What are these coming to do?" He answered, "These are the horns which scattered Judah, so that no man raised his head; and these have come to terrify them, to cast down the horns of the nations who lifted up their horns against the land of Judah to scatter it."

A measuring line

2ᵇ And I lifted my eyes and saw, and behold, a man with a measuring line in his hand! Then I said, "Where are you going?" And he said to me, "To measure Jerusalem, to see what is its breadth and what is its length." And behold, the angel who talked with me came forward, and another angel came forward to meet him, and said to him, "Run, say to that young man, 'Jerusalem shall be inhabited as villages without walls, because of the multitude of men and cattle in it. For I will be to her a wall of fire round about, says the LORD, and I will be the glory within her.' "

Ho! ho! Flee from the land of the north, says the LORD; for I have spread you abroad as the four winds of the heavens, says the LORD. Ho! Escape to Zion, you who dwell with the daughter of Babylon. For thus said the LORD of hosts, after his glory sent me to the nations who plundered you, for he who touches you touches the apple of his eye: "Behold, I will shake my hand over them, and they shall become plunder for those who

served them. Then you will know that the LORD of hosts has sent me. Sing and rejoice, 10 O daughter of Zion; for lo, I come and I will dwell in the midst of you, says the LORD. And many nations shall join themselves to 11 the LORD in that day, and shall be my people; and I will dwell in the midst of you, and you shall know that the LORD of hosts has sent me to you. And the LORD will inherit Judah as 12 his portion in the holy land, and will again choose Jerusalem."

Be silent, all flesh, before the LORD; for he 13 has roused himself from his holy dwelling.

The trial of the high priest

Then he showed me Joshua the high priest 3 standing before the angel of the LORD, and Satan standing at his right hand to accuse him. And the LORD said to Satan, "The 2 LORD rebuke you, O Satan! The LORD who has chosen Jerusalem rebuke you! Is not this a brand plucked from the fire?" Now 3 Joshua was standing before the angel, clothed with filthy garments. And the angel 4 said to those who were standing before him, "Remove the filthy garments from him." And to him he said, "Behold, I have taken your iniquity away from you, and I will clothe you with rich apparel." And I said, 5 "Let them put a clean turban on his head." So they put a clean turban on his head and clothed him with garments; and the angel of the LORD was standing by.

And the angel of the LORD enjoined Joshua, 6 "Thus says the LORD of hosts: If you will 7 walk in my ways and keep my charge, then you shall rule my house and have charge of my courts, and I will give you the right of access among those who are standing here. Hear now, O Joshua the high priest, you and 8 your friends who sit before you, for they are men of good omen: behold, I will bring my servant the Branch. For behold, upon the 9 stone which I have set before Joshua, upon a single stone with seven facets, I will engrave its inscription, says the LORD of hosts, and I will remove the guilt of this land in a single day. In that day, says the LORD of hosts, 10 every one of you will invite his neighbour under his vine and under his fig tree."

A golden lampstand

And the angel who talked with me came 4 again, and waked me, like a man that is wakened out of his sleep. And he said to me, 2 "What do you see?" I said, "I see, and behold, a lampstand all of gold, with a bowl

on the top of it, and seven lamps on it, with
seven lips on each of the lamps which are on
3 the top of it. And there are two olive trees by
it, one on the right of the bowl and the other
4 on its left." And I said to the angel who
talked with me, "What are these, my lord?"
5 Then the angel who talked with me answered
me, "Do you not know what these are?" I
6 said, "No, my lord." Then he said to me,
"This is the word of the LORD to Zerub'-
babel: Not by might, nor by power, but by
7 my Spirit, says the LORD of hosts. What are
you, O great mountain? Before Zerub'babel
you shall become a plain; and he shall bring
forward the top stone amid shouts of 'Grace,
8 grace to it!'" Moreover the word of the
9 LORD came to me, saying, "The hands of
Zerub'babel have laid the foundation of this
house; his hands shall also complete it. Then
you will know that the LORD of hosts has sent
10 me to you. For whoever has despised the day
of small things shall rejoice, and shall see the
plummet in the hand of Zerub'babel.
"These seven are the eyes of the LORD,
which range through the whole earth."
11 Then I said to him, "What are these two
olive trees on the right and the left of the
12 lampstand?" And a second time I said to
him, "What are these two branches of the
olive trees, which are beside the two golden
pipes from which the oil*c* is poured out?"
13 He said to me, "Do you not know what these
14 are?" I said, "No, my lord." Then he said,
"These are the two anointed who stand by
the Lord of the whole earth."

A flying scroll

5 Again I lifted my eyes and saw, and behold,
2 a flying scroll! And he said to me, "What do
you see?" I answered, "I see a flying scroll;
its length is twenty cubits, and its breadth
3 ten cubits." Then he said to me, "This is the
curse that goes out over the face of the whole
land; for every one who steals shall be cut off
henceforth according to it, and every one
who swears falsely shall be cut off henceforth
4 according to it. I will send it forth, says the
LORD of hosts, and it shall enter the house of
the thief, and the house of him who swears
falsely by my name; and it shall abide in his
house and consume it, both timber and
stones."

The woman in the ephah

5 Then the angel who talked with me came
forward and said to me, "Lift your eyes, and
see what this is that goes forth." And I said,
"What is it?" He said, "This is the ephah
that goes forth." And he said, "This is their
iniquity*d* in all the land." And behold, the
leaden cover was lifted, and there was a
woman sitting in the ephah! And he said,
"This is Wickedness." And he thrust her
back into the ephah, and thrust down the
leaden weight upon its mouth. Then I lifted
my eyes and saw, and behold, two women
coming forward! The wind was in their
wings; they had wings like the wings of a
stork, and they lifted up the ephah between
earth and heaven. Then I said to the angel
who talked with me, "Where are they taking
the ephah?" He said to me, "To the land of
Shinar, to build a house for it; and when this
is prepared, they will set the ephah down
there on its base."

Four chariots

And again I lifted my eyes and saw, and
behold, four chariots came out from between
two mountains; and the mountains were
mountains of bronze. The first chariot had
red horses, the second black horses, the third
white horses, and the fourth chariot dappled
grey*e* horses. Then I said to the angel who
talked with me, "What are these, my lord?"
And the angel answered me, "These are
going forth to the four winds of heaven, after
presenting themselves before the LORD of all
the earth. The chariot with the black horses
goes toward the north country, the white
ones go toward the west country,*f* and the
dappled ones go toward the south country."
When the steeds came out, they were
impatient to get off and patrol the earth.
And he said, "Go, patrol the earth." So they
patrolled the earth. Then he cried to me,
"Behold, those who go toward the north
country have set my Spirit at rest in the
north country."

THE NEW JERUSALEM

A coronation

AND the word of the LORD came to me:
"Take from the exiles Heldai, Tobi'jah,
and Jedai'ah, who have arrived from
Babylon; and go the same day to the house of
Josi'ah, the son of Zephani'ah. Take from
them silver and gold, and make a crown,*g*
and set it upon the head of Joshua, the son of
Jehoz'adak, the high priest; and say to him,

c Cn: Heb *gold*   *d* Gk Compare Syr: Heb *eye*   *e* Compare Gk: The meaning of the Hebrew word is uncertain
f Cn: Heb *after them*   *g* Gk Mss: Heb *crowns*
4.3, 11–14: Rev 11.4.   4.10: Rev 5.6.   6.1–3: Rev 6.2–8.   6.5: Rev 7.1.
6.12: Is 4.2; Jer 23.5; 33.15; Zech 3.8.

'Thus says the LORD of hosts, "Behold, the man whose name is the Branch: for he shall grow up in his place, and he shall build the 3 temple of the LORD. It is he who shall build the temple of the LORD, and shall bear royal honour, and shall sit and rule upon his throne. And there shall be a priest by his throne, and peaceful understanding shall be 4 between them both." ' And the crown[h] shall be in the temple of the LORD as a reminder to Heldai,[i] Tobi′jah, Jedai′ah, and Josi′ah[j] the son of Zephani′ah. 5 "And those who are far off shall come and help to build the temple of the LORD; and you shall know that the LORD of hosts has sent me to you. And this shall come to pass, if you will diligently obey the voice of the LORD your God."

True righteousness

7 In the fourth year of King Darius, the word of the LORD came to Zechari′ah in the fourth day of the ninth month, which is Chislev. 2 Now the people of Bethel had sent Share′zer and Reg′em-mel′ech and their men, to en- 3 treat the favour of the LORD, and to ask the priests of the house of the LORD of hosts and the prophets, "Should I mourn and fast in the fifth month, as I have done for so many 4 years?" Then the word of the LORD of hosts 5 came to me: "Say to all the people of the land and the priests, When you fasted and mourned in the fifth month and in the seventh, for these seventy years, was it for me 6 that you fasted? And when you eat and when you drink, do you not eat for your- 7 selves and drink for yourselves? When Jerusalem was inhabited and in prosperity, with her cities round about her, and the South and the lowland were inhabited, were not these the words which the LORD pro- claimed by the former prophets?"

8 And the word of the LORD came to 9 Zechari′ah, saying, "Thus says the LORD of hosts, Render true judgments, show kindness 10 and mercy each to his brother, do not oppress the widow, the fatherless, the sojourner, or the poor; and let none of you devise evil against his brother in your 1 heart." But they refused to hearken, and turned a stubborn shoulder, and stopped 2 their ears that they might not hear. They made their hearts like adamant lest they should hear the law and the words which the LORD of hosts had sent by his Spirit through the former prophets. Therefore great wrath 3 came from the LORD of hosts. "As I called, and they would not hear, so they called, and I would not hear," says the LORD of hosts,

"and I scattered them with a whirlwind 14 among all the nations which they had not known. Thus the land they left was desolate, so that no one went to and fro, and the pleasant land was made desolate."

The faithful city

And the word of the LORD of hosts came to 8 me, saying, "Thus says the LORD of hosts: I 2 am jealous for Zion with great jealousy, and I am jealous for her with great wrath. Thus 3 says the LORD: I will return to Zion, and will dwell in the midst of Jerusalem, and Jeru- salem shall be called the faithful city, and the mountain of the LORD of hosts, the holy mountain. Thus says the LORD of hosts: Old 4 men and old women shall again sit in the streets of Jerusalem, each with staff in hand for very age. And the streets of the city shall 5 be full of boys and girls playing in its streets. Thus says the LORD of hosts: If it is marvel- 6 lous in the sight of the remnant of this people in these days, should it also be marvellous in my sight, says the LORD of hosts? Thus says 7 the LORD of hosts: Behold, I will save my people from the east country and from the west country; and I will bring them to dwell 8 in the midst of Jerusalem; and they shall be my people and I will be their God, in faithfulness and in righteousness."

Thus says the LORD of hosts: "Let your 9 hands be strong, you who in these days have been hearing these words from the mouth of the prophets, since the day that the founda- tion of the house of the LORD of hosts was laid, that the temple might be built. For 10 before those days there was no wage for man or any wage for beast, neither was there any safety from the foe for him who went out or came in; for I set every man against his fellow. But now I will not deal with the 11 remnant of this people as in the former days, says the LORD of hosts. For there shall be a 12 sowing of peace; the vine shall yield its fruit, and the ground shall give its increase, and the heavens shall give their dew; and I will cause the remnant of this people to possess all these things. And as you have been a byword of 13 cursing among the nations, O house of Judah and house of Israel, so will I save you and you shall be a blessing. Fear not, but let your hands be strong."

For thus says the LORD of hosts: "As I 14 purposed to do evil to you, when your fathers provoked me to wrath, and I did not relent, says the LORD of hosts, so again have I 15 purposed in these days to do good to Jeru- salem and to the house of Judah; fear not.

h Gk: Heb crowns   i With verse 10: Heb Helem   j With verse 10: Heb Hen

16 These are the things that you shall do: Speak the truth to one another, render in your gates judgments that are true and make for peace, 17 do not devise evil in your hearts against one another, and love no false oath, for all these things I hate, says the LORD."

18 And the word of the LORD of hosts came to 19 me, saying, "Thus says the LORD of hosts: The fast of the fourth month, and the fast of the fifth, and the fast of the seventh, and the fast of the tenth, shall be to the house of Judah seasons of joy and gladness, and cheerful feasts; therefore love truth and peace.

20 "Thus says the LORD of hosts: Peoples shall yet come, even the inhabitants of many 21 cities; the inhabitants of one city shall go to another, saying, 'Let us go at once to entreat the favour of the LORD, and to seek the LORD 22 of hosts; I am going.' Many peoples and strong nations shall come to seek the LORD of hosts in Jerusalem, and to entreat the favour 23 of the LORD. Thus says the LORD of hosts: In those days ten men from the nations of every tongue shall take hold of the robe of a Jew, saying, 'Let us go with you, for we have heard that God is with you.' "

Look to the Lord

9　　　　An Oracle
The word of the LORD is against the land of Hadrach
　　and will rest upon Damascus.
For to the LORD belong the cities of Aram,[k]
　　even as all the tribes of Israel;
2 Hamath also, which borders thereon,
　　Tyre and Sidon, though they are very wise.
3 Tyre has built herself a rampart,
　　and heaped up silver like dust,
　　and gold like the dirt of the streets.
4 But lo, the Lord will strip her of her possessions
　　and hurl her wealth into the sea,
　　and she shall be devoured by fire.

5 Ash'kelon shall see it, and be afraid;
　　Gaza too, and shall writhe in anguish;
　　Ekron also, because its hopes are confounded.
The king shall perish from Gaza;
　　Ash'kelon shall be uninhabited;
6 a mongrel people shall dwell in Ashdod;
　　and I will make an end of the pride of Philistia.
7 I will take away its blood from its mouth,

and its abominations from between its teeth;
it too shall be a remnant for our God;
　　it shall be like a clan in Judah,
　　and Ekron shall be like the Jeb'usites.
Then I will encamp at my house as a guard,
　　so that none shall march to and fro;
no oppressor shall again overrun them,
　　for now I see with my own eyes.

The king of peace

Rejoice greatly, O daughter of Zion!
　　Shout aloud, O daughter of Jerusalem!
Lo, your king comes to you;
　　triumphant and victorious is he,
humble and riding on an ass,
　　on a colt the foal of an ass.
I will cut off the chariot from E'phraim
　　and the war horse from Jerusalem;
and the battle bow shall be cut off,

and he shall command peace to the nations;
his dominion shall be from sea to sea,
　　and from the River to the ends of the earth.

As for you also, because of the blood of my covenant with you,
　　I will set your captives free from the waterless pit.
Return to your stronghold, O prisoners of hope;
　　today I declare that I will restore to you
　　· double.
For I have bent Judah as my bow;
　　I have made E'phraim its arrow.
I will brandish your sons, O Zion,
　　over your sons, O Greece,
　　and wield you like a warrior's sword.

Then the LORD will appear over them,
　　and his arrow go forth like lightning;

---

[k] Cn: Heb the eye of Adam (or man)
8.16: Eph 4.25.　9.9: Mt 21.5; Jn 12.15.

the Lord GOD will sound the trumpet,
  and march forth in the whirlwinds of the
    south.
5 The LORD of hosts will protect them,
  and they shall devour and tread down
    the slingers;[l]
  and they shall drink their blood[m] like wine,
    and be full like a bowl,
  drenched like the corners of the altar.

He will save his people

6 On that day the LORD their God will save
    them
  for they are the flock of his people;
  for like the jewels of a crown
    they shall shine on his land.
7 Yea, how good and how fair it shall be!
  Grain shall make the young men
    flourish,
  and new wine the maidens.

10 Ask rain from the LORD
  in the season of the spring rain,
  from the LORD who makes the storm
    clouds,
  who gives men showers of rain,
  to every one the vegetation in the field.
2 For the teraphim utter nonsense,
  and the diviners see lies;
  the dreamers tell false dreams,
    and give empty consolation.
  Therefore the people wander like sheep;
    they are afflicted for want of a shepherd.

3 "My anger is hot against the shepherds,
  and I will punish the leaders;[n]
  for the LORD of hosts cares for his flock,
    the house of Judah,
  and will make them like his proud steed
    in battle.
4 Out of them shall come the cornerstone,
    out of them the tent peg,
  out of them the battle bow,
    out of them every ruler.
5 Together they shall be like mighty men in
    battle,
    trampling the foe in the mud of the
      streets;
  they shall fight because the LORD is with
    them,
  and they shall confound the riders on
    horses.

Judah and Israel

6 "I will strengthen the house of Judah,
  and I will save the house of Joseph.
  I will bring them back because I have
    compassion on them,

and they shall be as though I had not
    rejected them;
  for I am the LORD their God and I will
    answer them.
Then E'phraim shall become like a mighty 7
    warrior,
  and their hearts shall be glad as with
    wine.
Their children shall see it and rejoice,
  their hearts shall exult in the LORD.

"I will signal for them and gather them in, 8
  for I have redeemed them,
  and they shall be as many as of old.
Though I scattered them among the 9
    nations,
  yet in far countries they shall remember
    me,
  and with their children they shall live
    and return.
I will bring them home from the land of 10
    Egypt,
  and gather them from Assyria;
and I will bring them to the land of Gilead
    and to Lebanon,
  till there is no room for them.
They shall pass through the sea of Egypt,[o] 11
  and the waves of the sea shall be
    smitten,
  and all the depths of the Nile dried up.
The pride of Assyria shall be laid low,
  and the sceptre of Egypt shall depart.
I will make them strong in the LORD   12
  and they shall glory[p] in his name,"
                              says the LORD.

Their glory is despoiled

Open your doors, O Lebanon,   11
  that the fire may devour your cedars!
Wail, O cypress, for the cedar has fallen, 2
  for the glorious trees are ruined!
Wail, oaks of Bashan,
  for the thick forest has been felled!
Hark, the wail of the shepherds,   3
  for their glory is despoiled!
Hark, the roar of the lions,
  for the jungle of the Jordan is laid
    waste!

Thus said the LORD my God: "Become 4
shepherd of the flock doomed to slaughter.
Those who buy them slay them and go 5
unpunished; and those who sell them say,
'Blessed be the LORD, I have become rich';
and their own shepherds have no pity on
them. For I will no longer have pity on the 6
inhabitants of this land, says the LORD. Lo, I
will cause men to fall each into the hand of
his shepherd, and each into the hand of his

---

[l] Cn: Heb *the slingstones* [m] Gk: Heb *be turbulent* [n] Or *he-goats* [o] Cn: Heb *distress* [p] Gk: Heb *walk*

king; and they shall crush the earth, and I will deliver none from their hand."

7 So I became the shepherd of the flock doomed to be slain for those who trafficked in the sheep. And I took two staffs; one I named Grace, the other I named Union. 8 And I tended the sheep. In one month I destroyed the three shepherds. But I became impatient with them, and they also detested 9 me. So I said, "I will not be your shepherd. What is to die, let it die; what is to be destroyed, let it be destroyed; and let those that are left devour the flesh of one 10 another." And I took my staff Grace, and I broke it, annulling the covenant which I had 11 made with all the peoples. So it was annulled on that day, and the traffickers in the sheep, who were watching me, knew that it was the 12 word of the LORD. Then I said to them, "If it seems right to you, give me my wages; but if not, keep them." And they weighed out as 13 my wages thirty shekels of silver. Then the LORD said to me, "Cast it into the treasury"*q*—the lordly price at which I was paid off by them. So I took the thirty shekels of silver and cast them into the treasury*q* in 14 the house of the LORD. Then I broke my second staff Union, annulling the brotherhood between Judah and Israel.

15 Then the LORD said to me, "Take once more the implements of a worthless shep- 16 herd. For lo, I am raising up in the land a shepherd who does not care for the perishing, or seek the wandering,*r* or heal the maimed, or nourish the sound, but devours the flesh of the fat ones, tearing off even their hoofs.

17 Woe to my worthless shepherd,
who deserts the flock!
May the sword smite his arm
and his right eye!
Let his arm be wholly withered,
his right eye utterly blinded!"

A reeling city

12 An Oracle
The word of the LORD concerning Israel: Thus says the LORD, who stretched out the heavens and founded the earth and formed 2 the spirit of man within him: "Lo, I am about to make Jerusalem a cup of reeling to all the peoples round about; it will be against Judah also in the siege against Jerusalem. 3 On that day I will make Jerusalem a heavy stone for all the peoples; all who lift it shall grievously hurt themselves. And all the nations of the earth will come together 4 against it. On that day, says the LORD, I will

strike every horse with panic, and its rider with madness. But upon the house of Judah I will open my eyes, when I strike every horse of the peoples with blindness. Then 5 the clans of Judah shall say to themselves, 'The inhabitants of Jerusalem have strength through the LORD of hosts, their God.'

"On that day I will make the clans of Judah 6 like a blazing pot in the midst of wood, like a flaming torch among sheaves; and they shall devour to the right and to the left all the peoples round about, while Jerusalem shall still be inhabited in its place, in Jerusalem.

"And the LORD will give victory to the tents 7 of Judah first, that the glory of the house of David and the glory of the inhabitants of Jerusalem may not be exalted over that of Judah. On that day the LORD will put a 8 shield about the inhabitants of Jerusalem so that the feeblest among them on that day shall be like David, and the house of David shall be like God, like the angel of the LORD, at their head. And on that day I will seek to 9 destroy all the nations that come against Jerusalem.

A day of mourning

"And I will pour out on the house of David 10 and the inhabitants of Jerusalem a spirit of compassion and supplication, so that, when they look on him whom they have pierced, they shall mourn for him, as one mourns for an only child, and weep bitterly over him, as one weeps over a first-born. On that day the 11 mourning in Jerusalem will be as great as the mourning for Hadad-rim'mon in the plain of Megid'do. The land shall mourn, each 12 family by itself; the family of the house of David by itself, and their wives by themselves; the family of the house of Nathan by itself, and their wives by themselves; the 13 family of the house of Levi by itself, and their wives by themselves; the family of the Shim'e-ites by itself, and their wives by themselves; and all the families that are left, 14 each by itself, and their wives by themselves.

A cleansing fountain

"On that day there shall be a fountain**13** opened for the house of David and the inhabitants of Jerusalem to cleanse them from sin and uncleanness.

"And on that day, says the LORD of hosts, I 2 will cut off the names of the idols from the land, so that they shall be remembered no more; and also I will remove from the land the prophets and the unclean spirit. And if 3

q Syr: Heb *to the potter* *r* Syr Compare Gk Vg: Heb *the youth*
11.12–13: Mt 26.15; 27.9. 12.10: Jn 19.37.

any one again appears as a prophet, his father and mother who bore him will say to him, 'You shall not live, for you speak lies in the name of the LORD'; and his father and mother who bore him shall pierce him through when he prophesies. On that day every prophet will be ashamed of his vision when he prophesies; he will not put on a hairy mantle in order to deceive, but he will say, 'I am no prophet, I am a tiller of the soil; for the land has been my possession[s] since my youth.' And if one asks him, 'What are these wounds on your back?' he will say, 'The wounds I received in the house of my friends.'"

"Awake, O sword, against my shepherd,
      against the man who stands next to me,"
            says the LORD of hosts.
"Strike the shepherd, that the sheep may
            be scattered;
      I will turn my hand against the little
            ones.
In the whole land, says the LORD,
      two thirds shall be cut off and perish,
      and one third shall be left alive.
And I will put this third into the
            fire,
      and refine them as one refines silver,
      and test them as gold is tested.
They will call on my name,
      and I will answer them.
I will say, 'They are my people';
      and they will say, 'The LORD is my
            God.'"

The city saved

4 Behold, a day of the LORD is coming, when the spoil taken from you will be divided in the midst of you. For I will gather all the nations against Jerusalem to battle, and the city shall be taken and the houses plundered and the women ravished; half of the city shall go into exile, but the rest of the people shall not be cut off from the city. Then the LORD will go forth and fight against those nations as when he fights on a day of battle. On that day his feet shall stand on the Mount of Olives which lies before Jerusalem on the east; and the Mount of Olives shall be split in two from east to west by a very wide valley; so that one half of the Mount shall withdraw northward, and the other half southward. And the valley of my mountains shall be stopped up, for the valley of the mountains shall touch the side of it; and you shall flee as you fled from the earthquake in the days of Uzzi'ah king of Judah. Then the LORD your[t] God will come, and all the holy ones with him.[u]

On that day there shall be neither cold nor 6 frost.[v] And there shall be continuous day (it 7 is known to the LORD), not day and not night, for at evening time there shall be light.

On that day living waters shall flow out 8 from Jerusalem, half of them to the eastern sea and half of them to the western sea; it shall continue in summer as in winter.

Lord of all

And the LORD will become king over all the 9 earth; on that day the LORD will be one and his name one.

The whole land shall be turned into a plain 10 from Geba to Rimmon south of Jerusalem. But Jerusalem shall remain aloft upon its site from the Gate of Benjamin to the place of the former gate, to the Corner Gate, and from the Tower of Han'anel to the king's wine presses. And it shall be inhabited, for there 11 shall be no more curse;[w] Jerusalem shall dwell in security.

And this shall be the plague with which the 12 LORD will smite all the peoples that wage war against Jerusalem: their flesh shall rot while they are still on their feet, their eyes shall rot in their sockets, and their tongues shall rot in their mouths. And on that day a great panic 13 from the LORD shall fall on them, so that each will lay hold on the hand of his fellow, and the hand of the one will be raised against the hand of the other; even Judah will fight 14 against Jerusalem. And the wealth of all the nations round about shall be collected, gold, silver, and garments in great abundance. And a plague like this plague shall fall on the 15 horses, the mules, the camels, the asses, and whatever beasts may be in those camps.

Universal worship

Then every one that survives of all the 16 nations that have come against Jerusalem shall go up year after year to worship the King, the LORD of hosts, and to keep the feast of booths. And if any of the families of 17 the earth do not go up to Jerusalem to worship the King, the LORD of hosts, there will be no rain upon them. And if the family 18 of Egypt do not go up and present themselves, then upon them shall[x] come the plague with which the LORD afflicts the nations that do not go up to keep the feast of booths. This shall be the punishment to 19

[s] Cn: Heb for man has caused me to possess   [t] Heb my   [u] Gk Syr Vg Tg: Heb you
[v] Compare Gk Syr Vg Tg: Heb uncertain   [w] Or ban of utter destruction   [x] Gk Syr: Heb shall not
13.7: Mt 26.31; Mk 14.27.   14.8: Ezek 47.1–12; Rev 22.1–2.   14.11: Rev 22.3.
14.18–19: Is 19; Jer 46; Ezek 29–32.

Egypt and the punishment to all the nations that do not go up to keep the feast of booths.

An age of holiness

20 And on that day there shall be inscribed on the bells of the horses, "Holy to the LORD." And the pots in the house of the LORD shall be as the bowls before the altar; and every pot in Jerusalem and Judah shall be sacred to the LORD of hosts, so that all who sacrifice may come and take of them and boil the flesh of the sacrifice in them. And there shall no longer be a trader in the house of the LORD of hosts on that day.

THE BOOK OF
MALACHI

THE oracle of the word of the LORD to Israel by Mal'achi.[a]
2　"I have loved you," says the LORD. But you say, "How hast thou loved us?" "Is not Esau Jacob's brother?" says the LORD.
3 "Yet I have loved Jacob but I have hated Esau; I have laid waste his hill country and
4 left his heritage to jackals of the desert." If Edom says, "We are shattered but we will rebuild the ruins," the LORD of hosts says, "They may build, but I will tear down, till they are called the wicked country, the people with whom the LORD is angry for
5 ever." Your own eyes shall see this, and you shall say, "Great is the LORD, beyond the border of Israel!"
6 "A son honours his father, and a servant his master. If then I am a father, where is my honour? And if I am a master, where is my fear? says the LORD of hosts to you, O priests, who despise my name. You say,
7 'How have we despised thy name?' By offering polluted food upon my altar. And you say, 'How have we polluted it?'[b] By thinking that the LORD's table may be
8 despised. When you offer blind animals in sacrifice, is that no evil? And when you offer those that are lame or sick, is that no evil? Present that to your governor; will he be pleased with you or show you favour? says
9 the LORD of hosts. And now entreat the favour of God, that he may be gracious to us. With such a gift from your hand, will he show favour to any of you? says the LORD of
10 hosts. Oh, that there were one among you who would shut the doors, that you might not kindle fire upon my altar in vain! I have no pleasure in you, says the LORD of hosts, and I will not accept an offering from your
11 hand. For from the rising of the sun to its setting my name is great among the nations, and in every place incense is offered to my name, and a pure offering; for my name is great among the nations, says the LORD of hosts. But you profane it when you say that 12 the LORD's table is polluted, and the food for it[c] may be despised. 'What a weariness this 13 is,' you say, and you sniff at me,[d] says the LORD of hosts. You bring what has been taken by violence or is lame or sick, and this you bring as your offering! Shall I accept that from your hand? says the LORD. Cursed 14 be the cheat who has a male in his flock, and vows it, and yet sacrifices to the Lord what is blemished; for I am a great King, says the LORD of hosts, and my name is feared among the nations.

"And now, O priests, this command is for 2 you. If you will not listen, if you will not lay 2 it to heart to give glory to my name, says the LORD of hosts, then I will send the curse upon you and I will curse your blessings; indeed I have already cursed them, because you do not lay it to heart. Behold, I will 3 rebuke your offspring, and spread dung upon your faces, the dung of your offerings, and I will put you out of my presence.[e] So shall 4 you know that I have sent this command to you, that my covenant with Levi may hold, says the LORD of hosts. My covenant with 5 him was a covenant of life and peace, and I gave them to him, that he might fear; and he

---

[a] Or my messenger　[b] Gk: Heb thee　[c] Heb its fruit, its food　[d] Another reading is it
[e] Cn Compare Gk Syr: Heb and he shall bear you to it
1.2-3: Rom 9.13.　1.2-5: Is 34; 63.1-6; Jer 49.7-22; Ezek 25.12-14; 35; Amos 1.11-12; Obad.

feared me, he stood in awe of my name. True instruction[f] was in his mouth, and no wrong was found on his lips. He walked with me in peace and uprightness, and he turned many from iniquity. For the lips of a priest should guard knowledge, and men should seek instruction[f] from his mouth, for he is the messenger of the LORD of hosts. But you have turned aside from the way; you have caused many to stumble by your instruction;[f] you have corrupted the covenant of Levi, says the LORD of hosts, and so I make you despised and abased before all the people, inasmuch as you have not kept my ways but have shown partiality in your instruction."[f]

One Father

Have we not all one father? Has not one God created us? Why then are we faithless to one another, profaning the covenant of our fathers? Judah has been faithless, and abomination has been committed in Israel and in Jerusalem; for Judah has profaned the sanctuary of the LORD, which he loves, and has married the daughter of a foreign god. May the LORD cut off from the tents of Jacob, for the man who does this, any to witness[g] or answer, or to bring an offering to the LORD of hosts!

And this again you do. You cover the LORD's altar with tears, with weeping and groaning because he no longer regards the offering or accepts it with favour at your hand. You ask, "Why does he not?" Because the LORD was witness to the covenant between you and the wife of your youth, to whom you have been faithless, though she is your companion and your wife by covenant. Has not the one God made[h] and sustained for us the spirit of life?[i] And what does he desire? Godly offspring. So take heed to yourselves, and let none be faithless to the wife of his youth. "For I hate[j] divorce, says the LORD the God of Israel, and covering one's garment with violence, says the LORD of hosts. So take heed to yourselves and do not be faithless."

You have wearied the LORD with your words. Yet you say, "How have we wearied him?" By saying, "Every one who does evil is good in the sight of the LORD, and he delights in them." Or by asking, "Where is the God of justice?"

"Behold, I send my messenger to prepare the way before me, and the Lord whom you seek will suddenly come to his temple; the messenger of the covenant in whom you delight, behold, he is coming, says the LORD of hosts. But who can endure the day of his coming, and who can stand when he appears?

"For he is like a refiner's fire and like fullers' soap; he will sit as a refiner and purifier of silver, and he will purify the sons of Levi and refine them like gold and silver, till they present right offerings to the LORD. Then the offering of Judah and Jerusalem will be pleasing to the LORD as in the days of old and as in former years.

"Then I will draw near to you for judgment; I will be a swift witness against the sorcerers, against the adulterers, against those who swear falsely, against those who oppress the hireling in his wages, the widow and the orphan, against those who thrust aside the sojourner, and do not fear me, says the LORD of hosts.

Return to me

"For I the LORD do not change; therefore you, O sons of Jacob, are not consumed. From the days of your fathers you have turned aside from my statutes and have not kept them. Return to me, and I will return to you, says the LORD of hosts. But you say, 'How shall we return?' Will man rob God? Yet you are robbing me. But you say, 'How are we robbing thee?' In your tithes and offerings. You are cursed with a curse, for you are robbing me; the whole nation of you. Bring the full tithes into the storehouse, that there may be food in my house; and thereby put me to the test, says the LORD of hosts, if I will not open the windows of heaven for you and pour down for you an overflowing blessing. I will rebuke the devourer[k] for you, so that it will not destroy the fruits of your soil; and your vine in the field shall not fail to bear, says the LORD of hosts. Then all nations will call you blessed, for you will be a land of delight, says the LORD of hosts.

Final triumph

"Your words have been stout against me, says the LORD. Yet you say, 'How have we spoken against thee?' You have said, 'It is vain to serve God. What is the good of our keeping his charge or of walking as in mourning before the LORD of hosts? Henceforth we deem the arrogant blessed; evildoers not only prosper but when they put God to the test they escape.'"

---

[f] Or law [g] Cn Compare Gk: Heb arouse [h] Or has he not made one?
[i] Cn: Heb and a remnant of spirit was his [j] Cn: Heb he hates [k] Or devouring locust
3.1: Mt 11.10; Mk 1.2; Lk 1.17, 76; 7.27. **3.2:** Rev 6.17.

16 Then those who feared the LORD spoke with one another; the LORD heeded and heard them, and a book of remembrance was written before him of those who feared the
17 LORD and thought on his name. "They shall be mine, says the LORD of hosts, my special possession on the day when I act, and I will spare them as a man spares his son who
18 serves him. Then once more you shall distinguish between the righteous and the wicked, between one who serves God and one who does not serve him.

4[1] "For behold, the day comes, burning like an oven, when all the arrogant and all evildoers will be stubble; the day that comes shall burn them up, says the LORD of hosts, so that it will leave them neither root nor
2 branch. But for you who fear my name the sun of righteousness shall rise, with healing in its wings. You shall go forth leaping like calves from the stall. And you shall tread 3 down the wicked, for they will be ashes under the soles of your feet, on the day when I act, says the LORD of hosts.

A call to remembrance

"Remember the law of my servant Moses, the statutes and ordinances that I commanded him at Horeb for all Israel.

"Behold, I will send you Eli′jah the prophet 5 before the great and terrible day of the LORD comes. And he will turn the hearts of fathers 6 to their children and the hearts of children to their fathers, lest I come and smite the land with a curse." [m]

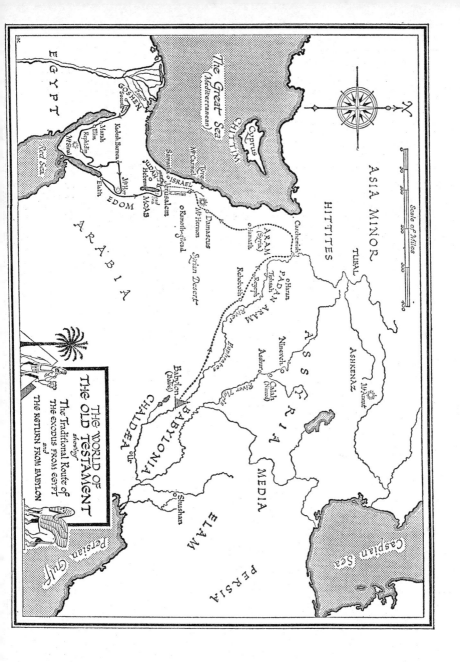

THE WORLD OF
THE OLD TESTAMENT
showing
The Traditional Route of
THE EXODUS FROM EGYPT
and
THE RETURN FROM BABYLON

THE WORLD OF
THE NEW TESTAMENT
showing
Saint Paul's Journey
to
ROME

THE NEW COVENANT

Commonly Called

THE

NEW TESTAMENT

Of Our Lord And Saviour
Jesus Christ

Revised Standard Version

TRANSLATED FROM THE GREEK

BEING THE VERSION SET FORTH A.D. 1611

REVISED A.D. 1881 AND A.D. 1901

COMPARED WITH THE MOST ANCIENT AUTHORITIES

AND REVISED A.D. 1946

"What is your life?" James **4,** 13–14

HK   BETHLEHEM

THE GOSPEL ACCORDING TO

MATTHEW

THE book of the genealogy of Jesus Christ, the son of David, the son of Abraham.

2 Abraham was the father of Isaac, and Isaac the father of Jacob, and Jacob the father of 3 Judah and his brothers, and Judah the father of Perez and Zerah by Tamar, and Perez the father of Hezron, and Hezron the father of 4 Ram,*a* and Ram*a* the father of Ammin′adab, and Ammin′adab the father of Nahshon, and 5 Nahshon the father of Salmon, and Salmon the father of Bo′az by Rahab, and Bo′az the father of Obed by Ruth, and Obed the father 6 of Jesse, and Jesse the father of David the king.

And David was the father of Solomon by 7 the wife of Uri′ah, and Solomon the father of Rehobo′am, and Rehobo′am the father of Abi′jah, and Abi′jah the father of Asa,*b* 8 and Asa*b* the father of Jehosh′aphat, and Jehosh′aphat the father of Joram, and Joram 9 the father of Uzzi′ah, and Uzzi′ah the father of Jotham, and Jotham the father of Ahaz, 10 and Ahaz the father of Hezeki′ah, and Hezeki′ah the father of Manas′seh, and Manas′seh the father of Amos,*c* and Amos*c* 11 the father of Josi′ah, and Josi′ah the father of Jechoni′ah and his brothers, at the time of the deportation to Babylon.

12 And after the deportation to Babylon: Jechoni′ah was the father of She-al′ti-el,*d* and She-al′ti-el*d* the father of Zerub′babel, and Zerub′babel the father of Abi′ud, and 13 Abi′ud the father of Eli′akim, and Eli′akim the father of Azor, and Azor the father of 14 Zadok, and Zadok the father of Achim, and Achim the father of Eli′ud, and Eli′ud the 15 father of Elea′zar, and Elea′zar the father of Matthan, and Matthan the father of Jacob, and Jacob the father of Joseph the husband 16 of Mary, of whom Jesus was born, who is called Christ.

So all the generations from Abraham to 17 David were fourteen generations, and from David to the deportation to Babylon fourteen generations, and from the deportation to Babylon to the Christ fourteen generations.

THE BIRTH OF JESUS

NOW the birth of Jesus Christ*e* took place 18 in this way. When his mother Mary had been betrothed to Joseph, before they came together she was found to be with child of the Holy Spirit; and her husband Joseph, 19 being a just man and unwilling to put her to shame, resolved to divorce her quietly. But 20 as he considered this, behold, an angel of the Lord appeared to him in a dream, saying, "Joseph, son of David, do not fear to take

---

a Greek *Aram* *b* Greek *Asaph* *c* Other authorities read *Amon* *d* Greek *Salathiel*
e Other ancient authorities read *of the Christ*
1.1-17: Lk 3.23-38. 1.3-6: Ruth 4.18-22; 1 Chron 2.1-15. 1.11: 2 Kings 24.14; Jer 27.20.
1.18: Lk 1.26-38.

Mary your wife, for that which is conceived
21 in her is of the Holy Spirit; she will bear a
son, and you shall call his name Jesus, for he
22 will save his people from their sins." All this
took place to fulfil what the Lord had spoken
by the prophet:
23   "Behold, a virgin shall conceive and bear a
son,
and his name shall be called Emman'u-el"
24 (which means, God with us). When Joseph
woke from sleep, he did as the angel of the
25 Lord commanded him; he took his wife, but
knew her not until she had borne a son; and
he called his name Jesus.

Wise men from the East

2 Now when Jesus was born in Bethlehem of
Judea in the days of Herod the king, behold,
wise men from the East came to Jerusalem,
2 saying, "Where is he who has been born king
of the Jews? For we have seen his star in the
3 East, and have come to worship him." When
Herod the king heard this, he was troubled,
4 and all Jerusalem with him; and assembling
all the chief priests and scribes of the people,
he inquired of them where the Christ was to
5 be born. They told him, "In Bethlehem of
Judea; for so it is written by the prophet:
6   'And you, O Bethlehem, in the land of
Judah,

are by no means least among the rulers of
Judah;
for from you shall come a ruler
who will govern my people Israel.' "
Then Herod summoned the wise men 7
secretly and ascertained from them what
time the star appeared; and he sent them 8
to Bethlehem, saying, "Go and search diligently for the child, and when you have
found him bring me word, that I too may
come and worship him." When they had 9
heard the king they went their way; and lo,

Frankincense

the star which they had seen in the East went
before them, till it came to rest over the place
where the child was. When they saw the 10
star, they rejoiced exceedingly with great joy;
and going into the house they saw the child 11
with Mary his mother, and they fell down
and worshipped him. Then, opening their
treasures, they offered him gifts, gold and
frankincense and myrrh. And being warned 12
in a dream not to return to Herod, they
departed to their own country by another
way.

1.21: Lk 2.21; Jn 1.29; Acts 13.23.   **1.23:** Is 7.14.   **2.1:** Lk 2.4–7; 1.5.
2.2: Jer 23.5; Zech 9.9; Mk 15.2; Jn 1.49; Num 24.17.   **2.5:** Jn 7.42.   **2.6:** Mic 5.2.   **2.11:** Mt 1.18; 12.46.
2.12: Mt 2.22; Acts 10.22; Heb 11.7.

The flight to Egypt

13 Now when they had departed, behold, an angel of the Lord appeared to Joseph in a dream and said, "Rise, take the child and his mother, and flee to Egypt, and remain there 14 till I tell you; for Herod is about to search for the child, to destroy him." And he rose and took the child and his mother by night, and 15 departed to Egypt, and remained there until the death of Herod. This was to fulfil what the Lord had spoken by the prophet, "Out of Egypt have I called my son."
16 Then Herod, when he saw that he had been tricked by the wise men, was in a furious rage, and he sent and killed all the male children in Bethlehem and in all that region who were two years old or under, according to the time which he had ascertained from 17 the wise men. Then was fulfilled what was spoken by the prophet Jeremiah:
18   "A voice was heard in Ramah,
  wailing and loud lamentation,
  Rachel weeping for her children;
  she refused to be consoled,
  because they were no more."

The return to Nazareth

19 But when Herod died, behold, an angel of the Lord appeared in a dream to Joseph in Egypt, saying, "Rise, take the child and his 20 mother, and go to the land of Israel, for those who sought the child's life are dead." And 21 he rose and took the child and his mother, and went to the land of Israel. But when he 22 heard that Archela'us reigned over Judea in place of his father Herod, he was afraid to go there, and being warned in a dream he withdrew to the district of Galilee. And he 23 went and dwelt in a city called Nazareth, that what was spoken by the prophets might be fulfilled, "He shall be called a Nazarene."

BAPTISM AND TEMPTATION

John the Baptist

3 IN those days came John the Baptist, preaching in the wilderness of Judea, 2 "Repent, for the kingdom of heaven is at hand." For this is he who was spoken of by 3 the prophet Isaiah when he said,

An eastern winnowing fork   Matt 3, 12

2.15: Hos 11.1; Ex 4.22.   2.18: Jer 31.15.   2.19: Mt 1.20; 2.13.   2.23: Is 11.1; Lk 1.26; Mk 1.24.
3.1–12: Mk 1.3–8; Lk 3.2–17; Jn 1.6–8, 19–28.   3.2: Mt 4.17; Dan 2.44; 4.17; Mt 10.7.   3.3: Is 40.3.

"The voice of one crying in the wilderness:
Prepare the way of the Lord,
make his paths straight."

4 Now John wore a garment of camel's hair, and a leather girdle around his waist; and his
5 food was locusts and wild honey. Then went out to him Jerusalem and all Judea and all
6 the region about the Jordan, and they were baptized by him in the river Jordan, confessing their sins.

7 But when he saw many of the Pharisees and Sad′ducees coming for baptism, he said to them, "You brood of vipers! Who warned
8 you to flee from the wrath to come? Bear
9 fruit that befits repentance, and do not presume to say to yourselves, 'We have Abraham as our father'; for I tell you, God is able from these stones to raise up children to
10 Abraham. Even now the axe is laid to the root of the trees; every tree therefore that does not bear good fruit is cut down and thrown into the fire.
11 "I baptize you with water for repentance, but he who is coming after me is mightier than I, whose sandals I am not worthy to carry; he will baptize you with the Holy
12 Spirit and with fire. His winnowing fork is

heavens were opened[f] and he saw the Spirit of God descending like a dove, and alighting on him; and lo, a voice from heaven, saying, 17 "This is my beloved Son,[g] with whom I am well pleased."

His temptation

Then Jesus was led up by the Spirit into the 4 wilderness to be tempted by the devil. And 2 he fasted forty days and forty nights, and afterward he was hungry. And the tempter 3 came and said to him, "If you are the Son of God, command these stones to become loaves of bread." But he answered, "It is 4 written,

'Man shall not live by bread alone,
but by every word that proceeds from the mouth of God.'"

in his hand, and he will clear his threshing floor and gather his wheat into the granary, but the chaff he will burn with unquenchable fire."

The baptism of Jesus

13 Then Jesus came from Galilee to the Jordan
14 to John, to be baptized by him. John would have prevented him, saying, "I need to be baptized by you, and do you come to me?"
15 But Jesus answered him, "Let it be so now; for thus it is fitting for us to fulfil all
16 righteousness." Then he consented. And when Jesus was baptized, he went up immediately from the water, and behold, the

A wilderness

f Other ancient authorities add *to him*　　*g* Or *my Son, my* (or *the*) *Beloved*
3.4: 2 Kings 1.8; Zech 13.4; Lev 11.22.　**3.7:** Mt 12.34; 23.33; 1 Thess 1.10.　**3.9:** Jn 8.33; Rom 4.16.
3.10: Mt 7.19.　**3.12:** Mt 13.30.　**3.13–17:** Mk 1.9–11; Lk 3.21–22; Jn 1.31–34.
3.17: Mt 12.18; 17.5; Mk 9.7; Lk 9.35; Ps 2.7; Is 42.1.　**4.1–11:** Mk 1.12–13; Lk 4.1–13; Heb 2.18; 4.15.
4.2: Ex 34.28; 1 Kings 19.8.　**4.4:** Deut 8.3.

5 Then the devil took him to the holy city, and
6 set him on the pinnacle of the temple, and
said to him, "If you are the Son of God,
throw yourself down; for it is written,

'He will give his angels charge of you,'
and

'On their hands they will bear you up,
lest you strike your foot against a stone.' "
7 Jesus said to him, "Again it is written, 'You
shall not tempt the Lord your God.' "

Again, the devil took him to a very high 8
mountain, and showed him all the kingdoms
of the world and the glory of them; and he 9
said to him, "All these I will give you, if you
will fall down and worship me." Then Jesus 10
said to him, "Begone, Satan! for it is written,

'You shall worship the Lord your God
and him only shall you serve.' "
Then the devil left him, and behold, angels 11
came and ministered to him.

Galilean fishermen

WORK IN GALILEE

12 NOW when he heard that John had been
13 arrested, he withdrew into Galilee; and
leaving Nazareth he went and dwelt in
Caper'na-um by the sea, in the territory of
14 Zeb'ulun and Naph'tali, that what was
spoken by the prophet Isaiah might be
fulfilled:
15 "The land of Zeb'ulun and the land of
Naph'tali,
toward the sea, across the Jordan,
Galilee of the Gentiles—
16 the people who sat in darkness
have seen a great light,

and for those who sat in the region and
shadow of death
light has dawned."
From that time Jesus began to preach, 17
saying, "Repent, for the kingdom of heaven
is at hand."

The first disciples

As he walked by the Sea of Galilee, he saw 18
two brothers, Simon who is called Peter and
Andrew his brother, casting a net into the
sea; for they were fishermen. And he said to 19

4.5: Mt 27.53; Neh 11.1; Dan 9.24; Rev 21.10.   4.6: Ps 91.11–12.   4.7: Deut 6.16.   4.10: Deut 6.13; Mk 8.33.
4.11: Mt 26.53; Lk 22.43.   4.12: Mk 1.14; Lk 4.14; Mt 14.3; Jn 1.43.   4.13: Jn 2.12; Mk 1.21; Lk 4.23.
4.15: Is 9.1–2.   4.17: Mk 1.15; Mt 3.2; 10.7.   4.18–22: Mk 1.16–20; Lk 5.1–11; Jn 1.35–42.

them, "Follow me, and I will make you
20 fishers of men." Immediately they left their
21 nets and followed him. And going on from
there he saw two other brothers, James the
son of Zeb'edee and John his brother, in the
boat with Zeb'edee their father, mending
22 their nets, and he called them. Immediately
they left the boat and their father, and
followed him.

Jesus begins his ministry

23 And he went about all Galilee, teaching in
their synagogues and preaching the gospel of
the kingdom and healing every disease and
24 every infirmity among the people. So his
fame spread throughout all Syria, and they
brought him all the sick, those afflicted with
various diseases and pains, demoniacs, epi-
leptics, and paralytics, and he healed them.
25 And great crowds followed him from Galilee
and the Decap'olis and Jerusalem and Judea
and from beyond the Jordan.

"Blessed are those who mourn, for they 4
shall be comforted.
"Blessed are the meek, for they shall inherit 5
the earth.
"Blessed are those who hunger and thirst 6
for righteousness, for they shall be satisfied.
"Blessed are the merciful, for they shall 7
obtain mercy.
"Blessed are the pure in heart, for they shall 8
see God.
"Blessed are the peacemakers, for they shall 9
be called sons of God.
"Blessed are those who are persecuted for 10
righteousness' sake, for theirs is the kingdom
of heaven.
"Blessed are you when men revile you and 11
persecute you and utter all kinds of evil
against you falsely on my account. Rejoice 12
and be glad, for your reward is great in
heaven, for so men persecuted the prophets
who were before you.
"You are the salt of the earth; but if salt 13
has lost its taste, how shall its saltness be
restored? It is no longer good for anything
except to be thrown out and trodden under
foot by men.
"You are the light of the world. A city set 14
on a hill cannot be hid. Nor do men light a 15
lamp and put it under a bushel, but on a
stand, and it gives light to all in the house.
Let your light so shine before men, that they 16
may see your good works and give glory to
your Father who is in heaven.
"Think not that I have come to abolish the 17
law and the prophets; I have come not to

SERMON ON THE MOUNT

5 SEEING the crowds, he went up on the
mountain, and when he sat down his
2 disciples came to him. And he opened his
mouth and taught them, saying:
3 "Blessed are the poor in spirit, for theirs is
the kingdom of heaven.

abolish them but to fulfil them. For truly, I 18
say to you, till heaven and earth pass away,
not an iota, not a dot, will pass from the law
until all is accomplished. Whoever then 19
relaxes one of the least of these commandments and teaches men so, shall be called

4.23-25: Mk 1.39; Lk 4.15, 44; Mt 9.35; Mk 3.7-8; Lk 6.17. 5.1-12: Lk 6.17, 20-23; Mk 3.13; Jn 6.3.
5.3: Mk 10.14; Lk 22.29. 5.4: Is 61.2; Jn 16.20; Rev 7.17. 5.5: Ps 37.11. 5.6: Is 55.1-2; Jn 4.14; 6.48-51.
5.8: Ps 24.4; Heb 12.14; 1 Jn 3.2; Rev 22.4. 5.10: 1 Pet 3.14; 4.14.
5.12: 2 Chron 36.16; Mt 23.37; Acts 7.52; 1 Thess 2.15; Jas 5.10. 5.13: Mk 9.49-50; Lk 14.34-35.
5.14: Eph 5.8; Phil 2.15; Jn 8.12. 5.15-16: Lk 11.33; Mk 4.21; 1 Pet 2.12. 5.18: Lk 16.17; Mk 13.31.
5.19: Jas 2.10.

Lamp and bushel measure Matt 5, 15

least in the kingdom of heaven; but he who does them and teaches them shall be called 10 great in the kingdom of heaven. For I tell you, unless your righteousness exceeds that of the scribes and Pharisees, you will never enter the kingdom of heaven.

The new law

21 "You have heard that it was said to the men of old, 'You shall not kill; and whoever kills 22 shall be liable to judgment.' But I say to you that every one who is angry with his brother[h] shall be liable to judgment; whoever insults[i] his brother shall be liable to the council, and whoever says, 'You fool!' shall be liable to 23 the hell[j] of fire. So if you are offering your gift at the altar, and there remember that your brother has something against you, 24 leave your gift there before the altar and go; first be reconciled to your brother, and then 25 come and offer your gift. Make friends quickly with your accuser, while you are going with him to court, lest your accuser hand you over to the judge, and the judge to 26 the guard, and you be put in prison; truly, I say to you, you will never get out till you have paid the last penny.

27 "You have heard that it was said, 'You shall 28 not commit adultery.' But I say to you that every one who looks at a woman lustfully has already committed adultery with her in his 29 heart. If your right eye causes you to sin,

pluck it out and throw it away; it is better that you lose one of your members than that your whole body be thrown into hell.[j] And if 30 your right hand causes you to sin, cut it off and throw it away; it is better that you lose one of your members than that your whole body go into hell.[j]

"It was also said, 'Whoever divorces his 31 wife, let him give her a certificate of divorce.' But I say to you that every one who 32 divorces his wife, except on the ground of unchastity, makes her an adulteress; and whoever marries a divorced woman commits adultery.

"Again you have heard that it was said to 33 the men of old, 'You shall not swear falsely, but shall perform to the Lord what you have sworn.' But I say to you, Do not swear at all, 34 either by heaven, for it is the throne of God, or by the earth, for it is his footstool, or by 35 Jerusalem, for it is the city of the great King. And do not swear by your head, for you 36 cannot make one hair white or black. Let 37 what you say be simply 'Yes' or 'No'; anything more than this comes from evil.[k]

"You have heard that it was said, 'An eye 38 for an eye and a tooth for a tooth.' But I say 39 to you, Do not resist one who is evil. But if any one strikes you on the right cheek, turn to him the other also; and if any one would 40 sue you and take your coat, let him have your cloak as well; and if any one forces you to go 41 one mile, go with him two miles. Give to 42 him who begs from you, and do not refuse him who would borrow from you.

"You have heard that it was said, 'You shall 43 love your neighbour and hate your enemy.' But I say to you, Love your enemies and pray 44 for those who persecute you, so that you may 45 be sons of your Father who is in heaven; for he makes his sun rise on the evil and on the good, and sends rain on the just and on the unjust. For if you love those who love you, 46 what reward have you? Do not even the tax collectors do the same? And if you salute 47 only your brethren, what more are you doing than others? Do not even the Gentiles do the same? You, therefore, must be perfect, 48 as your heavenly Father is perfect.

Real religion

"Beware of practising your piety before **6** men in order to be seen by them; for then

[h] Other ancient authorities insert *without cause*   [i] Greek says *Raca to* (an obscure term of abuse)
[j] Greek *Gehenna*   [k] Or *the evil one*
5.21: Ex 20.13; Deut 5.17; 16.18.   5.25-26: Lk 12.57-59.   5.27: Ex 20.14; Deut 5.18.
5.29-30: Mk 9.43-48; Mt 18.8-9.   5.31-32: Lk 16.18; Mk 10.11-12; Mt 19.9; 1 Cor 7.10-11; Deut 24.1-4.
5.33-37: Mt 23.16-22; Jas 5.12; Lev 19.12; Num 30.2; Deut 23.21.   5.35: Is 66.1; Acts 7.49; Ps 48.2.
5.38: Ex 21.24; Lev 24.20; Deut 19.21.
5.43-42: Lk 6.29-30; 1 Cor 6.7; Rom 12.17; 1 Pet 2.19; 3.9; Prov 24.29.
5.43-48: Lk 6.27-28, 32-36; Lev 19.18; Prov 25.21-22.   5.48: Lev 19.2.   6.1: Mt 23.5.

you will have no reward from your Father who is in heaven.

2 "Thus, when you give alms, sound no trumpet before you, as the hypocrites do in the synagogues and in the streets, that they may be praised by men. Truly, I say to you, 3 they have their reward. But when you give alms, do not let your left hand know what 4 your right hand is doing, so that your alms may be in secret; and your Father who sees in secret will reward you.

5 "And when you pray, you must not be like the hypocrites; for they love to stand and pray in the synagogues and at the street corners, that they may be seen by men. Truly, I say to you, they have their reward. 6 But when you pray, go into your room and shut the door and pray to your Father who is in secret; and your Father who sees in secret will reward you.

7 "And in praying do not heap up empty phrases as the Gentiles do; for they think that they will be heard for their many words. 8 Do not be like them, for your Father knows 9 what you need before you ask him. Pray then like this:

Our Father who art in heaven,
Hallowed be thy name.
10   Thy kingdom come,
Thy will be done,
On earth as it is in heaven.
11   Give us this day our daily bread;[l]
12   And forgive us our debts,
As we also have forgiven our debtors;
13   And lead us not into temptation,
But deliver us from evil.[m]

14 For if you forgive men their trespasses, your 15 heavenly Father also will forgive you; but if you do not forgive men their trespasses, neither will your Father forgive your trespasses.

16 "And when you fast, do not look dismal, like the hypocrites, for they disfigure their faces that their fasting may be seen by men. Truly, I say to you, they have their reward. 17 But when you fast, anoint your head and 18 wash your face, that your fasting may not be seen by men but by your Father who is in secret; and your Father who sees in secret will reward you.

19 "Do not lay up for yourselves treasures on earth, where moth and rust[n] consume and 20 where thieves break in and steal, but lay up for yourselves treasure in heaven, where

neither moth nor rust[n] consumes and where thieves do not break in and steal. For where 21 your treasure is, there will your heart be also.

"The eye is the lamp of the body. So, if 22 your eye is sound, your whole body will be full of light; but if your eye is not sound, 23 your whole body will be full of darkness. If then the light in you is darkness, how great is the darkness!

"No one can serve two masters; for either 24 he will hate the one and love the other, or he will be devoted to the one and despise the other. You cannot serve God and mammon.

True wisdom

"Therefore I tell you, do not be anxious 25 about your life, what you shall eat or what you shall drink, nor about your body, what you shall put on. Is not life more than food, and the body more than clothing? Look at 26 the birds of the air: they neither sow nor reap nor gather into barns, and yet your heavenly Father feeds them. Are you not of more value than they? And which of you by being 27 anxious can add one cubit to his span of life?[o] And why are you anxious about 28 clothing? Consider the lilies of the field, how they grow; they neither toil nor spin; yet 29 I tell you, even Solomon in all his glory was not arrayed like one of these. But if God so 30 clothes the grass of the field, which today is alive and tomorrow is thrown into the oven, will he not much more clothe you, O men of little faith? Therefore do not be anxious, 31 saying, 'What shall we eat?' or 'What shall we drink?' or 'What shall we wear?' For the 32 Gentiles seek all these things; and your heavenly Father knows that you need them all. But seek first his kingdom and his 33 righteousness, and all these things shall be yours as well.

"Therefore do not be anxious about 34 tomorrow, for tomorrow will be anxious for itself. Let the day's own trouble be sufficient for the day.

"Judge not, that you be not judged. For 7 with the judgment you pronounce you will 2 be judged, and the measure you give will be the measure you get. Why do you see the 3 speck that is in your brother's eye, but do not notice the log that is in your own eye? Or 4 how can you say to your brother, 'Let me

[l] Or *our bread for the morrow*   [m] Or *the evil one.* Other authorities, some ancient, add, in some form, *For thine is the kingdom and the power and the glory, for ever. Amen.*   [n] Or *worm*   [o] Or *to his stature*
6.4: Col 3.23–24.   6.5: Mk 11.25; Lk 18.10–14.   6.7: 1 Kings 18.25–29.   6.8: Mt 6.32; Lk 12.30.
6.9–13: Lk 11.2–4.   6.13: 2 Thess 3.3; Jn 17.15; Jas 1.13.   6.14–15: Mt 18.35; Mk 11.25; Eph 4.32; Col 3.13.
6.16: Is 58.5.   6.18: Mt 6.4, 6.   6.19–21: Mt 6.4, 6.   6.19–21: Mt 12.33–34; Mk 10.21; 1 Tim 6.17–19; Jas 5.1–3.
6.22–23: Lk 11.34–36; Mt 20.15; Mk 7.22.   6.24: Lk 16.13.
6.25–33: Lk 12.22–31; 10.41; 12.11; Phil 4.6; 1 Pet 5.7.   6.26: Mt 10.29.   6.27: Ps 39.5.
6.29: 1 Kings 10.4–7.   6.30: Mt 8.26; 14.31; 16.8.   6.33: Mt 19.28; Mk 10.29–30; Lk 18.29–30.
7.1–2: Lk 6.37–38; Mk 4.24; Rom 2.1; 14.10.   7.3–5: Lk 6.41–42.

take the speck out of your eye,' when there is
5 the log in your own eye? You hypocrite,
first take the log out of your own eye, and
then you will see clearly to take the speck out
of your brother's eye.

6 "Do not give dogs what is holy; and do not
throw your pearls before swine, lest they
trample them under foot and turn to attack
you.

7 "Ask, and it will be given you; seek, and
you will find; knock, and it will be opened to
8 you. For every one who asks receives, and he
who seeks finds, and to him who knocks it
9 will be opened. Or what man of you, if his
son asks him for bread, will give him a
10 stone? Or if he asks for a fish, will give him a
11 serpent? If you then, who are evil, know
how to give good gifts to your children, how
much more will your Father who is in heaven
12 give good things to those who ask him! So
whatever you wish that men would do to you,
do so to them; for this is the law and the
prophets.

13 "Enter by the narrow gate; for the gate is
wide and the way is easy,[p] that leads to
destruction, and those who enter by it are
14 many. For the gate is narrow and the way is
hard, that leads to life, and those who find it
are few.

15 "Beware of false prophets, who come to you
in sheep's clothing but inwardly are ravenous
16 wolves. You will know them by their fruits.
Are grapes gathered from thorns, or figs
17 from thistles? So, every sound tree bears
good fruit, but the bad tree bears evil fruit.
18 A sound tree cannot bear evil fruit, nor can a
19 bad tree bear good fruit. Every tree that does
not bear good fruit is cut down and thrown
20 into the fire. Thus you will know them by
their fruits.

21 "Not every one who says to me, 'Lord,
Lord,' shall enter the kingdom of heaven, but
he who does the will of my Father who is in
22 heaven. On that day many will say to me,
'Lord, Lord, did we not prophesy in your
name, and cast out demons in your name,
and do many mighty works in your name?'
23 And then will I declare to them, 'I never
knew you; depart from me, you evildoers.'

24 "Every one then who hears these words of
mine and does them will be like a wise man
25 who built his house upon the rock; and the
rain fell, and the floods came, and the winds
blew and beat upon that house, but it did not
fall, because it had been founded on the

Matt 7, 16

rock. And every one who hears these words 26
of mine and does not do them will be like a
foolish man who built his house upon the
sand; and the rain fell, and the floods came, 27
and the winds blew and beat against that
house, and it fell; and great was the fall of
it."

And when Jesus finished these sayings, the 28
crowds were astonished at his teaching, for 29
he taught them as one who had authority,
and not as their scribes.

MARVELLOUS DEEDS

Power over disease

WHEN he came down from the moun- **8**
tain, great crowds followed him; and 2
behold, a leper came to him and knelt before
him, saying, "Lord, if you will, you can make
me clean." And he stretched out his hand 3
and touched him, saying, "I will; be clean."
And immediately his leprosy was cleansed.
And Jesus said to him, "See that you say 4
nothing to any one; but go, show yourself to
the priest, and offer the gift that Moses
commanded, for a proof to the people."[q]

[p] Other ancient authorities read *for the way is wide and easy*   [q] Greek *to them*
7.7-11: Lk 11.9-13; Mk 11.24; Jn 15.7; 16.23-24; Jas 4.3; 1 Jn 3.22; 5.14.   **7.12**: Lk 6.31.
7.13-14: Lk 13.23-24; Jer 21.8; Deut 30.19; Jn 14.6; 10.7.
7.15: Mt 24.11, 24; Ezek 22.27; 1 Jn 4.1; Jn 10.12.
7.16-20: Lk 6.43-44; Mt 12.33-35; Mt 3.10; Jas 3.12; Lk 13.7.
7.21: Lk 6.46.   **7.22-23**: Lk 13.26-27; Ps 6.8.   **7.24-27**: Lk 6.47-49; Jas 1.22-25.
7.28-29: Mk 1.22; Lk 4.32; Mt 11.1; 13.53; 19.1; 26.1.   **8.2-4**: Mk 1.40-44; Lk 5.12-14.
8.2: Mt 9.18; 15.25; 18.26; 20.20; Jn 9.38.   **8.4**: Mk 3.12; 5.43; 7.36; 8.30; 9.9; Lev 14.2.

5 As he entered Caper′na-um, a centurion
6 came forward to him, beseeching him and
saying, "Lord, my servant is lying paralysed
7 at home, in terrible distress." And he said to
8 him, "I will come and heal him." But the
centurion answered him, "Lord, I am not
worthy to have you come under my roof; but
only say the word, and my servant will be
9 healed. For I am a man under authority,
with soldiers under me; and I say to one,
'Go,' and he goes, and to another, 'Come,'
and he comes, and to my slave, 'Do this,' and
10 he does it." When Jesus heard him, he
marvelled, and said to those who followed
him, "Truly, I say to you, not even′ in Israel
11 have I found such faith. I tell you, many will
come from east and west and sit at table with
Abraham, Isaac, and Jacob in the kingdom of
12 heaven, while the sons of the kingdom will be
thrown into the outer darkness; there men
13 will weep and gnash their teeth." And to the
centurion Jesus said, "Go; be it done for you
as you have believed." And the servant was
healed at that very moment.

14 And when Jesus entered Peter's house, he
saw his mother-in-law lying sick with a fever;
15 he touched her hand, and the fever left her,
16 and she rose and served him. That evening
they brought to him many who were possessed with demons; and he cast out the
spirits with a word, and healed all who were
17 sick. This was to fulfil what was spoken by
the prophet Isaiah, "He took our infirmities
and bore our diseases."

Power over men

18 Now when Jesus saw great crowds around
him, he gave orders to go over to the other
19 side. And a scribe came up and said to him,
"Teacher, I will follow you wherever you
20 go." And Jesus said to him, "Foxes have
holes, and birds of the air have nests; but the
Son of man has nowhere to lay his head."
21 Another of the disciples said to him, "Lord,
22 let me first go and bury my father." But
Jesus said to him, "Follow me, and leave the
dead to bury their own dead."

Power over nature

23 And when he got into the boat, his disciples
24 followed him. And behold, there arose a
great storm on the sea, so that the boat was

being swamped by the waves; but he was
asleep. And they went and woke him,
saying, "Save, Lord; we are perishing." And
he said to them, "Why are you afraid, O men
of little faith?" Then he rose and rebuked
the winds and the sea; and there was a great
calm. And the men marvelled, saying,
"What sort of man is this, that even winds
and sea obey him?"

Power over demons

And when he came to the other side, to the
country of the Gadarenes,⁸ two demoniacs
met him, coming out of the tombs, so fierce
that no one could pass that way. And
behold, they cried out, "What have you to do
with us, O Son of God? Have you come
here to torment us before the time?" Now a
herd of many swine was feeding at some
distance from them. And the demons
begged him, "If you cast us out, send us
away into the herd of swine." And he said to
them, "Go." So they came out and went
into the swine; and behold, the whole herd
rushed down the steep bank into the sea, and
perished in the waters. The herdsmen fled,
and going into the city they told everything,
and what had happened to the demoniacs.
And behold, all the city came out to meet
Jesus; and when they saw him, they begged
him to leave their neighbourhood.

Power to forgive sins

And getting into a boat he crossed over and 9
came to his own city. And behold, they 2
brought to him a paralytic, lying on his bed;
and when Jesus saw their faith he said to the
paralytic, "Take heart, my son; your sins are
forgiven." And behold, some of the scribes 3
said to themselves, "This man is blaspheming." But Jesus, knowingᵗ their thoughts, 4
said, "Why do you think evil in your hearts?
For which is easier, to say, 'Your sins are 5
forgiven,' or to say, 'Rise and walk'? But 6
that you may know that the Son of man has
authority on earth to forgive sins"—he then
said to the paralytic—"Rise, take up your
bed and go home." And he rose and went 7
home. When the crowds saw it, they were 8
afraid, and they glorified God, who had
given such authority to men.

ʳ Other ancient authorities read *with no one*   ⁸ Other ancient authorities read *Gergesenes;* some, *Gerasenes*
ᵗ Other ancient authorities read *seeing*
8.5–13: Lk 7.1–10; Jn 4.46–53.   8.11–12: Lk 13.28–29; Is 49.12; 59.19; Mal 1.11; Ps 107.3.
8.12: Mt 13.42, 50; 22.13; 24.51; 25.30; Lk 13.28.   8.14–16: Mk 1.29–34; Lk 4.38–41; Mt 4.23–24.
8.17: Is 53.4.   8.18–22: Lk 9.57–60; Mk 4.35; Lk 8.22.   8.22: Mt 9.9; Jn 1.43; 21.19.
8.23–27: Mk 4.36–41; Lk 8.22–25.
8.26: Mt 6.30; 14.31; 16.8.   8.28–34: Mk 5.1–17; Lk 8.26–37.
8.29: Judg 11.12; 2 Sam 16.10; Mk 1.24; Jn 2.4.   9.1–8: Mk 2.1–12; Lk 5.17–26.
9.2: Mt 9.22; Mk 6.50; 10.49; Jn 16.33; Acts 23.11; Lk 7.48.

Tax collectors and sinners are called

9 As Jesus passed on from there, he saw a man called Matthew sitting at the tax office; and he said to him, "Follow me." And he rose and followed him.

10 And as he sat at table[u] in the house, behold, many tax collectors and sinners came and sat down with Jesus and his disciples. 11 And when the Pharisees saw this, they said to his disciples, "Why does your teacher eat with tax collectors and sinners?" 12 But when he heard it, he said, "Those who are well have no need of a physician, but those who are sick. 13 Go and learn what this means, 'I desire mercy, and not sacrifice.' For I came not to call the righteous, but sinners."

Signs of change

14 Then the disciples of John came to him, saying, "Why do we and the Pharisees fast,[v] 15 but your disciples do not fast?" And Jesus said to them, "Can the wedding guests mourn as long as the bridegroom is with them? The days will come, when the bridegroom is taken away from them, and then 16 they will fast. And no one puts a piece of unshrunk cloth on an old garment, for the patch tears away from the garment, and a 17 worse tear is made. Neither is new wine put into old wineskins; if it is, the skins burst, and the wine is spilled, and the skins are destroyed; but new wine is put into fresh wineskins, and so both are preserved."

Signs of faith

18 While he was thus speaking to them, behold, a ruler came in and knelt before him, saying, "My daughter has just died; but come and lay your hand on her, and she will 19 live." And Jesus rose and followed him, with 20 his disciples. And behold, a woman who had suffered from a hemorrhage for twelve years came up behind him and touched the fringe 21 of his garment; for she said to herself, "If I only touch his garment, I shall be made 22 well." Jesus turned, and seeing her he said, "Take heart, daughter; your faith has made you well." And instantly the woman was 23 made well. And when Jesus came to the ruler's house, and saw the flute players, and 24 the crowd making a tumult, he said,

"Depart; for the girl is not dead but sleeping." And they laughed at him. But 25 when the crowd had been put outside, he went in and took her by the hand, and the girl arose. And the report of this went 26 through all that district.

And as Jesus passed on from there, two 27 blind men followed him, crying aloud, "Have mercy on us, Son of David." When 28 he entered the house, the blind men came to him; and Jesus said to them, "Do you believe that I am able to do this?" They said to him, "Yes, Lord." Then he touched their eyes, 29 saying, "According to your faith be it done to you." And their eyes were opened. And 30 Jesus sternly charged them, "See that no one knows it." But they went away and spread 31 his fame through all that district.

As they were going away, behold, a dumb 32 demoniac was brought to him. And when 33 the demon had been cast out, the dumb man spoke; and the crowds marvelled, saying, "Never was anything like this seen in Israel." But the Pharisees said, "He casts 34 out demons by the prince of demons."

JESUS AND HIS APOSTLES

AND Jesus went about all the cities and 35 villages, teaching in their synagogues and preaching the gospel of the kingdom, and healing every disease and every infirmity. When he saw the crowds, he had 36 compassion for them, because they were harassed and helpless, like sheep without a shepherd. Then he said to his disciples, 37 "The harvest is plentiful, but the labourers are few; pray therefore the Lord of the 38 harvest to send out labourers into his harvest."

Names of the twelve

And he called to him his twelve disciples 10 and gave them authority over unclean spirits, to cast them out, and to heal every disease and every infirmity. The names of the 2 twelve apostles are these: first, Simon, who is called Peter, and Andrew his brother; James the son of Zeb'edee, and John his brother; Philip and Bartholomew; Thomas and 3 Matthew the tax collector; James the son of Alphaeus, and Thaddaeus;[w] Simon the 4

u Greek reclined   v Other ancient authorities add much or often
w Other ancient authorities read Lebbaeus or Lebbaeus called Thaddaeus

9.9–13: Mk 2.13–17; Lk 5.27–32; 15.1–2; 7.34.   9.13: Hos 6.6; Mt 12.7; 1 Tim 1.15.
9.14–17: Mk 2.18–22; Lk 5.33–39; 18.12.   9.18–26: Mk 5.21–43; Lk 8.40–56.
9.18: Mt 8.2; 15.25; 18.26; 20.20; Jn 9.38.   9.20: Num 15.38; Deut 22.12; Mt 14.36; Mk 3.10.
9.22: Mk 10.52; Mt 7.50; 17.19; Mt 15.28; 9.29.   9.27–31: Mt 20.29–34.
9.32–34: Lk 11.14–15; Mt 12.22–24; Mk 3.22; Jn 7.20.   9.35: Mt 4.23; Mk 6.6.
9.36: Mk 6.34; Mt 14.14; 15.32; Num 27.17; Zech 10.2.   9.37–38: Lk 10.2; Jn 4.35.
10.1–4: Mk 6.7; 3.16–19; Lk 9.1; 6.14–16; Acts 1.13.

Cananaean, and Judas Iscariot, who betrayed him.

Their mission

5 These twelve Jesus sent out, charging them, "Go nowhere among the Gentiles, and enter 6 no town of the Samaritans, but go rather to 7 the lost sheep of the house of Israel. And preach as you go, saying, 'The kingdom of 8 heaven is at hand.' Heal the sick, raise the dead, cleanse lepers, cast out demons. You received without pay, give without pay. 9 Take no gold, nor silver, nor copper in your

Shekel and half-shekel

10 belts, no bag for your journey, nor two tunics, nor sandals, nor a staff; for the 11 labourer deserves his food. And whatever town or village you enter, find out who is worthy in it, and stay with him until you 12 depart. As you enter the house, salute it. 13 And if the house is worthy, let your peace come upon it; but if it is not worthy, let your 14 peace return to you. And if any one will not receive you or listen to your words, shake off the dust from your feet as you leave that 15 house or town. Truly, I say to you, it shall be more tolerable on the day of judgment for the land of Sodom and Gomor′rah than for that town.

16 "Behold, I send you out as sheep in the midst of wolves; so be wise as serpents and 17 innocent as doves. Beware of men; for they will deliver you up to councils, and flog you 18 in their synagogues, and you will be dragged before governors and kings for my sake, to bear testimony before them and the Gen- 19 tiles. When they deliver you up, do not be anxious how you are to speak or what you are to say; for what you are to say will be given to

you in that hour; for it is not you who speak, 20 but the Spirit of your Father speaking through you. Brother will deliver up brother 21 to death, and the father his child, and children will rise against parents and have them put to death; and you will be hated by 22 all for my name's sake. But he who endures to the end will be saved. When they perse- 23 cute you in one town, flee to the next; for truly, I say to you, you will not have gone through all the towns of Israel, before the Son of man comes.

"A disciple is not above his teacher, nor a 24 servant *x* above his master; it is enough for 25 the disciple to be like his teacher, and the servant *x* like his master. If they have called the master of the house Be-el′zebul, how much more will they malign those of his household.

"So have no fear of them; for nothing is 26 covered that will not be revealed, or hidden that will not be known. What I tell you in 27 the dark, utter in the light; and what you hear whispered, proclaim upon the house-tops. And do not fear those who kill the 28 body but cannot kill the soul; rather fear him who can destroy both soul and body in hell. *y* Are not two sparrows sold for a penny? And 29 not one of them will fall to the ground without your Father's will. But even the 30 hairs of your head are all numbered. Fear 31 not, therefore; you are of more value than many sparrows. So every one who acknow- 32 ledges me before men, I also will acknow-ledge before my Father who is in heaven; but 33 whoever denies me before men, I also will deny before my Father who is in heaven.

"Do not think that I have come to bring 34 peace on earth; I have not come to bring peace, but a sword. For I have come to set a 35 man against his father, and a daughter against her mother, and a daughter-in-law against her mother-in-law; and a man's foes 36 will be those of his own household. He who 37 loves father or mother more than me is not worthy of me; and he who loves son or daughter more than me is not worthy of me; and he who does not take his cross and follow 38 me is not worthy of me. He who finds his life 39 will lose it, and he who loses his life for my sake will find it.

"He who receives you receives me, and he 40 who receives me receives him who sent me.

x Or *slave* *y* Greek *Gehenna*
10.5: Lk 9.52; Jn 4.9; Acts 8.5, 25. **10.6:** Mt 15.24; 10.23. **10.7-8:** Lk 9.2; 10.9-11; Mt 4.17.
10.9-14: Mk 6.8-11; Lk 9.3-5; 10.4-12; 22.35-36. **10.10:** 1 Cor 9.14; 1 Tim 5.18. **10.14:** Acts 13.51.
10.15: Mt 11.24; Lk 10.12; Jude 7; 2 Pet 2.6. **10.16:** Lk 10.3; Gen 3.1; Rom 16.19.
10.17-22: Mk 13.9-13; Lk 12.11-12; 21.12-19; Jn 16.2. **10.18:** Acts 25.24-26. **10.20:** Jn 16.7-11.
10.21: Mt 10.35-36; Lk 12.52-53. **10.22:** Jn 15.18; Mt 24.9. **10.23:** Mt 16.27; 1 Thess 4.17.
10.24: Lk 6.40; Jn 13.16; 15.20. **10.25:** Mt 9.34; 12.24; Mk 3.22; Lk 11.15; 2 Kings 1.2.
10.26-33: Lk 12.2-9. **10.26:** Mk 4.22; Lk 8.17; Eph 5.13. **10.28:** Heb 10.31. **10.31:** Mt 12.12.
10.32: Mk 8.38; Lk 9.26; Rev 3.5; 2 Tim 2.12. **10.34-36:** Lk 12.51-53; Mt 10.21; Mk 13.12; Mic 7.6.
10.37-39: Lk 14.25-27; 17.33; 9.23-24; Mt 16.24-25; Mk 8.34-35; Jn 12.25.
10.40: Lk 10.16; Jn 13.20; Gal 4.14; Mk 9.37; Mt 18.5; Lk 9.48.

Sparrows Matt 10, 29

11 He who receives a prophet because he is a prophet shall receive a prophet's reward, and he who receives a righteous man because he is a righteous man shall receive a righteous 42 man's reward. And whoever gives to one of these little ones even a cup of cold water because he is a disciple, truly, I say to you, he shall not lose his reward."

11 And when Jesus had finished instructing his twelve disciples, he went on from there to teach and preach in their cities.

JESUS AND THE BAPTIST

2 NOW when John heard in prison about the deeds of the Christ, he sent word by 3 his disciples and said to him, "Are you he who is to come, or shall we look for 4 another?" And Jesus answered them, "Go 5 and tell John what you hear and see: the blind receive their sight and the lame walk, lepers are cleansed and the deaf hear, and the dead are raised up, and the poor have good 6 news preached to them. And blessed is he who takes no offence at me."

7 As they went away, Jesus began to speak to the crowds concerning John: "What did you go out into the wilderness to behold? A reed 8 shaken by the wind? Why then did you go out? To see a man[z] clothed in soft raiment? Behold, those who wear soft raiment are in 9 kings' houses. Why then did you go out?

To see a prophet?[a] Yes, I tell you, and more than a prophet. This is he of whom it is 10 written,
'Behold, I send my messenger before thy face,
who shall prepare thy way before thee.'
Truly, I say to you, among those born of 11 women there has risen no one greater than John the Baptist; yet he who is least in the kingdom of heaven is greater than he. From 12 the days of John the Baptist until now the kingdom of heaven has suffered violence,[b] and men of violence take it by force. For all 13 the prophets and the law prophesied until John; and if you are willing to accept it, he is 14 Eli'jah who is to come. He who has ears to 15 hear,[c] let him hear.

"But to what shall I compare this genera- 16 tion? It is like children sitting in the market places and calling to their playmates,
'We piped to you, and you did not dance; 17 we wailed, and you did not mourn.'
For John came neither eating nor drinking, 18 and they say, 'He has a demon'; the Son of 19 man came eating and drinking, and they say, 'Behold, a glutton and a drunkard, a friend of tax collectors and sinners!' Yet wisdom is justified by her deeds."[d]

JESUS AND HIS OPPONENTS

THEN he began to upbraid the cities 20 where most of his mighty works had been done, because they did not repent. "Woe to 21 you, Chora'zin! woe to you, Beth-sa'ida! for if the mighty works done in you had been done in Tyre and Sidon, they would have repented long ago in sackcloth and ashes. But I tell you, it shall be more tolerable on 22 the day of judgment for Tyre and Sidon than for you. And you, Caper'na-um, will you be 23 exalted to heaven? You shall be brought

A penny Matt 10, 29

z Or *What then did you go out to see? A man . . .*
a Other ancient authorities read *What then did you go out to see? A prophet?*
b Or *has been coming violently*   c Other ancient authorities omit *to hear*
d Other ancient authorities read *children* (Luke 7.35)
10.42: Mk 9.41; Mt 25.40.   11.1: Mt 7.28; 13.53; 19.1; 26.1.   11.2-19: Lk 7.18-35.
11.3: Mk 1.7-8; Hab 2.3; Jn 11.27.   11.5: Is 35.5-6; 61.1; Lk 4.18-19.   11.9: Mt 14.5; 21.26; Lk 1.76.
11.10: Mal 3.1; Mk 1.2.   11.12-13: Lk 16.16.   11.14: Mal 4.5; Mt 17.10-13; Jn 1.21; Lk 1.17.
11.15: Mt 13.9, 43; Mk 4.23; Rev 13.9; 2.7.   11.16-19: Lk 7.31-35. 11.20-24: Lk 10.13-15.

down to Hades. For if the mighty works done in you had been done in Sodom, it 24 would have remained until this day. But I tell you that it shall be more tolerable on the day of judgment for the land of Sodom than for you."

The hidden truth revealed

25 At that time Jesus declared, "I thank thee, Father, Lord of heaven and earth, that thou hast hidden these things from the wise and understanding and revealed them to babes; 26 yea, Father, for such was thy gracious will.ᵉ 27 All things have been delivered to me by my Father; and no one knows the Son except the Father, and no one knows the Father except the Son and any one to whom the Son 28 chooses to reveal him. Come to me, all who labour and are heavy laden, and I will give 29 you rest. Take my yoke upon you, and learn from me; for I am gentle and lowly in heart, 30 and you will find rest for your souls. For my yoke is easy, and my burden is light."

Jesus challenged

12 At that time Jesus went through the grain-fields on the sabbath; his disciples were hungry, and they began to pluck ears of grain 2 and to eat. But when the Pharisees saw it, they said to him, "Look, your disciples are doing what is not lawful to do on the 3 sabbath." He said to them, "Have you not read what David did, when he was hungry, 4 and those who were with him: how he entered the house of God and ate the bread of the Presence, which it was not lawful for him to eat nor for those who were with him, 5 but only for the priests? Or have you not read in the law how on the sabbath the priests in the temple profane the sabbath, 6 and are guiltless? I tell you, something 7 greater than the temple is here. And if you had known what this means, 'I desire mercy, and not sacrifice,' you would not have con- 8 demned the guiltless. For the Son of man is lord of the sabbath."

9 And he went on from there, and entered 10 their synagogue. And behold, there was a man with a withered hand. And they asked him, "Is it lawful to heal on the sabbath?" so 11 that they might accuse him. He said to them, "What man of you, if he has one sheep and it

falls into a pit on the sabbath, will not lay hold of it and lift it out? Of how much more value is a man than a sheep! So it is lawful to do good on the sabbath." Then he said to 1 the man, "Stretch out your hand." And the man stretched it out, and it was restored, whole like the other. But the Pharisees went 1 out and took counsel against him, how to destroy him.

Jesus, aware of this, withdrew from there. 1 And many followed him, and he healed them all, and ordered them not to make him 1 known. This was to fulfil what was spoken 1 by the prophet Isaiah:

"Behold, my servant whom I have 1 chosen,
    my beloved with whom my soul is well pleased.
I will put my Spirit upon him,
    and he shall proclaim justice to the Gentiles.
He will not wrangle or cry aloud,   1
    nor will any one hear his voice in the streets;
he will not break a bruised reed   2
    or quench a smouldering wick,
till he brings justice to victory;
    and in his name will the Gentiles 2
    hope."

False charges

Then a blind and dumb demoniac was 2 brought to him, and he healed him, so that the dumb man spoke and saw. And all the 2 people were amazed, and said, "Can this be the Son of David?" But when the Pharisees 2 heard it they said, "It is only by Be-el′zebul, the prince of demons, that this man casts out demons." Knowing their thoughts, he said 2 to them, "Every kingdom divided against itself is laid waste, and no city or house divided against itself will stand; and if Satan 2 casts out Satan, he is divided against himself; how then will his kingdom stand? And if I 2 cast out demons by Be-el′zebul, by whom do your sons cast them out? Therefore they shall be your judges. But if it is by the Spirit 2 of God that I cast out demons, then the kingdom of God has come upon you. Or 2 how can one enter a strong man's house and plunder his goods, unless he first binds the strong man? Then indeed he may plunder his house. He who is not with me is against 3

ᵉ Or so it was well-pleasing before thee
11.24: Mt 10.15; Lk 10.12.   11.25-27: Lk 10.21-22.   11.25: 1 Cor 1.26-29.
11.27: Jn 3.35; 5.20; 13.3; 7.29; 10.15; 17.25; Mt 28.18.   11.29: Jn 13.15; Phil 2.5; 1 Pet 2.21; Jer 6.16.
12.1-8: Mk 2.23-28; Lk 6.1-5.   12.1: Deut 23.25.   12.3: 1 Sam 21.1-6; Lev 24.9.   12.5: Num 28.9-10.
12.6: Mt 12.41-42; Lk 11.31-32.   12.7: Hos 6.6; Mt 9.13.   12.8: Jn 5.1-18; 7.19-24; 9.1-41.
12.9-14: Mk 3.1-6; Lk 6.6-11.   12.11: Lk 14.5.   12.12: Mt 10.31.
12.14: Mk 14.1; Jn 7.30; 8.59; 10.39; 11.53.   12.15-16: Mk 3.7-12; Lk 6.17-19.   12.18-21: Is 42.1-4.
12.22-29: Mk 3.22-27; Lk 11.14-22.   12.22: Mt 9.32-33.   12.24: Mt 9.34; 10.25; Jn 7.20; 8.52; 10.20.
12.30: Lk 11.23; Mk 9.40.

me, and he who does not gather with me scatters. Therefore I tell you, every sin and blasphemy will be forgiven men, but the blasphemy against the Spirit will not be forgiven. And whoever says a word against the Son of man will be forgiven; but whoever speaks against the Holy Spirit will not be forgiven, either in this age or in the age to come.

"Either make the tree good, and its fruit good; or make the tree bad, and its fruit bad; for the tree is known by its fruit. You brood of vipers! how can you speak good, when you are evil? For out of the abundance of the heart the mouth speaks. The good man out of his good treasure brings forth good, and the evil man out of his evil treasure brings forth evil. I tell you, on the day of judgment men will render account for every careless word they utter; for by your words you will be justified, and by your words you will be condemned."

Demand for a sign

Then some of the scribes and Pharisees said to him, "Teacher, we wish to see a sign from you." But he answered them, "An evil and adulterous generation seeks for a sign; but no sign shall be given to it except the sign of the prophet Jonah. For as Jonah was three days and three nights in the belly of the whale, so will the Son of man be three days and three nights in the heart of the earth. The men of Nin'eveh will arise at the judgment with this generation and condemn it; for they repented at the preaching of Jonah, and behold, something greater than Jonah is here. The queen of the South will arise at the judgment with this generation and condemn it; for she came from the ends of the earth to hear the wisdom of Solomon, and behold, something greater than Solomon is here.

"When the unclean spirit has gone out of a man, he passes through waterless places seeking rest, but he finds none. Then he says, 'I will return to my house from which I came.' And when he comes he finds it empty, swept, and put in order. Then he goes and brings with him seven other spirits more evil than himself, and they enter and dwell there; and the last state of that man becomes worse than the first. So shall it be also with this evil generation."

The mother and brothers of Jesus

While he was still speaking to the people, 46 behold, his mother and his brothers stood outside, asking to speak to him.[f] But he 48 replied to the man who told him, "Who is my mother, and who are my brothers?" And 49 stretching out his hand toward his disciples, he said, "Here are my mother and my brothers! For whoever does the will of my 50 Father in heaven is my brother, and sister, and mother."

PARABLES OF THE KINGDOM

THAT same day Jesus went out of the **13** house and sat beside the sea. And great 2 crowds gathered about him, so that he got into a boat and sat there; and the whole crowd stood on the beach.

The sower

And he told them many things in parables, 3 saying: "A sower went out to sow. And as he 4 sowed, some seeds fell along the path, and the birds came and devoured them. Other 5 seeds fell on rocky ground, where they had not much soil, and immediately they sprang up, since they had no depth of soil, but when 6 the sun rose they were scorched; and since they had no root they withered away. Other 7 seeds fell upon thorns, and the thorns grew up and choked them. Other seeds fell on 8 good soil and brought forth grain, some a hundredfold, some sixty, some thirty. He 9 who has ears,[g] let him hear."

Then the disciples came and said to him, 10 "Why do you speak to them in parables?" And he answered them, "To you it has been 11 given to know the secrets of the kingdom of heaven, but to them it has not been given. For to him who has will more be given, and 12 he will have abundance; but from him who has not, even what he has will be taken away. This is why I speak to them in parables, 13 because seeing they do not see, and hearing they do not hear, nor do they understand. With them indeed is fulfilled the prophecy of 14 Isaiah which says:

'You shall indeed hear but never under-
        stand,
    and you shall indeed see but never
        perceive.

---

f Other ancient authorities insert verse 47, *Some one told him, "Your mother and your brothers are standing outside, asking to speak to you"*   *g* Other ancient authorities add here and in verse 43 *to hear*
12.31-32: Mk 3.28-30; Lk 12.10.   **12.33-35:** Lk 6.43-45; Mt 7.16-20; Jas 3.11-12; Mt 15.18.
12.38-42: Lk 11.16, 29-32; Mk 8.11-12; Mt 16.1-4; Jn 2.18; 6.30; 1 Cor 1.22.   **12.40:** Jon 1.17.
12.41: Jon 3.5.   **12.42:** 1 Kings 10.1-10; 2 Chron 9.1-12.   **12.43-45:** Lk 11.24-26; 2 Pet 2.20.
12.46-50: Mk 3.31-35; Lk 8.19-21.   **12.46:** Jn 2.1-12; 19.25-27; 7.1-10; Mk 6.3; 1 Cor 9.5.
12.50: Jn 15.14.   **13.1-9:** Mk 4.1-9; Lk 8.4-8; 5.1-3.   **13.10-13:** Mk 4.10-12; Lk 8.9-10.
13.12: Mk 4.25; Lk 8.18; Mt 25.29; Lk 19.26.   **13.14-15:** Is 6.9-10; Mk 8.18; Jn 12.39-41; Acts 28.26-27.

15 For this people's heart has grown dull,
    and their ears are heavy of hearing,
    and their eyes they have closed,
  lest they should perceive with their
      eyes,
    and hear with their ears,
  and understand with their heart,
    and turn for me to heal them.'
16 But blessed are your eyes, for they see, and
17 your ears, for they hear. Truly, I say to you,
many prophets and righteous men longed to
see what you see, and did not see it, and to
hear what you hear, and did not hear it.

18, "Hear then the parable of the sower. When
19 any one hears the word of the kingdom and
does not understand it, the evil one comes
and snatches away what is sown in his heart;
20 this is what was sown along the path. As for
what was sown on rocky ground, this is he
who hears the word and immediately receives
21 it with joy; yet he has no root in himself, but
endures for a while, and when tribulation or
persecution arises on account of the word,
22 immediately he falls away.[h] As for what was
sown among thorns, this is he who hears the
word, but the cares of the world and the
delight in riches choke the word, and it

proves unfruitful. As for what was sown on
good soil, this is he who hears the word and
understands it; he indeed bears fruit, and
yields, in one case a hundredfold, in another
sixty, and in another thirty."

The weeds

Another parable he put before them, saying,
"The kingdom of heaven may be compared
to a man who sowed good seed in his field;
but while men were sleeping, his enemy
came and sowed weeds among the wheat, and
went away. So when the plants came up and
bore grain, then the weeds appeared also.
And the servants[i] of the householder came
and said to him, 'Sir, did you not sow good
seed in your field? How then has it weeds?'
He said to them, 'An enemy has done this.'
The servants[i] said to him, 'Then do you
want us to go and gather them?' But he said,
'No; lest in gathering the weeds you root up
the wheat along with them. Let both grow
together until the harvest; and at harvest
time I will tell the reapers, Gather the weeds
first and bind them in bundles to be burned,
but gather the wheat into my barn.'"

Mustard seed

Another parable he put before them, saying,
"The kingdom of heaven is like a grain of
mustard seed which a man took and sowed in
his field; it is the smallest of all seeds, but
when it has grown it is the greatest of shrubs
and becomes a tree, so that the birds of the
air come and make nests in its branches."

Leaven

He told them another parable. "The
kingdom of heaven is like leaven which a
woman took and hid in three measures of
meal, till it was all leavened."
All this Jesus said to the crowds in parables;
indeed he said nothing to them without a
parable. This was to fulfil what was spoken
by the prophet:[j]
"I will open my mouth in parables,
  I will utter what has been hidden since the
    foundation of the world."

The weeds explained

Then he left the crowds and went into the
house. And his disciples came to him,
saying, "Explain to us the parable of the
weeds of the field." He answered, "He who

h Or stumbles   i Or slaves   j Other ancient authorities read the prophet Isaiah
13.16–17: Lk 10.23–24; Jn 8.56; Heb 11.13; 1 Pet 1.10–12.   13.18–23: Mk 4.13–20; Lk 8.11–15.
13.22: Mt 19.23; 1 Tim 6.9–10, 17.   13.24–30: Mk 4.26–29.   13.31–32: Mk 4.30–32; Lk 13.18–19; Mt 17.20.
13.33: Lk 13.20–21; Gal 5.9; Gen 18.6.   13.34: Mk 4.33–34; Jn 10.6; 16.25.   13.35: Ps 78.2.

8 sows the good seed is the Son of man; the field is the world, and the good seed means the sons of the kingdom; the weeds are the
9 sons of the evil one, and the enemy who sowed them is the devil; the harvest is the close of the age, and the reapers are angels.

10 Just as the weeds are gathered and burned with fire, so will it be at the close of the age.
11 The Son of man will send his angels, and they will gather out of his kingdom all causes
12 of sin and all evildoers, and throw them into the furnace of fire; there men will weep and
13 gnash their teeth. Then the righteous will shine like the sun in the kingdom of their Father. He who has ears, let him hear.

Treasures

44 "The kingdom of heaven is like treasure hidden in a field, which a man found and covered up; then in his joy he goes and sells all that he has and buys that field.
45 "Again, the kingdom of heaven is like a
46 merchant in search of fine pearls, who, on finding one pearl of great value, went and sold all that he had and bought it.

The drag-net

47 "Again, the kingdom of heaven is like a net which was thrown into the sea and gathered
48 fish of every kind; when it was full, men drew it ashore and sat down and sorted the
49 good into vessels but threw away the bad. So it will be at the close of the age. The angels will come out and separate the evil from the
50 righteous, and throw them into the furnace of fire; there men will weep and gnash their teeth.
51 "Have you understood all this?" They
52 said to him, "Yes." And he said to them, "Therefore every scribe who has been trained for the kingdom of heaven is like a householder who brings out of his treasure what is new and what is old."

REJECTION

AND when Jesus had finished these 53 parables, he went away from there, and 54 coming to his own country he taught them in their synagogue, so that they were astonished, and said, "Where did this man get this wisdom and these mighty works? Is not this 55 the carpenter's son? Is not his mother called Mary? And are not his brothers James and Joseph and Simon and Judas? And are not 56 all his sisters with us? Where then did this man get all this?" And they took offence at 57 him. But Jesus said to them, "A prophet is not without honour except in his own country and in his own house." And he did 58 not do many mighty works there, because of their unbelief.

FROM PLACE TO PLACE

AT that time Herod the tetrarch heard 14 about the fame of Jesus; and he said to 2 his servants, "This is John the Baptist, he has been raised from the dead; that is why these powers are at work in him." For 3 Herod had seized John and bound him and put him in prison, for the sake of Hero'di-as, his brother Philip's wife;[k] because John said 4 to him, "It is not lawful for you to have her." And though he wanted to put him to 5 death, he feared the people, because they held him to be a prophet. But when Herod's 6 birthday came, the daughter of Hero'di-as danced before the company, and pleased Herod, so that he promised with an oath to 7 give her whatever she might ask. Prompted 8 by her mother, she said, "Give me the head of John the Baptist here on a platter." And 9 the king was sorry; but because of his oaths and his guests he commanded it to be given; he sent and had John beheaded in the prison, 10 and his head was brought on a platter and 11 given to the girl, and she brought it to her mother. And his disciples came and took the 12 body and buried it; and they went and told Jesus.

To a lonely place

Now when Jesus heard this, he withdrew 13 from there in a boat to a lonely place apart. But when the crowds heard it, they followed him on foot from the towns. As he went 14 ashore he saw a great throng; and he had compassion on them, and healed their sick.

k Other ancient authorities read his brother's wife
13.38: Jn 8.44; 1 Jn 3.10.   13.41: Mt 24.31.   13.42: Mt 13.50; 8.12; 22.13; 24.51; 25.30; Lk 13.28.
13.47-50: Mt 13.40-42.   13.53: Mt 7.28; 11.1; 19.1; 26.1.   13.54-58: Mk 6.1-6; Lk 4.16-30.
14.1-2: Mk 6.14-16; Lk 9.7-9; Mk 8.28.   14.3-4: Mk 6.17-18; Lk 3.19-20; Lev 18.16; 20.21.
14.5-12: Mk 6.19-29.   14.13-21: Mk 6.32-44; Lk 9.10-17; Jn 6.1-13; Mt 15.32-38.

Five thousand fed

15 When it was evening, the disciples came to him and said, "This is a lonely place, and the day is now over; send the crowds away to go into the villages and buy food for them- 16 selves." Jesus said, "They need not go away; 17 you give them something to eat." They said to him, "We have only five loaves here and 18 two fish." And he said, "Bring them here to 19 me." Then he ordered the crowds to sit down on the grass; and taking the five loaves and the two fish he looked up to heaven, and blessed, and broke and gave the loaves to the disciples, and the disciples gave them to the 20 crowds. And they all ate and were satisfied. And they took up twelve baskets full of the 21 broken pieces left over. And those who ate were about five thousand men, besides women and children.

Walking on the sea

22 Then he made the disciples get into the boat and go before him to the other side, while he 23 dismissed the crowds. And after he had dismissed the crowds, he went up into the hills by himself to pray. When evening 24 came, he was there alone, but the boat by this time was many furlongs distant from the land,^{l} beaten by the waves; for the wind was 25 against them. And in the fourth watch of the night he came to them, walking on the sea. 26 But when the disciples saw him walking on the sea, they were terrified, saying, "It is a 27 ghost!" And they cried out for fear. But immediately he spoke to them, saying, "Take heart, it is I; have no fear." 28 And Peter answered him, "Lord, if it is you, 29 bid me come to you on the water." He said, "Come." So Peter got out of the boat and 30 walked on the water and came to Jesus; but when he saw the wind,^{m} he was afraid, and beginning to sink he cried out, "Lord, save 31 me." Jesus immediately reached out his hand and caught him, saying to him, "O man 32 of little faith, why did you doubt?" And when they got into the boat, the wind 33 ceased. And those in the boat worshipped him, saying, "Truly you are the Son of God."

At Gennesaret

34 And when they had crossed over, they came 35 to land at Gennes'aret. And when the men

of that place recognised him, they sent round to all that region and brought to him all that were sick, and besought him that they might 36 only touch the fringe of his garment; and as many as touched it were made well.

Then Pharisees and scribes came to Jesus 15 from Jerusalem and said, "Why do your 2 disciples transgress the tradition of the elders? For they do not wash their hands when they eat." He answered them, "And 3 why do you transgress the commandment of God for the sake of your tradition? For God 4 commanded, 'Honour your father and your mother,' and, 'He who speaks evil of father or mother, let him surely die.' But you say, 5 'If any one tells his father or his mother, What you would have gained from me is given to God,^{n} he need not honour his father.' So, for the sake of your tradition, 6 you have made void the word^o of God. You 7 hypocrites! Well did Isaiah prophesy of you, when he said:

'This people honours me with their lips, 8
    but their heart is far from me;
in vain do they worship me, 9
    teaching as doctrines the precepts of men.' "

And he called the people to him and said to 10 them, "Hear and understand: not what goes 11 into the mouth defiles a man, but what comes out of the mouth, this defiles a man." Then 12 the disciples came and said to him, "Do you know that the Pharisees were offended when they heard this saying?" He answered, 13 "Every plant which my heavenly Father has not planted will be rooted up. Let them 14 alone; they are blind guides. And if a blind man leads a blind man, both will fall into a pit." But Peter said to him, "Explain the 15 parable to us." And he said, "Are you also 16 still without understanding? Do you not see 17 that whatever goes into the mouth passes into the stomach, and so passes on?^{p} But what 18 comes out of the mouth proceeds from the heart, and this defiles a man. For out of the 19 heart come evil thoughts, murder, adultery, fornication, theft, false witness, slander. These are what defile a man; but to eat with 20 unwashed hands does not defile a man."

Tyre and Sidon

And Jesus went away from there and 21 withdrew to the district of Tyre and Sidon.

---

^{l} Other ancient authorities read *was out on the sea* ^{m} Other ancient authorities read *strong wind*
^{n} Or *an offering* ^{o} Other ancient authorities read *law* ^{p} Or *is evacuated*
14.19: Mk 14.22; Lk 24.30.   14.22-23: Mk 6.45-46; Jn 6.15-17.   14.24-33: Mk 6.47-52; Jn 6.16-21.
14.26: Lk 24.37.   14.29: Jn 21.7.   14.31: Mt 6.30; 8.26; 16.8.   14.33: Mt 28.9, 17.
14.34-36: Mk 6.53-56; Jn 6.22-26.   14.36: Mk 3.10; Num 15.38; Mt 9.20.   15.1-20: Mk 7.1-23.
15.4: Ex 20.12; Deut 5.16; Ex 21.17; Lev 20.9.   15.8-9: Is 29.13.   15.11: Acts 10.14-15; 1 Tim 4.3.
15.13: Is 60.21; Jn 15.2.   15.14: Lk 6.39; Mt 23.16, 24; Rom 2.19.
15.19: Gal 5.19-21; 1 Cor 6.9-10; Rom 14.14.   15.21-28: Mk 7.24-30.

And behold, a Canaanite woman from that region came out and cried, "Have mercy on me, O Lord, Son of David; my daughter is severely possessed by a demon." But he did not answer her a word. And his disciples came and begged him, saying, "Send her away, for she is crying after us." He answered, "I was sent only to the lost sheep of the house of Israel." But she came and knelt before him, saying, "Lord, help me." And he answered, "It is not fair to take the children's bread and throw it to the dogs." She said, "Yes, Lord, yet even the dogs eat the crumbs that fall from their master's table." Then Jesus answered her, "O woman, great is your faith! Be it done for you as you desire." And her daughter was healed instantly.

By the Sea of Galilee

And Jesus went on from there and passed along the Sea of Galilee. And he went up into the hills, and sat down there. And great crowds came to him, bringing with them the lame, the maimed, the blind, the dumb, and many others, and they put them at his feet; and he healed them, so that the throng wondered, when they saw the dumb speaking, the maimed whole, the lame walking, and the blind seeing; and they glorified the God of Israel.

Four thousand fed

Then Jesus called his disciples to him and said, "I have compassion on the crowd, because they have been with me now three days, and have nothing to eat; and I am unwilling to send them away hungry, lest they faint on the way." And the disciples said to him, "Where are we to get bread enough in the desert to feed so great a crowd?" And Jesus said to them, "How many loaves have you?" They said, "Seven, and a few small fish." And commanding the crowd to sit down on the ground, he took the seven loaves and the fish, and having given thanks he broke them and gave them to the disciples, and the disciples gave them to the crowds. And they all ate and were satisfied; and they took up seven baskets full of broken pieces left over. Those who ate were four thousand men, besides women and

children. And sending away the crowds, he got into the boat and went to the region of Mag'adan.

And the Pharisees and Sad'ducees came, and to test him they asked him to show them a sign from heaven. He answered them,[q] "When it is evening, you say, 'It will be fair weather; for the sky is red.' And in the morning, 'It will be stormy today, for the sky is red and threatening.' You know how to interpret the appearance of the sky, but you cannot interpret the signs of the times. An evil and adulterous generation seeks for a sign, but no sign shall be given to it except the sign of Jonah." So he left them and departed.

When the disciples reached the other side, they had forgotten to bring any bread. Jesus said to them, "Take heed and beware of the leaven of the Pharisees and Sad'ducees." And they discussed it among themselves, saying, "We brought no bread." But Jesus, aware of this, said, "O men of little faith, why do you discuss among yourselves the fact that you have no bread? Do you not yet perceive? Do you not remember the five loaves of the five thousand, and how many baskets you gathered? Or the seven loaves of the four thousand, and how many baskets you gathered? How is it that you fail to perceive that I did not speak about bread? Beware of the leaven of the Pharisees and Sad'ducees." Then they understood that he did not tell them to beware of the leaven of bread, but of the teaching of the Pharisees and Sad'ducees.

The great confession

Now when Jesus came into the district of Caesare'a Philippi, he asked his disciples, "Who do men say that the Son of man is?" And they said, "Some say John the Baptist, others say Eli'jah, and others Jeremiah or one of the prophets." He said to them, "But who do you say that I am?" Simon Peter replied, "You are the Christ, the Son of the living God." And Jesus answered him, "Blessed are you, Simon Bar-Jona! For flesh and blood has not revealed this to you, but my Father who is in heaven. And I tell you, you are Peter,[r] and on this rock[s] I will build my church, and the powers of death[t] shall not

q Other ancient authorities omit the following words to the end of verse 3   r Greek Petros   s Greek petra
t Greek the gates of Hades.   15.24: Mt 10.6, 23.   15.25: Mt 8.2; 18.26; 20.20; Jn 9.38.   15.28: Mt 9.22, 28; Mk 10.52; Lk 7.50; 17.19.
15.29-31: Mk 7.31-37.   15.32-39: Mk 8.1-10; Mt 14.13-21.   15.32: Mk 9.36.
16.1-4: Mk 8.11-12; Lk 11.16, 29; 12.54-56; Mt 12.38-39; Jn 2.18; 6.30.   16.4: Jon 3.4-5.
16.5-12: Mk 8.13-21.   16.6: Lk 12.1.   16.8: Mt 6.30; 8.26; 14.31.   16.9: Mt 14.17-21.
16.10: Mt 15.34-38.   16.13-16: Mk 8.27-30; Lk 9.18-21.   16.14: Mt 14.2; Mk 6.15; Lk 9.7-8; Jn 1.21.
16.16: Mt 1.16; Jn 11.27; 1.49.   16.17: 1 Cor 15.50; Gal 1.16; Eph 6.12; Heb 2.14.
16.18: Jn 1.40-42; 21.15-17; 1 Cor 15.5.

THE PROVINCES OF PALESTINE

prevail against it. I will give you the keys of the kingdom of heaven, and whatever you bind on earth shall be bound in heaven, and whatever you loose on earth shall be loosed in heaven." Then he strictly charged the disciples to tell no one that he was the Christ.

True discipleship

From that time Jesus began to show his disciples that he must go to Jerusalem and suffer many things from the elders and chief priests and scribes, and be killed, and on the third day be raised. And Peter took him and began to rebuke him, saying, "God forbid, Lord! This shall never happen to you." But he turned and said to Peter, "Get behind me, Satan! You are a hindrance[u] to me; for you are not on the side of God, but of men."

Then Jesus told his disciples, "If any man would come after me, let him deny himself and take up his cross and follow me. For whoever would save his life will lose it, and whoever loses his life for my sake will find it. For what will it profit a man, if he gains the whole world and forfeits his life? Or what shall a man give in return for his life? For the Son of man is to come with his angels in the glory of his Father, and then he will repay every man for what he has done. Truly, I say to you, there are some standing here who will not taste death before they see the Son of man coming in his kingdom."

The transfiguration

7 And after six days Jesus took with him Peter and James and John his brother, and led them up a high mountain apart. And he was transfigured before them, and his face shone like the sun, and his garments became white as light. And behold, there appeared to them Moses and Eli'jah, talking with him. And Peter said to Jesus, "Lord, it is well that we are here; if you wish, I will make three booths here, one for you and one for Moses and one for Eli'jah." He was still speaking, when lo, a bright cloud overshadowed them, and a voice from the cloud said, "This is my beloved Son,[v] with whom I am well pleased;

listen to him." When the disciples heard 6 this, they fell on their faces, and were filled with awe. But Jesus came and touched them, 7 saying, "Rise, and have no fear." And when 8 they lifted up their eyes, they saw no one but Jesus only.

And as they were coming down the moun- 9 tain, Jesus commanded them, "Tell no one the vision, until the Son of man is raised from the dead." And the disciples asked 10 him, "Then why do the scribes say that first Eli'jah must come?" He replied, "Eli'jah 11 does come, and he is to restore all things; but 12 I tell you that Eli'jah has already come, and they did not know him, but did to him whatever they pleased. So also the Son of man will suffer at their hands." Then the 13 disciples understood that he was speaking to them of John the Baptist.

An afflicted boy cured

And when they came to the crowd, a man 14 came up to him and kneeling before him said, "Lord, have mercy on my son, for he is an 15 epileptic and he suffers terribly; for often he falls into the fire, and often into the water. And I brought him to your disciples, and 16 they could not heal him." And Jesus 17 answered, "O faithless and perverse genera- tion, how long am I to be with you? How long am I to bear with you? Bring him here to me." And Jesus rebuked him, and the 18 demon came out of him, and the boy was cured instantly. Then the disciples came to 19 Jesus privately and said, "Why could we not cast it out?" He said to them, "Because of 20 your little faith. For truly, I say to you, if you have faith as a grain of mustard seed, you will say to this mountain, 'Move hence to yonder place,' and it will move; and nothing will be impossible to you."[w]

In Galilee

As they were gathering[x] in Galilee, Jesus 22 said to them, "The Son of man is to be delivered into the hands of men, and they 23 will kill him, and he will be raised on the third day." And they were greatly dis- tressed.

---

[u] Greek *stumbling block*   [v] Or *my Son, my* (or *the*) *Beloved*
[w] Other ancient authorities insert verse 21, "*But this kind never comes out except by prayer and fasting*"
[x] Other ancient authorities read *abode*
16.19: Is 22.22; Rev 1.18; Mt 18.18; Jn 20.23.   **16.20:** Mt 8.4; Mk 3.12; 5.43; 7.36; 9.9.
16.21-28: Mk 8.31-9.1; Lk 9.22-27.   **16.21:** Mt 17.22-23; 20.17-19; Lk 17.25; Mt 17.12; 26.2.   **16.23:** Mt 4.10.
16.24-26: Mt 10.38-39; Lk 14.27; 17.33; Jn 12.25.   **16.27:** Mt 10.33; Lk 12.9; 1 Jn 2.28; Rom 2.6; Rev 22.12.
16.28: Mt 10.23; 1 Cor 16.22; 1 Thess 4.15-18; Rev 1.7; Jas 5.7.
17.1-9: Mk 9.2-10; Lk 9.28-36; 2 Pet 1.17-18.   **17.1:** Mt 26.37; Mk 5.37; 13.3.
17.5: Mt 3.17; Is 42.1; Ps 2.7; Jn 12.28.   **17.9:** Mt 8.4; Mk 3.12; 5.43; 7.36.
17.10-13: Mk 9.11-13; Mt 11.14; Mal 4.5.   **17.12:** Mt 16.21; 17.22; 20.17; 26.2; Lk 17.25.
17.14-18: Mk 9.14-27; Lk 9.37-43.   **17.19-21:** Mk 9.28-29.
17.20: Lk 17.6; Mt 21.21; Mk 11.22-23; 1 Cor 13.2; Mk 9.23.
17.22-23: Mk 9.30-32; Lk 9.43-45; Mt 16.21; 20.17-19; 26.2.

A city by the Sea of Galilee

24 When they came to Caper'na-um, the collectors of the half-shekel tax went up to Peter and said, "Does not your teacher pay the 25 tax?" He said, "Yes." And when he came home, Jesus spoke to him first, saying, "What do you think, Simon? From whom do kings of the earth take toll or tribute? 26 From their sons or from others?" And when he said, "From others," Jesus said to him, 27 "Then the sons are free. However, not to give offence to them, go to the sea and cast a hook, and take the first fish that comes up, and when you open its mouth you will find a shekel; take that and give it to them for me and for yourself."

Jesus and his disciples

18 At that time the disciples came to Jesus, saying, "Who is the greatest in the kingdom 2 of heaven?" And calling to him a child, he 3 put him in the midst of them, and said, "Truly, I say to you, unless you turn and become like children, you will never enter 4 the kingdom of heaven. Whoever humbles himself like this child, he is the greatest in the kingdom of heaven.

5 "Whoever receives one such child in my 6 name receives me; but whoever causes one of these little ones who believe in me to sin,^{y} it would be better for him to have a great millstone fastened round his neck and to be drowned in the depth of the sea.

"Woe to the world for temptations to sin!^{z} For it is necessary that temptations come, but woe to the man by whom the temptation comes! And if your hand or your foot causes you to sin,^{y} cut it off and throw it from you; it is better for you to enter life maimed or lame than with two hands or two feet to be thrown into the eternal fire. And if your eye causes you to sin,^{y} pluck it out and throw it from you; it is better for you to enter life with one eye than with two eyes to be thrown into the hell^a of fire.

"See that you do not despise one of these little ones; for I tell you that in heaven their angels always behold the face of my Father who is in heaven.^{b} What do you think? If a man has a hundred sheep, and one of them has gone astray, does he not leave the ninety-nine on the hills and go in search of the one that went astray? And if he finds it, truly, I say to you, he rejoices over it more than over the ninety-nine that never went astray. So it is not the will of my^c Father who is in heaven that one of these little ones should perish.

"If your brother sins against you, go and tell him his fault, between you and him alone. If he listens to you, you have gained your brother. But if he does not listen, take one or two others along with you, that every

^{y} Greek *causes . . . to stumble* ^{z} Greek *stumbling blocks* ^{a} Greek *Gehenna* ^{b} Other ancient authorities add verse 11, *For the Son of man came to save the lost* ^{c} Other ancient authorities read *your*
17.24: Ex 30.13; 38.26.   17.25: Rom 13.7; Mt 22.17–21.   17.27: Mt 5.29; 18.6–9; Jn 6.61; 1 Cor 8.13.
18.1–5: Mk 9.33–37; Lk 9.46–48.   18.3: Mk 10.15; Lk 18.17; 1 Pet 2.2.   18.5: Mt 10.40; Lk 10.16; Jn 13.20.
18.6–9: Mk 9.42–48; Lk 17.1–2.   18.8–9: Mt 5.29–30; 17.27.   18.10: Acts 12.11.   18.11: Lk 19.10.
18.12–14: Lk 15.3–7.   18.15–17: Lk 17.3; 1 Cor 6.1–6; Gal 6.1; Jas 5.19–20; Lev 19.17; Deut 19.15.

word may be confirmed by the evidence of two or three witnesses. If he refuses to listen to them, tell it to the church; and if he refuses to listen even to the church, let him be to you as a Gentile and a tax collector. Truly, I say to you, whatever you bind on earth shall be bound in heaven, and whatever you loose on earth shall be loosed in heaven. Again I say to you, if two of you agree on earth about anything they ask, it will be done for them by my Father in heaven. For where two or three are gathered in my name, there am I in the midst of them."

Then Peter came up and said to him, "Lord, how often shall my brother sin against me, and I forgive him? As many as seven times?" Jesus said to him, "I do not say to you seven times, but seventy times seven.[d]

"Therefore the kingdom of heaven may be compared to a king who wished to settle accounts with his servants. When he began the reckoning, one was brought to him who owed him ten thousand talents;[e] and as he could not pay, his lord ordered him to be sold, with his wife and children and all that he had, and payment to be made. So the servant fell on his knees, imploring him, 'Lord, have patience with me, and I will pay you everything.' And out of pity for him the lord of that servant released him and forgave him the debt. But that same servant, as he went out, came upon one of his fellow servants who owed him a hundred denarii;[f] and seizing him by the throat he said, 'Pay what you owe.' So his fellow servant fell down and besought him, 'Have patience with me, and I will pay you.' He refused and went and put him in prison till he should pay the debt. When his fellow servants saw what had taken place, they were greatly distressed, and they went and reported to their lord all that had taken place. Then his lord summoned him and said to him, 'You wicked servant! I forgave you all that debt because you besought me; and should not you have had mercy on your fellow servant, as I had mercy on you?' And in anger his lord delivered him to the jailers,[g] till he should pay all his debt. So also my heavenly Father will do to every one of you, if you do not forgive your brother from your heart."

Beyond the Jordan

Now when Jesus had finished these sayings, **19** he went away from Galilee and entered the region of Judea beyond the Jordan; and large **2** crowds followed him, and he healed them there.

And Pharisees came up to him and tested **3** him by asking, "Is it lawful to divorce one's wife for any cause?" He answered, "Have **4** you not read that he who made them from the beginning made them male and female, and said, 'For this reason a man shall leave **5** his father and mother and be joined to his wife, and the two shall become one'?[h] So **6** they are no longer two but one.[h] What therefore God has joined together, let no man put asunder." They said to him, "Why **7** then did Moses command one to give a certificate of divorce, and to put her away?" He said to them, "For your hardness of heart **8** Moses allowed you to divorce your wives, but from the beginning it was not so. And I **9** say to you: whoever divorces his wife, except for unchastity,[i] and marries another, commits adultery."[j]

The disciples said to him, "If such is the **10** case of a man with his wife, it is not expedient to marry." But he said to them, **11** "Not all men can receive this precept, but only those to whom it is given. For there are **12** eunuchs who have been so from birth, and there are eunuchs who have been made eunuchs by men, and there are eunuchs who have made themselves eunuchs for the sake of the kingdom of heaven. He who is able to receive this, let him receive it."

Then children were brought to him that he **13** might lay his hands on them and pray. The disciples rebuked the people; but Jesus said, **14** "Let the children come to me, and do not hinder them; for to such belongs the kingdom of heaven." And he laid his hands on **15** them and went away.

The rich young ruler

And behold, one came up to him, saying, **16** "Teacher, what good deed must I do, to have eternal life?" And he said to him, "Why do **17** you ask me about what is good? One there is who is good. If you would enter life, keep the commandments." He said to him, **18**

---

[d] Or *seventy-seven times*   [e] This talent was probably worth about £350
[f] The denarius was worth about seventeen pence   [g] Greek *torturers*   [h] Greek *one flesh*
[i] Other ancient authorities, after *unchastity*, read *makes her commit adultery*
[j] Other ancient authorities insert *and he who marries a divorced woman commits adultery*
18.18: Mt 16.19; Jn 20.23.   **18.19-20:** Mt 7.7; 21.22; Jas 1.5-7; 1 Jn 5.14; Jn 14.13.
18.21-22: Lk 17.4; Gen 4.24.   **18.23:** Mt 25.19.   **18.25:** Lk 7.42.   **18.26:** Mt 8.2.   **18.35:** Mt 6.14.
19.1: Mt 7.28; 11.1; 13.53; 26.1.   **19.1-9:** Mk 10.1-12.   **19.5:** Gen 1.27; 2.24; Eph 5.31; 1 Cor 6.16.
19.7: Deut 24.1-4.   **19.9:** Mt 5.32; Lk 16.18; 1 Cor 7.10-13.   **19.11:** 1 Cor 7.7-9.
19.13-15: Mk 10.13-16; Lk 18.15-17; Mt 18.2-3; 1 Cor 14.20.
19.16-22: Mk 10.17-22; Lk 18.18-23.   **19.16:** Lk 10.25; Lev 18.5.
19.18: Ex 20.12-16; Deut 5.16-20; Rom 13.9; Jas 2.11.

"Which?" And Jesus said, "You shall not kill, You shall not commit adultery, You shall not steal, You shall not bear false
19 witness, Honour your father and mother, and, You shall love your neighbour as
20 yourself." The young man said to him, "All these I have observed; what do I still lack?"
21 Jesus said to him, "If you would be perfect, go, sell what you possess and give to the poor, and you will have treasure in heaven;
22 and come, follow me." When the young man heard this he went away sorrowful; for he had great possessions.

23 And Jesus said to his disciples, "Truly, I say to you, it will be hard for a rich man to
24 enter the kingdom of heaven. Again I tell you, it is easier for a camel to go through the eye of a needle than for a rich man to enter
25 the kingdom of God." When the disciples heard this they were greatly astonished,
26 saying, "Who then can be saved?" But Jesus looked at them and said to them, "With men this is impossible, but with God all
27 things are possible." Then Peter said in reply, "Lo, we have left everything and followed you. What then shall we have?"
28 Jesus said to them, "Truly, I say to you, in the new world, when the Son of man shall sit on his glorious throne, you who have followed me will also sit on twelve thrones,
29 judging the twelve tribes of Israel. And every one who has left houses or brothers or sisters or father or mother or children or lands, for my name's sake, will receive a
30 hundredfold,[k] and inherit eternal life. But many that are first will be last, and the last first.

Labourers in the vineyard

20 "For the kingdom of heaven is like a householder who went out early in the morning to hire labourers for his vineyard.
2 After agreeing with the labourers for a denarius[l] a day, he sent them into his
3 vineyard. And going out about the third hour he saw others standing idle in the
4 market place; and to them he said, 'You go into the vineyard too, and whatever is right I
5 will give you.' So they went. Going out again about the sixth hour and the ninth
6 hour, he did the same. And about the eleventh hour he went out and found others standing; and he said to them, 'Why do you

A denarius

stand here idle all day?' They said to him, 7 'Because no one has hired us.' He said to them, 'You go into the vineyard too.' And 8 when evening came, the owner of the vineyard said to his steward, 'Call the labourers and pay them their wages, beginning with the last, up to the first.' And when those 9 hired about the eleventh hour came, each of them received a denarius. Now when the 10 first came, they thought they would receive more; but each of them also received a denarius. And on receiving it they grumbled 11 at the householder, saying, 'These last 12 worked only one hour, and you have made them equal to us who have borne the burden of the day and the scorching heat.' But he 13 replied to one of them, 'Friend, I am doing you no wrong; did you not agree with me for a denarius? Take what belongs to you, and 14 go; I choose to give to this last as I give to you. Am I not allowed to do what I choose 15 with what belongs to me? Or do you begrudge my generosity?'[m] So the last will 16 be first, and the first last."

And as Jesus was going up to Jerusalem, he 17 took the twelve disciples aside, and on the way he said to them, "Behold, we are going 18 up to Jerusalem; and the Son of man will be delivered to the chief priests and scribes, and they will condemn him to death, and deliver 19 him to the Gentiles to be mocked and scourged and crucified, and he will be raised on the third day."

Mother of James and John

Then the mother of the sons of Zeb′edee 20 came up to him, with her sons, and kneeling before him she asked him for something. And he said to her, "What do you want?" 21 She said to him, "Command that these two sons of mine may sit, one at your right hand

[k] Other ancient authorities read *manifold*   [l] The denarius was worth about seventeen pence
[m] Or *is your eye evil because I am good?*
19.19: Lev 19.18; Mt 22.39.   19.21: Lk 12.33; Acts 2.45; 4.34; Mt 6.20.
19.23-26: Mk 10.23-27; Lk 18.24-27.   19.26: Gen 18.14; Job 42.2.
19.27-30: Mk 10.28-31; Lk 18.28-30; Mt 4.18-22.   19.28: Lk 22.30; Mt 20.21; Rev 3.21.
19.30: Mt 20.16; Lk 13.30.   20.1: Mt 21.28, 33.   20.8: Lev 19.13; Deut 24.15.   20.13: Mt 22.12; 26.50.
20.15: Mt 6.23; Mk 7.22; Deut 15.9.   20.16: Lk 13.30; Mt 19.30; Mk 10.31.
20.17-19: Mk 10.32-34; Lk 18.31-34; Mt 16.21; 17.12, 22-23; 26.2.
20.20-24: Mk 10.35-41.   20.20: Mt 8.2; 9.18; 15.25; 18.26; Jn 9.38.   20.21: Mt 19.28.

22 and one at your left, in your kingdom." But Jesus answered, "You do not know what you are asking. Are you able to drink the cup that I am to drink?" They said to him, "We 23 are able." He said to them, "You will drink my cup, but to sit at my right hand and at my left is not mine to grant, but it is for those for whom it has been prepared by my Father." 24 And when the ten heard it, they were 25 indignant at the two brothers. But Jesus called them to him and said, "You know that the rulers of the Gentiles lord it over them, and their great men exercise authority over 26 them. It shall not be so among you; but whoever would be great among you must be 27 your servant, and whoever would be first 28 among you must be your slave; even as the Son of man came not to be served but to serve, and to give his life as a ransom for many."

Two blind men

And as they went out of Jericho, a great 29 crowd followed him. And behold, two blind 30 men sitting by the roadside, when they heard that Jesus was passing by, cried out,[n] "Have mercy on us, Son of David!" The crowd 31 rebuked them, telling them to be silent; but they cried out the more, "Lord, have mercy on us, Son of David!" And Jesus stopped 32 and called them, saying, "What do you want me to do for you?" They said to him, 33 "Lord, let our eyes be opened." And Jesus 34 in pity touched their eyes, and immediately they received their sight and followed him.

IN JERUSALEM

Triumphal entry

21 AND when they drew near to Jerusalem and came to Beth'phage, to the Mount of Olives, then Jesus sent two disciples, 2 saying to them, "Go into the village opposite you, and immediately you will find an ass tied, and a colt with her; untie them and 3 bring them to me. If any one says anything to you, you shall say, 'The Lord has need of them,' and he will send them immediately." 4 This took place to fulfil what was spoken by the prophet, saying,

5   "Tell the daughter of Zion,
    Behold, your king is coming to you,
    humble, and mounted on an ass,
    and on a colt, the foal of an ass."

6 The disciples went and did as Jesus had 7 directed them; they brought the ass and the colt, and put their garments on them, and he 8 sat thereon. Most of the crowd spread their garments on the road, and others cut branches from the trees and spread them on 9 the road. And the crowds that went before him and that followed him shouted, "Hosanna to the Son of David! Blessed is he who comes in the name of the Lord! Hosanna 10 in the highest!" And when he entered Jerusalem, all the city was stirred, saying, "Who 11 is this?" And the crowds said, "This is the prophet Jesus from Nazareth of Galilee."

Cleansing of the temple

And Jesus entered the temple of God[o] and 12 drove out all who sold and bought in the temple, and he overturned the tables of the money-changers and the seats of those who sold pigeons. He said to them, "It is written, 13 'My house shall be called a house of prayer'; but you make it a den of robbers."

And the blind and the lame came to him in 14 the temple, and he healed them. But when 15 the chief priests and the scribes saw the wonderful things that he did, and the children crying out in the temple, "Hosanna to the Son of David!" they were indignant; and 16 they said to him, "Do you hear what these are saying?" And Jesus said to them, "Yes; have you never read,

    'Out of the mouth of babes and sucklings
    thou hast brought perfect praise'?"
And leaving them, he went out of the city to 17 Bethany and lodged there.

The barren fig tree

In the morning, as he was returning to the 18 city, he was hungry. And seeing a fig tree by 19 the wayside he went to it, and found nothing on it but leaves only. And he said to it, "May no fruit ever come from you again!" And the fig tree withered at once. When the 20 disciples saw it they marvelled, saying, "How

[n] Other ancient authorities insert *Lord*   [o] Other ancient authorities omit *of God*
20.22: Mt 26.39; Jn 18.11.   20.23: Acts 12.2; Rev 1.9; Mt 13.11.   20.25–28: Mk 10.42–45; Lk 22.25–27.
20.26: Mt 23.11; Mk 9.35; Lk 9.48.   20.28: Mt 26.28; 1 Tim 2.5–6; Jn 13.15–16; Tit 2.14; 1 Pet 1.18.
20.29–34: Mk 10.46–52; Lk 18.35–43; Mt 9.27–31.   21.1–9: Mk 11.1–10; Lk 19.29–38; Jn 12.12–18.
21.5: Is 62.11; Zech 9.9.   21.8: 2 Kings 9.13.   21.9: Ps 118.26; Lk 2.14; Mt 21.15; 23.39.
21.11: Jn 6.14; 7.40; Acts 3.22; Mk 6.15; Lk 13.33.
21.12–13: Mk 11.15–17; Lk 19.45–46; Jn 2.13–17; Ex 30.13; Lev 1.14.   21.13: Is 56.7; Jer 7.11.
21.15: Lk 19.39; Mt 21.9.   21.16: Ps 8.2.   21.17–19: Mk 11.11–14; Lk 13.6–9.   21.20–22: Mk 11.20–24.

21 did the fig tree wither at once?" And Jesus answered them, "Truly, I say to you, if you have faith and never doubt, you will not only do what has been done to the fig tree, but 22 even if you say to this mountain, 'Be taken up and cast into the sea,' it will be done. And whatever you ask in prayer, you will receive, if you have faith."

Jesus in the temple

23 And when he entered the temple, the chief priests and the elders of the people came up to him as he was teaching, and said, "By what authority are you doing these things, 24 and who gave you this authority?" Jesus

and he went to the first and said, 'Son, go and work in the vineyard today.' And he 2 answered, 'I will not'; but afterward he repented and went. And he went to the 3 second and said the same; and he answered, 'I go, sir,' but did not go. Which of the two 3 did the will of his father?" They said, "The first." Jesus said to them, "Truly, I say to you, the tax collectors and the harlots go into

answered them, "I also will ask you a question; and if you tell me the answer, then I also will tell you by what authority I do 25 these things. The baptism of John, whence was it? From heaven or from men?" And they argued with one another, "If we say, 'From heaven,' he will say to us, 'Why then 26 did you not believe him?' But if we say, 'From men,' we are afraid of the multitude; 27 for all hold that John was a prophet." So they answered Jesus, "We do not know." And he said to them, "Neither will I tell you by what authority I do these things.
28 "What do you think? A man had two sons;

the kingdom of God before you. For John 32 came to you in the way of righteousness, and you did not believe him, but the tax collectors and the harlots believed him; and even when you saw it, you did not afterward repent and believe him.

The wicked tenants

"Hear another parable. There was a 33 householder who planted a vineyard, and set a hedge around it, and dug a wine press in it, and built a tower, and let it out to tenants, and went into another country. When the 34

21.21: Mt 17.20; Lk 17.6; 1 Cor 13.2; Jas 1.6.   21.22: Jn 14.13–14; 16.23.
21.23–27: Mk 11.27–33; Lk 20.1–8; Jn 2.18–22.   21.26: Mt 11.9; 14.5; Lk 1.76.   21.28: Mt 20.1; 21.33.
21.32: Lk 7.29–30.   21.33–46: Mk 12.1–12; Lk 20.9–19; Is 5.1–7.   21.34: Mt 22.3.

season of fruit drew near, he sent his servants
35 to the tenants, to get his fruit; and the
tenants took his servants and beat one, killed
36 another, and stoned another. Again he sent
other servants, more than the first; and they
37 did the same to them. Afterward he sent his
son to them, saying, 'They will respect my
38 son.' But when the tenants saw the son, they
said to themselves, 'This is the heir; come,
39 let us kill him and have his inheritance.' And
they took him and cast him out of the
40 vineyard, and killed him. When therefore
the owner of the vineyard comes, what will
41 he do to those tenants?" They said to him,
"He will put those wretches to a miserable
death, and let out the vineyard to other
tenants who will give him the fruits in their
seasons."
42 Jesus said to them, "Have you never read in
the scriptures:

'The very stone which the builders
rejected
has become the head of the corner;
this was the Lord's doing,
and it is marvellous in our eyes'?

43 Therefore I tell you, the kingdom of God
will be taken away from you and given to a
nation producing the fruits of it." *p*
45 When the chief priests and the Pharisees
heard his parables, they perceived that he
46 was speaking about them. But when they
tried to arrest him, they feared the multitudes, because they held him to be a prophet.

The wedding garment

22 And again Jesus spoke to them in parables,
2 saying, "The kingdom of heaven may be
compared to a king who gave a marriage feast
3 for his son, and sent his servants to call those
who were invited to the marriage feast; but
4 they would not come. Again he sent other
servants, saying, 'Tell those who are invited,
Behold, I have made ready my dinner, my
oxen and my fat calves are killed, and
everything is ready; come to the marriage
5 feast.' But they made light of it and went off,
one to his farm, another to his business,
6 while the rest seized his servants, treated
7 them shamefully, and killed them. The king
was angry, and he sent his troops and
destroyed those murderers and burned their
8 city. Then he said to his servants, 'The
wedding is ready, but those invited were not
9 worthy. Go therefore to the thoroughfares,
and invite to the marriage feast as many as

you find.' And those servants went out into 10
the streets and gathered all whom they
found, both bad and good; so the wedding
hall was filled with guests.
"But when the king came in to look at the 11
guests, he saw there a man who had no
wedding garment; and he said to him, 12
'Friend, how did you get in here without a
wedding garment?' And he was speechless.
Then the king said to the attendants, 'Bind 13
him hand and foot, and cast him into the
outer darkness; there men will weep and
gnash their teeth.' For many are called, but 14
few are chosen."

Taxes to Caesar

Then the Pharisees went and took counsel 15
how to entangle him in his talk. And they 16
sent their disciples to him, along with the
Hero'di-ans, saying, "Teacher, we know that
you are true, and teach the way of God
truthfully, and care for no man; for you do
not regard the position of men. Tell us, 17
then, what you think. Is it lawful to pay
taxes to Caesar, or not?" But Jesus, aware of 18
their malice, said, "Why put me to the test,
you hypocrites? Show me the money for the 19
tax." And they brought him a coin. *q* And 20
Jesus said to them, "Whose likeness and
inscription is this?" They said, "Caesar's." 21
Then he said to them, "Render therefore to
Caesar the things that are Caesar's, and to
God the things that are God's." When they 22
heard it, they marvelled; and they left him
and went away.

Silencing the Sadducees

The same day Sad'ducees came to him, who 23
say that there is no resurrection; and they
asked him a question, saying, "Teacher, 24
Moses said, 'If a man dies, having no
children, his brother must marry the widow,
and raise up children for his brother.' Now 25
there were seven brothers among us; the first
married, and died, and having no children
left his wife to his brother. So too the second 26
and third, down to the seventh. After them 27
all, the woman died. In the resurrection, 28
therefore, to which of the seven will she be
wife? For they all had her."
But Jesus answered them, "You are wrong, 29
because you know neither the scriptures nor
the power of God. For in the resurrection 30
they neither marry nor are given in marriage,

p Other ancient authorities add verse 44, *"And he who falls on this stone will be broken to pieces; but when it falls on any one, it will crush him"* *q* Greek *a denarius*
21.41: Mt 8.11; Acts 13.46; 18.6; 28.28. 21.42: Ps 118.22-23; Acts 4.11; 1 Pet 2.7. 22.1-10: Lk 14.16-24.
22.3: Mt 21.34. 22.10: Mt 13.47. 22.12: Mt 20.13; 26.50.
22.13: Mt 8.12; 13.42, 50; 24.51; 25.30; Lk 13.28. 22.15-22: Mk 12.13-17; Lk 20.20-26.
22.15: Mk 3.6; 8.15. 22.21: Rom 13.7. 22.23-33: Mk 12.18-27; Lk 20.27-38. 22.23: Acts 4.1-2; 23.6-10.
22.24: Deut 25.5.

31 but are like angels[r] in heaven. And as for the resurrection of the dead, have you not read
32 what was said to you by God, 'I am the God of Abraham, and the God of Isaac, and the God of Jacob'? He is not God of the dead,
33 but of the living." And when the crowd heard it, they were astonished at his teaching.

A challenge to the Pharisees

34 But when the Pharisees heard that he had silenced the Sad'ducees, they came together.
35 And one of them, a lawyer, asked him a
36 question, to test him. "Teacher, which is the
37 great commandment in the law?" And he said to him, "You shall love the Lord your God with all your heart, and with all your
38 soul, and with all your mind. This is the
39 great and first commandment. And a second is like it, You shall love your neighbour as
40 yourself. On these two commandments depend all the law and the prophets."
41 Now while the Pharisees were gathered together, Jesus asked them a question,
42 saying, "What do you think of the Christ? Whose son is he?" They said to him, "The
43 son of David." He said to them, "How is it then that David, inspired by the Spirit,[s] calls him Lord, saying,
44   'The Lord said to my Lord,
      Sit at my right hand,
      till I put thy enemies under thy feet'?
45 If David thus calls him Lord, how is he his
46 son?" And no one was able to answer him a word, nor from that day did any one dare to ask him any more questions.

The great denunciation

23 Then said Jesus to the crowds and to his
2 disciples, "The scribes and the Pharisees sit
3 on Moses' seat; so practise and observe whatever they tell you, but not what they do;
4 for they preach, but do not practise. They bind heavy burdens, hard to bear,[t] and lay them on men's shoulders; but they themselves will not move them with their finger.
5 They do all their deeds to be seen by men; for they make their phylacteries broad and
6 their fringes long, and they love the place of honour at feasts and the best seats in the

synagogues, and salutations in the market 7 places, and being called rabbi by men. But 8 you are not to be called rabbi, for you have one teacher, and you are all brethren. And 9 call no man your father on earth, for you have one Father, who is in heaven. Neither 10 be called masters, for you have one master, the Christ. He who is greatest among you 11 shall be your servant; whoever exalts himself 12 will be humbled, and whoever humbles himself will be exalted.

"But woe to you, scribes and Pharisees, 13 hypocrites! because you shut the kingdom of heaven against men; for you neither enter yourselves, nor allow those who would enter to go in.[u] Woe to you, scribes and Pharisees, 15 hypocrites! for you traverse sea and land to make a single proselyte, and when he becomes a proselyte, you make him twice as much a child of hell[v] as yourselves.

"Woe to you, blind guides, who say, 'If any 16 one swears by the temple, it is nothing; but if any one swears by the gold of the temple, he is bound by his oath.' You blind fools! For 17 which is greater, the gold or the temple that has made the gold sacred? And you say, 'If 18 any one swears by the altar, it is nothing; but if any one swears by the gift that is on the altar, he is bound by his oath.' You blind 19 men! For which is greater, the gift or the altar that makes the gift sacred? So he who 20 swears by the altar, swears by it and by everything on it; and he who swears by the 21 temple, swears by it and by him who dwells in it; and he who swears by heaven, swears 22 by the throne of God and by him who sits upon it.

"Woe to you, scribes and Pharisees, 23 hypocrites! for you tithe mint and dill and cummin, and have neglected the weightier matters of the law, justice and mercy and faith; these you ought to have done, without neglecting the others. You blind guides, 24 straining out a gnat and swallowing a camel!

"Woe to you, scribes and Pharisees, 25 hypocrites! for you cleanse the outside of the cup and of the plate, but inside they are full of extortion and rapacity. You blind Phari- 26 see! first cleanse the inside of the cup and of the plate, that the outside also may be clean.

---

[r] Other ancient authorities add *of God*   [s] Or *David in the Spirit*
[t] Other ancient authorities omit *hard to bear*
[u] Other authorities add here (or after verse 12) verse 14, *Woe to you, scribes and Pharisees, hypocrites! for you devour widows' houses and for a pretence you make long prayers; therefore you will receive the greater condemnation*   [v] Greek *Gehenna*

22.32: Ex 3.6.   22.33: Mt 7.28.   22.34–40: Mk 12.28–34; Lk 20.39–40; 10.25–28.   22.35: Lk 7.30; 11.45; 14.3.
22.37: Deut 6.5.   22.39: Lev 19.18; Mt 19.19; Gal 5.14; Rom 13.9; Jas 2.8.
22.41–46: Mk 12.35–37; Lk 20.41–44.   22.44: Ps 110.1; Acts 2.34–35; Heb 1.13; 10.13.
22.46: Mk 12.34; Lk 20.40.   23.4: Lk 11.46; Acts 15.10.   23.5: Mt 6.1, 5, 16; Ex 13.9; Deut 6.8; Mt 9.20.
23.6–7: Mk 12.38–39; Lk 20.46; 14.7–11; 11.43.   23.8: Jas 3.1.
23.11: Mt 20.26; Mk 9.35; 10.43; Lk 9.48; 22.26; Lk 14.11; 18.14; Mt 18.4; 1 Pet 5.6.
23.13: Lk 11.52.   23.15: Acts 2.10; 6.5; 13.43.   23.16–22: Mt 5.33–37; 15.14.   23.17: Ex 30.29.
23.21: 1 Kings 8.13; Ps 26.8.   23.23–24: Lk 11.42; Lev 27.30; Mic 6.8.   23.25–26: Lk 11.39–41; Mk 7.4.

Dill v. 23

27 "Woe to you, scribes and Pharisees, hypocrites! for you are like whitewashed tombs, which outwardly appear beautiful, but within they are full of dead men's bones 28 and all uncleanness. So you also outwardly appear righteous to men, but within you are full of hypocrisy and iniquity.

29 "Woe to you, scribes and Pharisees, hypocrites! for you build the tombs of the prophets and adorn the monuments of the 30 righteous, saying, 'If we had lived in the days of our fathers, we would not have taken part with them in shedding the blood of the 31 prophets.' Thus you witness against yourselves, that you are sons of those who 32 murdered the prophets. Fill up, then, the 33 measure of your fathers. You serpents, you brood of vipers, how are you to escape being 34 sentenced to hell?[v] Therefore I send you prophets and wise men and scribes, some of whom you will kill and crucify, and some you will scourge in your synagogues and perse-35 cute from town to town, that upon you may come all the righteous blood shed on earth, from the blood of innocent Abel to the blood of Zechari'ah the son of Barachi'ah, whom you murdered between the sanctuary and the 36 altar. Truly, I say to you, all this will come upon this generation.

37 "O Jerusalem, Jerusalem, killing the prophets and stoning those who are sent to you! How often would I have gathered your children together as a hen gathers her brood 38 under her wings, and you would not! Behold, your house is forsaken and desolate.[w] 39 For I tell you, you will not see me again, until you say, 'Blessed is he who comes in the name of the Lord.'"

Destruction of the temple

Jesus left the temple and was going away, 24 when his disciples came to point out to him the buildings of the temple. But he answered 2 them, "You see all these, do you not? Truly, I say to you, there will not be left here one stone upon another, that will not be thrown down."

As he sat on the Mount of Olives, the 3 disciples came to him privately, saying, "Tell us, when will this be, and what will be the sign of your coming and of the close of the age?" And Jesus answered them, "Take 4 heed that no one leads you astray. For many 5 will come in my name, saying, 'I am the Christ,' and they will lead many astray. And 6 you will hear of wars and rumours of wars; see that you are not alarmed; for this must take place, but the end is not yet. For nation 7 will rise against nation, and kingdom against kingdom, and there will be famines and earthquakes in various places: all this is but 8 the beginning of the sufferings.

"Then they will deliver you up to tribu-9 lation, and put you to death; and you will be hated by all nations for my name's sake. And 10 then many will fall away,[x] and betray one another, and hate one another. And many 11 false prophets will arise and lead many astray. And because wickedness is multi-12 plied, most men's love will grow cold. But 13 he who endures to the end will be saved. And this gospel of the kingdom will be 14 preached throughout the whole world, as a testimony to all nations; and then the end will come.

[v] Greek *Gehenna*   [w] Other ancient authorities omit *and desolate*   [x] Or *stumble*
23.27-28: Lk 11.44; Acts 23.3; Ps 5.9.   23.29-32: Lk 11.47-48; Acts 7.51-53.   23.33: Mt 3.7; Lk 3.7.
23.34-36: Lk 11.49-51; 2 Chron 36.15-16.   23.34: Mt 10.17, 23.
23.35: Gen 4.8; Heb 11.4; Zech 1.1; 2 Chron 24.21.   23.36: Mt 10.23; 16.28; 24.34.   23.37-39: Lk 13.34-35.
23.38: 1 Kings 9.7; Jer 22.5.   23.39: Mt 21.9; Ps 118.26.   24.1-35: Mk 13.1-31; Lk 21.1-33.
24.2: Mt 26.61; 27.39-40; Lk 19.44; Jn 2.19.   24.3: Lk 17.20; Mt 13.39, 40, 49; 28.20; 16.27.
24.5: Mt 24.11, 23-24; 1 Jn 2.18.   24.6-7: Rev 6.3-8, 12-17; Is 19.2.   24.9: Mt 10.17-18, 22; Jn 15.18; 16.2.
24.13: Mt 10.22; Rev 2.7.   24.14: Mt 28.19; Rom 10.18.

The desolating sacrilege

15 "So when you see the desolating sacrilege spoken of by the prophet Daniel, standing in the holy place (let the reader understand),
16 then let those who are in Judea flee to the
17 mountains; let him who is on the housetop
18 not go down to take what is in his house; and let him who is in the field not turn back to
19 take his mantle. And alas for those who are with child and for those who give suck in
20 those days! Pray that your flight may not be
21 in winter or on a sabbath. For then there will be great tribulation, such as has not been from the beginning of the world until now,
22 no, and never will be. And if those days had not been shortened, no human being would be saved; but for the sake of the elect those
23 days will be shortened. Then if any one says to you, 'Lo, here is the Christ!' or 'There he
24 is!' do not believe it. For false Christs and false prophets will arise and show great signs and wonders, so as to lead astray, if possible,
25 even the elect. Lo, I have told you before-
26 hand. So, if they say to you, 'Lo, he is in the wilderness,' do not go out; if they say, 'Lo, he is in the inner rooms,' do not believe it.
27 For as the lightning comes from the east and shines as far as the west, so will be the
28 coming of the Son of man. Wherever the body is, there the eagles[v] will be gathered together.

The coming of the Son of man

29 "Immediately after the tribulation of those days the sun will be darkened, and the moon will not give its light, and the stars will fall from heaven, and the powers of the heavens
30 will be shaken; then will appear the sign of the Son of man in heaven, and then all the tribes of the earth will mourn, and they will see the Son of man coming on the clouds of
31 heaven with power and great glory; and he will send out his angels with a loud trumpet call, and they will gather his elect from the four winds, from one end of heaven to the other.
32 "From the fig tree learn its lesson: as soon as its branch becomes tender and puts forth
33 its leaves, you know that summer is near. So also, when you see all these things, you know
34 that he is near, at the very gates. Truly, I say to you, this generation will not pass away till all these things take place. Heaven and earth 35 will pass away, but my words will not pass away.

"But of that day and hour no one knows, 36 not even the angels of heaven, nor the Son,[z] but the Father only. As were the days 37 of Noah, so will be the coming of the Son of man. For as in those days before the 38 flood they were eating and drinking, marrying and giving in marriage, until the day when Noah entered the ark, and they did not 39 know until the flood came and swept them all away, so will be the coming of the Son of man. Then two men will be in the field; one 40 is taken and one is left. Two women will be 41 grinding at the mill; one is taken and one is left. Watch therefore, for you do not know 42 on what day your Lord is coming. But know 43 this, that if the householder had known in what part of the night the thief was coming, he would have watched and would not have let his house be broken into. Therefore you 44 also must be ready; for the Son of man is coming at an hour you do not expect.

"Who then is the faithful and wise servant, 45 whom his master has set over his household, to give them their food at the proper time? Blessed is that servant whom his master 46 when he comes will find so doing. Truly, I 47 say to you, he will set him over all his possessions. But if that wicked servant says 48 to himself, 'My master is delayed,' and 49 begins to beat his fellow servants, and eats and drinks with the drunken, the master of 50 that servant will come on a day when he does not expect him and at an hour he does not know, and will punish[a] him, and put him 51 with the hypocrites; there men will weep and gnash their teeth.

The ten maidens

"Then the kingdom of heaven shall be 25 compared to ten maidens who took their lamps and went to meet the bridegroom.[b] Five of them were foolish, and five were 2 wise. For when the foolish took their lamps, 3 they took no oil with them; but the wise 4 took flasks of oil with their lamps. As the 5 bridegroom was delayed, they all slumbered and slept. But at midnight there was a cry, 6 'Behold, the bridegroom! Come out to meet

---

v Or *vultures*   z Other ancient authorities omit *nor the Son*   a Or *cut him in pieces*
b Other ancient authorities add *and the bride*

24.15: Dan 9.27; 11.31; 12.11.   24.17-18: Lk 17.31.   24.19: Lk 23.29.   24.21: Dan 12.1; Joel 2.2.
24.26-27: Lk 17.22-24; Rev 1.7.   24.28: Lk 17.37; Job 39.30.
24.29: Rev 8.12; Is 13.10; Ezek 32.7; Joel 2.10-11; Zeph 1.15.   24.30: Mt 16.27; Dan 7.13; Rev 1.7.
24.31: I Cor 15.52; I Thess 4.16; Is 27.13; Zech 9.14.   24.34: Mt 16.28.   24.35: Mt 5.18; Lk 16.17.
24.36: Acts 1.6-7.   24.37-39: Lk 17.26-27; Gen 6.5-8; 7.6-24.   24.40-41: Lk 17.34-35.
24.42: Mk 13.35; Lk 12.40; Mt 25.13.   24.43-51: Lk 12.39-46.
24.43: I Thess 5.2; Rev 3.3; 16.15; 2 Pet 3.10.   24.45: Mt 25.21, 23.   24.49: Lk 21.34.
24.51: Mt 8.12; 13.42, 50; 22.13; 25.30; Lk 13.28.   25.1: Lk 12.35-38; Mk 13.34.   25.2: Mt 7.24-27.

7 him.' Then all those maidens rose and
8 trimmed their lamps. And the foolish said to
the wise, 'Give us some of your oil, for our
9 lamps are going out.' But the wise replied,
'Perhaps there will not be enough for us and
for you; go rather to the dealers and buy for
10 yourselves.' And while they went to buy, the
bridegroom came, and those who were ready
went in with him to the marriage feast; and
11 the door was shut. Afterward the other
maidens came also, saying, 'Lord, lord, open
12 to us.' But he replied, 'Truly, I say to you, I
13 do not know you.' Watch therefore, for you
know neither the day nor the hour.

The talents

14 "For it will be as when a man going on a
journey called his servants and entrusted to
15 them his property; to one he gave five
talents,[c] to another two, to another one, to
each according to his ability. Then he went
16 away. He who had received the five talents
went at once and traded with them; and he

A talent

made five talents more. So also, he who had 17
the two talents made two talents more. But 18
he who had received the one talent went and
dug in the ground and hid his master's
money. Now after a long time the master of 19
those servants came and settled accounts
with them. And he who had received the five 20
talents came forward, bringing five talents
more, saying, 'Master, you delivered to me
five talents; here I have made five talents
more.' His master said to him, 'Well done, 21
good and faithful servant; you have been
faithful over a little, I will set you over much;
enter into the joy of your master.' And he 22
also who had the two talents came forward,
saying, 'Master, you delivered to me two
talents; here I have made two talents more.'
His master said to him, 'Well done, good and 23
faithful servant; you have been faithful over a
little, I will set you over much; enter into the
joy of your master.' He also who had 24
received the one talent came forward, saying,
'Master, I knew you to be a hard man,
reaping where you did not sow, and gathering where you did not winnow; so I was 25
afraid, and I went and hid your talent in the
ground. Here you have what is yours.' But 26
his master answered him, 'You wicked and
slothful servant! You knew that I reap
where I have not sowed, and gather where I
have not winnowed? Then you ought to 27
have invested my money with the bankers,
and at my coming I should have received
what was my own with interest. So take the 28
talent from him, and give it to him who has
the ten talents. For to every one who has will 29
more be given, and he will have abundance;
but from him who has not, even what he
will be taken away. And cast the worthless 30
servant into the outer darkness; there men
will weep and gnash their teeth.'

The judgment

"When the Son of man comes in his glory, 31
and all the angels with him, then he will sit
on his glorious throne. Before him will be 32
gathered all the nations, and he will separate
them one from another as a shepherd separates the sheep from the goats, and he will 33
place the sheep at his right hand, but the
goats at the left. Then the King will say to 34
those at his right hand, 'Come, O blessed of
my Father, inherit the kingdom prepared for
you from the foundation of the world; for I 35
was hungry and you gave me food, I was
thirsty and you gave me drink, I was a

[c] This talent was probably worth about £350
25.10: Rev 19.9. 25.11-12: Lk 13.25; Mt 7.21-23. 25.13: Mt 24.42; Mk 13.35; Lk 12.40.
25.14-30: Lk 19.12-28. 25.19: Mt 18.23. 25.21: Lk 16.10; Mt 24.45. 25.29: Mt 13.12; Mk 4.25; Lk 8.18.
25.30: Mt 8.12; 13.42, 50; 22.13; Lk 13.28. 25.31: Mt 16.27; 19.28. 25.32: Ezek 34.17.
25.34: Lk 12.32; Mt 5.3; Rev 13.8; 17.8. 25.35-36: Is 58.7; Jas 1.27; 2.15-16; Heb 13.2; 2 Tim 1.16.

36 stranger and you welcomed me, I was naked and you clothed me, I was sick and you visited me, I was in prison and you came to
37 me.' Then the righteous will answer him, 'Lord, when did we see thee hungry and feed
38 thee, or thirsty and give thee drink? And when did we see thee a stranger and welcome
39 thee, or naked and clothe thee? And when did we see thee sick or in prison and visit
40 thee?' And the King will answer them, 'Truly, I say to you, as you did it to one of the least of these my brethren, you did it to
41 me.' Then he will say to those at his left hand, 'Depart from me, you cursed, into the eternal fire prepared for the devil and his
42 angels; for I was hungry and you gave me no food, I was thirsty and you gave me no drink,
43 I was a stranger and you did not welcome me, naked and you did not clothe me, sick and in prison and you did not visit me.'
44 Then they also will answer, 'Lord, when did we see thee hungry or thirsty or a stranger or naked or sick or in prison, and did not
45 minister to thee?' Then he will answer them, 'Truly, I say to you, as you did it not to one of the least of these, you did it not to
46 me.' And they will go away into eternal punishment, but the righteous into eternal life."

THE DEATH OF JESUS

26 WHEN Jesus had finished all these say-
2 ings, he said to his disciples, "You know that after two days the Passover is coming, and the Son of man will be delivered up to be crucified."
3 Then the chief priests and the elders of the

people gathered in the palace of the high priest, who was called Ca'iaphas, and took 4 counsel together in order to arrest Jesus by stealth and kill him. But they said, "Not 5 during the feast, lest there be a tumult among the people."

The anointing at Bethany

Now when Jesus was at Bethany in the 6 house of Simon the leper, a woman came up 7 to him with an alabaster jar of very expensive ointment, and she poured it on his head, as he sat at table. But when the disciples saw it, 8 they were indignant, saying, "Why this waste? For this ointment might have been 9 sold for a large sum, and given to the poor." But Jesus, aware of this, said to them, "Why 10 do you trouble the woman? For she has done a beautiful thing to me. For you always 11 have the poor with you, but you will not always have me. In pouring this ointment on 12 my body she has done it to prepare me for burial. Truly, I say to you, wherever this 13 gospel is preached in the whole world, what she has done will be told in memory of her."

The betrayal

Then one of the twelve, who was called 14 Judas Iscariot, went to the chief priests and 15 said, "What will you give me if I deliver him to you?" And they paid him thirty pieces of silver. And from that moment he sought an 16 opportunity to betray him.

The last supper

Now on the first day of Unleavened Bread 17 the disciples came to Jesus, saying, "Where will you have us prepare for you to eat the passover?" He said, "Go into the city to 18 such a one, and say to him, 'The Teacher says, My time is at hand; I will keep the passover at your house with my disciples.'" And the disciples did as Jesus had directed 19 them, and they prepared the passover.
When it was evening, he sat at table with 20 the twelve disciples;[d] and as they were 21 eating, he said, "Truly, I say to you, one of you will betray me." And they were very 22 sorrowful, and began to say to him one after another, "Is it I, Lord?" He answered, "He 23 who has dipped his hand in the dish with me, will betray me. The Son of man goes as it is 24

[d] Other authorities omit *disciples*
25.40: Mt 10.42; Mk 9.41; Heb 6.10; Prov 19.17.   25.41: Mk 9.48; Lk 16.23; Rev 20.10.
25.46: Dan 12.2; Jn 5.29.   26.1: Mt 7.28; 11.1; 13.53; 19.1.   26.2-5: Mk 14.1-2; Lk 22.1-2; Jn 11.47-53.
26.6-13: Mk 14.3-9; Jn 12.1-8; Lk 7.36-38.   26.11: Deut 15.11.   26.12: Jn 19.40.
26.14-16: Mk 14.10-11; Lk 22.3-6.   26.15: Ex 21.32; Zech 11.12.   26.17-19: Mk 14.12-16; Lk 22.7-13.
26.18: Mt 26.45; Jn 7.6; 12.23; 13.1; 17.1.   26.19: Mt 21.6; Deut 16.5-8.
26.20-24: Mk 14.17-21; Lk 22.14, 21-23; Jn 13.21-30.
26.24: Ps 41.9; Lk 24.25; 1 Cor 15.3; Acts 17.2-3; Mt 18.7.

written of him, but woe to that man by whom the Son of man is betrayed! It would have been better for that man if he had not been born." Judas, who betrayed him, said, "Is it I, Master?"*e* He said to him, "You have said so."

Now as they were eating, Jesus took bread, and blessed, and broke it, and gave it to the disciples and said, "Take, eat; this is my body." And he took a cup, and when he had given thanks he gave it to them, saying, "Drink of it, all of you; for this is my blood of the*f* covenant, which is poured out for many for the forgiveness of sins. I tell you I shall not drink again of this fruit of the vine until that day when I drink it new with you in my Father's kingdom."

And when they had sung a hymn, they went out to the Mount of Olives. Then Jesus said to them, "You will all fall away because of me this night; for it is written, 'I will strike the shepherd, and the sheep of the flock will be scattered.' But after I am raised up, I will go before you to Galilee." Peter declared to him, "Though they all fall away because of you, I will never fall away." Jesus said to him, "Truly, I say to you, this very night, before the cock crows, you will deny me three times." Peter said to him, "Even if I must die with you, I will not deny you." And so said all the disciples.

Arrest and trial

Then Jesus went with them to a place called Gethsem'ane, and he said to his disciples, "Sit here, while I go yonder and pray." And taking with him Peter and the two sons of Zeb'edee, he began to be sorrowful and troubled. Then he said to them, "My soul is very sorrowful, even to death; remain here, and watch*g* with me." And going a little farther he fell on his face and prayed, "My Father, if it be possible, let this cup pass from me; nevertheless, not as I will, but as thou wilt." And he came to the disciples and found them sleeping; and he said to Peter, "So, could you not watch*g* with me one hour? Watch*g* and pray that you may not enter into temptation; the spirit indeed is willing, but the flesh is weak." Again, for the second time, he went away and prayed, "My Father, if this cannot pass unless I drink it,

thy will be done." And again he came and found them sleeping, for their eyes were heavy. So, leaving them again, he went away and prayed for the third time, saying the same words. Then he came to the disciples and said to them, "Are you still sleeping and taking your rest? Behold, the hour is at hand, and the Son of man is betrayed into the hands of sinners. Rise, let us be going; see, my betrayer is at hand."

While he was still speaking, Judas came, one of the twelve, and with him a great crowd with swords and clubs, from the chief priests and the elders of the people. Now the betrayer had given them a sign, saying, "The one I shall kiss is the man; seize him." And he came up to Jesus at once and said, "Hail, Master!"*e* And he kissed him. Jesus said to him, "Friend, why are you here?"*h* Then they came up and laid hands on Jesus and seized him. And behold, one of those who were with Jesus stretched out his hand and drew his sword, and struck the slave of the high priest, and cut off his ear. Then Jesus said to him, "Put your sword back into its place; for all who take the sword will perish by the sword. Do you think that I cannot appeal to my Father, and he will at once send me more than twelve legions of angels? But how then should the scriptures be fulfilled, that it must be so?" At that hour Jesus said to the crowds, "Have you come out as against a robber, with swords and clubs to capture me? Day after day I sat in the temple teaching, and you did not seize me. But all this has taken place, that the scriptures of the prophets might be fulfilled." Then all the disciples forsook him and fled.

Then those who had seized Jesus led him to Ca'iaphas the high priest, where the scribes and the elders had gathered. But Peter followed him at a distance, as far as the courtyard of the high priest, and going inside he sat with the guards to see the end. Now the chief priests and the whole council sought false testimony against Jesus that they might put him to death, but they found none, though many false witnesses came forward. At last two came forward and said, "This fellow said, 'I am able to destroy the temple of God, and to build it in three days.'" And the high priest stood up and said, "Have you no answer to make? What is it that these

e Or *Rabbi* *f* Other ancient authorities insert *new* *g* Or *keep awake* *h* Or *do that for which you have come*
26.26-29: Mk 14.22-25; Lk 22.17-19; 1 Cor 10.16; 11.23-26; Mt 14.19; 15.36.
26.28: Heb 9.20; Mt 20.28; Mk 1.4; Ex 24.6-8.
26.30-35: Mk 14.26-31; Lk 22.33-34, 39; Jn 14.31; 18.1; 13.36-38. 26.31: Zech 13.7; Jn 16.32.
26.32: Mt 28.7, 10, 16. 26.36-46: Mk 14.32-42; Lk 22.40-46. 26.38: Jn 12.27; Heb 5.7-8.
26.39: Jn 18.11; Mt 20.22. 26.41: Mt 6.13; Lk 11.4. 26.42: Jn 4.34; 5.30; 6.38.
26.45: Mt 26.18; Jn 12.23; 13.1; 17.1. 26.47-56: Mk 14.43-50; Lk 22.47-53; Jn 18.2-11.
26.50: Mt 20.13; 22.12. 26.52: Gen 9.6; Rev 13.10. 26.55: Lk 19.47; Jn 18.19-21.
26.57-75: Mk 14.53-72; Lk 22.54-71; Jn 18.12-27.
26.61: Mt 24.2; 27.40; Acts 6.14; Jn 2.19.

63 men testify against you?" But Jesus was silent. And the high priest said to him, "I adjure you by the living God, tell us if you 64 are the Christ, the Son of God." Jesus said to him, "You have said so. But I tell you, hereafter you will see the Son of man seated at the right hand of Power, and coming on 65 the clouds of heaven." Then the high priest tore his robes, and said, "He has uttered blasphemy. Why do we still need witnesses? You have now heard his blas- 66 phemy. What is your judgment?" They 67 answered, "He deserves death." Then they spat in his face, and struck him; and some 68 slapped him, saying, "Prophesy to us, you Christ! Who is it that struck you?"

69 Now Peter was sitting outside in the courtyard. And a maid came up to him, and said, "You also were with Jesus the Galilean." 70 But he denied it before them all, saying, "I 71 do not know what you mean." And when he went out to the porch, another maid saw him, and she said to the bystanders, "This man 72 was with Jesus of Nazareth." And again he denied it with an oath, "I do not know the 73 man." After a little while the bystanders came up and said to Peter, "Certainly you are also one of them, for your accent betrays 74 you." Then he began to invoke a curse on himself and to swear, "I do not know the man." And immediately the cock crowed. 75 And Peter remembered the saying of Jesus, "Before the cock crows, you will deny me three times." And he went out and wept bitterly.

27 When morning came, all the chief priests and the elders of the people took counsel 2 against Jesus to put him to death; and they bound him and led him away and delivered him to Pilate the governor.

3 When Judas, his betrayer, saw that he was condemned, he repented and brought back the thirty pieces of silver to the chief priests 4 and the elders, saying, "I have sinned in betraying innocent blood." They said, "What is that to us? See to it yourself." 5 And throwing down the pieces of silver in the temple, he departed; and he went and 6 hanged himself. But the chief priests, taking the pieces of silver, said, "It is not lawful to put them into the treasury, since they are 7 blood money." So they took counsel, and bought with them the potter's field, to bury

strangers in. Therefore that field has been 8 called the Field of Blood to this day. Then 9 was fulfilled what had been spoken by the prophet Jeremiah, saying, "And they took the thirty pieces of silver, the price of him on whom a price had been set by some of the sons of Israel, and they gave them for the 10 potter's field, as the Lord directed me."

Jesus before Pilate

Now Jesus stood before the governor; and 11 the governor asked him, "Are you the King of the Jews?" Jesus said to him, "You have said so." But when he was accused by the 12 chief priests and elders, he made no answer. Then Pilate said to him, "Do you not hear 13 how many things they testify against you?" But he gave him no answer, not even to a 14 single charge; so that the governor wondered greatly.

Now at the feast the governor was accus- 15 tomed to release for the crowd any one prisoner whom they wanted. And they had 16 then a notorious prisoner, called Barab'bas.[i] So when they had gathered, Pilate said to 17 them, "Whom do you want me to release for you, Barab'bas[i] or Jesus who is called Christ?" For he knew that it was out of envy 18 that they had delivered him up. Besides, 19 while he was sitting on the judgment seat, his wife sent word to him, "Have nothing to do with that righteous man, for I have suffered much over him today in a dream." Now the 20 chief priests and the elders persuaded the people to ask for Barab'bas and destroy Jesus. The governor again said to them, 21 "Which of the two do you want me to release for you?" And they said, "Barab'bas." Pilate said to them, "Then what shall I do 22 with Jesus who is called Christ?" They all said, "Let him be crucified." And he said, 23 "Why, what evil has he done?" But they shouted all the more, "Let him be crucified."

So when Pilate saw that he was gaining 24 nothing, but rather that a riot was beginning, he took water and washed his hands before the crowd, saying, "I am innocent of this man's blood;[j] see to it yourselves." And all 25 the people answered, "His blood be on us and on our children!" Then he released for 26 them Barab'bas, and having scourged Jesus, delivered him to be crucified.

Then the soldiers of the governor took Jesus 27 into the praetorium, and they gathered the

i Other ancient authorities read Jesus Barabbas
j Other authorities read this righteous blood or this righteous man's blood
26.63: Mt 27.11; Jn 18.33.   26.64: Mt 16.28; Dan 7.13; Ps 110.1.   26.65: Num 14.6; Acts 14.14; Lev 24.16.
26.75: Mt 26.34.   27.1-2: Mk 15.1; Lk 23.1; Jn 18.28.   27.3-10: Acts 1.16-20.   27.3: Mt 26.15; Ex 21.32.
27.6: Deut 23.18.   27.9: Zech 11.12-13; Jer 32.6-15; 18.2-3.
27.11-26: Mk 15.2-15; Lk 23.3, 18-25; Jn 18.29-19.16.   27.14: Lk 23.9; Mt 26.62; Mk 14.60; 1 Tim 6.13.
27.19: Lk 23.4.   27.21: Acts 3.13-14.   27.24: Deut 21.6-9; Ps 26.6.   27.25: Acts 5.28; Josh 2.19.
27.27-31: Mk 15.16-20; Lk 23.11; Jn 19.2-3.

28 whole battalion before him. And they
29 stripped him and put a scarlet robe upon
him, and plaiting a crown of thorns they put
it on his head, and put a reed in his right
hand. And kneeling before him they mocked
30 him, saying, "Hail, King of the Jews!" And
they spat upon him, and took the reed and
31 struck him on the head. And when they had
mocked him, they stripped him of the robe,
and put his own clothes on him, and led him
away to crucify him.

The crucifixion

32 As they were marching out, they came upon
a man of Cyre'ne, Simon by name; this man
33 they compelled to carry his cross. And when
they came to a place called Gol'gotha (which
34 means the place of a skull), they offered him
wine to drink, mingled with gall; but when
35 he tasted it, he would not drink it. And when
they had crucified him, they divided his
36 garments among them by casting lots; then
they sat down and kept watch over him
37 there. And over his head they put the charge
against him, which read, "This is Jesus the
38 King of the Jews." Then two robbers were
crucified with him, one on the right and one
39 on the left. And those who passed by
40 derided him, wagging their heads and saying,
"You who would destroy the temple and
build it in three days, save yourself! If you
are the Son of God, come down from the
41 cross." So also the chief priests, with the
42 scribes and elders, mocked him, saying, "He
saved others; he cannot save himself. He is
the King of Israel; let him come down now
from the cross, and we will believe in him.
43 He trusts in God; let God deliver him now, if
he desires him; for he said, 'I am the Son of
44 God.'" And the robbers who were crucified
with him also reviled him in the same
way.
45 Now from the sixth hour there was darkness
46 over all the land[k] until the ninth hour. And
about the ninth hour Jesus cried with a loud
voice, "Eli, Eli, la'ma sabach-tha'ni?" that
47 is, "My God, my God, why hast thou
forsaken me?" And some of the bystanders
hearing it said, "This man is calling
48 Eli'jah." And one of them at once ran and
took a sponge, filled it with vinegar, and put
49 it on a reed, and gave it to him to drink. But
the others said, "Wait, let us see whether
50 Eli'jah will come to save him."[l] And Jesus

cried again with a loud voice and yielded up
his spirit.
51 And behold, the curtain of the temple was
torn in two, from top to bottom; and the
52 earth shook, and the rocks were split; the
tombs also were opened, and many bodies of
the saints who had fallen asleep were raised,
53 and coming out of the tombs after his
resurrection they went into the holy city and
54 appeared to many. When the centurion and
those who were with him, keeping watch
over Jesus, saw the earthquake and what took
place, they were filled with awe, and said,
"Truly this was the Son[m] of God!"
55 There were also many women there, looking on from afar, who had followed Jesus
from Galilee, ministering to him; among
56 whom were Mary Mag'dalene, and Mary the
mother of James and Joseph, and the mother
of the sons of Zeb'edee.

The burial

57 When it was evening, there came a rich man
from Arimathe'a, named Joseph, who also
58 was a disciple of Jesus. He went to Pilate and
asked for the body of Jesus. Then Pilate
59 ordered it to be given to him. And Joseph
took the body, and wrapped it in a clean linen
60 shroud, and laid it in his own new tomb,
which he had hewn in the rock; and he rolled
a great stone to the door of the tomb,
61 and departed. Mary Mag'dalene and the
other Mary were there, sitting opposite the
sepulchre.
62 Next day, that is, after the day of Preparation, the chief priests and the Pharisees
63 gathered before Pilate and said, "Sir, we
remember how that impostor said, while he
was still alive, 'After three days I will rise
64 again.' Therefore order the sepulchre to be
made secure until the third day, lest his
disciples go and steal him away, and tell the
people, 'He has risen from the dead,' and the
65 last fraud will be worse than the first." Pilate
said to them, "You have a guard[n] of soldiers;
66 go, make it as secure as you can."[o] So they
went and made the sepulchre secure by
sealing the stone and setting a guard.

The resurrection

Now after the sabbath, toward the dawn 28
of the first day of the week, Mary Mag'dalene and the other Mary went to see the

---

[k] Or *earth* [l] Other ancient authorities insert *And another took a spear and pierced his side, and out came water and blood* [m] Or *a son* [n] Or *Take a guard* [o] Greek *know*
27.32: Mk 15.21; Lk 23.26; Jn 19.17; Heb 13.12.   27.33–44: Mk 15.22–32; Lk 23.33–39; Jn 19.17–24.
27.35: Ps 22.18.   27.39: Ps 22.7–8; 109.25.   27.40: Mt 26.61; Acts 6.14; Jn 2.19.
27.45–56: Mk 15.33–41; Lk 23.44–54; Jn 19.28–30.   27.46: Ps 22.1.   27.48: Ps 69.21.
27.51: Heb 9.8; 10.19; Ex 26.31–35; Mt 28.2.   27.54: Mt 3.17; 17.5.   27.56: Lk 24.10.
27.57–61: Mk 15.42–47; Lk 23.50–56; Jn 19.38–42; Acts 13.29.   27.63: Mt 16.21; 17.23; 20.19.
27.66: Mt 27.60; 28.11–15.   28.1–8: Mk 16.1–8; Lk 24.1–9; Jn 20.1–2.   28.1: Lk 8.2; Mt 27.56.

2 sepulchre. And behold, there was a great earthquake; for an angel of the Lord descended from heaven and came and rolled 3 back the stone, and sat upon it. His appearance was like lightning, and his raiment 4 white as snow. And for fear of him the guards trembled and became like dead men. 5 But the angel said to the women, "Do not be afraid; for I know that you seek Jesus who 6 was crucified. He is not here; for he has risen, as he said. Come, see the place where 7 he*p* lay. Then go quickly and tell his disciples that he has risen from the dead, and behold, he is going before you to Galilee; there you will see him. Lo, I have told 8 you." So they departed quickly from the tomb with fear and great joy, and ran to tell 9 his disciples. And behold, Jesus met them and said, "Hail!" And they came up and took hold of his feet and worshipped him. 10 Then Jesus said to them, "Do not be afraid; go and tell my brethren to go to Galilee, and there they will see me."

11 While they were going, behold, some of the guard went into the city and told the chief priests all that had taken place. And when 12 they had assembled with the elders and taken counsel, they gave a sum of money to the soldiers and said, "Tell people, 'His disciples 13 came by night and stole him away while we were asleep.' And if this comes to the 14 governor's ears, we will satisfy him and keep you out of trouble." So they took the money 15 and did as they were directed; and this story has been spread among the Jews to this day.

Now the eleven disciples went to Galilee, to 16 the mountain to which Jesus had directed them. And when they saw him they wor- 17 shipped him; but some doubted. And Jesus 18 came and said to them, "All authority in heaven and on earth has been given to me. Go therefore and make disciples of all 19 nations, baptizing them in the name of the Father and of the Son and of the Holy Spirit, teaching them to observe all that I have 20 commanded you; and lo, I am with you always, to the close of the age."

CAPERNAUM

THE GOSPEL ACCORDING TO

MARK

THE beginning of the gospel of Jesus Christ, the Son of God.[a]
2 As it is written in Isaiah the prophet,[b]
"Behold, I send my messenger before thy face,
who shall prepare thy way;
3 the voice of one crying in the wilderness:
Prepare the way of the Lord,
make his paths straight—"
4 John the baptizer appeared[c] in the wilderness, preaching a baptism of repentance
5 for the forgiveness of sins. And there went out to him all the country of Judea, and all the people of Jerusalem; and they were baptized by him in the river Jordan, confess-
6 ing their sins. Now John was clothed with camel's hair, and had a leather girdle around his waist, and ate locusts and wild honey.
7 And he preached, saying, "After me comes he who is mightier than I, the thong of whose sandals I am not worthy to stoop down and
8 untie. I have baptized you with water; but he will baptize you with the Holy Spirit."
9 In those days Jesus came from Nazareth of Galilee and was baptized by John in the
10 Jordan. And when he came up out of the water, immediately he saw the heavens opened and the Spirit descending upon him
11 like a dove; and a voice came from heaven,

"Thou art my beloved Son;[d] with thee I am well pleased."
12 The Spirit immediately drove him out into
13 the wilderness. And he was in the wilderness forty days, tempted by Satan; and he was with the wild beasts; and the angels ministered to him.

JESUS IN GALILEE

14 NOW after John was arrested, Jesus came into Galilee, preaching the gospel
15 of God, and saying, "The time is fulfilled, and the kingdom of God is at hand; repent, and believe in the gospel."

The first disciples

16 And passing along by the Sea of Galilee, he saw Simon and Andrew the brother of Simon casting a net in the sea; for they were
17 fishermen. And Jesus said to them, "Follow me and I will make you become fishers of
18 men." And immediately they left their nets
19 and followed him. And going on a little farther, he saw James the son of Zeb'edee and John his brother, who were in their boat
20 mending the nets. And immediately he called them; and they left their father

[a] Other ancient authorities omit *the Son of God*   [b] Other ancient authorities read *in the prophets*
[c] Other ancient authorities read *John was baptizing*   [d] Or *my Son, my* (or *the*) *Beloved*
1.2–8: Mt 3.1–12; Lk 3.2–16; Jn 1.6, 15, 19–28.   **1.2:** Mal 3.1; Mt 11.10; Lk 7.27.   **1.3:** Is 40.3.
1.4: Acts 13.24.   **1.9–11:** Mt 3.13–17; Lk 3.21–22; Jn 1.29–34.   **1.11:** Ps 2.7; Is 42.1.
1.12–13: Mt 4.1–11; Lk 4.1–13.   **1.14–15:** Mt 4.12–17; Lk 4.14–15.
1.16–20: Mt 4.18–22; Lk 5.1–11; Jn 1.40–42.

Zeb'edee in the boat with the hired servants, and followed him.

In Capernaum

21 And they went into Caper'na-um; and immediately on the sabbath he entered the 22 synagogue and taught. And they were astonished at his teaching, for he taught them as one who had authority, and not as the 23 scribes. And immediately there was in their 24 synagogue a man with an unclean spirit; and he cried out, "What have you to do with us, Jesus of Nazareth? Have you come to destroy us? I know who you are, the Holy 25 One of God." But Jesus rebuked him, saying, "Be silent, and come out of him!" 26 And the unclean spirit, convulsing him and crying with a loud voice, came out of him. 27 And they were all amazed, so that they questioned among themselves, saying, "What is this? A new teaching! With authority he commands even the unclean 28 spirits, and they obey him." And at once his fame spread everywhere throughout all the surrounding region of Galilee.

29 And immediately he* left the synagogue, and entered the house of Simon and Andrew, 30 with James and John. Now Simon's mother-in-law lay sick with a fever, and 31 immediately they told him of her. And he came and took her by the hand and lifted her up, and the fever left her; and she served them.

32 That evening, at sundown, they brought to him all who were sick or possessed with 33 demons. And the whole city was gathered 34 together about the door. And he healed many who were sick with various diseases, and cast out many demons; and he would not permit the demons to speak, because they knew him.

35 And in the morning, a great while before day, he rose and went out to a lonely place, 36 and there he prayed. And Simon and those 37 who were with him followed him, and they found him and said to him, "Every one is searching for you."

A preaching tour

38 And he said to them, "Let us go on to the next towns, that I may preach there also; for 39 that is why I came out." And he went throughout all Galilee, preaching in their synagogues and casting out demons.

40 And a leper came to him beseeching him,

and kneeling said to him, "If you will, you can make me clean." Moved with pity, he stretched out his hand and touched him, and said to him, "I will; be clean." And immediately the leprosy left him, and he was made clean. And he sternly charged him, and sent him away at once, and said to him, "See that you say nothing to any one; but go, show yourself to the priest, and offer for your cleansing what Moses commanded, for a proof to the people."*/ But he went out and began to talk freely about it, and to spread the news, so that Jesus* could no longer openly enter a town, but was out in the country; and people came to him from every quarter.

Jesus forgives sins

And when he returned to Caper'na-um 2 after some days, it was reported that he was at home. And many were gathered together, 2 so that there was no longer room for them, not even about the door; and he was preaching the word to them. And they came, 3 bringing to him a paralytic carried by four men. And when they could not get near him 4 because of the crowd, they removed the roof above him; and when they had made an opening, they let down the pallet on which the paralytic lay. And when Jesus saw their 5 faith, he said to the paralytic, "My son, your sins are forgiven." Now some of the scribes 6 were sitting there, questioning in their hearts, "Why does this man speak thus? It 7 is blasphemy! Who can forgive sins but God alone?" And immediately Jesus, perceiving 8 in his spirit that they thus questioned within themselves, said to them, "Why do you question thus in your hearts? Which is 9 easier, to say to the paralytic, 'Your sins are forgiven,' or to say, 'Rise, take up your pallet and walk'? But that you may know that the 1c Son of man has authority on earth to forgive sins"—he said to the paralytic—"I say to 11 you, rise, take up your pallet and go home." And he rose, and immediately took up the 12 pallet and went out before them all; so that they were all amazed and glorified God, saying, "We never saw anything like this!"

He went out again beside the sea; and all the 13 crowd gathered about him, and he taught them. And as he passed on, he saw Levi the 14 son of Alphaeus sitting at the tax office, and he said to him, "Follow me." And he rose and followed him.

---

* Other ancient authorities read *they* / Greek *to them* * Greek *he*
1.21-22: Mt 7.28-29; Lk 4.31-32. **1.23-28**: Lk 4.33-37. **1.24**: Jn 6.69. **1.29-31**: Mt 8.14-15; Lk 4.38-39.
1.32-34: Mt 8.16-17; Lk 4.40-41. **1.35-38**: Lk 4.42-43. **1.39**: Mt 4.23-25; Lk 4.44.
1.44: Lev 13.49; 14.2-32. **1.40-45**: Mt 8.2-4; Lk 5.12-16. **2.3-12**: Mt 9.2-8; Lk 5.18-26. **2.12**: Mt 9.33.
2.14-17: Mt 9.9-13; Lk 5.27-32.

Jesus eats with sinners

15 And as he sat at table in his house, many tax collectors and sinners were sitting with Jesus and his disciples; for there were many who 16 followed him. And the scribes of[h] the Pharisees, when they saw that he was eating with sinners and tax collectors, said to his disciples, "Why does he eat[i] with tax collectors 17 and sinners?" And when Jesus heard it, he said to them, "Those who are well have no need of a physician, but those who are sick; I came not to call the righteous, but sinners."

18 Now John's disciples and the Pharisees were fasting; and people came and said to him, "Why do John's disciples and the disciples of the Pharisees fast, but your 19 disciples do not fast?" And Jesus said to them, "Can the wedding guests fast while the bridegroom is with them? As long as they have the bridegroom with them, they cannot 20 fast. The days will come, when the bridegroom is taken away from them, and then 21 they will fast in that day. No one sews a piece of unshrunk cloth on an old garment; if he does, the patch tears away from it, the new 22 from the old, and a worse tear is made. And no one puts new wine into old wineskins; if he does, the wine will burst the skins, and the wine is lost, and so are the skins; but new wine is for fresh skins."[j]

In the grainfields

23 One sabbath he was going through the grainfields; and as they made their way his 24 disciples began to pluck ears of grain. And the Pharisees said to him, "Look, why are they doing what is not lawful on the sab-25 bath?" And he said to them, "Have you never read what David did, when he was in need and was hungry, he and those who were 26 with him: how he entered the house of God, when Abi'athar was high priest, and ate the bread of the Presence, which it is not lawful for any but the priests to eat, and also gave it 27 to those who were with him?" And he said to them, "The sabbath was made for man, 28 not man for the sabbath; so the Son of man is lord even of the sabbath."

A sabbath day

3 Again he entered the synagogue, and a man was there who had a withered hand. And 2 they watched him, to see whether he would heal him on the sabbath, so that they might accuse him. And he said to the man who had 3 the withered hand, "Come here." And he 4 said to them, "Is it lawful on the sabbath to do good or to do harm, to save life or to kill?" But they were silent. And he looked around 5 at them with anger, grieved at their hardness of heart, and said to the man, "Stretch out your hand." He stretched it out, and his hand was restored. The Pharisees went out, 6 and immediately held counsel with the Hero'di-ans against him, how to destroy him.

Jesus withdrew with his disciples to the sea, 7 and a great multitude from Galilee followed; also from Judea and Jerusalem and Idume'a 8 and from beyond the Jordan and from about Tyre and Sidon a great multitude, hearing all that he did, came to him. And he told his 9 disciples to have a boat ready for him because of the crowd, lest they should crush him; for 10 he had healed many, so that all who had diseases pressed upon him to touch him. And whenever the unclean spirits beheld 11 him, they fell down before him and cried out, "You are the Son of God." And he strictly 12 ordered them not to make him known.

The twelve apostles

And he went up into the hills, and called to 13 him those whom he desired; and they came to him. And he appointed twelve,[k] to be 14 with him, and to be sent out to preach and 15 have authority to cast out demons: Simon 16 whom he surnamed Peter; James the son of 17 Zeb'edee and John the brother of James, whom he surnamed Boaner'ges, that is, sons of thunder; Andrew, and Philip, and 18 Bartholomew, and Matthew, and Thomas, and James the son of Alphaeus, and Thaddaeus, and Simon the Cananaean, and Judas 19 Iscariot, who betrayed him.

Then he went home; and the crowd came 20 together again, so that they could not even eat. And when his friends heard it, they 21 went out to seize him, for they said, "He is beside himself." And the scribes who came 22 down from Jerusalem said, "He is possessed by Be-el'zebul, and by the prince of demons he casts out the demons." And he called 23 them to him, and said to them in parables, "How can Satan cast out Satan? If a 24

h Other ancient authorities read and   i Other ancient authorities add and drink
j Other ancient authorities omit but new wine is for fresh skins
k Other ancient authorities add whom also he named apostles
2.16: Acts 23.9.   2.18-22: Mt 9.14-17; Lk 5.33-38.   2.20: Lk 17.22.   2.23-28: Mt 12.1-8; Lk 6.1-5.
2.23: Deut 23.25.   2. 26: 1 Sam 21.1-6; 2 Sam 8.17.   2.27: Ex 23.12; Deut 5.14.   3.1-6: Mt 12.9-14; Lk 6.6-11.
3.2: Lk 11.54.   3.6: Mk 12.13.   3.7-12: Mt 4.24-25; 12.15-16; Lk 6.17-19.   3.8: Mt 11.21.
3.10: Mk 5.29, 34; 6.56.   3.12: Mk 1.25.   3.13: Mt 5.1; Lk 6.12.   3.14-15: Mt 10.1.
3.16-19: Mt 10.2-4; Lk 6.14-16; Acts 1.13.   3.19: Mk 2.1; 7.17.   3.20: Mk 6.31.
3.21: Mk 3.31-35; Jn 10.20.   3.22-27: Mt 12.24-29; Lk 11.15-22.   3.22: Mt 9.34; 10.25.

kingom is divided against itself, that
25 kingdom cannot stand. And if a house is
divided against itself, that house will not be
26 able to stand. And if Satan has risen up
against himself and is divided, he cannot
27 stand, but is coming to an end. But no one
can enter a strong man's house and plunder
his goods, unless he first binds the strong
man; then indeed he may plunder his house.
28 "Truly, I say to you, all sins will be forgiven
the sons of men, and whatever blasphemies
29 they utter; but whoever blasphemes against
the Holy Spirit never has forgiveness, but is
30 guilty of an eternal sin"—for they had said,
"He has an unclean spirit."

The mother and brothers of Jesus

31 And his mother and his brothers came; and
standing outside they sent to him and called
32 him. And a crowd was sitting about him;
and they said to him, "Your mother and your
33 brothers[l] are outside, asking for you." And
he replied, "Who are my mother and my
34 brothers?" And looking around on those who
sat about him, he said, "Here are my mother
35 and my brothers! Whoever does the will of
God is my brother, and sister, and mother."

Parables of the kingdom

4 Again he began to teach beside the sea.
And a very large crowd gathered about him,
so that he got into a boat and sat in it on the
sea; and the whole crowd was beside the sea
2 on the land. And he taught them many
things in parables, and in his teaching he said
3 to them: "Listen! A sower went out to
4 sow. And as he sowed, some seed fell along

the path, and the birds came and devoured
it. Other seed fell on rocky ground, where it 5
had not much soil, and immediately it sprang
up, since it had no depth of soil; and when 6
the sun rose it was scorched, and since it had
no root it withered away. Other seed fell 7
among thorns and the thorns grew up and
choked it, and it yielded no grain. And other 8
seeds fell into good soil and brought forth
grain, growing up and increasing and yielding thirtyfold and sixtyfold and a hundredfold." And he said, "He who has ears to 9
hear, let him hear."
And when he was alone, those who were 10
about him with the twelve asked him concerning the parables. And he said to them, 11
"To you has been given the secret of the
kingdom of God, but for those outside
everything is in parables; so that they may 12
indeed see but not perceive, and may indeed
hear but not understand; lest they should
turn again, and be forgiven." And he said to 13
them, "Do you not understand this parable?
How then will you understand all the parables? The sower sows the word. And these 14
are the ones along the path, where the word 15
is sown; when they hear, Satan immediately
comes and takes away the word which is
sown in them. And these in like manner are 16
the ones sown upon rocky ground, who,
when they hear the word, immediately
receive it with joy; and they have no root in 17
themselves, but endure for a while; then,
when tribulation or persecution arises on
account of the word, immediately they fall
away.[m] And others are the ones sown among 18
thorns; they are those who hear the word,
but the cares of the world, and the delight in 19
riches, and the desire for other things, enter
in and choke the word, and it proves
unfruitful. But those that were sown upon 20
the good soil are the ones who hear the word
and accept it and bear fruit, thirtyfold and
sixtyfold and a hundredfold."
And he said to them, "Is a lamp brought in 21
to be put under a bushel, or under a bed, and
not on a stand? For there is nothing hid, 22

[l] Other early authorities add *and your sisters*   [m] Or *stumble*
3.27: Is 49.24–25.   3.28–30: Mt 12.31–32; Lk 12.10.   3.31–35: Mt 12.46–50; Lk 8.19–21.
4.1–9: Mt 13.1–9; Lk 8.4–8.   4.10–12: Mt 13.10–15; Lk 8.9–10.
4.11: 1 Cor 5.12–13; Col 4.5; 1 Thess 4.12; 1 Tim 3.7.   4.12: Is 6.9–10.   4.13–20: Mt 13.18–23; Lk 8.11–15.
4.21: Mt 5.15; Lk 8.16; 11.33.   4.22: Mt 10.26; Lk 8.17; 12.2.

except to be made manifest; nor is anything
23 secret, except to come to light. If any man
24 has ears to hear, let him hear." And he said
to them, "Take heed what you hear; the
measure you give will be the measure you
25 get, and still more will be given you. For to
him who has will more be given; and from
him who has not, even what he has will be
taken away."

26 And he said, "The kingdom of God is as if a
man should scatter seed upon the ground,
27 and should sleep and rise night and day, and
the seed should sprout and grow, he knows
28 not how. The earth produces of itself, first
the blade, then the ear, then the full grain in
29 the ear. But when the grain is ripe, at once
he puts in the sickle, because the harvest has
come."

30 And he said, "With what can we compare
the kingdom of God, or what parable shall
31 we use for it? It is like a grain of mustard
32 seed, which, when sown upon the ground, is
the smallest of all the seeds on earth; yet
when it is sown it grows up and becomes the
greatest of all shrubs, and puts forth large
branches, so that the birds of the air can
make nests in its shade."

33 With many such parables he spoke the word
34 to them, as they were able to hear it; he did
not speak to them without a parable, but
privately to his own disciples he explained
everything.

A storm on the lake

35 On that day, when evening had come, he
said to them, "Let us go across to the other
36 side." And leaving the crowd, they took him
with them, just as he was, in the boat. And
37 other boats were with him. And a great
storm of wind arose, and the waves beat into
the boat, so that the boat was already filling.
38 But he was in the stern, asleep on the
cushion; and they woke him and said to him,
"Teacher, do you not care if we perish?"
39 And he awoke and rebuked the wind, and
said to the sea, "Peace! Be still!" And the
40 wind ceased, and there was a great calm. He
said to them, "Why are you afraid? Have
41 you no faith?" And they were filled with
awe, and said to one another, "Who then is
this, that even wind and sea obey him?"

The country of the Gerasenes

5 They came to the other side of the sea, to
2 the country of the Ger'asenes. [n] And when

he had come out of the boat, there met him
out of the tombs a man with an unclean spirit,
who lived among the tombs; and no one 3
could bind him any more, even with a chain;
for he had often been bound with fetters and 4
chains, but the chains he wrenched apart,
and the fetters he broke in pieces; and no
one had the strength to subdue him. Night 5
and day among the tombs and on the mountains he was always crying out, and bruising
himself with stones. And when he saw Jesus 6
from afar, he ran and worshipped him; and 7
crying out with a loud voice, he said, "What
have you to do with me, Jesus, Son of the
Most High God? I adjure you by God, do
not torment me." For he had said to him, 8
"Come out of the man, you unclean spirit!"
And Jesus[o] asked him, "What is your 9
name?" He replied, "My name is Legion;
for we are many." And he begged[o] him 10
eagerly not to send them out of the country.
Now a great herd of swine was feeding there 11
on the hillside; and they begged him, "Send 12
us to the swine, let us enter them." So he 13
gave them leave. And the unclean spirits
came out, and entered the swine; and
the herd, numbering about two thousand,
rushed down the steep bank into the sea, and
were drowned in the sea.

The herdsmen fled, and told it in the city 14
and in the country. And people came to see
what it was that had happened. And they 15
came to Jesus, and saw the demoniac sitting
there, clothed and in his right mind, the man
who had had the legion; and they were
afraid. And those who had seen it told what 16
had happened to the demoniac and to the
swine. And they began to beg Jesus[p] to 17
depart from their neighbourhood. And as he 18
was getting into the boat, the man who had
been possessed with demons begged him that
he might be with him. But he refused, and 19
said to him, "Go home to your friends, and
tell them how much the Lord has done for
you, and how he has had mercy on you."
And he went away and began to proclaim in 20
the Decap'olis how much Jesus had done for
him; and all men marvelled.

The daughter of Jairus

And when Jesus had crossed again in the 21
boat to the other side, a great crowd gathered
about him; and he was beside the sea. Then 22
came one of the rulers of the synagogue,
Ja'irus by name; and seeing him, he fell at his

n Other ancient authorities read *Gergesenes*, some *Gadarenes*
o Greek *he*　*p* Greek *him*
4.23: Mt 11.15; Mk 4.9.　**4.24:** Mt 7.2; Lk 6.38.　**4.25:** Mt 13.12; 25.29; Lk 8.18; 19.26.
4.26–29: Mt 13.24–30.　**4.30–32:** Mt 13.31–32; Lk 13.18–19.　**4.34:** Mt 13.34; Jn 16.25.
4.35–41: Mt 8.18, 23–27; Lk 8.22–25.　**5.1–20:** Mt 8.28–34; Lk 8.26–39.　**5.7:** Acts 16.17; Heb 7.1; Mk 1.24.
5.20: Mk 7.31.　**5.21–43:** Mt 9.18–26; Lk 8.40–56.　**5.22:** Lk 13.14; Acts 13.15; 18.8, 17.

23 feet, and besought him, saying, "My little daughter is at the point of death. Come and lay your hands on her, so that she may be 24 made well, and live." And he went with him.

And a great crowd followed him and 25 thronged about him. And there was a woman who had had a flow of blood for 26 twelve years, and who had suffered much under many physicians, and had spent all that she had, and was no better but rather 27 grew worse. She had heard the reports about Jesus, and came up behind him in the crowd 28 and touched his garment. For she said, "If I touch even his garments, I shall be made 29 well." And immediately the hemorrhage ceased; and she felt in her body that she was 30 healed of her disease. And Jesus, perceiving in himself that power had gone forth from him, immediately turned about in the crowd, and said, "Who touched my garments?" 31 And his disciples said to him, "You see the crowd pressing around you, and yet you say, 32 'Who touched me?'" And he looked around 33 to see who had done it. But the woman, knowing what had been done to her, came in fear and trembling and fell down before him, 34 and told him the whole truth. And he said to her, "Daughter, your faith has made you well; go in peace, and be healed of your disease."

35 While he was still speaking, there came from the ruler's house some who said, "Your daughter is dead. Why trouble the Teacher 36 any further?" But ignoring*q* what they said, Jesus said to the ruler of the synagogue, "Do 37 not fear, only believe." And he allowed no one to follow him except Peter and James 38 and John the brother of James. When they came to the house of the ruler of the synagogue, he saw a tumult, and people weeping 39 and wailing loudly. And when he had entered, he said to them, "Why do you make a tumult and weep? The child is not dead 40 but sleeping." And they laughed at him. But he put them all outside, and took the child's father and mother and those who were with him, and went in where the child 41 was. Taking her by the hand he said to her, "Tal′itha cu′mi"; which means, "Little girl, 42 I say to you, arise." And immediately the girl got up and walked; for she was twelve years old. And immediately they were over- 43 come with amazement. And he strictly charged them that no one should know this, and told them to give her something to eat.

Rejection at Nazareth

He went away from there and came to his 6 own country; and his disciples followed him. And on the sabbath he began to teach in the 2 synagogue; and many who heard him were astonished, saying, "Where did this man get all this? What is the wisdom given to him? What mighty works are wrought by his hands! Is not this the carpenter, the son of 3 Mary and brother of James and Joses and Judas and Simon, and are not his sisters here with us?" And they took offence*r* at him. And Jesus said to them, "A prophet is not 4 without honour, except in his own country, and among his own kin, and in his own house." And he could do no mighty work 5 there, except that he laid his hands upon a few sick people and healed them. And he 6 marvelled because of their unbelief.

And he went about among the villages teaching.

Interior of a synagogue

The apostles sent out

And he called to him the twelve, and began 7 to send them out two by two, and gave them authority over the unclean spirits. He 8 charged them to take nothing for their journey except a staff; no bread, no bag, no money in their belts; but to wear sandals and 9 not put on two tunics. And he said to them, 10

q Or *overhearing.* Other ancient authorities read *hearing*   *r* Or *stumbled*
5.23: Mk 6.5; 7.32; 8.23; Acts 9.17; 28.8.   5.30: Lk 5.17.   5.34: Lk 7.50; Mk 10.52.
5.37: Mk 9.2; 13.3.   5.41: Lk 7.14; Acts 9.40.   5.43: Mk 1.43-44; 7.36.   6.1-6: Mt 13.53-58; Lk 4.16-30.
6.2: Mk 1.21; Mt 7.28.   6.3: Mt 11.6.   6.5: Mk 5.23; 7.32; 8.23.   6.6: Mt 9.35.
6.7-11: Mt 10.1, 5, 7-11; Lk 9.1-5.   6.7: Lk 10.1.

"Where you enter a house, stay there until 1 you leave the place. And if any place will not receive you and they refuse to hear you, when you leave, shake off the dust that is on 2 your feet for a testimony against them." So they went out and preached that men should 3 repent. And they cast out many demons, and anointed with oil many that were sick and healed them.

Herod's alarm

4 King Herod heard of it; for Jesus's[s] name had become known. Some[t] said, "John the baptizer has been raised from the dead; that 5 is why these powers are at work in him." But others said, "It is Eli'jah." And others said, "It is a prophet, like one of the prophets of 6 old." But when Herod heard of it he said, "John, whom I beheaded, has been raised." 7 For Herod had sent and seized John, and bound him in prison for the sake of Hero'di-as, his brother Philip's wife; because he 8 had married her. For John said to Herod, "It is not lawful for you to have your 9 brother's wife." And Hero'di-as had a grudge against him, and wanted to kill him. 10 But she could not, for Herod feared John, knowing that he was a righteous and holy man, and kept him safe. When he heard him, he was much perplexed; and yet he 11 heard him gladly. But an opportunity came when Herod on his birthday gave a banquet for his courtiers and officers and the leading 12 men of Galilee. For when Hero'di-as' daughter came in and danced, she pleased Herod and his guests; and the king said to the girl, "Ask me for whatever you wish, and 13 I will grant it." And he vowed to her, "Whatever you ask me, I will give you, even 14 half of my kingdom." And she went out, and said to her mother, "What shall I ask?" And she said, "The head of John the baptizer." 15 And she came in immediately with haste to the king, and asked, saying, "I want you to give me at once the head of John the Baptist 16 on a platter." And the king was exceedingly sorry; but because of his oaths and his guests he did not want to break his word to her. 17 And immediately the king sent a soldier of the guard and gave orders to bring his head. He went and beheaded him in the prison, 18 and brought his head on a platter, and gave it to the girl; and the girl gave it to her mother. 19 When his disciples heard of it, they came and took his body, and laid it in a tomb.

In a lonely place

The apostles returned to Jesus, and told 30 him all that they had done and taught. And 31 he said to them, "Come away by yourselves to a lonely place, and rest a while." For many were coming and going, and they had no leisure even to eat. And they went away 32 in the boat to a lonely place by themselves. Now many saw them going, and knew them, 33 and they ran there on foot from all the towns, and got there ahead of them. As he landed 34 he saw a great throng, and he had compassion on them, because they were like sheep without a shepherd; and he began to teach them many things.

Five thousand fed

And when it grew late, his disciples came to 35 him and said, "This is a lonely place, and the hour is now late; send them away, to go into 36 the country and villages round about and buy themselves something to eat." But he 37 answered them, "You give them something to eat." And they said to him, "Shall we go and buy two hundred denarii[u] worth of bread, and give it to them to eat?" And he 38 said to them, "How many loaves have you? Go and see." And when they had found out, they said, "Five, and two fish." Then he 39 commanded them all to sit down by companies upon the green grass. So they sat 40 down in groups, by hundreds and by fifties. And taking the five loaves and the two fish he 41

looked up to heaven, and blessed, and broke the loaves, and gave them to the disciples to set before the people; and he divided the two fish among them all. And they all ate and 42 were satisfied. And they took up twelve 43 baskets full of broken pieces and of the fish. And those who ate the loaves were five 44 thousand men.

Across the lake

Immediately he made his disciples get into 45 the boat and go before him to the other side,

---

[s] Greek *his* [t] Other ancient authorities read *he* [u] The denarius was worth about seventeen pence
6.11: Mt 10.14. 6.12–13: Mt 11.1; Lk 9.6. 6.13: Jas 5.14. 6.14–16: Mt 14.1–2; Lk 9.7–9, 19; Mt 21.11.
6.17–18: Mt 14.3–4; Lk 3.19–20. 6.19–29: Mt 14.5–12. 6.20: Mt 21.26. 6.23: Esth 5.3, 6.
6.30–31: Lk 9.10; Mk 3.20. 6.32–44: Mt 14.13–21; Lk 9.11–17; Jn 6.5–13; Mk 8.1–10; Mt 15.32–39.
6.34: Mk 9.36. 6.37: 2 Kings 4.42–44. 6.41: Mk 14.22; Lk 24.30–31. 6.45–52: Mt 14.22–33; Jn 6.15–21.

to Beth-sa'ida, while he dismissed the
46 crowd. And after he had taken leave of them,
47 he went into the hills to pray. And when
evening came, the boat was out on the sea,
48 and he was alone on the land. And he saw
that they were distressed in rowing, for the
wind was against them. And about the
fourth watch of the night he came to them,
walking on the sea. He meant to pass by
49 them, but when they saw him walking on the
sea they thought it was a ghost, and cried
50 out; for they all saw him, and were terrified.
But immediately he spoke to them and said,
51 "Take heart, it is I; have no fear." And he
got into the boat with them and the wind
52 ceased. And they were utterly astounded, for
they did not understand about the loaves, but
their hearts were hardened.

53 And when they had crossed over, they came
to land at Gennes'aret, and moored to the
54 shore. And when they got out of the boat,
55 immediately the people recognised him, and
ran about the whole neighbourhood and
began to bring sick people on their pallets to
56 any place where they heard he was. And
wherever he came, in villages, cities, or
country, they laid the sick in the market
places, and besought him that they might
touch even the fringe of his garment; and as
many as touched it were made well.

Growing opposition

7 Now when the Pharisees gathered together
to him, with some of the scribes, who had
2 come from Jerusalem, they saw that some of
his disciples ate with hands defiled, that is,
3 unwashed. (For the Pharisees, and all the
Jews, do not eat unless they wash their
hands,[v] observing the tradition of the elders;
4 and when they come from the market place,
they do not eat unless they purify[w] themselves; and there are many other traditions
which they observe, the washing of cups and
5 pots and vessels of bronze.[x]) And the Pharisees and the scribes asked him, "Why do
your disciples not live[y] according to the
tradition of the elders, but eat with hands
6 defiled?" And he said to them, "Well did
Isaiah prophesy of you hypocrites, as it is
written,
'This people honours me with their lips,
but their heart is far from me;
7 in vain do they worship me,

teaching as doctrines the precepts of
men.'
You leave the commandment of God, and 8
hold fast the tradition of men."
And he said to them, "You have a fine way 9
of rejecting the commandment of God, in
order to keep your tradition! For Moses 10
said, 'Honour your father and your mother';
and, 'He who speaks evil of father or mother,
let him surely die'; but you say, 'If a man 11
tells his father or his mother, What you
would have gained from me is Corban' (that
is, given to God)[z]—then you no longer 12
permit him to do anything for his father or
mother, thus making void the word of God 13
through your tradition which you hand on.
And many such things you do."
And he called the people to him again, and 14
said to them, "Hear me, all of you, and
understand: there is nothing outside a man 15
which by going into him can defile him; but
the things which come out of a man are what
defile him."[a] And when he had entered the 17
house, and left the people, his disciples asked
him about the parable. And he said to them, 18
"Then are you also without understanding?
Do you not see that whatever goes into a man
from outside cannot defile him, since it 19
enters, not his heart but his stomach, and so
passes on?"[b] (Thus he declared all foods
clean.) And he said, "What comes out of a 20
man is what defiles a man. For from within, 21
out of the heart of man, come evil thoughts,
fornication, theft, murder, adultery, covet- 22
ing, wickedness, deceit, licentiousness, envy,
slander, pride, foolishness. All these evil 23
things come from within, and they defile a
man."

Tyre and Sidon

And from there he arose and went away to 24
the region of Tyre and Sidon.[c] And he
entered a house, and would not have any one
know it; yet he could not be hid. But 25
immediately a woman, whose little daughter
was possessed by an unclean spirit, heard of
him, and came and fell down at his feet.
Now the woman was a Greek, a Syrophoeni'- 26
cian by birth. And she begged him to cast
the demon out of her daughter. And he said 27
to her, "Let the children first be fed, for it is
not right to take the children's bread and
throw it to the dogs." But she answered him, 28

[v] One Greek word is of uncertain meaning and is not translated   [w] Other ancient authorities read *baptize*
[x] Other ancient authorities add *and beds*   [y] Greek *walk*   [z] Or *an offering*
[a] Other ancient authorities add verse 16, "If any man has ears to hear, let him hear"   [b] Or *is evacuated*
[c] Other ancient authorities omit *and Sidon*

6.48: Mk 13.35.   6.50: Mk 9.2.   6.52: Mk 8.17.   6.53-56: Mt 14.34-36.   6.56: Mk 3.10; Mt 9.20.
7.1-15: Mt 15.1-11; Lk 11.38.   7.4: Mt 23.25; Lk 11.39.   7.5: Gal 1.14.   7.6-7: Is 29.13.
7.10: Ex 20.12; Deut 5.16; Ex 21.17; Lev 20.9.   7.17-23: Mt 15.15-20; Mk 4.10.
7.18-19: 1 Cor 10.25-27; Rom 14.14; Tit 1.15; Acts 10.15.   7.20-23: Rom 1.28-31; Gal 5.19-21.
7.22: Mt 6.23; 20.15.   7.24-30: Mt 15.21-28.

Syrian dogs

"Yes, Lord; yet even the dogs under the
9 table eat the children's crumbs." And he
said to her, "For this saying you may go your
way; the demon has left your daughter."
o And she went home, and found the child
lying in bed, and the demon gone.

The region of the Decapolis

1 Then he returned from the region of Tyre,
and went through Sidon to the Sea of
Galilee, through the region of the Decap'-
2 olis. And they brought to him a man who
was deaf and had an impediment in his
speech; and they besought him to lay his
33 hand upon him. And taking him aside from
the multitude privately, he put his fingers
into his ears, and he spat and touched his
34 tongue; and looking up to heaven, he sighed,
and said to him, "Eph'phatha," that is, "Be
35 opened." And his ears were opened, his
tongue was released, and he spoke plainly.
36 And he charged them to tell no one; but the
more he charged them, the more zealously
37 they proclaimed it. And they were astonished beyond measure, saying, "He has done
all things well; he even makes the deaf hear
and the dumb speak."

Four thousand fed

8 In those days, when again a great crowd had
gathered, and they had nothing to eat, he
called his disciples to him, and said to them,
2 "I have compassion on the crowd, because
they have been with me now three days, and
3 have nothing to eat; and if I send them away
hungry to their homes, they will faint on the
way; and some of them have come a long
4 way." And his disciples answered him,
"How can one feed these men with bread
5 here in the desert?" And he asked them,

"How many loaves have you?" They said,
"Seven." And he commanded the crowd to 6
sit down on the ground; and he took the
seven loaves, and having given thanks he
broke them and gave them to his disciples to
set before the people; and they set them
before the crowd. And they had a few small 7
fish; and having blessed them, he commanded that these also should be set before
them. And they ate, and were satisfied; and 8
they took up the broken pieces left over,
seven baskets full. And there were about 9
four thousand people. And he sent them 10
away; and immediately he got into the boat
with his disciples, and went to the district of
Dalmanu'tha.[d]

Dalmanutha

The Pharisees came and began to argue 11
with him, seeking from him a sign from
heaven, to test him. And he sighed deeply in 12
his spirit, and said, "Why does this generation seek a sign? Truly, I say to you, no sign
shall be given to this generation." And he 13
left them, and getting into the boat again he
departed to the other side.
Now they had forgotten to bring bread; and 14
they had only one loaf with them in the boat.
And he cautioned them, saying, "Take heed, 15
beware of the leaven of the Pharisees and the
leaven of Herod."[e] And they discussed it 16
with one another, saying, "We have no
bread." And being aware of it, Jesus said to 17
them, "Why do you discuss the fact that you
have no bread? Do you not yet perceive or
understand? Are your hearts hardened?
Having eyes do you not see, and having 18
ears do you not hear? And do you not
remember? When I broke the five loaves for 19
the five thousand, how many baskets full of
broken pieces did you take up?" They said
to him, "Twelve." "And the seven for the 20
four thousand, how many baskets full of
broken pieces did you take up?" And they
said to him, "Seven." And he said to them, 21
"Do you not yet understand?"

Bethsaida

And they came to Beth-sa'ida. And some 22
people brought to him a blind man, and
begged him to touch him. And he took the 23
blind man by the hand, and led him out of
the village; and when he had spit on his eyes
and laid his hands upon him, he asked him,

d Other ancient authorities read *Magadan* or *Magdala*   *e* Other ancient authorities read *the Herodians*
7.31-37: Mt 15.29-31.   7.32: Mk 5.23.   7.33: Mk 1.44; 5.43.   7.36: Mk 1.44; 5.43.
8.1-10: Mt 15.32-39; Mk 6.32-44; Mt 14.13-21; Lk 9.11-17; Jn 6.5-13.
8.11-12: Mt 16.1-4; 12.38-39; Lk 11.29.   8.13-21: Mt 16.4-12.   8.15: Lk 12.1; Mk 6.14; 12.13.
8.17: Mk 6.52; Jer 5.21; Is 6.9-10; Mt 13.10-15.   8.19: Mk 6.41-44.   8.20: Mk 8.1-10.
8.22-26: Mk 10.46-52; Jn 9.1-7.   8.22: Mk 6.45; Lk 9.10.   8.23: Mk 7.33; 5.23.

24 "Do you see anything?" And he looked up and said, "I see men; but they look like trees, 25 walking." Then again he laid his hands upon his eyes; and he looked intently and was 26 restored, and saw everything clearly. And he sent him away to his home, saying, "Do not even enter the village."

Caesarea Philippi

27 And Jesus went on with his disciples, to the villages of Caesare′a Philippi; and on the way he asked his disciples, "Who do men say that 28 I am?" And they told him, "John the Baptist; and others say, Eli′jah; and others 29 one of the prophets." And he asked them, "But who do you say that I am?" Peter 30 answered him, "You are the Christ." And he charged them to tell no one about him.

31 And he began to teach them that the Son of man must suffer many things, and be rejected by the elders and the chief priests and the scribes, and be killed, and after three 32 days rise again. And he said this plainly. And Peter took him, and began to rebuke 33 him. But turning and seeing his disciples, he rebuked Peter, and said, "Get behind me, Satan! For you are not on the side of God, but of men."

34 And he called to him the multitude with his disciples, and said to them, "If any man would come after me, let him deny himself 35 and take up his cross and follow me. For whoever would save his life will lose it; and whoever loses his life for my sake and the 36 gospel's will save it. For what does it profit a man, to gain the whole world and forfeit his 37 life? For what can a man give in return for 38 his life? For whoever is ashamed of me and of my words in this adulterous and sinful generation, of him will the Son of man also be ashamed, when he comes in the glory of his Father with the holy angels."

9 And he said to them, "Truly, I say to you, there are some standing here who will not taste death before they see the kingdom of God come with power."

The transfiguration

2 And after six days Jesus took with him Peter and James and John, and led them up a high mountain apart by themselves; and he was transfigured before them, and his garments became glistening, intensely white, as no fuller on earth could bleach them. And there appeared to them Eli′jah with Moses; and they were talking to Jesus. And Peter said to Jesus, "Master,[f] it is well that we are here; let us make three booths, one for you and one for Moses and one for Eli′jah." For he did not know what to say, for they were exceedingly afraid. And a cloud overshadowed them, and a voice came out of the cloud, "This is my beloved Son;[g] listen to him." And suddenly looking around they no longer saw any one with them but Jesus only.

And as they were coming down the mountain, he charged them to tell no one what they had seen, until the Son of man should have risen from the dead. So they kept the matter to themselves, questioning what the rising from the dead meant. And they asked him, "Why do the scribes say that first Eli′jah must come?" And he said to them, "Eli′jah does come first to restore all things; and how is it written of the Son of man, that he should suffer many things and be treated with contempt? But I tell you that Eli′jah has come, and they did to him whatever they pleased, as it is written of him."

And when they came to the disciples, they saw a great crowd about them, and scribes arguing with them. And immediately all the crowd, when they saw him, were greatly amazed, and ran up to him and greeted him. And he asked them, "What are you discussing with them?" And one of the crowd answered him, "Teacher, I brought my son to you, for he has a dumb spirit; and wherever it seizes him, it dashes him down; and he foams and grinds his teeth and becomes rigid; and I asked your disciples to cast it out, and they were not able." And he answered them, "O faithless generation, how long am I to be with you? How long am I to bear with you? Bring him to me." And they brought the boy to him; and when the spirit saw him, immediately it convulsed the boy, and he fell on the ground and rolled about, foaming at the mouth. And Jesus[h] asked his father, "How long has he had this?" And he said, "From childhood. And it has often cast him into the fire and into the water, to destroy him; but if you can do anything, have pity on us and help us." And Jesus said to him, "If you can! All things are possible to him who believes." Immediately the father

---

f Or *Rabbi*   *g* Or *my Son, my* (or *the*) *Beloved*   *h* Greek *he*
8.27–30: Mt 16.13–20; Lk 9.18–21; Jn 6.66–69.   8.28: Mk 6.14.   8.30: Mk 9.9; 1.34.
8.31–9.1: Mt 16.21–28; Lk 9.22–27.   8.33: Mt 4.10.   8.34: Mt 10.38; Lk 14.27.
8.35: Mt 10.39; Lk 17.33; Jn 12.25.   8.38: Mt 10.33; Lk 12.9.   9.1: Mk 13.30; Mt 10.23; Lk 22.18.
9.2–8: Mt 17.1–8; Lk 9.28–36.   9.2: Mk 5.37; 13.3.   9.3: Mt 28.3.
9.7: 2 Pet 1.17–18; Mt 3.17; Jn 12.28–29.   9.9–13: Mt 17.9–13; Lk 9.36.   9.9: Mk 8.30; 5.43; 7.36.
9.11: Mt 11.14.   9.12: Mk 8.31; 9.31; 10.33.   9.14–27: Mt 17.14–18; Lk 9.37–43.
9.23: Mt 17.20; Lk 17.6; Mk 11.22–24.

THE COUNTRY OF JESUS

of the child cried out[i] and said, "I believe;
25 help my unbelief!" And when Jesus saw
that a crowd came running together, he
rebuked the unclean spirit, saying to it, "You
dumb and deaf spirit, I command you, come
26 out of him, and never enter him again." And
after crying out and convulsing him terribly,
it came out, and the boy was like a corpse; so
27 that most of them said, "He is dead." But
Jesus took him by the hand and lifted him
28 up, and he arose. And when he had entered
the house, his disciples asked him privately,
29 "Why could we not cast it out?" And he
said to them, "This kind cannot be driven
out by anything but prayer."[j]
30 They went on from there and passed
through Galilee. And he would not have any
31 one know it; for he was teaching his disciples,
saying to them, "The Son of man will be
delivered into the hands of men, and they
will kill him; and when he is killed, after
32 three days he will rise." But they did not
understand the saying, and they were afraid
to ask him.

Capernaum

33 And they came to Caper'na-um; and when
he was in the house he asked them, "What
34 were you discussing on the way?" But they
were silent; for on the way they had discussed with one another who was the
35 greatest. And he sat down and called the
twelve; and he said to them, "If any one
would be first, he must be last of all and
36 servant of all." And he took a child, and put
him in the midst of them; and taking him in
37 his arms, he said to them, "Whoever receives
one such child in my name receives me; and
whoever receives me, receives not me but
him who sent me."
38 John said to him, "Teacher, we saw a man
casting out demons in your name,[k] and we
forbade him, because he was not following
39 us." But Jesus said, "Do not forbid him; for
no one who does a mighty work in my name
will be able soon after to speak evil of me.
40, For he that is not against us is for us. For
41 truly, I say to you, whoever gives you a cup
of water to drink because you bear the name
of Christ, will by no means lose his reward.
42 "Whoever causes one of these little ones
who believe in me to sin,[l] it would be better

for him if a great millstone were hung round
his neck and he were thrown into the sea.
And if your hand causes you to sin,[l] cut it 43
off; it is better for you to enter life maimed
than with two hands to go to hell,[m] to the
unquenchable fire.[n] And if your foot causes 45
you to sin,[l] cut if off; it is better for you to
enter life lame than with two feet to be
thrown into hell.[m],[n] And if your eye causes 47
you to sin,[l] pluck it out; it is better for you to
enter the kingdom of God with one eye than
with two eyes to be thrown into hell,[m] where 48
their worm does not die, and the fire is not
quenched. For every one will be salted with 49
fire.[o] Salt is good; but if the salt has lost 50
its saltness, how will you season it? Have
salt in yourselves, and be at peace with one
another."

JESUS IN JUDEA

Beyond the Jordan

A ND he left there and went to the region 10
of Judea and beyond the Jordan, and
crowds gathered to him again; and again, as
his custom was, he taught them.
And Pharisees came up and in order to test 2
him asked, "Is it lawful for a man to divorce
his wife?" He answered them, "What did 3
Moses command you?" They said, "Moses 4
allowed a man to write a certificate of
divorce, and to put her away." But Jesus 5
said to them, "For your hardness of heart he
wrote you this commandment. But from the 6
beginning of creation, 'God made them male
and female.' 'For this reason a man shall 7
leave his father and mother and be joined to
his wife,[p] and the two shall become one.'[q] So 8
they are no longer two but one.[q] What 9

[i] Other ancient authorities add *with tears*   [j] Other ancient authorities add *and fasting*
[k] Other ancient authorities add *who does not follow us*   [l] Greek *stumble*   [m] Greek *Gehenna*
[n] Verses 44 and 46 (which are identical with verse 48) are omitted by the best ancient authorities
[o] Other ancient authorities add *and every sacrifice will be salted with salt*
[p] Other ancient authorities omit *and be joined to his wife*   [q] Greek *one flesh*
9.30–32: Mt 17.22–23; Lk 9.43–45.   **9.31**: Mk 8.31; 10.33.   **9.32**: Jn 12.16.   **9.33–37**: Mt 18.1–5; Lk 9.46–48.
9.34: Lk 22.24.   **9.35**: Mk 10.43–44; Mt 20.26–27; 23.11; Lk 22.26.   **9.36**: Mk 10.16.
9.37: Mt 10.40; Lk 10.16; Jn 12.44; 13.20.   **9.38–40**: Lk 9.49–50; 11.23; Mt 12.30; Num 11.27–29.
9.41: Mt 10.42.   **9.42–48**: Mt 18.6–9; 5.29–30; Lk 17.1–2.   **9.48**: Is 66.24.   **9.49–50**: Mt 5.13; Lk 14.34–35.
9.50: Col 4.6; 1 Thess 5.13.   **10.1–12**: Mt 19.1–9.   **10.1**: Lk 9.51; Jn 10.40; 11.7.   **10.4**: Deut 24.1–4.
10.6: Gen 1.27; 5.2.   **10.7–8**: Gen 2.24.

therefore God has joined together, let not man put asunder."

¹⁰ And in the house the disciples asked him ¹¹ again about this matter. And he said to them, "Whoever divorces his wife and marries another, commits adultery against her; ¹² and if she divorces her husband and marries another, she commits adultery."

¹³ And they were bringing children to him, that he might touch them; and the disciples ¹⁴ rebuked them. But when Jesus saw it he was indignant, and said to them, "Let the children come to me, do not hinder them; for ¹⁵ to such belongs the kingdom of God. Truly, I say to you, whoever does not receive the kingdom of God like a child shall not enter ¹⁶ it." And he took them in his arms and blessed them, laying his hands upon them.

¹⁷ And as he was setting out on his journey, a man ran up and knelt before him, and asked him, "Good Teacher, what must I do to ¹⁸ inherit eternal life?" And Jesus said to him, "Why do you call me good? No one is good ¹⁹ but God alone. You know the commandments: 'Do not kill, Do not commit adultery, Do not steal, Do not bear false witness, Do not defraud, Honour your father and ²⁰ mother.'" And he said to him, "Teacher, all ²¹ these I have observed from my youth." And Jesus looking upon him loved him, and said to him, "You lack one thing; go, sell what you have, and give to the poor, and you will have treasure in heaven; and come, follow ²² me." At that saying his countenance fell, and he went away sorrowful; for he had great possessions.

²³ And Jesus looked around and said to his disciples, "How hard it will be for those who ²⁴ have riches to enter the kingdom of God!" And the disciples were amazed at his words. But Jesus said to them again, "Children, how ²⁵ hard it isʳ to enter the kingdom of God! It is easier for a camel to go through the eye of a needle than for a rich man to enter the ²⁶ kingdom of God." And they were exceedingly astonished, and said to him,ˢ "Then ²⁷ who can be saved?" Jesus looked at them and said, "With men it is impossible, but not with God; for all things are possible with ²⁸ God." Peter began to say to him, "Lo, we have left everything and followed you." ²⁹ Jesus said, "Truly, I say to you, there is no one who has left house or brothers or sisters or mother or father or children or lands, ³⁰ for my sake and for the gospel, who will not

receive a hundredfold now in this time, houses and brothers and sisters and mothers and children and lands, with persecutions, and in the age to come eternal life. But many ³¹ that are first will be last, and the last first."

On the way to Jerusalem

And they were on the road, going up to ³² Jerusalem, and Jesus was walking ahead of them; and they were amazed, and those who followed were afraid. And taking the twelve again, he began to tell them what was to happen to him, saying, "Behold, we are ³³ going up to Jerusalem; and the Son of man will be delivered to the chief priests and the scribes, and they will condemn him to death, and deliver him to the Gentiles; and they will ³⁴ mock him, and spit upon him, and scourge him, and kill him; and after three days he will rise."

The sons of Zebedee

And James and John, the sons of Zeb′edee, ³⁵ came forward to him, and said to him, "Teacher, we want you to do for us whatever we ask of you." And he said to them, "What ³⁶ do you want me to do for you?" And they ³⁷ said to him, "Grant us to sit, one at your right hand and one at your left, in your glory." But Jesus said to them, "You do not ³⁸ know what you are asking. Are you able to drink the cup that I drink, or to be baptized with the baptism with which I am baptized?" And they said to him, "We are ³⁹ able." And Jesus said to them, "The cup that I drink you will drink; and with the baptism with which I am baptized, you will be baptized; but to sit at my right hand or at ⁴⁰ my left is not mine to grant, but it is for those for whom it has been prepared." And when ⁴¹ the ten heard it, they began to be indignant at James and John. And Jesus called them to ⁴² him and said to them, "You know that those who are supposed to rule over the Gentiles lord it over them, and their great men exercise authority over them. But it shall not ⁴³ be so among you; but whoever would be great among you must be your servant, and ⁴⁴ whoever would be first among you must be slave of all. For the Son of man also came ⁴⁵ not to be served but to serve, and to give his life as a ransom for many."

ʳ Other ancient authorities add *for those who trust in riches* ˢ Other ancient authorities read *to one another* **10.11:** Mt 5.32; Lk 16.18; 1 Cor 7.10–11; Rom 7.2–3. **10.13–16:** Mt 19.13–15; 18.3; Lk 18.15–17. **10.16:** Mk 9.36. **10.17–31:** Mt 19.16–30; Lk 18.18–30. **10.17:** Lk 10.25; Mk 1.40. **10.19:** Ex 20.12–16; Deut 5.16–20. **10.21:** Mt 6.20; Lk 12.33; Acts 2.45; 4.34–35. **10.28:** Mk 1.16–20. **10.30:** Mk 6.33. **10.31:** Mt 20.16; Lk 13.30. **10.32–34:** Mt 20.17–19; Lk 18.31–34. **10.33:** Mk 8.31; 9.12; 9.33. **10.34:** Mk 14.65; 15.19, 26–32. **10.35–45:** Mt 20.20–28. **10.37:** Mt 19.28; Lk 22.30. **10.38:** Lk 12.50; Jn 18.11. **10.39:** Acts 12.2; Rev 1.9. **10.42–45:** Lk 22.25–27. **10.43:** Mk 9.35. **10.45:** 1 Tim 2.5–6.

Jericho

46 And they came to Jericho; and as he was leaving Jericho with his disciples and a great multitude, Bartimae'us, a blind beggar, the son of Timae'us, was sitting by the roadside. 47 And when he heard that it was Jesus of Nazareth, he began to cry out and say, "Jesus, Son of David, have mercy on me!" 48 And many rebuked him, telling him to be silent; but he cried out all the more, "Son of 49 David, have mercy on me!" And Jesus

stopped and said, "Call him." And they called the blind man, saying to him, "Take heart; rise, he is calling you." And throwing 50 off his mantle he sprang up and came to Jesus. And Jesus said to him, "What do you 51 want me to do for you?" And the blind man said to him, "Master,† let me receive my sight." And Jesus said to him, "Go your 52 way; your faith has made you well." And immediately he received his sight and followed him on the way.

Bethany

HOLY WEEK

Sunday

11 AND when they drew near to Jerusalem, to Beth'phage and Bethany, at the Mount of Olives, he sent two of his disciples, 2 and said to them, "Go into the village opposite you, and immediately as you enter it you will find a colt tied, on which no one has 3 ever sat; untie it and bring it. If any one says to you, 'Why are you doing this?' say, 'The Lord has need of it and will send it back here 4 immediately.'" And they went away, and found a colt tied at the door out in the open

street; and they untied it. And those who 5 stood there said to them, "What are you doing, untying the colt?" And they told 6 them what Jesus had said; and they let them go. And they brought the colt to Jesus, and 7 threw their garments on it; and he sat upon it. And many spread their garments on the 8 road, and others spread leafy branches which they had cut from the fields. And those who 9 went before and those who followed cried out, "Hosanna! Blessed is he who comes in the name of the Lord! Blessed is the 10 kingdom of our father David that is coming! Hosanna in the highest!"

And he entered Jerusalem, and went into 11

† Or *Rabbi*
10.46–52: Mt 20.29–34; Lk 18.35–43; Mk 8.22–26. **10.47:** Mt 9.27.
10.52: Mt 9.22; Mk 5.34; Lk 7.50; 8.48; 17.19. **11.1–10:** Mt 21.1–9; Lk 19.29–38. **11.4:** Mk 14.16.
11.7–10: Jn 12.12–15. **11.9:** Ps 118.26; Mt 21.15; 23.39. **11.11:** Mt 21.10–11, 17.

the temple; and when he had looked round at everything, as it was already late, he went out to Bethany with the twelve.

Monday

12 On the following day, when they came from
13 Bethany, he was hungry. And seeing in the distance a fig tree in leaf, he went to see if he could find anything on it. When he came to it, he found nothing but leaves, for it was not
14 the season for figs. And he said to it, "May no one ever eat fruit from you again." And his disciples heard it.

15 And they came to Jerusalem. And he entered the temple and began to drive out those who sold and those who bought in the temple, and he overturned the tables of the money-changers and the seats of those who
16 sold pigeons; and he would not allow any one
17 to carry anything through the temple. And he taught, and said to them, "Is it not written, 'My house shall be called a house of prayer for all the nations'? But you have
18 made it a den of robbers." And the chief priests and the scribes heard it and sought a way to destroy him; for they feared him, because all the multitude was astonished at
19 his teaching. And when evening came they[u] went out of the city.

Tuesday

20 As they passed by in the morning, they saw the fig tree withered away to its roots.
21 And Peter remembered and said to him, "Master,[v] look! The fig tree which you
22 cursed has withered." And Jesus answered
23 them, "Have faith in God. Truly, I say to you, whoever says to this mountain, 'Be taken up and cast into the sea,' and does not doubt in his heart, but believes that what he says will come to pass, it will be done for
24 him. Therefore I tell you, whatever you ask in prayer, believe that you receive it, and you
25 will. And whenever you stand praying, forgive, if you have anything against any one; so that your Father also who is in heaven may forgive you your trespasses."[w]
27 And they came again to Jerusalem. And as he was walking in the temple, the chief priests and the scribes and the elders came
28 to him, and they said to him, "By what authority are you doing these things, or who
29 gave you this authority to do them?" Jesus said to them, "I will ask you a question;

answer me, and I will tell you by what authority I do these things. Was the baptism 30 of John from heaven or from men? Answer me." And they argued with one another, "If 31 we say, 'From heaven,' he will say, 'Why then did you not believe him?' But shall we 32 say, 'From men'?"—they were afraid of the people, for all held that John was a real prophet. So they answered Jesus, "We 33 do not know." And Jesus said to them, "Neither will I tell you by what authority I do these things."

And he began to speak to them in parables.**12** "A man planted a vineyard, and set a hedge around it, and dug a pit for the wine press, and built a tower, and let it out to tenants, and went into another country. When the 2 time came, he sent a servant to the tenants, to get from them some of the fruit of the vineyard. And they took him and beat him, 3 and sent him away empty-handed. Again he 4 sent to them another servant, and they wounded him in the head, and treated him shamefully. And he sent another, and him 5 they killed; and so with many others, some they beat and some they killed. He had still 6 one other, a beloved son; finally he sent him to them, saying, 'They will respect my son.' But those tenants said to one another, 'This 7 is the heir; come, let us kill him, and the inheritance will be ours.' And they took him 8 and killed him, and cast him out of the vineyard. What will the owner of the 9 vineyard do? He will come and destroy the tenants, and give the vineyard to others. Have you not read this scripture: 10

A vineyard watchtower

[u] Other ancient authorities read *he*   [v] Or *Rabbi*   [w] Other ancient authorities add verse 26, "*But if you do not forgive, neither will your Father who is in heaven forgive your trespasses*"
11.12–14: Mt 21.18–19; Lk 13.6–9.   **11.15–18:** Mt 21.12–16; Lk 19.45–48; Jn 2.13–16.
11.17: Is 56.7; Jer 7.11.   **11.19:** Lk 21.37.   **11.20–25:** Mt 21.20–22; Mt 17.20; Lk 17.6.
11.24: Jn 14.13–14; 16.23; Mt 7.7–11.   **11.25:** Mt 6.14–15; 18.35.
11.27–33: Mt 21.23–27; Lk 20.1–8; Jn 2.18.   **12.1–12:** Mt 21.33–46; Lk 20.9–19; Is 5.1–7.
12.10–11: Ps 118.22–23; Acts 4.11; I Pet 2.7.

'The very stone which the builders rejected
has become the head of the corner;
11 this was the Lord's doing,
and it is marvellous in our eyes'?"

12 And they tried to arrest him, but feared the multitude, for they perceived that he had told the parable against them; so they left him and went away.

13 And they sent to him some of the Pharisees and some of the Hero′di-ans, to entrap him 14 in his talk. And they came and said to him, "Teacher, we know that you are true, and care for no man; for you do not regard the position of men, but truly teach the way of God. Is it lawful to pay taxes to Caesar, or 15 not? Should we pay them, or should we not?" But knowing their hypocrisy, he said to them, "Why put me to the test? Bring me 16 a coin,ˣ and let me look at it." And they brought one. And he said to them, "Whose likeness and inscription is this?" They said 17 to him, "Caesar's." Jesus said to them, "Render to Caesar the things that are Caesar's, and to God the things that are God's." And they were amazed at him.

18 And Sad′ducees came to him, who say that there is no resurrection; and they asked him a 19 question, saying, "Teacher, Moses wrote for us that if a man's brother dies and leaves a wife, but leaves no child, the manʸ must take the wife, and raise up children for his 20 brother. There were seven brothers; the first took a wife, and when he died left no 21 children; and the second took her, and died, leaving no children; and the third likewise; 22 and the seven left no children. Last of all the 23 woman also died. In the resurrection whose wife will she be? For the seven had her as wife."

24 Jesus said to them, "Is not this why you are wrong, that you know neither the scriptures 25 nor the power of God? For when they rise from the dead, they neither marry nor are given in marriage, but are like angels in 26 heaven. And as for the dead being raised, have you not read in the book of Moses, in the passage about the bush, how God said to him, 'I am the God of Abraham, and the 27 God of Isaac, and the God of Jacob'? He is not God of the dead, but of the living; you are quite wrong."

28 And one of the scribes came up and heard them disputing with one another, and seeing that he answered them well, asked him,

"Which commandment is the first of all?" Jesus answered, "The first is, 'Hear, O 29 Israel: The Lord our God, the Lord is one; and you shall love the Lord your God with 30 all your heart, and with all your soul, and with all your mind, and with all your strength.' The second is this, 'You shall love 31 your neighbour as yourself.' There is no other commandment greater than these." And the scribe said to him, "You are right, 32 Teacher; you have truly said that he is one, and there is no other but he; and to love him 33 with all the heart, and with all the understanding, and with all the strength, and to love one's neighbour as oneself, is much more than all whole burnt offerings and sacrifices." And when Jesus saw that he 34 answered wisely, he said to him, "You are not far from the kingdom of God." And after that no one dared to ask him any question.

And as Jesus taught in the temple, he said, 35 "How can the scribes say that the Christ is the son of David? David himself, inspired 36 byᶻ the Holy Spirit, declared,
'The Lord said to my Lord,
Sit at my right hand,
till I put thy enemies under thy feet.'
David himself calls him Lord; so how is he 37 his son?" And the great throng heard him gladly.

And in his teaching he said, "Beware of the 38 scribes, who like to go about in long robes, and to have salutations in the market places and the best seats in the synagogues and the 39 places of honour at feasts, who devour 40 widows' houses and for a pretence make long prayers. They will receive the greater condemnation."

And he sat down opposite the treasury, and 41 watched the multitude putting money into the treasury. Many rich people put in large sums. And a poor widow came, and put in 42 two copper coins, which make a penny. And 43 he called his disciples to him, and said to them, "Truly, I say to you, this poor widow has put in more than all those who are contributing to the treasury. For they all 44 contributed out of their abundance; but she out of her poverty has put in everything she had, her whole living."

And as he came out of the temple, one of his 13 disciples said to him, "Look, Teacher, what

---

ˣ Greek *a denarius*   ʸ Greek *his brother*   ᶻ Or *himself, in*
12.12: Mk 11.18.   12.13-17: Mt 22.15-22; Lk 20.20-26.   12.13: Mk 3.6; Lk 11.54.   12.17: Rom 13.7.
12.18-27: Mt 22.23-33; Lk 20.27-38.   12.19: Deut 25.5.   12.26: Ex 3.6.
12.28-34: Mt 22.34-40; Lk 20.39-40; 10.25-28.   12.29: Deut 6.4.
12.31: Lev 19.18; Rom 13.9; Gal 5.14; Jas 2.8.   12.33: 1 Sam 15.22; Hos 6.6; Mic 6.6-8; Mt 9.13.
12.35-37: Mt 22.41-46; Lk 20.41-44.   12.36: Ps 110.1; Acts 2.34-35; Heb 1.13.
12.38-40: Mt 23.5-7; Lk 20.46-47; 11.43.   12.41-44: Lk 21.1-4; Jn 8.20.
13.1-37: Mt 24; Lk 21.5-36.

wonderful stones and what wonderful build-
2 ings!" And Jesus said to him, "Do you see
these great buildings? There will not be left
here one stone upon another, that will not be
thrown down."

3 And as he sat on the Mount of Olives
opposite the temple, Peter and James and
4 John and Andrew asked him privately, "Tell
us, when will this be, and what will be
the sign when these things are all to be
5 accomplished?" And Jesus began to say to
them, "Take heed that no one leads you
6 astray. Many will come in my name, saying,
'I am he!' and they will lead many astray.
7 And when you hear of wars and rumours of
wars, do not be alarmed; this must take
8 place, but the end is not yet. For nation will
rise against nation, and kingdom against
kingdom; there will be earthquakes in
various places, there will be famines; this is
but the beginning of the sufferings.
9 "But take heed to yourselves; for they will
deliver you up to councils; and you will be
beaten in synagogues; and you will stand
before governors and kings for my sake, to
10 bear testimony before them. And the gospel
11 must first be preached to all nations. And
when they bring you to trial and deliver you
up, do not be anxious beforehand what you
are to say; but say whatever is given you in
that hour, for it is not you who speak, but the
12 Holy Spirit. And brother will deliver up
brother to death, and the father his child, and
children will rise against parents and have
13 them put to death; and you will be hated by
all for my name's sake. But he who endures
to the end will be saved.
14 "But when you see the desolating sacrilege
set up where it ought not to be (let the reader
15 understand), then let those who are in Judea
flee to the mountains; let him who is on the
housetop not go down, nor enter his house,
16 to take anything away; and let him who is in
the field not turn back to take his mantle.
17 And alas for those who are with child and for
18 those who give suck in those days! Pray that
19 it may not happen in winter. For in those
days there will be such tribulation as has not
been from the beginning of the creation
which God created until now, and never will
20 be. And if the Lord had not shortened the
days, no human being would be saved; but
for the sake of the elect, whom he chose, he
21 shortened the days. And then if any one says
to you, 'Look, here is the Christ!' or 'Look,
22 there he is!' do not believe it. False Christs

and false prophets will arise and show signs
and wonders, to lead astray, if possible, the
elect. But take heed; I have told you all 23
things beforehand.
"But in those days, after that tribulation, 24
the sun will be darkened, and the moon will
not give its light, and the stars will be falling 25
from heaven, and the powers in the heavens
will be shaken. And then they will see the 26
Son of man coming in clouds with great
power and glory. And then he will send out 27
the angels, and gather his elect from the four
winds, from the ends of the earth to the ends
of heaven.
"From the fig tree learn its lesson: as soon 28
as its branch becomes tender and puts forth
its leaves, you know that summer is near. So 29
also, when you see these things taking place,
you know that he is near, at the very gates.
Truly, I say to you, this generation will not 30
pass away before all these things take place.
Heaven and earth will pass away, but my 31
words will not pass away.
"But of that day or that hour no one knows, 32
not even the angels in heaven, nor the Son,
but only the Father. Take heed, watch;[a] for 33
you do not know when the time will come. It 34
is like a man going on a journey, when he
leaves home and puts his servants in charge,
each with his work, and commands the
doorkeeper to be on the watch. Watch 35
therefore—for you do not know when the
master of the house will come, in the
evening, or at midnight, or at cockcrow, or in
the morning—lest he come suddenly and 36
find you asleep. And what I say to you I say 37
to all: Watch."

Wednesday

It was now two days before the Passover 14
and the feast of Unleavened Bread. And the
chief priests and the scribes were seeking
how to arrest him by stealth, and kill him; for 2
they said, "Not during the feast, lest there be
a tumult of the people."

JERUSALEM
1¾
MILES
BETHANY

---

[a] Other ancient authorities add *and pray*
13.2: Lk 19.43-44; Mk 14.58; 15.29; Jn 2.19; Acts 6.14.   13.3: Mk 5.37; 9.2.   13.4: Lk 17.20.
13.6: Jn 8.24; 1 Jn 2.18.   13.9-13: Mt 10.17-22.   13.11: Jn 14.26; 16.7-11; Lk 12.11-12.   13.13: Jn 15.21.
13.14: Dan 9.27; 11.31; 12.11.   13.17: Lk 23.29.   13.22: Mt 7.15; Jn 4.48.
13.26: Mt 8.38; Mt 10.23; Dan 7.13.   13.30: Mk 9.1.   13.31: Mt 5.18; Lk 16.17.   13.32: Acts 1.7.
13.33: Eph 6.18; Col 4.2.   13.34: Mt 25.14.   13.35: Lk 12.35-40.   14.1-2: Mt 26.1-5; Lk 22.1-2; Jn 11.47-53.

Alabaster ware

3 And while he was at Bethany in the house of Simon the leper, as he sat at table, a woman came with an alabaster jar of ointment of pure nard, very costly, and she broke the jar 4 and poured it over his head. But there were some who said to themselves indignantly, 5 "Why was the ointment thus wasted? For this ointment might have been sold for more than three hundred denarii,*b* and given to the 6 poor." And they reproached her. But Jesus said, "Let her alone; why do you trouble her? She has done a beautiful thing to me. 7 For you always have the poor with you, and whenever you will, you can do good to them; 8 but you will not always have me. She has done what she could; she has anointed my 9 body beforehand for burying. And truly, I say to you, wherever the gospel is preached in the whole world, what she has done will be told in memory of her."

10 Then Judas Iscariot, who was one of the twelve, went to the chief priests in order to 11 betray him to them. And when they heard it they were glad, and promised to give him money. And he sought an opportunity to betray him.

Thursday

12 And on the first day of Unleavened Bread, when they sacrificed the passover lamb, his disciples said to him, "Where will you have us go and prepare for you to eat the pass-13 over?" And he sent two of his disciples, and said to them, "Go into the city, and a man carrying a jar of water will meet you; 14 follow him, and wherever he enters, say to the householder, 'The Teacher says, Where is my guest room, where I am to eat the 15 passover with my disciples?' And he will show you a large upper room furnished and 16 ready; there prepare for us." And the disciples set out and went to the city, and found

it as he had told them; and they prepared the passover.

17 And when it was evening he came with the twelve. And as they were at table eating, 18 Jesus said, "Truly, I say to you, one of you will betray me, one who is eating with me." 19 They began to be sorrowful, and to say to him one after another, "Is it I?" He said to 20 them, "It is one of the twelve, one who is dipping bread in the same dish with me. For 21 the Son of man goes as it is written of him, but woe to that man by whom the Son of man is betrayed! It would have been better for that man if he had not been born."

22 And as they were eating, he took bread, and blessed, and broke it, and gave it to them, and said, "Take; this is my body." And he 23 took a cup, and when he had given thanks he gave it to them, and they all drank of it. And 24 he said to them, "This is my blood of the*c* covenant, which is poured out for many. 25 Truly, I say to you, I shall not drink again of the fruit of the vine until that day when I drink it new in the kingdom of God."

26 And when they had sung a hymn, they went out to the Mount of Olives. And Jesus said 27 to them, "You will all fall away; for it is written, 'I will strike the shepherd, and the sheep will be scattered.' But after I am 28 raised up, I will go before you to Galilee." 29 Peter said to him, "Even though they all fall away, I will not." And Jesus said to him, 30 "Truly, I say to you, this very night, before the cock crows twice, you will deny me three times." But he said vehemently, "If I must 31

---

b The denarius was worth about seventeen pence   *c* Other ancient authorities insert *new*

14.3-9: Mt 26.6-13; Lk 7.36-38; Jn 12.1-8. **14.7:** Deut 15.11. **14.8:** Jn 19.40.
14.10-11: Mt 26.14-16; Lk 22.3-6. **14.12-16:** Mt 26.17-19; Lk 22.7-13.
14.17-21: Mt 26.20-25; Lk 22.14, 21-23; Jn 13.21-30; Ps 41.9.
14.22-25: Mt 26.26-29; Lk 22.17-19; 1 Cor 11.23-26. **14.22:** Mk 6.41; 8.6; Lk 24.30. **14.23:** 1 Cor 10.16.
14.24: Ex 24.8; Heb 9.20. **14.26-31:** Mt 26.30-35; Lk 22.39, 33-34. **14.27:** Zech 13.7; Jn 16.32.
14.28: Mk 16.7. **14.30:** Mk 14.66-72; Jn 13.36-38; 18.17-18, 25-27.

die with you, I will not deny you." And they all said the same.

32 And they went to a place which was called Gethsem'ane; and he said to his disciples, 33 "Sit here, while I pray." And he took with him Peter and James and John, and began to 34 be greatly distressed and troubled. And he said to them, "My soul is very sorrowful, even to death; remain here, and watch."[d] 35 And going a little farther, he fell on the ground and prayed that, if it were possible, 36 the hour might pass from him. And he said, "Abba, Father, all things are possible to thee; remove this cup from me; yet not what 37 I will, but what thou wilt." And he came

And they laid hands on him and seized him. 46 But one of those who stood by drew his 47 sword, and struck the slave of the high priest and cut off his ear. And Jesus said to them, 48 "Have you come out as against a robber, with swords and clubs to capture me? Day after 49 day I was with you in the temple teaching, and you did not seize me. But let the scriptures be fulfilled." And they all forsook 50 him, and fled.

And a young man followed him, with 51 nothing but a linen cloth about his body; and

and found them sleeping, and he said to Peter, "Simon, are you asleep? Could you 38 not watch[d] one hour? Watch[d] and pray that you may not enter into temptation; the spirit 39 indeed is willing, but the flesh is weak." And again he went away and prayed, saying the 40 same words. And again he came and found them sleeping, for their eyes were very heavy; and they did not know what to answer 41 him. And he came the third time, and said to them, "Are you still sleeping and taking your rest? It is enough; the hour has come; the Son of man is betrayed into the hands of 42 sinners. Rise, let us be going; see, my betrayer is at hand."

43 And immediately, while he was still speaking, Judas came, one of the twelve, and with him a crowd with swords and clubs, from the chief priests and the scribes and the 44 elders. Now the betrayer had given them a sign, saying, "The one I shall kiss is the man; 45 seize him and lead him away safely." And when he came, he went up to him at once, and said, "Master!"[e] And he kissed him.

they seized him, but he left the linen cloth 52 and ran away naked.

Friday

And they led Jesus to the high priest; and 53 all the chief priests and the elders and the scribes were assembled. And Peter had 54 followed him at a distance, right into the courtyard of the high priest; and he was sitting with the guards, and warming himself at the fire. Now the chief priests and the 55 whole council sought testimony against Jesus to put him to death; but they found none. For many bore false witness against him, and 56 their witness did not agree. And some stood 57 up and bore false witness against him, saying, "We heard him say, 'I will destroy this 58 temple that is made with hands, and in three days I will build another, not made with hands.'" Yet not even so did their tes- 59 timony agree. And the high priest stood up 60 in the midst, and asked Jesus, "Have you no answer to make? What is it that these men

[d] Or *keep awake* [e] Or *Rabbi*
14.32–42: Mt 26.36–46; Lk 22.40–46; Heb 5.7–8. 14.34: Jn 12.27.
14.36: Rom 8.15; Gal 4.6; Mk 10.38; Jn 18.11. 14.38: Mt 6.13; Lk 11.4.
14.43–50: Mt 26.47–56; Lk 22.47–53; Jn 18.2–11. 14.49: Lk 19.47; Jn 18.19–21.
14.53–65: Mt 26.57–68; Lk 22.54–55, 63–71; Jn 18.12–24. 14.58: Mk 13.2; 15.29; Acts 6.14; Jn 2.19.

61 testify against you?" But he was silent and made no answer. Again the high priest asked him, "Are you the Christ, the Son of the 62 Blessed?" And Jesus said, "I am; and you will see the Son of man sitting at the right hand of Power, and coming with the clouds 63 of heaven." And the high priest tore his mantle, and said, "Why do we still need 64 witnesses? You have heard his blasphemy. What is your decision?" And they all con- 65 demned him as deserving death. And some began to spit on him, and to cover his face, and to strike him, saying to him, "Prophesy!" And the guards received him with blows.

66 And as Peter was below in the courtyard, 67 one of the maids of the high priest came; and seeing Peter warming himself, she looked at him, and said, "You also were with the 68 Nazarene, Jesus." But he denied it, saying, "I neither know nor understand what you mean." And he went out into the gateway.*f* 69 And the maid saw him, and began again to say to the bystanders, "This man is one of 70 them." But again he denied it. And after a little while again the bystanders said to Peter, "Certainly you are one of them; for you are a 71 Galilean." But he began to invoke a curse on himself and to swear, "I do not know this 72 man of whom you speak." And immediately the cock crowed a second time. And Peter remembered how Jesus had said to him, "Before the cock crows twice, you will deny me three times." And he broke down and wept.

15 And as soon as it was morning the chief priests, with the elders and scribes, and the whole council held a consultation; and they bound Jesus and led him away and delivered him to Pilate. And Pilate asked him, "Are 2 you the King of the Jews?" And he answered him, "You have said so." And the 3 chief priests accused him of many things. And Pilate again asked him, "Have you no 4 answer to make? See how many charges they bring against you." But Jesus made no 5 further answer, so that Pilate wondered.

Now at the feast he used to release for them 6 one prisoner whom they asked. And among 7 the rebels in prison, who had committed murder in the insurrection, there was a man called Barab′bas. And the crowd came up 8 and began to ask Pilate to do as he was wont to do for them. And he answered them, "Do 9 you want me to release for you the King of the Jews?" For he perceived that it was out 10 of envy that the chief priests had delivered him up. But the chief priests stirred up the 11 crowd to have him release for them Barab′- bas instead. And Pilate again said to 12 them, "Then what shall I do with the man whom you call the King of the Jews?" And 13 they cried out again, "Crucify him." And 14 Pilate said to them, "Why, what evil has he done?" But they shouted all the more, "Crucify him." So Pilate, wishing to satisfy 15 the crowd, released for them Barab′bas; and having scourged Jesus, he delivered him to be crucified.

And the soldiers led him away inside the 16 palace (that is, the praetorium); and they called together the whole battalion. And 17 they clothed him in a purple cloak, and plaiting a crown of thorns they put it on him. And they began to salute him, "Hail, 18 King of the Jews!" And they struck his head 19 with a reed, and spat upon him, and they

---

f Or *fore-court*. Other ancient authorities add *and the cock crowed*
14.62: Dan 7.13; Mk 9.1; 13.26.   **14.63:** Acts 14.14; Num 14.6.   **14.64:** Lev 24.16.
14.66–72: Mt 26.69–75; Lk 22.56–62; Jn 18.16–18, 25–27; Mk 14.30.   **15.1:** Mt 27.1–2; Lk 23.1; Jn 18.28.
15.2–15: Mt 27.11–26; Lk 23.2–3, 18–25; Jn 18.29–19.16.
15.11: Acts 3.14.   **15.16–20:** Mt 27.27–31; Lk 23.11; Jn 19.2–3.

20 knelt down in homage to him. And when they had mocked him, they stripped him of the purple cloak, and put his own clothes on him. And they led him out to crucify him.

21 And they compelled a passer-by, Simon of Cyre′ne, who was coming in from the country, the father of Alexander and Rufus,

22 to carry his cross. And they brought him to the place called Gol′gotha (which means the

23 place of a skull). And they offered him wine mingled with myrrh; but he did not take it.

24 And they crucified him, and divided his garments among them, casting lots for them,

25 to decide what each should take. And it was the third hour, when they crucified him.

26 And the inscription of the charge against him

27 read, "The King of the Jews." And with him they crucified two robbers, one on his

29 right and one on his left.[g] And those who passed by derided him, wagging their heads, and saying, "Aha! You who would destroy

30 the temple and build it in three days, save yourself, and come down from the cross!"

31 So also the chief priests mocked him to one another with the scribes, saying, "He saved

32 others; he cannot save himself. Let the Christ, the King of Israel, come down now from the cross, that we may see and believe." Those who were crucified with him also reviled him.

33 And when the sixth hour had come, there was darkness over the whole land[h] until the

34 ninth hour. And at the ninth hour Jesus cried with a loud voice, "E′lo-i, E′lo-i, la′ma sabach-tha′ni?" which means, "My God, my

35 God, why hast thou forsaken me?" And some of the bystanders hearing it said,

36 "Behold, he is calling Eli′jah." And one ran and, filling a sponge full of vinegar, put it on a reed and gave it to him to drink, saying, "Wait, let us see whether Eli′jah will come to

37 take him down." And Jesus uttered a loud

38 cry, and breathed his last. And the curtain of the temple was torn in two, from top to

39 bottom. And when the centurion, who stood facing him, saw that he thus[i] breathed his last, he said, "Truly this man was the Son[j] of God!"

40 There were also women looking on from afar, among whom were Mary Mag′dalene, and Mary the mother of James the younger

41 and of Joses, and Salo′me, who, when he was in Galilee, followed him, and ministered to

him; and also many other women who came up with him to Jerusalem.

42 And when evening had come, since it was the day of Preparation, that is, the day before

43 the sabbath, Joseph of Arimathe′a, a respected member of the council, who was also himself looking for the kingdom of God, took courage and went to Pilate, and asked for the body of Jesus. And Pilate wondered

44 if he were already dead; and summoning the centurion, he asked him whether he was

A centurion

45 already dead.[k] And when he learned from the centurion that he was dead, he granted the body to Joseph. And he bought a linen

46 shroud, and taking him down, wrapped him in the linen shroud, and laid him in a tomb which had been hewn out of the rock; and he rolled a stone against the door of the tomb.

47 Mary Mag′dalene and Mary the mother of Joses saw where he was laid.

Sunday

16 And when the sabbath was past, Mary Mag′dalene, and Mary the mother of James,

---

[g] Other ancient authorities insert verse 28, *And the scripture was fulfilled which says, "He was reckoned with the transgressors"*
[h] Or *earth* [i] Other ancient authorities insert *cried out and* [j] Or *a son*
[k] Other ancient authorities read *whether he had been some time dead*
15.21: Mt 27.32; Lk 23.26; Rom 16.13. 15.22-32: Mt 27.33-44; Lk 23.33-39; Jn 19.17-24.
15.24: Ps 22.18. 15.29: Mk 13.2; 14.58; Jn 2.19. 15.31: Ps 22.7-8.
15.33-41: Mt 27.45-56; Lk 23.44-49; Jn 19.28-30. 15.34: Ps 22.1. 15.36: Ps 69.21. 15.38: Heb 10.19-20.
15.39: Mk 1.11; 9.7. 15.40: Jn 19.25. 15.41: Lk 8.1-3.
15.42-47: Mt 27.57-61; Lk 23.50-56; Jn 19.38-42; Acts 13.29. 15.42: Deut 21.22-23.
16.1-8: Mt 28.1-8; Lk 24.1-10; Jn 20.1-2. 16.1: Lk 23.56; Jn 19.39.

and Salo'me, bought spices, so that they 2 might go and anoint him. And very early on the first day of the week they went to the 3 tomb when the sun had risen. And they were saying to one another, "Who will roll away the stone for us from the door of the tomb?" 4 And looking up, they saw that the stone was 5 rolled back; for it was very large. And entering the tomb, they saw a young man sitting on the right side, dressed in a white 6 robe; and they were amazed. And he said to them, "Do not be amazed; you seek Jesus of Nazareth, who was crucified. He has risen, he is not here; see the place where they laid him. But go, tell his disciples and Peter that 7 he is going before you to Galilee; there you will see him, as he told you." And they went 8 out and fled from the tomb; for trembling and astonishment had come upon them; and they said nothing to any one, for they were afraid.[l]

[l] Other texts and versions add as Mk 16.9-20 the following passage:

9 *Now when he rose early on the first day of the week, he appeared first to Mary Magdalene, from whom he had cast out seven demons.* 10 *She went and told those who had been with him, as they mourned and wept.* 11 *But when they heard that he was alive and had been seen by her, they would not believe it.*

12 *After this he appeared in another form to two of them, as they were walking into the country.* 13 *And they went back and told the rest, but they did not believe them.*

14 *Afterward he appeared to the eleven themselves as they sat at table; and he upbraided them for their unbelief and hardness of heart, because they had not believed those who saw him after he had risen.* 15 *And he said to them, "Go into all the world and preach the gospel to the whole creation.* 16 *He who believes and is baptized will be saved; but he who does not believe will be condemned.* 17 *And these signs will accompany those who believe: in my name they will cast out demons; they will speak in new tongues;* 18 *they will pick up serpents, and if they drink any deadly thing, it will not hurt them; they will lay their hands on the sick, and they will recover."*

19 *So then the Lord Jesus, after he had spoken to them, was taken up into heaven, and sat down at the right hand of God.* 20 *And they went forth and preached everywhere, while the Lord worked with them and confirmed the message by the signs that attended it. Amen.*

Other ancient authorities add after verse 8 the following: *But they reported briefly to Peter and those with him all that they had been told. And after this, Jesus himself sent out by means of them, from east to west, the sacred and imperishable proclamation of eternal salvation.*

16.7: Mk 14.28; Jn 21.1-23; Mt 28.7.

NAZARETH

THE GOSPEL ACCORDING TO

LUKE

INASMUCH as many have undertaken
to compile a narrative of the things
which have been accomplished among
2 us, just as they were delivered to us by those
who from the beginning were eyewitnesses
3 and ministers of the word, it seemed good to
me also, having followed all things closely[a]
for some time past, to write an orderly
account for you, most excellent Theoph'ilus,
that you may know the truth concerning the
things of which you have been informed.

THE BIRTH AND BOYHOOD OF JESUS

5 IN the days of Herod, king of Judea, there
was a priest named Zechari'ah,[b] of the
division of Abi'jah; and he had a wife of the
daughters of Aaron, and her name was
6 Elizabeth. And they were both righteous
before God, walking in all the commandments and ordinances of the Lord blameless.
7 But they had no child, because Elizabeth was
barren, and both were advanced in years.
8 Now while he was serving as priest before
9 God when his division was on duty, according to the custom of the priesthood, it fell to
him by lot to enter the temple of the Lord
10 and burn incense. And the whole multitude
of the people were praying outside at the
11 hour of incense. And there appeared to him
an angel of the Lord standing on the right
12 side of the altar of incense. And Zechari'ah

was troubled when he saw him, and fear fell
upon him. But the angel said to him, "Do 13
not be afraid, Zechari'ah, for your prayer is
heard, and your wife Elizabeth will bear you
a son, and you shall call his name John.
And you will have joy and gladness,   14
  and many will rejoice at his birth;
for he will be great before the Lord,   15
  and he shall drink no wine nor strong
    drink,
and he will be filled with the Holy Spirit,
  even from his mother's womb.
And he will turn many of the sons of Israel 16
  to the Lord their God,
and he will go before him in the spirit and 17
  power of Eli'jah,
to turn the hearts of the fathers to the
  children,

[a] Or *accurately*   [b] Greek *Zacharias*
1.2: 1 Jn 1.1; Acts 1.21; Heb 2. 3.   **1.3:** Acts 1.1.   **1.4:** Jn 20.31.   **1.5:** Mt 2.1; 1 Chron 24.10; 2 Chron 31.2.
1.9: Ex 30.7.   **1.11:** Lk 2.9; Acts 5.19.   **1.13:** Lk 1.30, 60.   **1.15:** Num 6.3; Lk 7.33.
1.17: Mt 11.14; 17.13; Mal 4.5.

and the disobedient to the wisdom of the just,
to make ready for the Lord a people prepared."

18 And Zechari′ah said to the angel, "How shall I know this? For I am an old man, and my 19 wife is advanced in years." And the angel answered him, "I am Gabriel, who stand in the presence of God; and I was sent to speak to you, and to bring you this good news.

David; and the virgin's name was Mary. And he came to her and said, "Hail, O 28 favoured one, the Lord is with you!"[c] But 29 she was greatly troubled at the saying, and considered in her mind what sort of greeting this might be. And the angel said to her, 30 "Do not be afraid, Mary, for you have found favour with God. And behold, you will 31 conceive in your womb and bear a son, and you shall call his name Jesus.

The well at Nazareth

20 And behold, you will be silent and unable to speak until the day that these things come to pass, because you did not believe my words, 21 which will be fulfilled in their time." And the people were waiting for Zechari′ah, and they wondered at his delay in the temple. 22 And when he came out, he could not speak to them, and they perceived that he had seen a vision in the temple; and he made signs to 23 them and remained dumb. And when his time of service was ended, he went to his home.

24 After these days his wife Elizabeth conceived, and for five months she hid herself, 25 saying, "Thus the Lord has done to me in the days when he looked on me, to take away my reproach among men."

The annunciation

26 In the sixth month the angel Gabriel was sent from God to a city of Galilee named 27 Nazareth, to a virgin betrothed to a man whose name was Joseph, of the house of

He will be great, and will be called the Son 32 of the Most High;
and the Lord God will give to him the throne of his father David,
and he will reign over the house of Jacob 33 for ever;
and of his kingdom there will be no end."
And Mary said to the angel, "How can this 34 be, since I have no husband?" And the 35 angel said to her,
"The Holy Spirit will come upon you,
and the power of the Most High will overshadow you;
therefore the child to be born[d] will be called holy,
the Son of God.
And behold, your kinswoman Elizabeth in 36 her old age has also conceived a son; and this is the sixth month with her who was called barren. For with God nothing will be 37 impossible." And Mary said, "Behold, I am 38 the handmaid of the Lord; let it be to me according to your word." And the angel departed from her.

In those days Mary arose and went with 39

[c] Other ancient authorities add *"Blessed are you among women!"*   [d] Other ancient authorities add *of you*
1.18: Lk 1.34.   1.19: Dan 8.16; 9.21; Mt 18.10.   1.25: Gen 30.23; Is 4.1.   1.30: Lk 1.13.
1.31: Lk 2.21; Mt 1.21.   1.33: Mt 28.18; Dan 2.44.   1.34: Lk 1.18.   1.35: Mt 1.20.   1.37: Gen 18.14.

LUKE 2

839

haste into the hill country, to a city of Judah,
10 and she entered the house of Zechari′ah and
11 greeted Elizabeth. And when Elizabeth
heard the greeting of Mary, the babe leaped
in her womb; and Elizabeth was filled with
12 the Holy Spirit and she exclaimed with a
loud cry, "Blessed are you among women,
13 and blessed is the fruit of your womb! And
why is this granted me, that the mother of
14 my Lord should come to me? For behold,
when the voice of your greeting came to my
ears, the babe in my womb leaped for joy.
15 And blessed is she who believed that there
would be[e] a fulfilment of what was spoken to
her from the Lord."

The Magnificat

46 And Mary said,
"My soul magnifies the Lord,
47 and my spirit rejoices in God my Saviour,
48 for he has regarded the low estate of his
handmaiden.
For behold, henceforth all generations will
call me blessed;
49 for he who is mighty has done great things
for me,
and holy is his name.
50 And his mercy is on those who fear him
from generation to generation.
51 He has shown strength with his arm,
he has scattered the proud in the imagination of their hearts,
52 he has put down the mighty from their
thrones,
and exalted those of low degree;
53 he has filled the hungry with good things,
and the rich he has sent empty away.
54 He has helped his servant Israel,
in remembrance of his mercy,
55 as he spoke to our fathers,
to Abraham and to his posterity for ever."
56 And Mary remained with her about three
months, and returned to her home.
57 Now the time came for Elizabeth to be
58 delivered, and she gave birth to a son. And
her neighbours and kinsfolk heard that the
Lord had shown great mercy to her, and they
59 rejoiced with her. And on the eighth day
they came to circumcise the child; and they
would have named him Zechari′ah after his
60 father, but his mother said, "Not so; he shall
61 be called John." And they said to her,
"None of your kindred is called by this
62 name." And they made signs to his father,
inquiring what he would have him called.

And he asked for a writing tablet, and wrote, 63
"His name is John." And they all marvelled. And immediately his mouth was 64
opened and his tongue loosed, and he spoke,
blessing God. And fear came on all their 65
neighbours. And all these things were talked
about through all the hill country of Judea; 66
and all who heard them laid them up in their
hearts, saying, "What then will this child
be?" For the hand of the Lord was with
him.

The Benedictus

And his father Zechari′ah was filled with 67
the Holy Spirit, and prophesied, saying,
"Blessed be the Lord God of Israel, 68
for he has visited and redeemed his people,
and has raised up a horn of salvation for us 69
in the house of his servant David,
as he spoke by the mouth of his holy 70
prophets from of old,
that we should be saved from our enemies, 71
and from the hand of all who hate us;
to perform the mercy promised to our 72
fathers,
and to remember his holy covenant,
the oath which he swore to our father 73
Abraham, to grant us 74
that we, being delivered from the hand of
our enemies,
might serve him without fear,
in holiness and righteousness before him 75
all the days of our life.
And you, child, will be called the prophet 76
of the Most High;
for you will go before the Lord to prepare
his ways,
to give knowledge of salvation to his 77
people
in the forgiveness of their sins,
through the tender mercy of our God, 78
when the day shall dawn upon[f] us from on
high
to give light to those who sit in darkness 79
and in the shadow of death,
to guide our feet into the way of peace."
And the child grew and became strong in 80
spirit, and he was in the wilderness till the
day of his manifestation to Israel.

In those days a decree went out from Caesar 2
Augustus that all the world should be enrolled. This was the first enrolment, when 2
Quirin′i-us was governor of Syria. And all 3
went to be enrolled, each to his own city.

---

e Or *believed, for there will be*
f Or *whereby the dayspring will visit.* Other ancient authorities read *since the dayspring has visited*
1.42: Lk 11.27–28. 1.46–55: 1 Sam 2.1–10. 1.47: 1 Tim 2.3; Tit 2.10; Jude 25.
1.55: Mic 7.20; Gen 17.7; 18.18; 22.17. 1.59: Lev 12.3; Gen 17.12. 1.63: Lk 1.13.
1.76: Lk 7.26; Mal 4.5. 1.77: Mk 1.4. 1.78: Mal 4.2; Eph 5.14. 1.79: Is 9.2; Mt 4.16. 1.80: Lk 2.40; 2.52.
2.1: Lk 3.1.

4 And Joseph also went up from Galilee, from the city of Nazareth, to Judea, to the city of David, which is called Bethlehem, because
5 he was of the house and lineage of David, to be enrolled with Mary, his betrothed, who
6 was with child. And while they were there,
7 the time came for her to be delivered. And she gave birth to her first-born son and wrapped him in swaddling cloths, and laid him in a manger, because there was no place for them in the inn.

The angels' song

8 And in that region there were shepherds out in the field, keeping watch over their flock by
9 night. And an angel of the Lord appeared to them, and the glory of the Lord shone around them, and they were filled with fear.
10 And the angel said to them, "Be not afraid; for behold, I bring you good news of a great
11 joy which will come to all the people; for to you is born this day in the city of David a
12 Saviour, who is Christ the Lord. And this will be a sign for you: you will find a babe wrapped in swaddling cloths and lying in a
13 manger." And suddenly there was with the angel a multitude of the heavenly host praising God and saying,
14   "Glory to God in the highest,
         and on earth peace among men with whom
            he is pleased!" [g]
15 When the angels went away from them into heaven, the shepherds said to one another, "Let us go over to Bethlehem and see this thing that has happened, which the Lord has
16 made known to us." And they went with haste, and found Mary and Joseph, and the
17 babe lying in a manger. And when they saw it they made known the saying which had
18 been told them concerning this child; and all

who heard it wondered at what the shepherds told them. But Mary kept all these things, 19 pondering them in her heart. And the 20 shepherds returned, glorifying and praising God for all they had heard and seen, as it had been told them.

And at the end of eight days, when he was 21 circumcised, he was called Jesus, the name given by the angel before he was conceived in the womb.

And when the time came for their purifica- 22 tion according to the law of Moses, they brought him up to Jerusalem to present him to the Lord (as it is written in the law of the 23 Lord, "Every male that opens the womb shall be called holy to the Lord") and to offer 24 a sacrifice according to what is said in the law of the Lord, "a pair of turtledoves, or two young pigeons."

The song of Simeon

Now there was a man in Jerusalem, whose 25 name was Simeon, and this man was right-eous and devout, looking for the consolation of Israel, and the Holy Spirit was upon him. And it had been revealed to him by the Holy 26 Spirit that he should not see death before he had seen the Lord's Christ. And inspired by 27 the Spirit[h] he came into the temple; and when the parents brought in the child Jesus, to do for him according to the custom of the law, he took him up in his arms and blessed 28 God and said,
      "Lord, now lettest thou thy servant depart 29
         in peace,
      according to thy word;
      for mine eyes have seen thy salvation   30
      which thou hast prepared in the presence 31
         of all peoples,
      a light for revelation to the Gentiles,   32
      and for glory to thy people Israel."
And his father and his mother marvelled 33 at what was said about him; and Simeon 34 blessed them and said to Mary his mother,
      "Behold, this child is set for the fall and
         rising of many in Israel,
      and for a sign that is spoken against
      (and a sword will pierce through your own 35
         soul also),
      that thoughts out of many hearts may be
         revealed."
And there was a prophetess, Anna, the 36 daughter of Phan'u-el, of the tribe of Asher; she was of a great age, having lived with her husband seven years from her virginity, and 37 as a widow till she was eighty-four. She did

g Other ancient authorities read *peace, good will among men*   *h* Or *in the Spirit*
2.4: Lk 1.27.   2.9: Lk 1.11; Acts 5.19.   2.11: Jn 4.42; Acts 5.31; Mt 16.16; Acts 2.36.
2.12: I Sam 2.34; 2 Kings 19.29; Is 7.14.   2.14: Lk 19.38; 3.22.   2.19: Lk 2.51.   2.21: Lk 1.59, 31; Mt 1.25.
2.22–24: Lev 12.2–8.   2.23: Ex 13.2, 12.   2.25: Lk 2.38; 23.51.   2.30: Is 52.10; Lk 3.6.
2.32: Is 42.6; 49.6; Acts 13.47; 26.23.   2.36: Acts 21.9; Josh 19.24; I Tim 5.9.

not depart from the temple, worshipping
38 with fasting and prayer night and day. And
coming up at that very hour she gave thanks
to God, and spoke of him to all who were
looking for the redemption of Jerusalem.
39 And when they had performed everything
according to the law of the Lord, they
returned into Galilee, to their own city,
40 Nazareth. And the child grew and became
strong, filled with wisdom; and the favour of
God was upon him.

The boyhood of Jesus

41 Now his parents went to Jerusalem every
42 year at the feast of the Passover. And when
he was twelve years old, they went up
according to custom; and when the feast was 43
ended, as they were returning, the boy Jesus
stayed behind in Jerusalem. His parents did
not know it, but supposing him to be in 44
the company they went a day's journey, and
they sought him among their kinsfolk and
acquaintances; and when they did not find 45
him, they returned to Jerusalem, seeking
him. After three days they found him in the 46
temple, sitting among the teachers, listening
to them and asking them questions; and all 47
who heard him were amazed at his understanding and his answers. And when they 48
saw him they were astonished; and his
mother said to him, "Son, why have you
treated us so? Behold, your father and I
have been looking for you anxiously." And 49
he said to them, "How is it that you sought
me? Did you not know that I must be in
my Father's house?" And they did not 50
understand the saying which he spoke to
them. And he went down with them and 51
came to Nazareth, and was obedient to them;
and his mother kept all these things in her
heart.
    And Jesus increased in wisdom and in 52
stature,[i] and in favour with God and man.

BAPTISM AND TEMPTATION

3 IN the fifteenth year of the reign of
Tibe'ri-us Caesar, Pontius Pilate being
governor of Judea, and Herod being tetrarch
of Galilee, and his brother Philip tetrarch of
the region of Iturae'a and Trachoni'tis, and
2 Lysa'ni-as tetrarch of Abile'ne, in the high-
priesthood of Annas and Ca'iaphas, the word
of God came to John the son of Zechari'ah in
3 the wilderness; and he went into all the
region about the Jordan, preaching a baptism
of repentance for the forgiveness of sins. As 4
it is written in the book of the words of Isaiah
the prophet,
    "The voice of one crying in the wilder-
          ness:
    Prepare the way of the Lord,
    make his paths straight.
    Every valley shall be filled,   5

[i] Or years
2.40: Judg 13.24; 1 Sam 2.26. 2.41: Deut 16.1–8; Ex 23.15. 2.48: Mk 3.31–35. 2.51: Lk 2.19.
2.52: Lk 1.80; 2.40. 3.1: Lk 23.1; 9.7; 13.31; 23.7. 3.2: Jn 18.13; Acts 4.6; Mt 26.3; Jn 11.49.
3.3–9: Mt 3.1–10; Mk 1.1–5; Jn 1.6, 23. 3.4–6: Is 40.3–5.

and every mountain and hill shall be
brought low,
and the crooked shall be made straight,
and the rough ways shall be made smooth;
6 and all flesh shall see the salvation of
God."

7 He said therefore to the multitudes that
came out to be baptized by him, "You brood
of vipers! Who warned you to flee from the
8 wrath to come? Bear fruits that befit repentance, and do not begin to say to yourselves,
'We have Abraham as our father'; for I tell
you, God is able from these stones to raise up
9 children to Abraham. Even now the axe is
laid to the root of the trees; every tree
therefore that does not bear good fruit is cut
down and thrown into the fire."

10 And the multitudes asked him, "What then
11 shall we do?" And he answered them, "He
who has two coats, let him share with him
who has none; and he who has food, let him
12 do likewise." Tax collectors also came to be
baptized, and said to him, "Teacher, what
13 shall we do?" And he said to them, "Collect
14 no more than is appointed you." Soldiers
also asked him, "And we, what shall we
do?" And he said to them, "Rob no one by
violence or by false accusation, and be content with your wages."

15 As the people were in expectation, and all
men questioned in their hearts concerning
John, whether perhaps he were the Christ,
16 John answered them all, "I baptize you with
water; but he who is mightier than I is
coming, the thong of whose sandals I am not
worthy to untie; he will baptize you with the
17 Holy Spirit and with fire. His winnowing
fork is in his hand, to clear his threshing
floor, and to gather the wheat into his
granary, but the chaff he will burn with
unquenchable fire."

18 So, with many other exhortations, he
19 preached good news to the people. But
Herod the tetrarch, who had been reproved
by him for Hero'di-as, his brother's wife, and
for all the evil things that Herod had done,
20 added this to them all, that he shut up John
in prison.

The baptism of Jesus

21 Now when all the people were baptized,
and when Jesus also had been baptized and
22 was praying, the heaven was opened, and the
Holy Spirit descended upon him in bodily
form, as a dove, and a voice came from
heaven, "Thou art my beloved Son;[j] with
thee I am well pleased."[k]

Family records

23 Jesus, when he began his ministry, was
about thirty years of age, being the son (as
24 was supposed) of Joseph, the son of Heli, the
son of Matthat, the son of Levi, the son
of Melchi, the son of Jan'na-i, the son of
25 Joseph, the son of Mattathi'as, the son of
Amos, the son of Nahum, the son of Esli, the
26 son of Nag'ga-i, the son of Ma'ath, the son of
Mattathi'as, the son of Sem'e-in, the son of
27 Josech, the son of Joda, the son of Jo-an'an,
the son of Rhesa, the son of Zerub'babel, the
28 son of Sheal'ti-el,[l] the son of Neri, the son of
Melchi, the son of Addi, the son of Cosam,
29 the son of Elma'dam, the son of Er, the son
of Joshua, the son of Elie'zer, the son of
Jorim, the son of Matthat, the son of Levi,
30 the son of Simeon, the son of Judah, the
son of Joseph, the son of Jonam, the son
31 of Eli'akim, the son of Me'le-a, the son of
Menna, the son of Mat'tatha, the son of
32 Nathan, the son of David, the son of Jesse,
the son of Obed, the son of Bo'az, the son
33 of Sala, the son of Nahshon, the son of
Ammin'adab, the son of Admin, the son of
Arni, the son of Hezron, the son of Perez, the
34 son of Judah, the son of Jacob, the son of
Isaac, the son of Abraham, the son of Terah,
35 the son of Nahor, the son of Serug, the son of
Re'u, the son of Peleg, the son of Eber, the
36 son of Shelah, the son of Ca-i'nan, the son
of Arphax'ad, the son of Shem, the son
37 of Noah, the son of Lamech, the son of
Methu'selah, the son of Enoch, the son
of Jared, the son of Maha'lale-el, the son of
38 Ca-i'nan, the son of Enos, the son of Seth,
the son of Adam, the son of God.

The temptation of Jesus

4 And Jesus, full of the Holy Spirit, returned
from the Jordan, and was led by the Spirit
2 for forty days in the wilderness, tempted by
the devil. And he ate nothing in those days;
and when they were ended, he was hungry.
3 The devil said to him, "If you are the Son of
God, command this stone to become
4 bread." And Jesus answered him, "It is
written, 'Man shall not live by bread
5 alone.'" And the devil took him up, and

[j] Or my Son, my (or the) Beloved   [k] Other ancient authorities read today I have begotten thee
[l] Greek Salathiel
3.6: Lk 2.30.   3.7: Mt 12.34; 23.33.   3.8: Jn 8.33, 39.   3.9: Mt 7.19; Heb 6.7-8.   3.11: Lk 6.29.
3.15: Acts 13.25; Jn 1.19-22.   3.16-18: Mt 3.11-12; Mk 1.7-8; Jn 1.26-27, 33; Acts 1.5; 11.16; 19.4.
3.19-20: Mt 14.3-4; Mk 6.17-18.   3.21-22: Mt 3.13-17; Mk 1.9-11; Jn 1.29-34.
3.21: Lk 5.16; 6.12; 9.18; 9.28; 11.1; Mk 1.35.   3.22: Ps 2.7; Is 42.1; Lk 9.35; Acts 10.38; 2 Pet 1.17.
3.23-38: Mt 1.1-17; Gen 5.3-32; 11.10-26; Ruth 4.18-22; 1 Chron 1.1-4, 24-28; 2.1-15.
3.23: Jn 8.57; Lk 1.27.   4.1-13: Mt 4.1-11; Mk 1.12-13.   4.2: Deut 9.9; 1 Kings 19.8.   4.4: Deut 8.3.

showed him all the kingdoms of the world in
6 a moment of time, and said to him, "To you
I will give all this authority and their glory;
for it has been delivered to me, and I give
7 it to whom I will. If you, then, will wor-
8 ship me, it shall all be yours." And Jesus
answered him, "It is written,
'You shall worship the Lord your God,
and him only shall you serve.' "
9 And he took him to Jerusalem, and set him
on the pinnacle of the temple, and said to
him, "If you are the Son of God, throw
yourself down from here; for it is written, 10
'He will give his angels charge of you, to
guard you,'
and 11
'On their hands they will bear you up,
lest you strike your foot against a stone.' "
And Jesus answered him, "It is said, 'You 12
shall not tempt the Lord your God.' " And 13
when the devil had ended every temptation, he
departed from him until an opportune time.

MESSAGE AND MISSION

14 AND Jesus returned in the power of the
Spirit into Galilee, and a report concerning him went out through all the sur-
15 rounding country. And he taught in their
synagogues, being glorified by all.

Jesus' proclamation

16 And he came to Nazareth, where he had
been brought up; and he went to the synagogue, as his custom was, on the sabbath
17 day. And he stood up to read; and there was
given to him the book of the prophet Isaiah.
He opened the book and found the place
where it was written,
18 "The Spirit of the Lord is upon me,
because he has anointed me to preach good
news to the poor.
He has sent me to proclaim release to the
captives
and recovering of sight to the blind,
to set at liberty those who are oppressed,
19 to proclaim the acceptable year of the
Lord."
20 And he closed the book, and gave it back to
the attendant, and sat down; and the eyes of
21 all in the synagogue were fixed on him. And
he began to say to them, "Today this scrip-
22 ture has been fulfilled in your hearing." And
all spoke well of him, and wondered at the
gracious words which proceeded out of his
mouth; and they said, "Is not this Joseph's
23 son?" And he said to them, "Doubtless you
will quote to me this proverb, 'Physician,
heal yourself; what we have heard you did at
Caper'na-um, do here also in your own
24 country.'" And he said, "Truly, I say to
you, no prophet is acceptable in his own
25 country. But in truth, I tell you, there were
many widows in Israel in the days of Eli'jah,
when the heaven was shut up three years and
six months, when there came a great famine
over all the land; and Eli'jah was sent to none 26
of them but only to Zar'ephath, in the land of
Sidon, to a woman who was a widow. And 27
there were many lepers in Israel in the time
of the prophet Eli'sha; and none of them was
cleansed, but only Na'aman the Syrian."
When they heard this, all in the synagogue 28
were filled with wrath. And they rose up and 29
put him out of the city, and led him to the
brow of the hill on which their city was built,
that they might throw him down headlong.
But passing through the midst of them he 30
went away.

At Capernaum

And he went down to Caper'na-um, a city 31
of Galilee. And he was teaching them on the
sabbath; and they were astonished at his 32
teaching, for his word was with authority.
And in the synagogue there was a man who 33
had the spirit of an unclean demon; and he
cried out with a loud voice, "Ah!ᵐ What 34
have you to do with us, Jesus of Nazareth?
Have you come to destroy us? I know who
you are, the Holy One of God." But Jesus 35
rebuked him, saying, "Be silent, and come
out of him!" And when the demon had
thrown him down in the midst, he came out
of him, having done him no harm. And they 36
were all amazed and said to one another,
"What is this word? For with authority and
power he commands the unclean spirits, and
they come out." And reports of him went 37
out into every place in the surrounding
region.
And he arose and left the synagogue, and 38
entered Simon's house. Now Simon's

ᵐ Or Let us alone
4.6: 1 Jn 5.19. 4.8: Deut 6.13. 4.10-11: Ps 91.11-12. 4.12: Deut 6.16. 4.13: Lk 22.28.
4.14: Mt 4.12; Mk 1.14; Mt 9.26; Lk 4.37. 4.15: Mt 4.23; 9.35; 11.1.
4.16-30: Mt 13.53-58; Mk 6.1-6; Acts 13.14-16. 4.18-19: Is 61.1-2. 4.22: Jn 6.42; 7.15.
4.23: Mk 1.21; 2.1; Jn 4.46. 4.24: Jn 4.44. 4.25: 1 Kings 17.1, 8-16; 18.1; Jas 5.17-18. 4.27: 2 Kings 5.1-14.
4.29: Acts 7.58; Num 15.35. 4.30: Jn 8.59; 10.39. 4.31-37: Mk 1.21-28.
4.32: Mt 7.28; 13.54; 22.33; Mk 11.18; Jn 7.46. 4.37: Lk 4.14; 5.15; Mt 9.26.
4.38-41: Mt 8.14-17; Mk 1.29-34.

mother-in-law was ill with a high fever, and
39 they besought him for her. And he stood
over her and rebuked the fever, and it left
her; and immediately she rose and served
them.
40 Now when the sun was setting, all those
who had any that were sick with various
diseases brought them to him; and he laid his
hands on every one of them and healed
41 them. And demons also came out of many,
crying, "You are the Son of God!" But he
rebuked them, and would not allow them to
speak, because they knew that he was the
Christ.
42 And when it was day he departed and went

And he sat down and taught the people from
the boat. And when he had ceased speaking, 4
he said to Simon, "Put out into the deep and
let down your nets for a catch." And Simon 5
answered, "Master, we toiled all night and
took nothing! But at your word I will let
down the nets." And when they had done 6
this, they enclosed a great shoal of fish; and
as their nets were breaking, they beckoned to 7
their partners in the other boat to come and
help them. And they came and filled both
the boats, so that they began to sink. But 8
when Simon Peter saw it, he fell down at
Jesus' knees, saying, "Depart from me, for I
am a sinful man, O Lord." For he was 9
astonished, and all that were with him, at the
catch of fish which they had taken; and so 10
also were James and John, sons of Zeb'edee,
who were partners with Simon. And Jesus
said to Simon, "Do not be afraid; henceforth
you will be catching men." And when they 11

into a lonely place. And the people sought
him and came to him, and would have kept
43 him from leaving them; but he said to them,
"I must preach the good news of the kingdom of God to the other cities also; for I was
44 sent for this purpose." And he was preaching in the synagogues of Judea.[n]

The first disciples

5 While the people pressed upon him to hear
the word of God, he was standing by the lake
2 of Gennes'aret. And he saw two boats by the
lake; but the fishermen had gone out of them
3 and were washing their nets. Getting into
one of the boats, which was Simon's, he
asked him to put out a little from the land.

had brought their boats to land, they left
everything and followed him.

Healing ministry

While he was in one of the cities, there came 12
a man full of leprosy; and when he saw Jesus,
he fell on his face and besought him, "Lord,
if you will, you can make me clean." And he 13
stretched out his hand, and touched him, saying, "I will; be clean." And immediately the
leprosy left him. And he charged him to tell no 14
one; but "go and show yourself to the priest,
and make an offering for your cleansing,

[n] Other ancient authorities read *Galilee*
4.42-43: Mk 1.35-38.   4.44: Mt 4.23; Mk 1.39; Mt 9.35.
5.1-11: Mt 4.18-22; Mk 1.16-20; Jn 1.40-42; 21.1-19.   5.3: Mt 13.1-2; Mk 4.1.
5.5: Lk 8.24, 45; 9.33, 49; 17.13.   5.12-16: Mt 8.1-4; Mk 1.40-45; Lk 17.11-19.   5.14: Lev 13.49; 14.2-32.

as Moses commanded, for a proof to the
5 people."⁰ But so much the more the report
went abroad concerning him; and great
multitudes gathered to hear and to be healed
16 of their infirmities. But he withdrew to the
wilderness and prayed.

17 On one of those days, as he was teaching,
there were Pharisees and teachers of the law
sitting by, who had come from every village
of Galilee and Judea and from Jerusalem;
and the power of the Lord was with him to
18 heal. ᵖ And behold, men were bringing on a
bed a man who was paralysed, and they
19 sought to bring him in and lay him before
Jesus;�q but finding no way to bring him in,
because of the crowd, they went up on the
roof and let him down with his bed through
20 the tiles into the midst before Jesus. And
when he saw their faith he said, "Man, your
21 sins are forgiven you." And the scribes and
the Pharisees began to question, saying,
"Who is this that speaks blasphemies? Who
22 can forgive sins but God only?" When Jesus
perceived their questionings, he answered
them, "Why do you question in your
23 hearts? Which is easier, to say, 'Your sins
are forgiven you,' or to say, 'Rise and walk'?
24 But that you may know that the Son of man
has authority on earth to forgive sins"—he
said to the man who was paralysed—"I say to
you, rise, take up your bed and go home."
25 And immediately he rose before them, and
took up that on which he lay, and went home,
26 glorifying God. And amazement seized
them all, and they glorified God and were
filled with awe, saying, "We have seen
strange things today."

The call of Levi

27 After this he went out, and saw a tax
collector, named Levi, sitting at the tax
office; and he said to him, "Follow me."
28 And he left everything, and rose and followed him.

And Levi made him a great feast in his 29
house; and there was a large company of tax
collectors and others sitting at tableʳ with
them. And the Pharisees and their scribes 30
murmured against his disciples, saying,
"Why do you eat and drink with tax collectors and sinners?" And Jesus answered 31
them, "Those who are well have no need of a
physician, but those who are sick; I have not 32
come to call the righteous, but sinners to
repentance."

And they said to him, "The disciples of 33
John fast often and offer prayers, and so do
the disciples of the Pharisees, but yours eat
and drink." And Jesus said to them, "Can 34
you make wedding guests fast while the
bridegroom is with them? The days will 35
come, when the bridegroom is taken away
from them, and then they will fast in those
days." He told them a parable also: "No one 36
tears a piece from a new garment and puts it
upon an old garment; if he does, he will tear
the new, and the piece from the new will not
match the old. And no one puts new wine 37
into old wineskins; if he does, the new wine
will burst the skins and it will be spilled, and
the skins will be destroyed. But new wine 38
must be put into fresh wineskins. And no 39
one after drinking old wine desires new; for
he says, 'The old is good.' "ˢ

Sabbath problems

On a sabbath,ᵗ while he was going through 6
the grainfields, his disciples plucked and ate
some ears of grain, rubbing them in their
hands. But some of the Pharisees said, 2
"Why are you doing what is not lawful to do
on the sabbath?" And Jesus answered, 3
"Have you not read what David did when he
was hungry, he and those who were with
him: how he entered the house of God, and 4
took and ate the bread of the Presence, which
it is not lawful for any but the priests to eat,
and also gave it to those with him?" And he 5
said to them, "The Son of man is lord of the
sabbath."

On another sabbath, when he entered the 6
synagogue and taught, a man was there
whose right hand was withered. And the 7
scribes and the Pharisees watched him, to see
whether he would heal on the sabbath, so
that they might find an accusation against
him. But he knew their thoughts, and he 8
said to the man who had the withered hand,

⁰ Greek to them   ᵖ Other ancient authorities read was present to heal them   q Greek him
ʳ Greek reclining   ˢ Other ancient authorities read better
Other ancient authorities read On the second first sabbath (on the second sabbath after the first)
5.15: Lk 4.14, 37; Mt 9.26.   5.16: Lk 3.21; 6.12; 9.18, 28; 11.1.   5.17-26: Mt 9.1-8; Mk 2.1-12; Jn 5.1-9.
5.17: Mt 15.1; Mk 5.30; Lk 6.19.   5.20: Lk 7.48-49.   5.27-32: Mt 9.9-13; Mk 2.13-17.   5.30: Lk 15.1-2.
5.32: 1 Tim 1.15.   5.33-38: Mt 9.14-17; Mk 2.18-22.   5.33: Lk 7.18; 11.1; Jn 3.25-26.
5.35: Lk 9.22; 17.22.   6.1-5: Mt 12.1-8; Mk 2.23-28.   6.1: Deut 23.25.   6.2: Ex 20.10; 23.12; Deut 5.14.
6.3: 1 Sam 21.1-6.   6.4: Lev 24.9.   6.6-11: Mt 12.9-14; Mk 3.1-6.

"Come and stand here." And he rose and
9 stood there. And Jesus said to them, "I ask
you, is it lawful on the sabbath to do good or
to do harm, to save life or to destroy it?"
10 And he looked around on them all, and said
to him, "Stretch out your hand." And he
11 did so, and his hand was restored. But they
were filled with fury and discussed with one
another what they might do to Jesus.

The twelve apostles

12 In these days he went out into the hills to
pray; and all night he continued in prayer to
13 God. And when it was day, he called his
disciples, and chose from them twelve, whom
14 he named apostles; Simon, whom he named
Peter, and Andrew his brother, and James
15 and John, and Philip, and Bartholomew, and
Matthew, and Thomas, and James the son of
Alphaeus, and Simon who was called the
16 Zealot, and Judas the son of James, and
Judas Iscariot, who became a traitor.
17 And he came down with them and stood on
a level place, with a great crowd of his
disciples and a great multitude of people
from all Judea and Jerusalem and the seacoast of Tyre and Sidon, who came to hear
18 him and to be healed of their diseases; and
those who were troubled with unclean spirits
19 were cured. And all the crowd sought to
touch him, for power came forth from him
and healed them all.

Jesus addresses his disciples

20 And he lifted up his eyes on his disciples,
and said:
"Blessed are you poor, for yours is the
kingdom of God.
21 "Blessed are you that hunger now, for you
shall be satisfied.
"Blessed are you that weep now, for you
shall laugh.
22 "Blessed are you when men hate you, and
when they exclude you and revile you, and
cast out your name as evil, on account of the
23 Son of man! Rejoice in that day, and leap for
joy, for behold, your reward is great in
heaven; for so their fathers did to the
prophets.
24 "But woe to you that are rich, for you have
received your consolation.
25 "Woe to you that are full now, for you shall
hunger.

"Woe to you that laugh now, for you shall
mourn and weep.
"Woe to you, when all men speak well of 26
you, for so their fathers did to the false
prophets.
"But I say to you that hear, Love your 27
enemies, do good to those who hate you,
bless those who curse you, pray for those 28
who abuse you. To him who strikes you on 29
the cheek, offer the other also; and from him
who takes away your cloak do not withhold
your coat as well. Give to every one who 30
begs from you; and of him who takes away
your goods do not ask them again. And as 31
you wish that men would do to you, do so to
them.
"If you love those who love you, what credit 32
is that to you? For even sinners love those
who love them. And if you do good to those 33
who do good to you, what credit is that to
you? For even sinners do the same. And if 34
you lend to those from whom you hope to
receive, what credit is that to you? Even
sinners lend to sinners, to receive as much
again. But love your enemies, and do good, 35
and lend, expecting nothing in return;[u] and
your reward will be great, and you will be
sons of the Most High; for he is kind to the
ungrateful and the selfish. Be merciful, even 36
as your Father is merciful.
"Judge not, and you will not be judged; 37
condemn not, and you will not be condemned; forgive, and you will be forgiven;
give, and it will be given to you; good 38
measure, pressed down, shaken together,
running over, will be put into your lap. For
the measure you give will be the measure you
get back."
He also told them a parable: "Can a blind 39
man lead a blind man? Will they not both
fall into a pit? A disciple is not above his 40
teacher, but every one when he is fully taught
will be like his teacher. Why do you see the 41
speck that is in your brother's eye, but do not
notice the log that is in your own eye? Or 42
how can you say to your brother, 'Brother,
let me take out the speck that is in your eye,'
when you yourself do not see the log that is in
your own eye? You hypocrite, first take the
log out of your own eye, and then you will see
clearly to take out the speck that is in your
brother's eye.
"For no good tree bears bad fruit, nor again 43
does a bad tree bear good fruit; for each tree 44
is known by its own fruit. For figs are not

u Other ancient authorities read *despairing of no man*
6.12-16: Mk 3.13-19; Mt 10.2-4; Acts 1.13.   6.12: Lk 3.21; 5.16; 9.18, 28; 11.1.
6.17-19: Mt 5.1-2; 4.24-25; Mk 3.7-12.   6.19: Mk 3.10; Mt 9.21; 14.36; Lk 5.17.   6.20-23: Mt 5.3-12.
6.22: 1 Pet 4.14; Jn 9.22; 16.2.   6.24-26: Lk 10.13-15; 11.38-52; 17.1; 21.23; 22.22.
6.24: Lk 16.25; Jas 5.1-5; Mt 6.2.   6.27-30: Mt 5.39-44; Rom 12.14, 17.   6.31: Mt 7.12.
6.32-36: Mt 5.44-48.   6.35: Mt 5.9.   6.37-38: Mt 7.1-2; Rom 2.1.   6.38: Mk 4.24; Acts 20.35.
6.39: Mt 15.14.   6.40: Mt 10.24-25; Jn 13.16; 15.20.   6.41-42: Mt 7.3-5.
6.43-45: Mt 7.18-19; 12.33-35; Jas 3.11-12.

gathered from thorns, nor are grapes picked from a bramble bush. The good man out of the good treasure of his heart produces good, and the evil man out of his evil treasure produces evil; for out of the abundance of the heart his mouth speaks.

⁵ "Why do you call me 'Lord, Lord,' and not ⁷ do what I tell you? Every one who comes to me and hears my words and does them, I will ⁸ show you what he is like: he is like a man building a house, who dug deep, and laid the foundation upon rock; and when a flood arose, the stream broke against that house, and could not shake it, because it had been ⁹ well built.ᵛ But he who hears and does not do them is like a man who built a house on the ground without a foundation; against which the stream broke, and immediately it fell, and the ruin of that house was great."

A Gentile believer

7 After he had ended all his sayings in the hearing of the people he entered Caper'- ² na-um. Now a centurion had a slave who was dearʷ to him, who was sick and at the ³ point of death. When he heard of Jesus, he sent to him elders of the Jews, asking him to ⁴ come and heal his slave. And when they came to Jesus, they besought him earnestly, saying, "He is worthy to have you do this for ⁵ him, for he loves our nation, and he built us ⁶ our synagogue." And Jesus went with them. When he was not far from the house, the centurion sent friends to him, saying to him, "Lord, do not trouble yourself, for I am not worthy to have you come under my roof; ⁷ therefore I did not presume to come to you. But say the word, and let my servant be ⁸ healed. For I am a man set under authority, with soldiers under me: and I say to one, 'Go,' and he goes; and to another, 'Come,' and he comes; and to my slave, 'Do this,' and ⁹ he does it." When Jesus heard this he marvelled at him, and turned and said to the multitude that followed him, "I tell you, not ¹⁰ even in Israel have I found such faith." And when those who had been sent returned to the house, they found the slave well.

The widow of Nain

¹¹ Soon afterwardˣ he went to a city called Na'in, and his disciples and a great crowd ¹² went with him. As he drew near to the gate of the city, behold, a man who had died was being carried out, the only son of his mother, and she was a widow; and a large crowd from the city was with her. And when the Lord ¹³ saw her, he had compassion on her and said to her, "Do not weep." And he came and ¹⁴ touched the bier, and the bearers stood still. And he said, "Young man, I say to you, arise." And the dead man sat up, and began ¹⁵ to speak. And he gave him to his mother. Fear seized them all; and they glorified God, ¹⁶ saying, "A great prophet has arisen among us!" and "God has visited his people!" And ¹⁷ this report concerning him spread through the whole of Judea and all the surrounding country.

The Baptist's question

The disciples of John told him of all these ¹⁸ things. And John, calling to him two of his ¹⁹ disciples, sent them to the Lord, saying, "Are you he who is to come, or shall we look for another?" And when the men had come ²⁰ to him, they said, "John the Baptist has sent us to you, saying, 'Are you he who is to come, or shall we look for another?'" In that hour ²¹ he cured many of diseases and plagues and evil spirits, and on many that were blind he bestowed sight. And he answered them, ²² "Go and tell John what you have seen and heard: the blind receive their sight, the lame walk, lepers are cleansed, and the deaf hear, the dead are raised up, the poor have good news preached to them. And blessed is he ²³ who takes no offence at me."

When the messengers of John had gone, he ²⁴ began to speak to the crowds concerning John: "What did you go out into the wilderness to behold? A reed shaken by the wind? What then did you go out to see? A ²⁵ man clothed in soft raiment? Behold, those who are gorgeously apparelled and live in luxury are in kings' courts. What then did ²⁶ you go out to see? A prophet? Yes, I tell you, and more than a prophet. This is he of ²⁷ whom it is written,

'Behold, I send my messenger before thy face,

ᵛ Other ancient authorities read *founded upon the rock*   ʷ Or *valuable*
ˣ Other ancient authorities read *Next day*
6.45: Mk 7.20.   **6.46:** Mt 7.21.   **6.47-49:** Mt 7.24-27; Jas 1.22-25.   **7.1-10:** Mt 8.5-10, 13; Jn 4.46-53.
7.5: Acts 10.2.   **7.11-17:** Mk 5.21-24, 35-43; Jn 11.1-44; 1 Kings 17.17-24; 2 Kings 4.32-37.
7.13: Lk 7.19; 10.1; 11.39; 12.42; 13.15; 17.5-6; 18.6; 19.8; 22.61; 24.3.
7.16: Lk 7.39; 24.19; Mt 21.11; Jn 6.14.   **7.18-35:** Mt 11.2-19.   **7.21:** Mt 4.23; Mk 3.10.
7.22: Is 29.18-19; 35.5-6; 61.1; Lk 4.18-19.   **7.27:** Mal 3.1; Mk 1.2.

who shall prepare thy way before thee.'
28 I tell you, among those born of women none
is greater than John; yet he who is least in the
29 kingdom of God is greater than he." (When
they heard this all the people and the tax
collectors justified God, having been bap-
30 tized with the baptism of John; but the
Pharisees and the lawyers rejected the purpose of God for themselves, not having been
baptized by him.)
31 "To what then shall I compare the men of
this generation, and what are they like?
32 They are like children sitting in the market
place and calling to one another,
'We piped to you, and you did not dance;
we wailed, and you did not weep.'
33 For John the Baptist has come eating no
bread and drinking no wine; and you say,
34 'He has a demon.' The Son of man has come
eating and drinking; and you say, 'Behold, a
glutton and a drunkard, a friend of tax
35 collectors and sinners!' Yet wisdom is justified by all her children."

In a Pharisee's house

36 One of the Pharisees asked him to eat with
him, and he went into the Pharisee's house,
37 and sat at table. And behold, a woman of the
city, who was a sinner, when she learned that
he was sitting at table in the Pharisee's house,
38 brought an alabaster flask of ointment, and
standing behind him at his feet, weeping, she
began to wet his feet with her tears, and
wiped them with the hair of her head, and
kissed his feet, and anointed them with the
39 ointment. Now when the Pharisee who had
invited him saw it, he said to himself, "If this
man were a prophet, he would have known
who and what sort of woman this is who is
40 touching him, for she is a sinner." And Jesus
answering said to him, "Simon, I have
something to say to you." And he answered,
41 "What is it, Teacher?" "A certain creditor
had two debtors; one owed five hundred
42 denarii, and the other fifty. When they could
not pay, he forgave them both. Now which
43 of them will love him more?" Simon
answered, "The one, I suppose, to whom he
forgave more." And he said to him, "You
44 have judged rightly." Then turning toward
the woman he said to Simon, "Do you see
this woman? I entered your house, you gave
me no water for my feet, but she has wet my
feet with her tears and wiped them with her
45 hair. You gave me no kiss, but from the time

I came in she has not ceased to kiss my feet.
You did not anoint my head with oil, but she
has anointed my feet with ointment. Therefore I tell you, her sins, which are many, are
forgiven, for she loved much; but he who is
forgiven little, loves little." And he said to
her, "Your sins are forgiven." Then those
who were at table with him began to say
among themselves, "Who is this, who even
forgives sins?" And he said to the woman,
"Your faith has saved you; go in peace."

The service of women

Soon afterward he went on through cities 8
and villages, preaching and bringing the
good news of the kingdom of God. And the
twelve were with him, and also some women 2
who had been healed of evil spirits and
infirmities: Mary, called Mag'dalene, from
whom seven demons had gone out, and 3
Jo-an'na, the wife of Chu'za, Herod's
steward, and Susanna, and many others, who
provided for them*y* out of their means.

Parable of the sower

And when a great crowd came together and 4
people from town after town came to him, he
said in a parable: "A sower went out to sow 5
his seed; and as he sowed, some fell along the
path, and was trodden under foot, and the
birds of the air devoured it. And some fell on 6
the rock; and as it grew up, it withered away,
because it had no moisture. And some fell 7
among thorns; and the thorns grew with it
and choked it. And some fell into good soil 8
and grew, and yielded a hundredfold." As
he said this, he called out, "He who has ears
to hear, let him hear."
And when his disciples asked him what this 9
parable meant, he said, "To you it has been 10
given to know the secrets of the kingdom of
God; but for others they are in parables, so
that seeing they may not see, and hearing
they may not understand. Now the parable 11
is this: The seed is the word of God. The 12
ones along the path are those who have
heard; then the devil comes and takes away
the word from their hearts, that they may not
believe and be saved. And the ones on the 13
rock are those who, when they hear the word,
receive it with joy; but these have no root,
they believe for a while and in time of
temptation fall away. And as for what fell 14
among the thorns, they are those who hear,

---

y Other ancient authorities read *him*

7.29–30: Mt 21.32; Lk 3.12.   7.33: Lk 1.15.   7.34: Lk 5.29; 15.1–2.
7.36–50: Mt 26.6–13; Mk 14.3–9; Jn 12.1–8.   7.36: Lk 11.37; 14.1.   7.39: Lk 7.16; 24.19; Mt 21.11; Jn 6.14.
7.42: Mt 18.25.   7.43: Lk 10.28.   7.48: Mt 9.2; Mk 2.5; Lk 5.20.   7.50: Mt 9.22; Mk 5.34; Lk 8.48.
8.1–3: Lk 4.15; Mk 15.40–41; Mt 27.55–56; Lk 23.49.   8.4–8: Mt 13.1–9; Mk 4.1–9.   8.8: Mt 11.15.
8.9–10: Mt 13.10–13; Mk 4.10–12; Is 6.9–10; Jer 5.21; Ezek 12.2.   8.11–15: Mt 13.18–23; Mk 4.13–20.
8.11: 1 Thess 2.13; 1 Pet 1.23.

storm of wind came down on the lake, and they were filling with water, and were in danger. And they went and woke him, 24 saying, "Master, Master, we are perishing!" And he awoke and rebuked the wind and the raging waves; and they ceased, and there was a calm. He said to them, "Where is your 25 faith?" And they were afraid, and they marvelled, saying to one another, "Who then is this, that he commands even wind and water, and they obey him?"

Casting out demons

Then they arrived at the country of the 26 Ger′asenes,[z] which is opposite Galilee. And 27 as he stepped out on land, there met him a man from the city who had demons; for a long time he had worn no clothes, and he lived not in a house but among the tombs. When he saw Jesus, he cried out and fell 28 down before him, and said with a loud voice, "What have you to do with me, Jesus, Son of the Most High God? I beseech you, do not torment me." For he had commanded the 29 unclean spirit to come out of the man. (For many a time it had seized him; he was kept under guard, and bound with chains and fetters, but he broke the bonds and was driven by the demon into the desert.) Jesus 30 then asked him, "What is your name?" And he said, "Legion"; for many demons had entered him. And they begged him not to 31 command them to depart into the abyss. Now a large herd of swine was feeding there 32 on the hillside; and they begged him to let them enter these. So he gave them leave. Then the demons came out of the man and 33 entered the swine, and the herd rushed down the steep bank into the lake and were drowned.

When the herdsmen saw what had hap- 34 pened, they fled, and told it in the city and in the country. Then people went out to see 35 what had happened, and they came to Jesus, and found the man from whom the demons had gone, sitting at the feet of Jesus, clothed and in his right mind; and they were afraid. And those who had seen it told them how he 36 who had been possessed with demons was healed. Then all the people of the sur- 37 rounding country of the Ger′asenes[z] asked him to depart from them; for they were seized with great fear; so he got into the boat and returned. The man from whom the 38 demons had gone begged that he might be with him; but he sent him away, saying,

but as they go on their way they are choked by the cares and riches and pleasures of life, 15 and their fruit does not mature. And as for that in the good soil, they are those who, hearing the word, hold it fast in an honest and good heart, and bring forth fruit with patience.

16 "No one after lighting a lamp covers it with a vessel, or puts it under a bed, but puts it on a stand, that those who enter may see the 17 light. For nothing is hid that shall not be made manifest, nor anything secret that shall 18 not be known and come to light. Take heed then how you hear; for to him who has will more be given, and from him who has not, even what he thinks that he has will be taken away."

19 Then his mother and his brothers came to him, but they could not reach him for the 20 crowd. And he was told, "Your mother and your brothers are standing outside, desiring 21 to see you." But he said to them, "My mother and my brothers are those who hear the word of God and do it."

Storm on the lake

22 One day he got into a boat with his disciples, and he said to them, "Let us go across to the other side of the lake." So they set 23 out, and as they sailed he fell asleep. And a

The Gerasene coast of the Sea of Galilee

39 "Return to your home, and declare how much God has done for you." And he went away, proclaiming throughout the whole city how much Jesus had done for him.

Jairus' daughter

40 Now when Jesus returned, the crowd welcomed him, for they were all waiting for 41 him. And there came a man named Ja'irus, who was a ruler of the synagogue; and falling at Jesus' feet he besought him to come to his 42 house, for he had an only daughter, about twelve years of age, and she was dying.

As he went, the people pressed round him. 43 And a woman who had had a flow of blood for twelve years[a] and could not be healed by 44 any one, came up behind him, and touched the fringe of his garment; and immediately 45 her flow of blood ceased. And Jesus said, "Who was it that touched me?" When all denied it, Peter[b] said, "Master, the multitudes surround you and press upon you!" 46 But Jesus said, "Some one touched me; for I perceive that power has gone forth from 47 me." And when the woman saw that she was not hidden, she came trembling, and falling down before him declared in the presence of all the people why she had touched him, and 48 how she had been immediately healed. And he said to her, "Daughter, your faith has made you well; go in peace."

49 While he was still speaking, a man from the ruler's house came and said, "Your daughter is dead; do not trouble the Teacher any 50 more." But Jesus on hearing this answered him, "Do not fear; only believe, and she shall 51 be well." And when he came to the house,

he permitted no one to enter with him, except Peter and John and James, and the father and mother of the child. And all were 52 weeping and bewailing her; but he said, "Do not weep; for she is not dead but sleeping." And they laughed at him, knowing that she 53 was dead. But taking her by the hand he 54 called, saying, "Child, arise." And her spirit 55 returned, and she got up at once; and he directed that something should be given her to eat. And her parents were amazed; but he 56 charged them to tell no one what had happened.

The apostles commissioned

And he called the twelve together and gave 9 them power and authority over all demons and to cure diseases, and he sent them out to 2 preach the kingdom of God and to heal. And 3 he said to them, "Take nothing for your journey, no staff, nor bag, nor bread, nor money; and do not have two tunics. And 4 whatever house you enter, stay there, and from there depart. And wherever they do 5 not receive you, when you leave that town shake off the dust from your feet as a testimony against them." And they departed 6 and went through the villages, preaching the gospel and healing everywhere.

Now Herod the tetrarch heard of all that 7 was done, and he was perplexed, because it was said by some that John had been raised from the dead, by some that Eli'jah had 8 appeared, and by others that one of the old prophets had risen. Herod said, "John I 9 beheaded; but who is this about whom I hear such things?" And he sought to see him.

[a] Other ancient authorities add *and had spent all her living upon physicians*
[b] Other ancient authorities add *and those who were with him*
8.40–56: Mt 9.18–26; Mk 5.21–43.   8.45: Lk 8.24.   8.46: Lk 5.17; 6.19.   8.48: Mt 9.22; Lk 7.50; 17.19;18.42.
8.56: Mt 8.4; Mk 3.12; 7.36; Lk 9.21.   9.1–6: Mt 10.1, 5, 7–11, 14; Mk 6.7–12; Lk 10.4–11.
9.5: Acts 13.51.   9.7–9: Mt 14.1–2; Mk 6.14–16; Lk 9.19.   9.9: Lk 23.8.

Five thousand fed

o On their return the apostles told him what they had done. And he took them and withdrew apart to a city called Beth-sa'ida. 1 When the crowds learned it, they followed him; and he welcomed them and spoke to them of the kingdom of God, and cured 2 those who had need of healing. Now the day began to wear away; and the twelve came and said to him, "Send the crowd away, to go into the villages and country round about, to lodge and get provisions; for we are here in a 3 lonely place." But he said to them, "You give them something to eat." They said, "We have no more than five loaves and two fish—unless we are to go and buy food for all 4 these people." For there were about five thousand men. And he said to his disciples, "Make them sit down in companies, about 5 fifty each." And they did so, and made them 6 all sit down. And taking the five loaves and the two fish he looked up to heaven, and blessed and broke them, and gave them to 7 the disciples to set before the crowd. And all ate and were satisfied. And they took up what was left over, twelve baskets of broken pieces.

The great confession

8 Now it happened that as he was praying alone the disciples were with him; and he asked them, "Who do the people say that I 9 am?" And they answered, "John the Baptist; but others say, Eli'jah; and others, that 0 one of the old prophets has risen." And he said to them, "But who do you say that I am?" And Peter answered, "The Christ of 1 God." But he charged and commanded 2 them to tell this to no one, saying, "The Son of man must suffer many things, and be rejected by the elders and chief priests and scribes, and be killed, and on the third day be raised."

3 And he said to all, "If any man would come after me, let him deny himself and take up 4 his cross daily and follow me. For whoever would save his life will lose it; and whoever 5 loses his life for my sake, he will save it. For what does it profit a man if he gains the whole world and loses or forfeits himself? 6 For whoever is ashamed of me and of my words, of him will the Son of man be ashamed when he comes in his glory and the glory of the Father and of the holy angels. But I tell you truly, there are some standing 27 here who will not taste death before they see the kingdom of God."

The transfiguration

Now about eight days after these sayings he 28 took with him Peter and John and James, and went up on the mountain to pray. And as he 29 was praying, the appearance of his countenance was altered, and his raiment became dazzling white. And behold, two men talked 30 with him, Moses and Eli'jah, who appeared 31 in glory and spoke of his departure, which he was to accomplish at Jerusalem. Now Peter 32 and those who were with him were heavy with sleep but kept awake, and they saw his glory and the two men who stood with him. And as the men were parting from him, Peter 33 said to Jesus, "Master, it is well that we are here; let us make three booths, one for you and one for Moses and one for Eli'jah"—not knowing what he said. As he said this, a 34 cloud came and overshadowed them; and they were afraid as they entered the cloud. And a voice came out of the cloud, saying, 35 "This is my Son, my Chosen;^{c} listen to him!" And when the voice had spoken, 36 Jesus was found alone. And they kept silence and told no one in those days anything of what they had seen.

v. 58

^{c} Other ancient authorities read *my Beloved*
9.10: Mk 6.30–31; Lk 10.17; Jn 1.44. **9.11–17**: Mt 14.13–21; Mk 6.32–44; Jn 6.1–14; Mk 8.4–10.
9.13: 2 Kings 4.42–44. **9.16**: Lk 22.19; 24.30–31; Acts 2.42; 20.11; 27.35.
9.18–21: Mt 16.13–20; Mk 8.27–30; Jn 1.49; 11.27; 6.66–69. **9.18**: Lk 3.21; 5.16; 6.12; 9.28; 11.1.
9.19: Lk 9.9; Mk 9.11–13. **9.22**: Mt 16.21; Mk 8.31; Lk 9.43–45; 18.31–34; 17.25.
9.23–27: Mt 16.24–28; Mk 8.34–9.1. **9.24–25**: Mt 10.38–39; Lk 14.27; 17.33; Jn 12.25.
9.26: Mt 10.33; Lk 12.9; 21.28. **9.27**: Lk 22.18; Mt 10.23; 1 Thess 4.15–18; Jn 21.22.
9.28–36: Mt 17.1–8; Mk 9.2–8; 2 Pet 1.17–18. **9.28**: Lk 8.51; 3.21; 5.16; 6.12; 9.18; 11.1.
9.30: Acts 1.9–11. **9.32**: Jn 1.14. **9.33**: Lk 5.5; 8.24, 45; 9.49; 17.13. **9.35**: Lk 3.22; Jn 12.28–30.
9.36: Mt 17.9; Mk 9.9–10.

37 On the next day, when they had come down from the mountain, a great crowd met him. 38 And behold, a man from the crowd cried, "Teacher, I beg you to look upon my son, for 39 he is my only child; and behold, a spirit seizes him, and he suddenly cries out; it convulses him till he foams, and shatters 40 him, and will hardly leave him. And I begged your disciples to cast it out, but they 41 could not." Jesus answered, "O faithless and perverse generation, how long am I to be with you and bear with you? Bring your son 42 here." While he was coming, the demon tore him and convulsed him. But Jesus rebuked the unclean spirit, and healed the boy, and 43 gave him back to his father. And all were astonished at the majesty of God.

The Passion foreshadowed

But while they were all marvelling at every-thing he did, he said to his disciples, "Let 44 these words sink into your ears; for the Son of man is to be delivered into the hands of men." But they did not understand this 45 saying, and it was concealed from them, that they should not perceive it; and they were afraid to ask him about this saying.

And an argument arose among them as to 46 which of them was the greatest. But when 47 Jesus perceived the thought of their hearts, he took a child and put him by his side, and 48 said to them, "Whoever receives this child in my name receives me, and whoever receives me receives him who sent me; for he who is least among you all is the one who is great."

John answered, "Master, we saw a man 49 casting out demons in your name, and we forbade him, because he does not follow with us." But Jesus said to him, "Do not forbid 50 him; for he that is not against you is for you."

ON THE WAY TO JERUSALEM

51 WHEN the days drew near for him to be received up, he set his face to go to 52 Jerusalem. And he sent messengers ahead of him, who went and entered a village of the 53 Samaritans, to make ready for him; but the people would not receive him, because his 54 face was set toward Jerusalem. And when his disciples James and John saw it, they said, "Lord, do you want us to bid fire come down from heaven and consume them?"[d] 55,But he turned and rebuked them.[e] And they 56 went on to another village.

Would-be disciples

57 As they were going along the road, a man said to him, "I will follow you wherever you 58 go." And Jesus said to him, "Foxes have holes, and birds of the air have nests; but the Son of man has nowhere to lay his head." 59 To another he said, "Follow me." But he said, "Lord, let me first go and bury my 60 father." But he said to him, "Leave the dead to bury their own dead; but as for you, go and proclaim the kingdom of God." 61 Another said, "I will follow you, Lord; but let me first say farewell to those at my 62 home." Jesus said to him, "No one who puts his hand to the plough and looks back is fit for the kingdom of God."

Seventy evangelists

After this the Lord appointed seventy[f] 10 others, and sent them on ahead of him, two by two, into every town and place where he himself was about to come. And he said to 2 them, "The harvest is plentiful, but the labourers are few; pray therefore the Lord of the harvest to send out labourers into his harvest. Go your way; behold, I send you 3 out as lambs in the midst of wolves. Carry 4 no purse, no bag, no sandals; and salute no one on the road. Whatever house you enter, 5 first say, 'Peace be to this house!' And if a 6 son of peace is there, your peace shall rest upon him; but if not, it shall return to you. And remain in the same house, eating and 7 drinking what they provide, for the labourer deserves his wages; do not go from house to house. Whenever you enter a town and they 8 receive you, eat what is set before you; heal 9 the sick in it and say to them, 'The kingdom of God has come near to you.' But whenever 10 you enter a town and they do not receive you, go into its streets and say, 'Even the dust of 11

[d] Other ancient authorities add as Elijah did
[e] Other ancient authorities add and he said, "You do not know what manner of spirit you are of; for the Son of man came not to destroy men's lives but to save them"   [f] Other ancient authorities read seventy-two
9.37–43: Mt 17.14–18; Mk 9.14–27.   9.43–45: Mt 17.22–23; Mk 9.30–32; Lk 9.22; 18.31–34; 17.25.
9.46–48: Mt 18.1–5; Mk 9.33–37.   9.48: Lk 10.16; Mt 10.40.   9.49–50: Mk 9.38–40; Lk 11.23.
9.49: Lk 5.5; 8.24, 45; 9.33; 17.13.   9.51–56: Mk 10.1; Lk 17.11; Jn 4.40–42.   9.52: Mt 10.5; Jn 4.4.
9.54: Mk 3.17; 2 Kings 1.9–16.   9.57–60: Mt 8.19–22.   9.61: 1 Kings 19.20; Phil 3.13.
10.1: Lk 9.1–2, 51–52; 7.13.   10.2: Mt 9.37–38; Jn 4.35.
10.3–12: Mt 10.7–16; Mk 6.8–11; Lk 9.2–5; 22.35–36.   10.5: 1 Sam 25.6.
10.7: 1 Cor 10.27; 9.14; 1 Tim 5.18; Deut 24.15.   10.11: Acts 13.51.

your town that clings to our feet, we wipe off against you; nevertheless know this, that the 2 kingdom of God has come near.' I tell you, it shall be more tolerable on that day for Sodom than for that town.

3 "Woe to you, Chora′zin! woe to you, Beth-sa′ida! for if the mighty works done in you had been done in Tyre and Sidon, they would have repented long ago, sitting in 4 sackcloth and ashes. But it shall be more tolerable in the judgment for Tyre and Sidon 5 than for you. And you, Caper′na-um, will you be exalted to heaven? You shall be brought down to Hades.

6 "He who hears you hears me, and he who rejects you rejects me, and he who rejects me rejects him who sent me."

Their return

7 The seventy*f* returned with joy, saying, "Lord, even the demons are subject to us in 8 your name!" And he said to them, "I saw Satan fall like lightning from heaven. 9 Behold, I have given you authority to tread upon serpents and scorpions, and over all the

power of the enemy; and nothing shall hurt 10 you. Nevertheless do not rejoice in this, that the spirits are subject to you; but rejoice that your names are written in heaven."

Thanksgiving

21 In that same hour he rejoiced in the Holy Spirit and said, "I thank thee, Father, Lord of heaven and earth, that thou hast hidden these things from the wise and understanding and revealed them to babes; yea, Father, 22 for such was thy gracious will.*g* All things have been delivered to me by my Father; and no one knows who the Son is except the Father, or who the Father is except the Son

and any one to whom the Son chooses to reveal him."

Then turning to the disciples he said pri- 23 vately, "Blessed are the eyes which see what you see! For I tell you that many prophets 24 and kings desired to see what you see, and did not see it, and to hear what you hear, and did not hear it."

The good Samaritan

And behold, a lawyer stood up to put him to 25 the test, saying, "Teacher, what shall I do to inherit eternal life?" He said to him, "What 26 is written in the law? How do you read?" And he answered, "You shall love the Lord 27 your God with all your heart, and with all your soul, and with all your strength, and with all your mind; and your neighbour as yourself." And he said to him, "You have 28 answered right; do this, and you will live." But he, desiring to justify himself, said to 29 Jesus, "And who is my neighbour?" Jesus 30 replied, "A man was going down from Jerusalem to Jericho, and he fell among robbers, who stripped him and beat him, and departed, leaving him half dead. Now by 31 chance a priest was going down that road; and when he saw him he passed by on the other side. So likewise a Levite, when he 32 came to the place and saw him, passed by on the other side. But a Samaritan, as he 33 journeyed, came to where he was; and when he saw him, he had compassion, and went to 34 him and bound up his wounds, pouring on oil and wine; then he set him on his own beast and brought him to an inn, and took care of him. And the next day he took out 35 two denarii*h* and gave them to the innkeeper, saying, 'Take care of him; and whatever more you spend, I will repay you when I come back.' Which of these three, do you 36 think, proved neighbour to the man who fell among the robbers?" He said, "The one 37 who showed mercy on him." And Jesus said to him, "Go and do likewise."

Martha and Mary

Now as they went on their way, he entered a 38 village; and a woman named Martha received him into her house. And she had a sister 39 called Mary, who sat at the Lord's feet and listened to his teaching. But Martha was 40

f Other ancient authorities read *seventy-two*   *g* Or *so it was well-pleasing before thee*
h The denarius was worth about seventeen pence
  10.12: Mt 11.24; Gen 19.24–28; Jude 7.   **10.13–15:** Mt 11.21–23; Lk 6.24–26.
10.16: Mt 10.40; 18.5; Mk 9.37; Lk 9.48; Jn 13.20; 12.48.   **10.18:** Rev 12.9; Jn 12.31.
10.20: Ex 32.32; Ps 69.28; Dan 12.1; Phil 4.3; Heb 12.23; Rev 3.5; 13.8; 21.27.
10.21–22: Mt 11.25–27.   **10.21:** 1 Cor 1.26–29.   **10.22:** Mt 28.18; Jn 3.35; 13.3; 10.15; 17.25.
10.23–24: Mt 13.16–17; Jn 8.56; Heb 11.13; 1 Pet 1.10–12.   **10.25–28:** Mt 22.34–39; Mk 12.28–31.
10.25: Mk 10.17; Mt 19.16; Lk 18.18.   **10.27:** Deut 6.5; Lev 19.18; Rom 13.9; Gal 5.14; Jas 2.8.
10.28: Lk 20.39; Lev 18.5.   **10.33:** Lk 9.51–56; 17.11–19; Jn 4.4–42.   **10.38–42:** Jn 12.1–3; 11.1–45.

THE CITIES OF JESUS

distracted with much serving; and she went to him and said, "Lord, do you not care that my sister has left me to serve alone? Tell her then to help me." But the Lord answered ₄₁ her, "Martha, Martha, you are anxious and troubled about many things; one thing is ₄₂ needful.ⁱ Mary has chosen the good portion, which shall not be taken away from her."

The Lord's prayer

11 He was praying in a certain place, and when he ceased, one of his disciples said to him, "Lord, teach us to pray, as John taught his ₂ disciples." And he said to them, "When you pray, say:
"Father, hallowed be thy name. Thy ₃ kingdom come. Give us each day our daily ₄ bread;ʲ and forgive us our sins, for we ourselves forgive every one who is indebted to us; and lead us not into temptation."

₅ And he said to them, "Which of you who has a friend will go to him at midnight and ₆ say to him, 'Friend, lend me three loaves; for a friend of mine has arrived on a journey, and ₇ I have nothing to set before him'; and he will answer from within, 'Do not bother me; the door is now shut, and my children are with me in bed; I cannot get up and give you ₈ anything'? I tell you, though he will not get up and give him anything because he is his friend, yet because of his importunity he will ₉ rise and give him whatever he needs. And I tell you, Ask, and it will be given you; seek, and you will find; knock, and it will be ₁₀ opened to you. For every one who asks receives, and he who seeks finds, and to him ₁₁ who knocks it will be opened. What father among you, if his son asks forᵏ a fish, will ₁₂ instead of a fish give him a serpent; or if he ₁₃ asks for an egg, will give him a scorpion? If you then, who are evil, know how to give good gifts to your children, how much more will the heavenly Father give the Holy Spirit to those who ask him!"

An evil generation

₁₄ Now he was casting out a demon that was dumb; when the demon had gone out, the dumb man spoke, and the people marvelled. ₁₅ But some of them said, "He casts out demons ₁₆ by Be-el′zebul, the prince of demons"; while others, to test him, sought from him a sign ₁₇ from heaven. But he, knowing their thoughts, said to them, "Every kingdom

divided against itself is laid waste, and house falls upon house. And if Satan also is divided ₁₈ against himself, how will his kingdom stand? For you say that I cast out demons by Be-el′zebul. And if I cast out demons by ₁₉ Be-el′zebul, by whom do your sons cast them out? Therefore they shall be your judges. But if it is by the finger of God that I cast out ₂₀ demons, then the kingdom of God has come upon you. When a strong man, fully armed, ₂₁

guards his own palace, his goods are in peace; but when one stronger than he assails him ₂₂ and overcomes him, he takes away his armour in which he trusted, and divides his spoil. He who is not with me is against me, ₂₃ and he who does not gather with me scatters.

"When the unclean spirit has gone out of a ₂₄ man, he passes through waterless places seeking rest; and finding none he says, 'I will return to my house from which I came.' And ₂₅ when he comes he finds it swept and put in order. Then he goes and brings seven other ₂₆ spirits more evil than himself, and they enter and dwell there; and the last state of that man becomes worse than the first."

ⁱ Other ancient authorities read *few things are needful, or only one* ʲ Or *our bread for the morrow*
ᵏ Other ancient authorities insert *bread, will give him a stone; or if he asks for*
10.41: Lk 7.13. **11.1:** Mk 1.35; Lk 3.21; 5.16; 6.12; 9.18, 28; 5.33; 7.18. **11.2-4:** Mt 6.9-13.
11.4: Mk 11.25; Mt 18.35. **11.5-8:** Lk 18.1-8. **11.9-13:** Mt 7.7-11.
11.9: Mt 18.19; 21.22; Mk 11.24; Jas 1.5-8; 1 Jn 5.14-15; Jn 15.7; 16.23-24.
11.14-23: Mt 12.22-30; 10.25; Mk 3.23-27. **11.14-15:** Mt 9.32-34.
11.16: Mt 12.38; 16.1; Mk 8.11; Jn 2.18; 6.30. **11.23:** Lk 9.50. **11.24-26:** Mt 12.43-45.

27 As he said this, a woman in the crowd raised her voice and said to him, "Blessed is the womb that bore you, and the breasts that you 28 sucked!" But he said, "Blessed rather are those who hear the word of God and keep it!"

29 When the crowds were increasing, he began to say, "This generation is an evil generation; it seeks a sign, but no sign shall be given to it 30 except the sign of Jonah. For as Jonah became a sign to the men of Nin'eveh, so will 31 the Son of man be to this generation. The queen of the South will arise at the judgment with the men of this generation and condemn them; for she came from the ends of the earth to hear the wisdom of Solomon, and behold, something greater than Solomon is here. 32 The men of Nin'eveh will arise at the judgment with this generation and condemn it; for they repented at the preaching of Jonah, and behold, something greater than Jonah is here.

33 "No one after lighting a lamp puts it in a cellar or under a bushel, but on a stand, that 34 those who enter may see the light. Your eye is the lamp of your body; when your eye is sound, your whole body is full of light; but when it is not sound, your body is full of 35 darkness. Therefore be careful lest the light 36 in you be darkness. If then your whole body is full of light, having no part dark, it will be wholly bright, as when a lamp with its rays gives you light."

In a Pharisee's house

37 While he was speaking, a Pharisee asked him to dine with him; so he went in and sat at 38 table. The Pharisee was astonished to see 39 that he did not first wash before dinner. And the Lord said to him, "Now you Pharisees cleanse the outside of the cup and of the dish, but inside you are full of extortion and 40 wickedness. You fools! Did not he who 41 made the outside make the inside also? But give for alms those things which are within; and behold, everything is clean for you.

42 "But woe to you Pharisees! for you tithe mint and rue and every herb, and neglect justice and the love of God; these you ought to have done, without neglecting the others. 43 Woe to you Pharisees! for you love the best seat in the synagogues and salutations in the market places. Woe to you! for you are like 44 graves which are not seen, and men walk over them without knowing it."

One of the lawyers answered him, 45 "Teacher, in saying this you reproach us also." And he said, "Woe to you lawyers 46 also! for you load men with burdens hard to bear, and you yourselves do not touch the burdens with one of your fingers. Woe to 47 you! for you build the tombs of the prophets whom your fathers killed. So you are wit- 48 nesses and consent to the deeds of your fathers; for they killed them, and you build their tombs. Therefore also the Wisdom of 49 God said, 'I will send them prophets and apostles, some of whom they will kill and persecute,' that the blood of all the prophets, 50 shed from the foundation of the world, may be required of this generation, from the 51 blood of Abel to the blood of Zechari'ah, who perished between the altar and the sanctuary. Yes, I tell you, it shall be required of this generation. Woe to you lawyers! for you 52 have taken away the key of knowledge; you did not enter yourselves and you hindered those who were entering."

As he went away from there, the scribes and 53 the Pharisees began to press him hard, and to provoke him to speak of many things, lying 54 in wait for him, to catch at something he might say.

The leaven of the Pharisees

In the meantime, when so many thousands 12 of the multitude had gathered together that they trod upon one another, he began to say to his disciples first, "Beware of the leaven of the Pharisees, which is hypocrisy. Nothing 2 is covered up that will not be revealed, or hidden that will not be known. Whatever 3 you have said in the dark shall be heard in the light, and what you have whispered in private rooms shall be proclaimed upon the housetops.

"I tell you, my friends, do not fear those 4 who kill the body, and after that have no more that they can do. But I will warn you 5 whom to fear: fear him who, after he has killed, has power to cast into hell;[l] yes, I tell you, fear him! Are not five sparrows sold for 6 two pennies? And not one of them is forgotten before God. Why, even the hairs 7

---

[l] Greek Gehenna

11.27: Lk 1.42; 23.29.   11.28: Lk 8.21; Jn 15.14.   11.29-32: Mt 12.39-42.
11.29: Mt 16.4; Mk 8.12; Lk 11.16; Jon 3.4-5.   11.31: 1 Kings 10.1-10; 2 Chron 9.1-12.   11.32: Mt 12.6.
11.33: Mt 5.15; Mk 4.21; Lk 8.16.   11.34-35: Mt 6.22-23.   11.37: Lk 7.36; 14.1.   11.38: Mk 7.1-5.
11.39-41: Mt 23.25-26.   11.39: Lk 7.13.   11.41: Tit 1.15; Mk 7.19.
11.42: Mt 23.23-24; Lev 27.30; Mic 6.8.   11.43: Mt 23.6-7; Mk 12.38-39; Lk 20.46.
11.44: Mt 23.27.   11.46: Mt 23.4.   11.47-48: Mt 23.29-32; Acts 7.51-53.
11.49-51: Mt 23.34-36.   11.49: 1 Cor 1.24; Col 2.3.   11.51: Gen 4.8; 2 Chron 24.20-21; Zech 1.1.
11.52: Mt 23.13.   12.1: Mt 16.6; Mk 8.15.   12.2-3: Mt 10.26-27; Mk 4.22; Lk 8.17; Eph 5.13.   12.4: Jn 15.14-15.   12.4-9: Mt 10.28-33.
12.5: Heb 10.31.   12.7: Lk 21.18; Acts 27.34; Mt 12.12.

of your head are all numbered. Fear not; you are of more value than many sparrows.

"And I tell you, every one who acknowledges me before men, the Son of man also will acknowledge before the angels of God; but he who denies me before men will be denied before the angels of God. And every one who speaks a word against the Son of man will be forgiven; but he who blasphemes against the Holy Spirit will not be forgiven. And when they bring you before the synagogues and the rulers and the authorities, do not be anxious how or what you are to answer or what you are to say; for the Holy Spirit will teach you in that very hour what you ought to say."

One of the multitude said to him, "Teacher, bid my brother divide the inheritance with me." But he said to him, "Man, who made me a judge or divider over you?" And he said to them, "Take heed, and beware of all covetousness; for a man's life does not consist in the abundance of his possessions." And he told them a parable, saying, "The land of a rich man brought forth plentifully; and he thought to himself, 'What shall I do, for I have nowhere to store my crops?' And he said, 'I will do this: I will pull down my barns, and build larger ones; and there I will store all my grain and my goods. And I will say to my soul, Soul, you have ample goods laid up for many years; take your ease, eat, drink, be merry.' But God said to him, 'Fool! This night your soul is required of you; and the things you have prepared, whose will they be?' So is he who lays up treasure for himself, and is not rich toward God."

The ravens and the lilies

And he said to his disciples, "Therefore I tell you, do not be anxious about your life, what you shall eat, nor about your body, what you shall put on. For life is more than food, and the body more than clothing. Consider the ravens: they neither sow nor reap, they have neither storehouse nor barn, and yet God feeds them. Of how much more value are you than the birds! And which of you by being anxious can add a cubit to his span of life?m If then you are not able to do as small a thing as that, why are you anxious about the rest? Consider the lilies, how they grow; they neither toil nor spin;n yet I tell

you, even Solomon in all his glory was not arrayed like one of these. But if God so clothes the grass which is alive in the field today and tomorrow is thrown into the oven, how much more will he clothe you, O men of little faith! And do not seek what you are to eat and what you are to drink, nor be of anxious mind. For all the nations of the world seek these things; and your Father knows that you need them. Instead, seek hiso kingdom, and these things shall be yours as well.

The little flock

"Fear not, little flock, for it is your Father's good pleasure to give you the kingdom. Sell your possessions, and give alms; provide yourselves with purses that do not grow old, with a treasure in the heavens that does not fail, where no thief approaches and no moth destroys. For where your treasure is, there will your heart be also.

"Let your loins be girded and your lamps burning, and be like men who are waiting for their master to come home from the marriage feast, so that they may open to him at once when he comes and knocks. Blessed are those servants whom the master finds awake when he comes; truly, I say to you, he will gird himself and have them sit at table, and he will come and serve them. If he comes in the second watch, or in the third, and finds them so, blessed are those servants! But know this, that if the householder had known at what hour the thief was coming, he would have been awake andp would not have left his house to be broken into. You also must be ready; for the Son of man is coming at an hour you do not expect."

Peter said, "Lord, are you telling this parable for us or for all?" And the Lord said, "Who then is the faithful and wise steward, whom his master will set over his household, to give them their portion of food at the proper time? Blessed is that servant whom his master when he comes will find so doing. Truly I tell you, he will set him over all his possessions. But if that servant says to himself, 'My master is delayed in coming,' and begins to beat the menservants and the maidservants, and to eat and drink and get drunk, the master of that servant will come on a day when he does not expect him and at

m Or to his stature   n Other ancient authorities read Consider the lilies; they neither spin nor weave
o Other ancient authorities read God's   p Other ancient authorities omit would have been awake and
12.9: Mk 8.38; Lk 9.26; 2 Tim 2.12.   12.10: Mt 12.31-32; Mk 3.28-29.
12.11-12: Mt 10.19-20; Mk 13.11; Lk 21.14-15.   12.15: 1 Tim 6.6-10.
12.20: Jer 17.11; Job 27.8; Ps 39.6; Lk 12.33-34.   12.22-31: Mt 6.25-33.
12.27: 1 Kings 10.1-10.   12.30: Mt 6.8.   12.32: Jn 21.15-17.   12.33-34: Mt 6.19-21; Lk 18.22.
12.35: Eph 6.14; Mt 25.1-13; Mk 13.33-37.   12.37: Jn 13.3-5; Mt 24.42; Lk 21.36.
12.39-40: Mt 24.43-44; 1 Thess 5.2; Rev 3.3; 16.15; 2 Pet 3.10.   12.42-46: Mt 24.45-51.   12.42: Lk 7.13.

an hour he does not know, and will punish[q]
47 him, and put him with the unfaithful. And
that servant who knew his master's will, but
did not make ready or act according to his
48 will, shall receive a severe beating. But he
who did not know, and did what deserved a
beating, shall receive a light beating. Every
one to whom much is given, of him will
much be required; and of him to whom men
commit much they will demand the more.
49 "I came to cast fire upon the earth; and
50 would that it were already kindled! I have a
baptism to be baptized with; and how I am
51 constrained until it is accomplished! Do you
think that I have come to give peace on
52 earth? No, I tell you, but rather division; for
henceforth in one house there will be five
divided, three against two and two against
53 three; they will be divided, father against son
and son against father, mother against
daughter and daughter against her mother,
mother-in-law against her daughter-in-law
and daughter-in-law against her mother-in-
law."
54 He also said to the multitudes, "When you
see a cloud rising in the west, you say at once,

'A shower is coming'; and so it happens.
55 And when you see the south wind blowing,
you say, 'There will be scorching heat'; and
56 it happens. You hypocrites! You know how
to interpret the appearance of earth and sky;
but why do you not know how to interpret
the present time?
57 "And why do you not judge for yourselves
58 what is right? As you go with your accuser
before the magistrate, make an effort to settle
with him on the way, lest he drag you to the
judge, and the judge hand you over to the
59 officer, and the officer put you in prison. I
tell you, you will never get out till you have
paid the very last copper."

A warning to the nation

There were some present at that very time 1
who told him of the Galileans whose blood
Pilate had mingled with their sacrifices. And 2
he answered them, "Do you think that these
Galileans were worse sinners than all the
other Galileans, because they suffered thus?
I tell you, No; but unless you repent you will 3
all likewise perish. Or those eighteen upon 4
whom the tower in Silo'am fell and killed
them, do you think that they were worse
offenders than all the others who dwelt in
Jerusalem? I tell you, No; but unless you 5
repent you will all likewise perish."
And he told this parable: "A man had a fig 6
tree planted in his vineyard; and he came
seeking fruit on it and found none. And he 7
said to the vinedresser, 'Lo, these three years
I have come seeking fruit on this fig tree, and
I find none. Cut it down; why should it use
up the ground?' And he answered him, 'Let 8
it alone, sir, this year also, till I dig about it
and put on manure. And if it bears fruit next 9
year, well and good; but if not, you can cut it
down.'"
Now he was teaching in one of the syna- 10
gogues on the sabbath. And there was a 11
woman who had had a spirit of infirmity for
eighteen years; she was bent over and could
not fully straighten herself. And when Jesus 12
saw her, he called her and said to her,
"Woman, you are freed from your infirmity." And he laid his hands upon her, and 13
immediately she was made straight, and she
praised God. But the ruler of the synagogue, 14
indignant because Jesus had healed on the
sabbath, said to the people, "There are six
days on which work ought to be done; come
on those days and be healed, and not on the
sabbath day." Then the Lord answered him, 15
"You hypocrites! Does not each of you on
the sabbath untie his ox or his ass from the
manger, and lead it away to water it? And 16
ought not this woman, a daughter of
Abraham whom Satan bound for eighteen
years, be loosed from this bond on the
sabbath day?" As he said this, all his 17
adversaries were put to shame; and all the
people rejoiced at all the glorious things that
were done by him.
He said therefore, "What is the kingdom of 18
God like? And to what shall I compare it?

q Or cut him in pieces
12.47-48: Deut 25.2-3; Num 15.29-30; Lk 8.18; 19.26.   12.49: Lk 22.15.   12.50: Mk 10.38-39; Jn 12.27.
12.51-53: Mt 10.34-36; Lk 21.16; Mic 7.6.   12.54-56: Mt 16.2-3.   12.57-59: Mt 5.25-26.   13.2: Jn 9.1-3.
13.6-9: Mt 21.18-20; Mk 11.12-14, 20-21.   13.7: Mt 3.10; 7.19; Lk 3.9.
13.14: Ex 20.9-10; Lk 6.6-11; 14.1-6; Jn 5.1-18.   13.15: Lk 7.13; 14.5; Mt 12.11.   13.16: Lk 19.9.
13.18-19: Mt 13.31-32; Mk 4.30-32.

9 It is like a grain of mustard seed which a man took and sowed in his garden; and it grew and became a tree, and the birds of the air made nests in its branches."

10 And again he said, "To what shall I compare the kingdom of God? It is like leaven which a woman took and hid in three measures of meal, till it was all leavened."

The narrow door

2 He went on his way through towns and villages, teaching, and journeying toward 3 Jerusalem. And some one said to him, "Lord, will those who are saved be few?" 4 And he said to them, "Strive to enter by the narrow door; for many, I tell you, will seek to 5 enter and will not be able. When once the householder has risen up and shut the door,

you will begin to stand outside and to knock at the door, saying, 'Lord, open to us.' He will answer you, 'I do not know where you 26 come from.' Then you will begin to say, 'We ate and drank in your presence, and you 27 taught in our streets.' But he will say, 'I tell you, I do not know where you come from; depart from me, all you workers of iniquity!' 28 There you will weep and gnash your teeth, when you see Abraham and Isaac and Jacob and all the prophets in the kingdom of God 29 and you yourselves thrust out. And men will come from east and west, and from north and south, and sit at table in the kingdom of 30 God. And behold, some are last who will be first, and some are first who will be last."

31 At that very hour some Pharisees came, and said to him, "Get away from here, for Herod 32 wants to kill you." And he said to them, "Go and tell that fox, 'Behold, I cast out demons and perform cures today and tomorrow, and 33 the third day I finish my course. Nevertheless I must go on my way today and tomorrow and the day following; for it

cannot be that a prophet should perish away from Jerusalem.'

Lament over Jerusalem

"O Jerusalem, Jerusalem, killing the pro- 34 phets and stoning those who are sent to you! How often would I have gathered your children together as a hen gathers her brood under her wings, and you would not! Behold, your house is forsaken. And I tell 35

you, you will not see me until you say, 'Blessed is he who comes in the name of the Lord!'"

Round a Pharisee's table

One sabbath when he went to dine at the 14 house of a ruler who belonged to the Pharisees, they were watching him. And behold, 2 there was a man before him who had dropsy. And Jesus spoke to the lawyers and Phari- 3 sees, saying, "Is it lawful to heal on the sabbath, or not?" But they were silent. 4 Then he took him and healed him, and let him go. And he said to them, "Which of 5 you, having an ass[r] or an ox that has fallen into a well, will not immediately pull him out on a sabbath day?" And they could not 6 reply to this.

Now he told a parable to those who were 7 invited, when he marked how they chose the places of honour, saying to them, "When you 8 are invited by any one to a marriage feast, do not sit down in a place of honour, lest a more eminent man than you be invited by him; and he who invited you both will come and 9 say to you, 'Give place to this man,' and then you will begin with shame to take the lowest

[r] Other ancient authorities read *a son*
13.20-21: Mt 13.33.   13.22: Lk 9.51; 17.11; 18.31; 19.11.   13.23-24: Mt 7.13-14; Jn 10.7.
13.25: Mt 25.10-12.   13.26-27: Mt 7.21-23; 25.41; Lk 6.46.   13.28-29: Mt 8.11-12.
13.30: Mt 19.30; Mk 10.31.   13.32: Heb 2.10; 7.28.   13.34-35: Mt 23.37-39; Lk 19.41.
13.35: Jer 22.5; Ps 118.26; Lk 19.38.   14.1: Lk 7.36; 11.37; Mk 3.2.   14.3: Mt 12.10; Mk 3.4; Lk 6.9.
14.5: Mt 12.11; Lk 13.15.   14.8: Prov 25.6-7; Lk 11.43; 20.46.

10 place. But when you are invited, go and sit in the lowest place, so that when your host comes he may say to you, 'Friend, go up higher'; then you will be honoured in the presence of all who sit at table with you. 11 For every one who exalts himself will be humbled, and he who humbles himself will be exalted."

12 He said also to the man who had invited him, "When you give a dinner or a banquet, do not invite your friends or your brothers or your kinsmen or rich neighbours, lest they also invite you in return, and you be repaid. 13 But when you give a feast, invite the poor, 14 the maimed, the lame, the blind, and you will be blessed, because they cannot repay you. You will be repaid at the resurrection of the just."

15 When one of those who sat at table with him heard this, he said to him, "Blessed is he who 16 shall eat bread in the kingdom of God!" But he said to him, "A man once gave a great 17 banquet, and invited many; and at the time for the banquet he sent his servant to say to those who had been invited, 'Come; for all is 18 now ready.' But they all alike began to make excuses. The first said to him, 'I have bought a field, and I must go out and see it; I 19 pray you, have me excused.' And another said, 'I have bought five yoke of oxen, and I go to examine them; I pray you, have me 20 excused.' And another said, 'I have married 21 a wife, and therefore I cannot come.' So the servant came and reported this to his master. Then the householder in anger said to his servant, 'Go out quickly to the streets and lanes of the city, and bring in the poor and 22 maimed and blind and lame.' And the servant said, 'Sir, what you commanded has 23 been done, and still there is room.' And the master said to the servant, 'Go out to the highways and hedges, and compel people to 24 come in, that my house may be filled. For I tell you, none of those men who were invited shall taste my banquet.' "

To a wayside crowd

25 Now great multitudes accompanied him; 26 and he turned and said to them, "If any one comes to me and does not hate his own father and mother and wife and children and brothers and sisters, yes, and even his own 27 life, he cannot be my disciple. Whoever does not bear his own cross and come after me, 28 cannot be my disciple. For which of you,

desiring to build a tower, does not first sit down and count the cost, whether he has enough to complete it? Otherwise, when he has laid a foundation, and is not able to finish, all who see it begin to mock him, saying, 'This man began to build, and was not able to finish.' Or what king, going to encounter another king in war, will not sit down first and take counsel whether he is able with ten thousand to meet him who comes against him with twenty thousand? And if not, while the other is yet a great way off, he sends an embassy and asks terms of peace. So therefore, whoever of you does not renounce all that he has cannot be my disciple.

"Salt is good; but if salt has lost its taste, how shall its saltness be restored? It is fit neither for the land nor for the dunghill; men throw it away. He who has ears to hear, let him hear."

Now the tax collectors and sinners were all 1 drawing near to hear him. And the Pharisees 2 and the scribes murmured, saying, "This man receives sinners and eats with them."

The lost sheep

So he told them this parable: "What man of 3 you, having a hundred sheep, if he has lost 4 one of them, does not leave the ninety-nine in the wilderness, and go after the one which is lost, until he finds it? And when he 5 has found it, he lays it on his shoulders, rejoicing. And when he comes home, he calls 6 together his friends and his neighbours, saying to them, 'Rejoice with me, for I have found my sheep which was lost.' Just so, I 7 tell you, there will be more joy in heaven over one sinner who repents than over ninety-nine righteous persons who need no repentance.

The lost coin

"Or what woman, having ten silver coins,[s] if 8 she loses one coin, does not light a lamp and sweep the house and seek diligently until she finds it? And when she has found it, she 9 calls together her friends and neighbours, saying, 'Rejoice with me, for I have found the coin which I had lost.' Just so, I tell you, 10 there is joy before the angels of God over one sinner who repents."

s The drachma, rendered here by *silver coin*, was about fourteen pence
14.11: Mt 23.12; Lk 18.14; Mt 18.4; 1 Pet 5.6.   14.12: Jas 2.2–4.   14.13: Lk 14.21.   14.15: Rev 19.9.
14.16–24: Mt 22.1–10.   14.20: Deut 24.5; 1 Cor 7.33.   14.21: Lk 14.13.   14.26–27: Mt 10.37–38.
14.27: Mt 16.24; Mk 8.34; Lk 9.23.   14.33: Lk 18.29–30; Phil 3.7.
14.34–35: Mt 5.13; Mk 9.49–50; Mt 11.15.   15.1–2: Lk 5.29–30; 19.7.   15.4–7: Mt 18.10–14.
15.7: Jas 5.20; Lk 19.10; 15.10.

The prodigal son

1 And he said, "There was a man who had
2 two sons; and the younger of them said to his
father, 'Father, give me the share of property
that falls to me.' And he divided his living
3 between them. Not many days later, the
younger son gathered all he had and took his
journey into a far country, and there he
4 squandered his property in loose living. And
when he had spent everything, a great famine

servants, 'Bring quickly the best robe, and
put it on him; and put a ring on his hand, and
shoes on his feet; and bring the fatted calf 23
and kill it, and let us eat and make merry; for 24
this my son was dead, and is alive again; he
was lost, and is found.' And they began to
make merry.

"Now his elder son was in the field; and as 25
he came and drew near to the house, he heard
music and dancing. And he called one of the 26
servants and asked what this meant. And he 27
said to him, 'Your brother has come, and
your father has killed the fatted calf, because

v. 6

arose in that country, and he began to be in
15 want. So he went and joined himself to one
of the citizens of that country, who sent him
16 into his fields to feed swine. And he would
gladly have fed on[t] the pods that the swine
17 ate; and no one gave him anything. But
when he came to himself he said, 'How many
of my father's hired servants have bread
enough and to spare, but I perish here with
18 hunger! I will arise and go to my father, and
I will say to him, "Father, I have sinned
19 against heaven and before you; I am no
longer worthy to be called your son; treat me
20 as one of your hired servants."' And he
arose and came to his father. But while he
was yet at a distance, his father saw him and
had compassion, and ran and embraced him
21 and kissed him. And the son said to him,
'Father, I have sinned against heaven and
before you; I am no longer worthy to be
22 called your son.'[u] But the father said to his

he has received him safe and sound.' But he 28
was angry and refused to go in. His father
came out and entreated him, but he answered 29
his father, 'Lo, these many years I have
served you, and I never disobeyed your
command; yet you never gave me a kid, that
I might make merry with my friends. But 30
when this son of yours came, who has
devoured your living with harlots, you killed
for him the fatted calf!' And he said to him, 31
'Son, you are always with me, and all that is
mine is yours. It was fitting to make merry 32
and be glad, for this your brother was dead,
and is alive; he was lost, and is found.' "

The dishonest steward

He also said to the disciples, "There was a **16**
rich man who had a steward, and charges
were brought to him that this man was
wasting his goods. And he called him and 2

[t] Other ancient authorities read *filled his belly with*
[u] Other ancient authorities add *treat me as one of your hired servants*
15.11: Mt 21.28.   **15.12:** Deut 21.15–17.   **15.22:** Gen 41.42; Zech 3.4.   **15.24:** 1 Tim 5.6; Eph 2.1; Lk 9.60.

said to him, 'What is this that I hear about you? Turn in the account of your steward-
3 ship, for you can no longer be steward.' And the steward said to himself, 'What shall I do, since my master is taking the stewardship away from me? I am not strong enough to
4 dig, and I am ashamed to beg. I have decided what to do, so that people may receive me into their houses when I am put
5 out of the stewardship.' So, summoning his master's debtors one by one, he said to the first, 'How much do you owe my master?'
6 He said, 'A hundred measures of oil.' And

Liquid measures

he said to him, 'Take your bill, and sit down
7 quickly and write fifty.' Then he said to another, 'And how much do you owe?' He said, 'A hundred measures of wheat.' He said to him, 'Take your bill, and write
8 eighty.' The master commended the dishonest steward for his prudence; for the sons of this world *v* are wiser in their own genera-
9 tion than the sons of light. And I tell you, make friends for yourselves by means of unrighteous mammon, so that when it fails they may receive you into the eternal habitations.
10 "He who is faithful in a very little is faithful also in much; and he who is dishonest in a
11 very little is dishonest also in much. If then you have not been faithful in the unrighteous mammon, who will entrust to you the true
12 riches? And if you have not been faithful in that which is another's, who will give you
13 that which is your own? No servant can serve two masters; for either he will hate the one and love the other, or he will be devoted to the one and despise the other. You cannot serve God and mammon."
14 The Pharisees, who were lovers of money,
15 heard all this, and they scoffed at him. But he said to them, "You are those who justify yourselves before men, but God knows your

hearts; for what is exalted among men is an abomination in the sight of God.
16 "The law and the prophets were until John; since then the good news of the kingdom of God is preached, and every one enters it
17 violently. But it is easier for heaven and earth to pass away, than for one dot of the law to become void.
18 "Every one who divorces his wife and marries another commits adultery, and he who marries a woman divorced from her husband commits adultery.

The rich man and Lazarus

19 "There was a rich man, who was clothed in purple and fine linen and who feasted sumptuously every day. And at his gate lay a poor
20 man named Laz'arus, full of sores, who
21 desired to be fed with what fell from the rich man's table; moreover the dogs came and licked his sores. The poor man died and was
22 carried by the angels to Abraham's bosom. The rich man also died and was buried; and
23 in Hades, being in torment, he lifted up his eyes, and saw Abraham far off and Laz'arus in his bosom. And he called out, 'Father
24 Abraham, have mercy upon me, and send Laz'arus to dip the end of his finger in water and cool my tongue; for I am in anguish in
25 this flame.' But Abraham said, 'Son, remember that you in your lifetime received your good things, and Laz'arus in like manner evil things; but now he is comforted here, and you are in anguish. And besides all
26 this, between us and you a great chasm has been fixed, in order that those who would pass from here to you may not be able, and none may cross from there to us.' And he
27 said, 'Then I beg you, father, to send him to my father's house, for I have five brothers, so
28 that he may warn them, lest they also come into this place of torment.' But Abraham
29 said, 'They have Moses and the prophets; let them hear them.' And he said, 'No, father
30 Abraham; but if some one goes to them from the dead, they will repent.' He said to him,
31 'If they do not hear Moses and the prophets, neither will they be convinced if some one should rise from the dead.'"

Take heed to yourselves

17 And he said to his disciples, "Temptations
to sin *w* are sure to come; but woe to him by
2 whom they come! It would be better for him

---

v Greek *age*　　*w* Greek *stumbling blocks*
16.8: 1 Thess 5.5; Eph 5.8; Lk 20.34; Jn 12.36.　**16.9**: Lk 12.33; 18.22.　**16.10**: Mt 25.21; Lk 19.17.
16.13: Mt 6.24.　**16.15**: 1 Sam 16.7; Prov 21.2; Acts 1.24; Lk 10.29.　**16.16**: Mt 11.12–13.
16.17: Mt 5.17–18; Lk 21.33.　**16.18**: Mt 5.31–32; 19.9; Mk 10.11–12; 1 Cor 7.10–11.
16.20: Jn 11.1–44; 12.1, 9.　**16.22**: Jn 13.23.　**16.25**: Lk 6.24.
16.29: Jn 5.45–47; Acts 15.21; Lk 4.17.　**16.30**: Lk 3.8; 19.9.　**17.1–2**: Mt 18.6–7; Mk 9.42; 1 Cor 8.12.

if a millstone were hung round his neck and he were cast into the sea, than that he should

3 cause one of these little ones to sin.[x] Take heed to yourselves; if your brother sins, rebuke him, and if he repents, forgive him;

4 and if he sins against you seven times in the day, and turns to you seven times, and says, 'I repent,' you must forgive him."

5 The apostles said to the Lord, "Increase our faith!" And the Lord said, "If you had faith as a grain of mustard seed, you could say to this sycamine tree, 'Be rooted up, and be planted in the sea,' and it would obey you.

7 "Will any one of you, who has a servant ploughing or keeping sheep, say to him when he has come in from the field, 'Come at once

8 and sit down at table'? Will he not rather say to him, 'Prepare supper for me, and gird yourself and serve me, till I eat and drink; and afterward you shall eat and drink'?

9 Does he thank the servant because he did

10 what was commanded? So you also, when you have done all that is commanded you, say, 'We are unworthy servants; we have only done what was our duty.'"

A grateful Samaritan

On the way to Jerusalem he was passing along between Samar'ia and Galilee. And as he entered a village, he was met by ten lepers,

13 who stood at a distance and lifted up their voices and said, "Jesus, Master, have mercy

14 on us." When he saw them he said to them, "Go and show yourselves to the priests."

15 And as they went they were cleansed. Then one of them, when he saw that he was healed, turned back, praising God with a loud voice;

16 and he fell on his face at Jesus' feet, giving

17 him thanks. Now he was a Samaritan. Then said Jesus, "Were not ten cleansed? Where

18 are the nine? Was no one found to return and give praise to God except this

19 foreigner?" And he said to him, "Rise and go your way; your faith has made you well."

The days of the Son of man

10 Being asked by the Pharisees when the kingdom of God was coming, he answered them, "The kingdom of God is not coming

11 with signs to be observed; nor will they say, 'Lo, here it is!' or 'There!' for behold, the

kingdom of God is in the midst of you."[y]

22 And he said to the disciples, "The days are coming when you will desire to see one of the days of the Son of man, and you will not see

23 it. And they will say to you, 'Lo, there!' or 'Lo, here!' Do not go, do not follow them.

24 For as the lightning flashes and lights up the sky from one side to the other, so will the Son

25 of man be in his day.[z] But first he must suffer many things and be rejected by this

26 generation. As it was in the days of Noah, so will it be in the days of the Son of man.

27 They ate, they drank, they married, they were given in marriage, until the day when Noah entered the ark, and the flood came

28 and destroyed them all. Likewise as it was in the days of Lot—they ate, they drank, they bought, they sold, they planted, they built,

29 but on the day when Lot went out from Sodom fire and brimstone rained from

30 heaven and destroyed them all—so will it be on the day when the Son of man is revealed.

31 On that day, let him who is on the housetop, with his goods in the house, not come down to take them away; and likewise let him who

32 is in the field not turn back. Remember

33 Lot's wife. Whoever seeks to gain his life will lose it, but whoever loses his life will

34 preserve it. I tell you, in that night there will be two men in one bed; one will be taken and

35 the other left. There will be two women grinding together; one will be taken and the

37 other left."[a] And they said to him, "Where, Lord?" He said to them, "Where the body is, there the eagles[b] will be gathered together."

Parables on prayer

18 And he told them a parable, to the effect that they ought always to pray and not lose

2 heart. He said, "In a certain city there was a judge who neither feared God nor regarded

3 man; and there was a widow in that city who kept coming to him and saying, 'Vindicate

4 me against my adversary.' For a while he refused; but afterward he said to himself, 'Though I neither fear God nor regard man,

5 yet because this widow bothers me, I will vindicate her, or she will wear me out by her

6 continual coming.'" And the Lord said, "Hear what the unrighteous judge says. And

7 will not God vindicate his elect, who cry to

[x] Greek *stumble*   [y] Or *within you*   [z] Other ancient authorities omit *in his day*
[a] Other ancient authorities add verse 36, "*Two men will be in the field; one will be taken and the other left*"
[b] Or *vultures*
17.3-4: Mt 18.15, 21-22.   17.5-6: Mt 17.20; 21.21; Mk 11.22-23.   17.8: Lk 12.37; Jn 13.3-5.
17.11: Lk 9.51; 13.22; 19.11.   17.12: Lev 13.45-46.   17.13: Lk 5.5; 8.24, 45; 9.33, 49.
17.14: Lk 5.14; Mt 8.4; Mk 1.44; Lev 14.2-32.   17.19: Mt 9.22; Mk 5.34; Lk 8.48; 18.42.
17.20: Lk 19.11; 21.7; Acts 1.6.   17.22: Mt 9.15; Mk 2.20; Lk 5.35.   17.23: Mt 24.23; Mk 13.21.
17.24: Mt 24.27; Rev 1.7.   17.25: Lk 9.22.   17.26-27: Mt 24.37-39; Lk 21.21.   17.32: Gen 19.26.
17.28-30: Gen 18.20-33; 19.24-25.   17.31: Mt 24.17-18; Mk 13.15-16; Lk 21.21.   17.32: Gen 19.26.
17.33: Mt 10.39; 16.25; Mk 8.35; Lk 9.24; Jn 12.25.   17.34-35: Mt 24.40-41.   17.37: Mt 24.28.
18.1-8: Lk 11.5-8.   18.6: Lk 7.13.   18.7: Rev 6.10; Mt 24.22; Rom 8.33; Col 3.12; 2 Tim 2.10.

him day and night? Will he delay long over
8 them? I tell you, he will vindicate them
speedily. Nevertheless, when the Son of
man comes, will he find faith on earth?"

9 He also told this parable to some who
trusted in themselves that they were right-
10 eous and despised others: "Two men went
up into the temple to pray, one a Pharisee
11 and the other a tax collector. The Pharisee
stood and prayed thus with himself, 'God, I
thank thee that I am not like other men,
extortioners, unjust, adulterers, or even like
12 this tax collector. I fast twice a week, I give
13 tithes of all that I get.' But the tax collector,
standing far off, would not even lift up his
eyes to heaven, but beat his breast, saying,
14 'God, be merciful to me a sinner!' I tell you,
this man went down to his house justified
rather than the other; for every one who
exalts himself will be humbled, but he who
humbles himself will be exalted."

Little children

15 Now they were bringing even infants to him
that he might touch them; and when the
16 disciples saw it, they rebuked them. But
Jesus called them to him, saying, "Let the
children come to me, and do not hinder
them; for to such belongs the kingdom of
17 God. Truly, I say to you, whoever does not
receive the kingdom of God like a child shall
not enter it."

A rich young ruler

18 And a ruler asked him, "Good Teacher,
19 what shall I do to inherit eternal life?" And
Jesus said to him, "Why do you call me
20 good? No one is good but God alone. You
know the commandments: 'Do not commit
adultery, Do not kill, Do not steal, Do not
bear false witness, Honour your father and
21 mother.' " And he said, "All these I have
22 observed from my youth." And when Jesus
heard it, he said to him, "One thing you still
lack. Sell all that you have and distribute to
the poor, and you will have treasure in
23 heaven; and come, follow me." But when he
heard this he became sad, for he was very
24 rich. Jesus looking at him said, "How hard it
is for those who have riches to enter the
25 kingdom of God! For it is easier for a camel
to go through the eye of a needle than for a
rich man to enter the kingdom of God."

Those who heard it said, "Then who can be
saved?" But he said, "What is impossible
with men is possible with God." And Peter
said, "Lo, we have left our homes and
followed you." And he said to them, "Truly,
I say to you, there is no man who has left
house or wife or brothers or parents or
children, for the sake of the kingdom of God,
who will not receive manifold more in this
time, and in the age to come eternal life."

An aside to the disciples

And taking the twelve, he said to them,
"Behold, we are going up to Jerusalem, and
everything that is written of the Son of man
by the prophets will be accomplished. For
he will be delivered to the Gentiles, and will
be mocked and shamefully treated and spit
upon; they will scourge him and kill him, and
on the third day he will rise." But they
understood none of these things; this saying
was hid from them, and they did not grasp
what was said.

On the Jericho road

As he drew near to Jericho, a blind man was
sitting by the roadside begging; and hearing
a multitude going by, he inquired what this
meant. They told him, "Jesus of Nazareth is
passing by." And he cried, "Jesus, Son of
David, have mercy on me!" And those who
were in front rebuked him, telling him to be
silent; but he cried out all the more, "Son of
David, have mercy on me!" And Jesus
stopped, and commanded him to be brought
to him; and when he came near, he asked
him, "What do you want me to do for you?"
He said, "Lord, let me receive my sight."
And Jesus said to him, "Receive your sight;
your faith has made you well." And immediately he received his sight and followed him,
glorifying God; and all the people, when they
saw it, gave praise to God.

Zacchaeus

He entered Jericho and was passing
through. And there was a man named
Zacchae'us; he was a chief tax collector, and
rich. And he sought to see who Jesus was,
but could not, on account of the crowd,
because he was small of stature. So he ran on
ahead and climbed up into a sycamore tree to

18.11: Mt 6.5; Mk 11.25.   18.12: Lk 5.33; 11.42.   18.14: Mt 18.4; 23.12; Lk 14.11; 1 Pet 5.6.
18.15-17: Mt 19.13-15; 18.3; Mk 10.13-16.   18.15-17: Mk 10.16-22; Mk 10.17-22.   18.18: Lk 10.25.
18.20: Ex 20.12-16; Deut 5.16-20; Rom 13.9; Jas 2.11.   18.22: Lk 12.33; Acts 2.45; 4.32.
18.24-27: Mt 19.23-26; Mk 10.23-27.   18.27: Gen 18.14; Job 42.2; Jer 32.17; Lk 1.37.
18.28-30: Mt 19.27-30; Mk 10.28-31; Lk 5.1-11.
18.31-34: Mt 20.17-19; Mk 10.32-34; Lk 9.22, 44-45; 17.25.
18.35-43: Mt 20.29-34; Mk 10.46-52; Mt 9.27-31; Mk 8.22; Jn 9.1-7.
18.42: Mt 9.22; Mk 5.34; 10.52; Lk 7.50; 8.48; 17.19.   19.1: Mk 10.46.

Sycamore

5 see him, for he was to pass that way. And when Jesus came to the place, he looked up and said to him, "Zacchae′us, make haste and come down; for I must stay at your 6 house today." So he made haste and came 7 down, and received him joyfully. And when they saw it they all murmured, "He has gone in to be the guest of a man who is a sinner." 8 And Zacchae′us stood and said to the Lord, "Behold, Lord, the half of my goods I give to the poor; and if I have defrauded any one of 9 anything, I restore it fourfold." And Jesus said to him, "Today salvation has come to this house, since he also is a son of Abraham. 10 For the Son of man came to seek and to save the lost."

Parable of the pounds

11 As they heard these things, he proceeded to tell a parable, because he was near to Jerusalem, and because they supposed that the kingdom of God was to appear immediately. 12 He said therefore, "A nobleman went into a far country to receive kingly power[c] and then 13 return. Calling ten of his servants, he gave them ten pounds,[d] and said to them, 'Trade 14 with these till I come.' But his citizens hated him and sent an embassy after him, saying, 'We do not want this man to reign over us.' 15 When he returned, having received the kingly power,[c] he commanded these servants, to whom he had given the money, to be called to him, that he might know what 16 they had gained by trading. The first came before him, saying, 'Lord, your pound has

made ten pounds more.' And he said to him, 17 'Well done, good servant! Because you have been faithful in a very little, you shall have authority over ten cities.' And the second 18 came, saying, 'Lord, your pound has made five pounds.' And he said to him, 'And you 19 are to be over five cities.' Then another 20 came, saying, 'Lord, here is your pound, which I kept laid away in a napkin; for I was 21 afraid of you, because you are a severe man; you take up what you did not lay down, and reap what you did not sow.' He said to him, 22 "I will condemn you out of your own mouth, you wicked servant! You knew that I was a severe man, taking up what I did not lay down and reaping what I did not sow? Why 23 then did you not put my money into the bank, and at my coming I should have collected it with interest?' And he said to 24 those who stood by, 'Take the pound from him, and give it to him who has the ten pounds.' (And they said to him, 'Lord, he 25 has ten pounds!') 'I tell you, that to every 26 one who has will more be given; but from him who has not, even what he has will be taken away. But as for these enemies of 27 mine, who did not want me to reign over them, bring them here and slay them before me.' "

IN JERUSALEM

Triumphal entry

AND when he had said this, he went on 28 ahead, going up to Jerusalem. When he 29 drew near to Beth′phage and Bethany, at the mount that is called Olivet, he sent two of the disciples, saying, "Go into the village 30 opposite, where on entering you will find a

c Greek *a kingdom*   d The mina, rendered here by *pound*, was equal to about £7
19.7: Lk 5.29–30; 15.1–2. 19.8: Lk 7.13; 3.14; Ex 22.1; Lev 6.5; Num 5.6–7. 19.9: Lk 3.8; 3.16; Rom 4.16. 19.11: Lk 9.51; 13.22; 17.11; 18.31; 9.27. 19.12–28: Mt 25.14–30. 19.12: Mk 13.34. 19.17: Lk 16.10. 19.26: Mt 13.12; Mk 4.25; Lk 8.18. 19.28: Mk 10.32. 19.29–38: Mt 21.1–9; Mk 11.1–10; Jn 12.12–18.

colt tied, on which no one has ever yet sat;
31 untie it and bring it here. If any one asks
you, 'Why are you untying it?' you shall say
32 this, 'The Lord has need of it.'" So those
who were sent went away and found it as he
33 had told them. And as they were untying the
colt, its owners said to them, "Why are you
34 untying the colt?" And they said, "The
35 Lord has need of it." And they brought it to
Jesus, and throwing their garments on the
36 colt they set Jesus upon it. And as he rode
along, they spread their garments on the
37 road. As he was now drawing near, at the
descent of the Mount of Olives, the whole
multitude of the disciples began to rejoice
and praise God with a loud voice for all the
38 mighty works that they had seen, saying,
"Blessed is the King who comes in the name
of the Lord! Peace in heaven and glory in
39 the highest!" And some of the Pharisees in
the multitude said to him, "Teacher, rebuke
40 your disciples." He answered, "I tell you, if
these were silent, the very stones would cry
out."
41 And when he drew near and saw the city he
42 wept over it, saying, "Would that even today
you knew the things that make for peace!
43 But now they are hid from your eyes. For
the days shall come upon you, when your
enemies will cast up a bank about you and
surround you, and hem you in on every side,
44 and dash you to the ground, you and your
children within you, and they will not leave
one stone upon another in you; because you
did not know the time of your visitation."

Jesus in the temple

And he entered the temple and began to 45
drive out those who sold, saying to them, "It 46
is written, 'My house shall be a house of
prayer'; but you have made it a den of
robbers."

And he was teaching daily in the temple. 47
The chief priests and the scribes and the
principal men of the people sought to destroy
him; but they did not find anything they 48
could do, for all the people hung upon his
words.

One day, as he was teaching the people in 20
the temple and preaching the gospel, the
chief priests and the scribes with the elders
came up and said to him, "Tell us by what 2
authority you do these things, or who it is
that gave you this authority." He answered 3
them, "I also will ask you a question; now
tell me, Was the baptism of John from 4
heaven or from men?" And they discussed 5
it with one another, saying, "If we say,
'From heaven,' he will say, 'Why did you not

19.32: Lk 22.13.   **19.34:** Lk 7.13.   **19.36:** 2 Kings 9.13.   **19.38:** Ps 118.26; Lk 13.35; 2.14.
19.39–40: Mt 21.15–16; Hab 2.11.   **19.41:** Lk 13.33–34.   **19.43:** Lk 21.21–24; 21.6; Is 29.3; Jer 6.6; Ezek 4.2.
19.44: 1 Pet 2.12.   **19.45–46:** Mt 21.12–13; Mk 11.15–17; Jn 2.13–17.   **19.47–48:** Mk 11.18; Lk 21.37; 22.53.
20.1–8: Mt 21.23–27; Mk 11.27–33.   **20.2:** Jn 2.18.

6 believe him ?' But if we say, 'From men,' all the people will stone us; for they are con-
7 vinced that John was a prophet." So they answered that they did not know whence it
8 was. And Jesus said to them, "Neither will I tell you by what authority I do these things."

The wicked tenants

9 And he began to tell the people this parable: "A man planted a vineyard, and let it out to tenants, and went into another country for a
10 long while. When the time came, he sent a servant to the tenants, that they should give him some of the fruit of the vineyard; but the tenants beat him, and sent him away
11 empty-handed. And he sent another servant; him also they beat and treated shamefully, and sent him away empty-handed.
12 And he sent yet a third; this one they
13 wounded and cast out. Then the owner of the vineyard said, 'What shall I do ? I will send my beloved son; it may be they will
14 respect him.' But when the tenants saw him, they said to themselves, 'This is the heir; let us kill him, that the inheritance may be
15 ours.' And they cast him out of the vineyard and killed him. What then will the owner of
16 the vineyard do to them? He will come and destroy those tenants, and give the vineyard to others." When they heard this, they said,
17 "God forbid!" But he looked at them and said, "What then is this that is written:
'The very stone which the builders rejected
has become the head of the corner' ?
18 Every one who falls on that stone will be broken to pieces; but when it falls on any one it will crush him."

Scribes and chief priests

19 The scribes and the chief priests tried to lay hands on him at that very hour, but they feared the people; for they perceived that he
20 had told this parable against them. So they watched him, and sent spies, who pretended to be sincere, that they might take hold of what he said, so as to deliver him up to the authority and jurisdiction of the governor.
21 They asked him, "Teacher, we know that you speak and teach rightly, and show no
22 partiality, but truly teach the way of God. Is it lawful for us to give tribute to Caesar, or
23 not?" But he perceived their craftiness, and
24 said to them, "Show me a coin.e Whose

likeness and inscription has it?" They said, "Caesar's." He said to them, "Then render 25 to Caesar the things that are Caesar's, and to God the things that are God's." And they 26 were not able in the presence of the people to catch him by what he said; but marvelling at his answer they were silent.

Sadducees

There came to him some Sad'ducees, those 27 who say that there is no resurrection, and 28 they asked him a question, saying, "Teacher, Moses wrote for us that if a man's brother dies, having a wife but no children, the manf must take the wife and raise up children for his brother. Now there were seven brothers; 29 the first took a wife, and died without children; and the second and the third took 30, her, and likewise all seven left no children 31 and died. Afterward the woman also died. 32 In the resurrection, therefore, whose wife 33 will the woman be? For the seven had her as wife."
And Jesus said to them, "The sons of this 34 age marry and are given in marriage; but 35 those who are accounted worthy to attain to that age and to the resurrection from the dead neither marry nor are given in marriage, for they cannot die any more, because they 36 are equal to angels and are sons of God, being sons of the resurrection. But that the 37 dead are raised, even Moses showed, in the passage about the bush, where he calls the Lord the God of Abraham and the God of Isaac and the God of Jacob. Now he is not 38 God of the dead, but of the living; for all live to him." And some of the scribes answered, 39 "Teacher, you have spoken well." For they 40 no longer dared to ask him any question.

David's son

But he said to them, "How can they say that 41 the Christ is David's son? For David him- 42 self says in the Book of Psalms,
'The Lord said to my Lord,
Sit at my right hand,
till I make thy enemies a stool for thy feet.' 43
David thus calls him Lord; so how is he his 44 son?"
And in the hearing of all the people he said 45 to his disciples, "Beware of the scribes, who 46 like to go about in long robes, and love salutations in the market places and the best seats in the synagogues and the places of

e Greek denarius f Greek his brother
20.6: Mt 14.5; Lk 7.29. 20.9-19: Mt 21.33-46; Mk 12.1-12. 20.9: Is 5.1-7; Mt 25.14.
20.16: Acts 13.46; 18.6; 28.28. 20.17: Ps 118.22-23; Acts 4.11; 1 Pet 2.6-7. 20.18: Is 8.14-15.
20.19: Lk 19.47. 20.20-26: Mt 22.15-22; Mk 12.13-17. 20.21: Jn 3.2. 20.25: Rom 13.7; Lk 23.2.
20.27-38: Mt 22.23-33; Mk 12.18-27. 20.27: Acts 4.1-2; 23.6-10. 20.28: Deut 25.5. 20.37: Ex 3.6.
20.39: Mk 12.28. 20.40: Mk 12.34; Mt 22.46. 20.41-44: Mt 22.41-45; Mk 12.35-37; Ps 110.1.
20.45-47: Mk 12.38-40; Mt 23.6-7; Lk 11.43; 14.7-11.

47 honour at feasts, who devour widows' houses and for a pretence make long prayers. They will receive the greater condemnation."

The widow's contribution

21 He looked up and saw the rich putting their 2 gifts into the treasury; and he saw a poor 3 widow put in two copper coins. And he said,

"Truly I tell you, this poor widow has put in 4 more than all of them; for they all contributed out of their abundance, but she out of her poverty put in all the living that she had."

Signs of the times

5 And as some spoke of the temple, how it was adorned with noble stones and offerings, 6 he said, "As for these things which you see, the days will come when there shall not be left here one stone upon another that will not 7 be thrown down." And they asked him, "Teacher, when will this be, and what will be the sign when this is about to take place?" 8 And he said, "Take heed that you are not led astray; for many will come in my name, saying, 'I am he!' and, 'The time is at 9 hand!' Do not go after them. And when you hear of wars and tumults, do not be terrified; for this must first take place, but the end will not be at once."

10 Then he said to them, "Nation will rise against nation, and kingdom against king-11 dom; there will be great earthquakes, and in various places famines and pestilences; and there will be terrors and great signs from 12 heaven. But before all this they will lay their hands on you and persecute you, delivering you up to the synagogues and prisons, and you will be brought before kings and gover-13 nors for my name's sake. This will be a time 14 for you to bear testimony. Settle it therefore in your minds, not to meditate beforehand 15 how to answer; for I will give you a mouth and wisdom, which none of your adversaries 16 will be able to withstand or contradict. You

will be delivered up even by parents and brothers and kinsmen and friends, and some of you they will put to death; you will be 17 hated by all for my name's sake. But not a 18 hair of your head will perish. By your 19 endurance you will gain your lives.

"But when you see Jerusalem surrounded 20 by armies, then know that its desolation has come near. Then let those who are in Judea 21 flee to the mountains, and let those who are inside the city depart, and let not those who are out in the country enter it; for these are 22 days of vengeance, to fulfil all that is written. Alas for those who are with child and for 23 those who give suck in those days! For great distress shall be upon the earth and wrath upon this people; they will fall by the edge of 24 the sword, and be led captive among all nations; and Jerusalem will be trodden down by the Gentiles, until the times of the Gentiles are fulfilled.

"And there will be signs in sun and moon 25 and stars, and upon the earth distress of nations in perplexity at the roaring of the sea and the waves, men fainting with fear and 26 with foreboding of what is coming on the world; for the powers of the heavens will be shaken. And then they will see the Son of 27 man coming in a cloud with power and great glory. Now when these things begin to take 28 place, look up and raise your heads, because your redemption is drawing near."

Look at the trees

And he told them a parable: "Look at the 29 fig tree, and all the trees; as soon as they 30 come out in leaf, you see for yourselves and know that the summer is already near. So 31 also, when you see these things taking place, you know that the kingdom of God is near. Truly, I say to you, this generation will not 32 pass away till all has taken place. Heaven 33 and earth will pass away, but my words will not pass away.

"But take heed to yourselves lest your 34 hearts be weighed down with dissipation and drunkenness and cares of this life, and that day come upon you suddenly like a snare; for 35 it will come upon all who dwell upon the face of the whole earth. But watch at all times, 36 praying that you may have strength to escape all these things that will take place, and to stand before the Son of man."

21.1-4: Mk 12.41-44.   21.5-23: Mt 24.1-19; Mk 13.1-17.   21.6: Lk 19.43-44; Mk 14.58; 15.29; Acts 6.14.
21.7: Lk 17.20; Acts 1.6.   21.8: Lk 17.23; Mk 13.21; 1 Jn 2.18.   21.10: 2 Chron 15.6; Is 19.2.
21.12-17: Mt 10.17-21.   21.12: Acts 25.24; Jn 16.2.   21.13: Phil 1.12.   21.14-15: Lk 12.11-12.
21.16: Lk 12.52-53.   21.17: Mt 10.22; Jn 15.18-25.   21.18: Lk 12.7; Mt 10.30; Acts 27.34; 1 Sam 14.45.
21.19: Mt 10.22; Rev 2.7.   21.20-22: Lk 19.41-44; 23.28-31; 17.31.   21.23: Lk 23.29.
21.24: Rom 11.25; Is 63.18; Dan 8.13; Rev 11.2.   21.25: Rev 6.12-13; Is 13.10; Joel 2.10; Zeph 1.15.   21.27: Mt 24.29-30; Mk 13.24-26.
21.25-27: Mt 24.29-30; Mk 13.24-26.   21.27: Dan 7.13-14.   21.28: Lk 18.7-8.
21.29-33: Mt 24.32-35; Mk 13.28-31.   21.32: Lk 9.27.   21.33: Lk 16.17.
21.34: Lk 12.45; Mk 4.19; 1 Thess 5.6-7.   21.36: Mk 13.33.

Visit to Olivet

And every day he was teaching in the temple, but at night he went out and lodged on the mount called Olivet. And early in the 38 morning all the people came to him in the temple to hear him.

DEATH AND RESURRECTION

2 NOW the feast of Unleavened Bread drew near, which is called the Passover. And the chief priests and the scribes were seeking how to put him to death; for they feared the people. 3 Then Satan entered into Judas called Iscariot, who was of the number of the 4 twelve; he went away and conferred with the chief priests and captains how he might 5 betray him to them. And they were glad, and 6 engaged to give him money. So he agreed, and sought an opportunity to betray him to them in the absence of the multitude.

The last supper

7 Then came the day of Unleavened Bread, on which the passover lamb had to be 8 sacrificed. So Jesus[g] sent Peter and John, saying "Go and prepare the passover for us, 9 that we may eat it." They said to him, 10 "Where will you have us prepare it?" He said to them, "Behold, when you have entered the city, a man carrying a jar of water will meet you; follow him into the house 11 which he enters, and tell the householder, 'The Teacher says to you, Where is the guest room, where I am to eat the passover with 12 my disciples?' And he will show you a large upper room furnished; there make ready." 13 And they went, and found it as he had told them; and they prepared the passover.

14 And when the hour came, he sat at table, 15 and the apostles with him. And he said to them, "I have earnestly desired to eat this 16 passover with you before I suffer; for I tell you I shall not eat it[h] until it is fulfilled in the 17 kingdom of God." And he took a cup, and when he had given thanks he said, "Take 18 this, and divide it among yourselves; for I tell you that from now on I shall not drink of the fruit of the vine until the kingdom of God 19 comes." And he took bread, and when he had given thanks he broke it and gave it to 21 them, saying, "This is my body.[i] But behold the hand of him who betrays me is with me

on the table. For the Son of man goes as it 22 has been determined; but woe to that man by whom he is betrayed!" And they began to 23 question one another, which of them it was that would do this.

A dispute also arose among them, which of 24 them was to be regarded as the greatest. And 25 he said to them, "The kings of the Gentiles exercise lordship over them; and those in authority over them are called benefactors. But not so with you; rather let the greatest 26 among you become as the youngest, and the leader as one who serves. For which is the 27 greater, one who sits at table, or one who serves? Is it not the one who sits at table? But I am among you as one who serves.

"You are those who have continued with 28 me in my trials; as my Father appointed a 29 kingdom for me, so do I appoint for you that 30 you may eat and drink at my table in my kingdom, and sit on thrones judging the twelve tribes of Israel.

g Greek *he*   h Other ancient authorities read *never eat it again*
i Other ancient authorities add *which is given for you. Do this in remembrance of me.* 20 *And likewise the cup after supper, saying, "This cup which is poured out for you is the new covenant in my blood.*
21.37: Lk 19.47; Mk 11.19. 22.1-2: Mt 26.2-5; Mk 14.1-2; Jn 11.47-53.
22.3-6: Mt 26.14-16; Mk 14.10-11; Jn 13.2. 22.7-13: Mt 26.17-19; Mk 14.12-16.
22.7: Ex 12.18-20; Deut 16.5-8. 22.8: Acts 3.1; Lk 19.29. 22.14: Mt 26.20; Mk 14.17; Jn 13.17.
22.15: Lk 12.49-50. 22.16: Lk 14.15. 22.17: Mt 26.27; Mk 14.23; 1 Cor 10.16. 22.18: Mt 26.29; Mk 14.25.
22.19: Mt 26.26; Mk 14.22; 1 Cor 10.16; 11.23-26; Lk 9.16.
22.21-23: Mt 26.21-24; Mk 14.18-21; Ps 41.9; Jn 13.21-30. 22.24: Lk 9.46; Mk 9.34.
22.25-27: Mt 20.25-28; Mk 10.42-45; Jn 13.3-16. 22.26: Lk 9.48. 22.28-30: Mt 19.28.
22.28: Lk 4.13; Heb 2.18; 4.15. 22.29: Mk 14.24; Heb 9.20. 22.30: Mk 10.37; Rev 3.21; 20.4.

31 "Simon, Simon, behold, Satan demanded
to have you,^{j} that he might sift you^j like
32 wheat, but I have prayed for you that your
faith may not fail; and when you have turned
33 again, strengthen your brethren." And he
said to him, "Lord, I am ready to go with
34 you to prison and to death." He said, "I tell
you, Peter, the cock will not crow this day,
until you three times deny that you know
me."
35 And he said to them, "When I sent you out
with no purse or bag or sandals, did you lack
36 anything?" They said, "Nothing." He said
to them, "But now, let him who has a purse
take it, and likewise a bag. And let him who
has no sword sell his mantle and buy one.
37 For I tell you that this scripture must be
fulfilled in me, 'And he was reckoned with
transgressors'; for what is written about me
38 has its fulfilment." And they said, "Look,
Lord, here are two swords." And he said to
them, "It is enough."

Gethsemane

39 And he came out, and went, as was his
custom, to the Mount of Olives; and the
40 disciples followed him. And when he came
to the place he said to them, "Pray that you
41 may not enter into temptation." And he
withdrew from them about a stone's throw,
42 and knelt down and prayed, "Father, if thou
art willing, remove this cup from me; nevertheless not my will, but thine, be done."
43 And there appeared to him an angel from
44 heaven, strengthening him. And being in an
agony he prayed more earnestly; and his
sweat became like great drops of blood falling
45 down upon the ground.^{k} And when he rose
from prayer, he came to the disciples and
46 found them sleeping for sorrow, and he said
to them, "Why do you sleep? Rise and pray
that you may not enter into temptation."

Betrayal and arrest

47 While he was still speaking, there came a
crowd, and the man called Judas, one of the
twelve, was leading them. He drew near to
48 Jesus to kiss him; but Jesus said to him,
"Judas, would you betray the Son of man
49 with a kiss?" And when those who were
about him saw what would follow, they said,

"Lord, shall we strike with the sword?"
And one of them struck the slave of the high
priest and cut off his right ear. But Jesus
said, "No more of this!" And he touched his
ear and healed him. Then Jesus said to the
chief priests and captains of the temple and
elders, who had come out against him, "Have
you come out as against a robber, with
swords and clubs? When I was with you day
after day in the temple, you did not lay hands
on me. But this is your hour, and the power
of darkness."

Peter's denial

Then they seized him and led him away,
bringing him into the high priest's house.
Peter followed at a distance; and when they
had kindled a fire in the middle of the
courtyard and sat down together, Peter sat
among them. Then a maid, seeing him as he
sat in the light and gazing at him, said, "This
man also was with him." But he denied it,
saying, "Woman, I do not know him." And
a little later some one else saw him and said,
"You also are one of them." But Peter said,
"Man, I am not." And after an interval of
about an hour still another insisted, saying,
"Certainly this man also was with him; for he
is a Galilean." But Peter said, "Man, I
do not know what you are saying." And
immediately, while he was still speaking, the
cock crowed. And the Lord turned and
looked at Peter. And Peter remembered the
word of the Lord, how he had said to him,
"Before the cock crows today, you will deny
me three times." And he went out and wept
bitterly.
Now the men who were holding Jesus
mocked him and beat him; they also blind-
folded him and asked him, "Prophesy! Who
is it that struck you?" And they spoke many
other words against him, reviling him.

Early morning trial

When day came, the assembly of the elders
of the people gathered together, both chief
priests and scribes; and they led him away to
their council, and they said, "If you are the
Christ, tell us." But he said to them, "If I
tell you, you will not believe; and if I ask you,
you will not answer. But from now on the

^{j} The Greek word for *you* here is plural; in verse 32 it is singular
^{k} Other ancient authorities omit verses 43 and 44
22.31: Job 1.6–12; Amos 9.9. 22.32: Jn 17.15; 21.15–17. 22.33–34: Mt 26.33–35; Mk 14.29–31; Jn 13.37–38.
22.35: Lk 10.4; Mt 10.9. 22.36: Lk 22.49–50. 22.37: Is 53.12. 22.39: Mt 26.30; Mk 14.26; Jn 18.1.
22.40–46: Mt 26.36–46; Mk 14.32–42; Heb 5.7–8. 22.40: Lk 11.4. 22.42: Mk 10.38; Jn 18.11; 5.30.
22.47–53: Mt 26.47–56; Mk 14.43–49; Jn 18.3–11. 22.49: Lk 22.38. 22.53: Lk 19.47.
22.54–55: Mt 26.57–58; Mk 14.53–54; Jn 18.12–16.
22.56–62: Mt 26.69–75; Mk 14.66–72; Jn 18.16–18, 25–27. 22.61: Lk 7.13; 22.34.
22.63–65: Mt 26.67–68; Mk 14.65; Jn 18.22–24. 22.66: Mt 26.57; Mk 14.53; Lk 22.54.
22.67–71: Mt 26.63–66; Mk 14.61–64; Jn 18.19–21.

Son of man shall be seated at the right hand of the power of God." And they all said, "Are you the Son of God, then?" And he said to them, "You say that I am." And they said, "What further testimony do we need? We have heard it ourselves from his own lips."

Jesus before Pilate

3 Then the whole company of them arose, and brought him before Pilate. And they began to accuse him, saying, "We found this man perverting our nation, and forbidding us to give tribute to Caesar, and saying that he himself is Christ a king." And Pilate asked him, "Are you the King of the Jews?" And he answered him, "You have said so." And Pilate said to the chief priests and the multitudes, "I find no crime in this man." But they were urgent, saying, "He stirs up the people, teaching throughout all Judea, from Galilee even to this place."

Before Herod

When Pilate heard this, he asked whether the man was a Galilean. And when he learned that he belonged to Herod's jurisdiction, he sent him over to Herod, who was himself in Jerusalem at that time. When Herod saw Jesus, he was very glad, for he had long desired to see him, because he had heard about him, and he was hoping to see some sign done by him. So he questioned him at some length; but he made no answer. The chief priests and the scribes stood by, vehemently accusing him. And Herod with his soldiers treated him with contempt and mocked him; then, arraying him in gorgeous apparel, he sent him back to Pilate. And Herod and Pilate became friends with each other that very day, for before this they had been at enmity with each other.

Pilate's judgment

Pilate then called together the chief priests and the rulers and the people, and said to them, "You brought me this man as one who was perverting the people; and after examining him before you, behold, I did not find this man guilty of any of your charges against him; neither did Herod, for he sent him back

to us. Behold, nothing deserving death has been done by him; I will therefore chastise him and release him."[l]

But they all cried out together, "Away with this man, and release to us Barab'bas"—a man who had been thrown into prison for an insurrection started in the city, and for murder. Pilate addressed them once more, desiring to release Jesus; but they shouted out, "Crucify, crucify him!" A third time he said to them, "Why, what evil has he done? I have found in him no crime deserving death; I will therefore chastise him and release him." But they were urgent, demanding with loud cries that he should be crucified. And their voices prevailed. So Pilate gave sentence that their demand should be granted. He released the man who had been thrown into prison for insurrection and murder, whom they asked for; but Jesus he delivered up to their will.

On the way to the cross

And as they led him away, they seized one Simon of Cyre'ne, who was coming in from the country, and laid on him the cross, to carry it behind Jesus. And there followed him a great multitude of the people, and of women who bewailed and lamented him. But Jesus turning to them said, "Daughters of Jerusalem, do not weep for me, but weep for yourselves and for your children. For behold, the days are coming when they will say, 'Blessed are the barren, and the wombs that never bore, and the breasts that never gave suck!' Then they will begin to say to the mountains, 'Fall on us'; and to the hills, 'Cover us.' For if they do this when the wood is green, what will happen when it is dry?"

Calvary

Two others also, who were criminals, were led away to be put to death with him. And when they came to the place which is called The Skull, there they crucified him, and the criminals, one on the right and one on the left. And Jesus said, "Father, forgive them; for they know not what they do."[m] And they cast lots to divide his garments. And the people stood by, watching; but the rulers scoffed at him, saying, "He saved others; let

---

l Here, or after verse 19, other ancient authorities add verse 17, *Now he was obliged to release one man to them at the festival*
m Other ancient authorities omit the sentence *And Jesus . . . what they do*
22.70: Lk 23.3; Mt 27.11.   23.1: Mt 27.1–2; Mk 15.1; Jn 18.28.   23.2: Lk 20.25.
23.3: Mt 27.11–12; Mk 15.2–3; Jn 18.29–38; Lk 22.70.   23.4: Lk 23.14, 22, 41; Mt 27.24; Jn 19.4, 6; Acts 13.28.
23.8: Lk 9.9; Acts 4.27–28.   23.9: Mk 15.5.   23.11: Mk 15.17–19; Jn 19.2–3.   23.14: Lk 23.4, 22, 41.
23.16: Lk 23.22; Jn 19.12–14.   23.18–23: Mt 27.20–23; Mk 15.11–14; Acts 3.13–14; Jn 18.38–40; 19.14–15.
23.23–25: Mt 27.26; Mk 15.15.   23.26: Mt 27.32; Mk 15.21; Jn 19.17.   23.28–31: Lk 21.23–24; 19.41–44.
23.33–39: Mt 27.33–44; Mk 15.22–32; Jn 19.17–24.   23.34: Acts 7.60; Ps 22.18.   23.35: Lk 4.23.

him save himself, if he is the Christ of God,
36 his Chosen One!" The soldiers also mocked
him, coming up and offering him vinegar,
37 and saying, "If you are the King of the Jews,
38 save yourself!" There was also an inscription over him,[n] "This is the King of the
Jews."

The penitent robber

39 One of the criminals who were hanged
railed at him, saying, "Are you not the
40 Christ? Save yourself and us!" But the
other rebuked him, saying, "Do you not fear
God, since you are under the same sentence
41 of condemnation? And we indeed justly; for
we are receiving the due reward of our deeds;
42 but this man has done nothing wrong." And
he said, "Jesus, remember me when you
43 come in your kingly power."[o] And he said to
him, "Truly, I say to you, today you will be
with me in Paradise."

After the crucifixion

It was now about the sixth hour, and there
was darkness over the whole land[p] until the
ninth hour, while the sun's light failed;[q] and
the curtain of the temple was torn in two.
Then Jesus, crying with a loud voice, said,
"Father, into thy hands I commit my
spirit!" And having said this he breathed his
last. Now when the centurion saw what had
taken place, he praised God, and said, "Certainly this man was innocent!" And all the
multitudes who assembled to see the sight,
when they saw what had taken place, returned home beating their breasts. And all
his acquaintances and the women who had
followed him from Galilee stood at a distance
and saw these things.

The burial

Now there was a man named Joseph from
the Jewish town of Arimathe′a. He was a
member of the council, a good and righteous
man, who had not consented to their purpose and deed, and he was looking for the
kingdom of God. This man went to Pilate
and asked for the body of Jesus. Then he
took it down and wrapped it in a linen
shroud, and laid him in a rock-hewn tomb,
where no one had ever yet been laid. It was
the day of Preparation, and the sabbath was
beginning.[r] The women who had come with
him from Galilee followed, and saw the
tomb, and how his body was laid; then they
returned, and prepared spices and ointments.
On the sabbath they rested according to the
commandment.

The resurrection

But on the first day of the week, at early
dawn, they went to the tomb, taking the
spices which they had prepared. And they
found the stone rolled away from the tomb,
but when they went in they did not find the
body.[s] While they were perplexed about
this, behold, two men stood by them in
dazzling apparel; and as they were frightened
and bowed their faces to the ground, the men
said to them, "Why do you seek the living
among the dead?[t] Remember how he told
you, while he was still in Galilee, that the
Son of man must be delivered into the hands
of sinful men, and be crucified, and on the
third day rise." And they remembered his

---

[n] Other ancient authorities add *in letters of Greek and Latin and Hebrew*   [o] Greek *kingdom*   [p] Or *earth*
[q] Or *the sun was eclipsed.* Other ancient authorities read *the sun was darkened*   [r] Greek *was dawning*
[s] Other ancient authorities add *of the Lord Jesus*   [t] Other ancient authorities add *He is not here, but has risen*
23.36: Mk 15.23; Ps 69.21.   **23.41:** Lk 23.4, 14, 22.   **23.43:** 2 Cor 12.3; Rev 2.7.
23.44-49: Mt 27.45-56; Mk 15.33-41; Jn 19.25-30.   **23.45:** Ex 26.31-35; Heb 9.8; 10.19.   **23.46:** Ps 31.5.
23.49: Lk 8.1-3; 23.55-56; 24.10.   **23.50-56:** Mt 27.57-61; Mk 15.42-47; Jn 19.38-42; Acts 13.29.
23.56: Mk 16.1; Ex 12.16; 20.10.   **24.1-9:** Mt 28.1-8; Mk 16.1-7; Jn 20.1, 11-13.   **24.6:** Lk 9.22; 13.32-33.

Luke 23, 45

9 words, and returning from the tomb they told all this to the eleven and to all the rest.
10 Now it was Mary Mag'dalene and Jo-an'na and Mary the mother of James and the other women with them who told this to the
11 apostles; but these words seemed to them an idle tale, and they did not believe them. "

On the way to Emmaus

13 That very day two of them were going to a village named Emma'us, about seven miles *v*
14 from Jerusalem, and talking with each other about all these things that had happened.
15 While they were talking and discussing together, Jesus himself drew near and went
16 with them. But their eyes were kept from
17 recognising him. And he said to them, "What is this conversation which you are holding with each other as you walk?" And
18 they stood still, looking sad. Then one of them, named Cle'opas, answered him, "Are you the only visitor to Jerusalem who does not know the things that have happened
19 there in these days?" And he said to them, "What things?" And they said to him, "Concerning Jesus of Nazareth, who was a prophet mighty in deed and word before
20 God and all the people, and how our chief priests and rulers delivered him up to be
21 condemned to death, and crucified him. But we had hoped that he was the one to redeem

Israel. Yes, and besides all this, it is now the third day since this happened. Moreover, 22 some women of our company amazed us. They were at the tomb early in the morning and did not find his body; and they came 23 back saying that they had even seen a vision of angels, who said that he was alive. Some 24 of those who were with us went to the tomb, and found it just as the women had said; but him they did not see." And he said to them, 25 "O foolish men, and slow of heart to believe all that the prophets have spoken! Was it not 26 necessary that the Christ should suffer these things and enter into his glory?" And 27 beginning with Moses and all the prophets, he interpreted to them in all the scriptures the things concerning himself.

So they drew near to the village to which 28 they were going. He appeared to be going further, but they constrained him, saying, 29 "Stay with us, for it is toward evening and the day is now far spent." So he went in to stay with them.

The evening meal

When he was at table with them, he took the 30 bread and blessed, and broke it, and gave it to them. And their eyes were opened and 31 they recognised him; and he vanished out of their sight. They said to each other, "Did 32 not our hearts burn within us while he talked to us on the road, while he opened to us the scriptures?"

The return to Jerusalem

And they rose that same hour and returned 33 to Jerusalem; and they found the eleven gathered together and those who were with them, who said, "The Lord has risen indeed, 34 and has appeared to Simon!" Then they 35 told what had happened on the road, and how he was known to them in the breaking of the bread.

The risen Christ appears

As they were saying this, Jesus himself 36 stood among them. *w* But they were startled 37 and frightened, and supposed that they saw a spirit. And he said to them, "Why are you 38 troubled, and why do questionings rise in your hearts? See my hands and my feet, that 39 it is I myself; handle me, and see; for a spirit has not flesh and bones as you see that I

u Other ancient authorities add verse 12, *But Peter rose and ran to the tomb; stooping and looking in, he saw the linen cloths by themselves; and he went home wondering at what had happened*
v Greek *sixty stadia*; some ancient authorities read *a hundred and sixty stadia*
w Other ancient authorities add *and said to them, "Peace to you!"*
24.10: Mk 16.1; Lk 8.1–3; Jn 20.2. **24.16:** Jn 20.14; 21.4. **24.19:** Mt 21.11; Lk 7.16; 13.33; Acts 3.22. **24.24:** Jn 20.3–10. **24.27:** Lk 24.44–45; Acts 28.23; 1 Pet 1.11. **24.28:** Mk 6.48. **24.30:** Lk 9.16; 22.19. **24.34:** 1 Cor 15.5. **24.36–43:** Jn 20.19–20, 27; Jn 21.5, 9–13; 1 Cor 15.5; Acts 10.40–41. **24.39:** 1 Jn 1.1.

41 have."ˣ And while they still disbelieved for joy, and wondered, he said to them, "Have 42 you anything here to eat?" They gave him a 43 piece of broiled fish, and he took it and ate before them.

You are my witnesses

44 Then he said to them, "These are my words which I spoke to you, while I was still with you, that everything written about me in the 45 law of Moses and the prophets and the psalms must be fulfilled." Then he opened 46 their minds to understand the scriptures, and said to them, "Thus it is written, that the Christ should suffer and on the third day rise 47 from the dead, and that repentance and forgiveness of sins should be preached in his name to all nations,ʸ beginning from Jeru-48 salem. You are witnesses of these things. 49 And behold, I send the promise of my Father upon you; but stay in the city, until you are clothed with power from on high."

The ascension

Then he led them out as far as Bethany, and 50 lifting up his hands he blessed them. While 51 he blessed them, he parted from them.ᶻ And 52 theyᵃ returned to Jerusalem with great joy, and were continually in the temple blessing 53 God.

ˣ Other ancient authorities add verse 40, *And when he had said this, he showed them his hands and his feet*
ʸ Or *nations. Beginning from Jerusalem you are witnesses*
ᶻ Other ancient authorities add *and was carried up into heaven*
ᵃ Other ancient authorities add *worshipped him, and*
24.44: Lk 24.26–27; Acts 28.23.   **24.46:** Hos 6.2; 1 Cor 15.3–4.   **24.47:** Acts 1.4–8; Mt 28.19.
24.49: Acts 2.1–4; Jn 14.26; 20.21–23.   **24.51:** Acts 1.9–11.   **24.52–53:** Acts 1.12–14.

The Great Sea

Sidon
Zarephath
Tyre

PHOENICIA

Mt Hermon
• Damascus

• Caesarea Philippi

GALILEE
Chorazin
Capernaum   • Bethsaida
Ptolemais   Magdala   *Sea of Galilee*
Cana   Tiberias   Gergesa
• Nazareth
• Nain

Mt Carmel

DE CAPOLIS

Caesarea

SAMARIA

• Samaria
Shechem   • Sychar

River Jordan

P E R Æ A

Joppa
Arimathea
Lydda   Ephraim   • Bethabara
Bethel
Emmaus   Jericho

■ Jerusalem
• Bethany

Azotus   • Bethlehem
JUDEA
• Gaza   • Hebron

Wilderness of Judea

Dead Sea

N

PALESTINE
in the time of
CHRIST

JERUSALEM

THE GOSPEL ACCORDING TO

JOHN

IN the beginning was the Word, and the Word was with God, and the Word was 2 God. He was in the beginning with 3 God; all things were made through him, and without him was not anything made that was 4 made. In him was life,[a] and the life was the 5 light of men. The light shines in the darkness, and the darkness has not overcome it.

6 There was a man sent from God, whose 7 name was John. He came for testimony, to bear witness to the light, that all might 8 believe through him. He was not the light, but came to bear witness to the light.

9 The true light that enlightens every man 10 was coming into the world. He was in the world, and the world was made through him, 11 yet the world knew him not. He came to his own home, and his own people received him 12 not. But to all who received him, who believed in his name, he gave power to 13 become children of God; who were born, not of blood nor of the will of the flesh nor of the will of man, but of God.

14 And the Word became flesh and dwelt among us, full of grace and truth; we have beheld his glory, glory as of the only Son from the Father. (John bore witness to him, 15 and cried, "This was he of whom I said, 'He who comes after me ranks before me, for he was before me.'") And from his fulness 16 have we all received, grace upon grace. For 17 the law was given through Moses; grace and truth came through Jesus Christ. No one has 18 ever seen God; the only Son,[b] who is in the bosom of the Father, he has made him known.

John the Baptist's testimony

And this is the testimony of John, when the 19 Jews sent priests and Levites from Jerusalem to ask him, "Who are you?" He confessed, 20 he did not deny, but confessed, "I am not the Christ." And they asked him, "What then? 21 Are you Eli′jah?" He said, "I am not." "Are you the prophet?" And he answered, "No." They said to him then, "Who are 22 you? Let us have an answer for those who

---

[a] Or *was not anything made. That which has been made was life in him* [b] Other ancient authorities read *God*
1.1: Gen 1.1; 1 Jn 1.1; Rev 19.13; Jn 17.5. **1.3**: Col 1.16; 1 Cor 8.6; Heb 1.2. **1.4**: Jn 5.26; 11.25; 14.6.
1.5: Jn 9.5; 12.46. **1.6**: Mk 1.4; Mt 3.1; Lk 3.3; Jn 1.19-23. **1.9**: 1 Jn 2.8.
1.12: Gal 3.26; Jn 3.18; 1 Jn 5.13. **1.13**: Jn 3.5; 1 Pet 1.23; Jas 1.18; 1 Jn 3.9.
1.14: Rom 1.3; Gal 4.4; Phil 2.7; 1 Tim 3.16; Heb 2.14; 1 Jn 4.2. **1.15**: Jn 1.30.
1.16: Col 1.19; 2.9; Eph 1.23; Rom 5.21. **1.17**: Jn 7.19. **1.18**: Ex 33.20; Jn 6.26; 1 Jn 4.12; Jn 3.11.
1.19: Jn 1.6. **1.20**: Jn 3.28. **1.21**: Mt 11.14; 16.14; Mk 9.13; Mt 17.13; Deut 18.15, 18.

sent us. What do you say about yourself?"
23 He said, "I am the voice of one crying in the wilderness, 'Make straight the way of the Lord,' as the prophet Isaiah said."
24 Now they had been sent from the Phari-
25 sees. They asked him, "Then why are you baptizing, if you are neither the Christ, nor Eli'jah, nor the prophet?" John answered 26 them, "I baptize with water; but among you stands one whom you do not know, even he 27 who comes after me, the thong of whose sandal I am not worthy to untie." This took 28 place in Bethany beyond the Jordan, where John was baptizing.

BEHOLD THE LAMB OF GOD

29 THE next day he saw Jesus coming toward him, and said, "Behold, the Lamb of God, who takes away the sin of the world!
30 This is he of whom I said, 'After me comes a man who ranks before me, for he was before
31 me.' I myself did not know him; but for this I came baptizing with water, that he might
32 be revealed to Israel." And John bore witness, "I saw the Spirit descend as a dove
33 from heaven, and it remained on him. I myself did not know him; but he who sent me to baptize with water said to me, 'He on whom you see the Spirit descend and remain, this is he who baptizes with the Holy Spirit.'
34 And I have seen and have borne witness that this is the Son of God."

The first disciples

35 The next day again John was standing with
36 two of his disciples; and he looked at Jesus as he walked, and said, "Behold, the Lamb of
37 God!" The two disciples heard him say this,
38 and they followed Jesus. Jesus turned, and saw them following, and said to them, "What do you seek?" And they said to him, "Rabbi" (which means Teacher), "where are
39 you staying?" He said to them, "Come and see." They came and saw where he was staying; and they stayed with him that day,
40 for it was about the tenth hour. One of the two who heard John speak, and followed him, was Andrew, Simon Peter's brother.
41 He first found his brother Simon, and said to him, "We have found the Messiah" (which
42 means Christ). He brought him to Jesus. Jesus looked at him, and said, "So you are Simon the son of John? You shall be called Cephas" (which means Peter[c]).
43 The next day Jesus decided to go to Galilee. And he found Philip and said to
44 him, "Follow me." Now Philip was from Beth-sa'ida, the city of Andrew and Peter.
45 Philip found Nathan'a-el, and said to him, "We have found him of whom Moses in the law and also the prophets wrote, Jesus of Nazareth, the son of Joseph." Nathan'a-el 46 said to him, "Can anything good come out of Nazareth?" Philip said to him, "Come and see." Jesus saw Nathan'a-el coming to him, 47 and said of him, "Behold, an Israelite indeed, in whom is no guile!" Nathan'a-el said 48 to him, "How do you know me?" Jesus answered him, "Before Philip called you, when you were under the fig tree, I saw you." Nathan'a-el answered him, "Rabbi, 49 you are the Son of God! You are the King of Israel!" Jesus answered him, "Because I 50 said to you, I saw you under the fig tree, do you believe? You shall see greater things than these." And he said to him, "Truly, 51 truly, I say to you, you will see heaven opened, and the angels of God ascending and descending upon the Son of man."

The first miracle

On the third day there was a marriage at 2 Cana in Galilee, and the mother of Jesus was there; Jesus also was invited to the marriage, 2 with his disciples. When the wine failed, the 3 mother of Jesus said to him, "They have no wine." And Jesus said to her, "O woman, 4 what have you to do with me? My hour has not yet come." His mother said to the 5 servants, "Do whatever he tells you." Now 6 six stone jars were standing there, for the Jewish rites of purification, each holding twenty or thirty gallons. Jesus said to them, 7 "Fill the jars with water." And they filled them up to the brim. He said to them, "Now 8 draw some out, and take it to the steward of the feast." So they took it. When the 9 steward of the feast tasted the water now become wine, and did not know where it came from (though the servants who had drawn the water knew), the steward of the feast called the bridegroom and said to him, 10 "Every man serves the good wine first; and when men have drunk freely, then the poor

c From the word for rock in Aramaic and Greek, respectively
1.23: Is 40.3; Mk 1.3; Mt 3.3; Lk 3.4.   1.26–27: Mk 1.7–8; Mt 3.11; Lk 3.16.   1.28: Jn 3.26; 10.40.
1.29: Jn 1.36; Is 53.7; Acts 8.32; 1 Pet 1.19; Rev 5.6; 1 Jn 3.5.   1.30: Jn 1.15.
1.32: Mk 1.10; Mt 3.16; Lk 3.22.   1.35: Lk 7.18.   1.40–42: Mt 4.18–22; Mk 1.16–20; Lk 5.2–11.
1.41: Dan 9.25; Jn 4.25.   1.42: Jn 21.15–17; 1 Cor 15.5; Mt 16.18.   1.43: Mt 10.3; Jn 6.5; 12.21; 14.8.
1.45: Lk 24.27.   1.46: Jn 7.41; Mk 6.2.   1.49: Ps 2.7; Mk 15.32; Jn 12.13.   1.51: Lk 3.21; Gen 28.12.
2.1: Jn 4.46; 21.2.   2.3: Jn 19.26; Mk 3.31.   2.4: Mk 1.24; 5.7; Jn 7.6, 30; 8.20.   2.6: Mk 7.3; Jn 3.25.

wine; but you have kept the good wine until
11 now." This, the first of his signs, Jesus did
at Cana in Galilee, and manifested his glory;
and his disciples believed in him.

After this he went down to Caper'na-um, 12
with his mother and his brothers and his
disciples; and there they stayed for a few
days.

THE FIRST PASSOVER

13 THE Passover of the Jews was at hand, and
14 Jesus went up to Jerusalem. In the
temple he found those who were selling oxen
and sheep and pigeons, and the money-
15 changers at their business. And making a
whip of cords, he drove them all, with the
sheep and oxen, out of the temple; and he
poured out the coins of the money-changers
16 and overturned their tables. And he told
those who sold the pigeons, "Take these
things away; you shall not make my Father's
17 house a house of trade." His disciples
remembered that it was written, "Zeal for
18 thy house will consume me." The Jews then
said to him, "What sign have you to show us
19 for doing this?" Jesus answered them,
"Destroy this temple, and in three days I will
20 raise it up." The Jews then said, "It has
taken forty-six years to build this temple, and
21 will you raise it up in three days?" But he
22 spoke of the temple of his body. When
therefore he was raised from the dead, his
disciples remembered that he had said this;
and they believed the scripture and the word
which Jesus had spoken.
23 Now when he was in Jerusalem at the
Passover feast, many believed in his name
24 when they saw the signs which he did; but

Jesus did not trust himself to them, because 25
he knew all men and needed no one to bear
witness of man; for he himself knew what
was in man.

Nicodemus

Now there was a man of the Pharisees, 3
named Nicode'mus, a ruler of the Jews.
This man came to Jesus[d] by night and said to 2
him, "Rabbi, we know that you are a teacher
come from God; for no one can do these
signs that you do, unless God is with him."
Jesus answered him, "Truly, truly, I say to 3
you, unless one is born anew,[e] he cannot see
the kingdom of God." Nicode'mus said to 4
him, "How can a man be born when he is
old? Can he enter a second time into his
mother's womb and be born?" Jesus 5
answered, "Truly, truly, I say to you, unless
one is born of water and the Spirit, he cannot
enter the kingdom of God. That which is 6
born of the flesh is flesh, and that which is
born of the Spirit is spirit.[f] Do not marvel 7
that I said to you, 'You must be born anew.'[g]
The wind[f] blows where it wills, and you hear 8
the sound of it, but you do not know whence
it comes or whither it goes; so it is with every

d Greek him   e Or from above   f The same Greek word means both wind and spirit
2.11: Jn 2.23; 3.2; 4.54; 6.2.   2.12: Mt 4.13; Jn 7.3; Mk 3.31.   2.13: Jn 6.4; 11.55; Deut 16.1–6; Lk 2.41.
2.14–16: Mt 21.12–13; Mk 11.15–17; Lk 19.45–46.   2.16: Lk 2.49.   2.17: Ps 69.9.
2.18: Mk 11.28; Mt 21.23; Lk 20.2.   2.19: Mk 14.58; Acts 6.14.   2.21: 1 Cor 6.19; Jn 8.57.
2.22: Jn 12.16; 14.26.   2.25: Jn 1.47; 6.61; 13.11; Mk 2.8.   3.1: Jn 7.50; 19.39; Jn 7.26.
3.2: Jn 2.11; 7.31; 9.16; Acts 10.38.   3.3: Jn 1.13; 1 Pet 1.23; Jas 1.18; 1 Jn 3.9.
3.5: Ezek 36.25–27; Eph 5.26; Tit 3.5.   3.6: 1 Cor 15.50.   3.8: Ezek 37.9.

9 one who is born of the Spirit." Nicode′mus
10 said to him, "How can this be?" Jesus
answered him, "Are you a teacher of Israel,
11 and yet you do not understand this? Truly,
truly, I say to you, we speak of what we
know, and bear witness to what we have
seen; but you do not receive our testimony.
12 If I have told you earthly things and you do
not believe, how can you believe if I tell you
13 heavenly things? No one has ascended into
heaven but he who descended from heaven,
14 the Son of man.⁹ And as Moses lifted up the
serpent in the wilderness, so must the Son of
15 man be lifted up, that whoever believes in
him may have eternal life."ʰ
16 For God so loved the world that he gave his
only Son, that whoever believes in him
17 should not perish but have eternal life. For
God sent the Son into the world, not to
condemn the world, but that the world might
18 be saved through him. He who believes in
him is not condemned; he who does not
believe is condemned already, because he has
not believed in the name of the only Son of
19 God. And this is the judgment, that the light
has come into the world, and men loved
darkness rather than light, because their
20 deeds were evil. For every one who does evil
hates the light, and does not come to the
21 light, lest his deeds should be exposed. But
he who does what is true comes to the light,
that it may be clearly seen that his deeds have
been wrought in God.

John the Baptist

22 After this Jesus and his disciples went into
the land of Judea; there he remained with
23 them and baptized. John also was baptizing
at Ae′non near Salim, because there was
much water there; and people came and were
24 baptized. For John had not yet been put in
prison.
25 Now a discussion arose between John's
26 disciples and a Jew over purifying. And they
came to John, and said to him, "Rabbi, he
who was with you beyond the Jordan, to
whom you bore witness, here he is, baptiz-
27 ing, and all are going to him." John
answered, "No one can receive anything
28 except what is given him from heaven. You
yourselves bear me witness, that I said, I am
not the Christ, but I have been sent before
29 him. He who has the bride is the bride-

groom; the friend of the bridegroom, who
stands and hears him, rejoices greatly at the
bridegroom's voice; therefore this joy of
mine is now full. He must increase, but I 30
must decrease."ⁱ
He who comes from above is above all; he 31
who is of the earth belongs to the earth, and
of the earth he speaks; he who comes from
heaven is above all. He bears witness to what 32
he has seen and heard, yet no one receives his
testimony; he who receives his testimony sets 33
his seal to this, that God is true. For he 34
whom God has sent utters the words of God,
for it is not by measure that he gives the
Spirit; the Father loves the Son, and has 35
given all things into his hand. He who 36
believes in the Son has eternal life; he who
does not obey the Son shall not see life, but
the wrath of God rests upon him.

The woman of Samaria

Now when the Lord knew that the Phari- 4
sees had heard that Jesus was making and
baptizing more disciples than John (although 2
Jesus himself did not baptize, but only his
disciples), he left Judea and departed again to 3
Galilee. He had to pass through Samar′ia. 4
So he came to a city of Samar′ia, called 5
Sy′char, near the field that Jacob gave to his
son Joseph. Jacob's well was there, and so 6
Jesus, wearied as he was with his journey, sat
down beside the well. It was about the sixth
hour.
There came a woman of Samar′ia to draw 7
water. Jesus said to her, "Give me a drink."
For his disciples had gone away into the city 8
to buy food. The Samaritan woman said to 9
him, "How is it that you, a Jew, ask a drink
of me, a woman of Samar′ia?" For Jews
have no dealings with Samaritans. Jesus 10
answered her, "If you knew the gift of God,
and who it is that is saying to you, 'Give me a
drink,' you would have asked him, and he
would have given you living water." The 11
woman said to him, "Sir, you have nothing

ⁿ Other ancient authorities add *who is in heaven*
ʰ Some interpreters hold that the quotation continues through verse 21
ⁱ Some interpreters hold that the quotation continues through verse 36
3.11: Jn 8.26; 1.18; 3.32.   **3.13:** Rom 10.6; Eph 4.9.   **3.14:** Num 21.9; Jn 8.28; 12.34.
3.16: Rom 5.8; 8.32; Eph 2.4; 1 Jn 4.9-10.   **3.17:** Jn 8.15; 12.47; Lk 19.10; 1 Jn 4.14.
3.19: Jn 1.4; 8.12; Eph 5.11, 13.   **3.21:** 1 Jn 1.6.   **3.22:** Jn 4.2.   **3.24:** Mk 1.14; 6.17-18.   **3.26:** Jn 1.7, 28.
3.27: 1 Cor 4.7.   **3.28:** Jn 3.16; 5.24.   **3.29:** Mk 2.19-20; Mt 25.1; Jn 15.11.   **3.31:** Jn 3.13; 8.23; 1 Jn 4.5.
3.32: Jn 3.11.   **3.36:** Jn 3.16; 5.24.   **4.1:** Jn 3.22.   **4.4:** Lk 9.52; 17.11.   **4.5:** Gen 33.19; 48.22; Josh 24.32.
4.9: Mt 10.5; Jn 8.48; Ezra 4.3-6.   **4.10:** Jn 7.37; Rev 21.6; 22.17.

to draw with, and the well is deep; where do 12 you get that living water? Are you greater than our father Jacob, who gave us the well, and drank from it himself, and his sons, and 13 his cattle?" Jesus said to her, "Every one 14 who drinks of this water will thirst again, but whoever drinks of the water that I shall give him will never thirst; the water that I shall give him will become in him a spring of water 15 welling up to eternal life." The woman said to him, "Sir, give me this water, that I may not thirst, nor come here to draw."

16 Jesus said to her, "Go, call your husband, 17 and come here." The woman answered him, "I have no husband." Jesus said to her "You are right in saying, 'I have no hus- 18 band'; for you have had five husbands, and he whom you now have is not your husband; 19 this you said truly." The woman said to him, "Sir, I perceive that you are a prophet. 20 Our fathers worshipped on this mountain; and you say that in Jerusalem is the place 21 where men ought to worship." Jesus said to her, "Woman, believe me, the hour is coming when neither on this mountain nor in 22 Jerusalem will you worship the Father. You worship what you do not know; we worship what we know, for salvation is from the 23 Jews. But the hour is coming, and now is, when the true worshippers will worship the Father in spirit and truth, for such the 24 Father seeks to worship him. God is spirit, and those who worship him must worship in 25 spirit and truth." The woman said to him, "I know that Messiah is coming (he who is called Christ); when he comes, he will show 26 us all things." Jesus said to her, "I who speak to you am he."

27 Just then his disciples came. They mar- velled that he was talking with a woman, but none said, "What do you wish?" or, "Why 28 are you talking with her?" So the woman left her water jar, and went away into the 29 city, and said to the people, "Come, see a man who told me all that I ever did. Can this 30 be the Christ?" They went out of the city and were coming to him.

31 Meanwhile the disciples besought him, 32 saying, "Rabbi, eat." But he said to them, "I have food to eat of which you do not know." 33 So the disciples said to one another, "Has 34 any one brought him food?" Jesus said to them, "My food is to do the will of him who 35 sent me, and to accomplish his work. Do you not say, 'There are yet four months, then comes the harvest'? I tell you, lift up your

eyes, and see how the fields are already white for harvest. He who reaps receives wages, 36 and gathers fruit for eternal life, so that sower and reaper may rejoice together. For 37 here the saying holds true, 'One sows and another reaps.' I sent you to reap that for 38 which you did not labour; others have laboured, and you have entered into their labour."

Many Samaritans from that city believed in 39 him because of the woman's testimony, "He told me all that I ever did." So when the 40 Samaritans came to him, they asked him to stay with them; and he stayed there two days. And many more believed because of 41 his word. They said to the woman, "It is no 42 longer because of your words that we believe, for we have heard for ourselves, and we know that this is indeed the Saviour of the world."

After the two days he departed to Galilee. 43 For Jesus himself testified that a prophet has 44 no honour in his own country. So when he 45 came to Galilee, the Galileans welcomed him, having seen all that he had done in Jerusalem at the feast, for they too had gone to the feast.

So he came again to Cana in Galilee, where 46 he had made the water wine. And at Caper'- na-um there was an official whose son was ill. When he heard that Jesus had come from 47 Judea to Galilee, he went and begged him to come down and heal his son, for he was at the point of death. Jesus therefore said to him, 48 "Unless you see signs and wonders you will not believe." The official said to him, "Sir, 49 come down before my child dies." Jesus said 50 to him, "Go; your son will live." The man believed the word that Jesus spoke to him and went his way. As he was going down, his 51 servants met him and told him that his son was living. So he asked them the hour when 52 he began to mend, and they said to him, "Yesterday at the seventh hour the fever left him." The father knew that was the hour 53 when Jesus had said to him, "Your son will live"; and he himself believed, and all his household. This was now the second sign 54 that Jesus did when he had come from Judea to Galilee.

At another festival

After this there was a feast of the Jews, and 5 Jesus went up to Jerusalem.

Now there is in Jerusalem by the Sheep 2 Gate a pool, in Hebrew called Beth-za'tha,[j]

---

[j] Other ancient authorities read Bethesda, others Bethsaida

4.14: Jn 6.35; 7.38. **4.15:** Jn 6.34. **4.18:** 2 Kings 17.24; Hos 2.7. **4.20:** Deut 11.29; Josh 8.33; Lk 9.53.
4.21: Jn 5.25; 16.2, 32; Mal 1.11. **4.22:** 2 Kings 17.28–41; Is 2.3; Rom 9.4. **4.24:** Phil 3.3. **4.26:** Jn 8.24.
4.29: Jn 7.26; Mt 12.23. **4.32:** Mt 4.4. **4.34:** Jn 5.30; 6.38; 17.4. **4.35:** Lk 10.2; Mt 9.37.
4.37: Job 31.8; Mic 6.15. **4.42:** 1 Jn 4.14; 2 Tim 1.10. **4.44:** Mk 6.4; Mt 13.57.
4.46: Jn 2.1–11; Mt 8.5–10; Lk 7.2–10. **4.48:** Dan 4.2; Mk 13.22; Acts 2.19; 4.30; Rom 15.19; Heb 2.4.
4.53: Acts 11.14. **4.54:** Jn 2.11. **5.2:** Neh 3.1; 12.39.

3 which has five porticoes. In these lay a
multitude of invalids, blind, lame, para-
5 lysed.[k] One man was there, who had been ill
6 for thirty-eight years. When Jesus saw him
and knew that he had been lying there a long
time, he said to him, "Do you want to be
7 healed?" The sick man answered him, "Sir,
I have no man to put me into the pool when
the water is troubled, and while I am going
8 another steps down before me." Jesus said
to him, "Rise, take up your pallet, and
9 walk." And at once the man was healed, and
he took up his pallet and walked.

10 Now that day was the sabbath. So the Jews
said to the man who was cured, "It is the
sabbath, it is not lawful for you to carry your
11 pallet." But he answered them, "The man
who healed me said to me, 'Take up your
12 pallet, and walk.'" They asked him, "Who
is the man who said to you, 'Take up your
13 pallet, and walk'?" Now the man who had
been healed did not know who it was, for
Jesus had withdrawn, as there was a crowd in
14 the place. Afterward, Jesus found him in the
temple, and said to him, "See, you are well!
Sin no more, that nothing worse befall you."
15 The man went away and told the Jews that it
16 was Jesus who had healed him. And this was
why the Jews persecuted Jesus, because he
17 did this on the sabbath. But Jesus answered
them, "My Father is working still, and I am
18 working." This was why the Jews sought all
the more to kill him, because he not only
broke the sabbath but also called God his
Father, making himself equal with God.

19 Jesus said to them, "Truly, truly, I say to
you, the Son can do nothing of his own
accord, but only what he sees the Father
doing; for whatever he does, that the Son
20 does likewise. For the Father loves the Son,
and shows him all that he himself is doing;
and greater works than these will he show
21 him, that you may marvel. For as the Father
raises the dead and gives them life, so also the
22 Son gives life to whom he will. The Father
judges no one, but has given all judgment to
23 the Son, that all may honour the Son, even as
they honour the Father. He who does not
honour the Son does not honour the Father
24 who sent him. Truly, truly, I say to you, he
who hears my word and believes him who
sent me, has eternal life; he does not come
into judgment, but has passed from death to
life.
25 "Truly, truly, I say to you, the hour is

coming, and now is, when the dead will hear
the voice of the Son of God, and those who
hear will live. For as the Father has life in 26
himself, so he has granted the Son also to
have life in himself, and has given him 27
authority to execute judgment, because he is
the Son of man. Do not marvel at this; for 28
the hour is coming when all who are in the
tombs will hear his voice and come forth, 29
those who have done good, to the resurrection of life, and those who have done evil, to
the resurrection of judgment.

"I can do nothing on my own authority; as I 30
hear, I judge; and my judgment is just,
because I seek not my own will but the will of
him who sent me. If I bear witness to 31
myself, my testimony is not true; there is 32
another who bears witness to me, and I know
that the testimony which he bears to me is
true. You sent to John, and he has borne 33
witness to the truth. Not that the testimony 34
which I receive is from man; but I say this
that you may be saved. He was a burning 35
and shining lamp, and you were willing to
rejoice for a while in his light. But the 36
testimony which I have is greater than that of
John; for the works which the Father has
granted me to accomplish, these very works
which I am doing, bear me witness that the
Father has sent me. And the Father who 37
sent me has himself borne witness to me.
His voice you have never heard, his form you
have never seen; and you do not have his 38
word abiding in you, for you do not believe

v. 39

k Other ancient authorities insert, wholly or in part, *waiting for the moving of the water;* [4] *for an angel of the Lord went down at certain seasons into the pool, and troubled the water; whoever stepped in first after the troubling of the water was healed of whatever disease he had*
5.8: Mk 2.11; Mt 9.6; Lk 5.24. **5.10:** Neh 13.19; Jer 17.21; Jn 7.23; 9.16; Mk 2.24. **5.14:** Mk 2.5.
5.17: Gen 2.3. **5.18:** Jn 7.1; 10.33. **5.19:** Jn 5.30; 8.28; 14.10. **5.20:** Jn 14.12.
5.21: Rom 4.17; 8.11; Jn 11.25. **5.23:** Lk 10.16; 1 Jn 2.23. **5.24:** Jn 3.18. **5.25:** Jn 4.21; 16.2, 32.
5.29: Dan 12.2; Acts 24.15; Jn 11.24; Mt 25.46; 1 Cor 15.52. **5.30:** Jn 5.19; 8.16; 6.38. **5.31–37:** Jn 8.14–18.
5.33: Jn 1.7, 19. **5.34:** 1 Jn 5.9. **5.36:** Jn 10.25; 14.11; 15.24; Mt 11.4.

39 him whom he has sent. You search the
scriptures, because you think that in them
you have eternal life; and it is they that bear
40 witness to me; yet you refuse to come to me
41 that you may have life. I do not receive glory
42 from men. But I know that you have not the
43 love of God within you. I have come in my
Father's name, and you do not receive me; if
another comes in his own name, him you will
44 receive. How can you believe, who receive
glory from one another and do not seek the
45 glory that comes from the only God? Do not
think that I shall accuse you to the Father; it
is Moses who accuses you, on whom you set
46 your hope. If you believed Moses, you
47 would believe me, for he wrote of me. But if
you do not believe his writings, how will you
believe my words?"

THE SECOND PASSOVER

6 AFTER this Jesus went to the other side of
the Sea of Galilee, which is the Sea of
2 Tibe′ri-as. And a multitude followed him,
because they saw the signs which he did on
3 those who were diseased. Jesus went up into
the hills, and there sat down with his dis-
4 ciples. Now the Passover, the feast of the
Jews, was at hand.

The bread of life

5 Lifting up his eyes, then, and seeing that a
multitude was coming to him, Jesus said to
Philip, "How are we to buy bread, so that
6 these people may eat?" This he said to test
him, for he himself knew what he would do.
7 Philip answered him, "Two hundred denarii[l]
would not buy enough bread for each of
8 them to get a little." One of his disciples,
Andrew, Simon Peter's brother, said to him,
9 "There is a lad here who has five barley
loaves and two fish; but what are they among
10 so many?" Jesus said, "Make the people sit
down." Now there was much grass in the
place; so the men sat down, in number about
11 five thousand. Jesus then took the loaves,
and when he had given thanks, he distributed
them to those who were seated; so also the
12 fish, as much as they wanted. And when
they had eaten their fill, he told his disciples,
"Gather up the fragments left over, that
13 nothing may be lost." So they gathered
them up and filled twelve baskets with
fragments from the five barley loaves, left by
14 those who had eaten. When the people saw
the sign which he had done, they said, "This

A street in Jerusalem

is indeed the prophet who is to come into the
world!"

Perceiving then that they were about to 1
come and take him by force to make him
king, Jesus withdrew again to the hills by
himself.

When evening came, his disciples went 1
down to the sea, got into a boat, and started 1
across the sea to Caper′na-um. It was now
dark, and Jesus had not yet come to them.
The sea rose because a strong wind was 1
blowing. When they had rowed about three 1
or four miles,[m] they saw Jesus walking on the
sea and drawing near to the boat. They were
frightened, but he said to them, "It is I; do 2
not be afraid." Then they were glad to take 2
him into the boat, and immediately the boat
was at the land to which they were going.

On the next day the people who remained 2
on the other side of the sea saw that there had
been only one boat there, and that Jesus had
not entered the boat with his disciples, but

l The denarius was worth about seventeen pence   m Greek *twenty-five or thirty stadia*
5.39: Lk 24.27; Acts 13.27.   **5.43:** Mt 24.5.   **5.45:** Jn 9.28; Rom 2.17.   **5.47:** Lk 16.29, 31.
6.1-13: Mt 14.13-21; Mk 6.32-44; Lk 9.10-17.   **6.5:** Jn 1.43; 12.21.   **6.8:** Jn 1.40; 12.22.   **6.9:** Jn 21.9-13.
6.14: Mt 21.11.   **6.15:** Jn 6.3; 18.36.   **6.16-21:** Mt 14.22-27; Mk 6.45-51.

that his disciples had gone away alone.
3 However, boats from Tibe′ri-as came near
the place where they ate the bread after the
4 Lord had given thanks. So when the people
saw that Jesus was not there, nor his disciples, they themselves got into the boats and
went to Caper′na-um, seeking Jesus.
5 When they found him on the other side of
the sea, they said to him, "Rabbi, when did
6 you come here?" Jesus answered them,
"Truly, truly, I say to you, you seek me, not
because you saw signs, but because you ate
7 your fill of the loaves. Do not labour for the
food which perishes, but for the food which
endures to eternal life, which the Son of man
will give to you; for on him has God the
8 Father set his seal." Then they said to him,
"What must we do, to be doing the works of
9 God?" Jesus answered them, "This is the
work of God, that you believe in him whom
10 he has sent." So they said to him, "Then
what sign do you do, that we may see, and
believe you? What work do you perform?
31 Our fathers ate the manna in the wilderness;
as it is written, 'He gave them bread from
32 heaven to eat.'" Jesus then said to them,
"Truly, truly, I say to you, it was not Moses
who gave you the bread from heaven; my
Father gives you the true bread from heaven.
33 For the bread of God is that which comes
down from heaven, and gives life to the
34 world." They said to him, "Lord, give us
this bread always."
35 Jesus said to them, "I am the bread of life;
he who comes to me shall not hunger, and he
36 who believes in me shall never thirst. But I
said to you that you have seen me and yet do
37 not believe. All that the Father gives me will
come to me; and him who comes to me I will
38 not cast out. For I have come down from
heaven, not to do my own will, but the will of
39 him who sent me; and this is the will of him
who sent me, that I should lose nothing of all
that he has given me, but raise it up at the
40 last day. For this is the will of my Father,
that every one who sees the Son and believes
in him should have eternal life; and I will
raise him up at the last day."
41 The Jews then murmured at him, because
he said, "I am the bread which came down
42 from heaven." They said, "Is not this Jesus,
the son of Joseph, whose father and mother
we know? How does he now say, 'I have
43 come down from heaven'?" Jesus answered
them, "Do not murmur among yourselves.
44 No one can come to me unless the Father

who sent me draws him; and I will raise him
up at the last day. It is written in the 45
prophets, 'And they shall all be taught by
God.' Every one who has heard and learned
from the Father comes to me. Not that any 46
one has seen the Father except him who is
from God; he has seen the Father. Truly, 47
truly, I say to you, he who believes has
eternal life. I am the bread of life. Your 48,
fathers ate the manna in the wilderness, and 49
they died. This is the bread which comes 50
down from heaven, that a man may eat of it
and not die. I am the living bread which 51
came down from heaven; if any one eats of
this bread, he will live for ever; and the bread
which I shall give for the life of the world is
my flesh."
The Jews then disputed among themselves, 52
saying, "How can this man give us his flesh
to eat?" So Jesus said to them, "Truly, 53
truly, I say to you, unless you eat the flesh of
the Son of man and drink his blood, you have
no life in you; he who eats my flesh and 54
drinks my blood has eternal life, and I will
raise him up at the last day. For my flesh is 55
food indeed, and my blood is drink indeed.
He who eats my flesh and drinks my blood 56
abides in me, and I in him. As the living 57
Father sent me, and I live because of the
Father, so he who eats me will live because of
me. This is the bread which came down 58
from heaven, not such as the fathers ate and
died; he who eats this bread will live for
ever." This he said in the synagogue, as he 59
taught at Caper′na-um.
Many of his disciples, when they heard it, 60
said, "This is a hard saying; who can listen to
it?" But Jesus, knowing in himself that his 61
disciples murmured at it, said to them, "Do
you take offence at this? Then what if you 62
were to see the Son of man ascending where
he was before? It is the spirit that gives life, 63
the flesh is of no avail; the words that I have
spoken to you are spirit and life. But there 64
are some of you that do not believe." For
Jesus knew from the first who those were
that did not believe, and who it was that
should betray him. And he said, "This is 65
why I told you that no one can come to me
unless it is granted him by the Father."
After this many of his disciples drew back 66
and no longer went about with him. Jesus 67
said to the twelve, "Will you also go away?"
Simon Peter answered him, "Lord, to whom 68
shall we go? You have the words of eternal
life; and we have believed, and have come to 69

6.27: Is 55.2.   **6.29:** 1 Thess 1.3; 1 Jn 3.23.   **6.30:** Mt 12.38; Mk 8.11.
6.31: Ex 16.4, 15; Num 11.8; Neh 9.15; Ps 78.24; 105.40.   **6.34:** Jn 4.15; Mt 6.11.   **6.35:** Jn 6.48–50; 4.14.
6.37: Jn 17.2.   **6.38:** Jn 4.34; 5.30.   **6.39:** Jn 17.12; 18.9.   **6.40:** Jn 5.29; 11.24; 6.54.   **6.42:** Lk 4.22; Jn 7.27.
6.44: Jer 31.3; Hos 11.4; Jn 12.32; 6.65.   **6.45:** 1 Thess 4.9; 1 Jn 2.27; Is 54.13.   **6.46:** Jn 1.18.
6.52: Jn 3.4; 4.9.   **6.56:** Jn 15.4; 1 Jn 3.24; 4.15.   **6.58:** Jn 6.41, 51.   **6.59:** Jn 6.25.   **6.61:** Mt 11.6.
6.62: Jn 3.13; 17.5.   **6.63:** 2 Cor 3.6; Jn 6.68.   **6.64:** Jn 2.25.   **6.65:** Jn 6.44; 3.27.   **6.68–69:** Mk 8.27–30.

The Sea of Galilee

know, that you are the Holy One of God."
70 Jesus answered them, "Did I not choose you,
71 the twelve, and one of you is a devil?" He
spoke of Judas the son of Simon Iscariot, for
he, one of the twelve, was to betray him.

The feast of Tabernacles

7 After this Jesus went about in Galilee; he
would not go about in Judea, because the
2 Jews[n] sought to kill him. Now the Jews'
3 feast of Tabernacles was at hand. So his
brothers said to him, "Leave here and go to
Judea, that your disciples may see the works
4 you are doing. For no man works in secret if
he seeks to be known openly. If you do these
5 things, show yourself to the world." For
even his brothers did not believe in him.
6 Jesus said to them, "My time has not yet
7 come, but your time is always here. The
world cannot hate you, but it hates me
because I testify of it that its works are evil.
8 Go to the feast yourselves; I am not[o] going
up to this feast, for my time has not yet fully
9 come." So saying, he remained in Galilee.
10 But after his brothers had gone up to the
feast, then he also went up, not publicly but
11 in private. The Jews were looking for him at
12 the feast, and saying, "Where is he?" And
there was much muttering about him among
the people. While some said, "He is a good
man," others said, "No, he is leading the
13 people astray." Yet for fear of the Jews no
one spoke openly of him.

About the middle of the feast Jesus went 14
up into the temple and taught. The Jews 15
marvelled at it, saying, "How is it that
this man has learning,[p] when he has never
studied?" So Jesus answered them, "My 16
teaching is not mine, but his who sent me; if 17
any man's will is to do his will, he shall know
whether the teaching is from God or whether
I am speaking on my own authority. He who 18
speaks on his own authority seeks his own
glory; but he who seeks the glory of him who
sent him is true, and in him there is no
falsehood. Did not Moses give you the law? 19
Yet none of you keeps the law. Why do you
seek to kill me?" The people answered, 20
"You have a demon! Who is seeking to kill
you?" Jesus answered them, "I did one 21
deed, and you all marvel at it. Moses gave 22
you circumcision (not that it is from Moses,
but from the fathers), and you circumcise a
man upon the sabbath. If on the sabbath a 23
man receives circumcision, so that the law of
Moses may not be broken, are you angry
with me because on the sabbath I made a
man's whole body well? Do not judge by 24
appearances, but judge with right judgment."

Some of the people of Jerusalem therefore 25
said, "Is not this the man whom they seek to
kill? And here he is, speaking openly, and 26
they say nothing to him! Can it be that the
authorities really know that this is the
Christ? Yet we know where this man comes 27
from; and when the Christ appears, no one

[n] Or *Judeans* [o] Other ancient authorities add *yet* [p] Or *this man knows his letters*
6.70: Jn 15.16, 19. **6.71:** Jn 13.2, 27; 17.12. **7.2:** Lev 23.34; Deut 16.16. **7.3:** Mk 3.21, 31; Mt 12.46.
7.6: Mt 26.18; Jn 2.4; 7.30. **7.7:** Jn 15.18–21. **7.12:** Jn 7.40–43. **7.13:** Jn 19.38; 20.19. **7.19:** Jn 1.17.
7.20: Jn 8.48; 10.20; Mt 11.18; Mk 3.22. **7.21:** Jn 5.2–9. **7.22:** Lev 12.3; Gen 17.10; 21.4.
7.23: Mk 3.5; Lk 13.12; 14.4. **7.24:** Jn 8.15; Is 11.3; Zech 7.9. **7.27:** Jn 6.42; 7.41; 9.29.

8 will know where he comes from." So Jesus proclaimed, as he taught in the temple, "You know me, and you know where I come from? But I have not come of my own accord; he who sent me is true, and him you 29 do not know. I know him, for I come from 30 him, and he sent me." So they sought to arrest him; but no one laid hands on him, 31 because his hour had not yet come. Yet many of the people believed in him; they said, "When the Christ appears, will he do more signs than this man has done?" 32 The Pharisees heard the crowd thus muttering about him, and the chief priests and 33 Pharisees sent officers to arrest him. Jesus then said, "I shall be with you a little longer, 34 and then I go to him who sent me; you will seek me and you will not find me; where I am 35 you cannot come." The Jews said to one another, "Where does this man intend to go that we shall not find him? Does he intend to go to the Dispersion among the Greeks 36 and teach the Greeks? What does he mean by saying, 'You will seek me and you will not find me,' and, 'Where I am you cannot come'?"

37 On the last day of the feast, the great day, Jesus stood up and proclaimed, "If any one 38 thirst, let him come to me and drink. He who believes in me, as*q* the scripture has said, 'Out of his heart shall flow rivers of living 39 water.'" Now this he said about the Spirit, which those who believed in him were to receive; for as yet the Spirit had not been given, because Jesus was not yet glorified. 40 When they heard these words, some of the people said, "This is really the prophet." 41 Others said, "This is the Christ." But some said, "Is the Christ to come from Galilee? 42 Has not the scripture said that the Christ is descended from David, and comes from Bethlehem, the village where David was?" 43 So there was a division among the people 44 over him. Some of them wanted to arrest him, but no one laid hands on him.

The officers then went back to the chief 45 priests and Pharisees, who said to them, "Why did you not bring him?" The officers 46 answered, "No man ever spoke like this man!" The Pharisees answered them, "Are 47 you led astray, you also? Have any of the 48 authorities or of the Pharisees believed in him? But this crowd, who do not know the 49 law, are accursed." Nicode′mus, who had 50 gone to him before, and who was one of them, said to them, "Does our law judge a 51 man without first giving him a hearing and learning what he does?" They replied, "Are 52 you from Galilee too? Search and you will see that no prophet is to rise from Galilee."*r*

The light of the world

Again Jesus spoke to them, saying, "I am 8 the light of the world; he who follows me will 12 not walk in darkness, but will have the light of life." The Pharisees then said to him, 13 "You are bearing witness to yourself; your testimony is not true." Jesus answered, 14 "Even if I do bear witness to myself, my testimony is true, for I know whence I have come and whither I am going, but you do not know whence I come or whither I am going. You judge according to the flesh, I judge no 15 one. Yet even if I do judge, my judgment is 16 true, for it is not I alone that judge, but I and he*s* who sent me. In your law it is written 17 that the testimony of two men is true; I bear 18 witness to myself, and the Father who sent me bears witness to me." They said to him, 19 therefore, "Where is your Father?" Jesus answered, "You know neither me nor my Father; if you knew me, you would know my Father also." These words he spoke in the 20 treasury, as he taught in the temple; but no one arrested him, because his hour had not yet come.

Again he said to them, "I go away, and you 21 will seek me and die in your sin; where I am going, you cannot come." Then said the 22

q Or *let him come to me, and let him who believes in me drink. As*
r Other ancient authorities add 7.53–8.11 either here or at the end of this gospel or after Luke 21.38, with variations of the text:
8 ⁵³ *They went each to his own house,* ¹ *but Jesus went to the Mount of Olives.* ² *Early in the morning he came again to the temple; all the people came to him, and he sat down and taught them.* ³ *The scribes and the Pharisees brought a woman who had been caught in adultery, and placing her in the midst* ⁴ *they said to him, "Teacher, this woman has been caught in the act of adultery.* ⁵ *Now in the law Moses commanded us to stone such. What do you say about her?"* ⁶ *This they said to test him, that they might have some charge to bring against him. Jesus bent down and wrote with his finger on the ground.* ⁷ *And as they continued to ask him, he stood up and said to them, "Let him who is without sin among you be the first to throw a stone at her."* ⁸ *And once more he bent down and wrote with his finger on the ground.* ⁹ *But when they heard it, they went away, one by one, beginning with the eldest, and Jesus was left alone with the woman standing before him.* ¹⁰ *Jesus looked up and said to her, "Woman, where are they? Has no one condemned you?"* ¹¹ *She said, "No one, Lord." And Jesus said, "Neither do I condemn you; go, and do not sin again."*
s Other ancient authorities read *the Father*
7.28: Jn 8.42. 7.29: Jn 8.55; 17.25; Mt 11.27. 7.30: Jn 7.44; 10.39; Mk 12.12; Jn 8.20.
7.31: Jn 8.30; 10.42; 11.45. 7.33: Jn 8.21; 12.35; 13.33; 14.19; 16.16–19.
7.35: Jas 1.1; 1 Pet 1.1; Jn 12.20; Acts 11.20. 7.37: Lev 23.36; Jn 4.10, 14. 7.38: Is 44.3; 55.1; 58.11.
7.39: Jn 20.22; 12.23. 7.40: Jn 1.21; Mt 21.11. 7.42: Mic 5.2; Mt 1.1; Lk 2.4. 7.44: Jn 7.30; 10.39.
7.46: Mt 7.28. 7.50: Jn 3.1; 19.39. 7.51: Deut 17.6; Ex 23.1. 7.52: 2 Kings 14.25.
8.12: Jn 9.5; 12.35; 1.4. 8.13–18: Jn 5.31–39. 8.15: Jn 7.24; 3.17. 8.16: Jn 5.30.
8.17: Deut 19.15; Mt 18.16. 8.19: Jn 14.7. 8.20: Mk 12.41; Jn 7.30. 8.21–22: Jn 7.33–36.

Jews, "Will he kill himself, since he says,
23 'Where I am going, you cannot come'?" He
said to them, "You are from below, I am
from above; you are of this world, I am not of
24 this world. I told you that you would die in
your sins, for you will die in your sins unless
25 you believe that I am he." They said to him,
"Who are you?" Jesus said to them, "Even
26 what I have told you from the beginning.[t] I
have much to say about you and much to
judge; but he who sent me is true, and I
declare to the world what I have heard from
27 him." They did not understand that he
28 spoke to them of the Father. So Jesus said,
"When you have lifted up the Son of man,
then you will know that I am he, and that I
do nothing on my own authority but speak
29 thus as the Father taught me. And he who
sent me is with me; he has not left me alone,
30 for I always do what is pleasing to him." As
he spoke, many believed in him.
31 Jesus then said to the Jews who had believed in him, "If you continue in my word,
32 you are truly my disciples, and you will know
the truth, and the truth will make you free."
33 They answered him, "We are descendants of
Abraham, and have never been in bondage to
any one. How is it that you say, 'You will be
made free'?"
34 Jesus answered them, "Truly, truly, I say to
you, every one who commits sin is a slave to
35 sin. The slave does not continue in the house
36 for ever; the son continues for ever. So if the
Son makes you free, you will be free indeed.
37 I know that you are descendants of
Abraham; yet you seek to kill me, because
38 my word finds no place in you. I speak of
what I have seen with my Father, and you do
what you have heard from your father."
39 They answered him, "Abraham is our
father." Jesus said to them, "If you were
Abraham's children, you would do what
40 Abraham did, but now you seek to kill me, a
man who has told you the truth which I
heard from God; this is not what Abraham
41 did. You do what your father did." They
said to him, "We were not born of fornication; we have one Father, even God."
42 Jesus said to them, "If God were your
Father, you would love me, for I proceeded
and came forth from God; I came not of my
43 own accord, but he sent me. Why do you not
understand what I say? It is because you
44 cannot bear to hear my word. You are of
your father the devil, and your will is to do
your father's desires. He was a murderer

from the beginning, and has nothing to do
with the truth, because there is no truth in
him. When he lies, he speaks according to
his own nature, for he is a liar and the father
of lies. But, because I tell the truth, you do 45
not believe me. Which of you convicts me of 46
sin? If I tell the truth, why do you not
believe me? He who is of God hears the 47
words of God; the reason why you do not
hear them is that you are not of God."
The Jews answered him, "Are we not right 48
in saying that you are a Samaritan and have a
demon?" Jesus answered, "I have not a 49
demon; but I honour my Father, and you
dishonour me. Yet I do not seek my own 50
glory; there is One who seeks it and he will
be the judge. Truly, truly, I say to you, if 51
any one keeps my word, he will never see
death." The Jews said to him, "Now we 52
know that you have a demon. Abraham died,
as did the prophets; and you say, 'If any one
keeps my word, he will never taste death.'
Are you greater than our father Abraham, 53
who died? And the prophets died! Who do
you claim to be?" Jesus answered, "If I 54
glorify myself, my glory is nothing; it is my
Father who glorifies me, of whom you say
that he is your God. But you have not 55
known him; I know him. If I said, I do not
know him, I should be a liar like you; but I
do know him and I keep his word. Your 56
father Abraham rejoiced that he was to see

A Levite and a priest

t Or *Why do I talk to you at all?*
8.23: Jn 3.31; 17.14; 1 Jn 4.5.   **8.24:** Jn 8.28; 4.26; 13.19; Mk 13.6.   **8.28:** Jn 3.14; 12.32.
8.30 Jn 7.31; 10.42; 11.45.   **8.31:** Jn 15.7; 2 Jn 9.   **8.32:** 2 Cor 3.17; Gal 5.1.   **8.33:** Mt 3.9; Gal 3.7.
8.34: Rom 6.16; 2 Pet 2.19.   **8.35:** Gen 21.10; Gal 4.30.   **8.41:** Deut 32.6; Is 63.16; 64.8.
8.42: Jn 13.3; 16.28.   **8.44:** 1 Jn 3.8, 15; Gen 3.4; 1 Jn 2.4; Mt 12.34.   **8.46:** 1 Jn 3.5; Jn 18.37.
8.48: Jn 7.20; 10.20; 4.9.   **8.53:** Jn 4.12.   **8.56:** Mt 13.17; Heb 11.13.

57 my day; he saw it and was glad." The Jews then said to him, "You are not yet fifty years 58 old, and have you seen Abraham?"*u* Jesus said to them, "Truly, truly, I say to you, 59 before Abraham was, I am." So they took up stones to throw at him; but Jesus hid himself, and went out of the temple.

9 As he passed by, he saw a man blind from 2 his birth. And his disciples asked him, "Rabbi, who sinned, this man or his parents, 3 that he was born blind?" Jesus answered, "It was not that this man sinned, or his parents, but that the works of God might be 4 made manifest in him. We must work the works of him who sent me, while it is day; 5 night comes, when no one can work. As long as I am in the world, I am the light of the 6 world." As he said this, he spat on the ground and made clay of the spittle and 7 anointed the man's eyes with the clay, saying to him, "Go, wash in the pool of Silo'am" (which means Sent). So he went and washed 8 and came back seeing. The neighbours and those who had seen him before as a beggar, said, "Is not this the man who used to sit and 9 beg?" Some said, "It is he"; others said, "No, but he is like him." He said, "I am the 10 man." They said to him, "Then how were 11 your eyes opened?" He answered, "The man called Jesus made clay and anointed my eyes and said to me, 'Go to Silo'am and wash'; so I went and washed and received my 12 sight." They said to him, "Where is he?" He said, "I do not know."

13 They brought to the Pharisees the man who 14 had formerly been blind. Now it was a sabbath day when Jesus made the clay and 15 opened his eyes. The Pharisees again asked him how he had received his sight. And he said to them, "He put clay on my eyes, and I 16 washed, and I see." Some of the Pharisees said, "This man is not from God, for he does not keep the sabbath." But others said, "How can a man who is a sinner do such signs?" There was a division among them. 17 So they again said to the blind man, "What do you say about him, since he has opened your eyes?" He said, "He is a prophet." 18 The Jews did not believe that he had been blind and had received his sight, until they called the parents of the man who had 19 received his sight, and asked them, "Is this your son, who you say was born blind? How 20 then does he now see?" His parents answered, "We know that this is our son, and 21 that he was born blind; but how he now sees

we do not know, nor do we know who opened his eyes. Ask him; he is of age, he will speak for himself." His parents said this because 22 they feared the Jews, for the Jews had already agreed that if any one should confess him to be Christ, he was to be put out of the synagogue. Therefore his parents said, "He 23 is of age, ask him."

So for the second time they called the man 24 who had been blind, and said to him, "Give God the praise; we know that this man is a sinner." He answered, "Whether he is a 25 sinner, I do not know; one thing I know, that though I was blind, now I see." They said to 26 him, "What did he do to you? How did he open your eyes?" He answered them, "I 27 have told you already, and you would not listen. Why do you want to hear it again? Do you too want to become his disciples?" And they reviled him, saying, "You are his 28 disciple, but we are disciples of Moses. We 29 know that God has spoken to Moses, but as for this man, we do not know where he comes from." The man answered, "Why, this is a 30 marvel! You do not know where he comes from, and yet he opened my eyes. We know 31 that God does not listen to sinners, but if any one is a worshipper of God and does his will, God listens to him. Never since the world 32 began has it been heard that any one opened the eyes of a man born blind. If this man 33 were not from God, he could do nothing." They answered him, "You were born in utter 34 sin, and would you teach us?" And they cast him out.

Jesus heard that they had cast him out, and 35 having found him he said, "Do you believe in the Son of man?"*v* He answered, "And who 36 is he, sir, that I may believe in him?" Jesus 37 said to him, "You have seen him, and it is he who speaks to you." He said, "Lord, I 38 believe"; and he worshipped him. Jesus 39 said, "For judgment I came into this world, that those who do not see may see, and that those who see may become blind." Some of 40 the Pharisees near him heard this, and they said to him, "Are we also blind?" Jesus said 41 to them, "If you were blind, you would have no guilt; but now that you say, 'We see,' your guilt remains.

The good shepherd

"Truly, truly, I say to you, he who does not **10** enter the sheepfold by the door but climbs in by another way, that man is a thief and a robber; but he who enters by the door is the 2

---

u Other ancient authorities read *has Abraham seen you?*   *v* Other ancient authorities read *the Son of God*
8.57: Jn 2.20.   8.58: Jn 1.1; 17.5, 24.   8.59: Jn 10.31; 11.8.   9.2: Lk 13.2; Acts 28.4; Ezek 18.20; Ex 20.5.
9.3: Jn 11.4.   9.4: Jn 11.9; 12.35.   9.5: Jn 1.4; 8.12; 12.46.   9.6: Mk 7.33; 8.23.   9.7: Lk 13.4.
9.16: Mt 12.2; Jn 5.9; 7.43; 10.19.   9.22: Jn 7.13; 12.42; Lk 6.22.   9.28: Jn 5.45.   9.38: Mt 28.9.
9.39: Jn 5.27; 3.19; Mt 15.14.   9.41: Jn 15.22.   10.2: Mk 6.34.

3 shepherd of the sheep. To him the gate-keeper opens; the sheep hear his voice, and he calls his own sheep by name and leads 4 them out. When he has brought out all his own, he goes before them, and the sheep 5 follow him, for they know his voice. A stranger they will not follow, but they will flee from him, for they do not know the voice 6 of strangers." This figure Jesus used with them, but they did not understand what he was saying to them.

7 So Jesus again said to them, "Truly, truly, I 8 say to you, I am the door of the sheep. All who came before me are thieves and robbers; 9 but the sheep did not heed them. I am the door; if any one enters by me, he will be saved, and will go in and out and find 10 pasture. The thief comes only to steal and kill and destroy; I came that they may have 11 life, and have it abundantly. I am the good shepherd. The good shepherd lays down his 12 life for the sheep. He who is a hireling and not a shepherd, whose own the sheep are not, sees the wolf coming and leaves the sheep and flees; and the wolf snatches them 13 and scatters them. He flees because he is a 14 hireling and cares nothing for the sheep. I am the good shepherd; I know my own and 15 my own know me, as the Father knows me and I know the Father; and I lay down my 16 life for the sheep. And I have other sheep, that are not of this fold; I must bring them also, and they will heed my voice. So there 17 shall be one flock, one shepherd. For this reason the Father loves me, because I lay 18 down my life, that I may take it again. No one takes it from me, but I lay it down of my own accord. I have power to lay it down, and I have power to take it again; this charge I have received from my Father."

19 There was again a division among the Jews 20 because of these words. Many of them said, "He has a demon, and he is mad; why listen 21 to him?" Others said, "These are not the sayings of one who has a demon. Can a demon open the eyes of the blind?"

The feast of the Dedication

22 It was the feast of the Dedication at Jeru-23 salem; it was winter, and Jesus was walking in the temple, in the portico of Solomon. 24 So the Jews gathered round him and said to him, "How long will you keep us in suspense? If you are the Christ, tell us 25 plainly." Jesus answered them, "I told you,

THE TEMPLE BUILDINGS

TOWER OF ANTONIA

Court of Gentiles

Court of Israel

Court of Priests

HOLY OF HOLIES

Altar

Court of Women

Court of Priests

GATE BEAUTIFUL

Court of Israel

Court of Gentiles

SOLOMON'S PORCH

and you do not believe. The works that I do in my Father's name, they bear witness to me; but you do not believe, because you do 26 not belong to my sheep. My sheep hear my 27 voice, and I know them, and they follow me; and I give them eternal life, and they shall 28 never perish, and no one shall snatch them out of my hand. My Father, who has given 29 them to me, [w] is greater than all, and no one is able to snatch them out of the Father's hand. I and the Father are one." 30

The Jews took up stones again to stone 31 him. Jesus answered them, "I have shown 32 you many good works from the Father; for which of these do you stone me?" The Jews 33 answered him, "We stone you for no good work but for blasphemy; because you, being a man, make yourself God." Jesus answered 34 them, "Is it not written in your law, 'I said,

[w] Other ancient authorities read *What my Father has given to me*
10.6: Jn 16.25.   **10.8:** Jer 23.1; Ezek 34.2.
10.11: Is 40.11; Ezek 34.11–16; Heb 13.20; 1 Pet 5.4; Rev 7.17; 1 Jn 3.16; Jn 15.13.   **10.15:** Mt 11.27.
10.16: Is 56.8; Jn 11.52; 17.20; Eph 2.13–18; 1 Pet 2.25.   **10.18:** Jn 14.31; 15.10; Phil 2.8; Heb 5.8.
10.19: Jn 7.43; 9.16.   **10.20:** Jn 7.20; 8.48; Mt 11.18.   **10.21:** Jn 9.32; Ex 4.11.   **10.23:** Acts 3.11; 5.12.
10.25: Jn 5.36; 10.38.   **10.26:** Jn 8.47.   **10.28:** Jn 17.2; 1 Jn 2.25.   **10.30:** Jn 17.21.   **10.31:** Jn 8.59; 11.8.
10.33: Lev 24.16; Mk 14.64.   **10.34:** Jn 8.17; Ps 82.6.

JOHN 11 889

5 you are gods'? If he called them gods to
whom the word of God came (and scripture
6 cannot be broken), do you say of him whom
the Father consecrated and sent into the
world, 'You are blaspheming,' because I
7 said, 'I am the Son of God'? If I am not
doing the works of my Father, then do not
8 believe me; but if I do them, even though
you do not believe me, believe the works,
that you may know and understand that the
Father is in me and I am in the Father."
9 Again they tried to arrest him, but he
escaped from their hands.
10 He went away again across the Jordan to the
place where John at first baptized, and there
11 he remained. And many came to him; and
they said, "John did no sign, but everything
that John said about this man was true."
12 And many believed in him there.

The Lord of life

11 Now a certain man was ill, Laz'arus of
Bethany, the village of Mary and her sister
2 Martha. It was Mary who anointed the Lord
with ointment and wiped his feet with her
3 hair, whose brother Laz'arus was ill. So the
sisters sent to him, saying, "Lord, he whom
4 you love is ill." But when Jesus heard it he
said, "This illness is not unto death; it is for
the glory of God, so that the Son of God may
be glorified by means of it."
5 Now Jesus loved Martha and her sister and
6 Laz'arus. So when he heard that he was ill,
he stayed two days longer in the place where
7 he was. Then after this he said to the
8 disciples, "Let us go into Judea again." The
disciples said to him, "Rabbi, the Jews were
but now seeking to stone you, and are you
9 going there again?" Jesus answered, "Are
there not twelve hours in the day? If any
one walks in the day, he does not stumble,
10 because he sees the light of this world. But if
any one walks in the night, he stumbles,
11 because the light is not in him." Thus he
spoke, and then he said to them, "Our friend
Laz'arus has fallen asleep, but I go to awake
12 him out of sleep." The disciples said to him,
"Lord, if he has fallen asleep, he will
13 recover." Now Jesus had spoken of his
death, but they thought that he meant taking
14 rest in sleep. Then Jesus told them plainly,
15 "Laz'arus is dead; and for your sake I am
glad that I was not there, so that you may
16 believe. But let us go to him." Thomas,
called the Twin, said to his fellow disciples,

"Let us also go, that we may die with
him."
Now when Jesus came, he found that 17
Laz'arus *x* had already been in the tomb four
days. Bethany was near Jerusalem, about 18
two miles *y* off, and many of the Jews had 19
come to Martha and Mary to console them
concerning their brother. When Martha 20
heard that Jesus was coming, she went and
met him, while Mary sat in the house.
Martha said to Jesus, "Lord, if you had been 21
here, my brother would not have died. And 22
even now I know that whatever you ask from
God, God will give you." Jesus said to her, 23
"Your brother will rise again." Martha said 24
to him, "I know that he will rise again in the
resurrection at the last day." Jesus said to 25
her, "I am the resurrection and the life; *z* he
who believes in me, though he die, yet shall
he live, and whoever lives and believes in me 26
shall never die. Do you believe this?" She 27
said to him, "Yes, Lord; I believe that you
are the Christ, the Son of God, he who is
coming into the world."
When she had said this, she went and called 28
her sister Mary, saying quietly, "The
Teacher is here and is calling for you." And 29
when she heard it, she rose quickly and went
to him. Now Jesus had not yet come to the 30
village, but was still in the place where
Martha had met him. When the Jews who 31
were with her in the house, consoling her,
saw Mary rise quickly and go out, they
followed her, supposing that she was going to
the tomb to weep there. Then Mary, when 32
she came where Jesus was and saw him, fell
at his feet, saying to him, "Lord, if you had
been here, my brother would not have
died." When Jesus saw her weeping, and the 33
Jews who came with her also weeping, he was
deeply moved in spirit and troubled; and he 34
said, "Where have you laid him?" They
said to him, "Lord, come and see." Jesus 35
wept. So the Jews said, "See how he loved 36
him!" But some of them said, "Could not he 37
who opened the eyes of the blind man have
kept this man from dying?"
Then Jesus, deeply moved again, came to 38
the tomb; it was a cave, and a stone lay upon
it. Jesus said, "Take away the stone." 39
Martha, the sister of the dead man, said to
him, "Lord, by this time there will be an
odour, for he has been dead four days."
Jesus said to her, "Did I not tell you that if 40
you would believe you would see the glory of
God?" So they took away the stone. And 41

x Greek *he* *y* Greek *fifteen stadia* *z* Other ancient authorities omit *and the life*
10.39: Jn 7.30; 8.59; Lk 4.30. 10.40: Jn 1.28. 10.42: Jn 7.31; 11.45. 11.1: Mk 11.1; Lk 10.38.
11.2: Jn 12.3; Lk 7.38; Mk 14.3. 11.4: Jn 9.3. 11.8: Jn 8.59; 10.31. 11.9: Jn 9.4; 12.35; Lk 13.33.
11.11: Mk 5.39; Acts 7.60. 11.16: Mt 10.3; Jn 20.24–28. 11.19: Job 2.11.
11.24: Dan 12.2; Jn 5.28; Acts 24.15. 11.25: Jn 1.4; 5.26; Rev 1.18. 11.26: Jn 6.47; 8.51. 11.27: Mt 16.16.
11.32: Jn 11.22. 11.35: Lk 19.41. 11.37: Jn 9.7. 11.38: Mt 27.60; Mk 15.46; Lk 24.2; Jn 20.1.
11.41: Jn 17.1; Mt 11.25.

Jesus lifted up his eyes and said, "Father, I
42 thank thee that thou hast heard me. I knew
that thou hearest me always, but I have said
this on account of the people standing by,
that they may believe that thou didst send
43 me." When he had said this, he cried with a
44 loud voice, "Laz′arus, come out." The dead
man came out, his hands and feet bound with
bandages, and his face wrapped with a cloth.
Jesus said to them, "Unbind him, and let
him go."

45 Many of the Jews therefore, who had come
with Mary and had seen what he did,
46 believed in him; but some of them went to
the Pharisees and told them what Jesus had
47 done. So the chief priests and the Pharisees
gathered the council, and said, "What are we
to do? For this man performs many signs.
48 If we let him go on thus, every one will
believe in him, and the Romans will come
and destroy both our holy place[a] and our
49 nation." But one of them, Ca′iaphas, who
was high priest that year, said to them, "You
50 know nothing at all; you do not understand
that it is expedient for you that one man
should die for the people, and that the whole
51 nation should not perish." He did not say
this of his own accord, but being high priest
that year he prophesied that Jesus should die
52 for the nation, and not for the nation only,
but to gather into one the children of God
53 who are scattered abroad. So from that day
on they took counsel how to put him to
death.

54 Jesus therefore no longer went about openly
among the Jews, but went from there to the
country near the wilderness, to a town called
E′phraim; and there he stayed with the
disciples.

The approaching Passover

55 Now the Passover of the Jews was at hand,
and many went up from the country to
Jerusalem before the Passover, to purify
56 themselves. They were looking for Jesus and
saying to one another as they stood in the
temple, "What do you think? That he will
57 not come to the feast?" Now the chief
priests and the Pharisees had given orders
that if any one knew where he was, he should
let them know, so that they might arrest him.

12 Six days before the Passover, Jesus came to
Bethany, where Laz′arus was, whom Jesus
2 had raised from the dead. There they made

Nard

him a supper; Martha served, and Laz′arus
was one of those at table with him. Mary 3
took a pound of costly ointment of pure nard
and anointed the feet of Jesus and wiped his
feet with her hair; and the house was filled
with the fragrance of the ointment. But 4
Judas Iscariot, one of his disciples (he who
was to betray him), said, "Why was this 5
ointment not sold for three hundred denarii[b]
and given to the poor?" This he said, not 6
that he cared for the poor but because he was
a thief, and as he had the money box he used
to take what was put into it. Jesus said, "Let 7
her alone, let her keep it for the day of my
burial. The poor you always have with you, 8
but you do not always have me."

When the great crowd of the Jews learned 9
that he was there, they came, not only on
account of Jesus but also to see Laz′arus,
whom he had raised from the dead. So the 10
chief priests planned to put Laz′arus also to
death, because on account of him many of 11
the Jews were going away and believing in
Jesus.

The next day a great crowd who had come 12
to the feast heard that Jesus was coming to
Jerusalem. So they took branches of palm 13
trees and went out to meet him, crying,
"Hosanna! Blessed is he who comes in the
name of the Lord, even the King of Israel!"

[a] Greek *our place*　[b] The denarius was worth about seventeen pence
11.42: Jn 12.30.　11.44: Jn 19.40; 20.7.　11.49: Mt 26.3.　11.52: Jn 10.16; 17.21.
11.55: Mt 26.1; Mk 14.1; Lk 22.1; Jn 13.1.　11.56: Jn 7.11.　12.1–8: Mt 26.6–13; Mk 14.3–9; Lk 7.37–38.
12.4: Jn 6.71; 13.26.　12.6: Lk 8.3.　12.7: Jn 19.40.　12.10: Mk 14.1.
12.12–15: Mt 21.4–9; Mk 11.7–10; Lk 19.35–38.　12.13: Ps 118.26; Jn 1.49.

The Mount of Olives

4 And Jesus found a young ass and sat upon it;
as it is written,
5 "Fear not, daughter of Zion;
behold, your king is coming,
sitting on an ass's colt!"
6 His disciples did not understand this at first;
but when Jesus was glorified, then they
remembered that this had been written of
7 him and had been done to him. The crowd
that had been with him when he called
Laz′arus out of the tomb and raised him
8 from the dead bore witness. The reason why
the crowd went to meet him was that they
9 heard he had done this sign. The Pharisees
then said to one another, "You see that you
can do nothing; look, the world has gone
after him."

10 Now among those who went up to worship
11 at the feast were some Greeks. So these
came to Philip, who was from Beth-sa′ida in
Galilee, and said to him, "Sir, we wish to see
12 Jesus." Philip went and told Andrew;
Andrew went with Philip and they told
13 Jesus. And Jesus answered them, "The hour
has come for the Son of man to be glorified.
14 Truly, truly, I say to you, unless a grain of
wheat falls into the earth and dies, it remains
15 alone; but if it dies, it bears much fruit. He
who loves his life loses it, and he who hates
his life in this world will keep it for eternal
16 life. If any one serves me, he must follow
me; and where I am, there shall my servant
be also; if any one serves me, the Father will
honour him.
17 "Now is my soul troubled. And what shall
I say? 'Father, save me from this hour'?
No, for this purpose I have come to this

hour. Father, glorify thy name." Then a 28
voice came from heaven, "I have glorified it,
and I will glorify it again." The crowd 29
standing by heard it and said that it had
thundered. Others said, "An angel has
spoken to him." Jesus answered, "This 30
voice has come for your sake, not for mine.
Now is the judgment of this world, now shall 31
the ruler of this world be cast out; and I, 32
when I am lifted up from the earth, will draw
all men to myself." He said this to show by 33
what death he was to die. The crowd 34
answered him, "We have heard from the law
that the Christ remains for ever. How can
you say that the Son of man must be lifted
up? Who is this Son of man?" Jesus said to 35
them, "The light is with you for a little
longer. Walk while you have the light, lest
the darkness overtake you; he who walks in
the darkness does not know where he goes.
While you have the light, believe in the light, 36
that you may become sons of light."
When Jesus had said this, he departed and
hid himself from them. Though he had done 37
so many signs before them, yet they did not
believe in him; it was that the word spoken 38
by the prophet Isaiah might be fulfilled:
"Lord, who has believed our report,
and to whom has the arm of the Lord been
revealed?"
Therefore they could not believe. For Isaiah 39
again said,
"He has blinded their eyes and hardened 40
their heart,
lest they should see with their eyes and
perceive with their heart,
and turn for me to heal them."

12.15: Zech 9.9. **12.16:** Mk 9.32; Jn 2.22. **12.20:** Jn 7.35; Acts 11.20. **12.21:** Jn 1.44; 6.5.
12.23: Jn 13.1; 17.1; Mk 14.35, 41. **12.24:** 1 Cor 15.36. **12.25:** Mt 10.39; Mk 8.35; Lk 9.24; 14.26.
12.27: Jn 11.33; Mt 26.38; Mk 14.34. **12.28:** Mk 1.11; 9.7. **12.31:** Jn 16.11; 2 Cor 4.4; Eph 2.2.
12.32: Jn 3.14; 8.28. **12.34:** Ps 110.4; Is 9.7; Ezek 37.25; Dan 7.14. **12.35:** Jn 7.33; 9.4; Eph 5.8; 1 Jn 2.11.
12.36: Lk 16.8; Jn 8.59. **12.38:** Is 53.1; Rom 10.16. **12.40:** Is 6.10; Mt 13.14.

41 Isaiah said this because he saw his glory and
42 spoke of him. Nevertheless many even of the
authorities believed in him, but for fear of
the Pharisees they did not confess it, lest they
43 should be put out of the synagogue: for they
loved the praise of men more than the praise
of God.
44 And Jesus cried out and said, "He who
believes in me, believes not in me but in him
45 who sent me. And he who sees me sees him
46 who sent me. I have come as light into the
world, that whoever believes in me may not
47 remain in darkness. If any one hears my
sayings and does not keep them, I do not
judge him; for I did not come to judge the
48 world but to save the world. He who rejects
me and does not receive my sayings has a
judge; the word that I have spoken will be his
49 judge on the last day. For I have not spoken
on my own authority; the Father who sent
me has himself given me commandment
50 what to say and what to speak. And I know
that his commandment is eternal life. What
I say, therefore, I say as the Father has
bidden me."

THE THIRD PASSOVER

13 NOW before the feast of the Passover,
when Jesus knew that his hour had
come to depart out of this world to the
Father, having loved his own who were in the
world, he loved them to the end.

The last supper

2 And during supper, when the devil had
already put it into the heart of Judas Iscariot,
3 Simon's son, to betray him, Jesus, knowing
that the Father had given all things into his
hands, and that he had come from God and
4 was going to God, rose from supper, laid
aside his garments, and girded himself with a
5 towel. Then he poured water into a basin,
and began to wash the disciples' feet, and to
wipe them with the towel with which he was
6 girded. He came to Simon Peter; and Peter
said to him, "Lord, do you wash my feet?"
7 Jesus answered him, "What I am doing you
do not know now, but afterward you will
8 understand." Peter said to him, "You shall
never wash my feet." Jesus answered him,
"If I do not wash you, you have no part in
9 me." Simon Peter said to him, "Lord, not
my feet only but also my hands and my
10 head!" Jesus said to him, "He who has

bathed does not need to wash, except for his
feet,[c] but he is clean all over; and you are
clean, but not all of you." For he knew who
was to betray him; that was why he said,
"You are not all clean."

When he had washed their feet, and taken
his garments, and resumed his place, he said
to them, "Do you know what I have done to
you? You call me Teacher and Lord; and
you are right, for so I am. If I then, your

In Jerusalem

Lord and Teacher, have washed your feet,
you also ought to wash one another's feet.
For I have given you an example, that you
also should do as I have done to you. Truly,
truly, I say to you, a servant[d] is not greater
than his master; nor is he who is sent greater
than he who sent him. If you know these
things, blessed are you if you do them. I am
not speaking of you all; I know whom I have
chosen; it is that the scripture may be
fulfilled, 'He who ate my bread has lifted his
heel against me.' I tell you this now, before
it takes place, that when it does take place

c Other ancient authorities omit *except for his feet*   d Or *slave*
12.41: Is 6.1; Lk 24.27.   12.42: Jn 9.22; Lk 6.22.   12.44: Mt 10.40; Jn 5.24.   12.45: Jn 14.9.
12.46: Jn 1.4; 8.12; 9.5.   12.47: Jn 3.17.   12.48: Mt 10.14-15.   13.1: Jn 11.55; 12.23; 16.28.
13.2: Jn 6.71; Mk 14.10.   13.5: Lk 7.44; 22.27.   13.8: Deut 12.12; Jn 3.5; 9.7.   13.11: Jn 13.2.
13.15: 1 Pet 2.21.   13.16: Mt 10.24; Lk 6.40.   13.17: Lk 11.28; Jas 1.25.   13.18: Ps 41.9.
13.19: Jn 14.29; 8.28.

you may believe that I am he. Truly, truly, I say to you, he who receives any one whom I send receives me; and he who receives me receives him who sent me."

When Jesus had thus spoken, he was troubled in spirit, and testified, "Truly, truly, I say to you, one of you will betray me." The disciples looked at one another, uncertain of whom he spoke. One of his disciples, whom Jesus loved, was lying close to the breast of Jesus; so Simon Peter beckoned to him and said, "Tell us who it is of whom he speaks." So lying thus, close to the breast of Jesus, he said to him, "Lord, who is it?" Jesus answered, "It is he to whom I shall give this morsel when I have dipped it." So when he had dipped the morsel, he gave it to Judas, the son of Simon Iscariot. Then after the morsel, Satan entered into him. Jesus said to him, "What you are going to do, do quickly." Now no one at the table knew why he said this to him. Some thought that, because Judas had the money box, Jesus was telling him, "Buy what we need for the feast"; or, that he should give something to the poor. So, after receiving the morsel, he immediately went out; and it was night.

When he had gone out, Jesus said, "Now is the Son of man glorified, and in him God is glorified; if God is glorified in him, God will also glorify him in himself, and glorify him at once. Little children, yet a little while I am with you. You will seek me; and as I said to the Jews so now I say to you, 'Where I am going you cannot come.' A new commandment I give to you, that you love one another; even as I have loved you, that you also love one another. By this all men will know that you are my disciples, if you have love for one another."

Simon Peter said to him, "Lord, where are you going?" Jesus answered, "Where I am going you cannot follow me now; but you shall follow afterward." Peter said to him, "Lord, why cannot I follow you now? I will lay down my life for you." Jesus answered, "Will you lay down your life for me? Truly, truly, I say to you, the cock will not crow, till you have denied me three times.

4 "Let not your hearts be troubled; believe[e] in God, believe also in me. In my Father's house are many rooms; if it were not so, would I have told you that I go to prepare a place for you? And when I go and prepare a 3 place for you, I will come again and will take you to myself, that where I am you may be also. And you know the way where I am 4 going."[f] Thomas said to him, "Lord, we do 5 not know where you are going; how can we know the way?" Jesus said to him, "I am 6 the way, and the truth, and the life; no one comes to the Father, but by me. If you had 7 known me, you would have known my Father also; henceforth you know him and have seen him."

Philip said to him, "Lord, show us the 8 Father, and we shall be satisfied." Jesus said 9 to him, "Have I been with you so long, and yet you do not know me, Philip? He who has seen me has seen the Father; how can you say, 'Show us the Father'? Do you not 10 believe that I am in the Father and the Father in me? The words that I say to you I do not speak on my own authority; but the Father who dwells in me does his works. Believe me that I am in the Father and the 11 Father in me; or else believe me for the sake of the works themselves.

"Truly, truly, I say to you, he who believes 12 in me will also do the works that I do; and greater works than these will he do, because I go to the Father. Whatever you ask in my 13 name, I will do it, that the Father may be glorified in the Son; if you ask[g] anything in 14 my name, I will do it.

"If you love me, you will keep my com- 15 mandments. And I will pray the Father, and 16 he will give you another Counsellor, to be with you for ever, even the Spirit of truth, 17 whom the world cannot receive, because it neither sees him nor knows him; you know him, for he dwells with you, and will be in you.

"I will not leave you desolate; I will come to 18 you. Yet a little while, and the world will see 19 me no more, but you will see me; because I live, you will live also. In that day you will 20 know that I am in my Father, and you in me, and I in you. He who has my com- 21 mandments and keeps them, he it is who loves me; and he who loves me will be loved by my Father, and I will love him and manifest myself to him." Judas (not 22 Iscariot) said to him, "Lord, how is it that you will manifest yourself to us, and not to

---

[e] Or *you believe* [f] Other ancient authorities read *where I am going you know, and the way you know*
[g] Other ancient authorities add *me*
13.20: Mt 10.40; Lk 10.16. **13.21–26:** Mt 26.21–25; Mk 14.18–21; Lk 22.21–23. **13.23:** Jn 19.26; 20.2; 21.7, 20.
13.26: Jn 6.71. **13.29:** Jn 12.6. **13.30:** Lk 22.53. **13.31–32:** Jn 17.1. **13.33:** 1 Jn 2.1; Jn 7.33.
13.34: Jn 15.12, 17; 1 Jn 3.23; 2 Jn 5; Lev 19.18; 1 Thess 4.9; 1 Pet 1.22; Heb 13.1; Eph 5.2; 1 Jn 4.10.
13.36: Jn 21.18; 2 Pet 1.14. **13.37–38:** Mt 26.33–35; Mk 14.29–31; Lk 22.33–34. **14.2:** Jn 13.33.
14.5: Jn 11.16. **14.6:** Jn 10.9; 1.4, 14. **14.9:** Jn 12.45. **14.11:** Jn 10.38.
14.13: Mt 7.7; Jn 15.7, 16; 16.23; Jas 1.5. **14.15:** Jn 15.10; 1 Jn 5.3; 2 Jn 6.
14.16: Jn 14.26; 15.26; 16.7; 1 Jn 2.1. **14.19:** Jn 7.33. **14.22:** Acts 1.13; 10.40–41.

The true vine

"I am the true vine, and my Father is the vinedresser. Every branch of mine that bears no fruit, he takes away, and every branch that does bear fruit he prunes, that it may bear more fruit. You are already made clean by the word which I have spoken to you. Abide in me, and I in you. As the branch cannot bear fruit by itself, unless it abides in the vine, neither can you, unless you abide in me. I am the vine, you are the branches. He who abides in me, and I in him, he it is that bears much fruit, for apart from me you can do nothing. If a man does not abide in me, he is cast forth as a branch and withers; and the branches are gathered, thrown into the fire and burned. If you abide in me, and my words abide in you, ask whatever you will, and it shall be done for you. By this my Father is glorified, that you bear much fruit, and so prove to be my disciples. As the Father has loved me, so have I loved you; abide in my love. If you keep my commandments, you will abide in my love, just as I have kept my Father's commandments and abide in his love. These things I have spoken to you, that my joy may be in you, and that your joy may be full.

"This is my commandment, that you love one another as I have loved you. Greater love has no man than this, that a man lay down his life for his friends. You are my friends if you do what I command you. No longer do I call you servants,[h] for the servant[i] does not know what his master is doing; but I have called you friends, for all that I have heard from my Father I have made known to you. You did not choose me, but I chose you and appointed you that you should go and bear fruit and that your fruit should abide; so that whatever you ask the

23 the world?" Jesus answered him, "If a man loves me, he will keep my word, and my 24 Father will love him, and we will come to him and make our home with him. He who does not love me does not keep my words; and the word which you hear is not mine but the Father's who sent me.

25 "These things I have spoken to you, while I 26 am still with you. But the Counsellor, the Holy Spirit, whom the Father will send in my name, he will teach you all things, and bring to your remembrance all that I have 27 said to you. Peace I leave with you; my peace I give to you; not as the world gives do I give to you. Let not your hearts be 28 troubled, neither let them be afraid. You heard me say to you, 'I go away, and I will come to you.' If you loved me, you would have rejoiced, because I go to the Father; for 29 the Father is greater than I. And now I have told you before it takes place, so that when it 30 does take place, you may believe. I will no longer talk much with you, for the ruler of this world is coming. He has no power over 31 me; but I do as the Father has commanded me, so that the world may know that I love the Father. Rise, let us go hence.

h Or slaves i Or slave
14.23: 1 Jn 2.24; Rev 21.3.   14.27: Jn 16.33; Phil 4.7; Col 3.15; Jn 20.19.   14.29: Jn 13.19.   14.30: Jn 12.31.
14.31: Mk 14.42; Jn 18.1.   15.1: Is 5.1–7; Ezek 19.10; Mk 12.1–9; Mt 15.13; Rom 11.17.   15.3: Jn 13.10.
15.4: Jn 6.56; 1 Jn 2.6.   15.7: Jn 14.13; 16.23; Mt 7.7; Jas 1.5.   15.8: Mt 5.16.   15.10: Jn 14.15; 1 Jn 5.3.
15.12: Jn 13.34.   15.13: Rom 5.7; Jn 10.11.   15.14: Lk 12.4.   15.16: Jn 6.70; 13.18; 14.13; 16.23.

Father in my name, he may give it to you.

7 This I command you, to love one another.
8 "If the world hates you, know that it has
9 hated me before it hated you. If you were of the world, the world would love its own; but because you are not of the world, but I chose you out of the world, therefore the world
10 hates you. Remember the word that I said to you, 'A servant[i] is not greater than his master.' If they persecuted me, they will persecute you; if they kept my word, they
11 will keep yours also. But all this they will do to you on my account, because they do not
12 know him who sent me. If I had not come and spoken to them, they would not have sin; but now they have no excuse for their sin.
13 He who hates me hates my Father also. If I
14 had not done among them the works which no one else did, they would not have sin; but now they have seen and hated both me and
15 my Father. It is to fulfil the word that is written in their law, 'They hated me without
16 a cause.' But when the Counsellor comes, whom I shall send to you from the Father, even the Spirit of truth, who proceeds from
17 the Father, he will bear witness to me; and you also are witnesses, because you have been with me from the beginning.

16 "I have said all this to you to keep you from
2 falling away. They will put you out of the synagogues; indeed, the hour is coming when whoever kills you will think he is offering
3 service to God. And they will do this because they have not known the Father, nor
4 me. But I have said these things to you, that when their hour comes you may remember that I told you of them.

"I did not say these things to you from the
5 beginning, because I was with you. But now I am going to him who sent me; yet none of
6 you asks me, 'Where are you going?' But because I have said these things to you,
7 sorrow has filled your hearts. Nevertheless I tell you the truth: it is to your advantage that I go away, for if I do not go away, the Counsellor will not come to you; but if I go, I
8 will send him to you. And when he comes, he will convince the world of sin and of
9 righteousness and of judgment: of sin,
10 because they do not believe in me; of righteousness, because I go to the Father,
11 and you will see me no more; of judgment, because the ruler of this world is judged.
12 "I have yet many things to say to you, but

you cannot bear them now. When the Spirit 13 of truth comes, he will guide you into all the truth; for he will not speak on his own authority, but whatever he hears he will speak, and he will declare to you the things that are to come. He will glorify me, for he 14 will take what is mine and declare it to you. All that the Father has is mine; therefore I 15 said that he will take what is mine and declare it to you.

"A little while, and you will see me no 16 more; again a little while, and you will see me." Some of his disciples said to one 17 another, "What is this that he says to us, 'A little while, and you will not see me, and again a little while, and you will see me'; and, 'because I go to the Father'?" They said, 18 "What does he mean by 'a little while'? We do not know what he means." Jesus knew 19 that they wanted to ask him; so he said to them, "Is this what you are asking yourselves, what I meant by saying, 'A little while, and you will not see me, and again a little while, and you will see me'? Truly, 20 truly, I say to you, you will weep and lament, but the world will rejoice; you will be sorrowful, but your sorrow will turn into joy. When a woman is in travail she has 21 sorrow, because her hour has come; but when she is delivered of the child, she no longer remembers the anguish, for joy that a child[j] is born into the world. So you have 22 sorrow now, but I will see you again and your hearts will rejoice, and no one will take your joy from you. In that day you will ask 23 nothing of me. Truly, truly, I say to you, if you ask anything of the Father, he will give it to you in my name. Hitherto you have asked 24 nothing in my name; ask, and you will receive, that your joy may be full.

"I have said this to you in figures; the hour 25 is coming when I shall no longer speak to you in figures but tell you plainly of the Father. In that day you will ask in my name; and I do 26 not say to you that I shall pray the Father for you; for the Father himself loves you, 27 because you have loved me and have believed that I came from the Father. I came from 28 the Father and have come into the world; again, I am leaving the world and going to the Father."

His disciples said, "Ah, now you are 29 speaking plainly, not in any figure! Now we 30 know that you know all things, and need none to question you; by this we believe that you came from God." Jesus answered them, 31

---

[i] Or slave　[j] Greek a human being

15.18: Jn 7.7; 1 Jn 3.13; Mt 10.22; 24.9.
15.20: Jn 13.16; Mt 10.24; 1 Cor 4.12; Acts 4.17; 1 Pet 4.14; Rev 2.3.　15.22: Jn 9.41.　15.25: Ps 35.19; 69.4.
15.26: Jn 14.16, 26; 16.7; 1 Jn 2.1; 5.7.　15.27: Jn 19.35; 21.24; 1 Jn 4.14.
16.2: Jn 9.22; Acts 26.9–11; Is 66.5.　16.5: Jn 7.33; 14.5.　16.7: Jn 14.16, 26; 15.26.　16.9: Jn 15.22.
16.10: Acts 3.14; 7.52; 1 Pet 3.18.　16.11: Jn 12.31.　16.14: Jn 7.39.　16.16–24: Jn 14.18–24.　16.20: Jn 20.20.
16.21: Is 13.8; Hos 13.13; Mic 4.9; 1 Thess 5.3.　16.24: Jn 14.14; 15.11.　16.25: Jn 10.6; Mt 13.34.

32 "Do you now believe? The hour is coming, indeed it has come, when you will be scattered, every man to his home, and will leave me alone; yet I am not alone, for the Father 33 is with me. I have said this to you, that in me you may have peace. In the world you have tribulation; but be of good cheer, I have overcome the world."

The prayer of Jesus

17 When Jesus had spoken these words, he lifted up his eyes to heaven and said, "Father, the hour has come; glorify thy Son 2 that the Son may glorify thee, since thou hast given him power over all flesh, to give eternal 3 life to all whom thou hast given him. And this is eternal life, that they know thee the only true God, and Jesus Christ whom thou 4 hast sent. I glorified thee on earth, having accomplished the work which thou gavest me 5 to do; and now, Father, glorify thou me in thy own presence with the glory which I had with thee before the world was made.
6 "I have manifested thy name to the men whom thou gavest me out of the world; thine they were, and thou gavest them to me, and 7 they have kept thy word. Now they know that everything that thou hast given me is 8 from thee; for I have given them the words which thou gavest me, and they have received them and know in truth that I came from thee; and they have believed that thou 9 didst send me. I am praying for them; I am not praying for the world but for those whom 10 thou hast given me, for they are thine; all mine are thine, and thine are mine, and I am 11 glorified in them. And now I am no more in the world, but they are in the world, and I am coming to thee. Holy Father, keep them in thy name, which thou hast given me, that 12 they may be one, even as we are one. While I was with them, I kept them in thy name, which thou hast given me; I have guarded them, and none of them is lost but the son of perdition, that the scripture might be ful- 13 filled. But now I am coming to thee; and these things I speak in the world, that they 14 may have my joy fulfilled in themselves. I have given them thy word; and the world has hated them because they are not of the world, 15 even as I am not of the world. I do not pray that thou shouldst take them out of the world, but that thou shouldst keep them 16 from the evil one.[k] They are not of the world, even as I am not of the world.

Sanctify them in the truth; thy word is truth. As thou didst send me into the world, so I have sent them into the world. And for their sake I consecrate myself, that they also may be consecrated in truth.
"I do not pray for these only, but also for those who believe in me through their word, that they may all be one; even as thou, Father, art in me, and I in thee, that they also may be in us, so that the world may believe that thou hast sent me. The glory which thou hast given me I have given to them, that they may be one even as we are one, I in them and thou in me, that they may become perfectly one, so that the world may know that thou hast sent me and hast loved them even as thou hast loved me. Father, I desire that they also, whom thou hast given me, may be with me where I am, to behold my glory which thou hast given me in thy love for me before the foundation of the world. O righteous Father, the world has not known thee, but I have known thee; and these know that thou hast sent me. I made known to them thy name, and I will make it known, that the love with which thou hast loved me may be in them, and I in them."

The betrayal

When Jesus had spoken these words, he 18 went forth with his disciples across the Kidron valley, where there was a garden, which he and his disciples entered. Now 2 Judas, who betrayed him, also knew the place; for Jesus often met there with his disciples. So Judas, procuring a band of 3 soldiers and some officers from the chief priests and the Pharisees, went there with lanterns and torches and weapons. Then 4 Jesus, knowing all that was to befall him, came forward and said to them, "Whom do you seek?" They answered him, "Jesus of 5 Nazareth." Jesus said to them, "I am he." Judas, who betrayed him, was standing with them. When he said to them, "I am he," 6 they drew back and fell to the ground. Again 7 he asked them, "Whom do you seek?" And they said, "Jesus of Nazareth." Jesus 8 answered, "I told you that I am he; so, if you seek me, let these men go." This was to fulfil 9 the word which he had spoken, "Of those whom thou gavest me I lost not one." Then 10 Simon Peter, having a sword, drew it and struck the high priest's slave and cut off his right ear. The slave's name was Malchus.

k Or from evil

16.32: Jn 4.23; Mk 14.27; Zech 13.7.   16.33: Jn 14.27; 15.18; Rom 8.37; 2 Cor 2.14; Rev 3.21.
17.1: Jn 11.41; 13.31.   17.5: Jn 1.1; 8.58; Phil 2.6.   17.9: Lk 22.32; Jn 14.16.
17.11: Phil 2.9; Rev 19.12; Rom 12.5; Gal 3.28; Jn 17.21.   17.12: Ps 41.9; Jn 6.70; 18.9.
17.14: Jn 15.19; 8.23.   17.21: Jn 10.38; 17.11.   17.24: Jn 1.14; 17.5; Mt 25.34.
18.1: Mt 26.30, 36; Mk 14.26, 32; Lk 22.39; 2 Sam 15.23.   18.3-11: Mt 26.47-56; Mk 14.43-50; Lk 22.47-53.
18.4: Jn 6.64; 13.1.   18.9: Jn 17.12; 6.39.

N

JERUSALEM
in the time
of
CHRIST

FORTRESS

THE TEMPLE

GETHSEMANE

GOLGOTHA

SOLOMON'S PORCH

COUNCIL CHAMBER

MACCABEAN PALACE

THEATRE   FORUM   MOUNT OF OLIVES

HEROD'S PALACE

HOUSE OF CAIAPHAS AND ANNAS

VALLEY
OF
KIDRON

THE UPPER ROOM

JERICHO ROAD

POOL OF SILOAM

VALLEY OF HINNOM

·HK·

11 Jesus said to Peter, "Put your sword into its sheath; shall I not drink the cup which the Father has given me?"

So the band of soldiers and their captain 12 and the officers of the Jews seized Jesus and bound him. First they led him to Annas; for 13

18.11: Mk 10.38; 14.36.   **18.12–13:** Mt 26.57; Mk 14.53; Lk 22.54; 3.2.

he was the father-in-law of Ca′iaphas, who
14 was high priest that year. It was Ca′iaphas
who had given counsel to the Jews that it was
expedient that one man should die for the
people.

15 Simon Peter followed Jesus, and so did
another disciple. As this disciple was known
to the high priest, he entered the court of the
16 high priest along with Jesus, while Peter
stood outside at the door. So the other
disciple, who was known to the high priest,
went out and spoke to the maid who kept the
17 door, and brought Peter in. The maid who
kept the door said to Peter, "Are not you also
one of this man's disciples?" He said, "I am
18 not." Now the servants[1] and officers had
made a charcoal fire, because it was cold, and
they were standing and warming themselves;
Peter also was with them, standing and
warming himself.

19 The high priest then questioned Jesus
20 about his disciples and his teaching. Jesus
answered him, "I have spoken openly to the
world; I have always taught in synagogues
and in the temple, where all Jews come
21 together; I have said nothing secretly. Why
do you ask me? Ask those who have heard
me, what I said to them; they know what I
22 said." When he had said this, one of the
officers standing by struck Jesus with his
hand, saying, "Is that how you answer the
23 high priest?" Jesus answered him, "If I
have spoken wrongly, bear witness to the
wrong; but if I have spoken rightly, why do
24 you strike me?" Annas then sent him bound
to Ca′iaphas the high priest.

25 Now Simon Peter was standing and warming himself. They said to him, "Are not you
also one of his disciples?" He denied it and
26 said, "I am not." One of the servants[1] of the
high priest, a kinsman of the man whose ear
Peter had cut off, asked, "Did I not see you
27 in the garden with him?" Peter again denied
it; and at once the cock crowed.

The trial

28 Then they led Jesus from the house of
Ca′iaphas to the praetorium. It was early.
They themselves did not enter the praetorium, so that they might not be defiled, but
29 might eat the passover. So Pilate went out to
them and said, "What accusation do you
30 bring against this man?" They answered
him, "If this man were not an evildoer, we
31 would not have handed him over." Pilate

said to them, "Take him yourselves and
judge him by your own law." The Jews said
to him, "It is not lawful for us to put any
man to death." This was to fulfil the word 32
which Jesus had spoken to show by what
death he was to die.

Pilate entered the praetorium again and 33
called Jesus, and said to him, "Are you the
King of the Jews?" Jesus answered, "Do 34
you say this of your own accord, or did others
say it to you about me?" Pilate answered, 35
"Am I a Jew? Your own nation and the
chief priests have handed you over to me;
what have you done?" Jesus answered, "My 36
kingship is not of this world; if my kingship
were of this world, my servants would fight,
that I might not be handed over to the Jews;
but my kingship is not from the world."
Pilate said to him, "So you are a king?" Jesus 37
answered, "You say that I am a king. For

[1] Or slaves

18.14: Jn 11.49–51.   **18.15–16:** Mt 26.58; Mk 14.54; Lk 22.54.
18.17–18: Mt 26.69–72; Mk 14.66–69; Lk 22.56–58.   **18.19–23:** Mt 26.59–66; Mk 14.55–64; Lk 22.67–71.
18.23: Mt 5.39; Acts 23.2–5.   **18.24:** Jn 18.13; Lk 3.2.   **18.25–27:** Mt 26.73–75; Mk 14.70–72; Lk 22.59–62.
18.28: Jn 11.55; Mt 27.1–2; Mk 15.1; Lk 23.1.   **18.29–38:** Mt 27.11–14; Mk 15.2–5; Lk 23.2–3.
18.32: Jn 3.14; 12.32.   **18.36:** Jn 6.15; Mt 26.53.   **18.37:** Jn 3.32; 8.14, 47; 1 Jn 4.6.

this I was born, and for this I have come into the world, to bear witness to the truth. Every one who is of the truth hears my voice." Pilate said to him, "What is truth?"

After he had said this, he went out to the Jews again, and told them, "I find no crime in him. But you have a custom that I should release one man for you at the Passover; will you have me release for you the King of the Jews?" They cried out again, "Not this man, but Barab′bas!" Now Barab′bas was a robber.

The crucifixion

9 Then Pilate took Jesus and scourged him. And the soldiers plaited a crown of thorns, and put it on his head, and arrayed him in a purple robe; they came up to him, saying, "Hail, King of the Jews!" and struck him with their hands. Pilate went out again, and said to them, "Behold, I am bringing him out to you, that you may know that I find no crime in him." So Jesus came out, wearing the crown of thorns and the purple robe.

Pilate said to them, "Here is the man!" When the chief priests and the officers saw 6 him, they cried out, "Crucify him, crucify him!" Pilate said to them, "Take him yourselves and crucify him, for I find no crime in him." The Jews answered him, 7 "We have a law, and by that law he ought to die, because he has made himself the Son of God." When Pilate heard these words, he 8 was the more afraid; he entered the prae- 9 torium again and said to Jesus, "Where are you from?" But Jesus gave no answer. Pilate therefore said to him, "You will not 10 speak to me? Do you not know that I have power to release you, and power to crucify you?" Jesus answered him, "You would 11 have no power over me unless it had been given you from above; therefore he who delivered me to you has the greater sin."

Upon this Pilate sought to release him, but 12 the Jews cried out, "If you release this man, you are not Caesar's friend; every one who

Roman soldiers

18.38–40: Mt 27.15–26; Mk 15.6–15; Lk 23.18–19; Acts 3.14.
19.2–3: Mt 27.27–31; Mk 15.16–20; Lk 22.63–65; 23.11.
19.4: Jn 18.38; 19.6; Lk 23.4.   19.7: Lev 24.16; Mk 14.61–64; Jn 5.18: 10.33.
19.11: Rom 13.1; Jn 18.28.   19.12: Lk 23.2.

makes himself a king sets himself against
13 Caesar." When Pilate heard these words, he
brought Jesus out and sat down on the
judgment seat at a place called The Pave-
14 ment, and in Hebrew, Gab′batha. Now it
was the day of Preparation of the Passover; it
was about the sixth hour. He said to the
15 Jews, "Here is your King!" They cried out,
"Away with him, away with him, crucify
him!" Pilate said to them, "Shall I crucify
your King?" The chief priests answered,
16 "We have no king but Caesar." Then he
handed him over to them to be crucified.
17 So they took Jesus, and he went out,
bearing his own cross, to the place called the
place of a skull, which is called in Hebrew
18 Gol′gotha. There they crucified him, and
with him two others, one on either side, and
19 Jesus between them. Pilate also wrote a title
and put it on the cross; it read, "Jesus of
20 Nazareth, the King of the Jews." Many of
the Jews read this title, for the place where
Jesus was crucified was near the city; and it
was written in Hebrew, in Latin, and in
21 Greek. The chief priests of the Jews then
said to Pilate, "Do not write, 'The King of
the Jews,' but, 'This man said, I am King of
22 the Jews.' " Pilate answered, "What I have
written I have written."
23 When the soldiers had crucified Jesus they
took his garments and made four parts, one
for each soldier; also his tunic. But the tunic
was without seam, woven from top to
24 bottom; so they said to one another, "Let us
not tear it, but cast lots for it to see whose it
shall be." This was to fulfil the scripture,
"They parted my garments among them,
and for my clothing they cast lots."
25 So the soldiers did this. But standing by
the cross of Jesus were his mother, and his
mother's sister, Mary the wife of Clopas, and
26 Mary Mag′dalene. When Jesus saw his
mother, and the disciple whom he loved
standing near, he said to his mother,
27 "Woman, behold, your son!" Then he said
to the disciple, "Behold, your mother!" And
from that hour the disciple took her to his
own home.
28 After this Jesus, knowing that all was now
finished, said (to fulfil the scripture), "I
29 thirst." A bowl full of vinegar stood there;
so they put a sponge full of the vinegar on
30 hyssop and held it to his mouth. When Jesus
had received the vinegar, he said, "It is
finished"; and he bowed his head and gave
up his spirit.

Since it was the day of Preparation, in order
to prevent the bodies from remaining on the
cross on the sabbath (for that sabbath was a
high day), the Jews asked Pilate that their
legs might be broken, and that they might be
taken away. So the soldiers came and broke
the legs of the first, and of the other who had
been crucified with him; but when they came
to Jesus and saw that he was already dead,
they did not break his legs. But one of the
soldiers pierced his side with a spear, and at
once there came out blood and water. He
who saw it has borne witness—his testimony
is true, and he knows that he tells the
truth—that you also may believe. For these
things took place that the scripture might be
fulfilled, "Not a bone of him shall be
broken." And again another scripture says,
"They shall look on him whom they have
pierced."
After this Joseph of Arimathe′a, who was a
disciple of Jesus, but secretly, for fear of the
Jews, asked Pilate that he might take away
the body of Jesus, and Pilate gave him leave.
So he came and took away his body.
Nicode′mus also, who had at first come to
him by night, came bringing a mixture of
myrrh and aloes about a hundred pounds'
weight. They took the body of Jesus, and
bound it in linen cloths with the spices, as is
the burial custom of the Jews. Now in the
place where he was crucified there was a
garden, and in the garden a new tomb where
no one had ever been laid. So because of the
Jewish day of Preparation, as the tomb was
close at hand, they laid Jesus there.

The resurrection

Now on the first day of the week Mary 2
Mag′dalene came to the tomb early, while it
was still dark, and saw that the stone had
been taken away from the tomb. So she ran, 2
and went to Simon Peter and the other
disciple, the one whom Jesus loved, and said
to them, "They have taken the Lord out of
the tomb, and we do not know where they
have laid him." Peter then came out with the 3
other disciple, and they went toward the
tomb. They both ran, but the other disciple 4
outran Peter and reached the tomb first; and 5
stooping to look in, he saw the linen cloths
lying there, but he did not go in. Then 6
Simon Peter came, following him, and went
into the tomb; he saw the linen cloths lying,

19.14: Mk 15.42; Jn 19.31, 42; Mk 15.25, 33. **19.17-24:** Mt 27.33-44; Mk 15.22-32; Lk 23.33-43.
19.24: Ex 28.32; Ps 22.18. **19.25:** Mt 27.55-56; Mk 15.40-41; Lk 23.49; Jn 2.3; Mk 3.31; Lk 24.18; Jn 20.1, 18.
19.26: Jn 13.23; 20.2; 21.20. **19.28-30:** Ps 69.21; Mt 27.45-50; Mk 15.33-37; Lk 23.44-46; Jn 17.4.
19.31: Deut 21.23; Ex 12.16. **19.34:** I Jn 5.6-8. **19.35:** Jn 15.27; 21.24.
19.36: Ex 12.46; Num 9.12; Ps 34.20. **19.37:** Zech 12.10. **19.38-42:** Mt 27.57-61; Mk 15.42-47; Lk 23.50-56.
19.39: Jn 3.1; 7.50. **19.40:** Mk 16.1; 14.8. **20.1-10:** Mt 28.1-8; Mk 16.1-8; Lk 24.1-10.
20.3-10: Lk 24.11-12.

and the napkin, which had been on his head, not lying with the linen cloths but rolled up in a place by itself. Then the other disciple, who reached the tomb first, also went in, and he saw and believed; for as yet they did not know the scripture, that he must rise from the dead. Then the disciples went back to their homes.

But Mary stood weeping outside the tomb, and as she wept she stooped to look into the tomb; and she saw two angels in white, sitting where the body of Jesus had lain, one at the head and one at the feet. They said to her, "Woman, why are you weeping?" She said to them, "Because they have taken away my Lord, and I do not know where they have laid him." Saying this, she turned round and saw Jesus standing, but she did not know that it was Jesus. Jesus said to her, "Woman, why are you weeping? Whom do you seek?" Supposing him to be the gardener, she said to him, "Sir, if you have carried him away, tell me where you have laid him, and I will take him away." Jesus said to her, "Mary." She turned and said to him in Hebrew, "Rab-bo'ni!" (which means Teacher). Jesus said to her, "Do not hold me, for I have not yet ascended to the Father; but go to my brethren and say to them, I am ascending to my Father and your Father, to my God and your God." Mary Mag'dalene went and said to the disciples, "I have seen the Lord"; and she told them that he had said these things to her.

On the evening of that day, the first day of the week, the doors being shut where the disciples were, for fear of the Jews, Jesus came and stood among them and said to them, "Peace be with you." When he had said this, he showed them his hands and his side. Then the disciples were glad when they saw the Lord. Jesus said to them again, "Peace be with you. As the Father has sent me, even so I send you." And when he had said this, he breathed on them, and said to them, "Receive the Holy Spirit. If you forgive the sins of any, they are forgiven; if you retain the sins of any, they are retained."

Now Thomas, one of the twelve, called the Twin, was not with them when Jesus came. So the other disciples told him, "We have seen the Lord." But he said to them, "Unless I see in his hands the print of the nails, and place my finger in the mark of the nails, and place my hand in his side, I will not believe."

Eight days later, his disciples were again in the house, and Thomas was with them. The doors were shut, but Jesus came and stood among them, and said, "Peace be with you." Then he said to Thomas, "Put your finger here, and see my hands; and put out your hand, and place it in my side; do not be faithless, but believing." Thomas answered him, "My Lord and my God!" Jesus said to him, "Have you believed because you have seen me? Blessed are those who have not seen and yet believe."

Now Jesus did many other signs in the presence of the disciples, which are not written in this book; but these are written that you may believe that Jesus is the Christ, the Son of God, and that believing you may have life in his name.

After this Jesus revealed himself again to **21** the disciples by the Sea of Tibe'ri-as; and he revealed himself in this way. Simon Peter, Thomas called the Twin, Nathan'a-el of Cana in Galilee, the sons of Zeb'edee, and two others of his disciples were together. Simon Peter said to them, "I am going fishing." They said to him, "We will go with you." They went out and got into the boat; but that night they caught nothing.

Just as day was breaking, Jesus stood on the beach; yet the disciples did not know that it was Jesus. Jesus said to them, "Children, have you any fish?" They answered him, "No." He said to them, "Cast the net on the right side of the boat, and you will find some." So they cast it, and now they were not able to haul it in, for the quantity of fish. That disciple whom Jesus loved said to Peter, "It is the Lord!" When Simon Peter heard that it was the Lord, he put on his clothes, for he was stripped for work, and sprang into the sea. But the other disciples came in the boat, dragging the net full of fish, for they were not far from the land, but about a hundred yards[m] off.

When they got out on land, they saw a charcoal fire there, with fish lying on it, and bread. Jesus said to them, "Bring some of the fish that you have just caught." So Simon Peter went aboard and hauled the net ashore, full of large fish, a hundred and fifty-three of them; and although there were so many, the net was not torn. Jesus said to them, "Come and have breakfast." Now none of the disciples dared ask him, "Who are you?" They knew it was the Lord.

---

m Greek two hundred cubits
20.9: Lk 24.26, 46.   20.12: Lk 24.4; Mt 28.5; Mk 16.5.   20.13: Jn 20.2.   20.14: Mt 28.9; Jn 21.4.
20.17: Jn 20.27; Mt 28.10; Jn 7.33.   20.18: Lk 24.10, 23.   20.19-20: Lk 24.36-39.   20.21: Jn 17.18; Mt 28.19.
20.22: Acts 2.4, 33.   20.23: Mt 16.19; 18.18.   20.24: Jn 11.16.   20.27: Lk 24.40.   20.29: 1 Pet 1.8.
20.30: Jn 21.25.   20.31: Jn 3.15.   21.2: Jn 11.16; 1.45; Lk 5.10.   21.3-6: Lk 5.3-7.   21.4: Jn 20.14; Lk 24.16.
21.5: Lk 24.41.   21.7: Jn 13.23; 19.26; 20.2; 21.20.

13 Jesus came and took the bread and gave it to
14 them, and so with the fish. This was now the
third time that Jesus was revealed to the
disciples after he was raised from the dead.

15 When they had finished breakfast, Jesus
said to Simon Peter, "Simon, son of John, do
you love me more than these?" He said to
him, "Yes, Lord; you know that I love you."
16 He said to him, "Feed my lambs." A second
time he said to him, "Simon, son of John, do
you love me?" He said to him, "Yes, Lord;
you know that I love you." He said to him,
17 "Tend my sheep." He said to him the third
time, "Simon, son of John, do you love
me?" Peter was grieved because he said to
him the third time, "Do you love me?" And
he said to him, "Lord, you know everything;
you know that I love you." Jesus said to
18 him, "Feed my sheep. Truly, truly, I say to
you, when you were young, you girded
yourself and walked where you would; but
when you are old, you will stretch out your
hands, and another will gird you and carry
19 you where you do not wish to go." (This he

said to show by what death he was to glorify
God.) And after this he said to him, "Follow
me."

Peter turned and saw following them the
disciple whom Jesus loved, who had lain
close to his breast at the supper and had said,
"Lord, who is it that is going to betray
you?" When Peter saw him, he said to
Jesus, "Lord, what about this man?" Jesus
said to him, "If it is my will that he remain
until I come, what is that to you? Follow
me!" The saying spread abroad among the
brethren that this disciple was not to die; yet
Jesus did not say to him that he was not to
die, but, "If it is my will that he remain until
I come, what is that to you?"

This is the disciple who is bearing witness
to these things, and who has written these
things; and we know that his testimony is
true.

But there are also many other things which
Jesus did; were every one of them to be
written, I suppose that the world itself could
not contain the books that would be written.

THE

ACTS OF THE APOSTLES

IN the first book, O The-oph′ilus, I have
dealt with all that Jesus began to
2   do and teach, until the day when he was
taken up, after he had given commandment
through the Holy Spirit to the apostles whom
3 he had chosen. To them he presented
himself alive after his passion by many
proofs, appearing to them during forty days,
4 and speaking of the kingdom of God. And
while staying[a] with them he charged them
not to depart from Jerusalem, but to wait for

the promise of the Father, which, he said,
"you heard from me, for John baptized with
water, but before many days you shall be
baptized with the Holy Spirit."

So when they had come together, they
asked him, "Lord, will you at this time
restore the kingdom to Israel?" He said to
them, "It is not for you to know times or
seasons which the Father has fixed by his
own authority. But you shall receive power
when the Holy Spirit has come upon you;

[a] Or eating

21.14: Jn 20.19, 26. 21.15: Jn 1.42; 13.37; Mk 14.29–31; Lk 12.32.
21.16: Mt 2.6; Acts 20.28; 1 Pet 5.2; Rev 7.17. 21.19: 2 Pet 1.14; Mk 1.17. 21.20: Jn 13.25.
21.22: 1 Cor 4.5; Jas 5.7; Rev 2.25; Mt 16.28. 21.24: Jn 15.27; 19.35. 21.25: Jn 20.30.
1.1: Lk 1.1–4. 1.4: Lk 24.49. 1.8: Lk 24.48–49.

and you shall be my witnesses in Jerusalem and in all Judea and Samar'ia and to the end 9 of the earth." And when he had said this, as they were looking on, he was lifted up, and a 10 cloud took him out of their sight. And while they were gazing into heaven as he went,

behold, two men stood by them in white robes, and said, "Men of Galilee, why do you 11 stand looking into heaven? This Jesus, who was taken up from you into heaven, will come in the same way as you saw him go into heaven."

THE CHURCH IN JERUSALEM

2 THEN they returned to Jerusalem from the mount called Olivet, which is near 13 Jerusalem, a sabbath day's journey away; and when they had entered, they went up to the upper room, where they were staying, Peter and John and James and Andrew, Philip and Thomas, Bartholomew and Matthew, James the son of Alphaeus and Simon the Zealot 14 and Judas the son of James. All these with one accord devoted themselves to prayer, together with the women and Mary the mother of Jesus, and with his brothers.

Peter's speech

5 In those days Peter stood up among the brethren (the company of persons was in all about a hundred and twenty), and said, 6 "Brethren, the scripture had to be fulfilled, which the Holy Spirit spoke beforehand by the mouth of David, concerning Judas who 7 was guide to those who arrested Jesus. For he was numbered among us, and was allotted 8 his share in this ministry. (Now this man bought a field with the reward of his wickedness; and falling headlong[b] he burst open in the middle and all his bowels 9 gushed out. And it became known to all the inhabitants of Jerusalem, so that the field was called in their language Akel'dama, that is, 10 Field of Blood.) For it is written in the book of Psalms,

'Let his habitation become desolate,
    and let there be no one to live in it';
and
'His office let another take.'

11 So one of the men who have accompanied us during all the time that the Lord Jesus went 12 in and out among us, beginning from the baptism of John until the day when he was taken up from us—one of these men must become with us a witness to his resurrec- 13 tion." And they put forward two, Joseph called Barsabbas, who was surnamed Justus, 14 and Matthi'as. And they prayed and said, "Lord, who knowest the hearts of all men, show which one of these two thou hast 15 chosen to take the place in this ministry and apostleship from which Judas turned aside, 16 to go to his own place." And they cast lots

for them, and the lot fell on Matthi'as; and he was enrolled with the eleven apostles.

Pentecost

When the day of Pentecost had come, they 2 were all together in one place. And suddenly 2 a sound came from heaven like the rush of a mighty wind, and it filled all the house where they were sitting. And there appeared to 3 them tongues as of fire, distributed and resting on each one of them. And they were 4 all filled with the Holy Spirit and began to speak in other tongues, as the Spirit gave them utterance.

Now there were dwelling in Jerusalem 5 Jews, devout men from every nation under heaven. And at this sound the multitude 6 came together, and they were bewildered, because each one heard them speaking in his own language. And they were amazed and 7 wondered, saying, "Are not all these who are speaking Galileans? And how is it that we 8 hear, each of us in his own native language? Par'thians and Medes and Elamites and 9 residents of Mesopota'mia, Judea and Cappado'cia, Pontus and Asia, Phryg'ia and 10 Pamphyl'ia, Egypt and the parts of Libya belonging to Cyre'ne, and visitors from Rome, both Jews and proselytes, Cretans and 11 Arabians, we hear them telling in our own tongues the mighty works of God." And all 12 were amazed and perplexed, saying to one another, "What does this mean?" But 13 others mocking said, "They are filled with new wine."

Peter's explanation

But Peter, standing with the eleven, lifted 14 up his voice and addressed them, "Men of Judea and all who dwell in Jerusalem, let this be known to you, and give ear to my words. For these men are not drunk, as you suppose, 15 since it is only the third hour of the day; but 16 this is what was spoken by the prophet Jo'el:

'And in the last days it shall be, God 17
    declares,
that I will pour out my Spirit upon all
    flesh,

---

b Or *swelling up*
1.9–12: Lk 24.50–53. 1.13: Mt 10.2–4; Mk 3.16–19; Lk 6.14–16. 1.16–19: Mt 27.3–10.
1.20: Ps 69.25; 109.8. 2.17–21: Joel 2.28–32.

PENTECOST

'EVERY NATION UNDER HEAVEN'

and your sons and your daughters shall
  prophesy,
and your young men shall see visions,
and your old men shall dream dreams;
18 yea, and on my menservants and my
  maidservants in those days
  I will pour out my Spirit; and they shall
  prophesy.'
19 And I will show wonders in the heaven
  above
  and signs on the earth beneath,
  blood, and fire, and vapour of smoke;
20 the sun shall be turned into darkness
  and the moon into blood,
  before the day of the Lord comes,
  the great and manifest day.
21 And it shall be that whoever calls on the
  name of the Lord shall be saved.'
22 "Men of Israel, hear these words: Jesus of
Nazareth, a man attested to you by God with
mighty works and wonders and signs which
God did through him in your midst, as you
23 yourselves know—this Jesus, delivered up
according to the definite plan and foreknow-
ledge of God, you crucified and killed by the
24 hands of lawless men. But God raised him
up, having loosed the pangs of death, because
it was not possible for him to be held by it.
25 For David says concerning him,
  'I saw the Lord always before me,
  for he is at my right hand that I may not be
  shaken;
26 therefore my heart was glad, and my
  tongue rejoiced;
  moreover my flesh will dwell in hope.
27 For thou wilt not abandon my soul to
  Hades,

  nor let thy Holy One see corruption.
  Thou hast made known to me the ways of 2
  life;
  thou wilt make me full of gladness with thy
  presence.'
  "Brethren, I may say to you confidently of 2
the patriarch David that he both died and
was buried, and his tomb is with us to this
day. Being therefore a prophet, and knowing 3
that God had sworn with an oath to him that
he would set one of his descendants upon his
throne, he foresaw and spoke of the resurrec- 3
tion of the Christ, that he was not abandoned
to Hades, nor did his flesh see corruption.
This Jesus God raised up, and of that we all 3
are witnesses. Being therefore exalted at the 3
right hand of God, and having received from
the Father the promise of the Holy Spirit, he
has poured out this which you see and hear.
For David did not ascend into the heavens; 3
but he himself says,
  'The Lord said to my Lord, Sit at my right
  hand,
  till I make thy enemies a stool for thy feet.' 35
Let all the house of Israel therefore know 36
assuredly that God has made him both Lord
and Christ, this Jesus whom you crucified."
  Now when they heard this they were cut to 37
the heart, and said to Peter and the rest of the
apostles, "Brethren, what shall we do?"
And Peter said to them, "Repent, and be 38
baptized every one of you in the name of
Jesus Christ for the forgiveness of your sins;
and you shall receive the gift of the Holy
Spirit. For the promise is to you and to your 39
children and to all that are far off, every one
whom the Lord our God calls to him." And 40

2.25-28: Ps 16.8-11. **2.30:** Ps 132.11. **2.31:** Ps 16.10. **2.34-35:** Ps 110.1. **2.39:** Is 57.19; Joel 2.32.

he testified with many other words and exhorted them, saying, "Save yourselves from this crooked generation." So those who received his word were baptized, and there were added that day about three thousand 2 souls. And they devoted themselves to the apostles' teaching and fellowship, to the breaking of bread and the prayers. 3 And fear came upon every soul; and many wonders and signs were done through the 4 apostles. And all who believed were together 5 and had all things in common; and they sold their possessions and goods and distributed 6 them to all, as any had need. And day by day, attending the temple together and breaking bread in their homes, they partook of food with glad and generous hearts, 7 praising God and having favour with all the people. And the Lord added to their number day by day those who were being saved.

At the gate of the temple

3 Now Peter and John were going up to the temple at the hour of prayer, the ninth hour. 2 And a man lame from birth was being carried, whom they laid daily at that gate of the temple which is called Beautiful to ask alms of those who entered the temple. 3 Seeing Peter and John about to go into the 4 temple, he asked for alms. And Peter directed his gaze at him, with John, and said, 5 "Look at us." And he fixed his attention upon them, expecting to receive something 6 from them. But Peter said, "I have no silver and gold, but I give you what I have; in the name of Jesus Christ of Nazareth, walk." 7 And he took him by the right hand and raised him up; and immediately his feet and ankles 8 were made strong. And leaping up he stood and walked and entered the temple with them, walking and leaping and praising 9 God. And all the people saw him walking 10 and praising God, and recognised him as the one who sat for alms at the Beautiful Gate of the temple; and they were filled with wonder and amazement at what had happened to him.

Peter's answer

11 While he clung to Peter and John, all the people ran together to them in the portico 12 called Solomon's, astounded. And when Peter saw it he addressed the people, "Men of Israel, why do you wonder at this, or why do you stare at us, as though by our own 13 power or piety we had made him walk? The God of Abraham and of Isaac and of Jacob,

the God of our fathers, glorified his servant[c] Jesus, whom you delivered up and denied in the presence of Pilate, when he had decided to release him. But you denied the Holy and 14 Righteous One, and asked for a murderer to be granted to you, and killed the Author of 15 life, whom God raised from the dead. To this we are witnesses. And his name, by faith 16 in his name, has made this man strong whom you see and know; and the faith which is through Jesus[d] has given the man this perfect health in the presence of you all.

"And now, brethren, I know that you acted 17 in ignorance, as did also your rulers. But 18 what God foretold by the mouth of all the prophets, that his Christ should suffer, he thus fulfilled. Repent therefore, and turn 19 again, that your sins may be blotted out, that times of refreshing may come from the presence of the Lord, and that he may send 20 the Christ appointed for you, Jesus, whom 21 heaven must receive until the time for establishing all that God spoke by the mouth of his holy prophets from of old. Moses said, 22 'The Lord God will raise up for you a prophet from your brethren as he raised me up. You shall listen to him in whatever he tells you. And it shall be that every soul that 23 does not listen to that prophet shall be destroyed from the people.' And all the 24 prophets who have spoken, from Samuel and those who came afterwards, also proclaimed these days. You are the sons of the prophets 25 and of the covenant which God gave to your fathers, saying to Abraham, 'And in your posterity shall all the families of the earth be blessed.' God, having raised up his servant,[c] 26 sent him to you first, to bless you in turning every one of you from your wickedness."

Peter and John imprisoned

And as they were speaking to the people, **4** the priests and the captain of the temple and the Sadducees came upon them, annoyed 2 because they were teaching the people and proclaiming in Jesus the resurrection from the dead. And they arrested them and put 3 them in custody until the morrow, for it was already evening. But many of those who 4 heard the word believed; and the number of the men came to about five thousand.

Peter's defence

On the morrow their rulers and elders and 5 scribes were gathered together in Jerusalem, with Annas the high priest and Caiaphas and 6 John and Alexander, and all who were of the

---

c Or child   d Greek him
2.44–45: Acts 4.32–35.   **3.13:** Ex 3.6; Is 52.13.   **3.22:** Deut 18.15–16.   **3.23:** Deut 18.19; Lev 23.29.
3.25: Gen 22.18.

7 high-priestly family. And when they had set them in the midst, they inquired, "By what power or by what name did you do this?"
8 Then Peter, filled with the Holy Spirit, said
9 to them, "Rulers of the people and elders, if we are being examined today concerning a good deed done to a cripple, by what means
10 this man has been healed, be it known to you all, and to all the people of Israel, that by the name of Jesus Christ of Nazareth, whom you crucified, whom God raised from the dead, by him this man is standing before you well.
11 This is the stone which was rejected by you builders, but which has become the head of
12 the corner. And there is salvation in no one else, for there is no other name under heaven given among men by which we must be saved."
13 Now when they saw the boldness of Peter and John, and perceived that they were uneducated, common men, they wondered; and they recognised that they had been with
14 Jesus. But seeing the man that had been healed standing beside them, they had
15 nothing to say in opposition. But when they had commanded them to go aside out of the council, they conferred with one another,
16 saying, "What shall we do with these men? For that a notable sign has been performed through them is manifest to all the inhabitants of Jerusalem, and we cannot deny it.

17 But in order that it may spread no further among the people, let us warn them to speak
18 no more to any one in this name." So they called them and charged them not to speak or
19 teach at all in the name of Jesus. But Peter and John answered them, "Whether it is right in the sight of God to listen to you
20 rather than to God, you must judge; for we cannot but speak of what we have seen
21 and heard." And when they had further threatened them, they let them go, finding no way to punish them, because of the people; for all men praised God for what had hap-
22 pened. For the man on whom this sign of healing was performed was more than forty years old.
23 When they were released they went to their friends and reported what the chief priests

and the elders had said to them. And when 24
they heard it, they lifted their voices together
to God and said, "Sovereign Lord, who didst
make the heaven and the earth and the sea
and everything in them, who by the mouth of 25
our father David, thy servant,[c] didst say by
the Holy Spirit,
'Why did the Gentiles rage,
  and the peoples imagine vain things?
The kings of the earth set themselves in 26
    array,
  and the rulers were gathered together,
against the Lord and against his
    Anointed'—[e]
for truly in this city there were gathered 27
together against thy holy servant[e] Jesus,
whom thou didst anoint, both Herod and
Pontius Pilate, with the Gentiles and the
peoples of Israel, to do whatever thy hand 28
and thy plan had predestined to take place.
And now, Lord, look upon their threats, and 29
grant to thy servants[f] to speak thy word with
all boldness, while thou stretchest out thy 30
hand to heal, and signs and wonders are
performed through the name of thy holy
servant[e] Jesus." And when they had prayed, 31
the place in which they were gathered together was shaken; and they were all filled
with the Holy Spirit and spoke the word of
God with boldness.
  Now the company of those who believed 32
were of one heart and soul, and no one said
that any of the things which he possessed was
his own, but they had everything in
common. And with great power the apostles 33
gave their testimony to the resurrection of
the Lord Jesus, and great grace was upon
them all. There was not a needy person 34
among them, for as many as were possessors
of lands or houses sold them, and brought
the proceeds of what was sold and laid it at 35
the apostles' feet; and distribution was made
to each as any had need. Thus Joseph who 36
was surnamed by the apostles Barnabas
(which means, Son of encouragement), a
Levite, a native of Cyprus, sold a field which 37
belonged to him, and brought the money and
laid it at the apostles' feet.

Ananias and Sapphira

But a man named Anani′as with his wife 5
Sapphi′ra sold a piece of property, and with 2
his wife's knowledge he kept back some of
the proceeds, and brought only a part and
laid it at the apostles' feet. But Peter said, 3
"Anani′as, why has Satan filled your heart to
lie to the Holy Spirit and to keep back part of
the proceeds of the land? While it remained 4

---

[c] Or child   [e] Or Christ   [f] Or slaves
4.11: Ps 118.22.   4.24: Ex 20.11; Ps 146.6.   4.25–26: Ps 2.1–2.   4.27: Ps 2.2; 2.1.   4.32–35: Acts 2.44–45.

unsold, did it not remain your own? And after it was sold, was it not at your disposal? How is it that you have contrived this deed in your heart? You have not lied to men but to 5 God." When Anani'as heard these words, he fell down and died. And great fear came 6 upon all who heard of it. The young men rose and wrapped him up and carried him out and buried him.

7 After an interval of about three hours his wife came in, not knowing what had hap-8 pened. And Peter said to her, "Tell me whether you sold the land for so much." 9 And she said, "Yes, for so much." But Peter said to her, "How is it that you have agreed together to tempt the Spirit of the Lord? Hark, the feet of those that have buried your husband are at the door, and they will carry 10 you out." Immediately she fell down at his feet and died. When the young men came in they found her dead, and they carried her out 11 and buried her beside her husband. And great fear came upon the whole church, and upon all who heard of these things.

12 Now many signs and wonders were done among the people by the hands of the apostles. And they were all together in 13 Solomon's Portico. None of the rest dared join them, but the people held them in high 14 honour. And more than ever believers were added to the Lord, multitudes both of men 15 and women, so that they even carried out the sick into the streets, and laid them on beds and pallets, that as Peter came by at least his 16 shadow might fall on some of them. The people also gathered from the towns around Jerusalem, bringing the sick and those afflicted with unclean spirits, and they were all healed.

The apostles imprisoned

17 But the high priest rose up and all who were with him, that is, the party of the Sad'ducees, 18 and filled with jealousy they arrested the apostles and put them in the common 19 prison. But at night an angel of the Lord opened the prison doors and brought them 20 out and said, "Go and stand in the temple and speak to the people all the words of this Life." And when they heard this, they 21 entered the temple at daybreak and taught.

Now the high priest came and those who were with him and called together the council and all the senate of Israel, and sent to the prison to have them brought. But 22 when the officers came, they did not find them in the prison, and they returned and reported, "We found the prison securely 23 locked and the sentries standing at the doors, but when we opened it we found no one inside." Now when the captain of the temple 24 and the chief priests heard these words, they were much perplexed about them, wondering what this would come to. And some one 25 came and told them, "The men whom you put in prison are standing in the temple and teaching the people." Then the captain with 26 the officers went and brought them, but without violence, for they were afraid of being stoned by the people.

And when they had brought them, they set 27 them before the council. And the high priest questioned them, saying, "We strictly 28 charged you not to teach in this name, yet here you have filled Jerusalem with your teaching and you intend to bring this man's blood upon us." But Peter and the apostles 29 answered, "We must obey God rather than men. The God of our fathers raised Jesus 30 whom you killed by hanging him on a tree. God exalted him at his right hand as Leader 31 and Saviour, to give repentance to Israel and forgiveness of sins. And we are witnesses to 32 these things, and so is the Holy Spirit whom God has given to those who obey him."

Gamaliel's speech

When they heard this they were enraged 33 and wanted to kill them. But a Pharisee in 34 the council named Gama'liel, a teacher of the law, held in honour by all the people, stood up and ordered the men to be put outside for a while. And he said to them, "Men of 35 Israel, take care what you do with these men. For before these days Theu'das arose, 36 giving himself out to be somebody, and a number of men, about four hundred, joined him; but he was slain and all who followed him were dispersed and came to nothing. After him Judas the Galilean arose in the 37 days of the census and drew away some of the people after him; he also perished, and all who followed him were scattered. So in the 38 present case I tell you, keep away from these men and let them alone; for if this plan or this undertaking is of men, it will fail; but if 39 it is of God, you will not be able to overthrow

5.30: Deut 21.22-23.

them. You might even be found opposing God!"

40 So they took his advice, and when they had called in the apostles, they beat them and charged them not to speak in the name of
41 Jesus, and let them go. Then they left the presence of the council, rejoicing that they were counted worthy to suffer dishonour for
42 the name. And every day in the temple and at home they did not cease teaching and preaching Jesus as the Christ.

The appointment of Stephen

6 Now in these days when the disciples were increasing in number, the Hellenists murmured against the Hebrews because their widows were neglected in the daily distribu-
2 tion. And the twelve summoned the body of the disciples and said, "It is not right that we should give up preaching the word of God to
3 serve tables. Therefore, brethren, pick out from among you seven men of good repute, full of the Spirit and of wisdom, whom we
4 may appoint to this duty. But we will devote ourselves to prayer and to the ministry of the
5 word." And what they said pleased the whole multitude, and they chose Stephen, a man full of faith and of the Holy Spirit, and Philip, and Proch'orus, and Nica'nor, and Timon, and Par'menas, and Nicola'us, a
6 proselyte of Antioch. These they set before the apostles, and they prayed and laid their hands upon them.

7 And the word of God increased; and the number of the disciples multiplied greatly in Jerusalem, and a great many of the priests were obedient to the faith.

8 And Stephen, full of grace and power, did great wonders and signs among the people.
9 Then some of those who belonged to the synagogue of the Freedmen (as it was called), and of the Cyre'nians, and of the Alexandrians, and of those from Cili'cia and Asia,
10 arose and disputed with Stephen. But they could not withstand the wisdom and the
11 Spirit with which he spoke. Then they secretly instigated men, who said, "We have heard him speak blasphemous words against
12 Moses and God." And they stirred up the people and the elders and the scribes, and they came upon him and seized him and
13 brought him before the council, and set up false witnesses who said, "This man never ceases to speak words against this holy place
14 and the law; for we have heard him say that this Jesus of Nazareth will destroy this place, and will change the customs which Moses

delivered to us." And gazing at him, all who 1 sat in the council saw that his face was like the face of an angel.

Stephen's speech

And the high priest said, "Is this so?" And 7
Stephen said: 2
"Brethren and fathers, hear me. The God of glory appeared to our father Abraham, when he was in Mesopota'mia, before he lived in Haran, and said to him, 'Depart from 3 your land and from your kindred and go into the land which I will show you.' Then he 4 departed from the land of the Chalde'ans, and lived in Haran. And after his father died, God removed him from there into this land in which you are now living; yet he gave 5 him no inheritance in it, not even a foot's length, but promised to give it to him in possession and to his posterity after him, though he had no child. And God spoke to 6 this effect, that his posterity would be aliens in a land belonging to others, who would enslave them and ill-treat them four hundred years. 'But I will judge the nation which 7 they serve,' said God, 'and after that they shall come out and worship me in this place.' And he gave him the covenant of circum- 8 cision. And so Abraham became the father of Isaac, and circumcised him on the eighth day; and Isaac became the father of Jacob, and Jacob of the twelve patriarchs.

"And the patriarchs, jealous of Joseph, sold 9 him into Egypt; but God was with him, and 10 rescued him out of all his afflictions, and gave him favour and wisdom before Pharaoh, king of Egypt, who made him governor over Egypt and over all his household. Now there 11 came a famine throughout all Egypt and Canaan, and great affliction, and our fathers could find no food. But when Jacob heard 12 that there was grain in Egypt, he sent forth our fathers the first time. And at the second 13 visit Joseph made himself known to his

7.2: Ps 29.3; Gen 11.31; 15.7.　**7.3:** Gen 12.1.　**7.4:** Gen 11.31; 15.7; 12.5.　**7.5:** Deut 2.5; Gen 12.7; 17.8.
7.6–7: Gen 15.13–14.　**7.7:** Ex 3.12.　**7.8:** Gen 17.10–14; 21.2–4; 25.26; 29.31–35; 30.1–24; 35.16–18, 23–26.
7.9: Gen 37.11, 28; 45.4.　**7.9–10:** Gen 39.2–3, 21.　**7.10:** Gen 41.40–46; Ps 105.21.
7.11: Gen 41.54–55; 42.5.　**7.12:** Gen 42.2.　**7.13:** Gen 45.1–4.

brothers, and Joseph's family became known
4 to Pharaoh. And Joseph sent and called to
5 him Jacob his father and all his kindred,
seventy-five souls; and Jacob went down into
Egypt. And he died, himself and our fathers,
6 and they were carried back to Shechem and
laid in the tomb that Abraham had bought
for a sum of silver from the sons of Hamor in
Shechem.
7 "But as the time of the promise drew near,
which God had granted to Abraham, the
8 people grew and multiplied in Egypt till
there arose over Egypt another king who had
9 not known Joseph. He dealt craftily with our
race and forced our fathers to expose their
10 infants, that they might not be kept alive. At
this time Moses was born, and was beautiful
before God. And he was brought up for
21 three months in his father's house; and when
he was exposed, Pharaoh's daughter adopted
him and brought him up as her own son.
22 And Moses was instructed in all the wisdom
of the Egyptians, and he was mighty in his
words and deeds.
23 "When he was forty years old, it came into
his heart to visit his brethren, the sons of
24 Israel. And seeing one of them being
wronged, he defended the oppressed man
and avenged him by striking the Egyptian.
25 He supposed that his brethren understood
that God was giving them deliverance by his
26 hand, but they did not understand. And on
the following day he appeared to them as
they were quarrelling and would have
reconciled them, saying, 'Men, you are
brethren, why do you wrong each other?'
27 But the man who was wronging his neighbour thrust him aside, saying, 'Who made
28 you a ruler and a judge over us? Do you
want to kill me as you killed the Egyptian
29 yesterday?' At this retort Moses fled, and
became an exile in the land of Mid'ian, where
he became the father of two sons.
30 "Now when forty years had passed, an
angel appeared to him in the wilderness of
Mount Sinai, in a flame of fire in a bush.
31 When Moses saw it he wondered at the sight;
and as he drew near to look, the voice of the
32 Lord came, 'I am the God of your fathers,
the God of Abraham and of Isaac and of
Jacob.' And Moses trembled and did not
33 dare to look. And the Lord said to him,
'Take off the shoes from your feet, for the
place where you are standing is holy ground.
34 I have surely seen the ill-treatment of my
people that are in Egypt and heard their

groaning, and I have come down to deliver
them. And now come, I will send you to
Egypt.'
35 "This Moses whom they refused, saying,
'Who made you a ruler and a judge?' God
sent as both ruler and deliverer by the hand
of the angel that appeared to him in the
36 bush. He led them out, having performed
wonders and signs in Egypt and at the Red
Sea, and in the wilderness for forty years.
37 This is the Moses who said to the Israelites,
'God will raise up for you a prophet from
38 your brethren as he raised me up.' This is he
who was in the congregation in the wilderness with the angel who spoke to him at
Mount Sinai, and with our fathers; and he
received living oracles to give to us. Our
39 fathers refused to obey him, but thrust him
aside, and in their hearts they turned to
40 Egypt, saying to Aaron, 'Make for us gods to
go before us; as for this Moses who led us out
from the land of Egypt, we do not know what
41 has become of him.' And they made a calf in
those days, and offered a sacrifice to the idol
and rejoiced in the works of their hands. But
42 God turned and gave them over to worship
the host of heaven, as it is written in the book
of the prophets:

'Did you offer to me slain beasts and
      sacrifices,
  forty years in the wilderness, O house of
      Israel?
And you took up the tent of Moloch,   43
  and the star of the god Rephan,
  the figures which you made to worship;
  and I will remove you beyond Babylon.'

44 "Our fathers had the tent of witness in the
wilderness, even as he who spoke to Moses
directed him to make it, according to the
45 pattern that he had seen. Our fathers in turn
brought it in with Joshua when they dispossessed the nations which God thrust out
before our fathers. So it was until the days of
46 David, who found favour in the sight of God
and asked leave to find a habitation for the
47 God of Jacob. But it was Solomon who built
48 a house for him. Yet the Most High does not
dwell in houses made with hands; as the
prophet says,

'Heaven is my throne,   49
  and earth my footstool.
What house will you build for me, says the
      Lord,
  or what is the place of my rest?
Did not my hand make all these   50
      things?'

7.14: Gen 45.9-10.   7.14-15: Deut 10.22.   7.16: Josh 24.32; Gen 50.13.   7.17-18: Ex 1.7-8.
7.19: Ex 1.10-11, 15-22.   7.20: Ex 2.2.   7.21: Ex 2.5-6, 10.   7.23-29: Ex 2.11-15.   7.29: Ex 2.22; 18.3-4.
7.30-34: Ex 3.1-10.   7.35: Ex 2.14.   7.36: Ex 7.3; 14.21; Num 14.33.   7.37: Deut 18.15, 18.   7.38: Ex 19.
7.39: Num 14.3-4.   7.40: Ex 32.1, 23.   7.41: Ex 32.4, 6.   7.42: Jer 19.13.   7.42-43: Amos 5.25-27.
7.44: Ex 25.9, 40.   7.45: Josh 3.14-17; Deut 32.49.   7.46: 2 Sam 7.8-16; Ps 132.1-5.   7.47: 1 Kings 6.
7.49-50: Is 66.1-2.

51 "You stiff-necked people, uncircumcised in heart and ears, you always resist the Holy Spirit. As your fathers did, so do you. 52 Which of the prophets did not your fathers persecute? And they killed those who announced beforehand the coming of the Righteous One, whom you have now be- 53 trayed and murdered, you who received the law as delivered by angels and did not keep it."

Death of Stephen

54 Now when they heard these things they were enraged, and they ground their teeth 55 against him. But he, full of the Holy Spirit, gazed into heaven and saw the glory of God, and Jesus standing at the right hand of God; 56 and he said, "Behold, I see the heavens opened, and the Son of man standing at the 57 right hand of God." But they cried out with a loud voice and stopped their ears and rushed together upon him. Then they cast 5 him out of the city and stoned him; and the witnesses laid down their garments at the feet of a young man named Saul. And as they 5 were stoning Stephen, he prayed, "Lord Jesus, receive my spirit." And he knelt down 6 and cried with a loud voice, "Lord, do not hold this sin against them." And when he had said this, he fell asleep.

And Saul was consenting to his death.   8

And on that day a great persecution arose against the church in Jerusalem; and they were all scattered throughout the region of Judea and Samar'ia, except the apostles. Devout men buried Stephen, and made great 2 lamentation over him. But Saul laid waste 3 the church, and entering house after house, he dragged off men and women and committed them to prison.

A city of Judea

THE CHURCH IN JUDEA AND SAMARIA

4 NOW those who were scattered went 5 about preaching the word. Philip went down to a city of Samar'ia, and proclaimed to 6 them the Christ. And the multitudes with one accord gave heed to what was said by Philip, when they heard him and saw the signs which he did. For unclean spirits came 7 out of many who were possessed, crying with a loud voice; and many who were paralysed or lame were healed. So there was much joy 8 in that city.

But there was a man named Simon who had 9

7.51: Ex 33.3, 5; Jer 9.26; 6.10; Num 27.14; Is 63.10.   8.1: Acts 11.19.

previously practised magic in the city and amazed the nation of Samar′ia, saying that he 10 himself was somebody great. They all gave heed to him, from the least to the greatest, saying, "This man is that power of God 11 which is called Great." And they gave heed to him, because for a long time he had 12 amazed them with his magic. But when they believed Philip as he preached good news about the kingdom of God and the name of Jesus Christ, they were baptized, both men 13 and women. Even Simon himself believed, and after being baptized he continued with Philip. And seeing signs and great miracles performed, he was amazed.

14 Now when the apostles at Jerusalem heard that Samar′ia had received the word of God, 15 they sent to them Peter and John, who came down and prayed for them that they might 16 receive the Holy Spirit; for it had not yet fallen on any of them, but they had only been baptized in the name of the Lord Jesus. 17 Then they laid their hands on them and they 18 received the Holy Spirit. Now when Simon saw that the Spirit was given through the laying on of the apostles' hands, he offered 19 them money, saying, "Give me also this power, that any one on whom I lay my hands 20 may receive the Holy Spirit." But Peter said to him, "Your silver perish with you, because you thought you could obtain the gift of God 21 with money! You have neither part nor lot in this matter, for your heart is not right 22 before God. Repent therefore of this wickedness of yours, and pray to the Lord that, if possible, the intent of your heart may 23 be forgiven you. For I see that you are in the gall of bitterness and in the bond of 24 iniquity." And Simon answered, "Pray for me to the Lord, that nothing of what you have said may come upon me."

25 Now when they had testified and spoken the word of the Lord, they returned to Jerusalem, preaching the gospel to many villages of the Samaritans.

Philip and an Ethiopian

26 But an angel of the Lord said to Philip, "Rise and go toward the south[g] to the road that goes down from Jerusalem to Gaza." 27 This is a desert road. And he rose and went. And behold, an Ethiopian, a eunuch, a minister of Canda′ce the queen of the Ethiopians, in charge of all her treasure, had come 28 to Jerusalem to worship and was returning; seated in his chariot, he was reading the 29 prophet Isaiah. And the Spirit said to Philip,

"Go up and join this chariot." So Philip ran 30 to him, and heard him reading Isaiah the prophet, and asked, "Do you understand what you are reading?" And he said, "How 31 can I, unless some one guides me?" And he invited Philip to come up and sit with him. Now the passage of the scripture which he 32 was reading was this:

"As a sheep led to the slaughter
or a lamb before its shearer is dumb,
so he opens not his mouth.
In his humiliation justice was denied him. 33
Who can describe his generation?
For his life is taken up from the earth."

And the eunuch said to Philip, "About 34 whom, pray, does the prophet say this, about himself or about some one else?" Then 35 Philip opened his mouth, and beginning with this scripture he told him the good news of Jesus. And as they went along the road they 36 came to some water, and the eunuch said, "See, here is water! What is to prevent my being baptized?"[h] And he commanded the 38 chariot to stop, and they both went down into the water, Philip and the eunuch, and he baptized him. And when they came up out 39 of the water, the Spirit of the Lord caught up Philip; and the eunuch saw him no more, and went on his way rejoicing. But Philip was 40 found at Azo′tus, and passing on he preached the gospel to all the towns till he came to Caesare′a.

Conversion of Saul

But Saul, still breathing threats and murder **9** against the disciples of the Lord, went to the high priest and asked him for letters to the 2 synagogues at Damascus, so that if he found any belonging to the Way, men or women, he might bring them bound to Jerusalem. Now 3 as he journeyed he approached Damascus, and suddenly a light from heaven flashed about him. And he fell to the ground and 4 heard a voice saying to him, "Saul, Saul, why do you persecute me?" And he said, "Who 5 are you, Lord?" And he said, "I am Jesus, whom you are persecuting; but rise and enter 6 the city, and you will be told what you are to do." The men who were travelling with him 7 stood speechless, hearing the voice but seeing no one. Saul arose from the ground; and 8 when his eyes were opened, he could see nothing; so they led him by the hand and brought him into Damascus. And for three 9 days he was without sight, and neither ate nor drank.

Now there was a disciple at Damascus 10

g Or at noon
h Other ancient authorities add all or most of verse 37, *And Philip said, "If you believe with all your heart, you may." And he replied, "I believe that Jesus Christ is the Son of God."*
8.21: Ps 78.37.   8.23: Is 58.6.   8.32–33: Is 53.7–8.   9.1–19: Acts 22.4–16; 26.9–18.

named Anani′as. The Lord said to him in a vision, "Anani′as." And he said, "Here I 11 am, Lord." And the Lord said to him, "Rise and go to the street called Straight, and inquire in the house of Judas for a man of Tarsus named Saul; for behold, he is 12 praying, and he has seen a man named Anani′as come in and lay his hands on him so 13 that he might regain his sight." But Anani′as answered, "Lord, I have heard from many about this man, how much evil he has done 14 to thy saints at Jerusalem; and here he has authority from the chief priests to bind all 15 who call upon thy name." But the Lord said to him, "Go, for he is a chosen instrument of mine to carry my name before the Gentiles 16 and kings and the sons of Israel; for I will show him how much he must suffer for the 17 sake of my name." So Anani′as departed and entered the house. And laying his hands on him he said, "Brother Saul, the Lord Jesus who appeared to you on the road by which you came, has sent me that you may regain your sight and be filled with the Holy 18 Spirit." And immediately something like scales fell from his eyes and he regained his 19 sight. Then he rose and was baptized, and took food and was strengthened.

For several days he was with the disciples 20 at Damascus. And in the synagogues immediately he proclaimed Jesus, saying, 21 "He is the Son of God." And all who heard him were amazed, and said, "Is not this the man who made havoc in Jerusalem of those who called on this name? And he has come here for this purpose, to bring them bound 22 before the chief priests." But Saul increased all the more in strength, and confounded the Jews who lived in Damascus by proving that Jesus was the Christ.

23 When many days had passed, the Jews 24 plotted to kill him, but their plot became known to Saul. They were watching the 25 gates day and night, to kill him; but his disciples took him by night and let him down over the wall, lowering him in a basket.

26 And when he had come to Jerusalem he attempted to join the disciples; and they were all afraid of him, for they did not believe that 27 he was a disciple. But Barnabas took him, and brought him to the apostles, and declared to them how on the road he had seen the Lord, who spoke to him, and how at

Damascus he had preached boldly in the name of Jesus. So he went in and out among 28 them at Jerusalem, preaching boldly in the 29 name of the Lord. And he spoke and disputed against the Hellenists; but they were seeking to kill him. And when the 30 brethren knew it, they brought him down to Caesare′a, and sent him off to Tarsus.

The state of the church

So the church throughout all Judea and 31 Galilee and Samar′ia had peace and was built up; and walking in the fear of the Lord and in the comfort of the Holy Spirit it was multiplied.

Peter's journeys

Now as Peter went here and there among 32 them all, he came down also to the saints that lived at Lydda. There he found a man 33 named Aene′as, who had been bedridden for eight years and was paralysed. And Peter 34 said to him, "Aene′as, Jesus Christ heals you; rise and make your bed." And immediately he rose. And all the residents of 35 Lydda and Sharon saw him, and they turned to the Lord.

9.24–25: 2 Cor 11.32–33.

gave her his hand and lifted her up. Then calling the saints and widows he presented her alive. And it became known throughout 42 all Joppa, and many believed in the Lord. And he stayed in Joppa for many days with 43 one Simon, a tanner.

Conversion of Cornelius

At Caesare′a there was a man named Cor-**10** nelius, a centurion of what was known as the Italian Cohort, a devout man who feared 2 God with all his household, gave alms liberally to the people, and prayed constantly to God. About the ninth hour of the day he saw 3 clearly in a vision an angel of God coming in and saying to him, "Cornelius." And he 4 stared at him in terror, and said, "What is it, Lord?" And he said to him, "Your prayers and your alms have ascended as a memorial before God. And now send men to Joppa, 5 and bring one Simon who is called Peter; he 6 is lodging with Simon, a tanner, whose house is by the seaside." When the angel who 7 spoke to him had departed, he called two of his servants and a devout soldier from among those that waited on him, and having related 8 everything to them, he sent them to Joppa.

The next day, as they were on their journey 9 and coming near the city, Peter went up on the housetop to pray, about the sixth hour. And he became hungry and desired some- 10 thing to eat; but while they were preparing it, he fell into a trance and saw the heaven 11 opened, and something descending, like a

6 Now there was at Joppa a disciple named Tabitha, which means Dorcas or Gazelle. She was full of good works and acts of 7 charity. In those days she fell sick and died; and when they had washed her, they laid her 8 in an upper room. Since Lydda was near Joppa, the disciples, hearing that Peter was there, sent two men to him entreating him, 9 "Please come to us without delay." So Peter rose and went with them. And when he had come, they took him to the upper room. All the widows stood beside him weeping, and showing coats and garments which Dorcas 10 made while she was with them. But Peter put them all outside and knelt down and prayed; then turning to the body he said, "Tabitha, rise." And she opened her eyes, 11 and when she saw Peter she sat up. And he

great sheet, let down by four corners upon
12 the earth. In it were all kinds of animals and
13 reptiles and birds of the air. And there came
a voice to him, "Rise, Peter; kill and eat."
14 But Peter said, "No, Lord; for I have never
eaten anything that is common or un-
15 clean." And the voice came to him again a
second time, "What God has cleansed, you
16 must not call common." This happened
three times, and the thing was taken up at
once to heaven.
17 Now while Peter was inwardly perplexed as
to what the vision which he had seen might
mean, behold, the men that were sent by
Cornelius, having made inquiry for Simon's
18 house, stood before the gate and called out to
ask whether Simon who was called Peter was
19 lodging there. And while Peter was pondering the vision, the Spirit said to him,
20 "Behold, three men are looking for you. Rise
and go down, and accompany them without
21 hesitation; for I have sent them." And Peter
went down to the men and said, "I am the
one you are looking for; what is the reason
22 for your coming?" And they said, "Cornelius, a centurion, an upright and God-
fearing man, who is well spoken of by
the whole Jewish nation, was directed by a
holy angel to send for you to come to his
23 house, and to hear what you have to say." So
he called them in to be his guests.
The next day he rose and went off with
them, and some of the brethren from Joppa
24 accompanied him. And on the following day
they entered Caesare′a. Cornelius was
expecting them and had called together his
25 kinsmen and close friends. When Peter
entered, Cornelius met him and fell down at
26 his feet and worshipped him. But Peter
lifted him up, saying, "Stand up; I too am a
27 man." And as he talked with him, he went in
28 and found many persons gathered; and he
said to them, "You yourselves know how
unlawful it is for a Jew to associate with or to
visit any one of another nation; but God has
shown me that I should not call any man
29 common or unclean. So when I was sent for,
I came without objection. I ask then why
you sent for me."
30 And Cornelius said, "Four days ago, about
this hour, I was keeping the ninth hour of
prayer in my house; and behold, a man stood
31 before me in bright apparel, saying, 'Cornelius, your prayer has been heard and your
alms have been remembered before God.

Send therefore to Joppa and ask for Simon
who is called Peter; he is lodging in the house
of Simon, a tanner, by the seaside.' So I sent
to you at once, and you have been kind
enough to come. Now therefore we are all
here present in the sight of God, to hear all
that you have been commanded by the
Lord."
And Peter opened his mouth and said:
"Truly I perceive that God shows no partiality, but in every nation any one who fears
him and does what is right is acceptable to
him. You know the word which he sent to
Israel, preaching good news of peace by
Jesus Christ (he is Lord of all), the word
which was proclaimed throughout all Judea,
beginning from Galilee after the baptism
which John preached: how God anointed
Jesus of Nazareth with the Holy Spirit and
with power; how he went about doing good
and healing all that were oppressed by the
devil, for God was with him. And we are
witnesses to all that he did both in the
country of the Jews and in Jerusalem. They
put him to death by hanging him on a tree;
but God raised him on the third day and
made him manifest; not to all the people but
to us who were chosen by God as witnesses,
who ate and drank with him after he rose
from the dead. And he commanded us to
preach to the people, and to testify that he is
the one ordained by God to be judge of the
living and the dead. To him all the prophets
bear witness that every one who believes in
him receives forgiveness of sins through his
name."
While Peter was still saying this, the Holy
Spirit fell on all who heard the word. And
the believers from among the circumcised

who came with Peter were amazed, because the gift of the Holy Spirit had been poured 6 out even on the Gentiles. For they heard them speaking in tongues and extolling God. 7 Then Peter declared, "Can any one forbid water for baptizing these people who have received the Holy Spirit just as we have?" 8 And he commanded them to be baptized in the name of Jesus Christ. Then they asked him to remain for some days.

Peter defends his action

11 Now the apostles and the brethren who were in Judea heard that the Gentiles also 2 had received the word of God. So when Peter went up to Jerusalem, the circumcision

3 party criticised him, saying, "Why did you go to uncircumcised men and eat with 4 them?" But Peter began and explained to 5 them in order: "I was in the city of Joppa praying; and in a trance I saw a vision, something descending, like a great sheet, let down from heaven by four corners; and it

came down to me. Looking at it closely I 6 observed animals and beasts of prey and reptiles and birds of the air. And I heard a 7 voice saying to me, 'Rise, Peter; kill and eat.' But I said, 'No, Lord; for nothing common 8 or unclean has ever entered my mouth.' But 9 the voice answered a second time from heaven, 'What God has cleansed you must not call common.' This happened three 10 times, and all was drawn up again into heaven. At that very moment three men 11 arrived at the house in which we were, sent to me from Caesare′a. And the Spirit told me 12 to go with them, making no distinction. These six brethren also accompanied me, and we entered the man's house. And he 13 told us how he had seen the angel standing in his house and saying, 'Send to Joppa and bring Simon called Peter; he will declare to 14 you a message by which you will be saved, you and all your household.' As I began to 15 speak, the Holy Spirit fell on them just as on us at the beginning. And I remembered the 16 word of the Lord, how he said, 'John baptized with water, but you shall be baptized with the Holy Spirit.' If then God gave the 17 same gift to them as he gave to us when we believed in the Lord Jesus Christ, who was I that I could withstand God?" When they 18 heard this they were silenced. And they glorified God, saying, "Then to the Gentiles also God has granted repentance unto life."

THE CHURCH IN ANTIOCH

19 NOW those who were scattered because of the persecution that arose over Stephen travelled as far as Phoeni′cia and Cyprus and Antioch, speaking the word to none except 20 Jews. But there were some of them, men of Cyprus and Cyre′ne, who on coming to Antioch spoke to the Greeks[i] also, preaching 21 the Lord Jesus. And the hand of the Lord was with them, and a great number that 22 believed turned to the Lord. News of this came to the ears of the church in Jerusalem, 23 and they sent Barnabas to Antioch. When he came and saw the grace of God, he was glad; and he exhorted them all to remain faithful to 24 the Lord with steadfast purpose; for he was a good man, full of the Holy Spirit and of faith. And a large company was added to the 25 Lord. So Barnabas went to Tarsus to look 26 for Saul; and when he had found him, he brought him to Antioch. For a whole year they met with[j] the church, and taught a large company of people; and in Antioch the disciples were for the first time called Christians.

Now in these days prophets came down 27 from Jerusalem to Antioch. And one of them 28 named Ag′abus stood up and foretold by the Spirit that there would be a great famine over all the world; and this took place in the days of Claudius. And the disciples determined, 29 every one according to his ability, to send relief to the brethren who lived in Judea; and 30

i Other ancient authorities read *Hellenists*   j Or *were guests of*
11.4–17: Acts 10.1–48.   11.16: Acts 1.5.   11.19: Acts 8.4.

Antioch in Syria

they did so, sending it to the elders by the hand of Barnabas and Saul.

Peter imprisoned in Jerusalem

12 About that time Herod the king laid violent hands upon some who belonged to the 2 church. He killed James the brother of John 3 with the sword; and when he saw that it pleased the Jews, he proceeded to arrest Peter also. This was during the days of 4 Unleavened Bread And when he had seized him, he put him in prison, and delivered him to four squads of soldiers to guard him, intending after the Passover to bring him out 5 to the people. So Peter was kept in prison; but earnest prayer for him was made to God by the church.

6 The very night when Herod was about to bring him out, Peter was sleeping between two soldiers, bound with two chains, and sentries before the door were guarding the 7 prison; and behold, an angel of the Lord appeared, and a light shone in the cell; and he struck Peter on the side and woke him, saying, "Get up quickly." And the chains 8 fell off his hands. And the angel said to him, "Dress yourself and put on your sandals." And he did so. And he said to him, "Wrap your mantle around you and follow me." 9 And he went out and followed him; he did not know that what was done by the angel was real, but thought he was seeing a vision.

When they had passed the first and the 10 second guard, they came to the iron gate leading into the city. It opened to them of its own accord, and they went out and passed on through one street; and immediately the angel left him. And Peter came to himself, 11 and said, "Now I am sure that the Lord has sent his angel and rescued me from the hand of Herod and from all that the Jewish people were expecting."

When he realised this, he went to the house 12 of Mary, the mother of John whose other name was Mark, where many were gathered together and were praying. And when he 13 knocked at the door of the gateway, a maid named Rhoda came to answer. Recognising 14 Peter's voice, in her joy she did not open the gate but ran in and told that Peter was standing at the gate. They said to her, "You 15 are mad." But she insisted that it was so. They said, "It is his angel!" But Peter 16 continued knocking; and when they opened, they saw him and were amazed. But 17 motioning to them with his hand to be silent, he described to them how the Lord had brought him out of the prison. And he said, "Tell this to James and to the brethren." Then he departed and went to another place.

Now when day came, there was no small stir 18 among the soldiers over what had become of Peter. And when Herod had sought for him 19 and could not find him, he examined the sentries and ordered that they should be put to death. Then he went down from Judea to Caesare′a, and remained there.

20 Now Herod was angry with the people of Tyre and Sidon; and they came to him in a body, and having persuaded Blastus, the king's chamberlain, they asked for peace, because their country depended on the king's

21 country for food. On an appointed day Herod put on his royal robes, took his seat upon the throne, and made an oration to

22 them. And the people shouted, "The voice of a god, and not of man!" Immediately an

23 angel of the Lord smote him, because he did not give God the glory; and he was eaten by worms and died.

24 But the word of God grew and multiplied.

The call of Barnabas and Saul

And Barnabas and Saul returned from[k] 25 Jerusalem when they had fulfilled their mission, bringing with them John whose other name was Mark.

Now in the church at Antioch there were 13 prophets and teachers, Barnabas, Symeon who was called Niger, Lucius of Cyre′ne, Man′a-en a member of the court of Herod the tetrarch, and Saul. While they were 2 worshipping the Lord and fasting, the Holy Spirit said, "Set apart for me Barnabas and Saul for the work to which I have called them." Then after fasting and praying they 3 laid their hands on them and sent them off.

46 — 48 A.D.

FIRST MISSIONARY JOURNEY

4 SO, being sent out by the Holy Spirit, they went down to Seleu′cia; and from there 5 they sailed to Cyprus. When they arrived at Sal′amis, they proclaimed the word of God in the synagogues of the Jews. And they had

John to assist them. When they had gone 6 through the whole island as far as Paphos, they came upon a certain magician, a Jewish

Coin of Cyprus (Claudius)

[k] Other ancient authorities read to

ANTIOCH of PISIDIA

Antioch

oPerga

7 false prophet, named Bar-Jesus. He was
with the proconsul, Sergius Paulus, a man of
intelligence, who summoned Barnabas and
Saul and sought to hear the word of God.
8 But El'ymas the magician (for that is the
meaning of his name) withstood them,
seeking to turn away the proconsul from the
9 faith. But Saul, who is also called Paul, filled
with the Holy Spirit, looked intently at him
10 and said, "You son of the devil, you enemy of
all righteousness, full of all deceit and villainy, will you not stop making crooked
11 straight paths of the Lord? And now,
behold, the hand of the Lord is upon you,
and you shall be blind and unable to see the
sun for a time." Immediately mist and
darkness fell upon him and he went about
seeking people to lead him by the hand.

Then the proconsul believed, when he saw 12
what had occurred, for he was astonished at
the teaching of the Lord.

Antioch of Pisidia

Now Paul and his company set sail from 13
Paphos, and came to Perga in Pamphyl'ia.
And John left them and returned to Jeru-
salem; but they passed on from Perga and 14

Coin of Antioch of Pisidia

came to Antioch of Pisid'ia. And on the
sabbath day they went into the synagogue
and sat down. After the reading of the law 15
and the prophets, the rulers of the synagogue
sent to them, saying, "Brethren, if you have
any word of exhortation for the people, say
it." So Paul stood up, and motioning with 16
his hands said:
"Men of Israel, and you that fear God,
listen. The God of this people Israel chose 17
our fathers and made the people great during
their stay in the land of Egypt, and with
uplifted arm he led them out of it. And for 18
about forty years he bore with[i] them in the

Perga

CYPRUS

Paphos

PAPHOS to PERGA

[i] Other ancient authorities read *cared for* (Deut 1.31)
13.10: Hos 14.9.   **13.17:** Ex 6.1, 6.   **13.18:** Deut 1.31.

19 wilderness. And when he had destroyed seven nations in the land of Canaan, he gave them their land as an inheritance, for about 20 four hundred and fifty years. And after that he gave them judges until Samuel the 21 prophet. Then they asked for a king; and God gave them Saul the son of Kish, a man 22 of the tribe of Benjamin, for forty years. And when he had removed him, he raised up David to be their king; of whom he testified and said, 'I have found in David the son of Jesse a man after my heart, who will do all 23 my will.' Of this man's posterity God has brought to Israel a Saviour, Jesus, as he 24 promised. Before his coming John had preached a baptism of repentance to all the 25 people of Israel. And as John was finishing his course, he said, 'What do you suppose that I am? I am not he. No, but after me one is coming, the sandals of whose feet I am not worthy to untie.'

26 "Brethren, sons of the family of Abraham, and those among you that fear God, to us has 27 been sent the message of this salvation. For those who live in Jerusalem and their rulers, because they did not recognise him nor understand the utterances of the prophets which are read every sabbath, fulfilled these 28 by condemning him. Though they could charge him with nothing deserving death, yet

29 they asked Pilate to have him killed. And when they had fulfilled all that was written of him, they took him down from the tree, and 30 laid him in a tomb. But God raised him from 31 the dead; and for many days he appeared to those who came up with him from Galilee to Jerusalem, who are now his witnesses to the 32 people. And we bring you the good news 33 that what God promised to the fathers, this he has fulfilled to us their children by raising Jesus; as also it is written in the second psalm,

'Thou art my Son,
today I have begotten thee.'

And as for the fact that he raised him from 34 the dead, no more to return to corruption, he spoke in this way,

'I will give you the holy and sure blessings of David.'

Therefore he says also in another psalm, 35

'Thou wilt not let thy Holy One see corruption.'

For David, after he had served the counsel of 36 God in his own generation, fell asleep, and was laid with his fathers, and saw corruption; but he whom God raised up saw no cor- 37 ruption. Let it be known to you therefore, 38 brethren, that through this man forgiveness of sins is proclaimed to you, and by him 39 every one that believes is freed from everything from which you could not be freed by the law of Moses. Beware, therefore, lest 40 there come upon you what is said in the prophets:

'Behold, you scoffers, and wonder, and 41 perish;

for I do a deed in your days,

a deed you will never believe, if one declares it to you.'"

As they went out, the people begged that 42 these things might be told them the next sabbath. And when the meeting of the 43 synagogue broke up, many Jews and devout converts to Judaism followed Paul and Barnabas, who spoke to them and urged them to continue in the grace of God.

The next sabbath almost the whole city 44 gathered together to hear the word of God. But when the Jews saw the multitudes, they 45 were filled with jealousy, and contradicted what was spoken by Paul, and reviled him. And Paul and Barnabas spoke out boldly, 46 saying, "It was necessary that the word of God should be spoken first to you. Since you thrust it from you, and judge yourselves unworthy of eternal life, behold, we turn to the Gentiles. For so the Lord has com- 47 manded us, saying,

'I have set you to be a light for the Gentiles,

that you may bring salvation to the uttermost parts of the earth.'"

And when the Gentiles heard this, they 48 were glad and glorified the word of God; and as many as were ordained to eternal life believed. And the word of the Lord spread 49 throughout all the region. But the Jews 50 incited the devout women of high standing and the leading men of the city, and stirred up persecution against Paul and Barnabas, and drove them out of their district. But 51 they shook off the dust from their feet against them, and went to Ico'nium. And the 52

13.19: Deut 7.1; Josh 14.1. 13.22: Ps 89.20; 1 Sam 13.14; Is 44.28. 13.24: Mk 1.1–4. 13.25: Jn 1.20; Mt 3.11; Mk 1.7; Lk 3.16. 13.26: Ps 107.20. 13.33: Ps 2.7. 13.34: Is 55.3. 13.35: Ps 16.10. 13.41: Hab 1.5. 13.47: Is 49.6.

disciples were filled with joy and with the Holy Spirit.

Iconium

14 Now at Ico'nium they entered together into the Jewish synagogue, and so spoke that a great company believed, both of Jews and of 2 Greeks. But the unbelieving Jews stirred up the Gentiles and poisoned their minds 3 against the brethren. So they remained for a long time, speaking boldly for the Lord, who bore witness to the word of his grace, granting signs and wonders to be done by 4 their hands. But the people of the city were divided; some sided with the Jews, and some 5 with the apostles. When an attempt was made by both Gentiles and Jews, with their rulers, to molest them and to stone them, 6 they learned of it and fled to Lystra and Derbe, cities of Lycao'nia, and to the sur- 7 rounding country; and there they preached the gospel.

Lystra

8 Now at Lystra there was a man sitting, who could not use his feet; he was a cripple from 9 birth, who had never walked. He listened to Paul speaking; and Paul, looking intently at him and seeing that he had faith to be made 10 well, said in a loud voice, "Stand upright on your feet." And he sprang up and walked. 11 And when the crowds saw what Paul had done, they lifted up their voices, saying in Lycao'nian, "The gods have come down to 12 us in the likeness of men!" Barnabas they called Zeus, and Paul, because he was the

Zeus and Hermes

chief speaker, they called Hermes. And the 13 priest of Zeus, whose temple was in front of the city, brought oxen and garlands to the gates and wanted to offer sacrifice with the people. But when the apostles Barnabas and 14 Paul heard of it, they tore their garments and rushed out among the multitude, crying, "Men, why are you doing this? We also are 15 men, of like nature with you, and bring you good news, that you should turn from these vain things to a living God who made the heaven and the earth and the sea and all that is in them. In past generations he allowed all 16 the nations to walk in their own ways; yet he 17 did not leave himself without witness, for he did good and gave you from heaven rains and fruitful seasons, satisfying your hearts with food and gladness." With these words they 18 scarcely restrained the people from offering sacrifice to them.

ANTIOCH to DERBE

oAntioch

Iconium

Lystra

Derbe

Derbe

9 But Jews came there from Antioch and Ico′nium; and having persuaded the people, they stoned Paul and dragged him out of the
10 city, supposing that he was dead. But when the disciples gathered about him, he rose up and entered the city; and on the next day he
11 went on with Barnabas to Derbe. When they

had preached the gospel to that city and had made many disciples, they returned to Lystra
22 and to Ico′nium and to Antioch, strengthening the souls of the disciples, exhorting them to continue in the faith, and saying that through many tribulations we must enter the
23 kingdom of God. And when they had appointed elders for them in every church, with prayer and fasting, they committed them to the Lord in whom they believed.

Antioch

24 Then they passed through Pisid′ia, and
25 came to Pamphyl′ia. And when they had spoken the word in Perga, they went down
26 to Attali′a; and from there they sailed to Antioch, where they had been commended to the grace of God for the work which they had
27 fulfilled. And when they arrived, they gathered the church together and declared all

that God had done with them, and how he had opened a door of faith to the Gentiles. And they remained no little time with the 28 disciples.

Council in Jerusalem

But some men came down from Judea and 15 were teaching the brethren, "Unless you are circumcised according to the custom of Moses, you cannot be saved." And when 2 Paul and Barnabas had no small dissension and debate with them, Paul and Barnabas and some of the others were appointed to go up to Jerusalem to the apostles and the elders about this question. So, being sent on their 3 way by the church, they passed through both Phoeni′cia and Samar′ia, reporting the conversion of the Gentiles, and they gave great joy to all the brethren. When they came 4 to Jerusalem, they were welcomed by the church and the apostles and the elders, and they declared all that God had done with them. But some believers who belonged to 5 the party of the Pharisees rose up, and said, "It is necessary to circumcise them, and to charge them to keep the law of Moses."

The apostles and the elders were gathered 6

ATTALIA to ANTIOCH

Attalia Perga Antioch

CYPRUS

14.19: 2 Cor 11.25. **15.1–30:** Gal 2.1–10.

7 together to consider this matter. And after there had been much debate, Peter rose and said to them, "Brethren, you know that in the early days God made choice among you, that by my mouth the Gentiles should hear 8 the word of the gospel and believe. And God who knows the heart bore witness to them, giving them the Holy Spirit just as he did to 9 us; and he made no distinction between us and them, but cleansed their hearts by faith. 10 Now therefore why do you make trial of God by putting a yoke upon the neck of the disciples which neither our fathers nor we 11 have been able to bear? But we believe that we shall be saved through the grace of the Lord Jesus, just as they will."

Judgment of James

12 And all the assembly kept silence; and they listened to Barnabas and Paul as they related what signs and wonders God had done 13 through them among the Gentiles. After they finished speaking, James replied, 14 "Brethren, listen to me. Symeon has related how God first visited the Gentiles, to take 15 out of them a people for his name. And with this the words of the prophets agree, as it is written,

16   'After this I will return,
    and I will rebuild the dwelling of David,
      which has fallen;
    I will rebuild its ruins,
    and I will set it up,
17   that the rest of men may seek the Lord,
    and all the Gentiles who are called by my
      name,
18   says the Lord, who has made these things
      known from of old.'

19 Therefore my judgment is that we should not trouble those of the Gentiles who turn to 20 God, but should write to them to abstain from the pollutions of idols and from unchastity and from what is strangled^m and 21 from blood. For from early generations

An ancient altar

Idols

Moses has had in every city those who preach him, for he is read every sabbath in the synagogues."

Letter to the churches

Then it seemed good to the apostles and the 22 elders, with the whole church, to choose men from among them and send them to Antioch with Paul and Barnabas. They sent Judas called Barsabbas, and Silas, leading men among the brethren, with the following 23 letter: "The brethren, both the apostles and the elders, to the brethren who are of the Gentiles in Antioch and Syria and Cili′cia, greeting. Since we have heard that some 24 persons from us have troubled you with words, unsettling your minds, although we gave them no instructions, it has seemed 25 good to us in assembly to choose men and send them to you with our beloved Barnabas and Paul, men who have risked their lives for 26 the sake of our Lord Jesus Christ. We have 27 therefore sent Judas and Silas, who themselves will tell you the same things by word of mouth. For it has seemed good to the 28 Holy Spirit and to us to lay upon you no greater burden than these necessary things: that you abstain from what has been sacri- 29 ficed to idols and from blood and from what is strangled^m and from unchastity. If you keep yourselves from these, you will do well. Farewell."

So when they were sent off, they went down 30

---

^{m} Other early authorities omit *and from what is strangled*
15.16–18: Amos 9.11–12; Jer 12.15; Is 45.21.

to Antioch; and having gathered the congregation together, they delivered the letter. And when they read it, they rejoiced at the exhortation. And Judas and Silas, who were themselves prophets, exhorted the brethren with many words and strengthened them.

And after they had spent some time, they 33 were sent off in peace by the brethren to those who had sent them.[n] But Paul and 35 Barnabas remained in Antioch, teaching and preaching the word of the Lord, with many others also.

49–52 A.D.

SECOND MISSIONARY JOURNEY

AND after some days Paul said to Barnabas, "Come, let us return and visit the brethren in every city where we proclaimed the word of the Lord, and see how they are." And Barnabas wanted to take with them John called Mark. But Paul thought best not to take with them one who had withdrawn from them in Pamphyl'ia, and had not gone with them to the work. And there arose a sharp contention, so that they separated from each other; Barnabas took Mark with him and sailed away to Cyprus, but Paul chose Silas and departed, being commended by the brethren to the grace of the Lord.

Churches revisited

And he went through Syria and Cili'cia, strengthening the churches.

And he came also to Derbe and to Lystra. A disciple was there, named Timothy, the son of a Jewish woman who was a believer; but his father was a Greek. He was well spoken of by the brethren at Lystra and Ico'nium. Paul wanted Timothy to accompany him; and he took him and circumcised him because of the Jews that were in those places, for they all knew that his father was a Greek. As they went on their way through the cities, they delivered to them for observance the decisions which had been reached by the apostles and elders who were at Jerusalem. So the churches were strengthened in the faith, and they increased in numbers daily.

And they went through the region of Phryg'ia and Galatia, having been forbidden by the Holy Spirit to speak the word in Asia. And when they had come opposite My'sia, they attempted to go into Bithyn'ia, but the Spirit of Jesus did not allow them; so, passing by My'sia, they went down to

Tro'as. And a vision appeared to Paul in the 9 night: a man of Macedo'nia was standing beseeching him and saying, "Come over to Macedo'nia and help us." And when he had 10 seen the vision, immediately we sought to go on into Macedo'nia, concluding that God had called us to preach the gospel to them.

Philippi

Setting sail therefore from Tro'as, we made 11 a direct voyage to Sam'othrace, and the following day to Ne-ap'olis, and from there 12 to Philippi, which is the leading city of the district[o] of Macedo'nia, and a Roman

---

[n] Other ancient authorities insert verse 34, *But it seemed good to Silas to remain there*
[o] The Greek text is uncertain

Philippi

colony. We remained in this city some days;
13 and on the sabbath day we went outside the
gate to the riverside, where we supposed
there was a place of prayer; and we sat down
and spoke to the women who had come
14 together. One who heard us was a woman
named Lydia, from the city of Thyati′ra, a
seller of purple goods, who was a worshipper
of God. The Lord opened her heart to give
15 heed to what was said by Paul. And when
she was baptized, with her household, she
besought us, saying, "If you have judged me
to be faithful to the Lord, come to my house
and stay." And she prevailed upon us.
16 As we were going to the place of prayer, we
were met by a slave girl who had a spirit of
divination and brought her owners much
17 gain by soothsaying. She followed Paul and
us, crying, "These men are servants of the
Most High God, who proclaim to you the
18 way of salvation." And this she did for many
days. But Paul was annoyed, and turned and
said to the spirit, "I charge you in the name
of Jesus Christ to come out of her." And it
came out that very hour.
19 But when her owners saw that their hope of
gain was gone, they seized Paul and Silas and
dragged them into the market place before
20 the rulers; and when they had brought them
to the magistrates they said, "These men are
21 Jews and they are disturbing our city. They
advocate customs which it is not lawful for us
22 Romans to accept or practise." The crowd
joined in attacking them; and the magistrates
tore the garments off them and gave orders to
23 beat them with rods. And when they had

inflicted many blows upon them, they threw
them into prison, charging the jailer to keep
them safely. Having received this charge, he 24
put them into the inner prison and fastened
their feet in the stocks.
But about midnight Paul and Silas were 25
praying and singing hymns to God, and the
prisoners were listening to them, and sud- 26
denly there was a great earthquake, so that
the foundations of the prison were shaken;
and immediately all the doors were opened
and every one's fetters were unfastened.
When the jailer woke and saw that the prison 27
doors were open, he drew his sword and was
about to kill himself, supposing that the
prisoners had escaped. But Paul cried with a 28
loud voice, "Do not harm yourself, for we are
all here." And he called for lights and 29
rushed in, and trembling with fear he fell
down before Paul and Silas, and brought 30
them out and said, "Men, what must I do to
be saved?" And they said, "Believe in the 31
Lord Jesus, and you will be saved, you and
your household." And they spoke the word 32
of the Lord to him and to all that were in his
house. And he took them the same hour of 33
the night, and washed their wounds, and he
was baptized at once, with all his family.
Then he brought them up into his house, and 34
set food before them; and he rejoiced with
all his household that he had believed in
God.
But when it was day, the magistrates sent 35
the police, saying, "Let those men go." And 36
the jailer reported the words to Paul, saying,
"The magistrates have sent to let you go;

now therefore come out and go in peace."
7 But Paul said to them, "They have beaten us publicly, unconditioned, men who are Roman citizens, and have thrown us into prison; and do they now cast us out secretly? No! let them come themselves and 8 take us out." The police reported these words to the magistrates, and they were afraid when they heard that they were 9 Roman citizens; so they came and apologised

Thessalonica and Beroea

Now when they had passed through **17** Amphip′olis and Apollo′nia, they came to Thessaloni′ca, where there was a synagogue of the Jews. And Paul went in, as was his **2** custom, and for three weeks *p* he argued with them from the scriptures, explaining and **3** proving that it was necessary for the Christ to suffer and to rise from the dead, and saying,

Thessalonica

to them. And they took them out and asked
o them to leave the city. So they went out of the prison, and visited Lydia; and when they had seen the brethren, they exhorted them and departed.

"This Jesus, whom I proclaim to you, is the Christ." And some of them were persuaded, **4** and joined Paul and Silas; as did a great many of the devout Greeks and not a few of the leading women. But the Jews were **5** jealous, and taking some wicked fellows of the rabble, they gathered a crowd, set the city in an uproar, and attacked the house of Jason, seeking to bring them out to the people. And when they could not find them, **6** they dragged Jason and some of the brethren before the city authorities, crying, "These men who have turned the world upside down have come here also, and Jason has received **7** them; and they are all acting against the decrees of Caesar, saying that there is

p Or *sabbaths*

The Acropolis, Athens

8 another king, Jesus." And the people and the city authorities were disturbed when they
9 heard this. And when they had taken security from Jason and the rest, they let them go.
10 The brethren immediately sent Paul and Silas away by night to Beroe′a; and when they
11 arrived they went into the Jewish synagogue. Now these Jews were more noble than those in Thessaloni′ca, for they received the word with all eagerness, examining the scriptures daily to see if these
12 things were so. Many of them therefore believed, with not a few Greek women of
13 high standing as well as men. But when the Jews of Thessaloni′ca learned that the word of God was proclaimed by Paul at Beroe′a also, they came there too, stirring up and
14 inciting the crowds. Then the brethren immediately sent Paul off on his way to the sea, but Silas and Timothy remained there.
15 Those who conducted Paul brought him as far as Athens; and receiving a command for Silas and Timothy to come to him as soon as possible, they departed.

Athens

16 Now while Paul was waiting for them at Athens, his spirit was provoked within him
17 as he saw that the city was full of idols. So he argued in the synagogue with the Jews and the devout persons, and in the market place every day with those who chanced to be
18 there. Some also of the Epicurean and Stoic philosophers met him. And some said, "What would this babbler say?" Others said, "He seems to be a preacher of foreign divinities"—because he preached Jesus and
19 the resurrection. And they took hold of him and brought him to the Are-op′agus, saying,

"May we know what this new teaching is which you present? For you bring some strange things to our ears; we wish to know therefore what these things mean." Now all the Athenians and the foreigners who lived there spent their time in nothing except telling or hearing something new.

Paul's address

So Paul, standing in the middle of the Are-op′agus, said: "Men of Athens, I perceive that in every way you are very religious. For as I passed along, and observed the objects of your worship, I found also an altar with this inscription, 'To an unknown god.' What therefore you worship as unknown, this I proclaim to you. The God who made the world and everything in it, being Lord of heaven and earth, does not live in shrines made by man, nor is he served by human hands, as though he needed anything, since he himself gives to all men life and breath and everything. And he made from one every nation of men to live on all the face of the earth, having determined allotted periods and the boundaries of their habitation, that they should seek God, in the hope that they might feel after him and find him. Yet he is not far from each one of us, for

'In him we live and move and have our being';

as even some of your poets have said,

'For we are indeed his offspring.'

Being then God's offspring, we ought not to think that the Deity is like gold, or silver, or stone, a representation by the art and imagination of man. The times of ignorance God overlooked, but now he commands all men everywhere to repent, because he has fixed a

17.24–25: Is 42.5.   17.28: Epimenides; Aratus, *Phaenomena*, 5.   17.31: Ps 9.8; 96.13; 98.9.

BEROEA to CORINTH

Beroea

Corinth

Athens

N

he went to see them; and because he was of 3 the same trade he stayed with them, and they worked, for by trade they were tentmakers. And he argued in the synagogue every 4 sabbath, and persuaded Jews and Greeks.

When Silas and Timothy arrived from 5 Macedo'nia, Paul was occupied with preaching, testifying to the Jews that the Christ was Jesus. And when they opposed and reviled 6 him, he shook out his garments and said to them, "Your blood be upon your heads! I am innocent. From now on I will go to the Gentiles." And he left there and went to the 7 house of a man named Titius[q] Justus, a worshipper of God; his house was next door to the synagogue. Crispus, the ruler of the 8 synagogue, believed in the Lord, together with all his household; and many of the Corinthians hearing Paul believed and were baptized. And the Lord said to Paul one 9 night in a vision, "Do not be afraid, but speak and do not be silent; for I am with you, 10 and no man shall attack you to harm you; for I have many people in this city." And he 11 stayed a year and six months, teaching the word of God among them.

But when Gallio was proconsul of Acha'ia, 12 the Jews made a united attack upon Paul and brought him before the tribunal, saying, 13 "This man is persuading men to worship God contrary to the law." But when Paul 14 was about to open his mouth, Gallio said to the Jews, "If it were a matter of wrongdoing or vicious crime, I should have reason to bear with you, O Jews; but since it is a matter of 15 questions about words and names and your own law, see to it yourselves; I refuse to be a judge of these things." And he drove them 16 from the tribunal. And they all seized 17 Sos'thenes, the ruler of the synagogue, and beat him in front of the tribunal. But Gallio paid no attention to this.

Ephesus

After this Paul stayed many days longer, 18 and then took leave of the brethren and sailed for Syria, and with him Priscilla and Aquila. At Cen'chre-ae he cut his hair, for he had a vow. And they came to Ephesus, and he left 19 them there; but he himself went into the synagogue and argued with the Jews. When 20 they asked him to stay for a longer period, he declined; but on taking leave of them he said, 21 "I will return to you if God wills," and he set sail from Ephesus. When he had landed at 22 Caesare'a, he went up and greeted the church, and then went down to Antioch.

day on which he will judge the world in righteousness by a man whom he has appointed, and of this he has given assurance to all men by raising him from the dead."

32 Now when they heard of the resurrection of the dead, some mocked; but others said, "We 33 will hear you again about this." So Paul went 34 out from among them. But some men joined him and believed, among them Dionys'ius the Are-op'agite and a woman named Dam'aris and others with them.

Corinth

18 After this he left Athens and went to 2 Corinth. And he found a Jew named Aquila, a native of Pontus, lately come from Italy with his wife Priscilla, because Claudius had commanded all the Jews to leave Rome. And

53-57 A.D.

THIRD MISSIONARY JOURNEY

23 AFTER spending some time there he departed and went from place to place through the region of Galatia and Phryg′ia, strengthening all the disciples.

24 Now a Jew named Apol′los, a native of Alexandria, came to Ephesus. He was an eloquent man, well versed in the scriptures.

25 He had been instructed in the way of the Lord; and being fervent in spirit, he spoke and taught accurately the things concerning Jesus, though he knew only the baptism of

26 John. He began to speak boldly in the synagogue; but when Priscilla and Aquila heard him, they took him and expounded to

27 him the way of God more accurately. And when he wished to cross to Acha′ia, the brethren encouraged him, and wrote to the disciples to receive him. When he arrived, he greatly helped those who through grace

28 had believed, for he powerfully confuted the Jews in public, showing by the scriptures that the Christ was Jesus.

Ephesus

19 While Apol′los was at Corinth, Paul passed through the upper country and came to Ephesus. There he found some disciples.

2 And he said to them, "Did you receive the Holy Spirit when you believed?" And they said, "No, we have never even heard that

3 there is a Holy Spirit." And he said, "Into what then were you baptized?" They said,

4 "Into John's baptism." And Paul said, "John baptized with the baptism of repentance, telling the people to believe in the one who was to come after him, that is, Jesus."

5 On hearing this, they were baptized in the

6 name of the Lord Jesus. And when Paul had laid his hands upon them, the Holy Spirit came on them; and they spoke with tongues

7 and prophesied. There were about twelve of them in all.

8 And he entered the synagogue and for three months spoke boldly, arguing and pleading

9 about the kingdom of God; but when some were stubborn and disbelieved, speaking evil of the Way before the congregation, he withdrew from them, taking the disciples with him, and argued daily in the hall of

Tyran′nus.[r] This continued for two years, so that all the residents of Asia heard the word of the Lord, both Jews and Greeks.

And God did extraordinary miracles by the hands of Paul, so that handkerchiefs or aprons were carried away from his body to the sick, and diseases left them and the evil spirits came out of them. Then some of the itinerant Jewish exorcists undertook to pronounce the name of the Lord Jesus over those who had evil spirits, saying, "I adjure you by the Jesus whom Paul preaches." Seven sons of a Jewish high priest named Sceva were doing this. But the evil spirit answered them, "Jesus I know, and Paul I know; but who are you?" And the man in whom the evil spirit was leaped on them, mastered all of them, and overpowered them, so that they fled out of that house naked and wounded. And this became known to all residents of Ephesus, both Jews and Greeks; and fear fell upon them all; and the name of the Lord Jesus was extolled. Many also of

Artemis of the Ephesians

---

r Other ancient authorities add *from the fifth hour to the tenth*

those who were now believers came, confess-
19 ing and divulging their practices. And a
number of those who practised magic arts
brought their books together and burned
them in the sight of all; and they counted the
value of them and found it came to fifty
20 thousand pieces of silver. So the word of
the Lord grew and prevailed mightily.

21 Now after these events Paul resolved in the
Spirit to pass through Macedo'nia and
Acha'ia and go to Jerusalem, saying, "After I
have been there, I must also see Rome."
22 And having sent into Macedo'nia two of his
helpers, Timothy and Eras'tus, he himself
stayed in Asia for a while.

Artemis of the Ephesians

23 About that time there arose no little stir
24 concerning the Way. For a man named
Deme'trius, a silversmith, who made silver
shrines of Ar'temis, brought no little busi-
25 ness to the craftsmen. These he gathered
together, with the workmen of like occupation, and said, "Men, you know that from
26 this business we have our wealth. And you
see and hear that not only at Ephesus but
almost throughout all Asia this Paul has
persuaded and turned away a considerable
company of people, saying that gods made
27 with hands are not gods. And there is danger
not only that this trade of ours may come into
disrepute but also that the temple of the great
goddess Ar'temis may count for nothing, and
that she may even be deposed from her
magnificence, she whom all Asia and the
world worship."

When they heard this they were enraged, 28
and cried out, "Great is Ar'temis of the
Ephesians!" So the city was filled with the 29
confusion; and they rushed together into
the theatre, dragging with them Ga'ius and
Aristar'chus, Macedo'nians who were Paul's
companions in travel. Paul wished to go in 30
among the crowd, but the disciples would
not let him; some of the A'si-archs also, who 31
were friends of his, sent to him and begged
him not to venture into the theatre. Now 32
some cried one thing, some another; for the
assembly was in confusion, and most of them
did not know why they had come together.
Some of the crowd prompted Alexander, 33
whom the Jews had put forward. And
Alexander motioned with his hand, wishing
to make a defence to the people. But when 34
they recognised that he was a Jew, for about
two hours they all with one voice cried out,
"Great is Ar'temis of the Ephesians!" And 35
when the town clerk had quieted the crowd,
he said, "Men of Ephesus, what man is there
who does not know that the city of the
Ephesians is temple keeper of the great
Ar'temis, and of the sacred stone that fell
from the sky?[s] Seeing then that these things 36
cannot be contradicted, you ought to be quiet
and do nothing rash. For you have brought 37
these men here who are neither sacrilegious
nor blasphemers of our goddess. If therefore 38
Deme'trius and the craftsmen with him have
a complaint against any one, the courts are
open, and there are proconsuls; let them
bring charges against one another. But if you 39
seek anything further,[t] it shall be settled in
the regular assembly. For we are in danger 40
of being charged with rioting today, there
being no cause that we can give to justify this

[s] The meaning of the Greek is uncertain   [t] Other ancient authorities read *about other matters*

41 commotion." And when he had said this, he dismissed the assembly.

Macedonia

20 After the uproar ceased, Paul sent for the disciples and having exhorted them took leave of them and departed for Macedo'nia. 2 When he had gone through these parts and had given them much encouragement, he 3 came to Greece. There he spent three months, and when a plot was made against him by the Jews as he was about to set sail for Syria, he determined to return through 4 Macedo'nia. Sop'ater of Beroe'a, the son of Pyrrhus, accompanied him; and of the Thessalo'nians, Aristar'chus and Secun'dus; and Ga'ius of Derbe, and Timothy; and the Asians, Tych'icus and Troph'imus.

Troas

5 These went on and were waiting for us at 6 Tro'as, but we sailed away from Philippi after the days of Unleavened Bread, and in five days we came to them at Tro'as, where we stayed for seven days. 7 On the first day of the week, when we were gathered together to break bread, Paul talked with them, intending to depart on the morrow; and he prolonged his speech until 8 midnight. There were many lights in the 9 upper chamber where we were gathered. And a young man named Eu'tychus was sitting in the window. He sank into a deep sleep as Paul talked still longer; and being overcome by sleep, he fell down from the third story 10 and was taken up dead. But Paul went down and bent over him, and embracing him said, "Do not be alarmed, for his life is 11 in him." And when Paul had gone up and had broken bread and eaten, he conversed with them a long while, until daybreak, and 12 so departed. And they took the lad away alive, and were not a little comforted.

Assos

13 But going ahead to the ship, we set sail for Assos, intending to take Paul aboard there; for so he had arranged, intending himself to 14 go by land. And when he met us at Assos, we took him on board and came to Mityle'ne. 15 And sailing from there we came the following day opposite Chi'os; the next day we touched at Samos; and *u* the day after that we came to 16 Mile'tus. For Paul had decided to sail past Ephesus, so that he might not have to spend time in Asia; for he was hastening to be at

Jerusalem, if possible, on the day of Pentecost.

Miletus

And from Mile'tus he sent to Ephesus and 17 called to him the elders of the church. And 18 when they came to him, he said to them: "You yourselves know how I lived among you all the time from the first day that I set foot in Asia, serving the Lord with all 19 humility and with tears and with trials which befell me through the plots of the Jews; how 20 I did not shrink from declaring to you anything that was profitable, and teaching you in public and from house to house, testifying both to Jews and to Greeks of 21 repentance to God and of faith in our Lord Jesus Christ. And now, behold, I am going 22 to Jerusalem, bound in the Spirit, not knowing what shall befall me there; except 23 that the Holy Spirit testifies to me in every city that imprisonment and afflictions await me. But I do not account my life of any 24 value nor as precious to myself, if only I may accomplish my course and the ministry which I received from the Lord Jesus, to testify to the gospel of the grace of God. And 25 now, behold, I know that all you among whom I have gone about preaching the kingdom will see my face no more. There- 26 fore I testify to you this day that I am innocent of the blood of all of you, for I did 27 not shrink from declaring to you the whole counsel of God. Take heed to yourselves and 28 to all the flock, in which the Holy Spirit has made you guardians, to feed the church of the Lord *v* which he obtained with his own blood. *w* I know that after my departure 29

---

u Other ancient authorities add *after remaining at Trogyllium*   *v* Other ancient authorities read *of God*
w Or *with the blood of his Own*

Tyre

fierce wolves will come in among you, not
30 sparing the flock; and from among your own
selves will arise men speaking perverse
things, to draw away the disciples after
31 them. Therefore be alert, remembering that
for three years I did not cease night or day to
32 admonish every one with tears. And now I
commend you to God and to the word of his
grace, which is able to build you up and to
give you the inheritance among all those who
33 are sanctified. I coveted no one's silver or
34 gold or apparel. You yourselves know that
these hands ministered to my necessities, and
35 to those who were with me. In all things I
have shown you that by so toiling one must
help the weak, remembering the words of the
Lord Jesus, how he said, 'It is more blessed
to give than to receive.' "
36 And when he had spoken thus, he knelt
37 down and prayed with them all. And they all
wept and embraced Paul and kissed him,
38 sorrowing most of all because of the word he
had spoken, that they should see his face no
more. And they brought him to the ship.

21 And when we had parted from them and set
sail, we came by a straight course to Cos, and
the next day to Rhodes, and from there to
2 Pat'ara.ˣ And having found a ship crossing
to Phoeni'cia, we went aboard, and set sail.

Tyre

3 When we had come in sight of Cyprus,
leaving it on the left we sailed to Syria, and
landed at Tyre; for there the ship was to
4 unload its cargo. And having sought out the
disciples, we stayed there for seven days.
Through the Spirit they told Paul not to go
5 on to Jerusalem. And when our days there

were ended, we departed and went on our
journey; and they all, with wives and children, brought us on our way till we were
outside the city; and kneeling down on the
beach we prayed and bade one another
farewell. Then we went on board the ship, 6
and they returned home.

Caesarea

When we had finished the voyage from 7
Tyre, we arrived at Ptolema'is; and we
greeted the brethren and stayed with them
for one day. On the morrow we departed 8
and came to Caesare'a; and we entered the
house of Philip the evangelist, who was one
of the seven, and stayed with him. And he 9
had four unmarried daughters, who prophesied. While we were staying for some days, a 10
prophet named Ag'abus came down from
Judea. And coming to us he took Paul's 11
girdle and bound his own feet and hands, and
said, "Thus says the Holy Spirit, 'So shall
the Jews at Jerusalem bind the man who
owns this girdle and deliver him into the
hands of the Gentiles.' " When we heard 12
this, we and the people there begged him not
to go up to Jerusalem. Then Paul answered, 13
"What are you doing, weeping and breaking
my heart? For I am ready not only to be
imprisoned but even to die at Jerusalem for
the name of the Lord Jesus." And when he 14
would not be persuaded, we ceased and said,
"The will of the Lord be done."

On to Jerusalem

After these days we made ready and went 15
up to Jerusalem. And some of the disciples 16
from Caesare'a went with us, bringing us to

ˣ Other ancient authorities add *and Myra*

the house of Mnason of Cyprus, an early
disciple, with whom we should lodge.

PAUL IN JERUSALEM

17 WHEN we had come to Jerusalem, the
18   brethren received us gladly. On the
following day Paul went in with us to James;
19 and all the elders were present. After
greeting them, he related one by one the
things that God had done among the Gen-
20 tiles through his ministry. And when they
heard it, they glorified God. And they said
to him, "You see, brother, how many
thousands there are among the Jews of those
who have believed; they are all zealous for
21 the law, and they have been told about you
that you teach all the Jews who are among
the Gentiles to forsake Moses, telling them
not to circumcise their children or observe
22 the customs. What then is to be done?
They will certainly hear that you have come.
23 Do therefore what we tell you. We have four
24 men who are under a vow; take these men
and purify yourself along with them and pay
their expenses, so that they may shave their
heads. Thus all will know that there is
nothing in what they have been told about
you but that you yourself live in observance
25 of the law. But as for the Gentiles who have
believed, we have sent a letter with our
judgment that they should abstain from what
has been sacrificed to idols and from blood
and from what is strangled[y] and from
26 unchastity." Then Paul took the men, and
the next day he purified himself with them
and went into the temple, to give notice when
the days of purification would be fulfilled
and the offering presented for every one of
them.

An uproar

When the seven days were almost com- 27
pleted, the Jews from Asia, who had seen
him in the temple, stirred up all the crowd,
and laid hands on him, crying out, "Men of 28
Israel, help! This is the man who is teaching
men everywhere against the people and the
law and this place; moreover he also brought
Greeks into the temple, and he has defiled
this holy place." For they had previously 29
seen Troph'imus the Ephesian with him in
the city, and they supposed that Paul had
brought him into the temple. Then all the 30
city was aroused, and the people ran
together; they seized Paul and dragged him
out of the temple, and at once the gates were
shut. And as they were trying to kill him, 31
word came to the tribune of the cohort that
all Jerusalem was in confusion. He at once 32
took soldiers and centurions, and ran down
to them; and when they saw the tribune and
the soldiers, they stopped beating Paul.
Then the tribune came up and arrested him, 33

The tower of the barracks

[y] Other early authorities omit *and from what is strangled*

and ordered him to be bound with two chains. He inquired who he was and what he 34 had done. Some in the crowd shouted one thing, some another; and as he could not learn the facts because of the uproar, he ordered him to be brought into the barracks. 35 And when he came to the steps, he was actually carried by the soldiers because of the 36 violence of the crowd; for the mob of the people followed, crying, "Away with him!"

Paul's defence

37 As Paul was about to be brought into the barracks, he said to the tribune, "May I say

them in the Hebrew language, they were the more quiet. And he said: "I am a Jew, born at Tarsus in Cili′cia, 3 but brought up in this city at the feet of Gama′liel, educated according to the strict manner of the law of our fathers, being zealous for God as you all are this day. I 4 persecuted this Way to the death, binding and delivering to prison both men and women, as the high priest and the whole 5 council of elders bear me witness. From them I received letters to the brethren, and I journeyed to Damascus to take those also

Tarsus

who were there and bring them in bonds to Jerusalem to be punished.
"As I made my journey and drew near to 6 Damascus, about noon a great light from heaven suddenly shone about me. And I fell 7 to the ground and heard a voice saying to me, 'Saul, Saul, why do you persecute me?' And 8 I answered, 'Who are you, Lord?' And he said to me, 'I am Jesus of Nazareth whom you are persecuting.' Now those who were 9 with me saw the light but did not hear the voice of the one who was speaking to me. And I said, 'What shall I do, Lord?' And 10 the Lord said to me, 'Rise, and go into Damascus, and there you will be told all that is appointed for you to do.' And when I 11 could not see because of the brightness of that light, I was led by the hand by those who were with me, and came into Damascus.
"And one Anani′as, a devout man according 12 to the law, well spoken of by all the Jews who lived there, came to me, and standing by me 13 said to me, 'Brother Saul, receive your sight.' And in that very hour I received my sight and saw him. And he said, 'The God 14

something to you?" And he said, "Do you 38 know Greek? Are you not the Egyptian, then, who recently stirred up a revolt and led the four thousand men of the Assassins out 39 into the wilderness?" Paul replied, "I am a Jew, from Tarsus in Cili′cia, a citizen of no mean city; I beg you, let me speak to the 40 people." And when he had given him leave, Paul, standing on the steps, motioned with his hands to the people; and when there was a great hush, he spoke to them in the Hebrew language, saying:

22 "Brethren and fathers, hear the defence which I now make before you." 2 And when they heard that he addressed

22.4-16: Acts 9.1-19; 26.9-18; Gal 1.14.

of our fathers appointed you to know his will, to see the Just One and to hear a voice from
15 his mouth; for you will be a witness for him to all men of what you have seen and heard.
16 And now why do you wait? Rise and be baptized, and wash away your sins, calling on his name.'
17 "When I had returned to Jerusalem and was praying in the temple, I fell into a trance
18 and saw him saying to me, 'Make haste and get quickly out of Jerusalem, because they will not accept your testimony about me.'
19 And I said, 'Lord, they themselves know that in every synagogue I imprisoned and beat
20 those who believed in me. And when the blood of Stephen thy witness was shed, I also was standing by and approving, and keeping
21 the garments of those who killed him.' And he said to me, 'Depart; for I will send you far away to the Gentiles.'"
22 Up to this word they listened to him; then they lifted up their voices and said, "Away with such a fellow from the earth! For he
23 ought not to live." And as they cried out and waved their garments and threw dust into the
24 air, the tribune commanded him to be brought into the barracks, and ordered him to be examined by scourging, to find out why
25 they shouted thus against him. But when they had tied him up with the thongs, Paul said to the centurion who was standing by, "Is it lawful for you to scourge a man who is a Roman citizen, and uncondemned?"
26 When the centurion heard that, he went to the tribune and said to him, "What are you about to do? For this man is a Roman
27 citizen." So the tribune came and said to him, "Tell me, are you a Roman citizen?"
28 And he said, "Yes." The tribune answered, "I bought this citizenship for a large sum."
29 Paul said, "But I was born a citizen." So those who were about to examine him withdrew from him instantly; and the tribune also was afraid, for he realised that Paul was a Roman citizen and that he had bound him.

Before the Sanhedrin

30 But on the morrow, desiring to know the real reason why the Jews accused him, he unbound him, and commanded the chief priests and all the council to meet, and he brought Paul down and set him before them.

23 And Paul, looking intently at the council, said, "Brethren, I have lived before God in
2 all good conscience up to this day." And the high priest Anani'as commanded those who stood by him to strike him on the mouth.

Then Paul said to him, "God shall strike 3 you, you whitewashed wall! Are you sitting to judge me according to the law, and yet contrary to the law you order me to be struck?" Those who stood by said, "Would 4 you revile God's high priest?" And Paul 5 said, "I did not know, brethren, that he was the high priest; for it is written, 'You shall not speak evil of a ruler of your people.'"
But when Paul perceived that one part were 6 Sad'ducees and the other Pharisees, he cried out in the council, "Brethren, I am a Pharisee, a son of Pharisees; with respect to the hope and the resurrection of the dead I am on trial." And when he had said this, a 7 dissension arose between the Pharisees and the Sad'ducees; and the assembly was divided. For the Sad'ducees say that there is 8 no resurrection, nor angel, nor spirit; but the Pharisees acknowledge them all. Then a 9 great clamour arose; and some of the scribes of the Pharisees' party stood up and contended, "We find nothing wrong in this man. What if a spirit or an angel spoke to him?" And when the dissension became 10 violent, the tribune, afraid that Paul would be torn in pieces by them, commanded the soldiers to go down and take him by force from among them and bring him into the barracks.
The following night the Lord stood by him 11 and said, "Take courage, for as you have testified about me at Jerusalem, so you must bear witness also at Rome."

A plot defeated

When it was day, the Jews made a plot and 12 bound themselves by an oath neither to eat nor drink till they had killed Paul. There 13 were more than forty who made this conspiracy. And they went to the chief priests 14 and elders, and said, "We have strictly bound ourselves by an oath to taste no food till we have killed Paul. You therefore, along with 15 the council, give notice now to the tribune to bring him down to you, as though you were going to determine his case more exactly. And we are ready to kill him before he comes near."
Now the son of Paul's sister heard of their 16 ambush; so he went and entered the barracks and told Paul. And Paul called one of the 17 centurions and said, "Bring this young man to the tribune; for he has something to tell him." So he took him and brought him to 18 the tribune and said, "Paul the prisoner called me and asked me to bring this young man to you, as he has something to say to you." The tribune took him by the hand, 19

and going aside asked him privately, "What
20 is it that you have to tell me?" And he said,
"The Jews have agreed to ask you to bring
Paul down to the council tomorrow, as
though they were going to inquire somewhat
21 more closely about him. But do not yield to
them; for more than forty of their men lie in
ambush for him, having bound themselves
by an oath neither to eat nor drink till they
have killed him; and now they are ready,
22 waiting for the promise from you." So the
tribune dismissed the young man, charging
him, "Tell no one that you have informed me
of this."
23 Then he called two of the centurions and
said, "At the third hour of the night get
ready two hundred soldiers with seventy
horsemen and two hundred spearmen to go
24 as far as Caesare'a. Also provide mounts for
Paul to ride, and bring him safely to Felix the
25 governor." And he wrote a letter to this
effect:

26 "Claudius Lys'ias to his Excellency the
27 governor Felix, greeting. This man was
seized by the Jews, and was about to be killed
by them, when I came upon them with the
soldiers and rescued him, having learned that
28 he was a Roman citizen. And desiring to
know the charge on which they accused him,
29 I brought him down to their council. I
found that he was accused about questions of
their law, but charged with nothing deserv-
30 ing death or imprisonment. And when it was
disclosed to me that there would be a plot
against the man, I sent him to you at once,
ordering his accusers also to state before you
what they have against him."
31 So the soldiers, according to their instructions, took Paul and brought him by night to
32 Antip'atris. And on the morrow they returned to the barracks, leaving the horsemen
33 to go on with him. When they came to
Caesare'a and delivered the letter to the
governor, they presented Paul also before
34 him. On reading the letter, he asked to what
province he belonged. When he learned that
35 he was from Cili'cia he said, "I will hear you

when your accusers arrive." And he commanded him to be guarded in Herod's
praetorium.

Paul before Felix

And after five days the high priest Anani'as 24
came down with some elders and a spokes-
man, one Tertul'lus. They laid before the
governor their case against Paul; and when 2
he was called, Tertul'lus began to accuse
him, saying:
"Since through you we enjoy much peace,
and since by your provision, most excellent
Felix, reforms are introduced on behalf of
this nation, in every way and everywhere we 3
accept this with all gratitude. But, to detain 4
you no further, I beg you in your kindness to
hear us briefly. For we have found this man 5
a pestilent fellow, an agitator among all the
Jews throughout the world, and a ringleader
of the sect of the Nazarenes. He even tried to 6
profane the temple, but we seized him.² By 8
examining him yourself you will be able to
learn from him about everything of which we
accuse him."
The Jews also joined in the charge, affirm- 9
ing that all this was so.
And when the governor had motioned to 10
him to speak, Paul replied:
"Realising that for many years you have
been judge over this nation, I cheerfully
make my defence. As you may ascertain, it is 11
not more than twelve days since I went up to
worship at Jerusalem; and they did not find 12
me disputing with any one or stirring up a
crowd, either in the temple or in the synagogues, or in the city. Neither can they 13
prove to you what they now bring up against
me. But this I admit to you, that according 14
to the Way, which they call a sect, I worship
the God of our fathers, believing everything
laid down by the law or written in the
prophets, having a hope in God which these 15
themselves accept, that there will be a resurrection of both the just and the unjust. So I 16
always take pains to have a clear conscience
toward God and toward men. Now after 17
some years I came to bring to my nation alms
and offerings. As I was doing this, they 18
found me purified in the temple, without any
crowd or tumult. But some Jews from
Asia—they ought to be here before you and 19
to make an accusation, if they have anything
against me. Or else let these men themselves 20
say what wrongdoing they found when I
stood before the council, except this one 21
thing which I cried out while standing

---

² Other ancient authorities add *and we would have judged him according to our law.* ⁷ *But the chief captain*
Lysias came and with great violence took him out of our hands, ⁸ *commanding his accusers to come before you.*

among them, 'With respect to the resurrection of the dead I am on trial before you this day.'"

22 But Felix, having a rather accurate knowledge of the Way, put them off, saying, "When Lys'ias the tribune comes down, I will decide your case." 23 Then he gave orders to the centurion that he should be kept in custody but should have some liberty, and that none of his friends should be prevented from attending to his needs.

24 After some days Felix came with his wife Drusil'la, who was a Jewess; and he sent for Paul and heard him speak upon faith in 25 Christ Jesus. And as he argued about justice and self-control and future judgment, Felix was alarmed and said, "Go away for the present; when I have an opportunity I will 26 summon you." At the same time he hoped that money would be given him by Paul. So he sent for him often and conversed with 27 him. But when two years had elapsed, Felix

was succeeded by Porcius Festus; and desiring to do the Jews a favour, Felix left Paul in prison.

Appeal to Caesar

25 Now when Festus had come into his province, after three days he went up to Jeru-2 salem from Caesare'a. And the chief priests and the principal men of the Jews informed 3 him against Paul; and they urged him, asking as a favour to have the man sent to Jerusalem, planning an ambush to kill him on the 4 way. Festus replied that Paul was being kept at Caesare'a, and that he himself intended to 5 go there shortly. "So," said he, "let the men of authority among you go down with me, and if there is anything wrong about the man, let them accuse him."

6 When he had stayed among them not more than eight or ten days, he went down to Caesare'a; and the next day he took his seat on the tribunal and ordered Paul to be 7 brought. And when he had come, the Jews who had gone down from Jerusalem stood about him, bringing against him many serious charges which they could not prove.

Paul said in his defence, "Neither against the 8 law of the Jews, nor against the temple, nor against Caesar have I offended at all." But 9 Festus, wishing to do the Jews a favour, said to Paul, "Do you wish to go up to Jerusalem, and there be tried on these charges before me?" But Paul said, "I am standing before 10 Caesar's tribunal, where I ought to be tried; to the Jews I have done no wrong, as you know very well. If then I am a wrongdoer, 11 and have committed anything for which I deserve to die, I do not seek to escape death; but if there is nothing in their charges against me, no one can give me up to them. I appeal to Caesar." Then Festus, when he had 12 conferred with his council, answered, "You have appealed to Caesar; to Caesar you shall go."

Now when some days had passed, Agrippa 13 the king and Berni'ce arrived at Caesare'a to welcome Festus. And as they stayed there 14 many days, Festus laid Paul's case before the king, saying, "There is a man left prisoner by Felix; and when I was at Jerusalem, the chief 15 priests and the elders of the Jews gave information about him, asking for sentence against him. I answered them that it was not 16 the custom of the Romans to give up any one before the accused met the accusers face to face, and had opportunity to make his defence concerning the charge laid against him. When therefore they came together 17 here, I made no delay, but on the next day took my seat on the tribunal and ordered the man to be brought in. When the accusers 18 stood up, they brought no charge in his case of such evils as I supposed; but they had 19 certain points of dispute with him about their own superstition and about one Jesus, who was dead, but whom Paul asserted to be alive. Being at a loss how to investigate these 20 questions, I asked whether he wished to go to Jerusalem and be tried there regarding them. But when Paul had appealed to be 21

kept in custody for the decision of the emperor, I commanded him to be held until I could send him to Caesar." And Agrippa 22 said to Festus, "I should like to hear the man myself." "Tomorrow," said he, "you shall hear him."

Paul before Agrippa

3 So on the morrow Agrippa and Berni'ce came with great pomp, and they entered the audience hall with the military tribunes and the prominent men of the city. Then by command of Festus Paul was brought in. 4 And Festus said, "King Agrippa and all who are present with us, you see this man about whom the whole Jewish people petitioned me, both at Jerusalem and here, shouting 5 that he ought not to live any longer. But I found that he had done nothing deserving death; and as he himself appealed to the 6 emperor, I decided to send him. But I have nothing definite to write to my lord about him. Therefore I have brought him before you, and, especially before you, King Agrippa, that, after we have examined him, I 7 may have something to write. For it seems to me unreasonable, in sending a prisoner, not to indicate the charges against him."

Paul's speech

26 Agrippa said to Paul, "You have permission to speak for yourself." Then Paul stretched out his hand and made his defence: 2 "I think myself fortunate that it is before you, King Agrippa, I am to make my defence today against all the accusations of the Jews, 3 because you are especially familiar with all customs and controversies of the Jews; therefore I beg you to listen to me patiently. 4 "My manner of life from my youth, spent from the beginning among my own nation and at Jerusalem, is known by all the Jews. 5 They have known for a long time, if they are willing to testify, that according to the strictest party of our religion I have lived as a 6 Pharisee. And now I stand here on trial for hope in the promise made by God to our 7 fathers, to which our twelve tribes hope to attain, as they earnestly worship night and day. And for this hope I am accused by 8 Jews, O king! Why is it thought incredible by any of you that God raises the dead? 9 "I myself was convinced that I ought to do many things in opposing the name of Jesus of 10 Nazareth. And I did so in Jerusalem; I not only shut up many of the saints in prison, by authority from the chief priests, but when they were put to death I cast my vote against 11 them. And I punished them often in all the synagogues and tried to make them blaspheme; and in raging fury against them, I persecuted them even to foreign cities. 12 "Thus I journeyed to Damascus with the authority and commission of the chief 13 priests. At midday, O king, I saw on the way a light from heaven, brighter than the sun, shining round me and those who journeyed with me. And when we had all fallen to the 14 ground, I heard a voice saying to me in the Hebrew language, 'Saul, Saul, why do you persecute me? It hurts you to kick against the goads.' And I said, 'Who are you, 15 Lord?' And the Lord said, 'I am Jesus whom you are persecuting. But rise and 16 stand upon your feet; for I have appeared to you for this purpose, to appoint you to serve and bear witness to the things in which you have seen me and to those in which I will appear to you, delivering you from the 17 people and from the Gentiles—to whom I send you to open their eyes, that they may 18 turn from darkness to light and from the power of Satan to God, that they may receive forgiveness of sins and a place among those who are sanctified by faith in me.'

"Wherefore, O King Agrippa, I was not 19 disobedient to the heavenly vision, but de- 20 clared first to those at Damascus, then at Jerusalem and throughout all the country of Judea, and also to the Gentiles, that they should repent and turn to God and perform deeds worthy of their repentance. For this 21 reason the Jews seized me in the temple and tried to kill me. To this day I have had the 22 help that comes from God, and so I stand here testifying both to small and great, saying nothing but what the prophets and Moses said would come to pass: that the Christ 23 must suffer, and that, by being the first to rise from the dead, he would proclaim light both to the people and to the Gentiles."

And as he thus made his defence, Festus 24 said with a loud voice, "Paul, you are mad; your great learning is turning you mad." But 25 Paul said, "I am not mad, most excellent Festus, but I am speaking the sober truth. For the king knows about these things, and 26 to him I speak freely; for I am persuaded that none of these things has escaped his notice, for this was not done in a corner. King 27 Agrippa, do you believe the prophets? I know that you believe." And Agrippa said to 28 Paul, "In a short time you think to make me a Christian!" And Paul said, "Whether short 29 or long, I would to God that not only you but also all who hear me this day might become such as I am—except for these chains."

Then the king rose, and the governor and 30 Berni'ce and those who were sitting with them; and when they had withdrawn, they 31 said to one another, "This man is doing nothing to deserve death or imprisonment." And Agrippa said to Festus, "This man 32 could have been set free if he had not appealed to Caesar."

26.9-18: Acts 9.1-8; 22.4-16.   26.16-17: Ezek 2.1, 3.   26.18: Is 42.7, 16.

59~62 A.D.

PAUL'S JOURNEY TO ROME

27 AND when it was decided that we should
sail for Italy, they delivered Paul and
some other prisoners to a centurion of the
2 Augustan Cohort, named Julius. And
embarking in a ship of Adramyt′tium, which
was about to sail to the ports along the coast
of Asia, we put to sea, accompanied by
Aristar′chus, a Macedo′nian from Thessa-
3 loni′ca. The next day we put in at Sidon;
and Julius treated Paul kindly, and gave him
leave to go to his friends and be cared for.
4 And putting to sea from there we sailed
under the lee of Cyprus, because the winds
5 were against us. And when we had sailed
across the sea which is off Cili′cia and
Pamphyl′ia, we came to Myra in Ly′cia.
6 There the centurion found a ship of
Alexandria sailing for Italy, and put us on
7 board. We sailed slowly for a number of
days, and arrived with difficulty off Cni′dus,
and as the wind did not allow us to go on, we
sailed under the lee of Crete off Salmo′ne.
8 Coasting along it with difficulty, we came to
a place called Fair Havens, near which was
the city of Lase′a.
9 As much time had been lost, and the voyage
was already dangerous because the fast had
10 already gone by, Paul advised them, saying,
"Sirs, I perceive that the voyage will be with
injury and much loss, not only of the cargo
11 and the ship, but also of our lives." But the
centurion paid more attention to the captain
and to the owner of the ship than to what
12 Paul said. And because the harbour was not

suitable to winter in, the majority advised to
put to sea from there, on the chance that
somehow they could reach Phoenix, a harbour of Crete, looking northeast and south-
east,[a] and winter there.

A storm

And when the south wind blew gently, 13
supposing that they had obtained their purpose, they weighed anchor and sailed along
Crete, close inshore. But soon a tempestuous 14
wind, called the northeaster, struck down
from the land; and when the ship was caught 15
and could not face the wind, we gave way to
it and were driven. And running under the 16
lee of a small island called Cauda,[b] we
managed with difficulty to secure the boat;
after hoisting it up, they took measures[c] to 17
undergird the ship; then, fearing that they
should run on the Syr′tis, they lowered the
gear, and so were driven. As we were 18
violently storm-tossed, they began next day
to throw the cargo overboard; and the third 19
day they cast out with their own hands the
tackle of the ship. And when neither sun nor 20
stars appeared for many a day, and no small
tempest lay on us, all hope of our being saved
was at last abandoned.
As they had been long without food, Paul 21
then came forward among them and said,
"Men, you should have listened to me, and
should not have set sail from Crete and
incurred this injury and loss. I now bid you 22

The Fair Havens

a Or *southwest and northwest*   *b* Other ancient authorities read *Clauda*   *c* Greek *helps* take heart; for there will be no loss of life among you, but only of the ship. For this 3 very night there stood by me an angel of the God to whom I belong and whom I worship, 4 and he said, 'Do not be afraid, Paul; you must stand before Caesar; and lo, God has 5 granted you all those who sail with you.' So take heart, men, for I have faith in God that 6 it will be exactly as I have been told. But we shall have to run on some island."

all to take some food, saying, "Today is the fourteenth day that you have continued in suspense and without food, having taken nothing. Therefore I urge you to take some 34 food; it will give you strength, since not a hair is to perish from the head of any of you." And when he had said this, he took 35 bread, and giving thanks to God in the presence of all he broke it and began to eat. Then they all were encouraged and ate some 36

PAUL'S JOURNEY to ROME

Ephesus
Colosse
Cnidus
Myra
Crete
Lasea Salmone
Cyprus
Sidon
Caesarea

The Great Sea

The shipwreck

27 When the fourteenth night had come, as we were drifting across the sea of A'dria, about midnight the sailors suspected that they were 28 nearing land. So they sounded and found twenty fathoms; a little farther on they sounded again and found fifteen fathoms. 29 And fearing that we might run on the rocks, they let out four anchors from the stern, and 30 prayed for day to come. And as the sailors were seeking to escape from the ship, and had lowered the boat into the sea, under pretence of laying out anchors from the bow, 31 Paul said to the centurion and the soldiers, "Unless these men stay in the ship, you 32 cannot be saved." Then the soldiers cut away the ropes of the boat, and let it go. 33 As day was about to dawn, Paul urged them

food themselves. (We were in all two 37 hundred and seventy-six[d] persons in the ship.) And when they had eaten enough, they 38 lightened the ship, throwing out the wheat into the sea.

Now when it was day, they did not recog- 39 nise the land, but they noticed a bay with a beach, on which they planned if possible to bring the ship ashore. So they cast off the 40 anchors and left them in the sea, at the same time loosening the ropes that tied the rudders; then hoisting the foresail to the wind they made for the beach. But striking a 41 shoal[e] they ran the vessel aground; the bow stuck and remained immovable, and the stern was broken up by the surf. The 42 soldiers' plan was to kill the prisoners, lest any should swim away and escape; but the 43 centurion, wishing to save Paul, kept them

d Other ancient authorities read *seventy-six* or *about seventy-six*   *e* Greek *place of two seas* from carrying out their purpose. He ordered those who could swim to throw themselves 44 overboard first and make for the land, and the rest on planks or on pieces of the ship. And so it was that all escaped to land.

Malta

28 After we had escaped, we then learned that 2 the island was called Malta. And the natives

escaped from the sea, justice has not allowed him to live." He, however, shook off the creature into the fire and suffered no harm. They waited, expecting him to swell up or suddenly fall down dead; but when they had waited a long time and saw no misfortune come to him, they changed their minds and said that he was a god.

Now in the neighbourhood of that place were lands belonging to the chief man of the

PAUL'S JOURNEY to ROME

showed us unusual kindness, for they kindled a fire and welcomed us all, because it had 3 begun to rain and was cold. Paul had gathered a bundle of sticks and put them on the fire, when a viper came out because of the 4 heat and fastened on his hand. When the natives saw the creature hanging from his hand, they said to one another, "No doubt this man is a murderer. Though he has

island, named Publius, who received us and entertained us hospitably for three days. It 8 happened that the father of Publius lay sick with fever and dysentery; and Paul visited him and prayed, and putting his hands on him healed him. And when this had taken 9 place, the rest of the people on the island who had diseases also came and were cured. They presented many gifts to us;[f] and when 10

---

[f] Or *honoured us with many honours*

we sailed, they put on board whatever we needed.

11 After three months we set sail in a ship which had wintered in the island, a ship of Alexandria, with the Twin Brothers as figurehead. 12 Putting in at Syracuse, we stayed there for three days. 13 And from there we made a circuit and arrived at Rhe′gium; and after one day a south wind sprang up, and on the second day we came to Pute′oli. 14 There we found brethren, and were invited to stay with them for seven days. And so we 15 came to Rome. And the brethren there, when they heard of us, came as far as the Forum of Ap′pius and Three Taverns to meet us. On seeing them Paul thanked God 16 and took courage. And when we came into Rome, Paul was allowed to stay by himself, with the soldier that guarded him.

Paul in Rome

17 After three days he called together the local leaders of the Jews; and when they had gathered, he said to them, "Brethren, though I had done nothing against the people or the customs of our fathers, yet I was delivered prisoner from Jerusalem into the hands of 18 the Romans. When they had examined me, they wished to set me at liberty, because there was no reason for the death penalty in 19 my case. But when the Jews objected, I was compelled to appeal to Caesar—though I had 20 no charge to bring against my nation. For this reason therefore I have asked to see you and speak with you, since it is because of the hope of Israel that I am bound with this 21 chain." And they said to him, "We have received no letters from Judea about you,

and none of the brethren coming here has reported or spoken any evil about you. But 22 we desire to hear from you what your views are; for with regard to this sect we know that everywhere it is spoken against."

When they had appointed a day for him, 23 they came to him at his lodging in great numbers. And he expounded the matter to them from morning till evening, testifying to the kingdom of God and trying to convince them about Jesus both from the law of Moses and from the prophets. And some were 24 convinced by what he said, while others disbelieved. So, as they disagreed among 25 themselves, they departed, after Paul had made one statement: "The Holy Spirit was right in saying to your fathers through Isaiah the prophet:

'Go to this people, and say,   26
You shall indeed hear but never under-
    stand,
and you shall indeed see but never per-
    ceive.
For this people's heart has grown dull,   27
and their ears are heavy of hearing,
and their eyes they have closed;
lest they should perceive with their eyes,
and hear with their ears,
and understand with their heart,
and turn for me to heal them.'

Let it be known to you then that this 28 salvation of God has been sent to the Gentiles; they will listen." [g]

And he lived there two whole years at his 30 own expense,[h] and welcomed all who came to him, preaching the kingdom of God and 31 teaching about the Lord Jesus Christ quite openly and unhindered.

Sidon

[g] Other ancient authorities add verse 29, *And when he had said these words, the Jews departed, holding much dispute among themselves*   [h] Or *in his own hired dwelling*
28.26–27: Is 6.9–10. **28.28:** Ps 67.2.

THE LETTER OF PAUL TO THE

ROMANS

PAUL, a servant^a of Jesus Christ, called to be an apostle, set apart for the 2 gospel of God which he promised beforehand through his prophets in the holy 3 scriptures, the gospel concerning his Son, who was descended from David according to 4 the flesh and designated Son of God in power according to the Spirit of holiness by his resurrection from the dead, Jesus Christ 5 our Lord, through whom we have received grace and apostleship to bring about the obedience of faith for the sake of his name 6 among all the nations, including yourselves who are called to belong to Jesus Christ;

7 To all God's beloved in Rome, who are called to be saints:

Grace to you and peace from God our Father and the Lord Jesus Christ.

THE GOSPEL OF SALVATION

8 FIRST, I thank my God through Jesus Christ for all of you, because your faith 9 is proclaimed in all the world. For God is my witness, whom I serve with my spirit in the gospel of his Son, that without ceasing I 10 mention you always in my prayers, asking that somehow by God's will I may now at 11 last succeed in coming to you. For I long to

see you, that I may impart to you some spiritual gift to strengthen you, that is, that 12 we may be mutually encouraged by each other's faith, both yours and mine. I want 13 you to know, brethren, that I have often intended to come to you (but thus far have been prevented), in order that I may reap some harvest among you as well as among the rest of the Gentiles. I am under obligation 14 both to Greeks and to barbarians, both to the wise and to the foolish: so I am eager to 15 preach the gospel to you also who are in Rome.

For I am not ashamed of the gospel: it is the 16 power of God for salvation to every one who has faith, to the Jew first and also to the Greek. For in it the righteousness of God is 17 revealed through faith for faith; as it is written, "He who through faith is righteous shall live."^b

The state of the world

For the wrath of God is revealed from 18 heaven against all ungodliness and wickedness of men who by their wickedness suppress the truth. For what can be known 19 about God is plain to them, because God has shown it to them. Ever since the creation of 20 the world his invisible nature, namely, his

---

^a Or *slave* ^b Or *The righteous shall live by faith*
1.1: Acts 9.15; 13.2; 1 Cor 1.1; 2 Cor 1.1; Gal 1.15. **1.5:** Acts 26.16–18; Rom 15.18; Gal 2.7, 9.
1.7: 1 Cor 1.3; 2 Cor 1.2; Gal 1.3; Eph 1.2; Phil 1.2; Col 1.2; 1 Thess 1.2; 2 Thess 1.2; 1 Tim 1.2; 2 Tim 1.2;
Tit 1.4; Philem 3; 2 Jn 3. **1.8:** Rom 16.19. **1.10:** Rom 15.23, 32; Acts 19.21.
1.13: Rom 15.22. **1.14:** 1 Cor 9.16. **1.16:** 1 Cor 1.18, 24.
1.17: Rom 3.21; Gal 3.11; Phil 3.9; Heb 10.38; Hab 2.4. **1.18:** Eph 5.6; Col 3.6. **1.20:** Ps 19.1–4.

eternal power and deity, has been clearly perceived in the things that have been made.
21 So they are without excuse; for although they knew God they did not honour him as God or give thanks to him, but they became futile in their thinking and their senseless minds
22 were darkened. Claiming to be wise, they
23 became fools, and exchanged the glory of the immortal God for images resembling mortal man or birds or animals or reptiles.
24 Therefore God gave them up in the lusts of their hearts to impurity, to the dishonouring
25 of their bodies among themselves, because they exchanged the truth about God for a lie and worshipped and served the creature rather than the Creator, who is blessed for ever! Amen.
26 For this reason God gave them up to dishonourable passions. Their women exchanged natural relations for unnatural,
27 and the men likewise gave up natural relations with women and were consumed with passion for one another, men committing shameless acts with men and receiving in their own persons the due penalty for their error.
28 And since they did not see fit to acknowledge God, God gave them up to a base mind
29 and to improper conduct. They were filled with all manner of wickedness, evil, covetousness, malice. Full of envy, murder, strife, deceit, malignity, they are gossips,
30 slanderers, haters of God, insolent, haughty, boastful, inventors of evil, disobedient to
31 parents, foolish, faithless, heartless, ruth-
32 less. Though they know God's decree that those who do such things deserve to die, they not only do them but approve those who practise them.

Jews as well as Gentiles

2 Therefore you have no excuse, O man, whoever you are, when you judge another; for in passing judgment upon him you condemn yourself, because you, the judge,
2 are doing the very same things. We know that the judgment of God rightly falls upon
3 those who do such things. Do you suppose, O man, that when you judge those who do such things and yet do them yourself, you
4 will escape the judgment of God? Or do you presume upon the riches of his kindness and forbearance and patience? Do you not know that God's kindness is meant to lead you
5 to repentance? But by your hard and

impenitent heart you are storing up wrath for yourself on the day of wrath when God's righteous judgment will be revealed. For he 6 will render to every man according to his works: to those who by patience in well- 7 doing seek for glory and honour and immortality, he will give eternal life; but for those 8 who are factious and do not obey the truth, but obey wickedness, there will be wrath and fury. There will be tribulation and distress 9 for every human being who does evil, the Jew first and also the Greek, but glory and 10 honour and peace for every one who does good, the Jew first and also the Greek. For 11 God shows no partiality.
All who have sinned without the law will 12 also perish without the law, and all who have sinned under the law will be judged by the law. For it is not the hearers of the law who 13 are righteous before God, but the doers of the law who will be justified. When Gentiles 14 who have not the law do by nature what the law requires, they are a law to themselves, even though they do not have the law. They 15 show that what the law requires is written on their hearts, while their conscience also bears witness and their conflicting thoughts accuse or perhaps excuse them on that day when, 16 according to my gospel, God judges the secrets of men by Christ Jesus.
But if you call yourself a Jew and rely upon 17 the law and boast of your relation to God and 18 know his will and approve what is excellent, because you are instructed in the law, and if 19 you are sure that you are a guide to the blind, a light to those who are in darkness, a 20 corrector of the foolish, a teacher of children, having in the law the embodiment of knowledge and truth—you then who teach 21 others, will you not teach yourself? While you preach against stealing, do you steal? You who say that one must not commit 22 adultery, do you commit adultery? You who abhor idols, do you rob temples? You who 23 boast in the law, do you dishonour God by breaking the law? For, as it is written, "The 24 name of God is blasphemed among the Gentiles because of you."
Circumcision indeed is of value if you obey 25 the law; but if you break the law, your circumcision becomes uncircumcision. So, if 26 a man who is uncircumcised keeps the precepts of the law, will not his uncircumcision be regarded as circumcision? Then 27 those who are physically uncircumcised but keep the law will condemn you who have the

1.21: Eph 4.17–18. **1.23:** Acts 17.29. **2.1:** Rom 14.22.
2.4: Eph 1.7; 2.7; Phil 4.19; Col 1.27. **2.6:** Mt 16.27; 1 Cor 3.8; 2 Cor 5.10; Rev 22.12.
2.11: Deut 10.17; 2 Chron 19.7; Gal 2.6; Eph 6.9; Col 3.25; 1 Pet 1.17. **2.12:** Rom 3.19; 1 Cor 9.21.
2.13: Jas 1.22–23, 25. **2.16:** Eccles 12.14; Rom 16.25; 1 Cor 4.5.
2.20: Phil 1.10. **2.20:** Rom 6.17; 2 Tim 1.13. **2.21:** Mt 23.3–4. **2.24:** Is 52.5. **2.25:** Jer 9.25.
2.26: 1 Cor 7.19; Acts 10.35. **2.27:** Mt 12.41.

28 written code and circumcision but break the
law. For he is not a real Jew who is one
outwardly, nor is true circumcision some-
29 thing external and physical. He is a Jew
who is one inwardly, and real circumcision is
a matter of the heart, spiritual and not
literal. His praise is not from men but from
God.

All are under the power of sin

3 Then what advantage has the Jew? Or
2 what is the value of circumcision? Much in
every way. To begin with, the Jews are
3 entrusted with the oracles of God. What if
some were unfaithful? Does their faith-
4 lessness nullify the faithfulness of God? By
no means! Let God be true though every
man be false, as it is written,
"That thou mayest be justified in thy
words,
and prevail when thou art judged."
5 But if our wickedness serves to show the
justice of God, what shall we say? That God
is unjust to inflict wrath on us? (I speak in a
6 human way.) By no means! For then how
7 could God judge the world? But if through
my falsehood God's truthfulness abounds to
his glory, why am I still being condemned as
8 a sinner? And why not do evil that good
may come?—as some people slanderously
charge us with saying. Their condemnation
is just.
9 What then? Are we Jews any better off?[c]
No, not at all; for I[d] have already charged
that all men, both Jews and Greeks, are
10 under the power of sin, as it is written:
"None is righteous, no, not one;
11 no one understands, no one seeks for God.
12 All have turned aside, together they have
gone wrong;
no one does good, not even one."
13 "Their throat is an open grave,
they use their tongues to deceive."
"The venom of asps is under their lips."
14 "Their mouth is full of curses and bitterness."
15 "Their feet are swift to shed blood,
16 in their paths are ruin and misery,
17 and the way of peace they do not know."
18 "There is no fear of God before their
eyes."
19 Now we know that whatever the law says it

speaks to those who are under the law, so that
every mouth may be stopped, and the whole
world may be held accountable to God. For 20
no human being will be justified in his sight
by works of the law, since through the law
comes knowledge of sin.

God's saving gift

But now the righteousness of God has been 21
manifested apart from law, although the law
and the prophets bear witness to it, the 22
righteousness of God through faith in Jesus
Christ for all who believe. For there is no
distinction; since all have sinned and fall 23
short of the glory of God, they are justified 24
by his grace as a gift, through the redemption
which is in Christ Jesus, whom God put 25
forward as an expiation by his blood, to be
received by faith. This was to show God's
righteousness, because in his divine forbearance he had passed over former sins; it 26
was to prove at the present time that he
himself is righteous and that he justifies him
who has faith in Jesus.
Then what becomes of our boasting? It is 27
excluded. On what principle? On the principle of works? No, but on the principle of
faith. For we hold that a man is justified by 28
faith apart from works of law. Or is God the 29
God of Jews only? Is he not the God of
Gentiles also? Yes, of Gentiles also, since 30
God is one; and he will justify the circumcised on the ground of their faith and the
uncircumcised through their faith. Do we 31
then overthrow the law by this faith? By no
means! On the contrary, we uphold the law.

The gift grasped by faith

What then shall we say about[e] Abraham, our 4
forefather according to the flesh? For if 2
Abraham was justified by works, he has
something to boast about, but not before
God. For what does the scripture 3
say? "Abraham believed God, and it was
reckoned to him as righteousness." Now to 4
one who works, his wages are not reckoned as
a gift but as his due. And to one who does 5
not work but trusts him who justifies the
ungodly, his faith is reckoned as righteousness. So also David pronounces a blessing 6

---

[c] Or at any disadvantage? [d] Greek we [e] Other ancient authorities read was gained by
2.28: Mt 3.9; Jn 8.39; Rom 9.6–7; Gal 6.15. 2.29: 2 Cor 3.6; Phil 3.3; Col 2.11; 1 Pet 3.4.
3.2: Ps 147.19; Rom 9.4. 3.4: Ps 51.4. 3.5: Rom 5.9; 6.19; 1 Cor 9.8; Gal 3.15. 3.8: Rom 6.1, 15.
3.9: Rom 1.18–32; 2.1–29; 11.32; 3.23. 3.10–12: Ps 14.1–3; 53.1–3. 3.13: Ps 5.9; 140.3. 3.14: Ps 10.7.
3.15–17: Is 59.7–8. 3.18: Ps 36.1. 3.19: Rom 2.12. 3.20: Ps 143.2; Acts 13.39; Gal 2.16; 3.11; Rom 7.7.
3.21: Rom 1.17; Phil 3.9; 2 Pet 1.1. 3.22: Rom 4.5; 9.30; 10.12; Gal 2.16. 3.23: Rom 3.9.
3.24: Rom 4.16; 5.9; Eph 2.8; Tit 3.7; Eph 1.7; Col 1.14; Heb 9.15. 3.26: 1 Jn 2.2; Col 1.20.
3.28: Acts 13.39; Rom 5.1; Eph 2.9. 3.29: Rom 9.24; Acts 10.34–35. 3.30: Rom 4.11–12, 16.
3.31: Rom 8.4; Mt 5.17. 4.2: 1 Cor 1.31. 4.3: Gen 15.6; Rom 4.9, 22; Gal 3.6; Jas 2.23. 4.4: Rom 11.6.
4.5: Rom 3.22.

upon the man to whom God reckons righteousness apart from works:

7 "Blessed are those whose iniquities are forgiven, and whose sins are covered;

8 blessed is the man against whom the Lord will not reckon his sin."

9 Is this blessing pronounced only upon the circumcised, or also upon the uncircumcised? We say that faith was reckoned to

10 Abraham as righteousness. How then was it reckoned to him? Was it before or after he had been circumcised? It was not after, but

11 before he was circumcised. He received circumcision as a sign or seal of the righteousness which he had by faith while he was still uncircumcised. The purpose was to make him the father of all who believe without being circumcised and who thus

12 have righteousness reckoned to them, and likewise the father of the circumcised who are not merely circumcised but also follow the example of the faith which our father Abraham had before he was circumcised.

13 The promise to Abraham and his descendants, that they should inherit the world, did not come through the law but through the

14 righteousness of faith. If it is the adherents of the law who are to be the heirs, faith is null

15 and the promise is void. For the law brings wrath, but where there is no law there is no transgression.

16 That is why it depends on faith, in order that the promise may rest on grace and be guaranteed to all his descendants—not only to the adherents of the law but also to those who share the faith of Abraham, for he is the

17 father of us all, as it is written, "I have made you the father of many nations"—in the presence of the God in whom he believed, who gives life to the dead and calls into

18 existence the things that do not exist. In hope he believed against hope, that he should become the father of many nations; as he had been told, "So shall your descendants be."

19 He did not weaken in faith when he considered his own body, which was as good as dead because he was about a hundred years old, or when he considered the barrenness of

20 Sarah's womb. No distrust made him waver concerning the promise of God, but he grew strong in his faith as he gave glory to God,

21 fully convinced that God was able to do what

22 he had promised. That is why his faith was

23 "reckoned to him as righteousness." But the words, "it was reckoned to him," were

24 written not for his sake alone, but for ours also. It will be reckoned to us who believe in

25 him that raised from the dead Jesus our Lord, who was put to death for our trespasses and raised for our justification.

Peace with God

5 Therefore, since we are justified by faith, we[f] have peace with God through our Lord

2 Jesus Christ. Through him we have obtained access[g] to this grace in which we stand, and we[h] rejoice in our hope of sharing

3 the glory of God. More than that, we[h] rejoice in our sufferings, knowing that

4 suffering produces endurance, and endurance produces character, and character

5 produces hope, and hope does not disappoint us, because God's love has been poured into our hearts through the Holy Spirit which has been given to us.

6 While we were yet helpless, at the right time

7 Christ died for the ungodly. Why, one will hardly die for a righteous man—though perhaps for a good man one will dare even to

8 die. But God shows his love for us in that while we were yet sinners Christ died for us.

9 Since, therefore, we are now justified by his blood, much more shall we be saved by him

10 from the wrath of God. For if while we were enemies we were reconciled to God by the death of his Son, much more, now that we are reconciled, shall we be saved by his life.

11 Not only so, but we also rejoice in God through our Lord Jesus Christ, through whom we have now received our reconciliation.

12 Therefore as sin came into the world through one man and death through sin, and so death spread to all men because all men

13 sinned—sin indeed was in the world before the law was given, but sin is not counted

14 where there is no law. Yet death reigned from Adam to Moses, even over those whose sins were not like the transgression of Adam, who was a type of the one who was to come.

15 But the free gift is not like the trespass. For if many died through one man's trespass, much more have the grace of God and the free gift in the grace of that one man Jesus

16 Christ abounded for many. And the free gift is not like the effect of that one man's sin. For the judgment following one trespass brought condemnation, but the free gift

f Other ancient authorities read *let us*   g Other ancient authorities add *by faith*   h Or *let us*
4.7: Ps 32.1-2.   4.11: Gen 17.10; Rom 3.22, 30.   4.13: Gen 17.4-6; 22.17-18; Gal 3.29.   4.14: Gal 3.18.
4.15: Gal 3.10.   4.17: Gen 17.5; Jn 5.21.   4.18: Gen 15.5.   4.19: Heb 11.12; Gen 17.17; 18.11.
4.22: Rom 4.3.   4.23-24: Rom 15.4; 1 Cor 9.10; 10.11.   4.25: Rom 8.32.   5.1: Rom 3.28.
5.2: Eph 2.18; 3.12; Heb 10.19-20.   5.3: Rom 5.11; 2 Cor 12.10; Jas 1.3.
5.5: Ps 119.116; Acts 2.33; Phil 1.20.   5.8: Jn 15.13; Rom 8.32; 1 Pet 3.18; 1 Jn 3.16; 4.10.
5.10: Rom 3.5, 24-25; Eph 1.7; 1 Thess 1.10.   5.10: Col 1.21.   5.11: Rom 5.3.
5.12: 1 Cor 15.21-22; Rom 6.23; Jas 1.15.   5.14: 1 Cor 15.22, 45.   5.15: Acts 15.11.   5.16: Rom 8.1.

following many trespasses brings justifi-
17 cation. If, because of one man's trespass,
death reigned through that one man, much
more will those who receive the abundance of
grace and the free gift of righteousness reign
in life through the one man Jesus Christ.
18 Then as one man's trespass led to condemnation for all men, so one man's act of
righteousness leads to acquittal and life for
19 all men. For as by one man's disobedience
many were made sinners, so by one man's
obedience many will be made righteous.
20 Law came in, to increase the trespass; but
where sin increased, grace abounded all the
21 more, so that, as sin reigned in death, grace
also might reign through righteousness to
eternal life through Jesus Christ our Lord.

Complete renewal

6 What shall we say then? Are we to con-
2 tinue in sin that grace may abound? By no
means! How can we who died to sin still live
3 in it? Do you not know that all of us who
have been baptized into Christ Jesus were
4 baptized into his death? We were buried
therefore with him by baptism into death, so
that as Christ was raised from the dead by
the glory of the Father, we too might walk in
newness of life.
5 For if we have been united with him in a
death like his, we shall certainly be united
6 with him in a resurrection like his. We know
that our old self was crucified with him so
that the sinful body might be destroyed, and
7 we might no longer be enslaved to sin. For
8 he who has died is freed from sin. But if we
have died with Christ, we believe that we
9 shall also live with him. For we know that
Christ being raised from the dead will never
die again; death no longer has dominion over

him. The death he died he died to sin, once 10
for all, but the life he lives he lives to God.
So you also must consider yourselves dead to 11
sin and alive to God in Christ Jesus.
Let not sin therefore reign in your mortal 12
bodies, to make you obey their passions. Do 13
not yield your members to sin as instruments
of wickedness, but yield yourselves to God as
men who have been brought from death to
life, and your members to God as instruments of righteousness. For sin will have no 14
dominion over you, since you are not under
law but under grace.
What then? Are we to sin because we are 15
not under law but under grace? By no
means! Do you not know that if you yield 16
yourselves to any one as obedient slaves, you
are slaves of the one whom you obey, either
of sin, which leads to death, or of obedience,
which leads to righteousness? But thanks be 17
to God, that you who were once slaves of sin
have become obedient from the heart to the
standard of teaching to which you were
committed, and, having been set free from 18
sin, have become slaves of righteousness. I 19
am speaking in human terms, because of
your natural limitations. For just as you
once yielded your members to impurity and
to greater and greater iniquity, so now yield
your members to righteousness for sanctification.
When you were slaves of sin, you were free 20
in regard to righteousness. But then what 21
return did you get from the things of which
you are now ashamed? The end of those
things is death. But now that you have been 22
set free from sin and have become slaves of
God, the return you get is sanctification and
its end, eternal life. For the wages of sin is 23
death, but the free gift of God is eternal life
in Christ Jesus our Lord.

A change of masters

Do you not know, brethren—for I am 7
speaking to those who know the law—that
the law is binding on a person only during his
life? Thus a married woman is bound by 2
law to her husband as long as he lives; but if
her husband dies she is discharged from the
law concerning the husband. Accordingly, 3
she will be called an adulteress if she lives
with another man while her husband is alive.
But if her husband dies she is free from that
law, and if she marries another man she is not
an adulteress.

5.19: Phil 2.8.   5.20: Rom 7.7–8; Gal 3.19; 1 Tim 1.14.   5.21: Rom 6.23.   6.1: Rom 3.8; 6.15.
6.2: Rom 7.4, 6; Gal 2.19; 1 Pet 2.24.   6.3: Acts 2.38; 8.16; 19.5.   6.4: Col 2.12.   6.5: 2 Cor 4.10; Col 2.12.
6.6: Rom 7.24; Col 2.13.   6.7: 1 Pet 4.1.   6.8: 2 Tim 2.11.   6.9: Acts 2.24; Rev 1.18.
6.11: Rom 7.4, 6; Gal 2.19; 1 Pet 2.24.   6.13: Rom 6.19; 7.5; 12.1.   6.14: Rom 8.2.   6.15: Rom 3.8; 6.1.
6.16: Mt 6.24; Jn 8.34; Rom 12.1.   6.18: Rom 8.2.   6.19: Rom 3.5; 6.13; 12.1.   6.20: Mt 6.24; Jn 8.34.
6.21: Rom 7.5; 8.6, 13, 21.   6.23: Rom 5.12, 21; Gal 6.7, 8.   7.2: 1 Cor 7.39.

Likewise, my brethren, you have died to the law through the body of Christ, so that you may belong to another, to him who has been raised from the dead in order that we may bear fruit for God. While we were living in the flesh, our sinful passions, aroused by the law, were at work in our members to bear fruit for death. But now we are discharged from the law, dead to that which held us captive, so that we serve not under the old written code but in the new life of the Spirit.

What then shall we say? That the law is sin? By no means! Yet, if it had not been for the law, I should not have known sin. I should not have known what it is to covet if sin. I do not understand my own actions. 15 For I do not do what I want, but I do the very thing I hate. Now if I do what I do not 16 want, I agree that the law is good. So then it 17 is no longer I that do it, but sin which dwells within me. For I know that nothing good 18 dwells within me, that is, in my flesh. I can will what is right, but I cannot do it. For I 19 do not do the good I want, but the evil I do not want is what I do. Now if I do what I do 20 not want, it is no longer I that do it, but sin which dwells within me.

So I find it to be a law that when I want to 21 do right, evil lies close at hand. For I delight 22 in the law of God, in my inmost self, but I 23

Street in a Roman city

the law had not said, "You shall not covet." But sin, finding opportunity in the commandment, wrought in me all kinds of covetousness. Apart from the law sin lies dead. I was once alive apart from the law, but when the commandment came, sin revived and I died; the very commandment which promised life proved to be death to me. For sin, finding opportunity in the commandment, deceived me and by it killed me. So the law is holy, and the commandment is holy and just and good.

Did that which is good, then, bring death to me? By no means! It was sin, working death in me through what is good, in order that sin might be shown to be sin, and through the commandment might become sinful beyond measure. We know that the law is spiritual; but I am carnal, sold under see in my members another law at war with the law of my mind and making me captive to the law of sin which dwells in my members. Wretched man that I am! Who will deliver 24 me from this body of death? Thanks be to 25 God through Jesus Christ our Lord! So then, I of myself serve the law of God with my mind, but with my flesh I serve the law of sin.

Life in the Spirit

There is therefore now no condemnation 8 for those who are in Christ Jesus. For the 2 law of the Spirit of life in Christ Jesus has set me free from the law of sin and death. For 3 God has done what the law, weakened by the flesh, could not do: sending his own Son in the likeness of sinful flesh and for sin,ⁱ he

ⁱ Or *and as a sin offering*
7.4: Rom 6.2, 11; Gal 2.19; Col 1.22. **7.5:** Rom 6.13, 21; 8.8; Jas 1.15.
7.7: Rom 3.20; 5.20; Ex 20.17; Deut 5.21. **7.8:** 1 Cor 15.56. **7.10:** Lev 18.5; Rom 10.5. **7.12:** 1 Tim 1.8.
7.14: 1 Cor 3.1. **7.15:** Gal 5.17. **7.22:** Ps 1.2. **7.23:** Gal 5.17. **7.24:** Rom 6.6; Col 2.11. **8.1:** Rom 5.16.
8.2: 1 Cor 15.45; Rom 6.14, 18. **8.3:** Acts 13.39; Heb 7.18; 10.1-2; Phil 2.7; Heb 2.14.

4 condemned sin in the flesh, in order that the just requirement of the law might be fulfilled in us, who walk not according to the flesh but
5 according to the Spirit. For those who live according to the flesh set their minds on the things of the flesh, but those who live according to the Spirit set their minds on the
6 things of the Spirit. To set the mind on the flesh is death, but to set the mind on the
7 Spirit is life and peace. For the mind that is set on the flesh is hostile to God; it does not
8 submit to God's law, indeed it cannot; and those who are in the flesh cannot please God.
9 But you are not in the flesh, you are in the Spirit, if the Spirit of God really dwells in you. Any one who does not have the Spirit
10 of Christ does not belong to him. But if Christ is in you, although your bodies are dead because of sin, your spirits are alive
11 because of righteousness. If the Spirit of him who raised Jesus from the dead dwells in you, he who raised Christ Jesus from the dead will give life to your mortal bodies also through his Spirit which dwells in you.
12 So then, brethren, we are debtors, not to the
13 flesh, to live according to the flesh—for if you live according to the flesh you will die, but if by the Spirit you put to death the
14 deeds of the body you will live. For all who are led by the Spirit of God are sons of God.
15 For you did not receive the spirit of slavery to fall back into fear, but you have received the spirit of sonship. When we cry, "Abba!
16 Father!" it is the Spirit himself bearing witness with our spirit that we are children of
17 God, and if children, then heirs, heirs of God and fellow heirs with Christ, provided we suffer with him in order that we may also be glorified with him.

A glory to be revealed

18 I consider that the sufferings of this present time are not worth comparing with the glory
19 that is to be revealed to us. For the creation waits with eager longing for the revealing
20 of the sons of God; for the creation was subjected to futility, not of its own will but by the will of him who subjected it in hope;
21 because the creation itself will be set free from its bondage to decay and obtain the
22 glorious liberty of the children of God. We know that the whole creation has been

groaning in travail together until now; and not only the creation, but we ourselves, who have the first fruits of the Spirit, groan inwardly as we wait for adoption as sons, the redemption of our bodies. For in this hope we were saved. Now hope that is seen is not hope. For who hopes for what he sees? But if we hope for what we do not see, we wait for it with patience.

Likewise the Spirit helps us in our weakness; for we do not know how to pray as we ought, but the Spirit himself intercedes for us with sighs too deep for words. And he who searches the hearts of men knows what is the mind of the Spirit, because[j] the Spirit intercedes for the saints according to the will of God.

We know that in everything God works for good[k] with those who love him,[l] who are called according to his purpose. For those whom he foreknew he also predestined to be conformed to the image of his Son, in order that he might be the first-born among many brethren. And those whom he predestined he also called; and those whom he called he also justified; and those whom he justified he also glorified.

More than conquerors

What then shall we say to this? If God is for us, who is against us? He who did not spare his own Son but gave him up for us all, will he not also give us all things with him? Who shall bring any charge against God's elect? It is God who justifies; who is to condemn? Is it Christ Jesus, who died, yes, who was raised from the dead, who is at the right hand of God, who indeed intercedes for us?[m] Who shall separate us from the love of Christ? Shall tribulation, or distress, or persecution, or famine, or nakedness, or peril, or sword? As it is written,
    "For thy sake we are being killed all the
        day long;
    we are regarded as sheep to be slaugh-
        tered."
No, in all these things we are more than conquerors through him who loved us. For I am sure that neither death, nor life, nor angels, nor principalities, nor things present, nor things to come, nor powers, nor height, nor depth, nor anything else in all creation,

---

j Or that   k Other ancient authorities read in everything he works for good, or everything works for good
l Greek God   m Or It is Christ Jesus . . . for us
8.4: Rom 3.31; Gal 5.16, 25.   8.5: Gal 5.19–25.   8.6: Rom 6.21; 8.13, 27; Gal 6.8.   8.8: Rom 7.5.
8.9: 1 Cor 3.16; 6.19; 2 Cor 6.16; 2 Tim 1.14.   8.10: Gal 2.20; Eph 3.17.   8.11: Jn 5.21.
8.13: Rom 8.6; Col 3.5.   8.14: Gal 5.18.   8.15: Rom 9.4; Gal 4.5–7; Mk 14.36.   8.16: Acts 5.32.
8.17: Gal 3.29; 4.7; 2 Cor 1.5, 7; 2 Tim 2.12; 1 Pet 4.13.   8.18: 2 Cor 4.17; Col 3.4; 1 Pet 5.1.
8.19: 1 Pet 1.7, 13; 1 Jn 3.2.   8.20: Eccles 1.2.   8.21: Acts 3.21; Rom 6.21; 2 Pet 3.13; Rev 21.1.
8.22: Jer 12.4, 11.   8.23: 2 Cor 1.22; 5.2, 4; Gal 5.5.   8.24: 2 Cor 5.7; Heb 11.1.
8.27: Ps 139.1–2; Lk 16.15; Rev 2.23; Rom 8.6, 34.   8.29: Rom 9.23; 11.2; 1 Pet 1.2, 20; Eph 1.5, 11.
8.31: Ps 118.6.   8.32: Jn 3.16; Rom 4.25; 5.8.   8.33: Lk 18.7; Is 50.8–9.   8.34: Rom 8.27.   8.36: Ps 44.22.
8.37: 1 Cor 15.57.

vill be able to separate us from the love of God in Christ Jesus our Lord.

THE PROBLEM OF THE JEWS

The rejection of Israel

I AM speaking the truth in Christ, I am not lying; my conscience bears me witness in the Holy Spirit, that I have great sorrow and unceasing anguish in my heart. For I could wish that I myself were accursed and cut off from Christ for the sake of my brethren, my kinsmen by race. They are Israelites, and to them belong the sonship, the glory, the covenants, the giving of the law, the worship, and the promises; to them belong the patriarchs, and of their race, according to the flesh, is the Christ. God who is over all be blessed for ever. [n] Amen.

But it is not as though the word of God had failed. For not all who are descended from Israel belong to Israel, and not all are children of Abraham because they are his descendants; but "Through Isaac shall your descendants be named." This means that it is not the children of the flesh who are the children of God, but the children of the promise are reckoned as descendants. For this is what the promise said, "About this time I will return and Sarah shall have a son." And not only so, but also when Rebecca had conceived children by one man, our forefather Isaac, though they were not yet born and had done nothing either good or bad, in order that God's purpose of election might continue, not because of works but because of his call, she was told, "The elder will serve the younger." As it is written, "Jacob I loved, but Esau I hated."

The problem

What shall we say then? Is there injustice on God's part? By no means! For he says to Moses, "I will have mercy on whom I have mercy, and I will have compassion on whom I have compassion." So it depends not upon man's will or exertion, but upon God's mercy. For the scripture says to Pharaoh, "I have raised you up for the very purpose of showing my power in you, so that my name may be proclaimed in all the earth." So then

he has mercy upon whomever he wills, and he hardens the heart of whomever he wills.

You will say to me then, "Why does he still 19 find fault? For who can resist his will?" But who are you, a man, to answer back to 20 God? Will what is moulded say to its moulder, "Why have you made me thus?" Has the potter no right over the clay, to make 21 out of the same lump one vessel for beauty and another for menial use? What if God, 22 desiring to show his wrath and to make known his power, has endured with much patience the vessels of wrath made for destruction, in order to make known the 23 riches of his glory for the vessels of mercy, which he has prepared beforehand for glory, even us whom he has called, not from the 24 Jews only but also from the Gentiles? As 25 indeed he says in Hose′a,

"Those who were not my people
I will call 'my people,'
and her who was not beloved
I will call 'my beloved.'"

"And in the very place where it was said to 26 them, 'You are not my people,'
they will be called 'sons of the living God.'"

And Isaiah cries out concerning Israel: 27 "Though the number of the sons of Israel be as the sand of the sea, only a remnant of them will be saved; for the Lord will execute his 28 sentence upon the earth with rigour and despatch." And as Isaiah predicted, 29
"If the Lord of hosts had not left us children,
we would have fared like Sodom and been made like Gomor′rah."

The divine justice of it

What shall we say, then? That Gentiles 30 who did not pursue righteousness have attained it, that is, righteousness through faith; but that Israel who pursued 31 righteousness which is based on law did not succeed in fulfilling that law. Why? 32 Because they did not pursue it through faith, but as if it were based on works. They have stumbled over the stumbling stone, as it is 33 written,
"Behold, I am laying in Zion a stone that will make men stumble,
a rock that will make them fall;
and he who believes in him will not be put to shame."

---

[n] Or Christ, who is God over all, blessed for ever
9.3: Ex 32.32.   **9.4:** Rom 3.2; 8.15.   **9.6:** Rom 2.28-29.   **9.7:** Gen 21.12; Heb 11.18.   **9.8:** Gal 3.29; 4.28.
9.9: Gen 18.10.   **9.10:** Gen 25.21.   **9.12:** Gen 25.23.   **9.13:** Mal 1.2-3.   **9.14:** 2 Chron 19.7.   **9.15:** Ex 33.19.
9.17: Ex 9.16.   **9.18:** Rom 11.7.   **9.20:** Is 29.16; 45.9.   **9.21:** 2 Tim 2.20.   **9.22:** Prov 16.4.   **9.23:** Rom 8.29.
9.24: Rom 3.29.   **9.25:** Hos 2.23; 1 Pet 2.10.   **9.26:** Hos 1.10.
9.27: Is 10.22-23; Gen 22.17; Hos 1.10; Rom 11.5; 2 Kings 19.4; Is 11.11.   **9.29:** Is 1.9.
9.30: Rom 3.22; 10.6, 20; Gal 2.16; 3.24; Phil 3.9; Heb 11.7.   **9.31:** Is 51.1; Rom 10.2-3; 11.7.
9.32: 1 Pet 2.8.   **9.33:** Is 28.16; Rom 10.11.

10 Brethren, my heart's desire and prayer to
2 God for them is that they may be saved. I
bear them witness that they have a zeal for
3 God, but it is not enlightened. For, being
ignorant of the righteousness that comes
from God, and seeking to establish their
own, they did not submit to God's righteous-
4 ness. For Christ is the end of the law, that
every one who has faith may be justified.
5 Moses writes that the man who practises the
righteousness which is based on the law shall
6 live by it. But the righteousness based on
faith says, Do not say in your heart, "Who
will ascend into heaven?" (that is, to bring
7 Christ down) or "Who will descend into the
abyss?" (that is, to bring Christ up from the
8 dead). But what does it say? The word is
near you, on your lips and in your heart (that
is, the word of faith which we preach);
9 because, if you confess with your lips that
Jesus is Lord and believe in your heart that
God raised him from the dead, you will be
10 saved. For man believes with his heart and
so is justified, and he confesses with his lips
11 and so is saved. The scripture says, "No one
who believes in him will be put to shame."
12 For there is no distinction between Jew and
Greek; the same Lord is Lord of all and
bestows his riches upon all who call upon
13 him. For, "every one who calls upon the
name of the Lord will be saved."
14 But how are men to call upon him in whom
they have not believed? And how are they to
believe in him of whom they have never
heard? And how are they to hear without a
15 preacher? And how can men preach unless
they are sent? As it is written, "How
beautiful are the feet of those who preach
16 good news!" But they have not all heeded
the gospel; for Isaiah says, "Lord, who has
17 believed what he has heard from us?" So
faith comes from what is heard, and what is
heard comes by the preaching of Christ.
18 But I ask, have they not heard? Indeed
they have; for
"Their voice has gone out to all the earth,
and their words to the ends of the world."
19 Again I ask, did Israel not understand?
First Moses says,
"I will make you jealous of those who are
not a nation;
with a foolish nation I will make you
angry."
20 Then Isaiah is so bold as to say,

"I have been found by those who did not
seek me;
I have shown myself to those who did not
ask for me."
But of Israel he says, "All day long I have
held out my hands to a disobedient and
contrary people."

The divine purpose in it

I ask, then, has God rejected his people?
By no means! I myself am an Israelite,
descendant of Abraham, a member of the
tribe of Benjamin. God has not rejected his
people whom he foreknew. Do you not know
what the scripture says of Eli′jah, how he
pleads with God against Israel? "Lord, they
have killed thy prophets, they have demolished thy altars, and I alone am left, and
they seek my life." But what is God's reply
to him? "I have kept for myself seven
thousand men who have not bowed the knee
to Ba′al." So too at the present time there is
a remnant, chosen by grace. But if it is by
grace, it is no longer on the basis of works;
otherwise grace would no longer be grace.
What then? Israel failed to obtain what it
sought. The elect obtained it, but the rest
were hardened, as it is written,
"God gave them a spirit of stupor,
eyes that should not see and ears that
should not hear,
down to this very day."
And David says,
"Let their feast become a snare and a trap,
a pitfall and a retribution for them;
let their eyes be darkened so that they
cannot see,
and bend their backs for ever."
So I ask, have they stumbled so as to fall?
By no means! But through their trespass
salvation has come to the Gentiles, so as to
make Israel jealous. Now if their trespass
means riches for the world, and if their
failure means riches for the Gentiles, how
much more will their full inclusion mean!
Now I am speaking to you Gentiles.
Inasmuch then as I am an apostle to the
Gentiles, I magnify my ministry in order to
make my fellow Jews jealous, and thus save
some of them. For if their rejection means
the reconciliation of the world, what will
their acceptance mean but life from the
dead? If the dough offered as first fruits is

10.2–4: Rom 9.31.   **10.3:** Rom 1.17.   **10.4:** Gal 3.24; Rom 3.22; 7.1–4.
10.5: Lev 18.5; Neh 9.29; Ezek 20.11, 13, 21; Rom 7.10.   **10.8:** Deut 30.12–13; Rom 9.30.   **10.8:** Deut 30.14.
10.9: Mt 10.32; Lk 12.8; Acts 16.31.   **10.11:** Is 28.16; Rom 9.33.
10.12: Rom 3.22, 29; Gal 3.28; Col 3.11; Acts 10.36.   **10.13:** Joel 2.32; Acts 2.21.
10.15: Is 52.7.   **10.16:** Is 53.1; Jn 12.38.   **10.18:** Ps 19.4; Col 1.6, 23.   **10.19:** Deut 32.21; Rom 11.11, 14.
10.20: Is 65.1; Rom 9.30.   **10.21:** Is 65.2.   **11.1:** 1 Sam 12.22; Jer 31.37; 33.24–26; 2 Cor 11.22; Phil 3.5.
11.2: Ps 94.14; 1 Kings 19.10.   **11.4:** 1 Kings 19.18.   **11.5:** 2 Kings 19.4; Is 11.11; Rom 9.27.
11.6: Rom 4.4.   **11.7:** Rom 9.18, 31; 11.25.   **11.8:** Is 29.10; Deut 29.4; Mt 13.13–14.   **11.9:** Ps 69.22–23.
11.11: Rom 10.19; 11.14.   **11.13:** Acts 9.15.   **11.14:** Rom 10.19; 11.11; 1 Cor 9.22.   **11.15:** Lk 15.24, 32.

holy, so is the whole lump; and if the root is holy, so are the branches.

The grafted tree

7 But if some of the branches were broken off, and you, a wild olive shoot, were grafted in their place to share the richness° of the olive 8 tree, do not boast over the branches. If you do boast, remember it is not you that support 9 the root, but the root that supports you. You will say, "Branches were broken off so that I 10 might be grafted in." That is true. They were broken off because of their unbelief, but you stand fast only through faith. So do not 1 become proud, but stand in awe. For if God did not spare the natural branches, neither 2 will he spare you. Note then the kindness and the severity of God: severity toward those who have fallen, but God's kindness to you, provided you continue in his kindness; 3 otherwise you too will be cut off. And even the others, if they do not persist in their unbelief, will be grafted in, for God has the 4 power to graft them in again. For if you have been cut from what is by nature a wild olive tree, and grafted, contrary to nature, into a cultivated olive tree, how much more will these natural branches be grafted back into their own olive tree.

5 Lest you be wise in your own conceits, I want you to understand this mystery, brethren: a hardening has come upon part of Israel, until the full number of the Gentiles 6 come in, and so all Israel will be saved; as it is written,

"The Deliverer will come from Zion,
he will banish ungodliness from Jacob";
27 "and this will be my covenant with them when I take away their sins."

28 As regards the gospel they are enemies of God, for your sake; but as regards election they are beloved for the sake of their fore-29 fathers. For the gifts and the call of God are 30 irrevocable. Just as you were once disobedient to God but now have received mercy 31 because of their disobedience, so they have now been disobedient in order that by the mercy shown to you they also may ᵖ receive 32 mercy. For God has consigned all men to disobedience, that he may have mercy upon all.

33 O the depth of the riches and wisdom and knowledge of God! How unsearchable are his judgments and how inscrutable his ways! 34 "For who has known the mind of the Lord,
or who has been his counsellor?"
35 "Or who has given a gift to him that he might be repaid?"
36 For from him and through him and to him are all things. To him be glory for ever. Amen.

CHRISTIAN LIVING

12 I APPEAL to you therefore, brethren, by the mercies of God, to present your bodies as a living sacrifice, holy and acceptable to God, which is your spiritual worship. Do 2 not be conformed to this world⁴ but be transformed by the renewal of your mind, that you may prove what is the will of God, what is good and acceptable and perfect.ʳ

3 For by the grace given to me I bid every one among you not to think of himself more highly than he ought to think, but to think with sober judgment, each according to the measure of faith which God has assigned him. For as in one body we have many 4 members, and all the members do not have the same function, so we, though many, are 5 one body in Christ, and individually members one of another. Having gifts that differ 6 according to the grace given to us, let us use them: if prophecy, in proportion to our faith; if service, in our serving; he who teaches, in 7 his teaching; he who exhorts, in his exhor-8 tation; he who contributes, in liberality; he who gives aid, with zeal; he who does acts of mercy, with cheerfulness.

Let love be genuine; hate what is evil, hold 9 fast to what is good; love one another with 10 brotherly affection; outdo one another in showing honour. Never flag in zeal, be 11 aglow with the Spirit, serve the Lord. Rejoice in your hope, be patient in tribu-12 lation, be constant in prayer. Contribute to 13 the needs of the saints, practise hospitality.

Bless those who persecute you; bless and do 14 not curse them. Rejoice with those who 15 rejoice, weep with those who weep. Live in 16 harmony with one another; do not be haughty, but associate with the lowly;ˢ never be conceited. Repay no one evil for evil, but 17 take thought for what is noble in the sight of all. If possible, so far as it depends upon 18

° Other ancient authorities read *rich root*   ᵖ Other ancient authorities add *now*   ⁴ Greek *age*
ʳ Or *what is the good and acceptable and perfect will of God*   ˢ Or *give yourselves to humble tasks*

11.20: 2 Cor 1.24.   11.25: 1 Cor 2.7–10; Eph 3.3–5, 9; Rom 9.18; 11.7; Lk 21.24.
11.26: Is 59.20–21.   11.27: Jer 31.33; Is 27.9.   11.32: Rom 3.9; Gal 3.22–29.   11.33: Col 2.3.
11.34: Is 40.13–14; 1 Cor 2.16.   11.35: Job 35.7; 41.11.   11.36: 1 Cor 8.6; 11.12; Col 1.16; Heb 2.10.
12.1: Rom 6.13, 16, 19; 1 Pet 2.5.   12.2: 1 Jn 2.15; Eph 4.23; 5.10.   12.4: 1 Cor 12.12–14; Eph 4.4, 16.
12.5: 1 Cor 10.17; 12.20, 27; Eph 4.25.   12.6–8: 1 Cor 7.7; 14.1–11; 1 Pet 4.10–11.
12.12: Acts 1.14; Rom 5.2; 1 Thess 5.17.   12.14: Mt 5.44; Lk 6.28.
12.16: Rom 11.25; 15.5; 1 Cor 1.10; 2 Cor 13.11; Phil 2.2; 4.2; Prov 3.7; 26.12.
12.17: Prov 20.22; 2 Cor 8.21; 1 Thess 5.15.   12.18: Mk 9.50; Rom 14.19.

19 you, live peaceably with all. Beloved, never avenge yourselves, but leave it[t] to the wrath of God; for it is written, "Vengeance is mine, 20 I will repay, says the Lord." No, "if your enemy is hungry, feed him; if he is thirsty, give him drink; for by so doing you will heap 21 burning coals upon his head." Do not be overcome by evil, but overcome evil with good.

Civil and social duties

13 Let every person be subject to the governing authorities. For there is no authority except from God, and those that exist have 2 been instituted by God. Therefore he who resists the authorities resists what God has appointed, and those who resist will incur 3 judgment. For rulers are not a terror to good conduct, but to bad. Would you have no fear of him who is in authority? Then do what is 4 good, and you will receive his approval, for he is God's servant for your good. But if you do wrong, be afraid, for he does not bear the sword in vain; he is the servant of God to execute his wrath on the wrongdoer. 5 Therefore one must be subject, not only to avoid God's wrath but also for the sake of 6 conscience. For the same reason you also pay taxes, for the authorities are ministers of God, attending to this very thing. 7 Pay all of them their dues, taxes to whom taxes are due, revenue to whom revenue is due, respect to whom respect is due, honour to whom honour is due.

8 Owe no one anything, except to love one another; for he who loves his neighbour has 9 fulfilled the law. The commandments, "You shall not commit adultery, You shall not kill, You shall not steal, You shall not covet," and any other commandment, are summed up in this sentence, "You shall love your neigh- 10 bour as yourself." Love does no wrong to a neighbour; therefore love is the fulfilling of the law.

11 Besides this you know what hour it is, how it is full time now for you to wake from sleep. For salvation is nearer to us now than 12 when we first believed; the night is far gone, the day is at hand. Let us then cast off the works of darkness and put on the armour of 13 light; let us conduct ourselves becomingly as in the day, not in revelling and drunkenness, not in debauchery and licentiousness, not in 14 quarrelling and jealousy. But put on the

Roman workmen

Lord Jesus Christ, and make no provision for the flesh, to gratify its desires.

Christian charity and unity

As for the man who is weak in faith, 1 welcome him, but not for disputes over opinions. One believes he may eat anything, 2 while the weak man eats only vegetables. Let 3 not him who eats despise him who abstains, and let not him who abstains pass judgment on him who eats; for God has welcomed him. Who are you to pass judgment on the servant 4 of another? It is before his own master that he stands or falls. And he will be upheld, for the Master is able to make him stand.

One man esteems one day as better than 5 another, while another man esteems all days alike. Let every one be fully convinced in his own mind. He who observes the day, 6 observes it in honour of the Lord. He also who eats, eats in honour of the Lord, since he gives thanks to God; while he who abstains, abstains in honour of the Lord and gives thanks to God. None of us lives to 7 himself, and none of us dies to himself. If we 8 live, we live to the Lord, and if we die, we die to the Lord; so then, whether we live or whether we die, we are the Lord's. For to 9

[t] Greek *give place*

12.19: Lev 19.18; Deut 32.35; Heb 10.30.   12.20: Prov 25.21–22; Mt 5.44; Lk 6.27.
13.1: Tit 3.1; 1 Pet 2.13–14; Prov 8.15; Jn 19.11.   13.3: 1 Pet 2.14.   13.4: 1 Thess 4.6.
13.7: Mt 22.21; Mk 12.17; Lk 20.25.   13.8: Mt 22.39–40; Rom 13.10; Gal 5.14; Col 3.14; Jas 2.8.
13.9: Ex 20.13–17; Deut 5.17–21; Lev 19.18; Mt 19.19.   13.10: Mt 22.39–40; Rom 13.8; Gal 5.14; Jas 2.8.
13.11: Eph 5.14; 1 Thess 5.6.   13.12: 1 Jn 2.8; Eph 5.11; 1 Thess 5.8.   13.13: 1 Thess 4.12; Gal 5.19–21.
13.14: Gal 3.27; 5.16.   14.3: Col 2.16.   14.5: Gal 4.10.   14.7: Gal 2.20; 2 Cor 5.15.   14.8: Phil 1.20.

this end Christ died and lived again, that he might be Lord both of the dead and of the living.

10 Why do you pass judgment on your brother? Or you, why do you despise your brother? For we shall all stand before the 11 judgment seat of God; for it is written,

"As I live, says the Lord, every knee shall bow to me,
and every tongue shall give praise[u] to God."

12 So each of us shall give account of himself to God.

The Christian spirit

13 Then let us no more pass judgment on one another, but rather decide never to put a stumbling block or hindrance in the way of a 14 brother. I know and am persuaded in the Lord Jesus that nothing is unclean in itself; but it is unclean for any one who thinks it 15 unclean. If your brother is being injured by what you eat, you are no longer walking in love. Do not let what you eat cause the ruin 16 of one for whom Christ died. So do not let 17 what is good to you be spoken of as evil. For the kingdom of God does not mean food and drink but righteousness and peace and joy in 18 the Holy Spirit; he who thus serves Christ is acceptable to God and approved by men. 19 Let us then pursue what makes for peace and 20 for mutual upbuilding. Do not, for the sake of food, destroy the work of God. Everything is indeed clean, but it is wrong for any one to make others fall by what he 21 eats; it is right not to eat meat or drink wine or do anything that makes your brother 22 stumble.[v] The faith that you have, keep between yourself and God; happy is he who has no reason to judge himself for what he 23 approves. But he who has doubts is condemned, if he eats, because he does not act from faith; for whatever does not proceed from faith is sin.[w]

15 We who are strong ought to bear with the failings of the weak, and not to please 2 ourselves; let each of us please his neighbour 3 for his good, to edify him. For Christ did not please himself; but, as it is written, "The reproaches of those who reproached thee fell 4 on me." For whatever was written in former days was written for our instruction, that by steadfastness and by the encouragement of

the scriptures we might have hope. May the 5 God of steadfastness and encouragement grant you to live in such harmony with one another, in accord with Christ Jesus, that 6 together you may with one voice glorify the God and Father of our Lord Jesus Christ.

For the glory of God

Welcome one another, therefore, as Christ 7 has welcomed you, for the glory of God. For 8 I tell you that Christ became a servant to the circumcised to show God's truthfulness, in order to confirm the promises given to the patriarchs, and in order that the Gentiles 9 might glorify God for his mercy. As it is written,

"Therefore I will praise thee among the Gentiles,
and sing to thy name";

and again it is said,   10
"Rejoice, O Gentiles, with his people";
and again,   11
"Praise the Lord, all Gentiles,
and let all the peoples praise him";
and further Isaiah says,   12
"The root of Jesse shall come,
he who rises to rule the Gentiles;
in him shall the Gentiles hope."

May the God of hope fill you with all joy and 13 peace in believing, so that by the power of the Holy Spirit you may abound in hope.

Personal messages

I myself am satisfied about you, my breth- 14 ren, that you yourselves are full of goodness, filled with all knowledge, and able to instruct one another. But on some points I have 15 written to you very boldly by way of reminder, because of the grace given me by God to be a minister of Christ Jesus to the 16 Gentiles in the priestly service of the gospel of God, so that the offering of the Gentiles may be acceptable, sanctified by the Holy Spirit. In Christ Jesus, then, I have reason 17 to be proud of my work for God. For I will 18 not venture to speak of anything except what Christ has wrought through me to win obedience from the Gentiles, by word and deed, by the power of signs and wonders, by 19 the power of the Holy Spirit, so that from Jerusalem and as far round as Illyr'icum I have fully preached the gospel of Christ, thus 20 making it my ambition to preach the gospel,

[u] Or confess   [v] Other ancient authorities add or be upset or be weakened
[w] Other authorities, some ancient, insert here Ch. 16.25–27
14.10: 2 Cor 5.10.   14.11: Is 45.23; Phil 2.10–11.   14.13: Mt 7.1; 1 Cor 8.13.   14.15: Rom 14.20; 1 Cor 8.11.
14.16: 1 Cor 10.30.   14.19: Mk 9.50; Rom 12.18; 1 Thess 5.11.   14.20: Rom 14.15; 1 Cor 8.9–12.
14.21: 1 Cor 8.13.   14.22: Rom 2.1.   15.3: Ps 69.9.   15.4: Rom 4.23–24; 1 Cor 9.10; 2 Tim 3.16.
15.5: Rom 12.16; 1 Cor 1.10; 2 Cor 13.11; Phil 2.2; 4.2.   15.9: Ps 18.49; 2 Sam 22.50.   15.10: Deut 32.43.
15.11: Ps 117.1.   15.12: Is 11.10; Mt 12.21.   15.16: Acts 9.15.   15.18: Rom 1.5; Acts 15.12; 21.19.
15.19: Acts 19.11; 2 Cor 12.12.   15.20: 2 Cor 10.15–16.

not where Christ has already been named,
21 lest I build on another man's foundation, but
as it is written,
"They shall see who have never been told
of him,
and they shall understand who have never
heard of him."
22 This is the reason why I have so often been
23 hindered from coming to you. But now, since
I no longer have any room for work in these
regions, and since I have longed for many
24 years to come to you, I hope to see you in
passing as I go to Spain, and to be sped on
my journey there by you, once I have
25 enjoyed your company for a little. At present, however, I am going to Jerusalem with
26 aid for the saints. For Macedo'nia and
Acha'ia have been pleased to make some
contribution for the poor among the saints at
27 Jerusalem; they were pleased to do it, and
indeed they are in debt to them, for if the
Gentiles have come to share in their spiritual
blessings, they ought also to be of service to
28 them in material blessings. When therefore I
have completed this, and have delivered to
them what has been raised,ˣ I shall go on by
29 way of you to Spain; and I know that when I
come to you I shall come in the fulness of the
blessingʸ of Christ.
30 I appeal to you, brethren, by our Lord Jesus
Christ and by the love of the Spirit, to strive
together with me in your prayers to God on
31 my behalf, that I may be delivered from the
unbelievers in Judea, and that my service for
32 Jerusalem may be acceptable to the saints, so
that by God's will I may come to you with
33 joy and be refreshed in your company. The
God of peace be with you all. Amen.

16 I commend to you our sister Phoebe, a
2 deaconess of the church at Cen'chre-ae, that
you may receive her in the Lord as befits the
saints, and help her in whatever she may
require from you, for she has been a helper of
many and of myself as well.
3 Greet Prisca and Aquila, my fellow workers
4 in Christ Jesus, who risked their necks for
my life, to whom not only I but also all the
5 churches of the Gentiles give thanks; greet
also the church in their house. Greet my
beloved Epae'netus, who was the first con-
6 vert in Asia for Christ. Greet Mary, who has
7 worked hard among you. Greet Androni'cus

and Ju'nias, my kinsmen and my fellow
prisoners; they are men of note among the
apostles, and they were in Christ before me.
Greet Amplia'tus, my beloved in the Lord. 8
Greet Urba'nus, our fellow worker in Christ, 9
and my beloved Stachys. Greet Apel'les, 10
who is approved in Christ. Greet those who
belong to the family of Aristobu'lus. Greet 11
my kinsman Hero'dion. Greet those in the
Lord who belong to the family of Narcis'sus.
Greet those workers in the Lord, Tryphae'na 12
and Tryphos'sa. Greet the beloved Persis,
who has worked hard in the Lord. Greet 13
Rufus, eminent in the Lord, also his mother
and mine. Greet Asyn'critus, Phlegon, 14
Hermes, Pat'robas, Hermas, and the brethren who are with them. Greet Philol'ogus, 15
Julia, Nereus and his sister, and Olym'pas,
and all the saints who are with them. Greet 16
one another with a holy kiss. All the
churches of Christ greet you.
I appeal to you, brethren, to take note of 17
those who create dissensions and difficulties,
in opposition to the doctrine which you have
been taught; avoid them. For such persons 18
do not serve our Lord Christ, but their own
appetites,ᶻ and by fair and flattering words
they deceive the hearts of the simple-
minded. For while your obedience is known 19
to all, so that I rejoice over you, I would have
you wise as to what is good and guileless as to
what is evil; then the God of peace will soon 20
crush Satan under your feet. The grace of
our Lord Jesus Christ be with you.ᵃ
Timothy, my fellow worker, greets you; so 21
do Lucius and Jason and Sosip'ater, my
kinsmen.
I Tertius, the writer of this letter, greet you 22
in the Lord.
Ga'ius, who is host to me and to the whole 23
church, greets you. Eras'tus, the city treasurer, and our brother Quartus, greet you.ᵇ

Now to him who is able to strengthen you 25
according to my gospel and the preaching of
Jesus Christ, according to the revelation of
the mystery which was kept secret for long
ages but is now disclosed and through the 26
prophetic writings is made known to all
nations, according to the command of the
eternal God, to bring about the obedience of
faith—to the only wise God be glory for 27
evermore through Jesus Christ! Amen.

ˣ Greek *sealed to them this fruit*   ʸ Other ancient authorities insert *of the gospel*
ᶻ Greek *their own belly* (Phil 3.19)   ᵃ Other ancient authorities omit this sentence
ᵇ Other ancient authorities insert verse 24, *The grace of our Lord Jesus Christ be with you all. Amen.*
15.21: Is 52.15.   **15.22:** Rom 1.13.   **15.23:** Acts 19.21; Rom 1.10–11; 15.32.   **15.24:** Acts 19.21; 24.17; 15.31.   **15.26:** 2 Cor 8.1–5; 9.2; 1 Thess 1.7–8.   **15.27:** 1 Cor 9.11.
15.28: Rom 15.24.   **15.29:** Acts 19.21.   **15.31:** 2 Thess 3.2; Rom 15.25–26; 2 Cor 8.4; 9.1.
15.32: Rom 1.10; Acts 19.21.   **15.33:** 2 Cor 13.11; Phil 4.9.   **16.3:** Acts 18.2.   **16.5:** 1 Cor 16.19.
16.16: 2 Cor 13.12; 1 Thess 5.26; 1 Pet 5.14.   **16.17:** Gal 1.8–9; 2 Thess 3.6, 14; 2 Jn 10.
16.19: Rom 1.8; 1 Cor 14.20.
16.20: 1 Cor 16.23; 2 Cor 13.14; Gal 6.18; Phil 4.23; 1 Thess 5.28; 2 Thess 3.18; Rev 22.21.
16.21: Acts 16.1.   **16.23:** 1 Cor 1.14.

THE FIRST LETTER OF PAUL TO THE

CORINTHIANS

PAUL, called by the will of God to be an apostle of Christ Jesus, and our brother Sos'thenes,

2 To the church of God which is at Corinth, to those sanctified in Christ Jesus, called to be saints together with all those who in every place call on the name of our Lord Jesus Christ, both their Lord and ours:

3 Grace to you and peace from God our Father and the Lord Jesus Christ.

4 I give thanks to God[a] always for you because of the grace of God which was given 5 you in Christ Jesus, that in every way you were enriched in him with all speech and all 6 knowledge—even as the testimony to Christ 7 was confirmed among you—so that you are not lacking in any spiritual gift, as you wait for the revealing of our Lord Jesus Christ; 8 who will sustain you to the end, guiltless in 9 the day of our Lord Jesus Christ. God is faithful, by whom you were called into the fellowship of his Son, Jesus Christ our Lord.

Divisions in the church

I appeal to you, brethren, by the name of 10 our Lord Jesus Christ, that all of you agree and that there be no dissensions among you, but that you be united in the same mind and the same judgment. For it has been reported 11 to me by Chlo'e's people that there is quarrelling among you, my brethren. What 12 I mean is that each one of you says, "I belong to Paul," or "I belong to Apol'los," or "I belong to Cephas," or "I belong to Christ." Is Christ divided? Was Paul crucified for 13 you? Or were you baptized in the name of Paul? I am thankful[b] that I baptized none of 14 you except Crispus and Ga'ius; lest any one 15 should say that you were baptized in my name. (I did baptize also the household of 16 Steph'anas. Beyond that, I do not know whether I baptized any one else.) For Christ 17 did not send me to baptize but to preach the gospel, and not with eloquent wisdom, lest the cross of Christ be emptied of its power.

For the word of the cross is folly to those 18

[a] Other ancient authorities read *my God*   [b] Other ancient authorities read *I thank God*
1.1: Rom 1.1; Acts 18.17.   **1.2:** Acts 18.1.   **1.3:** Rom 1.7.   **1.4:** Rom 1.8.   **1.8:** 1 Cor 5.5; 2 Cor 1.14.
1.9: Rom 8.28; 1 Jn 1.3.   **1.12:** 1 Cor 3.4; Acts 18.24; 1 Cor 3.22; Jn 1.42; 1 Cor 9.5; 15.5.
1.13: Mt 28.19; Acts 2.38.   **1.14:** Acts 18.8; Rom 16.23.   **1.16:** 1 Cor 16.15.
1.17: Jn 4.2; Acts 10.48; 1 Cor 2.1, 4, 13.

who are perishing, but to us who are being
19 saved it is the power of God. For it is
written,
> "I will destroy the wisdom of the wise,
> and the cleverness of the clever I will
> thwart."
20 Where is the wise man? Where is the
scribe? Where is the debater of this age?
Has not God made foolish the wisdom of the
21 world? For since, in the wisdom of God, the
world did not know God through wisdom, it
pleased God through the folly of what we
22 preach to save those who believe. For Jews
23 demand signs and Greeks seek wisdom, but
we preach Christ crucified, a stumbling
24 block to Jews and folly to Gentiles, but to
those who are called, both Jews and Greeks,
Christ the power of God and the wisdom of
25 God. For the foolishness of God is wiser
than men, and the weakness of God is
stronger than men.

26 For consider your call, brethren; not many
of you were wise according to worldly
standards, not many were powerful, not
27 many were of noble birth; but God chose
what is foolish in the world to shame the
wise, God chose what is weak in the world to
28 shame the strong, God chose what is low and
despised in the world, even things that are
29 not, to bring to nothing things that are, so
that no human being might boast in the
30 presence of God. He is the source of your
life in Christ Jesus, whom God made our
wisdom, our righteousness and sanctification
31 and redemption; therefore, as it is written,
"Let him who boasts, boast of the Lord."

The wisdom of God

2 When I came to you, brethren, I did not
come proclaiming to you the testimony[c] of
2 God in lofty words or wisdom. For I
decided to know nothing among you except
3 Jesus Christ and him crucified. And I was
with you in weakness and in much fear and
4 trembling; and my speech and my message
were not in plausible words of wisdom, but
in demonstration of the Spirit and power,
5 that your faith might not rest in the wisdom
of men but in the power of God.
6 Yet among the mature we do impart
wisdom, although it is not a wisdom of this

age or of the rulers of this age, who are
doomed to pass away. But we impart a secret 7
and hidden wisdom of God, which God
decreed before the ages for our glorification.
None of the rulers of this age understood 8
this; for if they had, they would not have
crucified the Lord of glory. But, as it is 9
written,
> "What no eye has seen, nor ear heard,
>   nor the heart of man conceived,
>   what God has prepared for those who love
>   him,"
God has revealed to us through the Spirit. 10
For the Spirit searches everything, even the
depths of God. For what person knows a 11
man's thoughts except the spirit of the man
which is in him? So also no one compre-
hends the thoughts of God except the Spirit
of God. Now we have received not the spirit 12
of the world, but the Spirit which is from
God, that we might understand the gifts
bestowed on us by God. And we impart 13
in words not taught by human wisdom but
taught by the Spirit, interpreting spiritual
truths to those who possess the Spirit.[d]
The unspiritual[e] man does not receive the 14
gifts of the Spirit of God, for they are folly to
him, and he is not able to understand them
because they are spiritually discerned. The 15
spiritual man judges all things, but is himself
to be judged by no one. "For who has 16
known the mind of the Lord so as to instruct
him?" But we have the mind of Christ.

But I, brethren, could not address you as 3
spiritual men, but as men of the flesh, as
babes in Christ. I fed you with milk, not 2
solid food; for you were not ready for it; and
even yet you are not ready, for you are still 3
of the flesh. For while there is jealousy and
strife among you, are you not of the flesh,
and behaving like ordinary men? For when 4
one says, "I belong to Paul," and another, "I
belong to Apol'los," are you not merely
men?
What then is Apol'los? What is Paul? 5
Servants through whom you believed, as the
Lord assigned to each. I planted, Apol'los 6
watered, but God gave the growth. So 7
neither he who plants nor he who waters is
anything, but only God who gives the
growth. He who plants and he who waters 8

---

[c] Other ancient authorities read *mystery* (or *secret*)
[d] Or *interpreting spiritual truths in spiritual language*; or *comparing spiritual things with spiritual*   [e] Or *natural*
1.19: Is 29.14.   **1.22:** Mt 12.38.   **1.23:** 1 Cor 2.2; Gal 3.1; 5.11.   **1.27:** Jas 2.5.
1.28: Rom 4.17.   **1.29:** Eph 2.9.
1.30: 1 Cor 4.15; Rom 8.1; 2 Cor 5.21; 1 Cor 6.11; 1 Thess 5.23; Eph 1.7, 14; Col 1.14; Rom 3.24.
1.31: Jer 9.24; 2 Cor 10.17.   **2.1:** 1 Cor 1.17.   **2.2:** Gal 6.14; 1 Cor 1.23.
2.3: Acts 18.1, 6, 12; 1 Cor 4.10; 2 Cor 11.30.   **2.4:** Rom 15.19; 1 Cor 4.20.   **2.5:** 2 Cor 4.7; 6.7; 1 Cor 12.9.
2.6: Eph 4.13.   **2.7:** Rom 8.29–30.   **2.8:** Acts 7.2; Jas 2.1.   **2.9:** Is 64.4; 65.17.
2.10: Mt 11.25; 13.11; 16.17; Eph 3.3, 5.   **2.12:** Rom 8.15.   **2.13:** 1 Cor 1.17.   **2.14:** 1 Cor 1.18; Jas 3.15.
2.15: 1 Cor 3.1; 14.37; Gal 6.1.   **2.16:** Is 40.13; Rom 11.34.   **3.1:** Rom 7.14; Heb 5.13.
3.2: Heb 5.12–13; 1 Pet 2.2.   **3.4:** 1 Cor 1.12.   **3.5:** 2 Cor 6.4; Eph 3.7; Col 1.25.
3.6: Acts 18.4–11, 24–27; 1 Cor 1.12.

are equal, and each shall receive his wages
9 according to his labour. For we are fellow
workers for God;/ you are God's field, God's
building.
10 According to the commission of God given
to me, like a skilled master builder I laid a
foundation, and another man is building
upon it. Let each man take care how he
11 builds upon it. For no other foundation can
any one lay than that which is laid, which is
12 Jesus Christ. Now if any one builds on the
foundation with gold, silver, precious stones,
13 wood, hay, stubble—each man's work will
become manifest; for the Day will disclose it,
because it will be revealed with fire, and the
fire will test what sort of work each one has
14 done. If the work which any man has built
on the foundation survives, he will receive a
15 reward. If any man's work is burned up, he
will suffer loss, though he himself will be
saved, but only as through fire.
16 Do you not know that you are God's temple
17 and that God's Spirit dwells in you? If any
one destroys God's temple, God will destroy
him. For God's temple is holy, and that
temple you are.
18 Let no one deceive himself. If any one
among you thinks that he is wise in this age,
let him become a fool that he may become
19 wise. For the wisdom of this world is folly
with God. For it is written, "He catches the
20 wise in their craftiness," and again, "The
Lord knows that the thoughts of the wise are
21 futile." So let no one boast of men. For all
22 things are yours, whether Paul or Apol′los or
Cephas or the world or life or death or the
23 present or the future, all are yours; and you
are Christ's; and Christ is God's.

4 This is how one should regard us, as
servants of Christ and stewards of the mys-
2 teries of God. Moreover it is required of
stewards that they be found trustworthy.
3 But with me it is a very small thing that I
should be judged by you or by any human
4 court. I do not even judge myself. I am not
aware of anything against myself, but I am
not thereby acquitted. It is the Lord who
5 judges me. Therefore do not pronounce
judgment before the time, before the Lord
comes, who will bring to light the things now
hidden in darkness and will disclose the
purposes of the heart. Then every man will
receive his commendation from God.

I have applied all this to myself and 6
Apol′los for your benefit, brethren, that you
may learn by us to live according to scripture,
that none of you may be puffed up in favour
of one against another. For who sees 7
anything different in you? What have you
that you did not receive? If then you
received it, why do you boast as if it were not
a gift?
Already you are filled! Already you have 8
become rich! Without us you have become
kings! And would that you did reign, so that
we might share the rule with you! For I 9
think that God has exhibited us apostles as
last of all, like men sentenced to death;
because we have become a spectacle to the
world, to angels and to men. We are fools for 10
Christ's sake, but you are wise in Christ. We
are weak, but you are strong. You are held in
honour, but we in disrepute. To the present 11
hour we hunger and thirst, we are ill-clad
and buffeted and homeless, and we labour, 12
working with our own hands. When reviled,
we bless; when persecuted, we endure; when 13
slandered, we try to conciliate; we have
become, and are now, as the refuse of the
world, the offscouring of all things.
I do not write this to make you ashamed, 14
but to admonish you as my beloved children. For though you have countless guides 15
in Christ, you do not have many fathers. For
I became your father in Christ Jesus through
the gospel. I urge you, then, be imitators of 16
me. Therefore I sent⁹ to you Timothy, my 17
beloved and faithful child in the Lord, to
remind you of my ways in Christ, as I teach
them everywhere in every church. Some are 18
arrogant, as though I were not coming to
you. But I will come to you soon, if the Lord 19
wills, and I will find out not the talk of these
arrogant people but their power. For the 20
kingdom of God does not consist in talk but
in power. What do you wish? Shall I come 21
to you with a rod, or with love in a spirit of
gentleness?

Moral disorders

It is actually reported that there is 5
immorality among you, and of a kind that is
not found even among pagans; for a man
is living with his father's wife. And you are 2
arrogant! Ought you not rather to mourn?

/ Greek God's fellow workers   ⁹ Or am sending
3.9: Is 61.3; Eph 2.20–22; I Pet 2.5.   3.10: Rom 12.3; I Cor 15.10.   3.11: Eph 2.20.   3.13: 2 Thess 1.7–10.
3.15: Job 23.10.   3.16: I Cor 6.19; 2 Cor 6.16.   3.18: Is 5.21; I Cor 8.2; Gal 6.3.   3.19: Job 5.13; I Cor 1.20.
3.20: Ps 94.11.   3.21: I Cor 4.6; Rom 8.32.   3.22: I Cor 1.12; Rom 8.38.   4.1: I Cor 9.17; Rom 11.25; 16.25.
4.4: 2 Cor 1.12.   4.5: Rom 2.16; I Cor 3.13; 2 Cor 10.18; Rom 2.29.
4.6: I Cor 1.19, 31; 3.19–20; 1.12; 3.4.   4.9: I Cor 15.31; 2 Cor 11.23; Rom 8.36; Heb 10.33.
4.10: I Cor 1.18; 2 Cor 11.19; I Cor 2.3; 13.9; I Cor 2.3.   4.11: Rom 8.35; 2 Cor 11.23–27
4.12: Acts 18.3; I Pet 3.9.   4.15: I Cor 1.30; Philem 10.   4.17: I Cor 16.10; Acts 16.1; I Cor 7.17.
4.21: 2 Cor 1.23.   5.1: Deut 22.30; 27.20.

Let him who has done this be removed from among you.

3 For though absent in body I am present in spirit, and as if present, I have already 4 pronounced judgment in the name of the Lord Jesus on the man who has done such a thing. When you are assembled, and my spirit is present, with the power of our Lord 5 Jesus, you are to deliver this man to Satan for the destruction of the flesh, that his spirit may be saved in the day of the Lord Jesus.[h]

6 Your boasting is not good. Do you not know that a little leaven leavens the whole 7 lump? Cleanse out the old leaven that you may be a new lump, as you really are unleavened. For Christ, our paschal lamb, 8 has been sacrificed. Let us, therefore, celebrate the festival, not with the old leaven, the leaven of malice and evil, but with the unleavened bread of sincerity and truth.

9 I wrote to you in my letter not to associate 10 with immoral men; not at all meaning the immoral of this world, or the greedy and robbers, or idolaters, since then you would 11 need to go out of the world. But rather I wrote[i] to you not to associate with any one who bears the name of brother if he is guilty of immorality or greed, or is an idolater, reviler, drunkard, or robber—not even to eat 12 with such a one. For what have I to do with judging outsiders? Is it not those inside the 13 church whom you are to judge? God judges those outside. "Drive out the wicked person from among you."

6 When one of you has a grievance against a brother, does he dare go to law before the 2 unrighteous instead of the saints? Do you not know that the saints will judge the world? And if the world is to be judged by you, are you incompetent to try trivial 3 cases? Do you not know that we are to judge angels? How much more, matters pertain-4 ing to this life! If then you have such cases, why do you lay them before those who are 5 least esteemed by the church? I say this to your shame. Can it be that there is no man among you wise enough to decide between 6 members of the brotherhood, but brother goes to law against brother, and that before unbelievers? 7 To have lawsuits at all with one another is defeat for you. Why not rather suffer 8 wrong? Why not rather be defrauded? But

you yourselves wrong and defraud, and that even your own brethren.

Do you not know that the unrighteous will 9 not inherit the kingdom of God? Do not be deceived; neither the immoral, nor idolaters, nor adulterers, nor homosexuals,[j] nor 10 thieves, nor the greedy, nor drunkards, nor revilers, nor robbers will inherit the kingdom of God. And such were some of you. But 11 you were washed, you were sanctified, you were justified in the name of the Lord Jesus Christ and in the Spirit of our God.

"All things are lawful for me," but not all 12 things are helpful. "All things are lawful for me," but I will not be enslaved by anything. "Food is meant for the stomach and the 13 stomach for food"—and God will destroy both one and the other. The body is not meant for immorality, but for the Lord, and the Lord for the body. And God raised the 14 Lord and will also raise us up by his power. Do you not know that your bodies are 15 members of Christ? Shall I therefore take the members of Christ and make them members of a prostitute? Never! Do you 16 not know that he who joins himself to a prostitute becomes one body with her? For, as it is written, "The two shall become one."[k] But he who is united to the Lord 17 becomes one spirit with him. Shun immor-18 ality. Every other sin which a man commits is outside the body; but the immoral man sins against his own body. Do you not know 19 that your body is a temple of the Holy Spirit within you, which you have from God? You are not your own; you were bought with a 20 price. So glorify God in your body.

Questions regarding marriage

Now concerning the matters about which **7** you wrote. It is well for a man not to touch a woman. But because of the temptation to 2 immorality, each man should have his own wife and each woman her own husband. The 3 husband should give to his wife her conjugal rights, and likewise the wife to her husband. For the wife does not rule over her own 4 body, but the husband does; likewise the husband does not rule over his own body, but the wife does. Do not refuse one another 5 except perhaps by agreement for a season, that you may devote yourselves to prayer; but then come together again, lest Satan

[h] Other ancient authorities omit *Jesus*   [i] Or *now I write*
[j] Two Greek words are rendered by this expression   [k] Greek *one flesh*
5.3: Col 2.5.   5.4: 2 Thess 3.6.   5.5: Mt 4.10; 1 Cor 1.8.   5.6: Gal 5.9.   5.8: Ex 12.19; 13.7; Deut 16.3.
5.9: 2 Cor 6.14.   5.10: 1 Cor 10.27.   5.11: 2 Thess 3.6; 1 Cor 10.7, 14, 20–21.   5.12: Mk 4.11.
5.13: Deut 17.7; 1 Cor 5.2.   6.1: Mt 18.17.   6.7: Mt 5.39–40.   6.9: 1 Cor 15.50.   6.11: Acts 22.16; Rom 8.30.
6.12: 1 Cor 10.23.   6.15: Rom 12.5; 1 Cor 12.27.   6.16: Gen 2.24; Mt 19.5; Mk 10.8; Eph 5.31.
6.17: Jn 17.21–23; Rom 8.9; Gal 2.20.   6.19: 1 Cor 3.16; Jn 2.21.   6.20: 1 Cor 7.23; Acts 20.28; Rom 12.1.
7.5: Ex 19.15.

tempt you through lack of self-control. I say this by way of concession, not of command. I wish that all were as I myself am. But each has his own special gift from God, one of one kind and one of another.

To the unmarried and the widows I say that it is well for them to remain single as I do. But if they cannot exercise self-control, they should marry. For it is better to marry than to be aflame with passion.

To the married I give charge, not I but the Lord, that the wife should not separate from her husband (but if she does, let her remain single or else be reconciled to her husband)—and that the husband should not divorce his wife. To the rest I say, not the Lord, that if any brother has a wife who is an unbeliever, and she consents to live with him, he should not divorce her. If any woman has a husband who is an unbeliever, and he consents to live with her, she should not divorce him. For the unbelieving husband is consecrated through his wife, and the unbelieving wife is consecrated through her husband. Otherwise, your children would be unclean, but as it is they are holy. But if the unbelieving partner desires to separate, let it be so; in such a case the brother or sister is not bound. For God has called us[l] to peace. Wife, how do you know whether you will save your husband? Husband, how do you know whether you will save your wife?

Only, let every one lead the life which the Lord has assigned to him, and in which God has called him. This is my rule in all the churches. Was any one at the time of his call already circumcised? Let him not seek to remove the marks of circumcision. Was any one at the time of his call uncircumcised? Let him not seek circumcision. For neither circumcision counts for anything nor uncircumcision, but keeping the commandments of God. Every one should remain in the state in which he was called. Were you a slave when called? Never mind. But if you can gain your freedom, avail yourself of the opportunity.[m] For he who was called in the Lord as a slave is a freedman of the Lord. Likewise he who was free when called is a slave of Christ. You were bought with a price; do not become slaves of men. So, brethren, in whatever state each was called, there let him remain with God.

Now concerning the unmarried, I have no command of the Lord, but I give my opinion as one who by the Lord's mercy is trustworthy. I think that in view of the impending[n] distress it is well for a person to remain as he is. Are you bound to a wife? Do not seek to be free. Are you free from a wife? Do not seek marriage. But if you marry, you do not sin, and if a girl marries she does not sin. Yet those who marry will have worldly troubles, and I would spare you that. I mean, brethren, the appointed time has grown very short; from now on, let those who have wives live as though they had none, and those who mourn as though they were not mourning, and those who rejoice as though they were not rejoicing, and those who buy as though they had no goods, and those who deal with the world as though they had no dealings with it. For the form of this world is passing away.

I want you to be free from anxieties. The unmarried man is anxious about the affairs of the Lord, how to please the Lord; but the married man is anxious about worldly affairs, how to please his wife, and his interests are divided. And the unmarried woman or girl is anxious about the affairs of the Lord, how to be holy in body and spirit; but the married woman is anxious about worldly affairs, how to please her husband. I say this for your own benefit, not to lay any restraint upon you, but to promote good order and to secure your undivided devotion to the Lord.

If any one thinks that he is not behaving properly toward his betrothed, if his passions are strong, and it has to be, let him do as he wishes: let them marry—it is no sin. But whoever is firmly established in his heart, being under no necessity but having his desire under control, and has determined this in his heart, to keep her as his betrothed, he will do well. So that he who marries his betrothed does well; and he who refrains from marriage will do better.

A wife is bound to her husband as long as he lives. If the husband dies, she is free to be married to whom she wishes, only in the Lord. But in my judgment she is happier if she remains as she is. And I think that I have the Spirit of God.

Social questions

Now concerning food offered to idols: we know that "all of us possess knowledge." "Knowledge" puffs up, but love builds up. If any one imagines that he knows something, he does not yet know as he ought to

[l] Other ancient authorities read _you_   [m] Or _make use of your present condition instead_   [n] Or _present_
7.7: 1 Cor 7.8; 9.5.   7.9: 1 Tim 5.14.   7.12: 2 Cor 11.17.   7.16: 1 Pet 3.1.
7.17: Rom 12.3; 1 Cor 14.33; 2 Cor 8.18; 11.28.   7.18: 1 Maccabees 1.15; Acts 15.1–2.
7.19: Gal 5.6; 6.15; Rom 2.25.   7.22: Jn 8.32, 36.   7.23: 1 Cor 6.20.   7.29: Rom 13.11–12; 1 Cor 7.31.
7.32: 1 Tim 5.5.   7.39: Rom 7.2.   7.40: 1 Cor 7.25.   8.1: Rom 15.14.   8.2: 1 Cor 3.18; 13.8, 9, 12.

3 know. But if one loves God, one is known by him.

4 Hence, as to the eating of food offered to idols, we know that "an idol has no real existence," and that "there is no God but 5 one." For although there may be so-called gods in heaven or on earth—as indeed there

The Greek gods Chronos and Apollo

6 are many "gods" and many "lords"—yet for us there is one God, the Father, from whom are all things and for whom we exist, and one Lord, Jesus Christ, through whom are all things and through whom we exist.

7 However, not all possess this knowledge. But some, through being hitherto accustomed to idols, eat food as really offered to an idol; and their conscience, being weak, is defiled.

8 Food will not commend us to God. We are no worse off if we do not eat, and no better 9 off if we do. Only take care lest this liberty of yours somehow become a stumbling block to 10 the weak. For if any one sees you, a man of knowledge, at table in an idol's temple, might he not be encouraged, if his conscience is 11 weak, to eat food offered to idols? And so by your knowledge this weak man is destroyed, 12 the brother for whom Christ died. Thus, sinning against your brethren and wounding their conscience when it is weak, you sin 13 against Christ. Therefore, if food is a cause of my brother's falling, I will never eat meat, lest I cause my brother to fall.

9 Am I not free? Am I not an apostle? Have I not seen Jesus our Lord? Are not you my 2 workmanship in the Lord? If to others I am not an apostle, at least I am to you; for you

are the seal of my apostleship in the Lord.
This is my defence to those who would examine me. Do we not have the right to our food and drink? Do we not have the right to be accompanied by a wife,[o] as the other apostles and the brothers of the Lord and Cephas? Or is it only Barnabas and I who have no right to refrain from working for a living? Who serves as a soldier at his own expense? Who plants a vineyard without eating any of its fruit? Who tends a flock without getting some of the milk?

Do I say this on human authority? Does not the law say the same? For it is written in the law of Moses, "You shall not muzzle an ox when it is treading out the grain." Is it for oxen that God is concerned? Does he not speak entirely for our sake? It was written for our sake, because the ploughman should plough in hope and the thresher thresh in hope of a share in the crop. If we have sown spiritual good among you, is it too much if we reap your material benefits? If others share this rightful claim upon you, do not we still more?

Nevertheless, we have not made use of this right, but we endure anything rather than put an obstacle in the way of the gospel of Christ. Do you not know that those who are employed in the temple service get their food from the temple, and those who serve at the altar share in the sacrificial offerings? In the same way, the Lord commanded that those who proclaim the gospel should get their living by the gospel.

But I have made no use of any of these rights, nor am I writing this to secure any such provision. For I would rather die than have any one deprive me of my ground for boasting. For if I preach the gospel, that gives me no ground for boasting. For necessity is laid upon me. Woe to me if I do not preach the gospel! For if I do this of my own will, I have a reward; but if not of my own will, I am entrusted with a commission. What then is my reward? Just this: that in my preaching I may make the gospel free of charge, not making full use of my right in the gospel.

For though I am free from all men, I have made myself a slave to all, that I might win the more. To the Jews I became as a Jew, in order to win Jews; to those under the law I became as one under the law—though not being myself under the law—that I might

o Greek *a sister as wife*

8.3: Gal 4.9; Rom 8.29. **8.4:** 1 Cor 10.19; Deut 6.4.
8.6: Mal 2.10; Eph 4.6; Rom 11.36; 1 Cor 1.2; Eph 4.5; Jn 1.3; Col 1.16. **8.7:** 1 Cor 8.4-5. **8.8:** Rom 14.17.
8.9: 1 Cor 8.10-11; Rom 14.1. **8.11:** Rom 14.15, 20. **8.12:** Mt 18.6; Rom 14.20. **8.13:** Rom 14.21.
9.1: 1 Cor 9.19; 2 Cor 12.12; 1 Thess 2.6; Acts 9.3, 17; 1 Cor 15.8. **9.4:** 1 Cor 9.14.
9.5: 1 Cor 7.7-8; Mt 12.46; 8.14; Jn 1.42. **9.6:** Acts 4.36. **9.9:** Deut 25.4; 1 Tim 5.18. **9.10:** 2 Tim 2.6.
9.11: Rom 15.27. **9.12:** 2 Cor 6.3. **9.13:** Deut 18.1. **9.14:** Mt 10.10; Lk 10.7-8.
9.15: 2 Cor 11.10. **9.17:** 1 Cor 4.1; Gal 2.7. **9.18:** 2 Cor 11.7. **9.20:** Rom 11.14.

win those under the law. To those outside the law I became as one outside the law—not being without law toward God but under the law of Christ—that I might win those outside 2 the law. To the weak I became weak, that I might win the weak. I have become all things to all men, that I might by all means 3 save some. I do it all for the sake of the gospel, that I may share in its blessings. 4 Do you not know that in a race all the runners compete, but only one receives the 5 prize? So run that you may obtain it. Every athlete exercises self-control in all things. They do it to receive a perishable wreath, but

6 we an imperishable. Well, I do not run aimlessly, I do not box as one beating the 7 air; but I pommel my body and subdue it, lest after preaching to others I myself should be disqualified.

10 I want you to know, brethren, that our fathers were all under the cloud, and all 2 passed through the sea, and all were baptized 3 into Moses in the cloud and in the sea, and 4 ate the same supernatural *p* food and all drank the same supernatural *p* drink. For they drank from the supernatural *p* Rock which followed them, and the Rock was Christ. 5 Nevertheless with most of them God was not pleased; for they were overthrown in the wilderness. 6 Now these things are warnings for us, not to 7 desire evil as they did. Do not be idolaters as some of them were; as it is written, "The people sat down to eat and drink and rose up 8 to dance." We must not indulge in immorality as some of them did, and twenty-9 three thousand fell in a single day. We must not put the Lord *q* to the test, as some of them 0 did and were destroyed by serpents; nor grumble, as some of them did and were 1 destroyed by the Destroyer. Now these things happened to them as a warning, but they were written down for our instruction, upon whom the end of the ages has come.

Therefore let any one who thinks that he 12 stands take heed lest he fall. No temptation 13 has overtaken you that is not common to man. God is faithful, and he will not let you be tempted beyond your strength, but with the temptation will also provide the way of escape, that you may be able to endure it. Therefore, my beloved, shun the worship of 14 idols. I speak as to sensible men; judge for 15 yourselves what I say. The cup of blessing 16 which we bless, is it not a participation *r* in the blood of Christ? The bread which we break, is it not a participation *r* in the body of Christ? Because there is one bread, we who 17 are many are one body, for we all partake of the one bread. Consider the practice of 18 Israel; are not those who eat the sacrifices partners in the altar? What do I imply 19 then? That food offered to idols is anything, or that an idol is anything? No, I imply that 20 what pagans sacrifice they offer to demons and not to God. I do not want you to be partners with demons. You cannot drink the 21 cup of the Lord and the cup of demons. You cannot partake of the table of the Lord and the table of demons. Shall we provoke the 22 Lord to jealousy? Are we stronger than he? "All things are lawful," but not all things 23 are helpful. "All things are lawful," but not all things build up. Let no one seek his own 24 good, but the good of his neighbour. Eat 25 whatever is sold in the meat market without raising any question on the ground of conscience. For "the earth is the Lord's, and 26 everything in it." If one of the unbelievers 27 invites you to dinner and you are disposed to go, eat whatever is set before you without raising any question on the ground of conscience. (But if some one says to you, 28 "This has been offered in sacrifice," then out of consideration for the man who informed you, and for conscience' sake—I mean his 29 conscience, not yours—do not eat it.) For why should my liberty be determined by another man's scruples? If I partake with 30 thankfulness, why am I denounced because of that for which I give thanks? So, whether you eat or drink, or whatever 31 you do, do all to the glory of God. Give no 32 offence to Jews or to Greeks or to the church of God, just as I try to please all men in 33 everything I do, not seeking my own advantage, but that of many, that they may be saved. Be imitators of me, as I am of Christ. **11**

p Greek *spiritual*   *q* Other ancient authorities read *Christ*   *r* Or *communion*
9.21: Rom 2.12, 14.   **9.22:** 2 Cor 11.29; Rom 15.1; 1 Cor 10.33; Rom 11.14.   **9.24:** Heb 12.1.
9.25: 2 Tim 2.5; 4.8; Jas 1.12; 1 Pet 5.4.   **10.1:** Rom 1.13; Ex 13.21; 14.22, 29.   **10.2:** Rom 6.3; Gal 3.27.
10.3: Ex 16.4, 35.   **10.4:** Ex 17.6; Num 20.11.   **10.5:** Num 14.29–30.   **10.6:** Num 11.4, 34.
10.7: Ex 32.4, 6.   **10.8:** Num 25.1–18.   **10.9:** Num 21.5–6.   **10.10:** Num 16.41, 49.   **10.13:** 1 Cor 1.9.
10.14: 1 Jn 5.21.   **10.16:** Mt 26.27–28; Acts 2.42.   **10.17:** Rom 12.5.   **10.18:** Lev 7.6.   **10.20:** Deut 32.17.
10.21: 2 Cor 6.16.   **10.22:** Deut 32.21; Eccles 6.10; Is 45.9.   **10.23:** 1 Cor 6.12; Phil 2.21.
10.26: Ps 24.1; 50.12.   **10.28:** 1 Cor 8.7, 10–12.   **10.32:** 1 Cor 8.13.   **10.33:** 1 Cor 9.22; Rom 15.2; 1 Cor 13.5.
11.1: 1 Cor 4.16.

Christian worship

2 I commend you because you remember me in everything and maintain the traditions 3 even as I have delivered them to you. But I want you to understand that the head of every man is Christ, the head of a woman is her husband, and the head of Christ is God. 4 Any man who prays or prophesies with his 5 head covered dishonours his head, but any woman who prays or prophesies with her head unveiled dishonours her head—it is the 6 same as if her head were shaven. For if a woman will not veil herself, then she should cut off her hair; but if it is disgraceful for a woman to be shorn or shaven, let her wear a 7 veil. For a man ought not to cover his head, since he is the image and glory of God; but 8 woman is the glory of man. (For man was not made from woman, but woman from 9 man. Neither was man created for woman, 10 but woman for man.) That is why a woman ought to have a veil[s] on her head, because of 11 the angels. (Nevertheless, in the Lord woman is not independent of man nor man of 12 woman; for as woman was made from man, so man is now born of woman. And all 13 things are from God.) Judge for yourselves; is it proper for a woman to pray to God with 14 her head uncovered? Does not nature itself teach you that for a man to wear long hair is 15 degrading to him, but if a woman has long hair, it is her pride? For her hair is given to 16 her for a covering. If any one is disposed to be contentious, we recognise no other practice, nor do the churches of God.

The Lord's supper

17 But in the following instructions I do not commend you, because when you come together it is not for the better but for the 18 worse. For, in the first place, when you assemble as a church, I hear that there are divisions among you; and I partly believe it, 19 for there must be factions among you in order that those who are genuine among you 20 may be recognised. When you meet together, it is not the Lord's supper that you 21 eat. For in eating, each one goes ahead with his own meal, and one is hungry and another 22 is drunk. What! Do you not have houses to eat and drink in? Or do you despise the church of God and humiliate those who have nothing? What shall I say to you? Shall I commend you in this? No, I will not.

For I received from the Lord what I also delivered to you, that the Lord Jesus on the night when he was betrayed took bread, and when he had given thanks, he broke it, and said, "This is my body which is for[t] you. Do this in remembrance of me." In the same way also the cup, after supper, saying, "This cup is the new covenant in my blood. Do this, as often as you drink it, in remembrance of me." For as often as you eat this bread and drink the cup, you proclaim the Lord's death until he comes.

Whoever, therefore, eats the bread or drinks the cup of the Lord in an unworthy manner will be guilty of profaning the body and blood of the Lord. Let a man examine himself, and so eat of the bread and drink of the cup. For any one who eats and drinks without discerning the body eats and drinks judgment upon himself. That is why many of you are weak and ill, and some have died.[u] But if we judged ourselves truly, we should not be judged. But when we are judged by the Lord, we are chastened[v] so that we may not be condemned along with the world.

So then, my brethren, when you come together to eat, wait for one another—if any one is hungry, let him eat at home—lest you come together to be condemned. About the other things I will give directions when I come.

Spiritual gifts

Now concerning spiritual gifts, brethren,1 I do not want you to be uninformed. You 2 know that when you were heathen, you were led astray to dumb idols, however you may have been moved. Therefore I want you to 3 understand that no one speaking by the Spirit of God ever says "Jesus be cursed!" and no one can say "Jesus is Lord" except by the Holy Spirit.

Now there are varieties of gifts, but the 4 same Spirit; and there are varieties of service, 5 but the same Lord; and there are varieties of 6 working, but it is the same God who inspires them all in every one. To each is given the 7 manifestation of the Spirit for the common good. To one is given through the Spirit 8 the utterance of wisdom, and to another the utterance of knowledge according to the same Spirit, to another faith by the same 9 Spirit, to another gifts of healing by the one Spirit, to another the working of miracles, 1

---

[s] Greek *authority* (the veil being a symbol of this)   [t] Other ancient authorities read *broken for*
[u] Greek *have fallen asleep* (as in Ch. 15.6, 20)   [v] Or *when we are judged we are being chastened by the Lord*
11.2: 2 Thess 2.15.   11.3: Eph 1.22; 4.15; 5.23; Col 1.8; 2.19.   11.5: Lk 2.36; Acts 21.9; 1 Cor 14.34.
11.7: Gen 1.26.   11.8: Gen 2.21–23.   11.9: Gen 2.18.   11.12: 2 Cor 5.18; Rom 11.36.   11.16: 1 Cor 7.17.
11.18: 1 Cor 1.10.   11.23: 1 Cor 15.3.   11.24–25: Mt 26.26–28; Mk 14.22–24; Lk 22.17–19; 1 Cor 10.16.
11.25: 2 Cor 3.6; Lk 22.20.   11.26: 1 Cor 4.5.   11.32: 1 Cor 1.20.   11.34: 1 Cor 4.19.   12.2: Eph 2.11–12.
12.3: Rom 10.9.   12.10: 1 Cor 14.26.

to another prophecy, to another the ability to distinguish between spirits, to another various kinds of tongues, to another the interpretation of tongues. All these are inspired by one and the same Spirit, who apportions to each one individually as he wills.

For just as the body is one and has many members, and all the members of the body, though many, are one body, so it is with Christ. For by one Spirit we were all baptized into one body—Jews or Greeks, slaves or free—and all were made to drink of one Spirit.

For the body does not consist of one member but of many. If the foot should say, "Because I am not a hand, I do not belong to the body," that would not make it any less a part of the body. And if the ear should say, "Because I am not an eye, I do not belong to the body," that would not make it any less a part of the body. If the whole body were an eye, where would be the hearing? If the whole body were an ear, where would be the sense of smell? But as it is, God arranged 18 the organs in the body, each one of them, as he chose. If all were a single organ, where 19 would the body be? As it is, there are many 20 parts, yet one body. The eye cannot say to 21 the hand, "I have no need of you," nor again the head to the feet, "I have no need of you." On the contrary, the parts of the body 22 which seem to be weaker are indispensable, and those parts of the body which we think 23 less honourable we invest with the greater honour, and our unpresentable parts are treated with greater modesty, which our 24 more presentable parts do not require. But God has so adjusted the body, giving the greater honour to the inferior part, that there 25 may be no discord in the body, but that the members may have the same care for one another. If one member suffers, all suffer 26 together; if one member is honoured, all rejoice together.

Now you are the body of Christ and 27 individually members of it. And God has 28 appointed in the church first apostles, second prophets, third teachers, then workers of miracles, then healers, helpers, administrators, speakers in various kinds of tongues. Are all apostles? Are all prophets? Are all 29 teachers? Do all work miracles? Do all 30 possess gifts of healing? Do all speak with tongues? Do all interpret? But earnestly 31 desire the higher gifts.

And I will show you a still more excellent way.

The more excellent way

If I speak in the tongues of men and of **13** angels, but have not love, I am a noisy gong or a clanging cymbal. And if I have pro- 2 phetic powers, and understand all mysteries and all knowledge, and if I have all faith, so as to remove mountains, but have not love, I am nothing. If I give away all I have, and if I 3 deliver my body to be burned,[w] but have not love, I gain nothing.

Love is patient and kind; love is not jealous 4 or boastful; it is not arrogant or rude. Love 5 does not insist on its own way; it is not irritable or resentful; it does not rejoice at 6 wrong, but rejoices in the right. Love bears 7 all things, believes all things, hopes all things, endures all things.

Love never ends; as for prophecies, they 8 will pass away; as for tongues, they will cease; as for knowledge, it will pass away.

HK

---

[w] Other ancient authorities read *body that I may glory*
12.12: Rom 12.4. **12.13:** Gal 3.28; Col 3.11; Eph 2.13–18; Jn 7.37–39.
12.27: Eph 1.23; 4.12; Col 1.18, 24; Eph 5.30; Rom 12.5. **12.28:** Eph 4.11; 2.20; 3.5.
13.1: Ps 150.5. **13.2:** I Cor 14.2; Mt 17.20; 21.21. **13.5:** I Cor 10.24. **13.7:** I Cor 9.12.

9 For our knowledge is imperfect and our
10 prophecy is imperfect; but when the perfect
11 comes, the imperfect will pass away. When I
was a child, I spoke like a child, I thought
like a child, I reasoned like a child; when I
12 became a man, I gave up childish ways. For
now we see in a mirror dimly, but then face
to face. Now I know in part; then I shall
understand fully, even as I have been fully
13 understood. So faith, hope, love abide, these
three; but the greatest of these is love.

The gift of tongues

14 Make love your aim, and earnestly desire
the spiritual gifts, especially that you may
2 prophesy. For one who speaks in a tongue
speaks not to men but to God; for no one
understands him, but he utters mysteries in
3 the Spirit. On the other hand, he who
prophesies speaks to men for their upbuild-
4 ing and encouragement and consolation. He
who speaks in a tongue edifies himself, but
5 he who prophesies edifies the church. Now I
want you all to speak in tongues, but even
more to prophesy. He who prophesies is
greater than he who speaks in tongues, unless
some one interprets, so that the church may
be edified.

6 Now, brethren, if I come to you speaking in
tongues, how shall I benefit you unless I
bring you some revelation or knowledge or
7 prophecy or teaching? If even lifeless
instruments, such as the flute or the harp, do
not give distinct notes, how will any one
8 know what is played? And if the bugle gives
an indistinct sound, who will get ready for
9 battle? So with yourselves; if you in a
tongue utter speech that is not intelligible,
how will any one know what is said? For
10 you will be speaking into the air. There are
doubtless many different languages in the
11 world, and none is without meaning; but if I
do not know the meaning of the language, I
shall be a foreigner to the speaker and the
12 speaker a foreigner to me. So with yourselves; since you are eager for manifestations
of the Spirit, strive to excel in building up
the church.
13 Therefore, he who speaks in a tongue
14 should pray for the power to interpret. For if
I pray in a tongue, my spirit prays but my
15 mind is unfruitful. What am I to do? I will
pray with the spirit and I will pray with the
mind also; I will sing with the spirit and I
16 will sing with the mind also. Otherwise, if
you bless *x* with the spirit, how can any one in
the position of an outsider *y* say the "Amen"
to your thanksgiving when he does not know

what you are saying? For you may give
thanks well enough, but the other man is not
edified. I thank God that I speak in tongues
more than you all; nevertheless, in church I
would rather speak five words with my mind,
in order to instruct others, than ten thousand
words in a tongue.

Brethren, do not be children in your
thinking; be babes in evil, but in thinking be
mature. In the law it is written, "By men of
strange tongues and by the lips of foreigners
will I speak to this people, and even then
they will not listen to me, says the Lord."
Thus, tongues are a sign not for believers but
for unbelievers, while prophecy is not for
unbelievers but for believers. If, therefore,
the whole church assembles and all speak in
tongues, and outsiders or unbelievers enter,
will they not say that you are mad? But if all
prophesy, and an unbeliever or outsider
enters, he is convicted by all, he is called to
account by all, the secrets of his heart are
disclosed; and so, falling on his face, he will
worship God and declare that God is really
among you.

What then, brethren? When you come
together, each one has a hymn, a lesson, a
revelation, a tongue, or an interpretation.
Let all things be done for edification. If any
speak in a tongue, let there be only two or at
most three, and each in turn; and let one
interpret. But if there is no one to interpret,
let each of them keep silence in church and
speak to himself and to God. Let two or
three prophets speak, and let the others
weigh what is said. If a revelation is made to
another sitting by, let the first be silent. For
you can all prophesy one by one, so that all
may learn and all be encouraged; and the
spirits of prophets are subject to prophets.
For God is not a God of confusion but of
peace.

As in all the churches of the saints, the
women should keep silence in the churches.
For they are not permitted to speak, but
should be subordinate, as even the law says.
If there is anything they desire to know, let
them ask their husbands at home. For it is
shameful for a woman to speak in church.
What! Did the word of God originate with
you, or are you the only ones it has reached?

If any one thinks that he is a prophet, or
spiritual, he should acknowledge that what I
am writing to you is a command of the Lord.
If any one does not recognise this, he is not
recognised. So, my brethren, earnestly
desire to prophesy, and do not forbid speaking in tongues; but all things should be done
decently and in order.

---

x That is, *give thanks to God*   *y* Or *him that is without gifts*
14.15: Eph 5.19; Col 3.16.   14.16: 1 Chron 16.36; Ps 106.48; Mt 15.36.   14.20: Eph 4.14.
14.21: Is 28.11–12.   14.26: Eph 5.19.   14.34: 1 Tim 2.11–12; 1 Pet 3.1.

The resurrection of the dead

15 Now I would remind you, brethren, in what terms I preached to you the gospel, which 2 you received, in which you stand, by which you are saved, if you hold it fast—unless you believed in vain. 3 For I delivered to you as of first importance what I also received, that Christ died for our 4 sins in accordance with the scriptures, that he was buried, that he was raised on the third 5 day in accordance with the scriptures, and that he appeared to Cephas, then to the 6 twelve. Then he appeared to more than five hundred brethren at one time, most of whom are still alive, though some have fallen 7 asleep. Then he appeared to James, then to 8 all the apostles. Last of all, as to one 9 untimely born, he appeared also to me. For I am the least of the apostles, unfit to be called an apostle, because I persecuted the church 10 of God. But by the grace of God I am what I am, and his grace toward me was not in vain. On the contrary, I worked harder than any of them, though it was not I, but the grace of 11 God which is with me. Whether then it was I or they, so we preach and so you believed. 12 Now if Christ is preached as raised from the dead, how can some of you say that there is 13 no resurrection of the dead? But if there is no resurrection of the dead, then Christ has 14 not been raised; if Christ has not been raised, then our preaching is in vain and your faith is 15 in vain. We are even found to be misrepresenting God, because we testified of God that he raised Christ, whom he did not raise 16 if it is true that the dead are not raised. For if the dead are not raised, then Christ has not 17 been raised. If Christ has not been raised, your faith is futile and you are still in your 18 sins. Then those also who have fallen asleep 19 in Christ have perished. If for this life only we have hoped in Christ, we are of all men most to be pitied. 20 But in fact Christ has been raised from the dead, the first fruits of those who have fallen 21 asleep. For as by a man came death, by a man has come also the resurrection of the 22 dead. For as in Adam all die, so also in 23 Christ shall all be made alive. But each in his own order: Christ the first fruits, then at his 24 coming those who belong to Christ. Then comes the end, when he delivers the kingdom to God the Father after destroying every rule 25 and every authority and power. For he must reign until he has put all his enemies under

his feet. The last enemy to be destroyed is 26 death. "For God*z* has put all things in 27 subjection under his feet." But when it says, "All things are put in subjection under him," it is plain that he is excepted who put all things under him. When all things are 28 subjected to him, then the Son himself will also be subjected to him who put all things under him, that God may be everything to every one. Otherwise, what do people mean by being 29 baptized on behalf of the dead? If the dead are not raised at all, why are people baptized on their behalf? Why am I in peril every 30 hour? I protest, brethren, by my pride in 31 you which I have in Christ Jesus our Lord, I die every day! What do I gain if, humanly 32 speaking, I fought with beasts at Ephesus? If the dead are not raised, "Let us eat and drink, for tomorrow we die." Do not 33 be deceived: "Bad company ruins good morals." Come to your right mind, and sin 34 no more. For some have no knowledge of God. I say this to your shame. But some one will ask, "How are the dead 35 raised? With what kind of body do they come?" You foolish man! What you sow 36 does not come to life unless it dies. And 37 what you sow is not the body which is to be, but a bare kernel, perhaps of wheat or of some other grain. But God gives it a body as 38 he has chosen, and to each kind of seed its own body. For not all flesh is alike, but there 39 is one kind for men, another for animals, another for birds, and another for fish. There are celestial bodies and there are 40 terrestrial bodies; but the glory of the celestial is one, and the glory of the terrestrial is another. There is one glory of the sun, and 41 another glory of the moon, and another glory of the stars; for star differs from star in glory. So is it with the resurrection of the dead. 42 What is sown is perishable, what is raised is imperishable. It is sown in dishonour, it is 43 raised in glory. It is sown in weakness, it is raised in power. It is sown a physical body, 44 it is raised a spiritual body. If there is a physical body, there is also a spiritual body. Thus it is written, "The first man Adam 45 became a living being"; the last Adam became a life-giving spirit. But it is not the 46 spiritual which is first but the physical, and then the spiritual. The first man was from 47 the earth, a man of dust; the second man is from heaven. As was the man of dust, so are 48 those who are of the dust; and as is the man

z Greek *he*
15.3: 1 Cor 11.23; 1 Pet 2.24; Is 53.5–12. **15.4:** Mt 16.21; Ps 16.8–9. **15.5:** Lk 24.34; Mt 28.17.
15.8: 1 Cor 9.1; Gal 1.16; Acts 9.3–6. **15.9:** Acts 8.3. **15.14:** 1 Thess 4.14. **15.18:** 1 Thess 4.16.
15.21: Rom 5.12. **15.22:** Rom 5.14–18. **15.23:** 1 Thess 2.19. **15.25:** Ps 110.1. **15.27:** Ps 8.6; Eph 1.22.
15.28: Phil 3.21. **15.30:** 2 Esdras 7.89. **15.31:** Rom 8.36. **15.32:** 2 Cor 1.8, 9; Is 22.13.
15.33: Menander, *Thais.* **15.34:** Rom 13.11. **15.36:** Jn 12.24. **15.38:** Gen 1.11. **15.42:** Dan 12.3.
15.45: Gen 2.7.

of heaven, so are those who are of heaven. 49 Just as we have borne the image of the man of dust, we shall[a] also bear the image of the 50 man of heaven. I tell you this, brethren: flesh and blood cannot inherit the kingdom of God, nor does the perishable inherit the imperishable.

51 Lo! I tell you a mystery. We shall not all 52 sleep, but we shall all be changed, in a moment, in the twinkling of an eye, at the last trumpet. For the trumpet will sound, and the dead will be raised imperishable, and 53 we shall be changed. For this perishable nature must put on the imperishable, and this mortal nature must put on immortality. 54 When the perishable puts on the imperishable, and the mortal puts on immortality, then shall come to pass the saying that is written:

"Death is swallowed up in victory."
55   "O death, where is thy victory?
O death, where is thy sting?"
56 The sting of death is sin, and the power of sin 57 is the law. But thanks be to God, who gives us the victory through our Lord Jesus Christ. 58 Therefore, my beloved brethren, be steadfast, immovable, always abounding in the work of the Lord, knowing that in the Lord your labour is not in vain.

Administrative and personal

16 Now concerning the contribution for the saints: as I directed the churches of Galatia, 2 so you also are to do. On the first day of every week, each of you is to put something aside and store it up, as he may prosper, so that contributions need not be made when I 3 come. And when I arrive, I will send those whom you accredit by letter to carry your gift 4 to Jerusalem. If it seems advisable that I should go also, they will accompany me. 5 I will visit you after passing through Macedo'nia, for I intend to pass through

Macedo'nia, and perhaps I will stay with you 6 or even spend the winter, so that you may speed me on my journey, wherever I go. For 7 I do not want to see you now just in passing; I hope to spend some time with you, if the Lord permits. But I will stay in Ephesus 8 until Pentecost, for a wide door for effective 9 work has opened to me, and there are many adversaries.

When Timothy comes, see that you put him 10 at ease among you, for he is doing the work of the Lord, as I am. So let no one despise 11 him. Speed him on his way in peace, that he may return to me; for I am expecting him with the brethren.

As for our brother Apol'los, I strongly 12 urged him to visit you with the other brethren, but it was not at all his will[b] to come now. He will come when he has opportunity.

Be watchful, stand firm in your faith, be 13 courageous, be strong. Let all that you do be 14 done in love.

Now, brethren, you know that the house- 15 hold of Steph'anas were the first converts in Acha'ia, and they have devoted themselves to the service of the saints; I urge you to be 16 subject to such men and to every fellow worker and labourer. I rejoice at the coming 17 of Steph'anas and Fortuna'tus and Acha'- icus, because they have made up for your absence; for they refreshed my spirit as well 18 as yours. Give recognition to such men.

The churches of Asia send greetings. 19 Aquila and Prisca, together with the church in their house, send you hearty greetings in the Lord. All the brethren send greetings. 20 Greet one another with a holy kiss.

I, Paul, write this greeting with my own 21 hand. If any one has no love for the Lord, let 22 him be accursed. Our Lord, come![c] The grace of the Lord Jesus be with you. 23 My love be with you all in Christ Jesus. 24 Amen.

---

[a] Other ancient authorities read *let us*   [b] Or *God's will for him*   [c] Greek *Maranatha*
15.51–52: 1 Thess 4.15–17.   15.54: Is 25.8.   15.55: Hos 13.14.   16.1: Acts 24.17.
16.2: Acts 20.7; 2 Cor 9.4–5.   16.3: 2 Cor 8.18–19.   16.5: Rom 15.26; Acts 19.21.   16.7: Acts 18.21.
16.8: Acts 18.19.   16.9: Acts 19.9.   16.10: Acts 16.1.   16.12: Acts 18.24.   16.13: Ps 31.24; Eph 6.10.
16.19: Acts 18.2; Rom 16.5.   16.20: Rom 16.16.   16.21: Col 4.18; Gal 6.11; 2 Thess 3.17.   16.22: Rom 9.3.
16.23: Rom 16.20.

THE SECOND LETTER OF PAUL TO THE
CORINTHIANS

PAUL, an apostle of Christ Jesus by the will of God, and Timothy our brother, To the church of God which is at Corinth, with all the saints who are in the whole of Acha'ia:

2 Grace to you and peace from God our Father and the Lord Jesus Christ.

Comfort in affliction

3 Blessed be the God and Father of our Lord Jesus Christ, the Father of mercies and God 4 of all comfort, who comforts us in all our affliction, so that we may be able to comfort those who are in any affliction, with the comfort with which we ourselves are com-5 forted by God. For as we share abundantly in Christ's sufferings, so through Christ we 6 share abundantly in comfort too.[a] If we are afflicted, it is for your comfort and salvation; and if we are comforted, it is for your comfort, which you experience when you patiently endure the same sufferings that we 7 suffer. Our hope for you is unshaken; for we know that as you share in our sufferings, you will also share in our comfort.

8 For we do not want you to be ignorant, brethren, of the affliction we experienced in Asia; for we were so utterly, unbearably 9 crushed that we despaired of life itself. Why, we felt that we had received the sentence of death; but that was to make us rely not on 10 ourselves but on God who raises the dead; he delivered us from so deadly a peril, and he will deliver us; on him we have set our hope 11 that he will deliver us again. You also must help us by prayer, so that many will give thanks on our behalf for the blessing granted us in answer to many prayers.

12 For our boast is this, the testimony of our conscience that we have behaved in the world, and still more toward you, with holiness and godly sincerity, not by earthly 13 wisdom but by the grace of God. For we write you nothing but what you can read and understand; I hope you will understand 14 fully, as you have understood in part, that you can be proud of us as we can be of you, on the day of the Lord Jesus.

15 Because I was sure of this, I wanted to come to you first, so that you might have a double pleasure;[b] I wanted to visit you on my way to 16 Macedo'nia, and to come back to you from Macedo'nia and have you send me on my way to Judea. Was I vacillating when I 17 wanted to do this? Do I make my plans like a worldly man, ready to say Yes and No at once? As surely as God is faithful, our word 18 to you has not been Yes and No. For the Son 19 of God, Jesus Christ, whom we preached among you, Silva'nus and Timothy and I, was not Yes and No; but in him it is always Yes. For all the promises of God find their 20 Yes in him. That is why we utter the Amen through him, to the glory of God. But it is 21 God who establishes us with you in Christ, and has commissioned us; he has put his seal 22 upon us and given us his Spirit in our hearts as a guarantee.

But I call God to witness against me—it was 23 to spare you that I refrained from coming to Corinth. Not that we lord it over your faith; 24 we work with you for your joy, for you stand firm in your faith.

For I made up my mind not to make you 2 another painful visit. For if I cause you pain, 2 who is there to make me glad but the one whom I have pained? And I wrote as I did, 3 so that when I came I might not be pained by those who should have made me rejoice, for I felt sure of all of you, that my joy would be the joy of you all. For I wrote you out of much 4 affliction and anguish of heart and with many tears, not to cause you pain but to let you know the abundant love that I have for you.

But if any one has caused pain, he has 5 caused it not to me, but in some measure —not to put it too severely—to you all. For 6 such a one this punishment by the majority is enough; so you should rather turn to forgive 7 and comfort him, or he may be overwhelmed by excessive sorrow. So I beg you to re-8 affirm your love for him. For this is why I 9 wrote, that I might test you and know whether you are obedient in everything. Any 10 one whom you forgive, I also forgive. What I have forgiven, if I have forgiven anything, has been for your sake in the presence of Christ, to keep Satan from gaining the 11 advantage over us; for we are not ignorant of his designs.

---

[a] Or *For as the sufferings of Christ abound for us, so also our comfort abounds through Christ*
[b] Other ancient authorities read *favour*
1.1: Eph 1.1; Col 1.1; 2 Cor 1.19; Acts 16.1; 18.1. **1.2:** Rom 1.7. **1.3:** Eph 1.3; 1 Pet 1.3; Rom 15.5. **1.4:** 2 Cor 7.6–7, 13. **1.16:** Acts 19.21. **1.19:** 1 Thess 1.1; Acts 15.22. **1.20:** 1 Cor 14.16; Rev 3.14.

Greek home life

12 When I came to Tro'as to preach the gospel
of Christ, a door was opened for me in the
13 Lord; but my mind could not rest because I
did not find my brother Titus there. So I took
leave of them and went on to Macedo'nia.

Triumph in Christ

14 But thanks be to God, who in Christ always
leads us in triumph, and through us spreads
the fragrance of the knowledge of him every-
15 where. For we are the aroma of Christ to
God among those who are being saved and
16 among those who are perishing, to one a
fragrance from death to death, to the other a
fragrance from life to life. Who is sufficient
17 for these things? For we are not, like so
many, pedlars of God's word; but as men of
sincerity, as commissioned by God, in the
sight of God we speak in Christ.

Proof of our ministry

3 Are we beginning to commend ourselves
again? Or do we need, as some do, letters of
2 recommendation to you, or from you? You
yourselves are our letter of recommendation,
written on your*c* hearts, to be known and
3 read by all men; and you show that you are a
letter from Christ delivered by us, written
not with ink but with the Spirit of the living
God, not on tablets of stone but on tablets of
human hearts.
4 Such is the confidence that we have through
5 Christ toward God. Not that we are sufficient of ourselves to claim anything as
coming from us; our sufficiency is from God,
6 who has qualified us to be ministers of a new
covenant, not in a written code but in the
Spirit; for the written code kills, but the
Spirit gives life.
7 Now if the dispensation of death, carved in

letters on stone, came with such splendour
that the Israelites could not look at Moses'
face because of its brightness, fading as this
8 was, will not the dispensation of the Spirit be
attended with greater splendour? For if
9 there was splendour in the dispensation of
condemnation, the dispensation of righteousness must far exceed it in splendour. Indeed,
10 in this case, what once had splendour has
come to have no splendour at all, because of
the splendour that surpasses it. For if what
11 faded away came with splendour, what is
permanent must have much more splendour.
Since we have such a hope, we are very
12 bold, not like Moses, who put a veil over his
13 face so that the Israelites might not see the
end of the fading splendour. But their minds
14 were hardened; for to this day, when they
read the old covenant, that same veil remains
unlifted, because only through Christ is it
taken away. Yes, to this day whenever
15 Moses is read a veil lies over their minds; but
16 when a man turns to the Lord the veil is
removed. Now the Lord is the Spirit, and
17 where the Spirit of the Lord is, there is
freedom. And we all, with unveiled face,
18 beholding*d* the glory of the Lord, are being
changed into his likeness from one degree of
glory to another; for this comes from the
Lord who is the Spirit.

Treasure in earthen vessels

Therefore, having this ministry by the
4 mercy of God,*e* we do not lose heart. We
2 have renounced disgraceful, underhanded
ways; we refuse to practise cunning or to
tamper with God's word, but by the open
statement of the truth we would commend
ourselves to every man's conscience in the
sight of God. And even if our gospel is
3 veiled, it is veiled only to those who are

c Other ancient authorities read *our*   *d* Or *reflecting*   *e* Greek *as we have received mercy*
2.12: Acts 16.8.   3.1: Acts 18.27; Rom 16.1; 1 Cor 16.3.   3.3: Ex 24.12; 31.18; 32.15-16; Jer 31.33.
3.6: Jer 31.31.   3.7: Ex 34.29-35.   3.17: Is 61.1-2.

4 perishing. In their case the god of this world has blinded the minds of the unbelievers, to keep them from seeing the light of the gospel of the glory of Christ, who is the likeness of 5 God. For what we preach is not ourselves, but Jesus Christ as Lord, with ourselves as 6 your servants*f* for Jesus' sake. For it is the God who said, "Let light shine out of darkness," who has shone in our hearts to give the light of the knowledge of the glory of God in the face of Christ.

7 But we have this treasure in earthen vessels, to show that the transcendent power belongs 8 to God and not to us. We are afflicted in every way, but not crushed; perplexed, but 9 not driven to despair; persecuted, but not forsaken; struck down, but not destroyed; 10 always carrying in the body the death of Jesus, so that the life of Jesus may also be 11 manifested in our bodies. For while we live we are always being given up to death for Jesus' sake, so that the life of Jesus may be 12 manifested in our mortal flesh. So death is at work in us, but life in you.

13 Since we have the same spirit of faith as he had who wrote, "I believed, and so I spoke," 14 we too believe, and so we speak, knowing that he who raised the Lord Jesus will raise us also with Jesus and bring us with you into 15 his presence. For it is all for your sake, so that as grace extends to more and more people it may increase thanksgiving, to the glory of God.

16 So we do not lose heart. Though our outer nature is wasting away, our inner nature is 17 being renewed every day. For this slight momentary affliction is preparing for us an eternal weight of glory beyond all compari-18 son, because we look not to the things that are seen but to the things that are unseen; for the things that are seen are transient, but the things that are unseen are eternal.

A house not made with hands

5 For we know that if the earthly tent we live in is destroyed, we have a building from God, a house not made with hands, eternal in 2 the heavens. Here indeed we groan, and long 3 to put on our heavenly dwelling, so that by putting it on we may not be found naked. 4 For while we are still in this tent, we sigh with anxiety; not that we would be un-clothed, but that we would be further clothed, so that what is mortal may be 5 swallowed up by life. He who has prepared

us for this very thing is God, who has given us the Spirit as a guarantee.

So we are always of good courage; we know 6 that while we are at home in the body we are away from the Lord, for we walk by faith, not 7 by sight. We are of good courage, and we 8 would rather be away from the body and at home with the Lord. So whether we are at 9 home or away, we make it our aim to please him. For we must all appear before the 10 judgment seat of Christ, so that each one may receive good or evil, according to what he has done in the body.

For the glory of God

Therefore, knowing the fear of the Lord, we 11 persuade men; but what we are is known to God, and I hope it is known also to your conscience. We are not commending our-12 selves to you again but giving you cause to be proud of us, so that you may be able to answer those who pride themselves on a man's position and not on his heart. For if 13 we are beside ourselves, it is for God; if we are in our right mind, it is for you. For the 14 love of Christ controls us, because we are convinced that one has died for all; therefore all have died. And he died for all, that those who 15 live might live no longer for themselves but for him who for their sake died and was raised.

A new creation

From now on, therefore, we regard no one 16 from a human point of view; even though we once regarded Christ from a human point of view, we regard him thus no longer. Therefore, if any one is in Christ, he is a new 17 creation;*g* the old has passed away, behold, the new has come. All this is from God, who 18 through Christ reconciled us to himself and gave us the ministry of reconciliation; that is, 19 God was in Christ reconciling*h* the world to himself, not counting their trespasses against them, and entrusting to us the message of reconciliation.

Ambassadors for Christ

So we are ambassadors for Christ, God 20 making his appeal through us. We beseech you on behalf of Christ, be reconciled to God. For our sake he made him to be sin 21

f Or slaves   *g* Or creature   *h* Or in Christ God was reconciling
4.4: Jn 12.31; Col 1.15.   4.6: Gen 1.3.   4.13: Ps 116.10.   4.14: 1 Thess 4.14.
5.10: Mt 16.27.   5.12: 2 Cor 3.1.   5.14: Rom 5.15; 6.6-7.   5.17: Rom 16.7; Gal 6.15.
5.18: 1 Cor 11.12; Col 1.20; Rom 5.10.   5.20: Eph 6.20.
5.21: Heb 4.15; 7.25; 1 Pet 2.22; 1 Jn 3.5; Acts 3.14.

who knew no sin, so that in him we might become the righteousness of God.

6 Working together with him, then, we entreat you not to accept the grace of God in 2 vain. For he says,
"At the acceptable time I have listened to you,
and helped you on the day of salvation."
Behold, now is the acceptable time; behold, 3 now is the day of salvation. We put no obstacle in any one's way, so that no fault 4 may be found with our ministry, but as servants of God we commend ourselves in every way: through great endurance, in 5 afflictions, hardships, calamities, beatings, imprisonments, tumults, labours, watching, 6 hunger; by purity, knowledge, forbearance, kindness, the Holy Spirit, genuine love, 7 truthful speech, and the power of God; with the weapons of righteousness for the right 8 hand and for the left; in honour and dishonour, in ill repute and good repute. We 9 are treated as impostors, and yet are true; as unknown, and yet well known; as dying, and behold we live; as punished, and yet not 10 killed; as sorrowful, yet always rejoicing; as poor, yet making many rich; as having nothing, and yet possessing everything.
11 Our mouth is open to you, Corinthians; our 12 heart is wide. You are not restricted by us, but you are restricted in your own affec-13 tions. In return—I speak as to children —widen your hearts also.

Entanglements

14 Do not be mismated with unbelievers. For what partnership have righteousness and iniquity? Or what fellowship has light with 15 darkness? What accord has Christ with Be'lial?[i] Or what has a believer in common 16 with an unbeliever? What agreement has the temple of God with idols? For we are the temple of the living God; as God said,
"I will live in them and move among them,
and I will be their God,
and they shall be my people.
17 Therefore come out from them,
and be separate from them, says the Lord,
and touch nothing unclean;
then I will welcome you,
18 and I will be a father to you,
and you shall be my sons and daughters,
says the Lord Almighty."

Since we have these promises, beloved, let 7 us cleanse ourselves from every defilement of body and spirit, and make holiness perfect in the fear of God.

Open your hearts to us; we have wronged 2 no one, we have corrupted no one, we have taken advantage of no one. I do not say this 3 to condemn you, for I said before that you are in our hearts, to die together and to live together. I have great confidence in you; I 4 have great pride in you; I am filled with comfort. With all our affliction, I am overjoyed.

The mission of Titus

For even when we came into Macedo'nia, 5 our bodies had no rest but we were afflicted at every turn—fighting without and fear within. But God, who comforts the down-6 cast, comforted us by the coming of Titus, and not only by his coming but also by the 7 comfort with which he was comforted in you, as he told us of your longing, your mourning, your zeal for me, so that I rejoiced still more. For even if I made you sorry with my letter, I 8 do not regret it (though I did regret it), for I see that that letter grieved you, though only for a while. As it is, I rejoice, not because you 9 were grieved, but because you were grieved into repenting; for you felt a godly grief, so that you suffered no loss through us. For godly grief produces a repentance 10 that leads to salvation and brings no regret, but worldly grief produces death. For see 11 what earnestness this godly grief has produced in you, what eagerness to clear yourselves, what indignation, what alarm, what longing, what zeal, what punishment! At every point you have proved yourselves guiltless in the matter. So although I wrote 12 to you, it was not on account of the one who did the wrong, nor on account of the one who suffered the wrong, but in order that your zeal for us might be revealed to you in the sight of God. Therefore we are comforted. 13
And besides our own comfort we rejoiced still more at the joy of Titus, because his mind has been set at rest by you all. For if I 14 have expressed to him some pride in you, I was not put to shame; but just as everything we said to you was true, so our boasting before Titus has proved true And his heart 15 goes out all the more to you, as he remembers the obedience of you all, and the fear and

i Greek *Beliar*
6.2: Is 49.8. 6.4: 2 Cor 4.8–11; 11.23–27. 6.5: Acts 16.23. 6.7: 2 Cor 10.4; Rom 13.12; Eph 6.11–12.
6.9: Rom 8.36. 6.10: Rom 8.32; 1 Cor 3.21. 6.11: Ezek 33.22; Is 60.5.
6.16: 1 Cor 10.21; 3.16; Ex 25.8; 29.45; Lev 26.12; Ezek 37.27; Jer 31.1. 6.17: Is 52.11.
6.18: Hos 1.10; Is 43.6. 7.2: 2 Cor 6.12–13. 7.3: 2 Cor 6.11–12. 7.5: 2 Cor 2.13; 4.8.
7.6: 2 Cor 2.13; 7.13–14. 7.8: 2 Cor 2.2. 7.12: 2 Cor 7.8; 2.3, 9.

trembling with which you received him. I rejoice, because I have perfect confidence in you.

God loves a cheerful giver

We want you to know, brethren, about the grace of God which has been shown in the churches of Macedo′nia, for in a severe test of affliction, their abundance of joy and their extreme poverty have overflowed in a wealth of liberality on their part. For they gave according to their means, as I can testify, and beyond their means, of their own free will, begging us earnestly for the favour of taking part in the relief of the saints—and this, not as we expected, but first they gave themselves to the Lord and to us by the will of God. Accordingly we have urged Titus that as he had already made a beginning, he should also complete among you this gracious work. Now as you excel in everything—in faith, in utterance, in knowledge, in all earnestness, and in your love for us—see that you excel in this gracious work also.

I say this not as a command, but to prove by the earnestness of others that your love also is genuine. For you know the grace of our Lord Jesus Christ, that though he was rich, yet for your sake he became poor, so that by his poverty you might become rich. And in this matter I give my advice: it is best for you now to complete what a year ago you began not only to do but to desire, so that your readiness in desiring it may be matched by your completing it out of what you have. For if the readiness is there, it is acceptable according to what a man has, not according to what he has not. I do not mean that others should be eased and you burdened, but that as a matter of equality your abundance at the present time should supply their want, so that their abundance may supply your want, that there may be equality. As it is written, "He who gathered much had nothing over, and he who gathered little had no lack."

But thanks be to God who puts the same earnest care for you into the heart of Titus. For he not only accepted our appeal, but being himself very earnest he is going to you of his own accord. With him we are sending the brother who is famous among all the churches for his preaching of the gospel; and not only that, but he has been appointed by the churches to travel with us in this gracious work which we are carrying on, for the glory

of the Lord and to show our good will. We intend that no one should blame us about this liberal gift which we are administering, for we aim at what is honourable not only in the Lord's sight but also in the sight of men. And with them we are sending our brother whom we have often tested and found earnest in many matters, but who is now more earnest than ever because of his great confidence in you. As for Titus, he is my partner and fellow worker in your service; and as for our brethren, they are messengers[j] of the churches, the glory of Christ. So give proof, before the churches, of your love and of our boasting about you to these men.

Now it is superfluous for me to write to you about the offering for the saints, for I know your readiness, of which I boast about you to the people of Macedo′nia, saying that Acha′ia has been ready since last year; and your zeal has stirred up most of them. But I am sending the brethren so that our boasting about you may not prove vain in this case, so that you may be ready, as I said you would be; lest if some Macedo′nians come with me and find that you are not ready, we be humiliated—to say nothing of you—for being so confident. So I thought it necessary to urge the brethren to go on to you before me, and arrange in advance for this gift you have promised, so that it may be ready not as an exaction but as a willing gift.

The point is this: he who sows sparingly will also reap sparingly, and he who sows bountifully will also reap bountifully. Each one must do as he has made up his mind, not reluctantly or under compulsion, for God loves a cheerful giver. And God is able to provide you with every blessing in abundance, so that you may always have enough of everything and may provide in abundance for every good work. As it is written,
"He scatters abroad, he gives to the poor;
his righteousness[k] endures for ever."
He who supplies seed to the sower and bread for food will supply and multiply your resources[l] and increase the harvest of your righteousness.[k] You will be enriched in every way for great generosity, which through us will produce thanksgiving to God; for the rendering of this service not only supplies the wants of the saints but also overflows in many thanksgivings to God. Under the test of this service, you[m] will glorify God by your obedience in acknowledging the gospel of

j Greek apostles   k Or benevolence   l Greek sowing   m Or they
8.3: 1 Cor 16.2.   8.4: Acts 24.17; Rom 15.31.   8.6: 2 Cor 8.16, 23; 2.13.   8.9: 2 Cor 6.10.
8.10: 2 Cor 9.2; 1 Cor 16.2–3.   8.15: Ex 16.18.   8.18: 2 Cor 12.18.   8.19: 1 Cor 16.3–4.   9.1: 2 Cor 8.4.
9.2: Rom 15.26; 2 Cor 8.10.   9.3: 1 Cor 16.2.   9.7: Prov 22.8 (Septuagint).   9.8: Eph 3.20.   9.9: Ps 112.9.
9.10: Is 55.10; Hos 10.12.   9.13: 2 Cor 8.4; Rom 15.31.

Christ, and by the generosity of your contri-
14 bution for them and for all others; while they
long for you and pray for you, because of the
15 surpassing grace of God in you. Thanks be
to God for his inexpressible gift!

Paul answers his opponents

10 I, Paul, myself entreat you, by the meekness
and gentleness of Christ—I who am humble
when face to face with you, but bold to you
2 when I am away!—I beg of you that when I
am present I may not have to show boldness
with such confidence as I count on showing
against some who suspect us of acting in
3 worldly fashion. For though we live in the
world we are not carrying on a worldly war,
4 for the weapons of our warfare are not
worldly but have divine power to destroy
5 strongholds. We destroy arguments and
every proud obstacle to the knowledge of
God, and take every thought captive to obey
6 Christ, being ready to punish every disobedience, when your obedience is complete.
7 Look at what is before your eyes. If any one
is confident that he is Christ's, let him
remind himself that as he is Christ's, so are
8 we. For even if I boast a little too much of
our authority, which the Lord gave for
building you up and not for destroying you, I
9 shall not be put to shame. I would not seem
10 to be frightening you with letters. For they
say, "His letters are weighty and strong, but
his bodily presence is weak, and his speech of
11 no account." Let such people understand
that what we say by letter when absent, we
12 do when present. Not that we venture to
class or compare ourselves with some of
those who commend themselves. But when
they measure themselves by one another, and
compare themselves with one another, they
are without understanding.
13 But we will not boast beyond limit, but will
keep to the limits God has apportioned us, to
14 reach even to you. For we are not over-
extending ourselves, as though we did not
reach you; we were the first to come all the
15 way to you with the gospel of Christ. We do
not boast beyond limit, in other men's
labours; but our hope is that as your faith
increases, our field among you may be
16 greatly enlarged, so that we may preach the
gospel in lands beyond you, without boasting
17 of work already done in another's field. "Let
18 him who boasts, boast of the Lord." For it is
not the man who commends himself that is
accepted, but the man whom the Lord
commends.

Street in a Greek city

I wish you would bear with me in a little 11
foolishness. Do bear with me! I feel a 2
divine jealousy for you, for I betrothed you
to Christ to present you as a pure bride to her
one husband. But I am afraid that as the 3
serpent deceived Eve by his cunning, your
thoughts will be led astray from a sincere and
pure devotion to Christ. For if some one 4
comes and preaches another Jesus than the
one we preached, or if you receive a different
spirit from the one you received, or if you
accept a different gospel from the one you
accepted, you submit to it readily enough. I 5
think that I am not in the least inferior to
these superlative apostles. Even if I am 6
unskilled in speaking, I am not in knowledge;
in every way we have made this plain to you
in all things.
Did I commit a sin in abasing myself so that 7
you might be exalted, because I preached
God's gospel without cost to you? I robbed 8
other churches by accepting support from
them in order to serve you. And when I was 9
with you and was in want, I did not burden
any one, for my needs were supplied by the
brethren who came from Macedo′nia. So I
refrained and will refrain from burdening
you in any way. As the truth of Christ is in 10
me, this boast of mine shall not be silenced in
the regions of Acha′ia. And why? Because I 11
do not love you? God knows I do!
And what I do I will continue to do, in 12

9.15: Rom 5.15–16. 10.1: 2 Cor 10.10. 10.2: 2 Cor 13.2, 10; 1 Cor 4.21. 10.6: 2 Cor 2.9. 10.7: 1 Cor 1.12.
10.10: 1 Cor 2.3. 10.15: Rom 15.20. 10.17: Jer 9.24. 11.1: 2 Cor 11.21. 11.2: Hos 2.19–20; Eph 5.26–27.
11.3: Gen 3.4. 11.4: Gal 1.6. 11.5: 2 Cor 12.11; Gal 2.6. 11.6: 1 Cor 1.17. 11.7: 2 Cor 12.13; 1 Cor 9.18.
11.8: Phil 4.15, 18. 11.10: 1 Cor 9.15. 11.11: 2 Cor 12.15. 11.12: 1 Cor 9.12.

order to undermine the claim of those who would like to claim that in their boasted mission they work on the same terms as we do. For such men are false apostles, deceitful workmen, disguising themselves as apostles of Christ. And no wonder, for even Satan disguises himself as an angel of light. So it is not strange if his servants also disguise themselves as servants of righteousness. Their end will correspond to their deeds.

Paul's defence

I repeat, let no one think me foolish; but even if you do, accept me as a fool, so that I too may boast a little. (What I am saying I say not with the Lord's authority but as a fool, in this boastful confidence; since many boast of worldly things, I too will boast.) For you gladly bear with fools, being wise yourselves! For you bear it if a man makes slaves of you, or preys upon you, or takes advantage of you, or puts on airs, or strikes you in the face. To my shame, I must say, we were too weak for that!

But whatever any one dares to boast of—I am speaking as a fool—I also dare to boast of that. Are they Hebrews? So am I. Are they Israelites? So am I. Are they descendants of Abraham? So am I. Are they servants of Christ? I am a better one—I am talking like a madman—with far greater labours, far more imprisonments, with countless beatings, and often near death. Five times I have received at the hands of the Jews the forty lashes less one. Three times I have been beaten with rods; once I was stoned. Three times I have been shipwrecked; a night and a day I have been adrift at sea; on frequent journeys, in danger from rivers, danger from robbers, danger from my own people, danger from Gentiles, danger in the city, danger in the wilderness, danger at sea, danger from false brethren; in toil and hardship, through many a sleepless night, in hunger and thirst, often without food, in cold and exposure. And, apart from other things, there is the daily pressure upon me of my anxiety for all the churches. Who is weak, and I am not weak? Who is made to fall, and I am not indignant?

If I must boast, I will boast of the things that show my weakness. The God and Father of the Lord Jesus, he who is blessed for ever, knows that I do not lie. At Damascus, the governor under King Ar'etas guarded the city of Damascus in order to seize me, but I was let down in a basket through a window in the wall, and escaped his hands.

I must boast; there is nothing to be gained by it, but I will go on to visions and revelations of the Lord. I know a man in Christ who fourteen years ago was caught up to the third heaven—whether in the body or out of the body I do not know, God knows. And I know that this man was caught up into Paradise—whether in the body or out of the body I do not know, God knows—and he heard things that cannot be told, which man may not utter. On behalf of this man I will boast, but on my own behalf I will not boast, except of my weaknesses. Though if I wish to boast, I shall not be a fool, for I shall be speaking the truth. But I refrain from it, so that no one may think more of me than he sees in me or hears from me. And to keep me from being too elated by the abundance of revelations, a thorn was given me in the flesh, a messenger of Satan, to harass me, to keep me from being too elated. Three times I besought the Lord about this, that it should leave me; but he said to me, "My grace is sufficient for you, for my power is made perfect in weakness." I will all the more gladly boast of my weaknesses, that the power of Christ may rest upon me. For the sake of Christ, then, I am content with weaknesses, insults, hardships, persecutions, and calamities; for when I am weak, then I am strong.

I have been a fool! You forced me to it, for I ought to have been commended by you. For I am not at all inferior to these superlative apostles, even though I am nothing. The signs of a true apostle were performed among you in all patience, with signs and wonders and mighty works. For in what were you less favoured than the rest of the churches, except that I myself did not burden you? Forgive me this wrong!

Here for the third time I am ready to come to you. And I will not be a burden, for I seek not what is yours but you; for children ought not to lay up for their parents, but parents for their children. I will most gladly spend and be spent for your souls. If I love you the more, am I to be loved the less? But granting that I myself did not burden you, I was crafty, you say, and got the better of you by guile. Did I take advantage of you through any of those whom I sent to you? I urged Titus to go, and sent the brother with him. Did Titus take advantage of you? Did

11.17: 1 Cor 7.12, 25.   11.19: 1 Cor 4.10.   11.23: Acts 16.23; 2 Cor 6.5.   11.24: Deut 25.3.
11.25: Acts 16.22; 14.19.   11.26: Acts 9.23; 14.5.   11.27: 1 Cor 4.11.   11.29: 1 Cor 9.22.
11.32-33: Acts 9.24-25.   12.4: Lk 23.43.   12.7: Job 2.6.   12.10: Rom 5.3; 2 Cor 6.4-5.   12.11: 2 Cor 11.5.
12.13: 2 Cor 11.7.   12.16: 2 Cor 11.9.   12.18: 2 Cor 2.13; 8.18.

we not act in the same spirit? Did we not take the same steps?

19 Have you been thinking all along that we have been defending ourselves before you? It is in the sight of God that we have been speaking in Christ, and all for your upbuild-

20 ing, beloved. For I fear that perhaps I may come and find you not what I wish, and that you may find me not what you wish; that perhaps there may be quarrelling, jealousy, anger, selfishness, slander, gossip, conceit,

21 and disorder. I fear that when I come again my God may humble me before you, and I may have to mourn over many of those who sinned before and have not repented of the impurity, immorality, and licentiousness which they have practised.

Paul's approaching visit

13 This is the third time I am coming to you. Any charge must be sustained by the evi-

2 dence of two or three witnesses. I warned those who sinned before and all the others, and I warn them now while absent, as I did when present on my second visit, that if I

3 come again I will not spare them—since you desire proof that Christ is speaking in me. He is not weak in dealing with you, but is

4 powerful in you. For he was crucified in weakness, but lives by the power of God. For we are weak in him, but in dealing with you we shall live with him by the power of God.

5 Examine yourselves, to see whether you are holding to your faith. Test yourselves. Do you not realise that Jesus Christ is in you?—unless indeed you fail to meet the

6 test! I hope you will find out that we have

7 not failed. But we pray God that you may not do wrong—not that we may appear to have met the test, but that you may do what is right, though we may seem to have failed.

8 For we cannot do anything against the truth,

9 but only for the truth. For we are glad when we are weak and you are strong. What we

10 pray for is your improvement. I write this while I am away from you, in order that when I come I may not have to be severe in my use of the authority which the Lord has given me for building up and not for tearing down.

11 Finally, brethren, farewell. Mend your ways, heed my appeal, agree with one another, live in peace, and the God of love

12 and peace will be with you. Greet one another with a holy kiss. All the saints greet you.

The grace of the Lord Jesus Christ and the love of God and the fellowship of[n] the Holy Spirit be with you all.

A Corinthian column

[n] Or *and participation in*

12.20: 2 Cor 2.1–4; 1 Cor 1.11; 3.3.   13.1: 2 Cor 12.14; Deut 19.15.   13.4: Phil 2.7–8; Rom 6.8.
13.10: 2 Cor 2.3.   13.12: Rom 16.16.   13.13: Phil 4.22.   13.14: Rom 16.20.

THE LETTER
OF PAUL TO THE

GALATIANS

PAUL an apostle—not from men nor through man, but through Jesus Christ and God the Father, who raised him 2 from the dead—and all the brethren who are with me,

To the churches of Galatia:

3 Grace to you and peace from God the 4 Father and our Lord Jesus Christ, who gave himself for our sins to deliver us from the present evil age, according to the will of our 5 God and Father; to whom be the glory for ever and ever. Amen.

Paul defends his authority

6 I am astonished that you are so quickly deserting him who called you in the grace of 7 Christ and turning to a different gospel—not that there is another gospel, but there are some who trouble you and want to pervert 8 the gospel of Christ. But even if we, or an angel from heaven, should preach to you a gospel contrary to that which we preached to 9 you, let him be accursed. As we have said before, so now I say again, If any one is preaching to you a gospel contrary to that which you received, let him be accursed.

10 Am I now seeking the favour of men, or of God? Or am I trying to please men? If I were still pleasing men, I should not be a servant[a] of Christ.

11 For I would have you know, brethren, that the gospel which was preached by me is not 2 man's[b] gospel. For I did not receive it from man, nor was I taught it, but it came through 3 a revelation of Jesus Christ. For you have heard of my former life in Judaism, how I persecuted the church of God violently and

tried to destroy it; and I advanced in Judaism 14 beyond many of my own age among my people, so extremely zealous was I for the traditions of my fathers. But when he who 15 had set me apart before I was born, and had called me through his grace, was pleased to 16 reveal his Son to[c] me, in order that I might preach him among the Gentiles, I did not confer with flesh and blood, nor did I go up 17 to Jerusalem to those who were apostles before me, but I went away into Arabia; and again I returned to Damascus.

Then after three years I went up to Jeru- 18 salem to visit Cephas, and remained with him fifteen days. But I saw none of the other 19 apostles except James the Lord's brother. (In what I am writing to you, before God, I 20 do not lie!) Then I went into the regions of 21 Syria and Cili′cia. And I was still not known 22 by sight to the churches of Christ in Judea; they only heard it said, "He who once 23 persecuted us is now preaching the faith he once tried to destroy." And they glorified 24 God because of me.

Then after fourteen years I went up again to **2** Jerusalem with Barnabas, taking Titus along with me. I went up by revelation; and I laid 2 before them (but privately before those who were of repute) the gospel which I preach among the Gentiles, lest somehow I should be running or had run in vain. But even 3 Titus, who was with me, was not compelled to be circumcised, though he was a Greek. But because of false brethren secretly 4 brought in, who slipped in to spy out our freedom which we have in Christ Jesus, that they might bring us into bondage—to them 5 we did not yield submission even for a

---

a Or *slave*   *b* Greek *according to man*   *c* Greek *in*
1.3: Rom 1.7.   1.4: Gal 2.20; 1 Tim 2.6.   1.5: Rom 16.27.   1.8: 2 Cor 11.4.   1.10: 1 Thess 2.4.
1.11: Rom 1.16–17.   1.13: Acts 8.3.   1.14: Acts 22.3.   1.15: Acts 9.1–19; Is 49.1; Jer 1.5.
1.18: Acts 9.26–30; 11.30.   2.1: Acts 15.2.   2.5: Acts 15.23–29.

moment, that the truth of the gospel might
6 be preserved for you. And from those who
were reputed to be something (what they
were makes no difference to me; God shows
no partiality)—those, I say, who were of
7 repute added nothing to me; but on the
contrary, when they saw that I had been
entrusted with the gospel to the uncircumcised, just as Peter had been entrusted with
8 the gospel to the circumcised (for he who
worked through Peter for the mission to the
circumcised worked through me also for the
9 Gentiles), and when they perceived the grace
that was given to me, James and Cephas and
John, who were reputed to be pillars, gave to
me and Barnabas the right hand of fellowship, that we should go to the Gentiles and
10 they to the circumcised; only they would
have us remember the poor, which very thing
I was eager to do.
11 But when Cephas came to Antioch I
opposed him to his face, because he stood
12 condemned. For before certain men came
from James, he ate with the Gentiles; but
when they came he drew back and separated
13 himself, fearing the circumcision party. And
with him the rest of the Jews acted in-
sincerely, so that even Barnabas was carried
14 away by their insincerity. But when I saw
that they were not straightforward about the
truth of the gospel, I said to Cephas before
them all, "If you, though a Jew, live like a
Gentile and not like a Jew, how can you
15 compel the Gentiles to live like Jews?" We
ourselves, who are Jews by birth and not
16 Gentile sinners, yet who know that a man is
not justified[d] by works of the law but
through faith in Jesus Christ, even we have
believed in Christ Jesus, in order to be
justified by faith in Christ, and not by works
of the law, because by works of the law shall
17 no one be justified. But if, in our endeavour
to be justified in Christ, we ourselves were
found to be sinners, is Christ then an agent of
18 sin? Certainly not! But if I build up again
those things which I tore down, then I prove
19 myself a transgressor. For I through the law
20 died to the law, that I might live to God. I
have been crucified with Christ; it is no
longer I who live, but Christ who lives in me;
and the life I now live in the flesh I live by
faith in the Son of God, who loved me and
21 gave himself for me. I do not nullify the
grace of God; for if justification[e] were
through the law, then Christ died to no
purpose.

Paul defends the truth of his message

O foolish Galatians! Who has bewitched
you, before whose eyes Jesus Christ was
publicly portrayed as crucified? Let me ask
you only this: Did you receive the Spirit by
works of the law, or by hearing with faith?
Are you so foolish? Having begun with the
Spirit, are you now ending with the flesh?
Did you experience so many things in
vain?—if it really is in vain. Does he who
supplies the Spirit to you and works miracles
among you do so by works of the law, or by
hearing with faith?
Thus Abraham "believed God, and it was
reckoned to him as righteousness." So you
see that it is men of faith who are the sons of
Abraham. And the scripture, foreseeing that
God would justify the Gentiles by faith,
preached the gospel beforehand to Abraham,
saying, "In you shall all the nations be
blessed." So then, those who are men of
faith are blessed with Abraham who had
faith.
For all who rely on works of the law are
under a curse; for it is written, "Cursed be
every one who does not abide by all things
written in the book of the law, and do
them." Now it is evident that no man is
justified before God by the law; for "He who
through faith is righteous shall live";[f] but the
law does not rest on faith, for "He who does
them shall live by them." Christ redeemed
us from the curse of the law, having become a
curse for us—for it is written, "Cursed be
every one who hangs on a tree"—that in
Christ Jesus the blessing of Abraham might
come upon the Gentiles, that we might
receive the promise of the Spirit through
faith.
To give a human example, brethren: no one
annuls even a man's will,[g] or adds to it, once
it has been ratified. Now the promises were
made to Abraham and to his offspring. It
does not say, "And to offsprings," referring
to many; but, referring to one, "And to your
offspring," which is Christ. This is what I
mean: the law, which came four hundred and
thirty years afterward, does not annul a
covenant previously ratified by God, so as to
make the promise void. For if the inheritance is by the law, it is no longer by
promise; but God gave it to Abraham by a
promise.
Why then the law? It was added because of
transgressions, till the offspring should come

---

[d] Or *reckoned righteous*; and so elsewhere   [e] Or *righteousness*   [f] Or *the righteous shall live by faith*
[g] Or *covenant* (as in verse 17)
2.6: Deut 10.17.   2.11: Acts 11.19–26.   2.16: Ps 143.2; Rom 3.20.   2.20: Gal 1.4.
3.6: Gen 15.6; Rom 4.3.   3.8: Gen 12.3; 18.18; Acts 3.25.   3.9: Rom 4.16.   3.10: Deut 27.26.
3.11: Hab 2.4; Rom 1.17; Heb 10.38.   3.12: Lev 18.5; Rom 10.5.   3.13: Deut 21.23.   3.16: Gen 12.7.
3.17: Ex 12.40.   3.18: Rom 11.6.   3.19: Rom 5.20.

to whom the promise had been made; and it was ordained by angels through an inter-
20 mediary. Now an intermediary implies more than one; but God is one.
21 Is the law then against the promises of God? Certainly not; for if a law had been given which could make alive, then righteousness would indeed be by the law.
22 But the scripture consigned all things to sin, that what was promised to faith in Jesus Christ might be given to those who believe.
23 Now before faith came, we were confined under the law, kept under restraint until faith
24 should be revealed. So that the law was our custodian until Christ came, that we might
25 be justified by faith. But now that faith has come, we are no longer under a custodian;
26 for in Christ Jesus you are all sons of God,
27 through faith. For as many of you as were baptized into Christ have put on Christ.
28 There is neither Jew nor Greek, there is neither slave nor free, there is neither male nor female; for you are all one in Christ
29 Jesus. And if you are Christ's, then you are Abraham's offspring, heirs according to promise.

4 I mean that the heir, as long as he is a child, is no better than a slave, though he is the
2 owner of all the estate; but he is under guardians and trustees until the date set by
3 the father. So with us; when we were children, we were slaves to the elemental
4 spirits of the universe. But when the time had fully come, God sent forth his Son, born
5 of woman, born under the law, to redeem those who were under the law, so that we
6 might receive adoption as sons. And because you are sons, God has sent the Spirit of his Son into our hearts, crying, "Abba!
7 Father!" So through God you are no longer a slave but a son, and if a son then an heir.
8 Formerly, when you did not know God, you were in bondage to beings that by nature are
9 no gods; but now that you have come to know God, or rather to be known by God, how can you turn back again to the weak and beggarly elemental spirits, whose slaves you
10 want to be once more? You observe days,
11 and months, and seasons, and years! I am afraid I have laboured over you in vain.
12 Brethren, I beseech you, become as I am, for I also have become as you are. You did
13 me no wrong; you know it was because of a bodily ailment that I preached the gospel to
14 you at first; and though my condition was a

trial to you, you did not scorn or despise me, but received me as an angel of God, as Christ Jesus. What has become of the satisfaction 15 you felt? For I bear you witness that, if possible, you would have plucked out your eyes and given them to me. Have I then 16 become your enemy by telling you the truth?[h] They make much of you, but for no 17 good purpose; they want to shut you out, that you may make much of them. For a 18 good purpose it is always good to be made much of, and not only when I am present with you. My little children, with whom I am 19 again in travail until Christ be formed in you! I could wish to be present with you 20 now and to change my tone, for I am perplexed about you.
Tell me, you who desire to be under law, do 21 you not hear the law? For it is written that 22 Abraham had two sons, one by a slave and one by a free woman. But the son of the 23 slave was born according to the flesh, the son of the free woman through promise. Now 24 this is an allegory: these women are two covenants. One is from Mount Sinai, bearing children for slavery; she is Hagar. Now 25 Hagar is Mount Sinai in Arabia;[i] she corresponds to the present Jerusalem, for she is in slavery with her children. But the Jerusalem 26 above is free, and she is our mother. For it is 27 written,
"Rejoice, O barren one that dost not bear;
   break forth and shout, thou who art not in
      travail;
for the desolate hath more children
   than she who hath a husband."
Now we,[j] brethren, like Isaac, are children of 28 promise. But as at that time he who was 29 born according to the flesh persecuted him who was born according to the Spirit, so it is now. But what does the scripture say? 30 "Cast out the slave and her son; for the son of the slave shall not inherit with the son of the free woman." So, brethren, we are not 31 children of the slave but of the free woman.

Paul commends the new life

For freedom Christ has set us free; stand 5 fast therefore, and do not submit again to a yoke of slavery.
Now I, Paul, say to you that if you receive 2 circumcision, Christ will be of no advantage to you. I testify again to every man who 3 receives circumcision that he is bound to keep the whole law. You are severed from 4 Christ, you who would be justified by the

h Or *by dealing truly with you*   i Other ancient authorities read *For Sinai is a mountain in Arabia*
j Other ancient authorities read *you*
3.21: Rom 8.2–4.   3.22: Rom 3.9–19; 11.32.   3.28: Rom 10.12.   4.3: Col 2.20.   4.6: Rom 8.15.
4.13: Acts 16.6.   4.19: 1 Cor 4.15.   4.22: Gen 16.15; 21.2, 9.   4.23: Rom 9.7–9.   4.27: Is 54.1.
4.29: Gen 21.9.   4.30: Gen 21.10–12.

5 law; you have fallen away from grace. For through the Spirit, by faith, we wait for the
6 hope of righteousness. For in Christ Jesus neither circumcision nor uncircumcision is of any avail, but faith working through love.
7 You were running well; who hindered you
8 from obeying the truth? This persuasion is
9 not from him who called you. A little leaven
10 leavens the whole lump. I have confidence in the Lord that you will take no other view than mine; and he who is troubling you will
11 bear his judgment, whoever he is. But if I, brethren, still preach circumcision, why am I still persecuted? In that case the stumbling
12 block of the cross has been removed. I wish those who unsettle you would mutilate themselves!

the like. I warn you, as I warned you before, that those who do such things shall not inherit the kingdom of God. But the fruit of 22 the Spirit is love, joy, peace, patience, kindness, goodness, faithfulness, gentleness, self- 23 control; against such there is no law. And 24 those who belong to Christ Jesus have crucified the flesh with its passions and desires.

If we live by the Spirit, let us also walk by 25 the Spirit. Let us have no self-conceit, no 26 provoking of one another, no envy of one another.

Brethren, if a man is overtaken in any 6 trespass, you who are spiritual should restore him in a spirit of gentleness. Look to yourself, lest you too be tempted. Bear one 2

Land-workers of Galatia

13 For you were called to freedom, brethren; only do not use your freedom as an opportunity for the flesh, but through love be
14 servants of one another. For the whole law is fulfilled in one word, "You shall love your
15 neighbour as yourself." But if you bite and devour one another take heed that you are not consumed by one another.
16 But I say, walk by the Spirit, and do not
17 gratify the desires of the flesh. For the desires of the flesh are against the Spirit, and the desires of the Spirit are against the flesh; for these are opposed to each other, to prevent you from doing what you would.
18 But if you are led by the Spirit you are not
19 under the law. Now the works of the flesh are plain: immorality, impurity, licentious-
20 ness, idolatry, sorcery, enmity, strife, jealousy, anger, selfishness, dissension, party
21 spirit, envy,^{k} drunkenness, carousing, and

another's burdens, and so fulfil the law of Christ. For if any one thinks he is some- 3 thing, when he is nothing, he deceives himself. But let each one test his own work, and 4 then his reason to boast will be in himself alone and not in his neighbour. For each 5 man will have to bear his own load.

Let him who is taught the word share all 6 good things with him who teaches.

Do not be deceived; God is not mocked, for 7 whatever a man sows, that he will also reap. For he who sows to his own flesh will from 8 the flesh reap corruption; but he who sows to the Spirit will from the Spirit reap eternal life. And let us not grow weary in well- 9 doing, for in due season we shall reap, if we do not lose heart. So then, as we have 10 opportunity, let us do good to all men, and especially to those who are of the household of faith.

^{k} Other ancient authorities add *murder*
5.6: 1 Cor 7.19; Gal 6.15.   **5.9:** 1 Cor 5.6.   **5.14:** Lev 19.18; Rom 13.8-10.   **5.17:** Rom 7.15-23.
5.19: Rom 1.28.

11 See with what large letters I am writing to
12 you with my own hand. It is those who want
to make a good showing in the flesh that
would compel you to be circumcised, and
only in order that they may not be persecuted
13 for the cross of Christ. For even those who
receive circumcision do not themselves keep
the law, but they desire to have you circumcised that they may glory in your flesh.
14 But far be it from me to glory except in the
cross of our Lord Jesus Christ, by which[1] the
world has been crucified to me, and I to the
world. For neither circumcision counts for 15
anything, nor uncircumcision, but a new
creation. Peace and mercy be upon all who 16
walk by this rule, upon the Israel of God.

Henceforth let no man trouble me; for I 17
bear on my body the marks of Jesus.

The grace of our Lord Jesus Christ be with 18
your spirit, brethren. Amen.

THE LETTER
OF PAUL TO THE
EPHESIANS

PAUL, an apostle of Christ Jesus by the
will of God,
To the saints who are also faithful[a] in
Christ Jesus:
2 Grace to you and peace from God our
Father and the Lord Jesus Christ.

The gospel of salvation

3 Blessed be the God and Father of our Lord
Jesus Christ, who has blessed us in Christ
with every spiritual blessing in the heavenly
4 places, even as he chose us in him before the
foundation of the world, that we should be
5 holy and blameless before him. He destined
us in love[b] to be his sons through Jesus
Christ, according to the purpose of his will,
6 to the praise of his glorious grace which he
7 freely bestowed on us in the Beloved. In him
we have redemption through his blood, the
forgiveness of our trespasses, according to
8 the riches of his grace which he lavished
9 upon us. For he has made known to us in all
wisdom and insight the mystery of his will,
according to his purpose which he set forth
in Christ as a plan for the fulness of time, to 10
unite all things in him, things in heaven and
things on earth.

In him, according to the purpose of him 11
who accomplishes all things according to the
counsel of his will, we who first hoped in 12
Christ have been destined and appointed to
live for the praise of his glory. In him you 13
also, who have heard the word of truth, the
gospel of your salvation, and have believed in
him, were sealed with the promised Holy
Spirit, which is the guarantee of our inheri- 14
tance until we acquire possession of it, to the
praise of his glory.

For this reason, because I have heard of 15
your faith in the Lord Jesus and your love[c]
toward all the saints, I do not cease to give 16
thanks for you, remembering you in my
prayers, that the God of our Lord Jesus 17
Christ, the Father of glory, may give you a
spirit of wisdom and of revelation in the
knowledge of him, having the eyes of your 18
hearts enlightened, that you may know what

---

[1] Or *through whom*   [a] Other ancient authorities read *who are at Ephesus and faithful*
[b] Or *before him in love, having destined us*   [c] Other ancient authorities omit *your love*
6.11: 1 Cor 16.21.   6.16: Ps 125.5.   1.3: 2 Cor 1.3.   1.6: Col 1.13.   1.7: Col 1.14.   1.10: Gal 4.4.
1.14: 2 Cor 1.22.   1.15: Col 1.9.   1.16: Col 1.3.   1.18: Deut 33.3.

is the hope to which he has called you, what are the riches of his glorious inheritance in 19 the saints, and what is the immeasurable greatness of his power in us who believe, according to the working of his great might 20 which he accomplished in Christ when he raised him from the dead and made him sit at 21 his right hand in the heavenly places, far above all rule and authority and power and dominion, and above every name that is named, not only in this age but also in that 22 which is to come; and he has put all things under his feet and has made him the head 23 over all things for the church, which is his body, the fulness of him who fills all in all.

The household of God

2 And you he made alive, when you were 2 dead through the trespasses and sins in which you once walked, following the course of this world, following the prince of the power of the air, the spirit that is now at work 3 in the sons of disobedience. Among these we all once lived in the passions of our flesh, following the desires of body and mind, and so we were by nature children of wrath, like 4 the rest of mankind. But God, who is rich in mercy, out of the great love with which he 5 loved us, even when we were dead through our trespasses, made us alive together with 6 Christ (by grace you have been saved), and raised us up with him, and made us sit with 7 him in the heavenly places in Christ Jesus, that in the coming ages he might show the immeasurable riches of his grace in kindness 8 toward us in Christ Jesus. For by grace you have been saved through faith; and this is not 9 your own doing, it is the gift of God—not because of works, lest any man should boast. 10 For we are his workmanship, created in Christ Jesus for good works, which God prepared beforehand, that we should walk in them.

11 Therefore remember that at one time you Gentiles in the flesh, called the uncircumcision by what is called the circumcision, which is made in the flesh by 12 hands—remember that you were at that time separated from Christ, alienated from the commonwealth of Israel, and strangers to the covenants of promise, having no hope and 13 without God in the world. But now in Christ Jesus you who once were far off have been 14 brought near in the blood of Christ. For he is our peace, who has made us both one, and has broken down the dividing wall of 15 hostility, by abolishing in his flesh the law of commandments and ordinances, that he

might create in himself one new man in place of the two, so making peace, and might 16 reconcile us both to God in one body through the cross, thereby bringing the hostility to an end. And he came and 17 preached peace to you who were far off and peace to those who were near; for through 18 him we both have access in one Spirit to the Father. So then you are no longer strangers 19 and sojourners, but you are fellow citizens with the saints and members of the household of God, built upon the foundation of the 20 apostles and prophets, Christ Jesus himself being the cornerstone, in whom the whole 21 structure is joined together and grows into a holy temple in the Lord; in whom you also 22 are built into it for a dwelling place of God in the Spirit.

The apostle of this gospel

For this reason I, Paul, a prisoner for Christ 3 Jesus on behalf of you Gentiles—assuming 2 that you have heard of the stewardship of God's grace that was given to me for you, how the mystery was made known to me by 3 revelation, as I have written briefly. When 4 you read this you can perceive my insight into the mystery of Christ, which was not 5 made known to the sons of men in other generations as it has now been revealed to his holy apostles and prophets by the Spirit; that 6 is, how the Gentiles are fellow heirs, members of the same body, and partakers of the promise in Christ Jesus through the gospel.

Of this gospel I was made a minister 7 according to the gift of God's grace which was given me by the working of his power. To me, though I am the very least of all the 8 saints, this grace was given, to preach to the Gentiles the unsearchable riches of Christ, and to make all men see what is the plan of 9 the mystery hidden for ages in ^{d} God who created all things; that through the church 10 the manifold wisdom of God might now be made known to the principalities and powers in the heavenly places. This was according 11 to the eternal purpose which he has realised in Christ Jesus our Lord, in whom we have 12 boldness and confidence of access through our faith in him. So I ask you not to^e lose 13 heart over what I am suffering for you, which is your glory.

Paul's prayer

For this reason I bow my knees before the 14 Father, from whom every family in heaven 15

^{d} Or by ^{e} Or I ask that I may not
1.20: Ps 110.1.   1.21: Col 1.6; 2.10, 15.   1.22: Ps 8.6; Col 1.19.   1.23: Rom 12.5; Col 2.17.   2.2: Col 1.13.
2.8: Gal 2.16.   2.12: Is 57.19.   2.17: Is 57.19.   3.2: Col 1.25.   3.6: Col 1.27.   3.9: Col 1.26.

16 and on earth is named, that according to the riches of his glory he may grant you to be strengthened with might through his Spirit 17 in the inner man, and that Christ may dwell in your hearts through faith; that you, being 18 rooted and grounded in love, may have power to comprehend with all the saints what is the breadth and length and height and 19 depth, and to know the love of Christ which surpasses knowledge, that you may be filled with all the fulness of God. 20 Now to him who by the power at work within us is able to do far more abundantly 21 than all that we ask or think, to him be glory in the church and in Christ Jesus to all generations, for ever and ever. Amen.

Paul's plea for unity

4 I therefore, a prisoner for the Lord, beg you to lead a life worthy of the calling to which 2 you have been called, with all lowliness and meekness, with patience, forbearing one 3 another in love, eager to maintain the unity 4 of the Spirit in the bond of peace. There is one body and one Spirit, just as you were called to the one hope that belongs to your 5 call, one Lord, one faith, one baptism, one 6 God and Father of us all, who is above all 7 and through all and in all. But grace was given to each of us according to the measure 8 of Christ's gift. Therefore it is said,

"When he ascended on high he led a host of captives,
and he gave gifts to men."

9 (In saying, "He ascended," what does it mean but that he had also descended into the 10 lower parts of the earth? He who descended is he who also ascended far above all the 11 heavens, that he might fill all things.) And his gifts were that some should be apostles, some prophets, some evangelists, some 12 pastors and teachers, for the equipment of the saints, for the work of ministry, for 13 building up the body of Christ, until we all attain to the unity of the faith and of the knowledge of the Son of God, to mature manhood, to the measure of the stature of the 14 fulness of Christ; so that we may no longer be children, tossed to and fro and carried about with every wind of doctrine, by the cunning of men, by their craftiness in 15 deceitful wiles. Rather, speaking the truth in love, we are to grow up in every way into him 16 who is the head, into Christ, from whom the whole body, joined and knit together by every joint with which it is supplied, when each part is working properly, makes bodily growth and upbuilds itself in love.

Christian living

Now this I affirm and testify in the Lord, 17 that you must no longer live as the Gentiles do, in the futility of their minds; they are 18 darkened in their understanding, alienated from the life of God because of the ignorance that is in them, due to their hardness of heart; they have become callous and have 19 given themselves up to licentiousness, greedy to practise every kind of uncleanness. You 20 did not so learn Christ!—assuming that you 21 have heard about him and were taught in him, as the truth is in Jesus. Put off your old 22 nature which belongs to your former manner of life and is corrupt through deceitful lusts, and be renewed in the spirit of your minds, 23 and put on the new nature, created after the 24 likeness of God in true righteousness and holiness.

Therefore, putting away falsehood, let 25 every one speak the truth with his neighbour, for we are members one of another. Be angry 26 but do not sin; do not let the sun go down on your anger; and give no opportunity to the 27 devil. Let the thief no longer steal, but 28 rather let him labour, doing honest work with his hands, so that he may be able to give to those in need. Let no evil talk come out of 29 your mouths, but only such as is good for edifying, as fits the occasion, that it may impart grace to those who hear. And do not 30 grieve the Holy Spirit of God, in whom you were sealed for the day of redemption. Let 31 all bitterness and wrath and anger and clamour and slander be put away from you, with all malice, and be kind to one another, 32 tenderhearted, forgiving one another, as God in Christ forgave you.

Therefore be imitators of God, as beloved 5 children. And walk in love, as Christ loved 2 us and gave himself up for us, a fragrant offering and sacrifice to God. But immorality and all impurity or covet- 3 ousness must not even be named among you, as is fitting among saints. Let there be no 4 filthiness, nor silly talk, nor levity, which are not fitting; but instead let there be thanksgiving. Be sure of this, that no 5 immoral or impure man, or one who is covetous (that is, an idolater), has any inheritance in the kingdom of Christ and of God. Let no one deceive you with empty 6 words, for it is because of these things that the wrath of God comes upon the sons of disobedience. Therefore do not associate 7 with them, for once you were darkness, but 8 now you are light in the Lord; walk as

4.2: Col 3.12-13.   4.8: Ps 68.18.   4.15: Col 1.18.   4.16: Col 2.19.   4.25: Zech 8.16; Rom 12.5.
5.2: Ex 29.18; Ezek 20.41.

9 children of light (for the fruit of light is found in all that is good and right and true), 10 and try to learn what is pleasing to the Lord. 11 Take no part in the unfruitful works of 12 darkness, but instead expose them. For it is a shame even to speak of the things that they 13 do in secret; but when anything is exposed by the light it becomes visible, for anything 14 that becomes visible is light. Therefore it is said,

"Awake, O sleeper, and arise from the dead,
and Christ shall give you light."

15 Look carefully then how you walk, not as 16 unwise men but as wise, making the most

cherishes it, as Christ does the church, because we are members of his body. "For 30 this reason a man shall leave his father and 31 mother and be joined to his wife, and the two shall become one." This is a great mystery, 32 and I take it to mean Christ and the church; however, let each one of you love his wife as 33 himself, and let the wife see that she respects her husband.

Domestic relationships

Children, obey your parents in the Lord, **6** for this is right. "Honour your father and 2 mother" (this is the first commandment with

Transport in the first century

of the time, because the days are evil. 17 Therefore do not be foolish, but understand 18 what the will of the Lord is. And do not get drunk with wine, for that is debauchery; but 19 be filled with the Spirit, addressing one another in psalms and hymns and spiritual songs, singing and making melody to the 20 Lord with all your heart, always and for everything giving thanks in the name of our Lord Jesus Christ to God the Father. 21 Be subject to one another out of reverence 22 for Christ. Wives, be subject to your hus- 23 bands, as to the Lord. For the husband is the head of the wife as Christ is the head of the church, his body, and is himself its 24 Saviour. As the church is subject to Christ, so let wives also be subject in everything to 25 their husbands. Husbands, love your wives, as Christ loved the church and gave himself 26 up for her, that he might sanctify her, having cleansed her by the washing of water with the 27 word, that he might present the church to himself in splendour, without spot or wrinkle or any such thing, that she might be holy and 28 without blemish. Even so husbands should love their wives as their own bodies. He who 29 loves his wife loves himself. For no man ever hates his own flesh, but nourishes and

a promise), "that it may be well with you and 3 that you may live long on the earth." Fathers, do not provoke your children to 4 anger, but bring them up in the discipline and instruction of the Lord. Slaves, be obedient to those who are your 5 earthly masters, with fear and trembling, in singleness of heart, as to Christ; not in the 6 way of eye-service, as men-pleasers, but as servants*f* of Christ, doing the will of God from the heart, rendering service with a good 7 will as to the Lord and not to men, knowing 8 that whatever good any one does, he will receive the same again from the Lord, whether he is a slave or free. Masters, do the 9 same to them, and forbear threatening, knowing that he who is both their Master and yours is in heaven, and that there is no partiality with him.

The armour of God

Finally, be strong in the Lord and in the 10 strength of his might. Put on the whole 11 armour of God, that you may be able to stand against the wiles of the devil. For we are not 12 contending against flesh and blood, but against the principalities, against the powers,

f Or *slaves*
5.16: Col 4.5. **5.19:** Col 3.16–17. **5.22–6.9:** Col 3.18–4.1. **5.31:** Gen 2.24. **6.2:** Ex 20.12. **6.3:** Deut 5.16.

against the world rulers of this present darkness, against the spiritual hosts of wicked-3 ness in the heavenly places. Therefore take the whole armour of God, that you may be able to withstand in the evil day, 4 and having done all, to stand. Stand therefore, having girded your loins with truth, and having put on the breastplate of righteous-5 ness, and having shod your feet with the 6 equipment of the gospel of peace; above all taking the shield of faith, with which you can quench all the flaming darts of the evil one. 7 And take the helmet of salvation, and the sword of the Spirit, which is the word of 8 God. Pray at all times in the Spirit, with all prayer and supplication. To that end keep alert with all perseverance, making supplica-9 tion for all the saints, and also for me, that

utterance may be given me in opening my mouth boldly to proclaim the mystery of the gospel, for which I am an ambassador in 20 chains; that I may declare it boldly, as I ought to speak.

Now that you also may know how I am and 21 what I am doing, Tych′icus the beloved brother and faithful minister in the Lord will tell you everything. I have sent him to you 22 for this very purpose, that you may know how we are, and that he may encourage your hearts.

Peace be to the brethren, and love with 23 faith, from God the Father and the Lord Jesus Christ. Grace be with all who love our 24 Lord Jesus Christ with love undying.

Phil 2, 15

THE LETTER
OF PAUL TO THE
PHILIPPIANS

PAUL and Timothy, servants*a* of Christ Jesus,
To all the saints in Christ Jesus who are at Philippi, with the bishops*b* and deacons:
2 Grace to you and peace from God our Father and the Lord Jesus Christ.

The heart of the apostle

I thank my God in all my remembrance of 3 you, always in every prayer of mine for you 4 all making my prayer with joy, thankful for 5 your partnership in the gospel from the first day until now. And I am sure that he who 6

a Or *slaves*   *b* Or *overseers*
6.14: Is 11.5; 59.17; 1 Thess 5.8.   **6.15:** Is 52.7.   **6.21–22:** Col 4.7–8.
1.1: Acts 16.1, 12–40; Rom 1.1; 2 Cor 1.1; Gal 1.10; Col 1.1; 1 Thess 1.1; 2 Thess 1.1; Philem 1.
1.2: Rom 1.7.   **1.6:** 1 Cor 1.8.

began a good work in you will bring it to
7 completion at the day of Jesus Christ. It is
right for me to feel thus about you all,
because I hold you in my heart, for you are
all partakers with me of grace, both in my
imprisonment and in the defence and con-
8 firmation of the gospel. For God is my
witness, how I yearn for you all with the
9 affection of Christ Jesus. And it is my prayer
that your love may abound more and more,
10 with knowledge and all discernment, so that
you may approve what is excellent, and may
be pure and blameless for the day of Christ,
11 filled with the fruits of righteousness which
come through Jesus Christ, to the glory and
praise of God.

12 I want you to know, brethren, that what has
happened to me has really served to advance
13 the gospel, so that it has become known
throughout the whole praetorian guard[c] and
to all the rest that my imprisonment is for
14 Christ; and most of the brethren have been
made confident in the Lord because of my
imprisonment, and are much more bold to
speak the word of God without fear.
15 Some indeed preach Christ from envy and
16 rivalry, but others from good will. The latter
do it out of love, knowing that I am put here
17 for the defence of the gospel; the former
proclaim Christ out of partisanship, not
sincerely but thinking to afflict me in my
18 imprisonment. What then? Only that in
every way, whether in pretence or in truth,
Christ is proclaimed; and in that I rejoice.
19 Yes, and I shall rejoice. For I know that
through your prayers and the help of the
Spirit of Jesus Christ this will turn out for
20 my deliverance, as it is my eager expectation
and hope that I shall not be at all ashamed,
but that with full courage now as always
Christ will be honoured in my body, whether
21 by life or by death. For to me to live is
22 Christ, and to die is gain. If it is to be life in
the flesh, that means fruitful labour for me.
23 Yet which I shall choose I cannot tell. I am
hard pressed between the two. My desire is
to depart and be with Christ, for that is far
24 better. But to remain in the flesh is more
25 necessary on your account. Convinced of
this, I know that I shall remain and continue
with you all, for your progress and joy in the
26 faith, so that in me you may have ample
cause to glory in Christ Jesus, because of my
coming to you again.
27 Only let your manner of life be worthy of
the gospel of Christ, so that whether I come
and see you or am absent, I may hear of you

that you stand firm in one spirit, with one
mind striving side by side for the faith of the
gospel, and not frightened in anything by 2
your opponents. This is a clear omen to
them of their destruction, but of your salvation, and that from God. For it has been 2
granted to you that for the sake of Christ you
should not only believe in him but also suffer
for his sake, engaged in the same conflict 3
which you saw and now hear to be mine.

The mind of Christ

So if there is any encouragement in Christ, 2
any incentive of love, any participation in the
Spirit, any affection and sympathy, complete 2
my joy by being of the same mind, having the
same love, being in full accord and of one
mind. Do nothing from selfishness or con- 3
ceit, but in humility count others better than
yourselves. Let each of you look not only to 4
his own interests, but also to the interests of
others. Have this mind among yourselves, 5
which you have in Christ Jesus, who, though 6
he was in the form of God, did not count
equality with God a thing to be grasped, but 7
emptied himself, taking the form of a servant,[d] being born in the likeness of men.
And being found in human form he humbled 8
himself and became obedient unto death,
even death on a cross. Therefore God has 9
highly exalted him and bestowed on him the
name which is above every name, that at the 10
name of Jesus every knee should bow, in
heaven and on earth and under the earth, and 11
every tongue confess that Jesus Christ is
Lord, to the glory of God the Father.

Therefore, my beloved, as you have always 12
obeyed, so now, not only as in my presence
but much more in my absence, work out your
own salvation with fear and trembling; for 13
God is at work in you, both to will and to
work for his good pleasure.

Do all things without grumbling or ques- 14
tioning, that you may be blameless and 15
innocent, children of God without blemish in
the midst of a crooked and perverse generation, among whom you shine as lights in the
world, holding fast the word of life, so that in 16
the day of Christ I may be proud that I did
not run in vain or labour in vain. Even if I 17
am to be poured as a libation upon the
sacrificial offering of your faith, I am glad
and rejoice with you all. Likewise you also 18
should be glad and rejoice with me.

I hope in the Lord Jesus to send Timothy to 19
you soon, so that I may be cheered by news of

[c] Greek *in the whole praetorium*   [d] Or *slave*
1.7: Acts 21.33; 2 Cor 7.3; Eph 6.20.   **1.10**: 1 Cor 1.8.   **1.12**: Lk 21.13.   **1.13**: Acts 28.30; 2 Tim 2.9.
1.19: Acts 16.7; 2 Cor 1.11.   **1.20**: Rom 14.8.   **1.21**: Gal 2.20.   **1.28**: 2 Thess 1.5.
1.30: Acts 16.19–40; 1 Thess 2.2.   **2.1**: 2 Cor 13.14.   **2.3–4**: Rom 12.10; 15.1–2.
2.5–8: Mt 11.29; 20.28; Jn 1.1; 2 Cor 8.9; Heb 5.8.   **2.9–11**: Rom 10.9; 14.9; Eph 1.20–21.
2.13: 1 Cor 15.10.   **2.15**: Mt 5.45, 48.

you. I have no one like him, who will be genuinely anxious for your welfare. They all look after their own interests, not those of Jesus Christ. But Timothy's worth you know, how as a son with a father he has served with me in the gospel. I hope therefore to send him just as soon as I see how it will go with me; and I trust in the Lord that shortly I myself shall come also. I have thought it necessary to send to you Epaphrodi'tus my brother and fellow worker and fellow soldier, and your messenger and minister to my need, for he has been longing for you all, and has been distressed because you heard that he was ill. Indeed he was ill, near to death. But God had mercy on him, and not only on him but on me also, lest I should have sorrow upon sorrow. I am the more eager to send him, therefore, that you may rejoice at seeing him again, and that I may be less anxious. So receive him in the Lord with all joy; and honour such men, for he nearly died for the work of Christ, risking his life to complete your service to me.

Paul and Christ

Finally, my brethren, rejoice in the Lord. To write the same things to you is not irksome to me, and is safe for you. Look out for the dogs, look out for the evil-workers, look out for those who mutilate the flesh. For we are the true circumcision, who worship God in spirit,[e] and glory in Christ Jesus, and put no confidence in the flesh. Though I myself have reason for confidence in the flesh also. If any other man thinks he has reason for confidence in the flesh, I have more: circumcised on the eighth day, of the people of Israel, of the tribe of Benjamin, a Hebrew born of Hebrews; as to the law a Pharisee, as to zeal a persecutor of the church, as to righteousness under the law blameless. But whatever gain I had, I counted as loss for the sake of Christ. Indeed I count everything as loss because of the surpassing worth of knowing Christ Jesus my Lord. For his sake I have suffered the loss of all things, and count them as refuse, in order that I may gain Christ and be found in him, not having a righteousness of my own, based on law, but that which is through faith in Christ, the righteousness from God that depends on faith; that I may know him and the power of his resurrection, and may share his sufferings, becoming like him in his death, that if possible I may attain the resurrection from the dead. Not that I have already obtained this or am

already perfect; but I press on to make it my own, because Christ Jesus has made me his own. Brethren, I do not consider that I have made it my own; but one thing I do, forgetting what lies behind and straining forward to what lies ahead, I press on toward the goal for the prize of the upward call of God in Christ Jesus. Let those of us who are mature be thus minded; and if in anything you are otherwise minded, God will reveal that also to you. Only let us hold true to what we have attained.

Brethren, join in imitating me, and mark those who so live as you have an example in us. For many, of whom I have often told you and now tell you even with tears, live as enemies of the cross of Christ. Their end is

destruction, their god is the belly, and they glory in their shame, with minds set on earthly things. But our commonwealth is in heaven, and from it we await a Saviour, the Lord Jesus Christ, who will change our lowly body to be like his glorious body, by the power which enables him even to subject all things to himself.

Paul and the Philippians

Therefore, my brethren, whom I love and long for, my joy and crown, stand firm thus in the Lord, my beloved.

I entreat Eu-o'dia and I entreat Syn'tyche to agree in the Lord. And I ask you also, true yokefellow, help these women, for they have laboured side by side with me in the gospel together with Clement and the rest of my fellow workers, whose names are in the book of life.

Rejoice in the Lord always; again I will say, Rejoice. Let all men know your forbear- ance. The Lord is at hand. Have no anxiety about anything, but in everything by prayer

---

e Other ancient authorities read *worship by the Spirit of God*
3.3: Rom 2.28–29; Gal 6.14–15.   **3.4–7:** Acts 8.3; 22.3–21; 23.6; 26.4–23; Rom 11.1; 2 Cor 11.18–31.
3.17: 1 Cor 4.15–17.   **3.21:** 1 Cor 15.35–58; Col 3.4.   **4.3:** Lk 10.20.   **4.6:** Mt 6.25–34.

and supplication with thanksgiving let your
7 requests be made known to God. And the
peace of God, which passes all understanding, will keep your hearts and your
minds in Christ Jesus.

Think about these things

8 Finally, brethren, whatever is true, whatever is honourable, whatever is just, whatever is pure, whatever is lovely, whatever is
gracious, if there is any excellence, if there is
anything worthy of praise, think about these
9 things. What you have learned and received
and heard and seen in me, do; and the God of
peace will be with you.

10 I rejoice in the Lord greatly that now at
length you have revived your concern for me;
you were indeed concerned for me, but you
11 had no opportunity. Not that I complain of
want; for I have learned, in whatever state I
12 am, to be content. I know how to be abased,
and I know how to abound; in any and all
circumstances I have learned the secret of
facing plenty and hunger, abundance and
want. I can do all things in him who
strengthens me.

Yet it was kind of you to share my trouble.
And you Philippians yourselves know that in
the beginning of the gospel, when I left
Macedo'nia, no church entered into partnership with me in giving and receiving except
you only; for even in Thessaloni'ca you sent
me help*f* once and again. Not that I seek the
gift; but I seek the fruit which increases to
your credit. I have received full payment,
and more; I am filled, having received from
Epaphrodi'tus the gifts you sent, a fragrant
offering, a sacrifice acceptable and pleasing
to God. And my God will supply every need
of yours according to his riches in glory in
Christ Jesus. To our God and Father be
glory for ever and ever. Amen.

Greet every saint in Christ Jesus. The
brethren who are with me greet you. All the
saints greet you, especially those of Caesar's
household.

The grace of the Lord Jesus Christ be with
your spirit.

THE LETTER
OF PAUL TO THE

COLOSSIANS

Grace to you and peace from God our
Father.

We always thank God, the Father of our
Lord Jesus Christ, when we pray for you,
because we have heard of your faith in Christ
Jesus and of the love which you have for all
the saints, because of the hope laid up for you
in heaven. Of this you have heard before in
the word of the truth, the gospel which has
come to you, as indeed in the whole world it
is bearing fruit and growing—so among
yourselves, from the day you heard and
understood the grace of God in truth, as you
learned it from Ep'aphras our beloved fellow
servant. He is a faithful minister of Christ on
our*a* behalf and has made known to us your
love in the Spirit.

And so, from the day we heard of it, we
have not ceased to pray for you, asking that
you may be filled with the knowledge of his
will in all spiritual wisdom and understanding, to lead a life worthy of the Lord, fully

PAUL, an apostle of Christ Jesus by the
will of God, and Timothy our brother,
2   To the saints and faithful brethren in
Christ at Colos'sae:

---

f Other ancient authorities read *money for my needs*   *a* Other ancient authorities read *your*
4.9: Rom 15.33.   4.10: 2 Cor 11.9.   4.13: 2 Cor 12.9.   4.16: Acts 17.1–9; 1 Thess 2.9.
4.23: Gal 6.18; Philem 25.   1.2: Rom 1.7.   1.3: Eph 1.16.   1.7: Col 4.12; Philem 23.   1.9: Eph 1.15–17.

pleasing to him, bearing fruit in every good work and increasing in the knowledge of God. May you be strengthened with all power, according to his glorious might, for all endurance and patience with joy, giving thanks to the Father, who has qualified us[b] to share in the inheritance of the saints in light. He has delivered us from the dominion of darkness and transferred us to the kingdom of his beloved Son, in whom we have redemption, the forgiveness of sins.

The supremacy of Christ

He is the image of the invisible God, the first-born of all creation; for in him all things were created, in heaven and on earth, visible and invisible, whether thrones or dominions or principalities or authorities—all things were created through him and for him. He is before all things, and in him all things hold together. He is the head of the body, the church; he is the beginning, the first-born from the dead, that in everything he might be pre-eminent. For in him all the fulness of God was pleased to dwell, and through him to reconcile to himself all things, whether on earth or in heaven, making peace by the blood of his cross.

And you, who once were estranged and hostile in mind, doing evil deeds, he has now reconciled in his body of flesh by his death, in order to present you holy and blameless and irreproachable before him, provided that you continue in the faith, stable and steadfast, not shifting from the hope of the gospel which you heard, which has been preached to every creature under heaven, and of which I, Paul, became a minister.

Now I rejoice in my sufferings for your sake, and in my flesh I complete what is lacking in Christ's afflictions for the sake of his body, that is, the church, of which I became a minister according to the divine office which was given to me for you, to make the word of God fully known, the mystery hidden for ages and generations[c] but now made manifest to his saints. To them God chose to make known how great among the Gentiles are the riches of the glory of this mystery, which is Christ in you, the hope of glory. Him we proclaim, warning every man and teaching every man in all wisdom, that we may present every man mature in Christ. For this I toil, striving with all the energy which he mightily inspires within me.

For I want you to know how greatly I strive 2 for you, and for those at La-odice'a, and for all who have not seen my face, that their hearts may be encouraged as they are knit together in love, to have all the riches of assured understanding and the knowledge of God's mystery, of Christ, in whom are hid all the treasures of wisdom and knowledge. I say this in order that no one may delude you with beguiling speech. For though I am absent in body, yet I am with you in spirit, rejoicing to see your good order and the firmness of your faith in Christ.

As therefore you received Christ Jesus the Lord, so live in him, rooted and built up in him and established in the faith, just as you were taught, abounding in thanksgiving.

The all-sufficiency of Christ

See to it that no one makes a prey of you by philosophy and empty deceit, according to human tradition, according to the elemental spirits of the universe, and not according to Christ. For in him the whole fulness of deity dwells bodily, and you have come to fulness of life in him, who is the head of all rule and authority. In him also you were circumcised with a circumcision made without hands, by putting off the body of flesh in the circumcision of Christ; and you were buried with him in baptism, in which you were also raised with him through faith in the working of God, who raised him from the dead. And you, who were dead in trespasses and the uncircumcision of your flesh, God made alive together with him, having forgiven us all our trespasses, having cancelled the bond which stood against us with its legal demands; this he set aside, nailing it to the cross. He disarmed the principalities and powers and made a public example of them, triumphing over them in him.[d]

Therefore let no one pass judgment on you in questions of food and drink or with regard to a festival or a new moon or a sabbath. These are only a shadow of what is to come; but the substance belongs to Christ. Let no one disqualify you, insisting on self-abasement and worship of angels, taking his stand on visions, puffed up without reason by his sensuous mind, and not holding fast to the Head, from whom the whole body, nourished and knit together through its joints and ligaments, grows with a growth that is from God.

If with Christ you died to the elemental spirits of the universe, why do you live as if

---

[b] Other ancient authorities read *you*   [c] Or *from angels and men*   [d] Or *in it* (that is, the cross)
1.13: Eph 1.21; 2.2.   **1.15:** 2 Cor 4.4.   **1.17:** Prov 8.22–31.   **1.18:** Eph 4.15.   **1.25:** Eph 3.2.
1.26: Eph 3.9.   **2.3:** Is 45.3.   **2.10:** Eph 1.21–22.   **2.15:** Eph 1.21.   **2.16:** Rom 14.1–12.
2.17: Eph 1.23.   **2.19:** Eph 1.22; 4.16.   **2.20:** Gal 4.3.

you still belonged to the world? Why do you
21 submit to regulations. "Do not handle, Do
22 not taste, Do not touch" (referring to things
which all perish as they are used), according
23 to human precepts and doctrines? These
have indeed an appearance of wisdom in
promoting rigour of devotion and self-
abasement and severity to the body, but they
are of no value in checking the indulgence of
the flesh.*

The new life in Christ

3 If then you have been raised with Christ,
seek the things that are above, where Christ
2 is, seated at the right hand of God. Set your
minds on things that are above, not on things
3 that are on earth. For you have died, and
4 your life is hid with Christ in God. When
Christ who is our life appears, then you also
will appear with him in glory.
5 Put to death therefore what is earthly in
you: immorality, impurity, passion, evil
desire, and covetousness, which is idolatry.
6 On account of these the wrath of God is
7 coming.ʲ In these you once walked, when
8 you lived in them. But now put them all
away: anger, wrath, malice, slander, and foul
9 talk from your mouth. Do not lie to one
another, seeing that you have put off the old
10 nature with its practices and have put on the

new nature, which is being renewed in
knowledge after the image of its creator.
Here there cannot be Greek and Jew, circumcised and uncircumcised, barbarian,
Scyth'ian, slave, free man, but Christ is all,
and in all.
Put on then, as God's chosen ones, holy and
beloved, compassion, kindness, lowliness,
meekness, and patience, forbearing one
another and, if one has a complaint against
another, forgiving each other; as the Lord
has forgiven you, so you also must forgive.
And above all these put on love, which binds
everything together in perfect harmony.
And let the peace of Christ rule in your
hearts, to which indeed you were called in
the one body. And be thankful. Let the
word of Christ dwell in you richly, as you
teach and admonish one another in all
wisdom, and as you sing psalms and hymns
and spiritual songs with thankfulness in your
hearts to God. And whatever you do, in
word or deed, do everything in the name of
the Lord Jesus, giving thanks to God the
Father through him.
Wives, be subject to your husbands, as is
fitting in the Lord. Husbands, love your
wives, and do not be harsh with them.
Children, obey your parents in everything,
for this pleases the Lord. Fathers, do not
provoke your children, lest they become

Ships of the period

e Or *are of no value, serving only to indulge the flesh*
ʲ Other ancient authorities add *upon the sons of disobedience*
2.22: Is 29.13; Mk 7.7.   **3.1:** Ps 110.1.   **3.10:** Gen 1.26.   **3.12-13:** Eph 4.2.   **3.16-17:** Eph 5.19.
3.18-4.1: Eph 5.22-6.9.

22 discouraged. Slaves, obey in everything those who are your earthly masters, not with eye-service, as men-pleasers, but in single-
23 ness of heart, fearing the Lord. Whatever your task, work heartily, as serving the Lord
24 and not men, knowing that from the Lord you will receive the inheritance as your reward; you are serving the Lord Christ.
25 For the wrongdoer will be paid back for the wrong he has done, and there is no partiality.

4 Masters, treat your slaves justly and fairly, knowing that you also have a Master in heaven.
2 Continue steadfastly in prayer, being
3 watchful in it with thanksgiving; and pray for us also, that God may open to us a door for the word, to declare the mystery of Christ, on
4 account of which I am in prison, that I may make it clear, as I ought to speak.
5 Conduct yourselves wisely toward out-
6 siders, making the most of the time. Let your speech always be gracious, seasoned with salt, so that you may know how you ought to answer every one.

7 Tych'icus will tell you all about my affairs; he is a beloved brother and faithful minister
8 and fellow servant in the Lord. I have sent him to you for this very purpose, that you may know how we are and that he may

encourage your hearts, and with him Ones'- 9 imus, the faithful and beloved brother, who is one of yourselves. They will tell you of everything that has taken place here.

Aristar'chus my fellow prisoner greets you, 10 and Mark the cousin of Barnabas (concerning whom you have received instructions —if he comes to you, receive him), and Jesus 11 who is called Justus. These are the only men of the circumcision among my fellow workers for the kingdom of God, and they have been a comfort to me. Ep'aphras, who is one of 12 yourselves, a servant[g] of Christ Jesus, greets you, always remembering you earnestly in his prayers, that you may stand mature and fully assured in all the will of God. For I 13 bear him witness that he has worked hard for you and for those in La-odice'a and in Hi-erap'olis. Luke the beloved physician 14 and Demas greet you. Give my greetings to 15 the brethren at La-odice'a, and to Nympha and the church in her house. And when this 16 letter has been read among you, have it read also in the church of the La-odice'ans; and see that you read also the letter from La-odice'a. And say to Archip'pus, "See 17 that you fulfil the ministry which you have received in the Lord."

I, Paul, write this greeting with my own 18 hand. Remember my fetters. Grace be with you.

g Or slave
3.23: Rom 12.11. 4.1: Lev 25.43, 53. 4.2: Rom 12.12. 4.5: Eph 5.16. 4.7–8: Eph 6.21-22.
4.9: Philem 10. 4.10–11: Acts 19.29; 27.2; Philem 24. 4.12: Col 1 7; Philem 23.
4.14: 2 Tim 4.10–11; Philem 24. 4.18: 1 Cor 16.21.

THE FIRST LETTER OF PAUL TO THE
THESSALONIANS

PAUL, Silva′nus, and Timothy,
To the church of the Thessalo′nians in
God the Father and the Lord Jesus
Christ:
Grace to you and peace.

Their faith and example

2 We give thanks to God always for you all,
constantly mentioning you in our prayers,
3 remembering before our God and Father
your work of faith and labour of love and
steadfastness of hope in our Lord Jesus
4 Christ. For we know, brethren beloved by
5 God, that he has chosen you; for our gospel
came to you not only in word, but also in
power and in the Holy Spirit and with full
conviction. You know what kind of men we
6 proved to be among you for your sake. And
you became imitators of us and of the Lord,
for you received the word in much affliction,
7 with joy inspired by the Holy Spirit; so that
you became an example to all the believers in
8 Macedo′nia and in Acha′ia. For not only has
the word of the Lord sounded forth from you
in Macedo′nia and Acha′ia, but your faith in
God has gone forth everywhere, so that we
9 need not say anything. For they themselves
report concerning us what a welcome we had
among you, and how you turned to God from
10 idols, to serve a living and true God, and to
wait for his Son from heaven, whom he
raised from the dead, Jesus who delivers us
from the wrath to come.

Their ties with the apostle

2 For you yourselves know, brethren, that our
2 visit to you was not in vain; but though we

had already suffered and been shamefully
treated at Philippi, as you know, we had
courage in our God to declare to you the
gospel of God in the face of great opposition.
For our appeal does not spring from error or 3
uncleanness, nor is it made with guile; but 4
just as we have been approved by God to be
entrusted with the gospel, so we speak, not to
please men, but to please God who tests our
hearts. For we never used either words of 5
flattery, as you know, or a cloak for greed, as
God is witness; nor did we seek glory from 6
men, whether from you or from others,
though we might have made demands as
apostles of Christ. But we were gentle[a] 7
among you, like a nurse taking care of her
children. So, being affectionately desirous of 8
you, we were ready to share with you not
only the gospel of God but also our own
selves, because you had become very dear to
us.

For you remember our labour and toil, 9
brethren; we worked night and day, that we
might not burden any of you, while we
preached to you the gospel of God. You are 10
witnesses, and God also, how holy and
righteous and blameless was our behaviour to
you believers; for you know how, like a father 11
with his children, we exhorted each one of
you and encouraged you and charged you to 12
lead a life worthy of God, who calls you into
his own kingdom and glory.

And we also thank God constantly for this, 13
that when you received the word of God
which you heard from us, you accepted it not
as the word of men but as what it really is,
the word of God, which is at work in you
believers. For you, brethren, became imita- 14
tors of the churches of God in Christ Jesus

a Other ancient authorities read *babes*
1.1: 2 Thess 1.1; 2 Cor 1.19; Acts 16.1; 17.1; Rom 1.7.   **1.2:** 2 Thess 1.3; 2.13; Rom 1.9.
1.3: 2 Thess 1.11; 1.3; Rom 8.25; 15.4; Gal 1.4.   **1.4:** 2 Thess 2.13; Rom 1.7; 2 Pet 1.10.
1.5: 2 Thess 2.14; Rom 15.19.   **1.6:** Col 2.2; 1 Thess 2.10; 1 Cor 4.16; 11.1; Acts 17.5–10; 13.52.
1.7: Rom 15.26; Acts 18.12.   **1.8:** 2 Thess 3.1; Rom 1.8.   **1.10:** Mt 3.7.   **2.2:** Acts 16.19–24; 17.1–9; Rom 1.1.
2.5: Acts 20.33.   **2.6:** 1 Cor 9.1.   **2.7:** 1 Thess 2.11; Gal 4.19.   **2.8:** 2 Cor 12.15; 1 Jn 3.16.   **2.11:** 1 Cor 4.14.
2.12: 1 Pet 5.10.   **2.13:** 1 Thess 1.2.   **2.14:** 1 Thess 1.6; 1 Cor 7.17; Gal 1.22; Acts 17.5; 2 Thess 1.4.

which are in Judea; for you suffered the same things from your own countrymen as they [15] did from the Jews, who killed both the Lord Jesus and the prophets, and drove us out, [16] and displease God and oppose all men by hindering us from speaking to the Gentiles that they may be saved—so as always to fill up the measure of their sins. But God's wrath has come upon them at last![b]

[17] But since we were bereft of you, brethren, for a short time, in person not in heart, we endeavoured the more eagerly and with great [18] desire to see you face to face; because we wanted to come to you—I, Paul, again and [19] again—but Satan hindered us. For what is our hope or joy or crown of boasting before our Lord Jesus at his coming? Is it not you? [20] For you are our glory and joy.

Timothy's visit

3 Therefore when we could bear it no longer, we were willing to be left behind at Athens [2] alone, and we sent Timothy, our brother and God's servant in the gospel of Christ, to establish you in your faith and to exhort you, [3] that no one be moved by these afflictions. You yourselves know that this is to be our [4] lot. For when we were with you, we told you beforehand that we were to suffer affliction; just as it has come to pass, and as you know. [5] For this reason, when I could bear it no longer, I sent that I might know your faith, for fear that somehow the tempter had tempted you and that our labour would be in vain. [6] But now that Timothy has come to us from you, and has brought us the good news of your faith and love and reported that you always remember us kindly and long to see [7] us, as we long to see you—for this reason, brethren, in all our distress and affliction we have been comforted about you through your [8] faith; for now we live, if you stand fast in the [9] Lord. For what thanksgiving can we render to God for you, for all the joy which we feel [10] for your sake before our God, praying earnestly night and day that we may see you face to face and supply what is lacking in your faith?

[11] Now may our God and Father himself, and [12] our Lord Jesus, direct our way to you; and may the Lord make you increase and abound in love to one another and to all men, as we

do to you, so that he may establish your [13] hearts unblamable in holiness before our God and Father, at the coming of our Lord Jesus with all his saints.

The new life

Finally, brethren, we beseech and exhort **4** you in the Lord Jesus, that as you learned from us how you ought to live and to please God, just as you are doing, you do so more and more. For you know what instructions [2] we gave you through the Lord Jesus. For [3] this is the will of God, your sanctification: that you abstain from immorality; that each [4] one of you know how to take a wife for himself in holiness and honour, not in the [5] passion of lust like heathen who do not know God; that no man transgress, and wrong his [6] brother in this matter,[c] because the Lord is an avenger in all these things, as we solemnly forewarned you. For God has not called us [7] for uncleanness, but in holiness. Therefore [8] whoever disregards this, disregards not man but God, who gives his Holy Spirit to you.

But concerning love of the brethren you [9] have no need to have any one write to you, for you yourselves have been taught by God to love one another; and indeed you do love [10] all the brethren throughout Macedo'nia. But we exhort you, brethren, to do so more and more, to aspire to live quietly, to mind your [11] own affairs, and to work with your hands, as we charged you; so that you may command [12] the respect of outsiders, and be dependent on nobody.

The coming of the Lord

But we would not have you ignorant, [13] brethren, concerning those who are asleep, that you may not grieve as others do who have no hope. For since we believe that [14] Jesus died and rose again, even so, through Jesus, God will bring with him those who have fallen asleep. For this we declare to you [15] by the word of the Lord, that we who are alive, who are left until the coming of the Lord, shall not precede those who have fallen asleep. For the Lord himself will descend [16] from heaven with a cry of command, with the archangel's call, and with the sound of the trumpet of God. And the dead in Christ will rise first; then we who are alive, who are left, [17] shall be caught up together with them in the

[b] Or *completely*, or *for ever*   [c] Or *defraud his brother in business*

2.15: Lk 24.20; Acts 2.23; 7.52.
2.16: Acts 9.23; 13.45, 50; 14.2, 5, 19; 17.5, 13; 18.12; 21.21, 27; 25.2, 7; 1 Cor 10.33; Gen 15.16; 1 Thess 1.10.
2.17: 1 Cor 5.3.   **2.19:** Phil 4.1; 1 Thess 3.13; 4.15; 5.23; Mt 16.27; Mk 8.38.
2.20: 2 Cor 1.14.   **3.1:** Phil 2.19; Acts 17.15.   **3.2:** 2 Cor 1.1; Col 1.1.   **3.3:** Acts 14.22.   **3.4:** 1 Thess 2.14.
3.5: Mt 4.3; Phil 2.16.   **3.6:** Acts 18.5.   **3.13:** 1 Cor 1.8; 1 Thess 2.19; 4.17.   **4.3:** 1 Cor 6.18.
4.4: 1 Cor 7.2; 1 Pet 3.7.   **4.11:** 2 Thess 3.12; Eph 4.28; 2 Thess 3.10–12.   **4.13:** Eph 2.12.
4.14: 2 Cor 4.14.   **4.16:** Mt 24.31; 1 Cor 15.23; 2 Thess 2.1.

clouds to meet the Lord in the air; and so we 18 shall always be with the Lord. Therefore comfort one another with these words.

5 But as to the times and the seasons, brethren, you have no need to have anything 2 written to you. For you yourselves know well that the day of the Lord will come like a 3 thief in the night. When people say, "There is peace and security," then sudden destruction will come upon them as travail comes upon a woman with child, and there will be 4 no escape. But you are not in darkness, brethren, for that day to surprise you like a 5 thief. For you are all sons of light and sons of the day; we are not of the night or of 6 darkness. So then let us not sleep, as others 7 do, but let us keep awake and be sober. For those who sleep sleep at night, and those who 8 get drunk are drunk at night. But, since we belong to the day, let us be sober, and put on the breastplate of faith and love, and for a 9 helmet the hope of salvation. For God has not destined us for wrath, but to obtain salvation through our Lord Jesus Christ, 10 who died for us so that whether we wake or 11 sleep we might live with him. Therefore encourage one another and build one another up, just as you are doing.

Be at peace

But we beseech you, brethren, to respect 12 those who labour among you and are over you in the Lord and admonish you, and to 13 esteem them very highly in love because of their work. Be at peace among yourselves. And we exhort you, brethren, admonish the 14 idle, encourage the fainthearted, help the weak, be patient with them all. See that none 15 of you repays evil for evil, but always seek to do good to one another and to all. Rejoice 16 always, pray constantly, give thanks in all 17, circumstances; for this is the will of God in 18 Christ Jesus for you. Do not quench the 19 Spirit, do not despise prophesying, but test 20, everything; hold fast what is good, abstain 21, from every form of evil. 22

May the God of peace himself sanctify you 23 wholly; and may your spirit and soul and body be kept sound and blameless at the coming of our Lord Jesus Christ. He who 24 calls you is faithful, and he will do it.

Brethren, pray for us. 25
Greet all the brethren with a holy kiss. 26
I adjure you by the Lord that this letter be 27 read to all the brethren.

The grace of our Lord Jesus Christ be with 28 you.

THE SECOND LETTER OF PAUL TO THE
THESSALONIANS

PAUL, Silva'nus, and Timothy,
To the church of the Thessalo'nians in God our Father and the Lord Jesus Christ:
2 Grace to you and peace from God the Father and the Lord Jesus Christ.

Joy in their faith

3 We are bound to give thanks to God always for you, brethren, as is fitting, because your faith is growing abundantly, and the love of every one of you for one another is increas-4 ing. Therefore we ourselves boast of you in the churches of God for your steadfastness and faith in all your persecutions and in the afflictions which you are enduring.

This is evidence of the righteous judgment 5 of God, that you may be made worthy of the kingdom of God, for which you are suffering—since indeed God deems it just to repay 6 with affliction those who afflict you, and to 7 grant rest with us to you who are afflicted, when the Lord Jesus is revealed from heaven with his mighty angels in flaming fire, inflic-8 ting vengeance upon those who do not know God and upon those who do not obey the gospel of our Lord Jesus. They shall suffer 9 the punishment of eternal destruction and exclusion from the presence of the Lord and from the glory of his might, when he comes 10 on that day to be glorified in his saints, and to be marvelled at in all who have believed, because our testimony to you was believed.

5.1: Acts 1.7.   **5.2:** 1 Cor 1.8.   **5.3:** 2 Thess 1.9.   **5.4:** 1 Jn 2.8; Acts 26.18.   **5.5:** Lk 16.8.
5.6: Rom 13.11; 1 Pet 1.13.   **5.7:** Acts 2.15; 2 Pet 2.13.   **5.8:** Eph 6.14, 17, 23; Rom 8.24.
5.9: 1 Thess 1.10; 2 Thess 2.13; Rom 14.9.
5.12: 1 Cor 16.18; 1 Tim 5.17; 1 Cor 16.16; Rom 16.6, 12; 1 Cor 15.10; Heb 13.17.   **5.13:** Mk 9.50.
5.14: Is 35.4; Rom 14.1; 1 Cor 8.7; 2 Thess 3.6, 7, 11.   **5.15:** Rom 12.17; 1 Pet 3.9.   **5.16:** Phil 4.4.
5.17: Eph 6.18.   **5.18:** Eph 5.20.   **5.19:** Eph 4.30.   **5.20:** 1 Cor 14.31.   **5.21:** 1 Cor 14.29; 1 Jn 4.1.
5.23: Rom 15.33.   **5.26:** Rom 16.16.   **5.27:** Col 4.16.   **5.28:** Rom 16.20; 2 Thess 3.18.
1.1: 1 Thess 1.1; 2 Cor 1.19; Acts 16.1.   **1.2:** Rom 1.7.   **1.3:** 1 Thess 1.2.   **1.8:** Gal 4.8.

1 To this end we always pray for you, that our God may make you worthy of his call, and may fulfil every good resolve and work of 2 faith by his power, so that the name of our Lord Jesus may be glorified in you, and you in him, according to the grace of our God and the Lord Jesus Christ.

The coming of the Lord

2 Now concerning the coming of our Lord Jesus Christ and our assembling to meet him, 2 we beg you, brethren, not to be quickly shaken in mind or excited, either by spirit or by word, or by letter purporting to be from us, to the effect that the day of the Lord has 3 come. Let no one deceive you in any way; for that day will not come, unless the rebellion comes first, and the man of lawlessness[a] 4 is revealed, the son of perdition, who opposes and exalts himself against every so-called god or object of worship, so that he takes his seat in the temple of God, proclaiming himself to 5 be God. Do you not remember that when I 6 was still with you I told you this? And you know what is restraining him now so that he 7 may be revealed in his time. For the mystery of lawlessness is already at work; only he who now restrains it will do so until he is out of 8 the way. And then the lawless one will be revealed, and the Lord Jesus will slay him with the breath of his mouth and destroy him 9 by his appearing and his coming. The coming of the lawless one by the activity of Satan will be with all power and with 10 pretended signs and wonders, and with all wicked deception for those who are to perish, because they refused to love the truth and so

be saved. Therefore God sends upon them a 11 strong delusion, to make them believe what is false, so that all may be condemned who did 12 not believe the truth but had pleasure in unrighteousness.

But we are bound to give thanks to God 13 always for you, brethren beloved by the Lord, because God chose you from the beginning[b] to be saved, through sanctification by the Spirit[c] and belief in the truth. To 14 this he called you through our gospel, so that you may obtain the glory of our Lord Jesus Christ. So then, brethren, stand firm and 15 hold to the traditions which you were taught by us, either by word of mouth or by letter. Now may our Lord Jesus Christ himself, 16 and God our Father, who loved us and gave us eternal comfort and good hope through grace, comfort your hearts and establish 17 them in every good work and word.

A closing appeal

Finally, brethren, pray for us, that the word 3 of the Lord may speed on and triumph, as it did among you, and that we may be delivered 2 from wicked and evil men; for not all have faith. But the Lord is faithful; he will 3 strengthen you and guard you from evil.[d] And we have confidence in the Lord about 4 you, that you are doing and will do the things which we command. May the Lord direct 5 your hearts to the love of God and to the steadfastness of Christ.

Now we command you, brethren, in the 6 name of our Lord Jesus Christ, that you keep away from any brother who is living in idleness and not in accord with the tradition

Eastern traders

[a] Other ancient authorities read *sin* [b] Other ancient authorities read *as the first converts* [c] Or *of spirit*
[d] Or *the evil one*
1.11: 1 Thess 1.3. **2.1:** 1 Thess 4.15–17. **2.2:** 2 Thess 3.17.
2.3: Eph 5.6–8; Dan 7.25; 8.25; 11.36; Rev 13.5; Jn 17.12. **2.4:** Ezek 28.2. **2.5:** 1 Thess 3.4.
2.8: Is 11.4. **2.9:** Mt 24.24; Jn 4.48. **2.11:** Rom 1.28. **2.13:** 2 Thess 1.3; Eph 1.4; 1 Pet 1.2.
2.15: 1 Cor 16.13; 11.2. **2.16:** 1 Thess 3.11; 1 Pet 1.3. **3.1:** 1 Thess 5.25; 1.8. **3.2:** Rom 15.31.
3.3: 1 Cor 1.9; 1 Thess 5.24. **3.6:** 1 Cor 5.4, 5, 11; 1 Thess 5.14.

7 that you received from us. For you yourselves know how you ought to imitate us; we
8 were not idle when we were with you, we did not eat any one's bread without paying, but with toil and labour we worked night and
9 day, that we might not burden any of you. It was not because we have not that right, but to give you in our conduct an example to
10 imitate. For even when we were with you, we gave you this command: If any one will
11 not work, let him not eat. For we hear that some of you are living in idleness, mere
12 busybodies, not doing any work. Now such persons we command and exhort in the Lord Jesus Christ to do their work in quietness

and to earn their own living. Brethren, do 13 not be weary in well-doing.

If any one refuses to obey what we say in 14 this letter, note that man, and have nothing to do with him, that he may be ashamed. Do 15 not look on him as an enemy, but warn him as a brother.

Now may the Lord of peace himself give 16 you peace at all times in all ways. The Lord be with you all.

I, Paul, write this greeting with my own 17 hand. This is the mark in every letter of mine; it is the way I write. The grace of our 18 Lord Jesus Christ be with you all.

THE FIRST LETTER OF PAUL TO
TIMOTHY

PAUL, an apostle of Christ Jesus by command of God our Saviour and of Christ Jesus our hope,
2 To Timothy, my true child in the faith: Grace, mercy, and peace from God the Father and Christ Jesus our Lord.

The Christian ministry

3 As I urged you when I was going to Macedo'nia, remain at Ephesus that you may charge certain persons not to teach any
4 different doctrine, nor to occupy themselves with myths and endless genealogies which promote speculations rather than the divine
5 training[a] that is in faith; whereas the aim of our charge is love that issues from a pure heart and a good conscience and sincere
6 faith. Certain persons by swerving from these have wandered away into vain discus-
7 sion, desiring to be teachers of the law, without understanding either what they are

saying or the things about which they make assertions.

Now we know that the law is good, if any 8 one uses it lawfully, understanding this, that 9 the law is not laid down for the just but for the lawless and disobedient, for the ungodly and sinners, for the unholy and profane, for murderers of fathers and murderers of mothers, for manslayers, immoral persons, 10 sodomites, kidnappers, liars, perjurers, and whatever else is contrary to sound doctrine, in accordance with the glorious gospel of the 11 blessed God with which I have been entrusted.

I thank him who has given me strength for 12 this, Christ Jesus our Lord, because he judged me faithful by appointing me to his service, though I formerly blasphemed and 13 persecuted and insulted him; but I received mercy because I had acted ignorantly in unbelief, and the grace of our Lord over- 14 flowed for me with the faith and love that are in Christ Jesus. The saying is sure and 15

---

[a] Or stewardship, or order
3.7: 1 Thess 1.6, 9.   3.8: 1 Thess 2.9; Acts 18.3; Eph 4.28.   3.9: 2 Thess 3.7.   3.10: 1 Thess 4.11.
3.11: 2 Thess 3.6.   3.12: 1 Thess 4.1, 11.   3.13: Gal 6.9.   3.16: Ruth 2.4.   3.17: 1 Cor 16.21.
3.18: Rom 16.20; 1 Thess 5.28.

worthy of full acceptance, that Christ Jesus came into the world to save sinners. And I 6 am the foremost of sinners; but I received mercy for this reason, that in me, as the foremost, Jesus Christ might display his perfect patience for an example to those who 7 were to believe in him for eternal life. To the King of ages, immortal, invisible, the only God, be honour and glory for ever and ever.*b* Amen.

8 This charge I commit to you, Timothy, my son, in accordance with the prophetic utterances which pointed to you, that inspired by them you may wage the good warfare, 9 holding faith and a good conscience. By rejecting conscience, certain persons have 10 made shipwreck of their faith, among them Hymenae'us and Alexander, whom I have delivered to Satan that they may learn not to blaspheme.

2 First of all, then, I urge that supplications, prayers, intercessions, and thanksgivings be 2 made for all men, for kings and all who are in high positions, that we may lead a quiet and peaceable life, godly and respectful in every 3 way. This is good, and it is acceptable in the 4 sight of God our Saviour, who desires all men to be saved and to come to the know- 5 ledge of the truth. For there is one God, and there is one mediator between God and men, 6 the man Christ Jesus, who gave himself as a ransom for all, the testimony to which was 7 borne at the proper time. For this I was appointed a preacher and apostle (I am telling the truth, I am not lying), a teacher of the Gentiles in faith and truth.

8 I desire then that in every place the men should pray, lifting holy hands without anger 9 or quarrelling; also that women should adorn themselves modestly and sensibly in seemly 10 apparel, not with braided hair or gold or pearls or costly attire but by good deeds, as 11 befits women who profess religion. Let a woman learn in silence with all submissive- 12 ness. I permit no woman to teach or to have 13 authority over men; she is to keep silent. For 14 Adam was formed first, then Eve; and Adam was not deceived, but the woman was de- 15 ceived and became a transgressor. Yet woman will be saved through bearing chil- dren,*c* if she continues*d* in faith and love and holiness, with modesty.

3 The saying is sure: If any one aspires to the office of bishop, he desires a noble task. 2 Now a bishop must be above reproach, the husband of one wife, temperate, sensible, 3 dignified, hospitable, an apt teacher, no

drunkard, not violent but gentle, not quarrel-some, and no lover of money. He must 4 manage his own household well, keeping his children submissive and respectful in every way; for if a man does not know how to 5 manage his own household, how can he care for God's church? He must not be a recent 6 convert, or he may be puffed up with conceit and fall into the condemnation of the devil;*e* moreover he must be well thought of by 7 outsiders, or he may fall into reproach and the snare of the devil.*e*

Deacons likewise must be serious, not 8 double-tongued, not addicted to much wine, not greedy for gain; they must hold the 9 mystery of the faith with a clear conscience. And let them also be tested first; then if they 10 prove themselves blameless let them serve as deacons. The women likewise must be 11 serious, no slanderers, but temperate, faith-ful in all things. Let deacons be the husband 12 of one wife, and let them manage their children and their households well; for those 13 who serve well as deacons gain a good standing for themselves and also great con-fidence in the faith which is in Christ Jesus.

I hope to come to you soon, but I am 14 writing these instructions to you so that, if I 15 am delayed, you may know how one ought to behave in the household of God, which is the church of the living God, the pillar and bulwark of the truth. Great indeed, we 16 confess, is the mystery of our religion:

He*f* was manifested in the flesh,
    vindicated*g* in the Spirit,
      seen by angels,
    preached among the nations,
    believed on in the world,
      taken up in glory.

The good minister

4 Now the Spirit expressly says that in later times some will depart from the faith by giving heed to deceitful spirits and doctrines of demons, through the pretensions of liars 2 whose consciences are seared, who forbid 3 marriage and enjoin abstinence from foods which God created to be received with thanksgiving by those who believe and know the truth. For everything created by God 4 is good, and nothing is to be rejected if it is received with thanksgiving; for then it is 5 consecrated by the word of God and prayer.

If you put these instructions before the 6 brethren, you will be a good minister of Christ Jesus, nourished on the words of the faith and of the good doctrine which you

---

b Greek *to the ages of ages*   *c* Or *by the birth of the child*   *d* Greek *they continue*   *e* Or *slanderer*
f Greek *Who*; other ancient authorities read *God*; others, *Which*   *g* Or *justified*
2.13: Gen 2.7, 21–22.   2.14: Gen 3.1–6.

7 have followed. Have nothing to do with godless and silly myths. Train yourself in 8 godliness; for while bodily training is of some value, godliness is of value in every way, as it holds promise for the present life and also for 9 the life to come. The saying is sure and 10 worthy of full acceptance. For to this end we toil and strive, [h] because we have our hope set on the living God, who is the Saviour of all men, especially of those who believe.

11, Command and teach these things. Let no 12 one despise your youth, but set the believers an example in speech and conduct, in love, in 13 faith, in purity. Till I come, attend to the public reading of scripture, to preaching, to 14 teaching. Do not neglect the gift you have, which was given you by prophetic utterance when the elders laid their hands upon you. 15 Practise these duties, devote yourself to them, so that all may see your progress. 16 Take heed to yourself and to your teaching; hold to that, for by so doing you will save both yourself and your hearers.

5 Do not rebuke an older man but exhort him as you would a father; treat younger men like 2 brothers, older women like mothers, younger women like sisters, in all purity.

3, Honour widows who are real widows. If a 4 widow has children or grandchildren, let them first learn their religious duty to their own family and make some return to their parents; for this is acceptable in the sight of 5 God. She who is a real widow, and is left all alone, has set her hope on God and continues in supplications and prayers night and day; 6 whereas she who is self-indulgent is dead 7 even while she lives. Command this, so that 8 they may be without reproach. If any one does not provide for his relatives, and especially for his own family, he has disowned the faith and is worse than an unbeliever.

9 Let a widow be enrolled if she is not less than sixty years of age, having been the wife 10 of one husband; and she must be well attested for her good deeds, as one who has brought up children, shown hospitality, washed the feet of the saints, relieved the afflicted, and devoted herself to doing good 11 in every way. But refuse to enrol younger widows; for when they grow wanton against 12 Christ they desire to marry, and so they incur condemnation for having violated their first 13 pledge. Besides that, they learn to be idlers, gadding about from house to house, and not only idlers but gossips and busybodies, 14 saying what they should not. So I would

have younger widows marry, bear children, rule their households, and give the enemy no occasion to revile us. For some have already 1 strayed after Satan. If any believing woman[i] 16 has relatives who are widows, let her assist them; let the church not be burdened, so that it may assist those who are real widows.

Let the elders who rule well be considered 1 worthy of double honour, especially those who labour in preaching and teaching; for 18 the scripture says, "You shall not muzzle an ox when it is treading out the grain," and, "The labourer deserves his wages." Never 19 admit any charge against an elder except on the evidence of two or three witnesses. As 20 for those who persist in sin, rebuke them in the presence of all, so that the rest may stand in fear. In the presence of God and of Christ 21 Jesus and of the elect angels I charge you to keep these rules without favour, doing nothing from partiality. Do not be hasty in 22 the laying on of hands, nor participate in another man's sins; keep yourself pure.

No longer drink only water, but use a little 23 wine for the sake of your stomach and your frequent ailments.

The sins of some men are conspicuous, 24 pointing to judgment, but the sins of others appear later. So also good deeds are con- 25 spicuous; and even when they are not, they cannot remain hidden.

Let all who are under the yoke of slavery **6** regard their masters as worthy of all honour, so that the name of God and the teaching may not be defamed. Those who have 2 believing masters must not be disrespectful on the ground that they are brethren; rather they must serve all the better since those who benefit by their service are believers and beloved.

Teach and urge these duties. If any one 3 teaches otherwise and does not agree with the sound words of our Lord Jesus Christ and the teaching which accords with godliness, he is puffed up with conceit, he knows 4 nothing; he has a morbid craving for controversy and for disputes about words, which produce envy, dissension, slander, base suspicions, and wrangling among men who 5 are depraved in mind and bereft of the truth, imagining that godliness is a means of gain. There is great gain in godliness with con- 6 tentment; for we brought nothing into the 7 world, and[j] we cannot take anything out of the world; but if we have food and clothing, 8 with these we shall be content. But those 9 who desire to be rich fall into temptation,

[h] Other ancient authorities read *suffer reproach*
[i] Other ancient authorities read *man or woman*; others, simply *man*
[j] Other ancient authorities insert *it is certain that*
5.18: Deut 25.4; 1 Cor 9.9; Mt 10.10; Lk 10.7; 1 Cor 9.14.   5.19: Deut 19.15.

into a snare, into many senseless and hurtful desires that plunge men into ruin and destruction. For the love of money is the root of all evils; it is through this craving that some have wandered away from the faith and pierced their hearts with many pangs.

Fight the good fight

But as for you, man of God, shun all this; aim at righteousness, godliness, faith, love, steadfastness, gentleness. Fight the good fight of the faith; take hold of the eternal life to which you were called when you made the good confession in the presence of many witnesses. In the presence of God who gives life to all things, and of Christ Jesus who in his testimony before Pontius Pilate made the good confession, I charge you to keep the commandment unstained and free from reproach until the appearing of our Lord Jesus Christ; and this will be made manifest at the proper time by the blessed and only Sovereign, the King of kings and Lord of lords, who alone has immortality and dwells 16 in unapproachable light, whom no man has ever seen or can see. To him be honour and eternal dominion. Amen.

The use of riches

As for the rich in this world, charge them 17 not to be haughty, nor to set their hopes on uncertain riches but on God who richly furnishes us with everything to enjoy. They 18 are to do good, to be rich in good deeds, liberal and generous, thus laying up for 19 themselves a good foundation for the future, so that they may take hold of the life which is life indeed.

O Timothy, guard what has been entrusted 20 to you. Avoid the godless chatter and contradictions of what is falsely called knowledge, for by professing it some have missed 21 the mark as regards the faith.

Grace be with you.

THE SECOND LETTER OF PAUL TO

TIMOTHY

PAUL, an apostle of Christ Jesus by the will of God according to the promise of the life which is in Christ Jesus,

2 To Timothy, my beloved child:

Grace, mercy, and peace from God the Father and Christ Jesus our Lord.

Timothy the beloved

3 I thank God whom I serve with a clear conscience, as did my fathers, when I
4 remember you constantly in my prayers. As I remember your tears, I long night and day
5 to see you, that I may be filled with joy. I am reminded of your sincere faith, a faith that dwelt first in your grandmother Lo'is and your mother Eunice and now, I am sure,
6 dwells in you. Hence I remind you to rekindle the gift of God that is within you
7 through the laying on of my hands; for God did not give us a spirit of timidity but a spirit of power and love and self-control.
8 Do not be ashamed then of testifying to our Lord, nor of me his prisoner, but take your share of suffering for the gospel in the power
9 of God, who saved us and called us with a holy calling, not in virtue of our works but in virtue of his own purpose and the grace which he gave us in Christ Jesus ages ago, and now has manifested through the appear- 10 ing of our Saviour Christ Jesus, who abolished death and brought life and immortality to light through the gospel. For 11 this gospel I was appointed a preacher and apostle and teacher, and therefore I suffer as 12 I do. But I am not ashamed, for I know whom I have believed, and I am sure that he is able to guard until that Day what has been entrusted to me.[a] Follow the pattern of the 13 sound words which you have heard from me, in the faith and love which are in Christ Jesus; guard the truth that has been en- 14 trusted to you by the Holy Spirit who dwells within us.

You are aware that all who are in Asia 15 turned away from me, and among them Phy'gelus and Hermog'enes. May the Lord 16 grant mercy to the household of Onesiph'- orus, for he often refreshed me; he was not ashamed of my chains, but when he arrived 17 in Rome he searched for me eagerly and found me—may the Lord grant him to find 18 mercy from the Lord on that Day—and you well know all the service he rendered at Ephesus.

a Or what I have entrusted to him
6.13: Jn 18.37. 1.5: Acts 16.1.

II Tim 1, 16

God's soldier and workman

2 You then, my son, be strong in the grace
2 that is in Christ Jesus, and what you have
heard from me before many witnesses entrust to faithful men who will be able to teach
3 others also. Take your share of suffer-
4 ing as a good soldier of Christ Jesus. No
soldier on service gets entangled in civilian
pursuits, since his aim is to satisfy the one
5 who enlisted him. An athlete is not crowned
6 unless he competes according to the rules. It
is the hard-working farmer who ought to

7 have the first share of the crops. Think over
what I say, for the Lord will grant you
understanding in everything.
8 Remember Jesus Christ, risen from the
dead, descended from David, as preached in
9 my gospel, the gospel for which I am suffering and wearing fetters like a criminal. But
10 the word of God is not fettered. Therefore I
endure everything for the sake of the elect,

that they also may obtain the salvation which
in Christ Jesus goes with eternal glory. The 11
saying is sure:
If we have died with him, we shall also live
with him;
if we endure, we shall also reign with him; 12
if we deny him, he also will deny us;
if we are faithless, he remains faithful— 13
for he cannot deny himself.
Remind them of this, and charge them 14
before the Lord[b] to avoid disputing about
words, which does no good, but only ruins
the hearers. Do your best to present yourself 15
to God as one approved, a workman who has
no need to be ashamed, rightly handling the
word of truth. Avoid such godless chatter, 16
for it will lead people into more and more
ungodliness, and their talk will eat its way 17
like gangrene. Among them are Hymenae'us
and Phile'tus, who have swerved from the 18
truth by holding that the resurrection is past
already. They are upsetting the faith of
some. But God's firm foundation stands, 19
bearing this seal: "The Lord knows those
who are his," and, "Let every one who
names the name of the Lord depart from
iniquity."
In a great house there are not only vessels 20
of gold and silver but also of wood and
earthenware, and some for noble use, some
for ignoble. If any one purifies himself from 21
what is ignoble, then he will be a vessel for
noble use, consecrated and useful to the
master of the house, ready for any good
work. So shun youthful passions and aim at 22
righteousness, faith, love, and peace, along
with those who call upon the Lord from a
pure heart. Have nothing to do with stupid, 23
senseless controversies; you know that they

b Other ancient authorities read God
2.19: Num 16.5; Is 26.13.

24 breed quarrels. And the Lord's servant must not be quarrelsome but kindly to every one, 25 an apt teacher, forbearing, correcting his opponents with gentleness. God may perhaps grant that they will repent and come to 26 know the truth, and they may escape from the snare of the devil, after being captured by him to do his will.[c]

Times of stress

3 But understand this, that in the last days 2 there will come times of stress. For men will be lovers of self, lovers of money, proud, arrogant, abusive, disobedient to their par- 3 ents, ungrateful, unholy, inhuman, implacable, slanderers, profligates, fierce, haters of 4 good, treacherous, reckless, swollen with conceit, lovers of pleasure rather than lovers 5 of God, holding the form of religion but denying the power of it. Avoid such people. 6 For among them are those who make their way into households and capture weak women, burdened with sins and swayed by various impulses, who will listen to anybody 7 and can never arrive at a knowledge of the truth. As Jannes and Jambres opposed 8 Moses, so these men also oppose the truth, men of corrupt mind and counterfeit faith; but they will not get very far, for their folly 9 will be plain to all, as was that of those two men.

Now you have observed my teaching, 10 my conduct, my aim in life, my faith, my patience, my love, my steadfastness, my 11 persecutions, my sufferings, what befell me at Antioch, at Ico′nium, and at Lystra, what persecutions I endured; yet from them all the Lord rescued me. Indeed all who desire to 12 live a godly life in Christ Jesus will be persecuted, while evil men and impostors 13 will go on from bad to worse, deceivers and deceived. But as for you, continue in what 14 you have learned and have firmly believed, knowing from whom you learned it and how 15 from childhood you have been acquainted with the sacred writings which are able to instruct you for salvation through faith in Christ Jesus. All scripture is inspired by 16

In an ancient library

God and[d] profitable for teaching, for reproof, for correction, and for training in
17 righteousness, that the man of God may be complete, equipped for every good work.

A farewell charge

4 I charge you in the presence of God and of Christ Jesus who is to judge the living and the dead, and by his appearing and his
2 kingdom: preach the word, be urgent in season and out of season, convince, rebuke, and exhort, be unfailing in patience and in
3 teaching. For the time is coming when people will not endure sound teaching, but having itching ears they will accumulate for themselves teachers to suit their own likings,
4 and will turn away from listening to the truth
5 and wander into myths. As for you, always be steady, endure suffering, do the work of an evangelist, fulfil your ministry.
6 For I am already on the point of being sacrificed; the time of my departure has
7 come. I have fought the good fight, I have finished the race, I have kept the faith.
8 Henceforth there is laid up for me the crown of righteousness, which the Lord, the righteous judge, will award to me on that Day, and not only to me but also to all who have loved his appearing.
9, Do your best to come to me soon. For
10 Demas, in love with this present world, has

deserted me and gone to Thessaloni′ca; Crescens has gone to Galatia,[e] Titus to Dalmatia. Luke alone is with me. Get Mark 11 and bring him with you; for he is very useful in serving me. Tych′icus I have sent to 12 Ephesus. When you come, bring the cloak 13 that I left with Carpus at Tro′as, also the books, and above all the parchments. Alexander the coppersmith did me great 14 harm; the Lord will requite him for his deeds. Beware of him yourself, for he 15 strongly opposed our message. At my first 16 defence no one took my part; all deserted me. May it not be charged against them! But the Lord stood by me and gave me 17 strength to proclaim the word fully, that all the Gentiles might hear it. So I was rescued from the lion's mouth. The Lord will rescue 18 me from every evil and save me for his heavenly kingdom. To him be the glory for ever and ever. Amen.

Greet Prisca and Aquila, and the household 19 of Onesiph′orus. Eras′tus remained at 20 Corinth; Troph′imus I left ill at Mile′tus. Do your best to come before winter. 21 Eubu′lus sends greetings to you, as do Pudens and Linus and Claudia and all the brethren.
The Lord be with your spirit. Grace be 22 with you.

THE LETTER OF PAUL TO
TITUS

P AUL, a servant[a] of God and an apostle of Jesus Christ, to further the faith of God's elect and their knowledge of the
2 truth which accords with godliness, in hope of eternal life which God, who never lies,
3 promised ages ago and at the proper time manifested in his word through the preaching with which I have been entrusted by command of God our Saviour;
4 To Titus, my true child in a common faith: Grace and peace from God the Father and Christ Jesus our Saviour.

Stewards of God

5 This is why I left you in Crete, that you might amend what was defective, and

appoint elders in every town as I directed you, if any man is blameless, the husband of 6 one wife, and his children are believers and not open to the charge of being profligate or insubordinate. For a bishop, as God's 7 steward, must be blameless; he must not be arrogant or quick-tempered or a drunkard or violent or greedy for gain, but hospitable, 8 a lover of goodness, master of himself, upright, holy, and self-controlled; he must 9 hold firm to the sure word as taught, so that he may be able to give instruction in sound doctrine and also to confute those who contradict it. For there are many insub- 10 ordinate men, empty talkers and deceivers, especially the circumcision party; they must 11 be silenced, since they are upsetting whole

[d] Or Every scripture inspired by God is also   [e] Other ancient authorities read Gaul   [a] Or slave

families by teaching for base gain what they have no right to teach. One of themselves, a prophet of their own, said, "Cretans are always liars, evil beasts, lazy gluttons." This testimony is true. Therefore rebuke them sharply, that they may be sound in the faith, instead of giving heed to Jewish myths or to commands of men who reject the truth. To the pure all things are pure, but to the corrupt and unbelieving nothing is pure; their very minds and consciences are corrupted. They profess to know God, but they deny him by their deeds; they are detestable, disobedient, unfit for any good deed.

Sound doctrine

But as for you, teach what befits sound doctrine. Bid the older men be temperate, serious, sensible, sound in faith, in love, and in steadfastness. Bid the older women likewise to be reverent in behaviour, not to be slanderers or slaves to drink; they are to teach what is good, and so train the young women to love their husbands and children, to be sensible, chaste, domestic, kind, and submissive to their husbands, that the word of God may not be discredited. Likewise urge the younger men to control themselves. Show yourself in all respects a model of good deeds, and in your teaching show integrity, gravity, and sound speech that cannot be censured, so that an opponent may be put to shame, having nothing evil to say of us. Bid slaves to be submissive to their masters and to give satisfaction in every respect; they are not to be refractory, nor to pilfer, but to show entire and true fidelity, so that in everything they may adorn the doctrine of God our Saviour.

For the grace of God has appeared for the salvation of all men, training us to renounce irreligion and worldly passions, and to live sober, upright, and godly lives in this world, awaiting our blessed hope, the appearing of the glory of our great God and Saviour[b] Jesus Christ, who gave himself for us to redeem us from all iniquity and to purify for himself a people of his own who are zealous for good deeds.

Declare these things; exhort and reprove with all authority. Let no one disregard you.

The way to live

Remind them to be submissive to rulers and authorities, to be obedient, to be ready for any honest work, to speak evil of no one, to avoid quarrelling, to be gentle, and to show perfect courtesy toward all men. For we ourselves were once foolish, disobedient, led astray, slaves to various passions and pleasures, passing our days in malice and envy, hated by men and hating one another; but when the goodness and loving kindness of God our Saviour appeared, he saved us, not because of deeds done by us in righteousness, but in virtue of his own mercy, by the washing of regeneration and renewal in the Holy Spirit, which he poured out upon us richly through Jesus Christ our Saviour, so that we might be justified by his grace and become heirs in hope of eternal life. The saying is sure.

I desire you to insist on these things, so that those who have believed in God may be careful to apply themselves to good deeds;[c] these are excellent and profitable to men. But avoid stupid controversies, genealogies, dissensions, and quarrels over the law, for they are unprofitable and futile. As for a man who is factious, after admonishing him once or twice, have nothing more to do with him, knowing that such a person is perverted and sinful; he is self-condemned.

When I send Artemas or Tych'icus to you, do your best to come to me at Nicop'olis, for I have decided to spend the winter there. Do your best to speed Zenas the lawyer and Apol'los on their way; see that they lack nothing. And let our people learn to apply themselves to good deeds,[c] so as to help cases of urgent need, and not to be unfruitful.

All who are with me send greetings to you. Greet those who love us in the faith.

Grace be with you all.

---

b Or *of the great God and our Saviour* c Or *enter honourable occupations*
1.12: Epimenides. **2.14**: Ps 130.8; Ezek 37.23; Deut 14.2.

THE LETTER OF PAUL TO
PHILEMON

PAUL, a prisoner for Christ Jesus, and Timothy our brother,

To Phile′mon our beloved fellow 2 worker and Ap′phia our sister and Archip′pus our fellow soldier, and the church in your house:

3 Grace to you and peace from God our Father and the Lord Jesus Christ.

4 I thank my God always when I remember 5 you in my prayers, because I hear of your love and of the faith which you have toward 6 the Lord Jesus and all the saints, and I pray that the sharing of your faith may promote the knowledge of all the good that is ours in 7 Christ. For I have derived much joy and comfort from your love, my brother, because the hearts of the saints have been refreshed through you.

8 Accordingly, though I am bold enough in Christ to command you to do what is re-9 quired, yet for love's sake I prefer to appeal to you—I, Paul, an ambassador*a* and now a 10 prisoner also for Christ Jesus—I appeal to you for my child, Ones′imus, whose father I 11 have become in my imprisonment. (For-merly he was useless to you, but now he is 12 indeed useful*b* to you and to me.) I am sending him back to you, sending my very 13 heart. I would have been glad to keep him with me, in order that he might serve me on your behalf during my imprisonment for the gospel; but I preferred to do nothing without 14 your consent in order that your goodness might not be by compulsion but of your own free will.

Perhaps this is why he was parted from you 15 for a while, that you might have him back for ever, no longer as a slave but more than a 16 slave, as a beloved brother, especially to me but how much more to you, both in the flesh and in the Lord. So if you consider me your 17 partner, receive him as you would receive me. If he has wronged you at all, or owes 18 you anything, charge that to my account. I, 19 Paul, write this with my own hand, I will repay it—to say nothing of your owing me even your own self. Yes, brother, I want 20 some benefit from you in the Lord. Refresh my heart in Christ.

Confident of your obedience, I write to you, 21 knowing that you will do even more than I say. At the same time, prepare a guest room 22 for me, for I am hoping through your prayers to be granted to you.

Ep′aphras, my fellow prisoner in Christ 23 Jesus, sends greetings to you, and so do 24 Mark, Aristar′chus, Demas, and Luke, my fellow workers.

The grace of the Lord Jesus Christ be with 25 your spirit.

---

a Or *an old man* *b* The name Onesimus means *useful* or (compare verse 20) *beneficial*
3: Rom 1.7. **4:** Rom 1.8. **10:** Col 4.9. **23:** Col 1.7; 4.12. **24:** Col 4.10, 14.

THE LETTER TO THE

HEBREWS

IN many and various ways God spoke of old to our fathers by the prophets; 2 but in these last days he has spoken to us by a Son, whom he appointed the heir of all things, through whom also he created the 3 world. He reflects the glory of God and bears the very stamp of his nature, upholding the universe by his word of power. When he had made purification for sins, he sat down at 4 the right hand of the Majesty on high, having become as much superior to angels as the name he has obtained is more excellent than theirs.

5 For to what angel did God ever say,
    "Thou art my Son,
        today I have begotten thee"?
Or again,
    "I will be to him a father,
        and he shall be to me a son"?
6 And again, when he brings the firstborn into the world, he says,
    "Let all God's angels worship him."
7 Of the angels he says,
    "Who makes his angels winds,
        and his servants flames of fire."
8 But of the Son he says,
    "Thy throne, O God,[a] is for ever and ever,
        the righteous sceptre is the sceptre of thy[b] kingdom.
9   Thou hast loved righteousness and hated lawlessness;
        therefore God, thy God, has anointed thee
        with the oil of gladness beyond thy comrades."
10 And,
    "Thou, Lord, didst found the earth in the beginning,
        and the heavens are the work of thy hands;
11   they will perish, but thou remainest;
        they will all grow old like a garment,
12   like a mantle thou wilt roll them up,

and they will be changed.[c]
But thou art the same,
    and thy years will never end."
But to what angel has he ever said, 13
    "Sit at my right hand,
        till I make thy enemies
        a stool for thy feet"?
Are they not all ministering spirits sent forth 14 to serve, for the sake of those who are to obtain salvation?

Therefore we must pay the closer attention 2 to what we have heard, lest we drift away from it. For if the message declared by 2 angels was valid and every transgression or disobedience received a just retribution, how 3 shall we escape if we neglect such a great salvation? It was declared at first by the Lord, and it was attested to us by those who heard him, while God also bore witness by 4 signs and wonders and various miracles and by gifts of the Holy Spirit distributed according to his own will.

For it was not to angels that God subjected 5 the world to come, of which we are speaking. It has been testified somewhere, 6
    "What is man that thou art mindful of him,
        or the son of man, that thou carest for him?
    Thou didst make him for a little while 7 lower than the angels,
        thou hast crowned him with glory and honour,[d]
    putting everything in subjection under his 8 feet."
Now in putting everything in subjection to him, he left nothing outside his control. As it is, we do not yet see everything in subjection to him. But we see Jesus, who for a little 9 while was made lower than the angels,

---

a Or *God is thy throne*   b Other ancient authorities read *his*   c Other ancient authorities add *like a garment*
d Other ancient authorities insert *and didst set him over the works of thy hands*
1.5: Ps 2.7; 2 Sam 7.14.   1.6: Deut 32.43 (Septuagint); Ps 97.7.   1.7: Ps 104.4.   1.8–9: Ps 45.6–7.
1.10–12: Ps 102.25–27.   1.13: Ps 110.1.   2.6–9: Ps 8.4–6.

crowned with glory and honour because of the suffering of death, so that by the grace of God he might taste death for every one.
10 For it was fitting that he, for whom and by whom all things exist, in bringing many sons to glory, should make the pioneer of their
11 salvation perfect through suffering. For he who sanctifies and those who are sanctified have all one origin. That is why he is not
12 ashamed to call them brethren, saying,

"I will proclaim thy name to my brethren,
in the midst of the congregation I will praise thee."

13 And again,

"I will put my trust in him."

And again,

"Here am I, and the children God has given me."

14 Since therefore the children share in flesh and blood, he himself likewise partook of the same nature, that through death he might destroy him who has the power of death, that
15 is, the devil, and deliver all those who through fear of death were subject to lifelong
16 bondage. For surely it is not with angels that

he is concerned but with the descendants of
17 Abraham. Therefore he had to be made like his brethren in every respect, so that he might become a merciful and faithful high priest in the service of God, to make expia-
18 tion for the sins of the people. For because he himself has suffered and been tempted, he is able to help those who are tempted.

Jesus and Moses

3 Therefore, holy brethren, who share in a heavenly call, consider Jesus, the apostle and
2 high priest of our confession. He was faithful to him who appointed him, just as
3 Moses also was faithful in^e God's house. Yet Jesus has been counted worthy of as much more glory than Moses as the builder of a
4 house has more honour than the house. (For

every house is built by some one, but the builder of all things is God.) Now Moses 5 was faithful in all God's house as a servant, to testify to the things that were to be spoken later, but Christ was faithful over God's^f 6 house as a son. And we are his house if we hold fast our confidence and pride in our hope.^g

Therefore, as the Holy Spirit says, 7
"Today, when you hear his voice,
do not harden your hearts as in the 8 rebellion,
on the day of testing in the wilderness,
where your fathers put me to the test 9
and saw my works for forty years.
Therefore I was provoked with that 10 generation,
and said, 'They always go astray in their hearts;
they have not known my ways.'
As I swore in my wrath, 11
'They shall never enter my rest.'"

Take care, brethren, lest there be in any of 12 you an evil, unbelieving heart, leading you to fall away from the living God. But exhort 13 one another every day, as long as it is called "today," that none of you may be hardened by the deceitfulness of sin. For we share in 14 Christ, if only we hold our first confidence firm to the end, while it is said, 15
"Today, when you hear his voice,
do not harden your hearts
as in the rebellion."

Who were they that heard and yet were 16 rebellious? Was it not all those who left Egypt under the leadership of Moses? And 17 with whom was he provoked forty years? Was it not with those who sinned, whose bodies fell in the wilderness? And to whom 18 did he swear that they should never enter his rest, but to those who were disobedient? So 19 we see that they were unable to enter because of unbelief.

Therefore, while the promise of entering his 4 rest remains, let us fear lest any of you be judged to have failed to reach it. For good 2 news came to us just as to them; but the message which they heard did not benefit them, because it did not meet with faith in the hearers.^h For we who have believed 3 enter that rest, as he has said,
"As I swore in my wrath,
'They shall never enter my rest,'"
although his works were finished from the foundation of the world. For he has 4 somewhere spoken of the seventh day in this way, "And God rested on the seventh day

5 from all his works." And again in this place he said,

"They shall never enter my rest."

6 Since therefore it remains for some to enter it, and those who formerly received the good news failed to enter because of disobedience,
7 again he sets a certain day, "Today," saying through David so long afterward, in the words already quoted,

"Today, when you hear his voice,
do not harden your hearts."

8 For if Joshua had given them rest, God[i]
9 would not speak later of another day. So then, there remains a sabbath rest for the
10 people of God; for whoever enters God's rest also ceases from his labours as God did from his.
11 Let us therefore strive to enter that rest, that no one fall by the same sort of disobedi-
12 ence. For the word of God is living and active, sharper than any two-edged sword, piercing to the division of soul and spirit, of joints and marrow, and discerning the
13 thoughts and intentions of the heart. And before him no creature is hidden, but all are open and laid bare to the eyes of him with whom we have to do.

Jesus our great high priest

14 Since then we have a great high priest who has passed through the heavens, Jesus, the Son of God, let us hold fast our confession.
15 For we have not a high priest who is unable to sympathise with our weaknesses, but one who in every respect has been tempted as we
16 are, yet without sinning. Let us then with confidence draw near to the throne of grace, that we may receive mercy and find grace to help in time of need.

5 For every high priest chosen from among men is appointed to act on behalf of men in relation to God, to offer gifts and sacrifices
2 for sins. He can deal gently with the ignorant and wayward, since he himself is
3 beset with weakness. Because of this he is bound to offer sacrifice for his own sins as
4 well as for those of the people. And one does not take the honour upon himself, but he is called by God, just as Aaron was.
5 So also Christ did not exalt himself to be made a high priest, but was appointed by him who said to him,

"Thou art my Son,
today I have begotten thee";
6 as he says also in another place,

"Thou art a priest for ever,
after the order of Melchiz'edek."

7 In the days of his flesh, Jesus[j] offered up prayers and supplications, with loud cries and tears, to him who was able to save him from death, and he was heard for his godly
8 fear. Although he was a Son, he learned
9 obedience through what he suffered; and being made perfect he became the source of
10 eternal salvation to all who obey him, being designated by God a high priest after the order of Melchiz'edek.
11 About this we have much to say which is hard to explain, since you have become dull
12 of hearing. For though by this time you ought to be teachers, you need some one to teach you again the first principles of God's
13 word. You need milk, not solid food; for every one who lives on milk is unskilled in the word of righteousness, for he is a child.
14 But solid food is for the mature, for those who have their faculties trained by practice to distinguish good from evil.

6 Therefore let us leave the elementary doctrines of Christ and go on to maturity, not laying again a foundation of repentance from dead works and of faith toward God, with
2 instruction[k] about ablutions, the laying on of hands, the resurrection of the dead, and
3 eternal judgment. And this we will do if God permits.[l] For it is impossible to restore again
4 to repentance those who have once been enlightened, who have tasted the heavenly gift, and have become partakers of the Holy
5 Spirit, and have tasted the goodness of the word of God and the powers of the age to
6 come, if they then commit apostasy, since they crucify the Son of God on their own account and hold him up to contempt. For
7 land which has drunk the rain that often falls upon it, and brings forth vegetation useful to those for whose sake it is cultivated, receives
8 a blessing from God. But if it bears thorns and thistles, it is worthless and near to being cursed; its end is to be burned.
9 Though we speak thus, yet in your case, beloved, we feel sure of better things that belong to salvation. For God is not so unjust
10 as to overlook your work and the love which you showed for his sake in serving the saints,
11 as you still do. And we desire each one of you to show the same earnestness in realising the full assurance of hope until the end, so
12 that you may not be sluggish, but imitators of those who through faith and patience inherit the promises.

i Greek *he* *j* Greek *he* *k* Other ancient manuscripts read *of instruction*
l Other ancient manuscripts read *let us do this if God permits*
4.5: Ps 95.11. 4.7: Ps 95.7–8. 4.10: Gen 2.2. 5.5: Ps 2.7. 5.6: Ps 110.4.
5.7: Mt 26.36–46; Mk 14.32–42; Lk 22.40–46. 5.9: Is 45.17. 5.10: Ps 110.4. 6.8: Gen 3.17–18.

13 For when God made a promise to Abraham,
14 since he had no one greater by whom to
15 swear, he swore by himself, saying, "Surely I
will bless you and multiply you." And thus
16 Abraham,[m] having patiently endured, obtained the promise. Men indeed swear by
a greater than themselves, and in all their
17 disputes an oath is final for confirmation. So
when God desired to show more convinc-
ingly to the heirs of the promise the unchangeable character of his purpose, he
18 interposed with an oath, so that through two
unchangeable things, in which it is impossible that God should prove false, we who
have fled for refuge might have strong
encouragement to seize the hope set before
19 us. We have this as a sure and steadfast
anchor of the soul, a hope that enters into the
20 inner shrine behind the curtain, where Jesus
has gone as a forerunner on our behalf,
having become a high priest for ever after the
order of Melchiz'edek.

Melchizedek

7 For this Melchiz'edek, king of Salem, priest
of the Most High God, met Abraham returning from the slaughter of the kings and
2 blessed him; and to him Abraham apportioned a tenth part of everything. He is first,
by translation of his name, king of righteousness, and then he is also king of Salem, that
3 is, king of peace. He is without father or
mother or genealogy, and has neither beginning of days nor end of life, but resembling
the Son of God he continues a priest for ever.
4 See how great he is! Abraham the patriarch
5 gave him a tithe of the spoils. And those
descendants of Levi who receive the priestly
office have a commandment in the law to
take tithes from the people, that is, from their
brethren, though these also are descended
6 from Abraham. But this man who has
not their genealogy received tithes from
Abraham and blessed him who had the
7 promises. It is beyond dispute that the
8 inferior is blessed by the superior. Here
tithes are received by mortal men; there, by
9 one of whom it is testified that he lives. One
might even say that Levi himself, who
receives tithes, paid tithes through Abraham,
10 for he was still in the loins of his ancestor
when Melchiz'edek met him.
11 Now if perfection had been attainable
through the Levitical priesthood (for under it
the people received the law), what further
need would there have been for another
priest to arise after the order of Melchiz'-

edek, rather than one named after the order
of Aaron? For when there is a change in the 12
priesthood, there is necessarily a change in
the law as well. For the one of whom these 13
things are spoken belonged to another tribe,
from which no one has ever served at the
altar. For it is evident that our Lord was 14
descended from Judah, and in connection
with that tribe Moses said nothing about
priests.

This becomes even more evident when 15
another priest arises in the likeness of
Melchiz'edek, who has become a priest, not 16
according to a legal requirement concerning
bodily descent but by the power of an
indestructible life. For it is witnessed of 17
him,
    "Thou art a priest for ever,
        after the order of Melchiz'edek."
On the one hand, a former commandment 18
is set aside because of its weakness and
uselessness (for the law made nothing 19
perfect); on the other hand, a better hope is
introduced, through which we draw near to
God.

And it was not without an oath. Those who 20,
formerly became priests took their office 21
without an oath, but this one was addressed
with an oath,
    "The Lord has sworn

High priest of the Levitical priesthood

[m] Greek he
6.13-14: Gen 22.16-17.   6.19: Lev 16.2.   6.20: Ps 110.4.   7.1-10: Gen 14.17-20.
7.11, 15, 17, 21: Ps 110.4.

and will not change his mind,
'Thou art a priest for ever.' "

22 This makes Jesus the surety of a better covenant.

23 The former priests were many in number, because they were prevented by death from
24 continuing in office; but he holds his priesthood permanently, because he continues for
25 ever. Consequently he is able for all time to save those who draw near to God through him, since he always lives to make intercession for them.

26 For it was fitting that we should have such a high priest, holy, blameless, unstained, separated from sinners, exalted above the
27 heavens. He has no need, like those high priests, to offer sacrifices daily, first for his own sins and then for those of the people; he did this once for all when he offered up
28 himself. Indeed, the law appoints men in their weakness as high priests, but the word of the oath, which came later than the law, appoints a Son who has been made perfect for ever.

Christ's supreme ministry

8 Now the point in what we are saying is this: we have such a high priest, one who is seated at the right hand of the throne of the Majesty
2 in heaven, a minister in the sanctuary and the true tent[n] which is set up not by man but by
3 the Lord. For every high priest is appointed to offer gifts and sacrifices; hence it is necessary for this priest also to have
4 something to offer. Now if he were on earth, he would not be a priest at all, since there are priests who offer gifts according to the law.
5 They serve a copy and shadow of the heavenly sanctuary; for when Moses was about to erect the tent,[n] he was instructed by God, saying, "See that you make everything according to the pattern which was shown
6 you on the mountain." But as it is, Christ[o] has obtained a ministry which is as much more excellent than the old as the covenant he mediates is better, since it is enacted on
7 better promises. For if that first covenant had been faultless, there would have been no occasion for a second.
8 For he finds fault with them when he says:
"The days will come, says the Lord,
when I will establish a new covenant with
the house of Israel
and with the house of Judah;
9 not like the covenant that I made with
their fathers
on the day when I took them by the hand
to lead them out of the land of Egypt;

for they did not continue in my covenant,
and so I paid no heed to them, says the
Lord.
This is the covenant that I will make with 10
the house of Israel
after those days, says the Lord:
I will put my laws into their minds,
and write them on their hearts,
and I will be their God,
and they shall be my people.
And they shall not teach every one his 11
fellow
or every one his brother, saying, 'Know
the Lord,'
for all shall know me,
from the least of them to the greatest.
For I will be merciful toward their 12
iniquities,
and I will remember their sins no more."
In speaking of a new covenant he treats the 13
first as obsolete. And what is becoming obsolete and growing old is ready to vanish away.

Now even the first covenant had regulations 9 for worship and an earthly sanctuary. For a 2 tent[n] was prepared, the outer one, in which were the lampstand and the table and the bread of the Presence;[p] it is called the Holy

Heb 9, 12

3 Place. Behind the second curtain stood a
4 tent[q] called the Holy of Holies, having the
golden altar of incense and the ark of the
covenant covered on all sides with gold,
which contained a golden urn holding the
manna, and Aaron's rod that budded, and
5 the tables of the covenant; above it were the
cherubim of glory overshadowing the mercy
seat. Of these things we cannot now speak in
detail.

6 These preparations having thus been made,
the priests go continually into the outer
7 tent,[q] performing their ritual duties; but into
the second only the high priest goes, and he
but once a year, and not without taking blood
which he offers for himself and for the errors
8 of the people. By this the Holy Spirit
indicates that the way into the sanctuary is
not yet opened as long as the outer tent[q] is
9 still standing (which is symbolic for the
present age). According to this arrangement,
gifts and sacrifices are offered which cannot
10 perfect the conscience of the worshipper, but
deal only with food and drink and various
ablutions, regulations for the body imposed
until the time of reformation.

11 But when Christ appeared as a high priest
of the good things that have come,[r] then
through the greater and more perfect tent[q]
(not made with hands, that is, not of this
12 creation) he entered once for all into the Holy
Place, taking[s] not the blood of goats and
calves but his own blood, thus securing an
13 eternal redemption. For if the sprinkling of
defiled persons with the blood of goats and
bulls and with the ashes of a heifer sanctifies
14 for the purification of the flesh, how much
more shall the blood of Christ, who through
the eternal Spirit offered himself without
blemish to God, purify your[t] conscience
from dead works to serve the living God.

15 Therefore he is the mediator of a new
covenant, so that those who are called may
receive the promised eternal inheritance,
since a death has occurred which redeems
them from the transgressions under the first
16 covenant.[u] For where a will[u] is involved, the
death of the one who made it must be
17 established. For a will[u] takes effect only at
death, since it is not in force as long as the
18 one who made it is alive. Hence even the
first covenant was not ratified without
19 blood. For when every commandment of the
law had been declared by Moses to all the
people, he took the blood of calves and goats,
with water and scarlet wool and hyssop, and
sprinkled both the book itself and all the
20 people, saying, "This is the blood of the

covenant which God commanded you."
And in the same way he sprinkled with the 21
blood both the tent[q] and all the vessels used
in worship. Indeed, under the law almost 22
everything is purified with blood, and
without the shedding of blood there is no
forgiveness of sins.

Thus it was necessary for the copies of the 23
heavenly things to be purified with these
rites, but the heavenly things themselves
with better sacrifices than these. For Christ 24
has entered, not into a sanctuary made with
hands, a copy of the true one, but into heaven
itself, now to appear in the presence of God
on our behalf. Nor was it to offer himself 25
repeatedly, as the high priest enters the Holy
Place yearly with blood not his own; for then 26

he would have had to suffer repeatedly since
the foundation of the world. But as it is, he
has appeared once for all at the end of the age
to put away sin by the sacrifice of himself.
And just as it is appointed for men to die 27
once, and after that comes judgment, so 28
Christ, having been offered once to bear the
sins of many, will appear a second time, not
to deal with sin but to save those who are
eagerly waiting for him.

For since the law has but a shadow of the 10
good things to come instead of the true form
of these realities, it can never, by the same
sacrifices which are continually offered year
after year, make perfect those who draw
near. Otherwise, would they not have ceased 2
to be offered? If the worshippers had once
been cleansed, they would no longer have
any consciousness of sin. But in these sacri- 3
fices there is a reminder of sin year after
year. For it is impossible that the blood of 4
bulls and goats should take away sins.

Consequently, when Christ[v] came into the 5
world, he said,
        "Sacrifices and offerings thou hast not
            desired,
        but a body hast thou prepared for me;

[q] Or *tabernacle*   [r] Other manuscripts read *good things to come*   [s] Greek *through*
[t] Other manuscripts read *our*   [u] The Greek word here used means both *covenant* and *will*   [v] Greek *he*
9.3: Ex 26.31–33.   **9.4:** Ex 30.1–5; 16.32–33; Num 17.8–10.   **9.7:** Lev 16.
9.13: Lev 16.6, 16; Num 19.9, 17–18.   **9.19–20:** Ex 24.6–8.   **10.5–9:** Ps 40.6–8.

6 in burnt offerings and sin offerings thou hast taken no pleasure.

7 Then I said, 'Lo, I have come to do thy will, O God,'
as it is written of me in the roll of the book.''

8 When he said above, ''Thou hast neither desired nor taken pleasure in sacrifices and offerings and burnt offerings and sin offerings'' (these are offered according to the law),

9 then he added, ''Lo, I have come to do thy will.'' He abolishes the first in order to

10 establish the second. And by that will we have been sanctified through the offering of the body of Jesus Christ once for all.

11 And every priest stands daily at his service, offering repeatedly the same sacrifices, which

12 can never take away sins. But when Christ[w] had offered for all time a single sacrifice for sins, he sat down at the right hand of God,

13 then to wait until his enemies should be

14 made a stool for his feet. For by a single offering he has perfected for all time those

15 who are sanctified. And the Holy Spirit also bears witness to us; for after saying,

16 ''This is the covenant that I will make with them
after those days, says the Lord:
I will put my laws on their hearts,
and write them on their minds,''

17 then he adds,
''I will remember their sins and their misdeeds no more.''

18 Where there is forgiveness of these, there is no longer any offering for sin.

Draw near in faith

19 Therefore, brethren, since we have confidence to enter the sanctuary by the blood of

20 Jesus, by the new and living way which he opened for us through the curtain, that is,

21 through his flesh, and since we have a great

22 priest over the house of God, let us draw near with a true heart in full assurance of faith, with our hearts sprinkled clean from an evil conscience and our bodies washed with pure

23 water. Let us hold fast the confession of our hope without wavering, for he who promised

24 is faithful; and let us consider how to stir up

25 one another to love and good works, not neglecting to meet together, as is the habit of some, but encouraging one another, and all the more as you see the Day drawing near.

26 For if we sin deliberately after receiving the knowledge of the truth, there no longer

27 remains a sacrifice for sins, but a fearful prospect of judgment, and a fury of fire

which will consume the adversaries. A man 28 who has violated the law of Moses dies without mercy at the testimony of two or three witnesses. How much worse punish- 29 ment do you think will be deserved by the man who has spurned the Son of God, and profaned the blood of the covenant by which he was sanctified, and outraged the Spirit of grace? For we know him who said, 30 ''Vengeance is mine, I will repay.'' And again, ''The Lord will judge his people.'' It 31 is a fearful thing to fall into the hands of the living God.

But recall the former days when, after 32 you were enlightened, you endured a hard struggle with sufferings, sometimes being 33

publicly exposed to abuse and affliction, and sometimes being partners with those so treated. For you had compassion on the 34 prisoners, and you joyfully accepted the plundering of your property, since you knew that you yourselves had a better possession and an abiding one. Therefore do not throw 35 away your confidence, which has a great reward. For you have need of endurance, so 36 that you may do the will of God and receive what is promised.
''For yet a little while, 37
and the coming one shall come and shall not tarry;
but my righteous one shall live by faith, 38
and if he shrinks back,
my soul has no pleasure in him.''
But we are not of those who shrink back and 39 are destroyed, but of those who have faith and keep their souls.

Examples of faith

11 Now faith is the assurance of things hoped
2 for, the conviction of things not seen. For by
it the men of old received divine approval.
3 By faith we understand that the world was
created by the word of God, so that what is
seen was made out of things which do not
appear.
4 By faith Abel offered to God a more
acceptable sacrifice than Cain, through
which he received approval as righteous,
God bearing witness by accepting his gifts;
he died, but through his faith he is still
5 speaking. By faith Enoch was taken up so
that he should not see death; and he was not
found, because God had taken him. Now
before he was taken he was attested as having
6 pleased God. And without faith it is impossible to please him. For whoever would draw
near to God must believe that he exists and
7 that he rewards those who seek him. By faith
Noah, being warned by God concerning
events as yet unseen, took heed and con-
structed an ark for the saving of his household; by this he condemned the world and
became an heir of the righteousness which
comes by faith.
8 By faith Abraham obeyed when he was
called to go out to a place which he was to
receive as an inheritance; and he went out,
9 not knowing where he was to go. By faith he
sojourned in the land of promise, as in a
foreign land, living in tents with Isaac and
Jacob, heirs with him of the same promise.
10 For he looked forward to the city which has
foundations, whose builder and maker is
11 God. By faith Sarah herself received power
to conceive, even when she was past the age,
since she considered him faithful who had
12 promised. Therefore from one man, and
him as good as dead, were born descendants
as many as the stars of heaven and as the
innumerable grains of sand by the seashore.
13 These all died in faith, not having received
what was promised, but having seen it and
greeted it from afar, and having acknowledged that they were strangers and exiles on
14 the earth. For people who speak thus make it
15 clear that they are seeking a homeland. If
they had been thinking of that land from
which they had gone out, they would have
16 had opportunity to return. But as it is, they
desire a better country, that is, a heavenly
one. Therefore God is not ashamed to be

called their God, for he has prepared for
them a city.
By faith Abraham, when he was tested, 17
offered up Isaac, and he who had received
the promises was ready to offer up his only
son, of whom it was said, "Through Isaac 18
shall your descendants be named." He 19
considered that God was able to raise men
even from the dead; hence, figuratively
speaking, he did receive him back. By faith 20
Isaac invoked future blessings on Jacob and
Esau. By faith Jacob, when dying, blessed 21
each of the sons of Joseph, bowing in worship over the head of his staff. By faith 22
Joseph, at the end of his life, made mention
of the exodus of the Israelites and gave
directions concerning his burial. *
By faith Moses, when he was born, was hid 23
for three months by his parents, because they
saw that the child was beautiful; and they
were not afraid of the king's edict. By faith 24
Moses, when he was grown up, refused to be
called the son of Pharaoh's daughter, choos- 25
ing rather to share ill-treatment than to enjoy the fleeting
pleasures of sin. He considered abuse 26
suffered for the Christ greater wealth than
the treasures of Egypt, for he looked to the
reward. By faith he left Egypt, not being 27
afraid of the anger of the king; for he
endured as seeing him who is invisible. By 28
faith he kept the Passover and sprinkled the
blood, so that the Destroyer of the first-born
might not touch them.
By faith the people crossed the Red Sea as if 29
on dry land; but the Egyptians, when they
attempted to do the same, were drowned. By 30
faith the walls of Jericho fell down after they
had been encircled for seven days. By faith 31
Rahab the harlot did not perish with those
who were disobedient, because she had given
friendly welcome to the spies.
And what more shall I say? For time 32
would fail me to tell of Gideon, Barak,
Samson, Jephthah, of David and Samuel and

---

x Greek *bones*

11.4: Gen 4.3–10.   11.5: Gen 5.21–24.   11.7: Gen 6.13–22.
11.8–9: Gen 12.1–8.   11.11: Gen 17.19; 18.11–14; 21.2.   11.12: Gen 15.5–6; 22.17; 32.12.
11.13: Ps 39.12; Gen 23.4.   11.16: Ex 3.6, 15; 4.5.   11.17: Gen 22.1–10.   11.18: Gen 21.12.
11.20: Gen 27.27–29, 39–40.   11.21: Gen 48; 47.31 (Septuagint).   11.22: Gen 50.24–25; Ex 13.19.
11.23: Ex 2.2; 1.22.   11.24: Ex 2.10, 11–15.   11.27: Ex 2.15.   11.28: Ex 12.21–28, 29–30.   11.29: Ex 14.21–31.
11.30: Josh 6.12–21.   11.31: Josh 2.1–21; 6.22–25.
11.32: Judg 6–8; 4–5; 13–16; 11–12; 1 Sam 16–30; 2 Sam 1–24; 1 Kings 1–2.11; 1 Sam 1–12; 15; 16.1–13.

33 the prophets—who through faith conquered kingdoms, enforced justice, received prom-
34 ises, stopped the mouths of lions, quenched raging fire, escaped the edge of the sword, won strength out of weakness, became mighty in war, put foreign armies to flight.
35 Women received their dead by resurrection. Some were tortured, refusing to accept release, that they might rise again to a better
36 life. Others suffered mocking and scourging,
37 and even chains and imprisonment. They were stoned, they were sawn in two,[v] they were killed with the sword; they went about in skins of sheep and goats, destitute, afflic-
38 ted, ill-treated—of whom the world was not worthy—wandering over deserts and mountains, and in dens and caves of the earth.
39 And all these, though well attested by their faith, did not receive what was promised,
40 since God had foreseen something better for us, that apart from us they should not be made perfect.

Run with perseverance

12 Therefore, since we are surrounded by so great a cloud of witnesses, let us also lay aside every weight, and sin which clings so closely, and let us run with perseverance the race that
2 is set before us, looking to Jesus the pioneer and perfecter of our faith, who for the joy that was set before him endured the cross, despising the shame, and is seated at the right hand of the throne of God.
3 Consider him who endured from sinners such hostility against himself, so that you
4 may not grow weary or faint-hearted. In your struggle against sin you have not yet resisted to the point of shedding your blood.
5 And have you forgotten the exhortation which addresses you as sons?—
    "My son, do not regard lightly the discipline of the Lord,
    nor lose courage when you are punished by him.
6 For the Lord disciplines him whom he loves,
    and chastises every son whom he receives."
7 It is for discipline that you have to endure. God is treating you as sons; for what son is there whom his father does not discipline?
8 If you are left without discipline, in which all have participated, then you are illegitimate
9 children and not sons. Besides this, we have

had earthly fathers to discipline us and we respected them. Shall we not much more be subject to the Father of spirits and live? For 10 they disciplined us for a short time at their pleasure, but he disciplines us for our good, that we may share his holiness. For the 11 moment all discipline seems painful rather than pleasant; later it yields the peaceful fruit of righteousness to those who have been trained by it.
    Therefore lift your drooping hands and 12 strengthen your weak knees, and make 13 straight paths for your feet, so that what is lame may not be put out of joint but rather be healed. Strive for peace with all men, and 14 for the holiness without which no one will see the Lord. See to it that no one fail to obtain 15 the grace of God; that no "root of bitterness" spring up and cause trouble, and by it the many become defiled; that no one be 16 immoral or irreligious like Esau, who sold his birthright for a single meal. For you know 17 that afterward, when he desired to inherit the blessing, he was rejected, for he found no chance to repent, though he sought it with tears.
    For you have not come to what may be 18 touched, a blazing fire, and darkness, and gloom, and a tempest, and the sound of a 19 trumpet, and a voice whose words made the hearers entreat that no further messages be spoken to them. For they could not endure 20 the order that was given, "If even a beast touches the mountain, it shall be stoned." Indeed, so terrifying was the sight that 21 Moses said, "I tremble with fear." But you 22 have come to Mount Zion and to the city of the living God, the heavenly Jerusalem, and to innumerable angels in festal gathering, and to the assembly[z] of the first-born who 23 are enrolled in heaven, and to a judge who is God of all, and to the spirits of just men made perfect, and to Jesus, the mediator of a 24 new covenant, and to the sprinkled blood that speaks more graciously than the blood of Abel.
    See that you do not refuse him who is 25 speaking. For if they did not escape when they refused him who warned them on earth, much less shall we escape if we reject him who warns from heaven. His voice then 26 shook the earth; but now he has promised, "Yet once more I will shake not only the earth but also the heaven." This phrase, 27 "Yet once more," indicates the removal of what is shaken, as of what has been made, in

---

v Other manuscripts add *they were tempted*   z Or *angels, and to the festal gathering and assembly*
11.33: Dan 6.   **11.34:** Dan 3.   **11.35:** 1 Kings 17.17–24; 2 Kings 4.25–37.
12.2: Ps 110.1.   **12.5–8:** Prov 3.11–12.   **12.12:** Is 35.3.   **12.13:** Prov 4.26 (Septuagint).
12.15: Deut 29.18 (Septuagint).   **12.16:** Gen 25.29–34.   **12.17:** Gen 27.30–40.
12.18–19: Ex 19.12–22; 20.18–21; Deut 4.11–12; 5.22–27.   **12.20:** Ex 19.12–13.   **12.21:** Deut 9.19.
12.24: Gen 4.10.   **12.25:** Ex 20.19.   **12.26:** Hag 2.6.

order that what cannot be shaken may 28 remain. Therefore let us be grateful for receiving a kingdom that cannot be shaken, and thus let us offer to God acceptable 29 worship, with reverence and awe; for our God is a consuming fire.

Instructions for Christian living

13 Let brotherly love continue. Do not neglect 2 to show hospitality to strangers, for thereby some have entertained angels unawares. 3 Remember those who are in prison, as though in prison with them; and those who are ill-treated, since you also are in the body. 4 Let marriage be held in honour among all, and let the marriage bed be undefiled; for God will judge the immoral and adulterous. 5 Keep your life free from love of money, and be content with what you have; for he has said, "I will never fail you nor forsake you." 6 Hence we can confidently say,

"The Lord is my helper,
I will not be afraid;
what can man do to me?"

7 Remember your leaders, those who spoke to you the word of God; consider the outcome 8 of their life, and imitate their faith. Jesus Christ is the same yesterday and today and 9 for ever. Do not be led away by diverse and strange teachings; for it is well that the heart be strengthened by grace, not by foods, which have not benefited their adherents. 10 We have an altar from which those who serve 11 the tent[a] have no right to eat. For the bodies of those animals whose blood is brought into the sanctuary by the high priest as a sacrifice 12 for sin are burned outside the camp. So

Jesus also suffered outside the gate in order to sanctify the people through his own blood. Therefore let us go forth to him 13 outside the camp, bearing abuse for him. For here we have no lasting city, but we seek 14 the city which is to come. Through him then 15 let us continually offer up a sacrifice of praise to God, that is, the fruit of lips that acknowledge his name. Do not neglect to do good 16 and to share what you have, for such sacrifices are pleasing to God.

Obey your leaders and submit to them; for 17 they are keeping watch over your souls, as men who will have to give account. Let them do this joyfully, and not sadly, for that would be of no advantage to you.

Pray for us, for we are sure that we have a 18 clear conscience, desiring to act honourably in all things. I urge you the more earnestly 19 to do this in order that I may be restored to you the sooner.

Now may the God of peace who brought 20 again from the dead our Lord Jesus, the great shepherd of the sheep, by the blood of the eternal covenant, equip you with everything 21 good that you may do his will, working in you[b] that which is pleasing in his sight, through Jesus Christ; to whom be glory for ever and ever. Amen.

I appeal to you, brethren, bear with my 22 word of exhortation, for I have written to you briefly. You should understand that our 23 brother Timothy has been released, with whom I shall see you if he comes soon. Greet all your leaders and all the saints. 24 Those who come from Italy send you greetings. Grace be with all of you. Amen. 25

---

a Or *tabernacle*   *b* Other ancient authorities read *us*
12.29: Deut 4.24.   13.2: Gen 18.1–8; 19.1–3.   13.5: Deut 31.6, 8; Josh 1.5.   13.6: Ps 118.6.
13.11, 13: Lev 16.27.   13.15: Lev 7.12; Is 57.19; Hos 14.2.   13.20: Is 63.11; Zech 9.11; Is 55.3; Ezek 37.26.

THE LETTER OF

JAMES

JAMES, a servant of God and of the Lord Jesus Christ,

To the twelve tribes in the Dispersion: Greeting.

Faith and humility

2 Count it all joy, my brethren, when you 3 meet various trials, for you know that the testing of your faith produces steadfastness. 4 And let steadfastness have its full effect, that you may be perfect and complete, lacking in nothing.

5 If any of you lacks wisdom, let him ask God, who gives to all men generously and 6 without reproaching, and it will be given him. But let him ask in faith, with no doubting, for he who doubts is like a wave of the sea that is driven and tossed by the 7,8 wind. For that person must not suppose that a double-minded man, unstable in all his ways, will receive anything from the Lord.

9 Let the lowly brother boast in his exalta-10 tion, and the rich in his humiliation, because like the flower of the grass he will pass away. 11 For the sun rises with its scorching heat and withers the grass; its flower falls, and its beauty perishes. So will the rich man fade away in the midst of his pursuits.

Enduring trial

12 Blessed is the man who endures trial, for when he has stood the test he will receive the crown of life which God has promised to 13 those who love him. Let no one say when he is tempted, "I am tempted by God"; for God cannot be tempted with evil and he himself 14 tempts no one; but each person is tempted when he is lured and enticed by his own 15 desire. Then desire when it has conceived gives birth to sin; and sin when it is full-grown brings forth death.

Do not be deceived, my beloved brethren. 16 Every good endowment and every perfect 17 gift is from above, coming down from the Father of lights with whom there is no variation or shadow due to change.[a] Of his 18 own will he brought us forth by the word of truth that we should be a kind of first fruits of his creatures.

True religion

Know this, my beloved brethren. Let every 19 man be quick to hear, slow to speak, slow to anger, for the anger of man does not work the 20 righteousness of God. Therefore put away 21 all filthiness and rank growth of wickedness and receive with meekness the implanted word, which is able to save your souls.

But be doers of the word, and not hearers 22 only, deceiving yourselves. For if any one is 23 a hearer of the word and not a doer, he is like a man who observes his natural face in a mirror; for he observes himself and goes 24 away and at once forgets what he was like. But he who looks into the perfect law, the law 25 of liberty, and perseveres, being no hearer that forgets but a doer that acts, he shall be blessed in his doing.

If any one thinks he is religious, and does 26 not bridle his tongue but deceives his heart, this man's religion is vain. Religion that is 27 pure and undefiled before God and the Father is this: to visit orphans and widows in their affliction, and to keep oneself unstained from the world.

Warning against partiality

My brethren, show no partiality as you hold 2 the faith of our Lord Jesus Christ, the Lord

---

a Other ancient authorities read *variation due to a shadow of turning*
1.10–11: Is 40.6–7.

2 of glory. For if a man with gold rings and in fine clothing comes into your assembly, and a poor man in shabby clothing also comes in, 3 and you pay attention to the one who wears the fine clothing and say, "Have a seat here, please," while you say to the poor man, 4 "Stand there," or, "Sit at my feet," have you not made distinctions among yourselves, and 5 become judges with evil thoughts? Listen, my beloved brethren. Has not God chosen those who are poor in the world to be rich in faith and heirs of the kingdom which he has 6 promised to those who love him? But you have dishonoured the poor man. Is it not the rich who oppress you, is it not they who drag 7 you into court? Is it not they who blaspheme that honourable name by which you are called?

8 If you really fulfil the royal law, according to the scripture, "You shall love your neigh-9 bour as yourself," you do well. But if you show partiality, you commit sin, and are 10 convicted by the law as transgressors. For whoever keeps the whole law but fails in one 11 point has become guilty of all of it. For he who said, "Do not commit adultery," said also, "Do not kill." If you do not commit adultery but do kill, you have become a 12 transgressor of the law. So speak and so act as those who are to be judged under the law 13 of liberty. For judgment is without mercy to one who has shown no mercy; yet mercy triumphs over judgment.

On faith and works

14 What does it profit, my brethren, if a man says he has faith but has not works? Can his 15 faith save him? If a brother or sister is 16 ill-clad and in lack of daily food, and one of you says to them, "Go in peace, be warmed and filled," without giving them the things 17 needed for the body, what does it profit? So faith by itself, if it has no works, is dead. 18 But some one will say, "You have faith and I have works." Show me your faith apart from your works, and I by my works will 19 show you my faith. You believe that God is one; you do well. Even the demons 20 believe—and shudder. Do you want to be shown, you foolish fellow, that faith apart 21 from works is barren? Was not Abraham our father justified by works, when he 22 offered his son Isaac upon the altar? You see that faith was active along with his works, 23 and faith was completed by works, and the scripture was fulfilled which says, "Abraham believed God, and it was reckoned to him as righteousness"; and he was called the friend

of God. You see that a man is justified by 24 works and not by faith alone. And in the 25 same way was not also Rahab the harlot justified by works when she received the messengers and sent them out another way? For as the body apart from the spirit is dead, 26 so faith apart from works is dead.

Control of the tongue

Let not many of you become teachers, my 3 brethren, for you know that we who teach shall be judged with greater strictness. For 2 we all make many mistakes, and if any one makes no mistakes in what he says he is a perfect man, able to bridle the whole body also. If we put bits into the mouths of horses 3

that they may obey us, we guide their whole bodies. Look at the ships also; though they 4 are so great and are driven by strong winds, they are guided by a very small rudder wherever the will of the pilot directs. So the 5 tongue is a little member and boasts of great things. How great a forest is set ablaze by a small fire! And the tongue is a fire. The tongue is an 6 unrighteous world among our members, staining the whole body, setting on fire the cycle of nature,[b] and set on fire by hell.[c] For 7 every kind of beast and bird, of reptile and sea creature, can be tamed and has been tamed by humankind, but no human being 8 can tame the tongue—a restless evil, full of deadly poison. With it we bless the Lord and 9 Father, and with it we curse men, who are made in the likeness of God. From the same 10 mouth come blessing and cursing. My brethren, this ought not to be so. Does a 11 spring pour forth from the same opening fresh water and brackish? Can a fig tree, my 12

brethren, yield olives, or a grapevine figs?
No more can salt water yield fresh.

False and true wisdom

13 Who is wise and understanding among
you? By his good life let him show his works
14 in the meekness of wisdom. But if you have
bitter jealousy and selfish ambition in your
hearts, do not boast and be false to the truth.
15 This wisdom is not such as comes down from
above, but is earthly, unspiritual, devilish.
16 For where jealousy and selfish ambition exist,
there will be disorder and every vile practice.
17 But the wisdom from above is first pure, then
peaceable, gentle, open to reason, full of
mercy and good fruits, without uncertainty or
18 insincerity. And the harvest of righteousness
is sown in peace by those who make peace.

Against friendship with the world

4 What causes wars, and what causes fight-
ings among you? Is it not your passions that
2 are at war in your members? You desire and
do not have; so you kill. And you covet[d] and
cannot obtain; so you fight and wage war.
3 You have not, because you do not ask.
You ask and do not receive, because you ask
wrongly, to spend it on your passions.
4 Unfaithful creatures! Do you not know that
friendship with the world is enmity with
God? Therefore whoever wishes to be a
friend of the world makes himself an enemy
5 of God. Or do you suppose it is in vain that
the scripture says, "He yearns jealously over
the spirit which he has made to dwell in
6 us"? But he gives more grace; therefore it
says, "God opposes the proud, but gives
7 grace to the humble." Submit yourselves
therefore to God. Resist the devil and he will
8 flee from you. Draw near to God and he will
draw near to you. Cleanse your hands, you
sinners, and purify your hearts, you men of
9 double mind. Be wretched and mourn and
weep. Let your laughter be turned to
mourning and your joy to dejection.
10 Humble yourselves before the Lord and he
will exalt you.
11 Do not speak evil against one another,
brethren. He that speaks evil against a
brother or judges his brother, speaks evil
against the law and judges the law. But if you
judge the law, you are not a doer of the law
12 but a judge. There is one lawgiver and judge,
he who is able to save and to destroy. But who
are you that you judge your neighbour?

Against the presumption of the rich

13 Come now, you who say, "Today or
tomorrow we will go into such and such a
town and spend a year there and trade and
14 get gain"; whereas you do not know about
tomorrow. What is your life? For you are a
mist that appears for a little time and then
15 vanishes. Instead you ought to say, "If the
Lord wills, we shall live and we shall do this
16 or that." As it is, you boast in your arrogance. All such boasting is evil. Whoever
17 knows what is right to do and fails to do it,
for him it is sin.

Against oppression by the rich

5 Come now, you rich, weep and howl for the
2 miseries that are coming upon you. Your
riches have rotted and your garments are
3 moth-eaten. Your gold and silver have
rusted, and their rust will be evidence against
you and will eat your flesh like fire. You
have laid up treasure[e] for the last days.
4 Behold, the wages of the labourers who
mowed your fields, which you kept back by
fraud, cry out; and the cries of the harvesters
have reached the ears of the Lord of hosts.
5 You have lived on the earth in luxury and in
pleasure; you have fattened your hearts in a
6 day of slaughter. You have condemned, you
have killed the righteous man; he does not
resist you.

Exhortation to patience

7 Be patient, therefore, brethren, until the
coming of the Lord. Behold, the farmer
waits for the precious fruit of the earth, being
patient over it until it receives the early and
8 the late rain. You also be patient. Establish
your hearts, for the coming of the Lord is at
9 hand. Do not grumble, brethren, against one
another, that you may not be judged; behold,
10 the Judge is standing at the doors. As an
example of suffering and patience, brethren,
take the prophets who spoke in the name of
11 the Lord. Behold, we call those happy who
were steadfast. You have heard of the
steadfastness of Job, and you have seen the
purpose of the Lord, how the Lord is
compassionate and merciful.
12 But above all, my brethren, do not swear,
either by heaven or by earth or with any
other oath, but let your yes be yes and your
no be no, that you may not fall under
condemnation.

---

d Or you kill and you covet *e Or will eat your flesh, since you have stored up fire*
4.6: Prov 3.34. **5.11:** Job 1.21–22; 2.10; Ps 103.8; 111.4. **5.12:** Mt 5.37.

The power of prayer

13 Is any one among you suffering? Let him
pray. Is any cheerful? Let him sing praise.
14 Is any among you sick? Let him call for the
elders of the church, and let them pray over
him, anointing him with oil in the name of
15 the Lord; and the prayer of faith will save the
sick man, and the Lord will raise him up; and
if he has committed sins, he will be forgiven.
16 Therefore confess your sins to one another,
and pray for one another, that you may be
healed. The prayer of a righteous man has
great power in its effects. Eli′jah was a man 17
of like nature with ourselves and he prayed
fervently that it might not rain, and for three
years and six months it did not rain on the
earth. Then he prayed again and the heaven 18
gave rain, and the earth brought forth its
fruit.

My brethren, if any one among you 19
wanders from the truth and some one brings
him back, let him know that whoever brings 20
back a sinner from the error of his way will
save his soul from death and will cover a
multitude of sins.

THE FIRST LETTER OF

PETER

PETER, an apostle of Jesus Christ,
To the exiles of the Dispersion in
Pontus, Galatia, Cappado′cia, Asia,
2 and Bithyn′ia, chosen and destined by God
the Father and sanctified by the Spirit for
obedience to Jesus Christ and for sprinkling
with his blood:
May grace and peace be multiplied to you.

Thanksgiving for the hope of salvation

3 Blessed be the God and Father of our Lord
Jesus Christ! By his great mercy we have
been born anew to a living hope through the
resurrection of Jesus Christ from the dead,
4 and to an inheritance which is imperishable,
undefiled, and unfading, kept in heaven for
5 you, who by God's power are guarded
through faith for a salvation ready to be
6 revealed in the last time. In this you rejoice,[a]
though now for a little while you may have
to suffer various trials, so that the genuine- 7
ness of your faith, more precious than gold
which though perishable is tested by fire,
may redound to praise and glory and honour
at the revelation of Jesus Christ. Without 8
having seen[b] him you[c] love him; though you
do not now see him you[c] believe in him and
rejoice with unutterable and exalted joy. As 9
the outcome of your faith you obtain the
salvation of your souls.

The prophets who prophesied of the grace 10
that was to be yours searched and inquired
about this salvation; they inquired what 11
person or time was indicated by the Spirit of
Christ within them when predicting the
sufferings of Christ and the subsequent
glory. It was revealed to them that they were 12
serving not themselves but you, in the things
which have now been announced to you by
those who preached the good news to you
through the Holy Spirit sent from heaven,
things into which angels long to look.

---

[a] Or *Rejoice in this*   [b] Other ancient authorities read *known*   [c] Or omit *you*
5.17: 1 Kings 17.1; 18.1; Lk 4.25.   5.18: 1 Kings 18.42.

A call to holy living

13 Therefore gird up your minds, be sober, set your hope fully upon the grace that is coming 14 to you at the revelation of Jesus Christ. As obedient children, do not be conformed to 15 the passions of your former ignorance, but as he who called you is holy, be holy yourselves 16 in all your conduct; since it is written, "You 17 shall be holy, for I am holy." And if you invoke as Father him who judges each one impartially according to his deeds, conduct yourselves with fear throughout the time of 18 your exile. You know that you were ransomed from the futile ways inherited from your fathers, not with perishable things such 19 as silver or gold, but with the precious blood of Christ, like that of a lamb without blemish 20 or spot. He was destined before the foundation of the world but was made manifest at 21 the end of the times for your sake. Through him you have confidence in God, who raised him from the dead and gave him glory, so that your faith and hope are in God. [d]

22 Having purified your souls by your obedience to the truth for a sincere love of the brethren, love one another earnestly from the 23 heart. You have been born anew, not of perishable seed but of imperishable, through 24 the living and abiding word of God; for

"All flesh is like grass
and all its glory like the flower of grass.
The grass withers, and the flower falls,
25   but the word of the Lord abides for ever."
That word is the good news which was preached to you.

The living stone and the holy nation

2 So put away all malice and all guile and 2 insincerity and envy and all slander. Like newborn babes, long for the pure spiritual milk, that by it you may grow up to salvation; 3 for you have tasted the kindness of the Lord. 4 Come to him, to that living stone, rejected by men but in God's sight chosen and 5 precious; and like living stones be yourselves built into a spiritual house, to be a holy priesthood, to offer spiritual sacrifices accep- 6 table to God through Jesus Christ. For it stands in scripture:

"Behold, I am laying in Zion a stone, a
    cornerstone chosen and precious,
and he who believes in him will not be put
    to shame."

7 To you therefore who believe, he is precious, but for those who do not believe,

"The very stone which the builders rejected
has become the head of the corner,"
and   8
"A stone that will make men stumble,
a rock that will make them fall";
for they stumble because they disobey the word, as they were destined to do.

But you are a chosen race, a royal priest- 9 hood, a holy nation, God's own people, [e] that you may declare the wonderful deeds of him who called you out of darkness into his marvellous light. Once you were no people 10 but now you are God's people; once you had not received mercy but now you have received mercy.

Beloved, I beseech you as aliens and exiles 11 to abstain from the passions of the flesh that wage war against your soul. Maintain good 12 conduct among the Gentiles, so that in case they speak against you as wrongdoers, they may see your good deeds and glorify God on the day of visitation.

Submission to the civil authorities

Be subject for the Lord's sake to every 13 human institution, [f] whether it be to the emperor as supreme, or to governors as sent 14 by him to punish those who do wrong and to praise those who do right. For it is God's 15 will that by doing right you should put to silence the ignorance of foolish men. Live as 16 free men, yet without using your freedom as a pretext for evil; but live as servants of God. Honour all men. Love the brother- 17 hood. Fear God. Honour the emperor.

The meaning of service

Servants, be submissive to your masters 18 with all respect, not only to the kind and gentle but also to the overbearing. For one is 19 approved if, mindful of God, he endures pain while suffering unjustly. For what credit is 20 it, if when you do wrong and are beaten for it you take it patiently? But if when you do right and suffer for it you take it patiently, you have God's approval. For to this 21 you have been called, because Christ also suffered for you, leaving you an example, that you should follow in his steps. He 22 committed no sin; no guile was found on his lips. When he was reviled, he did not revile 23 in return; when he suffered, he did not threaten; but he trusted to him who judges justly. He himself bore our sins in his body 24 on the tree, [g] that we might die to sin and live

[d] Or so that your faith is hope in God   [e] Greek a people for his possession   [f] Or every institution ordained for men
[g] Or carried up . . . to the tree
1.16: Lev 11.44-45.   1.24-25: Is 40.6-9.   2.3: Ps 34.8.   2.4: Ps 118.22; Is 28.16.   2.6: Is 28.16.   2.7: Ps 118.22.
2.8: Is 8.14-15.   2.9: Ex 19.5-6.   2.10: Hos 2.23.   2.22: Is 53.9.   2.24: Is 53.12 (Septuagint).   2.24-25: Is 53.5-6.

to righteousness. By his wounds you have
25 been healed. For you were straying like
sheep, but have now returned to the
Shepherd and Guardian of your souls.

Husbands and wives

3 Likewise you wives, be submissive to your
husbands, so that some, though they do not
obey the word, may be won without a word
2 by the behaviour of their wives, when they
3 see your reverent and chaste behaviour. Let
not yours be the outward adorning with
braiding of hair, decoration of gold, and
4 wearing of robes, but let it be the hidden
person of the heart with the imperishable
jewel of a gentle and quiet spirit, which in
5 God's sight is very precious. So once the
holy women who hoped in God used to
adorn themselves and were submissive to
6 their husbands, as Sarah obeyed Abraham,
calling him lord. And you are now her
children if you do right and let nothing
terrify you.
7 Likewise you husbands, live considerately
with your wives, bestowing honour on the
woman as the weaker sex, since you are joint
heirs of the grace of life, in order that your
prayers may not be hindered.

Christian sympathy

8 Finally, all of you, have unity of spirit,
sympathy, love of the brethren, a tender
9 heart and a humble mind. Do not return evil
for evil or reviling for reviling; but on the
contrary bless, for to this you have been
10 called, that you may obtain a blessing. For
"He that would love life
and see good days,
let him keep his tongue from evil
and his lips from speaking guile;
11 let him turn away from evil and do
right;
let him seek peace and pursue it.
12 For the eyes of the Lord are upon the
righteous,
and his ears are open to their prayer.
But the face of the Lord is against those
that do evil."

Suffering injustice and the example
of Christ

13 Now who is there to harm you if you are
14 zealous for what is right? But even if you do
suffer for righteousness' sake, you will be
blessed. Have no fear of them, nor be
15 troubled, but in your hearts reverence Christ

as Lord. Always be prepared to make a
defence to any one who calls you to account
for the hope that is in you, yet do it with
gentleness and reverence; and keep your 16
conscience clear, so that, when you are
abused, those who revile your good behaviour in Christ may be put to shame. For 17
it is better to suffer for doing right, if that
should be God's will, than for doing wrong.
For Christ also died[h] for sins once for all, the 18
righteous for the unrighteous, that he might
bring us to God, being put to death in the
flesh but made alive in the spirit; in which he 19
went and preached to the spirits in prison,
who formerly did not obey, when God's 20
patience waited in the days of Noah, during
the building of the ark, in which a few, that
is, eight persons, were saved through water.
Baptism, which corresponds to this, now 21
saves you, not as a removal of dirt from the
body but as an appeal to God for a clear
conscience, through the resurrection of Jesus
Christ, who has gone into heaven and is at 22
the right hand of God, with angels, authorities, and powers subject to him.

Renunciation of sin

Since therefore Christ suffered in the flesh,[i] 4
arm yourselves with the same thought, for
whoever has suffered in the flesh has ceased
from sin, so as to live for the rest of the time 2
in the flesh no longer by human passions but
by the will of God. Let the time that is past 3
suffice for doing what the Gentiles like to do,
living in licentiousness, passions, drunkenness, revels, carousing, and lawless idolatry.
They are surprised that you do not now join 4
them in the same wild profligacy, and they
abuse you; but they will give account to him 5
who is ready to judge the living and the
dead. For this is why the gospel was 6
preached even to the dead, that though
judged in the flesh like men, they might live
in the spirit like God.

The end of all things is at hand; therefore 7
keep sane and sober for your prayers. Above 8
all hold unfailing your love for one another,
since love covers a multitude of sins. Prac- 9
tise hospitality ungrudgingly to one another.
As each has received a gift, employ it for one 10
another, as good stewards of God's varied
grace: whoever speaks, as one who utters 11
oracles of God; whoever renders service, as
one who renders it by the strength which
God supplies; in order that in everything
God may be glorified through Jesus Christ.
To him belong glory and dominion for ever
and ever. Amen.

[h] Other ancient authorities read *suffered*   [i] Other ancient authorities add *for us*; some *for you*
3.6: Gen 18.12.   3.10–12: Ps 34.12–16.   3.14–15: Is 8.12–13.   3.20: Gen 6–8.

The privilege of suffering for Christ

12 Beloved, do not be surprised at the fiery
ordeal which comes upon you to prove you,
as though something strange were happening
13 to you. But rejoice in so far as you share
Christ's sufferings, that you may also rejoice
14 and be glad when his glory is revealed. If
you are reproached for the name of Christ,
you are blessed, because the spirit of glory[j]
15 and of God rests upon you. But let none of
you suffer as a murderer, or a thief, or a
16 wrongdoer, or a mischief-maker; yet if one
suffers as a Christian, let him not be
ashamed, but under that name let him glorify
17 God. For the time has come for judgment to
begin with the household of God; and if it
begins with us, what will be the end of those
18 who do not obey the gospel of God? And
"If the righteous man is scarcely saved,
    where will the impious and sinner
    appear?"
19 Therefore let those who suffer according to
God's will do right and entrust their souls to
a faithful Creator.

Exhortation to elders

5 So I exhort the elders among you, as a
fellow elder and a witness of the sufferings of
Christ as well as a partaker in the glory that is
2 to be revealed. Tend the flock of God that is
your charge,[k] not by constraint but will-
3 ingly,[l] not for shameful gain but eagerly, not
as domineering over those in your charge but
4 being examples to the flock. And when the
chief Shepherd is manifested you will obtain
5 the unfading crown of glory. Likewise you
that are younger be subject to the elders.
Clothe yourselves, all of you, with humility
toward one another, for "God opposes the
proud, but gives grace to the humble."

General exhortations

6 Humble yourselves therefore under the
mighty hand of God, that in due time he may
7 exalt you. Cast all your anxieties on him, for
8 he cares about you. Be sober, be watchful.
Your adversary the devil prowls around like a
roaring lion, seeking some one to devour.
9 Resist him, firm in your faith, knowing that
the same experience of suffering is required
10 of your brotherhood throughout the world.
And after you have suffered a little while, the
God of all grace, who has called you to his
eternal glory in Christ, will himself restore,
11 establish, and strengthen[m] you. To him be
the dominion for ever and ever. Amen.

12 By Silva'nus, a faithful brother as I regard
him, I have written briefly to you, exhorting
and declaring that this is the true grace of
13 God; stand fast in it. She who is at Babylon,
who is likewise chosen, sends you greetings;
14 and so does my son Mark. Greet one another
with the kiss of love.
Peace to all of you that are in Christ.

THE SECOND LETTER OF
PETER

SIMON Peter, a servant and apostle of
Jesus Christ,
To those who have obtained a faith of
equal standing with ours in the righteousness
of our God and Saviour Jesus Christ:[a]
2 May grace and peace be multiplied to you in
the knowledge of God and of Jesus our Lord.

Christian privileges and character

3 His divine power has granted to us all
things that pertain to life and godliness,
through the knowledge of him who called us
to[b] his own glory and excellence, by which he
4 has granted to us his precious and very great

[j] Other ancient authorities insert *and of power*   [k] Other ancient authorities add *exercising the oversight*
[l] Other ancient authorities add *as God would have you*
[m] Other ancient authorities read *restore, establish, strengthen and settle*
[a] Or *of our God and the Saviour Jesus Christ*   [b] Or *by*
4.14: Is 11.2.   4.18: Prov 11.31 (Septuagint).   5.5: Prov 3.34.   5.7: Ps 55.22.

promises, that through these you may escape from the corruption that is in the world because of passion, and become partakers of 5 the divine nature. For this very reason make every effort to supplement your faith with 6 virtue, and virtue with knowledge, and knowledge with self-control, and self-control with steadfastness, and steadfastness with 7 godliness, and godliness with brotherly affec- 8 tion, and brotherly affection with love. For if these things are yours and abound, they keep you from being ineffective or unfruitful in the knowledge of our Lord Jesus Christ. 9 For whoever lacks these things is blind and shortsighted and has forgotten that he was 10 cleansed from his old sins. Therefore, brethren, be the more zealous to confirm your call and election, for if you do this you 11 will never fall; so there will be richly provided for you an entrance into the eternal kingdom of our Lord and Saviour Jesus Christ.

Peter's approaching death

12 Therefore I intend always to remind you of these things, though you know them and are 13 established in the truth that you have. I think it right, as long as I am in this body,^{c} to 14 arouse you by way of reminder, since I know that the putting off of my body^c will be soon, as 15 our Lord Jesus Christ showed me. And I will see to it that after my departure you may be able at any time to recall these things.

Peter's witness and that of the prophets

16 For we did not follow cleverly devised myths when we made known to you the power and coming of our Lord Jesus Christ, 17 but we were eyewitnesses of his majesty. For when he received honour and glory from God the Father and the voice was borne to him by the Majestic Glory, "This is my beloved Son,^{d} with whom I am well 18 pleased," we heard this voice borne from heaven, for we were with him on the holy 19 mountain. And we have the prophetic word made more sure. You will do well to pay attention to this as to a lamp shining in a dark place, until the day dawns and the morning 20 star rises in your hearts. First of all you must understand this, that no prophecy of scrip- ture is a matter of one's own interpretation, 21 because no prophecy ever came by the

impulse of man, but men moved by the Holy Spirit spoke from God.^{e}

False teachers

But false prophets also arose among the 2 people, just as there will be false teachers among you, who will secretly bring in des- tructive heresies, even denying the Master who bought them, bringing upon themselves swift destruction. And many will follow 2 their licentiousness, and because of them the way of truth will be reviled. And in their 3 greed they will exploit you with false words; from of old their condemnation has not been idle, and their destruction has not been asleep.

For if God did not spare the angels when 4 they sinned, but cast them into hell^f and committed them to pits of nether gloom to be kept until the judgment; if he did not spare 5 the ancient world, but preserved Noah, a herald of righteousness, with seven other persons, when he brought a flood upon the world of the ungodly; if by turning the cities 6 of Sodom and Gomor′rah to ashes he con- demned them to extinction and made them an example to those who were to be ungodly; and if he rescued righteous Lot, greatly 7 distressed by the licentiousness of the wicked (for by what that righteous man saw and 8 heard as he lived among them, he was vexed in his righteous soul day after day with their lawless deeds), then the Lord knows how to 9 rescue the godly from trial, and to keep the unrighteous under punishment until the day of judgment, and especially those who 10 indulge in the lust of defiling passion and despise authority.

Bold and wilful, they are not afraid to revile the glorious ones, whereas angels, though 11 greater in might and power, do not pro- nounce a reviling judgment upon them before the Lord. But these, like irrational 12 animals, creatures of instinct, born to be caught and killed, reviling in matters of which they are ignorant, will be destroyed in the same destruction with them, suffering 13 wrong for their wrongdoing. They count it pleasure to revel in the daytime. They are blots and blemishes, revelling in their dissi- pation,^{g} carousing with you. They have eyes 14 full of adultery, insatiable for sin. They entice unsteady souls. They have hearts trained in greed. Accursed children! For- 15 saking the right way they have gone astray; they have followed the way of Balaam, the

^{c} Greek *tent* ^{d} Or *my Son, my* (or *the*) *Beloved*
^{e} Other authorities read *moved by the Holy Spirit holy men of God spoke* ^{f} Greek *Tartarus*
^{g} Other ancient authorities read *love feasts*
1.17–18: Mt 17.1–8; Mk 9.2–8; Lk 9.28–36.   **2.1–18:** Jude 4–16.   **2.5:** Gen 8.18; 6.6–8.   **2.6:** Gen 19.24.
2.7: Gen 19.16, 29.   **2.15:** Num 22.5, 7.

son of Be′or, who loved gain from wrong-
16 doing, but was rebuked for his own transgression; a dumb ass spoke with human voice
and restrained the prophet's madness.
17 These are waterless springs and mists
driven by a storm; for them the nether gloom
18 of darkness has been reserved. For, uttering
loud boasts of folly, they entice with licen-
tious passions of the flesh men who have
barely escaped from those who live in error.
19 They promise them freedom, but they themselves are slaves of corruption; for whatever
20 overcomes a man, to that he is enslaved. For
if, after they have escaped the defilements of
the world through the knowledge of our
Lord and Saviour Jesus Christ, they are
again entangled in them and overpowered,
the last state has become worse for them than
21 the first. For it would have been better for
them never to have known the way of
righteousness than after knowing it to turn
back from the holy commandment delivered
22 to them. It has happened to them according
to the true proverb, The dog turns back to
his own vomit, and the sow is washed only to
wallow in the mire.

The day of the Lord

3 This is now the second letter that I have
written to you, beloved, and in both of them
I have aroused your sincere mind by way of
2 reminder; that you should remember the
predictions of the holy prophets and the
commandment of the Lord and Saviour
3 through your apostles. First of all you must
understand this, that scoffers will come in
the last days with scoffing, following their
4 own passions and saying, "Where is the
promise of his coming? For ever since the
fathers fell asleep, all things have continued
as they were from the beginning of crea-
5 tion." They deliberately ignore this fact,
that by the word of God heavens existed long
ago, and an earth formed out of water and by
6 means of water, through which the world

that then existed was deluged with water and
perished. But by the same word the heavens 7
and earth that now exist have been stored up
for fire, being kept until the day of judgment
and destruction of ungodly men.

But do not ignore this one fact, beloved, 8
that with the Lord one day is as a thousand
years, and a thousand years as one day. The 9
Lord is not slow about his promise as some
count slowness, but is forbearing toward
you,[h] not wishing that any should perish, but
that all should reach repentance. But the day 10
of the Lord will come like a thief, and then
the heavens will pass away with a loud noise,
and the elements will be dissolved with fire,
and the earth and the works that are upon it
will be burned up.

The necessity of being prepared

Since all these things are thus to be dis- 11
solved, what sort of persons ought you to be
in lives of holiness and godliness, waiting for 12
and hastening[i] the coming of the day of God,
because of which the heavens will be kindled
and dissolved, and the elements will melt
with fire! But according to his promise we 13
wait for new heavens and a new earth in
which righteousness dwells.

Therefore, beloved, since you wait for 14
these, be zealous to be found by him without
spot or blemish, and at peace. And count the 15
forbearance of our Lord as salvation. So also
our beloved brother Paul wrote to you
according to the wisdom given him, speaking 16
of this as he does in all his letters. There are
some things in them hard to understand,
which the ignorant and unstable twist to
their own destruction, as they do the other
scriptures. You therefore, beloved, knowing 17
this beforehand, beware lest you be carried
away with the error of lawless men and lose
your own stability. But grow in the grace 18
and knowledge of our Lord and Saviour
Jesus Christ. To him be the glory both now
and to the day of eternity. Amen.

ℎ Other ancient authorities read *on your account*   ⁱ Or *earnestly desiring*
2.16: Num 22.21, 23, 28, 30–31.   2.22: Prov 26.11.   3.5–6: Gen 1.6–8; 7.11.   3.8: Ps 90.4.   3.12: Is 34.4.
3.13: Is 65.17; 66.22.

JOHN

THAT which was from the beginning, which we have heard, which we have seen with our eyes, which we have looked upon and touched with our hands, 2 concerning the word of life—the life was made manifest, and we saw it, and testify to it, and proclaim to you the eternal life which was with the Father and was made manifest 3 to us—that which we have seen and heard we proclaim also to you, so that you may have fellowship with us; and our fellowship is with the Father and with his Son Jesus Christ. 4 And we are writing this that our[a] joy may be complete.

God is light

5 This is the message we have heard from him and proclaim to you, that God is light and in 6 him is no darkness at all. If we say we have fellowship with him while we walk in darkness, we lie and do not live according to the 7 truth; but if we walk in the light, as he is in the light, we have fellowship with one another, and the blood of Jesus his Son 8 cleanses us from all sin. If we say we have no sin, we deceive ourselves, and the truth is not 9 in us. If we confess our sins, he is faithful and just, and will forgive our sins and cleanse 10 us from all unrighteousness. If we say we have not sinned, we make him a liar, and his word is not in us.

Obedience the proof of fellowship

2 My little children, I am writing this to you so that you may not sin; but if any one does

sin, we have an advocate with the Father, Jesus Christ the righteous; and he is the 2 expiation for our sins, and not for ours only but also for the sins of the whole world. And 3 by this we may be sure that we know him, if we keep his commandments. He who says "I 4 know him" but disobeys his commandments is a liar, and the truth is not in him; but 5 whoever keeps his word, in him truly love for God is perfected. By this we may be sure that we are in him: he who says he abides in 6 him ought to walk in the same way in which he walked.

Beloved, I am writing you no new com- 7 mandment, but an old commandment which you had from the beginning; the old commandment is the word which you have heard. Yet I am writing you a new com- 8 mandment, which is true in him and in you, because[b] the darkness is passing away and the true light is already shining. He who says he 9 is in the light and hates his brother is in the darkness still. He who loves his brother 10 abides in the light, and in it[c] there is no cause for stumbling. But he who hates his brother 11 is in the darkness and walks in the darkness, and does not know where he is going, because the darkness has blinded his eyes.

I am writing to you, little children, because 12 your sins are forgiven for his sake. I am 13 writing to you, fathers, because you know him who is from the beginning. I am writing to you, young men, because you have overcome the evil one. I write to you, children, because you know the Father. I write to you, 14 fathers, because you know him who is from the beginning. I write to you, young men,

---

[a] Other ancient authorities read *your* [b] Or *that* [c] Or *him*
1.1–2: Lk 24.39; Jn 1.1; 4.14; 15.27; 20.20, 25; Acts 4.20; 1 Jn 2.13. 1.4: Jn 15.11; 2 Jn 12. 1.5: 1 Jn 3.11.
1.6–8: Jn 3.21; 1 Jn 2.4, 11. 1.7: Rev 1.5. 1.10: 1 Jn 5.10. 2.1: Jn 14.16.
2.2: Jn 1.29; 3.14–16; 11.51–52; 1 Jn 4.10. 2.3: Jn 15.10. 2.4: 1 Jn 1.6–8; 4.20. 2.5: Jn 14.21, 23; 1 Jn 5.3.
2.6: Jn 13.15. 2.7: Jn 13.34. 2.8: Jn 8.12. 2.10–11: Jn 11.9–10; 1 Jn 1.6. 2.13: Jn 1.1; 1 Jn 1.1.

because you are strong, and the word of God abides in you, and you have overcome the evil one.

15 Do not love the world or the things in the world. If any one loves the world, love for 16 the Father is not in him. For all that is in the world, the lust of the flesh and the lust of the eyes and the pride of life, is not of the Father 17 but is of the world. And the world passes away, and the lust of it; but he who does the will of God abides for ever.

Warning against antichrists

18 Children, it is the last hour; and as you have heard that antichrist is coming, so now many antichrists have come; therefore we know 19 that it is the last hour. They went out from us, but they were not of us; for if they had been of us, they would have continued with us; but they went out, that it might be plain 20 that they all are not of us. But you have been anointed by the Holy One, and you all 21 know.[d] I write to you, not because you do not know the truth, but because you know it, 22 and know that no lie is of the truth. Who is the liar but he who denies that Jesus is the Christ? This is the antichrist, he who denies 23 the Father and the Son. No one who denies the Son has the Father. He who confesses the 24 Son has the Father also. Let what you heard from the beginning abide in you. If what you heard from the beginning abides in you, then you will abide in the Son and in the 25 Father. And this is what he has promised us,[e] eternal life.

26 I write to you about those who would 27 deceive you; but the anointing which you received from him abides in you, and you have no need that any one should teach you; as his anointing teaches you about everything, and is true, and is no lie, just as it has taught you, abide in him.

28 And now, little children, abide in him, so that when he appears we may have confidence and not shrink from him in shame at 29 his coming. If you know that he is righteous, you may be sure that every one who does right is born of him.

The children of God

3 See what love the Father has given us, that we should be called children of God; and so we are. The reason why the world does not know us is that it did not know him.

Beloved, we are God's children now; it does 2 not yet appear what we shall be, but we know that when he appears we shall be like him, for we shall see him as he is. And every one who 3 thus hopes in him purifies himself as he is pure.

Every one who commits sin is guilty of 4 lawlessness; sin is lawlessness. You know 5 that he appeared to take away sins, and in him there is no sin. No one who abides in 6 him sins; no one who sins has either seen him or known him. Little children, let no one 7 deceive you. He who does right is righteous, as he is righteous. He who commits sin is of 8 the devil; for the devil has sinned from the beginning. The reason the Son of God appeared was to destroy the works of the devil. No one born of God commits sin; for 9 God's[f] nature abides in him, and he cannot sin because he is[g] born of God. By this it 10 may be seen who are the children of God, and who are the children of the devil: whoever does not do right is not of God, nor he who does not love his brother.

For this is the message which you have 11 heard from the beginning, that we should love one another, and not be like Cain who 12 was of the evil one and murdered his brother. And why did he murder him? Because his own deeds were evil and his brother's righteous. Do not wonder, breth- 13 ren, that the world hates you. We know that 14 we have passed out of death into life, because we love the brethren. He who does not love remains in death. Any one who hates his 15 brother is a murderer, and you know that no murderer has eternal life abiding in him. By 16 this we know love, that he laid down his life for us; and we ought to lay down our lives for the brethren. But if any one has the world's 17 goods and sees his brother in need, yet closes his heart against him, how does God's love abide in him? Little children, let us not love 18 in word or speech but in deed and in truth.

By this we shall know that we are of the 19 truth, and reassure our hearts before him whenever our hearts condemn us; for God is 20 greater than our hearts, and he knows everything. Beloved, if our hearts do not condemn 21 us, we have confidence before God; and we 22 receive from him whatever we ask, because we keep his commandments and do what pleases him. And this is his commandment, 23 that we should believe in the name of his Son Jesus Christ and love one another, just as he has commanded us. All who keep his 24

---

d Other ancient authorities read you know everything   e Other ancient authorities read you
f Greek his   g Or for the offspring of God abide in him, and they cannot sin because they are
2.18: I Jn 4.3.   2.22: 2 Jn 7.   2.23: I Jn 4.15; 2 Jn 9.   2.27: Jn 14.26.   2.28: I Jn 4.17.
2.29: I Jn 3.7–10; 4.7.   3.1: Jn 1.12; 16.3.   3.5: Jn 1.29.   3.8: Jn 8.34, 44.   3.9: I Jn 5.18.   3.11: I Jn 1.5
3.13: Jn 15.18–19.   3.14: Jn 5.24.   3.15: Jn 8.44.   3.16: Jn 13.1; 15.13.   3.18: Jas 1.22.   3.21: I Jn 5.14.
3.23: Jn 6.29; 13.34; 15.17.   3.24: I Jn 4.13.

commandments abide in him, and he in them. And by this we know that he abides in us, by the Spirit which he has given us.

The spirit of truth and the spirit of error

4 Beloved, do not believe every spirit, but test the spirits to see whether they are of God; for many false prophets have gone out into the
2 world. By this you know the Spirit of God: every spirit which confesses that Jesus Christ
3 has come in the flesh is of God, and every spirit which does not confess Jesus is not of God. This is the spirit of antichrist, of which you heard that it was coming, and now it is in
4 the world already. Little children, you are of God, and have overcome them; for he who is in you is greater than he who is in the world.
5 They are of the world, therefore what they say is of the world, and the world listens to
6 them. We are of God. Whoever knows God listens to us, and he who is not of God does not listen to us. By this we know the spirit of truth and the spirit of error.

God is love

7 Beloved, let us love one another; for love is of God, and he who loves is born of God and
8 knows God. He who does not love does not
9 know God; for God is love. In this the love of God was made manifest among us, that God sent his only Son into the world, so that
10 we might live through him. In this is love, not that we loved God but that he loved us and sent his Son to be the expiation for our
11 sins. Beloved, if God so loved us, we also
12 ought to love one another. No man has ever seen God; if we love one another, God abides in us and his love is perfected in us.
13 By this we know that we abide in him and he in us, because he has given us of his own
14 Spirit. And we have seen and testify that the Father has sent his Son as the Saviour of
15 the world. Whoever confesses that Jesus is the Son of God, God abides in him, and he in
16 God. So we know and believe the love God has for us. God is love, and he who abides in love abides in God, and God abides in him.
17 In this is love perfected with us, that we may have confidence for the day of judgment, because as he is so are we in this world.
18 There is no fear in love, but perfect love casts out fear. For fear has to do with punishment, and he who fears is not perfected in

love. We love, because he first loved us. If 19 any one says, "I love God," and hates his 20 brother, he is a liar; for he who does not love his brother whom he has seen, cannot[h] love God whom he has not seen. And this 21 commandment we have from him, that he who loves God should love his brother also.

Every one who believes that Jesus is the 5 Christ is a child of God, and every one who loves the parent loves the child. By this we 2 know that we love the children of God, when we love God and obey his commandments. For this is the love of God, that we keep his 3 commandments. And his commandments are not burdensome. For whatever is born of 4 God overcomes the world; and this is the victory that overcomes the world, our faith. Who is it that overcomes the world but he 5 who believes that Jesus is the Son of God?

He who has the Son has life

This is he who came by water and blood, 6 Jesus Christ, not with the water only but with the water and the blood. And the Spirit 7 is the witness, because the Spirit is the truth. There are three witnesses, the Spirit, the 8 water, and the blood; and these three agree. If we receive the testimony of men, the 9 testimony of God is greater; for this is the testimony of God that he has borne witness to his Son. He who believes in the Son of 10 God has the testimony in himself. He who does not believe God, has made him a liar, because he has not believed in the testimony that God has borne to his Son. And this is 11 the testimony, that God gave us eternal life, and this life is in his Son. He who has the 12 Son has life; he who has not the Son of God has not life.

I write this to you who believe in the name 13 of the Son of God, that you may know that you have eternal life. And this is the 14 confidence which we have in him, that if we ask anything according to his will he hears us. And if we know that he hears us in 15 whatever we ask, we know that we have obtained the requests made of him. If any 16 one sees his brother committing what is not a mortal sin, he will ask, and God[i] will give him life for those whose sin is not mortal. There is sin which is mortal; I do not say that one is to pray for that. All wrongdoing is sin, 17 but there is sin which is not mortal.

[h] Other ancient authorities read *how can he*　[i] Greek *he*
4.3: 1 Jn 2.18.　4.5: Jn 15.19.　4.6: Jn 8.47.　4.7: 1 Jn 2.29.　4.9: Jn 3.16.　4.10: Jn 15.12; 1 Jn 4.19; 2.2.
4.12: Jn 1.18.　4.13: 1 Jn 3.24.　4.14: Jn 4.42; 3.17.　4.17: 1 Jn 2.28.　4.19: 1 Jn 4.10.
4.20: 1 Jn 2.4.　5.1: Jn 8.42.　5.3: Jn 14.15; 1 Jn 2.5; 2 Jn 6.　5.4: Jn 16.33.　5.6–8: Jn 19.34; 4.23; 15.26.
5.9: Jn 5.32, 36; 8.18.　5.10: 1 Jn 1.10.　5.12: Jn 3.36.　5.13: Jn 20.31.　5.14: Mt 7.7; 1 Jn 3.21.

18 We know that any one born of God does not sin, but He who was born of God keeps him, and the evil one does not touch him.

19 We know that we are of God, and the whole world is in the power of the evil one.

20 And we know that the Son of God has come and has given us understanding, to know him who is true; and we are in him who is true, in his Son Jesus Christ. This is the true God and eternal life. Little children, keep your-21 selves from idols.

THE SECOND LETTER OF
JOHN

THE elder to the elect lady and her children, whom I love in the truth, and not only I but also all who know 2 the truth, because of the truth which abides in us and will be with us for ever:

3 Grace, mercy, and peace will be with us, from God the Father and from Jesus Christ the Father's Son, in truth and love.

4 I rejoiced greatly to find some of your children following the truth, just as we have 5 been commanded by the Father. And now I beg you, lady, not as though I were writing you a new commandment, but the one we have had from the beginning, that we love 6 one another. And this is love, that we follow his commandments; this is the commandment, as you have heard from the beginning, 7 that you follow love. For many deceivers have gone out into the world, men who will not acknowledge the coming of Jesus Christ in the flesh; such a one is the deceiver and the antichrist. Look to yourselves, that you 8 may not lose what you *a* have worked for, but may win a full reward. Any one who goes 9 ahead and does not abide in the doctrine of Christ does not have God; he who abides in the doctrine has both the Father and the Son. If any one comes to you and does not 10 bring this doctrine, do not receive him into the house or give him any greeting; for he 11 who greets him shares his wicked work.

Though I have much to write to you, I 12 would rather not use paper and ink, but I hope to come to see you and talk with you face to face, so that our joy may be complete.

The children of your elect sister greet you. 13

THE THIRD LETTER OF
JOHN

THE elder to the beloved Ga'ius, whom I love in the truth.

2 Beloved, I pray that all may go well with you and that you may be in health; I 3 know that it is well with your soul. For I greatly rejoiced when some of the brethren arrived and testified to the truth of your life, 4 as indeed you do follow the truth. No greater joy can I have than this, to hear that my children follow the truth.

5 Beloved, it is a loyal thing you do when you render any service to the brethren, especially 6 to strangers, who have testified to your love before the church. You will do well to send them on their journey as befits God's 7 service. For they have set out for his sake and have accepted nothing from the 8 heathen. So we ought to support such men, that we may be fellow workers in the truth.

9 I have written something to the church; but Diot'rephes, who likes to put himself first, does not acknowledge my authority. So if I 10 come, I will bring up what he is doing, prating against me with evil words. And not content with that, he refuses himself to welcome the brethren, and also stops those who want to welcome them and puts them out of the church.

Beloved, do not imitate evil but imitate 11 good. He who does good is of God; he who does evil has not seen God. Deme'trius has 12 testimony from every one, and from the truth itself; I testify to him too, and you know my testimony is true.

I had much to write to you, but I would 13 rather not write with pen and ink; I hope to 14 see you soon, and we will talk together face to face.

Peace be to you. The friends greet you. 15 Greet the friends, every one of them.

a Other ancient authorities read *we*
5.18: Jn 17.15; 1 Jn 3.9. 5.20–21: Jn 17.3; Rev 3.7. 2 Jn 1: 3 Jn 1. 5: Jn 13.34. 6: 1 Jn 5.3.
7: 1 Jn 2.22. 12: 1 Jn 1.4; 3 Jn 13. 3 Jn 1: Acts 19.29; 2 Jn 1. 12: Jn 21.24. 13: 2 Jn 12.

THE LETTER OF

JUDE

JUDE, a servant of Jesus Christ and brother of James,

To those who are called, beloved in God the Father and kept for Jesus Christ:

2 May mercy, peace, and love be multiplied to you.

False teachers

3 Beloved, being very eager to write to you of our common salvation, I found it necessary to write appealing to you to contend for the faith which was once for all delivered to the 4 saints. For admission has been secretly gained by some who long ago were designated for this condemnation, ungodly persons who pervert the grace of our God into licentiousness and deny our only Master and Lord, Jesus Christ.[a]

5 Now I desire to remind you, though you were once for all fully informed, that he[b] who saved a people out of the land of Egypt, afterward destroyed those who did not 6 believe. And the angels that did not keep their own position but left their proper dwelling have been kept by him in eternal chains in the nether gloom until the judg-7 ment of the great day; just as Sodom and Gomor'rah and the surrounding cities, which likewise acted immorally and indulged in unnatural lust, serve as an example by undergoing a punishment of eternal fire.

8 Yet in like manner these men in their dreamings defile the flesh, reject authority, 9 and revile the glorious ones.[c] But when the archangel Michael, contending with the devil, disputed about the body of Moses, he did not presume to pronounce a reviling judgment upon him, but said, "The Lord 10 rebuke you." But these men revile whatever they do not understand, and by those things that they know by instinct as irrational 11 animals do, they are destroyed. Woe to them! For they walk in the way of Cain, and abandon themselves for the sake of gain to

Balaam's error, and perish in Korah's rebellion. These are blemishes[d] on your love 12 feasts, as they boldly carouse together, looking after themselves; waterless clouds, carried along by winds; fruitless trees in late autumn, twice dead, uprooted; wild waves of 13 the sea, casting up the foam of their own shame; wandering stars for whom the nether gloom of darkness has been reserved for ever.

It was of these also that Enoch in the 14 seventh generation from Adam prophesied, saying, "Behold, the Lord came with his holy myriads, to execute judgment on all, and to 15 convict all the ungodly of all their deeds of ungodliness which they have committed in such an ungodly way, and of all the harsh things which ungodly sinners have spoken against him." These are grumblers, mal-16 contents, following their own passions, loud-mouthed boasters, flattering people to gain advantage.

But you must remember, beloved, the 17 predictions of the apostles of our Lord Jesus Christ; they said to you, "In the last time 18 there will be scoffers, following their own ungodly passions." It is these who set up 19 divisions, worldly people, devoid of the Spirit. But you, beloved, build yourselves 20 up on your most holy faith; pray in the Holy Spirit; keep yourselves in the love of God; 21 wait for the mercy of our Lord Jesus Christ unto eternal life. And convince some, who 22 doubt; save some, by snatching them out of 23 the fire; on some have mercy with fear, hating even the garment spotted by the flesh.[e]

Now to him who is able to keep you from 24 falling and to present you without blemish before the presence of his glory with rejoicing, to the only God, our Saviour through 25 Jesus Christ our Lord, be glory, majesty, dominion, and authority, before all time and now and for ever. Amen.

---

[a] Or *the only Master and our Lord Jesus Christ*   [b] Ancient authorities read *Jesus* or *the Lord* or *God*   [c] Greek *glories*   [d] Or *reefs*   [e] The Greek text in this sentence is uncertain at several points
4–16: 2 Pet 2.1–18.   **7:** Gen 19.   **9:** Zech 3.2.   **11:** Gen 4.3–8; Num 22–24; 16.   **14–15:** Enoch 1.9.
23: Zech 3.3–4.

1026

Patmos — HK

THE
REVELATION TO JOHN

THE revelation of Jesus Christ, which God gave him to show to his servants what must soon take place; and he made it known by sending his angel to his 2 servant John, who bore witness to the word of God and to the testimony of Jesus Christ, 3 even to all that he saw. Blessed is he who reads aloud the words of the prophecy, and blessed are those who hear, and who keep what is written therein; for the time is near.

4 John to the seven churches that are in Asia:
Grace to you and peace from him who is and who was and who is to come, and from the seven spirits who are before his throne, 5 and from Jesus Christ the faithful witness, the first-born of the dead, and the ruler of kings on earth.
To him who loves us and has freed us from 6 our sins by his blood and made us a kingdom, priests to his God and Father, to him be glory and dominion for ever and ever. 7 Amen. Behold, he is coming with the clouds, and every eye will see him, every one who pierced him; and all tribes of the earth will wail on account of him. Even so. Amen.
8 "I am the Alpha and the Omega," says the Lord God, who is and who was and who is to come, the Almighty.

I John, your brother, who share with you in 9 Jesus the tribulation and the kingdom and the patient endurance, was on the island called Patmos on account of the word of God and the testimony of Jesus. I was in the 10 Spirit on the Lord's day, and I heard behind me a loud voice like a trumpet saying, "Write 11 what you see in a book and send it to the seven churches, to Ephesus and to Smyrna and to Per′gamum and to Thyati′ra and to Sardis and to Philadelphia and to La-odice′a."
Then I turned to see the voice that was 12 speaking to me, and on turning I saw seven golden lampstands, and in the midst of the 13 lampstands one like a son of man, clothed with a long robe and with a golden girdle round his breast; his head and his hair were 14 white as white wool, white as snow; his eyes were like a flame of fire, his feet were like 15 burnished bronze, refined as in a furnace, and his voice was like the sound of many waters; in his right hand he held seven stars, 16 from his mouth issued a sharp two-edged sword, and his face was like the sun shining in full strength.

1.4: Ex 3.14.   1.5: Ps 89.27.   1.6: Ex 19.6; Is 61.6.   1.7: Dan 7.13; Mt 24.30; Mk 14.62; Zech 12.10.
1.8: Ex 3.14.   1.13: Dan 7.13; 10.5.   1.15: Ezek 1.24.   1.16: Ex 34.29.

17 When I saw him, I fell at his feet as though dead. But he laid his right hand upon me, saying, "Fear not, I am the first and the last,
18 and the living one; I died, and behold I am alive for evermore, and I have the keys of
19 Death and Hades. Now write what you see, what is and what is to take place hereafter.
20 As for the mystery of the seven stars which you saw in my right hand, and the seven golden lampstands, the seven stars are the angels of the seven churches and the seven lampstands are the seven churches.

Letters to the seven churches

2 "To the angel of the church in Ephesus write: 'The words of him who holds the seven stars in his right hand, who walks among the seven golden lampstands.
2 " 'I know your works, your toil and your patient endurance, and how you cannot bear evil men but have tested those who call themselves apostles but are not, and found
3 them to be false; I know you are enduring patiently and bearing up for my name's sake,
4 and you have not grown weary. But I have this against you, that you have abandoned
5 the love you had at first. Remember then from what you have fallen, repent and do the works you did at first. If not, I will come to you and remove your lampstand from its
6 place, unless you repent. Yet this you have, you hate the works of the Nicola′itans, which
7 I also hate. He who has an ear, let him hear what the Spirit says to the churches. To him who conquers I will grant to eat of the tree of life, which is in the paradise of God.'
8 "And to the angel of the church in Smyrna write: 'The words of the first and the last, who died and came to life.
9 " 'I know your tribulation and your poverty (but you are rich) and the slander of those who say that they are Jews and are not, but
10 are a synagogue of Satan. Do not fear what you are about to suffer. Behold, the devil is about to throw some of you into prison, that you may be tested, and for ten days you will have tribulation. Be faithful unto death, and
11 I will give you the crown of life. He who has an ear, let him hear what the Spirit says to the churches. He who conquers shall not be hurt by the second death.'
12 "And to the angel of the church in Per′-gamum write: 'The words of him who has the sharp two-edged sword.
13 " 'I know where you dwell, where Satan's throne is; you hold fast my name and you did not deny my faith even in the days of An′tipas my witness, my faithful one, who

was killed among you, where Satan dwells. But I have a few things against you: you have 14 some there who hold the teaching of Balaam, who taught Balak to put a stumbling block before the sons of Israel, that they might eat food sacrificed to idols and practise immorality. So you also have some who hold the 15 teaching of the Nicola′itans. Repent then. If 16 not, I will come to you soon and war against them with the sword of my mouth. He who 17 has an ear, let him hear what the Spirit says to the churches. To him who conquers I will give some of the hidden manna, and I will give him a white stone, with a new name written on the stone which no one knows except him who receives it.'

THE SEVEN CHURCHES of ASIA

Pergamum
Thyatira
Sardis
Smyrna   Philadelphia
Ephesus   Laodicea
Patmos

"And to the angel of the church in 18 Thyati′ra write: 'The words of the Son of God, who has eyes like a flame of fire, and whose feet are like burnished bronze.
" 'I know your works, your love and faith 19 and service and patient endurance, and that your latter works exceed the first. But I have 20 this against you, that you tolerate the woman Jez′ebel, who calls herself a prophetess and is teaching and beguiling my servants to prac-tise immorality and to eat food sacrificed to idols. I gave her time to repent, but she 21 refuses to repent of her immorality. Behold, 22 I will throw her on a sickbed, and those who commit adultery with her I will throw into great tribulation, unless they repent of her doings; and I will strike her children dead. 23 And all the churches shall know that I am he who searches mind and heart, and I will give

1.17: Is 44.2, 6. 2.7: Gen 2.9. 2.8: Is 44.6. 2.10: Dan 1.12. 2.14: Num 31.16; 25.1–2. 2.17: Ps 78.24; Is 62.2. 2.18: Dan 10.6. 2.20: 1 Kings 16.31; 2 Kings 9.22, 30; Num 25.1. 2.23: Jer 17.10; Ps 62.12.

24 to each of you as your works deserve. But to the rest of you in Thyati′ra, who do not hold this teaching, who have not learned what some call the deep things of Satan, to you I say, I do not lay upon you any other burden;
25 only hold fast what you have, until I come.
26 He who conquers and who keeps my works until the end, I will give him power over the
27 nations, and he shall rule them with a rod of iron, as when earthen pots are broken in pieces, even as I myself have received power
28 from my Father; and I will give him the
29 morning star. He who has an ear, let him hear what the Spirit says to the churches.'

3 "And to the angel of the church in Sardis write: 'The words of him who has the seven spirits of God and the seven stars.
" 'I know your works; you have the name of
2 being alive, and you are dead. Awake, and strengthen what remains and is on the point of death, for I have not found your works
3 perfect in the sight of my God. Remember then what you received and heard; keep that, and repent. If you will not awake, I will come like a thief, and you will not know at
4 what hour I will come upon you. Yet you have still a few names in Sardis, people who have not soiled their garments; and they shall walk with me in white, for they are worthy.
5 He who conquers shall be clad thus in white garments, and I will not blot his name out of the book of life; I will confess his name
6 before my Father and before his angels. He who has an ear, let him hear what the Spirit says to the churches.'
7 "And to the angel of the church in Philadelphia write: 'The words of the holy one, the true one, who has the key of David, who opens and no one shall shut, who shuts and no one opens.
8 " 'I know your works. Behold, I have set before you an open door, which no one is able to shut; I know that you have but little power, and yet you have kept my word and
9 have not denied my name. Behold, I will make those of the synagogue of Satan who say that they are Jews and are not, but lie—behold, I will make them come and bow down before your feet, and learn that I have
10 loved you. Because you have kept my word of patient endurance, I will keep you from the hour of trial which is coming on the whole world, to try those who dwell upon the
11 earth. I am coming soon; hold fast what you have, so that no one may seize your crown.
12 He who conquers, I will make him a pillar in the temple of my God; never shall he go out of it, and I will write on him the name of

God, and the name of the city of my God, the new Jerusalem which comes down from my God out of heaven, and my own new name.
13 He who has an ear, let him hear what the Spirit says to the churches.'
14 "And to the angel of the church in La-odice′a write: 'The words of the Amen, the faithful and true witness, the beginning of God's creation.
15 " 'I know your works: you are neither cold nor hot. Would that you were cold or hot!
16 So, because you are lukewarm, and neither cold nor hot, I will spew you out of my
17 mouth. For you say, I am rich, I have prospered, and I need nothing; not knowing that you are wretched, pitiable, poor, blind,
18 and naked. Therefore I counsel you to buy from me gold refined by fire, that you may be rich, and white garments to clothe you and to keep the shame of your nakedness from being seen, and salve to anoint your eyes, that you
19 may see. Those whom I love, I reprove and
20 chasten; so be zealous and repent. Behold, I stand at the door and knock; if any one hears my voice and opens the door, I will come in to him and eat with him, and he with me. He
21 who conquers, I will grant him to sit with me on my throne, as I myself conquered and sat down with my Father on his throne. He who
22 has an ear, let him hear what the Spirit says to the churches.' "

A vision of heaven

4 After this I looked, and lo, in heaven an open door! And the first voice, which I had heard speaking to me like a trumpet, said, "Come up hither, and I will show you what
2 must take place after this." At once I was in the Spirit, and lo, a throne stood in heaven,
3 with one seated on the throne! And he who sat there appeared like jasper and carnelian, and round the throne was a rainbow that
4 looked like an emerald. Round the throne were twenty-four thrones, and seated on the thrones were twenty-four elders, clad in white garments, with golden crowns upon
5 their heads. From the throne issue flashes of lightning, and voices and peals of thunder, and before the throne burn seven torches of
6 fire, which are the seven spirits of God; and before the throne there is as it were a sea of glass, like crystal.
7 And round the throne, on each side of the throne, are four living creatures, full of eyes in front and behind: the first living creature like a lion, the second living creature like an ox, the third living creature with the face of a man, and the fourth living creature like a

2.26: Ps 2.8–9. **3.5**: Ex 32.32; Ps 69.28; Dan 12.1; Mt 10.32. **3.7**: Is 22.22. **3.9**: Is 60.14; 49.23; 43.4. **3.12**: Is 62.2; Ezek 48.35; Rev 21.2. **3.14**: Ps 89.28; Prov 8.22; Jn 1.1–3. **3.17**: Hos 12.8. **3.19**: Prov 3.12. **4.1**: Ex 19.16, 24. **4.2**: Ezek 1.26–28. **4.5**: Ex 19.16; Zech 4.2. **4.6**: Ezek 1.5, 18. **4.7**: Ezek 1.10.

8 flying eagle. And the four living creatures, each of them with six wings, are full of eyes all round and within, and day and night they never cease to sing,

"Holy, holy, holy, is the Lord God Almighty,
who was and is and is to come!"

9 And whenever the living creatures give glory and honour and thanks to him who is seated on the throne, who lives for ever and ever,
10 the twenty-four elders fall down before him who is seated on the throne and worship him who lives for ever and ever; they cast their crowns before the throne, singing,

11 "Worthy art thou, our Lord and God,
to receive glory and honour and power,
for thou didst create all things,
and by thy will they existed and were created."

The sealed scroll

5 And I saw in the right hand of him who was seated on the throne a scroll written within
2 and on the back, sealed with seven seals; and I saw a strong angel proclaiming with a loud voice, "Who is worthy to open the scroll and
3 break its seals?" And no one in heaven or on earth or under the earth was able to open the
4 scroll or to look into it, and I wept much that no one was found worthy to open the scroll
5 or to look into it. Then one of the elders said to me, "Weep not; lo, the Lion of the tribe of Judah, the Root of David, has conquered, so that he can open the scroll and its seven seals."

6 And between the throne and the four living creatures and among the elders, I saw a Lamb standing, as though it had been slain, with seven horns and with seven eyes, which are the seven spirits of God sent out into all
7 the earth; and he went and took the scroll from the right hand of him who was seated
8 on the throne. And when he had taken the scroll, the four living creatures and the twenty-four elders fell down before the Lamb, each holding a harp, and with golden bowls full of incense, which are the prayers
9 of the saints; and they sang a new song, saying,

"Worthy art thou to take the scroll and to open its seals,
for thou wast slain and by thy blood didst ransom men for God
from every tribe and tongue and people and nation,
10 and hast made them a kingdom and priests to our God,

and they shall reign on earth."

11 Then I looked, and I heard around the throne and the living creatures and the elders the voice of many angels, numbering myriads of myriads and thousands of thousands,
12 saying with a loud voice, "Worthy is the Lamb who was slain, to receive power and wealth and wisdom and might and honour
13 and glory and blessing!" And I heard every creature in heaven and on earth and under the earth and in the sea, and all therein, saying, "To him who sits upon the throne and to the Lamb be blessing and honour and glory and might for ever and ever!" And the
14 four living creatures said, "Amen!" and the elders fell down and worshipped.

Opening of the seals

6 Now I saw when the Lamb opened one of the seven seals, and I heard one of the four living creatures say, as with a voice of
2 thunder, "Come!" And I saw, and behold, a white horse, and its rider had a bow; and a crown was given to him, and he went out conquering and to conquer.

3 When he opened the second seal, I heard the second living creature say, "Come!"
4 And out came another horse, bright red; its rider was permitted to take peace from the earth, so that men should slay one another; and he was given a great sword.

5 When he opened the third seal, I heard the third living creature say, "Come!" And I saw, and behold, a black horse, and its rider had a balance in his hand; and I heard what
6 seemed to be a voice in the midst of the four living creatures saying, "A quart of wheat for a denarius,[a] and three quarts of barley for a denarius;[a] but do not harm oil and wine!"

7 When he opened the fourth seal, I heard the voice of the fourth living creature say,
8 "Come!" And I saw, and behold, a pale horse, and its rider's name was Death, and Hades followed him; and they were given power over a fourth of the earth, to kill with sword and with famine and with pestilence and by wild beasts of the earth.

9 When he opened the fifth seal, I saw under the altar the souls of those who had been slain for the word of God and for the witness
10 they had borne; they cried out with a loud voice, "O Sovereign Lord, holy and true, how long before thou wilt judge and avenge our blood on those who dwell upon the
11 earth?" Then they were each given a white robe and told to rest a little longer, until the number of their fellow servants and their

[a] The denarius was worth about seventeen pence
4.8: Is 6.2–3. 4.9: Ps 47.8. 5.1: Ezek 2.9; Is 29.11.
5.8: Ps 141.2. 5.9: Ps 33.3. 5.10: Ex 19.6; Is 61.6. 5.11: Dan 7.10. 6.2: Zech 1.8; 6.1–3.
6.6: 2 Kings 6.25. 6.8: Hos 13.14; Ezek 5.12. 6.10: Zech 1.12; Ps 79.5; Gen 4.10.

brethren should be complete, who were to be killed as they themselves had been.

12 When he opened the sixth seal, I looked, and behold, there was a great earthquake; and the sun became black as sackcloth,
13 and the full moon became like blood, and the stars of the sky fell to the earth as the fig tree sheds
14 its winter fruit when shaken by a gale; the sky vanished like a scroll that is rolled up, and every mountain and island was removed
15 from its place. Then the kings of the earth and the great men and the generals and the rich and the strong, and every one, slave and free, hid in the caves and among the rocks of
16 the mountains, calling to the mountains and rocks, "Fall on us and hide us from the face of him who is seated on the throne, and from
17 the wrath of the Lamb; for the great day of their wrath has come, and who can stand before it?"

Sealing the servants of God

7 After this I saw four angels standing at the four corners of the earth, holding back the four winds of the earth, that no wind might blow on earth or sea or against any tree.
2 Then I saw another angel ascend from the rising of the sun, with the seal of the living God, and he called with a loud voice to the four angels who had been given power to
3 harm earth and sea, saying, "Do not harm the earth or the sea or the trees, till we have sealed the servants of our God upon their
4 foreheads." And I heard the number of the sealed, a hundred and forty-four thousand sealed, out of every tribe of the sons of Israel,
5 twelve thousand sealed out of the tribe of Judah, twelve thousand of the tribe of Reuben, twelve thousand of the tribe of Gad,
6 twelve thousand of the tribe of Asher, twelve thousand of the tribe of Naph'tali, twelve
7 thousand of the tribe of Manas'seh, twelve thousand of the tribe of Simeon, twelve thousand of the tribe of Levi, twelve
8 thousand of the tribe of Is'sachar, twelve thousand of the tribe of Zeb'ulun, twelve thousand of the tribe of Joseph, twelve thousand sealed out of the tribe of Benjamin.
9 After this I looked, and behold, a great multitude which no man could number, from every nation, from all tribes and peoples and tongues, standing before the throne and before the Lamb, clothed in white robes,
10 with palm branches in their hands, and crying out with a loud voice, "Salvation belongs to our God who sits upon the throne,
11 and to the Lamb!" And all the angels stood

round the throne and round the elders and the four living creatures, and they fell on their faces before the throne and worshipped
12 God, saying, "Amen! Blessing and glory and wisdom and thanksgiving and honour and power and might be to our God for ever and ever! Amen."
13 Then one of the elders addressed me, saying, "Who are these, clothed in white robes, and whence have they come?" I said
14 to him, "Sir, you know." And he said to me, "These are they who have come out of the great tribulation; they have washed their robes and made them white in the blood of the Lamb.
15 Therefore are they before the throne of God,
and serve him day and night within his temple;
and he who sits upon the throne will shelter them with his presence.
16 They shall hunger no more, neither thirst any more;
the sun shall not strike them, nor any scorching heat.
17 For the Lamb in the midst of the throne will be their shepherd,
and he will guide them to springs of living water;
and God will wipe away every tear from their eyes."

Trumpet peals

8 When the Lamb opened the seventh seal, there was silence in heaven for about half an hour.
2 Then I saw the seven angels who stand before God, and seven trumpets were given to them.
3 And another angel came and stood at the altar with a golden censer; and he was given much incense to mingle with the prayers of all the saints upon the golden
4 altar before the throne; and the smoke of the incense rose with the prayers of the saints from the hand of the angel before God.
5 Then the angel took the censer and filled it with fire from the altar and threw it on the earth; and there were peals of thunder, loud noises, flashes of lightning, and an earthquake.
6 Now the seven angels who had the seven trumpets made ready to blow them.
7 The first angel blew his trumpet, and there followed hail and fire, mixed with blood, which fell on the earth; and a third of the earth was burnt up, and a third of the trees were burnt up, and all green grass was burnt up.

6.12: Joel 2.31; Acts 2.20.   6.13: Is 34.4.   6.15: Is 2.10.   6.16: Hos 10.8.   6.17: Joel 2.11; Mal 3.2.
7.1: Zech 6.5.   7.3: Ezek 9.4.   7.14: Dan 12.1; Gen 49.11.   7.16: Is 49.10; Ps 121.6.
7.17: Ezek 34.23; Ps 23.2; Is 25.8.   8.3: Amos 9.1; Ps 141.2.   8.5: Lev 16.12; Ezek 10.2.
8.7: Ex 9.23–25.

8 The second angel blew his trumpet, and
something like a great mountain, burning
9 with fire, was thrown into the sea; and a third
of the sea became blood, a third of the living
creatures in the sea died, and a third of the
ships were destroyed.

10 The third angel blew his trumpet, and a
great star fell from heaven, blazing like a
torch, and it fell on a third of the rivers and
11 on the fountains of water. The name of the
star is Wormwood. A third of the waters
became wormwood, and many men died of
the water, because it was made bitter.
12 The fourth angel blew his trumpet, and a
third of the sun was struck, and a third of the
moon, and a third of the stars, so that a third
of their light was darkened; a third of the day
was kept from shining, and likewise a third of
the night.
13 Then I looked, and I heard an eagle crying
with a loud voice, as it flew in midheaven,
"Woe, woe, woe to those who dwell on the
earth, at the blasts of the other trumpets
which the three angels are about to blow!"

9 And the fifth angel blew his trumpet, and I
saw a star fallen from heaven to earth, and he
was given the key of the shaft of the bottom-
2 less pit; he opened the shaft of the bottomless
pit, and from the shaft rose smoke like the
smoke of a great furnace, and the sun and
the air were darkened with the smoke from the
3 shaft. Then from the smoke came locusts on
the earth, and they were given power like the
4 power of scorpions of the earth; they were
told not to harm the grass of the earth or any
green growth or any tree, but only those of
mankind who have not the seal of God upon
5 their foreheads; they were allowed to torture
them for five months, but not to kill them,
and their torture was like the torture of a
6 scorpion, when it stings a man. And in those
days men will seek death and will not find it;
they will long to die, and death will fly from
them.

In appearance the locusts were like horses 7
arrayed for battle; on their heads were what
looked like crowns of gold; their faces were
like human faces, their hair like women's 8
hair, and their teeth like lions' teeth; they 9
had scales like iron breastplates, and the
noise of their wings was like the noise of
many chariots with horses rushing into
battle. They have tails like scorpions, and 10
stings, and their power of hurting men for
five months lies in their tails. They have as 11
king over them the angel of the bottomless
pit; his name in Hebrew is Abad´don, and in
Greek he is called Apol´lyon.[b]
The first woe has passed; behold, two woes 12
are still to come.
Then the sixth angel blew his trumpet, and 13
I heard a voice from the four horns of the
golden altar before God, saying to the sixth 14
angel who had the trumpet, "Release the
four angels who are bound at the great river
Euphra´tes." So the four angels were re- 15
leased, who had been held ready for the
hour, the day, the month, and the year, to kill
a third of mankind. The number of the 16
troops of cavalry was twice ten thousand
times ten thousand; I heard their number.
And this was how I saw the horses in my 17
vision; the riders wore breastplates the
colour of fire and of sapphire[c] and of
sulphur, and the heads of the horses were like
lions' heads, and fire and smoke and sulphur
issued from their mouths. By these three 18
plagues a third of mankind was killed, by the
fire and smoke and sulphur issuing from
their mouths. For the power of the horses is 19
in their mouths and in their tails; their tails
are like serpents, with heads, and by means
of them they wound.
The rest of mankind, who were not killed 20
by these plagues, did not repent of the works
of their hands nor give up worshipping
demons and idols of gold and silver and
bronze and stone and wood, which cannot
either see or hear or walk; nor did they 21
repent of their murders or their sorceries or
their immorality or their thefts.

The angel and the little scroll

Then I saw another mighty angel coming 10
down from heaven, wrapped in a cloud, with
a rainbow over his head, and his face was like
the sun, and his legs like pillars of fire. He 2
had a little scroll open in his hand. And he
set his right foot on the sea, and his left foot
on the land, and called out with a loud voice, 3
like a lion roaring; when he called out, the

[b] Or Destroyer   [c] Greek *hyacinth*
8.8: Jer 51.25.   8.10: Is 14.12.   9.2: Gen 19.28; Ex 19.18; Joel 2.10.   9.3: Ex 10.12-15.   9.4: Ezek 9.4.
9.6: Job 3.21.   9.7: Joel 2.4.   9.8: Joel 1.6.   9.9: Joel 2.5.   9.13: Ex 30.1-3.
9.20: Is 17.8; Ps 115.4-7; 135.15-17.

4 seven thunders sounded. And when the seven thunders had sounded, I was about to write, but I heard a voice from heaven saying, "Seal up what the seven thunders 5 have said, and do not write it down." And the angel whom I saw standing on sea and land lifted up his right hand to heaven 6 and swore by him who lives for ever and ever, who created heaven and what is in it, the earth and what is in it, and the sea and what is in it, that there should be no more delay, 7 but that in the days of the trumpet call to be sounded by the seventh angel, the mystery of God, as he announced to his servants the prophets, should be fulfilled.

8 Then the voice which I had heard from heaven spoke to me again, saying, "Go, take the scroll which is open in the hand of the angel who is standing on the sea and on the 9 land." So I went to the angel and told him to give me the little scroll; and he said to me, "Take it and eat; it will be bitter to your stomach, but sweet as honey in your 10 mouth." And I took the little scroll from the hand of the angel and ate it; it was sweet as honey in my mouth, but when I had eaten it 11 my stomach was made bitter. And I was told, "You must again prophesy about many peoples and nations and tongues and kings."

The angel and the temple

11 Then I was given a measuring rod like a staff, and I was told: "Rise and measure the temple of God and the altar and those who 2 worship there, but do not measure the court outside the temple; leave that out, for it is given over to the nations, and they will trample over the holy city for forty-two 3 months. And I will grant my two witnesses power to prophesy for one thousand two hundred and sixty days, clothed in sackcloth." 4 These are the two olive trees and the two lampstands which stand before the Lord of 5 the earth. And if any one would harm them, fire pours from their mouth and consumes their foes; if any one would harm them, thus 6 he is doomed to be killed. They have power to shut the sky, that no rain may fall during the days of their prophesying, and they have power over the waters to turn them into blood, and to smite the earth with every 7 plague, as often as they desire. And when they have finished their testimony, the beast that ascends from the bottomless pit will make war upon them and conquer them and 8 kill them, and their dead bodies will lie in the

street of the great city which is allegorically[d] called Sodom and Egypt, where their Lord was crucified. For three days and a half men 9 from the peoples and tribes and tongues and nations gaze at their dead bodies and refuse to let them be placed in a tomb, and those 10 who dwell on the earth will rejoice over them and make merry and exchange presents, because these two prophets had been a torment to those who dwell on the earth. But 11 after the three and a half days a breath of life from God entered them, and they stood up on their feet, and great fear fell on those who saw them. Then they heard a loud voice 12 from heaven saying to them, "Come up hither!" And in the sight of their foes they went up to heaven in a cloud. And at that 13 hour there was a great earthquake, and a tenth of the city fell; seven thousand people were killed in the earthquake, and the rest were terrified and gave glory to the God of heaven.

The second woe has passed; behold, the 14 third woe is soon to come.

The last trumpet's peal

Then the seventh angel blew his trumpet, 15 and there were loud voices in heaven, saying, "The kingdom of the world has become the kingdom of our Lord and of his Christ, and he shall reign for ever and ever." And the 16 twenty-four elders who sit on their thrones before God fell on their faces and wor- shipped God, saying, 17
"We give thanks to thee, Lord God Almighty, who art and who wast, that thou hast taken thy great power and begun to reign.
The nations raged, but thy wrath came, 18 and the time for the dead to be judged, for rewarding thy servants, the prophets and saints,
and those who fear thy name, both small and great,
and for destroying the destroyers of the earth."
Then God's temple in heaven was opened, 19 and the ark of his covenant was seen within his temple; and there were flashes of light- ning, loud noises, peals of thunder, an earth- quake, and heavy hail.

War in heaven

And a great portent appeared in heaven, a 12 woman clothed with the sun, with the moon

d Greek *spiritually*
10.5: Deut 32.40; Dan 12.7.   10.9: Ezek 2.8; 3.1-3.   10.11: Jer 1.10.   11.1: Ezek 40.3.
11.2: Zech 12.3; Is 63.18; Lk 21.24.   11.4: Zech 4.3, 11-14.   11.5: 2 Kings 1.10; Jer 5.14.
11.6: 1 Kings 17.1; Ex 7.17, 19.   11.7: Dan 7.3, 7, 21.   11.8: Is 1.9.   11.11: Ezek 37.5, 10.
11.12: 2 Kings 2.11.   11.15: Ps 22.28; Dan 7.14, 27.   11.18: Ps 2.1.
11.19: 1 Kings 8.1-6; 2 Maccabees 2.4-8.

under her feet, and on her head a crown of
2 twelve stars; she was with child and she cried
out in her pangs of birth, in anguish for
3 delivery. And another portent appeared in
heaven; behold, a great red dragon, with
seven heads and ten horns, and seven
4 diadems upon his heads. His tail swept
down a third of the stars of heaven, and cast
them to the earth. And the dragon stood
before the woman who was about to bear a
child, that he might devour her child when
5 she brought it forth; she brought forth a male
child, one who is to rule all the nations with a
rod of iron, but her child was caught up to
6 God and to his throne, and the woman fled
into the wilderness, where she has a place
prepared by God, in which to be nourished
for one thousand two hundred and sixty
days.
7 Now war arose in heaven, Michael and his
angels fighting against the dragon; and the
8 dragon and his angels fought, but they were
defeated and there was no longer any place
9 for them in heaven. And the great dragon
was thrown down, that ancient serpent, who
is called the Devil and Satan, the deceiver of
the whole world—he was thrown down to the
earth, and his angels were thrown down with
10 him. And I heard a loud voice in heaven,
saying, "Now the salvation and the power
and the kingdom of our God and the
authority of his Christ have come, for the
accuser of our brethren has been thrown
down, who accuses them day and night
11 before our God. And they have conquered
him by the blood of the Lamb and by the
word of their testimony, for they loved not
12 their lives even unto death. Rejoice then, O
heaven and you that dwell therein! But woe
to you, O earth and sea, for the devil has
come down to you in great wrath, because he
knows that his time is short!"
13 And when the dragon saw that he had been
thrown down to the earth, he pursued the
14 woman who had borne the male child. But
the woman was given the two wings of the
great eagle that she might fly from the
serpent into the wilderness, to the place
where she is to be nourished for a time, and
15 times, and half a time. The serpent poured
water like a river out of his mouth after the
woman, to sweep her away with the flood.
16 But the earth came to the help of the woman,
and the earth opened its mouth and swallowed the river which the dragon had poured
17 from his mouth. Then the dragon was angry
with the woman, and went off to make war

on the rest of her offspring, on those who
keep the commandments of God and bear
testimony to Jesus. And he stood[e] on the
sand of the sea.

War in the sea and on land

And I saw a beast rising out of the sea, with **13**
ten horns and seven heads, with ten diadems
upon its horns and a blasphemous name
upon its heads. And the beast that I saw was 2
like a leopard, its feet were like a bear's, and
its mouth was like a lion's mouth. And to it
the dragon gave his power and his throne and
great authority. One of its heads seemed to 3
have a mortal wound, but its mortal wound
was healed, and the whole earth followed the
beast with wonder. Men worshipped the 4
dragon, for he had given his authority to the
beast, and they worshipped the beast, saying,
"Who is like the beast, and who can fight
against it?"
And the beast was given a mouth uttering 5
haughty and blasphemous words, and it was
allowed to exercise authority for forty-two
months; it opened its mouth to utter blas- 6
phemies against God, blaspheming his name
and his dwelling, that is, those who dwell in
heaven. Also it was allowed to make war on 7
the saints and to conquer them.[f] And
authority was given it over every tribe and
people and tongue and nation, and all who 8
dwell on earth will worship it, every one
whose name has not been written before the
foundation of the world in the book of life of
the Lamb that was slain. If any one has an 9
ear, let him hear:

If any one is to be taken captive,   10
     to captivity he goes;
if any one slays with the sword,
     with the sword must he be slain.

Here is a call for the endurance and faith of
the saints.
Then I saw another beast which rose out of 11
the earth; it had two horns like a lamb and it
spoke like a dragon. It exercises all the 12
authority of the first beast in its presence,
and makes the earth and its inhabitants
worship the first beast, whose mortal wound
was healed. It works great signs, even 13
making fire come down from heaven to earth
in the sight of men; and by the signs which it 14
is allowed to work in the presence of the
beast, it deceives those who dwell on earth,
bidding them make an image for the beast
which was wounded by the sword and yet

---

[e] Other ancient authorities read *And I stood*, connecting the sentence with 13.1
[f] Other ancient authorities omit this sentence

12.2: Mic 4.10.   **12.3:** Dan 7.7.   **12.4:** Dan 8.10.   **12.5:** Is 66.7; Ps 2.9.   **12.7:** Dan 10.13.
12.9: Gen 3.1, 14–15; Zech 3.1.   **12.10:** Job 1.9–11.   **12.12:** Is 44.23; 49.13.   **12.14:** Dan 7.25; 12.7.
13.1: Dan 7.1–6.   **13.5:** Dan 7.8.   **13.7:** Dan 7.21.   **13.9:** Mk 4.23.   **13.10:** Jer 15.2.   **13.14:** Deut 13.1–5.

15 lived; and it was allowed to give breath to the image of the beast so that the image of the beast should even speak, and to cause those who would not worship the image of the
16 beast to be slain. Also it causes all, both small and great, both rich and poor, both free and slave, to be marked on the right hand or
17 the forehead, so that no one can buy or sell unless he has the mark, that is, the name of
18 the beast or the number of its name. This calls for wisdom: let him who has understanding reckon the number of the beast, for it is a human number, its number is six hundred and sixty-six. *g*

The Church triumphant

14 Then I looked, and lo, on Mount Zion stood the Lamb, and with him a hundred and forty-four thousand who had his name and his Father's name written on their fore-
2 heads. And I heard a voice from heaven like the sound of many waters and like the sound of loud thunder; the voice I heard was like the sound of harpers playing on their harps,
3 and they sing a new song before the throne and before the four living creatures and before the elders. No one could learn that song except the hundred and forty-four thousand who had been redeemed from the
4 earth. It is these who have not defiled themselves with women, for they are chaste; *h* it is these who follow the Lamb wherever he goes; these have been redeemed from mankind as first fruits for God and the
5 Lamb, and in their mouth no lie was found, for they are spotless.
6 Then I saw another angel flying in midheaven, with an eternal gospel to proclaim to those who dwell on earth, to every
7 nation and tribe and tongue and people; and he said with a loud voice, "Fear God and give him glory, for the hour of his judgment has come; and worship him who made heaven and earth, the sea and the fountains of water."
8 Another angel, a second, followed, saying, "Fallen, fallen is Babylon the great, she who made all nations drink the wine of her impure passion."
9 And another angel, a third, followed them, saying with a loud voice, "If any one worships the beast and its image, and receives a
10 mark on his forehead or on his hand, he also shall drink the wine of God's wrath, poured unmixed into the cup of his anger, and he

shall be tormented with fire and brimstone in the presence of the holy angels and in the presence of the Lamb. And the smoke of 11 their torment goes up for ever and ever; and they have no rest, day or night, these worshippers of the beast and its image, and whoever receives the mark of its name."
Here is a call for the endurance of the saints, 12 those who keep the commandments of God and the faith of Jesus.
And I heard a voice from heaven saying, 13 "Write this: Blessed are the dead who die in the Lord henceforth." "Blessed indeed," says the Spirit, "that they may rest from their labours, for their deeds follow them!"
Then I looked, and lo, a white cloud, and 14 seated on the cloud one like a son of man, with a golden crown on his head, and a sharp sickle in his hand. And another angel came 15 out of the temple, calling with a loud voice to him who sat upon the cloud, "Put in your sickle, and reap, for the hour to reap has come, for the harvest of the earth is fully ripe." So he who sat upon the cloud swung 16 his sickle on the earth, and the earth was reaped.
And another angel came out of the temple 17 in heaven, and he too had a sharp sickle. Then another angel came out from the altar, 18 the angel who has power over fire, and he called with a loud voice to him who had the sharp sickle, "Put in your sickle, and gather the clusters of the vine of the earth, for its grapes are ripe." So the angel swung his 19 sickle on the earth and gathered the vintage of the earth, and threw it into the great wine press of the wrath of God; and the wine press 20 was trodden outside the city, and blood flowed from the wine press, as high as a horse's bridle, for one thousand six hundred stadia. *i*

Then I saw another portent in heaven, great 15 and wonderful, seven angels with seven plagues, which are the last, for with them the wrath of God is ended.
And I saw what appeared to be a sea of glass 2 mingled with fire, and those who had conquered the beast and its image and the number of its name, standing beside the sea of glass with harps of God in their hands. And they sing the song of Moses, the servant 3 of God, and the song of the Lamb, saying,

"Great and wonderful are thy deeds,
    O Lord God the Almighty!
Just and true are thy ways,
    O King of the ages! *j*

g Other ancient authorities read *six hundred and sixteen*   *h* Greek *virgins*   *i* About two hundred miles
j Other ancient authorities read *the nations*
13.15: Dan 3.5.   **14.1:** Ezek 9.4.   **14.8:** Is 21.9.   **14.10:** Jer 51.7; Gen 19.24.   **14.11:** Is 34.10.
14.14: Dan 7.13.   **14.15:** Joel 3.13; Mt 13.30.   **14.20:** Joel 3.13.   **15.1:** Lev 26.21.
15.3: Ex 15.1; Ps 145.17.

4 Who shall not fear and glorify thy name, O Lord?
For thou alone art holy.
All nations shall come and worship thee,
for thy judgments have been revealed."

5 After this I looked, and the temple of the
6 tent of witness in heaven was opened, and out of the temple came the seven angels with the seven plagues, robed in pure bright linen, and their breasts girded with golden girdles.

7 And one of the four living creatures gave the seven angels seven golden bowls full of the wrath of God who lives for ever and ever;
8 and the temple was filled with smoke from the glory of God and from his power, and no one could enter the temple until the seven plagues of the seven angels were ended.

Visions of judgment

16 Then I heard a loud voice from the temple telling the seven angels, "Go and pour out on the earth the seven bowls of the wrath of God."

2 So the first angel went and poured his bowl on the earth, and foul and evil sores came upon the men who bore the mark of the beast and worshipped its image.

3 The second angel poured his bowl into the sea, and it became like the blood of a dead man, and every living thing died that was in the sea.

4 The third angel poured his bowl into the rivers and the fountains of water, and they
5 became blood. And I heard the angel of water say,

"Just art thou in these thy judgments,
thou who art and wast, O Holy One.
6 For men have shed the blood of saints and prophets,
and thou hast given them blood to drink.
It is their due!"

7 And I heard the altar cry,
"Yea, Lord God the Almighty,
true and just are thy judgments!"

The fourth angel poured his bowl on the 8 sun, and it was allowed to scorch men with fire; men were scorched by the fierce heat, 9 and they cursed the name of God who had power over these plagues, and they did not repent and give him glory.

The fifth angel poured his bowl on the 10 throne of the beast, and its kingdom was in darkness; men gnawed their tongues in anguish and cursed the God of heaven for 11 their pain and sores, and did not repent of their deeds.

The sixth angel poured his bowl on the 12 great river Euphra'tes, and its water was dried up, to prepare the way for the kings from the east. And I saw, issuing from the 13 mouth of the dragon and from the mouth of the beast and from the mouth of the false prophet, three foul spirits like frogs; for they 14 are demonic spirits, performing signs, who go abroad to the kings of the whole world, to assemble them for battle on the great day of God the Almighty. ("Lo, I am coming like a 15 thief! Blessed is he who is awake, keeping his garments that he may not go naked and be seen exposed!") And they assembled 16 them at the place which is called in Hebrew Armaged'don.

The seventh angel poured his bowl into the 17 air, and a great voice came out of the temple, from the throne, saying, "It is done!" And 18 there were flashes of lightning, loud noises, peals of thunder, and a great earthquake such as had never been since men were on the earth, so great was that earthquake. The 19 great city was split into three parts, and the cities of the nations fell, and God remembered great Babylon, to make her drain the cup of the fury of his wrath. And every 20 island fled away, and no mountains were to be found; and great hailstones, heavy as a 21 hundredweight, dropped on men from heaven, till men cursed God for the plague of the hail, so fearful was that plague.

Visions of doom

Then one of the seven angels who had the **17** seven bowls came and said to me, "Come, I will show you the judgment of the great harlot who is seated upon many waters, with 2 whom the kings of the earth have committed fornication, and with the wine of whose fornication the dwellers on earth have become drunk." And he carried me away in 3 the Spirit into a wilderness, and I saw a woman sitting on a scarlet beast which was full of blasphemous names, and it had seven

15.4: Jer 10.7; Ps 86.9–10. 15.5: Ex 40.34. 15.8: 1 Kings 8.10; Is 6.4; Ezek 44.4. 16.1: Is 66.6; Ps 69.24.
16.2: Ex 9.10–11; Deut 28.35. 16.3–4: Ex 7.17–21. 16.6: Ps 79.3. 16.7: Ps 119.137. 16.10: Ex 10.21.
16.12: Is 11.15–16. 16.13: 1 Kings 22.21–23; Ex 8.3. 16.15: 1 Thess 5.2. 16.16: 2 Kings 9.27.
16.17: Is 66.6. 16.18: Ex 19.16; Dan 12.1. 16.21: Ex 9.23. 17.1: Jer 51.13. 17.2: Is 23.17; Jer 25.15–16.

4 heads and ten horns. The woman was arrayed in purple and scarlet, and bedecked with gold and jewels and pearls, holding in her hand a golden cup full of abominations 5 and the impurities of her fornication; and on her forehead was written a name of mystery: "Babylon the great, mother of harlots and of 6 earth's abominations." And I saw the woman, drunk with the blood of the saints and the blood of the martyrs of Jesus.

7 When I saw her I marvelled greatly. But the angel said to me, "Why marvel? I will tell you the mystery of the woman, and of the beast with seven heads and ten horns that 8 carries her. The beast that you saw was, and is not, and is to ascend from the bottomless pit and go to perdition; and the dwellers on earth whose names have not been written in the book of life from the foundation of the world, will marvel to behold the beast, because it was and is not and is to come. 9 This calls for a mind with wisdom: the seven heads are seven hills on which the woman is 10 seated; they are also seven kings, five of whom have fallen, one is, the other has not yet come, and when he comes he must 11 remain only a little while. As for the beast that was and is not, it is an eighth but it belongs to the seven, and it goes to perdi- 12 tion. And the ten horns that you saw are ten kings who have not yet received royal power, but they are to receive authority as kings for 13 one hour, together with the beast. These are of one mind and give over their power and 14 authority to the beast; they will make war on the Lamb, and the Lamb will conquer them, for he is Lord of lords and King of kings, and those with him are called and chosen and faithful." 15 And he said to me, "The waters that you saw, where the harlot is seated, are peoples and multitudes and nations and tongues. 16 And the ten horns that you saw, they and the beast will hate the harlot; they will make her desolate and naked, and devour her flesh and 17 burn her up with fire, for God has put it into their hearts to carry out his purpose by being of one mind and giving over their royal power to the beast, until the words of God 18 shall be fulfilled. And the woman that you saw is the great city which has dominion over the kings of the earth."

18 After this I saw another angel coming down from heaven, having great authority; and the earth was made bright with his splendour. 2 And he called out with a mighty voice, "Fallen, fallen is Babylon the great!

It has become a dwelling place of demons, a haunt of every foul spirit, a haunt of every foul and hateful bird; for all nations have drunk[k] the wine of her 3 impure passion, and the kings of the earth have committed fornication with her, and the merchants of the earth have grown rich with the wealth of her wantonness."

Then I heard another voice from heaven 4 saying, "Come out of her, my people, lest you take part in her sins, lest you share in her plagues; for her sins are heaped high as heaven, 5 and God has remembered her iniquities. Render to her as she herself has rendered, 6 and repay her double for her deeds; mix a double draught for her in the cup she mixed. As she glorified herself and played the 7 wanton, so give her a like measure of torment and mourning. Since in her heart she says, 'A queen I sit, I am no widow, mourning I shall never see,' so shall her plagues come in a single day, 8 pestilence and mourning and famine, and she shall be burned with fire; for mighty is the Lord God who judges her."

And the kings of the earth, who committed 9 fornication and were wanton with her, will weep and wail over her when they see the smoke of her burning; they will stand off, 10 in fear of her torment, and say, "Alas! alas! thou great city, thou mighty city, Babylon! In one hour has thy judgment come." And the merchants of the earth weep and 11 mourn for her, since no one buys their cargo any more, cargo of gold, silver, jewels and 12 pearls, fine linen, purple, silk and scarlet, all kinds of scented wood, all articles of ivory, all articles of costly wood, bronze, iron and marble, cinnamon, spice, incense, myrrh, 13 frankincense, wine, oil, fine flour and wheat, cattle and sheep, horses and chariots, and slaves, that is, human souls. "The fruit for which thy soul longed has 14 gone from thee, and all thy dainties and thy splendour are lost to thee, never to be found again!" The merchants of these wares, who gained 15 wealth from her, will stand far off, in fear of her torment, weeping and mourning aloud,

k Other ancient authorities read *fallen by*
17.4: Jer 51.7.   17.8: Dan 7.3; Rev 3.5.   17.12: Dan 7.20–24.   17.14: Dan 2.47.   18.2: Is 21.9; Jer 50.39.
18.3: Jer 25.15, 27.   18.4: Is 48.20; Jer 50.8.   18.5: Jer 51.9.   18.6: Ps 137.8.   18.7: Is 47.8–9.
18.9: Ezek 26.16–17.   18.11: Ezek 27.36.   18.12: Ezek 27.12–13, 22.   18.15: Ezek 27.36, 31.

16 "Alas, alas, for the great city
  that was clothed in fine linen, in purple
    and scarlet,
  bedecked with gold, with jewels, and with
    pearls!
17 In one hour all this wealth has been laid
    waste."
  And all shipmasters and seafaring men,
  sailors and all whose trade is on the sea, stood
18 far off and cried out as they saw the smoke of
  her burning,

shall be heard in thee no more;
  for thy merchants were the great men of
    the earth,
  and all nations were deceived by thy
    sorcery.
  And in her was found the blood of 2
    prophets and of saints,
  and of all who have been slain on
    earth."

Songs of deliverance

After this I heard what seemed to be the 1
mighty voice of a great multitude in heaven,
crying,

No one buys their cargo any more. Rev **18,** 11

  "What city was like the great city?"
19 And they threw dust on their heads, as they
  wept and mourned, crying out,
    "Alas, alas, for the great city
    where all who had ships at sea grew rich by
      her wealth!
    In one hour she has been laid waste.
20 Rejoice over her, O heaven,
    O saints and apostles and prophets,
    for God has given judgment for you
      against her!"
21 Then a mighty angel took up a stone like a
  great millstone and threw it into the sea,
  saying,
    "So shall Babylon the great city be thrown
      down with violence,
    and shall be found no more;
22   and the sound of harpers and minstrels, of
      flute players and trumpeters,
      shall be heard in thee no more;
    and a craftsman of any craft
      shall be found in thee no more;
    and the sound of the millstone
      shall be heard in thee no more;
23   and the light of a lamp
      shall shine in thee no more;
    and the voice of bridegroom and bride

  "Hallelujah! Salvation and glory and
    power belong to our God,
  for his judgments are true and just;   2
  he has judged the great harlot who cor-
    rupted the earth with her fornication,
  and he has avenged on her the blood of his
    servants."
Once more they cried,   3
  "Hallelujah! The smoke from her goes up
    for ever and ever."
And the twenty-four elders and the four 4
living creatures fell down and worshipped
God who is seated on the throne, saying,
"Amen. Hallelujah!" And from the throne 5
came a voice crying,
  "Praise our God, all you his servants,
  you who fear him, small and great."
Then I heard what seemed to be the voice of 6

18.17: Is 23.14; Ezek 27.26–30.   **18.19:** Ezek 27.30–34.   **18.20:** Is 44.23; Jer 51.48.
18.21: Jer 51.63; Ezek 26.21.   **18.22:** Is 24.8; Ezek 26.13.   **18.23:** Jer 25.10.   **18.24:** Jer 51.49.
19.2: Deut 32.43.   **19.3:** Is 34 10.   **19.5:** Ps 115.13.

a great multitude, like the sound of many waters and like the sound of mighty thunderpeals, crying,

"Hallelujah! For the Lord our God the Almighty reigns.

Let us rejoice and exult and give him the glory,
for the marriage of the Lamb has come,
and his Bride has made herself ready;
it was granted her to be clothed with fine linen, bright and pure"—
for the fine linen is the righteous deeds of the saints.

And the angel said[l] to me, "Write this: Blessed are those who are invited to the marriage supper of the Lamb." And he said to me, "These are true words of God."

Then I fell down at his feet to worship him, but he said to me, "You must not do that! I am a fellow servant with you and your brethren who hold the testimony of Jesus. Worship God." For the testimony of Jesus is the spirit of prophecy.

Then I saw heaven opened, and behold, a white horse! He who sat upon it is called Faithful and True, and in righteousness he judges and makes war. His eyes are like a flame of fire, and on his head are many diadems; and he has a name inscribed which no one knows but himself. He is clad in a robe dipped in[m] blood, and the name by which he is called is The Word of God. And the armies of heaven, arrayed in fine linen, white and pure, followed him on white horses. From his mouth issues a sharp sword with which to smite the nations, and he will rule them with a rod of iron; he will tread the wine press of the fury of the wrath of God the Almighty. On his robe and on his thigh he has a name inscribed, King of kings and Lord of lords.

Then I saw an angel standing in the sun, and with a loud voice he called to all the birds that fly in midheaven, "Come, gather for the great supper of God, to eat the flesh of kings, the flesh of captains, the flesh of mighty men, the flesh of horses and their riders, and the flesh of all men, both free and slave, both small and great." And I saw the beast and the kings of the earth with their armies gathered to make war against him who sits upon the horse and against his army. And the beast was captured, and with it the false prophet who in its presence had worked the signs by which he deceived those who had received the mark of the beast and those who worshipped its image. These two were

thrown alive into the lake of fire that burns with brimstone. And the rest were slain by the sword of him who sits upon the horse, the sword that issues from his mouth; and all the birds were gorged with their flesh.

Then I saw an angel coming down from heaven, holding in his hand the key of the bottomless pit and a great chain. And he seized the dragon, that ancient serpent, who is the Devil and Satan, and bound him for a thousand years, and threw him into the pit, and shut it and sealed it over him, that he should deceive the nations no more, till the thousand years were ended. After that he must be loosed for a little while.

Then I saw thrones, and seated on them were those to whom judgment was committed. Also I saw the souls of those who had been beheaded for their testimony to Jesus and for the word of God, and who had not worshipped the beast or its image and had not received its mark on their foreheads or their hands. They came to life, and reigned with Christ a thousand years. The rest of the dead did not come to life until the thousand years were ended. This is the first resurrection. Blessed and holy is he who shares in the first resurrection! Over such the second death has no power, but they shall be priests of God and of Christ, and they shall reign with him a thousand years.

And when the thousand years are ended, Satan will be loosed from his prison and will come out to deceive the nations which are at the four corners of the earth, that is, Gog and Magog, to gather them for battle; their number is like the sand of the sea. And they marched up over the broad earth and surrounded the camp of the saints and the beloved city; but fire came down from heaven[n] and consumed them, and the devil who had deceived them was thrown into the lake of fire and brimstone where the beast and the false prophet were, and they will be tormented day and night for ever and ever.

Visions of glory

Then I saw a great white throne and him who sat upon it; from his presence earth and sky fled away, and no place was found for them. And I saw the dead, great and small, standing before the throne, and books were opened. Also another book was opened, which is the book of life. And the dead were judged by what was written in the books, by

---

l Greek *he said*   m Other ancient authorities read *sprinkled with*
n Other ancient authorities read *from God, out of heaven*, or *out of heaven from God*
19.7: Ps 118.24.   19.11: Ezek 1.1.   19.12: Dan 10.6.   19.15: Ps 2.9.
19.16: Deut 10.17; Dan 2.47.   19.17: Ezek 39.4, 17–20.
20.4: Dan 7.9, 22, 27.   20.8: Ezek 38.2, 9, 15.   20.9: 2 Kings 1.10–12.   20.11–12: Dan 7.9–10.

13 what they had done. And the sea gave up the dead in it. Death and Hades gave up the dead in them, and all were judged by what they 14 had done. Then Death and Hades were thrown into the lake of fire. This is the 15 second death, the lake of fire; and if any one's name was not found written in the book of life, he was thrown into the lake of fire.

A new heaven and earth

21 Then I saw a new heaven and a new earth; for the first heaven and the first earth had 2 passed away, and the sea was no more. And I saw the holy city, new Jerusalem, coming down out of heaven from God, prepared as a 3 bride adorned for her husband; and I heard a great voice from the throne saying, "Behold, the dwelling of God is with men. He will dwell with them, and they shall be his people,[o] and God himself will be with them;[p] 4 he will wipe away every tear from their eyes, and death shall be no more neither shall there be mourning nor crying nor pain any more, for the former things have passed away."

5 And he who sat upon the throne said, "Behold, I make all things new." Also he said, "Write this, for these words are 6 trustworthy and true." And he said to me, "It is done! I am the Alpha and the Omega, the beginning and the end. To the thirsty I will give water without price from the foun- 7 tain of the water of life. He who conquers shall have this heritage, and I will be his God 8 and he shall be my son. But as for the cowardly, the faithless, the polluted, as for murderers, fornicators, sorcerers, idolaters, and all liars, their lot shall be in the lake that burns with fire and brimstone, which is the second death."

9 Then came one of the seven angels who had the seven bowls full of the seven last plagues, and spoke to me, saying, "Come, I will show 10 you the Bride, the wife of the Lamb." And in the Spirit he carried me away to a great, high mountain, and showed me the holy city Jerusalem coming down out of heaven from 11 God, having the glory of God, its radiance like a most rare jewel, like a jasper, clear as 12 crystal. It had a great, high wall, with twelve gates, and at the gates twelve angels, and on the gates the names of the twelve tribes of the 13 sons of Israel were inscribed; on the east three gates, on the north three gates, on the south three gates, and on the west three

gates. And the wall of the city had twelve 1 foundations, and on them the twelve names of the twelve apostles of the Lamb.

And he who talked to me had a measuring 1 rod of gold to measure the city and its gates and walls. The city lies foursquare, its 1 length the same as its breadth; and he measured the city with his rod, twelve thousand stadia;[q] its length and breadth and height are equal. He also measured its wall, a 1 hundred and forty-four cubits by a man's measure, that is, an angel's. The wall was 1 built of jasper, while the city was pure gold, clear as glass. The foundations of the wall of 19 the city were adorned with every jewel; the first was jasper, the second sapphire, the third agate, the fourth emerald, the fifth 20 onyx, the sixth carnelian, the seventh chrysolite, the eighth beryl, the ninth topaz, the tenth chrysoprase, the eleventh jacinth, the twelfth amethyst. And the twelve gates were 21 twelve pearls, each of the gates made of a single pearl, and the street of the city was pure gold, transparent as glass.

And I saw no temple in the city, for its 22 temple is the Lord God the Almighty and the Lamb. And the city has no need of sun or 23 moon to shine upon it, for the glory of God is its light, and its lamp is the Lamb. By its 24 light shall the nations walk; and the kings of the earth shall bring their glory into it, and 25 its gates shall never be shut by day—and there shall be no night there; they shall bring 26 into it the glory and the honour of the nations. But nothing unclean shall enter it, 27 nor any one who practises abomination or falsehood, but only those who are written in the Lamb's book of life.

Then he showed me the river of the water of 22 life, bright as crystal, flowing from the throne of God and of the Lamb through the 2 middle of the street of the city; also, on either side of the river, the tree of life[r] with its twelve kinds of fruit, yielding its fruit each month; and the leaves of the tree were for the healing of the nations. There shall no more 3 be anything accursed, but the throne of God and of the Lamb shall be in it, and his servants shall worship him; they shall see his 4 face, and his name shall be on their foreheads. And night shall be no more; they 5 need no light of lamp or sun, for the Lord God will be their light, and they shall reign for ever and ever.

---

[o] Other ancient authorities read *peoples* [p] Other ancient authorities add *and be their God*
[q] About fifteen hundred miles
[r] Or *the Lamb. In the midst of the street of the city, and on either side of the river, was the tree of life,* etc.
20.15: Rev 3.5. **21.1:** Is 66.22. **21.2:** Rev 3.12. **21.3:** Ezek 37.27. **21.4:** Is 25.8; 35.10. **21.5:** Is 43.19.
21.6: Is 55.1. **21.7:** Ps 89.27-28. **21.8:** Is 30.33. **21.10:** Ezek 40.2. **21.12:** Ezek 48.30-35; Ex 28.21.
21.15: Ezek 40.5. **21.19:** Is 54.11-12. **21.23:** Is 24.23; 60.1, 19. **21.25:** Is 60.11. **21.27:** Is 52.1; Rev 3.5.
22.2: Gen 2.9. **22.3:** Zech 14.11. **22.4:** Ps 17.15.

The words of this book

And he said to me, "These words are trustworthy and true. And the Lord, the God of the spirits of the prophets, has sent his angel to show his servants what must soon take place. And behold, I am coming soon."

Blessed is he who keeps the words of the prophecy of this book.

I John am he who heard and saw these things. And when I heard and saw them, I fell down to worship at the feet of the angel who showed them to me; but he said to me, "You must not do that! I am a fellow servant with you and your brethren the prophets, and with those who keep the words of this book. Worship God."

And he said to me, "Do not seal up the words of the prophecy of this book, for the time is near. Let the evildoer still do evil, and the filthy still be filthy, and the righteous still do right, and the holy still be holy."

"Behold, I am coming soon, bringing my recompense, to repay every one for what he has done. I am the Alpha and the Omega, the first and the last, the beginning and the end."

Blessed are those who wash their robes,[s] 14 that they may have the right to the tree of life and that they may enter the city by the gates. Outside are the dogs and sorcerers and 15 fornicators and murderers and idolaters, and every one who loves and practises falsehood.

"I Jesus have sent my angel to you with this 16 testimony for the churches. I am the root and the offspring of David, the bright morning star."

The Spirit and the Bride say, "Come." 17 And let him who hears say, "Come." And let him who is thirsty come, let him who desires take the water of life without price.

I warn every one who hears the words of the 18 prophecy of this book: if any one adds to them, God will add to him the plagues described in this book, and if any one takes 19 away from the words of the book of this prophecy, God will take away his share in the tree of life and in the holy city, which are described in this book.

He who testifies to these things says, 20 "Surely I am coming soon." Amen. Come, Lord Jesus!

The grace of the Lord Jesus be with all the 21 saints.[t] Amen.

[s] Other ancient authorities read *do his commandments*
[t] Other ancient authorities omit *all*; others omit *the saints*
22.11: Dan 12.10. **22.12:** Is 40.10; Jer 17.10. **22.13:** Is 44.6; 48.12. **22.14:** Gen 2.9; 3.22.
22.16: Is 11.1, 10. **22.17:** Is 55.1. **22.21:** 2 Thess 3.18.

HOW OUR BIBLE

15th CENTURY
1454 THE INVENTION OF PRINTING in Europe increased book production, and the Renaissance stimulated further translation

16th CENTURY
The roman letter form, developed as a type-face, gradually replaced the use of 'black-letter' and made it possible to produce books smaller in size yet easier to read.
After years of opposition the Bible in English was set up in churches to the joy of the people

19th CENTURY
The Industrial Revolution enabled book production to meet the advance of popular education.
1804 The British and Foreign Bible Society was founded to encourage the wider circulation of the Scriptures. During this century of the pioneer missionaries, translations increased to more than 500

20th CENTURY
Through the Bible Societies Scriptures now go out into all the world in over 1000 languages

HEBREW

Hebrew scriptures were copied on scrolls by scribes down the centuries

Latin Manuscripts were copied and illuminated by monks from the 6th century onwards

BEDE d. 735
Anglo-Saxon St. John

ALFRED d. 899
Anglo-Saxon Psalms

LUTHER
German New Testament 1522

MILES COVERDALE
First printed English Bible 1535

THE GENEVA BIBLE
First small edition in roman type 1560

THE DOUAI-RHEIMS BIBLE
Roman Catholic version 1609

English Revised Version 1881-5

American Standard Version 1901

Revised Standard Version 1952

MODERN TRANSLATIONS